The

CHELSEA HOUSE LIBRARY
of LITERARY CRITICISM

The
CHELSEA HOUSE LIBRARY
of LITERARY CRITICISM

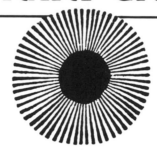

TWENTIETH-CENTURY BRITISH LITERATURE

Volume 3

General Editor

HAROLD BLOOM

1986
CHELSEA HOUSE PUBLISHERS
New York
New Haven   Philadelphia

MANAGING EDITOR
S. T. Joshi
ASSOCIATE EDITORS
Brendan Bernhard
Patrick Nielsen Hayden
Teresa Nielsen Hayden
Larson Powell
Daniel Carmi Sherer
Anna Williams
EDITORIAL COORDINATOR
Karyn Gullen Browne
EDITORIAL STAFF
Susan B. Hamburger
Perry King
Jeffrey Kosakow
RESEARCH
T. J. Chamberlain
Stephen Kent
PICTURE RESEARCH
Catherine Ruello
DESIGN
Susan Lusk

Printed and bound in the United States of
America.

Library of Congress Cataloging in Publication
Data

Twentieth-century British literature.
    (The Chelsea House library of literary
    criticism)
    Includes bibliographies and index.
    1. English literature—20th century—
History and criticism—Collected works.
2. Authors, English—20th century—
Biography—Dictionaries. 3. Criticism—United
States— Collected works. I. Bloom, Harold.
PR473.T84 1985   820'.9'0091
84-27428
ISBN 0-87754-811-O

Chelsea House Publishers
Harold Steinberg, Chairman & Publisher
Susan Lusk, Vice President
A Division of Chelsea House Educational
    Communications, Inc.

133 Christopher Street, New York, NY 10014

345 Whitney Avenue, New Haven, CT 06510

5014 West Chester Pike, Edgemont, PA 19028

Acknowledgments for selections used in this
volume commence on page 1880.

CONTENTS

The Index to this series, *Twentieth-Century British Literature*, appears in Volume 5.

ABBREVIATIONS

At	Atlantic	NR	New Republic
Ath	Athenaeum	NS	New Statesman
Bkm	Bookman (New York)	NSN	New Statesman and Nation
BkmL	Bookman (London)	NwA	New Age
CL	Canadian Literature	NYRB	New York Review of Books
CmQ	Cambridge Quarterly	NYTBR	New York Times Book Review
Cmty	Commentary	PBA	Proceedings of the British Academy
CoL	Contemporary Literature	Phil	Philosophy
CQ	Critical Quarterly	PoR	Poetry Review
Crit	Criticism	PR	Partisan Review
CR	Chicago Review	QR	Quarterly Review
DL	Dock Leaves	REL	Review of English Literature
Enc	Encounter	SA	Scientific American
Fndtn	Foundation	Salm	Salmagundi
FNW	Folios of New Writing	Scy	Scrutiny
FR	Fortnightly Review	SFS	Science-Fiction Studies
HdR	Hudson Review	Shen	Shenandoah
IM	Irish Monthly	SN	Studies in the Novel
IUR	Irish University Review	SoR	Southern Review
KR	Kenyon Review	Spec	Spectator
LM	London Mercury	SR	Saturday Review
Lon	London Magazine	SRL	Saturday Review (London)
LR	Literary Review	SSF	Studies in Short Fiction
LT	Listener	SwR	Sewanee Review
MCh	Modern Churchman	TCV	Twentieth Century Verse
MS	Moderna Språk	TLS	Times Literary Supplement
NA	Nation and Athenaeum	UTQ	University of Toronto Quarterly
NaR	National Review	VS	Victorian Studies

ILLUSTRATIONS

GEOFFREY HILL

1932–

Geoffrey Hill was born in Bromsgrove, Worcestershire, on June 18, 1932. After graduating with first class honors from Keble College, Oxford, in 1953, he taught English at the University of Leeds, and is currently a University Lecturer in English, and Fellow of Emmanuel College, Cambridge.

Hill first published poems as an undergraduate, and brought out his earliest collection, *For the Unfallen*, in 1959. He was soon recognized as a leading force in modern British poetry, receiving the Eric Gregory Award in 1961. His next major publication was *King Log* (1968), which gained him the Hawthornden Prize in 1969 and the Faber Memorial Prize in 1970. *Mercian Hymns*, a cycle of thirty prose poems, appeared in 1971, winning him further distinctions, including the Heinemann Award in 1972. American readers were introduced to Hill's poetry by the publication of *Somewhere Is Such a Kingdom* (1975), which incorporated his three earlier volumes, with an introduction by Harold Bloom. *Tenebrae* appeared in 1978, and the same year Hill's adaptation of Ibsen's *Brand* was performed at the National Theatre, London.

While the formal precision and rich cultural allusiveness of his work, which deals mainly with the past, have secured him a place at the forefront of contemporary British poetry, Hill is also a notable literary critic, and in 1984 published a collection of essays on literature and ideas under the title *The Lords of Limit*.

Hill has been a Fellow of the Royal Society of Literature since 1972, and in 1983 received the Loines Award and Special Citation for Poetry of the American Academy of Arts and Letters. He is married with two children.

CHRISTOPHER RICKS
"Cliché as 'Responsible Speech': Geoffrey Hill"

London Magazine, November 1964, pp. 96–101

Of all our present poets, Geoffrey Hill is the one who most persistently tackles the problem of what to do about dead language, clichés, the phrases which have gone sour, flat, or heartless on us. Of course there are good poets like Philip Larkin whose approach and style make it appropriate for them to take no notice. And again there is Donald Davie who, after providing the best modern criticism on the subject of dead metaphors, has now come to believe that the worst enemy just now is not such deadness but frantic liveliness, verbal fidgets, a high-pitched buzz of interference. Yet all the same the restoration of clichés is by no means a form of antiquarianism. Conspicuous consumption and planned obsolescence are features of the linguistic as well as the social scene. Words and idioms are created and worked to death with a ruthless speed that would have shocked a nineteenth-century poet—the process resembles one of those eerie films which speed up a flower's life from budding to withering. And the attempt to get the *New English Dictionary* up to date now recalls the doomed bustle of *Tristram Shandy*, falling further and further behind with its schedule because living is a brisker process than writing. If Eric Partridge were now compiling his *Dictionary of Clichés*, the result would have been a far fatter book. All of which means that we ought to take particular notice of a poet like Mr Hill who persists in his renovations with intelligence and passion. (And who writes some excellent poems meanwhile.) Anyone who thinks that there is still plenty of unspoilt language around, huge virgin forests, will find morbid any such dread of the dustbowl. The land-rich English used to be able to laugh at the Dutch: 'They with mad labour fish'd the land to shore.' Now that ours really is a tight little island, the Dutch seem sane.

One says 'renovations', because the poems in Hill's *For the Unfallen* and *Preghiere* are very different from those that simply incorporate clichés in order to be matey. Like everyone since Wordsworth, Hill agrees that it is necessary for poetry to be in a vital relation with the living speech of its own time. But he has argued, quite rightly, that this is not at all the same as believing that poetry need be chatty or full of gnarled rusticities. 'It seems to be a modern scholastic fallacy that "living speech" can be heard only in the smoke-room or in bed; in fact the clichés and equivocations of propaganda or of "public relations" are also part of the living speech of a society.' But the distinguishing characteristic of Hill's poetry is that it uses cliché for tragic rather than comic purposes. This is not to deny his strong vein of sardonic humour, which he shares with the writers he most admires: Ben Jonson ('profound parody'), Isaac Rosenberg ('macabre comedy'), Allen Tate ('dry pun') and Robert Lowell ('the lampoonist's art'). In his best poems there is a largeness of ambition at one with an amplitude of phrasing (lines which it is a pleasure to mouth)—qualities which are rare these days. Yet the largeness is saved from mere orotundity by the persistent invoking of our seedier world. Hill achieves dignity by rising above cliché; he achieves truthfulness by not eschewing cliché. What fascinates him is the appalling gulf between the way we usually mutter such-and-such a phrase and the way we might use it if the doors of perception were cleansed. Take the end of his fine poem, 'The Guardians', which tells how the old gather the bodies of the young (to me, the setting recalls the shore after a hideous sea-battle in Lucan's *Pharsalia*):

> There are silences. These, too, they endure:
> Soft comings-on; soft after-shocks of calm.
> Quietly they wade the disturbed shore;
> Gather the dead as the first dead scrape home.

'Scrape home' is a triumph. It is unforcedly literal, 'scrape' showing the dead body as like a keel that runs ashore, and 'home' being nothing but the truth. And in the gap between such a way of scraping home and our usual application (just winning, just safe, gulping with relief)—in that gap is the appalling heartbreak of the poem, the gap between what we expect of life and what we get. Pathos with dignity—there are not many poets now writing who can so command the combination.

But it would be as well to quote from Hill's essay on Ben Jonson to show that such effects are not accidental:

> In Marvell, as in Jonson, the perspective requires the utterance of deliberate cliché, but cliché rinsed and restored to function as responsible speech. . . . Jonson's language is frequently 'literary' in the best sense of the term. That is, its method requires that certain words and phrases, by constant repetition in popular literary modes, shall have been reduced to easy, unquestioned connotations. These connotations are then disturbingly scrutinized. Pope's 'Oblig'd by hunger and request of friends' requires for its effect the common formula of gentlemanly apologia, on the part of coy amateurs bringing out verse. It is 'hunger' that blasts the cliché into a new perspective.

And if anyone still doubted that Hill's words were apt to his practice, it would be necessary only to quote the extraordinary (and fascinating) notes which he provided for the revised edition of Kenneth Allott's *Penguin Book of Contemporary Verse*.

'A new perspective'—that is, something to break through our unseeing blandness. As with Lowell, the accusation of tastelessness is not thought to matter very much; it is not surprising that one of Hill's recent poems, 'The Humanist', suddenly erupts with '(Tasteless! tasteless!)'. So often have we seen St Sebastian pierced with arrows, that we cannot but be glazed to it, see it through glass. But not here:

> Naked, as if for swimming, the martyr
> Catches his death in a little flutter
> Of plain arrows. A grotesque situation,
> But priceless, and harmless to the nation.

'Catches his death' is certainly shockingly tasteless in its evocation of the common cold, but who could deny that it is altogether accurate as a description of Sebastian's way of death? And if it first of all tells the truth, what is the objection to its being shocking? Added to which, 'catches' certainly doesn't sneer at the martyr, since it implies his decisiveness, his skill and his power to will what God wills. The key-word is, of course, 'grotesque'—a range of conflicting emotions which is at work again on 'a little flutter'. Once more this is both literally accurate and desolatingly inadequate in its reduction of martyrdom to a petty thrill. (The rhyme *martyr* / *flutter* flaps with grim limpness.) The climax of these contrarieties is 'priceless'—is there any other epithet which we apply quite casually both to an invaluable work of art and to a preposterously comic situation? The woundingly comic effect here is achieved by a method resembling that which Hill pinpointed in Rosenberg's poetry, 'the skilful juxtaposing of elevated and banal diction'. Except that Hill outdoes this in skill, since we are given not juxtaposition but interpenetration: 'catches his death', like 'scrape home', is both elevated *and* banal. Hence the remarkable economy of Hill at his best. The ironic mode, as Yvor Winters has ruthlessly shown, is often a very wasteful one, since it spends words on doing something and then more words on undoing it. The simultaneous duplicity (in the best sense) of Hill's poems is a very different matter.

What lifts such effects above mere cleverness—though they are splendidly clever—is not only Hill's compassion and sense of grandeur. As always with a true poet, the linguistic concerns are a corollary of a way of looking at life. His praise of Jonson for a 'virtuous self-mistrust' has to be related to a persistent sense of the dangers lurking in ideals. He himself has offered the gloss on one of his phrases: ' "Our God scatters corruption" = "Our God puts corruption to flight" or "Our

God disseminates corruption".' His relationship to Christianity, as to all traditional systems and beliefs, is profoundly ambiguous, but not evasively or slily so: 'I want the poem to have this dubious end; because I feel dubious; and the whole business is dubious'. Undoubtedly such a habit of mind, or obsession, has—like all habits of mind—its inevitable limitations. There are many things in life that are not dubious, and Hill's temperament and mind are not suited to dealing with them. But he is still left with a gigantic field, and his own poetry (in the words he used of Lowell) is 'persistent in its manipulation of religious metaphor'. George Herbert's *The Sacrifice* is the greatest poem ever written in the mode which Hill most favours, and it seems to me a real tribute to Hill that one can mention Herbert with qualifications but without absurdity. Or look here, upon this passage:

> Who hath not . . .
> . . . let his spirit, like a demon-mole,
> Work through the clayey soil and gravel hard,
> To see scull, coffin'd bones, and funeral stole.

And on this:

> Before the scouring fires of trial-day
> Alight on men; before sleeked groin, gored head,
> Budge through the clay and gravel, and the sea
> Across daubed rock evacuates its dead.

Yes, Keats does come off best—with deceptive mildness he manages to make 'work through . . .' perform the task for which Hill has to call up 'budge through . . .' (fine though that is). But it is certainly something for Hill to have written lines that do not just curl up and die when juxtaposed with Keats. Not but what James Dickey was pitching it a bit high when he said of Hill's 'Genesis', 'I can think of no better compliment to pay Hill than to say I was all but persuaded that, were God a very talented young poet, the six days of the Creation might very well have been as the poem says they were'.

Sometimes Hill can find his doubts glinting in a single word, as in the opening of 'In Piam Memoriam':

> Created purely from glass the saint stands,
> Exposing his gifted quite empty hands
> Like a conjurer about to begin,
> A righteous man begging of righteous men.

'Purely': merely? with purity? The word refuses to plump. 'Gifted': talented? with a present? If his hands are empty, then such a saint is a bit of a disappointment; but then a conjurer is all the better for starting with frankly empty hands. What the context does is to give back to the 'conjurer' some of the dignity which he had in the old days when religion felt in no position to mock at magic—a conjurer used to be a man who could conjure up spirits. Dignity, but seen with a cold eye; the saint in the stained-glass window is a dubious figure (we are made aware of the doubt that lurks in 'stained'). He is 'a feature for our regard': for our respect? or because he is nice to look at? The dubiety makes for a poem of great economy and tolerance. I would prefer Hill as a man to be in one (dismissive) mind about the saint, but undeniably on this poetic occasion two minds are better than one.

In 'Ovid in the Third Reich', Hill has even been able to write a poem which says what can be said for those Germans who remained silent. The remarkable thing is that at the same time it says what must be said against them.

> Too near the ancient troughs of blood
> Innocence is no earthly weapon.

Eloquence is saved from becoming oratory because of the way in which that second line teeters on the edge of a collapse into self-pitying despair: 'Innocence is no earthly use'. But the (unspoken) cliché does offer a faint hope that innocence may be a heavenly weapon, or of heavenly use. Yet if the innocence of a German would not protect him, how much more must this have been true of a Jew?

> I have learned one thing: not to look down
> Too much upon the damned.

'Look down', with the uncertainty of 'despise' or 'see from Heaven'—and with a further uncertainty unfolding: is the reference to the traditional pastime of contemplating the tortures of the damned? Or are we speaking of a prudence that is by no means entirely ignoble, and that warns us against staring for ever at suffering? That way madness, or hardheartedness, lies. It is striking enough that Hill is able to write poems which say so much; what is even more striking is that the best of them are uncramped and unclogged, characterized indeed by an imaginative spaciousness.

It is of the nature of literary achievement that it can never get shot of a problem. And a talent as fiercely unaccommodating as Hill's does often leave a reader limping. His recent work seems to me too obdurately to have abandoned fluency in its determination to contract, to load every rift. The point seems virtually conceded when so young a poet publishes 'Two Fragmentary Variations' (five lines each) or 'The Assisi Fragments'. (Which is not to deny Hill's gifts as a sombre epigrammatist or emblem-writer in the seventeenth-century manner—see the uncollected 'Locust Songs', *Stand* V:2). The intricacy of syntax, or bullying of it, is becoming an entanglement, and the poems, though they still have force, no longer have so much momentum. 'Anguish bloated by the replete scream'. Replete, but bloated. And yet Lowell too is a poet who is always finding himself in an impasse, and then extraordinarily breaking free. Hill is a very harsh judge of his earlier work, but it would be a disaster if he were to underestimate the sheer loveliness—and fluency—of the end of 'Orpheus and Eurydice' (1958):

> Love goes, carrying compassion
> To the rawly-difficult;
> His countenance, his hands' motion,
> Serene even to a fault.

'Even to a fault' here blossoms wonderfully; it admits our doubts about an ideal of self-sacrificial love, and yet at the same time it offers an unforgettable sense of what true forgiveness is, 'serene even to a fault'. Whenever one feels any impatience with Hill's obscurity, or his massive withholding of judgement, or his simultaneous double-judgements, it would be as well to remember that at the very least his poems are, in both senses, 'serene even to a fault'.

JON SILKIN
"The Poetry of Geoffrey Hill"
British Poetry since 1960
eds. Michael Schmidt and Grevel Lindop
1972, pp. 143–64

I

The word "formal" in criticism often associates with ideas concerning metrical iambic, strict stanzaic form and rhyme, and the containment by these devices of whatever the poet has to say. It may be used approvingly, or, since the current has recently run more the other way, as a means of implying that a poet using these forms has little to say, and that his sensibility and imagination are insensitive, that the courage a poet needs in order to articulate what ought essentially to be

his way of exploring life is absent. As corollary to this, it is implied that only what is new in structure can sensitively and honestly engage this, since, it is argued, we are in the midst of such changes that only those forms originated by the poet in co-operation with his constantly changing environment can adequately express the new (as well as the past and hidden) in the tormenting life so many are forced to live.

The second position is persuasive, providing one keeps in mind the counter-balancing caveat that every more-or-less defined position provides the grounds for much bad work; and that even if the second position seems to account for a greater share of low-tension poetry, it is arguable that the position has helped into existence poetry that might not otherwise have got written (*vide* Alvarez writing of Plath and citing Lowell[1]). On the other hand one might ask what there is in such a position for Hill, whose work contrasts so strongly with, say, Ginsberg, and the Hughes of *Crow*.

There is, however, another way of defining "formal", which involves the origination of constraints and tensions with those forms themselves evolved by the concerns of the writer and his sensibility, as he or she worked these. One might say that a co-existing condition of the material evolving its forms involved, for this kind of formal writer, a productive impediment, a compacting of certain forms of speech, refracting the material into a mode of compression and close conjunction not normally found in speech, and which, probably, could not be found there. Such a definition, however, would imply that the mode of response, which could be brought to conscious active thought, was habitual to such a writer. The question of conjunction is especially important to such a poet as Hill, and in making these definitions, I have been trying to illustrate both a general type and identify a particular writer.

Such formality bears with its own problems. The payments on such a premium are continuous, and one way of apprehending this condition in Hill's work is to consider the variety of forms; to consider the restlessness within the variety. Formality of the first sort occurs with Hill's early poem "Genesis",[2] although here it seems that the formal iambic line, stanza, and section, are used to *express* that already stylised conception of earth's creation; and that the formality while representing such stylisation is already at odds with the central theme of the poem

> There is no bloodless myth will hold

and to a lesser extent with the sub-theme's concession

> And by Christ's blood are men made free.

Hill's "argument with himself" over formal means and expressiveness is already embryonically visible in the poem, but, for the moment, one might consider the difference in form between say this poem (and "In memory of Jane Fraser"—a poem he has had trouble with) and "September Song";[3] between that, and the unrhymed sonnets of "Funeral Music"[4] and between all these and the prose hymns (canticles) of *Mercian Hymns*.

Restlessness of forms is not something one would normally associate with Hill's work, but this is probably because the voice is unusually present and distinct. Sometimes it becomes over-distinctive, and this is usually the result of the formal means degenerating into mannerisms. Even so, a voice cannot itself provide more than a spurious unity, and to put on it work that is beyond its proper capacity produces the strain that exists in a fraction of Hill's work. This "mannered" and "mild humility", however, is more often disrupted by the variety of forms. Is it imaginative experimentation, or an inability to find one embracing and therefore controlling mode? It could be argued that such unity is undesirable, but I am suggesting that for a poet such as Hill, unity of form, as of thought and response, are important. This is why we have such apparently absolute control within each poem (or form) but such variety of form over the spread of his work so far. Each fragment of absoluteness represents a pragmatic concession to the intractable nature of the matter and response to it in each poem. One is glad that it is so, and it reflects the ongoing struggle between form, expressiveness, and the scrupulous attention Hill usually gives to his material, even when it is struggling against that oppressive attention so as to return an existence (in life) independent of his own.

II

Hill's use of language, and choice of words, has been noticed, often, one feels, to the detriment of his themes. One sympathises with the reviewers. The compressed language is intimately bound up with what it is conveying. This is true of many poets, but true to an unusual degree with Hill. It is true in another sense. The language itself is unlike most other writing current, and coupled with this is an unusually self-conscious pointing on the part of the poet to the language. This is not because he wishes to draw attention to it for its own sake, but because the language both posits his concerns, and is itself, in the way it is used, an instance of them. Moreover, his use of language is both itself an instance of his (moral) concerns; and the sensuous gesture that defines them. It is therefore difficult to speak of his themes without coming first into necessary contact with the language.

Hill's use of irony is ubiquitous, but is not, usually, of the non-participatory and mandarin sort. It articulates the collision of events, or brings them together out of concern, and for this a more or less regular and simple use of syntax is needed, and used.

> Undesirable you may have been, untouchable
>   you were not.

A concentration camp victim.[5] Even the "play" in the subtitle "born 19.6.32—deported 24.9.42" where the natural event of birth is placed, simply, beside the human and murderous "deported" as if the latter were of the same order and inevitability for the victim; which, in some senses, it was—even here, the zeugmatic wit is fully employed. The irony of conjuncted meanings between "undesirable" (touching on both sexual desire and racism) and "untouchable", which exploits a similar ambiguity but reverses the emphases, is unusually dense *and* simple. The confrontation is direct and unavoidable, and this directness is brought to bear on the reader not only by the vocabulary, but by the balancing directness of the syntax. This stanza contains one of Hill's dangerous words—dangerous because of its too-frequent use, and because these words sometimes unleash (though not here) a too evident irony:

> Not forgotten
>   or passed over at the proper time.

"Proper" brings together the idea of bureaucratically correct "as calculated" by the logistics of the "final solution" and the particular camp's timetable; it also contrasts the idea of the mathematically "correct" with the morally intolerable. It touches, too, on the distinction between what is morally right, and what is conventionally acceptable, and incidentally brings to bear on the whole the way in which the conventionally acceptable is often used to cloak the morally unacceptable. One of Hill's grim jokes, deployed in such a way that the laughter is precisely proportioned to the needs of ironic exposure. It is when the irony is in excess of the situation that

the wit becomes mannered. But here it does not. So the poem continues, remorselessly.

> As estimated, you died. Things marched,
>   sufficient, to that end.

One feels the little quibbling movement in

> As estimated, you died.

as, without wishing to verbalise it, Hill points to the disturbing contrast between the well-functioning time-table and what it achieved. "Things marched" has the tread of pompous authority, immediately, in the next line, qualified by the painfully accurate recognition that just so much energy was needed, and released, for the extermination. "Sufficient" implies economy, but it also implies a conscious qualification of the heavy, pompous tread of authority. The quiet function of unpretentious machinery fulfilled its programme, perhaps more lethally. One also notices here how the lineation gauges, exactly, the flow and retraction of meaning and impulse, and how this exact rhythmical flow is so much a part of the sensuous delivery of response and evaluation. It is speech articulated, but the lineation provides, via the convention of verse line-ending, a formal control of rhythm, and of sense emphasis, by locking with, or breaking, the syntactical flow. Thus in the third stanza the syntax is broken by the lineation exactly at those parts at which the confession, as it were, of the poem's (partial) source is most painful:

> (I have made
>   an elegy for myself it
>   is true)

The slightly awkward break after "it" not only forces the reading speed down to a word-by-word pace, in itself an approximation to the pain of the confession, but emphasises the whole idea. By placing emphasis on the unspecifying pronoun, Hill is able to say two things: that the elegy was made for himself (at least, in part) since in mourning another one is also commiserating with one's own condition.[6]

> When we chant
>   "Ora, ora pro nobis" it is not
>   Seraphs who descend to pity but ourselves.

But "it" may also refer to the whole event; I have made an elegy for myself, as we all do, but I have also made an elegy on a "true" event. True imaginatively, true in detailed fact; both for someone other than myself. Thus he is able to point to the difficulty of the poet, who wishes, for a variety of reasons, to approach the monstrousness of such events, but has compunction about doing so. He tactfully touches for instance on the overweening ambition of the poet who hitches his talent to this powerful subject, thereby giving his work an impetus it *may* not be fully entitled to, since, only the victim, herself, would be entitled to derive this kind of "benefit". But he also modestly pleads, I think, with "it/is true" that whatever the reasons for his writing such an elegy, a proper regard for the victim, a true and unambitious feeling, was present and used. I hope enough has been said here to point to Hill's use of irony at its best, and to indicate that the tact with which he uses language is not a convention of manners which he is inertly content to remain immersed in, but an active employment of the convention as it co-operates with his scrupulousness. The scrupulousness, like the pity, is in the language. The theme permeates it.

III

In pointing to the importance of the Imagist movement as it has affected English and American poetry, one is of course considering how central the image has become both in the writing, and for the considering, of twentieth-century poetry. What is strange about this is that apparently unrelated movements and poets apparently ignorant of each other were writing in modes which had certain formal elements in common. The hermetic poems of Ungaretti's earlier period as well as certain of Pound's and Eliot's earlier poems use the hard, clear image, seemingly as an instrument considered valuable for its own sake. In the expressionist poetry of Stramm, the images are used, as Michael Hamburger has indicated,[7] as the only needful flesh of the poem; the poem disdains the use of syntactical connections, thereby placing upon the image the whole burden of expressive meaning and impulse. To a lesser extent one finds this preoccupation with the image in Lorca; although even here one feels that sometimes the syntactical connections are used to lay stress on the image thereby placing on it a similar labour. The image becomes that point at which an ignition of all the elements of meaning and response takes place; that is, not only do the meanings and their impulses get expressed, but at that point are given their principal impetus. Even with the hard clear image calmly delivered this occurs. Hill has been both the innocent partaker and victim in this. He has used and been used. This is partly because of course the age as it were reeks of such practice. But with Hill one also feels that the choice has been made because he has come to recognise that the use of the image can properly communicate the intensity he wishes to express. Through it he can express the intensity, but fix it in such a way that it will evaluate the concerns of the poem it is embedded in without its intensity overruling the other parts. The intensity finds in its own kind of formality its own controlling expression. At the same time, the image as artefact has a perhaps satisfactory and not unmodest existence. It can be regarded, but it is also useful. Curiously enough, although the impression of imagery in Hill is, in my mind at least, strong, checking through the poetry, one is surprised at how controlled is the frequency of the kind of imagery I am thinking of. There are many instances of images used to represent objects, creatures, events. But it is as though the image whereby one object is enriched by the verbal presence of another, combined with it, and a third thing made—as though such a creation were recognised as so potentially powerful, and so open to abuse, that he was especially careful to use it sparingly. And he is, rightly, suspicious of offering confection to readers who enjoy the local richness without taking to them the full meaning of the poem, which is only susceptible to patience and a care for what it is as a whole thing. He says as much:

Anguish bloated by the replete scream. . . .
I could cry "Death! Death!" as though
To exacerbate that suave power;
But refrain. For I am circumspect,
Lifting the spicy lid of my tact
To sniff at the myrrh.[8]

The images have a richness, but here he is not so much reproaching himself for that, although he implies such a possibility, but rather for the perhaps evasive caution which is characterised by "tact". The self-questioning exposes further recessions of self-doubts and questions, themselves seen to be faintly absurd. There are other examples, however, of the kind of image I am describing:

Bland vistas milky with Jehovah's calm—[9]
and

cleanly
maggots churning spleen
to milk[10]

from a poem for another concentration camp victim, Robert Desnos; and

we are dying
to satisfy fat Caritas, those
Wiped jaws of stone[11]

and from the earlier Dr. Faustus:

A way of many ways: a god
Spirals in the pure steam of blood.[12]

What is noticeable about these images, chosen for the way in which they combine disparate elements, is their ferocity. Their expressiveness occurs at its fullest in the moment of sudden expansion, when the elements combine in often intolerable antipathy and produce judgements issuing from a disgust that has behind it a sense of outrage at this or that situation.

More often the images are "abstract", combinations of adjectives and nouns, whose conjunction is ironically disruptive, but with a similar moral evaluation intended. Thus in one of Hill's best shorter poems, "Ovid in the Third Reich", we again confront his justly obsessive concern with innocence, and its mutilation, or impossibility, within the context of human barbarism:

Too near the ancient troughs of blood
Innocence is no earthly weapon.[13]

The notion of innocence as a defence against earthly corruption has an ancient lineage; but here it is linked with the more combative "weapon", and in such a way as to suggest weapon in a very literal sense. Of what use is innocence in such a context? And: if it is of no use on earth, what is its use? Are we right to think of a condition as useless because inoperative on earth. And if thus inoperative, can it be so valued in a "heavenly" context? Hovering near the phrase "earthly weapon" is the phrase (no) "earthly good" with its worn-through substance, a little restored by Hill's regenerative irony. In these two lines Hill returns of course to the consideration of "Genesis":

There is no bloodless myth will hold.

(The "Ovid" poem suggests *to me* an Eichmann-like figure—not Eichmann—with whom the reader in his ordinariness and banality is invited to identify, thus being asked to make the connection with that other aspect of Eichmann, his evil. Ovid's exile may be seen to parallel our inability, or reluctance, to associate with guilt—in case we sully an innocence—already sullied.)

There are many examples of these "abstract" combinations, often zeugmatic in form (the device which has built into it a moral judgement). Thus

fastidious trumpets
Shrilling into the ruck[14]

and

my justice, wounds, love
Derisive light, bread, filth[15]

and, at the funeral of King Offa, the punning zeugma where the successive adjective suffers qualification by the former:

He was defunct. They were perfunctory.[16]

And again from *Mercian Hymns*, the man who has imagined, with ambiguous relish, a scene of torture

wiped his lips and hands. He strolled back to the
car, with discreet souvenirs for consolation.

"Discreet" is not an image precisely, but it produces an image of a man hiddenly guilty, voyeur upon his own imagination, which is, however, discreet in that it is secret. It has not tortured another's flesh.

In these instances, where Hill's intensity is released, I have tried to show that it is through images, of several kinds, that the sudden evaluative expansion occurs. Hill has more recently been concerned to accumulate meaning and response in a more gradual way. But, in the earlier work especially, the intense evaluation, response, judgement—all are released at that sudden moment of expansion which is the moment of visualisation. Hill's poetry has more often consisted of, not continuous narrative, but a conjunction of imagistic impulsions. A conjunction of intensities, sometimes sensuously rich, and nearly always scrupulously evaluative.

IV

The imagistic impulsion in Hill's work, as both imagistic and image-making, is of course related to the question of narrative and discursiveness. Imagism, considered as a reaction, developed out of an antipathy for the discursive nature of Victorian poetry. That was not the sum of its antipathies, but it is clear, from the principles and the practice, that Imagism constituted, among other things, an attempt to enact, rather than assert, a response. It wanted to cut from it those dilutions of response which had rendered a verse that was vaguely descriptive of states of feelings, and it found a method. It found in the image a pure answer. That is, it found in the image something that could not be adulterated. An image did not attempt to explain; it rendered the verbal equivalent of what was seen, and the more it rendered exactly what it saw, the better. Clearly this kind of antidote was needed in English poetry and we are still receiving its benefits. Yet the difficulty lay in that by nature, the hard, clear image, untroubled by a discursive reflectiveness, had little or no valency. It could only accommodate other images, perhaps of different intensities and implications, and it could not accommodate the syntax of argument or narrative. And despite what its claims implied, it could hardly accommodate connections of any kind; Imagism had to select very carefully indeed, and its methods could not easily be used without its being diluted. And at that stage in its development, to dilute its purity would have been to have annulled its impetus. What it gained in intensity it lost in its capacity to cope with a range of experience.

This is immediately apparent when we consider Imagism in relation to the war. This is not the place to speak in detail of, for instance, Aldington and Herbert Read, but, briefly, I should like to instance two very different poems by Read— "The Happy Warrior" and "The End of a War".[17] In the first, Read manages to make of his war experience an imagist poem. That is, he manages to make the "syntax" of Imagism render a particular set of very careful responses to combat, and to render, by implication, a set of arguments. But this is one instance, which, once done, could not be repeated. Moreover, the poem relies, for its deepest reading, on its being correlated with Wordsworth's poem "The Character of the Happy Warrior" of which it is also a criticism. But the fact that it needs, finally, this correlation with a poem that is anything but imagistic places Read's poem in a special relation to Imagism. Nothing like this that I know of in Imagist poetry had been done before, and one suspects that Read found his necessities out of what he called war's "terrorful and inhuman events".

In his autobiography, *The Contrary Experience*, Read wrote:

> I criticised [the Imagists] because in their manifestoes they had renounced the decorative word, but their sea-violets and wild hyacinths tend to become as decorative as the beryls and jades of Oscar Wilde. I also accused them of lacking that aesthetic selection which is the artist's most peculiar duty. . . . We were trying to maintain an abstract aesthetic ideal in the midst of terrorful and inhuman events.[18]

There is of course a skeletal narrative structure in "The Happy Warrior" but poems could hardly be written like that of any length and complexity. In his subsequent "war poems", those composing *Naked Warriors* (1919), we see Read introducing narrative, but the imagistic elements are much diluted by it, and in such a way as to enervate the poetry. In other words, Read had relied, as he had to, upon the imagistic elements to render intensity and expressiveness, but the collision of the two modes produced compromise. By the time Read came to write *The End of a War* (published 1933) he had worked out a solution; he pushed the narrative outside the poem, setting the scene and describing the events of the episode in a prefacing prose argument which, though essential to the reading of the poem, is in ambiguous relationship to it, and without any relationship to it structurally.

Hill is clearly a poet having little in common with Read, but he has, I think, similar problems engaging him. "Genesis" for instance is held together by using days of the week as a means of tabulating impulsions in sequence. The sequence of days is important to the poem structurally, and through it Hill tries to initiate an image of growing consciousness. Yet it is only a proper sequence as it refers back to God's six days of work. The poem itself does not have narrative coherence so much as a sequence of formulisations; in his subsequent work, Hill abandoned this kind of stylisation, and to a lesser extent, the incipient narrative structure.

With "Funeral Music", the prose note that at one time preceded the poem stands in similar elucidatory relation to it as Read's "Argument" does to "The End of a War". Less, perhaps, or perhaps less in Hill's mind, for the note has, in *King Log* itself, been placed at the end of the book, and separate from the poems, as though Hill were determined, with such a gesture, to make "Funeral Music" un-needful of any elucidatory material. The poems do not form a narrative sequence, although they lead through the battle (of Towton) into some deliberately incomplete attempts at evaluating the cost in both physical and spiritual excoriation. Evaluation is made partly by reference to a supposed, or possibly supposed, after-life, in which the ideals of an exemplary spiritual life would if anywhere be found; partly by reference to this, or to eternity, yet into which no sense of human evaluation can be extended with the certainty of finding corroborative "echoes". (Compare the following with the first stanza of "Ovid in the Third Reich".)

> If it is without
> Consequence when we vaunt and suffer, or
> If it is not, all echoes are the same
> In such eternity. Then tell me, love,
> How that should comfort us—[19]

Even supposed *notions* of an after-life, with its spiritual absolutes, are insufficient here since the first of the unrhymed sonnets opens in platonic supposition; that is, the platonic structure throws into ambiguity the question whether we are to suppose an after-life is to be believed in—does this by supplanting the idea of an after-life with its own metaphysical scheme. I am indicating here that in Hill's longer poems, sequences and extended work that demand some correspondingly developed structure, he meets the problem without conceding to narrative a function it might usefully fulfil in his work. Fearful of sacrificing the imagistic purity of his work, of sullying that compression, of impairing a dramatic enactment, or mimesis of psychological impulsions, he prefers to accumulate intensities than involve them in accumulating and continuous action. This may partly be due to the preference Hill shows for writing that, by dramatic mimesis, introduces to the reader internal impulsions rather than dramatic action. Thus in "Funeral Music", the battle of Towton, and its murderousness, is not encapsulated as dramatic action, but brooded on after the event, thereby allowing the external state of the field and the state of the mind experiencing and responding to it to meet. It is the self-questioning, the doubts, the beliefs half-held with a conviction of personal honesty, the motives and the state of the spirit, that interest Hill, rather than the shaping action of narrative. Nevertheless, these things too have their form of collision with other minds, and through action, alter and are altered. And they could also, I feel, build a narrative unity that Hill has only tentatively, if at all, used.

One of the most interesting and moving aspects of "Funeral Music" is its plainness. The images in the following passage do not fabricate either a local richness to colour-up the passage, nor is there an over-arching image employed supposedly to enlarge or make more significant the events and the responses to these of the observer-participant:

> "At noon,
> As the armies met, each mirrored the other;
> Neither was outshone. So they flashed and vanished
> And all that survived them was the stark ground
> Of this pain. I made no sound, but once
> I stiffened as though a remote cry
> Had heralded my name. It was nothing . . ."
> Reddish ice tinged the reeds; dislodged, a few
> Feathers drifted across; carrion birds
> Strutted upon the armour of the dead.[20]

An Ecclesiastes-like consideration of vanity moves in these first lines, located in the ironic flashing of the armies mirrored in each other's armour. But they do not see themselves; they see only the flash of their *own* pride by which they are, each of them, dazzled. Yet with an honesty that compels a grudging kind of admission, we are also told that theirs was a kind of sad "glory": "Neither was outshone". But this is also qualified by the other idea inherent in the phrase—that neither had more pride, nor was more capable of victory; what is impending is not the surfeiting of pride but its extinction in the futility of combat. If they mirror each other's pride they also mirror each other's destruction. The strutting carrion birds confirm this judgement.

Yet impressive as this is as narration implicated with judgement, and pity, there is also a turning inwards and sealing off from the outward visible of all this in the ambiguous "the stark ground/Of this pain". The ground is at once the actual ground where soldiers inflicted pain on each other; it is also, because of the disposition of the syntax, a kind of personification where the ground itself becomes absorbed in the huge lingering tremor of pain. This serves to incarcerate the reader, and perhaps the writer also, in an inescapable response, but it also fails, I think, to release him from a pre-occupation where the event has been so internalised that there results more response than event itself. The passage seems to recognise this by resuming its re-creation of the desolate battlefield. The sense of the pentameter, in these lines, and throughout the sequence, serves not merely a unifying function but as a framework within and around which Hill can make his supple impulses and retractions of rhythm:

> ". . . as though a remote cry
> Had heralded my name. It was nothing . . ."
> Reddish ice tinged the reeds; dislodged, a few
> Feathers drifted across.

The second line begins with a slow, regular pentameter; after the word "name", the expectations of the pentameter are reduced in the foreshortened remainder of the line, reducing exactly the expectations of the person in the *poem* as his

feelings are disappointed. In the next line the pentameter is extended. The other speaking voice is describing minute events on the surface of the battle-field. "Dislodged", in its participial form, is syntactically isolated, and mirrors the disconnectedness of the feathers, from a bird, or some martial plume, but reflects also the disconnectedness of the dead from the living. In the little halting movement at the end of the line, which the line-break emphasises, the temporary emphasis falls on "few" and thus serves to re-create sensuously the stillness of the battle-field which is

> its own sound
> Which is like nothing on earth, but is earth.[21]

These lines, from No. 3 of the sequence, serve to pre-resonate the irony of the situation, where the dead are unearthly (because of the possibility of the dead having an after-life) but are for us no more than the earth they have been reduced to by human action. Seen in this way, "Funeral Music" is, among other things, a consideration of war where "war", to use Clausewitz's strategy "is a continuation of state policy by other means". The sequence is at once an elegy of pity, an examination of pride, a self-examination of the responses appropriate to this apparent constant in human living. It is all these in relation to the question of whether suffering has any meaning in earthly life; and whether there exists some ideal platonic and/or spiritual system in which suffering, which is perhaps the only state during which we are innocent, can have a meaningful and positive place.

V

Sebastian Arrurruz ("The Songbook of Sebastian Arrurruz") was, as we now know, not an actual poet (1868–1922) who has bewilderedly survived into the twentieth century, but an invention that may have perplexed critics searching for the original work.

The poem makes use of the necessary "silence" surrounding the "original". The lack of information on the poet may obliquely refer to Arrurruz's own apprehension regarding the oblivion both of himself and his work, and is thus a wry part of the poems themselves. The poems composed by Arrurruz are also records of certain attitudes towards both the (discontinued) relationship with his mistress and to poetry. In a sense the poem, or group, is Hill's *Mauberley*. But where Pound is using himself, both for what he feels himself to be kin to as a poet, and for what the figure stands in contradistinction to in the effete and vulgar English culture, Hill's Sebastian (the saint pierced with arrows) is more separate from the poet who has shaped him.

Arrurruz (arrowroot) is a man pierced by the arrow (another's predation upon his relinquished mistress); the arrow remains rooted in him. He is also a man, the root of an arrow, himself equipped, organically, and with the incising gift of the poet. Both these, though, in the poem, are laconically expressed, and survive increasingly on the wryly self-regretful memory of what once obtained. But this double image, of potency, and the quite powerful if intermittent observation of it, serves to illustrate, among other things, the fate of The Poet surviving through two eras. The original potency may have had a bardic vigour unimpeded by a self-conscious and mocking observation of its impulsions; but the later work of Arrurruz that we are offered presents a considerable shift in temper and emphasis. In these poems we have, initially, not so much a man expressing passion as recollecting it:

> Ten years without you. For so it happens. . . .
> The long-lost words of choice and valediction.[22]

The energy is not in the passion itself, but re-located in the stare that recollects it, and which is itself observed. Arrurruz's writing is at once more complex than it was, and, significantly, more difficult to achieve. Whatever the auto-biographical references may amount to, Hill is clearly defining the poet's difficulties as he encounters an environment that is at once more self-conscious and less bardic. The attention is scrupulous and modern.

Arrurruz is of course a middle-ageing man, and knows it. Yet his struggles are not those of a defeated one.

> "One cannot lose what one has not possessed."
> So much for that abrasive gem.
> I can lose what I want. I want you.[23]

The first line is between inverted commas because it is a line from a poem he is writing or has perhaps recently completed. Either way the line is embedded in commentary by an older, more self-conscious, part of the man. "Coplas"—this is the first of four that constitute the poem—are "songs", perhaps somewhat lyrically un-selfregarding and unironic poems. They are also popular poems, often used to serenade the beloved. Some measure of Hill's irony here may be obtained by contrasting these simple definitions with the stance of the present Arrurruz's coplas which form neither a serenade, nor are popular, but unlyrical, allusive, and complex. The form is of course traditional and it has therefore accumulated to itself the energy of those poems which have earlier filled the form. But like so much else in the twentieth century, the traditional form has broken down. Or rather, not so much broken as become inappropriate; and not this, entirely, but that we have lost the ability to use the form. We have lost spontaneity.

Much of this centres in the phrase "abrasive gem". It is abrasive because it is a reminder of what he has lost. It is a gem beause it is a lyrical utterance faceted and cut like a jewel. Hill however uses "gem" to bring in other, colloquial meanings. Thus gem can mean a real beauty, but the poet can also, and certainly here does, mean it ironically and self-contemptuously. The self-contempt arises not only from his awareness of having lost his wife to another, but also of how his line of poetry untruthfully renders in lyrical terms a considerably unlyrical event. Arrurruz brings to his and our awareness the discontinuity between the two ways of looking at such an event, and the two ways of writing about it. There is no elegising or consolatory sweetness to be got; the paradox of Arrurruz's poem is still-born; and is replaced by the unparadoxical and unironical lack of consolation:

> I can lose what I want. I want you.

But in the second of the coplas there is already a modification of the harsh tone:

> Oh my dear one, I shall grieve for you
> For the rest of my life with slightly
> Varying cadence, oh my dear one.

The tone of this first line softens that of the previous copla's ending. He is, it seems, back in the convention of elegising the lost one. But the phrase "with slightly/varying cadence" tinges the whole with mockery. Is the irony conscious on Arrurruz's part, or is it reserved for the reader's inspection only? It hardly matters. The absurd monotony of such poetics is rendered, and we understand how the irony qualifies into clarity the whole situation. He is perhaps even beginning to write a poetry that feeds on such ironic awareness. Yet the irony cannot dissolve the passion, a crucial point for the poems that follow: "Half-mocking the half-truth." Michael Hamburger wrote of Hölderlin in *Reason and Energy* (pp. 17–18):

> Even before his enforced separation from Susette Gontard he had felt that his fate would be a tragic one. . . . Now he was to lose his last support

against the sense of personal tragedy. As he had foretold in 1798, all that remained was his art and the quite impersonal faith that sustained his art. . . . What Hölderlin did not know when he wrote this poem is that long after his heart had indeed died, as he says, his "mellow song" would continue; that the music of his strings *would* escort him down.

So with Arrurruz, in a way. Abandoned by his wife, musing with increasing, dilapidating irony on his loss, seeing that the earlier way of writing will fit neither the age, nor the event in his life, nor now his temperament, nothing it seems can prevent his gentle decline into oblivion. One might therefore expect the poems to degenerate, by mimesis, placing at the reader's disposal an irreversible picture of disintegration, among a flickering irony. This does not occur. What Arrurruz could not have foreseen, since he was engaged in it, was that his ironically truthful examination of the events in his life, including his poetry, would revitalise his art. For I take it that the succeeding poems of the "Songbook" are not only made of Arrurruz speaking but of his writing. If so, there is no failure, but rather, regeneration. In poem 5, Arrurruz can respond to, or write, a poem of genuine deprivation:

> I find myself
> Devouring verses of stranger passion
> And exile. The exact words
> Are fed into my blank hunger for you.[24]

A hunger that may not be fed; therefore blank. The crucial word, however, for the poet is "exact". The gaze has caught its truth. The reward is exactness, and its pain. Similarly in "A Song from Armenia":

> Why do I have to relive, even now,
> Your mouth, and your hand running over me
> Deft as a lizard, like a sinew of water?[25]

The emphatic, simplified movement of the song has returned, but this time filled with rich, *painful* memories, constantly reawakened, and admitted into his consciousness by the wry ironic truthfulness with which the mind regards such experience. It is not the distancing irony of the man who can afford irony because he is detached, but an irony created in pain. The relationship may have ceased, but the pain does not get subsumed in distance. There are two final twists to the "life", both occurring in the second of the prose poems which conclude the sequence:

> Scarcely speaking: it becomes as a
> Coolness between neighbours. Often
> There is this orgy of sleep. I wake
> To caress propriety with odd words
> And enjoy abstinence in a vocation
> Of now-almost-meaningless despair.[26]

"Orgy of sleep" oddly reverses the ironic vitality I have noticed, suggesting a dying inwards of life. The sexuality gets transcribed in a caressed "propriety". Yet the last word is despair. The registration is in the end one of feeling. Is there a further irony in that Arrurruz, caught up with an exact sense of it, can no longer make poems out of his pain because his equipment belongs to an earlier more rhetorical mode? I think not; although one can imagine that for Arrurruz this might often seem to have been the threat. As a latter-day saint, he experiences two temptations. One is to succumb to his earlier inexact rhetoric, as both an expression of and a response to his experience. The other is to create a distant and neutered irony from his pain. This latter gets suggested in "Postures". As it happens, Arrurruz succumbs to neither temptation.

VI

As with the Arrurruz sequence, the thirty prose poems that make up *Mercian Hymns* have a central figure from whom the poems depend, in this instance King Offa. Historically, as Hill tells us, Offa reigned over Mercia . . . in the years A.D. 757–796. During earlier medieval times he was already becoming a creature of legend. However the gloss is not entirely helpful in that the reader does not find a historical reconstruction of the King and his domain. Interleaved with a reconstruction of some of the King's acts are passages and whole poems concerned with the contemporary and representative figure Hill makes of himself. Why not? Additionally, the poem deliberately thwarts any attempt by the reader to keep his or her imagination safe in the past. The King himself, although rooted in the past, is to be "most usefully . . . regarded as the presiding genius of the West Midlands", and thus threads "his" way in and out of his past and our present. Hill makes quite sure we get this by offering, in the first Hymn, a description of the figure as

> King of the perennial holly-groves, the riven sand-
> stone: overlord of the M5: architect of the his-
> toric rampart and ditch.[27]

Nevertheless the historic facts of Offa the King are relevant, if tangled, and we should look at them. Entangled with them, however, are Hill's references themselves: (i) *Sweet's Anglo-Saxon Reader* (1950, pp. 170–80) and (ii) The Latin prose hymns or canticles of the early Christian Church; *The Penguin Book of Latin Verse* (1962, pp. xvii, 1v).

The interested reader will not be glad to discover that although there is a group of Hymns in Anglo-Saxon, quoted by Sweet, these texts are interlineally placed with the Latin taken from the *Vulgate*, of which these are literal and apparently not always accurate translations. Moreover it has been suggested that these translations embody no sense of the haecceity of the Mercian domain, or of the Anglo-Saxon world at large. That is, they were probably intended as instructional texts for the teaching of Latin. Moreover the two Vulgates are themselves of course translations from the Hebrew, the relevant Biblical references being made by Sweet at the head of each Anglo-Saxon translation (from the Latin). The first reference then suggests that, apart from some elaborate, heavy-witted joke, Hill's pointing to the Mercian Hymns indicates no more, as far as the Anglo-Saxon is concerned, than a homogeneity sanctioned by the Mercian dialect, a homogeneity that stems of course from a geographical area over which King Offa did rule, whose reign may or may not have witnessed these translations.

The second reference is as apparently oblique: "The 'Te Deum', a canticle in rhythmical prose, has been used in Christian worship from the fourth century to the present day. . . . As the Jewish psalter was the sole hymn-book of the early Church, it is not surprising that the 'Te Deum' is characterised throughout by the parallelism which is the basis of ancient Hebrew poetry."[28] As it happens, there appears to be no use of Hebrew parallelism in Hill's poems other than those traces which, through contact with the Bible, have crept into our speech and left there residually a few emphatic forms. Yet checking, in fact, through the relevant Biblical passages in Isaiah, Deuteronomy, Habakkuk, and Luke (which are the original texts for Sweet's Mercian Hymns) I found, almost by accident, and by linking my apprehension of rhythm in these English passages with the phrase quoted earlier—the "Te Deum", a canticle in rhythmical prose—I began to follow the point of the references, and even to give grudging assent to their obliquity.

It is helpful to remember that much of the *Old Testament* is, in the Hebrew, poetry, and that in rendering these translations in English of the Authorised Version, what is offered us is, precisely, "rhythmical prose". Moreover it is not merely rhythmical prose, but prose versions of poetry, although rendered, one feels, partly through the repetitions of parallelism, with emphatic *and* subtle rhythms. It is as if the exterior device of line ending, and all these devices contingent on this convention, have been discarded (not *entirely* true of *Mercian Hymns*); what is left, in the main, however, is the inherent structure itself, depending more than ever upon the rhythmical arrangement of the words. Greater stress may get laid on word-choice, and a closer attention is charged, perhaps, upon the meaning. These hopeful attempts at describing a prose poem, but in particular Hill's canticles, now offer the point of the references, since, without falling back on a description of his own method of writing, they allow the reader to pick up, in the best possible way, through example, the kind of poetry he is writing in *Mercian Hymns*. Moreover, although the Mercian dialect and the Anglo-Saxon language have little to do with the structure of the Hymns, and no comparison with the Anglo-Saxon will profitably help us in a reading of Hill's poems, I suggest that the Anglo-Saxon *Mercian Hymns* act as a historical filter for Hill. That is, they remind us that the Biblical transmissions which reach us additionally passed, for whatever reason, through the Mercian dialect, and that however indistinct the locality is now, and however restricted King Offa's jurisdiction may have been, Biblical contact was made via Mercia, which is also Offa's and Hill's locality.

As for the relevance of the Bible to King Offa, and both these to the character of Offa in Hill's poems, verse 21 from *Deuteronomy* 32 may help:

> They have moved me to jealousy with that which is
> not God; they have provoked me to anger with their
> vanities: and I will move them to jealousy with those
> which are not a people; I will provoke them to anger
> with a foolish nation.

In Hill's eighth poem:

> The mad are predators. Too often lately they harbour
> against us. A novel heresy exculpates all
> maimed souls. Abjure it! I am the King of
> Mercia, and I know. . . .
>
> Today I name them; tomorrow I shall express the
> new law. I dedicate my awakening to this
> matter.

It is useful to remember that while all of chapter 32 of *Deuteronomy* consists of God's words, Moses speaks them. They have the backing of God, but are vested in Moses' temporal authority. Of course, Moses the prime leader of Israel in a tight situation, had much to cope with, not least of all the comically frequent backsliding of the Israelites. But we recall that Moses was an autocratic ruler and, in this, had adequate sanction from the God of the *Old Testament*, who was jealous and wrathful. Curiously, those passages of the Bible translated into Anglo-Saxon stress, perhaps by accident, this aspect of God: provided we obey Him we shall find Him loving and protective: but should we not, we shall discover his wrath and punishments. The autocratic nature of such a God was perhaps a useful reminder, in that probably more anarchic period, that the nature and power of the Anglo-Saxon King was not unlike that of the Hebrew God.

R. W. Chambers in *Beowulf: An Introduction*[29] interestingly examines the character of King Offa II as well as the legends surrounding his supposed ancestor Offa I. He points to the shuffling of the deeds of the King onto his Queen by the monks of St. Alban's as a way of exonerating their benefactor of crime. Chambers speaks explicitly of "the deeds of murder which, as a matter of history, did characterise [King Offa II's] reign". History helps us to link the autocratic nature of God with King Offa, and see too what Hill has done with this in his *Mercian Hymns*.

Finally, I should quote from C. H. Sisson's Epigraph for *Mercian Hymns*:

> The conduct of government rests upon the same foundation and encounters the same difficulties as the conduct of private persons.

The quotation goes on to suggest that the technical aspects of government are frequently used to evade those moral laws which apply alike to individuals and governments.

The question of the private man and his public actions is one that Hill has already worked in "Ovid in the Third Reich". With such a figure as a king the question multiplies in direct ratio to the power of the king and his abuse of it. History suggests that Offa was a tyrant. In No. 7 ("The Kingdom of Offa"), a part of Offa's childhood, we have

> Ceolred was his friend and remained so, even after
>   the day of the lost fighter. . . .
>   Ceolred let it spin through a hole in the
>   classroom-floorboards. . . .
> After school he lured Ceolred, who was sniggering
>   with fright, down to the old quarries, and flayed him.

Then he continues with his play, alone. One cannot mistake the ferocity, or the egocentric peace of mind following it. Hill does not set out to establish the figure of a tyrant, since the sequence does not have that kind of narrative structure or intention. Yet in Offa's adult life the poems produce a similar ruthlessness to that of the child. Thus in dealing (in No. 11) with forgers of the realm's coinage:

> [the King's "moneyers"] struck with accountable
>   tact. They could alter the king's face.
> Exactness of design to deter imitation; mutilation if
>   that failed. . . .
> Swathed bodies in the long ditch; one eye upstaring.
>   It is safe to presume, here, the king's anger.

"Safe" underlies the irony and helps us to refer back to his "moneyers" who, alone, were free to alter, that is, flatter, the face. One is reminded of the monks rewriting the *Life* of King Offa their benefactor, by putting on his Queen the murder of his vassal, King Aethelbert. But the flattery tactfully (via Hill) points to the King's severity, if not cruelty. Of course we see here the attempt to establish in the kingdom the idea of money available only through productive work, and an attempt to establish a concept of lawfulness. Yet one is also aware of the naked word "moneyers", as opposed to the more neutral words available, with the suggestion that the King is, out of "good substance", making money. There are many qualifications here, and if the judgement is finally against Offa in the poem, there are mitigations. In poem 14, Offa assumes the role of powerful businessman:

> Dismissing reports and men, he put pressure on the
>   wax, blistered it to a crest. He threatened malefactors
>   with ash from his noon cigar.

The effect is one of humour, and opulence. The ritual "noon" cigar suggests the power of a minor potentate. The power has its reserves; yet in the obvious sense the vulgarity is miniature; he threatens with "ash". But ash, we recall, is what the concentration camp victims were reduced to. One notices the zeugma, with the built-in moral device. Men are dismissed as easily and thoughtlessly as reports (the line-split, male/factor,

emphasises this by means of the pun). The touch is light and has humour; but it engages the reader only to repel him.

There are other touches of opulence, of a more private kind, connected even more with the contemporary man than the king. He has been driving (in No. 17) through the beautiful "hushed Vosges". Some accident occurs with or between cyclists. It is unclear to me if it involves himself, as an adult, with these cyclists, or himself as a child with another cyclist, or whether Hill is merging both possibilities. In a sense it hardly matters. What is more important is the implied lack of compunction, whoever was to blame for the accident. The car "heartlessly" overtakes all this and

> He lavished on
> the high valleys its *haleine*.

By using, it would seem, the more delicate if exotic French for "breath", Hill is able to draw attention to the discrepancy between the beauty of the country he travels through, and the linked "heartlessness" of the pollution and lack of concern for the accident. The French word is beautiful, but cold, and lacks compunction in its erasure of concern.

Again in No. 18, we return to the problems of cruelty, with the contingent problem of the enjoyment of it:

> At Pavia, a visitation of some sorrow. Boethius'
>   dungeon. He shut his eyes. . . .
>   He willed the instruments of violence to
>   break upon his meditation. Iron buckles gagged;
>   flesh leaked rennet over them; the men stooped;
>   disentangled the body.
> He wiped his lips and hands. He strolled back to the
>   car, with discreet souvenirs for consolation and
>   philosophy.

The irony emerges. Boethius wrote his *De Consolatione Philosophiae* while imprisoned at Pavia. Still the tourist of the previous poem, the man visits Pavia with the conscious, formal intention of commiserating with Boethius' obscene death, and of wondering at the man who could console himself with philosophy at such a stage in his life. He wills himself to imagine the philosopher tortured, perhaps out of a dutiful compunction, but finds that, secretly, a part of him relishes the scene. "He wiped his lips and his hands". Both relish and guilt are here. The souvenirs are discreet because secret. He practises his enjoyment on no man's flesh. Yet there is a sense in which he is guilty, certainly, of unclean thoughts. The contrast between the cerebral and touristic appreciation of philosophy, and the voyeur's appreciation of cruelty, is notable. Rather, he is not only voyeur, but, in his relish, participator. "Flesh leaked rennet over them" is horrifying; the blood curdles under the extremity of the suffering; the blood is said to leak, uncontrollably, as if itself incontinent. The wracked body becomes truly pitiful. The buckles restrain the victim, and perhaps muffle his cries; they also choke. What is remarkable here, however, is that the scene and its relishing are admitted to. Admitted to, but hardly confessed. It is not so much a release from guilt as a judgement on the thought and its stimulation. And this judgement is as valid for the tourist as for the king:

> I have learned one thing: not to look down
> So much upon the damned[30]

One should be careful to avoid the impression that there is relish in Hill's re-creation of cruelty. The pity is not punctured carelessly over the Hymns, is some kind of reward to the reader, but it is present, and, in particular, in the finely intimate and tender No. 25:

> I speak this in memory of my grandmother, whose
> childhood and prime womanhood were spent in the
> nailer's darg.

And

> It is one
> thing to celebrate the "quick forge", another
> to cradle a face hare-lipped by the searing wire.

The insight is crucial to the tender pity. It is one thing to celebrate the dignity of labour, another to endure it in one's first maturity, especially when the work itself has caused the mutilation. Even the sound of the phrase "nailer's darg", the phrase isolated on a line of its own and following a rather rapid syllabic flow—the long-drawn vowel of "darg" expresses the reductive nature of the experience. The poem does not indulge in melancholy. It consistently touches on the harshness of the experience. The man is said to "brood" on Ruskin's text concerning labour. Ruskin's letter, which begins with reflections on a Worcestershire nail factory, is concerned with the immorality and hypocrisy of usury. Hill is suggesting, I imagine, that his grandmother's labour, with that of others, borrows money from her employer, and his profit on that represents his interest.

One has to finish. Offa dies and one is left with not so much the figure of a man, but an area, changing, and filled, on balance, with more distress than comfort, and "presided over" by a ruler and an ethos more cruel, more harsh, than severely just. Capricious, light, but capable of some consistent authority. One may feel that the work as a whole is perhaps too inconclusive. On the other hand, as Lawrence abjured the novelist, Hill finally refuses to tip the balance by putting his own thumb on the scales. He is concerned with how things are (and an evaluation of that), not firstly upon how they ought to be; although that perhaps also emerges.

Number 27 is not the last of the Hymns but I should like to indicate its diverse elements, and to suggest how the entire set of poems, as they draw to their end, contrive to echo their diversity within this one poem. At the funeral of King Offa an absurd composition of mourners, from all ages, attends:

> He was defunct. They were perfunctory.

The contrast is not only between the finality of death and the continuity of the living. There is an absurdity contingent on death, but this is not entirely it either. The comic element here mediates between the two and both eases and recognises the sharpness of the dividing line. Additionally, as Hill suggests, the more public and dignified the man who has died, the more absurd the situation, and the more susceptible to hypocrisy, since those intimate, mourning connections, do not, properly, exist. The pun joins the living recognitions with the dead man, only to distinguish finally, and for good. Then follows a last stanza of extraordinary beauty, in which nature mirrors the uprooting of the man. But even in the largeness of the event, death is seen to touch every creature. It is the leveller:

> Earth lay for a while, the ghost-bride of livid
> Thor, butcher of strawberries, and the shire-tree
> dripped red in the arena of its uprooting.

"Butcher of strawberries" carries the right amount of pathos. The innocent fruits are remarked on.

Notes

1. A. Alvarez, "Sylvia Plath: A Memoir" in *New American Review* 12, New York, 1971, pp. 26–27.
2. *For the Unfallen*, London, 1959; also Nos. 3, 11.
3. *King Log*, London, 1968.
4. *King Log*.
5. "September Song" (*King Log*).
6. See also No. 5 of "Funeral Music", a variation of this idea.
7. Michael Hamburger, *Reason and Energy*, London, 1957, pp. 219–22.
8. "Three Baroque Meditations" (2) (*King Log*).
9. "Locust Songs" (3) (*King Log*).
10. "Domaine Public" (*King Log*).
11. "Funeral Music" (2) (*King Log*).
12. "Dr. Faustus" (I) (*For the Unfallen*).
13. From *King Log*.
14. "Funeral Music" (2) (*King Log*).
15. "Men are a Mockery of Angels" (*King Log*).
16. No. 27 (*Mercian Hymns*).
17. Herbert Read, *Collected Poems*.
18. Herbert Read, *The Contrary Experience*, London, 1963, p. 176.
19. "Funeral Music" (8) (*King Log*).
20. "Funeral Music" (7) (*King Log*).
21. "Funeral Music" (3) (*King Log*).
22. "The Songbook of Sebastian Arrurruz" (1) (*King Log*).
23. "The Songbook" (2) (*King Log*).
24. "The Songbook" (5) (*King Log*).
25. "The Songbook" (9) (*King Log*).
26. "The Songbook" (II) (*King Log*).
27. *Mercian, Hymns* (1) London, 1971.
28. Edited by Frederick Brittain, *The Penguin Book of Latin Verse*, Harmondsworth, 1962, pp. xvi–xvii.
29. R. W. Chambers, *Beowulf: An Introduction*, Cambridge, 1932, see pp. 31–40.
30. "Ovid in the Third Reich" (*King Log*).

GEOFFREY THURLEY
From "The Legacy of Auden"
The Ironic Harvest
1974, pp. 154–57

Working on a smaller and smaller canvas, Geoffrey Hill has striven more rigorously and with more success than any of his contemporaries to realize the Empsonian ideal of a poetry of maximal, directed ambiguity. No poet of his time, on either side of the Atlantic, shows a more profound grasp of the working principles of the English language.[1] Moreover, the technical know-how is always mated with a stern seriousness, an impatience with any but the most ultimate and fundamental themes. Once more we note in English poetry of the middle twentieth century the same complex confusion of traditions: the emphasis upon irony here receives its strongest support, but informing it are the characteristically English modesty and sobriety. In some ways, in fact, Hill's poetry consummates the intellectualist tradition. Consummates, unfortunately, is quite the wrong word, with its associations of achieved release and fulfilment, not to say abandon. What Hill proves in the end is that the Empsonian obsession with consciously exploited ambiguity is ultimately stultifying: he succeeds in making room for the ambiguities at the expense of expression, so that for all the grandeur of his themes, he is like an expert with nothing to say. The verbal harmonies seem tendentiously 'accurate': 'fountains / Salt the sparse Haze' and the same poem has

> idyllic death
> Where fish at dawn ignite the powdery lake.

'Ignite', like 'salt' in the earlier example, is a typical piece of visual accuracy; but equally, both verbs are intended to hold resonance corresponding to and derived from the poem's theme announced in the title—'To the (supposed) Patron', and initiated in the first word, ('Prodigal'). The diction tells us throughout that the patron is the Man from Christ's parables and the puns and ambiguities re-enact the Rich Man's mortality. Thus, the Great Common-place enacted within the poem—the Rich Patron has to die no matter how suavely his wealth beguiles the fact into unconsciousness—invests the visually accurate verb, 'salt'—with its preservative significance, and at the end, the fish 'ignite', not only as their evanescent flashing suggests fire, to the eye, but as their fire suggests Life (though spuriously—this is the poem's irony) to the mind. The *mot juste* receives the support of the theme and works on two layers. This remorseless application of the Empsonian pun runs riot through Hill's otherwise sedate pages: the dead 'maintain their ground'; some are 'not past conceiving but past care'. The Shakespearean flavour of the latter example gives us the clue to Hill's derivation: Hill elaborates the weakness for a pun Johnson observed in Shakespeare into a poetic methodology. His should be—from the Empsonian point of view—the ideal poetry: it is all significance, every verb conceals its double meaning, and inserts its knife as the reader passes. If there is no absolute ambiguity of this kind, the verbs and adjectives are at least carefully precise: the 'dulled wood' of Christ's cross 'spat' blood on the stones. The salmon in 'Genesis' 'muscle', and the air contains 'wads' of sound. The expertise is considerable. So is that of the versification. Hill has studied carefully for example the art of exploiting the line-end to throw ironic or ambiguous emphasis onto particular words. Verb or adjective placed at the end of the line receives the weight and shadow of rhyme, yet always stands in danger of having its meaning or even its grammatical status altered by the following line:

> each deed
> Resurrecting those best dead
> Priests, soldiers and kings;

'dead' is first noun, then adjective qualifying 'priests, soldiers and kings'. We are forced to change our view of these dead: first they are the 'best' (of the dead), then quite the contrary, those who are best *when* dead. Fifty years ago Ezra Pound castigated the Georgians for concentrating on 'loveliness', on 'poetry', instead of keeping their eyes on the facts, and letting the poetry come in the back way, as it should: '. . . attempts to be poetic in some manner or other defeat their own end; whereas an intentness on the quality of the emotion to be conveyed makes for poetry.'[2]

Geoffrey Hill loads his poems with 'significance' rather as the Georgians loaded theirs with the 'poetic', with the result that poetry, and with it significance, often escapes him. A majority of his poems are about death. He writes epitaphs, some of them very fine. The lines for Osip Mandelstam, for example, move and are moved:

> And again I am too late. There go
> The salutes, dust-clouds and brazen cries.
> Images rear from desolation
> like ruins across a plain. . . .
> A few men glare at their hands, others
> Grovel for food in the roadside field.

This is subtle and fine, with no distracting pun under the stone.[3] The poem holds onto that grief Hill so often allows to slip between his too clenched fingers. In poetry, significance should accrue from the feeling; in Hill, the poetry exists for the 'significances'. These significances plate and coat the surface of verse concerned mostly with the great commonplace of Death. A stiff morbidity is conveyed, and no one knows more about the English language's stock of double meanings. Yet the final impression is of a man who chose his themes, or allowed them to be chosen for him, in the absence of any very compelling response to life of his own. 'Life' is precisely what Hill's poetry lacks. For life he substitutes gesture:

> But we are commanded
> To rise, when, in silence,
> I would compose my voice.

Literary attitudes of this kind are not to be struck after the fact: they should arise out of natural grief and what seems to the poet

an invisible and obvious mode of expression, which for some quality of emotion, crystallizes into the 'classic'.

The title of one of Hill's volumes, *For the Unfallen*, parallels that of one of Larkin's: *The Less Deceived*. For Hill, the living are merely those not yet dead, the Unfallen, for whom even now we ought to be composing epitaphs. For Larkin one can hope for nothing more than to be less deceived, less of a fool, than the others—the hearties, the bullies, the rulers, and the ruled. Both attitudes cohere within the ironist academy. Neither of the poets appears to have been shaped by Leavis, yet their acceptance of either defeat of the pyrrhic victory of self-awareness, does, I think, reflect his indirect influence.

Notes

1. Theodore Roethke comes, perhaps, closest to Hill.
2. Ezra Pound, *Make It New* (London, 1934), p. 162.
3. There is one, of course, on 'brazen'.

C. H. SISSON
"Geoffrey Hill"

Agenda, Autumn 1975, pp. 23–28

It is with some diffidence that I write about a poet eighteen years my junior. One's seniors one can take or leave. The road they have gone—or part of it—still stretches before one; they are on the way to being assimilated by the dead, who have seen it all, and by whom the overwhelming body of literature has been written. With one's juniors who do anything new—the only ones who are interesting—it is part of the scene one has missed that they are writing about. Because one has passed that way and not noticed, one is inclined in self-defence to say: It is not like that! But it may be, and one is helpless to judge.

In the case of Geoffrey Hill, I have to calculate: He was born in 1932, when I was already an undergraduate. When I was setting my eyes on Hitler and Goering, he was between two and three; when the war broke out, he was at seven, 'the age of reason; it ended as he entered upon the age of puberty. When he was twenty and published his first pamphlet of poems (with the Fantasy Press, 1952), I was about to write (though not to publish) *Christopher Homm*, which signified a pretension to view the whole of life, backwards and forwards. But Hill was already writing:

> By blood we live, the hot, the cold,
> To ravage and redeem the world:
> There is no bloodless myth will hold

—the last line a curiously Yeatsian statement of a Christian theme at which I was just belatedly arriving.

There are, however, about the approach to Hill's work, difficulties which are not age-bound and which, presumably, must be felt by some of his contemporaries and juniors. One such difficulty is—unless one should say, as one might of any writer who achieves his own distinction, *all* of them are—rooted in Hill's peculiar cast of mind. Here I would differentiate—though the difference is merely a help to getting on with my subject and has a very uncertain degree of validity—between the cast of mind which emerges in the poems and that of which we may have other evidences, particularly in the author's discursive writing. A recent, extremely interesting exhibition of the latter is the lecture on T. H. Green published in *Poetry Nation No. 4*. There is, in the first place, the characteristic, which it would be wrong to attribute solely to the nature of the subject-matter, or the academic milieu in which it was delivered, of an extreme meticulousness, what looks like a fear that some author quoted might be slightly misrepresented, or some idea picked up in the course of reading not precisely attributed. I have known similar manifestations in the transaction of business—which is hardly advanced by them; I remember a charming and intelligent civil servant who could hardly bring himself to give the general sense of an enactment, or of any provision in it, for fear that some shade of meaning might be lost, and so had recourse to quoting immense chunks from the depths of a fabulous memory. The effect is not the same in a piece of writing which does not aim at an immediate practical outcome, and it is a proper objective for philosophers and scholars to try to clear a little tidy space, here and there—if only temporarily—among the muddle of our terminologies. What is appropriate is a matter of context, and one can, for example, sympathise with the general sense of what Hill says in his essay in the special issue of *Agenda* on Rhythm (Vol. 10 No. 4—Vol. 11 No. 1) without thinking that John Stuart Mill had not got a point when he said that 'a certain laxity in the use of language must be borne with, if a writer makes himself understood', or that there is not a place, in the vast variety of human communication, for some of the looser forms of discursive writing from which Hill, being the man he is, quite properly shrinks.

Hill is fond of quoting Coleridge and one can see that he is, from one point of view, a natural follower of the author of those awesome *Note-Books*. He praises T. H. Green for demonstrating 'the pitch of attention at which the true (as apposed to the spectral) Coleridgean "clerisy" might be expected to work"; and it is apparently some sort of 'clerisy' he is addressing in his own discursive writings. What has all this to do with the poems? Something, for no-one tears himself apart entirely into prose and verse, but the connection is indirect. A case worth thinking about in this context is that of Valéry; one reason why he filled his *Cahiers* with such repetitive refinements must have been that he could not sleep in the morning.

If the fastidiousness which is evident in Hill's discursive writing has a part in determining the kind of poetry he writes, it is a relatively superficial part. For a man who published his first pamphlet at the age of twenty, and who is now forty-three, he has troubled the world with a very small bulk of poetry, and it can be said that there is nothing in his three volumes—*For the Unfallen* (1959), *King Log* (1968) and *Mercian Hymns* (1971)—which does not deserve close attention. The earliest surviving poems date from 1952. One of these, 'Holy Thursday', may I suppose be taken as confronting youthful experience as nakedly as any young poet might do:

> Naked, he climbed to the wolf's lair;
> He beheld Eden without fear,
> Finding no ambush offered there
> But sleep under the harbouring fur.

There is no trace of overwhelming; whatever the young man suffered, the *poet* holds the emotions in a perfect balance; a comparable case, in an earlier generation, is David Gascoyne. It is as if the shock of experience were received into a great volume of water, so that the surface trembling is no more than indicative. The fourth and last stanza of the poem reads:

> I have been touched with that fire,
> And have fronted the she-wolf's lair.
> Lo, she lies gentle and innocent of desire
> Who was my constant myth and terror.

There is already the—less visionary—maturity of the 'Coplas' in *King Log*:

> What other men do with other women
> Is for me neither orgy nor sacrament
> Nor a language of foreign candour

> But is mere occasion or chance distance
> Out of which you might move and speak my name
> As I speak yours

—which, like 'Holy Thursday', has a delicacy not to be taken for granted in the twentieth century. It is clear from the dating of the poems in *For the Unfallen* that the movement at this period is already away from the merely personal—and indeed even the poems of 1952 are too profoundly apprehended to be so described, for beyond a certain depth a common element appears. But the mode of presentation moves decisively towards myth, as later towards history—in both cases, as I read the poems, as towards repositories of the common experience which gives meaning to what we feel as individuals.

The centre-piece of *King Log* is perhaps 'Funeral Music', a sequence of unrhymed sonnets—or at any rate poems of fourteen lines—with allusion to the Wars of the Roses. In the essay appended to the volume Hill says that in this sequence he was 'attempting a florid grim music broken by grunts and shrieks', and he refers to a description of Eltham Palace, 'a perfect example of the ornate heartlessness of much mid-fifteenth century architecture', as 'pertinent'. I find these explanations curious, and perhaps see them as more significant than they are. They seem to imply a notion of the sequence as artifact, as something worked towards and built, which suggests a growing distance between the poetic impulse and the words which finally appear on the page—a gain in architectonics, perhaps, but at a price which is so often paid, by all but the greatest writers, in a loss of immediacy. This is no more than a suspicion of what—as I see it—would be an unfortunate direction. In fact 'Funeral Music' bristles with lines and phrases of indubitable directness:

> I made no sound, but once
> I stiffened as though a remote cry
> Had heralded my name.

Or

> Let mind be more precious than soul; it will not
> Endure

—which rings with a vibration which stretches from the deepest unspoken needs to the world of rational theological discourse.

The *Mercian Hymns* is in a manner the most accessible of Hill's books. I confess to a certain unhappiness about the prose poem in English. Hill had already attempted the *genre* in *King Log*, though the example there given—polished as one would expect from so accomplished a writer—is slight as compared with the chain of thirty poems which make up the *Hymns*. I suppose the classification of this work as 'prose' might be disputed, as one may dispute the point at which verse begins in the writings of David Jones; but the publisher and presumably the author accept this classification. Is the choice of prose a mark of growing deliberation and a gap between the conception and the performance? However that may be, the performance is indubitably poetic in its evocations and particularly in the freedom of the imagination under the polished surface. This is a world of metamorphoses, where Offa king of Mercia assumes a variety of shapes, with a life stretching over twelve centuries. As if to do penance for these excesses, the true prose author in Hill—a careful fact-finder and discourser—adds a series of notes which could claim a place beside those of Eliot on the *Waste Land*. The 'I believe I should acknowledge the sources' evidently comes from a depth of scruple which, besides producing such near-comedy as a page-reference to a book on coins to justify the inscription Offa Rex, watches over the whole of Hill's work, so that one feels as one reads it in the presence of a mind of extraordinary justness. A sense of this broods over the *Mercian Hymns*. The author holds in a steady gaze not only a series of complicated perspectives between past and present, but between public and private life. There is none of the special pleading which, for some, appears to disfigure the play of past and present in the work of David Jones. On the other hand, there is none of the splash of common life which gives movement to the interplay of past and present in Auden's early work—and surely one of his best—'Paid on Both Sides.'

The impressive series of—this time rhymed—sonnets, 'Lachrimae', which appeared in the Fifteenth Anniversary special issue of *Agenda*, is of very great interest as indicating another mode for this singularly direct mind which, none the less, seems impelled to seek indirect utterance. The 'seven tears shed in seven passionate Pavans' are shed with the aid of sources which include Dowland, Quevedo and Lope de Vega. The sub-title itself—chosen not invented, for it is from Dowland—has something of the baroque about it. There is in Hill a touch of the fastidiousness of Crashaw, which is that of a mind in search of artifices to protect itself against its own passions. Hill is perhaps the only contemporary poet in English to feel such an impulse, and this is an indication of his potentialities. Beside the 'Lachrimae' may be set 'Ad Incensum Lucernae', the text of a cantata by James Brown which was performed in Leeds in February, 1975. Hill wrote the words 'between October 1973 and February 1974, though some minor changes were made at a latter date'. Here Wordsworth, Giordano Bruno and Prudentius are summoned to bring grist to the mill—a phrase or a line or a sonnet for 'free translation'. John Attey comes, and sounds like a thrush in a library.

> 'Sweet was the song the Virgin sung
> When she to Bethlehem was come'.

Hill goes on, after Hildebert, 'c. 1100'—

> Our nature's ransom with the young
> Child and the ageless Seraphim.

Attey himself followed with—

> And was delivered of her Son,
> That blessed Jesus hath to name

—beside which Hill's lines look neither better nor worse than a bit of hymn-writing by J. M. Neale. Admittedly it is a hard test to set one's words beside the sung speech of the early seventeenth century. But one can ask, more generally, whether Hill's craving for a multiplicity of allusions, and his scholarly meticulousness in pointing to sources, may not as well hinder as help the kind of precision which is poetry. Yet it is a release which Hill appears to be seeking, turn where he will, and what puts him among the few contemporary writers who really matter is that the release he is seeking is not merely technical—though it is that—and not primarily his own—though it is that too.

HAROLD BLOOM
"Geoffrey Hill: The Survival of Strong Poetry"
Figures of Capable Imagination
1976, pp. 234–46

Strong poetry is always difficult, and Geoffrey Hill is the strongest British poet now alive, though his reputation in the English-speaking world is somewhat less advanced than that of several of his contemporaries. He should be read and studied for many generations after they have blent together, just as he should survive all but a handful (or fewer) of American poets now active. Such canonic prophecy is founded on the authority of his best work, as I have experienced it in the fifteen years since the publication of *For the Unfallen*, his first book. From his first poem, appropriately "Genesis," on through the *Mercian Hymns*, Hill has been the most Blakean of modern poets. But this is deep or true influence, or Blake's Mental Warfare, rather than the easy transmission of image, idea, diction and metric that superficially is judged to be poetic influence. The merely extrinsic influences on Hill's early verse are mostly American; I can detect the fierce rhetoric of Allen Tate, and the visionary intensities of Richard Eberhart, in some places. Yet the true precursor is always Blake, and the War in Heaven that the strong poet must conduct is fought by Hill against Blake, and against Blake's tradition, and so against Hill himself.

As a war of poetry against poetry, Hill's work testifies to the repressive power of tradition, but also to an immensely individual and deeply moving moral protest against tradition. Like the hero he celebrates in his masterpiece, the *Mercian Hymns*, Hill is a martyrologist. His subject is human pain, the suffering of those who both do and sustain violence, and more exactly the daemonic relationship between cultural tradition and human pain. Confronted by Hill's best poems, a reader is at first tempted to turn away, for the intellectual difficulty of the rugged, compressed verse is more than matched by the emotional painfulness and directness of Hill's vision. Hill does not comfort nor console, and offers no dialectic of gain through loss. His subject, like his style, is difficulty; the difficulty of apprehending and accepting moral guilt, and the difficulty of being a poet when the burden of history, including poetic history, makes any prophetic stance inauthentic. In more than twenty years of writing, Hill has given us three very slim volumes, not because his gift is sparse, but because he is too scrupulous to have allowed himself a less organized or less weighted utterance. There are no bad poems in Hill's three books, and so much is demanded of the reader, in concentration and in the dignity of a desperate humanism, that more productive poets are likely to seem too indulgent, by comparison. Hill does not indulge his reader, or himself, and just this remorseless concentration is Hill's assured greatness. The reader who persists will learn to read not only Hill, but other difficult and wholly indispensable poets as well, for only a poet as strong as Hill compels each of us to test his own strength as a reader, and so to test and clarify also our own relation to tradition.

Tradition, Freud surmised, was the cultural equivalent of repressed material in the consciousness of the individual. The role of repression in poetry was misunderstood by Freud and has been misunderstood by most of his followers. Freud thought that sublimation was the psychic defense that *worked*, whether in life or in literature, while repression invariably failed, since repression augmented the unconscious. But poetry *is* figurative language, and in poetry sublimation is accomplished through the self-limiting trope of metaphor, while repression is represented by the expansive trope of hyperbole, with all of its Sublime glories and Grotesque dangers. From the viewpoint of poetry, the "unconscious mind" is an oxymoron, since repressed material in poetry has no place to go but up, onto the heights of what Romanticism called the Imagination. Romantic Imagination, whether in Blake or Coleridge, does not represent a return of the repressed, but is identical with the process of repression itself.

An individual poetic imagination can defend itself against the force of another imagination only by troping, so that a successful defense against poetic tradition always answers repression by an increase in repression. The return of the repressed is only an utopian or apocalyptic dream much indulged in by Marxist speculation, and by assorted contemporary shamans who inspire what is still being termed a counterculture. Authentic poets show us that Emersonian Compensation is always at work in poetry as in life: nothing is got for nothing. What returns in authentic poetry is never the repressed, but rather the daemonic or uncanny element within repression, which poetic tradition has called by various names, including the Sublime, and the Imagination, both of them hyperbolical figurations for something that has no referential aspect or literal meaning, but that nevertheless guarantees the survival and continuity of poetic tradition. Poets and readers go on questing for one another in order to give a voice to this daemonic impulse that informs and purifies repression. "Purifies" here has no moral or spiritual meaning but refers rather to a process by which the daemonic is reconciled with the writing of poetry.

"Daemonic," in this sense, refers to a realm of power that invades the human world yet seems apart from human origins or human ends. In a very early poem, a visionary lyric in the mode of Eberhart, but like Eberhart reaching back to Blake's "Tyger," Hill laments the inadequacy of poetic language to tell his own experience of daemonic influx:

> I waited for the word that was not given,
>
> Pent up into a region of pure force,
> Made subject to the pressure of the stars;
> I saw the angels lifted like pale straws;
> I could not stand before those winnowing eyes
> And fell, until I found the world again.

Hill dislikes his early poems, yet they are not only permanent achievements but also quite essential for understanding all that comes after. "Genesis," for which he has a particular dislike, is superb in itself, a perfect "first" poem, and also a clear intimation of his largest debt to Blake's vision, which is the conviction that the Creation and the Fall were the same event. Another fine early poem, "In Memory of Jane Fraser" (which Hill evidently dislikes most, of all his work), speaks of a single, particular death as uncreating all of nature. For Hill, the natural world is, at best, "a stunned repose," a judgment that allies him to Blake rather than to Wordsworth, Shelley rather than to Keats. Hill's poem on the death of Shelley emphasizes the survival of the animal world, even as Shelley, the Modern Poet proper, or New Perseus, quests aimlessly, "clogged sword, clear, aimless mirror—/With nothing to strike at or blind/in the frothed shallows."

The themes and procedures of both Hill's books of short poems are summed up in what I judge to be his best single poem, the double-sonnet called "Annunciations." Though Hill transcends his own earlier mode in *Mercian Hymns* (as will be seen), "Annunciations" is so important a poem that I will discuss it at some length. A reader who can interpret "Annunciations" can learn to interpret the rest of Hill, and also acquire many insights that will aid in reading any truly difficult poetry of the Post-Romantic tradition. For, in "Annunciations," Hill wrote what later tradition may judge to have been the central shorter poem of his own generation, a poem that is itself a despairing poetics, and a total vision both of natural existence, and of the necessary limitations of what we have learned to call imagination.

An "annunciation" can be any proclamation, but despite Hill's plural title, the reverberation here depends upon the Annunciation proper, the announcement of the Incarnation by the Angel Gabriel in Luke 1:26–38. In some grim sense, Hill's starting-point is the festival (25 March) celebrating Gabriel's announcement. But "the Word" here is not the Logos, nor simply the words of poetry, all poetry, but the idealization of poetry that is so pervasive in Western tradition:

> The Word has been abroad; is back, with a tanned
>   look
> From its subsistence in the stiffening-mire.
> Cleansing has become killing, the reward
> More touchable, overt, clean to the touch.

This Word seems more a tourist than an Eliotic explorer; indeed a hygienic tourist-hunter. Returned, the questers sit together at a literary feast with their scholarly and critical admirers:

> Now, at a distance from the steam of beasts,
> The loathly neckings and fat shook spawn
> (Each specimen-jar fed with delicate spawn)
> The searchers with the curers sit at meat
> And are satisfied.

I do not know how to interpret this except as an attack upon everyone who has to do with poetry: poets, critics, teachers, students, readers. It is as though Yeats, after observing in vision his nymphs and satyrs copulating in the foam, his Innocents re-living their pain and having their wounds opened again, then attended a banquet in honor of his "News for the Delphic Oracle." The poem becomes a "specimen-jar," holding an aesthetic reduction of copulation and bleeding wounds. Is such an attack as Hill's legitimate, since it would apply as much to Homer as to any other poet? Is Hill attacking a false idealization of poetry or the *Ananke* that governs all poetry? The remainder of the first part of "Annunciations" will not answer these questions:

> Such precious things put down
> And the flesh eased through turbulence, the soul
> Purples itself; each eye squats full and mild
> While all who attend to fiddle or to harp
> For betterment, flavour their decent mouths
> With gobbets of the sweetest sacrifice.

Primarily this is Hill's uncompromising attack upon himself, for more even than Yeats, or even his contemporary Ted Hughes, he writes a poetry whose subject is violence and pain, thus accepting the danger of easing the flesh through a vision of turbulence. Much of the success with readers, particularly British readers, of the later Yeats and of Hughes is surely based upon feeding the reader's eye with imaginary lust and suffering until that eye "squats full and mild." Hill's attack upon "all who attend to fiddle or to harp/For betterment" is therefore an attack upon the most traditional, Aristotelian defense of poetry, an attack upon the supposed function of catharsis. Poems are "gobbets of the sweetest sacrifice," and readers flavor their mouths decently even as decent Christians swallow the bread of communion. It becomes clear that Hill is attacking, ultimately, neither poetry nor religion, but the inescapable element that always darkens tradition, which is that the living, feeding upon the repressions of the dead, repress further and so become the sustenance of the dead. Hill's "sacrifice" is what Nietzsche and Freud would have termed an Antithetical Primal Word, for it is debatable whether the victims commemorated by the poem, or the readers, are the "sacrifice."

The Antithetical Primal Word of the second part of "Annunciations" is of course "love," and here the majestic bitterness of the Sublime triumphs in and over Hill:

> O Love, subject of the mere diurnal grind,
> Forever being pledged to be redeemed,
> Expose yourself for charity; be assured
> The body is but husk and excrement.
> Enter these deaths according to the law,
> O visited women, possessed sons! Foreign lusts
> Infringe our restraints; the changeable

Soldiery have their goings-out and comings-in
Dying in abundance. Choicest beasts
Suffuse the gutters with their colourful blood.
Our God scatters corruption. Priests, martyrs,
Parade to this imperious theme: 'O Love,
You know what pains succeed; be vigilant; strive
To recognize the damned among your friends.'

If I could cite only one stanza by Hill as being wholly representative of him, it would be this, for here is his power, his despair and (in spite of himself) his Word, not in the sense of Logos but in the Hebraic sense of *davhar*, a word that is also an act, a bringing-forward of something previously held back in the self. This Word that rejects being a Word is a knowing misprision or mis-taking of tradition, but even the most revisionary of Words remains a Word, as Hill doubtless knows. Being willing to go on writing poems, however sparsely, is to believe that one possesses a Word of one's own to bring forward. When Hill says, "Our God scatters corruption," he means that the God of lovers (and of poets) is antithetical to Himself, that this God is the ambivalent deity of all Gnostics. I take it that "scatters" does not mean "drives away" but rather "increases" corruption by dispersal, which implies that "corruption" takes something of its root-meaning of "broken-to-pieces." Hill's subject then is the Gnostic or Kabbalistic "Breaking of the Vessels," the Fall that is simultaneously a Creation, as in his first, Blakean, chant-poem "Genesis."

Part II of "Annunciations" is thus more of a proclamation against Love than a prayer to Love. Love, addressed under its aspect of repetition, is urged to more honesty, and to a reductive awareness of the body. Corporeal passion lives and dies according to the old dispensation, or law, but Hill comes to proclaim a new Incarnation, which is only a Gnostic dying into yet more sexual abundance. As an incessant martyrologist, Hill grimly announces the imperious as against the imperial or Shakespearean theme. Love, who knows that pains only succeed or follow one another (but are never successful), is urged at least to distinguish its true martyrs among the panoply of its worshippers, and so recognize accurately its valid theme.

Repeated readings of "Annunciations" should clarify and justify Hill's densely impacted style, with its reliance upon figurations of hyperbole. Hill's mode is a negative or counter-Sublime, and his characteristic defense against the tradition he beautifully sustains and extends is an almost primal repression:

Not as we are but as we must appear,
Contractual ghosts of pity; not as we
Desire life but as they would have us live,
Set apart in timeless colloquy:
So it is required; so we bear witness,
Despite ourselves, to what is beyond us,
Each distant sphere of harmony forever
Poised, unanswerable

This is again a Gnostic sublimity. Blake could still insist that pity survived only because we kept on rendering others piteous, but Hill comes later, and for him the intoxication of belatedness is to know that our reality and our desire are both negated by our appearance as legatees. It is tradition that makes us into "contractual ghosts of pity." A Beautiful Necessity represses us, and makes us bear witness to a dead but still powerful transcendence. Hill characterizes one of his sequences as "a florid grim music" or an "ornate and heartless music punctuated by mutterings, blasphemies and cries for help." A baroque pathos seems to be Hill's goal, with the ornateness his tribute to tradition, and the punctuation of pathos his outcry against tradition. Hill's is clearly a poetics of pain, in which all the calamities of history become so many

poetic salutes, so many baroque meditations, always trapped in a single repetition of realization. Man is trapped "between the stones and the void," without majesty and without justice except for the errors of rhetoric, the illusions of poetic language. Like his own Sebastian Arrurruz, Hill's task is "to find value/In a bleak skill," the poet's craft of establishing true rather than false "sequences of pain."

"It must give pleasure," Stevens rightly insisted, and any critic responding to Hill should be prepared to say how and why Hill's poetry can give pleasure, and in what sense Hill's reader can defend himself from being only another decent mouth opened wide for the poetry-banquet. How is the reader to evade becoming "the (supposed) Patron" so bitterly invoked in the final poem of Hill's first book? The Gnostic answer, which is always a latecomer's answer, is that the reader must become not a patron but one of those unfallen who gave Hill's first book its title:

For the unfallen—the firstborn, or wise
Councillor—prepared vistas extend
As far as harvest; and idyllic death
Where fish at dawn ignite the powdery lake.

The final trope here is perhaps too Yeatsian, but the previous trope that gives back priority to the unfallen has a more High Romantic tenor, looking back to Keats' vision of Autumn. Hill cannot celebrate natural completion, but he always finds himself turning again "to flesh and blood and the blood's pain" despite his Gnostic desire to renounce for good "this fierce and unregenerate clay." Of his incessant ambivalence, Hill has made a strong poetry, one that battles tradition on tradition's own terms, and that attempts to make of its conscious belatedness an earliness. The accomplished reader responds to Hill's work as to any really strong poetry, for the reader too needs to put off his own belatedness, which is surely why we go on searching for strong poetry. We cannot live with tradition, and we cannot live without it, and so we turn to the strong poet to see how he acts out this ambivalence for us, and to see also if he can get beyond such ambivalence.

Hill begins to break through his own dialectics of tradition in *Mercian Hymns*, the sequence of prose-poems he published on the threshold of turning forty. His hero is Offa, an eighth century Midlands "king," who merges both into a spirit of place and into the poet celebrating him, particularly the poet-as-schoolboy, for *Mercian Hymns* is a kind of *Prelude*-in-little. Yet here the growth of a poet's mind is not stimulated by nature's teachings, but only by history and by dreams. Transcendence, for Hill, returned or re-entered the sublunary world in old tapestries, sculpture, and metal-work, but mostly in historicizing reverie, which is the substance of these hymns. With *Mercian Hymns*, Hill rather triumphantly "makes it new," and though the obsession with tradition is as strong, much of the ambivalence towards tradition is miraculously diminished. Indeed, certain passages in *Mercian Hymns* would approach sentimentality if the poet did not remain characteristically condensed and gnomic, with the familiar spectre of pain hovering uncannily close:

We have a kitchen-garden riddled with toy-shards,
with splinters of habitation. The children shriek
and scavenge, play havoc. They incinerate boxes,
rags and old tyres. They haul a sodden log, hung
with soft shields of fungus, and launch it upon
the flames.

Difficult as Hill was earlier, *Mercian Hymns*, despite the limpidity of its individual sections, is the subtlest and most oblique of his works. It is not only hard to hold together, but there is some question as to what it is "about," though the necessary answer is akin to *The Prelude* again; Hill has at last no subject but his own complex subjectivity, and so the poem is "about" himself, which turns out to be his exchange of gifts with the Muse of History (section X). I suggest that the structure and meaning of *Mercian Hymns* is best approached through its rhetoric, which as before in Hill is largely that of metaleptic reversal or transumption, the dominant trope of Post-Romantic poetry in English. For a full analysis of the trope and its poetic history, I must refer to my book, *A Map of Misreading* and give only a brief account here. Transumption is the trope of a trope, or technically the metonymy of a metonymy. That is, it tends to be a figure that substitutes an aspect of a previous figure for that figure. Imagistically, transumption from Milton through the Romantics to the present tends to present itself in terms of earliness substituting for lateness, and more often than not to be the figure that concludes poems. Translated into psychoanalytic terms, transumption is either the psychic defense of introjection (identification) or of projection (refusal of identity), just as metaphor translates into the defense of sublimation, or hyperbole into that of repression. The advantage of transumption as a concluding trope for belated poems is that it achieves a kind of fresh priority or earliness, but always at the expense of the presentness of the present or living moment. Hill is as transumptive a poet, rhetorically, as Milton or Wordsworth or Wallace Stevens, and so he too is unable to celebrate a present joy.

There is no present time, indeed there is no self-presence in *Mercian Hymns*. Though Hill's own note on the sequence betrays some anxiety about what he calls anachronisms, the genius of his work excludes such anxiety. Nothing can be anachronistic when there is no present:

> King of the perennial holly-groves, the riven sandstone: overlord of the M5: architect of the historic rampart and ditch, the citadel at Tamworth, the summer hermitage in Holy Cross: guardian of the Welsh Bridge and the Iron Bridge: contractor to the desirable new estates: saltmaster: money-changer: commissioner for oaths: martyrologist: the friend of Charlemagne.

> 'I liked that,' said Offa, 'sing it again.'

It is not that Offa has returned to merge with the poet, or that Hill has gone back to Offa. Hill and Offa stand together in a figuration that has introjected the past and the future, while projecting the present. Hill's epigraph, from the neglected poet and essayist, C. H. Sisson, analogizes his own conduct as private person and Offa's conduct of government, in all aspects of conduct having to do with "object and justification." Hill's struggle, as person and as poet, is with the repressive power of tradition, with the anxieties of history. Offa is seen by Hill as "the starting-cry of a race," as the master of a Primal Scene of Instruction, an imposition of order that fixates subsequent repression in others, which means to start an inescapable tradition. By reconciling himself with Offa, Hill comes close to accepting the necessary violence of tradition that earlier had induced enormous ambivalences in his poetry.

This acceptance, still somber but no longer grim, produces the dominant tone of *Mercian Hymns*, which is a kind of Wordsworthian "sober coloring" or "still sad music of humanity." But the sequence's vision remains Blakean rather than Wordsworthian, for the world it pictures is still one in which Creation and Fall cannot be distinguished, and at the end Offa is fallen Adam or every man: "he left behind coins, for his lodging, and traces of red mud." The reader sees that each hymn is like the inscription on one of Offa's hammered coins, and that these coins are literally and figuratively the price of a

living tradition, its perpetual balance of Creation and Fall. Hill has succeeded, obliquely, in solving his aesthetic-moral problem as a poet, but the success is as equivocal and momentary as the pun on "succeed" in "Annunciations." Hill now knows better "what pains succeed," and his moving sequence helps his readers to the same knowledge.

No critical introduction to a poet only just past forty in age can hope to prophesy his future development. I have seen no poems written by Hill since *Mercian Hymns*, but would be surprised if he did not return to the tighter mode of *For the Unfallen* and *King Log*, though in a finer tone. His achievement to date, as gathered in his volume, seems to me to transcend the more copious work of his contemporary rivals: Hughes, Gunn, Kinsella, Tomlinson, Silkin. Good as they are, they lack poetic strength when compared with Hill. He has the persistence to go on wrestling with the mighty dead—Blake, Wordsworth, Shelley, Yeats—and to make of this ghostly struggle a fresh sublimity. He is indeed a poet of the Sublime, a mode wholly archaic yet always available to us again, provided a survivor of the old line comes to us:

> Against the burly air I strode,
> Where the tight ocean heaves its load,
> Crying the miracles of God.

JOHN BAYLEY
"A Retreat or Seclusion:
Tenebrae of Geoffrey Hill"
Agenda, Spring 1979, pp. 38–42

Stephen Spender once made a distinction between opaque and transparent style. It works for poetry up to a point, and a lot of the poets and critics have suggested or implied it. In poetry there is a kind of style, hit on by individual talents in various ways, which seems fitted and apt to provide a strikingly clear medium for looking into a life and a consciousness, at the poet himself, his personality and preoccupation, and past the poet at the world in general, at ourselves. This sense of looking through and into is a particular feature of the way Lowell writes, and Berryman too; indeed it is the more common manner of poets today—good poets. Specific instances: it is the way we see through into such a poem as MacNeice's "The Mixer", or Larkin's "Dockery and Son".

Geoffrey Hill is quite outside this tradition. Every word in his poems gives the impression of having been carefully blocked in, as if it were a brick fitted into a solid structure; perhaps taken out again, scraped and examined, sometimes replaced. We can feel the process where Yeats—equally laborious—said we should not.

> A line will take us hours maybe
> But if it do not seem, a minute's thought
> Our stitching and unstitching has been nought.

This is a poetry to admire the outside of. Is there an inside? It's hard to say, because the subjects are not the sort that require it; we enjoy the feel of them, like the shade and patina on walls. The danger with this sort of poetry is that it is the kind that looks like poetry, which need not mean that it is not the real thing, but is bound to raise a certain sort of doubt.

> Slowly my heron flies
> pierced by the blade
> mounting in slow pain
> strikes the air with its cries
> goes seeking the high rocks
> where no man can climb
> where the wild balsam stirs
> by the little stream

the rocks the high rocks
are brimming with flowers
there love grows and there love
rests and is saved.

That's clear enough of course, even pellucid, but it's not the
kind of clarity we enter into without first enquiring how it's
done. It is a section of *The Pentecost Castle*, a poem in fifteen
such sections, whose texture is graceful and mystic. But I
cannot myself feel it to be much more than that, nor the rather
similar poem that follows, "Lachrimae or Seven tears figured
in seven passionate Pavans". Here is the opening of the fifth,
"Pavana Dolorosa".

Loves I allow and passions I approve;
Ash-Wednesday feasts, ascetic opulence,
the wincing lute so real in its pretence,
itself a passion amorous of love.

Self-wounding martyrdom, what joys you have,
true-torn among this fictive consonance,
music's creation of the moveless dance,
the decreation to which we all must move.

With the best will in the world I cannot feel anything much
except the deftness with which it is made, the effectiveness of
its look. The first line is beautifully modified from Robert
Southwell's line in "Mary Magdalen's Funeral Tears"—
"Passions I allow and loves I approve". "Fictive consonance"
and "decreation" have very much the look of words that we
have seen before in poetry, too often too lately. They give the
mystic appearance but not any feeling of a true and passionate
substance. Religion—if one may express it by that bald word—
is surely not Geoffrey Hill's poetic forte: obscure and inacces-
sive as they were, the Mercians had more life in them than the
Hymns. As Peter Levi said—a memorable sentence—of that
collection:

It's like a tree with fruit and branches, perfectly alive,
but without leaves.

With the next sectioned poem, "An Apology for the
Revival of Christian Architecture in England", things get
much better. The word architecture is significant: once
Geoffrey Hill is dealing, as it were, not only with poetic bricks
but with real ones, he seems much more at home. Is he
perhaps a poet of church observance and church atmosphere
rather than a religious poet? Certainly his sense of place, or not
so much of place itself as of the suitable topographics of piety, is
where he here seems most at home. In "Fidelities" the repose
of nuns in their convent is wonderfully imagined.

The wooden wings of justice borne aloof,
we close our eyes to Anselm and lie calm.
All night the cisterns whisper in the roof.

A perfect High Anglican touch somehow. All Geoffrey Hill's
gift of quiet but very consciously achieved decoration is here at
the proper disposition of his subject. As his

Reverend Mother, breakfastless, could feast her
constraint on terracotta and alabaster

so we can feast on the delicate relish of these poems and feel
ourselves in

the rooms of cedar and soft-thudding baize,
tremulous boudoirs where the crystals kissed
in cabinets of amethyst and frost.

The properties are in a sense those of Betjeman, but
distanced, remote, quite devoid of the vulgar emotional
humanity with which the Poet Laureate endows objects and
constructs from the past. This air of seeing interesting and
beautiful objects from a great distance is probably Geoffrey
Hill's special thing, and up to a point it is very successful; but

the trouble is that we seem to be seeing the author from a great
distance too; he seems to be keeping us so far away because he
does not want us to see through into him; and our impression is
that there might not in fact be much to see. That is not a
weakness but it may be a limitation of a sort; though I feel with
a sentiment of respect that Hill is not the sort of poet who
would be in the least interested in our reactions to him
personally, as a poet, rather than to the quality of his poetry.
The quality of remoteness in the lines may come from that.

One of the best "Apologies", which are in Sonnet form, is
the three part "Short History of British India". Faded groups
and portraits and ramshackle touches of the picturesque are
seen as if through the sad clear tunnel of a small telescope.

With indifferent aim
unleash the rutting cannon at the walls
of forts and palaces; pollute the wells.
Impound the memoirs for their bankrupt shame,
fantasies of true destiny that kills
"under the sanction of the English name".
Be moved by faith, obedience without fault,
the flawless hubris of heroic guilt,
the grace of visitation; and be stirred
by all her god-quests, her idolatries,
in conclave of abiding injuries,
sated upon the stillness of the bride.

That last line is a summation of a kind that would be
remarkable in any poet—the hidden suggestion of the child-
bride, stiff in the repose of heavy ornament, accepting without
expression or question—but it is the kind of concentration in
distance which Hill is peculiarly master of. On the other hand
"fantasies of true destiny that kills" and "the flawless hubris of
heroic guilt" seem to me phrases whose self-possession dominates at the expense of true meaning. And this tendency to
decline the close-up of meaning, as it were, is perhaps a
limitation in Hill and a source of weakness, though it is
presumption in the critic to remark on what the poet is no
doubt well aware of in his own way. One could put it crudely,
though, by saying that distance in Hill is a way of giving to pure
aesthetics an air of the moral. The aesthetic is notably
successful in the short poem "Florentines"—a frieze of warriors
"their feuds forgotten, remembered, forgotten". . . "The
stricken faces damnable and serene". "'Christmas Trees'", a
crystalline nine lines on Bonhoeffer, may be even more of a
masterpiece, but the payoff is a little too carefully calculated to
be wholly moving.

Against wild reasons of the state
his words are quiet but not too quiet.
We hear too late or not too late.

They could only have been written, though, by a very talented
and original poet.

ANDREW WATERMAN
"The Poetry of Geoffrey Hill"
British Poetry since 1970
eds. Peter Jones and Michael Schmidt
1980, pp. 85–102

Although time finally sifts matters justly, meanwhile too
many poets slog on turning the stuff out, and since only
so many among all who 'want to write' have even that talent,
their books receive tepid passes from reviewers for whom it is all
much of a muchness, themselves prone to lapse from their
crucial responsibility to be alert for the poets and poems of truly

enduring value. In this inevitable context, it is reassuring that over the twenty years since *For the Unfallen*, 1959, and still imperfectly, the exceptional excellence of Geoffrey Hill's poetry has come to receive acknowledgement.

In his poem 'The Cave of Making', W. H. Auden observed

After all, it's rather a privilege
   amid the affluent traffic
to serve this unpopular art which cannot be turned
   into
   background noise for study
or hung as a status trophy by rising executives,
   cannot be 'done' like Venice
or abridged like Tolstoy, but stubbornly still insists
   upon
   being read or ignored.

Truth particularly apt to Hill's poetry. No poetry, as Wordsworth put it, should 'level down/For the sake of being generally understood,' or wrongly conscious of audience court fashionable expectations and so perish with them; but Hill's is extraordinarily uncompromising, has a wholly self-preoccupied air; the reader may wander among its compelling splendours, but hardly feels invited or directly addressed. It is poetry intense with feeling, but not the accessible kinds arising directly from everyday experiences and relationships central in much of at least most poets' writing. The human content of Hill's poetry tends to be given elaborately remote frameworks: King Offa's Mercia and other recesses of history; religious concepts abstruse or arcane; the cryptic love of a fictive poet 'Sebastian Arrurruz'. Notes to Hill's latest collection *Tenebrae* declare 'Spanish and German poems have provided points of departure for several poems in this book'. While good poetry is owed attentive rereading, how far need we follow Hill into his historical, religious and foreign-language sources? Personally, I know some history, have an alert agnostic's understanding of Christian concepts and ritual, and no adequacy in any foreign language. But good poetry stands self-sufficiently free of whatever its origins. *Absalom and Achitophel*, *The Second Coming*, *The Waste Land*, would not exist without the constitutional controversy of Dryden's time, Yeats's idiosyncratic philosophy of gyres, and Eliot's reading in *From Ritual to Romance*, but the finished structures no longer depend upon the scaffolding necessary to get them up.

Altogether, the poet Hill insistently recalls is Eliot, whose own poetry magnificently passes what he defined as the 'test that genuine poetry can communicate before it is understood'. Hill's has comparable memorability: poems, lines, phrases, incise themselves on the imagination. Thus, the searing gnomic stanza from 'Dr Faustus' also made epigraph for *For the Unfallen*:

A beast is slain, a beast thrives.
Fat blood squeaks on the sand.
A blinded god believes
That he is not blind.

In *King Log*, Hill's 'Funeral Music' on the Wars of the Roses consummately realizes what his notes tell us he desiderated, 'a florid grim music broken by grunts and shrieks'; while '"Domaine Public"' has this image characteristically precise in its sensuous signification, about 'the Fathers':

How they
cultivate the corrupting flesh:
toothsome contemplation: cleanly
   maggots churning spleen
to milk.

The Arrurruz poems conjure fluently graphic immediacies:

Why do I have to relive, even now,
Your mouth, and your hand running over me
Deft as a lizard, like a sinew of water.

One can dip almost at random to find *Tenebrae* sustaining this ability to write poetry that stamps itself on the mind because definitively perfected:

the stale head
sauced in original blood; the little feast
foaming with cries of rapture and despair.
    ('A Pre-Raphaelite Notebook')

Whenever poetry has such power, pervasive through Hill's, almost by imaginative sleight to make the reader feel he has known always lines just read, this arises not only from vivid precision of denotation and image, but also from the poet commanding the movement of his verse in a subtle distinctive music. Hill's frequent poem-titles with musical reference are as wittingly chosen as Eliot's *Four Quartets*.

That his poetry *is* difficult has, inevitably yet surely shamefully, slowed and in some quarters apparently precluded its proper recognition. Hill is not mentioned in Donald Davie's *Thomas Hardy and British Poetry* and *The Poet in the Imaginary Museum*, in Ian Hamilton's *A Poetry Chronicle*, or in Jonathan Raban's *The Society of the Poem*, all generally perceptive on post-1950 poetry. Larkin's rise to due esteem was justly rapid, yet Larkin's own misrepresentation of Hill in his *Oxford Book of Twentieth-Century English Verse*, including only 'In Memory of Jane Fraser' about which Hill, when reprinting it amended as a 'penitential exercise' in *King Log* said 'I dislike the poem very much', seems as shabby as impercipient. But perhaps more characteristic through Hill's career has been the reaction typified by Kenneth Allott who introducing Hill in his *Penguin Book of Contemporary Verse* admitted 'I find the darkness of many of the poems so nearly total that I can see them to be poems only by a certain quality in their phrasing', understandable 'only in the sense that cats and dogs may be said to understand human conversations;' or by Alan Brownjohn reviewing *Mercian Hymns* for the *New Statesman* (6 August 1971) as the work of an 'implacably baffling talent', poetry that 'resists even several readings: yet the strange, ceremonial magnificence of it all is unmistakable'. Additional to the innate intricacy of Hill's poetic processes is his habit of frustrating most readers' expectations in the way defined by Gavin Ewart when, admiring *King Log*, he demurred 'yet contemporary life hardly exists in most of these poems, except by implication' (*London Magazine*, December 1968). Nor, though intensely aware of, and able poetically to realise, the power of the imagination significantly to mythicize untidy life, does Hill offer anything calculated so superficially to captivate as the instant cartoon-myth of Ted Hughes's *Crow* and other recent crass bestiaries, flinging the age an accelerated image of its own conventional grimace.

Yet, if very occasionally impenetrable, if sometimes as I think reading for example the striking 'Annunciations' in *King Log* excessive ellipsis grindingly short-circuits his lines as poetry, Hill's work everywhere convinces of its authenticity, and his difficulty need not be exaggerated. So much comes to mind as touchstones of a sensuous intellection healing that 'dissociation of sensibility' Eliot talked about, lucid enough even when at its highest pitch. Consider 'Te Lucis ante Terminum' from *Tenebrae*:

Centaury with your staunch bloom
you there alder beech you fern,
midsummer closeness my far home,
fresh traces of lost origin.

Silvery the black cherries hang
the plum-tree oozes through each cleft
and horse-flies siphon the green dung,
glued to the sweetness of their graft:

immortal transience, a 'kind
of otherness', self-understood,
BE FAITHFUL grows upon the mind
as lichen glimmers on the wood.

Certainly done with consummate economy, through to the
felicitous final simile finding graphic sensuous imagery for its
abstract concept, this poem yields with subtle clarity its sense:
that however passing life's shows, the proper fulfilling response
to recognizing this condition is an accepting fidelity, organically experienced, to what one is, and what is given, by which
word I mean both 'predicated' and 'bestowed'. Yet, 'midsummer closeness my far home': man, burdened with self-
consciousness as animals and plants are not, must start
spiritually remote from the desired condition, however immediately its manifestations surround him.

Much of Hill's poetry is religious, but if less amenable to
easy explication than, say, the later R. S. Thomas's religious
poetry, this is precisely because Hill gives complex spiritual
experience and questioning resonant realization, where
Thomas's poems spending most of their time telling us what
they are on about instead of getting on with being it, fall
towards the mere higher prattle of a metaphysically worried
man.

Fifteen years ago, in a *London Magazine* (November
1964) article on Hill's 'fiercely unaccommodating talent',
Christopher Ricks perceptively annotated early Hill's way of
exploiting tensioned ambiguities in particular words to bring
alive a complexly ambivalent attitude mingling faith and doubt
towards, for example, the pretensions represented by the
stained-glass saint in 'In Piam Memoriam':

Created *purely* from glass the saint stands,
Exposing his *gifted* quite empty hands
Like a conjurer about to begin,
A *righteous* man begging of *righteous* men.

My italics; and of course the conjurer simile too has divergent
implications. Ricks also drew attention to Hill's potent revivifi-
cation of cliché and phrases gone dead in everyday usage. The
poet is still doing these things in *Tenebrae*, where a line like
'the clock discounts us with a telling chime' ('The Eve of St.
Mark') fuses both. I would also note here Ricks's admirable
detailed elucidation of 'Ovid in the Third Reich', Hill's eight
brilliant lines encapsulating in a complex statement of enormous scope about the human condition, both what can be said
for, and what must be said against, those Germans who kept
passively silent under Hitler. While there is much more to Hill
than can be accommodated within Ricks's terrain of play on
ambiguity and cliché, it is in Hill certainly poetically no trivial
mannerism or flourish, but innate to his imaginative grasp of
life and centrally functional in articulating it. It enables, of
course, as well as the extraordinary resonance whereby wordplay irradiatingly informs Hill's image of that saint to make it a
vital focus for sinuous questionings, the exceptional economy
with which he gets large things said. Consider just the play on
'cultivate' in the fragment from ' "Domaine Public" ' I quoted
earlier. For Hill, as for Herbert or Marvell, ambiguity and
paradox are not tricks of rhetoric or decoration, but necessary
means of seizing and showing forth truths of life apprehended
as the complex thing it is, so requiring correspondingly subtle
use of language. Hill's 'difficulty' is demonstrably concomitant
to unusual ambitiousness of both theme and method: few poets
have begun a first collection with a shot at re-enacting the
Creation like Hill's 'Genesis'. That he poetically chews as
much as he bites off is not the least impressive thing about his
poetry. One trusts it, however baffled occasionally, because it is
never wantonly obscure or arbitrarily private, and its subtle

compressions function crucially to give significant and il-
luminative imaginative realization to large matters.

Hill is impressively enough intensively himself to stand
the comparison with Eliot. Both poets share historical awareness and perspective, and the poetic practice of bringing past
and present into fruitful juxtaposition; though here, I shall
argue, Hill's motives and effects generally differ from Eliot's.
Hill also has an Eliotian predilection for poetic strategies
calculated to achieve a seeming 'impersonality'. I am unim-
pressed by Eliot's argument in 'Tradition and the Individual
Talent' of his 'impersonal theory of poetry', with its precisely
meaningless postulation of complete separation between the
artist's human and creating self, which reflects Eliot's polemical stance against the Georgian fag-end of Romanticism; in
fact, Eliot's extraordinary poetic processes, whereby intensely
subjective fragments of creative or actual experience and
observation were slowly let aggregate and cohere within a
dominant imaginative field, so that 'Prufrock', 'Gerontion',
The Waste Land, achieve the paradox-form of Imagist epics,
show him an extreme Romantic. But his espousal of 'impersonality' does express also a genuine temperamental bias, one
Hill shares. Like *The Waste Land*, Hill's 'Funeral Music' and
Mercian Hymns assume at least some air of being objective
statements on the human condition delivered dispassionately
from God's right hand. Or, like Eliot with Prufrock, Gerontion, Tiresias, Hill masks utterance with personae discrete from
the authorial identity: King Offa, or in that oblique fiction 'The
Songbook of Sebastian Arrurruz' what Hill's notes tell us is 'an
apocryphal Spanish poet.' Thus much of Hill's poetry, like
early Eliot, becomes essentially dramatic. In *Tenebrae*, 'The
Pentecost Castle' sequence deploys seemingly various voices.
Even where, in his early work, in a thread woven through
Mercian Hymns, here and there in *Tenebrae* more intensely
than ever, Hill modulates into a personal 'I', the reader as with
Eliot's use of the pronoun in *Ash-Wednesday* or *Four Quartets*
feels its terms are sharply delimited by the poet, offer no
admission-key to his personality or autobiography. In Hill's
'Lachrimae' sonnets the 'I' is keenly insistent, yet never naked
of artifice, and incorporates voices, consciousnesses, other than
Hill's. One is Southwell's, the Elizabethan poet and Catholic
martyr who provides the sequence's epigraph. But consider the
apparently movingly direct and open final sestet of 'Lachrimae':

So many nights the angel of my house
has fed such urgent comfort through a dream,
whispered 'your lord is coming, he is close'

that I have drowsed half-faithful for a time
bathed in pure tones of promise and remorse:
'tomorrow I shall wake and welcome him.'

This, Hill tells us, is 'free translation of a sonnet by Lope de
Vega.' One does not doubt the feeling is validly Hill's, but so to
find for such unusually simple emotion a guise that at once
distances and confirmingly sanctions it is a radical characteristic of Hill's poetic temperament and strategy.

Again like Eliot, as well as masks of stance or personae
Hill appropriates to his purposes and makes distinguishingly his
own a range of poetic forms and manners, from the sonnet
sequence, through verse with a Metaphysical ground-bass, to
the prose-poems of *Mercian Hymns* and his recurrent Spanish
derivations. C. H. Sisson has noted (*Agenda*, 13:3, 1975) Hill's
'singularly direct mind which, none the less, seems impelled to
such indirect utterance.' Like Crashaw's, Sisson suggests, 'a
mind in search of artifices to protect itself against its own
passions.' No more than Eliot is Hill prone to offer personal
experience with open straightforwardness in the old-Romantic
or new-Confessional I-fall-upon-the-thorns-of-life-I-

bleed/My-mind's-not-right ways. His means are devious and oblique. His titles alone can be provocatively indirect: in *Tenebrae* the overall entitling of thirteen superb sonnets only loosely related and on the evidence of Hill's notes not homogeneous in conception, as 'An Apology for the Revival of Christian Architecture in England', seems less than inevitable. And yet, attentive reading shows any apparent 'impersonality' about Hill's poetry to be only his necessary guise or framework for a vision, a coherent array of attitudes and imaginative response, intensely subjective almost to idiosyncrasy.

If *For the Unfallen* was a first collection startling in the consummate finish of its writing and the amplitude of its aims, this sparing poet's next book, *King Log*, published nine years later in 1968, surpassed it in scope, penetration and mature poetic accomplishment. While in 'Ovid in the Third Reich' extreme compression superbly justifies itself, I would allow that occasionally elsewhere in *King Log* Hill's power-pack becomes a log-jam. In 'Annunciations', although such phrasing as 'the soul/Purples itself; each eye squats full and mild' stamps itself indelibly, and each line is in principle construable, the whole congestedly loses momentum. In 'The Stone Man', language like 'Words clawed my mind as though they had smelt/ Revelation's flesh. . . . The sun bellows over its parched swarms,' seems overpumped, even ludicrous. Intensity of feeling is pervasive through *King Log*, and the repelled notation in 'Annunciations' of 'the steam of beasts,/The loathly neckings and the fat shook spawn', expresses a disgust for the flesh and its appetites recurrent in Hill, though coolly enough revolved through different perspectives, as my earlier quotation from ' "Domaine Public" ' and the 'horse-flies siphon the green dung' image in 'Te Lucis ante Terminum' illustrate. But *King Log* frequently showed Hill in fluent relatively open style: in 'Cowan Bridge'; or 'Fantasia on "Horbury" ', that evoking a priest on a storm-threatened nineteenth-century West Riding day, his 'outworn pieties', how 'he will weaken, scribbling, at the end,/of unspeakable desolation. Really? Good Lord!' however concludes selfchasteningly:

> Consider him catspawed by an indolent poem,
> This place not of his choosing, this menace
>
> From concave stormlight a freak suggestion. . . .
> These heads of nettles lopped into the dust.

Then there is the delicate perception, feeling subdued to tones appropriately crepuscular, of 'Old Poet with Distant Admirers':

> What I lost was not part of this,
> The dark-blistered foxgloves, wet berries
> Glinting from shadow, small ferns and stones,
>
> Seem fragments, in the observing mind,
> Of its ritual power. Old age
> Singles them out, as though by first-light,
>
> As though a still life, presenting some
> Portion of the soul's feast, went with me
> Everywhere, to be hung in strange rooms,
> Loneliness being what it is.

The eleven Arrurruz poems intensify sexual passion precisely by stripping it of circumstantial documentation, an effect similar to Eliot's with sexual disgust in the three Thames-daughter songs in *The Waste Land*, where the nature of his achievement appears clearly from comparing the finished poem's 'Trams and dusty trees' quatrain with the eleven-line equivalent in Eliot's earlier draft, full of background information about the girl and her family. If Hill follows a similar instinct to forfeit a documentary kind of intelligibility to bare finally more illuminating intensities, his results equally justify themselves. Thus, when in an unsympathetic review (*New Statesman*, 5 January 1979) of *Tenebrae* I have come across

while writing this Craig Raine takes a sideswipe at the woman lamented in 'The Songbook of Sebastian Arrurruz' as 'shadowy', he seems wrong-headedly beside the point of Hill's psychologically subtle realizations of incandescent emotion. And within the sequence's cryptic framework and strategy, the writing is incisively fluent. The mistress-figure apart, one of the less-noticed poems, 'To His Wife', shows how the selectively sparing can intimate rich human substantiality:

> You ventured occasionally—
> As though this were another's house—
> Not intimate but an acquaintance
> Flaunting her modest claim; like one
> Idly commiserated by new-mated
> Lovers rampant in proper delight
> When all their guests are gone.

But it is the 'Funeral Music' sequence of eight unrhymed sonnets in *King Log* that marked a high point in Hill's poetic career. Here, the Wars of the Roses provide a gravitational field within which Hill can coherently cluster, explore, articulate, some of his huger themes and obsessions. The poems bear what Hill's notes term 'an oblique dedication' to three peers, variously representative of their time and encompassing humane and spiritual as well as ruthlessly worldly allegiances, all executed within the period. A central awareness in 'Funeral Music' is that medieval life was at once nasty brutish and short, and highly ritualized, ceremonious; fraught with spiritual aspirations liable to be broken with stark vividness on harsh and cruel actualities:

> The voice fragrant with mannered humility,
> With an equable contempt for this world,
> 'In honorem Trinitatis'. Crash. The head
> Struck down into a meaty conduit of blood.
> So these dispose themselves to receive each
> Pentecostal blow from axe or seraph,
> Spattering block-straw with mortal residue.

Everywhere, not through comment but by precise realization in the texture of his writing, Hill highlights the discrepancies, glaring in fifteenth-century life but by inference perennial, between the bloody and the formal, so that with two-way irony each becomes a criticism upon the other. His command of resonant ambiguity functions brilliantly to illumine the dichotomy: in 'dispose' in the passage just quoted; or 'scrape', hinting at 'bow and scrape', at the start of the second poem 'For whom do we scrape our tribute of pain. . . .' 'Funeral Music' alludes to the Battle of Towton in 1461, notorious for its carnage, and here Hill can particularly evoke the medieval mixture of ritual and butchery: 'fastidious trumpets shrilling into the ruck', the heraldic panoply and glitter of armies, resolves to 'reddish ice tinged the reeds'. The third poem achieves a pitch of suggestive definition quite exceptional in English battle-poetry:

> They bespoke doomsday and they meant it by
> God, their curved metal rimming the low ridge.
> But few appearances are like this. Once
> Every five hundred years a comet's
> Over-riding stillness might reveal men
> In such array, livid and featureless,
> With England crouched beastwise beneath it all.
> 'Oh, that old Northern business. . . .' A field
> After battle utters its own sound
> Which is like nothing on earth, but is earth,
> Blindly the questing snail, vulnerable
> Mole emerge, blindly we lie down, blindly
> Among carnage the most delicate souls
> Tup in their marriage-blood, gasping 'Jesus'.

A poetic style and tone Hill notes as 'ornate and heartless' is crucially instrumental to the total meaning of 'Funeral Music', implying, and through interrupting grunts and shrieks endorsing, a critique of its own limitations; and so effectively transcending these. Rarely is artifice so artfully significant; this is poetry of a formal magnificence that, in its own words, 'whines through the empyrean' aware, as that verb's connotations suggest, of its own ambivalence.

Beyond which, through the lives and times it articulates, 'Funeral Music' searingly meditates life's fundamental questions:

> Though I would scorn the mere instinct of faith,
> Expediency of assent, if I dared,
> What I dare not is a waste history.

Is all human effort, the expense of blood and spirit, in these or any other wars, or other human enterprise, finally terrifyingly meaningless? Life subject purely to logic, rationality, is definingly evoked as a stasis of beautiful sterility, a haunting inhuman impossibility:

> if intellect
> Itself were absolute law, sufficient grace,
> Our lives could be a myth of captivity
> Which we might enter: an unpeopled region
> Of ever new-fallen snow, a palace blazing
> With perpetual silence as with torches.

'Some parch for what they were'—yet neither does nostalgia, the yearning to start again pure, afford escape or exoneration. The figures Hill's poem meditates, whatever their temporal lives and desires, the meaning of their personal history or their time's, are now 'set apart in timeless colloquy' to 'bear witness' in the minds of those who contemplate them. Yet if for others they can thus remain, extracted from life's contingency, symbols to be given meaning as Hill's poetry has given it, still 'Funeral Music' closes insisting, in a strategy more powerfully enacting the poetic self-chastening of 'Fantasia on "Horbury"', that that is no consolation or succour to their mortal lives:

> If it is without
> Consequence when we vaunt and suffer, or
> If it is not, all echoes are the same
> In such eternity. Then tell me, love,
> How that should comfort us—or anyone
> Dragged unnerved out of this worldly place
> Crying to the end 'I have not finished.'

The grave abstractness of those lines is beautifully weighted by that personalizing 'love', that final cry, the more concrete of the alternative meanings contained in 'half-unnerved' and 'worldly place'.

Mercian Hymns, in 1971, surprised superficially by being a sequence of thirty prose-poems; thematically however it is consonant with 'Funeral Music': less intensively wrought, wider ranging, more sportive. It is no disadvantage to Hill's purposes that, Anglo-Saxon records belonging overwhelmingly to the later period of Wessex hegemony, and even archaeology having unearthed little, the powerful Mercian king Offa who controlled by conquest most of England and functioned as a European potentate, 'friend of Charlemagne', remains so sparsely documented, his testimony little more than his impressive money and the dyke he built against the Welsh:

> And it seemed, while we watched, he began to walk
>   towards us   he vanished
> he left behind coins, for his lodging, and traces of
>   red mud.

Thus hymn XXX. That the grandest worldly show is passing, is an awareness *Mercian Hymns* utters incisively as Shelley's 'Ozymandias'. Earth, the struggle to master it, and that all returns to it, is 'invested in mother earth' (IV), features

crucially through the sequence, its details delicately observed; Offa *Rex Totius Anglorum Patriae* is as transient as a snail that 'sugared its new stone' (XIV). Yet also Offa is something perennial, the 'creature of legend' Hill's notes tell us might 'in this sequence be regarded as the presiding genius of the West Midlands, his dominion enduring from the middle of the eighth century until the middle of the twentieth (and possibly beyond).' The final hymn's 'traces of red mud' intimate more than the historical Offa's grandiose dyke; Hymn I, listing his worldly attributes, has him also 'overlord of the M5 . . . contractor to the desirable new estates,' and gives clear guidance to Hill's framing strategy for the sequence, which is comprehensible enough. One should note though that if occasionally Hill collocates ancient and modern with the Eliotian motive of ironic contrast, as when suburban dwellings are named 'Ethandune', 'Catraeth', 'Maldon', 'Pengwern', generally his intention is the reverse, akin in its historical vision to that of David Jones in *In Parenthesis*: to suggest parallels, continuities. This allows him, through a book refreshingly humorous for Hill, to enjoy concocting anachronisms such as 'Merovingian car-dealers'; but the purpose is serious, and the vision coherent.

But the energies of *Mercian Hymns* flow not only along this axis between past and present, but concurrently along another vitally linking public and private worlds, those of temporal power and of a childhood evidently the poet's. Hill thus establishes a four-way system of metaphor of considerable resonance. And as with Joyce's equation of Leopold Bloom and Ulysses, the perspectives upon one another of past heroic modes and anti-heroic modern private life qualify the former, overtly present in Hill as not in *Ulysses*, as well as the latter, and finally inform and help understand both. Concerned with power and self-aggrandizement, Hill is interested not in their means and instruments, but the underlying subtle private impulses which will and energize them. Richly fruitful here is his use of childhood, which has its fantasies of power and command, whim, wanton cruelty, grievances, terrors, egotistic desires, but confined to expression objectively trivial. But if in adulthood such impulses obtain the means of power, there ensues inordinate enactment, most extremely exemplified in a Hitler, Stalin or Amin, perhaps bridled generally only insofar as given political systems check it. Hill clearly believes that power corrupts and absolute power corrupts absolutely; and Offa, whose early-medieval society desiderated military autocracy, becomes the type of a human phenomenon perennial if modulating its guises in the modern England of motorways, commerce and political democracy. Yet by implicating his own boyhood as a single child who 'fostered a strangeness; gave myself to unattainable toys' (VI) in his unsparing creation of this figure, Hill enables us to understand compassionately his common human nature. In Hymn VII we read: 'Coagulations of frogs: once, with branches and half-bricks, he battered a ditchful;' then,

> Ceolred was his friend and remained so, even after
> the day of the lost fighter: a biplane, already obsolete
> and irreplaceable, two inches of heavy snub silver.
> Ceolred let it spin through a hole in the classroom-
> floorboards, softly, into the rat-droppings and coins.
>
> After school he lured Ceolred, who was sniggering
> with fright, down to the old quarries, and flayed him.
> Then, leaving Ceolred, he journeyed for hours, calm
> and alone, in his private derelict sandlorry named
> *Albion*.

The various dimensions richly connect here: particularly charged is the last sentence, where that sandlorry given

England's name becomes receptacle for solitariness, fantasy, stasis, which comprehend child and king, past and present. Again, when in Hymn XIX Hill writes 'They haul a sodden log, hung with soft shields of fungus, and launch it upon the flames,' he is deploying metaphor to show that power is indeed child's play, transfiguring the latter into mimic enactment of Anglo-Saxon regal burial ritual.

Obviously Hill's strategy in *Mercian Hymns* allows enormous scope to his talent for verbal punning, refined and applied as felicitously as ever: the protagonist is a 'staggeringly-gifted child'; on his coins Offa appears 'cushioned on a legend', with a play on both 'cushioned' and the numismatic and larger meanings of 'legend'. Three of the hymns are about 'Offa's Coins': an arbitrary ruler's mark-making equivalent to the boy carving his name on desks. So, 'the masterful head emerges, kempt and jutting, out of England's well' (XIII), his name a 'best-selling brand, curt graffito. A laugh; a cough. . . . A specious gift. . . . The starting cry of a race. A name to conjure with.' (II). 'Hymns' implies, whatever else, celebration; yet Offa's legacy may be no more than—for the whole work's closing 'traces of red earth' bear another connotation—money and blood. Imagist epic seems an appropriate term for *Mercian Hymns*, where intensely worked and polished fragments cohere within a grand structure to intimate a vision of huge scope.

Tenebrae, the 1978 collection of Hill's subsequent work, shows some of his most purely beautiful writing in a return to traditional, rhymed forms, particularly the sonnet, by this poet always exceptionally intent on disciplining emotion. Much of the emotion in *Tenebrae* is religious, a desire trustingly to believe agonized by doubt; Hill's has always seemed perhaps a style learnt from a despair, and *Tenebrae* more than ever recalls Donne's observation, 'Grief brought to numbers cannot be so fierce,/For he tames it, that fetters it in verse.' But not only 'tames': also clarifyingly explores and articulates it as undisciplined utterance could not. And in any case, as 'Funeral Music' particularly, but his work pervasively, has shown, for Hill the tension between artifice of expression and immediacies of experience, which his poetic forms enact, is itself a central troubling theme in his engagement with the human condition. The nagging paradox is defined in the four-line poem closing both the title-sequence of *Tenebrae* and the book:

> Music survives, composing her own sphere,
> Angel of Tones, Medusa, Queen of the Air,
> and when we would accost her with real cries
> silver on silver thrills itself to ice.

Sharp as ever in *Tenebrae* is Hill's fearful awareness that in 'composing', conferring articulate order, whether in life or upon the materials of a poem, we abstract, petrify, real feelings, cries, within a realm inaccessible and unsuccouring to the actual contingent world we thus invade. The helpless gulf between the timeless yet literally unalive truth of our supreme imaginative constructs, and the timebound, transient anarchy of 'breathing human passion,' has always registered at the heart of our poetic tradition, in such works as Keats's 'Ode on a Grecian Urn' and Yeats's Byzantium poems. And Hill knows, as they did, and extendedly in his own terms Wallace Stevens, that our composed structures, however they chill and in a sense deny life, are also its supreme enduring expression, are moreover necessary, forms sustaining and generative of values in a world perhaps otherwise void of meaning. Always recognizing and often enacting the conflict between imaginative order and life's fearsome anarchy, Hill by giving each grave weight tensions a polarity which enricheningly energizes his poetry.

These considerations are especially relevant to the seven 'Lachrimae' sonnets, which take their epigraph—'Passions I allow, and loves I approve, onely I would wish that men would alter their object and better their intent'—and more, from Robert Southwell the Elizabethan Catholic poet who despising all things worldly composed his life towards martyrdom and in suffering torture and death achieved the consummation he devoutly wished. As sonnet 5, 'Pavana Dolorosa', puts it:

> Self-wounding martyrdom, what joys you have,
> true-torn among this fictive consonance,
> music's creation of the moveless dance,
> the decreation to which all must move,

A 'self-seeking hunter of forms', the martyr makes his real agony the focal point of a contrived artifice in which even his torturers are his collaborators, material for his composition; within which design, as Hill's earlier 'Ovid in the Third Reich' had it, 'They, in their sphere,/Harmonize strangely with the divine/Love.' So, 'Pavana Dolorosa' insists,

> None can revoke your cry.
> Your silence is an ecstasy of sound
> and your nocturnals blaze upon the day.

To express his sense of a resonance irrefutable and formally perfect found paradoxically through extinction at the worldly level 'Pavana Dolorosa' uses music and dance as analogy, a dimension of metaphor framing the whole 'Lachrimae' sequence, subtitled 'Seven tears figured in seven passionate Pavans' in allusion to the music of Southwell's Catholic contemporary John Dowland. Of course the relation between the violent human content and the poetry's formal qualities and tones of elaborate stately melancholy enacts the paradox at the heart of Hill's preoccupations: his skill at thus implicating form in theme is more intensively managed than in Keats's Ode or even Yeats's two hammered-gold Byzantium poems.

In Hill's first sonnet, 'Lachrimae Verae', Christ is addressed as

> the castaway of drowned remorse,
> you are the world's atonement on the hill.
> This is your body twisted by our skill
> into a patience proper for redress.

More 'fictive consonance', as Christ's body is not only literally 'twisted' to the Cross, but distorted by human concepts into a beautiful emblem for suffering: the fury and the mire of in this case possibly superhuman veins translated into an aesthetically satisfying image for our consolation. As 'Funeral Music' insisted, we perhaps abuse the lives we thus use 'set apart in timeless colloquy' to 'bear witness'; although in 'Lachrimae' complex considerations arise because the suffering contemplated is martyrdom, perhaps self-abuse when human like Southwell's, claiming divine nature and purposes when Christ's. Or attributed with them, 'twisted by our skill'; for this is a poetry of doubt. And in any case, perhaps in composing its own sphere wearing again the unconsoling face of Medusa, and icily inviolable when accosted with our real cries. The 'Lachrimae' sonnets certainly insist upon an unsatisfactory gulf between the poet and the saviour whose 'body moves but moves to no avail':

> I cannot turn aside from what I do;
> you cannot turn away from what I am.
> You do not dwell in me nor I in you. . . .
>   ('Lachrimae Verae')

Indeed, Hill's tone modulates into hostility, given ironic edge by the wordplay, in 'Lachrimae Coactae':

> You are the crucified who crucifies,
> self-withdrawn even from your own device,
> your trim-plugged body, wreath of rakish thorn.

And 'Martyrium' too shows distaste for this 'Jesus-faced' figure:

> Clamorous love, its faint and baffled shout,
> its grief that would betray him to our fear,
> he suffers for our sake, or does not hear
> above the hiss of shadows on the wheat.

That incorporation of 'amorous' into 'clamorous' love, in the context of a sequence throughout preoccupied with passion in both its religious and secular senses and the conflict and interplay between them, is characteristically masterly, and the last quoted line shows the incisive sensuousness repeatedly vivifying this poetry of abstract concepts. Like 'Funeral Music', 'Lachrimae' profoundly articulates a question acknowledged, for the closing sonnet translating Lope de Vega from which I have already quoted is a real human cry for a peace that passes understanding, as incapable of resolution: how far can composition, artifice, form, all imaginative mediation of life whether by poet or martyr, redeem and reconcile life's brute fact; how far, in reducing life to essence, are they its illusory shadows merely? Yet if art cannot cancel horrible realities it confers significance upon them: he who composes is forging in the smithy of his soul the uncreated conscience of his human race. As for words, as Saul Bellow's Moses Herzog puts it to himself, 'What can thoughtful people and humanists do but struggle towards suitable words? . . . I go after reality with language.' 'Lachrimae' exemplifies an art of language superbly self-reflexive, that questions critically what it is itself up to. The tensions between art as sublime significance and shadowy sublimation are done memorable justice; human passions, needs, fears, realize themselves through this poetry's smooth shapeliness like the glitter in shot silk.

That in 'Lachrimae' Hill's poetic manner adaptively assumes some characteristics of the Elizabethan Southwell about whom the preoccupations of the sequence gather, is of course an effect knowingly managed and part of the poetry's point; and given that it works, preempts Craig Raine's complaint (*New Statesman*, 5 January 1979) that 'the traditional diction makes for glum reading,' and his pejorative designation of Hill, a poet preoccupied with perennial man in temporal history, as 'archaeological'. The kind of languorous wordplay illustrated in some of my quotations from 'Lachrimae', typified by the close of 'Pavana Dolorosa',

> I founder in desire for things unfound.
> I stay amid the things that will not stay,

recurs in the book's title-sequence 'Tenebrae', where the second section is a tissue of it and the brief fourth has lines like 'Light of light, supreme delight;/Grace at our lips to our disgrace.' Distinct from the concentrated ambiguity within a single word or phrase by which Hill has always clarifyingly focused his understanding of life's paradoxes, this is less a 'metaphysical' than, consciously, a conventional Elizabethan kind of wordplay, a more decorative slow juggling of words to revolve their varieties of signification or merely achieve symmetries. Lines like Sidney's 'My heart was wounded with his wounded heart' or early Shakespeare's 'Light, seeking light, doth light of light beguile' would blend in harmoniously. Of course this, in collaboration with traditional verse forms, procures a fluency Hill occasionally forfeited in earlier books when compressing meaning as ruthlessly as those machines which crush scrapped cars to cubic inches. The euphuistic manner might lend itself to formulations superficially neat and reductive, but Hill employs it to purpose in specific poems, not self-indulgently; and if *Tenebrae* is throughout his most fluent collection, this is certainly not at the expense of the intensities which are this poet's hallmark, nor of that meticulously expressive articulation of syntax characterizing all his writing.

I do nevertheless find the 'Tenebrae' sequence a weak area in this collection, for overall it reads too much like Hill just letting his machinery tick over. And although in a way more enterprising, I cannot say that 'The Pentecost Castle' interests me greatly. Fluency, an exceptional openness of style for Hill, its short-lined stanzas certainly have. The notes to *Tenebrae* tell us that 'The Pentecost Castle' is 'particularly indebted' to Hill's reading of the *Penguin Book of Spanish Verse*, and browsing around that, with particular indebtedness in my case to the prose translations, I can see what Hill owes texturally, what has stimulated his poetry's tone, ballad musicality, temper, occasional piercing bitter-sweetness and glitter. These qualities acknowledged, there seems little more to say about 'The Pentecost Castle': although each section is tellingly charged with implication, I do not feel that as a whole the sequence shapes sufficiently into gathered articulation of the themes adumbrated in its epigraphs, from Simone Weil about love's egotism, and Yeats's 'It is terrible to desire and not possess, and terrible to possess and not desire.'

But generally *Tenebrae* sustains magnificently the development within continuity Hill's poetry has always achieved. Among several excellent individual poems are 'A Pre-Raphaelite Notebook', 'Te Lucis ante Terminum' which I have already discussed, 'Ave Regina Coelorum' brilliantly starting 'There is a land called Lost/at peace inside our heads', and 'Terribilis Est Locus Iste', dedicated to 'Gauguin and the Pont-Aven School' and effecting dextrous verbal capture of

> marginal angels lightning-sketched in red
> chalk on the month's accounts, or marigolds
> in paint runnily embossed.

Particularly, the thirteen sonnets, less intensively interrelated than those of 'Lachrimae', gathered under the devious title 'An Apology for the Revival of Christian Architecture in England', gravitating meditatively around Coleridge's hankering for 'the spiritual, Platonic old England,' mediate its personal, geographical and historical intimations in poetry as impressive as any Hill has written. The second sonnet, 'Damon's Lament for His Clorinda, Yorkshire 1654', exemplifies a lucidity, intensity and perfect pacing characterizing the sequence:

> The North Sea batters our shepherds' cottages
> from sixty miles. No sooner has the sun
> swung clear above earth's rim than it is gone.
> We live like gleaners of its vestiges
>
> knowing we flourish, though each year a child
> with the set face of a tomb-weeper is put down
> for ever and ever.

Anything but precious, Hill's fastidiousness of diction is as trenchant as it is elegant, as appears in his choice of verbs in this from the seventh sonnet 'Loss and Gain':

> brown stumps of headstones tamp into the ling
> the ruined and the ruinously strong.
> Platonic England grasps its tenantry
>
> where wild-eyed poppies raddle tawny farms
> and wild swans root in lily-clouded lakes.

But the final sonnet, 'The Herefordshire Carol', fittingly illustrates the kind of felicities abundant through this sequence, every sleight of phrase and cinematically sharp particular working within a poetry of packed lucidity to vitalize a delicate conception:

> So to celebrate that kingdom: it grows
> greener in winter, essence of the year;
> the apple-branches musty with green fur.
> In the viridian darkness of its yews

it is an enclave of perpetual vows
broken in time. Its truth shows disrepair,
disfigured shrines, their stones of gossamer,
Old Moore's astrology, all hallows,
the squire's effigy bewigged with frost,
and hobnails cracking puddles before dawn.
In grange and cottage girls rise from their beds
by candlelight and mend their ruined braids.
Touched by the cry of the iconoclast,
how the rose-window blossoms with the sun!

Hill's poetry here loses nothing in intensity for being more than usually at peace with the world. If an excitement of following it has been that its development from collection to collection is at once surprising and recognizably harmonious, in *Tenebrae*, his craftsmanship more adequate than ever to the intensity of his vision, and avoiding the occasional lockjaw hesitation of some of his earlier work, he has achieved his most eloquent poetry yet.

Generally, Hill's work, never condescending for the sake of yielding instant meaning, keeping aloof from superficialities of fashion and true to its imaginative temper and purposes, has through decades of much sloppy self-indulgent and makeshift writing, a certain literary chaos, conferred intellectual and emotional dignity on poetry. That in our place and time it exists, is an unqualified good for poetry and readers. Intricately exploring and enacting through diverse ramifications the central human tension between imaginative order and life's anarchy, employing a consummate technique commensurate with his ambitiousness, Hill like an old-timer panning for gold sifts life and language, prospecting among their silt for glinting richnesses. To borrow one of his own immaculately apt images, his poetry 'grows upon the mind/as lichen glimmers on the wood.'

CHRISTOPHER RICKS
"Geoffrey Hill 1: 'The Tongue's Atrocities'"
The Force of Poetry
1984, pp. 285–318

A principled distrust of the imagination is nothing new. One triumph of the imagination is that it can be aware of the perils of the imagination, the aggrandisements, covert indulgences, and specious claims which it may incite. Great art is often about the limits of what we should hope for even from the greatest of art, and among the many things which the imagination can realize on our behalf, one such is the limits of the sympathetic imagination.

A poem by Geoffrey Hill speaks of 'The tongue's atrocities' ('History as Poetry'), compacting or colluding the atrocities of which the tongue must speak, with the atrocities which—unless it is graced with unusually creative vigilance—it is all too likely to commit when it speaks of atrocities. For atrocity may get flattened down into the casually 'atrocious', or it may get fattened up into that debased form of imagination which is prurience. So the general burden of the imagination's self-scrutiny presses particularly upon all such art as contemplates (in both senses) atrocities.

In his literary criticism, Geoffrey Hill has worried at this, as when he praised the poetry with which Ben Jonson both fleshes and cauterizes the atrocities of imperial Rome: 'Jonson's qualifications worry the verse into dogs-teeth of virtuous self-mistrust';[1] and again when Hill praised the 'terrible beauty' of Yeats's 'Easter 1916': 'the tune of a mind distrustful yet envious, mistrusting the abstraction, mistrusting its own mistrust'.[2] This subject of much of Hill's criticism is the impulse of much of his

poetry. 'Annunciations: I' is about art as connoisseurship (for its creators as much as for its audiences or critics—Hill never makes a complacent distinction between the likes of him and the likes of us). 'The Humanist' and 'The Imaginative Life' are both impelled by virtuous self-mistrust; 'The Martyrdom of Saint Sebastian' bends its attention upon the glazing of the martyr's pains.

The act of imagining, and of inscribing in words, can so easily claim 'too much or too little'. The prose-poem which uses those words, 'Offa's Sword' (*Mercian Hymns*), ponders the great gift brought to Offa: 'The Frankish gift, two-edged, regaled with slaughter'. Regaled, with its regalia (and *regalo* means a gift); but 'regaled with slaughter' opens up a grim fissure—the poem uses the word 'fissured'—between the barbaric opulence and the jaded prurience: regaled with good stories, with Christmas fare (the poem speaks of 'Christ's mass'), and with deliciously domesticated slaughter. 'Two-edged'.

But let me quote Hill's most explicit imagining of prurience as imagination's dark double, 'Offa's Journey to Rome':

At Pavia, a visitation of some sorrow. Boethius'
dungeon. He shut his eyes, gave rise to a tower
out of the earth. He willed the instruments of
violence to break upon meditation. Iron buckles
gagged; flesh leaked rennet over them; the men
stooped, disentangled the body.

He wiped his lips and hands. He strolled back to the
car, with discreet souvenirs for consolation and
philosophy. He set in motion the furtherance of
his journey. To watch the Tiber foaming out
much blood.

See how 'gave rise to' is redeemed from its heartless officialese; and how the very instruments of imprisonment ought to have vomited (to have gagged in gagging him); and how the body becomes that of an unweaned calf, its rennet curdling; and how the poem itself honourably fears the feasting prurience of all such imaginings: 'He wiped his lips and hands'. Can we remember such things without reducing them to discreet souvenirs? Is even God above such diseased imaginings? God, 'voyeur of sacrifice'. But it is characteristic of Hill to have de-italicised the word 'voyeur' when he reprinted that poem after its first publication ('Locust Songs')[3]—who are the English to imply that voyeurism is foreign to them? A comment by Hill on 'Annunciations: II' might stand as an epigraph to all such poems of his: 'But I want the poem to have this dubious end; because I feel dubious; and the whole business is dubious'.[4]

Yet upon this ancient dubiety, which is not a failure of nerve but an acknowledgment of what a success of nerve might be, there has been urged in the last forty years a unique and hideous modern intensification. The Nazi extermination-camps are a horror which has been felt to dwarf all art and to paralyse all utterance. There would be something suspect about anybody who felt nothing of the impulse which voiced itself in George Steiner as 'The world of Auschwitz lies outside speech as it lies outside reason'.[5] But then this very impulse can uglily become a routine, a mannerism, or a cliché. There is something oppressively to-be-expected about beginning a book on *The Holocaust and the Literary Imagination* (1975)[6] with a chapter entitled 'In the Beginning Was the Silence', with its epigraph from Beckett: 'Speech is a desecration of silence', and with the first sentence invoking Adorno's cry that to write poetry after Auschwitz is barbaric. A poet may feel that not only is Auschwitz unspeakable but that this fear itself has become unsayable, so much said as scarcely to be accessible to feeling. There press upon all these grim doubts and realities both a harsh unignorability and a smoothly righteous triteness.

Geoffrey Hill was born in 1932. He is in my judgment the best of those English poets who entered into adult consciousness in the post-war, not the pre-war or the war-time, world. Poets just older than Hill—Philip Larkin, say—were in possession of a conscious experienced public conscience when the news and then the newsreels of Belsen and Auschwitz disclosed the atrocities. A poet of exactly Hill's age did not yet possess any such experienced conscience; Hill was thirteen in 1945, and he belongs to the generation whose awakening to the atrocity of adult life was an awakening to this unparalleled atrocity. It is true that no Englishman had ever before known anything like those newsreels, those photographs, those histories; but Englishmen older than Hill did not have this atrocity as their first introduction to atrocity. Hill wrote his first poems in the late 1940's; mercifully, there is every reason to believe that the poems were not bent upon the Nazi holocaust. But since then, he has written the deepest and truest poems on that holocaust: 'September Song', and 'Ovid in the Third Reich', as well as a few other poems on this atrocity which are honourable, fierce and grave: 'Two Formal Elegies', 'Domaine Public', and section IV in 'Of Commerce and Society':

Statesmen have known visions. And, not alone,
Artistic men prod dead men from their stone:
Some of us have heard the dead speak:
The dead are my obsession this week

But may be lifted away. In summer
Thunder may strike, or, as a tremor
Of remote adjustment, pass on the far side
From us: however deified and defied

By those it does strike. Many have died. Auschwitz,
Its furnace chambers and lime pits
Half-erased, is half-dead; a fable
Unbelievable in fatted marble.

There is, at times, some need to demonstrate
Jehovah's touchy methods, that create
The connoisseur of blood, the smitten man.
At times it seems not common to explain.

The dignified force of Hill's poetry on such atrocity is a matter of his grasping that the atrocity both is and is not unique, and that it presents to the imagination a challenge which likewise both is and is not unique. Hill does not permit the Jews' sufferings to be separated from or aloof from the other hideous sufferings which fill the air of the past and the present. It is characteristic of him that he should not countenance the well-meant but misguided turn which would monopolize the word 'holocaust' for the sufferings of the Jews. He does not withhold the word from the Jews (though not in the dangerous form 'the Holocaust'), and this not least because he feels dismay at the unjustly retributive irony of the word's etymology and its religious allegiance: 'A sacrifice wholly consumed by fire; a whole burnt offering'. But he would support neither monopoly nor pedantry, and he says of the Battle of Towton (Palm Sunday, 1461): 'In the accounts of the contemporary chroniclers it was a holocaust'.[7]

This poem, 'Statesmen have known visions . . .', is a poem which knows what it is up against. Its pained rhythms resist both a facile self-exculpation and a facile self-inculpation. 'The dead are my obsession this week': the rhythm is at once strong and strained, and it protects the groundedly sardonic against the ingratiatingly self-deprecating. It is doubly styptic. As is the turn which first grimly shrivels 'deified' down into 'defied' and then shrivels them both down to 'died'. 'Many have died'. 'Deified' into 'defied' is a genuine but precarious movement of the imagination; so the subsequent pared-down 'died' rightly does not disown it, but does place and weigh it. Against that laconic shrivelling root-simplicity is set the grossly

burgeoning unimaginability of Auschwitz, with the very sounds moving from delicacy ('a fable') into the fattened slabs of monumental evil:

a fable
Unbelievable in fatted marble.

For '*fatted mar* b*le*' is a distending of the word 'fable' into a sleek stoniness; and 'fatted' is the ancient sacrifice. To 'pass on the far side' may at the time be well-judged but may also later be harshly judged. The poem is forced to ask, at least, about the relation between the Jews and their God:

There is, at times, some need to demonstrate
Jehovah's touchy methods, that create
The connoisseur of blood, the smitten man.
At times it seems not common to explain.

For 'the smitten man' is a thrust at one of those moments when the God of the Jews moves in an appallingly mysterious way:

And a certain man of the sons of the prophets said unto his neighbour in the word of the Lord, Smite me, I pray thee. And the man refused to smite him. Then said he unto him, Because thou hast not obeyed the voice of the Lord, behold, as soon as thou art departed from me, a lion shall slay thee. And as soon as he was departed from him, a lion found him, and slew him. Then he found another man, and said, Smite me, I pray thee. And the man smote him, so that in smiting he wounded him. (*I Kings*, xx 37).[8]

'At times it seems not common to explain'. Which is not to say that the poem asks us to accept the cliché, the common explanation. For the 'unbelievable' is also the unexplainable, and the world of Hill's poem is completely different from the world of George Steiner's prose with its explanation of why all this befell the Jews: 'the blackmail of perfection' which the Jews three times visited upon Western life: the intolerable idealisms of, first, monotheism; then Christian adjuration; then messianic socialism. 'When it turned on the Jew, Christianity and European civilization turned on the incarnation—albeit an incarnation often wayward and unaware—of its own best hopes'.[9]

Statesmen have known visions. And, not alone,
Artistic men prod dead men from their stone.

Hill has pronounced

Two Formal Elegies
For the Jews in Europe
I

Knowing the dead, and how some are disposed:
Subdued under rubble, water, in sand graves,
In clenched cinders not yielding their abused
Bodies and bonds to those whom war's chance saves
Without the law: we grasp, roughly, the song.
Arrogant acceptance from which song derives
Is bedded with their blood, makes flourish young
Roots in ashes. The wilderness revives,

Deceives with sweetness harshness. Still beneath
Live skin stone breathes, about which fires but play,
Fierce heart that is the iced brain's to command
To judgment—(studied reflex, contained breath)—
Their best of worlds since, on the ordained day,
This world went spinning from Jehovah's hand.

II

For all that must be gone through, their long death
Documented and safe, we have enough
Witnesses (our world being witness-proof).
The sea flickers, roars, in its wide hearth.
Here, yearly, the pushing midlanders stand
To warm themselves; men, brawny with life,

Women who expect life. They relieve
Their thickening bodies, settle on scraped sand.
Is it good to remind them, on a brief screen,
Of what they have witnessed and not seen?
(Deaths of the city that persistently dies . . . ?)
To put up stones ensures some sacrifice.
Sufficient men confer, carry their weight.
(At whose door does the sacrifice stand or start?)

The first poem, which begins with the dangerous word 'Knowing', knows that our comprehension of it will have to be a matter of grasping it, with some of the urgent haste of such seizing. Like its creator, 'we grasp, roughly, the song'. *Roughly* as untenderly (how else can we resist the solicitations of a false tenderness—'Knowing the dead'? But, like Hill, we never did know them as people known to us; and a sense of threat swells within that other dark meaning of 'knowing the dead. . . .'— and what they are capable of). But *roughly*, too, as approximately (to hope for more than an honourable approximation in such a case would be dishonourable hubris).

There is an angry vibration in this response to the outraged dead. Life, bristling against injustice, quivers in the restive play upon *disposed*: 'Knowing the dead, and how some are disposed'—a disposition of mind, or the disposal of a body? Likewise in *subdued*: 'Subdued under rubble'—a crushed body, or a quietly stoical mind? The quivering of life is there again in the bitter archaism of 'war's chance': 'those whom war's chance saves'. For where in the world of technologized extermination is there even a memory of what was once true and poignant: 'The chance of war / Is equal and the slayer oft is slain' (*The Iliad*)?[10] There is the old sense of outrage felt yet once more, in the mingled gratitude to and warning to Voltaire: 'Their best of worlds'. There is the simultaneous delight and fear in 'This world went spinning from Jehovah's hand': spinning effortlessly into its ordained arc, or spinning away for ever from his hand?

In the second poem, there is the same glowering intensity alive to the terrible questions which ask what good it can do even to think on these things, truly knowing that it may well do ill. 'For all that must be gone through': for all which, or—with the known acknowledged *that* as either shouldered or shrugged off—'For all that must be gone through'. Gone through, as endured, or as wearisomely enumerated? How hostile the relation is between 'witness' and 'proof', held apart and together by their hyphen: 'witness-proof', and then between 'witness-proof' and fireproof or foolproof. What are we proofed in, armoured in, that we think we can witness, let alone bear witness to, such happenings? The 'midlanders', after all, are English tourists as well as Mediterranean natives. With the last line of the second poem, there ignites the fierceness which was smouldering in the first poem. For 'Without the law' had not forgotten Kipling's 'Recessional':

Such boastings as the Gentiles use,
    Or lesser breeds without the Law—
Lord God of Hosts, be with us yet,
    Lest we forget—lest we forget!

No tremor passes through Kipling's line: 'Still stands Thine ancient sacrifice'. Hill's final line has the tremor of genuine interrogation: '(At whose door does the sacrifice stand or start?)' 'The guilt of blood is at your door', wrote Tennyson. And *start* is a last twist: jump in shock (as against the stolid *stand*), or learn to begin? Hill, who says in another poem about the dead that 'Some, finally, learn to begin' ('The Distant Fury of Battle'), ends this poem with a sudden 'start'; he has brought us to the point at which we may indeed start.

These are poems which carry their weight, and they are substantially resistant, so there remain many serious questions as to how to construe and what to make of them. But I wish to move to a consideration which then bears on others of Hill's poems, a consideration which becomes manifest in the revisions which Hill made to this poem after its first publication. As originally published,[11] it had within brackets the dedication '(For the Jews of Europe)', and the second poem then ended with an extraordinary tour-de-force: of the last four lines, not only the first and the last were each within brackets, but so too were the second and the third. The poem ended with four successive lines each within brackets. Hill was right to think that his is a poetic gift which must be profoundly and variously alive to what simple brackets can do. He had been wrong to think that he could command to favourable judgment a concatenation of four lines, each bracketed, without his poem's indurating itself into mannerism and self-attention, a sequence of self-containednesses such as then seals the poem into self-congratulation. By removing the brackets from both the antepenultimate and the penultimate lines, he not only removed the oppression of paralysing self-consciousness, but also tautened the arc of the poem. For, unlike the first poem, the second has at last gravitated to couplets; against which there is now played a beautiful and complementary chiasmus, *a/b/b/ a*, in the sombre punctuation alone. Of the last four lines, the first and second, and then the third and fourth, rhyme together, but it is the second and third, and then the first and fourth, which punctuate together. The tensions of the last four lines now dispose themselves differently; less disruptedly, less fracturedly, and more finally, since chiasmus comprises an arc.

Brackets are a way of containing things and feelings, in both of the senses of containing: including and restraining. It is then a true sense of the metaphorical power even of ordinary punctuation which led Hill to have, as the only parenthesis within the first poem, the words '—(studied reflex, contained breath)—'. The parenthesis holds the breadth of the dead; we hold our breath, and contain ourselves, even as the speaking poet does, with his syntax suspended and his rhythm tensed (a steadying of the voice is necessary in 'contained breath', with its minute resistance to the iambic movement), so that, at once trained and spontaneous—'(studied reflex, contained breath)'—, the lines may 'command to judgment . . . Their best of worlds'.

There is a different kind of metaphorical life in the parenthesis in the second poem: '(our world being witness-proof)'. For here the brackets suggest the corrupt separateness of which contained breath is the pure counterpart; the brackets now act as a kind of proof or armour against all penetrative imagination, with *our world* fortified in blasé imperviousness by its brackets, unlike their open hope, 'Their best of worlds', 'This world'. The two other bracketings (two from what, as I have said, had been four) embody a move from one kind of musing, a brooding upon a paradox such as may be religious or religiose, musing into the truth-gathering or the wool-gathering of three dots: '(Deaths of the city that persistently dies. . . ?)'—a move from this kind of musing into something much sharper in sound and sense, a 'perplexed persistence', a baffled indictment: '(At whose door does the sacrifice stand or start?)'[12] Yet the end is at once curt and muted—muted by the inevitably receding or *recessional* quality of brackets as we read them.

But 'read them' is equivocal. Eyes and ears? Although our inner ear may divine a tone from such brackets, may sense a lowering of the timbre or pitch or tone or note or simply loudness, one of the important things about brackets is that they belong with those signs of punctuation which the voice cannot sufficiently utter. Hill's poetry makes weighty and delicate use of this very fact. Hugh Kenner has pointed out that you cannot say a footnote or an asterisk; I disagree with him about parentheses.

> The footnote's relation to the passage from which it depends is established wholly by visual and typographic means, and will typically defeat all efforts of the speaking voice to clarify it without visual aid. Parentheses, like commas, tell the voice what to do: an asterisk tells the voice that it can do nothing. You cannot read a passage of prose aloud, interpolating the footnotes, and make the subordination of the footnotes clear, and keep the whole sounding natural. The language has forsaken a vocal milieu, and a context of oral communication between persons, and commenced to take advantage of the expressive possibilities of technological space.[13]

This is entirely true of the footnote and the asterisk; perhaps the auditory imagination, when the eye reads such punctuation, hears something, calls up some tone to itself for what it is apprehending, but this auditory imagination is essentially private. You could not, in the manner of French dictation at school, read aloud such punctuation and elicit accurate transcriptions from your hearers, any more than you could of T. S. Eliot's spacing-punctuation in *The Waste Land*. The eye can here allow to enter its consciousness what the tongue cannot then utter.

But Kenner is wrong to set up the contrast: 'Parentheses, like commas,[14] tell the voice what to do: an asterisk tells the voice that it can do nothing'. For though a parenthesis is a syntactical unit, and of course the voice can make such a thing clear, a parenthesis is a syntactical unit which may be qualified by very different punctuations. *Parenthesis:* 'An explanatory or qualifying word, clause, or sentence inserted into a passage with which it has not necessarily any grammatical connexion, and from which it is usually marked off by round or square brackets, dashes, or commas' (*OED*). We use the word parenthesis both for the unit and for one of the many ways of indicating it, and the voice is not able to make adequately clear (adequate in both delicacy and clarity) whether the parenthesis is bracketed off, comma'd off, or dashed off. (Even apart from the fact that the voice cannot utter a square as against a round bracket.)[15] For although it may be true that such punctuation as is markedly durational may be uttered (a full stop is likely, though only likely, to mean a longer pause than a comma), the thing about brackets is that they are not essentially an indicator of duration. They indicate a relationship which may or may not have a durational dimension, and they speak to the eye and not to the ear. A poet who has a strong sense both of all that the voice can do and of all that it cannot, a poet who knows that the timing within a poem both is and is not a matter of tempo,[16] will be a poet who seizes upon the particular power of the bracket to incarnate something which commands a sense of the difference between what can be printedly read and what can be said.

It is Hill's 'September Song' which most fully realizes, in both senses, how much a simple point of punctuation may weigh.

September Song
born 19.6.32—deported 24.9.42

Undesirable you may have been, untouchable
you were not. Not forgotten
or passed over at the proper time.

As estimated, you died. Things marched,
sufficient, to that end.

Just so much Zyklon and leather, patented
terror, so many routine cries.

(I have made
an elegy for myself it
is true)

September fattens on vines. Roses
flake from the wall. The smoke
of harmless fires drifts to my eyes.

This is plenty. This is more than enough.

It is a poem which has elicited from Jon Silkin a sustained critical meditation, which I shall quote in its entirety:

> A concentration camp victim. Even the 'play' in the subtitle 'born 19.6.32—deported 24.9.42' where the natural event of the birth is placed, simply, beside the human and murderous 'deported' as if the latter were of the same order and inevitability for the victim; which, in some senses, it was—even here, the zeugmatic wit is fully employed. The irony of conjuncted meanings between 'undesirable' (touching on both sexual desire and racism) and 'untouchable', which exploits a similar ambiguity but reverses the emphases, is unusually dense *and* simple. The confrontation is direct and unavoidable, and this directness is brought to bear on the reader not only by the vocabulary, but by the balancing directness of the syntax. This stanza contains one of Hill's dangerous words—dangerous because of its too-frequent use, and because these words sometimes unleash (though not here) a too evident irony:
>
> > Not forgotten
> > or passed over at the proper time.
>
> 'Proper' brings together the idea of bureaucratically correct 'as calculated' by the logistics of the 'final solution' and the particular camp's timetable; it also contrasts the idea of the mathematically 'correct' with the morally intolerable. It touches, too, on the distinction between what is morally right, and what is conventionally acceptable, and incidentally brings to bear on the whole the way in which the conventionally acceptable is often used to cloak the morally unacceptable. One of Hill's grim jokes, deployed in such a way that the laughter is precisely proportionate to the needs of ironic exposure. It is when the irony is in excess of the situation that the wit becomes mannered. But here it does not. So the poem continues, remorselessly.
>
> > As estimated, you died. Things marched,
> > sufficient, to that end.
>
> One feels the little quibbling movement in
>
> > As estimated, you died.
>
> as, without wishing to verbalise it, Hill points to the disturbing contrast between the well-functioning time-table and what it achieved. 'Things marched' has the tread of pompous authority, immediately, in the next line, qualified by the painfully accurate recognition that just so much energy was needed, and released, for the extermination. 'Sufficient' implies economy, but it also implies a conscious qualification of the heavy, pompous tread of authority. The quiet function of unpretentious machinery fulfilled its programme, perhaps *more* lethally. One also notices here how the lineation guages, exactly, the flow and retraction of meaning and impulse, and how this exact rhythmical flow is so much a part of the sensuous delivery of response and evaluation. It is speech articulated, but the lineation provides, via the

convention of verse line-ending, a formal control of rhythm, and of sense emphasis, by locking with, or breaking, the syntactical flow. Thus in the third stanza the syntax is broken by the lineation exactly at those parts at which the confession, as it were, of the poem's (partial) source is most painful:

> (I have made
> an elegy for myself it
> is true)

The slightly awkward break after 'it' not only forces the reading speed down to a word-by-word pace, in itself an approximation to the pain of the confession, but emphasises the whole idea. By placing emphasis on the unspecifying pronoun, Hill is able to say two things: that the elegy was made for himself (at least, in part) since in mourning another one is also commiserating with one's own condition.

> When we chant
> 'Ora, ora pro nobis' it is not
> Seraphs who descend to pity but ourselves.
> ('Funeral Music:5')

But 'it' may also refer to the whole event; I have made an elegy for myself, as we all do, but I have also made an elegy on a 'true' event. True imaginatively, true in detailed fact; both for someone other than myself. Thus he is able to point to the difficulty of the poet, who wishes, for a variety of reasons, to approach the monstrousness of such events, but has compunction about doing so. He tactfully touches for instance on the overweening ambition of the poet who hitches his talent to this powerful subject, thereby giving his work an impetus it *may* not be fully entitled to, since, only the victim, herself, would be entitled to derive this kind of 'benefit'. But he also modestly pleads, I think, with 'it / is true' that whatever the reasons for his writing such an elegy, a proper regard for the victim, a true and unambitious feeling, was present and used.[17]

Silkin's sense of the poem is scrupulous and touching. The poem is indeed 'dense *and* simple'; so I should add that, for instance, the awful weight upon

> Not forgotten
> or passed over at the proper time

is instinct not only with the bitter reversal of the Passover (with its further flickering reminder that innocent Egyptians and not just guilty ones were smitten with the loss of their first-born), but also with the petty grievance of promotion denied: 'passed over'. Similar vibrations stir in the dehumanizing militaristic bureaucracy of 'Things marched', and in the tiny dubiety of 'Just so much . . .', where 'Just' is both the casually murderous 'Merely' and the meticulously murderous 'Precisely'. 'Zyklon' is then, in every sense, a word from—a wafting of poison gas from—a completely different world from that of everything else in the poem, unutterably alien and not just foreign; ugly; imperious (Hill had originally given it only a lower-case z, which too much lowered its hateful rank)—a word (is it a *word*, even?) which did not have this 'patented' sense until our time, scarcely belongs in the English language, and which is now for ever doomed to the detestation of one immediate association. There it is, capitalized, in this poem which has no name for the dead child. Then there is the sickening glissade from *leather* to *patented*, and the awful possibility of fatigued exasperation in 'so many routine cries'. Routine cries, to the camp's officials; can a poem raise itself above a routine cry?

The poem moves through from two groupings (they can't be called stanzas) which are 'you', through two which are 'I'

and 'my', to a bleak curt shaping (one line only) which is neither 'you' nor 'I'. 'This is plenty. This is more than enough'. This? This, as the smiling month of September, a mockery of that September in 1942, which itself had mocked the month of the Jewish New Year and of the Day of Atonement. The anger at the month is unjust, casting-about for a scapegoat: 'September fattens on vines'—again the basking fatness, being fattened for the kill, a fertilising richness. But then there is the other 'This'—This, as the attempt to speak of it (it, the further 'This,' the happening itself). Bitter at the ineffectuality of even its own best efforts, and so dismissing them curtly and yet with the reluctance of repetition: 'This is plenty. This is more than enough'. Plenty, as gratitude to nature's foison, but also as brusque slang; 'more than enough', as needing to end in something more English, an unillusioned understatement. The last line pounces, and yet its cadence doesn't fall into the trap which waits for the separate finality of that old reassurance, the clinching iambic pentameter. Partly this is a matter of the delicacy with which it both is and is not preceded by an iambic pentameter: 'The smoke / of harmless fires drifts to my eyes'. That is not one line, but one and a half; the cadence drifts across, and then what had been drifting suddenly clenches itself. Yet not into anything easily clinching, since the one line is both one and two in its structure: 'This is plenty. This is more than enough'. Behind the poet's pinched self-scrutiny, having to bite back, we should poignantly hear the age-old open-hearted fierce gratitude with which the Jews thank their God at Passover:

> If he had brought us forth out of Egypt but had not executed judgments upon the Egyptians, it would have been enough.
> If he had executed judgments upon the Egyptians, but had not executed judgments upon their gods, it would have been enough.
> If he had executed judgments upon their gods, but had not slain their first-born, it would have been enough.
> If he had slain their first-born, but had not bestowed their wealth on us, it would have been enough.
> If he had bestowed their wealth on us, but had not divided the sea for us, it would have been enough . . .[18]

Jon Silkin feels, and helps us feel, the central gravity of the three lines

> (I have made
> an elegy for myself it
> is true)

But I believe that it is crucial to them that they are in brackets. For it is this, and not their tone or syntax alone, which gives them that unique feeling of being at once a crux and an aside, at once an inescapable honourable admission and something which the poem may then honourably pass over. It is the brackets which embody the essential discrimination between the right and the wrong kind of detachment. Hopkins may tell his autumnal griever that she is grieving not for Goldengrove but for herself: 'It is Margaret you mourn for'. Hill acknowledges that he mourns for himself, but he refuses to make the total concession which would evacuate the whole matter; he does not say that he has made an elegy only for himself; and 'it is true'—which is unsayably punctuated so that only the eye can sense its utterance—is not only the concession, and not only an insistence that the deportation indeed happened, but also a quietly confident insistence that the elegy itself is true.

For its truth is partly that it embodies the truth that what happened was unspeakable, and at the heart of the poem is this moment of something that is perfectly lucid but unspeakable, unsayable. A man may write of it, and that is not nothing, but he cannot *speak* of it, any more than you can speak those brackets. If you know that there are brackets there, you can strain to hear them; and the eye may be deeply moved by the way in which the brackets lower the words within them down into silent depths. But they intimate an irreducible recalcitrance, of the kind which any true poem on such atrocities ought to intimate. 'The tongue's atrocities': but these bracketed words protect themselves against the tongue and its arts.

I have quoted Silkin on Hill; let me return the compliments by quoting some earlier criticism, Hill on Silkin, a passage which evokes something of the sense which a profound parenthesis may make within a poem:

> He is able to make his words hover and brood, often by re-iteration within and across the short line. The total effect is a curious amalgam of the forthright and the tentative. It is like a man facing his accusers; or like a man giving lessons in elementary logic; or like a man repeating to himself instructions for personal survival. The diffidence makes Silkin a 'man of his age', though his self-questioning is quite without the 'pawkiness' that can be so irritating in, say Philip Larkin or John Wain.[19]

Hill's parenthesis—bracketed parenthesis—in 'September Song' incorporates a true diffidence, an amalgam of the confessedly central with the proportionedly peripheral, 'a curious amalgam of the forthright and the tentative'. For the poet who used those words also said this:

> Language *contains* everything you want—history, sociology, economics: it is a kind of drama of human destiny. One thinks how it has been used and exploited in the past, politically and theologically. Its forthrightness and treachery are a drama of the honesty of man himself. Language reveals life.[20]

The forthright and the treacherous; the forthright and the tentative: these struggle in an art that tries to '*contain* everything'. '(Studied reflex, contained breath)'.

Yet this poet who knows about treachery, who knows that his line 'Our God scatters corruption' means both 'Our God puts corruption to flight' and 'Our God disseminates corruption',[21] is someone who knows that any device of language is an axis, not a direction. The very thing which may do such-and-such may do its opposite. So it must be added that, though it is true that the unsayableness of a typographical sign like a bracket may truly embody a recognition of the morally, spiritually and politically unspeakable, it is no less true that this very unspeakableness may choose exactly the same form: a voiceless and dehumanized 'language', denying the warm humanity of the voice and steeling its cold eye. What Kenner calls 'the expressive possibilities of technological space' have their appalling possibilities, in the technology for instance of extermination. So it is important that Hill's 'September Song' should incorporate both edges of this two-edged recognition, as it does in the italicised subheading (dedication? epigraph? subtitle?):

born 19.6.32—deported 24.9.42

For it is not only that though you may be able to say some italics (simply emphatic ones), you cannot say these; it is also that you can scarcely, without a terrible dehumanized bureaucratic numerateness, say '19.6.32' or '24.9.42'. A brutal official haste and economy lop off the centuries. The month in '24.9.42' can scarcely be felt to be the same month as September. 9 is unsayable (you may be saying *nine*); it is international, but with internationalism's anonymity and inhumanity; it is hatefully congruent with the calm hideous substitution of 'deported' for 'died' in the flat item. But then 'deported' amounted to 'died', and we are contemplating a repulsive travesty of the inscription on a memorial-stone. The effect is the counterpart, in its summoning up of professionalized dishonour, to Philip Larkin's title 'MCMXIV'. I cannot say MCMXIV; yet I cannot think it right of the B.B.C., in a reading of Larkin's poems, to say the title as '1914'. For what Larkin intimated, through those unsayable ancient numerals, was at once a continuity with age-old wars and a unique disjunction—both such as make 1914 the meeting of two eras. Larkin uses roman numerals for a departed honour; Hill uses modern numerals for a new dishonour. Moreover he made here a minute change to the punctuation after first publication;[22] instead of a bureaucrat's semi-colon, a stonemason's dash. The eye takes it in; in despairing of adequately, sufficiently, uttering it, the imagination creates something out of its own despair.

> (I have made
> an elegy for myself it
> is true)

For within the brackets there lurks another decent equivocation, another curious amalgam of the centrally forthright and the tangentially personal. I should like to come at it by way of one of the most moving entries in Dr Johnson's annals and prayers:

> Oct. 18. 1767 Sunday. Yesterday, Oct. 17 at about ten in the morning I took my leave for ever of my dear old Friend Catherine Chambers, who came to live with my Mother about 1724, and has been but little parted from us since. She buried my Father, my Brother, and my Mother. She is now fifty eight years old.
>
> I desired all to withdraw, then told her that we were to part for ever, that as Christians we should part with prayer, and that I would, if she was willing, say a short prayer beside her. She expressed great desire to hear me, and held up her poor hands, as she lay in bed, with great fervour, while I prayed, kneeling by her, nearly in the following words.
>
> Almighty and most merciful Father, whose loving kindness is over all thy works, behold, visit, and relieve this thy Servant who is grieved with sickness. Grant that the sense of her weakness may add strength to her faith, and seriousness to her Repentance. And grant that by the help of thy Holy Spirit after the pains and labours of this short life, we may all obtain everlasting happiness through Jesus Christ, our Lord, for whose sake hear our Prayers. Amen.
>
> Our Father.
>
> I then kissed her. She told me that to part was the greatest pain that she had ever felt, and that she hoped we should meet again in a better place. I expressed with swelled eyes and great emotion of tenderness the same hopes. We kissed and parted, I humbly hope, to meet again, and to part no more.

Nowhere do these moving words mention something which is at once properly central to Johnson's feelings and yet at the same time tangential to any such feelings: the fact that Johnson, like his dying Kitty Chambers, 'is now fifty eight years old'. 'After the pains and labours of this short life . . .': all human life is short, but it may feel the more short when you kneel beside someone of your own age who is dying. As Johnson composed his words and as he set them down (just a month after his 58th birthday), he must have thought of something which he did not mention, and his thoughts swell tacitly within his affecting prayer. And Geoffrey Hill, who was born in 1932, must he not have thought of something which he did not mention, when he wrote the simple evil headstone *born 19.6.32—deported 29.9.42?* Something at once central to his feelings and yet adventitious, tangential?

> (I have made
> an elegy for myself it
> is true)

It is the brackets, with the heart in hiding, which here 'come as near as may be to the impossible ideal of a silent eloquence',[23] and which make possible a mingling of the candid and the covert which is 'the true voice of feeling' partly because it acknowledges that some true feelings cannot exactly be voiced. Hill has noted, with good-natured scorn, that 'Henry Adams, it is true, remarked that "Beyond a doubt, silence is best"'.[24] But, for Hill, there are few truths which are beyond a doubt, and even the word *beyond* has its equivocation:

> so we bear witness,
> Despite ourselves, to what is beyond us,
> ('Funeral Music: 8')

Beyond us? Serenely out of our sphere, or exasperatingly out of our comprehension?—it's beyond me. But brackets may hint at something which is beyond us, but not beyond us; they can be at once tentative and forthright, a moment of silent eloquence and of 'contained breath'.

> But we are commanded
> To rise, when, in silence
> I would compose my voice.
> ('Men are a Mockery of
> Angels')

George Steiner must be speaking a truth when he says that 'the ineffable lies beyond the frontiers of the word',[25] but it may still be decent for a poet to seek the impossible ideal of a worded ineffability. What is 'beyond the frontiers' may be glimpsed in that special beyond/within which is parenthesis, a voice subdued to a kind of silence. T. S. Eliot allows us to hear this, when he encloses his paradox of silence and speech within the murmuring shell of brackets:

> At nightfall, in the rigging and the aerial,
> Is a voice descanting (though not to the ear,
> The murmuring shell of time, and not in any
> language)
> 'Fare forward, you who think that you are voyaging;'
> ('The Dry Salvages')

Hill, in his early poems, often drew upon this sense of the privileged paradoxicality of brackets, in their relation to silence. It could be an open juxtaposition, as in his beautiful early poem, published but uncollected, 'Summer Night':[26]

> The air yields to the nudging owl
> Stressing the dark with its long call
> Over the coppice and the pool:
> Silence has stirred inside this shell.
>
> The dark creaks like an empty house:
> (There is nothing, over the white fields, amiss)
> Though like the air the untroubled water flows,
> Time stands upon its toes.
>
> Overhead move the tense stars
> Stripping off such disguise
> As 'this will be' and 'this was.'
> There is not another moment to lose.

Silence, the shell, and the eerie security of the parenthesis: it may owe something to Eliot, but it earns enough to repay the debt. The end of another early uncollected poem, 'An Ark on the Flood',[27] owes too much to Melville, but even here there is life stirring within the collocation of 'ears . . . sound . . . mouths . . . silent' and the elegiac brackets:

> But Ishmael's ears are crippled to that sound,

> (O starry mouths amid the oozes drowned)
> The harp hangs silent from the windless tree.

Sometimes, even in tragic poems by Hill, the impulse seems to me to harden into mere mannerism, and there floats up the Rev. Dr. Edmund Law:

> According to Paley, the Bishop was once impatient at the slowness of his Carlisle printer. '"Why does not my book make its appearance?" said he to the printer. "My Lord, I am extremely sorry; but we have been obliged to send to Glasgow for a pound of parentheses."'[28]

I feel a disproportionate mannerism, for instance, throughout 'A Prayer to the Sun', particularly at the moment when the parenthesis

> (Hell is
> silent)

offers something which sounds flatly inured and impervious. There is more of a living cadence in the relation of the succeeding brackets (about 'mystery') to the way in which men 'Still leave much carefully unsaid', in the early uncollected poem 'For Isaac Rosenberg'.[29] Or in the later poem about another poet, 'Old Poet with Distant Admirers', with its final laconic deepening, from 'silence' to 'mouth' to 'death-songs' and then to the muted and altogether final parenthesis, at once tremulous and offhand:

> If
> I knew the exact coin for tribute,
> Defeat might be bought, processional
> Silence gesture its tokens of earth
> At my mouth: as in the great death-songs
> Of Propertius (although he died young).

Or there are the only brackets in the whole of the sequence *Mercian Hymns*, sealing the lips at the end of XXIV:

> Itinerant through numerous domains, of his lord's
> retinue, to Compostela. Then home for a
> lifetime
> amid West Mercia this master-mason as I
> envisage
> him, intent to pester upon tympanum and
> chancel-
> arch his moody testament, confusing warrior
> with
> lion, dragon-coils, tendrils of the stony vine.
>
> Where best to stand? Easter sunrays catch the ob-
> lique face of Adam scrumping through leaves;
> pale
> spree of evangelists and, there, a cross Christ
> mumming child Adam out of Hell
>
> ('Et exspecto resurrectionem mortuorum' dust in the
> eyes, on clawing wings, and lips)

The lips are sealed by the dust and by the brackets, somewhat as all sounds are muffled in the silent art-work which is masonry.[30] The shaping spirit of one imagination cannot be translated into the dimensions of another, any more than Latin can breathe within exactly the same world as what precedes it. Yet how creatively Hill translates into his religious art-world— '(. . . dust in the eyes, on clawing wings, and lips)'—the very different impulse of Eliot's evocation of a pagan art-world: '(Another hid his eyes behind his wing)'.

The maturing of Hill's achievement in an art of the parenthesis—a maturing technical and human, for as Eliot knew, we cannot say at what point technique begins or where it ends—comes with Hill's remarkable rotations of what Eliot had sensed as the life lived within the contained breath and silent eloquence of brackets. Perhaps the crucial moment was the grim turning of the tables upon Eliot, in the opening of Hill's 'Solomon's Mines':

Anything to have done!
(The eagle flagged to the sun)

—an allusion, presumably, to the wings which folded themselves around Eliot's notorious parenthesis in *Ash-Wednesday*:

(Why should the agèd eagle stretch its wings?)

—itself a strange sibling to that parenthesis of elegant pagan prurience in *The Waste Land*:

The Chair she sat in, like a burnished throne,
Glowed on the marble, where the glass
Held up by standards wrought with fruited vines
From which a golden Cupidon peeped out
(Another hid his eyes behind his wing)
Doubled the flames of sevenbranched candelabra

Certainly by the time of his poem 'Doctor Faustus', Hill had learnt, probably from Eliot, the various effects which a poet can gain from rhyming a word with its bracketed self, so that the rhyme is not truly a *rhyme*, and yet is gruesomely perfect, and yet is on a different plane or in a different dimension. In the first poem of 'Doctor Faustus', 'The Emperor's Clothes', there is no nakedness, and no candid child's voice to be heard:

There is no-one
Afraid or overheard, no loud
Voice (though innocently loud).

How oddly that second *loud* ends the poem, played against the brackets' pressure towards a feeling for the *sotto voce*. The insidious impalpability recalls one of Eliot's greatest triumphs, the astonishing play of the cadences and the sense against the punctuation's demands, in *The Waste Land*:

Only
There is shadow under this red rock,
(Come in under the shadow of this red rock),
And I will show you something different from either
Your shadow at morning striding behind you
Or your shadow at evening rising to meet you;
I will show you fear in a handful of dust.

The ear registers no disturbance, but the eye should be disturbed by its being so 'different' from the ear. For if there is one thing which would be thought to be stable, it is that if bracketed words are removed, there will be no stumble but an unbroken syntactical stride. Puttenham said of the parenthesis: 'when ye will seeme, for larger information or some other purpose, to peece or graffe in the middest of your tale an unnecessary parcel of speach, which neverthelesse may be thence without any detriment to the rest'.[31] Johnson defined a parenthesis as 'A sentence so included in another sentence, as that it may be taken out without injuring the sense of that which encloses it: commonly marked thus ( )'. So that when you exclude such 'intercluding' ('Parenthesis, an intercluding . . .'), your stride can pick up where it left off. Yet what happens if we exclude Eliot's intercluded parenthesis?

Only
There is shadow under this red rock,
And I will show you something different

The sense is so precarious as to sound deranged; so a reader is pressed to let the words '(Come in under the shadow of this red rock)' come in, or come out from the shadow of their brackets, in order that there may then be the sane sequence: 'Come in under the shadow . . . And I will show you'. It is a revolutionary moment in English poetry, in the mildness of its violence. Such a parenthesis deepens the meaning of Puttenham's definition of a parenthesis as 'your first figure of

tollerable disorder'. Eliot had not arrived at this eerie profundity in his original version of these lines, in 'The Death of St. Narcissus', where the sequence 'Come . . . And I will show you . . .' was not imperilled by any brackets.

I spoke of the broken syntactical stride not only because Eliot here speaks of 'striding', but also because there is a relation between these junctions and disjunctions and certain rhythmical triumphs which have fascinated Hill. Of the movement within Wordsworth's 'Ode: Intimations of Immortality', a movement from the 'weighed acknowledgment of custom's pressure':

Heavy as frost, and deep almost as life!

to the 'fresh time-signature' of

O joy! that in our embers
Is something that doth live

Hill has said:

Crudely stated, the difference is between being 'in' stride and 'out of' stride. The 'magical change' [quoting Hopkins] in the 'Immortality' Ode is perhaps the greatest moment in nineteenth-century English poetry; but in choosing this term one is suggesting restriction as well as potency. The recognition and the strategy to match the recognition—the cessation of 'stride', the moment of disjuncture, the picking up of fresh 'stride'—were of their very nature inimitable; they were of, and for, that moment.[32]

It is a creative disjuncture which Hill—like Eliot—effects, among other ways, through the imaginative use of mere brackets, such as give a different signature which is not exactly a matter of rhythm, or of timing, or of syntax, but a ghostlier demarcation.

In the essay from which I have quoted, 'Redeeming the Time', Hill considers the ways in which a particular passage by George Eliot suffers from having 'excluded the antiphonal voice of the heckler'; Hill imagines the heckler's interjections, and naturally intercludes them in brackets; and he is moved to quote what is for him (he alludes to it elsewhere) a crucial text from one of Coleridge's letters:

Of parentheses I may be too fond, and will be on my guard in this respect. But I am certain that no work of impassioned and eloquent reasoning ever did or could subsist without them. They are the *drama* of reason, and present the thought growing, instead of a mere *Hortus siccus*. (28 January 1810, to Thomas Poole).

Hill remarks: 'He surely foresaw the obligation to enact the drama of reason within the texture of one's own work, since nothing else would serve. His parentheses are antiphons of vital challenge'. Now it is evident that for Coleridge a parenthesis need not be something in brackets, and Hill is aware of the range and variety of the parenthetical. Yet one of the most obvious, and subtlest, forms of the parenthesis is simple brackets, and Hill is, as it happens, an especially keen observer of what other writers have done with brackets.

The bizarre scene in Jonson's *Catiline* is an awkward case for me, since it is not clear to me how an actress utters *brackets* exactly, but still the instance is potent enough, and Hill dourly delights in it:

Sempronia: I ha'beene writing all this night (and am
So very weary) unto all the *tribes*,
And *centuries*, for their voyces, to helpe Catiline
In his election. We shall make him *Consul*,
I hope, amongst us . . .

TWENTIETH-CENTURY BRITISH LITERATURE

Fulvia: Who stands beside?
    (Give me some wine, and poulder for my teeth.
Sempronia: Here's a good pearle in troth!
Fulvia: A pretty one.
Sempronia: A very orient one!) There are
    competitors . . .

                                        (II i)

On which Hill comments: 'The derangement is here stressed by the abrupt parenthesis of womanish trivia, chatter about pearls and dentrifice'.[33]

It is not only the 'parenthesis' there, but the word 'abrupt' which points towards one of Hill's convictions. For him, Hopkins is preeminently the poet of—in Hopkins's phrase— 'abrupt self', where *abrupt* is used 'both for a very technical thing and for a very spiritual or psychological thing';[34] and the abruptness manifests itself in movements of disjunction and junction such as brackets may encompass, as when Hopkins's power is for Hill eloquently realized in the final line of 'Carrion Comfort': '(my God!) my God'.[35]

Or there is this praise of Keith Douglas, and in particular of the poem 'Adams':

In it, Douglas swings abruptly from a description of the bird to the evocation of a (supposed) acquaintance, a dominating personality:

    Adams is like a bird;
    alert (high on his pinnacle of air
    he does not hear you, someone said).

Hill's bracketed '(supposed)' may remind us of the title of one of his best religious poems, 'To the (Supposed) Patron', wittily turning upon the God of love what the devout love-versifying seventeenth-century cleric was obliged to say of his loved one: 'To his (supposed) Mistresse'. What Hill responds to in Douglas's poem is partly the imaginative parenthesis, with its detached or pinnacled alertness and its strange relation to hearing and saying. Indeed, much of this essay by Hill on Douglas[36] is bent upon the taxing achievement of a decent detachment, a freedom from unjust appropriation of suffering and horror and war. Hill quotes from Douglas such things as 'We stood here on the safe side of it', and 'I in another place'; and this might call up the relation between the word 'safe' and the ensuing parenthesis in the second of Hill's 'Two Formal Elegies', or a sentence like this from his criticism: 'The prime significance of Swift's "sin of wit" is that it challenges and reverses in terms of metaphor the world's routine of power and, within safe parentheses, considers all alternatives including anarchy'.[37] Hill admires Douglas precisely for his sense that sometimes 'We stood here on the safe side of it'; 'You reach a new world'; 'I in another place'; 'the same hours':

Each of these phrases, far from asserting a 'unifying generalization' [quoting Ted Hughes] about experience, conveys a sense of alienation, exclusion, of a world with its own tragi-comic laws. . . . And much of the acuteness of the perception is in the recognition that not everyone has to go through with this; that two absolutely different worlds co-exist at about a day's journey from each other.

Yet a simple bracket may establish a co-existing zone which is only a contained breath away and yet which breathes the pure serene of another planet. '(There is nothing, over the white fields, amiss)'.

It is the hush of brackets which answers to Hill's deepest sense of things, or rather it is the antagonism between two different kinds of hush: the hush of contained breath, and the hush of contained anger or violence. The subject is that of one of the jealous coplas in Hill's 'Songbook of Sebastian Arrurruz':

It is to him I write, it is to her
I speak in contained silence. Will they be touched
By the unfamiliar passion between them?

That contained silence (which is both peace and war) may gravitate towards brackets: the contrariety is not unlike that which Eliot established with his four parentheses in 'The Love Song of J. Alfred Prufrock': the exasperated timorousness of

(They will say: 'How his hair is growing thin!')

and of the quick succession:

(They will say: 'But how his arms and legs are thin!')

heard against the awed erotic hush of imagining another's body:

Arms that are braceleted and white and bare
(But in the lamplight, downed with light brown hair!)

—and then, within twenty lines, the fourth and last parenthesis, cut down to a feebly factual baldness and to only a third of a line instead of the full parenthetical sigh:

Though I have seen my head (grown slightly bald)
    brought in upon a platter

Hill needs a comparable contrariety of impulses within the play of parentheses. The bitterly sardonic parenthesis can too easily become a métier for him.

Some keep to the arrangement of love
    (Or similar trust)

                    ('The Distant Fury of Battle')

The pun there on 'trust' is certainly true to the metaphorical ensconcement within the brackets: the security of loving trust, and the very different security of (as the lines unfold) a financial trust. But the effect is of a sudden gust of feeling; there is more to the related pun on 'trust' in 'Requiem for the Plantagenet Kings': 'At home, under caved chantries, set in trust . . .' 'Set in trust': Hill had originally published this as 'locked in trust';[38] either way, it is germane to his decision elsewhere to set, or lock, 'trust' within brackets. The comparison, when it comes to these sardonic turns, might be with the moment in Swift's 'Verses on the Death of Dr. Swift' which Hill praised:

My female Friends, whose tender Hearts
Have better learn'd to act their Parts
Receive the News in *doleful Dumps*,
'The Dean is dead *(and what is Trumps?)*'

'The rhyming wit', Hill remarks, 'itself works like a "trump" or triumph to snatch brilliant personal success from a position of elected disadvantage'.[39] But it is not only a rhyme, it is a rhyme within and without a bracket; the triumph is the fiercely witty sense that the brackets might better enclose what is really the parenthetical item, 'The Dean is dead'. As it stands, the aside—'(and what is Trumps?)'—is really the heart of the (heartless) matter, a point which flickers in Swift's having 'Trumps' as a bracketed rhyme-word and having the punning 'Hearts' ('whose tender Hearts') rhymingly out there in the open. What we see is the strange play of an utterly authentic voicing against a notation which defies exact vocalization.

Hill is aware that brackets, which can resist prurience (by detachment and a *cordon sanitaire*) can as easily encourage it (by snug smug private-booth gratifications of the secreted imagination). He has deplored 'the mild and modish pornography of Prior':

At last, I wish, said She, my Dear—
(And whisper'd something in his Ear.)

                    ('Paulo Purganti')

'Whisper'd something' is truly symptomatic of the mode and perhaps helps to explain by contrast the nature of Swift's verse, which cuts through that barrier of shame and coquetry where it is only too easy to excite a snigger with gestures of mock reticence.[40]

Yet there is a clear axis which connects Prior's bracketed ignobility of whispering-in-ears with Eliot's (and Hill's) bracketed nobility of such things,

> a voice descanting (though not to the ear,
> The murmuring shell of time, and not in any
>   language)

Hill often uses brackets to indict prurience, usually of a crueller sort than Prior's. It is there in the juxtaposition of one kind of imagination—sadistic relish—with an imagined bracketed silence:

>   we are dying
> To satisfy fat Caritas, those
> Wiped jaws of stone. (Suppose all reconciled
> By silent music; imagine the future
> Flashed back at us, like steel against sun,
> Ultimate recompense.)
>   ('Funeral Music:2')

(The right place for 'silent music' is there, within brackets.) The evocation of a prurience of violence is there too—again with a kind of rhyming at once totally overt (the same word repeated) and covert (one occurrence is within brackets)—when Hill contrasts the gross realities and the delicate prurient art:

> Now at a distance from the steam of beasts,
> The loathly neckings and fat shook spawn
> (Each specimen-jar fed with delicate spawn)
> The searchers with the curers sit at meat
> And are satisfied.
>   ('Annunciations:I')

It is the brackets which enforce the sense of being—this time corruptly—'at a distance', and which then themselves function as that 'specimen-jar' which they enclose. This same vigilance about prurience takes a very different tone when it imagines the heat—this time not steaming—which is immediately shaded by brackets, in one of Hill's prose-poems, 'A Letter from Armenia', a poem likewise about heat, delicacy, pillage, disasters, and glazings:

> So, remotely, in your part of the world:
> the ripe glandular blooms, and cypresses
> shivering with heat (which we have borne
> also, in our proper ways) I turn my mind
> towards delicate pillage, the provenance
> of shards glazed and unglazed, the three
> kinds of surviving grain. I hesitate amid
> circumstantial disasters. I gaze at the
>   authentic dead.

The tone of those lines could scarcely be more remote from, and yet the technical and emotional grounding has much in common with, Milton's great shading parenthesis in *Paradise Regained*, Satan's plea that Christ's reign

> Would stand between me and thy Fathers ire
> (Whose ire I dread more than the fire of Hell)
> A shelter and a kind of shading cool
> Interposition, as a summers cloud.
>   (iii 219–22)

The fire and the shade, and the forthright and the tentative, and the forthright and the treacherous, are alive in the interposition of the brackets.

Clearly there is an art, an allegiance, a strong choice of life, which will distrust any amalgam of the forthright and the tentative, or of the forthright and the treacherous. 'He disapproved of parentheses', says Boswell about Johnson, 'and I

believe in all his voluminous writings, not half a dozen of them will be found' (iv 190). But there is need for the art of dubiety as well as the art of indubitability, Hill has observed how Hopkins, 'against this specious flowing away . . . poised a faith and a technique',[41] and he has written eloquently about the meeting of a faith and a technique in Wordsworth:

> When Wordsworth says, of the female vagrant, that:
>> She ceased, and weeping turned away,
>> As if because her tale was at an end
>> She wept;—because she had no more to say
>> Of that perpetual weight which on her spirit lay
>
> he is indeed implying that words are 'in some degree mechanical' compared to the woman's action and suffering. But in order to bring out the difference Wordsworth puts in a collateral weight of technical concentration that releases the sense of separateness: the drag of the long phrasing across the formalities of the verse, as if the pain would drag itself free from the constraint. In 'as if' and 'because', pedantically isolating her, we glimpse the remoteness of words from suffering and yet are made to recognize that these words are totally committed to her existence. They are her existence. Language here is not 'the outward sign' of a moral action; it is the moral action.[42]

The sense of separateness, of isolation, of remoteness: these evoke a gulf between words and feelings as well as between the sufferer's feelings and the poet's. The scruple, the honesty, is in the compassionate separateness; and it is a compassionate (often fiercely so) separateness that Hill's simple subtle brackets can encompass. He is aware that just as there is a torrid art of prurience, so there is a frigid art of decorum, the wrong remoteness:

> A PASTORAL
>
> Mobile, immaculate and austere,
> The Pities, their fingers in every wound,
> Assess the injured on the obscured frontier;
> Cleanse with a kind of artistry the ground
> Shared by War. Consultants in new tongues
> Prove synonymous our separated wrongs.
>
> We celebrate, fluently and at ease.
> Traditional Furies, having thrust, hovered,
> Now decently enough sustain Peace.
> The unedifying nude dead are soon covered.
> Survivors, still given to wandering, find
> Their old loves, painted and re-aligned—
>
> Queer, familiar, fostered by superb graft
> On treasured foundations, these ideal features!
> Men can move with purpose again, or drift,
> According to direction. Here are statues
> Darkened by laurel; and evergreen names;
> Evidently-veiled griefs; impervious tombs.

Hill seeks something which both is and is not 'evidently-veiled', something truly and not falsely 'impervious'. It may be mediated through a resurrected cliché, as in the superimposition there of officious inquisitive solicitude upon Doubting Thomas: 'The Pities, their fingers in every wound'. Or it may be an art of the parenthesis. The composer of the words 'The tongue's atrocities' is the poet who writes, in 'The Lowlands of Holland', of Europe as

> Shrunken, magnified—(nest, holocaust)—

The double punctuation, dashes and brackets, as in '—(studied reflex, contained breath)—', points up the particular metaphoricality of the brackets, and what they enclose is then itself not just two but double. For 'nest' is both a natural security and a collusive treachery (a nest of vipers, thieves, or robbers); and 'holocaust' is both a reverential act and an evil totality of massacre. How unsettlingly the two words settle side by side, ensconced within the nest of their brackets: '—(nest, holocaust)—'. Yet even here Hill's art respects and fears much from the past. The Jewish God, the Christian poet, and the pagan legend met long ago in an earlier collocation of nest and holocaust, in *Samson Agonistes*:

> Like that self-begott'n bird
> In the *Arabian* woods embost,
> That no second knows nor third,
> And lay e're while a Holocaust

An art of the holocaust must also be an art of the phoenix. The first poem, 'Genesis' (1952), in Hill's first book of poems, *For the Unfallen* (1959), speaks of:

> A brooding immortality—
> Such as the charmed phoenix has
> In the unwithering tree.

Hill is a religious man without, it must seem, a religion; a profoundly honest doubter. 'The Pities, their fingers in every wound'; 'But I want the poem to have this dubious end; because I feel dubious; and the whole business is dubious'. So if we might suppose a patron for Hill, it might be Thomas.

CANTICLE FOR GOOD FRIDAY

> The cross staggered him. At the cliff-top
> Thomas, beneath its burden, stood
> While the dulled wood
> Spat on the stones each drop
> Of deliberate blood.
>
> A clamping, cold-figured day
> Thomas (not transfigured) stamped, crouched,
> Watched
> Smelt vinegar and blood. He,
> As yet unsearched, unscratched,
>
> And suffered to remain
> At such near distance
> (A slight miracle might cleanse
> His brain
> Of all attachments, claw-roots of sense)
>
> In unaccountable darkness moved away,
> The strange flesh untouched, carrion-sustenance
> Of staunchest love, choicest defiance,
> Creation's issue congealing (and one woman's).

A reader senses how bitterly 'cold-figured' is transfigured into the parenthetical '(not transfigured)'; and then how cleansingly the 'slight miracle' of brackets proffers, 'at such near distance', something which is at once 'attachments' and detachment; and then, finally, how simply and unutterably, with what gravity and awe the silent music sinks to the human mystery, the incarnation and the unparalleled muted glory of Mary:

> Creation's issue congealing (and one woman's).

The words are at once belated and perfectly timed; they are supremely weighed, with *issue* against the entrance into those brackets, brackets which may remind us not only of Hill's words 'In unaccountable darkness', but also of John Donne's words about Mary:

> Thou 'hast light in darke; and shutst in little roome,
> Immensity cloystered in thy deare wombe.
>
> ('La Corona:2. Annunciation')

All creation against—and yet not *against*—one woman. Those last three words incarnate a profound paradox, a crux and an aside, an admonition and a reassurance, such as allow Geoffrey

Hill to share the studied reflex and the contained breath of George Herbert.

Notes

1. (1960); *The Lords of Limit* (1984), p. 53.
2. '"The Conscious Mind's Intelligible Structure": A Debate', *Agenda*, 9:4–10:1 (1971–2), 23.
3. *Stand*, 5:2 (1961); then *King Log* (1968).
4. In *The Penguin Book of Contemporary Verse*, ed. Kenneth Allott (2nd edn, 1962), p. 393.
5. *Language and Silence* (1967), p. 146.
6. By Lawrence L. Langer (1975).
7. From the Essay accompanying 'Funeral Music', *King Log*.
8. Mr Brian Oxley drew my attention to I Kings, xx 37.
9. *In Bluebeard's Castle* (1971), p. 41.
10. *Iliad*, xviii 388; Bryant's translation (1870).
11. *Paris Review*, No. 21, Spring–Summer 1959.
12. With the bracketed 'door', compare the gates in 'Solomon's Mines', bracketed: '(Let the hewn gates clash to)'; and the bracketed 'citadels' in the house of 'Asmodeus'. T. S. Eliot shut his poem about himself with the bracketed line: '(Whether his mouth be open or shut)'.
13. *Flaubert, Joyce and Beckett: The Stoic Comedians* (1964), pp. 39–40.
14. A sharp piece of punctuation, and heir to Dryden's:

> Yet this I Prophesy; Thou shalt be seen,
> (Tho' with some short Parenthesis between:)
> High on the Throne of Wit;
>
> ('To Mr Congreve')

15. Much of the comedy of Laurence Sterne's punctuation is the play of the speaking voice against the typographical notation.
16. Hill has written of the 'timed and weighed' impropriety in Robert Lowell (*Essays in Criticism*, xiii, 1963, 188–97), and of the 'timed and placed' repetition in Jon Silkin (*Poetry and Audience*, 9:12, 1962, 5).
17. 'The Poetry of Geoffrey Hill', in *British Poetry since 1960*, ed. Michael Schmidt and Grevel Lindop (1972), pp. 145–7. Reprinted by kind permission of Jon Silkin.
18. I owe this point to Miss Aloma Halter and to Mrs. Nita Mandel.
19. 'The Poetry of Jon Silkin', *Poetry and Audience*, 9:12 (1962), 7.
20. Hill, as reported in *The Illustrated London News*, 20 August 1966.
21. In *The Penguin Book of Contemporary Verse*, p. 392.
22. *Stand*, 8:4 (1967); then *King Log*.
23. Donald Davie, *Articulate Energy* (1955), p. 25: 'As Miss Rosemond Tuve has said so well'.
24. (1972–3); *The Lords of Limit*, p. 84.
25. *Language and Silence*, p. 30.
26. *The Isis*, 19 November 1952.
27. *The Isis*, 10 March 1954; reprinted in *Oxford Poetry 1954*.
28. Boswell's *Life of Johnson*, ed. G. B. Hill and L. F. Powell (1934–50), iii 402 n.l.
29. *The Isis*, 20 February 1952; reprinted in *The Fantasy Poets, Number Eleven: Geoffrey Hill* (1952).
30. Seamus Heaney has a fine account of this poem, in 'Englands of the Mind', *Preoccupations* (1980), pp. 159–61.
31. *The Arte of English Poesie* (1589), III xiii.
32. (1972–3); *The Lords of Limit*, p. 97.
33. *The Lords of Limit*, p. 43.
34. Hill, interviewed by Hallam Tennyson (1977), for a B.B.C. programme on Hopkins.
35. *The Lords of Limit*, p. 102.
36. *Stand*, 6:4 (1963), 9, 11.
37. (1968); *The Lords of Limit*, p. 75.
38. *Paris Review*, No. 21 (Spring–Summer 1959); then *For the Unfallen* (1959).
39. *The Lords of Limit*, p. 71.
40. *The Lords of Limit*, p. 78.
41. Hill, interviewed by Hallam Tennyson.
42. (1975); *The Lords of Limit*, pp. 116–7.

RALPH HODGSON

1871–1962

Little is known of the early years of Ralph Hodgson, who avoided publicity and was always reticent about his private life. Born on September 9, 1871, in Darlington, County Durham, he ran away from school at the age of fifteen and spent two years in America before returning in 1891 to England, where he worked as an illustrator for newspapers and magazines. He began writing poetry in his thirties, but his first collection, *The Last Blackbird and Other Lines* (1907), was a failure, and he himself came to dislike it. In 1913 he founded a private press with two friends, and published his own poems as broadsides and chapbooks, enjoying a measure of success. In 1914 he won the Polignac Prize for his poems "The Bull" and "The Song of Honour," which were included in his *Poems 1917*, the volume for which he is best known. The brief celebrity brought by this book, and by his personal magnetism and lively conversation, is reflected in T. S. Eliot's "Lines to Ralph Hodgson Esqre."

In 1924 Hodgson took a position as lecturer in English at Sendai University, Japan, where he was awarded the Order of the Rising Sun on his retirement in 1938. Having taken up residence in the United States, he won a National Institute of Arts and Letters award in 1946, and in 1954 was honored in Britain with the Queen's Medal for Poetry. Merciless self-criticism kept his output small, and in 1958 he published only his third volume of poems, *The Skylark and Other Poems*, followed in 1961 by the comprehensive *Collected Poems*.

Hodgson, who was married three times, died on November 3, 1962, at his secluded home near Minerva, Ohio.

Personal

How delightful to meet Mr. Hodgson!
    (Everyone wants to know *him*)—
With his musical sound
And his Baskerville Hound
Which, just at a word from his master
Will follow you faster and faster
And tear you limb from limb.
How delightful to meet Mr. Hodgson!
Who is worshipped by all waitresses
(They regard him as something apart)
While on his palate fine he presses
The juice of the gooseberry tart.
How delightful to meet Mr. Hodgson!
    (Everyone wants to know *him*).
He has 999 canaries
And round his head finches and fairies
In jubilant rapture skim.
How delightful to meet Mr. Hodgson!
    (Everyone wants to meet *him*).

—T. S. ELIOT, "Lines to Ralph Hodgson Esqre."
(1933), *Collected Poems 1909–1962*, 1963, pp. 136–37

Hodgson was a man to my own mind, for we both preferred to talk of dogs and prizefighters instead of poets and poetry. He was very seldom seen without his dog, and the same words could be applied to him, with a little difference, as to the Mary of our childhood days, when we read—

And everywhere that Mary went,
    The lamb was sure to go.

The sight of Hodgson and his dog always reminded me of those words, altered to fit his particular case—

And everywhere that Hodgson went,
    The dog was sure to go.

. . . Only once, I believe, have Hodgson and I not agreed in our opinions. We had been talking of coloured men, and I, with the prejudice I had brought with me from America, was not speaking of them too kindly. On hearing this Hodgson said something about 'prejudice,' and giving them 'fair play.' When I heard this I was astonished, for even Hodgson had admitted that we in England were more lenient to coloured people than to our own. So I said, 'If I am prejudiced against them, you are prejudiced in their favour, and that is much worse. So when you say "fair play for coloured men," let me answer, "fair play for white men."'

However, this was a dangerous subject, and we changed it almost immediately. . . .

On one occasion we dined with one of Hodgson's best friends, who was also a great friend of mine. As Hodgson was a strict teetotaller, while we were drinking men, his friend and I began to wonder how Hodgson would be affected by drink. Seeing that Hodgson was such a furious and loud talker, and always gave one the impression that he was intoxicated, we came to the conclusion that drink would make him a melancholy whiner, and not the jolly, laughing man we saw at our side.

But we had no sooner brought this subject to an end than our friend, Hodgson's and mine, introduced the English novel in such a way that I became a little alarmed. For he began to express himself like this—'Now there lived down in Somersetshire a certain man, who was a Justice of the Peace and a Magistrate; that man's name was Henry Fielding, and he has been called "The Father of the English Novel."'

It was not long before he came to Richardson and others. When we were half-way through the dinner he was thoroughly enjoying himself on the subject of Dickens and Thackeray. At the end of the dinner he had come to Meredith and Thomas Hardy.

What Hodgson's real feelings were I cannot say, for he himself was a great and furious talker. That being the case, I feel certain that he could not have listened quietly and happily to the voice of another, for a whole hour too—not even when it was the voice of one of his very best friends. As for myself, being a man who always preferred to listen than to talk, and always happy if others saved me my tongue for drink and tobacco—as for myself, I was quite satisfied with what had happened. But when Hodgson and I were out of the restaurant and our mutual friend had gone, I said—'Do you know, Hodgson, that we have had a full and complete lecture on the English novel?'

When he heard this, Hodgson appeared to be rather uneasy, as though he had hoped that the fact had escaped my notice. However, true and faithful to his friends, Hodgson answered seriously indeed—'Yes, Davies, and wasn't it jolly good too!'—W. H. DAVIES, "A Poet and His Dog," *Later Days*, 1925, pp. 73–80

General

And now I've got to quarrel with you about the Ralph Hodgson poem ⟨"The Song of Honour"⟩: because I think it is banal in utterance. The feeling is there, right enough—but not in itself, only represented. It's like 'I asked for bread, and he gave me a penny'. Only here and there is the least touch of personality in the poem: it is the currency of poetry, not poetry itself. Every single line of it is poetic currency—and a good deal of emotion handling it about. But it isn't really poetry. I hope to God you won't hate me and think me carping, for this. But look

> the ruby's and the rainbow's song
> the nightingale's—all three

There's the emotion in the rhythm, but it's loose emotion, inarticulate, common—the words are mere currency. It is exactly like a man who feels very strongly for a beggar, and gives him a sovereign. The feeling is at either end, for the moment, but the sovereign is a dead bit of metal. And this poem is the sovereign. 'Oh, I do want to give you this emotion', cries Hodgson, 'I do'. And so he takes out his poetic purse, and gives you a handful of cash, and feels very strongly, even a bit sentimentally over it.

> the sky was lit
> The sky was stars all over it,
> I stood, I knew not why

No one should say 'I knew not why' any more. It is as meaningless as 'yours truly' at the end of a letter.
—D. H. LAWRENCE, Letter to Edward Marsh (Oct. 28, 1913), *The Letters of D. H. Lawrence*, Vol. 2, eds. George J. Zytaruk, James T. Boulton, 1981, pp. 92–93

Mr. Ralph Hodgson's much anthologized 'Bells of Heaven,' with its humanitarian appeal for 'wretched, blind pit-ponies and little hunted hares,' is easily recognizable as a black sheep of the Hodgson menagerie. It offends us certainly to think of pit-ponies being kept down in the dark until they lose the use of their eyes, and so it should; but not disproportionately to other crimes of civilization. Pit-ponies are more lovingly-treated than most of their kind above ground; so that, indeed, the pit-pony often shows fewer signs of wretchedness than the average miner or miner's wife and family. Thus the adjective 'wretched' can only apply fairly to certain particular pit-ponies who happen to be wretched: and the cause of their wretchedness is not specified. We would not insist on the weakness of 'wretched' if it were not matched by the 'little' hunted hares. The hares hunted are not singled out for sport *because* they are usually small in size. Nor should mere size in any case induce pity: mice are much smaller than hares and just as charming: but we destroy them without protest from Mr. Hodgson. Bugs are smaller still. The ugliness of hunting the hare is in the way that its wantonness is sportingly disguised, not in the relative *size* of man and hare: bigness in man does not mean relatively greater speed. The first part of the poem is:

> 'Twould ring the Bells of Heaven
> The wildest peal for years
> If Parson lost his senses
> And people came to theirs
> And he and they together
> Knelt down with angry prayers
> For tamed and shabby tigers
> And dancing dogs and bears.

The conceit about losing one's senses and coming to one's senses bears the whole burden of poeticality for this little piece and must be supposed to be wittily intended: but when one examines the antithesis it falls to pieces like the witticism of the dream examined in daylight. If Parson is at present *in* his senses, and 'people' are *out* of theirs, one would think that all that was necessary was for Parson to kneel down and say the necessary prayers, and for the people thereupon to come to their senses. No, Parson has first to *lose* his senses. But if Parson lost his senses there would be no sensible prayers. Mr. Hodgson probably intends that there is a callousness about Parson in his sensible moods that would allow such things to continue without protest. But if in Parson, why not in the Congregation? Why shouldn't they too lose their senses? If the first part of the antithesis is meant ironically, why not the second? Why should Parson come in for all the irony? And why should the bells of Heaven be so enthusiastically rung at the receipt of these prayers which are not contrite but definitely indignant, and addressed to the Deity. Must we suppose that the angelic bell-ringers dare to sympathize with 'people' in their new-found indignation, the Deity corresponding in callousness with His representative on earth, Parson? Must the Deity be persuaded to lose His senses in order to preserve the logic of Mr. Hodgson's humanitarianism?

This piece cannot be judged as poetry any more than 'Innisfree'; it has to be judged as propaganda verse. The first test of propaganda verse is whether it gives the message clearly: and we have found that 'The Bells of Heaven' are, in Mr. Hodgson's hands, cracked. The next test is whether its remedial suggestions are plausible. Now, there is figurative sense in Shelley's

> Men of England, wherefore plough
> For the lords who lay you low?

There is superficial sense in the temperance hymn beginning:

> Cold water is the best of drinks

There is even a homely if fanciful wisdom in the eighteenth-century catch:

> Slaves to the World should be tossed in a blanket
> If I might have my will.

But all that Mr. Hodgson can suggest to remedy the sufferings of (*a*) caged tigers, (*b*) performing bears and dogs, (*c*) pit-ponies, (*d*) hunted hares, is prayers to God by callous congregations miraculously converted to Sunday humanitarianism. The very inefficacy of the solution makes the poem delightful for anthology readers, for they realize that they are not expected to do anything for the poor animals but read it.
—LAURA RIDING, ROBERT GRAVES, "The Perfect Modern Lyric," *A Pamphlet against Anthologies*, 1928, pp. 105–8

The *Collected Poems* of Ralph Hodgson make up a slim volume. He did not start publishing until he was thirty-four. His first volume, *The Last Blackbird and Other Lines* (1907), was followed after ten years by *Poems* (1917) and, many years later, by *The Skylark and Other Poems* (privately printed, 1958). The reasons for this relatively late start, small production, and twenty-year silence between 1921 and 1941, when he published nothing even in magazines, are not known. One of them was probably his fastidious perfectionism.

None of the Georgian poets of nature was better informed about the animals and plants he described, and none was more tenderly sympathetic. None, moreover, took greater pains to find the exact epithet picturing their looks and doings. Yet Hodgson's poetry does not seem naturalistic, as does that of Thomas, Frost, or Blunden. The strengths of his art are imaginative vision and artifice. By "vision" I mean partly that he creates a world of fantasy ("Saint Athelstan," "The Royal Mails"), but much more than objects in his poetry are too artfully presented to seem quite real:

> Eve, with her basket, was
> Deep in the bells and grass,
> Wading in bells and grass
> Up to her knees.

This is a pastoral art, like Blunden's, but where Blunden resembles Cowper or John Clare, Hodgson is closer to the Blake of *Songs of Innocence*. He also resembles a fumigated, bird-watching Dowson, for his visionary simplicity is achieved by means of artistic self-consciousness and manipulation in an extreme degree.

In Hodgson's first volume the artifice is more obvious. We see firmly corseted quatrains, with compressed and inverted syntax, studied epithets, and a judicious intermixture of poetic and archaic vocabulary. One suspects that Hodgson at times was desperate for a subject. Hence, when he found one, he might work it up at excessive length or with excessive emotion. "An Elegy upon a Poem Ruined by a Clumsy Metre" prolongs humorous slightness into tedium. "The Missel Thrush" describes a bird in a thunderstorm with feelings that remind one of "The Wreck of the Deutschland." The trouble in both instances was probably the same: he had nothing to say, but wanted to write.

The *Poems* of 1917 are just as artificial, but the artifice forces itself less on our attention. Here Hodgson achieves a flowing grace and lightness of touch, a stylistic ease that harmonizes with his seeming simplicity of attitude and feeling. It is a completely self-aware simplicity, however, and evokes relatively complex states of mind. "Time, You Old Gipsy Man," for example, speaks of unresting time and evokes lapsed civilizations in long perspective. The theme usually weights and sobers poetry, but Hodgson handles it with swift, good-humored strokes and achieves a slight, blithe pathos:

> Time, you old gipsy man,
>   Will you not stay,
> Put up your caravan
>   Just for one day?
> . . .
> Last week in Babylon,
> Last night in Rome,
> Morning, and in the crush
> Under Paul's dome.

As with the art of de la Mare, such a poem depends on the knowing manipulation of poetic tradition and stock response. The finest example of this is "Eve," from which the first lines have already been quoted. Here Hodgson tells the biblical and Miltonic story of the fall of man as though it were a local village seduction. Eve is the innocent, "motherless" girl of melodrama and Satan the lewd "pretender." The charm of the poem lies partly in transposing the grand theme into locally familiar and miniature terms and partly in the naive speaker, who tells the story with open and full-hearted sympathy for the victim, as though he were watching a stage melodrama. By doing so, he keeps the reader at an emotional distance, following and responding to the story and yet appreciating the artist's control. The poem is deliberately minor and playful, yet

with pathos and horror. It is witty, poised, controlled, artificial, and evasive—evasive in that it would be impossible to say what Hodgson personally feels.—DAVID PERKINS, "The Georgian Poets," *A History of Modern Poetry*, 1976, pp. 222–24

CHARLES WILLIAMS
From "Ralph Hodgson"
Poetry at Present
1930, pp. 128–33

It may be supposed that when Giotto drew his famous circle there was very little for the draughtsmen of the neighbourhood to say about it. There the circle was.

Much the same is the natural feeling about Mr. Hodgson's poems. There is, for purposes of poetry, one book—the *Poems*—of sixty-two pages of text. Of these pages, making allowances for individual taste, perhaps ten or twelve are not quite so good as the other fifty. Another ten or twelve are as good as anything else in English lyric verse. And there, in a manner of speaking, we are.

It is, certainly, a particular kind of English lyric, and it has been described by Mr. Hodgson himself much better than anybody else could do it.

> Reason has moons, but moons not hers
>   Lie mirrored on her sea,
> Confounding her astronomers,
>   But O! delighting me.

These are the moons of a particular world of poetry—the world which is governed by the moon, and all the associations of the word in romantic poetry, the interior moon. Reason—land and sea—reflects a life not its own. Land and sea, for the metaphor could not be carried on to include all that it should include without enlarging it. The moon, of which those mirrored moons are images, has shone on wild dwellers in the air and the forest, on that strange and all but Platonic menagerie which goes in a shining procession through English verse. The Albatross perhaps leads them—Coleridge's albatross would be at home over Mr. Hodgson's ocean—but Shelley's skylark and Keats's nightingale are there, and Blake's lamb and tiger, and Darley's unicorn. Even before those great romantics a poet of another age had—in his only verse of that kind—summoned as beautiful an animal—

A milk-white hind, immortal and unchanged;

and Christopher Smart had called forth a mighty throng.

Mr. Hodgson has added another nightingale, who sings (like Patmore's—certainly the nightingale should be grateful to the poets) in Abyssinia, and a wren with it—

> The babble-wren and nightingale
> Sung in the Abyssinian vale
> That season of the year!—

and other beings too. Goldfinches (after which he names his own songs), 'a leopard bright as flame', 'a dotted serpent', 'the cinnamon bee',

> And everything that gleams or goes
> Lack-lustre in the sea.

But this bright and marvellous pageant meets another procession in his verse—the train of mortal animals, hurt or dying, the beasts on whom the sun and no unearthly moon pitilessly shines. The babble-wren and nightingale may be singing in Abyssinia, by Mount Abora; but some such 'singing-birds sweet' are also

> Sold in the shops
> For the people to eat,

Sold in the shops of
Stupidity Street.

Blake's tiger is near at hand, but so are the 'tamed and shabby tigers' of the creeping circuses of England.

The Bull to whom he gives a poem threatens the herd 'in the furnace of his look' (and the word seems strong enough here to describe Nebuchadnezzar's), but also he is a 'dupe of dream', old, abandoned, at the point of death. The 'loathly birds' that hover over him are direct neighbours of the 'goldfinches and other birds of joy' whom Mr. Hodgson's genius goes wonderfully snaring. Songs of innocence are interspersed with songs of experience. Fantasy and actuality go hand in hand, and both are real.

They are so real that here and there they almost act together. Which of them chose the adjective in that description of the serpent and Eve going

Down the dark path to
The Blasphemous Tree?

It is not given to every poet to find a new, appropriate, and surprising adjective for a noun which has been part of our common imaginative experience for centuries—new, at least, so far as our living poetry goes. But then the whole of that poem is a new presentation of the ancient myth; it is innocence—a rather childish innocence, certainly; not that of the Lady in 'Comus'—becoming, most unhappily, experience. There are two poems on that subject: one—'Eve'—in the terms of the old legend; one—'The Royal Mails'—a fable of Mr. Hodgson's own. In this a page is sent by a Prince 'of very famous fame' to carry letters to far-off cities, and allows himself to be deceived and robbed—like a score of others before him—by apparent merchants in the wood. It is his anguish which ends the prolonged lyric tale. The description of original happiness in both poems is exquisite—Eve

Wading in bells and grass
Up to her knees;

and the young boy starting

down the hill,
With Castle-bells and Fare-ye-wells
And bugles sweet and shrill,

which become at the end

Castle-bells and Fare-ye-wells
And hornets in his ear.

Nearly all Mr. Hodgson's other poems are expressions of one or other of those states. They are either about Beautysprite or 'wretched blind pit-ponies'; about the heartbreaking wonder of young love or the gipsy girl insulted by a loose-tongued man at a fair, about a soul stunned by 'the harmonious hymn of Being' or shocked by the stupidity of man. These things are not posed as philosophical opposites; they are loosed as poetic apprehensions. The infernal toast 'under the hill to-night' after Eve has eaten is no more and no less thrilling than 'the lyric might' of all creation in song.

The occasional phrases in which Mr. Hodgson suggests a belief in reconciliation are not perhaps his most successful. They have not his own peculiar and piercing ecstasy. When his mind is on the ecstasy (as in the poem called 'The Mystery') it does not communicate the thrill as it does when he is gazing at some actual or imagined example of it. Moments of anguish, however, moments of delight so intense as to be nearly anguish, are on almost every page; the less convincing poems are very rare, and in a poet less perfect than Mr. Hodgson would not be mentioned. But when he does not so much argue as assert, we tend to become restive.

God loves an idle rainbow
As much as labouring seas

Well, it's rather hard on the seas.

There is another miracle Mr. Hodgson has here and there worked, and that is the conquest of Time. One of his best-known poems is that which begins

Time, you old Gipsy-Man,
Will you not stay?

It is not in the least metaphysical; it has no relation to the Time in which Mr. de la Mare's poor Jim Jay got stuck. But it is extraordinarily effective; it really does communicate a sense of vast centuries in a few five- or six-syllabled lines. Another poem on Babylon is a protest against archaeologists and their excavations (here again we need not agree with the intellectual protest; after all, the Babylonians are not suffering as 'the wretched hunted hares' of 'The Bells of Heaven' are). But the two chief things in it are an eight-line picture of Babylon at its height and a ten-line picture of Babylon in the desert.

The soldier lad; the market wife;
Madam buying fowls from her;
Tip, the butcher's bandy cur;
Workmen carting bricks and clay;
Babel passing to and fro
On the business of a day
Gone three thousand years ago.

'But that', one's mind says, 'is not Babylon; no one ever talked of Madam and Tip in the city of Ashtoreth and such names. That is the life around us now. It is we who lived three thousand years'—and the verse has done its work. Within us is Babylon and contemporary London, and the whole airy curve of time that ends where it began. The period between is everything and nothing. And that is what one kind of poetry can do.

GEORGE BRANDON SAUL
From "Merlin's Flight: An Essay on Ralph Hodgson"
Withdrawn in Gold
1970, pp. 29–35

When the first of Hodgson's very small books, *The Last Blackbird and Other Lines*, appeared in 1907, the *Saturday Review* (whose files contain much of his verse) expressed a sarcastic anticipation of undeserved neglect which initial reception fully justified: one estimate, indeed, records a sale of only twenty copies; and the volume was practically forgotten until its reissue a decade later—and again in 1921. It contains, in "The Missel Thrush", what the just-named review calls its author's "first poem"; but, marred by diffuseness and occasional awkwardness, it is a volume that piques with promise more frequently than it satisfies with achievement. Nevertheless, no lover of Hodgson would willingly be without it.

For one thing, it is stamped with individuality, despite a few signs of indebtedness or "influence". "Lines" and "The Treasure-Box" do suggest Wordsworth pure and simple, as "The Pansy" of a later collection suggests Wordsworth with a fillip; "The Winds" has in "Night was rich / In eyes her own" an oblique reference to Bourdillon's "The night has a thousand eyes"; and a vaguely eighteenth century tone—or at least tincture—seems perceptible in spots, as in the slightly labored "An Elegy upon a Poem Ruined by a Clumsy Metre" and "The Vanity of Human Ambition and Big Behaviour", with its personifications and its mock-heroic characters, whose histories are presumed to illustrate the subject. But implied obligations are really inconsequential.

In the next place, the book testifies to a drily ironic sense of humor, especially in its epigrams; and it interests one because of its author's warming preoccupation with birds and bull terriers, his intimacy with the *little* lives of nature: an intimacy akin to W. H. Hudson's. And it is memorable for several poems that will resist all but the most ruthless critical assault: poems like the sombre "The Hammers"—like "Beauty Sprite", "The Linnet" (which arguing spirituality in life from the mere *fact* of linnets, is didacticism in the service of quiet ecstasy), "The Down by Moonlight"—a night pastoral whose "Old as the dark and concreate with Time" is one of Hodgson's most impressive lines, and "St. Athelstan". Of these, the last does invite the reflection that more directness in presentation would be desirable, as also more gracefulness in the use of preterit and historical present in juxtaposition. Yet the poem is true Hodgson in its handling of the ballad legacy; it has a moment of epic magnitude in "The sun fell like a god rebuked"; and its tragic story of how St. Athelstan came from heaven and sacrificed himself to a wolf to preserve the lost child of a searching shepherd is dramatically handled in a commentary that uses the question-and-answer formula effectively. "The Down by Moonlight", I may add, has the special appeal inherent in *terza rima*. And, indeed, Hodgson (herein markedly unusual among English poets of his time) uses regular or irregular *terza rima* also in four other poems of this volume ("The Sedge-Warbler", "The Missel Thrush", "The Winds", and "Holiday"), as if in agreement with the prosodist Schipper that the form is particularly appropriate to idyllic and meditative verse—though it does find only a brief and trimmed shadow ("February"—an amazing lyric in one sentence) in the later Hodgson, the adaptation in "To a Linnet" (1958) being really work of a half-century earlier than the publication date.

Without minimizing defects already remarked, it should in justice be added that there is something heartening, something suggestive of good-humored fortitude and joy, in this early verse (a quality also recognizable in "Ghoul Care", of the later *Poems*), as well as a rewarding share of good phrases and images: one can scarcely fail to respond to "the quiet owl-time" or the picture of "malice-eyed" Doubt madly riding "his midnight mare". Incidentally, it may be remarked for the sake of technicians that the verse of *The Last Blackbird* has by comparison with that of the later—and major—volume, *Poems*, a lower percentage of logical enjambement, a markedly higher frequency of cesuras, much less feminine ending and internal rhyme, decidedly more triple license, and a slightly higher percentage of initially truncated lines.

. . . *Poems*—its quality enormously out of proportion to its size—shows no signs of artistic immaturity: indeed, it approximates sheer lyrical perfection. And if it argues genius in "a narrow vessel", to adapt Francis Thompson's phrase, that genius is nevertheless exquisite in quality—and none the less remarkable because its bouquet may have been slow in ripening. For there is nothing in the entire volume (which is even architecturally absolutely "right") that the world would not be seriously poorer without: and that is something which, I think, could with equal confidence be asserted of very few other volumes of lyrics, if of any. And the emergent personality—a personality completely satisfied with the rich simplicities of life: the picture of a peasant bride in some old book to brood upon; "blue flowers and the merlin's flight / And the rime on the wintry tree"—is wholly engaging, while the metrical effects have a musical grace unsurpassed by that of even the finest madrigals.

It is pre-eminently the lyric romanticist who is here revealed: the poet, perpetually fresh and curiously timeless, who, it has been well said, "will not stay in a book". The poems almost insensibly sing themselves into the memory. And their complete lucidity and healthy character suggest by implicative example an anticipatory rebuke to the frenzied tides of self-communion, intellectual exhibitionism, cryptic intimation, self-pity gesturing in the hood of social sympathy, and political capering figuring as lyric wit which were shortly to inundate the poetic landscape.

The romanticist just specified is variously garbed in *Poems*: for example, as storyteller—in "The Royal Mails", the gentle history of a page unfortunately beguiled which has the pleasant shadow of Coleridge upon it; as dramatist—in the restrainedly passionate and perfect "The Gipsy Girl", which emphasizes anew what nourishment lyrical feeling gives both dramatic concept and dramatic speech; as humanitarian—in poems of crusading pity for beggars, for this world's Eves, for hungry, abused, and slaughtered animals; as painter—in "The Late, Last Rook" and elsewhere; as transcendentalist—in "Babylon" and "The Mystery":

> I did not pray Him to lay bare
> 　　The mystery to me,
> Enough the rose was Heaven to smell,
> 　　And His own face to see;

and as the rhapsodist who hears, in "The Song of Honour",

> 　　Earth's lowliest and loudest notes,
> 　　Her million times ten million throats
> 　　Exalt Him loud and long.

The poem last excerpted emphasizes Hodgson's rare capacity for simple unaffected ecstasy, for ecstasy more full-throated than that perceptible here is not to be found in recorded poetry: indeed, it is ecstasy piled upon ecstasy, suggestive in rhapsodic power of few things besides Francis Thompson's *Ode to the Setting Sun*, though certainly more lucid and breath-taking than even that. Incidentally, it was "The Song of Honour" which John Gould Fletcher, a minor American poet, falsely labelled "a direct transcription of Christopher Smart's 'Song to David'": "falsely" because—although his impulse to write the poem, which uses in several strophes Smart's stanzaic form, may have been ignited by the eighteenth century piece (obviously familiar as early as the "Vanity of Human Ambition . . .", of *The Last Blackbird*, if the suggestive "Xiphias", which recalls Smart's swordfish, be significant)—Hodgson does not even reflect his predecessor's basic concept or plan. Smart lists praisefully and moralistically God's creations and glorifies the Maker; Hodgson records the hymn of praise from all creation and, as Sir John Squire remarked, owes only "decently" to the madman.

It is observable that the romanticism of *Poems* (and one suspects this may be the real reason for Conrad Aiken's undervaluation of its author) is not of the dark-tinged variety. Indeed, it rarely records any voices out of ancient night such as, hearing, Chopin sometimes translated into musical tones and El Greco into color: it suggests, rather, the fundamentally unmorbid and self-reliant, sometimes joyous, answer to such voices—the answer of Mozart, of Il Tintoretto, occasionally even of Watteau. Hodgson does not evade the facts of sorrow and death and evil; he meets them with pity and sympathy and ironic fortitude, whether he is applauding the right anger of a gipsy girl in the face of lewd insult or grieving for "hungry sparrows in the snow". But folly and deliberate cruelty stir a cold fury—and then he writes (as previously "The Last Blackbird") "The Bells of Heaven" (its title also a phrase in "The Song of Honour"), or "Stupidity Street", that lyric which, in W. H. Chesson's just phrase, contains "all that is vital in the morality and mysticism of *The Rime of the Ancient Mariner . . .* condensed into twelve lines of accusation and threat". And in such instances he proves himself superior to most of his tribe in fusing the moral with the aesthetic aim and achieving that rare anomaly, propaganda which is also art. When the mood is milder, he writes "The Journeyman", a good example of his sardonic irony, or "Babylon", in which he pleads that both the dead past and its dead be allowed to remain undisturbed; but the results are of the same genre.

Most striking, perhaps, is his ability in *Poems* to evoke a picture which implies dramatization of a moral situation. This is not to name him a moralist in tone or method, but to recognize that, in the way of the greater poets, he defines situations which carry clear moral implications. I am thinking of certain of the poems just indicated—of "The Gipsy Girl" and "The Journeyman"—as well as of "The House across the Way" and, more broadly, "The Bull". But there are cases in which the statement is as specific as the crystallization of situation. Such a poem as "Eve", for instance, moderately labelled "the most fascinating poem of our time" by E. V. Lucas, has all the delicacy, the clarity of tone in its pictorial quality, of a canvas by Titian or da Vinci; it is charmingly simple, lacking even a modicum of the tinsel ornamentation which the best of the Pre-Raphaelite poets, whose finer gifts Hodgson shares, would probably have given it; but it presents the sorry old story of the temptation and fall in terms of a pity which *Genesis* does not reveal—and angrily follows this with an illustrative modern reference. Here the moralization is as explicit as anywhere, but the spell of the poem is strong enough to carry it. Similarly, the moralizations of "Stupidity Street" and "The Bells of Heaven" are triumphantly carried by sheer strength of angry feeling. Word-magic, the invocation of feeling, has a way of mocking all restrictive theorizing; and whereas such theorizing may reasonably enough condemn the Platonic justification of art and deplore pedestrian lessoning as tiresome, it must shrivel before the fury of a Swift or a Hodgson.

A. E. HOUSMAN

1859–1936

Alfred Edward Housman was born in Fockbury, Worcestershire, on March 26, 1859, and attended the nearby Bromsgrove School. In 1877 he won a scholarship to St. John's College, Oxford, where he met Moses Jackson, the great though secret and apparently unrequited love of his life. Although a brilliant student, Housman had little patience with required courses and failed to achieve a pass grade in his final examinations in 1881; returning the following year, he was awarded a pass degree.

In 1882 Housman took up an appointment at the Trade Marks Registry in London, where he shared accommodation for three years with Jackson and the latter's brother Adalbert. Proximity to the British Museum enabled him to continue his research as a classicist, and in the next decade he had twenty-five papers published, establishing an international reputation as a meticulous textual critic, which helped him to win the chair for Latin at University College, London, in 1892. An outpouring of lyric poetry in the next few years led to the collection *A Shropshire Lad* (1896), which slowly won him fame as a poet, but the bulk of his writing was of a scholarly nature, and his major publications were editions of Juvenal (1905), Manilius (1903–30), and Lucan (1926). In 1911 he advanced to the chair of Latin at Cambridge University, with a Fellowship at Trinity College.

Housman's second volume of poetry, *Last Poems*, appeared in 1922, in time for him to send a copy to the dying Moses Jackson. Though a lover of solitude and reserve, he was well known for his gastronomic expertise, nurtured by frequent trips to the Continent, and was much prized as an after-dinner speaker. He delivered the Leslie Stephen lecture at Cambridge in 1933, speaking on *The Name and Nature of Poetry*.

Housman died in Cambridge on April 30, 1936. After his death his brother and literary executor Laurence Housman edited *More Poems* (1936) and *Additional Poems*, in his *A. E. Housman: Some Poems, Some Letters and a Personal Memoir* (1937).

Personal

No one, not even Cambridge, was to blame
(Blame if you like the human situation):
Heart-injured in North London, he became
The Latin Scholar of his generation.

Deliberately he chose the dry-as-dust,
Kept tears like dirty postcards in a drawer;
Food was his public love, his private lust
Something to do with violence and the poor.

In savage foot-notes on unjust editions
He timidly attacked the life he led,
And put the money of his feelings on

The uncritical relations of the dead,
Where only geographical divisions
Parted the coarse hanged soldier from the don.

> —W. H. AUDEN, "A. E. Housman" (1939),
> *Collected Shorter Poems 1927–1957*, 1966,
> p. 126

Alfred Housman and I won open scholarships together at St. John Baptist's College, Oxford, at Midsummer 1877, and started residence on the same "stair" in the second quad the following October. Most of the scholarships at St. John's are appropriated to Merchants Taylor's School and their holders come up with friendships ready made; thus Housman and I from the first were thrown much together. My own success had been mainly in the essay paper; his was won on purely classical work and after a time, on the advice, I think, of Robinson Ellis, the editor of Catullus, he went for coaching to T. H. Warren, Fellow and Tutor, and subsequently President of Magdalen, in the hope of doing well for the Hertford, the University classical scholarship for men in their first or second year. The special gifts which subsequently made him such a fine textual critic did not help him for this, but I believe he was among the first five or six. His favourite English poet in these early days was Matthew Arnold, whose "Empedocles on Etna" he recommended to me as containing "all the law and the prophets." Among novelists his favourite was Thomas Hardy, and I think Hardy's influence went far deeper than Arnold's; but he read also Henry James, though with some affliction at his prolixity. After we had sat for classical Mods, in May, 1879, he stayed with me for the inside of a week in London and on four successive evenings we went together to see Irving and Ellen Terry in revivals of plays they had performed during the season. I think Housman was the most absorbed member of the audience.

Up to this time all had gone well with Housman at Oxford and I think he was quietly happy and was generally recognized in the College as exceptionally able. When he was in the mood he could recite to very restricted audiences humorous stories of his own making, which were made double humorous by his prim method of telling them. We had from the first taken many walks together and continued to do so in our third year, and began also to play elementary lawn tennis together in the College garden; otherwise I saw rather less of him as I had moved into the other quad. In our fourth year, however, when we had to go out of college, he and I and Moses Jackson, a delightful science scholar, took five rooms together in a picturesque old house in St. Giles', nearly opposite the college, now long ago displaced by academic buildings. After we had returned from dining in Hall, and had our coffee (neither Housman nor Jackson smoked), I mostly retired to work by myself in the lower sitting room, leaving the other two on the first floor. Jackson's was an absolutely safe first in science in the schools and had no need to read much in the evening. What and how much Housman read I don't know, but I was aware that he was working at Propertius as a recreation; also that he enjoyed W. H. Mallock's *Is Life Worth Living?*, and I think found this useful in writing his weekly essays for one of the College lecturers, to whom they were so diverting, that he does not seem to have questioned the adequacy of the knowledge on which they were based. In either the Lent or the Summer term of 1880, we had the College examination known as "collections" and it may have been then that the Senior Tutor began to suspect that Housman was not putting his back into his work for Greats, for at a lecture he made a harmless remark of Housman the occasion for informing him before us all that he was *not* a genius!

Like the college lecturer, I was so impressed with Housman's ability, that I took it for granted that he would do well in Greats, though he was obviously not specially interested in parts of the work. When however, some weeks after the written examinations, I went up to Oxford for my *viva*, the bewilderment of the examiners at finding themselves compelled, as they considered, to refuse even a pass to a man who had obtained a first in Mods, had caused enquiries to be made, which were now passed on to me, as to how it had come about that on some of the papers Housman had hardly attempted to offer any answers. What had he been doing? The only explanation I could offer at the time was that I believed he

might have occupied himself too much with the text of Propertius, and that remained the only explanation I could offer to myself or to anyone else, until in the emotion caused by the news of his death I realized that for a man who was, if not already a great scholar, at least a great scholar in the making, it was psychologically impossible to make the best of his knowledge on subjects in which he had lost interest.

It was necessary for Housman to get a degree to enable him to earn a living, so he took his Pass B.A. not without a mishap in one subject (I think political economy), and then after a temporary job as a schoolmaster, entered the Government Patent Office in 1882 as a Higher Division Clerk under the Playfair scheme, i.e. at a salary of £100 a year rising by triennial increments of £37 10s. to £400, as payment for a six hour day. This left him plenty of time for his own work, and if he had chosen he might easily have earned a supplementary income, either by his vein of extravagant humour or by elementary classical work. I doubt if he ever made the smallest effort to earn a penny in either way, but he soon became a frequent contributor of notes, chiefly emendations of corruptions in the texts of Horace, Propertius and the Greek tragedians, in the classical reviews. Fortunately Jackson had entered the Patent Office about the same time (in a better paid section, thanks to his science degree), and he and Housman lived together in rooms at Bayswater. I occasionally saw them, but I got it into my head that the sight of me reminded Housman of his troubles and was unwilling to thrust myself on him more than he might welcome. When, however, in 1890 I got together, for my bookseller-publisher, David Stott of Oxford Street, a selection of *Odes from Greek Dramatists*, with verse translations by English scholars, Housman came to my help with three renderings, from the *Septem contra Thebas* (1848–60), *Oedipus Coloneus* (1611–48), and *Alcestis* (962–1005), which should not be overlooked by his bibliographers. On two occasions he gave me the pleasure of helping him. The first time (1892), I did so with great diffidence, for what he asked was a testimonial from me in support of his application for the Professorship of Latin at University College, London, and I thought that I was much too inconspicuous for anything I could write to carry weight. However, he explained that he had influential backing as regards his competence as a Latin scholar, and all he wanted was a few words as to his power of expressing himself in English, and my various editings were enough to entitle me to testify to this; so I did as I was told. The second occasion came four years later, when *A Shropshire Lad*, under the name of *Terence*, was ready for publication. Housman knew that books of mine had been published by Messrs. Kegan Paul, Trench, Trubner and Co., who had gained rather a special reputation for bringing out prettily printed volumes of verse, and asked me to arrange with them for its publication at his expense. Of course there was no difficulty as to this (I think Housman put down £30 and got it back with a small profit), but my being entrusted with the manuscript led me to suggest that *Terence* was not an attractive title, and that in the phrase "A Shropshire Lad," which he had used in the poem, he had much a better one. He agreed at once, and I think the change helped.

After 1899, when I moved from Kensington to Wimbledon, I saw still less of Housman, though we occasionally corresponded and there was a jolly interlude when Jackson, who had left the Patent Office for the Headship of a native college in India, was home on leave, and he and Housman dined and slept in my house. When I retired to rest I found an apple-pie bed awaiting me and I think the Professor of Latin was a fellow victim, though I'm not quite sure that he wasn't an aggressor. Anyhow, we became very youthful and light-hearted. In 1911 I went up to Cambridge to hear his inaugural lecture in his second Professorship and was richly rewarded by the cry of pleasure with which I was greeted when he caught sight of me after it. I think that somehow my presence seemed to him a recognition that he had reached his haven at last. His final assurance as to this came when he was made an Honorary Fellow of his own Oxford College, and on going up to stay there received a great welcome, his genial response to which is still remembered. The last time I myself saw him was in 1934, when Cambridge honoured me with its Litt. D. on the occasion of the opening of the new University Library. There was a festive lunch at Kings, at which Housman was present, and in the course of it he came up to greet me with a pretty speech. He was already looking thin and tired, and I was not surprised to hear soon afterwards of the beginning of his illness. We did not see much of each other in these last years, but our friendship was undiminished. I owe him many and great debts, and am very grateful for being given this opportunity to acknowledge them.—A. W. POLLARD, "Some Reminiscences," *Alfred Edward Housman: Recollections*, 1936, pp. 30–33

I do not think any man could have gone so little out of his way to win affection as Housman; rather the contrary: he appeared neither to seek nor to expect affection; and when it came, and was beyond doubt, as in the case of R. V. Lawrence, he spoke of the acquisition, I vividly remember, with a naïveté that seemed to denote both an unusual occurrence and the intense pleasure it occasioned. If I am right in my conjecture that he purposely fought shy of giving or of awakening affection, it was assuredly not due to want of heart: no man, I am convinced, ever had more. It was and could only have been, that his excessive sensitiveness shrank from the possibility—to him it may have seemed the probability—of infidelity and disillusion-ment. He preferred to go without one of the most precious of this world's gifts rather than risk the pain of betrayal. It was this attitude perhaps that incited the flood of poetry in the nineties. Some outlet to his pent-up feelings must be found, and providentially the Muse was standing by to serve him.

When, one morning, in the visit before the last, disposed to intimacy as he had never before been, Housman told me he had never possessed but three friends—all, it is significant, associated with youth or early manhood. They were all now gone, and a note of exultation came into his voice as he spoke of his thankfulness for having outlived them. With a tenderness of passion utterly undisguised he went on to tell of the last of the three friends—a woman—recently dead. His voice faltered, his whole frame seemed shaken, as he told the brief story. He had loved and revered her from youth. In the earlier years companionship had been close and constant. Then distance and the exigencies of occupation had rendered meetings few and difficult, and of late years they had never met, he said bitterly, as a consequence of her having returned to her homeland, Germany, to end her days. The story closed with a thank God he had lived to know her safely laid to rest. He added—and for the first time his voice strengthened to a triumphant pitch—how comfortably he could meet death now his three friends were at peace.

In this deeply moving recital I particularly remarked a characteristic, more usual perhaps in women than in men, revealed on each of the two or three previous occasions when he indulged passionate utterance. His intensity of feeling was shown not by the use of emphatic words or declamatory expressions, but by the physical manifestations of a faltering voice, a flushed face, and an agitation of frame that gave the impression of a seething force restrained only by the exercise of

stern self-discipline, and not always successfully, for a visible tremor would momentarily escape. All else, in contrast to his demeanour when he expatiated on the trials of the Senate House lecture, was under complete and destinate control—a low even tone, measured speech, and words the fewest and most tempered possible.

In a letter dated November 1934, in which he said that life was bearable, but he did not want it to continue, he referred to 'the great and real troubles of my early manhood'. What they were, and which was most effectual in misshaping his life in after days, can, it appears, only be conjectured. . . . Hous-man's sister, Mrs. Symons, inferred that the lady I had mentioned in an article contributed to the *New Statesman and Nation* must be a family friend, much his senior, to whom she knew he had given his boyish devotion, but a devotion, she also knew, that had passed with boyhood. Of his affection for the German lady Mrs. Symons knew nothing; she had not the smallest conception that any intercourse between them had survived the first casual meeting, neither had she supposed it had given birth to aught beyond a pleasant, mutually enjoyable relationship. This appears to be the first indication that the young Housman, who had hitherto been the life and soul of his family's enterprises, the acknowledged leader, of whom they were all proud, to whom they were all devoted, was already taking the lonely path that was to lead him away from them, away from other human intimacies, and steadily into an ever-deepening isolation.

The 'great and real troubles' of which he spoke were, in so acutely sensitive a disposition, the main factor doubtless, but to me it seemed certain that another influence had played a decisive part. The longer I knew him, and the more I saw him in contact with people, not his colleagues only, the more I felt his very gifts and attainments—his wide and exact knowledge, his faultless memory, his swift repartee and merciless tongue— were an added source of estrangement. The most of folk stood in awe of him, preserved silence, and encouraged silence in him.—PERCY WITHERS, *A Buried Life: Personal Recollections of A. E. Housman*, 1940, pp. 128–31

We went up to the Nursing Home this afternoon and saw him lying in their little chapel—just a still form covered with a fine linen sheet over which was a gold and purple silk pall, and an alter behind. I uncovered his face and I thought he had not changed much since I last saw him twelve years ago. As Uncle Laurence said, his expression was "Imperious Roman," and it was a fine face with the lips and cheeks still holding colour in some mysterious way as if he were yet living. There was great composure and firmness of expression, and the look on the face was that of a man who had met the storms of life and faced and fought them. I cannot call it serene, it still held what I can only describe as a proud challenge—"I am captain of my soul and master of my fate; do your worst; I scorn you." Indeed, his features in death were a mirror of all he had suffered from life, and of his attitude to it—it was the face of an autocrat and an aristocrat facing a silly mob and defying it.

I placed my warm hand on his cool forehead in farewell, and we left.—N. V. H. SYMONS, "Farewell to A. E. H.," *Alfred Edward Housman: Recollections*, 1936, p. 60

Works

POETRY

When I examine my mind and try to discern clearly in the matter, I cannot satisfy myself that there are any such things as poetical ideas. No truth, it seems to me, is too precious, no observation too profound, and no sentiment too exalted to be expressed in prose. The utmost that I could admit is that some ideas do, while others do not, lend themselves kindly to poetical expression; and that these receive from poetry an enhancement which glorifies and almost transfigures them, and which is not perceived to be a separate thing except by analysis.

'Whosoever will save his life shall lose it, and whosoever will lose his life shall find it.' That is the most important truth which has ever been uttered, and the greatest discovery ever made in the moral world; but I do not find in it anything which I should call poetical. On the other hand, when Wisdom says in the Proverbs 'He that sinneth against me wrongeth his own soul; all they that hate me, love death,' that is to me poetry, because of the words in which the idea is clothed; and as for the seventh verse of the forty-ninth Psalm in the Book of Common Prayer, 'But no man may deliver his brother, nor make agreement unto God for him,' that is to me poetry so moving that I can hardly keep my voice steady in reading it. And that this is the effect of language I can ascertain by experiment: the same thought in the bible version, 'None of them can by any means redeem his brother, nor give to God a ransom for him,' I can read without emotion.

Poetry is not the thing said but a way of saying it. Can it then be isolated and studied by itself? for the combination of language with its intellectual content, its meaning, is as close a union as can well be imagined. Is there such a thing as pure unmingled poetry, poetry independent of meaning? . . .

My opinions on poetry are necessarily tinged, perhaps I should say tainted, by the circumstance that I have come into contact with it on two sides. . . . ⟨P⟩oetry is a very wide term, and inconveniently comprehensive: so comprehensive is it that it embraces two books, fortunately not large ones, of my own. I know how this stuff came into existence; and though I have no right to assume that any other poetry came into existence in the same way, yet I find reason to believe that some poetry, and quite good poetry, did. Wordsworth for instance says that poetry is the spontaneous overflow of powerful feelings, and Burns has left us this confession, 'I have two or three times in my life composed from the wish rather than the impulse, but I never succeeded to any purpose.' In short I think that the production of poetry, in its first stage, is less an active than a passive and involuntary process; and if I were obliged, not to define poetry, but to name the class of things to which it belongs, I should call it a secretion; whether a natural secretion, like turpentine in the fir, or a morbid secretion, like the pearl in the oyster. I think that my own case, though I may not deal with the material so cleverly as the oyster does, is the latter; because I have seldom written poetry unless I was rather out of health, and the experience, though pleasurable, was generally agitating and exhausting. If only that you may know what to avoid, I will give some account of the process.

Having drunk a pint of beer at luncheon—beer is a sedative to the brain, and my afternoons are the least intellectual portion of my life—I would go out for a walk of two or three hours. As I went along, thinking of nothing in particular, only looking at things around me and following the progress of the seasons, there would flow into my mind, with sudden and unaccountable emotion, sometimes a line or two of verse, sometimes a whole stanza at once, accompanied, not preceded, by a vague notion of the poem which they were destined to form part of. Then there would usually be a lull of an hour or so, then perhaps the spring would bubble up again. I say bubble up, because, so far as I could make out, the source of the suggestions thus proffered to the brain was an abyss

which I have already had occasion to mention, the pit of the stomach. When I got home I wrote them down, leaving gaps, and hoping that further inspiration might be forthcoming another day. Sometimes it was, if I took my walks in a receptive and expectant frame of mind; but sometimes the poem had to be taken in hand and completed by the brain, which was apt to be a matter of trouble and anxiety, involving trial and disappointment, and sometimes ending in failure. I happen to remember distinctly the genesis of the piece which stands last in my first volume. Two of the stanzas, I do not say which, came into my head, just as they are printed, while I was crossing the corner of Hampstead Heath between the Spaniard's Inn and the footpath to Temple Fortune. A third stanza came with a little coaxing after tea. One more was needed, but it did not come: I had to turn to and compose it myself, and that was a laborious business. I wrote it thirteen times, and it was more than a twelvemonth before I got it right.—A. E. HOUSMAN, *The Name and Nature of Poetry,* 1933, pp. 34–50

We may agree . . . that Housman is deeply in debt to classical tradition. But not to classical tradition alone. Some critics, indeed, think him very much a child of his time. He is said to be "ninetyish"—a term of strong disparagement to those who aspire to be fortyish—not so much in his poetic technique as in his outlook and emotions. It is true that he, like others in that distressing time of transition, could not help quarrelling with God for not existing, and that Arnold and Hardy were favourites of his youth; but his pessimism, though it bears some marks of the time, was the fruit of no literary fashion. His wisdom is described by one young writer as "trivial, tricked out with self-advertising stoicism"; and it is true that it is not altogether free—in the circumstances how could it be free?— from attitudinising. But, whatever its defects or lapses, it is his own. Wrung from "a stem that scored the hand", it is at its best original in this sense at least, that it has been deeply felt and bears the stamp of the mind that felt it.

Nor may Housman plausibly be classed as a "Georgian". Mr. ⟨Cyril⟩ Connolly detects in his poems certain "contemporary trends"—"imperialism (!), place-nostalgia, games, beer"— but, though I should deny that these things merely reflect literary fashions, the point is not worth powder and shot; and if a phrase here and there has a Georgian flavour, that does not affect one's broad impression that Housman stands strikingly apart from his contemporaries.

He himself, it is said, admitted the influence of the traditional ballads and the lyrics of Shakespeare and Heine; and this statement, though not exhaustive, conveys the main truth of the matter. If he was the product of a tradition, it was a tradition selected by himself. The few serious juvenilia which we possess give some hint of the more or less conventional apprenticeship which he served as a schoolboy and young man; but as his talent matured—and it was a talent to which maturity was essential—he discovered what he wanted and where to find it. What he learned, he learned rather by inquisition than infection. Even when he borrows a phrase, it is felt as a considered appropriation, not a vague reminiscence; and I think it significant that he borrows, in English, from a strictly limited field. The line "At to-fall of the day" is from Collins; "The slayers of themselves" adapts a line from the *Knight's Tale;* "And whistle and I'll be there" no doubt remembers Burns; and a few things are taken from English ballad or folksong. But, apart from these and one or two phrases of semi-proverbial currency, I can detect him borrowing, among the English poets, from Shakespeare and Milton alone. The only English book on which he draws deeply is the Bible.

Housman was not a revolutionary poet: his powers developed slowly, and very few of the poems which he himself printed were written before he was well on in his thirties. Literary, scholarly and late-ripening, he was inevitably deep in debt to his reading. What is significant is that his dependence was sufficiently discriminating to provide him with a foothold instead of a straitjacket. He is the opposite of the poet who lives as a blind parasite on his predecessors: he is the son who develops his father's business, not the son who sponges on his father's friends. Indeed, the metaphor is unfair to him, for he has chosen his line of business for himself. One may say of him, as of T. S. Eliot, that he has created his own tradition by selection, that he uses it, and does not simply allow it to use him. The man who has chosen and understood his masters has all the freedom he needs.

Admitting, therefore, Housman's debt to the past, one may still claim that his achievement was highly original. He discovered a technique which is so distinctive that some find it monotonous, though within its limits it has the subtlest variety. And he was not a technician alone. He did not begin to write well simply because he had at last learned to handle his tools of trade. A condition precedent to his mature work seems, if one may judge from somewhat conflicting evidence, to have been the emotional crisis over which he has drawn a veil; he knew, he said, that these poems were good because they were unlike anything he had done before; and we are even given to understand that parts of the best of them sprang full-formed from his solar plexus. One should perhaps make some allowance for Housman's ironic humour, and for the fact that public confessions are seldom exhaustive—at Cambridge. But I see no reason to doubt that his patroness, whether visceral or celestial, often made her visitations unimplored; that in much of his poetry the craftsmanship is unconscious, and subordinate to that inner force which would have made him a poet if he had been born to the plough.

Such arguments, of course, prove nothing: at best they may make one's impression more plausible. My impression—I need not say that it is not mine alone—is that Housman's poetry, though never iconoclastic, is one of the most distinctive things done in our time, so distinctive that one recognises with something of a shock a stanza or two in Arnold and Dr. Johnson that seem to anticipate the Housman ring. In Pound's phrase, he has "made it new", and in that broad sense at least he is a modern—one who has forged as well as filed.—IAN R. MAXWELL, "A. E. Housman," *Some Modern Writers*, 1940, pp. 55–57

SCHOLARSHIP

The death of A. E. Housman has started a lively debate on the merits, or faults, of his poetry. But scholarship was his chief concern, and for it he has received nothing but praise. He deserves better. Praise so perfunctory shows a lack of interest, and Housman was a stranger phenomenon as a scholar than as a poet. By the time of his death he had won a peculiar eminence in the world of learning. In early years he had been the bad boy of scholarship, who made fun of his elders and embarrassed scholars by what were thought deplorable exhibitions of bad taste. But he grew old, and age brought, as it will in England, respect. The rowdy of yesterday became the sage. His paradoxes were accepted as dogmas; his casual sayings were circulated with hushed reverence, and he became a figure of legend. Even the Germans knew of him.

Housman concerned himself with only a small department of classical scholarship. In a long life he edited three Latin poets, Manilius, Juvenal, and Lucan, and in editing them he confined his energies to establishing what he thought to be the correct text. His articles in learned journals were also concerned with textual criticism. He was, in every sense, a pure scholar. Whatever his tastes in reading may have been, in writing he showed himself singularly unsympathetic to many branches of classical learning. For literary criticism he displayed an open contempt. The descent of manuscripts left him cold, and he said that "*Überlieferungsgeschichte* is a longer and nobler name than fudge." He did not even claim to admire the poets whom he edited, but called Manilius "a fifth-rate author." But though he was narrow, he was extremely strong. In his chosen field he was a master. It is impossible to read anything that he wrote without admiring not only his untiring industry and remarkable organisation of knowledge but his piercing intelligence and matchless resource in devising solutions for difficulties. With new discoveries his interpretation was almost final in its acuteness and its mastery of all relevant evidence, so that, when he was confronted with hitherto unknown lines in the Oxford manuscript of Juvenal, he illustrated and explained them with an array of detail which requires neither supplement nor correction. He had a vast knowledge of classical literature, and he knew Latin as few can ever have known it. So, even if his solutions were sometimes wrong, he had always excellent reasons for them.

Housman, however, impressed others less by his actual performance, which could be properly appreciated only by a few experts, than by his personality. On every word that he wrote he left a unique imprint. This was partly a feat of style. His bold, clear, and resonant sentences stay in the memory as do those of no other scholar. But it is much more a triumph of personality. He had an extraordinary confidence in himself and a passionate belief in the importance of his subject. He felt that he was right, and that others were often wrong. Nor was he content to leave them alone. He persecuted them for their errors and hunted their heresies with a deadly fanaticism. If the dead displeased him, he said so, as of an earlier editor of Manilius: "If a man will comprehend the richness and variety of the universe, and inspire his mind with a due measure of wonder and of awe, he must contemplate the human intellect not only on its heights of genius but in its abysses of ineptitude; and it might be fruitlessly debated to the end of time whether Richard Bentley or Elias Stoeber was the more marvellous work of the Creator: Elias Stoeber, whose reprint of Bentley's text, with a commentary intended to confute it, saw the light in 1767 at Strasburg, a city still famous for its geese." But Housman's real concern was with the living. He saw them as the victims of detestable errors due to intellectual and moral defects. He attacked them with an anger which passed into a poisonous wit. In this mood he wrote: "I imagine that when Mr. Buecheler, when he first perused Mr. Sudhaus' edition of the *Aetna*, must have felt something like Sin when she gave birth to Death," or "He believes that the text of ancient authors is generally sound, not because he has acquainted himself with the elements of the problem, but because he would feel uncomfortable if he did not believe it; just as he believes, on the same cogent evidence, that he is a fine fellow, and that he will rise again from the dead." Those who read this in 1903 felt that a wild, angry demon had come into the quiet house of scholarship.

Housman was sure of himself, and he was not joking when he said: "Posterity should titter a good deal at the solemn coxcombries of the age which I have had to live through." He was equally sure that most of his fellow scholars were not only fools but knaves. Hard as he was on stupidity, he was even harder on what he believed to be dishonesty, laziness, sycophancy, and conceit. Against these failings, real or imagined, he thundered in Olympian anger. He had a peculiar gift for making the mistakes of editors look like vile sins. When someone attributed an unmetrical line to Propertius, Housman wrote: "This is the mood in which Tereus ravished Philomela: concupiscence concentrated on its object and indifferent to all beside." An editor of Lucilius, who complained of rashness in the work of some others, became an example of the hypocritical inconsistency of our ethical notions: "Just as murder is murder no longer if perpetrated by white men on black men or by patriots on kings; just as immorality exists in the relations between the sexes and nowhere else throughout the whole field of human conduct; so a conjecture is audacious when it is based on the letters preserved in a MS., and ceases to be audacious, ceases even to be called a conjecture, when, like these conjectural supplements of Mr. Marx's, it is based on nothing at all." The folly of editors made him reflect with bitter irony on the corruption of truth which it entailed: "In Association football you must not use your hands, and similarly in textual criticisms you must not use your brains. Since we cannot make fools behave like wise men, we will insist that wise men should behave like fools; by this means only can we redress the injustice of nature and anticipate the equality of the grave." In the small world of scholarship faults of intellect or character took on for Housman a cosmic significance, and he cursed them with the virulence of a Hebrew prophet.

There is wit in these curses, but there is no fun. Housman meant what he said. He stood for an ideal of impeccable scholarship, and anything with which he disagreed was a sin against it. His anger blasted many worthy scholars. In his own sphere he neither tolerated rivals nor admitted compromise. The truth obsessed him, and he was convinced that he was more usually in possession of it than anyone else. He can hardly be said to have furthered the general study of Latin in England. His standards were too high, his tastes too narrow, for others to share them. But he satisfied himself. His work was the expression of his belief: "The tree of knowledge will remain for ever, as it was in the beginning, a tree to be desired to make one wise."—C. M. Bowra, "The Scholarship of A. E. Housman," *Spec*, June 19, 1936, p. 1137

A critic once wrote of him as the first scholar in Europe. 'It is not true', said Housman, 'and if it were,——would not know it.' I did not ask whom he counted greater, but I have no doubt that he was thinking of Wilamowitz, of whom he always spoke with high regard. It was characteristic of him to dislike comparison with those he considered his superiors. 'I wish', he said to a pupil, 'they would not compare me with Bentley; Bentley would cut up into four of me', and Mr Percy Withers has recorded a conversation in which the same comparison, coming from an older man, was refused with more asperity:

> I chanced to remark that more than once in Cambridge he had been described in my hearing as the greatest scholar since Bentley. His face darkened, his whole frame grew taut, and in an angered voice he replied: 'I will not tolerate comparison with Bentley. Bentley is alone and supreme. They may compare me with Porson if they will—the comparison is not preposterous—he surpassed me in some qualities as I claim to surpass him in others.'

It is a pity that the remainder of the discussion, in which the qualities of Bentley and Porson were compared and illustrated, has perished, but it is not to be inferred that Housman claimed

equality with the latter. What he did claim is set out, though without reference to other scholars, in the retrospect in which he took leave of Manilius after more than a quarter of a century's work:

> To read attentively, think correctly, omit no relevant consideration, and repress self-will, are not ordinary accomplishments; yet an emendator needs much besides: just literary perception, congenial intimacy with the author, experience which must have been won by study, and mother wit which he must have brought from his mother's womb.
>
> It may be asked whether I think that I myself possess this outfit, or even most of it; and if I answer yes, that will be a new example of my notorious arrogance. I had rather be arrogant than impudent. I should not have undertaken to edit Manilius unless I had believed that I was fit for the task; and in particular I think myself a better judge of emendation, both when to emend and how to emend, than most others.

It is a claim which nobody conversant with his work is likely to dispute.—A. S. F. Gow, *A. E. Housman: A Sketch*, 1936, pp. 39–41

RANDALL JARRELL
"Texts from Housman"

Kenyon Review, Summer 1939, pp. 260–71

The logic poetry has or pretends to have generally resembles induction more than deduction. Of four possible procedures (dealing entirely with particulars, dealing entirely with generalizations, inferring the relatively general from the relatively particular, and deducing the particular from the more general), the third is very much the most common, and the first and second are limits which "pure" and didactic poetry timidly approach. The fourth is seldom seen. In this essay I am interested in that variety of the third procedure in which the generalizations are implicit. When such generalizations are simple ones, very plainly implied by the particulars of the poem, there will be little tendency to confuse this variety of the third procedure with the first procedure; when they are neither simple nor very plainly implied, the poem will be thought of as "pure" (frequently, "nature") poetry. This is all the more likely to occur since most "pure" poetry is merely that in which the impurity, like the illegitimate child of the story, is "such a little one" that we feel it ought to be disregarded. Of these poems of implicit generalization there is a wide range, extending from the simplest, in which the generalizations are made obvious enough to vex the average reader (some of the *Satires of Circumstance*, for instance), to the most complicated, in which they entirely escape his observation ("To the Moon"). The two poems of Housman's which I am about to analyze are more nearly of the type of "To the Moon."

II

Crossing alone the nighted ferry
With the one coin for fee,
Whom, on the wharf of Lethe waiting,
Count you to find? Not me.
The brisk fond lackey to fetch and carry,
The true, sick-hearted slave,
Expect him not in the just city
And free land of the grave.

The first stanza is oddly constructed; it manages to carry

over several more or less unexpressed statements, while the statement it makes on the surface, grammatically, is arranged so as to make the reader disregard it completely. Literally, the stanza says: *Whom do you expect to find waiting for you? Not me.* But the denying and elliptical *not me* is not an answer to the surface question; that question is almost rhetorical, and obviously gets a *me*; the *not me* denies *And I'll satisfy your expectations and be there?*—the implied corollary of the surface question; and the flippant and brutal finality of the *not me* implies that the expectations are foolish. (A belief that can be contradicted so carelessly and completely—by a person in a position to know—is a foolish one.) The stanza says: *You do expect to find me and ought not to* and *You're actually such a fool as to count on my being there?* and *So I'll be there, eh? Not me.*

Some paraphrases of the two stanzas will show how extraordinarily much they do mean; they illustrate the quality of poetry that is almost its most characteristic, compression. These paraphrases are not very imaginative—the reader can find justification for any statement in the actual words of the poem. (Though not in any part considered in isolation. The part as part has a misleading look of independence and reality, just as does the word as word; but it has only that relationship to the larger contexts of the poem that the words which compose it have to it, and its significance is similarly controlled and extended by those larger units of which it is a part. A poem is a sort of onion of contexts, and you can no more locate any of the important meanings exclusively in a part than you can locate a relation in one of its terms. The significance of a part may be greatly modified or even in extreme cases completely reversed by later and larger parts and by the whole. This will be illustrated in the following discussion: most of the important meanings attached to the first stanza do not exist when the stanza is considered in isolation.) And the paraphrases are not hypertrophied, they do not even begin to be exhaustive.

Stanza 1: Do you expect me to wait patiently for you there, just as I have done on earth? expect that, in Hell, after death, things will go on for you just as they do here on earth? that there, after crossing and drinking Lethe and oblivion, I'll still be thinking of human you, still be waiting faithfully there on the wharf for you to arrive, with you still my only interest, with me still your absolutely devoted slave,—just as we are here? Do you really? Do you actually suppose that you yourself, then, will be able to expect it? Even when dead, all alone, on that grim ferry, in the middle of the dark forgetful river, all that's left of your human life one coin, you'll be stupid or inflexible or faithful enough to *count* on (you're sure, are you, so sure that not even a doubt enters your mind?) finding me waiting there? How are we to understand an inflexibility that seems almost incredible? Is it because you're pathetically deluded about love's constancy, my great lasting love for you? (This version makes the *you* sympathetic; but it is unlikely, an unstressed possibility, and the others do not.) Or is it that you're so sure of my complete enslavement that you know death itself can't change it? Or are you so peculiarly stupid that you can't even conceive of any essential change away from your past life and knowledge, even after the death that has destroyed them both? Or is it the general inescapable stupidity of mankind, who can conceive of death only in human and vital terms? (Housman's not giving the reasons, when the reasons must be thought about if the poem is to be understood, forces the reader to make them for himself, and to see that there is a wide range that must be considered. This is one of the most important principles of compression in poetry; these implied foundations

or justifications for a statement might be called *bases*.) Are you actually such a fool as to believe that? So I'll be there? Not me. You're wrong. There things are really different.

One of the most important elements in the poem is the tone of the *not me*. Its casualness, finality, and matter-of-fact bluntness give it almost the effect of slang. It is the crudest of denials. There is in it a laconic brutality, an imperturbable and almost complacent vigor; it has certainly a sort of contempt. Contempt for what? Contempt at himself for his faithlessness? contempt at himself for his obsessing weakness—for not being faithless now instead of then? Or contempt at her, for being bad enough to keep things as they are, for being stupid enough to imagine that they will be so always? The tone is both threatening and disgusted. It shivers between all these qualities like a just-thrown knife. And to what particular denial does this tone attach? how specific, how general a one? These are changes a reader can easily ring for himself; but I hope he will realize their importance. Variations of this formula of alternative possibilities make up one of the most valuable resources of the poet.

The second stanza is most thoroughly ambiguous; there are two entirely different levels of meaning for the whole, and most of the parts exhibit a comparable stratification. I give a word-for-word analysis:

Do not expect me to be after death what I was alive and human: the *fond* (1. *foolish*; 2. *loving*—you get the same two meanings in the synonym *doting*) *brisk* (the normal meanings are favorable: *full of life, keenly alive or alert, energetic*; but here the context forces it over into *officious, undignified, solicitous, leaping at your every word*—there is a pathetic ignoble sense of it here) *lackey* (the most contemptuous and degrading form of the word *servant*: a servile follower, a toady) *to fetch and carry* (you thought so poorly of me that you let me perform nothing but silly menial physical tasks; thus, our love was nothing but the degrading relationship of obsequious servant and contemptuous master), *the true* (1. *constant, loyal, devoted, faithful*; 2. *properly so-called, ideally or typically such*—the perfectly slavish slave) *sick-hearted* (1. *cowardly*, disheartened in a weak discouraged ignoble way, as a Spartan would have said of helots, "These sick-hearted slaves"; 2. sick at heart at the whole mess, his own helpless subjection. There was a man in one of the sagas who had a bad boil on his foot; when he was asked why he didn't limp and favor it, he replied: "One walks straight while the leg is whole." If the reader imagines this man as a slave he will see sharply the more elevated sense of the phrase *sick-hearted slave*) *slave* (1. the conventional hardly meant sense in which we use it of lovers, as an almost completely dead metaphor; this sense has very little force here; or 2. the literal *slave*: the relation of slave to master is not pleasant, not honorable, is between lovers indecent and horrible, but immensely comprehensive—their love is made even more compulsive and even less favorable). But here I leave the word-by-word analysis for more general comment. I think I hardly need remark on the shock in this treatment, which forces over the conventional unfelt terms into their literal degrading senses; and this shock is amplified by the paradoxical fall through *just city* and *free land* into *the grave*. (Also, the effect of the *lackey—carry* and versification of the first line of the stanza should be noted.)

Let me give first the favorable literal surface sense of *the just city and free land of the grave*, its sense on the level at which you take Housman's Greek underworld convention seriously. The house of Hades is the *just city* for a number of reasons: in it are the three just judges; in it are all the exemplary convicts, from Ixion to the Danaides, simply dripping with justice; here justice is meted equally to the anonymous and rankless dead; there is no corruption here. It is the *free land* because here the king and the slave are equal (though even on the level of death as the Greek underworld, the horrid irony has begun to intrude—Achilles knew, and Housman knows, that it is better to be the slave of a poor farmer than king among the hosts of the dead); because here we are free at last from life; and so on and so on.

But at the deeper level, the *just* fastened to *city*, the *city* fastened to *grave*, have an irony that is thorough. How are we to apply *just* to a place where corruption and nothingness are forced on good and bad, innocent and guilty alike? (From Housman's point of view it might be called mercy, but never justice.) And the *city* is as bad; the cemetery looks like a city of the graves, of the stone rectangular houses—but a city without occupations, citizens, without life: a shell, a blank check that can never be filled out. And can we call a land *free* whose inhabitants cannot move a finger, are compelled as completely as stones? And can we call the little cave, the patch of darkness and pressing earth, the *land* of the grave?

And why are we told to expect him not, the slave, the lackey, in the just city and free land of the grave? Because he is changed now, a citizen of the Greek underworld, engrossed in its games and occupations, the new interests that he has acquired? O no, the change is complete, not from the old interests to new ones, but from any interests to none; do not expect him because he has ceased to exist, he is really, finally different now. It is foolish to expect *anything* of the world after death. But we can expect nothingness; and that is better than this world, the poem is supposed to make us feel; there, even though we are overwhelmed impartially and completely, we shall be free of the evil of this world—a world whose best thing, love, is nothing but injustice and stupidity and slavery. This is why the poet resorts to the ambiguity that permits him to employ the adjectives *just* and *free*: they seem to apply truly on the surface level, and ironically at the other; but in a way they, and certainly the air of reward and luck and approbation that goes with them, apply truly at the second level as well. This is the accusation and condemnation of life that we read so often in Housman: that the grave seems better, we are glad to be in it.

We ought not to forget that this poem is a love-poem by the living "me" of the poem to its equally living "you": *when we are dead things will be different—and I'm glad of it.* It is, considerably sublimated, the formula familiar to such connections: *I wish I were dead*; and it has more than a suspicion of the child's *when I'm dead, then they'll be sorry.* It is an accusation that embodies a very strong statement of the underlying antagonism, the real ambivalence of most such relationships. The condemnation applied to the world for being bad is extended to the *you* for not being better. And these plaints are always pleas; so the poem has an additional force. Certainly this particular-seeming little poem turns out to be general enough: it carries implicit in it attitudes (aggregates of related generalizations) toward love, life, and death.

III

It nods and curtseys and recovers
　　When the wind blows above,
The nettle on the graves of lovers
　　That hanged themselves for love.

The nettle nods, the wind blows over,
　　The man, he does not move,
The lover of the grave, the lover
　　That hanged himself for love.

This innocent-looking little nature poem is actually, I think, a general quasi-philosophical piece meant to infect the reader with Housman's own belief about the cause of any action. (I am afraid it is a judgment the reader is likely neither to resist nor recognize.) The nettle and the wind are Housman's specific and usual symbols. Housman's poetry itself is a sort of homemade nettle wine ("out of a stem that scored the hand/I wrung it in a weary land"); the nettle has one poem entirely to itself, XXXII in *New Poems*. No matter what you sow, only the nettle grows; no matter what happens, it flourishes and remains—"the numberless, the lonely, the thronger of the land." It peoples cities, it waves above the courts of kings; "and touch it and it stings." Stating what symbols "mean" is a job the poet has properly avoided; but, roughly, the nettle stands for the hurting and inescapable conditions of life, the prosperous (but sympathetically presented and almost admiringly accepted) evil of the universe—"great Necessity," if you are not altogether charmed by it. What the wind is Housman states himself (in "On Wenlock Edge the wind's in trouble,"; but it is given the same value in several other poems, notably "The weeping Pleiads wester"): the "tree of man" is never quiet because the wind, "the gale of life," blows through it always.

What I said just before the analysis of the first stanza of "Crossing alone the nighted ferry" is true here too; many of one's remarks about the first stanza of this poem will be plausible or intelligible only in the light of one's consideration of the whole poem. In the first line, *It nods and curtseys and recovers*, there is a shock which grows out of the contrast between this demure performance and its performer, the Housman nettle. The nettle is merely repeating above the grave, compelled by the wind, what the man in the grave did once, when the wind blew through him. So living is (we must take it as being) just a repetition of little meaningless nodding actions, actions that haven't even the virtue of being our own— since the wind forces them out of us; life as the wind makes man as the tree or nettle helpless and determined. This illustrates the general principle that in poetry you make judgments by your own preliminary choice of symbols, and force the reader who accepts the symbols to accept the judgments implicit in them. A symbol, like Bowne's "concept," is a nest of judgments; the reader may accept the symbols, and then be cautious about accepting judgments or generalizations, but the damage is done.

The images in the poem are quite general: "the nettle on the graves of lovers that hanged themselves for love" is not any one nettle, not really any particular at all, but a moderately extensive class. (If Housman were writing a pure poem, a nature poem, he would go about it differently; here the generality is insisted on—any lover, any nettle will do well enough: if you prove something for *any* you prove it for *all*, and Housman is arranging all this as a plausible *any*.) There is of course irony, at several levels, in a nettle's dancing obliviously (*nod* and *curtsey* and *recover* add up to *dance*) on the grave of the dead lover. All flesh is grass; but worse here, because the grass which is the symbol for transitoriness outlasts us. (The reader may say, remembering *The stinging nettle only will still be found to stand*: "But the nettle is a symbol of lasting things to Housman, not of transitory ones." Actually it manages for both here, for the first when considered as a common symbol, for the second when considered as Housman's particular one. But this ambiguity in symbols is frequent; without it they would be much less useful. Take a similar case, *grass*: this year's grass springs up and withers, and is shorter than man; but *grass*, all grass, lasts forever. With people we have different words for the two aspects, *men* and *man*. The whole business of thinking of the transitory grass as just the same more lasting than man—in one form or another, one of the stock poetic subjects—is a beautiful fallacy that goes like this: *Grass*—the year-after-year process—is more lasting than *men*; substituting *man* for *men* and this year's blade for the endless grass, you end by getting a proposition that everybody from Job on down or up has felt, at one time or another, thoroughly satisfactory.) Why a nettle to dance on the grave? Because in English poetry flowers grow on the graves of these lovers who have died for love, to show remembrance; Housman puts the nettle there, for forgetfulness. In the other poems the flower "meant" their love—here the nettle means it. All the nettle's actions emphasize its indifference and removedness. The roses in the ballads were intimately related to the lovers, and entwined themselves above the graves—the nature that surrounded the lovers was thoroughly interested in their game, almost as human as they; the nettle above this grave is alone, inhuman and casual, the representative of a nature indifferent to man.

The fifth and sixth lines of the poem are there mainly to establish this shocking paradox: here is a sessile thing, a plant, that curtseys and nods, while the man, the most thoroughly animate of all beings, cannot even move. Looked at in the usual way this is gloomy and mortifying, and that is the surface force it has here; but looked at in another way, Housman's way, there is a sort of triumph in it: the most absolute that man can know. That is what it is for Housman. Once man was tossed about helplessly and incessantly by the wind that blew through him—now the toughest of all plants is more sensitive, more easily moved than he. In other words, death is better than life, nothing is better than anything. Nor is this a silly adolescent pessimism peculiar to Housman, as so many critics assure you. It is better to be dead than alive, best of all never to have been born—said a poet approvingly advertised as seeing life steadily and seeing it whole; and if I began an anthology of such quotations there it would take me a long time to finish. The attitude is obviously inadequate and just as obviously important.

The triumph here leads beautifully into the poem's final statement: the triumph at being in the grave, one with the grave, prepares us for the fact that it was the grave, not any living thing, that the lover loved, and hanged himself for love of. The statement has some plausibility: hanging yourself for love of someone is entirely silly, so far as any possession or any furthering of your love is concerned, but if you are in love with death, killing yourself is the logical and obvious and only way to consummate your love. For the lover to have killed himself for love of a living thing would have been senseless; but his love for her was only ostensible, concealing—from himself too—the "common wish for death," his real passion for the grave.

But if this holds for this one case; if in committing this most sincere and passionate, most living of all acts (that is, killing yourself for love; nothing else shows so complete a contempt for death and consequences, so absolute a value placed on another living creature), the lover was deceiving himself about his motives, and did it, not for love of anything living, but because of his real love for death; then everybody must do everything for the same reason. (This is a judgment too exaggerated for anyone to expect to get away with, the reader may think; but judgments of life tend to this form—"Vanity, vanity, all is vanity.") For the lover is the perfectly simplified, extreme case. This is what is called a crucial experiment. (It is one of Mill's regular types of induction.) The logic runs: If you can prove that in committing this act—an act

about the motives of which the actor is so little likely to be deceived, an act so little likely to have the love of death as his motive—the actor was deceived, and had the love of death as his motive, then you can prove it for any other act the motive of which is more likely to be the love of death, and about the motives of which it is more likely that the actor might be deceived.

But for the conclusion to be true the initial premise must be true, the lover's one motive must have been the wish for death; and Housman has of course not put in even a word of argument for the truth of that premise, he has merely stated it, with the most engaging audacity and dogmatism—has stated it innocently, as a fact obvious as any other of these little natural facts about the wind and the nettle and the cemetery. He has produced it not as a judgment but as a datum, and the sympathetic reader has accepted it as such. He is really treating it as a percept, and percepts have no need for proof, they are neither true nor false, they are just there. If he had tried to prove the truth of the premise he would have convinced only those who already believed in the truth of the conclusion, and those people (i.e., himself) didn't need to be convinced. With the poem as it is, the reader is convinced; or if he objects, the poet can object disingenuously in return, "But you've made the absurd error of taking hypothetical reasoning as categorical. My form is: *If* A, *then* B; I'm not interested in *proving* A. Though, of course, if you decide to remove the *if*, and assert also; and A is awfully plausible, isn't it?—just part of the data of the poem; you could hardly reject it, could you?"

Two of the generalizations carried over by this poem—that our actions are motivated by the wish for death, that our ostensible reasons for acts are merely rationalizations, veneers of apparent motive overlying the real levels of motivation—are, in a less sweeping form, psychological or psychoanalytical commonplaces today. But I am not going to hold up Housman's poem as a masterly anticipation of our own discoveries; so far as I can see, Housman was not only uninterested but incapable in such things, and pulled these truths out of his pie not because of wit, but because of the perverse and ingenious obstinacy that pulled just such gloomy judgments out of any pie at all. Here the shock and unlikeliness of what he said were what recommended it to him; and the discovery that these have been mitigated would merely have added to his gloom.

J. P. SULLIVAN
From "'The Leading Classic of His Generation'"
Arion, Summer 1962, pp. 106–17

Academic England is as prone to snobbery as any other part of English life, and in Housman classicists have found an *arbiter elegantiae* of a most formidable sort. What was one man's choice of study, dictated by his own inclinations and his great if narrow talents, has been erected into a choice for a whole profession: his choice was 'those minute and pedantic studies in which I am fitted to excel and which give me pleasure.' Housman himself, it may be thought, was but negatively responsible for this: he had warned that 'Everyone has his favourite study, and he is therefore disposed to lay down, as the aim of learning in general, the aim which his favourite study seems specially fitted to achieve, and the recognition of which as the aim of learning in general would increase the popularity of that study and the importance of those who profess it.'[1]

Housman was in fact confirming for his period the criteria

of excellence which have dominated English classical studies since Bentley. Bentley—Porson—Housman, the tradition runs: these are the three luminaries of English classical studies, and these dictate the standards of classical prestige in Britain. Textual criticism is queen of classical studies, and those disciplines closest to it contend for the other places at court.

The four key documents for an understanding of Housman and his influence are the *Introductory Lecture* (1892), *The Application of Thought to Textual Criticism* (1921), *The Name and Nature of Poetry* (1933) and the biographical memoir of Arthur Platt (1927). Each of them raises issues of great importance, but one thing strikes the impartial reader immediately: 'the absolute honesty in the pursuit of truth' (D. S. Robertson), the 'fierce intellectual honesty which would neither condone nor extenuate' (A. Ker), these are by no means obvious qualities in the above pieces, and Housman himself described the first as 'rhetorical and not wholly sincere.'

Instead we meet with prejudiced and sometimes tendentious remarks or persuasive definitions which are still paraphrased by his admirers when criticising classical work which runs counter to the Housman tradition.

The *Introductory Lecture* ostensibly defends the Arts against the claims of Science. But the defence is not the personal or cultural benefits of humane studies, for Housman denies us any such responsibility, but the personal liberty of the Cyrenaic and the pragmatic value of any sort of truth. Knowledge is a good for man because it gives him pleasure and at most because 'it must in the long run be better to see things as they are than to be ignorant of them.' Any academic pursuits then which attract us personally have an equal claim on our attention and, by this reasoning, they should have equal honour in our universities. There is no conception of knowledge as an organized whole; there is no suggestion that some studies are more important or more valuable than others. Why certain literary studies, including classics, have a prestige not accorded to others is left unexplained. Prejudice and cant might be Housman's answer, for the humane benefits of academic classics seem negligible: few classical scholars get from their literary studies any just appreciation of literary excellence. This, according to Housman, requires congenital organs of literary perception, which are but rarely found and which may be stimulated by a small amount of classical training. Bentley is introduced as a prime example of a great scholar whose deficiency of taste is glaring:

> Turn what they will to Verse, their Toil is vain,
> Critics like me shall make it Prose again.

Ignoring Housman's view of the rarity of such organs of literary perception, which ties in with his romantic views on the rarity and nature of the true poet, one may see at once certain confusions in Housman's train of reasoning. To begin with, he seems to identify a classical training simply with the pursuit of knowledge, any sort of knowledge, and offers us the impression of a factual and almost scientific study. Secondly, he assumes that the study of classical literature, however pursued, is automatically a *literary* study; and so when certain practitioners like Bentley turn out defective in taste, he assumes that literary studies therefore cannot inculcate critical taste at all. This is not necessarily true, nor is the implication valid that Arnold's literary sense was refined by a very small amount of classical reading. Anyone who looks over Arnold's collected works will find there a self-education and a refining of method as rigorous as any. If Housman thought that Arnold's critical achievement was due to some divine natural gift, which required no training or hard work, he was mistaken.

Thirdly, Housman throughout the lecture assimilates humane studies to classical studies in England with their own particular tradition derived from Bentley. And it could be argued that this particular method of studying the classics does not 'beautify our inner natures' because it is not meant to and is not suitable for such a purpose, not because humane studies cannot of their nature pass on any cultural advantages.

Much of what Housman says is reminiscent of certain remarks of Macaulay, but Macaulay's diagnosis is different. Macaulay does not, like Housman, subscribe to the thesis that the organs of literary perception are rarely found in a man, that these organs, if they exist, are easily stimulated or that literary criticism is some god-given faculty which rises like genius in unpredictable places and times.

. . . But both Housman and Macaulay in their different ways support a later critic's contention that 'the common result of a classical education is to incapacitate from literature for life.' Whether the nature of classical study is such that this is inevitable or whether our present methods of study are at fault is another question.

Not surprisingly Housman begs this question in the interest of his own tastes. He does not pause to consider whether Arnold, Lessing and Goethe developed their faculties by any other study or whether in fact their study of classical *literature* may not have been as deep as his study of the classical tongues, but deep in a quite different way. Etymologists of English know much more about our language in one sense than many great writers, but it cannot be said that they know the language *better* than such writers or that they have worked harder at their studies. In effect, by denying any humanistic responsibility, Housman elevates his own practice into an ideal; it seems to follow that 'the minute and accurate study of the classical tongues affords Latin professors their only excuse for existing.' Yet this is neither obvious nor true, as the titles of many British chairs and faculties indicate (e.g., *Literae Humaniores* at Oxford and Professor of Humanity in Glasgow). Such titles look to other things as well, which should follow and complete 'the minute and accurate study' which is admittedly a prerequisite for any classical teaching or research. Who would suggest that all professors of English be Germanic philologists or experts on Elizabethan printing like Mr. Fredson Bowers?

In Housman's statement there is a confusion between education and research. Housman's indifferentism, his defence of the study of whatever attracts the scholar, is tempting and research institutions wisely follow this line; there is, however, no justification for its imposition on a system of education, for forcing the young to study literary texts in a way that attracts *us*.

Of course, Housman could weep over *Diffugere nives* and claim that it was the greatest poem in the language, and in private teaching no doubt literary judgments are made and offered to our pupils, but as serious literary discussion is not encouraged in our subject, there is no discipline and thus no check on the possible irresponsibility of such literary comment. The 'watery' or the 'dry' alternate in the education we offer. And it is only occasionally when some poor scholar unwittingly goes beyond his last and ventures to offer some literary comment on his author that we see the truth of Housman's remarks on the absolute poverty of literary comment by the trained classicist. The main disagreement with Housman centers on his inference that no training is possible or desirable even for those who have some native aptitude for literature. No one can become an artist without great native ability and some like the Douanier Rousseau and Grandma Moses have managed without training, but are art schools and artistic apprenticeships therefore useless?

Housman remarks: 'The majority of mankind, as is only natural, will be most attracted by those sciences which most nearly concern human life; those sciences which, in Bacon's phrase, are drenched in flesh and blood . . . The men who are attracted to the drier . . . sciences, say logic or pure mathematics or textual criticism, are likely to be fewer in number; but they are not to suppose that the comparative unpopularity of such learning renders it any the less worthy of pursuit.' Of course not, nor any the more worthy. But our attempt to impose, as a standard pattern, our own drier preferences on the education which we offer not only molds those who desire to excel in our subject and so perpetuates the tradition, but drives many students of equal intelligence and different aptitudes into subjects where their contribution to the common pursuit can be more profitably made. In Oxford, for instance, they betake themselves to logical analysis or epigraphy or some similar subject which bears a greater relation to the name and nature of philosophical and historical studies than textual criticism and the other ancillary studies do to the study of classical literature.

Housman's indifferentism is valid only if we think of personal satisfaction. By all means we should follow the direction of our aptitudes, but it is absurd to suggest, as Housman does, that there is no difference in value between one department of learning and another. This is not to deny the seeming fairmindedness of one of his concluding remarks. He remarked 'we can all dwell together in unity without crying up our own pursuits or depreciating the pursuits of others on factitious grounds.'

Some of the thoughts in *The Application of Thought to Textual Criticism* partly explain the honour paid to current philological practice. Housman, for all his own professed enjoyment, rather underestimates the pleasures of textual criticism and kindred studies: the delight in the limited problem satisfactorily solved with some approach to finality, the pleasure in bringing to bear a number of techniques and items of knowledge, the visual pleasures of palaeography, the ease of formulation, the multitude of guides, predecessors and advisors, the acceptability of the pursuit, its fertility in learned papers—all these adequately compensate for the rarity with which nowadays one's emendations are admitted to the text or one's vulnerability to superior scholars like Housman. Were textual criticism and exegesis *not* so pleasant (and prestigious), why would so many scholars be engaged in them? Why would there be so many articles and books containing nothing but textual notes and explications published, often when a full commentary is lacking on a certain author? This last, of course, requires a treatment of *all* the problems, not just the more soluble and congenial difficulties.

Housman however remarks, moderately enough, 'It has sometimes been said that textual criticism is the crown and summit of all scholarship. This is not evidently or necessarily true; but it is true that the qualities which make a critic, whether they are thus transcendent or no, are rare, and that a good critic is a much less common thing than, for instance, a good grammarian' (p. 133).

This rarity of the good critic (although at this time Housman was claiming for him little more than reason and commonsense) has imperceptibly led to the attribution to him of almost super-human qualities. Consider, for example, a recent remark made to the same body as Housman was addressing, the Classical Association, by the distinguished editor of Ovid, Mr. E. J. Kenney:

The editing of a classical text is a discipline that calls forth the widest possible range of knowledge and the richest possible combination of talents. The greatest practitioners of the past have been among the giants of scholarship.

The logical questions of definition we may leave aside but we should notice at least the high ambition of our studies that rigorously encourages only the widest possible range of knowledge and the richest possible combination of talents. Mr. Kenney's remark is similar to Housman's description of emending and judging emendations: 'To read attentively, think correctly, omit no relevant consideration, and repress self-will, are not ordinary accomplishments; yet an emendator needs much besides: just literary perception, congenial intimacy with the author, experience which must have been won by study, and mother wit which he must have brought from his mother's womb' (Pref. to Manilius V). And as historians and philosophers require emendations too we may add to the critic's equipment a sound knowledge of historical probability and history and an interest in philosophical problems and a feeling for the ways philosophers think.

Housman himself however refutes his idea of the critic by his own remarks on Bentley. Bentley would cut up into four critics like Housman and Housman refers to his 'unique originality and greatness' (p. 121), but he also speaks of 'Bentley's firm reliance on his own bad taste' and describes him as 'this tasteless and arbitrary pedant.'

Taste then is not such a necessary part of the critic's equipment in practice, even though it may be theoretically of advantage. And in Bentley's case Housman was careful not to go as far as Housman's admirers go in discussing *him*. Housman rightly confessed he was no literary critic, but did regard himself as a connoisseur—'I think I can tell good from bad in literature.' And eulogizers such as Percy Withers and D. S. Robertson describe him as 'exquisitely sensitive to literary values' or refer to 'the sureness of his aesthetic judgment.' His one venture into literary criticism ('referring opinions to principles and setting them forth so as to command assent,' as he defines it) will be examined later, but his claims to aesthetic judgment may be disposed of immediately. His taste was narrow and closely connected with the sort of poetry he wrote. Even within this range it was faulty. And although it was a definite taste, neither in his Manilius nor his Juvenal nor his Lucan can one see much scope for it or for that 'congenial' intimacy with an author that he regarded as a prerequisite for the emendator. Satire he classed with controversy and burlesque in *The Name and Nature of Poetry*; of Lucan he said 'his vocabulary is as commonplace as his diction.' Manilius was 'a facile and frivolous poet,' and the *Ibis* was Ovid's best work.

Prose he does not seem to have cared much for: so one might infer from his favorite authors. *Cranford* he described as 'one of the nicest stories ever written.' Other preferences were Sinclair Lewis, Theodore Dreiser, Edith Wharton, Anita Loos' *Gentlemen Prefer Blondes*, Josh Billings and Artemus Ward. Mark Twain he liked, but Henry James he read 'with some affliction at his prolixity.' His favorite English novelist was Thomas Hardy. His favorite English poet was originally Matthew Arnold, but he read Edgar Allan Poe (!), 'got more enjoyment from Edna St. Vincent Millay than from either Robinson or Frost'; Robert Bridges' *Shorter Poems* he called 'the most perfect single volume of verse ever published'; William Watson's *Wordsworth's Grave* was 'one of the precious things of English literature' and Masefield's plays 'are well worth reading and contain a lot that is good.'

All this may have the individuality of a poet's taste but even within these limits it is surely difficult to talk with conviction of his 'just literary perception' in preferring Millay to Frost or finding much merit in Poe (cf. his remarks on Poe's 'The Haunted Palace', p. 187). But the real insight into his literary judgments may be obtained from his notorious comments on Milton and Shakespeare in the *Introductory Lecture* (p. 10 ff.). And that this was no attempt to be merely shocking seems confirmed by a witness who reports: 'I have heard him say that it gave him no pleasure to read a play of Shakespeare's from beginning to end, for though some parts were magnificent, there were others so slovenly that the effect of the whole was disagreeable.'

It is now becoming clear what sort of taste this is. On one hand a belief in something like Valéry's *poésie pure* which may or may not be pure nonsense (cf. his remarks on a perfectly understandable song of Shakespeare's—*Take o take those lips away*, p. 189); on the other a very 'classical' preoccupation with form which leads him to say of Milton: 'The dignity, the sanity, the unfaltering elevation of style, the just subordination of detail, the due adaptation of means to ends, the high respect of the craftsman for his craft and himself, which ennoble Virgil and the great Greeks, are all to be found in Milton, and nowhere else in English literature are they all to be found.' Such remarks perhaps indicate why he says practically nothing of the poets of the post-war generation in England and seems scarcely to have known them: Eliot he seems to have approved of for writing sensibly on the poetry of *A Shropshire Lad*. A piece of adulation by A. Ker in the Memorial Edition of *The Bromsgrovian* is an adequate commentary on this taste by another classicist: 'There is no doubt that Housman's sober attention to form he owed to his classical reading; and in an age in which neglect of form seems the first requirement of a poet, he is likely to be discredited . . . It may well be that the lyric poets of the future, looking for these things in vain among the coteries of the twentieth century, will turn for their touchstone of literary merit, to the poetry of Housman.' *That* could only have been written by a classicist. The common element in Housman's literary judgments and such remarks as this from his admirers is what called forth once from a critic of classical education the following: 'The common result of a classical training (need it be said that there are, of course, exceptions) is to incapacitate from contact with literature for life. . . . The resulting "taste," "judgment" and "sense of fitness" (usually so strong in the "classic") are almost insuperable bars to the development of critical sensibility. For the "classic", Form is something that Flecker . . . has and Mr. Pound in *Hugh Selwyn Mauberley* most certainly hasn't.' (F. R. Leavis, *Education and the University*.)

Wisely then Housman disavows the title of literary critic in *The Name and Nature of Poetry*. Housman's conception of a literary critic is even more exalted than his or Mr. Kenney's conception of the textual critic (perhaps that is why one is a little shocked to find him mentioning Sir Walter Raleigh and A. C. Bradley in the same breath, p. 109):

'Whether the faculty of literary criticism is the best gift that Heaven has in its treasuries I cannot say; but Heaven seems to think so, for assuredly it is the gift most charily bestowed' (p. 168), and he says of Arthur Platt, 'He knew better than to conceive himself that rarest of all the great works of God, a literary critic' (p. 158).

Goethe, Lessing and Arnold, these are the mortals he admits to the literary pantheon as he put Scaliger, Bentley, Nicolaus Heinsius and others into his textual pantheon. But whereas the second, for all the aptitudes requisite in a textual critic, is allowed a goodly number of adequate scholars, the literary critic must be supreme or nowhere. The journeymen of classics must be scholars in Housman's sense or nothing. This deference to the heights of criticism is accompanied by sneers at anything else—'the usual flummery of the cobbler who is ambitious to go beyond his last.' Of Platt he says, 'he stuck to business as a scholar should, and preferred, as a man of letters will, the dry to the watery.' What exactly the scholar's last is, whether he be good cobbler or indifferent botcher, is clear from his remark to Platt that if he preferred one poet to another, then he was no true scholar.

The Name and Nature of Poetry is a strange but interesting document. It is valuable chiefly for the light it throws on Housman's taste and principles. One Cambridge critic lamented that it would take twelve years to undo the harm Housman had done in an hour. This is overestimating the influence of the classical scholar in the world of letters and Housman could do no harm to the criticism of classical authors: *cantabit vacuus coram latrone viator.*

Housman admits in this lecture that the good literature of several languages read for pleasure might do some good to the reader, 'must quicken his perception though dull, and sharpen his discrimination though blunt, and mellow the rawness of his personal opinions.' This is different stuff from what was implied in the *Introductory Lecture* about the effect of a classical education on those who lack the organs of literary perception. The contradiction is not formal but implicit.

In discussing poetry Housman's tendency towards persuasive definitions is as noticeable as in his definitions of the scholar and the literary critic. For Housman, as usual except in his textual work, is presenting a case or justifying a set of prejudices. Half the seventeenth and the eighteenth century are dismissed as almost barren of poetry in the highest sense, the latter on the extraordinary ground that the poetry of that age 'differed in quality . . . from the poetry of all those ages, whether modern or ancient, English or foreign, which are acknowledged as the great ages of poetry.' We soon see why. 'Poetry is not the thing said but a way of saying it. Can it then be isolated and studied by itself? For the combination of language with its intellectual content, its meaning, is as close a union as can well be imagined. Is there such a thing as pure unmingled poetry, poetry independent of meaning? . . . Even when poetry has a meaning, *as it usually has* [my italics], it may well be inadvisable to draw it out . . . "The Haunted Palace" is one of Poe's best poems so long as we are content to swim in the sensations it evokes and only vaguely to apprehend the allegory . . . Meaning is of the intellect, poetry is not[2] (p. 187). We soon find what poetry is of—'Poetry indeed seems to me more physical than intellectual.' Housman offers a set of physical reactions as a touchstone: that such reactions might be built up artificially by non-poetical feelings such as sentiment or familiarity he never considers. Obviously such feeling could be roused by cheap as well as good poetry. Like the mystic who *knows* he has seen God and cannot understand why his apprehension is not accepted as veridical by the rest of the world, Housman puts his faith in this purely personal criterion and shows how his vaunted taste can be stimulated by the tumpty-tump follies of Poe as well as by the songs of Shakespeare.

If, as seems clear, Housman's acquaintance with classical literature did not give him that fine aesthetic taste which is sometimes claimed for him, it must also be added that his acquaintance in general with the ancient world seems to have given him only that illiberal set of prejudices which the world associates with a certain type of headmaster, although these may be in part due to what Shackleton Bailey calls his lack of 'aptitude for broad generalization or for the arrangement of masses of uncoordinated material.' In a letter to Laurence Housman, he asserted 'civilization without slavery is impossible' and his brother glosses this as follows: 'In politics he stayed aloof, over the benefit of a democratic government being a complete sceptic. He even believed that slavery was essential to a well-governed state, but was so English in his preference that he probably considered England a better-governed country under democratic mismanagement than any other favoured with a form of despotism of which, theoretically, he more greatly approved.' Such remarks, from a professed admirer of Arnold, incidentally, seem to point to a complete isolation from life and a fundamental lack of that historical sense which a classical education is sometimes supposed to provide.

His biographical notice of Arthur Platt (pp. 154–160) allows us to see most clearly into the heart of the matter, although perhaps there is no key to Housman's character which can be cut entirely from his conscious motives and expressed views.[3] The piece on Platt is interesting; it is a sort of Grammarian's Funeral Oration and the subtle differences from the ethos of Browning's poem are well worth study. The remarks on Platt's scholarship and personality are generous and two of the comments in particular are illuminating for the light they throw on Housman:

'In literary comment he did not expatiate, although, or rather because, he was the most lettered scholar of his time. He stuck to business, as a scholar should, and preferred, as a man of letters will, the dry to the watery. He knew better than to conceive himself that rarest of all the works of God, a literary critic; but such remarks on literature as he did let fall were very different stuff from the usual flummery of the cobbler who is ambitious to go beyond his last' (p. 158). And: 'Nor were his studies warped and narrowed by ambition. A scholar who means to build himself a monument must spend much of his life in acquiring knowledge which for its own sake is not worth having and in reading books which do not in themselves deserve to be read . . .' (p. 159). The judgment of value implicit in this last statement, so at odds with the views of the *Introductory Lecture* is not my concern here; the real significance lies in the overt ambition it exudes. This, taken in conjunction with the earlier dogmatic definition of the scholar's function in the same piece—grammar, metrics, exegesis and textual criticism—explains much of Housman's theory and practice as well as the awed language he uses when talking of Bentley, the references to *lucida tela diei* and the adaptation of Arnold's description of Goethe, the physician of the Iron Age, to the healer of corrupt texts. This was Housman's own *métier*.

The energy which classical scholars have failed to devote to the nice discrimination of good and bad in the authors they study is usually spent on the nice discrimination in private of the merits and soundness of other scholars. Housman was no exception, and there is something egregiously childish in the prefaces with their mannered weighing of each critic's contribution to a text; on Bentley's Manilius he wrote 'Haupt alone has praised it in proportion to its merit . . . Had Bentley never edited Manilius, Nicolaus Heinsius would be the foremost critic of Latin poetry; but this is a work beyond the scope of even Heinsius. Great as was Scaliger's achievement, it is yet surpassed and far surpassed by Bentley's; Scaliger at the side of Bentley is no more than a marvellous boy' (p. 28). And examples might be multiplied.

Such praise of critics like Bentley naturally reflects glory on Housman's chosen line of study and Housman's own talents. Housman's genius was not for exploration, and he made nothing like the contribution of a Lachmann to textual science nor did he add a tithe of what, say, Milman Parry has added to our understanding of ancient literature. But in this matter reputation is not judged by impressive results or by large contributions to knowledge but by conformity to certain accepted criteria, criteria which Housman backed with the full force of his scholarly personality. Housman is offered to us as the model of the classical scholar, witness the eulogies I quoted earlier of the textual critic. Housman's ambition chose to build its monument in the narrow area where stand the monuments of Bentley and Porson and the smaller brasses of the English school of textual criticism. This is a closed world and within it the laudatory descriptions of its luminaries might be pardonably regarded by an outsider as appropriate only for some of our greatest English thinkers—*lucida tela diei* surely fits a Newton better than a Bentley. But a skillful walling off of classical reputation and scholarship from all comparison with other branches of study has produced some strange forced flowers of pride and reputation. The traditional regard for classical studies as a humane education bolsters this pride, even though the basis of that regard has passed away and the time has gone when our claims to intellectual merit were open to disinterested evaluation by more general criteria. Just as *we* cannot know what enormously high textual talents have been displayed in the study of Vedic texts, so the republic of letters cannot appreciate the high talents displayed in textual criticism of the classics nor evaluate this high intelligence and its contribution to culture. And of course by various self-denying ordinances no classical scholar has ever dared set himself up simultaneously as a man of letters and a great scholar—or if he has, he has never succeeded in impressing his peers in either field. It is this artificial situation which has to be taken into account when discussing Housman, and he should be set, not simply or solely in the context of classical studies, but in the context of a wider humane culture. Only then can an adequate evaluation of his contribution to the sum of things be made.

Notes

1. *A. E. Housman: Selected Prose*, ed. John Carter (Cambridge: Cambridge University Press, 1961), p. 2. All further references to this edition will occur parenthetically in the text.
2. It is, of course, obvious that such a belief in poetry as nonsense could not be applied to Latin poetry, for then the textual critic would have to acquiesce in some very strange things.
3. A more penetrating analysis, based on intuition and gossip, is to be found in W. H. Auden's sonnet on Housman, omitted from his collected shorter poems, no doubt because of one line which is admittedly in bad taste.

RICHARD WILBUR

From "Round about a Poem of Housman's"

The Moment of Poetry, ed. Don Cameron Allen

1962, pp. 78–91

One of my favorite poems of A. E. Housman is called "Epitaph on an Army of Mercenaries," and because it is a soluble problem in tact I want to discuss it here. Let me say it to you a first time in a fairly flat voice, so as to stress by *lack* of stress the necessity, at certain points, of making crucial decisions as to tone:

These, in the day when heaven was falling,
The hour when earth's foundations fled,

Followed their mercenary calling,
And took their wages and are dead.

Their shoulders held the sky suspended;
They stood, and earth's foundations stay;
What God abandoned, these defended,
And saved the sum of things for pay.

Perhaps the main decision to be made is, how to say those last two words, "for pay." Should they be spoken in a weary drawl? Should they be spoken matter-of-factly? Or should they be spat out defiantly, as if one were saying "Of *course* they did it for pay; what did you expect?" Two or three years ago, I happened to mention Housman's poem to a distinguished author who is usually right about things, and he spoke very ill of it. He found distasteful what he called its easy and sweeping cynicism, and he thought it no better, except in technique, than the more juvenile pessimistic verses of Stephen Crane. For him, the gist of the poem was this: "What a stinking world this is, in which what we call civilization must be preserved by the blood of miserable hirelings." And for him, that last line was to be said in a tone of wholesale scorn:

And saved the *sum of things* for *pay.*

I couldn't accept that way of taking the poem, even though at the time I was unprepared to argue against it; and so I persisted in saying Housman's lines to myself, in my own way, while walking or driving or waiting for trains. Then one day I came upon an excellent essay by Cleanth Brooks, which supported my notion of the poem and expressed its sense and tone far better than I could have done. Mr. Brooks likened Housman's Shropshire lads, so many of whom are soldiers, to those Hemingway heroes who do the brave thing not out of a high idealism but out of stoic courage and a commitment to some personal or professional code. Seen in this manner, Housman's mercenaries—his professional soldiers, that is—are not cynically conceived; rather their poet is praising them for doing what they had engaged to do, for doing what had to be done, and for doing it without a lot of lofty talk. If we understand the poem so, it is not hard to see what tones and emphases are called for:

These, in the day when heaven was falling
The hour when earth's foundations fled,
Followed their mercenary calling,
And took their wages and are dead.

Their shoulders held the sky suspended;
They stood, and earth's foundations stay;
What God abandoned, *these defended*,
And saved the sum of things for pay.

That is how I would read it, and I suspect that Mr. Brooks would concur. But now suppose that the distinguished author who thought the poem wholly cynical should not be satisfied. Suppose he should say, "Mr. Brooks' interpretation is very enhancing, and makes the poem far less cheaply sardonic; but unfortunately Mr. Brooks is being more creative than critical, and the poem is really just what I said it was."

There are a number of arguments I might venture in reply, and one would be this: Housman was a great classical scholar, and would have been particularly well acquainted with the convention of the military epitaph. His title refers us, in fact, to such poems of Simonides wrote in honor of the Spartans who fell at Thermopylae, or the Athenians who fought at the Isthmus. Those poems are celebratory in character, and so is Housman's. The sound and movement of Housman's poem accord, moreover, with the mood of plain solemnity which the convention demands. The tetrameter, which inclines by its nature to skip a bit, . . . is slowed down

here to the pace of a dead-march. The rhetorical balancing of line against line, and half-line against half-line, the frequency of grammatical stops, and the even placement of strong beats, make a deliberate movement inescapable; and this deliberate movement releases the full and powerful sonority which Housman intends. It is not the music of sardony.

The distinguished author might come back at me here, saying something like this: "No doubt you've named the right convention, but what you forget is that there are *mock*-versions of every convention, including this one. While Housman's mock-use of the military epitaph is not broadly comic but wryly subtle, it does employ the basic trick of high burlesque. Just as Pope, in his mock-epic *The Rape of the Lock*, adopts the tone and matter of Milton or Homer only to deflate them, so Housman sets his solemn, sonorous poem to leaking with the word 'mercenary,' and in the last line lets the air out completely. The poem is thus a gesture of total repudiation, a specimen of indiscriminate romantic irony, and it's what we might expect from the poet who counsels us to 'endure an hour and see injustice done,' who refers to God as 'whatever brute and blackguard made the world,' and who disposes of this life by crying, 'Oh, why did I awake? When shall I sleep again?'"

From now on I am going to play to win, and I shall not allow the distinguished author any further rebuttals. The answer to what he said just now is this: while Housman may maintain that "heaven and earth ail from the prime foundation," he consistently honors those who face up manfully to a bad world; and especially he honors the common soldier who, without having any fancy reasons for doing so, draws his mercenary "thirteen pence a day" and fights and dies. We find this soldier in such poems as "Lancer," or "Grenadier," and Housman always says to him,

dead or living, drunk or dry,
Soldier, I wish you well.

The mercenaries of the poem I've been discussing are enlisted from all these other soldier-poems, and though their deaths exemplify the world's evil, Housman stresses not that but the shining of their courage in the general darkness.

The poem is not a mock-version of the military epitaph; however, the distinguished author was right in feeling that Housman's poem is not so free of irony as, for instance, William Collins' eighteenth-century ode, "How sleep the brave . . ." These eight short lines do, in fact, carry a huge freight of irony, most of it implicit in a system of subtle echoes and allusions; but none of the irony is at the expense of the mercenaries, and all of it defends them against slight and detraction.

If one lets the eye travel over Housman's lines, looking for echo or allusion, it is probably line 4 which first arrests the attention:

And took their wages and are dead.

This puts one in mind of St. Paul's Epistle to the Romans, Chapter VI, where the Apostle declares that "the wages of sin is death." The implication of this echo is that paid professional soldiers are sinful and unrighteous persons, damned souls who have forfeited the gift of eternal life. That is certainly not Housman's view, even if one makes allowance for ironic exaggeration; and so we are forced to try and imagine a sort of person whose view it might be. The sort of person we're after is, of course, self-righteous, idealistic, and convinced of his moral superiority to those common fellows who fight, not for high and noble reasons, but because fighting is their job. Doubtless you've heard regulars of the American army subjected to just that kind of spiritual snobbery, and one readily finds analogies in other departments of life: think of the way professional politicians are contemned by our higher-minded citizens, while shiny-faced amateurs are prized for their wholesome incapacity. Spiritual snobs are unattractive persons under any circumstances, but they appear to especial disadvantage in Housman's poem. After all, they and their civilization were saved by the mercenaries—or professionals—who did their fighting for them, and that fact makes their scorn seem both ungrateful and hypocritical.

Housman's echo of St. Paul, then, leads us to imagine a class of people who look down on Tommy Atkins, and it also prompts us to defend Tommy Atkins against their unjust disdain. Let me turn now to some other echoes, to a number of Miltonic reverberations which are scattered throughout the poem. They all derive from some ten lines of the Sixth Book of *Paradise Lost*. That is the book about the war in heaven, wherein the good angels and the rebel angels fight two great and inconclusive engagements, after which the Messiah enters and single-handedly drives the rebels over the wall of heaven. It is probably not irrelevant to mention that the ruling idea of Book VI, the idea which all the action illustrates, is that might derives from right, and that righteousness therefore must prevail. Here is a passage which comes at the end of the second battle, when the good and bad angels are throwing mountains at each other:

> horrid confusion heapt
> Upon confusion rose: and now all Heav'n
> Had gone to wrack, with ruin overspread,
> Had not th' Almighty Father where he sits
> Shrin'd in his Sanctuary of Heav'n secure,
> Consulting on the sum of things, foreseen
> This tumult, and permitted all, advis'd.
> (668 ff.)

The sum of things means here the entire universe, including heaven and hell, and God is about to save the sum of things by sending his son against the rebel angels. Otherwise heaven might fall, and earth's foundations might flee. When the Messiah drives Satan and his forces over heaven's edge, and they begin their nine-day fall into hell, Milton gives us another passage which Housman has echoed:

> Hell heard the unsufferable noise, Hell saw
> Heav'n ruining from Heav'n, and would have fled
> Affrighted; but strict Fate had cast too deep
> Her dark foundations, and too fast had bound.
> (867 ff.)

It is quite plain that Housman is reminding his reader of Milton, and in particular of these two passages from Book VI, in which we find "the sum of things," fleeing foundations, and heaven in peril of falling. The ticklish question now is, how much of Milton should we put into Housman's poem; how detailed a comparison should we draw between the war in Milton's heaven and the battle in which Housman's mercenaries died? Should we, for instance, compare Housman's sacrificial mercenaries, whose deaths have preserved the sum of things, to the Son of God who won the war in heaven and later died on earth to save mankind? Housman is quite capable of implying such a comparison. In his poem "The Carpenter's Son," Christ is a Shropshire lad who dies on the gallows because he would not "leave ill alone." And in the poem "1887," Housman says this of the soldiers who have helped God save the Queen by dying in battle:

> To skies that knit their heartstrings right,
> To fields that bred them brave,
> The saviours come not home to-night:
> Themselves they could not save.

As Mr. Brooks points out in his essay, those last lines "echo the passage in the Gospels in which Christ, hanging on the cross, is taunted with the words: 'Others he saved; himself he cannot save.'" It appears, then, that in his "Epitaph on an Army of Mercenaries" Housman may be bestowing on his soldiers the ultimate commendation; he may be saying that their sacrifice, in its courage and in the scope of its consequences, was Christlike. For the rest, I should say that Housman's Miltonic allusions have a clear derogatory purpose, and that their function is once again to mock those who feel superior to the soldiers whom the poet wishes to praise. Housman mocks those who feel that they are on the side of the angels, that their enemies are devils, that God is their property and will defend the right, that heaven and earth depend upon their ascendancy and the prevalence of their lofty mores, yet who count in fact not on God or on themselves but on the courage of mercenaries whom they despise.

These smug people, whom the poem nowhere mentions but everywhere rebukes, are covertly attacked again in line five through an allusion to the eleventh labor of Heracles. In that enterprise, Heracles was out to secure the golden apples of the Hesperides, and he applied for the help of Atlas, the giant who supports the heavens on his shoulders. Atlas agreed to go and get the apples, if Heracles would temporarily take over his burden. When Atlas returned, he noticed that Heracles was supporting the heavens very capably, and it occurred to him that Heracles might well continue in the assignment. Had Heracles not then thought of a good stratagem, and tricked Atlas into reassuming the weight of the skies, he would have been the victim of the greatest buck-passing trick on record. What Housman is saying by way of this allusion is that the battle of his poem was won not on the playing fields of Eton but in the pastures of Shropshire, and that the Etonians, and the other pillars of the established order, transferred their burden in this case to the lowly professional army. Once we recognize Housman's reference, we can see again the extent of his esteem for the so-called mercenaries: he compares them to the great Heracles. And once we perceive that line five has to do with buck-passing, with the transference of a burden, we know where to place the emphasis. It should fall on the first word:

> *Their* shoulders held the sky suspended.

It was *they*, the mercenaries, and not the presumptive upholders of the right, who saved the day.

It seems to me that quite enough allusions have now been found; there may be others, but if so we don't need them for purposes of understanding. Nor, I think, do we need to consider the possible fiscal overtones of the words "saved" and "sum." It's true that in conjunction with the words "wages" and "pay," the phrase "saved the sum" has a slight clink of money in it, and one could probably think up an appropriate meaning for such a play on words. But readers and critics must be careful not to be cleverer than necessary; and there is no greater obtuseness than to treat all poets as Metaphysicals, and to insist on discovering puns which are not likely to be there.

What I've been trying to illustrate, no doubt too exhaustively, is how a reader might employ tact in arriving at a sure sense of an eight-line poem. Probably I've gone wrong here or there: I'm afraid, for one thing, that I've made the poem seem more English and less universal than it is. But I hope at any rate to have considered some of the things which need considering: the convention of the poem; the use of the convention; the sound, pace, and tone of the poem; its consistency with the author's attitudes and techniques in other poems; and the implicit argument of its allusions or echoes. Let me read it a last time:

These, in the day when heaven was falling,
The hour when earth's foundations fled,
Followed their mercenary calling,
And took their wages and are dead.

Their shoulders held the sky suspended;
They stood, and earth's foundations stay;
What God abandoned, these defended,
And saved the sum of things for pay.

Karl Shapiro has lately published in *Poetry* magazine a prose outburst with which I greatly sympathize and yet thoroughly disagree. I won't aim to answer it as a whole, because as he himself says it is too inconsistent to constitute a clear target. You can, within limits, argue with a wild man; wild men are simple; but there's no arguing with a subtle and reasonable man who is bent on being wild. Let me, however, quote one passage from Mr. Shapiro which bears on what I've been saying. He objects to the fact that in our country

> the only poetry that is recognized is the poetry that repeats the past, that is referential. It relates back to books, to other poetry, to names in the encyclopaedia. It is the poetry of the history-inhibited mind only, and as such it is meaningless to people who lack the training to read it. The Little Magazine, the avant-gardist, the culture academician base the esthetic experience on education. Whereas poetry needs not education or culture but the open perceptions of the healthy human organism.

Mr. Shapiro and I agree that a poem which refers to Romulus and Remus and the wolf will be meaningless, in part at least, to those who lack the training to read it. I disagree, however, with Mr. Shapiro's determination to hound that wolf out of poetry, to abolish the literary and historical past, to confine us to the modern city and declare the ruins off-limits. It would not be worth it to make poetry more generally usable at the cost of abridging the poet's consciousness.

I will say, parenthetically, that I wish the category of expertly-made popular poetry had not all but disappeared in this century. In the last century, the best poets did not hesitate to write on occasion simple songs, hymns, or story-poems which were instantly possessed and valued by a larger public. The author of *In Memoriam* also wrote the ballad of "The Revenge." Though societies were formed to unravel the knottier verses of Robert Browning, there are no knots in "The Pied Piper of Hamelin." I think too of James Russell Lowell's "Once to Every Man and Nation," and of Longfellow's "Paul Revere." These are all fine poems, and all of them are perfectly transparent. Perhaps it is their very transparency which has led critics and teachers to fall silent about them, there being no call for learned mediation; and perhaps that silence has helped many of our poets to forget that there is such a thing as a good popular poem.

But now let me take Housman's poem as a miniature specimen of what Mr. Shapiro calls "high art," and defend it against Mr. Shapiro. It is probably not Housman whom Mr. Shapiro is attacking, and yet the strictures might all apply to him. Mr. Shapiro talks as if a poem could be either referential or humanly vital, but not both. Surely you will agree that Housman's poem is both: it is a passionate celebration of courage, prompted one suspects by an immediate occasion; at the same time, and without any dampening of its urgency, it recalls a convention as old as the Greeks, and defends its heroes against detraction through liberal allusions to literature and myth. Mr. Shapiro says that to be referential is to "repeat the past"; Housman most certainly does not do that. What he does is to confront the present with a mind and heart which contain

the past. His poem does not knuckle under to a Greek convention, it makes use of that convention and much modifies it. His allusions do not "repeat" Milton and St. Paul, they bring them to bear upon a contemporary event, and in turn they bring that event to bear upon Milton and St. Paul. Milton's good angels are not, in Housman's poem, what they were in *Paradise Lost*; they are transformed by a fresh conjunction; and Housman implicitly quarrels both with the moral exclusiveness of St. Paul and with Milton's idea that righteousness must prevail.

I would uphold Housman's poem as a splendid demonstration of the art of referring. The poem requires a literate reader, but given such a reader it is eminently effective. I selected the poem for discussion precisely because, unlike most of Housman, it is capable of misinterpretation; nevertheless, as I've pointed out, a reader *can* arrive at a just sense of its tone and drift without consciously identifying any of its references. It *all but* delivers its whole meaning right away. One reason why Housman's allusions can be slow in transpiring, as they were for me, is that the words which point toward Milton or St. Paul—such words as "wages" or "earth's foundations"—are perfectly at home in the language of the poem as a whole; and this seems to me a great virtue. In a bad poem, there are often certain words which step out of line, wave their arms, and cry "Follow me! I have overtones!" It takes a master to make references, or what Robert Frost calls "displacements," without in any way falsifying the poem's voice, its way of talking. Now, as for the allusions proper, they are to the Bible, *Paradise Lost*, and Greek mythology, all of which are central to *any* version of our tradition, and in some degree familiar to every educated reader. So familiar are these sources that I'm sure Housman's allusions must unconsciously affect anyone's understanding of the poem, even upon a casual first reading. And I would say that our familiarity with the things to which Housman is referring justifies the subtlety and brevity of his echoes. The poem assumes that the words "wages" and "dead" will suffice to suggest St. Paul, and I think that a fair assumption.

Housman's allusions, once one is aware of them, are not decorative but very hard working. Their chief function is to supplement Housman's explicit praise of the mercenaries with implicit dispraise of their detractors, and so make us certain of the poem's whole attitude toward its subject. To achieve such certainty, however, one need not catch every hint, every echo; any *one* of Housman's references, rightly interpreted, will permit the reader to take confident possession of the poem. I like that. A poem should not be like a double-crostic; it should not be the sort of puzzle in which you get nothing until you get it all. Art doesn't or shouldn't work that way; we are not cheated of a symphony if we fail to react to some passage on the flute, and a good poem should yield itself more than once, offering the reader an early and sure purchase, and deepening repeatedly as he comes to know it better.

B. J. LEGGETT
From "The Poetry of Insight:
Persona and Point of View in Housman"
Victorian Poetry, Winter 1976, pp. 328–39

I am convinced that Housman's commentators have gone astray in pursuing the philosophy of his poetry, just as Housman believed Wordsworth's admirers were misdirected in concentrating on his philosophy of nature. In both cases we are confronted with a sense of the world which is beyond (or below) the intellect. That is, the poetry does not lend itself readily to philosophical schema or systemization. Further, Housman's poems are not frequently concerned with anything more than dramatizing the moment in which insight occurs. It is a commonplace of Housman criticism that he kept writing the same poem, and that poem most frequently is a means of placing the persona in a situation in which some vague sense of his condition is realized. The structures, the strategies of the poems, moreover, serve most often to convey the shock of recognition, the moment of insight.

The most obvious of Housman's strategies is the creation of a rustic persona—the Shropshire lad of the first volume—who controls the tone of almost the entire body of his verse, with the few exceptions in which the narrator is ill-defined or unimportant as a distinct voice. John Stevenson has examined both Housman's motives for this device and the character he has created in his perceptive essay "The Martyr as Innocent: Housman's Lonely Lad." His analysis indicates the value of an essentially naive speaker in dramatizing the characteristic movement from innocence to experience:

> The lad is variously the soldier, the lover, the "young sinner," and the rustic observer or commentator on life. In any of the roles, he is almost invariably characterized by his ingenuousness in the grip of a strong emotion, by what is often defined as on the threshold of discovery. He is awkward, but straight-forward in his actions, and always the process of discovery results in a revelation of some kind.[1]

Reading in the collected poems, one is struck not only with the frequency with which this revelatory moment is treated but also with the variety of effects Housman achieves with his rustic persona.

One may also note, in examining the best known of Housman's poems, the types of situations in which Housman involves his persona. A celebration of the fifty years that God has saved the Queen serves to remind him of the soldiers buried in foreign fields who shared the work with God, giving him a momentary glimpse of the mortality on which the permanence of the race is founded. A walk through the woods at Eastertide to observe the cherry in bloom produces a sudden intimation of mortality. The lad at two-and-twenty exclaims, of the transience of love, "And oh, 'tis true, 'tis true." A storm on Wenlock Edge, the site of an ancient Roman city, leads to the knowledge that "Then 'twas the Roman, now 'tis I." An athlete dying young, a funeral observed from Bredon Hill, the sounds of the soldiers' tread, the imagined last hour of a murderer who hangs at the stroke of nine—these are the occasions for the innocent's confrontation with the alien world of time and death.

But it is the manner in which Housman conveys to us the significance of the discovery that provides the force of many of his best poems. At times the poem depends on the paradox or irony of "To an Athlete Dying Young" or "1887," so much admired by the New Critics at the expense of the body of his verse. But he may also employ more subtle means in which no daring metaphors or metaphysical conceits are evident. Consider, for example, one of the most straightforward of the poems of A Shropshire Lad, "Loveliest of Trees," which has been generally admired. The tone of the poem clearly depends on the point of view of the naive persona, his essential innocence, and even his inability to articulate with any sophistication what he has discovered. His attitude is difficult to characterize, for it is not governed by pessimism or bitterness at his human state; Housman seems interested only in the

persona's discovery of his own mortality, and the poem is structured in such a manner as to make that discovery its central element. The poem depends to a great extent on a curious but obscure relationship between the sight of the cherry in bloom at Eastertide and a sense of human limitation. The first stanza concentrates wholly on the description of the cherry, "wearing white for Eastertide," and the second stanza on the persona's realization of his mortality. The casual connection between the two experiences is left unstated. Perhaps it is not capable of discursive statement. The lad's calculation of his threescore years and ten is handled in an almost neutral manner, with no betrayal of emotion:

> Now, of my threescore years and ten,
> Twenty will not come again,
> And take from seventy springs a score,
> It only leaves me fifty more.

There is more attention to arithmetic than to feeling here, much in the manner of Frost's "Stopping by Woods on a Snowy Evening," where the persona seems more involved with the owner of the woods and the horse than with the consequences of his experience. But in both cases the effect is the same. The poet escapes the danger of a maudlin treatment of a commonplace experience by the neutrality of tone and the attention to detail. John Ciardi has spoken of the duplicity of Frost's method, and the term is applicable here. In both cases, the force of the poem is greater than the occasion or the accumulation of details would seem to warrant. The opposite effect is sentimentality, a constant threat for poets like Frost and Housman who deal in potentially melodramatic situations.

The understatement of the last stanza provides an instance of Housman's characteristic treatment of the consequences of insight:

> And since to look at things in bloom
> Fifty springs are little room,
> About the woodlands I will go
> To see the cherry hung with snow.

The details of the stanza carry a significance hardly warranted by the commonplace sentiment they express or the bland language in which they are couched, and that is due almost entirely to the fact that they are now weighted by the persona's intuitive sense of his own mortality, introduced in stanza two. "Things in bloom" now suggest something of the vitality of life which has become more precious. The limitations of life are condensed into the almost trite phrase "little room," and the sense of death which now colors all living things is conveyed by the single description of the white blossoms of the cherry, "hung with snow." It is an effect which relies on what is unsaid, comparable to the similar conclusion of Frost's poem, "And miles to go before I sleep," although Frost's line seems almost heavy-handed in comparison. The poem relies also on its progressive structure and on metaphor and allusion, all of which warrant further discussion, but at the moment I should like to pursue the thematics of a poetry of insight, especially as it involves the problems of character and point of view.

It would be misleading to state that the point of view adopted by the persona in "Loveliest of Trees" is typical of that of the majority of Housman's poems. His reaction to the discoveries he makes in poem after poem varies from renewed vitality to melancholy. What remains constant is, however, the degree to which the poems depend for their effect on the character of the persona, his ability to voice afresh sentiments which in the mouth of a more sophisticated speaker would appear trite. Housman avoids the dangers of the trite, the sentimental, by separating himself from his poems through a created character, whereas a poet like Frost pretends actually to be the homely rustic speaker that the poem demands, a role Frost apparently found congenial to his public life as a poet. Housman's poetics are not elaborate enough to allow for Yeats's theory of the mask, but the result of the split between poet and persona produces a similar situation. His solution to the problems of personality and personae which Yeats spent a lifetime working out was simply to create the fiction of the Shropshire lad, substituting for the voice of the learned classical scholar whose reticence was almost legendary that of the rustic innocent, who declares,

> Some can gaze and not be sick,
> But I could never learn the trick.
> There's this to say for blood and breath,
> They give a man a taste for death.

The persona thus becomes a kind of Yeatsian mask or anti-self, the opposite of all that the poet represents in his private life.[2] The resulting tone, carefully cultivated, controls Housman's verse so pervasively that it has been tempting to blur the distinction between the personalities of poet and speaker. Such a crucial distinction has, of course, been an element of modern criticism for the past forty years, yet Housman criticism gives evidence that the formalist principle of the separation of poet and persona has been more often observed in theory than in practice.[3]

The nature of the persona we may expect to encounter in Housman's verse—initially the innocent confronted with the alien world, later the exile seeking to recapture his lost innocence—has been described in some detail. There is, moreover, the question of the persona's change throughout the sequence of A Shropshire Lad—he is certainly not a static character. But that is a related issue which I have attempted to treat elsewhere.[4] I should like to examine here another aspect of the persona, the effect of his presence in the poem as a whole. That is, what does Housman's art gain or lose by his use of the pastoral mask? It is a question which can be answered only by examination of individual poems, for the persona's presence is felt more strongly in some poems than in others. Housman rarely drops the mask, but sometimes it is crucial; at other times it seems only a habit of composition.

To look first at an instance in which the character and point of view of the speaker are decisive in determining the form of the poem, we may consider Lyric XXX of A Shropshire Lad, "Others, I am not the first." The poem has received little attention; it contains none of the obvious designs of irony or metaphor which would attract the notice of the formalists, and I suspect it would be set down as a relative failure by many, for its tone approaches that of "Could man be drunk for ever," a poem Cleanth Brooks condemns for its theatrical gestures and sentimentality.[5] There is a kind of theatricality in "Others, I am not the first," but one must be cautious in ascribing it to the poem as a whole, as opposed to its persona, who is presented as a young man dealing with his first taste of the desire and guilt which are the fruits of experience. His attempt to order his feelings and to relieve their intensity comprises the strategy of the poem:

> Others, I am not the first,
> Have willed more mischief than they durst:
> If in the breathless night I too
> Shiver now, 'tis nothing new.
> More than I, if truth were told,
> Have stood and sweated hot and cold,
> And through their reins in ice and fire
> Fear contended with desire.

> Agued once like me were they,
> But I like them shall win my way
> Lastly to the bed of mould
> Where there's neither heat nor cold.

The theme of private versus shared experience achieves a curious effect in the poem, for the speaker's determination to console himself with the knowledge that his feelings have been shared by other men serves only to reinforce the sense of their privacy. In the same way, the mental process, the argument of the poem, is continually undermined by its physical details. The fear and desire which contend in the reins, the seat of the passions, are stronger ultimately than the intellect, and they render the argument of the poem ineffectual. It is, in fact, an argument that cuts both ways; the attempt to escape the consequences of experience leads to the further revelation that such experience is the inescapable lot of the condition of man.

The poem is not quite as simple as it appears in paraphrase, but some measure of its complexity can be maintained only through the separation of persona and poet. The persona's response to his situation is obviously inadequate, as he casts about for ways to find release from his strong feelings. He reasons that he is no different from other men; he tries to take comfort in the thought that men die. But the poem as a whole, the poet's response to the experience, contrives to undermine the persona's strategy, as the poem reveals the weakness of his rationalizations by its concentration on the physical symptoms of his fear and desire. The poem reveals the inadequacy of the intellect, the domination of the feelings; and the conventional response of commentators to poems such as this—that Housman is advocating death as a release from the pain of life—misses the point for the very reason that it blurs the distinction between poet and speaker.

To label Housman's point of view adolescent, as has been frequently done, is to assume that he shares the innocence of the persona, but the effect of many poems depends on the exposure of such naiveté. "Is My Team Ploughing," for example, is constructed on the contrast between the knowledge, shared by the reader and poet, that life is transient, and the innocence maintained by a young man who has died believing that his girl and his best friend remain unchanged:

> 'Is my girl happy,
>   That I thought hard to leave,
> And has she tired of weeping
>   As she lies down at eve?'

> Ay, she lies down lightly,
>   She lies not down to weep;
> Your girl is well contented.
>   Be still, my lad, and sleep.

> 'Is my friend hearty,
>   Now I am thin and pine,
> And has he found to sleep in
>   A better bed than mine?'

> Yes, lad, I lie easy,
>   I lie as lads would choose;
> I cheer a dead man's sweetheart,
>   Never ask me whose.

There is, of course, no possibility of confusion here between the two points of view, since Housman has the youth speaking from the grave, but in poems such as "The Recruit" and "Oh see how thick the goldcup flowers" the point is made in less obvious ways. In "The Recruit" the sentiments of the persona are denied by the poem itself. He assures a young soldier that he will be long remembered in his home shire while the poem as a whole suggests the opposite.[6] In "Oh see how thick the goldcup flowers" the naiveté of the speaker is exploited in a seduction scene in which his expectations are dashed and his argument is turned against him.

There are, in fact, a great number of verses in Housman's collected poems which, because of the situations described, preclude an identification of poet and speaker, such as the following from *More Poems*:

My dreams are of a field afar
   And blood and smoke and shot.
There in their graves my comrades are,
   In my grave I am not.

I too was taught the trade of man
   And spelt the lesson plain;
But they, when I forgot and ran,
   Remembered and remain.

Whatever success the poem achieves obviously depends on the fictional background of the speaker's cowardice, his complicated attitude of regret and envy for his dead comrades, and all the trappings of war which provide the framework of the poem and which are clearly foreign to the classical scholar who wrote it. I would suggest that what is obvious here is operating in more complex ways in other poems. No matter what Housman's private compulsions for writing from the point of view of soldiers, murderers, dead men, and rustics, the use of such a point of view is a fact of his poetry, and it must be taken into account. If we examine not the personal basis for Housman's narrative devices but the results they achieve in the poetry, we are in a better position to understand his art. The poet's own emotional life, however fascinating, is at present beyond the reach of criticism.

It is clear Housman uses his lyrics to explore the obscure and unnamed feelings which give man a sense of his human state and that he treats the feelings as somehow prior to the intellect. The thesis of *The Name and Nature of Poetry*—that poetry is not of the intellect and that the intellect may hinder its production and retard its appreciation—whatever its value as a statement about art, is certainly a clue to Housman's method as an artist. It offers one explanation for his attraction to the sort of rustic persona who can express his passions without being able to account for them, and whose efforts to rationalize his situation are pitiably inadequate. In *The Name and Nature of Poetry* Housman reserves his greatest praise for William Blake, "the most poetical of all poets,"[7] and the *Songs of Innocence and Experience* is perhaps the closest prototype for Housman's own verse, although he chooses the adolescent rather than the child for his spokesman.

What Housman gains in his use of the Shropshire lad fiction may be further noted in observing that many of the most admired effects of his poems—the daring conceits, the paradoxes—are merely extensions of the point of view created through the innocent persona. To select one example, "The night is freezing fast" (*Last Poems*, XX) has been praised for its brilliant use of metaphor and handling of tone. Both may be traced to the speaker Housman has created for the occasion of the poem. It is the speaker's memory of his dead friend and the schoolboy attitude he adopts[8] which dictate the tone of the poem:

The night is freezing fast,
   To-morrow comes December;
      And winterfalls of old
Are with me from the past;
   And chiefly I remember
      How Dick would hate the cold.

Fall, winter, fall; for he
   Prompt hand and headpiece clever,

Has woven a winter robe,
   And made of earth and sea
      His overcoat for ever,
   And wears the turning globe.

One is reminded here of Wordsworth's "A Slumber Did My Spirit Seal," with its similar images of Lucy "Rolled round in earth's diurnal course, / With rocks, and stones, and trees." There is, however, one crucial difference. Wordsworth's persona views Lucy's return to nature as a tragic loss: "No motion has she now, no force; / She neither hears nor sees." He is the bereaved lover whose love had blinded him to Lucy's earthly nature: "She seemed a thing that could not feel / The touch of earthly years." The final image of his beloved helplessly spun by the forces of the earth reinforces his sudden recognition of the reality of death which his illusion of love's permanence had denied him. Housman's young speaker, on the other hand, seems incapable of that sort of recognition. He views Dick's death as a clever strategy for outwitting the cold. Rather than becoming the helpless victim of the impersonal turning globe, Dick is seen as triumphing over the misery of life. He has at last escaped the cold by making the earth his "overcoat for ever." In spite of the jesting tone, or perhaps because of it, the speaker's attitude toward death is essentially naive. It might be compared to that taken by Wordsworth's persona before he awoke to death's finality. Housman's speaker sees death only in terms of life. It is as if Dick, like Lucy, could not feel the touch of death. He attributes to Dick a will and a purpose which are obviously based on the memory of his personality when he was still alive: "Prompt hand and headpiece clever." Dick was a clever man, and his wit has finally paid off. In contrast of Wordsworth's persona, the speaker of "The night is freezing fast" displays no sense of the loss involved in death, but it is important to note that the poem, as opposed to the persona, does suggest such a loss. As Brooks notes, the gay tone "actually renders the sense of grief not less but more intense" (p. 69). He attributes this result to the fact that the tone is characteristic of the dead youth, and that may be a part of it. But what is more important in accounting for the paradoxical effect the poem achieves is the split between the persona's attitude and the attitude of the poem as a whole. The insufficiency of the persona's view of death is revealed in the same manner that the rhetoric of the funeral sermon is negated by the motionless corpse. We receive a sense of what death entails in a way that the speaker cannot. It is a curious and complex device, since it involves the assertion of two contradictory attitudes—gaiety and grief, triumph and defeat. The poem reveals perfectly how non-discursive elements may deny what, discursively, the persona asserts.

Housman achieves this effect in a number of poems about death. Although the "philosophy" of death in "To an Athlete Dying Young" has been discussed as an instance of Housman's perversity, no commentator, to my knowledge, has emphasized sufficiently that the attitude toward death taken in the poem is that of one of the dead athlete's friends, not that of the poet. Housman characterizes the speaker of the poem in several ways. In the first two stanzas he is pictured as one of the townsmen who has cheered the athlete to victory and who now, as one close to the dead youth, bears the coffin to the grave:

The time you won your town the race
We chaired you through the market-place;
Man and boy stood cheering by,
And home we brought you shoulder-high.

> To-day, the road all runners come,
> Shoulder-high we bring you home,
> And set you at your threshold down,
> Townsman of a stiller town.

The poem is thus a kind of graveside oration delivered by one of the lads who, presumably, "wore [his] honours out":

> Now you will not swell the rout
> Of lads that wore their honours out,
> Runners whom renown outran
> And the name died before the man.

Obviously, the speaker is acutely conscious of the transience of the "fields where glory does not stay," and one may assume that his sentiments are partly dictated by the difference he observes between the youth who died in his prime and himself. He is also characterized by the kind of schoolboy attitude seen in "Now the night is freezing fast." The expression "Smart lad" which begins line nine strikes me as typical of the kind of congratulatory phrase carried over from the playing fields, and it emphasizes the persona's rather commonplace analogy between life and a footrace.

Of course the entire oration develops the conceit that death is the final victory, "the road all runners come," offering a sense of permanence which man is denied in life. But the relationship between what the speaker asserts and what the poem conveys is remarkably close to that of "The night is freezing fast." The persona emphasizes in his graveside address the permanence achieved by the athlete, but the total effect of the poem is to reinforce a sense of transience, of the inescapable nature of change and death. The point I would emphasize is that the conceit of the poem, as in "The night is freezing fast," is developed from the character of the persona, his imagined relationship to the dead man, and the occasion of the poem. To equate his point of view with that of Housman is to confuse a technique by which the poet conveys a complex reaction to death with a philosophy, an abstract idea which has no meaning outside the poem.

Instances of this kind of tension between the persona's point of view and that suggested by the poem as a whole may be found throughout Housman's poetry, although it is clearly not the only effect he achieves with his fictional speaker. It is similar to the quality that Christopher Ricks has articulated, the disparity between *what is said* and *how* it is said, although Ricks looks only at how rhythm and style negate or temper what the poem would be saying in paraphrase. I am suggesting that the same sort of conflict extends to *what is said* once we recognize the division between the speaker of the poem and the poet who, in many cases, is exploiting the naiveté of his speaker. Ricks has analyzed the passages from other poets Housman quotes in *The Name and Nature of Poetry* to support his contention that disparities of feeling fascinated the poet, and he presents a convincing argument that Housman was attracted to a kind of poetry in which the feeling is strangely at odds with what is being asserted.

It seems clear that Housman achieved much the same result from his use of the mask of the rustic. The tension between the innocence of the persona and the sophistication of the poet is evident in many of his most successful poems. It is, however, a difficult tension to sustain, and Housman is not always successful with it. When he fails, the resulting tone gives the impression that it is the poet himself whose attitude is hopelessly childish and inadequate, and it is true that in some instances Housman found his poetic mask too congenial, so that he was unable to separate himself sufficiently from the Shropshire lad. Since his persona was, in Housman's words, "an imaginary figure with something of my temperament and

view of life,"[9] was perhaps too easy to blur the distinction. It might be argued, in fact, that the statement just quoted gives evidence that there was no distinction, but that is to confuse life and art, ideas with their expression. Housman stated in *The Name and Nature of Poetry* that "poetry is not the thing said but a way of saying it" (p. 187). Although we may have all shared, at times, the emotions expressed by Housman's persona, we would not ordinarily express them in the manner in which they are expressed by the rustic, and if we did create an "imaginary figure" to give vent to our emotions, we would no longer simply be expressing feeling but creating a fiction which would necessarily modify the feelings.

Readers who object to the "philosophy" of Housman's poetry are, in reality, objecting to the mode in which a view of life is being expressed, and they fail to take into account the narrative technique which Housman first employed for the poems of *A Shropshire Lad* and which carried over into the whole body of his poetry. To state the case in the most direct manner, if the feelings expressed in Housman's poetry seem to us adolescent, that is precisely because they are placed in the mouth of an adolescent. To insist on this point is not, however, to justify fully Housman's device of employing the rustic as his speaker. While it is the means by which he achieved his characteristic successes, it also imposes a severe limitation on his poetry.[10] It is primarily responsible for the limited range of his verse and its sameness of tone. What is missing in Housman is the range of voices and attitudes that we find in a poet like Yeats, and Yeats's status as a major poet owes a great deal to the fact that he was able to overcome, through his own self-criticism and through the system constructed about his theories of self and mask, the complex problems involved in the relationship between poet and persona.

Housman seems to have been uninterested in exploring such critical problems. His convictions about poetry and criticism precluded the sort of intellectual systems as well as the tendency toward self-analysis exhibited by Yeats. He subscribed to the Romantic notion that the peculiar function of poetry was "to transfuse emotion—not to transmit thought but to set up in the reader's sense a vibration corresponding to what was felt by the writer" (*SP*, p. 172). Holding such a belief, he was naturally drawn to devices and techniques which would enable him to deal with the deepest and most elementary human feelings, and his choice of the innocent as persona allowed him to explore a range of feelings revolving around man's first discovery of the world in which he finds himself. He owes much of his success as a poet to the manner in which he was able to exploit the relationship between poet and persona, but his status as a minor poet is also due in some measure to the restrictions imposed on his poetry by the nature of his persona.

Notes

1. *South Atlantic Quarterly*, 57 (1958), 77.
2. See John Stevenson, "The Ceremony of Housman's Style," *Victorian Poetry*, 10 (1972), 44–55: "He stands aside and lets the style become the mask by which he celebrates the ceremony of man's condition—the blight man was born for. Hence, the Shropshire setting, the rustic lad, the striving for the colloquial tone: the Kennedy Professor of Latin knew nothing of these country parts; he uses the setting to extinguish his personality in order to achieve the bardic tone of anonymity, to recapture what Mr. Richard Ellmann, writing of Yeats's style, describes as the 'traditionally authoritative manner of the poet.' The bardic position is always public (the ceremonial voice), and this stance is what Housman strives for in his poetry in order to hold in tension the double view of both innocence and experience" (p. 47).

3. For evidence of this see my *Housman's Land of Lost Content: A Critical Study of* A Shropshire Lad (Univ. of Tennessee Press, 1970), pp. 5–11.

4. See *Housman's Land of Lost Content*, esp. Chapters IV–VII.

5. "Alfred Edward Housman," in Christopher Ricks, ed., *A. E. Housman: A Collection of Critical Essays* (Prentice-Hall, 1968), pp. 65–66.

6. See "Housman's 'The Recruit'," *Explicator*, 25 (1965–66), Item 25.

7. *A. E. Housman: Selected Prose*, ed. John Carter (Cambridge Univ. Press, 1961), p. 189. All quotations from Housman's criticism are from this edition, hereafter cited as *SP*.

8. As Brooks notes. See "Alfred Edward Housman," pp. 68–69.

9. Quoted in Norman Marlow, *A. E. Housman: Scholar and Poet* (Univ. of Minnesota Press, 1958), p. 150.

10. See William R. Brashear, "The Trouble with Housman," *Victorian Poetry*, 7 (1969), 81–90: "Housman himself is largely responsible for the narrow reading of his poems. For the Shropshire pose is at once effective and misleading. It tends to draw attention too much to the 'local' . . . complaints of a melancholic and sensitive youth" (p. 82).

LAURENCE HOUSMAN

1865–1959

Laurence Housman, the younger brother of the poet A. E. Housman, was born in Bromsgrove, Worcestershire, on July 18, 1865. Instead of attending university, he went with his sister Clemence to London to study art, and by 1887 was building a reputation as a book designer and illustrator. His first writings were books of fairy tales, such as *A Farm in Fairy Land* (1894), which he illustrated himself, and poems, notably *Green Arras* (1895) and *Spikenard* (1898). His first novel, *An Englishwoman's Love-Letters*, was published anonymously in 1900, and created a sensation in England and America.

It is as a dramatist that Housman is best known, though he had to fight a lifelong battle against censorship because of his portrayal of religious figures and British royalty. The nativity play *Bethlehem* (1902) was the first play to be banned, and a play about Queen Caroline, *Pains and Penalties* (1911), suffered similarly. Housman's adaptation of Aristophanes' *Lysistrata*, produced in 1910, reflects his support of the women's suffrage movement, and he also wrote plays against the death penalty, and in favor of the Sinn Fein. A popular lecturer, he campaigned for causes including prison reform, pacifism, and freedom for India, and, himself a homosexual, served as Chairman of the British Society for the Study of Sex Psychology.

Housman achieved his greatest success with *The Little Plays of St. Francis* (1922) and his plays about Victoria and her age, notably *Victoria Regina* (1935), which was allowed public performance in 1937 after the centennial of the Queen's coronation. He also wrote many prose works, including the satirical novel *Trimblerigg* (1924), and a volume of memoirs, *The Unexpected Years* (1936), and edited his brother's unpublished poems. He lived with Clemence until her death in 1955, and died in Glastonbury on February 20, 1959.

Personal

During the 'nineties many books of verse were published; and out of them many mushroom reputations were made. John Lane had what he called his "nest of singing-birds," of whom, I imagine, only Francis Thompson would now count as important. In 1895 I became one of the ruck, and he published my first book of poems, *Green Arras*, with illustrations. Before submitting them I sent them to my brother Alfred for criticism; and his long critical notes which I still cherish were both kind and caustic. Thanks to him I left out several poems which I am now glad to have left out; had I accepted his advice without question, I should have left out a few more. I was just then designing book covers for John Lane; so naturally I did what I thought an extra-good one for myself. It was, at all events, very rich and elaborate. Alfred had not at that time published his own poems, but without having told us, was then writing them. Some years later I received from him a letter telling me how at a dinner his next-door neighbour "thought to interest me by talking about you and your poems. He said that he liked *Green Arras*: he added that *A Shropshire Lad* had a pretty cover. I am your affectionate brother. A. E. Housman. P. S. He did not say that the *Green Arras* had a pretty cover—nor *has* it.

"P. P. S. I was just licking the envelope when the following envenomed remark occurred to me: I had far far rather have my poems mistaken as yours, than your poems mistaken as mine."

As by that time we were constantly being taken for each other I had other letters from him of a like kind. Without malice he much enjoyed putting me in my place, though I was already sufficiently aware of it.

It was in the year following the publication of *Green Arras* that the bright blow descended upon me. I had begun in a small way to make a reputation for myself; there were just about a thousand people who liked my books sufficiently to buy them—my prose books that is to say; my poems were only wanted by about half that number. But this meant that publishers were willing to take what I brought them, though royalties usually did not begin with first sales. But I was happy, and hopeful, and prolific; and having the *Manchester Guardian* as a standby was able to indulge in the luxury of writing poems and stories which did not bring me much profit.

And then like a bolt from the blue out came *A Shropshire Lad*, and straightway, as an author with any individuality worth mentioning, I was wiped out. I became the brother of the *Shropshire Lad*, and for the next five years I laboured under the shadow of that bright cloud; then once more I got my own streak of the sunshine of popular favour: this time on a larger scale.

I came by it very easily, and very unexpectedly. I have always been a writer of letters, and of long ones; so, when I first thought of writing a book in the form of letters, I knew that I could do it quickly and easily. I had indeed already written a good number, to a domestic address but undomestic in character, which I could draw upon. A visit to Italy in 1899 provided me with a nucleus of material round which I had only to weave a story, or insert into it a plot. I happened to hit on one which mystified my readers (a concealed discovery of relationship within the prohibited degrees, preventing marriage); also (since a woman's love-letters followed by a man's name would have looked absurd) I had to choose anonymity, which made quite a lot of people think that the letters were genuine. With those two simple aids I wrote in a few weeks a book which, for a brief period, became the talk of the town. My agent, Pinker, hit on the ingenious device of planting the rather obvious fake on that most respectable and staid of publishers, Mr. John Murray, whose reputation seemed to guarantee authenticity. Thereupon, as soon as the book appeared, a feverish search for the author started and ran for nearly a year. Among the numerous authors suggested in the press three of almost diametrically opposed character were suggested: Mrs. Meynell, Marie Corelli, and Oscar Wilde.

The hunt was up before I knew. When the book had been published about a week—expecting nothing, but wishing to see if it was being properly announced—I turned one day to the advertisement columns of *The Times*, and there read Mr. John Murray's apologies to his readers for the book having sold out; a new issue was in the press, and would be ready immediately.

I went home feeling that my fortune was made, and bought myself an overcoat, such as I had never been able to afford before, and two beautiful Persian rugs.

A hectic time followed. The continued success of the book with its deluded public now depended upon secrecy; had my authorship been discovered, its main interest would have gone; and as I had not supposed it would have any success at all, I had told about thirty people. But they were friends and staunch; the quest grew rampant but they did not betray me. The secret was finally given away by a certain editor who had been told in strict confidence. At first it was not believed, for I had not written anything of the kind before; I was even accused of making fraudulent profit by deceptively sitting tight and saying nothing; but now with a fear that it had perhaps been "spoofed," the chatter-press, which had tumbled headlong into extravagant praise, began to hedge; memories were short, it must save itself from its own folly. . . .

Certain members of my own family had not been let into the secret: I cannot remember why. When it leaked out there was excitement, and a little resentment that they had not been told sooner.

To one member of the family I knew the book would not appeal; but Herbert, then about to start with his regiment for the field of action in the Transvaal from which he was not to return, expressed a great desire to read it. "After which," commented Alfred, "the Boers will have no terrors for him."

But the Mater, whose literary taste was influenced, if not entirely guided, by popular favour, was at last pleased with me. Only a short time before she had commented on my lack of success as a writer, and with a firm belief in my ability had told me where the fault lay. "The reason why your books don't succeed," she said, "is because you don't choose good titles. If you wrote one called 'Who stole the diamonds?' it would be

popular." She was probably right; unfortunately I could not see myself the writer of a book so named.

My titles were also charged against me by another member of the family; and it was not until I published *The Royal Runaway* that she admitted I had at last hit on an attractive one. Yet if there is one thing on which I pride myself it is my titles: *Gods and Their Makers, A Farm in Fairyland, The House of Joy, The Field of Clover, John of Jingalo, The Sheepfold, Trimblerigg, Cornered Poets, The Love Concealed, Palace Plays*, are all titles which, for the contents, could not I think be bettered.—LAURENCE HOUSMAN, "Bubble Reputation," *The Unexpected Years*, 1936, pp. 137–43

Works

DRAMA

No recent tendency has been more susceptible of amusing consequences than the sentimental attraction which the Victorian era has exercised upon the antinomian contemporary mind. Ten years ago to have been accused of mid-Victorian affiliations was equivalent to being uncomfortably ticketed as a curious anthropological specimen. It remained for Lytton Strachey and some others to discover the innate dignity of a Manx cat, and to transmute the Victorian label from a term in an evolutionary series into an order of merit. Thus it happens that an age whose pride it is that it has achieved a new dispensation, intellectual, political and social, has piously found esthetic enjoyment in the quaint antics of an uncloseted family skeleton.

The satiric intention and the sentimental climax of our Victorian renascence are inextricably mixed. Mr. Strachey's affair with the "Widow of Windsor," for example, began with a playful tweaking of the royal nose, and culminated in an impassioned kissing of her graciously forgiving fingers. So, too, with Laurence Housman, who proves by a preface to his "four plays of Victorian shade and character" (*Angels and Ministers*) that the delicate passion of middle age is not without its importunities. The bloom upon the grape, he tells us, fully appears only when it is ripe for death. "Just at this moment the Victorian age has that bloom upon it—autumnal, not spring-like—which, in the nature of things, cannot last. That bloom I have tried to illumine before time wipes it away. Under this rose-shaded lamp of history, domestically designed, I would have these old characters look young again, or not at least as though they belonged to another age."

But Mr. Housman has finely preserved the delicate balance of sentiment and humor; it has been a romantic experience to fall in love with his own youth, but one exquisitely productive of comedy. The pathos of distance is its own satiric commentary on the past, and contributes its bittersweet flavor to his adventure. Of the four plays, three are intimate glimpses of political personalities, and one, which the author terms a "peep-show in paradise," is a delicious thumbnail sketch of Victorian gentility as a philosophy.

In *The Queen: God Bless Her!* we find the august lady beneath a tent on the lawn of Balmoral, one hot Summer's day in 1877 when Lord Beaconsfield is expected. She is disturbed by two things—Gladstone's speeches and the attacks of a wasp upon a plate of peaches. Wasps, she observes, are like Adam and Eve, and she instructs John Brown to remove the fruit. "If God only done that," says John Brown, "maybe we'd still all be running about naked." "I'm glad He didn't, then," retorts the Queen. ". . . The fall made the human race decent, even if it did no good otherwise." Thus does Mr. Housman set the period before us at a stroke. Disraeli comes, a worn and tired old man, sophisticated, unctuous, flattering. But in playing upon the august lady's sentimental susceptibilities, his own are for one brief moment illuminated, and, with the half-calculated, half-sincere gesture of a toast and a shattered glass, reveals the palpitant romantic attachment which committed England to an imperialistic policy.

In *His Favorite Flower* Mr. Housman undertakes to explain the political myth which resulted in the observation of the anniversary of Disraeli's death as "Primrose Day." Disraeli, now out of power, an old, bedridden, querulous invalid, has had a woeful nightmare. He has dreamed himself pilloried before the House of Parliament, pelted with yellow primroses. He realized, in this dream, that his policies had all been proved wrong by time and the march of events. But the avalanche of hated primroses, instead of being a verdict of judgment, was the adulation of a people grateful to him for having put their money on the wrong horse! And it transpires that the cause of the nightmare is a bunch of yellow primroses sent him by an adoring Queen who believed them his favorite posy.

The third play, *The Comforter*, brings us to the Gladstones' sitting room to Downing Street on an evening in March, 1894, after the Cabinet has decided to resign. Gladstone has asked John Morley to break to Mrs. Gladstone the news of his final political defeat, and the play shows how the little old lady, who has spent her life "feeding a god on beef tea," accepts the failure of her most cherished ambition and succeeds in persuading her husband that his retirement from office is her happiness.

In these three plays, despite the "rose-shaded lamp," Mr. Housman has portrayed the veritable Victorians with consummate skill, etching with a sharp and cursive line the salient characteristics of a group of personalities who were the tragicomedians of their era. Disraeli, telling his physician: "If ever man blundered and fooled his countrymen into a false and fatal position, I was that man! It wasn't a question of right or wrong. In politics that doesn't really matter; you decide on a course, and you invent moral reasons for it afterward;" or John Morley asking Mrs. Gladstone whether she prays for Chamberlain as plain "Joe Chamberlain," or whether she puts in the "Mister"—such dexterous flashes as these reveal the mood of the Victorian mind. It is, however, in the fourth play, *Possession*, that Mr. Housman has given his most delicately ironic commentary on the period as a whole.

In *Possession* none of the characters is historical; they are merely representative of that great bulwark of Victorianism, the middle class. Reduced to its elemental situations, the plot is quite simple—merely a glance at the speculative possibilities resulting from the reunion of a respectable Victorian family in heaven. Respectability, conformity, orthodoxy, gentility—these, Mr. Housman implies, were the principal virtues in the Victorian code. Such being the case, what sort of heaven did the average Victorian imagination picture? Obviously, according to Mr. Housman, the heaven of worthy folk would be almost identically a continuation of their earthly life. There would, however, be one slight though important difference, conditioned by the Victorian theology. That difference would result from the fact that in heaven, at least, free will would operate. And Mr. Housman has made a subtly penetrating comedy out of the complete devastation produced in the social and family virtues of the Victorian era by the operation of a fundamental principle in Victorian belief.

Humor, as Mr. Housman's little book of comedies illustrates, is one of the most successful pathways to the past. In four brief episodes of the slightest texture he has succeeded in reviving the accent and the atmosphere of Victorian life. Implicit in them are moral, social and political values of the

period; its resolute faith in the authority of the individual conscience, its comfortable reliance on the political tradition of the status quo, its sentimental allegiance to the convention of gentility. That Mr. Housman has given us not a historical reconstruction of the era but rather a subtle expression of its spirit indicates that he is the artist rather than the craftsman.
—LLOYD R. MORRIS, "Angels, Puritans, and Playwrights," *NYTBR*, April 2, 1922, p. 10

In 1905 William Poel presented a play of his own called *The First Franciscans.* In itself, this piece has but little importance, but quite possibly Poel's innovating effort had some influence on Laurence Housman when, some seventeen years later, that author composed his *Little Plays of St Francis*, once very popular among readers and members of amateur acting groups, and not entirely forgotten even in our own times.

Since Housman is, so to say, the first "major" dramatist whom we have encountered in the minority field, and since he was a most prolific author, his plays may be taken as a picture in little of the many diverse interests displayed by his fellows during this period—and it may be added that it is impossible to assess the significance of these *Plays of St Francis* without relating them to the entire range of his other writings. . . . *Possession* . . . was a piece published in 1921, and almost two decades before, in 1902, his *Bethlehem* had been given a private performance in the hall of the Imperial Institute. For a few years after this it looked as though he might be thinking of shifting his theatrical allegiance from the amateurs to the professionals: a half-step in that direction was taken when he collaborated with Granville-Barker in writing *Prunella; or Love in a Dutch Garden*, certainly not a "commercial" piece but one which at least could be included in the Court's 1904 season; and a very definite stride followed when he made himself responsible for preparing the text of a "romantic opera", *The Vicar of Wakefield*, which, with music composed by Liza Lehmann, was produced at the Prince of Wales's Theatre in 1906. This toying with the commercial stage, however, did not last for long, and from 1910 onwards almost all his plays were "minority" in theme and structure. A "morality", *The Lord of the Harvest*, came in 1910, and a *Nazareth* in 1916; he penned several "fairy plays", a "political skit" called *Alice in Ganderland* (1911) and a collection of "dialogues", *Cornered Poets* (1929); rather unexpectedly he translated (with polite caution) Aristophanes' *Lysistrata* (1910) and, more predictably, dealt with some "tragic" classic material, *Apollo in Hades*, *The Death of Alcestis* and *The Doom of Admetus* (published as a "trilogy" in 1919). Although he must have been well aware that one of the Lord Chamberlain's fixed rules forbade the stage presentation of living or recent royalty, he spent time in penning his "defence of Queen Caroline", *Pains and Penalties* (1911), and this led him to his well-known one-acts showing episodes in the life of Queen Victoria. Others of his plays might be listed here, but these few selected titles are sufficient to indicate the diverse nature of his subject-matter and to demonstrate that his structural power never went beyond the limits of the one-act "episode". It is true that when *Pains and Penalties* was presented privately in 1911 it was described as a "four-act play", but, when it is compared with the *Victoria Regina* which was constructed from a number of his short sketches in 1935, it is patently clear that the dramatic architecture of both is the same.

Within this variegated pattern come the *Little Plays of St Francis* (1922), a collection which proved so attractive that many other playlets were added later to the original series of sixteen short episodes. Here we are carried back to the spirit of the earlier Nativity playlets. There is no cynicism here, no attempt to preach an author's personal philosophy. Housman's own claim that the *Little Plays* had been sincerely written in an attempt to "present a spiritual interpretation of character" may be taken at its face value, and it was this sincerity which gave them their appeal. As Granville-Barker observed, they were the result of the new conditions operative at that time, when there was an "unspringing all over England of bodies of people so hungry for a little simple, wholesome, unhocussed dramatic art, that, denied it by the professional producers, they are ready to see to the supply themselves".

Granville-Barker is correct in the presentation of his facts, yet two qualifications must be made concerning what he implies. First, while Housman's playlets on Franciscan legend deserve esteem for their simplicity and adroitness, they cannot be raised, as he here suggests, to the level of great dramatic achievements: whatever their virtues, they remain very much minority writings. And secondly, both here and in other related comments made by Granville-Barker we cannot accept his suggestion that the "professional producers" of that period had nothing of value to offer. A sense of balance must be maintained. On the one hand, there has to be clear recognition of what actually was accomplished by the minority playwrights, whether the unassuming and unambitious authors of little Nativity playlets or those, such as Laurence Housman, who were more "literary" in their approach, more varied in their themes and more skilful in the presentation of character. Yet, on the other hand, it must be admitted that "hocussing", the expert display of legerdemain, the conjuring skill of the dramatist, has always been an important part of the theatre's power and strength. Much of the professional dramatic fare put before West End audiences was certainly poor and shoddy and contemptible, but at the same time we must be prepared to admit that, even within areas where we might have expected the minority playwrights to have had especial advantages, professional West End authors catering for a general public often far exceeded their efforts. The truth of this becomes patently evident when a scrutiny is made of two other minority movements by no means unallied to that which encouraged the composition and performance of the Nativity and related playlets—and to these two movements Housman also may be taken as a guide. Towards the beginning of his dramatic career he had written two "fairy plays", *The Chinese Lantern* (1908) and *Bird in Hand* (1918), while in 1928 he published *Ways and Means: Five One Act Plays of Village Characters*. Thus does he introduce us to the Village Drama movement and the various attempts to establish a Children's Theatre. —ALLARDYCE NICOLL, "The Minority Drama," *English Drama 1900–1930: The Beginnings of the Modern Period*, 1973, pp. 237–40

OTHER WORKS

The distinction of Mr. Laurence Housman's workmanship, the nimbleness of his fancy, and the sombre strength of his imagination, must be patent to all readers of *Green Arras* and *Spikenard*. No one is more authentically a poet than he; yet the forms of thought which almost exclusively preoccupy him are to me so foreign, and, to be quite frank, so uninteresting, that I must own myself incapable of doing full justice even to his purely literary merits. He envisages the world from a point of view at which I cannot place myself, even in momentary make-believe. I lack all clue, in my own experience, to the processes of his mind. Consequently, I can but apologise in advance for the inadequate and perhaps utterly mistaken appreciation of his talent which is all I can offer. In the preface to his *All Fellows*, a book of prose legends "with insets of verse," Mr. Housman

says, "Unfortunately there are to be found, to sit in judgment, minds of a literal persuasion, that take from the artist his own soul, to set it in the image that he has made." In what I have to say I may fall into this error. But a single attitude of mind is so consistently maintained throughout Mr. Housman's verse, that it is impossible to conceive it a mere artistic pose.

On the contrary, it seems to me that sincerity is what distinguishes Mr. Housman from most of his school. His kinship with Rossetti, for example, is unmistakable; but what to Rossetti was mythology and decoration, is to Mr. Housman religion and tragic fact. His Catholicism is not like that of some other poets, a mere refuge from pantheism, a robe deliberately woven to clothe and confine an invisible, elusive deity. At the root of his thinking lies, I take it, a genuine Conviction of Sin. It is his instinct to prostrate and abase himself before the rulers of the universe, and to blame himself, not them, for whatever in himself he finds amiss. Not his to

> thank whatever gods there be
> For his unconquerable soul;

not his to

> step out in flesh and bone
> Manful like the man of stone.

It is his part rather to kiss the rod, and wreathe it in garlands of flowers; to groan in the fetters of flesh, while damascening their links. Life is to him a prison-house, and it does not occur to him to question the moral authority of the warrant that consigned him to it. The senses are tempters lurking in the darkness. He has not even the consolations of evangelical religion, the faith in another life and in personal salvation. He seems rather to conceive deity as the spirit of nothingness; to regard existence in itself as sin, and more especially the sense of beauty in existence; and to yearn for annihilation as the highest grace to which mankind, guilty of having been born, can possibly aspire. This spirit seems to me to inspire, not only his poems, but the designs which illustrate them: everywhere there is passionate depth of conception and great beauty of line; but everywhere there is a sense of oppression, of contortion, of grey gloom even in the sunshine, which not seldom results in a general effect of ugliness.—WILLIAM ARCHER, "Laurence Housman," *Poets of the Younger Generation*, 1902, pp. 196–97

The fairy-tale, like the question, bespeaks faith in the outcome of what is not yet evolved; and in their prime quality of illusory credibility, Mr. Housman's tales (in *Moonshine and Clover* and *A Doorway in Fairyland*) command belief. One reads eagerly until the end has been reached, infinitesimally disaffected by an occasional flaw. Although usually in the fairy-tale, good triumphs over evil and virtue is synonymous with beauty, an appearance of moral insouciance is essential; and in a number of these stories, one sees perhaps too plainly, the wish to bless. Also, evolving from an affection for the child mind and perhaps from a wish not to labour the matter, we have from time to time a kind of diminutive conversation as of an adult in the nursery, which is death to the illusion of make-believe. There is poetic security, however, in the statement, "he closed his eyes, and, with long silences between, spoke as one who prayed," and in the observation that Toonie's wife when her husband did not return, "became a kind of widow"; the pace is especially businesslike in this story of Toonie. Minute rapier-like shafts of crossing searchlights seem to play upon the "tight panting little bodies" whose sentinel Toonie outwitted, "picking him up by the slack of his breeches, so that his arms and legs trailed together along the ground." In "The Traveller's Shoes," one is infected with the poison of

Sister, sister; bring me your hair,
Of our mother's beauty give me your share.
You must grow pale, while I must grow fair!

. . . In these two books there is a disparity in favour of *Moonshine and Clover*, there being perhaps but one story in *A Doorway in Fairyland*, "The Ratcatcher's Daughter," which may surely be depended upon to remain in the mind. In this most civilized obverse of fox-hunting ethics, a gnome having got himself caught in a trap with a view to entrapping his captor, is found apparently "wriggling and beating to be free." As the price of freedom, he consents to give the ratcatcher all the gold in the world and to make his daughter pure gold so that the king's son will marry her. Then when the ratcatcher finds that the prince will marry her only in the event that she can be made natural, in order to effect a retransformation, he is obliged to relinquish to the gnome his last penny. "The White Doe" maintaining throughout the image of a creature springing this way and that across a narrow forest stream, "A Capful of Moonshine" with its theme of the man who wished to know "how one gets to see a fairy," "The Gentle Cockatrice" monumentally patient despite a recurring desire to identify its tail, and "The Man Who Killed the Cuckoo," are tales one does not forget. This Mr Badman's progress, told with a laconic wonder and embodying newly as it does, the moral contained in the story of Midas, is an account of a man who "lived in a small house with a large garden" and "took no man's advice about anything." Finding that the poisonous voice that he had disliked at a distance proceeded from himself, he "felt his eyes turning inwards, so that he could see into the middle of his body. And there sat the cuckoo." We find him eventually "sailing along under the stars," tied into a bed of cuckoo feathers, "complete and compact; and inside him was the feeling of a great windmill going round and round and round."

One must not monopolize; one need not avenge oneself; in improving the morals of the world, one should begin by improving one's own; these are the mordant preoccupations about which Mr Housman's fancy plays.—MARIANNE MOORE, "Gentle Sorcery," *Dial*, Sept. 1923, pp. 293–95

The title of Mr. Laurence Housman's selection of *War Letters of Fallen Englishmen* summons up a picture once customary— that of the subaltern, in his dugout or the best room of the farmhouse just beyond artillery range, rapidly censoring the company's letters. These usually amounted to a formidable heap, and the sight of it increased his instinctive disinclination to scan the private messages of others before scribbling his name and rank on the envelopes. If he glanced through one or two at random in order to ease his mind in respect of his responsibility, he did not expect to discover any great variation from those of previous occasions. There would be (in the perpetual indelible pencil) much the same good wishes to relatives and neighbours, the same homely forms of opening and ending, the same strings of capital letters (innocent riddles) below the signatures—and the same attempt to protect the person about to receive the letter from any realisation of war's ordeal. For various reasons, "the troops" had quite a passion for writing letters of this kind: the desire to keep in touch with their homes and all that home meant, the relief and solace that writing could give, the mere killing of time influenced them. Against the disadvantage of possible censorship might be placed the fact that active service letters went post free.

It is not this class of letters from the Front which supplies Mr. Housman's book. Few of his writers were "other ranks." Almost all were highly educated men who, even if they were not formally concerned with literature, commanded large resources of appropriate expression when they were impelled to put thoughts and experiences on paper. We cannot help feeling in every passage gathered by Mr. Housman the mental and spiritual grace of that generation, with some doubt as to whether it could be paralleled at the present date. At the time of the Crimean War the *Memorials of Captain Hedley Vicars* made an extraordinary appeal to the public, as revealing the exquisite and saintly personality of a most accomplished and gallant officer. Hedley Vicars would have found himself in worthy company in Mr. Housman's book, and could have enlarged even his range of sympathy in intimate talk with these later-fallen Englishmen. He, too, "considered war to be a dire calamity," but acknowledged an allegiance which overcame that aspect; they, no less knightly in their tenacious self-sacrifice, were profoundly eager to perceive the signs that war might become extinct altogether.

Had these letter-writers survived, the story of the War books would surely have been a very different one: for some of them must have resolved to continue for the general good the descriptions, the comments and the aspirations which they imparted under trying conditions to particular friends. Had Charles Sorley lived, what mood, what setting, what significance of the infantryman's life could have escaped his depicting? His letter of July 15, 1915, communicating with a wealth of original metaphor the normal sounds and sights of nightfall on the Flanders battlefield, is too long to quote; it is somewhere near the best of this kind of perpetuation achieved hitherto. One whose name is not so illustrious as Sorley's, C. C. Carver,—dead, like Sorley, at the age of twenty—also sent home the most vivid pictures in words, not to mention his casual-seeming but deep questionings on the War:

A sickly yellow moon is showing now, looking almost as jaded as we. Wearily I clamber upon a steed, once white, and with some half dozen of the rearguard set out for home. . . . A certain corner rounded, we breathe more freely. Along the cliff road till we are brought to halt by a "block" in the road ahead. On our left a steep and shell-pocked bank, over which the moon is peeping. To our right and below us is the river stretching across a vista of broken stumps, running water and shell pools, to the skeleton gleaming white of another village on the far bank. If only an artist could paint the grim scene now while the hand of war and death is still hovering over it. In our steel helmets and chain visors we somehow recall *Pilgrim's Progress*, armoured figures passing through the valley of the shadow. On—for Apollyon's talons are ever near. Steadily along the road, round curves and through a hollow, till we reach a point where some dead horses lie across the road. They were not there when we came up, and some ammunition-wagons, standing horseless, and sprinkled with earth from 5.9-inch crumps, tell their own story.

The old hands will mark many pages of the anthology as the living picture of War, that capricious phantom.

The immensity of war organisation, the incessant round of regimental duties, the apparent endlessness of the struggle, the severance of the soldier from "aids to reflection" and unrestricted intellectual interchange—these all, but most of all the exhausting demands made on physical and nervous energies, co-operated to transform the fighting man into a mechanical figure. Milton, in his "sweetest saddest" poem, has represented the conditions proper to unsphering the spirit of Plato and deciphering the entity of demons:

Let my lamp at midnight hour
Be seen in some high lonely tower
Where I may oft out-watch the Bear.

No such benefits blessed the student in charge of a battery or a company in the War; in some low and much-visited dugout he out-watched the hours for half a dozen reports, by the light of a candle. And still, this overtaxed and sleep-forsaken youth would be venturing shyly into Plato's company, or trying to discover what the demon was that presided over these colourless shell-holes and wooden crosses, and why he could do so. Mr. Housman's letter-writers often went far beyond the limits of the quarrel in which they had taken their stand; with heroic imagination, they worked towards a new earth which their acquaintance with war almost certainly told them they could not live to see. First of all, they saw both sides:

> I write this outside a German dugout wrecked by one of our sixty-pounders. The explosion has thrown five men lifeless down the stairway. Their boy officer, a young Absalom, is suspended downwards by one of his Bluchers from two viced beams in the roof. Get the harrowing details out of the mind; remember only the faithful service. It seems to me that so many of our journals urge the remembering of the worthlessness, the forgetting of the worth remembering. "Remember the *Lusitania*, remember Nurse Cavell." Rather keep them out of the mind. Heaven consists largely in thinking of mothers and wives and children and other things that are thus beautiful. Get the habit. Increase Heaven by thinking of the homely, fat but selfless Frau and the lad who hangs from the ceiling by his foot. Hell consists largely in thinking of our own nastiness. We cannot forget that even when forgiven, and so this Hell survives, but other people's nastiness we can forget quite easily.

And then, there was a wider vision still; sometimes it was in the spirit of Thomas Gray, in the final stanza of "The Bard"—a golden faith that, whoever lived, whoever died, whatever bombardments lacerated the earth, Nature's lights and shades would win at last.

> Children will play between the trenches as in a garden, hide in strange hollows where old fragments of iron peep out from a wilderness of poppies and cornflowers. Even in the shapeless ruins, where for the moment we are living, you may look up and see a swift dart from a cranny; and all is well.

That dream, in spite of the burnt-out desolation of the end of the War, has come true. Sometimes, the writers dip into the future, not sentimentally but philosophically:

> As for the future, I think it would be a mistake to expect this war to produce a revolution in human nature, and equally wrong to think nothing has been achieved if it doesn't. What I hope is that it will mark a distinct stage towards a more Christian conception of international relations. I'm afraid that for a long time to come there will be those who want to wage war and will have to be crushed with their own weapons. But I think this insane and devilish cult of war will be a thing of the past. War will only remain as an unpleasant means to an end.

It is tolerably easy, as years elapse, with war and post-war lessons in our minds, to advance such opinions; it was glorious in 1915 for the destined fighting man to turn aside from all his tribulations and speak with such a dignified, unhurried plainness of events to be.

The average age of the ninety-eight writers, men and women, of whose letters Mr. Housman has given us examples was twenty-nine years. The majority of them were junior officers. Many of the letters have not been published elsewhere. The term "Englishmen" in the title is to be interpreted broadly, "as applied to soldiers from all parts of the British Isles and the Overseas Dominions (and in at least one case from the United States) who fought under the British flag." The whole book, for which Mr. Housman and his helpers have deserved the fullest response, is of such a quality as always to stir the remembrance of "the hope and promise of youth, which the wastefulness of war has carried away."—EDMUND BLUNDEN, "Fallen Englishmen" (1930), *Votive Tablets*, 1931, pp. 363–67

W. H. HUDSON

1841–1922

William Henry Hudson was born on August 4, 1841, on a ranch near Buenos Aires owned by his parents, who had emigrated to Argentina from America in the 1830s. A rheumatic fever in adolescence left him with a permanently weak heart, but he led an active life working on his father's ranch and wandering about the pampas observing wildlife. In 1866 he was commissioned by the Smithsonian Institution to collect bird skins for scientific purposes, and from 1869 sent letters to the Zoological Society of London; these were published in the Society's *Proceedings*. Hoping to establish himself as a naturalist, he emigrated to England in 1874, but at first barely scraped a living selling essays and stories to magazines.

Hudson's first novel, *The Purple Land That England Lost* (1885), sold poorly, and *A Crystal Age* (1887) fared little better, but a series of books on birds in Argentina and Britain won him respect both as a naturalist and a writer in the 1890s; they include *The Naturalist in La Plata* (1892), *Idle Days in Patagonia* (1893), *Birds in London* (1898), and *Nature in Downland* (1900). Hudson's love of rambling and observing both wildlife and human life continued throughout his time in England, and as a member of the Society for the Protection of Birds he campaigned against the destruction of bird life.

W. H. HUDSON

A. E. HOUSMAN

RALPH HODGSON

LAURENCE HOUSMAN

ALDOUS HUXLEY

TED HUGHES

DOUGLAS HYDE

RICHARD HUGHES

After being naturalized in 1900, Hudson received a modest Civil List pension in 1901, which enabled him to continue his work free of financial worries. His most successful novel, *Green Mansions*, was published in 1904, and *A Shepherd's Life*, about life on the South Wiltshire Downs, in 1910. Increasing illness made Hudson's last years difficult and less productive, though he completed a volume about his childhood, *Far Away and Long Ago* (1918), before dying at his London home on August 18, 1922.

Personal

. . . ⟨A⟩fter my fifteenth anniversary, when I first began to reflect seriously on my future life, the idea still persisted that my perpetual delight in Nature was nothing more than a condition or phase of my child's and boy's mind, and would inevitably fade out in time. I might have guessed at an earlier date that this was a delusion, since the feeling had grown in strength with the years, but it was only after I took to reading at the beginning of my sixteenth year that I discovered its true character. One of the books I read then for the first time was White's *Selborne*, given to me by an old friend of our family, a merchant in Buenos Ayres, who had been accustomed to stay a week or two with us once a year when he took his holiday. He had been on a visit to Europe, and one day, he told me, when in London on the eve of his departure, he was in a bookshop, and seeing this book on the counter and glancing at a page or two, it occurred to him that it was just the right thing to get for that bird-loving boy out on the pampas. I read and re-read it many times, for nothing so good of its kind had ever come to me, but it did not reveal to me the secret of my own feeling for Nature—the feeling of which I was becoming more and more conscious, which was a mystery to me, especially at certain moments, when it would come upon me with a sudden rush. So powerful it was, so unaccountable, I was actually afraid of it, yet I would go out of my way to seek it. At the hour of sunset I would go out half a mile or so from the house, and sitting on the dry grass with hands clasped round my knees, gaze at the western sky, waiting for it to take me. And I would ask myself: What does it mean? But there was no answer to that in any book concerning the "life and conversation of animals." I found it in other works: in Brown's *Philosophy*—another of the ancient tomes on our shelves—and in an old volume containing appreciations of the early nineteenth-century poets; also in other works. They did not tell me in so many words that it was the mystical faculty in me which produced those strange rushes or bursts of feeling and lifted me out of myself at moments; but what I found in their words was sufficient to show me that the feeling of delight in Nature was an enduring one, that others had known it, and that it had been a secret source of happiness throughout their lives.

This revelation, which in other circumstances would have made me exceedingly happy, only added to my misery when, as it appeared, I had only a short time to live. Nature could charm, she could enchant me, and her wordless messages to my soul were to me sweeter than honey and the honeycomb, but she could not take the sting and victory from death, and I had perforce to go elsewhere for consolation. Yet even so, in my worst days, my darkest years, when occupied with the laborious business of working out my own salvation with fear and trembling, with that spectre of death always following me, even so I could not rid my mind of its old passion and delight. The rising and setting sun, the sight of a lucid blue sky after cloud and rain, the long unheard familiar call-note of some newly-returned migrant, the first sight of some flower in spring, would bring back the old emotion and would be like a sudden ray of sunlight in a dark place—a momentary intense joy, to be succeeded by ineffable pain. Then there were times when these two opposite feelings mingled and would be together in my mind for hours at a time, and this occurred oftenest during the autumnal migration, when the great wave of bird-life set northwards, and all through March and April the birds were visible in flock succeeding flock from dawn to dark, until the summer visitants were all gone, to be succeeded in May by the birds from the far south, flying from the antarctic winter.

This annual spectacle had always been a moving one, but the feeling it now produced—this mingled feeling—was most powerful on still moonlight nights, when I would sit or lie on my bed gazing out on the prospect, earth and sky, in its changed mysterious aspect. And, lying there, I would listen by the hour to the three-syllable call-note of the upland or solitary plover, as the birds went past, each bird alone far up in the dim sky, winging his way to the north. It was a strange vigil I kept, stirred by strange thoughts and feelings, in that moonlit earth that was strange too, albeit familiar, for never before had the sense of the supernatural in Nature been stronger. And the bird I listened to, that same solitary plover I had known and admired from my earliest years, the most graceful of birds, beautiful to see and hear when it would spring up before my horse with its prolonged wild bubbling cry of alarm and go away with swift, swallow-like flight—what intensity and gladness of life was in it, what a wonderful inherited knowledge in its brain, and what an inexhaustible vigour in its slender frame to enable it to perform that annual double journey of upwards of ten thousand miles! What a joy it would be to live for ages in a world of such fascinating phenomena! If some great physician, wise beyond all others, infallible, had said to me that all my doctors had been wrong, that, barring accidents, I had yet fifty years to live, or forty, or even thirty, I should have worshipped him and would have counted myself the happiest being on the globe, with so many autumns and winters and springs and summers to see yet.—W. H. HUDSON, "Loss and Gain," *Far Away and Long Ago*, 1918, pp. 322–26

He once proved to me that he knew better than I what bushes I had in my own hedges, though I had brushed them over and over again and I did not know that he had seen them at all, he having called on me when I was out. And similarly he proved to the *gauchos*—who, though they can tell a man from an ostrich at seven miles' distance, are singularly unobservant in small matters and can never be brought to see the difference between an *m* and an *n*—he proved to the *gauchos* of the pampas that the grass of the plains over which they galloped all day and the *ombu* trees under which they spent all their siestas and night hours, were not solid masses of green, like billiard cloths or the painted leaden trees that shelter tin soldiers. They had never noticed that and could not see it until he lent them his reading spectacles. Then they fell off their horses in amazement. So Hudson appeared to be full of the queerest knowledges, and, as he penetrated into the most unusual and dissimilar places, his range of those knowledges was extraordinary and disconcerting and made him a person very dangerous to argue with.

You walked beside him, he stalking along and, from far above you, Olympianly destroying your theories with accurate dogma. He was very tall, with the immense, lean frame of an old giant who has for long stooped to hear men talk. The muscles of his arms stood out like knotted cords. He had the

Spanish face and peaked grey beard of a Don Desperado of the Spanish Main; his features seemed always slightly screwed together like the faces of men looking to windward in a gale. He paused always for an appreciable moment before he spoke, and when he spoke he looked at you with a sort of humorous anticipation, as if you were a nice cockatoo whom he expected to perform amusing tricks. He was the gentlest of giants, although occasionally he would go astonishingly off the deep end, as when he would exclaim violently, 'I'm not one of you damned writers: I'm a naturalist from La Plata.' This he would put over with a laugh, for of course he did not lastingly resent being called the greatest prose writer of his day. But he had a deep, dark, permanent rage at the thought of any cruelty to birds.—FORD MADOX FORD, "W. H. Hudson," *Portraits from Life*, 1937, pp. 42–43

General

He is of course a distinguished naturalist, probably the most acute, broad-minded, and understanding observer of Nature, living. And this, in an age of specialism, which loves to put men into pigeon-holes and label them, has been a misfortune to the reading public, who seeing the label Naturalist, pass on and take down the nearest novel. Hudson has indeed the gifts and knowledge of a Naturalist, but that is a mere fraction of his value and interest. A really great writer such as this is no more to be circumscribed by a single word than America by the part of it called New York. The expert knowledge which Hudson has of Nature gives to all his work backbone and surety of fibre, and to his sense of beauty an intimate actuality. But his real eminence and extraordinary attraction lie in his spirit and philosophy. We feel from his writings that he is nearer to Nature than other men, and yet more truly civilised. The competitive, towny culture, the queer-up-to-date commercial knowingness with which we are so busy coating ourselves, simply will not stick to him. A passage in his *Hampshire Days* describes him better than I can: "The blue sky, the brown soil beneath, the grass, the trees, the animals, the wind, and rain, and stars are never strange to me; for I am in and of and am one with them; and my flesh and the soil are one, and the heat in my blood and in the sunshine are one, and the winds and the tempests and my passions are one. I feel the 'strangeness' only with regard to my fellow men, especially in towns, where they exist in conditions unnatural to me, but congenial to them. . . . In such moments we sometimes feel a kinship with, and are strangely drawn to, the dead, who were not as these; the long, long dead, the men who knew not life in towns, and felt no strangeness in sun and wind and rain." This unspoiled unity with Nature pervades all his writings; they are remote from the fret and dust and pettiness of town life; they are large, direct, free. It is not quite simplicity, for the mind of this writer is subtle and fastidious, sensitive to each motion of natural and human life; but his sensitiveness is somehow different from, also inimical to, that of us others, who sit indoors and dip our pens in shades of feeling. Hudson's fancy is akin to the flight of birds that are his special loves—it never seems to have entered a house, but since birth to have been roaming the air, in rain and sun, or visiting the trees and the grass. I not only disbelieve utterly, but intensely dislike, the doctrine of metempsychosis, which, if I understand it aright, seems the negation of the creative impulse, an apotheosis of staleness—nothing quite new in the world, never anything quite new—not even the soul of a baby; and so I am not prepared to entertain the whim that a bird was one of his remote incarnations; still, in sweep of wing, quickness of eye, and natural sweet strength of song he is not unlike a super-bird—which is a horrid image. . . .

Do we realize how far our town life and culture have got away from things that really matter; how instead of making civilisation our handmaid to freedom we have set her heel on our necks, and under it bite dust all the time? Hudson, whether he knows it or not, is now the chief standard-bearer of another faith. Thus he spake in *The Purple Land*: "Ah, yes, we are all vainly seeking after happiness in the wrong way. It was with us once and ours, but we despised it, for it was only the old common happiness which Nature gives to all her children, and we went away from it in search of another grander kind of happiness which some dreamer—Bacon or another—assured us we should find. We had only to conquer Nature, find out her secrets, make her our obedient slave, then the Earth would be Eden, and every man Adam and every woman Eve. We are still marching bravely on, conquering Nature, but how weary and sad we are getting! The old joy in life and gaiety of heart have vanished, though we do sometimes pause for a few moments in our long forced march to watch the labours of some pale mechanician, seeking after perpetual motion, and indulge in a little, dry, cackling laugh at his expense." And again: "For here the religion that languishes in crowded cities or steals shame-faced to hide itself in dim churches, flourishes greatly, filling the soul with a solemn joy. Face to face with Nature on the vast hills at eventide, who does not feel himself near to the Unseen?

> Out of his heart God shall not pass
> His image stampèd is on every grass."

All Hudson's books breathe this spirit of revolt against our new enslavement by towns and machinery, and are true Oases in an Age so dreadfuly resigned to the "pale mechanician."

But Hudson is not, as Tolstoi was, a conscious prophet; his spirit is freer, more wilful, whimsical—almost perverse—and far more steeped in love of beauty. If you called him a prophet he would stamp his foot at you—as he will at me if he reads these words; but his voice is prophetic, for all that, crying in a wilderness, out of which, at the call, will spring up roses here and there, and the sweet-smelling grass. I would that every man, woman and child in England were made to read him; and I would that you in America would take him to heart. He is a tonic, a deep refreshing drink, with a strange and wonderful flavour; he is a mine of new interests, and ways of thought instinctively right. As a simple narrator he is well-nigh unsurpassed; as a stylist he has few, if any, living equals. And in all his work there is an indefinable freedom from any thought of after-benefit—even from the desire that we should read him. He puts down what he sees and feels, out of sheer love of the thing seen and the emotion felt; the smell of the lamp has not touched a single page that he ever wrote. That alone is a marvel to us who know that to write well, even to write clearly, is a woundy business, long to learn, hard to learn, and no gift of the angels. Style should not obtrude between a writer and his reader; it should be servant, not master. To use words so true and simple, that they oppose no obstacle to the flow of thought and feeling from mind to mind, and yet by juxtaposition of word-sounds set up in the recipient continuing emotion or gratification—this is the essence of style; and Hudson's writing has preëminently this double quality. From almost any page of his books an example might be taken. Here is one no better than a thousand others, a description of two little girls on a beach: "They were dressed in black frocks and scarlet blouses, which set off their beautiful small dark faces; their eyes sparkled like black diamonds, and their loose hair was a wonder to see, a black mist or cloud about their heads and necks composed of threads fine as gossamer, blacker than jet and shining like spun glass—hair that looked as if no comb or brush could ever tame its beautiful wildness. And in spirit they were what they seemed; such a wild, joyous, frolicsome spirit, with such grace and fleetness, one does not look for in human beings, but only in birds or in some small bird-like volatile mammal—a squirrel or a spider-monkey of the tropical forest, or the chinchilla of the desolate mountain slopes; the swiftest, wildest, loveliest, most airy and most vocal of small beasties." Or this, as the quintessence of a sly remark: "After that Manuel got on to his horse and rode away. It was black and rainy, but he had never needed moon or lantern to find what he sought by night, whether his own house, or a fat cow—also his own, perhaps." So one might go on quoting felicity forever from this writer. He seems to touch every string with fresh and uninked fingers; and the secret of his power lies, I suspect, in the fact that his words: "Life being more than all else to me . . ." are so utterly true.

I do not descant on his love for simple folk and simple things, his championship of the weak, and the revolt against the cagings and cruelties of life, whether to men or birds or beasts, that springs out of him as if against his will; because, having spoken of him as one with a vital philosophy or faith, I don't wish to draw red herrings across the main trail of his worth to the world. His work is a vision of natural beauty and of human life as it might be, quickened and sweetened by the sun and the wind and the rain, and by fellowship with all the other forms of life—the truest vision now being given to us, who are more in want of it than any generation has ever been. A very great writer; and—to my thinking—the most valuable our Age possesses.—JOHN GALSWORTHY, "Foreword" to *Green Mansions*, 1916, pp. vi–xi

Hudson's work is of great and permanent value. He combines the priceless gift of seeing with the priceless gift of so vividly setting forth what he has seen that others likewise may see it. He is one of a very limited number of people—which include Knight, the author of the *Cruise of the Falcon*, and Cunninghame Graham—who have been able not only to appreciate the wild picturesqueness of the old time South American life, but to portray it as it should be portrayed. His writings come in that very small class of books which deserve the title of literature. To cultivated men who love life in the open, and possess a taste for the adventurous and the picturesque, they stand in a place by themselves. Herman Melville did for the South Sea whaling folk, and Ruxton did for the old time Rocky Mountain trappers, much what Hudson has done for the gaucho. He brings before us the wild rider of the pampas as Gogol brings before us the wild rider of the steppes. In addition he portrays the life of bird and beast as in more quiet lands they have been portrayed by White of Selborne and John Burroughs. The men, the horses, the cattle, the birds of the vast seas of grass, all are familiar to him. We see the rough work of the horsemen, and their rough play; the long, low, white house of the great ranch owner, solitary under the solitary ombu tree; and the squalid huts where the mounted laborers live and the squalid drinking booths where they revel. We see also the Indians standing erect on the bare backs of their horses to look across the waving plumes of the tall grass clumps; and we listen to the tremendous choral night-chant of huge bustard-like water fowl, whose kind is unknown in any Northern land. He tells of the fierce and bloody lawlessness of revolutionary strife. Above all, he puts before us the splendor and the vast loneliness of the country where this fervid life is led.—THEODORE ROOSEVELT, "An Introductory Note" to *The Purple Land*, 1916, pp. ix–x

To be specific, there are three W. H. Hudsons present and active in his books, and they may be clumsily denominated as the field naturalist pure and simple, the human-naturalist, and the super-naturalist. As the first of these—like the Gilbert White of the tortoise, the bee-boy, and the goat-sucker (or croon-owl or night-jar) that shook with its rattle the straw 'hermitage' in which he and his friends one summer evening sate drinking tea—Hudson watches, scrutinizes, plays 'I spy', and collects. He classifies and experiments. He is a child in the wilds of Nature, and by no means a dreamy child, taking notes. But whether it is the precision of his senses, of eye, ear, nose, hand, and tongue; or the ease with which he places, and bathes, so to speak, the object observed and examined, in its time, space and atmosphere; or the intimate companionableness of his solitude, that makes the reading of him, as compared with most writers of 'nature books', so peculiar a pleasure, it is impossible to say. These qualities are all of them in some degree necessary to any good book of this kind. Rather than any particular one of them being the secret leaven then, it is an elixir distilled from them all that is his own secret. And this is as difficult to analyse as the sheen of a starling's wing, or the dream of Spring upon the 'smiling face' of Winter.

When he speaks of the crystalline sparkle of a perfectly cooked potato; of the pale enamelled turquoise of an adder's belly, such as would have filled with joy and despair the heart of an old Chinese master-potter; or when he plucks rich clusters of elderberries to gratify his friend the pig; or refers casually to the grey of a jackdaw's eye, or to the cries of a heron; or retrieves the tragic fable of a squirrel from his earliest memories and adds to it a gloss out of mature experience; or as placidly and ripplingly as Coleridge's quiet-tuned brook gossips meanderingly on and on of worms and moles and wasps and sheep and foxes and moths and of the disreputable John-go-to-bed-at-noon—well, conjured up by his influence, there steals a spirit into our sophisticated minds that drinks it all in naïvely and wonderingly, and all but makes an 'actual' memory of it. It is then, in a momentary exaltation, that we are tempted to claim to be among the elect who (if not with the microscopical intensity of a Henri Fabre) are 'accustomed to watch insects closely and note their little acts', and who therefore must be possessed of some small share of 'ladies' brains', seeing that they are 'of a finer quality than men's'.

Children, chameleonic in attention though they may be, are often thus engrossed. Our medicine-man may survey us occasionally with some little attention; the novelist keeps a wary, divining, analytic eye on his fellows; the poet, like Patmore, focuses his gaze perhaps some few inches *beyond* the regarded face; the psychologist is an expert in reactions; the priest is a student of the soul. But how rarely is *any* such student of *humanity* even comparable to a Fabre; how rarely is even the confirmed and incorrigible introvert a Hudson! 'Ladies' brains' are notoriously in close connivance with their owners—according, that is, to man. Their surroundings, physical, social and mental, are dyed with themselves. And 'Woman of science' is still a novelty in phrases. So in part then must it be with Hudson and his fellow-devotees. The worms he dug up out of his friend's weedkiller-poisoned lawn are, as with Charles Darwin, red-hot poker in hand, or bassoon at lip, in an odd fashion *his* worms only. The toad, clearly of the same lineage as Gilbert White's, which he watched one day come shambling and panting down the hot stony dusty lane towards the peace, perfect peace, of the pool at its foot, is a toad unique and unprecedented. When he tells us of a pet lamb on the faraway and long-ago farm of his childhood that was wont to sleep and hunt and roister with its eight dogs, or of that adult sheep, also of Patagonia, that would devour tobacco and even books with a gusto shared only by the anatomist of melancholy and the historian of decadent Rome, even although his lamb may be of the species beloved of 'Mary', and his sheep as precisely similar to any other specimen of its species now abroad on the outskirts of Kensington Gardens as trotter is to trotter, yet both of them are as exclusively Hudson's sheep and Hudson's lamb as Alice's sage old bespectacled ewe with her knitting needles in the all-sorts shop was Lewis Carroll's. Even as eventual mutton their flavour, we fancy, would still have been his own. The objects and experiences, that is, which were common in his workaday life as a field-naturalist, however ordinary they may be in themselves (and any lucky anybody's for the asking), are almost always touched with the idiosyncratic. When these experiences, while still of the detective order, are strange and *uncommon*, he not only conveys them with an easy exactitude, he also dramatizes them. We are in his mind as we read, just as we are in the mind of Jessica sighing her love-reverie, 'In such a night . . .'

In what follows, his tiny dazzling humming bird lives for us as if we ourselves had thridded its native thickets, or as if we had discovered it at liberty in the cage of a poem. Moreover, we survey Hudson's face through *its* eyes:

> I have had one dart at me, invisible owing to the extreme swiftness of its flight, to become visible—to materialize, as it were—only when it suddenly arrested its flight within a few inches of my face, to remain there suspended motionless like a hover-fly on misty wings that produced a loud humming sound; and when thus suspended, it has turned its body to the right, then to the left, then completely round as if to exhibit its beauty—its brilliant scale-like feathers changing their colours in the sunlight as it turned. Then, in a few seconds, its curiosity gratified, it has darted away, barely visible as a faint dark line in the air, and vanished perhaps into the intricate branches of some tree, a black acacia perhaps, bristling with long needle-sharp thorns.

Again and again he repeats this achievement. As when, in describing the marvellous sixth sense of the bat, he stands, check cap on head, in a sunken lane at evening whirling his light cane around and above his head, while to and fro the flittermice veer and waver, and, in their hawking swoop into and *through* its scarcely-visible rotations, untouched, unscathed, unstartled! Or, again, as when the wife of 'a gentleman in a southern county', with a 'taste for adders and death's-head moths', emptied over him out of her cardboard box 'such as milliners and dressmakers use . . . a shower of living, shivering, fluttering, squeaking or creaking death's-head moths'. 'In a moment,' he says, 'they were all over me, from my head right down to my feet . . . so that I had a bath and feast of them.' Here again, for an instant, we seem to have pierced behind the veil of an alien life; the mere words momentarily illumine it, as may the flame of a singularly clear candle the objects in a dark and beautiful room.—WALTER DE LA MARE, "Naturalists" (1919), *Pleasures and Speculations*, 1940, pp. 55–59

He shared with Turgenev the quality that makes you unable to find out how he got his effects. Like Turgenev he was utterly undramatic in his methods, and his books have that same quality that have those of the author of *Fathers and Children*. When you read them you forget the lines and the print. It is as if a remotely smiling face looked up at you out of the page and told you things. And those things become part of your own experience. It is years and years since I first read *Nature in Downland*. Yet, as I have already said somewhere or other, the first words that I there read have become a part of my own life. They describe how, lying on the turf of the high sunlit downs above Lewes in Sussex, Hudson looked up into the perfect, limpid blue of the sky and saw, going to infinite distances one

behind the other, the eye picking up one, then another beyond it, and another and another, until the whole sky was populated . . . little shining globes, like soap bubbles. They were thistledown floating in an almost windless heaven.

Now that is part of my life. I have never had the patience—the contemplative tranquillity—to lie looking up into the heavens. I have never in my life done it. Yet that is I, not Hudson, looking up into the heavens, the eye discovering more and more tiny, shining globes until the whole sky is filled with them, and those thistle-seed globes seem to be my globes.

For that is the quality of great art—and its use. It is you, not another, who at night with the stars shining have leaned over a Venice balcony and talked about patines of bright gold; you, not anyone else, saw the parents of Bazarov realize that their wonderful son was dead. And you yourself heard the voice cry *Eli, Eli, lamma sabacthani!* . . . because of the quality of the art with which those scenes were projected.

That quality Hudson had in a supreme degree. He made you see everything of which he wrote, and made you be present in every scene that he evolved, whether in Venezuela or on the Sussex Downs. And so the world became visible to you and you were a traveller. It is almost impossible to quote Hudson *in petto*. He builds up his atmospheres with such little, skilful touches that you are caught into his world before you are aware that you have even moved. But you can't, just because of that, get his atmospheres fully without all the little touches that go to make them up. The passage that follows I selected by a process akin to that of the *sortes Virgilianae* of the ancients. I went in the dark to the shelf where my Hudsons are kept, took the book my hand first lighted on, and pushed my index finger into the leaves until it stopped on the passage I have written down here. It is from *Hampshire Days* and it is appropriate that it should be about his beloved birds. For Hudson watched birds with a passion that exceeded anything that he gave to any other beings . . . except to Rima of *Green Mansions*.

> The old coots would stand on the floating weeds and preen and preen their plumage by the hour. They were like mermaids for ever combing out their locks and had the clear stream for mirror. The dull-brown, white-breasted young coots, now fully grown, would meanwhile swim about picking up their own food. The moorhens were with them, preening and feeding, and one had its nest there. It was a very big and conspicuous nest, built up on a bunch of weeds, and formed, when the bird was on it, a pretty and curious object; for every day fresh, bright green sedge leaves were plucked and woven round it and on that high, bright green nest, as on a throne, the bird sat. And when I went near the edge of the water . . .

Don't you wish you knew what came next! . . . And don't you see the extraordinary skill with which the picture is built, and won't that picture be a permanent part of your mind's eye from now on? I don't suppose you would ever take the trouble to wade through rushes to the edge of clear water and stand for hours watching water birds in their domesticities. I know I never should, though I am never happy if I have not wild birds somewhere near me. But I have that picture and know now how water birds comport themselves when, like men after work sitting before their cottage doors, they take their ease in the twilight. And indeed, before I had half-finished transcribing that passage, I knew what was coming. I cannot have re-read *Hampshire Days* since just after it was republished in 1923, a year after Hudson's death. But when I had got as far as 'and had the clear stream for mirror' I knew what was coming—the high mound of the moorhen's nest decked out with bright green leaves.

Conrad—who was an even more impassioned admirer of Hudson's talent than am even I—used to say: 'You may try for ever to learn how Hudson got his effects and you will never know. He writes down his words as the good God makes the green grass to grow, and that is all you will ever find to say about it if you try for ever.'

That is true. For the magic of Hudson's talent was his temperament, and how or why the good God gives a man his temperament is a secret that will be for ever hidden . . . unless we shall one day have all knowledge. It is easy to say that the picture is made for you when those words 'and had the clear stream for mirror' are written. But why did Hudson select that exactly right image with which to get in his picture? His secrets were too well protected.—Ford Madox Ford, "W. H. Hudson," *Portraits from Life*, 1937, pp. 47–49

Works

As the clouded vision of the traveller to the Crystal Age clears, he finds himself received in a great Country House, which is inhabited by a large group of men and women who till the land and perform the simple operations of weaving and stonecutting and the like. All over the world, one gathers, these great country houses dot the landscape. Each of them is no weekend center of social life but a permanent home; indeed their permanence is almost past believing; for in each house traditions are carried back thousands of years. The great cities and the complicated metropolitan customs that they produced have long been wiped away, as one might wipe away mold. The world has been stabilized; the itch for getting and spending has disappeared. Our traveller must bind himself to work for a whole year in order to pay for the garments his house-mates weave for him, garments whose texture and cut have a classic turn.

This household, I say, is the social unit of the Crystal Age: the house-father administers the laws and customs, and he dispenses the punishment of seclusion when the visitor trespasses upon the code of the house. The house-mates work together, eat together, play together, and listen together to the music of a mechanical instrument called the musical sphere. At night they sleep in separate little cubicles which can be opened to the night air. The horses and dogs of the Crystal Age have a degree of intelligence which our common breeds do not possess, so that the horses all but harness themselves to the plow, and the dog teaches the traveller when to leave off working the animals. Each household has not merely its laws and traditions: it has its literature; its written history; and the very girl with whom the traveller falls in love bears a resemblance to the sculptured face of an unhappy house-mother who lived and suffered in the immemorial past. These houses, these families, these social relations are built for endurance. What is the secret of their strength?

The secret of our Crystal Age Utopia is the secret of the beehive: a queen bee. The Crystallites have done away with the difficulties of mating by appointing one woman, in every house, to be the house-mother, the woman whose capital duty is to carry on the family: the entire burden of each generation falls upon her shoulders, and in return for the sacrifice she is treated with the respect due to divinity, like the young man who was chosen in the Kingdom of Montezuma, as the tales have it, to represent the chief deity until at the end of a year he was disembowelled. The wish of a house-mother is a command; the word of the house-mother is law. For a year before her retirement as mother she is put into communion with the sacred books of the house, and has at her command a store of knowledge which the rest of the hive are not permitted to share. It is she who keeps burning the fires of life.

For all except the house-mother sex is a matter of purely physical appearance. The Crystallites, if we may speak irreverently, are "content with a vegetable love—which would certainly not suit me" nor, it appears, did it suit our traveller to the Crystal Age, when he discovers that his passion could never be reciprocated by his beloved, even if she so far transgressed the laws of the household as to give way to him. Against the appearance of passion and all the mortal griefs that it carries with it, the house-mother possesses a remedy. When in the murk of despair our traveller turns to her for advice and consolation, she gives him a phial of liquid. He drinks it in the belief that it will make him as free from passion as his housemates; and he is not deceived; for—he dies.

The social life of the household is not to be wrecked by the storms and stresses of the individual's passions. The engines of life are no longer dangerous: the fuel has been taken away! A "chill moonlight felicity" is all that remains.

There are times when one may look upon the whole adventure of civilized life as a sort of Odyssey of domestication; and in this mood the Crystal Age marks a terminus upon that particular aspect of the adventure. To the objection that this sort of utopia requires that we change human nature, the answer, in terms of modern biology, is that there is no apparent scientific reason why certain elements in human nature should not be selected and brought to the front, or why certain others should not be reduced in importance and eliminated. So, for all practical purposes, there is no apparent reason why human nature should not be changed, or why we should not be prepared to believe that in times past it has been changed—communities which selectively bred for pugnacity and aggression committing suicide and opening the way for communities which socially selected other traits that made for survival. It is possible that in times past man has done a great deal to domesticate himself and fit himself for harmonious social life; and a utopia which rests upon the notion that there should be a certain direction in our breeding is not altogether luny; indeed, is nowadays less so than ever before, for the reason that it is possible to separate romantic love from physical procreation without, as the Athenians did, resorting to homosexuality.

If *A Crystal Age* opens our minds to these possibilities it is not to be counted purely as a romance; in spite of the fact that as a romance it has passages that rival *Green Mansions*. Between the individual households and common marriages, the utopia of the beehive is a third alternative which possibly remains to be explored.—Lewis Mumford, *The Story of Utopias*, 1922, pp. 174–77

The innermost heart of *Green Mansions*, which are the forests of Mr. Hudson's book, is tender, is tranquil, is steeped in that pure love of the external beauty of things that seems to breathe upon us from the pages of Turgeniev's work. The charming quietness of the style soothes the hard irritation of our daily life in the presence of a fine and sincere, of a deep and pellucid personality. . . . *Green Mansions* comes to us with the tone of the elegy. There are the voices of the birds, the shadows of the forest leaves, the Indians gliding through them armed with their blowpipes, the monkeys peering sadly from above, the very spiders! The birds search for insects; spiders hunt their prey.

> Now as I sat looking down on the leaves and the small dancing shadow, scarcely thinking of what I was looking at, I noticed a small spider with a flat body and short legs creep cautiously out on to the upper surface of a small leaf. Its pale red colour, barred with velvet black, first drew my attention to it; for it was beautiful to the eye.

"It was beautiful to the eye," so it drew the attention of Mr. Hudson's hero. In that phrase dwells the very soul of the book whose voice is soothing like a soft voice speaking steadily amongst the vivid changes of a dream. Only you must note that the spider had come to hunt its prey, having mistaken the small dancing shadow for a fly, because it is there in the fundamental difference of vision lies the difference between book and book. The other type of novelist might say: "It attracted my attention because it was savage and cruel and beautiful only to the eye. And I have written of it here so that it may be hated and laughed at for ever. For of course being greedy and rapacious it was stupid also, mistaking a shadow for substance, like certain evil men, we have heard of, that go about crying up the excellence of the world."—JOSEPH CONRAD, "A Glance at Two Books," (1925), *Last Essays*, 1926, pp. 136–37

The first thing that strikes us as remarkable in *Green Mansions* is the fact that Hudson's projection of the figure of Rima has remained, and can remain, relatively acceptable, in a period more cynical and disabused than the one which first accorded her attention and appreciation. For contemporary taste rejects any symbolization of a natural force; this sort of symbolism has been worn threadbare and even reduced to complete vulgarity by simple-minded tales of this or that human being who has been nurtured by "savages." Anthropologists have cleared up any last illusions concerning the conditions of life in primitive surroundings; and any writer who ventures to deal with primitives must proceed with the utmost care, lest he push the reader's credulity over into realms of the comic. The modern reader is, moreover, bored and uneasy in the presence of any literary construction that hints of allegory.

Hudson skirts the very real difficulties involved in his narrative in several ways. In the first place, . . . the delicacy and sincerity of his style vivifies and makes credible everything it touches. Again, Rima, as Hudson presents her, is neither theatricalized into a supernatural deity nor prettified into a puppet. Her supernatural qualities are few. She was born in mystery and bears a few marks of strangeness, such as her wordless language and her cobweb dress. But she is human in every impulse. She is capable of love, of gaiety, of anger, of courage, and of sacrifice. She is as impulsive as she is shy. She is presented as one facet shining on the surface of "nature" as a whole, where much else is horror and darkness. And Hudson's attitude toward her, as expressed through Abel, is not one of blind adoration. Abel seeks her out and presents himself to her in the manner of a human suitor to a human beloved; he gives in to her whims in an understandable way; and he mourns and revenges her death in the most direct fashion.

The background to this love is thoroughly realistic: Nuflo's garrulous old age, the two lurching dogs, the details of food and drink and of the general problem of nourishment and of keeping alive in a tropical wilderness, as well as the pictures of Indian life, which range from the horrible to the ridiculous—all these are integral parts of the story. This mingling of humor and realism with fantasy saves the book from allegory's false and partial atmosphere. If there is a moral involved in this tale of action and of passion, of loss and quick revenge, of spiritual agony pushed to its limits, it is a moral pointed toward the impossibility of any human attempt to live according to an impossible ideal. Abel returns to humanity and to the acceptance of normal values after discovering that the world of the pure ideal is less a dream than a nightmare.

Rima certainly embodies the untouched crystal essence of young idealism. She is a distillation of the dreams of a young man who has chosen solitude as his métier; who from childhood has been content "to stand and stare" at the profusion of inhuman beauty in a country hardly touched by man's cultivating and civilizing hand. Rima remains in the memory, in spite of her recognizable human traits, as a translucent presence, as a voice and an echo—as an effect of tragic tenderness. And she dissolves into the tangled tropical light and shade because her creator asks us to share in his young imagination and his young passion.—LOUISE BOGAN, "Introduction" to *Green Mansions*, 1951, pp. viii–x

The Purple Land, which takes its reader galloping across the Banda Oriental as it appeared in the time of Hudson's youth, may best be classed as a tale of adventure. The far-flung pampas and widely scattered ranchos possess the appeal of distance and of frontier wildness; the natives are children of nature—the men, impulsive and picturesque, the women, mostly gracious and beautiful; and the hero frequently encounters not only the eager eye of discontented wives and lovelorn maidens, but, beset as his route was by revolutionary bands, the bright face of danger. The various adventures, amatory and otherwise, are presented with a broad humanity, an arch humor, and great gusto—a gusto wanting in most of Hudson's writings. Though the author disclaimed identity with his hero, he does not succeed in persuading all of us that Richard Lamb is not, to a certain degree, an imaginative projection of his youthful self—the self that so alertly and ardently looks out from the Smithsonian portrait.

The weakness of the beginning and, more pronounced, of the ending (the circumstances of Lamb's elopement and the extent of the penalty imposed are sensational enough to demand fuller treatment) results from the book's being originally part of a larger whole. The looseness of its structure, which at first glance gives one the impression of a series of character-sketches separated by an occasional story, may lead some, as it did Swinnerton, to deny *The Purple Land* sufficient design or meaning. But this very looseness, which is indeed not so great as that of the picaresque novel and is characteristic of the autobiographic technique, gives to the narrative a sense of naturalness that accounts for much of its charm. The personality of the hero is strong enough to hold the various sketches and stories together, and by the time one reaches the end, so fully has the locale been viewed in emotional and intellectual perspective, they take on meaning. Thus *The Purple Land* moves along on a thematic as well as on a story level.

The portrait of Lamb is painted in the virile, fluent manner of a Sorolla. General Coloma summarizes him well: "You are brave to rashness, abhor restraint, love women, and have a light heart. . . ." Since the "Oriental world is . . . an oyster only a sharp sword will serve to open," we even exult with him over the slaying of the cut-throat Gandara. His roaming eye, scarcely restrained by the thought of his wife waiting for him in Montevideo, marks him as a man more for amourettes than any grand passion; but, handsome and eloquent and daring, he is not altogether to blame for being irresistible to feminine hearts. "Love cometh up as a flower," he says in self-justification, "and men and charming women naturally flirt when brought together." His joining the hopeless rebel cause in order to redeem his pledge to Dolores and his rescuing of Demetria from the sinister Don Hilario do much to keep him in our good graces. To what extent the youthful Hudson shared these attributes, if not the adventures themselves, we cannot be sure. But the love of freedom, which had much to do with bringing Lamb into complete sympathy with the natives of the Banda Oriental, he did almost entirely share. The understanding and love of children, notable in the sketch of that forlorn little shepherdess, Anita, and the fanciful story of Alma and the white mist of Yí, is also Hudson's own, as is, of course, the accurate knowledge and panpsychic love of nature. "While the last rich flood of sunshine came over the earth from that red everlasting urn resting on the far horizon, I could," declares Lamb, "had I been alone, have cast myself upon the ground to adore the great God of Nature. . . ."—RICHARD E. HAYMAKER, "Novels and Tales," *From Pampas to Hedgerows and Downs: A Study of W. H. Hudson*, 1954, pp. 320–22

MERVIN NICHOLSON
From " 'What We See We Feel': The Imaginative World of W. H. Hudson"

University of Toronto Quarterly, Summer 1978, pp. 304–22

Green Mansions comes to mind when W. H. Hudson is mentioned. But Hudson, a man of many interests, wrote non-fiction as well as romance, combining, as H. J. Massingham says, a great variety of elements:

> the primitive with the man in advance of his time, the artist with the naturalist, the observer with the dreamer, the personal with the objective, the romantic with the realist, memory with spontaneity, fact with fantasy, self-expression with self-forgetfulness, the physical with the spiritual, the animist with the visionary, and what is perhaps most striking of all, the boy with the man.[1]

The opposed qualities make Hudson interesting. On the one hand, he produced books about nature, some of genuine scientific value; on the other, there is his 'romance of the tropical forest' *Green Mansions* with its haunting power and uninhibited passion. *Green Mansions*, in the words of Galsworthy's foreword, 'symbolises the yearning of the human soul for the attainment of perfect love and beauty in this life.'[2] The emphatic 'in this life' indicates that attainment is found here and now, if at all, so that there can be no contradiction between the precise observations of actual experience in the nature books and the larger-than-life saga of Rima and Mr Abel. The different elements of a writer are not mutually exclusive: they interpenetrate one another. Taking *Nature in Downland* as representative of Hudson's nature books, we find in it the same imaginative power giving shape and significance to ordinary experience that later produced the wider vistas of *Green Mansions*.

When we read *Nature in Downland* we are not exploring the geography of the South Downs, important as their natural history is, but an imaginative world which mediates between the hills traversed by Hudson in 1899–1900 and the romance domain over which Rima presides. Hudson sees a nature transmuted by feeling and organized by imagination, resulting in a structure of images and metaphoric ideas that identifies order and meaning in experience. *Nature in Downland* is not a simple record: the events are selected and handled in a specific way according to an imaginative conception of life. The book is doubly interesting because it illustrates how experience gets assimilated by the creative literary imagination, and because the themes informing this work of non-fiction reappear in the larger vision of *Green Mansions*. As *Nature in Downland* and *Green Mansions* are very different it seems that the variety is possible only because of the same imaginative power. To quote Galsworthy again, Hudson has in fiction and non-fiction alike 'a supreme gift of disclosing not only the thing he sees but the spirit of his vision. Without apparent effort he takes you with him into a rare, free, natural world, and always you are refreshed, stimulated, enlarged, by going there.'[3] What follows is a metaphoric map of that world as it appears in *Nature in Downland*.

I

The clues to the structure of imagery in non-fiction first appear in the writer's handling of metaphor. 'The Living Garment' in chapter 3 is the surface terrain, but the metaphor implies the existence of a being identical with earth and clothed by that garment. We find such a being in Hudson's description of the sloping hills:

> we have the succession of shapely outlines; the vast protuberances and deep divisions between, suggestive of the most prominent and beautiful curves of the human figure, and of the 'solemn slope of mighty limps asleep' . . . a Titanic woman reclined in everlasting slumber on the earth, her loose sweet-smelling hair lying like an old-world forest over leagues of ground.[4]

Hudson is somewhat defensive about this being because, in the age of realism in which he writes, seeing the hills as a gigantic woman is considered merely an associative fancy. But it is more than that. It 'is rather a startlingly vivid reminder that we ourselves are anthropomorphic and mythopoeic, even as our earliest progenitors were, who were earth-worshippers in an immeasurably remote past, before the heavenly powers existed' (23). We share with our remotest ancestors a mythopoeic power. The primitive religion it inspired has died, like the people who held it, but the power that created the religion survives for the simple reason that it is essential in our nature. The woman is asleep because metaphorically the power in us lies dormant.

The appearance of this goddess indicates just how near the surface of Hudson's thought the myth-making impulse is. Since she belongs to the imaginative background, the figure in the downs reappears only in the similes that help tie the non-fictional foreground to the poetic structure: 'above the dark green of the yews the round light-green summit is seen like a head crowned with a row of immense barrows' (210). The yew, tree of deathful repose, is appropriate for this quiescent being.

Presented early, the sleeping giantess occupies an important place in the structure of imagery. She may be termed a presiding figure, a figure that personifies the world in which it appears. Embodying in the most direct way the identity of man with nature which is the book's theme, she stands at the upper limit of Hudson's imaginative world, symbolizing the desire for perfect human freedom in and with creation, the world of 'wild nature . . . wide prospect . . . and full liberty to roam whithersoever we will' (21).

The imagination tends to work symmetrically; what we desire implies what we fear and reject. Hence the utter freedom and peace epitomized by the titanic woman in the hills implies an opposite pole of imprisonment and madness, so that we may expect to find a demonic figure embodying everything the giant is not, to mark a lower limit to Hudson's imaginative world. Near the end, in the detestable Chichester, the explorer of downland reaches this nadir:

> in a little while he will discern a huge recumbent form, paler in colour than the floor of rotting wood, the dripping stone walls, and vaulted roof—a stupendous human-shaped monster, like a Daniel Lambert increased to ten times his great size; his naked body and limbs extended on the black wet floor, apparently dead and swollen by death, but the head raised, supported by a hand and arm; the face, round as an ancient warrior's shield, but larger, turned to him, froth and yellow slime dropping from the obscene mouth, the wide bloodshot eyes fixed with a challenging gaze . . . in those pale blue watery orbs he will see visions appearing and vanish-

ing like lightning, an inconceivably rapid succession of faces, forms, events—wrecked lives of innumerable men, broken hearts, and homes made desolate; famine and every foul disease; feverish dreams and appetites, frantic passions, crimes, ravings of delirium, epilepsy, insanity; and strewn over all, the ashes of death . . . he has been face to face with a god, the only god known and worshipped by the people of this town. (246–7)

Stretched out like the female in the hills, this huge male divinity is also a presiding figure. He personifies the decay of city life, specifically liquor, worshipped for its power to hyperstimulate and numb. The claustrophobia expressed by the figure is the polar opposite of the limitless freedom associated with the goddess.⁵ Has Hudson slipped into some kind of temperance tract? The god of drink seems bizarre in a non-fictional account of Chichester. The purpose of the episode is to fill out the imaginative structure Hudson needs to organize and communicate his experience. The god marks the lower limit, as the goddess marks the upper limit, of Hudson's imaginative world.

These complementary figures may not be typical but they provide directions towards which everything in the book points. Between them lies the main body of *Nature in Downland*, consisting of a rambling account of the South Downs, focusing on the life to be found there—human, animal, vegetable, and even insect life. The narrator generates the sense of intimacy one feels for a welcome fellow-traveller; yet we never see him directly, and there remains something evasive about this solitary wanderer of the hills. One of the most modest writers in English history, Hudson conceals a very considerable skill behind the easy tone. His self-deprecation is a technique as ancient as rhetoric itself. The easygoing manner and modesty are calculated effects. He explains casually how (virtually by accident) he decided to write this 'small unimportant book' (6); the same tone continues to the end of 'this—well—this sort of thing' (260), as he describes the narrative. A calculated sinking typifies the method. For example, in 'Silence and Music' there is a striking description of the whinchat. Nothing arouses Hudson's feeling more than birds; we see it soar a hundred feet up, pouring out rapid shrill notes, with a powerful exhilarating effect, when Hudson abruptly breaks off: 'It is both dance and song, and a very pretty performance' (145)!

Nature in Downland is pervaded by the idea that the ordinary is really extraordinary. Hence the modesty is deceptive. Behind the associative, low-key rambling is an intense, even incommunicable vision. Hudson hints at the depth of 'what communion with nature really is to me' (259) but does not present it directly. The easygoing companion is only the visible aspect of a man from 'far away and long ago,' the solitary wanderer of romanticism who meets wonders, and perhaps horrors too, that effectively set him apart. Hence isolation seals up a vision that cannot be communicated directly in non-fiction. The same natural surrounding that inspires that vision is of no interest to many people, making Hudson's preference for solitude inevitable. Paradoxically anybody can share what Hudson found, but only through the love and knowledge of the apparently ordinary.

There are two principles in Hudson's imaginative thought that unite and organize his material. One is the idea of variety, the multiplicity of what we see in the range of our experience, the fact of many different things spread out in space, or what might be called the horizontal perspective. The other principle is intensity, the feeling or degree of attention that we devote to what we see, which makes up the vertical perspective. Since we feel what we see in Hudson, the two are metaphorically identical with each other. The horizontal perspective corresponds to the structure of imagery underlying the variety of *Nature in Downland*, while the vertical perspective corresponds to the incommunicable vision concealed and revealed in the relaxed tone of the narrator.

Hudson distinguishes between two attitudes towards life, both equally unacceptable, though they mislead in opposite directions. The first is a superficial interest that sees in living things only 'the image, the semblance' (97). Lacking fellow feeling for life, it experiences only one detached object after another. Hudson associates this attitude with works of art: people exposed to it become mere things or frozen surfaces, 'carvings and sculptures in a gallery.' The other attitude, extreme in the opposite way, regards the appearance as hiding some inner secret of identity to be pried open like an oyster. One sees without feeling; the second feels but does not see. Hudson associates the latter with De Quincey, one 'tormented' by 'gluttonism' (66) because incapable of fulfilment with things as they are. Continually searching but never satisfied, the 'gluttonist' suffers from one of the evils of modern life which Hudson visualizes as diseases: 'the modern curse or virus of restlessness and dissatisfaction with . . . life' (115). As extremes, the first attitude's paralyzing detachment and the second's tormented hunger meet in the disease-ridden god of Chichester.

As though espousing some *via media* of common sense, Hudson locates his own outlook between these two attitudes, claiming

> the mental attitude of the naturalist, whose proper study is not mankind but animals, including man; who does not wish to worry his brains overmuch, and likes to see very many things with vision a little clearer than the ordinary, rather than to see a very few things with preternatural clearness and miss all the rest. (98)

This modest-sounding statement implies a correspondence between the rejected attitudes and the horizontal and vertical perspectives. Separate the axes of experience and something goes wrong: variety without intensity produces the detached, objectifying attitude; intensity without variety becomes the gluttonist's struggle to penetrate a barren mystery. *Nature in Downland* does not objectify experience, nor is it primarily emotional. It is imaginative in nature. Hudson at first appears to aim at variety, on the one hand, but not that of a naturalist's catalogue or a series of isolated beautiful effects; and intensity, on the other hand, but not too much ('vision a little clearer' rather than 'preternatural clearness'). It sounds as if he wants moderate intensity and moderate variety at the same time, with the emphasis on variety, a goal tallying well with its modest expression.

But rejecting extremes (extremes are wrong because of what they miss or exclude) does not imply adopting a middle position. To Hudson everything in experience has value. He is really stressing the interdependence of the horizontal range of variety and the vertical perspective of intensity; he wants the maximum of both, not a little bit of each. This becomes clearer towards the end where he speaks of the various 'rural scenes and wild life' that make up his book, before mentioning the 'few faintly-traced lines' that hint at 'what communion with nature really is to me' (259). To grasp the intensity of that communion we must devote ourselves to the 'rural scenes,' the ordinary wild life of nature exactly as it is found. Then the paradox that the ordinary is miraculous begins to work and what we see expands into a feeling that liberates us in the fulfilment of desire.

II

Near the outset Hudson presents (in italics) his imaginative conception, *'what we see we feel'* (24). He derives the idea from Burke, one of the two really influential writers operating in this book, the other being Keats.[6] 'Feel' is a multiple pun. It denotes both 'touch' and 'experience' (as in Coleridge's 'I see, not feel, how beautiful they are!'). But the primary meaning for Hudson is the capacity of 'roaming corporeally' (24), as though by moving our eye across an object we also travel over it like a winged being. Hudson misunderstood the general theory of Burke's sublime and beautiful, mainly because he assimilated Burke's ideas to his own version of them. There is indeed an approximate sublime-beautiful contrast running all through *Nature in Downland*, but Hudson takes only one specific feature from the general theory: the metaphoric identity of sight and touch in the perception of the soft pleasing surfaces of beautiful objects. Then he applies this to what for Burke would be the sublime landscape of the hills. Hudson retains the sexual overtone implied by Burke's argument (as in sexual attraction, the soft visual appearance of the beautiful in Burke suggests how it feels to touch), in applying the sight-feeling identity to the gigantic—and female—body of the hills. Erotically based love is clearly an element in the creative mythopoeic imagination (one remembers Rima). Burke himself observes, 'the large and gigantic, though very compatible with the sublime, is contrary to the beautiful,' but adds: 'It is impossible to suppose a giant the object of love.'[7]

Burke's theory revolves around power. The beautiful object, before all else, is smaller and less powerful than we are, hence subject to our control. But the sublime, larger and more powerful than ourselves, would smash us if not separated by the safeguard of aesthetic distance. Burke's emphasis on terror indicates the dependence of his theory on power or force: essentially, the beautiful is weak, the sublime strong. Nothing could be more alien to Hudson's imaginative thought than the theory of power implicit in Burke. Instead of overwhelming force, Hudson's sublime is a larger identity that expands sensory experience; the beautiful is a bond of imaginative love and identification liberating even small objects into living relationship with us. The sublime enlarges us, while the beautiful expands the tiny and the insignificant. Sublime and beautiful are not opposed therefore: they differ from but are continuous with each other. The vertical perspective of intensity corresponds to Hudson's sublime, while the horizontal multitude of objects is the locale of the beautiful, and the one inevitably flows into the other.

Hudson's sublime has a liberating force associated with vast open space: 'among mountains, on moors, and in vast desolate marshes, on iron-bound coasts, and on wide seaside flats and saltings, and on level plains, I experience this same feeling of elation' (21). 'Elation' is the key; a gigantic horizon corresponds to 'elated,' literally lifted out or enlarged, sensation: the wider the landscape, therefore, the greater the feeling. Thus in climbing the high downs 'we have experienced that sense of freedom and elation which is the result of rising from a low level into a rarified atmosphere,' and we find that 'these purely physical sensations are succeeded by a higher, more enduring pleasure, which the mind receives from the prospect disclosed' (21). Hence climbing the high hills is metaphorically identical to sharpening the sensory powers, freedom being the 'subjective correlative' of wide open space: 'the freedom of an unenclosed country and of great hills' (265). It follows that freedom, purified sensory power, and the high hill country are metaphoric equivalents. To feel free is to see more, to find a larger nature. The image used for freedom is wide open space.

The first scene shows Hudson sitting on the plateau-like summit of Kingston Hill; he is not looking down at the view, as one might expect, but gazing upward, surprised by the unlooked for thistledown floating and shining in the sublime, clear blue space, and summing up emblematically his whole experience of downland. The scene is a vision of freedom. It introduces the structure of imagery while commencing the narrative. . . .

The opposite of freedom is imprisonment, a recurring theme in *Nature in Downland*. Thinkers of the imagination have always understood why stone walls do not a prison make: the feeling of claustrophobia is what makes a prison, not the formal paraphernalia of walls and bars. But walls and bars symbolize claustrophobia, and gaining unimpeded sensation feels like miraculous release from prison. This explains why Hudson often compares a sudden experience of joy or fresh sight with escaping from jail. The appearance of something new to see has the exhilaration of sudden freedom after captivity. Hudson actually meets a man just released from jail and promptly assimilates the fellow to his imagery of freedom, identifying him with 'the wild bird sing[ing] a new wonderful song' (163). The free flying bird is an image of human freedom in Hudson. Hence his anguish for a cooped-up owl (the 'feathered Dreyfus' in chapter 14) represents more than hatred of cruelty to animals, important as that is. For the caged bird belongs to the same world that the immured drink-god of Chichester embodies. Everywhere in Hudson is a keen awareness of the confining limits imposed on human life: 'if we could only go a little beyond our tether' (66). The tether goes back to Keats, whose Fancy, like a bird, must be untethered, escaping the 'mind's cage-door' to find fulfilment.

The more free, the more alive a thing is and the less mechanical or predictable. Hudson prizes spontaneity for the same reason that he left his walking tours unplanned:[8] the things that give life value come suddenly and from unexpected quarters. If receptive we are rewarded by delight that cannot be found in struggling for it. Life itself just happens; unplanned, yet the most precious of possessions, life is a free gift coming from nowhere and without our asking. Consequently, every valuable moment in Hudson is spontaneous and unexpected, new and therefore a surprise. This receptivity explains his fascination with any sudden motion, even when random. A quick wheeling movement always catches his attention, especially the swift flight of birds spontaneously taking to the air: 'suddenly, they are up again, an innumerable multitude of swiftly-rushing, twittering birdlings, brought, as it were, by a miracle into existence!' (222). Here sudden flight, birds, the miraculous, and life itself all fall into metaphoric alignment with one another. The emblem of *Nature in Downland*, the airborne thistledown seen from Kingston Hill, belongs to the same imagery, signifying the energy of pure life, 'springing spontaneously into existence' (4). Thistledown, flies, winged insects, even particles of dust attract Hudson's interest because of their random flight. But above all birds illustrate the free spontaneity of liberated existence. . . .

V

The imaginative world of *Nature in Downland* encompasses infinite desire and beauty, death, intensity, and man's relation to nature and time—themes that emerge with greater metaphoric clarity in the romance world of *Green Mansions*. The imaginative thought that flowers in *Green Mansions* is rooted in the earth of Hudson's actual experience. The compulsion to recreate memory, which gives both theme and narrative frame to *Green Mansions*, also appears in *Nature in Downland*, itself a recreation of remembered experience.

Recreation, in turn, is also communication. But here Hudson becomes the 'picture' and we the observer; hence the communication depends on our receptivity.

Hudson's vision seems remote at first, floating up from an era that looks idyllic compared with ours. But there is something important for us in Hudson. His concern for nature has now suddenly leapt into the centre of social imagination, as the ecological movement testifies. In the god of Chichester, furthermore, Hudson directly absorbs the claustrophobic panic and paralysis so universal today. *Nature in Downland* speaks with the voice of a profound sanity, neither disillusioned nor seduced by a facile rationalization of pain. To see accurately and feel the meaning of what we see shows us, on the one hand, the infinite value of life, and, on the other, its dangerous fragility. *Nature in Downland* exists because Hudson could not allow what he knew and loved to vanish; the same compulsion to prevent oblivion forms a theme of *Green Mansions*. It also, finally, explains Hudson's modesty, which is in part a refusal to accept the struggle necessary for preventing life from vanishing into nothingness. Perhaps there is wisdom here for a generation that could be the last.

Nature in Downland itself illustrates Hudson's principle that apparently minor things conceal great riches; the ordinary field in the parable hid a treasure. What we are really looking for may be close by, if we know how to feel what we see. At the end of *Nature in Downland* a Sussex villager explains how his region is the ultimate happiness, reminding us of the downland summer of Piers Plowman's heaven and also the words of a casual acquaintance earlier: 'If Heaven is like this, is must be a good place to be in' (110).

Notes

1. H. J. Massingham, 'W. H. Hudson,' in *English Critical Essays, Twentieth Century, Second Series*, ed Derek Hudson (London: Oxford University Press, 1958), p 57. W. J. Keith also comments on Hudson's variety: 'the mind that created Rima, the nature spirit of the tropical forest in *Green Mansions,* or the post-Ovidian fantasy of the boy metamorphosed into a wryneck in *Birds in Town and Village,* can also speculate about avian migration and develop theories of sense perception in *A Hind in Richmond Park': The Rural Tradition* (Toronto: University of Toronto Press, 1974), p 187. Keith's emphasis on Hudson's phrase *'what we see we feel'* has suggested my title.
2. John Galsworthy, Foreword to *Green Mansions* (New York: Random House, 1916; repr 1944), p viii.
3. Galsworthy, p vi.
4. W. H. Hudson, *Nature in Downland* [1900] (London: Dent, 1923), chap 2, pp 22–3. Subsequent page references are incorporated into the text.
5. See Robert Hamilton, *W. H. Hudson: The Vision of Earth* (London: Dent, 1946), who also discusses Hudson's imaginative response to Chichester, pp 75–7, as does Morley Roberts in his *W. H. Hudson: A Portrait* (London: Eveleigh Nash & Grayson, 1924), pp 147–8. Ruth Tomalin speaks of Hudson's 'passion for freedom' and contrasts it with the nightmare symbolized by Chichester in her *W. H. Hudson* (London: Witherby, 1954), pp 112–13.
6. See John T. Frederick, *William Henry Hudson* (New York: Twayne, 1972), p 80, where he notes the importance of the literary imagination in *Nature in Downland.* In his *From Pampas to Hedgerows and Downs* (New York: Bookman, 1954), pp. 109–11, Richard E. Haymaker also comments on the love and knowledge of literature, particularly Burke, in *Nature in Downland.*
7. Edmund Burke, *A Philosophical Enquiry into the Origin of Our Ideas of the Sublime and Beautiful*, ed J. T. Boulton (Notre Dame: University of Notre Dame Press, 1968), part IV, section xxiv, p 157.
8. Keith, p 175.

RICHARD HUGHES

1900–1976

Richard Arthur Warren Hughes was born in Weybridge, Surrey, on April 19, 1900, and was educated at Charterhouse and Oriel College, Oxford. As a student he was active in the Oxford literary scene, and the year of his graduation, 1922, saw the publication of *Gypsy Night and Other Poems* and the production of his one-act play, *The Sisters' Tragedy.* After graduating he traveled in Eastern Europe before settling in North Wales in 1923. There he helped to found the Portmadoc Players, and from 1924 to 1936 was vice-chairman of the Welsh National Theatre. *The Sisters' Tragedy and Three Other Plays*, including the first ever radio play, *Danger*, appeared in 1924.

Hughes's private income enabled him to travel widely, and his best-selling novel *A High Wind in Jamaica* (1929; in America, *The Innocent Voyage*) was begun on the Adriatic and completed in Connecticut. He also spent time in the Atlas Mountains, and in 1929 bought a house in Old Tangier; his stories about Morocco, *In the Lap of Atlas*, were edited by Richard Poole in 1979.

After marrying in 1932, Hughes lived in South Wales, where he wrote a second novel, *In Hazard* (1938). During World War II he served as an administrator at the Admiralty, for which he was made an MBE in 1946; with J. D. Scott he wrote a volume of the official history of the war, *The Administration of War Production* (1955). His major project in later life was a series of novels entitled "The Human Predicament," of which only *The Fox in the Attic* (1962) and *The Wooden Shepherdess* (1973) were completed. He also wrote children's stories, collected in *The Wonder Dog* (1977).

Richard Hughes died of leukemia on April 28, 1976.

A *High Wind in Jamaica* is one of the finest of the few truly original works of fiction that have appeared in the last few years. This is saying a great deal, for we are told that the bane of this generation, with its sweating and straining after originality, is that it rarely achieves much beyond sweat and strain. But with Mr. Hughes, originality shines in his work as naturally as the halo upon the head of a saint. He has just that sense of abnormality, that innocent callousness for which saints and children are notorious. One drops into his book as into fresh water that takes the breath away by its limpidity, freshness, and the masterly simplicity of its effects. This is a tropical morning:—

> The morning advanced. The heated air grew quite easily hotter, as if from some reserve of enormous blaze in which it could draw at will.

"Quite easily hotter"—Mr. Hughes, like those astounding days, can "quite easily" and "at will" rise, widen and deepen from subtlety to subtlety.

The scene is the Jamaica of the 'sixties. A family of English children are living in a wild part of the island in a wild tumbledown house. There is an atmosphere of ungoverned, animal enjoyment, for the whole scene in the island with its animals, negroes and forests, pools and lagoons for diving in, trees to climb, paths to explore, even to the increasing premonitions of earthquake and the final catastrophe of hurricane, is carefully seen with a child's eyes. Every word which would impose adult preoccupation, fear and moral feeling upon the scene is carefully eschewed. The world is the huge, slightly abnormal world of the detached and almost mindless wonder of little animals—and the little animals are the children. These opening pages in Jamaica are magnificent. They communicate a marvellous sense of beauty and power to the reader, as though he had gone back to the fresh and uncontaminated sources of his own life, his childhood, without using the sentimental ladder of adult memory to reach them. The ensuing pages in the pirates' ship are splendid too, but not quite so good.

The children, the eldest of whom is thirteen, and the rest from ten downwards, have been sent to England because of the catastrophe. They are captured by pirates and are transferred to the pirate ship. There they stay, enjoying themselves mightily and scarcely aware of the strangeness of their situation. This cargo of animal innocence most laughably embarrasses the pirates, especially the captain, who curses the day that he took such an inconvenient and happy cargo aboard. The story is not, however, primarily an adventure story. It is a most profound study of child character, without tears or complexes. Two thirds of the way through, there is a murder which I find very hard to believe in; and with the weight of this crime upon them, the succeeding pages lose their freshness. There is a note of adult bitterness. Towards the end when a steamer rescues the children Mr. Hughes' insight is rather too explanatory. To borrow from him a simile he most effectively uses for his children, his book is like a tadpole, all head and a lively body tapering away. But it is something like a work of genius. —V. S. PRITCHETT, "Three Exceptional Novels," *Spec*, Sept. 28, 1929, pp. 417–18

⟨A *High Wind in Jamaica*⟩ is an admirable novel. In fact, there are three approaches by which one is inclined to praise it as a book. To begin with, it is a poet's novel; and if only poets will turn to fiction in time the result is nearly always good. Like *The Memoirs of a Foxhunting Man*, this is the class of book in which the author has abandoned the hard conditions of his native element and migrated to a more generous climate with the wisdom he has learnt. But the writer is a modern rather than a Georgian poet, and the poetry of his novel is revealed,

not in style or language so much as by his observation, by that mixture of scientific accuracy and suppressed emotion, that French gift of spotting the unusual and inhuman in people and things, of describing it vividly, and leaving it at that. In a sense the book is a series of vignettes passionately observed, like the sketches, the ideas for poems, to be found in the notebooks of writers and artists. The art of the writer, however, is shown, not in the style so much as in the avoidance of style, in his skill in never "writing up" incidents which are preposterous enough in themselves, in always making the right transition from one extraordinary pen-picture to the next. It is the fashion for adventure stories to be rather spectacularly mousy. "What was Mr. Tippet's bewilderment at finding the sedate Miss Tuber, the fringe of her red petticoat oh, so exiguously showing, entirely surrounded by tarantulas, etc." Mr. Hughes, though deriving from Defoe, as must all writers of this genre, makes no attempt to keep up that brittle and disingenuous simplicity. The ease and the gusto with which he writes entirely obliterates the fantasy and sophistication so easily found in such a book. He is not only readable, but almost rattling in the way in which he carries one along. The third approach to his book is as a piece of research work into childhood, and that we will leave to the last.

A *High Wind in Jamaica* describes the adventures of a band of children who are sent home from that island by their parents after an earthquake and a hurricane. They are captured by pirates, the last pathetic buccaneers to linger unwittingly on the coast of Cuba into the Victorian period. In time they are rescued and brought home. The most original thing in the book is the melancholy satire with which the author enriches this Elizabethan remnant, their obsolete methods, their innocent ways, and their gradual victimisation by the children that they take on board. The scenery, the life at sea, the animals, from the pet cats and monkeys to the shoals of fishes and the sea-sick menagerie that is the pirates' only other prize, and the psychology of the pirates themselves are, too, all perfect in their way. Jamaica was once a romantic island, and the north shore, with its coral lagoons, maroon villages, a deserted eighteenth-century mansion like Rose Hall, must still be very like what it was in Mr. Hughes's time. Though (never having visited the island since 1860) he has yet been able to sublimate away the crust of upper Kipling classes uneasily reposing on a filling of small-town Americans and Portuguese Jews, and confine himself only to the tropic paradise restrained by village greens and church bells that the island ought to be. Earthquakes are the most evasive phenomena to describe, being so real yet so disappointing; but the account of this one, and of the high wind that follows it, seems the best in an unconradian way.

So much for the book as a novel—from that point of view A *High Wind* is vivid, exciting, delicate and swift. The strangeness is never exaggerated, the descriptions are exact as well as beautiful, there is nothing classy about the prose. Though anybody would enjoy A *High Wind* as fiction unless they disliked pirates, children, animals, satire and travellers' tales reinforced by modern sensibility, the inner significance will only exist to those who have been baffled by the child mind.

The difficulty of understanding children is really the difficulty of calculating the error when children begin to correlate what they think with what they are told they think, what they feel with what they ought to feel. At the same time children are voluble enough to give away a good deal of what is going on in their minds until the age at which the idea of gratitude is clapped on them by their parents like a butterfly net, and they subside into the guilty reticence of those who find it impossible to adapt their emotions to the belief that they exist to glorify those "who have done everything for them." Our age has been the first to really try to discover what children are like and not to substantiate what we hope they are; so, apart from Freud or behaviourists, a detached but sensitive poet, "not obscured," as Mr. Hughes puts it, "by an uprush of maternity to the brain," is most likely to get at the truth about children by animalising them intelligently or by studying them as primitive savages.

> Being nearly four years old, she was certainly a child: and children are human (if one allows the term "human" a wide sense): but she had not altogether ceased to be a baby: and babies, of course, are not human—they are animals and have a very ancient and ramified culture, as cats have, and fishes, and even snakes: the same in kind as these, but much more complicated and vivid, since babies are, after all, one of the most developed species of the lower vertebrates . . . Possibly a case might be made out that children are not human either: but I should not accept it. Agreed that their minds are not just more ignorant and stupider than ours, but differ in kind of thinking (are *mad*, in fact): but one can, by an effort of will and imagination, think like a child, at least in a partial degree—and even if one's success is infinitesimal it invalidates the case: while one can no more think like a baby, in the smallest respect, than one can think like a bee.

This passage seems the moral of the book, which is a study in the heartlessness, egotism, and animal grace of children not sophisticated by all the promises of the catechism. The three most striking qualities about children—real children, not Sonny Boy or Christopher Robin—are their exquisite sense of justice (in a complicated and legal rather than practical sense of the word), their amazing egotism and their perfect capacity for living in the present, which makes being with them like whirling with a flight of rooks over the fields which give them food. A writer cannot be great till he has created a universe of his own, yet children move effortlessly and with perfect modesty in theirs. The triumph of Mr. Hughes is that he has realised that children follow their elders about as affectionately as seagulls follow a ship. It is better to feed them and enjoy them through a telescope rather than imagine that we are receiving a gratitude which they do not feel for a benefit that we have not conferred. "The soft flesh and the sweet breath of children" was what Medea liked about them, and it is wisest to expect no more from them than that.

A *High Wind in Jamaica*, then, like *Gulliver's Travels*, may be read with delight for its story or with concern for the ethics which it describes. One cannot prophesy whether the manner or the matter will survive longest, but one wishes that the author would soon provide another picaresque novel, with more Antilles as its setting, and its subject, perhaps, that other mystery of childhood, which Remy de Gourmont states: "These little boys destined to become gross males, little girls whom time will turn into pretentious young ladies and rich middle-class brides—what pretty and delicate animals they are! How is it that these subtle creatures are so quickly transformed into imbeciles? Why should the flower of these fine, graceful plants be idiocy?"—CYRIL CONNOLLY, "The Innocent Voyage," NS, Oct. 5, 1929, p. 780

It is nine years since Mr. Richard Hughes published his former—and first—novel, A High Wind in Jamaica. Nine years is a long time: suppose only a mouse had emerged from the enormous gestation. A friendly critic opens the second novel 〈In Hazard〉—nervously. The first paragraph puts his mind at rest. Here is the old simplicity, surprise, outrageous humour.

Amongst the people I have met, one of those who stand out the most vividly in my memory is a certain Mr. Ramsay MacDonald. He was a chief engineer; and a distant cousin, he said, of Mr. J. Ramsay MacDonald, the statesman. He resembles his 'cousin' very closely indeed, in face and moustaches; and it astonished me at first to see what appeared to be my future Prime Minister, in a suit of overalls, crawling out of a piece of dismantled machinery with an air of real authority and knowledge and decision.

But the most outrageous quality of In Hazard is not its humour but its daring—to take the same subject as Conrad in Typhoon, the simple story of a hurricane and human endurance, to include even a shipload of Chinese; it would be foolhardy if it were not triumphantly justified.

Mr. Hughes himself describes the surface difference between the two tales: The 'Archimedes' is a large cargo steamer of nearly ten thousand tons belonging to a period which has charted weather like a continent. "The days of Conrad's Typhoon are past: the days when hurricanes pounced on shipping as unexpectedly as a cat on mice. For one thing, the mice know more than they used to know of the cat's anatomy, of the rules which govern its motion—and in addition to that, the cat has been belled." Meteorologists are on the watch: shipping send reports: gale warnings are broadcast. With immense skill and technical knowledge Mr. Hughes evokes our confidence in the great machine: we hear of the funnel-guys designed to stand a strain of a hundred tons: we are taken through the engine room by a man whose eye has been trained on nature—it is as if a bird-watcher had shifted his interest "from feathers to iron":

> You have seen, in a bush on a foggy day, the spider-runs among the branches? So, too, in an engine-room there are little metal runs at different levels and gossamer steel stairs, to carry you to whatever part you want of these huge iron lumps.

We learn the geography of a stokehold, the appearance of a propeller shaft, the purpose of tanks, and all this careful metallic framework for his tale is constructed in order that it may be startlingly shattered—by the sudden eccentricity of nature.

> The barometer had fallen to 26.9. So low a reading had never before been recorded for certain at sea . . . Precedents, book-knowledge, experience—they were no longer a guide. The air might now be expected to perform feats no living sailor had had to face before.

And so the 'Archimedes' suddenly, in the face of an unpredictable "sport" of nature ("Cannot understand your weather," another ship wirelessed back "a trifle huffily"), becomes as powerless as the little 'Nan-Shan,' and Captain Edwardes, with his radio reports, as impotent as Captain MacWhirr, who, it will be remembered, remarked vaguely, "There's some dirty weather knocking about," and read up the symptoms from a book in his cabin.

But the real difference between the two stories is this: that Conrad, unlike Mr. Hughes, was more interested in human beings than in the wild vagary of nature. The typhoon to him had the importance—and the unimportance—of a symbol. He speaks of Captain MacWhirr, that innocent and unimaginative commander with a bowler hat and an umbrella, as one

> who had sailed over the surface of the oceans as some men go skimming over the years of existence to sink gently into a placid grave, ignorant of life to the last,

without ever having been made to see all it may contain of perfidy, of violence, and of terror. There are on sea and land such men thus fortunate—or thus disdained by destiny or the sea.

His characters under that philosophic shadow live more intensely than those of Mr. Hughes. Conrad was a tragic poet, and Mr. Hughes is a rarer case in literature—a pure storyteller, unconcerned with anything but a succession of events, inventing with the greatest clarity and agility as if, like Scheherazade, he must save his neck from the sword. The poetry is in the observation, not in the feeling, and he observes his own inventions like a naturalist. If Conrad has something of Sophocles, Mr. Hughes has something of Fabre. And perhaps, too, something of Grimm—in what one may call the eccentricity of his invention (a junior officer at an American party finds himself alone with a naked girl, just as a character in Grimm might find a rabbit in her hair).

The pure story-teller is also heartless—the most appalling things happen in Grimm or the Arabian Nights—pity, remorse, anger have nothing to do with a succession of events. The little boy John in *A High Wind* falls out of a window and that's the end of him: the story goes on. The old chief, Ramsay MacDonald, after the 'Archimedes' has weathered the hurricane, falls asleep on the rail and drops overboard. Nothing is dwelt on, nothing impedes the story—except another story (I cannot help feeling the long byway into China and a Communist sailor's past life is a mistake), and in a world rather too warm with causes, affections, hatreds, ideologies, there is something icily refreshing in a writer who is concerned with nothing but things happening. If Mr. Hughes loses to Conrad in the vigour and vividness of characterisation, he answers Conrad's challenge magnificently in the description of the storm itself. Conrad's typhoon is a little blurred with rhetoric (Fabre could not have written of his ants so exactly if they had represented to him much more than ants): the 'Nan-Shan' is pounded and shattered with gigantic abstractions: we struggle in darkness with destiny for survival—but in the 'Archimedes' everything has the exactitude of a natural history, the excitement of a survivor's report, and the unexpectedness of a fable. One remembers the sudden appalling flight of the wild cats through the house before the hurricane in Jamaica, and one finds the same odd poetry here, the gentle acceptance of the eccentric fact, when he describes the 'Archimedes' as it enters the calmer centre of the hurricane:

> The whole ruin of the deck and upper-structures was covered with living things. Living, but not moving. Birds, and even butterflies and big flying grasshoppers. The tormented black sky was one incessant flicker of lightning, and from every mast-head and derrick-point streamed a bright discharge, like electric hair; but large black birds sat right amongst it, unmoving. High up, three john-crows sat on the standard compass. A big bird like a crane, looking as if its wings were too big for it when folded up, sat on a life-boat, staring through them moonily. Some herons even tried to settle on the ice-bulwarks, that were mostly awash; and were picked like fruit by the sharks. And birds like swallows: massed as if for migration. They were massed like that on every stay and handrail. But not for migration. As you gripped a hand-rail to steady yourself they never moved; you had to brush them off; when they just fell.

> —GRAHAM GREENE, "High Wind in the Caribbean," *Spec*, July 8, 1938, p. 68

Long awaited, much heralded, *The Fox in the Attic* is the first volume of a long historical novel of modern times called *The*

Human Predicament (The human predicament? Now which can that be?). It is impossible to judge a novel by a single part, particularly when it contains large numbers of plots and characters which are undeveloped, with no indication of what their development (if any) may be. Here the most interesting plot is about Hitler and the unsuccessful Munich *Putsch* of 1923, and the chief character appears to be Augustine Penry-Herbert, a rich misanthrope just young enough to have missed the war. He lives in Wales; has a sister married to a Liberal MP who lives in a house called Melton in Dorset and has servants with names like Trivett and Mr. Wantage; and goes to stay with some cousins in Bavaria, where he falls in love with a girl who goes blind at a party and is at once shoved into a convent. Hitler is one of the several foxes in the various attics in the book. There is a heavy use of coincidence and a good deal of even heavier philosophising: the theme seems to be the moral and political anarchy of a whole European generation brought up expecting to die at nineteen but reprieved by the Armistice. Perhaps something will be made of it in future volumes. The style is unfortunate: 'Now there was direct access—a direct union between the two of them through which great pulses of Mitzi's soul seemed to be pumped up his arm. . . .' Wow! And you know what he's doing? He's holding her arm on a walk through the snow!—JULIAN MITCHELL, "Everyman's Island," *Spec*, Oct. 6, 1961, p. 472

The scale of Mr. Hughes' attempt (in *The Fox in the Attic*) reminds one of other things—Dostoevsky, Tolstoy, and—especially—Hermann Broch's novel *The Sleepwalkers*, whose theme connecting characters is a thesis about the relation of modern architecture to life. These parallels make one a bit nervous. One wonders whether Mr. Hughes is not attempting to do something essentially Teutonic or Slavonic when really his gifts are those of a painter of landscapes and interiors. The German life he describes is of the kind which if it convinces does so because it seems so incredible that one reflects it must be possible—how else could Hitler and Ludendorff have happened? The real trouble is that Mr. Hughes' Germans and castle scenes seem only there, as it were, when Mr. Hughes is controlling them. Look round a corner of the Munich of 1923 and one might stumble into the Berlin of Mr. Issyvoo. But there are no corners. Hitler was in Munich in 1923, but so were Thomas, Klaus, and Erika Mann. Such people seem rigidly excluded from the intensely concentrated and concretised settings of Mr. Hughes. To think about the world of Thomas Mann's marvellous story, *Early Sorrow*, as happening contemporaneously with *The Fox in the Attic*, seems almost disloyal to Mr. Hughes' intensive build-up. On the other hand the Welsh and English scenes are brilliantly, surely, eloquently described and as full of air and implications of life beyond their particulars, as the German ones are lacking in these. —STEPHEN SPENDER, "The Miniature and the Deluge," *Enc*, Dec. 1961, p. 80

Lawrence Durrell and Evelyn Waugh have completed their very different multi-volumed projects, C. P. Snow and Anthony Powell continue their even vaster labors, and now Richard Hughes has entered the lists with *The Fox in the Attic*, the initial work of an ambitious sequence entitled *The Human Predicament*. Although Hughes' project differs from the others in its massive historical scope—which is, apparently, to be nothing less than the destiny of Europe between the two world wars—it shares with them a philosophical seriousness which aims to express a total and ordered vision of human personality and history. It is startling, in view of his previous work, to find Hughes mapping out this sort of territory for himself, but then it is surprising, at this point, to hear from him at all. The author, in 1928, of *A High Wind in Jamaica*, that curious and profound study of the mind of childhood which has established itself as a minor classic among modern novels, Hughes wrote a second novel in 1938 and then lapsed into more or less complete silence until *The Fox in the Attic*.

Set in 1923, *The Fox* deals with the disturbing but inconclusive experience of Augustine Penry-Herbert, an upper-class Englishman of liberal and humanitarian instincts, just young enough to have escaped active duty in the war. Involved by chance in the accidental death of a little girl near his Welsh estate, he goes to visit distant cousins in Bavaria in order to repair his shattered nerves. There, in a family as archetypally representative of the German aristocracy as Augustine and his family and friends are of the English, he discovers that the Germans are in fact different from the English (there is an amusing passage on his reaction to Baroque architecture); hears much about the violent political activities of a demagogue named Hitler, who is at the time engaged in carrying out his abortive *Putsch* in Munich; and falls in love with cousin Mitzi—who subsequently goes blind and is packed off to a convent. Disturbed and wretched, Augustine returns to England.

In its bare plot outline, *The Fox* is not a conspicuous departure from the manner of most serious modern fiction. There is a reliance on certain Victorian stock-properties (Hughes' great houses, whether English or German, always have a faint aura of Brontë which mingles strangely with his acridly modern preoccupations), but both its narrative detail and its texture reveal its fidelity to an older tradition: The conservative features of Hughes' novel.

Its wide scope, complex plot, and many sub-plots; its large cast of superficially but deftly drawn characters; its unabashed use of coincidence and its free assumption of omniscience— are inevitable products of a conception of personality and history which is to be, apparently, the ground-motif of the entire sequence. At the end of Part 1, just before Augustine's departure for Germany, Hughes halts the wheels of narrative and steps in *in propria persona* to enunciate his theories:

> Primitive man is conscious that the true boundary of his self is no tight little stockade round one lonely percieving "I," detached wholly from its setting: he knows there is always some overspill of self into penumbral regions—the perceiver's *footing* in the perceived. . . . But he knows also his self is not infinitely extensible either: on the contrary, his very identity with one part of his environment opposes him to the rest of it, the very friendliness of "this" implies a balancing measure of hostility in—and towards—"all that."

Retrospectively, *The Fox* explains World War I as the result of a collective re-drawing of the boundaries of selfhood, the creation, by both combatant groups, of a new beloved "we" and a new detested "they." This re-drawing was disastrous. "Suppose," says Hughes:

> . . . that in the name of emergent Reason the very we-they line itself within us had been deliberately so blurred and denied that the huge countervailing charges it once carried were themselves dissipated or suppressed? The normal penumbra of the self would then become a no-man's land: the whole self-conscious being is rendered unstable—it has lost its 'footing': the perceiver is left without emotional adhesion anywhere to the perceived, like a sea-anemone which has let go its rock.

Augustine typifies the class of reprieved young Englishmen for whom a secular religion of aloof and disengaged humanitarian-ism has replaced the discredited patriotic hysteria of the war

years. His is an unrooted ego. Mitzi, in her blindness, experiences an expansion of the "penumbra of selfhood" in which she loses herself in God. Adolf Hitler, at once product and symbol of cultural disintegration, confuses his personal ego with the will of history and the soul of the universe, and an unbalanced Europe careens toward the disaster which he epitomizes.

In his handling of the German scenes, Hughes shows admirable balance. He suggests incipient national neurosis without rendering his German characters either unbelievable or unsympathetic. Furthermore, he succeeds surprisingly in his boldest departures from contemporary narrative practice. We have grown unused to novels which are populated by scores of minor characters of quasi-Dickensian eccentricity and which present a complex plot articulated through a freely ranging focus of consciousness, but there is no reason not to applaud when a modern writer has both the courage and the skill to revive qualities of a past great age and come close to pulling it off.

The weaknesses of *The Fox* lie elsewhere—in its often undistinguished verbal texture, in its stiff and unwieldly use of symbols, and in its ultimate failure to provide, in Augustine, a hero who is believable. The intellectually provocative passages which I have quoted display the muddiness which sometimes afflicts the author's syntax, and the same defect contributes to his failure to make Augustine a personality or, indeed, anything except a conveniently—and incredibly—naïve observer. The "fox" of the title—variously identified with Hitler in hiding at Putzi Hanfstaengl's country house after the failure of the *Putsch* and with a paranoid young German in hiding in the attic of Augustine's cousins—never quite assumes validity as a symbol.

The Fox in the Attic is, of course, the prelude to an enormous work. It is possible that later volumes will bring much of it into retrospective focus. One thing is certain: Hughes has, despite his weaknesses, an intellectual power and a wealth of historical imagination which make it at least possible that he will end, by producing an important novel of ideas.—FRANK J. WARNKE, "Prologue to an Anatomy of Chaos," *NR*, April 23, 1962, pp. 29–30

Hughes says in a note that ⟨*The Fox in the Attic*⟩ is not a self-contained volume, but simply a length of novel which he decided to publish before the whole was finished, because he is such a slow writer. This characteristic is responsible also for the curious nature of his reputation; his has been for years a name more honored than spoken. He has written two other novels, *A High Wind in Jamaica* and *In Hazard*, the first over thirty and the second over twenty years old. These books are very distinguished, the second and less celebrated being the more completely achieved—it is an extraordinary and almost successful attempt to over-go Conrad on the hurricane at sea, and combines a striking immediacy of effect with the accomplishment of profounder purposes. As it seemed that these books would have no successor, *The Fox in the Attic*, is an uncovenanted boon to modern English fiction.

In his earlier work this very elaborate writer cultivated, when it suited him, a sort of ingenuousness, a let-me-tell-you-this-tale approach. There are reminiscences of this in *The Fox in the Attic*, though it is a sober, heavily-built piece, ambitious of permanence and grandeur. But if the scope is Tolstoyan, the manner is often more like Pasternak's, and there are carefully inlaid emblematic elements. These, however, do not prevent Hughes from speaking directly and at length to his thesis, his explanation of the human predicament; and there are two whole chapters in this volume which make no fictive gestures at all, but simply set forth this explanation.

So far as it has gone, Hughes's novel focusses strongly on what may for convenience be called the *ancien régime*, its privileges, its obligations, its changing posture, and the differences between English and German *Junker*. His hero, a young man named Augustine, inhabits "eremitically" a great house in Southwest Wales; but after being unjustly suspected by the working classes of having had a part in the death of a poor child, Augustine goes to live for a while in Bavaria with his German cousins, witnessing the early days of Nazism. In the opening chapter, which is certainly a fine achievement, Augustine (still nameless) carries home the dead girl's body, which he has found while shooting on the sea-marsh, on "a warm wet windless afternoon. . . . In a sodden tangle of brambles the scent of a fox hung, too heavy today to rise or dissipate." The fox (which also makes an appearance in a dream-sequence of *In Hazard*) is thus associated with death and the wish for death. Augustine finds himself alone in the house with the stiffened body, no longer child but total cadaver: "If (which God forbid) he had put it on again it would have fitted." This superbly careful opening inaugurates the double-plot of image and idea; for the novel is "about" death and selfhood.

Hughes's characters are "gentle" in an old complex sense—they can be placed, perhaps, by their loathing for even the best hotels, their slightly embarrassed dislike of the successful middle class. Augustine would, in his youth, like to break with the past, and finds it hard, for instance, to give orders to servants; but *noblesse oblige*, and "it's intolerable for the ruled themselves when the ruling class abdicates." Hughes has studied manners; the suggestion is that there are some social facts which no political upheaval can alter, just as the Freudian abolition of conscience does not save a beloved child from suffering bad dreams. After the two chapters of sermon, we move to the German house, where aristocracy, while much more closely united with religion, is inconceivable save in its military incarnation; where there is a kind of gentle brutality in the treatment of children, and a fierce sense of race. But in both countries there has grown up a separateness between people, a failure of the ego to merge its limits in other persons. The war itself was the world's revenge on these separated egos; hate poured in through the gaps left by love.

The Fox in the Attic is a very big, very systematic book, though it is not wonderfully good sport for those who like novels to be puzzles; Hughes is as open as he can be about a subject complex in itself and further complicated by disciplined feeling. Whether the disease of the social structure is correctly diagnosed as malignant egotism is a question to which the answer need be no simpler than the book; whether this is or isn't a magnificently good piece of a novel is an easier question, and the answer is, "it is."—FRANK KERMODE, *PR*, Summer 1962, pp. 467–68

His recently published novel, *The Fox in the Attic*, is the first of a group of novels to be called *The Human Predicament*. What he means by the latter title is something quite different from Malraux's *La Condition humaine*. It is not a question of disagreement but rather of the stance from which the subject is addressed. Malraux's title means what it is like to be human. Hughes's title means, I think, what it is like to be a Western human in the first half of the twentieth century. Malraux's world-view is radical and religious (or rather anti-religious). It is the Pascalian prison from which God has been subtracted. God is dead. Hughes is hoeing a different row. And God has very little to do with it—so far at least. Hughes's people are not

believers who have lost their faith, or even the sons of believers. They are Asquith liberals to whom nothing could matter less than God's death or survival. The question for the rebellious young man is not: after the death of God, what?—but, why does humanism lead to beastliness?

By "human predicament," Hughes is referring to the historical fix of Western man. What engages him first is the cataclysm of 1914 when, with the ultimate triumph of humanism clearly in sight, the West had its first *grand mal* convulsion. Why did it happen? And why, once it did, didn't everyone have the good sense to put an end to it? They didn't because they didn't want to. It was war one wanted. There is something worse than war. What?—for one thing, the creeping solipsism of the *pax Britannica*.

> Thus the day Belgium was invaded every caged ego in England could at last burst its false Cartesian bonds and go mafficking off into its long-abandoned penumbral regions towards boundaries new-drawn.

War is better than nothing.

The question is, why does humanism lead to beastliness? But for Hughes the question and the answer are non-radical. Malraux's *La Condition humaine* is an anthropology in the radical and European sense of the word. It speaks of what it is to be born a man, anywhere and at any time. Hughes's "human predicament" is an anthropology in the Anglo-American sense—which is to say, an ethnology. It is an historico-empirical enquiry into a segment of the culture toward the end of tracing out the proximate causes of a cultural phenomenon.

True, Hughes makes some general remarks about what makes men happy and what makes them miserable, but his frame of reference is genetic: casting about for answers, he finds it natural to look back to primitive man and natural to ask then, what went wrong? Like Malraux he is haunted by the loneliness of Western man, but very unlike Malraux and rather more like a Columbia professor of ethnology, he conceives a nostalgia for primitive wholeness.

> Primitive man is conscious that the true boundary of his self is no tight little stockade round one lonely perceiving "I," detached wholly from its setting: he knows there is always some overspill of self into penumbral regions—the perceiver's *footing* in the perceived. He accepts as naturally as the birds and beasts do his union with a part of his environment, and scarcely distinguishes that from his central "I" at all. . . .
> That primitive truth about selfhood we battle against at our peril. For the absolute solipsist—the self contained wholly within the ring-fence of his own minimal innermost "I" and for whom "we" and "my" are words quite without meaning—the asylum doors gape.

Hughes might agree with Eric Voegelin's characterization of the "twilit civilization of the cosmological myth"—but presumably he would not agree that man did well to put it behind him.

These sentences are part of a chapter of other such sentences—a chapter of straight-out theorizing set down bald as an egg right in the middle of an otherwise novelistic novel. Unlike the current French novelist whose novel is itself an ongoing exploration of reality, Hughes calls time out from his story to deliver a lecture. It is hard to know what to make of it. Perhaps *The Human Predicament* will be so big that a lecture will come across as but one more piece of epic furniture, like Tolstoy's theorizing about history. But here it gives the effect of breathlessness. It has been a long time between novels, one gathers, and Hughes has many things to say and can't wait. He wants to say how he sees things. . . .

Hughes has been compared to Tolstoy, perhaps because of Napoleon and Hitler and the big bites of history. Both novelists, too, work the empirical method of induction: from home and fireside and fictional family to large historical confrontations (Borodino, München), and on to even larger theories of history. But the comparison is silly—so far. Hughes's canvas is small and enigmatic rather than epic. Nicholas Rostov and Tsar Alexander very much belong to the same book, but I'm not sure Augustine and Hitler do. Yet it is

some measure of Hughes's powers that when Hitler does come on, there he is sure enough, in the round, as solid as nine-year-old Polly. But what are you going to do with Hitler in a novel? Maybe it will turn out that you can do it that simply: just put him in. Still it is in his treatment of Polly that he is most like Tolstoy. Tolstoy could tell what children and horses think. So can Hughes. His best trick is making a long cast at the goings-on inside someone else's head, an exotic someone like a child or a horse or a foreigner (an ordinary foreigner, not Hitler), and setting down what he finds out in good cranky idiomatic British English.—WALKER PERCY, "Hughes's Solipsism Malgré Lui," *SwR*, July–Sept. 1964, pp. 491–94

TED HUGHES

1930–

Edward James Hughes was born on August 17, 1930, in the West Yorkshire mill town of Mytholmroyd. He grew up roaming the local moors and farms and absorbing the dialect that would later inform his poetry. He was educated at Pembroke College, Cambridge, where, disillusioned with the way English was taught, he completed a B.A. in archaeology and anthropology, gaining a deep knowledge of world folklore. After a few odd jobs, he became a reader for Rank films and returned to writing poetry. In 1956 he married Sylvia Plath, and lived for two years with her in America; their personal and literary partnership ended in 1962, the year before Plath's suicide.

Hughes won both the first prize in the 1958 Guinness Poetry Awards and the New York City Poetry Center's First Publication Award for his book *The Hawk in the Rain* (1957). *Lupercal* (1960) brought him the Somerset Maugham Award and the Hawthornden Prize, and confirmed his status as a leading British poet. His prolific production since then includes prose and poetry for children, radio plays, reviews, and translations, including Seneca's *Oedipus*, produced at the National Theatre in London in 1968. He has also edited selections of poems by Shakespeare, Emily Dickinson, and Sylvia Plath, in addition to writing numerous volumes of verse of his own. Among his best-known works are *Wodwo* (1967), which includes poems, short stories, and a radio play, *Crow* (1970), *Crow Wakes* (1971), *Eat Crow* (1972), *Gaudete* (1977), *Cave Birds* (1978), and *Moortown* (1979). His experimental play *Orghast* was performed at the Fifth Festival of the Arts of Shiraz in Persepolis, Iran, in 1971. *Selected Poems 1957–1981* appeared in 1982.

Hughes has received many honors, including the Queen's Medal for Poetry in 1974. He was made an MBE in 1977, and in 1984 succeeded Sir John Betjeman as Poet Laureate. He has two children from his marriage to Plath, and married his second wife in 1970.

Personal

As I remember it, I met Sylvia ⟨Plath⟩ and her husband ⟨Ted Hughes⟩ in London in the spring of 1960. My first wife and I were living near Swiss Cottage, on the unsmart edge of literary Hampstead in a tall Edwardian building of particularly ugly red brick; it was the color of some old boiler that had been left out to rust for so long that even the brightness of decay had worn off. When we moved in, the place had just been converted by one of those grab-and-get-out property companies that did so well before the Rachman scandal. Naturally, they had made a shoddy job of it: the fittings were cheap and the finish awful; the window frames seemed too small for the brickwork around them and there were large, rough gaps at every joint. But we had sanded the floors and painted the place out in bright colors; then we bought bits and pieces from the junk-furniture dealers in Chalk Farm, and sanded and painted them, too. So in the end it seemed gay enough in a fragile, skin-deep way—just the place for the first baby, the first book, the first real unhappiness. By the time we left eighteen months later, there were gaping cracks in the outer wall where the new windows had been cut.

But by that time there were gaping cracks in our lives, too, so it all seemed to fit.

Since I was the regular poetry critic for *The Observer*, I saw few writers. To know whom I was reviewing seemed to make too many difficulties: nice men often write bad verse and good poets can be monsters; more often than not, both the man and his work were unspeakable. It seemed easier all around not to be able to put a face to the name, and judge solely on the printed page. I kept to my rule even when I was told that Ted Hughes was living nearby, just across Primrose Hill, with an American wife and a small baby. Three years before, he had brought out *The Hawk in the Rain*, which I admired greatly. But there was something about the poems which made me suspect that he wouldn't care what I thought. They seemed to emerge from an absorbed, physical world that was wholly his own; for all the technical skill deployed, they gave the impression that literary goings-on were no concern of the author. "Don't worry," I was told, "he never talks shop." I was also told that he had a wife called Sylvia, who also wrote poetry, "but"—and this was said reassuringly—"she's very sharp and intelligent."

In 1960 came *Lupercal*. I thought it the best book by a

young poet that I had read since I began my stint on *The Observer*. When I wrote a review to say so, the paper asked for a short piece about him for one of the more gossipy pages. I phoned him and we arranged to take our kids for a walk on Primrose Hill. It seemed like a nice, neutral idea.

They were living in a tiny flat not far from the Regent's Park Zoo. Their windows faced onto a run-down square: peeling houses around a scrappy wilderness of garden. Closer to the Hill, gentility was advancing fast: smart Sunday-newspaper real estate agents had their boards up, the front doors were all fashionable colors—"Cantaloupe," "Tangerine," "Blueberry," "Thames Green"—and everywhere was a sense of gleaming white interiors, the old houses writ large and rich with new conversions.

Their square, however, had not yet been taken over. It was dirty, cracked and rackety with children. The rows of houses that led off it were still occupied by the same kind of working-class families they had been built for eighty years before. No one, as yet, had made them chic and quadrupled their price—though that was to come soon enough. The Hugheses' flat was one floor up a bedraggled staircase, past a pram in the hall and a bicycle. It was so small that everything appeared to be sideways. You inserted yourself into a hallway so narrow and jammed that you could scarcely take off your coat. The kitchen seemed to fit one person at a time, who could span it with arms outstretched. In the living room you sat side by side, lengthwise, between a wall of books and a wall of pictures. The bedroom off it, with its flowered wallpaper, seemed to have room for nothing except a double bed. But the colors were cheerful, the knickknacks pretty, and the whole place had a sense of liveliness about it, of things being done. A typewriter stood on a little table by the window, and they took turns at it, each working shifts while the other minded the baby. At night they cleared it away to make room for the child's cot. Later they borrowed a room from another American poet, W. S. Merwin, where Sylvia worked the morning shift, Ted the afternoon.

This was Ted's time. He was on the edge of a considerable reputation. His first book had been well received and won all sorts of prizes in the States, which usually means that the second book will be an anticlimax. Instead, *Lupercal* effortlessly fulfilled and surpassed all the promises of *The Hawk in the Rain*. A figure had emerged on the drab scene of British poetry, powerful and undeniable. Whatever his natural hesitations and distrust of his own work, he must have had some sense of his own strength and achievement. God alone knew how far he was eventually going, but in one essential way he had already arrived. He was a tall, strong-looking man in a black corduroy jacket, black trousers, black shoes; his dark hair hung untidily forward; he had a long, witty mouth. He was in command.

. . . In varying degrees, both ⟨Sylvia Plath⟩ and ⟨Ted Hughes⟩ seemed to believe in the occult. As artists, I suppose, they had to, since both were intent on finding voices for their unquiet, buried selves. But there was, I think, something more to their belief than that. Ted has written that "her psychic gifts, at almost any time, were strong enough to make her frequently wish to be rid of them." That could simply have been her poet's knack of sensing the unspoken content of every situation and, later, her easy, instinctive access to her own unconscious. Yet although both of them talked often enough about astrology, dreams and magic—enough, anyway, to imply that this was not just a casually interesting subject—I had the impression that at heart their attitudes were utterly different. Ted constantly and carefully mocked himself and deflated his pretensions, yet there was always a sense of his being in touch with some primitive area, some dark side of the self which had nothing to

do with the young literary man. This, after all, was what his poems were about: an immediate, physical apprehension of the violence both of animal life and of the self—of the animality of the self. It was also part of his physical presence, a quality of threat beneath his shrewd, laconic manner. It was almost as though, despite all the reading and polish and craftsmanship, he had never properly been civilized—or had, at least, never properly believed in his civilization. It was simply a shell he sardonically put up with for the sake of convenience. So all that astrology, primitive religion and black magic he talked about, however ironically, was a kind of metaphor for the shaking but obscure creative powers he knew himself to possess. For this reason those dubious topics took on for him an immediacy which may not have implied any belief but which certainly transformed them into something beyond mere fad. Perhaps all I am describing is, quite simply, a touch of genius. But it is a genius that has little to do with the traditional Romantic concept of the word: with Shelley's canny otherworldliness or Byron's equally canny sense of his own drama. Ted, too, is canny and practical, like most Yorkshiremen, unwillingly fooled and with a fine, racing-mechanic's ear for the rumblings of the literary machine. But he is also, in a curiously complete way, an original: his reactions are always unpredictable, his frame of reference different. I imagine the most extreme example of this style of genius is Blake. But there are also many people of genius—perhaps the majority—who have almost nothing of that dislocating and dislocated quality: T. S. Eliot, for example, the Polish poet Zbigniew Herbert, John Donne and Keats—all men whose unusual creative intelligence and awareness seem not essentially at odds with the reality of their everyday worlds. Instead, their particular gift is to clarify and intensify the received world.—A. ALVAREZ, "Prologue: Sylvia Plath," *The Savage God*, 1970, pp. 3–6, 28–30

Edward James Hughes was born on 17 August 1930, in Mytholmroyd, deep in a sodden valley of the Yorkshire Pennines, near the Brontë country.

From the beginning, as he recalls in *Poetry in the Making*, he was fascinated by animals, first collecting toy lead animals until they went right round the fender, then drawing them and modelling them in plasticine, then acting as retriever when his older brother (who was later for a short time a gamekeeper) went shooting magpies, owls, rabbits, weasels, rats and curlews; and finally, and best, capturing them by writing poems about them.

Ted was the youngest of three children. His father, William Hughes, a carpenter, was one of the seventeen men from his entire regiment who returned from the Dardanelles. The boy's imagination was filled with images of Flanders in the First World War (vividly recalled in 'Out') which closely matched those implanted there by his own experience of the bone-strewn moors and the farms which fringed them.

The valley seemed always dark, under the shadow of a huge, almost vertical, looming cliff to the north, a mere corridor between the cotton towns of south Lancashire and the woollen towns of the West Riding, a shadow trap imposing on the growing boy the need to escape, upwards, onto the high moors, exposed and bleak. Hughes' spirit responded to that of the moors 'the peculiar sad desolate spirit that cries in telegraph wires on moor roads, in the dry and so similar voices of grouse and sheep, and the moist voices of curlews'.

Everything in West Yorkshire is slightly unpleasant. Nothing ever quite escapes into happiness. The people are not detached enough from the stone, as if they were only half-born from the earth, and the graves are too near the surface. A disaster seems to hang around in the air there for a long time. I can never escape the impression that the whole region is in mourning for the first world war. The moors don't escape this, but they give the sensation purely. And finally, in spite of it, the mood of moorland is exultant, and this is what I remember of it.

From there the return home was a descent into the pit, and after each visit I must have returned less and less of myself to the valley. This was where the division of body and soul, for me, began. ('The Rock')

This shut-in, in-bred, industrial community of the Calder Valley has bred strong values—dignity and decency, cleanliness and honesty, hard work and thrift, good neighbourliness, solidarity. This shaped Hughes, and he has much to be grateful for. But the opposite side of the coin is stifling respectability, a self-righteous and self-denying puritanism, and an aggressive self-congratulatory materialism and philistinism. Against the realities of work and muck and brass, all intellectual or artistic activity is traditionally scorned as effeminate and wasteful. For a child to use an unfamiliar word in the playground is to risk being mocked for having 'swallowed a dictionary'.

Yet the familiar words were a rich inheritance. The West Riding dialect has remained Hughes' staple poetic speech, concrete, emphatic, terse, yet powerfully, economically, eloquent. It is a speech in which a spade is called a spade; facts are looked in the face, especially the unpleasant facts; and a saving humour is never far from reach to ward off all self-indulgence, evasion or pretentiousness. The regional anthem of the West Riding is a comic song in dialect about a man who catches his death of cold on Ilkley Moor, is buried, eaten by worms, which are eaten by ducks, which are eaten by his mates. The song ends with the grisly pun:

That's wheer we gets us oan back.

When Hughes was seven, the family moved to Mexborough, in South Yorkshire, where his parents kept a newsagent's and tobacconist's shop until they returned to the Calder Valley in 1952. In Mexborough, like Lawrence before him in a similar area, Hughes was obliged to lead a double life, one with the town boys, sons of miners and railwaymen, the other in his bolt-hole—a nearby farm or a private estate with woods and a lake.

At fifteen he was writing poems, in galloping Kiplingesque rhythms, most of them about Zulus or the Wild West. One of his heroes, Carson McReared the terrible killer, the man with a hide like an armadillo, was 'shot to hell' in the Grand Canyon after shooting 1,200 men,

And knee deep in blood, where he had to paddle
Stood Diamond Ace, with an empty saddle.

A succession of perceptive English teachers at Mexborough Grammar School (culminating in John Fisher, who was able to do a great deal for him) fostered his interest in poetry. Before he left school, he had matured to the point where he could write these lovely lines:

O lady, consider when I shall have lost you
The moon's full hands, scattering waste,
The sea's hands, dark from the world's breast,
The world's decay where the wind's hands have
    passed,
And my head, worn out with love, at rest
In my hands, and my hands full of dust,
    O my lady.

('Song')

In 1948 Hughes won an Open Exhibition to Cambridge, but before taking it up he did two years of National Service as a ground wireless mechanic in the RAF on an isolated three-man radio station in east Yorkshire where he had 'nothing to do but read and reread Shakespeare and watch the grass grow'.

Hughes went up to Pembroke College, Cambridge, in 1951. His supervisor was M. J. C. Hodgart (an expert, of course, on the ballads) whom he found very sympathetic. He rarely attended lectures, though he occasionally went to hear F. R. Leavis whom he found fascinating and highly entertaining. But the intellectual ethos of Cambridge and of the English tripos in particular he found sterilizing, and wrote no more poetry. Hughes was probably speaking for himself in 'Dully Gumption's Addendum':

The colleges stooped over him and night after night
    thereafter
He dreamed the morphine of his Anglicising:
Dreamed his tongue uprooted, dreamed his body
    drawn and quartered
High over England and saw Thames go crawling
    from the fragments—
And fell, and lay his own gravestone, which went on
    all night
Carving itself in lordly and imperturbable English.
So he woke numbed.

W. S. Merwin has recorded a remarkable story:

At Cambridge he set out to study English Literature. Hated it. Groaned having to write those essays. Felt he was dying of it in some essential place. Sweated late at night over the paper on Dr. Johnson et al.— things he didn't want to read. One night, very late, very tired, he went to sleep. Saw the door open and someone like himself come in with a fox's head. The visitor went over to his desk, where an unfinished essay was lying, and put his paw on the papers, leaving a bloody mark; then he came over to the bed, looked down at Ted and said, 'You're killing us,' and went out the door. (Paul Carroll, *The Poem in Its Skin*, 1968, 149–50)

In his third year Hughes changed from English to Archaeology and Anthropology. His grounding in these disciplines has proved of immense and growing value in his creative work. His imagination is at home in the world of myth and folklore. Cambridge also gave him time to read a great deal.

Hughes graduated in June 1954, the same month in which his first poem appeared in a Cambridge periodical, 'The Little Boys and the Seasons' in *Granta* under the pseudonym Daniel Hearing. It is a pleasing poem, but too much under the influence of Dylan Thomas for the true Hughes to show through. During the next two years Hughes worked briefly as a rose-gardener, night-watchman in a steel works, zoo attendant, schoolteacher, and reader for J. Arthur Rank. Most of the time he lived in London or Cambridge, kept up his friendships there, and published a handful of poems in the Cambridge poetry magazines. In the early and middle fifties Cambridge was rich in budding poets, but the two Hughes poems published in the November 1954 number of *Chequer*, 'The Jaguar' and 'The Casualty', attracted an unusual amount of attention. The jaguar,

hurrying enraged
Through prison darkness after the drills of his eyes

was the first of Hughes' beast to be captured in all its vivid otherness in a poem. The last two stanzas were originally quite different from the version in *The Hawk in the Rain*. At the end it is the crowd of spectators who stare out through bars at the greater reality,

But what holds them from corner to corner swinging,
Swivelling the ball of his heel on the polished spot,
Jerking his head up in surprise at the bars
Has not hesitated in the millions of years,
And like life-prisoners they through bars stare out.

The central impulse of 'The Casualty' is also to lay open the reader to a wider, deeper reality than he is normally aware of. The witnesses

. . . stand, helpless as ghosts: in a scene
Melting in the August noon, the burned man
Bulks closer greater flesh and blood than their own

Early in 1956 Hughes and some of his friends decided to launch a poetry magazine of their own, the *St Botolph's Review*. The first and only issue contained four poems by Ted Hughes, 'Fallgrief's Girl-friends', 'Law in the Country of Cats', 'Soliloquy of a Misanthrope' and 'Secretary'. The Misanthrope looks forward to death when he will see 'every attitude showing its bone'. But he will 'thank God thrice heartily'

To be lying beside women who grimace
Under the commitments of their flesh,
And not out of spite or vanity.

Fallgrief is this same Misanthrope who, seeking to

stand naked
Awake in the pitch dark where the animal runs,

determines to choose 'a muck of a woman' to match 'this muck of man in this Muck of existence', but finds, by chance, 'a woman with such wit and looks He can brag of her in every company'.

At the party held to inaugurate the *St Botolph's Review*, on 25 February 1956, Hughes met Sylvia Plath and within four months he had married her.

Sylvia Plath was a Bostonian, two years younger than Hughes, at Newnham on a Fulbright. She had had an illustrious academic career, both at school and college. Her first published work appeared in 1950 in *Seventeen* and the *Christian Science Monitor*. In 1953 some of her poems were accepted by *Mademoiselle* and by *Harper's*. But between acceptance and publication had come her '6 month crash'—breakdown, attempted suicide, hospitalization—the experience she later recorded in her novel *The Bell Jar*. By 1956, however, her recovery seemed complete. She married Hughes not only because of their mutual attraction and shared commitment to poetry, but also because 'he was very simply the only man I've ever met whom I could never boss . . .' He seemed like a faun to her, able to call owls to him, able to teach her 'the vocabulary of woods and animals and earth'; she felt like 'adam's woman'. (*Letters Home*, 1975, 234–8) In May Sylvia wrote to her mother:

Ted has written many virile, deep banging poems . . . We love the flesh of the earth and the spirit of that thin, exacting air which blows beyond the farthest planets. All is learning, discovering, and speaking in a strong voice out of the heart of sorrow and joy.

(*Letters Home*, 248)

His was the stronger, surer poetic voice, and the immediate effect was of ventriloquism. Her 'Spinster', one of the first poems she wrote after their meeting, is a variation of his 'Secretary' and echoes the vocabulary of 'Fallgrief's Girl-friends':

But here—a burgeoning
Unruly enough to pitch her five queenly wits
Into vulgar motley—
A treason not to be borne. Let idiots
Reel giddy in bedlam spring:
She withdrew neatly.

And other poem of that period, 'Strumpet Song', ends with a passage of pure Hughes, the wrenched syntax, the savage consonants, the pounding monosyllables:

Walks there not some such one man
As can spare breath
To patch with brand of love this rank grimace
Which out from black tarn, ditch and cup
Into my most chaste own eyes
Looks up.

Hughes introduced her to the work of John Crowe Ransome, whom he and his friends admired unreservedly at that time, and for a while she adopted a few of his mannerisms. But Sylvia was, on the whole, resistant to influences, and the most important effect Hughes had on her was to increase her concentration on poetry and to supply her with a fully worked out belief in the poetic mythology of Robert Graves' *The White Goddess*.

Sylvia was able to act as a guide to American poetry for Hughes, and he could hardly have had a better one. Apart from Ransome he knew little of it at that time. Also she helped him to get his poems published, sending out beautifully typed manuscripts in a very efficient American way.

That summer of 1956, much of it spent in the Spanish fishing village of Benidorm, they began their remarkable creative partnership. Each had poems accepted by the *Nation*, *Poetry* and the *Atlantic*. Her scholarship was extended for a further year. They took a flat neighbouring Grantchester Meadows. He taught English and drama at a nearby secondary school. They would get up at five in the morning to do their own writing. By the time she graduated and they left for the United States in the spring of 1957, *The Hawk in the Rain* was finished.—KEITH SAGAR, "Beginnings," *The Art of Ted Hughes*, 1975, pp. 6–11

Works

Mr Ted Hughes is clearly a remarkable poet, and seems to be quite outside the currents of his time. His distinguishing power is sensuous, verbal and imaginative; at his best the three are fused together. His images have an admirable violence. Parrots 'shriek as if they were on fire'. The poet, drowning 'in the drumming ploughland', drags

Heel after heel from the swallowing of the earth's
mouth.

'The Jaguar' is a better poem than Rilke's much admired 'Panther'. The images are so vivid that a symbolic meaning springs from them whether it was intended to be there or not. Out of hawks and jaguars in their cages and macaws and winds Mr Hughes creates a world. The war poems at the end are very fine but the more sophisticated pieces are not nearly so good. A most surprising first book, and it leaves no doubt about Mr Hughes's powers.—EDWIN MUIR, *NS*, Sept. 28, 1957, p. 392

One sees the reason for the selectors of the Poetry Book Society and of the New York Poetry Center First Publication Award choosing *The Hawk in the Rain*, and it is not (one hastens to add) that Mr Auden is common to both panels. Violence and vigour of language—of which the book has plenty—are immediately attractive qualities, and many a poetic reputation has been founded on them and little else. Mr Hughes is a young English poet whose name has been whispered for some time by the knowing, but who by sagely publishing mainly in American periodicals now bursts with sudden effect on this side of the Atlantic.

He has, too, taken American poets as his models. The oblique, unexpected approach to his subjects, the poetically logical but rather underground movement of his poems, reveal him with more kinship to poets like Lowell and Wilbur than to his English contemporaries. The few poems of his I saw in periodicals did not favourably impress me. The energy of the diction seemed not quite to correspond to the energy of the poetic impulse: it is fatally easy, once the trick has been discovered, to use verbs like smash, crash, bang and hurl. And despite its knotted surface, one detected a certain sentimentality of feeling in the verse. These objections are less important when Mr Hughes is read in bulk. There are some very bad patches here: a refrain 'O my lady'; a last line 'Hearing the horizons endure'; similes like 'The house/Rang like some fine green goblet' (why green? why, indeed, fine?). But such things seem ill-judged rather than pretentious—the ill-judgment of a young poet who is preserving too many poems to make a first book. And one's interest is aroused and sustained even when a poem fails of its intended effect because it is almost always founded on the senses' response, particularly to seasons and weather:

> October is marigold, and yet
> A glass half full of wine left out
>
> To the dark heaven all night, by dawn
> Has dreamed a premonition
>
> Of ice across its eye as if
> The ice-age had begun its heave.

'Marigold' and 'heave' are not quite the words, nor 'dark heaven' the phrase, and a glass of water would have served, but one gets very well what Mr Hughes is conveying. And his best poems have a true originality of conception, and a density of execution which represents a real exploration of the complexities of the subjects.—ROY FULLER, *Lon*, Jan. 1958, pp. 61–62

In Ted Hughes's *The Hawk in the Rain*, winner of the YM-YWHA First Publication Award, the reader is kept at several removes from reality by layers of turbid metaphor. Here are two stanzas from a poem which compares choice to a midwife:

> Before choice's fairness
> Humanized both, barbarously you might
> Have made beast-death of the one a sacrifice
> To the god-head of the other, and buried its right
> Before it opened eyes to be emulous.
>
> But now that your twins wail, are wide-eyed—
> (Tugging between them some frivolous heirloom)
> You must cold murder the one and force-feed
> With your remorse the other and protect him from
> The vengeful voluble ghost of the twin dead.

Or, you should have made up your mind sooner.

Insight occurs in flashes. Of an old photograph, Ted Hughes writes, "Though their cocked hats are not now fashionable,/ Their shoes shine." He has a lover say, "When I walk about in my blood and the air/ Beside her". But his generalizations, such as "Love's a spoiled appetite for some delicacy", often appear more interesting than they are. Their wit and not their truth has enchanted the poet. Or so it seems when he illustrates and develops them, for in so doing he repeatedly distorts experience to make it fit. In "Incompatibilities" he explores the idea that desire, being of the spirit, separates persons as it draws them bodily together:

> their limbs flail
> Flesh and beat upon
> The inane everywhere of its obstacle,
>
> Each, each second, lonelier and further
> Falling alone through the endless
> Without-world of the other, though both here
> Twist so close they choke their cries.

This is, by the way, far from being the most over-written passage in the book.

Though such faults seem to be committed partly in order to provide excitement at the verbal level, there are other faults just at that level which take the excitement away. In this passage, for instance,

> The huge-eyed looming horde from
> Under the floor of the heart, that run
> To the madman's eye-corner came
> Deafening towards light, whereon,

the succession of last-foot caesuras has a deadening effect which the rhyme-word assonance only increases.

Though it offers us flashes of perception and sometimes elegance of structure, *The Hawk in the Rain* does not give us an important or, to the extent there is a difference, a finished poem.—GALWAY KINNELL, *Poetry*, June 1958, pp. 179–81

The new book (*Wodwo*) by Ted Hughes is terrifying, marvelous, macabre, and to me at least, not altogether comprehensible. This is not a charge of obscurity in the normal sense; indeed, it may reflect only upon my limitations as a reader. Mr. Hughes is largely concerned with Lawrencian darknesses and other kinds of darkness, and it is possibly a part of his strategy that everything should not be luminously clear. The book is composed of three parts: a section of poems, five short stories and a radio play, and a final section of poems. And the author has said that "the stories and the play may be read as notes, appendix and unversified episodes of the events behind the poems, or as chapters of a single adventure to which the poems are commentary and amplification. Either way, the verse and the prose are intended to be read together, as part of a single work." This may remind some readers of the technique of Robert Lowell's *Life Studies*, but reading through Hughes's book, I was reminded rather of a commentary I read somewhere on the Circe episode in Homer, suggesting that this was a disguised and sophisticated revelation of the rituals of certain Mystery Cults in which the initiate was made dramatically and terribly to confront his deepest animal nature. Something of this sort, elemental, harsh and ruthless, but not really bitter, is present, for example in the radio play, which is also strangely dream-like and almost surrealistic. It is set in the First World War, and two soldiers, Sergeant Massey and Ripley, seemingly the only survivors of a company wiped out by shelling, make a long and difficult journey on a secret mission through dangers and a landscape full of ghosts and corpses to a castle occupied by a Queen and her female retinue. The castle is filled with animal noises; the soldiers are invited to a banquet followed by a dance. Both of these events are part of a process of seduction to bestiality, disintegration and death; the sergeant succombs, Ripley resists, and at the every end somehow makes his way back to his own trenches, feeble and badly wounded, and we are allowed to suppose that the whole episode may have been the fevered fantasy of a wounded and dying man who makes a great last effort to pull himself back to life and safety. This, of course, is a crude and inadequate account. From the first, Hughes has been preoccupied essentially with human strength and weakness due to man's being both part of nature and apart from it by dint of his special human consciousness. This is a familiar theme of the nineteenth-century romantics, but Hughes adopts it to special and terrifying purposes of his own. His is largely a poetry of extreme situations or attitudes or pressures. His deservedly famous animal poems, for instance, are really emblematic of human postures and behavior. And the drama of his poems, indeed, of this whole book, consists in the frightening and insoluble paradox that man at his peril, possibly sometimes at the cost of his life, denies his animal nature, but at the same time that very nature, when it gets out of hand, makes him bestial and hateful and can also kill him. By the same token, man's consciousness, while useful, is also dangerous, and when divorced from his deepest nature is feeble and useless. There is a touching moment in the play when Ripley, full of energy and purpose, is told that he's been shot through the head. It is not the fact of this, but the knowledge or consciousness of it that immediately seems to paralyze him. At the banquet scene, the sergeant eats meat, which is somehow identified with the flesh of his dead comrades and the enemy he has killed. Ripley, on the other hand refuses, announcing that he is a vegetarian. It is true that he survives while the sergeant does not. But earlier in the book this wonderful poem appears, hinting, as it seems to me, at the other side of the picture.

A VEGETARIAN

Fearful of the hare with the manners of a lady,
Of the sow's loaded side and the boar's brown fang,

Fearful of the bull's tongue snaring and rending,
And of the sheep's jaw moving without mercy,

Tripped on Eternity's stone threshold.
Staring into the emptiness,
Unable to move, he hears the hounds of the grass.

There is more variety to this book than I have indicated here, but this seemed a convenient way to get at some central themes and preoccupations of Hughes's work. The poems are all wonderfully vigorous, and often quietly terrifying. They are not all easily accessible, but they are worth careful reading, and they reveal a tough, intricate and sensitive mind.—ANTHONY HECHT, *HdR*, Spring 1968, pp. 212–13

Wodwo, by Ted Hughes, is a mixed book, not only because it contains poems, a play, and five short stories, but because the quality, or rather the authenticity, of the writing fluctuates considerably. Hughes is a slick writer, in the sense that Stephen Spender was the slick writer of the Thirties. He can take the skills of modern verse, including the artifice of personal style, and do anything he likes with them. Thus in the poem called "The Green Wolf," for instance, he gives a new verbal surface, very sophisticated, to the ideas of our being devoured by summer's green rapacity—as hackneyed an idea as we have in English poetry. At first this sophisticated veneer is attractive, but after reading the poem two or three times I begin to feel that precisely this sophistication makes the poem a literary exercise, not a genuine experience; the poet, cool and ambitious, has set out to restore a hackneyed idea from desuetude, and I end by thinking the best pieces in the book are two short stories, "The Rain Horse" and "The Suitor." Yet I hesitate; in the case of Hughes I recognize that my taste may be too contrary at present, or too jaded, to respond to him. Certainly some of these poems are not as badly overwritten as others, certainly some are the best we have had from England recently: poems like "Pibroch" and "You Drive in a Circle." *Wodwo* is a book that most readers will wish to judge for themselves.—HAYDEN CARRUTH, *Poetry*, Sept. 1968, pp. 422–23

⟨Ted Hughes⟩ is the perfect English literary type, a man of immense literary sensitivity who can perceive the least nuance of literary fashion and put it to his own use. He can do this with every appearance of originality, since that is part of fashion. Yet I have always felt that his past work, except for two or three short stories, was original in appearance only, and that it was essentially a fabric of invention done to create that appearance. He is the journeyman *par excellence* of the English literary guild, with its emphasis on gamesmanship, cultism, and the

morality of leisure. His new book, *Crow*, was conceived as a joint project with the American artist Leonard Baskin, who strikes me as Hughes' perfect counterpart. Here we have, however, only part of the text and none of the drawings of the planned work. Crow is a mythological bird, done in the existential and expressionist traditions, to stand for the trials, courage, and humor of modern man. This is an extremely attractive idea to me; it goes near the heart of every tough and useful attitude in interpreting the experience of my lifetime. It is fable-making in a relevant modern form, and one can ask no more of any literature.

CROW'S SONG OF HIMSELF

When God hammered Crow
He made gold
When God roasted Crow in the sun
He made diamond
When God crushed Crow under weights
He made alcohol
When God tore Crow to pieces
He made money
When God blew Crow up
He made day
When God hung Crow on a tree
He made fruit
When God buried Crow in the earth
He made man
When God tried to chop Crow in two
He made woman
When God said, "You win, Crow,"
He made the Redeemer.

When God went off in despair
Crow stropped his beak and started in on the two
thieves.

It is audacious, it is true. But also easy, pat, and glib. The fable lacks the grain of authenticity, which can come in such a work only from a genesis in bedrock imaginative experience. Language is the clue, as always: that formulaic schoolboyish rhetoric, without verbal trust or affection. It is the same with substance. The ugliness, despair, and moral pain of the poetry are not genuine but derivative and predictable. Thirty-five years after *Man's Fate*, twenty-five after *The Plague*, fifteen after *The Tin Drum*, we have *Crow*, and it is a long descent. Existential agony has become as slick as Winnie-the-Pooh. We see from the jacket notes, in fact, that Hughes has written a number of children's books and that presumably this is how he makes his living. *Crow* has the qualities of children's literature, the same condescension not only toward the reader but, what is worse, toward the substance, toward the work itself; which is why the few good books for children were written for adults first. All at once I see what is wrong with most English writing I have read in the past fifteen years, and with much from before as well, large chunks of Auden and Spender, C. S. Lewis, Tolkien, Durrell—who knows where to stop?—Chesterton, Beerbohm, Peacock. They were all writing children's books for adults.—HAYDEN CARRUTH, *HdR*, Summer 1971, pp. 327–29

God knows I must be a weak little helpless person, but I can't take all this suffering any more. Every time I open Ted Hughes's latest book, there is something about testicles, bone-tissue or vomit. It's like watching *General Hospital*. And quite frankly what adds to my guilt about this cowardice is the fact that Hughes is only doing it for my *benefit*. He's not doing it for fame or for the money—his royalties are probably going to some important Wildlife Fund—he's only doing it to *help* us. There he is, hunched over his electric typewriter, the hair falling across his burning eyes, muttering all those Anglo-

Saxon rhythms in his rugged regional accent: he has taken all the suffering of the world upon his shoulders and offering it us, and for only £4.50! This is what life is all about! It's magnificent! He must be the greatest poet of his age!

At least that is what the newspaper-reviewers have been saying for some years now, ever since I was a boy and Ted Hughes was telling us the real truth about pigs, crows, elephants and jaguars. The reviewers liked him so much that even the academics felt they were missing something: he was put on the syllabus. But nothing could have prepared them for all the marvellous new anguish which Hughes has discovered; suddenly, with *Gaudete*, we are in man's country again where the true violence is. We began with *Fantasia*, and now we've got *The Exorcist*. Here at last it all hangs out, all the 'buckets of fresh blood', 'organs of horrific energy' and 'uncontrollable eyes'. Michael Winner would love this book.

Gaudete is really just an old-fashioned hymn in praise of violence. Here we have the famous poet, the unacknowledged legislator of his race, writing about men and women as though they had just stepped out of Pavlov's cages for a quick stroll around the cemetery. On the first page a Reverend Lumb finds himself in a mass-grave, among eye-pits and animal tendons and lizard figures; from pages 23 to 131 his demonic double assaults a number of parishioners in a number of ways; on page 35, Major Hagen clubs his pet labrador to death; on page 45 a young girl hangs herself; and on page 132 there is an orgiastic ritual, Hollywood style, in the basement of the local church where the ladies seem actually to be imitating Hughes's earlier poems by putting on animal masks. At last Hughes has learnt the lesson: suffering and pain are always boring, unless they can be made shocking.

In fact I think Ted Hughes simply wants to entertain us with some ordinary sex and violence, and it's rather unfair of his publishers to break the book up into a number of incomplete lines and describe it as 'a strange and powerful new poem'. Poetry it isn't:

> Lumb's face
> Contorts, transforming
> To a grotesque of swollen flesh
> A glistening friar-fat
> Gargoyle of screaming or laughter

Something has obviously gone wrong. Hughes was able to drag all those dumb animals into his act because they couldn't fight back. But it is one thing to treat animals as though they had human characteristics, it's quite another to treat human beings as if they were animals and reducing them, like a butcher, to lumps of tissue, bone, blood and sex. When a writer is possessed by images of gratuitous violence and sexual mayhem, he is forced to reduce both his language and his theme to lumpish vehicles of his obsessions. For all the reviewers' talk about 'apocalypse' and the 'human condition', it's really as if Ted Hughes had just rifled through a bestiary to pick up his characters. When a man talks about love, and ends up writing pornography, it has to be assumed that his writing has failed him. And here it has: there isn't a good line in the book.

In fact, the writing is so consistently heavy-handed, so trite and so clumsy that it has taken Hughes's rather elderly admirers a real effort of will to admire it. But they have managed the trick in the past: heavy writing can always be mistaken for serious writing, just as rhetoric can generally pass for poetry in a poor light. But surely not this time:

> Warms his calming hands
> Beneath her amply stylish coat.
> Her nerve-harrowed face
> Crisping towards a coarse harvest handsomeness
> Rests on his shoulder

It all sounds as if it had been lifted from a handbook for poets, a thesaurus of phrases only to be used in a real emergency. I was trying to remember when I last came across verse of this kind, and then it came to me: William McGonagall! Our taste in suffering may have changed—Hughes was called a 'survivor-poet' and the post of apocalypse, whereas Mr McGonagall specialised in train crashes or a large scale—but the clumsy rhetoric is much the same. *Gaudete* is a modern, and much longer, 'Tay-Bridge Disaster'. The prose is tired and hectoring, the verses are flaccid, and the lines so loosely arranged that they flop on top of each other. I do hope schoolmasters and provincial lecturers wake up to all this before our young people get the notion that suffering is somehow 'important', and that the worship of pain is the only true worship. Bad poetry can be corrosive, at least for a while.—PETER ACKROYD, "Agonising," *Spec*, June 11, 1977, p. 23

Rosetta, the tough and beautiful New York Jewess in *The Age of Anxiety*, solaces herself by imagining one of those landscapes 'familiar to readers of English detective stories', and peopling it with retired colonels, eccentric doctors, 'solitary women in country parishes', whose disquieting gifts beckon their chosen out from bars 'within a stone's throw of the sunlit water'. Rosetta's fantasies echo those potent and lighthearted ones of Auden's early poems.

But fantasy, in our time, takes itself more seriously, less hopefully. As a long and original narrative poem, *Gaudete* has something in common with *The Age of Anxiety*, something with *Under Milk Wood*; but Ted Hughes works with the astonishing verbal thrust and precision he has developed to make words 'more merciless and explicit than even the most daring fantasy'.

That phrase is used to describe the sight that confronts a young architect returning to his house 'up the fondly-designed cedar staircase', and finding his wife naked on a couch under the rector. It is by no means the only such confrontation in the poem; but it constitutes five of the most memorable and gripping pages in a compulsive sequence which one is unable to take one's eye off. Most uncommon for poetry; but this poem began as a film scenario, and Hughes shows the same powers that make Conrad, for instance, one of the most cinematic artists of detail—the scene is as taut, and perhaps as indulgent, too, as the stabbing of Mr Verloc in *The Secret Agent*. It also makes a psychological point: that a husband who is bored with the look of his wife's body sees it as wholly new and infinitely desirable when it is under someone else's.

The story is of the Polanski type now modish in all sorts of media. An Anglican clergyman is abducted by spirits, who create a duplicate in his place. The ministry of the new priest is one of love, and consists in copulating with all the women of his parish. Husbands eventually unite, and surprise him among his brides at a WI meeting where a wild orgy is in progress; and though he manages to escape, they eventually hunt him down and kill him. He and the casualties among his female followers are consumed in a funeral pyre—'the evidence has gone up'—and there is a finale of the poems his alter ego—or perhaps there was only one parson after all?—has written in the place to which he was spirited away. From these, it appears that he is not so good a poet as Hughes.

Equipped with the real Hughes's high magnification binoculars and hair-trigger style, we become fascinated voyeurs, focusing on repeated seductions, peering into interiors, prowling through clearings in woods past cows and couples, spring trees, moorhens, camps of nettles . . . Hughes has always been able to convey marvellously an awful, absorbed joylessness in nature, the hawk in the rain, the frenetic cuckoo, and the demented swift with its 'arrow-thwack into the eaves' (the swift poem was one of his best), the stare of the lizard, 'impotently severe'. A new wife, likewise, 'is disclosing her vowels, under a wide pink brim'; another 'puffs smoke, relaxes tensely'; a major's anger is 'like a frenzy of obsolete guns'. Absently searching for his car-keys, a man watches 'the mobs of young starlings struggling and squealing filthily in the clotted may-blossom, like giant blow-flies'.

The characters are speechless puppets, fuelled with insect lust, buzzing about, or sitting motionless, under their author's control. Hughes's has always been a reductive talent: here, he dispenses completely with humanity and the intellect, the memories and cultivations and constructions of the self. A. Alvarez has written that he is one of 'the select band of survivors-poets whose work is adequate to the destructive reality we inhabit'. Perhaps a poet gets the critic he deserves, but one hopes that such fashionable nonsense (what historical reality, with its diseases and wars and deaths in childbed, was not destructive?) is not believed by Hughes himself.

The facts, in any case, seem to me to point in exactly the opposite direction. This is poetry suited to a tepid, coddled, welfare society, dreaming of violence in front of the television screen, which is projecting its immaculate coloured detail, blood or sunburn, wildlife or underwater, superbly shot by telephoto lens.

May not the absence of humanity or intellect be the point—the goal and apogee of television art? Unfortunately, the poem has pretensions to both, in the same way that it is obligatory for any new film script today to suggest them. Meanings are hinted at: deep significances of religion and myth. They are, of course, brushed aside by a language that can conjure plain or exotic action so effortlessly, and which has at moments the genuine physical dimension of epic, and of what the ancient Greeks called 'smash and bash' poetry—the javelin entering Sarpedon, the arm torn from Grendel.

But epic narration is not perpetually frenetic—its calm is genuine and not 'relaxing tensely'—and its style continually returns to simplicity and obviousness, shaping the real matter of art and attaching it to a deep image of the human. As well as achieving, it seems to suffer and endure. Here, though, is a different sort of narrative, and Ted Hughes has never shown more virtuosity than in this remarkable poem, its operation the aim and target of the Major's Mannlicher .318.

> The crossed hairs have settled on Lumb's crown,
> And now the trigger
> Caresses in oil, and the kiss of sweetness jolts softly
>   through Hagen's bones.

A perfection of technical performance—poem, rifle—is identified with the closed circuit of sexual fantasy. It is curious, too, that the *Doppelgänger* theme here resembles that of Thom Gunn in *Jack Straw's Castle*, as if in both cases the poet and his medium were, in fact, obsessed with the completeness of their own identity. The myth also passes into the fact of a television image, which has no choice but to give the same maximum technical perfection: when the marvel is turned off the picture shrinks to a point and vanishes—all evidence gone up.—JOHN BAYLEY, "Smash and Bash," *LT*, June 2, 1977, p. 726

For those who sat through the *cinéma noir* of Ted Hughes's long poem, *Gaudete* (1977), his new collection, *Moortown*, will come as a welcome relief. Once again Hughes has returned to the source of his strength as a poet, the English countryside. The only problem is that he does not stay there long enough but soon wanders off into one or another mythic landscape where the resulting poems quickly become repetitive and facile. Yet the weak sections of *Moortown* do not distract from the book's better poems because the volume is actually a collection of four distinct sections, written (as far as I can tell from Harper & Row's scanty copyright information) over a period of about ten years. Of these sections the strongest is most certainly the title sequence which stands as one of the best things Hughes has ever written. I have always resisted the violent, sanguinary side of Hughes's imagination. In a way more typical of filmmakers like Peckinpah or De Palma than of a poet, Hughes uses sex and violence excessively in his work as a way to shock his readers into attention. The title sequence, "Moortown," is no exception to this rule. It contains enough blood, shit, piss, copulation, and afterbirth to satisfy the most scatalogically-minded twelve-year-old. And yet it is impossible to deny the cumulative power of the poems. Sex and violence are authentic parts of life, and these are the parts of experience that have exerted a lasting fascination on Hughes.

"Moortown" is a series of poems about a beef and sheep farm in Devon that Hughes worked with his late father-in-law, Jack Orchard. The poems chronicle a year of events on the farm against the changing backdrop of Devon. Hughes has always been drawn to writing about the nonhuman world, and so it is not surprising that the sheep, cows, and bulls dominate the poet's attention in this sequence. Hughes involves the reader so closely in a series of dramas involving animal births, deaths, diseases, and recoveries that towards the end, when he suddenly modulates into the human drama of his father-in-law's death, the effect is overwhelmingly tragic. The documentary, descriptive nature of the poem brings out a direct, unmediated pathos that shows the gentler side of Hughes's talent:

> And that is where I remember you,
> Skull-raked with thorns, sodden, tireless,
> Hauling bedded feet free, floundering away
> To check alignments, returning, hammering the
>   staple
> Into the soaked stake oak, a careful tattoo
> Precise to the tenth of an inch,
> Under December downpour, midafternoon
> Dark as twilight, using your life up.

Unfortunately the other three sections of *Moortown* do not measure up to the achievement of the first sequence. "Prometheus on his Crag," the second section, is Hughes at his worst—strident, abstract, and portentous. This sequence is full of passages like:

> A word
> A bitten-out gobbet of sun
> Buried behind the navel, unutterable.
> The vital, immortal wound.
> One nuclear syllable, bleeding silence.

The third section, "Earth Numb," is a miscellany of Hughes's recent work and includes some fine individual pieces like "Bride and Groom Lie Hidden for Three Days" and "Motorbike," but the bulk of it is mannered and strained. The last sequence, "Adam and the Sacred Nine," returns to the mythic manner of "Prometheus of His Crag" with only slightly better results. Perhaps I am deaf to the subtleties of such work, but to me it all sounds too "literary" in the worst sense of the word.—DANA GIOIA, *HdR*, Winter 1980, pp. 613–14

DERWENT MAY
From "Ted Hughes"
The Survival of Poetry, ed. Martin Dodsworth
1970, pp. 133–48

The most confident English poetry of the late 1950s was about a lack of confidence. In fact much of it set out, with considerable skill, precisely to undermine confidence: unsettling the reader and leaving him with the uncertainties that the poet had experienced. Something of this purpose runs almost everywhere, for example, in the poetry of D. J. Enright at that time. Enright constantly tempts the reader into assent to some high-minded denunciation or renunciation; then deftly brings up an aspect of the matter that has been overlooked, leaving the reader gently exposed as having reacted in a silly and superficial—and, above all, an over-confident—way. (Kingsley Amis, another characteristic poet of the period, uses the same device in the opening of his novel *One Fat Englishman*, where he lures the reader into sympathy with the witty anti-Americanism of his hero, before going on to show up the vulgarity and pettiness of that attitude.) The exposures are made in the name of humanity, tolerance, commonsense—all of which virtues they do admirably foster. But there is also in these writers an unmistakable sense of powerlessness when faced with the more intense feelings and desires of men. It is a powerlessness they hardly acknowledge themselves, however, since another strong suggestion present in their teaching is that intense feelings and desires must—and generally can—be indiscriminately given up and healthily forgotten. Here is a major difference between, say, Enright and Amis on the one hand, and Philip Larkin on the other. Larkin's poetry is often equally concerned with doubt, or at any rate with the moment of faltering confidence. But Larkin is not interested in teaching the desirability of strict self-criticism and control. His poetry of doubt is an openly poignant affair, a full rendering of situations in which the protagonist's history of inner conflicts and failures has left him grievously bewildered or resigned. These poems, while often portraying a state of 'powerlessness', nonetheless offer the compensating strength of a full and steady imaginative understanding of that state and all the feeling it entails, both for the protagonist and for the observer in the form of the reader.

Larkin stands out, in this way, as the most considerable poet of the time. But it can be judged how, even in its distinctive superiority, his poetry seemed to partake of the period's prevailingly sceptical character. It is against that background that the appearance of Ted Hughes's first book, *The Hawk in the Rain*, has to be seen. The book came out in 1957. At once it was evident that there was a gifted new poet on the scene who was prepared to make strong, confident assertions about the importance of strong—even confused or blind—feeling. And not only assertions; for the poems were often simply like assaults, designed to provoke the reader into vigorous—and in this poet's view, it seemed, perfectly healthy—responses of scarcely rational dismay or anger. *Lupercal* was the title of Hughes's second book, but what it suggests about the character of that volume could equally well be applied to *The Hawk in the Rain*: Lupercalia was a Roman festival at which the priests struck women to make them fertile.

One of the most tactically assured of these assaults is the poem in *The Hawk in the Rain*, 'October Dawn'.

> October is marigold, and yet
> A glass half full of wine left out
> To the dark heaven all night, by dawn
> Has dreamed a premonition

Of ice across its eye as if
The ice-age had begun its heave

'Marigold'—the adjective is brilliantly judged to conjure up the richly beautiful and benign character of the late autumn, pervasive inasmuch as one colour can stand for that whole character, yet as delicate and as unchallenging to human mastery as the single flower that the word could also stand for. And the second line of the same couplet, letting drop its defining references to the glass in the course of its steady progress towards the verb, throws out casually yet with perfect sureness a perspective in which human figures, intimate but unnamed, enjoy warmth, languor, carelessness, abundance. The 'dark heaven' of the next line is the bridge to the threatening evocation that the poem is, by contrast, going to be mainly concerned with. The dark heaven might, in the glow from the marigold, also be benign. But this suggestion is dispelled almost as soon as raised: in fact the darkness prefigures the assault to come. The ice is in fact the 'spearhead' of the returning ice-age.

> The lawn overtrodden and strewn
> From the night before

now suggests a scene not of careless pleasure but of panic-stricken flight. As the couplets spell out the increasing grip of ice on the land their half-rhymes mount a crescendo of creakings and crackings; until finally we read

> a fist of cold
> Squeezes the fire at the core of the heart,
> And now it is about to start.

The rapping full rhyme of the last couplet brings the preliminaries—the prophesying—sharply to an end, and simultaneously announces the beginning—left to the imagination—of a new, more terrible monotony.

These effects are achieved with a masterly instinct. Yet, although the emotions and sensations created in one by the poem are sharp and memorable, to scrutinize them is, after all, to find doubts coming in. On a banal factual level, to begin with, a frosty night in October would certainly be a clear night with stars, not a night with a 'dark heaven': a small point, but, I think, quite proper to notice, for the reflecting mind cannot help noticing it. Then the fantasy itself, powerfully evoked though it is, is on an instant's consideration just a tale to frighten us, without giving us any genuine grounds for fear. The return of the Mammoth and the Sabre-tooth, and *their* party (without wine-glasses)—

> Mammoth and Sabre-tooth celebrate
> Reunion . . . —

begin on reflection to take on a comic, nursery-rhyme aspect. In fact in the end one may begin to enjoy the poem again in a further way: as a witty example of the mock-sinister. But this appreciation continues to accord ill with the genuine feeling found at the beginning of the poem and the unmistakably seriously-intended—if unrewardingly vague—reference to 'the core of the heart' at the end.

Many of the assaults and arguments in *The Hawk in the Rain* are marked by this aggressive exaggeration that it is difficult after the first impact to take seriously, though one respects often in the same poems the justice—as it were, the sound theatrical imagination—with which the effects are managed: the impression the book made on its first appearance is wholly understandable. In 'The Dove Breeder' a full-rhyming four-stressed couplet again concludes the poem, this time with a statement that invites the reader to take up its crisp challenge. The earlier part of the poem describes, in unrhymed lines hovering between two and three stresses, how a hawk struck into a dovecote, and the effect it had on the dove-breeder. It is a sustained metaphor for the way in which love has struck into a man's life. The man's fate is elaborated with mock-sympathy:

> He will win no more prizes
> With fantails or pouters

The metaphor—if by this point it has a strong enough connection with its subject to be called that—seems to allude to the finicky, self-conscious relationships that have characterized the man's life before the catastrophe, and perhaps also to the conceited, coy women he has known. But there is a reversal of fate for the better:

> Now he rides the morning mist
> With a big-eyed hawk on his fist.

The last couplet thrusts the man's final condition cockily, almost insultingly, at the reader. It has a 'Go and do thou likewise *if thou canst!*' note about it. But if one should humbly ask what this evidently far superior condition that is being flaunted before one actually is, one has to put up with the fact that it is very ill-elaborated: it is some strong, steady, confident—but quite imprecisely rendered—emotional state. In the end the picture of the now tamed hawk—big-eyed, as opposed presumably to the small-eyed pigeons—sitting on the fist of the smug ex-breeder starts to take on a rather ludicrous air: who is the fantail or pouter now? In fact, of the poems in *The Hawk in the Rain* that aim to challenge or shock the reader, some which deliberately practise a comic exaggeration are the most wholly successful: like 'Soliloquy of a Misanthrope', which is hostile precisely to complacent smirks, and rejoices in the way that death forces its victims to recognize the undignified necessities of the flesh:

> Whenever I am got under my gravestone
> I shall thank God thrice heartily
> To be lying beside women who grimace
> Under the commitments of their flesh
> And not out of spite or vanity.

Some poems in *The Hawk in the Rain* engage more specifically in assertion and argument concerning the desirability of a certain kind of emotional and moral life. Two that seem to be presented as a pair, one following the other, are 'Egg-Head' and 'The Man Seeking Experience Enquires His Way of a Drop of Water'. They are about two contrasting kinds of self-assertion, that may remind us respectively of the way of life of the dove-breeder before and after the hawk struck. 'Egg-Head' represents, with explicit scorn, a man who establishes his individual existence in the world (his 'I am') by resisting all those experiences that might upset his settled and complacent ways. The poem begins with a list of objects, from the sea-bottom and the mountain peaks to a leaf, that might cause a man to be 'struck dead' at a glance. With a passing word of praise for those who dare to undergo such an experience, it then turns to describing the strategies of the resister, the egg-head—

> circumventing sleights
> Of stupefaction, juggleries of benumbing—

culminating in the need of the man's complacency to

> stop the looming mouth of the earth with a pin-
> Point cipher . . .

> and, opposing his eye's flea-red
> Fly-catching fervency to the whelm of the sun,
> Trumpet his own ear dead.

The second poem is about a man who is supposed to be learning a lesson from a water droplet—a lesson that the man in the previous poem would obviously not listen to. To this

man the water-drop seems to show how it is possible to go through extremes of experience and take full cognition of that experience—at the same time, casting benefits about one—and survive with unimpaired capacity to go on doing the same thing. The droplet has been in the Pacific depths of the Tuscarora and in a cup of tea, in the bodies of the sweating victor and the dead bird, in

> The abattoir of the tiger's artery,
> The slum of the dog's bowel.

It has 'travelled far and studied hard' and

> there is no place
> His bright look has not bettered.

But when the man asks the droplet to 'read us a lesson', an ironic note enters the poem. The man 'knows' his own nature is 'all droplet-kin'. But he has misjudged, at least in one respect. There is no response from the water-drop, which is, rather, like the new-born baby

> who lies long, long and frowningly
> Unconscious under the shock of its own quick.

Here too, then, we find a comic aspect to what might be taken for a wholly solemn poem. The conclusion does not seem to repudiate the man's dreams and ideals: the baby's—and one supposes by implication the droplet's—'I' is described in the last line as 'world-shouldering'. But the poet suggests that the shocks of experience of the kind the man wants do not issue in a reaction that can encompass reason or language. And that the man supposes they do is turned comically, if sympathetically, to his disadvantage. His words are like 'coy baby-talk'; he has a long way still to go.

In a good essay on Ted Hughes in *Essays in Criticism*, C. J. Rawson takes up argument with the poet over the scheme of values that these two poems seem to be advocating, and tries to show its limitations and inconsistencies. But I think that to do this is to put down an opponent of one's own devising. It is neither possible nor relevant to treat the 'arguments' in these poems as forms of sustained rational disquisition. There is neither evidence nor ratiocination offered here; nor, what is more, is there really any appeal *by demonstration* to our feelings. The first of the two poems is just a brilliant—and, taken in this way, also rather funny—display of abuse and verbal bullying from a wholly unargued viewpoint; the second might be described as a sort of awed comedy about fascinating but tantalisingly obscure ideas that the poet does not get down to scrutinising at all seriously in the end. At most we are left with hints at possibilities that we may be inspired to follow up.

More of Ted Hughes's work is marked by an extravagant but sardonic humour than has, I think, been stressed before (though, as we have seen, it sometimes shows lurches into portentousness that suggests he has not always been quite sure where the humour begins and ends). But *The Hawk in the Rain* also has some poems of a different kind that point forward to his finest work so far. (And here it must be said that his own work—particularly his most recent work—largely provides the criteria for the judgements made in this essay, just as, more widely, all literary judgements must finally proceed from a sense of what literature in fact has offered, an experience of the realisable achievements of literature being the only grounds for criticism at all.)

Any poem in some degree establishes simultaneously for the reader the presence of a speaker, and the independent presence of a situation external to the speaker to which he is responding. What characterizes Hughes's most remarkable poetry to date is the large part played in that 'external situation' by objects from nature—mountains, plants, birds—and the intricacy and force of the speaker's response to them. It is in these poems, rather than those more concerned with shock and assertion, that he most successfully conveys his sense of the importance of strong feelings and desires: important in some cases as being rewarding, in others simply as being present in human existence and necessary to recognize and cope with, and perhaps most often, in a tangled way, for both these reasons together.

The art of establishing those simultaneous presences is, all the same, only very intermittently present in Hughes's first two volumes. A good example is the title-poem of the first book. What such a poem calls for is a voice that in speaking of the objects it is concerned with conveys the speaker's reaction to them implicitly. The meaning-associations of the words, and their delivery under the thrust of the conventional rhythm and the supporting or contrary pull of the stresses normal to speech tax: these must offer as a composed whole a sense of the scene and its responsive occupant.

The poem 'The Hawk in the Rain' is the work of a poet prodigal with effects that are in this particular case over-employed: an undercommitted armoury, as it were. At the beginning the speaker energetically describes his own state as he crosses a ploughed field in the rain. But the rhythm crashes down with self-conscious heaviness on the key verbs and nouns, the alliteration echoes thunderously; the hyperboles come thick and fast, the double meanings ('habit', 'dogged grave') come to the surface and hesitate ineffectually there:

I drown in the drumming ploughland, I drag up
Heel after heel from the swallowing of the earth's
        mouth,
From clay that clutches my each step to the ankle
With the habit of the dogged grave.

I think one could extract a title and four lines from this poem that on their own would make a 'composed whole' saying almost as much as the whole poem as it stands is straining to say:

The Hawk

Effortlessly at height hangs his still eye . . .
That maybe in his own time meets the weather
Coming the wrong way, suffers the air, hurled upside
        down,
Fall from his eye, the ponderous shires crash on him.

These lines, though at first sight they might be thought almost pure imaginative description of the hawk's activity and experi-ence, are in fact quite as much concerned with the responding presence of the speaker. In the very act of describing the effortless hovering of the hawk, the stillness of its eye bent to look down on the farmland below, the speaker (and the reader as he 'becomes' the speaker) is gasping both with awe and with effort to mime the hawk hanging in the sky. 'Effortlessly': the first stress of the line demands, precisely, a sudden unexpected effort from one, the more to be sustained as there is not just the expected single unstressed syllable but three more unstressed syllables before the second stressed syllable comes, 'height'. This is followed immediately by a third stressed syllable, 'hangs', so that these last two syllables themselves hang, as it were, at the crest of the line, each with its initial 'h' demanding the lifting of the breath to the roof of the mouth so that both body and spirit are felt to rise with it. And after another unstressed syllable (which nevertheless begins again with the breath-lifting 'h') come two further isolated stressed syllables 'still eye'—a pair, again, that together would not normally both take a stress on them if the formal metre of the line did not, as here, compel it: so once more the effort is forced on the reader of, so to speak, holding the words in the air there, sharing with

the imaginary speaker *his* experience of sharing, with a kind of thrilled joy, the hawk's experience. Later in the poem we read:

                                        I
        strain towards the master-
Fulcrum of violence where the hawk hangs still

But this fact has already been wholly conveyed in the line I have been discussing.

In the other three lines I have extracted from 'The Hawk in the Rain' there is the same remarkable richness both of description and of response to what is described. The effect of the beginning of these does owe something to a contrast with what has gone directly before, so picking out the lines in this way diminishes them slightly. After the lines about the speaker 'straining towards the master-fulcrum of violence where the hawk hangs still' (these last three stressed words again seeming to reiterate the presence of the hawk poised in the air), the tone suddenly modulates into something quieter:

        That maybe in his own time meets the weather

There is a sudden easing of the strain—of the envy and emulation—here. The line lacks urgent stresses; the words are all either tentative or at any rate not bearing their full possible weight of meaning yet. 'In his own time' might suggest an act of choice on the hawk's part, rather than the comparison that is about to be made between the man's present experience and the hawk's in the future; 'meets', in 'meets the weather', again stands ambiguous for a moment—it too might suggest some act of choice, some agreeable encounter. So the sharp beginning of the next line puts the current of feeling in this poem at this moment dramatically in reverse:

        Coming the wrong way

There follows the brilliant impression of the hawk falling: the sky seeming to fall away under it, the ground below seeming to crash down on it. These two lines, far from either lacking strong stresses or placing them on words with no unstressed syllables either side, is filled with stresses and half-stresses whirling one after the other with no consonantal impediment. And just as the reader has lived with speaker and hawk through a sense of aspiring desire and mastery, so now he lives through a sense of terror and disaster.

Here, then, is that 'appeal by demonstration to our feelings' that I described as lacking in 'Egg-Head' and 'The Man Seeking Experience Enquires His Way of a Drop of Water'. It would obviously be quite wrong to suggest that the hawk in this poem, and the stones, animals, other birds and so on in other poems by Hughes, are simply there as vehicles for reflecting human situations in which they ultimately have no place. This poem would not have been possible without the existence of hawks—more specifically, of kestrels: the human sensations and emotions that the poem is about could only have been evoked by observation of the bird itself, and indeed to some extent by sympathetic feeling for it. Yet the poem, opening up as it does a shareable experience of a man living intensely through a certain situation, manages to establish a set of human possibilities for the feelings and the will, and of dangers and failures, that it might be possible to apply more largely, by making our own analogies, in our lives. Other poems in *The Hawk in the Rain* that recreate a response to natural phenomena—envy, in some cases, at unmatchable simplicity or ease, or in other cases fascination and fear at the fierce spectacle—are 'The Jaguar', 'The Horses', 'September', 'A Modest Proposal' and, perhaps best of all, 'Wind', where the constant flicker of humour at his own exaggeration lends, this time, a greater air of authority to the speaker's description of the wind's violence.

Lupercal, Ted Hughes's second book, published in 1960,

probably won greater acclaim than his first. To my mind, though, it does not show any great advance in the poet's powers of development or in his themes. There are forcefully-phrased pieces of thin argument or specious exhortation, dazzling curses and outbursts of hero-worship, but only a few poems in what I think is his most satisfying vein. The more aggressive poems assert points of view already familiar from *The Hawk in the Rain*. 'Strawberry Hill' is a zestful scarer: a symbolic 'stoat with the sun in its belly' who 'danced on the lawns' of Horace Walpole's Gothic castle but also 'bit through grammar and corset' was nailed to a door—

> But its red unmanageable life
> Has licked the stylist out of their skulls,
> Has sucked that age like an egg and gone off

Any number of vague threats are shaken at us in those two lines—all the forces of life and death at once, it seems. However, this poem, with its challenge to the playful macabre of Walpole's, does not lack its own lightness of touch—no stoat has licked the stylist out of Hughes's skull here; and the end of the poem, announcing the re-emergence of the stoat, takes quite an insouciant pleasure in the witty combination of rightness and arbitrariness in the word that provides its final half-rhyme:

> Has sucked that age like an egg and gone off
> Along ditches where flies and leaves
> Overpower our tongues, got into some grave—
> Not a dog to follow it down—
> Emerges, thirsting, in far Asia, in Brixton.

'Fourth of July' mocks contemporary America, where

> the mind's wandering elementals . . .
> Wait dully at the traffic crossing,
> Or lean over headlines, taking nothing in.

'The Good Life' sympathizes sardonically with a hermit who found that in his 'poor-bare' life his spirit was too occupied in patching his boot, and returned to the world again thinking

> Only a plump, cuffed citizen
> Gets enough quiet to hear God speak.

But he was disappointed there, too:

> Loud he prayed then; but late or early
> Never a murmur came to his need
> Save 'I'd be delighted.' and 'Yours sincerely',
> And 'Thank you very much indeed!'

These are impatient dismissals. But the alternatives to such lives that are offered in *Lupercal* are more deeply considered, if only in a handful of poems like—most impressively—'Thrushes' and 'November'. 'Thrushes' begins with a fine description of thrushes feeding on the lawn:

> More coiled steel than living—a poised
> Dark deadly eye, those delicate legs
> Triggered to stirrings beyond sense—with a start, a
>   bounce, a stab
> Overtake the instant and drag out some writhing
>   thing.

In this poem the contrast is made explicitly with men's usual inability to act with such speed, decisiveness and success: the birds display

> No indolent procrastinations and no yawning stares,
> No sighs or head-scratchings

The thought widens out in the second stanza, to compare Mozart's brain-mechanism with that of the thrushes, and to register awe at the similar efficiency of the shark

> That hungers down the blood-smell even to a leak of
>   its own
> Side and devouring of itself.

But on the whole these further reflections after the first stanza weaken the poem. There seems to be a confusion between different concepts of cause when Hughes asks:

> Is it their single-mind-sized-skulls, or a trained
> Body, or genius, or a nestful of brats
> Gives their days this bullet and automatic
> Purpose?

These are not equivalent alternatives. (There are also heavy, rather unsatisfactory Shakespearean echoes here—the 'bullet and automatic' purpose reminds one inescapably of Lady Macbeth's 'self and violent' hand.) And the last stanza again seems rather loosely to lump cerebration, doubt and emotional complexity together as enemies in man of his desire 'to be blent in the prayer'—itself a rather rough parallel to the thrush's and shark's unselfconsciousness.

In 'November', as in the title-poem of Hughes's first book, the speaker is describing an experience when out walking in the rain. This time it is another human being who provides the poet with an intimation of desirable life: a tramp seen sleeping in a ditch. But this is a classic case of a distinction without much difference. What the speaker sees of the tramp's behaviour is about as near to the instinctive life of animals as man can perhaps get. The sodden land, the mist on the thorn-bushes, the renewed fall of the rain's 'dragging grey columns'—these are superbly evoked in the poem. All that the speaker sees the tramp do, though, is described in five lines:

> A wind chilled,
> And a fresh comfort tightened through him,
> Each hand stuffed deeper into the other sleeve.
> His ankles, bound with sacking and hairy band,
> Rubbed each other, resettling

But it means this to the speaker:

> I thought what strong trust
> Slept in him—as the trickling furrows slept,
> And the thorn-roots in their grip on darkness.

The speaker runs on into a wood to get out of the rain, and there sees a gamekeeper's gibbet with owls, hawks, weasels, cats, crows on it. And in a fine conclusion he describes them.

> Some, stiff, weightless, twirled like dry bark bits
> In the drilling rain. Some still had their shape,
> Had their pride with it; hung, chins on chests,
> Patient to outwait these worst days that beat
> Their crowns bare and dripped from their feet.

This time no comparison or contrast is pressed: we are left—perfectly successfully—to feel for ourselves the fancifulness of the thought that the dead creatures are patient, and so feel also with a fresh shock the force of life in the man who might have seemed to be existing about as minimally as it is possible for a man to do. The movement of these last lines is especially beautiful, with the corpses' 'patience' already prefigured in the repetitions of structures and sounds—

> Some still had their shape,
> Had their pride with it; hung, chins on chests—

and the sense of the merciless beat of the rain in the last line and a half.

IAN HAMILTON
"Ted Hughes: *Crow*" (1971)
A Poetry Chronicle
1973, pp. 165–70

After *Lupercal*, Ted Hughes's bestiary seemed to be complete, and there was much wondering at the time (though more in private than in print) about where this gifted poet would go next. Beastless, would Hughes allow the fevered, apocalyptic rhetoric that had been ominously omnipresent in his first book, *A Hawk in the Rain*, to reassert itself or would he try to develop the naïve, generalizing commentaries on human conduct ('With man it is otherwise') that were inserted here and there in *Lupercal*? The justified suspicion was that in a period of tame, chatty, effortfully rationalistic verse, it was rather easy to overrate a poet who possessed even the beginnings of linguistic vigour; to mistake, in Hughes's case, a souped-up, ripplingly muscular, neo-Georgianism for something much more wise and novel than it really was.

At the same time, though, there was a general unwillingness among critics and reviewers to blur the advent of 'a poet of the first importance' (A. Alvarez) by making too much of such qualms; for example, by examining too closely the considerable discrepancy between the delicacy of Hughes's eye and the crudity of most of his ideas—by pointing out, in short, that if this poet were to apply to human beings even a fraction of the fond exactitude he brought to bear on animal behaviour, he would not find it possible to deal, as in *Lupercal* he almost exclusively did deal, in cartoons rather than in characters (the pimply clerk, the Mafeking colonel, the prize village boozer, and so on); cartoons employed, moreover, to support a vague, simple-mindedly asserted preference for the primitive, the brutal and the sudden as against (need one bother to trot out the hoary antitheses?) the cerebral, the sophisticated, the hesitant.

The absence from Hughes's work of any complex or subtle human personality continued to be worrying throughout the ambiguously aimed *Earth-Owl and Other Moon-People* and the somewhat thrown-together package of stories, plays and verse entitled *Wodwo*. In both books, Hughes's gift for fierce and thrilling natural observation was intermittently in evidence, but so too were his most striking faults: the flailingly portentous verbiage, the indulged relish for the violent and the painful, the deep authorial evasiveness, the ´skimped and shallow dealings with the human world, and so on. The problem of not having any more animals to write about he sinisterly solved by, quite simply, inventing imaginary ones or (as with his jaguar) revamping an old favourite. The horrific nursery frieze assembled in *Earth-Owl* was not just a marginal departure. It was a sketch of things to come, and the bursts of Gothickry that kept cropping up in *Wodwo*, rather suggested that Hughes, far from looking for a way of directing his linguistic gifts back to the human world (where, admittedly, they would need to have been refined, made more tentative, less self-admiring), was indeed seeking an area in which those gifts could be exercised even more randomly than hitherto. He was seeking, in short, a territory and a device which would enable him to unload his obsessions without requiring that he test them out, in any precise way, against reality.

The device and territory of *Crow* are perfectly chosen for this purpose. Crow's naturalistic presence, so far as he has one, allows some scope for Hughes's old bestiarizing gifts; his theological presence—he is simultaneously God's partner,

God's victim, God's godless Man—is vague and immense enough to permit unlimited portentousness; his human stance—tough, sardonic, blood-soaked—is so deliberately (and fashionably) cartoon-like for it to seem an irrelevance to complain of its utter superficiality.

The world that Crow moves in, is an emblem for, is drenched in blood, racked with agony, devastated by numerous varieties of violence. He views it with an eye proprietorial, laconically appalled yet also sadistically gratified. Standing for nothing, he can stand for anything, and moves effortlessly from God's right hand, through the Garden of Eden, to battlefields and blacknesses both old and new. The agent of evil or the principle of enduring, suffering humanity; the villain or the victim? Well, both, of course, for are they separable? Once this malleable symbolic function has been grasped, the reader can settle down to enjoy the creature's grisly travels; enjoy, indeed, a cosy, unperplexing wallow.

The majority of the poems in *Crow* are built on the catalogue, and sometimes the crescendo principle; the formula is simple and totally hospitable. Take a phrase like, for example: 'Black was the . . .' and invent resonant attachments to it. 'Black was the heart/Black the liver', 'Black the blood in its loud tunnel', 'Black the bowels packed in furnace/Black too the muscles'. When the animal anatomy is exhausted, move on to abundant Mother Nature: 'Black is the rock', 'Black is the otter's head'. Another method is the question and answer session, with either question or answer remaining constant throughout:

> Who owns these scrawny little feet? *Death.*
> Who owns this bristly scorched-looking face? *Death.*
> Who owns these still-working lungs? *Death.*
> Who owns this utility coat of muscles? *Death.*
> Who owns these unspeakable guts? *Death.*
> Where is the Black Beast?
> Crow, like an owl, swivelled his head.
> Where is the Black Beast?
> Crow hid in its bed, to ambush it.

Or, more sophisticated, there is the 'When the . . . then the . . .' strategy:

> When the owl sailed clear of tomorrow's conscience
> And the sparrow preened himself of yesterday's promises
> And the heron laboured clear of the Bessemer upglare
> And the bluetit zipped clear of lace panties
> And the woodpecker drummed clear of the rotovator and the rose-farm
> And the peewit tumbled clear of the laundromat
> When the bullfinch plumped in the apple bud
> And the goldfinch bulbed in the sun
> And the wryneck crooked in the moon
> And the dipper peered from the dewball.
> Crow spraddled head-down in the beach-garbage, guzzling a dropped ice-cream.

What these techniques have in common is that they grant total licence to the poet's freewheeling inventiveness; when he runs out of ingredients, the cake is baked. It is true to say of Hughes's list-poems in this book that each of them could be half-a-dozen lines shorter or half-a-dozen lines longer without being seriously damaged or enhanced. The formula depends on a mechanical, drugging repetition, and the last thing we are asked to do is respond to or examine the relevance and accuracy of individual components. Similarly, we need not look for any rhythmic subtlety, nor any pondered or incisive line-breaks; the liturgical scaffolding takes care of all that.

Just as we are not invited to make severe formal or rhythmic demands of these poems, similarly much of the actual language hardly bears examination. By employing rigid structural formulas and by making the most of Crow's own deflatingly ironic disposition (though how cumbersome so many of his ironies in fact are), Hughes manages to contain some of his rhetorical belligerence, but there can be no disguising the fact that the central energies of this book are, in their eager pursuit of blood and thunder, only minimally tempered by poetic caution—that caution which insists on trying to connect words to their full meanings. Take, as a sample of the book's bludgeoning behaviour, this (not exhaustive) list of blood-images and ask yourself if their progenitor need ever have seen anybody bleed; not, admittedly, a clinching test but one well worth applying to a work which has been credited with affording us *new* insights into our bloody selves: 'God bled, but with men's blood'; 'Blood blasts from the crown on his head in a column'; 'Blood was too like water'; 'Shock-severed eyes watched blood/Squandering as from a drain-pipe/Into the blanks between stars'; 'Screaming for Blood'; 'All this messy blood'; 'Black is the gall lying on the bed of the blood'; 'As he drowned in his own blood'; 'Blood her breasts her palms her brow all wept blood'; 'He stands trousered in blood and log-splits/The lolling body, bifurcates it/Top to bottom, kicks away the entrails—/Steps out of the blood-wallow'; 'His wife and children lie in their blood'; 'The suddenly dropped, heavily dropped/Star of blood on the fat leaf'; 'Drinking Beowulf's blood, and wrapped in his hide'; 'Smiles that went off with a mouthful of blood'; 'The pavement and the air and the light/Confined all the jumping blood/No better than a paper bag.'

One could compile a similar, similarly oppressive and similarly undisturbing, list involving Death or Disease (facile play with 'tattered guts', 'shattered brains' and 'death's mouldy tits' abounds), and one could point also to the book's key violent-verbs—stabbing, smashing, screaming, writhing, and so on. The measure of the sensibility behind the words is to be discovered in the way most of these words are mechanically chucked in, lazily relished, insultingly (to actual suffering) exploited.

One of the most significant poems in *Crow* is called 'Lovesong'; the described lovers are vampiric, gluttonous, destructive, bent on a brutal, absolute possession of each other. The significance of the poem is not in the black view it takes of human love (though this, as we have seen, is hardly insignificant) but in the way it (gluttonously, vampirically) piles blackness upon blackness, the way it seems—after the first dozen lines or so—to have moved far beyond any real gravity or wisdom into a horror-comic realm of barely controllable fascination with its own subject-matter. An important quality for poets is knowing exactly where to stop; this poem, like so many others in this brutal book, not only does not know, but does not care. It flogs on until it is drained, replete.

CALVIN BEDIENT
"Ted Hughes"
Eight Contemporary Poets
1974, pp. 95–118

Ted Hughes is our first poet of the will to live. Lawrence wrote of animal joy, a lighter, perhaps more fanciful thing. Robinson Jeffers picked up the topic occasionally, a hawk on his wrist, but was too eager, too clumsy, to master it. Hughes is its master and at the same time is mastered by it. The subject owns him, he is lord of the subject.

The will to live might seem the first and healthiest of subjects; in fact it is almost the last and most morbid. Men come to it after the other subjects have failed. It is the last stop—waterless, exposed—before nothingness. Civilization blows off, love and utopia evaporate, the interest the human mind takes in its own creations washes out, and there, its incisors bared, stands life, daring you to praise it.

Curiously, in an interview with Egbert Faas in *The London Magazine* (January 1971), Hughes speaks as if he were not at the very end but instead at some new beginning. Other poets, he says, suffer the disintegration of Christianity; he, by contrast, celebrates demonic force. More, he calls for a new ritual, a new whirring of 'the elemental power circuit of the Universe'. But we look at him and shy at the brutal light and conclude that he himself—he above all—is beyond the help of ritual. His hand is on the naked wire and he is held there helpless, a celebrant of a sort but a grimly desperate one. '. . . The whole and every individual', writes Schopenhauer, 'bears the stamp of a forced condition. . . .' It is Hughes's distinction to be the poet of this truth. As a thinker he is a hangman, not a priest.

Schopenhauer, Hughes notes, is the only philosopher he 'ever really read'—a case, no doubt, of bringing coals to Newcastle. Hughes would have come round to the same glowering pessimism on his own (and perhaps did), his school the animals. His work gives the impression—A. Alvarez notes the same of his presence—of a being congenitally indifferent to humanism, a mind on the outskirts of civilization, like a boy who skips school and spends the day, even the night, in the woods. That leaves the stars above, gleaming like the barrels of guns, and the animals below, jumping as if at the sound of shots.

In the beginning it was love—a boy's eager love, compounded of curiosity, possessiveness, and adventure. '. . . My interest in animals began when I began', Hughes writes in *Poetry Is* (a series of B.B.C. lectures originally published under the title *Poetry in the Making*). 'My memory goes back pretty clearly to my third year, and by then I had so many of the toy lead animals you could buy in shops that they went right round our flattopped fireplace fender, nose to tail. . . .' Later, at threshing time, Hughes would snatch mice from under the lifted sheaves till he had thirty or forty crawling inside the lining of his coat. Squirming life! Yet the animals—'the magpies and owls and rabbits and weasels and rats and curlews' his older brother shot—were just as exciting dead. 'He could not shoot enough for me.'

Then it was partisanship and envy, the steaming appetite cooling into respect. In the poems the animals re-emerged not as playthings but as the lords of death and life. In memory and imagination they were gods—or demons, no matter. In what did their superiority consist? In nothing so much as their lack of self-consciousness, of the sicknesses of the mind. No hesitation, no remorse, a mind all reflex, streamlined as a trigger—it began to look like the state before the fall.

In discovering his own death—so it would seem—Hughes concluded that the one thing that mattered was life: he became a worshipper of the claw. An animal's organs represent purely, as Schopenhauer said, 'the will to live in [its] particular circumstances'. Quick eyes, the trap jaw, the noose of the talon—these are forms of vital genius. The creature may be a poor thing of 'forced condition', but it is also a wire that will destroy, if it can, the first mouth that chews it. 'The universal desire for life' is a thing both driven and terrible. No poems so grim and airless, so remote from joy as Hughes's. But if this is life, so be it, he seems to say. Better to fight than die.

Signalling all to come, Hughes's first collected poem, the title piece of *The Hawk in the Rain* (1957), places man both literally and vitally below the hawk:

> I drown in the drumming ploughland, I drag up
> Heel after heel from the swallowing of the earth's
>   mouth,
> From clay that clutches my each step to the ankle
> With the habit of the dogged grave, but the hawk
> Effortlessly at height hangs his still eye

The hawk is 'a diamond point of will', the speaker is turning to mud. So runs the refrain of Hughes's poems, all written in furtive or open contempt for the human as the paltriest instance of the will to live, hence also of 'reality itself', as Schopenhauer would put it. We are all, says another poem, 'held in utter mock by the cats'. Nine to one.

Hughes is primarily a poet of the will to live at the phenomenal level of the leaping blood—which is almost to say at the poetic rather than the philosophical level of his theme. Only infrequently has he descended with Schopenhauer into the darkness below. Once in the somewhat Yeatsian 'Crow Hill':

> What humbles these hills has raised
> The arrogance of blood and bone,
> And thrown the hawk upon the wind,
> And lit the fox in the dripping ground.

Here he invites a glimpse into the vast desire that, in Schopenhauer's words, 'presses impetuously into existence under a million forms . . . eagerly grasping for itself every material of life'. In 'The Bull Moses', he goes down farther still:

> The brow like masonry, the deep-keeled neck:
> Something come up there onto the brink of the gulf,
> Hadn't heard of the world, too deep in itself to be
>   called to,
> Stood in sleep

He thus embodies, again in Schopenhauer's words, 'that which is no longer phenomenon, but thing in itself': the will as pure Cause, in trance at the centre of the world.

If Hughes scorns life, scorns it secretly, in part it is because this radical perspective lingers even in his daylight consciousness, like the black in a coal miner's skin. But he must live in the sun like everyone else; besides, his poet's senses pertinaciously buoy him up there; and there he feels forced to choose between the cat and the man.

To Hughes, the more terrible the beast the more admirable. The stabbing thrush, the slavering wolf, the meat-eating dragon-fly that 'stands in space to take aim', the hawk whose 'manners are tearing off heads', the pig whose 'bite is worse than a horse's', the jaguar waddling 'like a thick Aztec disemboweller', the rat with 'incisors bared to the night spaces, threatening the constellations', the tom that 'Will take the head clean off your simple pullet', the stoat 'Drinking the staring hare dry', the 'carrion-eating skate' with 'cupid lips in its

deathly belly'—these are the heroes of his world, his fierce bulwark against nothingness.

To Hughes the human has nothing whatever to recommend it: to be human is to start out *behind* the animals, like a one-legged man in a race. The human mind, for instance— what is it but a kind of missing leg, an ache where the amputated part had been? Not even in Lawrence does the intellect appear so repulsive as in 'Wings', Hughes's poem on Sartre, Kafka, and Einstein. Sartre 'regrows the world inside his skull, like the spectre of a flower', his hands meanwhile sinking 'to the status of flies'. As for Einstein, he has thought himself right out of being:

> The tired mask of folds, the eyes in mourning,
> The sadness of the monkeys in their cage—
> Star peering at star through the walls
> Of a cage full of nothing

'Poetry is nothing if not that', Hughes says in the Faas interview, 'the record of just how the forces of the Universe try to redress some balance disturbed by human error.' So 'Wings' would redress Einstein—rather like the robin that glimpses him walking ('—that was exciting!'). The poem is brilliant with negative grandeur. All the same, one wishes it were not trying so hard to snatch these pale worms from the ground. It wants to punish, to gobble. It is a gesture of contempt.

So mind, in Hughes, takes the sting out of a man. Women, too, incapacitate. They are formidable even though weak. Hughes seems to fear and hate them, like all would-be strong men—like the early Brecht, for instance. They are presented as stale, overpowering wombs, as in 'Crow and Mama', 'Revenge Fable', and 'Song for a Phallus'—mamas squatting on their little boys. Or they are head-swallowing vulvas:

> And Crow retched again, before God could stop
>   him.
> And woman's vulva dropped over man's neck and
>   tightened.
> The two struggled together on the grass.
> God struggled to part them, cursed, wept

Nothing more dangerous to an independent man. At their safest, in Hughes, women are grovelling whores, gravel under the male heel. In the radio play *The Wound*, the licentious queen and her ladies have 'faces like ear-wigs', they are 'maggots, writhing, squirming to split their seams—[a] carnivorous pile of garbage'. In truth this notion of female vileness is itself vile and we may be glad Hughes's world is ordinarily reserved for beasts and men.

Only two types of men survive Hughes's pitiless need for strength, the he-man and the artist. The first boasts what Norman O. Brown calls the 'simple health that animals enjoy, but not men'. The Vikings in 'The Warriors of the North' thaw 'at the red and black disgorging of abbeys, / The bountiful, cleft casks, / The fluttered bowels of the women of dead burghers' and Hughes cannot admire them enough. Then there is Dick Straightup—like a Western hero, too manly even to be sexual, despite his name:

> Past eighty, but never in eighty years—
> Eighty winters on the windy ridge
> Of England—has he buttoned his shirt or his jacket

'When I imagine one of those warriors in the room', Hughes writes almost girlishly in 'The Ancient Heroes and the Bomber Pilot', 'And hear his heart-beat burl . . . my heart / Is cold and small.' Or take Hughes's retired colonel, his 'face pulped scarlet with kept rage', a 'man-eating British lion / By a pimply age brought down':

Here's his head mounted, though only in rhymes,
Beside the head of the last English
Wolf (those starved gloomy times!)
And the last sturgeon of Thames.

A patriotic toast to a red neck.

For Hughes the he-man's shadow extends into the caves of sleep. To be able to curl up beyond all danger, to snore fearlessly—this is to be like the bull Moses, heavy and dark, a stone sunk beneath the frantic waters of conscious life. 'The unconscious part, the vegetative life with its ganglion system, into which in sleep the brain-consciousness disappears', notes Schopenhauer, 'is the common life of all.' Here there is safety, a red strength. Dick Straightup, a local legend, once

fell in the sleet, late,
Dammed the pouring gutter; and slept there; and,
    throughout
A night searched by shouts and lamps, froze,
Grew to the road with welts of ice. He has chipped
    out at dawn
Warm as a pie and snoring

Other poems sound the implications. In the masterpiece 'November' Hughes writes of the sleeping tramp: 'I thought what strong trust / Slept in him. . . .' Death would not think to stoop so low as that rainy ditch—think to descend there into 'the common life of all'. 'I swell in there, soaking', says the sleeper in 'Wino', a babe in the veined hot interior of the grape, his 'mulatto mother'. Then there are Hughes's witches, demonic queens of night and the common life,

Nightlong under the blackamoor spraddled,
Back beside their spouse by dawn

—women to whom the poet pays all the deference gentlemen once showed to ladies.

As for the artist, he has the steel of nature's involuntary will, he drops on the word, the note, the colour, as the hawk drops on the mouse. Like the thrush, he displays 'bullet and automatic / Purpose': 'Mozart's brain had it, and the shark's mouth / That hungers down the blood-smell even to a leak of its own / Side . . .' The artist works in a fearless, instinctual region of attack where no one heeds 'the minimum practical energy and illumination'—that curse of civilization. Here pleasure is like breakage, Dionysian. Dick and Jack and Dan, drunk themselves, 'sing, / Rightly too, the drunkenness of time'. And Beethoven, whalish of appetite, ugly of mug, laughs with 'black-mouth derisive' at nibbling and pretty aesthetes. '. . . I think of poems as a sort of animal', says Hughes, their stalker.

Though certainly it is easy to see why Hughes is criticized for violence, it isn't really violence he celebrates but an energy too strong for death. Hughes has even written one poem against violence, as if to clear his good name. In 'Wilfred Owen's Photographs' Parliament refuses to abolish the navy's cat-o-nine-tails until 'A witty profound Irishman calls / For a "cat" into the House, and sits to watch / The gentry fingering its stained tails.' True, the poem conveys contempt for the good men's queasiness. Yet its title, with its queer optimism, seems in earnest.

The closest poem to 'Wilfred Owen's Photographs' is 'Crow's Account of the Battle', which, however, is cynical about peace:

This had happened too often before
And was going to happen too often in future
And happened too easily
Bones were too like lath and twigs
Blood was too like water

Yet even in its regret over war the poem slings blood and

anguish like a clown slinging pies. The truth is that Hughes cannot avoid violence because life to him is a violent conception. And he wants to be on the winning side. His weakness is not violence but the absolute egotism of survival. It is the victor he loves, not war. He thrills to strength with all the envy, the trembling, of a mortal man.

But what is there to either win or lose? In truth, nothing: Hughes is a total nihilist. To keep death from drawing a black line and adding every effort up to zero is, for him, the whole sum of life. It is all a struggle against debit; the credit side is a blank.

Hughes is a nihilist on the scuffling, muscled side of nothingness, the opposite kind from, say, Philip Larkin, who has long since become a wise ghost. Larkin observes life half wistfully, half coldly, as if from the farther side; Hughes is in the midst of the battle, relishing its proof of the will not to die—the correct name of the will to live. Where Larkin has taken 'the grave's part', Hughes is terrified of 'the earth's mouth'. The latter fights shy of the border across which Larkin, glad to be reprieved from eating ash, has slipped almost gratefully.

The logic, of course, lies with Larkin. Hughes's 'wild rebellion' against nullity is, as Schopenhauer would put it, an 'irrational tendency'. It has no 'sufficient reason in the external world'. Driven out of the womb, it is our fate, according to Hughes's 'Existential Song', to run 'for dear life'—but not because life is dear, the running itself prevents that. In 'The Contender' the hero nails himself to life 'Though his body was sweeling away like a torrent on a cliff / Smoking towards dark gorges'. Nothing can budge him. Even 'through his atoms and decay' he grins into 'the ringing nothing'. What a hero! What a fool. For of course his trial of strength is 'senseless'. Several of Hughes's recent poems are full of grinning and black laughter. It is the sound of the will in the void.

Yet there is no telling life (at least not in Hughes) that it has nothing to lose. Waking up to itself in the middle of a race, it means to 'win'. So Hughes sides with the runners out front. Increasingly, though, he seems to have found himself among the losers—to have fallen behind with the weak who eat the dust.

His first two volumes vigorously champion animal wile. They represent a vomition of the human, of death. Hughes perches and gloats with the hawks, runs with the eaters not the eaten. To be sure, even so he cannot outrun himself. His human weakness nags like a tearful child stumbling behind. He is only a partisan, not one of the elect. In an unguarded moment, he even turns up his love of will and discloses its masochistic underside:

And we longed for a death trampled by such horses
As every grain of the earth had hooves and mane

All the same, life in these poems keeps its pride. Life is the side to be on. In 'November' even some of the gibbeted animals

still had their shape
Had their pride with it; hung, chins on chests,
Patient to outwait these worst days that beat
Their crowns bare and dripped from their feet.

In Hughes's two most recent volumes, by contrast, the pride has given way. Rigid and unliving, it was never more than a support to hold up the tunnel while the creature passed. Now the creature halts, terrified of the weight overhead. Living things begin to feel small. Even savage animals no longer save Hughes from himself; rather, his own frailty seeps into them. Hughes has gradually given himself up to his human problems, rather brilliantly.

In the first of these recent volumes, *Wodwo*, the poems

about animals are few. It is as if Hughes no longer knew how to pick the creatures up. More, when he does grab hold they are apt to turn and look at him with human eyes. Thus, where the wolf in the preceding volume, *Lupercal*, embodies feral energy, here it represents tormented mind: 'the wolf is small, it comprehends little', it goes 'to and fro, trailing its haunches and whimpering horribly'. The tracks of Hughes's animals now cross the inapprehensible. Metaphysical shock—Pip's madness—has broken their minds. Something like a rage of helplessness, of frustrated consequence, seems to set his skylarks 'Squealing and gibbering and cursing / Heads flung back . . . Like sacrifices set floating'. Something like a metaphysical masochism makes his gnats dance 'A dance giving their bodies to be burned', though 'their mummy faces will never be used'. Hughes's animals have discovered a world that doesn't need them.

In both *Wodwo* and the still more recent *Crow*, the principle of individuation thus does its work only too well. Anxiety begins to radiate from finiteness of being. The source, the mother, all comforting reason or ignorance of unreason, are lost. The nearly human wodwo observes: 'I seem / separate from the ground, and not rooted but dropped / out of nothing casually. . . .' All in all, it is as if the fountain of universal desire had been extinguished and the last drops were descending in isolation down the air.

Yet Hughes will resist this mood, will make or find life ebullient again. His gnats may complain that 'the one sun is too near / It blasts their song', but they add with braggadocio,

> That they are their own sun
> Their own brimming over
> At large in the nothing
> Their wings blurring the blaze

And though the skylark may gibber and scramble 'In a nightmare difficulty / Up through the nothing . . . As if it were too late, too late', it disappears heavenward all the same, leaving the sky 'blank open': 'Only the sun goes silently and endlessly on with the lark's song'. The bird, after all, is

> . . . shot through the crested head
> With the command, Not die
> But climb
> Climb
> Sing

Even the wodwo, with all his dullness, says, 'I'll go on looking'. Hughes's dependence on will is thus not altogether defeated. If Heidegger has begun to claim him, Schopenhauer claims him still. He is now metaphysically buoyant, now metaphysically low and fearful—a spurt of animal energy, or a mind deflating with a hiss of stale air.

Crow, especially, is a reel of attitudes. The title figure, nimbly embodying opposite extremes, is mythological in the sense that he is a vital yet fantastic being, at once animal and human. Hughes can colour him Schopenhauer, then Heidegger, or middle class, or elemental, or plain crow, and he will remain the same disturbing, curiously indismissible creature. He is Hughes's animal defiance and human jitters in one.

Because he is all the compulsion of instinct, Crow is 'stronger than death'—'evidently'. He is unthinking animal energy, as reflexive as water spat off a stove. He is also helpless animal appetite, unapologetic. 'In the beginning was Scream', and Crow, from the moment of his own beginning, screams for 'Blood / Grubs, crusts / Anything'. A blaze of animal egotism, he is the only creature in the world:

> His wings are the stiff back of his only book,
> Himself the only page—of solid ink

He gazes into time 'Like a leopard into a fat land'. Then he is

animal agility—cunning, amazing. Once Stone lumbered towards him, a mistake, for Stone has since 'battered itself featureless' while Crow has become a nimble monster. He can even outskip the flooding 'word'. Admire him, he will endure.

All this was implicit earlier in Hughes's roosting hawk:

> The sun is behind me.
> Nothing has changed since I began.
> My eye has permitted no change.
> I am going to keep things like this.

But the hawk was a hero and Crow . . . Crow is a necessary evil. Since he is its raw material, life, of course, cannot do without him; but that he should be the whole of it, as he threatens! He is matter inadequate to the good. He tries, oh how he tries, but he is—black. A further difference from the hawk: he knows shame. His every feather is 'the fossil of a murder', he feels 'Clothed in his conviction'. True, his guilt is mercifully unlocalized; but he is all the more disquieting for that: what he would do to the real Black Beast if he could find him!

When his anxiety deepens, Crow, without losing his crow's features, embodies empty human consciousness. '. . . the will to live does not appear in consequence of the world', said Schopenhauer, 'but the world in consequence of the will to live'; and perhaps this is echoed in 'Lonely Crow created the gods for playmates'. But for the rest lonely Crow is Heideggerean. For, having created the gods, he becomes the emptiness of the knower as against the fullness of the known. 'The mountain god tore free / And Crow fell back from the wall-face of mountains / By which he was so much lessened.' In the end he is 'his own leftover'. 'Mind is the negative', as Sartre put it. Knowledge is smoke, *being* the fuel. The knower walks out to the end of himself and then is only the distance between himself and what he knows. Hughes's 'Robin Song' laments:

> I am the lost child
>   Of the wind
>   *Who goes through me looking for something*
> else
>   *Who can't recognize me though I cry.*

Another twist and Crow is the finite beset by the Infinite. Now the sun is not behind but before him, burning. Like the wolf in *Wodwo* he is too little to understand:

> His utmost gaping of brain in his tiny skull
> Was just enough to wonder, about the sea,
> What could be hurting so much?

Great ego, famished spirit that he is, he resents being left out:

> Yet the prophecy inside him, like a grimace,
> Was I WILL MEASURE IT ALL AND OWN IT
>   ALL
> AND I WILL BE INSIDE IT
> AS INSIDE MY OWN LAUGHTER

At other moments, however, he pulls back:

> Crow saw the herded mountains, steaming in the
>   morning.
> . . . .
>
> He saw the stars, fuming away into the black,
>   mushrooms of the nothing forest, clouding their
>   spores, the virus of God.
> And he shivered with the horror of Creation.

It is better to be left out. . . .

Of course this very human Crow is a victim—the purest case. Like the next little 'man', he is fool enough to dream: 'Crow thought of a fast car— / It plucked his spine out, and left him empty and armless'. His mama holds on, holds on. His words won't keep things down. Manhattan buys out his song. And though God certainly loves him, 'Otherwise, he would have dropped dead', what then loves 'the shot-pellets / That dribbled from those strung-up mummifying crows?' No, the world's not right, at least for a crow. Fly, evade, still death will trip you up and dangle you from your one remaining claw, 'corrected'.

The theme of Hughes's recent work is, then, the dual horror of existence—that of the monstrous rage for life and that of being small, left out, emptily included. Double-barrelled, it hits a wide target and a poet who had once seemed limited to being the laureate of animals has developed (has suffered to develop) a significant scope. Not that his mind ranges free: it is part boot, part worm. Yet at least the brutal will to live, on the one hand, and the fear of both life and death, on the other, have the virtue of being essential truths. They comprehend, they are respectively, the first impulse and the first hesitation, the sun and the vapour of being. And of this frightening portion of existence—the struggle to live and the nothingness of life—Hughes is a jolting and original poet.

Hughes's style has changed almost from volume to volume. The reason is that his apprehension of his subject has altered also. His manner has bloated or grown lean, smoked up or illuminated, entirely as this changing apprehension has prompted. It could not have been otherwise: poetry is poignant understanding first, words second—though the words will seem always to race the understanding to the goal and get there in advance. The manner is a device for feeling the subject so fully, so precisely, that we will never forget it. But if it succeeds we will not forget the manner, either: it will cling to the subject, or to the memory, like a robe in the wind.

As it turned out, any early faith in Hughes's poetic ability was more than justified. And yet the praise that greeted his first volume, *The Hawk in the Rain* (1957), was not. Critics flocked to the book like ghosts to a pit of blood. Having been starved for violence, they found Hughes's violence—in Edwin Muir's word—'admirable'. The truth, I believe, is that nothing in the book could have turned out admirable, least of all the violence, because of Hughes's relation to his themes.

That relation is one of a sniggering voyeurism—a voyeurism of various forms of sensational extravagance. In fact the book can scarcely be said to have a subject, for extravagance is a romantic refusal of a subject, an excitation of the nerve ends. Here everything—war, childbirth, the weather, laughter, love—is galvanized into the improbable; even the prodigious wears a fright wig. Lovers like 'slavering' wolves yearn to 'sob contentment toward the moon'. A tight-buttocked secretary, if touched by a man, 'would shriek and weeping / Crawl off to nurse the terrible wound'. Jack Horner's 'hedge-scratched pig-splitting arm' grubs its nasty 'get' among the Virgin Mary's 'lilies'. Sympathies fasten 'like flies' to a crashed airman's blood but desert at the sight of his eye staring up from a handkerchief. In short, a puerile, dark titillation is the recurring note. The poems seem dreadfully knowing without displaying the least real knowledge of life.

Following suit, Hughes's manner is strained, pretentious, overexcited—a famine. Occasionally the phrases are welded in a series like brass knuckles: 'and I, / Bloodily grabbed dazed last-moment-counting / Morsel in the earth's mouth'. This leaves the mind stunned but empty. At the same time, the style affects elevation. For instance, 'Fair Choice' tells of 'Suave / Complicity with your vacillation / To your entire undoing'. A stanza in 'Egg-Head' runs:

Brain in deft opacities,
Walled in translucencies, shuts out the world's knocking
With a welcome, and to wide-eyed deafnesses
Of prudence lets it speak

The egg seems addled. All in all, it is as if Bully the giant had chosen to speak with the lexical mincingness of an Elizabethan page. The sensational embraces the precious, fulsomely. The language attempts to squeeze every thrill out of its subjects and yet be priggishly superior to them. It turns to Shakespeare as to stilts: 'Stamp was not current but they rang and shone / As good gold as any queen's crown'; 'Where admiration's giddy mannequin / Leads every sense to motley'. Here the barbarous aspires to the disquisitional.

Because of his false exploitative relation to his subject, Hughes can neither put word to word with any necessity nor make his poems pace, like animals, involuntarily. Concrete and abstract often mix *against* each other, like salt and sugar: 'blackouts of impassables'; 'their limbs flail / Flesh and beat upon / The inane everywhere of its obstacle'. Nor does concrete meet any more happily with concrete—a hammer 'knits', a jaguar hurries 'after the drills of his eyes / On a short fierce fuse'. As for the rhythm it is subject to cramps: '. . . Here's no heart's more / Open or large than a fist clenched'. At the other extreme it simply flops down: 'Love you I do not say I do or might either.' The volume is, all round, a disaster.

How remarkable that Hughes's next book, *Lupercal* (1960), should have proved an undeniable triumph. Like Larkin, Hughes is one of those poets who grow up miraculously between their first and second volumes. The second breaks like a new day and the old folly is abandoned.

If Hughes is a voyeur of violence in *The Hawk in the Rain*, in *Lupercal* he is a fearful lover of the will to live—a far profounder thing. Wading out at last beyond the froth of violent escapism, he is abruptly stunned by the elemental severity of his subject. His manner contracts at once, thoroughly penetrated by the ancient cold. Now he knows—where before he had been too glutted with sensation to inquire—that the tooth is the clue to existence. He hardens himself, he prepares for battle. Better to speak of *this* subject, he seems to have told himself, in a style as sharp and naked as an incisor.

The better poems in *Lupercal* have the waxy distinctness formed when the imagination presses down hard on actual things: they are taut and clean. In extreme contrast to the first volume, there is now no 'falsifying dream', no fancy or sensational indulgence, between 'hooked head and hooked feet'. The rhetorical fumes have lifted, revealing a world pristine and from the beginning, a world before which Hughes stands and looks, and looks again, matured by awe.

Where nothing in *The Hawk in the Rain* seems seriously observed, here no one can doubt that, if only within a narrow range, Hughes is an incomparable observer—that, for instance, he has seen pike more fully, boldly, and simply than anyone else:

Pike, three inches long, perfect
Pike in all parts, green tigering the gold.
Killers from the egg: the malevolent aged grin.
They dance on the surface among the flies.

Or move, stunned by their own grandeur,
Over a bed of emerald, silhouette
Of submarine delicacy and horror.
A hundred feet long in their world

Or doubt, either, that he has seen otters:

1315

Underwater eyes, an eel's
Oil of water body, neither fish nor beast is the otter:
Four-legged yet water-gifted, to outfish fish;
   With webbed feet and long ruddering tail
   And a round head like an old tomcat

or water lilies, or cats, or hawks, or pigs, or the 'month of the drowned dog', November:

   . . . The wind hardened;
A puff shook a glittering from the thorns,
And again the rains' dragging grey columns
   Smudged the farms. In a moment
   The fields were jumping and smoking

Or finally, his wonder edged with amusement, a bullfrog:

     you pump out
Whole fogs full of horn—a threat
As of a liner looming. True
That, first hearing you
Disgorging your gouts of darkness like a wounded
   god,
Not utterly fantastical I expected
(As in some antique tale depicted)
A broken-down bull up to its belly in mud,
Sucking black swamp up, belching out black cloud
And a squall of gudgeon and lilies.
    A surprise,
To see you, a boy's prize,
No bigger than a rat—all dumb silence
In your little old woman hands.

In all these instances, observation and imagination are so subtly merged that it would be arbitrary to separate them: their beauty is equally objective image and feeling. They display the unfaltering steps of a poet who has at last caught the scent of his destined subject. Now Hughes's words know how to act, where to strike, what to tell; now, it seems, everything is possible to him. To begin with, precision, as in 'submarine delicacy and horror'. Effortless grandeur: 'This evening, motherly summer moves in the pond'. Dramatic *frisson*, as when Cleopatra enjoins the asp, 'Drink me now, whole / With coiled Egypt's past; then from my delta / Swim like a fish toward Rome.' Telling metaphor: 'owlish moons', 'the welding cold', rain plastering the land 'till it was shining / Like hammered lead'. Haunting sensuousness: 'And lit the fox in the dripping ground'. Graceful plainness: 'the blue eye has come clear of time'. Quiet profundity of image, as in 'November', where, once again, the gibbeted owls, hawks, cats, weasels, and crows are 'Patient to outwait these worst days that beat / Their crowns bare and dripped from their feet'. Vocalic and alliterative music, as in the same lines. Imitative rhythm, as again in the persistent drip of these lines. Sybilline statement: 'The crow sleeps glutted and the stoat begins'. Merciless directness, as in 'View of the Pig': 'pink white eyelashes. / Its trotters stuck straight out.' And still other effects, a whole poetic cornucopia.

The richest poems of *Lupercal*—'An Otter', 'Pike', and 'November'—are boldly organized. Though they may seem random, in fact they possess a delicate and contingent unity. Each impression faces the same way, is part of a quivering shoal pointed towards some fountainhead of miraculous adaptation, or horror, or patience, as the case may be. Indeed, this method shows up throughout *Lupercal*, as if after *The Hawk in the Rain* Hughes had determined to throw out the brutal cables of discourse for more subtle and vibrant threads. The result is a remarkable increase in strength—poems lithe and swift and sinewy.

In *Lupercal* Hughes tightens himself like a spring; in his third volume, *Wodwo* (1967), he lets the spring go. He alters,

not in his truths, but again in his relation to them: now he throws himself on universal will, riding, not simply observing, energy. The stanza as a contracted ordering of lines gives way to the poem as a free space where life may run—the poems of *Lupercal* look neat on the page, many of those in *Wodwo* sprawl over it and leap down. The new space is almost frightening in its freedom: there seems to be nothing at all just beyond the lines, and nothing, too, in the frequent abrupt gaps between them. Still, having decided what is real, Hughes boldly runs with it. Here his imaginative awe is less contemplative than dramatic. Living things are seen often as from their struggling midst, in a flurry of perceptions.

The rhythm, generously empathic, seems regardless of itself. It is the shadow flying after the subject. It is notable less for exactitude than for a kind of frantic keeping up, as in 'Gnat-Psalm':

Dancing
Dancing
Writing on the air, rubbing out everything they write
Jerking their letters into knots, into tangles
Everybody everybody else's yoyo

If the movement ever *becomes* the subject, it is in the third section of 'Skylarks' and in 'Second Glance at a Jaguar'. The first could not be more exact, more inspired:

   I suppose you just gape and let your gaspings
   Rip in and out through your voicebox
                    O lark

   And sing inwards as well as outwards
   Like a breaker of ocean milling the shingle
                    O lark

   O song, incomprehensibly both ways—
   Joy! Help! Joy! Help!
                 O lark

We take our own breath with each 'O lark' and pause in admiration. The second poem, as it paces on and on menacingly in thirty-three consecutive lines, is perhaps too much of a *tour de force*. Still, its mimicry of its subject seems effortless, an instinctual meeting of poet and jaguar:

   Skinful of bowls, he bowls them,
   The hip going in and out of joint, dropping the spine
   With the urgency of his hurry
   Like a cat going along under thrown stones, under
     cover

The general effect of *Wodwo* is thus that of the will to live turned up to fever pitch. Even where energy is distanced, as in 'Stations' and parts of 'Scapegoats and Rabies', the irregular lines, the rubbed-out punctuation, the sudden drops, create an impression of near delirium, of a poetry and life more lost in space, with fewer bearings, than any poetry or life heretofore. The cause of this change in style, apart from the exploding empathy, is what we earlier spoke of as a new element of anguished consciousness. Even the empathic poems betray a scarcely containable anxiety. They jump and dart like animals, but like animals trying to outrun the end.

Much is sacrificed, something gained. Beauty is no longer (in Yeats's phrase) like a tightened bow. One delights in sweep and energy, not in delicate, indelible forms. Detail is lost, as in the whirr of the humming bird. Stop the poem, moreover, to look at the parts and they often seem less than choice, as in 'Ghost Crabs':

   All night, around us or through us,
   They stalk each other, they fasten on to each other,
   They mount each other, they tear each other to
     pieces,
   They utterly exhaust each other.

They are the powers of this world.
We are their bacteria

Hughes seems to lay about for phrases, not to care much about the words themselves. Hence the poems depend in large part on their surge and brilliance of conception; they must come down as wholes, like surf, if they are to move us at all. The exceptions are short pieces similar to the *Lupercal* poems: 'Thistles', 'Still Life', 'Wino', and 'Full Moon and Little Frieda' are perhaps the best of these, each being beautiful throughout. Still, the longer poems, however lacking in exquisiteness, are unlooked-for and compelling adventures. If often prose, they are *bursts* of prose in the stellar regions of poetry. There are few poems so headlong in our literature. Lawrence, Whitman, Williams—the points of comparison are few.

In truth, even the poems most like the *Lupercal* poems are a little sprung: the new virus, which undoes form, has just attacked them; they relax beyond the earlier elliptical brevity. For instance, 'Full Moon and Little Frieda' begins:

A cool small evening shrunk to a dog bark and the
    clank of a bucket—

And you listening.

The first line liberally gives the evening all the space from which it shrinks; the second confirms the shrinking, the intentness of the ear. Yet, as this example also shows, the poems have their economy, they are canny in form. 'Full Moon and Little Frieda', 'Wino', 'Thistles', 'Still Life', and 'Mountains' (except for its superfluous first three lines) are intelligently brief and almost tangibly rounded, and it would be difficult to say which of them ends the most wonderfully.

Certainly they differ enough from the longer poems— from 'The Howling of Wolves', 'Skylarks', 'Second Glance at a Jaguar', 'Gnat-Psalm', 'Wings', 'You Drive in a Circle', 'Ghost Crabs'—to make it wrong to weigh them together in the same basket. Are they superior to these? How easy to feel that Hughes's full energy and brilliance are not in them. Their form is consummate, but they are not his longest throw. His later style, though it stirs up more than it settles and elbows aside containment, yet spoils us a little for his earlier one—at least if we return to it still reeling from the wilder manner. The truth is that the poems have to be kept apart, like cats and dogs.

The poems in *Crow* (1970; Harper and Row published a slightly expanded edition in 1971) develop from the newer style, being slapdash, forceful, a little noisy and deaf in the ear, breathless. Now, however, the energy has largely dwindled to a nagging thing of the voice:

There was this hidden grin.
It wanted a permanent home. It tried faces
In their forgetful moments, the face for instance
Of a woman pushing a baby out between her legs
But that didn't last long the face
Of a man so preoccupied
With the flying steel in the instant
Of the car-crash he left his face
To itself that was even shorter

Hughes's new poems, like his first, are talk. 'They were usually something of a shock to write', he notes: but they sound like discourse all the same. As experiences most are no more dramatic than the Disney cartoons to which David Lodge has accurately compared them (*Critical Quarterly*, Spring 1971). They are flat if vehement, with only a murky profundity, like that of black marble. And sometimes Hughes has to drop the slab on your foot, at the end, to ensure a strong effect.

Yet what talk this is! It is so pell-mell, so bizarre, so knowingly black, that the reader cannot help but attend. One readily believes Hughes when he says that 'mostly they wrote themselves quite rapidly'. They are like fat thrown on the fire: ugly to both eye and ear, they yet spit and sizzle, are frantically there. They are fully as discordant and provoking as a crow's call—which, of course, is precisely their intention. And Hughes keeps throwing them out as if Crow were indeed real and sat hugely on the back of his chair, dictating.

Where the *Wodwo* manner confesses anxiety, the new manner reeks of disgust, races with horror. There is great cynicism in the style, which is slung out like hash. At this stage of case-hardened disillusion, so Hughes seems to say, words will all taste the same anyhow. The very indifference of the language is thus expressive. 'The first idea of *Crow*', Hughes observes, 'was originally just to write his songs, the songs that a Crow would sing. In other words, songs with no music whatsoever, in a super-simple and a super-ugly language which would in a way shed everything except just what he wanted to say without any other consideration. . . .' Thus, while the style of *Lupercal* is an attack of beauty on nihilism, the style of *Crow* is the croak of nihilism itself. Impossible to guess from these poems that Hughes could write such a line as 'Reeds, nude and tufted, shiver as they wade' (except for the beginning, here, of 'Dawn's Rose': 'Dawn's rose / is melting an old frost moon').

So this latest manner has its rationale, the spill of the words its compulsion. Still, in most of these poems Hughes wastes himself. A master of language who tosses words on the page—can any aesthetic justify this? Hughes explains that he relinquished the 'musically deeper world' of formal patterning 'to speak a language that raises no ghosts'—but in fact he mostly speaks prose, which is *all* ghost. Fresh and aggressive as his slants on his themes may be, his words themselves are frequently stale:

He wanted to sing very clear
But this tank had been parked on his voice
And his throttle was nipped between the Roman's
    Emperor's finger and thumb
Like the neck of a linnet
And King Kong in person
Held the loop of his blood like a garotte
While tycoons gambled with his glands in a fog of
    cigar smoke

This is to jumble old prose queerly rather than select words that will listen to themselves anew. The lines are striking, but in the manner of a deformed hand. Certainly there is nothing in them to make one wish to come back; they lack local genius. The same is true, we said, of the longer *Wodwo* poems, but in fact these last are somewhat happier in detail, less strained and grotesque, more often piercing, and more dramatic and deeply empathic besides. They have more sensual and formal richness than the poems in *Crow*.

Not that all is a loss here even as language. The detail in the first and better half of the volume comes forward a little further with each reading, winning one over. Even a wasted Hughes can prove very good. Consider 'Crow on the Beach':

Hearing shingle explode, seeing it skip,
Crow sucked his tongue.
Seeing sea-grey mash a mountain of itself
Crow tightened his goose-pimples

If these phrases do not exhilarate, neither do they bore; they have humour, freshness. Better still is 'Dawn's Rose', with its surprise and subtlety, its virtuoso comparisons:

Desolate is the crow's puckered cry
As an old woman's mouth
When the eyelids have finished
And the hills continue.

> A cry
> Wordless
> As the newborn baby's grieving
> On the steely scales.
>
> As the dull gunshot and its after-râle
> Among conifers, in rainy twilight.
>
> Or the suddenly dropped, heavily dropped
> Star of blood on the fat leaf.

Here each word counts. Other poems, too, revert to economy. 'Crow Sickened', 'Oedipus Crow', and 'Crow Blacker Than Ever', for instance, are stripped-down narratives. The first even drops the nominative pronoun, so ready a presence is Crow in these poems:

> Unwinding the world like a ball of wool
> Found the last end tied round his finger.
>
> Decided to get death, but whatever
> Walked into his ambush
> Was always his own body

Perhaps the best poem of all is 'Crow's Elephant Totem Song', a queer, delicious fable. It neither flags in tartness and beauty (ugly-beauty), nor violently plops, like many of these poems, on the decayed floor of nihilism:

> They Hyenas sang in the scrub   You are
>   beautiful—
> They showed their scorched heads and grinning
>   expressions
> Like the half-rotted stumps of amputations—
> We envy your grace
> Waltzing through the thorny growth
> O take us with you to the Land of Peaceful

Though this is grotesque, it is not with a vengeance. All these poems avoid the chief bane of the book, namely the list—a fatal device where brilliance of detail has been denied.

> Who owns these scrawny little feet? *Death.*
> Who owns this bristly scorched-looking face?
>   *Death.*
> Who owns these still-working lungs? *Death.*
> Who owns this utility coat of muscles? *Death.*
> Who owns these unspeakable guts? *Death.*

Etc., etc. The attention soon stops dead like chalk hitting a wet spot on the board.

Just as Hughes's words repeatedly sag into prose despite the lines on which they are hung, so his conceptions fall a little too readily into the mean slots of nihilism. In truth he now knows his own mind too well. He needs to pray, like Frost, to have some dust thrown in his eyes. And this is true even though the *Crow* poems crisscross one another. Both the nihilism of the tearing mouth and that of the 'nothinged' mind have become Hughes's familiars. How jolting were he now to write a poem as flexibly free of existential categories as 'An Otter'. He is in the double jeopardy of calling his shots beforehand and of shooting wildly for fear that he will. Often in *Crow* the intention is either patent, as in 'Examination at the Womb-Door', or frantically obscure, as in 'The Smile'. Most of the poems fall to either side of the richest poetry—poetry of conceptual but unconsummated imaginative experience.

Yet, raise objections against the *Crow* poems as we will, the volume itself, Crow-like, remains insistently standing before us, waiting to get its due. And perhaps the truth is just this, that it has to be read and considered as a whole. The poems, good and bad, add to one another; and Crow himself is somehow larger than their sum, so that the subtitle seems exact: 'From the Life and Songs of the Crow'.

In truth, the accumulative virtues are many: the subtle varieties of approach, the dogged essential probing, the metaphysical hopping about, the clever and fresh adaptation of cartoon techniques, the savage humour, the startling obliquities of attack, and, not least, the bristling fascination of Crow himself, the wealth of his black adventures and situations. Then, too, there is the new fearful beauty so randomly struck off, as in the lines on 'the herded mountains, steaming in the morning', or on strange unknown 'littleblood, hiding from the mountains in the mountains'; again in

> So Crow found Proteus—steaming in the sun.
> Stinking with sea-bottom growths
> Like the plug of the earth's sump-outlet.
> There he lay—belching quakily

and again in:

> the grass camps in its tussock
> With its spears and banners, at nightfall.
> . . .
>
> And I too am a ghost. I am the ghost
> Of a great general, silent at my chess.
> A million years have gone over
> As I finger one piece.
>
> The dusk waits.
>
> The spears, the banners, wait.

In sum, though the contents of *Crow* are far from being realized past change, the volume itself goes beyond what anyone else would be likely to conceive, let alone bring off. It has an impact that only a very remarkable and inventive talent could create.

What will Hughes do now, having worked his subject so near the philosophical bone? It is impossible to say; it cannot be an easy position to be in. Yet he has it in his favour that he has already displayed, several times over, a cunning for changing and still surviving as a poet—as if some aesthetic form of the will to live were ruthlessly pushing him on.

ROBERT STUART
"Ted Hughes"
British Poetry since 1970
eds. Peter Jones and Michael Schmidt
1980, pp. 75–84

Why has not England a great mythology? Our folklore has never advanced beyond daintiness and the greater melodies about our country-side have all issued through the pipes of Greece. Deep and true as the native imagination can be, it seems to have failed here. It has stopped with the witches and the fairies. It cannot vivify one fraction of a summer field, or give names to half a dozen stars. England still waits for the supreme moment of her literature—for the one poet who shall voice her. (E. M. Forster)

In his discussion of Ted Hughes's poetry in *The Art of the Real* (1977), Eric Homberger's obloquy stops little short of a fearsome tirade, bent, one feels, on connecting Hughes to his 'elemental power circuit' and to a voltage to dispatch him netherward to the dark world of the gods. There, Homberger suggests, Hughes might find much to disabuse himself about the nature of his preoccupation with elemental and primal forces; and his shamanistic return, if Homberger could conceive of such an event, might be with a 'new word' repentant and exclusively for *this* world, preferably enunciating a suitable political creed:

Socialism [writes Homberger] is one of the expressions of intense and reasonable desire to abate that 'elemental power circuit of the Universe' which regularly swept people into misery, sickness and death. That Hughes can so confidently dismiss it as a part of the hubris of an aggressive rationalism tells us something about the place that the sympathetic instinct occupies in his world-view. None—at least in theory.

Hughes, on the other hand (in the *New Statesman*, 6 September 1963), would have no truck with such a provisional myth-kit of survival, regarding socialism as 'the great "cooperatives" of non-competitive mutual parasitism', simply another grand advance on the rationalist humanist position, more irrefutable evidence with which to swell his own Book of Revelations. Yet, if we can see our way through Homberger's incessant barrage, there is much to sympathize with in his argument. Take, for example, the well-anthologized 'Hawk Roosting'.

In an interview with Egbert Faas, Hughes has commented on this poem: 'That bird is accused of being a fascist. . . . the symbol of some horrible totalitarian genocidal dictator. Actually what I had in mind was that in this hawk Nature is thinking. Simply Nature.' (*London Magazine*, January 1971.) Yet it takes little stretch of the imagination to fit the political interpretation to the poem. Indeed, by the lack of any note of ironic self-awareness, it seems almost to invite such an interpretation. The assertive personal pronouns and aggressive verbs toned in an unswerving and laconic mode, make the poem read almost as a personal declaration of Hughes' own position, unrepentantly aloof from the world, except in the occasional mindless forays and kills. Nevertheless, we should, I think, be duly cautious about falling too easily prey to the convenient option, most readily open to us now, of resurrecting the ghosts of Marinetti and Mussolini in such poems of Hughes which seem to exalt violence. If history should, at some future point, be diverted into a tyranny of authoritarianism from either political extreme, I doubt very much whether Hughes would have any colours to reveal.

Still, it is a common, even fashionable image of Hughes to see him wading bloody-toothed-and-clawed through the detritus of a collapsed civilization with a wry grin of satisfaction on his swarthy face. One wonders whether Hughes, imagining the possibilities of such a folk-devil myth, used it as a model for *Crow*, which some believe is his sharpest blade for making the critics smart and take stock of their position. And if Hughes has been more than once reviled by the critics, he has not been timid in his replies.

On the perennial question of 'violence' in his poetry, Hughes has remarked in the Faas interview, illustrating from Shakespeare's *Venus and Adonis*: 'Venus . . . if one reads between the lines eventually murdered Adonis . . . she murdered him because he rejected her. He was so desensitized, stupefied and brutalized by his rational scepticism, he didn't know what to make of her. He thought she was an ethical peril. He was a sort of modern critic in the larval phase. . . . a modern English critic. A typical modern Englishman.' One detects in this broadening to include the 'typical' English character an allusive Nietzscheanism: 'The man *who has become free*—and how much more the *mind* that has become free—spurns the sort of contemptible well-being dreamed of by shopkeepers, Christians, cows, women, Englishmen and other democrats. The free man is a *warrior*. How is freedom measured in individuals as in nations? By the resistance which has to be overcome, by the effort it costs to stay *aloft*.' (*Twilight of the Idols*.) But we should not align Hughes with the theories of *Übermensch* and the 'will to power', although there is

evidence of a Dionysian pessimism in his work. If that is true, we can readily see its antithesis, as perhaps Hughes does, personified in the typical English critic, as a *poverty of life* (Nietzsche, *The Gay Science*), a notion of art and knowledge as providing 'rest, peace, a smooth sea, delivery. . . .' a sense of comfortable inertia and complacency.

Though it is not within the scope of this essay to discuss the English critical tradition, it is a discussion worth bearing in mind when one considers Hughes's now notorious disclaimer in his Introduction to Keith Douglas's *Selected Poems* (1964), 'the terrible, suffocating, maternal octopus of ancient English poetic tradition', and the significance it has had in the development of his work. Yet, discernibly, many features of his disaffection with the English Liberal tradition emerge, paradoxically, out of the main concerns of that tradition. One only has to recall the attempts of the Modernists and pre-Modernists to reinvigorate language and form in order to restore some meaning to an otherwise complex and incomprehensible world, to discover many of Hughes's root preoccupations. Eliot, we remember, was there before him. Nevertheless, we can detect, even in Hughes's earliest work, an urgent attempt to restate these concerns.

Another well-anthologized poem is 'The Jaguar'. Formally, the poem appears well gauged and controlled to produce a maximum effect without threatening its overall cohesion. But one feels a progressive unease with the poem on each re-reading (a characteristic feeling with Hughes's poems), as if he had beckoned us over to the cage, then quite suddenly opened the door. For it is not a polite and ruminative diction that overwhelms us, but a solid phalanx of buffeting verbs and steel-heeled nouns in a jostling syntax, heftily thrown out in drummingly irregular three and four stressed lines. Like Lawrence, in *Sons and Lovers*, Hughes is concerned not to describe experience but to embody it wholly, in a tremendous exertion of will to expose '. . . . the very quivering tissue, the very protoplasm of life. . . .'. If one feels, at times, overwhelmed by Hughes's almost hedonistic relishing for the unharnessed elemental powers in all their 'conflagration and frenzy' and blood-bolted imagery, the reply we must expect from Hughes is that it is part evidence of the hubris of our liberal humanist outlook, our willingness to settle for a 'minimum practical energy and illumination.' It is a simple statement of faith—one to which we assent or dissent. No compromise is available to us.

Crow is no exception. In its burlesque of flamboyant rhetoric, precocious imagery and unpoeticalness, rather than providing a nostrum for our English malady it seems intent on worsening it—a strange physic indeed! But it is easy to treat *Crow* lightly and with the same ribald humour in which it is presented. Significantly, it is Hughes's first work to employ an elaborately conceived mythology, though how well it works in the end is debatable. In his essay 'Myth and History in Recent Poetry', in *British Poetry since 1960: A Critical Survey*, eds G. Lindop and M. Schmidt (1972), Terry Eagleton remarks on the Crow myth: 'Crow's triumph over the alienating casualties of history seems too cheaply bought: the inviolable security of myth has replaced, rather than confronted, the contingencies of history, as simple compensation.' But as a symbol, Crow's function is primarily to represent, not to confront, those contingencies. It is the mode of presentation to which we might finally take exception. Here is part of 'Crow's Account of the Battle'.

And when the smoke cleared it became clear
This had happened too often before
And was going to happen too often in the future

And happened too easily
Bones were too like lath and twigs
Blood was too like water
Cries were too like silence
The most terrible grimaces too like footprints in mud
And shooting somebody through the midriff
Was too like striking a match
Too like potting a snooker ball
Too like tearing up a bill
Blasting the whole world to bits
Was too like slamming a door

It is a glaringly unsubtle piece, dependent for its effect on a frenetic accumulation of physical images and a bludgeoning rhetorical tone. Argument rather by way of assault than persuasion. A long way, one might think, from the careful artifice and nuance of Geoffrey Hill's poetry. But whereas Hill runs the risk of an aesthetic ingrownness, Hughes, conversely, ventures too far into the other extreme, threatening total self-annihilation. There is little in the way of a conscious formal boundary or inner discipline. Consequently, what is depicted, rather than approximating to the fulness of the experience, instead veers off into meaninglessness and caricature—precisely the effect Hughes is after. For it is a minor triumph of *Crow* that Hughes manages to strike, with such devastating accuracy, the one discordant note in the human rhythm to release that suppressed and perverted part of our imagination over which we like to think we have achieved complete control. Far from being an historical, transcendent view of the world, *Crow* represents, in its total vision, history as the embodiment and expression of an alienated modern consciousness, questing vainly for access to a reality where the certainty of one's identity is not for ever turning to illusion and nightmare. But the overriding argument in *Crow* asserts that the defective imagination prevents ultimately its discovery, rising spectrally into the very medium in which are invested the hopes of such a discovery-language.

Crow
Decided to try words.

He imagined some words for the job, a lovely pack—
Clear-eyed, resounding, well-trained,
With strong teeth.
You could not find a better bred lot.

He pointed out the hare and away went the words
Resounding.
Crow was Crow without fail, but what is a hare?
It converted itself to a bunker.

The words circling, protesting, resounding.

Crow turned the words into bombs—they blasted the bunker.
The bits of bunker flew up—a flock of starlings.

Crow turned the words into shot-guns, they shot down the starlings.
The falling starlings turned into a cloudburst.

'. . . if thought corrupts language, language can also corrupt thought' wrote George Orwell in his essay *Politics and the English Language*. Hughes reminds us (in the *Listener*, 20 July 1970) that in parts of the narrative Crow has an ambition to become a man, though in fact, he never quite succeeds in this. The above poem, perhaps, is one instance of that attempt. But what for Orwell becomes a speculative truth and a way to fix and resolve the corruption, for Crow, half dressed in human consciousness, language becomes a horrifying chimera of violent metamorphoses, as the instinctive and rational parts of his consciousness are thrown against each other.

For Hughes, language is an intrinsic part of his vision, an organic monitor to record the gradual disintegration of society and civilization. With such a view of the world, it would seem best to remain silent but ever alert, as Hughes suggests, for the 'new word'. But it is an obvious fact that in *Crow* the 'new word' is not delivered up to us, or if it is, we are deafened to its sound by the nuclear blast which comes in 'Notes for a Little Play'. The bleakness of the vision and the lack of even a vestigial hope for redemption makes *Crow* at times unbearable. The sense of Hughes off-loading on to us the dead wood of our civilization makes even the humour of *Crow* seem weighted against us. For in its obviously ironic mode, it comes to represent for Hughes a personal refuge not from the world, but from its insanity—an insanity we alone are left to suffer. It is the unheuristic nature of the Crow myth, its inability to point towards a more heartening condition, that eventually threatens the myth with complete isolation.

What are we really to make of such poems as 'Glimpse', 'King of Carrion', 'Two Eskimo Songs' and finally "Little-blood"? If they represent a new mythology to replace the Christian one they do so without full awareness of the massive complexities—cultural, social and historical—that should inform such a task. That *Crow* is pre-eminently a psycho-mythological drama, should not automatically allow Hughes licence to ignore those other complexities. Of course, one might argue Hughes's direly pessimistic vision in a broader and more inclusive context by locating him in that nineteenth-century tradition of pessimism of which he seems so much a part ('We living, are out of life'—Conrad). In the interview with Egbert Faas Hughes commented that with *Crow* he 'projected too far into the future', and one can guess, as a consequence of this, that the dynamic of his imagination discovered new and hitherto unexplored areas into which he ventured perhaps too readily and impulsively. And there is much past as well as future in the poem.

In *Cave Birds*, Hughes has attempted to provide his explorations with a better sense of proportion and balance and has kept his eye firmly on his subject. The concerns of *Cave Birds* parallel and extend those of *Crow*, which is hardly surprising after the clear indication Hughes gave in the Faas interview that he had in mind enlarging upon the Crow myth. But unlike *Crow* the narrative of *Cave Birds* is clearer and better constructed. The protagonist is a Socratic Everyman figure, who remains intractable in his rational sceptical outlook. The narrative recounts his eventual psychic crisis and abduction by spectral birds into the underworld where he is tried for the crime of his outlook. Condemned to death, he goes on to experience a variety of bizarre ordeals and initiations, emerging finally in the form of a falcon. The drama is, of course, enacted in the form of a dream, in the incurably schizophrenic consciousness of the protagonist. But a more significant reading of the text is suggested by Baskin's own words that preface Keith Sagar's chapter on *Cave Birds* in *The Art of Ted Hughes* (1978): '. . . . . My owls of night and ignorance, genitaled and sexless, hulking, brooding, wailing and screeching, distorted into my vision of aggressive predatory tyranny.' The notion here of a fusion of pure instinctive aggression and perverse rationality seems to pervade *Cave Birds*:

When I said: 'Civilization,'
He began to chop off his fingers and mourn.
When I said: 'Sanity and again Sanity and above all Sanity,'
He disembowelled himself with a cross-shape cut.
I stopped trying to say anything.
But then when he began to snore in his death-struggle
The guilt came.
And when they covered his face I went cold.

The imagery here works more effectively than that of *Crow*. Its antiphonal voice, compassionate, even generous, permits rather than prevents the canting protests of 'civilization'. It displays rather than censures the self-inflicted suffering of our world, no longer with a tone of an embattled rhetoric, but one peculiarly composed, even humble. Is it, at last, Hughes admitting the possibility of innocence in guilt? Hughes seems close here to what he has discovered in the poetry of the European poets, particularly that of Vasko Popa:

> This helplessness in the circumstances has purged them of rhetoric. They cannot falsify their experience by any hopeful effort to change it. Their poetry is a strategy of making audible meanings without disturbing the silence, an art of homing in tentatively on vital scarcely perceptible signals, making no mistakes, but with no hope of finality, continuing to explore. Finally, with delicate manoeuvring, they precipitate out of a world of malicious negatives a happy positive. And they have created a small ironic space, a work of lyrical art, in which their humanity can respect itself. (*Vasko Popa, Selected Poems*, with Introduction by Ted Hughes, 1969)

Hughes comes close, but not always. Partly because, and for obvious reasons, his experience is historically different from theirs (he is not Milosz, after all), and partly, having something to do with that dissimilarity of experience, he falls short of their characteristic openness and simplicity, becoming at times involved with a dour and impenetrable abstractness.

One can admire the driving originality of Hughes's imagination and his reluctance to surrender the least meaning that might diffuse the energy of his perceptions. The compressed and highly charged metaphors seem to want to enthral rather than illuminate us with the awesome forms they invoke and upon which they gradually, almost tentatively, come to focus. The focus is kept teasingly blurred. Yet it is not a technical effect, part of the overall strategy of Hughes's art. It is more that Hughes himself is unable finally to adjust the lens to make those forms intelligible to us. In many ways, the density and unconnectedness of the metaphors explain his artistic predicament, acknowledging as he does the extraordinary fertile ground of his new imaginative experience but simultaneously discovering the inadequacy of language to give it direct and coherent expression. Consequently, in many poems we have a series of closed metaphors, each one suggesting a great occasion of insight, of imminent revelation, which is subsequently left in mid-air, as a new metaphor arrives, apparently nearer to the meaning of the experience under way:

> And suddenly you
> Have not a word to say for yourself.
>
> Only a little knife, a small incision,
> A snickety nick in the brain
> And you drop off like a polyp.
>
> Only a crumb of fungus,
> A pulp of mouldy tinder
> And you flare, fluttering, black-out like a firework.
>
> Who are you, in the nest among the bones?
> You are the shyest bird among birds.
> 'I am the last of my kind.'
> ('Only a Little Sleep, a Little Slumber')

The tensions set up in the language, though often threatening obscurity, are not the result of an excited over-indulgence, a sort of perverse linguistic filibustering. Rather, they derive their impulse from a genuine anxiety with the world in which the human consciousness can make only futile appeals to commonsense and reason—futile, because such appeals habitually reveal themselves as ultimately calamitous for us. Such are the horrors of the world, we try to exclude them from our minds, but always at our peril for they return more threateningly, agitating like an involuntary twitch in the corner of the eye:

> While I strolled
> Where a leaf or two still tapped like bluetits
> I met thin, webby rain
> And thought: 'Ought I to turn back, or keep going?'
> Her heart stopped beating, that second.
>
> As I hung up my coat and went through into the kitchen
> And peeled a flake off the turkey's hulk, and stood vacantly munching
> Her sister got the call from the hospital
> And gasped out the screech.
>
> And all the time
> I was scrubbing at my nails and staring through the window
> She was burning.
>
> Some, who had been close, walked away
> Because it was beyond help now.
> ('Something Was Happening')

The title of this poem could well stand as the motto of *Cave Birds*, for many of the poems exhibit a peculiar and uncanny resistance to full explication. They seem to exist in those areas of uncharted experience where one feels they can only be fully comprehended in their emotional and psychological impact, as if to seize upon any one aspect of their composition would be only to reveal the other areas of experience on which any single aspect depends wholly for its meaning. One wonders whether Hughes, whilst writing these poems, had in mind Marlow's comments on our 'inability to interpret aright the signs which experience (a mysterious thing in itself) makes to our understanding and emotion . . .' (Joseph Conrad, *Chance*). It is a difficult business indeed to come to any final decision as to whether or not Hughes himself has interpreted those signs aright. Once again, it is a simple note of faith, one which finds confirmation in our impressions or else does not.

Many of the same interpretative problems arise with *Gaudete*. It represents a further extension (though I hesitate to say refinement) of Hughes's previous mythopoeic ambitions, but with the difference that in *Gaudete* the mythology strives for an autonomy which before was only tentative. And finally it succeeds or fails on Hughes's terms only, as if we were placed in the wake of his mythologizing, obliged to gauge its aim and direction by an assortment of vaguely related events along the way. There is a narrative which is briefly summarized at the front of the book, but as one might suspect in such a lengthy work, it becomes considerably more complex and mystifying. This has to do with the lack of sufficient commentary on the action and pattern of events (it was originally conceived as a scenario for a film) and the problem of differentiating between the real and changeling Lumb. It has much to do with Hughes's own uncertainty about the nature of his mythology and how he might best develop it without baffling himself.

As a fiction, mythology is required to work within strictly defined limits and conventions, a fact Hughes acknowledged when he described Crow's folkloric origins in the Faas interview. But by attempting to use these conventions with mythological interests appropriate in modern context, Hughes seems to have taken a risk, trying to merge two very different cultural histories and world-views without fully considering the types of consciousness involved. Consequently (the schizoid mind of Lumb is an emblem of our perplexity) we are never given the opportunity of experiencing and therefore judging either the debilitating illusions of our own grim world or the spiritually 'reinvigorating' landscapes of Hughes's newly en-natured world. It is Hughes's belief that with the return of the Shaman—and we must presume Lumb is cast in this role—the effect on the audience will be cathartic, a profound refreshing of their deepest feelings. Is this the experience of *Gaudete?* Here is one initiation of our Shaman:

> Half a ton of guts
> Balloon out and drop on to Lumb.
> He fights in the roping hot mass.
> He pushes his head clear, trying to wipe his eyes
>   clear.
> Curtains of live blood cascade from the open bull
>   above him.
> Wallowing in the greasy pulps, he tries to crawl clear
> But men in bloody capes are flinging buckets of fresh
>   blood over him.
> Many bulls swing up, on screeching pulleys.
> Intestines spill across blood-flooded concrete.
>   ('Prologue')

Can we accept such verbal belchings as a serious offering of spiritual refreshment? One can appreciate Hughes's attempt to strip away the polite accessories of poetic language and restore its more vital mimetic speech-rhythms to give a sharper resonance and directness of address, but Hughes's voice keeps it on a too cramped and severe course. And when it does gain release, it achieves such an ecstatic rhetorical pitch that it seems close to bursting:

> She moves robed invisibly with gorgeous
>   richness.
> She knows she is burning plasma and infinitely tiny,
> That she and all these women are moving inside the
>   body of an incandescent creature of love,
> That they are brightening, and that the crisis is close,
> They are the cells in the glands of an inconceivably
>   huge and urgent love-animal

Those heaped-up adjectives give us little sense of the apparent-ly sublime sensual delight which Felicity is meant to be experiencing. Their straining abstractness seems rather to admit the inadequacy of the language, a falling short at the critical moment of spiritual orgasm. And all this happens in a Women's Institute, of all places! The failure is, and I return to an earlier point, that Hughes is unable to find a sufficiently plausible setting in which to enact his mythological drama. To thrust modern-day consciousness back into a pagan realm of mystery and magic in one violent turn of the imagination, and once there, attempt its renewal by a series of unnerving rituals, seems to require of us more than a suspension of disbelief. It must be with some relief that we come to the Epilogue where Lumb's poems are written out. And if they seem at all opaque in their meaning their translucency of feeling is wonderful compensation:

> The lark sizzles in my ear
> Like a fuse—
> A prickling fever
> A flush of the swelling earth—
> When you touch his grains, who shall stay?
> Over the lark's crested tongue
> Under the lark's crested head
> A prophecy
> From the core of the blue peace
> From the sapphire's flaw
> From the sun's blinding dust.

. . . out of a world of malicious negatives a happy positive'? Hughes seems to have achieved in this section what he has been after for so long—a quiet humility in awe of the majesty of the world, a renewed spirit happy to go on searching, exploring.

SEAMUS HEANEY
"Hughes and England"
The Achievement of Ted Hughes, ed. Keith Sagar
1983, pp. 14–21

One of the most precise and suggestive of T. S. Eliot's critical formulations was his notion of what he called 'the auditory imagination', 'the feeling for syllable and rhythm, penetrating far below the conscious levels of thought and feeling, invigorating every word; sinking to the most primitive and forgotten, returning to the origin and bringing something back', fusing 'the most ancient and the most civilised mentali-ty'. I presume Eliot was thinking here about the cultural depth-charges latent in certain words and rhythms, that binding secret between words in poetry that delights not just the ear but the whole backward and abysm of mind and body; thinking of the energies beating in and between words that the poet brings into half-deliberate play; thinking of the relationship between the word as pure vocable, as articulate noise, and the word as etymological occurrence, as symptom of human history, memory and attachments.

It is in the context of this auditory imagination that I wish to discuss the language of Ted Hughes, Geoffrey Hill and Philip Larkin. All of them return to an origin and bring something back, all three live off the hump of the English poetic achievement, all three, here and now, in England, imply a continuity with another England, there and then. All three are hoarders and shorers of what they take to be the real England. All three treat England as a region—or rather treat their region as England—in different and complementary ways. I believe they are afflicted with a sense of history that was once the peculiar afflication of the poets of other nations who were not themselves natives of England but who spoke the English language. The poets of the mother culture, I feel, are now possessed of that defensive love of their territory which was once shared only by those poets whom we might call colonial—Yeats, MacDiarmid, Carlos Williams. They are aware of their Englishness as deposits in the descending storeys of the literary and historical past. Their very terrain is becoming consciously precious. A desire to preserve indigen-ous traditions, to keep open the imagination's supply lines to the past, to receive from the stations of Anglo-Saxon confirma-tions of ancestry, to perceive in the rituals of show Saturdays and race-meetings and seaside outings, of church-going and marriages at Whitsun, and in the necessities that crave expression after the ritual of church-going has passed away, to perceive in these a continuity of communal ways, and a confirmation of an identity which is threatened—all this is signified by their language.

When we examine that language, we find that their three separate voices are guaranteed by three separate foundations which, when combined, represent almost the total resources of the English language itself. Hughes relies on the northern deposits, the pagan Anglo-Saxon and Norse elements, and he draws energy also from a related constellation of primitive myths and world views. The life of his language is a persistence of the stark outline and vitality of Anglo-Saxon that became the Middle English alliterative tradition and then went under-ground to sustain the folk poetry, the ballads, and the ebullience of Shakespeare and the Elizabethans. Hill is also sustained by the Anglo-Saxon base, but his proper guarantor is that language as modified and amplified by the vocabularies and values of the Mediterranean, by the early medieval Latin influence; his is to a certain extent a scholastic imagination founded on an England that we might describe as Anglo-Romanesque, touched by the polysyllabic light of Christianity but possessed by darker energies which might be acknowledged as barbaric. Larkin then completes the picture, because his proper hinterland is the English language Frenchified and turned humanist by the Norman conquest and the Renaissance, made nimble, melodious and plangent by Chaucer and Spenser, and besomed clean of its inkhornisms and its irrational magics by the eighteenth century.

And their Englands of the mind might be correspondingly characterised. Hughes' is a primeval landscape where stones cry out and horizons endure, where the elements inhabit the mind with a religious force, where the pebble dreams 'it is the foetus of God', 'where the staring angels go through', 'where all the stars bow down', where, with appropriately pre-Socratic force, water lies 'at the bottom of all things / utterly worn out utterly clear'. It is England as King Lear's heath which now becomes a Yorkshire moor where sheep and foxes and hawks persuade 'unaccommodated man' that he is a poor bare forked thing, kinned not in a chain but on a plane of being with the animals themselves. There monoliths and lintels. The air is menaced by God's voice in the wind, by demonic protean crow-shapes; and the poet is a wanderer among the ruins, cut off by catastrophe from consolation and philosophy. Hill's England, on the other hand, is more hospitable to the human presence. The monoliths make way for the keeps and chantries if also for the beheading block. The heath's loneliness is kept at bay by the natural magic of the grove and the intellectual force of the scholar's cell. The poet is not a wanderer but a clerk or perhaps an illuminator or one of a guild of masters: he is in possession of a history rather than a mythology; he has a learned rather than an oral tradition. There are wars, but there are also dynasties, ideas of inheritance and order, possibilities for the 'true governaunce of England'. His elegies are not laments for the irrevocable dispersal of the *comitatus* and the ring-river in the hall, but solemn requiems for Plantagenet kings whose murderous wars are set in a great pattern, to be understood only when 'the sea / Across daubed rocks evacuates its dead'. And Larkin's England similarly reflects features from the period that his language is hived off. His trees and flowers and grasses are neither animistic, nor hallowed by half-remembered druidic lore; they are emblems of mutabilitie. Behind them lies the sensibility of troubador and courtier. 'Cut grass lies frail; / Brief is the breath / Mown stalks exhale'; his landscape is dominated neither by the untamed heath nor the totemistic architectures of spire and battlement but by the civic prospects, by roofs and gardens and prospects where urban and pastoral visions interact as 'postal districts packed like squares of wheat'. The poet is no longer a bardic remnant nor an initiate in curious learning nor a jealous master of the secrets of a craft; he is a humane and civilised member of the customs service or the civil service or, indeed, the library service. The moon is no longer his white goddess but his poetic property; to be image rather than icon: 'high and preposterous and separate', she watches over unfenced existence, over fulfilment's desolate attic, over an England of department stores, canals and floatings of industrial froth, explosions in mines, effigies in churches, secretaries in offices; and she hauls tides of life where only one ship is worth celebration, not a Golden Hind or a Victory, but 'black-/Sailed unfamiliar, towing at her back / A huge and birdless silence'.

Hughes' sensibility is pagan in the original sense: he is a haunter of the *pagus*, a heath-dweller, a heathen; he moves by instinct in the thickets beyond the *urbs*; he is neither urban nor urbane. His poetry is as redolent of the lair as it is of the library. The very titles of his books are casts made into the outback of our animal recognitions. *Lupercal*, a word infested with wolfish stinks yet returning to an origin in Shakespeare's *Julius Caesar*: 'You all did see that on the Lupercal / I thrice presented him a kingly crown.' Yet the word passes back through Shakespeare into the Lupercal, a cave below the western corner of the Palatine Hill in Rome; and the Lupercal was also the festival held on 15 February when, after the sacrifice of goats and a dog, youths dressed only in girdles made from the skins of these victims ran about the bounds of the Palatine city, striking those whom they met, especially women, with strips of goatskin. It was a fertility rite, and it was also a ritual beating of the bounds of the city, and in a way Hughes' language is just this also. Its sensuous fetch, its redolence of blood and gland and grass and water, recalled English poetry in the fifties from a too suburban aversion of the attention from the elemental; and the poems beat the bounds of a hidden England in streams and trees, on moors and in byres. Hughes appeared like Poor Tom on the heath, a civilised man tasting and testing the primitive facts; he appeared as *Wodwo*, a nosing wild man of the woods. The volume *Wodwo* appeared in 1967 and carried as its epigraph a quotation from *Gawain and the Green Knight*, and that deliberate affiliation is instructive. Like the art of Gawain, Hughes' art is one of clear outline and inner richness. His diction is consonantal, and it snicks through the air like an efficient blade, marking and carving out fast definite shapes; but within those shapes, mysteries and rituals are hinted at. They are circles within which he conjures up presences.

Hughes' vigour has much to do with this matter of consonants that take the measure of his vowels like calipers, or stud the line like rivets. 'Everything is inheriting everything', as he says in one of his poems, and what he has inherited through Shakespeare and John Webster and Hopkins and Lawrence is something of that primary life of stress which is the quick of the English poetic matter. His consonants are the Norsemen, the Normans, the Roundheads in the world of his vocables, hacking and hedging and hammering down the abundance and luxury and possible lasciviousness of the vowels. 'I imagine this midnight moment's forest'—the first line of the well-known 'The Thought Fox'—is hushed, but it is a hush achieved by the quelling, battening-down action of the m's and d's and t's: I iMagine this MiDnighT MoMenT's foresT. Hughes' aspiration in these early poems is to command all the elements, to bring them within the jurisdiction of his authoritarian voice. And in 'The Thought Fox' the thing at the beginning of the poem which lives beyond his jurisdiction is characteristically fluid and vowelling and sibilant: 'Something else is alive' whispers of a presence not yet accounted for, a presence that is granted its full vowel music as its epiphany—'Something more near / Though deeper within darkness / Is entering the loneliness.' It is granted this dilation of its mystery before it is conjured into the possession of the poet-warden, the vowel-keeper; and its final emergence in the fully sounded i's and e's of 'an eye, / A widening deepening greeness,' is gradually mastered by the braking action of 'brilliantly, concentratedly', and by the shooting of the monosyllabic consonantal bolts in the last stanza:

> Till, with a sudden sharp hot stink of fox
> It enters the dark hole of the head.
> The window is starless still; the clock ticks,
> The page is printed.

Next a poem whose subject might be expected to woo the tender pious vowels from a poet rather than the disciplining consonants. About a 'Fern': 'Here is the fern's frond, unfurling a gesture'. The first line is an Anglo-Saxon line, four stresses, three of them picked out by alliteration; and although the frosty grip of those f's thaws out, the fern is still subsumed into images of control and discipline and regal authority:

> And, among them, the fern
> Dances gravely, like the plume
> Of a warrior returning, under the low hills,
> Into his own kingdom.

But of course we recognise that Hughes' 'Thistles' are vegetation more kindred to his spirit than the pliant fern. And when he turns his attention to them, they become reincarnations of the Norsemen in a poem entitled 'The Warriors of the North':

> Bringing their frozen swords, their salt-bleached
>   eyes, their salt-bleached hair,
> The snow's stupefied anvils in rows,
> Bringing their envy,
> The slow ships feelered Southward, snails over the
>   steep sheen of the water-globe.

and he imagines them resurrected in all their arctic mail 'into the iron arteries of Calvin', and into 'Thistles'. The thistles are emblems of the Hughes voice as I see it, born of an original vigour, fighting back over the same ground; and it is not insignificant that in this poem Hughes himself imagines the thistles as images of a fundamental speech, uttering itself in gutturals from behind the sloped arms of consonants:

> Every one a revengeful burst
> Of resurrection, a grasped fistful
> Of splintered weapons and Icelandic frost thrust up
> From the underground stain of a decayed Viking.
> They are like pale hair and the gutturals of dialect.
> Every one manages a plume of blood.
>
> Then they grow grey, like men.
> Mown down, it is a feud. Their sons appear,
> Stiff with weapons, fighting back over the same
>   ground.

The gutturals of dialect, which Hughes here connects with the Nordic stratum of English speech, he pronounces in another place to be the germinal secret of his own voice. In an interview published in the *London Magazine* in January 1971 he said:

> I grew up in West Yorkshire. They have a very distinctive dialect there. Whatever other speech you grow into, presumably your dialect stays alive in a sort of inner freedom . . . it's your childhood self there inside the dialect and that is possibly your real self or the core of it . . . Without it, I doubt if I would ever have written verse. And in the case of the West Yorkshire dialect, of course, it connects you directly and in your most intimate self to Middle English poetry.

In other words he finds that the original grain of his speech is a chip off the old block and that his work need not be a new planting but a new bud on an old bough. What other poet would have the boldness to entitle a collection *Wodwo*. Yet *Gawain and the Green Knight*, with its beautiful alliterating and illuminated form, its interlacing and trellising of natural life and mythic life, is probably closer in spirit to Hughes' poetry than Hughes' poetry is to that of his English contemporaries. Everything inherits everything—and Hughes is the rightful heir to this alliterative tradition, and to the cleaving simplicity of the Border ballad, which he elevates to the status of touchstone later in that same interview. He says that he started writing again in 1955:

> The poems that set me off were odd pieces by Shapiro, Lowell, Merwin, Wilbur and Crowe Ran-

som. Crowe Ransom was the one who gave me a model I felt I could use. He helped me get my words into focus . . . But this whole business of influences is mysterious . . . And after all the campaigns to make it new you're stuck with the fact that some of the Scots Border ballads still cut a deeper groove than anything written in the last forty years. Influences just seem to make it more and more unlikely that a poet will write what he alone could write.

What Hughes alone could write depended for its release on the discovery of a way to undam the energies of the dialect, to get a stomping ground for that inner freedom, to get that childhood self a disguise to roam at large in. Freedom and naturalness and homeliness are positives in Hughes' critical vocabulary, and they are linked with both the authenticity of individual poets and the genius of the language itself. Speaking of Keith Douglas in 1964, Hughes could have been speaking of himself; of the way his language and his imagination alerted themselves when the hunt for the poem in the adult world became synonymous with the hunt for the animal in the world of childhood, the world of dialect:

> The impression is of a sudden mobilising of the poet's will, a clearing of his vision, as if from sitting considering possibilities and impossibilities he stood up to act. Pictures of things no longer interest him much: he wants their substance, their nature and their consequences in life. At once, and quite suddenly, his mind is whole . . . He is a renovator of language. It is not that he uses words in jolting combinations, or with titanic extravagance, or curious precision. His triumph is in the way he renews the simplicity of ordinary talk . . . The music that goes along with this . . . is the natural path of such confident, candid thinking . . . A utility general purpose style that combines a colloquial prose readiness with poetic breadth, a ritual intensity of music with clear direct feeling, and yet in the end is nothing but casual speech.

This combination of ritual intensity, prose readiness, direct feeling and casual speech can be discovered likewise in the best poems of *Lupercal*, because in *Hawk in the Rain* and indeed in much of *Wodwo* and *Crow*, we are often in the presence of that titanic extravagance Hughes mentions, speech not so much mobilising and standing up to act as flexing and straining until it verges on the grotesque. But in poems like 'Pike', 'Hawk Roosting', 'The Bull Moses' and 'An Otter' we get this confident, speedy, hammer-and-tongs proficiency. And in this poem from *Wodwo*, called 'Pibroch', a poem uniquely Hughesian in its very title, fetching energy and ancestry from what is beyond the Pale and beneath the surface, we have the elements of the Scottish piper's *ceol mor*, the high style, implicit in words like 'dead', 'heaven', 'universe', 'aeon', 'angels', and in phrases like 'the foetus of God', 'the stars bow down'—a phrase which cunningly makes its cast and raises Blake in the pool of the ear. We have elements of this high style, ritual intensity, whatever you want to call it; and we have also the 'prose readiness', the 'casual speech' of 'bored', 'hangs on', 'lets up', 'tryout', and the workaday cadences of 'Over the stone rushes the wind', and 'her mind's gone completely'. The landscape of the poem is one that the Anglo-Saxon wanderer or seafarer would be completely at home in:

> The sea cries with its meaningless voice
> Treating alike its dead and its living,
> Probably bored with the appearance of heaven
> After so many millions of nights without sleep,
> Without purpose, without self-deception.

Stone likewise. A pebble is imprisoned
Like nothing in the Universe.
Created for black sleep. Or growing
Conscious of the sun's red spot occasionally,
Then dreamng it is the foetus of God.

Over the stone rushes the wind
Able to mingle with nothing,
Like the hearing of the blind stone itself.
Or turns, as if the stone's mind came feeling
A fantasy of directions.

Drinking the sea and eating the rock
A tree struggles to make leaves—
An old woman fallen from space
Unprepared for these conditions.
She hangs on, because her mind's gone completely.

Minute after minute, aeon after aeon,
Nothing lets up or develops.
And this is neither a bad variant nor a tryout.
This is where the staring angels go through.
This is where all the stars bow down.

Hughes attempts to make vocal the inner life, the simple being-
thereness, 'the substance, nature and consequence in life' of
sea, stone, wind and tree. Blake's pebble and tiger are shadowy
presences in the background, as are the landscapes of Anglo-
Saxon poetry. And the whole thing is founded on rock, that
rock which Hughes presented in his autobiographical essay as
his birthstone, holding his emergence in place just as his
headstone will hold his decease:

> This was the *memento mundi* over my birth; my
> spiritual midwife at the time and my godfather ever
> since—or one of my godfathers. From my first day it
> watched. If it couldn't see me direct, a towering
> gloom over my pram, it watched me through a
> species of periscope: that is, by infiltrating the very
> light of my room with its particular shadow. From
> my home near the bottom of the south-facing slope
> of the valley, the cliff was both the curtain and the
> backdrop to existence.

I quote this piece because it links the childhood core with the
adult opus, because that rock is the equivalent in its poetic
landscape of dialect in his poetic speech. The rock persists,
survives, sustains, endures and informs his imagination, just as
it is the bedrock of the language upon which Hughes founds his
version of survival and endurance.

HELEN VENDLER
"Raptures and Rendings"

New Yorker, December 31, 1984, pp. 66–72

The new Poet Laureate of England, Ted Hughes, now in
his mid-fifties, has written a water book, *River*, to match
his 1979 earth book, *Moortown*. In *Moortown*, Hughes' animal
surrogates were chiefly sheep and lambs; in *River*, they are fish,
eels, and insects. Hughes notices in nature what suits his
purpose: if he wants to wince at man's naïveté, he writes about
the innocent lamb ignorant of its fate; if he wants to write about
disability, he describes a dying insect. In "A March Calf," for
example (from the 1975 volume *Season-Songs*), Hughes is the
knowing speaker observing the lamb for the slaughter:

> Right from the start he is dressed in his best—his
>   blacks and his whites.
> Little Fauntleroy—quiffed and glossy . . .
>
> Hungry people are getting hungrier,
> Butchers developing expertise and markets,

But he just wobbles his tail—and glistens
Within his dapper profile
Unaware of how his whole lineage
Has been tied up.

In "A Cranefly in September" (from the same book), Hughes is
the "giant" who watches the crippled cranefly "with her
cumbering limbs and cumbered brain." He prophesies that

> Her jointed bamboo fuselage,
> Her lobster shoulders, and her face
> Like a pinhead dragon, with its tender mustache,
> And the simple colorless church windows of her
>   wings
> Will come to an end, in mid-search, quite soon.

Poems like these imply, as Hughes wishes to imply, that we,
too, are only animals in the universe, and live and die as
helplessly and as unavoidably as any other animal form. But
the poems shade rather too easily into a form of sadism.
Hughes no doubt means to include himself in the human
family of deceived lambs; but the writer of the poem is
undeceived, and the irony is tinged with the relish of superior
power, if only the superior power of knowledge. The giant who
watches the cranefly takes the diagnostic tone of a doctor
watching a terminal case: he "knows she cannot be helped in
any way." It is not Hughes' frustration at his own helplessness
that the poem illuminates but, rather, the triumph of his
biological knowledge:

> The calculus of glucose and chitin inadequate
> To plot her through the infinities of the stems.

For a long time, Hughes has represented himself as the
man who has seen into the bottomless pit of aggression, death,
murder, holocaust, catastrophe. There, in the pit, he has faced
not only the physical evils of mutilation and extinction but also
the moral squalor attending on the brute survival instinct, the
impulse to prey on others out of self-interest. His earlier
surrogate forms, the hawk and the crow—in *Lupercal* (1960)
and *Crow* (1971)—are his vehicles for facing base instinct.
Crow, for instance, watches a suicide; when it is over "And the
body lay on the gravel / Of the abandoned world . . . / Crow
had to start searching for something to eat." The hawk says, in
"Hawk Roosting":

> I kill where I please because it is all mine. . . .
> My manners are tearing off heads—
> The allotment of death.
> For the one path of my flight is direct
> Through the bones of the living. . . .
> I am going to keep things like this.

These are the poems of a man convinced that social hypocrisy
has prevented such unlovely truths from appearing in poetry
except in an "ethical" poetry condemning them. Hughes is
determined to unveil these instincts, to show himself and
others, through such animal surrogates, in the most predatory
and self-serving light. Needless to say, there is a self-sadism
here, which, when Hughes splits himself in two—the watcher
and the watched—turns into what appears to be sadism toward
the foolish lamb and the stumbling cranefly.

In fact, Hughes' gaze has been so relentlessly selective as
he looks at the world that all the arguments made against any
"naturalistic" writer apply to him. If a hundred lambs are
adequately born and one is not, Hughes' poem will savagely
concern itself with the exception. His anger against a world
containing stillbirths may be his conscious motive for writing;
but what reader will not see in "February 17th" (from
Moortown) Hughes' powerful imaginative appetite for naming
and ornamenting disaster? In the poem, Hughes, who has a

farm in Devon, tells us that he found one of his ewes with a half-born lamb "looking out" of her "back end":

> A blood ball swollen
> Tight in its black felt, its mouth gap
> Squashed crooked, tongue stuck out, black-purple,
> Strangled by its mother.

After trying in vain to pull the lamb out, Hughes fetched a razor, and

> Sliced the lamb's throat strings, levered with a knife
> Between the vertebrae and brought the head off
> To stare at its mother, its pipes sitting in the mud
> With all earth for a body.

Then, after decapitating the lamb, Hughes reached in to pull out the rest of it; it came (and the poem ends)

> In a smoking slither of oils and soups and syrups—
> And the body lay born, beside the hacked-off head.

To the argument "But that was exactly how it was" one can only put the counterargument: This is a poet who wants to write words like "blood ball swollen" and "sliced . . . throat strings" and "hacked-off head." Poems are, at one level, experiments in getting certain sounds and phrases and grammatical forms down on paper; and Hughes likes violent phrases, thick sounds, explosive verbs.

Hughes grew up, as every commentator on him remarks, with a sense of violence and death. This is attributed by Hughes himself, and by his critics, following him, to his having internalized his father's experience of the First World War. As the poems "Out" and "TV Off" tell us, the elder Hughes was wounded and left piled with the dead for two days; later, though outwardly healed, he never recovered from that memory of lying "Golden-haired, while his friend beside him / Attending a small hole in his brow / Ripened black." It may be true, as Hughes says, that "the shrapnel that shattered my father's paybook / Gripped me," and that Hughes' writing replays a child's monstrously enlarged imaginings of trench warfare, mutilation, and death. But something more has been added. Hughes mixes sexual intercourse into the brew of war and death, and his blighted imagination, though it occasionally mentions joy, tends to speak even of that with the exhaustion of one who knows all the moves in the erotic battle and finds a perverse fascination in the stylizations of victimage. In the new book, a damselfly who kills her mate during intercourse serves Hughes as a sexual symbol. She appears, in "Last Act,"

> Hover-poised, in her snakeskin leotards,
> A violet-dark elegance,
>
> Eyelash-delicate, a dracula beauty,
> In her acetylene jewels,
>
> Her mascara smudged, her veils shimmer-fresh.

Later, Hughes finds her murdered mate:

> A touch-crumple petal of web and dew—
> Midget puppet-clown, tranced on his strings.

Less violent matings interest Hughes proportionately less; he insists on demystifying "love" into its most aesthetically lethal biological instance. It cannot be aesthetic for Hughes, one suspects, without its fatality.

Hughes has by now found many ways to embody his wounded sense of the world: catastrophe (the stillborn lamb), predatory acts (by the hawk, by butchers), sexual victimage (the damselfly), suicide (Ophelia), and, in this book, hunting and fishing. He tears off the bandages to expose the "red unmanageable life," the raw flesh of existence. And he must find not only adequate emblems but adequate formal means. For him, this has meant putting the world into parables, which have an air of reducing things to their most basic terms. Here we are, for example, after the nuclear holocaust:

> The demolition is total
> Except for two strange items remaining in the
>   flames—
> Two survivors, moving in the flames blindly.
> Mutations—at home in the nuclear glare.
> Horrors—hairy and slobbery, glossy and raw.
> They sniff toward each other in the emptiness.
> They fasten together. They seem to be eating each
>   other.
> But they are not eating each other.
> They do not know what else to do.
> They have begun to dance a strange dance.

This, from the volume *Crow*, is disarmingly entitled "Notes for a Little Play." It uses, in a wholly mistaken portentousness, all the formal means of parable: a minimal number of actors and actions; an exaggerated plot (in which survivors immediately grapple in intercourse); a primerlike vocabulary ("See the mutants. See them slobber. See them fasten. See them dance"); an equally primitive syntax of short, unsubordinated, and atomized declarative sentences; and an impersonal point of view, which assumes that the anecdote has general applicability. The dangers and powers inherent in parables as representations of human life are self-evident; parables have appealed to stylists from Jesus to Kafka as an exercise in producing the greatest resonance with the fewest words. The irreducible child in Hughes, for whom reality is always large and looming, relishes parables as he relishes cartoon images.

In the new volume, cartoon appears in "Night Arrival of Seatrout" as a fantasy by a grimmer Disney. It is an autumn night, and Hughes fishes amid menacingly eroticized rural scenes:

> Honeysuckle hanging her fangs.
> Foxglove rearing her open belly.
> Dogrose touching the membrane.
>
> Through the dew's mist, the oak's mass
> Comes plunging, tossing dark antlers.

The seatrout leaps, snarls, and shivers; lobworms couple; earth sings under her breath.

> And out in the hard corn a horned god
> Running and leaping
> With a bat in his drum.

Though this would like to be pagan, it is in fact neo-pagan and symbolist, a "hard," revisionist view of Keats' apparently softer autumn. Hughes' neo-paganism was learned at Lawrence's knee, and his parables are Lawrentian, too. So are his repetitions (a formal means revived by Lawrence and frequent in Hughes):

> The river. . .
> Lay dark and grew darker. An evil mood
> Darkened in it. . . .
> Its darkness under roots . . .
> Was dark as blood,
> Rusty peaty blood-dark, old-blood dark.

"Dark," "darker," "darkened," "darkness," "dark," "blood-dark," "dark"—all these variants occur in eight lines, as though, in Lawrentian intensification, one could mesmerize oneself further into sensation by reiteration of a single hypnotic word. The hope of simplification through intensity explains as well Hughes' continued attachment to fixed, repeated sentence forms, as though a furrow once plowed could only be cut deeper and deeper.

On the other hand, against these simplifications of form and language, which play, we might say, the role of fate in

Hughes' universe (incorporating the immutable, the geometric, the rigid, the reduced, and the physical laws regulating space and time), there appear a number of variable forms, playing, we could say, the role of free will. It was in Hopkins that Hughes first found a model for this variable side of his otherwise obsessive nature—a side both visual and kinetic, and more animal than human. The intellectual side of Hughes is entirely aligned with fate; only his physical, sensual being escapes into freedom. In a remarkable poem on growing old, "October Salmon," Hughes sketches brilliantly the moment of male adolescence, remembering

> The eye of ravenous joy—king of infinite
> liberty
> In the flashing expanse, the bloom of sea-life,
> On the surge-ride of energy, weightless,
> Body simply the armature of energy
> In that earliest sea-freedom, the savage amazement
> of life.

This pure kinetic energy is often coarsened and brutalized by Hughes, when it is too theatrically tethered to his Celtic, even Scandinavian, gloom, or when it is too orgasmically "spasming" (his coinage) on the page, or when it is too imitatively re-creating Hopkins' larks and kestrels. But at its best, reined in, it gives Hughes' poems their tensile strength. Hughes has found it difficult in the past to moderate his touch. When he presses just hard enough, not too hard, he raises the English pastoral (Hopkins through Hardy through Lawrence) to a sharper and bleaker pitch. In "The Vintage of River Is Unending," Keatsian autumn—the ripeness, the grapevines, the sweetness, the gathered grain and swelling fruit, the weighted boughs, the river, the cider press—finds itself concentrated as in a burning glass in Hughes' praise of the river of being:

> Grape-heavy woods ripen darkening
> The sweetness.
>
> Tight with golden light
> The hills have been gathered.
>
> Granite weights of sun.
> Tread of burning days.
>
> Unending river
> Swells from the press
> To gladden men.

If this vocabulary of praise seems startling coming from the Hughes of wounds and blood, talon and fang, it is no less startling than Hughes' frequent abandon, in *River*, of the iron maiden of his habitual sentence structure. *River* is altogether a more flexible book, it seems to me, than its predecessors. Hughes is still recognizably himself in the thrust and momentum of his lines, in his choice of the animal world as human mirror, and in his interest in determined biological patterns. But he has readjusted his focus. As Crow, he was predatory and avian; as lamb, he was victim and mammal; now he goes lower on the evolutionary scale, and becomes eel, fish, insect. The cooling of the blood into a subaqueous current tempers Hughes' lines. They are still headstrong, still governed more by a linear sexual drive than by a spatial pooling; but they are driven less by the plunge and drive of instinctual will, more by the rhythms of biological birth and decay. Hughes seems to have decided, somewhat in the manner of Whitman, that if there ever was any death it led forth life. In the baldest statement of the book, Hughes hails, in italics, the river's perpetual "toilings of plasm" as the salmon spawn:

> *Only birth matters*
> Say the river's whorls.

Hughes' new vitalism participates in the same mystic obscurantism that animated his earlier convictions about rapacity and death. But because it exchanges the drilled bullet-gaze of Crow for a more sensuous, free-ranging, and associative registering of the natural scene, the vitalism seems more comprehensive and more adequate to natural existence, and even to human existence.

Hughes' father's nightmarish sense of war may have caused his son's obsession with death. But it is also possible, as Hughes suggests, that some quirk in his own makeup dictated his deathly sense of life, and drew him to others who carried death within them. In any case, Hughes often seems to have felt that, unlike ordinary people, he could not live but only imitate the actions of the living. "Life is trying to be life," he writes, in a poem of that title, but "death also is trying to be life":

> Death is in the sperm like the ancient mariner
> With his horrible tale.

Here, impersonally told, is Hughes' story of his own childhood, in the personage of "Death":

> It plays with dolls but cannot get interested.
> It stares at the windowlight and cannot make it out.
> It wears baby clothes and is patient.
> It learns to talk, watching the others' mouths.
> It laughs and shouts and listens to itself numbly.
> It stares at people's faces
> And sees their skin like a strange moon, and stares at
> the grass
> In its position just as yesterday.
> And stares at its fingers and hears: "Look at that
> child!"
> Death is a changeling
> Tortured by daisy chains and Sunday Bells. . . .
> Death only wants to be life. It cannot quite manage.

The subject may be "Death," but it is also Hughes' inner life:

> Death and Death and Death, it whispers
> With eyes closed, trying to feel life.

Perhaps the strenuousness and the forcing that can be felt in Hughes' poetry arise from the strain of death trying to feel life. His terrible emblems of life and death violently jammed together—the half-born dead lamb protruding from its mother, the live fish with a dead one stuck halfway down its gullet—represent the standoff in his own composition between his unusual physical strength and an underlying spiritual terror.

In the new book, Hughes tries to feel life through "the dance-orgy of being reborn," chiefly in the life cycle of the salmon. He writes of eggs and sperm, of salmon spawning, of insect copulation, of "exhumations and delirious advents." He rises to a rhapsody:

> And this is the liturgy
> Of the earth's tidings—harrowing, crowned—a
> travail
> Of raptures and rendings.

Around that climax are arranged, in this new volume, the tatters of man's mortal dress as it is about to be cast aside—leper-cloths, a frayed scarf, a mask, a shroud, the "crude paints and drapes" of death. Man becomes "death's puppet," and "the masks and regalia drift empty."

In the perfection of the river, all evil, says Hughes, is suspended. The river is the "primitive, radical / Engine of earth's renewal," washing everything to the pure ablution of the sea, "back to the sea's big re-think." In his early combination, in *Crow*, of powerful drama and fine-grained observation, Hughes had praised the power of human consciousness to rise above mortality:

> There was finally something
> The sun could not burn . . .
>
> Crow's eye-pupil, in the tower of its scorched fort.

But, on the evidence of his lifework, Hughes makes poems less to praise consciousness or to construct something beautiful than to reverse an evil spell. In "Stealing Trout on a May Morning" (from *Wodwo*, 1967), Hughes wrote down the deepest truth about his own poetic. As he stands deep in a river fishing, a flood of panic seizes him, "tearing the spirits from my mind's edge and from under." He is magically rescued from terror by the leap of a trout, which gets "a long look" at him. At that moment, the charm is wound up:

> So much for the horror:
> It has changed places.

Hughes' evil spirits have been cast out into the Gadarene swine of the objectified nature.

Hughes has gone about the world finding vessels in nature for his private horrors; once the poison is emptied into the natural vessel and the poem has fixed it there, the horror has changed placed—of course, only for a moment. For the spell to work, the poem has to be adequate to its object, one presumes; but, even so, the aesthetic end is subordinated to the therapeutic one. These priorities need to be reversed if the poems are to bear the strain well and long.

And it does seem as though a certain flagging in the horror had enabled Hughes to detach from his compulsive spell-casting and to look, at least sometimes, on his natural images with more reverie than exorcism. The most beautiful poem in *River*, to my mind, is "October Salmon," Hughes' long self-elegy, masked as an elegy for a dying salmon. I have already quoted some of its phrases; here is some of its long flow:

> Four years old at most, and hardly a winter at sea—
> But already a veteran,
> Already a death-patched hero. So quickly it's over!
> So briefly he roamed the gallery of marvels! . . .
> The mere hull of his prime, shrunk at shoulder and
>   flank,

> With the sea-going Aurora Borealis of his April
>   power—
> The primrose and violet of that first upfling in the
>   estuary—
> Ripened to muddy dregs,
> The river reclaiming his sea-metals.
> In the October light
> He hangs there, patched with leper-cloths.
> Death has already dressed him
> In her clownish regimentals, her badges and
>   decorations,
> Mapping the completion of his service,
> His face a ghoul-mask. . . .
> Yet this was always with him. This was inscribed in
>   his egg.
> This chamber of horrors is also home.
> He was probably hatched in this very pool. . . .
> All this, too, is stitched into the torn richness,
> The epic poise
> That holds him so steady in his wounds, so loyal to
>   his doom, so patient
> In the machinery of heaven.

The tonality of "epic poise" is new in Hughes. "October Salmon" was first published two years ago, in Hughes' *New Selected Poems*, but the tonality it embodies recurs throughout *River*, struggling for its poise against Hughes' equally recurrent, and more typical, violence and victimization. Hughes' remarkable adjectival gift and his propulsive rhythms may find a balance in epic poise. If they do, and if the obsessive rituals of the poetry are harmonized with aesthetic as well as therapeutic ends, Hughes may become an ampler poet of consciousness. Even if they do not, his glare into the machinery of evolutionary law results in a strong contemporary individual scanning of the rites of human life.

T. E. HULME

1883–1917

Thomas Ernest Hulme was born in Endon, North Staffordshire, on September 16, 1883. He entered St. John's College, Cambridge, in 1902, but was sent down in 1904 for reasons which remain unclear. Though he continued his studies at University College, London, he spent most of his time attending philosophy lectures in Cambridge, and left without a degree. In 1906 he visited Canada, working his way across the country and returning the following year via England to Brussels, where he studied French and German, poetry, and philosophy.

Back in London in 1908, Hulme, who lived on an allowance given him by an aunt, soon established himself as a leading figure in the city's intellectual life. As co-founder of the Poets' Club and as the center of a group of young intellectuals meeting at the Eiffel Tower café in Soho, he served as a conduit for Continental ideas, particularly those of Henri Bergson, and developed a theory of Imagism which was soon taken over by Ezra Pound. From 1911 to 1914 he presided over a brilliant salon at the Frith Street house of a close friend, Ethel Kibblewhite.

Hulme's interest in poetry was mainly theoretical, and he allowed only six of his poems to be published in his life time, five of them in the progressive journal *New Age* on January 25, 1912, under the title "The Complete Poetical Works of T. E. Hulme." By this time Hulme's energies were devoted to philosophy and aesthetics, and apart from regular essays in *New Age* his major publications were translations of Bergson's *Introduction to Metaphysics* (1913) and Georges Sorel's *Reflections on Violence* (1916). He attended a conference on philosophy in Bologna in 1911 and one on aesthetics in Berlin in 1912.

Hulme regarded World War I as a necessity, and enlisted on the outbreak of hostilities. Wounded in the trenches in 1915, he was killed by shellfire near Niewport on September 28, 1917. His papers on philosophy and aesthetics, edited by Herbert Read, were published as *Speculations* (1924), *Notes on Language and Style* (1929), and *Further Speculations* (1955).

MICHAEL ROBERTS
From "Hulme and Modern Poetry"
T. E. Hulme
1938, pp. 224–29

Hulme's dislike of the standard forms must be distinguished from the positive search for new cadences and sound patterns that was carried on by some of his contemporaries. In the poetic movement inaugurated by Hulme, Flint, Pound and Eliot there were two distinct tendencies; one towards a poetry depending mainly on images, and the other towards new cadences. The two are often lumped together as the free-verse movement, but Hulme was an innovator mainly in the matter of images, and only incidentally in musical form; Flint was more interested in the study of cadence, whereas Eliot's poetry is full of the sort of imagism that Hulme wanted, and is relatively conservative in the matter of verbal music. Eliot's rhythms are nearly all developments of standard rhythms, and much of his poetry is rhymed and uses familiar consonant-patterns.

Hulme's defence of free verse is not based on a liking for cadence or irregular rhythm: it arises from his conception of the proper subject-matter for modern poetry. In his *Lecture on Modern Poetry* he says that the old desire to make poetry imperishable and rigid was a result of the wish to make something durable amid the changing world, something like the Pyramids or the Trajan Column. That desire has now gone, he thinks, and 'We are no longer concerned that stanzas shall be shaped and polished like gems, but rather that some vague mood shall be communicated.' Whereas the old poetry dealt with the siege of Troy, the new deals (as G. K. Chesterton has said) with the emotions of a boy fishing. Furthermore, modern verse is to be read and not chanted: 'We have thus two distinct arts. The one intended to be chanted, and the other intended to be read in the study. . . . I am not speaking of the whole of poetry, but of this distinct new art which is gradually separating itself from the older one and becoming independent.

'I quite admit that poetry intended to be recited must be written in regular metre, but I contend that this method of recording impressions by visual images in distinct lines does not require the old metric system.'

The romantic poetry that Hulme disliked sprang from a desire to dramatize life and to exaggerate emotions, and for these purposes regular metres and heavy rhymes were useful. The new poetry that he hoped to see was to be more modest; and it was to aim solely at recording particular sensations: 'The first time I ever felt the necessity or inevitableness of verse, was in the desire to reproduce the peculiar quality of feeling which is induced by the flat spaces and wide horizons of the virgin prairie of western Canada.

'You see that this is essentially different to the lyrical impulse which has attained completion, and I think once and for ever, in Tennyson, Shelley and Keats. To put this modern conception of the poetic spirit, this tentative and half-shy manner of looking at things, into regular metre is like putting a child into armour.'[1]

Thus it seems to Hulme that there is a case for a kind of poetry that would be deliberately trivial, more concerned with exact physical observation and apt metaphor than with noble sentiments and imaginative insight. He flatly denies that poetry is related to religion, he attacks the idea of 'imagination', as used by Coleridge and Ruskin, and he asserts 'the particular verse we are going to get will be cheerful, dry and sophisticated, and here the necessary weapon of the positive quality must be fancy'.[2]

As a counter-blast to romantic vapourings, and as a description of one part of poetic technique, this is excellent, but as a theory of poetry, and as a forecast, it is poor stuff. The art of poetry cannot flourish unless people can appreciate poetry that is more concerned with a lady's shoe than with the starry heavens; but religion cannot flourish unless it has a language, and by Hulme's own argument that language must be poetry. As intuitions of the outer world need to be expressed in words, so also do moral and spiritual perceptions. Poetry is not religion, nor is it a substitute for religion: it is a medium through which we can express, among many other things, a religious intuition of the world; and without it religion is as inarticulate as physics would be without its mathematics. When we begin to write poetry, we are led to subjects such as the nature of man; and therefore the insight and sentiment that Hulme tried to keep out of poetry cannot be kept out. The device of defining imagination as a kind of more elaborate fancy does not succeed even with its author. Hulme claims that his 'classical' test of poetry does not depend at all on our sense of the importance of its subject-matter, but this is no more than a device for condemning poetry he does not like. As Pascal says: 'We only consult the ear because the heart is wanting. The rule is uprightness.'[3] Feelings about the value of human life, about suffering and love, about the value of simple enjoyment, and the nature of death, all the feelings Hulme distrusted whenever he recognized them, persist in coming. They can be modified by a changed outlook, but they are never abolished, and they demand expression in words.

If we turn to Hulme's own poetry, we find that it was far less trivial and particular than he believed. The infinite, kicked out of the front door, comes in at the back, and Hulme, without knowing it, writes poems that deal with important and universal subjects. We see this happening in a short poem called 'Above the Dock':

> Above the quiet dock in midnight,
> Tangled in the tall mast's corded height,
> Hangs the moon. What seemed so far away
> Is but a child's balloon, forgotten after play.

This certainly satisfies some of Hulme's criteria: it gives a definite picture and a neat analogy; it deals with simple and familiar things; but it is wrong to say that it does not drag in the infinite. In all Hulme's poems, the 'infinite' things—beauty, sky, moon and sea—appear, but where a romantic poet would try to make familiar things seem important by comparing them with moon or sea, Hulme reverses the effect and makes the infinite things seem small and homely by comparing them with a red-faced farmer, or a child's balloon, or a boy going home past the churchyard. This is the opposite of the romantic method, and it is easy enough to parody, but when it is done well its effects are as notable as those of romanticism, and perhaps not as different from them as Hulme thought.

The difference between Hulme's poetry and professed romantic poetry is not that the subject of Hulme's poetry is unimportant, but merely that its *explicit* subject is concrete and trivial. The underlying feeling and the latent meaning are as important as any 'emotion of the infinite' or romantic sense of wonder. But this is true of all good poetry: Hulme's criteria are among the technical tests of poetry, but these are not the only tests: the judgment of poetry cannot be wholly divorced from intellectual and moral judgments. Each of Hulme's poems implies a belief about the relation of religion to life, as a passage from Wordsworth might do, even if it were not one of the 'great' passages. A denial of the romantic view of life may be hard and sophisticated, but it is not unimportant. When Hulme, at the end of his description of the world as chaos, without order or purpose apart from the mind that sees it, tries to show how this view is acceptable to him, he falls into prose that is very near to poetry: 'A melancholy spirit, the mind like a great desert lifeless, and the sound of march music in the street, passes like a wave over that desert, unifies it, but then goes.'

This is the poetry of stoicism, not Christianity, but it is serious and imaginative, and it cannot be called cheerful, dry and fanciful.

Notes

1. 'Lecture on Modern Poetry.'
2. *Speculations*, 1924, p. 137.
3. Fragment 30.

CATHERINE NOTT
From "Mr. Hulme's Sloppy Dregs"
The Emperor's Clothes
1953, pp. 72–103

Hulme's *Speculations*, edited from notes and scattered material by Herbert Read, appeared posthumously not long after the end of the First World War, in which Hulme had been killed at the age of thirty-four. This book is a manifesto against all the humanist philosophies since the Renaissance.[1] Hulme, making the humanist test the disbelief, implicit or expressed, in the dogma of Original Sin, classifies them all as essentially one philosophy. He is not more precise than any of the writers who have succeeded him about what he really means by Original Sin, nor, I should say, theologically more accurate. In general, he couples the rather wide interpretation that man is radically imperfect, and needs God to achieve any ethical standard whatsoever, with a rather more definite dogmatism about the nature of the divine, its complete separation from the sphere of ordinary knowledge by a real and, as it were, chasmic discontinuity. This might not call for any very active criticism, other than the observation that it is a rather flatly dogmatic example of the Two Truths theory, if Hulme had drawn the logical conclusion from this concept of absolute discontinuity between the sphere of ethical and religious values, and that of scientific investigation—that there was no more therefore to be said, or known, about it. However, the bulk of Hulme's writings then follows, part of it æsthetic but most of it epistemological, which shows that Hulme himself did not allow the discontinuity, which he had posited, to trouble him and that the 'Keep Out' notice which this concept implied was meant only for humanistic, not for theological, reasoning. Hulme's æsthetic theory, particularly when it is about the nature of poetry, is acute though limited. It was part, I should say, of a then general valid reaction in the writing of poetry, and was therefore partly drawn from awareness of actual valuable practice among his contemporaries; while partly it gave them a reflective encouragement to continue in the same direction. This applies particularly to the Imagist poets with their insistence on concreteness and accuracy of description of the objects with which poetry deals, whether these objects are mental or physical. This, with its counterpart in Hulme, who narrows the æesthetic impulse to an urge for precision which can be said to have achieved its aim when we feel that the artist was actually and vividly in the presence of the object he describes, is true enough so far as it goes; and particularly in the case of poetry, which deals in words, it is a natural and healthy reaction when poets themselves have become infected by the historical tendency of language to become cloudy, hypostatised and meaningless—to detach itself, in short, from constant reference to experience. This means that in so far as Hulme and, for example, the Imagists were saying and doing anything valuable, they were simply reasserting the general nature of poetry, which of course has constantly to be reasserted, not only by movements or by critics, but by every poet, in so far as he is a poet, in his individual practice from day to day. It does not mean that the tissue of critical generalisation with which Hulme connected his æsthetic observations to his underlying philosophical concept was justified—any more than that the concept itself was verifiable. It was perfectly true that just before Hulme there was a confusion between poetry and mere emotion—perhaps partly due to 'War-poetry', which needed cleaning up, and that what passed as poetry was often vague, diffuse and sloppy, in short that verse-writers were dealing in poetically and semantically diseased language; but there is nothing in this to excuse a lot of critical language about Classicism and Romanticism which is also made semantically sloppy by these hypostatised concepts. For Hulme simply identifies Romanticism with the man-centred humanism which he hates and whose universal rejection he prophesies, and Classicism with the God-centred view of orthodox Christianity. This leads him to some odd sorting of poets and to some perhaps anxious subdivision of his own classes. Shakespeare, he says, for instance, is classical, but with a *dynamic* classicism; he is a classic of motion. Horace is still classical. This makes one wonder if there was also a special Harrowing of Hell for otherwise deserving literary men who were either pre-Christian or not clearly orthodox.

However, this view of the classical is the point of juncture between his æsthetics and his main philosophy. Good poets have throughout history practised in a way which agrees with Hulme's limited æsthetic, whether he would have called them classical or romantic. . . . What I wish to discuss here is Hulme's anti-humanistic contribution to neo-scholastism.

T. E. Hulme's work stands on a dogmatic basis, as I have indicated—the statement that man is a fallen and radically imperfect creature. This he calls the doctrine of Original Sin and characterises it as the central conception distinguishing the medieval Christian attitude to life from the humanist attitude which, so he says, has been dominant, to the point of completely unconscious acceptance, ever since the Renaissance. His work is also—with some striking variations which do not affect the underlying philosophical structure—based on the Two Truths theory. His method is to divide knowledge into three spheres, claiming an absolute discontinuity among them. The two extreme spheres are those of religion and inorganic science, while the middle one covers everything which we describe as biology or the social sciences. He gives the extreme spheres a kind of polar absoluteness. The idea of discontinuity here is simply another way of stating that we have two ways of knowing, each absolutely and equally valid *in its own sphere*. But the idea of the third or intermediate sphere, and particularly of its separation from the sphere of normal science, is of special interest because it is an expression of Hulme's wish to keep biology and the study of social phenomena 'pure' from scientific method, to preserve, in fact, the whole content of 'Human Nature' for the field of nescience. This wish is at least implicit in all scholastic and neo-scholastic thinking, and seems to be also the only ground on which that philosophy can re-erect itself.

But this idea of the third sphere concerned with the vital or what Hulme calls the 'loose' sciences (it is a 'muddy mixed zone' between two absolutes: this seems an example of what Richards calls emotive language) has another and more particular use in Hulme. For though, as I have said, the fundamental concepts of this manifesto against humanism are stated as flat dogma, Hulme intended to be the philosopher of the reaction which he helped to inaugurate—to erect an intellectual system designed to be tight against the encroachments which, for example, physical and astronomical science had been making for quite a long time. To do this he was prepared to make at least some show of meeting critical philosophy on its own empirical ground. He thought he had discovered the technique and the empirical basis in the philosophy of Bergson. His reasons for isolating "the muddy mixed zone of the loose sciences" which are concerned with life (he refers to them also as 'vital' to distinguish them from physical or mechanical) become clear. Certain basic concepts of scholastic theology have to be saved at all costs. For example, the concept of a fixed 'Human Nature' and at the same time the contradictory concept of an absolute Free Will. For the dogma of Original Sin is not only inextricably involved with these two, but, in particular, without Free Will in the absolute, it becomes a doctrine of despair from which it is very difficult to keep out some kind of determinism. It is interesting that Hulme with his sharp separation of the spheres of knowledge should have felt so much eagerness to put up a rational dialectic in this 'vital' sphere. He was relatively young, as well as ardent and militaristic, and this may have brought out a special moral and intellectual pride. Certainly his zeal seems to have been in the first place philosophical rather than salvationist and, unlike for instance Mr. Lewis and Miss Sayers, to be more expressive of the study, or at least of the drawing-room, than of the soap-box. In any case, Bergson provided him with an imposing terminology for this effort, which was not less hypostatical in the original than in Hulme's interpretation. . . .

It is not necessary here to go into the question of how far Bergson was influenced by, or in practical agreement with, the conception of an unconscious Self which arose in the contemporary psychology of Freud and Janet and to which he refers in *Matter and Memory*, or how far this conception can be used to give meaning to his Fundamental Self. It is only Hulme's interpretation and its purposes which matter here. Hulme's purpose is to combat mechanistic determinism and to save the doctrine of Free Will and the conception of unpredictability in the universe. Therefore if we could suppose, perhaps charitably, that, in giving some sort of account of Intuition and of the Fundamental Self, Hulme was only referring to the way in which unconscious processes become conscious—and not only creative and mathematical thinkers but most people of ordinary education are now familiar with this—we should still not have got very far with understanding Hulme's philosophical intentions. He says himself that there is nothing mysterious,

ineffable or infinite about either Intuition or the Fundamental Self. Intuition is a "perfectly normal and frequent phenomenon . . . in all probability any literary man or artist would understand—would grasp much more easily—what Bergson means by an intuition . . . nearly all of them constantly exercise the faculty." It is curious that Hulme did not observe that not only literary men and artists, but also intellectual and scientific thinkers, constantly exercise this faculty. In fact, the circulation between conscious and unconscious processes is characteristic of thinking of all kinds. We are all of us capable of a rapid, sometimes almost instantaneous, survey and summary of our mental events, in a direction in which we are practised, and have all of us experienced this. We can call this Intuition for conversational purposes, if we like, as long as we remember that it is indeed not a 'mysterious' or even a distinct 'faculty', nor one which peculiarly works on a material distinguishing itself from the rest of the circulation of mental life—what the Bergsonian Fundamental Self would have to be. It would perhaps be salutary to recall the expression 'A woman's intuition'. Surely this, if not totally 'mysterious'—let alone generally incompetent—clearly illustrates what I say: it is a quickening and sharpening of perceptiveness in a practised and interested direction.

I should say that, whether deliberately or not, Hulme leaves out the obvious fact that mental processes which he would describe as 'intellectual'—for example, analytical and scientific ones—work in the way I have discussed, exactly like creative or artistic ones, because he has to save Intuition and its counterpart, the Fundamental Self, so as to prevent the whole of Bergson's philosophy, and therefore the whole of the intellectual defence of dogmatism which he is trying to construct, from falling to pieces.

So this fundamental self has to exist and moreover it has to be free. To understand what Hulme means by freedom in the individual or unpredictability in the universe, we must go a little into the use he makes of Bergson's theory of time and change. The deterministic account of change, by which he means the mechanistic theory of the universe, that an infinite intelligence which knew all causes would be able to predict all effects, is only true, he says, if we admit that everything can really be analysed into separate elements so that change is only alteration in the position of particles. This applies if the knowing intellect is, as Hulme defines it, a faculty which operates only by 'spatial' unfolding. As already stated, this is a poor account of intellect and its operations.

"We have just seen," says Hulme, "that mental life at the level of the fundamental self cannot" be thus spatially analysed. We have just seen, on the contrary, I hope, that this Bergsonian concept has no apparent meaning, since the relationship of the Fundamental Self with the faculty of Intuition is the only evidence which Hulme has so far given for the existence of either. If Bergson was vaguely referring to what Freud and others have called the Unconscious, then it must be said that we only know about this at the level of the conscious (or Superficial) Self.

Nevertheless Hulme supposes that this Fundamental Self shows its freedom by changing in a way which will not fit in with the kind of conception the intellect forms of change. And "if we suppose," he says, "that free acts are possible, we are landed: it follows that real novelty is possible: that things can happen which could not have been foreseen even by an infinite intelligence." It may seem to be splitting hairs to say that the mere form of the last sentence is full of implication which is probably merely careless. But nothing whatsoever to do with real novelty, or things happening, can be said to follow from anything which 'we suppose' either about free acts on the part of the Fundamental Self, or indeed about infinite intelligence. But I believe that this construction, merely careless though it may be, is a minor illustration of the underlying confusion, which Hulme made equally with Bergson, between the totality of cause and effect, and an infinite intelligence which might be conceived to know that totality in an absolute sense.

The construction covers as usual a determination to attack the scientific method of understanding the universe. But the attack is not even well conceived. We have seen that the 'explicative' is not the sole or even the main way of knowing in the scientific sense. But it seems to be inexorably implied in both Hulme and Bergson that we are only free if we do not 'know' in this or indeed in any comprehensible sense. A free act is defined in effect as a non-intellectual and indeed unconscious act. The result is that Hulme's account of a determined universe lays altogether too much stress on the notion of an absolute predictability. . . .

Underneath the Hulme-Bergson ideas about predictability and novelty are all the usual misconceptions about the nature of knowledge—that it is not knowledge unless it is absolute, and that it is not scientific if it is not quantitative and dependent on measuring apparatus. He ignores the facts that science is a method of inquiry and that it refers to experience. There is an enormous range of scientific inquiry which produces an enormous body of verifiable information which is not affected, let alone invalidated, by the notion of universal predictability. The generalisations which result from scientific investigation into human life and behaviour on this planet, for instance in biology, medicine and psychology, are quite obviously verifiable or not. I mean that in these cases, as a mere minimum, it should be obvious to laymen, including Hulme, that the generalisations are verifiable or not, and claim to be knowledge only in so far as they are verifiable. If they are not verifiable, they can be, and are, continually set aside for others which are so.

The fundamental misconception is about the nature of intellectual process. According to Hulme, we cannot be said to 'know' anything in an intellectual sense, unless we know everything. We see now why the idea of infinite intelligence is really inseparable from that of an absolute predictability.

Hulme had put himself on an old and awkward spot. For in order to save the idea of 'novelty', of freedom in the universe, even an infinite intelligence would be liable to be suddenly caught out by arbitrary limitations. Anatole France (*Île des penguins*) put it in the mouth of the Lord, and in a nutshell:

> In order not to impair human liberty, I will be ignorant of what I know, I will thicken upon my eyes the veils I have pierced, and in my blind clearsightedness I will let myself be surprised by what I have foreseen.

Hulme and Bergson have done nothing more than uncover, without solving, the old dilemma of God's omniscience versus our freedom. From Hulme as a convinced theist entering the arena of empirical discussion we might justly have expected more. But from his account we can only conclude that freedom in the universe is a form of ignorance, and that the reality or objectivity of the universe essentially depends on being unknowable by the ordinary human method. . . .

It is Hulme's hope that we can "find the key to reality . . . in terms of mental life" because, he claims after Bergson, it is in mental life that we have an intuition of, we

directly know, real time, real change, therefore real freedom and the possibility of new creation, as opposed to the 'fixed future' of a universe mechanically conceived. The main distinction between the mental life of which we have an intuition and the mechanical world which we know by the intellect, and can also foreknow to a greater or lesser extent, is that the first is *vital*. There are two further important distinctions between a vital process and a mechanical one. The first is that the vital cannot be "dissected and spread out, without losing its vitality at least in that form". The second is that we don't quite *know* what goes on in a vital process; while, as far as the mechanical view is concerned "whether the complexity of life comes as the result of the working out of certain mechanical laws, or whether it is following a plan laid down for it, in both cases the future is fixed and could be known to an infinite intelligence. That is 'they don't exist in real time at all.'" (Does this refer to the *concepts* of law formed by mechanists and finalists or to life as dissected by them?)

It is clear that the first of Hulme's distinctions here rests entirely on a confusion caused by his own purely metaphoric account of intellect. If he were being merely anatomical we might agree, although without much enlightenment, that the vital cannot be "dissected and spread out without losing its vitality". But in Hulme's context the reference is to the behaviour of the intellect—it is the intellect's act of *knowing* which dissects and spreads out the vital.

It is therefore not at all remarkable that we 'cannot quite know what goes on in a vital process'. Let us, however, notice that this very ignorance is equated by Hulme with our possibility of freedom. In other words the fact that we do not know something is taken to prove that we know something else. This, as I have remarked above, is the typical philosophical procedure of theological and scholastic apologists. Finally the same concept that ignorance is freedom is implied again in the last quotation, where the possibility of absolute foreknowledge is equated with complete determinism.

If there were an 'infinite intelligence' with 'absolute foreknowledge' who had 'laid down a plan' for the universe to follow, I do not see how his plan could help taking real time. Surely Hulme's theology must have included the belief in some infinite intelligence of this sort? How is that to be saved from the fate of existing only in mechanical or mathematical time?

What Hulme has arrived at is that we know objective reality only through intuitive and unconscious processes (which I suppose would include some artistic ones). Intellectual, critical, scientific and conscious processes are subjective. By the time we can analyse our knowledge it has ceased to be knowledge. Knowledge would therefore, one supposes, be incommunicable and the intuitions of mystics are in the most favoured position. How much this resembles the anti-intellectualism of the Nazis and the 'knowing-together' of D. H. Lawrence, how redolent it is of blood and soil! How far from remarkable it is that Hulme was a professed militarist and that, for all his preferences for vital process he helped to inaugurate a cult for the non-vital in art! How unreason, in all its manifestations, yearns for death!

However, Hulme was not content to leave the world of apperception in the maya-like state to which he had reduced it. He was aware of his philosophical responsibilities and his duty to protect his intuitive pronouncements from too glaring a critical light, and so the verifying process of the intellect, its most important function, which had been thrown out like a bad angel, had to be summoned back to sign its own death warrant.

Hulme felt that, as far as the individual mind was concerned, he had 'refuted mechanism'. But on the other hand there might still be some people who would prefer to attribute subjectivity to our intuitive (or vital) processes, rather than to our intellectual awareness and analysis of the external world; who would still believe that that world could be most meaningfully and productively considered by intellectual methods, including the methods of calculation, as well as observation and generalisation; and who would claim that the 'feeling of free activity which you feel in a certain state of tension' tells us nothing positive or certain about the universe as a whole, nor indeed about anything external to the feeling, nor anything profoundly illuminating about the feeling itself.

. . . Both mechanism and finalism, as Hulme defines them, with their 'construction' and planning, are, I suggested, forms of the usual intellectual Aunt Sally. The intellect can only analyse, therefore it can only conceive of an organism, in this case, the eye, as an individual construct, or as part of a plan, of a wider construct. On the contrary, the Bergsonian view shows us the eye as the result of a simple unanalysable desire for vision, its degree of complexity being the result of the organisation which matter has received from that development and direction of consciousness. As this desire or impulse is simple and unanalysable, the investigations of the intellect, and therefore the observations of science, are automatically ruled out—and therefore, one would say, the empirical basis for the Bergsonian view of evolution. In fact, there is no empirical basis for Bergson's Creative Evolution. It is simply an analogy with what he imagines he discerns of free choice and consciousness, in introspection of his own mental life or fundamental self, or intensive manifold. An analogy in any case cannot be held to be evidence and, as we have seen in Hulme's account, there seems to be no kind of evidence that the fundamental self, if it exists, is free and unpredictable and no explanation of how it can be conscious.

All this however is the whole philosophical backing which Hulme provides for the essential concepts of scholastic orthodoxy—in particular for Free Will and the existence and freedom of God, implying the possibility of miraculous intervention—to which he hoped that the Bergsonian 'empirical' revelation of two kinds of knowledge would clear the way.

The chief dogmas of Catholic theology—those I have mentioned above and also, for instance, the doctrine of the Incarnation—cannot be proved empirically. Hulme, although he makes flat dogmatic statements about some of them, as we see in the first part of Read's edition of *Speculations*, particularly about Original Sin and the existence of God, is not so clear as, let us say, Mr. Eliot, on this inability. I have discussed him and his use of Bergson, for one important reason, because he illustrates a special confusion which has been and still is valuable to scholasticism. This confusion is between the fields of epistemology and of psychology. The confusion is implied already, I think, in the concepts, which theology puts all on the same dogmatic basis. For instance, Free Will, if it means human free will, is a psychological concept, whereas the existence of God is an epistemological one. The discussion about what I can know by logical implication, if anything, can never be quite on the same footing as that about what I can know, if anything, by introspection.

In the section on 'Humanism', Hulme has some interesting remarks about what he calls 'The Critique of Satisfactions'. He says, with much justification, that actual philosophy is not a pure but a mixed subject. Mixed up with the 'purely scientific and impersonal' method is something which aims to show what, according to the philosopher's conception, the world should be in reality:

. . . We should expect to find that consciously or unconsciously, the *final* picture (the philosopher) presents will to some degree or other *satisfy* him. It is these final pictures that make it true to say that there is a family resemblance between all philosophers since the Renaissance . . . the final pictures they present of man's relation to the world all conform to the same probably unconscious *standards* or *canons* of what is *satisfying*. . . . The philosophers share a view of what would be a satisfying destiny for man which they take over from the Renaissance. They are all satisfied with certain conceptions of the relations of man to the world. These *conclusions* are never questioned in this respect. Their truth may be questioned, but never their *satisfactoriness*. This ought to be questioned. This is what I mean by a *Critique of Satisfaction*.

We have sufficiently considered the epistemological, or what Hulme would himself have called the 'scientific' part of his own philosophy and we can now reasonably apply the Critique of Satisfaction to it. There are 'conclusions' at the end of *Speculations* but I think that we need not confine ourselves to these. As opposed to the post-Renaissance humanist philosophers whom he rounds up for punishment, Hulme was a quite overt apologist. He set out, not to analyse and reveal by implication, but to prove something. His 'conclusions' and therefore we must suppose his *satisfactions* are manifest from the first page. It may be true that, in so far as they do not maintain themselves as purely critical or analytical and semantic—this is certainly not Hulme's meaning, however—all philosophies are at least in part disguised psychologies.

We should ask ourselves whether or not Hulme did in fact mean *all* philosophies, including theological philosophy, or scholasticism. When we remember his division of knowledge which gives religion an absolute sphere of its own, and inorganic science another, we shall find ourselves justified in concluding that Hulme was ready to make an exception in favour of scholastic philosophy, and that his main object in trying to reduce all other philosophies to the same subjective level of psychological preference was that he wished to restore theology to its old position as 'Queen of the Sciences'. This is the Two Truths theory carried to its most extreme form. And in uncovering this wish, we also apply Hulme's Critique of Satisfaction to his own philosophy. It is not only subjectively a disguised indication of his own psychological processes—the will to power, the over-estimation of order, the preference for the hierarchical. But it is primarily a claim to be an objective and final psychology, to tell us the real and absolute nature of Man, and so to nullify the painstaking, tentative and scientific effort of human generations to tell us something humbler and more reliable about human motives and behaviour. In short, his whole work is aimed at annexing the terrain of the 'muddy mixed sciences' to the 'absolute' zone of religion.

Notes

1. It was the duty of every honest man to cleanse the world from these 'sloppy dregs' of the Renaissance, according to Hulme.

MURRAY KRIEGER
"T. E. Hulme: Classicism and the Imagination"
The New Apologists for Poetry
1956, pp. 31–45

Although modern criticism has done its most valuable work on the literary text, much of its emphasis and terminology has been greatly influenced by the psychological considerations about the creative imagination which have distinguished aesthetic thinking for the past century and a half. But it is not the "imagination" defined by traditional British philosophy which has held this key position. As the word was used from Hobbes to Locke and as it was used when Addison borrowed it from the latter for his *Spectator* papers on "The Pleasures of the Imagination," it had little which could inspire a literary criticism. Those twentieth-century theorists for whom the word has indicated a new direction have rather followed the example of Coleridge, who, seeing the inadequacy of a concept of imagination inhibited by a mechanical psychology of association, turned to the organicism of German transcendental philosophy. As a result, what served as imagination for Addison was from this time forward relegated to "fancy." Seen through the interests of twentieth-century critics, the meaning Coleridge attached to these two terms may be briefly summarized. "Imagination" is that spontaneous power of mind which allows it to express itself in a literally creative way; through imagination the mind infuses organic life into the lifeless mental impressions it has gathered from a lifeless world. "Fancy" is the faculty which, while it also chooses among the many impressions stored by the mind, remains essentially passive; bound by the law of association, it can only bind together additively the selections it has made from the mind's associative memories. For these critics, the imagination, thus derived from Coleridge, is the empowering faculty for our best poetry.[1]

The work of Coleridge was the culmination of the investigations of German aestheticians from Kant to Schelling, and it marked a new emphasis in thinking about art which would never allow the followers of Coleridge to return to the easy assurance of British empiricism. Its dominantly psychological interest may be seen in Coleridge's insistence that the question "What is poetry?" is almost the same as "What is a poet?" Of course these formulations left much to be done by any followers of Coleridge. For, as we shall see, all the questions about poetry that must be answered cannot be collapsed into the narrow dimensions of the poet's psychology. And in the criticism of a poem we must do more than attribute various of its parts to one or another faculty in a transcendental psychology.[2] Yet this is, for the most part, what Coleridge has left to us in his practical criticism. Later, when we come to consider what modern criticism has had to say about the aesthetic object, we shall be concerned with the ways devised by modern critics to judge literary texts objectively, without recourse to psychological speculations. Yet there too we shall see that the influence of Coleridge has been considerable, that often objective criteria have somehow been established through extensions of Coleridge's psychologizing. But here I shall restrict my concern to Coleridge's own field of special interest, to the question of the activity of the poet.

In contrast to these claims about the influence of Coleridge on twentieth-century theorists, it may justly be argued that in their battle against romanticism some of the most influential of modern critics have set themselves against the completely romantic Coleridgean imagination. It would be strange if they did not, in view of the avowed anti-romanticism of modern poetic theory. Indeed it is strange that Coleridge's theory is not more widely condemned by modern critics than it is. This condemnation is especially apparent in the theoretical tradition begun by T. E. Hulme. But even Hulme, who, as an anti-romantic, explicitly leads away from the Coleridgean imagination, must, as I shall show, end by returning to a markedly similar theory of poetic creativity.

Hulme feels that the essence of romanticism is located in its idolatry of the individual who, for the romantics, should have unlimited aspirations since he has unlimited powers.[3] The transcendental faculties given the individual by German Idealism and by Coleridge embody these unlimited powers and therefore must be denied by the classicist for whose advent Hulme prays. For the classicist, according to Hulme, sees man as an extremely limited being who needs all kinds of severely imposed disciplines if he is to function as he should in his proper sphere. Thus Hulme, defending the view of the classicist, rejects a concept of imagination which would substitute a monism for Christian dualism and would make of man a god. For the attribution to man of the power to create absolutely, *ex nihilo*, could mean little less. Thus Hulme explicitly calls for a poetry of fancy rather than the poetry of unbounded imagination which he feels contaminated English verse in the nineteenth and early twentieth centuries. He calls for a poetry that is formally precise and whose pretensions are limited to simple and vivid description. One might say he calls for a return to a theory of imitation and opposes the reigning theory of expression, the introduction of which was so largely Coleridge's responsibility.

But there is also a quite different side of Hulme. In his essay on Bergson, in which he expounds sympathetically the aesthetic of his master in philosophy, there is a description of the poet's activity that seems nearly as transcendental as Coleridge's.[4] Here Hulme distinguishes between intuition and stock perception and characterizes artistic creativity as the former. It is only the artist, he claims, who can break through the mere static recognition of the world about us which practical life demands; he alone can see through to the dynamic flux which characterizes essential reality. And as artist he makes this vision available to others who, without the artist, could never see beyond the stereotyped world of practicality.

This conception gives the poet a far higher and more romantic function than Hulme has assigned him in his severe "Romanticism and Classicism," which repeats, in more narrowly literary terms, the general argument of his more ambitious "Humanism and the Religious Attitude." For while Hulme, as influenced by Bergson, still wants the poet to be descriptive, he adds a metaphysical dimension to this objective. He would have the poet describe the world about him not merely as it seems to be but rather as it really is behind the veil that hides it from most of us. The poet must not give us as the world "the film of familiarity and selfish solicitude"[5] (note how apt this Coleridgean phrase is here) which our senses normally allow to us; rather he must give us the rare world beyond, which he somehow intuits. Now this is a handsome objective; and the intuitive faculty which is to fulfill it for Hulme seems not far removed from the imagination invoked by Coleridge.[6] Surely we may doubt the power of fancy to operate at these profound levels. Hence, we cannot accept Hulme's plea for a poetry of fancy and his condemnation of a poetry of imagination as his final or his only word. Similarly we may be disposed to categorize Hulme as a severe classicist who wants to return poetic theory to the well-ordered stalls of classical imitation from its chaotic refuge of romantic expressionism; but again Hulme's essay on Bergson should give us pause. For while the poet, as envisaged by Hulme in this essay, may in some metaphysical sense be said to imitate reality, only if we stretch the traditional meaning of the concept of imitation in an extraordinary way—one which would make it broad enough to accommodate anti-classicists as extreme as Schelling—can we make it apply here.

Of course, we can dismiss the entire problem by calling Hulme's two positions the damning inconsistency of a muddled mind. But even if this were true, as it very well may be, the problem simply takes another form, since we are still left with the need to account for this inconsistency if we are to see its significance for modern poetic theory. And Hulme's enormous influence on the direction this criticism has taken, an influence that stems from both aspects of his speculations, cannot be gainsaid. For, if we follow down the line that starts with Hulme, we find the same seemingly contradictory duality in most of its major exponents: an uncompromising prejudice against romanticism coupled with an invocation of romantic and Coleridgean concepts, even when Coleridge has been slandered by name. For example, the attraction of these critics to romantic theory is betrayed by their constant use of the now common "organic" concept in discussions of either creative activity or poetry itself, as they either use Coleridge's psychologizing or seek to transform it into objective criticism.

Thus, having forced a disjunction between romanticism and classicism, recent theorists, in the footsteps of Hulme, desire to justify classicism with the theoretical tools of romanticism, yet without permitting a reconciliation between the two. Perhaps their reasoning may become clearer if we examine, from another perspective, their general attitude toward this concept of imagination which some, like Hulme, explicitly reject even as they smuggle it into their theory. Of course, it must be admitted that other critics—I. A. Richards, Cleanth Brooks, and Robert Penn Warren particularly—hold Coleridge and his concept of imagination in high regard. And yet their theories are not necessarily much more similar to each other than they are to those of their critical brethren—like Hulme, Eliot, and Ransom—who have less esteem for the theory of Coleridge. In fact, although the former group of critics shares with Kenneth Burke, for example, its admiration for Coleridge, any one of this group is, in terms of poetic theory, perhaps more closely allied to any one of the latter group than he is to Burke.

To the overtly anti-Coleridgean critics, Coleridge's concept of imagination came swathed in the added meanings it had picked up during its use later in the nineteenth century. Writers like Ruskin had thought of themselves as Coleridgeans and had redefined imagination and fancy for their own uses. For Ruskin, the difference between the two consists mainly in the playfulness of fancy as against the dead earnestness of imagination, the finite as against the infinite.[7] No one who reads Coleridge closely, especially his practical criticism, can deny that this serious-playful dichotomy is involved in his own distinction between the two terms: witness his implied condemnation of the metaphysical poets as being fanciful rather than imaginative.[8] But if Coleridge's practical application of his theory displays this tendency to equate the imaginative with the serious, there is nothing in his theoretical statement of the distinction between imagination and fancy which demands this kind of application. The self-conscious, humorless seriousness which characterizes the so-called romantic disposition is what bothers the modern critic most, since because of it the romantic becomes vulnerable to irony by not being able to

supply his own. And the kind of poetry the romantic would try to justify with his theory would be of the unsmiling variety.

But the value of Coleridge's theory lies in its usefulness to those outside his period and beyond its attitudes; its value lies, as with every philosophical contribution, in whatever claim it can make about leading us toward solving the problems our experience sets for us. And the substance of his distinction does not concern seriousness and playfulness. His definition of imagination does not necessarily dictate against the poems of Donne, although it certainly may dictate, and rightfully so, against some of them. But what a Ruskin or a Carlyle did was to take the accidental aspects of Coleridge's definition—those whose applicability was completely controlled by the prejudices of Coleridge's own era—and to use them for the substantial aspects of his own definition, which he then assumed to be Coleridgean. And thus the serious and the witty came to characterize the imagination and the fancy, respectively.

This brief historical sketch is no mere digression. It partly reveals the reason that Hulme could throw out Coleridge and his imagination on one page and advocate similar aesthetic concepts on the next. Hulme was, in a way, repeating the error of Ruskin. Since he wanted above all a tough poetry—a poetry of wit, as his followers would say—obviously the imagination, with its meaning restricted to unleavened seriousness, would not do for him or his followers. If fancy allowed Hulme and his followers their conceits, then by all means they would take fancy. But when they examine the art of making witty verse, not only do they attribute to the poet the qualities Coleridge included in his concept of imagination, but they insist that only this kind of verse reveals these qualities; that, with few exceptions, the serious verse of the nineteenth-century variety, called imaginative by earlier Coleridgeans, reveals only those qualities that Coleridge relegated to fancy. Now this confusion does not necessarily imply that the distinction is a useless one. Rather two conclusions can be drawn from it: the obvious one is that judgments are so conditioned by epoch that it may seem at times almost futile even to strive for objectivity; a more important one is that neither imagination nor fancy has as its essential attribute the one bestowed on it by its most important post-Coleridgean definers—seriousness or playfulness, respectively—and, as a corollary, that only some quality which transcends these is basic to the meaning of imagination as this word has influenced our post-Coleridgean critical tradition.

Of course, this historical extenuation of Hulme's seeming inconsistencies does not reconcile them. Nor is it meant to. It cannot explain how Hulme, in his "Romanticism and Classicism," can deny to the poet the possibility of moving beyond the world about him and yet, in his "Bergson's Theory of Art," can import the term "intuition" to allow precisely for this possibility. Those who would defend Hulme's consistency may point out that, after all, his discussion in the closing pages of "Romanticism and Classicism" is carried on completely in the Bergsonian terms that characterize his other key essay. But this would hardly alter the charge. It would simply make the inconsistency more unforgivable, since now it would be seen to exist within the limits of a single brief essay.[9]

Other readers of Hulme may insist that I should not even have extenuated the charge to the extent I have done. In "Romanticism and Classicism," they can claim, Hulme clearly realizes that Coleridge's definitions of imagination and fancy are not Ruskin's. In fact Hulme, in quoting Ruskin's definitions of imagination, prefaces the quotations by conceding that Ruskin may be using the word in a highly distorted sense. He is quoting Ruskin, he tells us, to show us the romantic attitude, not to indicate anything about the concept of imagination.

Thus might one not say that the concept of imagination that is under attack by Hulme is far less parochial than Ruskin's, so that any subsequent invocation of this faculty constitutes far more serious an inconsistency than was suggested earlier? Before I can answer, however, several other considerations must enter which should clarify the precise nature of Hulme's inconsistency.

To begin with, although it is true that Hulme does not accept Ruskin's concept of imagination as necessarily identical with that of Coleridge (and it is the latter against which he intends to argue), he still carries along many of Ruskin's connotations in his own uses of the word. For example, late in the essay, when Hulme is discussing fancy, he says, "where . . . your only objection to this kind of fancy is that it is not serious in the effect it produces, then I think the objection to be entirely invalid." But an objection of this kind could come only from a defender of a concept of imagination that is close to Ruskin's. Elsewhere in this essay Hulme disparagingly characterizes all theories that derive from German romantic aesthetics as conceiving that the artist partakes in a vague infinite. Similarly, he says, although in another connection, ". . . there you seem to me to have the highest kind of verse, even though the subject be trivial and the emotions of the infinite far away." He distinguishes in yet another way between imagination and fancy: ". . . where you get this quality [of concrete and fresh imagery] exhibited in the realm of the emotions you get imagination, and . . . where you get this quality exhibited in the contemplation of finite things you get fancy." It is evident in these passages that Hulme considers the imagination to be distinguished from fancy because it is serious rather than witty, because it reveals the infinite rather than the limited, and because it deals with vague emotions rather than with concrete things. Now the former characteristics of these pairs follow from Ruskin's concept of imagination—and, to some extent, perhaps, from the imagination we could derive from Coleridge's practical criticism. But none of them appears as the defining quality of the imagination delineated in Coleridge's theory.

Yet at the end of the essay, when Hulme speaks of Coleridge's distinction between vital or organic complexity and mechanical complexity—which has seemed to be the essential feature of Coleridge's distinction between imagination and fancy—he treats this distinction sympathetically, strangely enough, and proceeds, on the basis of a careful analysis of this distinction, to outlaw romanticism and the poetry of the imagination. In other words, he seems to be defending organicism even as he attacks the romantic theory of imagination. Obviously Hulme does not intend to judge against this concept of imagination by using a law furnished him by this very concept. It should be clear, then, that Hulme is not defining imagination, as Coleridge originally did, in terms of the organic concept; that instead he is still characterizing the imagination largely by the traits attributed to it by Ruskin. In this way Hulme can both favor organicism and oppose the imagination, despite the fact that Coleridge's importance to us lies in the fact that he firmly identified the two. Further, in this last discussion, Hulme, as a faithful Bergsonian, uses "vital" complexity to characterize *all* art, in contrast to the mechanical complexity by which he characterizes the operations of the intellect. For he is as anxious to avoid "the old classical view," which defines beauty "as lying in conformity to certain standard fixed forms" (any such fixity would be abhorrent to Bergson), as he is to avoid "the romantic view which drags in the infinite." In a similar vein, Hulme earlier says of fancy that it "is not mere decoration added on to plain speech. Plain speech is essentially inaccurate. It is only by new metaphors,

that is, by fancy, that it can be made precise." Then he goes on to describe a form of fancy that is inferior to imagination. So here he is defining fancy (as "not mere decoration") in the very way that Richards and Brooks, for example, taking their lead from Coleridge, define imagination. For it is the concept of the functional, rather than the merely decorative, metaphor which characterizes that modern criticism which is admittedly Coleridgean.

It follows from these various passages, first, that the imagination excluded by Hulme is not excluded by reason of the definition Coleridge gave to it. On the contrary, the differentia established by Coleridge for the imagination is the very one Hulme uses to define all art—and here Hulme properly sees Coleridge and Bergson as agreeing. Secondly, Hulme's idea of fancy appears to be essentially no different from Coleridge's imagination, unless we import Ruskin's claims about the kinds of attitudes and subjects appropriate to each. In manner of operation, or in the kind of mental faculty involved, there is no important difference. To put it another way, if we look at the problem from the point of view of the Coleridgean imagination, Hulme is not actually calling for a different faculty; he is calling for a different use of the same faculty. He wants it to be addressed to different subject matter, to be at the service of different attitudes.

Hulme is reacting against a "Weltanschauung"[10] and a metaphysic more than against a literary theory. And this realization leads to another source of his confusion. In many of his essays Hulme uses the term "romanticism" to cover a multitude of sins. He collapses within this single term two quite antithetical movements, which would involve two quite different metaphysics and aesthetics. He often sees romanticism as best typified by the ideas behind the French Revolution—by what might be termed rationalistic progressivism. "Here is the root of all romanticism: that man, the individual, is an infinite reservoir of possibilities; and if you can so rearrange society by the destruction of oppressive order then these possibilities will have a chance and you will get Progress." He opposes to this political romanticism the belief in order and tradition, just as he opposes to the self-indulgent seriousness of literary romanticism the toughness of his proposed classical poetry.

But having established his definition of romanticism on the ideas, let us say, of a Thomas Paine, he proceeds to use the derogatory term to put what I shall term Germanic romanticism in its place.[11] But this is not entirely just. It perhaps springs from a confusion which commonly lumps all English and German romanticism together without first making the necessary distinctions. For example, Edmund Burke, who is indeed one of the earlier Germanic romantics, opposed to the rationalistic defenses of the French Revolution the very virtues—order and tradition—which Hulme claims to be the antidotes to romanticism. And the German romantics are equally conservative and equally traditional. Indeed, the number of converts they gave to Catholicism should certainly have pleased Hulme. With Burke they stood for the organic concept, which resists the mechanism of the rationalistic progressive. If segments of British romanticism were Godwinian, this is hardly reason to damn as a Godwinian anyone who has ever been called a romantic. Hulme has earned the right to condemn romanticism only by his arguments against the antitraditional progressives; he proceeds to prosecute the Germanic romantics (including, of course, Coleridge) on the wrong grounds, therefore. He would need a new series of objections to press the case. Similarly, when he disparages literary romanticism by citing its unleavened seriousness, we must conclude that he is unmindful of the sometimes tough-minded self-criticism of romantic irony (not entirely unlike the "irony" of modern criticism), which is displayed in some German romantic literature and proclaimed in much of its literary theory. Again he seems not to have realized sufficiently that much of English and Germanic romanticism has little in common beside the not very judiciously applied name.[12] In failing to classify the enemy more carefully, he fails also to note the points on which there may be some agreement between them and him. In his anxiety to make the romantic-classical cleavage too clean, he ignores certain all-important overlappings—all-important because so many of his followers are heavily dependent upon the romantic (Germanic romantic) concepts they have adapted to their own uses.

This is not to say that Hulme, had he seen the necessary distinctions among romantics, would have felt very much kinship with the Germanic variety. There still would remain the problem of metaphysics; and certainly few thinkers in the history of philosophy are more open to Hulme's charge that they "drag in the infinite" than these romantics are. Their frequent recourse to metaphysical monism, which would detract from God's transcendence in order to exalt His immanence, must have seemed sufficient reason for Hulme to give them the label of romanticism. And certainly they deserved it, at least on these grounds. But aesthetically, and often politically too, he would, and unconsciously did, find many of their ideas congenial to his own. And in his literary theory, like Bergson before him, he put their dynamic organicism to good use. Whether this organicism can flow consistently from Hulme's rigidly dualistic metaphysics is a question which need not concern us here.

While I may seem to have strayed a good distance from poetic creativity, I do not believe that I have. Surely the term "imagination," as conceived by Coleridge, is central to modern theoretical discussions of this problem. Now I have shown at the outset that Hulme, one of the pioneers of the movement under study, argued against this conception of imagination. And since critics in the wake of Hulme have, like him, been battling romanticism with the tools furnished them by romanticism, it seemed crucial to clarify the precise intellectual relationships between these critics and their romantic ancestor-enemies.

Several of the chapters which follow will be dedicated to proving that the duality I have been tracing in Hulme is hardly confined to him. We shall see many of his followers paralleling his attempt to make the best of two conflicting theoretical traditions. And they often do considerably less well with them than Hulme has done. For example, we shall shortly be concerned with the serious theoretical difficulties in the work of T. S. Eliot, in whom a classical interest, which demands an impersonal poetry that is "an escape from emotion . . . an escape from personality," is constantly accompanied by a romantically expressionistic interest, which calls for the famous objective correlative. If we assume for the moment what will be amply shown later—that similar and similarly serious difficulties exist in the work of Eliot and others—then it would seem clearly important to return to what has been said about Hulme to learn the precise direction his apparent inconsistencies have given to the more extensive and detailed poetic theories that followed.

Clearly it would seem that Hulme is trying to maintain a position which at once includes classical imitation and romantic expressionism, obedience to mechanical rules and individual creativity.[13] His distaste for nineteenth-century poetry, as well as for nineteenth-century criticism and philosophy, forces him to think of himself as a defender of another neoclassicism.

But at the same time his devotion to Bergson forces him to adopt the principle of an organicism or vitalism that must resist all fixity. To say merely that Hulme tries to stand between these extremes and to utilize the best that each has to offer would be radically incomplete; it would make of him no more than a reckless eclectic who would have little to contribute. Instead he made his way to a completely independent position which, to use his words again, avoids the "standard fixed forms" of "the old classical view" as well as "the romantic view which drags in the infinite." To clarify this position and the direction it has given, it is necessary to add yet another element to those shown to be at work so far.

As imagist, Hulme is especially concerned with language. We have seen that for Hulme, the disciple of Bergson, the poet must break through the stock recognitions which plague practical life and thus must make it possible for us to see things in their uniqueness. But Hulme does not allow these intuitions to take place in a vacuum; he is anti-romanticist enough not to believe in the self-sufficiency of the mind. Not only do intuitions take linguistic form, he claims, but they are dependent upon language. For just as most of us look at the world through stereotypes, so do we speak of the world through the equally fixed forms of language. Since thinking can take place only in a medium, it may very well be that we cannot have a fresh perception of the world unless we have first dislocated language in order to force fresh ways of expression from it. Thus, to the problem with which Hulme was seen to be concerned earlier—the artist's need to see the world in a new way—another must now be added which is perhaps prior to, or at least inseparable from, the first: the artist's need to use his language in a new way.

Here, in Hulme's insistence on the primary place of language in the poet's vision, is the clue to the most important difference between Coleridge's theory of imagination and Hulme's theory of intuition. I must postpone treating the total impact of this difference, however, until certain other views of creativity have been presented. But it is, as will appear later, a difference which has been of paramount significance in establishing a criticism that could, for the sake of insight-via-language, endorse poetic experiment even as, in the name of classical restraint, it forbade idiosyncratic recklessness.

Notes

1. For one of many such examples, see Cleanth Brooks, *The Well Wrought Urn* (New York, 1947), expecially pp. 17, 230–31.
2. See, for example, Coleridge's psychological treatment of Shakespeare as poet in *Coleridge's Essays and Lectures on Shakespeare and Some Other Old Poets and Dramatists* (London: J. M. Dent and Co., 1907), pp. 38–42; a somewhat similar faculty-analysis of Wordsworth appears in *Biographia Literaria*, ed. J. Shawcross (Oxford: Clarendon Press, 1907), I, 124–49.
3. *Speculations* (London: Routledge and Kegan Paul, Ltd., 1936), pp. 116–18. This collection is the source of all quotations from Hulme and all summaries of his position.
4. For Hulme's source see especially Henri Bergson, *Laughter: an Essay on the Meaning of the Comic*, trans. C. Bereton and F. Rothwell (New York, 1911).
5. *Biographia Literaria*, II, 6.
6. It is important, however, to note a significant difference involved in the relation of these faculties to the particular and the universal. In true German style, Coleridge often seems, like Schelling, to conceive of the universal as lying immanently within the particular. The poet's imagination, in dealing with the particular, can, through its creativity and its organic powers of unification, harmonize the concrete and the finite with the universal, the infinite, the real. But for Hulme, following Bergson, universals are not reality but are arid superimpositions upon reality which are demanded by our practical propensities. It is the uniquely particular—the dynamic, ever changing instantaneous—that is

the real, veiled from an action-ridden mankind. Thus the essential reality to which the Coleridgean imagination is to pierce is far removed from the fluid reality to which the Bergsonian intuition is to pierce. The similarity between the two faculties here being marked is one of function: each, as revelatory of the real, is our most significantly cognitive power. We may also see in the differing concept of the real given us by Bergson through Hulme a principal reason for the special concern of modern poetic criticism for freshness, precision, and concreteness.

7. *Modern Painters*, Part III, Chapter III.
8. *Biographia Literaria*, I, 15, 62.
9. In this entire discussion it may be well to recall Sir Herbert Read's claim in his introduction to *Speculations* (p. xv) that Hulme "was not, by design, a systematic thinker. He was, in one sense at least, a poet: he preferred to see things in the emotional light of a metaphor rather than to reach reality through scientific analysis." Even if this be the case, it nevertheless must be my task to examine his statements rigorously, however carelessly they may have been related to each other. It is the characteristic of many of the critics to be examined here that they are unsystematic by design. That is much of the reason that this study was deemed necessary. For whatever his design, a theoretical writer can be talked about only if we are aware of the justice he does to those obligations to logic which he incurs, willingly or not, when he begins to record his speculations. In the case of Hulme, however, it is true that his ambivalence is so baffling that I must move cautiously, making qualification upon qualification, if I am to avoid premature judgments and thus do him justice on the theoretical level.
10. This is the term used by Hulme. See *Speculations*, pp. 24–30.
11. I call it here "Germanic" rather than "German" romanticism because some non-Germans shared in the movement although the ideas were most fully explored by Germans.
12. While it may seem difficult to account for these oversights of Hulme in view of the fact that he spent time in Germany studying continually and profoundly, I do not believe his failure to make certain crucial distinctions among those whom he calls romantics can permit an alternative explanation.
13. Hulme's attempt to unite these positions is similar, often in detail as well as in principle, to Eliot's in his famous "Tradition and the Individual Talent."

FRANK KERMODE
From "T. E. Hulme"
Romantic Image
1957, pp. 124–32

For Hulme, the epoch of humanism, anti-religious in every department of life, but visibly so in art, was ending. He lavishes his contempt upon it; with a sort of doctrinaire fury he eliminates as bad and anti-religious (because on the side of life) even Michelangelo. Nor does he care for the kind of thing other Roman Catholics like—Fra Angelico, for instance. His Catholicism is intellectual in the extreme, almost to the point of being a dogmatic abstract from the religion; without its support he cannot have the world-picture he wants, but he will have none of its tenderness and sentiment. The art he cares for is that of the period which the Renaissance ended, an epoch which believed in Original Sin and produced, at its best, a geometric art quite distinct from the vitalism of Renaissance art, which ministered to the spectator's pleasure in being alive, his desire to be *acting*. The art of Byzantium abhors all this, being concerned with absolute non-human values; being life-alien, remote from organic life and even detesting it. This art resembled not that humanist art which began in Athens, but Egyptian religious sculpture and the art of primitive peoples. Geometrical abstraction is a characteristic of cultures which understand the human lot as tragic, and distinguish sharply between the human and the divine, never confusing them, as the 'vitalist' art he hated did. Hulme applies to philosophies

and art alike what he calls his *critique of satisfaction*. Never mind what the philosophers say, he advises; ask instead, what emotional requirement in themselves are they trying to satisfy. And all post-Renaissance philosophy is the same, so considered; it satisfies only the need for an assurance of human centrality. But new needs are now, he adds, appearing, and we are beginning, with Epstein and Wyndham Lewis, to get that anti-vitalist, geometric art of which the beginnings were to be perceived in Cézanne.

Whenever Hulme generalises about historical periods he goes wrong. The critique of satisfaction apparently fails to distinguish between Descartes and Schopenhauer, and it tells us that Hartley and the later Coleridge were seeking the same answers. It is impossible to understand how anybody who had read the *Essay on Man* could possibly regard Pope as exempt from the heresy (which Hulme called 'Romantic') of denying the *absolute* inaccessibility of ethics to the reason; Pope's trace of scepticism has very little to do with the chilly fideism of Hulme, and he has far more of Montaigne than Pascal in him. Much more important than the numerous minor objections of this sort that one could bring against Hulme is the well-established fact (ably presented in Michael Roberts's book) that he disastrously misrepresents Romantic philosophy. For Hulme, as we have seen, Romanticism was a calamity however you looked at it: politically, philosophically, aesthetically. It was the anthropocentric assumption of the Renaissance at the stage of mania, all Rousseauistic rubbish about personality, progress and freedom, all a denial of human limit and imperfection. (In fact it would be truer to say that the movement was obsessed by Original Sin than to say, as Hulme does, that it completely ignored it, and made life the measure of all values.) For Hulme, as for all seers, the moment at which he was thinking was the perfect one for seeing the whole matter in perspective, and so breaking history into two parts (Augustine to the Renaissance, the Renaissance to Hulme). He did not even see how inconsistent he was about Coleridge, whose 'vital' he sometimes uses in its original Coleridgean sense, and sometimes in Worringer's sense, with great confusion—a confusion, incidentally, which reflects the Paterian life-and-death ambiguity which we have already looked at, and which turns up again in the aesthetic of Vortex. Nor did he see how dependent he was upon the tradition he was attacking, despite his avowed and enormous debt to Bergson. In so far as he was merely doing propaganda for a new abstract art which had already got under way he was primarily a reporter of Worringer, and that is consistent and defensible as far as it goes, which is not so far as the main historical generalisation; but in so far as he was introducing a new 'classical' poetry—anti-humanist poetry he means, which is a pretty paradox in itself—his position is complex and unsatisfactory, because he has not found out what it really is. We shall see more clearly where he stood if we consider the theory of the image which is central to his whole aesthetic. It is closely related to the concept of discontinuity, with its attendant rejection of empathic, *vital* art; but, as we shall see, it fits much more neatly into the old Romantic-Symbolist theory with its dualist implication (*two* discontinuous orders related to reason and imagination) than into the triplex structure of his own Bergsonian-Pascalian hypothesis.

Let us, then, look at Hulme's requirements for good poetry. Negatively, it must not be concerned with the myth of human perfection or perfectibility in any form; it must accept the strict limitations of human powers, be life-alien. (Note that Hulme is evasive and inconsistent about Coleridge's Imagination, fearing that there is some connection between it and the hated divinisation of human intellect that denies limit; he seems to have been unaware of the controlling force over Coleridge's thought of his refusal to give up the doctrine of Original Sin, whatever metaphysical labour this refusal might involve him in. In fact Hulme's 'intellect' is much the same as the Coleridgean and Wordsworthian 'reason', the reflective faculty that partakes of death.) The acceptance of limit will at once cut out the ecstatic meaning and hysterical aspiration Hulme regards as characteristic of Romantic poetry. The first positive requirement is for *precise description* (Hulme might have reflected that it is also the first requirement of Wordsworth's *Preface* of 1815). For Hulme, however, this precision concerns the recording of images; and here we are at the core of Hulmian aesthetics.

Without pausing to comment upon its deficiencies, let us look at Hulme's distinction between prose and verse.

> In prose as in algebra concrete things are embodied in signs or counters which are moved about according to the rules, without being visualised at all in the process. There are in prose certain type situations and arrangements of words, which move as automatically into certain other arrangements as do functions in algebra. One only changes the X's and the Y's back into physical things at the end of the process. Poetry, in one aspect at any rate, may be considered as an effort to avoid this characteristic of prose. It is not a counter language, but a visible concrete one. It is a compromise for a language of intuition which would hand over sensations bodily. It always endeavours to arrest you, and to make you continuously see a physical thing, to prevent you gliding through an abstract process. It chooses fresh epithets and fresh metaphors, not so much because they are new, and we are tired of the old, but because the old cease to convey a physical thing and become abstract counters. A poet says a ship 'coursed the seas' to get a physical image, instead of the counter word 'sailed'. Visual meanings can only be transferred by the new bowl of metaphor; prose is an old pot that lets them leak out. Images in verse are not mere decoration, but the very essence of an intuitive language.

Presumably no one would now accept this as it is put; the semantics is, to say the least, naive, and Hulme's emphasis on the visual quality of all images (though not his insistence on their physical quality) has been outgrown. But that "images are the very essence of an intuitive language" is as much an assumption of modern criticism as of Coleridge's. Poetry, by virtue of the image, *is*; prose merely describes. One is end, the other means. What poetry seems to be *about* is therefore irrelevant to its value. "Subject doesn't matter." Poetry is bad when it directs the attention away from the physical uniqueness and oneness of the image (the poem itself of course is an image, if it is good) and enables the reader "to glide through an abstract process". It is concrete, because the Image can be represented only as concrete, and entirely devoid of discursive meanings and appeals to the intellect; it is the direct representation of what is intuited. Whether the poem is good or not depends upon the accuracy of the representation, and upon that alone.

> I always think that the fundamental process at the back of all the arts might be represented by the following metaphor. You know what I call architect's curves—flat pieces of wood with all different kinds of curvature. By a suitable selection from these you can draw approximately any curve you like. The artist I take to be a man who simply can't bear the idea of that 'approximately'. He will get the exact curve of what he sees whether it be an object or an idea in the mind.

Poems are concerned with intuited truth, not with what is discursively explicable by the reason. The mechanical can be measured in its own way, but the approximations which are all that way can offer in the aesthetic sphere are intolerable to the artist.

But this does not mean that good poems are about 'the infinite' or 'the ineffable'—that would be to fall into the Romantic heresy in a slightly different form. We return to Bergson's two orders. What *is* intuited in terms of the Image? In what circumstances does this act of intuition occur? Hulme's answer is Bergson's. The sphere in which intuition operates is that reality which is conceived "as a flux of interpenetrated elements unseizable by the intellect". What normally debars our entry into this sphere is the usual orientation of the human mind towards action. If that were not so we should have easy commerce with it, and there would be no need for art at all; as it is, the artist is "a man who is emancipated from the ways of perception engendered by action".

At this stage in the book it is hardly necessary to point out how richly 'Romantic' this formulation of the artist's function is, but it is worth emphasising that the twin concepts of isolation and image occur in Hulme as surely as in the poetry he despised. But we must return to the question of the intuited image.

Hulme's metaphysical justification of his image-theory is borrowed from Bergson. The human intellect tends to explain (*explico*, unfold) everything in a manner fitting its limitations; it analyses, because "that is the only way in which the intellect can deal with things"; "we reduce everything to extensive manifolds". We unfold everything out in space, and we tend to think that everything that cannot be so unfolded must be unknowable. But of course this is not so, and anybody can think of things which are somehow known but resist this form of knowing them. How do such things differ from the others which allow themselves to be treated as extensive manifolds? Bergson argues that such things, "while incomprehensible by our ordinary standards" are nevertheless finite. The nature of their complexity is qualitative, not quantitative; they simply do not yield to explanation, to discursive methods of analysis; they resist the intellect. Their parts are "interpenetrated in such a manner that they could not be separated or analysed out". And yet one should not even speak of parts, because the complex thing is a continuous whole, and it is impossible to conceive of its parts as having a separate existence. This is the intensive manifold, by the very terms of the argument impossible to define; it is accessible only to intuition, belonging to a different order of reality. It is "indescribable but not unknowable". The artist knows it; it is his Image. It is finite; hence the need for precision. Its meaning is the same thing as its form, and the artist is absolved from participation with the discursive powers of the intellect.

This theory, as Hulme explains it, makes a show of being in opposition to Romantic imprecision—hence the emphasis on finiteness, and the lack of reference to the third, Pascalian order—but in fact it is fundamentally a new statement of the old defence of poetry against positivism and the universe of death. It is a revised form of the old proclamation that poetry has special access to truth, and is not merely light entertainment for minds tired out by physics. Poets, excluded from action, are enabled to achieve the special form of cognition and pierce the veil and intuit truth; this is communicated in the Image.

And yet 'new' is certainly the wrong word for all this. Hulme himself recognises the essential similarity between his intuited manifold and Schopenhauer's Idea, arguing reasonably for the technical superiority of the later conception. And this similarity, from which Hulme draws no conclusion, is in a sense the key to a proper historical appraisal of Hulme on poetry. Bergson himself is the almost inevitable result of the nineteenth-century effort to find room for art amid the encroachments of science; and the aesthetic of the Symbolists is predominantly the artist's version of such anti-intellectualist concepts as the Idea of Schopenhauer. Hulme knew de Gourmont, but avoided his conclusion that the alternative to intellect was something more primitive; he avoids anything remotely resembling surrealism, and for the *rêve* so dear to Symbolism he substitutes his rather austere version, a higher but finite order of truth. To this extent there is justice in his claim that he is at war with Romantic imprecision; but it must be said that the term *rêve* covers many meanings, including that of a means of access to realms of truth habitually inaccessible, and Hulme's artist is really the Romantic *voyant* expressed in terms more agreeable to a man who disliked some kinds of philosophical language. Insist as he might on the *finite* nature of his intuited truth, it is only another version of that truth unavailable to science which was part of the whole protest against eighteenth-century 'uniformitarianism' (whether expressed as German 'organicism' or as something more characteristically English in the thought of Blake and Coleridge). To get the exact curve of the thing, insisting upon the imperviousness to paraphrase of the symbolic work of art (the 'aesthetic monad') was Mallarmé's business as much as Hulme's; in fact Mallarmé anticipates Hulme in various particulars, such as the theory that a poem must be read silently, and both writers were driven (Hulme in *Cinders*, his 'Notes for a new *Weltanschauung*') to the dance as a necessary emblem of the symbol. In short, the Hulmian Image—precise, orderly, anti-discursive, the product of intuition—is the Symbol of the French poets given a new philosophical suit. As a matter of aesthetic decency it may be that this was needed; but once it is granted that Hulme was trying to do much the same thing as Mallarmé, it becomes evident that he did not do it very well.

As I have said, Hulme falls instinctively into the image of the Dancer, and to complete the pattern he writes in 'Notes on Language and Style' of "the beauty of the feminine form . . . as a typical vesture or symbol of beauty herself", adding that

> Rossetti saw the spiritual element in face and form, and desired the spirit through his desire for the body, and at last did not know the one desire from the other, and pressed on, true mystic that he was, in ever-narrowing circles, to some third thing that seemed to lie behind both desires. 'Soul is form and doth the body make.'

The prose here is in the Paterian tradition, quite unlike Hulme's usual colloquial brightness; it could be Yeats. The quotation from a Renaissance poet (Spenser) is a borrowing from the enemy; Hulme must have realised, with his predecessors and successors, that there was matter in such poetry made to his hand (compare the vogue for Donne's passage on Elizabeth Drury). And the reference to Rossetti is surely significant. In matter and manner this short passage is pure Romantic. And Hulme was certainly sufficiently informed by *l'âme romantique* to see the affinity of his kind of thinking about poetry for mysticism and magic. He calls the Christian mystics "analogous to his own temper" (he would have been interested in the modern theory that much seventeenth-century poetry is technically based on prescribed methods of meditation) and he admires the "physical analogies" of the Neo-Platonists, which are in the end the *correspondance* of Baudelaire and the Magic of Yeats. Something of the sort is, of course, necessary to any Symbolist theory of poetry, for if you insist on calling paraphrase a heresy, if you insist that the common language of reason cannot achieve knowledge of the thing that the Image is, then you are forced to guard against the absolute surrender of the power of communicating by some theory explaining how your supra-rational knowledge can be shared. Hulme has not the Great Memory, and he has no theory of shared subliminal symbolisms; nor has he the modern veneration for the magic underworld of language, to be visited by all who can achieve the golden bough of a pun or an irony. Instead he has the Bergsonian Veil which the artist can pierce, to show what everybody could see if only they were likewise equipped. It is a High Dream perhaps, but a dream all the same; and the view that under certain conditions everybody can dream it is a magical view.

Hulme remained committed to this view so long as he persisted in his opinion of language as—in poetry—a mode of communicating *visual* images, "a compromise for a language of intuition—to make you continuously see a physical thing"; the poet strictly as *voyant*. There seems no doubt that the next step forward in Romantic aesthetic depended upon a new theory of language. Hulme was very deficient here, though there are possibilities in his work of a development which have rendered superfluous the awkward implications of the view he professed. The problem was to preserve the Symbol (the 'aesthetic monad', the Image alogical yet meaningful, or as Sir Herbert Read has recently called it, 'the poetic Gestalt') and yet to be rid of magic. This could not be done so long as the Image was thought of as a thing seen only, or so long as language was considered as a means of handing over visual concreteness only. In his anxiety to distinguish between symbolic and non-symbolic language Hulme commits himself absolutely to this visual hypothesis. His Symbol is a visual thing, and its opposite is just the dead sign of an abstract prose process. Professor Lehmann has pointed out very similar vagaries in earlier Symbolist attempts at a theory of language; Hulme's peculiar interests make his different, but only in detail.

ALDOUS HUXLEY

1894–1963

Born on July 26, 1894, in Laleham, Sussex, Aldous Leonard Huxley came from a family of distinguished scientists and writers. An eye disease in 1910 left him temporarily blind, forcing him to leave Eton and abandon hopes of becoming a doctor, but he recovered sufficiently to be able to read English literature at Balliol College, Oxford. After graduating, he married in 1919 and became a journalist.

Huxley's earliest literary work was poetry, including the volumes *The Burning Wheel* (1916) and *The Defeat of Youth* (1918), but it was the novels *Crome Yellow* (1921), *Antic Hay* (1923), and *Those Barren Leaves* (1925) which brought him to prominence. By 1925 he had also published three volumes of short stories and two volumes of essays, making this an extremely productive period. A journey round the world in 1925 led to the travel book *Jesting Pilate* (1926). Returning to England, Huxley became a close friend of D. H. Lawrence, whose letters he edited in 1932. The novel *Point Counter Point* appeared in 1928, followed by *Brave New World* in 1932 and *Eyeless in Gaza* in 1936.

In the 1930s Huxley lectured and wrote in favor of pacifism, and grew increasingly interested in mysticism and alternative medicine, particularly after emigrating to California in 1937. A system of eye training led to dramatic improvements in his vision, an experience recorded in *The Art of Seeing* (1943). In California he associated with Buddhist and Hindu groups, and in the 1950s experimented with hallucinogenic drugs such as LSD and mescalin, which he wrote about in *The Doors of Perception* (1954). Notable among his works on mysticism are *The Perennial Philosophy* (1946) and *Heaven and Hell* (1956). His later novels include *After Many a Summer* (1939), *Ape and Essence* (1948), and *Island* (1962). *Collected Essays* appeared in 1959.

Late in life Huxley received honors including an award from the American Academy of Letters in 1959 and election as a Companion of Literature of the British Royal Society of Literature in 1962. He died of cancer in California on November 22, 1963.

Personal

I first met Aldous Huxley in California, during the early summer of 1939. The Huxleys, Gerald Heard, and another close friend, named Christopher Wood, had moved out there from Europe to settle two years previously. They formed a group which had expanded to include some very different kinds of people: Charlie Chaplin, for example, and Krishnamurti, Anita Loos, Paulette Goddard, Edwin Hubble, Greta Garbo. One didn't think of Maria Huxley as being what is usually meant by a "great" hostess; yet, in her charmingly haphazard way—by accident, almost—she created some historic parties. At that period, the Huxleys lived in Santa Monica, not far from the beach, in an extraordinarily sinister house which was built and furnished in a style that I can best describe as log-cabin decadent. The place was so dimly illuminated that a lady to whom I had just been introduced once said to me, "Will you light my cigarette so I can see your face?" Its art treasures included a painting of a giant ape carrying off a virgin in torn veils, and several fetishistic pictures of "cruel" high-booted ladies, probably German in origin. Neither Maria nor Aldous seemed to have made any attempt to alter the decor, which had been dreamed up by their fun-loving landlord; their own lives were quite without relation to it, and they showed you around with civilized humor, as though they themselves were merely houseguests.

Aldous' physical appearance took me by surprise. I had expected somebody resembling the skinny, thickly bespectacled, spiderlike intellectual of the early photographs. (Or had I made my private image of the young author of *Crome Yellow*, *Antic Hay*, and *Point Counter Point* to match my opinion that nearly all of Huxley's best work was done in the latter, American half of his life.) In any case, the Aldous in his middle forties whom I now met in the flesh was slender but not at all skinny, and the insect look I had discovered in his photographs seemed to me to be more of a bird look, benevolent and quick with interest in his surroundings. He no longer wore spectacles. When he talked, his beautifully sensitive features seemed literally to shine with enthusiasm. He was interested in so many subjects that he could talk to anybody—anybody, that is, who was also interested. Thus he could thoroughly enjoy the company of children and teen-agers, scientists, ranchers, actresses, priests, and professors. It was only in the presence of the indifferent, the insincere, and the double-talker that he became uncomfortable and aloof.

Aldous' clothes were usually informal. But he wore everything well, and when he put on a suit, he looked marvelously distinguished. It was not in his character to be consciously dressy; but he was never careless, and I think he must have had a certain affection for some of the things he wore. For instance, he had kept a tie from Paris for more than twenty years and would remark that it was "like an early Rouault." . . .

Aldous and Maria both loved the desert. Indeed, Aldous was attached to California by a love for the terrain itself; this was perhaps his strongest reason for remaining here in later years. But life at Llano had its problems. The irrigation water was owned by a rancher who lived higher up the mountain; it was released into the garden along a system of ditches on certain days only, between certain hours. The Huxleys had their own gasoline engine for generating electric light. (To eliminate the fire hazard, it was sunk in a pit in the middle of the yard and covered by a trapdoor. On this trapdoor, Maria had placed an otherwise unwanted terra-cotta bust of Gerald Heard by way of ornament, and the pit was therefore known as "Gerald's Tomb.") Maria would beg you to use a candle if you wanted to read during the night. One night I forgot and flipped the light switch; the engine started with a clatter like a motorbike's and woke everybody else up.

Then there were the coyotes, who would send their bitches to lure away the male ranch dogs and then set on them and kill them. (A few ranch dogs were said to have been so big and strong that they killed their attackers and thereafter ran wild as leaders of the pack.) And there were the rattlesnakes; Aldous would go for long walks, and Maria was always afraid that one of them would lash out at him from underneath a mesquite bush. But the danger to which Aldous finally fell a victim was less apparent. One day, Maria found a pretty flower which had been washed down the hillside by a rainstorm. She planted it outside Aldous' study window. It proved to be a species of ragweed, and it gave him an allergic rash all over his body. This, I believe, was one of the several mishaps which made the Huxleys decide to give up the Llano house and return to live in Los Angeles.

Aldous was an exceptionally sensitive human instrument, and his health was correspondingly variable. One week he would look fresh and healthy and even robust; the next, wan, shattered, almost spectral. He suffered from all kinds of ailments, but they seemed to interest him quite as much as they distressed him. He would talk about them at length, objectively and without complaining. "I feel curiously *deconstellated*," he told me once, after being given a new type of shot. Both he and Maria were great connoisseurs of doctors; it sometimes seemed to their friends that they were prepared to consult absolutely anyone, at least once, in a spirit of disinterested experimentation.

Actually, this fearless curiosity was one of Aldous' noblest characteristics, a function of his greatness as a human being. Little people are so afraid of what the neighbors will say if they ask Life unconventional questions. Aldous questioned unceasingly, and it never occurred to him to bother about the neighbors. They laughed at him for consulting unlicensed healers and investigating psychic phenomena, and it was true that many of the healers proved to be wrong and many of the mediums frauds. That was unimportant from Aldous' point of view. For his researches also brought into his hands some very odd and precious pieces of the jigsaw puzzle of Truth, pieces that may not be officially fitted into the main pattern and recognized as scientifically respectable for many years to come.

Not long before my arrival in California, Heard and Huxley had met Swami Prabhavananda, a Hindu monk of the Ramakrishna Order, who had founded a center in Hollywood for the study and practice of Vedanta philosophy. Later, Heard introduced me to him. This was a contact which had far-reaching effects on the lives of all three of us. In Huxley's case, it was widely represented as the selling out of a once brilliant intellect. Huxley was alleged to have undergone a failure of nerve, to have relapsed into woolly-minded mysticism and embraced oriental mumbo jumbo. Well, that is old history now, and nothing to get heated about. At least it cannot be denied that Huxley's preoccupation with Vedanta inspired some of his best books.

In September, 1942, I heard Aldous make a personal statement to a small group of people on the relation between his concern with mystical religion and his art. I wrote down some of it verbatim, and I think it is well worth repeating here; the very artlessness of its expression, so unlike the lucidity and polish of Aldous' written work, seems to me to convey something of his live personality.

I came to this thing in a rather curious way, as a *reductio ad absurdum*. I have mainly lived in the world of intellectual life and art. But the world of knowing about things is unsatisfactory. It's no good knowing about the taste of strawberries out of a book. The more I think of art I realize that though artists do establish some contact with spiritual reality, they establish it unconsciously. Beauty is imprisoned, as it were, within the white spaces between the lines of a poem, between the notes of music, in the apertures between groups of sculpture. This function or talent is unconscious. They throw a net and catch something, though the net is trivial. . . . But one wants to go further. One wants to have a conscious taste of these holes between the strings of the net. . . .

Now, obviously, one could never possibly give it up.

That last sentence has the ring of an emotional intensity which Aldous very seldom displayed—to me, at any rate. In a world of backslappers and soul-barers, he avoided superfluous physical contacts and unasked-for confessions. When he was suffering the pain of Life most keenly, he said the least—during the worst days of the war, for example, or during Maria's slow death from cancer, or in the loss of his house and papers by fire. . . .

Aldous and Maria had seemed an inseparable couple. We all dreaded the long-term effects of bereavement on Aldous and were relieved when he married again. He seemed very happy as he told me about the wedding, which took place at a drive-in chapel at Yuma, Arizona, in March, 1956, with what Aldous described as "a broken-down cowboy" for a witness. "Really," he exclaimed, "there are so many delightful and intelligent and unusual people in the world!" Then—how characteristically— he added, "And so many unspeakably awful ones!"

In 1961, the house into which Aldous and Laura had moved after their marriage was destroyed by a brush fire. Driven by veering winds, the flames darted about the hillside with fiendish caprice; the house immediately behind the Huxleys' was unharmed. Certain journalists, with the unmotivated falsehood which sometimes makes their trade seem purely evil, wrote that Aldous had shed tears and had had to be restrained from rushing into the flames to rescue his archives. Aldous was naturally indignant about this. As a matter of fact, both Aldous and Laura behaved with a self-discipline worthy of an Asian philosopher; when they saw that the fire was out of control and that nothing more could be done, they got into their car and drove quietly away. Aldous told me, with ironical relish, that the television trucks arrived at least twenty minutes before the fire engines.

My final memories, except for the last one, are happy. After the fire, Aldous and Laura spent much of their time at the home of their friend Virginia Pfeiffer. She, too, had lost her house in the same fire and had moved, with magnificent assurance, into another quite nearby. Aldous went for walks around the Hollywood reservoir, with its wooded islands, which he had always loved; he was constantly busy on various literary projects; he had fun with Virginia's delightful adopted children; he and Laura traveled widely and returned to tell us stories of Brazil and India and Europe at pleasant supper parties. We heard rumors that he had had cancer of the tongue and been cured. I didn't inquire further because I didn't want to think about it. Then, on November 5, 1963, I visited him at the Cedars of Lebanon Hospital, where he had been taken for a few days of tests or treatment. Just before I went into his room, the surgeon told me that his condition was hopeless; the cancer was spreading rapidly.

Aldous looked like a withered old man, gray-faced, with dull blank eyes. He spoke in a low hoarse voice which was hard to understand. I had to sit directly facing him because it hurt him to turn his head. And yet, seeing what I saw and knowing what I knew, I could still almost forget about his condition while we talked, because his mind was functioning so well. I was nervous at first and talked at random. I mentioned Africa, and Aldous said that all the new African nations would soon be governed by their armies. I mentioned V. V. Rozanov's *Solitaria*, which I had just been reading. Aldous promptly quoted a passage from it, in which Rozanov says that "the private life is above everything . . . just sitting at home and even picking your nose, and looking at the sunset." I told him a silly story—not at all the kind of story I would normally have told him—about Our Lord and the Blessed Virgin playing golf. He laughed at it, quite heartily.

Laura had told me that Aldous did not realize how sick he was. But now he began to speak about old age, and I couldn't help suspecting that this was a kind of metaphor, a way of referring to his own death. He spoke of it almost with petulance, as a wretched hindrance which prevented you from working. He told me that he did not think he would ever write another novel. "I feel more and more out of touch with people." And he added that when one is old, one is absolutely cut off from the outside world. I told him, quite sincerely, that I have the impression that as I grow older my character gets worse and worse. This made him laugh a lot—not, I think, because he disbelieved me, but because he found the statement somehow reassuring. We parted almost cheerfully. I had hoped to see him at least once or twice again, but even the surgeon's prognosis was an overestimate. Aldous died that same month, on the twenty-second, not knowing that Kennedy had been shot that morning. It is good that he was no longer in the hospital but back in Virginia's home, with Laura by his side. And one of his fears, at least, was unfounded. He was able to work right up to the day before the end, dictating the last part of an article on Shakespeare. He was not accustomed to dictation, yet the flow of thought was as clear as always; only a couple of small corrections were necessary before it could be published.
—CHRISTOPHER ISHERWOOD, "Aldous Huxley in California," *At*, Sept. 1964, pp. 44–47

Now, as I write, memories of the early 1950s are beginning to return as well, though helter-skelter. A view of Aldous at the cinema is first to mind, though why there I am unable to say: with the exception of science documentaries—*The Sex Life of Lobsters* was a favourite—he loathed films. Is it because he seemed so lonely sitting in the front row? Or because of the comedy of his mumbling?—"inconceivable tripe," "monstrous oafs," "semi minus epsilons," I could hear as he wriggled and moaned. Ordinarily he watched the screen through his Chinese perforations, but when a pretty woman appeared he would switch to the magnifying glass; at a revival of *The Blue Angel* I remember him staring at Miss Dietrich's charms as intently as Emil Jannings himself. But Aldous only braved the cinema to accompany I⟨gor⟩ S⟨travinsky⟩, who, rather like Wittgenstein, would go to any movie, no matter how bad, as frequently as anyone could be found to take him.

And now a sheaf of pictures returns of Aldous listening to music, and these are all characteristic for music was the delight of his later life. But here the "I" intrudes. From 1952, Aldous attended rehearsals and concerts of pre-classical works which I conducted: Monteverdi's *Vespers*, the *Sinfoniae Sacrae* of Schütz, the Couperin *Tenebrae*, Bach cantatas; he was interested in but did not love new music—or, indeed, any music after Beethoven, with the exception of *Falstaff*—as much as most music before. In 1954 he fell under the spell of Gesualdo da Venosa, whose music I was then transcribing: he came to

rehearsals of our madrigal group, he translated the texts for us, and he even lectured at some of our concerts, on madrigal verse and on the musical history of the north Italian courts in the 16th century. I may indicate the quality of his musical ear by testifying that he was able to perform the speaker's part—though his voice was too subtle for it—in Schönberg's *Ode to Napoleon*. We worked on it for a time with a plan to record.

Another no less characteristic picture now reappearing is of Aldous the museum addict, his gracile and elastic-vertebrae back bent to an object which he studies like a bacteriologist through a pocket-glass held to his left eye. The museum might be the Huntington Library, in which I see him sloped over a manuscript of Hayden's *London Symphony* in the hand of Richard Wagner; or the Museum of Modern Art, in which he hated most of the pictures but to which he returned on every visit to New York, to see Monet's Water Lilies; the artist, being almost as blind as Aldous himself, had painted it to Aldous' scale, and here, uniquely, Aldous did not need his pocket-glass. (We were ever astonished at the reading and writing, proof-reading and manuscript-reading accomplished with that glass, incidentally; not until the last years did he begin to use dictaphones and tape-recorders.)

In another, but random, picture, I see Aldous threading his way through the thick of a Hollywood party—at Glenn Ford's, the last one I remember. He would wince from the jazz and the party voices, but fasten like an anthropologist to the film moguls and the actors with pink shirts and bare feet, and we could expect a lesson in the mores of these people at our next meeting, with a commentary of groans and comparisons to wilder New Guinea. But Aldous endured these affairs for other reasons, too, some of which, I suspect, were the starlets; in finding and physiologically appraising *them* his eyesight seemed to improve. In any case, he was surrounded at social events by adoring female flocks in which women in saris (mostly non-Indians) mixed with culture-struck nymphets for whom the strange charm of the English language (after the "beat" talk of their boy-friends) seemed to provide the initial attraction but who must eventually have felt some other awe as well in the presence of this shy but charismatic man.

I should add that Aldous was anthropologically interested in other types of juvenile delinquents than the luminaries of filmdom. I remember how he described his rescue by a mafia of neighbourhood boys from the fire that destroyed his house: "The gang warned me about fifteen minutes before the arrival of the TV camera-trucks which, in turn, were half an hour ahead of the fire-engines that could have saved the house. After the boys had guided me to safety, by the one passable street, I noticed that some familiar faces among them were absent. I said I was concerned about them, but the leader told me not to worry, that they were merely out starting more fires."

E morto il piccolo maestro Aldous Huxley, says the Rome newspaper, and even before the long drawl of his body is cold the reputation industry will have decided just how "*piccolo*" he was; will have attended to the summing-up—which is obituarese for hatcheting down, the denigrating epithet being so much easier to find than the epithet for the value quality. How boringly predictable it is, being exactly in accordance with the birth dates of the clerks who practise it. Aldous Huxley, a man gentle and good and a writer better than any who will literarily bury him, dear Aldous will be patted on the head and put away as an "era."

And what of myself, for I too am a clerk with a birthday, and an even unholier obituarist than the others? I know only that the man and his work can never come unjoined for me, and that the joining place is not on the bookshelf but in the heart. And I know that I will never read him again, for I could not bear to hear his voice, though I hear only that voice now, and it is the measure of the void.—ROBERT CRAFT, "With Aldous Huxley," *Enc*, Nov. 1965, pp. 15–16

On a typical London January evening thirty-five years ago, Aldous Huxley sailed into my view—and "sailed" is the word for it. An eight-year-old friendship with his brother Julian, the biologist, had led to my becoming the working editor of *The Realist*, a twelve-month-orbiting London literary magazine with an editorial board of such authors as H. G. Wells, Arnold Bennett, the two Huxleys, Rebecca West, Harold Laski, and another half-dozen originally bright advisers. *The Realist* carried no advertisements, paid no salaries, and delayed on all bills and authors' remittances. For that one year this unique monthly, like the primitive Montgolfier balloons, buoyed up by the hot air of literary reputations, held its inflated course. Among other not ephemeral contributions (one from Sigmund Freud), two successive issues carried the longest essay we were ever to print: a study of Blaise Pascal by Aldous Huxley. It was obvious that the aqua fortis of the *Crome Yellow* etchings and the full-scale engravings of *Point Counter Point* were being diluted by some more humane secretional doubt as to the certainty of human self-deceit. At the very close of *Those Barren Leaves* there was at least a hesitation in writing off the whole human drama as the idiot-told tale.

Beyond, then, knowing the curve of the Huxleyan corpus, the track of its projectiles, I had no knowledge of this mind. "Never diagnose without seeing the patient" is as sound advice for the student as for the physician, and Huxley was worth study as a presence quite as much as in his works: six feet four inches tall, eyes dilated through high-magnification lenses, broad, lofty forehead and, on the top of that, an outsize-brimmed felt hat. Before listening, one needed to take in. And his approach, his "port," had about it something of a galleon's. He came in, as it were, under full sail, a long coat billowing around him. The voice, however, was as neat as a seamstress's stitching. And, indeed, the long fingers made the precise movements of a needlewoman handling thread and seam. One would have expected from that leonine head (for the hat doffed showed the ancestral, Thomas Henry Huxley mane) at least an echo of the grandfather's roar.

Tone and diction matched the discourse, which was not only ironic and entertaining but fantastically informed. Our host—an old friend of us both—had asked no other guest. We stayed talking till past 1.00 A.M., when all buses had finished their routes, all taxis ceased their cruising. Consequently, each of us had before him a more than three-mile walk. To my surprise, for our directions were divergent, Huxley accompanied me all the way to my block of flats and then, changing tack, sailed off for another couple of miles of solitary striding to his own rooms. But not before he had invited me to another session the following week. After this, it was clear that he stood in need of someone who also took afternoon walks and who would in addition let him exercise the otherwise unexercised thinking of his mind.

He was never a conversationalist in the accepted sense of that word. Few fine writers are; still fewer fine thinkers. Both gifts demand sustained lucidity and precision. Good conversation does not ponder, is not prepared. It is a question of emotional rapport crossed with a certain irresponsibility only possible if friendship makes all guardedness unnecessary. Our host that first night, lately returned from America, had remarked, "On the west of the Atlantic conversation is croquet; here on the east it is still, and long may it remain, tennis." No man was better equipped than Huxley for conversational

croquet. When Sir Joshua Reynolds was commiserated with because Dr. Johnson snatched a subject Reynolds had opened, Reynolds smiled and said, "It was enough for me to knock and so bring the Doctor to the door." With modern writers such as G. B. Shaw and Aldous Huxley, it was enough to put the right coin in these encyclopedic juke boxes to be sure of a steady flow as lucid as anything on their printed pages—on many occasions, in fact, what one got was a word-perfect recitation from such texts.

Aldous Huxley was often accused of arrogance. He *was* fastidious. Frequently, when we were discussing some excellent, amiable, and informed persons whom we had agreed he should meet, and he had duly done so, he would exclaim, "But they *bore* me." And one realized that to a mind of his temper the distress caused by a flow of platitudes was akin to the inquisitional torture of a drop of water falling every second on top of the head, or Stravinsky's distress if made to sit through a concert of Balfe and Sullivan. As Konrad Lorenz, the master naturalist, has noted in his great studies of animals, the higher the nervous system the more what is mere weariness to lower beasts becomes an ever intenser exasperation of futility, bafflement, and frustration.

Huxley had to carry a further handicap. As a boy, he was determined to become an artist. During his adolescence, keratosis of the eyes spread extensively: at the height of the attack his blindness reached such a degree that, as he used to recall, finally the Ace of Spades was unrecognizable. With the stoical courage which his ancestry commanded and instructed, he surrendered art and turned to literature. But he still mounted watch at the small aperture through which a view of natural beauty and its reflections in art was obtainable. He was always attending art shows, revisiting the great galleries he loved and knew intimately, peering close up with an uncanny power of compositional attention at masterpieces from which the normal vision stands back, and writing with amazing perspicacity monographs on—for instance—intricate artists such as Pieter Bruegel the Elder or even Callot, the minute engraver. And, of course, his novels and essays have nearly all of them backgrounds of such memorable scenery that often these vistas still hang on in the mind's eye in their own right, wonderfully fresh, when the characters whose activities they were meant to frame have faded.

To quote perhaps the most successful of still living novelists, Somerset Maugham, "Aldous isn't a novelist just because he isn't interested in people." Maugham would own that his own interest was not necessarily, indeed seldom, sympathetic. But he certainly has been a master of that curiosity which makes the anatomist dissect with a deep fascination every contortion of viscera and convolution of brain. "Aldous"—and here again Maugham was an accurate diagnostician—"isn't interested in people because his real interest is in ideas." Huxley himself often allowed that this observation was accurate. But when I would urge him to confine himself to his highly influential essays, he would say, "Novels pay far better." It was true that his stories sold some ten times better than his dissertations, entertaining and instructive as these were. This may sound as though Huxley's main concern was not art but profit. And in a way that was true. But in a way that instead of being faintly false was secretively, unostentatiously noble. For he was a generous man and there were many demands from family and friends on his resources.

Huxley was in no respect a self-made man. Pretty certainly no one is. But compare him and his work with the effort and output of his old friend D. H. Lawrence, the coal miner, and it is clear not only that Huxley was a product of a particular and highly distinctive class but that his descent both on his father's and his mother's side brought down to him, and on him, a weight of intellectual authority and a momentum of moral obligation. Indeed, to understand Huxley's life in any detail—whether positive or negative, whether stoical acceptance or scornful rejection—one must realize how unique was his family's physical and social heredity.

Huxley, exposed to heavy ancestral pressures, told when young by his years-older brother Julian that he must never forget the intellectual nobility of his forefathers, might hold at bay his fate—but sooner or later he must confront his Doppelgänger. It was during this period in his life that he and I first met. *Point Counter Point*, a Book Society choice, had put him on the list of the profitable authors. It was *Crome Yellow* (to use Milton's phrase) "writ large." But whereas the personality that loomed in and out of these fantastic, acid stories was a caricature of Ottoline Morrell, now within the broad dimension of the full-scale novel Huxley had a gallery wherein all of his acquaintances could be paraded. D. H. Lawrence perhaps was let off most easily. (Not that that smoothed this gifted, sensitive collier. He took Huxley to task for making him out to be a pretentious preacher.) But Middleton Murry was pilloried.

. . . *Brave New World* he was working on when I was with him at his Riviera home in 1931. It dates today, for even he hadn't the layman's hardihood to foresee the atom bomb (though H. G. Wells, as the first World War broke out, had opened his current novel of the future with things shaken free by such a device). On the other hand, the aging Wells of the early '30s wrote Huxley an angry letter about *Brave New World*, charging him with treason to science, a defeatist pessimism.

Huxley was describing a future of physical health and also of the right of the individual not to be made to suffer—more, the right to differ, to secede, to have one's own reservation. *Brave New World* was not only more scientifically efficient, biologically equipped, and psychologically informed than were the societies of the Wellsian-Orwellian tradition, it was also far more tolerant: if you couldn't stand the conditioned-cum-glandularized state you were free to choose one of several islands where the balance between public efficiency and personal whim was more to your taste, more in the private person's favor. No dictator to date has approached such generous liberalism—nor, for that matter, has any one of the democratic nations. Yet, of course, *Brave New World*, though it showed those doubts of science's plenary inspiration (which naturally alarmed Wells), was on the other hand more to amuse the satirist than to encourage the dedicated forecaster and responsible extrapolative planner.

Many times we discussed the possibility of bringing *Brave New World* up to date, but like all such sketches it had become obsolete because of the growth and findings of subsequent research. Also, Huxley's own explorations and convictions had enlarged. He was becoming far more hopeful about the human spirit's capacity to grow. But proportionately there waned his hope that the men in power in the democracies would cease to drift. He was not a defeatist, an escapist, or a deserter. He was certain that armament could settle nothing and, even if the democracies beat their temporary foe, militarism would win and become ever more ineptly, obliteratingly violent.
—GEARLD HEARD, "The Poignant Prophet," *KR*, Winter 1965, pp. 50–57

General

. . . Aldous Huxley is a writer particularly accessible to the spirit of his time and by the middle twenties his period of dandyism was over. The influence of Mallarmé and Prufrock

waned and he set himself to moralise on the flux around him. Witty, serious, observant, well-read, sensitive and intelligent, there can have been few young writers as gifted as Huxley—as can be seen from his early stories, "Happily Ever-After," "Richard Greenow," "Little Mexican," "Young Archimedes" or *The Gioconda Smile*.

Yet he had the misfortune to suffer from what he considered, quoting Buddha, to be the deadliest of mortal sins, unawareness, for he was both unaware of his own nature as a writer and of the temptations into which he was falling. His nature was a very English one, that of the divided man, the lover of beauty and pleasure dominated by the puritan conscience. At first his dichotomy is apparent in his treatment of love. Love means everything to him but sex—and sex, although he is obsessed by it, is disgusting. The conflict is extended to become a warfare between the senses on one side and the intellect, generously moralising in the moment of victory, on the other until Huxley the intellectual pulls the lower self along like a man pulling a dog by a leash; there are glimpses of other dogs, lamp-posts, green grass, trousers and tree-trunks; then comes a jerk, "eyes look your last" and a scientific platitude.

It is a question whether anyone so at war with himself can be a novelist, for to the novelist a complete integration is necessary; the proper medium for the split-man is the *Journal Intime* or the *Dialogue*. *Ends and Means* owes its success to being a complete break with the novel for as a novelist, apart from being at war with himself, Huxley was hampered by his inability to create character or see a character except in an intellectual way.

The greatness of a novelist like Tolstoy is that he creates characters who being real creations are able to think and behave unlike themselves, to be false to type. Proust also had some of this greatness, and in English, Thackeray. But weaker novelists can only sling a few traits on to the characters they are depicting and then hold them there. "You can't miss So-and-so", they explain, "he stammers and now look, here he comes—'What's your name?' "S-s-s-so-and s-s-s-s-so.' There you see, what did I tell you!" Nearly all English novels are written to this prescription. Huxley suffers from the intellectual's difficulty of communicating with the people around him except through the intellect. In consequence the only people he can write about at length are those with whom he can carry on an intellectual discussion.

But the consequences of Huxley's *artistic* unawareness are more serious. He is a defaulting financier of the written word, and nobody since Chesterton has so squandered his gifts. A contract to produce two books a year forced him to vitiate that keen sense of words with which he started and as he had less to say, so, by a process which we have noticed, he took longer in which to say it. For such a writer who had to turn out 200,000 words a year, the Mandarin style was indispensable.

By dinner-time it was already a Story—*the latest addition* to Mary Amberley's *repertory. The latest,* and as good, it seemed to Antony's *critically attentive ear* as the *finest classics of the collection.* Ever since *he received her invitation,* he now realized, *his curiosity had been tinged* with a *certain vindictive hope* that she would have *altered for the worse, either relatively in his own* knowledgeable *eyes, or else absolutely* by reason of the *passage of these twelve long years;* would have degenerated from what she was, or what he had imagined her to be, at the time when he had loved her. Discreditably enough, *as he now admitted to himself, it was with a touch of disappointment* that he had found her *hardly changed from the Mary Amberley of his memories. She was forty-three. But her body was almost as slim as ever, and she moved with all the old swift agility. With something more than the old agility indeed;* for he had noticed that she was now agile on purpose, that she acted the part of one who is *carried away by a youthful impulse* to break into quick and violent motion—acted it, moreover, in circumstances where the impulse could not, if natural, possibly have been felt.

. . .

    After a lonely dinner—for Helen was keeping her room on *the plea of a headache*—Gerry went up to sit with Mrs. Amberley. He was *particularly charming that evening,* and so *affectionately solicitous that Mary forgot* all her *accumulated grounds* of complaint and *fell in love* with him *all over again,* and for *another set of reasons*—not because he was so *handsome, so easily and insolently dominating,* such a ruthless and *accomplished lover,* but because he was *kind, thoughtful, and affectionate,* was everything, *in a word,* she had previously known he wasn't.

    I quote these as examples of Huxley's writing, of the muse's revenge, but they also show the influence of Proust in all its flatulence. Thus, although the clichés I have italicised are examples of the lack of distinction in Huxley's writing, as is the use of unnecessary adverbs or the dogged repetition, the determination to hit the nail on the head and then hit it on the head and then hit it on the head, that vulgarity with which we are familiar yet there is also here the Proustian note: ". . . either relatively . . . or else absolutely . . . what she was, or what he had imagined her to be, etc." It is fake analysis and fatigued introspection, a frequent combination in Mandarinism at its worst.—CYRIL CONNOLLY, "The New Mandarins," *Enemies of Promise* (1938), 1948, pp. 52–54

The Classical and History Middle and Upper Eighth forms at St Paul's School were, in the middle and late 1920s, an unusually sophisticated establishment. This was not directly induced by the masters, who were (with one exception—an obscure, eccentric, devoted contemporary and follower of Lytton Strachey) solid, sentimental and unimaginative. While the most civilised among them recommended Shaw, Wells, Chesterton, Gilbert Murray, Flecker, Edward Thomas, Sassoon and the *London Mercury,* we read Joyce, Firbank, Edward Carpenter, Wyndham Lewis, Schiller's Logic, Havelock Ellis, Eliot, the *Criterion* and, under the impulsion of Arthur Calder-Marshall, whose elder brother was then in America and favoured them, the works of H. L. Mencken, Carl Sandburg, Sherwood Anderson; we also took an interest in Cocteau, *transition,* the early surrealists. We looked down on *Life and Letters,* edited by Desmond MacCarthy, as tame and conventional. Among our major intellectual emancipators were J. B. S. Haldane, Ezra Pound, Aldous Huxley.

    I cannot myself claim to have been liberated by anyone; if I was in chains then, I must be bound by them still. But, as men of letters—led by Voltaire, the head of the profession—rescued many oppressed human beings in the eighteenth century; as Byron or George Sand, Ibsen and Baudelaire, Nietzsche, Wilde and Gide and perhaps even Wells or Russell have done since, so members of my generation were assisted to find themselves by novelists, poets and critics concerned with the central problems of their day. Social and moral courage can, on occasion, exercise a more decisive influence than sensibility or original gifts. One of my own contemporaries, a man of exceptional honesty, intellectual power and moral responsiveness, inhibited and twisted by an uncertain social

position and bitter puritanism on the part of his father, was morally freed (as others have been by psychoanalysis, or Anatole France, or living among Arabs) by reading Aldous Huxley: in particular *Point Counter Point,* and one or two short stories. Light had been thrown for him on dark places, the forbidden was articulated, intimate physical experience, the faintest reference to which used to upset him profoundly and affect him with a feeling of violent guilt, had been minutely and fully described. From that moment my friend advanced intellectually, and has become one of the most admired and productive men of learning of our day. It is not this therapeutic effect, however, that appealed to the young men of my generation so much as the fact that Huxley was among the few writers who, with all his constantly commented upon inability to create character, played with ideas so freely, so gaily, with such virtuosity, that the responsive reader, who had learnt to see through Shaw or Chesterton, was dazzled and excited. The performance took place against a background of relatively few, simple, moral convictions; they were disguised by the brilliance of the technical accomplishment, but they were there, they were easily intelligible, and like a monotonous, insistent, continuous ground bass slowly pounding away through the elaborate intellectual display, they imposed themselves on the minds of the boys of seventeen and eighteen—still, for the most part, eager and morally impressionable, no matter how complex or decadent they may in their *naïveté* have conceived themselves to be. . . .

    The social world about which Huxley wrote was all but destroyed by the Second World War, and the centre of his interests appeared to shift from the external world to the inner life of men. His approach to all this remained scrupulously empirical, directly related to the facts of the experience of individuals of which there is record in speech or in writing. It was speculative and imaginative only in the sense that in his view the range of valuable human experience had often been too narrowly conceived; that the hypotheses and ideas which he favoured about men in their relations to each other and to nature, illuminated the phenomena commonly described as paranormal or supernormal better than much conventional physiology or psychology, tied as they seemed to him to be to inappropriate models. He had a cause and he served it. The cause was to awaken his readers, scientists and laymen alike, to the connections, hitherto inadequately investigated and described, between regions artificially divided: physical and mental, sensuous and spiritual, inner and outer. Most of his later writings—novels, essays, lectures, articles—revolved round this theme. He was a humanist in the most literal and honourable sense of that fearfully abused word; he was interested in, and cared about, human beings as objects in nature in the sense in which the *philosophes* of the eighteenth century had done. His hopes for men rested on the advance of self-knowledge: he feared that humanity would destroy itself by over-population or by violence; from this only greater self-understanding would save them—above all, understanding of the intimate interplay of mental and physical forces—of man's place and function in nature—on which so much alternate light and darkness seemed to him to have been cast both by science and by religion.

    He was sceptical of all those who have tried to systematise the broken glimpses of the truth that had been granted to mystics and visionaries, of whom he thought as uncommonly sensitive or gifted or fortunate men whose power of vision could be cultivated and extended by devoted, assiduous practice. He recognised no supernatural grace; he was not a theist, still less an orthodox Christian believer. In all his writings—whether inspired by Malthusian terrors, or by hatred of coercion and violence, or by opposition to what he called idolatry—the blind worship of some single value or institution to the exclusion of others, as something beyond rational criticism or discussion—or by Hindu and Buddhist classics, or by western mystics and writers gifted with capacity for spiritual or psychological insight—Maine de Biran, Kafka, Broch (Huxley was a remarkable discoverer of original talent)—or by composers, sculptors, painters, or by poets in all the many languages that he read well—whatever his purpose or his mood, he always returned to the single theme that dominated his later years: the condition of men in the twentieth century. Over and over again he contrasted on the one hand their new powers to create works of unheard-of power and beauty and live wonderful lives—a future far wider and more brilliant than had ever stretched before mankind—with, on the other hand, the prospect of mutual destruction and total annihilation, due to ignorance and consequent enslavement to irrational idols and destructive passions—forces that all men could in principle control and direct, as some individuals had indeed already done. Perhaps no one since Spinoza has believed so passionately or coherently or fully in the principle that knowledge alone liberates, not merely knowledge of physics or history or physiology, or psychology, but an altogether wider panorama of possible knowledge which embraced forces, open and occult, which this infinitely retentive and omnivorous reader was constantly discovering with alternate horror and hope.

His later works, novels and tracts—the frontiers were at times not clear—were everywhere respectfully received; respectfully, but without marked enthusiasm. Those who saw him as a latter-day Lucian or Peacock complained that the wit, the virtuosity, the play of facts and ideas, the satirical eye, had disappeared; that the sad, wise, good man who lived in California was but the noble ghost of the author who had earned himself an assured place in the history of English letters. In short, it was alleged that he had turned into a lay preacher, who, like other poets and prophets, had been abandoned by the spirit, so that, like Newton and Robert Owen, Wordsworth and Swinburne, he had ended with little to say, and went on saying it earnestly, honourably, tediously, to an ever-dwindling audience. Such critics were mistaken in at least one fundamental respect: if he was a prophet, he was so in a literal sense. Just as Diderot's *Le Rêve de d' Alembert* and the *Supplément au voyage de Bougainville* (particularly the former) anticipated biological and physiological discoveries of the nineteenth and twentieth centuries, and expressed in the form of audacious speculation some of the major advances in the natural sciences, so Aldous Huxley, with that special sensibility to the contours of the future which impersonal artists sometimes possess, stood on the edge of, and peered beyond, the present frontiers of our self-knowledge. He was the herald of what will surely be one of the great advances in this and following centuries—the creation of new psychophysical sciences, of discoveries in the realm of what at present, for want of a better term, we call the relations between body and mind; a field in which modern studies of myth and ritual, the psychological roots of social and individual behaviour, the relations of the physiological and the logical foundations of linguistics, as well as the phenomena of paranormal psychology, psychical therapy and the like, are but the earliest and most rudimentary beginnings.

Huxley was well aware of this. There is a sense in which he knew that he stood on the frontier between the old astrology that was passing and the new astronomy that was beginning in the sciences of man; and he therefore bore the frequent accusations of betraying his original rationalism in favour of a confused mysticism, of a sad collapse into irrationalism as a means of escape from his own private miseries and the bleakness of his particular world, of a weak abandonment of his old belief in the clear, the precise, the tangible, for the comforting obscurity of hazy, facile, pseudo-religious speculation—he bore these charges with great sweetness and patience. He was perfectly aware of what was being said: no one could have composed a better caricature of precisely these attitudes if he had wished. He persisted not because of some softening of a once gem-like intellect, but because he was convinced that his chosen field was the region in which the greatest and most transforming advance would be made by mankind. . . .

His warnings, whether in *Brave New World*, which is certainly the most influential modern expression of disillusionment with purely technological progress, or in his other novels and essays, and his premonitions, even at their flattest and least artistic, have enough genius to have created a new genre—the pessimistic, frightening Utopia—a vision of the unintended consequences of what a good many uncritical liberals and Marxists still conceive—in E. H. Carr's complacent words—as 'old-fashioned belief in progress'. These novels create a genuine uneasiness by getting near the bone (the rotting bone, he would have said) of the contemporary experience of the west. He was a victim of a deep and universal malaise, against which he rightly perceived that too many contemporary antidotes were and are useless because they are too practical and therefore too short-sighted, or operate with concepts which are too shallow, too crude and ephemeral, too vulgar and insulting to the nature of man, particularly to those—to him all-important—still concealed and neglected powers in it, about which he wrote. He was conscious of this fatal inadequacy in much contemporary politics, sociology and ethics. There is no coherent body of doctrine, no systematic exposition in his works. But that he had a sense of what men stood and stand in need of, and a premonition of the direction in which, if mankind survives at all, it will be moving—of that I feel convinced. If I am right, justice will one day be done to those very pages over which even his admirers at present shake their heads, some sadly, others patronisingly.—ISAIAH BERLIN, "Aldous Huxley" (1965), *Personal Impressions*, 1981, pp. 135–43

In all civilized communities, literary taste is bound to be, to some extent, institutionalized. A writer's work, even his minor work, will be gathered and published, and there will be a modest profit for those who do the gathering and publishing, even when he is manifestly not a living presence, when his words have no reverberation in living minds. So long as they once did! If there was ever a time when a generation of readers hurried out to buy each new book of this writer's because they felt that his work engaged itself directly with life as they were trying to live it. If he once passed into the bloodstream of his age to that extent, then he is of permanent interest, a 'classic,' however tiny his stature within the gigantic Parthenon of classics. His scattered writings will be published; libraries will order them so that their shelves will be complete; and, since they are available in libraries, they will be looked at by people confirming an old impression, or writing memoirs or theses; they will enter a twilight life that is better—every writer must feel—than no life at all.

Of course, given the vastness of literature and the enormous numbers who have tried their hand at writing, the proportion of writers who attain even this Hades-life is microscopic. That is why, in the last few years, I have felt a quiet satisfaction at watching the works of Aldous Huxley sail into this peaceful harbor. There have been times, since about 1955, when I wondered if he was going to disappear altogether. The world in which he grew up, and in which he knew his bearings, had vanished so utterly; the public who read him and made an idol of him had died off and not been replaced; he had left an England that no longer listened to him and settled in—of all places—California, one prophet amid a thousand self-appointed prophets. The targets of his early satire had become as remote as the targets of Pope and Swift; his later attempts to find a positive world-view seemed out of touch with the age or, as in the case of his brief flirtation with hallucinatory drugs, in touch with it only at its most pathetically mistaken.

With all this, Aldous Huxley deserves to live. He had, undeniably, first-rate gifts, even if they were gifts that never quite realized themselves. He was informed, speculative, intellectually hospitable; in his early days he had a pretty turn for satire; he retained to the end a useful sense of form, an instinct towards elegance. If there is not, in his long shelf of books, a single masterpiece, there are a number that live in the mind. *Brave New World*, which might have been his *Gulliver's Travels*, is unconvincing today because its picture of a future dominated by ease and plenty, by technology in the service of a fat-bellied hedonism, is so remote from the dark, hate-ridden barbarism that has actually resulted from twentieth-century scientific premises. But it is, in the terms of the 1920s, an interesting failure. *The Perennial Philosophy*, Huxley's attempt at a *Summa Philosophica* based on the entire range of his reading, shares the fate of most systems—after the lapse of a few years, it seems merely a monument to work for work's sake—but it speaks for the forties as the early satire speaks for the twenties. And the voluminous essays, though nothing they have to say seems important now, remain impressive in their willingness to find something to say about such a huge range of subjects—so much of history, of art, of literature, of manners and customs, of hagiography and mythology and psychology, fell under his restless eye.

In some ways, Huxley can be seen as a victim of family tradition. To be a scion of a famous intellectual dynasty is in itself a misfortune, for anyone who wants to do original work. The mandarin's robes are put on too early, the natural bearing gives way to the stiff gait on one From Whom Great Things Are Expected. In the case of the Huxleys, the particular tradition has been one of *haute vulgarisation*. Thomas Huxley was the most able of the exponents of Darwinism; his incisive and controversial writings helped the more purely speculative work of Darwin to do its work in the world, so that we still speak of 'Darwin and Huxley' as one might say 'Marx and Lenin.' Aldous Huxley's brother Julian, a biologist, has engaged for many years in a lucid and constructive popularization of scientific ideas; he became something of a national idol during the years of the BBC's pioneering discussion program, the 'Brains Trust,' during the war years. In the case of Aldous Huxley, one feels that the same family gifts were there, ready to be used, and that he spent his life in a search for some large and luminous idea, comparable with Darwinism, at whose service they might be put. He never found that idea; of the ideas that emerged in his lifetime, those in the sciences were too abstruse to be channeled into common thought, and those in politics, Fascism and the various forms of totalitarian Socialism, were too dull and brutal, too morally backward and intellectually bankrupt, to be worthy of the attention of a Huxley. There was, it is true, the quasi-science of psychology, and perhaps it should be placed to Huxley's credit that he had too much intelligence to become a vendor of the notions of either Freud or Jung. For a lifetime he wandered; he found here and there

an oasis in which to camp for the night, but he never came to a city.—JOHN WAIN, "Poems of a Prosaist," *NR*, Sept. 11, 1971, p. 27

Huxley's first reputation, achieved in the twenties, was as a bright young novelist, a wit who showed a fascination and disgust with human sexuality. But Huxley developed, as Wells essentially did not. Huxley's disgust came to be more a disgust with the discrepancy between spirituality and sexuality or, a later refinement, between aspiration and achievement. You recall the cruel joke at the end of *After Many a Summer*, when the price of immortality is shown to be humanity itself.

This Huxleyan obsession, if I may use that rather clinical word, mellowed to a feeling for the dichotomy between utopia and actuality. The discrepancy was embodied in a poem of Fulke Greville's, which Huxley was fond of quoting all his life:

Oh, wearisome condition of Humanity!
Born under one law, to another bound:
Vainly begot and yet forbidden vanity,
Created sick, commanded to be sound:
What meaneth Nature by these diverse Laws?
Passion and Reason, self division cause.

To escape this intolerable division, Huxley turned to the perennial philosophy, and then to mescalin. He wanted to see more, to see beyond our present frontiers, as Berlin puts it. His sight had always been a mystery. He was almost blind, and yet—Isherwood asked the question, among others, "How much did he actually see and how much did he *cognise?*" We should remember that the precision of Huxley's prose, perhaps more remarkable in essays than novels, was acquired by his having to read Braille—a way of appreciating the English language equivalent to swimming from Los Angeles to Hong Kong in order to get an idea of the size of the Pacific.

Plato never could visualise a state which did not rely on muscle-power. Huxley's utopias always require chemicals, either to dull or enhance the human spirit. *Brave New World* embodies the dichotomy Huxley experienced: the alternatives are a regimented and hedonistic utopia or a primitive life where art could exist, the Reason and Passion of Greville's poem.

The time came when Aldous Huxley was to dislike his remarkable novel for this very reason. Perhaps his personality was undergoing one of those mysterious changes of gear we experience now and again when he wrote a preface to an edition of *Brave New World* in 1946; he speaks then of "the most serious defect" in the story as the fact that "the Savage is offered only two alternatives, an insane life in Utopia, or the life of a primitive in an Indian village".

We will return to that remark. H.G. Wells preached against hedonism, although he was a bit of a hedonist himself. His Samurai in *A Modern Utopia* observe "an austere rule of living"—it's the first thing we hear about them. And they wear uniform, which we now find ominous, having a dislike even of armbands.

Huxley, in his final novel, *Island*, comes out in favour of hedonism. Of course it is a gentle hedonism; Huxley was a gentle person. Although we can see the similarity of Wells and Huxley as writers of utopias, they made, I believe, life-decisions which were diametrically opposed. Wells opted for Ego, Huxley for Self.

Incidentally, I believe that Iran has recently been caught in a similar dilemma of choice, the Shah representing a highly technological Ego, the Ayatollah Khomeini representing a backward-looking religious Self. Iran's conflict mirrors a torment working elsewhere; for in our present stage of development, the extremes are as extreme as anything in *Brave New World*: tanks and missiles—or public stoning of adulterers.

Let me give you a quotation from Huxley's *Doors of Perception* 1954, in which he speaks of what sounds like a mescalin vision but is not:

> I remember what an old friend, dead these many years, told me about his mad wife. One day in the early stage of the disease, when she still had her lucid intervals, he had gone to the hospital to talk to her about their children. She had listened for a while then cut him short. How could he bear to waste his time on a couple of absent children, when all that really mattered, here and now, was the unspeakable beauty of the patterns he made, in this brown tweed jacket, every time he moved his arms?

It sounds as if the poor mad woman is in an LSD state. But it is merely selfishness, the triumph of Self.

Huxley is not the only philosopher of this century to point to the alarming discrepancy between what—to use a shorthand invented by Arnold Toynbee—we can call the Head and the Heart. Shelley spoke of it at the beginning of last century, and of the need to get these two components of the human psyche to dwell in harmony. The Self had many indulgent centuries when it appeared in the ascendant, manifesting itself as religious persecution and denial of progress. Now the Ego, represented by the powers of technology, appears in the ascendant. Neither Self nor Ego—or Conscious and Unconscious, if you prefer those terms—can flourish alone. Each needs equal expression. If we are to be whole, we must allow equal expression to each.

These terms are possibly nebulous. Yet they may correspond to actual geographical locations in our brains. It may be that the outgoing Ego resides in the neocortex, the cerebrum, and the in-dwelling Self in the cerebellum.

Isaiah Berlin is a witness to Huxley's intense preoccupation with this question of balance in his later years. "He (Huxley) would speak—at least in public—of nothing but the need for the re-integration of what both science and life had divided too sharply: the restoration of human contact with non-human nature, the needs for antidotes to the lop-sided development of human beings."

This is a complex subject; I will not go deeper into it. I wish merely to make the point that Wells's killing off of our familiar animals, the dogs and cats which have accompanied *homo sapiens* from the beginnings of his journeyings, represents a wish to kill off the Self, in favour of a logical, rational, Ego-dominated system. Whereas the basic scheme of *Brave New World*, Huxley's contrasting of technological utopia with savage life, which he at one time tried to deny, is in fact a representation in dramatic terms, terms of metaphor, of the opposed Ego and the Self.

With this understanding, we can perceive that Huxley's last utopia, *Island*, is a brave attempt to draw up that peace treaty between the Head and the Heart for which we are seeking. Ultimately, Huxley will prove a wiser prophet than Wells.—BRIAN W. ALDISS, "The Hand in the Jar: Metaphor in Wells and Huxley," *Fndtn*, Sept. 1979, pp. 30–31

Works

NOVELS

Not everyone in 1923, not I for one, knew without recourse to the dictionary that a 'hey' or 'hay' was a country jig. As we sped from Blackwell's with our eagerly awaited copies of Mr Aldous Huxley's second novel ⟨*Antic Hay*⟩, its title suggested a neglected stable and, strange to recall, as we read it in that fragrant age, the tale did smack a little sour. To be quite accurate in reminiscence I got my own copy second-hand from the present literary critic of the *Daily Mail*—a young man already plainly destined for high position—and he passed it to me (for a financial consideration) saying I should find it 'dreary'. *Dreary!* Re-read now after all that has happened, after all that has been written, after all Mr Huxley has written, the book has the lilt of Old Vienna.

It is placed in London in springtime. The weather, page after page, is warm and airy and brilliant. Did we ever enjoy quite such a delightful climate? We certainly do not find it in modern fiction. And London is still in 1923 eminently habitable, a city of private houses and privates lives, leisurely, not too full even in the season, all leafy squares and stucco façades and Piranesan mewses. The pavements of Bond Street are 'perfumed', the shops are full of desirable goods. All one needs is a little money—not much; £300 a year is a competence, £5,000 is wealth—and that little is easily acquired by some whimsical invention such as a pair of pneumatic trousers. Regent Street is doomed but Verrey's is still open, open after luncheon until it is time to go out to tea. A few miles out in Surrey and Sussex an arcadian countryside is opening to the never-failing sun. Although all the inhabitants of this delicious city have been everywhere and speak every language they are thoroughly English, at home in their own capital. No character in *Antic Hay* ever uses the telephone. They write letters, they telegraph, they call, and there are always suitable servants to say 'not at home' to bores. It is Henry James's London possessed by carnival. A chain of brilliant young people linked and interlaced winds past the burnished front-doors in pursuit of happiness. Happiness is growing wild for anyone to pick, only the perverse miss it. There has been the single unpredictable, inexplicable, unrepeatable calamity of 'the Great War'. It has left broken hearts—Mrs Viveash's among them—but the other characters are newly liberated from their comfortable refuges of Conscientious Objection, to run wild through the streets.

The central theme of the book is the study of two falterers 'more or less in' their 'great task of happiness', Mrs Viveash and Theodore Gumbril. Everyone else, if young, has a good time. Two clowns, Lypiatt and Shearwater, get knocked about, but that is the clown's *métier*. Rosie is happy in her pink underclothes and her daze of romantic fantasy, picked up, rolled over, passed on, giving and gaining pleasure and all the time astutely learning the *nuances* of cultural advancement. Coleman is happy, uproariously blaspheming. Men rather like him turn up later in Mr Huxley's works, miserable men, haunted and damned. Coleman is boisterously happy, a sort of diabolic Belloc. And Mercaptan is happy, unambitious, sensual, accomplished, radiantly second-rate. He is a period piece, still in his twenties with the tastes and pretentions of ripe middle-age. They do not come like that today. Today one knows quite certainly that a young bachelor with a *penchant* for white satin sofas and *bibelots* would not be running after girls and, moreover, that though he might drop into idiomatic French, he would be quite incapable of writing grammatical English.

Mrs Viveash and Gumbril are the falterers in the Great Task and their situation is not quite desperate. She has her classic, dignified bereavement. Promiscuous sexual relations bore her. But she has, we are told, almost limitless power, power which, I must confess, has never much impressed me. She was 25 when I was 20. She seemed then appallingly mature. The girls I knew did not whisper in 'expiring' voices and 'smile agonizingly' from their 'death beds'. They grinned from ear to ear and yelled one's head off. And now thirty years on, when women of 25 seem to me moody children, I still cannot weep for Mrs Viveash's tragic emptiness.

Gumbril rejects the chance of a *Happy Hypocrite* idyll, of love, literally, in a cottage. But it would never have done. He is a clever, zestful cad. He would have been hideously bored in a week. He is off abroad to a wide, smiling continent full of wine and pictures and loose young women. He will be all right.

The story is told richly and elegantly with few of the interruptions which, despite their intrinsic interest, mar so much of Mr Huxley's story-telling. The disquisition on Wren's London should be in a book of essays but the parody of the night-club play is so funny that one welcomes its intrusion. The 'novel of ideas' raises its ugly head twice only, in the scenes with the tailor and the financier, crashing bores both of them but mere spectators at the dance. They do not hold up the fun for long.

And there is another delicious quality. The city is not always James's London. Sometimes it becomes Mediterranean, central to the live tradition. The dance winds through piazzas and alleys, under arches, round fountains and everywhere are the embellishments of the old religion. An ancient pagan feast, long christianized in name, is being celebrated in a christian city. The story begins in a school chapel, Domenichino's *Jerome* hangs by Rosie's bed, Coleman quotes the Fathers. There is an insistent undertone, audible through the carnival music, saying all the time, not in Mrs Viveash's 'expiring' voice, that happiness is a reality.

Since 1923 Mr Huxley has travelled far. He has done more than change climate and diet. I miss that undertone in his later work. It was because he was then so near the essentials of the human condition that he could write a book that is frivolous and sentimental and perennially delightful.—EVELYN WAUGH, "Youth at the Helm and Pleasure at the Prow," *Lon*, July 1955, pp. 51–53

To invite an Englishman of my age and background to write on *Point Counter Point* is almost equivalent to suggesting that he should indulge in a positive orgy of autobiography. Except perhaps marginally, I shall resist the temptation. I first read the novel in August, 1929, on the eve of my freshman year at university. I found it, as everyone else seems to have done, both shocking and exhilarating, a revelation, certainly the most remarkable novel I had experienced. By the age of eighteen, however, one cannot, even with the best will in the world, have read much, and in the years that followed, as I read more, and more deeply and in a more disciplined way, I found myself reacting against Huxley and *Point Counter Point* with what might have been a comparable passion to that with which I had espoused them had not Huxley, dimmed by later enthusiasms and preoccupations, suddenly become old hat and a bore.

Now, forty-nine years later, I find my feelings toward the author and his novel alike have changed again. The words "old hat" and "bore" seem grotesquely irrelevant; I am aware much more of a perennial quality in the best of his work, which for me must include *Point Counter Point*. Which is to say, I suppose, that the recognition of its classic status in English fiction has dawned upon me.

So I am now relatively undisturbed by the fact that, so far as its structure is concerned, Huxley may be in debt to André Gide. Though I still think Lewis's criticism, in *Men Without Art*, of the opening of the novel is just, there is much more to the work than the first chapter shows. Similarly, though I can feel the force of Arnold Kettle's criticism ("There is no respect for life in this novel and without such fundamental respect

words curdle and art cannot come into being."), it seems to me that Kettle's position is a dangerous one; one could banish Swift from the world of art on the same grounds; and I am not sure that Kettle's statement does not betray a failure to understand the novel and its intentions. And I am sad now that some years ago when I taught a course on the twentieth-century novel mainly for sophomores in an American university, students wanted to know why they had been made to read Huxley. They could, they said, have used their time better in reading more Lawrence and Joyce. They had received my hesitations, reservations, and strictures on Huxley much too uncritically to make me happy or leave me complacent.

For in fact the novel—whether successfully or not is for the moment beside the point—was surely written from an angle closely akin to Kettle's. In a sense, indeed, the weaknesses of the novel stem from its author's exaggerated respect for life. Its theme is explicitly stated in the epigraph from Fulke Greville:

Oh, wearisome condition of humanity,
Born under one law, to another bound,
Vainly begot and yet forbidden vanity,
Created sick, commanded to be sound.
    What meaneth nature by these diverse laws,
    Passion and reason, self-division's cause?

Huxley as the author sets out to heal this division in the human self, which is illustrated in numerous examples throughout the course of the novel. He is advocating balance by exhibiting for our benefit a gallery of men and women often of real distinction but characterized, all of them but two, by conspicuous lack of balance, and showing too the consequences of lack of balance. Plainly, even though drawn almost entirely from the upper class of London in the first years of the nineteen-twenties, the gallery depicted is meant to be representative of humanity generally. He is describing, in other words, the human condition. And he gives us in Mark Rampion, the character round whom all the other characters more or less revolve, the figure by comparison with which balance or the lack of it may be measured. We are plainly in the presence of a formidably ambitious work.

Huxley presents at least two versions of himself in the novel: Walter Bidlake, the Huxley of a decade or so before the publication of the book, the young man just down from Balliol who had worked for Murry on the *Athenaeum*; and Philip Quarles the novelist, who is a representation of Huxley at much the time of writing. The former, who is loved by a young woman who, in a phrase Huxley uses in an earlier novel, is a born murderee, lusts helplessly after another young woman, Lucy Tantamount, whom, intellectually, he recognizes is a vampire; he sees and approves the higher but follows the lower, and is powerless to do otherwise. Quarles, "an intellectual-aesthetic pervert" in Rampion's terms, can know the world and experience it only through his mind; an hypertrophied capacity for abstract thought has inhibited the feeling and the expression of emotion, so that he is unable, for instance, plainly to tell his wife of his love for her. Things outside the purely intellectual he can approach and interpret only through books and through his wife.

But I suspect that, besides these two, other characters in the novel are also versions of Huxley. Or, rather, he feels an imaginative sympathy for them so intense as to make it possible to say that in some sense he identifies himself with them. Obviously, he cannot be said literally to resemble Spandrell, who plainly derives from a knowledge of the life of Baudelaire. But time and again he makes an act of imaginative identity with Spandrell which confers upon the character a vitality which Rampion, for instance, never possesses. The same is true only to a less degree of Burlap, a figure the novelist holds in contempt, for which he shows no sympathy and presents wholly satirically. Yet, so strong is the sense of identity that one feels the novelist is satirizing in Burlap not himself certainly but aspects of himself that he is wholly conscious of.

One result of this identification is that these characters, Spandrell and Burlap and others from time to time, old Bidlake for instance and Illidge and Lord Edward intermittently, exist as figures rather larger than life size, as grand comic figures, as the characters of Dryden's *Absalom and Achitophel* do and some of Pope's characters and some of Dickens's. They do so, I suspect, for similar reasons. A love of his victims or at least a sneaking sympathy with them is probably essential to the successful satirist.

The point, however, I wish at the moment to make is that *Point Counter Point* is an intensely personal novel. Huxley, or variants of him (and he has only to look about him to find them, on all sides, for he sees his condition as a universal one), is his own guinea pig. He is in the position of the doctor who is called upon to heal himself. He knows, none better, health when he sees it and can identify it, unerringly, in one man, Rampion, and he knows the diagnosis of his own condition and its prognosis too. He puts himself on the operating table and bravely performs his self-surgery. But however bravely he performs, he cannot cure himself, and at the end of the operation he is in no better state than when he began, for the novel ends with a dramatized meditation of death—the death of little Phil Quarles in the agony of meningitis, the death of Webley by murder, the death of Spandrell, which is death by suicide in the guise of murder, the imminent death of old Bidlake by cancer—a meditation medieval in its intensity.

It is this sense we have of Huxley's passionate involvement in his own satire that gives *Point Counter Point* its power and dynamism and, I would say, its heroic quality. Huxley, it has been said often enough during the past half-century, overdoes the horrors. This is only to say that he will not burke the facts as he sees them. "If way to the better there be," wrote Hardy in a famous line, "it exacts a full look at the worst." Huxley takes that full look: it proves no way to the better. The worst remains. There is no final resolution, only: "suddenly there was no more music; only the scratching of the needle on the revolving disc."

For me, then, the overwhelming impression *Point Counter Point* makes is of Huxley's courage: unflinchingly, he has recognized the worst. All that is left for him is the statement of Fulke Greville's "wearisome condition of humanity." The unflinching acceptance is itself an example of point counter point.—WALTER ALLEN, *"Point Counter Point* Revisited," SN, Winter 1977, pp. 373–76

Chronic remorse, as all the moralists are agreed, is a most undesirable sentiment. If you have behaved badly, repent, make what amends you can and address yourself to the task of behaving better next time. On no account brood over your wrongdoing. Rolling in the muck is not the best way of getting clean.

Art also has its morality, and many of the rules of this morality are the same as, or at least analogous to, the rules of ordinary ethics. Remorse, for example, is as undesirable in relation to our bad art as it is in relation to our bad behaviour. The badness should be hunted out, acknowledged and, if possible, avoided in the future. To pore over the literary shortcomings of twenty years ago, to attempt to patch a faulty work into the perfection it missed at its first execution, to spend one's middle age in trying to mend the artistic sins committed and bequeathed by that different person who was oneself in

youth—all this is surely vain and futile. And that is why this new *Brave New World* is the same as the old one. Its defects as a work of art are considerable; but in order to correct them I should have to rewrite the book— and in the process of rewriting, as an older, other person, I should probably get rid not only of some of the faults of the story, but also of such merits as it originally possessed. And so, resisting the temptation to wallow in artistic remorse, I prefer to leave both well and ill alone and to think about something else.

In the meantime, however, it seems worth while at least to mention the most serious defect in the story, which is this. The Savage is offered only two alternatives, an insane life in Utopia, or the life of a primitive in an Indian village, a life more human in some respects, but in others hardly less queer and abnormal. At the time the book was written this idea, that human beings are given free will in order to choose between insanity on the one hand and lunacy on the other, was one that I found amusing and regarded as quite possibly true. For the sake, however, of dramatic effect, the Savage is often permitted to speak more rationally than his upbringing among the practitioners of a religion that is half fertility cult and half *Penitente* ferocity would actually warrant. Even his acquaintance with Shakespeare would not in reality justify such utterances. And at the close, of course, he is made to retreat from sanity; his native *Penitente*-ism reasserts its authority and he ends in maniacal self-torture and despairing suicide. "And so they died miserably ever after"—much to the reassurance of the amused, Pyrrhonic aesthete who was the author of the fable.

Today I feel no wish to demonstrate that sanity is impossible. On the contrary, though I remain no less sadly certain than in the past that sanity is a rather rare phenomenon, I am convinced that it can be achieved and would like to see more of it. For having said so in several recent books and, above all, for having compiled an anthology of what the sane have said about sanity and the means whereby it can be achieved, I have been told by an eminent academic critic that I am a sad symptom of the failure of an intellectual class in time of crisis. The implication being, I suppose, that the professor and his colleagues are hilarious symptoms of success. The benefactors of humanity deserve due honour and commemoration. Let us build a Pantheon for professors. It should be located among the ruins of one of the gutted cities of Europe or Japan, and over the entrance to the ossuary I would inscribe, in letters six or seven feet high, the simple words: SACRED TO THE MEMORY OF THE WORLD'S EDUCATORS. SI MONUMENTUM REQUIRIS CIRCUMSPICE.

But to return to the future . . . If I were now to rewrite the book, I would offer the Savage a third alternative. Between the utopian and the primitive horns of his dilemma would lie the possibility of sanity—a possibility already actualized, to some extent, in a community of exiles and refugees from the Brave New World, living within the borders of the Reservation. In this community economics would be decentralist and Henry-Georgian, politics Kropotkinesque and co-operative. Science and technology would be used as though, like the Sabbath, they had been made for man, not (as at present and still more so in the Brave New World) as though man were to be adapted and enslaved to them. Religion would be the conscious and intelligent pursuit of man's Final End, the unitive knowledge of the immanent Tao or Logos, the transcendent Godhead or Brahman. And the prevailing philosophy of life would be a kind of Higher Utilitarianism, in which the Greatest Happiness principle would be secondary to the Final End principle—the first question to be asked and answered in every contingency of life being: "How will this thought or action contribute to, or interfere with, the achievement, by me and the greatest possible number of other individuals, of man's Final End?"

Brought up among the primitives, the Savage (in this hypothetical new version of the book) would not be transported to Utopia until he had had an opportunity of learning something at first hand about the nature of a society composed of freely co-operating individuals devoted to the pursuit of sanity. Thus altered, *Brave New World* would possess an artistic and (if it is permissible to use so large a word in connection with a work of fiction) a philosophical completeness, which in its present form it evidently lacks.

But *Brave New World* is a book about the future and, whatever its artistic or philosophical qualities, a book about the future can interest us only if its prophecies look as though they might conceivably come true. From our present vantage point, fifteen years further down the inclined plane of modern history, how plausible do its prognostications seem? What has happened in the painful interval to confirm or invalidate the forecasts of 1931?

One vast and obvious failure of foresight is immediately apparent. *Brave New World* contains no reference to nuclear fission. That it does not is actually rather odd; for the possibilities of atomic energy had been a popular topic of conversation for years before the book was written. My old friend, Robert Nichols, had even written a successful play about the subject, and I recall that I myself had casually mentioned it in a novel published in the late twenties. So it seems, as I say, very odd that the rockets and helicopters of the seventh century of Our Ford should not have been powered by disintegrating nuclei. The oversight may not be excusable; but at least it can be easily explained. The theme of *Brave New World* is not the advancement of science as such; it is the advancement of science as it affects human individuals. The triumphs of physics, chemistry and engineering are tacitly taken for granted. The only scientific advances to be specifically described are those involving the application to human beings of the results of future research in biology, physiology and psychology. It is only by means of the sciences of life that the quality of life can be radically changed. The sciences of matter can be applied in such a way that they will destroy life or make the living of it impossibly complex and uncomfortable; but, unless used as instruments by the biologists and psychologists, they can do nothing to modify the natural forms and expressions of life itself. The release of atomic energy marks a great revolution in human history, but not (unless we blow ourselves to bits and so put an end to history) the final and most searching revolution.

This really revolutionary revolution is to be achieved, not in the external world, but in the souls and flesh of human beings. Living as he did in a revolutionary period, the Marquis de Sade very naturally made use of this theory of revolutions in order to rationalize his peculiar brand of insanity. Robespierre had achieved the most superficial kind of revolution, the political. Going a little deeper, Babeuf had attempted the economic revolution. Sade regarded himself as the apostle of the truly revolutionary revolution, beyond mere politics and economics—the revolution in individual men, women and children, whose bodies were henceforward to become the common sexual property of all and whose minds were to be purged of all the natural decencies, all the laboriously acquired inhibitions of traditional civilization. Between sadism and the really revolutionary revolution there is, of course, no necessary or inevitable connection. Sade was a lunatic and the more or

less conscious goal of his revolution was universal chaos and destruction. The people who govern the Brave New World may not be sane (in what may be called the absolute sense of that word); but they are not madmen, and their aim is not anarchy but social stability. It is in order to achieve stability that they carry out, by scientific means, the ultimate, personal, really revolutionary revolution.—ALDOUS HUXLEY, "Foreword" to *Brave New World*, 1946, pp. vii–xiii

The study of various touchstones in the history of man's search for the ideal commonwealth affords valuable insight into ideas and ideals that profoundly influenced the utopian thought of Aldous Huxley. *Brave New World*, *Ape and Essence*, and *Island* evidence their author's awareness of, and in many cases his dislike for, major phases in utopian literature. Early writings contain references to mythical islands and to a prehistoric Golden Age that provided a simple but an incredibly congenial life. Such a myth must surely suggest wishfulfillment and escapist tendencies. Especially in *Brave New World*, Huxley rejects primitivistic and pastoral perfection. Opposed to the escapist utopia of private pleasures is the ideal commonwealth established and maintained by careful regulation. This sort of utopia, of which Plato's *Republic* is the best known example, requires that the individual must offer much of his freedom for the privilege of living in the heavenly city and pursuing the good. Though the *Republic* is much more descriptive than prescriptive, Huxley strenuously objects to the work's seemingly authoritarian stance. He cannot accept the *Republic* as descriptive of the good, and he clearly cannot regard the work as a prescription for attaining desirable goals. According to Huxley's philosophy, it is an example of the type of utopia that must be avoided.

. . . Satire has always been a part of utopian thought. As numerous critics have observed, the very idea of creating a better world implies that there is something wrong with the present world. Many of the most enduring works in the utopian genre contain sharp criticisms of contemporary society. Instead of taking the reader to utopia and stressing the abuses of the outside world, however, writers of utopian literature began to emphasize the inhumanity of a "perfect" world and to suggest that contemporary society was pleasant by comparison. The twentieth-century dystopian view was not completely new; Aristophanes's anti-utopia is at least as old as the *Republic*. Swift and even More himself at times treated the concept of utopia satirically. For the first time in the history of utopian thought, however, the dystopian viewpoint displaced traditional utopianism as the most significant element in the philosophy of utopian speculations. Until the twentieth century, few authors had labored extensively over satires of utopia. Heretofore, utopia had been in large measure a good place to visit.

But it became increasingly and frighteningly apparent to writers like Huxley that, as Nicolas Berdiaeff remarks, utopia is realizable. Prefaced to *Brave New World* is a comment in French by Berdiaeff which insists that in the new century reasonable men may well search for a way to avoid "utopia" and return, instead, to a society that is less "perfect" but more free. *Brave New World* serves as a powerful warning that man may reach the so-often sought for state of the ideal commonwealth. Huxley's world-wide utopia, though, is considerably less desirable than Wells imagined that it might be. The novel is an attack upon utopianism—an attack that one cannot fully understand unless he has some knowledge of the utopian tradition and the works against which Huxley particularly campaigned. In effect, Huxley says that Plato's republic of rigid stability and unity—a society with little personal freedom and no innovation—is stagnant and unproductive. His literary assault upon the utopian tradition is sweeping and not entirely unjustified. Individuality does indeed frequently disappear behind a facade of utopian order and reason.

Huxley's other major target in *Brave New World* is the nineteenth-century utopia which assumes that scientific progress leads to an ideal world. Huxley, it becomes apparent, is fond of neither mechanization nor the concept of progress. He implies that wholesale industrialization creates men like machines and that too much stress upon progress unjustly sacrifices the here and now for the potentially better tomorrow. In *Brave New World* he rebels against the idea of progress and mechanization, and he disallows the very concept of utopia. Neither the primitive existence of the Indians, the ungoverned agricultural community of Alphas, nor the world-wide utopia can be defined as ideal. The society of A.F. 632 is "perfectly" terrifying to the creative individual who wishes to test the gates of heaven and hell, and who seeks to find doors of perceptions not conveniently opened for perverse purposes by the state. When pleasure and escape become unavoidable goals, Huxley reasons, the individual lives in a nightmarish ideal society that cannot allow him the right to be unhappy.

In his second dystopia, Huxley rescues society from utopia, but the cost is high. In *Ape and Essence* one sees an alternative that science and industry may provide. The inhabitants of twenty-second century America are even more perverse and pathetically ill-directed than Our Ford could have imagined. Still, there is some promise of a less abnormal life in the "Hot Community"—a community that does not treat sex and love animalistically as the early utopists often did.

It may seem curious that an author who so soundly denounces both traditional and most later utopian efforts could also create one, but Huxley's final utopian insight is predictable from his development toward a philosophy of escape. Huxley was bound ultimately to find his utopia, for he dwelled at length in the very nebulous land of negations. One gets only a hint in his dystopias of what their satisfactory commutation might be.

In many ways Huxley's last novel is traditionally utopian. The ideal commonwealth is an island populated by beautiful people and discovered by a traveller who, after being shipwrecked on paradise, uncovers the attributes of the ideal society—occasionally with skepticism but usually with joy. As Northrop Frye notes: "in utopian stories a frequent device is for someone, generally a first-person narrator, to enter the utopia and be shown around it by a sort of Intourist guide." In *Brave New World* it is the Savage who tours utopia. In *Ape and Essence* it is Dr. Alfred Poole who learns of modern conditions, and in *Island* Will Farnaby becomes a disciple of the Palanese system of values. As in *Utopia* and many other similar works, the skepticism of the central character is refuted by the unshakeable logic of a people accustomed to the ideal. Much unlike most utopias, however, the island society of Pala insists upon the rights of the individual for self-discovery, self-awareness, and self-satisfaction. The dominant atmosphere of Huxley's utopia suggests an insistence upon freedom, love, personal pleasures, and a mind-body interaction typical of *News from Nowhere* but completely atypical of most ideal commonwealths. The key to happiness on Pala is the here and now—not a vague promise of future happiness engendered by a trust in progress.

The examination of Huxley's three utopian novels against a background of the utopian tradition allows one to see more clearly those themes that influenced Huxley most. He shows the reader that the ends many utopists have sought, and not the means they employ to achieve these ends, are at fault. After

reading *Brave New World*, one might assume that Huxley feels that conditioning infants is always wrong. Upon perusing *Island*, however, one becomes aware that it is only the end toward which conditioning is directed in *Brave New World* that Huxley resents. In *Island*, conditioning for love and not for fear is endorsed. Similarly, after reading Huxley's depiction of the liberal sex practices of the brave new world and the "heat" period of 2108, one might conclude that the author is puritanical with respect to sex. But in *Island* each child is instructed in the yoga of love and is permitted at an early age to have sexual experiences. Again, it is the end toward which sex is directed in *Brave New World* and *Ape and Essence* that Huxley deplores. Meaningful sexual relationships, especially those involving a yoga of love, are applauded; only shallow, unthinking adventures in sex are condemned. The worst of the East and the West is discussed in *Ape and Essence*, but Huxley is strongly in favor of a meeting of the best aspects of the East and the West. In *Brave New World* artificial insemination and sperm banks lead to production-line people; in *Island* the same devices of science, employed for humane goals, improve the race. *Ape and Essence* and *Brave New World* are attacks upon man's use of technology. In *Island* science serves man; it does not control him. Similarly, *soma* is evil because it is used for escape; but *moksha*-medicine reveals reality.

The societies of *Brave New World* and *Ape and Essence* were directed toward goals which Huxley regards as unprofitable and frequently destructive to the human spirit. *Island*, on the other hand, describes a society with a sound sense of direction. The key to the change in Huxley's philosophy is found in the 1946 foreword to *Brave New World*. At one time, the author says, he considered man's choice to be between lunacy and insanity. But in his foreword an escape is briefly described. In such a community, Huxley states, "science and technology would be used as though, like the Sabbath, they had been made for man, not . . . as though man were to be adapted and enslaved to them. Religion would be the conscious and intelligent pursuit of man's Final End, the unitive knowledge of the immanent Tao or Logos, the transcendent Godhead or Brahman." Huxley declares that the general notion of a utopian escape was "in the back of my mind at that time [1946], and it has preoccupied me a good deal ever since." But in *Island* the final realization of the author's preoccupation occurs. It is evident, then, that Huxley's last novel is the result of a gradual progression of his utopian philosophy. Thus all three works are indicative of their creator's awareness of and his reaction to the utopian tradition.—WILLIAM W. MATTER, "The Utopian Tradition and Aldous Huxley," *SFS*, July 1975, pp. 146–50

In *Eyeless in Gaza* Anthony Beavis, whom I regard as Huxley's spokesman (the character's ideas conform closely to those of *Ends and Means*,) clarifies the ontological—as opposed to Mark Rampion's essentially moral—concept of personality:

> Now, human experience is analogous to matter. Analyze it—and you will find yourself in the presence of psychological atoms. A lot of these atoms constitute normal experience and a selection from normal experience constitutes 'personality.' Each individual atom is unlike normal experience and still more unlike personality. Conversely, each atom in experience resembles the corresponding atom in another. Viewed microscopically a woman's body is just like a washstand, and Napoleon's experience is just like Wellington's.

Thus the answer to the question as to "why we imagine that we have coherent experience and personality" lies with the fact that although we don't, "our minds work slowly and have very feeble powers of analysis." Although Beavis's theory permits him to avoid accountability for his moral and emotional failings, it must always be kept in mind that in the late twenties Huxley is dealing with two *distinct* perspectives on the self, one moral and psychological and the other ontological and ultimately mystical. Beavis will learn to integrate his personality on the moral-emotional level, but his basic premise of the inherently molecular structure of the self remains for Huxley an indisputable axiom.

In the eleventh chapter of *Eyeless in Gaza*, Huxley attempted to synthesize his thinking on the subject of the self or "personality" in a lengthy meditation recorded in Anthony Beavis's notebook. Anthony Beavis, after citing F. H. Bradley's *Appearance and Reality* and Hume's *Treatise*, turns to Blake and his doctrine of the states to resolve the problem of identity and the possibility of a more holistic conception of self:

> It was left to Blake to rationalize psychological atomism into a philosophical system. Man according to Blake (and, after him, according to Lawrence) is simply a succession of states. Good and evil can be predicted only of states, not of individuals, who in fact don't exist, except as places where the states occur. It is the end of personality in the old sense of the word.

He adds unexpectedly that Blake's concept of the states argues the appearance of a new kind of personality, the "total man" who exhibits two major traits: first, he is "the antithesis of . . . the fundamental Christian man of our history" and, second, he is nevertheless "the realization of that ideal personality conceived by the Jesus of the Gospel." In short, ontologically "the individual" does not exist except as a locus for the functioning of "states," but in the very same paragraph a "new kind of personality" is scrupulously defined in intensely moralistic and decidedly Victorian terms. The new personality is a very sharply contracted self conceived as inherently disinterested, passive in its receptivity to immediate experience, and characterized by humility and honesty. The important element in this concept of the self is its resounding negativity. The new man is "not interested," evinces a "refusal to exalt himself," lays "no lasting claims on anything," and is "not pharisaic." This of course would be a good description of one of George Eliot's or Dickens's self-renunciatory protagonists. Moreover, Huxley's ideal of a sensitive but passive alertness to immediate experience, coupled with a self-effacing humility, is profoundly un-Blakean in its neglect of the creative imagination and Blake's spirited endorsement of energy and self-assertion. There is, however, a subtle strategy behind Huxley's use of Blake.

Huxley's interpretation of Blake's concept of the states (set forth in Blake's *Milton* and *Jerusalem*) is somewhat skewed, emphasizing not only the transiency of the states but the disappearance of the individual as well. Blake vigorously stressed the potential infinity latent yet imperishable in every human being. Nevertheless, Blake did conceive of the self as constituting a series of states; that is, of static conditions that individuals are capable of transcending. For Blake a state is a fixed mental configuration, shaped and informed by specific societal, psychological, or political pressures, and as such can be recognized and then rejected by the individual. The personality or self, then, is governed by "the limitations of the given psychological socioeconomic state that a man inhabits at a certain time in a certain place," and is often emblematized in Huxley's novels by carefully circumscribed symbolic landscapes like the "realist's" Gog's Court, the romantic's Brighton

Pavilion, or Mark Staithes's barren house. Huxley's adoption of Blake's theory of the states permits him to argue for the deliberate creation of an enduring matrix of associated memories and feelings (i.e. personality) but to *limit* the integrity of that creation on the ontological level. Thus by defining the self in negative, sharply circumscribed terms, he avoids the inflated egoism of the baroque-romantic and the equally egocentric self-pity of the reverse romantic, whom Calamy in *Those Barren Leaves* condemns as hopelessly "sentimentalist." And in denying the absolute integrity of the individual on the ontological level, he has opened a window onto the absolute—so to speak. Just as life may exhibit a surface of diversity and flux, so too the mind is conceived as essentially dynamic. But underlying both is a *tertium quid* that only makes its presence felt when the exigent self disappears. —ROBERT S. BAKER, "The Descending Road of Modern History," *The Dark Historic Page*, 1982, pp. 128–30

Aldous Huxley's new novel, *Time Must Have a Stop*, is a good deal better than his last one, *After Many a Summer Dies the Swan*. For one thing, he has returned to Europe for his characters and his settings, and he is much more successful with the English intellectuals in the London and Florence of the twenties than he was, in the earlier book, with an American millionaire and his hangers-on. His people, in many cases, are still conventional figures of satire: the disgusting voluptuary who lives in Italy and talks about the art of life, the rude rich old lady who has a pet Pomeranian and raps out imperious orders, and an up-to-date version of the hard Gradgrind parent, who is a socialist instead of a utilitarian; but Huxley does not run here the same risk of an obvious and purely external caricature that he did in his California fantasia. Here there is much more that is piquant in the social observation, much more wit in the talk and the unspoken thoughts of the characters, much more novelty of invention in the action. And along with this there goes an improvement in his handling of the religious element which has lately come to figure in his fiction. Huxley's peculiar version of the life of contemplation and revelation was expounded in *After Many a Summer* by a boring non-satirical character who read homilies to the other characters with an insufferable air of quiet authority and who constantly made the reader feel that it would have been better if he, too, had been satirically treated as a typical California crank. But in this new novel these matters have been dramatized and incorporated in the story on the same level as the other material. The voluptuary dies of a stroke, and we follow him into the non-sensual world. We see him drift about the fringes of the Divine within its gravitational field; return at moments to communicate with his friends through the agency of an extremely stupid medium, who garbles what he is trying to say; and finally, shrinking from absorption in God, get himself born back into humanity in the body of a baby expected by the wife of one of the other characters. Now, one may not be prepared to accept Huxley's views about spiritualistic phenomena and the Platonic rebirth of souls, but the whole thing has been given plausibility—though queer, it is never creepy—by treating the disembodied vicissitudes of Eustace Barnack's soul in the same dry or droll way as the adventures of his consciousness while still in the flesh. The result of threading this in with the doings of the characters who are still alive is an effect which must be new in fiction. In its essentially rather dismal and dark-brown way, *Time Must Have a Stop* is quite a brilliant performance.

It is difficult, however, for Huxley to celebrate convincingly in a novel his present ideals of abnegation and withdrawal from the things of the world, just as it was for T. S. Eliot, in

Murder in the Cathedral, to celebrate the ideal of humility. These are virtues which—unlike some others: courage and brotherly love, for example—do not lend themselves to being illustrated in public by clever and accomplished writers, long admired and much in view. Just as Eliot's Thomas Becket becomes superior to the verge of snobbery in his perfect achievement of meekness, so Bruno Rontini, the contemporary saint of Huxley's latest novel, seems sometimes attainted by the smart virtuosity of so many of Huxley's other characters in his insight into other people's states of mind, his power to forecast what they are going to do and an ability to outmaneuver them morally which gives almost the impression of scoring off them—all talents that have something in common with those of the infallible detective that figures in so much mystery fiction. Aldous Huxley sharply criticizes Dante for carrying up into Heaven his partisan antagonisms and his pride, but the danger with Huxley himself is that he will turn Buddha, Pascal and St. John of the Cross into another neat performance for the salon. It must, however, be said that his descriptions of the dissociated trancelike states in which his characters sometimes feel or seem about to feel a super-corporeal union with God have a certain sound of authenticity and convince one that they are based on experience.

One's objection to what, at this point in his career, can only be called the moral teaching of Huxley is not that it is not derived from real states of exaltation, but that these states of exaltation themselves imply an incomplete experience of the earthly possibilities of human life. Huxley's satire has always been founded not only upon a distaste for humanity but also upon a real incapacity for understanding most of the things that seemed to other people important and exciting. It used to be fashionable to call him "intelligent," but he was never particularly intelligent. His habit of reading the *Encyclopaedia Britannica* gives the quality of his appetite for facts and ideas; his interest in the great intellectual movements that were bringing most light in his own time was on exactly the same level as his interest in a twelfth-century heresy, a queer species of carnivorous plant, a special variety of Romanesque architecture or a Greek poet surviving in fragments. Freud, Lenin, Einstein, Joyce—he sometimes expressed about them, in his casual essays, opinions as obtuse and philistine as those of the ordinary Fleet Street journalist. The new paths that they opened, the new hopes that they woke, were not opened or awakened for Huxley. For Huxley, in his satirical novels, the man whose imagination was aroused by, say, the quantum theory did not appear any more interesting than the old-fashioned pre-quantum mechanist, or the connoisseur of abstract painting than the fancier of Victorian bric-a-brac.

For the satirist, of course, this attitude may provide a basis for valid work. The Lilliputians of Swift seem too little, no matter what they do; the Bouvard and Pécuchet of Flaubert (invoked by one of the characters of *Time Must Have a Stop*) remain numskulls no matter what sciences or arts they think they are experimenting with. But Huxley is not, like Swift or Flaubert, complete and self-sufficient as a satirist. He has not even had the real love of writing, the power to express himself through art, of Evelyn Waugh or Ronald Firbank, the novels of both of whom may very well last longer than Huxley's. Merely a manipulator of Punch-and-Judy figures, he has inevitably to shake them off his hands and to use these hands in pulpit gestures as he comes forward to preach his way of life; and in this role his defects of intelligence again become fatally clear. We realize that his readiness to reject the world is due to his not knowing what is in it. That mixed and immature humanity which has been handled by the great artists and the great thinkers of his time—Huxley was not impressed by what they had been able to create from it because he had never had the

full sense of what that humanity was like and, hence, of what it might become. His whole ascetic system, for example, is arrived at by way of the conclusion that "the flesh," though theoretically to be tolerated as a device for perpetuating the species, can never, through sexual selection or through the idealizations of love, become a part of our higher activities. In this novel, sex is never represented as anything but cold or perverse. There is nothing beyond momentary pleasure in any of the amorous relations of *Time Must Have a Stop*. Of the fact that the relations between men and women are involved in everything humanity builds—in the forms of art, in the structure of thought, in the incitement to achievement and leadership—you will get no inkling from Huxley. This would be perfectly all right in a satire which did not purport to be anything else—the satirist has always the license to turn down the flame of life in order to let us take account more grimly of the mechanical aspect of the fixtures and the sordidness of the surrounding room; but it is very misleading in a fable which pretends to bring us solemnly to consider the fundamental problems of human behavior and destiny.

Aldous Huxley would probably say, in reply to the objection above, that it does not really matter what we build on this earth. Our retort would be: How does he know?, since he has taken little part in the building. His inability to build solidly in his novels is itself an evidence of this. You cannot live in them; the author himself has not lived in them. He has always found it easy to drop them in order to report on his spiritual progress. The epilogue to *Time Must Have a Stop* consists mostly of a series of *pensées*, the journal of the central character, a poet who is schooling himself in the discipline of self-renunciation. These last pages have a terseness of writing and an accent of moral sincerity that one has hardly found before in Huxley. But what sort of general validity can be expected of a set of principles derived from the diminished and distorted world invented by the author of this novel? Since the story is admittedly a satire, it should follow that a religious system deduced from the conduct of its characters is either not wholly serious or not susceptible of wide application.— EDMUND WILSON, "Aldous Huxley in the World beyond Time" (1944), *Classics and Commercials*, 1950, pp. 209–14

POETRY

Mr. Aldous Huxley is one of the most interesting of the new poets, partly because he has already written good poetry, but chiefly because he is a finer, richer poet in the making. But the emotional and intellectual elements in him have not yet been fused together into a malleable compound fit for the handling of the subjects which most often attract him. It naturally follows that it is the expression of an emotional or intellectual discord that he is most often prompted to express in verse. This is a characteristic common to many of the new poets. They can point to examples in past literature in which discords of that kind have flowered in poems of high excellence; the immense admiration which Donne's poems excite to-day springs from the need to point out to the world that the thing can indeed be done. But firstly, Donne was an exceptionally passionate poet, while most of our young contemporary poets (I am not thinking particularly of Mr. Huxley) are cold; and secondly, though Donne himself was subtle enough, his age was a comparatively naïve one. . . .

To return to Mr. Huxley. He has science in the blood. He is often preoccupied, as a poet, with experience as it may be felt in the light of science. This alone would make his work interesting; but, alas, it does not also make it beautiful. The fundamental reason why the ban has been removed from the expression of "ugliness" in literature, is that artists have so much new unconsecrated material to assimilate. But the poet with the imaginative digestion of a Lucretius has not yet emerged. Mr. Huxley, when he handles experience from this point of view, creates merely the grotesque or the curious; he is interested and excited himself, he takes a morose delectation in paining himself and his reader, but he is homesick all the time for the old mythological world. When he makes intellect the starting point of his inspiration, he allows his nerves (oh! fatal weakness!) to have the controlling influence on the result; he never rises to the peaks of contemplation. There is pathos in this failure; but it is a pathos that is interesting rather than satisfying. He relapses, after flutterings, upon the half-way ledge of irony, where he can perch and utter those mordant reflections which may be a relief to the poet himself, but can never raise the minds of others. Contrast his poem "Leda" with the series of poems in ⟨*Leda*⟩ called *Philosophers' Songs*. In "Leda" he is back in the old smooth, mythological world, consecrated by a thousand poets. He pays occasional tribute to ugly fact in the course of this poem, but he is at home while describing Leda with her maids bathing in Eurotas, her shining body and the clear deep pools! The modern terror of the too-perfect world makes him dwell longer, and more humorously, than his predecessors would have done, upon Jove tossing on his Olympian couch, tortured by his continence, and sending the searchlight of his glowing eye travelling over the earth below to find some object worthy of his god-like lust.

> Over the world his focussed passion flies
> Quicker than chasing sunlight on a day
> Of storm and golden April.

. . . In the centre of the book the reader will come across a preface, composed of separate reflections, in which the poet's aims and perplexities are obscurely set forth; where by means of an irritatingly allusive and imaged prose, for which Mallarmé's *Divagations* are a precedent, he asks himself what the task of the poet is. The first answer is: "Let us abandon ourselves to Time, which is beauty's essence"—that is to say, dwell pensively on the imperfection and the passing of happiness and all beautiful things. He brushes aside this answer: "If I have said 'Mortality is beauty,' it was a weakness." . . . If he has set up death and nothingness as an ideal (and in some of his poems his bitterness comes near to doing so), it is only his desperate mind that has desired it: "never my blood, whose pulse is a rhythm of the world." On the other hand, the pure imaginative ideal is equally unsatisfactory: "Beatrice lacks solidity, is as unresponsive to your kisses as mathematics" (Personally, I consider this a silly pronouncement); "she, too, is an oubliette, not a way of life." What, then, is the common measure, he asks? What is true poetry? He replies in a series of metaphors: "It is not the far-fetched, dear-bought gem; no pomander to be smelt only when the crowd becomes too stinkingly insistent." He wants poets to be "rather a rosy Brotherhood of Common Life, eating, drinking; marrying and giving in marriage; taking and taken in adultery; reading, thinking, and when thinking fails, feeling immeasurably more subtly, sometimes perhaps creating. . . . *Ventre à terre*, head in air—your centaurs are your only poets. Their hoofs strike sparks from the flints and they see both very near and immensely far."

Now, this is a robust poet's creed, and Mr. Huxley is not a robust poet—perhaps that is why this creed attracts him. True, he can not only waive away the pomander, but hold his nose and our noses, too, over the most complex and stenchful exhalations; he can keep his eyes without blenching on the most hideous sights and the most grating disappointments. But

the poetry that results? Those poems are the turnings and churnings of a queasy stomach. . . . Again, when science has suggested to him a theme on the prodigality of life ("The Fifth Philosopher's Song"), it is not to rejoice that he uses it, like one of "the rosy Brotherhood," but to lead up to a melancholy little quip that it was such a germ as produced himself by chance among a million that might have fertilised his mother's womb; instead, perchance, that of another Shakespeare, Newton, Donne. The mention of Donne brings me back to the point from which I started. Like Donne, like his centaur-poets, he would strike fire from flints (cutting facts), but . . . while the rebound from painful fact made Donne soar into a scholastic empyrean full of mystical conceits, it makes our modern poets dive instead into the dim confused underworld of the semi-conscious. That is the true "oubliette," not Dante's Heaven; and then—farewell, poet! But I have said enough to show that Mr. Aldous Huxley is a poet always interesting to the intellect and sometimes superbly satisfying to the æsthetic sense.—DESMOND MACCARTHY, "Mr. Aldous Huxley," *NS*, Sept. 4, 1920, pp. 595–97

. . . Huxley's verse . . . has mainly a historical and biographical interest. No one of my generation could fail to be touched rereading these yearnings after ideal love, this disgust at lust; the attempts, mainly with an outworn style, to bring modern properties and the intellectual life into verse. Mr Church is right in his introduction ⟨to *The Collected Poetry of Aldous Huxley*⟩ to point out Huxley's quality of innocence as a young man, an innocence all the more quaint in its alliance with the encyclopedic cleverness and the wish to shock. But he was rarely a poet who looked like staying the course, though one shouldn't underestimate the labour put into a number of extended pieces, and a good many idiosyncratic and original turns. However, I think it's true to say that what is really novel and striking here belongs properly to prose—the image, for example, of an unshaven face 'like a record in a musical box'.

Nevertheless, Huxley's interest in the potential scope of poetry stayed with him right until the end of his life, and one must pay proper tribute to it. There are two early essays on the subject—'Subject-Matter of Poetry' in *On the Margin* (1923) and 'And wanton optics roll the melting eye' in *Music at Night* (1931). The ideas here are gathered and amplified in the little book *Literature and Science* that he published in the year of his death. His main plea is for poets to feel science as they feel the traditional subjects of poetry, so that poetry may deal with it; and he points out that the commonly held notion that poets in this century have put back into poetry great tracts of life and thought for long considered inappropriate must be subject to severe qualification. The latter was a timely observation in 1923 and even in 1931, but it is extraordinary that *Literature and Science* fails to refer to Auden's remarkable work in the intervening years, to say nothing of other poets and critics of scientific temper, like Empson. Still, this book is well worth attention and, of course, it makes explicit what Huxley was trying to do in the side of his verse that we must find most interesting today.

Not until the final pages of his first collection (1916—published in Blackwell's 'Adventurers All' books, 'A Series of Young Poets Unknown to Fame') is there anything like the real Huxleyan tone and language:

> That glabrous dome that lifts itself so grand,
> There in the marish, is the omphalos,
> The navel, umbo, middle, central boss
> Of the unique, sole, true Cloud-Cuckoo Land.

The next volume, of 1918, is certainly an advance, but chiefly in technical adroitness (with it, he was promoted to

Blackwell's 'Initiates: a Series of Poetry by Proved Hands'). There is still the hankering after the resounding poetic 'touchstone' (he never lost this), but the greater skill and sophistication permits a number of successes—in the opening sonnet sequence, for instance, and the comparatively relaxed and colloquial poems like 'Crapulous Impression'. The Mallarmé translation, though perhaps now seeming impossibly 'poetic', was rightly celebrated.

The volume of 1920, *Leda*, is better still, and contains most of the lines by which he is remembered as a poet. In the interim he had become friendly with T. S. Eliot.

> There was his scar, a panel of old rose
> Slashed in the elegant buff of his trunk hose;
> Adonis punctured by his amorous boar,
> Permanent souvenir of the Great War.

Perhaps one is unjust in looking for influences: those lines come from a remarkable poem written to commemorate a friend killed in the war, and Huxley undoubtedly feels and reflects the excruciating pressures of the end of the conflict, though all he is able to express really successfully is irreverence and disgust:

> Seated upon the convex mound
> Of one vast kidney, Jonah prays
> And sings his canticles and hymns
> Making the hollow vault resound
> God's goodness and mysterious ways
> Till the great fish spouts music as he swims.

The last book, *The Cicadas and Other Poems*, is even more solid technically but, as it seems to me, essentially lifeless, Parnassian:

> I reach for grapes, but from an inward vine
> Pluck sea-cold nipples, still bedewed with brine.

Certainly throughout there has been no slackening of the effort to enlarge vocabulary, to import ideas and information from science and other disciplines. But Huxley infrequently escaped from the drawbacks (to which he affectionately drew attention in his essays) attaching to all those poets—such as Erasmus Darwin—whose diction was at odds with their subject-matter. What he was seeking is aptly and amusingly encapsulated in the prose quotation from Jules Verne that he used as epigraph to the essay of 1931: 'The sunrise was magnificent. The luminary of day, like a disc of metal gilded by the Ruolz process, came up from the Ocean, as from an immense voltaic bath.' We may feel that his verse never quite achieved the natural aplomb of this.

The end of the poetry more or less coincides with the end of Huxley's first fictional period—that is to say, with the publication of *Point Counter Point* (1928). What a dazzling, if over-forced, decade of creativity! Our reservations about the verse must be tempered with admiration for its prolixity, and in a time of enormous fictional and other output. I think the work of this decade will inevitably separate itself off from the later and, on the whole, disappointing books; and in that event the verse will play a minor but essential part in the reading of Huxley by future generations.—ROY FULLER, "Gilding by the Ruolz Process," *LT*, March 18, 1971, p. 343

PHILOSOPHY

Lord, Lord, you who know that my unworthiness to review this breviary of mystical touchstones ⟨*The Perennial Philosophy*⟩ is almost as great as Aldous Huxley's strivings to reach you by texts, precepts, and the will of those who could not love you half so much disliked they not existence more—Lord, hear out my complaint against this book, yet let me praise first the passion, the scope, the image of an ideal, with which it has

been made. Riding up and down the ladders of the steel cities, flung every day into a vortex of gas where eloquence is a trap to make us buy and words are used for what they will conceal, surrounded as we are by victims who suffer without a cause and the living who are steadily betrayed in an atmosphere of perfect good will, we can at least rejoice in a book which is addressed to the dignity of man and not his bitterness, to the imagination and not to the wise guy. There are visions recaptured in our day, Lord, which are irrelevant but not unmindful of what we are and how we live. How good it is to have these visions even if they lead us nobly nowhere on the path we have appointed since your son Luther's time! How good it is to be reminded that there is a wisdom of the heart which is not kindness but a deeper knowledge!

But irrelevant, Lord, irrelevant. In our day there are still many who seek you, you who are not the end of their seeking but the way in which they seek. Of these there are several kinds. First, there are those who own you in name, knock at your door familiarly as at a casket of jewels which will open at the magic word, and are useless to us and themselves. These are the eternal priests, the Petty Inquisitors, the magisterial believers; those who have taken shares in your unlimited company and are quick to feel everyone's guilt but their own. Their ways are benign, their politics are usually low, and they seek to make us meet you by rising from a Fall which is nowhere but in their conception of man. They still build Gothic in our time so that the least possible amount of light will be let into the greatest possible mass of doctrine, and in the same proportion as we suffer because you are so remote and so high, so they make a virtue of our difficulty in reaching you and a hierarchy in the social state is defended. Thus, you become King all the more as there will be many other Kings and Masters to appease before reaching you. I do not like these, Lord, and for the most part neither does your son Aldous. But he is not sure, he wavers. At times he seeks you so frantically on any ground that he joins forces with them. For he can never resist a theological statement perfectly expressed, and Lord, these men have furnished many beautiful statements, their prayer-books are chains of pearl, and Aldous is much taken with them. That is one of the many reasons why he does not love you well.

Then there are the people who seek you without often knowing that they do; or if they do know, properly think it more imperative to prove you than to invoke you—these are the men who speak at least one small portion of the truth so firmly that they are worth to us more than the saints and all the canons. These are the partisans for people, when they speak not in the name of the people but for all the rights of the living being; who know that all the truth of our condition would be more important to us than a new plan of reform, and even as they say *You are this and not the other*, or *You lie here without need; You hate too much and why do you hate at all?* bring you to us and love you best. These are the men—poets, doctors, revolutionaries, exiles—who have the insight to tell us that we are not innocent, and the courage to make us see that guilt is a sign and not a sentence. Often they deny you, and why should they not? Often they affirm you without words, and how better to worship you? They know that life is a problem, the setting of the problem honestly being the most human grace; that life is a poem, the measures of which are set by the depth and length of our awareness; but that it is only in specific problems and particular poems, fashioned by different men in various ways, that the bridge is crossed between insight and wisdom. But your son Aldous does not believe that these men know you and seek you. That is another reason why he does not love you well; he thinks you are above time, history, suffering. Lord, what else are you if you do not rise out of these?

Then there are the people who seek you because they are afraid—who pray to you in the dark because you are the dark; who hate themselves and therefore think that only you will love them; who use you for a thrill which they cannot define, for a service which they cannot use, to cover up a life which they do not live. These are not much, Lord, yet they are all of us; because we are men we seek out causes, and when we do not seek well we fall on you. Among these several types may be distinguished. There are those who are afraid and do not know; these seek you out by animism, by magic and spells, by indulgences to everyone but themselves. There are those who are afraid and know too well without binding their knowledge to men and to history: these are many in our time, Lord; they work by hatred, by deliberate myths, and by the false logic of sensationalism—to them the spasm is worth more than the life, is indeed higher than life. Finally, there are the men who are afraid because they are not attached to life, who think that life is something other than men, and men other than their "passions"; who are mystical not because the Godhead is in them or they in you, but because mysticism is symmetrical, severe, a dream in ideal forms that lifts us spasmodically above the murk. These are the men, Lord, who would seek in our condition to will us back to the ecstasies of men who lived in quite another; who think that the love of you is different in kind from the love of men for each other. These do not love at all; they recoil from the stink of life; for them life is raw and uninteresting, theories are graces, and if you must look at man, a rationalized description *ad hoc* from the latest findings in biology is so much more pleasing than failure, anxiety and natural bewilderment. Of such is your son Aldous: much-learned; deeply, deeply earnest, a true witness of our condition and an honest man, but helpless to help us, for he will not see where anything begins or why a belief in solutions is necessary even when no solution helps; and who seeks you now not as a son seeks a father, not as the lover seeks the beloved, but as the all-immaculate Idea, that which is highest because it is not-life, that which is most perfect and pleasing because it is so different from us.

Forgive me, Lord, but we are all there is. You exist because that is so, and you are perennial because we are so. Because we are alone, however, it does not follow that we are simple; because we are only men, it does not follow that you cannot be. As we imagined you, so we create you every day in the fire of every day; the creation is endless and complex, daily and minute—and that is your crown, as our need of each other, our seeking the truth of what lies beyond us as men through the knowledge of each other, is the material in it. Because eternity can be an experience, why should we forget that it begins as an idea in us, and that the idea is rooted in us as a child is rooted in desire? The seeking of the Godhead, the potential and imagined union, is real for some and not real for others; but it is most real, Lord, as a fable of man's knowledge of the mystery in which he lives and which every day he completes, transcends and begins again by being alive. Not so does your son Aldous see it. To him the Godhead is reached by escaping from "the lower self," by mortification of "self," by willing us to a higher state by saying that the lower is low, still lower, and should not exist. So sex is "discreditably low"; so "petty loves keep us from God" (as if our love of you were not the pettiest, shrewdest still!); so life is what it is in our century because men do not know "the way." Alas, Lord, they know and they do not know; but some men are tied vocationally to machines and many to ignorance and hatred; some are murdered because they are above the nation, and some because they have none; some have no time and some have no strength; many are foiled, and few are chosen.

Lord, you who condemned Aldous Huxley to dislike life and to write novels; to seek you in libraries and amid the fumes of Hollywood; to love the Indian scriptures but not the Indian masses; to know everything about man as a specimen and to believe so little in him, on sight, as an ultimately irreproachable being—Lord, will you not show him that all these texts are a defense against a real faith and not the road to one; that he really fails you most by failing us? Will you not show him that the Idea is not the pinnacle of thought as it rises into faith but the enemy of thought when it evades the life which grounds it? We have had enough, Lord, of "dying to self"; the self is still only honored or dishonored; it is not lived; and because it is not, there is not self-love either, but only a trembling to be what we are not and to deny what we are. And where we are denied, the love of you is gone forever.—ALFRED KAZIN, "Shortest Way to Nirvana," NR, Nov. 5, 1945, pp. 610–13

The perennial philosophy, says Huxley, is the metaphysic that recognizes a divine reality substantial to the world; a psychology that finds in the soul something similar to or even identical with divine reality; an ethic that places man's final end in the knowledge of the ground of all being. Such knowledge can be won by those who fulfil the conditions upon which alone it can be gained. It is a faculty which, as Plotinus says, "all possess but few use." Only the pure in heart and poor in spirit can come to unitive knowledge. All the exponents of the perennial philosophy agree that man is a kind of trinity composed of body, soul, and spirit. The distinction between soul and spirit is much emphasized by St. Paul, whose *pneuma*, as the Greek Fathers recognized, is almost identical with the Platonic *nous*, and, as Huxley insists, with the Indian *atman*. Christianity, he says, has been overlaid by an idolatrous preoccupation with events and things in time, regarded as intrinsically sacred and divine. The mystics have gone some way towards liberating it from this unfortunate servitude to historic fact. Modern idolaters of progress prefer an impossible existence on dry land to love, joy and peace in our native ocean.

The way of life may be summed up as charity, the marks of which are disinterestedness, tranquillity and humility. That disinterestedness, or as Huxley used to say non-attachment, as the root and flower of religion, is also the creed of Walter Lippmann.

Another important distinction is that between intellect (in the scholastic sense) and reason, between *nous* and *dianoia*. Neglect of this distinction had led to much ignorant censure of "Greek intellectualism," encouraged by modern pragmatism.

The doctrine of an evolving God, with a passionate concern not with eternity but with future time, has coloured not only such popular philosophy as that of Wells, but that of Alexander and other leaders of thought. It is not Christian. Bosanquet vainly protested that to throw our ideals into the future is the death of sane idealism. The temptation has been too strong. The future, as Anatole France says, is a convenient place in which to store our dreams.

The eternal Now is a consciousness; the temporal world is known, sustained and perpetually created by an eternal consciousness. Eternal life "stands in the knowledge" of the Godhead. Popular religion has forgotten eternity and occupied itself with events in time. "Into the yawning void thus created flowed the tide of political idolatry; of which the practical consequences are total war, revolution and tyranny." In the words of William Law, whose greatness Huxley appreciates, "religion in the hands of self serves only to discover vices of a worse kind than in nature left to itself. Pride, self-exaltation, hatred and persecution, under a cloak of religious zeal, will sanctify actions which nature left to itself would be ashamed to own."

This book, enriched by copious and well chosen quotations from the masters of the spiritual life, is probably the most important treatise on mysticism that we have had for many years. But many will think that it is more Buddhist than Christian. Crucial questions suggest themselves. Was the Christian revelation a mere disclosure of timeless truths, or do happenings in time affect supertemporal reality? Is the conflict with evil a real battle, still undecided? Is the growth of soul into spirit rightly described as self-noughting—*ich bin entworden*, as the German mystics said? Many of the Christian mystics have used this language. "Leave nothing of myself in me," Crashaw makes St. Teresa pray. But surely personality is enlarged, not transcended, as we advance in the spiritual life. Personality must be preserved, Plotinus says. δεῖ ἕκαστον ἕκαστον εἶναι. In the spiritual world, as he pictures it, we are transparent to each other, because there is no longer anything that separates us. But this does not mean that we are no longer ourselves.

The question comes to a head when we consider our relations to our "even-Christian," as Julian of Norwich puts it. "Until we put an end to particular attachments," Huxley says, "there can be no love of God with the whole heart." Is this true? There is, we remember, a text in the Gospels in which Christ bids us "hate" even our parents as the condition of being his disciples. If Christ ever said this, it is an example of the hyperbolical language which he permitted himself, like other popular preachers, to use without fearing that his words might be misunderstood. A cloistered contemplative might be free from particular attachments; but is this a counsel for persons living in the world? Can we love God without loving our brother also? And do not many of us arrive at the love of God through the purification and intensification of family and conjugal affection? What do we mean by the love of God? For myself, it means homage to the attributes of Love or Goodness, Truth and Beauty, in which the divine nature has been revealed to us, and gratitude for the response to private prayer, of which I have sometimes, less often than I could wish, been conscious. But the kind of isolation which some of the extreme mystics seem to recommend would be for me a fatal impoverishment of my spiritual life. "Do I wish to know anything except God and myself? Nothing," so Augustine once says. It is not true, unless we expand our notions both of God and self far beyond our customary use of the words. The negative road, if followed exclusively, leads to Nirvana, not to the Christian heaven or the intelligible world of the Platonists. The spiritual life, as lived on earth, must be a double movement of withdrawal and return.

There is one other curious feature in this book which may or may not have a vital connexion with Huxley's philosophy. He has studied psychical research, and believes that "laboratory tests" have established the reality of some beliefs which fifty years ago would have been stigmatized as foolish superstitions. He now believes not only in telepathy but in clairvoyance or second sight, miraculous cures, the power of predicting the future, and even in levitation. These "mystical phenomena," as they used to be called, are in his opinion on a lower level than spiritual religion, and are therefore, I suppose, irrelevant to the philosophy of mysticism, but on the material and psychical plane he believes them to be real. He speaks as a man of science, and would regard my incredulity as mere obstinacy; but though I try to keep an open mind about telepathy, of which I am still quite unconvinced, I do not believe a word of

all the rest. Either Christina Mirabilis and Home, the medium, flew without wings, or they did not. If they did, the law of gravitation is unreliable. If they did not, no doubt seeing is believing, but intelligent people may sometimes see things that are not there. I know of a case when two detectives flew howling from a ghost which was, literally, only moonshine. Crookes was an honest man and a real man of science, but he was not necessarily exempt from hallucinations. He chose as the motto for his coat of arms, *Ubi crux ibi lux*. His friends amended it to Ubi Crookes ibi Spooks.

I think Thomas Huxley would have spoken severely to his grandson.—W. R. INGE, "Discussion: *The Perennial Philosophy*," *Phil*, April 1947, pp. 67–70

This little book ⟨*Literature and Science*⟩ by the late Aldous Huxley is introduced as a contribution to the running fight between representatives of the "two cultures." Its opening words are: "Snow or Leavis? The bland scientism of *The Two Cultures* or, violent and ill-mannered, the one-track, moralistic literalism of [Leavis'] Richmond Lecture? If there were no other choice, we should indeed be badly off." Huxley was unfair to both parties: Snow has never maintained that science is the sole avenue to knowledge, nor has Leavis, for all his lifelong commitment to questions of "How to live?" ever denied science's rightful pretensions to insight in its own realm. Still, in proposing to bring the debate down to earth by using "terms more concrete," Huxley usefully diverted attention from personalities to the basic issues of the still controversial relations between the scientific and the literary modes of thought. Whether or not his own position constitutes "a more realistic approach to the subject," his elegant essay has the merit of raising important questions.

Huxley's discussion is controlled by a theme that was prominent in much of his writing. He always tended to see human beings as "multiple amphibians," living "at one and the same moment in four or five different and disparate universes" and therefore existing "in a chronic state of mild or acute civil war." For him man was the chronic schizophrenic. Tensions between man's animal nature and his spiritual aspirations, or between demands for social accommodation and a yearning for any kind of religious absolute, always fascinated Huxley and provided him, in a novel such as *Point Counter Point*, with a ready source of surrealistic juxtapositions. In the present book he concentrated for the most part on the ways in which the distinctive purposes of science and literature are displayed in correspondingly contrasted uses of language. "The aim of the scientist is to say only one thing at a time, and to say it unambiguously and with the greatest possible clarity. To achieve this, he simplifies and jargonizes. . . . At its most perfectly pure, scientific language ceases to be a matter of words and turns into mathematics." (May not the historian, the moralist or the philosopher also aspire to clarity and precision? And could mathematical symbolism, adrift from observational moorings, ever serve the purposes of an empirical science?) The "literary artist," it seems, is necessarily committed to ambiguity and "multiple meanings" (to saying several things at once and all unclearly?): "He purifies, not by simplifying and jargonizing, but by deepening and extending, by enriching with allusive harmonics, with overtones of association and undertones of sonorous magic."

Huxley dwelt appreciatively on the poet's devices: "mysterious implication . . . by means of the *mot juste*," metaphor, manipulation of syntax, "the magic of what may be called verbal recklessness" and so on. All the while, however, he was searching for what lies behind these verbal differences—some fundamental contrast between alternative yet complementary modes of understanding the universe and man's place in it. Meditating on the problem of the right "relationship between literature and science," he was led to answer some of the most controversial problems of the philosophies of the two disciplines. Reconciliation is achieved in the end by a mysticism that can find no better expression than references to "the Something whose dwelling is everywhere, the essential Suchness of the world, which is at once immanent and transcendent." Here there is a kind of "verbal recklessness," to employ Huxley's useful formula, that some readers may find less than satisfying. But Huxley's residual mysticism can be ignored without detriment to his enjoyable wit. Huxley may have been prone to substitute an epigram for an argument, but he was never dull.

With so much to appreciate, it may seem ungrateful to submit Huxley's philosophical framework to closer examination. Yet the effort is worthwhile, because this essay illustrates in an illuminating way the dangerous consequences of an oversimplified conception of the functions of both science and literature. Huxley set out from a plausible conception of these functions. Both science and literature, in their different ways, he says, concern themselves with the organization, expression and communication of "experiences" (a key word). This common purpose makes them partners, not competitors, in the struggle for mastery and comprehension of a reality that "remains forever whole, seamless and undivided." (How sharp a contrast he drew between the ultimate harmony and unity of reality and the strife-torn condition of man!) There is a crucial distinction, if only one of degree, in the different ways in which reality can manifest itself to the individual consciousness: "All our experiences are strictly private; but some experiences are less private than others." And so, as one might expect, science operates with "the more public of human experiences," literature and fine art with the "more private." The raw material of science, the more public experiences, are relatively "sharable," whereas the poet and novelist have the paradoxical task of trying to communicate what at best is essentially personal, private, "unsharable." The greatest art is committed to the absurdity of trying "to speak about the ineffable, to communicate in words what words were never intended to convey." Public and private, sharable and unsharable, routinely expressible and intrinsically ineffable—these contrasts ran through Huxley's thoughts and the phrases that mark them recur like incantations throughout.

Cetainly there is an initial plausibility in the notion of men using a raw material of "experiences" to fashion elaborate structures of science, literature and other modes of knowledge and insight. There could hardly fail to be some merit in a leading idea that has served the theoretical purposes of earlier empiricism and positivism. But the grand idea, in Huxley's simplified version, has the serious defect of bundling together, under the all-too-capacious title of "experience," everything that could loosely be said to belong to a person's "inner life," everything that in some sense happens consciously to him, including sensations, ideas, thoughts, beliefs, moods and so on. To realize how far the term "experience" is thereby stretched from its ordinary usage is to be armed against Huxley's metaphysics. Had Huxley seen that his label of "experience" would have to cover such disparate items as aesthetic judgments, moral insights, logical inferences—indeed everything that could conceivably be given linguistic expression—he might have been profoundly dissatisfied with his starting point.

The objection is not to an inept mode of expression but

rather to the distorted vision it encourages. What is notably unsatisfactory about this picture of the passive recipient of "experiences" is the gulf it sets between the received impression and its supposedly subsequent organization and conceptualization. (First the experience, then the *mot juste*.) Only the misleading enticements of the pictured experience-gatherer could have allowed Huxley, against what surely must have been his own better judgment, to make such remarks about poetical composition as this: "The ability to have poetical impressions is common. The ability to give poetical *expression* to poetical *im*pressions is very rare. Most of us can feel in a Keatsian way, but almost none of us can write in a Keatsian way" (that "almost none of us" is charming). This is about as plausible as saying that every man has the power to think in a Newtonian way, lacking only the power to express himself adequately. On this naïve view of the poet's labors it is hardly surprising that a gifted reader may be credited with the occasional power of having impressions "of a higher order of 'poeticalness' than those from which the writer set out." Unheard songs might indeed be the sweetest. Such a conception of literature, as "a device for inducing in the reader impressions of the same kind as those which served as raw materials for the finished product," encourages judgments as crude as the following: "The function of drama is to arouse and finally allay the most violent emotions"—a vulgarization of the ancient doctrine of catharsis that might well have made Aristotle shudder. By Huxley's criterion a public hanging would be high drama.

Still more indefensible, if possible, is the following characterization of the function of science: "The man of science observes his own and the reports of other people's more public experiences; conceptualizes them in terms of some language, verbal or mathematical, common to the members of his cultural group; correlates these concepts in a logically coherent system; then looks for 'operational definitions' of his concepts in the world of nature, and tries to prove, by observation and experiment, that his logical conclusions correspond to certain aspects of events taking place 'out there.'" How did this mythical scientist, confined within the world of "strictly private" experience, ever come to suspect the existence of other people and a world "out there"? And how did he ever come to control a language that, one might have supposed, could never be a private possession?

Any serious criticism of Huxley's offhand metaphysics might profitably start by challenging his notion of the contrast between the "private" and the "public." Philosophers who speak of the privacy of experiences have in mind a suppposed metaphysical barrier to the sharing of mental life: my pain cannot *be* yours, however it may resemble it, and the same is true of my glimpse of the setting sun or, for that matter, my thoughts about the civil rights bill. In this sense of "privacy" (a misleading one at best, in my opinion) the distinction admits of no degrees: it is senseless to say that your pain is *partly* mine or to allege that my pleasure at Huxley's remarks on obscenity will be *partly* shared by you—what is mine is mine and that is the end of the matter. (Huxley may have been thinking of this metaphysical conception when he said that all experience is *strictly* private.) Since Huxley in fact insisted on a distinction of degree, he must have also been relying on another sense of experience. Indeed, part of the time he had in mind the degree of uniformity of response to standard stimuli: "emotional experiences," he says, are more private than "sense experiences" because normal people may differ widely in the former although agreeing in the latter. It is to be doubted if Huxley is right about this in general; nearly all normal persons will be frightened by a lion's roar, whereas their observations of, say, a street accident are notoriously variable.

In any case, uniformity of response to stimuli is irrelevant to the admitted difficulty of unambiguously rendering attitudes and emotion. It can be granted that the literary artist has peculiar problems of communication. This has less to do, however, with an alleged idiosyncrasy of emotional response than with the absence of an established tradition of interpretation, criticism and evaluation. By restricting crucial observations to the registration of pointer readings, scientists can facilitate agreement between competent observers (although this model hardly fits scientific observation in general), but still more important is the established tradition of representation, explication and verification that on the whole ensures mutual comprehension and ultimate consensus.

The vaunted "objectivity" of science rests on an elaborately fashioned tradition of discussion, comparison of results and resolution of disagreement by methods acceptable to all members of the scientific community. What is most unsatisfactory about Huxley's conception of the supposed contrast between the "publicity" of science and the relative "privacy" of literature is that he abandons without discussion any hope of objectivity in the poet or novelist's judgment about life, condemning them to the precarious transmission of thrills and pangs. So far is this from being the case that all great literature aspires to make, in its own distinctive way, statements that are true, to present a view of life claiming the acceptance and allegiance of all who can understand. Here we are in what Leavis has called "the third realm," which is "neither merely private and personal nor public in the sense that it can be brought into the laboratory or pointed to. You cannot point to the poem; it is 'there' only in the re-creative response of individual minds to the black marks on the page."

Leavis makes the essential point when he adds that it is a "necessary faith" that the meaning of the poem is "something in which minds can meet." If we are to continue to use the overworked word "public" in a metaphorical sense, it had better stand for whatever can generate rational disagreement. In this sense literature is potentially as public as science. All of which Huxley implicitly recognized when he forgot his own theory of the relations between science and literature. When he spoke of Shakespeare making it possible for us to see "enlightening truth" or of literature as a device for "reporting the multifarious facts and expressing their various significances," he was far away from his simple metaphysical model and unconsciously slipped into common sense. In the realm of the "strictly private" there is neither truth nor facts, but everything is what it is and nothing more, devoid of significance, value and everything else that presupposes the existence of a community and a tradition. For all his occasional recognition of the power of great literature to teach as well as to give pleasure, Huxley leaves the large questions concerning the source of this power and its relation to the more purely intellectual resources of science very much of a mystery.

A disadvantage of Huxley's way of looking at these matters is that it encourages a tendency to attend excessively to the mechanism of literary expression ("verbal recklessness" and the like) in isolation from and in neglect of any context. Concentration on isolated examples of technique diverts attention from the far more important questions of the literary artist's over-all purpose and intention. It is perhaps significant that the numerous, and for the most part well-chosen, quotations with which Huxley's discussion is ornamented are left unidentified, except for rare cases where the publisher may have had

copyright problems; favorite tags like "purifying the language of the tribe" (an inept characterization of the writer's task at best) are used as if any educated reader might be expected to know their origin and intended meaning. The imputation, however flattering, is often unwarranted.

The same fragmented perspective led Huxley to conceive of the value of science for the writer as consisting mainly in scraps of curious information. (This "believe-it-or-not approach," which is congenial to someone like Huxley, who was a lifelong pilferer of encyclopedias, surely overstresses the element of the sensational in scientific discovery.) Thus we have a strange chapter in Huxley's book in which ornithological data concerning the nightingale are supposed to supply a writer with "potentially poetic raw material" that it would be "an act of literary cowardice" to ignore. But the relevant information is that, all the poets notwithstanding, the singing nightingale is a male, not a female, who sings "not in pain, not in passion, not in ecstasy, but simply in order to proclaim to other cock nightingales that he has staked out a territory and is prepared to defend it against all comers." It would be interesting to know how Huxley was able to deny the nightingale any access to relatively private experience, or how such a claim could be supported by scientific evidence. In any case, it is a curiously literal-minded conception of poetry that supposes the invocation to Philomela might conflict with and need to be checked by ornithological or ethological data. How odd to think of the poet's duty as that of "expressing simultaneously [there's the rub] the truth about nightingales, as they exist in their world of caterpillars, endocrine glands and territorial possessiveness, and the truth about human beings who listen to the nightingale's song"! Why not also the "truth" about the eaten caterpillar, as long as we are to be all-inclusive? Huxley complains that modern poets have been reprehensibly indifferent to the results of science, but poets might be excused for ignoring scraps of anthropomorphic chitchat about birds "proclaiming," "staking" and "defending" their "territories."

Of course, Huxley was not so silly as to take this oddly chosen example as paradigmatic; he also had his gaze fixed on the supposed "ethical and philosophical implications of modern science," which prove to be, as any follower of Huxley's pilgrimage through the assorted theologies might have expected, "more Buddhist than Christian, more Totemistic than Pythagorean and Platonic." Here Huxley is finding what he expected to find. Had he realized the extent to which science, for all its marvelous achievements, has no ethical or philosophical implications at all, he might have been even more hard put than he was to render an intelligible account of the mutual relations of scientist and poet. We may agree with Huxley that the man of letters could use "a general knowledge of science, a bird's-eye knowledge of what has been achieved in the various fields of scientific inquiry," and we can applaud his further demand that this needs to be supplemented by "an understanding of the philosophy of science." But the requisite philosophy of science will have to be something better than is to be found in this book. It would be agreeable if the literary man could have "an appreciation of the ways in which scientific information and scientific modes of thought are relevant to individual experience and the problems of social relationships, to religion and politics, to ethics and a tenable philosophy of life." But this is an ambitious syllabus of questions, to which Huxley provided only confused, if stimulating answers.—Max Block, "Aldous Huxley's View of the 'Two Cultures,'" SA, March 1964, pp. 141–44

D. S. SAVAGE
From "Aldous Huxley"
The Withered Branch
1950, pp. 129–55

The reputation of Aldous Huxley—that initial reputation, through which his claim upon popular esteem still persists—was made, it should be recollected, in the era of post-Great War 'disillusionment', whose predominant mood was faithfully reflected in the bright and bitter humour, the sardonic portrayal of human futility, which marked the early novels and tales. In his earlier days Huxley was read with enthusiasm by many of his contemporaries, not only in England, who felt that, in his sophisticated hedonism, his freedom from outworn loyalties, even his licence, he spoke for a generation. He was detached, ironical, and he knew how to be amusing with that wryness which revealed an awareness of the corruption at the bottom of the glass of pleasure.

Huxley's work as a whole has taken the form of a thinly disguised autobiographical sequence; its shape has been determined by its author's changing attitude to life, which has always found its corresponding intellectual expression (reviewers were wont, as a matter of course, to prostrate themselves before his overwhelming 'intellect'); and the problem for the critic lies in the difficulty of keeping a just balance between the attitude to life underlying and conditioning the specific artistic productions; these productions (the novels) themselves; and the resultant ideas which the novelist has abstracted, as it were, from the creative process, and which he now arrays formidably and somewhat menacingly before his public.

For, as it happens, that early entertainer ('that different person', Huxley writes in a recent new preface to one of his old novels, 'who was oneself in youth . . .') is a figure from whom the later and at first glance strangely altered Huxley would wish rather pointedly to dissociate himself. Today there confronts us, not the sardonic portraitist of futility, but the prophet and the philosopher of Enlightenment, of Liberation, through a species of contemplative mysticism, or mystical contemplation. And this prophet, or teacher, quite overshadows, if he has not finally liquidated, the artist.

What, in fact, is the nature of the teaching which emerges? It is rather a simple doctrine. Man's final end, according to Huxley's most recent work, a compendium entitled *The Perennial Philosophy* (1946), is nothing less than 'unitive love-knowledge of the Divine Ground', a knowledge which one must attain by 'making oneself loving, pure in heart and poor in spirit', through a 'discipline more arduous and unremitting than any imposed by ecclesiastical authority'—a discipline which involves indeed a total dying to self.

Salvation, deliverance, enlightenment are apostrophized; but always the emphasis, in this version of mysticism, is upon self-obliteration; and self-obliteration, it appears, in an impassive, non-personal, not-God (as with strange candour the 'Divine Ground' is here described). Time and all its works, being evil, must be annihilated: the goal is *Nirvana*, complete cessation of the pain which comes through individuation, separation from the abysmal One.

> Man must live in time in order to be able to advance into eternity, no longer on the animal, but on the spiritual level; he must be conscious of himself as a separate ego in order to be able consciously to transcend separate selfhood; he must do battle with the lower self in order that he may become identified with that higher Self within him, which is akin to the divine Not-Self; and finally he must make use of his

cleverness in order to pass beyond cleverness to the intellectual vision of Truth, the immediate, unitive knowledge of the divine Ground.

The mystics—Catholics, Quaker, Hindu, Buddhist, Taoist, Sufi, and the rest—have pointed out the way; Huxley annotates it: we refuse it at our peril.

Whether in fact the new doctrine can be so completely dissociated from its literary antecedents is something which we owe it to truth and to ourselves to investigate rather than to take on trust. A hundred years ago Søren Kierkegaard in a masterly essay categorically described the fundamental disorientation which afflicts all human existence not lived under the rubric, Faith, as the 'sickness unto death'; the sickness unto death being—despair. To designate Aldous Huxley as the novelist of despair—if despair is the emotional potentiation of futility, the central theme of his work—will seem unquestionably fitting to the earlier 'Pyrrhonic aesthete', and if it should arouse some surprise, here and there, when applied with even greater emphasis to the later Huxley, in his 'Perennial' avatar, that surprise will, I trust, be modified in the light of what is said below.

That there is, in reality, more than a marked affinity between Huxley's earlier and his later work and ideas we shall discover if, disregarding whatever overt attitudes the abstract theorist would have us accept, we scrutinize the underlying structure of the novelist's and the thinker's world. The fictional universe which he creates and populates possesses certain well-defined features which might all be said to be explicable in the light of a fundamental *discontinuity*. If we say of Huxley's characters that they are static and isolated, that a certain impersonal detachment shows itself in their creator's attitude towards them, and that at the same time their existence presumes a context of pointlessness, we shall have sketched a readily recognizable picture of Huxley's constant frame of reference. For, by a curious irony, while Huxley himself would claim a radical discontinuity between the divergent attitudes to life—'Pyrrhonic hedonism' and contemplative mysticism—which in turn grow out of and condition his earlier and his later work, in fact the two originate in a common dislocation of being: the one exaggeration of attitude finds its balancing counterpart in the other; and the irony is pointed in the fact that discontinuity itself can even be said to be the only continuous factor in decisive operation throughout Huxley's artistic career. Huxley's development follows not a spiral but an hour-glass pattern. The psychological structure underlying *Crome Yellow*, *Antic Hay*, and *Those Barren Leaves* becomes modified as the novelist's dissatisfaction with his non-committal relationship to life draws him towards a closer engagement, only to reassert itself with finality as he crosses over into a yet further detachment which is the obverse of the earlier attitude, and which reinforces its pronounced bias towards the impersonal, the non-human.

I

The mental structure upon which Huxley was to raise his successive fictional edifices is discoverable with little difficulty in his first novel, *Crome Yellow* (1921). A dualism of mind and matter, of spirit and body, of the ideal and the actual is fundamental to it, and is the source at once of Huxley's pessimism, of the purely static and episodic quality of his work, and of his humour. Futility and frustration, humorously presented, the disparity between intention and accomplishment, are the themes of this slight, episodic narrative which tells of a short holiday spent by a young poet, Denis, at the country house of Crome, during the course of which he encounters a succession of interestingly odd characters, is pursued by a young female while himself unsuccessfully pursuing another, and eventually allows himself to be bundled off for home just as he seems to be within reach of amorous success. The appropriate note is struck in the opening paragraph:

> Oh, this journey! It was two hours cut clean out of his life; two hours in which he might have done so much, so much—written the perfect poem, for example, or read the one illuminating book. Instead of which—his gorge rose at the smell of the dusty cushions against which he was leaning. . .

And it is maintained with fair consistency throughout. The character of Denis is indeterminate. He is young and very uncertain of his own feelings and beliefs, and is moreover somewhat isolated from human contacts. Denis's response to living is involuntarily moralistic; theoretically he is a hedonist:

> 'I've always taken things as they come,' said Anne. 'It seems so obvious. One enjoys the pleasant things, avoids the nasty ones. There's nothing more to be said.'
>
> 'Nothing—for you. But, then, you were born a pagan; I am trying laboriously to make myself one. I can take nothing for granted, I can enjoy nothing as it comes along. Beauty, pleasure, art, women—I have to invent an excuse, a justification for everything that's delightful. Otherwise I can't enjoy it with an easy conscience.
>
> '. . . Pleasure is one of the mystical roads to union with the infinite—the ecstasies of drinking, dancing, love-making. As for women, I am perpetually assuring myself that they're the broad highway to divinity. And to think that I'm only just beginning to see through the silliness of the whole thing!'

Of Huxley's two themes, the first, the disparity of the ideal and the actual, is expressed characteristically in the account from Mr. Wimbush's History of Crome, of the Elizabethan baronet's sanitary arrangements; 'the necessities of nature are so base and brutish that in obeying them we are apt to forget that we are the noblest creatures of the universe', so that accordingly the privy must be a book-lined room at the top of the house, commanding 'an extensive and noble prospect'. It finds expression also in the interpolated anecdote of the three lovely sisters who in public maintained a pretence of wan, etherial spirituality, while surreptitiously gorging themselves at elaborate private repasts in their chamber; while of the second, a deliberate hedonism coupled with an underlying sense of personal futility, Mr. Scogan in this novel is the mouthpiece:

> 'Worried about the cosmos, eh?' Mr. Scogan patted him on the arm. 'I know the feeling,' he said, 'It's a most distressing symptom. What's the good of continuing to function if one's doomed to be snuffed out at last along with everything else? Yes, yes. I know exactly how you feel. It's most distressing if one allows oneself to be distressed. But then why allow onself to be distressed? After all, we all know that there's no ultimate point. But what difference does that make?'

We shall see that throughout his successive works Huxley has never departed from these foundations.

Antic Hay (1923) is at once more serious and more farcical, a mordant blaze of characters and incidents against a starker background of futility. Yet there is a pronounced thread of morality running through the tale's desperate gaiety. When we are introduced first to Theodore Gumbril we find him 'speculating, in his rapid and rambling way, about the existence and the nature of God', and then, a little later,

disturbed by a pricking conscience over his 'first serious and deliberate lie'—in childhood.

The element of broad farce enters with Gumbril's invention and marketing of trousers with pneumatic seats. On the strength of his hopes from this venture he leaves his job as schoolmaster and embarks upon a random course of dissipation during which he encounters such exponents of depravity as Myra Viveash, whose voice 'seemed always on the point of expiring, as though each word were the last, uttered faintly and breakingly from a death-bed . . .'; Coleman, whose career of debauchery is carried out on principle and is accompanied by blasphemy; and Mr. Mercaptan, whose speciality is seduction according to the precepts of Crebillon *fils*, upon a white satin sofa in his tastefully decorated apartment. The thread of quasi-moral narrative—that which concerns Gumbril's relations of simple, genuine affection with the girl Emily, whom he is led to abandon at a whim of Mrs. Viveash's—is slight in proportion to the whole novel, which concerns the erratic futilities of Gumbril and the others as they are whirled around in the dry wind of boredom, vanity and despair.

Beneath the amusing surface there is a clear enunciation of the theme of futility:

> 'It's appalling, it's horrible,' said Gumbril at last, after a long, long silence, during which he had, indeed, been relishing to the full the horror of it all. Life, don't you know. . . .

And when, after his betrayal of Emily, he goes, with Mrs. Viveash, the dreary, anguished, pleasure-hunting round of night-clubs in an episode which palely reflects the Walpurgisnacht scenes of *Ulysses*, the night perpetuates itself with yet further revelations of human depravity and the farcical pointlessness of things, until finally:

> 'Tomorrow,' said Gumbril at last, meditatively.
> 'Tomorrow,' Mrs. Viveash interrupted him, 'will be as awful as today.' She breathed it like a truth from beyond the grave prematurely revealed, expiringly from her death-bed within.

Those Barren Leaves (1925), the novel following, is the first to be written from a serious questioning of life. Each of the major characters who are gathered at the wealthy Mrs. Aldwinkle's Italian villa—Calamy the disenchanted man of the world, whose temper provides a point of location for the mood of the book, Cardan, and Chelifer—shares with the other two a common disillusionment with the human state. But whereas Cardan has pursued to the end a course of genial parasitical pleasure-seeking, Chelifer is a self-torturing romantic who takes a perverse delight in seeking out and identifying himself with life's most dingy aspects, while Calamy himself has simply wearied of the amorous round of the idle, affluent set, and is on the verge of a vaguely-envisioned quest for the 'way'. . . .

Huxley's central character, whichever of his books we take up, is distinguished primarily by the fact that he places so little value upon his existence as a man that he is implicitly prepared to forgo his claim upon personal destiny and meaning, albeit with an uneasy conscience, for the immediate gain of a random succession of disrelated sensations. Inwardly inert, led this way and that by mere appetite, he becomes immersed consequently in a world which is deprived of value. Unaware that meaning and purpose do not reside as objective facts in the world of things but are interior realities which await for their realization upon interior dynamic movement, oblivious to the truth that personality is not a substance with which we are endowed by nature, but an inward integration which may be achieved only by the decisive choice of oneself, he arbitrarily attributes his own purposelessness to the universe as a whole. 'Hedonism' and 'futility' thus complement each other.

In *Crome Yellow* the chief character, Denis, is young, his hedonism an aspect of the common bewilderment of youth. Gumbril, in the second novel, is an older man, and hedonism gathers a cynical tinge, while futility is emphasized. Calamy, in the present novel, represents a further stage still—he is the disillusioned hedonist; and now the disparity of the Huxley world is presented from a new aspect. As a disillusioned hedonist Calamy has wearied of a life without *meaning*, he is beginning to look for another path, and hence the concept 'spirit' for the first time makes its appearance; but 'spirit' itself, superimposed upon the existing psychological pattern, takes the impress of the fundamental duality of mind, and appears as directly antithetical to 'matter', or 'the flesh', as something in some way beyond the limits of the sensual plane upon which human life is actually lived. Thus we find that Calamy unquestioningly assumes that the 'way' of which he is in quest must lie somewhere beyond the region of ordinary human experience, and that it is to be found in opposition to the path of sensual indulgence from which that experience is inseparable. . . .

This brings us at last to the structure of Huxley's novels, all of which—it is one of their principal defects—are remarkable for their lack of total dramatic movement and impetus. And this is precisely explicable as a consequence of the absence of dynamic movement in the mind of the novelist himself, a defect which is naturally communicated to his creatures, whose intercourse with each other, prepared and sustained by the accidents of social life, is virtually confined, as we have often heard it remarked, to sexuality and cerebration. No character in the course of this novel undergoes in the course of it any modifications of outlook or temperament, each remains immobile within the limits marked out for it from the first. Of Calamy, we know nothing of the particular events and motives which move him towards the tentative renunciation which begins to take effect at the novel's close. Mr. Cardan is a lay figure as rigid as any in a morality play, and Chelifer is a study only in deliberate self-stultification. And such figures as the doctrinaire socialist, Mr. Falx, and the preposterous Mrs. Aldwinkle herself, are merely caricatures sardonically sketched by the satirist of social types. Only with the immature—in this case with Irene and the young Lord Hovingden, in their naïvely innocent courtship, does the novelist show any movement of human sympathy. Between such inwardly static characters, it is clear, there can be no dramatic interplay and thus no movement of the novel as an entity. So that instead of the movement of life we are presented with episodes, blocks of incident and conversation broken up peremptorily by external change.

But this is something which deserves further exploration, for it is evidently bound up with the whole question of movement and purpose. Movement in a work of fiction is required, of course, to be significant—to bear some purposeful relation to an end. In that vivid portrayal of purposeless activity, *Antic Hay*, the dance of futility is necessarily non-dramatic and presupposes the stasis of character—which in turn is static just because, according to the context, the possibility of purposeful movement is non-existent; life itself is purposeless. In the succeeding novel there is some endeavour to move beyond this static condition dictated by life's total futility. Yet all that the novel succeeds in doing in this respect is to lay bare at great length the absolute cleavage between 'matter' and 'spirit' which underlies the idea of pointlessness.

Nowhere in it is there any questioning of the reality and the appropriateness of this dualism.

The novel ends inconclusively. Calamy retires to his mountain retreat, but it is uncertain whither his lonely quest will lead him; whether, indeed, it will lead anywhere. All we are told is that, looking at the distant skyline, he feels 'somehow reassured'.

II

That there is a progression of a sort within the first three novels is clear. And while *Point Counter Point* (1928) seems to show a divergence from what was later to appear as Huxley's main line of development, it nevertheless derives from the same basic pattern—though the emphasis is changed—while it continues the movement towards human responsibility already hinted at in the portrait of Calamy.

That *Point Counter Point* represents a movement away from the detached manipulation of puppet-characters towards a sympathetic approach to human life is a fact not entirely contradicted by the novel's ill-success in this aim, which is most signally exhibited by the emergence in its pages, for the first time, of a patently deliberate autobiographical character, the novelist Philip Quarles, whose personal views and problems, identical with Huxley's own, are placed directly before us.

The central problem in Philip Quarles's life is his personal isolation; 'All his life long he had walked in a solitude, in a private void, into which nobody, not his mother, not his friends, not his lovers had ever been permitted to enter.' Although, we are given to understand, he is a man of exceptional intellectual endowments, his convictions are fluid, his response to life indeterminate:

> If there was any single way of life he could lastingly believe in, it was that mixture of pyrrhonism and stoicism, which had struck him, an enquiring schoolboy among the philosophers, as the height of human wisdom and into whose mould of sceptical indifference he had poured his unimpassioned adolescence. Against the pyrrhonian suspense of judgment and the stoical imperturbability he had often rebelled. But had the rebellion ever been really serious? Pascal had made him a Catholic—but only so long as the volume of *Pensées* was open before him. There were moments when, in the company of Carlyle or Whitman or bouncing Browning, he had believed in strenuousness for strenuousness sake. And then there was Mark Rampion. After a few hours in Mark Rampion's company he really believed in noble savagery; he felt convinced that the proudly conscious intellect ought to humble itself a little and admit the claims of the heart, aye and the bowels, the loins, the bones and skin and muscles, to a fair share of life.

This last sentence provides the clue to the book's central 'idea'—a variation on the spirit-flesh duality, but with the scales weighted this time towards 'the flesh'—not now in the name of an irresponsible hedonism but of a biological vitalism obviously borrowed, in large measure, from D. H. Lawrence, who is caricatured admiringly in the novel in the painter, Mark Rampion, who preaches, in part, as follows:

> 'This damned soul,' he went on, 'this damned abstract soul—it's like a kind of cancer, eating up the real, human, natural reality, spreading and spreading at its expense. Why can't he be content with reality, your stupid old Beethoven? Why should he find it necessary to replace the real, warm, natural thing by

this abstract cancer of a soul? The cancer may have a beautiful shape; but, damn it all, the body's more beautiful. I don't want your spiritual cancer.'

. . . This novel, however, shows Huxley at his most inept. Badly constructed, incoherent, puerile in conception and presentation, and written in shoddy journalese, it reveals the fatal juvenility which, beneath the sophisticated surface, vitiates his understanding of life. The attempt to extend an inherently limited scope results in the crowding of the pages with flat caricatures of living personages, their characters and activites interpreted in terms no more searching than their relationship, 'wholesome' or 'perverted', to sex and physical life. With the conclusion of the novelette called *Brave New World* (1932)—a satirical projection into the future of the way of life implicit in a deliberate hedonism, which need not concern us here—the shadow of D. H. Lawrence lifts from Huxley's pages, and with his next work we are back to the main line of his development—to the haunting preoccupation with the futility of life and the possibility of finding a way of escape from its pointlessness and tedium.

III

Four years after *Brave New World* and eight after *Point Counter Point* there appeared Huxley's crucial novel, *Eyeless in Gaza* (1936); crucial, because it represents a direct attempt to deal with the problems raised by his earlier works, and because it stands at the mid-point of his career as a novelist. Here the characters, previously formalized to excess, gain in definition and humanity, and genuine drama begins to emerge, centring around the autobiographical figure of the writer, Anthony Beavis, and his movement from a self-indulgent, cynical detachment towards personal regeneration and the acceptance of human responsibility.

The autobiographical novelist-character in *Point Counter Point*, we have seen, was signally isolated from the world, from other persons. The following extract from his notebook links him indubitably with Anthony Beavis, who has come to precisely the same realization, and who, moreover, takes at last the hazardous step of implementing it in action:

> Till quite recently, I must confess [Philip Quarles writes] I took learning and philosophy and science— all the activities that are magniloquently lumped under the title of 'The Search for Truth'—very seriously. I regarded the Search for Truth as the highest of human tasks and the Searchers as the noblest of men. But in the last year or so I have begun to see that this famous Search for Truth is just an amusement, a distraction like any other, a rather refined and elaborate substitute for genuine living; and that Truth-Searchers become just as silly, infan-tile and corrupt in their way as the boozers, the pure aesthetes, the business men, the Good-Timers, in theirs. . . . Shall I ever have the strength of mind to break myself of these indolent habits of intellec-tualism and devote my energies to the more serious and difficult task of living integrally?

The personal theme of *Eyeless in Gaza* is Anthony's realization of the fatal error which has distorted and vitiated his life as a human being; but there is also an impersonal theme—that of the process of time. Once more the opening paragraph sets the key:

> The snapshots had become almost as dim as memories. This young woman who had stood in a garden at the turn of the century was like a ghost at cock-crow. His mother, Anthony Beavis recognized. A year or two, perhaps only a month or two, before she died. . . .

And the structure of the novel, the erratic alternation of pages from the remote past, the near past and the present of Anthony's history, while it reveals the temporal preoccupation, at the same time perfectly expresses the essential discontinuity of Anthony's existence as a result of his crucial, though always unacknowledged, refusal to go forward to claim his personal destiny as a human being, to 'become himself'.

Anthony has chosen not to be humanly responsible, chosen not only 'the part of the detached philosopher' but of the detached sensualist, desiring neither to love nor to be loved. The crisis in his life occurs on his forty-second birthday when with his mistress of the moment, Helen—who happens to be the daughter of a former mistress, Mary Amberley—he is lying on the roof of his retreat in southern France, 'in a golden stupor of sunlight and fulfilled desire'. Despite his volition, his wish to sever himself from his past and to live only in the immediate enjoyment of the present, perspectives of memory, invoked by this and that apparently trivial sense-association, persistently open up before him:

> Even the seemingly solid fragments of present reality are riddled with pitfalls. What could be more uncompromisingly *there*, in the present, than a woman's body in the sunshine? And yet it had betrayed him. The firm ground of its sensual im-mediacy and of his own physical tenderness had opened beneath his feet and precipitated him into another time and place. Nothing was safe. Even this skin had the scent of smoke under the sea. This living skin, this present skin; but it was nearly twenty years since Brian's death. . . . What if that picture gal-lery had been recorded and stored away in the cellars of his mind for the sole and express purpose of being brought up into consciousness at this present mo-ment? Brought up, today, when he was forty-two and secure, forty-two and fixed, unchangeably himself, brought up along with those critical years of his adolescence, along with the woman who had been his teacher, his first mistress, and was now a hardly human creature festering to death, alone, in a dirty burrow? And what if that absurd childish game with the flints had had a point, a profound purpose, which was simply to be recollected here on this blazing roof, now as his lips made contact with Helen's sun-warmed flesh? In order that he might be forced, in the midst of this act of detached and irresponsible sensuality, to think of Brian and of the things that Brian had lived for; yes, and had died for—died for, another image suddenly reminded him, at the foot of just such a cliff as that beneath which they had played as children in the chalk pit. Yes, even Brian's suicide, he now realized with horror, even the poor huddled body on the rocks, was mysteriously implicit in this hot skin.

Anthony's spiritual crisis, its antecedents and outcome, has been subterraneously prepared out of his unwilling but inescapable realization of the treacherous quality of time, with its accompaniments, age and death; and this is reproduced in the narrative, which takes us consecutively through various stages of Anthony's history, always returning to the point of departure—the sunlit roof. It is precipitated by the shock of an unexpected and startling incident. Out of an aeroplane flying immediately above there falls a yelping dog, to drop like a missile on to the roof, spattering the reclining lovers with its blood. Recovering from the shock, Anthony feebly passes it off as a joke, but 'for all answer, Helen covered her face with her hands and began to sob'. . . . This is the crisis which jerks Anthony into an abrupt awareness of his mistaken path. The rest of the novel conducts us through the corridors of Anthony's past history, his long, mistaken path being traced to its primal root in his early liaison with Mary Amberley, by whom he is idly prompted to betray his friend's trust and ultimately to cause Brian's suicide, by wantonly seducing the girl to whom he is betrothed, while concurrently, we are shown his later progress towards responsible participation in human affairs and the eventual acceptance of an ascetic, neo-Buddhist 'spirituality'.

The story, written with manifest sincerity, is a serious attempt to state a genuine human predicament and to find a way around it. Yet the statement, and the solution, when all is allowed, leave one with a disturbed feeling that all is not well, that somewhere there is a hiatus, a dislocation and a spiritual failure.

Anthony's conversion takes place at the point where he is made abruptly to realize that he has denied the inwardness of another person; that he has denied love for the sake of a detached sensuality. But as the narrative proceeds, we become aware that his personal discovery of love is turning from its proper object and becoming generalized, at first into hypothetical beneficence for humanity and at last into a cold moralism which derives its sanctions from a peculiarly impersonal metaphysic.

Returning to the antecedents of his conversion, we find that the tentative emotion of love (for Helen) becomes confused and finally submerged in the emotion of disgust (for Helen's mother, his once charming mistress, now a drunkard, a dope-addict, a squalid wreck). Simultaneously, this disgust fuses with the horror of time, of the accumulation of moments which leads inexorably to decay and death. The horror of time, as it accumulates in human life as age, is in turn associated with disgust for the physical body which experiences and expresses this accumulation. So that we are back at the position stated so clearly, eleven years before, in *Those Barren Leaves*. When, in his thirties, Anthony re-encounters Mary Amberley after an estrangement of more than ten years' duration, his predominant emotion is not pity but horror:

'Doing what one doesn't want,' she repeated, as though to herself. 'Always doing what one doesn't want.' She released his hand, and, clasping her own behind her head, leaned back against the pillows in the attitude, the known and familiar attitude, that in the Hôtel des Saints-Pères had been so delicious in its graceful indolence, so wildly exciting because of that white round throat stretched back like a victim's, those proffered breasts, lifted and taut beneath the lace. But today the lace was soiled and torn, the breasts hung tired under their own weight, the victim throat was no more a smooth column of white flesh, but withered, wrinkled, hollow between starting tendons.

She opened her eyes, and, with a start, he recognized the look she gave him as the same, identically the same look, at once swooning and cynical, humorous and languidly abandoned, as had invited him, irresistibly then, in Paris fifteen years ago. It was the look of 1913 in the face of 1928—painfully out of its context. He stared at her for a second or two, appalled; then managed to break the silence.

It becomes clear that Anthony's conversion is merely negatively and passively motivated. He has not sought reality and truth, but evaded them, until at last reality has found him and chased him—the analogy is his own—from his bolt-hole:

Even in the deepest sensual burrow, Anthony reflected as he walked back to his rooms, even in

the snuggest of intellectual other-worlds, fate could find one out. And suddenly he perceived that, having spent all his life trying to react away from the standards of his father's universe, he had succeeded only in becoming precisely what his father was—a man in a burrow. With this small difference, that in his case the burrow happened to be intermittently adulterous instead of connubial all the time; and that the ideas were about societies and not words. For the moment, he was out of his burrow—had been chased out, as though by ferrets. But it would be easy and was already a temptation to return.

Anthony is in fact seeking some way of *escape* from the conditions of human life rather than some way of positively transforming those conditions. And the spirituality which he is indicated as making his own towards the end of the book does actually fortify him, though with a shift of emphasis, in that very detachment and impersonality from which the incident of the dog and his emotional crisis has momentarily jolted him.

'God may or may not exist,' he writes in his diary. 'But there is the empirical fact that contemplation of the divinity—of goodness in its most unqualified form—is a method of realizing that goodness to some slight degree in one's life. . . .' His form of belief seems quite unashamedly chosen to conform to his own ingrained life-attitude:

God—a person or not a person? *Quien sabe?* Only revelation can decide such metaphysical questions. And revelation isn't playing the game—is equivalent to pulling three aces of trumps from up your sleeve.

Of more significance is the practical question. Which gives a man more power to realize goodness—belief in a personal or an impersonal God? Answer: it depends. Some minds work one way, some another. Mine, as it happens, finds no need, indeed, finds it impossible to think of the world in terms of personality.

And, appropriate to this central laxity, his new-found 'spirituality', so far from attending upon the wind that blows where it lists, resolves into the cataloguing of technicalities:

The fundamental problem is practical—to work out systems of psychological exercises for all types of men and women. Catholicism has many systems of mental power—Ignatian, Franciscan, Liguorian, Carmelite and so on. Hinduism, Northern, Southern and Zen Buddhism also have a variety of practices. There is a great work to be done here. Collecting and collating information from all these sources. Consulting books and, more important, people who have actually practised what is in the books, have had the experience of teaching novices. In time it might be possible to establish a complete and definite *Ars Contemplativa*. A series of techniques, adapted to every type of mind. Techniques for meditating on, communicating with and contemplating goodness. Ends in themselves and at the same time means for realizing some of that goodness in practice.

What better comment could be made on this than that which Anthony himself commits to his diary at one candid stage of his reflections:

Reflect that we all have our Poonas, bolt-holes from unpleasant reality. The danger, as Miller is always insisting, of meditation becoming such a bolt-hole. Quietism can be mere self-indulgence. Charismata like masturbations. Masturbations, however, that are dignified, by the amateur mystics who practise them, with all the most sacred names of religion and philosophy. 'The contemplative life.' It can be made a kind of high-brow substitute for Marlene Dietrich: a subject for erotic musings in the twilight.

IV

'Man', wrote Søren Kierkegaard in a famous definition, 'is spirit. But what is spirit? Spirit is the self'; and, further, 'eternity is essential continuity'. 'Selfness or personality,' according to Aldous Huxley in his last, mystical-didactic phase, is a '"stinking lump" . . . which has to be passionately repented of and completely died to before there can be any "true knowing of God in purity of spirit."' . . . Sin, for Huxley, is selfness. For Kierkegaard, as a Christian believer, sin is despair, and despair is precisely the dissociation, the dislocation of the self in its refusal to 'choose itself'—to put itself into inward motion and go forward to claim its unique destiny as a messenger of meaning to the world.

'When did the ego begin to stink?' asks a recent aesthetic sage, in a phrase which seems to have captured the public ear. Answer: *When it began to decompose.*

The later work of Aldous Huxley must be interpreted as a bitter diatribe against personality, which he sees as synonymous with selfness—selfness *when it begins to decompose.* . . .

A man who has never gone forward to claim his self, and achieve personality, can obviously never comprehend the meaning of personality, just as he can never understand the nature of communion and love. For him, personality *is* selfness, that dissolute conglomeration of appetites, volitions and perceptions which are functions of the body he is given by nature. And when the natural ego begins to disintegrate and to 'stink' beyond endurance there is only one course left—to get rid of it.

Not only must the sufferer withdraw from his offending self—he must withdraw from the world, from other persons, and finally from God. Huxley's mysticism is therefore a-historical, anti-personal and atheistic. The whole cosmic order is, in its eyes, a pointless and inexplicable escapade of an inert and irresponsible deity, or non-deity—an escapade from which we are called to 'liberate' ourselves with all possible speed, in order to turn to 'the pure One, the absolute not-God in whom we must sink from nothingness to nothingness [and who] is called in Mahayana Buddhism the Clear Light of the Void'. (*The Perennial Philosophy.*)

How is the novelist, the portraitist of human life and character, to work within this scheme? '. . . On the strictly human level, there was nothing that deserved to be taken seriously except the suffering men inflicted upon themselves by their crimes and follies . . .' reflects Huxley's Mr. Propter in the next novel, *After Many a Summer* (1939). 'No, a good satire was much more deeply truthful and, of course, much more profitable than a good tragedy. The trouble was that so few good satires existed, because so few satirists were prepared to carry their criticism of human values far enough.' A defect Huxley undertakes to remedy, for here criticism of human values is carried to the point of their complete abolition.

Huxley's basic dualism is here made unconditional. As a result we have on the one hand the group of puppet-characters—Jo Stoyte, the millionaire, whose palatial Californian residence is the scene of the novel, Dr. Obispo, the ruthless, scientific-minded sensualist, Jeremy Pordage, the ineffectual, flute-voiced littérateur from Oxford, Virginia Maunciple, the innocent-depraved little chorus-girl—puppets whose thoughts and actions bespeak their utter worthlessness and futility—and on the other the more than human,

withdrawn, contemplative-practical sage, Mr. Propter, the essentially static mouthpiece of Huxley's teachings on the futility of life on the 'strictly human level' and the necessity for a withdrawal from human life to 'the level of eternity'. Between the two poles significant movement is quite precluded. Life is a dance of puppets, grimly, savagely pointless.

The anti-personal bias of the novel is pronounced; thus Mr. Propter:

> Bondage is the life of personality, and for bondage the personal self will fight with tireless resourcefulness and the most sub born cunning. . . . The spirit is always willing; but the person, who is a mind as well as a body, is always unwilling—and the person, incidentally, is not weak but extremely strong.

This strange hatred of 'the stinking slough of our personality' is carried to the point of absurdity—

> 'Turn round, please.'
> Mr. Stoyte obeyed. The back, Dr. Obispo reflected, was perceptibly less revolting than the front. Perhaps because it was less personal.

The dislocation of being is expressed in the counterposing of a neutral, arid and abstract 'mysticism' on the one hand by a grossly material sensualism: life is separated into two mutually exclusive compartments. On the one hand—

> 'What is man?' he whispered to himself. . . . 'A nothingness surrounded by God, indigent and capable of God, filled by God if he so desires.' And what is this God of which men are capable? Mr. Propter answered with the definition given by John Tauler in the first paragraph of his *Following of Christ*. 'God is a being withdrawn from creatures, a free power, a pure working.' Man, then, is a nothingness surrounded by, and indigent of, a being withdrawn from creatures, a nothingness capable of free power, filled with a pure working if he so desires.

And the other:

> Through his dark glasses, Mr. Stoyte looked up at her with an expression of possessiveness at once gluttonous and paternal. Virginia was his baby, not only figuratively and colloquially, but also in the literal sense of the word. His sentiments were simultaneously those of the purest father-love and the most violent eroticism. . . .
> Delicious creature! The hand that had lain inert, hitherto, upon her knee, slowly contracted. Between the broad spatulate thumb and the strong fingers, what smoothness, what a sumptuous and substantial resilience!
> 'Jinny,' he said. 'My Baby!'

Mr. Propter's peculiarly arid and abstract mysticism has its end in 'a non-personal experience of timeless peace. Accordingly, non-personality, timelessness and peace are what it means. . . .' And it involves, centrally, a repudiation of, and an escape from, time:

> '. . . potential evil is *in* time; potential good isn't. The longer you live, the more evil you automatically come into contact with. Nobody comes automatically into contact with good. Men don't find more good merely by existing longer. . . . The solution is very simple and profoundly unacceptable. Actual good is outside time. . . . Time is potential evil, and craving converts the potentiality into actual evil. Whereas a temporal act can never be more than potentially

good, with a potentiality, what's more, that can't be actualized except out of time.'

Time as evil, once more, manifests in human life as age, physical decreptitude, death. Thus the thread of narrative depends primarily from Jo Stoyte's haunting fear of the grave, which causes him to employ Dr. Obispo upon researches into the possibilities of artificial longevity. Wound with this principal thread is the intermittent commentary on the human characters provided by the baboons in their enclosure outside the Stoyte mansion:

> To the right, on another shelf of rock, a formidable old male, leather-snouted, with the grey bobbed hair of a seventeenth-century Anglican divine, stood guard over his submissive female. . . . The coast was clear. The young male who had been looking for dandruff suddenly saw his opportunity. Chattering with excitement, he bounded down to the shelf on which, too frightened to follow her master, the little female was still squatting. Within ten seconds they had begun to copulate.
>   Virginia clapped her hands with pleasure. 'Aren't they cute?' she cried. 'Aren't they *human!*'

These threads wind together as the researches of Dr. Obispo coincide with Jeremy Pordage's discovery, among the ancient papers he is cataloguing for Jo Stoyte, that the eighteenth-century fifth earl of the all but extinct line of Gonister has in his old age been similarly experimenting with a diet of raw carps' guts, and has mysteriously arranged for his own counterfeit funeral. . . . The novel closes, bitingly acidulous, with Jo Stoyte's mentally preparing himself to accept the identical regime undergone by the fifth Earl.

That Huxley, driven by self-hatred and disgust with life, has reached a dead-end is finally demonstrated by his last, most tasteless production, *Time Must Have a Stop* (1945). Here the puppets, fixed in their unbreakable abstracts of human qualities, and offset by the static and detached figure of a pharisaical 'saint', exist at a remove from reality which gives the novel an air of complete futility to human experience. The 'saved' Bruno Rontini, like Mr. Propter a mere mouthpiece for Huxley's renunciatory gospel, is deprived of inward movement no less than the 'damned' puppet-characters immobilized in their habit of selfhood. In the previous novel, the only character not quite immune from 'the contagion of goodness' is the naïve and inarticulate Pete. It is no accident that for his hero this time Huxley should have chosen an adolescent (Sebastian Barnack is seventeen), that he should have involved him to his undoing for twenty-nine chapters in the depraved realm of 'the flesh' and then, by means of an abrupt hiatus, presented us, with the briefest of explanations, in the final chapter with a reformed and 'saintly' character, complete with copious extracts from those now all-too-familiar notebooks. For Huxley, as we have seen before, is for some reason at which one can only guess—we might label it 'arrested development'—at ease only with the immature. Incapable as he is of revealing the inner processes by which human beings come to inward maturity, even his supposedly adult characters remain adolescents upon whose juvenile responses has been superimposed arbitrarily the veneer of a quasi-adult sophistication and intellectuality.

Sensual depravity or an unreal 'spirituality'—down goes one scale heavily weighted with 'the flesh', and up goes the other with its insubstantial featherweight of spirit. The falsity to human experience of his naïve dislocation of being is paralleled in the novel both by the failure of its action to carry conviction and the air of unreality in which that action takes place. We can believe in the authenticity of Uncle Eustace's Italian villa, located, in accordance with Huxley's now pronounced retreat from history, in a dream-like nineteen-twenties, no more than we can accept the authenticity of Uncle Eustace himself or for that matter any of the book's characters. The vision, distorted for the satire of *After Many a Summer*, is here quite out of focus. The adult reader is utterly unable to make the required connection between Uncle Eustace's trivial sensualities—his cheerful over-indulgence in wine, women and cigars—and the bathetic solemnities of his post-mortem experiences in the spirit world when, after an evening of luxury, he dies on the seat of the toilet. And the anti-climax of the disembodied Uncle Eustace's eventual choice of reincarnation out of the 'living uterine darkness', the 'vegetative heaven' of Mme. Weyle, should serve, at least, in the mind of no uncommonly penetrating reader, to put Huxley's 'mysticism' in its proper, very humble place.

With this final novel, we may safely conclude, Huxley's career as a significant novelist of the modern plight has come to an end. It is an end implicit, like so many, in its beginning. The novelist of futililty, undergoing in mid-career a period in which the potentiality of meaning seemed for a time to offer itself—a potentiality accompanied by a realization of love and the value of human personality—has crossed over into positive accentuation of futility accompanied by a positive doctrine of non-attachment and impersonality. No hope of development here! And, necessarily, this positive acceptance of the meaninglessness of human life, the worthlessness of personality, has its implications for art. When human life is seen as intrinsically meaningless and evil, then the work of the novelist, whose task is to present a picture of that life in terms of its significance and value, is deprived of all justification. Art and life must be thrown overboard together.

R. C. ZAEHNER
From *Mysticism, Sacred and Profane*
1957, pp. 1–27

I. Mescalin

It is, of course, a well-known fact that certain drugs,—and among them one may include alcohol,—modify the normal human consciousness and produce what can literally be called ec-static states,—states in which the human ego has the impression that it escapes from itself and 'stands outside' itself. Indian hemp and hashish have long been used in the East to produce precisely such a result. In the West, however, it has never been taken for granted that such states are necessarily associated with religion, while in the East there have always been sober spirits who regarded such 'religion surrogates' with the gravest suspicion. Mr. Huxley appears to have no such scruples, for he implies unmistakably that what he experienced after taking mescalin was explicable in terms of 'contemplation at its height'.[1] Herein lies the importance of Mr. Huxley's thesis; praeternatural experience, whether produced by drugs or not, is equated with specifically religious experience.

It is essential that we should pause for a moment here in order to consider what Mr. Huxley and his friends understand by religion since, obviously, it is not what Protestant Christians normally understand by the word. Since the Reformation we have drifted more and more into a position of identifying religion with an ethical code; and despite the regrettable fact that the vast majority of those who call themselves Christians make no noticeable effort to follow the more difficult and paradoxical commandments of Our Lord, we like to think that the Christian ethic is the most perfect that has ever been propounded and that therefore Christianity is the best and for that reason the true religion. On turning to the Oriental religions, however, we will see that in India and in those parts of Asia which have come under Indian influence, such views are far from finding universal acceptance. Religion for the Hindu or Buddhist, we are repeatedly told by the modern advocates of those two religions, is primarily a matter of experience; it is not so much something to be believed as something to be lived. By belief or faith, too, they do not understand a series of propositions to which assent is given, they mean not only faith in, but contact with, a supra-sensory world. Religion, for them, is not so much something to be professed as something to be experienced; and such experience, in its higher forms, is usually called mystical experience. In the West the reverse is true: we have lost contact with the supra-sensory world to such an extent that many of us have come to deny it altogether. This is no place to discuss the effects of such an attitude on society at large; here we must be content to note that it leaves many people profoundly dissatisfied, and of these Mr. Huxley would seem to be a notable example.

Huxley's life would appear to have been one consistent revolt against the values of the nineteenth century, purely material values to which an air of respectability was lent by a decadent Christianity. Later in life he came into contact with the religious classics of the East which obviously attracted him strongly. Moreover, the fact that the Eastern religions had a far cleaner record than had Christianity in the matter of persecution, was one more point in their favour; and in the life of reflection, concentration, and contemplation which they stressed far more exclusively than did the Christian Church Huxley thought that at last he had found a sure anchor and lasting resting-place. Struck by the similarity of thought and expression he found in all the mystics, whether Hindu, Buddhist, Taoist, Muslim, or Christian, he reached the comforting conclusion that behind the great religions of the world there could be discerned a *philosophia perennis*, an ultimate truth of which all religions were only partial expressions. It was, however, the great religious systems of India which principally attracted him, particularly the Vedānta and those forms of Buddhism which are most akin to it. Just why this should have been it is difficult to say. Prima facie one might have supposed that his attraction was based on some profound religious experience and that this experience was felt to be in accordance with what the Vedānta taught rather than with what the Christian mystics described. Huxley himself, however, gives the lie to this in *The Doors of Perception*, for he there admits that until, thanks to mescalin, he came to know 'contemplation at its height', he had not in fact had any experience to which the word 'mystical' could possibly be applied. We can only conclude that Huxley's 'conversion' to a Vedāntin way of life was due to little more than a total rejection of everything that modern civilization stands for and to a deep-seated aversion to historical Christianity which, though it may not have directly given birth to the modern world, at least condoned it when it was born.

So it was that when Huxley came to take mescalin, his mind was permeated through and through with Vedāntin and Mahāyāna Buddhist ideas, and these ideas seem actually to have affected his vision; for as Baudelaire has rightly observed, drugs can add nothing new to a man, but can only raise to a higher power what is already within him.[2] . . .

The real importance of Huxley's book . . . is that in it the author clearly makes the claim that what he experienced under the influence of mescalin is closely comparable to a genuine mystical experience. If he is right, then it can only be said that the conclusions to be drawn from this are alarming. One thing seems certain; and that is that both the mescalin-taker who does not happen to be of a sceptical turn of mind and the mystic seem utterly convinced that their respective experiences are incomparably more real than their ordinary sense experiences. Moral problems, it is clear, have no meaning once one obtains this 'higher' vision, and personal relationships too cease to have any importance. The mundane world is transcended, and therefore what goes on there, or should we say, what appears to be going on there, can have no possible interest.

For the moment we are not concerned with the truth or falseness of these theories. In the past mystics, even in India, have been few and far between, and praeternatural experiences of any sort have been well out of the reach of the average man; and no visible harm has been done by the small band of ecstatics who had, or thought they had, transcended good and evil. The advent of mescalin in commercial quantities could change all that as Huxley sees, to my mind, all too clearly. The second part of his book treats with this question and draws the conclusion that mescalin is potentially a cure for the egocentricity of modern man just as religion was the recognized cure in the past. Obviously, if mescalin can produce the Beatific Vision here on earth,—a state that we had hitherto believed to have been the reward for much earnest striving after good,—the Christian emphasis on morality is not only all wrong but also a little naïve. Mescalin presents us not only with a social problem,—for how on earth could a society composed exclusively of ecstatics possibly be run?—but also with a theological problem of great magnitude. Mr. Huxley is to be thanked for having set the problem.

II. Mescalin Interpreted

In our last chapter we did little more than summarize Mr. Huxley's experiences under the influence of mescalin. It now remains for us to summarize the conclusions he draws from his experiences.

One thing is certain; and that is that Huxley was taken off his guard by his experiment and almost overwhelmed by it: and the reason for this appears to be that it was the first time he had had an experience of this kind. This is somewhat surprising: for it seemed natural to suppose that an author who has gone through all the outward manifestations of a religious conversion and who, ever since he published *Time Must Have a Stop*, has written about little except his new philosophy of life, must have gone through some supremely meaningful experience which occasioned his conversion and which led him to adopt the esoteric philosophy he has since favoured. This philosophy, which he calls the *philosophia perennis*, claims to be based on the experience of religious mystics of all nations and all faiths. It seemed, then, fair to assume that Huxley had had some praeternatural experience which, by enabling him to discern in all mystics an absolute unity of idea behind a considerable diversity of expression, had convinced him that what the mystics were trying to describe was essentially the same experience, however different the expression of it might be. It came, then, as something of a shock to the present author at least when he read that 'until this morning I had known contemplation only in its humbler, its more ordinary forms—as discursive thinking; as a rapt absorption in poetry or painting or music; as a patient waiting upon those inspirations, without which even the prosiest writer cannot hope to accomplish anything; as occasional glimpses, in nature, of Wordsworth's "something far more deeply interfused"; as systematic silence leading, sometimes, to hints of an "obscure knowledge"'.[3]

Huxley's concept of 'contemplation' seems to have been extremely wide, extending indeed to all the activities of normally educated and cultivated persons. It would never have occurred to the great majority of these to refer to their appreciation, rapt or otherwise, of poetry, painting, or music as 'contemplation', a term which has come to have religious overtones. Nor does the word naturally occur to one in connexion with discursive thinking,—a process which is generally regarded as being the reverse of contemplation. It seems, then, fairly clear that, before taking mescalin, Huxley had only the haziest notion of what 'contemplation', used in a religious sense, meant. On taking mescalin, he was pitchforked into a realm of experience about which he had written volumes, but which he appears never to have lived. He would, then, appear to have been converted to the *philosophia perennis* on purely intellectual grounds. Because there were certain common characteristics between the mystics of all religions, Huxley came to the conclusion that these common characteristics must represent one metaphysical truth. He does not seem to have realized that even in the writings of the mystics there are divergences not only of approach, which can be attributed to the different religious backgrounds on which they are grafted, but of substance; and that any arbitrary selection from their writings can demonstrate nothing except the subjective views of an individual. What attracted him in the mystics,— using this word in a wide sense for the moment,—was that one and all they claimed to have transcended the empirical 'self' and broken into a new and larger sphere of perception. Mysticism, so interpreted, could include not only the classical monistic mysticism of India, but the strictly pantheistic and 'pamphysistic' outpourings of, for instance, Walt Whitman: it could include not only those solipsistic Muslim mystics who identified themselves with God, but also pure visionaries who did no such thing, but lived in a different private universe of their own in the manner of William Blake. The only common factor between these different types of mysticism is that, one and all, they provide release from the everyday, humdrum existence of subject-object relationship and of what, for lack of a better word, we must continue to call the individual 'ego'. That it was precisely such release from the 'ego' that Huxley was in search of, emerges clearly from the epilogue of *The Doors of Perception.*

'That humanity at large will ever be able to dispense with Artificial Paradises seems very unlikely. Most men and women lead lives at the worst so painful, at the best so monotonous, poor and limited that the urge to escape, the longing to transcend themselves if only for a few moments, is and has always been one of the principal appetites of the soul.'[4] This is rather a bold generalization; but it is a generalization that is typical of the intellectual and particularly of the intellectual who has been born and bred in an industrial civilization. The 'urge to escape' is, of course, the mainspring of Gnosticism, and particularly of Manichaeanism which described the body as a 'carrion and a prison', a satanic substance in which the heavenly soul was unnaturally confined.[5] Mānī, like the founders of practically all heresies, as opposed to the founders of religions that last, was an intellectual; and his religion, in common with the other Gnostic sects, made an immediate appeal to the intelligentsia. His was a religion, exclusively, of escape and release: and in this he was catering for that 'urge to escape' which, according to Huxley, is and always has been one of the principal appetites of the human soul.

This is one point of view. Another has been expressed as follows: 'It is no good telling people that life is "pain" if they persist in regarding it as "fun", just as it is no good asking them if they are saved if they have not the slightest idea of what on earth they are supposed to be saved from, and would not in any case want to be saved from "it" even if they knew what "it" was

supposed to be.'[6] This is a view which I expressed three years ago; and I still believe that it is more true than that expressed by Huxley, at least as far as this country is concerned, and that Huxley greatly exaggerates this urge to escape and longing to transcend ourselves. Fundamentally this is only true of the neurotic: it is not true of what William James called the 'healthy-minded', a class to which even now, I am optimistic enough to believe, the great majority of the human race still belongs.

Huxley's outlook is preconditioned by his intellectualism. In the best tradition of intellectuals he started off as a rebel. His rebellion seems to have gone through two stages: first he revolted against the established form of society and its conventions, and when this revolt only involved him in new and deeper bondages, he rose in revolt against and from himself. The second rebellion really developed out of the first; for, as Huxley himself says in *Ends and Means,*[7] although the revolt against the 'political and economic system' may have been justified on the ground that it was unjust, he and his friends had nothing to put in its place. It was a revolt into meaninglessness; and it is not in the nature of persons so markedly cerebral as Huxley to live in a vacuum for long. His revolt against sexual morality was equally unrewarding, as, in the long run, it always is. It is easy to become impatient with the Evangelical Counsel of chastity, and it is even easier to flout it and tread it under foot. Huxley, however, found that by so doing he enmeshed and entangled himself further in the material world which nauseated him and from which even then he longed to escape. He slowly came to realize, what all the great religions have always taught, that bondage to the passions is as harsh a slavery as that imposed by any political system. Or, to put it in a more practical way, in the long run it is less trouble to be chaste. Huxley's whole career then predisposed him to conversion to a type of religion that would provide him with a way of escape from a world into which he had found it so extraordinarily difficult to fit himself. He had, it seems, not been a happy man; and because he was both unhappy and introspective, he needed a philosophy or religion that would deliver him from both his unhappiness and himself. Being a highly intelligent man he realized that the unhappiness and the self were in some way connected; and this is the beginning of religion. What Huxley calls the 'poisonous fruits' of the philosophy of meaninglessness forced him to look beyond himself for something a little more satisfactory. Realizing that preoccupation with self is the source of all unhappiness, he turned towards the two religions which made this connexion most clear,—Hinduism and Buddhism. He was right to do this: for though the Gospels teach that one must die to oneself in order to live, this is only one of many Christian teachings, whereas both Hinduism and Buddhism regard the elimination of the ego as the *sine qua non* of 'liberation' or 'enlightenment' and never tire of saying so. Moreover, a return to Christianity would have been difficult for Huxley since he remembered it only as something dry, moralistic, and pharisaical, as part and parcel of an inhuman and mechanistic society against which he, like Kierkegaard before him, had revolted. There would have been no sense in returning to a religion that seemed to have become ossified into a not very indispensable adjunct of a questionable social system. There was the further point too that Christianity was far less clear in teaching that unhappiness and the ego are one and the same thing than was either Buddhism or Hinduism. There are, of course, texts in the Gospels which say very nearly this; but modern Christianity has not been at great pains to emphasize them. Buddhism, on the other hand, emphasizes and constantly reiterates that since all phenomenal things are impermanent and in perpetual flux, there can be no real happiness in them, and that impermanence is therefore identical with pain. The cause of pain is 'craving', and release from pain can only be obtained by stamping out all craving, that is, by suppressing all desire. It is against this background that Huxley can write of the urge to escape and the longing to transcend oneself as being one of the principal appetites of the soul. That mescalin provided Huxley with such an escape is absolutely obvious from what he writes. And because it did so for him, he assumes that it will do so for everyone else, provided they have not had a recent attack of jaundice, that their livers are in order, and that they are not a prey to constant worry.

It does not appear to have occurred to Mr. Huxley that even in our modern civilization there are still people whose 'selves' are uncomplicated and tolerably decent. These persons may be irreligious in Huxley's sense of the word 'religious', in that they feel no need to escape from themselves into another less personal world. I am not referring to what the late Mr. Coomaraswamy, an eminent exponent of the *philosophia perennis*, used to call the 'spiritual proletariat' who have been brutalized by industrialism and its attendant materialism into complete forgetfulness of all spiritual values. These present a very real problem, but we must not digress to consider their plight, for, though they probably do not know it, plight it is. I am thinking rather of those genuinely carefree, generous persons whom everyone likes and who do good to others, not by any conscious effort, but by simply being what they are. Speaking in accordance with Christian theology this would mean such people from whom the sacrament of Baptism really does seem to have washed away the stain of original sin. Such people are saved, *salvi facti sunt*, they have been made whole. These do not feel any need for escape, nor can they be attracted by any religion which offers them only this (though I do not suggest for a moment that Hinduism and Buddhism have nothing further to offer, for obviously they have): for they have been made whole, and it is only what is partial or maimed that can feel the need for completion. Thus for them the word 'escape' has very little meaning.

In the order of Nature Man alone is endowed with reason; he alone is a 'rational animal' as Aristotle long ago observed; and it is because he has the power to reason that he is both puzzled and frightened by the prospect of death which seems to make nonsense of all human endeavour. The fear of death lies at the root of religion. Yet there are many people who are quite conscious of the fact that they must die and are nevertheless quite content that a lifetime should be granted them in which to develop into what they potentially are. This process has been described by Jung as 'becoming what one is',[8] and it has been beautifully put by Oscar Wilde (of all people) in the following passage:

> It will be a marvellous thing—the true personality of man—when we see it. It will grow naturally and simply, flowerlike, or as a tree grows. It will not be at discord. It will never argue or dispute. It will not prove things. It will know everything. And yet it will not busy itself about knowledge. It will have wisdom. Its value will not be measured by material things. It will have nothing. And yet it will have everything, and whatever one takes from it, it will still have, so rich will it be. It will not be always meddling with others, or asking them to be like itself. It will love them because they will be different. And yet while it

will not meddle with others, it will help all, as a beautiful thing helps us, by being what it is. The personality of man will be very wonderful. It will be as wonderful as the personality of a child.[9]

Here we have the obverse of Huxley's 'urge to escape'. Huxley sees salvation as an escape from self, as the annihilation of the ego and merging into a greater entity which he calls Mind at Large. Wilde sees it as a natural growth of the whole individual personality to its full stature in which soul, mind, and body all develop along their own lines, not encroaching on one another but balancing one another. In such a description as Wilde has given of the 'true personality of man' Christians can, without irreverence, recognize Adam as he emerged from the hand of God, Adam as we still see him painted on the ceiling of the Sistine Chapel. When we come to consider the Hindu mystics with their use of the word 'self' (*ātman-*) both for what Huxley calls the 'Not-self' and for the individual soul, the relevance of this passage will become apparent.

Before proceeding to the discussion of Huxley's experiences after taking mescalin and before seeking to explain it by similar experiences which others have had, and before we attempt to fit it into a general pattern, it would be as well to summarize the conclusions that Huxley has himself drawn from his excursion into the extra-temporal world and to study his recommendations for the greater use of drugs in the furtherance of the happiness of the human race. These recommendations and conclusions will be found in the epilogue to *The Doors of Perception*. They are remarkable. But nowhere does Huxley seem to face up to the main problem: what is the relationship between the ecstasies of persons of heroic sanctity and those of the mescalin-taker?

In the concluding section of his book Huxley implies that the taking of drugs is, or should be, part and parcel of all religion; and on this basis he criticizes Christianity for not 'baptizing' mescalin or similar drugs and incorporating them into Christian worship. This sounds outrageous: but it is not really so if we continue to bear in mind his major premiss that 'the urge to escape from selfhood and the environment is in almost everyone almost all the time'.[10] The premiss seems false, for it does not correspond to observed fact; and it would be only side-stepping the issue to say that this 'urge' is more often than not unconscious, since until the urge has been brought up into consciousness, it cannot be stated that it is there at all. The premiss should be emended to some such formula as this: 'the urge to escape selfhood and the environment (which are two very different things) is in almost every introspective introvert who is naturally retiring, over-cerebral, and over-sensitive, and who has been brought up in a materialist and industrialized environment, almost all the time'. If we are prepared to 'emend' the premiss in this way, Huxley's panacea for society becomes intelligible,—except, of course, that we can no longer speak of society as such, but only of a limited number of hyper-civilized persons in search of their soul. In lumping together 'the urge to escape from selfhood' and 'the urge to escape from the environment' Huxley is confusing two quite separate things. It is what William James calls the 'sick soul' which longs to escape from itself, and it is what Coomaraswamy calls the 'spiritual proletariat' that aspires to escape from its environment. This 'proletariat' now forms a large part of any industrial society. Its members are occupied in doing intrinsically boring jobs, and if they seek relief in the cinema, television, and the 'comics', they do so not in order to escape from themselves, but in order to project themselves into what seems to them a more meaningful existence. Their plight is the exact opposite of that of the neurotic intellectual; for the latter lives by and on introspection and is bound, sooner or later, to long to escape from a subject that has become a monomania, whereas the former has not yet got as far as finding a 'self' from which he could wish to escape. He feels no urge to escape from himself, only an urge to escape from the dullness of everyday life in which no 'self' of any sort has any chance to develop.

On the subject of how mescalin could be utilized for the good of humanity, Huxley's ideas appear to be extraordinarily confused. He oscillates in the most alarming manner between identifying the mescalin experience with the Beatific Vision on the one hand and regarding it as a safe substitute for alcohol on the other. The baffled reader finds himself wondering whether he regards the highest states of the mystics as being not only comparable to, but identical with, the effects of alcohol and drugs, or not. 'The Beatific Vision, *Sat Chit Ananda*, Being-Awareness-Bliss—for the first time I understood, not on the verbal level, not by inchoate hints or at a distance, but precisely and completely what those prodigious syllables referred to.' This is what he says on pages 12–13. If this means anything, then surely it must mean that what he was experiencing at the time was a near approximation to what Christians call the Beatific Vision and what the Hindus mean by *Sat Chit Ananda.* . . .

The confusion of thought that mescalin seems to have induced in Mr. Huxley is best illustrated in the epilogue. For here he says: 'I am not so foolish as to equate what happens under the influence of mescalin or of any other drug, prepared or in the future preparable, with the realization of the end and ultimate purpose of human life: Enlightenment, the Beatific Vision.'[11] It should merely be regarded, he says, as 'what Catholic theologians call "a gratuitous grace", not necessary to salvation but potentially helpful and to be accepted thankfully, if made available'. This is indeed a serious modification of his former position; and it is a modification by which he seems to stand. Yet from this it follows that intoxication of any sort must also be a 'gratuitous grace', and in so far as the Church teaches that the fruit of the vine and the beverages that derive from it are a gift of God and to be enjoyed in moderation, this view does not seem to be objectionable. His position, however, becomes much more shaky when he assails the Church for not enlivening her ceremonies with a little sacramental mescalin as the 'Native American Church' apparently does.

Huxley's impatience with the tedium and dullness of the average Christian service is comprehensible enough; and the dullness of our services and of our priests and pastors has done perhaps more than anything to empty the churches in this country. As Huxley's plea for sacramental mescalin, quixotic though it may be, all too clearly shows, the Churches in England are leaving unsatisfied a human religious need more genuinely felt, albeit often unconsciously, than the urge simply to escape from self, I mean the need to get into contact with the Divine Reality or what is felt to be such. How deep this need is has been sufficiently illustrated by the astonishing success that Dr. Billy Graham enjoyed in this country. Dr. Graham was able to attract record crowds of people not normally interested in religion simply because he had found a way of cutting through the fog of dullness with which modern Christianity has succeeded in obfuscating the most moving and prodigious 'myth' of all time.

. . . It would . . . be a grave mistake to underrate the

challenge thrown down by Mr. Huxley and by many who think like him. What, then, is this challenge? It is this: that religion is a matter of experience, almost of sensation; that religious experience means 'mystical' experience; and that mystical experiences are everywhere and always the same. Acting on this assumption Huxley first became interested in the Vedānta philosophy of the Hindus since only in that philosophy is praeternatural experience, deduced from the contents of the Upanisads, made the basis of all speculation. This teaching, in its extreme form, is the philosophy, not so much of the oneness of all things, but of the actual identity of the individual soul with the *Brahman* which can best be translated as 'the Absolute'. All mystical experience, according to this school of thought, ultimately leads to this identity,—a conclusion that Westerners may find suprising. By a mystical experience Huxley seems to understand not only the experiences of all the recognized mystics, but experiences such as his own under the influence of mescalin; and, since he is honest, he would be forced to add, the experiences of madness. . . . It is not for nothing that Huxley said that he thought he knew what it felt like to be mad.

It is not easy to see what Huxley's intention was when he wrote *The Doors of Perception*: for hitherto he had been one of the most stubborn defenders of what he calls the *philosophia perennis*, that philosophy which maintains that the ultimate truths about God and the universe cannot be directly expressed in words, that these truths are necessarily everywhere and always the same, and that, therefore, the revealed religions which so obviously differ on so many major points from one another, can only be relatively true, each revelation being accommodated to the needs of the time and the place in which it was made and adapted to the degree of spiritual enlightenment of its recipients. Thus, as Coomaraswamy, another exponent of the *philosophia perennis*, has said, the only real heresy is to maintain that one religion only is in exclusive possession of the truth. All are rather facets of the same truth, this truth being presented in a different manner at different times in accordance with the spiritual development of the society to which it is directed. The truth itself is that experienced by the mystics whose unity of thought and language is said to speak for itself.

Notes

1. Cf. *The Doors of Perception*, London, Chatto and Windus, 1954, p. 31.
2. *Le Poème du Haschisch*, iii. in *Œuvres*, Bibliothèque de la Pleiade, Paris, Gallimard, 1954, p. 445.
3. *The Doors of Perception*, p. 31.
4. Ibid., p. 49.
5. See H.-C. Puech, *Le Manichéisme, son fondateur, sa doctrine*, Publications du Musée Guimet, Paris, 1949, pp. 82–83: cf. R. C. Zaehner, *Zurvan, a Zoroastrian Dilemma*, Oxford, 1955, p. 169.
6. Id., *Foolishness to the Greeks*, Oxford, 1953, p. 14.
7. In Collected Edition, London, Chatto and Windus, 1948, pp. 275 ff.
8. C. G. Jung, *Principles of Practical Psychotherapy*, in Collected Works, vol. xvi, London, Routledge and Kegan Paul, 1954, p. 10.
9. From *The Soul of Man under Socialism*, New Collected Edition, London, Collins, 1948, p. 1023.
10. *The Doors of Perception*, p. 50.
11. Ibid., p. 58.
12. A. K. Coomaraswamy, *The Bugbear of Literacy*, London, Dobson, 1949, p. 49.

FRANK BALDANZA
From *"Point Counter Point:*
Aldous Huxley on 'The Human Fugue'"

South Atlantic Quarterly, Spring 1959, pp. 249–57

In *Point Counter Point* the vehicle for Huxley's method and the embodiment of his introspective activity is the novelist Philip Quarles, at once a portrait of himself and an outlet for his preoccupations. And it is in the journal of Quarles, quoted sporadically in the novel, that we find Huxley's speculations on the suitability of musical structure for the novel of ideas.

The first thing Huxley saw was that if one or the other of the two elements of the novel of ideas—the ideas themselves or the depiction of humanity—had to be sacrificed, then humanity would have to go: "The chief defect of the novel of ideas is that you must write about people who have ideas to express—which excludes all but about .01 per cent of the human race." But it is out of such a dilemma that his most brilliant inspiration came, one that enabled him not only to preserve both elements, but to make them mutually complementary and functional. It was in the example of music that he found a structural analogy which retained intellectual order and complexity without sacrificing emotional connotation. And, like Virginia Woolf, T. S. Eliot, and E. M. Forster, it is to Beethoven he turns for all his illustrations. Although the soirée in the opening passages of the novel is dominated by a performance of Bach's Suite in B minor, it is Beethoven's A minor Quartet which motivates Spandrell's suicide at the end, and it is Beethoven's B flat major and C sharp minor Quartets and the Diabelli variations that Huxley invokes for illustrations on how fiction might be "musicalized."

Abrupt transitions and subtle modulations from one mood to another are two of the basic devices he discusses. He means to reproduce, in the sequence of scenes in a novel, "majesty alternating with a joke" as in the first movement of the B flat major Quartet. Translated into literary terms, "While Jones is murdering a wife, Smith is wheeling the perambulator in the park." And toward the end of this novel, a lover arriving for a tryst is cracked on the head by an Indian club; as one of his murderers peruses the advertisements in a copy of V*ogue*, Burlap seduces Beatrice Gilray, Philip goes to a Satie concert, and Elinor rushes to the country to the bedside of her dying son. As the boy dies, Arkwright frets because the father is thus prevented from writing a preface to a new illustrated pornographic book he is publishing. But Huxley considered the modulations and subtle variations to be at once more "interesting" and more "difficult" than the abrupt transitions. The latter effect he hoped to gain by either having similar characters performing dissimilar acts or having dissimilar characters caught in parallel situations. Obviously in order to gain all these effects, he needed a large and varied gallery of types, which he apparently drew from his own experience, since this novel is often treated as a *roman à clef*.

The basic theme of the novel is provided by the outlook of Mark Rampion, a figure modeled after Huxley's admired friend, D. H. Lawrence. All the other characters of the novel are ranged about Rampion and his situation; perhaps the surest sign of this arrangement is Rampion's detachment from all the rest, who are related to each other by complicated ties of blood, intimacy, and friendship. In fact, although the novel has little enough plot in the conventional sense, Rampion simply appears at Sbisa's restaurant where he pontificates on his theories, but he takes no direct hand in any significant action in the book.

In a whole range of sexual frenzy, only Rampion and his wife Mary were satisfactorily adjusted, although their bickering relationship is a kind of contrapuntal balance of opposites. The theory that summarizes Mark's appeal to Mary, and which also stands as the basic theme for which all else in the book is a variation, is:

"Civilization is harmony and completeness. Reason, feeling, intinct, the life of the body—Blake managed to include and harmonize everything. Barbarism is being lop-sided. You can be a barbarian of the intellect as well as of the body. A barbarian of the soul and the feelings as well as of sensuality. Christianity made us barbarians of the soul and now science is making us barbarians of the intellect."

Certainly the theory has a recognizable relation to the ideas of D. H. Lawrence, who fascinated Huxley as a person.

What interests us at the moment is the suitability of this philosophy as a basic structural theme on which to work variations. In commenting on the theme of the Diabelli variations, Huxley says: "The whole range of thought and feeling, yet all in organic relation to a ridiculous little waltz tune. Get this into a novel." If one needs only "a ridiculous little waltz tune," then we should not be perturbed at either the inadequacy or the triteness of the philosophy because it is the number and variety of the variations, and the range of thought and feeling which the variations embrace, that constitute the artist's aim. Let us take the catalogue in the order in which it is presented in Rampion's speech ("reason, feeling, instinct, the life of the body") and note the ways in which Huxley varies each of these qualities in the lives of his characters.

Philip's interest in biology symbolizes the overdevelopment of his intellect and the consequent neglect of instinct and feeling in his relations with his wife. Frustrated by years of attempting to maintain an intimate relation with a nearly ghostly abstraction of a man (and even having failed to interest him in extramarital affairs as a therapeutic measure), she turns in revulsion to Everard Webley, the exact opposite of her husband. Webley's green-shirt fascist organization is a perfect channel for his blustering emotionalism: in contrast to Philip's orderly deductions, Webley's speech in Hyde Park represents the quintessence of antirational *non sequitur*. Elinor, however, finds herself incapable of surrendering to Webley: although she is thrillingly moved by the spectacle of his speech, her reason interrupts again and again to remind her that he really considers love to be "just an occasional brief violence in the intervals of business," and not a whole-hearted passion that integrally informs one's entire life. Elinor stands as a kind of bridge between the two men and although she incorporates a wholesome balance of the elements that Rampion finds in Blake, she is foiled by the lopsidedness of the people she associates with. Thus the three characters represent a kind of triadic variation on the reason-emotion theme.

While the contrasts offered by these three characters sufficiently illustrate the theme of the balance of reason and emotion, we rely more on the author's word as far as instinct is concerned. Suffice it to say that instinct is a quality which blends in a harmonious balance with the other qualities in the well-integrated characters like Mark Rampion and Elinor Quarles, and it also goes along with the more lovable traits of those who live almost entirely in their emotions, like John Bidlake. But instinct is found less and less frequently in the intellectually obsessed and unbalanced characters, until it disappears totally with such a person as Philip or Illidge, the Communist, who has overdeveloped his reasoning faculties.

It is when sensual indulgence enters as a factor that the

real complexity of the interrelation of these qualities is evident. Where the body is totally incapacitated, as is the case with Lord Gattenden, one passes his time seeking out mathematical proofs for the existence of God. Together with Lord Edward, he is as lifeless as it is possible to be without actually dying. Old John Bidlake, the sybaritic painter who is widely known for his fleshy and voluptuous nudes, makes his love "straightforwardly, naturally, with the good animal gusto of a child of nature." But when this same child of nature approaches death toward the end of the book, his panic fear of doctors and the elaborately circumscribed net of superstitions that controls his emotions show him to be a spiritual and rational savage.

However, his conversation with his former mistress, Lady Edward, at least reveals that he is capable of emotional attachments; when he turns to address her daughter, Lucy Tantamount, he faces a purer sensualist than even he could have conceived. Lucy, while she represents a kind of debauched jazz-age youth, also stands in Huxley's schematic arrangement as the extreme in dedication to nervous titillation, at the opposite pole from Lord Gattenden and Lord Edward, her father. She surrounds herself obsessively with company, regardless of its quality, and refuses to break up any party until dawn. "She could pursue her pleasure as a man pursues his, remorselessly, single-mindedly, without allowing her thoughts and feelings to be in the least involved." She takes Walter Bidlake as a lover only after her maddening regime of all-night table- and club-hopping drives him to several desperate and passionate attempts at physical attack. Surprised and delighted, she indulges him until his true character as a mawkish and ineffectual sentimentalist manifests itself. Lucy, who began going to the theater at the age of six, and who finds all balls uniformly dull, has exhausted all other sensations except those centering around cruelty. If she is not the victim of violence and capriciousness (as it at first appeared she would be with Walter) then she must inflict it on others, as in her fiendishly detailed description to the distraught Walter of her street encounter in Paris with the violent and olive-skinned Neapolitan.

Walter's attraction to Lucy was coincidental with his abandonment of Marjorie Carling, a timid and whey-faced woman very like himself, without the spiritual resources to use her intelligence effectively, and without the will to follow out her commitment to a life of sensual indulgence. Both Marjorie and Walter consequently get the worst of the four realms— intellectually frustrated, emotionally riddled by feelings of inferiority and guilt, instinctually hesitant and bungling, and physically discomfited, Marjorie by her unwelcome pregnancy and Walter by his bitter longing for the perverse and elusive Lucy.

An even subtler variation is attained in the depiction of Maurice Spandrell and Denis Burlap, both of whom are harried by pseudo-religious convictions but in different directions. They are distinguished from the preceding characters in that they indulge in reason, feeling, instinct, and the life of the body in a fairly balanced manner; neither of them concentrates exclusively on one of the faculties at the expense of the others. Subconsciously or not, both Burlap and Spandrell are committed to a quest for spiritual experience, deriving directly in Spandrell's case from Oedipean sources, and it becomes clear enough in the course of the novel that this drive is the one that vitiates and distorts their sensual lives and makes them such monsters of hypocrisy. Although it is clear, too, that Huxley has not always looked this dourly on man's need for God, the position fits well in the D. H. Lawrence–Rampion code that dominates this particular novel.

For a variation on both Burlap and Spandrell, Huxley manages to have the latter run into Carling, Marjorie's estranged husband, at a pub. Although deserted by his wife for drunken brutality, he drowns his sorrows in alcohol while he lectures the barmaid (who has the temerity, after his fifth whiskey, to call him "young Sacramento") on the inviolability of the sacrament of marriage.

But such a schematization of Huxley's method obscures the major effect he was seeking, the sense of progression and suspension as the themes work themselves out. To gain a sense of this buoyant plasticity as it manifests itself in the novel, we shall have to turn to the second of the devices we mentioned earlier, having similar characters doing dissimilar things and having dissimilar characters caught in similar situations. It is by the multiple ironies involved in these complex contrasts that the most subtle and elegant counterpoint is attained in the novel.

Thus Walter Bidlake's affair with Marjorie Carling, a high-minded and spiritual relation, contrasts with his frenzied pursuit of Lucy Tantamount, an affair that only the very late Roman empire could appreciate. The attraction and repulsion he feels for both women simultaneously symbolizes the split in his nature between allegiance to spiritual and physical values. And Illidge's humanitarian love of mankind expresses itself as surely in his biological researches as his hatred for the upper classes does in his high-principled murder of Everard Webley. Another purposefully muddled person, Denis Burlap, works at his major opus on St. Francis, but takes time out for childlike romps in the bathtub with his secretary.

However, the basic structural unit of this novel is the "scene," an afternoon or an evening during which a group of contrasting characters gather for conversation. And it is in playing one scene off against another, or in breaking up one scene by interspersed passages from other scenes, that Huxley gains his major ironic variations and shows dissimilar persons performing similar acts.

A miniature example of contrast in scenes is in Elinor's return from her first meeting with Webley after the Quarles's trip to India. She has determined to tell Philip about Webley's attraction for her in order to stimulate him to jealously and, perhaps, to love; he, however, is so deeply immersed in a manual of biology that he hardly hears what she says. Later in the book, he attempts to seduce the talkative Comtesse d'Exergillod, but learns in the process that she only flirts in order to be able to talk about—but never to do anything about—love. When he returns home, humiliated and angry with himself, Elinor retaliates, unconscious of the total irony of the situation, by immersing herself in a book and refusing to listen to his confidences. But behind the irony of situation is a more complex irony of meaning; Elinor is attracted by the real brutality of Webley, and just as effectually repelled by it when he attempts to actually embrace her; Philip, the over-civilized intellectual, attempts to fake out brutality in his advances to Molly d'Exergillod, but she perversely proves herself even more civilized in her shocked panegyric on Platonic love.

Of greater importance in terms of the total work are the grand "units" of scenes, such as the one that opens the novel. During the musicale, various contrasts occur; Illidge, the Communist, is introduced not only to reactionary military gentlemen, but even to the fascist Webley. Later, he expatiates on his bitter hatred of the rich to Walter Bidlake, who was harried during his ride on the tube to Tantamount House by *his* hatred of the poor. Just as Bidlake on the the tube thought back to the disgusting charity visits he made as a child to poor tenants' cottages with his mother, so Illidge now thinks back over the life of the poor as exemplified in his own childhood.

Then come in swift alternations a series of fragmentary conversations at Sbisa's, each of which is interrupted by a "going home" scene as one character after another comes home from the Tantamount musicale. In the same manner that Virginia Woolf organized *Mrs. Dalloway* a few years earlier, Huxley uses general contemporaneity as the means to shift from one group of characters to another and to embroider his ironic and thematic meanings. But in contrast with Mrs. Woolf's, Huxley's art is predominantly objective, and he embodies his meaning in conversation to such a degree that he simply uses the listings and turnings of the talk at Tantamount House or at Sbisa's to dictate the content of the intermezzi.

And of course there is a subtler and more detailed counterpoint of ideas running through the novel which does not find expression in major scenes. Illidge, the Communist, detests the virtues of wealth and good breeding—"disinterestedness, spirituality, incorruptibility, refinement of feeling, and exquisiteness of taste." Later, and for totally different reasons, Lucy Tantamount, the compulsive aristocratic slummer, mutters about her mother's "bear garden" soirées, in perfect accidental agreement with Illidge: "'There's nothing I hate more than the noise of cultured, respectable, eminent people, like these creatures.'"

In addition to all of these fairly obvious correspondences and variations, all of which center about specific ideas, Huxley also repeats abstract behavior patterns from scene to scene. For example, Marjorie, in the opening scene, pleads with Walter to stay at home with her; he offers all sorts of excuses and rationalizations, but finishes by acquiescing in her demand; however, by this time, Marjorie has begun to feel guilty about her insistence, and now they argue on opposite sides of the issue, she insisting he go and he adamantly determined to stay. The same pattern occurs between Walter and Burlap when Walter asks for a raise in salary; the interview ends with Walter elaborately rejecting the proffered raise and Burlap magnanimously bestowing it. Thus Huxley has twice reproduced the "hour-glass" pattern in which each character at the end of the scene holds the position occupied by the opposing character at the opening of the scene.

The opposite pattern for a scene is one in which both characters hold the same position simultaneously but for different reasons: after Elinor and Philip have quarreled in Chapter XXIV about the proper way to rear their child, each has misgivings and each suppresses an impulse to apologize to the other.

In addition to these structural devices, Huxley employs, again as did Virginia Woolf in *Mrs. Dalloway*, flashbacks which taken together form counterpoints played off against present developments in the novel. A series of eight recollections, for example, explores the courtships of various couples.

The end of the novel, initiated with Chapter XXXII, consists of a series of variations on the theme of death. We saw earlier that the first symposium in Sbisa's gave Rampion the opportunity to expose his philosophy, which we took as the basic theme of the book; the second symposium was devoted to predestination and to determining to what degree an individual shapes events to resemble his own character. Now the third of the great symposia which state philosophical possibilities that events in the novel bear out occurs again at Sbisa's; and again Rampion has the rostrum, with death as his subject. While this unit is composed of more scattered and discrete scenes than the opening unit that centered around the musicale at Tantamount House, it is richer in meaning and fuller in complexity,

depending as it does on all kinds of pre-established orientations on the part of the reader which Huxley could not avail himself of at the opening of the novel.

It is in Rampion's final philippic that we have the definitive statement of his humanistic values, and as we read it, we need to keep in mind what Huxley said earlier about art as a way of presenting "the human fugue":

> "After all, the only truth that can be of any interest to us, or that we can know, is a human truth. And to discover that, you must look for it with the whole being, not with a specialized part of it. What the scientists are trying to get at is non-human truth. . . . By torturing their brains they can get a faint notion of the universe as it would seem if looked at through non-human eyes. What with their quantum theory, wave mechanics, relativity, and all the rest of it, they do really seem to have got a little way outside humanity. Well, what the devil's the good of that?"

It is, by implication, only the completely balanced artist (Rampion draws and paints in addition to writing) who has a full view of life from a human point of view; any distortion or perversion leads inevitably to death.

The inevitability of death is at the same time in the process of being demonstrated as the novel closes. As little Phil suffers excruciatingly, Huxley contrasts the attitudes of old John Bidlake who is apparently dying of intestinal cancer and of the querulous elder Quarles who convinces himself with a flurry of self-pity that he is dying in order not to have to face the rages of Gladys Helmsley, his abandoned Cockney mistress. The death of young Philip comes as a kind of senseless and unmerited horror, accompanied by gruesome suffering, hopeful rallyings, and final despair. The murder of Webley, as he eagerly arrives at the Quarles home, gives Huxley a major opportunity for a disquisition on death. When Beatrice Gilray's ascent in the office of the *Literary World* is finally climaxed by her surrender to Burlap's caresses (aptly compared, given the preoccupation with death, to an inflated rubber glove used at seances to represent caresses from The Beyond), Ethel Cobbett is dismissed. Her consequent suicide is a kind of bitter and backhanded assertion of her idealism, as is the suicide of Spandrell to the closing strains of the Beethoven piece. His tentative prodding of the dead Webley's eye with his heel was a final attempt, like his premeditated seductions, to prove that there was a final horor that would assert its opposite, the existence of God. Having been foiled in this search all along, and knowing that, as Rampion had just said, he would be rejected from heaven at the ending of the Beethoven ersatz heaven, he took the only logical step left.

THEODOR W. ADORNO
"Aldous Huxley and Utopia"
Prisms (1967)
trs. Samuel and Shierry Weber

1981, pp. 97–117

One of the far-reaching effects of the European catastrophe was to create in America a social type which had never before existed there—the intellectual emigré. Those who came to the new world in the nineteenth century were lured by the unlimited possibilities it offered. They emigrated to make their fortunes or at least find enough to make ends meet, something they could not achieve in the overpopulated European countries. The interests of self-preservation were stronger than those of preserving the self, and the rapid economic growth of the United States took place under the aegis of the same principle that drove the emigrant across the ocean. The newcomer strove for successful adjustment; critical attitudes on his part might have compromised the prospects and the claim to legitimacy of his own efforts. Neither their backgrounds nor their position in the social process enabled the new arrivals to avoid being overpowered by the turbulent struggle for the maintenance of life. Any utopian hopes they might have attached to their resettlement took on a different character in the new context of the saga of struggling upwards, the horizon of a still uncharted existence, the prospect of advancing from dish-washer to millionaire. The skepticism of a visitor like De Tocqueville, who a century ago already perceived the element of unfreedom in unrestrained equality, remained the exception; opposition to what in the jargon of German cultural conservatism was called 'Americanism' was to be found in Americans like Poe, Emerson, and Thoreau rather than in the new arrivals. A hundred years later it was no longer individual intellectuals who emigrated but the European intelligentsia as a whole, by no means only the Jews. They sought not to live better but to survive; opportunities were no longer unlimited, and thus the necessity for adjustment which prevailed in the sphere of economic competition extended implacably to them. In place of the wilderness which the pioneer intended to open up spiritually as well as materially and through which he was to accomplish his spiritual regeneration, there has arisen a civilization which absorbs all of life in its system, without allowing the unregimented mind even those loopholes which European laxness left open into the epoch of the great business concerns. It is made unmistakably clear to the intellectual from abroad that he will have to eradicate himself as an autonomous being if he hopes to achieve anything or be accepted as an employee of the super-trust into which life has condensed. The refractory individual who does not capitulate and completely toe the line is abandoned to the shocks which the world of things, concentrated into gigantic blocks, administers to whatever does not make itself into a thing. Impotent in the machinery of the universally developed commodity relation, which has become the supreme standard, the intellectual reacts to the shock with panic.

Huxley's *Brave New World* is a manifestation of this panic, or rather, its rationalization. The novel, a fantasy of the future with a rudimentary plot, endeavours to comprehend the shocks through the principle of the disenchanted world, to heighten this principle to absurdity, and to derive the idea of human dignity from the comprehension of inhumanity. The point of departure seems to be the perception of the universal similarity of everything mass-produced, things as well as human beings. Schopenhauer's metaphor of nature as a manufactured article is taken literally. Teeming herds of twins are prepared in test tubes: a nightmare of endless doubles like that which the most recent phase of capitalism has spawned into everyday life, from regulated smiles, the grace instilled by charm schools, to the standardized consciousness of millions which revolves in the grooves cut by the communications industry. The here and now of spontaneous experience, long corroded, is stripped of its power; men are no longer merely purchasers of the concerns' mass-produced consumption goods but rather appear themselves to be the deindividualized products of the corporations' absolute power. To the panicked eye, observations that resist assimilation petrify into allegories of catastrophe; it sees through the illusion of the harmlessness of everyday life. For it, the model's commercial smile becomes what it is, the contorted grin of the victim. The more than thirty years since the book's appearance have provided more than sufficient verifica-

tion: small horrors such as the aptitude tests for elevator boys which detect the least intelligent, and visions of terror such as the rational utilization of corpses. If, in accordance with a thesis of Freud's *Group Psychology and Ego Analysis*, panic is the condition in which powerful collective identifications disintegrate and the released instinctual energy is transformed into raw anxiety, then the person seized by panic is capable of innervating the dark basis of the collective identification—the false consciousness of individuals who, without transparent solidarity and blindly subjected to images of power, believe themselves one with the whole whose ubiquity stifles them.

Huxley is free from the foolhardy sobriety which emerges from even the worst situations with a temporizing. 'It's not all that bad'. He makes no concessions to the childish belief that the alleged excesses of technical civilization will be ironed out automatically through irresistible progress, and he scorns the consolation upon which exiles so readily seize: the notion that the frightening aspects of American civilization are ephemeral relics of its primitiveness or potent safeguards of its youth. We are not permitted to doubt that American civilization has not only not lagged behind that of Europe but has indeed forged ahead of it, while the Old World diligently emulates the New. Just as the world-state of *Brave New World* knows only artificially maintained differences between the golf courses and experimental stations of Mombasa, London, and the North Pole, Americanism, the butt of parody, has taken over the world. And that world supposedly resembles the utopia whose realization, as the epigraph from Berdyaev indicates, is foreseeable in the light of technology. But, by extension, it becomes hell; Huxley projects observations of the present state of civilization along the lines of its own teleology to the point where its monstrous nature becomes immediately evident. The emphasis is placed not so much on objective technological and institutional elements as on what becomes of human beings when they no longer know need. The economic and political sphere as such recedes in importance. It is stipulated only that there is a thoroughly rationalized class system on a planetary scale and totally planned state capitalism, that total domination goes along with total collectivization, and that a money economy and the profit motive persist.

'Community, Identity, and Stability' replaces the motto of the French Revolution. Community defines a collectivity in which each individual is unconditionally subordinated to the functioning of the whole (the question of the point of this whole is no longer permitted or even possible in the New World). Identity means the elimination of individual differences, standardization even down to biological constitution; stability, the end of all social dynamics. The artfully balanced situation is an extrapolation from certain indications of a reduction in the economic 'play of forces' in late capitalism—the perversion of the millennium. The panacea that guarantees social stasis is 'conditioning'. The expression is a product of biology and behaviouristic psychology, in which it signifies the evocation of particular reflexes or modes of behaviour through arbitrary transformations in the environment, through control of the conditions; and it has made its way into colloquial American English as the designation for any kind of scientific control over the conditions of life, as in 'air-conditioning'. In *Brave New World* conditioning means the complete preformation of human beings through social intervention, from artificial breeding and technological direction of the conscious and unconscious mind in the earliest stages of life to 'death conditioning', a training that purges children of the horror of death by parading the dying before their eyes while they are being fed candy, which they then forever after associate with death. The ultimate effect of conditioning, which is in fact adjustment come into its own, is a degree of introjection and integration of social pressure and coercion far beyond that of the Protestant ethic; men resign themselves to loving what they have to do, without even being aware that they are resigned. Thus, their happiness is firmly established subjectively and order is maintained. Conceptions of a merely external influence of society upon individuals, through agencies like psychology or the family, are recognized to be obsolete. What today has already happened to the family is inflicted upon it once again in *Brave New World*, from above. As children of society in the literal sense, men no longer exist in dialectical opposition to society but rather are identical with it in their substance. Compliant exponents of the collective totality in which all antitheses have been absorbed, they are 'socially conditioned' in a non-metaphorical sense, not merely adjusted secondarily to the dominant system through 'development'.

The system of class relationships is made eternal and biological: directors of breeding assign each person to a caste designated by a Greek letter while he is still an embryo. Through an ingenious method of cell division, the common people are recruited from identical twins, whose physical and intellectual growth is stunted through an artificial addition of alcohol to the blood. That is, the reproduction of stupidity, which previously took place unconsciously under the dictates of material necessity, must be taken in hand by triumphant mass civilization now that scarcity could be eliminated. The rational fixation of irrational class relations indicates their superfluity. Today class lines have already lost their 'natural' character, an illusion created during the undirected history of mankind, so that classes can be perpetuated only through arbitrary selection and co-option, only through administrative differentiations in the distribution of the social product. By depriving lower-caste embryos and infants of oxygen in the Hatching and Conditioning Centres of *Brave New World*, the directors create an artificial slum atmosphere. In the midst of unlimited possibility they organize degradation and regression. Such regression, however, devised and automatically induced by the totalitarian system, is truly total. Huxley, who knows his way around, points out the signs of mutilation in the upper class as well: 'Even alphas have been conditioned.' Even the minds of those who credit themselves with being individuals are caught up in standardization by virtue of their identification with the 'in-group'. They automatically produce the judgments to which they have been conditioned, rather like the member of the present upper middle class who babbles that the real problem is not material circumstances but a religious regeneration or who insists that he cannot understand modern art. Non-comprehension becomes a virtue. Two lovers from the upper caste fly over the Channel in stormy weather, and the man wishes to delay the flight so as to escape from the crowds and be alone with his beloved for a longer time, closer to her and more himself. In response to her reluctance, he asks whether she understands his wish. ' "I don't understand anything," she said with decision, determined to preserve her incomprehension intact.' Huxley's observation does more than just point up the *rancune* that the statement of the most modest truth provokes in persons who can no longer allow such statements lest their equilibrium be disturbed. It diagnoses a powerful new taboo. The more the existing society, through its overwhelming power and hermetic structure, becomes its own ideological justification in the minds of the disillusioned, the more it brands as sinners all those whose thoughts blaspheme against the notion that what is, is right—just because it exists. They live in airplanes but heed the command, tacit like all genuine taboos,

'Thou shalt not fly'. The gods of the earth punish those who raise themselves above the earth. Avowedly anti-mythological, the pact with the existing order restores mystic power. Huxley demonstrates this in the speech of his characters. The idiocy of mandatory small talk, conversation as chatter, is discretely pursued to the extreme. The phenomenon has long since ceased to be a mere consequence of conventions intended to prevent conversation from becoming narrow shop talk or unabashed presumption. Rather, the degeneration of talk is due to objective tendencies. The virtual transformation of the world into commodities, the predetermination by the machinery of society of everything that is thought or done, renders speaking illusory; under the curse of perpetual sameness it disintegrates into a series of analytic judgments. The ladies of *Brave New World*—and in this case extrapolation is hardly required—converse only as consumers. In principle, their conversation concerns nothing but what is in any case to be found in the catalogues of the ubiquitous industries, information about available commodities. Objectively superfluous, it is the empty shell of dialogue, the intention of which was once to find out what was hitherto unknown. Stripped of this idea, dialogue is ripe for extinction. People completely collectivized and incessantly communicating might as well abandon all communication at once and acknowledge themselves to be the mute monads they have been surreptitiously since the beginnings of bourgeois society. They are swallowed up in archaic childlike dependency.

They are cut off both from the mind, which Huxley rather flatly equates with the products of traditional culture, exemplified by Shakespeare, and from nature as landscape, an image of creation unviolated by society. The opposition of mind and nature was the theme of bourgeois philosophy at its peak. In *Brave New World* they unite against a civilization which lays hands on everything and tolerates nothing which is not made in its own image. The union of mind and nature, conceived by idealist speculation as the supreme reconciliation, now becomes the absolute opposition to absolute reification. Mind, the spontaneous and autonomous synthesis achieved by consciousness, is possible only to the extent to which it is confronted by a sphere outside its grasp, something not categorically predetermined—'nature'. And nature is possible only to the extent to which mind knows itself as the opposite of reification, which it transcends instead of enthroning it as nature. Both are vanishing: Huxley is well acquainted with the latest-model average citizen who contemplates a bay as a tourist attraction while seated in his car listening to radio commercials. Not unrelated is hatred of things past. The mind itself seems a thing of the past, a ridiculous addition to the glorified facts, to the given, whatever it may be, and what is no longer around becomes bric-à-brac and rubbish. 'History is bunk' an expression attributed to Ford, relegates to the junkpile everything not in line with the most recent methods of industrial production, including, ultimately, all continuity of life. Such reduction cripples men. Their inability to perceive or think anything unlike themselves, the inescapable self-sufficiency of their lives, the law of pure subjective functionalism—all result in pure desubjectivization. Purged of all myths, the scientifically manufactured subject-objects of the anti-*Weltgeist* are infantile. In line with mass culture, the half-involuntary, half-organized regressions of today finally turn into compulsory ordinances governing leisure time, the 'proper standard of infantile decorum', Hell's laughter at the Christian dictum, 'If you do not become as little children. . . .' The blame rests with the substitution of means for all ends. The cult of the instrument, cut off from every objective aim (in *Brave New World*, the implicit religion of today—the auto—becomes literal with Ford for Lord and the sign of the Model T for that of the cross), and the fetishistic love of gadgetry, both unmistakable lunatic traits ingrained in precisely those people who pride themselves on being practical and realistic, are elevated to the norm of life. But that substitution is also in force in areas of the *Brave New World* where freedom seems to have won out. Huxley has recognized the contradiction that in a society where sexual taboos have lost their intrinsic force and have either retreated before the permissibility of the prohibited or come to be enforced by external compulsion, pleasure itself degenerates to the misery of 'fun' and to an occasion for the narcissistic satisfaction of having 'had' this or that person. Through the institutionalization of promiscuity, sex becomes a matter of indifference, and even escape from society is relocated within its borders. Physiological release is desirable, as part of hygiene; accompanying feelings are dispensed with as a waste of energy without social utility. On no account is one to be moved. The original bourgeois *ataraxia* now extends to all reactions. In infecting eros it turns directly against what was once the highest good, subjective eudaemonia, for the sake of which purgation of the passions was originally demanded. In attacking ecstasy it strikes at all human relations, at every attempt to go beyond a monadological existence. Huxley recognizes the complementary relationship of collectivization and atomization.

His portrayal of organized orgiastics, however, has an undertone which casts doubt upon his satirical thesis. In its proclamation of the bourgeois nature of what claims to be unbourgeois, the thesis itself becomes ensnared in bourgeois habits. Huxley waxes indignant at the sobriety of his characters but is inwardly an enemy of intoxication, and not only that from narcotics, which he earlier condemned, thus endorsing the prevailing attitude. Like that of many emancipated Englishmen, his consciousness is preformed by the very Puritanism he abjures. He fails to distinguish between the liberation of sexuality and its debasement. In his earlier novels libertinism already appears, as it were, as a localized thrill without an aura—not unlike the way men in so-called 'masculine' cultures habitually speak of women and love with a gesture in which pride at having won the sovereignty that enables them to discuss such matters is inevitably mixed with contempt. In Huxley everything occurs on a more sublimated level than in the Lawrence of the four-letter words, but everything is also more thoroughly repressed. His anger at false happiness sacrifices the idea of true happiness as well. Long before he acknowledged Buddhist sympathies, his irony displayed, especially in the self-denunciation of the intellectual, something of the sectarianism of the raging penitent, a quality to which his writing is usually immune. The flight from the world leads to the nudist colony, which destroys sexuality by over-exposure. Despite the pains Huxley takes to depict the pre-mass-civilization world of the Savage (who is brought to the Brave New World as a relic of humanity), as being distorted, repellent, and insane in its own way, reactionary elements find their way into his portrayal. Freud is included among the anathematized figures of modernity, and at one point he is equated with Ford. He is made a mere efficiency expert of the inner life. With all too genial scorn he is credited with having been the first to discover 'the appalling dangers of family life'. But this is in fact what he did, and historical justice is on his side. The critique of the family as the agent of oppression, a theme familiar to the English opposition since Samuel Butler, emerged just at the time when the family had lost its economic basis and, with it, its last legitimate right to determine human development, becoming a neutralized monstrosity of the sort Huxley so incisively exposes in the sphere of official religion.

Huxley ascribes to the world of the future the encouragement of infantile sexuality, in complete misunderstanding, incidentally, of Freud, who all too orthodoxly adhered to instinctual renunciation as a pedagogical aim. But Huxley himself sides with those who are less concerned with the dehumanization of the industrial age than with the decline of its morals. Whether happiness is dependent upon the existence of prohibitions to be broken is an endless dialectical question, but the novel's mentality distorts the question into an affirmative answer, into an excuse for the perpetuation of obsolete taboos—as if the happiness produced by the transgression of taboos could ever legitimate the taboo, which exists not for the sake of happiness but for its frustration. It is true that the regularly occurring communal orgies of the novel and the prescribed short-term change of partners are logical consequences of the jaded official sexual routine that turns pleasure to fun and denies it by granting it. But precisely in the impossibility of looking pleasure in the eye, of making use of reflection in abandoning one's whole self to pleasure, the ancient prohibition for which Huxley prematurely mourns continues in force. Were its power to be broken, were pleasures to be freed of the institutional reins which bind it even in the 'orgy-porgy', Brave New World and its fatal rigidity would dissolve. Its highest moral principle, supposedly, is that everyone belongs to everyone, an absolute interchangeability that extinguishes man as an individual being, liquidates as mythology his claim to exist for his own sake, and defines him as existing merely for the sake of others and thus, in Huxley's mind, as worthless. In the foreword he wrote after the war for the American edition, Huxley claimed, as the ancestor of this principle, de Sade's statement that the rights of man include the absolute sexual disposition of all over all. In this, Huxley sees the foolishness of consequent reasoning consummated. But he fails to see that the heretical maxim is incompatible with his world-state of the future. All dictators have proscribed libertinage, and Himmler's much cited SS-studs were its piously patriotic opposite. Domination may be defined as the disposition of one over others but not as the complete disposition of all over all, which cannot be reconciled with a totalitarian order. This is even more true of work relations than of sexual anarchy. A man who existed only for the sake of others, an absolute ζῷον Πολιτικον, would, to be sure, have lost his individual self, but he would also have escaped the cycle of self-preservation which maintains the Brave New World as well as the old one. Pure fungibility would destroy the core of domination and promise freedom. The weakness of Huxley's entire conception is that it makes all its concepts relentlessly dynamic but nevertheless arms them against the tendency to turn into their own opposites.

The *scène à faire* of the novel is the erotic collision of the two 'worlds': the attempt of the heroine, Lenina, a well-groomed and polished American career woman, to seduce the Savage, who loves her, in a way consonant with the mores of the conscientiously promiscuous. Her opponent belongs to the type of shy, aesthetic youth, tied to his mother and inhibited, who prefers to enjoy his feeling through contemplation rather than expression and who finds satisfaction in the lyrical transfiguration of the beloved. This type, incidentally, is bred at Oxford and Cambridge no less than are Epsilons in test tubes, and it belongs to the sentimental standbys of the modern English novel. The conflict arises from the fact that John feels the pretty girl's matter-of-fact abandonment to be a debasement of his sublime passion for her and runs away. The effectiveness of the scene works against its thesis. Lenina's artificial charm and cellophane shamelessness produce by no means the unerotic effect Huxley intended, but rather a highly seductive one, to which even the infuriated cultural savage succumbs at the end of the novel. Were Lenina the imago of Brave New World, it would lose its horror. Each of her gestures, it is true, is socially preformed, part of a conventional ritual. But because she is at one with convention down to her very core, the tension between the conventional and the natural dissolves, and with it the violence in which the injustice of convention consists; psychologically, poor conventionality is always the mark of unsuccessful identification. The concept of convention does not survive its opposite. Through total social mediation, from the outside, as it were, a new immediacy, a new humanity, would arise. American civilization shows no lack of tendencies in this direction. But Huxley construes humanity and reification as rigid opposites, in accordance with the tradition of the novel, which has as its object the conflict of human beings with rigidified conditions. Huxley cannot understand the humane promise of civilization because he forgets that humanity includes reification as well as its opposite, not merely as the condition from which liberation is possible but also positively, as the form in which, however brittle and inadequate it may be, subjective impulses are realized, but only by being objectified. All the categories examined by the novel, family, parents, the individual and his property, are already products of reification. Huxley curses the future with it, without realizing that the past whose blessing he invokes is of the same nature. Thus he unwittingly becomes the spokesman of that nostalgia whose affinity to mass culture his physiognomic eye so acutely perceives in the test-tube song: 'Bottle of mine, it's you I've always wanted! Bottle of mine, why was I ever decanted? . . . There ain't no Bottle in all the world Like that dear little Bottle of mine.'

The Savage's outburst against his beloved, then, is not so much the protest of pure human nature against the cold impudence of fashion, as was perhaps intended; rather, poetic justice turns it into the aggression of the neurotic who, as the Freud whom Huxley treats rather shabbily could easily have told him, is motivated in his frantic purity by repressed homosexuality. He shouts abuse at the girl like the hypocrite who trembles with rage at things he has to forbid himself. By putting him in the wrong, Huxley distances himself from social criticism. Its actual advocate in the novel is Bernard Marx, an Alpha-Plus who rebels against his own conditioning, a skeptically compassionate caricature of a Jew. Huxley is well aware that Jews are persecuted because they are not completely assimilated and that precisely for this reason their consciousness occasionally reaches beyond the social system. He does not question the authenticity of Bernard's critical insight. But the insight itself is attributed to a sort of organic inferiority, the inevitable inferiority complex. At the same time, following the time-honoured model, Huxley charges the radical Jewish intellectual with vulgar snobbism and, ultimately, with reprehensible moral cowardice. Ever since Ibsen's invention of Gregers Werle and Stockmann, actually since Hegel's philosophy of history, bourgeois cultural politics, claiming to survey and speak for the whole, has sought to unmask anyone who seeks to change things as both the genuine child and the perverse product of the whole which he opposes, and has insisted that the truth is always on the side of the whole, be it against him or present in him. As novelist, Huxley proclaims his solidarity with this tradition; as prophet of civilization, he detests the totality. It is true that Gregers Werle destroys those he seeks to save, and no one is free from the vanity of Bernard Marx who, in raising himself above the general stupidity, thereby imagines himself untainted by it. But the view which evaluates phenomena externally, in a detached, free, superior way, deeming itself above the limitations of negation and the arbitration of the dialectic, is for this very reason neither one of truth nor one of justice. A just reflection should not delight in the inadequacy of things which are better in order to compromise them before things which are worse, but should draw from inadequacy additional strength for indignation. The forces of negativity are underestimated in order to render them impotent. But it befits this position that what is set up as positive and absolute against the dialectic is no less powerless. When, in his crucial conversation with the World Controller Mond, the Savage declares, 'What you need is something with tears for a change,' his deliberately insolent exaltation of suffering is not merely a characteristic of the obdurate individualist. It evokes Christian metaphysics, which promises future salvation solely by virtue of suffering. But, despite all appearances to the contrary, the novel is informed by an enlightened consciousness in which Christian metaphysics no longer dares to assert itself. Hence the cult of suffering becomes an absurd end in itself. It is a mannerism of an aestheticism whose ties to the powers of darkness cannot be unknown to Huxley; Nietzsche's 'Live dangerously', which the Savage proclaims to the resigned, hedonistic World Controller, was a perfect slogan for the totalitarian Mussolini, himself a World Controller of a similar sort.

In a discussion of a biological paper which the World Controller has suppressed, the all too positive core of the novel becomes clearly visible. It is 'the sort of idea that might easily de-condition the more unsettled minds among the higher castes—make them lose their faith in happiness as the Sovereign Good and take to believing instead, that the goal was somewhere beyond, somewhere outside the present human sphere; that the purpose of life was not the maintenance of well-being, but some intensification and refinement of consciousness, some enlargement of knowledge'. However pallid and diluted or cleverly prudent the formulation of the ideal may be, it still does not escape contradiction. 'Intensification and refinement of consciousness' or 'enlargement of knowledge' flatly hypostatize the mind in opposition to praxis and the fulfilment of material needs. For mind by its very nature presupposes the life-process of society and especially the division of labour, and all mental and spiritual contents are intentionally related to concrete existence for their 'fulfilment'. Consequently, setting the mind in an unconditional and atemporal opposition to material needs amounts to perpetuating ideologically this form of the division of labour and of society. Nothing intellectual was ever conceived, nor even the most escapist dream, whose objective content did not include the transformation of material reality. No emotion, no part of the inner life ever existed that did not ultimately intend something external or degenerate into untruth, mere appearance, without this intention, however sublimated. Even the selfless passion of Romeo and Juliet, which Huxley considers something like a 'value', does not exist autarchically, for its own sake, but becomes spiritual and more than mere histrionics of the soul only in pointing beyond the mind towards physical union. Huxley unwittingly reveals this in portraying their longing, the whole meaning of which is union. 'It was the nightingale and not the lark' is inseparable from the symbolism of sex. To glorify the aubade for the sake of its transcendent quality without hearing in the transcendence itself its inability to rest, its desire to be gratified, would be as meaningless as the physiologically delimited sexuality of *Brave New World*, which destroys any magic which cannot be conserved as an end in itself. The disgrace of the present is not the preponderance of so-called material culture over the spiritual—in this complaint Huxley would find unwelcome allies, the Arch-Community-

Songsters of all neutralized denominations and world views. What must be attacked is the socially dictated separation of consciousness from the social realization its essence requires. Precisely the *chōrismos* of the spiritual and the material which Huxley's *philosophia perennis* establishes, the substitution of an indeterminable, abstract 'goal somewhere beyond' for 'faith in happiness', strengthens the reified situation Huxley cannot tolerate: the neutralization of a culture cut off from the material process of production. 'If a distinction between material and ideal needs is drawn,' as Max Horkheimer once put it, 'there is no doubt that the fulfilment of material needs must be given priority, for this fulfilment also involves . . . social change. It includes, as it were, the just society, which provides all human beings with the best possible living conditions. This is identical with the final elimination of the evil of domination. To emphasize the isolated, ideal demand, however, leads to real nonsense. The right to nostalgia, to transcendental knowledge, to a dangerous life cannot be validated. The struggle against mass culture can consist only in pointing out its connection with the persistence of social injustice. It is ridiculous to reproach chewing gum for diminishing the propensity for metaphysics, but it could probably be shown that Wrigley's profits and his Chicago palace have their roots in the social function of reconciling people to bad conditions and thus diverting them from criticism. It is not that chewing gum undermines metaphysics but that it *is* metaphysics—this is what must be made clear. We criticize mass culture not because it gives men too much or makes their life too secure—that we may leave to Lutheran theology—but rather because it contributes to a condition in which men get too little and what they get is bad, a condition in which whole strata inside and out live in frightful poverty, in which men come to terms with injustice, in which the world is kept in a condition where one must expect on the one hand gigantic catastrophes and on the other clever elites conspiring to bring about a dubious peace.' As a counterweight to the sphere of the satisfaction of needs, Huxley posits another, suspiciously similar to the one the bourgeoisie generally designates as that of the 'higher things'. He proceeds from an invariant, as it were biological concept of need. But in its concrete form every human need is historically mediated. The static quality which needs appear to have assumed today, their fixation upon the reproduction of the eternally unchanging, merely reflects the character of production, which becomes stationary when existing property relations persist despite the elimination of the market and competition. When this static situation comes to an end needs will look completely different. If production is redirected towards the unconditional and unlimited satisfaction of needs, including precisely those produced by the hitherto prevailing system, needs themselves will be decisively altered. The indistinguishability of true and false needs is an essential part of the present phase. In it the reproduction of life and its suppression form a unity which is intelligible as the law of the whole but not in its individual manifestations. One day it will be readily apparent that men do not need the trash provided them by the culture industry or the miserable high-quality goods proffered by the more substantial industries. The thought, for instance, that in addition to food and lodging the cinema is necessary for the reproduction of labour power is 'true' only in a world which prepares men for the reproduction of their labour power and constrains their needs in harmony with the interests of supply and social control. The idea that an emancipated society would crave the poor histrionics of Lametta or the poor soups of Devory is absurd. The better the soups, the more pleasant the renuncia-

tion of Lametta. Once scarcity has disappeared, the relationship of need to satisfaction will change. Today the compulsion to produce for needs mediated and petrified by the market is one of the chief means of keeping everyone on the job. Nothing may be thought, written, done, or made that transcends a condition which maintains its power largely through the needs of its victims. It is inconceivable that the compulsion to satisfy needs would remain a fetter in a changed society. The present form of society has in large measure denied satisfaction to the needs inherent in it and has thus been able to keep production in its control by pointing to these very needs. The system is as practical as it is irrational. An order which does away with the irrationality in which commodity production is entangled but also satisfies needs will equally do away with the practical spirit, which is reflected even in the non-utilitarianism of bourgeois *l'art pour l'art*. It would abolish not merely the traditional antagonism between production and consumption but also its most recent unification in state capitalism, and it would converge with the idea that, in the words of Karl Kraus, 'God created man not as consumer or producer but as man'. For something to be useless would no longer be shameful. Adjustment would lose it meaning. For the first time, productivity would have an effect on need in a genuine and not a distorted sense. It would not allay unsatisfied needs with useless things; rather, satisfaction would engender the ability to relate to the world without subordination to the principle of universal utility.

In his critique of false needs Huxley preserves the idea of the objectivity of happiness. The mechanical repetition of the phrase, 'Everybody's happy now', becomes the most extreme accusation. When men are products of an order based on denial and deception, and that order implants imaginary needs in them, then the happiness which is defined by the satisfaction of such needs is truly bad. It is a mere appendage of the social machinery. In a totally integrated world which does not tolerate sorrow, the command from Romans (xii.15), 'Weep with the weeping,' is more valid than ever, but 'Be joyous with the joyful' has become a gory mockery—the job the order permits the ordered feeds on the perpetuation of misery. Hence the mere rejection of false happiness has a subversive effect. Lenina's reaction when the Savage finds an idiotic film obnoxious, 'Why did he go out of his way to spoil things?' is a typical manifestation of a dense network of deception. 'One shouldn't spoil it for the others' has always been one of the stock maxims of those who spoil it for the others. But at the same time the description of Lenina's irritation provides the basis for a criticism of Huxley's own attitude. He believes that by demonstrating the worthlessness of subjective happiness according to the criteria of traditional culture he has shown that happiness as such is worthless. Its place is to be taken by an ontology distilled from traditional religion and philosophy, according to which happiness and the objective good are irreconcilable. A society which wants nothing but happiness, according to Huxley, moves inexorably into insanity, into mechanized bestiality. But Lenina's overzealous defensiveness betrays insecurity, the suspicion that her kind of happiness is distorted by contradictions, that it is not happiness even by its own definition. No pharisaical recollection of Shakespeare is necessary to become aware of the fatuousness of the feelies and of the 'objective despair' of the audience which participates in it. That the essence of the film lies in merely duplicating and reinforcing what already exists, that it is glaringly superfluous and senseless even in a leisure restricted to infantility, that its duplicative realism is incompatible with its claim to be an aesthetic image—all this can be seen in the film itself, without recourse to dogmatically cited *vérités éternelles*. The holes in the vicious circles which Huxley draws with so much care are due not to inadequacies in his imaginative construction but to the conception of a happiness subjectively consummate but objectively absurd. If his critique of subjective happiness is valid, then his idea of a hypostatized objective happiness removed from the claims of humanity must be ideological. The source of untruth is the separation of subjective and objective, which has been reified to a rigid alternative. Mustapha Mond, the *raisonneur* and devil's advocate of the book, who embodies the most articulate self-consciousness of *Brave New World*, formulates the alternative. To the Savage's protest that man is degraded by total civilization he replies, 'Degrade him from what position? As a happy, hard-working, goods-consuming citizen he's perfect. Of course, if you choose some other standard than ours, then perhaps you might say he was degraded. But you've got to stick to one set of postulates.' In this image of the two sets of postulates, exhibited like finished products between which one must choose, relativism is apparent. The question of truth dissolves into an 'if-then' relation. Similarly, isolated by Huxley, the values of death and interiority fall prey to pragmatization. The Savage reports that he once stood on a cliff with outstretched arms in burning heat in order to feel what it was like to be crucified. Asked for an explanation, he gives the curious answer: 'Because I felt I ought to. If Jesus could stand it, and then, if one has done something wrong . . . Besides, I was unhappy, that was another reason.' If the Savage can find no other justification for his religious adventure, the choice of suffering, than the fact that he has suffered, he can hardly contradict his interviewer, who argues that it is more reasonable to take *Soma*, the euphoria-producing cure-all drug, to dissolve one's depressions. Irrationally hypostatized, the world of ideas is demoted to the level of mere existence. In this form, it continually demands justification according to merely empirical norms and is prescribed for the sake of precisely that happiness which it is supposed to negate.

The crude alternative of objective meaning and subjective happiness, conceived as mutually exclusive, is the philosophical basis for the reactionary character of the novel. The choice is between the barbarism of happiness and culture as the objectively higher condition that entails unhappiness. 'The progressive domination of nature and society,' Herbert Marcuse argues, 'does away with all transcendence, physical as well as psychical. Culture, the all-embracing title for one side of the opposition, subsists upon lack of fulfilment, longing, faith, pain, hope, in short, on that which does not exist but leaves its mark in reality. That means, however, that culture exists on the basis of unhappiness.' The kernel of the controversy is the hard and fast disjunction that one cannot be had without the other, technology without death conditioning, progress without manipulated infantile regression. However, the honesty of the thought expressed in the disjunction is to be distinguished from the moral constraint of ideology. Today, only conformism could acquiesce in considering objective insanity to be a mere accident of historical development, for retrogression is essential to the consistent development of domination. Theory is not free to choose good-naturedly that which suits it in the course of history and to omit the rest. Attempts to come up with a *Weltanschauung* which takes a 'positive attitude' to technology but advocates that it ought to be given meaning provide shallow comfort and serve merely to reinforce an affirmative work morale which is itself highly questionable. Nevertheless, the pressure that *Brave New World* exerts on everyone and everything is conceptually incompatible with the deathlike stasis that makes it a nightmare. It is no accident that all the

major figures in the novel, even Lenina, show signs of subjective derangement. The alternative is false. The perfectly self-contained state which Huxley depicts with such grim satisfaction transcends itself not by virtue of an ineffective melange of desirable and reprehensible elements brought in from the outside, but by virtue of its objective nature. Huxley is aware that historical tendencies realize themselves behind men's backs. For him the essential tendency is the self-estrangement and perfected externalization of the subject, which makes itself into a mere means in the absence of any end whatsoever. But he makes a fetish of the fetishism of commodities. In his eyes the character of commodities becomes ontic and self-subsistent, and he capitulates to this apparition instead of seeing through it as a mere form of consciousness, false consciousness which would dissolve with the elimination of its economic basis. Huxley does not admit that the phantasmagoric inhumanity of *Brave New World* is actually a relation between human beings, a relation of social labour which is not aware of its own nature—that the totally reified man is one who has been blinded to himself. Instead, he pursues in succession various unanalysed surface phenomena, such as 'the conflict between men and machine'. Huxley indicts technology for something which does not, as he believes (and in this he follows the tradition of romantic philistinism), lie in its essential nature, which is the abolition of labour. It is rather a result of the involvement of technology in the social relations of production; this insight, moreover, is implicit throughout the novel. Even the incompatibility of art and mass production today does not originate in technology as such but rather in the need of these irrationally persisting social relations to maintain the claim to individuation (in Benjamin's words, an 'aura') which is only honoured in the breach. Even the process for which Huxley censures technology, the displacement of ends by means to the point where the latter becomes completely independent of the former, does not necessarily eliminate ends. Precisely in art,[1] where consciousness makes use of unconscious channels, blind play with means can posit and unfold ends. The relation of means and ends, of humanity and technology, cannot be regulated through ontological priorities. Huxley's alternative amounts to the proposition that mankind should not extricate itself from the calamity. Humanity is placed before the choice between regression to a mythology questionable even to Huxley and progress towards total freedom of consciousness. No room is left for a concept of mankind that would resist absorption into the collective coercion of the system and reduction to the status of contingent individuals. The very construction which simultaneously denounces the totalitarian world-state and glorifies retrospectively the individualism that brought it about becomes itself totalitarian. In that it leaves no escape open, this conception itself implies the thing that horrifies Huxley, the liquidation of everything that is not assimilated. The practical consequence of the bourgeois 'Nothing to be done', which resounds as the novel's echo, is precisely the perfidious 'You must adjust' of the totalitarian Brave New World. The monolithic trend and the linear concept of progress, as handled in the novel, derive from the restricted form in which the productive forces developed in 'pre-history'. The inevitable character of the negative utopia arises from projecting the limitations imposed by the relations of production (the enthronement of the productive apparatus for the sake of profit) as properties of the human and technical productive forces *per se*. In prophesying the entropy of history, Huxley succumbs to an illusion which is necessarily propagated by the society against which he so zealously protests.

Huxley criticizes the positivistic spirit. But because his

criticism confines itself to shocks, while remaining immersed in the immediacy of experience and merely registering social illusions as facts, Huxley himself becomes a positivist. Despite his critical tone, he is in basic agreement with descriptively oriented cultural criticism, which, in lamenting the inexorable decline of culture, provides a pretext for the strengthening of domination. In the name of culture, civilization marches into barbarism. Instead of antagonisms, Huxley envisages something like an intrinsically non-self-contradictory total subject of technological reason, and correspondingly, a simplistic total development. Such conceptions belong to the currently fashionable ideas of 'universal history' and 'style of life' which are part of the cultural façade. Although he gives an incisive physiognomy of total unification, he fails to decipher its symptoms as expressions of an antagonistic essence, the pressure of domination, in which the tendency to totalization is inherent. Huxley expresses scorn for the phrase, 'Everybody's happy nowadays'. But the essence of his conception of history, which is better revealed by its form than by the events which make up its content, is profoundly harmonious. His notion of uninterrupted progress is distinguished from the liberalist idea only in emphasis, not through objective insight. Like a Benthamite liberal, Huxley foresees a development to the greatest happiness of the greatest number, but it discomfits him. He condemns *Brave New World* with the same common sense whose prevalence there he mocks. Hence, throughout the novel there emerge unanalysed elements of that worn-out *Weltanschauung* which Huxley deplores. The worthlessness of the ephemeral and the catastrophic nature of history are contrasted to that which never changes—the *philosophia perennis*, the eternal sunshine of the heavenly realm of ideas. Accordingly, exteriority and interiority move into a primitive antithesis: men are the mere objects of all evil, from artificial insemination to galloping senility, while the category of the individual stands forth with unquestioned dignity. Unreflective individualism asserts itself as though the horror which transfixes the novel were not itself the monstrous offspring of individualist society. The spontaneity of the individual human being is eliminated from the historical process while the concept of the individual is detached from history and incorporated into the *philosophia perennis*. Individuation, which is essentially social, reverts to the immutability of nature. Its implication in the network of guilt was discerned by bourgeois philosophy at its zenith, but this insight has been replaced by the empirical levelling of the individual through psychologism. In the wake of a tradition whose predominance provokes resistance more readily than it invites respect, the individual is immeasurably exalted as an idea while each individual person is convicted of moral bankruptcy by the epigones of disillusioned romanticism. The socially valid recognition of the nullity of the individual turns into an accusation levelled against the overburdened private individual. Huxley's book, like his entire work, blames the hypostatized individual for his fungibility and his existence as a 'character mask' of society rather than as a real self. These facts are attributed to the individual's inauthenticity, hypocrisy, and narrow egoism, in short, to all those traits which are the stock-in-trade of a subtle, descriptive ego psychology. For Huxley, in the authentic bourgeois spirit, the individual is both everything—because once upon a time he was the basis of a system of property rights—and nothing, because, as a mere property owner, he is absolutely replaceable. This is the price which the ideology of individualism must pay for its own untruth. The novel's *fabula docet* is more nihilistic than is acceptable to the humanity which it proclaims.

Here, however, Huxley does not do justice to the very facts on which he puts his positivistic emphasis. *Brave New World* shares with all fully worked-out utopias the character of vanity. Things have developed differently and will continue to do so. It is not the accuracy of imagination which fails. Rather the very attempt to see into the distant future in order to puzzle out the concrete form of the non-existent is beset with the impotence of presumption. The antithetical component of the dialectic cannot be conjured away syllogistically, for example by means of the general concept of enlightenment. Such an approach eliminates the very material which provides the moving force of the dialectic—those elements that are external to the subject and are not already 'spiritual' and transparent. No matter how well equipped technologically and materially, no matter how correct from a scientific point of view the fully drawn utopia may be, the very undertaking is a regression to a philosophy of identity, to idealism. Hence the ironic 'accuracy' for which Huxley's extrapolations strive does his utopia no service. For however surely the unselfconscious concept of total enlightenment may move towards its opposite, irrationality, it is nevertheless impossible to deduce from the concept itself whether this will occur and if so, whether it will stop there. The looming political catastrophe can hardly fail to modify the escape route of technical civilization. *Ape and Essence* is a somewhat hasty attempt to correct a mistake which derives not from insufficient knowledge of atomic physics but from a linear conception of history, a mistake which thus cannot be corrected by the elaboration of additional material. Where the plausibility of *Brave New World's* prognoses was oversimplified, those of Huxley's second book dealing with the future bear the stigma of improbability (as, for instance, the devil cult). These characteristics can scarcely be defended in the midst of a novel which is realistic in style by allusions to philosophical allegory. But the ideological bias of the conception revenges itself in this inevitability of error. There is an unwitting resemblance to the member of the upper middle class who solemnly insists that it is not in his own interest but in that of all mankind that he advocates the continuance of a profit economy. Men are not yet ready for socialism, the argument runs; if they no longer had to work, they wouldn't know what to do with their time. Such platitudes are not only compromised by the usage to which they are put; they are also completely devoid of truth, since they both reify 'men' in general and hypostatize the observer as a disinterested judge. But this coldness is deeply embedded in Huxley's conceptual framework. Full of fictitious concern for the calamity that a realized utopia could inflict on mankind, he refuses to take note of the real and far more urgent calamity that prevents the utopia from being realized. It is idle to bemoan what will become of men when hunger and distress have disappeared from the world. For although Huxley can find nothing more to criticize in this civilization than the boredom of a never-never land which is in principle unattainable anyway, it is by virtue of the logic of this civilization that the world is subject to hunger and distress. All his indignation at the calamitous state of things notwithstanding, the basis of Huxley's attitude is a conception of a history which takes its time. Time is made responsible for that which men must accomplish. The relation to time is parasitical. The novel shifts guilt for the present to the generations of the future. This reflects the ominous 'It shall not be otherwise' which is the end-product of the basic Protestant amalgamation of introspection and repression. Because mankind, tainted with original sin, is not capable of anything better in this world, the bettering of the world is made a sin. But the novel does not draw its life from the blood of the unborn.

Despite many ingenuities of execution, it fails because of a basic weakness—an empty schematism. Because the transformation of men is not subject to calculation and evades the anticipating imagination, it is replaced by a caricature of the men of today, in the ancient and much abused manner of satire. The fiction of the future bows before the omnipotence of the present; that which does not yet exist is made comic through its resemblance to that which already is, like the gods in Offenbach operettas. The image of the most remote is replaced by a vision of that which is closest to hand, seen through inverted binoculars. The formal trick of reporting future events as though they had already happened endows their content with a repulsive complicity. The grotesqueness that the present assumes when confronted with its own projection into the future provokes the same laughs as naturalistic representations with enlarged heads. The pathetic notion of the 'eternally human' resigns itself to the less humane one of the normal man of yesterday, today, and tomorrow. It is not for its contemplative aspect as such, which it shares with all philosophy and representation, that the novel is to be criticized, but for its failure to contemplate a praxis which could explode the infamous continuum. Man's choice is not between individualism and a totalitarian world-state. If the great historical perspective is to be anything more than the *Fata Morgana* of the eye which surveys only to control, it must open on to the question of whether society will come to determine itself or bring about terrestrial catastrophe.

Notes

1. Schumann writes somewhere that in his youth he devoted his attention to his instrument, the piano—the means, whereas in his maturity his interest was purely in music—the end. But the unquestionable superiority of his early works to his late ones cannot be divorced from the incessantly productive imaginative richness of his use of the piano, which produces the chiaroscuro, the broken harmonic colour, indeed the density of the compositional structure. Artists do not realize 'the idea' merely by themselves; it is far more the result of technological achievements, often of aimless play.

DOUGLAS HYDE

1860–1949

Douglas Hyde was born in County Roscommon, Ireland, on January 17, 1860. From the age of seven he learned Irish from local country men and women, and by 1877 was writing anti-English verses in Irish, first publishing in *The Shamrock* in 1879–82. Descended from a line of Protestant clergymen, he entered Trinity College, Dublin, in 1880 to study divinity, but later transfered to law school, receiving his LL.D. in 1886.

After an early phase of radical and militant nationalism, Hyde dedicated himself to the achievement of Irish unity through reviving interest in the country's language and culture. To this end he recorded poems and stories told to him by the old, generally illiterate countryfolk in volumes including *Beside the Fire* (1890), *Love Songs of Connacht* (1893), and *The Religious Songs of Connacht* (1906). His general practice in these books was to publish the Irish text, together with a literal prose translation in Anglo-Irish, and a free verse rendering. In 1898 Hyde met Yeats's patroness, Lady Gregory, and collaborated with her and Yeats in writing a series of plays in Irish, beginning with *Casadh an tSugan (The Twisting of the Rope)* (1901), the first Irish play produced in any theatre. Further plays include *The Marriage* (1902) and *The Lost Saint* (1903). Hyde also wrote the first *Literary History of Ireland*, published in 1899.

As president of the Gaelic League from 1893 to 1915, Hyde succeeded in creating a great popular movement, unifying the different factions in Ireland. *Mo Turus go hAmerice* (1937) recalls his successful fund-raising and lecture tour of the United States in 1905–6. Ousted by Sinn Fein revolutionaries in 1915, Hyde distanced himself from politics and concentrated on scholarly work on Irish literature and folklore, and on teaching modern Irish at University College, Dublin. He retired in 1932, but in 1938 was called upon to serve as the first president of Eire, a position he held until 1945. Hyde suffered a stroke in 1940, and died on July 12, 1949.

Personal

One morning Lady Gregory, Dr. Hyde, and myself, wandered through one of the beautiful old gardens. She named over the names of this, that, and the other flower until Hyde said that if she just wrote down the names there was matter for a sonnet ready for Yeats. Yeats was very happy there, and he had just finished a poem on "The Seven Woods of Coole", and he was so pleased with it that he kept murmuring it over and over again, and these lines from it have remained in my memory still:—

> I have heard the pigeons of the Seven Woods
> Make their faint thunder, and the garden bees
> Hum in the lime-tree flowers; and put away
> The unavailing outcries and the old bitterness
> That empty the heart . . .
> I am contented, for I know that Quiet
> Wanders laughing and eating her wild heart
> Among pigeons and bees

Yeats, Hyde, and I used to sit up every night until one or two in the morning, talking, it seems to me, about everything and everybody under the sky of Ireland, but chiefly about the Theatre of which Yeats's mind was full. These were wonderful nights, long nights filled with good talk, Yeats full of plans for the development of the Theatre. The mornings were devoted to work, the afternoons to out-of-doors, and the evenings to the reading of scenarios for plays, the reading of short plays in English by Lady Gregory and in Irish by Hyde. Lady Gregory and Hyde read out to us from time to time their translations of Irish songs and ballads, in the beautiful English of her books and of Hyde's *Love Songs of Connacht*. Yeats and Lady Gregory made a scenario of a play and Hyde spent three afternoons "putting the Irish on it". She has written how one morning she went for a long drive to the sea, leaving Hyde with a bundle of blank paper before him. When she returned in the evening, Dr. Hyde had finished the play and was out shooting wild duck. This play was *The Lost Saint*. Dr. Hyde put the hymn in the play into Irish rhythm the next day while he was watching for wild duck beside the marsh. He read out the play to us in the evening, translating it back into English as he went along, and Lady Gregory has written how "we were all left with a feeling as if some beautiful white blossom had suddenly fallen at our feet".—JOHN QUINN, (1911), cited in Lady Gregory, *Seventy Years: Being the Autobiography of Lady Gregory*, 1974, pp. 379–80

Douglas Hyde was at Coole in the summer of 1899. Lady Gregory, who had learnt Gaelic to satisfy her son's passing desire for a teacher, had founded a branch of the Gaelic League; men began to know the name of the poet whose songs they had sung for years. Lady Gregory and I wanted a Gaelic drama, and I made a scenario for a one-act play founded upon an episode in my *Stories of Red Hanrahan*; I had some hope that my invention, if Hyde would but accept it, might pass into legend as though he were a historical character. In later years Lady Gregory and I gave Hyde other scenarios and I always watched him with astonishment. His ordinary English style is without charm; he explores facts without explaining them, and in the language of the newspapers—Moore compared one of his speeches to frothing porter. His Gaelic, like the dialect of his *Love Songs of Connacht*, written a couple of years earlier, had charm, seemed all spontaneous, all joyous, every speech born out of itself. Had he shared our modern preoccupation with the mystery of life, learnt our modern construction, he might have grown into another and happier Synge. But emotion and imagery came as they would, not as he would; somebody else had to put them together. He had the folk mind as no modern man has had it, its qualities and its defects, and for a few days in the year Lady Gregory and I shared his absorption in that mind. When I wrote verse, five or six lines in two or three laborious hours were a day's work, and I longed for somebody to interrupt me; but he wrote all day, whether in verse or prose, and without apparent effort. Effort was there, but in the unconscious. He had given up verse writing because it affected his lungs or his heart. Lady Gregory kept watch, to draw him from his table after so many hours; the gamekeeper had the boat and the guns ready; there were ducks upon the lake. He wrote in joy and at great speed because emotion brought the appropriate word. Nothing in that language of his was abstract, nothing worn-out; he need not, as must the writer of some language exhausted by modern civilization, reject word after word, cadence after cadence; he had escaped our perpetual, painful, purification.—W. B. YEATS, "Dramatis Personae" (1935), *Autobiographies*, 1955, pp. 438–40

Works

Dr. Hyde's volume of translations, *Love Songs of Connacht*, is one of those rare books in which art and life are so completely blended that praise or blame become well nigh impossible. It is so entirely a fragment of the life of Ireland in the past that if we praise it we but praise Him who made man and woman, love and fear, and if we blame it we but waste our breath upon

the Eternal Adversary who has marred all with incompleteness and imperfection. The men and women who made these love songs were hardly in any sense conscious artists, but merely people very desperately in love, who put their hopes and fears into simple and musical words, or went over and over for their own pleasure the deeds of kindness or the good looks of their sweethearts. One girl praises her lover, who is a tailor, because he tells her such pretty lies, and because he cuts his cloth as prettily as he tells them, and another cannot forget that hers promised her shoes with high heels. Nor is any little incident too slight to be recorded if only it be connected in some way with the sorrow or the hope of the singer. One poor girl remembers how she tossed upon her bed of rushes, and threw the rushes about because of the great heat.

These poems are pieced together by a critical account, which is almost as much a fragment of life as are the poems themselves. Dr. Hyde wrote it first in Gaelic, of that simple kind which the writers of the poems must have thought, and talked, and then translated poems and prose together, and now we have both English and Gaelic side by side. Sheer hope and fear, joy and sorrow, made the poems, and not any mortal man or woman, and the veritable genius of Ireland dictated the quaint and lovely prose. The book is but the fourth chapter of a great work called *The Songs of Connacht*. The preceding chapters are still buried in Irish newspapers. The third chapter was about drinking songs, and the present one begins: "After reading these wild, careless, sporting, airy drinking songs, it is right that a chapter entirely contrary should follow. Not careless and light-hearted alone is the Gaelic nature, there is also beneath the loudest mirth a melancholy spirit, and if they let on (pretend) to be without heed for anything but sport and revelry, there is nothing in it but letting on (pretence). The same man who will today be dancing, sporting, drinking, and shouting, will be soliloquising by himself to-morrow, heavy and sick and sad in his poor lonely little hut, making a croon over departed hopes, lost life, the vanity of this world, and the coming of death. There is for you the Gaelic nature, and that person who would think that they are not the same sort of people who made those loud-tongued, sporting, devil-may-care songs that we have been reading in the last chapter, and who made the truly gentle, smooth, fair, loving poems which we will see in this part, is very much astray. The life of the Gael is so pitiable, so dark and sad and sorrowful, and they are so broken, bruised, and beaten down in their own land and country that their talents and ingenuity find no place for themselves, and no way to let themselves out but in excessive, foolish mirth or in keening and lamentation. We shall see in these poems that follow, more grief and trouble, more melancholy and contrition of heart, than of gaiety or hope. But despite that, it is probably the same men, or the same class of men, who composed the poems which follow and the songs which we have read. We shall not prove that, and we shall not try to prove it, but where is the person who knows the Gaeldom of Erin and will say against (or contradict) us in this? They were men who composed many of the songs in the last chapter, but it is women who made many of the love-songs, and melodious and sorrowful they made them," and in like fashion the critical account flows on, a mountain stream of sweet waters. Here and there is some quaint or potent verse, like a moss-covered stone or jutting angle of rushes. Thus, for instance, lamented some girl long ago. "My heart is as black as a sloe, or as a black coal that would be burnt in a forge, as the sole of a shoe upon white halls, and there is great melancholy over my laugh. My heart is bruised, broken, like ice upon the top of water, as it were a cluster of nuts after their breaking, or a young maiden after her marrying. My love is of the colour of the raspberry on a fine sunny day, of the colour of the darkest heath berries of the mountain; and often has there been a black head upon a bright body. Time it is for me to leave this town. The stone is sharp in it, and the mould is cold; it was in it I got a voice (blame) without riches and a heavy word from the band who backbite. I denounce love; woe is she who gave it to the son of yon woman, who never understood it. My heart in my middle, sure he has left it black, and I do not see him on the street or in any place."

   . . . As for me, I close the book with much sadness. Those poor peasants lived in a beautiful if somewhat inhospitable world, where little had changed since Adam delved and Eve span. Everything was so old that it was steeped in the heart, and every powerful emotion found at once noble types and symbols for its expression. But we—we live in a world of whirling change, where nothing becomes old and sacred, and our powerful emotions, unless we be highly-trained artists, express themselves in vulgar types and symbols. The soul then had but to stretch out its arms to fill them with beauty, but now all manner of heterogeneous ugliness has beset us. A peasant had then but to stand in his own door and think of his sweetheart and of his sorrow, and take from the scene about him and from the common events of his life types and symbols, and behold, if chance was a little kind, he had made a poem to humble generations of the proud. And we—we labour and labour, and spend days over a stanza or a paragraph, and at the end of it have made, likely as not, a mere bundle of phrases. Yet perhaps this very stubborn uncomeliness of life, divorced from hill and field, has made us feel the beauty of these songs in a way the people who made them did not, despite their proverb:

     A tune is more lasting than the song of the birds,
     A word is more lasting than the riches of the world.

We stand outside the wall of Eden and hear the trees talking together within, and their talk is sweet in our ears.—W. B. YEATS, "Old Gaelic Love Songs" (1893), *Uncollected Prose*, Vol. 1, ed. John P. Frayne, 1970, pp. 292–95

As an objective job of literary scholarship, A *Literary History of Ireland* comes off fairly well by present-day standards. Hyde was honest in admitting that pre-Patrician history in Ireland is dependent on accounts given in twelfth- and thirteenth-century manuscripts and that the early history of Ireland is "a mass of pseudo-historic narrative and myth, woven together into an apparently homogenous whole, and all now posing as real history." He was properly guarded in his estimate of any pre-Christian Irish pantheon, suggesting that although it may have been as highly organized as the Scandinavian, Ireland's early and complete conversion to Christianity had meant that only traces of its pagan deities remain. He admitted quickly that Irish genealogies that purport to go back to Adam "must be untrue inventions . . . we grant it." But he also argued that whereas Irish history prior to 300 B.C. is uncertain, the four great race stems converge within reach of the historical period—most importantly, the Eremon stem, which converges in Niall of the Nine Hostages, who came to the throne in 356, and Cairbre of the Liffey, who became High King in 267. He warned that for all their unreliability, the genealogical books *were* kept from the earliest introduction of the art of writing and probably kept with greater accuracy than any other records of the past. He was conservative in assessing the role of the Druids on the grounds that proof is lacking for some of their practices. In a chapter entitled "The Irish Elysium and Belief in Rebirth" he revealed that of sixty folk tales that he had collected "from the lips of the peasantry," roughly five contained allusions to a belief in another world full of life under the water and perhaps four spoke of a life inside the hills. He declared that early Irish skill in metal and jewel-working, gold ornaments, and objects of clay and bronze argues for their seizing on the invention of writing and keeping their annals and genealogies all the more accurately because of the advanced state of their culture. He did a workmanlike job of the puzzle of the three Patricks and the poems and literature ascribed to that saint, although he seemed more comfortable with Columcille, a saint whose historicity is unquestioned and whose own poems Hyde could translate. He surveyed the monastic schools of the sixth and seventh centuries adequately for his time. Looking at the pagan elements in early Irish literature, he called on foreign scholars' opinions to reinforce his belief that the Irish poems and sagas offer a genuine picture of pagan life in Europe "such as we look for in vain elsewhere." He placed great faith in the long Celtic memory as it worked to preserve early tales and legends. The Heroic or Red Branch Cycle to Hyde seemed to deal with the very history of the Milesians, the present Irish race; he wrote, "for the first time we seem at least to find ourselves on historic ground." In a twenty-page chapter on the *Táin* Hyde complained that there is a "great deal of verbiage and piling up [of] rather barren names" but granted that the epic has some well-conceived and well-executed incidents. Altogether Hyde devoted nearly seventy pages to the Red Branch material. . . .

   Hyde repeatedly reminded readers of the *Literary History* of the shattering blows struck against native Irish letters by the English beginning with the invasion of 1169: "that permanent war . . . which almost from its very commencement, *thoroughly arrested Irish development and disintegrated Irish life.*" His case for the steady destruction of all things Irish ranged from indictments of the Ordnance Survey for "Englishing" Irish place names of historic significance to laughing contempt for Trinity's ignorance of all things Irish. He related that when the subject of the Vice-Chancellor's prize in English verse was announced to be "Deirdre" it was found "that the students did not know what the word meant, or what Deirdre was, whether animal, vegetable, or mineral." Looking at his own time and particularly the scene in his native Connacht, Hyde blamed the loss of the language on the apathy of clergy who preached in English, the dislike of the Anglo-Irish gentry for spoken Irish, and the efforts of the National Board of Education to extirpate the national language. His final lament was for the rotting manuscripts that neither children nor adults had respect for, since they were written in a language worth nothing in their society.—GARETH W. DUNLEAVY, "The End of a Ship Is Wreckage," *Douglas Hyde*, 1974, p. 73–77

ERNEST BOYD
From "Douglas Hyde"
Ireland's Literary Renaissance (1916)
1922, pp. 64–79

It will be the duty of the historian of the Gaelic Movement in Ireland to render justice to the achievement of Douglas Hyde, whose life has been devoted to the restoration of the Gaelic language and literature. In a study of the Literary Revival, concerning itself solely with Anglo-Irish literature, there can be no question of even attempting to give adequate consideration to his work. In a sense, Hyde represents a tendency opposed in principle, if not in fact, to the creation of a national literature in the English language. In a famous lecture delivered to the Irish National Literary Society in

Dublin, shortly after its foundation, he pleaded for "the necessity of de-Anglicising Ireland," and his constant purpose has been to effect the object which he defined on that occasion. He has been the organiser of a vast propaganda on behalf of all that is Irish, music, literature, games and customs of every kind. He was careful in 1892 to explain that work of de-Anglicisation was not "a protest against imitating what is best in the English people," but was "to show the folly of neglecting what is Irish, and hastening to adopt, pell-mell, and indiscriminately, everything that is English, simply because it *is* English." Since then, however, his more enthusiastic disciples have swept away these limits, and have championed everything that is Irish, simply because it *is* Irish. Consequently, they incline to view with suspicion the growth of Anglo-Irish literature, on the ground that it is written in an alien language, and has, in some cases, been primarily addressed to the British, rather than the Irish public. Language, it is argued, is the sign and symbol of nationality, and there can be no literature expressive of Irish nationality which is not in the Irish language.

Whether Hyde himself is entirely in agreement with this application of his teaching, it is impossible to say. If we may accept the statements of competent critics, his best work, plays, poems, and fairy tales, has been in Gaelic, while such of it as has been conceived in English is devoted to the history and vindication of the claims of Gaelic literature. Exception must be made of the three original poems published in 1895, together with some verse translations, under the title *The Three Sorrows of Story-telling*. The first of these, "Deirdre," was a prize poem, which obtained the Vice-Chancellor's prize in Dublin University, and possesses all the merits and defects peculiar to that order of composition. The same may be said of the other two stories, "The Children of Lir," and "The Fate of the Children of Tuireann," which were written about the same time. Perhaps the most significant feature of "Deirdre" is that a poem upon an essentially Irish theme should have been presented and found favour in a University which, at that time, was definitely hostile to de-Anglicised Ireland and, in the person of two of its most distinguished professors, had publicly expressed its contempt for the ancient literature of the country. In the same year, however, Hyde published his *Story of Gaelic Literature*, an admirable sketch, which was elaborated and ultimately appeared in 1899 as *The Literary History of Ireland*. This is Hyde's most important original work in English. For the first time a connected and adequate survey had been made of literary evolution of Gaelic Ireland. Hitherto Gaelic literature had only secured a few incidental pages or chapters in the works of such Irish antiquarians as O'Curry, for the necessarily rough and imperfect catalogues of Bishop Nicholson in the early part of the eighteenth century, and of Edward O'Reilly at the beginning of the nineteenth, can hardly be described as histories in the proper sense of the term. Hyde's book was the first of its kind and, apart from its value to the student of Gaelic literature, was a fine piece of propaganda. With such a demonstration of the diversity and importance of the old literature, it was no longer possible to dismiss the claims of the Language Movement. Hyde answered, once and for all, the objection of his more educated opponents that the Irish language did not repay study because it had no literature. *The Literary History of Ireland* placed within the reach of the general public the facts which had previously been vaguely admitted, or denied from hearsay. After its publication very little was heard about the "barbarians" who were supposed to have constituted Gaelic Ireland, and whose literature was alleged to be disgusting or negligible. . . .

In addition to the material derived from the old Gaelic literature, the Revival has found in the folk-lore and folk-songs of the peasantry a valuable deposit of literary ore which was in danger of being lost owing to the disappearance of Gaelic. This vast unwritten literature was cherished solely by the Irish-speaking country folk, and the diminution of the latter threatened it with oblivion. It was natural that Douglas Hyde, having set himself to restore the Gaelic language, should have been keenly sensible of the value of these songs and stories, which contained, as it were, the sparks of the tradition which he was endeavouring to fan into flame. He began at an early date to collect Gaelic folk-lore, and rapidly established a reputation as the foremost authority in this branch of Irish literature. As a folklorist he has exercised a very special influence upon the Literary Revival. Like his first volume of folktales, *Leabhar Sgeuluigheachta*, published in 1889, most of his work has been written in Gaelic, for the force of personal example has been conspicuous in his propaganda on behalf of the Language Movement. In order, however, to reach those less proficient than himself, he adopted in many cases the plan of giving parallel versions, Irish on the one side and the English translation on the other. *Beside the Fire*, the *Love Songs of Connacht* and the *Religious Songs of Connacht* were published in this fashion, and it is these three works, which must directly affect the development of Anglo-Irish literature. This is not the place to consider Hyde's achievement in Gaelic, but his translations in the three volumes referred to have a significance which must command attention in any study of the Literary Revival.

Prior to 1890 various efforts had been made to preserve something of Irish folk-lore, but it was not until the appearance in that year of *Beside the Fire*, that any serious contribution in the English language was made to the subject. As far back as 1825, Crofton Croker had published *Fairy Legends and Traditions of the South of Ireland*, a work whose literary charm has been widely recognised, but whose scientific value is as slight as that of the collections of Kennedy, Lady Wilde and Curtin, which succeeded it. In none of these is it possible to discover the sources from which the stories have been collected, nor can one be certain how far the originals have been followed, and to what extent the groundwork has been elaborated by the authors. The folk-tales suffered in many ways by this treatment. Their origins were lost, and they became dissociated from the soil from which they sprang by the fact that interest inevitably shifted from the stories themselves to the manner and style of their narration. As Hyde pointed out, it was essential that folk-lore should not be divorced from its original expression in language. It is easy, therefore, to understand why his first *Book of Folk Stories (Leabhar Sgeuluigheachta)* should have appeared in Irish, for it is in the old language that the folk-tales and songs are remembered. Except in those districts where English displaced Irish at such an early date that education and reading had not time to thrust themselves between the people and their spoken literature, the Gaelic stories did not pass into the new language. Consequently the rapidly declining population of native Irish speakers constituted the source of Hyde's researches. . . .

Beside the Fire, while it showed the author's preoccupation with the scientific use of Anglo-Irish, did not contain the elements necessary for so complete a transfiguration of this speech as the Literary Revival has witnessed. What was there suggested, and very cautiously outlined, did not wait long for complete realisation. In 1893, *The Love Songs of Connacht* came as a double revelation, first, of the beauties of folk-poetry, and, secondly, of the charm of Gaelicised English. Adopting the same methods as when collecting the prose-tales published three years before, Hyde had obtained from the lips of the Connacht peasantry, and from old manuscripts hitherto neglected, a number of charming folk-songs in danger of being lost. *The Songs of Connacht* originally appeared in serial form in *The Nation*, and later, in *The Weekly Freeman*, the first chapter being published in 1890. There were seven chapters entitled, respectively, "Carolan and His Contemporaries," "Songs in Praise of Women," "Drinking Songs," "Love Songs," "Songs Ascribed to Raftery" and two chapters of "Religious Songs." Of these, only Chapters IV, V, VI and VII were translated and published in book form. A concluding chapter containing "Keenes and Laments" was to have completed the work, but so far it has never been published. This work attaches to that of Sigerson's *Poets and Poetry of Munster*, in that it performs for Connacht the same service as the older work did for Munster. Continuing the method initiated by Sigerson, Hyde attempts in more than half of these translations to reproduce the rhyme and metres of the original Gaelic. His verse renderings are frequently very beautiful, and, although his best poetry has been written in Gaelic, these translations prove that he can use the English language with real skill and delicacy. *The Love Songs of Connacht* were supplemented some years later by *Songs Ascribed to Raftery* in 1903 and in 1906 by *The Religious Songs of Connacht*. These volumes represent a most valuable treasury of folk-poetry, and will rank with the work of Mangan and Sigerson as the repository of the best that could be saved of the old Gaelic tradition while still living. The gathering of these portions of a great heritage was the saving of the still smouldering ashes from which a new flame could be kindled. . . .

The name of Douglas Hyde has naturally been more prominently associated with the Gaelic Movement than with the Literary Revival. As a Gaelic writer he has attained a distinction which considerably enhances the force and value of his propaganda. The Revival, however, must always count him a powerful influence. It has derived strength and support from the collateral effect of Hyde's labours for the restoration of Gaelic, and to his direct collaboration it owes in part, if not entirely, some of its most fortunate achievements. The fundamental importance of the *Songs of Connacht* in the evolution of our contemporary literature has been insufficiently understood by the general public. Once Hyde had set the example, the possibilities of Gaelic-English were realised by the other writers, and greater credit has fallen to the better-known work of his successors. Lady Gregory, notably, employed his method in *Cuchulain of Muirthemne* and *The Book of Saints and Wonders*, with such effect that it is frequently forgotten how O'Grady preceded her by a quarter of a century, in the field of legend, and Hyde by ten years, in the use of Anglo-Irish idiom. It is interesting, therefore, to refer to the testimony of W. B. Yeats, who wrote some fifteen years ago, when Douglas Hyde was helping to create an Irish theatre:

> These plays remind me of my first reading of *The Love Songs of Connacht*. The prose parts of that book were to me, as they were to many others, the coming of a new power into literature. . . . I would have him keep to that English idiom of the Irish-thinking people of the West. . . . It is the only good English spoken by any large number of Irish people to-day, and one must found good literature on a living speech.

If peasant speech has now become an accepted convention of the Irish theatre, it is because the younger dramatists have confined themselves almost exclusively to the writing of peasant plays, both these mutually dependent facts being due

to the prestige conferred upon the *genre* by Synge. His plays removed this speech from all the associations of low comedy and buffoonery which clung to it, and established the dignity and beauty of Anglo-Irish. While he consummated the rehabilitation of the idiom, the process had been definitely inaugurated by Douglas Hyde. *The Love Songs of Connacht* were the constant study of the author of *The Playboy*, whose plays testify, more than those of any other writer, to the influence of Hyde's prose. In thus stimulating the dramatist who was to leave so deep a mark upon the form of the Irish Theatre, Douglas Hyde must be counted an important force in the evolution of our national drama. Without injustice to the labours of W. B. Yeats, it may be said that the success of his efforts would not have been complete but for Synge. Had it not been for Hyde, the latter's most striking achievement might never have been known.

ANGUS ROBERTSON
From "Dr Douglas Hyde"
Children of the Fore-World
1933, pp. 103–9

Until a few years ago I was only in a position to admire Dr Douglas Hyde at a distance. I looked upon him then, and I do now, as a central force in the whole Celtic movement. When I came in personal contact with him that impression was decidedly confirmed. Miss Susan L. Mitchell, in her book on George Moore, introduces the following appropriate and richly deserved encomium: 'We know what Ireland owes to Hyde's fiery spirit, his immense courage, his scholarship, his genius for organization, his sincerity, his eloquence, and the kindness of his heart'. These words carry no suspicion of flattery; they are pertinent to the man and his work. It is not alone Ireland's debt; the area is wider. Literature which he has largely enriched is his province, while the indents of his services are marked with purple and gold in the geography of universal culture.[1]

There is a certain belief—perhaps justified—that all Celts have a 'fiery spirit'. But they are not always credited with using that spirit in righteous causes. Results, however, and the accommodations of history have shown that Dr Hyde's fiery spirit was logical in inception and in the method of its application. He found the Irish language weltering to extinction. As a scholar he realized the condition as a potential loss to literature. As a patriot, fully aware of the servitude of his country to alien bonds, he visualized in its revival a latent instrument for the unification of Ireland. His convictions along those lines were strong—strong in reasoned impulse, strong in resource, and his determination was equal to his conviction. I hope no consideration will ever be permitted to temporize with that view.

Ireland can only retrace and consolidate the spirit of her early cultural achievements through the medium of her native speech—the liquid soulful mother-tongue of saints and scholars.[2] What Ireland once contributed towards the spiritual elevation of mankind Ireland may and can do again. But it must be Ireland, not Ulster and Ireland. Ulster will be wise to read the signs of the Zodiac. The lion and tiger of the circus were but improvised Irishmen. Nevertheless, Irishmen must remove the reproach of pit and gallows in their contacts with other civilizations.

Dr Hyde never suffered from what one might call a disparity of political illusions; judge and jury were in accord with his appeal. No one knew better than he that an armed conflict with Great Britian foredoomed Ireland to privations and misery—with the prospect of self-government prejudiced for an incalculable period. Other circumstances, however, arose which anticipated his calculations; and the birth of Saorstat Eireann followed. He is now in a position of being able to refer to the event as unprecedented in history, by the fact that less than four hundred citizens fell in the struggle for national independence.

Of course there were excesses, deplorable excesses, always have been and will be when a nation resists passive or real tyranny by lethal agencies. Excesses followed upon Wat Tyler and Jack Cade; and there were excesses when King Edward slaughtered the Welsh bards.[3] The struggles of Wallace were not exempt in our Scotland. Barns as well as castles were fired, and English inmates perished in the flames.

I daresay when the news of these happenings reached the ears of self-centred burghers sitting by their ale in London inns, they would denounce the so-called barbarous Scots in some such manner as this: 'Look at those brutal savages in Scotland. We are administering their country with justice; we have prevented them from slitting each other's throats; not perhaps a wise intervention, the more throats slit the better. We have placed the power of law and order in every shire. We have removed our neighbour's landmarks. We have gone farther: to save the rebellious ingrates the burden of kingship, our Royal hammerer destroyed their national records as well as removed all symbols of native sovereignty.[4] What is our thanks?—Our judges are martyred, our garrisons massacred, our governors held to ransom'. But what Caledonian today will condemn the methods of those who led the van towards the independence of Scotland?

I am glad Dr Douglas Hyde was not an active politician. Had he been, the probability is I should never have come across him—at any rate, not on this planet. For in all likelihood he would have met a summary dispatch at the hands of some irresponsible on one or other side of the contending zealots. His simple-heartedness saved him for the benefit of the humanities and spiritual uplift of the Celtic cause. How could we spare the author of *Love Songs of Connacht* for a grey dawn and a firing squad? Then take him at his *Three Sorrows of Story-telling*, which he turned into orthodox English iambics, and you have a key to the 'kindness of heart' alluded to by Miss Mitchell. 'The cold and cruel fate that overtook the Children of Lir

> is the saddest and softest tale
> That ever harper harped, or wordful poet
> With union assonance and fall of tone,
> Marking the marvel of the honey verse
> With lines of long alliterative words,
> And sweet compacted syllables, and feet
> Increasing upon feet, e'er framed in song'.

That is a reflex of Dr Hyde not at his best, but as if preparing a canvas for the larger vista—the carrying of the reader's kindled fancy into a world of mysticism, love, song and the softest music of invisible genii. 'But of enchantments such as Aefi played on the De Danann children we could tell stories to keep you listening many days'. And so he could and

has. . . . The enchantments are in his pen, the beautiful thing is in his soul, charm is in his personality while his ring of sincerity—apprehensive patriotism—silences the sceptic and melts opposition into a warm glow of solid sympathy and admiration. Let us remember for a moment that Dr Douglas Hyde is a Protestant, and that four-fifths of Ireland is Catholic, and it will immediately suggest itself that only genius allied to a magnetic personality could appreciably account for his widespread fruitful influence.

Notes

1. 'Douglas Hyde, the man who drew out of the gutter where we ourselves had flung her the language of our country, and set a crown upon her; who by sheer force of personality created the movement in Ireland for the revival of Gaelic, blowing with a hot enthusiasm on that dying spark of nationalism and recalling it to life. Those who know *The Love Songs of Connacht* will not need to be told that here was the soul of a poet. The movement he blasted out of the rock of Anglo-Irish prejudice is his epic'.—Susan L. Mitchell: *Life of George Moore* (1916).

2. The saturnine Swift is of a different mind respecting the Irish language, when he writes: 'It would be a noble achievement to abolish the Irish language in the kingdom, so far, at least, as to oblige all the natives to speak only English on every occasion of business, in shops, markets, fairs, and other places of dealing; yet I am wholly deceived if this might not be effectively done in less than half an age, and at a very trifling expense; for as such I look upon a tax of six thousand pounds a year, to accomplish so great a work'.— Swift's *Works* (1814), vol. xiii, p. 66.

   In a *History of Dublin* published in London in 1818, it is stated that Irish was still the vernacular language of three millions of people in Ireland.

3. We are told by Froissart that Edward, the Black Prince—the flower of English knighthood—superintended the butchery at Limoges of three thousand unresisting captives, men, women, and children, many of whom vainly kneeled to him for mercy.

   From the period that Adrian IV (Nicholas Breakspeare)—the only Englishman to occupy the papal throne—handed Ireland over to the unscrupulous machinations of Henry Second, is well-nigh 800 years of government enormities unparalleled in history. This note, I am afraid, is induced through the reading of J. Morrison Davidson's—he calls himself *Scottisimus Scotorum*—*The Book of Erin*, which I defy the most complacent anti-Irish, pro-Saxon, or any son of Ashtaroth to go through with a steady pulse.

   'Despotism', says the liberator St Just, 'consists in putting in force against the people a will in opposition to theirs'. 'When legislation', he thunders in another place, 'rivets a chain to the feet of a free citizen, enslaving him in spite of the rights of nature, eternal justice rivets the last links of that chain round the tyrant's neck'. Curran accused the English government of planning the leasing of Ireland to a company of Jews to be administered by tax-gatherers and excisemen 'If I were an Irishman I would be a rebel!' wrote the gallant Sir John Moore while on active service in Ireland. It is said of Lecky's *History of Ireland* that it made a Home Ruler of everyone who read it but the author.

4. 'Our King Edward the First, having claimed the sovereignty of Scotland, made a most miserable havoc of the histories and laws of that kingdom; hoping, that, in a short time, nothing should be found in all that country, but what carried an English name and face'.—Bishop Nicolson, quoted in John Jamieson: *Historical Account of the Culdees* (1811), p. 313.

CHRISTOPHER ISHERWOOD

1904–1986

Christopher William Bradshaw-Isherwood was born into an old and distinguished family in High Lane, Cheshire, on August 26, 1904. After attending Repton School, he entered Corpus Christi College, Cambridge, in 1923, but grew disillusioned with his studies and left without a degree. He worked briefly as a secretary and private tutor, and after publishing his first novel, *All the Conspirators*, in 1928, studied medicine for a year at King's College, London. In 1929 he visited his friend W. H. Auden in Berlin, and, feeling released there from social and sexual inhibitions, returned to live and teach in the German capital from 1930 to 1933. His second novel, *The Memorial*, appeared in 1932, followed in 1935 by *The Last of Mr. Norris*. After 1933 Isherwood traveled in Europe, supporting himself as a journalist, and in 1938 he visited China with Auden; the two writers had already collaborated on several plays, and recorded their travels in *Journey to a War* (1939).

In 1939 Isherwood emigrated to the United States, where he completed *Goodbye to Berlin* (1939) and became a declared pacifist. Settling in California, he began scriptwriting for Hollywood and converted to Vedantism. From 1943 to 1945 he edited the periodical *Vedanta and the West*, and in 1944 produced a translation of the *Bhagavad Gita* with his guru, Swami Prabhavananda; further translations of Hindu texts followed. Another novel, *Prater Violet*, appeared in 1945, and subsequent travels in South America are the basis of *The Condor and the Cows* (1949). Isherwood was elected to the National Institute of Arts and Letters in 1949, and from 1959 to 1967 taught at a number of Californian universities.

In the 1970s Isherwood, whose relationship with Don Bachardy dates back to 1953, became a leading spokesman for the gay liberation movement. His later novels include *Down There on a Visit* (1962) and *A Meeting by the River* (1967). In more recent years he turned increasingly to autobiography, notably in *Christopher and His Kind* (1976) and *My Guru and His Disciple* (1980).

Christopher Isherwood died on January 4, 1986, in Santa Monica, California.

Personal

Who is that funny-looking young man so squat with a top-
    heavy head
A cross between a cavalry major and a rather prim landlady
Sitting there sipping a cigarette?
A brilliant young novelist?
You don't say!

Sitting in the corner of the room at a party, with his hair neatly
    brushed, quite clean
Or lying on the beach in the sun
Just like the rest of the crowd
Just as brown, no, browner
Anonymous, just like us.

Wait a moment

Wait till there's an opening in the conversation, or a chance to
    show off
And you strike like a lobster at a prawn
A roar of laughter. Aha, listen to that
Didn't you fool them beautifully,
Didn't they think you were nobody in particular,
That landlady
That major
Sold again.

With your great grey eyes taking everything in,
And your nicely creased trousers
Pretending to be nobody, to be quite humdrum and harmless
All the time perfectly aware of your powers
You puff-adder
You sham.

And your will, my word!
Don't you love to boss just everybody, everybody
To make all of us dance to your tune
Pied Piper

At an awkward moment.
Turning on your wonderful diplomacy like a fire-hose
Flattering, wheedling, threatening,
Drenching everybody.
Don't you love being ill,
Propped up on pillows, making us all dance attendance.
Do you think we don't see
Fussy old Major
Do you think we don't know what you're thinking
'I'm the cleverest man of the age
The genius behind the scenes, the anonymous dictator
Cardinal Mazarin
Myecroft Holmes
Lawrence of Arabia
Lady Asquith
Always right.'

And if anything goes wrong,
If absolutely the whole universe fails to bow to your command
If there's a mutiny in Neptune
A revolt in one of the farthest nebulae
How you stamp your bright little shoe
How you pout
House-proud old landlady
At times I could shake you
Il y a des complaisances que je déteste.
Yet how beautiful your books are
So observant, so witty, so profound
And how nice you are really
So affectionate, so understanding, so helpful, such wonderful
    company
A brilliant young novelist?
My greatest friend?
Si, Signor.

Standing here in Dover under the cliffs, with dotty England
  behind you
And challenging the provocative sea
With your enormous distinguished nose and your great grey
  eyes
Only 33 and a real diplomat already
Our great ambassador to the mad.

Use your will. We need it.

> —W. H. AUDEN, Poem for Isherwood (1937),
> cited in Brian Finney, *Christopher Isherwood:*
> *A Critical Biography*, 1979, pp. 287–89

We discussed all this at great length, but I don't think we had
ever any serious intention of literally sitting down to write the
book. Quite apart from mere laziness, it hardly seemed
necessary: indeed, it would have spoilt all our pleasure. As long
as *Mortmere* remained unwritten, its alternative possibilities
were infinite; we could continue, every evening, to improvise
fresh situations, different climaxes. We preferred to stick to the
Hynd and Starn stories, and to make utterly fantastic plans for
the edition-de-luxe: it was to be illustrated, we said, with real
oil paintings, brasses, carvings in ivory or wood; fireworks
would explode to emphasize important points in the narrative;
a tiny gramophone sewn into the cover would accompany the
descriptive passages with emotional airs; all the dialogue would
be actually spoken; the different pages would smell appropriately, according to their subject-matter, of grave-clothes,
manure, delicious food, burning hair, chloroform or expensive
scent. All copies would be distributed free. Our friends would
find attached to the last page, a pocket containing banknotes
and jewels; our enemies, on reaching the end of the book,
would be shot dead by a revolver concealed in the binding.

—CHRISTOPHER ISHERWOOD, *Lions and Shadows*, 1938, p. 70

It is difficult to realize that Isherwood is already in his middle
sixties; certainly he gives the sense of having more to produce.
He seems to remain so consistently open to experience, all
experiences, from drugs to the arduous discipline of religious
devotion. One wonders, it is true, what he can possibly be like,
and reads with fascination this description of him by Robert
Craft, composed in 1949:

> Virginia Woolf's likening Isherwood to a jockey is
> perfect. Not the clothes, of course . . . but the
> stature, bantam weight, somewhat too short legs and
> disproportionately, even simianly long arms.
> . . . One easily sees Isherwood, or sees how Mrs.
> Woolf saw him, whether at the pari-mutuel window
> or the furlong post, as an ornament of the track and
> the turf.
>
>   His manner is casual, vagabondish, lovelorn.
> One does not readily imagine him in a fit of anger, or
> behaving precipitately, or enduring extended states of
> great commotion. At moments he might be thinking
> of things beyond and remote, from which the
> conversation brusquely summons him back to earth.
> But he is a listener and observer—he has the
> observer's habit of staring—rather than a prepounder
> and expatiator, and his trance-like eyes will see more
> deeply through, and record more essential matter
> about us than this verbosity of mine is doing about
> him. At the same time, his sense of humor is very
> ready. He maintains a chronic or semipermanent
> smile (a network of small creases about the mouth),
> supplementing it with giggles and an occasional full-
> throttle laugh, during which the tongue lolls. (This
> happens as he tells a story of why he is no longer
> invited to Chaplin's: "Someone had said I had peed

> on the sofa there one night while plastered.") But he
> is not at ease in spite of drollery. Underneath
> . . . are fears, the uppermost of which might well
> be of a musical conversation or high general conver-
> sation about The Arts.

Now, Craft writes in 1968, "of the old circle of California
friends, only Christopher Isherwood survives," and Craft and
Igor Stravinsky dedicate *Retrospectives and Conclusions* to
him.

He is indeed a survivor. His has been a life of extraordinary adventure, accomplishment, and love: he seems to have
meant much to many people. It is, in a sense, ironic that he
does not have a central place in the literature of our time, but
exists peripherally, still spoken of as one of the Auden,
Spender, MacNeice group, or remembered only as the creator
of Sally Bowles. But we must remind ourselves that, after all,
his life and art seem to have worked continuously toward the
extinction of personality, the chief mark of the religion he
adopted in 1940 and has practiced for thirty years. In all the
articles he has written about Vedanta he has mentioned the
symbolic nature of work, the necessity of ignoring its reception,
which is not one's business. If his religion of Vedanta simply
has not worked when incorporated wholesale into his novels (as
in *A Meeting by the River*) it appears to have worked well
enough in his life and therefore indirectly in his art. Certainly
it is essential for anyone who would understand him to realize
that his religious conversion has made him closer to, not more
distant from, the problems of his time.

For he has been, as Angus Wilson has said, close to the
moral center of his generation. "Again and again," Wilson
writes, "Berlin, America, California and the Ghita—he has
stepped over the edge that we have run away from, yet his
literary stature has grown and so, too, has the depth of vision he
offers us. . . . For those of us who cling to our more rational,
provincial and conventional ways," the maddening thing is not
only, as Wilson suggests, that our mixed reaction of jealousy,
admiration, disapproval, and embarrassment is precisely that
"with which we should receive a saint if ever we should meet
one." Maddening, too, is the realization that in failing to
appreciate Isherwood we have failed to understand ourselves.

—CAROLYN HEILBRUN, *Christopher Isherwood*, 1970, pp.
45–46

General

In England the ablest exponents of the colloquial style among
younger writers are Christopher Isherwood and George Orwell,
both left-wing and both, at the present level of current English,
superlatively readable. Here is an experiment:

> The first sound in the mornings was the clumping of
> the mill-girls' clogs down the cobbled street. Earlier
> than that, I suppose, there were factory whistles
> which I was never awake to hear. There were
> generally four of us in the bedroom, and a beastly
> place it was, with that defiled impermanent look of
> rooms that are not serving their rightful purpose.
> One afternoon, early in October, I was invited to
> black coffee at Fritz Wendel's flat. Fritz always
> invited you to "black coffee" with emphasis on the
> black. He was very proud of his coffee. People used
> to say it was the strongest in Berlin. Fritz himself was
> dressed in his usual coffee-party costume—a thick
> white yachting sweater and very light blue yachting
> trousers. You know how it is there early in Havana,
> with the bums still asleep against the walls of the
> buildings; before even the ice wagons come by with
> ice for the bars? Well we came across the square from

the dock to the Pearl of San Francisco to get coffee. My bed was in the right-hand corner on the side nearest the door. There was another bed across the foot of it and jammed hard against it (it had to be in that position to allow the door to open), so that I had to sleep with my legs doubled up; if I straightened them out I kicked the occupant of the other bed in the small of the back. He was an elderly man named Mr. Reilly. He greeted me with his full-lipped luscious smile.

"'Lo, Chris!"

"Hullo, Fritz. How are you?"

"Fine." He bent over the coffee-machine, his sleek black hair unplastering itself from the scalp and falling in richly scented locks over his eyes. "This darn thing doesn't go," he added.

We sat down and one of them came over.

"Well," he said.

"I can't do it," I told him. "I'd like to do it as a favour. But I told you last night I couldn't."

"You can name your own price."

"It isn't that. I can't do it. That's all. How's business?" I asked.

"Lousy and terrible." Fritz grinned richly.

Luckily he had to go to work at five in the morning so I could uncoil my legs and have a couple of hours proper sleep after he was gone.

This passage is formed by adding to the first three sentences of Orwell's *Road to Wigan Pier* the first five sentences of Isherwood's *Sally Bowles* and then the first two sentences of Hemingway's *To Have and Have Not*. I have woven the beginning of the three stories a little further. Next three sentences by Orwell, then dialogue by Isherwood to "added", by Hemingway to "That's all", by Isherwood to "richly" and last sentence by Orwell again. The reader can now go on with whichever book he likes best, Orwell and his bed, Fritz and his coffee, or Harry Morgan and Havana. As Pearsall-Smith says of modern writers: "The diction, the run of phrase of each of them seems quite undistinguishable from that of the others, each of whose pages might have been written by any one of his fellows."

This, then, is the penalty of writing for the masses. As the writer goes out to meet them half-way he is joined by other writers going out to meet them half-way and they merge into the same creature—the talkie journalist, the advertising, lecturing, popular novelist.

The process is complicated by the fact that the masses, whom a cultured writer may generously write for, are at the moment overlapped by the middle-class best-seller-making public and so a venal element is introduced.

According to Gide, a good writer should navigate against the current; the practitioners in the new vernacular are swimming with it; the familiarities of the advertisements in the morning paper, the matey leaders in the *Daily Express*, the blather of the film critics, the wisecracks of newsreel commentators, the know-all autobiographies of political reporters, the thrillers and 'teccies, the personal confessions, the *I was a so-and-so*, and *Storm over such-and-such*, the gossip-writers who play Jesus at twenty-five pounds a week, the straight-from-the-shoulder men, the middlebrow novelists of the shove-halfpenny school, are all swimming with it too. For a moment the canoe of an Orwell or an Isherwood bobs up, then it is hustled away by floating rubbish, and a spate of newspaper pulp. . . .

I have discussed the situation with Isherwood, whom I regard as a hope of English fiction and I have suggested how dangerous that fatal readability of his might become. The first person singular of the German stories, Herr Christoph, or Herr Issyvoo, is the most persuasive of literary salesmen—one moment's reading with him and one is tobogganing through the book, another second and one has bought it—but he is persuasive because he is so insinuatingly bland and anonymous, nothing rouses him, nothing shocks him. While secretly despising us he could not at the same time be more tolerant; his manners are charming and he is somehow on our side against the characters—confidential as, when playing with children, one child older or less animal than the rest, will suddenly attach itself to the grown-ups and discuss its former playmates.

Now for this a price has to be paid; Herr Issyvoo is not a dumb ox, for he is not condemned to the solidarity with his characters and with their background to which Hemingway is bound by his conception of art, but he is much less subtle, intelligent and articulate than he might be. In the little knitted skein from the three books it will be remembered that not only was the language almost identical and the pace the same but the three "I's" of Isherwood, Orwell and Hemingway were also interchangeable; three colourless reporters.

In Isherwood's earlier *The Memorial* however, there is no first person. The hero is a character who is more favoured than the others, and in the Berlin diary *(New Writing*, No. 3) the first person singular, unhampered by the conventions of fiction, at once postulates a higher level of culture and intelligence, and possesses a richer vocabulary. In conversation, Isherwood, while admitting the limitations of the style he had adopted, expressed his belief in construction as the way out of the difficulty. The writer must conform to the language which is understood by the greatest number of people, to the vernacular, but his talent as a novelist will appear in the exactness of his observation, the justice of his situations and in the construction of his book. It is an interesting theory, for construction has for long been the weak point in modern novels. It is the construction that renders outstanding *The Memorial, Passage to India*, and *Cakes and Ale*.

But will the construction, however rigid and faultless, of future books, if they are written in what will by then be an even more impoverished realist vocabulary, contribute enough to set those books apart from the copies made by the ever-growing school of imitators? At present it is impossible to tell; the path is beset by dangers; it is fortunate that Isherwood, who possesses the mastery of form, the imaginative content of a true novelist, is able to see them.—CYRIL CONNOLLY, "Predicament," *Enemies of Promise*, 1938, pp. 70–76

Isherwood has always been fond of playing with variations on his own name—Christoph, Herr Issyvoo, Curaçao Chris, Kreestoffer Ischervood, Christophilos—as if he were repeating his mantra, the holy name given to a disciple at his initiation by his guru. In one form or another his name must appear scores of times in his work. This obsession with his name provides a clue to what, fundamentally, he has been trying to achieve in his books; a further clue being his own casual remark; 'As a matter of fact, of course, my work is all part of an autobiography . . .'

George in *A Single Man*, looking into the bathroom mirror before shaving, sees not so much a face as the expression of a predicament; and in each of his books Isherwood has tried to give expression to his own personal predicament at a given moment of time. In his fiction, the two travel books—even the Ramakrishna biography—his object, explicit or implicit, has been to find an answer to the question: Who am I? His books are the result of a search for personal identity and should be seen as a complex, composite autobiography, a life's work-in-progress.

Although he has received little serious critical attention, he possesses to a remarkable degree the faculty of engaging the affection of his readers, of getting his personality across to them. The announcement of each new book is the occasion for pleasurable anticipation. Never a writer to repeat himself, it would be rash to forecast what he will choose to write in the future, but the occasional pieces which have appeared over the years in magazines and symposia are well worth collecting.

In a much-quoted passage from *Lions and Shadows* he contrasts the natures of the Truly Strong Man and the Truly Weak Man:

> 'The truly strong man', calm, balanced, aware of his strength, sits drinking quietly in the bar; it is not necessary for him to try and prove to himself that he is not afraid, by joining the foreign Legion, seeking out the most dangerous wild animals in the remotest tropical jungles, leaving his comfortable home in a snowstorm to climb the impossible glacier. In other words, the Test exists only for the Truly Weak Man: no matter whether he passes it or whether he fails, he cannot alter his essential nature. The Truly Strong Man travels straight across the broad America of normal life, taking always the direct, reasonable route. But 'America' is just what the truly weak man, the neurotic hero, dreads. And so, with immense daring, with an infinitely greater expenditure of nervous energy, money, time, physical and mental resources, he prefers to attempt the huge northern circuit, the laborious, terrible north-west passage, avoiding life; and his end, if he does not turn back, is to be lost for ever in the blizzard and the ice.

Isherwood's work records an attempt to make the huge northern circuit, avoiding the broad America of normal life. He has never lost the sense of the 'two sides', of the Enemy plotting day and night against 'our side'. He has chosen as his subject the underworld 'down there', the private hells of the truly weak, the police-hating, the rejected. Writing about the world from the viewpoint of the Outsider, he enables us to see a little more clearly the nature of our own, the human, predicament. In this he resembles Auden's ideal Novelist:

> For, to achieve his lightest wish, he must
> Become the whole of boredom, subject to
> Vulgar complaints like love, among the Just
> Be just, among the Filthy filthy too,
> And in his own weak person, if he can,
> Must suffer dully all the wrongs of Man.

> —JOHN WHITEHEAD, "Christophananda: Isherwood at Sixty," *Lon*, July 1965, pp. 99–100

. . . ⟨I⟩n talking or writing about Isherwood, one has the uncomfortable feeling that something not quite possible to say remains to be said; the element of charm is elusive. Born in the year Chekhov died, Isherwood resembles him in curious ways, and in more than being a fellow writer who once studied medicine: The warmth is implicit but not easily available—detachment gets in the way; the fusion of the subjective and the objective is original; and the lie is temperamentally the greatest sin in the moral register. Chekhov's voyage to Sakhalin Island bears a resemblance, not in kind but in motive, to Isherwood's trips to China and South America, and Chekhov's letters to Isherwood's autobiographical writing. In Isherwood's work, a magic potion of history and invention, the voice is clear, and, no matter how many times we hear it, it always seems to be speaking for the first time.—HOWARD MOSS, "Christopher Isherwood: Man and Work," *NYTBR*, June 3, 1979, p. 43

Works

Those who know Mr. Isherwood only as the part-author of *The Ascent of F6* will be agreeably surprised by the quality of his autobiography; those who know him only as the author of *Mr. Norris Changes Trains*, slightly disappointed; but all may pardonably be perplexed that he should be at pains to excavate the roots of a career which can hardly be in its full leaf. Of recent years several young men, headed by Mr. Beverley Nichols, have written autobiographies, moved by the desire to record anecdotes of their notable contemporaries while they are still fresh in their minds and still marketable. Mr. Isherwood has not attempted this. The characters of his story are shrouded in a pseudonymity which, for the present reviewer at any rate, is impenetrable. Who is the dapper medical student, the Don Juan of Holland Park Rink, who is now a fashionable novelist? Who the imaginative schoolmaster who, it is ironically recorded, found "a formula which would transform" his "private fancies and amusing freaks and bogies . . . not hidden in the mysterious emblems of Dürer or the prophetic utterances of Blake . . . but quite clearly set down . . . in the pages of Lenin and Marx"? The reader may ask in vain, for the answer is not of importance. The book is exclusively about Mr. Isherwood; it is written to explain how he became a novelist. The thesis—and the author, if no one else, is entitled to regard it as important—is that once Mr. Isherwood was a prig suffering from persecution mania. For relief in this disorder the author and his similarly afflicted chum discovered a variety of fanciful evasions; these comprise the bulk of the book; no biographer of the Strachey school was ever more ruthless in diagnosing affectation, pretension, humbug and secret fear in his subject than is Mr. Isherwood in his earlier self; indeed he seems to take such relish in the exposure that the reader may at moments doubt whether the transformation has been complete. Has Mr. Isherwood found his "formula"? The diction of the psychoanalyst still hangs about the narrative like exhaust-gas in a country lane. For example, the book is called *Lions and Shadows*, the title of an earlier, discarded novel. This story of a boy who was prevented by ill-health from going to a public school was symptomatic of an irrational interest in school life which consumed Mr. Isherwood during his days at Cambridge. A psychoanalyst has told him—and he appears to attach some value to the suggestion—that this obsession arose through his subconscious disappointment at having missed military service: "The Censor" conveniently substituted School for War and motorbike for gunfire in Isherwood's mind. It would be an impertinence in the case of a more reticent writer, but Mr. Isherwood, who has exposed so much of his subconsious for sale, cannot complain if a more prosaic suggestion is made. Is it not more plausible that he was missing family life? He appears to have been an only child brought up in a home where nothing excited his imagination; his friends at school and at the University took the places of brothers and sisters but did so inadequately. The particular weaknesses which so much upset Mr. Isherwood's adolescence may be traced in a milder form in almost everyone who has had a lonely nursery.

There is a laudable freedom from stylishness about Mr. Isherwood's way of writing which now and then degenerates into the use of words like "sufficient" and "alcohol." The book is readable and, though now ashamed of them, he is able to communicate some of the charm of his undergraduate intimacies. The reviewer may have given the impression that this is a vain book; it is not. Mr. Isherwood clearly is not, like so many women novelists, concerned with the importance of himself or his writing, competitively, as against rivals. It is simply that he has the naivety to pursue in public the wholly personal researches which occupied others, at his age, in private. It is fair to hope that, when he has "found his formula," this *Lions and Shadows* will embarrass him as much as its predecessor.—EVELYN WAUGH, "Author in Search of a Formula," *Spec*, March 25, 1938, p. 538

Mr. Isherwood's diary (*Journey to a War*) covers the spring of 1938, and is for the most part in the form of a day-to-day record. He and Mr. Auden travelled from Hong-kong to Canton, thence to Hankow and Chengchow, where the railway branches East and West to Suchow and Sian; here they visited the North battle-line; thence they returned to Shanghai, visiting the South front on their way. It is needless to say that their journey involved many inconveniences and some danger; at one stage they fell in with Mr. Peter Fleming, and with him evacuated Meiki a few hours before the Japanese moved in. There are inevitably a few passages of the kind which begin: "My feet now utterly collapsed," but the majority of the pages deal with sleeping-cars, mission-stations, consulates and universities. They travelled in a sensible way, accepting the comforts that were offered. These comforts have now become tolerably familiar to English readers; we have already shared the kindly domestic life that flourishes in the missions among bombs and bandits; we know that the papists will give you a drink, and the adventists will not; we have, vicariously, fumbled for adequate courtesies to exchange with Chinese officials.

There is only one portrait in Mr. Isherwood's collection that does not recall a familiar type; that is the host of the Journey's End Hotel, Mr. Charleton, and for the few pages of his appearance the narrative suddenly comes to life, and one is reminded that Mr. Isherwood is not only the companion of Mr. Auden, but the creator of Mr. Norris and Miss Bowles. Not that his work ever falls below a high literary standard. It is admirable. The style is austerely respectable; not only does he seldom use a *cliché*, he never seems consciously to avoid one; a distinction due to a correct habit of thought. Anyone of decent education can revise his work finding alternatives for his *clichés*; a good writer is free from this drudgery; he thinks in other terms. Mr. Isherwood writes a smooth and accurate kind of demotic language which is adequate for his needs; he never goes butterfly-hunting for a fine phrase. It is no fault of his technique that *Journey to a War* is rather flat; he is relating a flat experience, for he is far too individual an artist to be a satisfactory reporter. The essence of a journalist is enthusiasm; news must be something which excites him, not merely something he believes will excite someone else. Mr. Isherwood—all honour to him for it—has no news sense. In particular, he is interested in people for other reasons than their notoriety. The quality which makes Americans and colonials excel in news-reporting is the ease with which they are impressed by fame. Mr. Isherwood met nearly all the public characters in his district; he felt it his duty as a war correspondent to be interested in them. But they were bores—or rather the kind of contact a foreign journalist establishes with a public character is boring—and he is too honest a writer to disguise the fact. Nowhere in China did he seem to find the particular kind of stimulus that his writing requires.—EVELYN WAUGH, "Mr. Isherwood and Friend," *Spec*, March 24, 1939, pp. 496–98

Christopher Isherwood is principally known in America as a collaborator with W. H. Auden in several satirical plays. Only one of his novels has been published here, *The Last of Mr. Norris*, and this did not attract much attention. Mr. Isherwood

has remained the least known of that group of young English writers which includes Auden, Spender, MacNeice and Lewis.

This new book (*Goodbye to Berlin*) puts him clearly before us, and we see that any previous impression based on his work with Auden was bound to be misleading. Mr. Isherwood is not a poet, and his gifts are of a totally different kind from those of the other members of the group. He does not come out very well in these plays, because they demand of him a kind of generalized fantasy for which his mind is too classical. His real field is social observation; and in this field it would not be too much to say that he is already, on a small scale, a master.

Goodbye to Berlin is a chronicle—a sort of journal which expands into short stories—of ordinary life in Berlin just before the advent of the Nazis. (*The Last of Mr. Norris* is a part of the same series and ought to be read with the later book.) You see the working class, the underworld, the well-to-do Jews, the miscellaneous inmates of a cheap boarding house. Mr. Isherwood, unlike most Englishmen abroad, has studied the life of the people from the bottom instead of from the top, and with an eye singularly free for an Englishman from national or social bias.

This eye of Mr. Isherwood's is accurate, lucid, and cool; and it is a faculty which brings its own antidote to the hopelessness and horror he describes. His theme in *Mr. Norris* was the decay and degradation of the culture of upper-class Europe; yet he managed to be effective where the ordinary Marxist cartoon of the bourgeois esthete fails, precisely by presenting Mr. Norris as a figure of high comedy. Mr. Norris is damned but he is human. Let us not be hysterical about him: the artist must neither weep nor enter. Really to *see* Mr. Norris is to put him outside oneself and yet to leave him in the world of men. So in *Goodbye to Berlin*—which does not contain, however, any creation so brilliant as Mr. Norris—"Sally Bowles" is the story of a cabaret singer who fails to make good in Berlin because she is lacking in those careerist instincts to which the future in Germany belongs; "The Nowaks" is a story of the collapse of the morale of the German working class; "The Landauers" is a story of the doom of the Jews. Yet the writer has turned upon all these miseries a light which interpenetrates them completely and shows everything in daylight outlines, everything in proper proportion; a just and humane comprehension which, remaining unmuddied by the nightmares of the frightened, the darkness of the minds of the dying, never gives way to sentimentality or melodrama, even of the grim revolutionary brand. To have done this is in itself to have scored a kind of victory at a moment when such victories count even more than they always do.

Christopher Isherwood's prose is a perfect medium for his purpose. It has the "transparency" which the Russians praise in Pushkin. The sentences all get you somewhere without your noticing that you are reading them; the similes always have point without ever obtruding themselves before the object. You seem to look right through Isherwood and to see what he sees.—EDMUND WILSON, "Isherwood's Lucid Eye," *NR*, May 17, 1939, p. 51

Mr Isherwood's creative dilemma is an excruciating one. He wants to demonstrate that hell, like love, is not hereafter; it is a portable void that exists in time. But can a novelist properly deal with a state of alienation? His job is to record the multiplicity of the world and even perhaps seem to rejoice in it. Mr Isherwood's solution is to see the multiplicity as a set of disguises; a viable fictional aim is the stripping off of these to show the one great tired face. Chrissie, Herr Issyvoo, Bradshaw—all these have been allomorphs of a recording eye, though the novelist's trick—despite the 'I am a camera' disclaimer—was to flash the illusion of a genuine identity. In

Down There on a Visit trickery becomes irony. 'Down there' is 'down here', and we cannot visit where we already are. The circumference is crammed with characters; sink a shaft from each, though, and you arrive at a common centre—the hell of isolation, universal and single.

In *A Single Man* Mr Isherwood concentrates openly on this hell and calls on the unities of time and space to help hold the lamp. The rich variety of the world shrinks to the freeway and the supermarket. Here is a day in the life of George, a middle-aged Englishman who lectures at a Californian university. He lives alone, since Jim, whom he loved, is dead. Jim meant the whole of life, symbolized in the small menagerie they had, now dispersed. The bridge that connects George with his two-car bar-and-barbecue neighbours is sagging. Mr Strunk, who stands for all of them, says George is *queer*. Mrs Strunk, more charitable, a reader of popular psychology, says, in effect: 'Here we have a misfit, debarred for ever from the best things of life, to be pitied, not blamed'.

But George's aloneness doesn't go far enough. Nor does the fact that he belongs (as the Jews and Negroes and Commies belong) to a minority necessarily ennoble him. At the end of his lecture on *After Many a Summer* he tells his students that persecution makes the minorities nastier, hating not only the majority but the other minorities. 'Do you think it makes people nasty to be loved? You know it doesn't! Then why should it make them nice to be loathed?' The minorities put on protective, apotropaic clothing, and it is Mr Isherwood's grimly humorous task to strip George naked. He sits on the john after breakfast and carries his bared buttocks to the ringing telephone. In the gym, where he goes for his daily work-out, he finds comfort, a sense of community, in the common stripped condition: the pot belly and the athlete's muscles enter a democracy rather than an agape. At night he swims naked with one of his students, Kenny. Kenny puts him to bed, drunk, in clean pyjamas, but he wakes to throw them off and, the alcohol itching in his groin, masturbate. He masturbates to the image of 'the fierce hot animal play' of two students he has seen earlier on the tennis court. 'George hovers above them, watching; then he begins passing in and out of their writhing, panting bodies. He is either. He is both at once'.

Even now the nakedness is not complete. After the metaphorical death of the orgasm, the sham death of sleep, comes the true, but hypothetical, death of the body. This trilogy of deaths is the final ritual of stripping. Isherwood has told his entire story in the present tense, which lends itself to hypothesis. The day itself is a ritual covering an emptiness. Jim is dead and cannot be replaced. Charlotte, another British expatriate, offers herself, but George doesn't want a sister; Kenny, an Alcibiades with towel-chlamys slipping from his shoulder, flirts at offering himself, but George doesn't want a son. The hell of isolation can accept no palliatives.

What sounds like an intense book is, as we must expect from Isherwood, tense only in its economy. The language makes no big gestures, and some of the most telling effects are produced by ellipsis. But, as in *The World in the Evening* and *Down There on a Visit*, one sometimes has a feeling that one is being deliberately put at one's ease: Quakerism may embarrass, and so may homosexuality; let us make no protestations; let us neither raise nor lower our voices. Not that I think the homosexuality of this novel is one of its main issues: the love for dead Jim is the love for dead anyone; the particular loneliness may serve as an emblem for the loneliness of all single men, those smallest of minorities. And yet, since much of Isherwood's reputation rests on his skill at finding a shorthand for rendering the external world, and since no

observer of that world can really be a camera, we sometimes find our taste assaulted. When Kenny's blanket slips, we are told: 'At this moment he is utterly, dangerously charming'. He is not. Isherwood sometimes forgets to suffer dully the wrongs of which *all* men are capable. His job is to probe at the cavity which sleeps, unsensed, in even the most comfortable member of the majority. In other words, we don't want a limited hell. But that we so rarely stand outside and twitch our noses at a man who is George, and not a George who is man, is a testimony to Isherwood's undiminished brilliance as a novelist.—ANTHONY BURGESS, "Why, This Is Hell," *LT*, Oct. 1, 1964, p. 514

Isherwood's most recent novel, A *Meeting by the River* (1967), is a failure, an attempt to use insufficiently digested material gathered on a visit to a monastery in India. Unable to find the proper narrative technique, as in *A Single Man*, Isherwood falls back on letters which are unsuccessful on even the most superficial level: in an age of telephone calls and jet flights, it is simply improbable that the two brothers in the book would write, for the few days they are together, as compulsively as Clarissa Harlowe. The brother who is about to take his final vows as a monk falls back, sinfully, upon a diary to enable us to learn what we must know. The other brother, a worldly publisher stopping over on his way to Japan for a meeting that could certainly have been more conveniently held in another place at another time, is married and in love with a boy. We see the effect these two have on one another, chiefly the effect the monk has on his worldly brother. Again, the trouble is with sainthood: Isherwood can beautifully represent the charming, lying, ultimately life-enhancing, married, boy-loving publisher. But the connections and repercussions between the two men are insufficiently dramatized. Isherwood might have made a documentary, a sort of travel book, of this material; a novel is impossible, not least because the setting is so exotic as to become invisible. There is a mother (who worries about sanitation and is carefully lied to by her sons), a wife, and two little girls, but all the female characters are offstage, and the reader cannot avoid the conviction that the life of the novel should have taken place in their presence.—CAROLYN HEILBRUN, *Christopher Isherwood*, 1970, p. 44

In *Ramakrishna and His Disciples*, a biography of the 19th-century Indian saint, Christopher Isherwood makes a distinction between two religious approaches: discrimination and devotion. Discrimination eschews the loving worship of deities and concentrates instead on a more disciplined meditation on the unity that underlies experience. Devotion, by contrast, is more relaxed, more human, more homespun; as Isherwood puts it, "Devotion comes more naturally to the great majority of mankind. . . . For most of us it is the easier and safer path, because discrimination demands a most powerful will and strict austerity, and its occupational risk is pride."

My Guru and His Disciple is a contemporary work of devotional literature, but not in the dry, hagiographic sense. Rather, it is a sweetly modest and honest portrait of Isherwood's spiritual instructor, Swami Prabhavananda, the Hindu priest who guided Isherwood for some 30 years. It is also a book about the often amusing and sometimes painful counterpoint between worldliness and holiness in Isherwood's own life. Sexual sprees, all-night drinking bouts, a fast car ride with Greta Garbo, script-writing conferences at M-G-M, intellectual sparring sessions with Bertolt Brecht alternated with nights of fasting at the Vedanta Center, a six-month period of celibacy and sobriety and the pious drudgery of translating (in collaboration with the Swami) the *Bhagavad-Gita*. Seldom has a single man been endowed with such strong drives toward both sensuality and spirituality, abandon and discipline; out of the passionate dialectic between these drives, *My Guru and His Disciple* has been written.

This is a book uniquely devoid of pretension, either literary or personal—as though Isherwood at 75 has finally achieved the dissolution of egotism that is the goal of Vedanta, the philosophy of the ancient Sanskrit texts, the Vedas. The method of the book is to introduce terse diary entries from long ago into more ruminative commentary written now; this bifocal approach allows Isherwood to see both close and far and to spot his own vanity or good-heartedness through either the lens of the past or the present. Like all truly honest people, he is as ready to praise as to blame himself.

What emerges is a record of a religious adventure that would have delighted Kierkegaard, for Isherwood rejects conventional piety—all the humdrum apparatus of worship—in favor of a direct, even jaunty appreciation of how preposterous, certainly precarious, spirituality can be today. No other writer I'm aware of has so accurately rendered what it would be like to sit down one day on the floor to meditate—to be a clever, upper-class Englishman, a socialist and a skeptic, a handsome party-boy, a celebrated novelist who sits down and begins to meditate for the very first time. A few of us, I suppose, have had highly colored fantasies of abandoning our lives and entering a Zen or Trappist monastery, but our daydreams seldom get beyond the dramatic renunciation scene and the frozen *tableau vivant* of the praying monk or nun on the rice mat or prie-dieu. What Isherwood has detailed in precise stages are his four decades of actually trying to put this dream into action.

In 1939 Isherwood emigrated from England and settled in Los Angeles, where he worked as a film writer and continued to turn out novels (those he discusses in this memoir are *Down There on a Visit* and *A Meeting by the River*). Los Angeles during the war years, of course, was the artistic and intellectual capital of the world thanks to such expatriates as Mann, Stravinsky, Schönberg, Brecht and Adorno. Through two of his brilliant fellow expatriates, Aldous Huxley and Gerald Heard, Isherwood became acquainted with Swami Prabhavananda, a priest who had been sent by his monastery in India to Los Angeles as a missionary. At first their relationship was tentative, but over the years it became a true father-son bond. The quality of his guru's love—undemanding and never varying—was what became most useful to Isherwood. As he writes: "I personally am a devotee first and a Vedantist second. I flatter myself that I can discriminate—bowing down to the Eternal which is sometimes manifest to me in Swami, yet feeling perfectly at ease with him, most of the time, on an ordinary human basis. My religion is almost entirely what I glimpse of Swami's spiritual experience."

Isherwood's devotion to his teacher, however, never obscures his vision of the Swami's faults and foibles—his chain-smoking, his occasional laxness about monastic discipline, his fiery Indian nationalism and his moments of preening over his famous disciples. But even these shortcomings sometimes seem to be glimpses of the playful, childlike, even irresponsible nature of divinity—the boy Khrishna sporting in the river with his maidens.

At times I found this book too enamored of its own plain style; although a seeker after wisdom may free himself of the senses, the writer mustn't. As Sartre once said, "In the eyes of God, Who cuts through appearances and goes beyond them, there is no novel, no art, for art thrives on appearances." Similarly, I sometimes longed for Isherwood even in this work of nonfiction to describe his characters and settings more fully.

On another level, I wanted Isherwood to relate his religion to his politics. He has certainly been active throughout his life in various progressive movements from socialism to pacifism and gay liberation, but I kept wondering how he reconciled such activities with his other-worldly beliefs. India itself, with its sanctity and its suffering, seems a very symbol of this contradiction.

Nevertheless, I am grateful to this book for its candor and sincerity. In these pages Isherwood has reinvented the spirit of devotion for the modern reader. If I had to propose a candidate for canonization, Isherwood—wry, self-conscious, scrupulously honest—would get my vote.—EDMUND WHITE, "A Sensual Man with a Spiritual Quest," *NYTBR*, June 1, 1980, p. 9

JOHN LEHMANN
From "Refitting the Novel"
New Writing in Europe
1940, pp. 47–55

The experience which Spender and Auden received, at an impressionable age, of the conditions of life and the political struggle in Central Europe strongly influenced the development of their art. The same experience had an equally great influence on Christopher Isherwood, whose work many critics have held to offer the greatest promise for the future of our imaginative literature among all the younger novelists. Isherwood has only written five books, and it was not until his third novel was published in 1935, *Mr. Norris Changes Trains*, that a wider public than that interested in experimental "vanguard" literature began to see how gifted and original an author had appeared upon the scene. *Mr. Norris Changes Trains* was the first of a series of works which had pre-Hitler Berlin as their background. *The Nowaks*, by general consent one of the first long short-stories that have been written since the last war, followed it in the first number of *New Writing* in the autumn of 1936; *Sally Bowles* appeared as a booklet by itself in 1937; *A Berlin Diary* and *The Landauers* in later numbers of *New Writing*; and in 1939 all these pieces were collected together and published with two others as a more or less consecutive narrative under the title of *Goodbye to Berlin*. Isherwood's original idea, as he explains himself in the preface, was to write one long novel, a panorama of Berlin life in the five years which preceded the Nazis' seizure of power, to be called *The Lost*. After Isherwood had left Germany in 1933, this idea was finally abandoned and the material was broken up; *Mr. Norris* absorbed the main bulk of it, but any one who reads *Goodbye to Berlin* at the same time will catch glimpses of the bigger work which never materialised.

One cannot help being disappointed at this failure; but each of these fragments is nevertheless complete in itself, and taken together they still form a most impressive achievement. Before considering them in detail, however, I must go back to Isherwood's earlier novels, *All the Conspirators* and *The Memorial*. When they first came out, these books were little read, though the latter received high praise from several of the more intelligent reviewers; it was only after the success of the Berlin stories that a sort of posthumous glow of fame began to be directed on to them. That this process repeats itself again and again in the history of literary reputations is cold comfort for young writers struggling at the moment under the icy wind of the critics' and the public's indifference.

All the Conspirators is in any case not the sort of book with which a writer goes straight to "the heart of the public." It is the book of a young man who is stunting; he finds he is clever enough to do all sorts of rather surprising tricks with his machine, loops the loop recklessly and just misses the top of the grandstand as he hurtles down at the crowd in an almost perpendicular dive. In writing, however, unlike aeronautics, it is not the crowd but only the few with a real passion for literary experiment who can understand these stunts. Isherwood himself has admirably described some of its weaknesses in *Lions and Shadows:*

> I had improved it I hoped. What Chalmers called 'stage directions' ('he said,' 'she answered,' 'he smiled,' 'they both laughed') had been cut down to a minimum—indeed, it was now very nearly impossible to guess which of the characters was supposed to be speaking: and there were several 'thought-stream' passages in the fashionable neo-Joyce manner which yielded nothing, in obscurity, to the work of the master himself.

But in spite of all this, in spite of the artificiality of the book and the rather meagre interest of the theme, certain qualities were already in evidence which were to develop into the unique gifts of the mature writer. The dialogue, to begin with, is speedy, colloquially natural and trim; Isherwood had digested his Hemingway well. There are also passages which show an extraordinary humour of the fantastic, reappearing in *Mr. Norris* and *Sally Bowles* and some of the plays written in collaboration with Auden, a sort of high-speed clowning which is very rare in the modern novel, rare indeed anywhere except in revue and cabaret of the cleverest sort. And finally there are flashes of exciting psychological intuition, quite beyond the range of the average first novel. It is interesting to note, in this connection, that a theme which bobs up again and again in the later work is already present, even dominating: the struggle between the sensitive, rather neurotic young man and his home, his mother, for emancipation. *All the Conspirators* is an excellent study of the moment in a middle-class young man's life, when he feels he must break away or die.

To read the first few pages of *The Memorial* after *All the Conspirators* is to see at once that Isherwood has learnt a lot about style in the interval, though neither his dialogue nor his descriptive passages have the precision and memorableness they were to acquire in the Berlin stories. In this second book, Isherwood gives a hint of something it would have been difficult to guess from the first: that he is capable of developing into a great tragic writer. He describes the origins of the book amusingly enough in *Lions and Shadows:*

> It was to be about war: not the War itself, but the effect of the idea of 'War' on my generation. . . . I would tell the story of a family; its births and deaths, ups and downs, marriages, feuds and love affairs. . . . No more drawing-room comedies for me. I was out to write an epic; a potted epic; an epic disguised as a drawing-room comedy.

Rather too grand a plan, one might be forgiven for thinking, for a young novelist's second attempt. But the astonishing thing is, how nearly Isherwood succeeds. The book is short, rather less than seventy thousand words; and yet one is left at the end with the impression of something very close to epic. As one reads he compels one to feel, with steadily growing intensity, that the end of an epoch is at hand, that the War left an immense wound in the body of English society which is incurable for the generation which experienced it. He never says so in so many words, because he is too good an artist, though he puts it briefly into the mouth of a trivial character at the very end of the last scene; but episodes are carefully chosen to give the effect of frustration and restless

dissatisfaction; everywhere the ghost of the past is lurking near. There is often a curious similarity of feeling with Auden's first book of poems in 1930, a fact which is illuminated by the description in *Lions and Shadows* of their very close contact at the time.

The Memorial is an uneven book; the latter part is much more skilfully managed than the early scenes; there is too little "flow," the characters, particularly in the topsy-turvy time-scheme Isherwood has adopted, are confusing; too much action has to be carried by internal monologue, and the balance between the monologue, the descriptive passages and the dialogue is unsatisfactory. There is again some excellent psychological observation, but here and there one cannot help feeling that certain groups of people are imperfectly observed and digested. All these faults disappear in the next book, *Mr. Norris Changes Trains,* and the desire to write simply, avoiding the ornate and obscure, with a vocabulary as close to the colloquial as possible, is now completely fulfilled; and the sense of the wider social background is deeper and more perfectly expressed. It is impossible, however, to consider *Mr. Norris* by itself; it only falls into perspective when viewed with *Goodbye to Berlin* as part of the one greater, albeit incomplete, design.

The Lost is not merely remarkable from the artistic point of view; it has a claim to be considered one of the few successful solutions in the whole literature produced by the movement I am considering, of the problem of reconciling the claims of the artist and the claims of the moralist. And by "moralist" I mean here one who is aware of, and in the deepest layers of his nature condemns, social injustice and the phenomena of social decay, and sees at the same time that there are forces emerging in the pattern of history to challenge them. Christopher Isherwood never allowed himself in his prose works to be swept away by the impetus of the movement into letting propaganda get the upper hand of art; but the *implication* of his work is revolutionary, as for instance the Russian nineteenth-century novelist Turgenev's work was, and acts on the imagination in a way entirely beyond the scope of the writer who is thinking of politics, or some political party's line, first, and art second. This may sound strange to those who from reading *Mr. Norris* and *Sally Bowles* have received the impression that he is essentially a witty and improper writer who cares only for his comedy effects. Isherwood's love of absurdity may get the better of him from time to time, but these works are really serious, even tragic, and only the strength of the Puritan tradition in our literature can account for their being so misunderstood.

Isherwood was one of the first prose artists of his generation to receive the full impact of Europe as the Fascist tidal wave began to roll over it, and one of the very few who neither turned their backs on the catastrophe to write of other subjects nor were deflected by it—and one must remember the enormous pressure of political persuasion that was at work at the time—into more obviously propagandist and party activities. Instead, he absorbed the whole scene into his imagination, without a single hiccup of indigestion that one can detect. *The Lost* displays a wide panorama of the life of Berlin, from the houses of the rich middle-classes and the night-clubs they frequented to the lodging-houses of students and tarts and the poorest working-class tenements, from glimpses of parties in the gardens of wealthy suburban villas to demonstrations of Social-Democratic and Communist workers' organisations and outbreaks of Nazi violence in the streets. And this panorama is not a vivid but shapeless congestion of impressions, as is so often the result when a young author sets out with bold schemes to describe life from every side, but well-planned with every part conceived in relation to the whole,—to the underlying master-theme of social illness and approaching social conflict. The peculiar individuality of Isherwood as an artist is, however, shown in his choice of chief characters in such a scheme. He avoids revolutionaries, even average "men of good will"—though "I" in the whole series represents just such an average man with a more than averagely sharp eye—who eventually see through and learn to despise the shams of the world's workings. He almost invariably prefers, on the contrary, to take eccentric and fantastic characters as his central pivots, the extreme products of the anarchy and pathological condition of modern society; he delightedly drops them into his collecting bottle like rare "sports" among butterflies or beetles and studies them with a care that is curiously tender while it is merciless. Such is Mr. Norris himself, the nervous adventurer with an Edwardian fastidiousness of manners and culture and irregular sexual tastes, who has dabbled in every kind of crooked business where he could pick up a living and who ends by dabbling in political and military spying. Such are Sally Bowles, the cabaret artiste who abandons a respectable middle-class home in England to lead a demi-mondaine existence in Berlin, and is always being absurdly duped in her hunt for lovers who can bring her notoriety or riches; Otto, the good-looking son of proletarian parents, whom conceit, unemployment, and success in the night-clubs have corrupted into an irresponsible dream-existence; Baron Pregnitz with his minor political ambitions and secret fantasy obsession of an island world where he is for ever leader of a heroic band of adolescents; and many other characters from every layer of Berlin life.

It is true that Isherwood is often so entertained by his own creations that he seems in the end to fall in love with them and let the broader pattern go hang. The end of *Mr. Norris* is pure comedy; and this is bound to come as a shock to any one who was even remotely connected with the fateful crisis in the history of Europe which forms the near background of the book, and in which Isherwood has made it perfectly clear that his central character has played an entirely ignoble part. The emotions prepared in such a reader are indignation, horror and pity; and yet one is forced to read the last few pages shaking with laughter. While this is a source of disappointment to one part of Isherwood's public, I cannot help suspecting that it is the secret of his popularity with the other. The corrective, however, is given by the cumulative effect when *Mr. Norris* is read in conjunction with *Goodbye to Berlin*; and in general when he is dealing with his "cases" he takes the greatest care to relate them to the general stream of events and the social background. His "time-notes" are as deliberate, but much more effective because much less pretentious and more artistically woven into the narrative, than Dos Passos's staccato interpolations of the "camera eye" and other tricks. I take an example at random from the middle of *Mr. Norris*:

> Berlin was in a state of civil war. Hate exploded suddenly, without warning, out of nowhere; at street corners, in restaurants, cinemas, dance-halls, swimming-baths; at midnight, after breakfast, in the middle of the afternoon. Knives were whipped out, blows were dealt with spiked rings, beer-mugs, chair-legs or leaded clubs; bullets slashed the advertisements on the poster-columns, rebounded from the iron roofs of latrines. In the middle of a crowded street a young man would be attacked, stripped, thrashed and left bleeding on the pavement; in fifteen seconds it was all over and the assailants had disappeared. Otto got a gash over the eye with a razor in a battle on a fair-ground near the Cöpernicker-strasse. The doctor put in three stitches and he was in

hospital for a week. . . . And morning after morning, all over the immense, damp, dreary town and the packing-case colonies of huts in the suburb allotments, young men were waking up to another workless empty day to be spent as they could best contrive; selling bootlaces, begging, playing draughts in the hall of the Labour Exchange, hanging about urinals, opening the doors of cars, helping with crates in the markets, gossiping, lounging, stealing, overhearing racing tips, sharing stumps of cigarette-ends picked up in the gutter, singing folk-songs for groschen in courtyards and between stations in the carriages of the Underground Railway. After the New Year, the snow fell, but did not lie; there was no money to be earned by sweeping it away. The shopkeepers rang all coins on the counter for fear of forgers. Frl. Schroeder's astrologer foretold the end of the world. 'Listen,' said Fritz Wendel, between sips of a cocktail in the bar of the Eden Hotel, 'I give a damn if this country goes Communist. What I mean, we'd have to alter our ideas a bit. Hell, who cares?'

Another example will show how tactfully he relates the "I" of his stories to the Berlin scene. He goes to a working-class meeting to hear Mr. Norris speak in defence of the Chinese masses:

> What struck me most was the fixed attention of the upturned rows of faces; faces of the Berlin working-class, pale and prematurely lined, often haggard and ascetic, like the heads of scholars, with thin, fair hair brushed back from their broad foreheads. They had not come here to see each other or to be seen, or even to fulfil a social duty. They were attentive but not passive. They were not spectators. They participated, with a curious, restrained passion, in the speech made by the red-haired man. He spoke for them, he made their thoughts articulate. They were listening to their own collective voice. At intervals they applauded it, with sudden, spontaneous violence. Their passion, their strength of purpose elated me. I stood outside it. One day, perhaps, I should be with it, but never of it. At present I just sat there, a half-hearted renegade from my own class, my feeling muddled by anarchism talked at Cambridge, by slogans from the confirmation service, by the tunes the band played when father's regiment marched to the railway station, seventeen years ago. And the little man finished his speech and went back to his place at the table amidst thunders of clapping.

This is brilliantly observed, and entirely convincing. The same can be said of the final example I have chosen, which also shows Isherwood's skill in the handling of even the smallest dramatic scenes, and the deep humanism which informs all his work. "I" is staying with the working-class family of the Nowaks, in their tenement, and the father begins to hold forth after dinner:

> 'What I say is—' Herr Nowak put down his knife and fork and wiped his moustaches carefully on the back of his hand: 'we're all equal as God made us. You're as good as me. I'm as good as you. A Frenchman's as good as a German. You understand what I mean?'
>
> 'Take the war, now—' Herr Nowak pushed back his chair from the table: 'One day I was in a wood. All alone, you understand. Just walking through the wood by myself, as I might be walking down the street. . . . And suddenly—there before me, stood a Frenchman. Just as if he'd sprung out of

the earth. He was no further away from me than you are now.' Snatching up the breadknife from the table, he held it before him, in a posture of defence, like a bayonet. He glared at me from beneath his bushy eyebrows, re-living the scene: 'There we stand. We look at each other. That Frenchman was as pale as death. Suddenly he cries: "Don't shoot me!" Just like that.' Herr Nowak clasped his hands in a piteous gesture of entreaty. The breadknife was in the way now: he put it down on the table. '"Don't shoot me! I have five children"' . . . Well, I look at him and he looks at me. Then I say: "Ami." (That means friend.) And then we shake hands.' Herr Nowak took my hand in both of his and pressed it with great emotion. 'And then we begin to walk away from each other— backwards; I didn't want him to shoot me in the back.' Still glaring in front of him, Herr Nowak began cautiously retreating backwards, step by step, until he collided violently with the sideboard.

These extracts can only give a taste of the high qualifications which Christopher Isherwood possesses simply as an artist. His prose is easy and flowing, not a word is wasted, and everything is seen in precise and daylight-clear shape. He has an extraordinary flair for dialogue, for creating a character almost entirely by the way in which he is made to speak, though the added touches of description with their fresh and unexpected choice of words and metaphors are never superfluous. It is little wonder that he has always had a weakness for films, and has been employed in Hollywood as well as English studios on both scenario and directing work. It is perhaps not altogether fanciful to see in the development of his art a steady approach to "film quality": read *The Nowaks* with this in mind, and you will see how easy it is to imagine it on the screen almost without alteration.

Since the publication of *Goodbye to Berlin*, Isherwood has written no more novels; one can only hope that he will soon find his inspiration again, as those—and they are many—who believe that he is one of the very few young writers who have it in them to equal, in new ways, the masterpieces of the past in English fiction, feel that as yet he has only given a brilliant opening display.

There is one work, however, published in 1939, which is of particular interest as an indication of both the strength and the weakness of Isherwood as a writer. This is *Journey to a War*, an account of a visit to China and the Chinese front against the Japanese invaders by Isherwood and Auden in collaboration. In the plays which these two wrote together—to which I shall turn in my next chapter—the division of authorship is not at all easy to determine; but in *Journey to a War* it is quite clear, though not explicitly stated, that Isherwood is entirely responsible for the travel-diary sections. They show all the wit, the love of the absurd, the sharp observation and telling descriptive notes of both scenes and persons which distinguished *The Lost*, and there are moments when Isherwood gets very moving effects with even greater economy and restraint than before. They are a further, and more direct, tribute to the popular cause than any of the Berlin pieces. But they pose a crucial question: will Isherwood's talents eventually be canalised into a less exacting art than the writing of novels and stories? The convergence of journalism, or reportage, and fiction towards one another in the movement of the 'thirties, is one of its most striking features. . . . Isherwood is an excellent example of this tendency at its best, but its dangers are great and it would be a disaster if he were to become one of its victims. The diary-form, as he showed in the two sections of *A Berlin Diary*, suits him perfectly, and plot has not been his strongest point. And

yet, when one considers his real successes in construction, such as *The Nowaks*, one begins to see how much will be lost if he concentrates in the future on the development of diary notes.

V. S. PRITCHETT
"Books in General"
New Statesman, August 23, 1952, pp. 213–14

Looking forward from the novels of the Twenties to those of today, the change that strikes one is that, after two major evasions, the novelist has become a human being again. One is always hoping that this will turn out to be the large advantage it ought to be. Back in the Twenties, it used to be quite correctly said, the subject of the important novels was the writer writing. If he used the first person singular, he could no longer be Mr. Maugham's man of the world and the possibility of becoming Emile Brontë's housekeeper, Dickens's growing boy or Wells's ever expanding ego, was out of the question. The "I" had become a specialist in sensibility who saw himself judged only by other writers and for him, the supreme significance of the world was that of a work of art. One hardly needs to point out that this is the whole subject of Proust, the Gide of the *Les Faux Monnayeurs*, and of Virginia Woolf; and a good defence of the attitude is that, after 1914, it was the most exacting available, and literature must always take the most exacting course.

The break in the Thirties, indeed, occurred because life had again become more exacting than writing; but after all the attacks on "the ivory tower" during the Thirties, one's impression is that the structure stood up pretty well. It merely changed occupiers. The aesthete gave place to the reporter, to a figure who was really no more "in life" than the aesthete had been. The reporter merely *seemed* more committed because he got around. He had put the ivory tower on wheels. Human beings were significant only when they were news: in Isherwood's *Goodbye to Berlin* one of his stupid pupils asks him why he is living in Germany and he astounds her by replying that the German situation is the most interesting one in Europe at that time.

A valuable and, I think, disconcerting book could be written about the reporter in the literature of the last twenty years. I hope that the scores of students who take this as a subject for their Ph.D.'s will notice that the reporter has an assumed personality. He is probably first cousin to the gangster rising to power by the expert use of sawn-off feelings. There is the streak of Hamlet in him: the guilt in being on the spot but outside the struggle. There is the relief of having a rudimentary or ventriloqual personality only. There is the excitement of a new technique, for the reporter of the Thirties pretended to be a camera. I quote again from the opening of Isherwood's *Goodbye to Berlin*:

> I am a camera with its shutter open, quite passive recording not thinking. Recording the man shaving at the window opposite and the woman in the kimono washing her hair. Some day, all this will have to be developed, carefully printed and fixed.

In Isherwood one sees the interaction of the reporter and the artist at its most delicate.

Goodbye to Berlin, *Mr. Norris* and *The Memorial* have just been republished and we can see that if the camera was passive, the invisible cameraman was not. One can say, in a general way, I think, of all the talents of the Thirties that they floated in the air, and that Isherwood's sketches and novels, if we except *The Memorial*, seem to be hanging in an alarming void. They are suspended there from the pathos of Isherwood's personal loneliness. The loneliness of his characters—which is really his own imposed upon them—is the quality that makes them distinctive to him as a writer. His characters are tragic, squalid, comical *because* he is cut off from them. In this respect his compassion is the measure of his fundamental indifference to them, and this accounts for a frightening quality in his intimacy, his friendliness and his sudden laughter as a writer. Though they may flutter away on their mysterious compulsions, Frl. Schroeder, Mr. Norris, the exquisite Sally Bowles live only as they divert *him* or the Nowaks as they move his indignation and pity. They were to have formed part of a long episodic novel called *The Lost* and one can guess that the personal tie turned out to be too weak for the sustaining of a long book.

But if we never get at what Mr. Norris and the horrible Schmidt were like together, or what it was like to have an affair with Sally Bowles, we do get a brilliant collection of guesses. The shutter of the camera moves fast. From the spurt of Mr. Norris's match in the train to the rage of Frau Nowak in her kitchen, we see life in the continuous, delicate surprise of its instants. We see as fast as the writer's eye blinks and Isherwood was wonderfully adroit in placing himself with unobtrusive impudence in the best positions for seeing. He is, perhaps, too shamelessly the stooge in Mr. Norris, and I think, a little too knowing and pointed; on the other hand, even here, the cameraman has variety and surprise in his own character. It is a considerable moment in the history of first person narrations when Chris arrives at the drunken party and does not recognise his own state until he sees in a mirror that he has just walked through the streets wearing a false nose. Chris and Issyvoo are witty light creations, perfect in their touch, and they make the poker faces, the putty mugs of what Mr. Cyril Connolly called the "you-men" look stodgy and opaque.

A writer is driven by his own devils and it is idle for the critic to moralise about him; but if we turn back from Isherwood's German writing to the earlier novel *The Memorial* we see how more soundly based, from a novelist's point of view, it really is. Here, in fact, is the true novelist, young, full and already mature. His personal loneliness is populated by his people, and he has the aptitude (which distinguishes the novelist from other writers) for showing people living in one another's lives.

> But Maurice, as if he knew of this jealousy, always turned its edge by making reference, in front of Gerald and Tommy, to times when he and Eric had been together and the Ramsbothams had not been there. So that, if Gerald talked too much about the famous car they were building, in which they hoped to do a hundred, and which greatly interested Maurice, Maurice would nevertheless keep chipping in with "you remember last Friday, Eric, when you said so and so."

The Memorial gains from the minutely gathered unity of the English scene. We are to see the twilight of a rich family, the break up of a social order between 1919 and 1929, and although the underlying inference is political, this view is not pressed to the vicious point of the single explanation. These "bourgeois in decay" are stronger than they look because they inherit the old human acceptance of the inevitability of change. Lily and Mary, the pietist of the past and the post-war rebel, have the diverse resources of their native independence. Whatever else may be said of them, they win the self-sustaining victories of tenacity. When Lily hands on the Jacobean silver, she is performing a satisfying act of faith. And then, at different

dates in the story of these characters, we are able to compare their present with their future. Compassion is aroused because we know all, from their point of view and from the point of view of others. It rises because the judgment on people must, perforce, be endless.

Sex has been played low in this novel, possibly because of the difficulty of writing about homosexual love in 1932, but marriage and heterosexual love are played down also. This is not a disadvantage; for we are back in the centre of English fiction: the iron of sociability, the relationships of persons not souls. The tortures of the young, indeed the tortures of the older people, are not those of the passions, but come largely from the question of what constitutes good behaviour. Have I been selfish? Was I vile to Mummy? Do they like me? Will you stop being a bad influence? Was I just when I thought this of him or her? Is Lily being difficult, or is Mary insensitive? The middle-class preoccupation with considerateness is seen to be at the heart of the great worries of middle-class society. All this to-ing and fro-ing of conscience is animated by the most astonishingly fluid novelist, a kind of invisible man, who enters all his characters unnoticed and becomes like some grave imp inside them. Again, the personal loneliness of the writer is assimilated—as it is *not* in the expatriate works—by the peculiar loneliness natural to English life, where so much has to be privately reckoned, where there is so often a pause before the embarrassed kiss. Isherwood travelled best when he stood still as a novelist and found countries in his people. The long central episode in this book, which slowly unfolds the family drive to the War Memorial and its dedication, is in the English tradition at its sober and ironical best; and the general picture of the middling generation who have lost sons or fortune in the war and the new, car-mad generation who have succeeded them, comes closer to the reality of that time, than the angry visual satire of the writers of the previous decade. His youths messing about at home on empty Sundays or crashing cars on the Newmarket road, are various and distinguishable. Isherwood somehow manages to catch their speech and their follies and regards them without censoriousness. An ancient mind, clear and resilient in judgment, accompanies the light heart. He is equipped with the gift of a lively and premature old age.

The Memorial is a recognisable England of that decade and not an England inherited from literature. It gains indeed from its sense of news and the fading of news, which is nevertheless never allowed to overlie the permanent interests of the novelist. He escapes the Coward touch: I mean that he escapes the aggressive fallacy, the weakness for including irrelevant material in an attempt to be "fair." The dogmatism of the later Thirties has not falsified the picture. Of course, the book has not real shape. It is simply five or six adroitly arranged slices of life, an episodic novel with the episodes artfully placed in the wrong order. The only major weakness is an attempt to give a sort of unity to the book by the final *liaison de convenance* between the homosexual ex-war hero and a middle-aged woman painter, but the couple are shadowy—and the woman is as agreeable and unconvincing as any nice woman one does not know very well.

These two are granted a tenuous satisfaction, which is given to none of the others, because they have decided to be eccentric and are outside. They are making a virtue of being lost. They are thought of as being people who have "faced up," whereas—and this is a dogma of the Thirties—those who have not noticed the necessity of "facing up" become known as "shady." Mr. Norris is the comic king of shadiness. He is forgiven because he is criminally shady. We are moving towards that phase of contemporary literature in which the novelist looks for more sinners to forgive. The more difficult task, of course, is to endure and forgive the righteous. In the midst of these lapsing figures stands the neat, yet personally unruffled instrument, the camera eye of Mr. Isherwood. The instrument that was to be used by others mainly for events he has applied more cunningly, more subtly than any of his contemporaries, to the private lives of human beings. It was a remarkable adaptation of means and when we look back upon *The Memorial* we see what a novelist was lost when "the situation" elsewhere always seemed to him "more interesting" than the one at home.

ANGUS WILSON
"The New and the Old Isherwood"
Encounter, August 1954, pp. 62–68

" 'I 'll even forgive myself. As a matter of fact, I just have. Do you know something, Jane,' I said, as I emptied my glass, 'I really do forgive myself, from the bottom of my heart.' " So speaks Stephen, the central character of Christopher Isherwood's new novel, *The World in the Evening*, and on these words the book ends. Forgiveness of oneself is, of course, a spiritual state highly to be desired; but for those who accept the idea of personal guilt—and Mr. Isherwood belongs firmly to the generation of the guilt-acceptors—the deliberate statement of self-forgiving is an act of high seriousness. The slightest hint of triviality either in the conviction of sin or in the belief in its atonement is liable to produce an inelegant impression upon those who are asked to witness the confession. It is an embarrassment which I feel sure Mr. Isherwood must often have shared with his more discriminating contemporaries at those widely publicised intimate "sharings" of the Oxford Group in the early thirties. It was not so much the sincerity of the groupers that was doubted as their inadequacy to support the spiritual responsibilities they had assumed. It is exactly some such chasm between high intention and inadequate capacity that will, I am afraid, disturb Mr. Isherwood's admirers who have waited so long for this novel, and will, no doubt, delight his critics who have waited equally long to say "I told you so."

This failure in central purpose is particularly sad because *The World in the Evening* shows no decline in Mr. Isherwood's powers; indeed, in the understanding of certain human relationships and, above all, in technical control both of range and of organisation, it shows, I think, a very considerable advance. Nevertheless he has tried to stick out his spiritual neck a great deal further than it will stretch, and, by so doing, he has, I'm afraid, "asked for it." Mr. Isherwood's attainments entitle him to serious criticism. It is, therefore, I think necessary to examine this central failure in his work, where with a lesser writer one could merely expatiate on the incidental merits of the work and disregard the total intention. It is my purpose, then, in this article to begin with the brickbats and to end with the bouquets which Mr. Isherwood's extraordinary powers of entertainment and high technical achievement must always command.

Mr. Isherwood, of course, may argue that he is no longer writing of "Herr Issyvoo" or "William Bradshaw," that his new hero Stephen is the creature of his own imagination, not a convenient cover name for autobiographical reporting. To the extent that his new novel has, I imagine, drawn more deeply upon his invention than his earlier work, this is true. Nevertheless it is impossible not to equate his hero's spiritual odyssey with his own. Mr. Isherwood's conversion is, no doubt,

of vital importance to him, but *The World in the Evening* fails to communicate its urgency. A great deal of the novel is highly entertaining, much of it is percipient, some of it very moving, but it is not important at the level to which it aspires. This does not seem to me in the least degree surprising. Nothing in Mr. Isherwood's earlier work suggested that either his intellectual powers or his emotional strength would sustain a novel of the kind that could satisfy Dr. Leavis' criteria. To succeed in the portrayal of a man's progress from an undeveloped state of emotional parasitism to the inner conviction of a total and satisfying meaning in life that allows him to forgive even himself would require, surely, either the tornado of Dostoevsky's emotions sweeping good and evil alike before it, or the enveloping calm of Tolstoy. No one in his senses could have supposed that Mr. Isherwood could create an Alyosha, Myshkin, or a Bezukhov. Unfortunately, Stephen is a peculiarly feeble vehicle for the expression of spiritual truth. There is, of course, nothing unacceptable in presenting the spiritual progress of a feeble personality, even if it be only from minus six to minus four, but the author must be fully aware of the smallness of his compass.

Mr. Isherwood is, I suspect, only a very little conscious of the triviality of Stephen's story. He is afraid on occasion, I think, that he may seem to have lost his sense of proportion, but this is no real conviction, it is rather the embarrassment of any convert when he appears before his former friends in his new role. Whatever happens it must not seem that grace has robbed him of his sense of humour, finding God must at all costs be shown to be tremendous fun. Of course, Mr. Isherwood is too perceptive, too sophisticated not to see how unbecoming this archness is in other godly folk. We are given many examples of the irritating little jokes which the Pennsylvania Quakers employ to humanise their rectitude. Nevertheless, when he is ill at ease with his own theme, he uses exactly the same tactic, though the archness and charm are more worldly, more *New Yorker* than those of his Quaker characters. The most distressing example of this comes with his hero's final confession of self-forgiveness which I have already quoted. This episode is either the crux of the whole theme or it is nothing; yet the author is careful to present it at the end of a conversation between Stephen and his wife when both are "high" after a few cocktails. It is true that all we have learnt of Stephen tells us that he might not be able to say such a thing unless he were drunk, but Mr. Isherwood somehow contrives to present this circumstance as charmingly excusing the confession, when clearly it either needs no excuse or it should not have been made at all.

The truth is that Mr. Isherwood is not much at ease with "goodness" and "good people." In his earliest novel, *All the Conspirators*, the conventionally "good" were the targets of an irony which owed a lot to the ethics of Forster. They were the ununderstanding, the blundering, the philistine, the deadening forces in life. Conventional morality in the hands of the hero's mother and her elderly City friend was simply a weapon to deny the young self-expression and to treat themselves to the pleasures of self-inflicted martyrdom. This deadly, selfish, conventional goodness which Isherwood understood very well and ridiculed most entertainingly is continued in the character of Lily in *The Memorial*—once again the hero's mother. But in that novel, which owed so much to Virginia Woolf, we get his first presentation of a less conventional goodness which we are meant to respect. The presentation of the character of Mary shows the influence of Mrs. Woolf—"Coming down the gas-lit mews with three beer bottles under her arm, Mary experienced, as often before, a pang of love for her home. My dear little house, she thought." Mary is a more middle class, consciously Bohemian kind of woman than Mrs. Ramsay would have cared for, but the mould is similar. The most striking feature of the character, however—and this Mrs. Woolf would have found very alien—is the self-consciously jolly, leg-pulling sort of way in which she protects her emotions, her "goodness" from the world. "More work for the troops," she says, "Be little heroes won't you, and help your old Ma?" or, dealing with a heartbroken girl, "'Ave a drop of Mother's curse?" Mary of *The Memorial* is really the last "good" character in Mr. Isherwood's work until *The World in the Evening*. She is an Understander, an Acceptor—"Had Mary ever, during her whole life, had any really absurd, old-fashioned, stupid prejudice? Had she ever hated anybody?" In all the Berlin stories that followed, the Understanding and Accepting were done by Mr. Isherwood himself, and very brilliantly, if a little self-consciously, he did them. With his new novel, "good" characters appear again and once more they hide their emotions in the same rather embarrassing "chaffing" way. It is as though the author had communicated his own unease at the spectacle of "goodness" to his characters. There has always been a certain preoccupation with the ethics of his public school days about Mr. Isherwood's work, the first two novels are thick with it and it even obtrudes into so unlikely a situation as the story about Rügen Island. Its last imprint is left, I think, in this sort of self-deprecating facetiousness in which his "good" characters talk. It is a version of the traditional "chaffing" and "rotting" with which the cricket-captain hero of the school disguises—and I fear, all too often advertises—his merits. I do not think that Mr. Isherwood has ever quite lost his idolatry of that school hero.

There is one outstanding example of this sort of embarrassing facetious "goodness" in *The World in the Evening*. Among the characters who are on the side of the angels are two "queers"—a doctor and his painter boy-friend. They are not sure possessors of the inner light, but, nevertheless, the honesty of their relationship and their troubled but persistent fight to come to terms with life are among the most important factors that aid the hero, Stephen, in his own awakening. From their first appearance, the tone of their relationship is set in this awful, self-consciously humorous key. "'Bob's one of the Dog People' [says his lover]. 'Even when he talks English, he has a thick Airedale accent. Sometimes, he does nothing but growl for days on end.' 'Yeah,' said Bob, grinning. 'When Charles and I met, I bit him and he got rabies. He's been crazy like this ever since.'" And again, "'I paint with my paw,' said Bob 'in various styles. I'm the canine Cézanne, the pooch Picasso, the mongrel Matisse.' 'Sure, you are,' Charles patted Bob's shoulder, as though he were trying to sooth an hysterical patient. 'And the tyke Toulouse-Lautrec.'" People in love do, of course, have the habit of facetious back-chatting, though the more discriminating naturally avoid imposing it on others. To say that all those who do not have the good taste, the consideration, to keep such exchanges for their hours of privacy are inferior people would be snobbish and untrue. But Mr. Isherwood puts forward this awful dialogue—a proper subject for satire—as a badge of their "goodness." The reason, I think, for this extraordinary lapse of judgement is a curious confusion in his mind between "goodness" and "cosiness." Wherever the good are found in life, he seems to say, there you can be cosy.

This is the more peculiar because, in general, his puritan conscience will not allow him to accept the more simple, less self-conscious forms of happiness. There is a passage in *The World in the Evening* when Stephen and his first wife Elizabeth are on their honeymoon in Paris. I have seldom read a more successful account of unselfconscious, transcendent human happiness than this. Of course, happiness of this kind does not usually endure. Mr. Isherwood, however, is almost savage in his assertion of its insecurity. I find it difficult to understand how anyone, who can describe so exactly a genuine if impermanent happiness of this kind, is able at the same time to treat respectfully the awful substitute cosiness I have described above.

The answer lies partly, perhaps, in Mr. Isherwood's general disregard for intellectual competence. The intellect plays almost no part in his scheme. There is an awful passage in the book when the doctor, Charles, tells Stephen his philosophy of life. It revolves around the idea of a high sort of "camp" which is the mark of true artistic greatness. "High Camp is the emotional basis of the Ballet, for example, and of course of Baroque Art. You see, true High Camp always has an underlying seriousness. You can't camp about something you don't take seriously. You're not making fun of it; you're making fun out of it. You're expressing what's serious to you in terms of fun and artifice and elegance. Baroque is largely camp about religion. The Ballet is camp about love." He goes on to give a list of the great campers—Mozart, El Greco, Dostoevsky, Freud; but not Beethoven, Flaubert, or Rembrandt. This sort of arrant nonsense should never be treated seriously, but I fear it is not only Charles and Stephen who do so, but Isherwood himself. It is a nice, cosy substitute for thought.

The element of cosiness is very important in Mr. Isherwood's work. It is a somewhat smug emotion. It is already there, as I have said, in the character of Mary in *The Memorial*. It is there obliquely in *Mr. Norris*, *Sally Bowles*, and *The Nowaks*. Sally Bowles is quite a nice bitch, Arthur Norris a rather less nice scoundrel, and Otto Nowak a good-looking boy who is hardly nice at all. Mr. Isherwood is fully alive to all this and he presents them brilliantly. Nevertheless there is ultimately a certain false cosiness even in these Berlin stories. We are left with the feeling, not that these characters have been sentimentalised, but that somehow, because Herr Issyvoo is so understanding a man, we have been privileged to get on to cosy terms with people whom we would otherwise have found worthless. There is nothing against liking bad people as I am sure Isherwood does. Still less against finding the inevitable elements of good in them. But there is something a bit disturbingly smug about doing so in a cosy, happy family way. It is this cosiness which throws out the balance of *The World in the Evening*. It is at its worst in the character of Sarah, who is the true vessel of spiritual light in the book. Sarah is the adopted aunt of the hero, who, after the death of his parents, made a home for him. She is an elderly Quakeress full of good works, wise platitudes, everyday little jokes. As such, she is adequately drawn and no more. As such, she might have been left. But Mr. Isherwood had to make her the source of inner light, a source taken for granted by the hero and then suddenly realised as the central spring of his regeneration. This element of sanctity hidden by everyday Marthaism entirely fails to convince. Let me quote the moment at which her sanctity reveals itself. It is told to Stephen by Gerda, Sarah's German refugee protégée, whose husband Peter is in the hands of the Nazis. "'We are sewing to make clothes,' says Gerda, 'and suddenly I cannot go on. I stop. I am crying so much that I cannot see the needle. . . . And, Stephen, do you know what was so strange? All the time that I am crying, Sarah is sitting, and still sewing, and she says nothing. . . . At first I think that she has not noticed. . . . And then I know that she knows—all what I am feeling, everything. She is with me so close, although she has not moved. It is as if she holds my hands. . . . The room gets very still. . . . And it was then that I knew that it is all right . . . even if Peter is not safe, even if the worst happens to him and to me. . . . Sarah made me know it. . . . Then she looks up and says—you will never guess—she says, "I think I will make us some hot chocolate." That was all.'" It just does not do, I think. The note of cosiness, of the homely vessel of spiritual depths is overdone. It is, in fact, in the two principal characters chosen to expound the theme that *The World in the Evening* breaks down. Sarah, the true saint, may be as homely as you like; Stephen, the saint in travail, may be feeble and ineffectual; but we must be convinced that beneath the deceptive outward symbols there lies an inward grace of wisdom and strength, and we are not.

I have chosen to criticise at length the central failure of Mr. Isherwood's new novel, not only because his previous work gives him a right to serious criticism, but because I think that in all other respects *The World in the Evening* is an important advance on his previous novels. He has pretended to too much, but if he had not done so, I doubt if he could have made such a step forward. It is often the case when a good writer enters a new phase of creation. If Mr. Isherwood is not deterred by the criticism he will certainly receive, *The World in the Evening* points, I believe, to future novels with all the excellence of his old work and a considerably increased range.

After the criticism I have made, a reader may well ask in what the advance in Mr. Isherwood's work lies. First, I should like to mention one of the greatest qualities shown in *The World in the Evening*. If the author pretends to too much spiritually, he is admirably aware of his experiential limitations. This, I am sure, is a great strength in a writer. For Isherwood the important experiences happened before 1939 and he uses that period to illustrate his present position. Many critics at the moment—and I am among them—are anxious to see the contemporary scene exploited more in the contemporary novel. But that pious wish should surely not destroy our capacity for appreciating novels which satisfactorily exploit the immediate past. Many great writers have written solely out of their early experience. Mr. Isherwood has settled in post-war America, but the core of his imaginative life is still in pre-war Europe and nothing but praise should go to him for recognising this.

Now for the extraordinary advances I think he has made. I said earlier that they lay in two fields—the understanding of personal relationships and the extension of technical range. The two things are, of course, tied together. The growth of his understanding of people has demanded a corresponding growth of technique, and wonderfully, I think, he has responded to the demand.

Let me deal first with the increase of imaginative range. Mr. Isherwood has always had a powerful sense of place and time, of exact situation and the unspoken implications of such a situation. In the new novel he encompasses literary London of the late twenties, a young man's Paris of the same period, Bavaria with Nazism in the wings, Austria of the nineteen-thirties' intellectual pleasure-seeker, Mediterranean lotus land with the Spanish War offstage, and Hollywood when the War was still not America's affair. This is a very wide range and he never goes wrong. Ultimately, however, Mr. Isherwood is even more a novelist of character than of place. In *The World in the Evening* there are two major characters who seem to me more deeply felt and more truly realised than anything he has done previously: they are the two wives of Stephen—Elizabeth and Jane. The relation between Stephen and these two women is

the first serious attempt of Mr. Isherwood to explore the complex patterns of emotional love. The love-hate relationships of mothers and sons were skilfully, if rather one-sidedly, treated in his first two novels. The pathos and absurdity of homosexual obsession with heterosexual boys or men is well drawn in Edward in *The Memorial* or in the Rügen Island story, but any reciprocal sexual relationship has always been treated sketchily up to now. The success, therefore, of the analysis of Stephen's relationship with his wives, the sympathy and clarity with which these are analysed, is a great triumph for the author. Not a little of this success, I think, is due to the fact that both Elizabeth and Jane have, in quite different ways, a great deal that is unpleasant in them.

Elizabeth, the sensitive novelist of the twenties and thirties, owes a lot, I would imagine, to the journals of Katherine Mansfield and the personality of Virginia Woolf. It is very difficult to portray a writer, particularly one for whom, as was so often the case in those decades, life and letters were so curiously intermingled. Elizabeth is beautifully done. The intense egoistic preoccupation with life's meaning to *her*, the clinging to life combined with the neurotic and hypochondriac preoccupation with death, the awful paradox of a tired, ageing woman genuinely committed to a world of high, sensual values—all this is entirely convincingly presented. I was reminded so often of the last days of George Eliot in Cross' life. The pathos of Elizabeth's passion for her very young husband, her natural desire that his emotional dependence on her should increase, her high-minded attempt to free him from it as she is dying, are excellently brought to their fulfilment in the futile little episode of his unfaithfulness with a young man, Michael. The whole of this part of the book could not, I think, be better done.

If Elizabeth is a quite new extension of Mr. Isherwood's range, Jane is an improvement on an old theme. She is, in great degree, Sally Bowles seen again, but in *The World in the Evening* Mr. Isherwood has lost that satisfaction in standing apart, and that equal satisfaction with being cosy with the disreputable, which tinged so much of his earlier work with a sort of ironic sentimentalism. Jane is at once less of a bitch than Sally Bowles and also less sentimentalised. In Jane, I think, Mr. Isherwood, without altogether realising it, has drawn a very human, pleasant young woman who stands out above all his cosy saints.

As striking as this extension in emotional range is the corresponding growth of technique. Mr. Isherwood's previous novels have made few demands on his technical skill. *All the Conspirators* was a slight but admirable first novel *à la* Forster. *The Memorial* with its abrupt changes of scene and viewpoint was a rather slavish imitation of Mrs. Woolf. After these imitated constructions, he found his own standing in the camera-eye reportage of the Berlin novels, with their novel introduction of himself as central figure. He became absolute master of this form, but for those who regret that he has not remained faithful to it—and there are always admirers who do not want an artist to develop beyond the range of their own nostalgic admiration—it should be sufficient to recall the failure of *Prater Violet* which showed that Mr. Isherwood had done all he could with this form. And now, in *The World in the Evening*, he uses the Woolfian technique of change of time and place, of memory, journals, and letters with a logicality of sequence and a unification of purpose that makes the reading of the novel, even where its central theme is weakest, an absolute delight. Though one may doubt that the finished garment is the holy robe he intended to weave, the skill with which each thread is woven into the other in an intricate scheme is enough, I feel sure, to decide that Mr. Isherwood has not failed in his promise and that he promises even more for the future.

STEPHEN SPENDER
"Isherwood's Heroes"
New Republic, April 16, 1962, pp. 24–25

In an obvious sense this novel ⟨*Down There on a Visit*⟩ is a return to the early Isherwood. It is written in the first person, the narrator is Isherwood, and the character of a Berlin boy, Waldemar, is a thread connecting episodes dealing with the other main characters. Isherwood returns here to the method which served him so well in the Berlin stories, picturing people in situations which are microcosms of his view of the world through three decades: the late twenties, the thirties, and the forties.

A difference from the earlier stories is that Isherwood gives here a much more complex self-portrait. In Berlin, he was, as it were, looking at his characters; here, to some extent they are looking at him. There are also the present Isherwoods of various phases, looking back at several past Isherwoods. The view of the author as camera, observing his "real" characters, and remaining detached is seen in retrospect to have a fiction within the fiction. The new Isherwood connives in the behavior of his characters. This novel reminds one of the title of his first: *All the Conspirators*.

In several respects this is probably Isherwood's best novel. It offers the sheer pleasure of writing completely personal and yet completely controlled, radiant with observation, never wasting a word, funny and sympathetic. The more there is of it, the better. Whereas the earlier novels were fixed to their place, Berlin mostly, and their time, the thirties, *Down There on a Visit* extends over the author's whole adult life, and across half the world, from London to California.

On the other hand, the use of the self-regarding autobiographical method on this scale seems something of an expedient, a return to an earlier method because of the comparative failure of the conventionally objective method of *The World in the Evening*. One hopes that this novel is intermediary to some further solution of his problem of how to approach his material without obtruding too much his self, which at times becomes felt by both writer and reader as a burden.

The advantage of the Isherwood self-portrait is that it is so enjoyable. The main disadvantage is that, despite the writer's heroic effort to maintain all at the same time several perspectives in portraying himself, he deprives the reader of perspectives by which he can judge the Isherwood world. At every turn the reader finds himself being unable to separate the views and personality which are Isherwood from the view of life which is the novel.

The most obvious instance of this difficulty is in the simple matter of truth. The writer calls himself by his own name, he gives extracts from a journal which he was keeping "at the time," and in which these very characters (and some even more verifiable) appear. One assumes that some things are real, others invented. But which? Although fiction may be as true as history, there are (as one knows well when children tell tales) different kinds of truth, and one wants to be able to distinguish one from the other. Moreover, if in a novel the narrator is himself, the historic background itself, and the characters described at least partly *them*selves, there is a probability that the "real" characters are in some ways changed in order to spare people's real feelings. In parts of this novel (particularly in the account of Ambrose) one has the feeling that punches are being pulled, and that the writer is embarrassed by the inability to report things which, in fact, would make Ambrose much more convincing as fiction. So, paradoxically, Ambrose becomes a conventional aesthete of fiction just because he was "drawn closely" from a real person. A reviewer of this book is bound, I think, to feel a bit apologetic, because he is constantly being put in the position of finding that in writing about the book he is writing about the author. One of the entirely admirable things about this novel is that it is extremely honest, and that the new Isherwood is completely unself-sparing in his portrait of himself. But a difficulty of his method is that the chief fault which he describes in his own character—namely, that he is not really involved, that he is only "down here on a visit"—easily becomes confused with limitations in the novel.

Since there is always a suggestion in Isherwood's work (as in Forster's and Auden's early writings) that the world is divided into friends and enemies, these are friends. This is not obvious in the first story, *Mr. Lancaster*, in which the young Isherwood, conceited and superior, visits a relative who manages the office of a shipping line in Hamburg, and who bombastically acts out before Isherwood the role of his self-importance. But Mr. Lancaster dies and Isherwood realizes that Mr. Lancaster's true condition was despair.

The young Isherwood thinks that because Mr. Lancaster is a grotesque, he is therefore not to be regarded as a living person, but as a kind of dummy. But it was the young Isherwood whose arrogance gave him a certain deadness in his not perceiving that Mr. Lancaster was a living being. In Ambrose one learns more about the qualities which are needed to make a person "alive," and thus unlike the stuffy English he has left behind him, who are exemplary corpses. Ambrose is an aesthete, self-exiled from the England of Cambridge "hearties" who broke up his rooms, on his Greek island: a "Shakespearean king" of "the kind that got themselves exiled" and "have favorites." His chief favorite is an effete Greek boy called Aleko. It is the loneliness, concealed but unwavering will, courage, gaiety and gentleness of Ambrose which give him, in the Isherwood world, the quality of being one who has chosen, at whatever price, his own life. He could have been a Cambridge don, in that carved stone cemetery. It is significant that in the last, and best, story, the hero Paul, the intermittent dope addict, ex-paid-boy-friend of the rich is also compared to a king. It is the perverse strength of will which enables Paul to renounce this past, became a saint of the camp for pacifists, be ascetic, and then turn back to the long journey to the end of the night which is drug-taking, that makes him a lord on life.

Apart from *Mr. Lancaster*, this book is then about Isherwood's heroes. His relationships with them are a mixture of real affection and mutual esteem, tinged with a streak of competitiveness (naturally all people who in their minds set others tests want to pass themselves). When Mr. Lancaster dies he has scored against Isherwood by proving that he was desperately lonely; when Isherwood leaves the Greek island Ambrose scores heavily because he pretends not to care; when Isherwood gives Paul $10,000 he is submitting him to a test which he secretly feels Paul is bound to lose. In the long run, of course, everyone has scored and we are reminded of the early Auden poem in which the "ruined boys" get the prizes (there is a great deal of school mythology here). This novel is a pantheon for dead Paul, dead Ambrose, and even dead Mr. Lancaster. One is brought back to another early Isherwood title: *The Memorial*.

To a greater or less degree what the characters have here in common is that they are addicts. The positive aspect of an addict is, of course, his addiction: drink and boys with Ambrose, dope with Paul, his own image with Mr. Lancaster, sex with Waldemar. The negative aspect is that being fully committed to his addiction, the addict does not have to feel committed to anything else, not to other people, and still less to their boring morality, their "causes," etc. In fact, addicts have their own kind of moral superiority, because having become attached to a fragment of reality (Ambrose's island) they have a lofty disregard for nearly everything else (England left behind).

The significance of Mr. Isherwood's title *Down There on a Visit* is self-ironic, but the irony is ambiguous. It derives from one of the best scenes in the book, when Isherwood, wishing to please Paul, suggests that he too should take opium, and Paul, who is far away down his hallucinatory tunnel, roars with laughter, and exclaims:

So you want to try it? *Once! One pipe!* Or a dozen pipes, for that matter! You're exactly like a tourist who thinks he can take in the whole of Rome in one day. You know, you really *are* a tourist, to your bones. I bet you're always sending post cards with 'Down here on a visit' on them.

The accusation of course is revelatory, on one level only, of the addict's moral superiority. But, on the other level, where it is so difficult to distinguish the character and behavior of Isherwood the self-portrait from what one feels about his novel, it suggests that this book only visits the edge of horrors. It deals with a terrible period, and it mentions all the names and times: Berlin, September, 1939, the Nazis, 1940. These characters and their reactions somehow, in their own behavior, reflect these realities. There is everything to be said for Isherwood's method of reducing too gigantic events to small points of consciousness, but nevertheless with these characters somehow we do feel that we are only "down there on a visit" and that we have been spared the worst reality. There are—on the reduced scale of what goes on down there—no crabs, no bombs, no prison camps. The beatings, indulged in by one of the lesser characters, are just for fun. It is true that the Nazi horrors echo through these pages, and it is true that Isherwood is terrified of the approaching war. In a scene that took place in Athens and is reported on the island, one of Ambrose's "subjects" is hit on the head with a bottle, and permanently injured; but Ambrose does not take this seriously, and there is a feeling that the reader shouldn't either. The Nazis are there like a nagging conscience, the war is there like a nightmare which will become real, but in fact no one down there is going to be involved.

Possibly it is part of Isherwood's purpose to convey just this. The extracts from his journals of Vedantist philosophy suggest that he does not believe evil is real. In that case, however, one should surely see the worst as the worst, in order to be sure it is not evil. What is most lacking in this novel is a black sheep who is black to Isherwood, and not just apparently black, as seen by the "squares," so as to be seen as white by Isherwood.

Possibly this book is a preliminary for a novel which will really visit Hell. I feel that despite his almost compulsive pulling of punches, Isherwood may one day write such a novel, and perhaps it is the involvement of the projected Isherwood character with the portraits of semi-real people, which has here prevented him from going much further into the abyss than he does, even in *Paul*—the story where there are glimpses of how much further he might go.

W. H. AUDEN
"The Diary of a Diary"
New York Review of Books, January 27, 1972, pp. 19–20

In reading Mr. Isherwood's latest book—since in it he always refers to himself as Christopher, I shall henceforth call him by his first name—it may be helpful to recall the three crises through which, according to Erik Erikson, anybody who merits an autobiography must pass: the crisis of Identity, the crisis of Generativity, and the crisis of Integrity. Roughly speaking, these occur in youth, middle age, and old age respectively, but they usually overlap, and the intensity and duration of each varies from individual to individual.

In the identity crisis, the young man is trying to find the answer to the question, "Who am I *really*, as distinct from what others believe or desire me to be?" This is a crisis of consciousness. The Generativity crisis is a crisis of conscience. The question now to be answered is: "I have done this and that, my acts have affected others in this way or that. Have I done well or ill? Can I justify the influence that, intentionally or unintentionally, I have had on others?" Both the Identity and Generativity crises are preoccupied with freedom and choice. The Integrity crisis of old age is concerned with fate and necessity. As Mr. Erikson puts it, it demands:

the acceptance of one's one and only life-cycle as something that had to be and that, by necessity, permitted of no substitutions. The knowledge that an individual life is the accidental coincidence of but one life-cycle with but one segment of history.

As I read it, *Kathleen and Frank* is Christopher's attempt, wholly successful in my opinion, to solve his Integrity crisis. As he himself writes in his Afterword:

Christopher saw how heredity and kinship create a woven fabric: its patterns vary, but its strands are the same throughout. Impossible to say exactly where Kathleen and Frank and Richard and Christopher begin; they merge into each other. . . . Christopher has found that he is far more closely interwoven with Kathleen and Frank than he had supposed, or liked to believe.

And as he went on reading he made another discovery. If these diaries and letters were part of his project, he was part of theirs; for they in themselves were a project too. . . .

By now Christopher's project has become theirs. . . . For once the Anti-Son is in perfect harmony with his Parents, for he can say, "Our will be done!" Kathleen and Frank will seem at first to be their story rather than his. . . . Perhaps, on closer examination, this book may prove to be chiefly about Christopher.

Since I am Christopher's junior by only two and a half years, I am bound, of course, to compare his situation with my own. Thus I cannot imagine myself keeping a personal diary. In mine I enter only social engagements, lately the death of friends; when in the city, household incidents like getting the bathroom wash-basin unclogged; when in the country, natural phenomena like the weather, the first cuckoo, or the first strawberries. But then my professional preoccupation is with verse, not prose. With novelists it is evidently otherwise. It is a well-known fact that Christopher keeps a journal which his friends and admirers all look forward to reading some day. It now appears that he must have inherited this habit from his mother, for the core of his book is a diary which she started as a young girl and continued to keep until, in her seventies, a stroke made writing impossible.

The trouble for the reader of a diary who does not know its author personally is that he can only judge it firstly by its entertainment value—it must amuse him, and, secondly, by its historical value, the light it sheds upon the social mores and political events of the time in which it was written. I must frankly confess that, taken by itself, that is to say, without Christopher's comments and explanations, I do not think Kathleen's diary very interesting. For example, one expects from a diarist traveling in foreign countries vivid descriptions of the landscape and acute observations about the inhabitants. These Kathleen cannot provide. The only observation of hers that amused me was her preference—she was a stanch monarchist—for the royal splendor of Madrid to the "republican dullness" of Paris. When she does comment on public events, which is not very often, her remarks are too typical of her class to be considered her own.

What does, however, remain most impressive after one reads Christopher's description of her parents, Emily and Frederick, is that she grew up to be so "normal," not a wild neurotic, for both of them, it seems, were monsters. Emily, says Christopher, was

a great psychosomatic virtuoso who could produce high fevers, large swellings, and mysterious rashes within the hour; her ailments were roles into which she threw herself with abandon.

One is not surprised to learn that in later life, Kathleen was so suspicious of "illness" that Christopher had almost to die of blood poisoning before he could convince her that he was not being hysterical.

Frederick was a possessive bully with a deplorable passion for photography. (Since I consider the two most evil technical inventions so far to have been the internal combustion engine and the camera, I must also deplore Christopher's interest in the movies.)

In adolescence Christopher rebelled, very naturally, against Kathleen's cult of the past, but I'm not sure that he realizes even now that this was no personal idiosyncrasy; that, had he been in her situation, he would probably have felt the same nostalgia. If she looked back on the early years of her marriage in Wyberslegh Hall as the happiest days of her life, what could be more natural? It was clearly a very cozy home, much more than Marple, and later, owing to Frank's military duties, they had often to find temporary homes. Then, in 1915, she became a widow, and what widow can find much cause in rejoicing in either the present or the future?

Kathleen and Frank first met in 1893, their engagement was officially announced in 1903, they were married on March 12, 1903, and Christopher was born on August 26, 1904. Kathleen, it seems, had previously been in love with a young man generally referred to as "The Child," who jilted her when neither she nor her friends expected her to get married. Their courtship was prolonged and not without its sticky moments. In the first place, Frank had very little money. Then the very fact that they shared many interests, e.g., literary, made it difficult for them both to decide whether it would not be better if their relationship remained one of brother and sister rather than husband and wife. Fortunately, they finally opted for the second, and it is clear that their married life was exceptionally happy.

Of the two, Frank was the odd character. Though by profession a soldier, Frank had a passion for music—he played the piano very well—play-acting, including playing female roles, and knitting socks, even when on duty. I would have

expected his letters to be more "amusing" performances than they are, but it seems that only when telling stories or writing letters to Christopher could he really let himself go. Though he sometimes doubted if soldiering was his real vocation—shortly before World War I he seriously thought of resigning from his regiment—one's final impression is that he was not a misfit in the army. There is, for example, no evidence that his personal tastes ever caused him social embarrassment in an officer's mess. And in one letter, after complaining about his situation, he had to add:

However, there are moments when one feels quite military. Did I tell you about the little man who rushed up to me the other day and told me that he had made enquiries of the sergeants in the Volunteers, and he heard I was likely to be most popular—that what the men liked was a real officer who, when they came in from drill, said something which made their bosoms swell. I can't imagine myself doing this at all!

Then, whatever motives he may have had for sometimes wishing he were a civilian, one of them was certainly not the fear of getting killed. The young Christopher wove a myth about his dead father as the Anti-Hero, but it is obvious that he must have been a very brave man. He first saw battle in the Boer War, when he might very easily have got killed, in which case neither Christopher nor this book would exist. Luckily, he only caught typhoid fever and was invalided home. Then came World War I and in 1915 he was killed.

It seems clear that it was mainly from Frank that Christopher inherited his imaginative gifts. I'm sorry that he did not also inherit his love of music. I am also sorry, as a good little Episcopalian like Kathleen, that he did inherit Papa's addiction to esoteric religions. Frank took up theosophy and Christopher Vedanta. In the matter of religion I think I was luckier in my youth than he was. I should guess that the church Kathleen attended twice on Sundays was Broad if not Low. My parents, fortunately, were High, so that my first experiences of divine worship were of exciting dramatic rituals. I was even a boat-boy.

For selfish reasons I wish Christopher had said a little more about his experiences at St. Edmund's School, Hindhead, where we first met in 1915. He was known to us then as "Beesh," a contraction of Bradshaw Isherwood, and I can personally vouch for his linguistic and imaginative precocity, for it was from his lips that I heard the first witty remark in my life. We were out together on a Sunday walk in the Surrey landscape. "God," he said, "must have been tired when He made this country." About our headmaster "Ciddy" he is not quite fair. It is true that, since they were cousins, their relationship was bound to be difficult. It is also true that Ciddy's temperament was not of the kind that inspires affection in the young. I must say, however, that he was a brilliant teacher to whom I owe a great deal. Incidentally, last October I attended a luncheon in London at which the guests of honor were Miss Mons and Miss Rosa, both, I am happy to say, in fine fettle.

I myself never saw either Wyberslegh or Marple, and the only member of Christopher's family I ever met, outside of Kathleen, was his Uncle Henry, about whom I once wrote a slightly improper poem.

His descriptions of the family and their life in Cheshire are, however, fascinating both personally and historically. Marple Hall was said to be haunted, and both Christopher and Richard had experiences there that were clearly paranormal, i.e., no rational explanation for them is convincing. About one point I am curious. Kathleen seems never to have accepted her father and mother-in-law as friends, she always referred to them by their surnames. I cannot help wondering if the cause for this was not class consciousness. Her father, Frederick, was, or had been, in the wine business, that is to say, "in trade." In England at that time, both the landed gentry and the professional middle class looked down on those "in trade," those in business or in industry, as being not quite gentlemen, however rich they might be.

I have two little bones to pick, one with the author, the other with the publisher. The narrative would be easier to follow if the former had provided genealogical tables and the latter had printed at the top of each page the year with which it is concerned.

A fine book though. I cannot imagine any reader, whatever his social background, not being enthralled by it.

GORE VIDAL
From "Christopher Isherwood's Kind" (1976)
The Second American Revolution
1982, pp. 45–52

C hristopher and His Kind describes Isherwood's life from 1929 to 1939. The narrative (based on diaries and written, generally, in the third person) takes up where *Lions and Shadows* ends with "twenty-four-year-old Christopher's departure from England on March 14, 1929, to visit Berlin for the first time in his life." The book ends a decade later when Isherwood emigrates to the United States. Of *Lions and Shadows*, Isherwood says that it describes his "life between the ages of seventeen and twenty-four. It is not truly autobiographical, however. The author conceals important facts about himself . . . and gives his characters fictitious names." But "The book I am now going to write will be as frank and factual as I can make it, especially as far as I myself am concerned." He means to be sexually candid; and he is. He is also that rarest of creatures, the objective narcissist; he sees himself altogether plain and does not hesitate to record for us the lines that the face in the mirror has accumulated, the odd shadow that flaws character.

I have just read the two memoirs in sequence and it is odd how little Isherwood has changed in a half century. The style is much the same throughout. The shift from first to third person does not much alter the way he has of looking at things and it is, of course, the *precise* way in which Isherwood perceives the concrete world that makes all the difference. He is particularly good at noting a physical appearance that suggests, through his selection of nouns, verbs, a psychic description. This is from *Lions and Shadows*:

> [Chalmers] had grown a small moustache and looked exactly my idea of a young Montmartre poet, more French than the French. Now he caught sight of us, and greeted me with a slight wave of the hand, so very typical of him, tentative, diffident, semi-ironical, like a parody of itself. Chalmers expressed himself habitually in fragments of gestures, abortive movements, half-spoken sentences.

Then the same sharp eye is turned upon the narrator:

> Descending the staircase to the dining-room, I was Christopher Isherwood no longer, but a satanically proud, icy, impenetrable demon; an all-knowing, all-pardoning savior of mankind; a martyr-evangelist of the tea-table, from which the most atrocious drawing-room tortures could wring no more than a polite proffer of the buttered scones.

This particular *auteur du cinéma* seldom shoots a scene without placing somewhere on the set a mirror that will record the *auteur* in the act of filming.

At the time of the publication of *Lions and Shadows* in 1938, Isherwood was thirty-four years old. He had published three novels: *All the Conspirators, The Memorial, Mr. Norris Changes Trains.* With Auden he had written the plays *The Dog beneath the Skin* and *The Ascent of F6.* Finally, most important of all, the finest of his creations had made a first appearance in *Mr. Norris Changes Trains*; with no great fuss or apparent strain, Isherwood had invented Isherwood. The Isherwood of the Berlin stories is a somewhat anodyne and enigmatic narrator. He is looking carefully at life. He does not commit himself to much of anything. Yet what might have been a limitation in a narrator, the author, rather mysteriously, made a virtue of.

Spender describes Isherwood in Berlin as occasionally "depressive, silent or petulant. Sometimes he would sit in a room with Sally Bowles or Mr. Norris without saying a word, as though refusing to bring his characters to life." But they were very much *his* characters. He lived "surrounded by the models for his creations, like one of those portraits of a writer by a bad painter, in which the writer is depicted meditating in his chair whilst the characters of his novels radiate round him under a glowing cloud of dirty varnish. . . ." Isherwood had rejected not only the familiar, cozy world of Cambridge and London's literary life but also the world of self-conscious aestheticism. He chose to live as a proletarian in Berlin where, Spender tells us, "He was comparatively poor and almost unrecognized. His novel, *All the Conspirators*, had been remaindered," Spender notes yet again. Nevertheless, Spender realized that Isherwood

> was more than a young rebel passing through a phase of revolt against parents, conventional morality, and orthodox religion. . . . He was on the side of the forces which make a work of art, even more than he was interested in art itself. . . . His hatred of institutions of learning and even of the reputation attached to some past work of art, was really hatred of the fact that they came between people and their direct unprejudiced approach to one another.

In *Lions and Shadows* Isherwood writes of school, of friendships, of wanting to be . . . well, Isherwood, a character not yet entirely formed. Auden appears fairly late in the book though early in Isherwood's life: they were together at preparatory school. Younger than Isherwood, Auden wanted "to become a mining engineer. . . . I remember him chiefly for his naughtiness, his insolence, his smirking tantalizing air of knowing disreputable and exciting secrets." Auden was on to sex and the others were not.

Auden and Isherwood did not meet again for seven years. "Just before Christmas, 1925, a mutual acquaintance brought him in to tea. I found him very little changed." Auden "told me that he wrote poetry nowadays: he was deliberately a little over-casual in making this announcement. I was very much surprised, even rather disconcerted." But then, inevitably, the Poet and the Novelist of the age formed an alliance. The Poet had further surprises for the Novelist. Auden's "own attitude to sex, in its simplicity and utter lack of inhibition, fairly took my breath away. He was no Don Juan: he didn't run around hunting for his pleasures. But he took what came to him with a matter-of-factness and an appetite as hearty as that which he showed when sitting down to dinner."

Art and sex: the two themes intertwine in Isherwood's memoirs but in the first volume we do not know what the sex was all about: the reticences of the Thirties forbade candor.

Now in *Christopher and His Kind*, Isherwood has filled in the blanks; he is explicit about both sex and love. Not only did the Poet and the Novelist of that era lust for boys, there is some evidence that each might have echoed Marlowe's mighty line: I have found that those who do not like tobacco and boys are fools.

"The book I am now going to write will be as frank and factual as I can make it, especially as far as I myself am concerned." Then the writer shifts to the third person: "At school, Christopher had fallen in love with many boys and been yearningly romantic about them. At college he had at last managed to get into bed with one. This was due entirely to the initiative of his partner, who, when Christopher became scared and started to raise objections, locked the door and sat down firmly on Christopher's lap." For an American twenty-two years younger than Christopher, the late development of the English of that epoch is astonishing. In Washington, D.C., puberty arrived at ten, eleven, twelve, and sex was riotous and inventive between consenting paeds. Yet Tennessee Williams (fourteen years my senior) reports in his *Memoirs* that neither homo- nor heterosexuality began for him until his late twenties. On the other hand, he did not go to a monosexual school as I did, as Isherwood and his kind did.

Isherwood tells us that "other experiences followed, all of them enjoyable but none entirely satisfying. This was because Christopher was suffering from an inhibition, then not unusual among upper-class homosexuals; he couldn't relax sexually with a member of his own class or nation. He needed a working-class foreigner." Germany was the answer. "To Christopher, Berlin meant Boys." Auden promptly introduced him to the Cosy Corner, a hangout for proletarian youths, and Christopher took up with a blond named Bubi, "the first presentable candidate who appeared to claim the leading role in Christopher's love myth."

John Lehmann's recently published "novel" *In the Purely Pagan Sense* overlaps with Isherwood's memoirs not only in time and place but in a similar sexual preoccupation. "I was obsessed," writes Lehmann's narrator, "by the desire to make love with boys of an entirely different class and background. . . ." This desire for differentness is not unusual: misalliance has almost always been the name of the game hetero or homo or bi. But I suspect that the upper-middle-class man's desire for youths of the lower class derives, mainly, from fear of his own class. Between strongly willed males of the Isherwood-Auden sort, a sexual commitment could lead to a psychic defeat for one of the partners.

The recently published memoirs of Isherwood's contemporary Peter Quennell (*The Marble Foot*) describe how an upper-class *heterosexual* English writer was constantly betrayed by women of his own class. Apparently, Quennell is much too tender, too romantic, too . . . well, feminine to avoid victimization by the ladies. A beautiful irony never to be understood by United Statesmen given to the joys of the sexual majority is that a homosexualist like Isherwood cannot with any ease enjoy a satisfactory sexual relationship with a woman because he himself is so entirely masculine that the woman presents no challenge, no masculine hardness, no exciting *agon*. It is the heterosexual Don Juan (intellectual division) who is the fragile, easily wounded figure, given to tears. Isherwood is a good deal less "feminine" (in the pre-women's lib sense of the word) than Peter Quennell, say, or Cyril Connolly or our own paralyzingly butch Ernest Hemingway.

Isherwood describes his experiments with heterosexuality: "She was five or six years older than [Christopher], easygoing, stylish, humorous. . . . He was surprised and amused to find how easily he could relate his usual holds and movements to his unusual partner. He felt curiosity and the fun of playing a new game. He also felt a lust which was largely narcissistic. . . ." Then: "He asked himself: Do I now want to go to bed with more women and girls? Of course not, as long as I can have boys. Why do I prefer boys? Because of their shape and their voices and their smell and the way they move. And boys can be romantic. I can put them into my myth and fall in love with them. Girls can be absolutely beautiful but never romantic. In fact, their utter lack of romance is what I find most likeable about them." There is a clear-eyed normality (if not great accuracy) about all this.

Then Isherwood moves from the personal to the general and notes the lunatic pressure that society exerts on everyone to be heterosexual, to deny at all costs a contrary nature. Since heterosexual relations proved to be easy for Isherwood, he could have joined the majority. But he was stopped by Isherwood the rebel, the Protestant saint who declared with the fury of a Martin Luther: "even if my nature were like theirs, I should still have to fight them, in one way or another. If boys didn't exist, I should have to invent them." Isherwood's war on what he has called, so aptly, "the heterosexual dictatorship" has been unremitting and admirable.

In Berlin Isherwood settled down with a working-class boy named Heinz and most of *Christopher and His Kind* has to do with their life together during the time when Hitler came to power and the free and easy Berlin that had attracted Isherwood turned ugly. With Heinz (whose papers were not in order), Isherwood moved restlessly about Europe: Copenhagen, Amsterdam, the Canary Islands, Brussels. In the end Heinz was trapped in Germany, and forced to serve in World War II. Miraculously, he survived. After the war, Isherwood met Heinz and his wife—as pleasant an end as one can imagine to any idyll of the neo-Wagnerian age.

Meanwhile, Isherwood the writer was developing. It is during this period that the Berlin stories were written; also, *Lions and Shadows*. Also, the collaboration with Auden on the last of the verse plays. Finally, there is the inevitable fall into the movies . . . something that was bound to happen. In *Lions and Shadows* Isherwood describes how "I had always been fascinated by films. . . . I was a born film fan. The reason for this had, I think, very little to do with 'Art' at all; I was, and still am, endlessly interested in the outward appearance of people—their facial expressions, their gestures, their walk, their nervous tricks. . . . The cinema puts people under a microscope: you can stare at them, you can examine them as though they were insects."

Isherwood was invited to write a screenplay for the director "Berthold Viertel [who] appears as Friedrich Bergmann in the novelette called *Prater Violet*, which was published twelve years later." Isherwood and the colorful Viertel hit it off and together worked on a film called *Little Friend*. From that time on the best prose writer in English has supported himself by writing movies. In fact, the first Isherwood work that I encountered was not a novel but a film that he wrote called *Rage in Heaven*: at sixteen I thought it splendid. "The moon!" intoned the nutty Robert Montgomery. "It's staring at me, like a great Eye." Ingrid Bergman shuddered. So did I.

It is hard now for the young who are interested in literature (a tiny minority compared to the young who are interested in that flattest and easiest and laziest of art forms: the movies) to realize that Isherwood was once considered "a hope of English fiction" by Cyril Connolly, and a master by those of us who grew up in World War II. I think the relative neglect of Isherwood's work is, partly, the result of his expatriation. With

Auden, he emigrated to the United States just before the war began, and there was a good deal of bitter feeling at the time (they were clumsily parodied by the unspeakable Evelyn Waugh in *Put Out More Flags*). Ultimately, Auden's reputation was hardly affected. But then poets are licensed to be mad, bad, and dangerous to read, while prose writers are expected to be, if not responsible, predictable.

In America Isherwood was drawn first to the Quakers; then to Vedanta. Lately, he has become a militant spokesman of Gay Liberation. If his defense of Christopher's kind is sometimes shrill . . . well, there is a good deal to be shrill about in a society so deeply and so mindlessly homophobic. In any case, none of Isherwood's moral preoccupations is apt to endear him to a literary establishment that is, variously, academic, Jewish/Christian, middle-class, and heterosexual. Yet he has written some of his best books in the United States, including the memoir at hand and the novels *A Single Man* and *A Meeting by the River*. Best of all, he still views the world aslant despite long residence in Santa Monica, a somber place where even fag households resemble those hetero couples photographed in *Better Homes and Gardens*, serving up intricate brunches 'neath the hazel Pacific sky.

What strikes me as most remarkable in Isherwood's career has not been so much the unremitting will to be his own man as the constant clarity of a prose style that shows no sign of slackness even though the author is, astonishingly, in his seventies. There is a good deal to be said about the way that Isherwood writes, particularly at a time when prose is worse than ever in the United States, and showing signs of etiolation in England. There is no excess in an Isherwood sentence. The verbs are strong. Nouns precise. Adjectives few. The third person startles and seduces, while the first person is a good guide and never coy.

Is the Isherwood manner perhaps *too* easy? Cyril Connolly feared that it might be when he wrote in *Enemies of Promise* (1938): "[Isherwood] is persuasive because he is so insinuatingly bland and anonymous, nothing rouses him, nothing shocks him. While secretly despising us he could not at the same time be more tolerant. . . . Now for this a price has to be paid; Herr Issyvoo" (Connolly is contemplating Isherwood's Berlin stories) "is not a dumb ox, for he is not condemned to the solidarity with his characters and with their background to which Hemingway is bound by his conception of art, but he is much less subtle, intelligent and articulate than he might be." Isherwood answered Connolly: "In conversation, Isherwood . . . expressed his belief in construction as the way out of the difficulty. The writer must conform to the language which is understood by the greatest number of people, to the vernacular, but his talent as a novelist will appear in the exactness of his observation, the justice of his situations and in the construction of his book."

Isherwood has maintained this aesthetic throughout a long career. When he turned his back on what Connolly termed Mandarin writing, he showed considerable courage. But the later Isherwood is even better than the early cameraman because he is no longer the anonymous, neutral narrator. He can be shocked; he can be angry.

In *Christopher and His Kind*, Isherwood wonders what attitude to take toward the coming war with Germany. "Suppose, Christopher now said to himself, I have a Nazi Army at my mercy. I can blow it up by pressing a button. The men in the army are notorious for torturing and murdering civilians—all except one of them, Heinz. Will I press the button? No—wait: Suppose I know that Heinz himself, out of cowardice or moral infection, has become as bad as they are

and takes part in all their crimes? Will I press that button, even so? Christopher's answer, given without the slightest hesitation, was: Of course not." That is the voice of humanism in a bad time, and one can only hope that thanks to Christopher's life and work, his true kind will increase even as they refuse, so wisely, to multiply.

JAMES FENTON
"A Backward Love"
New Review, March 1977, pp. 41–43

There is a kind of autobiographical study, semi-novelistic in form, confessional in tone, at which the English seem to excel. Edmund Gosse perhaps founded the tradition with *Father and Son*. J. R. Ackerley contributed, most notably with *My Father and Myself*. V. S. Pritchett belongs to the heterosexual branch of the tradition, Christopher Isherwood to the 'musical', or homosexual, tendency. Isherwood admired Ackerley, wrote reviews for him in the *Listener*, and, as his latest book tells us, had plans to imitate him at an early stage in his career. As he wrote in a letter to Spender:

> If we do go to Greece, I shall write a book as much like *Hindoo Holiday* as possible. This will pay for everything for the next ten years.

Hindoo Holiday represents the lighter, more novelistic vein in this particular tradition: *My Father and Myself*, which remained unpublished until Ackerley's death, is more confessional. Isherwood has experimented with the form throughout his life. It has often been practically impossible to tell what is 'novel' in his work from what is pure autobiography. *Lions and Shadows*, which described his life from Repton through Cambridge and up to his departure for Berlin, contains a warning to the reader. We are to read the book as a novel. And yet it contains no fictional characters—or at least no wholly fictional characters. One suspects that to Isherwood the notion of writing fiction is bound up with evasiveness. He is not really, or not willingly, a novelist at all. If free to do so, he will prefer to confess.

Christopher and His Kind begins where *Lions and Shadows* left off, and ends in 1939 with Auden and Isherwood arriving in New York. It therefore covers the most interesting creative period of the author's life: *The Memorial, Mr Norris Changes Trains, Lions and Shadows, Goodbye to Berlin*, the collaboration with Auden on the three plays and *Journey to a War*, and the periods of his life described in *Prater Violet* and parts of *Down There on a Visit*. It is a marvellous book, superlatively good. One starts out eagerly but very soon slows down. There are, after all, only 250 pages, and it may be years before the sequel. Indeed no sequel, one feels, could match this volume for the intrinsic interest of the material. For Auden and Isherwood this was a miraculous decade. No doubt they knew it. On a visit to Amsterdam, Auden inscribed a visitors' book with a quotation from Ilya Ehrenburg:

> Read about us and marvel!
> You did not live in our time—be sorry!

The Isherwood of today tries to disabuse the reader of any too romantic notion he might have caught from the Berlin stories:

> In his two novels about Berlin, Christopher tried not only to make the bizarre seem humdrum but the humdrum seem bizarre—that is, exciting. He wanted his readers to find excitement in Berlin's drab streets and shabby crowds, in the poverty and dullness of the overgrown Prussian provincial town which had become Germany's pseudo-capital. Forty

years later, I can claim that the excitement has been created—largely by all those others who have reinterpreted Christopher's material; actresses and actors, directors and writers. Christopher was saying, in effect: 'Read about us and marvel! You did not live in our time—be sorry!' And now there are young people who agree with him. 'How I wish I could have been with you there!' they write. This is flattering but also ironic; for most of them could no more have shared Christopher's life in Berlin than they could have lived with a hermit in the desert. Not because of any austerities Christopher endured. Because of the boredom.

This is a charming and modest disclaimer, and not quite sincere, since it is perfectly obvious that Berlin was fascinating to Isherwood. Why else was he so keen, as he tells us earlier in the book, to keep Spender away from Berlin, in case Spender should scoop him by writing Berlin stories and rushing them into print? (They had a row, during which Spender said, 'If we're going to part, at least let's part like men.' To which Isherwood replied: 'But Stephen, we *aren't* men.')

As the extract above shows, Isherwood writes about himself in the third person. The 'Christopher' of the Thirties is treated as an historical character, about whom the 'I' of the Seventies is writing the memoir. The device is a constant reminder of Isherwood's sense of distance from his former self—but it is an irritating device. Sometimes it breaks down:

> When someone told Christopher he was a monster— it happened now and then—he would protest, and feel secretly flattered. The word sounds rather romantic. But here I am confronted by the reality of Christopher's monster behaviour—his tears followed by cold calculation—and it shocks me, it hurts my self-esteem, even after all these years! The more reason for recording it.

Nothing would be lost, one feels, by abandoning this double-vision, which clogs up perfectly simple sentences: 'As far as I know, Mr Lindsay neither read Christopher nor cared what he wrote.' Why not 'As far as I know, Mr Lindsay neither read me nor cared what I wrote'? In some passages the distinction is useful, but not here. And besides, Isherwood does not distinguish between, say, the Spender of the Thirties and the contemporary figure of the same name. The device is illogical. This may not matter, but I found it an unnecessary hurdle. The double vision only works when you learn to ignore it.

It is, however, a typically Isherwood device. It is part of the fascination with himself (Gore Vidal has called him 'the objective narcissist') which lies behind the best of his work. There is always something odd about his first persons. The original problem began with *Mr Norris*. Should the Narrator be a homosexual? Isherwood tells us that he wanted to concentrate on the character of Mr Norris, and therefore felt that the Narrator had to be as unobtrusive as possible:

> For example, the Narrator is at a Beethoven concert, he sees and smells a juicy steak in a restaurant, he wakes in the night to feel his cheek being licked by a non-venomous snake. The ordinary reader, being convinced of the Narrator's ordinariness, will take it for granted that he is feeling pleasure in the first instance, appetite in the second and terror and disgust in the third.
>
> But suppose that the Narrator shows no pleasure in the music? Suppose that he shows disgust on seeing and smelling the meat? Suppose that he shows no fear of the snake and even starts to pet it? Suppose, in other words that he proves himself to be a tone-deaf, vegetarian herpetologist? The ordinary reader

may be repelled by, or sympathetic to such a Narrator's reactions, but he will never be able to identify with him. He will always remain aware that the Narrator is an individual who is very different from himself.

This is part of the reason for the Narrator's sexlessness in *Mr Norris*. Isherwood dared not make him a homosexual, scorned to make him a heterosexual, and ended up with the curiously ambiguous figure who became famous. Few characters in contemporary literature have had such a varied and interesting sexual career as the narrator of the Berlin stories:

> In the film of *I Am a Camera*, Christopher gets drunk and tries to rape Sally. She resists him. After this, they are just good friends. In the musical play *Cabaret*, the male lead is called Clifford Bradshaw. He is an altogether heterosexual American; he has an affair with Sally and fathers her child. In the film of *Cabaret*, the male lead is called Brian Roberts. He is a bisexual Englishman; he has an affair with Sally and, later, with one of Sally's lovers, a German baron. At the end of the film, he is eager to marry Sally. But Sally reminds him of his lapse and hints that there may be others in the future. Brian's homosexual tendency is treated as an indecent but comic weakness to be snickered at, like bedwetting.

The tart phraseology of the final passage ('Sally reminds him of his *lapse*') is typical of Isherwood's militant attitude toward the subject of homosexuality. It is the one matter on which he permits himself any great degree of bitterness (although there is a trace of resentment in his comparison between E. M. Forster and Cyril Connolly as friends: Forster's friendship, we learn, would never desert you, however much your talent diminished). It is the one question which he will treat as a Cause. Others may desert the Cause, for marriages with girls who 'understand', are 'different', and will look back on their homosexual phases as periods of immaturity. Isherwood despises these desertions, one can see. He cannot even bring himself to marry Erika Mann, who needs to change her nationality. He is afraid that 'somebody, somewhere, might suspect him of trying to pass as a heterosexual'. When Auden agrees to marry Erika, Isherwood feels envious:

> Sir Wystan had won the glory of a knight errant who rescues the lady from the monster. Nevertheless, (Christopher) never seriously regretted his own decision.

Incidentally, the marriage between Auden and Erika was preceded by an unfortunate hitch, not described in this book. Erika took the Malvern train to meet Auden, but instead of waiting for Great Malvern station got out at Malvern Link. A single man was standing on the platform. Erika threw her arms around the astonished individual and said: 'My dear, it is so kind of you to marry me!'

If Auden's attitude to marriage in those days was more relaxed than Isherwood's, he was nevertheless, during the Thirties, a militant misogynist. This will appear when Edward Mendelson publishes a longish poem that Auden wrote in Brussels, New Year's Eve, 1938. The professor has told me that Auden wanted in later years to publish the poem, but wished first of all to tone down the misogynism. Certainly, although Auden never deserted the Cause, his attitude to his own homosexuality came to differ sharply from Isherwood's. He was once arguing with Chester Kallman on the question—is homosexuality a sin? Auden said: 'My dear, of course it's a sin. All we can hope is that Miss God will forgive us.' As for marriage, he *did* once again become quietly engaged, during the period of his life on Ischia. The lady in question, however, began to see that the idea was hopeless when he said:

'. . . and it'll be so nice to have a son. You realise we will *have* to call him Chester.'

In their public writings of the Thirties, Auden and Isherwood were unable to be open about the Cause. This created more problems for Isherwood than it did for Auden. The poet was able to remain obscure, or ambiguous. The very sexlessness of the pronouns 'I' and 'You' made it possible to write a famous homosexual love poem like 'Lay your sleeping head', without making it necessarily homosexual at all. Modernity and vatic privacy also came to the rescue. Whereas for Isherwood it was necessary either to be evasive or to shock the world. Auden could, in general, get away with murder— and he knew it. Whereas the Novelist had to learn 'how to be plain and awkward':

> For, to achieve his lightest wish, he must
> Become the whole of boredom, subject to
> Vulgar complaints like love, among the Just
> Be just, among the Filthy filthy too,
> And in his own weak person, if he can,
> Dully put up with all the wrongs of Man.

The last three lines of the sonnet ('The Novelist') illustrate Auden's greater room for manoeuvre, since they contain a private joke about venereal disease, from which Isherwood had just been suffering.

Since Auden's death, Isherwood has been at greater liberty to let us in on some of the other private jokes, which are worth knowing. It's worth knowing for instance that the 'Letter to a Wound' in *The Orators* was about a rectal fissure from which Auden suffered.

> In restaurants I used to find myself drawing pictures
> of you on the bottom of table mats. 'Who'll ever
> guess what that is?' Once, when a whore accosted
> me, I bowed, 'I deeply regret it, Madam, but I have a
> friend.' Once I carved on a seat in the park 'We have
> sat here. You'd better not.'

And it is particularly interesting to be given the key to the poem 'This Loved One'. Isherwood's first great love in Berlin, a boy called Bubi, is described as representing The German Boy, The Blond. Isherwood sees him as the exemplar of his race, and of foreignness in general. Bubi sees himself as 'The Wanderer, The Lost Boy, homeless, penniless . . . roaming the earth.' But:

> Wystan wasn't at all impressed by Bubi's performance
> as The Wanderer. Yet, largely to please Christopher,
> he wrote a beautiful poem about Bubi, *This Loved
> One*.

One thinks—hang on a moment, I don't remember the poem being about a boyfriend. Turning it up, one is at first surprised. (This is the 1930 version, without a later alteration and Prof. Mendelson's misprint.)

> Before this loved one
> Was that one and that one
> A family
> And history
> And ghost's adversity
> Whose pleasing name
> Was neighbourly shame.
> Before this last one
> Was much to be done,
> Frontiers to cross
> As clothes grew worse
> And coins to pass
> In a cheaper house
> Before this last one
> Before this loved one.

> Face that the sun
> Is supple on
> May stir but here
> Is no new year;
> This gratitude for gifts is less
> Than the old loss;
> Touching is shaking hands
> On mortgaged lands;
> And smiling of
> This gracious greeting
> 'Good day. Good luck'
> Is no real meeting
> But instinctive look
> A backward love.

The poem has hitherto inspired some very non-committal interpretations. John Fuller, in the *Reader's Guide*, is reticent. Monroe K. Spears comments:

> It uses no abstractions, though it generalises, and its
> level is the psychological-political: there is a constant
> ambiguity as to whether the new love is a person or a
> new form of society, and the point seems to be that it
> is both, that love and politics are intimately related
> (as in Blake and Lawrence). Frontiers must be
> crossed and ghosts defied if there is to be hope of
> anything other than a 'backward love'.

Although it is unfair to attack Spears with the benefit of Isherwood's significant clue, it is clear that he has missed the point of the poem. His talk of a political aspect seems fanciful. The poem is obscure, but not in a political direction. How does it now read? Auden is alluding, in the first stanza, to previous, surreptitious affairs—reminding the lover (Isherwood) of his previous partners. 'Frontiers to cross' can be read either literally—you have to come to Berlin in order to find this loved one—or metaphorically, in the sense of making approaches to would-be lovers. 'And coins to pass / In a cheaper house'— rough trade. The second stanza contains a massive qualification: watch out, it seems to say, you may be stirred by this new love, but it's not the Real Thing, 'no real meeting'. Since Auden was writing for a coterie, and since he was usually aware of any possible *double entendre* (although years later he became embarrased at having written the line 'Make a vineyard of the curse'), there must surely be a reference to sodomy in the expression 'A backward love'. Beautiful as the poem is, it seems to say: 'Though you have now found a boy you love more than any of your previous friends, do not imagine that this is the genuine love to which you aspire.'

I have gone into some detail about this poem partly in order to illustrate how rapidly critical works on the Thirties are becoming outdated. The publication of *Christopher and His Kind* will cause a shift of emphasis in our understanding of both Auden and Isherwood, and our appreciation of the significance of Berlin. There is no doubt that, as more suppressed poems, letters and memoirs of the period are published, as the Thirties begin to receive the sort of attention already given to the Twenties, the categories we have used, and the judgments we have accepted, will have to be changed. For instance, the notion of an English Auden, then the break with politics, leading to the American-style, religious, right wing Auden, it never made much sense, and what Isherwood tells us here (his Auden is deeply religious even in the Thirties) undermines it even further. The author of 'Spain' does not, years later, go back on his former beliefs: he writes the poem while the very experiences which have shocked and disillusioned him—the burning of churches by the Republicans— are fresh in his mind. No wonder he disliked the poem later. It was written at the very moment of defection.

As for the famous decision to go to America, the attendant circumstances arc sct out here. It turns out, of course, not to have been A Decision to Emigrate Once and For All, but the latest of a series of wanderings around the globe. Isherwood's great love, Heinz, had accompanied him on many of these, in an attempt to avoid the draft in Germany. Finally, unable to change his nationality or seek asylum in Britain, Heinz is arrested by the Gestapo; in a short while, he will be fighting for Hitler. Isherwood contemplates the consequences of this fact. He realises that he could never fight against an army in which Heinz is fighting. He therefore realises, by a series of logical extensions, that he must be a pacifist. As to Russia, the laws enacted against homosexuality there in 1934 mean that he cannot, honestly, support the Party Line any more. And yet it is not until the boat trip to America that he finally comes out with the truth:

> One morning, when they were walking on the deck, Christopher heard himself say: 'You know, it just doesn't mean anything to me any more—the popular front, the party line, the anti-fascist struggle. I suppose they're okay but something's wrong with me. I simply cannot swallow another mouthful.' To which Wystan answered: 'Neither can I.'

Auden had not liked to admit the fact to Isherwood before. Now he did so, telling him about the significance of his experience in Spain.

Isherwood's candour and perceptiveness have never been better deployed than in the final sections of this book, where he relates the story of losing Heinz, and builds up to the departure for the States. Indeed, it is delightful to find him writing here as well as he had ever written. *Christopher and His Kind* is the fruit of a brilliant Indian summer. One wishes its author all the best, and hopes that the weather holds.

PAUL PIAZZA
From "The Hero"
Christopher Isherwood: Myth and Anti-Myth
1978, pp. 150–61

Though radically different in technique, *A Single Man* and *A Meeting by the River* both point to an extra dimension, a "superconscious, extraphenomenal" aspect in reality. In *A Single Man*, Isherwood presents a day in the life of a Truly Lonely Man, George, a middle-aged homosexual and professor of English literature. George is very much like Jones or Smith or Brown, for his life is not particularly rich or luminous: if he is different, it is only in degree. His homosexuality, his education, his pathetic mourning for Jim, his dead lover, actually intensify George's very human condition of loneliness. The spiritual, even mystical aspects of George's life are suggested by Isherwood who, throughout the novel, sustains a delicate dialogue with the reader. Isherwood's description of George's late-night encounter with Kenny, one of his students, as a symbolic Platonic dialogue, defines the book's narrative method: a symbolic dialogue between the author as a kind of guru and the reader as a disciple meditating on the ephemera of George's day.[1]

George has no idea that his confusion and monotony contain mystical ramifications; he is the early Isherwood hero as he might have been without Isherwood's conversion. The dialogue remains between author and auditor only—George is unaware of his dimensions. In *A Meeting by the River*, two brothers hold another "dialogue" which is vividly reported through the book's epistolary format. The sparks struck by the clashing diary entries of Oliver, preparing to take vows in a Hindu monastery, and the letters of Patrick, his entrepreneur brother, kindle the reader's awareness of the suprasensible. Here both brothers seek religious experience, Oliver deliberately and Patrick unwittingly.

A Single Man[2] begins with George's awakening: fitfully, almost resentfully, George emerges from the pacific oblivion of sleep:

> Waking up begins with saying *am* and *now*. That which has awoken then lies for a while staring up at the ceiling and down into itself until it has recognized *I*, and therefore deduced *I am, I am now. Here* comes next, and is at least negatively reassuring; because *here*, this morning, is where it has expected to find itself: what's called *at home*. (SM 9)

"It" rises, empties its bladder, weighs itself, gazes into the mirror:

> What it sees there isn't so much a face as the expression of a predicament. Here's what it has done to itself, here's the mess it has somehow managed to get itself into during its fifty-eight years; expressed in terms of a dull, harassed stare, a coarsened nose, a mouth dragged down by the corners into a grimace. . . . (SM 10)

Isherwood's use of the first person plural pronoun formally begins the dialogue with the reader: "The creature we are watching will struggle on and on until it drops. Not because it is heroic. It can imagine no alternative" (SM 10). The "creature" obediently washes, shaves, brushes its hair, because it accepts its responsibility to the Others, and "it is even glad it has its place among them. . . ." It even knows its name: "It is called George" (SM 11). Isherwood's opening sentences, which at first lack a personal subject, mirror the circular journey of George's day: from unconsciousness, to self-awareness, back to the lack of personhood, the Vedantist ideal.

As George prepares for his day, Isherwood's use of the second person pronoun involves the reader in George's musings:

> He crosses the front room, which he calls his study, and comes down the staircase. The stairs turn a corner; they are narrow and steep. You can touch both handrails with your elbows, and you have to bend your head, even if, like George, you are only five eight. This is a tightly planned little house. . . . there is hardly room enough to feel lonely. Nevertheless . . . (SM 12)

Addressing the reader, Isherwood recreates George's hidden life with Jim:

> Think of two people, living together day after day, year after year, in this small space, standing elbow to elbow cooking at the same small stove, squeezing past each other on the narrow stairs, shaving in front of the same small bathroom mirror, constantly jogging, jostling, bumping against each other's bodies by mistake or on purpose, sensually, aggressively, awkwardly, impatiently, in rage or in love—think what deep though invisible tracks they must leave, everywhere, behind them. . . . here, nearly every morning . . . George, having reached the bottom of the stairs, has this sensation of suddenly finding himself on an abrupt, brutally broken off, jagged edge—as though the track had disappeared down a landslide. It is here that he stops short and knows, with a sick newness, almost as though it were for the first time: Jim is dead. Is dead. (SM 12–13)

Throughout George's day, Isherwood continues the dialogue with the reader, sometimes by direct questions: "He has gone deep down in himself. What is he up to?" (SM 36); "But does George really hate all these people?" (SM 40). Sometimes Isherwood uses the second person pronoun: "No sooner have you turned off the freeway onto San Tomas Avenue than you are back into the tacky sleepy slowpoke Los Angeles of the thirties" (SM 41). Sometimes he employs an informal manner to maintain the dialogue; after the class's discussion of Huxley's novel, Isherwood introduces their comments in the following informal manner: "Here are some of its [the class's] findings . . ."(SM 68).

George lives apart from others, his distorted life a Giacometti study in personal distance, the void in which men suffer remote from their fellows. A paragraph from *The Reptonian*, March 1922, outlines George's predicament. Isherwood probably read the article and perhaps even subconsciously culled his title from it:

> The individual man cares much more for the things that touch his individuality than for those that touch his manhood . . . there is many a prig and many a fool who possesses so large a love of mankind that he has not a grain of his tender emotion to spare for a single man. And Humanity and the single man are divided by the largest gulf; the single man is the smallest integral division of humanity. . . .[3]

In the first half of the novel, George is certainly the "smallest integral division of humanity." Toward the end of the novel, however, the single man advances toward a letting go of consciousness and of self and toward a merging with Being Itself.

As day declines, the pace of the novel slackens. Changes of scene occur less frequently, less suddenly. The high point of George's waking day is the symbolic dialogue with Kenny. This leads to their sacramental swim in the sea, symbolic of death and prologue to George's actual death.

In a beach bar, the Starboard Side Inn where he first met Jim, George runs into Kenny Potter. Kenny, who has been dumped by his girl friend, had been particularly kind to George earlier in the day: he had sought out his companionship after class and, in a boyish gesture, had bought George a yellow pencil sharpener. In the bar, George buys Kenny a drink; as they drink and talk, their conversation approaches the symbolic Platonic dialogue:

> . . . not a Platonic dialogue in the hair-splitting, word-twisting, one-up-to-me sense; not a mock-humble bitching match; not a debate on some dreary set theme. You can talk about anything and change the subject as often as you like. In fact, what really matters is not what you talk about, but the being together in this particular relationship. (SM 154)

George cannot imagine such a relationship with a woman "because women can only talk in terms of the personal" (SM 154). Nor with a man of his own age, unless there were "some sort of polarity; for instance, if he was a Negro" (SM 154). The dialogue partners must be opposites, for by its nature the dialogue is impersonal, symbolic, an encounter in which "you can say absolutely anything. Even the closest confidence, the deadliest secret, comes out objectively as a mere metaphor or illustration which could never be used against you" (SM 155). In the case of George and Kenny, the polarity is age and youth.

The two achieve the phatic communication attained by Christopher and Bergmann, though here it is not a father-son relationship but, as Isherwood notes, an age-youth symbolic relationship. "George can almost feel the electric field of the dialogue surrounding and irradiating them. . . . As for

Kenny, he looks quite beautiful. *Radiant with rapport . . .*" (SM 155). George even passes the Test Kenny proposes:

> "Let's go swimming," says Kenny abruptly, as if bored by the whole conversation.
> "All right."
> Kenny throws his head right back and laughs wildly. "Oh—that's terrific."
> "What's terrific?"
> "It was a test. I thought you were bluffing, about being silly. So I said to myself, I'll suggest doing something wild, and if he objects—if he even hesitates—then I'll know it was all a bluff." (SM 160–61)

Unlike Christopher in *Down There on a Visit* whose response to the proffered opium was a qualified "one pipe," George responds wholeheartedly. Thus George and Kenny, age and youth, bolt for the ocean, stripping as they go, and pitch themselves into the surf. The moment is jubilant and unconscious, a madcap midnight escapade which Isherwood turns into a religious experience, symbolic of George's and Kenny's mergings with the Greater Consciousness, for which both yearn. Isherwood's syntax—the long, right-branching second sentence—and the diction—"blackness," "mysteriously," "awfully"—communicate the mystical quality of the experience:

> As for George, these waves are much too big for him. They seem truly tremendous, towering up, blackness unrolling itself out of blackness, mysteriously and awfully sparkling, then curling over in a thundering slap of foam which is sparked with phosphorus. (SM 162)

Immersed in phosphorus, George laughs at the sparks all over his body, which seems "bejeweled. . . . Laughing, gasping, choking, he is too drunk to be afraid . . ." (SM 162). George, "intent upon his own rites of purification . . . wide-open-armed" receives "the stunning baptism of the surf. Giving himself to it utterly, he washes away thought, speech, mood, desire, whole selves, entire lifetimes . . ." (SM 162–63). And then, foreshadowing the book's conclusion, a prodigious wave roars forward, as climactic as death, as great as Being Itself, and swallows the single man into its mysterious utter vastness:

> And now, suddenly, here is a great, an apocalyptically great wave, and George is way out, almost out of his depth, standing naked and tiny before its presence, under the lip of its roaring upheaval and the towering menace of its fall. He tries to dive through it—even now he feels no real fear—but instead he is caught and picked up, turned over and over and over, flapping and kicking toward a surface which may be either up or down or sideways, he no longer knows. (SM 163)

By his imagery Isherwood shows that George is completely given over to Being Itself—George now possesses what he sought for in Jim, what he seeks for in Kenny, who he hopes will be another Jim—but he is singularly unaware of this. As one critic writes, "It is fitting that we never know his [George's] final name. Neither does he."[4] Nonetheless George's search for something better gives him kinship with Isherwood's saint.

Kenny finally drags George out of the ocean, and both stumble toward George's house. In drunken clarity, George divines why Kenny was in the Starboard Side Inn—he wanted to talk to him:

> "The point is, you came to ask me about something that really *is* important. . . . You want me to tell you *what I know*. . . . Oh Kenneth, Kenneth, believe me—there's nothing I'd rather do! But I can't. I quite literally can't. Because, don't you see, *what I know is what I am?*" (SM 176)

And what he is, George insists, Kenny must find out for himself, for George is like a book that must be read in order to discover its contents: "A book can't read itself to you. It doesn't even know what it's about. I don't know what I'm about" (SM 176). Kenny, George vatically rages on, is the single boy he has met on campus who could know what George is about. Could Kenny be another Jim? Unfortunately no, for Kenny cannot be bothered to read George and will commit the inexcusable triviality of calling him a dirty old man, thus diverting this potentially precious night into a flirtation:

> "You don't like that word, do you? But it's the word. It's the enormous tragedy of everything nowadays: flirtation. Flirtation instead of fucking, if you'll pardon my coarseness. All any of you ever do is flirt. . . . And miss the one thing that might really—and, Kenneth, I do not say this casually—*transform your entire life—*" (SM 176–77)

George then passes out, his state of unconsciousness rendered in imagery which echoes Blake's suicide attempt and harkens back to the midnight swim:

> For a moment, Kenny's face is quite distinct. It grins, dazzlingly. Then his grin breaks up, is refracted, or whatever you call it, into rainbows of light. The rainbows blaze. George is blinded by them. He shuts his eyes. And now the buzzing in his ears is the roar of Niagara. (SM 177)

Later, George awakens to find a coy note from Kenny; then, before falling asleep, he enjoys an intense sexual climax by masturbating. He begins by conjuring Kenny and his girlfriend, then Kenny and a tennis player he had watched earlier that day; they flirt, grapple, flirt. Because Kenny does not take himself seriously, George substitutes the other tennis player, and, finally, comically, himself: "He is either. He is both at once. Ah—it is so good! Ah—ah . . . !" (SM 180). Then, slowly, George submerges into the ocean of unconsciousness from which he originally surfaced. George sinks deeper; only "Partial surfacing. . . . Partial emergings, just barely breaking the sheeted calm of the water. Most of George remaining submerged in sleep" (SM 181). George's brain, barely awash, cognizes darkly, not in its daytime manner, for now, incapable of decision, it can become aware of certain decisions not yet formulated: "Decisions that are like codicils which have been secretly signed and witnessed and put away in a most private place to wait the hour of their execution" (SM 181). In a catechetical question-answer format similar to Bloom and Stephen's post-brothel dialogue in *Ulysses* (though Isherwood's diction is infinitely simpler), George reviews his day, his life. Unlike Kenny, George resolves that he will not flirt with life, that he will find another Jim, that he will not truckle to old age:

> *Why does George believe he will find him* [Jim]?
> He only knows that he must find him. He believes he will because he must.
> *But George is getting old. Won't it very soon be too late?*
> Never use those words to George. He won't listen. He daren't listen. Damn the future. Let Kenny and the kids have it. Let Charley keep the past. George clings only to Now. It is Now that he must find another Jim. Now that he must love. Now that he must live. (SM 182)

Isherwood begins to close the circle toward which the story line has been curving since its beginning. As in *Prater Violet*, the book concludes with a Vedantist epiphany, particularly trenchant here because both the ocean imagery and the dialogue technique are resumed. With "this body known as George's" (SM 183) asleep, Isherwood asks, "But *is* all of George altogether present here?" (SM 183). He answers his question with an extended analogy which summarizes George's entire day:

> Up the coast a few miles north, in a lava reef under the cliffs, there are a lot of rock pools. You can visit them when the tide is out. Each pool is separate and different, and you can, if you are fanciful, give them names. . . . Just as George and the others are thought of, for convenience, as individual entities, so you may think of a rock pool as an entity; though, of course, it is not. The waters of its consciousness—so to speak—are swarming with hunted anxieties, grim-jawed greeds, dartingly vivid intuitions, old crusty-shelled rock-gripping obstinacies, deep-down sparkling undiscovered secrets, ominous protean organisms motioning mysteriously, perhaps warningly, toward the surface light. (SM 183–84)

For the rock-pool image, Isherwood is clearly indebted to Cyril Connolly's 1936 novel *The Rock Pool*. There Connolly uses the rock pool as a metaphor for his protagonist's impersonal observation of a colony of decadent artists. Searching for a viewpoint, Connolly's narrator settles on ". . . *The Rock Pool*—a microcosm cut off from the ocean . . . aquarium similes were the rage now. . . ."[5] Isherwood, however, converts the image into a rich religious parable. Just as the ocean floods the rock pools at the end of the day, so over George and the others in sleep comes "that other ocean—that consciousness which is no one in particular but which contains everyone and everything, past, present and future, and extends unbroken beyond the uttermost stars" (SM 184). Extending his analogy, Isherwood prepares for George's death by describing the mysterious dying of the rock-pool creatures. In the dark of the full flood, surely some of the creatures are "lifted from their pools to drift far out over the deep waters" (SM 184), never to return again. What can they tell us about their nocturnal journey? "Is there, indeed, anything for them to tell—except that the waters of the ocean are not really other than the waters of the pool?" (SM 184). Centering the reader's attention back on George's body, Isherwood uses the imagery of a ship and its crew which easily doubles as medical terminology:

> Within this body on the bed, the great pump works on and on, needing no rest. All over this quietly pulsating vehicle the skeleton crew make their tiny adjustments. As for what goes on topside, they know nothing of this but danger signals, false alarms mostly: red lights flashed from the panicky brain stem, curtly contradicted by green all clears from the level-headed cortex. But now the controls are on automatic. The cortex is drowsing. (SM 184–85)

Isherwood then invites the reader to fantasize George's death ("Just let us suppose, however . . ." [SM 185]). Isherwood ironically traces its beginning to the moment in which George felt most alive: his first glorious meeting with Jim in the Starboard Side Inn.

> Let us then suppose that, at the same instant, deep down in one of the major branches of George's coronary artery, an unimaginably gradual process began. Somehow—no doctor can tell us exactly why—the inner lining begins to become roughened. . . . Thus, slowly, invisibly, with the utmost discretion and without the slightest hint of those old fussers in the brain, an almost indecently melodramatic situation is contrived: the formation of the atheromatous plaque. (SM 185)

Again Isherwood invites the reader to imagine George's death: "Let us suppose this, merely. . . . This thing is wildly improbable. You could bet thousands of dollars against its happening, tonight or any night. And yet it *could*, quite possibly, be about to happen—within the next five minutes" (SM 185–86). Together both writer and reader put George to death: "Very well—let us suppose that this is the night, and the hour, and the appointed minute" (SM 186). Isherwood traces the gradual necrosis of George's body by beginning with his favorite word, the word on which he based his life:

> *Now*—
> The body on the bed stirs slightly, perhaps; but it
> does not cry out, does not wake. (SM 186)

Cortex and brain stem are murdered in the blackout . . . throttled out of their oxygen . . . the lungs go dead, their power line cut. The great ship of George's body founders, sinks, as "one by one, the lights go out and there is total blackness" (SM 186).

What about George the single man? His body "is now cousin to the garbage in the container on the back porch. Both will have to be carted away and disposed of, before too long" (SM 186), for George's spirit can no longer associate with what lies on the bed. It must, at long last, follow the current of George's life and merge with the Greater Consciousness— what, as Isherwood has shown throughout the novel, George has yearned and searched for in the wrong places and by the wrong methods. In death, George is no longer the single man.

Who is George? Isherwood's Everyman: for in his humanity and desire for wholeness, George is no different from anyone else. Thus Isherwood's dialogue, which George thinks must be conducted by opposites, is resolved into a unity. The protagonist and the reader, as well as the novelist, do not "differ in kind, but only in degree."

Notes

1. Concerning the narrative technique in *A Single Man*, Isherwood writes: "The story is told in the present tense by a non-personal seemingly disembodied narrator who never says 'I' and addresses the reader with the air of a surgeon lecturing to medical students during an operation. The 'patient' is the chief character, George. The narrator knows everything that George feels and thinks and is present with him at all times. But he is not a part of George. Indeed it will be possible for George to die while the narrator looks on and describes his death to the reader." (Leon Surmelian, *Techniques of Fiction Writing*, p. 80.) As the novel progresses, however, I think Isherwood's medical lecturer goes far beyond the bounds of case history—in fact, the surgeon reveals extensive knowledge of the spirit, and for this reason I have preferred to call him a kind of guru.
2. *A Single Man* (New York: Simon and Schuster, 1964).
3. *The Reptonian*, XLV (March 1922).
4. George Greene, "Crying for Help," *The Commonwealth*, LXXXI (October 2, 1964), 53.
5. Cyril Connolly, *The Rock Pool* (1936; rpt. New York: Atheneum, 1968), p. 4.

CLAUDE J. SUMMERS
From "Evil Mothers and Truly Weak Men"
Christopher Isherwood
1980, pp. 63–69

I sherwood's collaborations with W. H. Auden in writing three experimental verse dramas and a remarkable travel book earned him the reputation of ideological commitment in an intensely political decade. But the artistic union of the decade's finest poet and its most sensitive prose stylist did not produce great literature, at least in part because of the overtly

political stance the collaborators assumed. They so heavy-handedly imposed political dogma upon the plays that dramatic development and thematic coherence suffered.

With the exception of *Journey to a War*, the Auden-Isherwood collaboration yielded work less satisfying than that produced by either writer separately. As Stephen Spender observes, "most of the poetry in these plays is inferior to the poetry of Auden's single poems; no character in them has the subtlety and profundity of characters in Mr. Isherwood's novels."[1]

The plays, written for Rupert Doone's Group Theatre, are frankly experimental reactions against traditional dramatic realism.[2] They incorporate elements of the political cabaret, German expressionism, the fairy tale, and the pantomime, while deliberately eschewing subtlety in both characterization and theme. Auden declared that "the development of the film has deprived drama of any excuse of being documentary. . . . The subject of drama. . . . is the commonly known, the universally familiar stories of the society or generation in which it is written. . . . the drama is not suited to the analysis of character, which is the province of the novel. Dramatic characters are simplified, easily recognisable and over life-size."[3] However serious as an attempt to make a moribund theater relevant as a forum for the exploration of contemporary issues, Auden's concept of the new drama actually rendered superfluous his collaborator's special talents for ironic observation and for shrewd insight into individual motivation.

The Dog beneath the Skin, or Where Is Francis?, produced in 1936, is an exuberant satire of contemporaneous political confusion. It is frequently very funny, but it lacks a sure sense of direction and, as a consequence, its effects are often adolescent. The episodic plot traces the mythic quest of Alan Norman in his search for a missing heir, Sir Francis Crewe. Accompanied by a dog, Alan travels through Europe, visiting a reactionary monarchy and a lunatic fascist state. He returns to England, where he finds fascism in his native village and discovers that the object of his quest has been with him all along, disguised as the dog Francis.

After a general denunciation—"most of you will die without ever knowing what your leaders are really fighting for or even that you are fighting at all"—Alan, Francis, and a handful of villagers depart to become "a unit in the army of the other side." Unfortunately, the "other side" is so imprecisely identified as to convict the play of superficiality in its political analysis.

The Ascent of F6, published in 1936 but not produced until 1937, is an altogether more serious poetic drama. It moves beyond topical satire to explore the nature of the will to power. The play's external plot is organized around the international competition to scale a politically significant mountain straddling the border of two colonies, British Sudoland and Ostnian Sudoland. In developing this plot, the play exposes the corruption of politics and the emptiness of contemporary daily life, the latter creating the public's voracious appetite for heroes. After much reluctance, Michael Ransom agrees to lead the British climbing expedition, and the journey up the mountain is paralleled by Ransom's interior journey of self-discovery.

Ransom, whose name suggests his sacrificial role, is modeled on T. E. Lawrence, whom Isherwood described in 1937 as having "suffered, in his own person, the neurotic ills of an entire generation."[4] Ransom's decision to undertake the climb is motivated not by the jingoistic appeals of his brother, the prime minister, but by his attachment to his mother. A reincarnation of the Evil Mother, Mrs. Ransom is finally exposed as her son's personal Demon. After losing all the members of his climbing party, Ransom reaches the summit of F6, where, in an expressionistic delirium, he confronts the phantoms of his guilt. The hallucination culminates in the appearance of his mother as a young woman. He dies with his head buried in her lap.

The most fully developed character in the Auden-Isherwood plays, Michael Ransom is an intriguing study in heroism. His mother tells him, "you were to be the truly strong." But on his quest he exposes himself as one more version of the Truly Weak Man. He discovers that he is as flawed in his personal life as, more obviously, his brother is in his public life. Ransom is corrupted both by allowing himself to be used for imperialistic interests and by sacrificing others in the course of his personal quest for power.

The play is brilliantly unified by patterns of linguistic and structural echoes, but its discovery of the will to power in an Oedipal source is both annoyingly simplistic and unconvincingly realized. *The Ascent of F6* is, in fact, a deeply flawed play, confused as well as confusing. But for all its obvious faults, the work remains fascinating in its haunting exploration of the will to power; and its recreation of the Evil Mother and the Truly Weak Man link it firmly to the Isherwood canon.

The final play of the Auden-Isherwood collaboration, *On the Frontier*, is less experimental and more unified than its two predecessors. Produced in 1938, the play's obsession with war has an immediacy that partially compensates for the crudity of its characterization and the predictability of its politics. Creating two mythic states, the monarchist Ostnia and the fascist Westland, the play savagely indicts nationalism and looks forward to a future city where "the will of love is done." The plot traces the movement of the two countries toward a war that channels the energies of workers away from the class struggle and into a self-defeating xenophobia.

The effect of the war is imaginatively portrayed by the simultaneous reactions of two families on the stage, one occupying the Ostnian side of the frontier, the other the Westland side, each oblivious of the other. The Westland son and the Ostnian daughter love each other, but they are unable to cross the artificial boundaries of hysteria and hatred erected by nationalism. They embrace only after death in an embarrassingly sentimental *Liebestod*.

On the Frontier is subtitled "a melodrama." The term fairly acknowledges the play's exaggerated emotion, stock characterization, and comic-strip simplicity. All the characters are stereotypes, including the fascist Leader, who is yet another Truly Weak Man. Much the most intriguing character, because more subtly drawn and more fully human, is Valerian, the power-hungry capitalist. Unfortunately, the two lovers are the most insipid of characters. Since they carry the burden of the play's version of a better world, the Just City comes dangerously close to the platitudinous. Although it lacks the zany fun of *The Dog beneath the Skin* and the poetic complexity of *The Ascent of F6*, *On the Frontier* successfully depicts the dangers of nationalism and of propaganda; and it effectively portrays the metaphorical boundaries that separate countries, classes, and individuals.

Journey to a War is the only really distinguished product of the Auden-Isherwood collaboration, and its success may result from a strict division of labor, one that allowed each partner to exploit his individual strengths. The book resulted from a commission by two publishing houses, Random House of New York and Faber & Faber of London, to write a travel book about the East. The collaborators decided to go to China and report on the Sino-Japanese War. They left London in January 1938 and returned at the end of July. The book appeared in 1939 and consists of four separate but related parts: prefatory sonnets by Auden, a "Travel-Diary" written by Isherwood and based on journals kept by both travelers, a group of photographs taken by Auden, and "In Time of War," a sonnet sequence with verse commentary by Auden.

The "Travel Diary" is by far the longest section of the book. Its particularity complements the universality of Auden's poetry: it documents the specific journey and the reactions of the two individual travelers in concrete detail, while Auden's poems take as their subject the generalized question of war in the abstract. Significantly, both men abandon the ideological rhetoric that burdens the plays. They are clearly committed to the Chinese cause, but their political point of view is the liberal humanism saluted in Auden's dedicatory sonnet, "To E. M. Forster": "You promise still the inner life shall pay." Like Forster, Auden and Isherwood calculate the cost of war in terms of its destructiveness to the human spirit; but the younger men also endorse their mentor's faith, expressed in *Howards End*, that "There are moments when the inner life actually 'pays,' when years of self-scrutiny, conducted for no ulterior motive, are suddenly of practical use."[5]

The personal response to war, its impact on the inner life, is indeed the prevailing theme of the book. Isherwood's wonderful description of a Japanese air raid weaves into the apparently objective reporting a personal response that colors the whole:

> The searchlights criss-crossed, plotting points, like dividers; and suddenly there they were, six of them, flying close together and high up. It was as if a microscope had brought dramatically into focus the bacilli of a fatal disease. They passed, bright, tiny, and deadly, infecting the night. . . . It was as tremendous as Beethoven, but *wrong*—a cosmic offence, and an insult to the whole of Nature and the entire earth. I don't know if I was frightened. Something inside me was flapping about like a fish.

The personal element is also emphasized by the concurrent development of an emerging portrait of Auden as the Truly Strong Man, the foil to Isherwood's self-portrait as a Truly Weak Man. The contrast is apparent in the following passage: "I slept uneasily that night—in my trousers and shirt: not wishing to have to leave the train and bolt for cover in my pajamas. Auden, with his monumental calm, had completely undressed."

The "Travel-Diary" is studiedly antiheroic in its presentation of war. With characteristic understatement and ironic humor, Isherwood continually explores the nature of war. He searches for a definition that will embrace war's absurdity, stupidity, pettiness, and monotony as well as its suffering and waste:

> War is bombing an already disused arsenal, missing it, and killing a few old women. War is lying in a stable with a gangrenous leg. War is drinking hot water in a barn and worrying about one's wife. War is a handful of lost and terrified men in the mountains, shooting at something moving in the undergrowth. War is waiting for days with nothing to do; shouting down a dead telephone; going without sleep, or sex, or a wash. War is untidy, inefficient, obscure, and largely a matter of chance.

The strength of the diary is that it creates from the narrow experience of two naive young men—limited by their own ignorance and fears and dependent on translators and bureaucrats—a vivid account of the human realities of war.

Notes

1. Stephen Spender, "The Poetic Dramas of W. H. Auden and Christopher Isherwood," *New Writing*, NS 1 (London: Hogarth, 1938), pp. 102–103.
2. For an account of the collaboration on the plays and of each author's individual contribution to them, see Edward Mendelson, "The Auden-Isherwood Collaboration," *Twentieth Century Literature* 22 (1976): 276–85. For an account of the Group

Theatre, see Julian Symons, *The Thirties: A Dream Revolved* (London: Faber, 1960; reprinted 1975), pp. 76–84.
3. W. H. Auden, "I Want the Theatre to Be . . . ," theater program, Group Theatre Season 1935; reprinted in Hynes, *The Auden Generation*, p. 399.
4. Isherwood, review of A. W. Lawrence, ed., *T. E. Lawrence by His Friends*, in *The Listener*, 17 (1937): 1170; reprinted in *Exhumations*, p. 24.
5. E. M. Forster, *Howards End* (London: Edward Arnold, 1910; reprinted New York: Vintage, 1960), p. 195.

W. W. JACOBS

1863–1943

William Wymark Jacobs was born in East London on September 8, 1863. The son of a wharf-manager in the Port of London, he grew up in the company of longshoremen and sailors, who provided the material for much of his fiction. After attending several private schools, he joined the Savings Bank Department of the Civil Service as a clerk, a job he greatly disliked. His earliest professional writing was accepted by *The Idler* and *To-day*, both edited by Jerome K. Jerome, who became a lifelong friend.

Jacobs achieved immediate success with his collection of stories *Many Cargoes* (1896), but published two further books, *The Skipper's Wooing* (1897) and *Sea Urchins* (1898), before committing himself to full-time writing. His humor made him a popular and successful author, though he also excelled in the uncanny, as in his most famous story, "The Monkey's Paw," which first appeared in *The Lady of the Barge* (1902). Jacobs wrote a stage version of this tale with Louis N. Parker, and it has been filmed several times and adapted for radio. His other collections of short stories include *Light Freights* (1901), *Sailors' Knots* (1909), *Deep Waters* (1919), and *Sea Whispers* (1926). Among his five novels are *A Master of Craft* (1900), and *The Castaways* (1916).

A shy and modest man, Jacobs married in 1900 and had five children. He lived for a time near Epping Forest, and then in Berkhamsted, before returning to London, where he died on September 1, 1943.

Personal

Jacobs was born in 1863 and began his career with a proper sense of the earnestness of life as we have made it by going as a clerk into the Savings Bank Department of the Post Office. If only he had stayed there and gone on diligently looking after the financial interests of the million he could have risen to such eminence that an O.B.E. or even a knighthood might have been his portion. But the humorist in him broke out and he took to writing short stories in his spare time; I remember the joy I had in reading the very earliest of them in Jerome's magazines *To-day* and *The Idler*, back in the '90's; and he went on doing this and became a boon and a blessing and a healthful antidote to the sort of literature that was plentiful in those days that are supposed to have been given over to the decadents, and a boon and a blessing he remains to a generation that has need of all the happiness it can get. Our various Governments that, of recent years, have showered honours lavishly on men who have never done any of us any good, have discreetly passed him by; but you will notice that such glittering rewards are never offered to humorists, perhaps because the powers that be think, like Lord Froth in Congreve's comedy, that laughter "is such a vulgar expression of the passion—everybody can laugh"; or perhaps because they have some instinct of self-defence and a hazy subconsciousness that one touch of humour makes the whole world kin, and too much of it would shatter the last absurdities of our sorry social scheme and puncture the possibilities of flashy distinction that are still open to ambitious politicians. Anyhow, as I say, apart from due wages, Jacobs has received no reward to date, except the admiration and affection of many thousands of readers, and, moreover, I am certain he does not covet any other. . . .

In all ⟨his⟩ novels and stories Jacobs has been as faithful to the docks and wharves and waterside districts of London and Essex as Hardy has been to Wessex and, allowing for some farcical extravagances of incident, his quaint old salts and the famous Night Watchman are as true to life as are the peasants of the Wessex novels. A born Londoner, they tell me, and I should have been surprised to hear otherwise, that Jacobs spent much of his younger days in and about the riverside places and little coast towns with whose atmosphere and picturesque personalities his books have made us familiar; that he used to voyage aboard such Thames barges and coasting schooners as glide through his pages, and was on terms of intimacy, ashore and at sea, with those captains, mates, able seamen, cabin boys, watchmen, publicans and other lively sinners whom he has introduced to us with such insight and imaginative humour that nowadays we feel almost as intimate with them as he is. You cannot easily fit him into that rough and hearty environment, and you picture him to yourself a slim, slight, boyish figure, oddly contrasting with his robust companions, a quiet, grave, reticent looker-on at the game, an acute observer, a chief amongst them making mental notes that, though he did not know it at the time, he would in due course print.

He had that boyishness of figure and general appearance,

M. R. James

W. W. Jacobs

Christopher Isherwood

JEROME K. JEROME

HENRY ARTHUR JONES

STORM JAMESON

PAMELA HANSFORD JOHNSON

that thoughtful gravity and shyness of manner when I first saw him at a public dinner soon after *At Sunwich Port* had given everybody something fresh to laugh over; and, except that his close, smooth hair is changing to an iron-grey, he has them all yet. Nobody seeing him at one of the dinners of the pleasant Bohemian club where he is occasionally to be seen, and not knowing who he was, would ever guess that he was one of the greatest of living humorists; they would far more likely fancy he was a venturesome young curate who, coming unwontedly into unconventional surroundings, that his flock might even consider slightly wicked, had discreetly laid his clerical garb aside and dressed appropriately as one of the ungodly for the occasion. He is a delightfully witty speaker, when he can be persuaded to speak, but that is rarely; I doubt whether any author of his distinction, or of half his distinction, is more seldom heard or seen in public places. He makes his home well away from London, at Berkhamsted, and I have heard from one of his admirers who visited the little Hertfordshire town (where that other quiet man, Cowper, was born), that he collogued with a prominent native who knew no more than the name of Jacobs and was surprised to hear that the tenant of Beechcroft was a famous author. He is as unobtrusive as Tennyson pretended to be; for, having a sense of humour, he does not cultivate eccentricities of behaviour, not even to the extent of going about clothed like a stage brigand.—ARTHUR ST. JOHN ADCOCK, "William Wymark Jacobs," *The Glory That Was Grub Street*, 1928, pp. 148–52

General

Jacobs had the fortune to grasp a small, fixed world at its moment of ripeness and decline, a time always propitious to the artist. A Thames-side clerk, Jacobs knew the wharves where the small coasting ships and land-hugging barge fleets tied up on their rounds between London and the wizened, rosy little towns of the Essex estuaries. This was a fading traffic: the cement, the flour, the bricks, the road flints, were more and more being diverted to the railway; the small mills and shippers were being devoured by the larger firms; the little towns with their raucous taverns and fighting inhabitants had already quietened; and unemployable and unspeakable old men sat on the posts of the empty quays, refining upon their memories of a past, spicy in its double dealing, prone to horseplay and cheered by the marital misfortunes of others. . . .

Material of this kind dates when it is used realistically and it would be simple to show that Jacobs draws the working-class and the lower middle-class as they were before even the Nineties; and treats them as comics for reasons that are, unconsciously, political. It is certain that Polly and Kipps, for example, are greater characters than the Night-watchman or thick-headed knockabouts like Ginger Dick, simply because Wells relates them to something larger than themselves. That is to attribute no artistic falsity to Jacobs's characters; they are merely limited and within those limits they are perfect. Jacobs's general impression of the poor is sound; the psychology of sailors, shopkeepers and so on is exact. And one important aspect of working-class character, or at any rate of male character when very ordinary men are thrown together, is strongly brought out and justifies his intricate plots from Nature; I refer to the observation that the rapid, oblique leg-pulling talk, with its lies and bland assertions which no one believes, is part of the fine male art of cutting a figure and keeping your end up. The plots in Jacobs are the breath of the fantasticating life of men. They are superior to the plots of a writer like O. Henry. They spring naturally from the wits of the characters as trickery comes naturally to cardsharpers; they seem to pour off the tongue.

The flavour and the skill of Jacobs are of course all in the handling of the talk. At first sight the talk looks like something merely funny in itself; but Jacobs had the art of adding the obstacle of character to narrative:

"Come here," said the mate sternly.
The boy came towards him.
"What were you saying about the skipper?" demanded the other.
"I said it wasn't cargo he was after," said Henry.
"Oh, a lot you know about it!" said the mate.
Henry scratched his leg but said nothing.
"A lot you know about it!" repeated the mate in rather a disappointed tone. Henry scratched the other leg.
"Don't let me hear you talking about your superior officer's affairs again," said the mate sharply. "Mind that!"
"No sir," said the boy humbly. "It ain't my business of course."
"What ain't your business?" said the mate carelessly.
"His," said Henry.

There is no doubt that Jacobs is one of the supreme craftsmen of the short story. It is extraordinary that he should have brought such pellucid economy to material that was, on the face of it, stuff for schoolboys, or the Halls; but in doing so, he transformed it. The comic spirit was perhaps his thwarted poetry. He knew his limits. The only carelessness or rather the only indifference in his work appears in his novels. Of these *A Master of Craft* suggests a partial attempt at the Mean Street realism of the period; and a desire to go beyond his range; it contains a lady-killing skipper—instead of the usual skipper-killing lady—and he is, for Jacobs, an ugly character. Jacobs shows his wounds a little in this book; but, for some reason, he slips back into his shell. I think we may be glad he decided to remain in the ivory fo'c'sle. The artificial, the almost pastoral Jacobs of *Dialstone Lane* is more satisfying. The spring sunlight of pure malice and self-possessed sentiment gleams on this story about three gullible townsmen who dream of going to sea; and the story has two immortally awful wives in it: the oppressed and the oppressor. But it is a major error in the plot that the dream voyage actually takes place. Jacobs would never have been so slapdash in a short story.—V. S. PRITCHETT, "W. W. Jacobs," *Books in General*, 1953, pp. 235–41

In 1944, having won a prize in the caucus race of youth club life, I was asked to nominate the book of my choice. I named an anthology of W. W. Jacobs short stories. In time the book vanished into that limbo which serves as the repository for all the unwanted artefacts in the universe. Whatever happened, I still sometimes wonder, to my suede shinpads, my monthly editions of *The Ring*, my George IV silver threepenny bit? Once they were deeply cherished, but that didn't save them. As for Jacobs, I think I must have passed him on with some disdain to a younger cousin even less literary than I was; perhaps I exchanged them at our local secondhand shop for Leacock or Ellery Queen. The point is that in 1944 Jacobs's books were still popular enough for an unintellectual adolescent to be interested in him. He had died in the previous year, so perhaps I saw an obituary somewhere which tickled my fancy. That was thirty years ago, and today Jacobs has become so remote and obscure a figure as to have joined the nostalgia trade, a relic from a vanished world who now requires for his survival the resolute revivalism of Hugh Greene.

Greene in his introduction (to Jacobs's *Selected Short*

Stories) defines the recurrent Jacobs character, Bob Pretty, as "surely one of the great comic characters of English literature". Arnold Bennett once coupled Jacobs with Aristophanes; Evelyn Waugh described him as "a pure artist"; Wodehouse said that Jacobs "represented to me perfection"; Edmund Wilson called him "a writer of distinction". With these praises ringing in your ears, now go out and try to find any of Jacobs's books in the shops. The most surprising thing about Greene's gesture is not its chivalric intent or the sentimental recollection which inspired it, but that the gesture should have been necessary at all. But then middle-brow magazine fiction of the type in which Jacobs specialised has been unfashionable for too long now for any but the very hardiest spirits to survive, and Jacobs has not been one of them. It is sometimes said, usually by boobies, that this kind of literature has been usurped by the telly-drama, when the truth is that the average telly-drama, having no literary antecedents of any kind, could not possibly have usurped anything or anybody except its own asinine self. Where in TV fiction would a character open an episode by remarking, "Sailormen 'ave their faults, I'm not denying it. I used to 'ave myself when I was at sea"?

Structurally Jacobs derives from the old O. Henry formula where the plot is a reversal of what we are supposed to expect. Most of the cockney vernacular tales follow an identical pattern. Somebody sees an easy touch and tries to keep it from his greedy friends; they cheat and connive to diddle him out of his good fortune; the good fortune turns out to be bad news; the biter is bit. The pervading atmosphere is one of cheerfully callous amorality; there are no finer feelings in a Jacobs short story, and all his women are sadistic termagants whose intractable viciousness provides decent men with the diversion of the only really important blood sport, which is avoiding getting married. In one Jacobs story in Greene's selection, the nastiest practical joke a man can think of is to leave his friend lots of money in his will provided he weds the first woman who asks him. Notice that Jacobs takes it for granted that whoever she is, she will turn out to be a pest.

Within the narrow scope of his style, Jacobs manipulated the strings with considerable wit. Take the story 'The Money Box', where the premise is so commonplace that the rest of us probably thought of it ourselves years ago. Two sailors decide to try to save their shore-leave money by depositing it with an old salt who will dole it out, a bit every day, and thereby make it last. The first thought to occur to us is that Jacobs will make the old salt abscond with the funds, but this he does not do. Then the two young men demand their money in one lump, and the old boy refuses. They threaten violence. So far the story has proceeded along predictably humdrum lines. But now watch what Jacobs does with the situation. He makes the two desperately thirsty young men pawn their spare clothes to raise the wind. This gives them the idea of stealing the old man's clothes and pawning those too, thereby bringing off the double ploy of raising money and gaining revenge. After they have pawned the clothes and spent the money, the old man tells them that their money is stitched into the lining of the very coat they have pawned. So the old man takes *their* clothes and pawns them so as to redeem his own coat, which they must agree to if they want their money back. The story ends with the two sailors trapped naked in their own bedroom for three days. Perhaps that sort of thing will never win a literary prize, but it takes some working out and putting down. Jacobs apparently wrote at a snail's pace of a hundred words a day, and the proof that his travail was worth it is contained in the pages of Greene's volume, which conveys a charming illusion of casual chat flowing easily off the page into the mind's eye. I have an idea that this kind of honest craftsmanship is not to be sneezed

at, and that much modern fiction is bedevilled by the deafening sound of sneezing on all sides. In a fortnight I hope to return to the theme of Hugh Greene among the Edwardians; for the moment the hedonistic reader could do worse than dip into the Wapping pubs and whopping lies of W. W. Jacobs's canny maritime drunks.—BENNY GREEN, "Wapping Lies," *Spec*, July 19, 1975, p. 85

Works

I have been reading a new novel by Mr. W. W. Jacobs—*Salthaven*. It is a long time since I read a book of his. Ministries have fallen since then, and probably Mr. Jacobs' prices have risen—indeed, much has happened—but the talent of the author of *Many Cargoes* remains steadfast where it did. *Salthaven* is a funny book. Captain Trimblett, to excuse the lateness of a friend for tea, says to the landlady: "He saw a man nearly run over!" and the landlady replies: "Yes, but how long would that take him?" If you ask me whether I consider this humorous, I reply that I do. I also consider humorous this conversational description of an exemplary boy who took to "Sandford and Merton" "as a duck takes to water": "By modelling his life on its teaching" (says young Vyner) "he won a silver medal for never missing an attendance at school. Even the measles failed to stop him. Day by day, a little more flushed than usual, perhaps, he sat in his place until the whole school was down with it, and had to be closed in consequence. Then and not till then did he feel that he had saved the situation." I care nothing for the outrageous improbability of any youthful son of a shipowner being able to talk in the brilliant fashion in which Mr. Jacobs makes Vyner talk. Success excuses it. *Salthaven* is bathed in humour.

At the same time I am dissatisfied with *Salthaven*. And I do not find it easy to explain why. I suppose the real reason is that it discloses no signs of any development whatever on the part of the author. Worse, it discloses no signs of intellectual curiosity on the part of the author. Mr. Jacobs seems to live apart from the movement of his age. Nothing, except the particular type of humanity and environment in which he specializes, seems to interest him. There is no hint of a general idea in his work. By some of his fellow-artists he is immensely admired. I have heard him called, seriously, the greatest humourist since Aristophanes. I admire him myself, and I will not swear that he is not the greatest humourist since Aristophanes. But I will swear that no genuine humourist ever resembled Aristophanes less than Mr. Jacobs does. Aristophanes was passionately interested in everything. He would leave nothing alone. Whereas Mr. Jacobs will leave nearly everything alone. Kipling's general ideas are excessively crude, but one does feel in reading him that his curiosity is boundless, even though his taste in literature must infallibly be bad. "Q." is not to be compared in creative power with either of these two men, but one does feel in reading him that he is interested in other manifestations of his own art, that he cares for literature. Impossible to gather from Mr. Jacobs' work that he cares for anything serious at all; impossible to differentiate his intellectual outlook from that of an average reader of the *Strand Magazine!* I do not bring this as a reproach against Mr. Jacobs, whose personality it would be difficult not to esteem and to like. He cannot alter himself. I merely record the phenomenon as worthy of notice.—ARNOLD BENNETT, "W. W. Jacobs and Aristophanes" (1908), *Books and Persons*, 1917, pp. 53–55

In the early lines of W. W. Jacobs' "The Monkey's Paw," an altogether chilling story, is embedded the germ of the entire story. Mr. White and his son Herbert were playing chess, the father,

(1) who possessed ideas about the game involving radical changes, (2) putting his king into . . . sharp and unnecessary perils. . . .

"Hark at the wind," said Mr. White, who, (3) having seen a fatal mistake after it was too late, (4) was amiably desirous of preventing his son from seeing it.

Contained in this passage are four elements that foreshadow the action of the story, although Jacobs is never heavy-handed in working out the tale as a projection of its opening paragraphs. The obvious parallel to the game of chess, is, of course, the game of life. While Mr. White's choosing a small sum (two hundred pounds) when he made his first wish on the monkey's paw might make him seem less than radical, we must remember that he snatched the paw from the fire when the old soldier tossed it there. Had White been one merely to accept life, he would have taken the soldier's advice and let the paw burn.

The second element, that of putting his king into "sharp and unnecessary peril," comes with the first wish. White had no way of knowing that he was endangering Herbert's life in requesting the £200, but the soldier's demeanor when he told of the magical powers of the paw should have warned a less radical man to let the paw burn. As it turned out, the £200 wished for came as an indemnity for Herbert, who was killed when he fell into some working machinery. While the Gothic tone of the story is not such that one would expect a pun on the "sharp" peril, certainly the peril was *unnecessary*. White planned to use the £200 requested to pay off the mortgage, but there was no urgent need for it to be paid off immediately.

White's seeing a fatal mistake after it was too late was the third element. The fatal mistake here is not the death of his son, however, but something even more terrible—the resurrection of his son with his face still mangled from the machinery. When Mrs. White insisted that White make a second wish—to bring Herbert back—White feared that the wish might bring the son back mutilated. Nevertheless, his fear of his wife caused him to make the second wish. It was only much later, when they heard a noise at the door, that White sensed it was his mutilated son and frantically sought the paw to make a third wish.

This wish—that Herbert be dead again—was an acting out of the fourth element. But it is not the son he is preventing from seeing the fatal mistake this time. It is his wife, who is not aware that the second wish did not include the request that Herbert be restored whole. The third wish prevented the heartstruck mother from seeing the hideous creature outside the door.

Thus in the opening two paragraphs, Jacobs has given us a *micro*-story which contains all the elements of the *macro*-story, if one may use those terms. Still his symbolic foreshadowing is not heavy-handed. The use of the words "amiably desirous" to describe White's efforts to prevent his son from seeing his mistake, for instance, would seem incongruous were they to describe his effort to prevent his wife from seeing their son. Indeed, despite the symbolic relationship of the chess game to the story proper, Jacobs handled it in such a sophisticated manner that the effect of the game on the reader is suggestive, hinting of the dangers implicit in Mr. White's radical ideas about the game—of life, while at the same time giving us with a few bold strokes a preliminary sketch of the central character in the story.—JOSEPH H. HARKEY, "Foreshadowing in 'The Monkey's Paw,'" *SSF*, Fall 1969, pp. 653–54

J. B. PRIESTLEY
From "Mr. W. W. Jacobs" (1923)
Figures in Modern Literature
1924, pp. 103–14

If Mr. W. W. Jacobs' stories had been concerned with absinthe and prostitution instead of beer and matrimony; if they had first appeared in the *Pale Review* instead of the *Strand Magazine*, and had been afterwards brought out in small private editions instead of such-and-such a sevenpenny or shilling series; if, in short, they had succeeded in depressing a handful instead of amusing a multitude of readers, then the very persons who never mention Mr. Jacobs would long ago have called him a great artist. Delicate appreciations of his art would have made their appearance in our English literary journals, and superior persons in America, following their usual custom, would have produced thesis after thesis analysing his technique. Actually, Mr. Jacobs is not, of course, a great artist, but, nevertheless, he is an artist, and now that he has entertained us for so long, there is perhaps no danger in calling him one. No doubt most capable readers have long since recognized this fact, but they do not seem to have thought it a subject worth discussion, and in all probability simply because Mr. Jacobs happens to be very popular. Literary conditions are becoming so topsy-turvy that popularity is almost a short cut to critical oblivion: it is as if the critics and the railway-bookstall clerks had agreed to divide contemporary literature between them and not encroach upon each other's territory. Of this popularity there can be no question; it began with the publication of his first book, nearly thirty years ago, and it is not yet at an end. If, as Coleridge (who would modify his statement if he lived to-day) once remarked, an author can be said to have achieved fame when his books are to be found in obscure country inns, then Mr. Jacobs is indeed famous. We have found him in the remotest little inns and have blessed the kindly or forgetful traveller that left him there; we have pounced upon him in the bookshelves of spare bedrooms here, there, and everywhere; the night-watches have often found us listening to the night-watchman; Ginger Dick, Peter Russet, and old Sam Small have gone with us and "fleeted the time" on the longest railway journeys; and we have sneaked into the company of the old man at the "Cauliflower," and Bob Pretty and the rest, many a time when our reputations, bank-balances, and families demanded that we should be otherwise engaged. For my own part, I am ready to confess that I could not name more than one-third of our author's volumes and could not say which story is in which volume, and yet I must have read most of his stories over and over again at odd times, and am quite ready to read them all over again. Mr. Jacobs has no message for the age; he has not imagined any Utopias, nor even invented a new religion; he has not helped to solve any of our more urgent problems, except that of obtaining liquid refreshment at a minimum of cost; no transatlantic critic has yet written an essay on the "Something-ism of Jacobs," comparing him with Strindberg and Wedekind; and yet he need not despair. He has the satisfaction of knowing that he has only to leave one of his volumes in the same room with any normal English-speaking person, and that person, opening the book and coming across some such beginning as this:

"Strength and good-nature"—said the night-watchman, musingly, as he felt his biceps—"strength and good-nature always go together. Sometimes you find a strong man who is not good-natured; but then, as everybody he comes in contack with is, it comes to the same thing.

"The strongest and kindest-'earted man I ever come across was a man o' the name of Bill Burton, a shipmate of Ginger Dick's. For that matter 'e was a shipmate o' Peter Russet's and old Sam Small's too. . . ."

will be compelled to settle himself (and perhaps herself) down, neglect his business, and read and enjoy to the end. And at the end, such a reader, hurrying to take up the threads of business again, will not find the world a worse place than it appeared to him when he began; his wits will have been sharpened, and he will have been mellowed and heartened by laughter. Certainly, Mr. Jacobs, perched though he is on the dubious heights of popularity, need not despair.

The few little notices of Mr. Jacobs one has seen here and there have always pointed out that his youth was spent in the neighbourhood of the London docks, and the writers would seem to imagine that by hanging about the waterside and keeping his ears open, a man can almost automatically become the author of *Many Cargoes* and *Old Craft.* Clearly this will not do. Mr. Jacobs' knowledge of sailors and the seafaring life in general has obviously played its part in his authorship, but it does not explain him. Mr. Conrad and Mr. H. M. Tomlinson, I take it, know a great deal about the sea and the docks, but they are no more capable of writing, say "The Skipper's Wooing" than Mr. Jacobs is of writing *Nostromo* or *London River.* One writer, talking about the way in which he used to meet our author occasionally at literary gatherings in the late 'nineties, remarks: "Obviously the men and women that he met on these occasions were of little use to him in his stories. Not one of us understood the difference between a barque and a schooner; we knew something about Guy de Maupassant and Flaubert, but nothing about marline-spikes or capstans. Where W. W. Jacobs got his intricate nautical knowledge from I know not. He never paraded it: he never said 'Avast there' or 'Shiver my timbers'" . . . But Mr. Jacobs is not a Clark Russell with a little comedy added, and it is quite possible that in order to appreciate him to the full it is more important to know something about Maupassant than it is to know something about a marline-spike. Actually, only about one-half of his stories deal with the adventures of sailormen, and even then the adventures usually take place ashore; while the rest have nothing whatever to do with the sea, though for the most part they find their characters in classes not far removed from that of the common sailor. Among this latter group is that series, spreading from volume to volume, which is supposed to be told to successive travellers by the old man (that adept at obtaining drink and tobacco at other people's expense without any apparent loss of dignity) at the "Cauliflower Inn" at Claybury, that series which might be called the epic of Bob Pretty, most ingenious of village rascals. I would not willingly alienate any fellow-enthusiast's sympathies at the outset by a too rash assertion of my own preferences; but I am not sure that these Bob Pretty stories are not among the very best things that Mr. Jacobs has done. Who could forget, having once read, that episode of the Prize Hamper, when the great Bob not only succeeded in winning the hamper, but also managed to obtain its value in money as well from the unsuccessful competitors; or that of the poaching, when the keepers rescued nothing more than a sack of cabbages from the middle of a very cold and muddy pond; or that encounter between Bob and the unfortunate conjurer who tried to do the famous watch trick?

These frequent references to the sea are important because they tend to show that Mr. Jacobs, when he has been approached at all by criticism, has been approached from the wrong direction. He has actually been mistaken for a realist. Such writers probably imagine that captains of small coasting vessels, when they come ashore, are immediately plunged into the most astonishing and farcical intrigues involving an imaginary rich uncle from New Zealand and what not; that a pint or two of ale given to any lighterman or bargee will result in funny tales of plot and counterplot that only need a touch here and there to make them into the most delicious short stories. But not only is Mr. Jacobs not a reporter, but an artist; he is also, in his own way, a most finished, conscientious and delicate artist. He is himself such a master of craft that if you take from him nearly everything that usually goes with his work, that is, his humour, his dexterity in certain kinds of comic dialogue and narrative, his knowledge of the habits and the point of view of certain classes, if you take away all this, he will yet produce an excellent short story of quite a different kind. He has not a sufficiently poetic mind, not enough acquaintance with those borderland states of the human spirit, to write a horror story of the highest class, but, nevertheless, in "The Monkey's Paw," and some other similar things, he has done very well. This incomplete but sufficiently astonishing success in work so far removed from that which we usually associate with his name must be largely set down to the credit of his technique; it is one proof of his mastery of form. And it is this, along with his very fine sense of humour, that has made him the excellent short story writer he is, so that any reference to particularly favourable opportunities for observing and reporting will not explain him. It is worth recollecting that at the time Mr. Jacobs began writing definitely localized fiction was becoming the fashion; every new novelist had to have his own particular district; London was being cut and carved and slices of it were being served out to ambitious young writers. Mr. Zangwill was given the Jewish quarters, Mr. Morrison took the East End, Mr. Pett Ridge claimed the suburbs, and so on; thus it fell out that Mr. Jacobs, having written a few stories of seafaring men, was presented with Wapping, Rotherhithe, and the docks. This part of the world, with the addition of a few sleepy little coast towns, his Sunwich Ports, and the village of Claybury, served its purpose as a kind of map reference to the setting of his stories; but actually, like most original writers, he was soon busily engaged creating a world of his own. . . .

This world of Mr. Jacobs, which is not unlike a tiny part of the Dickens world all cleaned up, painted, and burnished, is a very pleasant one indeed, so pleasant as a background to our imagination that some of the pleasure we get from these stories is nothing more nor less than the poetical pleasure we always get from what is called "atmosphere." It is a little world from which all the darker shades have been banished, a world filled with sleepy little ports, tiny coasting vessels, trim cottages that usually have a rose-garden or "a small, brick-paved yard, in which trim myrtles and flowering plants stand about in freshly ochred pots" and perhaps "neatly grained shutters and white steps and polished brass knockers," happy little taverns ("an old-world bar, with its loud-ticking clock, its Windsor chairs, and its cracked jug full of roses"), pretty, saucy girls with a string of admirers, comic policemen, love-lorn intriguing third mates, henpecked sea-captains, and philosophical night-watchmen. Here, in this bright limited world, with all its properties ready to be set on the stage in a few seconds, at once false and true, and certainly very English, is a delightful setting for comedy. Into this setting Mr. Jacobs projects what we may call farces, for we must now pass from setting to plot, and Mr. Jacobs' plots, the bare action of his little stories, for the most part belong to the realm of stage farce. There is an ingenious little plan to deceive some one or other, a great many lies are told, and then in the end, as a rule, the biter himself is bitten. Very often the plan involves an imaginary wealthy uncle or a mythical long-lost son, or, if not these, then either a legacy, a fortune-teller, a pretended deed of heroism, or a comic feud with the police. And nearly always these little plots of his are fantastic, artificial, and deliberately, shall we say, standardized, so that once we are in the Jacobs world we know exactly what kind of queer action people will take. A summary of one or two of the stories will do more to show the character of the action than pages of explanation. Thus, an impudent second officer, walking ashore, spies a very pretty girl, and learns that she and her mother, a widow, live alone, and also that she had a brother who went to sea many years before and never returned. Having learned this and a few other particulars, the young man boldly marches up to the door and announces himself as the long-lost brother and son. His impudence carries him through at first, but he is asked to call again, and when he does so, a huge woman, the charwoman of the house, promptly rushes in and claims him as her long-lost husband. The women have won the day. Again, two young men, one a dashing sergeant and the other a rather staid civilian, are rivals for the hand of a girl who has a taste for heroes. Her father, who wishes his daughter to marry the civilian, persuades the latter that his best plan is to save some one from drowning (the sergeant cannot swim), and, in order to make sure there is some one to save, to push his rival into the water when they are all strolling along the quay on the following Sunday afternoon. The plan is accepted, but actually it is the father himself who is pushed into the water and saved from drowning, and his subsequent conduct, in its seeming ingratitude, comes in for a good deal of comment. Again, there is the strong man whom the night-watchman was on the point of introducing to us above; he who was amazingly powerful, but very sociable and good-humoured. Unfortunately, when he went out with Ginger Dick and the rest, he would never touch beer, which he said had a bad effect upon him, but only such slops as lemonade. Finally, however, his friends persuaded him to drink as they did, and the unhappy sequel was that he proved to be very nasty indeed in liquor, giving them all a good hiding and creating an uproar wherever he went. The following day, Ginger Dick and the other, not relishing his companionship, tell him that a certain landlord he encountered the night before is dying from the effect of his boisterous social methods. This ruse, however, only makes a desperate man of him, and he proceeds to further his chances of escaping by tying up his friends one by one as they come into the room, and going off with their money. This is farce worked out like neat little problems in algebra.

M. R. JAMES

1862–1936

The son of an Anglican priest, Montague Rhodes James was born on August 1, 1862, in Goodnestone, Suffolk. Though high-spirited and lively, he exhibited precocious antiquarian interests while at Temple Grove preparatory school and Eton, immersing himself in the study of medieval manuscripts and Biblical apocrypha. He entered King's College, Cambridge, in 1882, and after graduating stayed on to become a Fellow in 1887. In his illustrious career he rose to be Provost of King's from 1905 to 1918 and Vice-Chancellor of the University from 1913 to 1915, but took greater pride in his function as Director of the Fitzwilliam Museum from 1893 to 1908 and in his service on the University Press and Library Syndicates. Though he never married, he played a leading role in Cambridge literary and convivial societies, and in the vacations enjoyed cycling tours with friends in Britain and France.

In 1918 James was appointed Provost of Eton, and in later years served on several Royal Commissions, and was appointed a Trustee of the British Museum. He was made a Commander of the Order of Leopold for his aid to Belgian refugees in World War I, and received the Order of Merit in 1930.

James's scholarly work gained him great respect, especially in the fields of codicology, Christian art, and Biblical research. He catalogued many manuscript collections, including those of the Fitzwilliam Museum, most of the Cambridge colleges, and Canterbury, and was well known particularly for his version of *The Apocryphal New Testament* (1924). He reached a wider audience as a master of the ghost story in his volumes *Ghost Stories of an Antiquary* (1904), *More Ghost Stories of an Antiquary* (1911), *A Thin Ghost* (1919), and *A Warning to the Curious* (1925). His *Collected Ghost Stories* appeared in 1931, and his memoirs, *Eton and Kings*, in 1926.

James continued as Provost of Eton until his death on June 12, 1936.

Personal

I was never one of his closest intimates, but he did not mind being questioned about his opinions, and I gained some impressions. He was a devoted son of the Church of England, and would describe himself as protestant, though he liked a grave and dignified ceremonial: he had some sympathy with the tractarians, but none with 'the ritualists': in politics uninterested, but faintly conservative. As a smoker—and he smoked a good deal—his tastes, at any rate in his Cambridge days, were to me extraordinary. There are many men who care neither for cigars nor cigarettes, and I know others who, even at a College Feast, would with a word of apology light a pipe when the rest started their cigars; but I do not think that I ever knew another man who only liked *new* briar pipes. Most of us regard a new pipe as something to be coaxed into friendliness after some period of discomfort, and greatly regret when old age breaks it up or makes necessary to discard it because it has become irremediably foul; but M. R. J. enjoyed a pipe only when it was new, and laid it aside in favour of a successor just at the moment when most of us would be beginning to enjoy it.

His holidays were greatly occupied in the exploration of provincial France, his immediate and expressed intent being to visit all the French Cathedrals, including of course those which were suppressed at the Revolution. He said that he did not know Notre-Dame, but he had of course been there: it was only that he had a considerable distaste for Paris. I said to him once that I believed that I had seen one French Cathedral that he had not. 'Which?' 'Nice.' 'Well, I think that you will continue to have the advantage of me there.' When he could not or did not go to France, the Suffolk of his ancestry and his early years was perhaps the most frequent scene of his wanderings, often (as in France) on a bicycle, and he frequently crossed the border into Norfolk. I think he would very gladly have allowed himself to be described as a man 'of the Eastern Counties'. . . .

The War broke out towards the end of the first year of his Vice-Chancellorship, and I well remember his speech on 1 October, 1914, as he took up the second. I was Proctor at the time, and stood very near him as he spoke; these are some of his words:

> The remembrance of what has been brilliant or sorrowful in the three terms has paled, for the time at least, before the events of the Long Vacation. The University meets in such circumstances as it has never known. We shall be few in number, and perpetually under the strain of a great anxiety. We may be exposed to actual peril: in any case we must look forward to straitened resources and, what is more, personal sorrows. Yet there is no doubt that we are bound to carry on our work; for by it we can render definite service to the nation. Our part, while we encourage all of our students who are capable of doing so to serve their country, and while we surrender to that service many valued teachers, is to prepare more men—especially in our medical schools—for rendering active help, and to keep alive that fire of 'education, religion, learning, and research' which will in God's good time outburn the flame of war. Let us devote ourselves to making useful men of the new generation. Let us confine our own controversies within the narrowest limits, and be ready if necessary to postpone them altogether. Let our advanced work—however irrelevant it may seem to the needs of the moment—be unremittingly and faithfully pursued.

(The University did not carry out his advice wholeheartedly, for a successful agitation to remove compulsory Greek from the Little-go was begun before its younger members were back from war work: but by that time the Provost had left Cambridge.)

The present Vice-Provost of King's, Dr. J. H. Clapham, says with truth 'War he took simply and vehemently'. He had always been fond of all things French (except Paris) and disliked most things German (except their scholarship), and merely found his natural feelings heightened and corroborated: but I do not think that I ever heard him say anything bitter, though indignation was vehement enough. Cambridge was comparatively quiet in the early War years, before it was so successfully made into a training camp for cadets, and he worked steadily at manuscripts and various archaeological questions.—STEPHEN GASELEE, "Montague Rhodes James," *PBA*, 1936, pp. 424–28

Works

SCHOLARSHIP

On Apocrypha I should think he made the greatest advance since the days of Fabricius (though Fabricius was more a collector and bibliographer than an investigator), and M.R.J.'s work is of the kind that is, so far as we can see, permanent. But I suppose that his work on medieval manuscripts is, really, even much more important than his identification, publication, and criticism of Apocrypha, and he acquired for the purpose an exceptional knowledge of medieval iconography, derived both from MSS. and from sculptures; and developed a special interest in tracing the homes and movements of the written books. Here, while we are astounded by the vast sum of his descriptions and identifications, the very amount of them makes it inevitable that there should be small imperfections: some of these were due to his handwriting, which was only good if he tried hard, and positively cruel for the compositor, and to the fact, which he admitted, that he was by no means a perfect proof-reader. 'The printer', I have heard him say, 'read Holy Trinity the first time I wrote Holy Family in a description of an illumination, and then put Holy Trinity each time I used the other phrase: and I fear that I removed none of these misprints from my proofs.' But no true scholar would have it otherwise; there has never been before, and probably there will never be again, a single man with the same accomplishment and combination of memory, palaeography, medieval learning, and artistic knowledge, and it was better for such studies that he should extend his cataloguing over almost the whole English treasures of this kind, and get his results printed and accessible to the scholars of the present and future, than that he should confine himself to a few manuscripts or collections and attain absolute accuracy and completeness in his description of them. Further, in his editions of a few illuminated manuscripts of the very first class, as in the books he edited for the Roxburghe Club, he showed that he was capable of perfect description when he had an object really worthy of his highest powers. Many of his accounts of manuscripts will have to be worked over again by specialists of the future: but to him will be due the fact that they are known and available to the specialists at all. In scholarship comparisons are even more difficult than in other qualities and attainments: he had not the lightning flashes of insight of Walter Headlam, or the deadly precision of Housman; but I consider him in *volume* of learning the greatest scholar it has been my good fortune to know.—STEPHEN GASELEE, "Montague Rhodes James," *PBA*, 1936, pp. 431–33

With his immense knowledge of the Victorian novel he never wrote the final survey. With his uncanny knowledge of Scripture in the Bible he gave his overwhelming instinct to the Apocrypha, both of New and Old Testament, with lingering research into lost and suspected books. Bible readers have been puzzled by reference to a Book of Japhet which no one has read. Apocrypha—the 'hidden' Scriptures were the romance of his life while as for the Apocalyptic or 'revelations' his devotion was such that the Oxford Orator in administering his degree referred to him as 'apocalypticotatos,' the single word which might have been found on his heart or been engraved on his tomb. In a childhood dream he found himself opening a shiny Folio Bible with an unknown book included with a Hebrew name.

When it was necessary to advance a thesis for a Fellowship if he were to remain at King's he restored a lost *Apocalypse of Peter* from the dead. With a half a dozen surviving clues he 'wove a web of considerable size.' But who was to say he was right until 'a few years later a large piece of the text, found in

Egypt in 1884, was printed and served to confirm my main guesses or conclusions.' In this there were accounts of Heaven and Hell which resembled an early foresight of Dante. The catalogue of torments is, however, concluded by comfortable words when our Lord promises St Peter that all sinners will be saved by the prayers of the righteous. Salvation all round may have been a little too much for the early Christians so Peter ordered this *Revelation* to be hidden in a box that foolish men may not see it; Monty's impression being the author 'tried to break the dangerous doctrine of the ultimate salvation of sinners gently to his readers.'

In the first centuries Christians were crazy in their search for new Gospels, spurious Acts, and more and more exciting Revelations, at least more than was known to the Angels in Heaven. To Monty 'as folklore and romance they are precious and to the lover of mediæval literature and art they reveal the solution of many a puzzle.'

For instance St Augustine's reference to the gardener's daughter who died at St Peter's prayer! This was a mystery till an *Epistle of Titus* was found which told how a gardener begged Peter's prayers for the best the Lord could give. The girl fell dead! When Peter restored her to life it turned out it would have been the best for her after all—for she was promptly ruined by a slave in the house.

One apocryphal legend, the *Domine quo vadis*, became as well known as anything in the Gospels, thanks to a Polish novelist. Monty's translation of the original passage is worth giving in its simplicity:

And as Peter went forth of the City he saw the Lord entering into Rome and when he saw Him he said: Lord whither thus? And the Lord said unto him: I go into Rome to be crucified. And Peter said unto Him: Yea Peter I am crucified again. And Peter came to himself.

This is the Apocrypha at its most picturesque and whether true or not carried its lesson like much of what Jerome rejected. Monty could talk freely about the Gelasian Decree which had early listed books which dropped unfortunately out of circulation. He thought their most sensational entry referred to 'the Book of Og the Giant who is said by the heretics to have fought with a Dragon after the Flood'—an unnoticed mention of some Loch Ness monster? To him the most thrilling lore was the *Gospel of the Hebrews* which no doubt contained the matrix of the early Gospels. Though the famous story of the woman taken in adultery does not appear in St John's Gospel and is set aside by modern translators—Monty pointed out that Papias had found it in the *Gospel of the Hebrews*. How interesting he found the *Acts of Pilate*, so seldom read by ecclesiasts. They supply a keen touch of irony when the astounded Jews interviewed the soldiers whose watch was so unsuccessful at the tomb. On hearing what the soldiers had to say, the Jews closed down the argument by asserting: As the Lord *liveth*, we believe you not! As a way of contradicting the Resurrection it sounds like an Irish bull.

Perhaps most interesting it was to tread the by-paths of lost Scripture with Monty and to learn that when Pilate asked our Lord what was Truth? He remained not silent but offered a superb answer replying: 'Truth is of Heaven,' whereat Pilate said: 'Is there not Truth upon earth?' and Jesus said unto Pilate: 'Thou seest how they which speak the Truth are judged upon earth.'

Surely the irony of such a dialogue remains too splendid to be lost.

In the end Monty wrote a Lost Apocrypha of the Old Testament for the S.P.C.K. and an Apocrypha of the New Testament for the Clarendon Press. At any rate William Hone's once popular volume was for ever replaced by a masterpiece. —SHANE LESLIE, "Montague Rhodes James," *QR*, Jan. 1966, pp. 51–53

GHOST STORIES

The art of Dr. James is by no means haphazard, and in the preface to ⟨*More Ghost Stories of an Antiquary*⟩ he has formulated three very sound rules for macabre composition. A ghost story, he believes, should have a familiar setting in the modern period, in order to approach closely the reader's sphere of experience. Its spectral phenomena, moreover, should be malevolent rather than beneficent; since *fear* is the emotion primarily to be excited. And finally, the technical patois of "occultism" or pseudo-science ought carefully to be avoided, lest the charm of casual verisimilitude be smothered in unconvincing pedantry.

Dr. James, practicing what he preaches, approaches his themes in a light and often conversational way. Creating the illusion of every-day events, he introduces his abnormal phenomena cautiously and gradually; relieved at every turn by touches of homely and prosaic detail, and sometimes spiced with a snatch or two of antiquarian scholarship. Conscious of the close relation between present weirdness and accumulated tradition, he generally provides remote historical antecedents of his incidents; thus being able to utilise very aptly his exhaustive knowledge of the past, and his ready and convincing command of archaic diction and colouring. A favourite scene for a James tale is some centuried cathedral, which the author can describe with all the familiar minuteness of a specialist in that field.

Sly humorous vignettes and bits of lifelike genre portraiture and characterisation are often to be found in Dr. James's narratives, and serve in his skilled hands to augment the general effect rather than to spoil it, as the same qualities would tend to do with a lesser craftsman. In inventing a new type of ghost, he has departed considerably from the conventional Gothic tradition; for where the older stock ghosts were pale and stately, and apprehended chiefly through the sense of sight, the average James ghost is lean, dwarfish, and hairy—a sluggish, hellish night-abomination midway betwixt beast and man— and usually *touched* before it is *seen*. Sometimes the spectre is of still more eccentric composition; a roll of flannel with spidery eyes, or an invisible entity which moulds itself in bedding and shows a *face of crumpled linen*. Dr. James has, it is clear, an intelligent and scientific knowledge of human nerves and feelings; and knows just how to apportion statement, imagery, and subtle suggestion in order to secure the best results with his readers. He is an artist in incident and arrangement rather than in atmosphere, and reaches the emotions more often through the intellect than directly. This method, of course, with its occasional absences of sharp climax, has its drawbacks as well as its advantages; and many will miss the thorough atmospheric tension which writers like Machen are careful to build up with words and scenes. But only a few of the tales are open to the charge of tameness. Generally the laconic unfolding of abnormal events in adroit order is amply sufficient to produce the desired effect of cumulative horror—H. P. LOVECRAFT, "The Modern Masters," *Supernatural Horror in Literature* (1927), 1973, pp. 101–2

English literature has always been haunted. From Grendel's cave to the blood-boultered imaginings of Kyd and Tourneur, and on again through the declamatory phantasmagoria of Restoration tragedy to the Wardour Street diabolics of Walpole and Monk Lewis, and thus to the Provost of Eton and the matter in hand—this is a long road, as these random landmarks suggest. But all along it there are supernatural echoes, and their evocation has seldom gone unapplauded. It is strange that a theme so universally recurrent, so certain of its appeal (which was once, and perhaps still is, stimulated by a strong oral tradition), has so seldom inspired technical perfection in its treatment. You will protest that there are plenty of good ghost stories; but nine out of your ten instances will prove to have been memorable only for their plot, their matter. The ghost story which you praise as an artistic whole is rare indeed. For, while there is no theme which requires, for true excellence, more delicacy in the handling, there is at the same time none more self-reliant, more capable of achieving, independently of the writer's craft, a measure of dramatic effect by virtue of its own inherent sensationalism. In this, and as far as I know in this alone, the supernatural resembles the obscene.

Dr. James, whose four volumes of ghost stories are now issued for the first time under one cover, has long been an acknowledged master of his craft: unrivalled at his best, for consistent merit never approached. "There is no receipt for success in this form of fiction," he says in his preface. And to be sure you cannot cabin horror in a formula; the raising of hair, unlike the raising of chickens, salaries, and hearty laughs, cannot be taught through a correspondence course. But although Dr. James' subtle methods hardly lend themselves to analysis, some of the foundations of his pre-eminence do become apparent from a study of this book, its monument.

His first secret is tact. I say tact rather than restraint because he can and does pile on the agony when his sense of the dramatic tells him to. (You remember, I dare say, what happened to Anders Bjornsen's face? . . . "the flesh of it was sucked away off the bones.") It is tact, a guileless and deadly tact, that gauges so nicely the force of half-definitions, adjusting the balance between reticence and the explicit so that our imaginations are ever ready to meet his purpose half-way. The best story in this book is "'Oh, Whistle, and I'll Come to You, My Lad'"; we never know what it was that answered Mr. Parkins' whistle, but we are not likely to forget that when it attacked him, substituting bed-clothes from an empty bed for the essential vesture of creation, it revealed "a horrible, an intensely horrible, face *of crumpled linen.*" That is the stuff of nightmares.

There are other constant ingredients in Dr. James' most potent magic. One, inevitably, is the background of learning to his stories. Though in his Preface he makes light of his "ostensible erudition," his knowledge of the Unknown is, if I may say so, sufficiently well-simulated to lend an air of authenticity and, sometimes, to serve the purposes of innuendo. His narrative has always a kind of dry naturalism which lends perspective to the action. He shows at times something of the same imaginative adaptability, the same power of suddenly bringing home the implications of an abnormal situation by reference to the trivial, which Swift showed when he made Gulliver notice the Brobdignagian pores. Add to all this an eye for, rather than a preoccupation with, character—particularly well-developed in the case of what our less democratic ancestors persisted in calling the "low characters"—and you will have excused, if not wholly explained, your surrender to the fascination of these stories.

When Dr. James errs, it is always on the side of reticence. "Casting the Runes," for instance, should carry a stronger climax after its delicate overture of horror, which is one of the best things in the book. But this is backhanded criticism and premises praise. Overstatement has been the besetting sin of

the ghost story since the statue at Otranto began to bleed at the nose, and Dr. James will have nothing to do with it, even in its emasculated modern form, which spells thing with a capital T and has a great camp-following of dots.

I detect in his later stories a certain leniency, a tendency to let the reader off lightly. There are signs that he finds it increasingly hard to take the creatures of his fancy seriously; like Prospero, he retires more and more into the benevolent showman. In such a master this is perhaps a venal fault. Far less easy to forgive is his answer to the self-imposed question: "Am I going to write any more ghost stories?" Who ever heard of Prospero breaking his staff after only four acts? I think Dr. James will find that his laconic "Probably not" has turned all his readers, for once, into critics.—PETER FLEMING, "The Stuff of Nightmares," *Spec*, April 18, 1933, p. 633

M. R. James adapted a variety of time-hallowed themes from folklore and legend, myth and ballad, and his stories are largely constructed from such traditional elements. Recognizing this process, he wrote: 'I have tried to make my ghosts act in a way not inconsistent with the rules of folklore.' His ability to manipulate familiar material is everywhere in evidence; so too is his scholarly interest in it. In 1914 he edited that strange hotchpotch of legend and learning, Walter Map's *De Nugis Curialium*, which contains several stories of the returning dead, and he published a group of medieval ghost stories he had unearthed in the *English Historical Review* in 1922. He had also read many nineteenth-century ghost stories, both fictional and veridical, his favourite author being Joseph Sheridan Le Fanu, whose imaginative treatment of Irish folklore he greatly admired. He found in the ballad a useful source of supernatural episodes, and was particularly interested in the Danish and Breton versions. It is worthwhile, in the light of his interest in the ballad, to consider how far his own narrative technique was influenced by it. The prosaic, matter-of-fact tone with which natural and supernatural events alike are presented, the build-up of suspense by steps, the overall importance of the action and the subordination of characteriza-tion to it, the stiff and conventional nature of the character-drawing, and perhaps above all, the sense of a background of shared traditional beliefs conveying further implications to the audience—all these qualities are present in James's work. We need to know something of the hats o' the birk and the red cock to understand the events of 'The Wife of Usher's Well', just as we need to know something of the associations of witches and ash-trees for 'The Ash-Tree' to work on us as its author intends. It may be that the self-effacing story-teller, the impersonal narrative technique and the extensive use of understatement were characteristics that James took over from the ballad, the supreme form for a tale of terror, as the Romantic poets had realized.

Much of the effect of his stories depends on our recognizing certain archetypal patterns of temptation and vengeance as typifying the workings of the supernatural world. The different allusions in a single story do not derive from any one origin, however, but from a compound of sources both in literature and folklore. It is often difficult to distinguish these elements completely, since ancient beliefs survive in a variety of contexts. In '"Oh, Whistle, and I'll Come to You, My Lad"' the malevolent spirit that appears in response to Parkins' blowing the whistle may be connected with the sailors' superstition about whistling on deck, the prototype of which is at least as old as Homer, and Odysseus' *contretemps* with the bag of winds. Witches, too, traditionally had power over the winds, as Shakespeare showed in *Macbeth*. As late as 1814 wise women sold winds to sailors, for in that year Walter Scott recorded buying one from a certain Bessie Miller of Stromness, Orkney. In the course of the story, the Colonel points out that Northern Europeans still believe that a sudden wind has been whistled for, adding 'there's generally something at the bottom of what these country-folk hold to'. Thus the very antiquity of a superstition is put forward as some sort of evidence of its validity. The horrible thing that responds to the summons is bodiless, as traditionally spirits often were, so it has to assume the body of bedlinen.

It first appears on the beach as Parkins returns from the Templars' Church, having found, but not yet blown, the whistle: 'an indistinct personage who seemed to be making great efforts to catch up with him, but made little, if any progress.' The sight of this figure throws up a completely new and quite different literary allusion, this time to Bunyan's Apollyon, which Parkins involuntarily associates with the distant pursuer, wondering what he would do

> . . . if I looked back and caught sight of a black figure sharply defined against the yellow sky, and saw that it had horns and wings? I wonder whether I should stand or run for it. Luckily that gentleman behind is not of that kind, and seems to be about as far off now as when I saw him first.

The spirit's identity becomes clearer in Parkins' subsequent dream of flight along the beach. Its failure to catch up with him on that first afternoon had been due to the fact that he had not yet actually blown the whistle, thus placing himself, both literally and metaphorically, within its reach. Another significant literary reference lies in the title, taken from a song of Burns, the refrain of which has a distinctly sinister ring:

> Though father and mother and brother go mad,
> Oh, whistle and I'll come to ye, my lad.

This elaborate network of allusion helps to provide a focus for our fears, which are themselves the more alarming for being vaguely familiar. The superstitions and quotations exploited here seem to lend an air of almost historical verification to the evil spirit that comes, just as the Sortes Biblicae in 'The Ash-Tree', or the quotations from Ecclesiasticus and Isaiah at the end of 'Canon Alberic's Scrapbook' convince by apparently supplying evidence from the Book of Truth itself.—JULIA BRIGGS, "No Mere Antiquary: M. R. James," *Night Visitors: The Rise and Fall of the English Ghost Story*, 1977, pp. 132–34

JACK SULLIVAN
From "The Antiquarian Ghost Story: Montague Rhodes James"
Elegant Nightmares: The English Ghost Story from Le Fanu to Blackwood
1978, pp. 69–90

"Count Magnus," from M. R. James's *Ghost Stories of an Antiquary*, is haunted not only by its own ghosts, but by the ghost of Sheridan Le Fanu. Mr. Wraxall, the hero of the tale, dooms himself by peering at a terrifying sarcophagus engraving which should have remained unseen and opening an obscure alchemy volume which should have remained closed. By doing these things, he inadvertently summons the author of the alchemy treatise, the dreaded Count Magnus, from the sarcophagus. To make matters worse, he also summons the count's hooded, tentacled companion. Anyone who has read Le Fanu's "Green Tea" knows that such creatures are easier summoned than eluded. Mr. Wraxall flees across the Continent, but his pursuers are always close behind. They arrive at

his remote country house in England before he does and wait for him there. Not surprisingly, he is found dead. At the inquest, seven jurors faint at the sight of the body. The verdict is "visitation of God," but the reader knows that he had been visited by something else.

In both incident and vision, "Count Magnus" is darkened by the shadow of Le Fanu. The basic dynamic of the story, the hunt, is symbolized by the sarcophagus engraving:

> Among trees, was a man running at full speed, with flying hair and outstretched hands. After him followed a strange form; it would be hard to say whether the artist had intended it for a man, and was unable to give the requisite similitude, or whether it was intentionally made as monstrous as it looked. In view of the skill with which the rest of the drawing was done, Mr. Wraxall felt inclined to adopt the latter idea.[1]

Upon reading this insidiously understated passage, the reader who is familiar with Le Fanu immediately knows two things: that the fleeing figure will soon be Mr. Wraxall himself and that the outcome of the pursuit will be fatal for him. Such a reader will not be surprised by the mysterious illogic of the plot, the absence of any moral connection between the hunter and the hunted. Mr. Wraxall is no Gothic villain or Fatal Man; he is a singularly unremarkable, almost anonymous character. He resembles several Le Fanu characters (especially in "Green Tea" and "Schalken the Painter") in that he is a pure victim, having done nothing amiss other than reading the wrong book and looking at the wrong picture. We are told in an ironic passage that "his besetting fault was clearly that of over-inquisitiveness, possibly a good fault in a traveler, certainly a fault for which this traveler paid dearly in the end" (100). We are not told why he is any more overly inquisitive than James's other antiquaries, many of whom are never pursued. The narrator sums up the problem near the end of the story: "He is expecting a visit from his pursuers—how or when he knows not—and his constant cry is 'What has he done?' and 'Is there no hope?' Doctors, he knows, would call him mad, policemen would laugh at him. The person is away. What can he do but lock his door and cry to God?" (118). This fragmented summary of Mr. Wraxall's final entries in his journal suggests that the horror of the situation is in the chasm between action and consequence. In the fictional world of Le Fanu and James, one does not have to be a Faust, a Melmoth, or even a Huckleberry Finn to be damned. The strategy of both writers is the same: to make the reader glance nervously around the room and say, "If this could happen to him, it could happen to me."

The style also owes much to Le Fanu. In an odd sense, "Count Magnus" is more in the Le Fanu manner than Le Fanu. James's use of innuendo and indirection is so rigorous that it hides more than it reveals. Le Fanu creates a balance between uneasy vagueness and grisly clarity. But James tilts the balance in favor of the unseen. Tiny, unsettling flashes of clarity emerge from the obscurity, but usually in an indirect context. We are allowed to see the protruding tentacle of one of the robed pursuers, for example—but only in the engraving, not in the actual pursuit. In the most literal sense, these are nameless horrors.

James also follows Le Fanu's example in his use of narrative distance, again transcending his model. Le Fanu separates himself from his material through the use of elaborate, sometimes awkward prologues and epilogues which filter the stories through a series of editors and narrators. Sometimes, as in "Mr. Justice Harbottle," the network of tales within tales results in a narrative fabric of considerable complexity. In "Count Magnus," the narrator is an anonymous editor who has access to the papers Mr. Wraxall was compiling for a travelogue. The story consists of paraphrases and direct quotations from these papers, a device which gives the narrative a strong aura of authenticity. The transitions from one document to the other, occurring organically within the text, are smooth and unobtrusive. They are also strangely impersonal, as if the teller in no way wishes to commit himself to his tale.

James's reticence probably relates as much to personal temperament as to the aesthetic problem of how to write a proper ghost story. It is commonly accepted, largely because of the work of James and Le Fanu, that indirection, ambiguity, and narrative distance are appropriate techniques for ghostly fiction.[2] (Material horror tales, such as Wells's "The Cone" and Alexander Woollcott's "Moonlight Sonata," are another matter.) Supernatural horror is usually more convincing when suggested or evoked than when explicitly documented. But James's understated subtlety is so obsessive, so paradoxically unrestrained that it feels like an inversion of the hyperbole of Poe or Maturin. I find his late work increasingly ambiguous and puzzling, sometimes to the point of almost total mystification. It is as if James is increasingly unwilling to deal with the implications of his stories. What begins as a way of making supernatural horror more potent becomes a way of repressing or avoiding it. Often he appears to be doing both at once, creating a unique chill and tension. . . .

On rare occasions, James makes manifesto-like statements about the need for linguistic economy. The Ezra Pound of ghost story writers, James once criticized Poe for his "vagueness"; for his lack of toughness and specific detail; for the "unreal" quality of his prose.[3] The charge is similar to Pound's denigration of Yeats's early poems. Actually, Poe and James were attempting very different things. Poe's tales are not ghostly but surreal. They immerse themselves in the irrational, whereas James's tales only flirt with it. The power of James lies in his ability to set up a barrier between the empirical and the supernatural and then gradually knock it down—to move subtly from the real to the unreal and sometimes back again. The distinction between the two is much more solid than in Poe, where nightmare and reality constantly melt into one another. James's stories assume a strong grounding in empirical reality. In this context, his refusal to accept the existence of ghosts until he encounters "conclusive evidence" is consistent with the attitude of his stories. The stories are consciously addressed to skeptical readers, readers with a twentieth (or eighteenth) century frame of reference. In making us momentarily accept what we instinctively disbelieve, the burden falls heavily on the language. The way to reach such a reader, James implies, is through clarity and restraint: the hyperbole and verbal effusiveness of the Gothic writers are to be strictly avoided, as are the "trivial and melodramatic" natural explanations of Lord Lytton and the neo-Gothic Victorians.[4] To James, both overwriting and natural explanations in ghost stories are related forms of cheating. Although James usually avoids issuing these anti-Gothic manifestoes, he indirectly pans the Gothic tradition in the introduction to the *Collected Ghost Stories* by refusing to acknowledge any literary debt to it. . . .

One exception to James's habitual terseness can be found in the descriptions of some of his settings. If the present is lacking, the past is always alive. Whenever James describes an antiquarian lore which provides the settings for all of his stories, his prose instantly becomes crowded with historical or scholarly detail. The opening paragraphs in "Lost Hearts" and "The Ash-Tree" are learned, graceful little essays on styles of architecture in the early and late eighteenth centuries as they

relate to the houses in the stories. They provide no "atmosphere," at least not in the Gothic sense which James so despised, and no ominous forebodings (which come later). Indeed the narrator of "The Ash-Tree" admits that the entire opening section is a "digression." These stories are saturated with nostalgia, yet never in a propagandistic context. In contrast to the stories of Machen and Blackwood, there are no Yeatsian spokesmen for the glories of the past. The emptiness of the present and richness of the past are implied by the distinct absence of the one and overwhelming presence of the other, but James never forces his fetish for the old down the reader's throat.

The paradox in James is that this very oldness is invariably a deadly trap. If antiquarian pursuits provide the only contact with life, they also provide an immediate contact with death. Even in tales where there is no dramatic coffin-opening scene, there is always an implicit analogy between digging up an art object and digging up a corpse. In the antiquarian tale, evil is something old, something which should have died. Old books are especially dangerous as talismanic summoners of this evil. The danger is trickier in James than in similar evil-book tales by James's contemporaries in that neither the nature nor titles of the books necessarily betrays their lethal potential. Chambers's *The King in Yellow*, Yeats's *Alchemical Rose*, and Lovecraft's *Necronomicon* (all imaginary books) are works with spectacularly demonic histories which the collector in a given story opens at his own risk. But James's collectors are liable to get in trouble by opening almost anything. In "The Uncommon Prayer Book," a remarkable rag-like monstrosity is summoned by a psalm (admittedly a "very savage psalm") in an eighteenth-century prayerbook. For James's antiquaries, even the Holy Scriptures can become a demonic text. Undermining the very thing they celebrate, the plots seem to symbolize, perhaps unconsciously, the futility of the entire antiquarian enterprise.

In a curious way, the style reinforces this contradiction. The most striking aspect of this style, even more striking than its ascetic brevity and clarity, is the gap between tone and story. This gap is especially telling in the more gruesome tales. In "Wailing Well," a small boy is tackled and brought down, much as in a football game, by an entire field of vampires. He is found hanging from a tree with the blood drained from his body, but he later becomes a vampire himself, hiding out with his new friends in a haunted well. (James wrote this cheerful tale for the Eton College troop of Boy Scouts.) More gruesome yet is "Lost Hearts," which tells of an antiquary who, in following an ancient prescription, seeks an "enlightenment of the spiritual faculties" through eating the hearts of young children while they are kept alive. (James is as unsparing of children as Le Fanu.) In the end, the children rise from the grave to wreak a bloody, predictably poetic justice. In both stories, the style is distinguished by a detachment, an urbanity, and a certain amount of Edwardian stuffiness which are entirely at odds with the nastiness of the plots. The narrators seem determined to maintain good manners, even when presenting material they know to be in irredeemably bad taste. Alternating between casualness and stiffness, chattiness and pedantry, James's narrators maintain an almost pathological distance from the horrors they recount. This contradiction between scholarly reticence and fiendish perversity becomes the authenticating mark of the antiquarian ghost story. For James's narrators, sophisticated literary techniques are a form of exorcism in a world filled with hidden menace. To stare the menace in the face is unthinkable; to convert it into a pleasant ghost story is to momentarily banish it. The reader, however, experiences an inversion of this process: the very unwillingness of the narrators to face up to implied horrors makes the stories all the more chilling and convincing.

James disguises unpleasantness in several ingenious ways. Narrative coolness in one disguise, but he sometimes builds others directly into the plot. There is a whole class of stories in which the dark center is enclosed, and occasionally buried, by several layers of supernatural apparatus. These stories move toward a gradual uncovering of the layers, but the anticipated climax, the final revelation, is less compelling than the means of arriving at it. The disguises do not appear in the form of occult mystification, as in the *Mythologies* of Yeats—James almost never uses elaborate occult material; nor do they appear in the form of complex visionary mechanisms, as in the Georgian fantasies of Dunsany and de la Mare. Like everything in James, the device is disarmingly straightforward rather than metaphysical. It involves the re-evoking, not of an actual supernatural being, as in "Count Magnus," but of a supernatural melodrama from the past. The twist in these stories is that the art object acts not as a mere catalyst, but as the substance of the experience. Although the scene itself is invariably grotesque and horrifying, the interest lies in the eccentricity of the mode of perception. Moreover, the antiquary is not physically threatened: he is a mortified, though by no means unwilling, spectator. . . .

If James is not a major writer, he nevertheless deserves a larger audience than he currently enjoys.[5] His fictional palate is admittedly restricted, even in comparison with other writers of ghostly tales. His stories have considerable power, but only muffled reverberation. He exhibits little of Henry James's psychological probity, none of Poe's Gothic extravagance, none of Yeats's passion—but he delivers a higher percentage of mystery and terror than any of these. If he is merely a sophisticated "popular" writer, content with manipulating surfaces, those very surfaces are potent and suggestive.

James is far more innovative than he pretends to be. In R. H. Malden's preface to *Nine Ghosts*, he reminds us that James "always regarded" Le Fanu as "The Master."[6] Yet Malden also speaks of a distinct James "tradition," implying that James refined, modified, and transgressed Le Fanu's precepts in ways profound enough to set James apart as an original. He brought to the ghost story not only a new antiquarian paradigm of setting and incident, but also a new urbanity, suaveness, and economy. To a contemporary audience, conditioned by the monotonous brutality of so many occult novels and films, James's use of subtlety to evoke ghostly horror is likely to seem as radical and puzzling as ever. Both academics and popular readers tend to associate supernatural horror in fiction with hyperbole, capitals, promiscuous exclamation marks, and bloated adjectives. Yet the field is crowded with undeservedly obscure writers—L. T. C. Rolt, E. G. Swain, R. H. Malden, Ramsey Campbell, H. R. Wakefield, Russell Kirk, Arthur Gray, Elizabeth Bowen, and Robert Aickman, among many others—who follow James's example.

James also gave the ghost story a new theme. His ghosts materialize not so much from inner darkness or outer conspiracies as from a kind of antiquarian malaise. Remaining modestly within the confines of popular entertainment, his fiction nevertheless shows how nostalgia has a habit of turning into horror. This is a distinct departure from Poe, where antiquarian pursuits are tied to sensationally deranged psyches such as Roderick Usher's. In James, the antiquaries are stolidly normal, and their ghosts are real. Above all, James's collectors clearly enjoy what they are doing: those who survive these stories would not dream of giving up their arcane pursuits simply because they were almost swallowed up by unearthly presences.

But the real enjoyment is ours. As readers, we can immerse ourselves in the process of discovery without taking any risks. We can even indulge in expecting the worst. Alfred Hitchcock has often said that terror and suspense grow not out of shock and surprise, but out of thickening inevitability.[7] James, who had already learned this lesson from Le Fanu, is careful to keep us one step ahead of the character so that the dreams and premonitions are as eerie as the apparitions they announce. This is the delightful paradox of James's ghost stories: the more of his stories we read and reread, the more we know what to expect, but that very reservoir of expectations infuses each reading with added menace. The sheer pleasure of these gentlemanly horror tales continually rejuvenates itself.

Notes

1. M. R. James, *Collected Ghost Stories* (London: Arnold, 1931; rpt. New York: St. Martin's Press, 1974), pp. 112–113. Further quotations from James's stories will be documented by citing page numbers from the text.
2. Even H. P. Lovecraft comments on the appropriateness of these techniques, despite his failure to use them in his own fiction. See Lovecraft, *Supernatural Horror in Literature*.
3. From an interview with James included in a review of *Madam Crowl's Ghost* published in the *Morning Post*, 9 October 1923, p. 11.
4. James, "Prologue," Sheridan Le Fanu, *Madam Crowl's Ghost and Other Tales of Mystery* (London: G. Bell, 1923), p. vii.
5. Though interest in James appears to be growing, it is still nowhere near as large as interest in the Lovecraft circle or in contemporary writers such as William Blatty, Thomas Tryon, and Stephen King.
6. R. H. Malden, "Preface," *Nine Ghosts* (London: Arnold, 1943), p. 5.
7. Alfred Hitchcock, "Preface," *Fourteen of My Favourites in Suspense*, ed. Alfred Hitchcock (New York: Dell, 1959), p. 9.

STORM JAMESON

1891–

Margaret Storm Jameson was born into a family of shipbuilders in Whitby, Yorkshire, on January 8, 1891. After taking a B.A. in English at Leeds University, she gained an M.A. from King's College, London, in 1914, and found work as an advertising copywriter. From 1919 to 1921 she was editor of the *New Commonwealth*, and she was later the English representative of Alfred A. Knopf publishers of New York.

The Pot Boils (1919) was the first of Jameson's many novels. Her family background contributed to the trilogy *The Triumph of Time* (1932), but in spite of the strength of her Yorkshire roots she is far from insular. As president of the English Centre of P.E.N. from 1938 to 1945, she toured Central and Eastern Europe before World War II, and during the war was an outspoken anti-Nazi, vigorous in her support of exiled writers. In 1948 she taught at the University of Pittsburgh.

In the 1930s Jameson wrote several novels under the pseudonyms James Hill and William Lamb. Notable among the novels published in her own name are *A Day Off* (1933), *Farewell, Night: Welcome, Day* (1939), *Cousin Honoré* (1941), *A Cup of Tea for Mr. Thorgill* (1957), *The Road from the Monument* (1962), *The White Crow* (1968), and *There Will Be a Short Interval* (1973). She has also translated short stories by Maupassant, and in 1970 published her autobiography, *Journey from the North*, and a volume of essays on the novel, *Parthian Words*. *Speaking of Stendhal* appeared in 1979.

Jameson received the Calabrian International Prize in 1972, and a P.E.N. Award in 1974. She was made an honorary member of the American Academy and Institute of Arts and Letters in 1978. She married her second husband, Professor Guy Chapman, in 1924, and after his death edited his autobiography, *A Kind of Survivor* (1975).

Personal

How many times have I drawn back from an underworld darkness I fear, closing my long-sighted eyes, blocking my keen ears? Possibly the journey backwards, against the current, through the tangled roots of withdrawals, evasions, lies, was from the start no good. I may have pursued a phantom: the person I made bit by bit out of my fears and greeds—that fake, that *construction*—may have strangled whatever infant reality once existed.

When I was a child I had already cut my stick to be famous. I was born as stubborn as the hardest wood and unwilling to learn what bored me. I read for pleasure and, now and then, to astonish my teachers by seeming to know more than I did. (One day, during a visit home, I was turning the pages of an old encyclopædia my mother bought when we were children. I found words—*Good*—*Yes, I see*—*To be looked into*—pencilled in a large perfectly round hand beside the articles on Plato, Hegel, Kant, Leibnitz and some others, and remembered the afternoon when I decided to read the philosophers, all of them: filled with excitement I began by reading about them, and chased them through the eleven large volumes with baffled patience.) As I look over my shoulder, the years divide: beginning in eternity, I came early into the suburbs of time. The years from my twelfth are marked off by public examinations that fell in December and June; I went at these like a man cutting steps in a rock face—they were my road to the world. I had no guide but my devouring ambition—not a guide, a thorn in my flesh, a fever.

More than anyone I knew then, I wanted to live. My hunger was a wild animal in my senses and brain. Perhaps its violence defeated it. The savage beast was probably blind.

I am deeply convinced—so deeply that it will be no use citing against me married women who are famous scientists or architects or financiers—that a woman who wishes to be a creator of anything except children should be content to be a nun or a wanderer on the face of the earth. She cannot be

writer and woman in the way a male writer can be also husband and father. The demands made on her as a woman are destructive in a peculiarly disintegrating way—if she consents to them. And if she does not consent, if she cheats . . . a sharp grain of guilt lodges itself in her, guilt, self-condemnation, regret, which may get smaller, but never dissolves.

Yet I could have managed my double life better than I did. A choice—in spite of the error of an early disastrous marriage—was possible. I could have chosen the monk and let the restless greedy mountebank starve. Even to refuse to choose is a choice. Say I *chose* to drift, to let the mountebank make a hare of the monk and debauch the writer, and the monk trip up the poor restless mountebank, in a perpetual bedlam. But why? Why construct round myself something more intricate than any abstract sculpture, and again and again, sitting silent and unmoving, hammer on it in impotent rage, shout unheard, weep inwardly tears as bitter as gall? Why?

'It is a strange madness,' Petrarch told his travel-worn secretary, 'to be forever sleeping in a strange bed.' The secretary, a good one, could not bear not to go away, he left and came back more than once. Petrarch himself never stayed long in one place.

Alive in me forever, ports not touched at, voyages not made.

Years ago I said Yes when I should have said No. That Yes took me out of my way. But it was I who said it. And I who, long before that moment, encouraged the birth of the smiling fake other people, beginning with my mother, drew out of me to take my place. I *am* my choice. I am what I made of my original condition.

Ah, say it, say it. You had not the courage to choose the creature you were born, avid *to get away*, to be perpetually footloose, without responsibilities, material or human. This famished *vagus*, as indisciplined, graceless, arrogant, as his mediæval kind, clown, spendthrift, gay, eager to be amused, has made antic hay of my life without doing himself any good. I clipped his nails. If he drove me to a series of departures, I hamstrung him by clumsy attempts to live what my forbears called a decent life, tearing pieces out of myself to make the remnant match, compromising, dancing like a bear, speaking softly. I could pretend I did it because I was ashamed to disappoint human beings who depended on me—including the one who is the salt and armature of my life. It would be only half true. The habit is only a few years younger than I am.

Robert Graves is of the poetic opinion that only the baser sort among the dead rush to drink from Lethe. Perhaps—but there may be no other way of reconciling me with myself. As the old women say: What you can't forgive, forget. The grain of guilt is still there. Look for it in my dust.

The early sun of my setting-out was a cold northern sun—sun and salt, a great deal of salt, in the air, on the lips. My confidence was limitless and absurd. It took a long time, years, to vanish out of sight, its place taken by a blind patience—promised in the persistence of a six-months-old child climbing stairs she was beaten for climbing, six attempts, six beatings, before her baffled young mother threw her into her cot to sleep it off. Today I feel my knees failing me before those stairs, but there is no escaping them. How many times, how many more times, before, unforgiven, I find my way back? I have the gross strength of my original hunger. Punished—sometimes justly—I get up and start again, always with less ease. I know whom I have to thank for my power of resistance, for the habit of enduring, the habit and pleasure of hiding behind lies, dissimulation, tricks.

I am writing this at a table of plain wood. Just now, when I ran my hand along the edge, a tiny splinter caught the edge of my palm. Pulling it out, I felt a wave of happiness, even gaiety. It had not come from one of those exultant moments when, dropping with sleep, alone in some cold room, I stumbled on words that I believed came from a centre of my body rather than my brain, but it belonged to that family. Another instant and I had it . . . I am in the kitchen of my mother's house, facing an iron range, the curtains drawn across the window on my right, one weak lamp throwing its yellow hoop on the square of cardboard under my hand. The calendar I am making for my mother in the hope of pleasing her and being praised has the months, days, figures, copied in red and green ink, and the wide margins filled in with an intricate pattern of small blue flowers, each petal painted separately with the point of the finest brush, scores of flowers, hundreds of petals. Slowly adding flower to flower, stopping only for a second to pull out the splinter my left hand has picked up from the rough edge of the table, I am happy, my God how happy.

Surely, somehow, it is still alive, the gaiety, the simple patience?

Of course. How else could you live?—STORM JAMESON, *Journey from the North*, Vol. 2, 1970, pp. 379–81

General

Storm Jameson . . . has portrayed the final overwhelming sorrow of the matriarch—the eternal mother doomed to see her glorious dream hanging upon a cross. She does her portrait with the restraint of the English writer, as well as with the English writer's brooding awareness of history. It is writing such as follows after emotional torture and belongs to the stillness that comes after pain, when the human spirit has learned to accept its burden of disappointment. It is writing which is characteristic of thoughtful women living through colossal tragedy. Tragedy pressed down upon the women who were emotionally mature during the war in England. They saw

everything taken from them. The incidental new freedom it brought to women meant nothing to them. They were too old and too mature to be taken in by the enthusiasm of something that appeared to be new. They had learned that there was no such thing as freedom for women; that women were bound to the race, and that women suffered acutely when the race entered upon a period of calamity; and that no amount of work and no amount of success in that work could ever make for a woman compensation for the descent of the race into hell. A whole generation of men had been swept out of the stream of living. And a whole generation of women were left who could do nothing but stand and watch the stream go on past them. The matriarchs had nothing to do but to look at the emptiness of everything. Life had no need of them any more. Yet they themselves went on living with the terrible attachment of life which is in women. It is so hard for them to die. For women have been endowed by their biology with some awful power to remain alive when every reason for living has gone, and all that there is for them to do is to watch by the empty tomb. Storm Jameson is the very voice of these bereft matriarchs. Though the individual woman she drew had everything for awhile that a woman could desire, she came in the end to have nothing, and the story took its emotional urge not from the beginning but the end of Mary Hervey's life. It is—the whole trilogy—an attempt to provide a negative kind of compensation to women. It says to the childless woman that it is all useless, anyway—that life itself is not worthy of motherhood—that the lines of life will never follow the pattern of the matriarch. Mary Hervey was wrong, she is saying, and wrong upon three counts. She looked for happiness; she worked like a man; she believed in the destiny of the family. There is no happiness except in short moments of illusion, and these must be paid for by the suffering that haunts all happiness. No woman could work like a man. Her whole nature asked only for racial blossoming and the peace that it needs. Children born to a career woman have their teeth on edge because they were not born in peace. No woman should seek to order the destinies of a group of associated individuals. She was no appointed vice-regal to God. She was only a vessel of the race. Her mission was fulfilled when her last baby was weaned; life might go on from then, but it could only go in watchful contemplation. For from her nothing more was to be expected.

It is a portrait taken at a long view. It is far-seeing. It is spiritually remote. It is intellectually composed. It is work that could only have come from a generation of women who had to become remote and composed. And this is true whether or not Storm Jameson herself is remote and composed out of personal necessity. The real writer draws from the population of his or her time the subconscious fiber of thought. We see again and again instances of books held back in their publication until the immediately appointed time, and marked cases of authors who seem to be caught in their creativeness by an inertia of waiting. This is because the real writer is essentially subjective to the race and seems to receive in some strange way from the undercurrents of life unspoken messages of desire. It is in response to these messages that their books are written, laboriously put together from peculiar, hardly touched substance within themselves, or torn out of them in agony which is of the spirit and tears the spirit as human birth tears the body of a woman. Storm Jameson is unquestionably one of those psychically obedient writers, weaving in and out of herself texts that belong to the race.

She writes simply and yet on a grand scale. She has made no attempt to be smart and modish. She does not experiment with style. She is preeminently the sensible middle-class woman of England, devoted to wearable tweeds and sturdy shoes and the traditions of her class and her race and her time. No light remarks fall from her. No passing mode snaps her into its restless cynical pattern. George Eliot could have read her books with understanding. And so also will some unknown woman years from now. It is work of painstaking balance and genuine humanity. As such it belongs to women of all centuries.—MARGARET LAWRENCE, "Matriarchs," *The School of Femininity*, 1963, pp. 228–30

⟨Storm Jameson⟩ is easily placed as the latest exponent of the English family chronicle and the person who has probably brought that particular mode of narration to its highest perfection. In a series of five books she has delineated the affairs of a shipbuilding family and has maintained through successive generations the traditions of English pride, shyness, obstinacy, consideration, and general intrinsic worth. In many respects she is a modernized Galsworthy. Her people are truly complicated individuals, the tangles of sentiment are intricate, and the modern scene is described with some sympathy for its changed codes.

Mrs. Jameson's faults are closely linked with the exigencies of chronicle-writing. Since family traits and the opposition of temperaments are the essential elements, the novelist must "heighten our interest in the characters of his story, so that we care intensely what happens to them. He must introduce delays, surprises, bewilderments." What Mrs. Jameson says of one of Bennett's novels is applicable to her own characters:

> These men and women, so calmly and faithfully going about their little daily tasks, are the battle-grounds of terrific forces. Love, jealousy, passion, hatred, courage, daring—all the monstrous emotions of a Webster play are here at work.

It is obvious that for such dramatic effects as Mrs. Jameson desires, the psychology is likely to be synthetic, the pictures picturesque. And yet in her effort to catch the flavor of successive generations Mrs. Jameson is successful. Ford Madox Ford has guided her in understanding the period of the war and the postwar days. She states that in his four Tietjens novels (concluding with *The Last Post*, 1928) he has

> succeeded in creating a picture of the years between 1912 and 1926 which wipes out (as a flame from a furnace would wipe out the light of a candle) such a picture as that drawn by Mr. Galsworthy in *The White Monkey* and *The Silver Spoon*. No other work . . . has so imprisoned the restless and violent spirit of those years when the ground moved under our feet.

In her own delineations of postwar attitudes Mrs. Jameson is generally unsentimental and aware, though by no means bold. Like Ford she gives an intimation that integrity and the finer English qualities are their own justification. To make life "clear and meaningful," she holds, is as little as you can do for the average reader. He must be given "something to take away into his own private corner. Some word to live by. Some spark at which to warm himself."

Mrs. Jameson's first trilogy was centered about the life of Mary Hervey. In *The Lovely Ship* (1927) her life is carried through the trials of two marriages and the birth of three children. In *The Voyage Home* (1930) she is, at forty-five, the owner and director of great shipbuilding yards, which she was left by Mark Henry Garton. Finally, in *A Richer Dust* (1931), she is an old woman, inflexible in will but frustrated in her desire to have a grandson carry on the business and unwilling to effect a reconciliation with her daughter, Sylvia Russell. The greater part of this volume is concerned with the unhappy marriage of Mary's grandson, Nicholas Roxby, and his disorientated postwar years. The trilogy was republished, 1932, in a single volume, *The Triumph of Time*.

The second trilogy concerns the fortunes of Mary's granddaughter, Hervey Russell, daughter of the unreconciled Sylvia. In *That Was Yesterday* (1932), *Company Parade* (1934), and *Love in Winter* (1935), Hervey's unhappy married life is traced. At the age of thirty she goes to live with Nicholas Roxby. The last two volumes give a vivid picture of demoralized postwar London.

In 1936 Mrs. Jameson wrote something of a thriller in portraying England under native fascist rule. Liberalism is gone and gentlemen beggars walk the streets. An enthusiastic dictator, Hillier, supplies the catchwords that inspire the young with ideals of sacrifice and national purity. Only the mutterings of submerged but unconquered Communists suggest that the seeds of a subsequent revolt are already present. *In the Second Year* has been unfavorably compared with Sinclair Lewis' *It Can't Happen Here* (1935). The Lewis influence is obvious. —WILLIAM C. FRIERSON, "Diffusion, 1929–1940," *The English Novel in Transition: 1885–1940*, 1942, pp. 311–14

Works

The Clash suffers from a stridency of mind and imagination which prejudice the reader against recognising that there is some very fine stuff in this novel. Throughout the book the action is constantly held up while there enters Tilburina, mad, in white satin. Miss Jameson is a person of enormous horsepower, and she occasionally puts this extraordinary force into drawing the conventional figures of the worst sort of fiction. With a gesture of energy that leads one to expect another *Wuthering Heights* she trots out again that cursed beautiful brave child, who steps forward from the shadow of the curtains when the vicar is attempting to comfort the bereaved family with talk of the will of God, and says in her clear treble, "He is a beast, that God," and who rushes out on the moors after she has heard the Moonlight Sonata played for the first time and is found at dawn high on the crags sleeping in the arms of the village harlot. Later on she writes of an aviator who "flew drunk rather than sober and he flew always with genius. He was swarthy and dark-browed, a giant with the ankles and wrists of a dancer. Women adored him for his insolent courtesy and for his eyes, which were the blue of rain-wet hyacinths." A girl's dream, a girl's dream. Nevertheless, in spite of a deal of this sort of thing (even including a Spanish dancer) there is real talent here. There is a description of the life that centred round an aerodrome where both American and English pilots were stationed which is brilliantly astute. The account of the Senator trying to unfurl the Stars and Stripes and keep command of his patriotic relative clauses is a curiously humorous production for a writer who elsewhere seems to have no sense of humour whatsoever. And the core of the story, the passion for a base and noisy man with power, which visits like a plague a woman who is married to a good and fastidious man who is without power, is described with great wisdom. There is a specially remarkable passage when the loquacious Texan picks up a pamphlet in Elizabeth's drawing-room and rants about it ("This country is rotten with Socialism," he observed, "your traditions are about to be strangled and turned out of their old home by a gang of sexless, immoral eaters of filth. To me a Socialist is a cross between a rattlesnake and a damned fool. And to all decent Americans. If we had the writer of this—indecency—over there we'd know how to deal with him.") and Elizabeth loathingly looks down on the bottomless pit of his folly, and at the same time sicklily recognises that even this knowledge of him does not break his power over her. Miss Jameson is a writer without literary taste, and that is a defect which does not correct itself. But it looks in this book as if she was developing a curious emotional clairvoyance which would make her novels worth reading.—REBECCA WEST, "Notes on Novels," *NS*, May 27, 1922, p. 213

In a fine, formal, eighteenth-century prose, with fewer adjectives to the book than the average writer uses in a chapter, Storm Jameson has written three long stories and issued them under the title *Women against Men*. The title holds the only misleading words in the volume. The women of these stories are no more against men than they are against other women, or against the scheme of the universe, and the title, with its hint of fusty feminism, gives no promise of the real character of the book. For at last here are stories about women by a woman which are honest and unsentimental.

Miss Jameson may have to suffer for "speaking out" like this. She has been as plain-spoken about her heroines as about those at whose hands they suffered. This means that none of the stories offers any restful oasis for illusions, no nook in which the tender-hearted can rest. The tawdry vulgarian of "Delicate Monster", a woman novelist who turns her lovers and friends into "copy" and uses lovers, husbands, child, and friend without scruple is one thing. We have all had the pleasure of disliking these villainesses before. But what of the heroine—herself a writer, the childhood friend of the "monster", the narrator of the story? She is drawn as relentlessly as Victoria. Belonging in many ways to a higher order of being, more sensitive, frequently scrupulous, by preference fastidious, when she is robbed of her husband by her predatory friend she shows traits as inadmirable as any of Victoria's own: under jealousy she sets traps, indulges in hysterics, reads letters and notebooks. But how dreadful! you may exclaim. Does Miss Storm Jameson believe that decent women are like this? Read the story; if at the conclusion you still hold that Storm Jameson is unfair or inaccurate you are one of two things: one of them is "remarkably fortunate".

The second story is as unlike the first as possible. "The Single Heart" is a love story of a girl who, falling in love with a young workman after her marriage, spends the rest of her life and all her strength to get the man she loves, and to keep him. It is unbearably poignant; Storm Jameson has done studies of jealousy before, but none as good as this. The lover, whom Emily marries after her husband's early death, and whose career she promotes to her own last breath, deceives her again and again; and again and again she takes him back to her arms in spite of her agonizing jealousy. If that were all, we should feel that we had heard this story of a betrayed and noble woman more than once before: but Miss Jameson goes on to tell us that Emily had steadily deceived both her lover and her husband, feeling not the least scruple about it, hardly realizing that she was doing it, since she felt that she was acting to her lover's advantage. Yet her heart is very nearly broken when she discovers that Evan has been consoling himself trivially while she travels in America with her husband.

This is abandoning conventional novel psychology with a vengeance; yet it is done so well that you accept all the testimony. The three main characters are, under different aspects, detestable, admirable, and pathetic. Miss Jameson does not underline the irony or palliate the double-dealing: she tells what one woman in love was like, and draws a good portrait. Again, if you are able to finish "The Single Heart" convinced that Emily is not recognizably feminine, you are, to say the least of it, lucky.

The last story in the book is "A Day Off." In its way it is as

successful as the other two, and, since the specimen of femininity being examined in this case is an aging streetwalker, it is likely to get more wholehearted approval than the other two tales. For some time it has been a literary fashion to be frank about such poor drabs: so much so that the critics know now that such honesty is all right, and one out of every two reviewers will undoubtedly hold that Miss Jameson has been at her most effective in capturing the essence of the dimwitted, distraught creature whose last lover has deserted her. It seems to me to have less of the bitter, tonic and bracing aftereffect than either of the other two.—DOROTHEA BRANDE, "Five Novels," *Bkm*, Jan. 1933, pp. 86–87

Company Parade is a novel of the peace, or—as Miss Jameson would probably prefer to describe it—of the lull between European wars. Its background could scarcely be more depressing; Miss Jameson and her characters seem to live and breathe under the shadow of an approaching conflict, and can talk and think of little else. The idiocy of politicians, the villainy of armament manufacturers, the apathy and criminal stupidity of the upper and middle classes haunt the narrative like a bad dream or a bad smell; and it is only now and then, with the slightly shamefaced air of a dilettante caught in the act, that the reader is able to remind himself that human beings, even today, still experience moments of rare and precious happiness, and that so illogical is our human composition that it is still possible to derive pleasure from these moments, though the were- or war-wolf is scratching at the door and every newspaper that slips through the letter-box contains an account of some fresh revolting atrocity. . . .

Thus speaks the "bourgeois intellectual." There are some of us for whom the mind is its own place, for whom the most important events are still primarily subjective, and for whom personal salvation must come—not from without, from participation in a new and improved social order, but from within, whose "Kingdom of Heaven" (such as it is) will never quite merge its frontiers in any Union of Socialist Soviet Republics. But Miss Jameson is a novelist with a message. Her message is one with which few readers of *The New Statesman and Nation* will find it difficult to sympathise; though I think they may agree that her indignation has not yet been assimilated by the literary medium through which it is set forth and that, so iterated and reiterated, used to colour paragraph after paragraph, line after taut resentful line, it tends to lose the immediacy of its first effect. On the Embankment, she scents a future cataclysm. . . . Well, granted the huddled, shapeless derelicts, heaped up on the benches, under the bluish glare of the arc-lamps, the reflection is plausible and does her credit; but when one of her characters is discovered eating chicken cutlets "in a restaurant in which even the plates witnessed to the death of society"—they had been "stamped by sweated Czech workers with patterns which satisfied the American importer's idea of French peasant art"—I cannot help wishing that she would allow society to expire in peace. Nero, with his Stradivarius on the heights of the Palatine, is the type of artist for whom personally I have a sneaking regard.

To stress the social and political side of Miss Jameson's narrative is to draw attention to a very important and perhaps slightly over-obtrusive aspect of her book, but does not help to explain the energy and resourcefulness with which the narrative itself is conducted. Miss Jameson is an extremely practised writer, and her account of Hervey Russell's struggle against poverty, obscurity and a foolish, weak-willed, unprincipled and unfaithful husband—the type of husband with whom feminine fiction has made us painfully familiar—is written in a convincing and lucid style. Yet the impression left by the book is

disappointing. Miss Jameson has attempted to give us a panorama of contemporary life. Up to a point she has succeeded; but beyond that point—the point at which observation becomes interpretation and clever reporting art—her imaginative grasp of her subject-matter does not extend. The reader may agree with her dominant thesis; but he will close the volume in much the same state as he started reading it.
—PETER QUENNELL, "New Novels," *NSN*, March 31, 1934, p. 488

JAMES GINDIN
From "Storm Jameson and the Chronicle"
Centennial Review, Fall 1978, pp. 403–8

A chronicle, more shapeless than most, written in the 1920's and '30's, as yet little known or seldom discussed in this country, is Storm Jameson's series of novels centering on the family that begins with Mary Hervey, born Mary Hansyke, who heads a large shipbuilding firm and shipping line on the north Yorkshire coast during a long stretch of late Victorian and Edwardian time. Within the past two years or so, Berkley Medallion Books has published seven of these novels in paperback: *The Lovely Ship, The Voyage Home, A Richer Dust, The Captain's Wife* (entitled *Farewell Night, Welcome Day* in England), *That Was Yesterday, Company Parade,* and *Love in Winter.* The first three of the novels were planned as a trilogy. Later novels extended the series, three of them described by Ms. Jameson only a few years ago (she is now eighty-seven) as part "of an unfinished series." The series is even less confined than this suggests, for the character of Mary Hervey Russell, called Hervey, the granddaughter of Mary Hansyke and the character who is the author's persona, as well as a number of characters outside the family, appear and are central to several of Ms. Jameson's later novels, novels written during the 1940's outside the boundaries of this series. Nevertheless, the seven novels now available in paperback do comprise a relatively coherent chronicle covering roughly the years from 1840 to 1930, tracing the three generations from the grandmother's leadership of the shipping firm through the intermediate generation's rebellion to the development of Hervey as a novelist.

Exciting plots through turbulent generations, in the manner of Taylor Caldwell, do not distinguish Ms. Jameson's chronicle. The episodes, particularly in the first novel, are simply a stringing together of exterior events, recordings of marriages, deaths, and careers that often seem too derivative of earlier novels (some of the first novel sounds like a pastiche of eighteenth century novels, a part of the second like a less compressed version of Sophia's disillusionment in the Paris portions of Bennett's *The Old Wives' Tale*). Not until *That Was Yesterday,* the fifth in the series as Berkley has reprinted it (although written fourth, originally published in 1932—the novel Berkley places fourth, in order to follow the chronology of events in the family because it deals centrally with Hervey's mother, is *The Captain's Wife,* another fine novel, which was not published until 1939, after the rest of the series had been finished), when Hervey herself becomes the central character and perspective, does the treatment of character deepen and the connection of the individual with history develop a particular and complicated resonance. Ms. Jameson herself has, more tersely, recently written as much, that "My earliest novels are not worth reading," and she lists *That Was Yesterday* as the first to be written that is now "worth looking at." Like some of Thomas Hardy's early chronicles, *The Trumpet-Major* or *Under the Greenwood Tree*, set in the distance of the origins of his world before he was born, Ms. Jameson's early novels, although with less distinctive originality than Hardy's, have a rather remote charm but suffer from a lack of intensity in contrast with the later ones.

The principal justification for the earlier novels is retrospective, the locus for attitudes and incidents later seen to be crucial for Hervey. The second novel, *The Voyage Home,* details the long incident in which Sylvia, Mary Hansyke's daughter, rebels against her mother and runs off to Dieppe with an aging charmer who has long sponged off the family. He leaves her in Dieppe, unmarried, because he's heard hints of gold mines in South Africa, and she, distraught, marries the first respectable man she sees, the unsuccessful captain of one of her mother's lesser ships. When, back in England, Mary refuses to give Sylvia's husband an executive job with the shipping line, Sylvia refuses to see or speak to her again. The lasting split between mother and daughter reverberates through all the subsequent novels, causes Hervey (Sylvia's daughter) to be brought up close to poverty, her brother to welcome flying and danger in the First World War as his only possible relief from apprenticeship to his father, creates a sense of constant grudging emotion and self-assertion, operating through the novels much in the same way that Soames Forsyte's raping of Irene in Galsworthy's *Man of Property* influences so many of the characters and events in the last novels of *The Forsyte Saga.* The continuity of the novels also allows the reader to see how Hervey gradually assumes something of her grandmother's force and identity, although the two meet only once. In that one incident, Hervey, then a scholarship student at the university, comes to ask her grandmother for a job, confident that, in spite of her technical ignorance and her shy awkwardness, she could learn to build ships. She is brusquely refused. The incident is told from three different perspectives in three different novels, her grandmother's, Hervey's, and that of Nicholas, the young cousin with whom, after each has been bruised by a bad marriage, Hervey later falls in love. Each perspective is a past, a set of relationships, a combination of generosities and guilts, almost a novel in itself, and each plays off ironically against the others throughout the chronicle. The chronicle multiplies the possibilities for ironies that depend on history, contrasts and identities that the characters only gradually, if ever, discover, each generation tending to simplify the ones before in order to define itself. Hervey never fully recognizes that the grandmother she has invented, the Victorian woman of steadfast principles and certainties, is a fiction, that the real woman, in her own terms, was as uncertain, as ambivalent, as full of guilt, as Hervey is herself.

Line by line, Storm Jameson's writing is sometimes untidy, uneven, especially in the earlier novels. The author sometimes loads the situation clumsily: "If she had been more experienced, she would have known that . . . ;" sometimes, she engages in a form of premonitory melodrama: "It was, though she did not know it, the last time she would step out of the dark side-street into the Place Verte"; self-pity can occasionally dwarf a passage of the persona's recollections. A portrait of the writer and rambunctious intellectual with whom Nicholas's young wife runs off for a temporary affair seems too obviously, too long-windedly, and too vituperatively modelled on the physiognomy and character of H. G. Wells. Ms. Jameson is much better with long descriptions of landscapes, the history and composition of towns, and the succession of small houses and furnished rooms in which Hervey lives during her first marriage, following her husband to various military posts in England later in the war, and, on her own, after the war, with her child, working at an advertising job in London and beginning to write novels. Like Bennett, Ms. Jameson is a splendid materialist, conveying the fabric and textures of domestic life in the past. She also is at her best in detailing the long complexities of relationships, as in the penetrating treatment of the slow dissolution of Hervey's first marriage in *That Was Yesterday* and subsequent novels. Their marriage erodes through living in a shabby housing estate outside of Liverpool as he takes his first job as an indigent teacher in a bad school, through the upheavals of war and different attitudes toward it, through changing social and political convictions, through the hostility of his wealthier family sending him back to Oxford for another career, and through their mutual infidelities. Yet the process of unraveling is protracted by each partner's dependence, his on her competence and her vulnerability to his weakness and his feckless rebellions, hers on his exterior manner of smooth assurance, but even more deeply on her own guilt and her own control. The reasons for prolonging the break are given far more painful intensity than is the collapse of the marriage itself. Ms. Jameson achieves a similar acuity and density in depicting Hervey's relationship with her mother. Sylvia begins by treating her first-born with severity, taking out her resolve to be independent from her mother on her daughter. She breeds, in Hervey, a tremendous desire both to please others and to go her own way, developing into ambition that would compensate her mother for a thwarted life. As the two characters, in superficial ways very different, build their defenses against each other, they reveal an intense, grudging, deep, almost unspoken respect for one another. Hervey comes, with great difficulty, to understand the self-defeating mother so unlike herself, as she never understood the grandmother she resembled. Storm Jameson works all these generational complexities of her characters' relationships with considerable skill.

Since the characters are always both within and reacting against their worlds, the chronicle also achieves and communicates a sense of history, less intimately the history of the nineteenth century, more immediately and intensively that surrounding the First World War. Before the war, all the sensible people cannot see how the murder of an obscure Archduke can possibly lead to general war, regard the welcoming of war, on the part of jingoists or old men in clubs who will not have to fight, as outrageous. Yet, as the war begins, in spite of her scorn for the jingoists, the women who hand out white feathers to young men not in uniform, and the complacent certain that the war will end in glorious victory by Christmas, Hervey, living on the housing estate, is not a pacifist either. From the perspective of 1932, when *That Was Yesterday* was published, "We are all conscientious objectors now (except some politicians, some parsons, most of the newspaper proprietors, and a few respectable morons of both sexes) but in those days pacifists were few and disgusting. Hervey had never spoken to one." As the war progresses, as she meets pacifists and the casualty lists increase (including several friends from college and her brother), Hervey begins to sort out varieties of non-combatants: those who are pacifists from abstract conviction, often remote and as militant in their own way as the war's enthusiasts; those simply revolted by the casualty lists and the endless and useless struggle; those, like her young husband who stays out as long as he can and finally finds a post as an equipment officer who never leaves England, without convictions, who preserve their own safety as best they can. Hervey recognizes that the war has "become a condition of life as impersonal as the weather," and, although attracted to pacifism, she cannot wholeheartedly embrace it because the war is so deeply and entirely there:

> I loathe war. I'm glad some few people are having the hardness to deny it. The only thing is—*I* can't deny it. It's like asking me to deny myself. I'm in the war, whether I like it or not. The whole of my generation is in it. It will blot us out.

War, unlike energy crises, imposes necessary conditions for its duration, temporarily obscures individual effort or conviction. After the war, as the later novels in the series show, Hervey's generation retains its singularity, not that all its members are identical (some respond by retreat, some by devotion to Communism as the force of the future, some by aggressive admiration for the new tyrants who, like Mussolini or the National Socialists in Germany, seek to control and impose themselves on history—the most difficult response to maintain is sane and liberal concern), but that all have been so indelibly marked by the war.

JEROME K. JEROME

1859–1927

Jerome Klapka Jerome was born in Walsall, Staffordshire, on May 2, 1859, and grew up in the East End of London. Because of the poverty of his parents he received little formal education, and became a clerk in 1873. After the death of his parents he took up acting with touring companies, but returned to London penniless at the age of nineteen. Having tried journalism and teaching, he returned to clerking and began to send contributions to magazines. His humorous essays on theater life were accepted by *The Play*, and in 1885 appeared in book form as *On the Stage—and Off*. A second series of essays was collected as *The Idle Thoughts of an Idle Fellow* (1886), and Jerome diversified by writing with some success for the stage. By 1888, he was able to become a full-time writer, marry, and settle down to the comforts of Victorian middle-class life.

A trip on the Thames provided the basis for Jerome's greatest success, *Three Men in a Boat* (1889), and a journey to Oberammergau to see the passion play resulted in *The Diary of a Pilgrimage* (1890). In the following decade most of his energies were devoted to the theatre, with *The Prude's Progress* enjoying a six-month run in 1895, and to the editorship of *The Idler* and

To-day. A libel suit in 1897 forced him to sell his interests in these magazines, and for much of the rest of his life he was paying off legal debts. A cycling holiday in Germany is recorded in *Three Men on the Bummel* (1900), and Jerome liked the country well enough to take up residence in Dresden for two years. He was much fêted in Germany, in America (which he toured in 1908 and 1911), and in Russia.

Jerome was much saddened by World War I, and after a brief spell in the French Ambulance Unit returned to England to appeal for a reasonable peace. After the war he lived mainly in London; he died on June 14, 1927.

Notable among Jerome's later works are the play *The Passing of the Third Floor Back* (1908), the novels *Paul Kelver* (1902), *They and I* (1909), and *Anthony John* (1923), and a volume of memoirs, *My Life and Times* (1926).

General

Jerome gives us very good specimens of the ordinary language of the Victorian era. His style is not surprisingly original, but he shows a remarkable talent in rendering with perfect accuracy the characteristic talk of different classes of society. The persons he introduces to us need only utter a few words, before we are able to form a conception of their social position, their degree of culture, etc.; very often we get in this manner a clue also to their character. The author has led an exceptionally varied life—in his early years he was at different times a clerk, a teacher, an actor, a journalist. He had, accordingly, frequent opportunities of communicating with individuals of different social position and different culture, and of studying their languaage. He does not aim at grammatical peculiarities, elaborate phrases, or rare expressions; his language is the average language of his own time, acutely observed and faithfully rendered. Giving us thus a true and varied image of the talk of different classes and trades.—OLOF E. BOSSON, "Preface" to *Slang and Cant in Jerome K. Jerome's Works*, 1911, pp. 5–6

The Idle Thoughts of an Idle Fellow, in 1889, gave ⟨Jerome⟩ a popular vogue: *Three Men in a Boat*, in the same year, made him one of the most widely-read authors in the world. Its facetious humours, its jokes about house-maid's knee, falling into rivers, getting wet through sleeping out, and men making messes of their cooking, were of their period, the period of *Happy Thoughts*, and *My Lady Nicotine*; the burlesque beautiful passages would have been good had a shade more trouble been taken with them. The book would hardly get a start now, the atmosphere having changed. Of Jerome's later works the most successful was *The Passing of the Third Floor Back*, a sentimental religious play which the genius of Sir J. Forbes Robertson made seem better than it was; but the best was *Paul Kelver*, a semi-autobiographical novel which never had the success it deserved. Jerome was at one time editor of *The Idler* (with Robert Barr), and then of *To-day*, both lively though ephemeral publications with a Bohemian tone.—UNSIGNED, *LM*, July 1927, p. 229

. . . ⟨I⟩t is certain that those who know Jerome only as a humorist only half know him. I remember going in 1890, I think it was to Terry's theatre, and laughing all through an evening at his joyously irresponsible farce, *New Lamps for Old*; but in 1907 I saw another side of him when I went to the first night of that story of Christ in a London lodging-house, the most poignant and beautiful of his plays, *The Passing of the Third Floor Back*. Like every humorist, he takes life seriously; no man lacking a sense of humour can do that; unless he can also see the fun of things he cannot rightly see the sadness of them—he attaches importance to trifles, mistakes pomposity for dignity, finds occasion for gravity in matters that are inherently laughable, imagines that wealth or inherited honour exalts him, condescends to patronise where he should be humble enough to pity and be kind, and is never able to feel the tie of common brotherhood that evens the odds between all who are mortal. You have to be humourless before you can be proud, and any sort of pride walls you in and keeps you ignorant of life outside your own.

You will find Jerome's more serious moods breaking through at intervals in his two *Idle Thoughts* books; in most of his humorous books; and they prevail, with a leaven of humour, in such of his novels as *Anthony John*, *All Roads Lead to Calvary*, in that best and most quietly humorous and charming of them, *Paul Kelver*, and in certain of his short stories, notably in the delicately wrought, tenderly imaginative "John Ingerfield"; they prevail, too, in the vigorous, outspoken articles he wrote on social problems of his day. Next to its abounding humour, the constant note in his work is a broad sympathy with all sorts and conditions of humanity, a sensitive understanding of the wrongs and disadvantages under which the less fortunate of us have to live and labour.—ARTHUR ST. JOHN ADCOCK, "Jerome K. Jerome," *The Glory That Was Grub Street*, 1928, pp. 167–68

Successful as *Three Men in a Boat* was, it was far from being Jerome's only or most characteristic work. In the essays he wrote between 1889 and 1905 and which he included in *The Idle Thoughts of an Idle Fellow*, *Second Thoughts of an Idle Fellow*, and *American Wives and Others*; in the travel sketches that filled *Diary of a Pilgrimage* and *Three Men on Wheels*, accounts of journeys to Oberammergau and the Black Forest; as well as in *Novel Notes*, a book about four men attempting to write a novel together and getting nowhere because they are too busy exchanging anecdotes, Jerome revealed a genuine gift for highlighting, in brief span, the more ridiculous aspects of the society of his day. With tolerance and a style of humor that owed much to Dickens and Mark Twain and more to Jerome's innate sense of absurdity, he wrote of the problems of husbands, of tourists, of the human animal trapped in the drawing room. It is these brief pieces, together with two short stories from the same period, which make up this representative selection of Jerome's work; together, they allow us a remarkably informal visit with a civilized and genuinely funny man.

The essay, of course, no longer exists in the form in which it was practiced in Jerome's day, and to a new generation, accustomed to the modern article with its burden of facts and heavy weight of responsibility, it may come as a surprise that only sixty years ago a man could write for the sheer amusement of the thing; could write, for instance, a piece on evergreens that turned out to be about men and bulldogs and courage, or one on teakettles that had nothing to do with teakettles at all. In its time, however, the essay was that most perfect of art forms, a chance for the author to speak his mind on any subject at all without being taken too seriously, and authors have been mourning its passing ever since.

Jerome was one of its most successful practitioners, as proved by the extent to which his own character comes through. We know him at once. He is the man whose chair always tips over, who forgets the name of the person he has just met, whose well-meant advice is always taken wrong and upon whose toes some child is always standing. Both in his candid confession of social blunders and in his occasional irascibility, he is completely likable and surprisingly modern.

He is also a man of wide human sympathies, whose advice is equal to the most perplexing of situations: how to deal with waiters, how to sleep in a German bed (by sleeping on the floor), how to go to pieces in a rocking chair, how to select a fiancée (easier if chosen from the few than from the many), how to be original, how to approach a pawnshop, how to speak to a baby if you are not sure of its sex. In all this foolishness there are many classic scenes: of Jerome's aunt sailing up the street with a bulldog beneath her crinoline, of an omelette ordered in pantomime, of an utterly demolishing bicycle-repair job that ends in complete disorder.

Here too are problems of a national character, for Jerome was a frequent traveler and keen observer. He sees American marriages threatened by wives traveling on their husband's money, and ponders the troublesome implications of German dueling ("How German Students Amuse Themselves"). With penetrating insight he forecasts, twelve years before it happened, the type of revolution that would come to Russia. And in an illuminating essay ("The New Utopia") that suggests Wells and Orwell, he depicts the regimented world of 1984.

But Jerome is most himself, and most amusing, when he is dealing with the contemporary social scene. He contrasts fictional woman with her real-life British counterpart; deplores the rules of society that frown on honesty and reward cheerful lying; and examines, critically, the current build-it-yourself fad. As a former actor he is amused by the British theatre (why are peasants so clean on the stage and so untidy off?), by the time-scheme of opera (do people really like statuary?). But perhaps most devastating is his analysis of the Victorian character itself. He presents the subject playfully, but in "The Poor," with its attack on ladies' charity, and in "Joe Smith and Mr. Smythe," with its Jekyll-and-Hyde motif, he lays bare, perhaps unconsciously, some of the problems of that troubled age. In the world of Jerome, men are always ready for a vacation from marriage, and one senses the undertones of our contemporary marital scene.

If Jerome is fully aware of human frailty, he has a soft spot for ghosts and animals. His ghosts, freed from earthly concerns, are full of fun and misleading information, and his animals always seem more alive than the more sentimentally depicted creatures of his time. In the story of the dog that saved its money or of the cat that played two families against one another, he sees the animal in all its lovable one-up-manship, and animal lovers have reason to be grateful.

From this it is but a step to probing human nature, and no one who reads Jerome can fail to be aware of the melancholy that descends upon him at times and is the reverse side of his hilarity. If the author of *Three Men in a Boat* sees life as absurd, the author of the mystical *The Passing of the Third Floor Back* is deeply troubled by its absurdity. Why must people spend their lives enslaved in unworthy roles? Why is the world a vanity fair in which good perishes and evil persists? What will outlast time? What is the reason for life? These are the questions of the man in the street, but that does not mean they are not profound. Jerome raises the basic questions of life, and there are no answers except that given at the end of "The New Utopia," where everyday life rises with all its noise and color, "fighting, striving, living." To Jerome, life itself, with all its failings, is its own justification.

His is therefore basically an accepting voice, saying yes to life—for all his complaints—because it cannot be other than it is. In this basic tolerance, as well as in the clarity with which he states it, Jerome is very much our contemporary in spite of the sixty years that have elapsed since these selections first appeared.

It is, of course, easy to say that Jerome's world of hansom cabs, four-wheelers, and trips up the Thames is not our world, and it is true that the costumes and social conventions have changed. Human nature, nevertheless—Jerome's real subject—remains the same. Husbands still try to fix furnaces and have ambitions of writing a book, and wives persist in arriving at the theatre late. Change the clothing slightly, and Jerome, confronted with a newborn baby to hold, is Benchley or Thurber or many a contemporary humorist faced with the same situation.—ROBERT HUTCHINSON, "Introduction" to *The Humorous World of Jerome K. Jerome*, 1962, pp. vi–viii

Works

To tell the truth, we hardly know what to make of *Three Men in a Boat*, of which we have no desire to make much, either good or ill. It is not a piece of fiction, as might be supposed, since the author goes out of his way to say in a preface that "its pages form a record of events that really happened." Again, "George and Harris and Montmorency"—that is the dog, a fox terrier—"are not poetic ideals, but things of flesh and blood." There can be no meaning in these words unless we are intended to understand that the book is a more or less realistic account of what it professes to describe—a week's trip, in early summer, on the Thames. The events are, obviously, exaggerated for purposes of humour, but they seem to be real events. "Other works," says Mr. Jerome, "may excel this in depth of thought and knowledge of human nature; other books may rival it in originality and size; but for hopeless and incurable veracity nothing yet discovered can surpass it." On the whole, after reading *Three Men in a Boat*, we come to the conclusion that this is not intended for irony. These are what French novelists call "documents"; this is the genuine relation of a passage in the lives of actual people. We are face to face with a British species of the genus which has produced Amiel and Marie Bashkirtseff. Let not Mr. Jerome think us unkind in making a few reflections on his volume from this point of view. It is the only point of view from which it appears to us to be interesting; and if we do not consider it as "documents" we shall not consider it at all.

The whole chronicle is an account of how the author and two young friends went up the Thames from Kingston to Oxford, and back so far as Pangbourne, in a double-sculling skiff. It reproduces all the minute adventures of such a summer outing, mildly describes, for the thousandth time, but in a novel spirit, the objects on the shore, and is written entirely in colloquial clerk's English of the year 1889, of which this is an example taken at random:—

> She was nuts on public-houses, was England's Virgin Queen. There's scarcely a pub. of any attractions within ten miles of London that she does not seem to have looked in at, or stopped at, or slept at, some time or other. I wonder now, supposing Harris, say, turned over a new leaf, and became a great and good man, and got to be Prime Minister, and died, if they would put signs over the public-houses that he had patronized. "Harris had a glass of bitter in this house"; "Harris had two of Scotch cold here in the summer of '88"; "Harris was chucked from here in December 1886."

This is not funny, of course; to do Mr. Jerome justice it is not intended to be particularly funny; but it is intensely colloquial, and, as an attempt to reproduce, without any kind of literary admixture, the ordinary talk of ordinary young people of to-day, it seems to us remarkable, especially as the whole book is kept at the same simple and yet abnormal level of style. It will be observed that in this short passage just quoted there are no less than six phrases which would be wholly unintelligible to a foreigner thoroughly conversant with the English of books, and yet not one of the six is in the least strained, or, though vulgar, would offer the least difficulty to a Londoner. For the future student of late Victorian slang, *Three Men in a Boat* will be invaluable, if he is able to understand it, and if, by the time he flourishes, the world of idle youth has not entirely forgotten what a "bally tent" and "sunday-school slops" and "a man of about number one size" are. In some of the sporting newspapers slang of this kind, and indeed of a much worse kind, may be discovered, but we do not recollect to have met any other book entirely written in it. In a sense, too, *Three Men in a Boat* is a much truer specimen of lower middle-class English than are the paragraphs in the coloured newspapers, because they are exaggerated and non-natural, while Mr. Jerome is amazingly real. That it was worth doing, we do not say; indeed, we have a very decided opinion that it was not. But the book's only serious fault is that the life it describes and the humour that it records are poor and limited, and decidedly vulgar. It is strange that a book like *Three Men in a Boat*, which is a *tour de force* in fun of a certain kind, should leave us with a sigh on our lips at the narrowness and poverty of the life it only too faithfully reflects. The illustrations, which are reproduced in some ineffectual modern process, go very well with the text, and are not less modern or faithful or incongruous. The figures in the really clever design on p. 71 give with complete accuracy, and without the least caricature, the outward appearance in the present year of grace of the sort of young men who figure in the pages of *Three Men in a Boat*. How droll and old-fashioned both will seem before the twentieth century opens!—UNSIGNED, *SRL*, Oct. 5, 1889, pp. 387–88

Mr. Jerome K. Jerome has followed his entertaining *Three Men in a Boat* with *Three Men on Wheels*, a story which is supposed to take the heroes of the earlier book on a bicycle trip through the Black Forest—we say suppose, because whenever there is any prospect of their getting too far toward their destination Mr. Jerome steps in with an anecdote or the narrative of some former experience of one of the trio until, when the end is reached, the reader lays the volume aside with a vague sort of wonder what the Black Forest really had to do in the matter. The book bears the imprint of Messrs. Dodd, Mead and Company, and is not at all bad reading for the lazy months of the year. The print is good and large, and there are no heavy arguments or long sentences. To us it is a book of considerable interest. In fact, we may say that it is in one respect a work of high art, and we hasten to acclaim Mr. Jerome and to express our profound admiration for that facility which enables him to spread a chapter of rather thin humour over two hundred and ninety-nine pages.—UNSIGNED, *Bkm*, July 1900, p. 410

Some great men are never found out. From that fate Mr. Jerome has escaped. Over his buried merit it will not be necessary to raise the tardy bust. Is he not saluted by the *Times* and other gallopers of fame as the successor of Dickens? How did they penetrate his disguise? I fear he was careless. Dickens wrote *David Copperfield*, and *David Copperfield* is an autobiography. Mr. Jerome wrote *Paul Kelver*, and *Paul Kelver* is an autobiography. A clear clue! There are others, too numerous to specify. (See the puppets' passion.) One, however, is frank to the verge of rashness. "I am not Doady," says Dan, "who always seems to me to have been somewhat of a—he reminds me of you, Paul, a little." Purblind is the critic who cannot take that hint and better it. The thing is a syllogism. Paul is Doady, and Doady is Dickens. Mr. Jerome is Paul, therefore Mr. Jerome is Dickens the Second, Q.E.D. The only question is, Which? Some will say, Dickens; others will say, Mr. Jerome; I say nothing.

One thing bewilders me. Is Mr. Jerome a humourist or is he not? I desire a plain answer to that plain question. It seems that he has cast humour behind him, and that this is a "serious novel." If so, how can it be Dickensian? For Dickens was a humourist. A friend suggests that *Paul Kelver* is a parody of *David Copperfield*. There may be something in that. Mr. Jerome is "beside" Dickens all the time, and *Paul Kelver* might be described as "issuing, derived and proceeding from" *David Copperfield*. It is true that Paul is not born with a caul, but that is the only missing trait. He is haunted by Dickensian ghosts. Even "the old House" in the Prologue talks Dickens. The "man in grey" is mildly Micawberish. There are ferociously honest men and insipidly angelic women. There are Mrs. Peedles, Minipin, Jarman, the O'Kelly, the Signora, Rosina Sellars, Uncle Gutton, Aunt Gutton, a watery-eyed young man, a fat young lady, a thin young lady, actors and actresses, painters, law-writers, playwriters, doctors, editors, commission agents, barmaids and members of other trades and professions mentioned in the London Directory. Then there are slabs of sentiment and hunks of love. As Paul says, "it is a curious sort of love." "The Making of Love" is a wonderful chapter. Paul stands "over against" Barbara, his arm "resting upon the dial's stone column" in a Marcus Stone garden. "The sun was sinking, casting long shadows on the velvety grass, illuminating with a golden light her upturned face." Paul begins his oration thus: "I would you were some great queen of olden days." All he wants is to "touch now and then at rare intervals with my lips your hand, kiss in secret the glove you had let fall, the shoe you had flung off." Or, in the alternative, he would she were a "priestess in some temple of forgotten gods, where I might steal at daybreak and at dusk to gaze upon your beauty; kneel with clasped hands, watching your sandalled feet coming and going about the altar steps; lie with pressed lips upon the stones your trailing robes had touched." But the base and brutal Barbara rejects the devout lover. "I shall be a countess, Paul, the Countess Huéscar," with elopements and infidelities "now and then at rare intervals." On the whole, this chapter supports Paul's apothegm, "once a humourist, always a humourist." Hal's dying confession removes all reasonable doubt. "I dared not kiss her for fear of waking her; but a stray lock of her hair—you remember how long it was?—fell over the pillow, nearly reaching to the floor. I pressed my lips against it, where it trailed over the bedstead, till they bled. I have it still upon my lips, the mingling of the cold iron and the warm, soft, silken hair."

Now there are three ways of interpreting Jeromean art, (1) to take it seriously, (2) to take it as unconscious humour, or (3) take it as conscious humour. On the whole, I prefer the third. *Paul Kelver* is a clever parody of Dickens, and a clever burlesque of popular fiction. The passages I have quoted are the quintessence of satirical caricature. They satirise not only the popular novelist, but the readers of the popular novelist. So innocent are the critics that they have mistaken the caricature for the thing caricatured. So infantile is the public that it has devoured four editions of the caricature without having discovered that Mr. Jerome is making fun of them and of their idols!—JAMES DOUGLAS, *Bkm*, Nov. 1902, pp. 367–77

Three Men in a Boat. (To say nothing of the dog), I wrote at Chelsea Gardens, up ninety-seven stairs. But the view was worth it. We had a little circular drawing-room—I am speaking now as a married man—nearly all windows, suggestive of a lighthouse, from which we looked down upon the river, and over Battersea Park to the Surrey hills beyond, with the garden of old Chelsea Hospital just opposite. Fourteen shillings a week we paid for that flat: two reception-rooms, three bedrooms and a kitchen. One was passing rich in those days on three hundred a year: kept one's servant, and sipped one's Hennessy's "Three Star" at four and twopence the bottle. I had known Chelsea Gardens for some time. Rose Norreys, the actress, had a flat there, and gave Sunday afternoon parties. She was playing then at the Court Theatre with Arthur Cecil and John Clayton. Half young Bohemia used to squeeze itself into her tiny drawing-room, and overflow into the kitchen. Bald or grey-headed they are now, those of them that are left. Bernard Partridge and myself were generally the last to leave. One could not help loving her. She was a strange spiritual creature. She would have made a wonderful Joan of Arc. She never seemed to grow up. I was rehearsing a play at the Vaudeville Theatre, when a boy slipped into my hand the last letter I had from her. The boy never said whom it was from; and I did not open it till the end of the act, some two hours later. It was written in pencil, begging me to come to her at once. She had rooms in Great Portland Street in a house covered with ivy. A small crowd was round the door when I got there; and I learned she had just been taken away to Colney Hatch asylum. I never could bring myself to go and see her there. She had kind women friends—Mrs. Jopling Rowe, the artist, was one—who watched over her. I pray her forgiveness.

I did not intend to write a funny book, at first. I did not know I was a humorist. I never have been sure about it. In the Middle Ages, I should probably have gone about preaching and got myself burnt or hanged. There was to be "humorous relief"; but the book was to have been *The Story of the Thames*, its scenery and history. Somehow it would not come. I was just back from my honeymoon, and had the feeling that all the world's troubles were over. About the "humorous relief" I had no difficulty. I decided to write the "humorous relief" first—get it off my chest, so to speak. After which, in sober frame of mind, I could tackle the scenery and history. I never got there. It seemed to be all "humorous relief." By grim determination I succeeded, before the end, in writing a dozen or so slabs of history and working them in, one to each chapter, and F. W. Robinson, who was publishing the book serially, in *Home Chimes*, promptly slung them out, the most of them. From the beginning he had objected to the title and had insisted upon my thinking of another. And half-way through I hit upon *Three Men in a Boat*, because nothing else seemed right.

There wasn't any dog. I did not possess a dog in those days. Neither did George. Nor did Harris. As a boy I had owned pets innumerable. There was a baby water-rat I had caught in a drain. He lived most of his time in my breast pocket. I would take him to school with me; and he would sit with his head poking out between my handkerchief and my coat so that nobody could see him but myself, and look up at me with adoring eyes. Next to my mother, I loved him more than anybody in the world. The other boys complained of him after a time, but I believe it was only jealousy. I never smelt anything. And then there was a squirrel—an orphan—that I persuaded a white rabbit to adopt, until he bit one of his foster-brothers; and a cat that used to come to the station to meet me.

But it never ran to a dog. Montmorency I evolved out of my inner consciousness. There is something of the dog, I take it, in most Englishmen. Dog friends that I came to know later have told me he was true to life.

Indeed, now I come to think of it, the book really was a history. I did not have to imagine or invent. Boating up and down the Thames had been my favourite sport since I could afford it. I just put down the things that happened.—JEROME K. JEROME, "More Literary Reminiscences," *My Life and Times*, 1926, pp. 106–8

'Three, I have always found, makes good company. Two grows monotonous, and four or over breaks up into groups.' (Jerome)

Nonetheless, three did prove to be quite a crowd. The idea was that in the early spring of 1889 this trio of eminently respectable pillars of the middle-class community should take a boat at Kingston, thenceforth to float wherever fancy might take them—which very nearly turned out to be Oxford and back. The book Jerome had in mind was to be called *The Story of the Thames*, a history, with one or two anecdotes: however, this is not the book that developed.

There was much preparation to be done before the trip could get under way. Jerome was very big on preparation. The three met one evening to plan the thing out, and to decide when best they could jettison their jobs, for George Wingrave was by now the manager of a bank, and Carl Hentschel was very actively engaged in his father's photography business—his father being the very Hentschel who perfected the technique of photo-etching, the process by which photographs could be printed in newspapers. Jerome was now freelance, it was true, but he was also married, and therefore diplomatic timing became an issue; the Thames trip, of course, was to be work and by no means play.

All three had been up the river before, and none was as inexperienced as the eventual narrative would lead the reader to believe. Something of the earlier boating ventures can be learnt from *Three Men in a Boat* itself, the anecdotes, of course, only very slightly coloured. To say this invokes the same ironic tone as employed by Jerome himself during the course of the preface of the book. 'Its pages', he says, 'form the record of events that really happened. All that has been done is to colour them; and for this, no extra charge has been made. George and Harris and Montmorency are not poetic ideals, but things of flesh and blood—especially George, who weighs about twelve stone.' With this preface, and by means of the use of the first person and diary-like mode of writing, Jerome seeks to impress upon us the veracity of the incidents, and he continues to do so throughout the narrative. And, up to a point, it is so. Wingrave, Hentschel and Jerome really did go up the river, several times, and doubtless many amusing occurrences befell them. *Three Men in a Boat* is an amalgam of all these—although very largely the story of the present trip—together with a very goodly portion indeed of the exaggerations and inventions of the raconteur. It is difficult—one might say impossible—to disentangle the real from the imaginary.

Accepting, then, that the work is fiction loosely based on fact it is suitable to chart the course of the real expedition of 1889 with the aid of the adventures of the (semi-fictional) three men—George (Wingrave), Harris (Hentschel), and 'J'—for as the author himself tells us yet again, and this time in his much later autobiography, 'Now I come to think of it, the book really was a history. I did not have to imagine or invent . . . I just put down the things that happened.' . . .

The book was published in the summer of 1889, when Jerome was just thirty. The dark green volume landed on the desks of the literary editors, and possibly because the author's name was not completely unknown, or because the work had already gained some sort of reputation through its serial publication, they noticed it. But not in the way Jerome would have liked. They were alternately haughty and condescending, pompous and cruel, uncomprehending and dismissive; in short, the critics hated it. 'One might have imagined—to read some of them—' JKJ recalled in his memoirs, 'that the British Empire was in danger.' . . .

The Great British Public, on the other hand, could not get enough of it. They took *Three Men in a Boat* to their hearts, and did the decent thing by buying it up in very large quantities, causing Arrowsmith the publisher to remark in later years: 'I can't imagine what becomes of all the copies of that book I issue. I often think the public must eat them.' The books were certainly devoured and inwardly digested, for it became quite the indoor sport of 1889 to quote extracts to one another, and to read aloud passages at soirées until either the audience or the stout party of narrator could no longer delay a collapse. And of course the public loved it for the very reasons that the critics loathed it: it was modern, vulgar, of the people, and written in the very way, as the *Saturday Review* indicated, in which people spoke. And the public could recollect no other book like it: it was new, and very, very fresh. Quite apart from the style, the characters were found to be human to the point of near-total deficiency. They were vain, selfish, prey to all the weaknesses and, on the whole, pretty useless at most things; the self-deprecating English, therefore, identified wholly. The anecdotes were of an everyday nature, though told with a true narrator's style, and the relish of a humorist. A really funny book was as rare then as it always is, and the public valued it. The entire concept of a holiday of which a good deal was spent immersed in some abysmal misery or other was so absolutely likable and familiar; that the holiday ended early, in the rain and with relief was sheer perfection: it was a very English book. . . .

To sum up, it was a gentle and ironic book, much given to digression, and yet written in a very tight and economical style. Its success depends largely upon the adroit alternation of exaggeration and understatement which—as V S Pritchett put it—'runs like a rheumatism through English humour'. The book never went out of print. It has been filmed three times—once in 1920, during Jerome's lifetime, again in 1933, and once more in 1956, by which time the English edition had sold three million copies, and was still selling at the rate of fifteen thousand a year. It became a 'Penguin', of course, and it was added—appropriately enough—to the 'Everyman' library. In very recent times appreciation was shown by Tom Stoppard, who adapted it for television. As Jerome said in a preface for a later edition: 'So much for testimonials. It remains only to explain the merits justifying such an extraordinary success. I am quite unable to do so.' Indeed, he could hardly recall having written it: 'I remember only feeling very young and absurdly pleased with myself for reasons that concern only myself. It was summer time, and London is so beautiful in summer. It lay beneath my window a fairy city veiled in golden mist, for I worked in a room high above the chimney pots; and at night the lights shone far beneath me, so that I looked down as into an Aladdin's cave of jewels. It was during those summer months I wrote this book; it seemed the only thing to do.'
—JOSEPH CONNOLLY, *Jerome K. Jerome: A Critical Biography,* 1982, pp. 52–53, 74–77

MAX BEERBOHM
From "A Deplorable Affair" (1908)
Around Theatres (1924)
1930, pp. 516–19

In the provinces, recently, he produced a play by Mr. Henry James—a play that was reported to be a great success. It would be a privilege to produce a play by Mr. Henry James, even though the play failed utterly. In its failure, it would be more interesting, and would bring higher esteem to its producer, than any number of successful plays by second-rate men. Having produced Mr. James' play with success, what does Mr. Forbes-Robertson do so soon as he comes to London? Apparently in doubt whether Mr. James be good enough for the metropolis, he gives us Mr. Jerome Klapka Jerome. This tenth-rate writer has been, for many years, prolific of his tenth-rate stuff. But I do not recall, in such stuff of his as I have happened to sample, anything quite so vilely stupid as *The Passing of the Third Floor Back*. I do not for a moment suppose that Mr. Forbes-Robertson likes it one whit more than I do. And I wish his pusillanimity in prostituting his great gifts to it were going to be duly punished. The most depressing aspect of the whole matter is that the play is so evidently a great success. The enthusiasm of a first-night audience is no sure gauge of success. Nor is the proverbial apathy of a second-night audience a sure gauge of failure. It was on the second night that I saw *The Passing of the Third Floor Back*; and greater enthusiasm have I seldom seen in a theatre. And thus I am brought sharply up against that doubt which so often confronts me: what can be hoped of an art which must necessarily depend on the favour of the public—of such a public, at least, as ours? Good work may, does sometimes, succeed. But never with the degree of success that befalls twaddle and vulgarity unrelieved. Twaddle and vulgarity will have always the upper hand.

The reformation of a bad person by a supernatural visitor is a theme that has often been used. Mr. Jerome, remembering the converted miser in "A Christmas Carol," and the converted egoist in "A Message from Mars," and many a similar convert, was struck by the bright idea that the effect would be just a dozen times as great if there were a dozen converts. So he has turned a supernatural visitor loose in a boarding-house inhabited by a round dozen of variously bad people—"A Satyr," "A Snob," "A Shrew," "A Painted Lady," "A Cheat," and so on. Now, supposing that these characters were life-like, or were amusing figments of the brain, and supposing that we saw them falling, little by little, under the visitor's spell, till gradually we were aware that they had been changed for the better, the play might be quite a passable affair. But to compass that effect is very far beyond Mr. Jerome's power. He has neither the natural talent nor the technical skill that the task requires. There is not a spark of verisimilitude in the whole dozen of characters. One and all, they are unreal. Mr. Jerome shows no sign of having ever observed a fellow-creature. His characters seem to be the result solely of a study of novelettes in the penny weekly papers, supplemented by a study of the works of Mr. Jerome K. Jerome. Take Major Tompkins, and his wife and daughter, for example. Could anything be more trite and crude than their presentment? Major and Mrs. Tompkins are anxious to sell their daughter for gold to an elderly man. "His very touch," says the daughter, according to custom, "is loathsome." The Major persists and says—what else could a stage-major say?—"Damn your infernal impudence!" The unnatural mother tries to persuade the unwilling daughter to wear a more décolleté dress. The daughter, of course, loves a young painter in a brown velveteen jacket; but she is weak and worldly, and she is like to yield to the importunities of the elderly man. The young painter—but no, I won't bore you by describing the other characters: suffice it that they are all ground out of the same old rusty machine that has served "The Family Herald" and similar publications for so many weary years. Mr. Jerome's humour, however, is his own, and he plasters it about with a liberal hand. What could be more screamingly funny than the doings at the outset? The landlady pours tea into the decanter which is supposed to hold whisky, on the chance that the drunken boarder won't notice the difference. Then she goes out, and the servant drinks milk out of the jug and replenishes the jug with water. Then *she* goes out, and the "Painted Lady" come in and steals a couple of fresh candles from the sconces on the piano and substitutes a couple of candle ends. Then *she* goes out, and the Major comes in and grabs the biscuits off the plate and drops them into his hat. Then *he* goes out, and the "Cad" and the "Rogue" come in and unlock the spirit-case with an illicit key and help themselves to what they presently find is tea. He's inexhaustibly fertile in such sequences is Mr. Jerome K. Jerome. When the "Passer-by" knocks at the front-door, and is admitted with a limelight full on his (alas, Mr. Forbes-Robertson's) classic countenance, the sequences set in with an awful severity. The beneficent stranger has one method for all evildoers, and he works it on every one in turn, with precisely the same result. He praises the landlady for her honesty; then the landlady is ashamed for her dishonesty and becomes honest. He praises the Major for his sweet temper; then the Major is ashamed of his bad temper, and becomes sweet-tempered. He praises the "Painted Lady" for her modesty in not thinking herself beautiful without paint; then the "Painted Lady" is ashamed of her paint, and reappears paintless. He praises—but again I won't bore you further. You have found the monotony of the foregoing sentences oppressive enough. Picture to yourselves the monotony of what they describe! For a period of time that seemed like eternity, I had to sit knowing exactly what was about to happen, and how it was about to happen, and knowing that as soon as it had happened it would happen again. The art of dramaturgy, some one has said, is the art of preparation. In that case Klapka is assuredly the greatest dramatist the world has ever known. It is hard to reconcile this conclusion with the patent fact that he hasn't yet mastered the rudiments of his craft.

The third and last act of the play, like the second, consists of a sequence of interviews—next man, please!—between the visitor and the other (now wholly reformed) persons of the play. Steadily, he works through the list, distributing full measure of devastating platitudes, all the way. The last person on the list, the Major's daughter, says suddenly "Who are you?" The visitor spreads his arms, in the attitude of "The Light of the World." The Major's daughter falls on her knees in awe. When the visitor passes out through the front-door, a supernatural radiance bursts through the fan-light, flooding the stage; and then the curtain comes slowly down. Well, I suppose blasphemy pays.

PAMELA HANSFORD JOHNSON

1912–1981

Pamela Hansford Johnson was born in London on May 29, 1912, and after the death of her father in 1923 grew up with her mother in poor circumstances in the London suburbs. Leaving school at sixteen, she worked as a secretary while continuing her education on her own and associating with other young writers. After her volume of poems, *Symphony for Full Orchestra*, was published in 1934, she was briefly engaged to Dylan Thomas, who suggested the title of her first novel, *This Bed Thy Centre* (1935).

Like other writers of her generation, Johnson actively supported the Spanish loyalists, and in London worked in left-wing organizations. She edited the weekly *Chelsea Democrat*, and contributed to other journals and magazines. From the 1940s she was a frequent broadcaster with the BBC.

Johnson was both versatile and prolific, writing short stories, essays, and literary criticism in addition to her twenty-seven novels. Her early reputation was enhanced by the "Helena" trilogy, including *Too Dear for My Possessing* (1940), *An Avenue of Stones* (1947), and *A Summer to Decide* (1948); after the publication of *An Impossible Marriage* (1954) and *The Last Resort* (in America, *The Sea and the Wedding*, 1957), she was widely regarded as one of the finest British novelists of the time. Notable among her later novels are *The Survival of the Fittest* (1968) and *The Good Listener* (1975). Her non-fiction includes studies of Thomas Wolfe and Proust, and a discussion of the problem of evil, *On Iniquity* (1967).

Johnson married scholar and novelist C. P. Snow in 1950, wrote several plays with him, and traveled in the Soviet Union, Canada, and the United States. She received a number of honorary degrees, and was made a CBE in 1975. She died on June 19, 1981, after the publication that year of her last novel, *The Bonfire*.

Personal

Halperin: . . . When did you first meet Charles ⟨C. P. Snow⟩?

Lady Snow: We first met through writing letters. I was a reviewer on the *Liverpool Post*, and I reviewed *Strangers and Brothers*—which I thought was the most original, most personality-laden of any novel I had read in a long time. So I praised it up to the skies. At that time he was getting a very sparse press, apart from a rave review of Desmond MacCarthy in the *Sunday Times*. Charles wrote to me and said how much he enjoyed my review in the *Liverpool Post*. And then we had a literary correspondence for a long time. And we first met in 1941 in Stewart's of Piccadilly. He was a don. I had given birth to Andy, so it was getting on for late summer. I had lunch with him and was very intrigued by it. I thought how clever he was—and how shabby.

Halperin: What else do you remember about that first meeting?

Lady Snow: A discussion about *Le Rouge et le noir*. I didn't like it very much, and he did. Anyway, we went through some of our literary ideas, and decided to continue it on paper. And we did, for quite a long time.

Halperin: Through letters?

Lady Snow: Yes. I met him very rarely during the war—only when he was free, or I was.

Halperin: Did you fall in love with him or he with you right away?

Lady Snow: That was years later, really years later.

Halperin: You and Charles were married nearly ten years after you first met, is that right?

Lady Snow: Yes. We were married in 1950, and we met in 1941.

Halperin: So for the first few years this was a literary correspondence course, so to speak?

Lady Snow: Yes. Then we took to meeting, now and again, when he could spare the time. And when I came back to London in 1946, it was much easier.

Halperin: Now you at that time were living with your first husband and your family?

Lady Snow: My first husband was in the war. At the time we were living in Staines, in Middlesex, where I'd gone to avoid the worst of the bombing. I avoided the worst of the bombs, but not many.

Halperin: Was your house there bombed?

Lady Snow: Nearby.

Halperin: Can you describe the course that your relationship with Charles took? How did it arrive at marriage?

Lady Snow: Some years after the war my marriage with my first husband broke up; and that was very sad, because we'd had a happy marriage. When the war ended we found we'd developed new interests—that we weren't interested in the same things. Gradually we came to the conclusion to break up.

Halperin: Did you decide to break up before Charles came into the picture, or afterwards?

Lady Snow: Afterwards.

Halperin: Was your first marriage already on its way—

Lady Snow: It was still stable.

Halperin: Deciding to marry Charles was how you made up your mind ultimately to end the first marriage?

Lady Snow: Ultimately, yes.

Halperin: Did your first husband fight the case, or was it amicable?

Lady Snow: It was an amicable arrangement, as far as these things can ever be. They're terribly sad.

Halperin: Do you ever see your first husband?

Lady Snow: Oh yes, I see him whenever he's over here. I write to him constantly. And my sons like to see him.

Halperin: How and when and where was the decision to marry taken? Did Charles propose to you?

Lady Snow: I think it was agreed. I don't know if he actually proposed; I can't remember that. Anyway, we were married in 1950, in July.

Halperin: It's been a successful marriage, hasn't it?

Lady Snow: Yes.

Halperin: I gather from each of you that, both emotionally and professionally, it has worked very well.

Lady Snow: Yes. We have a good working marriage.

Halperin: Why is that, do you think? Isn't it very rare for people who are working more or less in the same field to stay married to each other?

Lady Snow: We don't compete. That's the most important thing. If you start competing in a marriage like that, it's sunk. The great thing is not to compete at all. And we've never been jealous of each other. I have no reason to be jealous of him and he has no reason to be jealous of me. We both take an enormous interest in each other's work, and there's never a dull moment. There's always something to talk about. One of us is writing a book or the other is, or a book's coming out, and there's all that excitement, and disappointment, and bitter tension—but it doesn't worry us.

Halperin: When you first met, you were much better known as a writer than he was, isn't that right?

Lady Snow: Oh, I was then.

Halperin: And was there a sense that you were advising him, or that he was coming to you for advice? Or has it always been mutual—

Lady Snow: It was always a kind of mutual thing. I quite understood that I might be well known at that time, but that he was going to be much better known.

Halperin: Did you always think so?

Lady Snow: Yes, I always thought so. . . .

Halperin: Which of your novels is his favourite, do you happen to know?

Lady Snow: Well, two: *The Last Resort* and *The Unspeakable Skipton.*

Halperin: And how much give and take is there? Do you read each other's manuscripts, for example?

Lady Snow: Yes we do, but in rather large blocks: about 30,000 words. We always read the other's work as it's going on. He's just read a chunk of mine, but only 15,000 this time, and said he likes it, and that's given me an enormous lift and helped me to go on.

Halperin: When he doesn't like something he says so, presumably?

Lady Snow: He says so, yes.

Halperin: And you are the same with his work?

Lady Snow: It's the same. Once upon a time we both used to take it rather badly and sulk a little bit; but that soon wore out, and we took each other's advice, and on the whole it was good advice.

Halperin: Can you remember specific things he changed, or did something you advised, in his books?

Lady Snow: No, I don't think I can. They're all small things—little things in the manuscript, no big changes.

Halperin: How about in reverse? Have you made significant changes in your work which he suggested?

Lady Snow: Not significant changes, but he has given me ideas. He gave me an idea for *The Humbler Creation*. He said if I was so interested in the church, why didn't I write about it, and that was an enormous help. He's done that. But on the whole, no. He makes little changes, but they're very important. . . .

Halperin: Has he suggested any titles for you?

Lady Snow: Oh, he's suggested titles for me. *The Last Resort* he suggested, I think, which is a sort of pun; and he suggested *An Impossible Marriage*.

Halperin: Well, there really has been quite a lot to give and take.

Lady Snow: Quite a lot of give and take. It gives us great pleasure.

Halperin: Yes, it must. Does it go down to the level of, say, making stylistic suggestions?

Lady Snow: Yes.

Halperin: Is that in fact a chief part each of you plays—as a kind of editor of each other's manuscripts?

Lady Snow: Not the chief one, but part of it. I mean, he was reading mine through for stylistic things yesterday, which gave me an immense amount of help—little things, tiny things. You wouldn't realise, they're so small.

Halperin: Can you give me just one example, so I know what you mean? An adjective—

Lady Snow: Adjectives, or something he thinks I've repeated, an expression I've used twice. He does it very well. . . .

Halperin: How accurate is the picture given in your book *Important to Me* of your life when you first came to London?

Lady Snow: Pretty straight: very straight, I think.

Halperin: You've probably been asked this question before—but not by me, so let me ask it now. Why didn't you and Dylan Thomas marry? I presume he asked?

Lady Snow: Oh yes, it was plain that we should marry. In fact we'd got to the state of putting up, or going to put up, the banns in the Chelsea registry office, but we both thought the better of it, and we drifted. I think Dylan got into a circle of his own friends, and he would never introduce one old friend to one new friend, never. So he kept me in a separate compartment, and I got rather tired of that. And then he started to live the wildly bohemian life in Chelsea, which I didn't fall in with, and so we drifted—very painfully, from my point of view, but we did drift.

Halperin: How old were you then?

Lady Snow: Twenty-two. I was two years older than Dylan.

Halperin: Were you absolutely convinced that he was going to be a first-rate poet?

Lady Snow: Yes: absolutely.

Halperin: But probably not a first-rate husband?

Lady Snow: No. I couldn't have drunk all he did.

Halperin: Even then it appeared that he was going to drink himself into a bad—

Lady Snow: Yes, it did. But at that time he boasted about it more than he drank. I mean, he used to pretend to be awfully drunk when he wasn't at all. He'd go out to the King's Head and the Six Bells; he'd then come back and say he was drunk, which he was not—but it impressed his friends. Then it became real.

Halperin: He wound up actually acting out the role he had only played?

Lady Snow: Yes.

Halperin: Why do you think he drank so much, or pretended to?

Lady Snow: It's very hard to tell like that. I've no idea.

Halperin: What was the source of his appeal for you?

Lady Snow: He was a very alluring young man, and he had this beautiful voice, and wonderful eyes. And he was wonderfully verbal; he verbalised everything beautifully. I think everybody who met him at that time fell for him.

Halperin: At what point did you stop being intimate with him—in your mid-twenties?

Lady Snow: Oh no, earlier. We only had this long affair—a quite innocent one, incidentally—for about a year and a half. The war separated us, really, when he got into it. I got married myself, and he was married to Caitlin, and we only met very occasionally. I only saw him once after the war, and then I didn't recognise him, he'd got so fat. . . .

Halperin: Among other writers, what literary influences on your work would you say were paramount? Beyond the fact that you've read most of Charles's manuscripts, at least from the time you were married, has his work actually influenced you as a writer?

Lady Snow: No. I think we could both say that. No, I've been more influenced by people like Proust, whose way of looking at people interests me. They're not in style these days. It's like looking round a gallery, and seeing sculptures coming through different doors—seeing them all the way around.

Halperin: Any others significant enough to mention, besides Proust? Thomas Wolfe, perhaps?

Lady Snow: He wasn't an influence.

Halperin: But when you write a book about someone, you obviously feel something about the subject.

Lady Snow: Oh, I felt very strongly about him. In fact, he was a wonderful person for us to follow when we were all young. He was a young person's writer, of course. Now, I don't read him nearly so easily.

Halperin: When I was 20 I thought he was the greatest. When you were 20, who were you reading?

Lady Snow: James Joyce.

Halperin: And T.S. Eliot?

Lady Snow: Not particularly. I didn't read Eliot much. When I think back to all that, I was reading Donne and George Herbert and all those people.—JOHN HALPERIN, "Appendix: Conversation with Lady Snow," *C. P. Snow: An Oral Biography*, 1983, pp. 248–67

General

Miss Hansford Johnson belongs to that group of writers—they are perhaps most to be envied—whose fame has climbed slowly on the wings of each new achievement. In the past ten years she has become well known to the reading public as a novelist of great craftsmanship and distinction and to readers of the weeklies as one of the best contemporary reviewers of novels in the language. She is a profound moralist, though of a deliberately unpretentious kind, and each of her books is at bottom concerned with a moral situation. Yet each, at the same time, has been an attempt to master some technical problem. For, in spite of her great gifts as a critic and her deep involvement with the theatre—her essay on "The Future of Prose Drama," published as an introduction to her play *Corinth House*, is the best thing that has been written on the aesthetics of contemporary drama—it is with the art of fiction that she is primarily concerned. Where others have merely dogmatized, pooh-poohed or aired their fancies about the novel, she has genuinely mediated and practised.

Though her own interests in literature lean towards the bizarre—she had given us the most perceptive criticism of Miss Compton-Burnett's novels that has ever been written—it is in her comments on life as lived out by her characters that she excels. She has done this nowhere better than in *An Avenue of Stone* and its successor, *A Summer to Decide*, and also in her last book, *The Last Resort*—a novel conceived on a smaller scale but containing much superb characterization with its accompanying and unique gloss on the fruits of human action.

An Avenue of Stone lies at the centre of all Miss Hansford Johnson's fiction. In this novel and in its dying tigress of a heroine, Helena Archer, all her energy as an artist and her moral attention as an observer are concentrated. It is a book filled with a great urgency, like an angry sky, and its background—the strange post-war London of scarcities and points, regrets for lost *camaraderie* and good times—is brilliantly filled in and related to the immediate human situation. The theme—betrayal of the first-rate or the good in heart by the warped, the hangers-on or the discomfited—is one that absorbs this writer; she has returned to it many times, particularly in the play, *Corinth House*, in which a basic situation similar to Balzac's immortal *Le Curé de Tours* is lifted into metaphysical melodrama of a high order through the two antagonists' agreement to share their complementary guilt together. *An Avenue of Stone* is in no sense melodramatic: it is a plain, unvarnished study of human temperaments acting out their needs and jealousies on one another.—UNSIGNED, "A Corvo of Our Day," *TLS*, Jan. 9, 1959, p. 18

The novels of Pamela Hansford Johnson are the basic material of the publisher looking for a well-made, intelligent novel that stands the chance of a book club selection and will go well with a public that wants its fiction neither light nor heavy. It is the kind of fiction that keeps the novel going in between the valleys and the peaks. It handles ideas in terms of the people involved; it rarely aims at abstractions, and the conflicts themselves are those one encounters in daily life. Emotions are of course played down; there are few powerful climaxes, few dramatic intensities that would weight the novel unduly. In brief, the novelist makes no attempt to exceed the tight, well-controlled world over which he or she is a master.

The themes of Miss Johnson's novels demonstrate the ordinary world in which her characters are immersed. In *An Impossible Marriage* (1954), for example, she is concerned with a marriage that does not work; the situation, the characters themselves, the incidents that display their incompatibility are all commonplace. What significance the novel does have is simply its toned-down, day-to-day cataloguing of why and how a marriage fails—the direct appeal to a middle-class female audience is clear. In *The Sea and the Wedding*, published two years later, Miss Johnson centers on the relationship between Celia Baird and Eric Aveling, principally their hopeless love affair while Eric's wife is slowly dying, their inability to marry once she has died, and Celia's attempt to find happiness at any price, which she does by marrying a homosexual friend, Junius. This novel is somewhat spicier than the previous, including as it does the illicit affair and the homosexuals around Junius.

To take one more of Miss Johnson's novels, the one with perhaps the most exotic content: *The Unspeakable Skipton* (1959) features a rogue who lives in Bruges and tries to cadge his way through life, much as Cary's picaresque Gulley Jimson in *The Horse's Mouth*. Miss Johnson has turned the painter Gulley into the writer Skipton, a man who must live by his wits. The central character is a man who believes so strongly in himself that he will do anything to insure the opportunity for his art to mature. In presenting Skipton and his world, however, Miss Johnson avoids the larger issue suggested by the introduction of a confidence man: that is, coming to terms with the confidence man as he tries to disguise his various shifts from illusion to reality.—FREDERICK R. KARL, "Composite," *A Reader's Guide to the Contemporary English Novel*, 1961, pp. 275–76

. . . ⟨Robert⟩ Liddell, whose attitude towards fiction almost out-Jameses James's in its austerity and is altogether too limiting for my taste, preaches what he calls the 'pure novel', 'concentrating on human beings and their mutual reactions'. 'So rare is such concentration in the English novel', he goes on, 'that any writer who conscientiously practises it is almost sure to be accused of "imitating Jane Austen" whether their minds are alike or not.' In fact, at that point Liddell is writing upon I. Compton-Burnett, whose mind he finds in many ways like Jane Austen's. . . .

Pamela Hansford Johnson's view on the novel are nothing like Liddell's, yet it seems to me that, on his definition, she too can be considered a pure novelist. She too brings to its contemplation of human beings and their mutual reactions a rare degree of concentration. Like Liddell, Miss Hansford Johnson is a learned novelist: she is an expert on Dickens, can meet the Proust scholars on their own ground, and has sympathies wide enough to take in Thomas Wolfe and I. Compton-Burnett, on both of whom she has written persuasively. And all this seems relevant to her own fiction. She has been a professional novelist for many years now; *This Bed Thy Centre* (1935), a study of working-class life in south London, written when she was twenty-two, remains one of the most interesting first novels of the thirties. But through the years her talents have steadily deepened and her insights broadened until now she writes with complete authority. By that I mean that, having read her, one feels that the whole truth has been told about the characters and the situations in which they find themselves. One has a sense of her complete knowledge of them, and this sense is the effect, it seems to me, of her technical mastery and of her moral discriminations.

Such novels as *The Last Resort* (1956) and *The Humbler Creation* (1959), render beautifully the complexities, the discontinuities, the contradictions of human behaviour and the necessary recognition of the frustrations attendant upon it. They seem to me to have the sad, honest, lucid acceptance of life we find in George Eliot, and, like George Eliot, Pamela Hansford Johnson is concerned, in her later novels at any rate, with the problem of right doing, of duty. The central character of *The Humbler Creation* is an Anglican parson, vicar of an unfashionable London parish, saddled with a silly neurotic wife and with too many family burdens, a good man tempted into the sin of love outside his marriage. But this is very much to over-simplify, for in these novels complexity of detail is everything, and it is through the complexity that the author's discrimination asserts itself.

So, in *The Last Resort*, it is possible to isolate the moral element that sunders the two lovers in the words of one of them:

'Underneath it is all the undertow of the Ten Commandments. They make dreadful fools of us. They're like our grandmother's sideboard, which we don't use any more, but can't bring ourselves to sell. There it is, all the time, weighing us down from the attic or biding its time in the cellar.'

But beyond this is the whole intricate pattern of character-relations and the events that spring out of them, a pattern that has to be intricate in order acceptably to suggest the complexity of life itself. This is essential to Miss Hansford Johnson's purpose, and she achieves it. In *The Last Resort* particularly she is, one is persuaded, seeing life steadily and, if not whole, seeing sufficient of it to stand for the whole. She persuades us of this by the sobriety of her realism, her ability to render specific places and their inhabitants, by her sure grasp of her characters, who are many and diverse and who are never seen statically but are always capable of surprising us with new facets of their personalities, and, not less important, by her tone. In this novel, Pamela Hansford Johnson uses a narrator, a novelist who is the friend and confidant of the main actors. As an example of the tone:

> It occurred to me, as the train drew out beyond the downs, that she was of the company of those who can make and keep resolutions which must change a whole life; a member of that most incomprehensible of companies, in which are the martyrs and the saints. For most of us can conceive the noble idea, suggest it to ourselves, even go so far as to begin to put it into practice: but the secret planner of the mind knots the invisible safeguards, weaves the safety-net beneath us. We are in no danger of falling too far. We do not quite speak the irrevocable word: we only suggest that we are about to speak it. We envy the saints and martyrs, sometimes with passion: we long to match them. At moments we believe that there is, between them and ourselves, only a filament thin as the spider's, and that if we can make the one supreme effort of will we shall send it torn and floating into the air. But it is in the difference between the desire and the performance that the mystery lies, the mystery we shall never solve. The vast majority of us are expert recanters; we can do it with infinite grace and the minimum of blameworthiness when the time is ripe. During the whole period in which we are planning our gesture of complete self-abnegation, of total change, the daemon inside us keeps up its perpetual murmur, 'Stop! You're not quite committed'; when the time comes, we ourselves say, 'Stop!'—in the human voice.

In *The Last Resort* it became apparent that she was steadily extending the range of her fiction. It is not that the types she describes, or their milieus, are new; but she makes them new: the retired, angry, self-absorbed doctor, his wife neurotically possessive of her daughter, the homosexual architect, and the rest. She sees all round them and catches them in a new light, in a new significance, so that in the end they are somehow bigger, richer as emblems of the human condition, than one might expect them to be. And what is strikingly absent from their delineation is what Norman Douglas called 'the novelist's touch', the falsification of life through failure to realize 'the complexities of the ordinary human mind'.

How much Pamela Hansford Johnson is extending her range may be seen in the novel that followed *The Last Resort—The Unspeakable Skipton* (1959). Her subject here is the paranoiac artist. Familiar enough in life, in fiction treatment of him has been mainly marginal. In life the great exemplar is Frederick Rolfe, 'Baron Corvo', and Miss Hansford Johnson has admittedly drawn on him for her portrait of Daniel Skipton, Knight of the Most Noble Order of SS. Cyril and Methodius. But Rolfe is no more than the starting-point: Skipton exists in his own right and in our time, a separate creation.

Skipton is a monster. We see him in his austere garret in Bruges writing blackguarding letters to his long-suffering publisher even while trying to borrow from him; we see him attempting to blackmail the elderly cousin who has never met him and who makes him an allowance out of sheer kindliness. He scours the town for English tourists to pimp for. He is a monster of satanic egoism, and with diabolical glee he translates all who offend him—by their mere existence—into figures of fun, effigies of depravity, that go straight into his interminable, unpublishable novel. A monster—and yet, as

Miss Hansford Johnson reveals him, the mind, called to pass judgment, wavers. That ferocious anal-eroticism, that passion for cleanliness, that revulsion from the contacts of the flesh, don't they come very near to a perverted saintliness? And certainly the intransigence of his appalling lunatic self-regard makes him almost one of the saints of art.

Skipton is a splendid comic creation; and yet, without abating the rigour of her sardonic comedy, Pamela Hansford Johnson brings out the full pathos of the poor wretch and his fate, which is in essence that of the dedicated artist who is devoid of talent. She embodies his fate in a plot marked by continuously amusing invention and by a set of characters that are excellent foils to him. And the setting of the novel, Bruges with its bells and its canals, places the comedy in a further dimension of poetry.—WALTER ALLEN, "War and Post-War: British," *The Modern Novel*, 1964, pp. 257–60

Admirers of the work of Pamela Hansford Johnson (Lady Snow) have not always seen a preoccupation with the problems of right-doing, sometimes resolving itself into questions of the final sanctions of morality, which lies hidden under the complexities of her novels, as well as their wit, accurate reportage, and delight in the surface of life. Her first book, *This Bed Thy Centre*, appeared when she was only twenty-two, but its recent reissue reminds us that she has been pretty consistent in her preoccupation with moral dilemmas. *The Humbler Creation* presents an Anglican clergyman who is saintly but, driven by the intolerable frustrations of his family life, falls into adultery. As with Graham Greene (whom she in no way really resembles) we are tempted towards moral judgements that orthodoxy would not condone. *The Last Resort* seems to touch a theological level with its rumination (in the person of the narrator) on the difference between ourselves and the company of the saints and martyrs: they commit themselves to the big terrible decisions; we hold back. And however amoral and free we like to think ourselves, there are always nagging doubts about the religious furniture that lies, gathering dust but still very solid, up there in the attic. *An Error of Judgement* deals with a consultant physician who has done fine work and is revered by his patients. But he is aware that he took up medicine only because pain fascinates him: his profession could be a means of inflicting it, or at least withholding its palliatives. He abandons his practice and takes to a job whose altruism seems obvious—trying to rehabilitate delinquent youth. But he meets one young man who has committed a sadistic crime of particular ghastliness; he has not been caught, he is quite ready to commit the same crime again. Like a vet, the doctor 'puts down' the young brute with brandy and sleeping tablets. What sort of judgement do we make? The orthodox answer is not satisfactory, but could any answer be? No novel of any complexity can ever have the directness of a moral tract, but the virtue of Pamela Hansford Johnson's work often lies in its power to present the great issues nakedly—forcing us not so much to a decision as to a realization of the hopelessness of decisions. If, that is, we are not saints and martyrs.

I ought to stress that all Miss Hansford Johnson's novels are notable for a kind of grave lightness of touch, they are never without humour. Her comic gifts are seen as well as anywhere in *The Unspeakable Skipton*, whose hero is a mad, egoistical novelist working on a book that will never end and never be published. All kinds of beastliness are, to him, in order if they provide material for his fiction: like Dante, he puts his enemies in hell. There is nothing good about him, and yet there is this monstrous dedication of art which lifts him to a kind of empyrean: he is as far above ordinary decent plodders through life as the saints and martyrs are. He is, perhaps, a devil, and is not a devil a perverted angel—having more traffic with the divine order than people who are not Skipton and are all too speakable?—ANTHONY BURGESS, "Good and Evil," *The Novel Now*, 1967, pp. 66–67

Works

. . . ⟨T⟩here have been major-domos in the English novel, of whom Dickens was only the greatest, and they were of a tradition that was not discredited until after the 1914–18 war. Miss Hansford Johnson vigorously reasserts it. In her title, *An Impossible Marriage*, she tells you what you are going to receive, and thereafter is continually at your side, explaining and embellishing, in case some beauty should be missed.

> "You know I like you, don't you, Chris? You know that what I'm saying's really for the best?"
>
> "Things that are for the best always means the worst for somebody," I said, and was astonished by my own epigram.

From that short passage, how many novelists would have struck out the last seven words? Yet the effect of them is delightful; and Miss Johnson creates equally successful effects, by the same method, in passages of serious emotion. For instance, she makes her heroine, Christine, tell how Ned, the "impossible" husband, "put his head on my shoulder and began to cry." And this is not only a matter of how Christine felt, but also of how Miss Johnson's readers, of whatever sex and culture, ought to feel about a man crying. Miss Johnson tells them. She does it very well.

To risk such a method today you have got to be able. This author's special ability is a buoyant sense of situation. Her period here is the no-man's-land between the Twenties and Thirties, and a particular pocket of that territory: not the Bright Young Things, but the Nice Young Things. The BYTs had parents who had already despaired, but the NYTs were still growled at—"You young people want everything your own way," and "You young people think you can break marriages as easily as breaking teacups"—when, primly and dimly, they edged towards emancipation. Miss Johnson has a set of them, middle-class and moderately impoverished, in Clapham; the "blind date" their novelty, the Charleston their mania, the ukulele their fashion. This is all tremendously real; and the hierarchic travel-agency office in which Christine works as "Junior" is not less real.

Miss Johnson fails to check in herself a suave prodigality of style that was one cause of the revolt against the major-domo succession. She has "jewelled pincers" (of Outer London), "a moment of drenching terror and joy" (love), "the lightning-edged scarlet of pain" (pain). Often she lingers when she *ought* to hurry away. This is only a sort of carelessness. Yet it has allowed her to end this carrying and vital novel on a commonplace note. Christine has a new husband, and is happy. That is all right. But the language in which Miss Johnson makes Christine describe her good fortune is so careless—"blobby," I kept thinking—as to produce a commonplace and smug effect, that seems to ask for a closer type, a narrower column, and a shinier page.—GILES ROMILLY, NSN, April 3, 1954, pp. 445–46

Of the half dozen of her novels I have read, *The Sea and the Wedding* comes close to being the best: everything in it is sharply observed and finely ordered, down to the very title— that is, the real title, *The Last Resort*, which refers equally to the book's world, a seaside resort hotel filled with the left-overs of a dying middle class, and its chief character, a girl who ends by marrying a homosexual for a reason the author drives home in the book's last sentence: "She had added beneath her name

[on a post card] . . . in a spurt of unquellable pride in having some kind of country she could call her own, 'Evans.'" There is real pathos and irony in this ending, and it illuminates the book's social judgments in a variety of ways, but it has an even greater interest than those.

It was, I think, Virginia Woolf who pointed out that, since most of the novels have been written by men; women are in much the situation of Samuel Butler's Devil in his quarrel with God, who, as Butler pointed out, had also written all the books. This is as much a woman's book as a Hemingway novel is a man's. Its men, for all that they are extremely convincing externally, are emotionally about as convincing as Hemingway's women; they are, I take it, women's men. Its women strike me as terrible beyond belief, but I am prepared to believe they are what women really are, creatures with an "unquellable pride in having some kind of country [they can] call [their] own." The most impressive instances of this need are given by the narrator, because she is a normative character whose experience presumably enters the book only to provide occasions for the main characters. We are not, therefore, to consider it abnormal that, when her husband writes her that he is mildly ill in New York with virus pneumonia, she is reduced to hysteria and can only be calmed by a trans-Atlantic telephone call. On another occasion she has a miscarriage; "after that I wanted . . . simply to be alone with Gerard and to assure myself that this failure had not spoiled me for him." Any man's blood must, I think, run cold at the thought of being Gerard, faced with the appalling possessiveness of a demand to be needed which is so exclusive as that.

All the women in the book are like that. They feel on the grand scale, feel largely in relation to the minutely analysed battle of conquest for their chosen countries, and, in the last resort, choose to live with men who hate them, as the heroine's mother does, or to marry a man whose need for them is marginal, as the heroine does, rather than to have no country to call their own. It seems to me a terrifying vision, and it is made more terrible by the sanity and the supreme intelligence with which the novel represents the world in which these women live.—ARTHUR MIZENER, KR, Summer 1957, pp. 488–89

Her new book, *The Unspeakable Skipton*, is . . . a surprise, since it is so unlike anything that she has written before. The same qualities are there, the same crisp, business-like style shot through with flashes of poetry, the same wit, the same pointed observation of what one of her characters in a previous book has called "the routine experiences of life." Yet the essence of this novel is that it is so outside Miss Hansford Johnson's usual routine, so unanchored to the hard, determinate realities of time, love, marriage and money that form the staple of that trilogy of which *An Avenue of Stone* is the centrepiece. Her new novel is an hilarious comedy, an episodic study of a Rolfe-like castaway, living on his wits and feeding on his hates beneath the towers of Bruges—a favourite ambience of his creator, who has elsewhere celebrated "the bells that seemed to chime under water, the narrow streets with their blinded windows, the cobbles, the bad astringent smell of the canals and the fish market, and the sweet smell of the limes and the pollard elms . . . the green quays in summer and the frozen lakes in winter. . . ." Bruges fits the unspeakable Skipton like a glove. . . .

It is pertinent to say . . . how brilliantly yet soundly Miss Hansford Johnson has always handled the sexual side of the human comedy through its whole gamut, from calf love to an old woman's quasi-maternal passion of a devious and spineless young man. Here again, her very unobtrusive skill— coupled with her refusal to theorize about sex in the manner of so many windier and less conscientious practitioners of the novel—has led to her not receiving proper recognition. In her preface to *Corinth House* she makes a point that might be pondered by all creative writers when she remarks that it is important for playwrights (and this applies just as well to novelists):

> not to let themselves be constrained by the fear of psychological cliché from studying situations of very diverse and mysterious human interest. When the work of Freud and Jung first became available to the English common reader, many writers believed that somehow or other all the answers had been supplied to all the questions, and that no field of the mind remained for them to explore. The hypnosis of this first hasty conclusion is now beginning to wear off; but we are still liable to be frightened away by the threat of the mechanical psychological explanation, usually a sexual cliché. The writer eager to explore some out-of-the-way facet of human relationships ought not to let himself be blackmailed into dropping the idea by fear of comment either from the amateur or professional psychologist.

The writer has acted on her own good advice in the case of Skipton's own sexual satisfactions. It would have been so easy, so much of a psychological cliché, to reproduce life and create him a homosexual after the manner of the Baron himself. Instead, he is a *voyeur* of a rare and rarefied kind, seeing the genial coke-washer and the black-browed Walloon as "the billowy god sinking down upon the helpless breast of the daughter of Thestius, the wife of Tyndarus, making her one with whiteness as a cloud obliterates into itself the peak of a mountain." This is the point at which the artist, by his imaginative apprehension of human beings and their eternally mysterious and diverse permutations, genuinely enhances life. . . .

So poor Skipton, swindled, ruined and shown up, lies down to die. Though his creator has spared us nothing of his awfulness, at the end of the book we take leave of him feeling the comically malignant but indestructible heroism of the man—a narcissist of Don Juan proportions, hero of a thousand self-fascinations:

> When the pain moderated, he remembered his dream. The last quartettes of Beethoven. And it seemed to him, in an uprush of certitude, that thus he had brought his work to a climax: that nothing he had ever done his whole life through had been designed for any purpose but to save that work: and that the work itself justified his every action, each action was a humble stone in the erection of the final edifice. . . . If he were going to be ill they should not know it, they should not batten upon his weakness. They should not peer pop-eyed upon him, lay their sausage-fingers upon his pulse, quack about doctors. His body was, as it had always been, his own affair. He had loved only through his eyes. He had never allowed his flesh to be polluted either by human affection or human concern. He pulled the smelly sheets to the bridge of his nose, drew his knees up into his stomach.

In her foreword to the book its author declares that "I have always wanted to write a study of an artist's paranoia . . . in Daniel Skipton I have tried to . . . make a living figure out of what I have learned and can imagine of this special sub-branch of the artistic life." She has succeeded far beyond her aims, and, in doing so, immeasurably extended her own frontiers as an artist. It would perhaps be truer to say that she has added a new comic dimension to her work, for those frontiers were already extensive enough.

In lighting out for such new territory, *The Unspeakable Skipton* necessarily contains little of Miss Hansford Johnson's great primary quality as a writer of fiction—her distinction as a moralist. But she has confected an admirable short tragicomedy, and again shown herself as interesting a novelist as any in the country.—UNSIGNED, "A Corvo of Our Day," *TLS*, Jan. 9, 1959, p. 18

The Good Husband falls squarely into the Austen tradition; a cool anatomy of the selfish lives of comfortably off young people, jolted into a sense of others (hence into 'real' relationship) by small domestic events, a jealous quarrel, a mother's death. There are hints of a larger dimension now and then:

> 'Listen, dears,' Ann said, 'we simply must change the subject, even by an effort of will. There's a war in Vietnam. Let's talk about that.'

But nobody had anything to say about Vietnam. These are people who never take a bus or Tube, whose children are cared for by nannies until they go off to boarding school, for whom work at the BBC materializes whenever they feel a need to be 'doing' something, whose clothes are worth noting. Products of the economic expansion of the 1960s, they are probably destined to learn something about real life in the collapse of the 1970s. (Pamela Hansford Johnson is fond of trilogies, and this is the second novel for Toby Roberts, 'a young man of his time,' risen from his modest SE1 origins, by way of Cambridge, to an apparently secure career in merchant banking.) A bit disappointed by the lack of substance in *The Good Husband* (and irritated by the increasingly complacent Toby) I looked back at an early novel of Pamela Hansford Johnson's, *An Impossible Marriage* (in my 1955 reprint), which was as marvellous as I remembered—a beautifully rendered study of much the same kind of novelistic material, a group of young friends making their way in the world, false starts at love and marriage, the soul struggling to free itself from convention, from its own mistakes. Well, I shall wait for the next instalment.—JUDITH CHERNAIK, "Sacred Cows," *Lon*, Dec. 1978–Jan. 1979, pp. 129–30

ISABEL QUIGLEY
Pamela Hansford Johnson
1968, pp. 5–8, 43–45

I

Pamela Hansford Johnson was once described by *The Times Literary Supplement* as one of the writers who are 'perhaps most to be envied' for being one of those 'whose fame has grown on the wings of each new achievement'. Since the middle 'thirties she has been a full-time writer; yet in spite of the easy professionalism these three decades have given her, each new book of hers is still an 'achievement' in the sense that it takes a new direction, enlarges her scope, does not repeat past successes or styles and never succeeds in pigeon-holing her, in stamping her as a particular brand of writer. She commands respect because she never uses a formula or a gimmick; in a sense because she has never written a spectacular best-seller, and is never considered as the author of a single book, but must be judged for her work as a whole. From the first—and her first novel, written at the age of twenty-two, still seems remarkable—she spoke with a voice that was distinct, that belonged to no particular school or group, that reflected only her self, her background and experience; all of which were, in a way, individual, untypical.

Critics who know nothing about her life sometimes make

the mistake of supposing that, like so many women, she writes directly from experience, from a lifetime spent in a single atmosphere, at a single social level. An American reviewing *The Last Resort* described her, with hilarious inexactness, as a typical product of the narrow upper-middle-class world described in it; anyone reading, say, *The Humbler Creation* might be forgiven for supposing she had spent a lifetime married to a vicar in a rundown London parish. Admittedly, she has moved in wider circles than most women; has known several social worlds, where many women know only the one they are born or marry into—which often means the same one; has travelled widely and moved among very different people from the narrowly 'literary' ones that women writers so often mix with. Yet her grasp of all these milieux is exact: she seems to achieve, in a number of fields, the sort of familiarity most women get only through a lifetime's experience.

It might be argued that she achieves this familiarity through the normal tools of the novelist: good eyes and ears, and an uncommonly sharp and subtle understanding of human nature. But her strong point, too, has always been social description, atmosphere, situation, a sense of how things feel, look, taste and sound in a particular group, at a particular level: her people are always part of the wider world they live in, they are professionally, socially, externally recognizable, as well as personally known and understood. Personal relations matter, of course, they even matter supremely to the people involved in them; but her people live a good deal in the world of telegrams and anger, they are conditioned by money and jobs and responsibilities and all the external pressures of work, friends, background, family, old loyalties. No one lives in a vacuum, no one nurses feelings in isolation from the rest of life, untouched by responsibility for others.

All this makes Pamela Hansford Johnson unlike the woman novelist who, from Jane Austen downwards, has stuck to what might roughly be called a woman's world, has seen things from a strictly feminine, even domestic, point of view. Probably the best of these novelists in England today is Elizabeth Taylor, who writes brilliantly about the small social circle she knows, and sticks as closely as Jane Austen to themes and characters she can handle, without going outside it. Miss Hansford Johnson does not see the world from a specifically feminine point of view, certainly not from a sheltered social position: she can even write credibly in the first person as a man—an unusual achievement for a woman. As an artist she is able to forget her sex, as she is able, in a sense, to enter backgrounds she cannot know as intimately as she appears to.

This empathy, both social and psychological, this way of entering all kinds of people and of varied social worlds, is something found in another unclassifiable novelist who also seems to cover a wider social field than he can know from long personal experience, at least: Graham Greene. Significantly, Anthony Burgess has compared him with Pamela Hansford Johnson, though for another reason—for what he calls the 'light gravity' they share, a way of overlaying a basic seriousness and moral preoccupation with an entertaining style and often even a lighthearted air. Mr Greene, like Miss Hansford Johnson, is a chameleon-narrator: he takes the colour of his characters and their surroundings, and you can no more tell with him than you can with her just what the 'real', objective background was, where direct experience begins and ends. Her first novel one feels, perhaps inevitably, is based on direct experience, socially at least; and one admires the restraint with which she keeps to a narrow path without narrowing the vision to match it. But with the other novels it is hard to tell just where her own standpoint is, just how much of it she herself

has lived through. She is detached from her characters and situations in a way that hides her own personality; one does not identify her with this or that attitude, or feel—as nearly always happens with women novelists, even at the level of George Eliot or Charlotte Brontë—'of course, that must have been her idea of herself', idealized, perhaps, but taking her particular standpoint, seeing things from her particular age group, or social group, or feminine standpoint.

The action of the novels is mostly ordinary, in the sense of unadventurous; at times it is even domestic; but it often happens to people when they are in an extraordinary situation, a state of crisis, a moral dilemma. Moral choice is sometimes a central part of the action; but more often it is a moral situation, a confused moral struggle or argument, a case of moral support or betrayal. Yet these situations and choices and struggles are always presented in terms of recognizable everyday life, life at a particular moment and in a particular place, with surroundings one can see exactly and talk one can hear around one. Life is seen neither romantically nor grandiosely; yet it has a certain grandeur in its moments of personal triumph, in the personality of some of its own people, in the warmth and pathos of relationships. It may be desperate, but it is never drab.

Here, again, Pamela Hansford Johnson is untypical in that she deals with situations that are untypical, 'unfictional' in the sense that they have not the neat, ready-made air of so many chosen by novelists. Her lovers, for instance, are not necessarily young or attractive; people of many varied ages can love, depend on one another, desperately need one another; good people may need bad ones, worthy people be infatuated with wastrels (from Sid in *The Trojan Brothers* to Helena or Charmian in the trilogy, the decent person obsessed with the indecent, with the totally unworthy object of love, is a recurrent figure in her novels). Even in the first novels, when almost inevitably it was a case of boy meeting girl, there were no conclusions, solutions, or happy endings. Even when she was still at an age to be moulded by it herself, Miss Hansford Johnson could stand outside the ideas of her time and background, criticise the sort of education (or lack of it) that made a girl totally unready for marriage. The ability to 'belong', atmospherically, to a particular place, class or age-group never means that she is confined to the standards of that particular group: time and distance become integral parts of the action, so that, while one has a vivid sense of a particular moment, one has an equally strong sense of a later judgement, a distancing and re-living of what happened then. Even in the earliest books everything was seen as fluid with possibilities, the present opening into the future; life was never a series of compartments, fixed and sealed by a particular situation. Things were always relative, becoming, unfinished, open to every sort of possibility. . . .

II

Some novelists are predictable, they move forward in a straight line; but not Pamela Hansford Johnson. None of her novels repeats what its predecessor has done, or even repeats the manner and methods of its predecessor. Although there are links and patterns one can trace between them, situations that repeat themselves, relationships that clearly mean much to her, each one is a new departure. After more than twenty years as a 'straight' novelist, she turned to the satirical *Skipton*, which may be her best novel; after *Skipton* she went back to realism of the most moving, feeling sort in *The Humbler Creation*; then to a kind of metaphysical social comedy, or mixture of two *genres*: the philosophical and inquiring, and the near-thriller, socially observant, sharp, exciting. Then she was back with the Skipton characters, and something of the Skipton manner.

Always she has been a novelist of minutely exact observation, pin-pointing exactly this or that class, time or age-group; yet within that class, time or age-group always dealing with people who are intensely individual, quite outside the run of fictional characters that can be labelled hero, heroine, young, old. Indeed her most memorable characters are the eccentrics, the outsize outsiders, who fit nowhere, certainly no exact category: Helena, glowing with a half-absurd youthful radiance into old age; Dorothy Merlin, hag who finally gains a certain pathos; Skipton, voyeur, snob, beggar, unspeakable yet somehow, if not exactly grand, at least grandiose in his forlornness; Kate in *The Humbler Creation*, aggressive, frustrated by more than sexual loneliness, pathetically in love with her bedraggled journalist; even Celia of *The Last Resort*, bossy and moneyed, an oddity with a certain tragic grace. One remembers their worlds, for Pamela Hansford Johnson is a social novelist; but one remembers even more vividly their presences, their personalities—indeed, with a talent for catching likenesses one might sketch any one of them. And it is they, more strongly than their exactly observed surroundings, that give the novels their particular atmosphere and presence, that make the weather seem serene or threatening, sunny or oppressive, that alter the world to their image. This is not the mild talent called character-drawing; it is the creation of people who live outside the novels' pages, who enrich our knowledge of others. It is probably the most creative—the most importantly creative—of the novelist's gifts: the ability to fashion people we come to know more vividly and closely and fruitfully than we know most of our friends, people full grown, credible, feeling, responsive, whose unmentioned feelings we can gauge, whose undescribed reactions we can always imagine, who do not fade and diminish when we shut the book.

DAVID JONES

1895–1974

The son of a Welshman, David Jones was born on November 1, 1895, in Brockley, Kent, a suburb of London. From an early age his mother encouraged him in his drawing, and from 1909 to 1914 he studied at the Camberwell School of Art. In World War I he served in the trenches with the Royal Welsh Fusiliers, an experience that marked him for many years. After the war he attended Westminster Art School, and after converting to Roman Catholicism in 1921 he joined Eric Gill at Ditchley; there he trained as an engraver, and later illustrated *The Rime of the Ancient Mariner* and *Gulliver's Travels*. In 1924 he visited Gill at Capel-y-Ffin, Wales, and the following years saw his gradual emergence as a painter. Intense artistic activity and constant travels in Britain and abroad were disrupted by nervous breakdowns, but he exhibited work at the Venice Biennial International Exhibition of Fine Arts in 1934, and later enjoyed solo exhibitions in Britain.

Jones spent ten years writing his long poem *In Parenthesis* (1937); praised by T. S. Eliot, it won the Hawthornden Prize in 1938. His second long, fragmentary poem, *The Anathemata* (1952), made him the first European recipient of the Russell Loines Award in 1954. Further honors followed, with a CBE in 1955, and a D. Litt. from the University of Wales in 1960. Jones continued to paint, but became better known as a writer; later publications include the prose collection *Epoch and Artist* (1959), *The Fatigue* (1965), *The Tribune's Visitation* (1969), and *The Sleeping Lord* (1974).

After World War II Jones lived alone in Harrow, making rare public appearances. He was made a Companion of Honour in June 1974, and died later that year, on October 28.

Personal

He gave the impression of Blakean innocence and his water-colours, more than his poems perhaps, recalled the lines:

And I plucked a hollow reed
And I made a rural pen,
And I stained the water clear
And I wrote my happy songs.

After this superficial impression followed the far deeper one that David Jones' real inner life was that of a poet who had been an infantryman in the trenches during the First World War. Nearly all survivors who were at the Western Front for any length of time (I think particularly of poets—Robert Graves, Siegfried Sassoon, Edmund Blunden, Ivor Gurney) were, I should say, men apart, in some way dedicated by that tragedy, afflicted by an inner wound from which they never wholly recovered (perhaps this is the true cause of the wound of the Fisher King in *The Waste Land*). In the lives of these former soldiers this wound was sacred, tragic and singing.

Later, reading *In Parenthesis*, I felt that David Jones belonged to a company of men whom, through this poem, he had mythologized and made holy. His letters show that he thought constantly about the war, even up to the last week of his life. The war meant to him the Western Front and the Royal Welsh Fusiliers in which he was a private. In his poetry (or prose poetry) the men of his regiment, their words, deeds and accoutrements become absorbed into the 'signs' of the Celtic culture, as also into the patterns of living of soldiers in Roman times and in Shakespeare's historical plays. . . .

As a man, and perhaps as a writer, he does not seem to fall into the category of literary man, man of letters, poet even. My wife and I once had occasion to take Igor Stravinsky to see him in the room where he lived towards the end of his life in a convent at Harrow. When we left, Stravinsky remarked that it had seemed to him like visiting a holy man in his cell. David Jones would sometimes fish out from under his bed a very old gramophone of the kind that winds up with a handle, and play on it a worn record of plain-song Gregorian chant, almost inaudible to us through the rasp of the steel needle, while with hands clasped across his knees and an expression of bliss on his face, he swayed to and fro to the imagined music.—STEPHEN SPENDER, "Preface" to *Introducing David Jones: A Selection of His Writings*, 1980, pp. 9–11

Works

Am I dotty? For some fifteen years now Mr. David Jones has made me ask myself this question. When *In Parenthesis* came out in 1938, I thought it—I think so still—the greatest book about the First World War that I had read. But nobody seemed to notice or write about it. Having lived with *The Anathemata* for the last ten months, I feel as certain as one can feel of anything that it is one of the most important poems of our time. But where are the bells? Where are the cannon? . . .

Joyce certainly, and Dante probably, have had a hand in Mr. Jones' development, but his style is in no sense an imitation. Nor is this verse as "free" as at a superficial glance it looks. Mr. Jones is not a Welshman for nothing. Welsh poetry is famous for its use of internal rhyme and assonance, and a careful examination of the last quotation, for example, will disclose similar subtleties. Like Joyce, Mr. Jones uses a very wide vocabulary; like Joyce and Dante his poem is full of riddles which require considerable erudition to solve: unlike Joyce and Dante, however, he accompanies his text with his own commentary notes. . . .

T. S. Eliot, Marianne Moore, William Empson (and Coleridge one might add) have supplied notes to their poems, but none of them to anything like the same degree as David Jones, and *The Anathemata* raises as never before the question whether a poem can be good which cannot be understood without them. One must begin by distinguishing between riddle, which is, I believe, a fundamental element in poetry, and obscurity, which is an æsthetic vice. Every crossword-puzzle addict (it is curious that it should so often be precisely he who objects most violently to puzzles in poetry) knows the difference: when, having failed to get a word, he looks at the answer next week, he says either "What a fool I was. Of course that's it," or "The clue was unfair. Four or five other words would fit it equally well."

Yet the same man, when he comes to a line in a poem which he finds difficult, is apt to accuse the poet of making fun of him out of conceit, of sneering at his lack of knowledge or sensibility, when, in fact, the poet is only trying to give him fun. If a poet hesitates to add an explanatory note, his hesitation often arises from the same neighbourly feeling which restrains a man, looking over the shoulder of a fellow clubman as he does his weekly crossword, from telling him the answers. To be laughed at for not knowing something is not nearly so insulting as having one's ignorance falsely assumed and being informed of what one knows already.

While the riddle element has always existed in poetry, the disappearance of a homogeneous society with a common cult, a common myth, common terms of reference, has created difficulties in communication for the poet which are historically new and quite outside his control. The poet—and each one of his readers—is a particular man; none of them can become a generalised type. As Mr. Jones says in his introduction:

> The poet may feel something with regard to Penda the Mercian and nothing with regard to Darius the Mede. In itself that is a limitation, it might be regarded as a disproportion; no matter, there is no help—he must work within the limits of his love. There must be no mugging-up, no 'ought to know' or

'try to feel'; for only what is actually loved and known can be seen *sub specie aeternitatis*. The muse herself is adamant about this: she is indifferent to what the poet may wish he could feel, she cares only for what he in fact feels.

The question then arises whether a reader is entitled to retort: "It so happens that Darius means a lot to me and Penda nothing. I can only read about what I love and know."

If, as I believe, the reader is not entitled to this retort, it is because of a fundamental difference between the imaginative activity of making and that of reading. If the poet can only make a living work out of what he knows and loves, it is only a living work that the reader can, and with much less difficulty than one might suppose, translate and understand in terms of his own, different yet analogous, love and knowledge. The Darius-loving reader is able to see his hero in the poet's Penda because, and only because, the latter is a creation of love. . . .

Mr. Jones has set out to write a poem which should be at once epic, contemporary, and Christian. It would be interesting, on another occasion, to compare *The Anathemata* with another poem which is epic and contemporary, but religiously excludes any religious references whatsoever, St. Jean Perse's *Vents*. Something has already been said about the problems of a contemporary epic; the peculiar and paradoxical relation, for a poet who is a Christian, between his art and his faith raises all kinds of other fascinating questions. Is all "Christian" poetry, for example, necessarily and profoundly, a joke? Is it possible, in poetry, to speal of God the Father without making him indistinguishable from Zeus, or of God the Son without making him into another culture-hero like Dionysus or Hercules? If it is not possible, does it matter? But a review is not the place to discuss such matters. I can only conclude by reiterating my profound admiration for this work and expressing the hope that many others will come to share it.—W. H. AUDEN, "A Contemporary Epic," *Enc*, Feb. 1954, pp. 67–71

The Anathemata, by David Jones, gives little ground of comparison with the other books this review is about, being no collection of lyrics but a long poem in eight sections. The conception it displays of what a poet is, and what his tradition, is in some sense ancient and bardic; he is the personified voice of a particular culture. But because there are now so many cultures, none of them intimately known to the others and none which can be commanding except in despite of its particularities, the voice of the bard is now attended by a long, intelligent preface and a myriad footnotes. It is a poem, with all this apparatus (and illustrations by the author), capable of exercising an antiquarian rather than a poetic fascination; and I ought confess at once having fallen into this trap, if it is a trap, and liking, on the whole, the explanations better than what they explain.

First as to the title. In antiquity the word had a double sense, referring equally to holy and accursed things, the common element (as in a word like *sacer*) being that the things were *set apart*. Only the second meaning is preserved in our "anathemas," but Mr. Jones draws for his purpose on the other English plural form, "anathemata," which preserves the ancient ambiguity and which he uses to mean "the blessed things that have taken on what is cursed and the profane things that somehow are redeemed . . . things that are the signs of something other, together with those signs that not only have the nature of a sign, but are themselves, under some mode, what they signify." The poem, subtitled "fragments of an attempted writing," "has no plan, or at least is not planned. If it has a shape it is chiefly that it returns to its beginning. It has themes and a theme even if it wanders far." It is about "one's own 'thing,' which *res* is unavoidably part and parcel of the Western Christian *res*," further modified by the author's being "a Londoner, of Welsh and English parentage, of Protestant upbringing, of Catholic subscription." The poem is written to be spoken aloud. About the poet's function Mr. Jones has this to say:

> Rather than being a seer or endowed with the gift of prophecy, he is something of a vicar whose job is legatine—a kind of Servus Servorum to deliver what has been delivered to him, who can neither add to nor take from the deposits. It is not that that we mean by "originality." There is only one tale to tell even though the telling is patient of endless development and ingenuity and can take on a million variant forms.

The poet, on this view, is the reciter of the ritual which keeps the world in being; but because the ritual these days has either fallen in disuse or is used for limited purposes (religion, ironically, having become a limited purpose), the poet must also be a rediscoverer, reedifier who causes the purified and idealized history recited in the ritual to be freshly seen as penetrating and modifying our secular or supposed secular concerns—which is, after all, exactly what was proposed, and achieved, by Dante. Mr. Jones is aware of the immensity of the task, of difficulties which Dante faced and overcame, but also of many which, at this distance, it does not appear that Dante had to deal with. But it is a question, beyond that, whether the attempt in its nature may ever be unplanned or random, whether the assumption, to begin with, of *ruins* does not in a degree dishonor or make unavailing whatever fragments may be shored against them.

This poem, a continuous meditation in free verse and prose, presents us with an enormously detailed world chiefly composed of those artefacts nearest to the heroic life of the past; with an easy familiarity the poet or his anonymous characters talk the honorable craftsmen's languages of old techniques neglected or lost: architecture, shipbuilding, manufacture of sieging engines. Thematically, through all this, the ancient Mediterranean *res* is absorbed into the matter of Britain, pagan antiquity into Catholicism—*Teste David cum Sibylla*, as it is written at the head of the poem. By the familiar Catholic argument that anything which is not Catholic is merely a natural prevision and inadequate vision of what is Catholic, even the geology of Great Britain is pictured as preparing itself for a sacred task as the matrix of the cultural form: "This is how Cronos reads the rubric, *frangit per medium*, when he breaks his ice like morsels, for the therapy and fertility of the landmasses," a figure explained by the following note: "See the rubric directing the celebrant at the point of the Mass called the Fraction: 'he . . . takes the host and breaks it in half (*frangit per medium*) over the chalice.' Cf. also Psalm CXLVII, 17, Bk. of Com. Pr. version. 'He casteth forth his ice like morsels: who is able to abide his frost?'"

Now it is perfectly part of Mr. Jones' business in the poem to present us with this connection, if he can, as a *fait accompli*; and, facing an audience which cannot unaided make such connections, to explain them in a note. He splendidly, unfailingly, anticipates our great ignorance, but does not care to anticipate our resistance. So far as his poem is a religious testament, that is entirely up to him, but so far as we may speak of poetry I'd contend that this connection, and others like it, is arbitrary and does not strike, when understood, as an illumination; and that the poem largely fails of conviction because it is undramatic in small things as in general outline—which doesn't prevent it from being often very interesting, but with,

for me, as I said before, an antiquarian and rather epicurean interest.

The distinction defines itself pretty precisely in the language and the verse. The book brings back into use, in great numbers, weird and wonderful words:

> Carlings or athwart her
> horizontaled or an-end
>   tabernacled and stepped
> or stanchioned and 'tween decks.
>   Stayed or free.
> Transom or knighthead.
> Bolted, out in the channels or
> battened in, under the king-plank.
> Hawse-holed or lathed elegant for an after baluster
>   cogginged, tenoned, spiked
> plugged or roved
>   or lashed.

But it does not always appear that all this is doing much more than "talking the way a shipwright (or his hardware catalogue) would be expected to talk." Nor is it particularly convincing, on the same line, that the Goddess should be represented as a Cockney girl if she must also be a Cockney girl philologist, folklorist, antiquarian, much in the manner of the historical novelist: ". . . on m'own name-day captain, the day the British Elen found the Wood—Ceres big moon half ris beyond her own Cornhill, behind de Arcubus as chimes *I do not know*. . . ."

And the verse, or verse-and-prose, with all its beautiful things, suffers similarly from arbitrariness and want of dramatic tension; its particular beauties want a common rhythmic beauty to play against. The incantatory tone, which when one reads aloud is seen to be a sort of substitute for a formal verse, is for all its interspersed erudition and colloquialism capable of no great variation, nor does the considerable amount of informal riming and chiming (if, as the notes warn us, we pronounce the Welsh aright) make up for a certain inherent want of energy in the verse and syntax.

Still, the explicit intention is to write "fragments," and if you take it that way there is a great deal here to wonder at and care for, though housed, perhaps, more in a museum than in a poem; a particular freshness, delicacy and clarity now and then emerges from a speech which is by nature and intention somewhat pedantic:

> so Iuppiter me succour!
> they do garland them with Roman roses and do have
>   stitched
> on their zoomorphic apparels and vest 'em gay for
>   Artemis.
>   When is brought in her stag to be pierced,
> when is bowed his meek head between the porch and
>   the
> altar, when is blowed his sweet death at the great
>   door, on the
> day before the Calends o' Quintilis.

> —HOWARD NEMEROV, "Seven Poets and the Language," *SwR*, 1954, pp. 313–16

There are two questions which people are given to asking, often in a peremptory tone, about certain modern works of literature. The first is: "Is this poetry or prose?"—with the implication that it is neither. The second question is: "What is this book about?"—with the implication that it is not really about anything. A good deal of time, which one would prefer to spend otherwise, can be devoted to trying to explain to such people that the questions are unimportant, even if not meaningless. These questions were asked about David Jones's *In Parenthesis*.

But people like to classify: and *In Parenthesis* was not so difficult to classify as his second book, *The Anathemata*. *In Parenthesis* could be regarded as a "war book", a book about the first world war; even though the author had said "I did not intend this as a 'War Book'—it happens to be concerned with war". The distinction is important. But if *In Parenthesis* was a 'War Book', then, people could say, it was probably intended to be prose, even though you could not take the typography as a reliable guide. But as for *The Anathemata*, it is certainly not a 'War Book', so what *is* it about? Now, Mr. David Jones is exceptional amongst writers of works of imagination, in writing for his own books introductions which do introduce, which explain to the reader what he is doing—if the reader is prepared to study them carefully and to believe that the author means what he says. *The Anathemata*, he says, is "about one's own thing, which *res* is unavoidably part and parcel of the Western Christian *res*, as inherited by a person whose perceptions are totally conditioned and limited by and dependent upon his being indigenous to this island."

Now that the first generation of "obscure" writers, those who survive, is approaching old age, the accusation of "obscurity" can no longer be employed so effectively for dismissing the work of younger men. And it might at last be worth while for some critic to ask whether there may not have been some cause of obscurity other than wilfulness or charlatanism. My own belief is that we, including David Jones, have all been desperately anxious to communicate, and maddened by the difficulty of finding a common language. May not the malady perhaps be in the reader, rather than in the writer, unless it is a malady of the world to-day from which we all suffer? In the preface to *The Anathemata* David Jones shows himself aware of this problem. "There have been culture-phrases," he says, "in which the maker and the society in which he lived shared an enclosed and common background, where the terms of reference were common to all. It would be an affectation to pretend that such was our situation to-day".

He is, in this context, justifying his Notes. *The Anathemata* is unusual, in my experience of long poems with notes, in having notes which really do give useful information. I recommend reading the book three times: first, rapidly without reading the notes: second, slowly and reading the notes with great care; third, at a normal pace, having become so familiar with the notes as hardly to look at them. I am aware that very few books are worth so much trouble, and that very few readers are capable of taking so much trouble. There may still be, however, even amongst readers capable of such mental exertion, some who will say: "I don't think this book is meant for *me*; there's too much that's Welsh and too much that's Catholic—but I dare say it would mean a lot to a Welsh Roman Catholic!" Well, if I thought the book was only for Welsh Roman Catholics, I should not have the impudence to talk about it. The book is, as the author says, about his own *thing*. Every author of works of imagination is trying to tell us about the world as he sees it. Nowadays, the more such a writer has to communicate, the more difficulty he may have in communicating it. So he must endeavour to convey a sense of his own private world—the world *he* lives in—*the* world as he has experienced it; he must turn that world inside out for you to look at, as if he was emptying his pockets on the table in front of you. Would you be annoyed to find that the contents of his pocket differed from yours? I am thinking of several other writers of major importance, besides David Jones. It seems to me that if we approach these authors in the right way we shall find that in coming to understand the different worlds in which

each of them lives, we shall, each of us, come to know more about his own. And this is, at least, a surcease of solitude.
—T. S. ELIOT, "A Note on *In Parenthesis* and *The Anathemata*," DL, Spring 1955, pp. 21–23

JOHN HOLLOWAY
From "A Perpetual Showing:
The Poetry of David Jones"
The Colours of Clarity
1964, pp. 115–23

Jones's elaborate descriptive passages, elaborately woven if you like, are no more than one band in a capacious verbal spectrum. The richly humdrum, the plain and moving ('he turned between where bees hived, between low plants, to his presbytery'), the coarsely vernacular, all have their places too.

But there is another kind of ambition at work in the poem: to tell not merely a plain and moving, nor even a brilliant and colourful tale, but one radiant also in depth.

> Every man's speech and habit of mind were *a perpetual showing*: now of Napier's expedition, now of the Legions at the Wall . . . now of Coel Hên

And this perpetual showing is what Jones has taken his stand by. So, when a cockney soldier has been speaking of his regiment's battle-honours, 'Private Dai' replies:

> My fathers were with the Black Prinse [sic] of wales . . .
> I was the spear in Balin's hand
>   that made waste King Pellam's land . . .
> On Badon hill . . .
> We staked trip-wire as a precaution at
> Troy Novaunt . . .
> I saw Him die

I telescope from 300 lines; but this long 'boasting' passage, in one sense authentically bardic (Jones's notes refer the reader to Widsith, Taliessin, and Christ's 'before Abraham was, I am') represents a recurrent movement in the work. The reader, however, is not at ease. No question that this movement adds to the seriousness of the undertaking, and intellectually to its depth and range and interest. No doubt that it keeps one thinking busily. But busy thought is not an invitation characteristic of poetry (though of course compatible with those invitations); and these recessions into radiant depth leave a sense of something at once willed and wrenched.

I leave that last word unexplained, because *The Anathemata* makes it clearer as it does everything else. Of the two works, the later one is perhaps the less successful, but it is much the more ambitious, and what it attempts is deeply and centrally significant. Many writers bemoan, but when it comes to the test most evade, the crisis of culture in our time, *The Anathemata* tries to meet it, answer it, on what we have almost lost the very sight of: a scale commensurate with what is at issue. The poem, that is to say, attempts the authentic and traditional task of epic: to show a people itself from the very roots. In a society which has miniaturized its poems almost as much as its radios, this deserves salutation and gratitude whether it succeeds or fails; it is central, inescapable, the act of a major figure.

The poem's guiding intention, then, is to recover, and thereby of course *re*-create to the extent even of in part creating, the myths or rather the Myth of Britain. In the early sections there is a shadowy thread of narrative, evoking (the just word) the pre-history of northern Europe, and the early settlement of the island (in which Brut our legendary eponymous hero, the early Tyrian traders, perhaps Augustine or Joseph of Arimathea, perhaps Christ himself, seem to play interchanging roles). Narrative extends into Anglo-Saxon times, but disappears as the poem moves to Albion and the apotheosis of London (it is this remarkable section which makes one speak of the creation of myth as well as of its re-creation). The later sections of the poem comprise a dithyrambic celebration of the ship, the siege-engine and the cross as recurrent and once more interchangeable symbols of the national *Mythos*, and finally a celebration of Christ's life and meaning in which Christian, classical, Arthurian and a good deal else converge and run into each other.

'Modernist' in its rejection of narrative, the poem is also modernist in the detail of its technical resource. This, the title proves. 'I mean by my title as much as it can be made to mean, or can evoke or suggest, however obliquely.' Those words are enough by themselves, of course, to place Jones historically. By 'Anathemata' he means whatever enters the dimension of the mythical in that it has *mana*: is ambivalently numinous in a by now familiar sense. That he adds six other meanings to this basic one merely illustrates the plethoric quality of the poem—'evoke or suggest, however obliquely'—about which there is more to say. Like many of us, Jones believes that

> on the couch of time
> departed myth
> left ravished fact

The nineteenth century was a lesion when society broke with myth and settled for formulae. The aim of the poem is to repair the break, re-energizing the world of atrophied legend until the numinous is once again luminous, and the plain man conscious of a radiance which surrounds the plain facts of life with haloes of mythical meaning receding into each other until they interplay and almost interchange. 'The complete consort dancing together.'

Eliot's words strike home; for just as *In Parenthesis* triangulated, one could say, from the matter of the later war poets and the technique of the 'Modernists', so *The Anathemata* triangulates from the Modernists' later work. Those who jib at this do so because they suppose such triangulation to be a recipe for poetic success ('to go back to Pound and Eliot and go on from there', one English critic formulated the recipe recently) instead of simply one form of recent historical development. Jones's poem performs this triangulation in that, while its basic drive is towards a recovered sense of tradition and continuity (so much part of the *Quartets*), it conducts its main enterprise, like the *Cantos*, by amassing an encyclopaedia of recondite particulars which, again like the *Cantos* to a considerable extent, it presents in what Pound called 'the mode of super-position': a juxtaposing which, in intention anyhow, by-passes logic and reverberates through the imagination direct.

So here, again much abridged, is Christ's 'Boast' from *The Anathemata*, to set beside those of Widsith, Taliessin and Private Dai:

> *Alpha es et O*
>   that which
> the whole world cannot hold.
> Atheling to the heaven-king.
> Harrower of Annwn.
> Freer of the Waters.
> Chief Physician and
> *dux et pontifex.*
> Gwledig Nefoedd and
> Walda of *every* land
> *et vocabitur* WONDERFUL

> Coming with great power
>   Twelve *legiones* . . .
>   For an anamnesis of whom
> is said daily
>   at the stone:
> *hostiam immaculatam*
>   aberth pur, aberth glân.
>   Lar of Lares Consitivi
>   Himself the Lar and the garner . . .
>   Out from the mother (coronate of the daughter)
>   bearing the corn-stalks.
>   Exact Archon (by whom Astraea on Themis)
>   Lord Paraclete of the Assize—
> Yet who alone is named MISERICORS.

Clearly, when Jones says that poetry is 'occupied with the embodiment and expression of the mythus and deposits comprising (a nation's) cultural complex', he means it; and his notes on this passage help those who need help—and who does not?—to pick up the references to the Celtic Hades, the Percival myth, the Anglo-Saxon world, the Mass, and lastly Christ as identified with Persephone-Triptolemus in both their agricultural and Rhadamanthine aspects.

But the question is, whether when all this 'recession and thickness', this 'totality of connotation' has been reread and run over and run together, we are left with poetry or with something else. It happens that Welsh words, which totally gravel many English readers, and the pronunciation of which Jones has to provide, syllable by syllable, in his footnotes, look no more outlandish to me than English ones (which is not to say that I am proficient in that language). But if this qualification is an irrelevance with regard to me, so it is with regard to him. The passage I have just quoted is venial over Welsh, but it certainly begins to show that constant leaning on Celtic legend, Welsh language, and Roman ritual, which in the end seems to introduce into the poem a radical distortion and asymmetry, a lapse from objective to subjective, public to idiosyncratic and private, and which I had in mind when I used the word 'wrenched' earlier on. And this is wholly at odds with the status and intention of epic which the poem indisputably claims. Nor is this in any way a matter of the critic's subjectivity against the author's, of the former telling the latter what to write about. It is to challenge the general validity, as a resurrection of the *mythos* of the people of Britain (or let us say England and Wales) of a work which tracks down every London city parish, but is silent over Durham, Canterbury, Winchester and the great wool churches; which is full of Geoffrey of Monmouth and the *Mabinogion*, but barely hints at Shakespeare; or which draws on the Mass of St Gabriel and the Feast of the Exaltation of the Cross, but makes nothing of St Aidan, Ockham, Wycliff, the English Prayer Book, or the Authorized Version.

The point could be put another way: as a radical divergence between performance and programme; for the programme is clearly laid down in the *Preface*, and it is there that the careful reader can see 'We' turning into 'I', and 'the embodiment and expression of the mythus and deposits comprising that cultural complex' to which *artists in general* belong, to 'matters of all sorts which, by a kind of quasi-free association, are apt to stir in my mind at any time'; and turn out to come from (among other sources, some of them no less eccentric, in the strict sense of that word) a catalogue of Welsh samplers and a guide-book to the Isle of Wight.

This is meant as condemnation only within limits. 'Quasi-free association', 'what I have written has no plan, or rather is not planned . . . what goes before conditions what comes after and *vice versa*' are not recipes for badness. The point is merely that they are not recipes for epic, for a national mythos. They are, in fact, something like recipes for Modernist poetry; and their provenance, back to Mallarmé's 'suggérer, voilà le rêve', is familiar. But since the time of Mallarmé, the poetry of evoke-however-obliquely has undergone a curious transformation from 'alchimie du *verbe*' (the phrase is not of course Mallarmé's) almost to its opposite: an evoking and suggesting which employs Pound's 'mode of super-position' for *items of fact alone*, presented in a language-texture of as it were zero density. This fact might be traced in the *Cantos*. True, certain areas of life cannot ever but call out from the *miglior fabbro* a marvellous felicity that Jones never comes near ('The cut cool of the air,/ Blossoms cut on the wind, by Helios / Lord of the light's edge': 29 . . . 'To see the light pour, / that is, towards sinceritas / of the word': 99). But there are Saharan stretches of the middle Cantos where anything that anyone could call a poetic texture of language is replaced by the mode of super-position operating either polyglot-wise between languages themselves, or between massive *blocs* of allegedly significant fact (Chinese, American, Italian history for example). Inter-inanimating life is to stream from Ens not Logos.

So with the passage from *The Anathemata* quoted above: the reader can go back to it if he is in doubt. And so with most though not quite all of the poem. The alchemy which is to make the worlds of Celtic, Saxon, Roman, Hebrew and Greek myth inter-penetrate and grow radiant lies in their perpetual showing in closest juxtaposition. Until, at its most clotted and forced, the poem has passages like:

> And then he must . . . relate in a clear high voice from his Aramean brut [*sic*], how that within six months from the beginning of the Sixth Age of the World, our divine Ymherawdr Octavian, ever august, of the blood of the progenitress the Purifier, Turner of Hearts and of Mars Pencawr (the *old* Pantocrator) . . .

At this stage it is right (once one has drawn breath) to look once more at

> on the couch of time
> departed myth
> left ravished fact

The underlying metaphor has gone wrong. Jones cannot have meant to suggest that myth was the Tarquin. Subtle exactness of metaphor is only one kind of local life in poetry; but the flaw, even if a small one, is perhaps revealing. A poem is a perpetual making as well as showing.

Ultimately, much of the interest of *The Anathemata* is that besides being a poem of great originality, of immense if bewildered learning, and of serious and unusual relevance to the cultural problems of our time, it also enables its readers to reflect on, and comprehend with a new clarity, something of the ultimate limits of the technical resources within which it is written: resources, that is, among those most characteristic of Modernist poetry, which our pundits scold us for not following on from, though often they have conspicuously not followed on from it themselves.

For the fact—learnable from the *Quartets*, where it is provided for, from the *Cantos*, where over long stretches it is not, and from *The Anathemata*, which does indeed 'go on from there'—is that erudition, with all that that implies of quotation, cross-reference, allusion, comparison, or a hail, simply, of recondite and piquant minute particulars—erudition and super-position *are not in themselves poetic activities at all*. It is obvious as soon as it is stated. Of these north and south poles of the Eliot-Pound achievement, the first is not the natural staple, and the second not the natural mode, of the poetic imagination. The natural staple of the poetic imagina-

tion is not facts but language, and its natural mode of expression is the complex with inevitable development and thence organic unity. This the author of *Widsith* had not forgotten. Widsith's boast was that of the bard as a realized character, and was integral with everything in his nature, mood and status. Private Dai (shadowiest of people in any case) was here only a mouthpiece for the author at his perpetual showing. In the end, all the immense elaboration of *The Anathemata* reduces to something very simple: to one relation repeated over and over, an endless catachresis of *hinted identity*, thrown off from a diffused agitation of particulars, a quasi-free association, a recession and thickness, a transfinite array of not-plannednesses. And by itself the mode of super-position can produce nothing but hinted identity or its opposite, a kind of hinted contrast. It is not an organizing relation, but a non-organizing one. Unless it is the servant of a deeper architectonic—and it is this, and nothing other than this, which can enrich the verbal texture of a literary work in a meaningful way—baldest accretion is what the mode of super-position naturally and characteristically creates, and the limit of its unaided powers.

If this train of thought is right, it explains a major though in a way paradoxical fact about *The Anathemata*. Which is, that although its *himmlische Länge* of what I should like to call *Mars-Pencawr-the-old-Pantocrator* texture constitutes a work of deep seriousness, and high interest, one for the existence of which everyone who cares about society or thinks about poetry should be grateful, *The Anathemata*, save for a handful of rather striking and very uncharacteristic passages, is poetically a work of almost astonishing boredom. The author, who is a large-minded man, admits this possibility in his Preface; but he cannot have recognized how large boredom bulks in his poem. Boredom, mind you, strictly from the standpoint of poetry: from another standpoint the London material, for example, or that about ships, is absorbing, and everywhere the work invites a busy mental activity with which boredom in the general sense cannot co-exist. But almost throughout, there is a radical disregard of what busy mental activities belong with and are compatible with the life of the imagination, and the inextricable vision-and-delight which are the signs of that life. To make this criticism is not of course to lament mere difficulty, which in this day and age would be fatuous. It is to identify, within the difficulty, first an idiosyncrasy, and ultimately a kind of erudite triteness, which do not create poetry but preclude it.

Some will give this judgment less weight (and some, I hope, more) because if we have to judge the *Cantos* as a single poem 109 or more sections long, I should say something like the same thing of that work also. Compared with *The Anathemata*, the passages in the *Cantos* about which it is imperative to say something else are longer and more numerous, their local merit is much greater, and their contribution to the whole work therefore perhaps of another order. Moreover, there is in the *Cantos* (though sadly obscured enough), a glowingly rewarding sense of something more important and central than the life of myth; it is, if you like, the myth of life—how life works, what men do and are like, how good and evil enter their enduring labours. I find more of this in *In Parenthesis* than in *The Anathemata*, and that is largely why I like it better.

Saying these things does not of course range one with those who seem to repudiate Modernism in poetry: of these we have a number in England, like Mr Macbeth with his predilection for Lascelles Abercrombie, or Mr Larkin with his for Stevie Smith. It attempts to recognize how certain of the techniques of Modernism naturally have a limit to their potential. We should make points of the same kind if we tried to explain why God is the worst part of *Paradise Lost*, why Pope fails with Homer, why English Romantic poets failed in drama; and it is a measure of the interest of David Jones's two works that they call out reflection at this level, lighting up the intrinsic powers of the tools of poetry, which constitute one of the fundamentals of the art, perhaps the most fundamental of all.

BERNARD BERGONZI
From "Remythologizing: David Jones' *In Parenthesis*"
Heroes' Twilight:
A Study of the Literature of the Great War
1980, pp. 202–12

Jones is concerned to restore the mythology of heroism, but with crucial differences. Whereas earlier literary representations of the hero, from Renaissance drama to the poetry of the early days of the Great War, had been rooted in an implicit but assured complex of assumptions and attitudes that were shared by the writer and his readers, Jones, writing in a post-heroic phase, has laboriously to construct an *ad hoc* frame of reference from his acquaintance with literature, showing the continuity of human attitudes in the conditions of battle. And this demonstration, this concrete embodiment of experience, is in no way rhetorical or assertive; thus, it is at the opposite pole from the expressions of the heroic mode that we find in the speeches of Tamburlaine or Hotspur, or, for that matter, in the sonnets of Rupert Brooke. It is unique and non-generalizable, valid only for Jones's particular purposes in writing *In Parenthesis.*

This uniqueness means that the quality of epic that some critics have discovered in *In Parenthesis*, notably Mr. John H. Johnston in his *English Poetry of the First World War* (1964), needs to be discussed with some qualifications. As I have already suggested, in writing about Manning's *Her Privates We*, the private soldier's experience of total immersion in a vast inhuman process gave more scope for epic understanding than the officers' narratives; and this is true, also, of *In Parenthesis*; indeed, both Manning and Jones share a common element in their use of Shakespeare's picture of the soldier's life as a substratum in their narratives. Undoubtedly Jones does move towards the level of epic, in that he reproduces a sense of shared experience and transcends the limitations of the purely individual standpoint. But true epic, I take it, reaches out beyond the personal to appeal to a system of public and communal values which are ultimately collective, national, and even cosmic. And this Jones does not do; he may feel that Celtic myth is central and not peripheral to his understanding of British tradition, and he may have some success in persuading a discerning reader that this is so. Nevertheless, such knowledge will not already be there to provide a ready response in the consciousness of most of his readers. Quite apart from an author's subject-matter and treatment, the question of epic involves the author's relation with his audience. Jones, in this respect, was no differently placed from other twentieth-century *avant-garde* artists with a strictly minority appeal. Although he aspires towards the impersonality of epic, his perceptions remain individual, rooted in the accidents of his own experience and reading. One can reasonably doubt whether the conditions for epic—the existence of a shared scheme of communal values and assumptions—are ever likely to be fulfilled in modern society.

In Parenthesis remains, however, the nearest equivalent to an epic that the Great War produced in English. It is far more objective than the wartime poetry or the novels and memoirs of the 'twenties. . . .

Jones is distinguished from the poets who wrote during the course of the war both by his impersonality and by the far wider emotional range of his work. As Mr. John H. Johnston has observed, 'Unlike Owen, Jones found little poetry in pity; pity was an emotion that might be aroused under certain circumstances, but the full reality of war was much too complex to be viewed through the eyes of pity alone.' Jones was, however, very aware of the sacrificial elements in the soldiers' experience, which he understood in Christian terms. Johnston acutely remarks:

> Positive, aggressive heroism of the epic character is seldom possible in modern war; a man may perform valiantly in action, but for every valiant moment there are weeks of inactivity, boredom, suffering, and fear. Thus the virtues of the modern infantryman are Christian virtues—patience, endurance, hope, love—rather than the naturalistic virtues of the epic hero.

As we have seen, this concept of the Christian hero had already been foreshadowed in Ford Madox Ford's Tietjens. Jones admits in his preface that the period of the war he was writing about—the early months of 1916—was still amenable to such treatment: it had not become entirely mechanized and depersonalized. Whether he could have written similarly about the post-Somme phase, so much more massive in its brutality, which produced the other war poets, is open to doubt.

Again, Jones resembles his contemporaries in seeing the actualities of the war against a background of traditional values, but differs from them in his manner of doing so. He looks much farther back than the nostalgically recalled Home Counties pastoral scenes of the Georgians, or even than Ford's Yorkshire squirearchy. Jones feels that his roots are British rather than narrowly English, and emphasizes the Romano-British elements in the national character (surviving in mythology if not in continuing social forms) rather more strongly than the Anglo-Saxon and subsequent strains. Thus, Jones establishes a comprehensive though eclectic frame for his action, whose closest parallel is perhaps to be found in the vision of the British past in Kipling's *Puck of Pook's Hill* (1906). As I have suggested, the degree of Jones's cultural eclecticism may, for many readers unfamiliar with his material, tend to obscure his comprehensiveness, though this difficulty diminishes on successive readings of *In Parenthesis*. In one other important respect, Jones's method differs from that of other war poets and prose writers: whereas they establish contrasts, whether nostalgic or ironical, between the past and the realities of the Front, Jones is concerned always to find parallels, to emphasize the underlying unity rather than the discontinuity of experience.

That Jones establishes this unity rather too easily is a point that might be urged against him by his critics. His achievement in *In Parenthesis* is increasingly recognized, but some readers may incline towards D. J. Enright's rather unfavourable comment that *In Parenthesis* is:

> a consciously 'literary' work: its style, tapestried and 'modernistic' at the same time, is at odds with its subject-matter (infantry life on the Western Front), and the allusions to ancient Welsh poetry and Celtic myths with their explanatory but not always justificatory footnotes rob the account of most of its immediacy.[1]

This is a curiously superficial comment from a normally penetrating critic. If Jones has succeeded (as I would claim) then his style is not at odds with but expresses in depth his subject-matter (it is hard to see that any given subject inescapably *demands* one style rather than another). Enright's crucial point is his assumption that 'immediacy' is, or should be, the principal criterion of literary merit, at least in the literature of war. Jones, as I hope to have shown, possesses as much concrete 'immediacy' as his more avowedly realistic contemporaries, though he uses this as one element in a complex of modes. The supremacy of the 'immediate' was part of the implicit aesthetic of Imagism as well as of naturalistic fiction, and as a doctrine it has become a little threadbare; it should at least be justified and not merely asserted. It is one of the characteristics of the major work of art that it can modify habitual responses and in some measure impose the criteria by which it is to be assessed. This, I think, *In Parenthesis* succeeds

in doing; but like any major work it needs to be lived with before all its meanings become fully alive.

In a recent letter defending *In Parenthesis* against a Welsh critic, Mr. John Wain quoted Jorge Luis Borges's dictum that 'all literature begins in myth, and ends there'.[2] This forms an apt conclusion to my discussion of a work which blends myth and realism in a way that makes it one of the great achievements of the Modern Movement, and which, at the same time, has a rather greater depth of humanity than some other masterpieces of post-symbolist literature.

Notes

1. *The Pelican Guide to English Literature*, Vol. 7: *The Modern Age*, Boris Ford, ed., 1961, p. 169.
2. *Encounter*, July 1964, p. 94.

HENRY ARTHUR JONES

1859–1929

Born in Grandesborough, Buckinghamshire, on September 20, 1859, Henry Arthur Jones came from a lower-middle-class nonconformist family. Leaving school at twelve, he worked as a draper's assistant for six years while educating himself in literature, science and politics. On moving to London in 1869 he grew fascinated by the theatre, and began to write plays while working as a commercial traveler. In 1875 he married and took a house in Exeter, where his domestic drama *It's Only Round the Corner* (revised as *Harmony Restored*) was performed in 1878. After the London success of *A Clerical Error* the following year, Jones gave up trade and became a full-time writer.

The melodrama *The Silver King* (1882), written with Henry Herman, brought Jones financial security and critical acclaim. His later triumphs included *Saints and Sinners* (1884), *The Middleman* (1889), *The Case of Rebellious Susan* (1894), *The Liars* (1897), and *Mrs. Dane's Defence* (1900). Less successful at the time were *The Triumph of the Philistines* (1895) and *Michael and His Lost Angel* (1896).

Though Jones remained largely conventional and believed in the need to appeal to popular taste, he worked actively for theatre reform, and in 1895 published a collection of articles and speeches under the title *The Renascence of the English Drama*. He also labored for copyright laws and for a national theatre. He made several visits to America, and in 1907 was awarded an honorary degree by Harvard University.

A staunch patriot, Jones engaged in later life in vigorous polemics with Shaw and Wells, whose pacifism he regarded as a betrayal. His last years were embittered by a sense that British drama had left him behind. He died at his home in Hampstead on January 7, 1929.

To-day we look upon Mr. Henry Arthur Jones, as upon Sir Arthur Pinero, as one of our veteran dramatists. Once they were in the van of reform; once they stood almost alone as writers who sought to recover its old prestige for our drama, to make it once more an intelligent and a fine art, to relate it with modern life and thought and feeling. That was in the late eighties and the early nineties. Now other and younger men are taking up the torch from their hands. Not from Mr. Jones or his friendly rival do we expect the plays of to-morrow. To the credit of the former we can set a series of entertaining comedies of manners; his serious dramas were generally overtinged with melodrama and rhetoric, and when, after a rather prolonged absence from the London stage, he made his return with plays hall-marked with American approval, it was seen that in the interval his old faults had not been removed, his zeal had lost much of its freshness, and his schemes and characters had, to a large extent, become conventionalized. The movement which he did so much to set going a couple of decades ago has passed

him by, and our eyes turn for deliverance to the younger generation.

Still, though we can anticipate little from Mr. Jones now in the way of practical contributions to the theatre of ideas, we can promise ourselves gain from listening to the opinions a man of his considerable experience and patient idealism has formed as to the handicaps under which the drama labours in this country, and the way in which those obstacles might be overcome. Not only has the author of *The Liars* toiled hard and conscientiously at his craft, he has also been an assiduous and ardent propagandist in the interests of the drama. In lectures, in speeches, in magazine articles, he has hammered away at what should be—and are in other countries except England and America—commonplaces concerning the playwright's work and function. With a reiteration almost monotonous, he has urged the distinction between drama and popular entertainment: he has insisted that there ought to be close relations between drama and literature, and that the former deserves to be popularly recognized as one of the arts; he has protested against the notion that the English drama is "the instrument and creature and tributary and appurtenance of the English stage"; he has asked for conditions, whether brought about by the abolition of the Censorship or the establishment of repertory or municipal or State theatres, that will enable an author to handle the serious problems and passions of life and be freed from the tyranny of the schoolgirl and the sentimentalist.

Mr. Jones now collects the various public utterances and presents them under the title of *Foundations of a National Drama*. In only two of these papers is he found taking anything like recreation from the business of championing his art and pressing its claims; only twice does he abandon the mood of earnestness and the fervour of the orator for genial discourse on the extent to which real life can be expressed on the stage and the difficulties a dramatist encounters in delineating character. For the rest, at the American Universities, before learned societies, at the Oxford Union, among members of playgoers' societies, and in the monthly reviews he declaims on the points already mentioned with great earnestness, and, except when he attempts a heavy-handed humour, very cogently. The consequence is that, since his topics are few, and his thoughts have not materially changed during a number of years, he repeats himself in a way that would have been avoided had his volume been a consecutive treatise instead of a collection of scattered discourses.

There is another disadvantage associated with the issue of utterances ranging as these do over seventeen years, however they may be revised, enlarged, or corrected. Even in the world of the theatre circumstances are always changing, and surveys made in one decade are falsified by the progress of another. Mr. Jones's surveys of the condition of the drama, many of them ten years old, do not escape the fate of being thus out-dated. He almost writes sometimes as if the progress of our stage had stopped at the time he ceased to be one of its chief supporters, and he takes next to no account of that school of thoughtful young playwrights, including Mr. Galsworthy and Mr. Granville Barker, which makes us most hopeful of the future. He talks as if literature were still as divorced as ever from the drama, when men of letters like Mr. ⟨J. M.⟩ Barrie and the author of *Justice* ⟨John Galsworthy⟩ have equally high reputations as playwrights and novelists. He includes an article here on the chaos of the old licensing system long after the chief anomaly has been abolished. No small part of a paper dealing with 'Drama in the English Provinces in 1900,' he himself sees, needed correction in a supplementary chapter, yet in that chapter he makes but slight reference to what is the most significant feature in the development of our stage—the foundation in town after town of a repertory theatre. The time will probably come when the provinces will turn the tables on the capital, and, rejecting the fashions in plays London has long dictated to them, will—with a noble revenge—impose on London a drama that will be quick with thought and observation, with courage and humour. Mr. Jones tells us he is eager not to be thought a pessimist, but there are many signs of promise and advance which he has overlooked.

Let us freely admit, on the other hand, that this rhetorician has many grounds for dismay. It is a question, as he says, of supreme importance, how our populace spend their evening hours—the only hours in which many can be said really to live and the vast bulk of them, we must confess, pass that time in the sorriest entertainment. It is a fact that the habit of playgoing, as distinct from that of seeking amusement and an escape from life, is by no means increasing with the increase of pleasure-seekers. It is evident that even supporters of the drama are interested in the play rather as the vehicle for some popular favourite's acting than as an example of an art, a representation of life. It is also true that a National Theatre, were it built to-day, would find neither sufficiently versatile actors to hand nor, perhaps, a sufficient repertory of modern plays. Our public, let it be granted, has been debauched by spectacle and musical comedy; our more earnest playwrights are still hampered by the anachronism of the Censorship. Mr. Jones does not, and could hardly, exaggerate the significance of these drawbacks; but some of them are temporary. The main trouble is the omnipresence of a huge half-educated class which has no traditions as to entertainment, and accepts the worse because it has no knowledge of the better; nay, seems also to have infected its social superiors with its own viciousness of taste. The remedies, as Mr. Jones sees, are patience, organization, and the insistence of the cultivated playgoer on having his own needs met. Somehow or other the puritan and the superior person must be roped into the theatre, the lovers of stage art must found their own "théâtres intimes," the repertory system must be extended to London boroughs and suburbs, and the playgoer who wants a living drama must develope the propagandist spirit of the zealot in religion—must, in fact, imitate Mr. Jones's own restless enthusiasm.—UNSIGNED, *Ath*, Feb. 1, 1913, pp. 139–40

In the preface to his *Theatre of Ideas* Henry Arthur Jones, referring to his own experience, seems inclined to adopt the ancient heresy—beloved of most modern managers—that the public and the critics are incapable of appreciating really good plays, and that, therefore, to write or produce them generally results in waste of labor and money. He cannot seriously believe it. The ample success of his own best works is a sufficient refutation. Moreover, the acknowledged masterpieces of drama, adequately interpreted, have always been supported by the masses. Plays of great merit sometimes fall, undoubtedly, but it by no means follows that their failure must be attributed to their virtues. It might be hinted that authors are not always the least fallible judges of the absolute values of their own inventions. Mr. Jones, who is nothing if not self-reliant, would not subscribe to that notion. But on most theatrical subjects he speaks with great authority, and he is a fluent and entertaining writer. Skeptical as he is on some points, and radical on others, he is at heart an essential conservative. His contempt for faddists of all sorts, in and out of the theatre, is infinitely wholesome and refreshing. It is as an apostle of common-sense that he laments the disappearance of true burlesque from the stage. He professes an ambition to revive that form of pungent satire in order to assail the varieties of current humbug, impervious to the lighter shafts of comedy, with the savage strokes of the humorous bludgeon. He is, perhaps, somewhat too fond of that homely weapon. Some of his best work is at times married by over-emphasis. His burlesque sketch, *The Theatre of Ideas*, which he has cast in narrative instead of dramatic form, contains much robust and well-aimed satire, with some humorous illustrations not unworthy of their model; but it would be more effective if it were a little less extravagant. It could be greatly improved by judicious pruning and editing. His plea for the one-act play is timely, and it is to be hoped that he may be encouraged to continue his efforts in this direction. His *The Goal*, printed in the volume, was one of the most notable one-act pieces produced in the Princess Theatre, and is in many ways a striking and excellent bit of workmanship. *Her Tongue*, described as comedy, but really more akin to farce, tells how a silly woman frightened off a desirable wooer by foolish chatter.

Two-thirds of it is admirable, but in the end the designed effect is weakened, if not destroyed, by the undue prolongation and elaboration of a capital comic situation. In his little Cornish tragedy, *Grace Mary*, he ventures upon the dangerous expedient, in a modern play, of a speaking apparition. In itself, it is a moving and vigorously written tale. A puritanical old fisherman exacts from his daughter—to whom he is devoted—an oath that she will neither see nor listen to her drunken, ne'er-do-well lover. The latter, knowing her to be within hearing, vows to devote himself to eternal perdition if she will not come to him. Distracted by conflicting emotions, she dies of a broken heart, but her wraith appears to the frenzied lover and pledges him to reform, promising to rejoin him in the beyond. The piece exhibits literary and technical skill, and is theatrically and emotionally strong.—UNSIGNED, *Nation*, July 22, 1915, p. 128.

From the start Jones had upon him the council of good works. He was one of the first to realize the potency of the play in social reform. As a dramatist he seldom lets slip an opportunity to pass judgment on his fellows. This social-mindedness which he displays as a playwright characterizes all his thinking on the theatre. His first production in London had taken place the year in which Arnold had sounded his clarion, "The theatre is irresistible; organize the theatre." Thenceforward Jones devoted himself to this cause. Jones became a propagandist for the theatre in the same spirit in which Ruskin and Morris had become propagandists for art. He saw the social obligation of the dramatist, the social possibilities of the play, and he saw too that these obligations and opportunities were violated by the condition of the theatre in his time. He proceeded to make appeal on behalf of the theatre to the only powers that could bring forth a new theatre, the minds and the hearts of the people themselves.

The dramatist set himself to the solution of two problems in the organization of the theatre. The first of these is the official problem and has to do with the relationship between the theatre and the State. The second is the social problem and has to do with the building of a theatre in the midst of the new society of the world. Of these two the first is far less important than the second and more simple to handle. It is concerned with such matters as copyright protection, the licensing of theatres, the censorship, and projects of national support. The problems of copyright and music hall license were satisfactorily solved. Only the censorship and the problem of the national theatre are left to vex the dramatist. But the unofficial and social situation presents a permanent problem of increasing difficulty.

More vigorous and captious than the censorship of the king's reader of plays, is the censorship of the English audience. Mrs. Grundy, sitting in the pit of an English theatre, wields the final power over the dramatist's work. And the pit is no ready listener to any direct appeal, to any rational statement of the issues. Jones set himself first to find out what laws, if any, underlie the reactions of the public toward a play, and then to raise the standard of those laws by direct appeal.

In endeavoring to reach the ear and mind of the audience, Jones has used all the channels of publicity. He indulged in an advertising campaign in behalf of good plays. In this spirit he helped to establish the Playgoers Club in 1884, wrote articles in *The Nineteenth Century* and the *New Review*, prefaces to *Saints and Sinners* and *The Case of Rebellious Susan*, addressed audiences of workingmen and students in England and America, and engaged in debates in print and on the platform. In 1895 he issued *The Renascence of the English Drama* and in 1912 *Foundations of a National Drama*,

discussing in these volumes such subjects as drama and the mob, education and the theatre, religion, the provinces, and censorship.

The characteristics that Jones shows in his campaigning he shows also in his plays. His plays may be traced definitely to English root. He refers often contemptuously to the "lob-worm symbolic school" of Norwegian drama. Owing little to the Continent, outside of the stimulation of examples and a push toward a sex interest, his plays are in structure and character thoroughly English. Neither in thought nor in technique does he show more than a glimmer of the ideas for which Ibsen was striving. In spite of an appearance of revolt, his plays defend the *status quo*, they go down to no absolutes of judgment, they are pungent exposés of surfaces that involve no fundamental searching. Jones has given us a picture of the English mind of the time as confused and full of moral pockets as the original, and yet it is the best picture of the middle-class mind that we have in the theatre.

As a dramatist Jones subordinates everything to a sociological interest. Though he is interested in perfecting the instrument of his craft his intellectual prepossession seems to lie outside the art in the substance of society. For this reason his work has a certain tangential twist. He seems to be aiming at some point outside of the structure of the play itself. Most of his plays have a large and carefully worked out social background in which the action itself is dwarfed. When he builds a play around a character, that character is an embodied point of view, a crux in the social fabric. Jones's code of play construction is evolved from his own necessities rather than from a study of the well-made play or the codes of naturalism. For this reason his plays refuse to catalogue under schools or influences. He maintains throughout his career many of the characteristics of melodrama with which he began. His plays are spread over long spaces of time. The action seldom proceeds in sequence of events from beginning to end.

A mark of Jones's diagrammatic mind is found in his handling of characters. In trying to make his characters representative he has fallen into formulas. His favorite man seems to be a priestly ascetic, an artist, scientist, explorer, or minister who revolts against the frivolity of the age and yet is led with total lack of wisdom into the arms of folly. Another character is the middle-class tradesman, sufficiently prosperous, who has elected himself guardian of the morality of the community. Jones usually presents his tradesmen in groups and too often under their respectable robes they are badly spotted with sin. Above all Jones has prided himself on his women. He has given us all kinds of women except the "eternal womanly." Customary figures are a temperamental woman, a girl self-willed, a siren, an adventuress, a pagan, a woman misled by revenge, or ennui, or tipsy with frivolity. Frail as these women may be, Jones's strong man always succumbs to them. Last among his types is that of the aged baronet who has gone the *"fin de siècle"* pace and has come forth safe on the other side and is calm and understanding and helpful to mesdames and men. Adept at putting hand on shoulder, with plenty of time from great duties to patch up domestic rows, talkative fellows, these noblemen have a certain urbane charm.

In one particular sense Jones makes his structure typical of the time. The world he presents is a show world. Its doctrine is appearances. Its punishments are meted out to those who violate the code of front. It is not hypocrisy that he attacks but the assumption that anything else is the code. Hypocrisy is the means by which the ideal is kept alive. He takes the text of *The Triumph of the Philistines* from Ecclesiastes "Be not righteous overmuch; why should'st thou destroy thyself"; and from *The*

Pilgrim's Scrip for another play he quotes "Expediency is man's wisdom; doing right is God's." Taking this pragmatic doctrine, Jones adapts a code of playwriting to it. This code rejects the absolute values, asks no support from right or the sense of duty, but rests upon the law that only those who conform can be happy. The movement of most of Jones's plays is directed either to the weaving of a nice veil of appearances around dubious scenes or to showing that the bad appearances were misleading. The cardinal sins of society are in Jones's plays cardinals sins still. Courageous as he is in attacking the Philistine, he throws him no deep challenge of doctrine. Jones's doctrine of appearances is shown in the theatrical use he makes of confessions. As his final standard does not lie within the man but outside him, the final solution comes through adjustment not to one's own sense of right but to the crowd. It need not be said that the confession scenes of *Saints and Sinners* and *Michael and his Lost Angel* have a strong theatrical value. But they have another value. A public confession is an admission of the right of the crowd to an interest in the affair. Jones's confession scenes are surrenders to philistinism. In this way his social predilections extend even to his technique.—THOMAS H. DICKINSON, "Henry Arthur Jones," *The Contemporary Drama of England*, 1920, pp. 91–96

The position occupied by Jones proved to be peculiarly anomalous. In 1900 his *Mrs Dane's Defence* proved that his constructive power remained unimpaired, fully as expert as it had been in the past, and that his skill in the penning of tense, terse dialogue was even more adept than it had been before; and from the date when this play was presented to the public on until 1923 he continued to write prolifically for the stage, producing nearly thirty works of diverse kinds, some deeply serious, some entertainingly light. In themselves these facts might suggest that within this period his popularity and fame must have been second to none; yet the truth is that, however active and adroit he remained, whatever occasional successes he enjoyed, his previous firm grip on the public had been lost. Gradually—and increasingly as year succeeded year—this man who before the advent of the present century had been so largely responsible for arousing audiences to appreciation of new dramatic themes came to appear old-fashioned, and towards the close of his career he stood neglected, almost completely forgotten. In *Whitewashing Julia* (1903), despite its occasionally amusing situations, his familiar satire of moral hypocrisy seemed just a bit stupid; the artificialities of *Joseph Entangled* (1904) are more evident than its virtues; in *The Chevaleer* (1904) the presentation of the passing-by travelling showman gave to Arthur Bourchier one of his most effective parts, yet the general theme of the play was thought by many to be merely silly; we today may find a slight interest in *The Hypocrites* (1906), the more particularly since its plot anticipates those of two significant plays of 1912—Galsworthy's *The Eldest Son* and Houghton's *Hindle Wakes*—yet for us and for Jones's contemporaries alike the narrowness of his vision leaves his own scenes dull and ineffective. It is true that when *Dolly Reforming Herself* appeared in 1908 one still-esteemed critic (whom charity may here leave anonymous) referred to its "lifelike" characters, while one of his companions, equally distinguished, actually compared the author with Sheridan; it is also true that even now we can admit it as belonging to Jones's more successful efforts—yet at the same time there must be a more serious admission, that its planning is mechanical and its persons rather caricatures than characters. Nor can we accept the rather poor drama of provincial politics and rivalries, *Mary Goes First* (1913), as being, in the words of still

another well-known critic, a "notable achievement" in the style of "high comedy".

Jones, in fact, suffered the fate of not a few playwrights in the history of the theatre—men whose abilities by no means can be questioned, men whose purposes were sincere and serious, but at the same time men whose own intelligences were not deep and who, as a result, after making considerable impact in the theatre during their earlier days, soon found that the relatively simple things which they had preached were later become old-fashioned, obsolete and even at times not a little ridiculous. Fundamentally, the dominant "idea" which Jones constantly incorporated in his plays may be described simply as a hatred of hypocrisy; beyond this it proved difficult for him to go, while the hatred itself tended, as the years advanced, to become blindingly rigid. One really anonymous reviewer summed this up when, in 1907, he declared that Jones exhibited "a narrowness of mind exceeding . . . the narrowness of mind" which he set out to castigate. Certainly it must be admitted that among his later writings he composed some comedies in which he introduced divers versions of charming ladies who by the exercise of sheer audacity managed to get their own way in everything, or who were delightfully irresponsible over money matters, or who complicated the lives of all around them by their feminine whims and fancies and follies; also to be admitted is the fact that in these comedies appear several skilfully written scenes—yet, even so, there is comparatively little here that can be compared with what he had to offer earlier audiences in *The Masqueraders*, *The Triumph of the Philistines*, *Michael and His Lost Angel* and *The Liars*.—ALLARDYCE NICOLL, "The 'General' Drama," *English Drama 1900–1930: The Beginnings of the Modern Period*, 1973, pp. 337–39

A. E. MORGAN
From "Henry Arthur Jones"
Tendencies of Modern English Drama
1924, pp. 29–35

After writing some inconsiderable trifles Mr. Jones scored a tremendous theatrical success in 1882 with a full-blooded melodrama, *The Silver King*, of which he was the principal author. This doubtless filled his pocket, but it did not prevent him, as well it might, from becoming a dramatist; and in 1884 he produced *Saints and Sinners*. This play may not be great drama but it is of striking importance. It undoubtedly has many faults, but it stands almost alone in its day as marking the road along which English drama was to advance. In three respects it was in the van of dramatic development. In the first place it was a definite attempt to consider English life seriously on the stage. We have attempted to trace briefly the earlier efforts in this direction: we have seen the contributions of men like Jerrold, Boucicault and Robertson. Mr. Jones was now to carry English drama another step along the same road, and at the same time such a long step that he may be said to have initiated the vogue of modern serious drama.

Secondly, he held that drama had suffered by the discontinuance of the practice of printing plays. If the drama depends wholly on the theatre for its propagation the playwright will suffer perhaps excessive influence from stage conditions. Mr. Jones therefore published *Saints and Sinners*, and since then the practice has become prevalent, and to-day almost every dramatist who does not look merely for theatrical success issues his plays in book form.[1] This happy return to the fashion of the seventeenth and eighteenth centuries has done as much as anything to restore English drama to its place amongst the arts. Mr. Jones went further and wrote a preface. The interest and value of a preface as a means of communication between the author and the public has been demonstrated from Dryden to Mr. Shaw. There is perhaps a danger that the dramatist will tend to rely on the preface to explain what ought to be made clear in the play itself, or he may even become so much enamoured of preface writing that the play becomes a dramatic illustration of a prose treatise. Nevertheless the revival of prefaces has been another step in the direction of restoring seriousness to the dramatist's work and has given him an opportunity of discussing the function and nature of his art in a way impossible by any other means.

The third respect in which *Saints and Sinners* was an important influence was its onslaught on English middle class puritanism. In more recent times we have heard so much of this in drama that we have at length wearied. This theme has been one of the commonest in the drama for the past twenty-five years. Mr. Shaw has perhaps been the most potent influence in this matter, but Mr. Jones preceded him by many years. This play is a very pointed attack on the false religion and the commercialism of the English middle class. The Victorian ideal of social and religious respectability ran admirably in double harness with the belief in self-help, duty and the inherent virtue of work. Together they succeeded in building up a vast commercial system and producing wealth on a scale unequalled in the world's history. But if they ran well in double harness it was because each knew that it must mind its own business. As Mr. Jones says in the preface to his play, it is remarkable to notice the "ludicrous want of harmony, or apparently of even the most distant relation of any sort between a man's religious professions and his actions." In the play Hoggard and Prabble are deacons of the local Bethel, of which Jacob Fletcher is pastor. Hoggard is a tanner whose transactions are "businesslike," but his attempt to oppress the widow of his late partner comes to the knowledge of Fletcher. Fletcher is one of the trustees and is able to thwart his plans, but in the end he suffers cruel vengeance from Hoggard. Prabble, a grocer by trade, is not a hard villain like Hoggard, but a sneaking sanctimonious creature, much annoyed by the success of the new Co-operative Stores. As a matter of course he expects Pastor Fletcher to protect him from their dangerous competition. First we hear him complaining to Hoggard:

> *Prabble*: . . . I find the members of the congregation are going to the Stores, and I've asked Mr. Fletcher more than once to preach against them. I'm a grocer, and I've got eleven children, and how can I pay my rates and taxes and bring up my family if the Stores are allowed to undersell me, eh? I ask you as a member of the great tax-paying middle class.
> *Hoggard*: Very true, Prabble. The middle classes are the great backbone of this country. It's such men as you and I, Prabble, that are the source of England's greatness. We have made England what she is to-day.

This was good social criticism. It may seem somewhat threadbare to-day, but we must recollect that it is nearly forty years old. It is serious but it is not dull. The subtlety and irony, especially in Hoggard's last remark, are still fresh. At this point Fletcher arrives and again refuses to preach against the Stores. Prabble is genuinely unable to understand his objection. To him it is so obvious and clear:

> If I support your chapel, I expect you to get the congregation to support my shop. That's only fair.

Mr. Jones also directed the attack against the dullness and the repression which accompanied the hypocrisy and materialism of the society he was exposing. Fletcher's daughter, Letty, is oppressed by the drab and soulless philistinism of the puritan middle class provincial town in which they exist:

> *Letty*: . . . How sick I am of it all!
> *Jacob*: Sick of what, dear?
> *Letty*: Of this silly town, and our silly people. Everything in Steeplefold is so commonplace, and so respectable, and nothing ever happens, and you and I are buried under it all!

The play is in many ways open to censure. The plot is melodramatic, the incidents sensational and the characterization is often weakly conventional. The innocent daughter of a pious minister is seduced by a typical stage villain, one Captain Fanshawe. The true lover is a simple, honest young farmer, George Kingsmill, a stock pattern of virtue, forgiveness and chivalry. Troubles fall on the devoted head of the pious pastor in direct proportion to his goodness, and sentiment recruits our emotions for the cause of virtue. We have the satisfaction of seeing the cruel Hoggard hunted as a criminal; Fanshawe meets an appropriately sudden death; George Kingsmill returns in the nick of time before the curtain falls finally. But despite all that is false and unreal there is no question that Mr. Jones had found the right road. The fact that he was not afraid to forgot the conventional happy ending showed that he was a man of some courage. The death of Letty in the final scene was, to say the least, unconventional. Ten years later English dramatists dared to write a domestic tragedy, but it was a novelty in 1884.

As we have already suggested, it was in his belief in drama as a great art that Mr. Jones was a revolutionist. Not content to accept the current attitude towards drama as merely the means of three hours' amusement in the theatre, he wanted to restore it to its high place as a great form of art and as a criticism of life. There is no reason to believe that he would have denied the necessity that drama should please, or that it should provide amusement. Art may be serious without being sombre, and it was for a serious drama that Mr. Jones was fighting. The preface is very illuminating on this point. There he accounts for "the comparative intellectual and literary degradation of the modern drama for two or three generations past" by reference "to the fact that plays have been chiefly considered and exploited from their purely theatrical side." He realized fully that a play is not the same as life, and he did not fail to understand the great difference between realism and reality. His contention was that the English drama instead of being merely "the art of sensational and spectacular illusion . . . the art of building up an ingenious Chinese puzzle of comic or thrilling situations" should be "mainly and chiefly the art of representing English life."

The real question is whether we go to the theatre to escape from life, or whether, on the contrary, we go to see a picture of the life we know, or recognize imaginatively as true, and so take pleasure in studying it as the dramatist displays it before our eyes. For a hundred years or more the former theory of drama had prevailed. Mr. Jones led the way towards the new ideal, and thus infused modern drama with one of its most vitalizing qualities. Robertson and the Bancrofts had tried to give reality by purely mechanical means. Mr. Jones recognized that something more fundamental was necessary. "It is of the smallest moment to be 'true to nature' in such mint and cummin of the stage as the shutting of a door with a real lock, in the observation of niceties of expression and behaviour . . . it is . . . of the smallest moment to be 'true to nature' in these, if the playwright is false to nature in all the great verities of the heart and spirit of man."[2] He was far-sighted enough to see that the movement of the age was towards "a steadfast and growing attempt to treat the great realities of our modern life upon our stage, to bring our drama into relation with our literature, our religion, our art and our science, and to make it reflect the main movements of our national thought and character."[3] *Saints and Sinners* was an honest, if faulty, attempt to do this.

Mr. Jones has written many and diverse plays, some better and some worse; but none is so important in the development of dramatic tendencies as *Saints and Sinners. Judah* (1890) is an exceedingly interesting study of the stern religious conscience of English puritanism in Judah himself. Melodrama is disappearing and the satire is less crude. The material is tragic, but the dénouement is happy. It is an example of that genre which was to be known as "drama"—the modern attempt to meet the need which had been supplied by the tragi-comedy of an earlier day. In *The Middleman* (1889) he had returned to the theme of English commercialism. In *The Masqueraders* (1894) he made a violent attack on the hollow mockery of marriage and the sham life in high society. In 1896 was produced one of his most ambitious and perhaps his greatest play, *Michael and His Lost Angel*. The influence of Ibsen and the repercussion of the work of Sir Arthur Pinero are apparent in this drama, which is frankly tragic. Leaving on one side the irrelevant grounds on which the play was originally attacked, in particular its supposed irreverence for religion, one feels that it lacks the stuff of great tragedy. Aubrie Lesden is a subtle piece of characterization, but she is too small a human soul to bear the burden of real tragedy, and the hero, Michael Faversham, is at best a stiff and somewhat bloodless creature. *Saints and Sinners* is undoubtedly more faulty as a play, but it is a more

striking landmark in dramatic development. By the date of *Michael and His Lost Angel* domestic tragedy was almost a re-established form. We shall see very shortly what important work Sir Arthur Pinero had contributed to this genre by 1896. This play does not therefore demand the same attention that we bestowed on the early tragedy. It is intrinsically superior, but from an evolutionary point of view it must be regarded not as the first of a species but as a more highly developed example of a type which was revolutionary in its novelty in 1884 but which had reached its dull middle age by 1896.

In his later work Mr. Jones has often fallen under the sway of the aristocratic ideal, if one may so term it. In some of his most striking drama he has utilized the middle class life of the provinces as dramatic material, but in many of his plays he has preferred to take as his theme the lives of the richest and most select grade of society. Such a milieu is suitable for comedy, but even in his plays which are designed perhaps primarily for comic effect Mr. Jones is rarely able to escape a certain earnestness of purpose. *The Masqueraders* and *The Liars* (1897) are two good examples of ostensibly comic plays unmistakably marked by serious intention.

Notes

1. It should be explained that the play was published only in 1891. One of the most potent reasons for not publishing plays was the inadequacy of the Copyright regulations as between this country and U.S.A. The acting rights of a published play could not be secured in America. This was a great hardship which was removed by the American Copyright Act of 1891. Thenceforward dramatists could publish without fear of losing American stage rights.
2. Jones, H. A. Introd. to English translation of P. A. Filon, *The English Stage*, 1897, p. 12.
3. Jones, H. A. Introd. to English translation of Filon, *The English stage*, p. 15.

JAMES JOYCE

1882–1941

James Augustine Aloysius Joyce was born on the outskirts of Dublin on February 2, 1882. The oldest of ten children, he began his education at a Jesuit boarding school, but when his father could no longer afford the fees he transferred to the Jesuit Belvedere College in Dublin. As a student at University College, Dublin, he distanced himself from religion and from nationalist literary and political movements and distinguished himself academically. After graduating in 1902 he went to Paris to study medicine, supporting himself by teaching English, but returned to Dublin the following year to be with his dying mother. He began work on his autobiographical first novel and on short stories, and in 1904 met a woman from Galway, Nora Barnacle; when he returned to the continent he took her with him, though they married only in 1931 to protect their children's rights. Settling in Trieste in 1905, Joyce taught at the Berlitz School of Languages, numbering among his pupils the Italian novelist Italo Svevo. The First World War forced the family to move to Zürich in 1915.

Joyce's first book, a collection of short poems entitled *Chamber Music*, was published in 1907, followed by the collection of short stories *Dubliners* in 1914. Ezra Pound arranged for *A Portrait of the Artist as a Young Man* to be published in *The Egoist* in 1914–15, and the novel appeared in book form in 1916. Joyce's financial difficulties were eased somewhat by a Civil List grant that year and by the support of Harriet Shaw Weaver, editor of *The Egoist*.

In Zürich Joyce organized a company of Irish actors, who gave the first performance of his play *Exiles* (1918). In 1920 he moved to Paris on the urging of Pound; the serial publication of *Ulysses* in *The Little Review* in New York was halted that year because of an obscenity suit. The court scandal did Joyce little harm; his fame was, if anything, enhanced by a reputation for pornographic prose. *Ulysses* was finally published in Paris on his fortieth birthday, in 1922, but remained banned for many years in England and America. In the following years Joyce worked on his final novel, published in instalments as *Work in Progress* from 1928; it appeared complete as *Finnegans Wake* in 1939. His life at this time was darkened by severe eye problems, for which he had eleven operations between 1917 and 1930, and by the deteriorating mental health of his daughter. World War II forced him to leave Paris for Zürich, where he died on January 13, 1941.

General

WILLIAM YORK TINDALL
From "Myth and Symbol"
James Joyce:
His Way of Interpreting the Modern World
1950, pp. 95–105

S tephen Dedalus is fascinated by "suck," the word for water down a drain in the Wicklow Hotel. For more curious words he ransacks Skeat's *Etymological Dictionary*, adds them to his treasure house, and, taking them out, repeats them again and again. Although Stephen agrees that words are receptacles for thought, they acquire for him another value. Becoming intercessors, they stand between himself and reality. Through their agency alone he has "glimpses of the real world about him." Words do more than reveal that reality. They create it, and, as if God's compasses, draw significant form.

Like Rabelais, Joyce made grotesque catalogues of words. Like Nashe and Shakespeare, enamored of words in the age of discovery, he delighted in abundance. He called Shakespeare, whom he admired less as playwright than as poet, a "lord of language," richer than Dante and better to have on a desert island. Detesting "vague words for a vague emotion," he admired the precision of Flaubert. The Male Brutes who appear before unmanned Mr. Bloom in the brothel have only one thing to say. "Good!" they say. That is the *mot juste.* When the printers objected to the word "bloody" in the manuscript of *Dubliners*, Joyce replied that bloody is the one word in the language that can create the effect he wanted.

As he admired the words of other artists, so he exulted in his own command of what he considered the greatest of powers. To Eugene Jolas he announced: "I can do anything with language." His study of archaic language and his notes on living language in street or pub had made him master of all verbal effects from the divine speech of thunder to "lowquacity." The words "Sechseläuten" and "Lebensquatsch," which occur throughout *Finnegans Wake*, are examples of both kinds. Sechseläuten is the spring festival of Zürich, and Lebensquatsch or life's muddle is the interpretation by a Zürich waitress of Joyce's demand for lemon squash. He once told Frank Budgen that he had been working all day at two sentences of *Ulysses*: "Perfume of embraces all him assailed. With hungered flesh obscurely, he mutely craved to adore." When asked if he was seeking the *mot juste*, Joyce replied that he had the words already. What he wanted was a suitable order.

He composed a novel as great poets compose their poems. Under his hand all the resources of word, rhythm, and tone conspired to create intricate beauty. His novels are more like poems or symphonies or statues than like ordinary novels. Maybe they are not novels at all but works of their own kind like *Tristram Shandy* or *Gargantua*, which we call novels for want of a word for them. We must approach Joyce's greater works as we would a poem or a symphony. That reader who read *Ulysses* as if it were a common thing would be disappointed.

According to Ernst Cassirer's *Language and Myth*, words, which precede things in our minds, are the only way of knowing things. It is only after naming a thing that we control it. Therefore primitive men confused words with things, and, attributing magic power to words, used them for ritual or incantation. Since the power of the real thing was contained in its name, the word, as the power of powers, became God or His source or His creative instrument, and the agent for transforming chaos into cosmos. From this holy origin the word developed into a sign or symbol for something else, and, divested of potency in modern times, became a convenience. But the artist, recovering the ancient veneration of the word, recovers something of its potency. He uses it with reverence but without the limitations that surrounded his ancestors. What was once the means of practical magic becomes through his conscious control the means of aesthetic magic. Unlike a savage, the artist knows the word as the mind's revelation and the revelation of external reality.

What is true of the word is true of myth. Myth and language, Cassirer says, have a common origin in metaphor or analogy. Word, myth, and metaphor, coming from man's own being, are not imitations of nature. Each of them is a way of conceiving it, and each is a form of expression. What these expressive forms say cannot be said in terms of other things; for each of these forms gives its own insight into reality. Joyce, the master of words and analogies, was foremost among those who, reviving myth, have used its insights for modern art.

Ulysses is modelled more or less loosely upon an ancient myth. Joyce's Homeric parallel, as it is called, was the first of his devices to become known. Joyce told Valéry Larbaud, who told the world; and Stuart Gilbert gave more than enough weight to the details. We know, therefore, that each of Joyce's main characters corresponds to one of Homer's. Bloom is Ulysses, Stephen is Telemachus, and Mrs. Bloom, who stays at home with the suitors, is Penelope. Her concern with metempsychosis supports the Homeric parallel by suggesting that Joyce's characters are the reincarnation of Homer's. Like the *Odyssey*, *Ulysses* is divided into three parts: the hunt of Telemachus for his father, the wanderings of Odysseus, and the return to Ithaca. Each episode of *Ulysses* corresponds to an episode of the *Odyssey*. But these episodes do not occur in the original order, for other than Homeric considerations helped to determine Joyce's structure. As he used Vico for *Finnegans Wake*, so for *Ulysses* he used Homer. To some extent structural devices, both Vico and Homer were of more use as expressive analogies. By references and hints, that are sometimes grotesque or trivial in character, Joyce suggests Homer. It is Homer's function to suggest in turn the central themes of *Ulysses*.

When the Citizen in Barney Kiernan's pub throws the biscuit tin at Mr. Bloom, he is parodying the Cyclops, but the Cyclops supports Joyce's point about Irish nationalism. Mr. Bloom's cigar, that corresponds to the stake with which

Odysseus blinded the one-eyed giant, typifies Joyce's way of suggesting this reciprocal relationship between the ancient world and Dublin. "You don't grasp my point," says Homeric Mr. Bloom. Gerty MacDowell and Nausicaa, those lovely seaside girls, help each other on their beaches to confirm the nature of woman. Metaphors of wind and all the winds of rhetoric make the newspaper office as windy as the home of Aeolus and our world.

Sometimes Joyce's characters play double parts. Mrs. Bloom, as both Penelope and Calypso, brings her husband home while keeping him abroad. In the fourth chapter, Calypso is symbolized by the picture Mr. Bloom has cut out from *Photo Bits*, but in the picture of that nymph he sees Mrs. Bloom. The ancient mariner in the cabman's shelter is a surrogate for Mr. Bloom. As Odysseus tells lies to Eumaeus about his voyages, so the dubious sailor tells lies to the belated company. Buck Mulligan, the "usurper" of the first chapter, is one of the suitors who keep Telemachus from his heritage and waste his substance. Yet Mulligan is one of the few in Dublin who have not enjoyed Mrs. Bloom.

In the third chapter, where the shifting sands suggest Proteus, Stephen is not only Telemachus searching the flux for a father but he is Menelaus as well, attempting to hold slippery reality in his hands. Change is symbolized by more than sand and tide. Words change, as every philologist knows, and all other things, assuming disguises, are "clutched at, gone, not here." The wonderful dog, trotting on twinkling shanks at the lacefringe of the tide, parodies the shapes of Proteus. A hare, a buck, a bear, a wolf, a calf, and a panther by turns, the dog at last sniffs rapidly "like a dog." The owners of this dog seem gypsies because Proteus is Egyptian. Stephen's changing mind passes from gypsies and Egyptians to gypsy-words:

> White thy fambles, red thy gan
> And thy quarrons dainty is.

These words, which, when looked up, are not half so bad as they sound, are by Richard Head, whose strange seventeenth-century verses invite Stephen to compose verses of his own. "Here. Put a pin in that chap," he says in the endeavor to fix Protean flux by art.

The "old chap picking his tootles" in the Burton restaurant, where Mr. Bloom goes in hope of food, suggests the cannibalism of Homer's Laestrygonians, and so does the limerick about the reverend Mr. MacTrigger, the missionary had by his flock for lunch. The man-eating Laestrygonians themselves, descending from their cliffs upon the black ships of Odysseus, are represented by the gulls, swooping from their heights about Anna Liffey to pounce on Mr. Bloom's Banbury cakes. For the curious ways in which Joyce recalls Scylla and Charybdis and other Homeric episodes one may consult Stuart Gilbert and Frank Budgen.

Victor Bérard's theory about the Semitic origins of the *Odyssey* increased, for Joyce, the likeness of Odysseus and Mr. Bloom. Not, of course, that Odysseus was a Jew, but he is the hero of a more or less Phoenician document in which a Jew could feel at home or away from it. "Jewgreek is greekjew. Extremes meet," says Lynch in the Circe episode or the scene in Bella Cohen's brothel. To strengthen the parallel Joyce also compares Bloom with those other restless Semites Sinbad the Sailor and the Wandering Jew.

Although an extraordinary linguist, Joyce knew little Greek—as we might expect of one who specialized in patristic Latin and modern languages. "*Oinopa ponton*" from the *Odyssey* and "polyfizzyboisterous seas" from the *Iliad* are embedded in *Ulysses* and *Finnegans Wake*, but these are the most familiar of Homeric tags. Buck Mulligan's "*thalatta*" is not Homeric Greek. There is enough of Homer around, however, to keep the attentive reader aware that in some sense *Ulysses* is a modern version of an ancient myth. To find in what sense *Ulysses* is a myth we must define myth.

Myth is the most difficult thing in the world. One man's definition contradicts another's, but most definers agree that since myth is pre-logical, it all but evades our thought. Many with whom Joyce was familiar—Vico, Frazer, Jung, and Lévy-Bruhl—had theories about myth. . . .

It may be possible to reconcile . . . discouraging differences of opinion, especially those of the psychoanalysts and the anthropologists, and to arrive at a workable definition ⟨of myth⟩. Since the psychoanalysts are concerned with the individual and the anthropologists with society, there could be less contradiction between their ideas than they think. European literary myth, which is what we are after, may serve individual and social purposes at once. Expressing the individual, it may unite the group. Here is a composite definition, which, although incomplete and doing justice to neither side, seems as good as any: Myth is a dreamlike narrative in which the individual's central concerns are united with society, time, and the universe. Both expression and sanction, it organizes experience, uniting fact with imagination, the conscious with the unconscious, the present with the past, man with nature, and the individual with the group. It gives values to reality and makes one feel at home. Allusions to the *Odyssey* do not make *Ulysses* mythical. *Ulysses* is mythical because it is a narrative which, while uniting Joyce with tradition, projects his central concerns.

Joyce considered Homer's myth the complete expression of man. In the departure of a family man from his home and in his return Joyce saw everybody's pattern. By adapting this general pattern to his own purposes, Joyce provided support for himself. Lonely and eccentric, he could feel one with mankind. His exile seemed only a departure to be followed by return. Away from home, he could feel at home. In the hunt of Telemachus for his father, Joyce found sanction for himself as artist. Telemachus can represent not only man's search for social support but the artist's search for humanity. Finding his father, Telemachus fulfills the wish of every man and every artist. Exile, home, humanity, and art, Joyce's concerns, found expression in Homer's *Odyssey*.

But the Homeric pattern is only one level of the narrative Joyce composed. Another level is the Christian pattern. As we have seen, Bloom is not only Odysseus but Jesus-God. These traditional levels, however, are less important than the main level of Joyce's myth: the story of Stephen Dedalus and Mr. Bloom in Dublin or the present, the particular, and the personal. *Ulysses* is a narrative composition of three levels, to which, by allusion, Joyce added others of less importance. His myth is not the *Odyssey* but *Ulysses*.

Stephen had served Joyce in an earlier myth. *A Portrait of the Artist* embodies the myth of Daedalus. Finding expression for himself in the eighth book of *Metamorphoses*, Joyce connected Ovid's myth with personal history. References to the fabulous artificer throughout *A Portrait of the Artist* and in *Ulysses*, before its climax, justify exile and explain frustration. The myth of Stephen and Daedalus, projecting Joyce's quarrel with society, expressed his condition and his desire. This composite myth united him with other exiles. All artists of the past century, or all whom he admired, composed a group in which, by no means least, he took his place. Any tradition was comforting. But to express fulfillment he had to exchange a parallel no longer adequate for that of Telemachus and Odysseus.

As the artist, ill at ease apart from society, finds justification in myth, society, feeling guilt for its treatment of the artist, finds similar justification. W. S. Gilbert's *Patience*, or the myth of the artist in reverse, defends Philistine contempt of art and sanctions exile. The artist is exiled because he is a sham. For a time Bunthorne can fool the ladies. But, finding him out, they turn with rewards to Archibald, who not only puts on commonplace pants but writes commonplace verses and will, no doubt, write books of the month. They turn also to heavy dragoons, but that is only natural. This opera, revived from time to time to support our ritual, delights us with music and, like all myths, with truth.

In the Circe or brothel episode of *Ulysses*, Stephen says, "The rite is the poet's rest." Joyce's support of the artist's ritual continues through the first half of *Finnegans Wake* in the story of exiled Shem. But, becoming one with his social brother, Shem takes his place in a larger tradition than that of exile. Becoming one with mankind, he takes his place in time. *Finnegans Wake* is the myth of eternal history. Joyce's narrative of the Earwicker family in the cycles of time sanctions humanity. Uniting the temporal and the eternal, the unconscious and the conscious, the individual and the universal, and all other opposites, it is perhaps the most comprehensive of myths.

Joyce built his earlier myths upon a foundation of ancient myth. The foundation of *Finnegans Wake* is philosophical. *Finnegans Wake* is not myth because it embodies Vico's cycles or Bruno's contraries but because it projects by narrative Joyce's central concerns and those of other men. In the course of this narrative he alludes to all the myths, legends, and fairy tales of the world: Leda and the Swan, Cinderella, Mutt and Jeff. Such parallels give richness and depth to the narrative. The sweet vision of the twenty-eight girls is projected as a fairy tale of Lady Shortbred in her Sundae dress and of Prince Le Monade, who serves not only as lemonade in this candied fantasy but as Bruno's monad or elementary form. The mythical stories of the Prankquean and of the Norwegian captain, both of whom go and return three times, are original variations on an old pattern. Implying death and birth again, most great myths are cyclical. *Finnegans Wake* is in the great tradition.

A myth composed by a modern artist, however, is different from ancient myth. More conscious for one thing, and more private for another, modern myth seems more elaborate and contrived than myths of the past. It was in part to remedy this defect that Joyce used old myths for new narratives. Familiar myth, moreover, guarantees a public level for new myth.

A measure of the difference between Joyce and the primitive myth-maker is provided by Joyce's attitude. The combination of heroic Odysseus with bourgeois Mr. Bloom, of Nausicaa with Gerty MacDowell, or of Daedalus with Stephen is not without ironic purpose or effect. The primitive mind is innocent of irony. At best, whether ironic or solemn, the modern myth is pseudomyth. But its function for the maker is identical with that of ancient myth. And if, like Joyce's myths, the modern myth has a public level, it can do for us what myths did for our ancestors. *Ulysses* and *Finnegans Wake* have a social function; for modern man needs to be assured of his humanity.

Joyce was but one of many who revived old myths in order to make new ones. Yeats drew upon Leda and the Swan and Dove and Virgin to furnish the great wheel of history, and all reviving gods attend its revolutions. D. H. Lawrence drew upon Genesis, the fantasies of Wagner, and the myths of ancient Mexico for his novels. These narratives of death and rebirth contain a private level—not altogether without social

meaning—of the little black, horse-loving proletarian who always runs off with the duchess. And in *The Waste Land* Eliot combined the quest for the Grail and the resurrection of Frazer's gods with a suggested narrative of modern London. Overtones of Dante and the Christian myth found more emphatic, but still indirect, expression in *Four Quartets*, where cycles of time lead us to the point of eternity. These works are like Joyce's works in kind. Not all good literature of our time is myth, but much of it seems to be or, at least, to be trying to be.

MARSHALL McLUHAN
From "James Joyce: Trivial and Quadrivial"
Thought, Spring 1953, pp. 75–87

We've had our day at triv and quad and writ our bit as
    intermidgets.

Many people would probably welcome an elucidation of Joyce's celebrated retort to a critic of his puns: "Yes, some of them are trivial and some of them are quadrivial." For, as usual, Joyce was being quite precise and helpful. He means literally that his puns are crossroads of meaning in his communication network, and that his techniques for managing the flow of messages in his network were taken from the traditional disciplines of grammar, logic, rhetoric, on one hand, and of arithmetic, geometry, music, and astronomy, on the other.

Language as Model of Culture

At the time when Joyce was studying the trivium with the Jesuits there had occurred in the European world a rebirth of interest in the traditional arts of communication. Indirectly, this had come about through the reconstruction of past cultures as carried on by nineteenth-century archaeology and anthropology. For these new studies had directed attention to the role of language and writing in the formation of societies and the transmission of culture. And the total or gestalt approach natural in the study of primitive cultures had favored the study of language as part of the entire cultural network. Language was seen as inseparable from the tool-making and economic life of these peoples. It was not studied in abstraction from the practical concerns of society.

It was at this time that Vico came into his own. At the beginning of the eighteenth century Vico's *Scienza Nuova* had proposed language as the basis for anthropology and a new science of history. Extant languages, he argued, could be regarded as working models of all past culture, because language affords an unbroken line of communication with the totality of the human past. The modalities of grammar, etymology and word-formation could be made to yield a complete account of the economic, social and spiritual adventures of mankind. If geology could reconstruct the story of the earth from the inert strata of rock and clay, the *scienza nuova* could do much better with the living languages of men. Previously, historians had attempted to create working models of some segment of the human past in their narratives. These were necessarily hypothetical structures eked out by scraps of recorded data. The new historian need never attempt again to revivify the past by imaginative art, because it is all present in language. And it is present, Joyce would add, as a newsreel represents actual events. We can sit back and watch the "all night news reel" of *Finnegans Wake* reveal as interfused the whole human drama past and present. This can be done by directing an analytical camera-eye upon the movements within and between words.

The Work of the Symbolists

Joyce came to this kind of awareness through the symbolists. It is typical of them that vers libre, for example, should be a return to the formal rhythms of early litanies, hymns, and to the psalter. But going with this liturgical bias in art was a new sense of the neglected resources of classical rhetoric. Until the eighteenth century, rhetoric had been taught much as Cicero and Quintilian had presented it. But the ancient linguistic theory which had supported the rhetorical structure had receded. Newtonian science knocked ancient rhetoric off its much reduced pedestal by making the spatial and pictorial aspects of the external world supreme. So that from Thomson to Tennyson poets are concerned to establish and communicate states of mind in terms of external landscape. Psychology is managed in terms of external landscape. Psychology is managed in terms of space. The dimensions of time, tradition, and language are given minimal scope. But it was precisely to these neglected aspects of art and language that the later nineteenth century was turning. And the symbolists habitually work in terms of an interior landscape in which by the juxtaposition of more than one time (e.g., the opening of "Prufrock" or *The Waste Land* of Mr. Eliot) the poet reacquires his proprietorship of the human past.

It is necessary to see the century of neglect of the ancient trivium in order to explain how the revival of the trivium could have been what it was. The new context provided by anthropology and modern psychology really put grammar, logic, and rhetoric in an ancient rather than in a medieval or Renaissance context. Modern linguistic theory is quite sympathetic to the semimagical views of the ancients. Our idea of language as gesture, as efficacious, and as representing a total human response, is a much better base for a study of the figures and arts of speech than any merely rationalistic approach can provide. But for Mallarmé, Valéry, Joyce, and Eliot the figures of rhetoric are discriminated as notable postures of the human mind. The linguistic studies of Edward Sapir and B. L. Whorf have lately shown that language is not only the storehouse of scientific thought. All actual and potential scientific theories are implicit in the verbal structure of the culture associated with them. By 1885 Mallarmé had formulated and utilized in his poetry these concepts about the nature of language uniting science and philology, which nowadays are known as "metalinguistics." However, these views of languages were commonplaces to Cratylus, Varro, and Philo Judaeus. They were familiar to the Church Fathers, and underlay the major schools of scriptural exegesis. If "four-level exegesis" is back in favor again as the staple of the "new criticism," it is because the poetic objects which have been made since 1880 frequently require such techniques for their elucidation. *Finnegans Wake* offers page by page much of the labyrinthine intricacy of a page of the Book of Kells. And the central feature of the *Wake* is the exegesis of a letter dug up by the musical fowl Belinda. Pope wrote A *Key to the Lock* by way of an elaborate exegesis of the symbolic senses of his poem. Joyce made his poem in the shape of the key which unlocks it. But for Joyce as much as for St. Augustine the trivial and quadrivial arts form a harmony of philology and science which is indispensable to the exegetist of scripture and of language, too.

St. Augustine

One way of seeing how ancient philology was linked to the quadrivial arts is found in St. Augustine's treatise *De Musica*, which is a discussion of metrics, astronomy and prosody. In the milieu of St. Augustine it was natural to consider metrics in relation to numbers and arithmetic, for the entire order of the cosmos was supposed to be based on number just as all earthly music was but an approximation to the music of the spheres. Music was, esthetically speaking, the meeting place of poetics and mathematics, of grammatica and astronomy. Each letter of the alphabet had its numerical power attached to it quite as definitely as Rimbaud joined vowel and color. So that to speak of medieval illumination, as Ruskin did, as the art of color chords would have seemed as trite and obvious to St. Augustine as it is basic for the work of Joyce. For example, one of the most persistent and deeply embedded motifs in *Ulysses* is that of the "series of empty fifths" which Stephen plays on Bella Cohen's piano, expounding their ritual perfection "because the fundamental and the dominant are separated by the greatest possible interval which . . . is the greatest possible ellipse. Consistent with the ultimate return. The Octave . . . What went forth to the ends of the world to traverse not itself. God, the sun, Shakespeare, a commercial traveller . . . The longest way round is the shortest way home." The musical chord is a means of linking with the stages of human apprehension, the growth of the soul, the movement of the sun through the zodiacal signs, the Incarnation and Ascension, the mental labyrinth of art and the cloacal labyrinth of commerce. Nor are these diverse themes merely introduced casually in the Circe episode. They pervade this epic which unites the trivial and quadrivial arts by means of the same solar ritual which underlies Homeric and other epic structures. Every incident becomes a point crossed and recrossed by the seven arts. For example, the above theme of the return and the commercial traveller recurs in the Ithaca episode in connection with Bloom as the Wandering Jew. The "technic" of the episode is "catechism (impersonal)."

> Would the departed never nowhere nohow reappear?
> Ever he would wander, selfcompelled, to the extreme limit of his cometary orbit, beyond the fixed stars and variable suns and telescopic planets, astronomical waifs and strays, to the extreme boundary of space passing from land to land, among peoples, amid events. Somewhere imperceptibly he would hear and somehow reluctantly, suncompelled, obey the summons of recall.

Astronomy is operative in two modes in *Ulysses*, an Eastern and a Western mode, as befits a work which follows the course of the rising and setting sun. Moreover, the opening episode of the book, organized in accord with the art of theology, is liturgical. One of the little epics contained analogously within the larger action of *Ulysses* concerns the wanderings of a cake of lemon soap purchased by Bloom early in the day. At one level the soap is a comic and cloacal variant on the ritual labyrinth traversed by Bloom that day (Pope's *Rape of the Lock* is a similar comic epic ending in a similar apotheosis). The soap says from the heavens:

> We're a capital couple are Bloom and I;
> He brightens the earth, I polish the sky.

At another level the soap is a sign of grace uniting earthly and stellar, hermetic and astrologic, East and West labyrinths. These two levels of reality, which are in conflict all during Bloomsday, are thus reconciled among the stars. In the same context Dante is invoked obliquely as another sign of the reconciliation of Bloom and Stephen. For Dante, like Joyce and Eliot, employs grace to reconcile East and West. Reconciliation is not merging, however. This is made explicit in the Ithaca episode where Bloom's "Eastern" creed of perfectibility, "vital growth through convulsions of metamorphosis" is counterpointed with Stephen's "Western" way: "He affirmed his significance as a conscious rational animal proceeding syllogistically from the known to the unknown and a conscious rational reagent between a micro- and macrocosm ineluctably constructed upon the incertitude of the void." These two labyrinths are counterpointed throughout *Ulysses*. The one is "Eastern," hermetic, earthly and cloacal, proceeding by peristaltic convulsions to metamorphosis (e.g., the Marxian materialistic dialectic of history). The other is "Western," a cognitive labyrinth cognizant and constitutive of the word and of analogy. As a true analogist Joyce attempts no reduction of these realities, but orders their ineluctable modalities to the reconciliation of vision rather than of fusion. But, roughly, the two modes correspond to quadrivium and trivium.

Ulysses as concerned primarily with Bloom carries him over the sea of matter. His quest is social, ethical, political, in contrast to the spiritual quest of Stephen. Joyce pursues a rigorous classical decorum in his delineation of these themes which can best be enjoyed by a reader possessing some acquaintance with the traditional scope of the trivium and the quadrivium. As St. Thomas says (*De Trinitate* V, 3) "These subjects are known as the trivium and quadrivium because by them, as if by certain roads, the eager mind enters into the secrets of philosophy." They are propaedeutic to other studies.

If St. Augustine's *De Musica* affords a view of the traditional way of seeing the relation between metrics and astronomy, his *De Doctrina Christiana* links the trivium and quadrivium to the business of scriptural exegesis and sacred oratory. It amounts to an adaptation of the Ciceronian ideal of the *doctus orator* to the new tasks of the Christian theologian and teacher.

The Level of Rhetoric

In this regard Cicero's *De Oratore* is itself a charter of classical humanism, an attempt to unify the Graeco-Roman culture in a vision of the ideal orator. As such it underlies not only St. Augustine and St. Jerome but most medieval and Renaissance books of advice to princes and courtiers. However, it is far from being a mere resumé of ancient cultural ideals, for Cicero is consciously pre-Socratic in his bias. His synthesis is directed to the end of forming the perfect man of action rather than the man of speculation and science. He is Isocratean and Sophist, therefore, rather than Socratic or Platonic and Aristotelian. This preference, as well as the conflict it involves, has dominated the culture of Western Europe until today. Joyce gives these themes full play in his work. His Bloom is Homer's prudent "man of many devices" and he is also Cicero's orator.

Since the principal sphere of rhetoric and social guidance is advertising in these latter days of the Gutenberg era, Bloom is presented as a copywriter and canvasser for ads. He is peripatetic, encyclopedic, and able, like Cicero's orator, to speak eloquently on all subjects. As the Citizen says in the Cyclops episode:

I declare to my antimacassar if you took up a straw from the bloody floor and if you said to Bloom: *Look at, Bloom, Do you see that straw? That's a straw.* Declare to my aunt he'd talk about it for an hour so he would and talk steady.

At this particular moment Bloom is elsewhere examining *The Awful Disclosures of Maria Monk* and Aristotle's *Metaphysics*. As type of the encyclopedic and prudent citizen Bloom's network of communication stretches from heaven to earth and includes especially all aspects of corporate social life. With respect to the conditions of modern life Joyce characterizes Bloom with exact classical decorum as the perfect rhetorician and type of Homer's "man of many devices."

What were habitually his final meditations? Of some one sole unique advertisement to cause passers to stop in wonder, a poster novelty, with all extraneous accretions excluded, reduced to its simplest and most efficient terms not exceeding the span of casual vision and congruous with the velocity of modern life.

The ideal orator will be a man of encyclopedic knowledge because learning precedes eloquence. And because he will be the type of the perfect citizen he will be eloquent about everything which concerns corporate life. But eloquence implies great tact, a sense of the propriety of word and thing as befits each contingency. Bloomsday is a prolonged demonstration of Bloom's learned sense of decorum. But decorum in language or action is of all things, observed Aristotle, in common with antiquity, the hardest thing to hit, calling, as it does, for an agile perception and adjustment to the fluctuating circumstances of times, places, and persons.

Joyce underlines the skill of Bloom's social decorum in a peculiarly witty way. Homer's Odysseus learns from Circe that after passing the Sirens there were two courses open to him. One is by way of the Wandering Rocks, which Jason alone had passed in the Argo. The other is the way of Scylla and Charybdis, rock and whirlpool. Odysseus avoids the labyrinth of the Wandering Rocks. But Bloom navigates both labyrinths safely, thus excelling Odysseus. The Rocks are citizens and society seen in abstraction as mindless, Martian mechanisms. The "stone" men are children of the sun, denizens of space, exempt from time, and linked with the Druidic culture. Opposed to them are "The Dead" (see last story in *Dubliners*) children of the moon, the Celtic twilight ("cultic twalette"), moving in the aquacities of time, memory, and sentiment. On these dual labyrinths of stone and water Joyce has built almost every line he has written. And all the antithetic pairs of the *Wake* embrace these polarities as H.C.E. bricklayer and A.L.P. river, male and female; Shem and Shaun, poet and policeman. Since, moreover, the letters of the alphabet are easily polarized in the same way, it is a matter of main consequence to recognize their hermetic signatures in order to get around in the *Wake*.

In the same episode of the Wandering Rocks there is another aspect of decorum seen in the contrasting monologues of Stephen and Bloom. The leaping movement of Stephen's wide-ranging thoughts counterpoint the slow-footed earth-bound progress of Bloom as each threads his way through a world of contrived illusions and fake identities.

Level of the Poet and Being

If Bloom represents the actualized modern embodiment of classical decorum in *Ulysses*, Stephen illustrates the sense in which the poet is dispensed from the bonds of social decorum. The Aeolus or newspaper episode in which the art is rhetoric shows Stephen declining the editorial invitation to a journalistic career. The episode opens with an evocation of the stone-steel labyrinth of the Dublin trainway system and then shifts to the analogous network of movable type and the world of spatial communication controlled by the press. (Mr. Eliot's *Coriolan* poems traverse the same labyrinths of spatial organization represented by government in a technological age.) By counterpoint, this episode concerned with the spatial power and emptiness of the press, proceeds by reminiscences of great orations (communication in time) and moves backwards out of the one-day press world to the stone labyrinth of Sinai and the Mosaic fables of the law. Professor MacHugh recalls "a speech made by John F. Taylor at the college historical society" in a debate about the revival of the Irish tongue. Taylor's argument is that "had the youthful Moses listened to and accepted that view of life (i.e., the Egyptian-English view of Hebrew-Irish culture and language). . . . He would never have spoken with the Eternal amid lightnings on Sinai's mountaintop nor ever have come down with the light of inspiration shining in his countenance, and bearing in his arms the tables of the law graven in the language of the outlaw."

That this speech has the same central role in *Ulysses* as the Anna Livia passage in the *Wake* may be concluded from the fact that they are the only two passages that Joyce ever consented to record for gramophone. Stephen's comment on this speech is his "parable of the plums," after which the group noisily recedes from the stone-steel labyrinth of the press world to the aquatic labyrinth of the pub. In the *Wake* Shem the penman is, like Moses, an "outlex." The seer cannot be a rhetor. He does not speak for effect, but that we may know. He is also an outlet, a shaman, a scapegoat. And the artist, in order that he may perform his katharsis-purgative function, must mime all things. (The katharsis-purgative role of the Herculean culture-hero dominates the nightworld of the *Wake* where the hero sets Alpheus, the river of speech and collective consciousness, to the task of cleansing the Augean stables of thought and feeling.) As mime, the artist cannot be the prudent and decorous Ulysses, but appears as a sham. As sham and mime he undertakes not the ethical quest but the quest of the great fool. He must become all things in order to reveal all. And to be all he must empty himself. Strictly within the bounds of classical decorum Joyce saw that, unlike the orator, the artist cannot properly speak with his own voice. The ultimate artist can have no style of his own but must be an "outlex" through which the multiple aspects of reality can utter themselves. That the artist should intrude his personal idiom between thing and reader is literally impertinence. Decorum permits the artist as a young man *(The Portrait)* to speak with his master's voice—the voice of Pater, his father in art. (Joyce like Chesterton delighted in the multivalent wit of nature and reality so that, no matter how far-fetched his analogues and paradoxes, they are never concocted nor forced. They not only bear but require intent scrutiny.)

Whereas the ethical world of *Ulysses* is presented in terms of well-defined human types the more metaphysical world of the *Wake* speaks and moves before us with the gestures of being itself. It is a nightworld and, literally, as Joyce reiterates, is "abcedminded." Letters ("every letter is a godsend"), the frozen, formalized gestures of remote ages of collective experience, move before us in solemn morrice. They are the representatives of age-old adequation of mind and things, enacting the drama of the endless adjustment of the interior acts and dispositions of the mind to the outer world. The drama of cognition itself. For it is in the drama of cognition, the stages of apprehension, that Joyce found the archetype of poetic imitation. He seems to have been the first to see that the dance of being, the nature imitated by the arts, has its primary analogue in the activity of the exterior and interior senses. Joyce was aware that this doctrine (that sensation is imitation because the exterior forms are already in a new matter) is implicit in Aquinas. He made it explicit in *Stephen Hero* and the *Portrait*, and founded his entire poetic activity on *these* analogical proportions of the senses.

Delivery

The doctrine of decorum, the foundation of classical rhetoric, is a profoundly analogical doctrine, so that to discuss it as it operates in Joyce is to be at the center of his communication network. In *Ulysses* each character is discriminated by his speech and gestures, and the whole work stands midway between narrative and drama. But the *Wake* is primarily dramatic and the techniques proper to this form are taken from the fourth part of rhetoric, "pronuntiatio" or action and delivery. This division of rhetoric was a crux of communication theory in former times, being the crossroads of rhetoric, psychology, and other disciplines. St. Thomas discusses the issue, for example (*Summa Theologica* I, 57, 4, ad 3), apropos of the modes of communication between men and angels:

> Since, therefore, the angels know corporeal things and their dispositions, they can thereby know what is passing in the appetite or in the imaginative apprehension of brute animals, and even of man, in so far as man's sensitive appetite sometimes acts under the influence of some bodily impression.

The analogical relation between exterior posture and gesture and the interior movements and dispositions of the mind is the irreducible basis of drama. In the *Wake* this appears everywhere. So that any attempt to reduce its action, at any point, to terms of univocal statement, results in radical distortion. Joyce's insistence on the "abcedminded" nature of his drama can be illustrated from his attitude to the alphabet throughout. He was familiar with the entire range of modern archaeological and anthropological study of pre-alphabetic syllabaries and hieroglyphics, including the traditional kabbalistic lore. To this knowledge he added the Thomistic insights into the relation of these things with mental operations. So that the polarity between H.C.E. and A.L.P. involves, for one thing, the relation between the agent and possible intellect. H.C.E. is mountain, male and active. A.L.P. is river, female and passive. But ALP equals mountain and historically "H" is interfused with "A," and "A" is both ox-face and plough first of arts and letters; so that, dramatically, the roles of HCE and ALP are often interchangeable. Punning on "Dublin," he constantly invites us to regard his drama as the story of "doublends joined." Irremediably analogical, Joyce's work moves as naturally on the metaphysical as on the naturalistic plane.

The Liturgical Level

But there is always the liturgical level as well. Nothing Joyce ever wrote lacks that dimension. One significance of Stephen's surname Dedalus (the French form of Daedalus) is that Daedalus, the inventor of the labyrinth, was accredited with having been the first to reduce the ancient initiation rituals to the form of art. That is to say, Daedalus was the first to grasp the relation between the pagan rebirth rituals and the labyrinthine retracings of the artistic process. The pagan rituals were imitations of nature *in sua operatione*, because the soul imprisoned in existence could only be released by retracing the stages of its fall and descent through the various degrees of material being. Necessarily, therefore, all artistic imitation first arose from the pagan liturgies or mysteries. If Daedalus was the first to note this relation, Joyce was the first to see in these ancient rituals of descent and return the perfect externalization, in drama and gesture, of the stages of human apprehension. The retracing of any moment of cognition will thus provide the unique artistic form of that moment. And its art form coincides with its quiddity, except that the artist arrests what is otherwise fleeting. (M.D. Chénu, O.P., has explained the larger pattern of the *Summa* of St. Thomas to be based on the Neo-Platonic theme of emanation and return which pagan rituals have derived and expressed in the pattern of solar movement: "This brief scheme . . . is utilized by St. Thomas not as a commodious frame in which he can dispose at his pleasure the immense material of his sacred doctrine, but as an order of knowledge, which produces intelligibility at the heart of revealed truth" [*Cross Currents* II 2, p. 72]).

It is the liturgical sense of Joyce that enables him to manipulate such encyclopedic lore, guided by his analogical awareness of liturgy as both an order of knowledge and an order of grace.

In this respect it could be suggested that Austin Farrer's *A Rebirth of Images* (Dacre Press, 1949), which is a commentary on the Book of Revelation, is probably the ideal introduction to the work of Joyce. His conclusions are relevant to the Joycean procedure: "If John is keeping so many concerns in mind, following the symbolical week and the sacred year, the scheme of traditional eschatology, of Christ's prophecy, and of multiple Old Testament typology, how can he move at all, and how can he keep his pattern firm? The diagram supplies the answer [a diagram of the Hebrew plus the Christian liturgical year laid out on the zodiacal plan]. He makes each movement of the poem by working round the diagram: each such movement, or group of such movements, is a day in the week, a quarter of the year, and so on—he will never get lost. The diagram, as St. John comes back over it, retains the enrichments of meaning with which the previous movements have overlaid it. These afford materials for the fresh movement and give rise to that continually varied embellishment of a standing cyclic pattern which is the literary miracle of the Apocalypse. . . . St. John started with the diagram ready drawn . . . it was not enough to contemplate the diagram; the diagram must, as it were, be persuaded to speak, and, in its own order, to reveal its mysteries. As the mind passed over and over it, the several stages of ascent were built up . . . until the World to Come burst on the seer's vision, charged with the weight of all he had seen by the way.

"What it is so hard for us to recover is the thought-world in which the diagram, and the diagram simply, could be viewed as a sacred and illuminating thing." But such a thought-world is entirely congenial to the twentieth century as its art and criticism testify. Representative as he is of that return to the plenary scope of patristic exegesis, Dr. Farrer unintentionally provides a splendid introduction to Joyce (as Joyce does to these other fields). This can perhaps be taken as a mark of the profound coherence of modern culture when viewed at its best levels.

The Cyclic Pattern

As Hugh Kenner indicated in his essay on the *Portrait*, the first page provides the standing cyclic pattern which is the track which Joyce traverses over and over again with deepening awareness and ever richer epiphanies of being. That track is the order of the expanding sensuous, moral and intellectual development of a human being. It is an order of knowledge. Because it is a standing cycle, Joyce can record the growth of an artist's mind as a portrait rather than a narrative. In *Ulysses* Bloom's day is a solar cycle including the social and political dimensions. *Finnegans Wake* is a full-scale liturgical cycle involving the total experience of the race. The *Wake* follows the track of the Christian liturgical year, but at any moment the four quarters of this track may shift to H.C.E.'s four-poster bed or to the four evangelists. It is at some moments a hippodrome, at another a conducted tour of a museum, or a radio-television network. The use of these analogous patterns as projective techniques is parallel to what Dr. Farrer notes in St. John: "For the already written part of his work becomes formative of the rest. . . . In writing the Candlestick-vision, he underwent the control of Zecariah and Daniel, in writing the Seven Messages he underwent the control of the Candlestick-vision. . . . The vision thrust upon him the symbol of the

lamps and stars, and of their mysterious equivalence. . . . Passing back over the text of the vision, he heard in it the messages of Christ to the Seven Churches. . . . The meaning of the Name works itself out in the short pattern of the Greeting, Doxology, Advent, Promise and Amen . . . the short pattern has set forth the Name, but a longer pattern must set forth the short pattern. . . . The fulfilment must begin in further oracle or vision."

STEPHEN HEATH
From "Ambiviolences: Notes for Reading Joyce" (1972)
Post-Structuralist Joyce
eds. Derek Attridge and Daniel Ferrer
1984, pp. 31–47

For the Ancients the verb 'to read' had a meaning that is worth recalling and bringing out with a view to an understanding of literary practice. 'To read' was also 'to pick up', 'to pluck', 'to keep a watch on', 'to recognize traces', 'to take', 'to steal'. 'To read' thus denotes an aggressive participation, an active appropriation of the other. 'To write' would be 'to read' become production, industry: writing-reading, paragrammatic activity, would be the aspiration towards a total aggressiveness and participation. (Julia Kristeva[1])

The prouts who will invent a writing there ultimately is the poeta, still more learned, who discovered the raiding there originally. That's the point of eschatology our book of kills reaches for now in soandso many counterpoint words. (*FW* 482.31–4)

Reading Joyce remains a problem. This can be seen easily enough from the two rigorously complementary poles of critical reaction to *Finnegans Wake*: the first, faced with the specific practice of writing in Joyce's text and thus with the impossibility of converting that text into a critical object, rejects it as 'aberration'; the second, seeking to preserve Joyce's text for criticism, finds itself obliged to that end to 'reduce' its writing to the simple carrier of a message (a meaning) that it will be the critic's task to 'extract from its enigmatic envelope'. The writing of *Finnegans Wake*, however, work *in progress* ('wordloosed over seven seas' (*FW* 219.16)), develops according to a fundamental incompletion; the text produces a derisive hesitation of sense, the final revelation of meaning being always for 'later'.[2] The writing opens out onto a multiplicity of fragments of sense, of possibilities, which are traced and retraced, colliding and breaking ceaselessly in the play of this text that resists any homogenization. As 'collideorscape' (*FW* 143.28), *Finnegans Wake* is the space of a writing-reading, of an ambiviolence ('Language this allsfare for the loathe of Marses ambiviolent [. . .]' (*FW* 518.2)), disturbing the categories that claim to define and represent literary practice, leaving the latter in ruins, and criticism too. Already at the time of the composition of *Ulysses* Joyce spoke of the '*scorching*' effect of his writing: 'each successive episode, dealing with some province of artistic culture (rhetoric or music or dialectic), leaves behind it a burnt up field'.[3] In its activity, the writing scorches a path 'outside' these fields, continually destroying itself as object.

Reading *Finnegans Wake* is thus necessarily that aggressive participation described by Kristeva. What is in question is not what Beckett called 'a rapid skimming and absorption of the scant cream of sense' on the basis of 'a tertiary or quartary conditioned reflex of dribbling comprehension',[4] but entry into a world that 'is, was and will be writing its own wrunes for ever' (*FW* 19.35–6). Where criticism *ex*plicates, opening out the folds of the writing in order to arrive at the meaning, *Finnegans Wake* is offered as a permanent *inter*plication, a work of folding and unfolding in which every element becomes always the fold of another in a series that knows no point of rest. The fourth section of the book gives a whole range of discursive explications of the Letter but the latter exhausts them all (and *not* vice versa), running through them and encompassing them in the materiality of the letters of the text itself, holding them in that derisive hesitation referred to earlier. It is in relation to this activity that we should understand the description of the book as 'sentenced to be nuzzled over a full trillion times for ever and a night till his noddle sink or swim by that ideal reader suffering from an ideal insomnia' (*FW* 120.12–14). The text is never closed and the 'ideal reader' will be the one who accedes to the play of this incompletion, placed in 'a situation of writing',[5] ready no longer to master the text but now to become its actor.

I. *Against Continuity*

The brief mention of this problem of reading allows the recognition of the limitations of this essay. Its aim is a preliminary disengagement of the possibility of reading Joyce and it is thus no more than a few notes, grouped under various headings, *towards* that reading. In which respect, there is a further aspect of the general problem of reading that should be given some consideration here and that will provide a starting point for this work of disengagement.

It was stressed above that a text such as *Finnegans Wake* is not to be read according to a process of unification. The text is not homogeneous, but ceaselessly discontinuous, a hesitation of meaning into the perpetual 'later'. It is in this context that the further aspect of the problem of reading is posed—that of the manner in which the whole body of Joyce's work is to be read. This can, in fact, be immediately recast into the question as to whether it is possible to succeed, against the pressure of a criticism founded on continuity and identity (grasped above all in the construction of the Author-source), in reading that body of work itself according to a radical discontinuity that will allow an attention to the specificity of the practices of each text. It is hardly necessary to recall the multitude of critical studies that derive the whole of the work from 'aesthetic theories' extracted more or less opportunely from *Stephen Hero* or *A Portrait of the Artist as a Young Man*, thus offering to solve what is supposed to be 'the enigma of continuity in Joyce's work'. What is needed, against all attempts to locate some 'style' of the Author (traceable through the work as the area of some spiritual development), is the operation of a reading that, on the contrary, will remain attentive to the writing of each text in order to consider them in their totality as network of specific practices.

It is worth asking, indeed, how exactly it would be possible to speak of Joyce's style. Pound recognized the difficulty posed by Joyce's writing in this respect and expressed his irritation with *Ulysses* for this very reason: 'Also even the assing girouette of a postfuturo Gertrudo Steino protetopublic dont demand a new style per chapter. If a classic author "shows steady & uniform progress" from one oeuvre to ensanguined next, may be considered ample proof of non-stagnation of cerebral Rodano—flaming Farinatas included—.[6] Beckett, more succinctly, in an acrostic on Joyce's name written two years before the publication of *Finnegans Wake*, spoke of Joyce's 'sweet noo style';[7] the newness, the point at which Joyce is *not* Pound's 'classic author', lying in the no-ness, the discontinuity of Joyce's writing in which no one style can be traced. It is

tempting to give as a definition of the effect of the practice of writing operated in Joyce's works the fact that it is impossible to parody Joyce, to parody *Joyce* (in striking contrast to what might be done with a contemporary such as Lawrence). Parody, of course, is a mode of stylistics: the gathering together of the marks of an individuality—the style of an author—and the subsequent reproduction of that individuality. In Joyce's work, however, parody finds no simple point of attachment: where is Joyce's style? in which of the sections of *Ulysses*? what marks of individuality are to be gathered together from the conjunction of 'Ivy Day in the Committee Room' and the 'Night Studies' section of *Finnegans Wake*? In place of style we have *plagiarism*: Joyce does not express himself as the confident subject of a style; he runs through a multiplicity of styles, of orders of discourse, plagiastically open to a whole range of cultural forms that are stolen and broken in the perpetual fragmentation of the writing—a process in which the 'declamatory personality' (Flaubert's term)[8] founders in the vacillation of the play of forms, sliding through them and retraceable only in the terms of sham and forgery, terms to which we will need to return.

Joyce's works do not, therefore, form a 'portrait' of the 'Artist' to be explained or derived in univocal fashion from a supposed biography; nor is *A Portrait of the Artist as a Young Man* the source of a perennial 'Joycean aesthetic' that can account for the whole of Joyce's writing (it is significant that studies of Joyce based on this premiss are almost invariably led to reject or simply ignore *Finnegans Wake*). Joyce himself often insisted forcefully on the breaks between his various works (during the writing of *Finnegans Wake* he would ask pointedly to be told who had written *Ulysses*)[9] and that insistence deserves to be remembered. The texts should not be read as the spiritual biography of a full sourceful subject (the Author) but as a network of paragrammatic interrelations constructed in a play of reassumption and destruction, of pastiche and fragmentation. One level of this interrelation will be described here by placing the texts in conjunction with one another according to their specific practices of what will be called 'strategies of hesitation'.[10]

II. *Strategies of Hesitation*

Jung recognized in Joyce's writing a powerful effect of negation, *Ulysses* being received by him indeed as 'bloße Negation'.[11] This recognition, usually in the form of a violent attack, was applied to each of Joyce's texts from *Dubliners*, the negativity of which led to the physical destruction of several editions, to *Finnegans Wake*, widely received as the vicious and aberrant destruction of literature, Jung having already called *Ulysses* a backside of art ('die Kunst der Rückenseite, oder die Rückseite der Kunst').[12] Literature is, indeed, a crucial focus of this force of negation: paralysis of stereotype and repetition, 'literature', a term already diminishing in value in the early writings, becomes in *Finnegans Wake*, via the passage from letter to litter, 'litterature'.[13] The early importance of Ibsen for Joyce is the degree to which his work offers the difference between a paralysed literature and a drama that seems, according to the convention of that literature, to demonstrate, scandalously, the extent of that paralysis. Hence the title of the paper on Ibsen written in 1900, 'Drama and Life'; instead of literature and stereotype, drama *and* life, the exposure of the real paralysis then received inevitably as an act of negation.

This is the context of the necessity of the strategies of hesitation of Joyce's texts. Gripped in a general paralysis, Joyce's writing is obliged to effect a constant activity of refusal of available meanings, explications, discursive forms, all the very texture of the paralysis. It is precisely the evasion and baffling of the available, the given, its hesitation, to which the writing of Joyce's early texts is devoted and which defines their negativity.

Dublin is here the wasteland, the centre of what Eliot described in his review of *Ulysses* as 'the immense panorama of futility and anarchy which is contemporary history':[14] 'that city seemed to me the centre of paralysis', 'that hemiplegia or paralysis which many consider a city'.[15] Given this paralysis, how can the writing develop its demonstration without, in so doing, itself falling into the snares of sense, fixing itself within the blanket of that paralysis, repeating its very terms? how can it baffle the expectations of reading within which the paralysis is blindly enclosed? how can it hesitate these expectations and their sense and realize that negativity noted by Jung? Joyce's writing explores various procedures in response to these problems.

One such procedure is that of epiphany, of the kind that Joyce had at one time the habit of jotting down in a notebook; the definition of a climactic moment of paralytic banality by its copying down in writing. The process of copying down is to be understood literally, since the matter copied in this kind of epiphany is as often as not a fragment of dialogue[16]—an indication of the extent to which the spread of paralysis is located in the thickening weft of sense, stifling in its all-envelopingness. (Note too how much of the writing of *Stephen Hero* and *A Portrait of the Artist as a Young Man* is made up of citations of instances of discourse, from the sermon to the brief epiphanies that reappear in the former novel.)[17] This procedure is extended in *Dubliners* in the writing of 'Ivy Day in the Committee Room', organized through the recitation of a series of commonplaces (of 'idées reçues') the stringing together of which mimes with smothering clarity the blanket of paralysis.[18]

Dubliners, in fact, extends the procedure of the epiphany into a second, more general procedure within which it can be contained. This is the development of a kind of 'colourless' writing (that zero degree of writing described by Barthes) which can be held at the same level as the repetition of fragments of discourse, framing them in an absence of any principle (of organization, of order) or, more exactly, in the signification of its purpose to remain silent, outside commentary, interpretation, *parole*. Joyce, with great precision, refers to this as 'a style of scrupulous meanness'.[19] A further procedure, that of *A Portrait*, is to rend the blanket of sense through the production of the counter-text of the fiction of the artist and his 'voluntary exile'; his para-doxical status forming a contra-position to the realm of the doxa within the interstices of which the writing can, hesitatingly, proceed.

What has to be understood is the way in which these procedures respond to the problem posed as to the position from which the writing is developed, the way in which, that is, they are operative as strategies of hesitation. How is the writing to develop without fixing itself within the whole paralysis? From the position of the Stephen of *A Portrait*? Assuredly not—Stephen has no simple reality as some liberating character. The answer lies not in any position, but precisely in the strategies, in the absence of any position, in the continual hesitation effected by the writing. It has already been said that the writing of *A Portrait* proceeds not from the position of Stephen but, as it were, in the 'between' of that position and its opposite. The strategies of hesitation place Joyce's writing not in some fixed outside (the illusion of 'Reality') but within a continual process of fragmentation, destruction, hesitation. This is the rigour of Joyce's writing; its development of a suspension of sense. Thus, in the epiphanies and the scrupu-

lous meanness of *Dubliners*, the strategy of the copy determines precisely an absence of sense. It is this that is found so disturbing in the majority of the pieces in *Dubliners*; there is no *context*. The copy empties of reference, leaving a colourless and embarrassing platitude. 'Ivy Day in the Committee Room' *resists* meaning; flat and disruptive, the copy is self-sufficient, is itself the 'test'—the source of all the irony.[20]

The possibility of irony developed within these strategies of hesitation is crucial. Traditionally, irony is a mode of confidence and fixation, elaborated from a stable position to which it constantly refers in its critique of deviations from that position. Joyce's irony (the term is kept here for convenience and also for the kind of emphasis it finds in the writings of Nietzsche—it would perhaps be preferable to replace it by the term "hecitency', the significance of which in Joyce's writing will be seen below) lacks any centre of this kind; it knows no fixity, and its critique is not moral, derived from some sense, but self-reflexive, a perpetual displacement of sense in a play of forms without resolution. This irresolution is the very wager of *A Portrait*; the carrying through of two fictions, that of the doxa (Dublin, the Church, the family) and that of the paradoxa (the artist), without the writing being committed to either. The writing of the book is thus a tourniquet between the two fictions and it is in this mobility that the writing hesitates irresolvably. Consider in this respect the celebrated juxtaposition at the end of the fourth and the beginning of the fifth sections of the climactic moment of the vision of the girl wading and the description of Stephen in the kitchen:

> He climbed to the crest of the sandhill and gazed about him. Evening had fallen. A rim of the young moon cleft the pale waste of sky like the rim of a silver hoop embedded in grey sand; and the tide was flowing in fast to the land with a low whisper of her waves, islanding a few last figures in distant pools.

> He drained his third cup of watery tea to the dregs and set to chewing the crusts of fried bread that were scattered near him, staring into the dark pool of the jar. The yellow dripping had been scooped out like a boghole, and the pool under it brought back to his memory the dark turfcoloured water of the bath in Clongowes. The box of pawntickets at his elbow had just been rifled and he took up idly one after another in his greasy fingers the blue and white dockets (*P* 187–8)

The sudden inversion, from the distant pools created by the whispering waves to the pool under the boghole of the dripping, from the young moon cleaving the pale waste of sky to greasy fingers fondling pawntickets, in short from one writing to another, creates an expectation of irony. This expectation is baffled, however, by the absence of the sense to which the irony could be reduced; does the juxtaposition work for Stephen (showing the unbearableness of his position and the necessity for a justified exile) or against him (deflating the misty languor of the celtic twilight)? Critics continue to argue now one way, now the other, producing two versions of the book according to the tenets of classic irony. It is exactly this bafflement, this confusion (in the same way that *Dubliners* provokes a confusion in reading), that is the strategy of hesitation of *A Portrait*, that is the production of its irony of suspended sense.

The importance of Flaubert's writing for Joyce in this respect is evident (Flaubert was one of the three or four writers whose works Joyce claimed to have read in their entirety).[21] The strategy of *A Portrait*, indeed, finds a certain parallel in *Madame Bovary* with its play between the position of Emma and that of Charles, Homais and Yonville in general. Not the least of Pound's insights with regard to Joyce's work was his recognition of the possibility of this reference to Flaubert in the strategies of Joyce's writing; in *Dubliners* he found that 'English prose catches up with Flaubert'[22] and he continually insisted on a parallel between *Ulysses* and *Bouvard et Pécuchet*; 'He has done what Flaubert set out to do in *Bouvard et Pécuchet*, done it better, more succinct. An epitome.'[23] It is the reference to *Bouvard et Pécuchet* that is crucial, for the strategy of that text is again that of the copy developed as the process of a vertiginous hesitation ('in such a way that the reader does not know, yes or no, whether he is being made a fool of').[24] Hesitation, held in the strategy of style (in Flaubert's sense), stands against the stupidity of conclusiveness ('stupidity consists in wishing to conclude; we are a thread and we want to know the pattern'),[25] of fixity, of the myth of the absolute centre, the itinerary of which is that of Bouvard and Pécuchet, ever in search of the final copy, the original Truth, until they too become the compilators of the mythologies of others, lost in the play of the copy like Flaubert himself. Where is 'Flaubert' in *Bouvard et Pécuchet?* The definition of the artist as God remaining 'within or behind or beyond or above his handiwork, invisible, refined out of existence, indifferent, paring his fingernails', taken over from Flaubert in *A Portrait*,[26] is to be read, in relation to Joyce's writing, in this connection: it is not, in this relation, a question of the artist as substantial subject dominating everything from the fixity of his position, but of the absence of any position, an indifference which is here an illimitation, a perpetual movement of difference (in the very movement of hesitation) in which the subject is no longer visible, is dispersed in the writing.

In the typology of these strategies of hesitation sketched here, *Ulysses* represents at once a further extension of this irony of 'hecitency' (it is *Ulysses* that Pound likens to *Bouvard et Pécuchet*) and, in this extension, the decisive definition of a practice of writing-reading in which the subject is desubstantialized through fragmentation into the multiple processes of its inscription. (Shaw was right to talk of the negativity of *Ulysses* in relation to its treatment of the human subject.)

A mark of this new level of the activity of the writing is what Broch called the urge for totality in *Ulysses* ('Totalitätsanspruch')[27] and what Joyce described as encyclopaedism: 'It is an epic of two races (Israelite-Irish) and at the same time the cycle of the human body as well as a little story of a day (life). [. . .] It is also a sort of encyclopaedia. My intention is to transpose the myth *sub specie temporis nostri*. Each adventure (that is, every hour, every organ, every art being interconnected and interrelated in the structural scheme of the whole) should not only condition but even create its own technique. Each adventure is so to say one person although it is composed of persons—as Aquinas relates of the angelic hosts.'[28] There is scarcely need to elaborate on this description; the complexity of the development of Joyce's scheme is sufficiently well known from the indications given in the table of 'correspondences' drawn up by Joyce for Herbert Gorman and in Stuart Gilbert's book on *Ulysses* written under Joyce's supervision. What is perhaps not sufficiently recognized, indeed, is how little Gilbert's book *explains*; on the contrary, in strict accordance with Joyce's strategies of hesitation (compare in this respect the Ithaca section of *Ulysses*, Joyce's favourite) it enumerates and lists; in response to questions (interrogations of sense) it catalogues, it gives, that is, the beginnings of the series of elements that that writing of *Ulysses* perpetually unfolds. The aim of the writing of *Ulysses* is the achievement of a multiplicity of levels of narrative (of 'adventure') and inter-

reference (the permutations available in the reading of the correspondences), the interplay of which will be the fragmentation of every particular one. (The grossest, and commonest, misreading of *Ulysses* is that which derives a single realist narrative of Bloom and Stephen and, with this as centre of reference, explains or abandons the writing.) It is in this multiplicity of levels that the urge for totality is to be understood. *Ulysses* is written as a *repertoire* of fictions: the writing passes across a range of fictions, of forms, juxtaposing and breaking them in a ceaseless narration. The movement from morning to night is the reality of this passage *across* of the writing in which the subject, in the hesitation, in the demonstration of fictions and the themes that demonstration invokes—birth/death, order/chaos, etc.—is lost in its ceaseless reinscription in a totality of possibilities (the writing of the interplay of Bloom and Stephen plays its part in this dissolution). Jung saw clearly in his account of the negativity of *Ulysses* how this passage across fictions was a strategy for the disengagement from sense, for a process of hesitation the self-reflexive effect of which was not the fixing of any sense in the commitment to a single fiction, but an attention to the logic of fictions and to the position of the construction of the subject within that logic: 'I sincerely hope that *Ulysses* is not symbolic, for if it were it would have failed in its purpose.'[29]

III. Context/Intertext

One of the key stresses of Nietzsche's work may be summarized by the following: 'Because we have to be stable in our beliefs if we are to prosper, we have made the "real" world a world not of change and becoming, but one of being.'[30] The apparatus of a vraisemblable, the given series of beliefs defining the '"wahre" Welt', functions as a self-perpetuating stabilization, converting the world into a realm of essence (whether theological or the fixed 'Reality' of mechanistic materialism). It is this stability that is shattered by the writing of Joyce's texts in their definition of a logic of fictions, not of truths; their attention to what is called in *Finnegans Wake* 'the fictionable world' (*FW* 345.36). *Finnegans Wake*, transforming the 'real Matter-of-Fact' of realist writing into a 'matter of fict' or 'mere matter of ficfect' (*FW* 532.29), is the negation of any vraisemblable. The writing ceaselessly violates (this is its *ambiviolent* activity) the principles of identity and non-contradiction, effecting an infinitization of fictions, of possibilities: 'we are in for a sequentiality of improbable possibles though possibly nobody after having grubbed up a lock of cwold cworn aboove his subject probably in Harrystotalies or the vivle will go out of his way to applaud him on the onboiassed back of his remark for utterly impossible as are all these events they are probably as like those which may have taken place as any others which never took person at all are ever likely to be' (*FW* 110.15–21).

Crucial to the action of a vraisemblable is the definition of a context of reference, producing, according to a process of limitation (effected in discourse by conventions of genre, style and so on), a fixed meaning. Joyce's texts, by contrast, in their unstabilization, their 'hecitency', refer not to a context—and thus not to a 'Reality' (the context defined by the vraisemblable being received precisely as *unique*, as *essence*)—but to an intertext. In these texts, that is, the context is splintered into a multiplicity of instances of discourse, fragments of sense; into a plurality, or dialogue, irreducible to the single line of a truth, as, for instance, that of realist writing naturalized, according to the context of a vraisemblable, as monologue of 'Reality'. The practice of writing-reading in Joyce's texts is the recognition of the text not as absolute origin or source (expression of 'Reality', expression of the Author, etc.) but as intertextual space, dialogue of forms which write it as it writes them. The urge for

totality defined by Broch in relation to *Ulysses* is the acknowledgement of the problem of intertextuality. Writing, no
longer seen as unique expression, becomes an activity of
assemblage, of reading (again in the sense on which Kristeva
insists), in which activity the writing subject itself is dispersed
in a plurality of possible positions and functions, read within
the orders of discourse. *Finnegans Wake* comments exactly on
the multiplicity of 'identities in the writer complexus (for if the
hand was one, the minds of active and agitated were more than
so)' (*FW* 114.33–5).

Joyce declared himself 'quite content to go down to
posterity as a scissors and paste man for that seems to me a
harsh but not unjust description'.[31] The reference is to the
literal activity of assemblage that characterizes, in part and in
differing ways, the writing of *Ulysses* and of *Finnegans Wake*.
The term 'litterature' might be adopted here in the precise
reference it finds in Carroll's preface to 'Sylvie and Bruno',
where the genesis of writing is linked to the idea of assemblage,
to the possession by the subject of a 'huge unwieldy mass of
litterature' in which he is lost (how can he wield it?).[32] The
following are two examples of this 'litterature' in relation to
Joyce's writing (the first concerns *Ulysses*, the second *Finnegans Wake*):

> I have seen him collect in the space of a few hours
> the oddest assortment of material: a parody on the
> *House that Jack built*, the name and action of a
> poison, the method of caning boys on training ships,
> the wobbly cessation of a tired unfinished sentence,
> the nervous trick of a convive turning his glass in
> inward-turning circles, a Swiss music-hall joke turn-
> ing on a pun in Swiss dialect, a description of the
> Fitzsimmons shift.[33]

> the books I am using for the present fragment which
> include Marie Corelli, Swedenborg, St Thomas, the
> Sudanese War, Indian outcasts, Women under En-
> glish Law, a description of St Helena, Flammarion's
> The End of the World, scores of children's singing
> games from Germany, France, England and Italy
> and so on. . . .[34]

This heterogeneous material has no value of unity of meaning
in Joyce's writing (where could this unity lie between 'Women
under English Law' and 'The End of the World' or between
'the method of caning boys on training ships' and 'a Swiss
music-hall joke turning on a pun in Swiss dialect'?). The value
is to be found in the heterogeneity, in the very distance
between these diverse elements that the writing will cross in a
ceaseless play of relations and correspondences in which every
element becomes the fiction of another. The unity of these
elements is not, then, as is generally supposed, one of content,
of meaning, but one grasped at the level of their reality as
forms, as fictions. What is constructed in the play of their
interrelations in the writing is a discontinuity in progress, a
constant displacement from fiction to fiction. It is this
discontinuity that realizes the negativity of Joyce's writing.
There is no fiction, no level of narrative, that 'stops' the others
(as a context 'stops' the multiple possibilities of meaning, the
play of the signifier, thus avoiding the loss of the meaning).
The irony of *Ulysses* is that of this perpetual displacement,
that, briefly noted by Kristeva, of the capture of 'a meaning
always already old, always already exceeded, as funny as it is
ephemeral'.[35] It is in these terms that Joyce's irony is not, as in
the case of the classic tradition of irony, contextual, but,
exactly, intertextual, a strategy of hesitation opening onto 'a
finally real text . . . the current letter of meaning finally
formulated and played'.[36] . . .

VI. *The Spiral*

Flaubert planned a novel to be called *La Spirale*.[37] That
title might be given to the body of Joyce's work, marking the
action of that discontinuity described above. Is it not precisely
as a spiral that the succession of Joyce's works should be
conceived? They represent not a line of development but a
ceaseless work of return and disengagement, of dissemination,
each text reinscribing the others to achieve a distance of
parody, derision, anecdote (what is *Ulysses* for *Finnegans Wake*
if not an anecdote?). The *Scribbledehobble* workbook, written
round about 1924 and having a claim to be considered as one
of Joyce's finest texts, is divided into sections with headings
made up of titles of previous texts and, in the case of *Ulysses*, of
episodes of previous texts. Each section is more or less filled
with words, phrases, occasional sequences of phrases, related
in various ways (via parody, commentary, extension, thematic,
aleation) with the previous texts. In the explicitness of its
organization, *Scribbledehobble* provides a perfect image of the
Joycean spiral; a return across earlier writings but in order to
open a distance, the circle not closing but disengaging a new
activity of writing.

The spiral of Flaubert's title referred to the narrative of one
particular text. His projected novel was to be an attempt to
confound in a single narrative line—that of the story of a
painter—the 'real' and the 'imaginary', the events of everyday
and the dreams and visions provoked by hashish, the confusion
finally putting into question their habitual easy distinction.
The spiral described the succession of stages undergone by the
painter in the process of this confusion, culminating in a
dramatic conclusion: 'The conclusion is that: happiness consists in being Mad (or what is thus so called), that is to say, in
seeing the True, the whole of time, the absolute—'.[38]

Flaubert's plan finds in some sort a realization in *Ulysses*
in the succession of 'streams of consciousness' that interfold
and come together in an action which, in the 'nighttown'
section, spills out of the limitation of any 'person' or 'Reality'.
The image of the spiral is not, however, to be reduced to a
single level of narrative—one amongst many others—of *Ulysses*. It is, in fact, precisely the multiplicity of levels that gives
the spiral of the text, producing as it does neither the enclosing
cohesion of a circular movement nor the unfolding and
revelation of a meaning on a line of development but a spiral, a
constant displacement of possibilities of reading. The spiral is
then the realization of the urge for totality in *Ulysses*. The folly
of the book is its desire to 'voir le Vrai, l'ensemble du temps,
l'absolu': its absolute, however, is not the theological stasis of a
fixed Absolute but the absolute of possibles, the incessant
movement of forms, the spirals of returns and recommence-
ments in which meaning is always 'later'.

The image of the spiral finds a precise reference in Joyce's
writing, that of the historical theory of Vico with its conception
of the spiral of *corsi* and *ricorsi*. This reference, as is well
known, is basic to the writing of *Finnegans Wake*, which makes
the 'real world', the stable fixity of realist writing, the 'reel
world' (*FW* 64.25–6), forming and reforming in a play of
difference and repetition, the 'seim anew' (*FW* 215.23). This
movement of 'vicous circles' (*FW* 134.16)—'by a commodius
vicus of recirculation' (*FW* 3.02)—is, as was Vico's work in its
opposition to the unidimensional linear progress of the Enlightenment version of history, an opposition to the writing of
history as the straight unfolding of a single line of development.
'The June snows was flocking in thuckflues on the hegelstomes'
(*FW* 416.32–3); disorder and discontinuity ('June snows')
opposes the order and continuity of Hegel's writing of the
process of the realization of Geist. The characteristic of Joyce's

writing is, in Beckett's words, 'the absolute absence of the Absolute'.[39] The discontinuity is the mark of this absence, an anti-synthesis: 'What a meanderthalltale to unfurl and with what an end in view of squattor and anntisquattor and postproneauntisquattor!' (*FW* 19.25-7). The synthesis is continually *postponed* in the 'meanderthalltale', meaning is deferred. 'The Vico road goes round and round to meet where terms begin' (*FW* 452.21-2).

'To meet where terms begin' may be read as an appeal not to a simple circularity[40] but to a primitive level (as 'meanderthalltale' appeals to neanderthal). This primitive level is to be understood in thinking the foundation of history eternally and contrapuntally present in the spiralling movement of *corsi* and *ricorsi* and given in language as the history of that history. For Vico the spiral is definable exactly in terms of stages of language and the historical humanities are to be included in the general science of philology. Vico's 'new science' is a passage across history in the interests of the disengagement of the logic of the movement of history; 'the ideal history of the eternal laws over which run the facts of all nations'.[41] This logic functions as a structural model which gives the intelligibility of any particular historical fact, that fact actualizing one among the multiplicity of virtualities present in the structure. The importance of this for Joyce's writing is evident. Where realist writing had made of history the fixed point of its representations, realized in narratives supported by the context of a vraisemblable that defined and ratified their typicality, their 'truth', Joyce's writing is concerned, like that of Vico, with a history of forms of intelligibility. In a very early essay Joyce had written of 'history or the denial of reality, for they are two names for the one thing';[42] the reality of Joyce's writing will be its attention to forms, no longer to 'Reality' but to the history of fictions. The history of Joyce's writing is not that produced by a context but that grasped in its realization of the intertext as scansion of fictions. It is in this sense that Joyce's writing is an interrogation of 'origins', of the 'reality' 'before' history as the very possibility of its foundation, of, in fact, the 'time' of language with which—this was Vico's central theme—history begins and which—a further Viconian theme—is perpetually present in every act of language, the horizon of its intelligibility. The spiral of Joyce's writing, finally, is the process of this interrogation.

Notes

Page references to Joyce's works refer to the following editions:

    A *Portrait of the Artist as a Young Man*: in *The Essential Joyce*, ed. Harry Levin, Penguin Books, 1963.

    Finnegans Wake: The Viking Press, 1939.

    Letters: Vol. I, ed. Stuart Gilbert, 1957, Vols. II and III, ed. Richard Ellmann, 1966, Faber & Faber and The Viking Press.

1. Julia Kristeva, *Semeiotiké: recherches pour une sémanalyse* (Paris: Seuil, 1969), p. 181.
2. Lautréamont's 'plus tard', in a passage where he promises the reader revelation 'at the end of your life' and 'even perhaps at the end of this stanza' but certainly for 'later'; Lautréamont, *Oeuvres complètes*, ed. Maurice Saillet (Paris: Livre de poche, 1963), pp. 268-9.
3. Joyce, letter to Harriet Shaw Weaver, 20 July 1919; *Letters*, I, 129.
4. Samuel Beckett, 'Dante . . . Bruno. Vico . . . Joyce', in *Our Exagmination Round His Factification for Incamination of* Work in Progress (Paris: Shakespeare and Co., 1929), p. 13.
5. Cf. Roland Barthes, *L'Empire des signes* (Geneva: Skira, 1970), p. 11.
6. Ezra Pound, letter to Joyce, 10 June 1919; *Pound/Joyce*, ed. Forrest Read (London: Faber & Faber, 1968), p. 157.
7. Beckett, 'Home Olga'; cit. Richard Ellmann, *James Joyce* (New York: Oxford University Press, 1959), p. 714.
8. Flaubert, letter to Louise Colet, 27 March 1852; *Correspondance*, deuxième série (Paris: Conard, 1926), p. 379.
9. Svevo records his surprise at discovering on a visit to Paris at the time of the writing of *Finnegans Wake* that 'L'*Ulisse* per Joyce non esiste più'; 'James Joyce', in Italo Svevo, *Saggi e pagine sparse* (Verona: Mondadori, 1954), p. 231.
10. It might be noted here that Vico, a key reference for Joyce's writing, argues in the third section of the *Scienza Nuova* ('Della discoverta de vero Omero') against the assumption of Homer as individual genius. Homer is to be seen rather as a poetical 'character' open to the totality of forms of his culture, which find supreme articulation in 'his' poems. Writer of the modern *Odyssey*, Joyce is likewise a 'character' in this sense, a disposition of forms.
11. C. G. Jung, 'Ulysses. Ein Monolog', *Wirklichkeit der Seele* (Zurich: Rascher, 1934), p. 150. The reception of *Ulysses* as negation was very general: cf., for example, G. B. Shaw, 'In Ireland they try to make a cat cleanly by rubbing its nose in its own filth. Mr Joyce has tried the same treatment on the human subject', letter to Sylvia Beach, 10 October 1921; *Letters*, III, 50; E.M. Forster, 'It is a dogged attempt to cover the universe with mud, an inverted Victorianism, an attempt to make crossness and dirt succeed where sweetness and light failed, a simplification of the human character in the interests of Hell', *Aspects of the Novel* (London: E. Arnold, 1927), p. 158.
12. Jung, 'Ulysses. Ein Monolog', p. 148.
13. 'But by writing thithaways end to end and turning, turning and end to end hithaways writing and with lines of litters slittering up and louds of latters slettering down, the old semetomplace and jupetbackagain from tham Let Rise till Hum Lit. Sleep, where in the waste is the wisdom?' (*FW* 114.16-20)
14. T. S. Eliot, 'Ulysses, Order and Myth' (1923), in *James Joyce: Two Decades of Criticism*, ed. Seon Givens (New York: Vanguard Press, 1948), p. 201.
15. Joyce, letter to Grant Richards, 5 May 1906; *Letters*, II, 134; letter to Constantine P. Curran, undated (1904?); *Letters*, I, 55.
16. Cf. epiphanies nos. I, II, III, IV, V, VI, VIII, IX, XI, XIII, XVIII, XXI, *Epiphanies*, ed. O. A. Silverman (Buffalo: Buffalo University Press, 1956). Reference might also be made in connection with this procedure to Swift's A *Complete Collection of Genteel and Ingenious Conversation* and, above all, to Flaubert's compilation of the *Dictionnaire des idées reçues*.
17. As is well known, *Stephen Hero* contains a longish discussion of the epiphany between Stephen and Cranly, in which it is given certain aesthetic justifications (held within the play of a perpetually vacillating irony). What is in question in the present discussion is the procedure of the epiphany as demonstrated in Joyce's recording-writing of epiphanies.
18. Remember also in this context the dizzying assemblage of fragments into a kind of staccato narrative of disrupting triviality in the 'Eumaeus' section of *Scribbledehobble*: 'chaff: stayed to tea and later proposed marriage; lady's affections went astray: under rather a cloud: wicked untruth: met a man, had a drop of port wine and remembered no more: inspired statement: ugly wound: angry boil: denied all knowledge of the matter', etc.; Scribbledehobble: *The Ur-Workbook for* Finnegans Wake, ed. T. E. Connolly (Evanston: Northwestern University Press, 1961), p. 150.
19. Joyce, letter to Grant Richards, 5 May 1906; *Letters*, II, 134.
20. 'Ivy Day in the Committee Room' was the piece in *Dubliners* that gave Joyce most satisfaction; cf. letter to Grant Richards, 20 May 1906; *Letters*, I, 62. It may be noted that Joyce proposed copying as the way to evaluate a work of art: 'the way to test a work of art is to copy out a page of it'; cit. R. Ellmann, *James Joyce*, p. 622. The valid work will be that which can support this reinscription, which *can* be copied without provoking the nausea of stereotype and repetition.
21. Stuart Gilbert, *James Joyce's Ulysses* (London: Faber & Faber, 1952), p. 92.
22. Pound, 'Past History' (1933), *Pound/Joyce*, p. 248.
23. Pound, 'Joyce' (1920), ibid., p. 139 (cf. pp. 194, 200f., 250).
24. Flaubert, letter to Louis Bouillet, *Correspondance*, deuxième série, 4 September 1850, p. 238.
25. Ibid., p. 239.

26. P337; cf. Flaubert, *Correspondance, troisième série* (Paris; Conard, 1927), *pp.* 61–2.

27. Hermann Broch, letter to Dr Daniel Brody, 19 October 1934; *Briefe von 1929 bis 1951* (Zürich: Rhein-Verlag, 1957), p. 102.

28. Joyce, letter to Carlo Linati, 21 September 1920; *Letters*, I, 146–7.

29. Jung, '*Ulysses*. Ein Monolog', p. 157.

30. F. Nietzsche, *Der Wille zur Macht, Gesammelte Werke*, vol. 19 (Munich, 1926), p. 24.

31. Joyce, letter to George Antheil, 3 January 1931; *Letters*, I, 297.

32. Cf. *The Complete Works of Lewis Carroll* (London: Nonesuch, 1939), p. 257.

33. Frank Budgen, *James Joyce and the Making of* Ulysses (London: Grayson, 1934), p. 176.

34. Joyce, letter to Harriet Shaw Weaver, 4 March 1931; *Letters*, I, 302.

35. Julia Kristeva, 'Comment parler à la littérature', *Tel Quel* 47 (Autumn, 1971), p. 40.

36. Philippe Sollers, *Logiques* (Paris: Seuil, 1968), p. 110. Dublin for Joyce is exactly a heterogeneity (as witness the 'Wandering Rocks' section of *Ulysses* or the organization of the pieces in *Dubliners*). Mention is often made of Joyce's letters to his Aunt Josephine requesting the verification of details relating to Dublin life—as, for example, the famous query as to whether or not it would be 'possible for an ordinary person to climb over the area railings of no 7 Eccles street', letter to Mrs William Murray, 2 November 1921; *Letters*, I, 175. These requests—many of which, it should be noted, are for details directly relating to forms of discourse (e.g. 'please send me a bundle of other novelettes and any penny hymnbook you can find', letter to Mrs William Murray, 5 January 1920; *Letters*, I, 135)—do not identify *Ulysses* as a prime example of realist writing. What Joyce demands, in connection with the 'Totalitätsanspruch', is the maximum number of reports on 16 June 1904 in order to provide for one level of the totality of his text. Dublin, which is ceaselessly a question of identity, 'Dyoublong?' (*FW* 13.04), is at the same time 'Echoland!' (*FW* 13.05), network of fictions, of resonances in which the subject is 'listened'.

37. 'La Spirale', *Carnets et projets, Oeuvres de Gustave Flaubert*, vol. 18 (Lausanne: Editions Rencontre, 1965), pp. 34–7.

38. Ibid., p. 36

39. 'Dante . . . Bruno, Vico . . . Joyce', p. 22.

40. Vico's spiral contains a conception of progress. 'His cycle, in truth, is more aptly described as a spiral, for though each stage is repeated in the next cycle, it is repeated on a higher level'; Bruce Mazlish, *The Riddle of History* (New York: Harper & Row, 1966), p. 41. Gilbert writes that 'after each epoch of dissolution and reconstruction, a fragment of the advance gained by each spent wave is conserved, for there is a slowly rising tide in human history' and adds as a footnote 'I doubt if the author of *Ulysses* endorsed Vico's optimistic belief in "progress"'; *James Joyce's* Ulysses, p. 50. Following the sense of this, Umberto Eco states that Joyce equates Vico's theory with the 'oriental theme of the circular character of everything [. . .] The "development" aspect is sacrificed to circular identity, to the continual repetition of original archetypes'; *L'Oeuvre ouverte* (Paris: Seuil, 1965), p. 262. The debate, perhaps, needs simply to be disrupted with Joyce's 'It's a wheel, I tell the world, *And* it's all *square*'; letter to Harriet Shaw Weaver, 16 April 1927; *Letters*, I, 251. Note also that no more than Joyce's does Vico's movement imply the culmination of a synthesis—*verum* is realized only *partially* in different ages—and that it too is the manifestation of a logic, what Eco calls 'original archetypes'. More importantly, as will be stressed below, the attention of Joyce's writing is on the side of the signifier, the reading of a totality of historical forms through which the writing passes and only within the movement of which, in the play of difference and repetition, can any 'origin' be conceived.

41. G. Vico, *Principi di scienza nuova* (1744), *Opere*, vol. 1 (Verona: Mondadori, 1957), p. 546.

42. 'James Clarence Mangan' (1902), *The Critical Writings of James Joyce*, ed. Ellsworth Mason and Richard Ellmann (London: Faber & Faber, 1959), p. 81.

UMBERTO ECO
From "The Early Joyce"
The Aesthetics of Chaosmos:
The Middle Ages of James Joyce, tr. Ellen Esrock
1982, pp. 1–8, 23–30

> Steeled in the school of the old Aquinas.
> (James Joyce, "The Holy Office")

The term "poetics" has acquired many meanings during the centuries. Aristotle's *Poetics* is an answer to both the questions "What is Art?" and "How does one make a work of art?" The modern philosophical tradition has preferred to define the theoretical answer to the first question as "aesthetics" and to utilize "poetics" in order to describe the program of a single artist or a particular artistic school. In this context, "poetics" addresses the question "How does one make a work of art according to a personal program and an idiosyncratic world view?" The more recent definition by the Prague Linguistic School considers "poetics" as the study of "the *differentia specifica* of verbal behavior."[1] In other words, "poetics" is the study of the structural mechanism of a given text which possesses a self-focusing quality and a capacity for releasing effects of ambiguity and polysemy.

Joyce plays with all these notions of poetics throughout his works; he interweaves questions as to the concept of art, the nature of his personal artistic program, and the structural mechanisms of the texts themselves. In this respect all of Joyce's works might be understood as a continuous discussion of their own artistic procedures.

A *Portrait* is the story of a young artist who wants to write A *Portrait*; *Ulysses*, a little less explicit, is a book which is a model of itself; *Finnegans Wake* is, above all, a complete treatise on its own nature, a continuous definition of "the Book" as the *Ersatz* of the universe. The reader, therefore, is continually tempted to isolate the poetics proposed by Joyce in order to define, in Joycean terms, the solutions that Joyce has adopted.

Although one can discuss the poetics of Horace, Boileau, or Valéry without referring to their creative works, Joyce's poetics cannot be separated from Joyce's texts. The poetics themselves form an intimate part of the artistic creation and are clarified in the various phases of the development of his opus. The entire Joycean project might thus be seen as the development of a poetics, or rather, as the dialectical movement of various opposite and complementary poetics—the history of contemporary poetics in a game of oppositions and continuous implications.

Among the numerous cultural influences upon the young Joyce, we note three major lines which appear in all his works. On one count, we find the influence of Aquinas, thrown into crisis but not completely destroyed by the reading of Bruno and, on another, the influence of Ibsen, with a call for closer ties between art and life. Finally, we note the influence of the symbolist poets, with the aesthetic ideal of a life devoted to art and of art as a substitute for life, and with their stimulus to resolve the great problems of the spirit in the laboratory of language.[2] These contrasting influences from different centuries were assimilated within a framework that grew increasingly concerned with the problems of contemporary culture, from the psychology of the unconscious to the physics of relativity. The staggering quantity of Joyce's reading and the diversity of his interests opened the way to his discovery of new dimensions of the universe.

Approached in this way, our research needs a guiding

thread, a line of investigation, an operative hypothesis. We take, therefore, the opposition between a classical conception of form and the need for a more pliable and "open" structure of the work and of the world. This can be identified as a dialectic of order and adventure, a contrast between the world of the medieval *summae* and that of contemporary science and philosophy.

Joyce himself authorizes us to use this dialectical key. The Joycean detachment from the familiar clarity of the schoolmen and his choice of a more modern and uneasy problematic is actually based on the Brunian revelation of a dialectic of contraries, on the acceptance of the *coincidentia oppositorum* of Cusano. Art and life, symbolism and realism, classical world and contemporary world, aesthetic life and daily life, Stephen Dedalus and Leopold Bloom, Shem and Shaun, order and possibility are the continuous terms of a tension that has its roots in this theoretical discovery. In Joyce's works the very crisis of late scholasticism is accelerated and therein a new cosmos is born.

But this dialectic is not perfectly articulated; it does not have the balance of those ideal triadic dances upon which more optimistic philosophies build legends. While Joyce's mind brings this elegant curve of oppositions and mediations to its limits, his unconscious agitates like the unexpressed memory of an ancestral trauma. Joyce departs from the *summa* to arrive at *Finnegans Wake*, from the ordered cosmos of scholasticism to the verbal image of an expanding universe. But his medieval heritage, from which his movements arise, will never be abandoned. Underneath the game of oppositions and resolutions in which the various cultural influences collide, on the deepest level, is the radical opposition between the medieval man, nostalgic for an ordered world of clear signs and the modern man, seeking a new habitat but unable to find the elusive rules and thus burning continually in the nostalgia of a lost infancy.

We would like to demonstrate that the definitive choice is not made and that the Joycean dialectic, more than a mediation, offers us the development of a continuous polarity between Chaos and Cosmos, between disorder and order, liberty and rules, between the nostalgia of Middle Ages and the attempts to envisage a new order. Our analysis of the poetics of James Joyce will be the analysis of a moment of transition in contemporary culture.

The Catholicism of Joyce

I will tell you what I will do and what I will not do. I will not serve that in which I no longer believe whether it call itself my home, my fatherland or my church: and I will try to express myself in some mode of life or art as freely as I can and as wholly as I can, using for my defence the only arms I allow myself to use—silence, exile, and cunning (P 247).

With Stephen's confession to Cranly, the young Joyce proposes his own program of exile. The assumptions of Irish tradition and Jesuitical education lose their value as rules. Thus Joyce abandons the faith but not religious obsession. The presence of an orthodox past reemerges constantly in all of his work under the form of a personal mythology and with a blasphemous fury that reveals its affective permanence. Critics have spoken a great deal of Joyce's "Catholicism." The term appropriately reflects a mentality which rejects dogmatic substance and moral rules yet conserves the exterior forms of a rational edifice and retains its instinctive fascination for rites and liturgical figurations. Evidently, we are dealing with a fascination *à rebours*; speaking about Catholicism in connection with Joyce is a bit like speaking about filial love in

connection with Oedipus and Jocasta. When Henry Miller insults Joyce, calling him the descendant of a medieval erudite with "priest's blood" and speaking of his hermit's morality with the onanistic mechanism that such a life comports, he identifies, with paradoxical treachery, a distinctive feature of Joyce. Similarly, when Valéry Larbaud remarks that *A Portrait* is closer to Jesuitical casuistry than to French naturalism, he says nothing that the average reader has not already sensed. But *A Portrait* reflects something more. The narration which is tuned to liturgical time, the taste for sacred oratory and moral introspection convey not only the mimetic instincts of the narrator but also an all-pervasive psychological mood. The style, imitating that of a rejected position, does not succeed as an indictment of Catholicism. It was not by chance that Thomas Merton converted to Catholicism upon reading *A Portrait*, thereby taking a road opposite that of Stephen's. This was possible not because the ways of the Lord are infinite but because the ways of Joycean sensibility are strange and contradictory, with the Catholic thread surviving in a vague, abnormal manner.

Buck Mulligan opens *Ulysses* with his *"Introibo ad altare Dei,"* and the Black Mass is placed at the center of the work. The erotic ecstasy of Bloom and his lewd and platonic seduction of Gerty MacDowell are in counterpoint with the moments of the Eucharistic ceremony performed in the church near the beach of Reverend Hughes. The macaronic Latin that appears at the end of *Stephen Hero*, which returns in *A Portrait* and appears here and there in *Ulysses*, reflects not only the speech patterns of the medieval *Vagantes* but also the patterns of their conceptual thought. Like those who abandon a discipline but not its cultural baggage, with Joyce there remains the sense of a curse celebrated according to a liturgical ritual. "Come up you, fearful jesuit," Mulligan shouts to Stephen and later clarifies, "Because you have the cursed jesuit strain in you, only it's injected the wrong way . . . ." And in *A Portrait*, Cranly observes the curious fact that Stephen's mind is saturated with the religion that he supposedly rejects.

Similarly, references to the liturgy of the Mass appear in the most unexpected ways at the center of the puns which are woven throughout *Finnegans Wake*:

(enterellbo add all taller Danis) (336.02). . . . Per omnibus secular seekalarum (81.08). . . . meac Coolp, (344.31) . . . meas minimas culpads! (483.35). . . . Crystal elation! Kyrielle elation! (528.09). . . . Sussumcordials (453.26). . . .— Grassy ass ago (252.13). . . . Eat a missal lest (456.18). . . . Bennydick hotfoots onimpudent stayers! (469.23). . . .

Here one can discern the pure taste for assonance and parody. In light of this ambivalent relationship with Catholicism, the two symbolic superstructures imposed upon *Ulysses* and *Finnegans Wake* appear clearer. The triangle of Stephen-Bloom-Molly becomes the image of the Trinity; H. C. Earwicker acquires the symbolic role of the scapegoat who assumes within himself the whole of humanity ("Here Comes Everybody"), fallen and saved by a resurrection. Stripped of any precise theological nature, involved in all myths and religions, the symbolic figure of HCE assumes coherence by respect of an ambiguous relationship to a Christ who is deformed by historical awareness and identified with the very process of history (see Henry Morton Robinson, "Hardest Crux Ever," in *A James Joyce Miscellany*; Second Series, ed. Marvin Magalaner, Carbondale: Southern Illinois University Press, 1959). In the heart of this same evolving cycle of human history, the author feels as victim and logos, *"in honour bound to the cross of your own cruelifiction."*

But the displays of Joycean Catholicism develop along more than one line. If we find, on one side, this almost unconscious, obsessive ostentation, somewhat *mal tournée*, then on the other we detect a mental attitude that is valuable at the level of operative efficacy. On the one hand, a mythical obsession, on the other, a way of organizing ideas. Here, the deposit of symbols and figures is filtered and brought to play within the framework of another faith; there, a mental habit is placed in the service of a heterodox *Summulae*. This is the second moment of Joycean Catholicism—the moment of medieval scholasticism.

Joyce attributes to Stephen "a genuine predisposition in favour of all but the 'premises of scholasticism'" (*SH* 77). According to Harry Levin, the tendency for abstraction reminds us continuously that Joyce reaches aesthetics through theology. Joyce loses his faith but remains faithful to the orthodox system. Even in his mature works, Joyce often seems to have remained a realist in the most medieval sense of the word (Harry Levin, *James Joyce: A Critical Introduction*, Norfolk, CT: New Directions, 1941, p. 25).

This mental structure is not exclusively a characteristic of the young Joyce who is still close to the Jesuitical influence, for the syllogistic style of reasoning survives even in *Ulysses*, if only as the distinctive mark of a pattern of thinking. As an example, consider the monologue in the third chapter or the discussion in the library. Also in *A Portrait*, though Stephen is joking by speaking in macaronic Latin, it is with maximum seriousness that he asks these kinds of questions: is baptism by mineral water valid? does the theft of a sterling and the acquisition of a fortune from it require one to restore the sterling or the entire fortune? And with greater problematic acuteness, he asks the following: if a man hacking randomly at a block of wood makes the image of a cow, is that image a work of art? These questions are of the same family as those posed by the scholastic doctors debating the *questiones quodlibetales* (one of these, by Aquinas, asks in what way the human will is most strongly determined—by wine, women, or love of God). And of a more direct scholastic origin, less influenced by counter-reformist casuistry than the preceding, is the question that Stephen asks himself: is the portrait of Mona Lisa good by the fact that I desire to see it?

It is thus necessary to ask how much of the scholasticism of the young Joyce is substantial and how much is only superficial—a mischievous taste for contamination or an attempt to smuggle revolutionary ideas under the cape of Doctor Angelicus (the technique that Stephen frequently utilizes with the college professors).

Stephen confesses to having read "only a garner of slender sentences from Aristotle's poetics and psychology and a *Synopsis philosophiae scholasticae ad mentem divi Thomae.*" The question that must be asked is whether or not Stephen is lying. It is of little help to discuss Joyce's reading material while he was in Paris. There is the confession to Valéry Larbaud that "il passait plusieurs heures chaque soir à la bibliothèque Ste. Geneviève lisant Aristote et St. Thomas d'Aquin." But we know the Joycean ability in mystifying his friends. His "Paris Notebook" shows that he studied the Aristotelian definitions of pity and terror, rhythm, and imitation of nature by art. This would suggest that Joyce had probably read excerpts from the *Poetics*. Where St. Thomas is concerned, the quotations in the "Pola Notebook" ("Bonum est in quo tendit appetitum [*sic*]" and "Pulcera [*sic*] sunt quae visa placent") are both misquoted, and the definition of the three conditions of Beauty in *A Portrait* is linguistically correct but abridged. From this we

infer that Joyce had probably never read directly from the texts of Aquinas.[3]

The Medieval Model

What is meant by the affirmation that Joyce remained medievally minded from youth through maturity? In reading all of Joyce it is possible to single out thousands of situations in which he uses terms drawn from the medieval tradition, arguments accorded to a technique from medieval literature and philosophy. At this point, it may be helpful to construct an abstract model of the medieval way of thinking in order to demonstrate how Joyce adapts it point by point. While the medieval thought process is certainly more complex than the proposed outline, so too is Joyce. The point of this exercise is to summarily indicate the presence of medieval patterns in the mental economy of our author.

The medieval thinker cannot conceive, explain, or manage the world without inserting it into the framework of an Order, an Order whereby, quoting Edgard de Bruyne, "les êtres s'emboîtent les uns dans les autres." The young Stephen at Clongowes Wood College conceives of himself as a member of a cosmic whole—"Stephen Dedalus—Class of Elements—Clongowes Wood College—Sallins—County of Kildare—Ireland—Europe—The World—The Universe." *Ulysses* demonstrates this same concept of order by the choice of a Homeric framework and *Finnegans Wake* by the circular schema, borrowed from Vico's cyclical vision of history.

The medieval thinker knows that art is the human way to reproduce, in an artifact, the universal rules of cosmic order. In this sense art reflects the artist's impersonality rather than his personality. Art is an *analogon* of the world. Even if Joyce had discovered the notion of impersonality in more modern authors such as Flaubert, it goes without saying that his enthusiasm for this theory had medieval sources.

This framework of Order provides an unlimited chain of relations between creatures and events. Quoting Alanus ab Insulis:

> Omnis mundi creatura
> quasi liber et pictura
> nobis est in speculum.
>
> Nostrae vitae, nostrae mortis
> nostri status, nostrae sortis
> fidele signaculum.

It is the mechanism which permits epiphanies, where a thing becomes the living symbol of something else, and creates a continuous web of references. Any person or event is a cypher which refers to another part of the book. This generates the grid of allusions in *Ulysses* and the system of puns in *Finnegans Wake*. Every word embodies every other because language is a self-reflecting world. Language is the dream of history telling itself to itself. Language is a book readable by an ideal reader affected by an ideal insomnia. If you take away the transcendent God from the symbolic world of the Middle Ages, you have the world of Joyce. This operation, however, is performed by the most medieval thinkers of the Renaissance—Giordano Bruno and Nicola da Cusa, both masters to Joyce. The world is no longer a pyramid composed of continual transcendent displacements but a self-containing circle or spiral. . . .

Epiphany: From Scholasticism to Symbolism

The concept, not the term, "epiphany" reached Joyce from Walter Pater or, more explicitly, from that "Conclusion" to the *Studies in the History of the Renaissance* which had so great an influence on English culture between the two centuries. Rereading the pages of Pater, we realize that the analysis of the various moments in the process of the epiphanization of reality proceeds in a way that is analogous to the Joycean analysis of the three criteria of beauty. In Joyce, however, the object of analysis is a stable and objective given, while in Pater, it is the elusive flow of reality. It is not by chance that the famous "Conclusion" begins with a quotation from Heraclitus.

For Pater, reality is the sum of forces and elements that fade away as soon as they arise; they are made tangible and embodied in a troublesome presence only by our superficial experience, but when subjected to deeper reflection, they dissolve and their cohesive force is instantly suspended. We are then in a world of incoherent, flashing, unstable impressions. Habit is broken, everyday life dissolves, and only singular moments remain, seizable for an instant then immediately vanishing. In every moment, the perfection of a form appears in a hand or in a face; some tonality on the hill or on the sea is more exquisite than the rest; some state of passion or vision or intellectual excitement is "irresistibly real and attractive for us—for that moment only." Afterwards the moment has vanished, but for that moment only life has taken on a value, a reality, a reason. Not the fruit of experience, but experience itself is the end. To maintain this ecstasy would be "the success of life."

In this portrait of Pater is the English *fin de siècle* aesthete and his day-by-day strain to capture the fugitive and exquisite instant. In Joyce this heredity is purified of such delicacy and languor; Stephen Dedalus is not Marius the Epicurean. Nonetheless, the influence of the page cited above is quite vivid. Thus we realize that the entire scholastic framework that Stephen has erected to support his aesthetic perspective is used only to sustain a romantic idea of the poetic word as revelation and the poet as the only one who can give a reason to things, a meaning to life, a form to experience, a finality to the world.

Stephen's reasoning, crammed with Thomistic quotations, tends toward this resolution. In fact, only in the light of this resolution does one find real value in the various affirmations concerning the nature of the poet and the imagination that are found in Stephen's discussions and in the early writings of Joyce.

> The poet is the intense centre of the life of his age to which he stands in a relation than which none can be more vital. He alone is capable of absorbing in himself the life that surrounds him and of flinging it abroad again amid planetary music. When the poetic phenomenon is signalled in the heavens . . . it is time for the critics to verify their calculations in accordance with it. It is time for them to acknowledge that here the imagination has contemplated intensely the truth of the being of the visible world and that beauty, the splendour of truth, has been born (*SH* 80).

The poet is thus the one who, in a moment of grace, discovers the profound soul of things, and he is the one who makes them *exist* solely through the poetic word. Epiphany is thus a way of discovering reality and, at the same time, a way of defining reality through discourse. This conception develops somewhat from *Stephen Hero* to *A Portrait*. In the first book, the epiphany is still a way of seeing the world and thus a type of intellectual and emotional experience. Such experiences are represented in the sketches that the young Joyce gathers in his notebook *Epiphanies*—pieces of conversation that serve to identify a character, a tic, a typical vice, an existential experience. They are the rapid and imponderable visions that are noted in *Stephen Hero*—a conversation between two lovers overheard by chance on a foggy evening that gives Stephen "an impression keen enough to afflict his sensitiveness" (*SH* 211),

or the clock in the customs which is suddenly epiphanized and, without apparent reason, becomes "important." But why, and for whom? Pater offers an answer—*for the aesthete*, at the very moment when he seizes the event at a level beyond its habitual evaluation. Various pages in *A Portrait* seem directly inspired by this idea:

> His thinking was a dusk of doubt and selfmistrust lit up at moments by the lightnings of intuition, but lightnings of so clear a splendour that in those moments the world perished about his feet as if it had been fireconsumed: and thereafter his tongue grew heavy and he met the eyes of others with unanswering eyes for he felt that the spirit of beauty had folded him round like a mantle and that in revery at least he had been acquainted with nobility.
>
> . . . he found himself glancing from one casual word to another on his right or left in stolid wonder that they had been so silently emptied of instantaneous sense until every mean shop legend bound his mind like the words of a spell and his soul shrivelled up, sighing with age as he walked on in a lane among heaps of dead language (*P* 177–79).

Sometimes the image is more rapid: the vision of the reverend Stephen Dedalus, the *Mulier cantat*, an odor of rotten cabbage. The insignificant thing takes on importance. In *Stephen Hero* these are the cases in which there seems to be a tacit agreement between the aesthete and reality. These are also the cases in which *A Portrait* most clearly shows itself as the ironic and affectionate report of those inner experiences which, in *Stephen Hero*, were the unique moments, the central moments of the aesthetic experience as identified with the experience of life.

But between *Stephen Hero* and the final draft of *A Portrait* about ten years intervene. Situated in the middle is the experience of *Dubliners*. Each short story of this collection appears like a vast epiphany, or at least the arrangements of the events tend to resolve themselves in an epiphanic experience. But it is no longer a question of a rapid and momentary note-taking, an almost stenographic relationship to life experience. Here fact and emotional experience are isolated and, through the careful strategy of narrative technique, are placed "montage-style" at the culminating part of the story where they become climax, summary, and judgment of the entire situation.

In this way the epiphanies of *Dubliners* are key moments that arise in a realistic context. They consist of common facts or phrases but acquire the value of a moral symbol, a denunciation of a certain emptiness of existence. The vision of the old dead priest in the first story, the squalid inanity of Corley with his smile of triumph while showing the little coin in "Two Gallants," the final crying of Chandler in "A Little Cloud," and the solitude of Duffy in "A Painful Case" are all brief moments that turn moral situations into metaphors as the result of an accent placed imperceptibly upon them by the narrator.

Thus, at this point in his artistic maturation Joyce seems to achieve that at which the aesthetics of *Stephen Hero* merely hinted:

> the artist who could disentangle the subtle soul of the image from its mesh of defining circumstances most exactly and "re-embody" it in artistic circumstances chosen as the most exact for it in its new office, he was the supreme artist (*SH* 78).

In *A Portrait* the epiphany is no longer an emotional moment that the artistic word helps to recall but an operative moment of art. It founds and institutes, not a way to perceive but a way to produce life. At this point Joyce abandons the word "epiphany" for it suggests a moment of vision in which *something shows itself;*[4] what now interests him is the act of the *artist who shows something* by a strategic elaboration of the image. Stephen truly becomes "a priest of eternal imagination, transmuting the daily bread of experience into the radiant body of everliving life" (*P* 221).

This affirmation acquires meaning in *Stephen Hero*, for whom the classical style, "the syllogism of art, the only legitimate process from one world to another," is by nature "mindful of limitations" and "chooses rather to bend upon these present things and so to work upon them and fashion them that the quick intelligence may go beyond them to their meaning which is still unuttered" (*SH* 78). Art does not record; rather, it produces epiphanic visions in order to make the reader seize the "inside true inwardness of reality" across the "sextuple gloria of light actually retained."

The paramount example of epiphany in *A Portrait* is that of the seabird girl. It is no longer a question of a fleeting experience that can be written down and communicated by brief hints. Here reality is epiphanized through the verbal suggestions of the poet. The vision, with all its potential for the revelation of a universe resolved in beauty, in the pure aesthetic emotion, acquires its full importance only in the total and unalterable structure of the page.

At this point the last suspicion of Thomism is radically discarded and the categories of Aquinas reveal themselves as they were understood by the young artist—as a useful launching pad, a stimulating interpretive exercise whose sole purpose is to serve as the departure point for another solution. Although the epiphanies in *Stephen Hero*, identified with a discovery of reality, still retain a connection with the scholastic concept of *quidditas*, the artist now builds his epiphanic vision from the objective context of events—by connecting isolated facts in new relationships through a completely arbitrary poetic catalysis. An object does not reveal itself because of its verifiable, objective structure but because it becomes the symbol of an interior moment in Stephen.

Why does it become a symbol? The object which is epiphanized has no reasons for its epiphany other than the fact that it has been epiphanized. Both before and after Joyce, contemporary literature offers examples of this type. We notice that the fact is never epiphanized because it is worthy of being epiphanized. On the contrary, it appears worthy of being epiphanized because, in fact, it *has been* epiphanized. In pages like Montale's *Vecchi versi*, for example, the moth that beats against the lamp and sinks upon the table "pazza aliando le carte" does not have any right to survival in our memory other than in the force of a fact that has survived other facts. Only after it has become *gratuitously* important can an epiphanic fact overload itself with meaning and become a symbol.

This is not an example of the revelation of a thing itself in its objective essence, *quidditas*, but the revelation of what the thing means to us in that moment. It is the value bestowed on the thing at that moment which actually *makes* the thing. The epiphany confers upon the thing a value which it did not have before encountering the gaze of the artist. In this respect the doctrine of epiphany and *radiance* is clearly in opposition to the Thomist doctrine of *claritas*. Aquinas maintains a surrender to the object and its splendor. Joyce uproots the object from its usual context, subjecting it to new conditions and conferring upon it new splendor and value as the result of a creative vision.

In this light even the *integritas* can be understood as a type of choice, a perimeter, as we have said, not so much following

the contours of the given object as conferring outlines upon the chosen object. The epiphany is now the result of an art that dismantles reality and reshapes it according to new means. The evolution from the early writings, still anchored to an Aristotelian principle, to those of *A Portrait* is now complete.

Upon review of these texts in terms of the early Joycean aesthetics, we notice that in the "Pola Notebook" of 1904 Joyce again attempts to determine the phases of ordinary perception and, within it, the moment which offers the possibility of aesthetic enjoyment. Joyce thereby identifies two fundamental activities in the act of apprehension; the first is that of simple perception and the second that of "recognition" in which the perceived object is judged satisfactory and therefore beautiful and pleasing (even if it is an ugly object, it is judged beautiful and pleasing insofar as it is perceived as a formal structure). In these notes Joyce is more scholastic than he perhaps thought himself to be, posing the old question as to the "transcendental" properties of Being. He asks whether beauty is a quality that is coessential with all Being and whether every object is beautiful insofar as it is a form embodied in a determined matter and perceived through these structural characteristics— be it a flower, a monster, a moral act, a stone, a table. St. Thomas would have fully subscribed to these convictions, for which reason it is so difficult to individuate, from the point of view of Scholastic aesthetics, a specific "aesthetic" experience from the aesthetic quality of each common experience. Joyce therefore concludes that "even the most hideous object may be said to be beautiful for this reason as it is *a priori* said to be beautiful insofar as it encounters the activity of simple perception" (*CW* 147).

Joyce proposes the following solution in order to distinguish the aesthetic experience from the "normal" one: the second activity of apprehension carries a third, that of "satisfaction" in which the perceptual process is wholly fulfilled. From the intensity and duration of this satisfaction, one measures the aesthetic validity of the thing contemplated. With this, Joyce again approaches the Thomist position in which the beautiful object would be that "in cujus aspectu seu cognitione quietetur appetitus," and the fullness of aesthetic perception would consist in a sort of *pax*, a contemplative gratification. This *pax* can be easily identified with the concept of aesthetic "stasis" in the "Paris Notebook," in which Joyce resolves the Aristotelian idea of "catharsis."

Joyce takes no interest in the medico-psychological interpretation of catharsis as a Dionysiac experience, a purification effected through the kinetic stimulations of passion in order to obtain a purgation through shock. By catharsis, Joyce means the *arrest* of the feelings of pity and terror and the rising of joy. It is a rationalistic interpretation of the Aristotelian concept. At the appropriate moments, passions will be exorcized, detached from the mind of the audience and made "objective" in the pure dramatic texture of the plot. In a certain sense, these passions will be "defamiliarized" and rendered universal, thereafter "impersonal." It is understandable how Stephen Dedalus, who defends so vigorously the impersonality of art, finds himself attracted by this interpretation and makes it his own in *Stephen Hero*.

Although it appears unaltered in its surface form, the conception has radically changed from the early writings to *A Portrait*. In *A Portrait* the aesthetic joy and the stasis of passions become "the luminous silent stasis of esthetic pleasure." The terminology charges the concept with new implications. This static pleasure is not the purity of rational contemplation but the thrill in the face of mystery, the tension of sensitivity at the limits of the ineffable. Walter Pater, the symbolists, and D'Annunzio have replaced Aristotle.

In order to make this transition, Joyce needs to reconceptualize the mechanism of aesthetic perception and the nature of the perceived object. This happens in the theory of *claritas* and in the development of the idea of epiphany. Pleasure is no longer given by the fullness of an objective perception but by the subjective translation of an imponderable moment of experience. By a stylistic strategy, one thereby translates an actual experience into a linguistic equivalent of reality. The medieval artist was the servant of things and their laws, charged to create the work according to given rules. The Joycean artist, last inheritor of the romantic tradition, elicits meanings from a world that would otherwise be amorphous and, in so doing, masters the world of which he becomes the center.

Throughout A *Portrait*, Joyce thus debates a series of unresolved contradictions. Stephen, steeled in the school of the old Aquinas, rejects both the faith and the lessons of the master, modernizing the scholastic categories by instinct, without even realizing it. He does this by drawing upon an idea that is present in contemporary culture and that deeply influenced him. This is the romantic concept of the poetic act as the foundation and resolution of the world. Through this romanticism, the world is denied as a place of objective relationships and is conceived instead as a network of subjective connections established through the poetic act.

Could this poetic theory suffice one who has absorbed the lesson of Ibsen in order to find a way of clarifying, through art, the laws that govern human events? Could it suffice someone nourished by a scholastic way of thinking, a mode of thought which is a continuous invitation to order, to clear and qualifiable structure rather than lyrical and evanescent allusion?

In other words, Joyce, who began his career of aesthete with an essay titled, "Art and Life" and who found in Ibsen a profound relationship between the artistic work and moral experience, seems to reject any link between art and life in A *Portrait*. As his heritage of decadentism, he recognizes the only livable life to be the one which lives on the pages of the artist. If Joyce had stopped with A *Portrait*, nothing in the aesthetic formulation of the book could have been criticized and the aesthetics of Stephen would have been identified with those of the author. But from the moment that Joyce proposes to write *Ulysses*, he reveals the deep conviction that if art is a shaping activity, "the human disposition of sensible matter for an aesthetic end," then the exercise of shaping must be applied to a well-determined material, the tissue itself of the real events, psychological phenomena, moral relations, that is, to the whole of society and culture.[5] Thus Stephen's aesthetics will not entirely be the aesthetics of *Ulysses*. In fact, what Joyce states concerning *Ulysses* goes beyond the well-defined borders of the philosophical categories and the cultural choices of the young artist.

Joyce knew this and, in fact, A *Portrait* does not claim to

be the aesthetic manifesto of Joyce but the portrait of a Joyce who no longer existed when the author had finished this ironic, autobiographical sketch and begun *Ulysses*. In the third chapter of the book, Stephen is walking along the beach and remembers his own youthful projects, "remember your epiphanies on green oval leaves. . . ."

Naturally, many of the major aesthetic pivots of the early Joyce remain valid in his successive works. But the aesthetics of the first two books remain exemplary under another aspect; they propose, in all its significance, the conflict between a world thought *ad mentem divi Thomae* and the need for a contemporary sensibility. This conflict will be fatally repeated in the two successive works in a different form. It is the conflict of a traditional order and a new vision of the world, the conflict of the artist who tries to give form to the chaos in which he moves yet finds in his hands the instruments of the old Order which he has not yet succeeded in replacing.

Notes

The following abbreviations and editions of Joyce's works have been used in this article: P: A *Portrait of the Artist as a Young Man*, ed. Richard Ellmann (New York: Viking, 1963); SH: *Stephen Hero*, ed. John J. Slocum and Herbert Cahoon (Norfolk, CT: New Directions, 1944, 1963); FW: *Finnegans Wake* (New York: Viking, 1939, and London: Faber & Faber, 1939).

1. Roman Jakobson, "Closing Statements: Linguistics and Poetics," in *Style in Language*, ed. T. A. Sebek (Cambridge, MA: MIT Press, 1960).

2. See "The Study of Languages" (*The Critical Writings of James Joyce*, ed. Ellsworth Mason and Richard Ellmann. [New York: Viking, 1959], Chapter III), in which Joyce (1898–99, at the age of sixteen) already outlines his main lines of thought: 1) the discourse must maintain "even in moments of the greatest emotion an innate symmetry"; 2) "the higher grades of language . . . are . . . the champion and exponents . . . of Truth"; 3) "in the history of words there is much that indicates the history of men." These three remarks can be read as the program of the three major works, A *Portrait*, *Ulysses*, and the *Wake*.

3. As for Joyce's Aristotelian and Thomistic readings, see *Critical Writings*; Richard Ellmann, *James Joyce* (New York: Oxford University Press, 1959); William T. Noon, *Joyce and Aquinas* (New Haven: Yale University Press, 1957); John J. Slocum and Herbert Cahoon, A *Bibliography of James Joyce (1882–1941)* (New Haven: Yale University Press, 1953).

4. According to Noon (1957, p. 71), the notion of epiphany came to Joyce through the interpretation of Aquinas' *claritas* proposed by De Wulf in 1895; the entire argument is based on the fact that De Wulf uses the word "epiphenomenon" in order to designate the aesthetic quality of an object. There is not, on the contrary, however, any proof that Joyce had read De Wulf; on the contrary, there is proof that Joyce had read D'Annunzio's *Il fuoco* (see Ellmann, 1959, pp. 60–61). The first part of *Il fuoco* is entitled "Epifania del fuoco." A term-to-term comparison between D'Annunzio's work and A *Portrait* reveals astounding stylistic and lexical affinities. See Umberto Eco, "Joyce et D'Annunzio," *L'Arc* 36 (1968), special issue on James Joyce.

5. Cf. S. L. Goldberg, *The Classical Temper* (London: Chatto & Windus, 1961), namely the chapter "Art and Life."

Dubliners

BREWSTER GHISELIN

From "The Unity of Joyce's *Dubliners*"

Accent, Spring 1956, pp. 75–86

The idea is not altogether new that the structure of James Joyce's *Dubliners*, long believed to be loose and episodic, is really unitary. In 1944, Richard Levin and Charles Shattuck made it clear that the book is "something more than a

collection of discrete sketches." In their essay "First Flight to Ithaca: A New Reading of Joyce's *Dubliners*," they demonstrated that like the novel *Ulysses* the stories of *Dubliners* are integrated by a pattern of correspondence to the *Odyssey* of Homer. To this first demonstration of a latent structural unity in *Dubliners* must be added the evidence of its even more full integration by means of a symbolic structure so highly organized as to suggest the most subtle elaborations of Joyce's method in his maturity.

So long as *Dubliners* was conceived of only as "a straight

work of Naturalistic fiction," the phrase of Edmund Wilson characterizing the book in *Axel's Castle*, its unity could appear to be no more than thematic. The work seemed merely a group of brilliant individual stories arranged in such a way as to develop effectively the import which Joyce himself announced, but did not fully reveal, in describing the book as "a chapter of the moral history of my country" and in suggesting that his interest focused upon Dublin as "the centre of paralysis." As Harry Levin explained in his introduction to *The Portable Joyce*, "The book is not a systematic canvass like *Ulysses*; nor is it integrated, like the *Portrait*, by one intense point of view; but it comprises, as Joyce explained, a series of chapters in the moral history of his community; and the episodes are arranged in careful progression from childhood to maturity, broadening from private to public scope."

So narrow an understanding of *Dubliners* is no longer acceptable. Recent and steadily increasing appreciation of the fact that there is much symbolism in the book has dispelled the notion that it is radically different in technique from Joyce's later fiction. During the past six or eight years a significant body of critics, among them Caroline Gordon, Allen Tate, and W. Y. Tindall, have published their understanding that the naturalism of *Dubliners* is complicated by systematic use of symbols, which establish relationships between superficially disparate elements in the stories. Discussion of "The Dead," for example, has made it obvious that the immobility of snowy statues in that story is symbolically one with the spiritual condition of Gabriel Conroy turned to the wintry window at the very end of *Dubliners* and with the deathly arrest of paralysis announced on the first page of the book. In the light of this insight other elements of the same pattern, such as the stillness of the girl frozen in fear at the end of the fourth story, virtually declare themselves.

Such images, significantly disposed, give a firm symbolic texture and pattern to the individual stories of *Dubliners* and enhance the integrity of the work as a whole. But no constellation, zodiac, or whole celestial sphere of symbols is enough in itself to establish in the fifteen separate narratives, each one in its realistic aspect a completely independent action, the embracing and inviolable order of full structural unity. That is achieved, however, by means of a single development, essentially of action, organized in complex detail and in a necessary, meaningful sequence throughout the book. Because this structure is defined partly by realistic means, partly by symbols, much of it must remain invisible until the major symbols in which it defines itself are recognized, as too few of them have been, and displayed in their more significant relationships. When the outlines of the symbolic pattern have been grasped, the whole unifying development will be discernible as a sequence of events in a moral drama, an action of the human spirit struggling for survival under peculiar conditions of deprivation, enclosed and disabled by a degenerate environment that provides none of the primary necessities of spiritual life. So understood, *Dubliners* will be seen for what it is, in effect, both a group of short stories and a novel, the separate histories of its protagonists composing one essential history, that of the soul of a people which has confused and weakened its relation to the source of spiritual life and cannot restore it.

In so far as this unifying action is evident in the realistic elements of the book, it appears in the struggle of certain characters to escape the constricting circumstances of existence in Ireland, and especially in Dublin, "the centre of paralysis." As in *A Portrait of the Artist as a Young Man*, an escape is envisaged in traveling eastward from the city, across the seas to the freedom of the open world. In *Dubliners*, none of Joyce's protagonists moves very far on this course, though some aspire to go far. Often their motives are unworthy, their minds are confused. Yet their dreams of escape and the longing of one of them even to "fly away to another country" are suggestive of the intent of Stephen Dedalus in *A Portrait* to "fly by those nets," those constrictions of "nationality, language, religion," which are fully represented in *Dubliners* also. Thus, in both books, ideas of enclosure, of arrest, and of movement in space are associated with action of moral purport and with spiritual aspiration and development.

In *Dubliners*, the meaning of movement is further complicated by the thematic import of that symbolic paralysis which Joyce himself referred to, an arrest imposed from within, not by the "nets" of external circumstance, but by a deficiency of impulse and power. The idea of a moral paralysis is expressed sometimes directly in terms of physical arrest, even in the actual paralysis of the priest Father Flynn, whose condition is emphasized by its appearance at the beginning of the book and is reflected in the behavior of Father Purdon, in the penultimate story "observed to be struggling up into the pulpit" as if he were partially paralyzed. But sheer physical inaction of any kind is a somewhat crude means of indicating moral paralysis. Joyce has used it sparingly. The frustrations and degradations of his moral paralytics are rarely defined in physical stasis alone, and are sometimes concomitant with vigorous action. Their paralysis is more often expressed in a weakening of their impulse and ability to move forcefully, effectually, far, or in the right direction, especially by their frustration in ranging eastward in the direction of release or by their complete lack of orientation, by their failure to pass more than a little way beyond the outskirts of Dublin, or by the restriction of their movement altogether to the city or to some narrow area within it.

The case of the boy in the first story, "The Sisters," is representative. Restive under the surviving influence of his dead mentor Father Flynn, yet lost without him, and resentful of the meager life of the city, he only dreams vaguely and disturbingly of being in a far country in the East, and wakes to wander in the city that still encloses him. At the end of the story he sits among hapless women, all immobile and disconsolate, in the dead priest's own room, in the very house where the priest has died, near the center of the center of paralysis. His physical arrest and his enclosure are expressive, even apart from a knowledge of the rich symbolism which qualifies them in ways too complicated to consider at this stage in discussion. Bereft of spiritual guidance, and deprived of the tension of an interest that has been primary in his life, he sits confused and in isolation, unsustained by the secular world about him, unstirred by anything in the natural world, moved only by a fleeting sense of life still in the coffin in the room overhead, a doubt and a hope like a faint resurgence of faith, instantly dispelled.

It should be no surprise to discover in a book developing the theme of moral paralysis a fundamental structure of movements and stases, a system of significant motions, countermotions, and arrests, involving every story, making one consecutive narrative of the surge and subsidence of life in Dublin. In the development of the tendency to eastward movement among the characters of *Dubliners*, and in its successive modifications, throughout the book, something of such a system is manifest. It may be characterized briefly as an eastward trend, at first vague, quickly becoming dominant, then wavering, weakening, and at last reversed. Traced in rough outline, the pattern is as follows: in a sequence of six stories, an impulse and movement eastward to the outskirts of the city or beyond; in a single story, an impulse to fly away upward out of a confining situation near the center of Dublin; in a sequence of four stories, a gradual replacement of the impulse eastward by an impulse and movement westward; in three stories, a limited activity confined almost wholly within the central area of Dublin; and in the concluding story a movement eastward to the heart of the city, the exact center of arrest, then, in vision only, far westward into death.

Interpreted realistically, without recourse to symbol, this pattern may show at most the frustration of Dubliners unable to escape eastward, out of the seaport and overseas, to a more living world. An orientation so loosely conceived seems quite unsuited to determine a powerful organization of form and meaning. Understood in its symbolic import, however, the eastward motion or the desire for it takes on a much more complicated and precise significance.

Orientation and easting are rich in symbolic meanings of which Joyce was certainly aware. An erudite Catholic, he must have known of the ancient though not invariable custom of building churches with their heads to the east and placing the high altar against the east wall or eastward against a reredos in the depths of the building, so that the celebrant of the mass faced east, and the people entered the church and approached the altar from the west and remained looking in the same direction as the priest. He knew that in doing so they looked toward Eden, the earthly paradise, and he may have felt, like Gregory of Nyssa, that the force of the sacramental orientation was increased by that fact. Perhaps he did not know that the catechumens of the fourth century turned to the west to renounce Satan and to the east to recite the creed before they stepped into the baptismal font, to receive the sacrament that opens the door of spiritual life. Probably he did know that Christ returning for the Last Judgment was expected to come from the east. And he must have shared that profound human feeling, older than Christianity, which has made the sunrise immemorially and all but universally an emblem of the return of life and has made the east, therefore, an emblem of beginning and a place of rebirth. Many times Joyce must have seen the sun rise out of the Irish Sea, washed and brilliant. He could not have failed to know that washing and regeneration are implicit in the sacrament of baptism, and he may have known that in the earlier ages of Christianity baptism was called Illumination. He could not have failed, and the evidence of his symbolism in *Dubliners* shows that he did not fail, to see how a multitude of intimations of spiritual meaning affected the eastward aspirations and movements of characters in his book, and what opportunity it afforded of giving to the mere motion of his characters the symbolic import of moral action.

In constructing *Dubliners*, Joyce must have responded to the force of something like the whole body of insights of which these are representative. For these insights, with some others closely associated with them, are the chief light by which we shall be enabled to follow the development of what I have called the unifying action of *Dubliners* and, through understanding the structure of the book, to penetrate to its central significance. The unity of *Dubliners* is realized, finally, in terms of religious images and ideas, most of them distinctively Christian.

Among these the most important for the immediate purpose of understanding are the symbols, sacraments, and doctrines of the Catholic Church, especially its version of the ancient sacraments of baptism and the sacrificial meal and its concepts of the soul's powers, its perils, and its destiny. In terms of the religious ideas with which Joyce was most familiar the basic characteristics of his structural scheme are readily definable, and some of them are not definable otherwise. The unifying action may be conceived of, oversimply yet with essential accuracy, as a movement of the human soul, in desire of life, through various conditions of Christian virtue and stages of deadly sin, toward or away from the font and the altar and all the gifts of the two chief sacraments provided for its salvation, toward or away from God. In these ideas all the most essential determinants of the spiritual action which makes of *Dubliners* one consecutive narrative are represented: its motivation, its goal and the means of reaching it, and those empowering or disempowering states of inmost being which define the moral conditions under which the action takes place.

The states of being, of virtue and sin, are doubly important. For in *Dubliners* the primary virtues and sins of Christian tradition function both in their intrinsic character, as moral manifestations and determinants of behavior, and structurally in defining the order of the separate stories and in integrating them in a significant sequence. Thus they are one means of establishing the unity of the book, a simple but not arbitrary or wholly superficial means, supplementing with structural reinforcement and with a deepening of import that more fundamental pattern of motions and arrests already touched upon.

Like the booklong sequence of movements and stases, the various states of the soul in virtue and sin form a pattern of strict design traceable through every story. Each story in *Dubliners* is an action defining amid different circumstances of degradation and difficulty in the environment a frustration or defeat of the soul in a different state of strength or debility. Each state is related to the preceding by conventional associations or by casual connections or by both, and the entire sequence represents the whole course of moral deterioration ending in the death of the soul. Joyce's sense of the incompatibility of salvation with life in Dublin is expressed in a systematic display, one by one in these stories, of the three theological virtues and the four cardinal virtues in suppression, of the seven deadly sins triumphant, and of the deathly consequence, the spiritual death of all the Irish. Far more than his announced intention, of dealing with childhood, adolescence, maturity, and public life, this course of degenerative change in the states of the soul tends to determine the arrangement of the stories in a fixed order and, together with the pattern of motions and arrests, to account for his insistence upon a specific, inalterable sequence.

Although Joyce's schematic arrangement of virtues and sins in *Dubliners* does not conform entirely to the most usual order in listing them, it does so in the main. In the first three stories, in which the protagonists are presumably innocent, the theological virtues faith, hope, and love, in the conventional order, are successively displayed in abeyance and finally in defeat. In the fourth story, the main character, Eveline, lacking the strength of faith, hope, and love, wavers in an effort to find a new life and, failing in the cardinal virtue of fortitude, remains in Dublin, short of her goal and weakened in her spiritual powers and defenses against evil. In the fifth through the eleventh stories the seven deadly sins, pride, covetousness, lust, envy, anger, gluttony, and sloth, are portrayed successively in action, usually in association with other sins adjacent in the list. The seven stories devoted to the sins occupy exactly the central position in the book. The sequence of their presentation is the most conventional one, except for the placing of anger before gluttony, a slight and not unique deviation. Gluttony is strongly represented, moreover, in the usual position, the fifth place, by means of the drunkenness of the central character Farrington, as well as in the sixth. And in the sixth place gluttony is defined in the attitudes and behavior of others than the main character, Maria, who is interested in food and much concerned with it rather than avid of it. Her quiet depression is more truly expressive of her essential state of soul; and in it another sin that appears rarely in lists of the seven is apparent, the sin of tristitia, or gloominess, sometimes substituted for the similar sin of sloth. Joyce's intent seems to have been to create here a palimpsest, inscribing three sins in the space afforded for two. The effect has been to reduce gluttony to secondary importance while giving it full recognition in both of its aspects as overindulgence in drinking as well as in eating. The sequence of sins completes Joyce's representation of the defeat of the soul in its most inward strength and prepares for its failure in the exercise of rational powers. Alienated wholly from God, it cannot act now even in expression of the natural or cardinal virtues, in the words of Aquinas "the good as defined by reason." In the twelfth through the fourteenth stories, the subversion of the cardinal virtues of justice, temperance, and prudence, and the contradiction of reason, upon which they are based, is displayed in those narratives that Joyce intended to represent "public life" in Ireland. Justice, the social virtue regulating the others, comes first in the group. The placing of prudence or wisdom last instead of first, the commonest position, is perhaps influenced by the sequence of appearance in these stories of those hindrances of the spirit in Ireland, the "nets" of "nationality, language, religion." The order, moreover, is climactic. Certainly the culminating subversion of the three virtues is represented in the third story of this group, "Grace," in the sermon of "a man of the world" recommending worldly wisdom for the guidance of "his fellowmen." In the fifteenth and last story of *Dubliners*, no virtue or sin is given such attention as to suggest its predominance. Perhaps that virtue of magnanimity which Aristotle added to the group of four named by the Greeks is displayed in abeyance in Gabriel Conroy's self-concern, but recovered at last in his final self-abnegation and visionary acceptance of the communion of death. Perhaps merely the consequences of moral degeneration are to be discerned in the final story, the completion of spiritual disintegration, death itself.

The pattern of virtues and sins and the spatial pattern of motions and arrests in *Dubliners* are of course concomitant, and they express one development. As sin flourishes and virtue withers, the force of the soul diminishes, and it becomes more and more disoriented, until at the last all the force of its impulse toward the vital east is confused and spent and it inclines wholly to the deathly west. All this development is embodied, realistically or symbolically, in the experience of the principal characters as they search for vital satisfaction either in spiritual wholeness or in personal willfulness, apprehending the nature of their goal and their immediate needs truly or falsely, moving effectually toward the means of spiritual enlargement or faltering into meanness and withdrawing into a meager and spurious safety, seeking or avoiding the sacred elements of the font and the altar, those ancient Christian and pre-Christian means of sustaining the life of the spirit through lustration, regeneration, illumination, and communion. The unifying pattern of motions and arrests is manifested, story by story, in the action of the principal figure in each, as he moves in relation to the orient source and to the sacramental resources of spiritual life, expressing in physical behavior his moral condition of virtue or sin and his spiritual need and desire. His activity, outwardly of the body, is inwardly that of the soul, either advancing more or less freely and directly eastward or

else confined and halted or wandering disoriented, short of its true goal and its true objects the water of regeneration and the wine and bread of communion, the means of approach to God, and often in revulsion from them, accepting plausible substitutes or nothing whatever.

In *Dubliners* from first to last the substitutes are prominent, the true objects are unavailable. The priest in the first story, "The Sisters," has broken a chalice, is paralyzed, and dies; he cannot offer communion, and an empty chalice lies on his breast in death. The food and drink obtained by the boy whose friend he has been are unconsecrated: wine and crackers are offered to him solemnly, but by secular agents. Again and again throughout *Dubliners* such substitutes for the sacred elements of the altar recur, always in secular guise: "musty biscuits" and "raspberry lemonade," porter and "a caraway seed." Suggestions less overt are no less pointed. The abundant table in "The Dead," loaded with food and with bottled water and liquors, but surrounded by human beings gathered together in imperfect fellowship, emphasizes the hunger of the soul for bread and wine that can nourish it, rather than the body, and assuage its loneliness through restoring it to the communion of love. The symbolism of baptismal water likewise enforces the fact of spiritual privation. In "The Sisters" the secular baptism of a cold bath is recommended by the boy's uncle as the source of his strength. Less certainly symbolic, but suggestive in the context, is the fact that the body of the priest is washed by a woman, a point that Joyce thought important enough to define by explicit statements in two passages. In the house where the priest has lived and died, his sisters keep a shop where umbrellas, devices for rejecting the rain of heaven, are sold and re-covered. The open sea, the great symbol of the font in *Dubliners*, is approached by many of the central characters, longed for, but never embarked upon, never really reached. Canal, river, and estuary are crossed; Kingstown Harbor is attained, but the vessel boarded in the harbor is lying at anchor. When, in fear of drowning, the reluctant protagonist of the fourth story, "Eveline," hangs back refusing to embark on an ocean voyage, she may be understood to have withdrawn as at the brink of the baptismal font, for by her action she has renounced that new life which she had looked forward to attaining through moving eastward out of Dublin Bay on the night sea. The idea of her deprivation is reinforced by her final condition, of insensate terror, the reverse of spiritual refreshment and illumination.

Though the spiritual objects that are imaged in these substitutes represent the gifts of the two chief sacraments of the Church, baptism, the first in necessity, and the Eucharist, the first in dignity, there is no suggestion in *Dubliners* that the soul's needs can be supplied by the Church, in its current condition. The only scene in a church, in the story "Grace," implies exactly the opposite, for the sermon of Father Purdon is frankly designed to serve the purposes of those who "live in the world, and, to a certain extent, for the world." The Church is secularized, and it shares in the general paralysis. Its failure in the lives of Joyce's Dubliners is emphasized by the irony that although the nature of the soul has not altered and the means of its salvation retain their old aspect, its needs must be satisfied in entire dissociation from the Church.

Since those needs cannot be satisfied in Ireland, as Joyce represents it in *Dubliners*, the soul's true satisfaction cannot be exhibited in the experience of those who remain in Ireland. It can only be simulated and suggested, either in their relation to those secular substitutes for spiritual things that intimate the need for baptism and communion or in their turning toward the soul's orient, the symbolic east, variously imaged. Some of

Joyce's dissatisfied characters, such as Little Chandler, suppose that they can change their condition by escaping from Ireland eastward across the sea to another life in a different place. Physically their goal must be another country; spiritually it has the aspect of a new life. The association functions symbolically. Throughout *Dubliners*, one of the symbolic images of the spiritual goal is a far country. Like the symbols of water, wine, and bread, the far country images the soul's need for life that cannot be attained in Ireland.

Apparently it is not easily attainable outside of Ireland either. Those Dubliners who have reached England or the Continent, characters such as Gabriel Conroy or Ignatius Gallaher, the journalist whom Little Chandler envies because he has made a life for himself in London, show by their continuing to behave like other Dubliners that to be transported physically overseas is not necessarily to find a new life, or to be changed essentially at all. No doubt their failure to change means that the whole of Europe is secularized, perhaps the whole world. Still more, it emphasizes the subjective nature of the attainment symbolized by arrival in a far country. A new condition of inward life is the goal; not a place, but what the place implies, is the true east of the soul. The far countries reached by the boy in "The Sisters" and sought by the boy in "Araby," perhaps the same boy, are not in the world. In one story he dreams of being in an eastern land which he thinks, not very confidently, is Persia. In the other he goes to a bazaar bearing the "magical name" *Araby*, a word casting "an Eastern enchantment." In both stories the far country is probably the same, that fabulous Arabia which is associated with the Phoenix, symbol of the renewal of life in the resurrection of the sun. To the dreamer it suggests a journey and strange customs, but he cannot conceive its meaning. The meaning is plain, however, to the reader aware of the symbols: the boy has looked inward toward the source of his own life, away from that civilization which surrounds him but does not sustain him. The same import, with further meaning, is apparent in the later story. The response of the boy to the name *Araby* and his journey eastward across the city define his spiritual orientation, as his response to the disappointing reality of the bazaar indicates his rejection of a substitute for the true object of the soul's desire.

The sea too, like the image and idea of a far country, symbolizes the orient goal of life. It may of itself, as water, suggest the baptismal font. And in any case it must tend strongly to do so because of the sacramental import of water established by other water symbolism throughout *Dubliners*. The element itself is highly significant, and the great image of it is the sea, the water of liberating voyage and of change and danger, of death and resurrection. The sheer physical prominence of the sea eastward from Dublin colors the east with the significance of baptismal water. In turn the sea is colored by the significance of the east. The altar, even more immediately than the font, is implied in the concept of orientation.

Perhaps in the symbol of the sea in *Dubliners* the identification of the two chief sacraments should be understood. Their identification would not be altogether arbitrary. For the close relationship and even the essential similarity of the two sacraments is suggested in several ways, apart from their association with the east: by their interdependence in fulfillment of a spiritual purpose; by the invariable mixture of a few drops of water with the wine in the chalice; and above all by the concept of rebirth, in which the font is profoundly associated with the altar, the place where Christ is believed to be reborn at the consecration of the divine sacrifice. That Joyce could make the identification is plain from his having merged font with altar in *Finnegans Wake*, in the conception of the "tubbathaltar" of Saint Kevin Hydrophilos. Going "westfrom" toward a suitable supply of water, and showing his sense of the importance of orientation by genuflecting seven times eastward, Saint Kevin fills up his device of dual function, in "ambrosian eucharistic joy of heart," and sits in it. Though Joyce may not have been ready, so early as in *Dubliners*, to identify font with altar, he has developed a body of symbolism which intimately involves them, and possibly merges them, in the symbol of the orient sea.

In that spatial pattern in which the unity of *Dubliners* is expressed as an action, the orient goal is no one simple thing. It is a rich complex of associated ideas and images, only outwardly a place or places, intrinsically a vital state of being, a condition of grace conferred and sustained, presumably, by all the means of grace. Perhaps the main aspect of the symbolic orient, however, is of the eastward sea, its richest and most constantly represented image. The sea is the image most clearly opposable to that deadly contrary of the symbolic orient in all its import of spiritual life, that deathly state of moral disability, which Joyce conceived to be dominant in Ireland and centered in Dublin. The opposition is basic and clear in *Dubliners* of the eastward sea to the westward land, of ocean water to earth, of movement to fixation, of vital change to passivity in the status quo, of the motion toward new life to the stasis of paralysis in old life ways.

S. L. GOLDBERG
From "The Development of the Art:
Chamber Music to *Dubliners*"
James Joyce
1962, pp. 36–40

W hatever influences may be detected in *Dubliners*—and Chekhov, Maupassant, George Moore, and Flaubert have all been mentioned[1]—and however easy it has since become to write the same kind of stories, it is nevertheless a remarkable achievement for a writer in his early twenties. The stories are by no means simple naturalistic sketches, as some have thought them; nor, on the other hand, are they structures of infinitely complex "symbolism."[2] Each brings a limited area of experience to sharp focus, renders visible its "whatness," and does so with an economical, concentrated purposefulness that gives the realistic details their full metaphorical import. Joyce had learned his craft. What is more, the stories are lightly but suggestively related, so that the book is something more than merely a sum of its parts.

The opening sentences of the first story, "The Sisters," as we gradually come to realise, are something like a statement of the major themes of the whole book:

> There was no hope for him this time: it was the third stroke. Night after night I had passed the house (it was vacation time) and studied the lighted square of the window: and night after night I had found it lighted in the same way, faintly and evenly. If he was dead, I thought, I would see the reflection of candles on the darkened blind, for I knew that two candles must be set at the head of a corpse. He had often said to me: 'I am not long for this world,' and I had thought his words idle. Now I knew they were true. Every night as I gazed up at the window I said softly to myself the word *paralysis*. It had always sounded strangely in my ears, like the word *gnomon* in the Euclid and the word *simony* in the Catechism. But

now it sounded to me like the name of some maleficent and sinful being. It filled me with fear, and yet I longed to be nearer to it and to look upon its deadly work.

The terms "paralysis" and "simony" (more discursively defined in *Stephen Hero*) suggest the pervasive moral condition, the "maleficent and sinful being," exposed in story after story.[3] "Gnomon" suggests their artistic method, by which the whole is suggested by the part or (as with the gnomon on a sun-dial) the light by its shadow: the simple but effective metaphor of light/darkness is used in many of the stories.

In this first story, the old priest's physical paralysis becomes the mark of his failure of courage before the divine mystery he had tried to serve, and of his consequent resignation to hopelessness and death. In "An Encounter," the paralysis is that of diseased obsession. The unruly, romantic, adventurous spirit of the boy, seeking a larger freedom of life, encounters only the maleficent disorder of the old pervert; yet although he fears it, he outwits it: courage wins him his freedom. In "Araby," the boy's romantic longings at last collapse and yet triumph in the darkened hall of the bazaar; the chink of money and the inane chatter there come to represent the materialistic "simony" which (even in his own desires) at once betrays his foolish ideals and is itself exposed by their innocent "folly." And so on through the book. The stories become images: of paralysed automatism of the will, the paralysing hand of the past, a paralysing feebleness of moral imagination, a simoniac-al willingness to buy and sell the life of the spirit, timidity, frustration, self-righteousness, fear of convention, fear of sin, hypocrisy, vulgarity, pettiness. Each, with a fine dexterity, vivisects its material to lay bare the moral disease that distorts it to its present shape.

The metaphor of vivisection is Joyce's own,[4] and it describes perfectly the art of such stories as "Two Gallants" or "Ivy Day in the Committee Room" or "Grace," an art swift, sharp, accurate, with every stroke deliberately measured. The tone is flat, grimly reticent; the style distant; the observation and metaphorical detail so consistently pointed that they achieve a kind of wit. Yet the success is not consistent. Some stories are too intent upon their analytical purposes. The formal neatness of "Eveline," "After the Race," "The Boarding House," and "Counterparts," for instance, is so obvious and oversimplifying, that the art comes to seem almost program-matic. These stories lack the vital detail pressing *against* the author's scalpel, and they also lack the author's rather malicious enjoyment both of his material and of his skill in dealing with it, which enliven "Two Gallants," "Ivy Day," "Grace," or even "A Little Cloud," "Clay," and "A Mother." But then, as all these images of spiritual decay succeed each other, we may well begin to question the mood of the book generally. Is not its tone, indeed its whole attitude to life, perhaps too insistently, and too constrictingly, "vivisective"?

Our answer inevitably reflects our view of Joyce's work as a whole. To some critics, *Dubliners* is a dispassionate, morally realistic account of modern life, Joyce's discovery of his lifelong attitude (ironical exposure) to his lifelong subject ("paralysis"

and alienation). To others, his irony is "romantic," built upon the contrast between the individual's desires or feelings and the sordid realities of the modern world. To others again, his irony is only a device (like Chekhov's) for heightening the pity and terror of life.[5] Clearly, there are grounds for each of these judgments; but we also have to remember Joyce's relative immaturity when he wrote *Dubliners* and not be surprised if the book betrays it. Even while recognising the artistic success, we must also appreciate its limitations—not least because both help to explain Joyce's further development. And, not unnatur-ally, the limitations are very much those revealed more blatantly in *Stephen Hero*: an uncertain grasp of the values by which others are criticised, a vagueness about the genuine "life" by which simony and paralysis are constantly measured, a tendency to oversimplify reality in the process of exposing it.

It is not that the stories fail to imply the importance of courage, self-knowledge, fulfilment, freedom, or even the plainer domestic virtues; nor do they lack pity of a kind. But the comparison with Chekhov (or *Ulysses* for that matter) shows how little these values mean in *Dubliners*, how little it reveals what they might *be* in the actual experience of ordinary people, how complacent is its superior viewpoint. Some of the stories do reach towards a more self-critical, more specific, and hence (to that degree) deeper insight: "Araby," for example, "The Boarding House," "A Painful Case," and (most notably) "The Dead"—each, incidentally, the last in its respective group (childhood, adolescence, maturity, and public life).[6] But "Araby," for all its tone of mature wisdom, remains slightly evasive about how compromised the boy's romanticism really is; "The Boarding House" can only gesture vaguely towards the interconnexions between the mother's "simoniacal" plotting and the possibilities of life opening before her daughter as a result, symbolically suggesting only enough to make us realise how little the art realises (here and elsewhere) of the complicat-ing paradoxes of life.

Notes

1. M. Magalaner and R. M. Kain, *Joyce: the Man, the Work, the Reputation*, New York 1956, pp. 58 ff.; Allen Tate, "Three Commentaries," in *Sewanee Review*, LVIII (1950), p. 1. But cp. Richard Ellmann, *James Joyce*, New York 1959, p. 171n.
2. See Magalaner and Kain, *Joyce*, pp. 68 ff. Other "symbolic" explications may be found in B. Ghiselin, "The Unity of James Joyce's *Dubliners*," in *Accent*, XVI (1956), pp. 75 ff., 196 ff.; M. Magalaner, *Time of Apprenticeship: The Fiction of the Young James Joyce*, New York and London 1959, ch. 3; W. Y. Tindall, *A Reader's Guide to James Joyce*, New York 1959, ch. 1; but as criticisms of *literature* most of these strike me as either irrelevant or unconvincing.
3. Cp. A. Ostroff, "The Moral Vision in *Dubliners*," in *Western Speech*, XX (1956), pp. 196 ff.
4. *Stephen Hero*, ed. Theodore Spencer, London 1944; New York 1955; London 1956; p. 190 (186).
5. E.g. Hugh Kenner, *Dublin's Joyce*, London 1955, ch. 5; Harry Levin, *James Joyce, A Critical Introduction*, Norfolk, Conn. 1941, p. 41; Magalaner and Kain, *Joyce*, p. 62.
6. *Epiphanies*, ed. O. A. Silverman, Lockwood Memorial Library, University of Buffalo, 1956, p. 216.

A Portrait of the Artist as a Young Man

HUGH KENNER

From "The *Portrait* in Perspective"
Dublin's Joyce (1955)
1956, pp. 112–33

Linking Themes

I n the . . . *Portrait* Joyce abandoned the original intention (in *Stephen Hero*) of writing the account of his own escape from Dublin. One cannot escape one's Dublin. He recast Stephen Dedalus as a figure who could not even detach himself from Dublin because he had formed himself on a denial of Dublin's values. He is the egocentric rebel become an ultimate. There is no question whatever of his regeneration. "Stephen no longer interests me to the same extent [as Bloom]," said Joyce to Frank Budgen one day. "He has a shape that can't be changed."[1] His shape is that of aesthete. The Stephen of the first chapter of *Ulysses* who "walks wearily", constantly "leans" on everything in sight, invariably sits down before he has gone three paces, speaks "gloomily", "quietly", "with bitterness", and "coldly", and "suffers" his handkerchief to be pulled from his pocket by the exuberant Mulligan, is precisely the priggish, humourless Stephen of the last chapter of the *Portrait* who cannot remember what day of the week it is, P206/201,[2] sentimentalizes like Charles Lamb over the "human pages" of a second-hand Latin book, P209/204, conducts the inhumanly pedantic dialogue with Cranly on mother-love, P281/271, writes Frenchified verses in bed in an erotic swoon, and is epiphanized at full length, like Shem the Penman beneath the bedclothes, F176,[3] shrinking from the "common noises" of daylight:

> Shrinking from that life he turned towards the wall, making a cowl [!] of the blanket and staring at the great overblown scarlet flowers of the tattered wallpaper. He tried to warm his perishing joy in their scarlet glow, imaging a roseway from where he lay upwards to heaven all strewn with scarlet flowers. Weary! Weary! He too was weary of ardent ways. (P260/252.)

This new primrose path is a private Jacob's ladder let down to his bed now that he is too weary to do anything but go to heaven.

To make epic and drama emerge naturally from the intrinsic stresses and distortions of the lyric material meant completely new lyric techniques for a constation exact beyond irony. The *Portrait* concentrates on stating themes, arranging apparently transparent words into configurations of the utmost symbolic density. Here is the director proposing that Stephen enter the priesthood:

> The director stood in the embrasure of the window, his back to the light, leaning an elbow on the brown crossblind, and, as he spoke and smiled, slowly dangling and looping the cord of the other blind, Stephen stood before him, following for a moment with his eyes the waning of the long summer daylight above the roofs or the slow deft movements of the priestly fingers. The priest's face was in total shadow, but the waning daylight from behind him touched the deeply grooved temples and the curves of the skull. (P178/175.)

The looped cord, the shadow, the skull, none of these is accidental. The "waning daylight," twice emphasized, conveys that denial of nature which the priest's office represented for Stephen; "his back to the light" co-operates toward a similar effect. So "crossblind": "blind to the cross";[4] "blinded by the cross". "The curves of the skull" introduces another death-image; the "deathbone" from Lévy-Bruhl's Australia, pointed by Shaun in *Finnegans Wake*, F193, is the dramatic version of an identical symbol. But the central image, the epiphany of the interview, is contained in the movement of the priest's fingers: "slowly dangling and looping the cord of the other blind." That is to say, coolly proffering a noose. This is the lyric mode of *Ulysses'* epical hangman, "The lord of things as they are whom the most Roman of Catholics call *dio boia*, hangman god", U210/201.[5]

The Contrapuntal Opening

According to the practice inaugurated by Joyce when he rewrote "The Sisters" in 1906, the *Portrait*, like the two books to follow, opens amid elaborate counterpoint. The first two pages, terminating in a row of asterisks, enact the entire action in microcosm. An Aristotelian catalogue of senses, faculties, and mental activities is played against the unfolding of the infant conscience.

> Once upon a time and a very good time it was there was a moocow coming down along the road and this moocow that was down along the road met a nicens little boy named baby tuckoo. . . .
> His father told him that story: his father looked at him through a glass: he had a hairy face.
> He was baby tuckoo. The moocow came down along the road where Betty Byrne lived: she sold lemon platt.
>   *O, the wild rose blossoms*
>   *On the little green place.*
> He sang that song. That was his song.
>   *O, the green wothe botheth.*
> When you wet the bed, first it is warm then it gets cold. His mother put on the oilsheet. That had the queer smell.

This evocation of holes in oblivion is conducted in the mode of each of the five senses in turn; hearing (the story of the moocow), sight (his father's face), taste (lemon platt), touch (warm and cold), smell (the oil-sheet). The audible soothes: the visible disturbs. Throughout Joyce's work, the senses are symbolically disposed. Smell is the means of discriminating empirical realities ("His mother had a nicer smell than his father," is the next sentence), sight corresponds to the phantasms of oppression, hearing to the imaginative life. Touch and taste together are the modes of sex. Hearing, here, comes first, via a piece of imaginative literature. But as we can see from the vantage-point of *Finnegans Wake*, the whole book is about the encounter of baby tuckoo with the moocow: the Gripes with the mookse.[6] The father with the hairy face is the first Mookse-avatar, the Freudian infantile analogue of God the Father.

In the *Wake*

> Derzherr, live wire, fired Benjermine Funkling outa th'Empyre, sin right hand son. (F289.)

Der Erzherr (arch-lord), here a Teutonic Junker, is the God who visited his wrath on Lucifer; the hairy attribute comes through via the music-hall refrain, "There's hair, like wire, coming out of the Empire."

Dawning consciousness of his own identity ("He was baby tuckoo") leads to artistic performance ("He sang that song. That was his song.") This is hugely expanded in chapter IV:

> Now, as never before, his strange name seemed to him a prophecy . . . of the end he had been born

to serve and had been following through the mists of childhood and boyhood, a symbol of the artist forging anew in his workshop out of the sluggish matter of the earth a new soaring impalpable imperishable being. (P196/192.)

By changing the red rose to a green and dislocating the spelling, he makes the song his own ("But you could not have a green rose. But perhaps somewhere in the world you could." P8/13.)

His mother had a nicer smell than his father. She played on the piano the sailor's hornpipe for him to dance. He danced:

> *Tralala lala,*
> *Tralala tralaladdy,*
> *Tralala lala,*
> *Tralala lala.*

Between this innocence and its Rimbaudian recapture through the purgation of the *Wake* there is to intervene the hallucination in Circe's sty:

> *The Mother: (With the subtle smile of death's madness.)* I was once the beautiful May Goulding. I am dead. . . .
> *Stephen: (Eagerly.)* Tell me the word, mother, if you know it now. The word known to all men. . . .
> *The Mother: (With smouldering eyes.)* Repent! O, the fire of hell!
>
> (U565/547.)

This is foreshadowed as the overture to the *Portrait* closes:

> He hid under the table. His mother said:
> —O, Stephen will apologise.
> Dante said:
> —O, if not, the eagles will come and pull out his eyes.—
>
> > Pull out his eyes,
> > Apologise,
> > Apologise,
> > Pull out his eyes.
> >
> > Apologise,
> > Pull out his eyes,
> > Pull out his eyes,
> > Apologise.

The eagles, eagles of Rome, are emissaries of the God with the hairy face: the punisher. They evoke Prometheus and gnawing guilt: again-bite. So the overture ends with Stephen hiding under the table awaiting the eagles. He is hiding under something most of the time: bedclothes, "the enigma of a manner", an indurated rhetoric, or some other carapace of his private world.

Theme Words

It is through their names that things have power over Stephen.

> —The language in which we are speaking is his before it is mine. How different are the words *home*, *Christ*, *ale*, *master*, on his lips and on mine! I cannot speak or write these words without unrest of spirit. His language, so familiar and so foreign, will always be for me an acquired speech. I have not made or accepted its words. My voice holds them at bay. My soul frets in the shadow of his language. (P221/215.)

Not only is the Dean's English a conqueror's tongue; since the loss of Adam's words which perfectly mirrored things, all language has conquered the mind and imposed its own order, askew from the order of creation. Words, like the physical world, are imposed on Stephen from without, and it is in their canted mirrors that he glimpses a physical and moral world

already dyed the colour of his own mind since absorbed, with language, into his personality.

> Words which he did not understand he said over and over to himself till he had learnt them by heart; and through them he had glimpses of the real world about him. (P68/70.)

Language is a Trojan horse by which the universe gets into the mind. The first sentence in the book isn't something Stephen sees but a story he is told, and the overture climaxes in an insistent brainless rhyme, its jingle corrosively fascinating to the will. It has power to terrify a child who knows nothing of eagles, or of Prometheus, or of how his own grown-up failure to apologise will blend with gathering blindness.

It typifies the peculiar achievement of the *Portrait* that Joyce can cause patterns of words to make up the very moral texture of Stephen's mind:

> Suck was a queer word. The fellow called Simon Moonan that name because Simon Moonan used to tie the prefect's false sleeves behind his back and the prefect used to let on to be angry. But the sound was ugly. Once he had washed his hands in the lavatory of the Wicklow hotel and his father pulled the stopper up by the chain after and the dirty water went down through the hole in the basin. And when it had all gone down slowly the hole in the basin had made a sound like that: suck. Only louder.
>
> To remember that and the white look of the lavatory made him feel cold and then hot. There were two cocks that you turned and the water came out: cold and hot. He felt cold and then a little hot: and he could see the names printed on the cocks. That was a very queer thing. (P6/12.)

"Suck" joins two contexts in Stephen's mind: a playful sinner toying with his indulgent superior, and the disappearance of dirty water. The force of the conjunction is felt only after Stephen has lost his sense of the reality of the forgiveness of sins in the confessional. The habitually orthodox penitent tangles with a God who pretends to be angry; after a reconciliation the process is repeated. And the mark of that kind of play is disgraceful servility. Each time the sin disappears, the sinner is mocked by an impersonal voice out of nature: "Suck!"

This attitude to unreal good and evil furnishes a context for the next conjunction: whiteness and coldness. Stephen finds himself, like Simon Moonan,[7] engaged in the rhythm of obedience to irrational authority, bending his mind to a meaningless act, the arithmetic contest. He is being obediently "good". And the appropriate colour is adduced: "He thought his face must be white because it felt so cool."

The pallor of lunar obedient goodness is next associated with damp repulsiveness: the limpness of a wet blanket and of a servant's apron:

> He sat looking at the two prints of butter on his plate but could not eat the damp bread. The table-cloth was damp and limp. But he drank off the hot weak tea which the clumsy scullion, girt with a white apron, poured into his cup. He wondered whether the scullion's apron was damp too or whether all white things were cold and damp. (P8/13.)

Throughout the first chapter an intrinsic linkage, white-cold-damp-obedient, insinuates itself repeatedly. Stephen after saying his prayers, "his shoulders shaking", "so that he might not go to hell when he died", "curled himself together under the cold white sheets, shaking and trembling. But he would not go to hell when he died, and the shaking would stop." P16/20. The sea, mysterious as the terrible power of God, "was cold day and night, but it was colder at night", P14/19; we are reminded of Anna Livia's gesture of submission: "my cold father, my cold mad father, my cold mad feary father", F628. "There was a cold night smell in the chapel. But it was a holy smell", P14/19. Stephen is puzzled by the phrase in the Litany of the Blessed Virgin: Tower of Ivory. "How could a woman be a tower of ivory or a house of gold?" He ponders until the revelation comes:

> Eileen had long white hands. One evening when playing tig she had put her hands over his eyes: long and white and thin and cold and soft. That was ivory: a cold white thing. That was the meaning of *Tower of Ivory*. (P36/40.)

This instant of insight depends on a sudden reshuffling of associations, a sudden conviction that the Mother of God, and the symbols appropriate to her, belong with the cold, the white, and the unpleasant in a blindfold morality of obedience. Contemplation focussed on language is repaid:

> *Tower of Ivory. House of Gold.* By thinking of things you could understand them. (P45/48.)

The white-damp-obedient association reappears when Stephen is about to make his confession after the celebrated retreat; its patterns provide the language in which he thinks. Sin has been associated with fire, while the prayers of the penitents are epiphanized as "soft whispering cloudlets, soft whispering vapour, whispering and vanishing." P164/163. And having been absolved:

> White pudding and eggs and sausages and cups of tea. How simple and beautiful was life after all! And life lay all before him. . . .
> The boys were all there, kneeling in their places. He knelt among them, happy and shy. The altar was heaped with fragrant masses of white flowers: and in the morning light the pale flames of the candles among the white flowers were clear and silent as his own soul. (P168/166.)

We cannot read *Finnegans Wake* until we have realized the significance of the way the mind of Stephen Dedalus is bound in by language. He is not only an artist; he is a Dubliner.

The Portrait as Lyric

The "instant of emotion", P251/244, of which this 300–page lyric is the "simplest verbal vesture" is the exalted instant, emerging at the end of the book, of freedom, of vocation, of Stephen's destiny, winging his way above the waters at the side of the hawklike man: the instant of promise on which the crushing ironies of *Ulysses* are to fall. The epic of the sea of matter is preceded by the lyric image of a growing dream: a dream that like Richard Rowan's in *Exiles* disregards the fall of man; a dream nourished by a sensitive youth of flying above the sea into an uncreated heaven:

> The spell of arms and voices: the white arms of roads, their promise of close embraces and the black arms of tall ships that stand against the moon, their tale of distant nations. They are held out to say: We are alone—come. And the voices say with them: We are your kinsmen. And the air is thick with their company as they call to me, their kinsman, making ready to go, shaking the wings of their exultant and terrible youth. (P298/288.)

The emotional quality of this is continuous with that of the *Count of Monte Cristo*, that fantasy of the exile returned for vengeance (the plot of the *Odyssey*) which kindled so many of Stephen's boyhood dreams:

> The figure of that dark avenger stood forth in his mind for whatever he had heard or divined in

childhood of the strange and terrible. At night he built up on the parlour table an image of the wonderful island cave out of transfers and paper flowers and strips of the silver and golden paper in which chocolate is wrapped. When he had broken up this scenery, weary of its tinsel, there would come to his mind the bright picture of Marseilles, of sunny trellises and of Mercedes. (P68/70.)

The prose surrounding Stephen's flight is empurpled with transfers and paper flowers too. It is not immature prose, as we might suppose by comparison with *Ulysses*. The prose of "The Dead" is mature prose, and "The Dead" was written in 1908. Rather, it is a meticulous pastiche of immaturity. Joyce has his eye constantly on the epic sequel.

> He wanted to meet in the real world the unsubstantial image which his soul so constantly beheld. He did not know where to seek it or how, but a premonition which led him on told him that this image would, without any overt act of his, encounter him. They would meet quietly as if they had known each other and had made their tryst, perhaps at one of the gates or in some more secret place. They would be alone, surrounded by darkness and silence: and in that moment of supreme tenderness he would be transfigured. (P71/73.)

As the vaginal imagery of gates, secret places, and darkness implies, this is the dream that reaches temporary fulfilment in the plunge into profane love, P113/114. But the ultimate "secret place" is to be Mabbot Street, outside Bella Cohen's brothel; the unsubstantial image of his quest, that of Leopold Bloom, advertisement canvasser—Monte Cristo, returned avenger, Ulysses; and the transfiguration, into the phantasmal dead son of a sentimental Jew:

> *Against the dark wall a figure appears slowly, a fairy boy of eleven, a changeling, kidnapped, dressed in an Eton suit with glass shoes and a little bronze helmet, holding a book in his hand. He reads from right to left inaudibly, smiling, kissing the page.* (U593/574.)

That Dedalus the artificer did violence to nature is the point of the epigraph from Ovid, *Et ignotas animum dimittit in artes*; the Icarian fall is inevitable.

> In tedious exile now too long detain'd
> Dedalus languish'd for his native land.
> The sea forclos'd his flight; yet thus he said,
> Though earth and water in subjection laid,
> O cruel Minos, thy dominion be,
> We'll go through air; for sure the air is free.
> *Then to new arts his cunning thought applies,*
> *And to improve the work of nature tries.*

Stephen does not, as the careless reader may suppose, become an artist by rejecting church and country. Stephen does not become an artist at all. Country, church, and mission are an inextricable unity, and in rejecting the two that seem to hamper him, he rejects also the one on which he has set his heart. Improving the work of nature is his obvious ambition ("But you could not have a green rose. But perhaps somewhere in the world you could"), and it logically follows from the aesthetic he expounds to Lynch. It is a neo-platonic aesthetic; the crucial principle of epiphanization has been withdrawn. He imagines that "the loveliness that has not yet come into the world", P297/286, is to be found in his own soul. The earth is gross, and what it brings forth is cowdung; sound and shape and colour are "the prison gates of our soul"; and beauty is something mysteriously gestated within. The genuine artist reads signatures, the fake artist forges them, a process adumbrated in the obsession of Shem the Penman (from *Jim the*

Penman, a forgotten drama about a forger) with "Macfear-some's Ossean", the most famous of literary forgeries, studying "how cutely to copy all their various styles of signature so as one day to utter an epical forged cheque on the public for his own private profit." F181.

One can sense all this in the first four chapters of the *Portrait*, and *Ulysses* is unequivocal:

> Fabulous artificer, the hawklike man. You flew. Whereto? Newhaven-Dieppe, steerage passenger. Paris and back. (U208/199.)

The Stephen of the end of the fourth chapter, however, is still unstable; he had to be brought into a final balance, and shown at some length as a being whose development was virtually ended. Unfortunately, the last chapter makes the book a peculiarly difficult one for the reader to focus, because Joyce had to close it on a suspended chord. As a lyric, it is finished in its own terms; but the themes of the last forty pages, though they give the illusion of focussing, don't really focus until we have read well into *Ulysses*. The final chapter, which in respect to the juggernaut of *Ulysses* must be a vulnerable flank, in respect to what has gone before must be a conclusion. This problem Joyce didn't wholly solve; there remains a moral ambiguity (how seriously are we to take Stephen?) which makes the last forty pages painful reading.

Not that Stephen would stand indefinitely if *Ulysses* didn't topple him over; his equilibrium in Chapter V, though good enough to give him a sense of unusual integrity in University College, is precarious unless he can manage, in the manner of so many permanent undergraduates, to prolong the college context for the rest of his life. Each of the preceding chapters, in fact, works toward an equilibrium which is dashed when in the next chapter Stephen's world becomes larger and the frame of reference more complex. The terms of equilibrium are always stated with disquieting accuracy; at the end of Chapter I we find:

> He was alone. He was happy and free: but he would not be anyway proud with Father Dolan. He would be very quiet and obedient: and he wished that he could do something kind for him to show him that he was not proud. (P64/66.)

And at the end of Chapter III:

> He sat by the fire in the kitchen, not daring to speak for happiness. Till that moment he had not known how beautiful and peaceful life could be. The green square of paper pinned round the lamp cast down a tender shade. On the dresser was a plate of sausages and white pudding and on the shelf there were eggs. They would be for the breakfast in the morning after the communion in the college chapel. White pudding and eggs and sausages and cups of tea. How simple and beautiful was life after all! And life lay all before him. (P168/166.)

Not "irony" but simply the truth: the good life conceived in terms of white pudding and sausages is unstable enough to need no underlining.

The even-numbered chapters make a sequence of a different sort. The ending of IV, Stephen's panting submission to an artistic vocation:

> Evening had fallen when he woke and the sand and arid grasses of his bed glowed no longer. He rose slowly and, recalling the rapture of his sleep, sighed at its joy. (P201/197.)

—hasn't quite the finality often read into it when the explicit parallel with the ending of II is perceived:

> He closed his eyes, surrendering himself to her, body and mind, conscious of nothing in the world but the dark pressure of her softly parting lips. They pressed upon his brain as upon his lips as though they were the vehicle of a vague speech; and between them he felt an unknown and timid pressure, darker than the swoon of sin, softer than sound or odour. (P114/115.)

When we link these passages with the fact that the one piece of literary composition Stephen actually achieves in the book comes out of a wet dream ("Towards dawn he awoke. O what sweet music! His soul was all dewy wet", P254) we are in a position to see that the concluding "Welcome, O life!" has an air of finality and balance only because the diary-form of the last seven pages disarms us with an illusion of auctorial impartiality.

Controlling Images: Clongowes and Belvedere

Ego *vs.* authority is the theme of the three odd-numbered chapters, Dublin *vs.* the dream that of the two even-numbered ones. The generic Joyce plot, the encounter with the alter ego, is consummated when Stephen at the end of the book identifies himself with the sanctified Stephen who was stoned by the Jews after reporting a vision (Acts VII, 56) and claims sonship with the classical Daedalus who evaded the ruler of land and sea by turning his soul to obscure arts. The episodes are built about adumbrations of this encounter: with Father Conmee, with Monte Cristo, with the whores, with the broad-shouldered moustached student who cut the word "Foetus" in a desk, with the weary mild confessor, with the bird-girl. Through this repeated plot intertwine controlling emotions and controlling images that mount in complexity as the book proceeds.

In chapter I the controlling emotion is fear, and the dominant image Father Dolan and his pandybat; this, associated with the hangman-god and the priestly denial of the senses, was to become one of Joyce's standard images for Irish clericalism—hence the jack-in-the-box appearance of Father Dolan in Circe's nightmare imbroglio, his pandybat cracking twice like thunder, U547/531. Stephen's comment, in the mode of Blake's repudiation of the God who slaughtered Jesus, emphasizes the inclusiveness of the image: "I never could read His handwriting except His criminal thumbprint on the haddock."

Chapter II opens with a triple image of Dublin's prepossessions: music, sport, religion. The first is exhibited via Uncle Charles singing sentimental ballads in the outhouse; the second via Stephen's ritual run around the park under the eye of a superannuated trainer, which his uncle enjoins on him as the whole duty of a Dubliner; the third via the clumsy piety of Uncle Charles, kneeling on a red handkerchief and reading above his breath "from a thumb-blackened prayerbook wherein catchwords were printed at the foot of every page." P67/69. This trinity of themes is unwound and entwined throughout the chapter, like a net woven round Stephen; it underlies the central incident, the Whitsuntide play in the Belvedere chapel (religion), which opens with a display by the dumb-bell team (sport) preluded by sentimental waltzes from the soldier's band (music).

While he is waiting to play his part, Stephen is taunted by fellow-students, who rally him on a fancied love-affair and smiting his calf with a cane bid him recite the *Confiteor*. His mind goes back to an analogous incident, when a similar punishment had been visited on his refusal to "admit that Byron was no good". The further analogy with Father Dolan is obvious; love, art, and personal independence are thus united in an ideogram of the prepossessions Stephen is determined to cultivate in the teeth of persecution.

The dream-world Stephen nourishes within himself is played against manifestations of music, sport, and religion throughout the chapter. The constant ironic clash of Dublin *vs.* the Dream animates chapter II, as the clash of the ego *vs.* authority did chapter I. All these themes come to focus during Stephen's visit with his father to Cork. The dream of rebellion he has silently cultivated is externalized by the discovery of the word *Foetus* carved in a desk by a forgotten medical student:

> It shocked him to find in the outer world a trace of what he had deemed till then a brutish and individual malady of his own mind. His monstrous reveries came thronging into his memory. They too had sprung up before him, suddenly and furiously, out of mere words. (P101/102.)

The possibility of shame gaining the upper hand is dashed, however, by the sudden banal intrusion of his father's conversation ("When you kick out for yourself, Stephen, as I daresay you will one of these days, remember, whatever you do, to mix with gentlemen . . ."). Against the standards of Dublin his monstrous reveries acquire a Satanic glamour, and the trauma is slowly diverted into a resolution to rebel. After his father has expressed a resolve to "leave him to his Maker" (religion), and offered to "sing a tenor song against him" (music) or "vault a fivebarred gate against him" (sport), Stephen muses, watching his father and two cronies drinking to the memory of their past:

> An abyss of fortune or of temperament sundered him from them. His mind seemed older than theirs: it shone coldly on their strifes and happiness and regrets like a moon upon a younger earth. No life or youth stirred in him as it had stirred in them. He had known neither the pleasure of companionship with others nor the vigour of rude male health nor filial piety. Nothing stirred within his soul but a cold and cruel and loveless lust. (P107/108.)

After one final effort to compromise with Dublin on Dublin's terms has collapsed into futility ("The pot of pink enamel paint gave out and the wainscot of his bedroom remained with its unfinished and illplastered coat", P110/111), he fiercely cultivates his rebellious thoughts, and moving by day and night "among distorted images of the outer world", P111/112, plunges at last into the arms of whores. "The holy encounter he had then imagined at which weakness and timidity and inexperience were to fall from him", P112/113, finally arrives in inversion of Father Dolan's and Uncle Charles' religion: his descent into night-town is accompanied by lurid evocations of a Black Mass (Cf. *Ulysses*, 583/565):

> The yellow gasflames arose before his troubled vision against the vapoury sky, burning as if before an altar. Before the doors and in the lighted halls groups were gathered arrayed as for some rite. He was in another world: he had awakened from a slumber of centuries. (P113/114.)

Controlling Images: Sin and Repentance

Each chapter in the *Portrait* gathers up the thematic material of the preceding ones and entwines them with a dominant theme of its own. In chapter III the fear-pandybat motif is present in Father Arnall's crudely materialistic hell, of which even the thickness of the walls is specified; and the Dublin-*vs.*-dream motif has ironic inflections in Stephen's terror-stricken broodings, when the dream has been twisted into a dream of holiness, and even Dublin appears transfigured:

> How beautiful must be a soul in the state of grace when God looked upon it with love!
> Frowsy girls sat along the curbstones before their

baskets. Their dank hair trailed over their brows. They were not beautiful to see as they crouched in the mire. But their souls were seen by God; and if their souls were in a state of grace they were radiant to see; and God loved them, seeing them. (P162/160.)

A *rapprochement* in these terms between the outer world and Stephen's desires is too inadequate to need commentary; and it makes vivid as nothing else could the hopeless inversion of his attempted self-sufficiency. It underlines, in yet another way, his persistent sin: and the dominant theme of chapter III is Sin. A fugue-like opening plays upon the Seven Deadly Sins in turn; gluttony is in the first paragraph ("Stuff it into you, his belly counselled him"), followed by lust, then sloth ("A cold lucid indifference reigned in his soul"), pride ("His pride in his own sin, his loveless awe of God, told him that his offence was too grievous to be atoned for"), anger ("The blundering answer stirred the embers of his contempt for his fellows"); finally, a recapitulation fixes each term of the mortal catalogue in a phrase, enumerating how "from the evil seed of lust all the other deadly sins had sprung forth", P120/120.

Priest and punisher inhabit Stephen himself as well as Dublin: when he is deepest in sin he is most thoroughly a theologian. A paragraph of gloomy introspection is juxtaposed with a list of theological questions that puzzle Stephen's mind as he awaits the preacher:

> Is baptism with mineral water valid? How comes it that while the first beatitude promises the kingdom of heaven to the poor of heart, the second beatitude promises also to the meek that they shall possess the land? . . . If the wine change into vinegar and the host crumble into corruption after they have been consecrated, is Jesus Christ still present under their species as God and as man?
> —Here he is! Here he is!
> A boy from his post at the window had seen the rector come from the house. All the catechisms were opened and all heads bent upon them silently. (P120/120.)

Wine changed into vinegar and the host crumbled into corruption fits exactly the Irish clergy of "a church which was the scullery-maid of Christendom". The excited "Here he is! Here he is!" following hard on the mention of Jesus Christ and signalling nothing more portentous than the rector makes the point as dramatically as anything in the book, and the clinching sentence, with the students suddenly bending over their catechisms, places the rector as the vehicle of pandybat morality.

The last of the theological questions is the telling question. Stephen never expresses doubt of the existence of God nor of the essential validity of the priestly office—his *Non serviam* is not a *non credo*, and he talks of a "malevolent reality" behind these appearances P287/277—but the wine and bread that were offered for his veneration were changed into vinegar and crumbled into corruption. And it was the knowledge of that underlying validity clashing with his refusal to do homage to vinegar and rot that evoked his ambivalent poise of egocentric despair. The hell of Father Arnall's sermon, so emotionally overwhelming, so picayune beside the horrors that Stephen's imagination can generate, had no more ontological content for Stephen than had "an eternity of bliss in the company of the dean of studies", P282/273.

The conflict of this central chapter is again between the phantasmal and the real. What is real—psychologically real, because realized—is Stephen's anguish and remorse, and its context in the life of the flesh. What is phantasmal is the "heaven" of the Church and the "good life" of the priest. It is only fear that makes him clutch after the latter at all; his reaching out after orthodox salvation is, as we have come to expect, presented in terms that judge it:

> The wind blew over him and passed on to the myriads and myriads of other souls, on whom God's favour shone now more and now less, stars now brighter and now dimmer, sustained and failing. And the glimmering souls passed away, sustained and failing, merged in a moving breath. One soul was lost; a tiny soul; his. It flickered once and went out, forgotten, lost. The end: black cold void waste.
>
> Consciousness of place came ebbing back to him slowly over a vast tract of time unlit, unfelt, unlived. The squalid scene composed itself around him; the common accents, the burning gasjets in the shops, odours of fish and spirits and wet sawdust, moving men and women. An old woman was about to cross the street, an oilcan in her hand. He bent down and asked her was there a chapel near. (P162/160.)

That wan waste world of flickering stars is the best Stephen has been able to do towards an imaginative grasp of the communion of Saints sustained by God; "unlit, unfelt, unlived" explains succinctly why it had so little hold on him, once fear had relaxed. Equally pertinent is the vision of human temporal occupations the sermon evokes:

> What did it profit a man to gain the whole world if he lost his soul? At last he had understood: and human life lay around him, a plain of peace whereon antlike men laboured in brotherhood, their dead sleeping under quiet mounds. (P144/143.)

To maintain the life of grace in the midst of nature, sustained by so cramped a vision of the life of nature, would mean maintaining an intolerable tension. Stephen's unrelenting philosophic bias, his determination to understand what he is about, precludes his adopting the double standard of the Dubliners; to live both the life of nature and the life of grace he must enjoy an imaginative grasp of their relationship which stunts neither. "No one doth well against his will," writes Saint Augustine, "even though what he doth, be well;" and Stephen's will is firmly harnessed to his understanding. And there is no one in Dublin to help him achieve understanding. Father Arnall's sermon precludes rather than secures a desirable outcome, for it follows the modes of pandybat morality and Dublin materiality. Its only possible effect on Stephen is to lash his dormant conscience into a frenzy. The description of Hell as "a strait and dark and foul smelling prison, an abode of demons and lost souls, filled with fire and smoke", with walls four thousand miles thick, its damned packed in so tightly that "they are not even able to remove from the eye the worm that gnaws it", is childishly grotesque beneath its sweeping eloquence; and the hair-splitting catalogues of pains—pain of loss, pain of conscience (divided into three heads), pain of extension, pain of intensity, pain of eternity—is cast in a brainlessly analytic mode that effectively prevents any corresponding Heaven from possessing any reality at all.

Stephen's unstable pact with the Church, and its dissolution, follows the pattern of composition and dissipation established by his other dreams: the dream for example of the tryst with "Mercedes", which found ironic reality among harlots. It parallels exactly his earlier attempt to "build a breakwater of order and elegance against the sordid tide of life without him", P110/111, whose failure, with the exhaustion of his money, was epiphanized in the running-dry of a pot of pink enamel paint. His regimen at that time:

> He bought presents for everyone, overhauled his rooms, wrote out resolutions, marshalled his books up and down their shelves, pored over all kinds of price lists

is mirrored by his searching after spiritual improvement:

> His daily life was laid out in devotional areas. By means of ejaculations and prayers he stored up ungrudgingly for the souls in purgatory centuries of days and quarantines and years. . . . He offered up each of his three daily chaplets that his soul might grow strong in each of the three theological virtues. . . . On each of the seven days of the week he further prayed that one of the seven gifts of the Holy Ghost might descend upon his soul. (P170–167.)

The "loan bank" he had opened for the family, out of which he had pressed loans on willing borrowers "that he might have the pleasure of making out receipts and reckoning the interests on sums lent" finds its counterpart in the benefits he stored up for souls in purgatory that he might enjoy the spiritual triumph of "achieving with ease so many fabulous ages of canonical penances". Both projects are parodies on the doctrine of economy of grace; both are attempts, corrupted by motivating self-interest, to make peace with Dublin on Dublin's own terms; and both are short-lived.

As this precise analogical structure suggests, the action of each of the five chapters is really the same action. Each chapter closes with a synthesis of triumph which the next destroys. The triumph of the appeal to Father Conmee from lower authority, of the appeal to the harlots from Dublin, of the appeal to the Church from sin, of the appeal to art from the priesthood (the bird-girl instead of the Virgin) is always the same triumph raised to a more comprehensive level. It is an attempt to find new parents; new fathers in the odd chapters, new objects of love in the even. The last version of Father Conmee is the "priest of the eternal imagination"; the last version of Mercedes is the "lure of the fallen seraphim". But the last version of the mother who said, "O, Stephen will apologise" is the mother who prays on the last page "that I may learn in my own life and away from home and friends what the heart is and what it feels". The mother remains.

The Double Female

As in *Dubliners* and *Exiles*, the female role in the *Portrait* is less to arouse than to elucidate masculine desires. Hence the complex function in the book of physical love: the physical is the analogue of the spiritual, as St. Augustine insisted in his *Confessions* (which, with Ibsen's *Brand*, is the chief archetype of Joyce's book). The poles between which this affection moves are those of St. Augustine and St. John: the Whore of Babylon and the Bride of Christ. The relation between the two is far from simple, and Stephen moves in a constant tension between them.

His desire, figured in the visions of Monte Cristo's Mercedes, "to meet in the real world the unsubstantial image which his soul so constantly beheld" draws him toward the prostitute ("In her arms he felt that he had suddenly become strong and fearless and sure of himself", P114/114) and simultaneously toward the vaguely spiritual satisfaction represented with equal vagueness by the wraithlike E—— C——, to whom he twice writes verses. The Emma Clery of *Stephen Hero*, with her loud forced manners and her body compact of pleasure, S66/56, was refined into a wraith with a pair of initials to parallel an intangible Church. She is continually assimilated to the image of the Blessed Virgin and of the heavenly Bride. The torture she costs him is the torture his apostasy costs him. His flirtation with her is his flirtation with Christ. His profane villanelle draws its imagery from religion—the incense, the eucharistic hymn, the chalice—and her heart, following Dante's image, is a rose, and in her praise "the earth was like a swinging swaying censer, a ball of incense", P256/248.

The woman is the Church. His vision of greeting Mercedes with "a sadly proud gesture of refusal":

—Madam, I never eat muscatel grapes. (P68/71.)

is fulfilled when he refuses his Easter communion. Emma's eyes, in their one explicit encounter, speak to him from beneath a cowl, P76/78. "The glories of Mary held his soul captive", P118/118, and a temporary reconciliation of his lust and his spiritual thirst is achieved as he reads the Lesson out of the Song of Solomon. In the midst of his repentance she functions as imagined mediator: "The image of Emma appeared before him," and, repenting, "he imagined that he stood near Emma in a wide land, and, humbly and in tears, bent and kissed the elbow of her sleeve", P132/131. Like Dante's Beatrice, she manifests in his earthly experience the Church Triumphant of his spiritual dream. And when he rejects her because she seems to be flirting with Father Moran, his anger is couched in the anti-clerical terms of his apostasy: "He had done well to leave her to flirt with her priest, to toy with a church which was the scullery-maid of Christendom", P258/250.

That Kathleen ni Houlihan can flirt with priests is the unforgivable sin underlying Stephen's rejection of Ireland. But he makes a clear distinction between the stupid clericalism which makes intellectual and communal life impossible, and his long-nourished vision of an artist's Church Triumphant upon earth. He rejects the actual for daring to fall short of his vision.

The Final Balance

The climax of the book is of course Stephen's ecstatic discovery of his vocation at the end of chapter IV. The prose rises in nervous excitement to beat again and again the tambours of a fin-de-siècle ecstasy:

His heart trembled; his breath came faster and a wild spirit passed over his limbs as though he were soaring sunward. His heart trembled in an ecstasy of fear and his soul was in flight. His soul was soaring in an air beyond the world and the body he knew was purified in a breath and delivered of incertitude and made radiant and commingled with the element of the spirit. An ecstasy of flight made radiant his eyes and wild his breath and tremulous and wild and radiant his windswept limbs.

—One! Two! . . . Look out!—

—O, Cripes, I'm drownded!—(P196/192.)

The interjecting voices of course are those of bathers, but their ironic appropriateness to Stephen's Icarian "soaring sunward" is not meant to escape us: divers have their own "ecstasy of flight", and Icarus was "drownded". The imagery of Stephen's ecstasy is fetched from many sources; we recognize Shelley's skylark, Icarus, the glorified body of the Resurrection (cf. "His soul had arisen from the grave of boyhood, spurning her graveclothes", P197/193) and a tremulousness from which it is difficult to dissociate adolescent sexual dreams (which the Freudians tell us are frequently dreams of flying). The entire eight-page passage is cunningly organized with great variety of rhetoric and incident; but we cannot help noticing the limits set on vocabulary and figures of thought. The empurpled triteness of such a cadence as "radiant his eyes and wild his

breath and tremulous and wild and radiant his windswept limbs" is enforced by recurrence: "But her long fair hair was girlish: and girlish, and touched with the wonder of mortal beauty, her face", P199/195. "Ecstasy" is the keyword, indeed. This riot of feelings corresponds to no vocation definable in mature terms; the paragraphs come to rest on images of irresponsible motion:

He turned away from her suddenly and set off across the strand. His cheeks were aflame; his body was aglow; his limbs were trembling. On and on and on and on he strode, far out over the sands, singing wildly to the sea, crying to greet the advent of the life that had cried to him. (P200/196.)

What "life" connotes it skills not to ask; the word recurs and recurs. So does the motion onward and onward and onward:

A wild angel had appeared to him, the angel of mortal youth and beauty, an envoy from the fair courts of life, to throw open before him in an instant of ecstasy the gates of all the ways of error and glory. On and on and on and on! (P200/196.)

It may be well to recall Joyce's account of the romantic temper:

. . . an insecure, unsatisfied, impatient temper which sees no fit abode here for its ideals and chooses therefore to behold them under insensible figures. As a result of this choice it comes to disregard certain limitations. Its figures are blown to wild adventures, lacking the gravity of solid bodies. (S78/66.)

Joyce also called *Prometheus Unbound* "the Schwärmerei of a young jew".

And it is quite plain from the final chapter of the *Portrait* that we are not to accept the mode of Stephen's "freedom" as the "message" of the book. The "priest of the eternal imagination" turns out to be indigestibly Byronic. Nothing is more obvious than his total lack of humour. The dark intensity of the first four chapters is moving enough, but our impulse on being confronted with the final edition of Stephen Dedalus is to laugh; and laugh at this moment we dare not; he is after all a victim being prepared for a sacrifice. His shape, as Joyce said, can no longer change. The art he has elected is not "the slow elaborative patience of the art of satisfaction". "On and on and on and on" will be its inescapable mode. He does not *see* the girl who symbolizes the full revelation; "she seemed like one whom magic had changed into the likeness of a strange and beautiful seabird", P199/195, and he confusedly apprehends a sequence of downy and feathery incantations. What, in the last chapter, he does see he sees only to reject, in favour of an incantatory "loveliness which has not yet come into the world", P197/286.

The only creative attitude to language exemplified in the book is that of Stephen's father:

—Is it Christy? he said. There's more cunning in one of those warts on his bald head than in a pack of jack foxes.

His vitality is established before the book is thirty pages under way. Stephen, however, isn't enchanted at any time by the proximity of such talk. He isn't, as a matter of fact, even interested in it. Without a backward glance, he exchanges this father for a myth.

Notes

1. Frank Budgen, *James Joyce and the Making of* Ulysses (Grayson and Grayson, London).

2. *A Portrait of the Artist as a Young Man*, American edition by Modern Library; English edition by Jonathan Cape.

3. *Finnegans Wake*, American edition by Viking Press; English edition by Faber and Faber.

4. —You want me, said Stephen, to toe the line with those
   hypocrites and sycophants in the college. I will never do so.
   —No. I mentioned Jesus.
   —Don't mention him. I have made it a common noun. They
   don't believe in him; they don't observe his precepts.
   (*Stephen Hero*, American edition by New Directions,
   p. 141; English edition by Jonathan Cape, p. 124.

5. *Ulysses*, American edition by Modern Library; English edition by
   John Lane, the Bodley Head.

6. Compare the opening sentences: "Eins within a space, and a
   wearywide space it wast, ere wohned a Mookse", F152. Mookse is
   moocow plus fox plus mock turtle. The German "Eins" evokes
   Einstein, who presides over the interchanging of space and time;
   space is the Mookse's "spatialty".

7. Joyce's names should always be scrutinized. Simon Moonan: moon:
   the heatless (white) satellite reflecting virtue borrowed from Simon
   Peter. Simony, too, is an activity naturally derived from this
   casually businesslike attitude to priestly authority.

Ulysses

EDMUND WILSON
From "James Joyce"
Axel's Castle
1931, pp. 202–17

II

To describe ⟨*Ulysses* in light of its Homeric parallel⟩ gives no idea of what it is really like—of its psychological and technical discoveries or of its magnificent poetry.

Ulysses is, I suppose, the most completely "written" novel since Flaubert. The example of the great prose poet of Naturalism has profoundly influenced Joyce—in his attitude toward the modern bourgeois world and in the contrast implied by the Homeric parallel of *Ulysses* between our own and the ancient world, as well as in an ideal of rigorous objectivity and of adaptation of style to subject—as the influence of that other great Naturalistic poet, Ibsen, is obvious in Joyce's single play, *Exiles*. But Flaubert had, in general, confined himself to fitting the cadence and the phrase precisely to the mood or object described; and even then it was the phrase rather than the cadence, and the object rather than the mood, with which he was occupied—for mood and cadence in Flaubert do not really vary much: he never embodies himself in his characters nor identifies his voice with theirs, and as a result, Flaubert's own characteristic tone of the sombre-pompous-ironic becomes, in the long run, a little monotonous. But Joyce has undertaken in *Ulysses* not merely to render, with the last accuracy and beauty, the actual sights and sounds among which his people move, but, showing us the world as his characters perceive it, to find the unique vocabulary and rhythm which will represent the thoughts of each. If Flaubert taught Maupassant to look for the definitive adjectives which would distinguish a given cab-driver from every other cab-driver at the Rouen station, so Joyce has set himself the task of finding the precise dialect which will distinguish the thoughts of a given Dubliner from those of every other Dubliner. Thus the mind of Stephen Dedalus is represented by a weaving of bright poetic images and fragmentary abstractions, of things remembered from books, on a rhythm sober, melancholy and proud; that of Bloom by a rapid staccato notation, prosaic but vivid and alert, jetting out in all directions in little ideas growing out of ideas; the thoughts of Father Conmee, the Rector of the Jesuit college, by a precise prose, perfectly colorless and orderly; those of Gerty-Nausicaa by a combination of school-girl colloquialisms with the jargon of cheap romance; and the ruminations of Mrs. Bloom by a long, unbroken rhythm of brogue, like the swell of some profound sea.

Joyce takes us thus directly into the consciousness of his characters, and in order to do so, he has availed himself of methods of which Flaubert never dreamed—of the methods of Symbolism. He has, in *Ulysses*, exploited together, as no writer had thought to do before, the resources both of Symbolism and of Naturalism. Proust's novel, masterly as it is, does perhaps represent a falling over into decadence of psychological fiction: the subjective element is finally allowed to invade and to deteriorate even those aspects of the story which really ought to be kept strictly objective if one is to believe that it is actually happening. But Joyce's grasp on his objective world never slips: his work is unshakably established on Naturalistic foundations. Where *A la recherche du temps perdu* leaves many things vague—the ages of the characters and sometimes the actual circumstances of their lives, and—what is worse—whether they may not be merely bad dreams that the hero has had; *Ulysses* has been logically thought out and accurately documented to the last detail: everything that happens is perfectly consistent, and we know precisely what the characters wore, how much they paid for things, where they were at different times of the day, what popular songs they sang and what events they read of in the papers, on June 16, 1904. Yet when we are admitted to the mind of any one of them, we are in a world as complex and special, a world sometimes as fantastic or obscure, as that of a Symbolist poet—and a world rendered by similar devices of language. We are more at home in the minds of Joyce's characters than we are likely to be, except after some study, in the mind of a Mallarmé or an Eliot, because we know more about the circumstances in which they find themselves; but we are confronted with the same sort of confusion between emotions, perceptions and reasonings, and we are likely to be disconcerted by the same sort of hiatuses of thought, when certain links in the association of ideas are dropped down into the unconscious mind so that we are obliged to divine them for ourselves.

But Joyce has carried the methods of Symbolism further than merely to set a Naturalistic scene and then, in that frame, to represent directly the minds of his different characters in Symbolistic monologues like "Mr. Prufrock" or "L'Après-midi d'un faune." And it is the fact that he has not always stopped here which makes parts of *Ulysses* so puzzling when we read them for the first time. So long as we are dealing with internal monologues in realistic settings, we are dealing with familiar elements merely combined in a novel way—that is, instead of reading, "Bloom said to himself, 'I might manage to write a story to illustrate some proverb or other. I could sign it, Mr. and Mrs. L. M. Bloom,'" we read, "Might manage a sketch. By Mr. and Mrs. L. M. Bloom. Invent a story for some proverb which?" But as we get further along in *Ulysses*, we find the realistic setting oddly distorting itself and deliquescing, and we are astonished at the introduction of voices which seem to belong neither to the characters nor to the author.

The point is that of each of his episodes Joyce has tried to make an independent unit which shall blend the different sets of elements of each—the minds of the characters, the place where they are, the atmosphere about them, the feeling of the time of day. Joyce had already, in *A Portrait of the Artist*, experimented, as Proust had done, in varying the form and style of the different sections to fit the different ages and phases of his hero—from the infantile fragments of childhood impressions, through the ecstatic revelations and the terrifying nightmares of adolescence, to the self-possessed notations of hood. But in A *Portrait of the Artist*, Joyce was presenting everything from the point of view of a single particular character, Dedalus; whereas in *Ulysses* he is occupied with a number of different personalities, of whom Dedalus is no longer the centre, and his method, furthermore, of enabling us to live in their world is not always merely a matter of making us shift from the point of view of one to the point of view of another. In order to understand what Joyce is doing here, one must conceive a set of Symbolistic poems, themselves involving characters whose minds are represented Symbolistically, depending not from the sensibility of the poet speaking in his own person, but from the poet's imagination playing a rôle absolutely impersonal and always imposing upon itself all the Naturalistic restrictions in regard to the story it is telling at the same time that it allows itself to exercise all the Symbolistic privileges in regard to the way it tells it. We are not likely to be prepared for this by the early episodes of *Ulysses*: they are as sober and as clear as the morning light of the Irish coast in which they take place: the characters' perceptions of the external world are usually distinct from their thoughts and feelings about them. But in the newspaper office, for the first time, a general atmosphere begins to be created, beyond the specific minds of the characters, by a punctuation of the text with newspaper heads which announce the incidents in the narrative. And in the library scene, which takes place in the early afternoon, the setting and people external to Stephen begin to dissolve in his apprehension of them, heightened and blurred by some drinks at lunch-time and by the intellectual excitement of the conversation amid the dimness and tameness of the library—"Eglintoneyes, quick with pleasure, looked up shybrightly. Gladly glancing, a merry puritan, through the twisted eglantine." Here, however, we still see all through Stephen's eyes—through the eyes of a single character; but in the scene in the Ormond Hotel, which takes place a couple of hours later—our reveries absorb the world about us progressively as daylight fades and as the impressions of the day accumulate—the sights and sounds and the emotional vibrations and the appetites for food and drink of the late afternoon, the laughter, the gold-and-bronze hair of the barmaids, the jingling of Blazes Boylan's car on his way to visit Molly Bloom, the ringing of the hoofs of the horses of the viceregal cavalcade clanging in through the open window, the ballad sung by Simon Dedalus, the sound of the piano accompaniment and the comfortable supper of Bloom—though they are not all, from beginning to end, perceived by Bloom himself—all mingle quite un-Naturalistically in a harmony of bright sound, ringing color, poignant indistinct feeling and declining light. The scene in the brothel, where it is night and where Dedalus and Bloom are drunk, is like a slowed-up moving-picture, in which the intensified vision of reality is continually lapsing into phantasmagoric visions; and the let-down after the excitement of this, the lassitude and staleness of the cabmen's shelter where Bloom takes Stephen to get him some coffee, is rendered by a prose as flavorless, as weary and as banal as the incidents which it reports. Joyce has achieved here, by different methods, a relativism like that of Proust: he is reproducing in literature the different aspects, the different proportions and textures, which things and people take on at different times and under different circumstances.

III

I do not think that Joyce has been equally successful with all these technical devices in *Ulysses*; but before it will be possible to discuss them further, we must approach the book from another point of view.

It has always been characteristic of Joyce to neglect action, narrative, drama, of the usual kind, even the direct impact on one another of the characters as we get it in the ordinary novel, for a sort of psychological portraiture. There is tremendous vitality in Joyce, but very little movement. Like Proust, he is symphonic rather than narrative. His fiction has its progressions, its developments, but they are musical rather than dramatic. The most elaborate and interesting piece in *Dubliners*—the story called "The Dead"—is simply a record of the modification brought about during a single evening in the relations of a husband and wife by the man's becoming aware, from the effect produced on the woman by a song which she has heard at a family party, that she has once been loved by another man; A *Portrait of the Artist as a Young Man* is simply a series of pictures of the author at successive stages of his development; the theme of *Exiles* is, like that of "The Dead," the modification in the relations of a husband and wife which follows the reappearance of a man who has been the wife's lover. And *Ulysses*, again, for all its vast scale, is simply the story of another small but significant change in the relations of yet another married couple as a result of the impingement on their household of the personality of an only slightly known young man. Most of these stories cover a period of only a few hours, and they are never carried any further. When Joyce has explored one of these situations, when he has established the small gradual readjustment, he has done all that interests him.

All, that is, from the point of view of ordinary incident. But though Joyce almost entirely lacks appetite for violent conflict or vigorous action, his work is prodigiously rich and alive. His force, instead of following a line, expands itself in every dimension (including that of Time) about a single point. The world of *Ulysses* is animated by a complex inexhaustible life: we revisit it as we do a city, where we come more and more to recognize faces, to understand personalities, to grasp relations, currents and interests. Joyce has exercised considerable technical ingenuity in introducing us to the elements of his story in an order which will enable us to find our bearings: yet I doubt whether any human memory is capable, on a first reading, of meeting the demands of *Ulysses*. And when we reread it, we start in at any point, as if it were indeed something solid like a city which actually existed in space and which could be entered from any direction—as Joyce is said, in composing his books, to work on the different parts simultaneously. More than any other work of fiction, unless perhaps the *Comédie humaine*, *Ulysses* creates the illusion of a living social organism. We see it only for twenty hours, yet we know its past as well as its present. We possess Dublin, seen, heard, smelt and felt, brooded over, imagined, remembered.

Joyce's handling of this immense material, his method of giving his book a shape, resembles nothing else in modern fiction. The first critics of *Ulysses* mistook the novel for a "slice of life" and objected that it was too fluid or too chaotic. They did not recognize a plot because they could not recognize a progression; and the title told them nothing. They could not even discover a pattern. It is now apparent, however, that *Ulysses* suffers from an excess of design rather than from a lack of it. Joyce has drawn up an outline of his novel, of which he has allowed certain of his commentators to avail themselves, but which he has not allowed them to publish in its entirety (though it is to be presumed that the book on *Ulysses* which Mr. Stuart Gilbert has announced will include all the information contained in it); and from this outline it appears that Joyce has set himself the task of fulfilling the requirements of a most complicated scheme—a scheme which we could scarcely have divined except in its more obvious features. For even if we had known about the Homeric parallel and had identified certain of the correspondences—if we had had no difficulty in recognizing the Cyclops in the ferocious professional Fenian or Circe in the brothel-keeper or Hades in the cemetery—we should never have suspected how closely and how subtly the parallel had been followed—we should never have guessed, for example, that when Bloom passes through the National Library while Stephen is having his discussion with the literary men, he is escaping, on the one hand, a Scylla—that is, Aristotle, the rock of Dogma; and, on the other, a Charybdis—Plato, the whirlpool of Mysticism; nor that, when Stephen walks on the seashore, he is reënacting the combat with Proteus—in this case, primal matter, of whose continual transformations Stephen is reminded by the objects absorbed or washed up by the sea, but whose forms he is able to hold and fix, as the Homeric Proteus was held and vanquished, by power of the words which give him images for them. Nor should we have known that the series of phrases and onomatopoetic syllables placed at the beginning of the Sirens episode—the singing in the Ormond Hotel—and selected from the narrative which follows, are supposed to be musical themes and that the episode itself is a fugue; and though we may have felt the ironic effect of the specimens of inflated Irish journalism introduced at regular intervals in the conversation with the patriot in the pub—we should hardly have understood that these had been produced by a deliberate technique of "gigantism"—for, since the Citizen represents the Cyclops, and since the Cyclops was a giant, he must be rendered formidable by a parade of all the banalities of his patriotic claptrap swollen to gigantic proportions. We should probably never have guessed all this, and we should certainly never have guessed at the ingenuity which Joyce has expended in other ways. Not only, we learn from the outline, is there an elaborate Homeric parallel in *Ulysses*, but there is also an organ of the human body and a human science or art featured in every episode. We look these up, a little incredulously, but there, we find, they all actually are—buried and disguised beneath the realistic surface, but carefully planted, unmistakably dwelt upon. And if we are tipped off, we are able further to discover all sorts of concealed ornaments and emblems: in the chapter of the Lotos-Eaters, for example, countless references to flowers; in the Laestrygonians, to eating; in the Sirens, puns on musical terms; and in Æolus, the newspaper office, not merely many references to wind but, according to Mr. Gilbert—the art featured in this episode being Rhetoric—some hundred different figures of speech.

Now the Homeric parallel in *Ulysses* is in general pointedly and charmingly carried out and justifies itself: it does help to give the story a universal significance and it enables Joyce to show us in the actions and the relations of his characters meanings which he perhaps could not easily have indicated in any other way—since the characters themselves must be largely unaware of these meanings and since Joyce has adopted the strict objective method, in which the author must not comment on the action. And we may even accept the arts and sciences and the organs of the human body as making the book complete and comprehensive, if a little laboriously systematic—the whole of man's experience in a day. But when we get all these things together and further complicated by the virtuosity of the technical devices, the result is sometimes baffling or confusing. We become aware, as we examine the outline, that when we went through *Ulysses* for the first time, it was these organs and arts and sciences and Homeric correspondences which sometimes so discouraged our interest. We had been climbing over these obstacles without knowing it, in our attempts to follow Dedalus and Bloom. The trouble was

that, beyond the ostensible subject and, as it were, beneath the surface of the narrative, too many other subjects and too many different orders of subjects were being proposed to our attention.

It seems to me difficult, then, not to conclude that Joyce elaborated *Ulysses* too much—that he tried to put too many things into it. What is the value of all the references to flowers in the Lotos-Eaters chapter, for example? They do not create in the Dublin streets an atmosphere of lotus-eating—we are merely puzzled, if we have not been told to look for them, as to why Joyce has chosen to have Bloom think and see certain things, of which the final explanation is that they are pretexts for mentioning flowers. And do not the gigantic interpolations of the Cyclops episode defeat their object by making it impossible for us to follow the narrative? The interpolations are funny in themselves, the incident related is a masterpiece of language and humor, the idea of combining them seems happy, yet the effect is mechanical and annoying: in the end we have to read the whole thing through, skipping the interpolations, in order to find out what has happened. The worst example of the capacities for failure of this too synthetic, too systematic, method seems to me the scene in the maternity hospital. I have described above what actually takes place there as I have worked it out, after several readings and in the light of Joyce's outline. The Oxen of the Sun are "Fertility"—the crime committed against them is "Fraud." But, not content with this, Joyce has been at pains to fill the episode with references to real cattle and to include a long conversation about bulls. As for the special technique, it seems to me in this case not to have any real appropriateness to the situation, but to have been dictated by sheer fantastic pedantry: Joyce describes his method here as "embryonic," in conformity to the subject, maternity, and the chapter is written as a series of parodies of English literary styles from the bad Latin of the early chronicles up through Huxley and Carlyle, the development of the language corresponding to the growth of the child in the womb. Now something important takes place in this episode— the meeting between Dedalus and Bloom—and an important point is being made about it. But we miss the point because it is all we can do to follow what is happening at the drinking-party, itself rather a confused affair, through the medium of the language of the *Morte d'Arthur*, the seventeenth-century diaries, the eighteenth-century novels, and a great many other kinds of literature in which we are not prepared at the moment to be interested. If we pay attention to the parodies, we miss the story; and if we try to follow the story, we are unable to appreciate the parodies. The parodies have spoiled the story; and the necessity of telling the story through them has taken most of the life out of the parodies.

Joyce has as little respect as Proust for the capacities of the reader's attention; and one feels, in Joyce's case as in Proust's, that the *longueurs* which break our backs, the mechanical combinations of elements which fail to coalesce, are partly a result of the effort of a supernormally energetic mind to compensate by piling things up for an inability to make them move.

We have now arrived, in the maternity hospital, at the climactic scenes of the story, and Joyce has bogged us as he has never bogged us before. We shall forget the Oxen of the Sun in the wonderful night-town scene which follows it—but we shall be bogged afterwards worse than ever in the interminable let-down of the cabman's shelter and in the scientific question-and-answer chapter which undertakes to communicate to us through the most opaque and uninviting medium possible Dedalus's conversation with Bloom. The night-town episode itself and Mrs. Bloom's soliloquy, which closes the book, are, of course, among the best things in it—but the relative proportions of the other three latter chapters and the jarring effect of the pastiche style sandwiched in with the straight Naturalistic seem to me artistically absolutely indefensible. One can understand that Joyce may have intended the colorless and tiresome episodes to set off the rich and vivid ones, and also that it is of the essence of his point of view to represent the profoundest changes of our lives as beginning naturally between night and morning without the parties' appreciating their importance at the time; but a hundred and sixty-one more or less deliberately tedious pages are too heavy a dead weight for even the brilliant flights of the other hundred and ninety-nine pages to carry. Furthermore, Joyce has here half-buried his story under the virtuosity of his technical devices. It is almost as if he had elaborated it so much and worked over it so long that he had forgotten, in the amusement of writing parodies, the drama which he had originally intended to stage; or as if he were trying to divert and overwhelm us by irrelevant entertainments and feats in order that we might not be dissatisfied with the flatness—except for the drunken scene—of Dedalus's final meeting with Bloom; or even perhaps as if he did not, after all, quite want us to understand his story, as if he had, not quite conscious of what he was doing, ended by throwing up between us and it a fortification of solemn burlesque prose—as if he were shy and solicitous about it, and wanted to protect it from us.

WILLIAM EMPSON
From "The Theme of *Ulysses*"

Kenyon Review, Winter 1956, pp. 26–39

What I have to say cannot help sounding a bit odd. It sounds both rather improper in itself and also a rather unhigh-minded view to take of the great book *Ulysses*. But I have long thought that my view of that book is not only much less dismal than what critics usually say about it but also allows you to think that the author had decent feelings in writing it, instead of very nasty ones. Let me recall that the book describes one day in the life of Stephen Dedalus, who was the hero of a previous book by Joyce called *Portrait of the Artist as a Young Man*, so Stephen in *Ulysses* has to be Joyce himself on June 16th 1904. He appears in the book *Ulysses* to be accepting friendship from the man Bloom, a coarse and depressed advertising agent who soon becomes much more funny and interesting and agreeable than Stephen; but in the whole last third of the book this offer of friendship is becoming more and more of a failure, till the heroic young author walks away into the night. Bloom is married to a well-known professional singer, and the marriage has got into great confusion, and he offers to put Stephen to bed with his wife, not in actual words but extremely plainly; and his chief reason is that he wants to get rid of her present lover, Blazes Boylan, the worst man in Dublin. The last chapter of the book is a vast monologue by the wife Molly thinking in bed; she is now looking forward to pleasure with Stephen, whom her husband has described to her before going to sleep, but also as her chapter goes on she expresses a surprising amount of emotional dependence upon her reliable husband. As for Bloom, the book has already made him reflect that he will be almost in despair if Stephen doesn't come back. However, Stephen, even though we have seen him refuse everything and everybody else in Dublin, and he has nowhere to sleep, let alone any source of money, has walked out on them at two in the morning. I think it is true to say that

every one of the critics, all these years, has assumed that both the Blooms are deluded when they hope that Stephen will come back to them. This of course has made all the critics think the book frightful, whether they admire it or denounce it; both sides take for granted that it is not merely pointless but as one might say nerve-rackingly and needlingly pointless, saying nothing except that nothing in Dublin was good enough for the young Joyce. It would be fun to give a lot of quotations from critics, but I haven't time.

Now, I think this basic assumption about the book completely wrong. It is meant to be a very gay book, and a lot of it actually is so funny that I can't read it aloud at home of an evening, as I have sometimes tried to do, without breaking down and going into fits. You and I may think he makes Dublin seem sordid and dismal, but we need to realize that Joyce didn't think that himself; after 1904, the year of the story, he chose to be in exile for almost all the rest of his life, but he stuck to saying he had never felt at home except in Dublin. Now there is nothing in the book to stop you from assuming, what seems natural if you start from this point of view, that Stephen *did* go to bed with Molly, very soon after the one day of the book; and, what is more, that Joyce when he looks back thinks it probably saved his life and anyhow made it possible for him to become the great author who tells the story. Joyce was a very self-important man, as he had to be to do what he did, and he was also fanatically devoted to making his art tell the essential truth. He would never have turned the final book of his autobiography into a mere description of how sickeningly mean-minded and nasty he had been when he was young. He knew he was doing that too; he said to a friend who saw the work in progress, "I haven't let this young man off lightly, have I?" For that matter, there is a photograph of Joyce taken in 1904 which makes me feel sure that the later Joyce made him look much worse than he was.[1] As the book shows the young man, he is downright dangerous; he is on the edge either of lunacy or crime. But that is why the young man needed what happened to him on the day of the novel; after that he turned into the novelist Joyce, an extremely fixed and reliable character, and there was no further development of his character that Joyce felt any duty to put in a book, ever after. You see, the first thing about his attitude to writing novels is that they ought to tell the essential truth. But here, as he was writing about himself, he had another duty, to hide the people he was really talking about. In this second duty, so far as I can make out, he succeeded completely; the Dubliners are wonderful gossips, but they have never found out.

We need therefore to consider Joyce's own life at the time. The day of the novel *Ulysses* is June 16th 1904, and that June was when he first met the lady who ran away with him from Ireland the following October, and remained his devoted wife through all his future troubles (incidentally her relations gave enough money at a crucial point to keep the family alive). Now in the rejected first version of the *Portrait of the Artist*, some of which happens to have survived, he describes how the young man became fond of a respectable young girl and expressed this by waylaying her in the street and saying that if she would go to bed with him at once he would fall in love with her later. It seems she didn't take this too solemnly but felt she couldn't have any more to do with him. We hear a good deal in his books about the brothels then in Dublin, and the peculiar mixture of fascination and disgust which he felt for the girls there. Now, for any young man, this makes a confusing experience when he passes on to try to deal with a respectable girl, but much more so for the young Joyce, who was in revolt against all convention, because such a man refuses to try out the accepted rules. Molly would be the first woman not a prostitute he had ever been to bed with, and this would be a very decisive thing in his life, one might almost say his first real sexual experience. Molly was not too hampering for him, she wouldn't tie him down; but she was peaceful and domestic, she was earning her own living, and above all she would never put up with being despised. I tell you the first thing Molly would do; she would make him wash.[2] He spends a lot of time, as part of his general revolt, boasting that he hasn't washed for a year or some such period. Now it is very unlikely that he could have got his future wife to trust him so deeply as to run away with him unless he had had some such experience with an older woman first. Stephen as we meet him in *Ulysses* could not have induced a reliable level-headed girl to do that; she would have realized that he was already jeering at her, even though he didn't want to.

I have gone into all this at perhaps tiresome length because I believe it is the fundamental human point of the novel. When Joyce came to look back on his life, a number of years later, having finished the book *Dubliners* in the mean time, he thought, "How did it happen? How did I get out with body and soul alive from that appalling situation?" And then he thought, "What made it possible, the turning point, was that first minor affair with old Molly." This was a delightful conclusion for the novelist, because he could go ahead with a clear conscience, and tell the truth, and the more he invented things to hide the real individuals the better. On this view, the whole idea that the story of *Ulysses* was meant to feel "bitter," with nothing ever happening, in fact *not* an epic,[3] is simply a delusion which the critics copy out from one another.

This much I think can't help being true, but there is another half of the story in *Ulysses* which I am less sure of. It is in the book, my question is whether it really happened; and the chief reason for thinking it did is that Joyce seems so very incapable of inventing it. You understand, I am now going further: I am postulating *two* happy endings for a story which has long been regarded as consecrated to frustration. Bloom is described, with startling literary power so that there is no doubt about it, as having a very specific neurosis: the death of his infant son ten years before gave him a horror of the business of having a child so that he can't try to have another one. At the same time he longs to have a son, and so does Molly; both of them, during their private reflections in the book, are made to express this with dreadful pathos. (By the way, I have no patience with critics who say it is impossible ever to tell whether Joyce means a literary effect to be ironical or not; if they don't know this part isn't funny, they ought to.) Bloom is not impotent or homosexual or afraid of Molly; he has simply this special trouble which has long upset his home life. He feels that if he could plant on her a lover he was fond of, who would even take his advice instead of jeering at him, he could even now have this son himself by his wife; and after that was over, and the present jam in his married life was broken, so his incessantly calculating mind begins to reflect, he might even fix Molly by marrying Stephen to their daughter Milly. That would be the best thing for Milly too; and if you could only get Stephen to be a reliable concert singer he would be a very useful man to have in the house. Now Joyce very nearly did become a concert singer, and was extremely proud of his voice, though he couldn't afford to have it fully trained. He failed in an audition for the profession after the day of the book. And we gather the main job of Bloom is as an entrepreneur for his wife's jobs as a singer, though the rude Blazes Boylan is doing it at present; so Bloom is in a position to make serious offers to Stephen. Some critics have described this sordid beast Bloom

as trying to drag the great genius Joyce down into the mud, but Joyce didn't look at it like that, very reasonably. When Bloom says to Stephen, in effect, "I am only trying to save you for my own advantage," he is showing good feeling and good manners; in a way it is true, but he is going very far out of his way to do it. And music is one of the few positive arts in the curious world of the book; everybody takes singing extremely seriously. If you join the sexual story onto the whole position of the characters, you needn't think it so very scabrous. We know that in the end Joyce didn't go in for singing, but the offer he describes as being made to him was a serious one all round.

Now, an enormous background of symbolism is piled up behind this personal story, or rather this preparation for a story; about mother-goddesses and fertility cults, about the son who has renounced his father and is searching for a spiritual father, about the father looking for a son, about what Shakespeare meant by the *Sonnets* and by *Hamlet*, and of course about the *Odyssey* itself. All this background seems fussy and pedantic until you realize that it builds up the terrible refusal to choose, done by Stephen in the Question and Answer chapter. This comes just before the final chapter, given to Molly. A parody of both scientific and legal styles of writing makes it almost impossible to find out what Bloom and Stephen are feeling about each other, or even saying to each other. Joyce said that this chapter was the Ugly Duckling of his book, meaning of course that in the end it would be recognized as a swan. The chapter certainly need not be taken to mean that Stephen will never accept; surely the chief point of it is that in real life he couldn't decide, at such a peculiarly exhausting moment. The drama of the thing is left entirely hanging in suspense. But at any rate a real offer is being made; there is no need for critics to say that nothing but grim acceptance of the sordid common-place is going on all through the last third of the book.

As to the parallel with the *Odyssey*, which is made prominent in the title, that seems merely tiresome if it is only supposed to be what is called irony, that is, a joke because it doesn't fit; the point of it, I think, is that it was the only way left for Joyce to hint that there *would* be a happy ending for Ulysses-Bloom. In fact this is what makes the book an epic. Joyce can't do it any other way if he is to keep to his rigid convention of one day and also keep to his theory that the author must not speak in person. The book is like the Ibsen Problem Plays which he greatly admired; the aim is to thrust on the reader a general problem, so one mustn't make it easy for the reader by ending with a particular solution. The reason for dragging in Shakespeare and the Sonnets, which happens chiefly when Stephen tries to get advance payment for an article on Shakespeare by talking about him in the library chapter, is simply that the reader needs this amount of help to understand the book; the situation that Joyce is leading up to is one that hardly any other author has handled, whereas something like it does happen to crop up in the Shakespeare Sonnets. And then, the reason for the magnificent but over-laboured chapter in the maternity hospital is that the book is leading up to Ulysses-Bloom recovering his son. And so forth. All this is evident, but critics usually deal with it by saying that the relation of a spiritual father to his spiritual son was what Joyce meant. But Joyce would have laughed at that; it could only mean to him a priest, and he was cross with priests; he had himself refused to become one. Only a real son would count, and he has labored to present a special psychology for Bloom which makes a real son a possible result of this day. To be sure, the novel does not ask you to believe that Bloom *did* have a son, but it does expect you to believe that on this day Bloom is getting a real opportunity to produce a son; the problem as it is shown to you is not trivial. Nor is there anything in the book to make you assume, as the critics regularly do, that Bloom must have lost his opportunity.

Such is my general opinion about the book, and I ought now to present at least a little evidence for it. The bit about Stephen's Doom, in the Question and Answer chapter, seems a good example. I might first say that, early in the book, Stephen has struggled to remember, while alone on the beach, a dream he had last night which is in effect the Bloom Offer; he feels a certain fear about what the dream meant. Joyce, as well as Stephen, was a quaintly superstitious man who would regard a prophetic dream as a serious part of the build-up. Towards the end of the book the exhausted Stephen, already drunk and half starving and half mad with remorse, and then knocked out by a soldier, has been searched out and picked up and taken home by Bloom, who is a Jew, and given cocoa; then Stephen sings a savage ballad about the Christian boy who went into the Jew's house and was killed by the Jew's daughter. This is his habit, and does not mean serious anti-semitic feelings; as soon as he revived, he would insult anybody who was helping him, in the simplest way he could. Then, in the appalling style of this chapter, we have (and I quote):

> Condense Stephen's commentary.
> One of all, the least of all, is the victim predestined. Once by inadvertence, twice by design he challenges his destiny. It comes when he is abandoned and challenges him reluctant and, as an apparition of hope and youth, holds him unresisting. It leads him to a strange habitation, to a secret infidel apartment, and there, implacable, immolates him, consenting.

This handsome paragraph has rather little to do with the song, and I think it must mean that Stephen will consent to the Bloom Offer, though he is automatically nasty about it. You may naturally think that he won't do it if he thinks it is a doom. But the reader has had some acquaintance with him by this time, and every time he has seen a doom he has run into it as fast as he could go. Why should we suppose he will keep away from this particularly interesting doom? I would take a small bet that he didn't.

So far as one can make out, Stephen rambles on drunkenly saying what is "condensed" in this answer, while the hurt Bloom is silent. Then there seems to be a long pause, while this insult makes Bloom think about his own daughter. (You understand I am trying to interpret this frightful text.) The next words are Bloom inviting Stephen to stay the night, and Stephen is shocked by this kindness into rather more decent behavior.

> Was the proposal of asylum accepted?
> Promptly, inexplicably, with amicability, gratefully it was declined.

So Bloom gives him back the bit of money he had saved him from throwing away, and Stephen then promises to come back and clear up for Molly the Italian pronunciation of the concert songs she sings in Italian. The promise is expressed so very obscurely, and has been so much ignored by critics, that it needs quoting. It goes like this:

> What counterproposals were alternately advanced, accepted, modified, declined, restated in other terms, reaccepted, ratified, reconfirmed?
> To inaugurate a prearranged course of Italian instruction, place the residence of the instructed. To inaugurate a course of vocal instruction, place the residence of the instructress. To inaugurate a series of static, semistatic and peripatetic intellectual dialo-

gues, places the residence of both speakers (if both speakers were resident in the same place), the Ship hotel and tavern, the . . .

and so on, a farcical list of other places. It does look as if Stephen was bored and irritated by the efforts of poor Bloom to pin him down about these intellectual talks. But we must remember the meaning of the word *counterproposal*, which Joyce would not simply get wrong, especially when he is claiming to be pedantic. The proposal was made by Bloom, to stay the night; the counterproposal was therefore made by Stephen, to come later and improve Molly's Italian; this was ratified and reconfirmed. The tactless Bloom then suggested that Molly as a professional singer could train Stephen for that career, which would offend Stephen, so he is rude about it. But he urgently needs something to do, now that he has thrown up his job; he is very scornful of other people who break their promises, and he has just made a promise; and he has not yet met Molly, though he has heard so much about her. Surely the Bloom Offer would at least excite curiosity. I think he refuses to stay the night merely because he wants to meet her first on some other footing than that of waif and stray; it would be very like his habitual pride. We need not suppose he thinks he is too grand or too high-class to do anything with the Bloom couple except tell lies to them; that is not the way Stephen's pride works, or Joyce's either.

The difficulty about *Ulysses*, as is obvious if you read the extremely various opinions of critics, is that, whereas most novels tell you what the author expects you to feel, this one not only refuses to tell you the end of the story, it also refuses to tell you what the author thinks would have been a good end to the story. A critic of *Ulysses* always holds a theory about the intention of Joyce in *Ulysses*, without realizing that he is holding it. Most of the critics who have hated the book, and also the American Judge who allowed the book into the States, which he did on the ground that it is emetic rather than aphrodisiac, seem to hold what I call the Jeer Theory; that is, they think there really was a couple, whom we may call the Ur-Blooms, who tried to be kind to the young Joyce, and as a result the elder Joyce spent at least ten years in trying to make them look immortally ridiculous and disgusting. No wonder these readers think Joyce a pretty disgusting author; no other objection to the morality of the book is half so serious as that one. I think Joyce simply miscalculated there; he did not foresee that people would read him like that, chiefly because it was so remote from his own sentiments. Most critics who have accepted him, so far as one can make out, have adopted what I call the Remorse Theory; that is, they think there was a Bloom Offer, and that Joyce rejected it, and perhaps went on feeling he couldn't have done anything but reject it, but even so came to feel he was a cad about rejecting it, and perhaps that somehow it could have been accepted in a better world. This gives you a decent moral basis for reading the book, as far as the author is concerned, but it makes the book seem very dismal or even self-torturing. I am assuming that we cannot hold the Pure Invention Theory, which critics in their tactful way usually take for granted; I do not believe Joyce was capable of inventing such a good story, as it works out; the unearthly shocking surprise with which all the theorizing of the book at last becomes solid, as an actual homely example, hard to know what to make of. We have only to peep into *Finnegans Wake*, where Joyce clearly was trying to invent a story, to see how extremely short of novelistic invention he was in his otherwise wonderful equipment. For that matter his behavior in later life doesn't suggest the Pure Invention Theory at all, and positively refutes the Remorse Theory; he expected all his friends to come on Bloomsday for a sort of private Christmas and celebrate it in a farcical but rejoicing manner. As soon as you look at the matter from that angle, which most critics have refused to do, it seems clear the Acceptance Theory holds the field.

I am also rejecting the Pure Epiphany Theory, which some critics have deduced because Joyce himself said that a novel ought to give an Epiphany. I agree that this opinion of Joyce is important, because it shows he didn't think a novel ought to be pointless. But, the way the critics take it, even a tiny contact with the young Joyce is supposed to have been enough to bring happiness to the Blooms. This school makes great play with Bloom asking his wife for breakfast in bed next morning, just before he goes to sleep; it is supposed to show he has become a man again; but it seems a natural thing to do, after he has had such a hard day. He isn't shown as afraid of his wife, except in his nightmares; in fact the Citizen says he bullies her. What is wrong with him is a more specific psychological trouble. In any case, this theory, though it doesn't make the author malicious or poisoned, surely makes him ridiculously vain about his influence as a young man; he might as well have called the book *Pippa Passes*. There is, I would agree, a strand of silliness in the mind of Joyce, but nothing near as bad as that.

A great deal of the difficulty of writing the book, and indeed I think its peculiar form, came from the fact that he had already told the reader he is writing about his own life. Surely this made it very hard to tell what he thought the essential part of his own story without dragging in the originals of the Blooms. I make no doubt that they were extremely different from the Bloom couple in the book; for one thing, I think making them Jewish was part of the business of laying a false trail. The whole game of keeping his secret while telling the truth on such a big scale was obviously a great spur to his invention, and also gave him a great deal of innocent glee. This also, I think, explains another rather puzzling aspect of the book. Once you realize that he has got hold of a subject of great interest, in fact one which novelists do not dare to treat, it does seem absurd to have hidden it completely from practically all readers while getting himself banned for years on completely irrelevant grounds of petty indecency. But he wanted to do both; his novel was meant to be the last word all round, the last word in using rude words, and also the last word in the problem novel treating a profound subject which would gradually open itself to posterity. You may well ask why I should suppose that the critics have all been wrong for so long; the answer is that Joyce felt he had to arrange things like that, and the business of doing it gave him a very exhilarating sense of glory.

Well, I do not expect to get agreement on this subject; many very keen minds have been at work for twenty years on what the intention of *Ulysses* can be. But my theory does at least prevent the book from seeming a record piece of dismal sustained nagging; and also I turn the puzzle into something which the mind of Joyce, always a straightforwardly well-intentioned mind unless he was kicking back at a supposed enemy, would have enjoyed doing.[4] It may well be true that Joyce hadn't had enough experience of the Bloom situation to finish the book properly; that is, he did go to bed with the original Molly, but he felt afterwards that he hadn't been friends enough with her husband. So then he tried to work out the Bloom situation as far as he could just because other novelists had funked it. But I think it equally likely that the original Bloom couple did have a son as a result of this incident, a son by Bloom, who will now be about fifty, and that is why Joyce always felt such glee about the whole affair. Joyce

might have said what Jane Austen said on a similar occasion; Jane Austen has just remarked, at the end of *Northanger Abbey*, that the rich young man in her story wanted to marry the heroine merely because she had recklessly shown she was fond of him, and then Jane Austen says:

> It is a new circumstance in romance, I acknowledge; but if it be as new in common life, the credit of a wild imagination will at least be all my own.

Notes

1. *James Joyce's Dublin*, by Patricia Hutchins. Grey Walls Press, 1950.
2. A correspondent, after this was broadcast, thought Molly would be too dirty to bother; but the cautious Bloom seems to doubt at one point whether she would find Stephen clean enough. By the way if, as we are told, Joyce was in fact at this time greatly enjoying the swimming, that is all the more reason to think the detail has some purpose.
3. It seems he vowed in about 1904 that he would write an epic of Dublin after ten years; he settled down to the final version of *Ulysses* in 1914, and recalled the vow in the book.
4. "If there is any difficulty in reading what I write it is because of the material I use. In my case the thought is always simple."

RICHARD ELLMANN
"The Growth of Imagination"
James Joyce
1959, pp. 302–9

> the childman weary, the manchild in the womb.
> *(Ulysses* (722 [697])[1])

The agitation of Joyce's feelings during his visit to Dublin in 1909 laid bare for a moment topics of that conversation with himself which, like Yeats, he never ceased to conduct. One was his bond to Dublin, which his books indicate he thoroughly understood. Although Stephen Dedalus in both *Stephen Hero* and *A Portrait* assumes his isolation, he surrounds himself with friends and family to whom he can confide it. When he rebels he hastens to let them know of his rebellion so that he can measure their response to it. He searches for disciples who must share his motives vicariously. As he demands increasing allegiance from them, step by step, he brings them to the point where they will go no further, and their refusal, half-anticipated, enables him to feel forsaken and to forsake them. He buys his own ticket for Holyhead, but claims to have been deported. Yet his mother prepares his clothing for the journey; she at any rate does not break with him. Of this young man it may be safely predicted that he will write letters home.

Joyce's life wears a similar aspect. Having stomped angrily out of the house, he circled back to peer in the window. He could not exist without close ties, no matter in what part of Europe he resided; and if he came to terms with absence, it was by bringing Ireland with him, in his memories, and in the persons of his wife, his brother, his sister. So in later life, when asked if he would go back to Ireland, he could reply, 'Have I ever left it?' In memory his closest ties to the past were with the scenes of his early childhood. This childhood was dominated rhetorically by his father, but emotionally by his mother with her practicality, her unquenchable indulgence, her tenacity, even her inveterate pregnancy. As a small boy he had gone to her to ask that she examine him in his school work; as a young man, the letters from Paris in 1902 and 1903 confirm, he asked her support for his ambitions and ideas. His confidences went to his mother, not to his father, a man (as his sister May remembered) impossible to confide in.

His attitude toward his mother is clarified by his attitude toward Nora Barnacle. In the letters he sent to Nora in that discomposed summer of 1909, there are many testimonies that Joyce longed to reconstitute, in his relation with her, the filial bond which his mother's death had broken. Explicitly he longs to make their relationship that of child and mother, as if the relationship of lovers was too remote. He covets an even more intimate dependence: 'O that I could nestle in your womb like a child born of your flesh and blood, be fed by your blood, sleep in the warm secret gloom of your body!'[2]

Joyce seems to have thought with equal affection of the roles of mother and child. He said once to Stanislaus about the bond between the two, 'There are only two forms of love in the world, the love of a mother for her child and the love of a man for lies.' In later life, as Maria Jolas remarked, 'Joyce talked of fatherhood as if it were motherhood.'[3] He seems to have longed to establish in himself all aspects of the bond of mother and child. He was attracted, particularly, by the image of himself as a weak child cherished by a strong woman, which seems closely connected with the images of himself as victim, whether as a deer pursued by hunters, as a passive man surrounded by burly extroverts, as a Parnell or a Jesus among traitors. His favorite characters are those who in one way or another retreat before masculinity, yet are loved regardless by motherly women.

The sense of his family life as warm and tranquil, which was established in Joyce's mind during his earliest years, was disturbed for him by his father's irresponsibility. To some extent John Joyce served his son as model, for he continually tried his wife's steadfastness, which however proved equal to every challenge, including the drunken attempt on her life. James, contesting for his mother's love, learned to use the same weapons with a difference. A merely good boy would have been submerged, unable to compete with his father in the inordinate demands upon a mother's affection, but a prodigal son had a better chance. His mother must be encouraged to love him more than his father because he was just as errant and much more gifted, so more pitiable and lovable. For his irresponsibility was the turbulence of genius, motivated— unlike his father's—by courage rather than by failure.[4] At first it took the form of arousing his mother to question his conduct. His answers proved surprisingly sweeping and persuasive. Then he tried her further: John Joyce had been anticlerical, James exceeded him by becoming irreligious.

This change, which was not easy for him to undergo, presented an added complication. For one thing, in the figure of the Virgin he had found a mother image which he cherished. He had gone to prostitutes and then prayed to the Virgin as later he would drum up old sins with which to demand Nora's forgiveness; the Virgin's love, like his mother's and later his wife's, were of a sort especially suited to great sinners. But there was an aspect of Irish Catholicism which he was glad to abandon. It was not a mother church but a father church, harsh, repressive, masculine. To give it up was both consciously and unconsciously to offer his mother's love its supreme test, for his mother was deeply religious. She was disconcerted but did not abandon him. Yet her death not long after one of his open defiances of her belief seemed a punishment; he felt as if he had killed her by trying her too far. This thought he confided to Nora, who called him reproachfully, 'Woman-killer.'[5]

When Joyce met Nora Barnacle in 1904, it was not enough for her to be his mistress; she must be his queen and even his goddess; he must be able to pray to her. But to gain all her love, and so increase her perfection, he must make sure she will accept even the worst in him. He must test her by making her his wife without calling her that, by denying legal sanction to the bond between them, just as in dealing with his mother he had wanted her to acknowledge him as her son even though in so many ways he was not filial. Nora Barnacle passed this test easily, no doubt aware that their attachment was indispensable to him. Then he tried her further, not by flouting her religion, which she did not care deeply about, but by doubting her fidelity. That the accusation might be false did not deter him; in a way, it encouraged him, for if he was accusing her falsely he could be, when reassured of her innocence, more humble and so more childlike than before. When this test too was surmounted, Joyce made a final trial of her: she must recognize all her impulses, even the strangest, and match his candor by confiding in him every thought she has found in herself, especially the most embarrassing. She must allow him to know her inmost life, to learn with odd exactitude what it is to be a woman. This test, the last, Nora passed successfully later in 1909. In so doing she accepted complicity, she indulged his reduction of her motherly purity just as she had indulged his insistence upon that purity. Joyce's letters during his two subsequent absences from her in Trieste were full of thoughts about 'adoration' and 'desecration' of her image, extravagant terms that he himself applied.

What was unusual about his attitude was not that he saw his wife as his mother or that he demanded inordinate fulfillment of either role. The novelty lay in his declining to confuse the two images and instead holding them remorsefully apart, opposing them to each other so that they became the poles of his mind. He was thereby enabled to feel that with Nora, as with his mother, he was a prodigal son, full of love and misbehavior; he was pleased that she 'saw through him,' as he said, and detected the boy in the man. This view of himself he encouraged. In *Ulysses* and *Finnegans Wake* he apportioned womanhood in its sexual aspect to Molly Bloom, and in its maternal aspect to Anna Livia Plurabelle. But he understood and marveled that Nora had no sense of the dichotomy that bothered him. He represented her attitude, which he took to be feminine in general, when Molly, though primarily the sensualist, thinks of Stephen Dedalus as child and as lover, without incompatibility, and Anna Livia, though primarily the mother, recollects her once passionate attachment to her husband.

Joyce studied his mental landscape and made use of it in his books. *Dubliners* is written on the assumption that Ireland is an inadequate mother, 'an old sow who eats her farrow,' and he associates himself with the masticated children. As he wrote to George Goyert, the book did not describe the way 'they' are in Dublin, but they way 'we' are.[6] We are foolish, comic, motionless, corrupted; yet we are worthy of sympathy too, a sympathy which, if Ireland denies us, the international reader may give. But the reader must be tested like a loving mother by an errant child, must be forced to see the ugly, undecorated reality before he is allowed to extend his pity, a pity compounded of outraged affection, amusement, and understanding.

Joyce's own preoccupations emerge through the impersonal façade of *Dubliners*. Two stories, 'A Mother' and 'The Boarding House,' portray mothers who fail in their role by browbeating, a type Joyce could never endure. 'The Dead' represents in Gretta a woman with genuine maternal sympathy, which she extends both to the dead boy who loved her and to her inadequate husband. She overwhelms Gabriel's sexual passion by letting her thoughts dwell upon the boy, with whom Gabriel at the last associates himself. Other stories, especially 'Araby' and 'Ivy Day in the Committee Room,' play on the theme of the loss of warmth in the past: the bazaar closed, the radiant image of Parnell chilled by small feelings. Throughout the book the women usually hold together when the men do not, 'The Sisters' in that they survive so solidly their brother the priest, Chandler's wife in 'A Little Cloud' in her relegation of her husband in favor of her child. Yet there is pity for them too, especially for those who, like Corley's girl in 'Two Gallants,' like 'Eveline,' like Maria in 'Clay,' cannot achieve full maternal being, and for Gretta in 'The Dead' because of her inevitably lost girlhood. In the book women act (or fail to act) the mother, men drink, children suffer.

To write A *Portrait of the Artist as a Young Man* Joyce plunged back into his own past, mainly to justify, but also to expose it. The book's pattern, as he explained to Stanislaus, is that we are what we were; our maturity is an extension of our childhood, and the courageous boy is father of the arrogant young man. But in searching for a way to convert the episodic *Stephen Hero* into A *Portrait of the Artist*, Joyce hit upon a principle of structure which reflected his habits of mind as extremely as he could wish. The work of art, like a mother's love, must be achieved over the greatest obstacles, and Joyce, who had been dissatisfied with his earlier work as too easily done, now found the obstacles in the form of a most complicated pattern.

This is hinted at in his image of the creative process. As far back as his paper on Mangan, Joyce said that the poet takes into the vital center of his life 'the life that surrounds it, flinging it abroad again amid planetary music.' He repeated this image in *Stephen Hero*, then in A *Portrait of the Artist* developed it more fully. Stephen refers to the making of literature as 'the phenomenon of artistic conception, artistic gestation and artistic reproduction,' and then describes the progression from lyrical to epical and to dramatic art:

> The simplest epical form is seen emerging out of lyrical literature when the artist prolongs and broods upon himself as the centre of an epical event and this form progresses till the centre of emotional gravity is equidistant from the artist himself and from others. The narrative is no longer purely personal. The personality of the artist passes into the narration itself, flowing round and round the persons and the action like a vital sea. . . . The dramatic form is reached when the vitality which has flowed and eddied round each person fills every person with such vital force that he or she assumes a proper and intangible esthetic life. . . . The mystery of esthetic like that of material creation is accomplished.[7]

This creator is not male but female; Joyce goes on to borrow an image of Flaubert by calling him a 'god,'[8] but he is really a goddess. Within this womb creatures come to life. No male intercession is necessary even; as Stephen says, 'In the virgin womb of the imagination the word was made flesh.'

Joyce did not take up such metaphors lightly. His brother records that in the first draft of A *Portrait*, Joyce thought of a man's character as developing 'from an embryo' with constant traits. Joyce acted upon this theory with his characteristic thoroughness, and his subsequent interest in the process of gestation, as conveyed to Stanislaus during Nora's first pregnancy, expressed a concern that was literary as well as anatomical. His decision to rewrite *Stephen Hero* as A *Portrait* in five chapters occurred appropriately just after Lucia's birth. For A *Portrait of the Artist as a Young Man* is in fact the gestation of a soul, and in the metaphor Joyce found his new principle of order. The book begins with Stephen's father and, just before the ending, it depicts the hero's severance from his mother. From the start the soul is surrounded by liquids, urine,

slime, seawater, amniotic tides, 'drops of water' (as Joyce says at the end of the first chapter) 'falling softly in the brimming bowl.' The atmosphere of biological struggle is necessarily dark and melancholy until the light of life is glimpsed. In the first chapter the foetal soul is for a few pages only slightly individualized, the organism responds only to the most primitive sensory impressions, then the heart forms and musters its affections, the being struggles toward some unspecified, uncomprehended culmination, it is flooded in ways it cannot understand or control, it gropes wordlessly toward sexual differentiation. In the third chapter shame floods Stephen's whole body as conscience develops; the lower bestial nature is put by. Then at the end of the fourth chapter the soul discovers the goal towards which it has been mysteriously proceeding—the goal of life. It must swim no more but emerge into air, the new metaphor being flight. The final chapter shows the soul, already fully developed, fattening itself for its journey until at last it is ready to leave. In the last few pages of the book, Stephen's diary, the soul is released from its confinement, its individuality is complete, and the style shifts with savage abruptness.[9]

The sense of the soul's development as like that of an embryo not only helped Joyce to the book's imagery, but also encouraged him to work and rework the original elements in the process of gestation. Stephen's growth proceeds in waves, in accretions of flesh, in particularization of needs and desires, around and around but always ultimately forward. The episodic framework of *Stephen Hero* was renounced in favor of a group of scenes radiating backwards and forwards.[10] In the new first chapter Joyce had three clusters of sensations: his earliest memories of infancy, his sickness at Clongowes (probably indebted like the ending of 'The Dead' to rheumatic fever in Trieste), and his pandying at Father Dolan's hands. Under these he subsumed chains of related moments, with the effect of three fleshings in time rather than of a linear succession of events. The sequence became primarily one of layers rather than of years.

In this process other human beings are not allowed much existence except as influences upon the soul's development or features of it. The same figures appear and reappear, the schoolboy Heron for example, each time in an altered way to suggest growth in the soul's view of them. Eileen Vance, a partner in childhood games, becomes the object of Stephen's adolescent love poems; the master of Clongowes reappears as the preacher of the sermons at Belvedere.[11] The same words, 'Apologise,' 'admit,' 'maroon,' 'green,' 'cold,' 'warm,' 'wet,' and the like, keep recurring with new implications. The book moves from rudimentary meanings to more complex ones, as in the conceptions of the call and the fall. Stephen, in the first chapter fascinated by unformed images, is next summoned by the flesh and then by the church, the second chapter ending with a prostitute's lingual kiss, the third with his reception of the Host upon his tongue. The soul that has been enraptured by body in the second chapter and by spirit in the third (both depicted in sensory images) then hears the call of art and life, which encompass both without bowing before either, in the fourth chapter; the process is virtually complete. Similarly the fall into sin, at first a terror, gradually becomes an essential part of the discovery of self and life.

Now Stephen, his character still recomposing the same elements leaves the Catholic priesthood behind him to become 'a priest of eternal imagination, transmuting the daily bread of experience into the radiant body of everlasting life.' Having listened to sermons on ugliness in the third chapter, he makes his own sermons on beauty in the last. The Virgin is transformed into the girl wading on the strand, symbolizing a more tangible reality. In the last two chapters, to suit his new structure, Joyce minimizes Stephen's physical life to show the dominance of his mind, which has accepted but subordinated physical things. The soul is ready now, it throws off its sense of imprisonment, its melancholy, its no longer tolerable conditions of lower existence, to be born.

Joyce was obviously well-pleased with the paradox into which his method had put him, that he was, as the artist framing his own development in a constructed matrix, his own mother. The complications of this state are implied in Stephen's thought of himself as not his parents' true son, but a foster-son.[12] In *Ulysses* Joyce was to carry the method much further; he makes that book the epic of the whole human body, the womb being the organ only of the *Oxen of the Sun* episode. In that episode, as Joyce said later,[13] Stephen is again the embryo. But, in a parody of the method of *A Portrait*, Stephen emerges not to life but to Burke's pub. The theme of *Ulysses*, Joyce intimates, is reconciliation with the father. Of course, the father whom Joyce depicts in Bloom is in almost every way the opposite of his own father, and is much closer to himself.[14] Insofar as the movement of the book is to bring Stephen, the young Joyce, into *rapport* with Bloom, the mature Joyce, the author becomes, it may be said, his own father. Stephen is aware enough of the potential ironies of this process to ponder all the paradoxes of the father as his own son in the Trinity, and of Shakespeare as both King Hamlet and Prince Hamlet. Yet the book is not without its strong woman; Bloom is appropriately under the influence of his wife, whom he dissatisfies (to some extent intentionally), and wishes to bring Stephen under her influence too.

In both these books Joyce seems to reconstitute his family relationships, to disengage himself from the contradictions of his view of himself as a child and so to exploit them, to overcome his mother's conventionality and his father's rancor, to mother and father himself, to become, by the superhuman effort of the creative process, no one but James Joyce.

Notes

1. *Ulysses*, Random House and Modern Library, 1961, and John Lane, The Bodley Head, 1969.
2. See Joyce's letter of September 2, 1909, Ellmann 1959, pp. 296–7.
3. Interview with Mrs. Maria Jolas, 1953.
4. Joyce writes of Mr Dedalus in *Stephen Hero* (New Directions, 1955, p. 110; Jonathan Cape, 1956, p. 115), 'He had his son's distaste for responsibility without his son's courage.'
5. Joyce, *Exiles* (1951), 118 (Joyce's notes for the play). The expression is also used by Bertha in the play itself (*The Portable James Joyce*, ed. Harry Levin, Viking Press, 1949), 617[432]).
6. Letter to Georg Goyert, October 19, 1927, *Letters of James Joyce*, Vol. III, ed. Richard Ellmann 1966, The Viking Press and Faber & Faber.
7. *A Portrait of the Artist as a Young Man* in *The Portable James Joyce* and *The Essential James Joyce* (Jonathan Cape, 1948).
8. Stephen says the artist is 'like the God of the creation,' remaining 'within or behind or beyond or above his handiwork, invisible, refined out of existence, paring his fingernails.' But Lynch sardonically qualifies this statement by saying, 'Trying to refine them [the fingernails] also out of existence.' Stephen makes no reply. *A Portrait* (481–2 [336–7]).
9. For a fuller explanation, see R. Ellmann, *Ulysses on the Liffey* (1972), esp. the discussions of *Scylla and Charybdis*, 81–9, of *Oxen of the Sun*, 133–40, and of *Eumaeus*, 151–5.
10. It is a technique which William Faulkner was to carry even further in the opening section of *The Sound and the Fury*, where the extreme disconnection finds its justification, not, as in Joyce, in the haze of childhood memory, but in the blur of an idiot's mind. Faulkner, when he wrote his book, had read *Dubliners* and *A Portrait*; he did not read *Ulysses* until a year later, in 1930, but

knew about it from excerpts and from the conversation of friends. He has said that he considered himself the heir of Joyce in his methods in *The Sound and the Fury*. Interview with William Faulkner, 1958.
11. In both these instances Joyce changed the actual events. His freedom of recomposition is displayed also in the scene in the physics classroom in *A Portrait* (453[319]), where he telescopes two lectures, one on electricity and one on mechanics, which as Professor Felix Hackett remembers, took place months apart. Moynihan's whispered remark, inspired by the lecturer's discussion of ellipsoidal balls, 'Chase me, ladies, I'm in the cavalry!', was in fact made by a young man named Kinahan on one of these occasions. In the same way, as J. F. Byrne points out in *Silent Years*, 33–5, the long scene with the dean of studies in *A Portrait* (446–51 [313–17]) happened not to Joyce but to him; he told it to Joyce and was later displeased to discover how his innocent description of Father Darlington lighting a fire had been converted into a reflection of Stephen's strained relations with the Church.
12. *A Portrait*, 349 (248).
13. See his letter to Frank Budgen, Ellmann 1959, pp. 489–90, and the discussion of *Finnegans Wake*, p. 729.
14. Pp. 384–5.

CLEANTH BROOKS

From "Joyce's *Ulysses*:
A Symbolic Poem, Biography, or Novel?"

Imagined Worlds, eds. Maynard Mack and Ian Gregor

1968, pp. 419–23, 432–38

Is James Joyce's *Ulysses* a novel—interpret the term with as much latitude as you like? Or is it a kind of ragbag of Joyce's personal memories, inspired doodlings, speculations, private jokes, and scattered observations on Dublin life as it was lived in the early nineteen hundreds? Some of Joyce's Dublin acquaintances and friends, like Oliver St. John Gogarty (transmogrified in the novel into Buck Mulligan) have contended that to look for any consistent or over-all meaning is silly. Those that do so are "victims of a gigantic hoax, of one of the most enormous leg-pulls in history". But the general view has been quite otherwise. In that view, *Ulysses* is an ordered and intricately organized masterpiece. Indeed it is usually accorded the treatment given to a sacred book. A painfully careful exegesis is regarded as appropriate to these Joycean scriptures, which have been diligently searched in order to discover proof texts, to recover hidden meanings, to unravel cryptic allusions, and, more ambitiously, to develop a systematic symbolism.

The appearance of Robert M. Adams' *Surface and Symbol* a few years ago raised a good many questions about the consistency of the symbolism of *Ulysses*. As Richard Ellmann has said, after Adams' exploration of the relation of fact and fiction in this work, "everyone will have to reconsider his position about *Ulysses*".

What Adams shows is that "there is no proper fictional reason for some of the things that are said and done" in *Ulysses*. Some of the items are found to lack any symbolic import whatever. For example, the winners in the bicycle race that is held on Bloom's Day are mentioned by name and some commentators have tried to find special meanings in the names that Joyce chose for them. Is, for example, the name of the winner, J. A. Jackson, an "enigmatic allusion" to the author himself, viz. James Augustine Joyce, the son of Jack Joyce? Such an interpretation has been proposed. But Adams shows that Joyce copied the names from a newspaper account of a race that actually took place in Dublin on 16 June 1904. Adams is able indeed to prove that the newspaper that Joyce used was the *Irish Independent*, for the name of one of the riders, J. B. Jones, as printed in that paper, looks—probably because the type was dirty—"remarkably like 'Jeffs' ", the name that Joyce uses in *Ulysses*. In this instance, the symbol-hunter would be very much in the plight of the fabled cornet-player who was unfortunate enough to mistake a fly speck on his score for a musical note.

Usually, however, Joyce did not slavishly follow his sources but reworked the materials he derived from them very freely indeed. Yet the motive determining his alterations and transpositions is not always easy to discern. Often there seems to be no "fictional reason" served by the changes. There may be personal reasons: occasionally Joyce seems to be simply venting his dislike of a Dublin acquaintance as when, for example, he calls a priest whom he knew, and whom Adams is able to identify, "Father Purdon", assigning to him "deliberately, the name of a street in the red-light district of Dublin". In other instances the alterations serve to develop a private joke, and often a joke so private that only a Dubliner of the time and in the know would find it comprehensible. Adams, it should be said, is not particularly worried by Joyce's propensity to insert his signature thus into odd corners of his canvas or to work into it his little private ceremonies and rituals. Yet Adams does question, and properly, "a general principle of construction not very economical of the general reader's time, and not very neat so far as the economy of forces within the novel is concerned".

It is the latter point, of course, that is finally important. Conceivably the scholars some day may have succeeded in annotating all the private allusions and in solving all the riddles, but in so far as such material cannot be related to the import of the novel—in so far as it has no "fictional reason" behind it—then so much the worse for *Ulysses* as a work of fiction.

Because the prime critical sin of our day—certainly the currently fashionable sin—is "symbol-mongering", and because critics too often seize upon any item that seems invitingly "symbolic" or that evokes something remembered from *The Golden Bough*, we have had a proliferation of *Ulysses* "symbols", some of them clearly possessing no genuine relation to the work. Against this kind of reading, *Surface and Symbol* serves as a powerful counterblast. Adams has shown that some of the matter in *Ulysses* is mere connective tissue, some of it is not even healthy connective tissue. This or that suspicious lump, under his probing, turns out to be simply as excrescence, a wart, or, if deeper below the surface, a mere tumour, serving no function even though it may be harmless and benign. Such elements in *Ulysses* may represent bits of the author's private life, elements that he has not been able—or perhaps has not taken the trouble—to transmute into the fictional fabric. Or, to change the metaphor, such elements may be regarded as odd pieces of scaffolding, necessary perhaps for Joyce's rather peculiar method of composition, but once composition has been completed, serving no function, constituting no part of the total architecture, though still firmly attached to the permanent structure.

But the reader may ask, are you sure that you really understand Joyce's architecture? Isn't it possible that someone whose head was filled with preconceived notions about what a novel ought to be might mistake for bits of leftover scaffolding what are actually essential parts of the building? That indeed is the question. How does one determine what is integral and what is not? What is the organizing principle of *Ulysses*? Mr. Adams' essential contribution is to show that odd bits of scaffolding do remain—i.e., J. B. Jeffs or J. B. Jones—that some parts of *Ulysses* are merely surface and have no symbolic reference. Mr. Adams has also thrown suspicion on a still larger number of allegedly symbolic items by showing that the

symbolic patterns they seem to suggest either peter out to nothing when one explores them further, or else require so much elaboration and so many esoteric references that the law of diminishing returns sets in.

On the more positive side, however, Adams is less helpful. He fails to discern some of the symbolic patterns that are really there. The section of *Surface and Symbol* entitled "Dog-God" is an instance. Adams begins this part of his book by referring to Joyce's well-known fear and hatred of dogs. He goes on to sum up what is known about the real life antecedents of the Citizen's dog Garryowen. The incident on the beach, recounted in the third chapter, in which Stephen sees the live dog sniff at the body of the dead dog is referred to Mulligan's earlier characterization of Stephen as a "dogsbody". Furthermore, Adams sees that the various references to dogs in *Ulysses* are connected in some way with spelling "God" backwards when the black mass is celebrated in the Circe chapter. The general inversion of the sacred rites converts "God" into "dog"—a matter most apposite to the pattern of Stephen's thoughts as developed in the earlier chapters of *Ulysses*.

In Adams' view, however, no really meaningful pattern emerges from the references to dogs; he finds the mention of them in *Ulysses* to be "surely random". The distant bark of a dog that is heard at the end of the Circe chapter may be read, Adams tells us, "if one wishes, as a pathetic picture of God in the modern world, where truth cries out in the streets and no man regards it". But Adams quite properly sees little point in pressing this particular notion. Even the fact that Rudy's conception is occasioned by Molly's sexual stimulation at seeing two dogs copulating doesn't seem to him to have any "crucial symbolic significance". If it does have, it is "buried in an oddly out-of-the-way corner of the book structure."

In his attempt to discover whether the references to dogs mean anything in particular in this novel, Adams considers the associations of Odysseus with the dog and with other animals, the pig and the fox. He is also driven back into speculations about what books on the subject Joyce might have read, including quite remarkable lexicons such as Selig Korn's *Etymologisch-symbolisch-mythologisches Real-Wörterbuch zum Handgebräuche für Bibelforscher, Archäologen und bildende Künstler* (Stuttgart, 1843) and Oskar Seyffert's *Lexikon der klassischen Altertumskunde*. Adams' conclusion is cautiously, but rather disappointingly, inconclusive. Joyce, he finds, digs up various traditional properties for Odysseus and Telemachus. For these he sometimes found "brilliant applications—parodic, serious, symbolic, superficial . . . but sometimes he did not. Quite sensibly he continued to use them anyway, whether or no; and left the reader to find or neglect the application, according to his temperament."

I think that one can make more of Joyce's use of dogs than Adams has done and that one can show that the development of symbols and the interrelating of them are more coherent and even more traditional than a good deal of Joyce criticism would lead us to believe. . . .

The question put some pages earlier was whether *Ulysses* can be read as a novel. The reader's answer will depend upon whether he can discern a pattern of meaning that grows out of the thoughts and actions of the various characters. The first chapters, as I have tried to show, do yield a pattern of meaning, and one which, if it does demand a sensitive and careful reading, and if it does require that the reader should know something about the Mass, and that he have at least a bowing acquaintance with such historical figures as Matthew Arnold, Pyrrhus, Oscar Wilde, and Bishop Berkeley, does not require any encyclopedic scholarship. More important still, it does not require that the reader have the key or code to a private and esoteric set of "symbols".

Stephen's irritation at Buck and his resentment of Haines are indeed unreasonable, though understandable. The author has made it plain that we are not asked to agree with Stephen or to give him more than "dramatic" sympathy. Moreover, Stephen's gloomy thoughts and his bitter speculations are related to a more general state of affairs: they have relevance to the culture of our age, and they are used to throw light upon a climate of opinion that characterizes modern civilization.

The opening chapters of *Ulysses* give us a brilliant dramatization of, among other things, the alienation of the sensitive artist in our day. Stephen's case is, of course, special. It is related to his personal circumstances: his education by the Jesuits, his bitterness at his poverty, and his hurt at the recent death of his mother. But his case, special as it is, is related to general and universal problems including the relation of science, poetry, and religion seen in the post-Arnoldian world. Stephen has won a Pyrrhic victory. He has decided not to join Buck and Haines at The Ship at half-past noon and he has resolved not to return to the Tower that evening. He will break off his connection with Buck Mulligan. If this will cost him a place to sleep, so be it.

How is this pattern of meaning developed in the subsequent chapters? How is Stephen related to Bloom and what part does Bloom play in this emerging pattern of meanings? What finally is the total meaning of the novel? In a short essay, one can only sketch very general directions. Moreover, *Ulysses* is such a rich novel that one does not want to risk oversimplifying it or reducing it to an abstract theme. Perhaps the most concise way to indicate the pattern of meaning that develops in the novel is to make some comments upon the meaning of Stephen and Bloom. What occurs when these polar extremes are connected? What currents leap across from one to the other? Or does anything leap across? In my own view, no transaction takes place. The total meaning of the novel, so it seems to me, has to be one that accepts this obvious fact.

In spite of the many attempts to show that Stephen and Bloom achieve some sort of real communication, I think that the case is not proved. On this point I would agree with Harry Levin's early and excellent introductory study (*James Joyce*, 1941) and with Adams in his *Surface and Symbol*. There is no real communication between the two men. How could there be? Stephen and Bloom speak different languages. Indeed, these polar, antithetical men come closest to a meeting of minds in an incident that occurs in the Circe chapter. When Bloom and Stephen both look into the mirror in Mrs. Cohen's establishment, each sees not his own face but the face of Shakespeare, "beardless . . . rigid in facial paralysis, crowned by the reflection of the reindeer antlered hatrack." If one can accept the fact that they are "seeing things" in this chapter of hallucinations, there is perfectly good reason to account for their seeing this face. Stephen can see himself reflected in Shakespeare because for him Shakespeare is the type of the artist. Stephen conceives that Shakespeare, like himself, lacked appreciation, was betrayed, and had to live by Stephen's own code of silence, cunning, and exile. As for Bloom, Shakespeare, like himself, was a cuckold and a kind of commercial traveller.

The vision of Shakespeare that unites Stephen and Bloom has welled up, as it were, out of the subconscious, bypassing the medium of words. Yet the shared perception hardly amounts to communication, for presumably neither man knows that the perception is shared—that his opposite is seeing Shakespeare too.

Why is it that so many commentators have felt that Stephen and Bloom simply must have something to say to each other, something that will alter the lives of both? The demand has arisen from the very fact of polarity. Stephen and Bloom so completely divide the world of man between themselves that each obviously needs the other: either standing alone is incomplete. Yet the reader's sense that the two men ought to join forces or become atoned one with the other does not mean that they do. To argue that since an atonement is desirable it must occur takes the intent for the deed. In fact, it does more: it makes an assumption about the author's intent that cannot be supported by the author's text.

A complicating factor has been the prominence given in *Ulysses* to the theme of paternity. It has been argued that Bloom, throughout the day, is the only person who takes a fatherly interest in Stephen. Indeed, according to this argument Bloom proves himself to be Stephen's spiritual father. Yet it is a very obtuse special pleading that can make the argument that Bloom is the only person who is kind to Stephen during the day. Miles Crawford, the newspaper editor, Professor McHugh, Mr. Deasy the schoolmaster—all of them recognize Stephen's talent and express a wish to help him. Even Buck Mulligan, it is plain, thinks of him as a kind of genius and wishes him well.

Stephen does indeed need a father, but the father whom he has already chosen for himself is his namesake, Dedalus, the fabulous artificer. In any case, Bloom's efforts to engage Stephen's interests do not get very far. Stephen, tired and bored, rejects them politely, and finally, when Bloom suggests that Stephen spend the night with him, Stephen again politely but firmly rejects the invitation.

For the sake of argument, however, let us assume that the meeting of Stephen and Bloom is productive of something. What did it produce? Is there any evidence that Bloom's life has been changed by the meeting? It is true that in the Oxen of the Sun chapter, we are told that one of the dreams that Bloom has had argues that he is in for a change. But the only change that he finds when he returns home is a rearrangement of the furniture. He bumps into a walnut sideboard which is not in its accustomed place, thanks to Molly's altered notions of where it and other pieces of furniture should be. But apparently this is all that has been altered in the Bloom household. Bloom does request Molly to make breakfast for him the next morning, and several commentators have rather desperately interpreted this modest request as betokening that Bloom will become from now on master in his own house. It would be nice to think that the worm has finally turned, but the logic of the book would indicate that no real change in his relation to Molly has occurred or can occur.

Yet so insistent has been the urge to endow the meeting of Bloom and Stephen with significance that various expedients have been used to get over the obvious fact that they have nothing to say to each other and that nothing happens. One stratagem has been to point to "symbolic" communion or communication. In the kitchen of Bloom's house Stephen and Bloom have a cup of cocoa together. Since Joyce refers to the cocoa as "Epps's massproduct", it is evident to some readers that what really is being celebrated in the kitchen is a symbolic equivalent of the Mass, a rite of communion.

To take another instance: stepping out of the kitchen, Stephen and Bloom urinate in the garden, an act that is said to symbolize fertility. As they do so, they gaze upward and see the lighted window of Molly's bedroom. She is a kind of fertility goddess who presides over the scene. Stephen has found his true Muse and will become the writer that he ought to be. Thus, what does not occur in the thoughts and actions of the characters may still occur symbolically, and what occurs symbolically must be true.

A second strategy for proving that something does come out of the meeting of Stephen and Bloom is to make Stephen Dedalus and James Joyce interchangeable. The argument runs this way: since Stephen is an expression of Joyce as a young man, anything that happened to or was true of Joyce can be attributed to Stephen.

When Stephen leaves Bloom, after declining Bloom's offer of hospitality, where does he go? He has resolved not to return to the Tower. Where did he sleep that night? What happened to him? We are not told. The novel does not take his career any further. On the other hand, we know that James Joyce did indeed survive his experiences in Ireland, went to live on the Continent, and wrote *Ulysses*. Joyce did develop, was turned into a man by his marriage to Nora, and put away the rather brittle aestheticism of Stephen Dedalus. By a kind of illicit transfer from the realm of biography to that of fiction, various things that are true of Joyce can be attributed to Stephen Dedalus. W. Y. Tindall puts the matter quite explicitly in *James Joyce: His Way of Interpreting the Modern World*. He writes: "The encounter with Bloom has changed Stephen's inhumanity to humanity. The egotist has discovered charity, the greatest of virtues, and compassion for mankind . . . 'Pity', Stephen says in *A Portrait of the Artist*, "is the feeling which arrests the mind in the presence of whatsoever is grave and constant in human suffering and unites it with the human sufferer'. He now discovers what this means, and, leaving Bloom, he goes away to write *Ulysses*." But the "he" who left Bloom with "*Liliata rutilantium*" still ringing in his head was Stephen, and the "he" who wrote *Ulysses* was James Joyce. For all we know, Stephen Dedalus never wrote any fiction at all.

What, then, is one to say about *Ulysses* as a novel? When one reviews the various attempts to elucidate the meaning of *Ulysses* it quickly becomes apparent that the red herring lying across the path is Joyce's own biography together with his own incidental comments about *Ulysses*. It is this material that has put most of the hounds off the true scent. One readily grants that *Ulysses* bears a very special relationship to Joyce's biography, and further that all sorts of parallels exist between Joyce and Stephen and between Joyce and Bloom, for that matter. I think also that one has to accept the fact that the structure is intricate, and that there are levels of meaning which will elude readers who are not in possession of certain specialized bodies of knowledge. Thus, in the earlier chapters the various heresies concerning the doctrine of the Trinity are used to comment upon Buck and Stephen and on the modern world generally. Averroes and Moses Maimonides, "flashing in their mocking mirrors the obscure soul of the world, a darkness shining in brightness which brightness could not comprehend", reverse St. John's account of the Logos, as a "light shining in the darkness" which the darkness could not comprehend. They also comment further upon the Christian scheme which has permeated Stephen's thought but which for him has now become emptied of reality.

Most readers will not be able or willing to pursue these more delicate ramifications. And they need not: the general import of the novel will come through even though the reader has to regard Aquinas, Averroes, and Aristotle as simply part of the equipment of Stephen's mind and thus dramatically appropriate to his brooding meditations. Furthermore, one has to concede the fact that *Ulysses* is a kind of private logbook and spiritual diary containing Joyce's own personal revenges on particular people, his private jokes, and allusions to incidents and happenings that had some particular meaning for him. On this general point, Adams's book has been decisive.

Yet when all is said and done, *Ulysses* is not simply a catchall into which Joyce stuffed such materials. Nor is it merely or even primarily a Joycean riddle. It is a novel, and yields, in spite of its special difficulties, the sort of knowledge about ourselves and about our world that any other authentic novel does yield.

Among other things, *Ulysses* is a novel about the rift in modern civilization—as reflected in the attitudes of an intransigent and sensitive and brilliant young artist, of a good-natured, rather bumbling, bourgeois citizen, and of a sceptical, practical, "natural" female like Molly Bloom, who is fascinated by men but who is also amused by them, and in some sense rather contemptuous of them and the elaborate intellectual structures that they insist upon raising. There is a great deal of comedy in *Ulysses*, though it does not bar out pathos. There is some very brilliant and searching satire.

The fabric of the book is intricate. The tone is of an equivalent complexity. Commentators, in their anxiety to find a happy ending, have insisted on the book's compassion and on its final optimism, have oversimplified and probably distorted its meaning. In any case, whatever conclusions about the meaning of this novel we are to draw will require testing against the fictional structure—will have to be matched with what can actually be found in the novel. Too often the commentator has argued in effect that the meaning of *Ulysses* is the development of James Joyce, and if we venture to ask why it is so important to learn about the artistic development of James Joyce, we are told that this is important because James Joyce was able to write *Ulysses*. The hopelessly circular nature of this argument needs no comment.

HÉLÈNE CIXOUS
From "The Language of Reality"
The Exile of James Joyce, tr. Sally A. J. Purcell
1972, pp. 673–79, 699–702

After the moral history of *Dubliners*, after the spiritual gestation of the archetypal artist and the discovery of the subject's own style, after the skilfully demonstrated statement that the Artist creates, starting from his inner exile, a work outside which (or far from which) he stands, Joyce wrote *Ulysses*, the work which reconciles unity and multiplicity to an end which is both realistic, moral, and universal. The Artist is both within and without, and the style of the object responds to that of the subject. The relationships of symbolism and realism are modified, sometimes to such an extent that the code and the message, the surface and the depths, are confused with one another. That object of realism is not "reality," for the reality of Ireland is only a part of an infinitely larger whole. *Ulysses* is not the modern *Odyssey*; the Odysseyan symbolism with its network of correspondences leads scarcely further than an ethical statement, and in fact the *Odyssey* is also part of an infinitely larger whole, taking on its meaning from that whole (all Western culture, its historical duration, and its myths) and from its relationship with the concrete reality of the here and now. The best definition of Joyce's intentions is to be found in a letter he wrote to Carlo Linati:

> I think that in view of the enormous bulk and the more than enormous complexity of my three times blasted novel it would be better to send you a sort of summary-key-skeleton-scheme, for your personal use only. . . . I have given only catchwords in my

scheme but I think you will understand it all the same. It is an epic of two races (Israelite-Irish) and at the same time the cycle of the human body as well as a little story of a day (life). . . . For seven years I have been working at this book—blast it! It is also a sort of encyclopaedia. My intention is to transpose the myth *sub specie temporis nostri*. Each adventure (that is, every hour, every organ, every art being interconnected and interrelated in the structural scheme of the whole) should not only condition but even create its own technique. Each adventure is so to say one person although it is composed of persons—as Aquinas relates of the angelic hosts.[1]

Joyce's programme, in its methodical formulation and with its encyclopaedic intention, is in its universality nothing less than a project to write the book of books, to find a form or "structural scheme" in which everything may be said in relation to everything, in which each component part (art, organ, hour, etc.) should create its own language. This monstrous epiphany is to be the total manifestation of reality through language.

The first point to notice is the idea of a "summa," a mediaeval idea from which Joyce takes the concept of totality, while abandoning its content, that order and hierarchy which made the correspondence-system possible; the form of the summa is dictated by the demands of language. Joyce rejects the idea of one unique style, one author's commentary, and replaces it by a multiplicity of styles. At the very most, he admits that the word "style" may have a meaning. He explains to Miss Weaver that it is the mode of language of any one generation, thereby reducing it to the garment of writing, not even the garment of thought; by this he means that the men of any given generation will command the same resources of language, drawn from their vocabulary, and that in this sense one can speak of the purple style of the symbolist decadents, or of the style of the generation of Pope. But when "style" is meant as a purely formal and objective term, it is simply the historical aspect of the language, that which permits the reader to date the work. Apart from this meaning (in which style appears as that which is not the man, but that which is the age in which he lives, the very reverse of the original expression), he always insisted, in the explanations given to friends while the work was in progress, on the primordial function of the "multilanguage" of *Ulysses*: "The task I set myself technically in writing a book from eighteen different points of view and in as many styles. . . ."[2]

There might seem to be some contradiction here, in that the idea of totality is limited by the order Joyce has chosen, in that there are to be eighteen styles and no more. The traditional idea of style is indeed destroyed, but it is replaced, given the artifice of the choosing of the eighteen styles, by an experimental style which is a kind of summa of all styles, including the philological parody of the English language from its origins to the present day. He does this in one chapter alone, 'Oxen of the Sun,' whose corresponding co-ordinates are in themselves a comic metaphor of what Joyce considers literature to be; the organ of this chapter in which literary style develops like a technical embryo is the womb.[3]

Yet *Ulysses* may further be a summa of all possibilities of literary representation, a kind of critical anatomy of genres, myths, and modes; in this way the work becomes a part of culture, if only with purpose of destroying it from within, for "each successive episode, dealing with some province of artistic culture, (rhetoric or music or dialectic) leaves behind it a burnt up field."[4]

The context of experiences is always the same, that of culture as expressed through language and, through culture only, a very definite vision of the universe in its spatio-temporal categories. This limitation is expressed in the choice itself of a unity of time and space: "everything" happens in one single day, in one place, and Joyce remains in the main stream of Western thought, with its vision of the world always directed towards the One or the Absolute.

This multiplicity caught in unity permits the author-as-demiurge to withdraw, leaving reality to speak its own language. There is sometimes a perfect equation established between the code and the message it conveys, between the world and the way in which it is expressed, which may go so far as to include phonetic mimicry like that of the four words spoken by the tide: "seesoo, hrss, rsseeiss, ooos. Vehement breath of waters amid seasnakes, rearing horses, rocks. In cups of rocks it slops: flop, slop, slap: bounded in barrels. And, spent, its speech ceases" (*Ulysses*, p. 52). But there is still, of necessity, a permanent presence, a witness of reality, one who hears this language. In the 'Proteus' chapter, everything passes through Stephen's consciousness; but Stephen is not the author of the chapter, he exists in the flux of reality as do the objects which he perceives. In fact, the author and the character are replaced in *Ulysses* by a new sort of subject, who participates in both the action and the creation; the epiphany is still there, but an enlarged, totalitarian epiphany that includes space and all moments. It ensures the harmony of this chaotic universe by wrapping it in a "verbal clothing". The epiphany-as-cosmos allows for the depersonification of art in *Ulysses*.

A work such as *Ulysses* was only possible in a prolongation of *Portrait*, and by means of greater flexibility in the technique of the epiphany, which becomes a focus of metamorphoses, the meeting-point of *stasis* and *movens* where they unite for an instant, the brilliant reconciliation of contraries; *Ulysses*, freed from the limitations imposed by the single gaze of the artist, can include the sounds of the everyday world and of the elements, individual images and images from myth, banal moments and moments from Biblical legend. Objects are given speech: the cat, the church bell, the beach strewn with shells, the mirror and its glancing reflections, can all speak. The art of *Ulysses* is not only impersonal, but also often depersonified. The depersonified passages by finding verbal expression take their places in the general established order, and at the same time ensure its mobility and freedom. The ultimate function of the epiphany is to express the mobility that exists within the order Joyce has fixed, and this function of mediation between subject and object is precisely that which Joyce in his earliest aesthetic allotted to the artist himself. The language of epiphany has become the vital centre of art; through it, what was hallucination in *Portrait* becomes a liberation of subjective and objective reality in *Ulysses*. When Stephen at the beginning of the 'Proteus' chapter says that "the soul is in a manner all that is," we can see from this wider conception of the "soul" how far he has progressed, and how much the idealistic definition of existence has been expanded. The "soul" is here understood in the sense of the Aristotelian "form".

Everything that is also caught in the "form of forms," which is the summa, *Ulysses*. The "hero" of *Ulysses* is the "form of forms," just as the "hero" of *Finnegans Wake* is not the dreamer but the dream in which he is dreaming (just, indeed, as Alice is "dreamed" by the King, according to Lewis Carroll's formal logic). When the human mind is embodied as part of the world, persons and objects may be of equivalent status; Stephen's mind, on the beach, eventually scatters his thoughts about like sand. Bloom, who is more closely sympathetic to the animal kingdom, is so near to the seagulls or to the cat that he reaches a kind of communion with them, foreshadowing the abolition of the function of difference between the world and the self which occurs in the 'Circe' episode. In 'Calypso,' Bloom is in a state of osmosis with the cat:

—Mkgnao!
—O, there you are, Mr. Bloom said, turning from the fire.
The cat mewed in answer and stalked again stiffly round a leg of the table, mewing. Just how she stalks over my writingtable. Prr. Scratch my head. Prr. (*Ulysses*, p. 54)

"My table and "my" head do not refer to the same subject; the cat-as-object enters the porous consciousness of the subject in such a way that the first person may indifferently be Bloom or the cat, in the same speech. Bloom-as-cat links up with Molly-as-cat, her mewings and sighs echoing this first scene, and "she" may mean either Molly or the cat in this monologue of Bloom, as he goes about the feeding of his pets:

She didn't like her plate full. Right. . . .
—Milk for the pussens, he said.
—Mrgknao! the cat cried. . . .
She understands all she wants to. Vindictive too. Wonder what I look like to her. Height of a tower? No, she can jump me.
. . . She might like something tasty. Thin bread and butter she likes in the morning. Still perhaps: once in a way.
He said softly in the bare hall:
—I am going round the corner. Be back in a minute.
And when he had heard his voice say it he added:
—You don't want anything for breakfast?
A sleepy soft grunt answered:
—Mn.
No. She did not want anything. (*Ulysses*, pp. 54–5)

Gradually, objects are drawn into the epiphany, which becomes full of memories, associating the present with the past, memory with hope, and Dublin with Gibraltar. There are certain focal points which direct and hold the reader's attention, as though to continue the first form of the epiphany, that of the image isolated from reality and set in a context which it illumined and which caused its soul to show forth clearly; they may be words, such as "parallax" or "metempsychosis," which (as in *Portrait*) are planted in reality and then germinate and branch out to form recurring psychological themes. Or they may be snatches of song which play the role taken in *Portrait* by such phrases as "Tower of Ivory" and "House of Gold". Examples of these latter are the song "All is lost now" and the aria *Vorrei e non vorrei* from *Don Juan*, which is quoted with a mistake in it that reveals the whole of Molly's intrigue with Boylan. Other focal points may be mistakes such as that made by Bloom's secret correspondent Martha Clifford, who writes "world" instead of "word"; the sentence "I do not like this other world" becomes allegorical, and allows a transition to take place from "word" to "world". It acts, in fine, as a disguised epiphany, a signal from Joyce to the attentive reader. More and more, objects are becoming signs, though these were still rare in *Portrait*. They are often mysterious: for instance, Bloom carries a potato around with him all day in his pocket, and when he gives it to a young prostitute in the house of Bella Cohen or Circe he explains that it is a talisman, for good luck. The contents of his pockets, indeed, would deserve an inventory to themselves—not a realistic one like that made of

Gulliver's pockets by the Lilliputians, but a symbolic, and epiphanic, list. The soap he buys for Molly eventually turns into the moon, Molly's bed creaks all day long, and the newspapers sum up the immediate present. Some insignificant details seem to secrete a kind of mystery, and an abundance of small unexplained elements makes up the substance of everyday life, in which, as in the substance of culture, Joyce carves strange, unexpected shapes.

There is an intellectual order hidden within and beyond the apparent chaos of details. Just as Saint Thomas trained Stephen's mind for its conflicts in *Portrait*, here in *Ulysses* we find Aristotle, or rather Aristotle as revived, contradicted, or, on occasions, supported by his Semitic disciples Averroes and Maimonides. The philosophical key to *Ulysses* is certainly borrowed from the Stagirite, and it opens the two worlds, that of the possibles and that of the actual, the gap between which Stephen is trying to bridge. Furthermore, and as always in this work where everything follows two paths, that of Stephen and that of Bloom, if Stephen is thinking in fashions which agree or disagree with Aristotle, Bloom is to be seen, in a way both comical and unexpected, as the living object of a demonstration of a particular Aristotelian mode of being. Aristotle is no more important to the pattern of *Ulysses* than Saint Thomas was to that of *Portrait*, but he is present in *Ulysses* as master of the stability of the world, in relation to whom the apparent instability of *Ulysses* takes on its full meaning.

If one could speak of a philosophy of Joyce that informs his poetics, one would have to define it as "anti-history," with its basis in the permanent nature of art. Aristotle's causality serves Joyce's aesthetic purposes, but, although he was able to be a Thomist without involving himself in any profession of faith, he had to oppose Aristotle insofar as the latter's theory of the actualisation of possibles produced in him a movement of metaphysical rebellion. Joyce's reply is an ambiguous one: he knows himself to be the product of the Aristotelian world-vision, but he feels much closer, by a spiritual affinity, to Aristotle's Semitic commentators Averroes and Maimonides.

These two are spiritual brothers of Stephen. Joyce was probably acquainted with them through the intermediary of another of his allies, the rebellious thinker Ernest Renan, whose works he still read with excitement when he was living in Italy.[5] The dark-eyed philosophers, contemporaries and enemies, played the same chess-games with the truth as did Stephen and Joyce; both, as readers and commentators of Aristotle, sought to establish an enlightened humanism at the crossroads between history and theology, between Faith and Reason.

Form as Immediate Message

. . . Once one has registered the fact that *Ulysses* is a book of consciousness, history ceases to exist. The reduction of chronological and objective time is expressed as an image by the compression of all time into one single day, 16 June 1904, all the hours of which are lived through as experience but at different depths and to different rhythms. The space of reality is, as we have said, that of one consciousness which is globally and cosmically inclusive, so that events in outer or inner worlds have the same spatio-temporal setting and attributes. Finally, because the characters are not identified by an omniscient Author but represented by whatever they think or say, the reader eventually becomes unable to distinguish where he is, in whose mind or at what time in that mind. In effect, everyone has two languages; the one carries along with it the specific signs of the individual's existence and thought as they are in the present, but marked by the past, in a form that is absolutely personal and recognisable, while the other is the common language of the senses, of permeability to daily life—the colourless language of indifference common to all of the inhabitants of the same city, who are all informed to much the same extent of those facts and circumstances which do not affect their personal lives.

In the outside world, which is embodied in the crowd of all Dubliners, the mass of citizens who are seen in groups in a pub or hospital waitingroom or cemetery is divided into individuals—but only their names differentiate them, because they are all alike and all like Dublin. Their language is superficial, their speeches interchangeable, and the reader has to pay very close attention in order to see how the roles are distributed among these minor characters. Similarly, in the inner world in which Bloom, Stephen, and Molly move (accompanied occasionally and briefly by other individuals who suddenly impinge on their consciousness, such as the two Siren-barmaids, glimpsed for the time of a sigh and no more), images, facts, or events may be encountered in exactly the same way by Bloom's mind and by Stephen's mind, as though the universal consciousness were really a continuous space permitting any idea to be thought, without telepathy, by anyone. This notion indicates that the author's vision of reality has nothing left in common with the traditional arrangement usual in novels. And if a thought is no longer the property of one particular ego, then the sum of all thoughts is reality, and Bloom, Molly, and Stephen are nothing more than objects of cognition floating in a *continuum*—a not inconceivable situation, and one which is basically the same as that of Alice when she learns that she is being "dreamed" by someone else; this is where the dream of *Finnegans Wake* begins.

Nevertheless, Joyce does not carry this technique of interpenetrability to its limits: only in the 'Circe' episode are the boundaries of the self shattered, as the experience of dissolution is dramatised in a kind of play whose theme is guilt. The polycentricity of this play is apparently polarised and made to focus on one of the two minds which act as the stage for their hallucinations, but in fact the space in which they occur is not separated from the surroundings in the way the normally perceived world is separated from and arranged round the observer. There is no "omphalos," as Mulligan would say, precisely because 'Circe' represents an attack upon the unity of the theological world with its single centre; Joyce is attempting to set up a vision of his own, ex-centric as far as the Creation is concerned, a world which can escape from the Absolute which rules the world God has created. Everything which usually constitutes or contributes to the traps and nets in which God holds the world and the mind captive, subjected to his Presence and Omnipotence, is endangered by Joyce's art—spatial orientation, currents in time, duration and evolution, dialogue which supposes a relationship between two people and hence a space established firmly between two fixed points, and grammar that imprisons words between the rails of reason, obedient to the laws of the divine Logos. All these suffer in Joyce's world.

Joyce also tries to replace the imagery common to Western thought, with its implications of a beginning and an end, a here and a there, a past and a present, a self and an other, by a world without history, a continuous world of osmosis. Space is then no longer defined by personal landmarks, and one's surroundings are not a line separating the known and visible from a beyond which is different and strange. The outlines of reality become blurred, the horizon clouds over, and people and things can appear to us without being subjected to our minds' usual process of examination and recognition; races, knowledge, cultures, personal histories, childhood memories, desires, all mingle, with no concern for the normal boundaries of mine and thine, *hic* and *ille*, *tunc* and *nunc*. This is not chaos, but the polycentricity that has replaced egocentricity or theocentricity. Even Bloom and Stephen only succeed in directing the disorder to a limited extent; their minds interpenetrate, and fantasies move from one to the other, without at once being noticed. Life and death communicate in the vertiginous movements of the *danse macabre*.

In *Ulysses* the devaluation of space and that of time are parallel processes; 'Circe' inverts the spatio-temporal manifestation of Stephen's reason that took place in 'Proteus'. As soon as doubt affects the *nacheinander* and the *nebeneinander*, everything may become reversible or simulated, even life and death, age and youth, male and female, here and there, yesterday and tomorrow. Logic leaps in any direction, and no-one is concerned with contradiction. The lack of continuity between the perceived reality and that which it impresses on the mind is replaced by continuity of such a kind that characters can move freely about on a continuous stage. Here, for instance, causality can do away with the temporal interval which generally separates cause from its consequence, and either manifest both simultaneously or invert the logical order and make the effect seem the cause.

It is thus possible to dismember history and time, conjugating past and future in the present tense, and even going so far as to attribute to the dead past an imaginary future which contradicts the real past, permitting, for example, the final apparition of Rudy, Bloom's son who died at the age of eleven days.

Notes

1. *Letters*, vol. I, ed. S. Gilbert (New York, 1959), pp. 146–7, 21 Sept. 1920.
2. Ibid., p. 167.
3. Bloom, Stephen, and the medical students meet at the maternity hospital at ten in the evening. Stephen as artist is in a sense the apostle of fecundity, but as prodigal son is the enemy of Ireland and of every mother-figure; he conducts a discussion about life and death and man's last end. Parodying Aristotle again, he remarks, "What of those Godpossibled souls that we nightly impossibilise, which is the sin against the Holy Ghost, Very God, Lord and Giver of Life?" (*Ulysses*, Shakespeare and Co., Paris, 1922, p. 383.)
4. *Letters*, vol. I, p. 129, 20 July 1919.
5. There was virtually no available translation of the two philosophers, except one into French, but Joyce was able to make use of Saint Thomas' commentaries on them and of other works of scholastic philosophy.

Finnegans Wake

MARGOT NORRIS
From "Technique"
The Decentered Universe of Finnegans Wake:
A *Structuralist Analysis*
1974, pp. 119–40

Deconstruction

When Samuel Beckett wrote of *Work in Progress*, "Here form *is* content, content *is* form,"[1] he seemed to beg the same question that Yeats so wisely left in rhetorical form at the end of "Among Schoolchildren." Beckett goes on to support his comment by noting, "His writing is not *about* something; *it is that something itself*. . . . When the sense is sleep, the words go to sleep. . . . When the sense is dancing, the words dance." True, of course, but the same could be said even more convincingly about *Ulysses*, particularly the *tour de force* of "Oxen of the Sun," and the musical form of "Sirens." Questions of content and form in *Finnegans Wake* must at least explain its difference from *Ulysses*, and this difference is quite simple. Whatever its mythical underpinnings, *Ulysses* is about three people, Stephen Dedalus, Leopold Bloom, and Molly Bloom, in Dublin, Ireland on 16 June 1904. On Bloomsday, every 16 June, we can take Bloomsday pilgrimages in Dublin because we know exactly where Bloom spent his entire day. In fact, we know Bloom as well as we are ever likely to know any fictional character. On the other hand, Nathan Halper notwithstanding, we don't know when Earwicker dreams, or if he dreams, or if his name is really Humphrey (it could be Harold) Chimpden Earwicker (it could be Porter or Coppinger or O'Reilly). We know that Molly is voluptuous, but Earwicker's hunchback, for all we know, could merely be that suspicious parcel he is sometimes reported to be toting around. The major difference between *Ulysses* and *Finnegans Wake* is clearly that in *Ulysses* we can be certain of most things, whereas in *Finnegans Wake* we must be uncertain. The greatest critical mistake in approaching *Finnegans Wake* has been the assumption that we can be certain of who, where, and when everything is in the *Wake*, if only we do enough research. The discovery that Maggie is ALP may be true enough, but it doesn't mean anything. ALP is also Kate, the old slopwoman, and Isabel, the daughter, and Biddie Doran, the hen, in a way that Molly Bloom is decidedly *not* Mrs. Riordan, or Milly, or Josie Breen.

In the course of several chapters, I have examined this lack of certainty in every aspect of the work. Events in *Finnegans Wake* repeat themselves as compulsively as Scheherazade did, spinning her tales, until there are so many versions of the event that one can no longer discover the "true" one. Wakean events can reverse themselves so that we do not know if father seduces daughter or daughter tempts father. The Wakean family is therefore in chaos because, through incest and parricide, family roles and family relationships are violated in such a way that figures can no longer be defined. Consequently identities are unstable and interchangeable, and the self is constantly alienated from itself and fails to know itself. This self-alienation is manifested in a language which is devious, which conceals and reveals secrets, and therefore, like poetry, uses words and images that can mean several, often contradictory, things at once.

The formal elements of the work, plot, character, point of view, and language, are not anchored to a single point of reference, that is, they do not refer back to a center. This condition produces that curious flux and restlessness in the work, which is sensed intuitively by the reader and which the *Wake* itself describes as follows.

> Every person, place and thing in the chaosmos of Alle anyway connected with the gobblydumped turkery was moving and changing every part of the time: the travelling inkhorn (possibly pot), the hare and turtle pen and paper, the continually more and less intermisunderstanding minds of the anticollaborators, the as time went on as it will variously inflected, differently pronounced, otherwise spelled, changeably meaning vocable scriptsigns. (*Wake*, New York: Viking, 1971, 118. 21)

The substitutability of parts for one another, the variability and uncertainty of the work's structural and thematic elements, represent a decentered universe, one that lacks the center that defines, gives meaning, designates, and holds the structure together—by holding it in immobility. Samuel Beckett acknowledges this when he calls the book a purgatorial work for its lack of any Absolute.[2]

The literary heterodoxy of *Finnegans Wake* is the result of Joyce's attack on the traditional concept of structure itself. This attack was not isolated, but belonged to an "event" or "rupture" in the history of the concept of structure, which, according to philosopher Jacques Derrida, took place in the history of thought sometime in the late nineteenth and early twentieth centuries. The destructive impact of this "event" becomes clear only in view of the history of metaphysics, which Derrida characterizes as belief in being as "presence." "The whole history of the concept of structure, before the rupture I spoke of, must be thought of as a series of substitutions of center for center, as a linked chain of determinations of the center."[3]

A clear illustration of this historic concept of structure can be found in T. E. Hulme's influential work, *Speculations*. Hulme evaluated Classicism and Romanticism, whose dialectics he regarded as forming the basis of the history of art, in terms of a single fundamental premise: that belief in a Deity constitutes the fixed part of man's nature.[4] Hulme denounced Romanticism as the displacement of that fixed belief in Deity from the religious sphere, to which it properly belongs, to the human sphere, that is, the belief in man as a god. Fundamental to Hulme's tenets is, therefore, the notion of a center according to which man defines himself; the issue is merely who or what shall occupy that center.

The "rupture" in the history of structure—brought about, as Derrida says, by our being self-consciously forced to "think the structurality of structure"—results in the idea of a structure in which presence is not so much absent as unlocatable. The center is ex-centric, and the structure is determined not by presence but by play. This "rupture" is manifested most purely in certain destructive discourses of the early twentieth century.

> Where and how does this decentering, this notion of the structurality of structure, occur? . . . I would probably cite the Nietzschean critique of metaphysics, the critique of the concepts of being and truth, for which were substituted the concepts of play, interpretation, and sign (sign without truth present); the Freudian critique of self-presence, that is, the critique of consciousness, of the subject, of self-identity and of self-proximity or self-possession; and, more radically, the Heideggerean destruction of metaphysics, of onto-theology, of the determination of being as presence.[5]

Among these destructive discourses of the early twentieth century, *Finnegans Wake* served as a literary exemplar, and in doing so inaugurated a new concept of literary structure, which itself could not be deciphered so long as critical formalism was ruled by concepts like Hulme's.

As an artist deeply concerned with the philosophical implications of the creative process, Joyce must have faced the special difficulties of trying to create something truly "new" in his last work. He was clearly aware of a problem whose linguistic and anthropological implications are of great interest at the present time: that the *Weltanschauung* of a writer is limited by the language he employs. The image of Shem writing with his own shit on his own body about himself indicates not only the scatological and solipsistic nature of the creative act, but also the entrapment in what is apparently a closed system. The writer who tries to escape the epistemology of his culture is confronted by a language embedded with inherited concepts; to criticize these concepts he must still make use of a language in which they are embedded. Jacques Derrida writes, "It is a question of putting expressly and systematically the problem of the status of a discourse which borrows from a heritage the resources necessary for the deconstruction of that heritage itself."[6] In other words, a "new" literary vision that seeks to critique previous literary modes must use the tools of those same modes—language, concepts, themes, conventions—in the process of the critique itself. William Carlos Williams describes this frustration in *Spring and All*, where the artist imaginatively annihilates the universe to create it anew, only to discover that "EVOLUTION HAS REPEATED ITSELF FROM THE BEGINNING. . . . In fact now, for the first time, everything IS new. . . . The terms 'veracity', 'actuality', 'real', 'natural', 'sincere' are being discussed at length, every word in the discussion being evolved from an identical discussion which took place the day before yesterday."[7] To outflank this contradiction, Joyce needed to decenter the literary structure, a process that would affect every aspect of the work so radically as to make it unique in literary history. The traditional concept of structure, which implied a center or presence, also implied a formal wholeness of the work of art, in which each of the particular elements referred always back to the center. Decentering of the structure, then, suggests another, as yet uncategorizable sense of form—which modern poets often call "open" in contrast to "closed," but which is more conveniently defined here as "freeplay." Jacques Derrida describes this freeplay of a decentered system of language as follows. "This field is in fact that of *freeplay*, that is to say, a field of infinite substitutions in the closure of a finite ensemble. This field permits these infinite substitutions only because it is finite, that is to say, because instead of being an inexhaustible field, as in the classical hypothesis, instead of being too large, there is something missing from it: a center which arrests and founds the freeplay of substitutions."[8] The freeplay of elements in *Finnegans Wake* has long been recognized without pursuit of its implications for the total structure of the work. William York Tindall writes, "As God's world, created by the Word, is an endless arrangement and rearrangement of ninety-six elements—give or take a couple—so Joyce's closed system is an endless arrangement and rearrangement of a thousand and one elements that, whatever their multiplicity, are limited in number."[9]

It is freeplay that makes characters, times, places, and actions interchangeable in *Finnegans Wake*, that breaks down the all-important distinction between the self and the other, and that makes uncertainty a governing principle of the work. In order to effect this "new" decentered literary structure and to implement freeplay not only in the themes of the work but in the language as well, Joyce instituted two major techniques: a new application of "imitative form," and a building technique I will call *bricolage*, borrowing a term from anthropologist Lévi-Strauss.

Imitative Form

Finnegans Wake includes those imitative techniques so successfully employed in *Ulysses*: the imitation of printed formats as in "Aeolus" and the "Triv and Quad" chapter (II.2), the imitation of sounds in "Sirens" and "Anna Livia Plurabelle" (I.8), and the imitation of pedagogical modes as in the catechism of "Eumaeus" and the quiz show of I.6. But the *Wake* language far surpasses the experiments of *Ulysses* as a type of verbal simulation. The stylistic incorporation of the novel's themes depends on the most fundamental correspondence between social and linguistic structures. The law of man and the law of language are homologous systems because they share an identical unconscious structure. The father's symbolic function as figure of the law is therefore analogous to the semantic function of language, which assigns to lexical items their meanings and their grammatical functions. The primordial law of the father, the incest taboo and the kinship regulations, function like those laws of phonological combination which permit certain sounds to be combined only in certain ways in the formation of words, and those laws of syntax that regulate the relationships of words in the formation of the sentence.[10] That the theme of the fallen father, the fallen God, has linguistic repercussions is suggested in the *Wake* itself ("Gwds with gurs are gttrdmmrng. Hlls vlls. The timid hearts of words all exeomnosunt" [258.1]). The vowels are here the "timid hearts of words" which flee with the defeated gods: the words can no longer be spoken, like many of the words in the *Wake*, and their meaning becomes dislocated, uncertain. The familial/linguistic correspondence is also revealed in the passage that describes the shooting of the Russian General, a type of parricide (*"The abnihilisation of the etym by the grisning of the grosning of the grinder of the grunder of the first lord of Hurtreford expolodotonates through Parsuralia with an ivanmorinthorrorumble fragoromboassity amidwhiches general uttermosts confusion are preceivable moletons skaping with mulicules"* [353.22]). The "etym," or word, is also "etymon," which, as the primary word from which a derivative is formed, corresponds to father. Although the construction of the phrase, "abnihilisation of the etym," is essentially ambiguous—it is not clear whether "etym" is the subject or object of the action implied in abnihilisation, or a creation out of nothing—the implication is that in either case, the fall of the father creates first of all noise, an "ivanmorinthorrorumble fragoromboassity." The equation of word and void occurs also in a parody of St. John's gospel prologue in II.2 ("In the buginning is the woid, in the muddle is the sounddance and thereinofter you're in the unbewised again" [378.29]). If the father signifies the semantic function of language, the act of giving names to things or assigning meanings to words, then the fall of the father in *Finnegans Wake* signifies that severing of words from their referents which creates a linguistic freeplay, a "sounddance," or "variously inflected, differently pronounced, otherwise spelled, changeably meaning vocable scriptsigns" (118.26), and therefore one is clearly in the "unbewised," the unproven (German: *Beweis*), the uncertain, again. Hugh Kenner, after quoting a sentence from the *Wake*, remarks, "It is worse than useless to push this toward one or the other of the meanings between which it hangs; to paraphrase it, for instance, in terms of porter being uncorked and poured. It is equally misleading to scan early drafts for the author's intentions, on the assumption that a 'meaning' got buried by elaboration. Joyce worked seventeen years to push the work away from 'meaning,' adrift into language; nothing is to be gained by trying to push it back."[11]

If the ultimate meaningful word is the theological Logos, the Word of John's prologue, then its antithesis might be Stephen's recurrent notion in *Ulysses* ("God: noise in the street" [*U*, p. 186]). The fall of the father, which marks the disjunction of word from meaning, results in noise, as the *Wake* passage cited earlier seems to suggest. The *Wake* repeats Stephen's concept of God as a noise in the street and amplifies it to thematic proportions. At the end of II.1, there appears a litany which includes the invocation, "Loud, hear us!/Loud, graciously hear us!" (258.25). The substitution of "Loud" for "Lord" is, of course, consistent with the Wakean proposition that the voice of God, the voice of the father, is the sound of thunder, and that the thunder announces the father's fall (cf. 3.15). Other associations of the father's fall with noise include reference to the tower of Babel: the fallen giant MacCool, marking with his body the geography of Dublin, is described as an "overgrown babeling" (6.31), a fallen tower of Babel or babbling baby. Both babble, the first speech of the infant man, and thunder, the first word of God to postlapsarian man, represent sound without meaning or signification.

The events of *Finnegans Wake* are steeped in noise: the crash of falling towers, bridges, men, Wall Street, and civilizations; the clamor of countless battles; the boisterous happenings in Earwicker's pub; the angry invectives of quarreling antagonists. As someone says in the midst of the drunken shouting and raucous merrymaking at Finn MacCool's wake, "E'erawhere in this whorl would ye hear sich a din again?" (6.24). Furthermore, the gossip, rumor, and slander discussed in the previous section illustrate an archaic definition of the word "noise" as "common talk, rumor, evil report, or scandal"—a definition that still survives in the dual meaning of the word "report." In its perfect fusion of noise and rumor, *Finnegans Wake* resembles nothing so much as Chaucer's *The House of Fame*.

The noise that characterizes the thematic events of *Finnegans Wake* is expressed stylistically by a number of technical devices. There are many "voices" in the *Wake*—numerous utterances by the various figures, frequently unidentified, and often seeming to occur all at once, like many people shouting and clamoring simultaneously ("Mulo Mulelo! Homo Humilo! Dauncy a deady O! Dood dood dood! O Bawse! O Boese! O Muerther! O Mord! . . . Malawinga! Malawunga! Ser Oh Ser! See ah See! Hamovs! Hemoves! Mamor!" [499.5]) In addition, any given utterance can be considered to contain a number of voices, as Clive Hart notes, "In theory, highly controlled choral speaking by a small group would be the only satisfactory solution to the problem of how to read *Finnegans Wake* aloud, each speaker adhering to one 'voice' of the counterpoint and using the appropriate accent and stress."[12] Stylistically, however, the *Wake* not only simulates the sound of "noise," as in the onomatopoeic thunder, but the concept of noise as an obstruction to the understanding of a message, as well. As a principle of information theory, noise is any interference in the transmission of information. "Whatever medium is used for the purpose of transmitting information, it will be subject to various unpredictable physical disturbances, which will obliterate or distort part of the message and thus lead to the loss of information. If the system were free of redundancy, the information lost would be irrecoverable."[13] If we grant that little information is transmitted to the reader of *Finnegans Wake* even when we disregard the interference

generated by the labyrinthian progress of the narrative or the interference inherent in the linguistic distortions, another rationale for the work's length and extraordinary redundancy becomes apparent. Joyce clearly followed a sound principle of information theory in *Finnegans Wake*: a work with an unprecedented amount of "interference" requires an unprecedented amount of seemingly gratuitous repetition in compensation.

The familial/linguistic homology can be most simply illustrated with reference to simple grammatical slot and filler technique. The family consists of certain slots or positions which are occupied by certain individuals—for example, slot F (father) is occupied by HCE, Slot M (mother), by ALP, slot D (daughter), by Isabel. The incest taboo decrees that slot M can be filled by any woman except Isabel, the daughter, HCE's mother or sister, and so on. The laws that govern the combinations of sounds in words, or words in sentences, work in a similar manner. In the potential English word "—lan" for example, the initial slot cannot be filled by the sounds of "m," "n," "d," "t," "r," or "v." In the sentence "The —— told us," the slot may *not* be filled by another article like "a" or "an," a preposition like "into" or "from," a pronoun like "she," or even a proper noun like "George." In other words, the social structure of the family and the linguistic structure of the sentence is intelligible only if certain laws of combination are observed. The theme of incest in *Finnegans Wake* is stylistically simulated in a language that violates linguistic laws of combination, that is, phonotactic or syntactic laws.

While the rules of permissible phonological combinations must account for all the actual words in the English lexicon, they also encompass words that are not, in fact, actualized in the language, but could be without violating these rules. John Lyons notes some interesting applications of these "potential" words.

> Many of the non-occurrent combinations of phonemes would be accepted by native speakers as more 'normal' than others; they are, not only easily pronounceable, but in some way similar in form to other words of the language. . . . It is noticeable, for instance, and it has often been pointed out, that writers of nonsense verse (like Lewis Carroll or Edward Lear) will create 'words' which almost invariably conform to the phonological structure of actual words in the language; and the same is true of brand-names invented for manufactured products.[14]

The bulk of Joyce's "nonsense" words in the *Wake* are such potential English words: "flosting" (501.33) and "marracks" (15.36), for example. In many words, however, the combination of sounds is quite impossible in English: "tuvavnr" (54.15), "dgiaour" (68.18), "stlongfella" (82.13), "trwth" (132.5), "tsifengtse" (299.26), "remoltked" (333.13), or "grianblachk" (503.23).

The task confronting Joyce in letting the language reflect a universe whose structure is determined by substitutions and freeplay, is to deconstruct the language itself. Of course, this involves the paradox of critical language, the need to use language to represent the deconstruction of language. One of the strategies Joyce uses to communicate a deconstructed language involves his interesting manipulation of structure words. Structure words—articles, prepositions, auxiliaries, intensifiers, and the like—have essentially no semantic content but act like the mortar that holds the lexical bricks of the sentence in place. Sometimes Joyce substitutes descriptive words for these structural items as in "How wooden I not know it" (16.33) and "you skull see" (17.18), where "wooden" and "skull" replace "wouldn't" and "shall" in the auxiliary slots in the sentence. The *Wake* sentences are now ungrammatical, but they still communicate because the reader unconsciously recognizes the slot and knows the correct filler. Such substitutions also occur frequently in cases not involving structure words. For example, the items "who eight the last of the goosebellies" (142.2) and "were we bread by the same fire" (168.8), show questionable substitutions in slots that are usually occupied by verbs.

Besides filling linguistic slots with impermissible fillers, Joyce further disrupts linguistic structure by ignoring internal junctures. Internal junctures, the meaningful pauses between words, are treated as suprasegmental phonemes in modern linguistics because they function to distinguish the meanings of otherwise identical units, as for example the joke in W. C. Fields's *The Dentist*, where there is confusing talk of either "an ice man" or "a nice man." In the *Wake* we find such expressions as "an earsighted view" (143.9) and "the course of his tory" (143.12)—irregular expressions produced by incorrect junctures. Joyce also used junctures to perform such interesting substitutions as "to be cause" (16.18), "dumptied the wholeborrow of rubbages on to soil here" (17.4), and "they are in surgence" (17.25). He clearly realized that many prefixes sound like prepositions. So the "be" of "because" becomes a verb on the order of "to be sure"; the "to" of "onto" becomes an infinitive that changes "soil" from a noun to a verb; and the prefix "in" of "insurgence" becomes a preposition that changes the meaning of "are" from "may be identified with" to "are located."

Violations of junctures also produce other interesting linguistic aberrations. The expression, "how he stud theirs" (234.10), probably derives from an artificial juncture in the resonant "how he stutters." "As bold and as madhouse a bull in a meadows" (353.13) ignores the junction between "mad as" to create "madhouse." An interesting case of overlap occurs in the expression, "pleasekindly communicake with the original sinse we are only yearning" (239.1), where the juncture can come either before or after "sinse" depending on whether it is read as "sins" or as "since." These examples demonstrate how syntactic disruption produces the uncertainty and ambiguity that must characterize a decentered language.

Joyce introduces ungrammaticality into *Finnegans Wake* deliberately. The expression, "after having said your poetry," is quite all right, while "after having sat your poetries" (435.26) is ungrammatical because "sat" is an obligatory intransitive and cannot take a direct object. To return to the correspondence between social and linguistic structures in *Finnegans Wake*, we can charge much of the thematic confusion and ambiguity to a kind of ungrammaticality. For example, a very common basic sentence pattern, illustrated as "——— kills ———" shows the importance of syntactic structure. When Alice reads the nonsense poem "Jabberwocky" in *Alice in Wonderland*, she knows, without understanding all the words, "*somebody* killed *something*: that's clear, at any rate."[15] Yet it is precisely these crucial relations between subjects and objects that are often deliberately ambiguous in *Finnegans Wake*. As with Oedipus and Laius, father-son enmity is complex and Laius tries to kill Oedipus as surely as Oedipus does kill him. So in *Finnegans Wake*, there is enough confusion to have to ask "who struck Buckley though nowadays as thentimes every schoolfilly . . . knows as yayas is yayas how it was Buckleyself . . . struck and the Russian generals, da! da!, instead of Buckley who was caddishly struck by him when be herselves" (101.15). The many reversible actions in *Finnegans Wake* serve precisely to make distinctions between subjects and objects difficult. The questions that surround the sin in Phoenix Park are reduced

continually to this kind of ambiguity: Did HCE seduce the girls or did the girls tempt HCE? Did HCE watch the girls urinate or did the girls watch HCE deliberately expose himself? Did ALP start the wars and deluge that mark the collapse of civilization, or did she merely clean up the rubbish afterwards? Did Shem forge the Letter or did Shaun steal the Letter from Shem? The subject/object confusions are types of thematic ambiguity that approximate the syntactic ambiguity of the language.

Joyce's inclusion of multitudinous fragments of foreign languages in the *Wake* is also consistent with the principle of freeplay. Unlike artificial or "auxiliary" languages whose purpose is to overcome the Babelian diversity of national languages, Joyce's "mutthering pot" (20.7) in the *Wake* appears to be a dump or rubbish heap like ALP's scavenger sack, in which the fragments merely mix and mingle to be distributed anew. Citing examples, Ronald Buckalew notes, "Joyce's foreign language is often distorted and mixed to produce puns and jokes."[16] The mixing of various languages in the same work may represent a type of linguistic miscegenation that imitates the thematic incest. The parallel is not inappropriate, particularly since we speak of the historical development of languages in terms of the relationships of language "families."

Joyce once wrote of *Finnegans Wake*, "What the language will look like when I have finished I don't know. But having declared war I shall go on *jusqu'au bout*."[17] If Joyce violates the laws of language, he does no more than to adapt the language to a vision in which law has been supplanted by play—a linguistic freeplay that is the fertile ground for new semantic and syntactic forms, for a thoroughgoing linguistic originality.

Bricolage

Richard Ellmann aptly describes *Finnegans Wake* as "a wholly new book based upon the premise that there is nothing new under the sun."[18] This paradox is clearly the crux of the philosophical problem that Joyce set out to solve in *Finnegans Wake*. Hart and Atherton attribute Joyce's artistic dependence on the inherited matter of the cultural and personal past to a sense of religious prohibition, a guilt which Joyce associated with the creative process. However, judging from the profanity which, no doubt, qualifies *Finnegans Wake* as one of the most aggressively sacrilegious books in the language, the notion of Joyce's fearing "the presumption of human attempts at creation"[19] is untenable.

More plausibly, Joyce realized that he could not escape his debt to the culture, the language, and the literature. The well-known works on comparative mythology, which so influenced Eliot and Yeats, impressed Joyce also with the persistence of mythic structures, as we know from *Ulysses*. The artist has no choice but to plunder his heritage, and Joyce, at least, acknowledges the debt grandly, calling *Finnegans Wake* an "epical forged cheque" (181.16) and "the last word in stolentelling" (424.35).

To confront this dilemma, Joyce resorts to a technical method which critics have already identified in their comparisons of *Finnegans Wake* to the "objet trouvé" collage. "Bits and pieces are picked up and incorporated into the texture with little modification, while the precise nature of each individual fragment is not always of great importance."[20] Borrowing a term which Lévi-Strauss applies to mythical thought and mythological activity in *The Savage Mind*, this practice of using bits and pieces of heterogeneous materials without regard to their specific function, may be called *bricolage*. Joyce once asked his Aunt Josephine, send "any news you like, programmes, pawntickets, press cuttings, handbills. I like reading them."[21] Joyce is like Lévi-Strauss's *bricoleur*, collecting and saving things "on the principle that 'they may always come in handy,'"[22] That Joyce's method certainly approximated that of the *bricoleur* is most evident in his voluminous working notebooks for the *Wake*, crammed as these are with list upon list of apparently unrelated words, phrases, snatches of thought, and bits of data.[23]

More important than Joyce's writing practice, however, is the way in which this method, *bricolage*, allows Joyce to liberate materials from their old contexts, to juxtapose them freely, and allow them to enter into new and unexpected combinations with each other. Lévi-Strauss writes of the *bricoleur*, "Now, the characteristic feature of mythical thought, as of 'bricolage' on the practical plane, is that it builds up structured sets, not directly with other structured sets but by using the remains and debris of events: in French 'des bribes et des morceaux,' or odds and ends in English, fossilized evidence of the history of an individual or a society."[24]

Some of Joyce's puns and verbal jokes demonstrate this technique of salvaging bits and pieces for new purposes and uses. In *Ulysses*, the pornographic *Ruby, the Pride of the Ring* becomes a ruby ring which Bloom slips romantically on Josie Breen's finger during the Nighttown hallucinations (*U*, p. 445). Our understanding of Joyce's use of the battle of Waterloo in the *Wake* will be little improved by checking up on facts in a history book. In *bricoleur* fashion, Joyce uses the event as it comes to hand, and what seems to interest him chiefly is the word-play potential which makes the battleground the site of urinating girls. The Crash of Wall Street resulted in the Great Depression, and if it is a giant or an egg that falls from the wall, then the economic disaster of the thirties becomes merely an enormous imprint of the fallen giant's body on the topography of Dublin.

Finnegans Wake is unmistakably original—and just as self-consciously unoriginal. In its bizarre, distorted language are lodged all of Joyce's immense, but thoroughly familiar, preoccupations: the Dublin of his youth, familial relationships, sexual obsessions, bits of military and political history, allusions to a multitude of literary works, sacred books, arcane writings, old myths, fables, fairy tales, children's games, songs, riddles, and great quantities of talk. . . .

When Joyce wanted to write an epic about common, modern man, he took Homer's *Odyssey* and systematically inverted its values and deflated its dimensions. Yet the result was not an anti-epic, nor is Bloom an anti-hero. Joyce had used a structured set to build up another structured set, in the language of Lévi-Strauss. The result was a work with an almost identical structure but a different ambience; *Ulysses* is simply a modern epic.

When Joyce first began *Finnegans Wake*, he sorted out the unused notes from *Ulysses* and exhumed old anecdotes and tales.[25] The materials for the new book were already in existence—unlike *Portrait*, his later works were not autobiographical and we have no fiction about his mature life on the continent. But he used these worn things freely as we can see from his transformation of the sources. As in the dream, where trivial details are invested with important values, Joyce sometimes took the least important details of stories—for example, the quarreling adult brothers, Joe and Alphy, form "Clay," and the fighting child twins, Jacky and Tommy from "Nausicaa," —removed them from their old contexts, and made them into major configurations in *Finnegans Wake*. Joyce eschewed an established model, a structured set, in favor of using bits and pieces, "a jetsam litterage of convolvuli of times lost or strayed, of lands derelict and of tongues laggin too" (292.15). He wrote to Harriet Shaw Weaver, "The construction is quite different

from *Ulysses* where at least the ports of call were known beforehand."[26]

The *bricoleur* does not begin, like the engineer, with a fully conceived project, a detailed model whose actualization depends on the procurement of tools and materials precisely designed for the purposes of the project. The *bricoleur* uses whatever is at hand for his tools and materials, and the result of his labors will never conform exactly to his original aim, which is sketchy at best.[27] As a result, the project of the *bricoleur* proceeds like an organic growth; Joyce often spoke of *Finnegans Wake* as though it had an independent life of its own, as though it achieved its form without his direction or intervention.[28] Perhaps the difference between Joyce's method in *Portrait* and in *Finnegans Wake* can be described by the different meanings that the important word "forge" holds for each work: in *Portrait*, Joyce fashions and tempers his elements into an impeccably designed artifact; in the *Wake*, he uses essentially devious means, compared with those of the artisan, to create an impressively original design, which on closer inspection consists of unaltered and familiar pieces of junk, borrowed or stolen from the smithies of countless others ("The prouts who will invent a writing there ultimately is the poeta, still more learned, who discovered the raiding there originally. That's the point of eschatology our book of kills reaches for now in soandso many counterpoint words. What can't be coded can be decorded if an ear aye seize what no eye ere grieved for" (482.31).

Like the *Book of Kells*, which weaves an imaginative graphic text from the pretext of the Gospels, *Finnegans Wake* is woven from a multitude of earlier literatures. Implied in this process is a plunder ("the raiding there originally"), the hoax of Father Prout. The countless modern versions of ancient myths and themes is proof not of the barrenness of the modern imagination, but of the limited vision of human life permitted the artist. A breaking up of the old structures and recombination of the bits and pieces is the only mode of escape. Eliot suggests as much in *The Wasteland* when he writes, "These fragments I have shored against my ruins." William Carlos Williams speaks of it also in relation to Joyce's style in *Work in Progress*. "If to achieve truth we work with words purely, as a writer must, and all the words are dead or beautiful, how then shall we succeed any better than might a philosopher with dead abstractions or their configurations? . . . There must be something new done with the words. Leave beauty out, or, conceivably, one might begin again, one might break them up to let the staleness out of them as Joyce, I think, has done."[29]

The technique of *bricolage* is most striking at the level of words themselves, where it consists of breaking up words and phrases and reassembling them as they come to hand, without regard to their original functions. A phrase like "goat along nose" (413.28) takes the expressions "God alone knows" and "got a long nose" and invests them simultaneously in the words "goat" and "along" which have nothing to do with either of them, but which refer to earlier pasture jargon, "kidding" and "together." Grammatically the phrase is meaningful only if we picture a goat at the side of a nose—a novel image indeed, God knows, the result of *bricolage*.

As a result of *bricolage*, the reader of *Finnegans Wake* is required to learn to read all over again, both at the word level and at the greater level of myths and themes. In fact, the process of learning to read may be that primitive act suggested in the coding/decoding passage (482.31) as the raiding (reading) there originally, "reading" in the full sense of the German word *lese*, which is both a reading and a gathering. The reader, like the artist and the *bricoleur*, works by putting one thing with another as it comes to hand, like the child who first learns to read ("We are once amore as babes awondering in a wold made fresh where with the hen in the storyaboot we start from scratch" [336.16]).

In constructing a work from its fragments, broken up and considered with an innocent and unbiased eye, Joyce must have learned again what poets may have forgotten, but what contemporary linguists are now teaching: the significance of linguistic structure. The form of the language is learned unconsciously—even young children who have never heard of an "article" know that "the ball" is correct while "ball the" is not. Throughout *Finnegans Wake*, at all levels of construction, Joyce makes structure meaningful, makes it communicate quite independently of content. Therefore, it is fitting that Joyce ends *Finnegans Wake* with a structure word, pure and simple. Although it is commonly supposed to be so, I recall no conclusive evidence that the last word of the book connects with the first to form a complete circle. But even if it does, the last "the" stands alone at the end of the work, completely devoid of semantic meaning, and followed only by the remaining blank paper of the page. For "the," although it means nothing in itself, means something in relation to other words. Its sole purpose is to anticipate the next word, to guarantee that something will follow, something definite and particular. The "the" at the end of *Finnegans Wake* anticipates nothing—a definite nothing, the void, the silence, the death of ALP.

The problems of deconstruction in *Finnegans Wake* are not without implications for critics and criticism of the work. A commentator on *Finnegans Wake* ignores at her or his peril the fact that the book is itself about the quest for truth, the "true" facts, the correct interpretation, the "authentic" version, and that it purposefully levels all such pretensions. The results of critical efforts are not important in the *Wake*, but rather the compulsions and motives of the questors, their styles and methods, their quarrels, their self-justifications, and their own implication in the object of their study. Hermeneutics is an important issue in *Finnegans Wake*. It is possible, therefore, that just as Joyce provided for diverse interpretations of the hen's Letter or ALP's "mamafesto" I.7 of the *Wake* itself, so he provided for diverse interpretations of *Finnegans Wake*. *Our Exagmination Round His Factification for Incamination of Work in Progress* is a veritable extension of *Work in Progress*. While Joyce merely supervised the work of the "twelve Marshals"[30] and allowed them to write serious critical essays, he collected these into a volume that belongs nicely to the *Wake*. Besides the Wakean title, which Joyce invented and to which there is reference in the work itself (284.20), the number of essays corresponds to the number of customers and judges in the *Wake*, to the twelve apostles, twelve jurors, and so on. *Our Exagmination* was designated with a symbol (○), a designation not unlike those belonging to the *Wake* (□) and the members of the Earwicker "doodles" family: HCE (m), ALP (Δ), Mamalu-jo (×) (see 299. F4). Another projected book of four essays, to correspond to the four annalists, historians, teachers, and evangelists in the work was designated as ×, but was never produced. Joyce included two letters of protest in *Our Exagmination*, one of them the priceless contribution of Vladimir Dixon, which, of course, was Joyce's own. Nothing could be more Wakean than this self-reflexive act of writing a letter to oneself about oneself.

By writing *Finnegans Wake* as he did, Joyce confirmed the impossibility of metalanguage, that is, the impossibility of making a critique in language of the epistemology embedded in language. This problem applies also to commentary *on* the *Wake*. It is difficult to write or talk about *Finnegans Wake* in conventional language. Wakean titles of critical studies, *Eternal Geomater* and *Joyce-Again's Wake*, for example, and often the text itself—"The hen's 'culdee sacco of wabbash' (210.1) does not sound too hopeful, nor does the prospect of 'potluck' for her children 'for evil and ever'" (210.5–6), writes Tindall[31]—confirm the dependence of the critic on *Wake* language. Perhaps *Wake* critics and their interpretations form merely one dimension in the infinite regress that characterizes the hermeneutic theme of *Finnegans Wake*. Perhaps like the *Wake* citizenry itself, we investigate the sin in Phoenix Park, wondering what happened, trying to identify the principals, quarreling among ourselves, coming up with conflicting and contradictory versions, engaged in a love/hate relationship with the father, Joyce, and all the while examining insomniacally the seemingly unintelligible Letter under lamplight, muttering softly, "Bethicket me for a stump of a beech if I have the poultriest notions what the farest he all means" (112.5).

Notes

1. Samuel Beckett et al., *Our Exagmination Round His Factification for Incamination of Work in Progress* (New York: New Directions Books, 1962), p. 14.
2. Ibid., p. 22.
3. Jacques Derrida, "Structure, Sign, and Play in the Discourse of the Human Sciences," in Richard Macksey and Eugenio Donato, eds., *The Languages of Criticism and the Sciences of Man: The Structuralist Controversy* (Baltimore: The Johns Hopkins University Press, 1970), p. 249.
4. T. E. Hulme, *Speculations*, ed. Herbert Read (New York: Harcourt, Brace and Company, 1924), p. 117.
5. Derrida, p. 249–50.
6. Ibid., p. 252.
7. William Carlos Williams, *Imaginations*, ed. Webster Schott (New York: New Directions Books, 1970), p. 93.
8. Derrida, p. 260.
9. William York Tindall, *A Reader's Guide to* Finnegans Wake (New York: Farrar, Straus and Giroux, 1969), p. 15.
10. Lacan, "The Function of Language in Psychoanlaysis," in Anthony Wilden, *The Language of the Self* (Baltimore: The Johns Hopkins University Press, 1968), p. 40.
11. Hugh Kenner, *Dublin's Joyce* (Boston: Beacon Press, 1956), p. 304.
12. Clive Hart, *Structure and Motif in* Finnegans Wake (London: Faber and Faber, 1962), p. 36.
13. John Lyons, *Introduction to Theoretical Linguistics* (New York: Cambridge University Press, 1968), p. 88.
14. Ibid., p. 120.
15. Lewis Carroll, "Alice in Wonderland," in *The Annotated Alice*, ed. Martin Gardner (Cleveland: The World Publishing Company, 1963), p. 197.
16. Ronald Buckalew, "Night Lessons on Language," in Michael H. Begnal and Fritz Senn, eds., *A Conceptual Guide to* Finnegans Wake (University Park: Pennsylvania State University Press, 1974), p. 105.
17. James Joyce, *Letters of James Joyce*, ed. Stuart Gilbert (New York: Viking Press, 1966), 1: 237. From a letter to Harriet Shaw Weaver dated 11 November 1925.
18. Richard Ellmann, *James Joyce* (New York: Oxford University Press, 1965), p. 558.
19. Hart, p. 44.
20. Ibid., p. 35.
21. Joyce, *Letters*, 1: 194. From a letter to Mrs. William Murray dated 10 November 1922.
22. Claude Lévi-Strauss, *The Savage Mind* (Chicago: University of Chicago Press, 1969), p. 18.
23. David Hayman describes how Joyce wrote the draft for the introduction of II.2, working directly from the notes in his workbook. "Of the 266 words in the completed first draft approximately 132 can be traced directly to the notes." See "'Scribbledehobbles' and How they Grew: A Turning Point in the Development of a Chapter," in Jack P. Dalton and Clive Hart,

eds., *Twelve and a Tilly* (Evanston, Ill.: Northwestern University Press, 1965), p. 110.
24. Lévi-Strauss, *The Savage Mind*, p. 21.
25. Ellmann, p. 558.
26. Joyce, *Letters*, 1: 204. Letter to Harriet Shaw Weaver dated 9 October 1923.
27. Lévi-Strauss, *The Savage Mind*, p. 21.
28. Joyce, *Letters*, 1: 204.
29. William Carlos Williams, from "William Carlos Williams on Joyce's Style," in Robert Deming, ed., *James Joyce: The Critical Heritage*, 2 vols. (New York: Barnes & Noble, 1970), 1: 377.
30. Ellmann, p. 626.
31. Tindall, p. 145.

DAVID A. WHITE
From "The Reality of Flux"
The Grand Continuum:
Reflections on Joyce and Metaphysics
1983, pp. 29–40, 51–53

One of the most frequently quoted phrases in *Finnegans Wake* is "the book of Doublends Jined," a locution which contains, among other things, perhaps the first explicit mention of the *Wake*'s circular structure. Here Joyce intimates that once the reader joins the double ends of the sentence which "begins" on the last page and "ends" on the first, the *Wake* will start repeating itself, thus becoming a work without beginning and without end. However, the sentence in which this phrase appears is equally important. It reads:

> So you need hardly spell me how every word will be bound over to carry three score and ten toptypsical readings throughout the book of Doublends Jined (may his forehead be darkened with mud who would sunder!) till Daleth, mahomahouma, who oped it closeth thereof the. Dor. (20.13–18)

Here we are notified that "every word" in the *Wake* will have multiple readings, in fact, the same number of readings as the biblical life span of the ideal reader who devotes his life to the *Wake*—threescore and ten. What verges on an Old Testament curse enjoins us to accept the fact that every word (not just the puns) will stand for an indefinitely large number of meanings. Assuming that the threatened mud of this curse will move us to seek a lifetime's worth of meaning in the *Wake*, only death itself closes the door on the subsequent search. *Finnegans Wake* will then become our wake as well.

All conventional semantic limits of language have thus been virtually eliminated in the *Wake*. Each linguistic element will concurrently convey many meanings and point to many possible referents. From the standpoint of literary style, this internal complexity establishes a seemingly endless horizon of literary significance. And from the standpoint of metaphysics, this concurrence of untold meanings and referents all within one word testifies to the fact that a condition of flux has been established between the surface significance of the word or phrase and the meanings and referents incorporated within each such linguistic component. Once this condition of flux has been set into play, any attempt to stabilize the flux at a point somewhere short of its proper dimensions (if, indeed, the notion of "dimension" can be applied in this context) risks distorting the full meaning of each word in the *Wake*'s fluid prose.

This prescriptive warning about the limitless semantic and denotative range of the *Wake*'s language should be taken seriously. It will compel us to strain our literary sensibilities and intelligence to the utmost in order to discern nuances and connections which may not be visible when the text is read as literature is usually read. Why should we undertake an exercise apparently fated to fall short of anything like completion if our knowledge remains less extensive than that of the *Wake*'s author? This question is answered in the course of the *Wake* and the answer concerns the very nature of reality itself. For the prescriptive declamation announcing the *Wake*'s semantic fluidity receives a full-fledged, if intermittently expressed, metaphysically descriptive underpinning. The language of the *Wake* assumes its unique form because that language has been integrated within a metaphysical structure in which the forms of reality as we commonly experience them no longer apply. Language becomes out of joint with our present sense of reality precisely to mirror the out-of-joint condition of reality itself. It is an especially profound index of the *Wake*'s genius that its concern for evoking totality includes a statement of the abstract conditions which must be met before that totality can assume the stylistic form that it displays.

How shall we begin to substantiate this assertion? One pair of metaphysical concepts crucial to this type of analysis is motion and rest. However, to stipulate a definite point of departure when the inquiry intends to deal with metaphysical fundamentals is to risk the charge of arbitrariness. After all, one could argue that some other concept or pair of concepts is as crucial as motion and rest, if not more so. As we shall see, textual reasons can provide good grounds for this selection, but in any case motion and rest will be complemented by three other notions of commensurate generality—identity and difference, space and time, cause and effect. A comprehensive exploration of the *Wake* using these four pairs of concepts will indicate how the distinctive totality to the *Wake*'s linguistic world has been made accessible through metaphysical determination.

Each of the four pairs of concepts establishes its own special place as a metaphysical guidepost and also blends with the others so that their collective presence can be felt throughout the *Wake*. To appreciate the absolute pervasiveness of these principles, we must set our metaphysical ear at the highest possible pitch. Each sentence in the *Wake* must be read as if it were a potential metaphysical microcosm unto itself. Some sentences, especially long and complex ones, will provide examples of the full panorama of the notions to be sketched below. But once every sentence, regardless of length and complexity, assumes its role in the four parts of the *Wake*, the comprehensiveness of the *Wake*'s metaphysical vision will become undeniable. . . .

Identity and Difference

The *Wake*'s form seems to dissolve before our very eyes, assuming of course that the metaphysics of the *Wake*'s content applies to the *Wake* itself as an entity affected by that content. This peculiar self-reflexivity epitomizes the extent to which the *Wake* attacks apparently solid and sacrosanct metaphysical principles. The fundamental presence of a one at rest (for example, the *Wake* itself) in continuous tension with the many in motion (for example, all possible meanings of the *Wake*) permeates all other subsequent distinctions and concepts purporting to differentiate a formless flux into recognizable shapes and individuals. Consider, for example, that distinction between an entity being the same as itself and irreducibly different from its opposite. Surely no metaphysical principle is more self-evident. And yet the *Wake* does not agree. Thus, the "equals of opposites, evolved by a onesame power of nature or of spirit" are nonetheless "polarized for reunion by the symphysis of their antipathies" (92.9, 11–12). Opposites, whether subjectively conceived or putatively objective realities, spring from that one and the same power of nature by which all things flow. As a result, opposites become synthesized and fused with nature ("symphysis"), the flowing womb of all, however antithetical and polarized these opposites may be with respect to one another.

The same point may be educed from this delightfully penetrating passage, somersaulting with reversed Latin pronouns and phrases and plays on the name of the philosopher Bruno:

> When himupon Nola Bruno monopolises his ego-bruno most unwillingly seses by the mortal powers alionola equal and opposite brunoipso, *id est,* eternally provoking alio opposite equally as provoked as Bruno at being eternally opposed by Nola. (488.7–11)

The conflict within the individual ego of Bruno is no less intensely universal ("eternally" occurs twice in this passage) than was the warlike strife between the duo of Muta and Juva cited earlier. Apparently the author of the *Wake* sensed that keeping a flux flowing fluidly forever is no facile feat.

Identity and difference are an especially basic set of opposites, and therefore we should expect that their disappearance into an even more primal flux will not be easy. For example, the need to maintain the stability of identity is found in the description of HCE: "An imposing everybody he always indeed looked, constantly the same as and equal to himself and magnificently well worthy of any and all such universalisation" (32.19–21). But if all opposites, regardless of their metaphysical primordiality, are nullified by continually flowing into their own counterparts, then it should also come as no great surprise that the identity of HCE as well as any other distinct individual will dissolve itself into pure difference, or difference without apparent limitation. Such fragmentation occurs when HCE becomes transmogrified into myriad characters (as he is on pages 58–61) and when he is displaced geographically all over the globe (as he is on pages 552–55). The question then arises whether the phrase "the same as and equal to" can be predicated of such a multiform being. It seems that the fact of difference of this epic sort must surely swamp the claim of identity. For in what sense is it possible to assert that the many is identical to HCE if the difference between what HCE is and what he (she? it?) is not can no longer be preserved?

Nevertheless, for all its concerted emphasis on flux and the implications of flux, the *Wake* does not ignore the need to counterbalance the formless sweep. Note the parenthetical remark, uttered as if the author were speaking to himself, that "you must, how, in undivided reawlity draw the line somewhawre" (292.31–32). And again, in what appears to be a tone of self-admonition—"there is a limit to all things so this will never do" (119.8–9). And to reinforce the necessary presence of individual identity in even the most fluid of contexts—"But there's a little lady waiting and her name is A.L.P. And you'll agree. She must be she" (102.22–23). Short but rhythmic sentences and a lack of puns make it difficult to miss the relevant metaphysical point. If ALP is she, then surely HCE is he—and if she is she and he is he, then perhaps these twain will never merge to the point of losing their distinctive individuality. To conclude on a hopeful metaphysical note, "we only wish everyone was as sure of anything in this watery world" (452.29–30). But can the possibility of difference, both in the metaphysically abstract and in the concretely actual, still be maintained?

It is perhaps worth emphasizing that from the standpoint of traditional modes of thought, difference is metaphysically no less fundamental than identity. Persons, places and things differ from one another. I am not identical to my typewriter, nor is either identical to the room in which I work. But if everything is really in a condition of metaphysical flux, then at some point it will become impossible to determine precisely what differentiates that aspect of the flux which appears to be me from that aspect of the flux which appears to be my typewriter. We may speak of the difference between entity X and entity Y, but ultimately there is no ground, according to the *Wake,* for believing that any real difference between these two entities actually exists.

This implication of the flux principle receives a distinctively Joycean enunciation in the following text:

> Whence it is a slopperish matter, given the wet and low visibility (since in this scherzarade of one's thousand one nightinesses that sword of certainty which would identifide the body never falls) to idendifine the individuone. (51.3–6)

Arising from the context of the Arabian nights, dream language transforms the literary charade of Scheherazade's thousand and one nighttime tales into a metaphysical denial of the possibility of individuation. The sword of certainty, deftly eluded by these coy linguistic spells, fails to make an indentation on her body. And, by metaphysical extension, this same sword now neither identifies nor defines any one individual being so that identity can be predicated of it. That scientific sword which, upon descent, would cut off a portion of the flux so that it became a "this" rather than a "that" just hangs there suspended while everything passing beneath its sharp potentially defining edge remains essentially formless.

The phrase "idendifine the individuone" is, as it were, a particulary effective stroke. Something must be identified as *an* entity before it can be defined as a being of this or that type. The two processes, identification and definition, are normally distinguished from one another in philosophy, with identification primarily described in terms of perception and definition usually based on the adoption of a certain conceptual scheme. The *Wake* verbally merges the two processes into one undifferentiated activity, then casts doubt on the very possibility of that activity being performed on all bodies, just as it has been left unperformed on the undented body of Scheherazade.

At this point, we might stubbornly maintain that the *Wake* seems to be gnawing away at the pen from which it took shape, not to mention at the instrument of rationality and purpose guiding that pen. For of all the many paradoxical ramifications consequent upon the principle of universal flux, that just described is surely the most quixotic and the most unsettling. But there are other effects which, although perhaps less dizzying, are equally far-reaching and important for extending the universality of the flux principle into the region of identity and difference. For example, the flux principle also makes its presence felt in terms of what might be called the infinite relativity of beings. Each entity in the world of the *Wake* "flows" into each and every other entity in the sense that the identification of *this* being also establishes a concurrent set of relations with all that is *other than* this being. Because of this peculiar omnivorousness, each apparently distinct referent in the *Wake* readily yields itself to something other than itself, with language merely serving as the external manifestation of this process of dissolution rather than its sole underlying source.

Consider one apparently clear-cut example of preserved difference—it seems evident that the identity of one self differs from the identity of another self. I am not James Joyce. Joyce is not Nicholas of Cusa, the twelfth-century philosopher. Or is he?

Now let the centuple celves of my egourge as
Micholas de Cusack calls them,—of all of whose I in
my hereinafter of course by recourse demission me—
by the coincidance of their contraries reamalgamerge
in that identity of undiscernibles. (49.33–36; 50.1)

The cell of my self includes far more than a centuple of other
selves, just as the number of meanings read into each word in
the *Wake* far exceeds threescore and ten. My ego urges me into
becoming an "I" whose being transcends the limits of the "I"
which I now believe myself to be. A male becomes a
"sonhusband," a female becomes a "daughterwife" (627.1,2);
indeed, all differences between the sexes are now groundless
since, Teutonically speaking, "himundher" (92.9) describes
what we all are. Thus, "I is a femaline person" (251.31) follows
logically from the fact that I am "manorwombanborn" (55.10),
a metaphysical process occurring regardless of whether or not
the individual self has even the barest inklings of such extensive
self-differentiation. However contrary these multiple selves
may appear, either in company with that "I" which I call
myself or with any other self, they nonetheless remain
"coincidancing" within whatever surface limitations pertain to
this or that individual ego. This union does not simply
amalgamate contraries, nor does it reamalgamate them; rather,
contraries are "reamalgamerged" so that the metaphysically
sensitive reader of the *Wake* becomes subject to as many self-
transformations as do the central characters (character?) of the
Wake itself. For "*Shem and Shaun*," the "*shame that sunders
em*" (526.14) has no justification, whether in the parlance of
printing or in the traditional modes of metaphysics.

Universal flux has dissolved all real differences between
individual beings, thereby setting into motion an unending
series of fluid relations among all apparently discrete beings.
This particular repercussion assumes special prominence in
considering the self as one kind of being. It seems true to say
that an individual self apprehends other selves as other by
existing in relation to those selves. The more individual egos a
given self has experienced, the more the limits of that self are
extended. Now to affirm that I experience many selves other
than my own ego presupposes that I can relate to all these selves
in some way; however, I must retain the unique reality of my
ego as distinct from these other selves in order to preserve the
difference between myself and others. To the extent that a
reader of the *Wake* merges with, say, HCE in the experience of
reading about that character, to that extent an identity of sorts
exists between these two selves. The reader *is*, in some sense,
HCE (just as, in some sense, HCE *is* the reader). The same
sort of identity emerges whenever two individual characters
interact with one another within the metaphysical confines of
the *Wake*. Yet surely no one would think of denying that
however engrossed one becomes in the *Wake*, the reader and
HCE remain distinct individuals of vastly different metaphysical types. And similar considerations would seem to apply
within the *Wake*. But precisely to what extent do individual
characters in the *Wake* remain individual in any discernible
sense?

This problem concerns the fact that the limits necessary to
establish the difference between selves (or between literary
characters) begin to blur because of the omnipresence of the
flux. Should the metaphysics of the *Wake* be extended to the
point where the individuality of no character can be preserved?
If so, then in effect everyone is no one, since anyone is really
the same as everyone else, given that the very possibility of
difference between or among them has been ruled out by
implication. The apparently indeterminate limits of the flux
must be settled somehow not simply for the sake of pursuing

the question as having intrinsic metaphysical interest, but more
importantly in order to determine the status of individual
characters in the *Wake* (if, indeed, there be any). We must
therefore discover, if possible, the extent to which the flux
principle can admit of real differentiation. The greater the
degree of differentiation, the greater the possibility for preserving the uniqueness of individual characters within the flux.
After all, whenever days were nights and nights days (549.6), it
would be impossible to tell the difference between being awake
and being asleep, not to mention the impossibility of ever really
knowing what's what. . . .

Cause and Effect

The twin notions of cause and effect have undergone
rough treatment at the hands of modern philosophers. David
Hume initiated the attack by arguing that the concept of
causality was simply the result of habit ingrained in the minds
of those who believed that they detected causes in the external
world. And more than a few contemporary philosophers have
suggested that the word "cause" has become so encrusted with
meanings that it can no longer be credited with any kind of
philosophical respectability. Despite such assaults, however,
cause and effect remain deeply embedded in ordinary human
consciousness. And they must remain just as embedded in the
consciousness of philosophers when they are dealing with the
everyday non-philosophical world.

The fixed quality of causality, like time and space, also
comes under critical fire in the *Wake*, although attacks depend
upon the prior cogency of more fundamental metaphysical
principles and notions. For example, the common-sense idea
that a cause generates an effect, and thus must temporally
precede that effect, receives several severe jolts. As one should
expect by now, attacks on causality originate as implications
from the structure of time as defined in the *Wake*. Consider the
following quasi-axiomatic claim: "we have occasioning cause
causing effects and affects occasionally recausing altereffects"
(482.36–483.1). Now from the standpoint of traditional
metaphysics, one effect can cause another effect only if an
effect resulting from a prior cause becomes a cause of
subsequent effect. But the *Wake* suggests here that an effect can
"recause" an "altereffect," a metaphysical possibility realizable
on the supposition that the notion of a causal order necessarily
moving in only one direction has been thrown into question.
And that is precisely what the *Wake* has done.

In the normal run of events, nothing can be both cause
and effect at the same time and in the same respect. But here,
as elsewhere, normality has run its course. Let us reflect on this
remarkably convoluted aside: "For was not just this in effect
which had just caused that the effect of that which it had caused
to occur?" (92.33–34). First of all, one might object that this
particular locution is a prime example for Burgess's reading of
the *Wake* as, in part, high-level gibberish; consequently, such
language should never be taken as anything more than a
playful romp through the often bewildering logic of cause and
effect. But if we examine this comment carefully, we discern
that the infinitive "to occur" terminates a line of thought which
virtually identifies cause with effect and effect with cause. The
temporal element in this utterance is intriguing and instructive—the repeated pluperfects direct the reader to reorient the
temporality of the effect so that it becomes prior to the cause,
thus reversing the traditionally understood order. If, however, a
cause does not precede an effect on temporal grounds, then
apparently any cause can be seen as an effect and any effect can
be seen as a cause. A distinction between the two concepts
becomes almost impossible to establish. And if cause cannot be
distinguished from effect, then all causes are effects and all

effects are causes, and thus the concept of cause preceding effect has no metaphysical significance.

The dissolution of causality as a potential explanation for the universal turbulence of the *Wake* highlights the systematic disintegration of those notions which from the metaphysical backdrop for the *Wake's* epic narrative. Let them again pass in review. The preponderance of motion over rest results in the incapacity of preserving identity over difference. With difference overwhelming identity, it then becomes impossible to conceive of time (as well as everything else) as anything other than a continually undifferentiated flow, conveniently labeled "the present" for the sake of preserving time's most manifest appearance. And without a differentiated past, present, and future within which to locate and order serially the cause/effect relation, there is no telling what may happen to whom, when, where, and why. How then is the reader of the *Wake*, existing in a non-*Wake* reality which typically makes more metaphysical sense than not, to intuit a correlation between that reality etched in stability and the riotous tumult which the *Wake* celebrates with such metaphysical meticulousness? Perhaps the very language of this topsy-turvy world presents some kind of secret haven for the reader who senses the tension between the two worlds. But on the other hand, perhaps the stylistic subtleties of the *Wake* plunge the reader even deeper into its constantly revolving metaphysical flux. The quest for some sort of stability must therefore be carried still further, now moving into the world of words themselves.

PATRICK KAVANAGH

1904–1967

Patrick Kavanagh was born on October 21, 1904, in Inniskeen, County Monaghan, Ireland. After leaving school in 1916 he continued his education by reading widely in the classics of English literature and in contemporary magazines. Like his father, he worked as a cobbler, and after 1926 as a farmer. His first poems were published in the *Irish Weekly Independent* in 1928, and in 1929 in the *Irish Statesman*, whose editor A.E. (George William Russell) encouraged and advised his work.

Kavanagh's first book, *Ploughman and Other Poems* (1936), sold well in London and Dublin, and established his reputation as a peasant poet; it was followed in 1938 by the autobiographical work *The Green Fool.* After visits to Dublin and London he moved to Dublin to further his literary career, though he regretted leaving the countryside and his farm. He won the A.E. Memorial Prize in 1939, but had to struggle to make ends meet as a journalist. His long poem *The Great Hunger* was published in 1942, followed by more poems in *A Soul for Sale* (1947) and a novel, *Tarry Flynn* (1948), which was banned by the Irish censors; it was, however, as a vigorous and often acerbic critic of Irish culture and society that he achieved notoriety. His attacks reached their peak in *Kavanagh's Weekly*, edited with his brother, which failed after thirteen issues in 1952.

A rather slanted article on him provoked Kavanagh to a libel suit in 1954, which proved a disastrous failure. The following year he was operated on for lung cancer, and after a surprising recovery entered a more restrained phase. Seeking to regain prestige, he published the successful *Come Dance with Kitty Stobling and Other Poems* in 1960, but declining health made him despondent and unproductive in his remaining years. After completing *Self Portrait* (1964) he produced the selections *Collected Poems* (1964) and *Collected Pruse* [*sic*] (1967). He died on November 30, 1967.

A short series of quotations will show how casually Mr. Kavanagh (in *Tarry Flynn*) makes his assertions about Tarry's spiritual strength. It pains as well as vexes that the author cares to tell us these things about his hero but doesn't seem to care the slightest bit about convincing us of their truth:

As (his mother) went down the road he could feel the power of her ruthless organising mind trying to throw a flame over his life.

She couldn't see that apparent indifference and laziness was not laziness but the enchantment of the earth over him, and the wonder of a strange beauty revealed to him.

Tarry wasn't being let into the secret at all. The mother was making a child of him, an irresponsible child—and all because he was able to see the wild and wonderful meaning in the commonest things of earth.

If any man of them in that country were to open his eyes, if the fog in which they lived lifted, they would be unable to endure the futility of it all. Their courage was the courage of the blind. But Tarry had seen beyond the fog the Eternal light shining on the stones.

At one point Mr. Kavanagh does explicitly mention that his hero is unusually self-centered, but Tarry knows he is and (for our greater distress)—

he knew that he had his justification. There were some people who were fit for nothing else but to sympathise, but a man like himself had a dispensation from such side-tracking activities.

A man who had seen the ecstatic light of Life in stones, on the hills, in leaves of cabbages and weeds was not bound by the pity of Christ.

Or was he?

If he were, how much that was great in literature and art would be lost. He justified himself by the highest examples he knew of.

This passage goes on:

Is self-pity not pity for mankind as seen in one man? He had it all off. But, O God! if he could only transport himself down the years, three years into the future when all would be forgotten. The present tied him in its cruel knots and dragged him through bushes and briars, stones and weeds on his mouth and nose—

but, if that brings us closer to the anguish, no step is taken towards self-knowledge. In none of these cases does Mr. Kavanagh go on to say more about the vision of "the Eternal light." The only support that these crucial and unconvincing assertions get within the novel is from the details that are given now and again about Tarry's physical work, and that support isn't nearly enough: the details only explain how it was that Tarry and Mr. Kavanagh could tell themselves this particular story. . . .

Tarry Flynn is disappointing because Mr. Kavanagh had a subject. Even in the document as it stands one is in touch with something both real and different, which makes one think. The novel is also disappointing, to this reader at any rate, because it has made him look at the author's poetry with a colder eye. What, then, is wrong with Mr. Kavanagh's idea of the 'imagination' as the faculty of seing the eternal beauty and the permanent laws of life in small everyday objects? The perceptions come, momentarily and without notice, in a condition of inner stillness, when the perceiver is unegotistic and able to go outwards with unusual clarity. It therefore isn't quite fair to say that this faculty has *nothing* in common with what Shelley called imagination. The only thing wrong with Mr. Kavanagh's idea is that he doesn't allow for the unavoidable condition, that the richness of what is found in the small and the everyday will depend upon the richness of what is brought to them. Mr. Kavanagh somehow makes his momentary states of inner peace an excuse—and afterwards a defence—for refusing experience. His idea of the value of 'imagination' is an idea that he can *rest* on these small moments he has had. And resting on them and making them part of his self-justification he inevitably becomes the self-centred writer whom Shelley's words do fit. But the consequence of the fact that "Even the teeming pot was very important" is not that the person with the power to find that out doesn't need to attend to greater things: it is that he should find more than other people in those greater things. And his possession of his initial gift itself will not be secure if he doesn't make this natural progress in life. (He can only not make it, of course, through fear, wilful perversity, misunderstanding or fundamental lack of vitality—mixed in whatever proportions.)

Inevitably, then, the more successful of Mr. Kavanagh's poems are very short, inevitably more of these are about the eternal beauty than about the eternal laws of life, and inevitably the poems about that beauty talk about it more often than they render it. Inevitably, also, the great majority of these more successful poems are in Mr. Kavanagh's first volume of poetry (*Ploughman and Other Poems*, 1936), which takes up the first 23 pages of the 200-page *Collected Poems*. Effective recognition of the laws of life is all too clearly absent from the later long poems that attempt to deal with human affairs of some moment—absent, even, from "The Great Hunger." This ambitious work (of 1942) may be the poem of Mr. Kavanagh's best-known in this country (it was singled out by Mr. Charles Tomlinson in the last volume of the Pelican Guide) and it is certainly a more determined and impressive effort than *Tarry Flynn*. But its bitter account of Patrick Maguire's unfulfilled bachelor life on his farm, *all* in terms of the influence of his strong-willed mother and the hard, narrow community behind

her, is unconvincing and untragic in a very similar way. The self-pity is only sharper and more innocently wholehearted: the poem is more moving but not in the way of art. The fundamental procedure in those early short poems concerned with presenting a swift vision of an eternal beauty is that of the passage from *Tarry Flynn* quoted at the head of this review: the physical facts are simply stated and are then laid *alongside* a simple statement not so much of their spiritual significance as of the fact that they have spiritual significance; and the poem works, when there is any question of its working, if this second statement comes with the right delicate surprise to excite the reader's mind into seeing the two things fuse together. A reader who has discovered from *Tarry Flynn* how much blarney Mr. Kavanagh is capable of is likely to lose something of whatever confidence he had in the success of these poems. But the best poems are about small actions, not small observations, and here the simple description simultaneously suggests the more or less unstated larger significance. This is more comfortable, since the small action exists in its own right and doesn't have to be taken any further beyond itself or taken any more seriously than the reader is willing to take it. It is also more interesting, since there is more knowledge of life in it. Here I quote "Beech Tree" as illustration rather the stronger "Crossed Furrows" because the lapse in the last two lines here helps to make another necessary point.

> I planted in February
> A bronze-leafed beech,
> In the chill brown soil
> I spread out its silken fibres.
> Protected it from the goats
> With wire netting
> And fixed it firm against
> The worrying wind.
> Now it is safe, I said,
> April must stir
> My precious baby
> Into greenful loveliness.
> It is August now, I have hoped
> But I hope no more—
> My beech tree will never hide sparrows
> From hungry hawks.

Why shouldn't Mr. Kavanagh achieve perfection when he writes so briefly and with such simplicity and naturalness? He hardly ever—in my opinion never—does achieve perfection. Such faults as the *gauche* flatness of this poem's conclusion seem to come from a lack of strong inspiration. The poet is neither uninspired nor falsely inspired: he simply hasn't any urgent concern to get the poem perfectly right. And in his later poetry the slackness grows markedly. Throughout Mr. Kavanagh's writing the reader will have some sense, smaller or greater, of *idling*.

The genuineness of Mr. Kavanagh's start as a poet and his relative innocence in his self-misdirection, which makes the failure a more poignant one, mean that he can be quite attractive in later squibs about the Dublin literary world. There may have been some egotistic disappointment but it wasn't all that. However, his satire has little bite.

Is it the fact that *even so* Mr. Kavanagh distinguishes himself above most contemporary English poets by his simplicity and naturalness and distinguishes himself above Mr. Larkin, who *has* these qualities, by trying to say something that was more worth saying?—J. M. NEWTON, "Patrick Kavanagh's Imagination," *Delta*, Autumn 1965, pp. 5–8

Kavanagh saw 'Irishness' as 'a form of anti-art'; as a pernicious kind of provincialism, a playing up to an Anglo-American image of Ireland. For this reason such exploiters and exporters of it as Brendan Behan were to Kavanagh anathema.

The Ireland presented by Kavanagh is penny plain and unsentimental as a shovel. It is to be found in his two major pieces, a long poem called *The Great Hunger* (1942) and the autobiographical novel *Tarry Flynn* (1948). The central figure of the poem is an old peasant farmer, Maguire ('that man on a hill whose spirit/Is a wet sack flapping about the knees of time'). Though entirely contemporary in conception and treatment, here is a Wordsworthian portrait—like *Michael* but with less unction; Maguire is not as unendurably admirable a character. The theme may be bleak—the history of a life cheated and defeated by unsensational but inexorable frustrations—

> No crash,
> No drama.
> This is how his life happened.
> No mad hooves galloping about in the sky,
> But the weak, washy way of true tragedy—
> A sick horse nosing around in the meadow for a clean
>   place to die.

Yet the poem remains genial, even gay. In *Tarry Flynn* the basic situation—the constrictions and futility of a bucolic existence—is the same but in this case the victim (like Kavanagh himself) escapes to the big city. The two works are complementary, and together make a stereoscopic vignette of the reality of the human condition, not only in a particular time and place—rural Ireland of the thirties—but (and this is not too large a claim) all times and places. Stereoscopic because *The Great Hunger* looks at the subject from the tragic and *Tarry Flynn* from the comic angle. While the poem has its share of comic vision the novel is pure comedy throughout, just as Joyce's *Ulysses* is comedy; ironic and deadpan, and so involved with the texture of the life it depicts that some have not recognized it as such. *Tarry Flynn* has never really received its due, though it has been several times reprinted and even turned into a play. . . .

'Now there is no one,' somebody said to me in Dublin after his death. It was the general feeling; for fifteen years Kavanagh had been Dublin's unacknowledged legislator. His throne-room (at least when I saw him there in 1960) was McDaid's bar off Grafton Street, and later the Bailey, owned by his friend John Ryan, where now stands enshrined the front door of 7 Eccles Street. Here Kavanagh was to be found almost any day, hunched characteristically—an elbow gripped in either hand—at one of the small oval screwed-down iron tables; which in his case would be supporting a ball of whisky and a glass of bicarbonate. Tourists would come to McDaid's just to look at him and hear the great voice 'reminiscent of a load of gravel sliding down a quarry' . . . Dr Johnson's subjugation of London seems the nearest parallel to Kavanagh's conquest of Dublin: an analogue not so far-fetched as might seem. Both were pub-men, both of formidable physical presence accentuated by a touch of the uncouth and by characteristic mannerisms; both devastating in argument, capable of bludgeoning an opponent into silence with some unanswerable aphorism whose weight derived from a massive uncommonsense, experience of life, and fundamental spiritual integrity. It was not wit: just that one had to recognize the truth when one heard it.—DAVID WRIGHT, "Patrick Kavanagh," *Lon*, April 1968, pp. 23–28

———

JOHN JORDAN
From "Mr. Kavanagh's Progress"
Studies, Autumn 1960, pp. 296–304

The Green Fool cannot be written off as a young man's aberration. It is Mr Kavanagh's most successful attempt at sustained prose narrative, to my mind of greater merit than the novel *Tarry Flynn* (The Pilot Press 1948) which covers a deal of the same ground. The latter book has perhaps more cohesion but it is rather more self-regarding, and lacks the bright and clear transfer effects of *The Green Fool*. And in this openly autobiographical book there are laid bare the elements of Kavanagh, the pieties and predispositions which have been the sustenance of his talent and the architecture of its products. In his later verse, Mr Kavanagh has not been afraid of walking naked, as in the beautiful poem 'I Had a Future', of which more later. The chief value of *The Green Fool* may be the revelation, almost embarrassingly authentic, of a mind at once cunning and naive, suspicious and trusting. I suppose the unsatisfactory term 'peasant' has to be brought in, sooner or later. *The Green Fool* demonstrates how devious the mind of the peasant can be, and yet how simple when it is released from traditional bondages of land and cattle and family. But it is Mr Kavanagh's mind I am trying to write about, and only quotation and commentary can illustrate that.

Even in this early book there are inklings of his later strengths as a poet. Here he is on the subject of a pig-killing.

> It was a memorable morning; the blood of dawn was
> being poured over the hills and of that other blood we
> only thought how much black-pudding it would
> make. Our talk had the romantic beauty of reality.
> We were as close to life and death as we could be.

I can think of no other writer who could get away with a phrase like 'the romantic beauty of reality'. But in no other writer would so flabby a phrase have the backing of a red sky at morning juxtaposed with the blood of stuck-pigs. It will be seen, I hope, that Mr Kavanagh has adhered, increasingly through the years, to the extreme form of the doctrine of 'meanest flower' as subject-matter for the imagination. Much of this essay will be given to demonstration of his growing awareness of his own inmost preoccupation, and of his attempts, sometimes successful, to create poems, emblematic or discursive, on the theme of ripening consciousness. It might be said as a general proposition of any worthwhile poet, that he struggles to establish to his own satisfaction the nature of reality. Mr Kavanagh's peculiar status as a poet depends very largely on the freshness of his rediscovery of an axiom. He is archetypical. . . .

Almost all the most recent poems of quality in *Kitty Stobling* are further, more complex attempts to attain a kind of passing self-knowledge. In the superbly jazzy 'Auditors In' he writes,

> From the sour soil of a town where all roots canker
> I turn away to where the Self reposes
> The placeless Heaven that's under all our noses
> Where we're shut from all the barren anger,
> No time for self-pitying melodrama

leading to the wry gravity of the conclusion,

> I am so glad
> To come so accidentally upon
> My Self at the end of a tortuous road
> And have learned with surprise that God
> Unworshipped withers to the Futile One.

Mr Kavanagh's Self is a very different one from that in *A Soul for Sale*, but he still has links with the man who praised 'the undying difference in the corner of a field'. This is best illustrated from the sonnet 'The Hospital', appearing here with some, to my mind, dubious revisions. I quote the sestet as it appeared in *Nimbus*.

> This is what love does to things: the Rialto Bridge,
> The main gate that was bent by a heavy lorry,
> The seat at the back of a shed that was a suntrap.
> Naming these things is the love-act and its pledge;
> For we must set in words the mystery without
>   claptrap,
> Experience so light-hearted appears transitory.

In *Kitty Stobling* the last two lines run,

> For we must record love's mystery without claptrap,
> Snatch out of time the passionate transitory.

The first emendation is acceptable, the second disastrous. For a rediscovered truth—that experience *appears* transitory to the outgoing heart—is substituted the cliché of art eternizing the moment. But even in its new version the sonnet is not alone masterly in its control of speech-rhythms, but most moving as a declaration of faith in life.

There are others in this book:

> Gather the bits of road that were
> Not gravel to the traveller
> But eternal lanes of joy
> On which no man who walks can die.
> Bring in the particular trees
> That caught you in their mysteries,
> And love again the weeds that grew
> Somewhere specially for you.
> Collect the river and the stream
> That flashed upon a pensive theme,
> And a positive world make,
> A world man's world cannot shake,
> And do not lose love's resolution
> Though face to face with destitution.
>
>   ('Prelude')

Love is the theme of this book ultimately, love for life as it is, not as it might have been, or ought to be, or might well be in the near future. And how many fruitful statements Mr Kavanagh makes in naming his great discovery:

> To look on is enough
> In the business of love
>   ('Is')

Again,

> I will have love, have love
> From anything made of
> And life with a shapely form
> With gaiety and charm
> And capable of receiving
> With grace the grace of living
> And wild moments too
> Self when freed from you.
>   ('The Self-slaved')

Kitty Stobling contains several botched poems—'In Memory of My Mother' collapses one word from the end—but as a whole it stands out as that rarest of achievements, a book of verse which manifestly indicates an integrated personality, rather than an album of shots from various angles. This is Kavanagh, nor are we out of him.

As against this, there are some suggestions that Mr Kavanagh has not yet expunged from his thinking and his writing certain gritty elements. I am *not* thinking of the enchanting 'House Party to Celebrate the Destruction of the Roman Catholic Church in Ireland', a lampoon in the grand style rising to the final searing indictment of pinchbeck liberalism:

> In far off parishes of Cork and Kerry
> Old priests walked homeless in the winter air
> As Seamus poured another pale dry sherry.

What I have called the 'gritty elements' in the poet's thinking are best seen at their clogging process, whenever he writes about his vision of the Eternal Feminine. I'm afraid that Mr Kavanagh collapses irremediably into sentimentality when he proclaims his image of woman as warm, intuitive, uncomplicated, comprehensive of the poet, as distinct from calculating shallow man. The image is as valid potentially as any other, but he has not as yet succeeded in presenting it satisfactorily. It is seen as its lachrymose worst in a poem not reprinted in the new book, 'God in Woman':

> While men the poet's tragic light resented,
> The spirit that is woman caressed his soul.

It mars an already uneasily poised poem, 'Intimate Parnassus':

> It is not cold on the mountain, human women
> Fall like ripe fruit, while mere men
> Are climbing out on dangerous branches
> Of banking, insurance and shops;

The convenient, over-cosy dichotomy suggests a temperamental fixation, the kind of fixation which makes for bad verse unless chastened by the discipline of self-knowledge. This dichotomy may be seen in a less explicit form in 'If Ever You Go to Dublin Town' an inferior ballad in which Mr Kavanagh refurbishes an old fustian icon of the poet as solitary, eccentric, head-in-the-air, but withal tenderhearted:

> He had the knack of making men feel
> As small as they really were
> Which meant as great as God had made them
> But as males they disliked the air.

Why male, wherefore base? This kind of implied dogma is of course one of the varieties of sentimentality and such a disrupter of poetry.

I will just touch on another variety of sentimentality to which Mr Kavanagh is prone, a kind which might be traced to one of his chief strengths, the re-burnishing of the banal.

The sonnet 'Lines Written on a Seat on the Grand Canal, Dublin' is a beautifully spikey tribute to his ravishment by the ordinary—until the last two lines:

> O commemorate me with no hero-courageous
> Tomb—just a canal-bank seat for the passer-by.

There is here, I submit, a double failure of language and feeling. That infernal word 'just' cheapens the poet's wish into a wheedling petition—'just' a song at twilight or a penny for a poor blind man. But it is the 'passer-by' that does the real harm. Between the poet and the object-experience falls the shadow of a cliché sentiment, posthumous contact with the undying generations. Yet, apart from the exigencies of rhyme, it is fairly obvious that Mr Kavanagh was aiming at no more than the kind of tentacular simplicity he achieves through 'naming' objects; but to adapt from the book's title poem, he is here ceasing to be 'namer' and becoming 'the beloved'.

Mr Kavanagh's defects are grave. A catalogue of them would include over-reliance on portentous abstractions, the mandarin platitude (see for both, 'The One'), an uneasy acquaintance with Greek mythology (he must never again mention Parnassus, in any form), and a habit of trailing his coat unnecessarily—this mars the sonnet 'Dear Folks' ('the laughter-smothered courage,/The Poet's'). But for me the defects are often in themselves contributory to the success of individual poems, breaking up the light and refracting it. And he can make high capital out of jagged verbal effects, out of a kind of shrewd and tender clumsiness:

> Leafy-with-love banks and the green waters of the
>   canal
> Pouring redemption for me, that I do
> The Will of God, wallow in the habitual, the banal,
> Grow with nature again as before I grew.

and again:

> The gravel in the yard was pensive annoyed to be
>   crunched
> As people with problems in their faces drove in in
>   cars
> Yet I with such solemnity around me refused to be
>   bunched
> In fact was inclined to give the go-by to bars.

Mr Kavanagh now speaks in a manner that leads us to await, constantly, surprises of language and rhythm, and no-one with an ear for rhyme can fail to be enchanted by his skill in breaking down cliché associations. In fact he is a major craftsman in words. As for his substantive values, it is sufficient for the time being to recognize that he is, first and foremost, a celebrant of life.

TERENCE BROWN

From "Conclusion: With Kavanagh in Mind"
Northern Voices: Poets from Ulster

1975, pp. 216–21

Patrick Kavanagh, the son of a country shoemaker in Inniskeen, Co. Monaghan, was born three years before MacNeice and Hewitt. His development as a poet was inevitably affected by provincial ignorance of literary traditions and possibilities. His youthful imagination was nurtured in the pages of the school anthologies, and a persistent tendency in his poetry to over-literary diction and effects must be related to these early intimations as to the nature of poetic achievement. He began—writing ballads, occasional poems, and literary effusions—almost as naïvely as did any forgotten local poet or versifying weaver. Yet from a very early point in his career Kavanagh revealed an unconventional quality of imagination. In an early poem such as 'Shancoduff' the poet's sense of landscape and nature is bleakly and uncompromisingly his own, uncontaminated by any provincial urge to satisfy literary ambitions in the employment of conventional pastoral properties.

> My black hills have never seen the sun rising,
> Eternally they look north towards Armagh.
> Lot's wife would not be salt if she had been
> Incurious as my black hills that are happy
> When dawn whitens Glassdrummond chapel.
> My hills hoard the bright shillings of March
> While the sun searches in every pocket.
> These are my Alps and I have climbed the Matter-
>   horn
> With a sheaf of hay for three perishing calves
> In the field under the Big Forth of Rocksavage.
> The sleety winds fondle the rushy beards of Shanco-
>   duff
> White cattle-drovers sheltering in the Featherna
>   Bush
> Look up and say: 'Who owns them hungry hills
> That the water-hen and snipe must have forsaken?
> A poet? Then by heavens he must be poor'
> I hear and is my heart not badly shaken?[1]

The poet here realises his own territory with an open-eyed understanding which transcends realism in its vision of complicated loyalty and acceptance. The poet does not sentimentalise or simplify his material but allows love, loneliness, poverty, 'the usual barbaric life of the Irish country poor', to determine the poem's complex emotional structure. In this book I have spoken of some Irish poets' inability or refusal to come to terms with urban experience and complexity. The inference was not, it is important to point out, that rural experience lacks complexity. Clearly, as a poem such as 'Shancoduff' demonstrates, it does not. Rather, the countryside represented for some Irish poets a retreat (though some of the more propagandist poets wished to project their rural version of Irish identity into a political future) from the contemporary, the actual, to what they imagined were the simple permanencies of rural life. In Kavanagh's poem these are by no means simple.[2] The poet's native region can, if his imaginative powers are sufficient and self-confidently exercised, offer the poet a richly fruitful field for mature poetic harvesting. The poet can be imaginatively self-sufficient within his parish. Kavanagh perceptively distinguished between parochialism and provincialism:

> Parochialism and provincialism are direct opposites.
> A provincial is always trying to live by other people's
> loves, but a parochial is self-sufficient. A great deal of
> this parochialism with all its intended intensities and
> courage continued in rural Ireland up till a few years
> ago and possibly will continue in some form for
> ever . . .
>   My idea of a cultural parochial entity was the
> distance a man would walk in a day in any direction.
> The centre was usually the place where oneself lived
> though not always.
>   For me, my cultural parish was certain hills that
> I could see from my own hills. The ordinary bicycle
> did not change these dimensions; for though one
> seldom explored the full extent of one's parish on
> foot, one could and did so on the bicycle. And those
> bicycle journeys that I made to the limits of my
> kingdom were the greatest adventures of my life.[3]

It is from such self-sufficient parochialism that a poem like 'Shancoduff' emerges.

But Kavanagh did not stay in Monaghan. A provincial urge to be where the poet's activity might be more recognised than in Inniskeen took him first to London in 1937 and then, in 1939, to Dublin, where he spent most of his remaining life.

For Kavanagh Dublin was a trauma which eventually bore fruit in his remarkable late poetry. In Dublin he was the provincial who could achieve some success as a peasant poet in a literary climate which esteemed the value of bog-wisdom without much unsentimental knowledge of rural realities. Some of the poems in his first volume, *Ploughman and Other Poems* (1936), would have satisfied the fashionable taste for unreal Irish pastoralism, but Kavanagh very quickly rejected the opportunity for success as Dublin's peasant poet and as a contributor to a conventional Irish literature. 'My misfortune as a writer', he wrote later, 'was that atrocious formula which was invented by Synge and his followers to produce an Irish literature.'[4] He came to feel with increasing violence that the 'so-called Irish Literary Movement which purported to be frightfully Irish and racy of the Celtic soil was a thorough-going English-bred lie':[5]

> The important thing about this idea of literature was
> how Irish was it. No matter what sort of trash it was,
> if it had the Irish quality. And that Irish quality
> simply consisted in giving the English a certain
> picture of Ireland. The English love 'Irishmen' and
> are always on the look-out for them.[6]

In 1942 Kavanagh wrote *The Great Hunger*, that massive anti-pastoral, that anguished denunciation of the spiritual starvation of Irish country life. The work is obviously one of the most powerful by an Irish poet since Yeats, yet Kavanagh was later to reject it, as he rejected the pastoralism implicit in some of his early work. He declared that 'it lacks the nobility and repose of poetry'.[7] It is the poetry of reaction, of response to a problem that accepts the terms in which the problem is posed. It is poetry with palpable design, poetry with intention. Kavanagh was later to feel there was 'some kinetic vulgarity in it' and that 'all action is vulgar'.[8] Many of his subsequent rather febrile satiric pieces are equally 'vulgar' in Kavanagh's sense, without even the violent passion of passages in *The Great Hunger*—'the queer and terrible things'—which stamp themselves on the reader's memory with a force of great conviction. The satiric poems are the poet's splenetic, even peevish, reactions to the spiritually debased conditions of Dublin's bourgeois culture where provincialism was the primary determinant of the citizen's awareness.

It was Kavanagh's major achievement that he transcended the provincial-urban waste of spirit to write, late in his life, a number of city-inspired poems which establish his own parish of the imagination. Poems such as 'October', 'Canal Bank Walk', 'Lines Written on a Seat on the Grand Canal', and 'The Hospital' stand out amid much chaff as the true grain of achieved individual celebratory vision, arrived at against all the odds. 'The Hospital' is a poem that deserves much attention.

> A year ago I fell in love with the functional ward
> Of a chest hospital: square cubicles in a row
> Plain concrete, wash basins—an art lover's woe,
> Not counting how the fellow in the next bed snored.
> But nothing whatever is by love debarred,
> The common and banal her heat can know.
> The corridor led to a stairway and below
> Was the inexhaustible adventure of a gravelled yard.
> This is what love does to things: the Rialto Bridge,
> The main gate that was bent by a heavy lorry,
> The seat at the back of a shed that was a suntrap.
> Naming these things is the love-act and its pledge;
> For we must record love's mystery without claptrap,
> Snatch out of time the passionate transitory.[9]

In this poem the poet writes in celebration not out of a desire to solve some problem or to resolve some tension. No troubled insecurity about personal identity disturbs its 'noble repose': it contains the minutiae of the urban everyday within a formal harmony that bespeaks a spiritual self-confidence which is a balance of strength and humility. The poem, for all the quietism of its explicit statement, gives this reader a sense of great imaginative energy. This may perhaps be explained by the fact that the poem is a sonnet. A heightened response to individual moments, to 'spots in time', to epiphanies, is frequent in modern poetry, but the containing of such moments within the rich formality of a traditional complex form is not conventional. A sense of vision and control combine to suggest imaginative energies of a quite unusual degree.

Furthermore, the diction is colloquial and direct, while the verbal music is ornate, almost Tennysonian (note the rounded vowel music of the 'o's' and 'a's'), binding the banal and the elevated in a mysterious synthesis. In such a poem modern urban experience is bathed in the poet's visionary light: its complexity is not denied (the poem suggests pain, boredom, ugliness) but a strange simplicity of statement can comprehend its conditions.

The poem is rich in a further, satisfying manner. That the poet should have chosen the sonnet, that European and English form, to write a poem that transcends the conditions of his own bitter, difficult Irish experience is a cultural fact of intriguing significance. Equally it is an illumination to see what Kavanagh can make, in this and some of his other later poems, of the sonnet form, and what he can make that form contain. What has customarily been an aristocratic or portentous form is made amenable, without incongruity, to Dublin's Rialto Bridge and a man snoring in a hospital bed. Such a poem may therefore be read as cultural paradigm. The poet, without any sense of inferiority, can employ what forms he chooses, borrowing from such traditions as seem appropriate the means to express his parochial vision without any provincial insecurity.

In 1949 Roy McFadden wrote:

> We shall not find a unified movement in our poetry until we have achieved a pattern of living which we can call our own (something very different from a political programme); and the achievement of that pattern is as much the responsibility of the poet as of anyone else.[10]

In revealing the possibility of a self-confident imagining that can combine the urbane and the colloquial, the sophisticated with the local, Kavanagh, although he chose late in life to ignore history, may have more to say to our historic condition in Ulster and in Ireland than any number of political programmes or problem-possessed poets. He reveals to us the quality of a free form of life, an independent pattern of living.

Notes

1. *Collected Poems*, London: MacGibbon & Kee, 1964, 30.
2. Kavanagh once remarked: 'There is a thing which is often said that is the thing about the simplicity of the countryman and his language minted direct from experience . . . There are as I say quite a lot of these freshly minted images but on the whole when the Irish country person or ordinary person whether of town or country utters himself he is anything but simple.' ('Return in Harvest' in *November Haggard*, ed. Peter Kavanagh, New York, 1971, 33.)
3. *November Haggard*, 69–70.
4. Note to the *Poetry Book Society Bulletin* (Jun. 1960), quoted by Alan Warner, *Clay Is the Word*, Dublin: The Dolmen Press, 1973, 28.
5. *Self-Portrait*, Dublin: The Dolmen Press, 1964, 9.
6. Warner, op. cit., 28.
7. *Self-Portrait*, 27.
8. *November Haggard*, 15.
9. *Collected Poems*, 153.
10. McFadden, Editorial, *Rann*, No. 4 (Spring 1949), 1–2.

MARGARET KENNEDY

JAMES JOYCE

PATRICK KAVANAGH

RUDYARD KIPLING

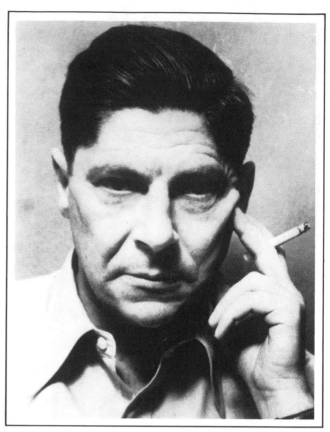

ARTHUR KOESTLER

PHILIP LARKIN

THOMAS KINSELLA

SHEILA KAYE-SMITH

1887–1956

The daughter of a doctor, Sheila Kaye-Smith was born in Hastings, Sussex, on February 4, 1887. Her mother was of mixed Scottish and Huguenot descent, and Kaye-Smith was brought up a Methodist. She grew up in Sussex, gaining an intimate knowledge of its landscape, people, and history, and was educated at Hastings and St. Leonards Ladies' College until 1905; already in her school years she wrote prolifically.

Kaye-Smith's first published novel, *The Tramping Methodist,* was published in 1908, but she enjoyed her first real success with *Sussex Gorse* (1916). In 1918 she was received into the Anglo-Catholic Church, and in 1924 married an Anglican priest, Theodore Penrose Fry. The couple visited Italy in 1928, and converted to Roman Catholicism the following year. Having bought a farm, "Little Doucegrove," in Hastings, they built a Catholic chapel in 1935 and led a quiet and contented life there.

Notable among Kaye-Smith's more than thirty novels are *Tamarisk Town* (1919), *Green Apple Harvest* (1920), *Joanna Godden* (1921), *The End of the House of Alard* (1923), *Shepherds in Sackcloth* (1930), *Susan Spray* (1931), *The Lardners and the Laurelwoods* (1948), *Mrs. Gailey* (1951), and *The View from the Parsonage* (1954). She also wrote several volumes of poetry, including *Saints in Sussex* (1923), and three autobiographical works, notably *Three Ways Home* (1937).

Sheila Kaye-Smith died at her home on January 14, 1956.

Personal

My output of fiction is rather like an iceberg; by far the greater part of it is out of sight. The visible part consists of twenty-two published novels, but invisible under the water lies the mass of my forty-two "composed" novels, and the thirteen novels I wrote during my last two years at school. The latter did not in any way approach the length of the former—in fact, strictly speaking, they were not novels at all, as the longest does not run to more than twenty thousand words, and the shortest works out at scarcely more than half that. Nevertheless, as I wrote at least six a year, this was no mean effort for a schoolgirl who has to fit her writing into her ordinary school routine, including three hours' daily music practice. In fact, looking back on it now from my present rate of achievement, I don't know how I did it.

But I did it, because I have all the volumes in proof—dozens of green exercise books—"fifty pages for one penny"—darkened with pencil and smeary with india-rubber. I wrote entirely for my own private pleasure without a thought of publication, though I was still determined to be a famous author one day. I read some of the tales to my sister, and of one I made a fair copy, bound it and presented it to my mother; but in each case this happened some time after the work was finished. When it was new and fresh in my consciousness I could not bear any eye to see it but my own.

Of these thirteen novelettes four are staged in Devonshire, and the rest belong to Sussex. All except two are historical. I was a devourer of historical novels, especially those written by Edna Lyall, who had almost as devastating an effect on my literary style at this period as she had once had on my religious beliefs. All without any exception are tales of gloom and woe. One or two are allowed a happy ending, but they all abound in death scenes, partings, swoonings, fightings, frustrations, and undying regrets. In this they were not unlike the Scottish stories. My muse was always melancholy, and at this age I had no interest in humour at all—regarding it as something occasionally inevitable in private life, but always degraded and having no place in superior fiction.

These schoolgirl stories are obvious predecessors of my first two published novels—*The Tramping Methodist* and *Starbrace*. Not only are these both historical, but one of them deals with a subject that had already filled half a dozen of the penny exercise books. I had written two highwayman tales called respectively *Sion Hall* and *Merriment Farm*, and in *Starbrace* I deliberately used again scenes and characters that seemed as good to me at twenty-one as they had seemed at sixteen.

Re-reading those early works to-day, I am struck by their sentimentality, their unreality, their third-hand impression of everything except the country outside Hastings. Of character-drawing there is hardly a vestige—the characters, men and women alike, are all dressed-up schoolgirls, except perhaps the highwaymen, who, being drawn entirely from my imagination without any help from Edna Lyall, come a little closer to life as it may have been. The stories themselves are unlikely and badly constructed, though here some of the faults may be due to lack of revision. Occasionally there is a well-imagined if badly executed scene or situation, and often a real feeling for beauty and history in the Sussex country-side. But certainly my first two published novels, crude as they are, are master-pieces in comparison. One might say that the chief promise of those schoolgirl tales lies in the fact that they were written—that I should have had the perseverance and devotion to cover all those endless sheets of paper without any encouragement beyond that given me by my own naïve delight in my performance.

I do not know when I first came to think of publication. I certainly had no idea of it when I started to write my first published novel, *The Tramping Methodist.* I can remember exactly how that novel began—there is the clearest picture of it in my mind.

I am lying in bed—in a high, shapeless feather bed—in a room in a farm-house known as Botvyle. The window looks into a farmyard, and at right-angles to it "the old part of the house" juts out. The blind is drawn, but through its papery paleness I can see the outline of the old black and white gable, and on the peak of the gable sits the shadow of a robin. At that moment a number of vague things rush together in my mind—

they have been lying scattered about it for some time, but now they suddenly cohere into a purpose. I shall write a novel called *The Romance of a Methodist*, all about the wanderings of a Methodist preacher through the country I love best—Brede, Ewhurst, Ticehurst and the Rother Valley, and perhaps away across the Kent Ditch to Rolvenden and Benenden and Tenterden. . . . It shall be a real, full-length novel, filling at least ten of the penny exercise books, and when it is finished I shall make a fair copy of it, with red-ink margins, as I made of *Iden*, and give it to my mother. I shall illustrate it, too, with photographs, and there shall be a robin in it.

I cannot remember exactly how or when this purpose changed to the more ambitious one of writing the book for publication. But change it did, as well as the title, at some time and for some reason in the course of the following year. I told nobody of my plan either before or after it changed. Everyone was used to seeing me writing, and everyone knew better than to ask me what I was writing about.—SHEILA KAYE-SMITH, *Three Ways Home*, 1937, pp. 46–51

General

Those of us who started to publish novels a few years before the War have, I think, always been handicapped. The generation before us—the Bennett Wells Galsworthy generation—had a settled world to get their pictures from. The generation after us—Virginia Woolf, Aldous Huxley, David Garnett—were able to give colour to all the mad ideas of that extraordinary post-war period without an embarrassing consciousness of a world that had once been alive to them and now was dead. It has been Sheila Kaye-Smith's virtue, as I think it has been the virtue of Francis Brett-Young and Frank Swinnerton, to make her novels timeless. That is not to say that the post-war generation may not, for the moment, think her novels old-fashioned both in aim and technique, but it means, I believe, that fifty years from now she will still be readable when many of the novelists of this particular 'moment' will be old-fashioned.

She deals in timeless things, the soil, trees, rivers, corn, food and drink. She has timeless themes, birth, death, love, jealousy, patience, maternity, friendship. In those books of hers that I like best—*Joanna Godden, Sussex Gorse, Green Apple Harvest, The George and the Crown*—she touches one's heart very deeply as though one were hearing news of one's own kin.

But best of all, she is a creator of a little world. If there is one certain passport for a novelist towards immortality, I think it is this—that in these books a world is created, a world with its own towns, streams, roads, hills, farms and ancient houses, a world whose citizens have a cosmic life of their own, a life related to other worlds but coloured uniquely in their own colour.

She is one of the very few living novelists in England who have done this—Galsworthy and Bennett, E. M. Forster, Brett-Young, very few more.

I am also old-fashioned enough to like her work because she has a tale to tell. Although I care also for the modern type of novel that deals mainly in ideas, I find that, for re-reading, a tale is an advantage. Ideas, or rather the latest shaping of them, have an odd way of suddenly withering so that when you turn your back to them they have the yellow air of a faded photograph.

Sheila Kaye-Smith because she is old-fashioned is never out of fashion. Her characters are true of any time and all time. Her England is immortal and she is always a creator.—HUGH WALPOLE, "Sheila Kaye-Smith: A Note," *Sheila Kaye-Smith*, 1929, pp. 7–9

⟨A⟩t their best Sheila Kaye-Smith's novels, though they do not surprise, have the merit of an honest and faithful reporting on experience. Her Sussex is realistically presented, her subject matter being for the most part the lives and ambitions of small farmers; and, although she has a love for old customs and traditions, she accepts the twentieth-century world without complaint (in this an exception among rural writers) though not without criticism. In *The End of the House of Alard* (1923), one of her more popular and more stereotyped novels, she portrays an ancient aristocratic family adapting to change through the various compromises and revolts of the younger generation. The eldest son, putting the estate before personal inclination, deserts his true love and marries money. The theme is Trollopian though the resolution—suicide—is not. One of the daughters turns down the man she loves because he is not good enough for the family, while her younger sister marries a local farmer and has to adjust her life accordingly. The youngest son becomes a garage hand and, later, a monk: on his accession to the title he decides to sell the estate. There is a constant stress on the stultifying nature of mere conformity to tradition, a serious questioning of such values as family loyalty. But in the sequel, *The Ploughman's Progress* (1933), Gervase Alard's altruistic action comes in for sharp criticism. As one of the independent farmers writes to him,

> You took the land away from the squires to give it to the yeomen, but I don't suppose you will be broken-hearted to hear that the yeomen have found your gift too expensive and have in their turn handed it over to the speculative builder (on the edges) and to desolation (in the midst).

This book, a thoughtful treatment of the changing agricultural conditions of the time, is a characteristic rural novel of the 1930s; but the conventional incidents and characterisation make it compare unfavourably with the less obviously polished work of A. G. Street and Adrian Bell. . . .

Sheila Kaye-Smith's writing has the merit of evoking not only a contemplative's feeling for landscape but also the actual feel of working the land. *Joanna Godden* is a faithfully drawn picture of a young woman farmer; indeed, it contains more than the portrait of Joanna herself, and portrays a whole community, the other marsh farmers, the clergy, the labourers, the squires, as well as the impact of the world of the town, above all the world of social fashion as mediated through Joanna's younger sister Ellen, whom she succeeds in educating into a way of thought and feeling hostile to all that the farm stands for. The world of the farm is the world of honesty, of work as a source of life and not simply as a means towards it: it represents the positive in the author's scale of values. In a characteristic passage she portrays both Joanna and that for which she stands:

> Father Lawrence came to see her one April day when the young lambs were bleating on the sheltered innings and making bright clean spots of white beside the ewes' fog-soiled fleeces, when the tegs had come down from their winter keep inland, and the sunset fell in long golden slats across the first water-green grass of spring. The years had aged him more than they had aged Joanna—the marks on her face were chiefly weather marks, token of her exposure to marsh suns and winds, and of her own ruthless applications of yellow soap. Behind them was a little of the hardness which comes when a woman has to fight many battles and has won her victories, largely through the sacrifice of her resources. The lines on his face were mostly those of his own humour and other people's sorrows, he had exposed himself perhaps not enough to the weather and too much to

the world, so that where she had fine lines and a fundamental hardness, he had heavy lines like the furrows of a ploughshare, a softness beneath them like the fruitful soil that the share turns up.

This is beautifully done: two worlds of experience are here related and shown to be complementary. Sheila Kaye-Smith's own Christian convictions are, however, subdued to a more general concern with the values of a Christian humanism—her study of religious fanaticism in *Green Apple Harvest*, for example, has more to do with its effects on her pitiful protagonist than with the rights and wrongs of his belief. Where her own specific convictions obtrude they are ecclesiastical, as in the portrait of the young Anglo-Catholic priest in *The End of the House of Alard* and of the older one in *Shepherds in Sackcloth* (1930), which are sympathetic accounts of the impact made by the Oxford Movement in the country districts. . . .

Sheila Kaye-Smith was the first twentieth-century English novelist to attempt an entirely naturalistic picture of the rural community. In comparing her novels with those of Eden Phillpotts and John Trevena one is aware not only of her greater literary proficiency and tact, but also of a fundamental difference in approach. Sheila Kaye-Smith's Sussex is far less isolated from the contemporary urban world than are Phillpotts's and Trevena's Devonshire and Cornwall. Partly, of course, this is a matter of geography: the landscape configuration produces a different kind of peasant type. But it is also a matter of the way in which the rural community are presented. In the novels of Phillpotts and Trevena the peasant figures are drawn more than life-size, but Sheila Kaye-Smith's farmers and labourers are part of the same social world and moral world as her squires and parsons. And this difference is reflected in the technique, style and presentation of her novels, which are indistinguishable from others of the same period on more urban or psychological themes. As Katherine Mansfield shrewdly observed, reviewing *Green Apple Harvest*, two hands were at work:

> One is the country hand, scoring the dialect, and the other is the town hand, hovering over the wild flowers and pointing out the moon like the 'blown petal' of a cherry tree.

Whereas Phillpotts and Trevena, and even Walpole, have a sense of inner purpose, of private vision and creative obsession, the world of Sheila Kaye-Smith opens out to nothing beyond itself. Balanced, likable, observant within limits, and highly readable, her books in the end fail to put the rural theme to more than a local and particular use. They remain regional in interest just as they are regional in setting.—GLEN CAVALIERO, "Literary Regionalism: Hugh Walpole, Sheila Kaye-Smith," *The Rural Tradition in the English Novel 1900–1930*, 1977, pp. 73–80

Works

Were Miss Kaye-Smith a painter, we should be inclined to say that we do not feel she has yet made up her mind which it is that she wishes most to paint—whether landscape or portraits. Which is it to be? Landscape—the blocking-in of a big difficult scheme, the effort required to make it appear substantial and convincing, the opportunity it gives her for the bold, sweeping line—it is plain to see how strongly this attracts her. Portraits—there is a glamour upon the human beings she chooses which fascinates her, and which she cannot resist. Why should she not be equally at home with both? What is her new novel *Tamarisk Town* but an attempt to see them in relation to each other? And yet, in retrospect, there is her town severely and even powerfully painted, and there are her portraits, on the same canvas, and yet so out of it, so separate that the onlooker's attention is persistently divided—it flies between the two, and is captured by neither.

Her theme is the development of a small Sussex town into a select seaside resort, patronized by the wealthy and aristocratic, not on account of its natural beauties alone, but because of the taste and judgment with which its reformation has been achieved. There is a time when it seems established in its enchanting prosperity for ever, but the hour of its triumph contains the seeds of its downfall. Very gradually, and then more swiftly, it is attacked by vulgarians, who are allowed to have their way, until at the end, wretched, shoddy, decayed little place that it is become, it is the scene of a brawl between drunken trippers. *Sic transit gloria Marlingate.*

It is, of course, absurd to imagine that Marlingate could grow, come to flower, blow to seed, without the aid of man, and yet at the moments when Miss Kaye-Smith is least conscious of the forces that govern it, she is at her happiest. Wandering at will in the Assembly rooms, in the beautiful little Town Park, along the white, gleaming parade, in the woods at French Landing, her style is very natural and unforced, and, until the beginning of the disintegrating process, her touch is light. But, after all, this is only the landscape half. Let us examine the 'portraits.' The chief is Edward Moneypenny, creator of Marlingate, who, at the age of twenty-eight, is in a position powerful enough to determine the future of the town. This curious young man, with his shock of white hair, coal-black eyes and black side whiskers, is, for all his cynical aloofness, in love with Marlingate; we are to believe that, until he meets with the little wild governess, he has never known what it was to feel for anything more responsive than a new block of houses or a bandstand. But she, Morgan, Morgan le Fay, running out of the wood with dead leaves in her hair, very nearly makes havoc of his resolute ambition in the old, old way.

> . . . She had crept towards him, drooping like a wild hyacinth in her blue gown. Then suddenly she flung her body straight, flung back her head, her arms were round him soft and strong as fox-glove stalks, and her hair, falling loose, trailed on his lips till it tasted sweet as syllabub.

But while she is still a woodland elf, his old love wins:

> He turned back to Marlingate, as a man who has left his work to watch from the window an organ-grinder with a performing monkey turns to his desk again.

Years pass, and all his dreams are realized. Royalty has put its special blessing upon Marlingate, and Moneypenny is Mayor, in cocked hat and black and crimson robes. And this is the hour chosen by the enchantress for her return—in scarlet. 'Crimson and silky, a peony trailing its crinkled petals . . . it came.'

This time the long, slanting eyes eat him up with their spells, and she has her way with him.

> Then she dropped her sunshade, which rolled in a whirl of scarlet down the slope, like a poppy falling, and stretching out her hands, took his white, struggle-worn face into their cool palms, drawing it down to her silent mouth.

It is a matter for wonder that, in spite of all the many pages describing the progress of their guilty love, in spite of the tremendous pains taken by the author to depict the agonies of Moneypenny upon his discovering that sweet Morgan le Fay holds in contempt, nay hates, his beloved Marlingate, and the other tremendous pains taken to show Morgan's despair upon realizing that Edward will not flee with her to foreign parts— we are never once moved by these two creatures. Marionettes they are, and marionettes they remain, jigging in a high fierce light that Miss Kaye-Smith would convince us is the fire of passion, until the last puppet-quarrel and the last glimpse of the heroine, 'half under the water, half trailing on the rock . . . something which, from the top of the cliff, looked like a dead crimson leaf.' This extreme measure is for love of Moneypenny, who, at first, is properly grateful for his freedom. Again he is a man like a town walking, until one day he is filled with the idea that his first love is fattening upon the dead body of his second love, and that, after all, a woman is more to be desired than bricks and mortar. This starts working passion number three—he will kill that which killed her, and so have his revenge.

Here, to our thinking, the book ends. All that is going to happen has happened; we are at the top of the hill. Below us lies Marlingate, in its prosperity, 'lying there licked by the sun,' and gazed upon by the man who has made it, and is about to unmake it. But the author is, if we may be pardoned the expression, as fresh as when she started. New characters appear—a wife for Moneypenny, a little wooden son who has time to grow up and marry the daughter of Morgan le Fay (so like, yet so unlike) and to live his father's history all over again before Marlingate is destroyed. And the years roll by, unbroken, heavy, like waves slapping against the promenade, the vulgar pier, before Miss Kaye-Smith is content to leave Marlingate to its fate.

How does it happen that a writer, obviously in love with writing, is yet not curious? This is the abiding impression left us by Miss Kaye-Smith; she is satisfied to put into the mouths and the hearts and minds of her characters the phrase, the emotion, the thought that 'fits' the situation, with the result that it does not seem to matter whether they speak, feel or think. Nothing is gained by it. They are just what they are. The plot's the thing—and having decided upon it she gets her team together and gives out the parts. There is but to speak them. And into the hand of Morgan le Fay she thrusts a scarlet umbrella, she throws a cherry cloak about her and clothes her in a scarlet dress—and sets her going.—KATHERINE MANS-FIELD, "A Landscape with Portraits" (1919), *Novels and Novelists*, ed. J. Middleton Murry, 1930, pp. 77–80

. . . *Susan Spray* . . . is set back in time and the setting was taken from the laboring classes. But it is built upon a theme which belongs to all time and all classes of women. Susan Spray was a girl who was reared in an atmosphere of poverty and religious excitement. She manifested early in her childhood a tendency to play for attention. The only audience she could have was the audience of the little religious sect to which her parents belonged. She made the most of it. She saw remarkable visions. She spoke in the meeting. She married a man who admired her. The play for attention went on apace. Though the author does not say so in plain language, it is inferred that Susan's marriage was no great upheaval of passion to her. The man died. Her baby died. Had the baby lived, all her dissatisfaction would have veered into a Messianic fixation upon the child. She was injured at childbirth and could have no more children. The visions and the preaching continued. Then she met a he-man who took her to London with him, amused her, and gave her emotional heaven and emotional hell, and generally treated her to a period of intense femininity. She did no preaching during that time. The man was unfaithful and she left him, and all her visions returned. Step

by step she rose to them and became a power in the religious form to which she was accustomed. The man was presumably drowned at sea and Susan found another man who had money enough to endow her with a temple for her adherents and the position of religious authority and utter superiority which she craved. Just before her marriage to this man she learned that the other man had not been drowned, but so intense was her need for the attention she would get from her temple and her leadership that she went through a bigamous marriage and trusted to her luck to see her through. For by this time she was in the full power of her fantasy and saw herself anointed by God, and in no need, therefore, to trouble about the small laws of mankind regarding marriage.

This is a powerfully drawn portrait of abnormal functioning in woman as related to sexual and play satisfaction. Susan was the plain girl child. It was her only chance for attention and she took it. It was suspended while she was living with her second husband. It was resumed in a revenge-defense mechanism when he failed her. Her whole life after him was to be a revenge-defense mechanistic gesture. She insulted him by her bigamous marriage. She became, according to her own lights and in the only way open to her, a famous woman. Sheila Kaye-Smith by this portrait proclaimed herself a deep student of women and of their psychology. It is probably the history of many women who have achieved fame or what approaches fame in their own immediate circle. It portrays unquestionably the preliminary stages of the development of religious matriarchy in a woman. For indubitably Susan Spray would come to rule her believers with the matriarchal rod. It opens up a whole field of speculation upon the data behind any woman who in our time has reached a pinnacle of power in religious sects and their platforms. It is, for all its literary power, a grave study of matriarchal danger. Step by step Susan was led to see herself as the center of a group. From a simple need for attention she moved out into a complex need for dominance until the whole universe so far as she was concerned had to revolve around her satisfaction.

Though the story is set back in an earlier century in its time element, it belongs to the present because of one unescapable fact—the lost generation of men—and the corresponding generation of women who are under the necessity of finding abnormal satisfaction. Whether in religion, in business, in the professions, or in the community life generally, there is full cause for the development of matriarchy in women. Power is relatively easy to get. And the matriarchal temperament slips up on women almost imperceptibly. Professions such as all the amplifications of social service lie temptingly open to women in which they can so easily forget the fine art of minding one's own business. Social service is only a step or so away from community control, and community control is only a step behind a matriarchal society and government. It might be admirable. Certainly it would be a change. But every woman who heads that way should be under the compulsion of studying her own private affairs and determining the position of the thin line between her own need of dominance and the good of the public. And the greatest help in this lies in the tentative doctrines of the Viennese school of psychotherapy. So much is this true that unquestionably the whole development of the present phase of the feminist movement will lie in the acceptance, whether partial or whole, or the negation, whether partial or whole, of these tenets by women.—MARGARET LAWRENCE, "Matriarchs," *The School of Femininity*, 1936, pp. 236–39

G. B. STERN
"The Heroines of Sheila Kaye-Smith"
Yale Review, October 1925, pp. 204–8

The heroines of Sheila Kaye-Smith's novels pass before me slowly, one by one, as in a procession. Shadows, at first; but they grow stronger; their outlines clearer. It is almost inconceivable that the creator of those first unreal, bloodless puppets, Ruth of *The Tramping Methodist*, Theodora of *Starbrace*, Maggie and Lorena of *The Challenge to Sirius*, should also be the creator of—Joanna Godden, most of her readers will cry exultantly, as this brilliant buxom woman-farmer, with the ambitions of a man, and a woman's soul, tender and white and hidden as the inside of a horse-chestnut in October, pauses for a moment in the centre of the stage along which the procession is trooping; pauses, conscious that she, of all the others, is likeliest to live and be remembered. Joanna Godden!—but quite alone in my own corner, unheard, perhaps, in the universal shout of admiration, I shall be piping the name of my own favorite, Morgan Wells, who was loved by the mayor of Tamarisk Town.

Ruth, Theodora, Emily—no, they died quickly, for they were woven painfully, laboriously, out of the author's mind, never from pure inspiration. She had as yet no interest in drawing women. Her men, from the very beginning, were full-fledged, full-blooded, lusty creatures, with will and force and personality that swept the story along to its usual tragic end; for the early Sheila Kaye-Smith revelled in tenebrous glooms and horrors. In six or seven novels her heroines, though differing a little in individuality from book to book, were yet entirely subservient; to use stage jargon, their appointed part was to "feed" the man; to serve him, to help him towards achievement or failure.

The first attempt, a gallant but unsuccessful one, to create a heroine who should not be entirely of plasticine, was in *Isle of Thorns*. Sally Odiarne was unsuccessful because she was cheap and tawdry, and smelt of the Chelsea studio, whereas she was meant to be modern, vivid, and adventurous. Yet in her you might recognize that dawning interest in woman as a separate entity from man, that was to lead presently to Morgan Wells, Joanna Godden, and Stella Mount. In *Three against the World* the wistful little school-girl, Tony, is hardly a bright enough candle to draw the eye in a book which in itself was so far below the standard of all the other books to come, that we marvelled at that masterpiece, *Sussex Gorse*, published directly afterwards. *Sussex Gorse* enshrines no one heroine, but a group of women who are all interesting, except Alice Jury, who might officially claim the title of heroine, but reveals herself as merely bright and ladylike, and what, in our childhood, we used to call "preachy-preachy." It is pleasant, even luxurious, nowadays, to dwell on these inadequate figures among Sheila Kaye-Smith's characters; while saving up, as a child saves up the currants from the cake, our knowledge of her successes in the future. Naomi, the wife of Reuben Backfield, who patiently has to bear him son after son until she sinks under the weight and dies, might be taken as symbolical of the author's queer sadic delight in showing woman the victim of man's more cosmic ambitions. We have had this theme sounded before; it was to be sounded again, even after Naomi had been sacrificed to the great boor, Boarzell. Maggie, in *The Challenge to Sirius*, was equally sacrificed to Frank's lust for travel and experience. Morgan, in *Tamarisk Town*, saddest victim of all to Money-penny's frantic desire to be sponsor of a fashionable seaside town. Finally, in *The End of the House of Alard*, Stella Mount had to be set aside to suffer, while the last squire clung

obdurately to his last lands. It is of significant interest that never once does the ambition of the man, to which is sacrificed the heart and individuality of the woman, take the form of art. Most women novelists are especially fond of showing art as an altar, and love the votive offering; but all these lusty strenuous adventurers go stumbling and swinging after the soil and the stars, fighting, and religion, and the soil again.

The most vivid little sketch of a woman in Miss Kaye-Smith's earlier novels is in *Sussex Gorse*—Reuben Backfield's second wife, Rose; pretty Rose, with her longings for trivial jollities, and happiness that was all of the flesh. Rose was altogether sensual, and altogether charming; she belongs to the group who find their joy in things they may touch, in things they may see, most certainly in lips they may kiss. There is something in all of us that responds to the irresponsible heroine. Not so many books ahead, in *The End of the House of Alard*, we are to discover, in Stella Mount, a perfect blend of the heroine who loves spiritual things, and the heroine who loves material things; but then, they were still sharply divided; the author had not yet conceived the subtle art of mingling body and soul. In her next book after *Sussex Gorse*, *The Challenge to Sirius*, we encounter again one of those terrible lapses into gentility; Lorena, a ladylike young woman with a pale pure profile, and that ingratiating type of thin Italian voice at the piano, which one associates, somehow, with a swanlike neck and drooping eyelids.

Then we pass on into *Little England*. There are three women in *Little England*: Thyrza, Ivy, and Nell; country women, and farm women. Thyrza was well done; she was a maternal woman; you could picture her always with both lover and child lying softly in the crook of her arm. And so, indeed, we leave her, in the last lines of this, the most tender of all Sheila Kaye-Smith's books; and find ourselves face to face with *Tamarisk Town*.

I have often marvelled whence exquisite Morgan le Fay came dancing down into the author's mind. She is less a heroine, in the familiar sense of the word, than the spirit of all intangible romance and beauty, that sometimes steals very near to a man, and then, when he puts out his hand for it, melts away again. For Edward Moneypenny, Mayor of Marlingate, was after solid and yet frangible things. His dream and his ambition were municipal translations of Reuben Backfield's; Reuben had desired to tame the untamed moor and grow oats upon its stoniest crest; Moneypenny dreamed and schemed for a fair town beside the sea, and to this end he sat upon town councils, and examined maps for the erection of an esplanade and a band-stand. Morgan Wells was a little governess who married another town councillor, after Moneypenny had set her aside; developed graciously into a Lady of the mid-Victorian Period; and then threw herself down from the edge of a cliff into the sea, because Moneypenny had broken through her spells, and she could not bear to live and watch his love grow worldly-cold. The deep interest of this portrait is that suddenly, quite suddenly and perfectly, Sheila Kaye-Smith has realized woman-alive! It was a paradox that her first real woman should hardly be a woman at all, but the embodiment of her creed that a woman in man's life stands for something that takes him away from his appointed task, whatever that may be. Morgan stands for the wild woods, and the wild sea; when she dies, halfway through the book, the pages die with her, and become dead and flabby. She lives again in the end, when we realize that she, and not the town, has triumphed; that all his life long, Moneypenny has lacked her, as a man who cannot live by roofs and chimneys alone.

It is impossible, in a few lines, to recall the many pictures of Morgan le Fay, delicate brilliant pictures, that we carry away with us, a precious freight, from the reading of *Tamarisk Town.* Leave her then for her great contrast, Joanna Godden.

Between the two, lay *Green-Apple Harvest*; but in *Green-Apple Harvest* no woman matters vitally except Gipsy Hannah, who, again voicing and re-emphasizing the creed, is less of an individual than a symbol of the warm flesh. It is curious how many of the women, though none of the men, in these novels, could take part in old morality plays, as abstract virtues or vices.

But Joanna Godden, beyond all doubt or argument, is neither victim, spirit, temptation, nor is she submissive in any way to a man's central figure. She, for the first time in all this procession of heroines, is the actual book itself, from beginning to end; a woman who, with all her domineering will and mind and energies, was bent on becoming a farmer, and was beaten again and again by being too much woman; and who finally, at the end, became a heroine, in the word's finest aspect, in that she was given strength for a renunciation beyond that of man in any of the books. For not only did she renounce her farm and her lands, but also her deeply valued respectability, and her hope of marriage with "the little singing clerk," so that she might devote all that was left of her life to her illegitimate child. Joanna was symbolic of nothing; she was very much flesh and blood, with her hot, practical speech; her pride in glowing colors, and fine clothes, and good eating; in the smack of vulgarity in nearly all her doings. At times, when Joanna was most loudly trying, one could sympathize quite poignantly even with the priggish and refined younger sister, Ellen Godden. Yet we love Joanna, and grant her literature's immortality, for two simple strong reasons; that she was human, and that she blundered.

"What you are doesn't matter in love, but it matters in marriage." So spoke Ernley Munk, with a flash of wisdom, in *The George and the Crown*—and that is why the heroine of Sheila Kaye-Smith's latest novel is not the principal woman character, the ubiquitous Belle Shackford, an untidy, beautiful blowse, without much meaning to her emotional gestures, selfishly grabbing at love's physical warmth and possession, caring little whom she sacrificed, and with no ideals to turn passion's fire and flame into steadfast starshine; but Rose Falla, the child whom Daniel Sheather marries during his brief sojourn in Sark. Rose is like an exquisite tender gift, to us as well as to her husband. And when he loses her, we sigh, bereaved as he is; more bereaved, indeed, for Daniel finds comfort again: "Was it indeed true, then, that the woman of his dream who sat in an inn stable with her child upon her knee, was not Belle, nor even Rose, but just any woman, every woman, whose heart was warm and whose eyes were kind?"

Again and again, in the last group of Sheila Kaye-Smith's books, we have been startled by achievement which her early books taught us to believe could never be hers. Stella Mount is the reply to those who, while admitting Morgan to be an elfin sprite of the woods, and Joanna a strapping woman of the soil, yet asserted that she had not the power to present to us a normally attractive, human girl of her own class. The unspoken challenge was accepted, and the result was the heroine of "The End of the House of Alard." Stella is too recent a creation to need much recalling. She was ardently religious, but her religion did not make her dreary, for hers was also a gay, yet eminently decent, outlook on the world; she is, indeed, in spirit, the very best type of the gallant modern girl; when her heart is broken, she can still crank up the engine of her father's motor-car, because she knows it has to be done. Her naïve lack of respect for the dignity of the Alard family was delicious; though she had enough imagination to love the home of the Sussex squires, which was crumbling into financial ruin; enough human recklessness not to worry if it did crumble, so long as she and Peter might marry and "be together always," which was her sweeter substitute for "live happy ever after."

Margaret Kennedy

1896–1967

The daughter of a distinguished lawyer, Margaret Kennedy was born in London on April 23, 1896. After attending Cheltenham College, she studied history at Somerville College, Oxford; on graduating in 1919, she rejoined her parents in St. Ives, Cornwall, and wrote a textbook on modern European history. Turning to fiction, she published *The Ladies of Lyndon* in 1923, and the following year enjoyed an overwhelming success with *The Constant Nymph*. After her marriage to a lawyer in 1925, she spent most of the rest of her life in Kensington, London.

Red Sky at Morning appeared in 1927, followed by a sequel to *The Constant Nymph, The Fool of the Family* (1930). Apart from novels, Kennedy wrote plays, notably *Escape Me Never* (1933), and from 1938 to 1950 was mainly occupied with film work. *Troy Chimneys* (1953) won her the James Tait Black Award. She was also active as a critic, writing a biography, *Jane Austen*, in 1950, and a study of fiction and its status, *The Outlaws on Parnassus* (1958).

After the death of her husband in 1964 Kennedy moved to Oxfordshire, where she died on July 31, 1967.

Miss Kennedy has undertaken (in *The Constant Nymph*) to describe the conflict between the ferocious egotism of the creative artist and those who are the unfortunate victims of his love, and though she begins in the mood of sophisticated farce, with a description of the disorganized household of another artist, she means to rise to a considerable height in the description of passion and to achieve a moving pathos through presenting the fate of two women condemned to love this man of no passion save the passion for music. Yet she does not, so it seems to me, do either of these things supremely well. The desired fusion does not take place. What we get is only a preliminary farce succeeded by a tragedy which would be readily seen to be executed in a manner no more than reasonably competent were it not for the piquancy of the contrast and the fact that such a contrast happens to have a very definite appeal to contemporary taste.

In the case of Mr. Huxley it is impossible to separate his farce from his tragedy or to treat them other than as parts of the same whole, and in the case of Mr. Arlen—though his passion seems to me a good deal less genuine—the same thing is true. But *The Constant Nymph* falls apart, so that if one is to discuss it one must discuss its farce and its drama as separate entities. The first is undoubtedly good. The section which deals with the family known as "Sanger's Circus," and describes in its full development that tendency toward bad manners which the cultivation of music, even more than the cultivation of any of the other arts, seems to produce, is effective and funny; but the fun soon dies away and the author enters upon a serous analysis of artistic ruthlessness which is sometimes good and sometimes, especially when it is presented, through the action of the characters, stiffly unreal. The persons are all of heroic stature and they are mastered, so we are told, by volcanic passions; but it is difficult for the reader to feel them, and we are compelled—a fatal thing for a novel—to take the author's word for their existence. When we are told, for instance, that almost at first sight an English girl of conventional upbringing falls desperately in love with our hero and wishes to marry him a few days later we have nothing except the word of the author to make it seem credible, in spite of the fact that upon a belief in this passion hangs the whole effect of the story. Thus we are given the outline of a great novel, but that outline is not filled by living characters or surrounded by that atmosphere of convincing passion which alone could achieve the effect contemplated. When, for example, the author says:

> With an increasing disgust she listened to their conversation. Tony jested with the men, while old Rachel, with hoarse chuckles, supplied occasional anecdotes which always smacked of her calling. Even in the impudent, childish remarks thrown in by Teresa and Sebastian, there was the same want of decorum,

her method is dangerously like that of Mr. Savonarola Brown, who wrote in his stage directions: "Enter Boccaccio and Benvenuto Cellini, making remarks highly characteristic of themselves, but hardly audible in the terrific thunderstorm." And surely no one who had not taken very good care to forestall an accusation of intolerable naïveté would dare, as Miss Kennedy does, to precipitate her catastrophe by having one of the heroines die suddenly of a convenient heart failure just as she is eloping with the hero.

The trouble with Miss Kennedy seems to me not that she lacks talent but that she has very definitely fallen between two stools, that she has failed to make up her mind soon enough whether she wished to write a tragic farce or a genuinely heroic novel of the sort which she ends by attempting. Evidently she is familiar with the work of the contemporary English sophisticates; but if she has not already done so she might profitably read Jacob Wassermann's *The Goose Man*. It is a novel which deals with a theme almost identical with hers, and it does all the things which her novel does not. To read it is to believe it, as one must of necessity believe those things which one has experienced; to read *The Constant Nymph* is no more than to be told that certain things took place. The difference is the difference between a great novel and one which, whatever intelligence it may reveal, is not in the most important sense a novel at all.—Joseph Wood Krutch, "A Minority Report," *Nation*, April 15, 1925, p. 434

Few aspects of Anglo-Saxon art plead for critical satire so urgently as the English School of Oratorio Musicians. We have seen these august gentlemen, interrupting their composition of a Chorus of High Priests to partake of tea and toast within their cloistered gardens. We have watched them at their daughters' ballad concerts, nodding happily at the hopeful development of home-grown talent. We have read letters to their publishers, promising a complete fair copy of Boadicea's Victory within ten days, and begging that two hundred impressions shall be delivered in ample time for the joint choirs to get into training for Michaelmas. Choral unions, female quartets that play from three to six on alternate Wednesdays, competitive soirées where the prize goes to the hostess bagging the largest lion: we have known them all and waited for some skilled ironic pen.

And now Miss Margaret Kennedy writes a novel ⟨*The Constant Nymph*⟩ so fearlessly unrespectable in its sympathies, so alluring in its characterizations, so romantic and so true that all England buys it, reads it, and promptly bursts into smiles of wholesome bitterness.

Cleverly Miss Kennedy has made her musical genius an Englishman, Albert Sanger, asserting at the outset that he "was barely known to the musical public of Great Britain" since that public is "disinclined to believe that great men are occasionally born in Hammersmith." More cleverly still she has presented the home surroundings of her hero as a thoroughly disorganized chalet in the Austrian Tyrol, where the children of two wives and a mistress of the great Sanger help him to his death on page 76 in an atmosphere of untidy petticoats, irregular brandy and inadequate pork.

The rest of the book shows the spirit of Sanger, brutal, passionate, disorderly, and sound, chafing at the small satisfactions of England. Sanger is dead, but his influence is alive and at war. And though this main struggle never for a moment loses its central place on Miss Kennedy's stage, it winds about itself the garb of fiction, and beguiles the reader with many personalities and at least one acute triangle.

Sanger's disciple, Lewis Dodd—also, cleverly, an Englishman—marries the charming English bourgeois cousin of some of the Sanger children and goes to live in a well-ordered house at Strand-on-the-Green. Three of the children are sent to English schools where "they can turn out a splendid type." But the buoyant natures of Tessa and Lina and Sebastian will not bear such an imprint. They run away. Even Strand-on-the-Green is better than enforced hockey and Jardins sous la Pluie played fortissimo in an adjacent cubicle.

They bring back to Lewis a vivid picture of the life he has left, of the genius to which he may become untrue. His wife, Florence, scents the dissatisfaction, and tracks it down with Anglo-Saxon thoroughness into personal rivalry. Lewis must be in love with Tessa. Her jealousy is fanned by two factors: her own love for her husband and her knowledge that she has not understood him. As an alumna of the English School of Oratorio Musicians she has tried to lionize him, and he will not be lionized. Her consistent persecution of her little rival precipitates the final and fatal elopement. The curtain falls and the struggle is undecided. Genius has escaped the shackles of convention and order to fall by its own impotence.

It is not often that the author allows her thesis a naked demonstration, but in one scene the fiction is stripped down and the main issue shines out. Florence Dodd has traced her husband to the home of his old associates:

Music, with all these people, came first; that was why they talked about it as if nobody else had any right to it. Once Florence had liked them all too well; now that she understood them better she was frightened of them. She wanted to challenge them, to make a demonstration of her power, to call them back to that world of necessity and compromise which they so sublimely ignored, but with which they would ultimately have to reckon. After all she was the strongest. She had order and power on her side. They were nothing but a pack of rebels.

An author who can so clearly state one cause, and yet throw her sympathy and hero worship to the other has herself solved a compromise. She has written a satirical novel, and securely pinioned her subject to the wall for all to laugh at, and yet she has lured a public composed largely of such subjects to read her book and thus to laugh at themselves.

Given such a large order to fill, it is small wonder that Miss Kennedy has relegated literary style to the background. At her hands the English language becomes a serviceable medium, coin of the realm, useful as a means to an end. And if her shillings and pence transfer easily into marks or francs and buy for the reader convincing pictures of Munich and Brussels, she is tempted to satisfaction. Why should they also jingle as numismatic curios?

Though said to be under thirty, Miss Kennedy can bring to her characters a sympathy that magnifies its object without distortion. Her situations are developed with humor and her descriptions with restraint. A Russian ballet master is writing to his wife:

> "Spring has already come to this charming valley, and the meadows round me are full of . . ."
> He had a look at the meadows around him, but could not determine what it was that filled them. There were a lot of blue flowers and some yellow, but as these were neither camellias nor gardenias he could not put a name to them. He compromised:
> "full of a thousand blooms of every color."

Similarly is her dialogue a significant and transparent lens by which her characters are elucidated. She refrains from saying things about people which they themselves do not say. A single exception has been found in the profanity of the young Sangers. The reader is continually told of their lewd habits of speech, but rarely given a chance to hear more than an isolated "damn."

One other fault casts a small shade on the book's importance: its inappropriate and banal title. *The Constant Nymph* suggests a pastoral lyric, a romantic glimpse into a post-war drawing-room, even a ballerina's tragedy, but it does not convey the bitter fight between talent and genius, the harsh contrast between orderly, constructive calm and high revolt. Is this perhaps another subtle bit of compromise, one final bait to invite the bourgeoisie to their own funeral? For its success, at least, whether accidental or intended, one must admit appreciation.—MARY ELLIS OPDYCKE, NR, April 15, 1925, pp. 12–13

Here is Miss Margaret Kennedy's new novel ⟨*Red Sky at Morning*⟩, and one naturally asks oneself, Is it as good as *The Constant Nymph*, or less good, or better? A difficult question to answer. Certainly no book could make a more difficult debut than *Red Sky at Morning*, following and necessarily challenging comparison with a novel that was at once a popular success and a *succès d'estime*. The books have certain resemblances; *The Constant Nymph* opened, and its successor closes, with a large group of people compressed into surroundings too narrow for them. The friction engendered by this compression set in motion the earlier story and is instrumental in bringing about the catastrophe in this. For it is of the essence of Miss Kennedy's view of life that her characters are always in opposition to each other, and to intensify their mutual uncongeniality she naturally places them in circumstances in which they cannot possibly get out of each other's way.

Monk's Hall is a slightly more artificial rendezvous than Sanger's Chalet. The inmates of the latter were loosely bound together by ties of consanguinity; they lived under a patriarchal system. But Monk's Hall was a caprice of William Crowne's. He had plenty of money and little idea of what to do with it: so he bought the house which should have gone to his cousin Trevor, and established there not only Trevor, but a large company of unsuccessful and second-rate artists with their wives, mistresses and children. Not least important of these was his own wife Tilli, a sinister figure who seems to have married him out of an obscure wish to revenge herself on the whole male sex. A few miles away is the "other house," Water Hythe, the home of Catherine, Trevor's mother and William's aunt, a stronghold of Victorian respectability and intolerant conventionality. Catherine wishes that these leavings of Bohemia and riff-raff of the studios could be cleared out of Monk's Hall; but from convenience, from inertia, from positive malevolence, they continue to stay on. But they might have gone, and as the sufferings born of a distasteful contiguity grow apace, one asks oneself, Would they really have stayed, would common little Sally have lingered on to swallow Catherine's polite insults, would Trevor have stayed on, merely to be near Tilli, whom, though her lover, he really loathed?

Perhaps the answer to this lies in the consideration that while the World plays a part in *Red Sky at Morning*, and the Flesh a greater one, the Devil has perhaps the largest rôle of all. Several of the characters, Tilly, Sally, sometimes even Trevor and Catherine herself, seem to be animated by pure wickedness; there is something, malignant in their egoism, their extreme wilfulness. They are as dark and purposeful as beasts of prey. Beside them the Crowne twins, William and Emily, children of a murderer and brought up in the shadow of their father's crime, seem like angels of light: William is positively Shelleyan in his ignorance of base motives and his natural proclivity towards good ones.

Emily, whether as brilliant youthful poetess or dull safe wife of a country clergyman (as she became), is a less distinct figure. The Crownes begin by dominating the book. We see them taking the world by storm with their agreeable manners and their specious talents; we see them in their pathetic partnership, standing four-square to the hostility of the world which had petted and grown tired of them, which never forgot their origin nor would let them forget it. We see how the alliance is broken up, and how, lacking each other's support, they make a poor thing of their lives, one a tragic thing, the other a dull one. And we see, very horribly, the peculiarities of Norman Crowne beginning to stir in the too docile character of William.

Thus the Crownes are the thread on which the story is hung, but a thread which, till the final pages, becomes increasingly concealed and overlaid. In itself, the last scene is quite strong enough to end any book, so brief and cold and deadly is it. But its effect is a little weakened by the fact that, when it comes, not William, but the community at Monk's Hall, is beginning to usurp the centre of the stage. The dénouement seems meant for the other, earlier William, not this later one scarcely visible beneath the press of his creatures and dependents. Nor does it exactly clear up the Monk's Hall situation, except on the principle that so foul a sky clears not without a storm. And it makes it a little difficult to trace the figure in Miss Kennedy's carpet, for a figure we are determined to see, even if she has been equally resolute in leaving the figure out. Considered as a work of art the book shows its predecessor's merits, and shows them intensified. It creates a world of living people, who lend themselves to the imagination and at the same time compel it. They are people who can be talked about and discussed as though they were actually alive. They are so vital, so full of themselves at every moment, that their most casual encounter is a crisis. With the possible exception of William, they accumulate personality as the story goes on instead of shedding it, as happens to the characters of so many authors. They have immense momentum and solidity. But they seem to end with themselves.

Unlike Tessa, William Crowne is not a figure to which emotion naturally attaches itself, nor is there among the characters (as far as I could see) one who, by the possession of some universal, extra-personal attribute (such as Tessa's devotion) brings the whole bitter, melancholy, unforgettable story into a cadence which the lover of life can realize and take heart from. The antagonisms between human beings are presented with unremitting force, particularly the antagonism (if such it be) between the present and the previous generation. It is as though Miss Kennedy had been anxious to acquit herself of a charge of sentimentality, and gone to the further extreme. *Red Sky at Morning*, as its name suggests, is a book heavy with menace, doom and despair. It is intensely interesting and provocative; one's armour of emotional security is for ever being pierced by its darts, one's memory is dyed by its vivid colours. It establishes Miss Kennedy's reputation on an even firmer basis than did *The Constant Nymph*; for here we are in no danger of being beguiled into the indulgence of those emotions which, while we have them, minister to our self-complacency, assure us of charitable impulses, and persuade us to see the author's greatness reflected in our own. Miss Kennedy does not tempt us to identify ourselves with her characters, and if we did we should get no self-satisfaction. We could no more project ourselves into the story, for the sake of increasing our self-esteem or living a denied romantic existence remote from our own, than we could insinuate ourselves into the marble of the Venus of Milo and conceive ourselves equally beautiful and equally adored. Certainly *Red Sky at Morning* extends no consolation for and escape from life. It stands on its own merits, and they are of the first order.—L. P. HARTLEY, *SRL*, Nov. 5, 1927, pp. 628–30

The problem of what to do next after a popular success is almost insoluble. There are only three courses for a serious author: to try to write another, to try to win back the public of his early work, or to stop writing altogether. In the first case the new popular success is nearly always a failure; and where it succeeds, only condemns the author to a groove so that every book he writes must be exactly like his last; in the second he has to face the disappointment of the vast body of trash-reading public who admire a good book for the wrong reasons; and in the third he is condemned to watch the rise of new constellations as he prods the cattle on his farm.

There is no tragedy like that of the unintentional best seller. At first the boom is a delight. It is only afterwards that there seems something wrong; that the stupidity of the admirers finally discounts their praise, and that the protests of dogmatic readers, who do not usually read at all, begin to bully the author, and make him feel he is now an accepted entertainer, who having had his supper, is henceforth expected to sing. Meanwhile the early worshippers have left in a body—rats

indignant to remain on so unsinkable a ship. This is the public who will decide the fate of the author's sequel, and this is the public before which Miss Kennedy now appears.

Red Sky at Morning is not such a good book as *The Constant Nymph*, and yet it is a book that has certainly demanded progress to write. *The Constant Nymph* revealed a balance of qualities, a proportion very rare in that kind of work; it was obvious that Miss Kennedy could probably only proceed by stressing some particular side, her humour, her wit, her sentimentality, or her respect for life. *Red Sky at Morning* is about the same theme as *The Constant Nymph*, the sad fate of genius at the hands of vulgarity. The children of a brilliant murderer and of a successful critic are brought up together; all are literary, but the first two are rich and unpractical, the others scheming and poor. In post-War London, and at a country retreat, the genius is robbed by his cynical cousin whom finally he shoots for making love to his wife. There is no radical change to the moral of *The Constant Nymph*. There is even a transplanted Sanger's Circus, a brother and sister to play Lewis and Tessa, a husband like Jacob, a wife like Florence, and a great deal about implicit intimacy, destroyed by the second-rate contacts of life. The book has less charm, less economy, and less clearness than *The Constant Nymph*; the brother and sister are too unreal, the wife of one is too squalid, and the husband of the other too dull. The Sanger's Circus is almost intolerable when composed of needy grown-ups, transplanted to a Cotswold Valley. There is no character that is really sympathetic, but this one must excuse because it is the surest way in which the public will be discarded, the huge sentimental public, which it is a mark of genius to have bitten off but which it would be proof of a miracle to be able to chew.

Though the book as a whole is packed and blurred, the workmanship itself stands very high. The dialogue, the descriptions of English scenery, and the Greek chorus reflections on the theme are really an improvement on *The Constant Nymph*, and the details of the book reveal infinite care. The management of the title and of the allusions to the toy theatre are perfect examples of tragic irony; and the humour and insight of the author are delicate and sure. The ugly ducklings are too ugly for this to be a popular book, but what is rare in this kind of sequel, it is undoubtedly a promising one.

A Long Week-End is a story of two lovers and their frustrated attempt at consummation. The moral ending is a little thin, as if designed to placate some imaginary critic, but the manner of the story is perfect, and the comedy is delightfully told. It is important because it differs in kind from her other work and suggests that Miss Kennedy should perhaps let geniuses take care of themselves. These Ariel spirits battered by the world are finding too many biographers, while the brother and sister theme is likely to be sentimental unless it is carried to the lengths of Ford. Everyone, however, can look forward to Miss Kennedy's next book more than they will enjoy reading this, and meanwhile be glad to welcome her back to her early public, uninjured after her breathless but exciting outing in the larger world.—CYRIL CONNOLLY, *NS*, Nov. 12, 1927, p. 143

NICOLA BEAUMAN
From "Introduction"
The Ladies of Lyndon
1981, pp. ix–xix

Margaret Kennedy's name is inextricably linked with the title of her bestselling novel *The Constant Nymph*. Published in 1924 when she was twenty-eight, it soon, after six weeks of sluggish sales, caught the public imagination so forcibly that over the next five years a million copies were sold. The reviews, apart from a couple by two septuagenarian 'men of letters', were not particularly favourable and publicity as we know it did not exist; yet it touched a chord in the same way as did, for example, *The Four Feathers, Lost Horizon, The Citadel* or *Rebecca*.

To the eternal dismay of publishers, bestsellers are almost always chance creations and there is no obvious reason why *The Constant Nymph* was so hugely successful. Two things helped: the unforgettable Sanger family, and the intense passion with which the novel is imbued. Not the passion of sexuality, despair or longing but the passion of life (what used to be called spirit) and each individual manifestation of it. The underlying message of the book is that spirit and integrity are the only values worth holding out for, and the Sanger family are shown doing just that.

This same theme had already been explored by Margaret Kennedy in her first novel, written a year previously, called *The Ladies of Lyndon*. Considered as a novel, as a work of art, it is undoubtedly superior. And yet it too received lukewarm reviews, sank without trace during the winter of 1923–4 and only sold a magnificent 10,000 copies a year or two later, after the success of the second novel. Even then many readers concurred with the writer in *The New York Times* who observed that 'many persons who joined in praising *The Constant Nymph* will buy *The Ladies of Lyndon* and feel themselves to have been woefully sold'.

Modern readers will find the first novel far richer, more moving and certainly less sentimental. Margaret Kennedy herself always had an especial fondness for it in the way that people tend to for their first creations, whether works of art or children. She once told a reporter that 'the memory of its appearance is sweeter even than the success of *The Constant Nymph*'. And this was not merely because she had fulfilled a twenty-year-long ambition to write (and publish) a novel; it was surely because in her heart she knew that the first novel had fewer of the qualities that appeal to the mass reading public but more to recommend it as a carefully crafted work of fiction. The lightness of her touch, her shrewd social comment and clear, often ironic insight into human nature are here displayed to perfection. *The Ladies of Lyndon* also has its own special interest for us as a period piece, as an early statement of the clash between the Edwardian and the post-war age.

. . . For a first novel, written by someone in her mid-twenties, it is extraordinarily rich in theme and subtle in overtone; in some ways Margaret Kennedy never did anything quite so accomplished again. The novel is one of social comedy rather than plot. The central 'lady' is Agatha Clewer, née Cocks, who married in haste and repents at leisure, a repentance that is activated partly by her own dawning self-knowledge and partly by her newly recognised love for her cousin. The other main character is James, her brother-in-law, who is a budding painter of genius treated by his family as not only beyond the pale socially but also as a near half-wit.

Reviewers at the time treated the Agatha theme as most important, but in Margaret Kennedy's mind James mattered most. *Queen* magazine reported:

> The idea for *The Ladies of Lyndon* arose from a children's party where Miss Kennedy met a little boy who was considered mentally deficient. He was having a sad time with the other children, so she took him into another room and played the gramophone to him and found that he could hum perfectly all the tunes she played, though he was not more than three years old. That made her consider the possibility of a

child quite different from others, perhaps with genius in his strangeness, who might be treated kindly, but in quite the wrong way, by those in charge of him. Not his mother, but possibly a stepmother. And so James in *The Ladies of Lyndon* came to literary life. 'I meant to make James the central character of the book,' said Miss Kennedy, 'But I did not have the courage of my convictions and he was swallowed up by Agatha and the others. If I were to re-write it, it would be different.'

As the novel turned out, Agatha was definitely the central character. Having married promptly and well she has, by 1914, transformed herself into the young Lady Clewer dispensing tea under the cedar tree to young men in white flannels, effortlessly radiating charm, sympathy and beauty. At first only her cousin Gerald with whom she had once had a brief but happy flirtation wonders whether 'she might be wasting a very exceptional brain in this futile life of hers'. Slowly she begins to realise that her 'soul was gone, dead and buried beneath the gorgeousness of Lyndon', that she and the other 'ladies' had become 'perfect monuments of conspicuous waste'.

James plays an important part in her 'sentimental journey'. He realised on her wedding-day that the eighteen-year-old bride had been bred to look upon marriage as 'after all, a duty to one's neighbour and not a personal affair'. '"Here! What are you frightened of?" Turning to rebuff his foolishness, she was silenced by his expression. In that ugly countenance she perceived so much gravity, indignation and concern that she was mute.' But she shrugs him off and only gradually comes to accept him as the most sensible person she knows, the only one to have retained his sanity and individuality. The climax of the book is when she defends his engagement to Dolly the housemaid: 'This was an open defection and was felt as such by the company.' Ironically, Dolly turns out to be far more of a lady than any of her relations-by-marriage.

Agatha begins to see herself as potentially something other than a beautiful but marble monument, dependent on the deference of others for her own self-esteem, her spirit dead to art, feelings, moral values and tenderness. During the war she has the 'volcanic notion' of trying to work in a canteen and, confusedly, assumes that true love is sufficiently expressed in financial sacrifice. In trying to ignore her expensive upbringing she is also trying to run away from the world of Lyndon where people never speak directly to one another but, inevitably, plunge into the accustomed 'abyss of irritation, suspicion, veiled criticism, secret conclaves, tactful hints and plain speaking'.

For Lyndon is the villain of the book. It is all external trappery, obsessed with appearance and display, luxurious rather than beautiful. Just as, in Paris, James discovered that 'the ones who drew worst talked most' so at Lyndon the lusher the exterior the shallower the reality. As, for example, the library: 'seldom used by the household', crammed with books, yet none of them straightforward enough to provide the simple facts for a lecture on Dante at the Village Institute.

And it is Lyndon which is the symbol of the change which creeps over both Agatha and the world: after the war it represents the sloughed-off skin of England's past. It can no longer be the greedy, devouring 'shrine of ease' it has once been. It can either disintegrate, adjust to the 'sensible' values of post-war life or become a Braxhall. This is the house built by Sir Thomas Bragge in 1919 which 'marked monumentally, the excessive prosperity of Sir Thomas during the war with Germany'. He is a 'new gentleman' and, to Agatha's distress, 'proclaimed blatantly an ideal of life which, in her own household, was discreetly and beautifully intimated'.

As a character, the Profiteer, he is drawn with crude strokes and there is a rather distressing hint of anti-semitism in the tone used by Margaret Kennedy to describe him. But there is nothing crude in the handling of the most richly comic scene in the book, the unveiling of the frescoes which he has commissioned from James. And he and Cynthia, with their quite unashamed worship of luxury, provide a wonderful foil to Agatha's painfully awakening spirit.

The war is shown to have wrought enormous, totally unexpected changes. Lyndon has to change, Agatha changes, the Sir Thomas Bragges of this world are in the ascendant, John contracts his eventually fatal strained heart as a result of gas poisoning. Even James is 'taken up'. As Lois remarks: '"James has improved a lot lately . . . Besides, all the canons of artistic taste have changed so much lately. It's the war, you know".' James resists attempts to turn him into the 'tame family genius' and baffles his family by living domestically in Hampstead rather than in romantic squalor in a one-room studio—which course of action would have been considered more conventional.

Agatha too tries to adapt herself, to bridge the gap between the two worlds she sees to each side of her. But the conflict between the artists and the moneyed, the sensitive and the insensitive, the cultured and the philistine is well-nigh inevitable. It is a conflict which has often been described in fiction, the most obvious parallels (because they too use a large house as hero/villain) being *Mansfield Park* and *Howards End*. The former explores the opposing pull of principles and worldliness, the latter, which was published when Margaret Kennedy was in her early teens, describes the struggle, either futile or dependent on compromise, to connect the world of 'telegrams and anger' with the world which holds personal relations paramount. Virginia Woolf too was ever conscious of the apartness of the two worlds believing that 'the gulf we crossed between Kensington and Bloomsbury was the gulf between respectable mummified humbug & life crude & impertinent perhaps, but living'.

It was this theme, as well as that of the 'genius' in society, which was re-explored with even more obvious point and such public success in *The Constant Nymph*. In this novel, the father of the family, a musical genius, dies early on and his children are left to wade in the murky waters of the real, orderly, civilised world, a world which had hitherto been hidden from them in their unfettered life on an Austrian alp. There the constraints of civilisation had been completely ignored in deference to the sacred worship of music. But in South Kensington music was granted its appropriate place in the scheme of things, it was 'only part of the supreme art, the business of living beautifully'.

The core of *The Constant Nymph* is the contrast between Tessa (the nymph) who brings her direct and innocent view of the world to bear on Kensington values and Florence, who is trying to subdue the whole Sanger family with those values. Both women love Lewis Dodd, the musical genius who adopts Sanger's mantle and who, misguidedly, married Florence without recognising that it is really the adolescent Tessa who is his destiny. And both women are crushed by him in the end, his wife because she is turned from a naïve Cambridge girl into an embittered woman trying to subdue Lewis's spirit with the values of 'decency and humanity and civilisation' and Tessa

because she is physically crushed by the onslaught of the real world on 'the wild, imaginative solitude of her spirit'.

Time after time Margaret Kennedy describes women who lack the inner strength to forge their own destinies, who are at the mercy of their circumstances, domestic responsibilities or inner natures. Agatha has been stifled by her mother and her life is subtly sabotaged by her mother-in-law's interference. There is the memorable scene at Braxhall where the two older women parry verbal blows and finally 'Marian, having eased her bosom of some of her furniture, departed'. The theme of sabotaging mothers is also central to the later novel *Together and Apart* (1936), where again home truths administered for people's own good render a death blow to something precious and living—a happy marriage.

Another theme throughout Margaret Kennedy's early novels is the weariness of the married woman who wishes that she could escape from the myriad of people, objects and chores which depend on her for their life's blood, who feels that somehow life has passed her by yet has no clear idea of what she wants out of it. A character in *Return I Dare Not* (1931) thinks dejectedly:

> She must go to Mrs Duckett's Registry again on Monday. She must make a list of all the things to be done on Monday . . . laundry . . . teeth . . . shoes . . . Ada . . . it was damned unfair! For nearly half her life she had been smothered under teeth and laundries, when really she was not that sort of person at all. She had married too young. She had never lived her life. They (some hidden influences, not specified) ought not to have allowed her to marry so young.

And Agatha too felt the same ensnared feelings, though hers were more of the soul since the everyday harmony of her family's material world was not her responsibility.

But it seems that Margaret Kennedy, although preoccupied with the imprisoned woman, did not have those feelings herself—she always put her work first and there is an element of contempt, certainly not of sympathy, in her descriptions of subjugated women. It is the rebels, the Sangers and James's of this world, who have her sympathy—they, as she, took their art deeply seriously. . . .

Although the fourteen novels after the first two all sold respectably, and some were Book Society choices, in a way she never did anything as good again. A *Long Time Ago* (1932), *Together and Apart* (1936) and *The Midas Touch* (1938) are in the next rank, all three novels having many outstanding qualities. She continued to publish good fiction until 1964, but somehow, whether it was chance or the effect of success or the responsibilities of marriage, something disappeared from her writing. Not the wit, not the eye for social comedy, and not the range; but the Forsterish ironic understatement, the suggestions of profundity and the tragic overtones were never recaptured in quite the same way. And perhaps the intelligence of the writing and the deftness of form displayed in *The Ladies of Lyndon* will bring it a new popularity; to set it, after nearly sixty years, against Huxley's famous *Antic Hay* published in the same month is an instructive experience, for there is little doubt which has greater staying power. The comedy, the insight and the sombre conclusion make this novel memorable, on its own terms a work of fiction of a high order.

THOMAS KINSELLA

1928–

Thomas Kinsella was born in Dublin on May 4, 1928. After attending local schools he entered University College, Dublin, but abandoned a science scholarship there to join the Irish Civil Service in 1946. He began writing poetry shortly before 1950, and published his first book, *Starlit Eye*, in 1952. *Poems* followed in 1956, *Another September*, for which he received a Guinness Award, in 1958, and *Downstream* in 1962.

In 1965 Kinsella was elected to the Irish Academy of Letters, and resigned from the Department of Finance to take up a position as artist-in-residence at Southern Illinois University. Since 1970 he has been Professor of English at Temple University in Philadelphia.

Kinsella's later publications include *Nightwalker and Other Poems* (1968), *Notes from the Land of the Dead* (1972), *Song of the Night and Other Poems* (1978), *Poems 1956–1973* (1980), and *One Fond Embrace* (1981). Most of his longer poems have been issued separately before collection by the Peppercanister Press, which he founded in Dublin in 1972. He is also a director of the Dolmen Press and the Cuala Press, and has translated older Irish literature, notably the twelfth-century *Thirty Three Triads* (1955), *The Táin* (1969), and *An Duanaire* (1981), an anthology of poems from 1600 to 1900. He received the Denis Devlin Memorial Award in 1967 and 1970 and Guggenheim Fellowships in 1968 and 1971.

Kinsella married in 1955 and has three children.

Of the young poets in Ireland today the most interesting is Thomas Kinsella, whose work is beginning to filter into English anthologies. Mr. Kinsella already encompasses "large" statements with a considerable degree of control: usually because they are sanctioned by image and situation, by context. His outstanding weakness at the moment is a tendency to luxuriate in gestures of romantic isolation:

> My quarter-inch of cigarette
> Goes flaring down to Baggot Street,
> Mission accomplished. Those who trod,
> Today, that stone it dies on, lie
> Companionably asleep, in God
> Locking their property. All that I
> Am sure of in this jaded night
> Is the slow explosion of my pulse
> In a wrist with poet's cramp, a tight
> Beat tapping out endless calls
> Into the dark, as the alien
> Garrison in my blood
> Keeps constant contact with the main
> Mystery, not to be understood.

The rhyming "I" is such a blatant whine, set off in its isolation against "companionably" and "God." The death of the cigarette is *his* death, etc. etc. The emotional issue is forced in "jaded": "explosion" is designed less to "render the thing" than to coax the reader to sympathise with the hyper-sensitive Poet; and all in the service of the capitalised "Mystery." Mr. Kinsella is probably writing too much and too fluently: he could learn a great deal from Mr. Clarke's *Ancient Lights* or from the austere poems of Yvor Winters. In the meantime, however,—and since we can hardly claim Donald Davie as Irish property— Mr. Kinsella is our White Hope.—DENIS DONOGHUE, "Irish Writing," *Month*, March 1957, p. 185

DONALD T. TORCHIANA
From "Contemporary Irish Poetry"
Chicago Review, 1964, pp. 160–64

Kinsella's decided but unflamboyant concern for poetry, his excellent translations from Gaelic verse, his quiet self-assurance may well mark him as part of Ireland's new breed— the highly educated and cultured specialist. Just as Gaelic and Catholic as their peasant forebearers, these young pro-consuls are nevertheless at home anywhere in the English-speaking world, not to mention the Continent and even the underdeveloped countries. This new breed mans UN posts, guides the fortunes of Aer Lingus, does scientific research at Cal Tech or MIT when not holding a chair at UCD, UCC or UCG. They are mild, cosmopolitan, and sure as steel. There is something awesome about them, awesome in the way that Kevin O'Higgins, their great predecessor, struck Yeats. They have borne out the great if somewhat deflected promise of the original Free State. The astonishing quality in O'Higgins, and in Ireland's new young men, is an unflinching singleness of purpose that combines with a relaxed and good-humored exterior. These stem, I think, from a prescribed and religious education in a country where finances are slim, where personal life remains hidden, indirect, insinuating. From whence, nevertheless, there seems to flower an awareness of the world's flow, a shrewd pragmatism, and yet withal an easy set of assumptions about our final ends, a certainty about Christian principles, that make them terrors at the bargaining table. And what is a Russian but an Irishman with his heels in the air?

If this is possible, Kinsella might be called their poet. His forte is the long poem. He does not falter. He is calm but never dull. He is contemporary in his idiom and display of psychic fireworks. A Dubliner born, Kinsella also offers the Dubliner's mock-resignation and self-laughter than can be misunderstood as British offhandedness were they not so grimly and historically Irish. But let me see if I can point out some of this in "Baggot Street Deserta" and "A Country Walk."

"Baggot Street Deserta" is the more interior of the two poems. Near midnight, the poet gazes out his window upon the empty Baggot Street—Dublin's art quarter. His mood is a complicated one of boredom, passion, and loss. Even more, it also includes the Irish artist's peculiar "call of exile, half-/Buried longing, half/serious Anger and the rueful laugh." The burden that Kinsella fleshes out before our eyes is that of the ever-present past, here fed upon by an unflinching, verse-making heart. Yet he does not stop, as do so many contemporary poets, by merely dramatizing the fact that

> Versing, like an exile, makes
> A virtuoso of the heart,
> Interpreting the old mistakes
> And discords in a work of Art
> For the One, a private masterpiece
> Of doctored recollections.

Nor does he halt in the piercing light of hindsight. For if the poet and his lucubrations are gladdened or saved or made whole it is by the radiance or clarification in the italicized line: *Endure and let the present punish.* True, the poem does tend to inflict on us a didacticism peculiarly dry yet sentimental popularized by Auden and now, seemingly, part of the bag of tricks belonging to most British poets. Still and all, the last lines of the poem infuse the local overtones of "flight," "alien garrison" and "border-marches" cleverly and naturally enough to insinuate a sensibility unmistakably Irish. At the same time, the reader is forcibly confronted with the universal problem of the contemporary poet and the Reality—to echo Yeats:

> Fingers cold against the sill
> Feel, below the stress of flight,
> The slow implosion of my pulse
> In a wrist with poet's cramp, a tight
> Beat tapping out endless calls
> Into the dark, as the alien
> Garrison in my own blood
> Keeps constant contact with the main
> Mystery, not to be understood.
> Out where imagination arches
> Chilly points of light transact
> The business of the border-marches
> Of the Real, and I—a fact
> That may be countered or may not—
> Find their privacy complete.

But in the two remaining lines, we catch the symbolic arch of the imagination that the poem itself has also cunningly traced, or transacted, between the poet, the streets of memory, and Dublin—ultimately the Ireland that feeds the River Liffey which pours into the sea and so touches all men. And so the poem has insisted from the beginning:

> A mile away the river toils
> Its buttressed fathoms out to sea;
> Tucked in the mountains, many miles
> Away from its roaring outcome, a shy
> Gasp of waters in the gorse
> Is sonnetting origins. Dreamers' heads
> Lie mesmerized in Dublin's beds
> Flashing with images, Adam's morse.

"A Country Walk" is a meditation on Ireland's history, more truly perhaps Kinsella's personal musing on the rebelly yet treacherously Irish Ireland. The poem very literally yet magically takes us on a pilgrimage, through the legendary rural stations of Ireland's cross, to the holy well of imagination. All the bloody historical landscape is there intermingling with the endless rooks, drizzle, cattle, ruined towers, the abandoned barracks, castles, brewery, the distant railroad, the everpresent steeple. The first appropriate memory is of twin brothers in mortal combat. There follow the massacring Normans, Cromwell's crew, the penal days and the men of 1798, right down to the last deluded patriot, dead and buried, who followed "the phantom hag,/Tireless Rebellion," only to be killed by the Black and Tans. Then brother fought brother once more during the Civil War, and now, after that "trenchcoat playground," there's the "gombeen jungle." The evidence?

> Around the corner, in an open square,
> I came upon the sombre monuments
> That bear their names: MacDonaugh & McBride,
> Merchants; Connolly's Commercial Arms . . .
> Their windows give me back my stolid self
> In attitudes of staring as I placed
> Their otherworldly gloom, reflected light
> Playing on lens and raincoat stonily.
> I turned away. Down the sloping square
> A lamp switched on above the urinal;
> Across the silent handball alley eyes
> That never looked on lover measured mine
> Over the Christian Brothers' frosted glass
> And turned away.

And yet and yet, for all the perennial disappointment of Irish historical realities, the land survives, the waters spill on, in hatred and in love, the evening star rises in a light of green and gold, momentary and always. Watching a river, spanned beneath his feet, Kinsella ends by giving us the consolations of the flowing waters of history:

> their shallow, shifting world
> Slid on in troubled union, forging together
> Surfaces that gave and swallowed light;
> And grimly the flood divided where it swept
> An endless debris through the failing dusk
> Under the thudding span beneath my feet.
> *Venit Hesperus;*
> In green and golden light; bringing sweet trade,
> The inert stirred. Heart and tongue were loosed:
> 'The waters hurtled through the flooded night . . .'

And so, at last, modern Ireland, in Tom Kinsella's poetry, begins to come to terms with itself.

CALVIN BEDIENT
From "Thomas Kinsella"
Eight Contemporary Poets
1974, pp. 119–38

Perhaps the most seriously talented Irish poet since Yeats, Thomas Kinsella gives us (like glimpses of a shabby backyard) the expectable battered grief over his country's failing heroic spirit. At the same time he displays a steadily increasing scepticism about life itself: an appalled perspective from which even heroism is just tearing. Life for Kinsella is both a moral hell of blind eating, of eating 'pain in each other', and a metaphysical void consisting of the treacherous anterior negation of natural hopes. He thus comprehends the opposing nihilist realms of Hughes and Larkin; but where the other poets colonize them, he simply finds himself from time to time in each. He has little philosophical ambition or curiosity; he rather takes off and unpacks what he feels, itemizing the heavy load. Doubly cursed, an Irishman, a modern man, he walks the earth—guilt and weariness freezing his animal faith—as if it were an overnight moon.

> There is nothing here for sustenance.
> Unbroken sleep were best.
> Hair. Claws. Grey.
> Naked. Wretch. Wither.[1]

Naming the first and last things in their inexorable order, the final six words, hopeless in parataxis, are Kinsella's latest Summa. If they form a graph of the essential Victorian nightmare, it is a nightmare seen now in the grey light of day, without believing resistance, as the ageing view their face in the morning mirror.

The interest—certainly the *achievement*—of Kinsella's work lie in his resistance to this scepticism. Viewed so much from inside, his 'nightnothing' has, as was said, little intellectual consequence. But in countering it he exemplifies—not least in his carefully wrought poetry—the strength and resourcefulness of the constructive will. He has even sought heroic images of a being at once passionate and ordered—images of secular and vital grace. These have not survived in his poetry, nor were they necessary to it, but the will which underlay them was. Making use of his bile, the same will has also informed his attacks on Ireland.

Kinsella's problem as a poet has been to weigh his depression honestly against the truth that, without an animal adherence to life, however wrathful, balked, pained, poetry has no reason to exist. His difficult achievement has been the creation of a dozen or more poems of vital necessity, poems passionately ordered without special pleading on the part of the will.

. . . ⟨I⟩n *Downstream* (1962) Kinsella emerged as a master not of slick verse but—more saddened, more naked, more groping—of a poetry of subdued but unrelenting power. And so he continued to prove in the short sequence *Wormwood* (1966) and the cumulative volume *Nightwalker and Other Poems* (1967). Here surfaced a poetry that, if almost completely without a surprising use of words, all being toned to a grave consistency, has yet the eloquence of a restrained sorrow, a sorrow so lived-in that it seems inevitable. With its sensitive density of mood, its un-self-conscious manner, there is nothing in this poetry for other poets to imitate. Its great quality is the modesty and precision of its seriousness.

Consider 'Tara', in which this modesty is the more apparent because the subject itself is all mist and quietness. Alluding to, rueing, accepting Ireland's extinguished glory, the poem imitates as well the smoking transitoriness of all things. Here the past seems to survive as the debris of a dream:

> The mist hung on the slope, growing whiter
> On the thin grass and dung by the mounds;
> I hesitated at the dyke, among briars.
> Our children picked up the wrapped flasks, capes and
>   baskets
> And we trailed downward among whins and thrones
> In a muffled dream, guided by slender axe-shapes.
> Our steps scattered on the soft turf, leaving
> No trace, the children's voices like light.
> Low in the sky behind us, a vast silver shield
> Seethed and consumed itself in the thick ether.
> A horse appeared at the rampart like a ghost,
> And tossed his neck at ease, with a hint of harness.[2]

The poem shows an art beyond and indifferent to surface excitement. Everything here is 'muffled', even the metre, which, despite the stresses, seems softened, diffused by the long clauses. The very absence of rhyme enforces the impression of obscured forms and fastenings. The gentle way the words and lines are bound intimates acquiescence in decay. The alliteration, at the same time that it holds a few of the words together, also enacts disintegration, as when the *s* in 'sky', after extending the shield to vastness by continuing through 'vast silver shield', makes it simmer in 'Seethed and consumed itself' until lost in the thick *th* of 'thick ether'; and at the end its principle of

repetition itself hints of harness. So too the diction, precise but not uncaged, not striking, without ambition to stop time, to move or amaze it into amnesty. All in all, here where axe-shapes give directions, where the heroic shield of time itself looks fatally compromised by the mist, the lines trail with the picnic party down the obliterating path of history.

This is a depression so calm, so stable, that it is something new in poetry in English, newly beautiful, newly quiet. All Kinsella's finest poems are written in partial forfeiture to the inevitable destruction of life and pleasure. His art is like the wintered grapevines that growers sheathe in ice to keep off the still colder frost. Thus not only the subtle linkage of his sounds but his imagery has the beauty of stolen fruit—is precious because limited, taken at risk. Here is the close of the long, austere elegy for a fisherman, 'The Shoals Returning':

> The shale-grass shivers around him.
> He turns a shrunken mask
> Of cheekbone and jawbone
> And pursed ancient mouth
> On the sea surface.
> A windswept glitter of light
> Murmurs toward the land.
> His eyes, out of tortoise lids,
> Assess the crystalline plasm,
> Formations of water
> Under falls of air.[3]

The writing is as reticent as the elegized subject, here recalled like a revenant to the 'ravenous element', the scene of his life and death. Difficult not to imagine his eyes, however reptilian, however claimed and changed by his work on the sea, humbly, humanly delighting in the beauty even of the realm in which his spirit will be, has been, 'eaten / In the smell of brine and blood'—the very beauty so cautiously intimated by the lines, as a child gives but a glimpse of a possession he fears to lose, of a possession he fears. Here again is the astringent sensuousness found so often in contemporary British poets—poets as sensitive, as poignant as any but more canny before the threats of pain than most, more concerned to get themselves through. So the lines invite just so much joy in appearance as we can stand to lose, if we must lose it. For instance, 'crystalline' evokes sparkling light and voluptuous glassiness but also the minerally cold and static, which leaves us estranged. And 'plasm' speaks not only of rich glutinous substance but of living material horrifyingly uncontained. Again, 'Formations of water' is determinedly abstract while 'falls of air' activates and beautifies the most abstract of elements—the second phrase supplying what the first withholds and supplying it, moreover, as an unlooked-for gift, the kind we can afford to do without.

At the same time that Kinsella's art claps a stoic hand to the mouth of grief, stands aloof from defeat, proves reticent almost beyond resistance, the salvage work of his images, his craftsmanship, the elegant immaculateness of his style, his meticulous if severe structures, imply a protest against the waste, any waste, of existence. This protest is the pale light shed by the pewter of his lines. . . .

In 'Nightwalker',[4] by contrast, the structure mirrors 'madness within' and 'madness without'. The fourteen-page monologue of an official in the Department of Finance (as Kinsella had been) out exercising 'Shadowy flesh', walking the streets of Dublin under the 'fat skull' of the moon, seeing television watchers 'snuggle in their cells / Faintly luminous, like grubs', recalling 'Bruder and Schwester—Two young Germans' wanting earlier in the day 'to transfer investment income', their faces 'livid with little splashes / Of blazing fat', and spinning stunningly bilious fables of Ireland's destiny of self-sabotage, the poem is powerfully harsh with contemptuous hopelessness, regret for lost heroism, loathing for 'Massed human wills'—its moon a horrifying 'hatcher of peoples'. Here, with aching lungs, Irish poetry comes abreast of *The Waste Land* and *Hugh Selwyn Mauberley*. It has been thrown with the centrifugal flight of a culture losing its provincial integrity, its safety, into that modern space in which, however populous, the individual finds himself receding from everyone. In particular, Kinsella, like his predecessors, looks on his own culture as a moral catastrophe, an alien unreason that, since it contaminates him, is not alien enough. His poem has the extreme bitterness of a man who finds that the last refuge of his virtue is his despair. If more continuous, less allusive and difficult than *The Waste Land*, its structure similarly expresses, through slips and shifts, both uncontrollable cultural disintegration and personal misery, the spirit writhing to find a tenable position. It, too, alternates with disconcerting unpredictability—with intent method—between objectivity and subjective theatre, nightmare, jagged emotionalism. The fuses overload, the truth flashes, is a truth grown monstrous.

In one sense 'Nightwalker' is even more 'modern' than *The Waste Land*, forty years more advanced in despair. And yet, probably for the same reason, it is aesthetically wearier. Like Robert Lowell's poetry it brings out by contrast the experimental brightness, the sophisticated buoyancy of Eliot's great poem. With its cool, modelled precision and showmanship, *The Waste Land* now looks like the work of a lively young poet (convalescent though Eliot may have been, and assisted by Pound) completely on top of his material and out to dazzle the wizened eyes of English poetry—and Pound's poem has the same Yankee energy. 'Nightwalker' is certainly deft and, for a work coming out of the English tradition (Eliot's poem rather broke into it), undeniably bold. And yet properly, given the defeatist mood it assumes, its manner is less invented than that of *The Waste Land* or even *Hugh Selwyn Mauberley*. It is a masterful constellation of familiar styles, restively twisting from one to the other, finding none sufficient, ringing each with parody—now bitter-sweetly lyrical, now prosaic, now metatheatrical, now luridly expressionistic, now satirical. Moreover, the same grey tone prevails throughout, so that the various styles all but blur into one. The language, though characteristically meticulous, shaped, poised, is not exquisite. It is sculptured from dour pumice stone, not Poundian 'alabaster', and is too morose for the '"sculpture" of rhyme'. The words seem dragged down by the lagging blank verse. And the verse itself, if formal, scarcely credits measure. As *traditional* form it is as perfunctory, as much a habit no longer believed in, as exercise for 'Shadowy flesh' or government service. In all, the poem is stalled between anxiety and saturnine resignation, aesthetic adventurousness and aesthetic doldrums—but powerfully stalled, like a dream from which the dreamer wants to wake.

The triumph of 'Nightwalker' as a construction is that, for all its splintered logic, its associative jerks between narrative and hallucinatory fantasy, the pressure never lets up, everything having equally a note of corrosive misery, the terror of an abscess that is too full. Endlessly resourceful, thoroughly worked out and worked over despite its lived-out nausea, *felicitously* flaring, like the final, futile straining of the stork's wings as it alights, the odyssey over, it stands as a rebuke to the country its author loves, scorns, regrets: the country that has, in its ill fortune, the good fortune to arouse so *much* regret.

So it is that, whether on the fields of his sounds, his diction, his images, or his structures, Kinsella's love of heroic human character, of natural beauty, his love-hatred of Ireland, above all his love of the blown glass of words, wars with his

scepticism and depression. And so it is that the poems face at once towards their own extinction and towards a defiance of human defeat. This is art at the crossroads, going out, turning back, ambiguously arrested like a raised arm that could either be greeting or fending off. Yet we cannot really regret a poetry able to discover, in its straits, such lines as 'Formations of water / Under falls of air', such structures as those of '"To Autumn"' or 'Ritual of Departure', such new mottling of familiar resources as moves us in 'Nightwalker'. The poems display the poet's *traditional* ability to join words with the intelligence, the just-born, unguessably old infusing spirit, the care and control, that the rest of the world seems increasingly without.

And yet, as was observed, Kinsella does not leave it to his art alone to exemplify the passionate order that is at once his answer to scepticism and, in its absence, the greatest reason for it. Several of his poems, among them some of his best, are intent to conjure into existence, or to happen upon, to seize, instances and models in life itself of vital poise.

The best, longest, and most ambitious of these are 'Downstream', 'A Country Walk', and 'Phoenix Park', and perhaps it is no accident that all three—together with Larkin's 'Whitsun Weddings' and Graham's 'The Nightfishing'—illustrate a new kind of reflective poem, the modern poem of travel. Like certain earlier poems—Gray's 'Eton Ode', for instance, or Wordsworth's 'Tintern Abbey'—these face a solitary consciousness towards place and time yet do not, as it were, sit still, are not even ostensibly at rest, but move through the world, continually stimulated to new observations, reactions, associations. Cast through space, these poems bring a flutter to the tentativeness of consciousness, which they heighten. They ride on motion the way, and at the same time as, the mind floats on duration. Informed by our contemporary hypersensitivity to the moment, they say that life is only here and now, and fleeting, a thing that *cannot* stand still; and more, that space is as unfathomably deep as time, is time's body, but at least outside ourselves, both mercifully and cruelly outside. The poems increase the sense of exposure to existence as actual travel renews and magnifies the sensation of living.

And in so doing they seem to draw Kinsella out to the front of himself in expectation, curiosity, involvement in life—an involvement lacking energy in the other poems, discouraged, but here released as if by the momentous motion of the poems. In consequence Kinsella's personal presence proves surprisingly pressing and immediate. He is there before us as a chaos in search of an order. Indeed, his poems, being singlehanded attempts to haul his existence into unity, seem more American than Irish and by the same token more Irish than English. They rise from a nearly insurmountable interior isolation, from a scepticism of the social world so total that the poet seems all but lost in himself; and yet he comes out, all the same, to forge or claim as his own some image of order in the world. (All this is true of 'Nightwalker', too, except that it is heroic only in its craft and residual wrath and that, instead of seeking passionate being, it digs into life, in its own passion, with the nails of despair.)

In 'Downstream' and 'A Country Walk' the one answer to the devastations of history—an answer so slight as to be pathetic, so beautiful as to steel hope—is the sight of, a momentary empathy with, an instance of vital serenity in nature. The speaker in the first poem, rowing with an unidentified companion through a narrowing channel full of the sly intimations of dusk, a channel spectral, besides, with recollections of the Second World War, finds himself downstream indeed from 'the primal clarities' of the Greco-Christian past; and finally his skiff is sped into the Mill-Hole, 'a pit of night'—an emblem of modern history, 'the cold fin / Turning in its heart.' For him (as for most modern artists) the centre of gravity has shifted downward into terror:

> The river bed
> Called to our flesh. Across the water skin,
> Breathless, our shell trembled. The abyss[5]

It is just here, however, beside what the first, longer version identifies as a former religious retreat 'Where teacher and saint declined in ghostly white, / Their crosses silent in a hush of wills', that the speaker discerns, drifting in living white on 'pure depth' itself, an emblem of vital order:

> A milk-white breast . . .
> A shuffle of wings betrayed with feathery kiss
> A soul of white with darkness for a nest.
> The creature bore the night so tranquilly
> I lifted up my eyes[6]

For a moment the old stability of nature, the unconscious trust achieved through ages of struggle, quiets the human will. Here, without sacrificing itself, life attains grace. Opposites kiss, fear sleeps. Vitality and order have been reconciled.

In 'A Country Walk' the example of ideal order, more obviously dynamic, more troubled in its serenity, is the river to which the speaker comes after escaping 'the piercing company of women': a river that, 'Under a darkening and clearing heaven', its 'face a-swarm', its 'thousand currents . . . Kissing, dismembering', sliding in 'troubled union', giving and swallowing light, relieves the great sickness from his feeling. Poetry recognizing its own in this passionate dispassion, this restless calm, 'Heart and tongue were loosed: / "The waters hurtle through the flooded night. . . ."'

Here is the releasing order missing from the 'gombeen jungle' of the proximate town square, from turbulent sexual relations, from historical Ireland, whose monuments to violence the speaker has passed, and finally from the town as seen earlier from a hill top, 'mated, like a fall of rock, with time'. Here, on the other hand, is the stir and impulse missing from the priest glimpsed a moment before, his 'eyes / That never looked on lover' measuring the speaker's 'Over the Christian Brothers' frosted glass', and from the three cattle seen at the outset, soothing as they were, indeed in another world, as they

> turned aside
> Their fragrant bodies from a corner gate
> And down the sucking chaos of a hedge
> Churned land to liquid in their dreamy passage[7]

Here in the river under Hesperus in 'green and golden light', not human and yet not in another sphere, here in the river running like the thousand currents of a man's life, is the identity of power with form, the rare and wonderful balance that satisfies flesh and spirit alike, killing the misery in the excess of either, one with the reason of the soul.

These poems are wholly in accord with themselves, their conscious appreciation of united flow and pattern, impulse and rest, being implicit, evident, admirable in their very procedures—certified by them, emulated. Even as 'Downstream' sends the speaker out in search of order—readying him through the enchantment of movement, half mesmeric, half anticipatory, for an image that will strike with the enlarged force of the images in dreams yet not endure because, like a dream image, an effect of time and need—all its fears and horrors prepare and unconsciously call out for the moment when the swan startles with its almost perfect, its vitally stirring, peace. And then when the rock where the speaker seeks a landing place towers and blots the heavens, to which the sight of the swan had involuntarily directed his eyes, order alluding to order, the

poem is over, ending as it has to in the actual darkness here below. The poem never fixes on anything and yet it is all as continuous and determined and beautiful as the unwinding of a lustrous grey cloth, a cloth that darkens, like the twilight, as it unfolds. Just as the movement of the poem merges the interest of the local and fugitive with the fascination of movement itself, so the implicit life of every image is one with the import of the poem as a whole. And 'A Country Walk', through the protagonists' furious or envious notice of objects, picks up and bears along the outer world as casually yet peremptorily as a river gathers debris, and at the end, having swollen to its utmost capacity, seems to pour in silence past its own last words. Neither poem wills its order, or they will it without willfulness. Everything in them coheres yet not as if by conscious effort.

Meanwhile, their style, classical in its gravity and poise, itself reconciles emotion and order. The blank verse of 'A Country Walk', disturbed yet distinct as a pattern, is at once intent and dreamy, exact and elegant, vigorous and serene, as in these lines on the town,

> Below me, right and left, the valley floor
> Tilted in a silence full of storms;
> A ruined aqueduct in delicate rigor
> Clenched cat-backed, rooted to one horizon

or these,

> A line of roofs
> Fused in veils of rain and steely light
> As the dying sun struck it huge glancing blows

or here,

> Then came harsh winters, motionless waterbirds,
> And generations that let welcome fail

or (it is hard to stop quoting from this immaculate poem) the exquisite line,

> The littered fields where summer broke and fled[8]

The style of 'Downstream', less concentrated, without angry edge, is detached and yet mimetic in its flow, line by line, stanza through stanza. Indeed, perhaps never has *terza rima* been given such a 'liquid grip':

> Again in the mirrored dusk the paddles sank.
> We thrust forward, swaying both as one.
> The ripples scattered to the ghostly bank
> Where willows, with their shadows half undone,
> Hung to the water, mowing like the blind.
> The current seized our skiff. We let it run
> Grazing the reeds, and let the land unwind
> In stealth on either hand[9]

Few of the lines, few of the stanzas, are stopped; the verse flows, yet not evenly, halting again and again internally, as if in sudden and momentary releases from the current. The writing is eloquent without being luxurious, with merely the rich sufficiency that flowing water itself seems to possess. The metre adds sway, the rhymes sink 'as one', like the paddles. And the stanzas themselves are held together in one stream by the interlinking rhymes as well as by *enjambement*. The style kisses, dismembers; bears tormented consciousness tranquilly along. . . .

Unfortunately, what Kinsella's most recent volume, *New Poems* (1973), reveals is that the death of the will to order is just as likely as its excess to lead to washed-out, unwilling writing. The new poems envince an extreme depression of his art and spirit. The dejection once held back by the poet's pride in his own mastery now meets with little resistance, seems to have soaked right through the forms and language. After his effort in 'Phoenix Park' to rise from despair, Kinsella has slumped back into defeatism with a vengeance. Discouraged by the world, the new poetry stagnates in tired literary fantasy ('I saw, presently, it was a cauldron: / ceaselessly over its lip a vapour of forms / curdled, glittered and vanished . . . I confess / my heart, as I stole through to my enterprise, / hammered in fear'), or revisits actual scenes with the bleary eyes of a malcontent. Though the volume contains effective lines and passages, notably in 'The Liffey Hill', 'A Selected Life', 'Touching the River', 'The Route of the Táin', the poems on childhood, and the uncharacteristically graphic 'Crab Orchard Sanctuary: Late October',

> The lake water lifted a little and fell
> doped and dreamy in the late heat.
> The air at lung temperature—like the end of the
> world[10]

still as a whole it seems the work of a poet for whom no strong sensation remains.

Indeed, in opening at last the trunk of his childhood, Kinsella seems to have discovered, like Larkin, an *initial* void: 'Not even in my mind / has one silvery string picked / a single sound. And it will never.' His animal faith—so he now interprets it—was all along like wet wood that the world failed to ignite. Dour adults towering about him like headstones, he could not see *life* except as the little that waited, grumbling, on this side of death, the visible, grievous side. . . . 'All Is Emptiness / and I Must Spin' runs one of his titles—and in parts of these poems Kinsella is in truth reduced to writing for the mere form of it. Beyond every emotion that attaches to the world—beyond even nostalgia and anger, the respective last stands of Larkin and Hughes—he seems unable to judge his own creativity. . . .

Yet even in *New Poems*, however unsure and intermittent, one passion in Kinsella remains: the passion for selectivity and movement, for 'putting together'.[11] It has gone pale, you may think—and certainly the passages of fantasy are sickly. But reread the poems, make yourself as patient as water on a windless day, and you find that, for the most part, the passion has only grown more delicate, gaining in refinement what it loses in force. Kinsella is still an artist, his poems 'a labour', as he says of his rescue-work translation of *The Táin*, 'of some kind of love'. Suffocating under his depression but still alive is the desire to pay homage to art, nature, courage, love—to everything great. 'Certain gaps in ourselves', he remarks in his superbly intelligent and sensitive lecture 'The Irish Writer', 'can swallow up all the potentiality in the world', and though Kinsella is in danger of leaving nothing *outside* himself, still he haunts the edge of potentiality, observant if no longer hopeful. If his new art, for instance 'The Liffey Hill', really *is* new—at least as new as Lowell's *For the Union Dead*—the reason lies in his spiritual extremity. His tenuous structures are the metonyms of a spirit on the verge of disintegration. All the same, our wish for Kinsella as a poet must be that the protesting animal in him will regain its strength; the security of his touch depends on it, as does the vigour of his art, its bruised bloom.

Notes

1. "Survivor," *New Poems* (Dublin: Dolmen Press, 1973), p. 38.
2. *Nightwalker* (Dublin: Dolmen Press, 1967), p. 18.
3. *Nightwalker*, p. 33.
4. Ibid., p. 53.
5. Ibid., p. 98.
6. Ibid., p. 98.
7. *Downstream* (Dublin: Dolmen Press), 1962, p. 45.
8. Ibid., p. 45.
9. Ibid., p. 98.
10. *New Poems*, p. 73.
11. *New Poems*, p. 61.

RUDYARD KIPLING

1865–1936

Rudyard Kipling was born on December 30, 1865, in Bombay, where his father was a professor at the School of Art. His early years were happy, but he suffered greatly after being taken at the age of six to England, and left by his parents in the charge of a stern disciplinarian. His schooldays ended in 1882, and he returned to India to work as a journalist for the *Civil and Military Gazette* in Lahore. Apart from news items, he contributed poems, collected in *Departmental Ditties* (1886), and short stories, published in *Plain Tales from the Hills* (1888) and subsequent successful volumes. In 1887 he joined the *Pioneer* in Allahabad, and saw more of the country before leaving India in 1889 to travel via America to England.

Taking up residence in London, Kipling soon made an impact on the literary scene with the reissue of his Indian stories and the publication of *Life's Handicap* (1891). That year Kipling made an extended voyage for reasons of health, visiting India for the last time before returning to England to marry an American, Caroline Balestier, in 1892, and traveling with her to settle in Vermont. *Barrack-Room Ballads* appeared in 1892, the short stories *Many Inventions* in 1893, *The Jungle Book* in 1894, and its sequel in 1895, but these productive years in America ended when Kipling quarreled with his brother-in-law and returned to England in 1896.

After 1898 Kipling frequently wintered in South Africa, and he was outspoken in his support of England in the Boer War. In later years he remained staunchly imperialist in outlook, harboring an idealistic vision of the white man's mission, though he declined the many honors offered him by the state, including knighthoods and the Order of Merit. He did accept the Nobel Prize for Literature in 1907 and various honorary degrees. After World War I, in which his son died, he felt increasingly isolated, though he enjoyed the respect and friendship of George V. He died a few days before the king on January 18, 1936, and was buried in Poets' Corner, Westminster Abbey.

Notable among Kipling's later works are the novel *Kim* (1901), the *Just So Stories* (1902), *Puck of Pook's Hill* (1906), *Rewards and Fairies* (1910), *The Years Between* (1919), and the autobiographical *Something of Myself*, published posthumously in 1937.

Personal

(August 11, 1906)

This morning's cables contain a verse or two from Kipling, voicing his protest against a liberalizing new policy of the British government which he fears will deliver the balance of power in South Africa into the hands of the conquered Boers. Kipling's name, and Kipling's words always stir me now, stir me more than do any other living man's. But I remember a time, seventeen or eighteen years back, when the name did not suggest anything to me and only the words moved me. At that time Kipling's name was beginning to be known here and there, in spots, in India, but had not traveled outside of that empire. He came over and traveled about America, maintaining himself by correspondence with Indian journals. He wrote dashing, free-handed, brilliant letters but no one outside of India knew about it.

On his way through the State of New York he stopped off at Elmira and made a tedious and blistering journey up to Quarry Farm in quest of me. He ought to have telephoned the farm first; then he would have learned that I was at the Langdon homestead, hardly a quarter of a mile from his hotel. But he was only a lad of twenty-four and properly impulsive and he set out without inquiring on that dusty and roasting journey up the hill. He found Susy Crane and my little Susy there, and they came as near making him comfortable as the weather and the circumstances would permit.

(August 13, 1906)

The group sat on the veranda and while Kipling rested and refreshed himself he refreshed the others with his talk, talk of a quality which was well above what they were accustomed to, talk which might be likened to footprints, so strong and definite was the impression which it left behind. They often spoke wonderingly of Kipling's talk afterward, and they recognized that they had been in contact with an extraordinary man, but it is more than likely that they were the only persons who had perceived that he was extraordinary. It is not likely that they perceived his full magnitude, it is most likely that they were Eric Ericsons who had discovered a continent but did not suspect the horizonless extent of it. His was an unknown name and was to remain unknown for a year yet, but Susy kept his card and treasured it as an interesting possession. Its address was Allahabad.

No doubt India had been to her an imaginary land up to this time, a fairyland, a dreamland, a land made out of poetry and moonlight for the Arabian Nights to do their gorgeous miracles in; and doubtless Kipling's flesh and blood and modern clothes realized it to her for the first time and solidified it. I think so because she more than once remarked upon its incredible remoteness from the world that we were living in, and computed that remoteness and pronounced the result with a sort of awe, fourteen thousand miles, or sixteen thousand, whichever it was. Kipling had written upon the card a compliment to me. This gave the card an additional value in Susy's eyes, since as a distinction it was the next thing to being recognized by a denizen of the moon.

Kipling came down that afternoon and spent a couple of hours with me, and at the end of that time I had surprised him as much as he had surprised me, and the honors were easy. I believed that he knew more than any person I had met before,

and I knew that he knew I knew less than any person he had met before—though he did not say it and I was not expecting that he would. When he was gone, Mrs. Langdon wanted to know about my visitor. I said, "He is a stranger to me but he is a most remarkable man—and I am the other one. Between us, we cover all knowledge; he knows all that can be known, and I know the rest."

He was a stranger to me and to all the world, and remained so for twelve months, then he became suddenly known and universally known. From that day to this he has held this unique distinction: that of being the only living person, not head of a nation, whose voice is heard around the world the moment it drops a remark, the only such voice in existence that does not go by slow ship and rail but always travels first-class by cable.

About a year after Kipling's visit in Elmira, George Warner came into our library one morning in Hartford, with a small book in his hand, and asked me if I had ever heard of Rudyard Kipling. I said, "No."

He said I would hear of him very soon, and that the noise he was going to make would be loud and continuous. The little book was the *Plain Tales* and he left it for me to read, saying it was charged with a new and inspiriting fragrance and would blow a refreshing breath around the world that would revive the nations. A day or two later he brought a copy of the London *World* which had a sketch of Kipling in it, and a mention of the fact that he had traveled in the United States. According to this sketch he had passed through Elmira. This remark, added to the additional fact that he hailed from India, attracted my attention—also Susy's. She went to her room and brought his card from its place in the frame of her mirror, and the Quarry Farm visitor stood identified.

I am not acquainted with my own books but I know Kipling's—at any rate I know them better than I know anybody else's books. They never grow pale to me; they keep their color; they are always fresh. Certain of the ballads have a peculiar and satisfying charm for me. To my mind, the incomparable Jungle Books must remain unfellowed permanently. I think it was worth the journey to India to qualify myself to read *Kim* understandingly and to realize how great a book it is. The deep and subtle and fascinating charm of India pervades no other book as it pervades *Kim*; *Kim* is pervaded by it as by an atmosphere. I read the book every year and in this way I go back to India without fatigue—the only foreign land I ever daydream about or deeply long to see again.—MARK TWAIN, "Various Literary People" (1906), *Mark Twain in Eruption*, ed. Bernard De Voto, pp. 309–12

What did we talk of? So many things that it is difficult to summarise them. Chiefly they had to do with the soul and the fate of man. Rudyard, apparently, cannot make up his mind about these things. On one point, however, he is perfectly clear. I happened to remark that I thought that this world was one of the hells. He replied that he did not *think*, he was *certain* of it. He went on to show that it had every attribute of a hell, doubt, fear, pain, struggle, bereavement, almost irresistible temptations springing from the nature with which we are clothed, physical and mental suffering, etc., etc., ending in the worst fate that man can devise for man, Execution! As for the future he is inclined to let the matter drift. He said what he has often said to me before, that what he wants is a 'good long rest'. I asked him if he wished for extinction and could contemplate without dismay separation eternal from all he loved—John for instance. He replied that he was never happier than when he knew that as a child his boy was asleep in the next room—why therefore should he mind it in the grave, or words to that effect. I pushed the subject and found that he does not really want to go out, only to *rest*. I pointed out that his notion was futile since if he rested for a million years or for a minute, it would make no difference to him in a state of unconsciousness, should he awake after all. Here he agreed. The upshot of it is that he is no unbeliever, only like the rest of us, one who knows nothing and therefore cannot understand.

Like myself he has an active faith in the existence of a personal devil and thinks (I gathered) that much which is set down to God is really attributable to that personality who at present cannot be controlled *even* by God, at least not altogether. He holds that the story of Pharaoh is being repeated in the case of the Germans. God is 'hardening' their heart, to their ultimate destruction. His humility is very striking. We were talking of our failings. I said that what grew on me from day to day was a sense of my own utter insufficiency, of complete humiliation both in the case of those things that I had done and left undone, and of the knowledge of sin ingrained in my nature which became more and more apparent to me as I approached the end of my days. He answered that it was absolutely the same with himself in every sense and detail and proceeded to speak very strongly on the matter, pointing out how we were subject to different weaknesses and temptations at the various periods of life. I commented on the fact that he had wide fame and was known as 'the great Mr Kipling', which should be a consolation to him. He thrust the idea aside with a gesture of disgust. 'What is it worth—what *is* it all worth?' he answered. Moreover he went on to show that anything which any of us did *well* was no credit to us: that it came from somewhere else: 'We are only telephone wires.' As an example he instanced (I think) 'Recessional' in his own case, and *She* in mine. '*You* didn't write *She*, you know,' he said. 'Something wrote it through you!' or some such words.—H. RIDER HAGGARD, *The Private Diaries of Sir H. Rider Haggard 1914–1925* (entry for May 22, 1918), ed. D. S. Higgins, 1980, pp. 135–36

With the generosity that always overflowed from his heart, AE helped all the young Irish poets of his time. There was a melody in his verse like the echo of bells, and to hear him reading them in his organ voice was an experience the world has lost. He was one of the kindest men I have ever known. The kindest was Kipling. And it is sad that a bit of politics should ever have drifted a cloud between these two, dark upon AE's side though bright on Kipling's; for, though he had not known AE, he had read a poem of mine in the *Times* when AE died, and I remember his sympathetic words to me about it when walking in the garden of his beautiful house at Burwash. That house now belongs to the nation, like some lovely shell from the Indian Ocean from which the pearl has been taken.

The zest that Kipling had for everything in the world shone back on the world from him, and none of the scenes that he knew seem quite the same now that that light has gone from them. One came to Batemans at the bottom of a little valley through a door in a wall, then over a lovely lawn down a paved path to the hall door of the house, of which I will attempt no inventory, but will mention the Spanish leather with which the walls of the dining room were hung, and all the pictures done by Kipling's father in clay for *Kim*, which hung all along the dark old panels of the staircase.

Another thing that I remember in that house was the magic-alphabet necklace that was kept in the temple of Tegumai in *Just So Stories*: all the charms in the necklace had been collected and put together and given to Kipling by a friend of both of us, Sir Percy Bates of the Cunard line. In that house too were all Kipling's manuscripts and the illustrations he did for them. I don't think he showed us any of these, but after he had died, when we went for the last time to Batemans, Mrs. Kipling showed them all to my wife and me. And it was then that she told us that he never minded any criticism of his writing, but that he took great pride in his pictures.

On one side of the house were smooth lawns with a pond in them, and one huge willow, and a row of lime trees with bare trunks higher than one's head, and above that neatly clipped foliage, so that it all gave the appearance of a hedge floating in air.

The garden paths were made of old millstones from the ruined mills of Sussex. But I am writing about the shell, and not the pearl that was Kipling's genius, which used to sparkle from his blue eyes with a zest like that of a boy planning a huge joke. Perhaps any tales about Kipling, even trivial ones, are of interest, and something in him must have lifted one of them above triviality for me to remember it from another century. When I first met Kipling in Africa during the Boer War, he told of how the farmers made their hedges somewhere near the Cape. They made them out of the ribs of whales. He said that he had written his name on one of the ribs. I am afraid that autograph will not have survived the time and the weather of more than half a century. But Kipling's name is indelibly written on something more lasting than whalebones.—LORD DUNSANY, "Four Poets," *At*, April 1958, p. 78

General

The prevailing force in my undergraduate days was not Socialism but Kiplingism. Our set was quite exceptional in its socialistic professions. And we were all, you must understand, very distinctly Imperialists also, and professed a vivid sense of the "White Man's Burden."

It is a little difficult now to get back to the feelings of that period; Kipling has since been so mercilessly and exhaustively mocked, criticised and torn to shreds;—never was a man so violently exalted and then, himself assisting, so relentlessly called down. But in the middle nineties this spectacled and moustached little figure with its heavy chin and its general effect of vehement gesticulation, its wild shouts of boyish enthusiasm for effective force, its lyric delight in the sounds and colours, in the very odours of empire, its wonderful discovery of machinery and cotton waste and the under officer and the engineer, and "shop" as a poetic dialect, became almost a national symbol. He got hold of us wonderfully, he filled us with tinkling and haunting quotations, he stirred Britten and myself to futile imitations, he coloured the very idiom of our conversation. He rose to his climax with his "Recessional," while I was still an undergraduate.

What did he give me exactly?

He helped to broaden my geographical sense immensely, and he provided phrases for just that desire for discipline and devotion and organised effort the Socialism of our time failed to express, that the current socialist movement still fails, I think, to express. The sort of thing that follows, for example, tore something out of my inmost nature and gave it a shape, and I took it back from him shaped and let much of the rest of him, the tumult and the bullying, the hysteria and the impatience, the incoherence and inconsistency, go uncriticised for the sake of it:—

Keep ye the Law—be swift in all obedience—
Clear the land of evil, drive the road and bridge the
    ford,
Make ye sure to each his own
That he reap where he hath sown;
By the peace among Our peoples let men know we
    serve the Lord!

And then again, and for all our later criticism, this sticks in my mind, sticks there now as quintessential wisdom:

The 'eathen in 'is blindness bows down to wood an'
    stone;
'E don't obey no orders unless they is 'is own;
'E keeps 'is side-arms awful: 'e leaves 'em all about
An' then comes up the regiment an' pokes the
    'eathen out.

    All along o' dirtiness, all along o' mess,
    All along o' doin' things rather-more-or-less,
    All along of abby-nay, kul, an' hazar-ho,
    Mind you keep your rifle an' yourself jus' so!

It is after all a secondary matter that Kipling, not having been born and brought up in Bromstead and Penge, and the war in South Africa being yet in the womb of time, could quite honestly entertain the now remarkable delusion that England had her side-arms at that time kept anything but "awful." He learnt better, and we all learnt with him in the dark years of exasperating and humiliating struggle that followed, and I do not see that we fellow learners are justified in turning resentfully upon him for a common ignorance and assumption. . . .—H. G. WELLS, "Adolescence," *The New Machiavelli*, 1910, pp. 120–21

. . . Kipling has committed one of the most serious sins against his calling which are possible for an imaginative writer. He has resisted his own sense of life and discarded his own moral intelligence in favor of the point of view of a dominant political party. To Lord Roberts and Joseph Chamberlain he has sacrificed the living world of his own earlier artistic creations and of the heterogeneous human beings for whom they were offered as symbols. Here the constraint of making the correct pro-imperialist point is squeezing out all the kind of interest which is proper to a work of fiction. Compare a story of the middle Kipling with a story by Stephen Crane or Joseph Conrad, who were dealing with somewhat similar subjects. Both Conrad and Crane are pursuing their independent researches into the moral life of man. Where the spy who is the hero of *Under Western Eyes* is a tormented and touching figure, confused in his allegiances by the circumstances of his birth, a secret agent in Kipling must invariably be either a stout fellow, because his ruses are to the advantage of the British, or a sinister lying dog, because he is serving the enemy. Where the killing of 'The Blue Hotel' is made to implicate everybody connected with it in a common human guilt, a killing in a story by Kipling must absolutely be shown to be either a dastardly or a virtuous act.

To contrast Kipling with Conrad or Crane is to enable us to get down at last to what is probably the basic explanation of the failure of Kipling's nerve. He lacked faith in the artist's vocation. We have heard a good deal in modern literature about the artist in conflict with the bourgeois world. Flaubert made war on the bourgeois; Rimbaud abandoned poetry as piffling in order to realize the adventure of commerce; Thomas Mann took as his theme the emotions of weakness and defeat of the artist overshadowed by the business man. But Kipling neither faced the fight like Flaubert, nor faced the problem in his life like Rimbaud, nor faced the problem in his art like Mann. Something in him, something vulgar in the middle-class British way, something perhaps connected with the Methodist ministers who were his grandfathers on both sides, a tradition which understood preaching and could understand craftsmanship, but had a good deal of respect for the powers that governed the material world and never thought of putting the artist on a par with them—something of this sort at a given point prevented Kipling from playing through his part, and betrayed him into dedicating his talents to the praise of the practical man. Instead of *becoming* a man of action like Rimbaud, a course which shows a boldness of logic, he fell into the ignominious rôle of the artist who prostrates his art before the achievements of soldiers and merchants, and who is always declaring the supremacy of the 'doer' over the man of ideas.

The results of this are very curious and well worth studying from the artistic point of view—because Kipling, it must always be remembered, was a man of really remarkable abilities. Certain of the symptoms of his case have been indicated by George Moore and Dixon Scott, whose discussions of him in *Avowals* and *Men of Letters* are among the few first-rate pieces of criticism that I remember to have seen on the subject. George Moore quotes a passage from *Kim*, a description of evening in India, and praises it for 'the perfection of the writing, of the strong masculine rhythm of every sentence, and of the accuracy of every observation'; but then goes on to point out that 'Mr. Kipling has seen much more than he has felt,' that 'when we come to analyze the lines we find a touch of local color not only in every sentence, but in each part between each semicolon.' So Scott diagnoses admirably the mechanical ingenuity of plot that distinguishes the middle Kipling. 'Switch,' he says, 'this imperatively map-making, pattern-making method upon . . . the element of human nature, and what is the inevitable result? Inevitably, there is the same sudden stiffening and formulation. The characters spring to attention like soldiers on parade; they respond briskly to a sudden description; they wear a fixed set of idiosyncrasies like a uniform. A mind like this *must* use types and set counters; it feels dissatisfied, ineffective, unsafe, unless it can reduce the fluid waverings of character, its flitting caprices and twilit desires, to some tangible system. The characters of such a man will not only be definite; they will be definitions.' And he goes on to show how Kipling's use of dialect makes a screen for his relinquishment of his grip on the real organism of human personality: 'For dialect, in spite of all its air of ragged lawlessness, is wholly impersonal, typical, fixed, the code of a caste, not the voice of an individual. It is when the novelist sets his characters talking the King's English that he really puts his capacity for reproducing the unconventional and capricious on its trial. Mr. Kipling's plain conversations are markedly unreal. But honest craftsmanship and an ear for strong rhythms have provided him with many suits of dialects. And with these he dresses the talk till it seems to surge with character.'

The packed detail, the automatic plot, the surfaces lacquered with dialect, the ever-tightening tension of form, are all a part of Kipling's effort to impose his scheme by main force. The strangest result of this effort is to be seen in a change in the subject matter itself. Kipling actually tends at this time to abandon human beings altogether. In that letter of Henry James in which he speaks of his former hope that Kipling might grow into an English Balzac, he goes on: 'But I have given that up in proportion as he has come steadily from the less simple in subject to the more simple—from the Anglo-Indians to the natives, from the natives to the Tommies, from the Tommies to the quadrupeds, from the quadrupeds to the fish, and from the fish to the engines and screws.' This increasing addiction of Kipling to animals, insects and machines is evidently to be explained by his need to find characters which will yield themselves unresistingly to being presented as parts of a system. In the *Jungle Books*, the animal characters are each one all of a piece, though in their ensemble they still provide a variety, and they are dominated by a 'Law of the Jungle,' which lays down their duties and rights. The animals have organized the Jungle, and the Jungle is presided over by Mowgli in his function of forest ranger, so that it falls into its subsidiary place in the larger organization of the Empire.

Yet the *Jungle Books* (written in Vermont) are not artistically off the track; the element of obvious allegory is not out of place in such fairy tales. It is when Kipling takes to contriving these animal allegories for grown-ups that he brings up the reader's gorge. What is proved in regard to human beings by the fable called 'A Walking Delegate,' in which a pastureful of self-respecting horses turn and rend a yellow loafer from Kansas, who is attempting to incite them to rebellion against their master, Man? A labor leader and the men he is trying to organize are, after all, not horses but men. Does Kipling mean to imply that the ordinary working man stands in the same relation to the employing and governing classes as that in which the horse stands to its owner? And what is proved by 'The Mother Hive,' in which an invasion of wax-moths that ruin the stock of the swarm represents the infiltration of socialism? (Compare these with that more humane fable of 1893, 'The Children of the Zodiac,' which deals with gods become men.) And, though the discipline of a military unit or of the crew of a ship or a plane may provide a certain human interest, it makes us a little uncomfortable to find Kipling taking up locomotives and representing '.007' instead of the engineer who drives it as the hero of the American railroad; and descending even to the mechanical parts, the rivets and planks of a ship, whose drama consists solely of being knocked into place by the elements so that it may function as a co-ordinated whole.—EDMUND WILSON, "The Kipling That Nobody Read," *The Wound and the Bow,* 1941, pp. 149–54

What is it . . . that makes Kipling so extraordinary? Is it not that while virtually every other European writer since the fall of the Roman empire has felt that the dangers threatening civilization came from *inside* that civilization (or from inside the individual consciousness), Kipling is obsessed by a sense of dangers threatening from *outside*?

Others have been concerned with the corruptions of the big city, the *ennui* of cultured mind; some sought a remedy in a return to Nature, to childhood, to Classical Antiquity; others looked forward to a brighter future of liberty, equality and fraternity: they called on the powers of the subconscious, or prayed for the grace of God to irrupt and save their souls; they called on the oppressed to arise and save the world. In Kipling there is none of this, no nostalgia for a Golden Age, no belief in Progress. For him civilization (and consciousness) is a little citadel of light surrounded by a great darkness full of malignant forces and only maintained through the centuries by everlasting vigilance, will-power and self-sacrifice. The philosophers of the Enlightenment shared his civilization-barbarism antithesis, but their weapon was reason, *i.e.*, coming to consciousness, whereas for Kipling too much thinking is highly dangerous, an opening of the gates to the barbarians of melancholia and doubt. For him the gates are guarded by the conscious Will (not unlike the Inner Check of Irving Babbitt). . . .

Given such a situation, the important figure in society is, of course, the man on guard, and it is he who, in one form or another, from the sentry on the Afghanistan frontier to the gardener

> Grubbing weeds from gravel paths with broken
>   dinner knives

is the Kipling hero. Unlike the epic hero, he is always on the *defensive*. Thus Kipling is interested in engineering, in the weapons which protect man against the chaotic violence of nature, but not in physics, in the intellectual *discovery* that made the weapons possible.

His ethics and his politics are those of a critical emergency, which is why it is impossible to classify them under conventional party labels, for they presuppose a state where differences of opinion are as irrelevant as they are to a soldier in a foxhole, and, in so far as they apply at all, apply to everyone, Democrat, Nazi or Communist.

Of the guardians, Kipling has profound understanding. He knows that most of them are prodigal sons, given to drink and fornication, acquainted with post-dated checks, now cruel, now sentimental, and he does not try to present them as nice people. But when he turns from them to the Sons of Mary whom they are paid to guard (the shift from religious to social meaning is significant), this vision becomes dim and his touch uncertain, for his interest is not really in them, but only in their relation to the sons of Martha; so that what he sees is either too soft, the exile's nostalgic daydream of Mom and the roses round the door, or too hard, the sentry's resentful nightmare of the sleek and slack stay-at-homes dining and wining while he and his sufferings are forgotten.

Kipling has been rightly praised for his historical imagination, but it is questionable if historical is the right word. If by history we mean *irreversible* temporal changes as contrasted with the cyclical and reversible changes of Nature, then Kipling's imaginative treatment of the past is an affirmation of Nature and a denial of History, for his whole concern is to show that the moment of special emergency is everlasting:

> As it will be in the future, it was at the birth of
>   Man—
> There are only four things certain since Social
>   Progress began:
> That the Dog returns to his Vomit and the Sow
>   returns to her Mire,
> And the Burnt Fool's bandaged finger goes wabbling
>   back to the Fire.

But if Nature and History are the same, how can Nature and Man, the Jungle and the City, be opposed to each other, as Kipling is clearly certain that they are? If one asks him "What is civilization?" he answers, "The People living under the Law, who were taught by their fathers to discipline their natural impulses and will teach their children to do the same":

> This we learned from famous men,
>   Knowing not its uses,
> When they showed, in daily work
> Man must finish off his work—
> Right or wrong his daily work
>   And without excuses

in contrast to the barbarian who is at the mercy of his selfish appetites. But if one asks him "What is this Law and where does it come from?" he refers one back to Nature, to the Darwinian law of the Jungle, "Be Fit," or to the Newtonian law of the Machine:

> We are not built to comprehend a lie
> We can neither love nor pity nor forgive
> If you make a slip in handling us, you die

One might almost say that Kipling had to concentrate his attention and ours upon the special emergency in order to

avoid the embarrassment of this paradox, for it is precisely when We are threatened by Them that we can naturally think of the ethical relation between Me and You as one of self-sacrifice, and the ethical relation between Us and Them as one of self-interest. It is precisely when civilization is in mortal danger that the immediate necessity to defend it has a right to override the question of just what it is we are defending.
—W. H. AUDEN, "The Poet of the Encirclement," NR, Oct. 25, 1943, pp. 579–80

The basis of action in the Kipling story is not fundamentally political in character: nor is the empire there as a symbol of the author's confidence either in a dynamic progress or in the viability of the British way of life. Indeed the very possibility of creative achievement is spurned:

> It is but the shifting of a little dirt. Let the dirt dig in
> the dirt if it pleases the dirt . . .

His is a pessimistic vision: and though on occasion he may pay lip-service to an idea of progress it is never more than this and is always fitful and without intrinsic value.

To him as to Conrad the end of action was to be found in the preservation of the individual's identity and self-consciousness. In his activity man realises his own potential for selfhood and is objectified. To fortify himself he conspires with others to erect certain codes and institutions in a large-scale repeat of the exercise, so that he is able to reappropriate to himself their substantial existence and through them come to have a definite place in the world and *be* something.

This 'concept' of action is what firmly allies Kipling to the anti-positivist school of social thinkers. Man's conduct was not determined by a universal law but by a non-rational, highly subjective, psychological need: and for Kipling, as for others, that need was emphatically the reassurance of his own moral integrity.

It is quite clear from this why the criterion of moral action for Kipling should be whether or not it is structural: he would, one feels, have readily subscribed to Fichte's interpretation of man's relationship to society:

> The social impulse . . . belongs to the fundamen-
> tal impulse of man. It is man's vocation to live in
> Society—he *must* live in Society;—he is no complete
> man, but contradicts his own being, if he live in a
> state of isolation . . .

So Kipling found himself totally committed to a principle of order and stability through a massive opposition to the entropic or disintegrative forces of the universe. To the effects of this on his art I have already alluded in the preceding pages of this chapter. Of the ironic, even cynical, detachment of sympathy which was one of its consequences I might offer just two reminders:

> . . . one cannot visit a loafer in the Serai by day.
> Friends buying horses would not understand it.

> He was going to marry Miss Castries, and the
> business was his own business . . . with a man in
> this condition mere words only fix him in his
> purpose. Of course he cannot see that marriage in
> India does not concern the individual but the
> Government he serves.

Implicit in this sort of action is the 'illusion of a mastered destiny', in Conrad's phrase: the illusion that a human determination of events is possible. But, like Conrad, he never forgets that it *is* an illusion, fostered to conceal the chaos that lies beneath.

Like one of the greatest social thinkers in the anti-positivist tradition, Georges Sorel—whom he resembles far more closely than he does Durkheim—he has something approaching a horror of what this distinguished contemporary described as 'natural nature'. To Sorel 'natural nature' was 'a mysterious even malignant Fate, an arbitrary and meaningless force that constantly threatens to overwhelm the spheres conquered by human reason'. And the particular mode of Sorel's response to the threat strengthens the affinity, for he sought the antidote in 'artificial nature', which was the construction imposed on the chaos of reality by scientists and technicians in order to tame it. This, as I have tried to point out, is precisely the *métier* of the Kipling character: his heroes are all, in this sense, scientists and technicians.

The analogy with Sorel's response to nature illuminates another of Kipling's interests which finds expression in his stories: his fascination with the world of machinery in tales like 'The Ship That Found Herself' and '.007'. The machine was one of the most powerful adjuncts of man's efforts to command through the creation of an 'artificial nature'. Henry James failed to understand this when he complained of Kipling's 'deterioration':

> . . . he has come steadily from the less simple in
> subject to the more simple—from the Anglo-Indians
> to the natives, from the natives to the Tommies, from
> the Tommies to the quadrupeds, from the quad-
> rupeds to the fish, and from the fish to engines and
> screws.

And Edmund Wilson simplifies grossly for the same reason, explaining Kipling's increasing addiction to 'animals, insects and machines' as the expression of a need to find 'characters which will yield themselves unresistingly to being presented as parts of a system'. In fact, to Kipling as to Sorel the machine is a major expression of man's ability to understand and control the forces of nature.

One can go further still in the analogy between Sorel and Kipling: for the role that empire plays in the latter's fiction would identify it in Sorel's terminology as one of the great creative myths. A myth to Sorel was the indispensable incentive to action: 'We do nothing great', he writes, 'without the help of warmly-coloured and clearly-defined images, which absorb the whole of our attention.' And he quotes with approval a remark from Newman's *Grammar of Assent*:

> Strictly speaking, it is not imagination that causes
> action; but hope and fear, likes and dislikes, appetite,
> passion, affection, the strings of selfishness and self-
> love. What imagination does for us is to find a means
> of stimulating those motive powers; and it does so by
> providing a supply of objects strong enough to
> stimulate them.

To Sorel the value of the myth did not in the slightest depend on the actual attainment of the professed ends but on the movement itself.

Both Sorel and Kipling were very well aware that man 'would probably never abandon his inertia if he had a perfectly clear view of the future': action, courage in the face of destructiveness, could only be sustained by the help of these evocative illusions. And for Kipling, the challenge of Empire had just such a function. For it offered, to adapt another of Conrad's remarks, the barbed hook of action baited not only with the illusion of progress but also with a multiplicity of self-gratifying images such as, 'la mission civilisatrice', the White Man's Burden, the Man of Destiny and so on. Certainly it provided man with an image 'towards which he could work in the fulfilment of his own possibilities'.

So well does this fit the theory of myths that when Sorel is found mourning the extinction of 'the heroic myths which had such great popularity at the beginning of the nineteenth century' we might question whether Victorian England with the powerful assistance of Rudyard Kipling had not found themselves another in the idea of empire.—ALAN SANDISON, "Rudyard Kipling: The Imperial Simulacrum," *The Wheel of Empire*, 1967, pp. 109–12

Works

PROSE

The peculiar quality of *The Jungle Books* consists in the fusion of three worlds. First of all, there is the child's play-world, where all is really subject to his pastime. It is essentially a homely world, and the good beasts have prototypes in the child's daily life. The identification of the similarity in the difference is part of the pleasure. Baloo is the conscientious, solicitous, elderly schoolmaster; but what enchanting lessons he teaches! From him Mowgli learns the master-words of all the tribes in the jungle. Mother and Father Wolf live in recognizable domesticity with their four cubs—who, apparently, like grown-up Victorian sons, remain under the family roof for years—but their delightful home is a cave. The heavy Sea-Catch, with his bristling moustache, and his gentle mate, Matkah, reflect another kind of parental grouping, and it is with warm satisfaction that the child reads how Sea-Catch flings himself into the battle on Kotick's side with the shout: 'Don't tackle your father, my son; he's with you.' To this world belong, in the first instance, the pass-words and taboos of the jungle, which are entirely congenial to a child's imagination. This is the part of the books that grew from the remembered children's stories of Kipling's youth, the Freemason lions and the boy who lived with wolves.

The second world, which it is impossible to distinguish from the first by the material it is built of, is the world of the fable proper. The elements of moral instruction, which are certainly not alien to a child's world, are systematized. The beasts, without discarding pleasingly incongruous habits of their own, are plainly representative of human traits and conditions, and we are never oblivious of their counterparts in the world of men. They are grouped into arrangements that point a moral, and the moral may extend beyond a child's comprehension, though it should not lie wholly outside it. In *The Jungle Books* the fable comes and goes, and sometimes lies like a transparent glaze over the adventures. The examples are best found in the Mowgli tales, where we move, most of the time, in a self-consistent animal world; where human beings play a large part in the story, as in '"Rikki-tikki-tavi"', the conditions for fable are less good. In 'Kaa's Hunting', however, the fable and the play-world are inextricably fused. The Bandar-log, the monkey-peoples, who sympathize with Mowgli when he is under punishment and abduct him into the tree-tops, are primarily figures in a thrilling and grim story. The green roads through the trees, along which they take Mowgli, his presence of mind when he gives the master-word to Chil the Kite and bids him mark his trail—this is the stuff of the play-world, raised to an exciting pitch by wonder. But very early and easily, before the adventures begin, the Bandar-log—irresponsible, chattering, without law or shame or memory—are seen as the antithesis to jungle-righteousness, and their dangerous futility is brought out by their doings at Cold Lairs. The adult reader can find the Bandar-log elsewhere in Kipling's writings and read how Frankwell Midmore was saved from one tribe of them. He has a clue in their self-comforting cry: 'What the Bandar-log think now the Jungle will think to-morrow'; but this, in its immediate meaning, is not beyond the child, and at no time does the allegory press too hard. Baloo and Bagheera,

fighting for their lives in the moonlight at Cold Lairs, are the beloved beasts in peril, the companions of the man-cub in the play-world; when they become the mouthpieces of the Law, and Mowgli has to learn that sorrow never turns aside punishment, it seems to the child a suitable law in this sort of world; the types and morals are fully absorbed into the story. In 'The King's Ankus' Kipling takes a version of a wide-spread moral apologue, which Chaucer had used for his *Pardoner's Tale*, and combines it with a tale of hidden treasure and the following of a trail. The failure of Mowgli, the fosterling of wolves, to comprehend the value of the cumbrous jewelled ankus, for which men kill each other, serves the same purpose as the Pardoner's sermon. The power of the ancient tale sends a cold breath of awe through the narrative. In '"Tiger-Tiger!"' the fable-elements are more insistent. The young wolves desert their old leader to accept Shere Khan's demoralizing advice, and, at the end, when Shere Khan's skin is pegged out on the Council Rock, they illustrate a Wordsworthian moral—'Me this uncharted freedom tires'. At times, especially near the beginning of the series, before the jungle world has grown into full imaginative authority, the human counterparts of the doings of the pack show too clearly. In the matter of the taboo against killing man the wolves are human enough to give an idealistic reason for what is a measure of plain self-interest.

More important than these two worlds, however, is what I can only call the world of the wild and strange, the ancient and the far. It includes myth, but extends beyond it. There are not very many pages of strictly mythological imagination in *The Jungle Books*. There is Hathi's tradition of how Fear came, a more mysterious *Just So* story, told in the setting of the Water-Truce; there is Kotick's search for the shore where man has never come to destroy the seals—a combination of Leif Eirikson's Wonder-Strands with the Islands of the Blest; and there is, in the later Mowgli tales, the majestic shadow of Adam, King of the Jungle. It is, however, only a shadow; for Mowgli moves in place and time, suffers the ill-temper of Buldeo and the stones of the man-pack, lets Messua comb his hair, and speeds her to the unknown English at Kanhiwara. He has drawn the milk of a woman and a wolf. Messua thinks him a wood-god; but to children he is more like a boy who is helped by kingly beasts in a fairy-tale. He has a fairy-tale extension of power, and his communion with his foster-brothers, which makes old Muller of 'In the Rukh' describe him as before the Stone Age, is to the child another magic power. . . .

But the true *utile dulci* of the children's book is not attained unless it conveys intimations of obligations and passions outside the reach of a child's experience. *The Jungle Books* do this again and again. Sometimes, though not always, a clue may be laid in his hand, or a violent action may be attenuated for his behoof. When Mowgli's bitterness against the man-pack, who have stoned him, doubles his bitterness against the young wolves, who hate him because he has taken thorns out of their feet, he resolves: 'Now I will hunt alone', and his mood is brought nearer to a child's level by the title of his 'Song against People'. When in his revenge he lets in the jungle on the village, no human blood is shed. Nevertheless, here and in 'Kaa's Hunting' and 'The King's Ankus' and 'Red Dog', there is a strong note of the terrible, and the corpse-laden waters of the Mutiny in 'The Undertakers' are horrible enough, even when reduced by distance in the relishing memory of the gluttonous old crocodile. Here the note is macabre, but in 'Red Dog' it is heroic. The hunting-grounds of Mowgli's pack are over-run by the inferior but vastly more numerous pack of the Dholes from the Deccan, and the wolves fight to the death for their lairs and their cubs. Only the confidence that comes from moving for a long time in a powerful and coherent world of the imagination could have enabled Kipling to write this tale at this pitch. It is extraordinarily—almost blindly—bold, and courts every disaster; and yet I do not think it can be read without emotion by any except such as are unable to read these tales at all. We are presented with the ancient patterns of desperate valour—the threat of the barbarian horde, the sacrificial exploit, the fight in the narrow place, the death of the old leader—in terms which, if we stop to think, are wholly artificial. But we do not stop to think, because the patterns are too strong. The same thing happens in Professor Tolkien's *Lord of the Rings*. The spells work. It is very odd that they do, and a strong note of surprise was perceptible in the reviews of Professor Tolkien's great imaginative story. In 'Red Dog', Won-Tolla, the maimed Outlier, whose mate and cubs have been killed by the horde and who asks only to fight them and die, runs three-legged along the river bank, as his enemies come downstream, taunting them and playing 'his horrible sport'. Considering what parallels such an episode must recall, it is odd that Won-Tolla holds his place as an adequate symbol. The language of the battle is wolf-metaphor. 'The bone is cracked', says Phaon, as the Dholes give back. There is no attempt to obscure the growling, biting, worrying pack, and the tale ends with the cold requiem of Chil the Kite as his hosts drop to their feast. But before that Won-Tolla has died on his slain enemy, and Mowgli has held up Akela to sing his death-song. It is carried through with astonishing conviction and intensity, and with an elevation that does not flag. The laws of life and death have their way with Mowgli's brethren, and the child learns all this from the shelter of a fairy-tale.

The last tale, 'The Spring Running', where Mowgli goes back to his human kindred, is written with a delicate mixture of humour and pathos. At last the Time of New Talk, which sends the wild creatures singing and roving through the jungle and incites even Bagheera to undignified antics, touches the young man. 'Red Dog' could be told through bare facts; but to convey the compulsion that is driving Mowgli, which neither he nor the child who reads about him understands, Kipling has to move indirectly. Mowgli wonders if he has eaten poison; his unhappiness covers him as water covers a log, and the tears that Raksha, his wolf-mother, has told him are the signs of manhood, come to his eyes, for 'It is hard to cast the skin', says Kaa. But he has seen the young girl walk through the crops, and he goes with the favour of the jungle and—such is the reconciling nature of the fairy-tale—with the company of his four-footed foster-brothers. The young child accepts his departure as he accepts Hiawatha's, as another obscure necessity of the strange life of men, and responds to the high mournfulness of the farewell; and the acceptance of uncomprehended necessity is no bad preparation for life.—J. M. Tompkins, "Tales for Children," *The Art of Rudyard Kipling*, 1959, pp. 66–71

⟨Edmund⟩ Wilson disposes of Kipling's novel ⟨*Kim*⟩ by arguing that there must be an inescapable conflict between the Indians and British. Kim, the white orphan, has escaped into native life and becomes simultaneously a neophyte in the British secret service and the disciple of the Lama. "Now what the reader tends to expect is that Kim will come eventually to realise that he is delivering into bondage to the British invaders those whom he has always considered his people." But, he complains, the conflict never materialises and the discrepancy between the Lama's search for salvation and Kim's disreputable mundane activities remains unresolved. No doubt this is what a courageous liberal writing at a time when Gandhi and

Congress were struggling for Indian independence did expect, but such a conflict is imposed by the critic on the novel. No doubt the future life of a young agent would have entailed confounding Indian resistance to the British, but this is an *ex post facto* judgment, and in the novel such a career is depicted as the maintenance of that minimum of order such as is necessary to prevent foreign intrigue, frontier invasions, and injustice by native princes and to permit the joyous, noisy, pullulating mess of Indian life on the Great Trunk Road to continue. Secret services in general since the rise of communist and fascist regimes, and the British secret service in particular since Buchan, Sapper, and other best-sellers for many weary years used it as a vehicle, have little to recommend them in the eyes of the liberal: unhappily they are necessary and in Kipling's India the secret service formed part of that ideal of minimal government—of a handful of officials and a few brigades of troops—which is some degrees better than a full-scale military occupation and a bureaucracy of spies coming not as single sorrows but in M.V.D. battalions. This conflict cannot arise within the terms of the book because the hierarchy of religion and life which is implicit in every description of Indian or English society allots a place to each character which he is compelled to occupy. Born white, Kim can no more become an Indian than the Lama can reverse the Wheel of Life and become a merchant. Just as Tolstoy's characters in *War and Peace* find rest when they realise their essential being and their place and duties, so Kim has to discover the exact slot into which his own tiny personality must fit in the bewildering variety of human beings who pass their transitory lives in the Indian sub-continent.

There can then be no conflict in deciding what role to play in life. Kim and the Lama each has his vocation, Kim to govern, the Lama to achieve Nirvana. These vocations are not contradictory but complementary. Kim and the Lama are the two sides of the coin of man's duty on earth. Both are engaged on a search for reality through knowledge, Kim to find his niche on earth and to discover what he really is, the Lama to find the sacred river on whose banks he will be freed from sin. Both have much to learn. Kim has to endure the humiliation and boredom of being transformed into an Englishman in cantonment and school and has then to master the mysteries of his craft. The Lama, who has realised that God cannot be approached solely through adherence to the reformed laws of his monastery in Tibet, has to experience what other people are and what position they occupy on the Wheel of Life; and whereas at the beginning of the story he blessed the Amritzar courtesan for her alms—"She has acquired merit. Beyond doubt it was a nun"—he has learnt much by the end.

The conflict lies elsewhere, and the fact that it materialises late and is not inevitable is the weakness of the book. The conflict is born of the loyalty of Kim and the Lama to their separate vocations and of their love for each other. When Kim and the Babu have thwarted the two foreign spies, Kim is faced with the dilemma on the one hand of being loyal to his trust, delivering the papers speedily and safely to his chiefs and helping his fellow agent the Babu; and on the other of succouring the Lama who is exhausted by the realisation that he has sinned through pride in his prowess in climbing among the hills and through anger against the Russian officer who struck him. Under this physical and mental strain Kim breaks down and weak with illness staggers out to sleep in the life-giving dust. When he wakes the cog-wheel of his soul has fallen into place and connects with the Wheel of Life on which he and all other beings are bound. Meanwhile the Lama too has been torn with conflict. For while Kim was ill, he stumbled into a brook and found at last his sacred river. In a trance he left the illusions of Time and Space and saw the whole world within the Soul and drew near to the Great Soul. "'Then a voice cried: "What shall come to the boy if thou art dead?" and I was shaken back and forth in myself with pity for thee; and I said: "I will return to my *chela* lest he miss the Way."' Upon this my Soul . . . withdrew itself from the Great Soul with strivings and yearning and retchings and agonies not to be told . . . I pushed aside world upon world for thy sake.'" At the moment of union with Nirvana, the Lama renounces for love his soul's desire.

Kim and the Lama each pursue different kinds of knowledge and neither desires or pretends to understand the other's mind. Both find enlightenment and freedom—the comprehension of the order of things—through love. Kim's love for the Lama makes the Sahiba, the woman of Shamlegh, and Mahbub Ali all love him; the Lama's love for Kim makes Mahbub Ali, who despises the Lama as an unbeliever and a madman, resist the temptation to pillage the Sahiba's household. But the Babu—the only babu whom Kipling drew with affection—does not know love: he is "too good Herbert Spencerian." For only those who are loyal to people, as distinct from ideas, can love.

Such was Kipling's scheme of things. It rests on a highly articulated functional analysis of society in which none but socialised individuals exist. From the analysis proceeds a conservative theory of human existence and political life. This in turn is modified by an awareness of spiritual facts such as repentance, forgiveness, love, and supernatural (or inexplicable) forces which can mitigate the harshness of existence, however little Kipling is willing to allow his readers to forget the harshness. Kipling is almost the sole analogue in England at the turn of the century to Durkheim and Weber and the German and Italian thinkers (whom H. Stuart Hughes treats in his book *Consciousness and Society*) who were in revolt against mid-nineteenth century constructs of the individual and society. He was not a social Darwinist as Wells argued; his understanding of social forces was original and was not as superficial as has been imagined. The charge that he has no mind must be mitigated. He was one of the *cleverest* of Victorian writers.—NOEL ANNAN, "Kipling's Place in the History of Ideas," VS, June 1960, pp. 342–44

. . . ⟨T⟩he offhand, laconic, matter-of-fact, conversational tone of *Plain Tales from the Hills*, the little asides or pieces of intimate information that remind the insider of what he and the author already know, and impress the outsider with that shared knowledge that constitutes a world—these and the continual understatement, the continual contrast of form and content, the continual "writing short," all help to give the stories their particular force. Only six or eight of the forty *Plain Tales from the Hills* are very good stories, and yet somehow the whole book is better than the best of the stories, and gives the reader a surprisingly vivid and comprehensive feeling of the society that produced it. "Lispeth" is a succinct and conclusive anecdote of the betrayal of a native girl—whom Kipling treats with thorough imaginative sympathy—by English hypocrisy, the Protestant, missionary self-righteousness and self-centeredness that Kipling had so early learned to detest; what the story ironically doesn't say, its entire absence of any palliation or justification of what happens, help to give it its attractive, slightly mannered, concise elegance. Kipling's account of the servant's child who, like a bowerbird, makes his queer little pebble-and-glass-and-feather constructions among the castor-oil bushes of the garden is also notable for what it doesn't say: "The Story of Muhammad Din," a plain,

representative anecdote, quite moving and quite unsentimental, seems to me the best of Kipling's early stories about children. (Stories like "Wee Willie Winkie," "His Majesty the King," and "Tods' Amendment"—what you can call, with rough accuracy, Kipling's Little Lord Fauntleroy pieces—are sentimental contrivances that worked with our grandparents and no longer work with us; we have our own.) "A Bank Fraud" is a queerly touching story, ambiguous as life, about the children of darkness being wiser in their generation than the children of light; the "savage self-conceit" of the harshly unworldly accountant, the elaborate, unthanked, unmotivated kindness of the worldly manager, as he sits obediently "reading the Bible and grim 'Methody' tracts" to the dying man, and plans each day's consoling lies—the whole thing is very human and very appealing, down to its last two-faced sentence. "False Dawn," the story of a picnic and a proposal, with complications, makes a reader feel that he has been dipped into Anglo-Indian society for a night, without reservations: by the end of it he is willing to repeat admiringly, with the narrator: "I never knew anything so un-English in my life." It has, perhaps, more sensory immediacy than any of the other *Plain Tales*—or, at least, than any except "In the House of Suddhoo": this presentation of a séance in a native house, and the hodgepodge of attitudes and emotions that goes with it, has at its best an uncanny actuality—Kipling's description of the seal cutter's "unspeakable triple crawl," of the "lip-lip-lapping" of the baby's head in the basin, comes almost too close for comfort. Even the most knowing Anglo-Indians are not much more than accidents at the edge of *this* world. "Jews in Shushan" (it is not actually one of the *Plain Tales* but is so understated, so decidedly "written short," that I always mistakenly remember it as one, along with "At the Pit's Mouth") is a grim, wry little story of the precariousness of life for some other accidents powerless within a large and deadly world; Kipling's picture of the "meek bill-collector at his work, nostrils dilated, lips drawn back over his teeth, and his hands upon a half-maddened sheep" is something else that comes uncomfortably close, and helps to give the story its ambiguous actuality. "At the Pit's Mouth" is a poker-faced story in which all the lines are thrown away. Its organization is as exact as its pictures of the Simla Cemetery, the accident on the Himalayan-Tibet Road, are arresting; the whole story has an unpitying finality about it. It is one of the best and is decidedly the most unpleasant of all Kipling's stories of illicit affairs—it is queer to remember that these were one of his specialties in his early twenties, just as stories actually or ostensibly for children became one of his specialties in his thirties and early forties, and were replaced for the rest of his life by entirely adult stories. "The Man Who Would Be King" is an effective, rather showy adventure story that seems to me romantic in the bad sense of the word; its frame of Indian events is more plausible and attractive than its central action in Kafiristan, which requires a great deal of willing credulity on the reader's part. Many anthologists seem to have said about it, "I guess we'd better put in 'The Man Who Would Be King' for Kipling"; yet, effective as it is, is it really one of his best stories? When I was a boy I used to read, in a magazine called *Adventure*, stories by a thoroughly Kipling-esque writer named Talbot Mundy; it seems to me that "The Man Who Would Be King" is closer to the best of those stories than it is to the best of Kipling's.—RANDALL JARRELL, "In the Vernacular" (1963), *Kipling, Auden & Co.*, 1980, pp. 353–54

'The Man Who Would Be King', the best of the stories Kipling wrote in India, must conclude any study of his apprenticeship, not only because of its brilliance, but because in a sense it embodies and sums up Kipling's attitude to India and the role of the British in the land they had conquered. The story is susceptible of innumerable interpretations: in its mysterious way it is concerned with issues larger than the adventures of a pair of English ne'er-do-wells in the unexplored hills of Kafiristan. Nevertheless, the form of the tale is straightforward. Dravot and Carnehan are tragic figures, conquerors who, like Tamburlaine, conceive the ambition of becoming emperors. They are above the common run of mankind; they are as strong and vigorous as Mulvaney, as subtle at disguise as Strickland, as worldly and cynical as McIntosh Jellaludin. With courage and luck they pile success upon success until they become gods in the eyes of their primitive subjects. But in the end they violate the conditions of their success. Dravot overreaches himself in wanting to take a wife from among his subjects, and his failure of judgment causes him to pull down upon his own head the frail structure his courage and ambition have reared.

Like 'A Wayside Comedy', 'The Man Who Would Be King' is peculiarly Indian in the moral experiment to which its heroes are subjected. 'A Wayside Comedy', however, displays Anglo-Indians in a state of paralysis. Isolated in the remote valley of Kashima, the heirs of the conquerors are unable to enjoy the fruits of conquest. They are a far-flung patrol of an army of occupation, but they lack the inner strength to survive the rigours of such a calling; India is too much for them. In a sense, 'The Man Who Would Be King' looks back to an earlier generation, a generation less troubled by boredom, isolation, and responsibility. Dravot and Carnehan recapitulate the British conquest. Like Clive and the great generals who followed him, they prove that a disciplined native army, provided with effective weapons, is a match for a much larger force of untrained tribesmen. Like the great Anglo-Indian administrators, they find the land divided by petty rulers: they put an end to internecine war, establish the pax Britannica, and win the support of tribesmen who prefer subjection to anarchy. Even their motives show the odd mixture of patriotism and personal ambition that characterized the men who conquered the world for England: '". . . we'd be an Empire. When everything was shipshape, I'd hand over the crown—this crown I'm wearing now—to Queen Victoria on my knees, and she'd say: 'Rise up, Sir Daniel Dravot.'"'

Why, then, does this simulacrum of the Indian Empire fall and crush its makers? The meaning of Dravot's and Carnehan's failure is complex. On the one hand, they have effected their conquest under false pretences. They have concealed from their people the real significance of the Masonic Mark; '"'Only the Gods know that,'"' says Billy Fish; '"'We thought you were men till you showed the Sign of the Master.'"' In Kipling's stories deceit is often a risky business: the truth that underlies situations and men has a powerful tendency to manifest itself. Kafiristan, like India, is a place of extremes; circumstances corrode and destroy false appearances. On the other hand, Dravot and Carnehan succeed as gods and fail only when their manhood is revealed. One of the many ironies of the story is provided by Carnehan's perpetual awareness of his rough-and-tumble background, his continual reduction of their royal acts to the terms he best understands. And so, when Dravot proposes to take a wife—'"'A Queen out of the strongest tribe, that'll make them your blood-brothers, and that'll lie by your side and tell you all the people thinks about you and their own affairs'"'—Carnehan can see it only in terms of a casual liaison with a native girl: '"'Do you remember that Bengali woman I kept at Mogul Serai when I was a platelayer?' says I. 'A fat lot o' good she was to me.'"' Dravot is justifiably angered by the comparison; and yet Peachey is not entirely wrong about Dravot's motives: rather,

he is oversimplifying them. Dravot's desire for a queen is more than lust and more than political strategy; in a sense, it is one of those gestures towards a real contact with the conquered land that occur in *Plain Tales* and always come to nothing. Like the British in India, Dravot and Carnehan can move just so far in the direction of acclimatizing themselves to Kafiristan before they are forcibly reminded that an immense gulf lies between them and their subjects. Reducing the problem to his own simple terms, Carnehan sums it up thus: '"'There's no accounting for natives. This business is our 'Fifty-seven.'"' It is appropriate that Dravot, the unsuccessful builder of a bridge between races, should die as he does, hurled into a chasm from a broken bridge, a bridge that has been destroyed by the tribesmen he has tried to civilize and enlighten.—LOUIS L. CORNELL, "A Vision of India," *Kipling in India*, 1966, pp. 161–64

POETRY

⟨The *Barrack-Room Ballads*⟩ are a statement of Tommy's case as powerful and convincing as it is passionate and sincere. This may not be the real Tommy in his totality. Mr. Kipling, with commendable modesty, leaves that to the decision of Tommy himself, who alone can tell him if what he has written is 'true.' But there can be no mistake about the fact that this is at least the *Wahrheit und Dichtung*—the truth and the poetry—of Tommy, and to have added this to a like achievement concerning Anglo-India, and a certain portion of India, is a record of which any man under thirty might be proud. The *Barrack-Room Ballads* have caught on, as the Americans say, even more decisively than the Anglo-Indian stories, and they have already had an ample, perhaps too ample a measure of justice done to them. In one way they are Mr. Kipling's most genuine personal expression. He threw away the scabbard when he wrote them, and came to the test with those of us who had complained that his earlier work was as good as his latest, and that the bolt seemed shot. Certainly the result proves that, whether or not the bolt was shot in his prose, it was not in his verse, and it is freely to be admitted that he has not only turned back upon himself and put his ancient speech to fresh rhyme and rhythm, but has also struck out notes entirely new. There is only one word for the *Ballads*, viewed from the calmer point of view of criticism, and that is 'taking.' They are wonderfully and tremendously taking. The very cockney *canaillerie* of the dialect in which Tommy is made to express himself has the true contagion of the best music-hall patter song of the hour. The question that arises, of course, is: 'But is this product good enough, strong enough, verifiable enough to last?' No single ballad has had such a *furore* of success as 'Fuzzy-Wuzzy.' A snatch, a line here and there, seems already to have passed into our daily speech, but has it passed permanently? Is not the hour close at hand in which we shall all be hopelessly sick of '"E's a daisy, 'e's a ducky, 'e's a lamb! / 'E's a injia-rubber idiot on the spree'? or of 'We never got a ha'porth's change of 'im: / 'E squatted in the scrub an' 'ocked our 'orses, / 'E cut our sentries up at Suakim, / An' 'e played the cat an' banjo with our forces'?

Doggerel, clever doggerel, attractive doggerel, but doggerel so much above the best of the music-hall as to win it a time-honoured place—inspired doggerel, in a word? Ah, that is less certain! The more often one reads these *Ballads*, the thinner and thinner appear the worst of them, the more and more dubious all but one or two of the very best; and as for the 'other verses,' the twenty poems that follow them up, there are some of them so appallingly bad that they paralyse all efforts at consideration. When you have taken out three or four, the others are simply non-existent. The drop in Mr. Kipling is always straight from the stars into the puddles. He has no middle place, no gradual process of descent. And yet this is not quite so, for at least half a dozen instances could be quoted of his success at spoiling good work by flaws in workmanship, or by his uncertainty of touch. But then his uncertainty of touch is perpetual. It is rarely that he is quite sure how he is working, that he entirely transfuses his material. Take his use of allegory. Could anything be more stupidly and annoyingly obscure than 'The Three Captains'? The whole matter treated of was quite ephemeral, and one may almost say quite personal. He makes an elaborate allegory of it where his letch for technical terms runs riot. Even in the 'Galley Slave,' his one success in this style, he cannot help trying to show us how well up he is in nautical phraseology, as if in an allegory any pressure of the symbolism were not the most obvious futility. Of course, when he attempts direct portrayal, he doses us with his peculiar pedantries to the top of his bent. The *Bolivar* doesn't drift seven days and seven nights merely: she drifts to the Start, because everybody ought to know that the Start is a bit of local colour. Her 'coal and fo'c'sle are short'; her 'bulkheads fly'; she 'hogs' and 'sags' and 'races'; the seas pound at her 'strake'; the Lord, it is hoped, has 'his thumb on the plummer-block' and so on. Clever, isn't it? But (as Mr. Kipling says the devil keeps inquiring), 'Is it art?' To tell the simple truth, it reads rather more like juvenile vanity. Or, again, there is the equal uncertainty of touch which afflicts him when he attempts to write with an assured poetical diction. The 'Ballad of East and West' is such an attempt, and it is the least like a failure of them all. ('The English Flag' is a remarkable instance of how he *can* fail when he really makes up his mind to show us that he is a master of style *quâ* style.) It is, indeed, curious to note how he can write, even in work that has stirred him, galvanised conventionalism side by side with the most vivid and actual realism. Yet he does it again and again. The magnanimous Afghan of this Ballad, for instance, 'whistles his only son,' who, like unto the good young only sons of all the robber chiefs in our more or less pseudo-literature, and also unto our old, old poetic friend the eagle or the hawk or the falcon, or any other member of the *genus raptor*, 'drops from the mountain crest.' Then Mr. Kipling suddenly looks at him as he is, and describes him in one admirable line like this:

He trod the ling like a buck in spring, and he looked
    like a lance at rest.

Fancy that being the line that follows and rhymes with the venerable crest-dropping business! It is almost as bad as the terrible second couplet in the fifth stanza of the 'Galley Slave.'

So much, then, for the outer shape taken by his limitations. The shape they take in the essential qualities of his spirit and intellect is far more disconcerting, because in his happier moments, with thought and emotion at the white-heat, he again and again transcends his tricks of inferior workmanship; but it is, indeed, rarely that he ever quite transcends his tricks of clap-trap sentiment. 'Gunga Din' is one of the very finest of the *Ballads*; it is not too much to say of it that it comes very near being a little masterpiece of its kind. He gives the picture of the 'regimental bhisti,' the devoted 'limpin' lump of brick-dust,' who 'didn't seem to know the use of fear' in his thankless duty of water-carrier to the men, fighting or wounded, on the march, or in camp, or under fire. The particular Tommy who tells the story relates how, when he dropped behind the fight, 'with a bullet where his belt-plate should 'a' been,' it was the inevitable Gunga Din who spied him first, lifted up his head, plugged his wound, gave him a drink, and finally carried him away to a dooli. At this point a bullet comes and drills Gunga Din clean; but, none the less, he

puts Tommy safe inside, and, just before rendering up the ghost,

    I 'ope you liked your drink,' sez Gunga Din!

Could a falser note have been struck? Of course, Gunga Din never said anything of the kind. It was Mr. Rudyard Kipling who said it, because it was one of those superficially smart things which he and his friends, the groundlings, cannot resist. Again and again he does it. The fat Babu Harendra sends the head of a Burman dacoit chief in a packet to an English officer who had, in a moment of baffled impotence, promised 'a hundred' for it; and this is the way the Babu Harendra Mukerji opens his letter:

    Dear Sir—I have honour to send, as you said,
    For final approval (see under) Boh's Head.

Of course, that 'for final approval (see under)' was never written by the Babu. The real writer was *aut Kipling aut diabolus*. Now, what is the good of giving an intensely realistic picture, crammed with technical terms and concentrated characterisation, to end it up with a piece of burlesque like this?— FRANCIS ADAMS, "Mr. Rudyard Kipling's Verse" (1893), *Essays in Modernity*, 1899, pp. 202–8

A . . . definitely unfavorable opinion of his poetry, repeated until it has become a *cliché*, is that the only ideas which he expresses are narrowly intolerant and jingoistic. "The English Flag" is cited as triumphant evidence that he regards his own nation as superior to all others, and three or four bitter occasional poems on British relations with Russia, Germany, and Ireland bespeak a degree of prejudice. It is not usually, however, held a sin in a poet to be a good patriot, or even to express vigorously one-sided views on contemporary events. Such controversial pieces are nearly always bad poetry, being dated and shackled by the topicality of both their subject and their excitement, but Milton, Wordsworth, Shelley, and many others have been guilty of thus giving way to intemperate utterance on passing quarrels, without being eternally stigmatized. With them we readily ignore the offending pages; but for Kipling, though the proportion of bad poems is no greater, there is no leniency.

The fact too often overlooked is that Kipling, instead of being a mouthpiece of jingoistic imperialism, is a vigorous critic of it. His intense devotion to his empire and his high ideal for it make him all the more uncomfortable to the orthodox exponents of British supremacy. The whole caste of Anglo-Indian army and civil service officers still regard him with thinly-veiled hatred for the impudent revelations of their follies with which he began his career, and they are prone to insinuate that he was subversively sympathetic with the native life. Other undesirable types of the "empire-builder" caste are unsparingly displayed in "The Broken Men" and "Gentlemen Rankers". His poems of the common soldier were the first step toward that poetic championing of the underdog in our social system, which has since been exploited by Masefield; and the frank record of the Tommy's point of view regarding his shilling a day from the Widow of Windsor is generally blamed for Kipling's exclusion from the inheritance of Tennyson's laureate crown. In the orgy of national pride at the diamond jubilee, "Recessional" sounded a clear warning against militaristic pretension.

As a matter of fact, tolerance is the very foundation stone of his creed, and human brotherhood is his ideal—not, to be sure, the apotheosis of mediocrity implied in communistic doctrines, but a brotherhood which admits individualism. His opposition to socialistic levelling, as uttered in "Macdonough's Song", "A Servant When He Reigneth", and one or two other poems, arises from his conviction that such a government would be more intolerant and oppressive than any other. But to any artificial barriers of race or religion, to any attempts at coercion, he is vigorously hostile. Again and again he shows that respect or love can surmount racial differences. Some of his most popular pieces enforce this fact—"Gunga Din", "Fuzzy-Wuzzy," "Mandalay". The universally quoted—and universally misinterpreted—text of "The Ballad of East and West" sums up his view: when he says, "East is East and West is West, and never the twain shall meet", he is not emphasizing the color line, the incompatibility of character and outlook of the two races—utterly the reverse. Preparing for an emphatic contrast, his first line is intended to state the mere physical fact of geography, and then follows the assertion that such material boundaries mean nothing to the human spirit:

> But there is neither East nor West, Border, nor
> Breed, nor Birth,
> When two strong men stand face to face, though they
> come from the ends of the earth!

—LIONEL STEVENSON, "The Ideas in Kipling's Poetry," *UTQ*, July 1932, pp. 470–72

HENRY JAMES
"Introduction"
Mine Own People
1891, pp. 1–19

It would be difficult to answer the general question whether the books of the world grow, as they multiply, as much better as one might suppose they ought, with such a lesson of wasteful experiment spread perpetually behind them. There is no doubt, however, that in one direction we profit largely by this education: whether or not we have become wiser to fashion, we have certainly become keener to enjoy. We have acquired the sense of a particular quality which is precious beyond all others—so precious as to make us wonder where, at such a rate, our posterity will look for it, and how they will pay for it. After tasting many essences we find freshness the sweetest of all. We yearn for it, we watch for it and lie in wait for it, and when we catch it on the wing (it flits by so fast) we celebrate our capture with extravagance. We feel that after so much has come and gone it is more and more of a feat and a *tour de force* to be fresh. The tormenting part of the phenomenon is that, in any particular key, it can happen but once—by a sad failure of the law that inculcates the repetition of goodness. It is terribly a matter of accident; emulation and imitation have a fatal effect upon it. It is easy to see, therefore, what importance the epicure may attach to the brief moment of its bloom. While that lasts we all are epicures.

This helps to explain, I think, the unmistakable intensity of the general relish for Mr. Rudyard Kipling. His bloom lasts, from month to month, almost surprisingly—by which I mean that he has not worn out even by active exercise the particular property that made us all, more than a year ago, so precipitately drop everything else to attend to him. He has many others which he will doubtless always keep; but a part of the potency attaching to his freshness, what makes it as exciting as a drawing of lots, is our instinctive conviction that he cannot, in the nature of things, keep that; so that our enjoyment of him, so long as the miracle is still wrought, has both the charm of confidence and the charm of suspense. And then there is the further charm, with Mr. Kipling, that this same freshness in such a very strange affair of its kind so mixed and various and cynical, and, in certain lights, so contradictory of itself. The extreme recentness of his inspiration is as enviable as the tale is startling that his productions tell of his being at home, domesticated and initiated, in this wicked and weary world. At times he strikes us as shockingly precocious, at others as serenely wise. On the whole, he presents himself as a strangely clever youth who has stolen the formidable mask of maturity and rushes about, making people jump with the deep sounds, the sportive exaggerations of tone, that issue from its painted lips. He has this mark of a real vocation, that different spectators may like him—must like him, I should almost say—for different things; and this refinement of attraction, that to those who reflect even upon their pleasures he has as much to say as to those who never reflect upon anything. Indeed there is a certain amount of room for surprise in the fact that, being so much the sort of figure that the hardened critic likes to meet, he should also be the sort of figure that inspires the multitude with confidence—for a complicated air is, in general, the last thing that does this.

By the critic who likes to meet such a bristling adventurer as Mr. Kipling I mean of course the critic for whom the happy accident of character, whatever form it may take, is more of a bribe to interest than the promise of some character cherished in theory—the appearance of justifying some foregone conclusion as to what a writer of a book "ought," in the Ruskinian sense, to be; the critic, in a word, who has, *à priori*, no rule for a literary production but that it shall have genuine life. Such a critic (he gets much more out of his opportunities, I think, than the other sort) likes a writer exactly in proportion as he is a challenge, an appeal to interpretation, intelligence, ingenuity, to what is elastic in the critical mind—in proportion indeed as he may be a negation of things familiar and taken for granted. He feels in this case how much more play and sensation there is for himself.

Mr. Kipling, then, has the character that furnishes plenty of play and of vicarious experience—that makes any perceptive reader foresee a rare luxury. He has the great merit of being a compact and convenient illustration of the surest source of interest in any painter of life—that of having an identity as marked as a window-frame. He is one of the illustrations, taken near at hand, that help to clear up the vexed question in the novel or the tale, of kinds, camps, schools, distinctions, the right way and the wrong way; so very positively does he contribute to the showing that there are just as many kinds, as many ways, as many forms and degrees of the "right," as there are personal points in view. It is the blessing of the art he practices that it is made up of experience conditioned, infinitely, in this personal way—the sum of the feeling of life as reproduced by innumerable natures; natures that feel through all their differences, testify through their diversities. These differences, which make the identity, are of the individual; they form the channel by which life flows through him, and how much he is able to give us of life—in other words, how much he appeals to us—depends on whether they form it solidly.

This hardness of the conduit, cemented with a rare assurance, is perhaps the most striking idiosyncrasy of Mr. Kipling; and what makes it more remarkable is that accident of his extreme youth which, if we talk about him at all, we can not affect to ignore. I cannot pretend to give a biography or a chronology of the author of *Soldiers Three*, but I cannot overlook the general, the importunate fact that, confidently as he has caught the trick and habit of this sophisticated world, he has not been long of it. His extreme youth is indeed what I may call his window-bar—the support on which he somewhat rowdily leans while he looks down at the human scene with his pipe in his teeth; just as his other conditions (to mention only some of them), are his prodigious facility, which is only less remarkable than his stiff selection; his unabashed temperament, his flexible talent, his smoking-room manner, his familiar friendship with India—established so rapidly, and so completely under his control; his delight in battle, his "cheek" about women—and indeed about men and about everything; his determination not to be duped, his "imperial" fibre, his love of the inside view, the private soldier and the primitive man. I must add further to this list of attractions the remarkable way in which he makes us aware that he has been put up to the whole thing directly by life (miraculously, in his teens), and not by the communication of others. These elements, and many more, constitute a singularly robust little literary chapter (our use of the diminutive is altogether a note of endearment and enjoyment) which, if it has the rattle of high spirits and is in no degree apologetic or shrinking, yet offers a very liberal pledge in the way of good faith and immediate performance. Mr. Kipling's performance comes off before the more circumspect have time to decide whether they like him or not, and if you have seen it once you will be sure to return to the show. He makes us prick up our ears to the good news that in the smoking-room too there may be artists; and indeed to an intimation still more refined—that the latest development of the modern also may be, most successfully, for the canny artist to put his victim off his guard by imitating the amateur (superficially, of course) to the life.

These, then, are some of the reasons why Mr. Kipling may be dear to the analyst as well as, M. Renan says, to the simple. The simple may like him because he is wonderful about India, and India has not been "done"; while there is plenty left for the morbid reader in the surprises of his skill and the *fioriture* of his form, which are so oddly independent of any distinctively literary note in him, any bookish association. It is as one of the morbid that the writer of these remarks (which doubtless only too shamefully betray his character) exposes himself as most consentingly under the spell. The freshness arising from a subject that—by all good fortune I do not mean to under-estimate—has never been "done," is after all less of an affair to build upon than the freshness residing in the temper of the artist. Happy indeed is Mr. Kipling, who can command so much of both kinds. It is still as one of the morbid, no doubt— that is, as one of those who are capable of sitting up all night for a new impression of talent, of scouring the trodden field for one little spot of green—that I find our young author quite most curious in his air, and not only in his air, but in his evidently very real sense, of knowing his way about life. Curious in the highest degree and well worth attention is such an idiosyncrasy as this in a young Anglo-Saxon. We meet it with familiar frequency in the budding talents of France, and it startles and haunts us for an hour. After an hour, however, the mystery is apt to fade, for we find that the wondrous initiation is not in the least general, is only exceedingly special, and is, even with this limitation, very often rather conventional. In a word, it is with the ladies that the young Frenchman takes his ease, and more particularly with ladies selected expressly to make this attitude convincing. When *they* have let him off, the dimnesses too often encompass him. But for Mr. Kipling there are no dimnesses anywhere, and if the ladies are indeed violently distinct they are not only strong notes in a universal loudness. This loudness fills the ears of Mr. Kipling's admirers (it lacks sweetness, no doubt, for those who are not of the number), and there is really only one strain that is absent from it—the voice, as it were, of the civilized man; in whom I of course also include the civilized woman. But this is an element

that for the present one does not miss—every other note is so articulate and direct.

It is a part of the satisfaction the author gives us that he can make us speculate as to whether he will be able to complete his picture altogether (this is as far as we presume to go in meddling with the question of his future) without bringing in the complicated soul. On the day he does so, if he handles it with anything like the cleverness he has already shown, the expectation of his friends will take a great bound. Meanwhile, at any rate, we have Mulvaney, and Mulvaney is after all tolerably complicated. He is only a six-foot saturated Irish private, but he is a considerable pledge of more to come. Hasn't he, for that matter, the tongue of a hoarse siren, and hasn't he also mysteries and infinitudes almost Carlylese? Since I am speaking of him I may as well say that, as an evocation, he has probably led captive those of Mr. Kipling's readers who have most given up resistance. He is a piece of portraiture of the largest, vividest kind, growing and growing on the painter's hands without ever outgrowing them. I can't help regarding him, in a certain sense, as Mr. Kipling's tutelary deity—a landmark in the direction in which it is open to him to look furthest. If the author will only go as far in this direction as Mulvaney is capable of taking him, (and the inimitable Irishman is, like Voltaire's Habakkuk, *capable de tout*), he may still discover a treasure and find a reward for the services he has rendered the winner of Dinah Shadd. I hasten to add that the truly appreciative reader should surely have no quarrel with the primitive element in Mr. Kipling's subject-matter, or with what, for want of a better name, I may call his love of low life. What is that but essentially a part of his freshness? And for what part of his freshness are we exactly more thankful than for just this smart jostle that he gives the old stupid superstition that the amiability of a story-teller is the amiability of the people he represents—that their vulgarity, or depravity, or gentility, or fatuity are tantamount to the same qualities in the painter itself? A blow from which, apparently, it will not easily recover is dealt this infantine philosophy by Mr. Howells when, with the most distinguished dexterity and all the detachment of a master, he handles some of the clumsiest, crudest, most human things in life—answering surely thereby the play-goers in the sixpenny gallery who howl at the representative of the villain when he comes before the curtain.

Nothing is more refreshing than this active, disinterested sense of the real; it is doubtless the quality for the want of more of which our English and American fiction has turned so wofully stale. We are ridden by the old conventionalities of type and small proprieties of observance—by the foolish baby-formula (to put it sketchily) of the picture and the subject. Mr. Kipling has all the air of being disposed to lift the whole business off the nursery carpet, and of being perhaps even more able than he is disposed. One must hasten of course to parenthesize that there is not, intrinsically, a bit more luminosity in treating of low life and of primitive man than of those whom civilization has kneaded to a finer paste; the only luminosity in either case is in the intelligence with which the thing is done. But it so happens that, among ourselves, the frank, capable outlook, when turned upon the vulgar majority, the coarse, receding edges of the social perspective, borrows a charm from being new; such a charm as, for instance, repetition has already despoiled it of among the French—the hapless French who pay the penalty as well as enjoy the glow of living intellectually so much faster than we. It is the most inexorable part of our fate that we grow tired of everything, and of course in due time we may grow tired even of what explorers shall come back to tell us about the great grimy condition, or, with unprecedented items and details, about the grey middle state which darkens into it. But the explorers, bless them! may have a long day before that; it is early to trouble about reactions, so that we must give them the benefit of every presumption. We are thankful for any boldness and any sharp curiosity, and that is why we are thankful for Mr. Kipling's general spirit and for most of his excursions.

Many of these, certainly, are into a region not to be designated as superficially dim, though indeed the author always reminds us that India is above all the land of mystery. A large part of his high spirits, and of ours, comes doubtless from the amusement of such vivid, heterogenous material, from the irresistible magic of scorching suns, subject empires, uncanny religions, uneasy garrisons, and smothered-up women—from heat and color and danger and dust. India is a portentous image, and we are duly awed by the familiarities it undergoes at Mr. Kipling's hand and by the fine impunity, the sort of fortune that favors the brave, of *his* want of awe. An abject humility is not his strong point, but he gives us something instead of it— vividness and drollery, the vision and the thrill of many things, the misery and strangeness of most, the personal sense of a hundred queer contacts and risks. And then in the absence of respect he has plenty of knowledge, and if knowledge should fail him he would have plenty of invention. Moreover, if invention should ever fail him, he would still have the lyric string and the patriotic chord, on which he plays admirably; so that it may be said he is a man of resources. What he gives us, above all, is the feeling of the English manner and the English blood in conditions they have made at once so much and so little their own; with manifestations grotesque enough in some of his satiric sketches and deeply impressive in some of his anecdotes of individual responsibility.

His Indian impressions divide themselves into three groups, one of which, I think, very much outshines the others. First to be mentioned are the tales of native life, curious glimpses of custom and superstition, dusky matters not beholden of the many, for which the author has a remarkable *flair*. Then comes the social, the Anglo-Indian episode, the study of administrative and military types, and of the wonderful rattling, riding ladies who, at Simla and more desperate stations, look out for husbands and lovers; often, it would seem, and husbands and lovers of others. The most brilliant group is devoted wholly to the common soldier, and of this series it appears to me that too much good is hardly to be said. Here Mr. Kipling, with all his off-handedness, is a master; for we are held not so much by the greater or less oddity of the particular yarn—sometimes it is scarcely a yarn at all, but something much less artificial—as by the robust attitude of the narrator, who never arranges or glosses or falsifies, but makes straight for the common and the characteristic. I have mentioned the great esteem in which I hold Mulvaney—surely a charming man and one qualified to adorn a higher sphere. Mulvaney is a creation to be proud of, and his two comrades stand as firm on their legs. In spite of Mulvaney's social possibilities, they are all three finished brutes; but it is precisely in the finish that we delight. Whatever Mr. Kipling may relate about them forever will encounter readers equally fascinated and unable fully to justify their faith.

Are not those literary pleasures after all the most intense which are the most perverse and whimsical, and even indefensible? There is a logic in them somewhere, but it often lies below the plummet of criticism. The spell may be weak in a writer who has every reasonable and regular claim, and it may be irresistible in one who presents himself with a style corresponding to a bad hat. A good hat is better than a bad one, but a conjurer may wear either. Many a reader will never be able to say what secret human force lays its hand upon him when Private Ortheris, having sworn "quietly into the blue sky," goes mad with homesickness by the yellow river and raves for the basest sights and sounds of London. I can scarcely tell why I think "The Courting of Dinah Shadd" a masterpiece (though, indeed, I can make a shrewd guess at one of the reasons), nor would it be worth while perhaps to attempt to defend the same pretension in regard to "On Greenhow Hill"—much less to trouble the tolerant reader of these remarks with a statement of how many more performances in the nature of "The End of the Passage" (quite admitting even that they might not represent Mr. Kipling at his best) I am conscious of a latent relish for. One might as well admit while one is about it that one has wept profusely over "The Drums of the Fore and Aft," the history of the "Dutch courage" of two dreadful dirty little boys, who, in the face of Afghans scarcely more dreadful, saved the reputation of their regiment and perished, the least mawkishly in the world, in a squalor of battle incomparably expressed. People who know how peaceful they are themselves and have no bloodshed to reproach themselves with needn't scruple to mention the glamor that Mr. Kipling's intense militarism has for them, and how astonishing and contagious they find it, in spite of the unromantic complexion of it—the way it bristles with all sorts of ugliness and technicalities. Perhaps that is why I go all the way even with "The Gadsbys"—the Gadsbys were so connected (uncomfortably, it is true) with the army. There is fearful fighting—or a fearful danger of it—in "The Man Who Would Be King"; is that the reason we are deeply affected by this extraordinary tale? It is one of them, doubtless, for Mr. Kipling has many reasons, after all, on his side, though they don't equally call aloud to be uttered.

One more of them, at any rate, I must add to these unsystematized remarks—it is the one I spoke of a shrewd guess at in alluding to "The Courting of Dinah Shadd." The talent that produces such a tale is a talent eminently in harmony with the short story, and the short story is, on our side of the Channel and of the Atlantic, a mine which will take a great deal of working. Admirable is the clearness with which Mr. Kipling perceives this—perceives what innumerable chances it gives, chances of touching life in a thousand different places, taking it up in innumerable pieces, each a specimen and an illustration. In a word, he appreciates the episode, and there are signs to show that this shrewdness will, in general, have long innings. It will find the detachable, compressible "case" an admirable, flexible form; the cultivation of which may well add to the mistrust already entertained by Mr. Kipling, if his manner does not betray him, for what is clumsy and tasteless in the time-honored practice of the "plot." It will fortify him in the conviction that the vivid picture has a greater communicative value than the Chinese puzzle. There is little enough "plot" in such a perfect little piece of hard representation as "The End of the Passage," to cite again only the most salient of twenty examples.

But I am speaking of our author's future, which is the luxury that I mean to forbid myself—precisely because the subject is so tempting. There is nothing in the world (for the prophet) so charming as to prophesy, and as there is nothing so inconclusive the tendency should be repressed in proportion as the opportunity is good. There is a certain want of courtesy to a peculiarly contemporaneous present even in speculating, with a dozen differential precautions, on the question of what will become in the later hours of the day of a talent that has got up so early. Mr. Kipling's actual performance is like a tremendous walk before breakfast, making one welcome the idea of the meal, but consider with some alarm the hours still to be traversed. Yet if his breakfast is all to come, the indications are that he will be more active than ever after he has had it. Among these indications are the unflagging character of his pace and the excellent form, as they say in athletic circles, in which he gets over the ground. We don't detect him stumbling; on the contrary, he steps out quite as briskly as at first, and still more firmly. There is something zealous and craftsman-like in him which shows that he feels both joy and responsibility. A whimsical, wanton reader, haunted by a recollection of all the good things he has seen spoiled; by a sense of the miserable, or, at any rate, the inferior, so many continuations and endings, is almost capable of perverting poetic justice to the idea that it would be even positively well for so surprising a producer to remain simply the fortunate suggestive, unconfirmed and unqualified representative of what he has actually done. We can always refer to that.

ROBERT BUCHANON
From "The Voice of 'The Hooligan'"

Contemporary Review, December 1899, pp. 777–83

The English public's first knowledge of Mr. Rudyard Kipling was gathered from certain brief anecdotal stories and occasional verses which began to be quoted about a decade ago in England, and which were speedily followed by cheap reprints of the originals, sold on every bookstall. They possessed one not inconsiderable attraction, in so far as they dealt with a naturally romantic country, looming very far off to English readers, and doubly interesting as one of our own great national possessions. We had had many works about India— works of description and works of fiction; and a passionate interest in them, and in all that pertained to things Anglo-Indian, had been awakened by the Mutiny; but few writers had dealt with the ignobler details of military and civilian life, with the gossip of the mess-room and the scandal of the governmental departments. Mr. Kipling's little kodak-glimpses, therefore, seemed unusually fresh and new; nor would it be just to deny them the merits of great liveliness, intimate personal knowledge, and a certain unmistakable, though obviously Cockney, humour. Although they dealt almost entirely with the baser aspects of our civilisation, being chiefly devoted to the affairs of idle military men, savage soldiers, frisky wives and widows, and flippant civilians, they were indubitably bright and clever, and in the background of them we perceived, faintly but distinctly, the Shadow of the great and wonderful national life of India. At any rate, whatever their merits were, and I hold their merits to be indisputable, they became rapidly popular, especially with the Newspaper Press, which hailed the writer as a new and quite amazing force in literature. So far as the lazy public was concerned, they had the one delightful merit of extreme brevity; he that ran might read them, just as he read *Tit-bits* and the Society newspapers, and then treat them like the rose in Browning's poem—

Smell, kiss, wear it,—at last throw away!

Two factors contributed to their vogue: first, the utter apathy of general readers, too idle and uninstructed to study works of any length or demanding any contribution of serious thought on the reader's part, and eager for any amusement which did not remind them of the eternal problems which once beset Humanity; and second, the rapid growth in every direction of the military or militant spirit, of the Primrose League, of aggression abroad, and indifference at home to all religious

ideals—in a word, of Greater Englandism, or Imperialism. For a considerable time Mr. Kipling poured out a rapid succession of these little tales and smoking-room anecdotes, to the great satisfaction of those who loved to listen to banalities about the English Flag, seasoned with strong suggestions of social impropriety, as revealed in camps and barracks and the boudoirs of officers' mistresses and wives. The things seemed harmless enough, if not very elevating or ennobling. Encouraged by his success, the author attempted longer flights, with very indifferent results; though in the *Jungle Books*, for example, he got near to a really imaginative presentment of fine material, and if he had continued his work in that direction criticism might have had little or nothing to say against him. But in an unfortunate moment, encouraged by the journalistic praise lavished on certain fragments of verse with which he had ornamented his prose effusions, he elected to challenge criticism as a Poet—as, indeed, the approved and authoritative Poet of the British Empire;—and the first result of this election, or, as I prefer to call it, this delusion and hallucination, was the publication of the volume of poems, partly new and partly reprinted, called *Barrack-Room Ballads*.

I have said that Mr. Kipling's estimate of himself as a poet was a delusion; it was no delusion, however, so far as his faith in the public was concerned. The book was received with instantaneous and clamorous approval; and, once again, let me pause to admit that it contained, here and there, glimpses of a real verse-making faculty—a faculty which, had the writer been spiritually and intellectually equipped, might have led to the production of work entitled to be called "poetry." On the very first page, however, the note of insincerity was struck, in a dedication addressed to Mr. Wolcott Balestier, but recognised at once as having done duty for quite a different purpose— resembling in this respect the famous acrostic of Mr. Slum, which, although written to fit the name of "Warren," became at a pinch "a positive inspiration for Jarley." This dedication, with its false feeling and utterly unsuitable imagery, suggests the remark *en passant* that Mr. Kipling's Muse alternates between two extremes—the lowest Cockney vulgarity and the very height of what Americans call "high-falutin'"—so that when it is not setting the teeth on edge with the vocabulary of the London Hooligan it is raving in capital letters about the Seraphim and the Pit and the Maidens Nine and the Planets. . . .

That we might be in no doubt about the sort of thinker who was claiming our suffrages, Mr. Kipling printed at the end of his book certain other lyrics not specially devoted to the military. The best of these, the "Ballad of the *Bolivar*," is put into the mouth of seven drunken sailors "rolling down the Ratcliffe Road drunk and raising Cain," and loudly proclaiming, with the true brag and bluster so characteristic of modern British heroism, how "they took the (waterlogged) *Bolivar* across the Bay." It seems, by the way, a favourite condition with Mr. Kipling, when he celebrates acts of manly daring, that his subjects should be mad drunk, and, at any rate, as drunken in their language as possible. But this ballad may pass, that we may turn to the poem "Cleared," in which Mr. Kipling spits all the venom of Cockney ignorance on the Irish party, *à propos* of a certain Commission of which we have all heard, and while saying nothing on the subject of forged letters and cowardly accusations, affirms that Irish patriots are naturally and distinctively murderers, because in the name of patriotism murders have now and then been done. He who loves blood and gore so much, who cannot even follow the soldier home into our streets without celebrating his drunken assaults and savageries, has only hate and loathing for the unhappy Nation which has suffered untold wrong, and which, when all is said and done, has struck back so seldom. In the poem which follows, "An Imperial Rescript," he protests with all his might against any bond of brotherhood among the Sons of Toil, pledging the Strong to work for and help the Weak. Here, as elsewhere, he is on the side of all that is ignorant, selfish, base, and brutal in the instincts of Humanity. . . .

The truth is, however, that these lamentable productions were concocted, not for sane men or self-respecting soldiers, not even for those who are merely ignorant and uninstructed, but for the "mean whites" of our eastern civilisation, the idle and loafing Men in the Street, and for such women, the well-drest Doll Tearsheets of our cities, as shriek at their heels. Mr. Kipling's very vocabulary is a purely Cockney vocabulary, even his Irishmen speaking a dialect which would cause amazement in the Emerald Isle but is familiar enough in Seven Dials. Turning over the leaves of his poems, one is transported at once to the region of low drinking-dens and gin-palaces, of dirty dissipation and drunken brawls; and the voice we hear is always the voice of the soldier whose God is a Cockney "Gawd," and who is ignorant of the aspirate in either Heaven or Hell. Are there no Scotchmen in the ranks, no Highlanders, no men from Dublin or Tipperary, no Lancashire or Yorkshire men, no Welshmen, and no men of any kind who speak the Queen's English? It would seem not, if the poet of "The Sergeant's Weddin'" is to be trusted. Nor have our mercenaries, from the ranks upwards, any one thing, except brute courage, to distinguish them from the beasts of the field. This, at least, appears to be Mr. Kipling's contention, and even in the Service itself it seems to be undisputed.

How, then, are we to account for the extraordinary popularity of works so contemptible in spirit and so barbarous in execution? In the first place, even fairly educated readers were sick to death of the insincerities and affectations of the professional "Poets," with one or two familiar exceptions, and failing the advent of a popular singer like Burns, capable of setting to brisk music the simple joys and sorrows of Humanity, they turned eagerly to any writer who wrote verse, doggerel even, which seemed thoroughly alive. They were amused, therefore, by the free-and-easy rattles, the jog-trot tunes, which had hitherto been heard only in the Music-halls and read only in the sporting newspapers. In the second place, the spirit abroad to-day is the spirit of ephemeral Journalism, and whatever accords with that spirit—its vulgarity, its flippancy, and its radical unintelligence—is certain to attain tremendous vogue. Anything that demands a moment's thought or a moment's severe attention, anything that is not thoroughly noisy, blatant, cocksure, and self-assertive, is *caviare* to that Man in the Street on whom cheap Journalism depends, and who, it should be said *en passant*, is often a member of smart Society. In the third place, Mr. Kipling had the good, or bad, fortune to come at the very moment when the wave of false Imperialism was cresting most strongly upward, and when even the great organs of opinion, organs which, like the *Times*, subsist entirely on the good or bad passions of the hour, were in sore need of a writer who could express in fairly readable numbers the secret yearnings and sympathies of the baser military and commercial spirit. Mr. Kipling, in a word, although not a Poet at all in the true sense of the word, is as near an approach to a Poet as can be tolerated by the ephemeral and hasty judgment of the day. His very incapacity of serious thought or deep feeling is in his favour. He represents, with more or less accuracy, what the Mob is thinking, and for this very reason he is likely to be forgotten as swiftly and summarily as he has been applauded, nay, to be judged and condemned as

mean and insignificant on grounds quite as hasty as those on which he has been hailed as important and high-minded. Savage animalism and ignorant vainglory being in the ascendant, he is hailed at every street-corner and crowned by every newspaper. To-morrow, when the wind changes, and the silly crowd is in another and possibly saner temper, he is certain to fare very differently. The misfortune is that his effusions have no real poetical quality to preserve them when their momentary purpose has been served. Of more than one poet of this generation it has been said that "he uttered nothing base." Of Mr. Kipling it may be said, so far at least as his verses are concerned, that he has scarcely on any single occasion uttered anything that does not suggest moral baseness, or hover dangerously near it.

G. K. CHESTERTON
From "On Mr. Rudyard Kipling and Making the World Small"
Heretics
1905, pp. 42–51

The first and fairest thing to say about Rudyard Kipling is that he has borne a brilliant part in thus recovering the lost provinces of poetry. He has not been frightened by that brutal materialistic air which clings only to words; he has pierced through to the romantic, imaginative matter of the things themselves. He has perceived the significance and philosophy of steam and of slang. Steam may be, if you like, a dirty by-product of science. Slang may be, if you like, a dirty by-product of language. But at least he has been among the few who saw the divine parentage of these things, and knew that where there is smoke there is fire—that is, that wherever there is the foulest of things, there also is the purest. Above all, he had had something to say, a definite view of things to utter, and that always means that a man is fearless and faces everything. For the moment we have a view of the universe, we possess it.

Now, the message of Rudyard Kipling, that upon which he has really concentrated, is the only thing worth worrying about in him or in any other man. He has often written bad poetry, like Wordsworth. He has often said silly things, like Plato. He has often given way to mere political hysteria, like Gladstone. But no one can reasonably doubt that he means steadily and sincerely to say something, and the only serious question is, What is that which he has tried to say? Perhaps the best way of stating this fairly will be to begin with that element which has been most insisted by himself and by his opponents—I mean his interest in militarism. But when we are seeking for the real merits of a man it is unwise to go to his enemies, and much more foolish to go to himself.

Now, Mr. Kipling is certainly wrong in his worship of militarism, but his opponents are, generally speaking, quite as wrong as he. The evil of militarism is not that it shows certain men to be fierce and haughty and excessively warlike. The evil of militarism is that it shows most men to be tame and timid and excessively peaceable. The professional soldier gains more and more power as the general courage of a community declines. Thus the Pretorian guard became more and more important in Rome as Rome became more and more luxurious and feeble. The military man gains the civil power in proportion as the civilian loses the military virtues. And as it was in ancient Rome so it is in contemporary Europe. There never was a time when nations were more militarist. There never was a time when men were less brave. All ages and all epics have sung of arms and the man; but we have effected simultaneously the deterioration of the man and the fantastic perfection of the arms. Militarism demonstrated the decadence of Rome, and it demonstrates the decadence of Prussia.

And unconsciously Mr. Kipling has proved this, and proved it admirably. For in so far as his work is earnestly understood the military trade does not by any means emerge as the most important or attractive. He has not written so well about soldiers as he has about railway men or bridge builders, or even journalists. The fact is that what attracts Mr. Kipling to militarism is not the idea of courage, but the idea of discipline. There was far more courage to the square mile in the Middle Ages, when no king had a standing army, but every man had a bow or sword. But the fascination of the standing army upon Mr. Kipling is not courage, which scarcely interests him, but discipline, which is, when all is said and done, his primary theme. The modern army is not a miracle of courage; it has not enough opportunities, owing to the cowardice of everybody else. But it is really a miracle of organization, and that is the truly Kiplingite ideal. Kipling's subject is not that valour which properly belongs to war, but that interdependence and efficiency which belongs quite as much to engineers, or sailors, or mules, or railway engines. And thus it is that when he writes of engineers, or sailors, or mules, or steam-engines, he writes at his best. The real poetry, the "true romance" which Mr. Kipling has taught, is the romance of the division of labour and the discipline of all the trades. He sings the arts of peace much more accurately than the arts of war. And his main contention is vital and valuable. Everything is military in the sense that everything depends upon obedience. There is no perfectly epicurean corner; there is no perfectly irresponsible place. Everywhere men have made the way for us with sweat and submission. We may fling ourselves into a hammock in a fit of divine carelessness. But we are glad that the net-maker did not make the hammock in a fit of divine carelessness. We may jump upon a child's rocking-horse for a joke. But we are glad that the carpenter did not leave the legs of it unglued for a joke. So far from having merely preached that a soldier cleaning his side-arm is to be adored because he is military, Kipling at his best and clearest has preached that the baker baking loaves and the tailor cutting coats is as military as anybody.

Being devoted to this multitudinous vision of duty, Mr. Kipling is naturally a cosmopolitan. He happens to find his examples in the British Empire, but almost any other empire would do as well, or, indeed, any other highly civilized country. That which he admires in the British army he would find even more apparent in the German army; that which he desires in the British police he would find flourishing in the French police. The ideal of discipline is not the whole of life, but it is spread over the whole of the world. And the worship of it tends to confirm in Mr. Kipling a certain note of worldly wisdom, of the experience of the wanderer, which is one of the genuine charms of his best work.

The great gap in his mind is what may be roughly called the lack of patriotism—that is to say, he lacks altogether the faculty of attaching himself to any cause or community finally and tragically; for all finality must be tragic. He admires England, but he does not love her; for we admire things with reasons, but love them without reasons. He admires England because she is strong, not because she is English. There is no harshness in saying this, for, to do him justice, he avows it with his usual picturesque candour. In a very interesting poem, he says that—

If England was what England seems
—that is, weak and inefficient; if England were not what (as he believes) she is—that is, powerful and practical—

How quick we'd chuck 'er! *But she ain't!*
He admits, that is, that his devotion is the result of a criticism, and this is quite enough to put it in another category altogether from the patriotism of the Boers, whom he hounded down in South Africa. In speaking of the really patriotic peoples, such as the Irish, he has some difficulty in keeping a shrill irritation out of his language. The frame of mind which he really describes with beauty and nobility is the frame of mind of the cosmopolitan man who has seen men and cities.

For to admire and for to see,
For to be'old this world so wide.
He is a perfect master of that light melancholy with which a man looks back on having been the citizen of many communities, of that light melancholy with which a man looks back on having been the lover of many women. He is the philanderer of the nations. But a man may have learnt much about women in flirtations, and still be ignorant of first love; a man may have known as many lands as Ulysses, and still be ignorant of patriotism.

Mr. Rudyard Kipling has asked in a celebrated epigram what they can know of England who know England only. It is a far deeper and sharper question to ask, "What can they know of England who know only the world?" for the world does not include England any more than it includes the Church. The moment we care for anything deeply, the world—that is, all the other miscellaneous interests—becomes our enemy. Christians showed it when they talked of keeping one's self "unspotted from the world;" but lovers talk of it just as much when they talk of the "world well lost." Astronomically speaking, I understand that England is situated on the world; similarly, I suppose that the Church was a part of the world, and even the lovers inhabitants of that orb. But they all felt a certain truth—the truth that the moment you love anything the world becomes your foe. Thus Mr. Kipling does certainly know the world; he is a man of the world, with all the narrowness that belongs to those imprisoned in that planet. He knows England as an intelligent English gentleman knows Venice. He has been to England a great many times; he has stopped there for long visits. But he does not belong to it, or to any place; and the proof of it is this, that he thinks of England as a place. The moment we are rooted in a place, the place vanishes. We live like a tree with the whole strength of the universe.

The globe-trotter lives in a smaller world than the peasant. He is always breathing an air of locality. London is a place, to be compared to Chicago; Chicago is a place, to be compared to Timbuctoo. But Timbuctoo is not a place, since there, at least, live men who regard it as the universe, and breathe, not an air of locality, but the winds of the world. The man in the saloon steamer has seen all the races of men, and he is thinking of the things that divide men—diet, dress, decorum, rings in the nose as in Africa, or in the ears as in Europe, blue paint among the ancients, or red paint among the modern Britons. The man in the cabbage field has seen nothing at all; but he is thinking of the things that unite men—hunger and babies, and the beauty of women, and the promise or menace of the sky. Mr. Kipling, with all his merits, is the globe-trotter; he has not the patience to become part of anything. So great and genuine a man is not to be accused of a merely cynical cosmopolitanism; still, his cosmopolitanism is his weakness. That weakness is splendidly expressed in one of his finest poems, "The Sestina of the Tramp-Royal," in which a man declares that he can endure anything in the way of hunger or horror, but not permanent presence in one place. In this there is certainly danger. The more dead and dry and dusty a thing is the more it travels about; dust is like this and the thistle-down and the High

Commissioner in South Africa. Fertile things are somewhat heavier, like the heavy fruit trees on the pregnant mud of the Nile. In the heated idleness of youth we were all rather inclined to quarrel with the implication of that proverb which says that a rolling stone gathers no moss. We were inclined to ask, "Who wants to gather moss, except silly old ladies?" But for all that we begin to perceive that the proverb is right. The rolling stone rolls echoing from rock to rock; but the rolling stone is dead. The moss is silent because the moss is alive.

BONAMY DOBRÉE
From "Rudyard Kipling" (1927)
The Lamp and the Lute
1929, pp. 45–61

Mr. Kipling has so scrupulously winnowed the elements of his art, that his candour has deceived many into thinking him too nearly a simpleton to yield much that can be of use to them in exploring life. They are inclined to take too literally Mr. Max Beerbohm's vision of him dancing a jig with Britannia upon Hampstead Heath (after swapping hats with her), and have thought her as much belittled by his bowler as he is made ridiculous by her helmet. But it is really only the high finish of his art which makes him seem to lack subtlety, for he does not display the workings of his mind, his doubts, his gropings. He drives his thought to a conclusion; and it is only when it has reached to force of an intuition, of an assent in Newman's meaning of the word, that he clothes it in appropriate symbols.

He is, one may perhaps claim, romantic by impulse; but then he tries his romance seven times in the fire of actuality, and brings it to the clearness of crystal. Romance, for him, does not lie in yearning, but in fruition: it is not a vague beacon floating in a distant void. It may be

A veil to draw 'twixt God his Law
And Man's infirmity,

but that particular throwing up of the sponge, that sort of beglamouring of facts, is not permanently to his taste. What is more to the credit of romance, in his view, is that, by imagination, and faith, it brings up the 9:15. Yet if that were the end, romance itself would be a trivial thing to make such a pother about, even if bringing up the 9:15 does stand for building cities and conquering continents. For even these things are not, in themselves, of vast worth to Mr. Kipling: they are of value only in so far as they are the mechanism which brings action into play. For in the scheme of things as he sees it, action is of the first and final importance, since it is action alone which can make real for man that 'reality', as we say, which is, perhaps, no more than a dream in the mind of Brahma. So small a matter as

the every day affair of business, meals and
clothing
Builds a Bulkhead 'twixt Despair and the Edge of
Nothing,

for man is playing a Great Game of 'To Be, or Not to Be' in the face of an indifferent universe, a universe as indifferent as Hardy's. So man must work, since 'For the pain of the soul there is, outside God's Grace, but one drug; and that is a man's craft, learning, or other helpful motion of his own mind'; and by the last Mr. Kipling means action, since thought by itself is incomplete, and is only made whole through doing.

It is in the story 'The Children of the Zodiac' that Mr. Kipling seems most wholly to express his view; and there we

read, 'You cannot pull a plough,' said the bull, with a little touch of contempt, 'I can, and that prevents me thinking of the Scorpion,' namely death. But that is not action as a form of running away from thought, but rather identifying oneself with the material of thought. There is a touch of the tragic about Mr. Kipling. But even so the problem is not so clear and shallow that it can be solved easily, for disillusion lurks even behind useful action, and the void may still be there:

As Adam was a-working outside of Eden-Wall,
He used the Earth, he used the Seas, he used the Air
and all;
And out of black disaster
He arose to be the master
Of Earth and Water, Air and Fire,
But never reached his heart's desire!
(The Apple Tree's cut down!)

This disillusion also, it is plain, must be warded off, otherwise work (which is salvation) will not take place; and the Children of the Zodiac did not succeed in warding it off until they had learnt to laugh. Therefore Mr. Kipling also laughs, sometimes to ease his bitterness in this way, but oftener to do more than this; he laughs, not the Bergsonian laughter of social adjustment, but the impassioned, defiant laughter of Nietzsche; not the rectifying laughter of comedy, but the healing laughter of farce. Whence 'Brugglesmith', 'The Village That Voted the Earth Was Flat', and the immortal, the Puck-like Pyecroft. Man must laugh lest he perish, just as he must work if he is to exist at all.

Yet it must not be thought that by work Mr. Kipling means fuss and hurry; he will have nothing to do with 'indecent restlessness'. As to the battle of life, that good old comforter, he remarks that 'The God who sees us all die knows that there is far too much of that battle', and the man who created Kim's lovable lama is not blind to the possibility that his own means of defeating emptiness and evading the fear of death may be vanity. There is a rift somewhere, and Ganesh in 'The Bridge-Builders' may after all be right in regarding the toil of men but as 'dirt digging in the dirt'. There is, indeed, another possibility, and the problem is neatly put in the *Bhagavadgītā*, where Arjuna says: 'Oh Krishna, thou speakest in paradoxes, for first thou dost praise renunciation, and then praisest thou the performance of service through actions. Pray which of them has the greater merit?' It is only after some hesitation that Krishna answers, 'Verily, I say unto thee, that of the two, the performance of service is preferable to the renunciation of action.'

But there must be something behind action to justify it, and with Mr. Kipling it is a love of loyalty which reinforces his philosophy of action. First of all there is that of man to man, a loyalty born of understanding of a man's work, and the wholeness of his character. But personal loyalty, if infinitely valuable, is also horribly rare, and Mr. Kipling has no exaggerated faith in it; he has come not to hope overmuch of man. 'The raw fact of life,' Pharaoh Akhenaton told him, 'is that mankind is just a little lower than the angels, but if you begin by the convention that men are angels, they will assuredly become bigger beasts than ever.' And loyalty is an angelic quality.

This takes us a long way from the 'personal relation', which, as we shall see, figures so large in recent literature; and, indeed, what distinguishes Mr. Kipling from so many present-day writers is precisely that he does not attempt to break down man's loneliness, seeing only futility in the balm of the 'personal relation'.

> Chase not with undesired largesse
>   Of sympathy the heart
> Which, knowing her own bitterness
>   Presumes to dwell apart.

That is why, when Mulvaney told him the story of 'The Courting of Dinah Shadd', the catastrophic tale of his wooing, Mr. Kipling said nothing; he gave him a hand, which can help, but cannot heal: for at the moment when a man's black hour descends upon him, he has to fight it out alone. 'When I woke I saw Mulvaney, the night dew-gemming his moustache, leaning on his rifle at picket, lonely as Prometheus on his rock, with I know not what vultures tearing his liver.'

But since man is thus unavoidably lonely among men, there is another loyalty to serve as a spring of action, and that is a devotion to something each man must conceive of as bigger than himself. Power man has, yet

>   It is not given
>   For goods or gear
>   But for the Thing,

whatever the Thing may be. Mr. Kipling does not even admit the last infirmity of noble mind, for fame does not count. Thus more than sympathy, admiration, and love, go out from him to obscure men with whom 'heroism, failure, doubt, despair, and self-abnegation' are daily matters, and about whom the official reports are silent. His heart is given at once to any person who strives to do a thing well, not for praise, but through sheer love of the craftsman. For him, as for Parolles, self-love is 'the most inhibited sin in the canon'; and, after all, 'one must always risk one's life or one's soul, or one's peace—or some little thing.'

Here then, we see the scale of Mr. Kipling's values. First it is essential to accept the world for what it is with no romantic illusions, to play the man while the odds are eternally and crushingly against you. It is hopeless to try to alter the world. even if you are capable of adding to it, if yours is not the appointed time your work will be sacrificed, as the medieval priest in *Debits and Credits* had to smash his microscope, and the Elizabethan seaman in *Rewards and Fairies* had to abandon his idea of iron ships: the time was not yet. But man must not complain, nor ask for life's handicap to be reduced. '"My right!" Ortheris answered with deep scorn. "My right! I ain't a recruity to go whining about my rights to this and my rights to that, just as if I couldn't look after myself. My rights! 'Strewth A'mighty! I'm a man".' It is that kind of individuality, that kind of integrity, proud and secure in its own fortress, which constitutes the aristocracy which alone is worth while, which alone can play the Great Game of actuality.

An aristocrat is, for Mr. Kipling, one who, whatever his race or caste or creed, has a full man within him: Ortheris, Tallantire of the frontier district, Mahbub Ali, M'Andrew, a whole host of them, all are aristocrats, as is Hobden the labourer, with his sardonic smile at the changes of landlords and the unchangeableness of things. They are aristocrats because they care little for themselves in comparison with what they stand for, because they are generous, and play the Great Game with laughter on their lips, seeking nobody's help, and claiming no reward. 'First a man must suffer, then he must learn his work, and the self-respect that that knowledge brings.' Never mind if he is a failure, a tramp, or a drunkard, he may yet be an aristocrat, if he keeps himself whole, and does not set an undue value upon his feelings. This band of chosen naturally hates the intriguers of Simla, or the Tomlinsons, who, when they die in their houses in Berkeley Square, deserve neither heaven nor hell. It despises the self-styled 'intellectuals' who 'deal with people's insides from the point of view of men who have no stomachs'. It loathes the rabble which whimpers, and the elements which ruin the industrious hive, crying to the workers, 'Come here, you dear downy duck, and tell us about your feelings.' The mob which denies the loneliness of man is hateful to it, for the mob has accomplished nothing, and always defiles what it cannot understand. Thus Mr. Kipling's Utopia, unlike Mr. Well's, is one where privacy must not be violated, and where men slink away when they find themselves part of a crowd, loathing the claims of 'the People', who can be crueller than kings. Moreover, Mr. Kipling has only contempt for those who would marshal and pigeon-hole mankind, making it nicely tidy and neat; he feels they are ignorant of men, shallow in their analysis of motives, 'since the real reasons which make or break a man are too absurd or too obscene to be reached from the outside.' And it follows that for him 'social reform' is the selfish game of the idle.

With this aristocratic preference there goes, as so often, a sense of some Divine Ruler, for to whom else is man to dedicate his work? But Mr. Kipling has no especial choice in this direction, is no sectarian, thinking that 'when a man has come to the turnstiles of Night, all the creeds in the world seem to him wonderfully alike and colourless'. He asks of a creed only that it shall give a man the virtues he admires. 'I tell you now that the faith that takes care that every man shall keep faith, even though he may save his soul by breaking faith, is the faith for a man to believe in.' He has small opinion of Christianity because it has not eliminated the fear of the end, so that the Western world 'clings to the dread of death more closely than to the hope of life'. However, he is very tender to other people's beliefs, for men, after all, need a respite. Thus he writes of a Burmese temple, that 'Those that faced the figures prayed more zealously than the others, so I judged that their troubles were the greater'. For when all has been written and acted, his own faith also may be subject to disillusion; so with perfect consistency he may urge us 'be gentle while the heathen pray to Buddha at Kamakura'.

This, oddly enough, brings us back to Hampstead Heath, for once we speak of Mr. Kipling's religion, we speak of the British Empire. Mr. Beerbohm was cruel in his caricature, but also wittier than he appears at first sight, for he made Mr. Kipling look a little unhappy at having thus blatantly to parade the lady of his homage. Yet one must agree that Mr. Kipling cannot be dissociated from the British Empire. It would almost seem that his mission was to bind it together in one blood-brotherhood, a purposive Masonic lodge, whose business it is to cleanse the world of shoddy. Nor can he altogether escape the suspicion of having been dazzled by it. He is enraptured by the vision of men clean of mind and thew, clear of eye and inward sight, spreading over the earth, their lands bound by the ships which fly over the sea like shuttles, weaving the clan together. His is no mere politician's picture of red on the map, since Britannia for him is a goddess. She is a goddess not only by the fact of her being, but in her nature, for she exacts much toil from her votaries, much of the silent endurance, abnegation, and loyalty that he loves. The Empire then is to be cherished, not so much because it is in itself an achievement, but because, like old Rome, it is the most superb instrument to cause men to outface the universe, assert himself against vacancy. Since it unifies the impulses needed to do this, it is Mr. Kipling's Catholic Church.

These things being, apparently, the basis of Mr. Kipling's thought (though the Empire is, strictly speaking, only an accident, an expression rather than a necessity), we may now ask ourselves, honestly facing the risk of being impudent and unduly probing, of what impulses this thought is the satisfaction. And at the foundation of his philosophic love of action we are tempted to find that pining for action men often have, when, for one reason or another, it is denied them. He sometimes comes near to blaspheming against his art, echoing James Thomson's

> Singing is sweet, but be sure of this;
> Lips only sing when they cannot kiss,

as though the mere act of writing were itself proof of impotence or frustration. This is not a final attitude, but it indicates what may lie behind Mr. Kipling's adoration of perfectly insufferable and not altogether real subalterns, and others, who in various degrees (so long as it is not from offices) handle the affairs of the world.

Yet, ultimately, he is too good a craftsman, too whole an artist, not to see that God, or whatever other name he may be known by, is to be praised in more ways than the obvious. Nevertheless, he now and again reaches out for support to the knowledge that he also is playing the great game, if not of the universe, at least of the world, and is as worthy of a number as Kim, Mahbub Ali, or Hurree Babu:

> Who once hath dealt in the widest game
>   That all of a man can play,
> No later love, no larger fame
>   Will lure him long away.
> As the war-horse smelleth the battle afar,
>   The entered Soul, no, less
> He saith 'Ha! Ha!' where the trumpets are
>   And the thunders of the Press.

Such an attitude permanently held would be far too jejune to produce the real intensity of vision we get from Mr. Kipling; and luckily for us, he has at bottom that worship of his own craft he so much admires in others. Addressing his God, his subtilized Jehovah, who judges man by his deeds, he says:

> Who lest all thought of Eden fade
>   Bring'st Eden to the craftsman's brain,
> God-like to muse on his own trade,
>   And Man-like stand with God again.

There he is the priest of the Mysterious Will, who causes all things to come in their due time; but one feels he still sometimes needs to justify his work to himself. He is urged to make it plain that all his stories are parables. Thus:

> When all the world would have a matter hid,
>   Since truth is seldom friend to any crowd,
> Men write in fable, as old Æsop did,
>   Jesting at that which none will name aloud.
> And this they needs must do, or it will fall
>   Unless they please, they are not heard at all.

It is clear that for Mr. Kipling, art is not an escape: it is a precision of bare facts, which his art must make palatable.

Further, since the choice of a goddess does not lie altogether within a man's mental scope, we may seek in Mr. Kipling's impulses the reason for his profound satisfaction in the Empire, and his need to assert it. Perhaps the most important of these is his craving to belong to something, a love, not of 'the little platoon', to use Burke's phrase, but of the large regiment. 'It must be pleasant to have a country of one's own to show off,' he remarks. Indeed, his craving for roots makes even the deck of a P. and O. British soil; British, not English, because he is a citizen of the Empire, not of England alone: for if it were essential to be the latter, he would be partly dispossessed. Having spent so many of his early years in India, he is not wholly of England: indeed, India is the place where he really belongs. When, for instance, in 1913, he visited Cairo, he wrote: 'It is true that the call to prayer, the cadence of some of the street cries, and the cut of some of the garments differed a little from what I had been brought up to; but for the

rest, the shadow on the dial had turned back twenty degrees for me, and I found myself saying, as perhaps the dead say when they have recovered their wits, "This is my real world again!"' But he is not an Indian, he is an Englishman; therefore, to be an integral whole, he must at all costs make England and the Empire one.

His love of the Empire, and his admiration for those virtues it brings out in men, makes him apt to find qualities in Englishmen only which really exist in all races; and this is part of the deformation Mr. Kipling the artist has at times undergone at the hands of Mr. Kipling the man of action, who found his weapon in the press, and his altar in the Empire. If there had been no daily, or weekly, or monthly papers, he might have remained a priest; but in his middle days he fell into the encouraging hands of W. E. Henley, then, in 1893, editing *The National Observer*. Though this gave his talent scope, it meant that instead of speaking only to those who would understand his very special philosophy, he began to proselytize, and shout too loud into the deaf ears of Demos. His work suffered by the accidents of time and circumstance, by the mischance that he was born into an age of magazines and newspapers, when the listeners are the many, and not the aristocrats to whom he naturally belongs. It took him, with his slightly unhappy expression, on to Hampstead Heath. A change came over his work, and the echo of the voice of Henley 'throwing a chest' (another man of action to whom action was denied) is every now and again heard between the lines. In 1893 he published *Many Inventions*, a rich, varied, and mature work which might be singled out as the best volume of his stories, unless *Life's Handicap* be preferred; but from that year, when he joined Henley, his writing took on a more obviously didactic hue, and we have *The Day's Work*, such parables as 'A Walking Delegate', that tale of perfectly dutiful horses kicking the Trades-Union-Agitator horse; and later, the terrible jingo outbursts of the Boer War. In 1887, or thereabouts, he was writing his delightful *Letters of Marque*, with their profound tolerance of India: in 1907 he wrote for *The Morning Post* the clangorous *Letters to the Family*. The man who had in earlier years remarked 'He began to understand why Boondi does not encourage Englishmen', could later complain 'Yet South Africa could even now be made a tourists' place—if only the railroad and the steamship lines had faith'. That is shocking. It is true that he always loved the Empire, but not in the Hampstead Heath way; and surely it was the exigencies of this later didactic journalism which turned him from a priest into an advance booking agent, and forced him into too extravagant a statement of 'British' qualities. He does not, however, in all his work assume that these are the monopoly of the British, for he awards his due to the Frenchman and the Sikh, and even to the Bengali, when he really gives rein to his profound instincts, and forgets the thunders of the press. Therefore the distortion does not matter in the long run, for time and again he gives us things of a breadth and a peculiar grip we get from no other writer of his generation.

The accidents, then, of Mr. Kipling's attitude may be dismissed, to allow us to return to his intuitions, and proceed to the next step in our analysis, namely, a consideration of what symbols he has chosen to clothe his intuitions in. He has usually chosen men and women to body forth his notions—his plots have no great symbolic importance; and thus his people, as is always the case in really creative art, represent something beyond themselves. They are not merely vehicles for an idle tale. Where he has chosen other material, as in 'The Mother Hive', or 'The Ship That Found Herself', he has failed, as any one is bound to do. An apologue always smacks of the schoolroom, and it is worth noticing that these stories belong to his most didactic period. He is not quite at his ease there, his assent is a little forced; but when his intuition was whole, as in *Kim*, in which the artist conquers the moralist and buries him deep under ground, he is nothing short of superb: his symbols clothe his intuition so that we take it for flesh and blood. That is, we work from life to the thought, and not from the thought to life, as we do with lesser artists, who have ideas they wish to impose upon life. Mr. Kipling's failures occur either when his shallower, demagogue nature takes charge, and we are conscious of didacticism; or where the intuition is uncompleted. It is uncompleted in two sets of instances: the first where women are concerned, whence Mrs. Hauksbee, Mrs. Gadsby, and others, where the symbols are vulgar because the intuition is false (there is a reservation to be made in the case of the woman in the last story in *Debits and Credits*); the second is in the mysterious world of unreality which he feels about him, but which he has not resolved within himself: hence such failures—one must here defy popular opinion—as 'They', and 'The Brushwood Boy'. There the symbols are sentimental because the intuition is feeble.

So far an attempt has been made to define Mr. Kipling's philosophic apparatus; but without delight, and perhaps an attitude of praise, there can be no great art after his manner, and these he has abundantly. A *Diversity of Creatures*; that is not only the title of a book, it is a phrase which occurs often in other of his volumes, and he often thanks God for the variety of his beings. He is an apt illustration for those who claim that only by adoring what is can one add to life; and *quia multum amavit* is a passport to his heaven. He revels in men so long as they are positive, since it is only by his deeds that man can exist. Also, with a generous sensuality which rejects no physical sensation, he loves 'the good brown earth', especially the smells that it produces, West or East. With all these likes, with his keen senses, his recognition of adventure in life and his feeling of romance in works, and his zestful following of men on their occasions lawful and unlawful, he has God's plenty within him.

Thus it is that his best symbols also have God's plenty within them. It is noticeable that they are not like those of Tchekov, say, or of Henry James, since different symbols correspond with different intuitions, and his are not theirs. There is nothing rarefied about them. Mr. Kipling's live close to the ground, and he has frequented the more primitive sort of men because 'all the earth is full of tales to him who listens and does not drive the poor away from his door. The poor are the best of tale-tellers, for they must lay their ear to the ground every night.' He met a hundred men on the road to Delhi, and they were all his brothers, since they lived close to the actualities that can be handled. They were the people in *Kim*, there were Peachey Carnehan and Daniel Dravot (in 'The Man Who Would Be King'); there were forgotten toilers in out-stations, and above all there were Mulvaney, Ortheris, and Learoyd. Nor must it pass unnoticed that all his three soldiers had trodden paths of bitterness ('first a man must suffer'), and were at times subject to an overwhelming sorrow akin to madness, the sorrow of disillusion. They are of value as symbols precisely because they have outfaced much. They were none of them obviously successful, for Mr. Kipling despises success except that which consists in keeping one's soul intact. Whence his sympathy for those who are broken because they are too positive, such as the sometime Fellow of an Oxford college who had passed 'outside the pale', for the lighthouse man who went mad because of the infernal streakiness of the tides, and even for Love o' Women. In such cases, where human beings seem wholly to live the life of the symbol and to exist as a quality, Mr. Kipling is content that men should be no more than a part of the earth; he is happy to be their interpreter, and give them their place as players of the Great Game.

T. S. ELIOT
From "Rudyard Kipling"
A Choice of Kipling's Verse
1941, pp. 5–36

There are several reasons for our not knowing Kipling's poems so well as we think we do. When a man is primarily known as a writer of prose fiction we are inclined—and usually, I think, justly—to regard his verse as a by-product. I am, I confess, always doubtful whether any man can so divide himself as to be able to make the most of two such very different forms of expression as poetry and imaginative prose. I am willing to pay due respect, for instance, to the poetry of George Meredith, of Thomas Hardy, of D. H. Lawrence as part of their *œuvre*, without conceding that it is as good as it might have been had they chosen to dedicate their whole lives to that form of art. If I make an exception in the case of Kipling, it is not because I think he succeeded in making the division successfully, but because I think that, for reasons which it will be partly the purpose of this essay to put forward, his verse and his prose are inseparable; that we must finally judge him, not separately as a poet and as a writer of prose fiction, but as the inventor of a mixed form. So a knowledge of his prose is essential to the understanding of his verse, and a knowledge of his verse is essential to the understanding of his prose. In so far therefore as I concern myself here with his verse by itself, it is only with the aim of restoring it to its place afterwards and seeing the total work more clearly. In most studies of Kipling that I have read, the writers seem to me to have treated the verse as secondary, and in so doing to have evaded the question—which is, nevertheless, a question that everyone asks—whether Kipling's verse really is poetry; and, if not, what it is.

The starting point for Kipling's verse is the motive of the ballad-maker; and the modern ballad is a type of verse for the appreciation of which we are not provided with the proper critical tools. We are therefore inclined to dismiss the poems, by reference to poetic criteria which do not apply. It must therefore be our task to understand the type to which they belong, before attempting to value them: we must consider what Kipling was trying to do and what he was not trying to do. The task is the opposite of that with which we are ordinarily faced when attempting to defend contemporary verse. We expect to have to defend a poet against the charge of obscurity: we have to defend Kipling against the charge of excessive lucidity. We expect a poet to be reproached for lack of respect for the intelligence of the common man, or even for deliberately flouting the intelligence of the common man: we have to defend Kipling against the charge of being a 'journalist' appealing only to the commonest collective emotions. We expect a poet to be ridiculed because his verse does not appear to scan: we must defend Kipling against the charge of writing jingles. In short, people are exasperated by poetry which they do not understand, and contemptuous of poetry which they understand without effort; just as an audience is offended by a speaker who talks over its head, and by a speaker whom it suspects of talking down to it.

A further obstacle to the appreciation of many of Kipling's

poems is their topicality, their occasional character, and their political associations. People are often inclined to disparage poetry which appears to have no bearing on the situation to-day; but they are always inclined to ignore that which appears to bear only on the situation of yesterday. A political association may help to give poetry immediate attention: it is in spite of this association that the poetry will be read, if it is read, to-morrow. Poetry is condemned as 'political' when we disagree with the politics; and the majority of readers do not want either imperialism or socialism in verse. But the question is not what is ephemeral, but what is permanent: a poet who appears to be wholly out of touch with his age may still have something very important to say to it; and a poet who has treated problems of his time will not necessarily go out of date. Arnold's 'Stanzas from the Grande Chartreuse' voice a moment of historic doubt, recorded by its most representative mind, a moment which has passed, which most of us have gone beyond in one direction or another: but it represents that moment for ever.

We have therefore to try to find the permanent in Kipling's verse: but this is not simply to dissociate form from content. We must consider the content itself, the social and political attitude in its development; and, making an effort to detach ourselves from the assumptions of our own generation, enquire whether there is something more in Kipling than is expressed by Beerbohm's caricature of the Bank Holiday cornet virtuoso on the spree.

I

. . . There have been many writers of verse who have not aimed at writing poetry: with the exception of a few writers of humorous verse, they are mostly quickly forgotten. The difference is that they never did write poetry. Kipling does write poetry, but that is not what he is setting out to do. It is this peculiarity of intention that I have in mind in calling Kipling a 'ballad-writer' and it will take some time to make clear what I mean by that. For I am extending and also somewhat limiting the meaning of the word 'ballad'. It is true that there is an unbroken thread of meaning connecting the various kinds of verse to which the term 'ballad' has been applied. In the narrative Border Ballad, the intention is to tell a story in what, at that stage of literature, is the natural form for a story which is intended to arouse emotion. The poetry of it is incidental and to some extent unconscious; the form is short rhymed stanzas. The attention of the reader is concentrated on the story and the characters; and the ballad must have a meaning immediately apprehensible by its auditors. Repeated hearings may confirm the first impressions, may repeat the effect, but full understand-ing should be conveyed at one hearing. The metrical form must be of a simple kind which will not call attention to itself, but repetitions and refrains may contribute an incantatory effect. There should be no metrical complications correspond-ing to subtleties of feeling that cannot be immediately responded to. At another stage of culture—as in Anglo-Saxon and in the elaborate forms of Welsh—poetry develops a conscious virtuosity, requiring a virtuosity of appreciation on the part of the audience: the forms impose upon the bard restrictions and obstacles in overcoming which he exhibits his skill. It must be remembered that this sophistication is not only present in what we call 'modern' literature or in the later stages of development of classical literatures such as those of Latin, Greek, Sanskrit, Persian, or Chinese: it is a stage sometimes reached in the poetry of peoples of lower cultures. And on the other hand, ballad verse is not simply a stage in historical development: the ballad persists and develops in its own way, and corresponds to a permanent level of enjoyment of literature. There is always a potential public for the ballad: but

the social conditions of modern society make it difficult for the good ballad to be written. It is perhaps more difficult now than it was at the time when *Barrack-Room Ballads* were written: for Kipling had at least the inspiration and refreshment of the living music-hall.

In order to produce the contemporary ballad, it is of no particular help to hold advanced social views, or to believe that the literature of the future must be a 'popular' literature. The ballad must be written for its own sake and for its own purposes. It would be a mistake, also, and a supercilious kind of mistake, to suppose that the audience for balladry consists of factory workers, mill hands, miners and agricultural labourers. It does contain people from these categories, but the composition of this audience has, I suspect, no relation to any social and economic stratification of society. The audience for the more highly developed, even for the more esoteric kinds of poetry is recruited from every level: often the uneducated find them easier to accept than do the half-educated. On the other hand, the audience for the ballads includes many who are, according to the rules, highly educated; it includes many of the powerful, the learned, the highly specialised, the inheritors of prosperity. I do not mean to suggest that the two audiences ought to be, or must be, two worlds: but that there will be one audience capable only of what I may call ballad attention, and a smaller audience capable of enjoying both the ballad and the more difficult forms of poetry. Now it is to the ballad attention that Kipling addresses himself: but that does not mean that all of his poems appeal only on that level.

What is unusual about Kipling's ballads is his singleness of intention in attempting to convey no more to the simple minded than can be taken in on one reading or hearing. They are best when read aloud, and the ear requires no training to follow them easily. With this simplicity of purpose goes a consummate gift of word, phrase, and rhythm. There is no poet who is less open to the charge of repeating himself. In the ballad, the stanza must not be too long and the rhyme scheme must not be too complicated;[1] the stanza must be immediately apprehensible as a whole; a refrain can help to insist upon the identity within which a limited range of variation is possible. The variety of form which Kipling manages to devise for his ballads is remarkable: each is distinct, and perfectly fitted to the content and the mood which the poem has to convey. Nor is the versification too regular: there is the monotonous beat only when the monotonous is what is required; and the irregularities of scansion have a wide scope. One of the most interesting exercises in the combination of heavy beat and variation of pace is found in 'Danny Deever', a poem which is technically (as well as in content) remarkable. The regular recurrence of the same end-words, which gain immensely by imperfect rhyme (*parade* and *said*) gives the feeling of marching feet and the movement of men in disciplined formation—in a unity of movement which enhances the horror of the occasion and the sickness which seizes the men as individuals; and the slightly quickened pace of the final lines marks the change in movement and in music. There is no single word or phrase which calls too much attention to itself, or which is not there for the sake of the total effect; so that when the climax comes—

'What's that that whimpers over'ead?' said Files-on-
    Parade,
'It's Danny's soul that's passin' now,' the Colour-
    Sergeant said.

(the word *whimper* being exactly right) the atmosphere has been prepared for a complete suspension of disbelief.

It would be misleading to imply that all of Kipling's poems, or at least all that matter, are 'ballads': there is a great variety of kinds. I mean only that the approach to the understanding of what he was trying to do, in all his varied verse, is through the ballad motive. The best introduction, for my present purpose, is to call attention to a dozen or so particular poems representing his different types. For the reader to whom the ballad approach to poetry is the most natural, there is no need to show that Kipling's verse reaches from time to time the intensity of 'poetry': for such readers it is more useful to discuss the content, the view of life, and to overcome the prejudices which they may entertain against any verse which has a different subject matter or a different point of view from that which they happen to accept: to detach it, furthermore, from irrelevant association with subsequent events and attitudes. That I shall attempt in the next section. In choosing the examples which follow here, I have in mind rather the reader who, if he believes that Kipling wrote 'political jingles', stresses the word *jingles* rather than the word *political*.

The first impression we may take from inspection of a number of the poems chosen to show the variety, is that this variety is suspiciously great. We may, that is, fail to see in it more than the virtuosity of a writer who could turn his hand to any form and matter at will: we may fail to discern any unity. We may be brought to admit that one poem after another does, in one way or another, have its 'poetic' moment, and yet believe that the moments are only accidental or illusory. It would be a mistake to assume that a few poems can be chosen which are 'poetry', and that the rest, by implication, need not be read. A selection made in this way would be arbitrary, because there is no handful of poems which can be so isolated from the rest; it would be misleading because the significance of the 'poems' would be lost except with the background of the 'verse', just as the significance of the verse is missed except in the context of the prose. No part of Kipling's work, and no period of his work, is wholly appreciable without taking into account the others: and in the end, this work, which studied piecemeal appears to have no unity beyond the haphazard of external circumstances, comes to show a unity of a very complicated kind.

If, therefore, I call particular attention to 'Danny Deever' as a barrack-room ballad which somehow attains the intensity of poetry, it is not with the purpose of isolating it from the other ballads of the same type, but with the reminder that with Kipling you cannot draw a line beyond which some of the verse becomes 'poetry'; and that the poetry, when it comes, owes the gravity of its impact to being something over and above the bargain, something more than the writer undertook to give you; and that the matter is never simply a pretext, an occasion for poetry. There are other poems in which the element of poetry is more difficult to put one's finger on, than in 'Danny Deever'. Two poems which belong together are 'M'Andrew's Hymn' and 'The *Mary Gloster*'. They are dramatic monologues, obviously, as I have said, owing something to Browning's invention, though metrically and intrinsically ballads. The popular verdict has chosen the first as the more memorable: I think that the popular verdict is right, but just what it is that raises 'M'Andrew's Hymn' above The *Mary Gloster* is not easy to say. The rapacious old ship owner of the latter is not easily dismissed, and the presence of the silent son gives a dramatic quality absent from M'Andrew's soliloquy. One poem is no less successful than the other. If the M'Andrew poem is the more memorable, it is not because Kipling is more inspired by the contemplation of the success of failure than by that of the failure of success, but because there is greater poetry in the subject matter. It is M'Andrew who creates the poetry of Steam, and Kipling who creates the poetry of M'Andrew.

We sometimes speak as if the writer who is most consciously and painstakingly the 'craftsman' were the most remote from the interests of the ordinary reader, and as if the popular writer were the artless writer. But no writer has ever cared more for the craft of words than Kipling: a passion which gives him a prodigious respect for the artist of any art, and the craftsman of any craft[2] and which is perhaps involved in his respect for Free Masonry. The problems of the literary artist constantly recur in his stories:[3] in '"Wireless"', for instance, where the poor consumptive chemist's assistant is for a night identified with Keats at the moment of writing *The Eve of St. Agnes*; in '"The Finest Story in the World"', where Kipling takes the trouble to provide a very good poem, in rather free verse (the 'Song of the Galley Slaves') and a very bad poem in regular verse, to illustrate the difference between the poem which forces its way into the consciousness of the poet and the poem which the writer himself forces. The difference between the craft and the art of poetry is of course as difficult to determine as the difference between poetry and balladry. It will not help us to decide the place of Kipling in poetry: we can only say that Kipling's craftsmanship is more reliable than that of some greater poets, and that there is hardly any poem, even in the collected works, in which he fails to do what he has set out to do. The great poet's craft may sometimes fail him: but at his greatest moments he is doing what Kipling is usually doing on a lower plane—writing transparently, so that our attention is directed to the object and not to the medium. Such a result is not simply attained by absence of decoration—for even the absence of decoration may err in calling attention to itself—but by never using decoration for its own sake,[4] though, again, the apparently superfluous may be what is really important. Now one of the problems which arise concerning Kipling is related to that skill of craftsmanship which seems to enable him to pass from form to form, though always in an identifiable idiom, and from subject to subject, so that we are aware of no inner compulsion to write about this rather than that—a versatility which may make us suspect him of being no more than a performer. We look, in a poet as well as in a novelist, for what Henry James called the Figure in the Carpet. With the greatest of modern poets this Figure is perfectly manifest (for we can be sure of the existence of the Figure without perfectly understanding it): I mention Yeats at this point because of the contrast between his development, which is very apparent in the way he writes, and Kipling's development, which is only apparent in what he writes about. We expect to feel, with a great writer, that he *had* to write about the subject he took, and in that way. With no writer of equal eminence to Kipling is this inner compulsion, this unity in variety more difficult to discern.

I pass from the earlier ballads to mention a second category of Kipling's verse: those poems which arise out of, or comment upon topical events. Some of these, such as 'The Truce of the Bear', in the form of an apologue, do not aim very high. But to be able to write good verse to occasion is a very rare gift indeed: Kipling had the gift, and he took the obligation to employ it very seriously. Of this type of poem I should put 'Gehazi'—a poem inspired by the Marconi scandals—very high, as a passionate invective rising to real eloquence (and a poem which illustrates, incidentally, the important influence of Biblical imagery and the Authorised Version language upon his writing). The poems on Canada and Australia, and the exequy on King Edward VII, are excellent in their kind, though not very memorable individually. And the gift for occasional verse is allied to the gift for two other kinds of verse in which Kipling excelled: the epigram and the hymn. Good epigrams in English are very few; and the great hymn writer is very rare. Both are extremely objective types of verse: they can and should be charged with intense feeling, but it must be a feeling that can be completely shared. They are possible to a writer so impersonal as Kipling: and I should like the reader to look attentively at the 'Epitaphs of the War'. I call Kipling a great hymn writer on the strength of 'Recessional'. It is a poem almost too well known to need to have the reader's attention called to it, except to point out that it is one of the poems in which something breaks through from a deeper level than that of the mind of the conscious observer of political and social affairs—something which has the true prophetic inspiration. Kipling might have been one of the most notable of hymn writers. The same gift of prophecy appears, on the political plane, in other poems, such as 'The Storm Cone', but nowhere with greater authority than in 'Recessional'.

It is impossible, however, to fit all of Kipling's poems into one or another of several distinct classes. There is the poem 'Gethsemane', which I do not think I understand, and which is the more mysterious because of the author's having chosen to place it so early in his collected edition, since it bears the sub-heading '1914–1918'. And there are the poems of the later period.

The verse of the later period shows an even greater diversity than the early poems. The word 'experimentation' may be applied, and honourably applied, to the work of many poets who develop and change in maturity. As a man grows older, he may turn to new subject-matter, or he may treat the same material in a different way; as we age we both live in a different world, and become different men in the same world. The changes may be expressed by a change of rhythm, of imagery, of form: the true experimentor is not impelled by restless curiosity, or by desire for novelty, or the wish to surprise and astonish, but by the compulsion to find, in every new poem as in his earliest, the right form for feelings over the development of which he has, as a poet, no control. But just as, with Kipling, the term 'development' does not seem quite right, so neither does the term 'experimentation'. There is great variety, and there are some very remarkable innovations indeed, as in 'The Way through the Woods' and in 'The Harp Song of the Dane Woman'—

> What is a woman that you forsake her,
> And the hearth-fire and the home-acre,
> To go with the old grey Widow-maker?

and in the very fine 'Runes on Weland's Sword'. But there were equally original inventions earlier ('Danny Deever'); and there are too, among the later poems, some very fine ones cast in more conventional form, such as 'Cold Iron', 'The Land', 'The Children's Song'.

I confess therefore that the critical tools which we are accustomed to use in analysing and criticising poetry do not seem to work; I confess furthermore that introspection into my own processes affords no assistance—part of the fascination of this subject is in the exploration of a mind so different from one's own. I am accustomed to the search for form: but Kipling never seems to be searching for form, but only for a particular form for each poem. So we find in the poems an extraordinary variety, but no evident pattern—the connection is to be established on some other level. Yet this is no display of empty virtuosity, and we can be sure that there is no ambition of either popular or esoteric success for its own sake. The writer is not only serious, he has a vocation. He is completely ambidexterous, that is to say completely able to express himself in verse or prose: but his necessity for often expressing the same thing in a story and in a poem is a much deeper necessity than that merely to exhibit skill. I know of no writer of such great gifts for whom poetry seems to have been more purely an

instrument. Most of us are interested in the form for its own sake—not apart from the content, but because we aim at making something which shall first of all *be*, something which in consequence will have the capability of exciting, within a limited range, a considerable variety of responses from different readers. For Kipling the poem is something which is intended to *act*—and for the most part his poems are intended to elicit the same response from all readers, and only the response which they can make in common. For other poets—at least, for some other poets—the poem may begin to shape itself in fragments of musical rhythm, and its structure will first appear in terms of something analogous to musical form; and such poets find it expedient to occupy their conscious mind with the craftsman's problems, leaving the deeper meaning to emerge, if there, from a lower level. It is a question then of what one chooses to be conscious of, and of how much of the meaning, in a poem, is conveyed direct to the intelligence and how much is conveyed indirectly by the musical impression upon the sensibility—always remembering that the use of the word 'musical' and of musical analogies, in discussing poetry, has its dangers if we do not constantly check its limitations: for the music of verse is inseparable from the meanings and associations of words. If I say, then, that this musical concern is secondary and infrequent with Kipling, I am not implying any inferiority of craftsmanship, but rather a different order of values from that which we expect to determine the structure of poetry. . . .

II

I have expressed the view that the variety of Kipling's verse, and its mutations from one period to another, cannot be accounted for, and given a unified pattern, by tracing development as we might with most poets. His development cannot be understood through his verse alone, because he was, as I said at the beginning, an integral prose-and-verse writer; and to understand changes we have to consider the prose and the verse together. Kipling appears first to be a writer of different phases and occupations, who in each phase is completely developed, who is never so committed to the pursuit of one verse form as to be prevented from moving to another. He is so different from other poets that the lazy critic is tempted merely to assert that he is not a poet at all, and leave it at that. The changes in his poetry, while they cannot be explained by any usual scheme of poetic development, can to some extent be explained by changes in his outward circumstances. I say 'to some extent', because Kipling, apparently merely the reflection of the world about him, is the most inscrutable of authors. An immense gift for using words, an amazing curiosity and power of observation with his mind and with all his senses, the mask of the entertainer, and beyond that a queer gift of second sight, of transmitting messages from elsewhere, a gift so disconcerting when we are made aware of it that thenceforth we are never sure when it is *not* present: all this makes Kipling a writer impossible wholly to understand and quite impossible to belittle.

Certainly an exceptional sensitiveness to environment is the first characteristic of Kipling that we notice; so that on one level, we may trace his course by external circumstances. What life would have made of such a man, had his birth, growth, maturity and age all taken place in one set of surroundings, is beyond speculation: as life directed, the result was to give him a peculiar detachment and remoteness from all environment, a universal foreignness which is the reverse side of his strong feeling for India, for the Empire, for England and for Sussex, a remoteness as of an alarmingly intelligent visitor from another planet. He remains somehow alien and aloof from all with which he identifies himself. The reader who can get a little distance—but not deep enough—below the level of Kipling's popularity as a teller of tales and reciter of ballads, and who has a vague feeling of something underneath, is apt to give the wrong explanation of his own discomfort. I have tried to disturb the belief that Kipling is a mere writer of jingles: we must now consider whether these 'jingles' are, in a denigratory sense, 'political'.

To have been born in India and to have spent the first remembered years there, is a circumstance of capital importance for a child of such impressionability. To have spent the years from seventeen to twenty-four earning his living there, is for a very precocious and observant young man an important experience also. The result is, it seems to me, that there are two strata in Kipling's appreciation of India, the stratum of the child and that of the young man. It was the latter who observed the British in India and wrote the rather cocky and acid tales of Delhi and Simla, but it was the former who loved the country and its people. In his Indian tales it is on the whole the Indian characters who have the greater reality, because they are treated with the understanding of love. One is not very loving between seventeen and twenty-four. But it is Purun Bhagat, it is the four great Indian characters in *Kim* who are real: the Lama, Mahbub Ali, Hurree Chunder Mookerjee, and the wealthy widow from the North. As for the Britons, those with whom he is most sympathetic are those who have suffered or fallen— McIntosh Jellaludin has learned more than Strickland.[5] Kipling is of India in a different way from any other Englishman who has written, and in a different way from that of any particular Indian, who has a race, a creed, a local habitation and, if a Hindu, a caste. He might almost be called the first citizen of India. And his relation to India determines that about him which is the most important thing about a man, his religious attitude. It is an attitude of comprehensive tolerance.[6] He is not an unbeliever—on the contrary, he can accept all faiths: that of the Moslem, that of the Hindu, that of the Buddhist, Parsee or Jain, even (through the historical imagination) that of Mithra: if his understanding of Christianity is less affectionate, that is due to his Anglo-Saxon background—and no doubt he saw enough in India of clergy such as Mr. Bennett in *Kim*.

To explain Kipling's feeling for the Empire, and his later feeling for Sussex, as merely the nostalgia of a man without a country, as the need for support felt by the man who does not belong, would be a mistake which would prevent us from understanding Kipling's peculiar contribution. To explain away his patriotic feeling in this way is only necessary for those who consider that such feeling is not a proper theme for verse. There are perhaps those who will admit to expression in poetry patriotism on the defensive: Shakespeare's Henry V is acceptable, in his otherwise embarrassing grandiloquence, because the French army was a good deal bigger than the English force, even though Henry's war could hardly be described as a defensive one. But if there is a prejudice against patriotic verse, there is a still stronger prejudice against imperial patriotism in verse. For too many people, an Empire has become something to apologise for, on the ground that it happened by accident, and with the addition that it is a temporary affair anyway and will eventually be absorbed into some universal world association: and patriotism itself is expected to be inarticulate. But we must accustom ourselves to recognising that for Kipling the Empire was not merely an idea, a good idea or a bad one; it was something the reality of which he felt. And in his expression of his feeling he was certainly not aiming at flattery of national, racial or imperial vanity, or attempting to propagate a political

programme: he was aiming to communicate the awareness of something in existence of which he felt that most people were very imperfectly aware. It was an awareness of grandeur, certainly, but it was much more an awareness of responsibility.

There is the question of whether 'political' poetry is admissible; there is the question of the way in which Kipling's political poetry is political; there is the question of what his politics were; and finally, there remains the question of what we are to say of that considerable part of his work which cannot, by any stretch of the term, be called political at all.

It is pertinent to call attention to one other great English writer who put politics into verse—Dryden. The question whether Kipling was a poet is not unrelated to the question whether Dryden was a poet. The author of *Absalom and Achitophel* was satirising a lost cause in retrospect, and he was on the successful side; the author of *The Hind and the Panther* was arguing a case in ecclesiastical politics; and both of these purposes were very different from that which Kipling set himself. Both of Dryden's poems are more political in their appeal to the reason than any of Kipling's. But the two men had much in common. Both were masters of phrase, both employed rather simple rhythms with adroit variations; and by both the medium was employed to convey a simple forceful statement, rather than a musical pattern of emotional overtones. And (if it is possible to use these terms without confusion) they were both classical rather than romantic poets. They arrive at poetry through eloquence; for both, wisdom has the primacy over inspiration; and both are more concerned with the world about them than with their own joys and sorrows, and concerned with their own feelings in their likeness to those of other men rather than in their particularity. But I should not wish to press this likeness too far, or ignore the great differences: and if Kipling suffers in some respects by the comparison, it must be remembered that he has other qualities which do not enter into it at all.

Kipling certainly thought of verse as well as prose as a medium for a public purpose; if we are to pass judgment upon his purpose, we must try to set ourselves in the historical situations in which his various work was written; and whether our prejudice be favourable or antagonistic, we must not look at his observations of one historical situation from the point of view of a later period. Also, we must consider his work as a whole, and the earlier years in the light of the later, and not exaggerate the importance of particular pieces or phrases which we may not like. Even these may be misinterpreted. Mr. Edward Shanks, who has written the best book on Kipling that I have read (and whose chapter on 'The Prophet of Empire' resumes Kipling's political views admirably) says of the poem called 'Loot' (a soldier ballad describing the ways of extorting hidden treasure from natives): 'this is wholly detestable, and it makes the commentator on Kipling turn red when he endeavours to explain it'. This is to read an attitude into the poem which I had never suspected. I do not believe that in this poem he was commending the rapacity and greed of such irregularities, or condoning rapine. If we think this, we must also presume that 'The Ladies' was written to glorify miscellaneous miscegenation on the part of professional soldiers quartered in foreign lands. Kipling, at the period to which these poems belong, undoubtedly felt that the professional ranker and his officers too were unappreciated by their peaceful countrymen at home, and that in the treatment of the soldier and the discharged soldier there was often less than social justice: but his concern was to make the soldier known, not to idealise him. He was exasperated by sentimentalism as well as by depreciation or neglect—and either attitude is liable to evoke the other.

I have said that in Kipling as a poet there is no development, but mutation; and that for the development we must look to changes in the environment and in the man himself. The first period is that of India; the second that of travel and of residence in America; the third is that of his settlement in Sussex. These divisions are obvious: what is not so obvious is the development of his view of empire, a view which expands and contracts at the same time. He had always been far from uncritical of the defects and wrongs of the British Empire, but held a firm belief in what it should and might be. In his later phase England, and a particular corner of England, becomes the centre of his vision. He is more concerned with the problem of the soundness of the *core* of empire; this core is something older, more natural and more permanent. But at the same time his vision takes a larger view, and he sees the Roman Empire and the place of England in it. The vision is almost that of an idea of empire laid up in heaven. And with all his geographical and historical imagination, no-one was farther than he from interest in men in the mass, or the manipulation of men in the mass: his symbol was always a particular symbol. The symbol had been, at one time, such men as Mulvaney or Strickland: it became Parnesius and Hobden. Technical mechanics do not lose their charm for him; wireless and aviation succeed steam, and in one of his most other-worldly stories— 'They'—a considerable part is played by an early, and not very reliable, model of a motor-car: but Parnesius and Hobden are more important than the machines. One is the defender of a civilisation (of a civilisation, not of civilisation in the abstract) against barbarism; the other represents the essential contact of the civilisation with the soil.

I have said that there is always something alien about Kipling, as of a visitor from another planet; and to some readers he may still seem alien in his identification of himself with Sussex. There is an element of *tour de force* in all his work, which makes some readers uncomfortable: we are always suspicious of people who are too clever. Kipling is apt to arouse some of the same distrust as another great man who was alien in a very different way, and on a more worldly level—though he too had his vision of empire and his flashes of profound insight. Even those who admire Disraeli most may find themselves more at ease with Gladstone, whether they like the man and his politics or not. But Disraeli's foreignness was a comparatively simple matter. And undoubtedly the difference of early environment to which Kipling's foreignness is due gave him an understanding of the English countryside different from the understanding of a man born and brought up in it, and provoked in him thoughts about it which the natives would do well to heed.

It may well be unfortunate for a man's reputation that he should have great success early in life, with one work or with one type of work: for then his early work is what he is remembered by, and people (critics, sometimes, most of all) do not bother to revise their opinions in accordance with his later work. With Kipling, furthermore, a prejudice against the content may combine with a lack of understanding of the form to produce an inconsistent condemnation. On the ground of content, he is called a Tory; and on the ground of style, he is called a journalist. Neither of these terms, to be sure, need be held in anything but honour: but the former has come to acquire popular odium by a vulgar identification with a nastier name: to many people a critical attitude towards 'democracy' has come to imply a friendly attitude towards fascism—which, from a truly Tory point of view, is merely the extreme degradation of democracy. Similarly the term 'journalist', when applied to anyone not on the staff of a newspaper, has come to connote truckling to the popular taste of the moment. Kipling was not even a Tory, in the sense of one giving unquestioning loyalty to a political party: he can be called a Tory in a sense in which only a handful of writers together with a number of mostly inarticulate, obscure and uninfluential people are ever Tories in one generation. And as for being a journalist (in the sense mentioned above) we must keep in mind that the causes he espoused were not popular causes when he voiced them; that he did not aim to idealise either border warfare or the professional soldier; that his reflections on the Boer War are more admonitory than laudatory. It may be proposed that, as he dwelt upon the glory of empire, in so doing he helped to conceal its more seamy side: the commercialism, exploitation and neglect. No attentive reader of Kipling can maintain, however, that he was unaware of the faults of British rule: it is simply that he believed the British Empire to be a good thing, that he wished to set before his readers an ideal of what it should be, but was acutely aware of the difficulty of even approximating to this ideal, and of the perpetual danger of falling away even from such standard as might be attained. I cannot find any justification for the charge that he held a doctrine of race superiority. He believed that the British have a greater aptitude for ruling than other people, and that they include a greater number of kindly, incorruptible and unselfseeking men capable of administration; and he knew that scepticism in this matter is less likely to lead to greater magnanimity than it is to lead to a relaxation of the sense of responsibility. But he cannot be accused of holding that any Briton, simply because of his British race, is necessarily in any way the superior or even the equal of an individual of another race. The types of men which he admires are unlimited by any prejudice; his maturest work on India, and his greatest book, is *Kim*.

The notion of Kipling as a popular entertainer is due to the fact that his works have been popular and that they entertain. However, it is permitted to express popular views of the moment in an unpopular style: it is not approved when a man holds unpopular views and expresses them in something very readable. I do not wish to argue longer over Kipling's early 'imperialism', because there is need to speak of the development of his views. It should be said at this point, before passing on, that Kipling is not a doctrinaire or a man with a programme. His opinions are not to be considered as the antithesis of those of Mr. H. G. Wells. Mr. Wells's imagination is one thing and his political opinions another: the latter change but do not mature. But Kipling did not, in the sense in which that activity can be ascribed to Mr. Wells, think: his aim, and his gift, is to make people see—for the first condition of right thought is right sensation—the first condition of understanding a foreign country is to smell it, as you smell India in *Kim*. If you have seen and felt truly, then if God has given you the power you may be able to think rightly.

The simplest summary of the change in Kipling, in his middle years, is 'the development of the imperial imagination into the historical imagination'. To this development his settling in Sussex must have contributed to no small degree: for he had both the humility to subdue himself to his surroundings, and the freshness of vision of the stranger. My references here will be to stories rather than to poems: that is because the later unit is a poem and a story together—or a story and two poems—combining to make a form which no-one has used in the same way and in which no-one is ever likely to excel him. When I speak of 'historical imagination' I do not assume that there is only one kind. Two different kinds are exemplified by

Victor Hugo and Stendhal in their accounts of the battle of Waterloo. For the first it is the charge of the Old Guard, and the sunken road of Ohain; for the latter it is Fabrice's sudden awareness that the little pattering noise around him is caused by bullets. The historian of one kind is he who gives life to abstractions; the historian of another kind may imply a whole civilisation in the behaviour of a single individual. Mr. Wells can give an epic grandeur to the accumulation of an American fortune; Mr. Lytton Strachey (to name a lesser figure) gave reality to the great by dilating upon their foibles. Kipling's imagination dwells on the particular experience of the particular man, just as his India was realised in particular men. In '"The Finest Story in the World"' there appears the same passion for the exact detail that is given scope in his studies of machinery. The Greek galley is described from the point of view of the galley slave. The ship was 'the kind rowed with oars, and the sea spurts through the oar-holes, and the men row sitting up to their knees in water. Then there's a bench running down between the two lines of oars, and an overseer with a whip walks up and down the bench to make the men work. . . . There's a rope running overhead, looped to the upper deck, for the overseer to catch hold of when the ship rolls. When the overseer misses the rope once and falls among the rowers, remember the hero laughs at him and gets licked for it. He's chained to his oar, of course—the hero . . . with an iron band round his waist fixed to the bench he sits on, and a sort of handcuff on his left wrist chaining him to the oar. He's on the lower deck where the worst men are sent, and the only light comes from the hatchways and through the oar-holes. Can't you imagine the sunlight just squeezing through between the handle and the hole and wobbling about as the ship moves?'

The historical imagination may give us an awful awareness of the extent of time, or it may give us a dizzy sense of the nearness of the past. It may do both. Kipling, especially in *Puck of Pook's Hill* and *Rewards and Fairies*, aims I think to give at once a sense of the antiquity of England, of the number of generations and peoples who have laboured the soil and in turn been buried beneath it, and of the contemporaneity of the past. Having previously exhibited an imaginative grasp of space, and England in it, he now proceeds to a similar achievement in time. The tales of English history need to be considered in relation to the later stories of contemporary Sussex, such as 'An Habitation Enforced,' 'My Son's Wife', and 'The Wish House', together with 'They' in one aspect of this curious story. Kipling's awareness and love of Sussex is a very different affair from the feeling of any other 'regional' writer of comparable fame, such as Thomas Hardy. It is not merely that he was highly conscious of what ought to be preserved, where Hardy is the chronicler of decay: or that he wrote of the Sussex which he found, where Hardy wrote of the Dorset that was already passing in his boyhood. It is, first, that the conscience of the 'fabulist' and the consciousness of the political and historical imagination are always at work. To think of Kipling as a writer who could turn his hand to any subject, who wrote of Sussex because he had exhausted his foreign and imperial material, or had satiated the public demand for it, or merely because he was a chameleon who took his colour from environment, would be to miss the mark completely: this later work is the continuation and consummation of the earlier. The second peculiarity of Kipling's Sussex stories I have already touched upon, the fact that he brings to his work the freshness of a mind and a sensibility developed and matured in quite different environment: he is discovering and reclaiming a lost inheritance. The American Chapins, in 'A Habitation Enforced', have a passive role: the protagonist in the story is the house and the life that it

implies, with the profound implication that the countryman belongs to the land, the landlord to his tenants, the farmer to his labourers and not the other way about. This is a deliberate reversal of the values of industrial society. The Chapins, indeed (except for the point of their coming from a country of industrialised mentality) are a kind of mask for Kipling himself. He is also behind the hero of a less successful story in the same group, 'My Son's Wife'. (I call this story less successful because he seems to point his moral a little too directly, and because the contrast between the garrulous society of London—or suburban—intellectuals and the speechless solicitor's daughter who likes hunting is hammered with too great insistence. The contrast between a bucolic world in which the second rate still participates in the good, and an intellectual world in which the second rate is usually sham and always tiresome, is not quite fair. The animus which he displays against the latter suggests that he did not have his eye on the object: for we can judge only what we understand, and must constantly dine with the opposition.) What is most important in these stories, and in 'The Wish House', and in 'Friendly Brook', is Kipling's vision of the people of the soil. It is not a Christian vision, but it is at least a pagan vision—a contradiction of the materialistic view: it is the insight into a harmony with nature which must be re-established if the truly Christian imagination is to be recovered by Christians. What he is trying to convey is, again, not a programme of agrarian reform, but a point of view unintelligible to the industrialised mind. Hence the artistic value of the *obviously* incredible element of the supernatural in 'The Wish House', which is exquisitely combined with the sordid realism of the women of the dialogue, the country bus, the suburban villa, and the cancer of the poor.

This hard and obscure story has to be studied in relation to the two hard and obscure poems . . . which precede and follow it, and which would be still more hard and obscure without the story. We have gone a long way, at this stage, from the mere story teller: a long way even from the man who felt it his duty to try to make certain things plain to his countrymen who would not see them. He could hardly have thought that many people in his own time or at any time would take the trouble to understand the parables, or even to appreciate the precision of observation, the calculating pains in selecting and combining elements, the choice of word and phrase, that were spent in their elaboration. He must have known that his own fame would get in the way, his reputation as a story teller, his reputation as a 'Tory journalist', his reputation as a facile writer who could dash off something about what happened yesterday, his reputation even as a writer of books for children which children liked to read and hear.

I return to the beginning. The late poems like the late stories with which they belong, are sometimes more obscure, because they are trying to express something more difficult than the early poems. They are the poems of a wiser and more mature writer. But they do not show any movement from 'verse' to 'poetry': they are just as instrumental as the early work, but now instruments for a matured purpose. Kipling could handle, from the beginning to the end, a considerable variety of metres and stanza forms with perfect competence; he introduces remarkable variations of his own; but as a poet he does not revolutionize. He is not one of those writers of whom one can say, that the *form* of English poetry will always be different from what it would have been if they had not written. What fundamentally differentiates his 'verse' from 'poetry' is the subordination of musical interest. Many of the poems give, indeed, judged by the ear, an impression of the mood, some are distinctly onomatopoeic: but there is a harmonics of poetry which is not merely beyond their range—it would interfere with the intention. It is possible to argue exceptions; but I am speaking of his work as a whole, and I maintain that without understanding the purpose which animates his verse as a whole, one is not prepared to understand the exceptions.

I make no apology for having used the terms 'verse' and 'poetry' in a loose way: so that while I speak of Kipling's work as verse and not as poetry, I am still able to speak of individual compositions as poems, and also to maintain that there is 'poetry' in the 'verse'. Where terminology is loose, where we have not the vocabulary for distinctions which we feel, our only precision is found in being aware of the imperfection of our tools, and of the different senses in which we are using the same words. It should be clear that when I contrast 'verse' with 'poetry' I am not, *in this context*, implying a value judgement. I do not mean, here, by verse, the work of a man who would write poetry if he could: I mean by it something which does what 'poetry' could not do. The difference which would turn Kipling's verse into poetry, does not represent a failure or deficiency: he knew perfectly well what he was doing; and from his point of view more 'poetry' would interfere with his purpose. And I make the claim, that in speaking of Kipling we are entitled to say '*great* verse'. What other famous poets should be put into the category of great verse writers is a question which I do not here attempt to answer. That question is complicated by the fact that we should be dealing with matters as imprecise as the shape and size of a cloud or the beginning and end of a wave. But the writer whose work is *always* clearly verse, is not a great verse writer: if a writer is to be that, there must be some of his work of which we cannot say whether it is verse or poetry. And the poet who could not write 'verse' when verse was needed, would be without that sense of structure which is required to make a poem of any length readable. I would suggest also that we too easily assume that what is most valuable is also most rare, and vice versa. I can think of a number of poets who have written great poetry, only of a very few whom I should call great verse writers. And unless I am mistaken, Kipling's position in this class is not only high, but unique.

Such reflections could be pursued indefinitely: but this essay is intended as an introduction: if it assists the reader to approach Kipling's verse with a fresh mind, and to regard it in a new light, and to read it as if for the first time, it will have served its purpose.

Notes

1. Though Kipling could manage even so difficult a form as the sestina: see 'Sestina of the Tramp-Royal'.
2. 'The Bull That Thought' in the bull-ring 'raged enormously; he feigned defeat; he despaired in statuesque abandon, and thence flashed into fresh paroxysms of wrath—but always with the detachment of the true artist who knows that he is but the vessel of an emotion whence others, not he, must drink'.
3. In 'Proofs of Holy Writ' (a story published in the *Sussex* edition only), Shakespeare and Jonson discuss a problem of choice of words put before them by one of the translators of the King James Bible.
4. The great speech of Enobarbus in *Antony and Cleopatra* is highly decorated, but the decoration has a purpose beyond its own beauty.
5. On the subject of Kipling's ethics, and the types of man which he holds up for respect, see a valuable essay by Mr. Bonamy Dobree in *The Lamp and the Lute*. My only criticism of this essay is that it does not take full account of Kipling's later work.
6. Not the tolerance of ignorance or indifference. See 'The Mark of the Beast', which those who do not believe in the existence of the Beast probably consider a beastly story.

GEORGE ORWELL
From "Rudyard Kipling" (1942)
Dickens, Dali and Others
1946, pp. 140–53

It was a pity that Mr. Eliot should be so much on the defensive in the long essay with which he prefaces this selection of Kipling's poetry,[1] but it was not to be avoided, because before one can even speak about Kipling one has to clear away a legend that has been created by two sets of people who have not read his works. Kipling is in the peculiar position of having been a byword for fifty years. During five literary generations every enlightened person has despised him, and at the end of that time nine-tenths of those enlightened persons are forgotten and Kipling is in some sense still there. Mr. Eliot never satisfactorily explains this fact, because in answering the shallow and familiar charge that Kipling is a "Fascist," he falls into the opposite error of defending him where he is not defensible. It is no use pretending that Kipling's view of life, as a whole, can be accepted or even forgiven by any civilised person. It is no use claiming, for instance, that when Kipling describes a British soldier beating a "nigger" with a cleaning rod in order to get money out of him, he is acting merely as a reporter and does not necessarily approve what he describes. There is not the slightest sign anywhere in Kipling's work that he disapproves of that kind of conduct—on the contrary, there is a definite strain of sadism in him, over and above the brutality which a writer of that type has to have. Kipling *is* a jingo imperialist, he *is* morally insensitive and æsthetically disgusting. It is better to start by admitting that, and then to try to find out why it is that he survives while the refined people who have sniggered at him seem to wear so badly.

And yet the "Fascist" charge has to be answered, because the first clue to any understanding of Kipling, morally or politically, is the fact that he was *not* a Fascist. He was further from being one than the most humane or the most "progressive" person is able to be nowadays. An interesting instance of the way in which quotations are parroted to and fro without any attempt to look up their context or discover their meaning is the line from "Recessional," "Lesser breeds without the Law." This line is always good for a snigger in pansy-left circles. It is assumed as a matter of course that the "lesser breeds" are "natives," and a mental picture is called up of some pukka sahib in a pith helmet kicking a coolie. In its context the sense of the line is almost the exact opposite of this. The phrase "lesser breeds" refers almost certainly to the Germans, and especially the pan-German writers, who are "without the Law" in the sense of being lawless, not in the sense of being powerless. The whole poem, conventionally thought of as an orgy of boasting, is a denunciation of power politics, British as well as German. Two stanzas are worth quoting (I am quoting this as politics, not as poetry):

> If, drunk with sight of power, we loose
> Wild tongues that have not Thee in awe,
> Such boastings as the Gentiles use,
> Or lesser breeds without the Law—
> Lord God of hosts, be with us yet,
> Lest we forget—lest we forget!
>
> For heathen heart that puts her trust
> In reeking tube and iron shard,
> All valiant dust that builds on dust,
> And guarding, calls not Thee to guard,
> For frantic boast and foolish word—
> Thy mercy on Thy People, Lord!

Much of Kipling's phraseology is taken from the Bible,

and no doubt in the second stanza he had in mind the text from Psalm cxxvii.: "Except the Lord build the house, they labour in vain that build it; except the Lord keep the city, the watchman waketh but in vain." It is not a text that makes much impression on the post-Hitler mind. No one, in our time, believes in any sanction greater than military power; no one believes that it is possible to overcome force except by greater force. There is no "law," there is only power. I am not saying that that is a true belief, merely that it is the belief which all modern men do actually hold. Those who pretend otherwise are either intellectual cowards, or power-worshippers under a thin disguise, or have simply not caught up with the age they are living in. Kipling's outlook is pre-Fascist. He still believes that pride comes before a fall and that the gods punish *hubris*. He does not foresee the tank, the bombing plane, the radio and the secret police, or their psychological results.

But in saying this, does not one unsay what I said above about Kipling's jingoism and brutality? No, one is merely saying that the nineteenth-century imperialist outlook and the modern gangster outlook are two different things. Kipling belongs very definitely to the period 1885–1902. The Great War and its aftermath embittered him, but he shows little sign of having learned anything from any event later than the Boer War. He was the prophet of British Imperialism in its expansionist phase (even more than his poems, his solitary novel, *The Light That Failed*, gives you the atmosphere of that time) and also the unofficial historian of the British Army, the old mercenary army which began to change its shape in 1914. All his confidence, his bouncing vulgar vitality, sprang out of limitations which no Fascist or near-Fascist shares.

Kipling spent the later part of his life in sulking, and no doubt it was political disappointment rather than literary vanity that accounted for this. Somehow history had not gone according to plan. After the greatest victory she had ever known, Britain was a lesser world power than before, and Kipling was quite acute enough to see this. The virtue had gone out of the classes he idealised, the young were hedonistic or disaffected, the desire to paint the map red had evaporated. He could not understand what was happening, because he had never had any grasp of the economic forces underlying imperial expansion. It is notable that Kipling does not seem to realise, any more than the average soldier or colonial administrator, that an empire is primarily a money-making concern. Imperialism as he sees it is a sort of forcible evangelising. You turn a Gatling gun on a mob of unarmed "natives," and then you establish "the Law," which includes roads, railways and a court-house. He could not foresee, therefore, that the same motives which brought the Empire into existence would end by destroying it. It was the same motive, for example, that caused the Malayan jungles to be cleared for rubber estates, and which now causes those estates to be handed over intact to the Japanese. The modern totalitarians know what they are doing, and the nineteenth-century English did not know what they were doing. Both attitudes have their advantages, but Kipling was never able to move forward from one into the other. His outlook, allowing for the fact that after all he was an artist, was that of the salaried bureaucrat who despises the "box-wallah" and often lives a lifetime without realising that the "box-wallah" calls the tune.

But because he identifies himself with the official class, he does possess one thing which "enlightened" people seldom or never possess, and that is a sense of responsibility. The middle-class Left hate him for this quite as much as for his cruelty and vulgarity. All left-wing parties in the highly industrialised countries are at bottom a sham, because they make it their business to fight against something which they do not really wish to destroy. They have internationalist aims, and at the same time they struggle to keep up a standard of life with which those aims are incompatible. We all live by robbing Asiatic coolies, and those of us who are "enlightened" all maintain that those coolies ought to be set free; but our standard of living, and hence our "enlightenment," demands that the robbery shall continue. A humanitarian is always a hypocrite, and Kipling's understanding of this is perhaps the central secret of his power to create telling phrases. It would be difficult to hit off the one-eyed pacifism of the English in fewer words than in the phrase, "making mock of uniforms that guard you while you sleep." It is true that Kipling does not understand the economic aspect of the relationship between the highbrow and the blimp. He does not see that the map is painted red chiefly in order that the coolie may be exploited. Instead of the coolie he sees the Indian Civil Servant; but even on that plane his grasp of function, of who protects whom, is very sound. He sees clearly that men can only be highly civilised while other men, inevitably less civilised, are there to guard and feed them.

How far does Kipling really identify himself with the administrators, soldiers and engineers whose praises he sings? Not so completely as is sometimes assumed. He had travelled very widely while he was still a young man, he had grown up with a brilliant mind in mainly philistine surroundings, and some streak in him that may have been partly neurotic led him to prefer the active man to the sensitive man. The nineteenth-century Anglo-Indians, to name the least sympathetic of his idols, were at any rate people who did things. It may be that all that they did was evil, but they changed the face of the earth (it is instructive to look at a map of Asia and compare the railway system of India with that of the surrounding countries), whereas they could have achieved nothing, could not have maintained themselves in power for a single week, if the normal Anglo-Indian outlook had been that of, say, E. M. Forster. Tawdry and shallow though it is, Kipling's is the only literary picture that we possess of nineteenth-century Anglo-India, and he could only make it because he was just coarse enough to be able to exist and keep his mouth shut in clubs and regimental messes. But he did not greatly resemble the people he admired. I know from several private sources that many of the Anglo-Indians who were Kipling's contemporaries did not like or approve of him. They said, no doubt truly, that he knew nothing about India, and on the other hand, he was from their point of view too much of a highbrow. While in India he tended to mix with "the wrong" people, and because of his dark complexion he was wrongly suspected of having a streak of Asiatic blood. Much in his development is traceable to his having been born in India and having left school early. With a slightly different background he might have been a good novelist or a superlative writer of music-hall songs. But how true is it that he was a vulgar flag-waver, a sort of publicity agent for Cecil Rhodes? It is true, but it is not true that he was a yes-man or a time-server. After his early days, if then, he never courted public opinion. Mr. Eliot says that what is held against him is that he expressed unpopular views in a popular style. This narrows the issue by assuming that "unpopular" means unpopular with the intelligentsia, but it is a fact that Kipling's "message" was one that the big public did not want, and, indeed, has never accepted. The mass of the people, in the 'nineties as now, were anti-militarist, bored by the Empire, and only unconsciously patriotic. Kipling's official admirers are and were the "service" middle class, the people who read *Black-wood's*. In the stupid early years of this century, the blimps, having at last discovered someone who could be called a poet and who was on their side, set Kipling on a pedestal, and some of his more sententious poems, such as "If," were given almost Biblical status. But it is doubtful whether the blimps have ever read him with attention, any more than they have read the Bible. Much of what he says they could not possibly approve. Few people who have criticised England from the inside have said bitterer things about her than this gutter patriot. As a rule it is the British working class that he is attacking, but not always. That phrase about "the flannelled fools at the wicket and the muddied oafs at the goal" sticks like an arrow to this day, and it is aimed at the Eton and Harrow match as well as the Cup-Tie Final. Some of the verses he wrote about the Boer War have a curiously modern ring, so far as their subject-matter goes. "Stellenbosch," which must have been written about 1902, sums up what every intelligent infantry officer was saying in 1918, or is saying now, for that matter.

Kipling's romantic ideas about England and the Empire might not have mattered if he could have held them without having the class-prejudices which at that time went with them. If one examines his best and most representative work, his soldier poems, especially *Barrack-Room Ballads*, one notices that what more than anything else spoils them is an underlying air of patronage. Kipling idealises the army officer, especially the junior officer, and that to an idiotic extent, but the private soldier, though lovable and romantic, has to be a comic. He is always made to speak in a sort of stylised Cockney, not very broad but with all the aitches and final "g's" carefully omitted. Very often the result is as embarrassing as the humorous recitation at a church social. And this accounts for the curious fact that one can often improve Kipling's poems, make them less facetious and less blatant, by simply going through them and transplanting them from cockney into standard speech. This is especially true of his refrains, which often have a truly lyrical quality. Two examples will do (one is about a funeral and the other about a wedding):

> So it's knock out your pipes and follow me!
> And it's finish up your swipes and follow me!
>   Oh, hark to the big drum calling,
>   Follow me—follow me home!

and again:

>   Cheer for the Sergeant's wedding—
>   Give them one cheer more!
>   Grey gun-horses in the lando,
>   And a rogue is married to a whore!

Here I have restored the aitches, etc. Kipling ought to have known better. He ought to have seen that the two closing lines of the first of these stanzas are very beautiful lines, and that ought to have overriden his impulse to make fun of a working-man's accent. In the ancient ballads the lord and the peasant speak the same language. This is impossible to Kipling, who is looking down a distorting class-perspective, and by a piece of poetic justice one of his best lines is spoiled—for "follow me 'ome" is much uglier than "follow me home." But even where it makes no difference musically the facetiousness of his stage Cockney dialect is irritating. However, he is more often quoted aloud than read on the printed page, and most people instinctively make the necessary alterations when they quote him.

Can one imagine any private soldier, in the 'nineties or now, reading *Barrack-Room Ballads* and feeling that here was a writer who spoke for him? It is very hard to do so. Any soldier capable of reading a book of verse would notice at once that Kipling is almost unconscious of the class war that goes on in an army as much as elsewhere. It is not only that he thinks the soldier comic, but that he thinks him patriotic, feudal, a ready

admirer of his officers and proud to be a soldier of the Queen. Of course that is partly true, or battles could not be fought, but "What have I done for thee, England, my England?" is essentially a middle-class query. Almost any working man would follow it up immediately with "What has England done for me?" In so far as Kipling grasps this, he simply sets it down to "the intense selfishness of the lower classes" (his own phrase). When he is writing not of British but of "loyal" Indians he carries the "Salaam, sahib" motif to sometimes disgusting lengths. Yet it remains true that he has far more interest in the common soldier, far more anxiety that he shall get a fair deal, then most of the "liberals" of his day or our own. He sees that the soldier is neglected, meanly underpaid and hypocritically despised by the people whose incomes he safeguards. "I came to realise," he says in his posthumous memoirs, "the bare horrors of the private's life, and the unnecessary torments he endured." He is accused of glorifying war, and perhaps he does so, but not in the usual manner, by pretending that war is a sort of football match. Like most people capable of writing battle poetry, Kipling had never been in battle, but his vision of war is realistic. He knows that bullets hurt, that under fire everyone is terrified, that the ordinary soldier never knows what the war is about or what is happening except in his own corner of the battlefield, and that British troops, like other troops, frequently run away:

> I 'eard the knives be'ind me, but I dursn't face my
>   man,
> Nor I don't know where I went to, 'cause I didn't stop
>   to see,
> Till I 'eard a beggar squealin' out for quarter as 'e ran,
> An' I thought I knew the voice an'—it was me!

Modernize the style of this, and it might have come out of one of the debunking war books of the nineteen-twenties. Or again:

> An' now the hugly bullets come peckin' through the
>   dust,
> An' no one wants to face 'em, but every beggar must;
> So, like a man in irons, which isn't glad to go,
> They moves 'em off by companies uncommon stiff
>   an' slow.

Compare this with:

> Forward the Light Brigade!
> Was there a man dismayed?
> No! though the soldier knew
> Someone had blundered.

If anything, Kipling overdoes the horrors, for the wars of his youth were hardly wars at all by our standards. Perhaps that is due to the neurotic strain in him, the hunger for cruelty. But at least he knows that men ordered to attack impossible objectives *are* dismayed, and also that fourpence a day is not a generous pension.

How complete or truthful a picture has Kipling left us of the long-service, mercenary army of the late nineteenth century? One must say of this, as of what Kipling wrote about nineteenth-century Anglo-India, that it is not only the best but almost the only literary picture we have. He has put on record an immense amount of stuff that one could otherwise only gather from verbal tradition or from unreadable regimental histories. Perhaps his picture of army life seems fuller and more accurate than it is because any middle-class English person is likely to know enough to fill up the gaps. At any rate, reading the essay on Kipling that Mr. Edmund Wilson has just published,[2] I was struck by the number of things that are boringly familiar to us and seem to be barely intelligible to an American. But from the body of Kipling's early work there does seem to emerge a vivid and not seriously misleading picture of the old pre-machine-gun army—the sweltering barracks in Gibraltar or Lucknow, the red coats, the pipeclayed belts and the pillbox hats, the beer, the fights, the floggings, hangings and crucifixions, the bugle-calls, the smell of oats and horse-piss, the bellowing sergeants with foot-long moustaches, the bloody skirmishes, invariably mismanaged, the crowded troop-ships, the cholera-stricken camps, the "native" concubines, the ultimate death in the workhouse. It is a crude, vulgar picture, in which a patriotic music-hall term seems to have got mixed up with one of Zola's gorier passages, but from it future generations will be able to gather some idea of what a long-term volunteer army was like. On about the same level they will be able to learn something of British India in the days when motor-cars and refrigerators were unheard of. It is an error to imagine that we might have had better books on these subjects if, for example, George Moore, or Gissing, or Thomas Hardy, had had Kipling's opportunities. That is the kind of accident that cannot happen. It was not possible that nineteenth-century England should produce a book like *War and Peace*, or like Tolstoy's minor stories of army life, such as *Sebastopol* or *The Cossacks*, not because the talent was necessarily lacking but because no one with sufficient sensitiveness to write such books would ever have made the appropriate contacts. Tolstoy lived in a great military empire in which it seemed natural for almost any young man of family to spend a few years in the army, whereas the British Empire was and still is demilitarised to a degree which continental observers find almost incredible. Civilised men do not readily move away from the centres of civilisation, and in most languages there is a great dearth of what one might call colonial literature. It took a very improbable combination of circumstances to produce Kipling's gaudy tableau, in which Private Ortheris and Mrs. Hauksbee pose against a background of palm trees to the sound of temple bells, and one necessary circumstance was that Kipling himself was only half civilised.

Notes

1. A *Choice of Kipling's Verse* made by T. S. Eliot.
2. Published in a volume of collected essays, *The Wound and the Bow*.

C. S. LEWIS
From "Kipling's World"
Kipling Journal, September 1958, pp. 9–16

The earliest generation of Kipling's readers regarded him as the mouthpiece of patriotism and imperialism. I think that conception of his work is inadequate. Chesterton did a great service to criticism by contradicting it in a famous chapter of *Heretics*. In that chapter he finds the essential characteristics of Kipling's mind to be two. In the first place he had discovered, or rediscovered, the poetry of common things; had perceived, as Chesterton says, "the significance and philosophy of steam and of slang." In the second place, Kipling was the poet of discipline. Not specially, nor exclusively, of military discipline, but of discipline in every shape. "He has not written so well of soldiers," says Chesterton, "as he has of railwaymen or bridge-builders, or even journalists." This particular judgment may be disputed, but I feel no doubt at all that Chesterton has picked up the right scent.

To put the thing in the shortest possible way, Kipling is first and foremost the poet of work. It is really remarkable how poetry and fiction before his time had avoided this subject. They had dealt almost exclusively with men in their "private hours"—with love affairs, crimes, sport, illness, and changes of fortune. Mr. Osborne may be a merchant, but *Vanity Fair* has

no interest in his mercantile life. Darcy was a good landlord and Wentworth a good officer, but their activities in these capacities are all "off stage." Most of Scott's characters, except the soldiers, have no profession; and when they are soldiers the emphasis is on battles and adventures, not on the professional routine. Business comes into Dickens only in so far as it is criminal or comic. With a few exceptions, imaginative literature in the eighteenth and nineteenth centuries had quietly omitted, or at least thrust into the background, the sort of thing which, in fact, occupies most of the waking hours of most men. And this did not merely mean that certain technical aspects of life were unrepresented. A whole range of strong sentiments and emotions—for many men, the strongest of all—went with them. For, as Pepys once noted with surprise, there is great pleasure in talking of business. It was Kipling who first reclaimed for literature this enormous territory.

His early stories of Anglo-Indian society still conform to the older convention. They are about love affairs, elopements, intrigues, and domestic quarrels. They are indeed connected with his later and more characteristic work by a thread which I shall discuss presently; but on the surface they are a different kind of thing. The *Departmental Ditties* are much more typical of the author's real interests. The point about Potiphar Gubbins is not simply that he is a cuckold but that his horns bring him advancement in the Civil Service and that he builds very bad bridges. The sting of "The Story of Uriah" lies not merely in the wife's depravity but in the fact that the husband was sent, for her lover's convenience, to die at Quetta, "attempting two men's duty in that very healthy post." Exeter Battleby Tring, who really knows something about railways, has his mouth silenced with rupees in order that "the Little Tin Gods (long may their Highnesses thrive!)" may keep "their Circle intact." Boanerges Blitzen ruins his official career by exposing "office scandals" in the papers. The whole bitter little collection presents a corrupt society, not in its leisure, but in its official corruption. In his later work this preference for depicting men at their jobs becomes his most obvious characteristic. Findlayson's hopes and fears about his bridge, McPhee's attitude both to engines and owners, William the Conqueror's work in the famine district, a lighthouse-keeper at his post on a foggy night, Gisborne and his chief in the forest, McAndrew standing his watch—these are the things that come back to us when we remember Kipling; and there had really been nothing like them in literature before. The poems again and again strike the same note. Lord Dufferin (heavily influenced by Bishop Blougram) hands on the *arcana imperii* to Lord Lansdowne; the professional spies set out, "each man reporting for duty alone, out of sight, out of reach of his fellow"; the crew of the *Bolivar*, "mad with work and weariness," see "some damned Liner's lights go by like a grand hotel"; H. Mukerji ends with the Boh's head a covering letter in perfect Babu officialese; the fans and beltings in a munition factory roar round a widowed war worker. The rhythms of work—boots slogging along a road, the Harrild and the Hoe devouring "their league-long paper-bale," the grunting of a water-wheel—echo through Kipling's verse and prose as through no other man's. Even Mowgli in the end accepts a post in the Civil Service. Even "The Brushwood Boy" turns aside from its main theme to show how much toil its hero suffered and inflicted in the course of his professional career. Even when we are taken into the remote past, Kipling is not interested in imagining what it felt like to be an ancient and pagan man; only in what it felt like to be a man doing some ancient job—a galley slave, a Roman officer. How the light came in through the oar-holes in the galley—that little detail which everyone who had served in a galley would remember and which no one else would know—that is Kipling's quarry.

It would be quite a mistake, however, to accuse Kipling of swamping the human interest in his mass of material and technical detail. The detail is there for the sake of a human interest, but that human interest is one that no previous writer had done justice to. What Kipling chiefly communicates—and it is, for good and for ill, one of the strongest things in the world—is the peculiar relation which men who do the same work have to that work and to one another; the inescapable bond of shared experiences, and, above all, of shared hardships. It is a commitment for life:

> Oh, was there ever sailor free to choose,
> That didn't settle somewhere near the sea?
> We've only one virginity to lose,
> And where we lost it, there our hearts will be!

That is why in "Steam Tactics" Hinchcliffe, who, when starting on his leave, had "thanked his Maker that he wouldn't see nor smell nor thumb a runnin' bulgine till the nineteenth prox," nevertheless fell immediately to studying the engine of Kipling's steam-car.

For the same reason, Kipling, the old journalist, writes:

> But the Jew shall forget Jerusalem
> Ere we forget the Press.

In the next stanza he goes on to explain why. The man who has "stood through the loaded hour" and "lit his pipe in the morning calm"—who has, in fact, been through the nocturnal routine of producing a newspaper—"hath sold his heart." That is the whole point. We who are of one trade (whether journalists, soldiers, galley slaves, Indian Civilians, or what you will) know so many things that the outsiders will never, never understand. Like the two child lovers in *The Light That Failed*, "we belong." It is a bond which in real life sometimes proves stronger than any other:

> The men of my own stock
> They may do ill or well,
> But they tell the lies I am wonted to,
> They are used to the lies I tell;
> And we do not need interpreters
> When we go to buy and sell.

How true to life is the immediate alliance of the three journalists whom chance has thrown together in the story called "A Matter of Fact."

This spirit of the profession is everywhere shown in Kipling as a ruthless master. That is why Chesterton got in a very large part of the truth when he fixed on discipline as Kipling's main subject. There is nothing Kipling describes with more relish than the process whereby the trade-spirit licks some raw cub into shape. That is the whole theme of one of his few full-length novels, *Captains Courageous*. It is the theme of "The Centaurs," and of "Pharaoh and the Sergeant," and of "The 'Eathen." It is allegorically expressed in "The Ship That Found Herself." It is implicit in all the army stories and the sea stories; indeed, it may be thought that the author turns aside from his narrative rather too often to assure us that Mulvaney was invaluable for "licking the new batch of recruits into shape." Even when we escape into the jungle and the wolf pack we do not escape the Law. Until he has been disciplined—"put through it," licked into shape—a man is, for Kipling, mere raw material. "Gad," says Hitchcock to Findlayson in "The Bridge-builders," "what a Cooper's Hill cub I was when I came on the works." And Findlayson muses, "Cub thou wast; assistant thou art." The philosophy of the thing is summed up at the end of "A Walking Delegate," where the yellow horse (an agitator) has asked the old working horse, "Have you no respec' whatever for

the dignity o' our common horsehood?" He gets the reply, "Horse, sonny, is what you start from. We know all about horse here, an' he ain't any high-toned, pure-souled child of nature. Horse, plain horse, same ez you, is chock-full o' tricks an' meannesses an' cussednesses an' monkey shines. . . . That's horse, an' thet's about his dignity an' the size of his soul 'fore he's been broke an' raw-hided a piece." Reading "man" for "horse," we here have Kipling's doctrine of Man.

This is one of the most important things Kipling has to say and one which he means very seriously, and it is also one of the things which has aroused hatred against him. It amounts to something like a doctrine of original sin, and it is antipathetic to many modern modes of thought. Perhaps even more antipathetic is Kipling's presentation of the "breaking" and "raw hiding" process. In "His Private Honour" it turns out to consist of prolonged bullying and incessant abuse; the sort of bullying (as we learn from "The 'Eathen") which sends grown men off to cry in solitude, followed by the jeers of the old hands. The patient is not allowed to claim any personal rights whatever; there is nothing, according to Kipling, more subversive. To ask for justice is as the sin of witchcraft. The disaster in the poem called "That Day" began with the fact that "every little drummer 'ad 'is rights an' wrongs to mind." In contrast, "My rights," Ortheris answered with deep scorn, "my rights! I ain't a recruity to go whinin' about my rights to this an' my rights to that, just as if I couldn't look after myself. My rights! 'Strewth A'mighty. I'm a man."

Now there is no good whatever in dismissing this part of Kipling's message as if it were not worth powder and shot. There is a truth in it which must be faced before we attempt to find any larger truths which it may exclude. Many who hate Kipling have omitted this preliminary. They feel instinctively that they themselves are just the unlicked or unbroken men whom Kipling condemns; they find the picture intolerable, and the picture of the cure more intolerable still. To escape, they dismiss the whole thing as a mere Fascist or "public school" brutality. But there is no solution along those lines. It may (or may not) be possible to get beyond Kipling's harsh wisdom; but there is no getting beyond a thing without first getting as far. It is a brutal truth about the world that the whole everlasting business of keeping the human race protected and clothed and fed could not go on for twenty-four hours without the vast legion of hard-bitten, technically efficient, not-over-sympathetic men, and without the harsh processes of discipline by which this legion is made. It is a brutal truth that unless a great many people practised the Kipling *ethos* there would be neither security nor leisure for any people to practise a finer *ethos*. As Chesterton admits, "We may fling ourselves into a hammock in a fit of divine carelessness; but we are glad that the maker did not make the hammock in a fit of divine carelessness." In "The Proconsuls," speaking of those who have actually ruled with a strong hand, Kipling says:

> On the stage their act hath framed
> For thy sports, O Liberty!
> Doubted are they, and defamed
> By the tongues their act set free.

It is a true bill, as far as it goes. Unless the Kipling virtues—if you will, the Kipling vices—had long and widely been practised in the world we should be in no case to sit here and discuss Kipling. If all men stood talking of their rights before they went up a mast or down a sewer or stoked a furnace or joined an army, we should all perish; nor while they talked of their rights would they learn to do these things. And I think we must agree with Kipling that the man preoccupied with his own rights is not only a disastrous, but a very unlovely object;

indeed, one of the worst mischiefs we do by treating a man unjustly is that we force him to be thus preoccupied.

But if so, then it is all the more important that men should, in fact, be treated with justice. If we all need "licking into shape" and if, while undergoing the process, we must not guard our rights, then it is all the more important that someone else should guard them for us. What has Kipling to say on this subject? For, quite clearly, the very same methods which he prescribes for licking the cub into shape, "making a man of him" in the interests of the community, would also, if his masters were bad men, be an admirable method of keeping the cub quiet while he was exploited and enslaved for their private benefit. It is all very well that the colts (in "The Centaurs") should learn to obey Chiron as a means to becoming good cavalry chargers; but how if Chiron wants their obedience only to bring them to the knacker's yard? And are the masters never bad men? From some stories one would almost conclude that Kipling is ignorant of, or indifferent to, this possibility. In "His Private Honour" the old soldiers educate the recruits by continued bullying. But Kipling seems quite unaware that bullying is an activity which human beings *enjoy*. We are given to understand that the old soldiers are wholly immune to this temptation; they threaten, mock, and thrash the recruits only from the highest possible motives. Is this naïvety in the author? Can he really be so ignorant? Or does he not care?

He is certainly not ignorant. Most of us begin by regarding Kipling as the panegyrist of the whole imperial system. But we find, when we look into the matter, that his admiration is reserved for those in the lower positions. These are the "men on the spot"; the bearers of the burden; above them we find folly and ignorance; at the centre of the whole thing we find the terrible society of Simla, a provincial smart set which plays frivolously with men's careers and even their lives. The system is rotten at the head, and official advancement may have a *teterrima causa*. Findlayson had to see "months of office work destroyed at a blow when the Government of India at the last moment added two feet to the width of the bridge under the impression that bridges were cut out of paper!" The heart-rending death of Orde (one of Kipling's best tragic scenes) is followed by the undoing of his life's work when the ignorant Viceroy sends a Babu to succeed him. In "Tod's Amendment" disaster is averted by a child who knows what all the rulers of India (the "little Tin Gods") do not know. It is interesting to compare "The 'Eathen" with "The Sergeant's Wedding." In the one, the sergeants are benevolent despots—it is only the softness and selfishness of the recruit that make him think they are cruel tyrants. In the other, we have a sergeant who uses his position to make money by cheating the men. Clearly this sergeant would have just as strong a motive as the good ones for detesting privates who talked about their "rights and wrongs."

All this suggests that the disciplinary system is a very two-edged affair; but this does not in the least shake Kipling's devotion to it. That, he says in effect, is what the world always has been like and always will be like. Even in prehistoric times the astute person

> Won a simple Viceroy's praise
> Through the toil of other men.

And no one can rebuke more stunningly than Kipling those who exploit and frustrate the much-enduring "man on the spot":

> When the last grim joke is entered
> In the big black Book of jobs,
> And Quetta graveyards give again
> Their victims to the air,
> I shouldn't like to be the man
> Who sent Jack Barrett there.

But this makes no difference to the duty of the sufferer. Whatever corruptions there may be at the top, the work must go on; frontiers must be protected, epidemics fought, bridges built, marshes drained, famine relief administered. Protest, however well-grounded, about injustice, and schemes of reform, will never bring a ship into harbour or a train into the station or sow a field of oats or quell a riot; and "the unforgiving minute" is upon us fourteen hundred and forty times a day. This is the truest and finest element in Kipling; his version of Carlyle's gospel of work. It has affinities with Piers Plowman's insistence on ploughing his half-acre; but there are important differences.

The more Kipling convinces us that no plea for justice or happiness must be allowed to interfere with the job, the more anxious we become for reassurance that the work is really worthy of all the human sacrifices it demands. "The game," he says, "is more than the player of the game." But perhaps some games are and some aren't. "And the ship is more than the crew"—but one would like to know where the ship was going and why. Was its voyage really useful—or even innocent? We want, in fact, a doctrine of Ends. Langland could supply one. He knows how Do Well is connected with Do Better and Do Best; the ploughing of the half-acre is placed in a cosmic context and that context would enable Langland, in principle, to tell us whether any given job in the whole universe was true worship or miserable idolatry; it is here that Kipling speaks with an uncertain voice. For many of the things done by his Civil Servants the necessity is perhaps obvious; but that is not a side of the matter he develops. And he writes with equal relish where the ultimate ends of the work described are much less obvious. Sometimes his choice of sides seems to be quite accidental, even frivolous. When William the Conqueror met a schoolmaster who had to teach the natives the beauties of Wordsworth's *Excursion*, she told him, rather unnecessarily, "I like men who do things." Teaching English Literature to natives is not "doing things," and we are meant to despise that schoolmaster. One notes that the editor of the local paper, whom we met a few pages before, is visited with no similar ignominy. Yet it is easy enough to imagine the situations reversed. Kipling could have written a perfect Kipling story about two men in the Educational Department working eighteen hours a day to conduct an examination, with punkah flapping and all the usual background. The futility of the curriculum which makes them set Wordsworth to Indian schoolboys would not in the least have detracted from their heroism if he had chosen to write the story from that point of view. It would have been their professional grievance—ironically and stoically endured—one more instance of that irresponsible folly at the top which wastes and breaks the men who really do the work. I have a disquieting feeling that Kipling's actual respect for the journalist and contempt for the schoolmaster has no thought-out doctrine of ends behind it, but results from the accident that he himself worked for a newspaper and not for a school. And now, at last, I begin to suspect that we are finding a clue to that suffocating sensation which overtakes me if I read Kipling too long. Is the Kipling world really monstrous in the sense of being misshaped? How if this doctrine of work and discipline, which is so clear and earnest and dogmatic at the periphery, hides at the centre a terrible vagueness, a frivolity or scepticism?

Sometimes it hides nothing but what the English, whether fairly or unfairly, are inclined to call Americanism. The story called "Below the Mill Dam" is an instance. We are expected to rejoice that the native black rat should be superseded by the alien brown rat; that the mill wheel could be yoked to a dynamo and the countryside electrified. None of the questions which every thinking man must raise about the beneficence of this whole transition have any meaning for Kipling. They are to him mere excuses for idleness. "We have already learned six refined synonyms for loafing," say the waters; and, to the Wheel itself, "While you're at work you'll work." The black rat is to be stuffed. Here is the creed of Activism—of "Progress," hustle, and development—all blind, naked, uncritical of itself. Similarly in "The Explorer," while we admire the man's courage in the earlier stanzas, the end which he has in view gives us pause. His Holy Grail is simply the industrialization of the country he has discovered. The waterfalls are "wasting fifty thousand head an hour" and the forests are "axe-ripe"; he will rectify this. The End, here as in the Mill Dam story, may be a good one; it is not for me to decide. But Kipling does not seem to know there is any question. In "Bread upon the Waters" all the usual hardships are described and with all Kipling's usual relish; but the only end is money and revenge—though, I confess, a very excusable revenge. In "The Devil and the Deep Sea" the job, which is treated with his usual reverence, the game, which is still more than the player of the game, is merely the triumph of a gang of criminals.

This might be explained by saying that Kipling is not a moralist but a purely objective writer. But that would be false. He is eminently a moralist; in almost every story we are invited, nay forced, to admire and condemn. Many of the poems are versified homilies. That is why this chanciness or uncertainty about the end to which the moralism of his *bushido* is applied in any particular instance makes us uncomfortable. And now we must take a step further. Even Discipline is not a constant. The very people who would be cubs to be licked into shape in one story may, in another, be the heroes we are asked to admire.

NOEL ANNAN
From "Kipling's Place in the History of Ideas"
Victorian Studies, June 1960, pp. 327–40

II

The picture of India which Kipling painted in his first four volumes of short stories and in his earliest verse is that of a society which politically, nervously, physically, and spiritually quivered on the edge of a precipice. None of the conditions of life resembled those of England. Here Nature was inconceivably hostile. The pitiless sun spread famine and the rain floods, and cholera, fever, reptiles, and wild beasts brought death. Death was always at a man's elbow, and Anglo-Indians in remote villages met regularly to prove to each other that they were still alive. The very flowers, the hateful marigolds, were symbols of heat and death. Kipling did not personify Nature like Hardy: like a sociologist he took the environment as given and noted its effect upon men. In such a climate love was almost impossible. Young men slaving to save money in order to bring out their girl from England denied themselves the company or diversions which they needed in order to survive: either they died themselves or the girl succumbed or their children were the victims of the carelessness of their *ayah*. As often as not the girl in England had forgotten them long before they could pay her fare. So they turned to other men's wives or to the few daughters of their superiors. Yet what romance could blossom when everyone knew to the last rupee everyone else's income and prospects in this salaried class? Besides, in this world one could easily propose to the wrong girl in a dust-storm. Those who married fretted their hearts out as they saw their wives pine in the plains tortured by heat and illness. Or they sent them to Simla—to the scandal and adultery which boredom bred, a boredom in which adultery losts its romance and was founded on delusion. For what was there to talk about? In this world there was no art, no music, no books; there was only India.[1] Marriage frequently brought disaster. Those, like Captain Gadsby, who had private means, however loyal to their regiment, in the end sent in their papers for the sake of their wife and family. Those who had not, necessarily cut themselves off from the Indians: Strickland, the omniscient police officer, married, and now "he fills in his Departmental returns beautifully" ("Miss Youghal's Sais," *Plain Tales from the Hills*). In this world marriage halved a man's efficiency in his work.

Kipling then cast an admiring but piercing eye upon this work—the work of governing India. In England government whatever its faults achieved results. Did it in India? Come to Simla and see the high-ups entirely lacking that intimate knowledge which was needed to govern a country—men whose very children, like Tod, could better amend legislation because they mixed with Indian servants and knew more facts. Come to Simla and see the wives of the high-ups placing their fancy-men in the Secretariat at the expense of those who accumulated experience and knowledge in the Provinces. Come to Simla to see the full corruption of love, of marriage, of administration. Yet perhaps Simla was right. Not to take one's work too seriously was the only way of retaining sanity. Overwork, the endemic disease of the Indian civil servant, led to the collapse in health which spelt death; and why overwork when Pagett, M.P., appeared from Home to tell you in the heat of summer that you were overpaid? Overwork led to the mania whereby an official would spend weeks in plotting revenge upon another who had chaffed him for buying a crock of a horse. Why overwork administering justice in a country where witnesses to a murder could be bought for a few rupees, where the native police were frequently bribed, and where an English attempt to be "moral" could be defeated by a mixture of black magic, debt, and the virtual slavery of women which were integral to Indian life? Nothing changed in India "in spite of the shiny top-scum stuff that people call 'civilisation'" ("The Bisara of Pooree," *Plain Tales*). The Army was full of fine young officers, yet in the arithmetic of the frontier "two thousand pounds of education drops to a ten-rupee jezail" ("Arithmetic on the Frontier," *Departmental Ditties*); and was not the campaign likely to be mismanaged when the brigadier was out for a knighthood and the colonel for a medal and the Government wanted to spend as little money and excite as little comment as possible? The life of the private soldier was spent in early morning drill in cantonment followed by hours of insufferable *cafard* broken by a little quiet looting and torturing of Indians when the drink was in him; and it ended perhaps on a gallows hanged for a murder to which he had been driven by heat or by delusion. In this world delusion, not truth, made men act—the delusion that they were doing good, or fulfilling some mission, or giving someone his just deserts.

Kipling perceived that if the normal criteria of the Victorian novelist did not apply to Anglo-India, they applied still less to the Indians. Indians lived lives incomprehensible to white men because custom and religion imposed a code of behaviour different from theirs: the duty to kill another man in a blood-feud was called by the English murder and when the English imposed their culture in addition to their rule—when they sent missionaries to a village—confusion and resentment followed on both sides. Anglicisation of Indians was a delusion. British justice was an efficient machine which enabled the moneylender and landlord the keener to oppress the poor. Finally Kipling declared that no native could be trusted to rule because "he is as incapable as a child of understanding what authority means, or where is the danger of disobeying it" ("His Chance in Life," *Plain Tales*).

III

What then prevented such a society from going over the precipice? Kipling answered: religion, law, custom, convention, morality—the forces of social control—which imposed upon individuals certain rules which they broke at their peril. Conventions enabled men to retain their self-respect and even to live together under appalling circumstances. In "A Wayside Comedy" (*Wee Willie Winkie and Other Stories*), at a remote outpost inhabited by two Anglo-Indian couples and a bachelor, the first wife hates the bachelor for trying to seduce her; the second wife hates the first for rejecting the man who was her lover but has now left her; but the husbands see that life in this place and situation is possible only if everyone obeys the trivialities of existence. They have created a hell from which there is no escape; this is the only way to alleviate the torment. As a corollary, punishment must fall on those who break the conventions, and this partially explains why so many of Kipling's stories are concerned with scenes in which the individualist, the eccentric, the man who offends against the trivial rules of the club, are tarred and feathered with gleeful brutality. If the offender is not brought to heel, society will suffer. What brought about the situation described in "A Wayside Comedy"? The absence of one of the forces of social control: "all laws weaken in a small and hidden community where there is no public opinion." Kipling's favourite themes are those in which punishment falls on those who break the rules and disaster on those who do not know them.

He was hardly interested whether the customs or morality or religion were right or wrong. For him all that mattered was that they existed. The old sociologists, Comte and Spencer, informed him that science was true and religion false, and Kipling denounced them in "The Conversion of Aurelian McGoggin" (*Plain Tales*). In India God and souls existed because the culture and assumptions of the Indians were based on their existence. Religion was a social fact. One tenet of the liberal atheists, said Kipling, paraphrasing W. K. Clifford, "seemed to be that the one thing more sinful than giving an order was obeying it."[2] But in India order rested on hierarchy and authority and "the climate and the work are against playing bricks with words." Comte's Humanity bore no relation to the raw, brown, naked humanity which surrounded Kipling, who understood the social significance of religion in one sense far better than his great contemporary, the author of *The Golden Bough*. Writing in the afterglow of evolutionary theory, Frazer saw religion and magic as a kind of primitive science which would ultimately vanish as scientific knowledge spread. Kipling, on the other hand, like Weber, regarded the truth of religion as irrelevant because religion was a medium through which men expressed their aspirations and found solace when frustrated. There were many gods, and men changed and discarded them, as Weland Smith discovered and as Krishna warned his fellow deities. The forces of social control preserved man by constraining him.

The second part of Kipling's social theory emerges most clearly in the stories of his middle period. The forces of social control are harsh, but the burden of conformity can be alleviated by belonging to in-groups which protect their members from the outsiders who want to invade their privacy, and differentiate them by stamping them with the individuality of the group. Men belong involuntarily to their family or their school and choose other in-groups such as their craft or profession voluntarily. Each in-group teaches the rules by which society is governed. For Kipling, as for nearly all Victorians, the greatest of all involuntary in-groups is the family, the great protector against the world's hostility and the inculcator of love and decency. How closely (and absurdly) Kipling thought the well-being of the family was connected with the good of society may be deduced from one of the most dreadful sentences he ever wrote. When that paragon of virtue, the Brushwood Boy, returns to his ancestral home, his mother, wishing to spy out his intentions as regards marriage, takes him aside. "They talked for a long hour, as mother and son should, if there is to be any future for our Empire" ("The Brushwood Boy," *The Day's Work*). The dispensations of the family were too sacred to be recorded. The parting of children from their parents, the common lot of Anglo-Indians, was a blasphemy to Kipling, who remembered his own suffering. The family was the only place where affections between human beings could *safely* be displayed. His personal life, so carefully hidden in his autobiography, existed first within the orbit of his parents and his sister, to whom he was devoted, and then within that of his wife and children. Such happiness acquired the characteristics of a tabu and could not be profaned in speech.

The second involuntary in-group was the school which showed men what society was like. Kipling emphasised that this education was implicit and impersonal, not explicit and pedagogic. In *Stalky & Co.* the distinction is continually drawn between appearance and reality. The good-form, herd schoolboy is opposed to Stalky. The heavy priggish housemaster, Prout, with his self-conscious encouragement of games and house spirit is set against the realists Hartopp and the Chaplain, who expect boys to crib and bully. King, the best teacher (in the academic sense), with his passion for the Latin authors and the respectable English poets is regarded cynically by the heavy-lidded boys who know that he is hired to cram them for Sandhurst and that "all the rest's flumdiddle." Whereas King's ambition is to raise the standard and manners of the place to those of the great public schools, the common sense of the Head and the boys tells them that the Imperial Service College is a minor public school and "a limited liability company paying four per cent." The real patriot is the subaltern Toffee Crandall, not the Jelly-Bellied Flag-Flapper; the real enthusiasm for letters is not to be found among the Sixth Form swats but in Beetle, avidly reading his way through the Head's French yellow-backs and the metaphysical poets. Real education is what the boys teach each other in ways which the masters cannot. The in-group teaches spontaneously the way society works. The masters are powerless to diminish vice unless they work subtly unobserved through the boys' collective sense of rightness. Appeals to individual conscience are ineffective because they are "unreal," being based on an ideology—the ideology of public school "good form" behaviour—that does not spring from social facts but is imposed from without by abstract moralisers. Even the individuality of Stalky, McTurk, and Beetle does not grow from themselves but from the fact that they form an in-group within the macrocosm and are thus able to protect and assert themselves. As the self-made father of Harvey in *Captains Courageous* tells his son, schooling gives men the means to hurt their enemies more effectively. To acquire this power is a painful process and Kipling significantly describes it as learning "all the Armoured Man should know, Through his Seven Secret Years . . ."

("The Totem," *Limits and Renewals*). It consists in hardening the shell. Not to expect fairness was the mark of the "educated" man.[3] Stalky earned his name by seeing the facts as they were: by not being blinded by emotion or resentment, as Beetle frequently was, by never being "drawn" either by King or the Viceroy, and by rejecting the ideology of the public school or the army, which is a gloss put upon the facts by moralists who try to conceal the harsh truth about social relationships.

The true spirit of the public school or the army was not expressed in precepts and regulations. On the one occasion when Stalky abandoned his principles and on an emotional impulse took the lead in joining the volunteer cadet corps because he wanted to play at being a regular soldier, he was so disintegrated by the speech of the Jelly-Bellied Flag-Flapper that he broke up the cadet corps and burst into tears because he knew that he had been an instrument in profaning the sacred. Malinowski observed that precisely because savages understood that no magic or ritual could bring the dead back to life, the need for regulating emotion by ritual was all the stronger: death inspired such violent emotions that the tribe would be exposed to the danger of the frenzied grief of the bereaved unless such grief were canalised. Kipling similarly suggested that emotion which gushed uncontrolled was a menace permissible only to those who had no roots.

> Unless you come of the gipsy stock
>   That steals by night and day
> Lock your heart with a double lock
>   And throw the key away
> ("Gipsy Vans," *Debits and Credits*)

The voluntary in-groups repeat these lessons. The practical jokes in "The Rescue of Pluffles" or "Watches of the Night" (*Plain Tales*) exemplify the way in which the in-group educates. And they teach another. Self-discipline is needed to master a craft. Dick Helder in *The Light That Failed* was in danger of valuing success instead of his craft and had to learn the wisdom of the Maltese Cat or Mahbub Ali. Knowledge comes only to those who acquire it for its own sake. Kipling seems to suggest that he who had mastered a craft would possess insight into the workings of the world; or rather that discipline would regulate the mind and purge it of fancies and conceit so that it would intuitively distinguish the true from the false. This was why he so admired the "crafty" and desired to be on the inside, why he displayed his knowledge by throwing off aphorisms and proverbial wisdom, and why he was able through his gift of turning a casual acquaintance inside out to convey to his reader the technique of the forester, the engineer, the soldier, or the horse-coper. He was astonished on his return to London from India to find that his fellow-writers ignored contemporary French fiction, an essential instrument for mastering their craft. The knowledge learnt first-hand from the involuntary in-group or second-hand from those who discovered the secrets of other in-groups was the clue to social adjustment.

IV

There remains the last part of his sociology, the doctrine of the Law. All cultures exhibit common features and men in all ages have recognized that different societies owe obligations to each other. Although Kipling was not concerned with the rightness of the codes of in-groups or societies, he was not a moral relativist. British culture was superior to Indian only by virtue of its superior techniques and ability to rule: as Bagehot said, the British were superior because "they can beat [them] in war when they like; they can take from them anything they like, and kill any of them they choose."[4] Kipling, who had little love for the Christianity of the churches, implied that the

Indians were as superior to the British in religion as the British were to them in material power. Civilisation in all of its forms rested upon knowledge of the Law which transcended individual cultures. The Law, which appears in the form of a fable in the Jungle Books, consisted of those rules of conduct—the keeping of promises, loyalty to friends, bravery, generosity, respect for parents, and so on—which restrained men's egotism, which all races and creeds held were good, and which enabled the British soldier to recognise that Gunga Din was a better man that he. It follows that those who broke the Law were outside the pale of civilisation.

This theory of society contains within it two interesting modulations in the Conservative tradition. Ever since Burke conservative political thinkers have attacked deductive or "rationalist" political philosophy and in the past hundred years have often used Kant's distinction between Pure and Practical Reason as the foundation of their critique of knowledge. The argument is familiar. *Real* knowledge about things that matter—morals, behaviour, politics, and personal relations—is incapable of scientific analysis and can be acquired only be experience. To express a tradition of behaviour in rules or precepts is to devitalise it. Thus the folk-lore of Pook's Hill is a better guide to the feelings and needs of common people than abstract treatises on their rights or sanctimonious schemes for their improvement. Kipling suspected any belief that purported to have been formed by rational conviction and delighted in showing that such beliefs were either held for disreputable motives or were mere repetitions of formulae. An Indian's conversion to Christianity could never be more than skin-deep and a sophisticated Moslem's agnosticism would vanish at the sound of a religious riot. Social well-being depended not on abstract notions of justice but on the administration of people. The hard-bitten district officers such as Orde and Tallentire, who knew all the gossip of the area under their administrations, were contrasted with the bureaucrats and Radical politicians. To Kipling Josephine Butler's struggle for women's rights was an instance of abstract morality that had increased the rate of venereal disease in the army by forcing the military authorities to discontinue the medical inspection of prostitutes in licensed military brothels. Democracy and popular education were suspect in that they enabled people to cut loose from the conventions of their class which gave them stability and dignity. Whereas liberals regard class distinctions as fetters forged by society which prevent equals from shaking hands, conservatives regard them as valuable hall-marks enabling men to recognise how they stand in relation to each other. "Without Benefit of Clergy" (*Life's Handicap*) showed Kipling writing with sympathy of a liaison between an Englishman and an Indian woman; but the idyll ends with the death of wife and child and the demolition of the very house which they inhabited. The demolition symbolises the impossibility of fusing British and Indian culture through love. Love is not a supra-social attribute: as Malthus argued it is socialised by the institution of marriage. Since marriage in this case is impossible the separate cultures cannot be bridged by love. Nor could the English genius for government be transmitted by bureaucratic fiat to the Indians: only on the level of the Law where strength recognized strength could East and West meet.

Implicit, however, in the conservative theory of knowledge runs a deep distrust of science and the scientific method, which in late Victorian times was riding high on the crest of positivist philosophy and radicalism. Here Kipling added something new. As the bard of the engineer and protagonist of the new technology he would have nothing to do with the reactionary cant which maintains that science itself is an evil.

The evil lay only in claiming more for science than it can perform. It was a marvellous craft whose discoveries Kipling continually set in contrast to the as yet undiscovered. In "Wireless" (*Traffics and Discoveries*) the transmission of the human voice by the new invention was dwarfed by the extraordinary transferences in the thought of the tubercular chemist's assistant who spoke Keats's poetry. Science could never challenge "true" knowledge because it was true only for its own time and our science would appear to future generations as astrology did to us: discoveries in fact might be made too early and as in "The Eye of Allah" (*Debits and Credits*) might have to be suppressed because society was not yet able to assimilate them. The close connection between science and society was again picked up in "Unprofessional" (*Limits and Renewals*) where Kipling stressed that a new discovery in science would create a new social problem: Mrs. Berner tried to commit suicide *after* she was cured, a moral to those who imagined that a problem has only to be scientifically examined for the "correct" solution to be found. If Kipling admired the strides made in psychology and medicine and engineering, he also intended to demonstrate how limited were their potentiality and accuracy.[5]

The second modulation that Kipling made was in breaking with the older English conservatism which placed its trust in leadership by an aristocracy of birth. He belonged to the new conservatism of imperial adventure and to the new class of skilled workers, technicians, engineers, and public servants, products of the rapid class-differentiation in the second phase of the Industrial Revolution. His genius in describing the emotions of this class towards their work has diverted attention from his delight in the mess of cotton waste and oil and clinker generated by engines; his tramp steamers are held together by the proverbial piece of string and coaxed along by their engineers. This adds to his picture of society as ordered by laws but nevertheless as dynamic, bursting at the seams, untidy, full of rascals and shrewd men operating on a shoestring and ready to exploit any sucker. A world without hardness, a world in which fairness, in which men's rights were scrupulously weighed, would be for Kipling a devitalised world. Miss Tompkins points out that in Kipling's most famous anti-democratic tract, "As Easy as A.B.C." (*A Diversity of Creatures*), the utopian world governed by five dictators in which peace and plenty reign is afflicted by too much happiness and "the basic energy of life is failing in a world where men do not struggle and suffer to their full scope." Action, then, has a positive merit. The natural conflict of social forces within the state is to be regarded as a blessing, not as a curse, and happiness is only one of the many goals in life. Liberals regard men's happiness as the ideal to which all the sciences and arts minister: the forms of government which ensure his freedom, the drugs and psycho-analysis which cure his diseased body and mind, the economics which shows how the plenty which the applied sciences make possible can best be produced and distributed, are all called into being to increase his happiness. The conservative distrusts this word. In his worst moods he is apt to argue that the abolition of slavery is a piece of legislative legerdemain which in no way increases happiness because it does not change those social processes which determine whether a man is free in more than name: or he plays the game of *tu quoque* observing, like Kipling, that those who protested most loudly about British oppression of Indians were those most given to oppressing their housemaids.[6] But even when he admits that happiness is a reality, he defines it as a state of mind which comprehends where the self fits into the scheme of things and realises that spring cannot for ever be spring and that

winter succeeds autumn. Men are, however, incurably full of illusions and seldom contented with their lot. They should therefore be taught the terms on which they are allowed to rise and the upstart should be subjected to a course of indoctrination which will bring his ambition within bounds, and turn his children into gentlemen. A sequence of stories, from "The Walking Delegate" (*The Day's Work*) to "The Tie" (*Limits and Renewals*), all emphasise the necessity for men or animals to find their place and, if they have come up in the world, to be taught it. But when the individual has proved himself in his in-group and so long as he is not in the strict sense of the word an eccentric, then the more daring his behaviour and the more abundant his action, the greater is the addition of joy in the world. The baby of the mess could score off the Senior Subaltern, a scoundrel such as Dana Da could perpetrate monstrous deceptions, and Stalky could tweak the nose of authority. Stalky was the prototype of this socialised individualism. He acted beyond the formal law of army regulations and possessed the gift of seeing himself from the outside—in relation to society.[7] In Kipling's world the joy in action and its revitalising influence were the obverse of the suffering it caused. And suffering was inevitable. Political action is often not a choice between good and evil but between lesser and greater evil. This is one of the lessons, Miss Tompkins notes, that Puck teaches Dan: "We cannot judge men for what they do under duress; nor can we judge the Lord for imposing the duress by which such actions are enforced."

Puck of Pook's Hill is a study in the dynamics of culture and its tales are deliberately arranged unchronologically to illustrate the connection between social order and civilisation. The main theme is that the Sword led men to the Treasure, and the Treasure gave the Law. The two symbols of Power are civilised by the Law. The Norman stories present the picture of an England smitten by rebellion and riven between Norman and Saxon. How did order and civilisation collapse? The Roman stories provide the answer: the Wall, the symbol of civilisation, was then about to fall because Rome had lost its genius for government. The Norman De Aquila by his cunning and political wisdom is trying to unite the country. He marries his young knights to the conquered and does not hang but uses the rebels Fulke and Gilbert. " 'I am too old to judge or to trust any man', he said . . . De Aquila was right. One should not judge men." And this theme is repeated in "Hal o' The Draft" where the shrewd J.P. lets the smugglers go scot free: he does not want civil war in Sussex and a lot of nonsense talked about traitors. The last story cuts back to Magna Carta, the formal pronouncement of the English Law. Here Kipling introduces the theme of the Jew who alone understands money, the dangerous solvent of society. When the Danes returned from Africa with the Gold, all except the landless Thorkild of Borkum were infected by its presence. "Gold changes men altogether." But the rootless Jew knows that Gold is stronger than the Sword and can make and break kings. "That is *our* God in our captivity. Power to use!" And Kadmiel uses it to benefit his race by getting the barons to include even Jews under the provisions of Magna Carta.

Four orders of men appear; those like the Picts, slaves by Necessity, ground between the grindstones of Rome and the Winged Hats, and also slaves by nature, "too little to love or to hate"; the craftsmen of England, Hal the painter and Hobson the yeoman; the officers or administrators, Parnesius and Pertinax (the Ordes and Tallentires of yesterday) who know their province and their people; and Maximus and De Aquila, the politicians and governors. To test Parnesius' flexibility Maximus orders him to execute a soldier for trivial disobedience; he refuses, and Maximus tells him that he will never be a staff officer or rule a province for he lacks the will to please his superiors. Meanwhile the fairy theme illuminates a different order of reality. The fairies, gods of a bye-gone age who have come down in the world and learnt humility through misfortune, were worshipped in the days when man was the child of Nature. But when he discovered iron and believed himself to be her master they fell, and when the Reformation turned Englishmen's religion into hate they flitted. Now they are gone—but Puck bestowed a gift upon the descendants of the widow who gave them her blessing and the means to flit: in each generation one of her family will be a simpleton and blessed with the gift of insight into the ways of Nature to preserve the immemorial wisdom of the country and the rituals which descend from the runes on the sword and Mithraism through the religion of freemasonry.

The presence throughout of the children conveys the hope for the future. For beneath the solid trappings of Edwardian affluence Kipling scanned the future with anxious eyes. Would the Wall fall again before the democratic hordes of little men and the Prussian Winged Hats? Were not the younger rulers, F. E. Smith and the renegade conservative Winston Churchill, tainted by the ambition of Maximus? Were not the financiers manipulating trade and industry to their own ends—were not luxury and wealth corrupting the ruling class and turning their children into flannelled fools at the wicket? What then was the fate of England—an England rent by class warfare and in a few years' time to be meditating civil war in Ireland? Critics have pointed out that other writers also scanned the future.[8] *Heartbreak House, Howard's End,* and *Puck of Pook's Hill* are the attempts by a socialist, a liberal, and a conservative to discern England's destiny.

Notes

1. There were highly intelligent and able men in the Indian Civil Service; but their intelligence was brought to bear exclusively on their work or on their hobbies, rarely on general ideas.
2. Cf. W. K. Clifford, *Lectures and Essays* (1901), II, 44.
3. Who need not have been to a public school. Cf. Ortheris' scorn when in "His Private Honour" *(Many Inventions)* he rejects the suggestion that he could have stood on his right to get the officer who struck him cashiered. Kipling wrote *Stalky & Co.* on his return from America after the row with his brother-in-law in which he had stood on his rights and expected fairness.
4. Walter Bagehot, *Physics and Politics* (1872), p. 207. (He was referring to Australian aborigines.)
5. For similar reasoning about the place of science in history and thought by two modern conservatives see: Herbert Butterfield, *The Origins of Modern Science* (London, 1949) and Michael Oakeshott, "Rationalism in Politics," *Cambridge Journal,* I (1947), 81–98, 145–157.
6. *Something of Myself for My Friends* (London, 1937), p. 91.
7. Kipling was surprised when Dunsterville (Stalky) dispassionately admitted that the War Office was justified in dispensing with his services after he had pitched in a particularly hot letter on his return to England at the end of the Dunsterforce expedition *(Something of Myself for My Friends,* p. 28).
8. F. E. W. McDowell, "Technique, Symbol and Theme in *Heartbreak House,*" PMLA, LXVIII (1953), 335–356; Lionel Trilling, *E. M. Forster* (London, 1951), p. 102.

JOHN BAYLEY
From "The Puzzles of Kipling"
The Uses of Division
1976, pp. 51–62

Forster saw himself, as he said of Cavafy, 'at a slight angle to the world'. Lawrence too was in a sense at an angle,

though it was of course for him the proper and sacred relation to life. Both owe to this the unity and achievement of their writing personalities. A writer like Kipling, scattered among the contingencies of his time, and involved particularly in the technologies of militarism which had come to dominate the European scene, is in very different case. And yet the contrast does not now seem quite so clear as it did. It may even be, as I have been trying to suggest, that the achievement of Lawrence and Forster, as it has survived and matured, depends more than their admirers admit on aspects of their genius which they themselves would disown or refuse to recognize. Compared with Kipling, the black sheep of their era, they once seemed clear cases of enlightenment, of civilization and progress. Do they still?—or rather do their novels as we now read them seem so wholly separated from other sorts of inspired fantasy which have left a mark on the age and on later readers? Freud's favourite reading in his later years, *The Jungle Book,* has impressed itself on readers at one stage of their lives at least as deeply as the works of these more accepted masters.

Edmund Wilson, in *The Wound and the Bow,* suggested that Kipling is one of those artists whose skills attend disablement from a childhood trauma. Yet, though Kipling's desertion by his parents was in all likelihood more traumatic than the prolonged maternal domination to which Lawrence and Forster were subject, its influence on the pattern of his life and ideas seems in fact to have been much less clearly pronounced. Nor would it be true to say that Lawrence and Forster are exiles from their epoch while Kipling is inside and identified with his. All were rather leaders, or associated with leaders, of more or less exclusive groups who sought to influence the age. It is true that Kipling was absorbed by—even disintegrated by—his age, with more evident completeness than we can forgive a great writer for being, or accept that he should be, if we are to think of him as a great writer. He cannot be said to have belonged to his times in any conventional sense, for though his temperament and views were those of a great many other persons of his class and kind he went with embarrassing detail and enthusiasm into what they took for granted. He was always far too much for 'the Group' to be of it, and he was a lonelier figure than either Lawrence or Forster, though probably a more widely influential one.

His influence and his loneliness are closely connected, and make it immediately necessary to redefine what we understand by being 'lonely' in his case. For it is no use blinking the fact that in terms of sensibility he was not lonely at all; his feelings and responses coincided completely with those of a large and widespread social and class ethos, not with those of a cult group or 'inner ring'. The major disconcertment to many people in Kipling, and especially to *bien pensants* in our time, is to find so much intelligence in such an unlikely area of sensibility. The sensibility of that part of the tribe *is* coarse, is repellent—there is no doubt about it: but it cannot blunt the acuteness and the powers of observation which Kipling bestows on it. Indeed the coarser the feeling he shares, the finer the perception of it in his art—a rare and embarrassing conjunction. And so loneliness for Kipling is being far cleverer than the people whose sensibility he shares, and just as clever as the fellow-artists whose sensibilities cause them to shun him.

He fitted, in his own imagination and work, into a category which Lawrence in his correspondence with Dr Trigant Burrow (a sociologist rather surprisingly respected by Lawrence) called 'societal man'. That is to say Kipling took himself for granted but was fascinated by any social unit he sought to belong to, or saw himself as belonging to. He had no interest in himself as such, and had none of the two other writers' ability to project that self into an imagined social scene, dominate it and take it over. Why it is interesting, after this lapse of time, to look at him in the context, not of the literature of imperialism but of the solitary authentic consciousness in its self-created social setting, is because Kipling's answer to the problem of Hegelian awareness is not so much opposed to theirs as complementary to it. Kipling understands, no less than they, the symptoms of social neurosis, alienation and discontent, but the ways in which he puts these things into art suggest remedies of a wholly practical, non-visionary kind. Kipling's fantasies, like the notorious one of 'Mary Postgate', are always rooted in a well observed and understood social situation, and his solutions accept in practical fashion the limitations of that situation.

The odd thing about Kipling is that such a talent, at such a time, should not have been housed in an 'authentic consciousness', and in self-estrangement, but in a personality passionately committed to all the honest social and family values. In one sense the paradox was disabling, for it prevented him becoming—what Henry James thought he had it in him to be—'the English Balzac'. In fact it was James himself who can now be seen to qualify for something like that title: he was able to do so because he combined the strongest possible interest in social ties and commitments with an equally strong disinclination to involve himself in them. Kipling's involvement was complete, and it prevented him from standing far enough back to write a novel; the nearest he came to it was *Kim*, in which his absorption of India could be made use of in a superlatively vivid and fantastic retrospection.

Kipling was not only deeply and continuously involved in every aspect of English life and politics but he also believed in and practised the normal family virtues, affections and responsibilities. Balzac's form of detachment was irresponsibility. Exploiting his two mistress-mothers, both more than twenty years older than himself, pining for a third mistress who lived romantically on a Polish estate as big as a French department, Balzac was totally involved in those obsessions and appetites of living which he described, but not in its duties or abnegations. Kipling's curiosity in and relish for what made people and society tick was equally great, and so perhaps was his power to describe it—his dimension was as large and as vivid as Balzac's—but his personality was not up to his talents. He used to be considered a monster by liberal *bien pensants*—'horrible old Kipling' as Auden called him—but it would be nearer the mark to say that he was not monster enough, certainly not the kind of 'sacred monster' who could create on Balzac's scale. His personality was not commonplace, but it was kept, in what was perhaps a peculiarly English way, dutiful, careful, and ordinary. He revered 'the Gods of the Copy Book headings'.

Yet as an artist he was deeply divided, none the less, and the divisions may determine what we feel about his art. Forster's 'Only connect' does not at all apply; the unified and dominating consciousness, which we may see developing and forming itself during a writer's creative life, is conspicuously absent. In a suggestive essay on his later stories W. W. Robson made the point that his art

> does not in any very obvious sense show development . . . Masterpieces as assured as anything he ever wrote can be found, at any period of his work, side by side with very inferior things; and yet on these inferior things the same minuteness of skill and care seems to have been expended.

This is certainly a clue, and it may lead to a deduction that Robson does not make. For what he calls 'inferiority' is of strange importance in Kipling. It is not, as it would be with

other writers, a sign of failure of imagination, concentration or nerve, but is as determined and confident, as full of mastery, as the recognized excellence. It is a sign of his stature, as it is with Lawrence: perhaps, indeed, it is *the* sign of a writer who is important in the ways I have been trying to suggest.

Women in Love, I maintained, does not have the same qualities we associate with the idea of a 'masterpiece'; it is loosened and freed in its aesthetic structure by kinds of comedy, even of absurdity, in language and vision which are wholly Lawrentian but which yet do not strike us as belonging to Lawrence in the often oppressive way that his style and ideas can do. It may be that the gap between this vulnerable Lawrence and the armed and unified author getting the statue clean away from the marble is too great: we can't easily, in appreciation, assimilate the one to the other and find a proper home, as we do in the 'good' and the 'bad' alike of Hardy or of Kipling. That is because Lawrence is too intent on forcing everything into consciousness, and the same certainly cannot be said of Kipling, who more typically seems concerned to leave matters below the level of realization. This may be a weakness or it may not: Kipling is convinced that what is most important to social man is usually conditioned in him in ways that ought not to be disturbed or brought to light too much; a conviction difficult to reconcile with the ways in which art works as finding out, exploring and revealing. That is why the pay-off, in Kipling's narrative metaphysic, so often disappoints, seems either meagre or smart, and not rigorous enough.

But this applies more to what is usually thought of as good in his work than to what is considered bad. It is probably true that if we accept Kipling we are not all that much concerned with the difference between the two, granted always that both the good and the bad are concerned with the investigation of a social unit. And ultimately something of the same kind may happen with Lawrence, for the addict of both writers rapidly becomes indifferent to their doctrines—though he may remain very knowledgeable about them—and becomes hooked on something that is not exactly their 'art', but more their individual speech and their particular mode of self-revelation. Like Lawrence, also like Dickens, Kipling was essentially daemonic in temperament, though he preferred to think of his daemon not as the fire in his own belly, but as it were a powerful and senior colleague who lived in the next compound. He insisted, and over-insisted, on being an artist, but his place is more with these other daemonic creators who have no regard for art in the lamp and inkhorn sense in which Kipling liked to talk of it. It was as difficult for him to get outside himself, and to be the detached artist, as it was to get outside the packs and societies which he ran with and believed in.

For the writer who depends in one way or another on divisions, unresolved issues and confusions present in the completed work, detachment is in any case not possible. All he thinks and is shows all the time, and this is as true of the early tales in which Kipling is at school with de Maupassant as in the later ones, with their finicky techniques of the elliptic and absconded narrator. It is significant that Hemingway, who admired and learnt from Kipling, has none of this involuntary presentness. When he relaxed his revolutionary and immaculate technique of narrative mannerism he is revealed as a wordy bore, a mind and being at the end of the road. Kipling, like Lawrence, retains his mystery, his power to make us continue wondering about him. Kipling is too big to present a 'case', as Edmund Wilson tried to make him, and as Hemingway undoubtedly is. He goes on cropping up all over the place, even among the young Soviet intelligentsia, offering—in spite of the lack of bulk fiction in his varied work—his own odd version of God's plenty, and something for everyone, even his own variation on Lamb's ideal of 'the sanity of true genius'.

From his own fastidious angle, T. S. Eliot summed up much of what I have been trying to suggest when he said that the pleasure of reading Kipling was 'the pleasure of exploring a mind so very different from my own'. The compliment implicit in the word 'exploration' is a very considerable one. As in Browning's metaphor in 'Love in a Life' (and Browning was Kipling's favourite poet) we go from room to room through closed doors. In such a compartmented mind, of a kind familiar to us from daily human contact but not often met with in great writers—though Milton and Dickens both reveal it—we experience contradictions and prejudices which do not meet and examine one another except through our presence. Impulses like vindictiveness and forbearance, humility and strident assurance, appear to maintain a separate but equalizing pressure on the creative temperament. Though in story and character we are always in the presence, it is a presence that does not necessarily weigh upon us as that of much more enlightened authors may do; for the compartments act like a modern equivalent of what Keats called 'negative capability'. Kipling could certainly feel with an Iago and an Imogen, with a Learoyd and a Liza Rowntree, but the impulse to hate or to love which he depicts in such characters doesn't appear capable of meeting or recognition. To draw a crude parallel, he sometimes reminds us of a loving father who votes for hanging and flogging; and indeed as a man of his time that was what he was, and what he did.

In *The Wound and the Bow* Edmund Wilson compares Kipling, much to his disadvantage, with Yeats and with Henry James.

> Kipling *had* terribly shrunk . . . Whereas Yeats was playing out superbly the last act of a personal drama which he had sustained unembarrassed by public events, and Henry James was now seen in retrospect to have accomplished, in his long career, a prodigy of disinterested devotion to an art and a criticism of life.

A personal drama unembarrassed by public events suggests, rather more than Wilson perhaps intended, the fundamental and self-willed isolation of Yeats; and James, too might have smiled wryly at Wilson's compliment. The truth is, surely, that all three acted as they had to do and as their creative natures required, but the limitations are not necessarily on Kipling's side. His vulnerability was as intelligent as the dedication of Yeats and no less noble than James's abstinence. The loss of his son and daughter; his knowledge of hatred and vindictiveness and of their inevitability in any social group; his involvement in duty and unfreedom; his sense of attachment and forebearance, not as moral qualities or enlightened opinions, but as what was for him absolute needs, like the need to support order and be some kind of snob—these are the marks of Kipling's participation, as of many other persons', and that silent majority would no doubt endorse his view that in this way 'hearts, like muddy streams, cleanse themselves as they go forward'.

James in fact, in his subterraneous way, has an almost wholly deterministic view of the moral world. The hero of his story 'The Beast in the Jungle', knew his fate to be emptiness, not by reason of a noble abstinence, but because of his own egoism: that was the way he was. Kipling's remarkable late tale of a fantastic literary forgery, 'Dayspring Mishandled', resembles James's story in its bleak and subtle suggestion of the inability to be other than oneself. Its hero is a writer of historical potboilers who plans an elaborate revenge on a Chaucerian scholar who has done him a great injury: he composes and forges a superb fragment which he contrives that the scholar should discover; but when his enemy is delivered utterly into his hand he refrains from consummating his triumph, not through any free and virtuous moral choice—such things do not exist in Kipling's world—but because as an artist he cannot bear to see such a piece of work collapsed into the triviality of life.

The story is composed and highlighted with great care and cunning. And as often happens with Kipling this meticulousness emphasizes something both coarse and conventional in the selection of characters and in the concept itself. The woman whom the villain has 'wronged' has no proper specification, which implies that Kipling is too much of a gentleman to give her one; and though his discovery has brought him fame the villain dies of cancer without enjoying the knighthood he has got by it, while his wife, now Lady Castorley, prepares to remarry. We may be chilled by a callousness in the characters' behaviour which Kipling seems quite to take for granted, and perhaps repelled as well by the glib 'nature's revenge' in the ending. James, perhaps, could have given us a more artistic chill by delicately indicating and probing the ugliness in and beneath the seeming decorum of professional literary society. But Kipling's *donnée*, though so much like many of James's, draws us into a more memorable encounter, perhaps because he himself seems not wholly aware of the nature and meaning of the materials he is so meticulously handling—on this, as on other Kipling conundrums, we can never be quite sure. Characteristically he prefers to present himself as a technician rather than a creator: we can sometimes tell if something is important, deep down, from his light and offhand manner of talking about it.

And in fact the technical expertise and knowledge he prided himself on is often much more insecure than his instincts. There is an example in his memoir, *Something of Myself*, which has an odd bearing on 'Dayspring Mishandled', for it shows how sketchy was Kipling's actual knowledge of Chaucer. He relates, in that ebullient manner which is both stimulating and strangely repellent, how the *Manchester Guardian*, always hating his attitudes, managed in their reviews to find fault with everything he published. One of his later tales, 'The Wish House', earned their contempt by having a heroine obviously cribbed from Chaucer's Wife of Bath, down to the 'mormal on her shinne'. Kipling wrote to the paper

> and gave myself 'out—caught to leg'. The reply came from an evident human being . . . who was pleased with the tribute to his knowledge of Chaucer.

What Kipling did not appear to have realised was that he had compounded a howler—the 'mormal' belongs to the Cook in Chaucer's *Prologue*, not to the Wife of Bath. The incident shows not only Kipling's attitude to expertise, and to false expertise, but how some of his fascination comes from a kind of involuntary collusion by the reader in falsity got up so closely to resemble life that it sheds sudden and disconcerting light on Kipling's views *on* life. The gap between hand-rubbing accuracy and an over-casual tone holds the particular flavour of the Kipling experience, and like good journalism (no wonder Kipling felt kinship with the *Guardian* reviewer) it makes an immediate impression without much follow-through. The trouble with elaborations on reporting is that they are only true for a moment, where the 'story' and the reader intersect; and we often feel that what happened afterwards is no affair of Kipling's.

The really bizarre thing about this hypnotically untrustworthy innocence, which earned him in his time as many English-speaking readers as the Bible, is the way it is mixed in with a cunning ceremony—the literary equivalent of free-masonry. It is hinted that only initiates, those really in the know, can understand the Last Effects, the 'overlaid tints and textures', in his Burne-Jones picture vocabulary, 'which might or might not reveal themselves according to the shifting light of sex, youth and experience'. (Just conceivably his story about the *Guardian* man and Chaucer is intended to test the reader, with Kipling knowing what was wrong all the time, for he tells us in *Something of Myself* that he used when he was young to plumb the real knowledge of 'the Men of Letters' he met by misattributing quotations, and was seldom or never corrected.) In one of the South African stories, 'The Comprehension of Private Copper', clues are undoubtedly planted to show Sahibs in the know that Private Copper's captor, a renegade young Boer of English origin, has come in his speech and outlook, his consciousness of inferiority, to resemble a Eurasian, because the true Boers have denied him political rights and treated him as an inferior being. For Kipling (as for Lord Milner) this was the crux of the case against the Boers—to dissolve the reflexes of British superiority was the unforgivable sin—and, as Professor Bodelsen has pointed out, some verses called 'The Old Issue' introduce a sexual motif that the story completes. 'Deeper strikes the rottenness in the people's loins', because as helots they lose self-respect, and with it the will to power and the hegemony of race. Kipling was conditioned by his time, and by his varied experience, especially in India, and his understanding of these matters can be seen now to be exact and profound. However acute their intuition of a place—and Lawrence's could be astonishing—Lawrence and Forster were always visitors and tourists, whereas Kipling knew to the bone how men are set and moulded into the place where they must live and the job they must do.

But such knowledge is in its nature unprincipled. Its only real logic is the maintenance of British domination, because that domination was the best thing for the world in general, and for India or South Africa in particular. (As Marlowe observes without irony in Conrad's *Heart of Darkness*, where the map is red you can be sure that good work is being done there.) But in terms of Kipling's art this lack of moral logic or external insight (Kipling loathed principles or beliefs unearned in the conditioning of action) is not important. What is important is that a story which may seem morally deplorable, even indefensible, can none the less be a work of art in the Tolstoyan sense. Kipling's art effects may stop on the page, but not the moral of his art; and its lack of abstract ethic provides a sort of challenge. Why is it wrong for Boers to treat English *uitlanders* as an inferior class, and right for the English to do the same to natives and Eurasians? Why is it right to drop bombs that may kill German civilians, and vile of them to kill our children by the same means? Of course there is no answer and Kipling does not pretend that there is; unlike racial theorists he never tried to justify himself—the feeling of the tribe was what counted. But equally of course we ask the question, because the stories—so far from requiring we should—cannot, by reason of their peculiar power, prevent us.

This, with a vengeance, is to trust the tale and not the teller. A late tale from *Limits and Renewals*, a companion of 'Dayspring Mishandled', is a case in point. 'The Tie', deplored by Mr Robson as 'negligible and unpleasant', is about a fraudulent contractor of the 1914 war who is only saved from violence at the hands of some young officers by the old school tie he is wearing. Conditioning tells, in a manner that is as explosively satirical in effect as it is—presumably—merely genial and admonitory in intention. Such tales are able to reach into us through outrage, whereas the *Puck* series, in which the 'tints and textures' are all methodically and insipidly overlaid, are by this comparison lacking in the secret dynamic, and are parables too consciously intended to be read on more than one level. But in these tales knowledge is not imparted by an author outside; Kipling has no Lawrentian intelligence to place, define and assign from a position of isolated integrity. Light does not come from outside—it dawns inside the locked compartments of assumption and prejudice which the daemon makes us enter, and it is arguable that the more apparently awful the stories, the further they reach in our hearts and minds, if we let them.

One of the Plain Tales from the Hills, as 'awful' as 'The Tie', but written something like forty years earlier, makes much the same point as the later story, and forces us equally to understand by participation in the society described. A young English civil servant is determined to marry a Portuguese Eurasian girl and is 'saved' by his colleagues, who kidnap him before the wedding can take place. There is a gruesome equability in the narration. The Eurasian is both good and beautiful, and the pink and white English girl who will subsequently be chosen for the promising young man will be without interest: between them there will evidently be, as is fitting, no real sympathy or emotion. But things are as they are, and the relation in the tale between Kipling's gleeful acceptance of the situation, and his cool understanding of it, is charged with his special kind of disturbing vitality; just how much so we can see if we compare it with the similar themes that Somerset Maugham was going to handle. In terms of so tricky a theme Maugham's enlightened views are as repellent as his detachment; though he is a far from negligible writer his authorial attitudes are all too simply egoistic. Maugham annoyed Colonials who found themselves and the tales they had told him in his stories; but Kipling must have embarrassed his contemporaries in India very much more, and more subtly. For they had always taken tacitly for granted what he now exuberantly took for granted in print, and the demonstration is far more unsettling than any satire, especially to the community so equivocally endorsed by Kipling's art.

Kipling's involvement here is not so unlike that of Tolstoy in *War and Peace* and *Anna Karenina*. Tolstoy's enthusiasm for the manners and assumptions of his class and kind is subjected to a massive process of self-analysing and self-revealing detail and is both more lyric and more epic to the extent that Tolstoy is by far the greater genius. But the Rostovs' ball, Stiva's lunch-party, the great reception for Bagration, show Tolstoy as emphatically on the side of a way of life as Kipling is, and this emphasis could be said to be just as damaging, not only in retrospect but in the eyes of those associates of his who realized—as which of them, however obscurely, did not?—that such a mode of being depended both for its confidence and for its private validity on *not* being publicized in this way. We know that Tolstoy's peers privately resented his magnificent process, and we may assume that Kipling's had the same reservations about his more specific and workaday one. In both authors there is the same secret sense of the injustice of the world, and of where they stand in relation to it, and to its necessities.

The daemon knew more than the journalist and spokesman for imperialism, and certainly had more human sympathy: when Kipling tries to show sympathy in person he almost always fails and is not infrequently embarrassing. His apologists today make the mistake of supposing that it was Kipling himself—as it might be Lawrence or Forster—who could be an independent judge, accepting, so to speak, the laws of Israel, but retaining and demonstrating his own values—

values more like their own. But there are no values for him outside the pack. It has been suggested that a criticism is passed on 'the great game' of the secret service in *Kim*, by means of the figures of the Lama and the Babu, but the Lama is really only a case of self-indulgence on Kipling's part. As a Tibetan monk, of an exotically unknown and therefore uninferior race and religion, the Lama is excused from real participation in society. We can see Kipling clearly—too clearly—in these moments of humanity, but we cannot see him at all when he is writing about what really inspired him.

ARTHUR KOESTLER

1905–1983

Born in Budapest on September 5, 1905, Arthur Koestler grew up bilingual in Hungarian and German. His family moved to Vienna in 1914, and Koestler studied at a polytechnic college there from 1922 until 1926, when he abandoned his studies and traveled to Palestine as a Zionist extremist. In 1927 he became a correspondent for the German Ullstein newspapers, and was posted to Paris in 1929 before moving to Berlin in 1930 as a science editor. He joined the Communist Party at the end of 1931, and this cost him his job the following year. After an extended visit to the Soviet Union he worked as a propagandist in Paris, and became the Spanish correspondent of the London *News Chronicle* during the Civil War. Captured by fascist forces, he was held for three months under sentence of death, but was released following British pressure. He resigned from the Communist Party in 1938, and was later a prominent and influential anti-Communist. In 1940 he was interned in a French prison camp for aliens; after his release he joined the French Foreign Legion, and, deserting, escaped to England, where he worked during the war for the Ministry of Information.

Koestler's early writings, including the novels *The Gladiators* (1939) and *Darkness at Noon* (1940), were in German, but he took up the English language in *Arrival and Departure* (1943). The essays *The Yogi and the Commissar* appeared in 1945, followed by a Zionist novel, *Thieves in the Night* (1946) and a historical study of Zionism and Palestine, *Promise and Fulfilment* (1949). Although he continued to write fiction, including *The Age of Longing* (1951) and *The Call Girls* (1972), most of his later writings were on science, art, and parapsychology; notable among his works of non-fiction are *The Sleepwalkers* (1959), *The Act of Creation* (1964), and *The Ghost in the Machine* (1967).

After World War II Koestler lived in Britain, except for brief periods in France and America. His many distinctions included a CBE in 1972 and a C.Lit. in 1974. Vice-President of the Voluntary Euthanasia Society, and suffering from Parkinson's disease and leukemia, he committed suicide with his third wife, Cynthia, on March 3, 1983, in London.

GEORGE ORWELL
"Arthur Koestler" (1944)
Dickens, Dali and Others
1946, pp. 185–201

One striking fact about English literature during the present century is the extent to which it has been dominated by foreigners—for example, Conrad, Henry James, Shaw, Joyce, Yeats, Pound and Eliot. Still, if you chose to make this a matter of national prestige and examine our achievement in the various branches of literature, you would find that England made a fairly good showing until you came to what may be roughly described as political writing, or pamphleteering. I mean by this the special class of literature that has arisen out of the European political struggle since the rise of Fascism. Under this heading novels, autobiographies, books of "reportage," sociological treatises and plain pamphlets can all be lumped together, all of them having a common origin and to a great extent the same emotional atmosphere.

Some of the outstanding figures in this school of writers are Silone, Malraux, Salvemini, Borkenau, Victor Serge and Koestler himself. Some of these are imaginative writers, some not, but they are all alike in that they are trying to write contemporary history, but *unofficial* history, the kind that is ignored in the text-books and lied about in the newspapers. Also they are all alike in being continental Europeans. It may be an exaggeration, but it cannot be a very great one, to say that whenever a book dealing with totalitarianism appears in this country, and still seems worth reading six months after publication, it is a book translated from some foreign language. English writers, over the past dozen years, have poured forth an enormous spate of political literature, but they have produced almost nothing of æsthetic value, and very little of historical value either. The Left Book Club, for instance, has been running ever since 1936. How many of its chosen volumes can you even remember the names of? Nazi Germany, Soviet Russia, Spain, Abyssinia, Austria, Czechoslovakia—all that these and kindred subjects have produced, in England, are slick books of reportage, dishonest pamphlets in which propaganda is swallowed whole and then spewed up again, half digested, and a very few reliable guide-books and text-books. There has been nothing resembling, for instance, *Fontamara* or *Darkness at Noon*, because there is almost no English writer to whom it has happened to see totalitarianism from the inside. In Europe, during the past decade and more, things have been happening to middle-class people which in England do not even happen to the working class. Most of the European writers I mentioned above, and scores of others like them, have been obliged to break the law in order to engage in politics at all; some of them have thrown bombs and fought in street-battles, many have been in prison or the concentration camp, or fled across frontiers with false names and forged passports. One cannot imagine, say, Professor Laski indulging in activities of that kind. England is lacking, therefore, in what one might call concentration-camp literature. The special world created by secret police forces, censorship of opinion, torture and frame-up trials is, of course, known about and to some extent disapproved of, but it has made very little emotional impact. One result of this is that there exists in England almost no literature of disillusionment about the Soviet Union. There is the attitude of ignorant disapproval, and there is the attitude of uncritical admiration, but very little in between. Opinion on the Moscow sabotage trials, for instance, was divided, but divided chiefly on the question of whether the accused were guilty. Few People were able to see that, whether justified or not, the trials were an unspeakable horror. And English disapproval of the Nazi outrages has also been an unreal thing, turned on and off like a tap according to political expediency. To understand such things one has to be able to imagine oneself as the victim, and for an Englishman to write *Darkness at Noon* would be as unlikely an accident as for a slave-trader to write *Uncle Tom's Cabin*.

Koestler's published work really centres about the Moscow trials. His main theme is the decadence of revolutions owing to the corrupting effects of power, but the special nature of the Stalin dictatorship has driven him back into a position not far removed from pessimistic Conservatism. I do not know how many books he has written in all. He is a Hungarian who usually writes in German, and five books have been published in England: *Spanish Testament*, *The Gladiators*, *Darkness at Noon*, *The Scum of the Earth*, and *Arrival and Departure*. The subject-matter of all of them is similar and none of them ever escapes for more than a few pages from the atmosphere of nightmare. Of the five books, the action of three takes place entirely or almost entirely in prison.

In the opening months of the Spanish Civil War Koestler was the *News Chronicle's* correspondent in Spain, and early in 1937 he was taken prisoner when the Fascists captured Malaga. He was nearly shot out of hand, then spent some months imprisoned in a fortress, listening every night to the roar of rifle fire as batch after batch of Republicans was executed, and being most of the time in acute danger of execution himself. This was not a chance adventure which "might have happened to anybody," but was in accordance with Koestler's life style. A politically indifferent person would not have been in Spain at that date, a more cautious observer would have got out of Malaga before the Fascists arrived, and a British or American newspaper man would have been treated with more consideration. The book that Koestler wrote about this, *Spanish Testament*, has remarkable passages, but apart from the scrappiness that is usual in a book of reportage, it is definitely false in places. In the prison scenes Koestler successfully establishes the nightmare atmosphere which is, so to speak, his patent, but the rest of the book is too much coloured by the Popular Front orthodoxy of the time. One or two passages even look as though they had been doctored for the purposes of the Left Book Club. At that time Koestler still was, or recently had been, a member of the Communist Party, and the complex politics of the Civil War made it impossible for any Communist to write quite honestly about the internal struggle on the Government side. The sin of nearly all left-wingers from 1933 onwards is that they have wanted to be anti-Fascist without being anti-totalitarian. In 1937 Koestler already knew this, but did not feel free to say so. He came much nearer to saying it—indeed, he did say it, though he put on a mask to do so—in his next book, *The Gladiators*, which was published about a year before the war and for some reason attracted very little attention.

The Gladiators is in some ways an unsatisfactory book. It is about Spartacus, the Thracian gladiator who raised a slaves' rebellion in Italy round about 65 B.C., and any book on such a subject is handicapped by challenging comparison with *Salammbô*. In our own age it would not be possible to write a book like *Salammbô*, even if one had the talent. The great thing about *Salammbô*, even more important than its physical detail, is its utter mercilessness. Flaubert could think himself into the stony cruelty of antiquity, because in the mid-nineteenth century one still had peace of mind. One had time to travel in the past. Nowadays the present and the future are too terrifying to be escaped from, and if one bothers with history it is in order to find modern meanings there. Koestler makes Spartacus into an allegorical figure, a primitive version of the proletarian dictator. Whereas Flaubert has been able, by a prolonged effort of the imagination, to make his mercenaries truly pre-Christian, Spartacus is a modern man dressed up. But this might not matter if Koestler were fully aware of what his allegory means. Revolutions always go wrong—that is the main theme. It is on the question of *why* they go wrong that he falters, and his uncertainty enters into the story and makes the central figures enigmatic and unreal.

For several years the rebellious slaves are uniformly successful. Their numbers swell to a hundred thousand, they overrun great areas of Southern Italy, they defeat one punitive expedition after another, they ally themselves with the pirates who at that time were the masters of the Mediterranean, and finally they set to work to build a city of their own, to be named the City of the Sun. In this city human beings are to be free and equal, and above all, they are to be happy: no slavery, no hunger, no injustice, no floggings, no executions. It is the dream of a just society which seems to haunt the human imagination ineradicably and in all ages, whether it is called the Kingdom of Heaven or the classless society, or whether it is thought of as a Golden Age which once existed in the past and from which we have degenerated. Needless to say, the slaves fail to achieve it. No sooner have they formed themselves into a community than their way of life turns out to be as unjust, laborious and fear-ridden as any other. Even the cross, symbol of slavery, has to be revived for the punishment of malefactors. The turning-point comes when Spartacus finds himself obliged to crucify twenty of his oldest and most faithful followers. After that the City of the Sun is doomed, the slaves split up and are defeated in detail, the last fifteen thousand of them being captured and crucified in one batch.

The serious weakness of this story is that the motives of Spartacus himself are never made clear. The Roman lawyer Fulvius, who joins the rebellion and acts as its chronicler, sets forth the familiar dilemma of ends and means. You can achieve nothing unless you are willing to use force and cunning, but in using them you pervert your original aims. Spartacus, however, is not represented as power-hungry, nor, on the other hand, as a visionary. He is driven onwards by some obscure force which he does not understand, and he is frequently in two minds as to whether it would not be better to throw up the whole adventure and flee to Alexandria while the going is good. The slaves' republic is in any case wrecked rather by hedonism than by the struggle for power. The slaves are discontented with their liberty because they still have to work, and the final break-up happens because the more turbulent and less civilised slaves, chiefly Gauls and Germans, continue to behave like bandits after the republic has been established. This may be a true account of events—naturally we know very little about the slave rebellions of antiquity—but by allowing the Sun City to be destroyed because Crixus the Gaul cannot be prevented from looting and raping, Koestler has faltered between allegory and history. If Spartacus is the prototype of the modern revolutionary—and obviously he is intended as that—he should have gone astray because of the impossibility of combining power with righteousness. As it is, he is an almost passive figure, acted upon rather than acting, and at times not convincing. The story partly fails because the central problem of revolution has been avoided or, at least, has not been solved.

It is again avoided in a subtler way in the next book, Koestler's masterpiece, *Darkness at Noon*. Here, however, the story is not spoiled, because it deals with individuals and its interest is psychological. It is an episode picked out from a background that does not have to be questioned. *Darkness at Noon* describes the imprisonment and death of an Old Bolshevik, Rubashov, who first denies and ultimately confesses to crimes which he is well aware he has not committed. The grown-upness, the lack of surprise or denunciation, the pity and irony with which the story is told, show the advantage, when one is handling a theme of this kind, of being a European. The book reaches the stature of tragedy, whereas an English or American writer could at most have made it into a polemical tract. Koestler has digested his material and can treat it on the æsthetic level. At the same time his handling of it has a political implication, not important in this case but likely to be damaging in later books.

Naturally the whole book centres round one question: Why did Rubashov confess? He is not guilty—that is, not guilty of anything except the essential crime of disliking the Stalin regime. The concrete acts of treason in which he is supposed to have engaged are all imaginary. He has not even been tortured, or not very severely. He is worn down by solitude, toothache, lack of tobacco, bright lights glaring in his eyes, and continuous questioning, but these in themselves would not be enough to overcome a hardened revolutionary. The Nazis have previously done worse to him without breaking his spirit. The confessions obtained in the Russian State trials are capable of three explanations:

(1) That the accused were guilty.
(2) That they were tortured, and perhaps blackmailed by threats to relatives and friends.
(3) That they were actuated by despair, mental bankruptcy and the habit of loyalty to the Party.

For Koestler's purpose in *Darkness at Noon* (1) is ruled out, and though this is not the place to discuss the Russian purges, I must add that what little verifiable evidence there is suggests that the trials of the Old Bolsheviks were frame-ups. If one assumes that the accused were not guilty—at any rate, not guilty of the particular things they confessed to—then (2) is the common-sense explanation. Koestler, however, plumps for (3), which is also accepted by the Trotskyist Boris Souvarine, in his pamphlet *Cauchemar en URSS*. Rubashov ultimately confesses because he cannot find in his own mind any reason for not doing so. Justice and objective truth have long ceased to have any meaning for him. For decades he has been simply the creature of the Party, and what the Party now demands is that he shall confess to non-existent crimes. In the end, though he has had to be bullied and weakened first, he is somewhat proud

of his decision to confess. He feels superior to the poor Czarist officer who inhabits the next cell and who talks to Rubashov by tapping on the wall. The Czarist officer is shocked when he learns that Rubashov intends to capitulate. As he sees it from his "bourgeois" angle, everyone ought to stick to his guns, even a Bolshevik. Honour, he says, consists in doing what you think right. "Honour is to be useful without fuss," Rubashov taps back; and he reflects with a certain satisfaction that he is tapping with his pince-nez while the other, the relic of the past, is tapping with a monocle.

Like Bukharin, Rubashov is "looking out upon black darkness." What is there, what code, what loyalty, what notion of good and evil, for the sake of which he can defy the Party and endure further torment? He is not only alone, he is also hollow. He had himself committed worse crimes than the one that is now being perpetrated against him. For example, as a secret envoy of the Party in Nazi Germany, he has got rid of disobedient followers by betraying them to the Gestapo. Curiously enough, if he has any inner strength to draw upon, it is the memories of his boyhood when he was the son of a landowner. The last thing he remembers, when he is shot from behind, is the leaves of the poplar tree on his father's estate. Rubashov belongs to the older generation of Bolsheviks that was largely wiped out in the purges. He is aware of art and literature, and of the world outside Russia. He contrasts sharply with Gletkin, the young G.P.U. man who conducts his interrogation, and who is the typical "good Party man," completely without scruples or curiosity, a thinking gramophone. Rubashov, unlike Gletkin, does not have the Revolution as his starting-point. His mind was not a blank sheet when the party got hold of it. His superiority to the other is finally traceable to his bourgeois origin.

One cannot, I think, argue that *Darkness at Noon* is simply a story dealing with the adventures of an imaginary individual. Clearly it is a political book, founded on history and offering an interpretation of disputed events. Rubashov might be Trotsky, Bukharin, Rakovsky or some other relatively civilised figure among the Old Bolsheviks. If one writes about the Moscow trials one must answer the question, "Why did the accused confess?" and which answer one makes is a political decision. Koestler answers, in effect, "Because these people have been rotted by the Revolution which they served," and in doing so he comes near to claiming that revolutions are of their nature bad. If one assumes that the accused in the Moscow trials were made to confess by means of some kind of terrorism, one is only saying that one particular set of revolutionary leaders has gone astray. Individuals, and not the situation, are to blame. The implication of Koestler's book, however, is that Rubashov in power would be no better than Gletkin: or rather, only better in that his outlook is still partly pre-revolutionary. Revolution, Koestler seems to say, is a corrupting process. Really enter into the Revolution and you must end up as either Rubashov or Gletkin. It is not merely that "power corrupts": so also do the ways of attaining power. Therefore, all efforts to regenerate society *by violent means* lead to the cellars of the Ogpu. Lenin leads to Stalin, and would have come to resemble Stalin if he had happened to survive.

Of course, Koestler does not say this quite explicitly, and perhaps is not altogether conscious of it. He is writing about darkness, but it is darkness at what ought to be noon. Part of the time he feels that things might have turned out differently. The notion that So-and-so has "betrayed," that things have only gone wrong because of individual wickedness, is ever present in left-wing thought. Later, in *Arrival and Departure*, Koestler swings over much further towards the anti-revolutionary position, but in between these two books there is another, *The Scum of the Earth*, which is straight autobiography and has only an indirect bearing upon the problems raised by *Darkness at Noon*. True to his life style, Koestler was caught in France by the outbreak of war and, as a foreigner and a known anti-Fascist, was promptly arrested and interned by the Daladier Government. He spent the first nine months of war mostly in a prison camp, then, during the collapse of France, escaped and travelled by devious routes to England, where he was once again thrown into prison as an enemy alien. This time he was soon released, however. The book is a valuable piece of reportage, and together with a few other scraps of honest writing that happened to be produced at the time of the debacle, it is a reminder of the depths that bourgeois democracy can descend to. At this moment, with France newly liberated and the witch-hunt after collaborators in full swing, we are apt to forget that in 1940 various observers on the spot considered that about forty per cent. of the French population was either actively pro-German or completely apathetic. Truthful war books are never acceptable to non-combatants, and Koestler's book did not have a very good reception. Nobody came well out of it—neither the bourgeois politicans, whose idea of conducting an anti-Fascist war was to jail every left-winger they could lay hands on, nor the French Communists, who were effectively pro-Nazi and did their best to sabotage the French war effort, nor the common people, who were just as likely to follow mountebanks like Doriot as responsible leaders. Koestler records some fantastic conversations with fellow-victims in the concentration camp, and adds that till then, like most middle-class Socialists and Communists, he had never made contact with real proletarians, only with the educated minority. He draws the pessimistic conclusion: "Without education of the masses, no social progress; without social progress, no education of the masses." In *The Scum of the Earth* Koestler ceases to idealise the common people. He has abandoned Stalinism, but he is not a Trotskyist either. This is the book's real link with *Arrival and Departure*, in which what is normally called a revolutionary outlook is dropped, perhaps for good.

Arrival and Departure is not a satisfactory book. The pretence that it is a novel is very thin; in effect it is a tract purporting to show that revolutionary creeds are rationalisations of neurotic impulses. With all too neat a symmetry, the book begins and ends with the same action—a leap into a foreign country. A young ex-Communist who has made his escape from Hungary jumps ashore in Portugal, where he hopes to enter the service of Britain, at that time the only power fighting against Germany. His enthusiasm is somewhat cooled by the fact that the British consulate is uninterested in him and almost ignores him for a period of several months, during which his money runs out and other astuter refugees escape to America. He is successively tempted by the World in the form of a Nazi propagandist, the Flesh in the form of a French girl, and—after a nervous breakdown—the Devil in the form of a psycho-analyst. The psycho-analyst drags out of him the fact that his revolutionary enthusiasm is not founded on any real belief in historical necessity, but on a morbid guilt complex arising from an attempt in early childhood to blind his baby brother. By the time that he gets an opportunity of serving the Allies he has lost all reason for wanting to do so, and he is on the point of leaving for America when his irrational impulses seize hold of him again. In practice he cannot abandon the struggle. When the book ends, he is floating down in a parachute over the dark landscape of his native country, where he will be employed as a secret agent of Britain.

As a political statement (and the book is not much more), this is insufficient. Of course it is true in many cases, and it may be true in all cases, that revolutionary activity is the result of personal maladjustment. Those who struggle against society are, on the whole, those who have reason to dislike it, and normal healthy people are no more attracted to violence and illegality than they are by war. The young Nazi in *Arrival and Departure* makes the penetrating remark that one can see what is wrong with the left-wing movement by the ugliness of its women. But after all, this does not invalidate the Socialist case. Actions have results, irrespective of their motives. Marx's ultimate motives may well have been envy and spite, but this does not prove that his conclusions were false. In making the hero of *Arrival and Departure* take his final decision from a mere instinct not to shirk action and danger, Koestler is making him suffer a sudden loss of intelligence. With such a history as he has behind him, he would be able to see that certain things have to be done, whether our reasons for doing them are "good" or "bad." History has to move in a certain direction, even if it has to be pushed that way by neurotics. In *Arrival and Departure* Peter's idols are overthrown one after the other. The Russian Revolution has degenerated, Britain, symbolised by the aged consul with gouty fingers, is no better, the international class-conscious proletariat is a myth. But the conclusion (since, after all, Koestler and his hero "support" the war) ought to be that getting rid of Hitler is still a worth-while objective, a necessary bit of scavenging in which motives are almost irrelevant.

To take a rational political decision one must have a picture of the future. At present Koestler seems to have none, or rather to have two which cancel out. As an ultimate objective he believes in the Earthly Paradise, the Sun State which the gladiators set out to establish, and which has haunted the imagination of Socialists, anarchists and religious heretics for hundreds of years. But his intelligence tells him that the Earthly Paradise is receding into the far distance and that what is actually ahead of us is bloodshed, tyranny and privation. Recently he described himself as a "short-term pessimist." Every kind of horror is blowing up over the horizon, but somehow it will all come right in the end. This outlook is probably gaining ground among thinking people: it results from the very great difficulty, once one has abandoned orthodox religious belief, of accepting life on earth as inherently miserable, and on the other hand, from the realisation that to make life livable is a much bigger problem than it recently seemed. Since about 1930 the world has given no reason for optimism whatever. Nothing is in sight except a welter of lies, hatred, cruelty and ignorance, and beyond our present troubles loom vaster ones which are only now entering into European consciousness. It is quite possible that man's major problems will *never* be solved. But it is also unthinkable! Who is there who dares to look at the world of to-day and say to himself, "It will always be like this: even in a million years it cannot get appreciably better"? So you get the quasi-mystical belief that for the present there is no remedy, all political action is useless, but that somehow, somewhere in space and time, human life will cease to be the miserable brutish thing it now is.

The only easy way out is that of the religious believer, who regards this life merely as a preparation for the next. But few thinking people now believe in life after death, and the number of those who do is probably diminishing. The Christian churches would probably not survive on their own merits if their economic basis were destroyed. The real problem is how to restore the religious attitude while accepting death as final.

Men can only be happy when they do not assume that the object of life is happiness. It is most unlikely, however, that Koestler would accept this. There is a well-marked hedonistic strain in his writings, and his failure to find a political position after breaking with Stalinism is a result of this.

The Russian Revolution, the central event in Koestler's life, started out with high hopes. We forget these things now, but a quarter of a century ago it was confidently expected that the Russian Revolution would lead to Utopia. Obviously this has not happened. Koestler is too acute not to see this, and too sensitive not to remember the original objective. Moreover, from his European angle he can see such things as purges and mass deportations for what they are; he is not, like Shaw or Laski, looking at them through the wrong end of the telescope. Therefore he draws the conclusion: This is what revolutions lead to. There is nothing for it except to be a "short-term pessimist," *i.e.* to keep out of politics, make a sort of oasis within which you and your friends can remain sane, and hope that somehow things will be better in a hundred years. At the basis of this lies his hedonism, which leads him to think of the Earthly Paradise as desirable. Perhaps, however, whether desirable or not, it isn't possible. Perhaps some degree of suffering is ineradicable from human life, perhaps the choice before man is always a choice of evils, perhaps even the aim of Socialism is not to make the world perfect but to make it better. All revolutions are failures, but they are not all the same failure. It is his unwillingness to admit this that has led Koestler's mind temporarily into a blind alley and that makes *Arrival and Departure* seem shallow compared with the earlier books.

ROBERT BEUM
"Epigraphs for Rubashov: Koestler's *Darkness at Noon*"
Dalhousie Review, Spring 1962, pp. 86–91

Darkness at Noon was a timely book, it was highly praised and, wonder of wonders, not overpraised. In 1940 the immediate enemy was fascist, and the price of immediacy was league with that different order of New Order farther east. But we were beginning to see the latter for what it was. Western European and American naiveté was disappearing—not, of course, as rapidly or as pervasively as was necessary. Soviet participation in the seizure of Poland, and the unprovoked attack on Finland, had rendered the revolutionary claim to humanist idealism finally ludicrous, and brought, or in some cases acted as the catalyst which brought, a host of converts to the West. The image of modern totalitarianism had become, in Newman's phrase, a real rather than a merely notional apprehension: Berlin and Moscow were particulars of the same essence. Koestler's novel provided a look at the totalitarian structure from the inside, from the point of view of only slightly fictionalized personal involvement, rather than in terms of expository or homiletic or allegorical presentation of ideology and machination. Two decades later, the book is unworn. It is standard reading in the curricula of university courses in The Modern Novel and in Philosophy in Literature; it circulates well in libraries, even in those of small and modest towns.

The book stands in the great tradition of Russian psychological and metaphysical fiction, the tradition of Tolstoi and Dostoevski. To my mind—to make at once a strict normative judgment—it does not come up to *Anna Karenina* or to *The Brothers Karamazov* or even to *Crime and Punishment*. It is more of a special adventure than the first; its scope is not as great as that of the second; and it is philosophically and psychologically less complex than either of the Dostoevski books. Yet it belongs with them (not only normatively but, interestingly enough, thematically as well with the latter two). It seems to me immensely superior to our modern allegories of the new order's utopias—to *Brave New World* and *1984*. Over these and other such books, it has the inevitable advantage of realism over allegory, of present over possible horror, of character over counter, and of internal conflict and intense conflict of wills over developed and rather panoramic external adventure. And yet critics have not, I think, wholly understood the rationale of its success. There are two insufficiently examined critical assumptions about its unweakening appeal: it is, we are reminded, a political book, and politics still engulfs us; and the book is a study of a thoroughly modern consciousness, rendered by the most adroit modern fictional techniques descending from James, Ford, Conrad, and Joyce. The explanations are true, but are not the truth. We are perhaps as weary of politics as we are caught up in it, and yet the most politics-jaded reader turns or returns to *Darkness at Noon*. This fact argues against the first point, but only apparently in favour of the second: the book is a triumph of technique and of subject, but the modernity of both technique and subject has been overstated. Koestler's novel is also an old-fashioned—I would say, distinctly classic—triumph. I am as yet undecided about our mania for seizing upon and hailing as a justification of modernism any and every instance of competent writing which is in part modern in theme and in treatment; it may reveal an enormous insecurity and emptiness, or it may not: but in any case it is not shrewd to us.

I want only to correct our inclination to view the book as an absolute triumph of the absolutely modern in conception and execution. A masterwork of modern fictional technique it certainly is—in some respects. The narrative is pared down to essentials. What goes on in Rubashov's mind and heart—his ideas and attitudes and the incidents of his past seen in retrospect—have great vitality because one senses, from the beginning, that they will determine his relationship to death and his soul's final relationship to his life. The very fact of his confinement and the virtual certainty of his imminent liquidation lend all of Rubashov's reflections and all of the retrospective narrative a power they would not have in more detached circumstances. The book opens without preliminaries; the reader is at once imprisoned with Rubashov. And from there to the last sentence, the restricted point of view is utilized for the unity and concentration which it so well affords. Description, narration, and analysis develop only as a consequence of some action of Rubashov's. Thus, Koestler does not offer independent descriptions of the prison, but sees them through Rubashov's eyes, and then only after the prisoner has come into a mood or situation which would logically cause him to be looking about. Such a technique allows the novelist freedom from excessive delineation; the sole concern is with elementary and symbolic imagery that has stuck in Rubashov's mind. The technique of utter sparseness and the device of somnambulistic flashback and of stream-of-consciousness are undeniably modern. But of course they are all the more effective in a book which at the same time observes the unities of action and place strictly, and the unity of time almost as punctiliously. Nor should we fail to see the importance of plot in the old-fashioned sense. True, much of the action has already occurred before the book begins, but it is offered to us (through Rubashov's reveries) as background; we are not able to understand Rubashov without these incidents from his past, and some of them, such as his friendship with Bogrov and his affair with Arlova, bear directly upon the catastrophe. For that matter, though, there occur within the prison itself incidents that produce or help to produce significant inward change: the Bogrov incident contributes powerfully to Rubashov's disaffection, and the grillings weaken his spirit (and body) and cloud his mind significantly. It might be said, too, that the very inaction of the story is in this case active, because it is intense; since the relative inaction is a consequence of imprisonment, the slightest bodily and sequential actions take on a dramatic vividness and create suspense (since the most trivial and routine actions become necessary and, in many cases, are at the same time dangerous to the prisoners). Besides this, there is suspense throughout—not so much about Rubashov's fate as about its shape. The book affords little comfort for champions of the plotless novel.

Rubashov himself is only modern in the sense that Dostoevski characters are modern. He holds the grey values of a subtle mind and Alexandrian age; not even by the end of the book is he able to define with anything like perfect clarity his reasons for dying in the manner he chooses or to arrive at any final judgment on the nature of man or even of his own soul. But he is not more complex than Raskolnikov or Ivan Karamazov. He is certainly as classic a protagonist as ever entered a tragedy. He has magnitude of soul, maturity, intellectual power, and loyalty. He even fulfils one of those qualifications held by Aristotle to be necessary to the tragic figure but neglected assiduously by almost all gifted modern writers: he is a man of official responsibility, of the state. His weakness lies, of course, in his past sins against humanity (in the name of humanity) and against his own soul. But he commands the attention and respect so naturally and easily granted a leader, and his suffering and his end elicit feelings not far below wonder. His humiliation and punishment at the hands of the regime, and the fact that he chooses the most difficult rather than the easiest way in his confessions and at the trial, elicit a response to the god in man. He is, in fact, one of the very few twentieth-century protagonists whose consciousness is modern and intellectually compelling and who remains at the same time the type of the classic hero.

Thus the structure of the novel is that of tragedy, and it is better than any tragedy the modern stage has seen. But the philosophical ideas themselves, insofar as they have a bearing on Rubashov's fate and ultimate decisions and attitudes, are of no small interest, and they receive a development which they could not properly receive in a tragic drama. Curiously enough, these ideas, and Rubashov's changing feelings about them, achieve much of their distinctness and power through Koestler's technique—a technique of old-fashioned rhetoric— of breaking the book into distinct sections, each treating with one idea and one inner change, and of prefacing each section with one or more highly functional epigraphs. These sententiae are the very themes, and they stick in the mind, haunting it and keeping it on track, like motifs of grave music, or like scriptural texts incessantly charged by the homily. While it is true that Rubashov dies—as the intellectual often dies— without final certainties, it is also true that he has come a long way toward repudiating the totalitarian doctrine that the end justifies the means, and toward confirming the existence of a spiritual reality in man which is violated by a religion of expediency. The five epigraphs mark the stages of Rubashov's spiritual development during his imprisonment.

The first of them, Saint-Just's remark that "Nobody can rule guiltlessly", defines Rubashov's original attitude toward the employment of heartless means in order to attain a seemingly utopian end. It is a mild and abstract remark; it seems almost a commonplace. And of an abstract character is Rubashov's attitude toward such things as his deposition of Richard and of Little Loewy, and his sacrifice of Arlova. These seem to him small sacrifices toward a utopian gain. But Rubashov is able to regard these deaths in the abstract only because he did not witness them in person or even realize them imaginatively (being caught up continually in official business). His devotion to pure reason and expediency, and his absence from the scenes, allowed their deaths an abstract quality which made them relatively easy to justify.

A shallower novelist would have set Rubashov to brooding on these responsibilities, with a view toward repentance, immediately upon his confinement in the prison. But human psychology does not always proceed in such a straight line. Instead, the prisoner launches out upon an even more elaborate philosophical exposition of the doctrine of justification of means by ends. The second of the epigraphs is a quotation (from Dietrich von Nieheim, Bishop of Verden in 1411) which endorses the totalitarian dogma from a medieval Christian point of view: "When the existence of the Church is threatened, she is released from the commandments of morality . . . the use of every means is sanctified, even cunning, treachery, violence, simony, prison, death. For all order is for the sake of the community, and the individual must be sacrificed to the common good." At the beginning of this section of the book, Rubashov is discovered writing on the Marxist theory of "consequent logic." His abstractions have not yet been sufficiently challenged.

A challenge does occur in this second section, however: Rubashov's dear and longtime comrade, Bogrov, who shares Rubashov's status as a political prisoner, is taken to execution, and for once Rubashov is physically confronted with the spectacle—and a particularly horrible spectacle—of a close friend, transformed by torture into something sub-human, being dragged to his death. The ghost of Arlova appears. And at last "physical liquidation" has become death after torture. Rubashov's revulsion is not at all inconsistent with his past hardness toward political death: he is now dangerously skeptical of the dogmas which could keep it abstract, and he is personally confronted and involved.

But once again his course is not to be in a straight line. Partly through Ivanov's arguments in favor of confession, and through his personal apologies for the Bogrov incident, Rubashov's horror is mitigated, and he half surrenders to Ivanov's suggestions. At the opening of "The Third Hearing" he is again elaborating a doctrine of expediency to which the epigraph from Machiavelli is most appropriate: "Occasionally words must serve to veil the facts. But this must happen in such a way that no one becomes aware of it; or, if it should be noticed, excuses must be at hand to be produced immediately." An additional quotation, however, introduces a new note: "But let your communication be, Yea, yea; Nay, nay: for whatsoever is more than these cometh of evil." This verse from Matthew is interpreted (in the orthodox tradition, at least) as a counsel of humility, admonishing the prideful oath and the prideful defending of oneself from one's accusers; behind it lies the notion that reason, as applied toward solving human problems, only conjoins with evil unless it is continually adjusted to revealed love and meaning. Rubashov comes to adopt the first position and is, at the end of the book, groping uncertainly toward the second. Realizing, first of all, that he will not find Gletkin's narrow and doctrinaire intellect amenable to a detailed defense of his true position, and secondly, that in actuality he *is* guilty—of Richard, of Little Loewy, of Arlova and others—and thereby does not deserve the luxury of defending himself, he more and more relinquishes his opportunities to answer the accusations. At the trial, he relinquishes his opportunities, and answers, for the most part, in simple agreement with the charges—"Yea, yea." In his last hours he clearly refutes his—and Marxism's—position that man is capable of solving his problems by will and reason alone. He notes that wherever the scalpel of reason has been applied, in the Marxist rebuilding of society, to lift a cancer from the body of humanity, another festering sore has immediately replaced the old one. He is not at all clear, of course, about alternatives.

In the final section, Rubashov is also brought to realize the entanglement of means and ends: the key line of the epigraph is, "Each different path brings other ends in view." The spuriousness of Ivanov's clever and seemingly humanitarian argument justifying massive experimentation with human lives and societies is now clearly revealed: massive coercion and the abstract, automatic destruction of human lives, so debase the souls of the manipulators that the ends themselves are inevitably transformed, the experimenters no longer being capable of their once lofty (if mistaken) aims.

Yet Rubashov's disaffection is not absolute. There is in this section ample evidence that his going through with the public trial and his acceptance of all accusation still, in part, represent his hope that such a submission will somehow and perhaps remotely be of value to the old aims of the Party. This submission, this loyalty, is entirely possible to a mind which gave even Gletkin the benefit of the doubt, which saw him as a new Neanderthal Man, but as perhaps a Neanderthal ultimately of use to the original character of Marxist aims. Carefully formulated and disciplined ideals are not readily lost, especially in the absence of any positive witness to another faith; and after the exhausting interrogations, Rubashov is scarcely in a condition to be absolute about anything. On the other hand, it is clear that the greatest single motive behind Rubashov's having chosen the ordeal of prolonged confrontation and of relative silence then and at the trial is his distinct sense of guilt. He reminds one of Dmitri Karamazov confessing to spurious crimes as atonement for his actual and lesser crimes. Rubashov's struggle to redefine his relation to the Party, to the world, and to eternity, which is the whole subject of this novel, ends in a manner not unfamiliar to tragedy. He has discovered his own ego, and to a certain extent his own soul. He has overcome self-interest, he has begun to free himself from a narrow, self-contradictory deterministic philosophy, and has experienced, if only somnambulistically, "the oceanic sense," the darkness of the soul obscurely seeking its home.

KATHLEEN NOTT
"Koestler and His Critics"

Encounter, February 1968, pp. 76–81

Arthur Koestler's less favourable reviewers sometimes suggest that in working out the nature and probable destiny of mankind he is working out himself and his own problems. This suggestion, rather more often than not, comes from the scientific side. In all fields, it is a common enough strategy where a defensive need is felt.

> "His attacks, growing ever more violent in this book on those with whom he disagrees, may reflect some of his own uncertainties." (Dr. William Sargant, *Spectator*)

> ". . . Much of the biologism of this and other of his recent books is mere accretion concealing his own experiential progress. A rational Marxist, disappoint-

ed by irrational Marxists, aghast at the irrational destruction around and inside himself, turning to psycho-analysis, examining yoga, winding up in pharmacology . . . he presents a thread of experience to which theories adhere on all sides." (Dr. Alex Comfort, *Guardian*)

In one important sense, it is fair to say that Koestler's "personality" (and its development) is the king-pin of his splendid structure, *The Sleepwalkers* (1959), *The Act of Creation* (1964), and now *The Ghost in the Machine*. But it is the objective, not the private person which matters. Koestler continues to work out, not his emotions, but his ideas. In particular, he has been trying throughout the trilogy to found a more reasonable, indeed a more "scientific," belief about human nature and its potentialities than he (with others) has been able to find in the creeds and ideologies listed by Dr. Comfort, many of which have hardened into dogma. The present book carries the quest into sciences, near-sciences, and some possibly pseudo-sciences, into biology, psychology, and linguistics, as they affect the study and understanding of our human selves. That he may be passionately committed to his disagreements does not make them irrational: and their expression, though often satirical, is not violent. So what is the problem? That he feels, or that he disagrees?

Scientists themselves are not without passions and sometimes it appears, passionately resent "amateur" poaching on specialist preserves. The tone of Sir Peter Medawar's review of *The Act of Creation (New Statesman,* June 1964) was in parts highly personal and almost aggrieved, with the complaint that Koestler didn't understand the scientific mentality because he couldn't grasp the scientist's natural pride, chiefly in achieving priority. This (according to Professor Medawar) must drive him to seek only the "soluble," and to avoid a reach that might "exceed his grasp." Professor Medawar himself, in other essays, has described the scientific imaginative process in terms which are not sharply different from Koestler's. But in this review he hardly seems to be clearly distinguishing the scientist's typical mentality from the social and competitive epiphenomena of his research. It appeared to me at the time that he could not accept the kind of book Koestler is trying to write, nor the kind of person nor the kind of intellectual attitude it reflects. The result may be, perhaps unwittingly, a defensive projection, either personal or professional.[1]

Two quotations from the recent press about *The Ghost in the Machine* may be illuminating. Charles Rycroft (a psychologist) writes in *New Society:* ". . . in one respect his exposition is naughty. He *assumes* [my italics] that there is a Scientific Establishment with an entrenched belief in 'the naïvely mechanistic world-view of the nineteenth century'. . . ." In fact, Koestler knows and shows that many professional scientists, as well as others with scientific training, seek a much more holistic insight than is now common, into both the human being and the methods and framework of science. He cites, for instance, Professors Michael Polanyi and L. L. Whyte. Those whom he attacks, particularly the Behaviourists and some neo-Darwinians, if not quite stuck in 19th-century mechanism (generally because their philosophic interest is not strong anyway) certainly haven't got quite away from it.

Rycroft also says that Koestler, "although he doesn't quite say so . . . is a neo-vitalist." This suggests that Rycroft has missed the main structural conception of the whole book, which doesn't depend on a sort of neo-vitalistic pat-ball answer to 19th-century mechanism. The attack on Behaviourism is a war waged against the whole concept of randomness which dominates not only neo-Darwinian theory but also provides the ideological background to the most influential forms of Anglo-American psychology and philosophy.

On previous experience, one other quotation (from a balanced but on the whole friendly review in the *Times Literary Supplement* of 2 November 1967) sounds like reliable prophecy: "The general purpose . . . will madden some (especially the specialist—who resents this kind of adventurousness and takes issue on detail). . . ."

One or two reviewers started up speculation about the significance of Koestler's "personality" in his own work. Alex Comfort, once again, "can't help respecting Koestler the encyclopaedist"; John Raymond in the *Financial Times* (admitting he himself has little or no scientific education) calls him a polymath. These innocent and probably ungrudging compliments may still be typical of our intellectually foggy climate. Koestler comes originally from the "isolated continent" where, in many countries, being a polymath is respected and is even an expected standard. A scholar is expected to have a large range of understanding in a wide variety of subjects and to be able to connect them and discuss them intelligently. Moreover, speculation is respectable. Maybe the English have a special need to be taught a God's Eye view. We are in many ways still a tight (and now hallucinated) little island, and we are only cosy with the "piecemeal." This has had its advantages, in law and even, no doubt—anyway at some periods—in philosophy and science. But we mustn't enviously conclude, because a writer or thinker believes that there are large questions of essential human interest—and even asks some of them—that he is unwilling or unable to put his generalisations as far as possible to the test.

The insular, specialist, piecemeal approach may for the time have passed its peak of value: particularly because, as I believe with Koestler, there really is a Behaviourist tide in psychology and philosophy which responds to and demands an atomist and reductive background. Hence it is an actual resistance-movement to a more organic conception of human life, habits and origins. It fits in well with specialist resentment and with the specialist implication that no one is yet in a position to generalise about the meaning and value of science as a human activity. But this is just something we cannot afford to wait for; we need Koestler's sort of "amateur"—if I called him that, as some scientists do, I should imply a compliment.

This holistic approach, in general and in particular applications, is what Koestler thinks we need and he is trying to provide it and to give it scientific warrant. He is not afraid to speculate, and we should be grateful to him, if for nothing else, for trying to "free the continent." (Let it be mentioned, in passing, but relevantly, that he is a "one-culture man"; that is, he can reasonably be interpreted as implying that the "Cultures", from whichever side, ought to be the "Humanities.")

A general outlook such as this would surely be seen to entail a diametrical and dynamic opposition to Behaviourism and all its proliferations. Nevertheless, some of Koestler's critics, informed or otherwise, think this is either "naughty" of him, irrelevant, or (perhaps less ingenuously) "old hat." Professor Medawar (in the quoted earlier review) refers to Koestler's "love-hate" relationship with the Behaviourists. Dr. Sargant suggests that the Behaviourists with "their exciting, new and effective treatments of the mind" aren't being quite fairly done by—and that Koestler just wilfully *prefers* his own "holonic" account: ("holonic" here refers to Koestler's concept of "holons," not to "holism"). Koestler himself, no doubt from experience in discussion and conversation, anticipates in this book what might be called a pro-Behaviourist filibuster of criticisms—and has founded a *Society for the Prevention of Cruelty to Dead Horses*.

I believe, with Koestler, that Behaviourism is in fact a live horse, fresh in all senses; and I even wish he had been able to chase it further afield. He has some reference to the Behaviourist parallels in contemporary British philosophy (and of course has borrowed his title from Gilbert Ryle, reasonably suspected of verbal Behaviourism). There is a kind of double irony in the borrowing: for it is really the Behaviourists who are haunted by the "ghost" and make the most strenuous efforts to exorcise it. The rest of us know that by "mind," "person," "consciousness" and so on, we can be quite content to mean necessary organising functions without which, to put it all at the lowest level, we could hardly communicate with our fellows.

I wish Koestler had been able to say more about Behaviourist incursions into aesthetics and psychotherapy: for these topics are at least vivid illustrations of a whole new and very active philosophy of existence which is permeating all our thinking (and in the case of Behaviour-therapy is likely to have profound and undesirable consequences in social philosophy.)

Koestler's endeavour is to rescue us from "ratomorphic" psychology and philosophy while remaining within a strictly biological framework:

> I do not believe that we can formulate the simplest questions . . . without the help of the sciences of life. But it must be a true science of life, not the antiquated slot-machine model. . . . We shall not be able to ask the right questions until we have replaced that rusty idol by a new, broader conception of the living organism.

This new conception is what the first part of the book is about, worked out in detail, with remarkable parallels and analogies. The *TLS* reviewer thought that the wealth of analogy and illustration befogged the argument (could this be anti-polymathism?). But Koestler's central conception would be weakened if it were not traced, as it is, in a ramified pattern of great richness. The same reviewer faintly complains that Koestler's summaries at the end of chapters and an appendix which gives a complete abstract of his holon-hierarchy argument, are suspicious—showing that "the argument is not all that simple." I don't see why it should be. I found the appendix completely clarifying and the summaries, particularly for easy back-reference, obliging and helpful.

> The organism in its structural aspect is not an aggregation of elementary parts, and in its functional aspects not a chain of elementary units of behaviour. . . . Parts and wholes in an absolute sense do not exist in the domain of life. . . .

The "holon" is the part which *is* always still a whole—"which displays both the autonomous properties of wholes and the dependent properties of parts." This facing-both-upwards-and-downwards in the hierarchic organisation, Koestler calls the "Janus-principle."

> More generally, the term "holon" may be applied to any stable biological or social sub-whole which displays rule-governed behaviour and/or structural Gestalt-constancy. Thus organelles and homologous organs are evolutionary holons; morphogenetic fields are ontogenetic holons; the ethologist's "fixed action-patterns" and the sub-routines of acquired skills are behavioural holons; phonemes, morphemes, words, phrases, are linguistic holons; individuals, families, tribes, nations are social holons.

It is clear that this holonistic structure is taken as applying not only to the biological world (which includes, as above, all the fields of living behaviour and skills, from language, to individuals in their "tribes") but also to the natural and physical world. An atom is also a "holon." And indeed a point in Appendix I claims the intention of reconciling the atomistic and holistic approaches.

So how does Koestler deal with the question of distinguishing between non-life and life, or between the animal and the human? There can be no doubt that he is profoundly concerned with the second of these questions (that doesn't make him a neo-vitalist)—particularly with the attributes of purpose and freedom which we commonly regard as almost defining the human.

His answer about "freedom" is to be found in the Janus-concept itself. All organisms (including ourselves) are governed from "above" (from the higher levels of the social hierarchy) by fixed rules: but we are inherently endowed with "flexible strategies"; we can autonomously or reciprocally adapt the environmental conditions we meet.

> There is a significant analogy in physics. . . . The geometrical structure of a crystal is represented by fixed rules; but crystals growing in a saturated solution will reach the same final shape by different pathways. . . . In this and many other well-known phenomena we find the self-regulatory properties of biological holons foreshadowed on an elementary level.

"Freedom," then, is a graduated continuity throughout the universe. But this "freedom" has to be translated into terms of "consciousness" and "purpose." In spite of the "naughtiness" attributed to him by the *TLS* reviewer, Koestler has plenty of anti-randomist scientists and biologists on his side. As E. W. Sinnott wrote, "purpose is 'the directive activity shown by individual organisms that distinguishes living things from inanimate objects.' "

This section concludes: "The Purposer is each and every individual organism, from the inception of life, which struggled and strove to make the best of its limited opportunities."

So, after all, "purpose" begins with "life" and does not depend on a natural-physical continuity. And we can't help being puzzled about how "purpose" becomes a moral notion—unless it is specifically human and individual.

Koestler admits the problem and answers as follows:

> . . . if we assume that there exists a continuous scale of gradations, from the sentience of primitive creatures, through various degrees of consciousness, to full self-awareness, then the experimental biologist's challenge to the concept of individuality poses a genuine dilemma. The only solution seems to be . . . to get away from the concept of the individual as a monolithic structure, and to replace it by the concept of the individual as an open hierarchy whose apex is for ever receding, striving towards a state of complete integration which is never achieved.

But also, it would seem, to get away from the concept of the *individual* as the centre of freedom, choice, purpose—and of "humanity" or *human being*. Whose freedom? and what purpose? It appears that the only real room is at the top. And that the state of complete integration which the individual has to strive for, is not *first* with himself, but with his group-hierarchy (whatever that may be).

Certainly Koestler heavily stresses what appears to be the contrary point of view—that infinitely more of our human troubles come from our urge to integrate ourselves with groups, than from our instinctual self-assertive tendencies. But still I do not think that I am doing him an injustice. His "anti-rodent" operation against the Behaviourists is a brilliant triumph. But there comes a point where the other rats-in-the-maze get in—those of the Evolutionary Futurists—who cannot help thinking collectivistically and who, if they're not careful, will finish up occupying a primitive cell in the world-brain of Teilhard.

It seems to be very difficult to steer a course between the atomistic-mechanistic, and the semi-mystical "integrative" idea of mankind—to think philosophically in terms of human beings, men and women, as individual organisms. Even the Existentialists who are claiming to do just that, do not bring it off in their academic statements. If we will not think of human life as a mechanical assemblage or move towards the "rato-morphic" conception of human beings, we start to think and plan for the Species-as-a-whole and to take the funicular line towards perfectibility and Point Omega.

Koestler is very well aware of this dilemma; but I do not think he altogether escapes it. Admittedly he rejects the "jolly vein" of the Evolutionary Progressivists (Huxley, Waddington, Teilhard) and adds, with perfect justice, that he is well able to do so because "having written such a lot about the creative side of man, I can hardly be accused of belittling his achievements."

Nevertheless, even with Koestler, the ordinary "human being" gets lost, and with him the possibility of a genuine, a realistic psychology. Isn't it a fact of observation, not merely an article of faith, that the human being cannot be fully described in a biological or physiological language? Not because he has inside him an irreducible spiritual homunculus, but because a generalising collectivistic language is unsuitable. And so if you can't have a "scientific" psychology of the individual, you can't have a "scientific" morality either.

It is this identification of "human beings" with their Species, I believe, which makes the conclusion of Koestler's book—a minor section which contains his proposed treatment for "our predicament"—unsatisfying.

Koestler's diagnosis of "Man's" predicament is that there is a built-in fight between the old brain and the new cortex. It is not just that the old brain is an old ignoble savage, for many animal communities and many primitive societies are peaceful.

> We can reformulate Lorenz's argument by saying that, from the very beginning of the manufacture of weapons, *man's instinct and intellect fell out of step*. The *invention* of weapons and tools was . . . the combined achievement of brain and hand. . . . But the *use* to which the weapons were put, was dependent on . . . instinct and emotion—on the old brain.

Evolution can and does take wrong turnings even in the minimal necessities for preserving a species—Koestler gives many illuminating examples. But with us, the very thing that gives us our uniqueness and our capacity for survival, astronomically higher than that of any other species, also intensifies our doom-potential. We have a unique gift—"our" Brain—the model of all computers, which should solve all our problems. But we have another "uniqueness," too—we don't know how to make full or proper use of it.

This thesis about "brain-potential" is also strongly favoured by Evolutionary Humanists (and other Futurists): and with the same insistence on "*Man's*" brain. But they hardly ever commit themselves to telling us what is a useful "use." So that even if we could suppose that we all have this master-computer—and only have to learn or to be taught how to use it—we have no idea at all how this could be of benefit to the

Species. (The serious brain-potential thesis is perhaps not all that different from newspaper generalisations about the Species: *i.e.*, "our" intellectual powers have outrun "our" moral and spiritual powers, as if Tom, Dick and Harry had each personally, in a variant of Original Sin, committed the Theory of Relativity!)

Evolution, according to Koestler, has made us an "insane giant," bent on self-destruction, who can't be argued with— "Sweet reason has failed." It is the biochemists who will now have to get to work and produce some nostrum, analogous to a biological mutation, which will harmonise the old brain with the new. Koestler believes that this will be gladly received, without pressure either from politicians or from the boffin "apex of the hierarchy"—because people will realise in increasing numbers how much better, freer and happier they feel with it, and how much more able to make use of their innate powers, intellectual and spiritual. (And he *doesn't* mean "Pop-Nirvana.")

Koestler, with good reason, genuinely feels that time is running short. Particularly after a devastating and in many ways convincing analysis of the root causes of our global predicament, he may feel that *some* solution, something that looks like a hope, ought to be offered. But with the greatest respect to a brilliant and fascinating book, I think he has gone off track: and that the simple but essential cause is thus confusing the Species with the individual. Characteristically the members of the Species are personally immature if not retarded. But very many are ordinary *normal* people, who like life and like going on living, and would live and let live. And they do not live beyond their intellectual and psychological income: which means, of course, that they dodge social responsibility and group-integration as much as they are allowed to.

Surely the real human problem is much as Shelley stated it: *the good want power, the powerful goodness want* (for "good" today, read, comparatively unpushing). It may be that "insane giants" take power; but *they* won't take any mutatory pill, and they will be the last people to think they might need it.

What really human morality can the Species—necessarily in scientific language—preach to itself? Nothing, it seems, but the absolute value of survival, at all costs, including the sacrifice of the creative benefit of human intra-psychic conflict. We may reasonably claim that it is the syntheses coming out of the antitheses (as Koestler, for one, has pre-eminently shown) that really advance the human (individual and creative) mind—and so lift the species a slipping, but constantly repeated step. Dare one say it—if survival isn't going to be qualitative and help select the truly human definition, do we and should we care all that much—or pretend to care? People care as far as they can feel and see—generally not beyond their immediate progeny. Why should they care? An abstract concern with an unknowable future species, whether it comes from scientists, from do-gooders, from priests or politicians, is always a bit suspect. It can be a substitute altruism which helps to hide our mortality from our egos: and our helplessness too.

Like most people I haven't the faintest idea what might save the Species. Like most people I probably don't want to be too much bothered with problems I can't solve. I see "insane giants" all over the place and wish *they* would take a pill. And sometimes on good days I think I discern little greennesses which suggest to me that the meek—I mean by this all those who can at whatever level maintain passive but intelligent resistance—might, by sitting on their bottoms, here, there, and everywhere (but of course also in front of Pentagons and Downing Streets) just manage to inherit the earth.

Notes

1. This projective attitude is much more obvious, and much more objectionable, in Leslie Fiedler's astounding, irrelevant and prolonged yelp of fury about *The Ghost in the Machine*, in the *New Statesman* (27 October 1967). The burden of his complaint is that Koestler is moved by hatred and resentment of youth and its Pop-Culture, with which Fiedler seems to identify himself. In the 1930s, it seems, Koestler spoke for youth (when presumably they both were young). The only rational connecting point (which Fiedler misses) is that Koestler dissociates his own biological-mutatory "pharmacology" from the drugs in present cultural favour. In the *New Statesman* of 10 November Koestler has replied, pointing out among other things that his interests have simply moved on since the '30s. Why should anyone object to somebody growing (or growing up)?

BERNARD CRICK
From "Koestler's Koestler"
Partisan Review, 1982, pp. 279–83

Koestler's prewar books told in sturdy prose fascinating stories about his own adventures. When he comes to write in English, it is a workmanlike, even at times lively, prose, occasionally even florid, but certainly with little of the vivid feeling for a new language shown by Conrad or the sharp simplicity of Orwell's use of his native tongue. Personally, I don't find much difference between his own first writing in English and the earlier translations of his German or French (not Hungarian of course): it is almost as if he modelled his prose on his last translator. Before the war, then, he wrote well about his own experiences and matters arising from them— especially well about extreme psychological states; but he had also written, though no examples here ⟨in *Bricks to Babel*⟩, with some authority on scientific matters as the science correspondent of the biggest German newspaper chain in the 1920s. So when he returns to write about science, though now in books and on themes of his own choosing, he is speculative, most certainly, but not amateur or eccentric; and if he is selective in his use of evidence, he is a good reporter of what "challenging" research and theories he reads: he can both understand and popularize scientific literature. Thus, there is both more continuity in his writing than first appears to be the case or than he is prepared to acknowledge.

Add to this the fact that his novels have all dealt well with the character and ideological contradictions of a central hero or antihero, as well as with extreme situations, but they have shown neither psychological depth nor complexity in the interrelations of the characters. Indeed, the minor characters are all ideological or social types, neither interacting upon nor modifying each other's characters: they break or bust each other, or some escape and others remain unchanged. Reflective and revealing autobiography, then, beyond telling a good public tale of important and exciting public events, is not likely to be his strongest card as a writer. He may simply be well aware of this—no skeletons to hide, simply an old craftsman's dialectic awareness of his professional strengths and weaknesses. The one clear thread in all the variety of his themes, and linking closely his two periods, is that he has been a professional reporter of mighty themes, but always using his pen for his career, considering carefully his subject matter and his changing audiences.

This is perhaps why so many of us are still uneasy and uncertain about Koestler. His themes are great themes, but he is not a great writer, if in some sense great writing becomes, whether as political or scientific writing, an end in itself. He always demands our agreement or disagreement, not our appreciation—although we should appreciate very greatly the skill and cultural role of such writing, admitting that it is not great literature. I think of Koestler as one might think of Orwell if he had never written *Animal Farm* and *Nineteen Eighty-Four*. The claim for literary greatness could not be made, but he would still have been a figure—like Koestler—of extraordinary interest and importance.

What, however, if the content, if the message, is the thing? What emerges in his later, more difficult writings is both compelling and tantalizing. What is compelling is his humanistic tone, even at times when journalistic cadences slip in. He sees the humor as well as the seriousness of life. Life is serious, not simply in how we react to each other, a purely humanistic position, but in how we must, he still believes, search for an overall synthesis or sense of purpose in humanity. He is an individualist who has come utterly to reject hedonism or utilitarianism in favor of a long-term responsibility for improving the human species.

In a paper of 1969, he identified "four outstanding, pathological symptoms reflected in the disastrous history of our species." They are (i) the "ubiquitous ritual" of human sacrifice; (ii) that "*homo sapiens* is virtually unique in the animal kingdom in his lack of instinctive safeguards of his own species"; (iii) "the chronic, quasi-schizophrenic split between reason and emotion, between man's rational faculty and his irrational, affect-bound beliefs"; and (iv) "the striking disparity between the growth curves of science and technology on the one hand and of ethical conduct on the other." And in *The Ghost in the Machine*, he set out a physiological hypothesis about the differential evolution of the brain in support of the third and fourth points.

It could of course be objected that the species has survived and flourished despite all this; that "disastrous history" is not a descriptive summary but an emotive prophecy; that "ethics" is not something for which a "growth curve" can be plotted, still less, extrapolated from; and that anthropological-physiological hypotheses are interesting as hypotheses, but virtually untenable, not established theories that could guide public policy and medical research. Koestler, I repeat, had real scientific training but, nonetheless, obvious tricks of the journalist creep in. He talks about "conspecifics," an easy piece of impressive jargon, though he immediately says in plain English, "members of his own species." This is a small and innocent example. I get more worried when he talks about "neuro-physiological *evidence*" for a "schizopsychology" in the human evolutionary process, without reminding his readers that such "evidence" is only inference from untested and contentious hypotheses.

Yet one admires his courage and explicit determination to show that a genuine intellectual must take his stand in two cultures. How much more interesting he still is than C. P. Snow ever was. Reading Koestler never makes one snooze, though my schizopsychology comes out in an occasional desire to throw the book out of the window, but then to run down and pick it up again, hoping that nothing *disastrous* has happened to it, only some rich, disfiguring marks of human tragedy from which to fashion a significant anecdote. In other words, I prefer Koestler the skeptic, telling his tale of Malraux's suddenly saying at a Writer's Congress in Moscow, after hearing countless speeches promising universal happiness in a brave new world: "'And what about a child run over by a tram-car?' There was a pained silence; then somebody said, amid general approbation: 'in a perfect, planned socialist transport system, there will be no accidents.'" This is better, to my taste, than the man who likes to be the H. G. Wells of the intellectual

upper middle classes rather than of the self-taught lower middle classes.

So an assessment of Koestler's peculiar genius is difficult. Have any of us ever read all his books? And there is the journalism as well as the books. His own sense of achievement is shown clearly in the selection of this book. He probably disappoints his old readers or the young who read his old novels by calling fully half of *Bricks to Babel* his "Search of Synthesis," and presenting there mainly the scientific writings. But in terms of the sheer bulk of this scientific writing, the first half of the book, "In Search of Utopia," is in fact disproportionate. He would like to be remembered as a scientific thinker; but he is too good a professional writer not to realize where his greater effect and following still lie. So he presents his literary past fully and does not appear to rewrite. No Audenesque problems here.

The extracts from the novels fit in easily with the nonfictional works. The value of *Darkness at Noon* and *Arrival and Departure* is in their authenticity. Camus's *The Rebel* is a better philosophical analysis of the totalitarian mind, but it is too abstract for most readers, just as Arendt's *Origins of Totalitarianism* is too pedantic and monumental. Even Orwell's *Nineteen Eighty-Four*, impossible though it is to put down, can be brushed aside as a nightmare or diminished as an overdrawn satire on postwar Britain. Koestler knows what he was talking about and is hard to diminish; he is easier to ignore or foolishly dismiss in New York as a nice "cold war warrior" or in London as "too clever by half." The issue in the 1940s, as the Party hacks and the fellow travelers put it, was only whether he was a liar or not. And plainly he wasn't.

This very factualness is both the clue to and the continuity in his achievement. It is not an esthetic achievement. We read his books for their matter and to learn something from them. This too links the old with the New Koestler. We should read the new scientific Koestler just as we read the earlier political novels: because he is talking about something we need to know, but all the time aware that it is a prince of journalists, a cosmic reporter, the doyen of conferenceurs, who is addressing us as an audience, mingling, like any good feature writer, personal angles with hard information. We open the quality press and we are informed, stimulated, but always on our guard. He writes columns as big and bustling as Babel, not monographs.

Whether or not Koestler himself believes that he has philosophical or scientific originality (as did Wells, alas) is irrelevant. I hope he doesn't, but it really doesn't matter. He is one of the greatest intellectual popularizers of our time, the interpreter for one set of intellectuals of the concepts of another. And his genuine cosmopolitan stance has been earned and not easily achieved. One Koestler speaks more for human unity, despite his rationalist assault on the cult of Zen and the pretensions of Gandhi, than a dozen committees of UNESCO. He deeply appreciates national cultural differences, but attaches little value to them and adopts each in turn with a kind of ironic affection.

Ultimately, he should be pleased with himself as the super-reporter. What he has now given us is, in fact, in its temporal order and with its headnotes, a remarkably full and clear picture of the public activities of his life. The rest is silence.

To end, most tentatively, on a mischievous or an affectionate thought? His last novel was a rather lightweight, merry satire called *The Call Girls*: those great men, mainly, who wait for the letter or the phone to summon them to Alpbach, Pugwash, Villa Bellagio (the Rockefeller Foundation's earthly paradise), or wherever, the eternal conference round of internationally famous intellectuals. It was a very knowing satire. How often had he played that game himself, as perhaps a widely translated professional writer must. He may have grown weary of it, found it no longer useful to him, or even risen above it; but in the end I suspect that the old journalist simply had to report on the institution: to send it up simply by describing it. It was like that. He was a great descriptive writer. But what they were probably all talking about were themes as vast, but at times possibly as vapid, as some of his "fate of the species" books.

Surely it will be, rightly or wrongly, his earlier political books for which he will be best and longest remembered. He told the tale so compellingly of how a man came to look for utopias, but finally grew skeptical of political activity, except for small clear things: like abolition of capital punishment. It might fairly be objected that between utopianism and skepticism lies the whole range of practical politics, from the conservative to the democratic socialist. Orwell thought that

Koestler should have explored the nature of a non-utopian political theory. But Koestler was not a political thinker. And no man, not even Koestler, can do everything. Koestler had a tendency to dramatize things to extremes, the Yogi or the commissar, and to exclude obvious mundane middles. He was a reporter of great themes, however. If there were no immediate utopias to observe in the 1950s from that Graf Zeppelin still hovering over polar extremes, he would have to report on the evolution of the species itself. I cannot evaluate his success or not in this matter, only share a common skepticism, but with a shameful sense of not being brave or rash enough to try myself. But it does not diminish or change his earlier work, and one has to hope that he himself takes this view, either at peace with himself in his old age or properly proud of all the bricks he made so skillfully and in such difficulties as a great and dedicated professional writer and superjournalist.

PHILIP LARKIN

1922–1985

Philip Arthur Larkin was born on August 9, 1922, in Coventry, Warwickshire. After attending the King Henry VIII School in Coventry, he studied English at St. John's College, Oxford, graduating with first class honors in 1943. He became a librarian, and since 1955 has been in charge of the library at the University of Hull.

Larkin's first book of poems, *The North Ship*, appeared in 1945, followed by the novels *Jill* in 1946 and *A Girl in Winter* in 1947. A second collection of poems, *The Less Deceived* (1955), brought him a wider audience, and secured his inclusion in Robert Conquest's anthology *New Lines* (1956). *The Whitsun Weddings* (1964) won him the Queen's Gold Medal and the triennial Arts Council Prize, and *High Windows* (1974) was recognized with the Loines Award. He was made a CBE in 1975 and a C.Lit in 1978. Though regarded by many as the foremost contemporary British poet, his always meager output of carefully crafted poems appears to have dried up completely in recent years.

Larkin was jazz correspondent of the *Daily Telegraph* from 1961 to 1971, and a selection of his work in this capacity appeared as *All What Jazz?* (1970). In jazz, as in religion and politics, he allied himself with the traditional, and his edition of *The Oxford Book of Twentieth Century Verse* (1973) was controversial on account of its conservative slant. His most recent publication was a collection of essays, *Required Writing* (1983), which won him the W. H. Smith Literary Award.

Philip Larkin died in Hull on December 2, 1985.

Contemporary British verse of wit is both seductive and repulsive. Developing a taste for it is like falling in love with a brilliant, sensitive woman who, however, demands oceans of sympathy because she has the usual troubles of life. Then, it is really insular, British in a special sort of way, idiosyncratic as a family joke. That is good; art should, certainly, grow out of the specifics of a life-style—and damn the ponderous seekers after "universality"! Still, you can't help thinking of Lawrence's "The English are so nice!" and his picture of the British bourgeois:

Nicely groomed, like a mushroom
standing there so sleek and erect and eyeable—
and like a fungus, living on the remains of bygone
    life.

Or Auden's picture of the invalidism of middle-class British society, with its obvious similarity to Lord Chatterley's condition—

I don't want any more hugs;
Make me some fresh tea, fetch me some rugs.

It is the disproportionate infusion of self-pity, I suppose, that makes the difference at this moment. The tragic and revolutionary perspectives of the great generation of modern poets begin to seem archaic to people embroiled in the petty particulars of welfare-state planning. Most of their passion now goes into self-loathing at being part of a protected, routine system of minimum standards and into indignation that Albion's sacred landscape is being "modernized." That the new security represents at least a minimal triumph after age-long struggle and sacrifice causes no exultation. That millions in the world are really, and horribly, suffering seems not to inhibit her complaints one whit. (But that is a commonplace of life—the well-fed and hearty demanding compassion of the starving or the deathly ill. One is reminded of that famous scene in Proust where the Duke complains to the dying Swann that "I had a wretched lunch this morning" and that the Duchess "is not nearly so strong as people think.") Nevertheless, all this is part of the idiom in England today; and it is authenticity of voice that makes a poetry live, whatever we may think of what the voice is saying. . . .

Philip Larkin is a representative of the younger group of self-snubbers and self-loathers (to whom, nevertheless, it has never occurred to put down their wretched mirrors) who have recently risen to the fore in English letters. He is forever promising to be a wit and then appealing to the reader to pity him instead. It is another turn on that *petty* bitterness about life that Betjeman too sometimes exhibits—not a world's sorrow and loss of meaning, but the sullenness of a man who finds squalor in his own spirit and fears to liberate himself from it:

> Why should I let the toad *work*
> Squat on my life? . . .
> Ah, were I courageous enough
> To shout *Stuff your pension!*
> But I know, all too well, that's the stuff
> That dreams are made on:
> For something sufficiently toad-like
> Squats in me, too;
> Its hunkers are heavy as hard luck,
> And cold as snow.
>
> ("Toads")

As in *Look Back in Anger* or *Lucky Jim*, the speaker's assumption that he is in an inescapable predicament will seem to Americans more stubborn than unavoidable. Larkin's poems of refusal to participate—such as "Reasons for Attendance" and "Places, Loved Ones"—have an air of spurious self-alienation, as opposed to a poem like Edwin Muir's "The Interrogation" whose tragic authority derives from awareness of the myriads whom war and authoritarian militarism have deprived of birthright and identity. In the new British atmosphere a writer can speak of his childhood, as Larkin does in "Coming," as "a forgotten boredom," and have it accepted as a self-evident truth. He can write, seriously:

> Sex, yes, but what
> Is sex? Surely, to think the lion's share
> Of happiness is found by couples—sheer
> Inaccuracy, as far as I'm concerned

There is a good deal of this kind of defiant beating-down of straw men, in the vein of the posturings of a precocious pubescent in revolt against the prospect of happiness. But another side to Larkin appears in poems like "Dry-Point," "Myxomatosis," and "Going." The querulous whine and the limp squeak of defiance have disappeared, the poems are much more impersonal, and we can see from them that there is something of a deep, end-of-a-civilization sadness behind the talkative self-analyses and the almost silly little manifestoes. "Dry-Point" is perhaps the best poem in the book and immensely suggestive in the way its images carry through a feeling of men's helplessness within history. At endlessly recurrent crucial moments we are compelled to action amid an exalted vision which deserts us immediately the action is completed, and the dream of a concentrated, glowing perfection immune to historical destiny remains remote as ever.

> The wet spark comes, the bright blown walls collapse,
> But what sad scapes we cannot turn from then:
> What ashen hills! what salted, shrunken lakes! . . .
> And how remote that bare and sun-scrubbed room,
> Intensely far, that padlocked cube of light.

The spiritual dolor of "Dry-Point" comes not from the explicit meaning of its succession of evocative images, but from the character and arrangement of the images themselves. The abstract patterning here gathers the feeling for which Larkin strives in his lesser poems into its richest expression. He is able, thus, not only to speak sharply and springily about what he feels his predicament to be, but in poems like "Deceptions" and "Church Going" he hits a rather satisfying middle ground.

The first, like Betjeman's "An Incident in the Early Life of Ebenezer Jones, Poet, 1828," is a gesture of keen sympathy toward the suffering of violated innocence. The second, which may be contrasted with Betjeman's propagandistic church pieces, is a moving consideration by the poet—merciless toward his own ignorance and incomplete commitments—of what churches mean to him. The British are generally better at this kind of contemplative verse-exposition than we are. It's their language, and they are well-trained at using it to be subtly lucid about things. They do not, it is true, have our knack, improvised under pressure, of beating hell out of, and passion into, the language by main force.—M. L. ROSENTHAL, "Tuning In on Albion," *Nation*, May 16, 1959, pp. 457–58

The pieties of the Movement were as predictable as the politics of the thirties' poets. They are summed up at the beginning of Philip Larkin's 'Church Going':

> Hatless, I take off
> My cycle-clips in awkward reverence.

This, in concentrated form, is the image of the post-war Welfare State Englishman: shabby and not concerned with his appearance; poor—he has a bike, not a car; gauche but full of agnostic piety; underfed, underpaid, overtaxed, hopeless, bored, wry. This is . . . an attempt to show that the poet is not a strange creature inspired; on the contrary, he is just like the man next door—in fact, he probably *is* the man next door.

Now, I am wholly in favour of restoring poetry to the realm of common sense. But there is always the delicate question of how common common sense should be. All three negative feed-backs work, in their different ways, to preserve the idea that life in England goes on much as it always has, give or take a few minor changes in the class system. The upper-middle class, or Tory, ideal—presented in its pure crystalline form by John Betjeman—may have given way to the predominantly lower-middle class, or Labour, ideal of the Movement and the Angries, but the concept of gentility still reigns supreme. And gentility is a belief that life is always more or less orderly, people always more or less polite, their emotions and habits more or less decent and more or less controllable; that God, in short, is more or less good.

It is a stance which is becoming increasingly precarious to maintain. That the English have succeeded so long owes a good deal to the fact that England is an island; it is, literally, insulated from the rest of the world. But since the First World War, that insulation has slowly broken down. . . . What, I suggest, has happened in the last half century is that we are gradually being made to realize that all our lives, even those of the most genteel and enislanded, are influenced profoundly by forces which have nothing to do with gentility, decency or politeness. Theologians would call these forces evil, psychologists, perhaps, libido. Either way, they are the forces of disintegration which destroy the old standards of civilization. Their public faces are those of two world wars, of the concentration camps, of genocide, and the threat of nuclear war. . . .

I am not suggesting that modern English poetry, to be really modern, must be concerned with psychoanalysis or with the concentration camps or with the hydrogen bomb or with any other of the modern horrors. I am not suggesting, in fact, that it *must* be anything. For poetry that feels it has to cope with pre-determined subjects ceases to be poetry and becomes propaganda. I am, however, suggesting that it drop the pretence that life, give or take a few social distinctions, is the same as ever, that gentility, decency and all the other social totems will eventually muddle through.

What poetry needs, in brief, is a new seriousness. I would define this seriousness simply as the poet's ability and willingness to face the full range of his experience with his full intelligence; not to take the easy exits of either the conventional response or choking incoherence. Believe in it or not, psychology has left its mark on poetry. First, the writer can no longer deny with any assurance the fears and desires he does not wish to face; he knows obscurely that they are there, however skilfully he manages to elude them. Second, having acknowledged their existence, he is no longer absolved from the need to use all his intelligence and skill to make poetic sense of them. Since Freud, the late Romantic dichotomy between emotion and intelligence has become totally meaningless.

This position had, I think, already been partially assumed by T. S. Eliot when he wrote *The Waste Land*. The poem follows, with great precision and delicacy, the movement of a psyche, not just of a society, in the process of disintegration. Eliot's talk of classicism, like his use in the poem of literature and theology, was an elaborate and successful defence which forced impersonality on a deeply personal and painful subject. . . .

But to walk naked is, of course, no guarantee of achievement in the arts—often the contrary. Several pieces in (Robert Lowell's) *Life Studies* fail for appearing more compulsively concerned with the processes of psychoanalysis than with those of poetry. Conversely, with their deliberate common sense and understatement, some of the Movement poets command, at their best, a self-contained strength and a concern for the discipline of verse which is vital if the art is to remain public. The question is the kind of success a style allows. Compare, for instance, Philip Larkin's 'At Grass' with Ted Hughes's 'A Dream of Horses':

AT GRASS

The eye can hardly pick them out
From the cold shade they shelter in,
Till wind distresses tail and mane;
Then one crops grass, and moves about
—The other seeming to look on—
And stands anonymous again.

Yet fifteen years ago, perhaps
Two dozen distances sufficed
To fable them: faint afternoons
Of Cups and Stakes and Handicaps,
Whereby their names were artificed
To inlay faded, classic Junes—

Silks at the start: against the sky
Numbers and parasols: outside,
Squadrons of empty cars, and heat,
And littered grass: then the long cry
Hanging unhushed till it subside
To stop-press columns on the street.

Do memories plague their ears like flies?
They shake their heads. Dusk brims the shadows.
Summer by summer, all stole away,
The starting-gates, the crowds and cries—
All but the unmolesting meadows.
Almanacked, their names live; they

Have slipped their names, and stand at ease,
Or gallop for what must be joy,
And not a fieldglass sees them home,
Or curious stop-watch prophesies:
Only the groom, and the groom's boy,
With bridles in the evening come.

Larkin's poem, elegant and unpretentious and rather beautiful in its gentle way, is a nostalgic re-creation of the Platonic (or *New Yorker*) idea of the English scene, part pastoral, part sporting. His horses are *social* creatures of fashionable race

meetings and high style; emotionally, they belong to the world of the R.S.P.C.A. It is more skilful but less urgent than 'A Dream of Horses':

We were born grooms, in stable-straw we sleep still,
All our wealth horse-dung and the combings of horses,
And all we can talk about is what horses ail.

Out of the night that gulfed beyond the palace-gate
There shook hooves and hooves and hooves of horses:
Our horses battered their stalls; their eyes jerked white.

And we ran out, mice in our pockets and straw in our hair,
Into darkness that was avalanching to horses
And a quake of hooves. Our lantern's little orange flare.

Made a round mask of our each sleep-dazed face,
Bodiless, or else bodies by horses
That whinnied and bit and cannoned the world from its place.

The tall palace was so white, the moon was so round,
Everything else this plunging of horses
To the rim of our eyes that strove for the shapes of the sound.

We crouched at our lantern, our bodies drank the din,
And we longed for a death trampled by such horses
As every grain of the earth had hooves and mane.

We must have fallen like drunkards into a dream
Of listening, lulled by the thunder of the horses.
We awoke stiff; broad day had come.

Out through the gate the unprinted desert stretched
To stone and scorpion; our stable-horses
Lay in their straw, in a hag-sweat, listless and wretched.

Now let us, tied, be quartered by these poor horses,
If but doomsday's flames be great horses,
The forever itself a circling of the hooves of horses.

The poem, by the standard of Hughes's best writing, is not all that good; it is less controlled than Larkin's and has a number of romantic, quasi-medieval trappings which verge on the pretentious. But it is unquestionably *about* something; it is a serious attempt to re-create and so clarify, unfalsified and in the strongest imaginative terms possible, a powerful complex of emotions and sensations. Unlike Larkin's, Hughes's horses have a violent, impending presence. But through the sharp details which bring them so threateningly to life, they reach back, as in a dream, into a nexus of fear and sensation. Their brute world is part physical, part state of mind.

They have, of course, their literary antecedents: the strange, savage horses which terrorize Ursula Brangwen at the end of *The Rainbow*. But this is part of their wider significance. Dr Leavis has come, apparently, to believe that D. H. Lawrence and T. S. Eliot represent the two warring and unreconcilable poles of modern literature. The best contemporary English verse, however, shows that their influences can be creatively reconciled. In the seriousness of what I have called the new depth poetry, the openness to experience, the psychological insight and integrity of D. H. Lawrence would, ideally, combine with the technical skill and formal intelligence of T. S. Eliot. If this were to happen, we would have contemporary work which, like Coleridge's Imagination, would reconcile 'a more than usual state of emotion with more than usual order'.

My own feeling is that a good deal of poetic talent exists in England at the moment. But whether or not it will come to anything largely depends not on the machinations of any literary racket but on the degree to which the poets can remain immune to the disease so often found in English culture: gentility.—A. ALVAREZ, "Beyond the Gentility Principle," *The New Poetry*, 1962, pp. 24–32

The publication of Philip Larkin's third book, *The Whitsun Weddings*, was awaited with genuine eagerness, by his enemies as well as his friends. In many ways it was an advance on *The Less Deceived*. That volume was generally agreed to be skilful and perceptive, to achieve nearly all that it seems to aim at, but the quarrel with Larkin has rarely been over individual poems which can be exposed as failures on their own terms—it has usually amounted to a total questioning of his narrow range of rather negative attitudes. He has been variously accused of provincialism, of arid reticence, of nourishing his sense of defeat to the point of fascinated self-parody.

Now it is certainly true that a poetry like his, which is aimed to expose a core of personal vacuity, of lapsed resentment at opportunities missed, privileges withheld and so on, will invariably run risks of this kind, always threatening to spread out into what will appear a desiccated self-regard. It was perhaps in order to counter such impressions that Larkin very often assumed the offhand, debunking stance that is so familiar in his earlier volume; a stance which generally has the effect of diffusing his personal predicament into an inclusive and unconvincing sneer at the Emotional Life (at 'Sex, yes, but what is sex?'), ranking it along with God and Art as just another tarnished absolute, a snare of affectation. Larkin to some extent gets round the unevenness of tone that must arise from this by projecting a *persona* who is seen to actively relish his impoverishment as 'undeceived', a mark of superiority over the herd. At the same time, of course, we are made to know that the poet sees through the rationalization he is promoting.

Very often Larkin's punchline will suggest a whole range of emotional possibilities which the rest of his poem has been careful to ignore. For instance, in the last lines of 'Poetry of Departures' the phrase 'a life reprehensibly perfect' not only completes the cycle of rather smug self-imprisonment which the poem has been plotting but also introduces a whole new dimension, of despair. The tongue is removed from the cheek and is given a sharp bite. This is the kind of thing, too, that happens in 'Church Going', where the final recognition of the church as a 'serious house on serious earth' is not so much a natural intensification of the irreverent early stanzas as a lofty rejection of their slick disengagement. It is almost as if the *persona* is being scolded by the poet.

The best poems in *The Less Deceived* are those like 'At Grass' where the poet has none of these problems of attitude but discovers an objective situation that can dramatize his sense of exclusion and defeat, or those like 'Next Please' where he attempts a kind of representative wisdom and operates from a rhetorical 'we'. Here his skill at maintaining a complex reflection through several elegant stanzas without cramping either his syntax or his natural speech movement is really remarkable. One can think of few contemporary poets who can manage this kind of writing without stuttering into the pompous or obvious. In Larkin, though, it seems effortless.

In *The Whitsun Weddings* volume Larkin allows these metaphoric and reflective gifts more scope than he did in *The Less Deceived*. Only now and then—in poems like 'Self's the Man' and 'A Study of Reading Habits', for example—does one discover the old self-deprecatory habit and in these it is handled with a light-hearted assertiveness that seems to signal the level

on which it is meant to be taken. Larkin's sense of pity is now extended to the 'cut-price crowd' with their manipulated desires and their shoddy festivals, and to individuals like Mr. Bleaney, from whom love has been withheld, or the widow in 'Love Songs in Age' whom it has cheated by promising to 'solve and satisfy/and set unchangeably in order'. Though Larkin is fairly caustic at the expense of that 'much-mentioned brilliance, love' and regularly discovers a pathos in the situation of those who have succumbed to it, his portrait of the loveless Mr. Bleaney is one of his most compelling. There is a sense in which Larkin's ubiquitous compassion tends to reduce people to the sum of their paraphernalia, but in this poem his observation and selection of detail is rigorous enough for this to be acceptable—Bleaney's tragedy is that he probably *can* be summed up in this way, by his flowered curtains, his saucer-souvenir, his four aways. The last two stanzas are expertly managed. They work into a suspended knottiness that is beautifully resolved by the poet's final intervention. It has not, we realize, been idle speculation—if the poet doesn't know about Bleaney, he does know about himself. The indentification is chillingly complete. Bleaney is in his coffin and the poet has inherited his 'hired box':

> But if he stood and watched the frigid wind
> Tousling the clouds, lay on the fusty bed
> Telling himself that this was home, and grinned
> And shivered, without shaking off the dread
> That how we live measures our own nature,
> And at his age having no more to show
> Than one hired box should make him pretty sure
> He warranted no better, I don't know.

But how might Bleaney have improved his situation? Not, from what we are told in other parts of the book, by reading, travel or marriage. Money? We never learn, in the title poem, if having the real thing instead of 'jewellery substitutes' would have helped. In 'Faith Healer' the suggestion seems to be that there is no getting away from that 'much-mentioned brilliance':

> in everyone there sleeps
> A sense of life lived according to love.
> To some it means the difference they could make
> By loving others, but across most it sweeps
> As all they might have done had they been loved.

This moving ambiguity runs throughout. On the one hand, there is 'everyone making love and going shares', love that is organized into the drudgery of marriage, that cheats and disappoints and is disproved by time. On the other, there is the isolation and discontent of those who have never had it, or who, rejecting it on these terms, seek it instead as 'an enormous yes' that can be intimated as forcefully by a pair of 'new, slightly out-moded shoes' as it can by 'wheat's restless silence'. The closing lines of the title-poem seems to contain and energize this conflict. The arrow shower is both ironic and visionary and being so can beautifully concentrate the strands of aspiration and defeat which are present in the dramatic commentary of which it is the superb climax:

> and it was nearly done, this frail
> Travelling coincidence; and what it held
> Stood ready to be loosed with all the power
> That being changed can give. We slowed again,
> And as the tightened brakes took hold, there swelled
> A sense of falling, like an arrow shower
> Sent out of sight, somewhere becoming rain.

Larkin is not always as skilful as he is here. He often delivers some terrible rhymes (easiest/honest/unrest/; lines/limousines etc.) and breaks his lines against the speech rhythm to achieve them, as in 'Sunny Prestatyn', where—in search of rhymes for 'sand' and 'poster'—he does this

> Behind her, a hunk of coast, a
> Hotel with palms
> Seemed to expand from her thighs and
> Spread breast-lifting arms.

He can also lapse into a rollicking Betjemanesque which does not suit him; though the worst example occurs in the second stanza of 'The Large Cool Store', which is, anyway, a rather silly poem about nighties.

On the whole, though, one can only welcome and admire this volume. It has all the virtues of *The Less Deceived* and very few of its faults. Larkin has extended his range of interests with admirable ease and seems no longer concerned to pose. There is no saying what he might go on to achieve.—IAN HAMILTON, "Philip Larkin" (1964), *A Poetry Chronicle*, 1973, pp. 134–38

In the '50s, Larkin, contributing to a Movement manifesto, wrote that he didn't know why most poetry had to be written. This might be the crash of the new wave, its puritanism and purism. I didn't think, though, that he was just applauding the Movement, its low-voiced insularity and lack of pretence. No style or school could have given his words their poignant severity, the music of Herbert, afflicted, amused, clear accents stiffening colloquial informality. What is technique with nothing said? We cannot do metre or speak to God as Herbert did. Larkin, like some other moderns, is particularly good at finding words for the instants of action, a person in his instant of time and place, colours that come once only.—ROBERT LOWELL, "Digressions from Larkin's *Twentieth-Century Verse*," *Enc*, May 1973, p. 68

A. ALVAREZ
From "Poetry of the 'Fifties: In England"

International Literary Annual, 1959, pp. 97–103

Had I been writing this article two or three years ago, there would have been every reason to be gloomy. There was, of course, plenty of verse being written and, with more or less heat, discussed. But even the stage managers of the dominant style found they could define it only by negatives. Here, for example, is Mr Robert Conquest, introducing his anthology *New Lines*:

> If one had briefly to distinguish this poetry of the 'fifties from its predecessors, I believe the most important general point would be that it submits to no great systems of theoretical contracts nor agglomerations of unconscious commands. It is free from both mystical and logical compulsions and—like modern philosophy—is empirical in its attitude to all that comes. This reverence for the real person or event is, indeed, a part of the general intellectual ambience . . . of our time. . . . On the more technical side, though of course related to all this, we see a refusal to abandon a rational structure and comprehensive language, even when the verse is most highly charged with sensuous or emotional intent. . . . What (these poets) do have in common is, perhaps, at its lowest little more than a negative determination to avoid bad principles. By itself that cannot guarantee good poetry. Still, it is a good deal. . . .

This, then, was 'The Movement' (that is the last time inverted commas will be needed for the name), a group of writers united by the negative determination to avoid bad habits. On one side of them was the rather esoteric University intellectualism represented best by William Empson's poetry. On the other was the deliberate Philistinism of Kingsley Amis's novels and light verse. No wonder the poetry often appeared a little wan and, in the effort to avoid wild emotional gestures, ended sometimes with cramp. It was a poetry of reaction, or, as John Wain once described it, of consolidation.

Why? Why this determination to underplay every hand? What was the Movement moving from? And what was it moving towards? It seemed as though the period and the poetry would be more likely to interest future literary historians than literary critics. So perhaps a little rough literary history might be useful.

The Movement's point of departure was, I think, the war. During the 'thirties, Auden used to describe the gathering political crisis in the intense, muffled language of neurosis. The more Europe split and crumbled, always just below the surface, the larger the neurotic fantasies loomed. So when the war finally broke out, poetry lurched into a kind of nervous breakdown. That is, it lurched into a world uncontrolled, overwhelming and private. I say 'poetry', not 'the poets', deliberately. For the peculiar thing about the work of this period was, for all the emotionalism, its sameness and unreality, much as Freud said that all cases are unique and alike. It reads as though Orwell's electronic poetry-making machine in *1984* had suddenly short-circuited; all the traditionally dramatic, and melodramatic, ingredients of verse—blood, guts, limbs, God, angels, stars, jewels, rocks, trees, flowers, the elements, storms, love, death, etc., etc.—were jostled together in hopeless confusion.

Not that the principle was necessarily wrong; every poet has to commit a certain violence upon language in order to make it take the exact form and pressure of his own sensibility. What mattered was the lack of principle. For all the words, words, words, and the occasional, inert fragments of unconscious symbolism, there was never any sign of a creative intelligence, ordering and judging and modulating the mass. In fact, with the exception of a few poets like F. T. Prince, Alun Lewis and Henry Reed, what was missing from the poetry of the 'forties was simply a voice, distinct, alive and humanly, reasonably speaking. Everyone was always shouting. It was all very portentous in its strained, bardic way, but what it portended never became clear. Behind these poets, of course, was Dylan Thomas; but what came naturally and powerfully to a Welsh spellbinder sounded, in his followers, about as convincing as *How Green Was My Valley* in repertory.

The Movement, then, was the reaction to this nervous breakdown. Its first aim was sanity (variously called 'common sense', 'honesty' and 'discipline'). Its second was to restore some of the status of the poet. For when the poets resigned their obligations to intelligence, the educated public responded by dismissing them from any serious consideration. They encouraged them in their various acts (Dylan Thomas was finally sacrificed to his) but they accorded no more than pitying tolerance to the monotonous attempts to dress hackneyed emotions in an elaborate verbiage, much as *Les Précieuses* were said to dress the legs of their tables in trousers for fear the vulgar truth should be seen. The poets of the Movement tried to have done with this by showing that poetry could be written by intelligent, educated people who respected both the intelligibility of their subjects and their audience's ability to read. It was a movement, in fact, back to those standards Eliot had demanded ('The only method', he once wrote, 'is to be very intelligent') and the whole movement of modern criticism substantiated. But it was to be done without any of the earlier experimentation; traditional means seemed, for the moment, safer. Hence the new reverence for the poems of Robert Graves and William Empson which combined this tough-minded intellectual discipline with a certain traditional regularity. That few of the Movement poets managed to live up to these standards is, for the moment, beside the point.

I have been using the past tense because the Movement has now ended and its poets have gone off on their separate ways. The convalescence after the breakdown, with its wanness and fear of exertion, is over. First sanity, then strength returns. And in this the Movement, for all its limitations and negatives, was immensely valuable. For at least it demanded that its poets should be able to do the elementary things: make sense and be technically adept. The standard of competence and the sense of responsibility in poetry are higher now than they were ten years ago. And that is something.

Rather belatedly, I should point out that, apart from these generalisations I am not trying to write an inclusive survey of recent poetry. A disproportionate number of volumes of verse is published each year and disproportionately few real poems come out of them. As for the real poets: even at the best of times, there are not likely to be more than two or three. A large survey of the more or less interesting poets, with a brief comment on each, would be at best invidious. Anyway, that is what the weekly reviews and the publishers' hand-outs are for. Instead, I want to talk about two of the younger poets who seem to me in their different ways to be significant. They are Philip Larkin and Thom Gunn. Mr Larkin's book, *The Less Deceived* (The Marvell Press), first appeared in 1955, but, because of the gang-warfare raging at that time, has hardly been written about in cold blood. I want to try to do so now because his poetry represents everything that was best in the Movement and at the same time shows what was finally lacking. Mr Gunn's first volume, *Fighting Terms* (Fantasy Press), came out in 1954, his second, *The Sense of Movement* (Faber & Faber), in 1957. Though he started from the Movement, Mr Gunn is now free of it and moving, I think, towards something new.

Mr Larkin is one of those poets continually needed by literature to preserve the standards for the rest. He is a poet, that is, of above all great technical accomplishment. His accomplishment, like De La Mare's, Graves's, or that of the rest of the Movement, is not specifically 'modern'. He takes the traditional forms of English verse and refines them to his own use, helped by but never overstepping their bounds of elegant clarity:

> Lots of folk live up lanes
>   With fires in a bucket,
> Eat windfalls and tinned sardines—
>   They seem to like it.
>
> Their nippers have got bare feet,
>   Their unspeakable wives
> Are skinny as whippets—and yet
>   No one actually *starves*.
>
> Ah, were I courageous enough
>   To shout *Stuff your pension!*
> But I know, all too well, that's the stuff
>   That dreams are made on.
>   ('Toads')

An enormous amount of skill has gone into making the verse sound as easy as that. The effect depends on the way the half-rhymes at once check and stress the colloquialism; in the same way, in the last stanza, the pun plays off the slang against the fine literary yearning. Mr Larkin is not often as witty as this, but the personal note of his best work is always a matter of this kind of ironic nostalgia, at once elegant and off-hand.

His constant theme is that of opportunities lost and modest proposals never made. It is a poetry of disappointment, forever celebrating those multitudinous denials needed if one is determined never to overstep any mark. In other words, it is a poetry of conformity. Not that Mr Larkin is pleased with his lot; on the contrary, it saddens him, even makes him, at times, mildly indignant. And this, apart from his skill and originality, is what makes him a poet of quite another colour from, say, Mr John Betjeman. He is pink not blue. Mr Betjeman, that is, is a great fan of the comfortable middle classes; and he loves them all the more because their lapses allow him to patronise them even as he sings his little hymns of praise. Mr Larkin, on the other hand, is so far from being a snob that he is constantly blaming himself for his least wavering from a kind of enlightened middle-class socialism. He writes as though he had been voluntarily nationalised. That is, as though he *sees* that a benignant Welfare State is a necessary and reasonable thing and uses all his intelligence to reconcile himself to the cosy anonymity that goes with it. But he is uneasy because, despite all his efforts, he can't quite manage the reconciliation. Take another look at that last stanza I quoted above; or at this, the end of a poem on passing through the town he was born in:

> 'You look as if you wished the place in Hell',
> My friend said, 'judging from your face.' 'Oh well,
> I suppose it's not the place's fault', I said.
> 'Nothing, like something, happens anywhere.'
>   ('I Remember, I Remember')

No, it's not the place's fault, it's his own. This is quite the opposite of the 'forties' conceit: 'I write verse. Therefore I am a genius. Therefore I do not have to make myself understood.' Mr Larkin is always accusing himself of a necessary timidity of one kind or another: emotional (the girls he might have proposed to), moral (the things he might have done and said), even physical (the places he might have gone to had he not liked his comforts). His reasonable intelligence, affirming he must make the best of what his timidity has brought him, pulls one way, his poetic intelligence, whispering of all the chances missed, pulls the other. Perhaps that is why he makes his poetry so difficult technically; it solaces his poetic intelligence.

Perhaps, too, this is why Mr Larkin becomes a little sentimental when he sets out to affirm things wholeheartedly. He often settles, I mean, for feelings that are too large, too easy and too vague. For example, in 'Lines on a Young Lady's Photograph Album', 'Maiden Name', 'Born Yesterday' and 'At Grass' he needs all his wry charm in order not to sound uncomfortably like Rupert Brooke. Even in his best poem, 'Church Going', he has to go through certain ritual motions before he can say his say. It is an ambitious poem that works up to a climax that satisfies all the ambitions:

> A serious house on serious earth it is,
> In whose blent air all our compulsions meet,
> Are recognised, and robed as destinies.
> And that much never can be obsolete,
> Since someone will forever be surprising
> A hunger in himself to be more serious,
> And gravitating with it to this ground,
> Which, he once heard, was proper to grow wise in,
> If only that so many dead lie round.

He is saying something original and serious with serenity, control and conviction. But before doing so, he has bent over backwards so as not to appear out of the ordinary. With that final stanza in mind, now read the beginning:

> Once I'm sure there's nothing going on
> I step inside, letting the door thud shut.
> Another church: matting, seats and stone,

And little books; sprawlings of flowers, cut
For Sunday, brownish now; some brass and stuff
Up at the holy end; the small neat organ;
And a tense, musty, unignorable silence,
Brewed God knows how long. Hatless, I take off
My cycle-clips in awkward reverence,

Move forward, run my hand around the font.
From where I stand, the roof looks almost new—
Cleaned, or restored? Someone would know: I don't.
Mounting the lectern, I peruse a few
Hectoring large-scale verses, and pronounce
'Here endeth' much more loudly than I'd meant.
The echoes snigger briefly. Back at the door
I sign the book, donate an Irish sixpence,
Reflect the place was not worth stopping for.

There are two things about this which, considering the assurance with which the poem ends, I find tiresome. First, there is Mr Larkin's insistence that he is an ordinary, agnostic chap like the rest of us ordinary, agnostic chaps:

Once I'm sure there's nothing going on . . .
        Hatless, I take off
My cycle-clips in awkward reverence . . .
        Someone would know: I don't.

Second, there is the element of good, clean fun: the business about 'Here endeth', or 'some brass and stuff (the crucifix?) Up at the holy end', or, alas, that 'Irish sixpence' (Mr Kingsley Amis would have used the traditional currency, a flybutton). But what kind of good, clean fun is this? In the introduction to *New Lines* that I quoted earlier, Mr Conquest invoked the influence of 'George Orwell, with his principle of real, rather than ideological honesty'. I suggest that Mr Larkin has Orwell in mind when he goes through these motions. But not Orwell's honesty. Instead, it is the thread that runs through all Orwell's work without ever becoming dominant: that element in him of the clear-eyed, candid, nonconformist schoolboy. Even in this otherwise excellent poem, Mr Larkin seems embarrassed to be caught taking anything seriously. So he has to assure us that he is not taken in before he can go on to affirm so beautifully what there is to be taken in by.

It is precisely because Mr Larkin has made such a constant and unpretentious effort to mould the difficulties of living with this seriousness and this embarrassment into a polished control, that he has been able to make real poetry out of the restrictions and deliberate ordinariness of the Movement. Whereas the other members having tried it therapeutically for a time have either given up verse altogether or gone on to write in some other way.

COLIN FALCK
"Philip Larkin" (1964)
The Modern Poet: Essays from the Review
ed. Ian Hamilton
1968, pp. 101–10

The hero of Philip Larkin's first novel dreams up a girl called Jill, and then tries to identify this beautiful unreality with a real girl who in some ways resembles her. The result is comic and sometimes very moving, but in terms of making contact with the real girl it is not a success.

Real life seems never to have borne very much relation to the idea that Larkin wanted to have of it, and the progress of his poetry since *The North Ship* is a kind of steady exorcising of romantic illusions, an ever-deepening acceptance of the ordinariness of things as they are. Or if not as they are, at least as they might seem to be, beyond all their dashed hopes and

"unreal wishes", to ordinary people. And yet at the same time the unreal wishes have continued to haunt this ordinary world and to make everything in it seem stale and impoverished.

Larkin's poems have nearly always turned on ideas, above all on ideas of love and death, and one of the differences between *The Whitsun Weddings* and the earlier books is that the ideas themselves are now presented without very much poetic adornment. Death, which was once

        a black-
Sailed unfamiliar, towing at her back
A huge and birdless silence

can now appear simply as "the only end of age" or "what is left to come"; and "that much-mentioned brilliance, love" is in fact mentioned by name a great many times throughout *The Whitsun Weddings*. The effect of this is to give real strength to some of the more autobiographical poems, and in "Dockery and Son", perhaps the best of these, the reflection on death grows out of the opening personal situation with a terrible bareness and clarity:

        Where do these
Innate assumptions come from? . . .
        looked back on, they rear
Like sand-clouds, thick and close, embodying
For Dockery a son, for me nothing.
Nothing with all a son's harsh patronage.
Life is first boredom, then fear.
Whether or not we use it, it goes,
And leaves what something hidden from us chose,
And age, and then the only end of age.

The starkness of these lines (and the way the poem breaks metre to accommodate them) seems to me something quite new in Larkin's poetry.

But this courting of abstract ideas has another result which is not so encouraging. It intensifies, almost to the point of absoluteness, the contrast between life as it is and life as it might (impossibly) be if only everything were different. And I think this may be the real difference between *The Whitsun Weddings* and the earlier poetry. It is love, more than anything else, which seems to concentrate our dreams of another and better life:

        In everyone there sleeps
A sense of life lived according to love.
To some it means the difference they could make
By loving others, but across most it sweeps
As all they might have done had they been loved.

Love promises "to solve, and satisfy, / And set unchangeably in order", and it should fall on us, "they say", "Like an enormous yes". Even the Modes for Night section of the large cool store can remind us "How separate and unearthly love is". Love, in fact, has to bear the heaviest load of our unreal wishes. But the contrast between the ideal and the ordinary is to be seen elsewhere too, and the "sharply-pictured groves / Of how life should be" in the poem about advertising have echoes in many other places. The girl in the "Sunny Prestatyn" poster was "too good for this life". Home is "A joyous shot at how things ought to be, / Long fallen wide". And all through the book there is a sense of "our live imperfect eyes / That stare beyond this world".

The title of the advertising poem, "Essential Beauty", is really more than a joke, because what all this adds up to is a kind of Platonism. Goodness, truth and beauty are not really to be found in the human world at all. The counterpart of such impossible idealism is that real human existence comes to seem quite meaningless. Even brute nature has its own laws and order, and even "our flesh / Surrounds us with its own decisions": but we can never share in this order ourselves. We remain

> ignorant of the way things work:
> Their skill at finding what they need,
> Their sense of shape, and punctual spread of seed,
> And willingness to change.

Our own lives are simply a "unique random blend / Of families and fashions". If we dedicate ourselves to finding out the meaning of things we shall end up watching

> the hail
> Of occurrence clobber life out
> To a shape no one sees

and with our faces "bent in / By the blows of what happened to happen". When we finally learn the mistake of having

> spent youth
> Tracing the trite, untransferable
> Truss-advertisement, truth

and discover that books are a load of crap, etc., half life is over and it is too late even to enjoy ourselves.

It is easy enough to sympathise with all this: perhaps everything really is pretty hopeless. But futile though life may be for the majority of people in our present society, it is not futile in principle in the way that Larkin makes it seem. By coming to rest so easily in this necessity, the necessity of life's meaninglessness, Larkin's poetry is most of the time a poetry of consolation. The grip of this deadening philosophy is not yet complete, though, and there are many poems where it is qualified or even held off altogether. It is this that makes "The Whitsun Weddings" itself so unusual. The end of this poem, with its thought "of London spread out in the sun, / Its postal districts packed like squares of wheat", its sense of "the power / That being changed can give", and its final image of the "arrow-shower / Sent out of sight, somewhere becoming rain", it unlike anything else in the book and succeeds, however fragilely, in overcoming the usual despair. Another poem, "Reference Back", concludes with the reflection that

> Truly, though our element is time,
> We are not suited to the long perspectives
> Open at each instant of our lives.
> They link us to our losses: worse,
> They show us what we have as it once was,
> Blindingly undiminished, just as though
> By acting differently we could have kept it so.

There is disillusion enough here, and yet there is hope too: the long perspectives are at least open, and the two very personal stanzas which lead up to this sad conclusion make it more of a reflection on one particular life than a judgement on life in general.

It is the autobiographical poems which stand up to Larkin's philosophy best, in fact. By developing out of a personal situation it can take on an existential force for the poet himself without at the same time imposing itself on everyone. This comes out best of all, perhaps, in "Dockery and Son", where the poem as a whole is so personal that the summing-up line "Life is first boredom, then fear" has all the force of a personal cry. In a poem like "Love Songs in Age", on the other hand, the poet is writing about someone else, and for all his sensitivity to this person's feelings at a particular moment the result is somehow generalized and sentimental: the sense of loss remains pure nostalgia, leading nowhere, and we may even find ourselves resenting the poet's too-easy familiarity with it in another person. When the emptiness and futility of the other person's life is as complete as it is in "Mr. Bleaney", of course, this question hardly arises: the sadness of Bleaney is that his life really can be summed up in his landlady's remarks and the few

bits and pieces of his "one hired box", and the only feelings we really experience are the poet's own incomprehension of what it must have felt like to be Bleaney and his horror at how much he has in common with him. The poem where Larkin comes nearest to capturing someone else's experience without being either patronising or sentimental is probably "Afternoons". The description here is precise and delicate—not least through being in free verse instead of the usual iambics—and goes well beyond a mere notation of the scenery:

> Summer is fading:
> The leaves fall in ones and twos
> From trees bordering
> The new recreation ground
> In the hollows of afternoons
> Young mothers assemble
> At swing and sandpit
> Setting free their children.

The degree of identification seems exactly right in this poem, and even in the concluding lines the language is poetic, interpreting the young mothers' situation without imposing any judgement on it:

> Their beauty has thickened.
> Something is pushing them
> To the side of their own lives.

There is something of Rilke's *Neue Gedichte* in this poem: it shows the rather special kind of success which is possible when the poet sets himself to write about the emotions of people he does not know. But it also shows how delicately this has to be done.

It is interesting that none of the poems in *The Whitsun Weddings* is autobiographical in the fullest sense—in the sense, that is, of presenting the poet as a poet and not simply as his usual bachelor persona. This is not surprising perhaps, because there is really no room for poets in the Platonic world that Larkin has committed himself to. In most of the poems which describe the world of ordinary people the poet appears either as an observer or not at all. In the one poem which is explicitly about the poet *qua* poet ("Send No Money") the concrete world itself disappears, and the result is a kind of moral tale, more than a little vicious in tone. (Compare this with its equivalent in *The Less Deceived*, "Reasons for Attendance".) The effectiveness of a poem like "Dockery and Son" comes in part from our awareness that the real man present is also a poet; but there is no indication of this in the poem (beyond the fact that it was written at all) and we really have to supply the information for ourselves.

I think Larkin's general conception of truth and reality accounts for much that is typical in his style. In all the poems in *The Whitsun Weddings* there is an extreme propriety of syntax and language which seems to have intellectual clarity as its ideal and to regard metaphor as something rather special. When the poems do leave the level of basic description it is most often by means of explicit simile. The effect of this is to preserve the appearance of language as somehow in itself literal and to lodge the poetry self-consciously in a grammatical device:

> Its postal districts packed like squares of wheat
> Here silence stands like heat
> As if out on the end of an event

But the distinction here is very rough, of course (and there would not be much room for poetry if it were otherwise). Who can say whether "Summer is fading" is literal or metaphorical? The point is only that Larkin writes most of the time as though the distinction was quite clear. And yet his most impressive lines actually come when he allows himself to unbend and to submit to more or less pure metaphor:

> Dark towns heap up on the horizon

Some of the most beautiful lines of all are in fact very meticulous in their grammar:

> A sense of falling, like an arrow-shower
> Sent out of sight, somewhere becoming rain.

> An immense, slackening ache,
> As when, thawing, the rigid landscape weeps

But their real power is in the metaphor they carry: "an arrow-shower . . . somewhere becoming rain", "the rigid landscape weeps".

These last examples are revealing in another way too. For want of any overall texture of metaphor, Larkin's poems usually fall into a pattern of description-plus-evaluation: it is nearly always the summarising argument which holds the poem together. (His earlier technique, on the other hand, was very often to build from a single metaphor, carrying it right through the poem like an argument.) One result of this is that it becomes necessary to attempt direct descriptions of emotions themselves, almost as if these were simply another kind of object, to be observed and recorded along with all the objects of the external world. The last two examples are both descriptions of this kind: of "a sense of falling", of "an immense slackening ache". That Larkin pushes through to poetry here is not surprising, perhaps, because it is only at points like these that this general approach permits of any subjectivity at all. If emotions are to be described, then it is crucial that they should be described well. But would it not be better to give up the general approach itself? It is not really a poem's job to describe emotions, any more than it is its job (merely) to describe anything else. A poem is an *expression* of an emotion, but this is quite another thing: it does not demand that any emotions should be mentioned at all. A poem can express emotion without talking about anything but trees or cities or other people. The very way in which Larkin succeeds in his direct attempts to describe emotions actually demonstrates the case against his method as a whole: in both of the above examples an emotion is finally expressed through a metaphor which takes in the outside world—"the rigid landscape weeps", "an arrow-shower . . . somewhere becoming rain"—and which carries a subjectivity deeper than any "sense of falling" or "immense slackening ache". There are times, on the other hand, when Larkin's most descriptive-looking lines do quiver towards a real intensive meaning. When he describes the women in "Faith Healing"—

> Moustached in flowered frocks they shake

—there is a genuine subjectivity in the description, and its effect is to make the accompanying reflection and philosophising seem almost unnecessary.

This basically descriptive approach, depending as it does on argument rather than the individual moment of perception, makes it easy to understand Larkin's adherence to very regular metres and rhyme-schemes. But it also goes some way to explaining that other hallmark of his style, the doubled adjective. "Frank submissive", "immense slackening", "unique random", "sweet commissioned": at their best they are words which have a good deal of tension between their central meanings, and they get their effect by being juxtaposed within a grammatical form which would as a rule be simply descriptive ("big red", etc.) or else banal ("wise old", etc.). It is one of the few imaginative techniques that remain for the poet who has committed himself to an external-descriptive view of language and the avoidance of metaphor.

I have said that Larkin's poetry is for the most part a poetry of consolation. In an article on "Poetry and Landscape in Present England" (*Granta*, 19 Oct. 1963) Donald Davie has praised Philip Larkin for the "humanism" with which he identifies himself with the ordinary life of this most industrialised of societies. "Precisely", Davie says, "because poem after poem since *The Waste Land* has measured our present (usually seen as depleted) against our past (usually seen as rich) Larkin's refusal to do this is thoroughly refreshing—at last, we recognise with relief, we can take all that for granted, take it as read." It seems to me that this is a mistake. There is not much doubt, perhaps, that the landscape of present-day England is more completely dominated by the urban-industrial way of life than that of any other country. But to extol the kind of poetry which takes this as its starting point and retains no serious urge to make discriminations is to surrender in advance to the scientific nightmare. By all means let us not retreat into the "nature" world of plants and animals and forget about humanity. But unless we are able to find and choose the natural from the unnatural in human life itself we are surely lost. We can accept modern civilisation in its entirety, as Larkin seems to, or we can reject it equally entirely (as the school of Leavis comes near to doing); but either way we are refusing the real choice between life and death, between good and evil. And if we do this, what we have to say will no longer seem very relevant to the people who still make these choices in their lives, because what we are refusing is human existence as such. Larkin has probably captured the feel of life as it is for a great many ordinary people much of the time, and this gives his poetry a certain kind of humanity. But he has done this only at the expense of a deeper and more important humanity, because he has done it ultimately at the expense of poetry. No doubt it is always important to maintain some general sense of what most other people's lives are like. But the poet cannot be content with this, and it might even be argued that it is not really his business *qua* poet at all, whatever might be expected of him as a novelist or as a human being. If there is really no beauty or truth or love to be found in the concrete here-and-now, however it might appear to ordinary people, then there is surely none to be found anywhere. The "other" Platonic truth, if it exists at all, is only the order which is to be found in the real world of existing things, and it is the poet, above all, who can be expected to find this order; and he will find it in his own experience. So that by identifying himself with the drab, fantasy-haunted world of the waste land Larkin has not only downgraded the whole of real existence against an impossible absolute standard, but has also cut the ground from under the poet's feet. The fantasy-world which he has elected to share has little to do with romanticism, because it destroys the very bridge which romanticism would construct between the ideal and the world which actually exists: the poet can no longer do anything to bring our dreams into relation with reality. The ideal, for Larkin, has become inaccessible, and being inaccessible it can only throw the real world into shadow instead of lighting it up from within. In the typical landscape of Larkin's poems the whole chiaroscuro of meaning, all polarities of life and death, good and evil, are levelled away. Farms, canals, building-plots and dismantled cars jostle one another indiscriminately—the view from the train window, with its complete randomness and detachment, is at the heart of Larkin's vision—and all of them are bathed in the same general wistfulness. There are no epiphanies. Love and death, though they are the controlling ideas of the poems, can never inflame the individual moments of existence; instead they simply diminish them, and the boredom of this diminished existence is invested with a kind of absolute necessity.

That Larkin himself is not oblivious to these questions is clear enough; and indeed no one really could be. The short poem "Water" ("If I were called in / To construct a religion / I should make use of water . . .") shows that he is able to see things symbolically and not only as part of the modern landscape; but there is a coyness about this poem which makes it hard to take very seriously. Asked to prophesy, I should see two possible lines of development in *The Whitsun Weddings*. The first is in the autobiographical bareness of "Dockery and Son", the second in the delicacy of a poem like "Afternoons". That the first can lead somewhere is clear enough from, for example, Robert Lowell's *Life Studies*; but I think it points ultimately to a dead end. This kind of bare utterance ("Life is first boredom, then fear", "My mind's not right", "I have wasted my life", etc.) must somehow, if it is to remain poetry and not psychology, maintain some outlet to the real world and be set off by an external vision of things. It is this which the second alternative promises more directly, both in its quality of language and in its relatively free verse form. Larkin has found a new kind of directness in this book, and some of his earlier single-metaphor poems now look decorative and "poetic" by comparison. But when the metaphor itself was open enough ("No Road" is one of the best) they could carry a richness of vision which it would be a pity to lose altogether ("To watch that world come up like a cold sun . . ."). I should like to think that something of this vision might now find its way into poems basically as simple and direct as "Afternoons".

In rejecting Larkin's particular brand of "humanism" I may seem to be asking for the kind of "right wing" violence to which D. H. Lawrence was sometimes led. I think perhaps I am. The last and truest humanism in art is the truthful expression of emotion, and this is something prior to all questions of politics: it concerns only the honesty or the corruption of our own consciousness. If this means barbarism, then let us have barbarism. Barbarism has come to be associated with obscurity, but no true expression can be really obscure. Let us have lucid barbarism. If we cannot face it in art, we shall have to face it soon enough in life. Should we really, in this post-Nazi age, be dismissing "solemn-sinister wreath-rubbish" in a piece of light verse? And does the Modes for Night counter really show "How separate and unearthly love is"?

PHILIP LARKIN
Interview with Ian Hamilton

London Magazine, November 1964, pp. 71–77

Hamilton: I would like to ask you about your attitude to the so-called 'modernist revolution' in English poetry; how important has it been to you as a poet?

Larkin: Well, granted that one doesn't spend any time at all thinking about oneself in these terms, I would say that I have been most influenced by the poetry that I've enjoyed—and this poetry has not been Eliot or Pound or anybody who is normally regarded as 'modern'—which is a sort of technique word, isn't it? The poetry I've enjoyed has been the kind of poetry you'd associate with me, Hardy pre-eminently, Wilfred Owen, Auden, Christina Rossetti, William Barnes; on the whole, people to whom technique seems to matter less than content, people who accept the forms they have inherited but use them to express their own content.

Hamilton: You don't feel in any way guilty about this, I

imagine; would you see yourself as rebelliously anti-modern—you have talked about the 'myth-kitty' and so on . . .

Larkin: What I do feel a bit rebellious about is that poetry seems to have got into the hands of a critical industry which is concerned with culture in the abstract, and this I do rather lay at the door of Eliot and Pound. I think that Eliot and Pound have something in common with the kind of Americans you used to get around 1910. You know, when Americans began visiting Europe towards the end of the last century, what they used to say about them was that they were keen on culture, *laughably* keen—you got jokes like 'Elmer, is this Paris or Rome?' 'What day is it?' 'Thursday.' 'Then it's Rome.'—you know the kind of thing. This was linked with the belief that you can order culture whole, that it is a separate item on the menu—this was very typically American, and German too, I suppose, and seems to me to have led to a view of poetry which is almost mechanistic, that every poem must include all previous poems, in the same way that a Ford Zephyr has somewhere in it a Ford T Model—which means that to be any good you've got to have read all previous poems. I can't take this evolutionary view of poetry. One never thinks about other poems except to make sure that one isn't doing something that has been done before—writing a verse play about a young man whose father has died and whose mother has married his uncle, for instance. I think a lot of this 'myth-kitty' business has grown out of that, because first of all you have to be terribly educated, you have to have read everything to know these things, and secondly you've got somehow to work them in to show that you are working them in. But to me the whole of the ancient world, the whole of classical and biblical mythology means very little, and I think that using them today not only fills poems full of dead spots but dodges the writer's duty to be original.

Hamilton: You are generally written up as one of the fathers of this so-called Movement; did you have any sense at the time of belonging to a group with any very definite aims?

Larkin: No sense at all, really. The only other writer I felt I had much in common with was Kingsley Amis, who wasn't really at that time known as a writer—*Lucky Jim* was published in 1954—but of course we'd been exchanging letters and showing each other work for a long time, and I think we laughed at the same things and agreed largely about what you could and couldn't write about, and so on. But the Movement, if you want to call it that, really began when John Wain succeeded John Lehmann on that B.B.C. programme; John planned six programmes called *First Readings* including a varied set of contributors—they weren't all Movementeers by any means. It got attacked in a very convenient way, and consequently we became lumped together. Then there was an article in *The Spectator* actually using the term 'Movement' and Bob Conquest's *New Lines* in 1956 put us all between the same covers. But it certainly never occurred to me that I had anything in common with Thom Gunn, or Donald Davie, for instance, or they with each other and in fact I wasn't mentioned at the beginning. The poets of the group were Wain, Gunn, Davie and, funnily enough, Alvarez.

Hamilton: To what extent, though, did you feel consciously in reaction against Thomas, the Apocalypse, and so on?

Larkin: Well, one had to live through the forties at one's most impressionable time and indeed I could show you, but won't, a lot of poems I wrote that you wouldn't—well, that were very much of the age. I wrote a great many sedulous and worthless Yeats-y poems, and later on far inferior Dylan Thomas poems—I think Dylan Thomas is much more difficult to imitate than Yeats—and this went on for years and years. It wasn't until about 1948 or 9 that I began writing differently, but it wasn't as any conscious reaction. It's just that when you start writing your own stuff other peoples' manners won't really do for it.

Hamilton: I would like to ask you about reviews of your work; do they bore you, do you find any of them helpful? In general, how do you react to what is said about you?

Larkin: Well, one can't be other than grateful for the kind things that are said. They make you wish you wrote better. Otherwise one tries to ignore it—critics can hinder but they can't help. One thing I do feel a slight restiveness about is being typed as someone who has carved out for himself a uniquely dreary life, growing older, having to work, and not getting things he wants and so on—is this so different from everyone else? I'd like to know how all these romantic reviewers spend their time—do they kill a lot of dragons, for instance? If other people do have wonderful lives, then I'm glad for them, but I can't help feeling that my miseries are over-done a bit by the critics. They may retort that they are over-done by me, of course.

Hamilton: You usually write in metre, but now and then you have rather freer poems. I wonder if you have any feeling of technical unrest, of being constricted by traditional forms. Do things like syllabics, projective verse, for instance, have any interest for you?

Larkin: I haven't anything very original to say about metre. I've never tried syllabics; I'm not sure I fully understand them. I think one would have to be very sure of oneself to dispense with the help that metre and rhyme give and I doubt really if I could operate without them. I have occasionally, some of my favourite poems have not rhymed or had any metre, but it's rarely been premeditated.

Hamilton: I'd like to ask you about the poem, 'Church Going', which has been taken fairly generally as a kind of 'representative attitude' poem, standing for a whole disheartened, debunking state of mind in post-war England. How do you feel about that poem, do you think that the things that have been said about it are true? How do you feel about its enormous popularity?

Larkin: In a way I feel what Hardy is supposed to have said about *Tess:* if I'd known it was going to be so popular I'd have tried to make it better. I think its popularity is somewhat due to extraneous factors—anything about religion tends to go down well; I don't know whether it expresses what people feel. It is of course an entirely secular poem. I was a bit irritated by an American who insisted to me it was a religious poem. It isn't religious at all. Religion surely means that the affairs of this world are under divine superveillance, and so on, and I go to some pains to point out that I don't bother about that kind of thing, that I'm deliberately ignorant of it—'Up at the holy end', for instance. Ah no, it's a great religious poem; he knows better than me—trust the tale and not the teller, and all that stuff.

Of course the poem is about going to church, not religion—I tried to suggest this by the title—and the union of the important stages of human life—birth, marriage and death—that going to church represents; and my own feeling that when they are dispersed into the registry office and the crematorium chapel life will become thinner in consequence. I certainly haven't revolted against the poem. It hasn't become a kind of 'Innisfree', or anything like that.

Hamilton: I have the feeling about it—this has been said often enough, I suppose—that it drops into two parts. The stanza beginning 'A serious house on serious earth it is' seems significantly different in tone and movement to the rest of the poem and it is almost as if it sets up a rejoinder to the attitudes that are embodied in the first part. And that the first part is not just about religious belief or disbelief, it's about the whole situation of being a poet, a man of sensibility, a man of learning even, in an age like ours—that it is all this exclusiveness that is being scoffed at in the first half—it is seriousness in general. Somehow the final stanzas tighten up and are almost ceremonial in their reply to the debunkery; they seem to affirm all that has been scoffed at, and are deliberately more poetic and dignified in doing so. In this sense it seems a debate between poet and *persona*. I'd like to know if you planned the poem as a debate.

Larkin: Well, in a way. The poem starts by saying, you don't really know about all this, you don't believe in it, you don't know what a rood-loft is—Why do you come here, why do you bother to stop and look round? The poem is seeking an answer. I suppose that's the antithesis you mean. I think one has to dramatize oneself a little. I don't arse about in churches when I'm alone. Not much, anyway. I still don't know what rood-lofts are.

Hamilton: A number of poems in *The Less Deceived* seem to me to carry a final kick in the head for the attitudes they have seemed to be taking up. In a poem like 'Reasons for Attendance', say, where you have that final 'Or lied'; somehow the whole poem doubles back on itself. What I want to know is how conscious you are of your poems plotting a kind of elaborate self-imprisonment. Do you feel, for instance, that you will ever write a more abandoned, naïve, kind of poetry where you won't, as it were, block all the loopholes in this way? I think this is why I prefer *The Whitsun Weddings* book, because it doesn't do this anything like as confidently.

Larkin: Well, I speak to you as someone who hasn't written a poem for eighteen months. The whole business seems terribly remote and I have to remember what it was like. I do think that poems are artificial in the sense that a play is artificial. There are strong second act curtains in poems as well as in plays, you know. I don't really know what a 'spontaneous' poem would be like, certainly not by me. On the other hand, here again I must protest slightly. I always think that the poems I write are very much more naïve—very much more emotional—almost embarrassingly so—than a lot of other people's. When I was tagged as unemotional, it used to mystify me; I used to find it quite shaming to read some of the things I'd written.

Hamilton: I didn't mean that there is not strong personal feeling in your poems, or that they don't have a strong confessional element. But what I do rather feel is that many of them carry this kind of built-in or tagged-on comment on themselves, and I wonder if you will feel able to dispense with this. I can see how this might mean being less alert, in a way, less adult and discriminating even. It's probably a stupid question.

Larkin: It's a very interesting question and I hadn't realised I did that sort of thing. I suppose I always try to write the truth and I wouldn't want to write a poem which suggested that I was different from what I am. In a sense that means you have to build in quite a lot of things to correct any impression of over-optimism or over-commitment. For instance, take love poems. I should feel it false to write a poem going overboard about someone if you weren't at the same time marrying them and setting up house with them, and I should feel bound to add what you call a tag to make it clear I wasn't, if I wasn't. Do you see what I mean? I think that one of the great criticisms of poets of the past is that they said one thing and did another, a false relation between art and life. I always try to avoid this.

Hamilton: I would like to ask you about your novels, and why you haven't written any more.

Larkin: Well, because I can't. As I may have said somewhere else, I wanted to be a novelist. I wrote one, and then I wrote another, and I thought, This is wonderful, another five years of this and I'll be in the clear. Unfortunately, that was where it stopped. I've never felt as interested in poetry as I used to feel in novels—they were more theatrical, if you know what I mean, you could do the strong second-act curtain even better. Looking back on them, I think they were over-sized poems. They were certainly written with intense care for detail. If one word was used on page 15 I didn't re-use it on page 115. But they're not very good novels. A very crude difference between novels and poetry is that novels are about other people and poetry is about yourself. I suppose I must have lost interest in other people, or perhaps I was only pretending to be interested in them.

Hamilton: There was a review recently in the *Times Literary Supplement* which gave this portrait of you as being some kind of semi-recluse, almost, deliberately withdrawing from the literary life, not giving readings, talks, and so on. I wonder to what extent this withdrawal from literary society is necessary to you as a writer; given that it is true, that is.

Larkin: I can't recall exactly what the *TLS* said, but as regards readings, I suppose I'm rather shy. I began life as a bad stammerer, as a matter of fact. Up to the age of 21 I was still asking for railway tickets by pushing written notes across the counter. This has conditioned me against reading in public—the dread that speech failure might come back again. But also, I'm lazy and very busy and it wouldn't give me much in the way of kicks. I think if there is any truth in this rumour or legend, it's because I do find literary parties or meetings, or anything that considers literature, in public, in the abstract rather than concretely, in private, not exactly boring—it is boring, of course—but unhelpful and even inimical. I go away feeling crushed and thinking that everyone is much cleverer than I am and writing much more, and so on. I think it's important not to feel crushed.

Hamilton: Following on, really, from the last question, I was going to ask you about that poem, 'Naturally the Foundation Will Bear Your Expenses'. . .

Larkin: Well, that was rather a curious poem. It came from having been to London and having heard that A had gone to India and that B had just come back from India; then when I got back home, happening unexpectedly across the memorial service at the Cenotaph on the wireless, on what used to be called Armistice Day, and the two things seemed to get mixed up together. Almost immediately afterwards *Twentieth Century* wrote saying that they were having a Humour number and would I send them something funny, so I sent that. Actually, it's as serious as anything I have written and I was glad to see that John Wain has picked this up, quite without any prompting from me, in an article in *The Critical Quarterly.* Certainly it was a dig at the middleman who gives a lot of talks to America and then brushes them up and does them on the Third and then brushes them up again and puts them out as a book with Chatto. Why he should be blamed for not sympathising with the crowds on Armistice Day, I don't quite know. The awful thing is that the other day I had a letter from somebody called Lal in Calcutta, enclosing two poetry books of his own and mentioning this poem. He was very nice about it, but I shall have to apologise. I've never written a poem that has been less understood; one editor refused it on the grounds, and I quote, that it was 'rather hard on the Queen'; several people have asked what it was like in Bombay! There is nothing like

writing poems for realizing how low the level of critical understanding is; maybe the average reader can understand what I say, but the above-average often can't.

Hamilton: I wonder if you read much foreign poetry?

Larkin: Foreign poetry? *No!*

Hamilton: Of contemporary English poets, then, whom do you admire?

Larkin: It's awfully difficult to talk about contemporaries, because quite honestly I never read them. I really don't. And my likes are really very predictable. You know I admire Betjeman. I suppose I would say that he was my favourite living poet. Kingsley Amis I admire very much as a poet as well as a novelist; I think he's utterly original and can hit off a kind of satiric poem that no-one else can (this is when he is being himself, not when he's Robert Graves). Stevie Smith I'm very fond of in a puzzled way. I think she's terribly good but I should never want to imitate her. Anthony Thwaite's last book seemed very sensitive and efficient to me. I think one has to be both sensitive and efficient. That's about as far as I can go. I don't mean I dislike everyone else, it's just that I don't know very much about them.

Hamilton: What about Americans?

Larkin: I find myself no more appreciative of Americans. I quite liked Lowell's *Life Studies* but his last book was all about foreign poets—well, I think that is the end; versions of other people's poems are poor substitutes for your own. Occasionally one finds a poem by Donald Justice or Anthony Hecht, but I don't know enough about them to comment. Actually, I like the Beat poets, but again I don't know much about them. That's because I'm fond of Whitman; they seem to me debased Whitman, but debased Whitman is better than debased Ezra Pound.

Hamilton: Do you have many poems you haven't collected? Are you more prolific than you seem to be?

Larkin: I'm afraid not. There was a whole period between *The North Ship* and *The Less Deceived* which produced a book with the portentous title of *In the Grip of Light*, which went round the publishers in the middle and late forties, but thank God nobody accepted it. Otherwise I hardly ever finish a poem that I don't publish.

Hamilton: One final, rather broad question. How would you characterize your development as a poet from *The North Ship* to *The Whitsun Weddings*?

Larkin: I suppose I'm less likely to write a really bad poem now, but possibly equally less likely to write a really good one. If you can call that development, then I've developed. Kipling said somewhere that when you can do one thing really well, then do something else. Oscar Wilde said that only mediocrities develop. I just don't know. I don't think I want to change; just to become better at what I am.

J. M. NEWTON
"'. . . And a More Comprehensive Soul'"

Cambridge Quarterly, Winter 1965–66, pp. 98–103

If Mr. Larkin is among the most widely praised of contemporary English writers of verse, the rare naturalness and simplicity of his manner in a number of poems partly justify the distinction. In these, his best poems, he certainly satisfies one of the demands that Wordsworth made of a poet: he is a man speaking to men. And, at a time when so much new verse gives the impression that it is being spoken only to other writers of minor verse (and perhaps to professional teachers of

English literature, with their victims!), a poem which speaks and moves like this comes as water in a desert:

> That Whitsun, I was late getting away:
>   Not till about
> One-twenty on the sunlit Saturday
> Did my three-quarters-empty train pull out,
> All windows down, all cushions hot, all sense
> Of being in a hurry gone

The naturalness would not be so exceptional if it were only in the language and not also, as it is, in the convincing use of verse. But is the water really refreshing when it is tasted? This third volume of poems, from the title-poem of which my quotation is drawn, is not different in kind from that previous volume which made Mr. Larkin's reputation, *The Less Deceived*, though it has less of fashionable poeticality and the poet's own comment on life comes out more plainly. It is clearer than ever that that comment fatally lacks all nobility. That should, at any rate, be clearer than ever, though it hasn't been much said. Many readers and reviewers must be so pleased to find *any* humanity in new verse that they don't question themselves closely about its quality. And Mr. Larkin is sometimes even spoken of as a representative voice and interpreter of our times, though I should have thought that to believe that was to be (at least) intellectually lazy. It is about time that Mr. Larkin's poetry was described as what it is, a limitedly personal poetry which, because the poet never struggles for any finer-than-average or even fine-as-average humanity in it, is of little or no use to anyone. Other words that Wordsworth used of the poet must sound merely cruel when quoted here—'a man . . . endowed with more lively sensibility, more enthusiasm and tenderness, who has a greater knowledge of human nature, and a more comprehensive soul, than are supposed to be common among mankind'—but the words may show up a radical self-contradiction in a poet who has a small natural gift but nevertheless seems to have nothing of this special endowment. (More lively sensibility, tenderness and enthusiasm show themselves, of course, not only directly but also in the quality of anger, grief, humour, etc.) In his best manner Mr. Larkin successfully gives the impression of being at his ease, a clear-minded, cool, mildly curious man, capable sometimes of mild feeling sometimes of mild shrewdness. But not only is he very restricted in the number and importance of the things he can say in this manner of negative virtues: the naturalness comes in the end to seem a little too studied, as if it were an evasion.

The lack of nobility has particularly to be noted and judged fatal because in most of his best poetry Mr. Larkin is a meditative poet preoccupied with ageing, death, and the boredom, emptiness and meaninglessness of life—of his own life, of modern life or of life in general. No deep or extensive knowledge of life is felt to be present that would justify the generalisations and effects of generalisation and there is no sense of a delicate, generous spirit struggling against defeat, let alone of a strong one. There is no clean feeling either of indignation or of regret. 'Et jadis fusmes si mignottes! . . .'— *that* is a very long way away. There is only a rather mean sourness and misery, and putting these into poetry seems to be the poet's way to feeling a little more comfortable and complacent with them. But there are degrees of uncleanliness. The lack of nobility is clearer in *The Whitsun Weddings* only because the need for it there is a more obvious one: the more frequently occurring brightness and cleverness in *The Less Deceived* are actually more ignoble. Since there is no clear break between the two volumes the distinction can be illustrated wholly from the present one. The feeling of compla-

cency is always greater, as in the following extract from 'Love Songs in Age', the more the writing is fashionably poetical. Here a widow has come across old songs and felt momentarily rejuvenated:

>   But, even more,
> The glare of that much-mentioned brilliance, love,
>   Broke out, to show
> Its bright incipience sailing above,
> Still promising to solve, and satisfy,
> And set unchangeably in order. So
>   To pile them back, to cry,
> Was hard, without lamely admitting how
> It had not done so then, and could not now.

Compare the more consistent plainness of the last lines of a poem which I think is one of Mr. Larkin's very best, 'Afternoons', a meditation on young mothers seen in a park in 'the hollows of afternoons':

>   Before them, the wind
>   Is ruining their courting-places
>
> That are still courting-places
> (But the lovers are all in school),
> And their children, so intent on
> Finding more unripe acorns,
> Expect to be taken home.
> Their beauty has thickened.
> Something is pushing them
> To the side of their own lives.

The poet is fashionably poetical when he is so would-be knowing and ironic and so conspicuously (and bogusly) concerned with being precise. For all that conspicuous concern, he is actually unable or unwilling to do ordinary justice to his widowed woman's recollection of love. There were many signs in *The Less Deceived* that Mr. Larkin was fundamentally a poet of very simple, not strong sentiment, covering up for some reason with a hollow-ringing jauntiness and smartness. Together with the welcome freedom from that the greater plainness of 'Afternoons' also brings solidity. Only the 'more unripe acorns' damage the conviction of reality, by heavy-handedness.

Another way of approaching the main point is to mark the distinction between poems in which Mr. Larkin meditates only by describing and poems (a smaller number) in which he meditates by discussing. The latter tend not to come off, and this in spite of the fact that the poet has so definite a gift for conversing easily in verse. A poem that begins with an unselfconsciousness that attracts and draws the reader into reflecting with the poet on his subject falls away at the end, sometimes disastrously. 'Toads Revisited', in the present volume, begins and ends like this:

> Walking round in the park
> Should feel better than work:
> The lake, the sunshine,
> The grass to lie on,
> Blurred playground noises
> Beyond black-stockinged nurses—
> Not a bad place to be.
> But it doesn't suit me . . .
>
> No, give me my in-tray,
> My loaf-haired secretary,
> My shall-I-keep-the-call-in-Sir:
> What else can I answer
>
> When the lights come on at four
> At the end of another year?
> Give me your arm, old toad;
> Help me down Cemetery Road.

At the same time as they disappoint the reader these poems show up a certain weakness in purposeful effort on the poet's part. Mr. Larkin doesn't seem very concerned to reach an adequate statement or resolution of any problem he sets himself. He follows out and articulates a train of thought and feeling with a moderately subtle accuracy, and with an effect of going somewhere, but that latter then proves to be only an effect: the poem isn't really going anywhere and was perhaps never meant to and a more or less banal conclusion abruptly or forcedly ends it. The poet seems to articulate only for the sake of articulating, perhaps because that gives him some compensating sense of mastery. He almost certainly turns and returns to subjects because they are his genuine worries, but that is all. The weakness in purpose is less obvious in some of the descriptive poems because there is not in them so clear a movement forward to be disappointed. The longest poem in *The Whitsun Weddings*, the title-poem, seems to me better than the famous 'Church Going' of *The Less Deceived*: it is not really so much less ambitious as it might seem and is almost entirely free of the nervous smartness that ruins the latter poem for me. ('Church Going' is in its substance so very near to being like the reflections and sentiments of a mild bore that I find the conceit of its smart manner very irritating). But even 'The Whitsun Weddings' is a little awkwardly top-heavy, the successful ending not being quite strong enough to give meaning to all the small well-rendered details that have preceded. These are again partly there for their own sakes and it is as if Mr. Larkin is deliberately and over-carefully going for the smallest things because of their easiness. It is notable, finally, that Mr. Larkin successfully moves between the inner experience and the observed appearances when the inner experience is his own or shared by him. When he makes the following reflections on the bridal couples who are all in the Whitsun train he is travelling in, he is unimaginative and unconvincing:

> none
> Thought of the others they would never meet
> Or how their lives would all contain this hour.

How did he know? And he is appealing to a lazily unthinking and ignorant response when he tries to call up an image of the bleakness of the young mothers' lives in 'Afternoons' with these lines:

> Behind them, at intervals,
> Stand husbands in skilled trades,
> An estateful of washing,
> And the albums, lettered
> *Our Wedding*, lying
> Near the television

It is not a dramatic poem, about the deadness of what a man sees when he is in low spirits.

The pleasure of recognising some well-caught externals of modern life in Mr. Larkin's poetry (as in Mr. Betjeman's) is partly a corrupt pleasure, because there is nothing underneath, just as the pleasure of recognising some of our own experience in Mr. Larkin's is partly corrupt because the experience is small, ordinary and depressed while it is not seen or felt in its relations with other experience. At best, though rarely, a very pale tenderness of feeling partly modifies the effect of the cold liveliness and observation and self-anxiety.

ANTHONY THWAITE
From "The Poetry of Philip Larkin"
The Survival of Poetry, ed. Martin Dodsworth
1970, pp. 37–55

There is a certain irony about sitting down to write a critical paper on the poetry of Philip Larkin, when one remembers some remarks of Larkin's about 'poetry as syllabus' and 'the dutiful mob that signs on every September'. Larkin needs no prolegomena, no exegesis: there is no necessary bibliography, no suggested reading, except the poems themselves. In a straightforward Wordsworthian sense, he is a man speaking to men (though his detractors might put it that he is too often simply a chap chatting to chaps). Although few of the poems need any background knowledge beyond that which any reader of English may be supposed to command, when such knowledge is necessary Larkin himself has generally provided it, in his rare but always relevant and commonsensical statements about his work. Beyond that, I can only stand witness to my conviction that he is our finest living poet—and not in any '*Victor Hugo, hélas*' sense—and go on to draw out and underline what seem to me to be his themes, his special voice and his peculiar excellences. . . .

The North Ship is now gently and self-deprecatingly dismissed by Larkin. Indeed, I want to make no great claims for it. It is interesting in the way that any considerable poet's juvenilia are interesting, with a phrase here, a line there, suggesting or prefiguring what was to come. Larkin has written:

> Looking back, I find in the poems not one abandoned self but several—the ex-schoolboy, for whom Auden was the only alternative to 'old-fashioned' poetry; the undergraduate, whose work a friend affably characterized as 'Dylan Thomas, but you've a sentimentality that's all your own'; and the immediately post-Oxford self, isolated in Shropshire with a complete Yeats stolen from the local girls' school.

I find few traces of Auden; certainly nothing as Audenesque as 'Ultimatum', though 'Conscript' has something of 'In Time of War' about it, particularly the first two stanzas:

> The ego's county he inherited
> From those who tended it like farmers; had
> All knowledge that the study merited,
> The requisite contempt of good and bad;
>
> But one Spring day his land was violated;
> A bunch of horsemen curtly asked his name,
> Their leader in a different dialect stated
> A war was on for which he was to blame

I can find nothing at all of Dylan Thomas; perhaps the friend whom Larkin quotes was commenting on poems which did not in fact get selected for *The North Ship*. It is true that a good deal of *Poetry Quarterly* and *Poetry London* in that 1943–53 decade was taken up with Dylanism, and it might be thought surprising that Larkin escaped it; but as he has said:

> The principal poets of the day—Eliot, Auden, Dylan Thomas, Betjeman—were all speaking out loud and clear, and there was no reason to become entangled in the undergrowth . . . except by a failure of judgement.

Admiration for Dylan Thomas didn't then, and doesn't now, necessarily carry in its wake base imitation.

But of Yeats there is a predominance in *The North Ship*:

> Not because I liked his personality or understood his ideas but out of infatuation with his music . . . In fairness to myself it must be admitted that it is a particularly potent music, pervasive as garlic, and has ruined many a better talent.

. . . In the 1966 re-publication of *The North Ship*, Larkin included an additional poem 'as a coda'. Rather, it is a prelude. In his preface to the Faber edition, he tells how in early 1946 he began to read Hardy's poems, having known him before only as a novelist: 'as regards his verse', Larkin says:

I shared Lytton Strachey's verdict that 'the gloom is not even relieved by a little elegance of diction'. This opinion did not last long; if I were asked to date its disappearance, I should guess it was the morning I first read 'Thoughts of Phena At News of Her Death'.

Larkin's added poem (XXXII in the re-published *The North Ship*) first appeared in the little pamphlet, *XX Poems*, which Larkin brought out at his own expense in 1951. (There were 100 copies of this pamphlet, most of them—as ruefully described by Larkin—sent to well-known literary persons, the majority of whom failed even to acknowledge it, presumably because he had under-stamped the envelopes at a time when the postal charges had just been increased. It was still possible to order it in early 1954, as I did through Blackwells in Oxford, and to pay 4/6d for it. Its present dealers' value has been quoted at £20.) The first stanza of the new poem immediately establishes not just the new presence of Hardy (it is in fact much less like Hardy than the Yeatsian pieces are like Yeats) but a new way in Larkin of finding and using material. The observation is exact, the framing of mood and incident within description makes a perfect fit:

> Waiting for breakfast, while she brushed her hair,
> I looked down at the empty hotel yard
> Once meant for coaches. Cobblestones were wet,
> But sent no light back to the loaded sky,
> Sunk as it was with mist down to the roofs.
> Drainpipes and fire-escape climbed up
> Past rooms still burning their electric light:
> I thought: Featureless morning, featureless night.

What Hardy taught Larkin was that a man's own life, its suddenly surfacing perceptions, its 'moments of vision', its most seemingly casual epiphanies (in the Joycean sense), could fit whole and without compromise into poems. There did not need to be any large-scale system of belief, any such circumambient framework as Yeats constructed within which to fashion his work: Larkin has dismissed all that as the 'myth-kitty'. Like Parolles in *All's Well*, he seems to say: 'Simply the thing I am shall make me live.' As Larkin himself put it in a radio programme on Hardy:

> When I came to Hardy it was with the sense of relief
> that I didn't have to try and jack myself up to a
> concept of poetry that lay outside my own life . . .
> One could simply relapse back into one's own life
> and write from it.

Looking again at 'Waiting for Breakfast', one sees that what it turns into is an address to the Muse, though in no sense that that habitual Muse-invoker, Robert Graves, would accept. The 'I' of the poem has spent the night with a girl, and his mood is one of almost surprised disbelief that he is so happy:

> Turning, I kissed her,
> Easily for sheer joy tipping the balance to love.

Yet whatever sparks the poet into writing poems doesn't seem to start from such a mood. 'Perfection of the life, or of the work': one is pushed back to Yeats again, to the sort of conundrum he poses there. Will absorption in the girl and in the happiness she seems to bring stifle his poems?

> Are you jealous of her?
> Will you refuse to come till I have sent
> Her terribly away, importantly live
> Part invalid, part baby, and part saint?

This is the first poem of Larkin's maturity, and it links interestingly with the earliest poem in *The Less Deceived*: 'Wedding-Wind', which also dates from 1946. But there is one large difference. The voice of the poem here is in no useful sense that of the poet: a woman on the morning after her wedding night is wonderingly turning over the fact of her happiness, with the force of the high wind 'bodying-forth' not only the irrelevance of such violent elements to the new delight she has found, but also the way in which the whole of creation seems somehow to be in union with her state:

> Can it be borne, this bodying-forth by wind
> Of joy my actions turn on, like a thread
> Carrying beads? Shall I be let to sleep
> Now this perpetual morning shares my bed?
> Can even death dry up
> These new delighted lakes, conclude
> Our kneeling as cattle by all-generous waters?

'Wedding-Wind' is the only completely happy poem of Larkin's, the only one in which there is a total acceptance of joy. Perhaps that is why it is liked by some people who otherwise find him too bleak a poet for their taste. Yet it is happy, joyous, without being serene: it implies, in its three closing questions, the impermanence of the very happiness it celebrates, the possibility of its being blown and scattered, made restless as the horses have been and

> All's ravelled under the sun by the wind's blowing.

The poem's three questions remind one of the three questions at the end of 'Waiting for Breakfast', suggesting that the balance of 'sheer joy' can as easily be tipped in the other direction.

This emotional wariness, which can too easily—and inaccurately—be labelled as pessimism, is at the roots of Larkin's sensibility. Its fine-drawn expression can be found in most of the poems in *The Less Deceived* and *The Whitsun Weddings*. And it is at this point, when Larkin in 1946 wrote 'Waiting for Breakfast' and 'Wedding-Wind', that it seems unprofitable to go on examining his poems in a supposed chronological order of composition; for from now on the personality is an achieved and consistent one, each poem re-stating or adding another facet to what has gone before. Critics who tried to sniff out 'development' when *The Whitsun Weddings* followed nine years after *The Less Deceived*, or who showed disappointment when they found none, were wasting their time or were demonstrating that Larkin was at no time their man. The sixty-one poems in these two books, and the handful that have appeared in periodicals since, make a total unified impact. There have been rich years and lean years (Larkin's remark that he writes about four poems a year shouldn't be taken too literally in any statistical sense), but only quantitatively.

Yet though there has been no radical development in Larkin's poetry during these years, the number of tones and voices he has used has been a great deal more varied than some critics have given him credit for. The 'emotional wariness' can in some of the poems be better defined as an agnostic stoicism, close to the mood (though not to the origin of that mood) of Arnold's 'Dover Beach'. And what he is both agnostic and stoical about is time, the passing of time, and 'the only end of age': death. Indeed, if it had not been used perfectly properly for another literary achievement (and in any case Larkin might reject it as being too presumptuously resonant), 'The Music of Time' could serve as a title for all Larkin's post-1946 poetry.

There are poems in which time, and death as the yardstick of time, are seen in an abstract or generalized context: 'Ignorance', 'Triple Time', 'Next, Please', 'Nothing to Be Said', 'Going', 'Wants', 'Age'. They are abstract or generalized in that they don't start from some posited situation, though their language and imagery are concrete enough: the street, sky and landscape of 'Triple Time', the 'armada of promises' of 'Next, Please', the quickly shuffled references ('Small-statured cross-faced tribes/And cobble-close families/In mill-towns on dark mornings') of 'Nothing to be Said'. All our hours, however we spend them,

> advance
> On death equally slowly.
> And saying so to some
> Means nothing; others it leaves
> Nothing to be said.

This great blankness at the heart of things has to be endured—that is what I meant by stoicism. We bolster up our ignorance, and make ourselves able to bear our long diminution and decay, by being busy with the present and—when we are young—dreaming about the future:

> An air lambent with adult enterprise.

So, too, we look at the past, and cling to and preserve those bits of it that belong to us, which we call our memories. It is no accident that of the jazz which Larkin regards with such enthusiasm, it is the blues that he writes about with most feeling (in his prose pieces, that is; for example, in his record reviews in the *Daily Telegraph*. Only one poem, 'For Sidney Bechet', celebrates this 'natural noise of good'). For the blues are thick with the searchings and regrets of memory.

In an often-quoted statement made in 1955, Larkin said:

> I write poems to preserve things I have seen/thought/ felt (if I may so indicate a composite and complex experience) both for myself and for others, though I feel that my prime responsibility is to the experience itself, which I am trying to keep from oblivion for its own sake. Why I should do this I have no idea, but I think the impulse to preserve lies at the bottom of all art.

More recently, commenting on *The Whitsun Weddings* in the Poetry Book Society Bulletin, he wrote:

> Some years ago I came to the conclusion that to write a poem was to construct a verbal device that would preserve an experience indefinitely by reproducing it in whoever read the poem.

Though he went on to qualify this, the 'verbal pickling' (as he put it) is seen to be the process at work in many of his best and best-known poems: in his two most sustained efforts, 'Church Going' and 'The Whitsun Weddings', and also in 'Mr Bleaney', 'Reference Back', 'I Remember, I Remember', 'Dockery and Son', and elsewhere. All of these start from some quite specifically recalled incident which becomes, through the course of the poem, 'an experience' in the sense intended by Larkin in that prose note. A casual dropping-in to a deserted church; a long train-journey on Whit Saturday; the taking of new lodgings; a visit home to one's widowed mother; another train-journey, which takes one through one's long-abandoned birthplace; a visit in middle age to one's old college at Oxford—these 'human shows' inhabit an area Hardy would have recognized, and each both preserves the experience and allows it to move out into other areas not predicted by the casually 'placing' opening lines. Indeed, in several of them the placing, the observation, is steadily sustained for a great part of the poem, as if the 'impulse to preserve' were determined to fix and set the moment with every aspect carefully delineated, every shade faithfully recorded. I remember Larkin writing to tell me, when I was about to produce the first broadcast reading (in fact the first public appearance) of 'The Whitsun Weddings', that what I should aim to get from the actor was a level, even a plodding, descriptive note, until the mysterious last lines, when the poem should suddenly 'lift off the ground':

> there swelled
> A sense of falling, like an arrow-shower
> Sent out of sight, somewhere becoming rain.

'Impossible, I know,' he said comfortingly; though I think that first reader (Gary Watson) made a very fair approximation to it.

If 'The Whitsun Weddings' is a poem of one carefully held note until the very end, 'Church Going' is more shifting in its stance and tone. Both poems are written in long, carefully-patterned rhyming stanzas (Larkin once said to me that he would like to write a poem with such elaborate stanzas that one could wander round in them as in the aisles and side-chapels of some great cathedral), but whereas each ten-line stanza of 'The Whitsun Weddings' seems caught on the pivot of the short four-syllable second line, pushing it forward on to the next smooth run, the nine-line stanza of 'Church Going' is steady throughout, the iambic pentameter having to hold together—as it successfully does—the three unequal sections: the first two stanzas, easy, colloquial, mockingly casual; then the four stanzas of reflection and half-serious questioning, becoming weightier and slower as they move towards the rhetorical solidity of the final stanza's first line:

> A serious house on serious earth it is

'Church Going' has become one of the type-poems of the century, at the very least 'the showpiece of the "New Movement"', as G. S. Fraser put it; much discussed in every sixth-form English class and literary extension-course, anthologized and duplicated, so that I sometimes feel it has become too thoroughly institutionalized and placed. Larkin has quoted Hardy's supposed remarks (on *Tess*) on the subject: 'If I'd known it was going to be so popular, I'd have tried to make it better,' and one senses a wry surprise in that, as one does in his comment that after it was initially published in the *Spectator* (after first being lost, and then held in proof, for about a year), he 'had a letter from one of the paper's subscribers enclosing a copy of the Gospel of St John':

> In fact it has always been well liked. I think this is because it is about religion, and has a serious air that conceals the fact that its tone and argument are entirely secular.

Here Larkin is perfectly properly fending off the common misconception that it is a 'religious' poem. It is not so, in any dogmatic or sectarian sense. It dips not even the most gingerly of toes into metaphysics, makes not even the most tentative gestures towards 'belief' ('But superstition, like belief, must die'). What it does do is to acknowledge the human hunger for order and ritual (such as go with 'marriage, and birth, / And death, and thoughts of these'), and to recognize the power of the past, of inherited tradition, made emblematic in this abandoned piece of ground,

> Which, he once heard, was proper to grow wise in,
> If only that so many dead lie round.

But 'Church Going' is not a perfect poem, though a fine one, and it is not Larkin's best. Donald Hall has maintained that it would be a better one if it were cut by a third, and without accepting that kind of drastic surgery (American editors have a reputation for being the 'heaviest' in the world, leaning on their authors in a way that has more to do with power than with support) it is fair to say that it has some amusing but distracting divagations—particularly in the middle section—of a sort which one doesn't find in the equally circumstantial but more unified 'Whitsun Weddings'. That Irish sixpence, for example—many readers don't know whether they are supposed to laugh here or not (many do in any case); but if the ruined church which started the poem off was in Ireland, as Larkin in a broadcast said it was, wouldn't it make a difference? Does he mean to demonstrate the sort of unthinking piety that agnostics hold to out of habit, or is he chalking up another mild self-revelatory bit of schoolboyish japing, as in the mouthing of 'Here endeth' from the lectern? (What Larkin intends of *that* performance comes out very clearly in his Marvell Press recording.) One doesn't know; and in a poem so specific this is a flaw.

To go on about the Irish sixpence at such length may well seem absurdly trivial, but the uncertainty it suggests is not unique in the poem. One has the feeling that Larkin knows more than he chooses to admit, with the pyx brought in so effortlessly and the rood-lofts sniggeringly made much of: naming them implies knowledge of what they are, and one doesn't need to be a 'ruin-bibber, randy for antique' to recognize such things. They are part of one's general store of unsorted knowledge, like knowing who A. W. Carr or Jimmy Yancey (or, indeed, Sidney Bechet) were. Here, without much relish, I am drawn into mildly deploring what might be called the Yah-Boo side of Larkin's work—a side not often apparent, which he shares sporadically with his admired (and admiring) fellow-undergraduate and old friend from St John's, Kingsley Amis. (Incidentally, *XX Poems* was dedicated to Amis, and Amis dedicated *Lucky Jim* to Larkin.) The 'filthy Mozart' type of jeer is never given the extended outing with Larkin that it is with Amis, and one has to be aware of personae and so forth, but the edgy and gratuitous coarseness of 'Get stewed. Books are a load of crap' and 'What does it mean? Sod all' have always made me wince a bit. This might show a feeble prudishness in me, but rather I feel that Larkin's poems can get by without such manly nudging.

It could be argued that these things are part of Larkin's apt contemporary tone; certainly he has such a tone, more usefully heard in 'Mr Bleaney', 'Toads', 'Toads Revisited', 'Reasons for Attendance', 'Poetry of Departures', and most startlingly in 'Sunny Prestatyn'. In this last poem the calculated violence seems exactly and inevitably matched with the brutalizing of the language: those lunging monosyllables are dead right—and 'dead' is right too. 'A hunk of coast' is drawn into the stabbing words that follow—'slapped up', 'snaggle-toothed and boss-eyed', 'Huge tits and a fissured crotch', 'scrawls', 'tuberous cock and balls', 'a knife/Or something to stab right through'. Like the faded photographs that must lie behind 'MCMXIV', like the medieval figures in 'An Arundel Tomb' that 'Time has transfigured into . . . untruth', the blandishments of the girl on the poster have (with the help of human agency) been reduced to the wrecks of time. As in the lines of the body, in 'Skin', she is the end-product

> Of the continuous coarse
> Sand-laden wind, time.

'Sunny Prestatyn' is the most extreme of Larkin's poems about diminution, decay, death. Elsewhere, he more often brings to them what—in a review of Betjeman's poems—he has called 'an almost moral tactfulness'. 'Faith Healing', 'Ambulances', 'Love Songs in Age', 'At Grass', 'An Arundel Tomb', the more recent and uncollected 'Sad Steps'—all, with perhaps the exception of the last, stand at a reserved but certainly not unfeeling distance from their ostensible subjects. In the broadcast I have already quoted from, Larkin said:

'I sometimes think that the most successful poems are those in which subjects appear to float free from the preoccupations that chose them, and to exist in their own right, reassembled—one hopes—in the eternity of imagination.' And he went on to say, introducing 'Love Songs in Age':

'I can't for the life of me think why I should have wanted to write about Victorian drawing-room ballads: probably I must have heard one on the wireless, and thought how terrible it must be for an old lady to hear one of these songs she had learnt

as a girl and reflect how different life had turned out to be.' 'How different life had turned out to be'—here time is shown as the gradual destroyer of illusions. Like the advertisement hoardings in 'Essential Beauty', showing us serenely and purely 'how life should be', the old sheet music summons up and sets blankly before us two things: that lambent air which the future promised, and that present which has hardened 'into all we've got/And how we got it.' ('Dockery and Son'.) Christopher Ricks (who has written particularly well on Larkin) has pointed out how in 'Love Songs in Age' the three sentences of the poem gradually narrow down, from the expansive openness of the first, with its careful proliferation of detail and its almost mimetic lyricism ('Word after sprawling hyphenated word'), through the briefer concentration on 'that much-mentioned brilliance, love', to the blank acknowledgement that love has indeed not solved or satisfied or 'set unchangeably in order':

> So
> To pile them back, to cry,
> Was hard, without lamely admitting how
> It had not done so then, and could not now.

That last sentence, so much less serpentine than the others, seems the last brief twist of the knife.

Ricks has also pointed out one of the hallmarks of Larkin's style: those negatives which define the limits and shades of the world, and which coldly confront our flimsy illusions. *Un, in, im, dis*—with such small modifiers Larkin determines the edges of things, which blur into

> the solving emptiness
> That lies just under all we do.

So we find *unfakable, unspoilt, undiminished, unmolesting, unfingermarked, unhindered, unchangeably,* set against *unsatisfactory, unlucky, unworkable, unswept, uninformed, unanswerable, unrecommended, untruthful* and *untruth. Imprecisions, imperfect, incomplete* and *inexplicable* jostle with *disbelief, disproved, disused* and *dismantled.* They seem to share something—in their modifying, their determination to record an exact shade of response rather than a wilder approximation—with another hallmark: those compounds which one begins to find as early as the poems in *The North Ship. Laurel-surrounded, fresh-peeled, branch-arrested, Sunday-full, organ-frowned-on, harsh-named, differently-dressed, luminously-peopled, solemn-sinister*—there are over fifty others in *The Less Deceived* and *The Whitsun Weddings* alone.

Compound-formations bring Hopkins to mind, though his are of course a good deal more strenuous and draw more attention to themselves than Larkin's. Yet Hopkins is, perhaps curiously, a poet Larkin much admires. Indeed, though he has been at some pains to admit how narrow his tastes in poetry are, Larkin's acknowledged enthusiasms show a wider range of appreciation than he seems to give himself credit for. Without at all being a regular pundit in the literary papers, he has written with warmth and depth about not only Hardy but also William Barnes, Christina Rossetti, Wilfred Owen, and among living poets, Auden (pre-1940), Betjeman and Stevie Smith. Not much of a common denominator there, and of them all it is only Hardy who seems to have left any trace on Larkin's own work, and that in no important verbal way. In fact Larkin is very much his own poet. His impressment into the Movement, in such anthologies as Enright's *Poets of the 1950s* and Conquest's *New Lines*, did no harm and may have done some good, in that it drew attention to his work in the way that any seemingly concerted action (cf. The Group) makes a bigger initial impact than a lone voice. But really he shares little with the 'neutral tone' of what have been called the Faceless Fifties: anonymity and impersonality are not at all characteristics of his work, and the voice that comes across is far more individual than those of such properly celebrated poets as Muir, Graves and R. S. Thomas, to pick three who have never (so far as I know) been accused of hunting with any pack or borrowing anyone's colouring.

The case against Larkin, as I have heard it, seems to boil down to 'provincialism' (Charles Tomlinson), 'genteel belly-aching' (Christopher Logue), and a less truculent but rather exasperated demur that any poet so negative can be so good (A. Alvarez). Well, he is provincial in the sense that he doesn't subscribe to the current cant that English poets can profitably learn direct lessons from what poetry is going on in Germany or France or Hungary or up the Black Mountain: poetry is, thank heaven, a long way from falling into an 'international style', such as one finds in painting, sculpture, architecture and music, and such validly 'international' pieces as I *have* seen (e.g. in concrete poetry) are at best peripherally elegant and at worst boring and pointless. 'Genteel bellyaching' and 'negative' are really making the same objection, the first more memorably and amusingly than the second. There is a sense in which Larkin does define by negatives; I have made the point already. He is wary in front of experience, as who should not be: one doesn't put in the same set of scales Auschwitz and the realization that one is getting older, or the thermo-nuclear bomb and the sense that most love is illusory. Yet the fact that Larkin hasn't, in his poems, confronted head-on the death camps or the Bomb (or Vietnam, or Che Guevara) doesn't make him, by definition, minor. His themes—love, change, disenchantment, the mystery and inexplicableness of the past's survival and death's finality—are unshakably major. So too, I think, are the assurance of his cadences and the inevitable rightness of his language at their best. From what even Larkin acknowledges as the almost Symbolist rhetoric of

> Such attics cleared of me! Such absences!

to the simple but remorseless

> They show us what we have as it once was,
> Blindingly undiminished, just as though
> By acting differently we could have kept it so

is a broad span for any poet to command. And those haunting closing lines to many poems ('Church Going', 'The Whitsun Weddings', 'No Road', 'Next, Please', 'Faith Healing', 'Ambulances', 'Dockery and Son', 'An Arundel Tomb', 'Sad Steps'—the list becomes long, but not absurdly so): they have an authentic gravity, a memorable persistence. I think that Larkin's work will survive; and what may survive is his preservation of 'the true voice of feeling' of a man who was representative of the mid-20th century hardly at all, except in negatives—which is, when you come to think about it, one way in which to survive the mid-20th century.

CALVIN BEDIENT
"Philip Larkin"
Eight Contemporary Poets
1974, pp. 69–94

English poetry has never been so persistently out in the cold as it is with Philip Larkin—a poet who (contrary to Wordsworth's view of the calling) rejoices not more but less than other men in the spirit of life that is in him. Frost is a perennial boy, Hardy a fighter, by comparison. The load of snow, soiled and old, stays on the roof in poem after poem and, rubbing a clear space at the window, Larkin is there to mourn once again a world without generative fire. Well, it is just as he

knew it would be, though now and then something surprising—a sheen of sunlight, some flutter of life—almost makes him wish for a moment that he could frolic out of doors.

Not that Larkin has wholly a mind of winter. A neighbourly snowman, he sometimes wears his hat tipped jauntily, and smiles and makes you laugh. Notice the drooping carrot nose in the mockingly titled 'Wild Oats':

> About twenty years ago
> Two girls came in where I worked—
> A bosomy English rose
> And her friend in specs I could talk to.
> Faces in those days sparked
> The whole shooting-match off, and I doubt
> If ever one had like hers:
> But it was the friend I took out,
>
> And in seven years after that
> Wrote over four hundred letters,
> Gave a ten-guinea ring
> I got back in the end, and met
> At numerous cathedral cities
> Unknown to the clergy. I believe
> I met beautiful twice. She was trying
> Both times (so I thought) not to laugh

In fact this is more lively than (say) the typical poem in *The Oxford Book of English Verse*. A witty and amiable snowman, then, with a clown's rueful sense of himself, and a clown's way of asking a genial tolerance for, indeed an easy complicity in, his ancient familiarity with defeat.

Yet where the clown, however little and stepped on, is indefatigably hopeful, Larkin is unillusioned, with a metaphysical zero in his bones. Larger than his world, outside it, he bears it before him, in chagrin, like a block of ice. While the clown is merely done to, Larkin in a sense does in the world, denying it every virtue in advance. Behind the paint a countenance of stone . . .

This dismissal of the world, at the same time as it ensures his nullity, is a proud, self-affirming act. Yet at times his complaint against life is precisely that it has never attempted to lure him. Its very indifference, its failure to have any use for him, makes him want to reject it. 'Life is first boredom', he writes in 'Dockery and Son', speaking of his own life but (so overwhelming is the tedium) generalizing, too. And in 'I Remember, I Remember', he elaborates devastatingly:

> By now I've got the whole place clearly charted.
> Our garden, first: where I did not invent
> Blinding theologies of flowers and fruits,
> And wasn't spoken to by an old hat.
> And here we have that splendid family
>
> I never ran to when I got depressed,
> The boys all biceps and the girls all chest,
> Their comic Ford, their farm where I could be
> 'Really myself'. I'll show you, come to that,
> The bracken where I never trembling sat,
>
> Determined to go through with it; where she
> Lay back, and 'all became a burning mist'.
> And, in those offices, my doggerel
> Was not set up in blunt ten-point, nor read
> By a distinguished cousin of the mayor,
>
> Who didn't call and tell my father *There
> Before us, had we the gift to see ahead*

Yet it is just this accident of temperament that brings Larkin into line with contemporary history—not with its actual resilience and stubborn energy but with its contagious fears: his very cells seeming formed to index the withering of the ideal, of romance, of possibility, that characterizes post-war thought. If Larkin is not merely admired but loved, it is partly because, finding poetry and humour even in sterility, he makes it bearable: he shows that it can be borne with grace and gentleness. He arrived at the right time to blend in with the disenfranchised youth of the Second World War ('At an age when self-importance would have been normal', he writes in the Preface to his novel *Jill*, 'events cut us ruthlessly down to size'). And although his depression, like Hardy's, is as if from before the ages, he has continued to seem the poet mid-century England required, his dogged parochialism reflecting the shrunken will of the nation, his bare details the democratic texture of the times.

Larkin's distinction from other nihilists lies in his domestication of the void: he has simply taken nullity for granted, found it as banal as the worn places in linoleum. Other nihilists, by comparison, are full of emotional and technical protest. With frighteningly poised hysteria, a Donald Barthelme dips his readers into a whirlpool of received pretensions that have just been dissolved by parody; a Robert Lowell is tragically grand, a Samuel Beckett savagely sardonic, a Harold Pinter sinister as a toyed-with knife . . . Larkin is plain and passive. Yet these qualities, far from letting him down, prove almost as striking as brilliant inventiveness—striking for their very simplicity. Characteristically Larkin presents not a 'world elsewhere' but life 'just here', denuded of libido, sentiment, obvious imaginative transvaluation. Like Hardy and Frost he uses imagination precisely in order to show what life is like when imagination is taken out of it.

> 'This was Mr Bleaney's room. He stayed
> The whole time he was at the Bodies, till
> They moved him.' Flowered curtains, thin and
>   frayed,
> Fall to within five inches of the sill,
>
> Whose window shows a strip of building land,
> Tussocky, littered. 'Mr Bleaney took
> My bit of garden properly in hand.'
> Bed, upright chair, sixty-watt bulb, no hook
>
> Behind the door, no room for books or bags—
> 'I'll take it'

In everything except effect, Larkin is thus the weakling of the current group of nihilists, or the pacifist, the one who never stands up to the niggling heart of existence, throwing down even the stones of fantasy, technical dazzle, fierce jokes—the devices of an adventurous imagination—as being in any case useless against the Goliath of the void. His achievement has been the creation of imaginative bareness, a penetrating confession of poverty.

This achievement came only with difficulty, Larkin respecting bareness so much and misapprehending the function of imagination so greatly that at first he tried to keep the two apart, like honour from shame. Imagination? The dubious water spilling over the dam the world erects in front of the ego. From the beginning Larkin was the sort of young man, old before his time, whose stern wish is to put aside childish things. 'Very little that catches the imagination', he says in *The London Magazine* of February 1962, 'can get its clearance from either the intelligence or the moral sense.' 'There is not much pleasure', he adds, 'to be got from the truth about things as anyone sees it. . . . What one does enjoy writing—what the imagination is only too ready to help with—is, in some form or other, compensation, assertion of oneself in an indifferent or hostile environment, demonstration . . . that one is in command of a situation, and so on.' The imagination, moreover, is a fetishist, 'being classic and austere, or loading every rift with ore . . . with no responsible basis or rational encouragement.'

Larkin's problem, then, has been to write in the grim countenance of these views, with their pride in naked endurance, their fierce modesty—his limited output no doubt confessing to the difficulty. And if at first he took up fiction as well as poetry, it was because of its traditional alliance with 'the truth about things'. His fiction became the exercise ground of his lucidity. Both *Jill* (1946) and *A Girl in Winter* (1947) creep coldly to their conclusions. Though necessarily works of imagination—works *conceived*—their conceptions are unexcited, even numb. Imagination, they imply, is nugatory, a nail scratching a dream on ice. And so they labour against themselves. Virtually nothing happens to their youthful protagonists; crocuses doomed to fill with snow, they have only to sense futility to give way to it. The pale Oxford undergraduate in the first learns from a visit to his home town, recently bombed, 'how little anything matters', 'how appallingly little life is'. Then a dream tells him that, 'whether fulfilled or unfulfilled', love dies. This is enough to destroy his desire for the innocent Jill. He decides to die, as it were, before his death, so as to die as little as possible. In *A Girl in Winter*, too, wartime lends plausibility to a disillusionment that in fact seems pursued. And again the most ordinary relationships fail, as if there were something radically wrong with the human heart. The heroine, Katherine, finally repudiates 'the interplay of herself and other people'. With resolution, not in self-pity, beyond calling back, even gratefully, she steps out into a lucid solitude. At the close she envisions the 'orderly slow procession', as of an 'ice floe', of her permanently frozen desires: 'Yet their passage was not saddening. Unsatisfied dreams rose and fell about them, crying out against their implacability, but in the end glad that such order, such destiny, existed. Against this knowledge the heart, the will, and all that made for protest, could at last sleep.' And so she chooses to abstain from life, convinced that the fruit is anyway infested.

Given not only these passive protagonists but a starved-sparrow manner and a merely *determined* disenchantment, totally lacking in the passion either of truth or regret, the novels could not help seeming too long, indeed superfluous after the drain pipes, the snow. Larkin had yet to see that his thorough disbelief in adventure—even a Beckett shows a taste for mock adventure—necessitated the briefest of literary forms, and that the surest way to make the humanly sterile emotionally forceful is to place it in the midst of a poem, where, dwarfed by the glorious remembrances of the medium, it can have a shivering significance.

Meanwhile his poetry was the lyrical run-off of his lucidity. The poems in *The North Ship* (1946) treat the same themes as the novels—a world eaten through at the root by time, the wisdom of taking 'the grave's part', the failure of love—with all the runaway outcry that the novels stiffly restrained. Seeking at once the altitudes of the great lyrists of his youth, Yeats and Dylan Thomas, Larkin rises too high for his leaden themes:

> I was sleeping, and you woke me
> To walk on the chilled shore
> Of a night with no memory,
> Till your voice forsook my ear
>
> Till your two hands withdrew
> And I was empty of tears,
> On the edge of a bricked and streeted sea
> And a cold hill of stars.

And again:

> And in their blazing solitude
> The stars sang in their sockets through the night:
> 'Blow bright, blow bright
> The coal of this unquickened world.'

So Larkin sings as the blade comes down, is ardent about the ice in the fire of youth. Fulsomely embracing poetry as a legitimized form of 'compensation', he wrote as if it were unnecessary to be sensible in it, permissible to speak of 'bricked and streeted' seas or of stars that, while blazing, begged to be ignited. A remarkable discrepancy: the novels prematurely grizzled, the poems puerile.

Larkin had yet to reconcile the supposed unpleasure of truth with the pleasure of imagination. This he was now to do abruptly, being one of those poets who undergo an almost magical transformation between their first and second volume. It was Hardy who showed him that imagination could treat 'properly truthful' themes truthfully yet with acute delicacy, deliberate power. Never mind that Hardy's poems are greyly literal: they get into you like a rainy day. 'When I came to Hardy', Larkin says, 'it was with the sense of relief that I didn't have to try and jack myself up to a concept of poetry that lay outside my own life—this is perhaps what I felt Yeats was trying to make me do. One could simply relapse back into one's own life and write from it.' Again: 'Hardy taught one to feel . . . and he taught one as well to have confidence in what one felt.'

In truth, Larkin's themes belong to that great negative order of ideas that has always proved the most potent in art. We cannot help ourselves: we home to tragedy—optimism in art commonly leaving us feeling deprived of some deeper truth. Nothing is of more initial advantage to a poet than a horizon of clouds. For pathos makes us irresistibly present to ourselves, silhouettes us against a backdrop of fate, renders us final for the imagination. And to achieve it Larkin, as he now saw, had only to 'feel'—feel simply, without exaggeration. This itself meant that he had to measure ordinary life, life as he knew it, with the rigour of regret. In his novels he had passed beyond protest into a limbo of resignation. In *The North Ship*, on the other hand, he had exhibited a preposterous surprise and anguish—as if sterility were not, after all, the scene on which his blind rose every morning. Now he needed to find a manner at once warm and cold, steeped in futility but not extinguished by it. He had to open bare cupboards that would speak of all that might have been in them.

And so he does in his second volume, *The Less Deceived* (1955), and again in his third and most recent, *The Whitsun Weddings* (1964). Here is 'As Bad as a Mile':

Watching the shied core
Striking the basket, skidding across the floor,
Shows less and less of luck, and more and more

Of failure spreading back up the arm
Earlier and earlier, the unraised hand calm,
The apple unbitten in the palm.

What redoubtable depths of acceptance in the calm of that unraised hand. Even so, the close-up of the unbitten apple proves affecting: if the poem is stoic about the end, it is without prejudice to the pleasure preceding it; it is stoic with regret. What is more, here Larkin brings the lofty literary sorrow of *The North Ship* down from 'black flowers', 'birds crazed with flight', and wintry drums, to the level of the everyday, where, no longer diffuse, it can be felt like pain in a vital organ. And, neither egoistic nor fetishistic, imagination has now become only a way the truth has of entering us all at once, swiftly and completely, in a context of value. Far from being an evasion of the truth, it is a hammer for the nail, the poignancy secreted in the prosaic.

Larkin's poems now take on the brute force of circumstantial evidence. Like sour smoke, the odour of actual days hangs about them. They have an unusual authenticity; they form a reliving. Even when the naming is general, it can have bite:

Home is so sad. It stays as it was left,
Shaped to the comfort of the last to go
As if to win them back. Instead, bereft
Of anyone to please, it withers so,
Having no heart to put aside the theft

And turn again to what it started as,
A joyous shot at how things ought to be,
Long fallen wide. You can see how it was:
Look at the pictures and the cutlery.
The music in the piano stool. That vase.

The final articles are as blunt as pointing fingers and, with the adjective *that*, the series ends in a conclusive jab. It amounts to instant trial and conviction. The vase stands exposed, empty as the atmosphere around it, coldly reduced to its potential function—a failure, a thing without love.

Many of Larkin's poems, however, have the specific density of descriptive detail—often autobiographical. Consider the first portion of 'Dockery and Son':

'Dockery was junior to you,
Wasn't he?' said the Dean. 'His son's here now.'
Death-suited, visitant, I nod. 'And do
You keep in touch with——' Or remember how
Black-gowned, unbreakfasted, and still half-tight
We used to stand before that desk, to give
'Our version' of 'these incidents last night'?
I try the door of where I used to live:
Locked. The lawn spreads dazzlingly wide.
A known bell chimes. I catch my train, ignored.
Canal and clouds and colleges subside
Slowly from view. But Dockery, good Lord,
Anyone up today must have been born
In '43, when I was twenty-one.
If he was younger, did he get this son
At nineteen, twenty? Was he that withdrawn

High-collared public-schoolboy, sharing rooms
With Cartwright who was killed? Well, it just shows
How much . . . How little . . . Yawning, I suppose
I fell asleep, waking at the fumes
And furnace-glares of Sheffield, where I changed,
And ate an awful pie, and walked along
The platform to its end to see the ranged
Joining and parting lines reflect a strong

    Unhindered moon

Here again pleasure and truth meet effortlessly. How casually the lawn and then the moon, both unhindered in beauty, set off hindered humanity. The detail is at once natural (though 'Death-suited' forces perception) and resonant. The poem has the simple fascination of an honestly reported life—even suggesting the moment to moment flow of consciousness. It possesses also a humble appeal of personality, a tone as unpressingly intimate as the touch of a hand on one's arm.

So it was that Larkin took the path of Edward Thomas, of Frost, of Hardy, and became a poet who looks at ordinary life through empty, silent air. His poems now sprang like snowdrops directly from the cruel cast of things, yet in themselves attaining beauty. And just as they now found their pathos in everyday things, so the void now spoke, in part, where day by day Larkin heard it, in the trite though sometimes pert and piquant language of the streets. Here was a language as sceptical as it was hardy, soiled with disappointment. Of a certain billboard beauty, 'Kneeling up on the sand / In tautened white satin', Larkin writes:

She was slapped up one day in March.
A couple of weeks, and her face
Was snaggle-toothed and boss-eyed;
Huge tits and a fissured crotch
Were scored well in, and the space
Between her legs held scrawls
That set her fairly astride
A tuberous cock and balls

Autographed *Titch Thomas*, while
Someone had used a knife
Or something to stab right through
The moustached lips of her smile.
She was too good for this life

By contrast, Larkin's words will not be too good for this life. They make room not only for the colloquial 'Or something' but—sympathetically—for words betraying the fascinated disgust of adolescent sexual emotion. Still, Larkin's regret that anything *should* be too good for this life shines through his contempt for the meretricious poster. He makes the common words sorrier than they know.

Larkin thus renews poetry from underneath, enlivening it with 'kiddies', 'stewed', 'just my lark', 'nippers', 'lob-lolly men', 'pisses', 'bash', 'dude', and more of the same. And yet his manner rises easily from the slangy to the dignified; its step is light, its range wide. Here it is as vernacular caricature, amused at itself:

When getting my nose in a book
Cured most things short of school,
It was worth ruining my eyes
To know I could still keep cool,
And deal out the old right hook
To dirty dogs twice my size

A degree up from this we find the almost aggressive slang of the poem on the billboard girl. Then comes the perky, street-flavoured simplicity of 'Toads', 'Wild Oats', 'Send No Money', or 'Self's the Man':

Oh, no one can deny
That Arnold is less selfish than I.
He's married a woman to stop her getting away
Now she's there all day

A step higher and the style rises from self-consciousness and begins to leave the street:

Talking in bed ought to be easiest,
Lying together there goes back so far,
An emblem of two people being honest

This is the plain style of most of Larkin's poems. And this plainness is sometimes heightened by rhythmical sculpturing, syntactical drama, or repetition, as in 'MCMXIV':

Never such innocence,
Never before or since,
As changed itself to past
Without a word—the men
Leaving the gardens tidy,
The thousands of marriages
Lasting a little while longer:
Never such innocence again

Whatever its degree of formality, the peculiarity of Larkin's style is an eloquent taciturnity: it betrays a reluctance to use words at all. If, as 'Ambulances' says, a 'solving emptiness . . . lies just under all we do', then Larkin's words, as if preparing to be swallowed up, will make themselves as lean as they can—nothingness, they assert, will not fatten on them. Indeed, they seem to have soaked a long age in a vinegar that dissolves illusions. Such is the impression they make in 'As Bad as a Mile', and here again in 'Toads Revisited':

Walking around in the park
Should feel better than work:
The lake, the sunshine,
The grass to lie on,

Blurred playground noises
Beyond black-stockinged nurses—
Not a bad place to be.
Yet it doesn't suit me

The short lines and clipped syntax suggest an almost painful expenditure of language. A head with a wagging tongue, they say, is time's fool. Larkin, of course, also writes in somewhat freer rhythms, as at the end of 'An Arundel Tomb'. But he always counts before he pays, and his more expansive effects bank on their moving contrast with his usual, slightly tough laconicism.

Larkin's laconicism also conveys the poverty of the sayable. That 'Life is slow dying', it implies, 'leaves / Nothing'—or almost nothing—'to be said'. He says little because he sees too much. Like Ted Hughes, he feels pressed back into himself by a vision of an unjustified and unjustifiable reality, but where this has finally provoked Hughes into desperate garrulity, it has all but frozen Larkin's mouth—two slender volumes since 1946; two interruptions of silence.

If Larkin relies on traditional form, it is partly out of the agreement of numbness and caution that we find in his style. Why seek new forms, he seems to ask, when there is nothing new under the sun? In any case, 'Content alone interests me', he says. 'Content is everything'. Like a man freezing to death in a snowstorm, refusing to be distracted by the beauty of the flakes, he resolves to be lucid to the last, his mind on the truth alone. And, paradoxically precisely this is why he writes in form. For, by virtue of its familiarity, traditional form, skilfully used, is all but transparent. (Only experimenters, antiformalists, and writers of verse make an *issue* of form.) At its finest, prosody is anyway meltingly one with the content; and Larkin is frequently a fine craftsman. So nothingness stares out of Larkin's poems undistracted, with a native starkness. Even the bodily warmth conveyed by rhythm is often restrained by nicely calculated metrical irregularity.

Yet form has also for Larkin its traditional function: not modest after all, it is an attempt at the memorable. If he writes, the reason is to silence death, if only with the fewest possible words. In a statement contributed to D. J. Enright's anthology, *Poets of the 1950's*, Larkin says: 'I wrote poems to preserve things I have seen/thought/felt (if I may so indicate a composite and complex experience) both for myself and for others, though I feel that my prime responsibility is to the experience itself, which I am trying to keep from oblivion for its own sake. Why I should do this I have no idea, but I think the impulse to preserve lies at the bottom of all art.' Nihilist though he is, he thus raises against nothingness—like every other literary nihilist, if more moderately—the combined plea and protest of his constructions, with their exemplary inner necessity, their perfection.

In sum, his forms are at the same time sorry to be there and insistently there. In his use of words and form alike, Larkin both defies and skulks before his nihilistic 'content', like an animal that, while shrinking back, offers to fight.

So it was that, without betraying his scruples, Larkin became a poignant and cohesive poet, his means the functional intelligence of his ends. More sophisticated writers have chided him for his poetic provinciality, but he is right, I think, to be as simple as he is. His poetry seems not only the necessary expression of his temperament but the very voice of his view of things, the pure expression of his aim—his purpose being not to make sterility whirl but precisely to make it stand still, freed from confusion, from the human fevers that oppose it. Far from adhering piously to English poetic tradition, he uses it for his own ends. The result, in any case, is a poetry of mixed formality and informality, mixed severity and charm, mixed humour and pathos, that carries a unique personal impress—a poetry that, for all its conservatism, is unconsciously, inimitably new.

Even *The Less Deceived* and *The Whitsun Weddings*, however, are somewhat subject to the 'poetic' toning up of *The North Ship*, and poems corrupted by self-pity appear side by side with the mature poems just described. A void with an ashen pallor—how resist rouging it, giving it dramatic visibility? Regret, in any case, touches us so nearly that it slips at the slightest urge into self-commiseration. At his weakest Larkin exploits this readiness for sorrow-suckling, for the histrionic; he tries for pathetic *effects*.

Of course, when a poem is so delightful as 'Days', criticism hesitates:

> What are days for?
> Days are where we live.
> They come, they wake us
> Time and time over.
> They are to be happy in:
> Where can we live but days?
>
> Ah, solving that question
> Brings the priest and the doctor
> In their long coats
> Running over the fields.

But those men in their long coats are too easy to summon over the fields: they border on the animated cartoon. Throwing us on the wretchedness of being passive before them, in need of them, they are more melodramatic than the truth. For all that its subject is 'days', the poem places itself so far from the quotidian that it can say, can picture anything without fearing contradiction from itself. The often admired 'Next, Please' also steps off from life into self-pity. The poem figures expectancy as a 'Sparkling armada of promises' that leaves us 'holding wretched stalks / Of disappointment'. But whatever were we waving at those ships? In the intoxication of its chagrin, the piece neglects propriety and probability. Even the final stanza, though grand, begets uneasiness:

> Only one ship is seeking us, a black-
> Sailed unfamiliar, towing at her back
> A huge and birdless silence. In her wake
> No waters breed or break.

This is a trifle too awesome, Death in makeup. Another admired poem, 'No Road', begins:

> Since we agreed to let the road between us
> Fall to disuse,
> And bricked our gates up, planted trees to screen us,
> And turned all time's eroding agents loose,
> Silence, and space, and strangers—our neglect
> Has not had much effect.
>
> Leaves drift unswept, perhaps; grass creeps unmown;
> No other change

What is really 'unmown' is the conceit—its leaves, grass, bricks, and trees lacking specific reference as metaphors. As in 'Next, Please', the vehicle is too much an end in itself. All three poems are rhetorical, written in emotional generality. Like still other pieces, including 'Whatever Happened?', 'Age', 'Triple Time', 'Latest Face', 'If, My Darling', and 'Arrivals, Departures', they stand at a remove from the literal, on a swaying rope bridge of tropes, dramatic but ill-supported.

Yet virtual fact is liable to the cosmetic impulse, too, as

witness so ostensibly autobiographical a poem as 'Church Going'. The first two stanzas, it is true, are everything these other poems are not:

> Once I am sure there's nothing going on
> I step inside, letting the door thud shut.
> Another church: matting, seats, and stone,
> And little books; sprawlings of flowers, cut
> For Sunday, brownish now; some brass and stuff
> Up at the holy end; the small neat organ;
> And a tense, musty, unignorable silence,
> Brewed God knows how long. Hatless, I take off
> My cycle-clips in awkward reverence,
>
> Move forward, run my hand around the font.
> From where I stand, the roof looks almost new—
> Cleaned, or restored? Someone would know: I don't.
> Mounting the lectern, I peruse a few
> Hectoring large-scale verses, and pronounce
> 'Here endeth' much more loudly than I'd meant.
> The echoes snigger briefly. Back at the door
> I sign the book, donate an Irish sixpence,
> Reflect the place was not worth stopping for.

Pungently detailed, this has a wonderful air of verisimilitude and candour. Except for 'Someone would know: I don't', the lines are free of padding, and the symbolism, as in the brownish flowers and 'Here endeth', is like an afterthought to the forcefully literal. Compare the middle of the poem, with its speculation about the time when churches will be out of use:

> Shall we avoid them as unlucky places?
>
> Or, after dark, will dubious women come
> To make their children touch a particular stone;
> Pick simples for a cancer; or on some
> Advised night see walking a dead one?
> Power of some sort or other will go on
> In games, in riddles, seemingly at random;
> But superstition, like belief, must die,
> And what remains when disbelief has gone?
> Grass, weedy pavement, brambles, buttress, sky,
>
> A shape less recognizable each week,
> A purpose more obscure. I wonder who
> Will be the last, the very last, to seek
> This place for what it was; one of the crew
> That tap and jot and know what rood-lofts were?
> Some ruin-bibber, randy for antique,
> Or Christmas-addict, counting on a whiff
> Of gowns-and-bands and organ-pipes and myrrh?

It is hard to say what is more forced here—the questions, or the assertions that 'power of some sort or other will go on' and that the church will be 'less recognizable each week', or the effort to imagine 'the very last' to seek its purpose. Like the consciously colourful detail at the close, all this is essentially idle, a fabrication. The poem picks up again as Larkin confronts the church in discovery and wonder:

> A serious house on serious earth it is,
> In whose blent air all our compulsions meet,
> Are recognized, and robed as destinies

But the effect is partly to make us regret all the more the triviality of the middle stanzas.

The impression of falseness is sometimes just as strong when Larkin sets his imaginative paints aside and attempts serious thought. Indeed, without much exaggeration it might be said that he is only poised and intelligent with particulars—abstractions tend to spill out of his hands. When he thinks, he often seems to be frowningly struggling to create a philosophical intricacy and importance. Here he is in 'Lines on a Young Lady's Photograph Album':

Those flowers, that gate,
These misty parks and motors, lacerate
Simply by being over; you
Contract my heart by looking out of date.

Yes, true; but in the end, surely, we cry
Not only at exclusion, but because
It leaves us free to cry. We know *what was*
Won't call on us to justify
Our grief, however hard we yowl across
The gap from eye to page

With 'Yes, true', you can virtually hear his voice leaving its natural home in particulars, growing thin and subject to confusion. As if driven to manufacture complexities, the lines suddenly snarl up what had been plain from the descriptive life of the poem. To say that the past leaves us 'free to cry' is to make a false conundrum of what has already been said simply: that it excludes us. The truly subtle idea in the passage—namely, that the past is forlorn because *excluded from us*—is obscured by the fussy thought. And meanwhile grace and measure are abandoned—'yowl' being especially awkward, an attempt to bring the blanched thought back into poetic animation.

'Dockery and Son' similarly gravels in 'philosophy'. Why, asks the speaker, did Dockery

> think adding meant increase?
To me it was dilution. Where do these
Innate assumptions come from? Not from what
We think truest, or most want to do:
Those warp tight-shut, like doors. They're more a
> style
Our lives bring with them: habit for a while,
Suddenly they harden into all we've got

And how we got it; looked back on, they rear
Like sand-clouds, thick and close, embodying
For Dockery a son, for me nothing,
Nothing with all a son's harsh patronage

Reasoning this through is at first like trying to put on a shirt with sewn sleeves—and finally we can only *grant* that such assumptions are 'innate' or distant from what we 'think truest'. (Innate assumptions are usually not all we have but what we wish we had: eternal life, supreme importance, a guiltless being. . . .) The simile of the sand-clouds is slipshod also. Until the last line, we are far from the brilliant beginning.

In the final stanza of 'Deceptions', the self-pity that permits such laxity lies still more forward, spoiling an even more exquisite poem. At the same time, it compares weakly with the epigraph from Mayhew's *London Labour and the London Poor*, a statement of bald power almost beyond art itself: 'Of course I was drugged, and so heavily I did not regain my consciousness till the next morning. I was horrified to discover that I had been ruined, and for some days I was inconsolable, and cried like a child to be killed or sent back to my aunt.' The stanza comments:

Slums, years, have buried you. I would not dare
Console you if I could. What can be said,
Except that suffering is exact, but where
Desire takes charge, readings will grow erratic?
For you would hardly care
That you were less deceived, out on that bed,
Than he was, stumbling up the breathless stair
To burst into fulfilment's desolate attic.

The final phrase, 'fulfilment's desolate attic', bears a Johnsonian indictment, irrevocably disabused, of the delusions of desire. But even granting the romantic assumption that the seducer made too much of his desire, what is its brief match flame compared to the conflagration of the girl's young life? We can hardly care either that the girl was the less deceived. The poem treats the misreading of desire as a tragedy. But nothing it says or implies supports so extravagant and self-condoling a view.

Yet, serious as they are, Larkin's defects are easily outbalanced by his virtues. Thus, though he may abandon an imaginary scene for questionable thought, he is also likely to have put us into that scene with as piercing a dramatic immediacy as any poet now writing. We have witnessed this in 'Church Going' and 'Dockery and Son'; and here is the first stanza of 'Deceptions':

Even so distant, I can taste the grief,
Bitter and sharp with stalks, he made you gulp.
The sun's occasional print, the brisk brief
Worry of wheels along the street outside
Where bridal London bows the other way,
And light, unanswerable and tall and wide,
Forbids the scar to heal, and drives
Shame out of hiding. All the unhurried day
Your mind lay open like a drawer of knives.

Imagination, said Emerson, is a sort of seeing that comes by 'the intellect being where and what it sees', and this happy definition highlights what is remarkable in the stanza. For the lines virtually *are* the original moment, as well as a beauty beyond it and compassion for it. 'Print', it is true, is lost in ambiguity (footprint? a picture-shape on the wall?) and indefinite in relation to the light described later; and 'scar' rather rushes a fresh wound. But almost everything else tells keenly—'The brisk brief / Worry of wheels' poignantly commenting on the girl's inconsolateness, 'bridal London' on her social ruin; 'Light, unanswerable and tall and wide' being unimprovable; and the simile of the drawer of knives, though risking melodrama, properly savage.

We touch here on gifts more specialized than the dramatic imagination, gifts for epithet and metaphor. Of course, in their own way, these too are dramatic, restoring a primal power to the language. We are all bees trapped behind the spotted glass of usage till the poet releases us to the air. And so Larkin releases us in these lines of 'Coming':

On longer evenings,
Light, chill and yellow,
Bathes the serene
Foreheads of houses.
A thrush sings,
Laurel-surrounded
In the deep bare garden,
Its fresh-peeled voice
Astonishing the brickwork . . .

'Chill and yellow' and 'fresh-peeled' are especially happy inventions. So again at the beginning of a recent poem, 'Dublinesque': 'Down stucco side-streets, / Where light is pewter. . . .' In another recent poem, 'The Cardplayers', the trees are—magnificently—'century-wide'. Spring, in the poem of that title, is 'race of water, / Is earth's most multiple, excited daughter'. Delightful in 'Broadcast' is the 'coughing from / Vast Sunday-full and organ-frowned-on spaces'. And what could be at once more homely and endearing than the 'loaf-haired secretary' of 'Toads Revisited'?

Larkin's imagination has also, of course, a turn for wit. At times he instinctively inhibits the sobbing in his strings by playing staccato. Consider the lover in 'Lines on a Young Lady's Photograph Album':

From every side you strike at my control,
Not least through these disquieting chaps who loll
At ease about your earlier days:
Not quite your class, I'd say, dear, on the whole

Or take the comic candour of 'Annus Mirabilis':

> Sexual intercourse began
> In nineteen sixty-three
> (Which was rather late for me)—
> Between the end of the *Chatterley* ban
> And the Beatles' first LP

Next time around the parenthesis reads, 'Though just too late for me', which gives the playfulness a fine grimace. These poems have the good grace of self-irony, a civilized lightness. Better still is the comedy—vigorous with universal truth—in 'Toads' and 'Toads Revisited'. With rising bravura the first begins:

> Why should I let the toad *work*
>   Squat on my life?
> Can't I use my wit as a pitchfork
>   And drive the brute off?
>
> Six days of the week it soils
>   With its sickening poison—
> Just for paying a few bills!
>   That's out of proportion

The second, with toad-eating helplessness, concludes:

> No, give me my in-tray,
> My loaf-haired secretary,
> My shall-I-keep-the-call-in-Sir:
> What else can I answer,
>
> When the lights come on at four
> At the end of another year?
> Give me your arm, old toad;
> Help me down Cemetery Road.

Entertaining though they are, these are works of the full imagination, more quickened than compromised by caricature. They are true and touching as well as spirited. One would be tempted to call the poisoning toad and the pitchfork the best comic conceit in modern poetry were not that of the old toad on Cemetery Road consummate to the point of tears. We are not far here from the world of fairy tales and have only to hear of Cemetery Road to fancy that, like the way through the woods to Grandmother's house, it has existed in the imagination for ever.

An unusual poet, reminding us on the one hand of the grand classical tradition and on the other of Beatrix Potter and Dorothy Parker, and all the while sounding like no one so much as himself! And Larkin has still other virtues. To begin with, there is, as we have seen, the instinctive adjustment of his means to his end, so that, for instance, he is one of the most pellucid of poets because nothing to him is more self-evident than nothingness. Then the unconscious rightness of his forms, 'Toads' being, for example, appropriately restless in alternating uneven trimeters and dimeters, 'Toads Revisited' properly more settled in its trimeters; 'Toads', again, troubled with alternating off-rhyme and 'Toads Revisited' calmer in off-rhymed couplets, full rhyme kept in reserve for the *entente cordiale* of 'toad' and 'Road'. There is the frequent perfection of his metrical spacing; the easy way his words fall together; the tang and unsurpassed contemporaneity of his diction and imagery; the fluent evolution of his poems. There is also his beautifully mild temper and his tenderness for those pushed 'To the side of their own lives'. Nor finally should we fail to add his facility at opening that scepticism about life which everyone closets in his bones.

Still, only at his best does Larkin make us grateful for what a human being can do with words. It is above all in 'Coming', 'Toads', 'Toads Revisited', 'At Grass', 'Here', 'The Whitsun Weddings', and 'An Arundel Tomb' (with two fairly recent poems, 'High Windows' and 'To the Sea', pressing near) that

he puts experience under an aspect of beauty, gracing and deepening it with the illusion of necessary form and producing the privileged sensation—perhaps illusory, perhaps not—of piercing through to a truth. It is in these poems, too, that, at once detached and concerned, he most frees us from self-pity without destroying feeling.

With the exception of 'Here' and 'Toads', these pieces display an exquisite stoic compassion for the littleness, the fragility, indeed the unlikelihood, of happiness. Even in 'Here', however, tenderness is implicit in the perception, the diction, the syntax. For instance, in 'Isolate villages, where removed lives / Loneliness clarifies', the lives are considerately enfolded by the clause at the same time that the line break removes and isolates them. But such tenderness is like water under ice. Where life is as raw, insufficient, and essentially lonely as it is in 'Here', better (so the poem implies) keep yourself inwardly remote, like the 'bluish neutral distance' of the sea. Though 'Here' is all one travelling sentence till it brakes in short clauses at the end, 'Swerving east, from rich industrial shadows' out finally to the 'unfenced existence' of the sea, emotionally it is one continuous 'freeze', since each successive 'here' is as barren, as without self-justification, as the rest. 'Here' leads us as far from ourselves, as far into objective reality, as we can go—to the sea that has nothing for us, 'Facing the sun, untalkative, out of reach'—then leaves us there, all but freed from desire and too well schooled by the accumulated evidence, too guarded, to be appalled. The poem is a masterpiece of stoicism.

The equally fine 'Coming' is as remarkable for its original conception as for the felicity (already sampled) of its similes. Indeed, the two prove inseparable in the second half of the poem:

> It will be spring soon,
> It will be spring soon—
> And I, whose childhood
> Is a forgotten boredom,
> Feel like a child
> Who comes on a scene
> Of adult reconciling,
> And can understand nothing
> But the unusual laughter,
> And starts to be happy.

Throwing us back into the vulnerable heart of childhood, into an ignorance not ignorant enough, the simile redeems an inevitably romantic subject by abrading it, complicating it with domestic truth. Nor could any comparison be at once so unexpected and convincing, giving exactly, as it does, the situation of being drawn into an emotion neither understood nor trusted yet beyond one's power to refuse, since the moment it comes it reveals itself as all, nearly all, of what was needed. The poem, if complete in itself, is also an expressive elaboration of its most poignant word, 'starts'. Too doubting and perplexed for rhyme or a long line, as slender as the inchoate joy it evokes, it is like the 'chill and yellow' light described at the outset, lyrically lovely yet inhibited—its recurring two beats like a heart quickened but still at the tentative start, the mere threshold, of happiness.

There is nothing tentative about 'At Grass', which celebrates the profound peace, the cold joy, in the relinquishment of labour and identity. The retired racehorses in the poem have stolen death from itself:

> The eye can hardly pick them out
> From the cold shade they shelter in,
> Till wind distresses tail and mane;
> Then one crops grass, and moves about
> —The other seeming to look on—
> And stands anonymous again

The early, strenuous days of the horses, full of 'Silks at the start' and 'Numbers and parasols', are later evoked with the same classical directness as this shaded scene, which has a clarity that leaves nothing between us and the subject. Like the horses the poem exists quietly, is envyingly 'at ease' in a pace slowed often enough by stressed monosyllables to seem tranced beyond all care. The rhyme, too, is spaced out placidly, making the stanzas like the 'unmolesting meadows'. (It does, however, cause an awkward syntactic inversion at the close: 'Only the groom, and the groom's boy, / With bridles in the evening come.') Because of its distanced subject and because the horses have both lived out and outlived their swiftness, the poem takes the sickness out of the desire for oblivion, offering in place of weariness a paradise of shade.

An even more exquisite poem is 'An Arundel Tomb', which begins:

> Side by side, their faces blurred,
> The earl and countess lie in stone,
> Their proper habits vaguely shown
> As jointed armour, stiffened pleat,
> And that faint hint of the absurd—
> The little dogs under their feet.

The lines rise to the ceremony of their occasion. So 'Side by side', each syllable royally weighted, is balanced by the four syllables of 'their faces blurred', the two phrases equal and graceful in their partnership but immobile as the effigies they describe. Through rhyme, the third line offers its arm to the second as they move in iambic procession. Then the time-softened long *i* stiffens into the short one, and the little dogs break into the sentence like an afterthought (which in fact they may originally have been). Modelled and exact in its rhythms, lovely, fresh, and affecting in its detail, tender in its deeply deliberated tone, holding the slow centuries in its hands, the poem is indeed very lovely, very moving. Unfortunately, it has need to be in order to humble its one defect: its manipulation of the subject for the sake of pathos. Noting 'with a sharp tender shock' that the earl and countess are holding hands, the poet says:

> They would not think to lie so long.
> Such faithfulness in effigy
> Was just a detail friends would see:
> A sculptor's sweet commissioned grace
> Thrown off in helping to prolong
> The Latin names around the base

But why would they not think to lie so long? If Larkin denies them intention, it is evidently to press his own, which is to view faithful love through the ironic and brittle glass of accident. One balks at this, censures it, and at the same time acknowledges, 'This is Larkin's most beautiful poem'.

Less exquisite but more substantial than 'An Arundel Tomb', 'The Whitsun Weddings' is distinguished for ease, poise, balance, and inclusiveness.

It has even more of England in it than 'Here', similarly taking us by train through the country and making its breadth and variety, its unfolding being, our own. The very movement is that of a leisurely if inexorable journey, the lines frequently pausing as if at so many stations, yet curving on in repeated *enjambements* past scenes swiftly but timelessly evoked, as though the stanzas themselves were the wide windows of a moving train:

> All afternoon, through the tall heat that slept
>   For miles inland,
> A slow and stopping curve southwards we kept.
> Wide farms went by, short-shadowed cattle, and
> Canals with floatings of industrial froth;

> A hothouse flashed uniquely: hedges dipped
> And rose: and now and then a smell of grass
> Displaced the reek of buttoned carriage-cloth
> Until the next town, new and nondescript,
> Approached with acres of dismantled cars

This is deft, light in depiction but strongly evocative. And the English themselves are as vividly present as their towns and countryside, indeed man himself is here in his several ages: the children in the platform wedding parties frowning as 'at something dull', the young men 'grinning and pomaded', the brides' friends staring after the departing trains as 'at a religious wounding', the married couples themselves boarding the carriages in distraction, the uncles shouting smut, the fathers looking as if they had 'never known / Success so huge and wholly farcical', and the mothers' faces sharing the bridal secret 'like a happy funeral'.

And the poet? By chance, he himself is there on the train that Whitsun as the eternal witness of the contemplative artist, inward with what he sees yet outside it precisely to the extent that he sees it. Single amid the married couples in the carriage, he is yet caught up by them, caught up *with* them ('We hurried towards London'), quickened into a sense of physical existence in time. On the other hand, with his indisplaceable knowledge of failure, absence, endings, he is the loneliness of contemplation lucid before the happy blindness of the body and its emotions. He knows he might well envy this happiness and yet he dwarfs it:

> Now fields were building-plots, and poplars cast
> Long shadows over major roads, and for
> Some fifty minutes, that in time would seem
> Just long enough to settle hats and say
>   *I nearly died,*
> A dozen marriages got under way.
> They watched the landscape, sitting side by side
> —An Odeon went past, a cooling tower,
> And someone running up to bowl—and none
> Thought of the others they would never meet
> Or how their lives would all contain this hour.
> I thought of London spread out in the sun,
> Its postal districts packed like squares of wheat:
> There we were aimed. And as we raced across
>   Bright knots of rail
> Past standing Pullmans, walls of blackened moss
> Came close, and it was nearly done, this frail
> Travelling coincidence; and what it held
> Stood ready to be loosed with all the power
> That being changed can give. We slowed again,
> And as the tightened brakes took hold, there swelled
> A sense of falling, like an arrow-shower
> Sent out of sight, somewhere becoming rain.

The poem throughout links beginnings to ends, ends to beginnings—as in its wedding parties 'out on the end of an event / Waving goodbye', its mingling of generations, and the stops and starts of the journey itself. And here at the close, at the same time that it gives the energy of life and the fruition of time their due, even as arrows speed and rain promises germination, it also makes us aware of inevitable dissolution, as arrows fall and rain means mould, dampness, the cold, the elemental. Like certain romantic poems—'The Echoing Green', 'Kubla Kahn', 'Intimations of Immortality', 'Among School Children'—the poem thus brings together, irreducibly, life in its newness and power and life in its decline and end. Nowhere else in his work (though 'To the Sea' marks a near exception) is Larkin so irresistibly drawn out to observe with an emotion close to happiness the great arena of life in its diversity and energy, undeluded though he is, doomed though he feels the energy to be.

'Poetry', St.-John Perse remarks, 'never wishes to be absence, nor refusal'; and certainly in 'The Whitsun Weddings' Larkin grants it the presence of the world, as he grants the world its presence. Yet even apart from 'The Whitsun Weddings' we would be without Larkin's poems the poorer by that much presence and that much love. Poet though he is of the essential absence of life from itself, he yet makes himself present as regret that it must be so; and for all his defeatism it is easy to find him a sympathetic figure as he stands at the window, trying not to cloud it with his breath, mourning the winter casualties, concerned to be there even though convinced beyond all argument that, like everything else, his concern is gratuitous.

CHRISTOPHER RICKS
"Philip Larkin: 'Like Something Almost Being Said'"
The Force of Poetry
1984, pp. 274–84

'The whole frame of the poem', said Donne, 'is a beating out of a piece of gold, but the last clause is as the impression of the stamp, and that is it that makes it current.' Larkin's endings are finely judged, and so he proved a just judge of a poet—Emily Dickinson—who, like Donne, inaugurated poems magnificently: 'Only rarely, however, did she bring a poem to a successful conclusion: the amazing riches of originality offered by the index of her first lines is belied on the page . . . Too often the poem expires in a teased-out and breathless obscurity.'[1] Larkin's poems do not expire. 'An Arundel Tomb' ends its volume, *The Whitsun Weddings*, and ends consummately.

AN ARUNDEL TOMB

Side by side, their faces blurred,
The earl and countess lie in stone,
Their proper habits vaguely shown
As jointed armour, stiffened pleat,
And that faint hint of the absurd—
The little dogs under their feet.

Such plainness of the pre-baroque
Hardly involves the eye, until
It meets his left-hand gauntlet, still
Clasped empty in the other; and
One sees, with a sharp tender shock,
His hand withdrawn, holding her hand.

They would not think to lie so long.
Such faithfulness in effigy
Was just a detail friends would see:
A sculptor's sweet commissioned grace
Thrown off in helping to prolong
The Latin names around the base.

They would not guess how early in
Their supine stationary voyage
The air would change to soundless damage,
Turn the old tenantry away;
How soon succeeding eyes begin
To look, not read. Rigidly they

Persisted, linked, through lengths and breadths
Of time. Snow fell, undated. Light
Each summer thronged the glass. A bright
Litter of birdcalls strewed the same
Bone-riddled ground. And up the paths
The endless altered people came.

Washing at their identity.
Now, helpless in the hollow of
An unarmorial age, a trough
Of smoke in slow suspended skeins
Above their scrap of history,
Only an attitude remains:

Time has transfigured them into
Untruth. The stone fidelity
They hardly meant has come to be
Their final blazon, and to prove
Our almost-instinct almost true:
What will survive of us is love.

It is hard to say just where the ending begins. Not with the last line, which is ushered in by a colon. Not with the last sentence, which begins in mid-line, in the second line of the last stanza, and which anyway is an elucidation of the riddling half-a-dozen words which precede it. Not with the last stanza, which might well (less well) have been self-contained but is ushered in by its colon. Yet if you work back within the penultimate stanza, you find that again the sentence-shape is played against the stanza-shape: this sentence too begins in the stanza's second line, and it begins with 'Now', intimating a retrospect as well as a prospect. But if you work still further back, you find that the previous sentence begins with 'And'. And this would not provide the marked inauguration of an ending . . . The poem speaks of prolonging, and is itself a tender prolongation. No stiffened pleats, no rigid persistence. In short, you cannot abbreviate the poem if you want to speak of its finality. Nevertheless:

Time has transfigured them into
Untruth. The stone fidelity
They hardly meant has come to be
Their final blazon, and to prove
Our almost-instinct almost true:
What will survive of us is love.

Love, not art, though it is art which tells us so.

The very last line has the apophthegmatic weight of classical art. Yet Larkin combines what in less good poets prove incompatible: the understandings both of classicism and of romanticism. It is a matter of tone, but the printed page, or rather the printed page of my discursive prose, is crude in its notation of intonations; it cannot but harden intimations into what Beckett, in *Company*, calls imperations: 'Same flat tone at all times. For its affirmations. For its negations. For its interrogations. For its exclamations. For its imperations. Same flat tone.' Still, to put it simply, Larkin's last line has at least two different possibilities of intonation. If you lay more weight on 'survive', you hear a classical asseveration—'What will *survive* of us is love'. Classical because what is meant by the less stressed 'us', taken in passing, is humanity at large, the largest community of all men and women; classical because of the transcending of individuality within commonalty. But the weight could, with equal propriety, be distributed differently; the words might be heard with more of their weight and salience devoted to 'us'—'What will survive of *us* is love'. This would be the weight of romantic apprehension; 'us', not as the unstressed and properly undifferentiated mankind, but as a particular 'us', here and now, moved not just personally but individually, particular visitors to a tomb or particular contemplators of one such visitor.

Romanticism's pathos of self-attention, its grounded pity for itself, always risks self-pity and soft warmth; classicism's stoicism, its grounded grief at the human lot, always risks frostiness. What Larkin achieves is an extraordinary complementarity; a classical pronouncement is protected against a carven coldness by the ghostly presence of an arching counter-thrust, a romantic swell of feeling; and the romantic swell is protected against a melting self-solicitude by the bracing counterthrust of a classical impersonality. The classical intonation for the line says something *sotto voce*: 'What will survive—and not just mount, shine, evaporate, and fall—of us is love'. The romantic intonation says something different *sotto voce*: 'What will survive of us—of us too, ordinary modern people in an unarmorial age, uncommemorated by aristocratic art or by a Latin inscription—is love'.

Nothing could be more effortlessly direct than such a line as 'What will survive of us is love' (there is nothing disingenuous about the poem's introducing it with a colon), and yet the line is an axis, with two directions. The dignity and pathos of this line which opens out at the end of 'An Arundel Tomb' flow from its being strictly ineffable; you cannot simultaneously utter both of these intonations, though in uttering it—or in hearing it with an inner ear—with one of the intonations, you should comprehend that it might be otherwise uttered. If you were to stress both 'survive' and 'us', the line would not survive the plethora; and if you were to stress neither, the line would not survive the inanition. The line's compactness is that two lines, identical in wording but not in intonation, occupy exactly the same space.

> Nature that hateth emptiness,
> Allows of penetration less.
> ('An Horatian Ode')

The penetration of Marvell's poetry was at one with its duality of wit, and there is a sombre wit in Larkin's line, wit as most comprehensively defined by T. S. Eliot in speaking of Marvell: 'It involves, probably, a recognition, implicit in the expression of every experience, of other kinds of experience which are possible.' The dignity of such wit comes from its conceding that the possibilities cannot all be made simultaneously explicit and yet that the magnanimous imagination can grant their existence; the pathos comes from the acknowledgement that we can entertain the thought of such a universal realm but cannot enter the realm itself.

> The trees are coming into leaf
> Like something almost being said.
> ('The Trees')

There is many a way in which things may almost be said. Absences, as in Larkin's poem of that title, make themselves felt; and 'Maiden Name' ends with a line the obvious rhyme for which has not been granted but left unsounded, silently wedded: 'With your depreciating luggage laden'. As with so much of Larkin, the art is a version of pastoral, an apprehension of poignant contraries. The last line of 'An Arundel Tomb' functions as in an inscription itself, lucid and gnomic, an oracular and honourable equivocation, its possibilities equally voiced. Like the Latin inscription spoken of within the poem, it entails some contrariety of looking and reading. The earl and countess would not have imagined the swift decay of the international language of commemoration: 'How soon succeeding eyes begin / To look, not read'.

Larkin's classical temper shows its mettle when he deplores modernism, whether in jazz, poetry, or painting: 'I dislike such things not because they are new, but because they are irresponsible exploitations of technique in contradiction of human life as we know it. This is my essential criticism of modernism, whether perpetrated by Parker, Pound or Picasso: it helps us neither to enjoy nor endure.'[2] Dr. Johnson compacted classicism into the confidence that men more often require to be reminded than informed, and it was Dr. Johnson of whom Larkin reminded us when he said that modernism

'helps us neither to enjoy nor endure'. 'The only end of writing is to enable the readers better to enjoy life or better to endure it.' Yet though Larkin's convictions are classical, his impulses are romantic; as in a great deal of romantic poetry, self-pity is a central concern and has to be watched lest it become the dominant impulse. The argument about Larkin is essentially as to whether his poems are given up to self-pity or given to a scrutiny of self-pity and in particular to an alert refusal of easy disparaging definitions of it. If we should love our neighbour as ourselves, why should we not be permitted to feel as sorry for ourselves as for our neighbour?

The objection to Shelley's torrid cry, 'I fall upon the thorns of life! I bleed!', is that it would sound coolly unconcerned if it were transposed to the third person plural: 'They fall upon the thorns of life! They bleed!' *Tiens*. Whereas the triumph of Larkin's ending to 'Afternoons' is that, though it is specifically about the young mothers and has no *œillade* of mirrored self-attention, it yet would not be an embarrassing or self-pitying reflection if it were turned to the first person.

> Their beauty has thickened.
> Something is pushing them
> To the side of their own lives.

To grow old is to be pushed to the side of your own life; something pushes all of us there, yet the somethings are different. The life to which you have given birth, a child, is a manifest and embodied something which pushes you to the side of your own life. But then your poem might push you there too. There is no sense of grievance or of being victimized, simply a flat fidelity. So if we were to transpose it into either a large commonalty, with 'them' meaning not only young mothers but all of us, the poem's way of speaking would be large enough to accommodate this; or if we were to imagine the 'them' contracted into any single one of us—'Something is pushing me / To the side of my own life'—Larkin's way of speaking would be strict enough, calm enough, to acknowledge the pity of it. The poetry is in the pity, for oneself no less than for others.

> *Poor soul,*
> They whisper at their own distress.
> ('Ambulances')

At, not *to,* though it is to their distress that they are moved to whisper.

Larkin's responsible control of tone includes the delegation of responsibility. In responses begin responsibilities, and the recognition, implicit in the expression of every experience, of other kinds of experience which are possible, informs Larkin's belief that for his poetry of lyric meditation the proper medium is the printed page, since there the words are not pressed to the either/or of utterance. The poet who wrote 'The Importance of Elsewhere' is alive to the importance of elsehow—a word from elsewhen which should not have been let die. Wittgenstein's duck/rabbit cannot simultaneously be seen as a duck and as a rabbit, however fast we click our focusing; yet it can be known to be also the other even while it is being seen as the one. What is a perceptual or philosophical trick or flick becomes in Larkin this version of pastoral. Hence Larkin's greatest soft sell, when he did his best to discourage prospective purchasers of his recording of *The Whitsun Weddings*; the form which solicited your order included Larkin's rumbling comedy:

> And what you gain on the sound you lose on the sense: think of all the mishearings, the 'their' and 'there' confusions, the submergence of rhyme, the disappearance of stanza-shape, even the comfort of knowing how far you are from the end!

For the sense of nearing a destination, something which is apprehended by sight quite differently from hearing, and which itself arrives at one of Larkin's great destinations, the end of 'The Whitsun Weddings': this sense is more than a comfort; it is a shaping spirit of imagination. Indeed, it is one of the paradoxes and strengths of his art that it is at once diversely idiomatic and yet in some crucial respects cannot be voiced at all. When a poetry-speaker on the B.B.C. ushers in a poem by saying '1914', you sympathize, since some title has to be given and he couldn't say 'MCMXIV'. Yet how much of the sense of loss is lost. How long the continuity was with ancient wars and with immemorial commemoration; how sharp is the passing of an era. 'Never such innocence again'.

Tact is necessary but insufficient, since there may still be an irreducible other sounding. The movement of a poem like 'Going, Going' ('Gone' has not gone, but will come soon, sadly) is one which gives a particular hinged stress to these lines:

> For the first time I feel somehow
> That it isn't going to last.

For the stress has to go, delicately, on 'isn't', not exactly where it would have gone if the lines had not been anticipated within the poem. 'That it *isn't*—contrary to what I had once thought—going to last'. For thirty lines earlier, the poem had kicked off with: 'I thought it would last my time'; and we find that we needed to carry responsibly and lastingly forward the memory of that launching, that attractive and good-humoured irresponsibility, so that this might brace the later moment with a salutary recognition, now that the crucial word 'last' (coming for the second time) demands the strongly conceded stress on 'isn't':

> For the first time I feel somehow
> That it isn't going to last.

The poem is going to.

It is a corollary that the moment at which a Larkin poem loses hold is likely to be one when a reader cannot make sense and sensibility of the relation between repetition and intonation. As, for me, just before the end of 'The Whitsun Weddings'. The newly-weds watched the landscape:

> —and none
> Thought of the others they would never meet
> Or how their lives would all contain this hour.
> I thought of London spread out in the sun,
> Its postal districts packed like squares of wheat:

I don't know how the man knows that none of them thought those things (and yet this itself doesn't seem to be up for scrutiny within the poem), and my unease is accentuated by my not being able to hear the relation between 'none thought' and 'I thought'. None thought this whereas I thought it, or whereas I thought something quite other? If there is no stress placed upon 'I' in 'I thought', the hinge turns idly; but if 'I' is at all stressed, what depends from the hinge? Pronouns, especially in their both contrasting and assimilating 'I' and others, are asked to take such weight in Larkin's poems that any factitious relationship (none thought / I thought?) does real damage.

The very structure of a poem like 'Mr Bleaney' turns upon the decision as to the precise degree of stress and precisely where to lay it. Once the speaker (so to speak) takes Mr Bleaney's place, the shape of the poem is simple: 'I know his habits' (this and that), and 'their yearly frame' (this, that, and the other):

> But if he stood and watched the frigid wind
> Tousling the clouds, lay on the fusty bed
> Telling himself that this was home, and grinned,
> And shivered, without shaking off the dread

> That how we live measures our own nature,
> And at his age having no more to show
> Than one hired box should make him pretty sure
> He warranted no better, I don't know.

But if he stood, as I do, and . . .: the plot of the poem asks some stress on *he*; and yet it is a stress that becomes increasingly and illuminatingly difficult to maintain with grace and exactitude as the final eight-line sentence rolls on. 'Telling *himself*'—as I tell *myself*: the antithesis-cum-assimilation may still be pointed up by the voice, but by the time we reach 'at his age', and 'make him pretty sure', and 'he warranted', the contrastive *I* has been dissolved to wan listlessness. At which point 'I' makes itself heard: 'I don't know'. But to accentuate this other arch of the structure (I know his habits, but these things I *don't* know) by coming down unignorably on 'don't' would be as coarsening as it would be to slight this structural turn.

Without the contrast furnished by 'I know his habits', there would be at the end a more mild puzzlement, equalizing the stresses within 'I don't know'; and this puzzlement must not be sacrificed to the more urgent fears (was he just like me? am I just like him?), since these last eight lines subtly twine an ordinary wondering and a morbid anxiety. Is the speaker imputing his own sensitivities and anxieties to Mr Bleaney, or is he acknowledging a true fellow-feeling? Any act of imagination risks the accusation that it is just an imputing of oneself, a sort of anthropomorphism, but then is this accusation too an unimaginative imputation? 'I don't know.' You must stress to some degree all three of those concluding words; yet you mustn't treat 'don't' as if it were not an unpriceable pivot. But then nor must you slight the first of persons, 'I', or the searching verb 'know'. 'Mr Bleaney' is one of Larkin's best poems, and it is natural that it should come to its consummation of 'incomplete unrest' with those three words: the pronoun which so often marks the crucial turn or takes the crucial stress in his poetry; the colloquial negative 'don't'; and the admission as to doubtful knowledge.

'Know' can function similarly at the start of a poem, as with 'Ignorance', where the first words might advance naturally towards a stress on nothing—'Strange to know *nothing*'—only then to be retrospectively reconsidered because of being followed by 'never to be sure / Of what is true or right or real'. For the succession asks that there be a stronger stress on 'know' than you could have known at the time:

> Strange to know nothing, never to be sure
> Of what is true or right or real,
> But forced to qualify *or so I feel*.

An equal stress on 'I' and 'feel'?

The start of 'Toads' offers a pronominal prospect which is likewise qualified as the poem moves on:

> Why should I let the toad *work*
> Squat on my life?

The general aggrievedness, which is at first all there is to go on, would stress 'should'—'Why *should* I?'. But it then turns out, as things continue, that there is a particular aggrievedness instead or as well, which means: 'Why should *I*, who am no fool, let the toad work squat on *my* life?' You can feel these challenging undulations of tone, idiomatic and yet unspeakable, in a stanza like this:

> Their nippers have got bare feet,
> Their unspeakable wives
> Are skinny as whippets—and yet
> No one actually *starves*.

This needs both the tone of matter-of-fact reportage, without argumentative stresses until the last word, and the pitching upon 'have' and 'Arc' which will bring out the concessive combativeness: 'True, their nippers *have* got bare feet, and their unspeakable wives *are*—oh yes—skinny as whippets—and yet . . .'. Larkin's accents are audible either as equable or as elbowing.

'Unspeakable': the negative prefix matters to Larkin for what it cannot but call up, and an unspoken but not unheard melody is one of his honest insinuations. The negative prefix may be markedly absent, as when Larkin musically imagines 'Mute glorious Storyvilles' ('For Sidney Bechet'), challenging us to sound the mute prefix *in*—or at least not to succumb to merely hitting upon 'glorious' as if this would make music or sense. Allusion like this (double or triple, since it plays upon Gray as well as upon Milton: 'Some mute inglorious Milton here may rest') always invites at least two effects of intonation: the voice must use its pitch so that it gives one kind of salience to the words that have been carried over unchanged, and it must use its stress so that it gives a different kind of salience to the words that have been changed and that therefore constitute the narrative of the matter. The opening of Edmund Blunden's best poem, 'Report on Experience', would not be sounded in the same way if it were not that the Psalmist were audible.

> I have been young, and now am not too old,
> And I have seen the righteous forsaken

'I have been young, and now am old: and yet saw I never the righteous forsaken . . .' So the tones of Blunden's lines must be something like this:

> 'I have been young, and now am' *not too* 'old',
> And I *have* 'seen the righteous forsaken'

A characteristic Larkin turn of phrase like 'the wind's incomplete unrest' ('Talking in Bed'[3]) alludes to the easy restfulness of the phrase 'a complete rest'—a phrase newly completed unrestfully. But uttering this—saying the words, as against imagining them—is not as easy as it sounds. If you stress the negative prefixes, '*in*complete *un*rest', you reduce the effect to that of a dig in the ribs; but if you don't stress them at all, you cut free from the tacit down-to-earth idiom which touchingly tethers the high fancy. Again, it is commonplace to meet a welcome, and easily said, but how do you say 'Meet a vast unwelcome' ('First Sight')? It asks a stress small enough to be no strain. Or there is the negative prefix at the very end of 'Spring'; 'Their visions mountain-clear, their needs immodest'. Our modest needs are one thing; our immodest needs would be something other than quite other, since immodest isn't exactly the opposite of modest. Yet the alighting upon the negative prefix must be delicate—must meet the modest needs of such exact art. Likewise with the felicity which ends a poem ('Wild Oats') with the line 'Unlucky charms, perhaps'. To stress the prefix would be to smirk, and to ignore it would be to wear a vacant look. Larkin's art is varying and almost invariably lovely, and a phrase like 'Unvariably lovely there' ('Lines on a Young Lady's Photograph Album') depends on 'unvariably' being a variation of the usual 'invariably', from which it differs as minutely and substantially as does T. S. Eliot's 'unsubstantial' ('Are become unsubstantial', in 'Marina') from 'insubstantial'. Larkin's too is a poetry in which things both great and small shine substantially expressed.

Notes

1. *New Statesman*, 13 March 1970; *Required Writing* (1983), p. 194.
2. *All What Jazz?* (1970), p. 17.
3. The whole poem may be found on p. 387.

MARY LAVIN

1912–

Mary Lavin was born of Irish parents on June 11, 1912, in East Walpole, Massachusetts. In 1921 her family returned to Ireland, where she was educated at the Loreto Convent School in Dublin. In 1930 she enrolled at University College, Dublin, and after gaining her M.A. in 1936 worked as a teacher while writing her Ph.D. dissertation. Her first short story, "Miss Holland," written in 1938, was published in *Dublin Magazine* the following year. After several further magazine publications in Ireland and America, her collection *Tales from Bective Bridge* appeared in 1942, winning her the James Tait Black Prize. A second volume, *The Long Ago*, was published in 1944. Though concentrating on short fiction, she wrote two novels in the following years, *The House in Clewe Street* (1945) and *Mary O'Grady* (1950).

After the death of her father in 1945 Lavin moved with her husband and two children to Bective, County Meath. Her husband died in 1954, and a personally difficult and creatively less productive time followed, until the publication of "The Living" in the *New Yorker* in 1958 and the receipt of a Guggenheim Fellowship in 1959, renewed in 1960. The collection *The Great Wave* (1961) brought her the Katherine Mansfield Prize, and after the appearance of *In the Middle of the Fields* (1967) she was awarded a D.Litt. from University College, Dublin. In the 1970s many honors followed, including the Eire Society Gold Medal in 1974, the Gregory Medal in 1975, and the American Irish Foundation Literary Award in 1979. She served as president of the Irish Academy of Writers from 1971 to 1975.

Lavin married her second husband in 1969, and lives in Bective and Dublin. Her more recent publications include the collections of short stories *Happiness* (1969), *A Memory* (1973), and *The Shrine* (1976).

. . . I once asked her to meet one or two writers in my house, and when one of them, a professor from Trinity College, afterwards read the only story of hers that as yet had been printed, he realized rather uncomfortably that those searching eyes must have gone right through him; it was rather as though he had come with his pockets full of all sorts of collected objects, and perhaps had a broken rib long ago mended, and had afterwards learned that he had been all the while exposed to the action of X-rays.

. . . ⟨M⟩y first impression when Mary Lavin sent me some of her work, an impression that I have never altered, was that I had no advice whatever to give her about literature; so I have only helped her with her punctuation, which was bad, and with her hyphens, about which she shares the complete ignorance that in the fourth decade of the twentieth century appears to afflict nearly everybody who writes. Only in these trivial matters do I feel that I know anything more about writing than Mary Lavin.

I have never had much to do with the classifying of writers, my attitude towards art having always been that of a child to a butterfly rather than that of an entomologist, that is to say a greater interest in its flashing beauty than in its Latin name; so that others will classify Mary Lavin's work, if it is necessary for it to be classified. To me she seems reminiscent of the Russians more than of any other school of writers and, with the exception of the gigantic Tolstoy, her searching insight into the human heart and vivid appreciation of the beauty of the fields are worthy in my opinion to be mentioned beside their work. Often, as I read one of her tales, I find myself using superlatives, and then wondering if such praise must not necessarily be mistaken, when applied to the work of a young and quite unknown writer. And yet are not such doubts as these utterly wrong-minded?

. . . ⟨R⟩ead these stories ⟨in *Tales from Bective Bridge*⟩ for yourselves, and see if again and again you do not find sentences which, if they had been translated from the Russian, would make you say that they do indeed show us that those writers understood life. I am reluctant to quote, because anything I would quote lies before you in this book, and because there are quotations which I might make from those tales which would seem to prove my point with almost unnecessary violence. But I suggest that a page should be taken at random from "The Green Grave and the Black Grave" and compared with a random page of any novelist of the present century, to see which page evokes with vividest pictures. . . .

She tells the stories of quite ordinary lives, the stories of people who many might suppose to have no story in all their experience; and when she tells these stories there may be some whose ears, attuned to the modern thriller, may suppose that they are not stories at all. The pivot of one of them for instance is where a fly thrown out of a cup of tea, "and celebrating his release a little too soon by sitting on a blade of grass rubbing his hands," is killed by a small dog. It may seem too tiny a thing to notice, and the man's life, which turns in another direction from that moment, may seem tiny and unimportant too, to any who may not reflect how hard it is for any of us to say what is important and what is not. Browning speaks of the gnats

that carry aloft
The sound they have nursed, so sweet and pure,
Out of a myriad noises soft,
Into a tone that can endure
Amid the noise of a July noon,

and many an ear must miss that tone, and many may miss the work of Mary Lavin. The bold plots and the startling events of the modern thriller are to these tales what a great factory is to the works of a gold watch. Those looking for great engines running at full blast might overlook the delicacy of the machinery of such a watch—Lord Dunsany, "A Preface" to *Tales from Bective Bridge*, 1942, pp. vii–xi

The literature of the Irish Literary Renaissance is a peculiarly masculine affair, and I fancy the same is true of most renaissance literatures. Almost of necessity they are the work of men of action disguised as men of thought, or of men of thought disguised as men of action. In such reckless adventures as donating a backward country with a literature it does not want, women must be left at home, or, at most, be permitted to bring food to the prison gates, because the explosion of a flying bishop can do them so much more damage than it can do to men. . . .

So an Irishman, readying the stories of Mary Lavin, is actually more at a loss than a foreigner would be. His not-so-distant political revolution, seen through her eyes, practically disappears from view. She has written only one story about it— 'The Patriot Son'—and from a patriotic point of view that is more than enough. It describes two young men, one a revolutionary, the other a mammy's boy who, despite his mother's scorn, admires the revolutionary from afar. When the revolutionary attempts to escape from his enemies the mammy's boy tries to shield him, but all that happens is that he rips himself on some barbed wire and meekly returns to the authority of Ma and the local police. What it was all about was apparently the attempted overthrow of the Irish matriarch, a type Miss Lavin seems to dislike, and we may consider it a failure as the matriarch persists. The point of view is perhaps too exclusively feminine, for as the story unfolds a man may be excused for thinking that the mammy's boy is a far better type than the revolutionary, Mongon, and might even feel inclined to pity any matriarch who in future tried to bully him.

But here, at least, the Irishman is on familiar ground, the ground of O'Flaherty and O'Casey. It is only when he turns to the other stories that he gets the real shock, for, though names, details, dialogue seem all of unimpeachable accuracy, he might as well be reading Turgenev or Lyseskov for the first time, overwhelmed by the material unfamiliarity of the whole background, versts, shubas, roubles and patronymics. First, there is the sensual richness, above all in the sense of smell. 'There was a queer pleasure, too, in smelling the children's soiled clothes and Tom's used shirts. Even the smell that would have turned her stomach as a girl had a curious warm fascination for her now, and in the evenings when the diapers were hanging by the fire to dry, with a hot steam going up from them, she shut her eyes and drew in a deep breath, and felt safe and secure and comforted.' Even the word 'diapers' in an Irish story is not more foreign than the feeling of that passage from 'The Inspector's Wife.' And surely, when one first read Russian fiction, there was nothing in it more startling in the way of psychology than this from 'The Nun's Mother':

Women had a curious streak of chastity in them, no matter how long they were married, or how ardently they loved. And so, for most women, when they heard that a young girl was entering a convent, there was a strange triumph in their hearts at once; and during the day, as they moved round the house, they felt a temporary hostility to their husbands, towards the things of his household, towards his tables and chairs; yes, indeed, down even to his dishes and dish-cloths.

As the last Emperor of Russia wrote in his diary on hearing of the Revolution, 'Nice goings-on!' I remember my dear Lady Gregory, and the mighty end of 'The Gaol Gate' and ask myself if this is indeed how most women feel. But then I remember the girl from the North Presentation Convent who came to the real gaol with the cake she had freshly baked, in the shopping bag on her arm, and, though she has been practically left out of modern Irish literature, I wonder if in fact this is not precisely how she does feel, and it seems as though a new dimension had been added to Irish literature. 'O'Flaherty, L. *see also* Lavin, M.'

A woman cannot afford to caricature herself as a man may do, and if she does, she is made to pay for it. It is a drawback to the Irish woman writer. But, on the other hand, a woman's ideas of success and failure need not necessarily be the same as man's. No man need regard himself as a failure if he has failed with women, but a woman does so almost invariably if she has failed with men. All through Mary Lavin's stories one is aware of a certain difference in values which finally resolves itself into an almost Victorian attitude to love and marriage, an attitude one would be tempted to call old-fashioned if it did not make the attitude of so many famous modern women writers seem dated.

. . . Miss Lavin is much more of a novelist in her stories than O'Flaherty, O'Faoláin, or Joyce, and her technique verges—sometimes dangerously—on the novelist's technique. That has its advantages, of course. In her later stories there is an authenticity and solidity that makes the work of most Irish writers seem shadowy; not the life of the mind interrupted by occasional yells from the kitchen, but the life of the kitchen suddenly shattered by mental images of extraordinary vividness which the author tries frantically to capture before the yells begin again. ('What Mummy needs,' her daughter once said when some kind friends advised her to marry again, 'is not a husband but a wife.') The only story in which she deliberately eschews the physical world is the fable of 'The Becker Wives' which she sets in a capital city that might be either Dublin or London, and among merchants whose names might be Irish or English, and, for all its brilliance and lucidity it seems to me only the ghost of a story, a Henry James fable without the excuse of James's sexual peculiarities. She has the novelist's preoccupation with logic, the logic of Time past and Time future, not so much the real short story teller's obsession with Time present—the height from which past and present are presumed to be equally visible. Sometimes she begins her stories too far back, sometimes she carries them too far forward, rarely by more than a page or two, but already in that space the light begins to fade into the calm grey even light of the novelist.

She fascinates me more than any other of the Irish writers of my generation because more than any of them, her work reveals the fact that she has not said all she has to say. Between 'Tales from Bective Bridge' published in 1943 and 'The Patriot Son' published in 1956, her stories have developed almost beyond recognition, and with her growing power has come a certain irritable experimentation, as in 'The Widow's Son' where she experiments dangerously with alternative endings and 'A Story with a Pattern' where she experiments with the guying of her audience in the manner of Molière in *L'Impromptu de Versailles*. Her most important work will, I fancy, be neither in the novel nor in the short story pure and simple. In the former she will be defeated by Irish society, whatever standard of values she chooses to judge it by, in the latter because in it she can never fully express her passionate novelist's logic. I should guess that her real achievements will all be done in the form of the *novella* in which she has done her finest work till now. But it will be a very different sort of *novella*, as different from 'Frail Vessel' as 'Frail Vessel' is from the *novellas* in *Tales from Bective Bridge*, more expansive,

more allusive, more calligraphic. In the remarkable group of stories of which 'Frail Vessel' is one, there seems to be the material of a long novel of provincial life, put aside not because Miss Lavin lacked time or enthusiasm but because it would be bound to raise the question I have discussed about the value of lives lived in that particular way, yet which continued to haunt her because whether or not this was life lived as a sensitive person would consider it worth living, it was still life lived, and lived intensely.—FRANK O'CONNOR, "The Girl at the Gaol Gate," *REL*, April 1960, pp. 25–33

In her work there is a whole range of characters who recoil from the more fullblooded implications of life and settle for a cool cloistered compromise; over against them stands an equal rank of figures who are characterized by their energetic commitment to the hot realities of living. Several of her stories enact the conflict between these two basic life attitudes and it is especially significant that in one of her very earliest stories 'Love Is for Lovers' the tension is quite clearly epitomized. Here Matthew, a character of the first type, is almost tempted from his ordered, emotionally tepid existence by a stiflingly full-blooded widow, Mrs. Cooligan, but he retreats quite deliberately into the cool cloister of his bachelorhood. As it is an early story the author presents the issues less subtly than in her subsequent work and the contrast is quite aggressively deliberate:

> Life was hot and pulsing and it brought sweat to the forehead. He didn't know anything about marriage, but it must be close and pulsing too . . . . Life was nauseating to him. Death was cool and fragrant. Of course, he had a long way to go before its green shade lengthened to reach him. But in the meantime he could keep away from the hot rays of life, as he had always done before he had got familiar with Rita.

Surely this is the death wish presented in a most assertive, not to say unnerving form. If it cropped up only in one early and rather clumsy story, one might dismiss it as a transitory if curious tangent of the author's creative imagination. But it re-emerges inexorably though more subtly through her later work: in the contrast between Miss Holland and her fellow lodgers; in the contrast between the prim and pathetic spinster and her father in 'A Single Lady'; in Daniel's rejection of the little servant girl in 'Posy'—where even the heroine's nickname is redolent of the life principle; in the disparity between the vigorous and sweating Magenta and the two pallid old maids; and more subtly in the contrast between Mamie Sully and Naida Paston in the two stories in which they appear. This persistent dichotomy could be expanded and developed. There is little doubt that the author is on the side of life despite the fact that many of its protagonists in her work are little short of repellent—Mamie Sully, Annie Bowles, Rita Cooligan—and many of its deniers are sympathetically, almost tenderly evoked—Naida Paston, Miss Holland, Matthew and Daniel. Again it is difficult to be sure whether the author is—however unconsciously—presenting the death wish as something central in the human condition or merely posing the question of its peculiar relevance to Ireland. It is sufficient here to note that the psychological tensions which surround it are a constant principle of energy in her creative consciousness.

The centre of her focus is the 'vagaries and contrarieties' of the human heart as seen in its small-town habitat. This is her objective correlative and it is on this murky prism that she concentrates the strongest creative light; it is here that her human concern is most sustained and urgent. Out of this material she builds not only the Grimes cycle but her only other related sequence of stories—those featuring Naida

Paston, Elgar and Mamie Sully—'The Convert', 'Limbo' and 'The Mouse', though in the last of these for some inscrutable reason she gives the characters new names.

Outside of this small-town ethos Miss Lavin has written accomplished and powerful stories but it is within it, one feels, that she is most consistently close to the hard core of the human predicament. 'The Great Wave' is more exotic and spectacular, more overwhelming in its symbolic overtones than say 'Frail Vessel', but it is also more remote from the authentic problems of living. With all its lyrical splendour it is really no more than an illuminated capital on the parchment of life. It is in the tedious and unadorned script of the Grimes history that life's meaning is to be read. It is the final proof of Miss Lavin's integrity as an artist that she has pursued this squalid chronicle with such relentless and minute concern and forced it to yield up its hidden and unexpected riches. Of course we must not be ungrateful that she has paused from time to time to give us such a finely worked capital as 'The Great Wave' or such diverting and irresponsible marginalia as 'My Vocatiton' or 'The Patriot Son'—that irreverent footnote to Irish revolutionary literature.—AUGUSTE MARTIN, "A Skeleton Key to the Stories of Mary Lavin," *Studies*, Winter 1963, pp. 403–5

I do not think a story always has to have a beginning, middle and end. To me, a story is more like an arrow in flight, or better still like a flash of forked lightning. You know the way a flash of lightning seems to be *all there on the sky* at once, beginning, middle and end, because it traces its path so fast? Of course, the work on a story is a different matter. The work has to begin and end but I am pretty sure that the entire content of a story is in my mind before I start but compressed—as if it were a small capsule. There is a story of mine called "The Living" (one I *do* like, by the way)—I had that story in my mind for years before I sat down to write it. It was filed away in the back of my mind, complete in all its parts. I write at a tremendous pace.

Yet, if I had not written it when I did, it would probably turn out more or less the same if I were to write it today.—MARY LAVIN, Interview by Catherine Murphy (1967), *IUR*, Autumn 1979, p. 267

The thing about Mary Lavin is that she knows how to start. Contrary to popular conviction, a tremendous number of people know where to chop it off—too many, in the short story: they write without conviction, but with excessive craftsmanship. They end with a *Q.E.D.* sort of flourish. Not in a pat way—that's temporarily out. But emphatically unemphatically, as if they had said something. All is insinuative, you see. Only they never got anything started in the first place. They pretend inscrutability. And hope.

Not so Mary Lavin. She gives at once the impression of knowing what she is going to do, having been caught up in one of those human entanglements which are not "way out," which we ourselves recognize as going on about us. Only she finds that which eludes us or which at least leaves us mentally and spiritually tongue-tied, so that we can formulate it neither to other people nor (more hopelessly graspingly) to ourselves. She can, and does. Typically, the prime matter is tenderness. We feel that she recollects in tranquillity, has it eventually all there, and talks it into her typewriter. "Mother," Mrs. Lavin begins in "Happiness"—so superb a story that it justly appears in both collections reviewed here—"had a lot to say."

So simple it is to begin a great short story—when you know where you are going. For in "Happiness" Mrs. Lavin is up to her old tricks only in the sense that life is tremendous and mighty in its sleight of hand. The story, like all of her stories, is disarmingly circumstantial. Mother is happy, although a loved husband has died. There are other *althoughs*, including a self-pitying grandmother—never named as such, for Mrs. Lavin

rarely names: she shows. "As the years went on, Grandmother had a new bead to add to her rosary: if only her friends were not all dead!" There it is. There is Wordsworthian simplicity, without the leech-gatherer bent double under his load of pompous pantheism. Grandmother demands. Mother gives, over and above, but not through masochistic submissiveness, and is abundant in generosity. She has taken her dying husband so many daffodils that she spills them all over the hospital hall. After her husband's death, she drives the family about Europe in an old inadequate car. Even in her attempts to escape, she is just this side of flamboyant. She can never be really flamboyant: she is too richly fine. She is this way in her close relationship, after her husband's death, with Father Hugh: so beautifully outgoing that she flows beyond any occasion for scandal; and in the very special love which she gives to the priest and which she teaches him to give to her, she makes him all the more a priest, all the more a man, all the more powerfully celibate.

Then, Mother herself comes to her end. She seems to be already looking into "God's exigent eyes." There are, of course, daffodils. Mother wants them not to be cloistered on the nuns' altar but to be sacramentals, sent and put to work among many people in the public ward. The gracious death of a gracious woman closes the gap: "Then her mind came back from the stark world of the spirit to the world where her body was still detained. . . ." Detained, but not debased. She has consideration for a daffodil on the floor: "Don't step on that one!" Remember the old nun for whom all things were so complete that, dying, she called out for the holy candles to be snuffed correctly? Mother has loved *genuinely* this world and its properties (sin is the abuse of good things, for there are no bad things); so she is equipped to love the other. We are shown, also, that she experiences suffering as a subordinate part of happiness, or a gap, maybe, a stretch of non-existence. She has brought things off splendidly, affirming, but with no cheap screeches. Affirming, she carries affirmation triumphantly over into death. " 'You've finished with this world, Mother,' she [her daughter] said, and, confident that her tidings were joyous, her voice was strong." Then, the last paragraph is quietly powerful. She grasps at her daughter's meaning. She sighs. There is nothing more now to say: it has been said. We are not told that she has found the meaning; we are shown: ". . . this time her head sank so deep into the pillow that it would have been dented had it been a pillow of stone." So near is strong emphasis to comedy—so emphatically does it not deteriorate.

So from the beginning the meaning has all been there. Only we hadn't got it until Mrs. Lavin guided us to it through circumstance and disarming detail. Otherwise, we would have seen only things and people, appearances, bread and wine. This story does not encourage the cheap vulgarity of tears. It is quiet.

Much time to one story; but this lady stirs you, and you give. Besides, this is the best of her stories that I have read. It is typical, but more so. Mrs. Lavin is the short story writer of our times who is capable of viewing philosophically, in the wide sense of the word, the relationship between life and death without being prosy or melodramatic. She knows that the two go together. She knows that in life we must always take life. In "A Tragedy" she pretends to give us a choice between loneliness and life on the one hand and death on the other. But she gives us no choice, and we don't want one. Life is potentiality, she insinuates, even on its loneliest, most nearly sordid, terms. And in "A Pure Accident," her fine study of a bulky, sad, pathetically, mentally foolish priest, she avoids easy brutal caricature. Instead, she shows her usual firm, restrained but genuine tenderness: here, too, even on the grubbiest level, life has its potentialities.

This must end—but just one more story, up there beside "Happiness": it is "Sunday Brings Sunday" and again, as in "The Cuckoo-Spit" although with quite different intentions, Mrs. Lavin uses nature. How strong a hold she has on its banal splendors and how stubbornly she sees them not in themselves but through people, moved by them to ends beyond pure nature's thrusts. But she is not overwhelmed by nature.

Indeed, she is never overwhelmed by anything. Life for her is always examining and finding, within the suggestive guidance of a large Catholic conception. Within Mrs. Lavin's stories, there is a cosmic awareness, something of grandeur. —John Hazard Wildman, "Beyond Classification: Some Notes on Distinction," *SoR*, Jan. 1973, pp. 240–42

Mary Lavin, whose fiction reflects the sights, smells, and sounds of places where she herself has lived and presents characters who follow patterns of life familiar to such places, has been called both a naturalist and an autobiographical writer. Because each of her stories is built around events that have a discernible beginning, middle, and end, she also has been described as an old-fashioned storyteller, comforting to readers who like to be assured that the universe is, after all, an orderly place. But Mary Lavin is also the writer who fascinated Frank O'Connor, because of her early capacity to suggest that she had not said all that she had to say. And V. S. Pritchett, intrigued by her "extraordinary sense that what we call real life is a veil", has described her as an artist who presents "the surface of life rapidly, but as a covering for something else."

All these statements about Mary Lavin's work are true. The surface of her fiction faithfully records details of an exterior reality through which men, women, and children who resemble people she has known move from yesterday to today to tomorrow. Hidden in their words, gestures, and observations, however, is that which extends beyond the limits of time, place, and individual character. What seems so solid and permanent in her stories is revealed, in afterthought, as fluid and temporal—the moment immobilized by the reader's willing suspension of disbelief in response to the artist's power to recreate milieu. What seems so fleeting and illusory is revealed as timeless—a fragment recognized, in afterthought, as essential human nature: The resulting interplay of universal sensibility and particular experience is what makes her work disarmingly simple on first reading, disturbingly complex on recollection, elusive, tantalizing, and seductive.—Janet Egleson Dunleavy, "The Fiction of Mary Lavin: Universal Sensibility in a Particular Milieu," *IUR*, Autumn 1977, p. 222

Mary Lavin's own observation of the force of the "intuitive imagination" suggests that her apprehension of a "plane of reality" beyond that known merely by observation and experience in analogous to these views. For instance, in the Preface to *Selected Stories*, she has commented,

> many of the things about which I wrote in the early years were not then experienced, and yet I think I wrote of them with greater ease and greater intensity than I did later. Intuitive imagination can focus more directly upon the object of its interest than memory or direct observation.

Moreover, the characteristic action of her stories of ordinary experience, the synthesis of external perceptions as these are modified by an individual's habitual process of feeling, accords with Tillyard's description of normal poetic process: imagination, interacting with consciousness, establishes in the individual a unity of normal "planes of reality."

However, the group of Miss Lavin's stories which involve experience encountered at a time of heightened imagination (in Tillyard's phrase, "when our normal equipoise is disturbed") does a good deal more. These stories describe an individual's apprehension of an extended dimension of reality, the "spiritual reality" whose existence is noted in Murry and Tillyard; they not only reaffirm the existence of this reality but also (despite Murry's view that "no veridical report [of it] can be given") suggest something of its precise link to the human imagination and its not always beneficent influence on human life. Primary suggestions include the views that this spiritual reality is the locus of the ongoing life force which fructifies the individual's imagination, enabling it to interact with his or her consciousness in the task of unifying individual experience; that under certain circumstances this force can so overcharge or intensify the process of imagination that the countering process of consciousness is overwhelmed; that with this overwhelming of consciousness comes a consequent blind and direct subjection to the dynamic of the extended dimension, a subjection which is ironically destructive, not vivifying, because individual human consciousness, the distinction of the species and the source of a person's active and evaluative comprehension of reality, has been replaced by a tyrannical life force quite indifferent to individual existence and to individual aspiration to complete development.

Miss Lavin's stories not only suggest these ideas but dramatize them with extraordinary imaginative, psychological, and artistic power. Her use of a dynamic developmental image or group of images to suggest the unifying of several planes of awareness in stories of ordinary existence such as "Lilacs" and "Brother Boniface" (Tillyard's "normal poetic method") is also the method of those of her stories which involve the extended dimension; the difference is that in the latter stories Miss Lavin seeks to encompass in a single unity that further plane of reality perceived by the roused imagination—parallel to Murry's world *sub specie aeterni*. This pursuit of the connection between the reality perceived under normal conditions of consciousness, the structure of which the individual feels he comprehends (however partial that comprehension may seem from another perspective), and the reality perceived by "even the simplest and most normal people" in heightened states of imagination, the structure of which is not fully apprehended and which is not comprehended at all, is present from the very first collection of stories and increases in importance with each succeeding volume.

. . . ⟨I⟩n "The Great Wave" as, indeed, throughout Miss Lavin's work, the fragility of the necessary partnership of imagination and consciousness is at its roots inescapable: to evade involvement with the ambiguous forces of the larger cosmos is to evade vital human life; to become involved with these forces is to risk being overwhelmed directly by them, drawn from the meaning and order of conscious life into a formless inhuman chaos. The human being of vital imagination exists, then, with an aware allegiance to conscious life in its fullness as his only bulwark; and that bulwark, "The Great Wave" implies, is arbitrarily subject to an unequal encounter with the ambiguous forces of a supra-human cosmos linked to his imagination. Miss Lavin's awareness of the power and indifference—even malignity—of this supra-human and influential cosmos would seem to be the foundation of her ironic vision, its existence casting into question the strength and pride of conscious human choice; her recognition of the courage of the men and woman of vital imagination who live at risk in the face of it is her testament to human beauty and value. —Catherine A. Murphy, "The Ironic Vision of Mary Lavin," *Mosaic*, Spring 1979, pp. 70–79

––––––––

ROBERT W. CASWELL
From "Irish Political Reality
and Mary Lavin's *Tales from Bective Bridge*"
Éire-Ireland, Spring 1968, pp. 50–60

The importance of Miss Lavin's first volume of stories, *Tales from Bective Bridge* (1943)—the year of the censorship debate over Eric Cross's *The Tailor and Anstey*—is due primarily to the way in which she retains certain ideas of Irish life with which we are familiar from the work of Moore, Joyce, and others, while at the same time she transforms these ideas into conceptions of a more than Irish value. In fact the transformation is so successful that, as she herself has said, her stories could take place anywhere. By not adhering to the "reality of politics," and by not exploiting nationalism in its widest sense, she risks losing the force of a specific Irish identity. So far she has not done so. Moreover, her approach enables her, even at the beginning of her work, to keep from coming enmeshed in certain images of Irish life that by now have become clichés.

To illustrate. The conflict in "Lilacs," the first story in *Tales from Bective Bridge*, arises from the desire of the daughters of Phelim and Rose Molloy, Kate and Stacy, to get rid of the dung in which their father trades. To Phelim as a young man, the dung is a source of income which will enable him to marry Rose. Later, it is a source of income for giving a fine education, including music lessons for Stacy, to his daughters. Moreover, to Phelim there is at times a natural beauty in the dung. When the young Rose protests that it is dirty stuff, he replies:

> 'I don't know so much about that,' said Phelim. 'There's a lot in the way you think about things. Do you know, Rose, sometimes when I'm driving along the road I look down at the dung that's into the road and I think to myself you couldn't ask much prettier than it, the way it flashes by under the horse's feet in pale gold rings.' Poor Phelim! There weren't many men would think of things like that.[1]

However, Rose "didn't like the smell of manure, then, anymore than after, but she liked Phelim" (p. 16). The remark helps to explain the title: the ideal, in this case love, and the real, in this case the wherewithal to support the love, are inextricably bound together; both, if life is to be something rich, must be accepted. Neither Kate nor Stacy ever realize this fact. After the death of the parents, Kate decides to expand the dung business so that she can make enough money to escape from the house she detests with a large dowry. Kate recognizes the necessity of coming to terms with the reality of the manure, of the necessity of using it to get the lilacs of freedom from the house and of marriage. However, she has no intention of coming to terms with the perennial fact of what is, to her, disgusting in life. It is something that she recognizes must be faced, made practical use of, and then put aside. This attitude is clear in the scene in which Stacy calls Kate's attention to the smell of Con O'Toole's pipe. To Stacy the smell is worse than that of the dung. Kate, who has not noticed the smell at first, laters says that

> 'It *is* disgusting. I'll make him give up using it as soon as we take up residence in Rowe House. But don't say anything to him. He mightn't take it well. Of course I can say anything I like to him. He'll take anything from me. But it's better to wait till after we're married and not come on him with everything all at once.' (p. 31)

The calculation, the slight harshness of tone, are sufficient to indicate the distance between Kate and Con, on the one hand, and Rose and Phelim on the other. The tone, clearly enough, reveals the author's attitude towards this manipulation of the real and the ideal. Kate's thinking, however, is probably the best modern way of dealing with what is nasty in life, but clearly her thinking does not possess the wholeness and beauty that is natural to Phelim, and that Rose could respond to and accept without deluding herself in the matter.

If life for Phelim and Rose is an indissoluble union of lilacs and dung, and if life for Kate is a task of making use of the dung to get the lilacs, however impaired they may be as a result of her attitude, for Stacy life must be all lilacs. She is less bothered by the social stigma of the dunghill than Kate is, but the odor from the manure, especially on the days when fresh manure is delivered, causes severe headaches. Because of them she can seclude herself in her room delivery days where at least she does not have to see the dung. It is Kate who notices Stacy's propensity for withdrawal from facing the unpleasant. At the time of Rose's death, Kate comments:

> No wonder Stacy had no lines on her face. No wonder she looked a child, in spite of her years. Stacy got out of a lot of worry, very neatly, by just flopping off in a faint. Poor Rose was washed, and her eyes shut and her habit put on her, before Stacy came round to her senses again. 'It looks as if you're making a habit of this,' said Kate, when Stacy fainted again, in the cemetery this time, and didn't have to listen, as Kate did, to the sound of the sods clodding down on the coffin. (p. 27)

Earlier, during one of her headache spells, Stacy has the following fantasy:

> . . . she lay in bed and thought of a big lilac tree sprouting up through the boards of the floor, bending the big bright nails, sending splinters of wood flying till they hit off the window-panes. The tree always had big pointed bunches of lilac blossom all over it; more blossoms than leaves. But the blossoms weighed down towards her where she lay shivering, and they touched her face. (p. 26)

There is a strangely erotic note in this passage, and the immensity of the somewhat phallic lilac tree here might suggest barrenness of physical love in her life. She is never paired with any male in the story. But however suggestive the fantasy may be along these lines, the main thrust of the story renders such an interpretation peripheral. More to the point is the destructiveness of the lilac tree and the unnaturalness of the blossoms outnumbering the leaves. It is the dream or ideal unhinged from the reality of the manure. This point is made final in the closing scene of the story. After Kate marries and moves out of the house, Stacy informs Jasper Kane, the family solicitor, that she is at last going to get rid of the dunghill. "But what will you live on, Miss Stacy?" he said (p. 32), and the story ends.

The implications in the line are various although they do not focus the entire story. Practical Jasper Kane literally points out a detail that the sensitive and impractical Stacy has simply never thought of, and the moment he does so the humor is delightful. The reader's answer to the question is, almost involuntarily, that she will live on lilacs, figuratively, of course, her day dreams—or perhaps her unused violin and piano? Impossible, and no doubt Jasper, as well as the reader, knows this even if Stacy does not. Clearly the course of Phelim, in making a living from the manure, which enabled him to marry Rose, and the course of Kate, in doubling the intake and sale of manure to insure a large dowry so that she could marry Con O'Toole, is preferable to Stacy's alternative. The sane thing for her to do is to deal in enough manure to make a living. The story, however, is more than a criticism or gentle mocking of the dreamer who gets unmoored from reality; the word "live" in the final sentence can carry more meaning than simply to make a living. Implicit in the word, although neither Jasper Kane nor Stacy seem aware of it, is the necessity for Stacy, if she is to have a life as meaningful as that of Phelim and Rose, with whom she is temperamentally akin, to find for herself the relationship, the abiding and necessary union, between the lilacs and the dung. Only in this way will her life, unlike that of Kate and Con, be a thing of beauty.

Had Miss Lavin fashioned the dung heap as an image of Ireland, and had she fashioned the lilacs as an ideal that was incompatible with life on the Irish dung heap, the story would be a variation on a familiar theme; presumably it would also be considered a work that adhered to the "reality of politics." What we have instead is a story that adheres to reality, Irish or otherwise.

. . . ⟨I⟩t is clear why O'Connor is correct in saying that "she has stood a little apart from the rest of us. . . ." The separation is even clearer if *Tales from Bective Bridge* is thought of in conjunction with Moore's *The Untilled Field*, Joyce's *Dubliners*, Corkery's *A Munster Twilight*, O'Faoláin's *A Midsummer Night's Madness*, O'Connor's *Guests of the Nation*, and O'Flaherty's *Spring Sowing*. From Moore to O'Flaherty we move in a fictional world that is dominated, to a greater or lesser extent, by the politics and nationalism of which O'Connor speaks. These two things dominated the life of the country, so naturally they dominated the life of the imagination. It need only be added that much of our image of Ireland is dominated by the work of these writers, and that much of our fascination with them is due to the singularness of the experiences depicted, or perhaps what to non-Irish readers is somewhat exotic. When that exotic note is missing, we are disappointed; we are not getting what we have come to expect from Irish writers. However, this note is present in *Tales from Bective Bridge* and in later works, but it is the *basso ostinato* of a much larger orchestration.

Tales from Bective Bridge is one of the truly significant volumes of short stories by an Irish writer, as important in its way as those which O'Connor singles out in *The Lonely Voice*: Moore's *The Untilled Field*, Joyce's *Dubliners*, and O'Flaherty's *Spring Sowing*—as important, but of course not as influential. Free of their domination, the stories indicated quite unconsciously a way out of the political and national trap that increasingly threatens an impasse for the Irish writer. One of the values of her way out is evident in the fact that her purely creative productivity is greater than that of her contemporaries or her near contemporaries. . . .

The best explanation of her especial orientation comes from an interview. Asked if she felt herself "part of a tradition of Irish writers," she replied:

> I do not feel aware of being a particularly Irish writer. Since I lived in Ireland for most of my life, the raw material was Irish. But I suppose that if I had not moved from Massachusetts at the age of ten, I would have written about Massachusetts and the people of Massachusetts. It is the people among whom we live that provide our objective correlative. They are our idiom. Anything I wanted to achieve was in the traditions of world literature. I did not read the Irish writers until I had already dedicated myself to the short story. Then I would have been a fool not to have studied them, masters as they were of the medium. I studied English and French in college and outside the curriculum I read widely among the Russians and the Americans. O'Connor, O'Faoláin, and O'Flaherty were only a part of literature as I thought of it. I had read Tchekov and Tourgeniev, Flaubert and Joyce and the shorter works of D. H. Lawrence, Tolstoy and Henry James. As for influences, perhaps I owed most to Edith Wharton, the pastoral works of George Sand, and especially Sarah Orne Jewett.[2]

Like Joyce, who also stood a little apart from the rest of them, she aimed for achievements "in the traditions of world literature."

The point, then, is that no matter how valid O'Connor's remark on the relationship of politics and Anglo-Irish literature may be, and no matter how much, as a result of achievements of the revival writers who adhered to "the immediate reality of politics," we have come to expect this relationship, we should not allow this orientation to affect our just appreciation of Irish writing that, as in the case Mary Lavin and others, is playing a different tune.

Notes

1. (London, 1945), p. 16. All quotations from *Tales from Bective Bridge* are from this edition.
2. *St. Stephen's* (Trinity Term, No. 12, 1967), 22.

D. H. LAWRENCE

1885–1930

David Herbert Lawrence was born in Eastwood, Nottinghamshire, on September 11, 1885. Conflicts between his father, a coalminer, and his mother, a former schoolteacher, were frequent in his childhood, and his mother held a dominant influence over him for many years. Leaving school at the age of sixteen, he became a clerk, but had to give up his job after three months because of pneumonia. After a few years as a pupil-teacher at local schools, he entered University College, Nottingham, in 1906, to study for a teacher's certificate, which he gained in 1908. Moving to London, he took a teaching position in Croydon, but devoted himself increasingly to writing, in which he was encouraged by Ford Madox Ford, who published his early poems in the *English Review*. Lawrence's mother died in December 1910, a month before the publication of his first novel, *The White Peacock*.

Giving up teaching to write full-time, Lawrence published another novel, *The Trespasser,* in 1912, the year in which he eloped to the Continent with Frieda Weekley, née von Richthofen. The couple traveled in Germany and Italy while Lawrence completed *Sons and Lovers* (1913) and worked on short stories, published in *The Prussian Officer* (1914), and plays, including *The Widowing of Mrs. Holroyd* (1914). After returning to England in 1914, they were married.

His German wife added to the suspicion with which Lawrence, outspoken in his opposition to World War I, was regarded. *The Rainbow* was seized and condemned as obscene after its publication in 1915, and arguments with literary friends and illness made the war years still harder, though Lawrence did manage to publish several volumes of poetry, including *Look! We Have Come Through!* (1917), and work on *Women in Love* (1920). After the war Lawrence returned with Frieda to Italy, where he spent time in Sicily and Sardinia, giving rise to the travel book *Sea and Sardinia* (1921). In 1922 he completed a collection of stories, *England, My England,* before traveling to America via Ceylon and Australia, which he wrote of in the novel *Kangaroo* (1923). Settling in Taos, New Mexico, he visited Mexico, the background for *The Plumed Serpent* (1926), and various parts of the United States. Increasingly ill, Lawrence was found to have tuberculosis, and returned to spend his last restless years in Europe. His most controversial novel, *Lady Chatterley's Lover,* was privately printed in 1928, but was widely banned for over thirty years. Lawrence also worked on paintings, exhibited in London in 1929; a number of these, too, were seized by court order as obscene.

With his health deteriorating, Lawrence entered a sanatorium in Vence, in the south of France, where he died on March 2, 1930.

Personal

To those who knew Lawrence, not *why,* but *that* he was what he happened to be, is the important fact. I remember very clearly my first meeting with him. The place was London, the time 1915. But Lawrence's passionate talk was of the geographically remote and of the personally very near. Of the horrors in the middle distance—war, winter, the town—he would not speak. For he was on the point, so he imagined, of setting off to Florida—to Florida, where he was going to plant that colony of escape, of which up to the last he never ceased to dream. Sometimes the name and site of this seed of a happier and different world were purely fanciful. It was called Rananim, for example, and was an island like Prospero's. Sometimes it had its place on the map and its name was Florida, Cornwall, Sicily, Mexico and again, for a time, the English countryside. That wintry afternoon in 1915 it was Florida. Before tea was over he asked me if I would join the colony, and though I was an intellectually cautious young man, not at all inclined to enthusiasms, though Lawrence had startled and embarrassed me with sincerities of a kind to which my upbringing had not accustomed me, I answered yes.

Fortunately, no doubt, the Florida scheme fell through. Cities of God have always crumbled; and Lawrence's city—his village, rather, for he hated cities—his Village of the Dark God would doubtless have disintegrated like all the rest. It was better that it should have remained, as it was always to remain, a project and a hope. And I knew this even as I said I would join the colony. But there was something about Lawrence which made such knowledge, when one was in his presence, curiously irrelevant. He might propose impracticable schemes, he might say or write things that were demonstrably incorrect or even, on occasion (as when he talked about science), absurd. But to a very considerable extent it didn't matter. What mattered was always Lawrence himself, was the fire that burned within him, that glowed with so strange and marvellous a radiance in almost all he wrote.

My second meeting with Lawrence took place some years later, during one of his brief revisitings of that after-war England, which he had come so much to dread and to dislike. Then in 1925, while in India, I received a letter from Spotorno. He had read some essays I had written on Italian travel; said he liked them; suggested a meeting. The next year we were in Florence and so was he. From that time, till his

death, we were often together—at Florence, at Forte dei Marmi, for a whole winter at Diablerets, at Bandol, in Paris, at Chexbres, at Forte again, and finally at Vence where he died.

In a spasmodically kept diary I find this entry under the date of December 27th, 1927: 'Lunched and spent the p.m. with the Lawrences. D.H.L. in admirable form, talking wonderfully. He is one of the few people I feel real respect and admiration for. Of most other eminent people I have met I feel that at any rate I belong to the same species as they do. But this man has something different and superior in kind, not degree.'

'Different and superior in kind.' I think almost everyone who knew him well must have felt that Lawrence was this. A being, somehow, of another order, more sensitive, more highly conscious, more capable of feeling than even the most gifted of common men. He had, of course, his weaknesses and defects; he had his intellectual limitations—limitations which he seemed to have deliberately imposed upon himself. But these weaknesses and defects and limitations did not affect the fact of his superior otherness. They diminished him quantitively, so to speak; whereas the otherness was qualitative. Spill half your glass of wine and what remains is still wine. Water, however full the glass may be, is always tasteless and without colour.

To be with Lawrence was a kind of adventure, a voyage of discovery into newness and otherness. For, being himself of a different order, he inhabited a different universe from that of common men—a brighter and intenser world, of which, while he spoke, he would make you free. He looked at things with the eyes, so it seemed, of a man who had been at the brink of death and to whom, as he emerges from the darkness, the world reveals itself as unfathomably beautiful and mysterious. For Lawrence, existence was one continuous convalescence; it was as though he were newly re-born from a mortal illness every day of his life. What these convalescent eyes saw his most casual speech would reveal. A walk with him in the country was a walk through that marvellously rich and significant landscape which is at once the background and the principal personage of all his novels. He seemed to know, by personal experience, what it was like to be a tree or a daisy or a breaking wave or even the mysterious moon itself. He could get inside the skin of an animal and tell you in the most convincing detail how it felt and how, dimly, inhumanly, it thought. Of Black-Eyed Susan, for example, the cow at his New Mexican ranch, he was never tired of speaking, nor was I ever tired of listening to his account of her character and her bovine philosophy.

'He sees,' Vernon Lee once said to me, 'more than a human being ought to see. Perhaps,' she added, 'that's why he hates humanity so much.' Why also he loved it so much. And not only humanity: nature too, and even the supernatural. For wherever he looked, he saw more than a human being ought to see; saw more and therefore loved and hated more. To be with him was to find oneself transported to one of the frontiers of human consciousness. For an inhabitant of the safe metropolis of thought and feeling it was a most exciting experience.

One of the great charms of Lawrence as a companion was that he could never be bored and so could never be boring. He was able to absorb himself completely in what he was doing at the moment; and he regarded no task as too humble for him to undertake, nor so trivial that it was not worth his while to do it well. He could cook, he could sew, he could darn a stocking and milk a cow, he was an efficient wood-cutter and a good hand at embroidery, fires always burned when he had laid them and a floor, after Lawrence had scrubbed it, was thoroughly clean. Moreover, he possessed what is, for a highly strung and highly intelligent man, an even more remarkable accomplishment: he knew how to do nothing. He could just sit and be perfectly content. And his contentment, while one remained in his company, was infectious.

As infectious as Lawrence's contented placidity were his high spirits and his laughter. Even in the last years of his life, when his illness had got the upper hand and was killing him inch-meal, Lawrence could still laugh, on occasion, with something of the old and exuberant gaiety. Often, alas, towards the end, the laughter was bitter, and the high spirits almost terrifyingly savage. I have heard him sometimes speak of men and their ways with a kind of demoniac mockery, to which it was painful, for all the extraordinary brilliance and profundity of what he said, to listen. The secret consciousness of his dissolution filled the last years of his life with an overpowering sadness. (How tragically the splendid curve of the letters droops, at the end, towards the darkness!) It was, however, in terms of anger that he chose to express this sadness. Emotional indecency always shocked him profoundly, and, since anger seemed to him less indecent as an emotion than a resigned or complaining melancholy, he preferred to be angry. He took his revenge on the fate that had made him sad by fiercely deriding everything. And because the sadness of the slowly dying man was so unspeakably deep, his mockery was frighteningly savage. The laughter of the earlier Lawrence and, on occasion, as I have said, even the later Lawrence was without bitterness and wholly delightful.

Vitality has the attractiveness of beauty, and in Lawrence there was a continuously springing fountain of vitality. It went on welling up in him, leaping, now and then, into a great explosion of bright foam and iridescence, long after the time when, by all the rules of medicine, he should have been dead. For the last two years he was like a flame burning on in miraculous disregard of the fact that there was no more fuel to justify its existence. One grew, in spite of constantly renewed alarms, so well accustomed to seeing the flame blazing away, self-fed, in its broken and empty lamp that one almost came to believe that the miracle would be prolonged, indefinitely. But it could not be. When, after several months of separation, I saw him again at Vence in the early spring of 1930, the miracle was at an end, the flame guttering to extinction. A few days later it was quenched.—ALDOUS HUXLEY, "Introduction" to *The Letters of D. H. Lawrence*, 1932, pp. 1263–67

Poste Restante!

So any knowing correspondent would have labeled the envelope of almost any letter he was addressing to D. H. Lawrence. *Poste restante*, or *Post-lagernd*, or *Hold until called for*—a half dozen languages, a dozen countries, but always the same admonition. How many postal clerks the world over must have observed it, wondered briefly or not wondered about the identity of the English mister, at last looked him in the face as they handed him his packet of accumulated mail, and then, once having seen this improbable addressee, thin and red and dusty and vivid, wondered about him indeed! Certainly the admonition on his letters was indispensable if the mail was by any chance to reach him. A paraphrased refrain of Lawrence's correspondence runs like this: We are here. . . . We leave tomorrow, write me at. . . . Everything changed, we are still here. . . . Tomorrow we may be off after all. . . . We are still here. . . . We are off at last, and in two days will be at. . . . We have come here instead. . . . We are leaving, I will send address.

The most casual leafing through of Lawrence's letters, the unpublished together with the published, invokes at once a sense of the relentlessness of his itinerant life, and ten different leafings through would produce ten catalogues of travel in general like the following, each different from the others only as to details of place. In 1918 Lawrence wrote from England, "Frieda is pretty well—wondering what is to become of us. There are primroses in the wood and avenues of yellow hazel catkins, hanging like curtains." In 1920, from Taormina: "At the moment I feel I never want to see England again—if I move, then further off, further off"; a few months later, from the Abruzzi: "I feel all unstuck, as if I might drift anywhere"; and eighteen months after that, from Taormina again, "Our great news is that we are going to Ceylon." Ceylon promptly proved unsatisfactory: "Here we are on a ship again—somewhere in a very big blue choppy sea with flying fishes sprinting out of the waves like winged drops, and a Catholic Spanish priest playing Chopin at the piano—very well—and the boat gently rolling. . . . We are going to Australia—Heaven knows why." Less than six months later, from Taos, New Mexico: "We got here last week and since then I have been away motoring for five days into the Apache country to see an Apache dance. It is a weird country, and I feel a great stranger still." The stay in New Mexico and Mexico was to be long enough to make of these places as much a home for Lawrence as any he was to know after his native Nottinghamshire, and yet, in 1924, inevitably, he writes: "We are packing up to leave here on Saturday. . . . It is time to go." England again, and then, in late 1925, from Spotorno, south of Genoa, "We got here yesterday—it's lovely and sunny, with a blue sea, and I'm sitting out on the balcony just above the sands, to write. Switzerland was horrid—I don't like Switzerland anyhow—in slow rain and snow. We shall find ourselves a villa here, I think, for the time." The time was short, as usual, and presently they were living outside Florence, and from there in 1927 he wrote: "I have put off coming to England. I just feel I don't want to come north—feel a sort of migration instinct pushing me south rather than north." But in the next year he wrote to Harry Crosby from Switzerland, "I suppose we shall stay a week or two, then perhaps move up the mountain a little higher—my woful [*sic*] bronchials! How are you and where are you and where are you going?" From the south of France less than a year before his death, Lawrence could still write, "I wonder where we shall ultimately settle! At the moment I feel very undecided about everything. I shall send an address as soon as I have one." And then in 1929 he had one, the last:

"We have got this little house on the sea for six months, so the address is good. It is a rocky sea, very blue, with little islands way out, and mountains behind Toulon—still a touch of Homer, in the dawn—we like it—& it is good for my health. . . ." But in less than six months the long, circling journey was over.

This odyssey that only death could end, as uneasy as it was adventurous, of the most restless spirit in a world that seems more stable than it is because his restlessness strides and flashes and flies across it—this odyssey, if we are to see it in its multiple and shifting details, demands an itinerary that is fixed at last in print; Lawrence's, more than any other modern literary life, should have a calendar.

The chief reason for this necessity is that all the time that Lawrence was moving, he was also writing, and the settings of his works follow upon the march of his feet. It is in no way surprising, of course, that a writer, and especially a novelist, should assimilate his travels in his works; but there is probably no other writer in literary history whose works responded so immediately to his geographical environment as Lawrence, and certainly there is no other modern writer to whose imagination "place" made such a direct and intense appeal, and in whose works, as a consequence, place usurps such a central role. Often it becomes the major character, as it were, Lawrence's arbiter, disposing of human destinies in accordance with the response that the human characters have made to itself, the nonhuman place. Or one may say that Lawrence's people discover their identities through their response to place, and that, having thus come upon their true selves, they mark out their fate and are able to pursue it to another place—factory or farm, city or country, north or south, England or Italy, Europe or America, death or life.—MARK SCHORER, "Lawrence and the Spirit of Place" (1956), *A D.H. Lawrence Miscellany*, ed. Harry T. Moore, 1959, pp. 280–82

General

It is no wonder that D. H. Lawrence should have written two penetrating studies of Melville, for Lawrence himself is, as far as I know, the only prophetic novelist writing today—all the rest are fantasists or preachers: the only living novelist in whom the song predominates, who has the rapt bardic quality, and whom it is idle to criticize. He invites criticism because he is a preacher also—it is this minor aspect of him which makes him so difficult and misleading—an excessively clever preacher who knows how to play on the nerves of his congregation. Nothing is more disconcerting than to sit down, so to speak, before your prophet, and then suddenly to receive his boot in the pit of your stomach. "I'm damned if I'll be humble after that," you cry, and so lay yourself open to further nagging. Also the subject matter of the sermon is agitating—hot denunciations or advice—so that in the end you cannot remember whether you ought or ought not to have a body, and are only sure that you are futile. This bullying, and the honeyed sweetness which is a bully's reaction, occupy between them the foreground of Lawrence's work; his greatness lies far, far back, and rests, not like Dostoevsky's upon Christianity, nor like Melville's upon a contest, but upon something aesthetic. The voice is Balder's voice, though the hands are the hands of Esau. The prophet is irradiating nature from within, so that every colour has a glow and every form a distinctness which could not otherwise be obtained. Take a scene that always stays in the memory: that scene in *Women in Love* where one of the characters throws stones into the water at night to shatter the image of the moon. Why he throws, what the scene symbolizes, is unimportant. But the writer could not get such a

moon and water otherwise; he reaches them by his special path which stamps them as more wonderful than any we can imagine. It is the prophet back where he started from, back where the rest of us are waiting by the edge of the pool, but with a power of re-creation and evocation we shall never possess.

Humility is not easy with this irritable and irritating author, for the humbler we get, the crosser he gets. Yet I do not see how else to read him. If we start resenting or mocking, his treasure disappears as surely as if we started obeying him. What is valuable about him cannot be put into words; it is colour, gesture and outline in people and things, the usual stock-in-trade of the novelist, but evolved by such a different process that they belong to a new world.—E. M. FORSTER, "Prophecy," *Aspects of the Novel*, 1927, pp. 143–44

I regard ⟨Lawrence⟩ as a very much greater genius, if not a greater artist, than Hardy. . . . Lawrence has three aspects, and it is very difficult to do justice to all. I do not expect to be able to do so. The first is the ridiculous: his lack of sense of humour, a certain snobbery, a lack not so much of information as of the critical faculties which education should give, and an incapacity for what we ordinarily call thinking. Of this side of Lawrence, the brilliant exposure by Mr. Wyndham Lewis in *Paleface* is by far the most conclusive criticism that has been made. Secondly, there is the extraordinarily keen sensibility and capacity for profound intuition—intuition from which he commonly drew the wrong conclusions. Third, there is a distinct sexual morbidity. Unfortunately, it is necessary to keep all of these aspects in mind in order to criticise the writer fairly; and this, in such close perspective, is almost impossible. I shall no doubt appear to give excessive prominence to the third; but that, after all, is what has been least successfully considered.

I have already touched upon the deplorable religious upbringing which gave Lawrence his lust for intellectual independence: like most people who do not know what orthodoxy is, he hated it. With the more intimate reasons, of heredity and environment, for eccentricity of thought and feeling I am not concerned: too many people have made them their business already. And I have already mentioned the insensibility to ordinary social morality, which is so alien to my mind that I am completely baffled by it as a monstrosity. The point is that Lawrence started life wholly free from any restriction of tradition or institution, that he had no guidance except the Inner Light, the most untrustworthy and deceitful guide that ever offered itself to wandering humanity. It was peculiarly so for Lawrence, who does not appear to have been gifted with the faculty of self-criticism, except in flashes, even to the extent of ordinary worldly shrewdness. Of divine illumination, it may be said that probably every man knows when he has it, but that any man is likely to think that he has it when he has it not; and even when he has had it, the daily man that he is may draw the wrong conclusions from the enlightenment which the momentary man has received: no one, in short, can be the sole judge of whence his inspiration comes. A man like Lawrence therefore, with his acute sensibility, violent prejudices and passions, and lack of intellectual and social training, is admirably fitted to be an instrument for forces of good or for forces of evil; or as we might expect, partly for one and partly for the other. A trained mind like that of Mr. Joyce is always aware what master it is serving; an untrained mind, and a soul destitute of humility and filled with self-righteousness, is a blind servant and a fatal leader. It would seem that for Lawrence any spiritual force was good, and that evil resided only in the absence of spirituality. Most people, no doubt, need to be aroused to the perception of the simple distinction between the spiritual and the material; and Lawrence never forgot, and never mistook, this distinction. But most people are only very little alive; and to awaken them to the spiritual is a very great responsibility: it is only when they are so awakened that they are capable of real Good, but that at the same time they become first capable of Evil. Lawrence lived all his life, I should imagine, on the spiritual level; no man was less a sensualist. Against the living death of modern material civilisation he spoke again and again, and even if these dead could speak, what he said is unanswerable. As a criticism of the modern world, *Fantasia of the Unconscious* is a book to keep at hand and re-read. In contrast to Nottingham, London or industrial America, his capering redskins of *Mornings in Mexico* seem to represent Life. So they do; but that is not the last word, only the first. The man's vision is spiritual, but spiritually sick. The dæmonic powers found an instrument of far greater range, delicacy and power in the author of "The Prussian Officer" than in the author of "A Group of Noble Dames"; and the tale which I used as an example ("The Shadow in the Rose Garden") can be matched by several others. I have not read all of his late and his posthumous works, which are numerous. In some respects, he may have progressed: his early belief in Life may have passed over, as a really serious belief in Life must, into a belief in Death. But I cannot see much development in *Lady Chatterley's Lover*. Our old acquaintance, the game-keeper, turns up again: the social obsession which makes his well-born—or almost well-born—ladies offer themselves to—or make use of—plebeians springs from the same morbidity which makes other of his female characters bestow their favours upon savages. The author of that book seems to me to have been a very sick man indeed.

There is, I believe, a very great deal to be learned from Lawrence, though those who are most capable of exercising the judgment necessary to extract the lesson, may not be those who are most in need of it. That we can and ought to reconcile ourselves to Liberalism, Progress and Modern Civilisation is a proposition which we need not have waited for Lawrence to condemn; and it matters a good deal in what name we condemn it. I fear that Lawrence's work may appeal, not to those who are well and able to discriminate, but to the sick and debile and confused; and will appeal not to what remains of health in them, but to their sickness. Nor will many even accept his doctrine as he would give it, but will be busy after their own inventions. The number of people in possession of any criteria for discriminating between good and evil is very small; the number of the half-alive hungry for any form of spiritual experience, or what offers itself as spiritual experience, high or low, good or bad, is considerable. My own generation has not served them very well. Never has the printing-press been so busy, and never have such varieties of buncombe and false doctrine come from it. *Woe unto the foolish prophets, that follow their own spirit, and have seen nothing! O Israel, thy prophets have been like foxes in the waste places. . . . And the word of the* LORD *came unto me, saying, Son of man, these men have taken their idols into their hearts, and put the stumbling-block of their iniquity before their face: should I be inquired of at all by them?*—T. S. ELIOT, *After Strange Gods*, 1934, pp. 62–67

SIR,—I never knew D. H. Lawrence well, but my memories, such as they are, date from the period so sympathetically and beautifully described in O. M.'s article. I, too, was shown the woods in spring and taken a walk near Arundel. Perhaps my character did not pass the test of the Sussex downs, anyhow I heard little from him in after years—only an occasional postcard.

The war tortured him but never paralyzed him; the tremendous nightmare chapter in *Kangaroo* is sufficient proof of that, and all through his later work the vitality continues. Now he is dead, and the low-brows whom he scandalized have united with the high-brows whom he bored to ignore his greatness. This cannot be helped; no one who alienates both Mrs. Grundy and Aspatia can hope for a good obituary Press. All that we can do—those of us who agree, as I do, with your correspondent Mr. Hellyar—is to say straight out that he was the greatest imaginative novelist of our generation. The rest must be left where he would have wished it to be left—in the hands of the young.—E. M. FORSTER, Letter to the Editor, *NA*, March 29, 1930, pp. 888

SIR,—Mr. E. M. Forster, in a letter in your issue of March 29th, says "straight out" that the late D. H. Lawrence was "the greatest imaginative novelist of our time."

I am the last person to wish to disparage the genius of Lawrence, or to disapprove when a writer of the eminence of Mr. Forster speaks "straight out." But the virtue of speaking straight out is somewhat diminished if what one speaks is not sense. And unless we know exactly what Mr. Forster means by *greatest*, *imaginative*, and *novelist*, I submit that this judgment is meaningless. For there are at least three "novelists" of "our generation"—two of whom are living—for whom a similar claim might be made.—T. S. ELIOT, Letter to the Editor, *NA*, April 5, 1930, p. 11

SIR,—Mr. T. S. Eliot duly entangles me in his web. He asks what exactly I mean by "greatest," "imaginative," and "novelist," and I cannot say. Worse still, I cannot even say what "exactly" means—only that there are occasions when I would rather feel like a fly than a spider, and that the death of D. H. Lawrence is one of these.—E. M. FORSTER, Letter to the Editor, *NA*, April 12, 1930, p. 45

SIR,—I am sorry Mr. Forster is unable to answer Mr. Eliot, but I daresay he is not very good at definition. Particularly I wanted to know what is meant by saying something "straight out." It is a phrase, I have noticed, frequently used by high-minded controversialists, apparently to give an air of nobility and audacity even to some exceptionally silly remark: but what precisely does it mean? I hoped also to discover what was meant by "high-brow." I used to surmise it meant an intelligent and well-educated person; but then what reason has Mr. Forster for supposing that such people have been unfair to the works of D. H. Lawrence? They have been critical; but then intelligent and well educated people are critical of Shakespeare, and of Mr. Forster, and even of themselves. Perhaps speaking "straight out" means merely being uncritical. That, I admit, is a quality which Mr. Forster may have reason to admire.—CLIVE BELL, Letter to the Editor, *NA*, April 19, 1930, pp. 76–77

SIR,—I cannot tell Mr. Clive Bell the meaning of "straight out" and "high-brow" until he has defined what he means by "meaning," but I would like to remind your other readers that my letter, which occasions his questions, was occasioned by the death of D. H. Lawrence. They may not have agreed with what I said, Mr. Adamson, for example, did not, but they will scarcely misunderstand it or bark their shins on every other word unless they are expert controversialists. These, very properly, form a race apart, with difficulties and methods of their own.

I should also like to make a suggestion about Lawrence, if your space allows. He was both a preacher and a poet, and some people, myself included, do not sympathize with the preaching. Yet I feel that without the preaching the poetry could not exist. With some writers one can disentangle the two, with him they are inseparable. As he grew older, he became more didactic and mannered, and, if one differed from him, more tiresome; but the poetry, also, was increasing in strength. *The Plumed Serpent* blares out explicitly what the snowdrops in *The White Peacock* shyly hinted at, yet, exquisite as were those early woodlands, they droop towards unreality beneath the sunlight of Mexico. In a sense he never developed. One can hear from the first what he is going to say. But one never knows what his own message will evoke in him, and although I cannot believe in it, I believe it was the mainspring of his greatness.—E. M. FORSTER, Letter to the Editor, *NA*, April 26, 1930, p. 109

The force which eventually produced Auschwitz, Hiroshima, and the present 'tension' seemed to break right over Lawrence, shattering the complex fabric of feeling, institutions, and nature which Burke had celebrated as the foundation of civilisation, and whose slow decay Lawrence had already studied in *The Rainbow*. It created not only the famous cries of the soul in the letters and in Chapter XII of *Kangaroo*: it transformed Lawrence from a symbolist experimenter in the traditional novel into the compulsive, chaotic, half-comic propagandist of the popular imagination . . . If the war made of the body of his subsequent work a kind of vast, sometimes incoherent *Waste Land*, the important point is that the effect is fully commensurate with the cause. If one takes World War I and its aftermath seriously, one must take seriously the Lawrence who spilled his awesome energy in reaction to it. One must take seriously precisely what alienates so many readers—the restless, angry disorder, and the interest in the kinds of savage energies that would fill the sudden chasm that the war had opened. The War made Lawrence an anarchist in all but the most literal political sense . . . To Lawrence, the use of poison gas or the 'bullying' of innocent civilians are essentially religious crimes which, like man's first fall, corrupt everything associated with them. A society which creates and exalts 'that huge obscene machine they called the war' immediately breaks its organic social contract, dissolves its most intimate bonds, and sends men back to their original experiencing selves. Amid such chaos, one can choose either shame or loneliness. *Any* conventional act means a 'completely base and obscene' surrender to 'the dream helplessness of the mass-psyche' . . .

This vision is the source of the moral and aesthetic freedom in the later Lawrence, which frequently irritates humanistic critics.—NEIL MYERS, "Lawrence and the War," *Crit*, Winter 1962, p. 44

For some time I read kilometers of English novels, among them the first edition of *Lady Chatterley's Lover*, published privately in Florence. Lawrence's works impressed me because of their poetic quality and a certain vital magnetism focused on the hidden relationships between human beings. However, it soon became clear to me that, for all his genius, he was frustrated by his passion for instructing the reader, like so many other great English writers. D. H. Lawrence sets up a course in sexual education that has almost nothing to do with what we learn spontaneously from love and life. He ended up boring me stiff, but this did not lessen my admiration for his tortured mystico-sexual search, all the more painful because it was so useless.—PABLO NERUDA, "Luminous Solitude," *Memoirs*, 1976, p. 93

The first thing that happened in the Industrial Revolution was that boys were pulled away from their fathers and other men,

and placed in schools. D. H. Lawrence described what this was like in his essay "Men Must Work and Women as Well." What happened to his generation, as he describes it, was the appearance of one idea: that physical labor is bad. Lawrence recalls how his father enjoyed working in the mines, enjoyed the camaraderie with the other men, enjoyed coming home and taking his bath in the kitchen. But in Lawrence's lifetime the schoolteachers arrived from London to teach him and his classmates that physical labor is a bad thing, that boys and girls both should strive to move upward into more "spiritual" work—higher work, mental work. With this comes the concept that fathers have been doing something wrong, that men's physical work is low, that the women are right in preferring white curtains and a sensitive, elegant life.

When he wrote *Sons and Lovers*, Lawrence clearly believed the teachers: he took the side of "higher" life, his mother's side. It was not until two years before he died, when he had tuberculosis in Italy, that he began to notice the vitality of the Italian working men, and to feel a deep longing for his own father. He began to realize it was possible that his mother hadn't been right on this issue.—ROBERT BLY, Interview by Keith Thompson, *NwA*, May 1982, p.37

Works

The *Love Poems*, if by that Mr. Lawrence means the middling-sensual erotic verses in this collection, are a sort of pre-raphaelitish slush, disgusting or very nearly so. The attempts to produce the typical Laurentine line have brought forth:

I touched her and she shivered like a dead snake.

which was improved by an even readier parodist, to

I touched her and she came off in scales.

Jesting aside, when Mr. Lawrence ceases to discuss his own disagreeable sensations, when he writes low-life narrative, as he does in "Whether or Not" and in "Violets," there is no English poet under forty who can get within shot of him. That Masefield should be having a boom seems, as one takes count of these poems, frankly ridiculous.

It is no more possible to quote from them as illustration than it would be to illustrate a Rembrandt by cutting off two inches of canvas. The first is in mood-ridden *chiaroscuro*, the characters being a policeman, his sweetheart, his mother, and a widow who has taken advantage of his excitement and by whom he has had a child. It is sullen and heavy, and as ugly as such a tale must be.

Yi, tha'rt a man, tha'rt a fine big man, but never a
　　baby had eyes
As sulky an' ormin as thine.
　　　I damn well shanna marry 'er,
　　　　　So chew at it no more,
　　　Or I'll chuck the flamin' lot of you—
　　　　　You needn't have swore.

So much for the tonality. Kipling has never done it as well in verse, though he gets something like the same range in his prose of "Bedelia Harrodsfoot." The comparison with Masefield is, as I have said, ridiculous. It is what Masefield would like to do and can not.

"Violets" presents two girls and another at the funeral of a young fellow who has died among

　　　Pals worse n'r any name as you could call.
Ah know tha liked 'im better nor me. But let
　Me tell thee about this lass. When you had gone
Ah stopped behind on t' pad i' th' drippin' wet
　An' watched what 'er 'ad on.

If this book does not receive the Polignac prize a year from this November, there will be due cause for scandal.

Mr. Lawrence was "discovered" by Ford Madox Hueffer during the latter's editorship of thc *English Review*, about four years ago. Some of his verses appeared then, and he has since made a notable reputation by his prose works, *The White Peacock* and *The Trespasser*.

His prose training stands him in good stead in these poems. The characters are real. They arc not stock figures of "the poor," done from the outside and provided with *cliché* emotions.

> I expect you know who I am, Mrs. Naylor!
> —Who yer are? yis, you're Lizzie Stainwright.
> An 'appen you might guess what I've come for?
> —'Appen I mightn't, 'appen I might.

Mr. Lawrence has attempted realism and attained it. He has brought contemporary verse up to the level of contemporary prose, and that is no mean achievement. These two poems at least are great art.—EZRA POUND, "Love Poems, and Others," *Poetry*, July 1913, pp. 149–51

Both *The Trespasser* and *The White Peacock* are early studies in mis-mating. These novels already foreshadow the born stylist and reveal Mr Lawrence as a writer of puzzling importance. But the mis-matings they portray remain obscurely motivated and therefore seem arbitrary; the psychological justification is often inadequate or obscure. We do not understand them, and hesitate to accept them. The same criticism applies to Mr Lawrence's play, *The Widowing of Mrs Holroyd*. We see that Mrs Holroyd hates her husband, but we do not see so clearly why her love for him has died, drunkard though he is. For the author, in spite of himself, has made him lovable notwithstanding his vices, so that his death comes as a sorrow and a rebuke to his wife. The play is more powerful than the novels if only because a livid hate expressed on the stage by an impassioned woman carries its own conviction.

Sons and Lovers marks an astonishing change in its author. If this slow-moving, profound, almost too inevitable study leaves the fascinated reader disturbed and exhausted, it is surely no less exhaustive of the author's true inwardness. Here Mr Lawrence has found the very core of himself; here he has dipped deep into his own childhood, setting down all that he ever knew or felt. We notice a sudden exquisite refinement of psychological texture, a new, painstaking reverence for the most subtle and intangible details of motivation. The problem of mis-mating is no longer studied in an already established marital relation; here it is not a matter of mis-mating at all but of a radical inability to mate. This inability Mr Lawrence seeks to explain entirely in terms of his hero's emotional relation to his parents. . . .

No summary can convey the pathos of *Sons and Lovers*. With all its power and its passion, it remains to a certain extent incomprehensible. We may, for the moment, accept it intuitively. But we hesitate to accept it in its implications. The very idea that an excess of mother love should prove so disastrous to an individual's fate seems monstrous. Instinctively we look upon this as an exceptional case, and fortify ourselves against it by calling the book morbid or perverse. Mr Lawrence himself has not come to our aid with any supplementary theory, nor, fortunately, does he weaken the natural eloquence of his artistry by any attempt to generalize.

How deeply felt, how little reasoned, the reaction has been with him may be gathered from a reading of his *Love Poems*. These astonishingly self-revealing lyrics repeat, with almost monotonous regularity, Paul's most intimate psychic conflicts. And it would not be at all difficult, going back now, to show that the earlier novels and the play are also, in their essence, nothing more than unclarified and fragmentary expressions of the same personal experience before Mr Lawrence had arrived at the searching and pitiless insight which in *Sons and Lovers* makes him such a memorable artist. Hatred of the father and too much love of the mother are the *leitmotifs* of everything this author has written.

In order to understand Mr Lawrence fully we must go beyond his works. Fiction is at best a specialized and limited way of conveying the truth. A novel based upon the truth of the evolutionary theory, poetically visioned by the author at a time when that theory was not yet a part of general knowledge, would, despite all artistic merit, leave a certain margin of incredulity until, let us say, Huxley's lectures had made evolution a household term. In precisely the same way our completer understanding of *Sons and Lovers* depends upon our knowledge of a theory. For without the Freudian psycho-sexual theories *Sons and Lovers* remains an enigma; with it we see that artist and scientist supplement each other, that each in his own way attests to the same truth.

The methods necessarily differ. Where Mr Lawrence particularizes so passionately Freud generalizes. Freud has proved beyond cavil that the parental influence regularly determines the mating impulse. The child's attachment to the parent of opposite sex becomes the prototype of all later love relations. The feeling is so strong and even fraught with such intense jealousy of the parent of the same sex, that all children seem to entertain conscious and unconscious fantasies in which the rival parent is either killed or removed. In the normal development this first infatuation is gradually obliterated from memory by widening associations and by transference, but the unconscious impress remains, so that every man tends to choose for his mate a woman who has associative connections for him with the early infantile image of his mother, while the woman also makes her choice in relation to her father. As soon as there is any disturbance of the balanced influence of both parents upon the child there follows an abnormal concentration upon the beloved parent. To such distortion of the normal erotic development Freud attaches the greatest importance, seeing in it the major cause of all neurotic disturbances.

Of this *Sons and Lovers* is an eloquent example. A distortion so great that it precludes all mating is not only prejudicial to the individual's true happiness but may lead to an atrophy of all initiative. Paul constantly associates the feeling of death with his inability to mate, and that too is psychologically sound. We recognize the Paul in us. For though we may dislike a happy ending in our novel, we cannot but prefer it in our lives.—ALFRED KUTTNER, *NR*, April 10, 1915, pp. 255–57

Our generation has chosen to see in *Lady Chatterley's Lover* only a convenient expression, in strong language, of its revolt from the white idealistic love of the past and a defiant justification of a life of free physical sensation. But if Lawrence had meant to justify mere sensation for its own sake he would have stopped with the descriptions of the physical acts. As it is, one French commentator at least has taken him to task for exalting sexual experience and enveloping it with mysticism.

If, to some, his work is nothing but crude realism, to others who know poetry it is more than that: the prose is lyrical as well as sensual, the descriptions full of sensitiveness as well as crudeness, of beauty as well as obscenity. A vigorous and impetuous style carries the weight of intense physical and imaginative emotions and in the end unites them in a brilliant fusion of physical-mysticism.

Why the crudeness and the obscenity of the language? Because Lawrence was preoccupied with his *beginning*, with making a new beginning in love. And first it was necessary to dethrone mentally directed love. Lawrence never tired of warning us that "the affinity of mind and personality is an excellent basis of friendship between the sexes, but a disastrous basis for marriage." Why? Because it often constitutes a denial of the deeper needs of our nature. So he pleads for an instinctive beginning. He gives us in *Lady Chatterley's Lover* an honest picture of all the aspects and moods of physical love. But he writes neither scientifically nor for the sake of pornography. Even when he is most naturalistic and apparently obscene there is a reason for the obscene words. They are the very words by which Lawrence believed one could alone renew contact with the reality of sexual passion, which the cult of idealism had distorted for us. His war was against evasive, reticent language, which makes for evasive, reticent living and thinking.

Love had been travestied by the idealists. By force of association the words they used aroused lofty exaltations or timorous reactions in the head which had no connection whatever with sensual love and were therefore "counterfeits." Lawrence took the naked words and used them because they conveyed realities which we were to live out not merely in action but in thought. For Lawrence did not mean *Lady Chatterley's Lover* to incite everyone to action in sex; only those who should act must. Modern psychology has told us what becomes of feelings which are not honestly and naturally lived out: they reappear later in perverted forms. It has also told us that no feeling can be awakened in us unless we have the roots of it in ourselves; no ideas can be put into our heads, they can only be developed when the seed of them is already growing in us. *Lady Chatterley's Lover* could do nothing but awaken those who desired to be awakened. For others, the experience has to be gone through, not with the body but with the mind. Lawrence says himself: "This is the real point of the book. I want men and women to be able to *think* sex, fully, completely, honestly and cleanly." Now this cannot be done if we are afraid of words.

When Lawrence had taken Lady Chatterley and Mellors back to the sources and basis of sexual love it was like his imaginative retrogression into the primitive, which, as we have seen, was not a permanent return but only a dipping back, to be refreshed at the source, in order that we might go forward again with renewed strength. In the book, Lady Chatterley and Mellors can go on, because of their fulfillment—she to motherhood, he to the building of their world together, and in the end both to chastity. For now there can be chastity between them. There are few endings as serene as the end of Mellors's letter to Lady Chatterley: "I love the chastity now that it flows between us . . . We could be chaste together . . . We really trust in the little flame, and in the unnamed gods that shield it from being blown out . . . So I believe in the little flame between us. For me it's the only thing in the world . . ."—ANAÏS NIN, "Lady Chatterley's Lover," *D. H. Lawrence: An Unprofessional Study* (1932), 1964, pp. 107–10

To say what one means in art is never easy, and the more intimately one is implicated in one's material, the more difficult it is. If, besides, one commits fiction to a therapeutic function which is to be operative not on the audience but on the author, declaring, as D. H. Lawrence did, that "One sheds one's sicknesses in books, repeats and presents again one's emotions to be master of them," the difficulty is vast. It is an acceptable theory only with the qualification that technique, which objectifies, is under no other circumstances so imperative. For merely to repeat one's emotions, merely to look into one's heart and write, is also merely to repeat the round of emotional bondage. If our books are to be exercises in self-

analysis, then technique must—and alone can—take the place of the absent analyst.

Lawrence, in the relatively late Introduction to his *Collected Poems*, made that distinction of the amateur between his "real" poems and his "composed" poems, between the poems which expressed his demon directly and created their own form "willy-nilly," and the poems which, through the hocus pocus of technique, he spuriously put together and could, if necessary, revise. His belief in a "poetry of the immediate present," poetry in which nothing is fixed, static, or final, where all is shimmeriness and impermanence and vitalistic essence, arose from this mistaken notion of technique. And from this notion, an unsympathetic critic like D. S. Savage can construct a case which shows Lawrence driven "concurrently to the dissolution of personality and the dissolution of art." The argument suggests that Lawrence's early, crucial novel, *Sons and Lovers*, is another example of meanings confused by an impatience with technical resources.

The novel has two themes: the crippling effects of a mother's love on the emotional development of her son; and the "split" between kinds of love, physical and spiritual, which the son develops, the kinds represented by two young women, Clara and Miriam. The two themes should, of course, work together, the second being, actually, the result of the first: this "split" is the "crippling." So one would expect to see the novel developed, and so Lawrence, in his famous letter to Edward Garnett, where he says that Paul is left at the end with the "drift towards death," apparently thought he had developed it. Yet in the last few sentences of the novel, Paul rejects his desire for extinction and turns towards "the faintly humming, glowing town," to life—as nothing in his previous history persuades us that he could unfalteringly do.

The discrepancy suggests that the book may reveal certain confusions between intention and performance.

The first of these is the contradiction between Lawrence's explicit characterizations of the mother and father and his tonal evaluations of them. It is a problem not only of style (of the contradiction between expressed moral epithets and the more general texture of the prose which applies to them) but of point of view. Morel and Lawrence are never separated, which is a way of saying that Lawrence maintains for himself in this book the confused attitude of his character. The mother is a "proud, *honorable* soul," but the father has a "small, *mean* head." This is the sustained contrast; the epithets are characteristic of the whole; and they represent half of Lawrence's feelings. But what is the other half? Which of these characters is given his real sympathy—the hard, self-righteous, aggressive, demanding mother who comes through to us, or the simple, direct, gentle, downright, fumbling, ruined father? There are two attitudes here. Lawrence (and Morel) loves his mother, but he also hates her for compelling his love; and he hates his father with the true Freudian jealousy, but he also loves him for what he is in himself, and he sympathizes more deeply with him because his wholeness has been destroyed by the mother's domination, just as his, Lawrence-Morel's, has been.

This is a psychological tension which disrupts the form of the novel and obscures its meaning, because neither the contradiction in style nor the confusion in point of view is made to right itself. Lawrence is merely repeating his emotions, and he avoids an austerer technical scrutiny of his material because it would compel him to master them. He would not let the artist be stronger than the man.

The result is that, at the same time that the book condemns the mother, it justifies her; at the same time that it shows Paul's failure, it offers rationalizations which place the failure elsewhere. The handling of the girl, Miriam, if viewed closely, is pathetic in what it signifies for Lawrence, both as man and artist. For Miriam is made the mother's scape-goat, and in a different way from the way that she was in life. The central section of the novel is shot through with alternate statements as to the source of the difficulty: Paul is unable to love Miriam wholly, and Miriam can love only his spirit. The contradictions appear sometimes within single paragraphs, and the point of view is never adequately objectified and sustained to tell us which is true. The material is never seen as material; the writer is caught in it exactly as firmly as he was caught in his experience of it. "That's how women are with me," said Paul. "They want me like mad, but they don't want to belong to me." So he might have said, and believed it; but at the end of the novel, Lawrence is still saying that, and himself believing it.

For the full history of this technical failure, one must read *Sons and Lovers* carefully and then learn the history of the manuscript from the book called *D. H. Lawrence: A Personal Record*, by one E. T., who was Miriam in life. The basic situation is clear enough. The first theme—the crippling effects of the mother's love—is developed right through to the end; and then suddenly, in the last few sentences, turns on itself, and Paul gives himself to life, not death. But all the way through, the insidious rationalizations of the second theme have crept in to destroy the artistic coherence of the work. A "split" would occur in Paul; but as the split is treated, it is superimposed upon rather than developed in support of the first theme. It is a rationalization made from it. If Miriam is made to insist on spiritual love, the meaning and the power of theme one are reduced; yet Paul's weakness is disguised. Lawrence could not separate the investigating analyst, who must be objective, from Lawrence, the subject of the book; and the sickness was not healed, the emotion not mastered, the novel not perfected. All this, and the character of a whole career, would have been altered if Lawrence had allowed his technique to discover the fullest meaning of his subject.—MARK SCHORER, "Technique as Discovery," *HdR*, Spring 1948, pp. 75–78

The writing of *Kangaroo* was an extraordinary *tour de force* of rapid composition, comparable with the almost fabulous creation of *Guy Mannering* in six weeks. Although some characters and episodes in the book are imaginary or transferred to Australia from elsewhere, much of the writing deals with Lawrence's experiences of Australia—with the unique result that he was remembering and setting down with extreme accuracy and vividness one set of experiences while actually undergoing others, themselves destined to be remembered and written as he found new ones. All that Australian part of the book was lived and written, not so much simultaneously, as successively during his brief visit. . . .

Kangaroo, then, is not one of Lawrence's worked-over novels, which he wrote and re-wrote over and over with such energy. It was "improvised", as most of his novels are, in the sense that he began to write the book without having planned it and without even knowing where it would take him. *Kangaroo*, like *Aaron's Rod*, he gave to the printer in its first draft, without bothering to reconstruct. What the book lacks in conventional form and grouping is more than atoned for by its magical freshness and vividness, that immediate feeling of life which Lawrence's writings had more abundantly than any author of his time. Nobody else gives you that sense that you yourself have actually experienced what he has written. An Australian friend, Mr. Adrian Lawlor, writes me that he has never seen that coast south of Sydney, but "after reading Lawrence, God! I've *been* there."

But the reader must be warned that some of these Australian characters and the scenes between people are wholly imagined or imaginatively transported from the outside world. Whenever Lawrence is evoking the Australian spirit of place and anonymous people going about their everyday lives and so coming casually in contact with Somers and Harriet, then it is all "real" as children say, it actually happened—the Sydney taximan, the garbage man, the bus conductor, and so on. But the named characters and all that happens with them were imagined. For in Australia Lawrence met nobody socially. "I don't present any letters of introduction, we don't know a soul on this side of the continent: which is almost a triumph in itself. For the first time in my life I feel how lovely it is to know nobody in the whole country: and nobody can come to the door, except the tradesmen who bring the bread and meat and so on, and who are very unobtrusive." Jack and Victoria and Jaz are probably founded on memories of Australians Lawrence met on liners between Naples and Sydney. Dr. Eder is said to have given hints for the character of Kangaroo, and though Lawrence vehemently denied this, the reason may have been the English novelist's dread of the libel action—particularly haunting to Lawrence who was accustomed to draw such recognisable yet unflattering portraits of his acquaintances. The minor character of William James is a recollection of Lawrence's days in Cornwall.

Yet so convincing are these imagined scenes that Lawrence was bitterly blamed for refusing to tell the dying 'Roo that he loved him—thought no such person and no such scene ever existed! Where did he get the vivid scenes of political contest between the Diggers and the socialists? Not from his favourite periodical, *The Sydney Bulletin*, for at that time no such political violence occurred in Australia. Probably they were a transference to the Australian scene of the bitter contests between fascists and communists Lawrence had seen in Italy in 1920–22. Lawrence himself was greatly interested in the nature of power, and many pages and scenes of *Kangaroo* will show the strange battle of wills between himself and his wife when, after nearly ten years marriage, he laboured and battled unavailingly to prove to her that the basis of marriage is not perfect love, but perfect submission of the wife to the husband. This Somers-Harriet contest is one of the major themes of the book, and marvellously true to the characters of Lawrence and his wife. But Lawrence, mistaking perhaps his power as a writer for power as a leader, was constantly brooding over the thought of himself as a leader of men in action—only to recoil violently and instinctively from any such part the moment he sensed—or his "daimon" sensed—that it would interfere with his power as a writer, which required pure individualism and isolation. Out of this in turn came the two astonishing chapters of reminiscence of Lawrence's life in wartime England when he felt himself threatened with having to submit to crude bullying power in the humblest of positions, and revolted angrily from the threat. In fact, he was never in any danger of conscription since he was so ill with comsumption that he was instantly exempted; but the spiritual battle was to be fought, and he did not shrink. As Lawrence Powell says, those two chapters are "an impassioned chronicle of the hatred and persecution visited upon individuals who do not succumb to the madness of wartime propaganda". But in the end as in the beginning, it must be insisted that, with all its other achievements, the supreme achievement of *Kangaroo* lies in its unforgettably vivid and accurate pictures of the Australian continent, in which no other English writer has approached Lawrence.—RICHARD ALDINGTON, "Introduction" to *Kangaroo*, 1951, pp. vii–x

The Lost Girl is indeed equally unlike *Sons and Lovers* and *The Rainbow*; it is unlike any other novel that Lawrence wrote. It suggests the work of an unsentimental, more subtle, and incomparably more penetrating Dickens, about whose humour, generous though it is, there is nothing soft, as there is nothing savage (though I find the Natcha Kee Tawara business irritating). As a rendering of English provincial life, it strikes one as what Arnold Bennett would have wished to have done, though, being the work of a great creative genius, it is utterly beyond Bennett's achievement. I am thinking of that main part of the book the scene of which is placed in England; the conclusion in the South Italian mountains (the note of it could not have been foreseen from the opening of the book) was obviously added after the war when Lawrence was in Italy or Sicily. What distinguishes *The Lost Girl*, then, is the lightness of Lawrence's personal engagement in it—the absence in it of the felt pressure of problems and personal urgencies: thinking of the prevailing comedy note, Lawrence himself, in a letter announcing that he has finished it, describes the book as "amusing." "It amuses me terribly," he says in that earlier letter (if we assume it to be about *The Lost Girl*), written in the last winter of the war.

It is amusing at a very high level. It contains plenty of acute social observation and of characteristic psychological insight. But, as the narrative proceeds and one thing comes after another, we realize that there is no compelling total significance in control.

In *Aaron's Rod*, which came out in 1921, we have again the full urgency of personal engagement, but we have it in a new way. Different as Laurentian art is from the Flaubertian, in *The Rainbow* and *Women in Love* Lawrence worked assiduously to achieve the impersonality of full creation. But in *Aaron's Rod* he is no longer very much preoccupied with this, though what he offers us is art or nothing—art challenging the maxim: "Never trust the artist, trust the tale." A desperately personal urgency, we know, provided theme and impulsion for *Sons and Lovers*; but that work in the final achieved form in which we have it offers the achieved insight into the "case," and the delicately verified exhibition of it; the author's judgment that the form is now right is his judgment that intelligence has successfully performed its office. *Aaron's Rod* is far more tentative, much more like an actual immediate living of the problem; something experimental embarked on in the expectation that the essential insight will have sufficiently clarified and established itself by the close, and that a sufficiently satisfactory close will present itself. The self-exploratory nature of the personal engagement is virtually stated at one point in the book, the occasion being the letter addressed by Aaron to Sir William Franks:

> Well, here was a letter for a poor old man to receive. But, in the dryness of his withered mind, Aaron got it out of himself. When a man writes a letter to himself, it is a pity to post it to somebody else. Perhaps the same is true of a book. (Chapter XVIII)

That last sentence has its clear significance: in writing his letter Aaron discovers what he feels and thinks, and Lawrence is writing *Aaron's Rod* as a kind of "letter" to himself.

The spirit of unembarrassed tentativeness in which he wrote the book proclaims itself in that lack of artistic providence which appears so unmistakably in the treatment of Jim Bricknell. So insistent a part do the oddities of this character play in the early pages of the book that we naturally assume that something is going to be done with him. But after punching Lilly in the wind in Chapter VIII he drops out. We remain convinced that Lawrence *had* been going to do something with him, but there has been a change of mind as the book has gone forward. Jim now figures merely as part of the representation of that artistic and intellectual Bohemia with which there is certainly some point in Aaron's having had his contacts. And of that representation in general we find that in other respects, too, it is calculated to prepare us for a development that actually we do not get. We come, in fact, to recognize in due course that in *Aaron's Rod* we are not reading a work of art of the order of *Women in Love*; there is nothing of that closeness of organization and density of significance, though what we are reading is certainly a most lively novel and a work of genius. The genius is irresistibly apparent in the rendering of the various scenes and episodes of Aaron's truancy. There are Sir William and Lady Franks and their houseparty at Novara; there are the street demonstration at Milan, and the meeting with Angus and Francis (Francis, that perfectly observed type of the artistic-intellectual nineteen-twenties in whom we recognize the Rico of "St. Mawr"); there is Aaron's railway journey with this distinguished pair to Florence; and at Florence there is the English-speaking colony, done with that incomparable rightness of touch which is Lawrence's—comedy too intelligent and sensitive and poised for malice or the satirical note (and placing the callowness of Forster's treatment of the theme in *A Room with a View*). And as one goes on recalling the things in which the genius of the novelist especially compels recognition, one realizes that their power is not, as a rule, at the same time some inevitability of significance in relation to the themes of the novel. We may see in them a relevance to those themes, but this does not strike us as having compelled their presence, or as explaining their life. Lawrence, we feel, would not have been at a loss to substitute things that would have done as well. We recognize, in fact, that what we have here is for the most part recent actual experience of Lawrence's own, directly rendered: it is just because its impact on him is fresh that it plays so large a part in the life of this novel.—F. R. LEAVIS, "Lawrence and Art," *D. H. Lawrence: Novelist*, 1956, pp. 22–25

Lawrence's last novel bears detailed and striking resemblances to his first, *The White Peacock*. Each has a gamekeeper, a wood, a lady who must choose between an industrial magnate and a "natural" man. But the two books contrast sharply in the way they turn out. In the earlier novel the lady chooses the magnate while the vital man sickens and dies. As a matter of fact, this pessimistic conclusion is doubled since no less than two men identified with the woods and fields, the farmer George Saxton and the gamekeeper Frank Annable, come to unhappy ends. But Mellors at the end of *Lady Chatterley's Lover* is still on his feet and, although gloomy enough about the future, can find the energy to set about planning a new life for himself and his mistress. Even in the letter that closes Lawrence's last novel, Mellors, despite his predictions of doom for modern industrial man, greets Connie hopefully and sets out his absurd program of salvation for the masses with conviction, if not with any idea that people are going to do what he suggests:

> If only they were educated to *live* instead of earn and spend, they could manage very happily on twenty-five shillings. If the men wore scarlet trousers as I said, they wouldn't think so much of money; if they could dance and hop and skip, and sing and swagger and be handsome, they could do with very little cash. And amuse the women themselves, and be amused by the women. They ought to learn to be naked and handsome, and to sing in a mass and dance the old group dances, and carve the stools they sit on, and embroider their own emblems. Then they wouldn't need money.

This boyish and anarchic dream of peace on an earth magically transformed from the cold, crowded, and raw place that it by and large is—and was when people still danced group dances and hopped and skipped—into an innocent and sensual Garden rejects tragic knowledge of man's difficult position in the world. It flies in the face of facts. It is immature. Nevertheless, Lawrence was well aware that no one but a Laurentian gamekeeper could believe in such a program. He did not want men of the twentieth century to don white jackets and scarlet trousers pulled tight across the buttocks. But he did want men and women of the "tragic" age to look at themselves and to raise the question of whether the tragic view of man's plight took full account of creative human possibilities. He wanted us to look at our maturity and to consider whether it did not become for some people a mask concealing deadness.

The genuine yet carefully restrained optimism of *Lady Chatterley's Lover* is founded on a belief that the world is alive and that aliveness is the only thing worth cherishing. Men and societies denying this fundamental fact will sicken and die. In *The White Peacock* the gamekeeper had remarked, "Tell a woman not to come in a wood till she can look at natural things—she might see something." Connie Chatterley, unlike the heroine of *The White Peacock*, does come into the woods and lingers there until she sees something. More clearly and more persuasively than in any previous novel, Lawrence brings the reader into touch with that vision, the mystery which, as one suspected from the beginning, was only of life itself.
—JULIAN MOYNAHAN, *"Lady Chatterley's Lover*: The Deed of Life," *ELH*, March 1959, pp. 89–90

In *Lady Chatterley's Lover*, Lawrence wrote fuller descriptions of the manifestations of love than had ever been written before in serious literature in English, and he put into the mouths of his characters words that are not used in the genteel society he had hated from the time when he was a miner's little boy.

It is ironic that one of the elder intellectuals to whom Lawrence had become cool, Edward Garnett, should have played so important a part in the gestation of *Lady Chatterley's Lover*. Garnett's son David had enjoyed the book, and Lawrence wrote to ask him whether his father, who had found *The Rainbow* too strong, would like to have a presentation copy of *Lady Chatterley*: "In my early days your father said to me, 'I should welcome a description of the whole act.'—which has stayed in my mind till I wrote this book."

Lawrence publicly explained his intentions in *Pornography and Obscenity* (1929), which he wrote after the criticisms of *Lady Chatterley* and the censorship troubles over the *Pansies* poems. In *Pornography and Obscenity*, Lawrence indicated the difference between the "mob" use of taboo words and the private, individual definitions of them. He believed that word-prudery was a mob-habit people needed to be shaken out of—he was against genuine pornography, which never came out into the open, which rubbed humanity's "dirty little secret." Some of these premises were repeated and deepened in the preface to the authorized Paris edition of the novel. This preface ("My Skirmish with Jolly Roger"), reprinted in expanded form as the book *A Propos of Lady Chatterley's Lover* (1930), surprisingly contained some praise of the Church because it had fostered the sense of the intrinsic rhythms of living and because it had established the idea of marriage for life. Lawrence again spoke for the "blood-stream" kind of sex, and spoke against its opposite, the destructive personal-nervous type of sex:

> The mind has an old grovelling fear of the body and the body's potencies. It is the mind we have to liberate, to civilize on these points. The mind's terror of the body has probably driven more men mad than

ever could be counted. The insanity of a great mind like Swift's is at least partly traceable to this cause. In the poem to his mistress Celia, which has the maddened refrain "But—Celia, Celia, Celia s***s," (the word rhymes with spits), we see what can happen to a great mind when it falls into panic. A great wit like Swift could not see how ridiculous he made himself. Of course Celia s***s! Who doesn't? And how much worse if she didn't. It is hopeless. And then think of poor Celia, made to feel iniquitous about her proper natural function by her "lover." It is monstrous. And it comes from having taboo words, and from not keeping the mind sufficiently developed in physical and sexual consciousness.

> In contrast to the puritan hush! hush!, which produces the sexual moron, we have the modern young jazzy and high-brow person who has gone one better, and won't be hushed in any respect, and just "does as she likes." From fearing the body, and denying its existence, the advanced young go to the other extreme and treat it as a sort of toy to be played with, a slightly nasty toy, but still you can get some fun out of it, before it lets you down. These young people scoff at the importance of sex, take it like a cocktail, and flout their elders with it. These young ones are advanced and superior. They despise a book like *Lady Chatterley's Lover*. It is much too simple and ordinary for them. The naughty words they care nothing about, and the attitude to love they find old-fashioned. Why make a fuss about it. Take it like a cocktail! The book, they say, shows the mentality of a boy of fourteen. But perhaps the mentality of a boy of fourteen, who still has a little natural awe and proper fear in fact of sex, is more wholesome than the mentality of the young cocktaily person who has no respect for anything and whose mind has nothing to do but play with the toys of life, sex being one of the chief toys, and who loses his mind in the process. Heliogabulus, indeed!

> So, between the stale grey puritan who is likely to fall into sexual indecency in advanced age, and the smart jazzy person of the young world, who says: "We can do anything. If we can think a thing we can do it," and then the low uncultured person with a dirty mind, who looks for dirt—this book has hardly a space to turn in. But to them all I say the same: Keep your perversions if you like them—your perversion of puritanism, your perversion of smart licentiousness, your perversion of a dirty mind. But I stick to my book and my position: Life is only bearable when the mind and the body are in harmony, and there is a natural balance between them, and each has a natural respect for the other.

—HARRY T. MOORE, *D. H. Lawrence: His Life and Works*, 1964, pp. 225–27

One of the triumphs of ⟨Lawrence's⟩ doctrine occurred, characteristically, when Lawrence brought a mind full of it, but still almost supernaturally quick in its response to life, here the life of a set of texts, to his critical work on American literature. During the war, mostly in Cornwall, he had been reading the American novelists and Whitman as a preparation for his hoped-for journey to the New World. Between August 1917 and February 1919 he wrote a dozen essays on these themes, eight of which were published in the *English Review*. He revised them drastically in Sicily (1920) and again in New Mexico in 1922–1923, to produce the version published in 1923 as *Studies in Classic American Literature*. The earlier version was published in 1962 as *The Symbolic Meaning*.

This version, though much less known and relatively hard to obtain, is much the finer. In the revision, Lawrence understandably altered some of his views: he now knew America, and the substitution of reality for myth meant some tempering of his praise, some changes in his judgments, even the introduction of a contemptuous note. What is almost totally harmful in the recasting of the work is the new tone of jeering journalism, and a sort of hysteria which Mr. Armin Arnold, who edited the earlier versions, attributes to the nervous tension of Lawrence's life in Taos . . . . Whatever the cause of the change of tone, the first version best illustrates how metaphysics could assist Lawrence's intellectual operations.

To Lawrence the Americans are strangers, and their literature cannot be considered apart from their place, the land from which they see and feel the world. His subject is "difference and otherness." American writers have sought to conceal that otherness, but their "art speech" gives them away; that is why we have to listen to that, to the tale and not to the teller. Already, by the late war years, Lawrence thought of art speech—imaginative fiction—as "a language of pure symbols," the "greatest universal language of mankind." The critic's job is to listen to this language, not to its author. In so doing Lawrence proved himself a critic of exceptional power.

For him the visible America is only a monstrous development of the old Europe, a product of the overdeveloped will, a mechanical democracy; but there remains under that false America a true one, slowly emerging—an Indian not a paleface America, which will express the land as its beasts and flowers express it. While we wait for the birth of this America we can study the progress of its white counterpart, which is transmuting men into machines and ghosts. There is Franklin, insentient to the living universe, "the gleaming Now," slave of the will he cultivated, enemy of the mystery of the Self. There is Crèvecoeur, rich in sensual understanding, capable of a "primal dark veracity," half in love with the Indian, with a tension between his idealism and his art that illustrates the dualism of Lawrence's great nerve centers. Fenimore Cooper calls forth another lecture on the solar plexus and lumbar ganglia, an early allusion to Saint John's Revelation as an allegory of the conquest of the sensual centers by the dynamic consciousness, and another to the Eleusinian mysteries. Cooper hints at American rebirth, the communion of white and red, the new "race-soul." The essays on Cooper are an astonishing achievement, a delicate, rapt symbolic interpretation of material few would have thought to promise much to an approach of this kind.

With Poe disintegration takes firm hold. He illustrates the process, which can in its way be beautiful, of dissolution. This is also part of the theme of the fine Hawthorne essay, so debilitated in the later version. It begins with the assertion that the primary or sensual mind progresses from myth to art, the reasoning mind from ancient cosmic theory to science; when these two are reconciled man can live in his fulness. Meanwhile, the nearest approach to a union is in art. Hawthorne illustrates the gap; "there is a discrepancy between his conscious understanding and his passional understanding." In *The Scarlet Letter* his attempt to be rational fails, and the book gives us, in spite of him, "the passional or primary account of the collapse of the human psyche in the white race," distorted in the same way as alchemy and astrology are distorted remains of an old knowledge of the organic universe. Thus Hawthorne's book, but not Hawthorne, recovers an ancient mode of sensual understanding, and Lawrence praises it unreservedly. Hawthorne's ethical intrusions, he insists, are precisely what the critic must discount. Trust the tale.

Sometimes the metaphysic stifles the intuitions, as when, in writing of Dana, Lawrence approves the flogging of the sailor as good for the lumbar-sacral ganglia of the victim, even if he has a "smarty back," and good for the captain, too, as proof that he's master. But this rarely happens, even in the demonstration that *Moby Dick* symbolizes the apocalyptic destruction of "sacral-sexual consciousness." Lawrence detests Melville's conscious symbolism; "his mind lags far, far behind his physical comprehension." But *Moby Dick*, as felt by Lawrence, still sounds like "one of the strangest and most wonderful books in the world."

Finally, Whitman, "the greatest of the Americans" and indeed "the greatest modern poet." Lawrence had over the years absorbed a good deal of Whitman; but now he sees him as ushering in the last stage of the reduction of the sensual to the spiritual, a process begun by Christianity and now reaching its end. Like the other moderns—French, Russian, English—he had art in the head. He conquers "the lower centres." He is the climax of the dying epoch of Love; he it is that captures the whale, "the pure sensual body of man." Whitman was wrong in making women purely functional—muscles and wombs— but right in stressing the importance of man acting womanless: "the polarity is between man and man. Whitman alone of all moderns has known this positively." The relationship between males is beyond marriage though it must coexist with marriage. The new epoch Whitman heralds will be an epoch of the love of comrades. By the time Lawrence wrote his final version of the essay he had changed his mind about comrades, and jeered at Whitman for believing in them, and in the future: "This awful Whitman. This post-mortem poet." Yet, for all his mistakes, his identification with Love, Whitman remains "the first white aboriginal" of America, the bearer of the necessary heroic message.

There are tiresome and even silly things in this book; but in its penetration of the texts, its concern for the spirit of place, it is a justification of the metaphysical fictions by which Lawrence did much of his thinking. The literary criticism is made part of the pattern of all his other interests. The later version of the book retains some of the good things from the earlier, and makes some points more precisely; but in shedding much of the metaphysic it acquires a chill sneering tone, and is often hideously written. The loss is great; though some romantic notions are excised—for example, the confidence that white men could be turned into Indians was qualified by Lawrence's experience in New Mexico—there is a baser kind of knowingness which is no gain. Basically the scheme is the same, and the Joachite Holy Ghost still presides:

> The Father had his day, and fell.
> The Son has had his day, and fell.
> It is the day of the Holy Ghost.

Lawrence had learned his own system. In some ways he makes it more flatly explicit: "The *Pequod* was the ship of the white American soul. She sank . . . ." And Whitman, constantly heckled, remains "a very great poet, of the end of life." *Studies in Classic American Literature* was still a powerful enough book to change the ways in which a nation reads its classics.
—FRANK KERMODE, "1917–1922," *D. H. Lawrence*, 1973, pp. 96–101

The Rainbow is an impressive fictional interpretation of a part of English social and cultural history over three generations, roughly from the 1840s to the second decade of the twentieth century. Dr Leavis has praised this aspect of the novel and shown how Lawrence is here the true inheritor of George Eliot, particularly the George Eliot of *Middlemarch*. But

Lawrence's novel is also, in intention at least, something more than imaginative social history. It aspires to the condition of myth: that is, it attempts to capture the essential rhythm of human experience not only in relation to fact and history, but in a larger relation to a trans-temporal order of being. This sounds portentous, but it is this latter ambition which imparts much of its distinctive quality to *The Rainbow*, and in attempting to fulfil it Lawrence more or less consciously casts the novel into the framework of a modern Genesis myth. The parallels between Lawrence's novel and biblical myth exist at many levels, from the structural to the stylistic. Perhaps the most obvious link is that suggested by the title. In the Old Testament the rainbow is a sign of the covenant God makes with Noah, a natural emblem of a supernatural bond. In Lawrence too the rainbow occurs at various key points in the novel, always with the suggestion of a two-way relationship, a bond between man and woman, or man and the world about him, or man and the larger non-human scheme of things. When Tom Brangwen is at a loss because of the strange mood of 'sombre exclusion' into which Lydia has fallen during her pregnancy, we are told 'He felt like a broken arch thrust sickeningly out from support.' This is perhaps the narrowest range of the symbol, whose widest occurs at the very end of the book, in Ursula's vision of the rainbow as 'the earth's new architecture . . . fitting to the over-arching heaven'.

As Tom Brangwen grows to maturity he acquires something of the stature of a biblical patriarch and his drunken speech at Anna's wedding has, paradoxically, something of prophetic dignity while at the same time faintly recalling the episode of the drunken Noah before his sons. His death reminds us that Lawrence is not simply leaning parasitically on the Genesis story in an effort to confer on his own myth a significance it does not intrinsically possess. Tom Brangwen's death indicates that the covenant is yet to be fulfilled. The life on Marsh Farm is on the one hand presented as something valuable and concretely achieved and therefore a norm, but on the other it is also something that can never be repeated, partly because individuals differ from one another but also because the circumstances of life change from generation to generation. The flood in which Tom is carried away is presented as a vast cataclysm, an act of God recalling that in the Old Testament.

Two other aspects of the relationship between *The Rainbow* and the Old Testament go nearer the heart of the novel. Alone among Lawrence's books this one spreads itself across several generations of human history, reproducing in miniature one of the basic rhythmic patterns of the Genesis story. But it is not simply the concern with generational rather than individual time which links the novel to the Bible. It is the preoccupation in both with what may be called the theme of salvation. The manner in which the bond with God is honoured or violated is the prime reason for the recounting of individual histories in the Old Testament. In much the same way, Lawrence's real concern is not with whether a given character is successful, happy or even 'good' in the ordinary sense of these words, but ultimately with whether he or she honours or betrays the bond with life, with the deepest springs of being. In this sense *The Rainbow* can be fairly described as a religious novel.

Particular allusions to the Bible are of course frequent throughout the book and the staple of its prose is a unique and generally successful variation on the rhythms of the Authorized Version. But these gain their true significance only when we realize that the novel and the Christian scriptures are so closely related because Lawrence is trying to define in imaginative terms his own essentially religious vision of life by bringing it

into an ever-changing relationship with the myths and dogmas of the religion in which, from early childhood, his consciousness has been steeped.—GAMINI SALGADO, "Story and Fable: The Biblical Framework," A *Preface to Lawrence*, 1982, pp. 110–11

WYNDHAM LEWIS
From "Love? What Ho! Smelling Strangeness"
Paleface
1929, pp. 174–96

I. 'We Whites, creatures of spirit.'—D. H. LAWRENCE.

I will now turn to Mr. D. H. Lawrence's account of the Mexican Indian ⟨in *Mornings in Mexico*⟩, and especially to his chapter 'Indians and Entertainment':

> It is almost impossible for the White people to approach the Indian without either sentimentality or dislike.

[Mr. Lawrence proves himself in this respect a *good White Man*, I think, in his book about the Indian. There is no sign of dislike, so he is the other sort of conventional White Man.]

> The common healthy vulgar White usually feels a certain native dislike of these drumming aboriginals.

Mr. Lawrence we can at once agree is not 'a common healthy vulgar White'; he has nothing very 'native' about him, either white or dark.

> The highbrow invariably lapses into sentimentalism like the smell of bad eggs.

Mr. Lawrence is a 'highbrow,' about that I think there cannot be two opinions. And a 'sentimentalism like the smell of bad eggs,' I am sorry to have to say, rises from all the work of Mr. Lawrence. It is all slightly 'high' and *faisandé* in a sentimental way.

Anyhow, far from 'disliking' the 'drumming' of these 'aboriginals,' there is no question that he likes it very much; and heavily implied in all his descriptions is the notion that these drumming and other 'native' habits are far superior to ours; the dark ones to the white. If we followed Mr. Lawrence to the ultimate conclusion of his romantic teaching, we should allow our 'consciousness' to be overpowered by the alien 'consciousness' of the Indian. And we know what he thinks that would involve: for he has told us that 'the Indian way of consciousness is different from and fatal to our way of consciousness.'

We will now turn to his account of the specific way in which this 'consciousness' of the Mexican Indian differs from ours.

The 'commonest entertainment among the Indians,' we are told (that is I suppose among the 'common healthy vulgar' Indians, if Mr. Lawrence's romantic soul could bring itself to admit that a Toltec or a Hopi *could* be 'common' or 'vulgar'), 'is singing round the drum, at evening.'

There are fishermen in the Outer Hebrides, he says, who do something of this sort, 'approaching the indian way,' but of course, being mere Whites, they do not reach or equal it. Still, the Outer Hebrideans do succeed in suggesting to Mr. Lawrence a realm inhabited by 'beasts that . . . stare through . . . vivid *mindless* eyes.' They do manage to become *mindless*: though not so *mindless* as the Indian, therefore inferior.

> This is *approaching* the Indian song. But even this is *pictorial, conceptual* far beyond the Indian point. *The Hebridean still sees himself human*, and *outside* the great naturalistic influences.

The poor White Hebridean still, alas, remains *human*, he is not totally *mindless*, though more nearly so than any other White Mr. Lawrence offhand can bring to mind.

The important thing to note in all these accounts is the insistence upon *mindlessness* as an essential quality of what is admirable. The Hebridean is not to be admired so much as the Mexican Indian because he still deals in 'conceptual,' 'pictorial' things; whereas the Mexican Indian is purely emotional—'musical,' in a word, in the Spengler sense. (For the full analysis of this type of thinking I refer you to *Time and Western Man*, where there is a detailed account of spenglerism.) And the first impulse to the anti-conceptualist, anti-intellectual, anti-pictorial point of view in philosophy, and thinking generally, was given by Bergson: just as in Berman's account of Behaviourism we saw him attributing the genesis of *Gestalt* to Bergson. So at last we know just where we are, philosophically, with Mr. Lawrence. Mr. D. H. Lawrence is a distinguished artist—member of the great and flourishing society of 'Emergent Evolution,' 'Creative Evolution,' 'Gestalt,' 'World-as-History,' etc. etc.

II. Mr. Lawrence a Follower of the Bergson-Spengler School.

I will go on quoting to show how completely Mr. Lawrence is beneath the spell of this evolutionist, emotional, non-human, 'mindless' philosophy: and how thoroughly he reads it into and applies it to the manifestations of the Indian 'consciousness.'

The Indian, singing, sings *without words or vision*.

I am italicizing the expressions that it is particularly necessary to mark in what I am quoting. How the attitude to 'words,' on the one hand, and to 'vision' and the things of vision, 'pictorial' things, on the other, is pure Spengler!

Face lifted and *sightless*, eyes half closed and *visionless*, mouth open and *speechless*, the *sounds* arise in his chest, from the *consciousness in the abdomen*.

A 'consciousness in the abdomen' or a visceral consciousness (which otherwise is 'sightless,' 'visionless,' and 'speechless') is what we commonly should call *unconsciousness*. And indeed that is what—if we were to capitalize it under one word—we should take as describing the kernel of this propagandist account. It is as a servant of the great *philosophy of the Unconscious* (which began as 'Will' with Schopenhauer, became 'The Philosophy of the Unconscious' with Von Hartmann, launched all that 'the Unconscious' means in Psychoanalysis, and was 'Intuition' for Bergson, which is 'Time' for Spengler, and 'Space-Time' for Professor Alexander) that Mr. Lawrence is writing.

'The consciousness in the abdomen' removes the vital centre into the viscera, and takes the privilege of leadership away from the hated 'mind' or 'intellect,' established up above in the head. . . .

IV. Communism, Feminism, and the Unconscious Found in the Mexican Indian by Mr. Lawrence.

One of the rhythmical patterns of 'sound' produced by the Indian the latter describes as a 'bear hunt,' Mr. Lawrence tells us.

'But,' says Mr. Lawrence, 'the man coming home from the bear hunt is any man, all men, the bear is any bear, every bear, all bear. *There is no individual, isolated experience*. It is the hunting . . . demon of manhood which has won against the . . . demon of all bears. The experience is generic, non-individual.'

So we reach Mr. Lawrence's *communism*, cast into the anthropologic moulds first prepared by Sir Henry Maine. For Mr. Lawrence is, in full hysterical flower, perhaps our most accomplished english communist. He is *the natural communist*, as it were, as distinguished from the indoctrinated, or theoretic, one.

(1) The Unconscious; (2) The Feminine; (3) The Communist; those are the main principles of action of the mind of Mr. Lawrence, linked in a hot and piping trinity of rough-stuff primitivism, and freudian hot-sex-stuff. With *Sons and Lovers*, his first book, he was at once hot-foot upon the fashionable trail of incest; the book is an eloquent wallowing mass of Mother-love and Sex-idolatry. His *Women in Love* is again the same thick, sentimental, luscious stew. The 'Homo'-motive, how could that be absent from such a compendium, as is the nature of Mr. Lawrence, of all that has long passed for 'revolutionary,' reposing mainly for its popular effectiveness upon the meaty, succulent levers of sex and supersex, to bait those politically-innocent, romantic, anglo-saxon simpletons dreaming their 'anglo-saxon dreams,' whether in America or the native country of Mr. Lawrence? The motif of the 'child-cult,' which is usually found prominently in any 'revolutionary' mixture, is echoed, and indeed screamed, wept and bellowed, throughout *Sons and Lovers*.

At first sight, I am afraid, many of the *rapprochements* that I make here may sound strained, since, I am sorry to say, if things do not lie obviously together and publish their conjunction explicitly and prominently, it is not considered quite respectable to suggest that they have any vital connection. The suggestion of anything 'illicit' shocks, even where ideas are concerned. That one idea should have a hidden liaison or be in communication with another idea, without ever approaching it in public, or any one even *mentioning them together*—that is the sort of thing that is never admitted in polite society.

So the majority of people are deeply unconscious of the affiliations of the various phenomena of our time, which on the surface look so very autonomous, and even hostile; yet, existing under quite a different label, in a quite different region of time and space, they are often closely and organically related to one another. If you test this you will be surprised to find how many things do belong together, in fact, in our highly contentious and separatist time.

Yet it is our business—especially, it appears, mine—to establish these essential liaisons, and to lay bare the widely-flung system of cables connecting up this maze-like and destructive system in the midst of which we live—destructive, that is of course, to something essential that we should clutch and be careful not to lose, on our way to the Melting-pot.

What, you might say, for instance, has Mr. Lawrence's remark about the 'mindlessness' of the Mexican songs got to do with communism? Or, again, 'mindlessness' or 'communism' to do with 'the Feminine Principle' (as opposed to the Masculine)? I can show you at once what 'mindlessness' has to do with 'communism.' I will quote the latest european advocate of Bolshevism, René Fülöp-Miller, from his book *The Mind and Face of Bolshevism*. It should really be called *The Face of Bolshevism*, since we learn that 'Mind' is of all things what Bolshevism is concerned to deny and prohibit. He is relating how the 'higher type of humanity' is to be produced, the super-humanity of which Bolshevism is the religion.

It is only by such external functions as the millions have in common, their uniform and simultaneous movements, that the many can be united in a higher unity: marching, keeping in step, shouting 'hurrah' in unison, festal singing in chorus, united attacks on the enemy, these are the manifestations of life which are to give birth to the new and superior type of humanity. *Everything that divides the many from each other, that fosters the illusion of the individual importance of man, especially the 'soul,' hinders this higher evolution and must consequently be destroyed . . .* organization is to be substituted for the soul . . . the vague mystery of the 'soul,' with that evil handed down from an accursed individualistic past.

Let us now continue with our quotations from Mr. Lawrence.

There is no individual, isolated experience. . . . It is an experience of the blood-stream, not of the mind or spirit. Hence the subtle incessant insistent rhythm of the drum, which is pulsated like a heart, and *soulless* and inescapable. Hence the strange blind unanimity of the . . . men's voices.

As you see, it might equally be Mr. Fülöp-Miller on the beauties of Bolshevism. The Mexican Indian of Mr. Lawrence is the perfect Bolshevik. The 'blind unanimity of the men's voices' (the 'keeping in step . . . festal singing in chorus' of Fülöp-Miller) assures 'soullessness.' The 'soul . . . must be destroyed' says the apostle of Bolshevism. '—— the Indian song is non-individual. . . . Strange clapping, crowing, gurgling sounds, in an unseizable subtle rhythm, the rhythm of the heart in her throes: . . . from an abdomen where the great bloodstream surges in the dark, and surges in its own generic experiences.'

To witness all this is, to Mr. Lawrence, heaven. '—— perhaps it is the most stirring sight in the world in the dark, near the fire, with the drums going,' etc. etc.

It is the dark blood falling back from the mind, from sight and speech and knowing, back to the great central source where is rest and unspeakable renewal.

On the same principle as 'Back to the Land,' the cry of Mr. Lawrence (good little Freudian that he has always been) is 'Back to the Womb!' For although a natural communist and born feminist, it required the directive brain of Freud and others to reveal him to himself.

'We Whites, creatures of spirit!' he cries. Ah, the 'strange' things we 'never realize'! (such as the 'strange falling back of the blood . . . the *downward* rhythm, the rhythm of pure forgetting and pure renewal').

What is *virtue* in woman? Mr. Lawrence becomes very Western at once, under the shadow of a kind of suffragist-chivalry, at the mere thought of 'Woman.'

'In woman [virtue] is the putting forth of all herself in a delicate, marvellous, sensitiveness, which draws forth the wonder to herself, etc.' (To 'draw the wonder to herself' is to be a witch, surely? So virtue and wickedness would get a little mixed up.)

What would the Indian think if he heard his squaw being written about in that strain?—'delicate, marvellous sensitiveness.' He would probably say 'Chuck it, Archie!' in Hopi. At least he would be considerably surprised, and probably squint very hard, under his 'dark' brows, at Mr. Lawrence. . . .

IX. *An Invitation to Suicide Addressed to the White Man.*

The emotion throughout the book from which I have quoted is the dogmatism of 'revolution,' of political revolution, to be precise. In contrast to the White Overlord of this world in which we live, Mr. Lawrence shows us a more primitive type of 'consciousness,' which has been physically defeated by the White 'consciousness,' and assures us that that defeated 'consciousness' is the better of the two. But, since the 'consciousness' of the Indian is death to the 'consciousness' of the White, and eventually, if it prevailed, to the White,

physically, as well, it is (however indirectly, and in the form of an entertainment, a book of 'fiction') an invitation to suicide addressed to the White Man. 'Give up, lay down, your White "consciousness,"' it says. 'Capitulate to the mystical communistic Pan of the Primitive Man! Be Savage!'

Not only the opposition as between beasts and men, or Black and White, is stressed (with, always, the rebellious hypnotic accompaniment of the revolutionary drum, the primitive tom-tom, and always, that is the important thing, all the sympathy of the reader engaged on the side of the oppressed and superseded, the under-dog—or, in the above instance, of the under-parrot); also we are taken into the dark-backward, to more exaggerated oppositions. Once we have got to the earliest birds, and, most ancient of all the dispossessed, the serpent (whom Mr. Lawrence sees biting his tail with an immemorial rage, and remarking, as he glances malevolently up at Man, 'I will bruise his heel!'), beyond this we reach *things*—beyond the earliest amœba. Mr. Lawrence does not take us as far as that. But the philosophers who mainly influence him do.

This will be without meaning perhaps for some readers. Elsewhere I have shown how *that* most fundamental of all revolutionary impulses works, too. Mr. Bertrand Russell, for instance, obedient to his liberalist traditions, which he imports into his physics, attempts to stir up the tables and chairs against us and lead them in revolt against the overweening overlord, Man, who sits upon them, and uses them to write books at, without even asking himself if they may not resent his behaviour, and have their private thoughts about *him*—as he flings himself down upon them, or rests his elbows upon them and scratches his head.

The reason why I direct an adverse analysis against this type of 'revolutionary' emotionality, is not, once more, because I believe that the White Man as he stands to-day is the last word in animal life, or in spiritual perfection, or that he is not often quite as ridiculous as Mr. Lawrence's parrots would have him, and in any case he is engaged in the road to the Melting-pot. I will not here enumerate my reasons for hostility where this revolutionary picture is concerned: I will say, only, that most Aztecs are probably fairly bored with being Aztecs: that the average Hopi, like the average cat, is rather negatively admirable and exceedingly mechanical: that admiration for savages and cats is really an expression of the worst side of the Machine Age—that Machine-Age Man is effusive about them *because they are machines* like himself; and Mr. Lawrence, at least, makes no pretence of admiring his savages because they are *free*—they are no longer for the contemporary 'revolutionary' doctrinaire 'the noble savage' in the rousseauesque or Fenimore Cooper sense, at least not for the best informed doctrinaire: and, lastly, what such gospels as those of Mr. Lawrence or of Sherwood Anderson really amount to is an emotional, and not quite disinterested, exaltation (indirectly) of the *average man*, l'homme moyen sensuel—though in this case *the average Hopi*.

I find the average White European (such as Chekov depicted) often exceedingly ridiculous, no doubt, but much more interesting than the average Hopi, or the average Negro. I would rather have the least man that *thinks*, than the average man that squats and drums and drums, with 'sightless,' 'soulless' eyes: I would rather have an ounce of human 'consciousness' than a universe full of 'abdominal' afflatus and hot, unconscious, 'soulless,' mystical throbbing.

VIRGINIA WOOLF
"Notes on D. H. Lawrence"
The Moment and Other Essays
1947, pp. 79–82

The partiality, the inevitable imperfection of contemporary criticism can best be guarded against, perhaps, by making in the first place a full confession of one's disabilities, so far as it is possible to distinguish them. Thus by way of preface to the following remarks upon D. H. Lawrence, the present writer has to state that until April 1931 he was known to her almost solely by reputation and scarcely at all by experience. His reputation, which was that of a prophet, the exponent of some mystical theory of sex, the devotee of cryptic terms, the inventor of a new terminology which made free use of such words as solar plexus and the like, was not attractive; to follow submissively in his tracks seemed an unthinkable aberration; and as chance would have it, the few pieces of his writing that issued from behind this dark cloud of reputation seemed unable to rouse any sharp curiosity or to dispel the lurid phantom. There was, to begin with, *Trespassers*, a hot, scented, overwrought piece of work, as it seemed; then *The Prussian Officer*, of which no clear impression remained except of starting muscles and forced obscenity; then *The Last Girl*, a compact and seamanlike piece of work, stuffed with careful observation rather in the Bennett manner; then one or two sketches of Italian travel of great beauty, but fragmentary and broken off; and then two little books of poems, *Nettles* and *Pansies*, which read like the sayings that small boys scribble upon stiles to make housemaids jump and titter.

Meanwhile, the chants of the worshippers at the shrine of Lawrence became more rapt; their incense thicker and their gyrations more mazy and more mystic. His death last year gave them still greater liberty and still greater impetus; his death, too, irritated the respectable; and it was the irritation roused by the devout and the shocked, and the ceremonies of the devout and the scandal of the shocked, that drove one at last to read *Sons and Lovers* in order to see whether, as so often happens, the master is not altogether different from the travesty presented by his disciples.

This then was the angle of approach, and it will be seen that it is an angle that shuts off many views and distorts others. But read from this angle, *Sons and Lovers* emerged with astonishing vividness, like an island from off which the mist has suddenly lifted. Here it lay, clean cut, decisive, masterly, hard as rock, shaped, proportioned by a man who, whatever else he might be—prophet or villain—was undoubtedly the son of a miner who had been born and bred in Nottingham. But this hardness, this clarity, this admirable economy and sharpness of the stroke are not rare qualities in an age of highly efficient novelists. The lucidity, the ease, the power of the writer to indicate with one stroke and then to refrain indicated a mind of great power and penetration. But these impressions, after they had built up the lives of the Morels, their kitchens, food, sinks, manner of speech, were succeeded by another far rarer, and of far greater interest. For after we have exclaimed that this coloured and stereoscopic representation of life is so like that surely it must be alive—like the bird that pecked the cherry in the picture—one feels, from some indescribable brilliance, sombreness, significance, that the room is put into order. Some hand has been at work before we entered. Casual and natural as the arrangement seems, as if we had opened the door and come in by chance, some hand, some eye of

astonishing penetration and force, has swiftly arranged the whole scene, so that we feel that it is more exciting, more moving, in some ways fuller of life than one had thought real life could be, as if a painter had brought out the leaf or the tulip or the jar by pulling a green curtain behind it. But what is the green curtain that Lawrence has pulled so as to accentuate the colours? One never catches Lawrence—this is one of his most remarkable qualities—'arranging'. Words, scenes flow as fast and direct as if he merely traced them with a free rapid hand on sheet after sheet. Not a sentence seems thought about twice: not a word added for its effect on the architecture of the phrase. There is no arrangement that makes us say: 'Look at this. This scene, this dialogue has the meaning of the book hidden in it.' One of the curious qualities of *Sons and Lovers* is that one feels an unrest, a little quiver and shimmer in his page, as if it were composed of separate gleaming objects, by no means content to stand still and be looked at. There is a scene of course; a character; yes, and people related to each other by a net of sensations; but these are not there—as in Proust—for themselves. They do not admit of prolonged exploration, of rapture in them for the sake of rapture, as one may sit in front of the famous hawthorn hedge in *Swann's Way* and look at it. No, there is always something further on, another goal. The impatience, the need for getting on beyond the object before us, seem to contract, to shrivel up, to curtail scenes to their barest, to flash character simply and starkly in front of us. We must not look for more than a second; we must hurry on. But to what?

Probably to some scene which has very little to do with character, with story, with any of the usual resting places, eminences, and consummations of the usual novel. The only thing that we are given to rest upon, to expand upon, to feel to the limits of our powers is some rapture of physical being. Such for instance is the scene when Paul and Miriam swing in the barn. Their bodies become incandescent, glowing, significant, as in other books a passage of emotion burns in that way. For the writer it seems the scene is possessed of a transcendental significance. Not in talk nor in story nor in death nor in love, but here as the body of the boy swings in the barn.

But, perhaps, because such a state cannot satisfy for long, perhaps because Lawrence lacks the final power which makes things entire in themselves, the effect of the book is that stability is never reached. The world of *Sons and Lovers* is perpetually in process of cohesion and dissolution. The magnet that tries to draw together the different particles of which the beautiful and vigorous world of Nottingham is made is the incandescent body, this beauty glowing in the flesh, this intense and burning light. Hence whatever we are shown seems to have a moment of its own. Nothing rests secure to be looked at. All is being sucked away by some dissatisfaction, some superior beauty, or desire, or possibility. The book therefore excites, irritates, moves, changes, seems full of stir and unrest and desire for something withheld, like the body of the hero. The whole world—it is a proof of the writer's remarkable strength—is broken and tossed by the magnet of the young man who cannot bring the separate parts into a unity which will satisfy him.

This allows, partly at least, of a simple explanation. Paul Morel, like Lawrence himself, is the son of a miner. He is dissatisfied with his conditions. One of his first actions on selling a picture is to buy an evening suit. He is not a member, like Proust, of a settled and satisfied society. He is anxious to leave his own class and to enter another. He believes that the middle class possess what he does not possess. His natural honesty is too great to be satisfied with his mother's argument that the common people are better than the middle class because they possess more life. The middle class, Lawrence feels, possess ideas; or something else that he wishes himself to have. This is one cause of his unrest. And it is of profound importance. For the fact that he, like Paul, was a miner's son, and that he disliked his conditions, gave him a different approach to writing from those who have a settled station and enjoy circumstances which allow them to forget what those circumstances are.

Lawrence received a violent impetus from his birth. It set his gaze at an angle from which it took some of its most marked characteristics. He never looked back at the past, or at things as if they were curiosities of human psychology, nor was he interested in literature as literature. Everything has a use, a meaning, is not an end in itself. Comparing him again with Proust, one feels that he echoes nobody, continues no tradition, is unaware of the past, of the present save as it affects the future. As a writer, this lack of tradition affects him immensely. The thought plumps directly into his mind; up spurt the sentences as round, as hard, as direct as water thrown out in all directions by the impact of a stone. One feels that not a single word has been chosen for its beauty, or for its effect upon the architect of the sentence.

SIMONE DE BEAUVOIR
"D. H. Lawrence or Phallic Pride"
The Second Sex (1949), tr. H. M. Parshley
1953, pp. 214–24

Lawrence is poles apart from a Montherlant. Not for him to define the special relations of woman and of man, but to restore both of them to the verity of Life. This verity lies neither in display nor in the will: it involves animality, in which the human being has his roots. Lawrence passionately rejects the antithesis: sex—brain; he has a cosmic optimism that is radically opposed to the pessimism of Schopenhauer; the will-to-live expressed in the phallus is joy, and herein should be the source of thought and action unless these are to be respectively empty concept and sterile mechanism. The sex cycle pure and simple is not enough because it falls back into immanence: it is a synonym of death; but still this mutilated reality, sex and death, is better than an existence cut off from the humus of the flesh. Man needs more than, like Antæus, to renew contact now and then with the earth; his life as a man should be wholly an expression of his virility, which immediately presupposes and demands woman. She is therefore neither diversion nor prey; she is not an object confronting a subject, but a pole necessary for the existence of the pole of opposite sign. Men who have misunderstood this truth, a Napoleon for example, have failed of their destiny as men: they are defectives. It is not by asserting his singularity, but by fulfilling his generality as intensely as possible that the individual can be saved: male or female, one should never seek in erotic relations the triumph of one's pride or the exaltation of one's ego; to use one's sex as tool of the will, that is the fatal mistake; one must break the barriers of the ego, transcend even the limits of consciousness, renounce all personal sovereignty. Nothing could be more beautiful than that little statue of a woman in labor: "A terrible face void, peaked, *abstracted almost into meaninglessness* by the weight of sensation beneath."[1]

This ecstasy is one neither of sacrifice nor abandon; there is no question of either of the two sexes permitting the other to swallow it up; neither man nor woman should seem like a "broken-off fragment" of a couple; the sex part is not a still aching scar; each member of the couple is a complete being, perfectly polarized; when one feels assured in his virility, the other in her femininity, "each acknowledges the perfection of the polarized sex circuit";[2] the sexual act is, without annexing, without surrender of either partner, a marvelous fulfillment of each one by the other. When Ursula and Birkin finally found each other, they gave each other reciprocally that stellar equilibrium which alone can be called liberty. "She was for him what he was for her, the immemorial magnificence of the *other reality*, mystic and palpable."[3] Having access to each other in the generous extortion of passion, two lovers together have access to the Other, the All. Thus with Paul and Clara in the moment of love:[4] "What was she? A strong, strange wild life, that breathed with his in the darkness through this hour. It was all so much bigger than themselves that he was hushed. They had met, and included in their meeting the thrust of the manifold grass-stems, the cry of the peewit, the wheel of the stars." Lady Chatterley and Mellors attained to the same cosmic joys: blending one with the other, they blend with the trees, the light, the rain. Lawrence develops his doctrine broadly in *The Defense of Lady Chatterley*: "Marriage is only an illusion if it is not lastingly and radically phallic, if it is not bound to the sun and the earth, to the moon, to the rhythm of the seasons, the years, the lustra, and the centuries. Marriage is nothing if it is not based on a correspondence of blood. For blood is the substance of the soul." "The blood of man and the blood of woman are two eternally different streams which cannot mix." That is why these two streams embrace the totality of life in their meanderings. "The phallus is a quantity of blood that fills the valley of blood in the female. The powerful stream of masculine blood overwhelms in its ultimate depths the grand stream of feminine blood . . . however, neither breaks through its barriers. It is the most perfect form of communion . . . and it is one of the greatest of mysteries." This communion is a miraculous enrichment of life; but it demands that the claims of the "personality" be abolished. When personalities seek to reach each other without renouncing themselves, as is common in modern civilization, their attempt is doomed to frustration. There is in such cases a sexuality "personal, blank, cold, nervous, poetic," which tends to disintegrate the vital stream of each. The lovers treat each other as instruments, engendering hate: so it is with Lady Chatterley and Michaelis; they remain shut up in their subjectivity; they can experience a fever such as alcohol or opium gives, but it is without object: they fail each to discover the reality of the other; they gain access to nothing. Lawrence would have condemned Costals without appeal. He has painted in the figure of Gerard, in *Women in Love*, one of these proud and egoistic males; and Gerard is in large part responsible for the hell into which he hurls himself with Gudrun. Cerebral, willful, he delights in the empty assertion of his ego and hardens himself against life: for the pleasure of mastering a fiery mare, he keeps her head at a gate behind which a train passes with thunderous commotion; he draws blood from her rebellious flanks and intoxicates himself with his own power. This will to domination abases the woman against whom it is exercised; lacking strength, she is transformed into a slave. Gerard leans over Pussum: "Her inchoate look of a violated slave, whose fulfillment lies in her further and further violation, made his nerves quiver . . . his was the only will, she was the passive substance of his will." That is a miserable kind of domination; if the woman is only a passive substance, what the male dominates is nothing. He thinks he is taking something, enriching himself: it is a delusion. Gerard takes Gudrun in his arms: "she was the rich, lovely substance of his being. . . . So she was passed away and gone in him, and he was perfected." But as soon as he quits her, he finds himself alone and empty; and the next day she fails to come to the rendezvous. If the woman is strong, the male demand arouses a similar, symmetrical demand in her; fascinated and rebellious, she becomes masochistic and sadistic in turn. Gudrun is overwhelmed with agitation when she sees Gerard press the flanks of the raging mare between his thighs; but she is agitated also when Gerard's nurse tells her "many's the time I've pinched his little bottom for him." Masculine arrogance provokes feminine resistance. While Ursula is conquered and saved by the sexual purity of Birkin, as Lady Chatterley was by that of the gamekeeper, Gerard drags Gudrun into a struggle without end. One night, unhappy, broken down by mourning for his father, he let himself go in her arms. "She was the great bath of life, he worshipped her. Mother and substance of all life she was. . . . But the miraculous, soft effluence of her breast suffused over him, over his seared, damaged brain, like a healing lymph, like a soft, soothing flow of life itself, perfect as if he were bathed in the womb again." That night they feel something of what a communion with woman could be; but it is too late; his happiness is vitiated, for Gudrun is not really present; she lets Gerard sleep on her shoulder, but she stays awake, impatient, separate. It is the punishment meted out to the individual who is a victim of himself: he cannot, being solitary, invade her solitude; in raising the barriers of his ego, he has raised those of the Other: he will never be reunited with her. At the end Gerard dies, killed by Gudrun and by himself.

Thus it would at first appear that neither of the two sexes has an advantage. Neither is subject. Woman is no more a mere pretext than she is man's prey. Malraux[5] notes that for Lawrence it is not enough, as it is for the Hindu, that woman be the occasion for contact with the infinite, like, for example, a landscape: that would be making an object of her, in another fashion. She is just as real as the man, and a real communion is what he should achieve. This is why the heroes who have Lawrence's approval demand from their mistresses much more than the gift of their bodies: Paul does not permit Miriam to give herself to him as a tender sacrifice; Birkin does not want Ursula to limit herself to seeking pleasure in his arms; cold or burning, the woman who remains closed up within herself leaves man to his solitude: he should repulse her. Both ought to give themselves body and soul. If this gift were made, they would remain forever faithful. Lawrence is a partisan of monogamous marriage. There is the quest for variety only if one is interested in the peculiarities of individuals; but phallic marriage is founded on generality. When the virility-femininity circuit is established, desire for change is inconceivable: it is a complete circuit, closed and definitive.

Reciprocal gift, reciprocal fidelity: have we here in truth the reign of mutuality? Far from it. Lawrence believes passionately in the supremacy of the male. The very expression "phallic marriage," the equivalence he sets up between "sexual" and "phallic," constitute sufficient proof. Of the two blood streams that are mysteriously married, the phallic current is favored. "The phallus serves as a means of union between two rivers; it conjoins the two different rhythms into a single flow." Thus the man is not only one of the two elements in the couple, but also their connecting factor; he provides their transcendence: "The bridge to the future is the phallus." For the cult of the Goddess Mother, Lawrence means to substitute a phallic cult; when he wishes to illuminate the sexual nature of the cosmos, it is not woman's abdomen but man's virility that he calls to mind. He almost never shows a man agitated by a woman; but time and again he shows woman secretly overwhelmed by the ardent, subtle, and insinuating appeal of the male. His heroines are beautiful and healthy, but not heady; whereas his heroes are disquieting fauns. It is male animals that incarnate the agitation and the powerful mystery of Life; women feel the spell: this one is affected by a fox, that one is taken with a stallion, Gudrun feverishly challenges a herd of young oxen; she is overwhelmed by the rebellious vigor of a rabbit.

A social advantage for man is grafted upon this cosmic advantage. No doubt because the phallic stream is impetuous, aggressive, because it spreads into the future—Lawrence explains himself but imperfectly—it is for man to "carry forward the banner of life";[6] he is intent upon aims and ends, he incarnates transcendence; woman is absorbed in her sentiment, she is all inwardness; she is dedicated to immanence. Not only does man play the active role in the sexual life, but he is active also in going beyond it; he is rooted in the sexual world, but he makes his escape from it; woman remains shut up in it. Thought and action have their roots in the phallus; lacking the phallus, woman has no rights in either the one or the other: she can play a man's role, and even brilliantly, but it is just a game, lacking serious verity. "Woman is really polarized downwards towards the center of the earth. Her deep positivity is in the downward flow, the moon-pull. And man is polarized upwards, toward the sun and the day's activity."[7] For woman "the deepest consciousness is in the loins and the belly."[8] If this is perverted and her flow of energy is upward, to the breast and head, woman may become clever, noble, efficient, brilliant, competent in the manly world; but, according to Lawrence, she soon has enough of it, everything goes pop, and she returns to sex, "which is her business at the present moment."[9] In the domain of action man should be the initiator, the positive; woman is the positive on the emotional level.

Thus Lawrence rediscovers the traditional bourgeois conception of Bonald, of Auguste Comte, of Clément Vautel. Woman should subordinate her existence to that of man. "She ought to believe in you, and in the deep purpose you stand for."[10] Then man will pay her an infinite tenderness and gratitude. "Ah, how good it is to come home to your wife when she *believes* in you and submits to your purpose that is beyond her. . . . You feel unfathomable gratitude to the woman who loves you."[11] Lawrence adds that to merit such devotion, the man must be genuinely occupied with a great design; if his project is but a false goal, the couple breaks down in low deceptiveness. Better to shut oneself up again in the feminine cycle of love and death, like Anna Karenina and Vronsky, Carmen and Don José, than to lie to each other like Pierre and Natasha.

But there is always this reservation: what Lawrence is extolling—after the fashion of Proudhon and Rousseau—is monogamous marriage in which the wife derives the justification of her existence from the husband. Lawrence writes as hatefully as Montherlant against the wife who wishes to reverse the roles. Let her cease playing the Magna Mater, claiming to have in her keeping the verity of life; monopolizing, devouring, she mutilates the male, causing him to fall back into immanence and turning him away from his purposes. Lawrence is far from execrating maternity: quite the contrary. He is glad to be flesh, he willingly accepts his birth, he is fond of his mother; mothers appear in his works as splendid examples of true femininity; they are pure renunciation, absolute generosity, all their living warmth is devoted to their children: they gladly accept their becoming men, they are proud of it. But one should fear the egoistic *amante* who would take a man back to his childhood; she hampers the *élan*, the flight of the male. "The moon, the planet of women, sways us back."[12] She talks unceasingly of love; but for her love is to take, it is to fill this void she feels within her; such love is close to hate. Thus Hermione, suffering from a terrible sense of deficiency because she has never been able to give herself, wants to annex Birkin. She fails. She tries to kill him, and the voluptuous ecstasy she feels in striking him is identical with the egoistic spasm of sex pleasure.[13]

Lawrence detests modern women, creatures of celluloid and rubber laying claim to a consciousness. When woman has become sexually conscious of herself, "there she is functioning away from her own head and her own consciousness of herself and her own automatic self-will."[14] He forbids her to have an independent sensuality; she is made to give herself, not to take. Through Mellors's mouth, Lawrence cries aloud his horror of lesbians. But he finds fault also with the woman who in the presence of the male takes a detached or aggressive attitude; Paul feels wounded and irritated when Miriam caresses his loins and says to him: "you are beautiful." Gudrun, like Miriam, is at fault when she feels enchanted with the good looks of her lover: this contemplation separates them, as much as would the irony of frozen intellectual females who find the penis comic or male gymnastics ridiculous. The eager quest for pleasure is not less to be condemned: there is an intense, solitary enjoyment that also causes separation, and woman should not strain for it. Lawrence has drawn numerous portraits of these independent, dominating women, who miss their feminine vocation. Ursula and Gudrun are of this type. At first Ursula is a monopolizer. "Man must render himself up to her. He must be quaffed to the dregs by her."[15] She will learn to conquer her desire. But Gudrun is obstinate; cerebral, artistic, she mildly envies men their independence and their chances for activity; she perseveres in keeping her individuality intact; she wants to live for herself; she is ironic and possessive, and she will always remain shut up in her subjectivity.

Miriam, in *Sons and Lovers*, is the most significant figure because she is the least sophisticated. Gerard is in part responsible for Gudrun's failure; but Miriam, as far as Paul is concerned, carries her weight of unhappiness alone. She too would rather be a man, and she hates men; she is not satisfied with herself as woman, she wants to "distinguish herself"; so the grand stream of life does not flow through her. She can be like a sorceress or a priestess, never like a bacchante; she is stirred by things only when she has re-created them in her soul, giving them a religious value: this very fervor separates her from life; she is poetical, mystical, maladjusted. "Her exaggerated effort locked itself . . . she was not awkward and yet she never made the right movement." She seeks inward joys, and reality frightens her; sexuality scares her; when she sleeps with Paul, her heart stands apart in a kind of horror; she is always consciousness, never life. She is not a companion; she refuses to melt and blend with her lover; she wishes to absorb him into herself. He is irritated by this desire of hers, he flies into a violent rage when he sees her caressing flowers: one would say that she wanted to tear out their hearts. He insults her: "You are a beggar of love; you have no need of loving, but of being loved. You wish to *fill yourself full of love* because you lack something, I don't know what." Sexuality was not made for filling voids; it should be the expression of a whole being. What women call love is their avidity before the virile force of which they want to take possession. Paul's mother thinks clearly regarding Miriam: "she wants all of him, she wants to extract him from himself and devour him." The young girl is glad when her friend is sick, because she can take care of him: she

pretends to serve him, but it is really a method of imposing her will upon him. Because she remains apart from Paul, she raises in him "an ardor comparable to fever, such as opium induces"; but she is quite incapable of bringing him joy and peace; from the depth of her love, within her secret self "she detested Paul because he loved her and dominated her." And Paul edges away from her. He seeks his equilibrium with Clara; beautiful, lively, animal, she gives herself unreservedly; and they attain moments of ecstasy which transcend them both; but Clara does not understand this revelation. She thinks she owes this joy to Paul himself, to his special nature, and she wishes to take him for herself. She fails to keep him because she, too, wants him all for herself. As soon as love is individualized, it is changed into avid egotism, and the miracle of eroticism vanishes.

Woman must give up personal love; neither Mellors nor Don Cipriano is willing to say words of love to his mistress. Terese, the model wife, is indignant when Kate asks her if she loves Don Ramón.[16] "He is my life," she replies; the gift she has yielded to him is something quite other than love. Woman should, like man, abdicate from all pride and self-will; if she incarnates life for the man, so does he for her; Lady Chatterley finds peace and joy only because she recognizes this truth: "she would give up her hard and brilliant feminine power, which fatigued and hardened her, she would plunge into the new bath of life, into the depths of its entrails where sang the voiceless song of adoration"; then is she summoned to the rapture of bacchantes; blindly obeying her lover, seeking not herself in his arms, she composes with him a harmonious couple, in tune with the rain, the trees, and the flowers of springtime. Just so Ursula in Birkin's arms renounces her individuality, and they attain to a "stellar equilibrium." But *The Plumed Serpent* best reflects Lawrence's ideal in its integrity. For Don Cipriano is one of those men who "carry forward the banners of life"; he has a mission to which he is so completely devoted that in him virility is transcended and exalted to the point of divinity: if he has himself anointed god, it is not a mystification; it is simply that every man who is fully man is a god; he merits therefore the absolute devotion of a woman. Full of Occidental prejudices, Kate at first refuses to accept this dependence, she clings to her personality and to her limited existence; but little by little she lets herself be penetrated by the great stream of life; she gives Cipriano her body and her soul. This is not a surrender to slavery; for before deciding to live with him she demands that he acknowledge his need for her; he does acknowledge it since in fact woman is necessary to man; then she agrees never to be anything other than his mate; she adopts his aims, his values, his universe. This submission is expressed even in their erotic relation; Lawrence does not want the woman to be tensed in the effort toward her acme of pleasure, separated from the male by the spasm that shakes her; he deliberately denies her the orgasm; Don Cipriano moves away from Kate when he feels her approaching that nervous enjoyment: "the white ecstasy of frictional satisfaction, the throes of Aphrodite of the foam"; she renounces even this sexual autonomy. "Her strange seething feminine will and desire subsided in her and swept away, leaving her soft and powerfully potent, like the hot springs of water that gushed up so noiseless, so soft, yet so powerful, with a sort of secret potency."[17]

We can see why Lawrence's novels are, above all, "guidebooks for women." It is much more difficult for woman than for man to "accept the universe," for man submits to the cosmic order autonomously, whereas woman needs the mediation of the male. There is really a surrender when for woman the Other takes the shape of an alien consciousness and will; on the contrary, an autonomous submission, as by man, remarkably resembles a sovereign decision. Either the heroes of Lawrence are condemned at the start, or from the start they hold the secret of wisdom;[18] their submission to the cosmos has been accomplished so long since, and they derive from it so much inner certainty, that they seem as arrogant as any proud individualist; there is a god who speaks through them: Lawrence himself. As for woman, it is for her to bow down before their divinity. In so far as man is a phallus and not a brain, the individual who has his share of virility keeps his advantages; woman is not evil, she is even good—but subordinated. It is once more the ideal of the "true woman" that Lawrence has to offer us—that is, the woman who unreservedly accepts being defined as the Other.

Notes

1. *Women in Love* (Modern Library, 1932), p. 88. (Italics mine.)
2. Ibid., p. 228.
3. Ibid., p. 366.
4. *Sons and Lovers* (Duckworth, 1913), p. 415.
5. Preface to *L'Amant de Lady Chatterley* (Gallimard, 1932).
6. *Fantasia of the Unconscious* (Thomas Seltzer, 1922), p. 138.
7. Ibid., p. 279.
8. Ibid., p. 279.
9. Ibid., p. 280.
10. Ibid., p. 285.
11. Ibid., pp. 287–8.
12. Ibid., p. 286.
13. *Women in Love*.
14. *Fantasia of the Unconscious*, p. 114.
15. *Women in Love*, p. 302.
16. *The Plumed Serpent* (Afred A. Knopf, 1951), p. 408.
17. Ibid., p. 422.
18. Excepting Paul of *Sons and Lovers*, the most alive of all of them. But this is the only one of the novels which shows us a masculine apprenticeship.

MONROE ENGEL
"The Continuity of Lawrence's Short Novels"

Hudson Review, Summer 1958, pp. 201–9

Lawrence's short novels are a special and sustained achievement belonging roughly to the last decade of his life. It is of course not clear at precisely what point the long story becomes the short novel, but with *The Fox* (1918–19; revised and lengthened in 1921), not only does Lawrence write a story that is appreciably longer than his earlier stories (about three times the length of "The Prussian Officer," for example), but he establishes certain themes—and, more peculiarly, certain patterns and devices for vivifying these themes—that become generic for his longer stories.

The Fox is written in a markedly objective style verging on irony, or a kind of satire with only the mutest comedy. The elastic fluency of the style also allows direct seriousness, even earnestness. The opening pages describe a peculiar state of disorder suggested by the facts that the two girls in the story are known by their surnames; that March, who had "learned carpentry and joinery at the evening classes in Islington," was "the man about the place;" and that on the farm, nothing prospers: the heifer gets through the fences, and the girls sell the cow—not insignificantly—just before it is to calf, "afraid of the coming event." The fowls are drowsy in the morning, but stay up half the night; and the fox carries them off at will. All in all, the girls "were living on their losses, as Banford said," and they acquired a "low opinion of Nature altogether."

This detailing of disorder is perhaps overdone, labored, and some other elements in the story seem too insisted on

also—a kind of heaviness from which the subsequent short novels do not suffer. For March—who is obviously from the first the more restive and saveable of the two girls—the fox represents an escape from her present deadening life, an escape conceived in increasingly sexual terms. "Her heart beats to the fox," she is "possessed by him." Then, when the young man appears, he is at once seen in foxy terms. He has "a ruddy, roundish face, with fairish hair, rather long, flattened to his forehead with sweat. His eyes were blue, and very bright and sharp. On his cheeks, on the fresh ruddy skin, were fine, fair hairs, like a down but sharper. It gave him a slightly glistening look." And he is the fabulous fox as well as the natural one, the sly predatory Reynard, for "Having his heavy sack on his shoulders, he stooped, thrusting his head forward. His hat was loose in one hand."

Most of the time though, the analogy is to the natural fox. The analogy is intentionally overt from the beginning. Lawrence says of the boy that "to March he was the fox;" and once March says to him, "I thought you were the fox." The effect then comes not from a hidden analogy suddenly bursting on the reader's consciousness with the force of discovery, but from the detailed accumulation of the analogy, supported by Lawrence's genius for the description of nature and animals.

The analogy, and March's sexual dream of the fox, are such that we quite accept the remark, late in the story, that March's upper lip lifts "away from her two white, front teeth, with a curious, almost rabbit-look . . . that helpless fascinated rabbit-look." And accept too the serious weight of sexual implication when she examines the dead fox, and to her hand "his wonderful black glinted brush was full and frictional, wonderful."

The boy's fox-likeness matters—given Lawrence's beliefs—in ways other than simply his vital quickness, or his sexual splendor. There is also "always . . . the same ruddy, self-contained look on his face, as though he were keeping himself to himself." The essential concerns in this story are more nearly simply sexual than in the later ones, but even here this self-contained boy says: "If I marry, I want to feel it's for all my life." And part of his claim to March is that there can be more permanence for her in a relationship with him than in one with Banford. The permanent marriage of two self-contained people is close to Lawrence's ideal.

For of course here as elsewhere, Lawrence is trying to render imaginatively what the relationship between the sexes is and might be, and the contest—between the boy and Banford—for March, is a contest that appears repeatedly, though in various guises, in Lawrence's work: a contest in which the new kind of lover must win the still neutral beloved from the claims of the old kind of love. Banford and March are held together by the old kind of love. Whether that love is also abnormal, is largely beside the point. It is not simply that March encases her soft flesh in manly dress for Banford, and shows it in female dress for the boy Henry—though this simple device has enormous and, once more, overt effect in the story. It is rather that March feels responsible for Banford's health and happiness and well-being, and feels safe and sane with her. Sanity and over-responsibility are the marks, in all the short novels, of the old love. It was from these self-destroying feelings that March "wanted the boy to save her."

With Henry—who kills Banford to free March for himself—she feels something else. The story is at its weakest in these final pages, expanded in Lawrence's 1921 revision, which attempt to get at what the nature of the new kind of relationship between man and woman will be. Lawrence, who wished to write social and prescriptive fiction, felt a responsibility to substantiate the better world he preached. A similar impulse and failure can be found in the final act of *Prometheus Unbound*. Each of Lawrence's short novels has this kind of visionary finale, but they become increasingly successful.

The Captain's Doll (1921) is in a similarly objective style, with the author detached even from the proponents of his thesis. But there is less bent of irony this time than of wonder, for *The Captain's Doll* is peculiarly a story about beauty. Again, the meaningful working of the story depends on an overt analogy—between Captain Hepburn and the doll portrait that Hannele makes of him, but doesn't make him into. For this time the analogy is a kind of anti-analogy—the doll is what Captain Hepburn must not become: "any *woman*, to-day," the Captain says, "no matter *how* much she loves her man—she could start any minute and make a doll of him. And the doll would be her hero; and her hero would be no more than her doll."

All these short novels make heavy use of analogy. This is the only one, however, in which the analogy is to an inanimate object, and the inanimate fixedness of the doll limits its range of usefulness. The use it has, though, is exact and startling, and is at least inherent in the first unseemly appearance of the doll, flourishing head downwards.

Again, as in *The Fox*, the story starts with disordered relationships, and the action concerns the choice a neutral person, Hannele, must make between conventional love and a new kind of relationship. But the choice as posed here is more complicated and rich than in *The Fox*. For one thing, conventional love is given formidable and deeply attractive proponents in Mitchka, the Regierungsrat, and Mrs. Hepburn, who has, in her husband's account of her at least, a quality of out-of-the-world or primitive magic that will recur in the subsequent short novels as a quality reserved for certain adherents of the new order only. Also, the new kind of relationship is suggested more exactly and coherently in *The Captain's Doll* than it was in *The Fox*, and is less simply sexual.

The dramatic acceptability of the doctrine in this story depends on its being given dramatic validity, rather than being merely sermonized as at the end of *The Fox*. It comes too from the substantial impressiveness of Hepburn as a character, and from his and the author's nearly painful sense of the pull and attractions of the old ways, and particularly of the moral painfulness of beauty. And on the lake, at the very end of the story, we even get a flash of what the life of Hepburn and Hannele may be together, united in this new kind of marriage.

In *The Ladybird* (1921–22), Lawrence told Middleton Murry he had "the quick of a new thing." The "quick" lies chiefly in the character of the Bohemian Count Dionys, who is a resurrected man in a more intellectual, varied, and charming way than Hepburn. Dionys, of course, is purposefully named; but he is the magic Pan, not the vulgar Bacchus.

Again the objective style verges on irony, but this time it is a grave kind of irony, as seen in the opening description of Lady Beveridge. The style is subtle, the exact weight of meaning unfixed. Nothing but such complex fluency of style could make the scenes between Daphne and Count Dionys—and particularly the climactic scene in Count Dionys' bedroom—convincing, and free from any air of the ludicrous.

Again—as in the two previous stories—there is a contest for the neutral soul: the soul of Lady Daphne. But the forces in this contest are not in each case single figures. Lady Beveridge and Basil are a team—the fully civilized or naturally repressed characters, bound to the old civilized kind of selfless love. This is in contrast to Lord Beveridge and Lady Daphne, who are *un*naturally repressed. Repressed, that is, in opposition to their own natures. With Lord Beveridge, the repression is nearly final, despite his choleric intransigence and personal integrity. But with Daphne it is not yet final. Even her body cannot accept it, is in disorder, as shown by the tendency to tuberculosis from which she suffers when under stress—a tendency, of course, that Lawrence also had, and which he seems often to have attributed to social causes, to his inability to find a healthy moral atmosphere in which to live. The character who has thrown off civilized repression, the other principal in the contest, is of course Count Dionys.

Perhaps the most remarkable scene in the active contest is the long debate on love between Count Dionys and Basil, the champion of conventional love, who has told Daphne that his love for her now is a sacrament, and that he considers himself an eager sacrifice to her, and could happily die on her altar. These champions of different attitudes toward love carry on their debate with Daphne sitting between them, finding it "curious that while her sympathy . . . was with the Count, it was her husband whose words she believed to be true." So the schism between her mind, educated to repression, and that other part of her which suffers under this repression, is made dramatically clear. It is an indication of the energy of the ideas and the fluency of the style, that this almost formal debate is always dramatic, never abstracted from the situation, and never tedious—even as is the nobly ludicrous debate between Hepburn and Hannele on the bus in *The Captain's Doll*.

Again animal analogy is important in the story—principally the ladybird analogy from which it gets its title. The ladybird, on the crest of Count Dionys' family, is, he thinks, a descendant of the Egyptian scarab. This leads to a deceptively casual and not quite open exchange:

"Do you know Fabre?" put in Lord Beveridge. "He suggests that the beetle rolling a little ball of dung before him, in a dry old field, must have suggested to the Egyptians the First Principle that set the globe rolling. And so the scarab became the creative principle—or something like that."

"That the earth is a tiny ball of dry dung is good," said Basil.

"Between the claws of a ladybird," added Daphne.

"That is what it is, to go back to one's origin," said Lady Beveridge.

"Perhaps they meant that it was the principle of decomposition which first set the ball rolling," said the Count.

"The ball would have to be *there* first," said Basil.

"Certainly. But it hadn't started to roll. Then the principle of decomposition started it." The Count smiled as if it were a joke.

"I am no Egyptologist," said Lady Beveridge, "so I can't judge."

The analogy between Count Dionys and this usefully destructive ladybird is admirably clear.

The place of magic—slight and off to one side in *The Captain's Doll*, and to the wrong side at that—is very important in *The Ladybird*. Not the occult theorizing about light and dark—recurrent in so much of Lawrence's fiction—but rather the magic that is conveyed by the songs in the story, the magic of personal power. When Daphne uses the Count's thimble, a German song occurs to her:

> Wenn ich ein Vöglein wär
> Und auch zwei Flüglein hätt'
> Flög ich zu dir—

This is obviously a song of the ladybird, though in her conscious mind Daphne labels it a song of longing for her absent husband. And Daphne is finally brought to the Count—resolving the schism between her conscious and unconscious will—by the "old songs of his childhood" that he sings, an "intense peeping . . . like a witchcraft . . . a ventriloquist sound or a bat's uncanny peeping . . . inaudible to any one but herself. . . . It was like a thread which she followed out of the world."

Again the resurrection to a new way is not easy, not a trick, but a painful, chastening separation of the self from the accustomed world and—most painfully, and for Daphne particularly—from its surface beauties. Yet at the end of *The Ladybird*, the reader is convinced that he has glimpsed in Daphne and Dionys some special capacity possessed neither by the other characters in the story, nor by himself.

In *St. Mawr* (1924) the objective style is at times a style of high comedy, and particularly when Mrs. Witt is on scene. Again, of course, the story depends on a central analogy, stressed by the title, between a human being and an animal. But the horse St. Mawr defines Rico not by similarity but by contrast. In this way, the analogy is something like that in *The Captain's Doll*. Once more the analogy is entirely overt, and is suggested or anticipated well before the horse even appears, in a horsey description of Rico in the second paragraph. Rico is all fraudulent play, never the real thing (Mr. Leavis has pointed to the significance of his playing at being an artist). Even his sexuality is bogus. His marriage with Lou is "a marriage . . . without sex"; and so there is brutal irony in the circumstance that he wears a ring, sent him by a female admirer, bearing a "lovely intaglio of Priapus under an apple bough." What Lou requires—and Rico is not at all—is a Dionys, the Pan of the dinner table conversation with the painter Cartwright.

The only men in this story who are at all Pan-like are Phoenix and Lewis, the two grooms, and Phoenix doesn't quite make it either. Lewis, however, is the real thing. He and St. Mawr both avoid physical contact with women because—presumably, and as he says—modern women are incapable of the proper and necessary respect for their husbands. Again, part of the real creative accomplishment of the story is that it can make ideas and notions that we might resist or find absurd out of context, convincing and moving in context. This is particularly true of the long conversation between Lewis and Mrs. Witt during the cross country ride they take together to save St. Mawr. The ride culminates with Lewis's refusal of Mrs. Witt's offer of marriage; but before this offer, which ends all exchange between them, Lewis has shown himself another of the Lawrence characters endowed with other-worldly magic. Mrs. Witt, who in her relations with every other man she'd ever known had "conquered his country," feels that Lewis looks "at her as if from out of another country, a country of which he was an inhabitant, and where she had never been." And this magic property is given simpler demonstration by Lewis's naive, stubborn, but only partially credulous talk about falling-stars and ash-tree seeds and the people of the moon. When he sees a falling-star, Lewis thinks to himself: *"There's movement in the sky. The world is going to change again. They're throwing something to us from the distance, and we've got to have it, whether we want it or not."*

St. Mawr is an ambitious story. In the disaster in which St. Mawr is disgraced, he is the figure of unrepressed man ridden by repressed man, Rico. The accident occurs, not fortuitously, when the horse shies at a dead snake. And—

supporting the same suggestions—this precipitates for Lou an overwhelming vision of evil.[1]

The magic and visionary qualities emerging through all the preceding short novels, dominate the middle and end of *St. Mawr*. The very end—the description of the deserted mountain ranch in the American Southwest—is a vision of the potential and possibility that Lawrence in his more optimistic thoughts about America considered it to possess. Lou Witt is not saved here, but is to be brought—possibly—to the condition that precedes any radically new life, a kind of exalted waiting, without sexuality or, really, any connection with other human beings. Lewis and St. Mawr—who has finally found his mate in a long-legged Texas mare: a touch that surely fails to add to the seriousness of the story—drop out before the end, and Phoenix, too, is in effect disposed of. The final pages—marred only at times by Lawrence's preachy vein—give an affecting picture of the beauty and effort of man's attempt to bring order into chaos. And we have here again the Shelleyan attempt to envision with some concreteness the condition abstractly prescribed.

The Man Who Died (1927) is entirely visionary and miraculous. Here the objective style is more formal, to help convey the quality of myth, and again analogy is important. At first Lawrence had called the story *The Escaped Cock*—a title that accentuates the analogy, as do the titles of the other short novels. As usual, the overt import of the analogy requires no expounding.

The theme of the resurrected man (and the Pan-Christ) had occurred in several of the other short novels, in different degrees of importance. Dionys is a resurrected man, coming back to life after being near death, and after considering himself dead and wishing his death. So too is Captain Hepburn in *The Captain's Doll*. In *St. Mawr*, Lou Witt—writing to her mother—says she wishes no more marriages, and understands "why Jesus said: *Noli me tangere.* Touch me not, I am not yet ascended unto the Father . . . That is all my cry to all the world." And this, of course, is the repeated cry of the man who had died.

It is unnecessary, here, to outline Lawrence's sexual prescriptions. But clearly of great moment in this story are the reverential and respecting wonder between the man and the priestess, and that they know and need to know so little about each other, thus retaining a kind of inviolate personal integrity. Nor is anything like mere sexuality being invoked—not, for example, the slavish sexuality of the slaves. And once more, the extraordinary beauty of the narrative, often gratuitous to its immediate intent, prevents import from becoming anything so meagre as doctrine.

These stories have a richness and intricacy—purposeful, and also nearly accidental virtues—that summary cannot suggest. What should be suggested is the achievement not only of form—which often appears to be lacking in the long novels of the same period—but of something very close to formula. There is a bold repetition—often with increasing evidence of intention—of certain elements, principally: the objective and fluent style; analogy—generally animal analogy; disordered relationships; the opposition of traditional love and a new kind of relationship between the sexes, dramatized by a contest between these forces for a neutral beloved; the use of magic; and the visionary ending, associated with the emergent theme of resurrection, and given final importance in *The Man Who Died*. Altogether, these short novels constitute an extraordinary body of imaginatively realized thesis fiction.

In the short novels, Lawrence puts into practice some of the objectives he sets himself in the letter to Edward Garnett defending the early draft of *The Rainbow,* and objecting to the practice of the great traditional novelists of fitting all their characters into a moral scheme. This moral scheme is, he says, "whatever the extraordinariness of the characters themselves, dull, old, dead." For himself, he wants to get away from "the old stable ego of the character," and make the characters, instead, fall into "some other rhythmic form, as when one draws a fiddlebow across a fine tray delicately sanded, the sand takes lines unknown."

For reasons having to do largely with the implications of length, these more formal principles of characterization may be more peculiarly suited to the short novel than to the long. In *The Fox,* the attempt to break the tyranny of the moral scheme is still flagrant and crude. But in the short novels that follow— particularly beginning with *The Ladybird* and its "quick of a new thing"—ego in any conventional sense is no longer the spring of action. Characters act instead in an intricate formal pattern, vivifying and responding to a central concern. The extremity of Lawrence's views required highly formal expression to be in any way acceptable, and the artifice of these short novels is nearly as formal as ballet or ritual dance.

Notes

1. It might, incidentally, be interesting to compare Lou's vision on the expedition to the Devil's Chair, and Mrs. Witt's related lassitude toward the end of the story, with the enervating vision of Mrs. Moore in *Passage to India,* after her visit to the Malabar caves. In a letter to Middleton Murry written just after he had completed *St. Mawr,* Lawrence says: ". . . the *Passage to India* interested me very much . . . the repudiation of our white bunk is genuine, sincere, and pretty thorough, it seems to me. Negative, yes. But King Charles must have his head off. Homage to the headsman."

W. H. AUDEN
"D. H. Lawrence"
The Dyer's Hand
1962, pp. 277–95

If men were as much men as lizards are lizards,
They'd be worth looking at.

The artist, the man who makes, is less important to mankind, for good or evil, than the apostle, the man with a message. Without a religion, a philosophy, a code of behavior, call it what you will, men cannot live at all; what they believe may be absurd or revolting, but they have to believe something. On the other hand, however much the arts may mean to us, it is possible to imagine our lives without them.

As a human being, every artist holds some set of beliefs or other but, as a rule, these are not of his own invention; his public knows this and judges his work without reference to them. We read Dante for his poetry not for his theology because we have already met the theology elsewhere.

There are a few writers, however, like Blake and D. H. Lawrence, who are both artists and apostles and this makes a just estimation of their work difficult to arrive at. Readers who find something of value in their message will attach unique importance to their writings because they cannot find it anywhere else. But this importance may be shortlived; once I have learned his message, I cease to be interested in a messenger and, should I later come to think his message false or misleading, I shall remember him with resentment and distaste. Even if I try to ignore the message and read him again as if he were only an artist, I shall probably feel disappointed because I cannot recapture the excitement I felt when I first read him.

When I first read Lawrence in the late Twenties, it was his message which made the greatest impression on me, so that it was his "think" books like *Fantasia on the Unconscious* rather than his fiction which I read most avidly. As for his poetry, when I first tried to read it, I did not like it; despite my admiration for him, it offended my notions of what poetry should be. Today my notions of what poetry should be are still, in all essentials, what they were then and hostile to his, yet there are a number of his poems which I have come to admire enormously. When a poet who holds views about the nature of poetry which we believe to be false writes a poem we like, we are apt to think: "This time he has forgotten his theory and is writing according to ours." But what fascinates me about the poems of Lawrence's which I like is that I must admit he could never have written them had he held the kind of views about poetry of which I approve.

Man is a history-making creature who can neither repeat his past nor leave it behind; at every moment he adds to and thereby modifies everything that had previously happened to him. Hence the difficulty of finding a single image which can stand as an adequate symbol for man's kind of existence. If we think of his ever-open future, then the natural image is of a single pilgrim walking along an unending road into hitherto unexplored country; if we think of his never-forgettable past, then the natural image is of a great crowded city, built in every style of architecture, in which the dead are as active citizens as the living. The only feature common to both images is that both are purposive; a road goes in a certain direction, a city is built to endure and be a home. The animals, who live in the present, have neither cities nor roads and do not miss them; they are at home in the wilderness and at most, if they are social, set up camps for a single generation. But man requires both; the image of a city with no roads leading away from it suggests a prison, the image of a road that starts from nowhere in particular, an animal spoor.

Every man is both a citizen and a pilgrim, but most men are predominantly one or the other and in Lawrence the pilgrim almost obliterated the citizen. It is only natural, therefore, that he should have admired Whitman so much, both for his matter and his manner.

> Whitman's essential message was the Open Road. The leaving of the soul free unto herself, the leaving of his fate to her and to the loom of the open road. . . . The true democracy . . . where all journey down the open road. And where a soul is known at once in its going. Not by its clothes or appearance. Not by its family name. Not even by its reputation. Not by works at all. The soul passing unenhanced, passing on foot, and being no more than itself.

In his introduction to *New Poems,* Lawrence tries to explain the difference between traditional verse and the free verse which Whitman was the first to write.

> The poetry of the beginning and the poetry of the end must have that exquisite finality, perfection which belongs to all that is far off. It is in the realm of all that is perfect . . . the finality and perfection are conveyed in exquisite form: the perfect symmetry, the rhythm which returns upon itself like a dance where the hands link and loosen and link for the supreme moment of the end . . . But there is another kind of poetry, the poetry of that which is at hand: the immediate present. . . . Life, the ever present, knows no finality, no finished crystallisation. . . . It is obvious that the poetry of the instant present cannot have the same body or the

same motions as the poetry of the before and after. It can never submit to the same conditions, it is never finished. . . . Much has been written about free verse. But all that can be said, first and last, is that free verse is, or should be, direct utterance from the instant whole man. It is the soul and body surging at once, nothing left out. . . . It has no finish. It has no satisfying stability. It does not want to get anywhere. It just takes place.

It would be easy to make fun of this passage, to ask Lawrence, for example, to tell us exactly how long an instant is, or how it would be physically possible for the poet to express it in writing before it had become past. But it is obvious that Lawrence is struggling to say something which he believes to be important. Very few statements which poets make about poetry, even when they appear to be quite lucid, are understandable except in their polemic context. To understand them, we need to know what they are directed against, what the poet who made them considered the principal enemies of genuine poetry.

In Lawrence's case, one enemy was the conventional response, the laziness or fear which makes people prefer second-hand experience to the shock of looking and listening for themselves.

Man fixes some wonderful erection of his own between himself and the wild chaos, and gradually goes bleached and stifled under his parasol. Then comes a poet, enemy of convention, and makes a slit in the umbrella; and lo! the glimpse of chaos is a vision, a window to the sun. But after a while, getting used to the vision, and not liking the genuine draft from chaos, commonplace man daubs a simulacrum of the window that opens into chaos and patches the umbrella with the painted patch of the simulacrum. That is, he gets used to the vision; it is part of his house decoration.

Lawrence's justified dislike of the conventional response leads him into a false identification of the genuine with the novel. The image of the slit in the umbrella is misleading because what you can see through it will always be the same. But a genuine work of art is one in which every generation finds something new. A genuine work of art remains an example of what being genuine means, so that it can stimulate later artists to be genuine in their turn. Stimulate, not compel; if a playwright in the twentieth century chooses to write a play in a pastiche of Shakespearian blank verse, the fault is his, not Shakespeare's. Those who are afraid of firsthand experience would find means of avoiding it if all the art of the past were destroyed.

However, theory aside. Lawrence did care passionately about genuineness of feeling. He wrote little criticism about other poets who were his contemporaries, but, when he did, he was quick to pounce on any phoniness of emotion. About Ralph Hodgson's lines

The sky was lit,
The sky was stars all over it,
I stood, I knew not why

he writes, "No one should say *I knew not why* any more. It is as meaningless as *Yours truly* at the end of a letter," and, after quoting an American poetess

Why do I think of stairways
With a rush of hurt surprise?

he remarks, "Heaven knows, my dear, unless you once fell down." Whatever faults his own poetry may have, it never puts on an act. Even when Lawrence talks nonsense, as when he asserts that the moon is made of phosphorous or radium, one is convinced that it is nonsense in which he sincerely believed. This is more than can be said of some poets much greater than he. When Yeats assures me, in a stanza of the utmost magnificence, that after death he wants to become a mechanical bird, I feel that he is telling what my nanny would have called "A story."

The second object of Lawrence's polemic was a doctrine which first became popular in France during the second half of the nineteenth century, the belief that Art is the true religion, that life has no value except as material for a beautiful artistic structure and that, therefore, the artist is the only authentic human being—the rest, rich and poor alike, are canaille. Works of art are the only cities; life itself is a jungle. Lawrence's feelings about this creed were so strong that whenever he detects its influence, as he does in Proust and Joyce, he refuses their work any merit whatsoever. A juster and more temperate statement of his objection has been made by Dr. Auerbach:

When we compare Stendhal's or even Balzac's world with the world of Flaubert or the two Goncourts, the latter seems strangely narrow and petty despite its wealth of impressions. Documents of the kind represented by Flaubert's correspondence and the Goncourt diary are indeed admirable in the purity and incorruptibility of their artistic ethics, the wealth of impressions elaborated in them, and their refinement of sensory culture. At the same time, however, we sense something narrow, something oppressively close in their books. They are full of reality and intellect, but poor in humor and inner poise. The purely literary, even on the highest level of artistic acumen, limits the power of judgment, reduces the wealth of life, and at times distorts the outlook upon the world of phenomena. And while the writers contemptuously avert their attention from the political and economic bustle, consistently value life only as literary subject matter, and remain arrogantly and bitterly aloof from its great practical problems, in order to achieve aesthetic isolation for their work, often at great and daily expense of effort, the practical world nevertheless besets them in a thousand petty ways.

Sometimes there are financial worries, and almost always there is nervous hypotension and a morbid concern with health. . . . What finally emerges, despite all their intellectual and artistic incorruptibility, is a strangely petty impression; that of an upper bourgeois egocentrically concerned over his aesthetic comfort, plagued by a thousand small vexations, nervous, obsessed by a mania—only in this case the mania is called "Literature." (*Mimesis.*)

In rejecting the doctrine that life has no value except as raw material for art, Lawrence fell into another error, that of identifying art with life, making with action.

I offer a bunch of pansies, not a wreath of immortelles. I don't want everlasting flowers and I don't want to offer them to anybody else. A flower passes, and that perhaps is the best of it. . . . Don't nail the pansy down. You won't keep it any better if you do.

Here Lawrence draws a false analogy between the process of artistic creation and the organic growth of living creatures. "Nature hath no goal though she hath law." Organic growth is a cyclical process; it is just as true to say that the oak is a potential acorn as it is to say the acorn is a potential oak. But the process of writing a poem, of making any art object, is not cyclical but a motion in one direction towards a definite end. As Socrates says in Valéry's dialogue *Eupalinos:*

The tree does not construct its branches and leaves; nor the cock his beak and feathers. But the tree and all its parts, or the cock and all his, are constructed by the principles themselves, which do not exist apart from the constructing. . . . But, in the objects made by man, the principles are separate from the construction, and are, as it were, imposed by a tyrant from without upon the material, to which he imparts them by acts. . . . If a man waves his arm, we distinguish this arm from his gesture, and we conceive between gesture and arm a purely possible relation. But from the point of view of nature, this gesture of the arm and the arm itself cannot be separated.

An artist who ignores this difference between natural growth and human construction will produce the exact opposite of what he intends. He hopes to produce something which will seem as natural as a flower, but the qualities of the natural are exactly what his product will lack. A natural object never appears unfinished; if it is an inorganic object like a stone, it is what it has to be, if an organic object like a flower, what it has to be at this moment. But a similar effect—of being what it has to be—can only be achieved in a work of art by much thought, labor and care. The gesture of a ballet dancer, for example, only looks natural when, through long practice, its execution has become "second nature" to him. That perfect incarnation of life in substance, word in flesh, which in nature is immediate, has in art to be achieved and, in fact, can never be perfectly achieved. In many of Lawrence's poems, the spirit has failed to make itself a fit body to live in, a curious defect in the work of a writer who was so conscious of the value and significance of the body. In his essay on Thomas Hardy, Lawrence made some acute observations about this very problem. Speaking of the antimony between Law and Love, the Flesh and the Spirit, he says

> The principle of the Law is found strongest in Woman, the principle of Love in Man. In every creature, the mobility, the law of change is found exemplified in the male, the stability, the conservatism in the female.
>
> The very adherence of rhyme and regular rhythm is a concession to the Law, a concession to the body, to the being and requirements of the body. They are an admission of the living positive inertia which is the other half of life, other than the pure will to motion.

This division of Lawrence's is a variant on the division between the City and the Open Road. To the mind of the pilgrim, his journey is a succession of ever-new sights and sounds, but to his heart and legs, it is a rhythmical repetition—tic-toc, left-right—even the poetry of the Open Road must pay that much homage to the City. By his own admission and definition Lawrence's defect as an artist was an exaggerated maleness.

Reading Lawrence's early poems, one is continually struck by the originality of the sensibility and the conventionality of the expressive means. For most immature poets, their chief problem is to learn to forget what they have been taught poets are supposed to feel; too often, as Lawrence says, the young man is afraid of his demon, puts his hand over the demon's mouth and speaks for him. On the other hand, an immature poet, if he has real talent, usually begins to exhibit quite early a distinctive style of his own; however obvious the influence of some older writer may be, there is something original in his manner or, at least, great technical competence. In Lawrence's case, this was not so; he learned quite soon to let his demon speak, but it took him a long time to find the appropriate style

for him to speak in. All too often in his early poems, even the best ones, he is content to versify his thoughts; there is no essential relation between what he is saying and the formal structure he imposes upon it.

> Being nothing, I bear the brunt
> Of the nightly heavens overhead, like an immense
>   open eye
> With a cat's distended pupil, that sparkles with little
>   stars
> And with thoughts that flash and crackle in far-off
>   malignancy
> So distant, they cannot touch me, whom nothing
>   mars.

A mere poetaster with nothing to say, would have done something about *whom nothing mars*.

It is interesting to notice that the early poems in which he seems technically most at ease and the form most natural, are those he wrote in dialect.

> I wish tha hadna done it, Tim,
>   I do, an' that I do,
> For whenever I look thee i'th' face, I s'll see
>   Her face too.
>
> I wish I could wash er off'n thee;
>   'Appen I can, if I try.
> But tha'll ha'e ter promise ter be true ter me
>   Till I die.

This sounds like a living woman talking, whereas no woman on earth ever talked like this:

> How did you love him, you who only roused
> His mind until it burnt his heart away!
> 'Twas you who killed him, when you both caroused
> In words and things well said. But the other way
> He never loved you, never with desire
> Touched you to fire.

I suspect that Lawrence's difficulties with formal verse had their origin in his linguistic experiences as a child.

> My father was a working man
>   and a collier was he,
> At six in the morning they turned him down
>   and they turned him up for tea.
>
> My mother was a superior soul
>   a superior soul was she,
> Cut out to play a superior role
>   in the god-damn bourgoisie.
>
> We children were the in-betweens,
>   Little non-descripts were we,
> In doors we called each other *you*
>   outside it was *tha* and *thee*.

In formal poetry, the role played by the language itself is so great that it demands of the poet that he be as intimate with it as with his own flesh and blood and love it with a single-minded passion. A child who has associated standard English with Mother and dialect with Father has ambivalent feelings about both which can hardly fail to cause trouble for him in later life if he should try to write formal poetry. Not that it would have been possible for Lawrence to become a dialect poet like Burns or William Barnes, both of whom lived before public education had made dialect quaint. The language of Burns was a national not a parochial speech, and the peculiar charm of Barnes' poetry is its combination of the simplest emotions with an extremely sophisticated formal technique: Lawrence could never have limited himself to the thoughts and feelings of a Nottinghamshire mining village, and he had neither the taste nor the talent of Barnes for what he scornfully called word games.

Most of Lawrence's finest poems are to be found in the volume *Birds, Beasts, and Flowers*, begun in Tuscany when he was thirty-five and finished three years later in New Mexico. All of them are written in free verse.

The difference between formal and free verse may be likened to the difference between carving and modeling; the formal poet, that is to say, thinks of the poem he is writing as something already latent in the language which he has to reveal, while the free verse poet thinks of language as a plastic passive medium upon which he imposes his artistic conception. One might also say that, in their attitude towards art, the formal verse writer is a catholic, the free verse writer a protestant. And Lawrence was, in every respect, very protestant indeed. As he himself acknowledged, it was through Whitman that he found himself as a poet, found the right idiom of poetic speech for his demon.

On no other English poet, so far as I know, has Whitman had a beneficial influence; he could on Lawrence because, despite certain superficial resemblances, their sensibilities were utterly different. Whitman quite consciously set out to be the Epic Bard of America and created a poetic *persona* for the purpose. He keeps using the first person singular and even his own name, but these stand for a *persona*, not an actual human being, even when he appears to be talking about the most intimate experiences. When he sounds ridiculous, it is usually because the image of an individual obtrudes itself comically upon what is meant to be a statement about a collective experience. *I am large. I contain multitudes* is absurd if one thinks of Whitman himself or any individual; of a corporate person like General Motors it makes perfectly good sense. The more we learn about Whitman the man, the less like his *persona* he looks. On the other hand it is doubtful if a writer ever existed who had less of an artistic *persona* than Lawrence; from his letters and the reminiscences of his friends, it would seem that he wrote for publication in exactly the same way as he spoke in private. (I must confess that I find Lawrence's love poems embarrassing because of their lack of reticence; they make me feel a Peeping Tom.) Then, Whitman looks at life extensively rather than intensively. No detail is dwelt upon for long; it is snapshotted and added as one more item to the vast American catalogue. But Lawrence in his best poems is always concerned intensively with a single subject, a bat, a tortoise, a fig tree, which he broods on until he has exhausted its possibilities.

A sufficient number of years have passed for us to have gotten over both the first overwhelming impact of Lawrence's genius and the subsequent violent reaction when we realized that there were silly and nasty sides to his nature. We can be grateful to him for what he can do for us, without claiming that he can do everything or condemning him because he cannot. As an analyst and portrayer of the forces of hatred and aggression which exist in all human beings and, from time to time, manifest themselves in nearly all human relationships, Lawrence is, probably, the greatest master who ever lived. But that was absolutely all that he knew and understood about human beings; about human affection and human charity, for example, he knew absolutely nothing. The truth is that he detested nearly all human beings if he had to be in close contact with them; his ideas of what a human relationship, between man and man or man and woman, ought to be are pure daydreams because they are not based upon any experience of actual relationships which might be improved or corrected. Whenever, in his novels and short stories, he introduces a character whom he expects the reader to admire, he or she is always an unmitigated humorless bore, but the

more he dislikes his characters the more interesting he makes them. And, in his heart of hearts, Lawrence knew this himself. There is a sad passage in *An Autobiographical Sketch*:

> Why is there so little contact between myself and the people I know? The answer, as far as I can see, has something to do with class. As a man from the working class, I feel that the middle class cut off some of my vital vibration when I am with them. I admit them charming and good people often enough, but they just stop some part of me from working.
>
> Then, why don't I live with my own people? Because their vibration is limited in another direction. The working class is narrow in outlook, in prejudice, and narrow in intelligence. This again makes a prison. Yet I find, here in Italy, for example, that I live in a certain contact with the peasants who work the land of this villa. I am not intimate with them, hardly speak to them save to say good-day. And they are not working for me. I am not their padrone. I don't want to live with them in their cottages; that would be a sort of prison. I don't idealise them. I don't expect them to make any millenium here on earth, neither now nor in the future. But I want them to be there, about the place, their lives going along with mine.

For the word *peasants*, one might substitute the words *birds, beasts and flowers*. Lawrence possessed a great capacity for affection and charity, but he could only direct it towards non-human life or peasants whose lives were so uninvolved with his that, so far as he was concerned, they might just as well have been nonhuman. Whenever, in his writings, he forgets about men and women with proper names and describes the anonymous life of stones, waters, forests, animals, flowers, chance traveling companions or passers-by, his bad temper and his dogmatism immediately vanish and he becomes the most enchanting companion imaginable, tender, intelligent, funny and, above all, happy. But the moment any living thing, even a dog, makes demands on him, the rage and preaching return. His poem about "Bibbles," "the walt whitmanesque love-bitch who loved just everybody," is the best poem about a dog ever written, but it makes it clear that Lawrence was no person to be entrusted with the care of a dog.

> All right, my little bitch.
> You learn loyalty rather than loving,
> And I'll protect you.

To which Bibbles might, surely, with justice retort: 'O for Chris-sake, mister, go get yourself an Alsatian and leave me alone, can't you.'

The poems in *Birds, Beasts, and Flowers* are among Lawrence's longest. He was not a concise writer and he needs room to make his effect. In his poetry he manages to make a virtue out of what in his prose is often a vice, a tendency to verbal repetition. The recurrence of identical or slightly varied phrases helps to give his free verse a structure; the phrases themselves are not particularly striking, but this is as it should be, for their function is to act as stitches.

Like the romantics, Lawrence's starting point in these poems is a personal encounter between himself and some animal or flower but, unlike the romantics, he never confuses the feelings they arouse in him with what he sees and hears and knows about them.

Thus, he accuses Keats, very justly, I think, of being so preoccupied with his own feelings that he cannot really listen to the nightingale. *Thy plaintive anthem fades* deserves Lawrence's comment: *It never was a plaintive anthem—it was Caruso at his jauntiest.*

Lawrence never forgets—indeed this is what he likes most about them—that a plant or an animal has its own kind of existence which is unlike and uncomprehending of man's.

It is no use my saying to him in an emotional voice:
'This is your Mother, she laid you when you were an
egg.'
He does not even trouble to answer: 'Woman, what
have I to do with thee?'
He wearily looks the other way,
And she even more wearily looks another way still.
("Tortoise Family Connections.")
But watching closer
That motionless deadly motion,
That unnatural barrel body, that long ghoul
nose . . .
I left off hailing him.
I had made a mistake, I didn't know him,
This grey, monotonous soul in the water,
This intense individual in shadow,
Fish-alive.
I didn't know his God.
("Fish.")

When discussing people or ideas, Lawrence is often turgid and obscure, but when, as in these poems, he is contemplating some object with love, the lucidity of his language matches the intensity of his vision, and he can make the reader *see* what he is saying as very few writers can.

Queer, with your thin wings and your streaming legs,
How you sail like a heron, or a dull clot of air.
("The Mosquito.")
Her little loose hands, and sloping Victorian
shoulders
("Kangaroo.")
There she is, perched on her manger, looking over
the boards into the day
Like a belle at her window.
And immediately she sees me she blinks, stares,
doesn't know me, turns her head and ignores
me vulgarly with a wooden blank on her face.
What do I care for her, the ugly female, standing up
there with her long tangled sides like an old rug
thrown over a fence.
But she puts her nose down shrewdly enough when
the knot is untied,
And jumps staccato to earth, a sharp, dry jump, still
ignoring me,
Pretending to look around the stall
Come on, you crapa! I'm not your servant.
She turns her head away with an obtuse female sort
of deafness, *bête.*
And then invariably she crouches her rear and makes
water.
That being her way of answer, if I speak to her.—
Self-conscious!
Le bestie non parlano, poverine! . . .
Queer it is, suddenly, in the garden
To catch sight of her standing like some huge
ghoulish grey bird in the air, on the bough of
the leaning almond-tree,
Straight as a board on the bough, looking down like
some hairy horrid God the Father in a William
Blake imagination.
Come, down, Crapa, out of that almond tree!
("She-Goat.")

In passages like these, Lawrence's writing is so transparent that one forgets him entirely and simply sees what he saw.

Birds, Beasts, and Flowers is the peak of Lawrence's achievement as a poet. There are a number of fine things in the later volumes, but a great deal that is tedious, both in subject matter and form. A writer's doctrines are not the business of a literary critic except in so far as they touch upon questions which concern the art of writing; if a writer makes statements about nonliterary matters, it is not for the literary critic to ask whether they are true or false but he may legitimately question the writer's authority to make them.

The Flauberts and the Goncourts considered social and political questions beneath them; to his credit, Lawrence knew that there are many questions that are more important than Art with an A, but it is one thing to know this and another to believe one is in a position to answer them.

In the modern world, a man who earns his living by writing novels and poems is a self-employed worker whose customers are not his neighbors, and this makes him a social oddity. He may work extremely hard, but his manner of life is something between that of a *rentier* and a gypsy, he can live where he likes and know only the people he chooses to know. He has no firsthand knowledge of all those involuntary relationships created by social, economic and political necessity. Very few artists can be *engagé* because life does not engage them: for better or worse, they do not quite belong to the City. And Lawrence, who was self-employed after the age of twenty-six, belonged to it less than most. Some writers have spent their lives in the same place and social milieu; Lawrence kept constantly moving from one place and one country to another. Some have been extroverts who entered fully into whatever society happened to be available; Lawrence's nature made him avoid human contacts as much as possible. Most writers have at least had the experience of parenthood and its responsibilities; this experience was denied Lawrence. It was inevitable, therefore, that when he tried to lay down the law about social and political matters, money, machinery, etc., he could only be negative and moralistic because, since his youth, he had had no firsthand experiences upon which concrete and positive suggestions could have been based. Furthermore, if, like Lawrence, the only aspects of human beings which you care for and value are states of being, timeless moments of passionate intensity, then social and political life, which are essentially historical—without a past and a future, human society is inconceivable—must be, for you, the worthless aspects of human life. You cannot honestly say, "This kind of society is preferable to that," because, for you, society is wholly given over to Satan.

The other defect in many of the later poems is a formal one. It is noticeable that the best are either of some length or rhymed; the short ones in free verse very rarely come off. A poem which contains a number of ideas and feelings can be organized in many different ways, but a poem which makes a single point and is made up of no more than one or two sentences can only be organized verbally; an epigram or an aphorism must be written either in prose or in some strictly measured verse; written in free verse, it will sound like prose arbitrarily chopped up.

It has always seemed to me that a real thought, not an argument can only exist in verse, or in some poetic form. There is a didactic element about prose thoughts which makes them repellent, slightly bullying, "He who hath wife and children hath given hostages to fortune." There is a point well put: but immediately it irritates by its assertiveness. If it were put into poetry, it would not nag at us so practically. We don't want to be nagged at. (Preface to "Pansies.")

Though I personally love good prose aphorisms, I can see what Lawrence means. If one compares

Plus ça change, plus c'est la même chose

with

The accursed power that stands on Privilege
And goes with Women and Champagne and Bridge
Broke, and Democracy resumed her reign
That goes with Bridge and Women and Champagne

the first does seem a bit smug and a bit abstract, while, in the second, the language dances and is happy.

The bourgeois produced the Bolshevist inevitably
As every half-truth at length produces the contradic-
tion of itself
In the opposite half-truth

has the worst of both worlds; it lacks the conciseness of the prose and the jollity of the rhymed verse.

The most interesting verses in the last poems of Lawrence belong to a literary genre he had not attempted before, satirical doggerel.

If formal verse can be likened to carving, free verse to modeling, then one might say that doggerel verse is like *objets trouvés*—the piece of driftwood that looks like a witch, the stone that has a profile. The writer of doggerel, as it were, takes any old words, rhythms and rhymes that come into his head, gives them a good shake and then throws them onto the page like dice where, lo and behold, contrary to all probability they make sense, not by law but by chance. Since the words appear to have no will of their own, but to be the puppets of chance, so will the things or persons to which they refer; hence the value of doggerel for a certain kind of satire.

It is a different kind of satire from that written by Dryden and Pope. Their kind presupposes a universe, a city, governed by, or owing allegiance to, certain eternal laws of reason and morality; the purpose of their satire is to demonstrate that the individual or institution they are attacking violates these laws. Consequently, the stricter in form their verse, the more artful their technique, the more effective it is. Satirical doggerel, on the other hand, presupposes no fixed laws. It is the weapon of the outsider, the anarchist rebel, who refuses to accept conventional laws and pieties as binding or worthy of respect. Hence its childish technique, for the child represents the naïve and personal, as yet uncorrupted by education and convention. Satire of the Pope kind says: "The Emperor is wearing a celluloid collar. That simply isn't done." Satiric doggerel cries: "The Emperor is naked."

At this kind of satiric doggerel, Lawrence turned out to be a master.

And Mr. Meade, that old old lily,
Said: "Gross, coarse, hideous!" and I, like a silly
Thought he meant the faces of the police court
officials
And how right he was, so I signed my initials.

But Tolstoi was a traitor
To the Russia that needed him most,
The great bewildered Russia
So worried by the Holy Ghost;
He shifted his job onto the peasants
And landed them all on toast.

Parnassus has many mansions.

ALFRED KAZIN
"Sons, Lovers and Mothers"
Partisan Review, Summer 1962, pp. 373–85

Sons and Lovers was published fifty years ago. In these fifty years how many autobiographical novels have been written by young men about the mothers they loved too well, about their difficulties in "adjusting" to other women, and about themselves as the sensitive writers-to-be who liberated themselves just in time in order to write their first novel? Such autobiographical novels—psychological devices they usually are, written in order to demonstrate freedom from the all-too-beloved mother—are one of the great symbols of our time. They are rooted in the modern emancipation of women. Lawrence himself, after a return visit in the 1920's to his native Nottinghamshire, lamented that the "wildness" of his father's generation was gone, that the dutiful sons in his own generation now made "good" husbands. Even working-class mothers in England, in the last of the Victorian age, had aimed at a "higher" standard of culture, and despising their husbands and concentrating on their sons, they had made these sons images of themselves. These mothers had sought a new dignity and even a potential freedom for themselves as women, but holding their sons too close, they robbed them of their necessary "wildness" and masculine force. So the sons grew up in bondage to their mothers, and the more ambitious culturally these sons were—Frank O'Connor says that *Sons and Lovers* is the work of "one of the New Men who are largely a creation of the Education Act of 1870"—the more likely they were to try for their emancipation by writing a novel. The cultural aspiration that explains their plight was expected to turn them into novelists.

Sons and Lovers (which is not a first novel) seems easy to imitate. One reason, apart from the relationships involved, is the very directness and surface conventionality of its technique. James Joyce's *A Portrait of the Artist As a Young Man*, published only three years after *Sons and Lovers*, takes us immediately into the "new" novel of the twentieth century. It opens on a bewildering series of images faithful to the unconsciousness of childhood. Proust, who brought out the first volume of his great novel, *A la recherche du temps perdu*, in the same year that Lawrence published *Sons and Lovers*, imposed so highly stylized a unity of mood on the "Ouverture" to *Du côté de chez Swann*, that these impressions of childhood read as if they had been reconstructed to make a dream. But *Sons and Lovers* opens as a nineteenth-century novel with a matter-of-fact description of the setting—the mine, the land-scape of "Bestwood," the neighboring streets and houses. This opening could have been written by Arnold Bennett, or any other of the excellent "realists" of the period whose work does not summon up, fifty years later, the ecstasy of imagination that Lawrence's work, along with that of Joyce and Proust, does provide to us. Lawrence is writing close to the actual facts. In his old-fashioned way he is even writing *about* the actual facts. No wonder that a young novelist with nothing but *his* own experiences to start him off may feel that Lawrence's example represents the triumph of experience. Literature has no rites in *Sons and Lovers*; everything follows as if from memory alone. When the struggle begins that makes the novel—the universal modern story of a "refined" and discontented woman who pours out on her sons the love she refuses the husband too "common" for her—the equally universal young novelist to whom all this has happened, the novelist who in our times is likely to have been all too mothered and fatherless, cannot help saying to himself—"Why can't I write this good a novel out of myself? Haven't I suffered as much as D. H. Lawrence and am I not just as sensitive? And isn't this a highly selective age in which 'sensitive' writers count?"

But the most striking thing about Lawrence—as it is about Paul Morel in *Sons and Lovers*—is his sense of his own authority. Though he was certainly not saved from atrocious suffering in relation to his mother, Lawrence's "sensitivity" was in the main concerned with reaching the highest and widest possible consciousness of everything—"nature," family, society, books—that came within his experience as a human being. His sense of his own powers, of himself as a "medium" through which the real life in things could be discovered for other people, was so strong that his personal vividness stayed with his earliest friends as a reminder of the best hopes of their youth; it was instantly recognized by literary people in London when they read his work. You can easily dislike Lawrence for this air of authority, just as many people dislike him for the influence that he exerted during his lifetime and that has grown steadily since his death in 1930. There is already an unmistakeable priggish conceit about Paul Morel in this novel. Here is a miner's son who is asked by his mother if his is a "divine discontent" and replies in this style: "Yes, I don't care about its divinity. But damn your happiness! So long as life's full, it doesn't matter whether it's happy or not. I'm afraid your happiness would bore me." But even this contains Lawrence's sense of his own authority. He saw his talent as a sacred possession—he was almost too proud to think of his career as a *literary* one. This sense of having a power that makes for righteousness—this was so strong in Lawrence, and so intimately associated with his mother's influence, that the struggle he describes in *Sons and Lovers*, the struggle to love another woman as he had loved his mother, must be seen as the connection he made between his magic "demon," his gift, and his relationship to his mother.

Freud once wrote that he who is a favorite of the mother becomes a "conqueror." This was certainly Freud's own feeling about himself. The discoverer of the Oedipus complex never doubted that the attachment which, abnormally protracted, makes a son feel that loving any woman but his mother is a "desecration," nevertheless, in its early prime features, gives a particular kind of strength to the son. It is a spiritual strength, not the masculine "wildness" that Lawrence was to miss in contemporary life. Lawrence's own feeling that he was certainly somebody, the pride that was to sustain him despite horribly damaged lungs through so many years of tuberculosis until his death at forty-five; the pride that carried him so far from a miner's cottage; the pride that enabled him, a penniless schoolteacher, to run off with a German baronness married to his old teacher and to make her give up her three children; the pride that thirty years after his death still makes him so vivid to us as we read—this pride had not its origin but its *setting*, in the fierce love of Mrs. Arthur Lawrence for "Bert," of Mrs. Morel for her Paul.

Lawrence, who was so full of his own gift, so fully engaged in working it out that he would not acknowledge his gifted contemporaries, certainly did feel that the "essential soul" of him as he would have said, his special demon, his particular gift of vision, his particular claim on immortality, was bound up with his mother. Not "love" in the psychological sense of conscious consideration, but love in the mythological sense of a sacred connection, was what Lawrence associated with his mother and Paul with Mrs. Morel. Lawrence's power over others is directly traceable to his own sense of the sacredness still possible to life, arising from the powers hidden in ordinary human relationships. The influence he had—if only temporar-

ily—even on a rationalist like Bertrand Russell reminds one of the hold he kept on socialist working-class people he had grown up with and who certainly did not share Lawrence's exalted individualism. Lawrence's "authority," which made him seem unbearably full of himself to those who disliked him, was certainly of a very singular kind. He had an implicit confidence in his views on many questions—on politics as on sex and love; he was able to pontificate in later life about the Etruscans, of whom he knew nothing, as well as to talk dangerous nonsense about "knowing through the blood" and the leader principle. Yet it is Lawrence's struggle to retain all the moral authority that he identified with his mother's love that explains the intensity of *Sons and Lovers*, as it does the particular intensity of Lawrence's style in this book, which he later criticized as too violent. Yet behind this style lies Lawrence's lifelong belief in what he called "quickness," his need to see the "shimmer," the life force in everything, as opposed to the "dead crust" of its external form. Destiny for Lawrence meant his privileged and constant sense of the holiness implicit in this recognition of the life force. Destiny also meant his recognition, as a delicate boy who had already seen his older brother Ernest (the "William" of *Sons and Lovers*) sicken and die of the struggle to attach himself to another woman, that his survival was somehow bound up with fidelity to his mother. Lawrence had absolute faith in his gift, but it was bound up with his physical existence, which was always on trial. He felt that it was in his mother's hands. The gift of life, so particularly precious to him after his near-fatal pneumonia at seventeen (when his brother died), could be easily lost.

With so much at stake, Lawrence put into ultimate terms, life or death, the struggle between Paul Morel's need to hold onto his mother and his desire to love Miriam Leivers as well. The struggle in *Sons and Lovers* is not between love of the mother and love of a young woman; it is the hero's struggle to *keep* the mother as his special strength, never to lose her, not to offend or even to vex her by showing too much partiality to other women. This is why the original of "Miriam Leivers," Jessie Chambers, says in her touching memoir (*D. H. Lawrence: A Personal Record:* by "E. T.") that she had to break with Lawrence after she had seen the final draft of the book, that "the shock of *Sons and Lovers* gave the death-blow to our friendship," for in that book "Lawrence handed his mother the laurels of victory."

That is indeed what Lawrence did; it would not have occurred to him to do anything else. And Jessie Chambers also honestly felt that she minded this for Lawrence's sake, not her own, since by this time there was no longer any question of marriage between them. Jessie, who certainly loved Lawrence for his genius even after she had relinquished all personal claim on him, had launched Lawrence's career by sending out his poems. When Lawrence, after his mother's death, wrote a first draft of *Sons and Lovers*, he was still unable to work out his situation in a novel. Jessie encouraged him to drop this unsatisfactory version of the later novel and to portray the emotional struggle directly. At his request, she even wrote out narrative sections which Lawrence revised and incorporated into his novel. (Lawrence often had women write out passages for his novels when he wanted to know how a woman would react to a particular situation; Frieda Lawrence was to contribute to his characterization of Mrs. Morel.) Lawrence sent Jessie parts of the manuscript for her comments and further notes. After so much help and even collaboration, Jessie felt betrayed by the book. Lawrence had failed to show, she said, how important a role the girl had played in the development of the young man as an artist. "It was his old inability to face his problem squarely. His mother had to be supreme, and for the sake of that supremacy every disloyalty was permissible."

Lawrence is quoted in Harry T. Moore's biography, *The Intelligent Heart*, as saying of Miriam-Jessie, she "encouraged my demon. But alas, it was me, not he, whom she loved. so for her too it was a catastrophe. My demon is not easily loved: whereas the ordinary me is. So poor Miriam was let down." Lawrence's tone is exalted, but he certainly justified himself in *Sons and Lovers* as a novelist, not as a "son." That is the only consideration now. Jessie Chambers herself became an embittered woman. She tried to find her salvation in politics, where the fierce hopes of her generation before 1914 for a new England were certainly not fulfilled. But Lawrence, taking the new draft of *Sons and Lovers* with him to finish in Germany after he had run off with Frieda, was able, if not to "liberate" himself from his mother in his novel, to write a great novel out of his earliest life and struggles.

That is the triumph Jessie Chambers would not acknowledge in *Sons and Lovers*, this she could not see—the Lawrence "unable to face his problem squarely" made a great novel out of the "problem," out of his mother, father, brother, the miners, the village, the youthful sweetheart. Whatever Jessie may have thought from being too close to Lawrence himself, whatever Lawrence may have said about his personal struggles during the six-week frenzy in which he launched the new draft, Lawrence felt his "problem" not as something to be solved, but as a subject to be represented. All these early experiences weighed on him with a pressure that he was able to communicate—later he called it "that hard violent style full of sensation and presentation." Jessie Chambers herself described Lawrence's accomplishment when she said, speaking of the new draft of *Sons and Lovers* that she drove Lawrence to write, "It was his power to transmute the common experiences into significance that I always felt to be Lawrence's greatest gift. He did not distinguish between small and great happenings. The common round was full of mystery, awaiting interpretation. Born and bred of working people, he had the rare gift of seeing them from within, and revealing them on their own plane."

Lawrence's particular gift was this ability to represent as valuable anything that came his way. He had the essential religious attribute of *valuing* life, of seeing the most trivial things as a kind of consecration. In part, at least, one can trace this to the poverty, austerity and simplicity of his upbringing. Jessie Chambers once watched Lawrence and his father gathering watercress for tea. "Words cannot convey Lawrence's brimming delight in all these simple things." Delight in simple things is one of the recurring features of the working-class existence described in *Sons and Lovers*. We can understand better the special value that Lawrence identified with his mother's laboriousness and self-denial in the scene where Mrs. Morel, wickedly extravagant, comes home clutching the pot that cost her fivepence and the bunch of pansies and daisies that cost her fourpence. The rapture of the commonest enjoyments and simplest possessions is represented in the mother and father as well as in the young artist Paul, the future D. H. Lawrence. This autobiographical novel rooted in the writer's early struggles is charged with feeling for his class, his region, his people. Lawrence was not a workingman himself, despite the brief experience in the surgical appliances factory that in the novel becomes Paul Morel's continued job. Chekhov said that the working-class writer purchases with his youth that which a more genteel writer is born with. But Lawrence gained everything, as a writer, from being brought up in the working class, and lost nothing by it. In *Sons and Lovers* he portrays the miners without idealizing them, as a socialist would; he relishes their human qualities (perhaps even a little jealously) and works them up as a subject for his art. He does not identify himself with them; his mother, too, we can be sure from the portrait of Mrs. Morel, tended to be somewhat aloof among the miners' wives. But Lawrence knows *as a writer* that he is related to working people, that he is bound up with them in the same order of physical and intimate existence, that it is workers' lives he has always looked on. Some of the most affecting passages in this novel are based on the force and directness of working-class speech. "'E's niver gone, child?" Morel says to his son when William dies. Paul answers in "educated" and even prissy English, but the voice of the miners, the fields and the kitchens is rendered straight and unashamed. Lawrence, who knew how much he had lost as a man by siding with his mother in the conflict, describes the miner Morel getting his own breakfast, sitting "down to an hour of joy," with an irresistible appreciation of the physical and human picture involved: "He toasted his bacon on a fork and caught the drops of fat on his bread; then he put the rasher on his thick slice of bread, and cut off chunks with a clasp-knife, poured his tea into his saucer, and was happy."

The writer alone in Lawrence redeemed the weakness of being too much his mother's son. We see the common round of life among the miners' families very much as the young Lawrence must have seen it, with the same peculiar directness. His mental world was startlingly without superfluities and wasted motions. What he wrote, he wrote. The striking sense of authority, of inner conviction, that he associated with his mother's love gave him a cutting briskness with things he disapproved. But this same immediacy of response, when it touched what he loved, could reach the greatest emotional depths. The description of William Morel's coffin being carried into the house is a particular example of this. "The coffin swayed, the men began to mount the three steps with their load. Annie's candle flickered, and she whimpered as the first men appeared, and the limbs and bowed heads of six men struggled to climb into the room, bearing the coffin that rode like sorrow on their living flesh." Lawrence's power to move the reader lies in this ability to summon up all the physical attributes associated with an object; he puts you into direct contact with all its properties *as* an object. Rarely has the realistic novelist's need to *present*, to present vividly, continually, and at the highest pitch of pictorial concentration—the gift which has made the novel the supreme literary form of modern times—rarely has this reached such intense clarity of representation as it does in *Sons and Lovers*. There are passages, as in Tolstoy, that make you realize what a loss to directness of vision our increasing self-consciousness in literature represents. Lawrence is still face to face with life, and he can describe the smallest things with the most attentive love and respect.

Lawrence does not describe, he would not attempt to describe, the object as in *itself* it really is. The effect of his prose is always to heighten our consciousness of something, to relate it to ourselves. He is a romantic—and in this book is concerned with the most romantic possible subject for a novelist, the growth of the writer's own consciousness. Yet he succeeded as a novelist, he succeeded brilliantly, because he was convinced that the novel is the great literary form, for no other could reproduce so much of the actual motion or "shimmer" of life, especially as expressed in the relationships between people. Since for Lawrence the great subject of literature was not the writer's own consciousness but consciousness between people, the living felt relationship between them, it was his very concern to represent the "shimmer" of life, the "wholeness"—

these could have been mere romantic slogans—that made possible his brilliance as a novelist. He was to say, in a remarkable essay called "Why The Novel Matters," that "Only in the novel are *all* things given full play, or at least, they may be given full play, when we realize that life itself, and not inert safety, is the reason for living. For out of the full play of all things emerges the only thing that is anything, the wholeness of a man, the wholeness of a woman, man alive, and live woman." It was *relationship* that was sacred to him, as it was the relationships *with* his mother, her continuing presence in his mind and life, that gave him the sense of authority on which all his power rested. And as a novelist in *Sons and Lovers* he was able to rise above every conventional pitfall in an autobiographical novel by centering his whole vision on character as the focus of a relationship, not as an absolute.

After *Sons and Lovers*, which was his attempt to close up the past, Lawrence was to move on to novels like *The Rainbow* (1915) and *Women in Love* (1920), where the "non-human in humanity" was to be more important to him than "the old-fashioned human element." The First World War was to make impossible for Lawrence his belief in the old "stable ego" of character. Relationships, as the continuing interest of life, became in these more "problematical," less "conventional" novels, a version of man's general relationship, as an unknown in himself, to his unexplained universe. But the emphasis on growth and change in *Sons and Lovers*, the great book that closes Lawrence's first period, is from the known to the unknown; as Frank O'Connor has said, the book begins as a nineteenth century novel and turns into a twentieth century one. Where autobiographical novels with a "sensitive" artist or novelist as hero tend to emphasize the hero's growth to self-knowledge, the history of his "development," the striking thing about *Sons and Lovers*, and an instance of the creative mind behind it, is that it does not hand the "laurels of victory" to the hero. It does not allow him any self-sufficient victory over his circumstances. With the greatest possible vividness it shows Paul Morel engulfed in relationships—with the mother he loves all too sufficiently, with the "spiritual" Miriam and Clara, neither of whom he can love whole-heartedly— relationships that are difficult and painful, and that Lawrence leaves arrested in their pain and conflict. When Jessie Chambers said of the first draft of *Sons and Lovers* that "Lawrence had carried the situation to the point of deadlock and had stopped there," she may have been right enough about it as an aborted novel. But Lawrence's primary interest and concern as a novelist, his sense of the continuing *flow* of relationship between people, no matter how unclear and painful, no matter how far away it was from the "solution" that the people themselves may have longed for, is what makes this whole last section of the novel so telling.

But of course it is the opening half of *Sons and Lovers* that makes the book great. The struggle between husband and wife is described with a direct, unflinching power. Lawrence does not try to bring anything to a psychological conclusion. The marriage is a struggle, a continuing friction, a relationship where the wife's old desire for her husband can still flash up through her resentment of his "lowness." That is why everything in the "common round" can be described with such tenderness, for the relationship of husband and wife sweeps into its unconscious passion everything that the young Lawrence loved, and was attached to. Living in a mining village on the edge of old Sherwood Forest, always close to the country, Lawrence was as intimate with nature as any country poet could have been, but he was lucky to see rural England and the industrial Midlands in relation to each other; the country

soothed his senses, but a job all day long in a Nottingham factory making out orders for surgical appliances did not encourage nature worship. "On the fallow land the young wheat shone silkily. Minton pit waved its plumes of white steam, coughed, and rattled hoarsely." Lawrence is a great novelist of landscape, for he is concerned with the relationships of people living on farms, or walking out into the country after the week's work in the city. He does not romanticize nature, he describes it in its minute vibrations. In *Sons and Lovers* the emotional effect of the "lyrical" passages depends on Lawrence's extraordinary ability to convey movement and meaning even in non-human things. But in this book nature never provides evasion of human conflict and is not even a projection of human feelings; it is the physical world that Lawrence grew up in, and includes the pit down which a miner must go every day. Paul in convalescence, sitting up in bed, would "see the fluffy horses feeding at the troughs in the field, scattering their hay on the trodden yellow snow; watch the miners troop home—small, black figures trailing slowly in gangs across the white field."

This miniature, exquisite as a Japanese watercolor, is typical of *Sons and Lovers*—the country lives and seethes, but it has no mystical value. It is the landscape of Nottinghamshire and Derbyshire, and in the book it is still what it was to Lawrence growing up in it, an oasis of refreshment in an industrial world. The countryside arouses young lovers to their buried feelings and it supplies images for the "quickness," the vital current of relationship, that Lawrence valued most in life. It is never sacred in itself. When you consider that this novel came out in 1913, at the height of the "Georgian" period, when so many young poets of Lawrence's generation were mooning over nature, it is striking that *his* chief interest is always the irreducible ambiguity of human relationships. Lawrence's language, in certain key scenes, certainly recalls the emotional inflation of fiction in the "romantic" heyday preceding the First World War. But the style is actually exalted rather than literary. There is an unmistakably scriptural quality to Lawrence's communication of extreme human feeling. Mr. Morel secretly cut young William's hair, and Mrs. Morel feels that "this act of masculine clumsiness was the spear through the side of her love." The Lawrences were Congregationalist, like American Puritans. They were close to the Lord. The strong sense of himself that Lawrence was always to have, the conviction that what he felt was always terribly important just in the way he felt it, is imparted to Mrs. Morel herself in the great scene in which the insulted husband, dizzy with drink, locks her out of the house. The description of Mrs. Morel's feelings is charged with a kind of frenzy of concern for her; the language sweeps from pole to pole of feeling. Mrs. Morel is pregnant, and her sense of her moral aloneness at this moment is overwhelming. "Mrs. Morel, seared with passion, shivered to find herself out there in a great white light, that fell cold on her, and gave the shock to her inflamed soul." Later we read that "After a time the child, too, melted with her in the mixing-pot of moonlight, and she rested with the hills and lilies and houses, all swum together in a kind of swoon."

In this key scene of the mother's "trouble" (which must have been based on things that Lawrence later heard from his mother), the sense we get of Mrs. Morel, humiliated and enraged but in her innermost being haughtily inviolate, gives us a sense of all the power that Lawrence connected with his mother and of the power in the relationship that flowed between them. In *Sons and Lovers* he was able to re-create, for all time, the moment when the sympathetic bond between them reached its greatest intensity—and the moment when her death broke it. Ever after, Lawrence was to try to re-create this living bond, this magic sympathy, between himself and life. He often succeeded in creating an exciting and fruitful version of it—in relationship to his extraordinary wife Frieda; to a host of friends, disciples, admirers and readers throughout the world; even to his own novels and stories, essays and articles and poems and letters. Unlike Henry James, James Joyce, Marcel Proust, T. S. Eliot, Lawrence always makes you feel that not art but the quality of the lived experience is his greatest concern. That is why it is impossible to pick up anything by him without feeling revivified. Never were a writer's works more truly an allegory of his life, and no other writer of his imaginative standing has in our time written books that are so open to life. Yet one always feels in Lawrence his own vexation and disappointment at not being able to reproduce, in the full consciousness of his genius, the mutual sympathy he had experienced with his mother. One even feels about Lawrence's increasing vexation and disappointment that it tore him apart physically, exhausted and shattered him. Wandering feverishly from continent to continent, increasingly irritable and vulnerable to every human defect and cultural complacency, he seems finally to have died for lack of another place to aim at; for lack, even, of another great fight to wage. His work itself was curiously never enough for him, for he could write so quickly, sitting anywhere under a tree, that the book seemed to fly out of his hand as soon as he had made it; and he was so much the only poet in his imaginative universe that he could not take other writers seriously enough to rejoice in his own greatness. He was searching, one feels, for something infinitely more intangible than fame, or a single person, or a "God"—he was searching for the remembered ecstasy of experience, the quality of feeling, that is even more evanescent than the people we connect with it. Lawrence kept looking for this even after he had reproduced it in *Sons and Lovers*, whose triumph as art was to give him so little lasting satisfaction. Art could not fulfill Lawrence's search, and only death could end it. But the ecstasy of a single human relationship that he tried to reproduce never congealed into a single image or idol or belief. Imaginatively, Lawrence was free; which is why his work could literally rise like a phoenix out of the man who consumed himself in his conflict with himself.

ADRIENNE RICH
From "Reflections on Lawrence"
Poetry, June 1965, pp. 219–25

Let it be said clearly: Lawrence is a major poet, and ⟨*The Complete Poems of D. H. Lawrence*⟩ fully reveals the quantity as well as the quality of his best poems. And the organic shape and movement of these poems has nothing mindless and happenstance about it: he knows what he is doing with line-length, with diction, with pause, repetition, termination.

Love, hate, the self. How repeatedly, in Lawrence, the longing for escape appears, escape of the kind Eliot meant when he said, "But of course, only those who have personality and emotions know what it is to want to escape from those things." Remarkable men, who see the nature of experience in almost mutually exclusive ways, have also their moments of consanguinity. Lawrence is forever searching for an inward zone of apartness. To be as private as an animal!

> You would think twice before you touched a weasel
>   on a fence
> as it lifts its straight white throat.

> Your hand would not be so flig and easy.
> Nor the adder we saw asleep with her head on her
>   shoulder,
> curled up in the sunshine like a princess;
> when she lifted her head in delicate, startled wonder
> you did not stretch forward to caress her . . .
>   ("'She Said as Well to Me'")

To exist in one's uniqueness, and still in profound relation to another—

> one clear, burnished, isolated being, unique,
> and she also, pure, isolated, complete,
> two of us, unutterably distinguished, and in unutter-
>   able conjunction.
>   ("Manifesto")

Love, the word itself, being today an emotional pantry even more than when Lawrence wrote, it's easy to read hate as the final destination of Lawrence's journey beyond love; to diagnose his "problem" even more crudely as fear of women, as embryonic Fascism, as egomania. But Lawrence knew the shallowness of pure ego-satisfaction for what it was: see for example the ironic little portraits in "True Love at Last" or "Ultimate Reality" or "Intimates" (all in *More Pansies*). And he knew the frenetic sterility of the soul that, like the little black dog in New Mexico, is "Such a waggle of love you can hardly distinguish one human from another." The naked irritability, and revulsion, that Lawrence felt in the face of many human contacts was the price he paid, and that we pay in suffering much of it through his poems, for his enormous sense of the possibilities inherent in human contacts and human separateness. At times it is paid brilliantly, in poems like "Frost Flowers"; elsewhere it simply devours the poem. Yet everywhere is evidence that he found man sacred in design even if degraded in execution. And nature, which he never sentimentalized, was always sacred to him. He was able to fuse them— the natural world and the possible nature of man—in poems which purify as they redefine love and sex in both their spasmodic and timeless modes:

> Go deeper than love, for the soul has greater depths;
> love is like the grass, but the soul is deep wild rock
> molten, yet dense and permanent.
> Go down to your deep old heart, woman, and lose
>   sight of yourself,
> And lose sight of me, the me whom you turbulently
>   loved.
> Let us lose sight of ourselves, and break the mirrors.
> But say, in the dark wild metal of your heart
> is there a gem, which came into being between us?
> is there a sapphire of mutual trust, a blue spark?
> Is there a ruby of fused being, mine and yours, an
>   inward glint?
>   ("Know Deeply, Know Thyself More Deeply")

And one style Lawrence never had, as poet or in life. His pride, his intolerance, stand invincibly opposed to the posture of the loving fool, the ironic self-depreciation of God's poor slob. There is something cleanly arrogant in Lawrence's bitterness, the astringency of a drop of pure alcohol. His vituperation is nearly always aimed at some form of self-indulgence, of narcissism, of emotional neurasthenia. He would have been ill at home in a society where people not only eat the ones they love but do so out of simplistic moral motives.

Pansies; More Pansies. The ones that get most often quoted and anthologized are the anti-bourgeois squibs, the outbursts against mass society, the machine, censorship. Lawrence himself fosters, in his prefaces, the notion that we have to do here with "a little bunch of fragments"; "casual thoughts". And in fact, while some of these crackle and sting with nervous wit, others are deliberate doggerel, Lawrence rhyming and fuming aloud. But a large number are poems, part of Lawrence's central achievement: e.g., the short series on "Touch," the poem "Know Deeply" quoted in part above, and the one just preceding it, "Fidelity." And some of the religious poetry:

> Who is it that softly touches the sides of my breast
> and touches me over the heart
> so that my heart beats soothed, soothed, soothed and
>   at peace?
> Who is it smooths the bed-sheets like the cool
> smooth ocean where the fishes rest on edge
> in their own dream?
> Who is it that clasps and kneads my naked feet, till
>   they unfold,
> till all is well, till all is utterly well? the lotus-lilies of
>   the feet!
> I tell you, it is no woman, it is no man, for I am
>   alone.

("There Are No Gods")

How many little anthologies could be put together out of the two *Pansies* volumes alone! anthologies compiled to prove almost anything for or against Lawrence. And of course, they would all be misleading. Because the total impression in the *Collected Poems* is the refusal to belong, to become anyone's pet D.H.L. or straw man. After all the memoirs, the letters, the photographs on sunny terraces, the *romans à clef* by other hands, the toilsome efforts to come to terms with him posthumously by those who knew him, the fact remains that we have long had an imperfect notion of Lawrence and a poorly balanced vision of his ideas. The use of the phrase "Lawrentian" to indicate a kind of primitivism; the odd assumption that Lawrence was attracted to political power or could have stomached any process of mob-manipulation; the belief that sexual union was for him a cure-all or an exclusive source of truth—these and other equally blurred gropings for a formula are gainsaid in the experience of the poetry in full.

> Oh leave off saying I want you to be savages.
> Tell me, is the gentian savage, at the top of its course
>   stem?
> Oh what in you can answer to this blueness?

Look! We Have Come Through! This sequence has more diversity of tone, intention, accent than any unified sequence of love poems since Shakespeare. In a literal sense the man and woman of *Look! . . .* are a microcosm, a world in which nearly everything happens. It is Lawrence's functional honesty that produces this variety, his rejection of the blandishments of false consistency, of turning a good face to the world. Compare "She Looks Back," a poem bitter at the division in the woman's soul, her longing for her children, with "Meeting among the Mountains," in which the face of a bullock-cart driver encountered "among the averted flowers" near a wayside crucifix seems to recall the woman's suffering husband. Neither poem is a vindication, nowhere in this series do we smell the odor of self-pity, or the lust to charm or wheedle. And, blisteringly close as these poems are to actual events, conversations, sufferings, you can feel the quality of the mind that could render its and another's anguish so precisely even while it was gradually inventing the texture and dimensions of the later great poetry concerned with love: "'She Said as Well to Me,'" "Manifesto," "Know Deeply," "Deeper Than Love," etc. If the poems are rooted in personal history they are also rooted in the development of a mind, for this hero of the instinctual was one of the most intelligent men of any time,

who knew that "The profoundest of all sensualities / is the sense of truth"; and that "All vital truth contains the memory of that for which it is not true."

Language. More than any other poet-novelist's, Lawrence's fiction and his poems breathe in the same language. It appears at first startlingly simple, direct, almost *naif* at moments, with its abrupt entrances and exits, its declarative sentences, its repetitions, with infinitesimal variations, of a word or a phrase. The directness and repetition are related to the English of the King James Version, more than to Imagist or Georgian poetry, as the editor of this edition rightly notes. But Lawrence's use of repetition is more than incantation. It has to do with his passionate grasp upon the physical world, as total as any in our language. With delicate, deliberate touch he palpates the physical shell or skin of reality until it seems to relax and fall open:

> Fig-trees, weird fig-trees
> Made of thick smooth silver,
> Made of sweet, untarnished silver in the sea-southern
>   air—
> I say untarnished, but I mean opaque—
> Thick, smooth-fleshed silver, dull only as human
>   limbs are dull
> With the life-lustre,
> Nude with the dim light of full, healthy life
> That is always half-dark,
> And suave like passion-flower petals,
> Like passion-flowers,
> With the half-secret gleam of a passion-flower hang-
>   ing from the rock,
> Great, complicated, nude fig-tree, stemless flower-
>   mesh,
> Flowerily naked in flesh, and giving off hues of life.

He was able to redeem the old words of richness, plenitude, light, and darkness in their primalness, through his insistence on keeping close to the power of the object, seeing it from every side (those suave, lustrous fig-trees become concretely absurd and admirable as the poem moves on, ending as the "equality-puzzle", the ego-mystery ironically perceived). To do this for language it is not enough to be "intoxicated with words"; one has to be intoxicated with things in their natures, their detail, their physical essences. And Lawrence was. If in "Bavarian Gentians" the words "dark", "blue", and "darkness" become key-notes to an hypnotic chant of passage, it is first of all because the living flower in its precise, physical truth hypnotizes Lawrence:

> ribbed and torch-like, with their blaze of darkness
>   spread blue
> down flattening into points, flattened under the
>   sweep of white day,
> torch-flower of the blue-smoking darkness, Pluto's
>   dark-blue daze

And as with language, so with the world: it was in a very real sense sacramentally that Lawrence saw what he saw. The poems that fail seem to be the ones where he failed to attach his vision to anything which could be thus seen; where all that is observable is his disgust and disappointment at loss of possibility, loss of potency. The language becomes thin, vituperative, loose as a torn sail flapping in a squall; the language of a man whose nerves are worn out.

> O cease to listen to the living dead.
> They are only greedy for your life!
> O cease to labour for the gold-toothed dead.
> they are so greedy, yet so helpless if not worked for.
> . . . .
> Don't ever be kind to the dead
> it is pandering to corpses,
> the repulsive, living fat dead.

In studying the complete work of a major poet, there is always a group of poems to which we revert over and over, not only for their individual force and beauty, but because through them we come to trust the entire *oeuvre*, to give a hearing to other poems less immediately attractive or accessible to us. It is as if we watched a man in certain situations and said: "There, the man who could do this, or that, is one to whom I can give credence in whatever he does; such a man has value for me even where I do not understand him or feel sympathy for his ideas." For me, a list of such poems by Lawrence would include, of the earlier poems, "End of Another Home Holiday," "The Collier's Wife," "Bei Hennef," "In the Dark," "Mutilation," "Sinners," "'She Said as Well to Me,'" "Frost Flowers"; most of *Birds, Beasts and Flowers*, but especially "Bare Almond-Trees," "Bare Fig-Trees," "Sicilian Cyclamens," "The Mosquito," "Man and Bat," "Peach," "Snake," "Baby Tortoise." It would also include "Man of Tyre," "There Are No Gods," "Know Deeply, Know Thyself More Deeply," "Swan," "Elemental," and the two late poems, "Bavarian Gentians" and "The Ship of Death." The last two poems alone, it seems to me, must persuade anyone that this poet's entire work bears listening to, that the full dimensions are worth having.

ANTHONY BURGESS
"Introduction"
D.H. Lawrence and Italy by D. H. Lawrence
1972, pp. vii–xiii

This trinity of travel books may be offered very reasonably as a unity. The unifying element is, however, less place than temperament. It is of less importance that we should be able to pencil an ellipse around Italy and her dependencies and neighbors, saying "D. H. Lawrence was here," than that we should take pleasure in the response of a highly idiosyncratic temperament to the impact of new places—any new places. This book should not be packed by intending tourists to the Mediterranean as a convenient guide to Italy, Sicily, and Sardinia—with a bit of Bavaria, the Tyrol, and Switzerland for good measure; as Lawrence says, "I am not Baedeker." But it is an indispensable guide to the sensibility of one of the most astonishing writers of our century. It is for visitors to Lawrence, a pretty large country, not for rubberneckers in mere southern Europe.

Moreover, the world which Lawrence describes has long disappeared—except, of course, for the unchanging human groundbass which is his main, perhaps only, concern. *Twilight in Italy* (an inept title, as Lawrence's biographer Richard Aldington says, for so sunlit a book) was first published in 1916, and it records aspects of the *vita nuova* that Lawrence was experiencing in 1912 and 1913. It was a happy, even ecstatic, time, though a penniless one. Lawrence, as a student in Nottingham, had fallen in love with the wife of Professor Weekley (author of *Adjectives and Other Words*) and persuaded her to elope with him. She was the aristocratic Frieda von Richthofen, cousin of the flying ace who was to be known as the Red Baron; he was a working-class intellectual with little more than an original mind and an appetite for life. He was, at the time of the experiences recounted in *Twilight in Italy*, responding with almost Adamic wonder to the new life and the new world of southern Europe. But his book is no river of uncritical lyricism. That sharp honesty which was to earn him hatred and suppression was early at work. He was in love with a German lady, but the *Westminster Gazette* rejected some of his

travel sketches as "too anti-German". And that very Lawrentian approach to the Tyrolean Christ-icons must have shocked plenty of the conventionally pious in 1913, when the *Gazette* published one of the versions of what is called here "The Crucifix across the Mountains."

The seven studies of life around Lake Garda, where Lawrence and Frieda lived from 1912 till the spring of 1913, may be regarded as devices for affirming the here-and-now while Lawrence, in the major work then proceeding, was being drawn back to his own past. For he was completing *Sons and Lovers* (of which Frieda started to write a parody called "Paul Morel, or Mother's Boy") as well as drafting *The Rainbow* and *The Lost Girl*. This was a period of immense creative activity for Lawrence, and that liveness of the sensorium and the imagination, given primarily to fiction, is manifested also in these essays, with their relish and humor and immense capacity for *rapport* with the mountains and the lakeside and the people.

Sea and Sardinia first appeared in 1921, when Lawrence and Frieda had been through the nightmare recorded so vividly in *Kangaroo*. Lawrence was now rejecting finally all ties with an England that had treated him with, it seemed, exemplary brutality. *The Rainbow* had been prosecuted for immorality in 1915; he had been humiliated and bullied by military authorities well aware that the state of his lungs rendered him unfit for the Army; he and Frieda had been expelled from Cornwall in 1917 on a suspicion of espionage. If England had no love either of him or of his writings, it was curiously reluctant to let him go into the exile he now passionately sought, and it was not until November 1919 that he was permitted to have a passport. From then on his estrangement was permanent. He made a few trips back to see family or friends, but his readership became mainly an American one—it was already, in the early days of the peace, drawing him out of a long penury—and his home was wherever his restlessness led him.

His brief winter trip to Sardinia (February 4–10, 1921) was born of such restlessness. Living in Taormina, on the eastern shore of Sicily, sick of a January in which "it thunders and lightnings for twenty-four hours and hailstorms continually," he could not really have expected to escape from winter weather in Sardinia. It is conceivable that he was sick of the other English-speaking exiles in Taormina, sick indeed of the whole of self-pitying postwar Europe (soon he was to go to Mexico by way of Ceylon and Australia), conducting the first of his searches for some unspoilt pocket of strangeness. Whatever the motive, the sea trip to Sardinia produced a small miracle of a book. A single week's visit was enough for him to extract the very essence of the island and its people, and six weeks were enough to set it all down in words—without a single note as an *aide-mémoire*. This feat anticipates a greater one, which still makes Australian writers gloomy—the re-creation of a whole continent, along with a wholly accurate prophecy of its political future, out of a few weeks' stay in a suburb of Sydney.

Etruscan Places is the last of all his travel books, which may be taken to include not only these Italian ones but also the novels *Kangaroo* and *The Plumed Serpent* (formal categories don't matter much in Lawrence), as well as *Mornings in Mexico*. As early as 1920 Lawrence had become fascinated by the Etruscans, but it was not until his return from Mexico in 1927 that he went, with his American friend Earl Brewster, to the sites of their lost and intriguing civilization—Cerveteri, Tarquinia, Grosseto, Volterra. He planned a bigger Etruscan book than the one we have, but he recognized that he could not compete—on the level of observation and scholarship—

with the authorities in whose work he had already read deeply—D. Randall-MacIver's *Villanovans and Early Etrus- cans*, Pericles Ducati's *Etruria Antica*, and the classic survey by the Englishman, and hence potential competitor, George Dennis. Lawrence always lacked the discipline and objectivity of approach which mark the true scholar. His book on European history, for instance, is more Lawrentian interpreta- tion than solid fact. Nevertheless, his highly idiosyncratic approach to the Etruscans has probably been more influen- tial—among nonspecialists, of course—than the works of the true scholars. There is special poignancy about *Etruscan Places*, the poignancy of our knowledge that a dying man is drinking from the founts of a civilization dedicated to life. He was a year or two off death when he wandered among the tombs of the Etruscans. The book itself was published posthumously, in 1932.

The Etruscan tombs have not changed, nor have the baroque churches and the legionaries' roads, but the Italy Lawrence knew is different in so many respects from the Italy of today that, entering his books, we enter a remote world which, to use a paradox, touches modernity only through its perennial antiquities. Travel was slow and painful, Mussolini had not yet taught the trains to run on time, there were no *autostrade* or Agip motels. The inn food was usually filthy—stewed-out- meat fibres, the skimmed meat fat used to warm over tired spinach—and the beds were dirty and verminous. Lawrence's journeys by post-bus or cold late train or on foot are in the great laborious tradition which produced genuine travel books—the eye slowly taking it all in, the aching feet imposing the leisure to observe the common people in the smoky inn kitchen. At the end of *Twilight in Italy* Lawrence is already sounding the note which was to become shrill in *Lady Chatterley's Lover*: under the vivid street faces of Milan he saw "the same purpose stinking in it all, the mechanizing, the perfect mechanizing of human life." Although he shows a certain minimal apprecia- tion of a good Italian automobile and a good Italian road, he would not, I think, have taken kindly to the delights of modern Italian travel, the despair at not being able to park in Spoleto, the abstract motor roads, and he would have raged at the industrial smog over Ravenna. He would see all this as the ultimate victory of Rome, that depersonalizing force which destroyed the Etruscans and threw up monsters like Mussolini.

For—in *Etruscan Places* most, but in the other books too at one level or another—Lawrence brings to the pageant of Mediterranean life an eye not wholly innocent. He has what he calls a philosophy, meaning a highly emotional conviction about the location of human values, and he tends to impose this—most often lightly, but occasionally with tub-thumping and boring earnestness—on what he observes. Instinct is more important than reason; the loins, not the brain, are the center of life; a mechanized civilization is evil. He went to the Etruscans longing to find that perfect "natural" people he had sought also in Mexico; he was, as he says, "instinctively attracted to them," and the Lawrentian instinct justifies everything, even the building of a big ramshackle philosophy. He can be bitterly sarcastic about what we may term anti- Etruscanism (meaning anti-life or anti-Quetzalcoatl or anti- Lawrence), either in a scientific historian like Mommsen ("Their existence was antipathetic to him. The Prussian in him was enthralled by the Prussian in the all-conquering Romans") or in the people who were ruled by "Messalina and Heliogabalus and such-like snowdrops" and, because the Etruscans were "vicious" (or life-loving), ruthlessly exter- minated their civilization. In the Etruscan remains he finds not just joy of life but the very Lawrentian metaphysic of

"phallism." As for anti-joy, anti-phallism, he was finding it as early as 1912 in those Tyrolean crucifixes: "This is the worship, then, the worship of death and the approaches to death, physical violence, and pain. There is something crude and sinister about it, almost like depravity, a form of reverting, turning back along the course of blood by which we have come." Everywhere he goes he finds symbols for his Manichaeism; even Sardinia and Italy are turned into facile emblems of the good and bad aspects of the human spirit. Lawrence was more a symbol-seeker than a thinker (indeed, he disapproved of thinking, except with the loins or instincts). He was, of course, that best kind of philosopher, a poet.

To say that these three books are "poetical" is not the best tribute to them, if by the term we mean the carefully, self- consciously finely wrought Paterian, or the turgid purple Ruskinian. But Lawrence's poetry is different from any other man's: it is not the result of the creative process, it is the creative process itself. We are always in the smithy, watching the verbal hammering. In his impatience to find the right phrase for his referent, Lawrence cannot be bothered to hide his false starts; nor can he trouble himself with well-balanced "literary" sentences. When he finds the *mot juste* he does not let it go; he invites us to walk round it and examine its justness. There is a sense of reading a private notebook; there is also a sense of hearing actual speech, complete with fractured syntax, repetition, slang, facetiousness, buttonholing, even bullying. This is especially true of *Sea and Sardinia*, perhaps the most charming of all the books Lawrence ever wrote, and certainly the one which gives the most charming—and quite unselfcon- sciously charming—portrait of Lawrence himself.

That Lawrence is an Englishman is always evident, but it is never evident that he is an Englishman who has abandoned, and been abandoned by, his country. There is something touching about the pawky patriotism with which, when Italians attack it, he defends England (only America and England have done well out of the war, say the Italians; here are Englishmen in Italy taking advantage of the *cambio* and exploiting us nice, good people, etc., etc.). More interesting and significant is the *kind* of Englishman Lawrence was—essentially an Educated working-man, the product of a "phatically" loquacious Mid- land mining community, not a cold, taciturn Southerner educated in an expensive, though austere, centre of learning, condescending, assured of certain certainties, including the British superiority to foreigners. Men like that, and especially women like that, are most apt to coo over Italian peasants and artisans; their condescension makes them *simpatici*. Lawrence never worries about being *simpatico* (was Dante *simpatico?*). He knows his own class, and he is not bemused by the Italian representatives of it. He is Bert Lawrence, the miner's son, packing bacon sandwiches ("good English bacon from Malta") and a thermosful of tea for the start of the Sardinian journey. If the little Sicilian bank clerks stare at the rucksack on his shoulder, then the hell with them. And yet no English traveller in Italy ever understood the bank clerks and the carpenters and the roadmenders better.

It is the anonymous people in these Italian books who have become immortal for us. Even the most horrible of them, like the innkeeper whose dirty waistcoat is an insult or the German Etruscan expert who sees nothing in the Etruscans, inhabit the back quarters of our memories and become confused with people we have met in actuality, not in books. The sharpness of Lawrence's eye is incredible, and his judgements are madly sane. The Sicilians are "so terribly physically all over one another. They pour themselves over the other like so much melted butter over parsnips. They catch each other under the chin, with a tender caress of the hand, and they smile with sunny melting tenderness into each other's faces." So they do, but who but Lawrence would have thought in terms of buttered parsnips? And who but he would have tried to explain the gross tenderness in terms of living under a volcano? "Naples and Catania alike, the men are hugely fat, with great macaroni paunches, they are expansive and in a perfect drip of casual affection and love. . . . They never leave off being amorously friendly with almost everybody, emitting a relentless physical familiarity that is quite bewildering to one not brought up near a volcano." This is the kind of atrocious false logic Lawrence loved to indulge in, but the falseness is always more persuasive than other men's cautious rationality.

Finally, there is what Lawrence renders so marvellously and so mysteriously—the spirit of place. This spirit, he says, "is a strange thing. Our mechanical age tries to override it. But it does not succeed. In the end the strange, sinister spirit of the place, so diverse and adverse in differing places, will smash our mechanical oneness into smithereens, and all that we think the real thing will go off with a pop, and we shall be left staring." What Lawrence means—and means when he talks of love and phallism and loins and instinct—is certain gods, unconquerable *numina*, which we oppose at our peril. It is the sense of these gods that permeates his writing and makes this little trilogy of travel books—so ordinary on the surface, so much the sort of thing an author will turn out for a living—rather awesome to read, as well as (which we may take for granted) brilliantly informative, educative, entertaining, and moving.

FRANK KERMODE
From "1913–1917"
D. H. Lawrence
1973, pp. 42–49

The Rainbow enacts the ages of Love and Law, and ends at the Pause before the next age (Lawrence probably drafted the blurb, which speaks of Ursula, at the end, "waiting at the advance post of our time to blaze a path into the future").[1] The first section of the book was almost certainly added to *Rainbow i*, and it is there to give flesh to the concept of the age of Law, of "blood-consciousness" under female threat. Of course, he then reworked the whole; Lawrence was not tacking something on, but modifying the whole structure, and aiming to achieve, in his final pages, that "Supreme Art" which, as the treatise claims, "knows the final reconciliation";[2] the rainbow is the Old Testament type of the epoch-making covenant. At the outset the men sit in a plenitude like that at the beginning of Job, at one with the oneness of the flesh and the world; but the women are beginning to look to them for something else, for something unlike the blood-peace they themselves possess; they want "another form of life" (I) and it seems that what they want is knowledge in their men, and a spiritual apartness, and a new kind of mutual awareness. They want men to be fighting "on the edge of the unknown."[3] The meeting with Lydia is enough to move Brangwen in that direction. Their struggles are proper to good marriage; as so often in Lawrence the marriage goes wrong before it goes very right, but it is a good marriage, though proper to its epoch. Neither feels the need to discover and cultivate a difficult regenerate and separate personality or he has no great need of it, and she, the aristocrat, has it already (unlike the Jews who ruined her father). In the next section there is not only a difference of personalities, there is a difference of epochs.

To speak thus of the opening of *The Rainbow* is to leave out all that gives flesh to the word; it is evident to everybody that Lawrence wrote it with an extraordinary devotion to the fullness of experience: the stormy night skies, the corn, the udders of cows, the bodies of men heavy with blood, the brooding eyes of the women—but also the behavior of the servant Tilly, and the passionately observed insecurities and certainties of the child—all this has a weight in the hand, a richly laborious craft, that tell us something of the deepest importance about Lawrence, namely the shortness of the passage between life and his art. Again and again he astonishes us with accuracy, with fullness, with the sense of an archaic life. His mind held remotely to the doctrine, intensely to the flow of the text which represented the odd angles, the peripeties, the ecstatic memories and climaxes of life. For in the time of *The Rainbow*, the power of doctrine was less and the fertility of textual invention greater. Yet deeply concealed as it is, there can be no doubt that there is a doctrinal skeleton in this first part of *The Rainbow*; and it was in the Hardy study that it was articulated. An example of the union of doctrine and "realist" narrative in this section might be the Swedenborgian proposition about marriage and angels, made by Brangwen at the wedding: it is part of the profuse provision of humorous authentication, yet it also remembers the suggestions in *Thomas Hardy* about spiritual evolution, and the hints at the Consummate Marriage.

We find the same situation, though with a difference, in the part which describes the love and marriage of Anna and Will. We are in a world (we nearly always are in Lawrence) where fathers, apprised of their daughters' intention to marry, ask questions about money, though it is also a world where their deeper resentments are recorded. It is a world where embraces in the stable are of bodies "keen and wonderful," touching in each other the center of reality yet sharing the world with coughing cows and stirring horses, breathing the sharp ammoniac air. Attention having been deflected, for various reasons, from Lawrence's most remarkable achievements in the rendering of sexual love, we may forget the beautiful accuracy of the opening pages of the chapter called "Anna Victrix," an account of the intoxication of early married love unmatched in fiction—deeply sensual but shading into the comic, it has a genuine archaic or ritual force—just as the passage concerning Will's attempted seduction of the shopgirl has an exactness and, indeed, elegance exceeding those of the comparable scenes in *Sons and Lovers*. Even Ursula's violence to her pupil, though related to doctrine, has veracity and fineness. There are moments in Lawrence when one remembers with pleasure that he insisted on his commonness; that he used with fineness the knowledge that gave him in his early days an ambiguous reputation among his upper-class acquaintances. When Rachel Annand Taylor said he "was definitely a cad," that he had "attained some culture the hard way" but still "there was some slum in him,"[4] she did not know she was alluding to the kind of power that Lawrence cut off when he was writing *The Trespasser* and admiring Rachel Annand Taylor, but turned on when he was about his serious business later. He had no "slum" in him, but he knew how men make love to girls in parks and stables, and he learned that this knowledge was not irrelevant.

Anna and her failed artist husband owe something to Hardy's Sue and Jude as Lawrence discusses them in *Thomas Hardy*, but there is a profound transformation. Will's reluctance to emerge from voluptuousness into separate male labor has its doctrinal side, but it is also a point at which the doctrine is confirmed by ordinary experience; so too with the pain and conflict of the marriage as it develops, with the deep lapse into voluptuousness after the shopgirl incident, and the final defeat of Will by Anna Victrix. It all fits the doctrine, yet it is also the kind of truth novels tell.

The Rainbow possesses a virtuoso range of tones, and the good reader will learn to interpret it with a parallel virtuosity. There are passages which have a kind of narrative singleness in itself highly satisfying—old Brangwen's address to his horse as he sets out for home, drunk in the deluge, or Will's chiding of the little Ursula in his kitchen garden, are examples of this basic novelistic power. In other places, the texture is much thicker. For example, the discussion between Will and Anna about the miracle at Cana: she forcing him out of his comfortable acceptance into an uncomfortable, unwelcome independence of spirit, wanting him at the rim, not at the axle, herself lapsing victorious, into the stasis of motherhood. The fifty pages of "Anna Victrix" are in themselves a remarkable demonstration of the use of doctrine to Lawrence as novelist. Will loses; the symbols he carves—his phoenix, his Adam and Eve—are rejected and ruined. In the cathedral—another chapter with a powerful thematic line—we may take Anna's jeering as part of the marital struggle, or as doctrinal; for in the Hardy study we learn that the medieval cathedrals are Monist, female tributes to the Law, denials of male separateness—except for the gargoyles; and the arguments about Will's passion for them, and about the sex of the gargoyles, mean much more to Lawrence than the occasion of a family dispute. So with the Lamb and Flag window in the parish church—to Anna "a silly absurd toy-lamb with a Christmas-tree flag ledged on its paw—and if it wants to mean anything else, it must look different from that" (VI), but to Will a symbol of Christ, of his innocence and sacrifice—of Love, in fact. To Lawrence, steeped in the symbolism of apocalypse, it is even more, being the emblem of the victorious Christ in the last days, and he places it here, ambiguously, in his own first apocalypse. It becomes part of the story of Anna Victrix, which is itself part of the story of the destruction of marriage and society by women denied their passive role by inactive husbands.

Such, then, are the deep harmonies of doctrine and narrative in this text. So flexible has Lawrence become that when we come on a passage of prose that seems to belong not to a novel but a treatise—when the text is subdued by a metaphysic—we can take it in our stride. There is a passage of this kind at the end of Chapter X—an Easter sermon on the Resurrection, occasioned by an account of how the Brangwen children responded to the liturgical year. Precisely because of the mobility of the text this does not strike us as intrusive; Lawrence has learned to accommodate metaphysic by extending rather than restricting the skills of the novelist. The confidence he has already acquired will prevent the reader from introducing the wrong kind of resistance at such points. This is also true of moments when the fiction tentatively explores obscure aspects of the theory, as in the Winifred Inger passages. Lawrence, his fierce separation of male from female established, wondered about the homosexual relations possible on either side of the divide. Himself attracted to men (though severe on sodomy) he speculated also about lesbianism. That he should do so seems well enough in tune. The range of the novel is great, and we have learned to be flexible, too.

The third section of *The Rainbow* consists of that part of the double novel which Lawrence introduced in order to prepare Ursula for her later encounter with Birkin. Skrebensky brings to her that admired aristocratic isolation, that maleness she associated with the sons of God who lay with the daughters of men, and were not the servile children of Adam. The necessary struggle, the necessary disillusion, that follow, are

certainly doctrinal, yet they count among the most magnificent of Lawrence's fictional achievements. The climactic scene of love-making on the dunes, Ursula mad, at her crisis, a harpy in the moonlight, is unlike anything in any other novel—easily represented, by those who will not trust Lawrence, as absurd and overwritten, but merely at the extreme range of the voice we can learn to trust, a voice capable of authenticating a hidden world of feeling and behavior, of which this is the edge. There can be no question, presumably, about the two stackyard scenes. Lawrence probably wrote the second (with Ursula and Skrebensky) first.

> There he saw, with something like terror, the great new stacks of corn glistening and gleaming transfigured, silvery and present under the night-blue sky, throwing dark, substantial shadows, but themselves majestic and dimly present. She, like glimmering gossamer, seemed to burn among them, as they rose like cold fires to the silvery-bluish air. All was intangible, a burning of cold, glimmering, whitish-steely fires. He was afraid of the great moon-conflagration of the cornstacks rising above him. His heart grew smaller, it began to fuse like a bead. He knew he would die (XI).

Ursula is seized by "a sudden lust," a cold, brilliant desire; again and again the language insists on cold crystalline brilliance, the salt destructiveness of all the powers that are hostile to living sex. A generation earlier Will and Anna went to the stackyard, lit by a golden moon, and put up sheaves together.

> The air was all hoary silver. . . . "You take this row," she said to the youth, and passing on, she stooped in the next row of lying sheaves, grasping her hands in the tresses of the oats, lifting the heavy corn in either hand, carrying it, as it hung heavily against her, to the cleared space, where she set the two sheaves sharply down, bringing them together with a faint, keen clash. Her two bulks stood leaning together. He was coming, walking shadowily with the gossamer dusk, carrying his two sheaves. She waited near-by. He set his sheaves with a keen, faint clash, next to her sheaves. They rode unsteadily. He tangled the tresses of corn. It hissed like a fountain. He looked up and laughed (IV).

And so on for several unfaltering pages, the moon revealing Anna, laying bare her bosom, before the clash of mouths and love declarations.

Friction is already, in the Hardy study, a word for the evil in a sexual relationship. But in the Anna passage the hiss and clash of the corn is a kind or organic premonition of sexual surrender. Her daughter, later to be called, by Rupert Birkin in his bitterness, a moon-goddess, is about to engage in an act of destruction, the description of which was a totally unprecedented task, but one for which Lawrence found the means. His Ursula is no suffragette, but a woman who finds only death in the old sexual order, a death reflected in the sight of England grown meager and paltry. Lawrence took his greatest risk with the conclusion, in the prose poem of Ursula and the horses, in the sickness which burns out an epoch in her life and England's—or so he allowed himself, at this time, to hope—thus preparing for the age of the Reconciler, who will bring the dualities into life-giving tension. The colliers—always for Lawrence men of another, darker life—wait in their warped and stiffened bodies for the great liberation; and over the sad corrupted landscape glows the premature rainbow.

> She knew that the sordid people who crept hard-scaled and separate on the face of the world's

corruption were living still, that the rainbow was arched in their blood and would quiver to life in their spirit, that they would cast off their horny covering of distintegration, that new, clean, naked bodies would issue to a new germination. . . . She saw in the rainbow the earth's new architecture (XVI).

That closing passage has images—of separateness, of beetlelike carapaces—that will persist in Lawrence as his mind grows darker; but although the doctrine suggested its form it is validated by the power of the fiction itself, by the confidence the text has taught us. F. R. Leavis called it "oddly desperate," a way of ending one book to get on to another in which there would be no such necessary lapses into the "wholly unprepared and unsupported."[5] This is surely wrong; the first version of apocalypse required such a conclusion, and it was well prepared. The book—it is still astonishing to reflect—was called filthy, partly because of the scene in which the pregnant Anna dances before a glass. It is the reaction of a mere consumer; Lawrence's readers must produce. They must also understand by remaking the metaphysic as it exists, not raw, but as part of the tissue of the narrative and the rhetoric, which are not subdued.

Notes

1. Harry T. Moore, *The Intelligent Heart* (New York, 1954), p. 254.
2. *Phoenix: The Posthumous Papers of D. H. Lawrence*, ed. Edward D. McDonald (New York, 1936), p. 516.
3. Edward H. Neils, ed., *D. H. Lawrence: A Composite Biography* (Madison, 1957), I, p. 162.
4. Ibid., pp. 137, 556.
5. *D. H. Lawrence, Novelist* (London, 1957), p. 148.

FRANK KERMODE
From "1913–1917"
D. H. Lawrence
1973, pp. 64–78

Women in Love is a unique masterpiece, but surely those who in their day failed to see this were forgivable. What we have taught ourselves to read as complexity presented itself as opinionated confusion; what seems audacious looked absurd. Thus a by no means imperceptive contemporary reviewer called Lawrence's muse "aesthetically unchaste"—"His genius has consorted with life and has acquired mystical imperfections, nailprints in the palms"; and another found that "some shocks make you giggle," especially "in the novel where all the characters suffer the pangs of dissolution several times a week." Middleton Murry's review, though hostile, was the first critique of the book to see its destructiveness: "Mr. Lawrence's consummation is a degradation, his passing beyond a passing beneath, his triumph a catastrophe."[1] Murry, who hated the book, understood it better than most; later he spoke of Lawrence as one of the few writers who "struggled with the spiritual catastrophe of the war in the depths of their souls. . . . They regard the war as a climacteric event, not only in their own subjective experience, but also in the spiritual history of the world. For them it marked the end of an epoch of the human consciousness." Hence the attempt in *Women in Love* to take us through a hideous but necessary process of dissolution. Lawrence, he assures us, bore him no grudge: "I had taken it seriously, and nobody else had done that."[2]

The metaphysic must indeed be taken seriously, but not simply extracted. "In his queer make-up," said Forster in his obituary, "things were connected, and . . . if he did not preach and prophesy he could not see and feel. . . . You cannot say, 'Let us drop his theories and enjoy his art,' because

the two are one."[3] Just as *Thomas Hardy* helped Lawrence to see the shape of *The Rainbow*—though that novel is by no means a simple vehicle for the *Hardy* ideas—so *Women in Love* needed its proper metaphysic. It is not a novel of extended arcs, as its predecessor is; it proceeds by awful discontinuous leaps; its progress enacts those desperate religious plunges into an unknown Lawrence so much wanted. Yet, like a great many others who have made or wanted to make such leaps, Lawrence was not deficient in common sense, even in intellectual and spiritual prudence. This is something one feels often in the poems, in his sudden ironies, in what Richard Hoggart calls his "nicely bloody-minded" tone: "We trust the visionary more because it's rooted in the solid and down-to-earth."[4] One of the achievements of the novel is to criticize the metaphysic, both by attacking Birkin and by obscuring doctrine with narrative symbolisms capable in their nature of more general and more doubtful interpretation. Just as Ursula and Gudrun were originally Frieda, though differentiated and transformed over the years, so Birkin was the voice of the hectoring preacher Lawrence, and is yet reviled, justly ridiculed, and in the end prevented by the narrative from being right and from being able to say he has come through.

We begin with the individual spirit, the race, and the world at the end of their tethers; we also begin with two intelligent provincial girls talking, at about the same level of seriousness as the sisters at the beginning of *Middlemarch*, about marriage—not wanting it, confused about it, but by no means in distress. They walk into the colliery landscape, chthonic, *post-mortem*, a landscape of ghouls, hideous but with a strange inhuman vitality. The machine has turned England and its people into this kind of underworld: the English have led the rush into dissolution. Before the first chapter is over, we have seen Gudrun choose Gerald, master of the ghouls, his icy beauty representing a Nordic depth of corruption; and we have seen Hermione as an image of the passional life corruptly led in the mind, and rejected by Birkin as he struggles against this corruption. The words "dissolution" and "corruption" haunt the book, and are closely associated with Hermione.

Though every major section in the novel is a new leap, Lawrence established certain recurrences of language and image which insure continuous narrative and doctrinal pressure; so that although we think of sections of the book—"Moony," "Water-Party," "Rabbit"—as having an unusual distinctness, we also remember it as a whole. To take one instance, the theme of Gerald's guilt. Much of the time Gerald is a plausibly sensible, amused figure; but at the outset we are reminded that he killed his brother, not because he thought, as did Birkin, that "People don't really matter," but in an accident. Birkin ponders this. "Is there no such thing as pure accident? Has everything that happens a universal significance? . . . He did not believe that there was any such thing as accident. It all hung together, in the deepest sense" (II). What he means is that the text of life is like that of a novel; that on some possible reading it all hangs together, every incident referable to some continuing encodement.[5] Two chapters later, Gudrun and Ursula revert to the topic. Gudrun finds such accidents more terrifying than murder, because murder is willed. "Perhaps there *was* an unconscious will behind it," says Ursula. They disagree, Gudrun savoring the terror of the meaningless. We are reminded of this earlier accident of Gerald's immediately before the accidental death of his sister, in "Water-Party"; he has declared his love for Gudrun, but walks beside her, "set apart, like Cain." Birkin and Ursula are discussing corruption, the "dark river of dissolution." The passage is pure doctrine ("we find ourselves part of the inverse process, the blood of destructive creation"—with which Gudrun and Gerald are specifically associated), and the associated imagery of marsh, serpent, swan, and lily is all there. Birkin will not quite agree that we are *all* "flowers of dissolution—*fleurs du mal*," at this end of the world, but he comes near to saying so, and Ursula is angry, chiding him as so often: "You only want us to know death." On this cue Gerald enters; two pages have passed since he was last in the text, under the name of "Cain."

Thus "everything hangs together," as Birkin had said; and the necessity that it should do so is behind Lawrence's emphasis on the novelty of his concept for form in fiction. Mere authenticity—the description of children, or the clothes at a fete—he could do as well as anybody; but in the matter of *hanging together* every book was a wholly new start. It is a view that Conrad, whom Lawrence never read well, would have shared; but the methods are different, and Lawrence's certainly implies a whole new approach to narrative. When the bodies are found, it is Gerald's sister who has drowned the young doctor; the whole history of his family is used to strengthen the narrative myth of Gerald, and so are his fight with the mare, his use of the slave girl Pussum, and, finally, his self-destruction in the heart not of African darkness but of Alpine cold, the icy dissolution of the Northern races.

Another recurrence of great importance in the matching of doctrine and novel is the insistence on Birkin's sickness and on his occasional strident absurdity. Already when we encounter him at the Shortlands wedding party he is slightly ridiculous, gulping champagne, and "thinking about race or national death." When he lectures Hermione in "Class-Room"—"We get it all in the head, really. You've got to lapse out before you can know what sensual reality is"—we are told that "He sounded as if he were addressing a meeting." His attack on piano-owning colliers (V) is qualified by Gerald's patient smile; Gerald may be one of the damned, but he is allowed to register amusement when the savior is silly. At Breadalby the "powerful, consuming, destructive mentality" which "emanates" from Joshua Mattheson (based on Russell) and Hermione (based on Lady Ottoline) also emanates from Birkin (based on Lawrence). Birkin feels he deserves Hermione's onslaught with the lapis-lazuli paperweight, though her assault is quite firmly related to her corrupt voluptuousness.

Later, Ursula takes over the role of Birkin's critic; she cuts the metaphysic down to novelistic size. However near death she may herself feel, she instinctively rejects the apocalyptic excesses of Birkin. When he longs for a new world purged of humanity she is attracted by the notion but rejects it: "She knew it could not appear so cleanly and conveniently. It had a long way to go yet, a long hideous way. Her subtle and demoniacal female soul knew it well." Humanity, says Birkin, "rots in the chrysalis, it will never have wings"—the kind of diffuse doctrinal generalization she can't stand, regarding it as venal immodesty, even as prostitution, since Birkin offered these essentially private meditations to all, indiscriminately: "she hated the Salvator Mundi touch" (XI).

". . . what *do* you believe in?" she asked, mocking. "Simply in the end of the world, and grass?"

He was beginning to feel a fool.

"I believe in the unseen hosts," he said.

"And nothing else? You believe in nothing visible, except grass and birds? Your world is a poor show."

"Perhaps it is," he said. . . .

Birkin is like the canary which thinks night has come when somebody puts a cloth over its small cage.

The chapter called "Moony" is famous as a doctrinal core, but it is worth looking at as an example of Lawrence's way of taming metaphysic by fiction. Ursula, finding the world "lapsing into a grey wish-wash of nothingness," thinks well of cows, on the Whitmanesque grounds that "they do not sweat and whine about their condition" (a famous passage in "Song of Myself" which is followed by another about the stallion, which Lawrence must have still had in his head when he wrote *St. Mawr*). In this mood of "contemptuous ridicule" for humanity, she comes upon Birkin throwing dead flowers and stones into a pool, and muttering "Cybele—curse her! The accursed *Syria Dea!*" Not surprisingly she finds this ridiculous. But Lawrence is giving Birkin, in this silly situation, many essential things to say. Characteristically, therefore, he makes Birkin absurd at the outset, brings in his doctrinal critic, and then tackles the enormous task of leaping from absurdity to power. At once he writes the superb passage about the reflected moon, "a white body of fire writhing and striving" as the stones shatter the surface of the water. Doctrine loses itself in pagan symbolism—the presence of the castrating moon-goddess may be shaken but not finally dispersed—and that, in turn, is lost in the virtuosity of the description of the interflow of light and dark on the water. Birkin and Ursula talk combatively, differing about love; she wants to surrender to it, he the equilibrium of separateness. Next day, Birkin remembers Halliday's African statue, beetle like, emblem of the sensual, of disintegration and dissolution: "the principle of knowledge in dissolution and corruption." The white races must undergo their version of the same process: "ice-destructive knowledge, snow-abstract annihilation." He thinks of Gerald, "omen of the universal dissolution into whiteness and snow."

This very complex passage is, of course, "metaphysical," but it also depends upon the recurrence of the statue, and the anticipation of the last scenes of the book. It is so constructed that many of its expressions are untranslatable directly into narrative or doctrine; what are the "dreadful mysteries, far beyond the phallic cult," and what, in addition to our too mental, too abstract civilization, is meant by the passage on racial death by frost? The whole thing has a deliberate afflatus, an incantatory haziness, as of apocalyptic preaching. But it is equally characteristic that Birkin switches his thought to a soul-equilibrium marriage with Ursula as an alternative to dissolution, and that he hurries over to her house to ask her to marry him. He is rejected; but Ursula, having fallen into a Gudrun-like contemptuous abstraction, swings round to the Birkin view that human beings, "painting the universe with their own image," are a blot on the true nonhuman universe. Yet she still wants of him complete surrender, abandon; he seeks "mutual union in separateness." She is still bound by the false fleshly notions of the old Law, still unprepared for the new union of Law and Love. Birkin himself goes straight into "Gladiatorial," his wrestling with Gerald, Gerald frictional, Birkin abstract, a strife for oneness between two men as different as man and woman, an exploration of intermediate sex and love which turns his thoughts back to Ursula: "Gerald was becoming dim again, lapsing out of him."

These chapters are full of metaphysic, but they transcend it; the risks they take are of implausible absurdity, and the power that enables Lawrence to take them successfully is the power not of a prophet but of a novelist, even in the matter of characterization. Ursula swings toward Gudrun, and Birkin to Gerald; then both achieve a certain release, and move together again. From what we know of them all, we can, if we wish, interpret this allegorically, and up to a point the text encourages this. But not to the extent that we forgot what Lawrence said in his letter to Garnett, and all the other things he says concerning the ways in which novels ought to shape themselves and their meanings. The metaphysic does not subdue, nor is it unchanged.

With Gudrun and Gerald, who do not directly voice or contest the metaphysic but are important in illustrating it, there are many instances of ambivalence. Gudrun is frictional, sensational, corrupted, and corrupting; how well, with her high clanging metallic voice, her art, her interest in the marshy water plants, her thrilled response to Gerald's imposing of his will on the mare, she complies with the theme of the river of dissolution. Yet she is also a charming girl, capable of intense sympathy with her sister, fond and even generous; it is she who saves the letter full of Birkinian metaphysic when Halliday and his friends are jeering at it in the Pompadour. As to Gerald, no occasion is lost of stressing his thematic significance: he is first described as having "something northern about him"—"In his clear northern flesh and his fair hair was a glisten like sunshine refracted through crystals of ice" (I)—and we are continually reminded of this "northern kind of beauty, like light refracted from snow" (XX). He first comes to Gudrun for love with churchyard clay on him, and the smell of dead flowers. Having imposed his will on the colliers as ruthlessly as on his mare, he stands with Gudrun under the railway arch—where these corrupted victims of the mechanical dissolution make love to their girls. Gudrun has always been sexually excited by colliers. At their love-making "she, subject, received him as a vessel filled with his bitter potion of death. . . . The terrible frictional violence of death filled her, and she received it in an ecstasy of subjection, in throes of acute, violent sensation" (XXIV). And he accepts her as Magna Mater, giver and renewer of his life.

Yet to find the house he had to ask the way of a stupid collier; and after this evil love-making he had, like any trivially illicit lover, to tiptoe downstairs at five in the morning, carrying his boots. Here, as in so many other of the pages concerning Gerald, we find, at the level of narrative, that union of the apocalyptic and the colloquial to which Kinkead-Weekes refers. Much the same kind of thing may be said of the artist Loerke. In the early drafts he was necessary to the racial aspect of Lawrence's apocalypse: a Jew, further gone in corruption than the rest of us, a Chamberlain Jew, corruptly female, pederastic, a devotee of the flow of dissolution. His views on art, hotly contested by Ursula, are powerfully opposed to life: decadent symbolism, the flesh represented geometrically, a Wyndham Lewis-like cult of death. He is, as Birkin and Gerald agree, a rat, a beetle, all corrupt ego. At the last moment, Lawrence incorporates into his account of Loerke the "terrible and dreadful" painting called "The Merry-Go-Round" by his friend the Jewish artist Mark Gertler. He admired it, called it "obscene . . . but then, since obscenity is the truth of our passion today, it is the only stuff of art." And he conjectures that Gertler is "absorbed in the violent and lurid processes of inner decomposition. . . . It would take a Jew to paint this picture. . . . You are of an older race than I, and in these ultimate processes you are beyond me . . . it will be left for the Jews to utter the great and final death-cry of this epoch. . . . But I think I am sufficiently the same, to be able to understand."[6] Later, Lawrence assured Gertler that Loerke was not he (490); but there can be no doubt that he saw the picture in terms of his racial theory, and so associated it with Loerke. What is interesting is that in the book he arranges a conflict between this art of dissolution, and the art which is "only the truth about the real world" (XXIX). Ursula tells

Loerke that he is "too far gone" to see that the second concept is the right one. The phrase is significant.

Gudrun is attracted to Loerke as to all manifestations of dissolution; he is illusionless, a "mud-child. He seemed to be the very stuff of the underworld of life. There was no going beyond him." He is in this sense reminiscent of the colliers who lust after Gudrun in her colored stockings, and she feels excited by him. Yet this "rat," this "gnawing little negation," with his "insect-like repulsiveness," is somehow made a man, and is the survivor in the clash with Gerald at the end. The scheme of the book called for a corrupt Jewish artist; the book makes that a wholly inadequate and "metaphysical" description of the result. Loerke is important as an agent of the plot; satisfying Gudrun's lust for dissolution, he motivates her rejection of Gerald; he sends Gerald off into his own realm of death and icy corruption. He is important to the metaphysic. But neither exigency can prevent his acquiring those qualities which belong to an art that has to do "with the real world."

Trust the tale, says Lawrence, and to make it trustworthy he gives us a Loerke whose connection with the metaphysic is usually ignored; some critics even find him an admirable character. It is the same throughout. We could make a table of Birkin's beliefs and relate them very closely to Lawrence's views on the impending end, on race, on the complementary flows of creation and dissolution, on true marital relations as "beyond love"—"star-equilibrium" (Carpenterian notion) with tension but no friction, spirit but no sensation. But the book does not exist to endorse these views; they are there in full strength, attended by the private system of images—rats, marsh, beetles, and so on—but the text is neither messianic nor mechanical nor even conclusive.

What saves it from being any of those things is its honest insistence on the power of a text to encompass absurdity, contradiction, tension. Its courage is remarkable. One scene after another—Birkin with the statuette in Halliday's flat, or "Gladiatorial"—tempts the absurd, but is forced through into meaning. Lawrence leaps precipitously from one emblematic scene to the next, chooses an image for his text, and overwhelms it with a novelist's not a preacher's passion. Consider "Rabbit." There is a clearly defined social situation: Gudrun is to be a teacher, her social situation is delicate; Winifred knows it. The French governess is envious or insolent. It might be a scene from a very conventional novel. But the rabbit, Bismarck, changes all that. There is a joke about cooking him, but he is a mystery, *ein Wunder*. Gudrun looks like a macaw, the governess is "a little French beetle." Bismarck is simply there to be drawn by the child. Then he exhibits his demoniacal power, a savagery that lacerates but satisfies Gerald and Gudrun. To make it work Lawrence had to use extreme imaginative force. Gerald brings "his free hand down like a hawk on the neck of the rabbit." Gudrun's seagull cry of excitement, the "obscene recognition" that passes between her and Gerald, his obscene solicitude for her scratch, the reaction of the child, and the superb bit of dialogue which ends the chapter, are all the rewards of an artistic, not a prophetic risk.

Many such linked parables make the book—"The Chair," for instance. Occasionally we may find that matters have grown too simple (the representation, in "Pompadour," of the old Café Royal as a "small slow central whirlpool of disintegration and dissolution" is an instance of mental bombast, "thoughts and images too great for the subject") but for the most part the writing is equal to the extraordinary demands made upon it. The chapter called "Excurse" illustrates most of the risks and achievements. Here is the climactic struggle—starting in a newfangled car at the side of the road. Ursula accuses Birkin of deathly obscenity, of loving in Hermione both the sham spirituality and the foul sex act: "You are so *perverse*, so death-eating," she says. They are interrupted by a passing bicyclist; and Birkin admits to himself his own degradation. She throws the jewels he has just given her—emblems of a warm creation—into the mud, and goes off, only to come back with a flower. That bicyclist is very typical of Lawrence. But the hardest part is to come: the love scene in the Saracen's Head, her fingers tracing the life flow in his thighs. At last, she is a daughter of man with one of the Sons of God. From somewhere "deeper than the phallic source" she gets the necessary knowledge of what lies beyond love and passion. They eat a large meal, plan the future, drive off (Birkin "like an Egyptian Pharaoh, driving the car. . . . He knew what it was to have the strange and magical current of force in his back and loins, and down his legs, force so perfect that it stayed him immobile, and left his face subtly, mindlessly smiling"). Then they make love in a dark forest, giving each other "the immemorial magnificence of mystic, palpable, real otherness." However, they remember to send Ursula's father a telegram, to say she will not be home that night, and make a respectable excuse.

It is in such passages that Lawrence dares the reader to take the profound for the ridiculous; the bicyclist, the meal, the telegram, are all there to remind one that this is life, not a scribble to be resolved by reference to some doctrine, not a fantasy either. It is quite understandable that the intense insistence on Birkin's buttocks (a blend of sexual reverie and doctrine) strikes some as very ridiculous, and even sympathetic readers may feel some strain. But this is how he does it, and given that it was something so unprecedented, so strange, there was evidently no other way. Metaphysically Lawrence is saying (what he was soon to express in another doctrinal work) that the source of resistance to the evil male surrender to the solar plexus, the lapse into the hated mother, was in the lumbar ganglia; separateness once established and venerated, the "immemorable magnificence" of that love act was possible. It is not like the intentions of most novelists, and the method is therefore totally idiosyncratic.

The same is true of "Continental," with its faintly comic presentation of a trip abroad as a great leap in the dark; it has to put the four principal characters into new relationships of great significance and complexity, and take many chances in the process. Yet this, and the concluding chapter, may be thought to represent Lawrence's power of complex narrative at its highest.

Of the acts of buggery in which all four characters appear to engage, two with benefit, two destructively, dissolutely—I shall say more in the pages on *Lady Chatterley's Lover*. Certainly they have something to do with the metaphysic: certainly in this version of Lawrence's apocalypse, it is necessary for those on the side of life to comply with dissolution in such a way that it is hard to distinguish them from the party of death. What is more important is the boldness with which Lawrence registers the schism between Gerald and Gudrun, the departure of Birkin and Ursula, and the encounter with the body of Gerald; that stiff body, its icy hair now literally frozen, glittering with frost. Birkin's "He should have loved me," and the final dialogue—the lovers parted again on the issue of the two kinds of love, the novel ending with its own equilibrium once more and finally disturbed—belong to what Lawrence meant by the art of the novel.

Philosophy, religion, science, they are all of them nailing things down, to get a stable equilibrium.

. . . But the novel, no. . . . If you try to nail anything down, in the novel, either it kills the novel, or the novel gets up and walks away with the nail. Morality in the novel is the trembling instability of the balance. When the novelist puts his thumb in the scale, to pull down the balance to his own predilection, that is immorality. . . . And of all the art forms, the novel most of all demands the trembling and oscillating of the balance.[7]

Women in Love has this instability. In life Lawrence was, it might seem, dangerously unstable at the time of its writing; but the book is unstable in exactly the sense he exigently demands of novels that are true, not false. The "metaphysic" was important to him, and, as he believed, to everybody; he could not enact primary human relationships without putting it in. Yet to be effective it must not be programmatic; whatever got through to the reader would come not from the prescriptions of philosophy or religion, but from a sense of the beneficent instability of the text into which he wove it. The effort was so enormous that he was never to put it forth with quite the same energy again.

Notes

1. These reviews were by Evelyn Scott in *The Dial*, an anonym in *Saturday Westminster Gazette*, and Middleton Murry in *The Nation and Athenaeum*; reprinted in R. P. Draper, *D. H. Lawrence: The Critical Heritage* (New York, 1970), pp. 162, 167, 172.
2. J. Middleton Murry, *Reminiscences of D. H. Lawrence* (London, 1933), pp. 247, 103.
3. Full text in Draper, op. cit., 343–47.
4. Richard Hoggart, quoted in *The Complete Poems of D. H. Lawrence*, ed. Vivian De Sola Pinto and F. Warren Roberts (New York, 1964), p. 15.
5. "In a novel, everything is relative to everything else, if that novel is art at all. There may be didactic bits, but they aren't the novel" (*Phoenix II: More Uncollected Writings*, ed. Warren Roberts and Harry T. Moore (New York, 1968), p. 416).
6. *The Collected Letters of D. H. Lawrence*, ed. Harry T. Moore (New York, 1962), pp. 477–78.
7. *Phoenix: The Posthumous Papers of D. H. Lawrence*, ed. Edward D. McDonald (New York, 1936), pp. 528–29.

WILLIAM H. PRITCHARD
"D.H. Lawrence: 1920–1930"
Seeing through Everything
1977, pp. 70–89

Lawrence doesn't fit in anywhere, refuses to be bracketed with postwar 'satirists', would make an unhappy consort with the Men of 1914 (he disliked *Ulysses*, thought Lewis a purely negative writer, seems not even to have bothered forming an opinion of Eliot's or Pound's work), and is neither sympathetic towards Bloomsbury nor nostalgic for the solid entertainments of Wells or Bennett. I speak here of the Lawrence who pronounced on these matters in essays, letters and the fiction written in that period from war's end and the publication of *Women in Love* (1920) to his death in 1930. This leaves out of account the great Lawrence; even if one can't decide finally whether *Women in Love* is more a work of inspiriting genius or a shrill and grotesque piece of murderous disintegration, *The Rainbow* and *Sons and Lovers* will remain and Lawrence be remembered as a great realistic novelist of the family and the sexual struggle. I feel less guilty than otherwise I might about confining my own commentary—much of it adverse—to the postwar, progressively embittered Lawrence, for two reasons: first that there is much fascination in sorting out conflicting responses to the stories, novels, poems, invectives and essays written from *Women in Love* until his death; second, that there has recently appeared an excellent discussion by Roger Sale of Lawrence's three major works—*Sons and Lovers, The Rainbow, Women in Love*—which makes the fullest, most convincingly imaginative defense and explanation of his career, as revealed in those books.[1]

On the other hand, Mr. Sale gives short shrift to Lawrence's work after *Women in Love*, indeed treats it as no more than a brief and largely unsatisfactory postscript to a completed story. A few tales and the book on American literature are all he cares to salvage from the general stridency and wreckage of those years. Such an accounting of a great artist's production, when it spans the years from age thirty-five to his death is not easy to understand and accept. Lawrence was dying, at least was seriously ill from 1925 on, was not acclaimed as a great writer by everyone, was harassed by censors and other culture-morons; still, others have been as ill, have suffered as many slings and arrows without causing us to invoke outrageous fortune as an answer to what went wrong in a writer during the years which should have been the most creatively distinguished ones of his life. Or perhaps nothing *did* go wrong, at least in the books which came from Lawrence's pen during this last decade. It is common to wish that he were less doggedly insistent in his saying of valuable things. It is also common to argue as John Carey has in the conclusion to his acute essay on Lawrence's 'doctrine', where after extracting and ridiculing that doctrine Carey pulls himself up a step short of total condemnation; even though abstractly conceived it may well be 'disgusting, dangerous or satanic', it becomes something else in the books themselves, namely 'alive':

> Extracted, schematized, it loses its shifting, paradoxical quality: the luminous visual and verbal power marshalled to attack the visual and verbal; the intellect deriding the intellect; the sensitivity and callousness fused together. It loses, too, its personality, its human smell—and that is a vital consideration, for it is the final paradox of Lawrence's thought that, separated from his warm, intense, wonderfully articulate being, it becomes the philosophy of any thug or moron.[2]

These two positions are not as far apart as at first they sound: one admires the good things Lawrence says but is put off by the messianic style; the other insists that the things he had to say are only good when they smell human and occur as the expression, in a book, of a 'warm, intense, wonderfully articulate being'. It is surely right to look for what is live and shifting and undeniably expressive of Lawrence's personality; such looking for and pointing out is to be preferred to further 'objective' analysis or readings of individual books. But when Lawrence of 1920–30 is inspected for moments when, in Carey's terms, the human smell is most evident, these moments very often turn out to be ones of rejection, disgust at others and at self expressed through the passionate but chilling cry of *noli me tangere*: moments in which the reek of the human reeks of the grave, where in the words of his fine poem 'Hymn to Priapus' Lawrence cannot 'And will not forget./The stream of my life in the darkness/Deathward set!'

In a review of Edward Dahlberg's *Bottom Dogs* written toward the end of Lawrence's life he made this judgement on a contemporary: 'Wyndham Lewis gives a display of the utterly repulsive effect people have on him, but he retreats into the intellect to make his display. It is a question of manners and manners. The effect is the same. It is the same exclamation: They stink! My God, they stink!' No one would deny that

Lewis created some unlovely specimens of things behaving like persons in his satiric fiction; but it is primarily in Lawrence's own writings from the 1920s that the really violent and reproachfully negative emotions are directed, in scorn and profound depression, at the way other people behave. A letter written on 22 December 1913, filled with acute comments about Walt Whitman, ended with Lawrence criticizing Whitman's generalizing rhetoric by saying that 'One *doesn't* feel like that—except in the moments of wide, gnawing desire when everything has gone wrong' and going on to speak of Whitman's poetry as "Just a self revelation of a man who could not live, and so had to write himself.' At the risk of being unfeelingly glib it is hard to avoid turning these remarks back on Post-*Women in Love* Lawrence, as when things went wrong—censorship, bodily decay, the deterioration of things with Frieda—his desire to set other people straight, to chastise the world for being out of step, reached its widest and most gnawing proportions. As the life became ever more dissatisfied, transient and tortured, so the books poured out faster, the 'self revelation' increased to epic scale. And the 'clear-sighted and mocking vivacity . . . quite without animus', which F. R. Leavis found in Lawrence's criticism and letters, more and more seems a figment of Leavis's imagination rather than anything encountered in the pages of Lawrence's books.

Of course if Leavis had found more 'animus' in Lawrence, less clear-sighted vision and more obsessive rage projected on his human surroundings, he could not have admired him as the apostle of health and sanity presented to us in the pages of *D.H. Lawrence: Novelist*. Yet whether or not we esteem Lawrence's work in the 1920s it is inescapably there, disturbing us by its refusal, its inability to be, among other things, great literature. For rather than appearing as Dr. Leavis's supreme novelist, the Lawrence of this decade often is scarcely a novelist at all, impatient with everything that makes the novel what it is and not another thing. This does not make his work less interesting. Twenty years after Leavis's book, we no longer have to answer, as he did, Eliot's charge that Lawrence was a corruptor, 'rotten and rotting others', by insisting that on the contrary he was the sanest and healthiest English writer of this century. Nor are his views now felt by the young to carry with them the possibilities for profound changes of conviction in regard to sexual and social behavior, although *Lady Chatterley's Lover* and *Women in Love* are read interestedly and argued about disinterestedly in university classrooms, without recriminations. This disinterestedness could be interpreted as a sign that Lawrence's power to convert is diminished; as one who twenty years ago thought he was converted, I do not lament this possibility, and think that present-day cooler heads may well be better readers of his books than I was.

Women in Love

One of the truths about *Women in Love* is true also of Lawrence's other prophetic fictions: that reading the novel over a period of years, one more and more treasures incidental things, while passing over the big moments with a sense that one has been there before. There is a chapter called 'Continental' which is not strictly necessary to develop the tale or characters but simply tells how Ursula and Birkin leave England and travel across Belgium. In the darkness they see the lights of Ghent station and Ursula is reminded of her childhood at the Marsh and her servant Tilly 'who used to give her bread and butter sprinkled with brown sugar in the old living-room where the grandfather clock had two pink roses in a basket painted above the figures on the face'. Now she is 'travelling into the unknown with Birkin, an utter stranger', and the distance between now and childhood 'was so great, that it seemed she had no identity, that the child she had been, playing in Cossethay churchyard, was a little creature of history, not really herself. In this lovely passage, and in much of the chapter, Lawrence reverts to a narrative not strikingly different from the one employed in *Sons and Lovers* and at times in *The Rainbow*, so it may be retrograde to admire it. Yet often-made claims that the central narrative technique of *Women in Love* is something we must appreciate in its own, new terms should not be too quickly accepted.

Lawrence tells us in the preface to *Women in Love* that we should approach our soul with a 'deep respect', that nothing in the passional self can be bad, and that 'This struggle for verbal consciousness should not be left out in art' since it is a great part of life. The last, strange sentence has its own art, reads as if 'art' is exactly the kind of finished thing liable to leave out the 'struggle for verbal consciousness'. By opting for a style that would express the 'pulsing, frictional to-and-fro which works up to culmination', the crucial struggle will be presented as it deserves to be. But Lawrence also adds, as if in nervous self-justification, that in portraying this struggle he is not out to superimpose a theory, rather to give us life as it is most deeply felt. This is exactly the way he talks in his preface to the American edition of *New Poems* (1918) which sets up the fluid pulse of his own Free verse in rather crude opposition to the fixities and rigidities of 'the old poetry', and puts life against death, the organic against the mechanical.

One sees why Lawrence insisted that he wasn't superimposing a theory, since he most surely had a theory about the nature and destiny of Gudrun and Gerald. Towards the end of *Women in Love*, in the 'Snowed Up' chapter where crucial steps in Gudrun's progression towards mechanical corruption and Gerald's towards polar annihilation have to be made, the narrator says with regard to Gudrun:

> Cross the threshold, and you found her completely, completely cynical about the social world and its advantages. Once inside the house of her soul, and there was a pungent atmosphere of corrosion, an inflamed darkness of sensation, and a vivid, subtle, critical consciousness, that saw the world distorted, horrific.

> What then, what next? Was it sheer blind force of passion that would satisfy her now? Not this, but the subtle thrills of extreme sensation in reduction. It was an unbroken will reacting against her unbroken will in a myriad subtle thrills of reduction, the last subtle activities of analysis and breaking down . . .

Aside from the crudity of its style—why should one *not* find fault with the unimaginative repetition of 'subtle', or the attempt to pass off 'pungent atmosphere of corrosion' as convincingly about anything?—the trouble with the passage is that only a few chapters before we have seen Ursula and Gudrun taking a last look at their parents' house and agreeing that they are not eager for another 'home':

> 'But a home, an establishment! Ursula, what would it mean?—think!'

> 'I know,' said Ursula, 'We've had one home—that's enough for me.'

> 'Quite enough,' said Gudrun.

> 'The little grey home in the west,' quoted Ursula ironically.

> 'Doesn't it sound grey, too,' said Gudrun grimly.

In 'Why the Novel Matters' Lawrence says that only in the Novel are 'all things given full play', that 'out of the full play of all things emerges the only thing that is anything, the wholeness of a man, the wholeness of a woman, man alive and live woman'. One must consult his own sense of what is or isn't full play, but I submit that something like it is heard in this exchange between the sisters and in Gudrun's final 'Doesn't it sound grey, too,' said 'grimly' but with a saving wit and sanity such as is found in Lawrence's best letters. By contrast, the other passage's insistence on how only the 'subtle thrills of extreme sensation is reduction' will satisfy her (and which the sculptor, Loerke, supposedly represents) sounds like a put-up job. Isn't it possible that a girl who was capable of making the remark about the greyness of a grey home in the west might possess the saving touch of complication which would allow her to be seen as more than illustrative of the 'vivid, subtle critical consciousness' that is wholly disintegrative and reductive?

Lawrence abuses Tolstoy (in 'Morality and the Novel') with respect to *Anna Karenina* and to the creation of Pierre, for putting his 'thumb on the scale' and interfering with life—the full play of all things; yet he could not heed his own warning in the books beginning with *Women in Love*. Gerald and Gudrun are hunted down and done in by an author who has imposed a scheme upon the novel that these characters are not permitted to disrupt. The freedom of disruption is reserved instead for Birkin and Ursula, and it is remarkable in the case of these successful lovers how their conversational and social individuation is so strong, their 'full play' so evident after prolonged struggle with each other. It even survives the embarrassing language Lawrence reaches for in the famous 'Excurse' chapter. The struggle for verbal consciousness with respect to Ursula and Birkin is present in carefully worked-out scenes where different ways of expression are tried out, rejected, come back to: in their struggle the novel succeeds in putting us in touch with the 'wholeness' of man alive and live woman. It is a tribute to Lawrence's full sense of life then that even though he writes about Birkin (in 'Excurse') that 'a lambent intelligence played secondarily about his pure Egyptian concentration in darkness' the book shucks off such cant; we *know* there is a truer reality of character here than any talk about 'suave loins of darkness' or 'pure mystic nodality of physical being' or 'star-equilibrium' can suggest. And there are poignant post-'Excurse' moments in the book, where it becomes clear that Lawrence can't bring Birkin and Ursula any closer together, where we know that even what they shared in 'Excurse' is only momentary and not enough—especially when something more, like Birkin's failed man-to-man relation with Gerald Crich, is contemplated.

With respect to Birkin and Ursula the book survives its doctrinal superimpositions; with respect to Gudrun and Gerald it does not, though there is much interesting analysis of Gerald in relation to industrial society, to family, and to the condition of England. What it's most difficult to excuse Lawrence for—particularly in the light of the books to come—is his badgering of characters, most blatantly evident in the case of Hermione Roddice. Although Lawrence is usually praised for his creation of this supposedly liberated woman who is but a mouthpiece for Birkin's doctrines, in fact the exposure of her is crude. As revealed most fully in the 'Classroom' chapter, Lawrence's method is to have Hermione go on at great length about how knowledge and the mind are killing us:

> Then, pulling herself together with a convulsed movement, Hermione resumed, in a sing-song, casual voice:

> 'But leaving me apart, Rupert; do you think the children are better, richer, happier, for all this knowledge; do you really think they are? Or is it better to leave them untouched, spontaneous? Hadn't they better be animals, simply animals, crude, violent *anything*, rather than this self-consciousness, this incapacity to be spontaneous?'

As she goes on and on, repeating the same catch-phrases, we are asked to notice 'a queer rumbling in her throat', a 'clenched' fist, 'like one in a trance', another 'convulsed movement of her body' all of which go to make up her 'queer rhapsody' which she 'drawls' to Ursula in a 'queer resonant voice'. Eventually, taking a deep breath, Birkin assumes command and destroys her, exposing the arguments as shibboleths only. Or so we are supposed to feel. In fact one finds oneself embarrassed and eventually annoyed at the slovenly butchering of Hermione. No worry about revealing 'the full play of all things' here—supposedly this woman is *only* a mouthpiece, wholly entranced by her own 'queer' rhapsody, incapable of a word of truth or honest response to anything. To take sides with Birkin and exult in his triumph is a debasement of intelligence; the triumph is hollow because the fight has been staged, allowed to be conducted only within certain rigidly circumscribed limits. Admittedly Lawrence does permit Hermione to bash Birkin with the piece of lapis lazuli not too long afterwards; and as long as we direct the blow towards Lawrence, as well as his hero, perhaps the writer is vindicated. But the book's 'satire', if meant to be a lively and engaging battle of wills and ideas, sadly fails to be such. The word for it instead is one Lawrence uses frequently and in this book— 'jeering'.

Women in Love is largely free of such jeering because Lawrence has not yet totally despaired of regenerative possibilities, perhaps even the creation between men and women of a new world—'the joint work of men and women' of which he spoke to Garnett in 1914 and which the novel set out to express. Seven years later, in another letter to Garnett (19 October 1921) the following postscript occurs: 'I hear I am in worse odour than ever, for *Women in Love*. But, pah! what do I care for all the *canaille.*' It was a refrain to be heard often over the remainder of his life. And the 'joint work of men and women' of which he spoke so hopefully in 1914, while struggling to realize it in his marriage to Frieda, might be recalled in juxtaposition with the following extract from a letter to Koteliansky in March 1919:

> I am not going to be left to Frieda's tender mercies until I am well again. She really is a devil—and I feel as if I would part from her for ever—let her go alone to Germany, while I take another road. For it is true, I have been bullied by her long enough. I really could leave her now, without a pang I believe. The time comes, to make an end, one way or another.

Look, we have come through, and I can't stand it. But somehow he kept going and in the grip of a 'wide, gnawing desire when everything has gone wrong' undertook a savage pilgrimage or, if one prefers, a journey with genius, while attempting (in his early phrase about *Sons and Lovers*) to shed his sickness in the books which he poured out.

1920–25

Lawrence's major fictional expression of these years I take to be *St. Mawr* (1925) which Leavis first proclaimed a masterpiece comparable with *The Waste Land* and is now included in the *Oxford Anthology of English Literature*. But before considering *St. Mawr* let us examine the tone and direction of certain essays and short novels which appeared during these post-*Women in Love* years. As the quotation from 'Why the Novel Matters' suggested, Lawrence as critic-philosopher of the form is in favour of Life, against rules and 'Thou Shalt Nots', against schemes of morality and superimposed systems of explanation; he is against the intellect of the novelist insofar as it tries to dictate to the passional self, tries to force the blood to obey its prescriptions. So Tolstoy cheated in *Anna Karenina* by making Anna pay, and created the 'dull'

Pierre in *War and Peace* who has too many ideas and is not 'quick' enough. He is also against too much 'purpose' in modern novelists: 'They've all got it: the same snivelling purpose. They're all little Jesuses in their own eyes, and their "purpose" is to prove it. Oh Lord!—*Lord Jim! Sylvestre Bonnard! If Winter Comes! Main Street! Ulysses! Pan!*' No attempt is made to elucidate the 'purpose' that somehow links Conrad to Sinclair Lewis, Joyce, and some others, but the jeering tone ('Oh Lord—*Lord Jim!*) is heard at length in the same essay ('The Novel', 1924) in Lawrence's baiting of 'Leo' (Tolstoy) and Leo's insufficiently alive creations—Pierre, and the Prince in *Resurrection*. This habit of jeering, of baiting and teasing authors had been fully developed in the just-published *Studies in Classic American Literature*, and there it often works brilliantly: destructively and amusingly in the Franklin essay; more complicatedly critical in the essays on two writers towards whom Lawrence had the deepest feelings—Melville and Whitman. Along with their harsh wit these essays reveal a critical disinterestedness and impersonality which, if it were general in Lawrence's work, would make him the great critic Leavis salutes.

But perhaps the American writers were sufficiently distant in time and space for Lawrence not to feel threatened by them or in competition with them. Not so with *Ulysses*, nor with Proust, who is jeered at along with other too 'personal' novelists because they keep writing about whether they feel twinges in their little toe. Even the Russians who admittedly meant so much to him come in for their licks: as early as 1916 he charged Tolstoy, Dostoyevsky, Turgenev, Chekhov (a 'Willy Wet-Leg') with showing 'a certain crudity and thick, uncivilised, insensitive stupidity about them', and he realizes 'how much finer and purer and more ultimate our own stuff is'. By the 1920s 'our own stuff' had pretty much boiled down to the works of D.H. Lawrence; even *A Passage to India*, just about the only novel by a contemporary Englishman Lawrence is caught admiring, makes him 'wish a bomb would fall and end everything. Life is more interesting in its undercurrents than in its obvious; and E. M. does see people, people and nothing but people: *ad nauseam*' (23 July 1924). Novels should be about something more than people, should be 'finer and purer and more ultimate' than those Russian novels with their 'certain crudity' perhaps smelling too much of people. Novelists should not, on the other hand, do dirt on life like Flaubert or Thomas Mann did, nor be deliberately dirty-minded like Joyce, nor be resigned like Arnold Bennett (who is referred to as 'a pig in clover') nor be clever and negative like Lewis or Huxley. At the same time Lawrence seems to have been impressed with his own work, particularly with *Women in Love* which he liked best, but also with *Lady Chatterley, The Man Who Died* and no doubt others. We can presume that he was attempting to transcend the limitations of other novelists and to create in his own works what he found lacking in theirs.

It would be easy but unprofitable to treat Lawrence's fiction during these years as failing to live up to his principles: no artist should be expected to practise what he preaches. Still it is instructive—perhaps only as illustrating the gap between promise and performance—to hear him loudly declaring (in 'Morality and the Novel', 1925) that if you try to 'nail anything down' in the novel it 'gets up and walks away with the nail', and that it is a sin for the novelist to put his 'thumb in the pan'. His own most recent novels, *Aaron's Rod* and *Kangaroo*, had shown a very heavy thumb in the pan indeed; nor was anyone likely to be unaware of doctrinal designs in his just-completed *The Plumed Serpent*. While essential reading for the student of Lawrence, these novels all seem to me disastrous ventures that no one would recommend to an ideal common reader. *Aaron's Rod* is shapeless and wandering, filled with invitations to connect a name with some real-life friend or enemy of Lawrence's, and of course providing (in the Aaron-Lilly relationship) the leader-follower business which interested Lawrence so much in those years and which now seems only dreary and embarrassing. *Aaron's Rod* begins wonderfully with the hero's walkout on his family, shocking yet natural in its execution. Later on there are some good moments in London and later still some interesting travelogue. But the whole doesn't add up to a novel; nor does *Kangaroo* which is part leader-follower dialectic, part good writing about Australia, plus the famous and detachable insert of Lawrence's nightmare physical examination for the army. And while *The Plumed Serpent* might appeal to some readers with anthropological interests or a soft spot in the heart for morning in Mexico, it seems to me at the very bottom of all Lawrence's work—an often hateful and more often boring tract. It must have been this book, or work related to it, which moved Wyndham Lewis to refer on a later occasion to the tiresomeness of Lawrence's 'arty voodooism'.

More attractive to our hypothetical common reader are the longer stories (or shorter novels) from these years, notably 'The Fox', 'The Captain's Doll', 'The Princess', and 'The Woman Who Rode Away'. The first two have been praised as masterpieces by Leavis, while Graham Hough puts 'The Woman Who Rode Away' at the very summit of Lawrence's art. All of them contain flashes of vivid creation, but they do not get up and walk away with the nail Lawrence has hammered through them. More troublingly, they set forth with evident sympathy, even with some relish on their author's part, certain aggressively cruel actions we are asked to assent to, or at least to believe have more 'life' in them than the deadness they sweep out of the way. It is not surprising that Kate Millett, preoccupied with hunting down Lawrence in *Sexual Politics*, should gleefully pounce on 'The Princess' with its dark-blooded rapist, Romero, who serves the prim Princess with what Lawrence evidently thinks she deserves. Nor that Millett should read 'The Woman Who Rode Away' as reminiscent of hard-core pornography in its carefully-graduated stripping-down of the woman in preparation for the final to-be-welcomed-as-her-destiny thrust of the dark-blooded Indian's knife. What price landscape, symbolic journeys, mythical translation beyond the social world, if to get them you have to endure a happening simply beyond sympathetic comprehension? One doesn't have to be a feminist to find it absurd, or to deplore our assumed situation as a watchful reader of all those Indians watching the white lady. No struggle towards verbal consciousness, no full play of all things: only a toneless narration, rhapsodic and drugged in its assent to the 'inevitable'.

The earlier short novels written in the backwash of *Women in Love* are much more humanly interesting; the possibility of love and marriage between man and woman was then still a real one in Lawrence's mind, and so he did not have to search out a character's fulfilment in the most remote, unhuman circumstances. Yet even here, in the social comedy of 'The Captain's Doll' which Leavis admires so much, or in the fine renderings of March, Banford and Henry in 'The Fox', a new relationship between man and woman is possible only after great violence has been done to the world, or to its representatives—like Banford or Mrs. Hepburn—who stands for oppression, morality and disapproval. For the liberation of March to occur, Banford has to be obliterated by a falling tree, cut down of course by March's lover Henry who had earlier

said to himself about Banford: 'You're a nasty little thing. I hope you'll be paid back for all the harm you've done me for nothing. I hope you will—you nasty little thing.' She is paid back with interest, and if the tale had ended there, as perhaps it should have, the shocked abruptness of the event might have discouraged questions about its meaning. As written, Lawrence goes on for a few pages in which March envies Banford and Henry wonders if he should have left them to kill each other. Still, 'The Fox' remains a memorable tale whose particularity is richer than its doctrinal reference. It says more than it means. 'The Captain's Doll' is much more the comedy of ideas with the lovers, Hepburn and Hannele, further exploring the proper relationship between man and wife which occupied Birkin and Ursula. For a short novel it seems curiously overextended, disposes of Hepburn's first wife by making her fall out of a window (a joke?) and is burdened by the rather tedious figure of Hepburn himself who spends much time peering solemnly at the stars through his telescope. By itself, without the fact of *Women in Love*, it would excite little interest.

St. Mawr

With *St. Mawr* the 'Lawrence problem' presents itself most fully for inspection. Leavis would have us admire its sardonic 'doing' of rootless London society, of Lou's husband 'being an artist', of the intensity and seriousness of Lawrence-Lou's awareness of modern sterility and her wish to live more deeply and passionately in a harmony of mind-and-blood consciousness. Richard Poirier has seen it as a moving example of the attempt to create a world elsewhere, through Lou's early imaginings of what the horse means and later through her attempt to articulate her feelings about 'wild America' on the farm in New Mexico. But as with the other tales, someone has to be got out of the way so that Lou can have her vision of at least possible liberation: in *St. Mawr* that someone is her husband Rico. Lawrence wastes no time in warming to the task; when Rico is introduced we are told that

> He was anxious for his future, and anxious for his place in the world, he was poor, and suddenly wasteful in spite of all his tension of economy, and suddenly spiteful in spite of all his ingratiating efforts, and suddenly ungrateful in spite of his burden of gratitude, and suddenly rude in spite of all his good manners, and suddenly detestable in spite of all his suave, courtier-like amiability.

With the exception of Lou's mother, Mrs. Witt, nobody in the tale, not even Lou herself, finds Rico 'detestable'. But Lawrence's thumb has tilted the pan at the outset: Rico is a pathetic, or detestable, contradiction; a thwarter of life, a purely social being and an unserious man. Since nobody in society will punish him, the novelist must put things to right—this is the sort of burden Lawrence takes on himself increasingly in his later fictions.

St. Mawr is everything Rico is not, yet is himself thwarted by Man, unfairly mastered by a race that has lost the capacity for true mastery. There is no mistaking the depth of Lou-Lawrence's feelings about St. Mawr; passages in which Lou thinks about or observes the stallion are expressed with a care and poignancy that deliberately contradict the slapdash casualness Lawrence affects in relation to the young people and to English society: 'Since she had really seen St. Mawr looming fiery and terrible in an outer darkness, she could not believe the world she lived in. She could not believe it was actually happening . . . the talk, the eating and drinking, the flirtation, the endless dancing: it all seemed far more bodiless and, in a strange way, wraithlike, than any fairy-story.' It is perhaps understandable then that when Lawrence attempts to embody Lou's feelings in pointed dialogue with her mother, some strain is felt; as in the following exchange about St. Mawr's Welsh groom, Lewis, whom Mrs. Witt has called stupid:

> 'No, mother, he's not stupid. He only doesn't care about our sort of things.'
>
> 'Like an animal! But what a strange look he has in his eyes! a strange sort of intelligence! and a confidence in himself. Isn't that curious, Louise, in a man with as little mind as he has?' . . .
>
> 'Why, mother!' said Lou impatiently. 'I think one gets so tired of your men with mind, as you call it. There are so many of that sort of clever men. And there are lots of men who aren't very clever, but are rather nice: and lots are stupid. It seems to me there's something else besides mind and cleverness, or niceness or cleanness. Perhaps it is the animal. Just think of St. Mawr! I've thought so much about him. We call him an animal but we never know what it means. He seems a far greater mystery to me than a clever man. He's a horse. Why can't one say in the same way, of a man: *he's a man?* There seems no mystery in being a man. But there's a terrible mystery in St. Mawr.'

After which Mrs. Witt is given, for her, an incredibly naïve line—'Man is wonderful because he is able to *think*'—which Lou has no trouble rounding on in the expected way.

It may be that in criticizing Lawrence here I simply reveal my own limitations as a clever man. But the exclamatory and thrilled air of it all is hard to accept. Though in other places Mrs. Witt is revealed to be a ruthless ironist and relentless wit, she here plays straight-woman to Lou's vision and is set up with extremely simpleminded lines. In a similar manner Lawrence sees to it that there is not the least hint of complication or mystery in the stage-Dean Vyner and his stuffy wife who preside over the small English parish where Lou and her mother are temporarily settled, nor in the fashionable young people who invite Lou and Rico about. With the hills of Wales as backdrop' one of the young set is allowed to say: 'I think this is the best age there ever was for a girl to have a good time in. I read all through H. G. Wells' history, and I shut it up and thanked my stars I live in nineteen-twenty odd, not in some other beastly date when a woman had to cringe before mouldy domineering men.' Thus Flora Manby's declaration, and one knows the response it invites—the lip curled in knowing contempt for this frivolous jazz-age young woman. Yet Lou Witt is only twenty-five herself; is there no human speech possible for a woman which is neither social inanities on one hand or world-weary, wholly disillusioned knowingness about men and horses on the other? Not, it seems, in the world of this cut-to-order fable.

The book's climax occurs on that same excursion along the Welsh border where Flora makes her declaration. St. Mawr rears; Rico, trying to regain control, pulls the horse over on top of him and injures his own leg. A recent book in discussing this scene typifies the academic acceptance of Lawrence which seems to me not only inadequate but pernicious. One of the young people has been demonstrating his superficiality by whistling a new dance tune:

> 'That's an awfully attractive tune,' Rico called.
> 'Do whistle it again, Fred. I should like to memorize it.'
>
> Fred began to whistle it again.
> At that moment St Mawr exploded again, shied

sideways as if a bomb had gone off, and kept backing through the heather.

> 'Fool!' cried Rico, thoroughly unnerved . . .

after which he pulls the horse over backwards on top of him. The critic (Keith Sagar) remarks that the real fools are those who whistle dance tunes—'Triviality in the face of life is what distinguishes them, the old effort at serious living given up'—and that (as Lou learns later) since what St. Mawr had reared at was an adder, 'In thwarting him, Rico has thwarted the deepest impulses. In this context St. Mawr's destructiveness is healthy.' When the tune-whistler, Fred Edwards, tries to help Rico by grabbing the reins, St. Mawr convulses again, and Lawrence says: 'Horror! The young man reeled backwards with his face in his hands. He had got a kick in the face. Red blood running down his chin!' About which Mr. Sagar simply comments: 'We cheer his kick in the face of the young man.'[3]

On the contrary, I should say that 'we cheer' only if we forget that novels are made out of words, if we see nothing embarrassing and crude in Lawrence's exclamatory, falsely-naïve rendering of that kick in the face. Or if, when 'It turned out that Rico had two broken ribs and a crushed ankle. Poor Rico, he would limp for life', we're quite willing to accept that fate as the right punishment for 'thwarting the deepest impulses'. A more ironic reader might ask, what price the deepest impulses, or how much does one deserve to be punished for whistling dance tunes once too often? And this is not even to consider the 'vision of evil' Lou has afterwards in which Lawrence loudly lays out the allegorical reference of events: 'Mankind, like a horse, ridden by a stranger, smooth-faced, evil rider. Evil himself, smooth-faced and pseudo-handsome, riding mankind past the dead snake, to the last break.' All this without the slightest regard for Lou's presumed consciousness, as her creator goes on to preach about Germany, Russia, Judas and various other matters.

The remarkable thing about *St. Mawr*, and about Lawrence generally as an artist, is that even after nailing down the book in such a way it goes on to become quite interesting: in conversations between Lou and Mrs. Witt; in Mrs. Witt's spiriting away of the horse accompanied by Lewis the groom; most of all in the long finale which relates the history of the ranch Lou buys and the confrontation between mother and daughter, between cynical nihilism and the still-struggling effort to create a new myth of 'wildness' in America. And again, as often in Lawrence, it is in the incidental pleasures, moments when the novelist seems relaxed, not pressing to make his big points, where truly the 'full play of all things' goes on. One should read him then in an uneasy doubleness of response, with a distrustful eye cocked at the doctrine and a disdain for the way it hobbles characters into the narrow confines of an author's will. But also with eyes open as, breathing more freely, he produces a matchless bit of nature or an undeniably strong whiff of despairing, hopeless sadness and impotence. This divided response will assure against assenting to academic readings like the just-instanced one, in which we find ourselves all too effortlessly on the right side, Lawrence's side. Surely he would not want us so easily there, would prefer us to be a bit insouciant, as one of his favorite words has it. Such insouciance characterizes perhaps the two best books he wrote during the years between *Women in Love* and *St. Mawr*—the studies in American literature and *Sea and Sardinia*. My preoccupation here with the novels and stories, and in the necessity of arguing with Lawrence, shouldn't obscure these important evidences that the writer is larger than the novelist.

Post-Mortem Effects

The novelist came back to life twice in the late 'twenties, in *Lady Chatterley's Lover* and at moments in *The Man Who Died*. With these affirmations of the phallic mystery, Lawrence celebrated his real subject once more, freed from doctrinal hagglings about Leader and Follower, wreaking less jeering vengeance on those who stood in the way of passional responses fully expressed. Yet there is a truth in Middleton Murry's review of *Lady Chatterley* (*Adelphi*, June 1929) which he termed 'for all its fiery purity' 'a deeply depressing book'. Murry was depressed because he understood Lawrence to be saying that the *only* sensitive awareness we need, and which is real, is awareness of the sexual mystery. All the eggs are there intensely gathered in one basket and presented to us with fervour and reverence. Do we accept them gratefully?

In addition to defenses of the novel against censorship, its merits as a work of art have recently been argued by Frank Kermode who is concerned to show how, triumphantly in *Women in Love* but often enough in the succeeding books, Lawrence's doctrine is resisted, even contradicted by the stuff of life incorporated in those books. Kermode sees *Lady Chatterley's Lover* as, despite serious lapses, a great achievement, and he calls *The Man Who Died* 'one of the most perfect of Lawrence's shorter fictions'. This is much more generous language than I myself should use about these last works; and Kermode has to work hard to make it stick, especially when discussing what until recently was not shared wisdom about *Lady Chatterley*—that Connie's shame is finally 'burned out' by an act of anal intercourse initiated by the resourceful gamekeeper. Kermode wants us to understand and accept the buggery, along with the initial paralysis of Clifford Chatterley (which readers have always and justly complained about as making things too easy by half) as apocalyptic symbols of the sort that Spenser and Milton used. He argues that

> . . . just as Lawrence himself recognised, when he read his first draft, that Chatterley's lameness symbolised 'the paralysis, the deeper emotional or passional paralysis, of most men of his sort and class today,' so we recognise the symbolism of Connie's rebirth. Both symbolisms belong to a metaphysic which Lawrence had long since internalised, and which the tale had, in its own way, to make objective. If we trust them it is because we trust the tale.

If Lawrence had, as on all evidence seems likely, 'internalised' the metaphysic of which these symbols are part, that seems to me regrettable, since as ideas or beliefs they are not very sturdy ones. More important though, is the 'tale' we are encouraged to trust somehow independent of the worth of these symbols or ideas? One might complain that, compared to tale-tellers like George Eliot, or James, or Arnold Bennett, Lawrence does not tell a very good tale here, that few readers move on breathlessly to find out what happens next—as they should do in Forster's ideal of the good story. Whatever connection there is between the ruined condition of industrial England and Sir Clifford's paralysis is of that 'symbolic' kind which the novel asserts rather than can possibly demonstrate; thus the lovers' word becomes desperately idyllic, pastoral right down to those famous garlands woven into pubic hair, and, not only from Middleton Murry's perspective, depressing.

It is depressing that Lawrence believes so relentlessly in symbols which exclude so much of life, of history, of friendship, tolerance, sympathy, good-humor, the minor Forsterian virtues Lawrence in *Lady Chatterley* is too busy to

practise or imagine. His fervent self-righteousness in the great cause makes us want to pick holes in his vision. He is against both the grey Puritan and the liberated smart youth of the 1920s; for he knows that 'Life is only bearable when the mind and body are in harmony, and there is a natural balance between them, and each has a natural respect for the other.' This sentiment, from 'Apropos *Lady Chatterley's Lover*', might be nodded at soberly, except that it goes along with an exultant kick at Swift, who supposedly was disturbed that 'Celia, Celia, Celia shits': 'A great wit like Swift could not see how ridiculous he made himself!' exclaims Lawrence with a ridiculous disregard for the excellently witty poem in which that refrain is sung by a hapless beau, and in which 'Swift' is not at all the horror-stricken figure Lawrence invents. It is Mellors rather, assuring Connie that 'if tha shits and if tha pisses' he wouldn't have it any other way, who is truly ridiculous and silly-sounding. Katherine Anne Porter was extremely perceptive when she complained in her 1961 *Encounter* essay on the book that the whole attempt to hallow 'dirty words', or to exalt bodily functions as marvelously natural and worthy of respect, was a mistake. In effect Miss Porter was saying that there is a gutter-side to life, a ribald, unsentimental lore that has grown up about certain functions which Swift made use of in his poem, and that there was something obscene about Lawrence trying to elevate and rescue them into natural acceptance, 'to purify and canonise obscenity . . . to take the low comedy out of sex'. Surely this is the most interesting question to ask about *Lady Chatterley's Lover* and one which a reader will answer as temperament directs.

More generally it involves one's attitude towards Romanticism in our century. As late as 1916 Lawrence could write about Swinburne that 'He is a great revealer, very great. I put him with Shelley as our greatest poet. He is the last fiery spirit among us . . .' Not quite the last, it turned out. It may well be that any attempt at 'objective' appraisal of Lawrence's work is doomed to failure. Roy Fuller was not speaking only for himself when in one of his Oxford poetry lectures he pointed out how his own relation to Lawrence began with a blind love affair with the books; after the affair ended and he fell out of love he was never able to look at them with the required dispassion. In late adolescence twenty-five years ago, one hitched one's wagon to Lawrence because he was a leader who knew how things should be revised, knew what was true and what false, what live and what dead. When thereafter one's life did not confirm these truths, one found other writers who talked in quite different ways and who did not even unanimously admire the fiery spirit of D. H. Lawrence. After the adverse criticism directed here against some key books in which the spirit reveals itself, it may seem disingenuous to end with a salute to Lawrence. But there are acceptable terms for this salute in another phrase of John Carey's, with whose remarks about Lawrence's doctrine we began. Speaking of *Paradise Lost* Carey says that it is 'great because it is objectionable. It spurs us to protest. Hence its continued life . . .' At least this kind of greatness the later Lawrence unarguably exhibits.

Notes

1. Roger Sale, *Modern Heroism* (University of California Press, 1973). My own discussion of *Women in Love*, though not as admiring of the book, owes much to him. I should also like to thank my colleagues Benjamin DeMott and G. Armour Craig for insights into *St. Mawr* and *Lady Chatterley's Lover* which I have made use of. Richard Poirier's discussion of *St. Mawr* is to be found in *A World Elsewhere* (Oxford, 1966); Frank Kermode's discussion of *Lady Chatterley's Lover* is in his *Lawrence* ('Modern Masters' Series, Fontana, 1973).

2. John Carey, 'D. H. Lawrence's Doctrine', in *D. H. Lawrence: Novelist, Poet, Prophet*, ed. Stephen Spender (London, 1973), pp. 122-34.
3. Keith Sagar, *The Art of D. H. Lawrence* (Cambridge, 1966), p. 155.

JOYCE CAROL OATES
"Lawrence's Götterdämmerung:
The Apocalyptic Vision of *Women in Love*" (1978)
Contraries
1981, pp. 141–70

And was he fated to pass away in this knowledge, this one process of frost-knowledge, death by perfect cold? Was he a messenger, an omen of the universal dissolution into whiteness and snow? (Birkin thinking of Gerald, *Women in Love*)

I

In a little-known story of Lawrence's called "The Christening" an elderly wreck of a man contemplates his illegitimate grandchild and attempts to lead his embarrassed and impatient household in a prayer in "the special language of fatherhood." No one listens, no one wishes to hear. He is rambling, incoherent, bullying even in his confession and self-abnegation, yet his prayer is an extraordinary one: he implores God to shield the newborn child from the conceit of family life, from the burden of being a *son* with a specific *father*. It was his own interference with his children, his imposition of his personal will, that damaged them as human beings; and he prays that his grandson will be spared this violation of the spirit. Half-senile he insists upon his prayer though his grown-up children are present and resentful:

"Lord, what father has a man but Thee? Lord, when a man says he is a father, he is wrong from the first word. For Thou art the Father, Lord. Lord, take away from us the conceit that our children are ours. . . . For I have stood between Thee and my children; I've had *my* way with them, Lord; I've stood between Thee and my children; I've cut 'em off from Thee because they were mine. And they've grown twisted, because of me. . . . Lord, if it hadn't been for me, they might ha' been trees in the sunshine. Let me own it, Lord, I've done 'em mischief. It would ha' been better if they'd never known no father."

Between the individual and the cosmos there falls the deathly shadow of the ego: the disheveled old man utters a truth central to Lawrence's work. Where the human will is active there is always injury to the spirit, always a perversion, a "twisting"; that human beings are compelled not only to assert their greedy claims upon others but to manipulate their own lives in accord with an absolute that has little to do with their deeper yearnings constitutes our tragedy. Is it a tragedy of the modern era; is it inevitably bound up with the rise of industry and mechanization? Lawrence would say that it is, for the "material interests" of which Conrad spoke so ironically are all that remain of spiritual hopes; God being dead, God being unmasked as a fraud, nothing so suits man's ambition as a transvaluing of values, the reinterpretation of religious experience in gross, obscene terms. Here is Gerald Crich, one of Lawrence's most deeply realized and sympathetic characters, surely an alter ego of his—

In his travels, and in his accompanying readings, he had come to the conclusion that the essential secret of life was harmony. . . . And he proceeded to put

his philosophy into practice by forcing order into the established world, translating the mystic word harmony into the practical word organisation.[1]

Harmony becomes *organization*. And Gerald dedicates himself to work, to feverish, totally absorbing work, inspired with an almost religious exaltation in his fight with matter. The world is split in two: on one side matter (the mines, the miners), on the other side his own isolated will. He wants to create on earth a perfect machine, "an activity of pure order, pure mechanical repetition"; a man of the twentieth century with no nostalgia for the superannuated ideals of Christianity or democracy, he wishes to found his eternity, his infinity, in the machine. So inchoate and mysterious is the imaginative world Lawrence creates for *Women in Love* that we find no difficulty in reading Gerald Crich as an allegorical figure in certain chapters and as a quite human, even fluid personality in others. As Gudrun's frenzied lover, as Birkin's elusive beloved, he seems a substantially different person from the Gerald Crich who is a ruthless god of the machine; yet as his cultural role demands extinction (for Lawrence had little doubt that civilization was breaking down rapidly, and Gerald is the very personification of a "civilized" man), so does his private emotional life, his confusion of the individual will with that of the cosmos, demand death—death by perfect cold. He is Lawrence's only tragic figure, a remarkable creation in a remarkable novel, and though it is a commonplace to say that Birkin represents Lawrence, it seems equally likely that Gerald Crich represents Lawrence—in his deepest, most aggrieved, most nihilistic soul.

Women in Love is an inadequate title. The novel concerns itself with far more than simply *women* in love; far more than simply women *in* love. Two violent love affairs are the plot's focus, but the drama of the novel has clearly to do with every sort of emotion, and with every sort of spiritual inanition. Gerald and Birkin and Ursula and Gudrun are immense figures, monstrous creations out of legend, out of mythology; they are unable to alter their fates, like tragic heroes and heroines of old. The mark of Cain has been on Gerald since early childhood, when he accidentally killed his brother; and Gudrun is named for a heroine out of Germanic legend who slew her first husband. The pace of the novel is often frenetic. Time is running out, history is coming to an end, the Apocalypse is at hand. *Dies Irae* and *The Latter Days* (as well as *The Sisters* and *The Wedding Ring*) were titles Lawrence considered for the novel, and though both are too explicit, too shrill, they are more suggestive of the chiliastic mood of the work (which even surprised Lawrence when he read it through after completion in November of 1916: it struck him as "end-of-the-world" and as "purely destructive, not like *The Rainbow*, destructive-consummating").[2]

Women in Love is a strangely ceremonial, even ritualistic work. In very simple terms it celebrates love and marriage as the only possible salvation for twentieth-century man and dramatizes the fate of those who resist the abandonment of the ego demanded by love: a sacrificial rite, an ancient necessity. Yet those who "come through"—Birkin and Ursula—are hardly harmonious; the novel ends with their arguing about Birkin's thwarted desire for an "eternal union with a man," and one is given to feel that the shadow of the dead man will fall across their marriage. And though the structure of the novel is ceremonial, its texture is rich, lush, fanciful, and, since each chapter is organized around a dominant image, rather self-consciously symbolic or imagistic; action is subordinate to theme. The perversity of the novel is such that its great subject of mankind's tragically split nature is demonstrated in the artwork itself, which is sometimes a fairly conventional novel with a forward-moving plot, sometimes a gorgeous, even outrageous prose poem on the order of the work Aloysius Bertrand and Charles Baudelaire were doing in the previous century. Birkin is sometimes a prophetic figure, and sometimes merely garrulous and silly; Ursula is sometimes a mesmerizing archetypal female, at other times shrill and possessive and dismayingly obtuse. In one of Lawrence's most powerful love scenes Gerald Crich comes by night to Gudrun's bedroom after his father's death and is profoundly revitalized by her physical love, but Gudrun cannot help looking upon him with a devastating cynicism, noting his ridiculous trousers and braces and boots, and she is filled with nausea of him despite her fascination. Gudrun herself takes on in Gerald's obsessive imagination certain of the more destructive qualities of the Magna Mater or the devouring female, and she attains an almost mythic power over him; but when we last see her she has become shallow and cheaply ironic, merely a vulgar young woman. It is a measure of Lawrence's genius that every part of his immensely ambitious novel works (with the possible exception of the strained chapter "In The Pompadour") and that the proliferating images coalesce into fairly stable leit-motifs: water, moon, darkness, light, the organic and the sterile.

Our own era is one in which prophetic eschatological art has as great a significance as it did in 1916; Lawrence's despairing conviction that civilization was in the latter days is one shared by a number of our most serious writers, even if there is little belief in the Apocalypse in its classical sense. The notion of antichrist is an archaic one, a sentiment that posits unqualified belief in Christ; and the ushering in of a violent new era, a millennium, necessitates faith in the transcendental properties of the world, or the universe, which contrast sharply with scientific speculations about the fate we are likely to share. Even in his most despairing moments Lawrence remained curiously "religious." It is a tragedy that Western civilization may be doomed, that a man like Gerald Crich must be destroyed, and yet—does it really matter? Lawrence through Birkin debates the paradox endlessly. He cannot come to any conclusion. Gerald is beloved, yet Gerald is deathly. Gerald is a brilliant young man, yet he is a murderer, he is suicidal, he is rotten at the core. It is a possibility that Birkin's passionate love for him is as foully motivated as Gudrun's and would do no good for either of them. *Can* human beings alter their fates? Though his pessimism would seem to undercut and even negate his art, Lawrence is explicit in this novel about his feelings for mankind; the vituperation expressed is perhaps unequaled in serious literature. Surely it is at the very heart of the work, in Birkin's strident ranting voice:

> "I detest what I am, outwardly. I loathe myself as a human being. Humanity is a huge aggregate lie, and a huge lie is less than a small truth. Humanity is less, far less than the individual, because the individual may sometimes be capable of truth, and humanity is a tree of lies. . . .
>
> I abhor humanity, I wish it was swept away. It could go, and there would be no *absolute* loss, if every human being perished to-morrow."

But Ursula also perceives in her lover a contradictory desire to "save" this doomed world, and characteristically judges this desire a weakness, and insidious form of prostitution. Birkin's perverse attachment to the world he hates is not admirable in Ursula's eyes, for Ursula is an ordinary woman but a fiercely intolerant creature who detests all forms of insincerity. She is Birkin's conscience, in a sense; his foil, his gadfly; a taunting form of himself. Yet later, immediately after Birkin declares that he loves her, she is rather disturbed by the starkly nihilistic

vision he sets before her; and indeed it strikes us as more tragic than that of Shakespeare:

> "We always consider the silver river of life, rolling on and quickening all the world to a brightness, on and on to heaven, flowing into a bright eternal sea, a heaven of angels thronging. But the other is our real reality . . . that dark river of dissolution. You see it rolls in us just as the other rolls—the black river of corruption. And our flowers are of this—our sea-born Aphrodite, all our white phosphorescent flowers of sensuous perfection, all our reality, nowadays."

Aphrodite herself is symptomatic of the death-process, born in what Lawrence calls the "first spasm of universal dissolution." The process cannot be halted. It is beyond the individual, beyond choice. It ends in a universal nothing, a new cycle in which humanity will play no role. The prospect is a chilling one and yet—*does* it really matter? Humanity in the aggregate is contemptible, and many people (like Diana Crich) are better off dead since their living has somehow gone wrong. No, Birkin thinks, it can't *really* matter. His mood shifts, he is no longer frustrated and despairing, he is stoical, almost mystical, like one who has given up all hope. For he has said earlier to Gerald, after their talk of the death of God and the possible necessity of the salvation through love, that reality lies outside the human sphere:

> "Well, if mankind is destroyed, if our race is destroyed like Sodom, and there is this beautiful evening with the luminous land and trees, I am satisfied. That which informs it all is there, and can never be lost. After all, what is mankind but just one expression of the incomprehensible. And if mankind passes away, it will only mean that this particular expression is completed and done. . . . Humanity doesn't embody the utterance of the incomprehensible any more. Humanity is a dead letter. There will be a new embodiment, in a new way. Let humanity disappear as quick as possible."

Lawrence's shifts in mood and conviction are passionate, even unsettling. One feels that he writes to discover what he thinks, what is thinking in him, on an unconscious level. Love is an ecstatic experience. Or is it, perhaps, a delusion? Erotic love is a way of salvation—or is it a distraction, a burden? Is it something to be gone through in order that one's deepest self may be stirred to life? Or is it a very simple, utterly natural emotion . . . ? (In *Sons and Lovers* Paul Morel is impatient with Miriam's near-hysterical exaggeration of ordinary emotions; he resents her intensity, her penchant for mythologizing, and finds solace in Clara's far less complex attitude toward sexual love.) Lawrence does not really know, regardless of his dogmatic remarks about "mind-consciousness" and "blood-consciousness." He cannot *know*; he must continually strive to know, and accept continual frustration.[3]

Tragedy for Lawrence arises out of the fatal split between the demands of the ego and those of the larger, less personal consciousness: we are crippled by the shadow of the finite personality as it falls across our souls, as the children of the old man in "The Christening" are crippled by his *particular* fatherliness. If at one point in history—during the great civilization of the Etruscans, for instance—there was a unity of being, a mythic harmony between man and his community and nature, it is lost to us now; the blighted landscapes in Beldover through which Lawrence's people walk give evidence that humanity is no longer evolving but devolving, degenerating. ("It is like a country in an underworld," says Gudrun, repulsed but fascinated. "The people are all ghouls, and everything is ghostly. Everything is a ghoulish replica of the real world . . . all soiled, everything sordid. It's like being mad, Ursula.") One England blots out another England, as Lawrence observes in *Lady Chatterley's Lover* some years later.

In Lawrence's work one is struck repeatedly by the total absence of concern for community. In the novels after *Sons and Lovers* his most fully developed and self-contained characters express an indifference toward their neighbors that is almost aristocratic. Both Anna and Will Brangwen of *The Rainbow* are oblivious to the world outside their household: the nation does not exist to them; there is no war in South Africa: they are in a "private retreat" that has no nationality. Even as a child Ursula is proudly contemptuous of her classmates, knowing herself set apart from them and, as a Brangwen, superior. She is fated to reject her unimaginative lover Skrebensky who has subordinated his individuality to the nation and who would gladly give up his life to it. ("I belong to the nation," he says solemnly, "and must do my duty by the nation.") Some years later she and Gudrun express a loathing for their parents' home that is astonishing, and even the less passionate Alvina Houghton of *The Lost Girl* surrenders to outbursts of mad, hilarious jeering, so frustrated is she by the limitations of her father's household and of the mining town of Woodhouse in general. (She is a "lost" girl only in terms of England. Though her life in a primitive mountain village in Italy is not a very comfortable one, it is nevertheless superior to her former, virginal life back in provincial England.)

Lawrence might have dramatized the tragedy of his people's rootlessness, especially as it compels them to attempt desperate and often quixotic relationships as a surrogate for social and political involvement (as in *The Plumed Serpent* and *Kangaroo*); but of course he could not give life to convictions he did not feel. The human instinct for something larger than an intense, intimate bond, the instinct for community, is entirely absent in Lawrence, and this absence helps to account for the wildness of his characters' emotions. (Their passionate narrowness is especially evident when contrasted with the tolerance of a character like Leopold Bloom of *Ulysses*. Leopold thinks wistfully of his wife, but he thinks also of innumerable other people, men and women both, the living and the dead; he is a man of the city who is stirred by the myriad trivial excitements of Dublin—an adventurer writ small, but not contemptible in Joyce's eyes. His obsessions are comically perverse, his stratagems pathetic. Acceptance by Simon Dedalus and his friends would mean a great deal to poor Bloom, but of course this acceptance will be withheld; he yearns for community but is denied it.)

For the sake of argument Gudrun challenges Ursula's conviction that one can achieve a new space to be in, apart from the old: "But don't you think you'll *want* the old connection with the world—father and the rest of us, and all that it means, England and the world of thought—don't you think you'll *need* that, really to make a world?" But Ursula speaks for Lawrence in denying all inevitable social and familial connections. "One has a sort of other self, that belongs to a new planet, not to this," she says. The disagreement marks the sisters' break with each other; after this heated discussion they are no longer friends. Gudrun mocks the lovers with her false enthusiasm and deeply insults Ursula. "Go and find your new world, dear. After all, the happiest voyage is the quest of Rupert's Blessed Isles."

Lawrence's utopian plans for Rananim aside, it seems obvious that he could not have been truly interested in establishing a community of any permanence, for such a community would have necessitated a connection between one generation and the next. It would have demanded that faith in a reality beyond the individual and the individual's impulses which is absent in Lawrence—not undeveloped so much as simply absent, undiscovered. For this reason alone he seems to us distinctly un-English in any traditional sense. Fielding and Thackeray and Trollope and Dickens and Eliot and Hardy and Bennett belong to another world, another consciousness entirely. (Lawrence's kinship with Pater and Wilde, his predilection for the intensity of the moment, may have stimulated him to a vigorous glorification of Nietzschean instinct and will to power as a means of resisting aestheticism: for there is a languid cynicism about Birkin not unlike that of Wilde's prematurely weary heroes.)

Halfway around the world, in Australia, Richard Somers discovers that he misses England, for it isn't freedom but mere *vacancy* he finds in this new, disturbingly beautiful world: the absence of civilization, of culture, of inner meaning; the absence of spirit.[4] But so long as Lawrence is in England he evokes the idea of his nation only to do battle with it, to refute it, to be nauseated by it. The upper classes are sterile and worthless, the working classes are stunted aborigines who stare after the Brangwen sisters in the street. Halliday and his London friends are self-consciously decadent—"the most pettifogging calculating Bohemia that ever reckoned its pennies." Only in the mythical structure of a fabulist work like *The Escaped Cock* can Lawrence imagine a harmonious relationship between male and female, yet even here in this Mediterranean setting the individual cannot tolerate other people, nor they him: "the little life of jealousy and property" resumes its sway and forces the man who died to flee. There is, however, no possibility of a tragic awareness in these terms; it is not tragic that the individual is compelled to break with his nation and his community because any unit larger than the individual is tainted and suspect, caught in the downward process of corruption.[5] The community almost by definition is degraded. About this everyone is in agreement—Clifford Chatterley as well as Mellors, Hermione as well as Ursula and Gudrun. Community in the old sense is based on property and possessions and must be rejected, and all human relationships not founded upon an immediate emotional rapport must be broken. "The old ideals are dead as nails—nothing there," Birkin says early in *Women in Love*. "It seems to me there remains only this perfect union with a woman—sort of ultimate marriage—and there isn't anything else." Gerald, however, finds it difficult to agree. Making one's life up out of a woman, one woman only, woman only seems to him impossible, just as the forging of an intense love-connection with another man—which in Lawrence's cosmology would have saved his life—is impossible.

"I only feel what I feel," Gerald says.

II

The core of our human tragedy has very little to do with society, then, and everything to do with the individual: with the curious self-destructive condition of the human spirit. Having rejected the theological dogma of original sin, Lawrence develops a rather similar psychological dogma to account for the diabolic split within the individual between the dictates of "mind-consciousness" and the impulses of "blood-consciousness." In his essay on Nathaniel Hawthorne in *Studies in Classic American Literature*, he interprets *The Scarlet Letter* as an allegory, a typically American allegory, of the consequences of the violent antagonism between the two ways of being. His explicitness is helpful in terms of *Women in Love*, where a rich verbal texture masks a tragically simple paradox. The cross itself is the symbol of mankind's self-division, as it is the symbol, the final haunting image, in Gerald Crich's life. (Fleeing into the snow, exhausted and broken after his ignoble attempt to strangle Gudrun, Gerald comes upon a half-buried crucifix at the top of a pole. He fears that someone is going to murder him. In terror he realizes "This was the moment when the death was uplifted, and there was no escape. Lord Jesus, was it then bound to be—Lord Jesus! He could feel the blow descending, he knew he was murdered.")

Christ's agony on the cross symbolizes our human agony at having acquired, or having been poisoned by, the "sin" of knowledge and self-consciousness. In the Hawthorne essay Lawrence says:

> Nowadays men do hate the idea of dualism. It's no good, dual we are. The cross. If we accept the symbol, then, virtually we accept the fact. We are divided against ourselves.
>
> For instance, the blood *hates* being KNOWN by the mind. It feels itself destroyed when it is KNOWN. Hence the profound instinct of privacy.
>
> And on the other hand, the mind and the spiritual consciousness of man simply *hates* the dark potency of blood-acts: hates the genuine dark sensual orgasms, which do, for the time being, actually obliterate the mind and the spiritual consciousness, plunge them in a suffocating flood of darkness.
>
> You can't get away from this.
>
> Blood-consciousness overwhelms, obliterates, and annuls mind-consciousness.
>
> Mind-consciousness extinguishes blood-consciousness, and consumes the blood.
>
> We are all of us conscious in both ways. And the two ways are antagonistic in us.
>
> They will always remain so.
>
> That is our cross.

It is obvious that Lawrence identifies with the instinct toward formal allegory and subterfuge in American literature. He understands Hawthorne, Melville, and Poe from the inside; it is himself he speaks of when he says of Poe that he adventured into the vaults and cellars and horrible underground passages of the human soul, desperate to experience the "prismatic ecstasy" of heightened consciousness and of love. And Poe knew himself to be doomed, necessarily—as Lawrence so frequently thought himself (and his race). Indeed, Poe is far closer to Lawrence than Hawthorne or Melville:

> He died wanting more love, and love killed him. A ghastly disease, love. Poe telling us of his disease: trying even to make his disease fair and attractive. Even succeeding. Which is the inevitable falseness, duplicity of art, American art in particular.

The inevitable duplicity of art: an eccentric statement from the man who says, elsewhere (in an essay on Walt Whitman), that the essential function of art is moral. "Not aesthetic, not decorative, not pasttime and recreation. But moral." Yet it is possible to see that the artist too suffers from a tragic self-division, that he is forced to dramatize the radically new shifting over of consciousness primarily in covert, even occult and deathly terms: wanting to write a novel of consummate health and triumph whose controlling symbol is the rainbow, writing in fact a despairing, floridly tragic and rather mad work that resembles poetry and music (Wagnerian music) far more than it resembles the clearly "moral" bright book of life that is the novel, Lawrence finds himself surprised and disturbed by the apocalyptic nature of this greatest effort, as if he had imagined he had written something quite different. The rhythm of Lawrence's writing is that of the American works he analyzes so irreverently and so brilliantly, a "disintegrating and sloughing of the old consciousness" and "the forming of a new consciousness underneath." Such apocalyptic books must be written because old things need to die, because the "old white psyche has to be gradually broken down before anything else can come to pass" (in the essay on Poe). Such art must be violent, it must be outlandish and diabolic at its core because it is revolutionary in the truest sense of the word. It is subversive, even traitorous; but though it seeks to overturn empires, its primary concerns are prophetic, even religious. As Lawrence says in the poem "Nemesis" (from *Pansies*), "If we do not rapidly open all the doors of consciousness/and freshen the putrid little space in which we are cribbed/the sky-blue walls of our unventilated heaven/will be bright red with blood." In any case the true artist does not determine the direction of his art; he surrenders his ego so that his deeper self may be heard. There is no freedom except in compliance with the spirit within, what Lawrence calls the Holy Ghost.

The suppressed Prologue to *Women in Love* sets forth the terms of Birkin's torment with dramatic economy.[6] "Mind-consciousness" and "blood-consciousness" are not mere abstractions, pseudo-philosophical notions, but bitterly existential ways of perceiving and of being. When Birkin and Gerald Crich first meet they experience a subtle bond between each other, a "sudden connection" that is intensified during a mountain-climbing trip in the Tyrol. In the isolation of the rocks and snow they and their companion attain a rare sort of intimacy that is to be denied and consciously rejected when they descend again into their usual lives. (The parallel with Gerald's death in the snow is obvious; by suppressing the Prologue and beginning with the chapter we have, "Sisters," in which Ursula and Gudrun discuss marriage and the home and the mining town and venture out to watch the wedding, Lawrence sacrificed a great deal. "Sisters" is an entirely satisfactory opening, brilliant in its own lavish way; but the Prologue with its shrill, tender, almost crazed language is far more moving.)

Preliminary to the action of *Women in Love*, and unaccountable in terms of *The Rainbow*, which centers so exclusively upon Ursula, is the passionate and undeclared relationship between Birkin and Gerald, and the tortured split between Birkin's spiritual and "sisterly" love for Hermione and his "passion of desire" for Gerald. Birkin is sickened by his obsession with Gerald; he is repulsed by his overwrought, exclusively mental relationship with Hermione (which is, incidentally, very close to the relationship of sheer nerves Lawrence discusses in his essay on Poe: the obscene love that is the "intensest nervous vibration of unison" without any erotic consummation). That Birkin's dilemma is emblematic of society's confusion in general is made clear, and convincing, by his immersion in educational theory. What is education except the gradual and deliberate building up of consciousness, unit by unit? Each unit of consciousness is the "living unit of that great social, religious, philosophic idea towards which mankind, like an organism seeking its final form, in laboriously growing," but the tragic paradox is that there *is* no great unifying idea at the present time; there is simply aimless, futile activity. For we are in the autumn of civilization, and decay, as such, cannot be acknowledged. As Birkin suffers in his awareness of his own deceitful, frustrated life, he tries to forget himself in work; but he cannot escape a sense of the futility to all attempts at "social constructiveness." The tone of the Prologue is dark indeed, and one hears Lawrence's undisguised despair in every line:

How to get away from this process of reduction, how escape this phosphorescent passage into the tomb, which was universal though unacknowledged, this was the unconscious problem which tortured Birkin day and night. He came to Hermione, and found with her the pure, translucent regions of death itself, of ecstasy. In the world the autumn itself was setting in. What should a man add himself on to?—to science, to social reform, to aestheticism, to sensationalism? The whole world's constructive activity was a fiction, a lie, to hide the great process of decomposition, which had set in. What then to adhere to?

He attempts a physical relationship with Hermione which is a cruel failure, humiliating to them both. He goes in desperation to prostitutes. Like Paul Morel he suffers a familiar split between the "spiritual" woman and the "physical" woman, but his deeper anxiety lies in his unacknowledged passion for Gerald Crich. Surely homoerotic yearning has never been so vividly and so sympathetically presented as it is in Lawrence's Prologue, where Birkin's intelligent complexity, his half-serious desire to rid himself of his soul in order to escape his predicament, and his fear of madness and dissolution as a consequence of his lovelessness give him a tragic depth comparable to Hamlet's. He *wants* to love women, just as he wants to believe in the world's constructive activity; but how can a man create his own feelings? Birkin knows that he cannot: he can only suppress them by an act of sheer will. In danger of going mad or of dying—of possibly killing himself—Birkin continues his deathly relationship with Hermione, keeping his homoerotic feelings to himself and even, in a sense, secret from himself. With keen insight Lawrence analyzes Birkin's own analysis of the situation. "He knew what he felt, but he always kept the knowledge at bay. His a priori were: 'I *should* not feel like this,' and 'It is the ultimate mark of my own deficiency, that I feel like this.' Therefore, though he admitted everything, he never really faced the question. He never accepted the desire, and received it as part of himself. He always tried to keep it expelled from him." Not only does Birkin attempt to dissociate himself from an impulse that *is* himself, he attempts to deny the femaleness in his own nature by objectifying (and degrading) it in his treatment of Hermione and of the "slightly bestial" prostitutes. It maddens him that he should feel sexual attraction for the male physique while for the female he is capable of feeling only a kind of fondness, a sacred love, as if for a sister. "The women he seemed to be kin to, he looked for the soul in them." By the age of thirty he is sickly and dissolute, attached to Hermione in a loveless, sadistic relationship, terrified of breaking with her for fear of falling into the abyss. Yet the break is imminent, inevitable—so the action of *Women in Love* begins.

A tragedy, then, of an informal nature, experimental in its gropings toward a resolution of the central crisis: how to integrate the male and female principles, how to integrate the organic and the "civilized," the relentlessly progressive condition of the modern world. It is not enough to be a child of nature, to cling to one's ignorance as if it were a form of blessedness; one cannot deny the reality of the external world, its gradual transformation from the Old England into the New, into an enthusiastic acceptance of the individual as an instrument in the great machine of society. When Hermione goes into her rhapsody about spontaneity and the instincts, echoing Birkin in saying that the mind is death, he contradicts her brutally by claiming that the problem is not that people have too much mind, but too little. As for Hermione herself, she is merely making words because knowledge means every-

thing to her: "Even your animalism, you want it in your head. You don't have to *be* an animal, you want to observe your own animal functions, to get a mental thrill out of them. . . . What is it but the worst and last form of intellectualism, this love of yours for passion and the animal instincts?" But it is really himself he is attacking: Hermione is a ghastly form of himself he would like to destroy, a parody of a woman, a sister of his soul.

Women in Love must have originally been imagined as Birkin's tragedy rather than Gerald's, for though Gerald feels an attraction for Birkin, he is not so obsessed with it as Birkin is; in the Prologue he is characterized as rather less intelligent, less shrewd, than he turns out to be in subsequent chapters. Ursula's role in saving Birkin from dissolution is, then, far greater than she can know. Not only must she arouse and satisfy his spiritual yearnings, she must answer to his physical desire as well: she must, in a sense, take on the active, masculine role in their relationship. (Significantly, it is Ursula who presses them into an erotic relationship after the death of Diana Crich and her young man. It is she who embraces Birkin tightly, wanting to show him that she is no shallow prude, and though he whimpers to himself, "Not this, not this," he nevertheless succumbs to desire for her and they become lovers. Had Ursula not sensed the need to force Birkin into a physical relationship, it is possible their love would have become as spiritualized, and consequently as poisoned, as Birkin's and Hermione's.) Ursula's role in saving Birkin from destruction is comparable to Sonia's fairly magical redemption of Raskolnikov in *Crime and Punishment*, just as Gerald's suicide is comparable to Svidrigaylov's when both men are denied salvation through women by whom they are obsessed. Though the feminine principle is not sufficient to guarantee eternal happiness, it is nevertheless the way through which salvation is attained: sex is an initiation in Lawrence, a necessary and even ritualistic *event* in the process of psychic wholeness. Where in more traditional tragedy—Shakespeare's *King Lear* comes immediately to mind—it is the feminine, irrational, "dark and vicious" elements that must be resisted, since they disturb the status quo, the patriarchal cosmos, in Lawrence it is precisely the darkness, the passion, the mind-obliterating, terrible, and even vicious experience of erotic love that is necessary for salvation. The individual is split and wars futilely against himself, civilization is split and must fall into chaos if male and female principles are opposed. Lawrence's is the sounder psychology, but it does not follow that his world view is more optimistic, for to recognize a truth does not inevitably bring with it the moral strength to realize that truth in one's life.

Birkin's desire for an eternal union with another man is thwarted in *Women in Love*, and his failure leads indirectly to Gerald's death. At least this is Birkin's conviction. "He should have loved me," he says to Ursula and she, frightened, replies without sympathy, "What difference would it have made!" It is only in a symbolic dimension that the men are lovers; consciously, in the daylight world, they are never anything more than friends. In the chapter "Gladiatorial" the men wrestle together in order to stir Gerald from his boredom, and they seem to "drive their white flesh deeper and deeper against each other, as if they would break into a oneness." The effort is such that both men lose consciousness and Birkin falls over Gerald, involuntarily. When their minds are gone their opposition to each other is gone and they can become united—but only temporarily, only until Birkin regains his consciousness and moves away. At the novel's conclusion Birkin is "happily" married, yet incomplete. He will be a reasonably content and normal man, a husband to the passionate Ursula, yet unfulfilled; and one cannot quite believe that his frustrated love for Gerald will not surface in another form. His failure is not merely his own but civilization's as well: male and female are inexorably opposed, the integration of the two halves of the human soul is an impossibility in our time.[7]

III

Hence the cruel frost-knowledge of *Women in Love*, the death by perfect cold Lawrence has delineated. Long before Gerald's actual death in the mountains Birkin speculates on him as a strange white wonderful demon from the north, fated like his civilization to pass away into universal dissolution, the day of "creative life" being finished. In *Apocalypse* Lawrence speaks of the long slow death of the human being in our time, the victory of repressive and mechanical forces over the organic, the pagan. The mystery religions of antiquity have been destroyed by the systematic, dissecting principle; the artist is driven as a consequence to think in deliberately mythical, archaic, chiliastic terms. How to express the inexpressible? Those poems in *Pansies* that address themselves to the problem—poems like "Wellsian Futures," "Dead People," "Ego-Bound," "Climb Down, O Lordly Mind," "Peace and War"—are rhetorical and strident and rather flat; it is in images that Lawrence *thinks* most clearly. He is too brilliant an artist not to breathe life even into those characters who are in opposition to his own principles. In a statement that resembles Yeats's (that the occult spirits of *A Vision* came to bring him images for his poetry) Lawrence indicates a surprising indifference to the very concept of the Apocalypse itself: "We do not care, vitally, about theories of the Apocalypse. . . . What we care about is the release of the imagination. . . . What does the Apocalypse matter, unless in so far as it gives us imaginative release into another vital world?"[8]

This jaunty attitude is qualified by the images that are called forth by the imagination, however: the wolfishness of Gerald and his mother; the ghoulishness of the Beldover miners; the African totems (one has a face that is void and terrible in its mindlessness; the other has a long, elegant body with a tiny head, a face crushed small like a beetle's); Hermione striking her lover with a paperweight of lapis lazuli and fairly swooning with ecstasy; Gerald digging his spurs into his mare's sides, into wounds that are already bleeding; the drowned Diana Crich with her arms still wrapped tightly about the neck of her young man; the demonic energy of Winifred's rabbit, and Gudrun's slashed, bleeding arm which seems to tear across Gerald's brain; the uncanny, terrifying soullessness of Innsbruck; the stunted figure of the artist Loerke; the final vision of Gerald as the frozen carcass of a dead male. These are fearful images, and what has Lawrence to set against them but the embrace of a man and a woman, a visionary transfiguration of the individual by love?—and even the experience of love, of passion and unity, is seen as ephemeral.

Birkin sees Gerald and Gudrun as flowers of dissolution, locked in the death-process; he cannot help but see Gerald as Cain, who killed his brother. Though in one way *Women in Love* is a naturalistic work populated with realistic characters and set in altogether probable environments, in another way it is inflexible and even rather austerely classical: Gerald is Cain from the very first and his fate is settled. Birkin considers his friend's accidental killing of his brother and wonders if it is proper to think in terms of *accident* at all. Has everything that happens a universal significance? Ultimately he does not believe that there is anything accidental in life: "it all hung together, in the deepest sense." (And it follows that no one is murdered accidentally: ". . . a man who is murderable is a man who in a profound if hidden lust desires to be murdered.") Gerald plainly chooses his murderer in Gudrun, and it is in the curious, misshapen form of Loerke that certain of Gerald's inclinations are given their ultimate realization. Gerald's glorification of the machine and of himself as a god of the machine is parodied by Loerke's inhuman willfulness: Gudrun sees him as the rock-bottom of all life. Unfeeling, stoic, he cares about nothing except his work, he makes not the slightest attempt to be at one with anything, he exists a "pure, unconnected will" in a stunted body. His very being excites Gerald to disgusted fury because he is finally all that Gerald has imagined for himself—the subordination of all spontaneity, the triumph of "harmony" in industrial organization.

Of the bizarre nightmare images stirred in Lawrence's imagination by the idea of the Apocalypse, Loerke is perhaps the most powerful. He is at once very human, and quite inhuman. He is reasonable, even rather charming, and at the same time deathly—a "mud-child," a creature of the underworld. His name suggests that of Loki, the Norse god of discord and mischief, the very principle of dissolution. A repulsive and fascinating character, he is described by Lawrence as a gnome, a bat, a rabbit, a troll, a chatterer, a magpie, a maker of disturbing jokes, with the blank look of inorganic misery behind his buffoonery. That he is an artist, and a homosexual as well, cannot be an accident. He is in Lawrence's imagination the diabolic alter ego who rises up to mock all that Lawrence takes to be sacred. Hence his uncanny power, his parodistic talent: he accepts the hypothesis that industry has replaced religion and he accepts his role as artist in terms of industry, without sentimental qualms. Art should interpret industry; the artist fulfills himself in acquiescence to the machine. Is there nothing apart from work, mechanical work?—Gudrun asks. And he says without hesitation, "Nothing but work!"

Loerke disgusts Birkin and Gerald precisely because he embodies certain of their own traits. He is marvelously self-sufficient; he wishes to ingratiate himself with no one; he is an artist who completely understands and controls his art; he excites the admiration of the beautiful Gudrun, and even Ursula is interested in him for a while. Most painful, perhaps, is his homosexuality. He is not divided against himself, not at all tortured by remorse or conscience. In the Prologue to the novel Birkin half-wishes he might rid himself of his soul, and Loerke is presented as a creature without a soul, one of the "little people" who finds his mate in a human being. It is interesting to note that the rat-like qualities in Loerke are those that have attracted Birkin in other men: Birkin has felt an extraordinary desire to come close to and to know and "as it were to eat" a certain type of Cornish man with dark, fine, stiff hair and dark eyes like holes in his head or like the eyes of a rat (see the Prologue); and he has felt the queer, subterranean, repulsive beauty of a young man with an indomitable manner "like a quick, vital rat" (see the chapter "A Chair"). The Nietzschean quality of Loerke's haughtiness and his loathing of other people, particularly women, remind us of the aristocratic contempt expressed by the middle-aged foreigner whom Tom Brangwen admires so much in the first chapter of *The Rainbow*: the man has a queer monkeyish face that is in its way almost beautiful, he is sardonic, dry-skinned, coldly intelligent, mockingly courteous to the women in his company (one of whom has made love with Tom previously), a creature who strangely rouses Tom's blood and who, in the form of Anna Lensky, will be his mate. There is no doubt but that Lawrence, a very different physical type, and temperamentally quite opposed to the cold, life-denying principle these men embody, was nevertheless powerfully attracted by them. There is an irresistible *life* to Loerke that makes us feel the strength of his nihilistic charm.

Surely not accidental is the fact that Loerke is an artist. He expresses a view of art that all artists share, to some extent, despite their protestations to the contrary. It is Flaubert speaking in Loerke, declaring art supreme and the artist's life of little consequence; when Loerke claims that his statuette of a girl on a horse is no more than an artistic composition, a certain form without relation to anything outside itself, he is echoing Flaubert's contention that there is no such thing as a subject, there is only style. ("What seems beautiful to me, what I should like to write," Flaubert said, in a remark now famous, "is a book about nothing, a book dependent on nothing external. . . .") Loerke angers Ursula by declaring that his art pictures nothing, "absolutely nothing," there is no connection between his art and the everyday world, they are two different and distinct planes of existence, and she must not confuse them. In his disdainful proclamation of an art that refers only to itself, he speaks for the aesthetes of the nineteenth century against whom Lawrence had to define himself as a creator of vital, moral, life-enhancing art. Though Lawrence shared certain of their beliefs—that bourgeois civilization was bankrupt, that the mass of human beings was hopelessly ignorant and contemptible—he did not want to align himself with their extreme rejection of "ordinary" life and of nature itself. (Too unbridled a revulsion against the world would lead one to the sinister self-indulgent fantasies of certain of the decadent poets and artists—the bizarre creations of Oscar Wilde and Huysmans and Baudelaire, and of Gustave Moreau and Odilon Redon and Jan Toorop among others.) Loerke's almost supernatural presence drives Ursula and Birkin away, and brings to the surface the destructive elements in the love of Gudrun and Gerald. He is an artist of decay: his effect upon Gudrun is like that of a subtle poison.

"Life doesn't *really* matter," Gudrun says. "It is one's art which is central."[9]

Symbolically, then, Gerald witnesses the destruction of his love, or of a part of his own soul, by those beliefs that had been a kind of religion to him in his operating of the mines. Lawrence himself plays with certain of his worst fears by giving them over to Loerke and Gudrun, who toy with them, inventing for their amusement a mocking dream of the destruction of the world: humanity invents a perfect explosive that blows up the world, perhaps; or the climate shifts and the world goes cold and snow falls everywhere and "only white creatures, polar-bears, white foxes, and men like awful white snow-birds, persisted in ice cruelty." It is Lawrence's nightmare, the Apocalypse without resurrection, without meaning; a vision as bleak and as tragically unsentimental as Shakespeare's.

IV

Only in parable, in myth, can tragedy be transcended. In that beautiful novella *The Escaped Cock*, written while Lawrence was dying, the Christian and the pagan mate, the male and the female come together in a perfect union, and the process of dissolution is halted. The man who had died awakes in his tomb, sickened and despairing, knowing himself moral, not the Son of God but no more than a son of man—and in this realization is his hope, his true salvation. He is resurrected to the flesh of his own body; through the warm, healing flesh of the priestess of Isis he is healed of his fraudulent divinity. "Father!" he cries in his rapture, "Why did you hide this from me?"

Poetic, Biblical in its rhythms, *The Escaped Cock* is an extraordinary work in that it dramatizes Lawrence's own sense of resurrection from near death (he had come close to dying several times) and that it repudiates his passion for changing the world. The man who had died realizes that his teaching is finished and that it had been a mistake to interfere in the souls of others; he knows now that his reach ends in his fingertips. His love for mankind had been no more than a form of egotism, a madness that would devour multitudes while leaving his own being untouched and virginal. What is crucified in him is his passion for "saving" others. Lawrence has explored the near dissolution of the personality in earlier works—in Ursula's illness near the end of *The Rainbow*, and in her reaction to Birkin's love-making in *Women in Love*; and in Connie Chatterley's deepening sense of nothingness before her meeting with Mellors—but never with such powerful economy as in *The Escaped Cock*. The man who had died wakes slowly and reluctantly to life, overcome with a sense of nausea, dreading consciousness but compelled to return to it and to his fulfillment as a human being. The passage back to life is a terrible one; his injured body is repulsive to him, as is the memory of his suffering. The analogy between the colorful cock and the gradually healing flesh of the man who had died is unabashedly direct and even rather witty. In this idyllic Mediterranean world a cock and a man are kin, all of nature is related, the dead Osiris is resurrected in the dead Christ, and the phenomenal world is revealed as the transcendental world, the world of eternity. Simply to live in a body, to live as a mortal human being—this is enough, and this is everything. Only a man who had come close to dying himself and who had despaired of his efforts to transform the human world could have written a passage like this, in awed celebration of the wonders of the existential world:

> The man who had died looked nakedly onto life, and saw a vast resoluteness everywhere flinging itself up in stormy or subtle wave-crests, foam-tips emerging out of the blue invisible, a black-and-orange cock, or the green flame tongues out of the extremes of the fig-tree. They came forth, these things and creatures of spring, glowing with desire and with assertion. . . . The man who had died looked on the great swing into existence of things that had not died, but he saw no longer their tremulous desire to exist and to be. He heard instead their ringing, defiant challenge to all other things existing. . . . And always, the man who had died saw not the bird alone, but the short, sharp wave of life of which the bird was the crest. He watched the queer, beaky motion of the creature. . . .
> And the destiny of life seemed more fierce and compulsive to him even than the destiny to death.

The man who had died asks himself this final question: *From what, and to what, could this infinite whirl be saved?*

The mystic certitude of *The Escaped Cock*, like the serenity of "The Ship of Death" and "Bavarian Gentians," belongs to a consciousness that has transcended the dualism of tragedy. The split has not been healed, it has simply been transcended; nearing death, Lawrence turns instinctively to the allegorical mode, the most primitive and the most sophisticated of all visionary expressions. *Women in Love* is, by contrast, irresolute and contradictory; it offers only the finite, tentative "resurrection" of marriage between two very incomplete people. Like Connie Chatterley and her lover Mellors, the surviving couple of *Women in Love* must fashion their lives in a distinctly unmythic, unidyllic landscape, their fates to be bound up closely with that of their civilization. How are we to escape history?—defy the death-process of our culture? With difficulty. In sorrow. So long as we live, even strengthened as we are by the "mystic conjunction," the "ultimate unison" between men and women, our lives are tempered by the ungovernable contingencies of the world that is no metaphor, but our only home.

Notes

1. All quotations from *Women in Love* are taken from the Modern Library edition.
2. *Collected Letters*, ed. Harry T. Moore (New York, 1962), pp. 482 and 519.
3. As Lawrence says in an essay about the writer's relationship to his own work: "Morality in the novel is the trembling instability of the balance. When the novelist puts his thumb on the scale, to pull down the balance to his own predilection, that is immorality. . . . And of all the art forms, the novel most of all demands the trembling and oscillating of the balance," *Phoenix: The Posthumous Papers of D. H. Lawrence* (London, 1936), p. 529.
4. Richard Somers is fascinated and disturbed by Australia, into which he has projected the struggle of his own soul. The bush has frightened him with its emptiness and stillness; he cannot penetrate its secret. At one point it seems to him that a presence of some sort lurks in the wilderness, an actual spirit of the place that terrifies him. As for the social and political conditions of Australia—what is more hopelessly uninteresting than accomplished liberty? (See *Kangaroo*, London, 1968, p. 33.)
5. That Lawrence might have dealt with the tragic implications of the individual's failure to find a home for himself in his own nation is indicated by remarks he makes elsewhere, for instance in the introductory essay, "The Spirit of Place," to *Studies in Classic American Literature*: "Men are free when they are in a living homeland, not when they are straying and breaking away. Men are free when they are obeying some deep, inward voice of religious belief. Obeying from within. Men are free when they belong to a living, organic, *believing* community, active in fulfilling some unfulfilled, perhaps unrealized purpose." The *Studies* were written between 1917 and 1923.
6. The Prologue is available in *Phoenix II* (New York, 1968) and in a recently published anthology, *The Other Persuasion*, ed. Seymour Kleinberg (New York, 1977).
7. It is interesting to note Lawrence's intense dislike of the very idea of homosexuality in women. Miss Inger of *The Rainbow* is revealed as a poisonous, corrupt woman who makes an ideal mate for Ursula's cynical uncle Tom Brangwen. Ursula had loved them both but when she realizes that they are in the "service of the machine," she is repulsed by them. "Their marshy, bitter sweet corruption came sick and unwholesome in her nostrils. . . . She would leave them both forever, leave forever their strange, soft, half-corrupt element" (*The Rainbow*, London, 1971, p. 351). In *Lady Chatterley's Lover* Mellors begins to rant about women he has known who have disappointed him sexually, and the quality of his rage—which must be, in part, Lawrence's—is rather alarming. He goes through a brief catalogue of unacceptable women, then says, "It's astonishing how Lesbian women are, consciously or unconsciously. Seems to me they're nearly all Lesbian." In the presence of such a woman, Mellors tells Connie, he fairly howls in his soul, "wanting to kill her" (*Lady Chatterley's Lover*, New York, 1962, p. 190).
8. *Phoenix*, pp. 293–94.
9. Gudrun is an artist of considerable talent herself, one who works in miniatures, as if wishing to see the world "through the wrong end of the opera glasses." It is significant that she expresses a passionate wish to have been born a man, and that she feels an unaccountable lust for deep brutality against Gerald, whom in another sense she loves. Far more interesting a character than her sister Ursula, Gudrun is fatally locked into her own willful instinct for making herself the measure of all things: her vision is anthropomorphic and solipsistic, finally inhuman. We know from certain of Lawrence's poems, particularly "New Heaven and Earth," that the "maniacal horror" of such solipsism was his own. He seems to have been driven nearly to suicide, or to a nervous breakdown, by the terrifying conviction that nothing existed beyond his own consciousness. Unlike Lawrence, who sickened of being the measure of all things, Gudrun rejoices in her cruel talent for reducing everyone and everything—robins as well as people—to size. Her love affair with Gerald is really a contest of wills; in her soul she is a man, a rival. Like one of the seductive chimeras or vampires in decadent art—in the paintings of Munch and in the writings of Strindberg—Gudrun sees her lover as an "unutterable enemy," whom she wishes to kiss and stroke and embrace until she has him "all in her hands, till she [has] strained him into her knowledge. Ah, if she could have precious *knowledge* of him, she would be filled . . ." (379). At the novel's end she has become so dissociated from her own feelings and so nauseated by life that she seems to be on the brink of insanity. It strikes her that she has never really lived, only worked, she is in fact a kind of clock, her face is like clock's face, a twelve-hour clock dial—an image that fills her with terror, yet pleases her strangely.

DAVID LODGE
"Comedy of Eros"

New Republic, December 10, 1984, pp. 96–100

The latest title in Cambridge University Press's ambitious scholarly edition of D. H. Lawrence's works is of exceptional interest, for what it gives us is not merely a more comprehensive view, through the recording of textual variants, of a familiar book, but virtually a new book, by one of the greatest writers of the twentieth century.

Mr Noon runs to nearly three hundred pages. The first third, Part I of the present volume, has been published before, as an "unfinished novel," in the posthumous collections *A Modern Lover* (1934) and *Phoenix II* (1968), but the longer (and more interesting) Part II was effectively lost for fifty years after Lawrence's death, and is published here for the first time. It is still an incomplete work (Lawrence envisaged a third part), and it is undoubtedly a flawed and broken-backed one—which was no doubt why he abandoned it. But it is nevertheless full of splendid scenes and passages which only Lawrence could have written. It is also of considerable biographical interest, since the second part is transparently based on Lawrence's elopement with Frieda Weekley in 1912, and its immediate sequel.

Lawrence began writing *Mr Noon* in November 1920, partly out of frustration with the slow progress of *Aaron's Rod*. "I can't end it . . . so I began a comedy, which I hope will end," he wrote to a correspondent at the time. Now, although there are certainly flashes of humor, especially of a sarcastic kind, in Lawrence's writing, comedy is not on the whole his forte, and it is hard to think of any major work by him that could be described generically as "comic." The first part of *Mr Noon* is not entirely successful in this respect, and the second part works better by trying less desperately to be funny. This entailed a considerable adjustment not only of tone, but of the character of the eponymous hero and the direction of his fortunes.

The Gilbert Noon of Part I, evidently based on a Nottinghamshire friend of Lawrence's, George Henry Neville, is a schoolteacher who gets into a compromising entanglement with another young schoolteacher, Emmie, through going too far in the ritual of "spooning." Spooning is to the youthful inhabitants of Woodhouse (a thinly disguised version of Lawrence's native Eastwood) what petting was (and perhaps still is) to the teenagers of small-town America: an almost institutionalized form of sexual play, ostensibly frowned upon but in practice tolerated, through which some relief is offered to adolescent eroticism without fundamentally threatening the mores of a puritanical and conservative society.

In Woodhouse the ritual has a special piquancy in being performed on Sunday evenings, when the young men loiter outside church and chapel to pick up their girlfriends as they emerge from evening service. Gilbert makes such a rendezvous with Emmie in the second chapter of the novel, entitled "Spoon," and before long is kissing and cuddling her in a corner of a passageway in the local Co-op Stores, conscious of several other couples sighing and rustling in the dark around him. Lawrence's evocation of these fragile moments of bliss, snatched from the cold rainy night and the encroaching threat of the working week, is vivid, but curiously equivocal in tone, at times mocking the lovers, at other times the reader: "Ah, dear reader, I hope you are not feeling horribly superior . . . you have never so much as seen a Co-op entry. But don't on that account sniff at Emmie."

Emmie is certainly well satisfied with Gilbert's spooning technique ("With his mouth he softly moved back the hair from her brow, in slow, dreamy movements, most faintly touching her forehead with the red of his lips . . ."), but Gilbert wants to go further. After escorting her home, he makes a clumsy attempt to possess her in a greenhouse. Interrupted *in flagrante delicto* by Emmie's suspicious father, Gilbert runs off into the night, furious and humiliated. Emmie also flees from her outraged parent, going to stay with her married brother, and taking to her bed with "neuralgia of the stomach"—or is it pregnancy? That possibility haunts Gilbert, for he would then be under pressure to do the decent thing by Emmie, and far from wanting to marry and settle down in the English Midlands he is now consumed by the desire to escape from this constricting milieu. When the local Education Committee starts an investigation into a complaint brought by Emmie's father, Gilbert impetuously resigns his post and visits Emmie to ascertain whether he can honorably leave her and go abroad to study. He is disconcerted to find a young man called Walter George paying court to Emmie.

> Emmie, we had forgotten to say, was engaged to Walter George all the time she was carrying on with Mr Noon. The fact so easily slipped her memory that it slipped ours.

Lawrence employs in *Mr Noon* an intrusive authorial voice reminiscent of nineteenth-century novelists like Thackeray, Dickens, and Trollope, frequently apostrophizing the "gentle reader," and sometimes breaking the frame of realistic illusion by drawing attention to the fictionality of his own text. I cannot recall his doing this anywhere else, and no doubt it developed from his professed aim of writing a comedy. The result, however, is often a tone of rather strained jocularity. After bringing Gilbert, Emmie, and Walter George together in a mutually embarrassing silence, he prays aloud for inspiration to continue the story:

> Oh Deus ex machina, get up steam and come to our assistance, for this obtuse-angled triangle looks as if it would sit there stupidly forever in the spare bedroom at Eakrast. Which would be a serious misfortune for us, who have to make our bread and butter chronicling the happy marriage and prize-taking cauliflowers of Emmie and Walter George, and the further lapses of Mr Noon.

But the deus ex machina does not materialize, and Lawrence winds up Part I abruptly. Emmie is married off to Walter George and drops out of the story. Another casualty is a character called Patty Goddard, a married but unfulfilled woman friend of Gilbert's, a "soft, full, strange, unmated Aphrodite of 40," who was evidently destined in the original conception of the novel to afford Gilbert a more satisfying sexual relationship than spooning with Emmie. Patty's role is taken over, in Part II, by Johanna Keighley, the German wife of

an English doctor working in America, and a very recognizable portrait of Frieda Lawrence. She breezes into Gilbert's life one night when he is looking after the Munich flat of his German professor (her brother-in-law), dazzles him with her ripe beauty, excites him with bold conversation about sex and love, and concludes their encounter by inviting him to her bed. It is a brilliantly written and totally convincing scene.

As Martin Green showed in his study of Frieda's intellectual milieu, *The Von Richthofen Sisters*, she and her friends were deeply influenced by the psychiatrist and one-time disciple of Freud, Otto Gross, who preached a gospel of sexual freedom. Frieda put it into practice by running away with Lawrence, and one of the most fascinating aspects of *Mr Noon* is the insight it gives us into the joys, discomforts, and stresses of that time for the two lovers: the hysterical telegrams from the outraged husband, the pressures brought to bear by the errant wife's highly respectable German relations, and the ups and downs of liberated sex—all described against the background of a Germany ominously full of marching soldiers, and a Tyrolean landscape dotted with accusing images of the crucified Christ.

It is curious how many important literary careers were founded on elopements—the Brownings, Marian Evans and George Lewes, James Joyce and Nora Barnacle come immediately to mind—but Lawrence and Frieda's was perhaps the most sensationally dramatic of all. The last section of *Mr Noon* describes a walk across the Alps from Bavaria into Italy that was actually undertaken by Lawrence and Frieda, and of which we have other accounts in his letters and essays. It has no practical point or cause. It is a symbolic journey, a rite of passage, confirming the lovers' break with their respective pasts, with the conventions and values of bourgeois society. The joys of love and companionship are expressed through their enthusiastic response to the beauty of the alpine landscape and its vegetation, but this is no sentimental idyll. Gilbert and Johanna fight and quarrel as well as make love; sleeping in a hay hut turns out to be an itchy and uncomfortable experience; and the horrors of privies in cheap lodging houses are not flinched from. Most startling of all these deviations from romantic cliché is Johanna's casual infidelity with a young American called Stanley, who, with his friend Terry, accompanies the lovers for part of their honeymoon hike.

As we know from other sources (notably David Garnett, the "Terry" of the story), this incident actually happened, the character of Stanley being based on Harold Hobson. Whether it was revealed and responded to as described in *Mr Noon*, we shall never know, but the account carries conviction. Gilbert, though deeply disturbed by Johanna's abrupt confession, rises to the challenge and magnanimously forgives her, but she resents his forgiveness.

> And half she felt enmeshed, even a little fascinated by his clear, strange, beautiful look of innocent exaltation. And half she hated him for it. It seemed so false and unmanly. Hateful unmanly unsubstantial look of beauty!
>
> "Well," she said. "It wasn't much, anyhow. It meant nothing to me. I believe he was impotent."
>
> Gilbert looked at her. This brought him to earth a little.

As Lindeth Vasey observes in her introduction, *Mr Noon* seems out of phase with the evolution of Lawrence's thought about relations between the sexes, which in the early '20s was turning away from the polarity-and-equilibrium concept of *Women in Love* toward the idea of charismatic leadership and the subordination of woman to man expounded in novels like *Kangaroo* and *The Plumed Serpent*. "Part II of *Mr Noon* thus appears as an elegiac backward glance to Lawrence's old belief in the primacy of the loving relationship between man and woman," she says, suggesting that this is why Lawrence abandoned the novel. But in another way *Mr Noon* looks forward to the more "tender" celebration of sexuality in *Lady Chatterley's Lover*. There is the same emphasis on marriage rather than promiscuity being the royal road to a sexual fulfillment seen ultimately as a religious mystery:

> The deep accustomedness of marriage is the only way of preparation. Only those who know each other in the intricate dark ways of physical custom can pass through the seven dark hells and the seven bright heavens of sensual fulfillment.

The seventh sexual act between Connie Chatterley and Mellors is, notoriously, anal, a form of intercourse to which, for reasons too complex to rehearse here, Lawrence attached a special significance; and there is an interesting hint at the same idea in the closing pages of *Mr Noon*, when "in the night one night he touched Johanna as she lay asleep with her back to him, touching him, and something broke alive in his soul that had been dead before."

Where *Mr Noon* scores over *Lady Chatterley's Lover* is precisely in the element of comedy which is so conspicuously lacking from the later novel. In Part I of *Mr Noon*, Lawrence strains too obviously for humor, but in Part II he uses it more subtly to temper and vary the rhapsodic and prophetic treatment of sexuality. There is, for example, a scene early in the relationship between Johanna and Gilbert, when they are surprised in bed together in the middle of the morning by an importunate caller, that is both funny and erotic—a rare combination in Lawrence. Feminists, too, will find *Mr Noon* more to their taste than *Lady Chatterley*, since Johanna is very much the sexual tutor of Gilbert, a virile but clumsy lover. Indeed, nowhere else in Lawrence's fiction is the allure of an unashamedly sexual woman so powerfully communicated; for example,

> Johanna was hovering in the doorway of her room as he went down the passage. A bright, roused look was on her face. She lifted her eyelids with a strange flare of invitation, like a bird lifting its wings.

Taken as a whole, *Mr Noon* is certainly no masterpiece, but it crackles with energy. It is a reckless, risky book that makes much of our own contemporary fiction seem over-anxious to please and impress. Its belated appearance is cause for gratitude and celebration.

T. E. LAWRENCE

1888–1935

Born on August 16, 1888, in Tremadoc, North Wales, Thomas Edward Lawrence was the second of five illegitimate sons; his parents lived together as man and wife, but Lawrence discovered the truth of their relationship—that his father had abandoned an earlier marriage—as a child. In 1896 the family settled in Oxford, where Lawrence attended the City of Oxford High School and Jesus College. He early developed a strong interest in medieval castles, which he studied on bicycle tours of England and France; in 1909 he made a walking tour in the Middle East in quest of Crusader ruins. After graduating from Oxford in 1910 he took part in archaeological excavations at Carchemish in Syria, where he soon became known for his understanding of the Arab workers, and for his use of their language and dress.

At the outbreak of World War I Lawrence joined Military Intelligence and was based for two years in Cairo. Having promoted the idea of using an Arab revolt against the Turks to further the British campaign, he joined Emir Feisal's forces in October 1916. Though officially a liaison officer between Feisal and the Allied command, he played a prominent role in the desert war, leading many guerrilla operations in the push from Mecca to Damascus. His rather romantic ideas were disturbed by what he saw and experienced of the realities of the war, and by his own part in its cruelties; in addition, at the end of the war he felt that the Arabs had been betrayed in their fight for independence by the colonial interests of Britain and France. As adviser to Feisal at the Paris Peace Conference in 1919, and adviser to Winston Churchill in the War Office in 1921 and 1922, he was able to press the cause for Arab hegemony in Iraq and Trans-Jordan.

By this time "Lawrence of Arabia" was already a legendary figure, and in an attempt to make clear (above all, to himself) the part he had played, Lawrence wrote his *Seven Pillars of Wisdom*, published in a limited edition in 1926. Seeking anonymity and peace of mind, he joined the Royal Air Force as John Hume Ross in 1922, and after being discovered and discharged he enlisted in the Royal Tank Corps under the name T. E. Shaw, transferring back to the Air Force in 1925. His years in the ranks are the basis of *The Mint* (1936). He also translated Homer's *Odyssey* for an edition published in 1934.

Lawrence retired from the Air Force in 1935. Three months later he was fatally injured in a motorcycle accident, dying on May 19, 1935.

One day not long after Allenby had captured Jerusalem, I happened to be in front of a bazaar stall on Christian Street, remonstrating with a fat old Turkish shopkeeper who was attempting to relieve me of twenty piasters for a handful of dates. My attention was suddenly drawn to a group of Arabs walking in the direction of the Damascus Gate. The fact that they were Arabs was not what caused me to drop my tirade against the high cost of dates, for Palestine, as all men know, is inhabited by a far greater number of Arabs than Jews. My curiosity was excited by a single Bedouin, who stood out in sharp relief from all his companions. He was wearing an agal, kuffieh, and aba such as are worn only by Near Eastern potentates. In his belt was fastened the short curved sword of a prince of Mecca, insignia worn by descendants of the Prophet.

Christian Street is one of the most picturesque and kaleidoscopic thoroughfares in the Near East. Russian Jews, with their corkscrew curls, Greek priests in tall black hats and flowing robes, fierce desert nomads in goatskin coats reminiscent of the days of Abraham, Turks in balloon-like trousers, Arab merchants lending a brilliant note with their gay turbans and gowns—all rub elbows in that narrow lane of bazaars, shops, and coffee-houses that leads to the Church of the Holy Sepulcher. Jerusalem is not a melting-pot. It is an uncompromising meeting-place of East and West. Here are accentuated, as if sharply outlined in black and white by the desert sun, the racial peculiarities of Christian, Jewish, and Mohammedan peoples. A stranger must, indeed, have something extraordinary about him to attract attention in the streets of the Holy City. But as this young Bedouin passed by in his magnificent royal robes, the crowds in front of the bazaars turned to look at him.

It was not merely his costume, nor yet the dignity with which he carried his five feet three, marking him every inch a king or perhaps a caliph in disguise who had stepped out of the pages of *The Arabian Nights*. The striking fact was that this mysterious prince of Mecca looked no more like a son of Ishmael than an Abyssinian looks like one of Stefansson's red-haired Eskimos. Bedouins, although of the Caucasian race, have had their skins scorched by the relentless desert sun until their complexions are the color of lava. But this young man was as blond as a Scandinavian, in whose veins flow viking blood and the cool traditions of fiords and sagas. The nomadic sons of Ishmael all wear flowing beards, as their ancestors did in the time of Esau. This youth, with the curved gold sword, was clean-shaven. He walked rapidly with his hands folded, his blue eyes oblivious to his surroundings, and he seemed wrapped in some inner contemplation. My first thought as I glanced at his face was that he might be one of the younger apostles returned to life. His expression was serene, almost saintly, in its selflessness and repose.

"Who is he?" I turned eagerly to the Turk profiteer, who could only manipulate a little tourist English. He merely shrugged his shoulders.

"Who could he be?" I was certain I could obtain some information about him from General Storrs, governor of the Holy City, and so I strolled over in the direction of his palace beyond the old wall, near Solomon's Quarries. General Ronald Storrs, British successor to Pontius Pilate, had been Oriental secretary to the high commissioner of Egypt before the fall of Jerusalem and for years had kept in intimate touch with the peoples of Palestine. He spoke Hebrew, Greek, Latin, and Arabic with the same fluency with which he spoke English. I knew he could tell me something about the mysterious blond Bedouin.

"Who is this blue-eyed, fair-haired fellow wandering about the bazaars wearing the curved sword of a prince of——?"

The general did not even let me finish the question but quietly opened the door of an adjoining room. There, seated at the same table where von Falkenhayn had worked out his unsuccessful plan for defeating Allenby, was the Bedouin prince, deeply absorbed in a ponderous tome on archæology.

In introducing us the governor said, "I want you to meet Colonel Lawrence, the Uncrowned King of Arabia."

He shook hands shyly and with a certain air of aloofness, as if his mind were on buried treasure and not on the affairs of this immediate world of campaigns and warfare. And that was how I first made the acquaintance of one of the most picturesque personalities of modern times, a man who will be blazoned on the romantic pages of history with Raleigh, Drake, Clive, and Gordon. . . .

The spectacular achievements of Thomas Edward Lawrence, the young Oxford graduate, were unknown to the public at the end of the World War. Yet, quietly, without any theatrical head-lines or fanfare of trumpets, he brought the disunited nomadic tribes of Holy and Forbidden Arabia into a unified campaign against their Turkish oppressors, a difficult and splendid stroke of policy, which caliphs, statesmen, and sultans had been unable to accomplish in centuries of effort! Lawrence placed himself at the head of the Bedouin army of the shereef of Mecca, who was afterward proclaimed king of the Hedjaz. He united the wandering tribes of the desert, restored the sacred places of Islam to the descendants of the Prophet, and drove the Turks from Arabia forever. Allenby liberated Palestine, the Holy Land of the Jews and Christians. Lawrence freed Arabia, the Holy Land of millions of Mohammedans.—LOWELL THOMAS, "A Modern Arabian Knight," *With Lawrence in Arabia*, 1925, pp. 3–10

This abridgment ⟨*Revolt in the Desert*⟩ of the famous *Seven Pillars* (itself an abridgment) contains as much of the immense original as anyone but an Imam has time to read. . . . The book does not, like the original, leave you with a sense of having spent many toilsome and fateful years in the desert struggling with Nature in her most unearthly moods, tormented by insomnia of the conscience: indeed it is positively breezy; but that will not be a drawback to people who, having no turn for "salutary self-torture," prefer a book that can be read in a week to one that makes a considerable inroad on a lifetime.

Among the uncommon objects of the worldside, the most uncommon include persons who have reached the human limit of literary genius, and young men who have packed into the forepart of their lives an adventure of epic bulk and intensity. The odds against the occurrence of either must be much more than a million to one. But what figure can estimate the rarity of the person who combines the two? Yet the combination occurs. . . . ⟨W⟩e have "Colonel Lawrence" (the inverted commas are his own) appearing first in the war news from Arabia as a personage rather more incredible than Prester John, and presently emerging into clear definition as the author of one of the great histories of the world, recording his own conquests at an age at which young company officers are hardly allowed to speak at the mess table.

The fate of the man who has shot his bolt before he is thirty, and has no more worlds to conquer, may be compared curiously with that of the genius who dies unwept, unhonored, and unsung, and is dug up and immortalized a century later. Nobody will ever be able to decide which is the more enviable. But it is mitigated if the hero has literary faculty as a second string to his bow; and Colonel Lawrence has this with a vengeance.

. . . The subjective side which gives Miltonic gloom and grandeur to certain chapters of *The Seven Pillars*, and of the seventy and seven pillars out of which they were hewn, plays no great part in this abridgment: Lawrence's troublesome conscience and agonizing soul give place here to his impish humor and his scandalous audacities; but it will interest the latest French school of drama to know that their effect remains, and imparts an otherwise unattainable quality to the work, even though they are not expressed.

The political side of the revolt, important and extraordinary as it is, need not be dwelt on here: it is now public property; and the value of the national service rendered by its author is patent to everybody, except, apparently, those whose function it is to give official recognition to such services. It is characteristic of the author and hero of this book that he has provided most effectively against the possibility of his ever making a farthing by it; and it is equally characteristic of the powers that be, to assume that he is amply provided for by it. He is left in his usual ultra-scrupulous attitude; but the nation can hardly claim to have left itself in a generous one. For it is England's way to learn young men not to know better than their elders. Nothing could have been more irregular than the methods by which Lawrence disabled Turkey in the Great War by hurling an Arab revolt on her rear; and to encourage and reward irregularity would be to set a bad example to the young.—GEORGE BERNARD SHAW, "The Latest from Colonel Lawrence," *Spec*, March 1927, p. 429

And now I want to draw your attention to another figure whose life's work was done in Palestine, and which like the work of Jesus reached its climax and its most creative stage during a period of some three years, the man whom all the world knows as Lawrence of Arabia, the greatest genius who ever sojourned for a time within the walls of this College, and probably the greatest who ever will sojourn here.

It is not for me to tell of his exploits, they are too well-known for that to be necessary. No did his genius appear so much in what he did as in how he did it. He made history; he changed the face of the Near East. I do not wish to suggest that he was a second Jesus, or that he was as great as Jesus, but his life, if not consciously modelled on that life, has many striking parrals, and what is more important, has many lessons for us.

. . . ⟨F⟩rom early days he became absorbed in the study of the past. The classics, archaeology, campaigns, old MSS., music, were to him meat and drink, not with a view only to his class in the Schools, but with a view to the understanding of life and obtaining complete harmony with it. From men too, men of all classes, he learnt the art of living. He says himself in his instructions to young officers, 'The beginning and the end of the secret of handling the Arabs is unremitting study of them.' It was his familiarity with their past history, with their present circumstances, and with their future hopes, his making of himself a complete Arab, which placed him in a position of such complete confidence in relation to them as no other Englishman . . . has ever enjoyed. He became the uncrowned King of Arabia: certainly at the end of the War there were no honours or prizes of war which could not have been his, but he refused them all. He despised the pomps and vanities of this world. He asked nothing for himself.

Like our Lord also his mind dwelt on the future as well as on the past and present. The whole time that he was leading his Arabs he was not thinking only of the immediate issues of the War, and the particular sector of the world battle-line on which he was fighting. He was thinking of and planning for the future of that great Arab people who in the world not only of politics but also of science, literature, art and religion have in the past played such an important part in the evolution of culture. It was, I suppose, disappointment at the result of the final

settlement after the War, and especially what he considered to be the treachery of the Allied Governments towards the Arabs, which made him retire from public life and seek refreshment in commonplace things.

This he did, as you all know, by enlisting, first in the Army, and then in the Air Force. This was an act, perhaps of self-discipline, certainly of an English gentleman. The man who, as I have said, could have had any honours and practically any position which he desired in the Army, in Government, or at the Universities, chose to become a private in the British Army. It was an act of self-abnegation, it was not cowardice, refusal to face up to the struggle. There in that work he found as much adventure, as much creative opportunity, as he had found in the desert. To be able to do that is true greatness.

. . . Like Paul, Lawrence was capable of becoming all things to all men. To the Arab he became an Arab, to the Private a Private, to men a man. His belief was that a man should become one with other men, but one better than they, better by merit, not by holding vantage positions over them. . . . He scorned competition of any kind excepting competition in well doing: throughout his career he strove only to reach a standard raised in his own mind, not to outreach other men.

Of his courage, enterprise, scholarship, and, according to those who knew him, his personal charm, I will not speak; I will just leave those few thoughts with you. In shaping life draw your inspiration from the past, but live adventurously and courageously in the present. No man did this more than Lawrence; he was no mere antiquarian, nor was he an idle dreamer. Seek first the Kingdom of God and His righteousness. 'Have this mind in you which was also in Christ Jesus: who, being in the form of God . . . humbled Himself, becoming obedient unto death.'—REV. L. B. CROSS, "Lawrence of Arabia," *MCh*, July 1935, pp. 236–42

In recent weeks a startling biographical controversy has been raised among publishing circles in New York and London. A British author, Richard Aldington, has pronounced publicly that the saga of T. E. Lawrence is a myth. Although Aldington's views are to be incorporated in a book, he cites as pre-publication evidence several physical inconsistencies, and numerous military and diplomatic discrepancies in Lawrence's own autobiography. Lawrence, Aldington insists, could not possibly have accomplished all that he claimed; the Lawrence legend was a deliberate fabrication of its principal. Rushing to the defense of Lawrence's reputation, a group of friends and admirers of the late Oxford classicist has contended that the weight of personal observation ought properly to be given precedence over documents and statistics. The final denouement of the palpably iconoclastic affair will not be known until Aldington's evidence is published and weighed against earlier testimony.

But if it is not yet possible to evaluate the personal exploits of T. E. Lawrence, the time clearly has arrived for an evaluation of the world T. E. Lawrence described. His luster, after all, derives not merely from victories to which he ostensibly led the Arabs, but also from the nobility with which he invested the Arab world. He himself wrote in his introduction to the *Seven Pillars of Wisdom:*

> It is intended to rationalize the campaign, that everyone may see how natural the success was and how inevitable, how little dependent on direction or brain, how much less on the outside assistance of the few British. It was an Arab war waged and led by Arabs for an Arab aim in Arabia.

"I meant to make a new nation," Lawrence wrote in the same account, "to restore a lost influence, to give twenty millions of Semites the foundation on which to build an inspired dream-palace of their national thoughts. So high an aim called out the inherent nobility of their minds, and made them play a generous part in events." Yet it is the irony of Lawrence's descriptive power that, although he portrays Feisal as the glittering reincarnation of Saladin, the Arab forays recalled by his talented pen are a chaos of cross-purposes and looting-parties. . . .

The image—the Lawrence-created image—of the forsaken Bedouin persisted beyond Paris to San Remo, where the claims of Feisal and his brothers were blandly ignored. The old unworkable promise of an immense Arab empire was abandoned for a series of mandates. The sons of the Sherif Hussein watched helplessly as the French railways bisected Arab Syria, and the Indian Government glutted Iraq with insufferably patronising civil servants (although Lawrence associated the perfidy with France, and ascribed genuinely tutorial motives to his own country). The photographs of Lawrence in this period reveal a little man, draped in the traditional Arab *kafiyah*, standing perplexed and shamefaced amidst a cluster of hearty, grinning colonial officials. For the better part of a decade, the spell of Lawrence's personality and prose sustained the classic portrait of the keen-visaged son of the desert, fighting a grim and lonely battle against Western politicians.

It is not without significance that the rise of Fascism on the one hand, and Zionism on the other, should have produced a subtle metamorphosis in the sponsorship of the Arab legend. By 1935 Lawrence himself had passed from the scene, the victim of a fatal motorcycle accident. It was not longer possible to continue to suffuse the Arab and his aspirations with grandeur and romance. . . .

The post-war era . . . has become the period for a re-evaluation of T. E. Lawrence's world. The year 1951, which witnessed the publication of David Garnett's warm testimonial, *The Essential T. E. Lawrence*, was the same year in which a skilled and hardened reporter, John Roy Carlson, was impelled to write a terrifying exposé of the Arab world—a volume entitled *From Cairo to Damascus*. It was the end and beginning of a legend. . . .

The difference was more than that of individuals. The stereotype has changed because the Near Eastern world has been found out. It is difficult to discover, in the accounts of such contemporary reporters as Carlson, even the vestige of that undulating grandeur, that austere dignity, that single-minded courage that glowed from the Arab image created by Lawrence. Carlson, Lengyel, Reynolds, and other recent observers are preoccupied with the filth of the Arab village, the scurviness of the Arab soldier, the bombast of the Arab officers, their raving addiction to Nazi slogans, the black medievalism of the effendi class. Their descriptions blot out the serene *Arabia Deserta* that elevated the classic rhythms of T. E. Lawrence, Gertrude Bell, and Ronald Storrs. The world they describe is dominated by a Holy Alliance called the Arab League; it is a landlord-ruled world of bilharziasis and trachoma, and it encompasses a *fellahin* population eighty-five percent of whom suffer from chronic malnutrition and venereal disease. The world is savagely exploited by Communist and Fundamentalist propagandists, maneuvered for dynastic purposes by calculating Hashemites. There is genuine liberalism in the Arab rectangle, too, a deep-rooted hunger for freedom and independence nursed tenaciously and heroically by students and teachers. But the progression toward freedom is but one slender strand in a larger tapestry of corruption and reaction; it is not the brilliant magic carpet on which T. E. Lawrence rode into battle. It is likely that the luminous Arab World of the *Seven Pillars of Wisdom* existed only for Lawrence and others who wished that it were so. The legend of Thomas Edward Lawrence may survive the scrutiny of historians. But it is not likely that the stylized world he described will linger much longer to bewitch the Western imagination.—HOWARD M. SACHAR, "The Declining World of T. E. Lawrence," *NR*, May 10, 1954, pp. 18–19

. . . The precocity of his childhood was followed by an arrested psychological development, leaving him with certain perpetually adolescent traits. He carried through life the self-consciousness which is characteristic of so many Englishmen, above all at the adolescent stage when in that environment nature and nurture are at cross-purposes. Some say he could not look another man in the eyes, and that his own eyes were in constant furtive movement. He had a low apologetic voice, a silly giggle, a schoolboy grin, a habit of playing stupid practical jokes, and above all a perpetual "kidding" so that "I could hardly tell my own self where the leg-pulling began or ended." . . .

The question is—how much of this ⟨Lawrence's statements about himself⟩ was genuine, how much pose? And do not start away from the world "pose" as unfair, a pre-judgment, an attributing of motive. It is Lawrence's own word for himself. Among the many, many things this self-absorbed man said about himself at various times, he wrote from Arabia towards the end of the war (July 1918) that the war-time things he had been doing "in fancy dress" were all "part of the pose"; adding, "how to reconcile it with the Oxford pose I know not." If words mean anything those words mean that he admitted two of the most important periods of his life—Oxford and the War—were play-acting, a pose. From this we may infer that he had little real and lasting conviction in either phase, whether intellectualist or military, he had no real centre to his being. Can a man be part adolescent and part adult? For, behind that mask, real or assumed, was a watchful and clever adventurer waiting always for the moment when he could assert his superior will, an almost fanatical will which had no other purpose than its self-assertion, and therefore took for granted that the moment of success was also the moment of feeling "absolutely bored." . . .

Lawrence had considerable gifts as a rhetorical and propagandist writer, though he lacked spontaneity and naturalness and the "tact of omission." He was a persuasive and plausible advocate with a decided taste and ability for descriptive writing. He was not naturally an observer, but could force himself to note and to remember when he felt that it was called for, and must have kept elaborate notes during 1917–18. (His private 1911 diary of his walk is one of the most jejune travel productions ever printed.) It is Lawrence's perpetual conscious effort to write up to this artificial level which puts a strain on the admiration of his readers. At the same time Lawrence was clever enough to see that his contemporaries were mostly in reaction against his models and striving for what is loosely called "realism." And so in a work which is almost all murex-tinted, we come upon anti-purple patches of horror or nastiness or brutality or sadism. Let me repeat that Lawrence said himself he only wrote well when he was excited, and that it was exactly such repulsive things which excited him, for though they are far from being the only well-written passages in his long book, they are the best in point of view of vividness and gusto. . . .

Guilt—that gives us the clue ⟨to Lawrence's neuroses⟩. Let us look back upon what we have learned by this long enquiry about him and his circumstances. He was, and knew that he was from an indeterminate but certainly early date, the child of an irregular union between an Anglo-Irish aristocrat and a girl of humble birth. Although there was the painful but far from uncommon circumstance of a former wife and children, this union—though unblessed by Church or State—was in all essentials a life-long marriage, fruitful in five gifted sons. Unluckily, the social and religious views of the protagonists, the prejudices of the age, and the alarmed interests of distinguished relatives, all combined to insist imperatively on the necessity for keeping the real relationship secret. Thus Lawrence grew up to bear the intolerable burden for a sensitive youth of a Guilty Secret, made no easier to bear from the fact that it had to be borne in Oxford, the heart of censorious academic and clerical respectability. Hence the solitude, the lack of society, the absence of girls in his youth. The impact on a gifted, hypersusceptible, extremely vain youth of learning that Guilty Secret must indeed have been shattering and heartbreaking.

. . . ⟨T⟩he whole situation becomes clear if we remember Lawrence's assertion that home life for him was intolerable, and realise the ferocity with which he blamed his parents for having children at all in their situation. Hence, in later life, the bitter antagonism to women as a sex, leading to a puritanical horror of normal sexual intercourse.

This impulse of refusal, of rejection, of wilful courting of plebeian degradation was linked with an irresistible and apparently contrary impulse to over-value himself and all he did and to persuade or to compel others to accept him at his own over-valuation. It is said—but I give this merely as common room gossip—that in the post-war days at Oxford, Lawrence made no attempt to maintain the Secret with his inmost group of friends, that indeed he would boast of it, saying he was born on Napoleon's birthday and that illegitimate children were often exceptionally gifted. Be that as it may, there can be no doubt that from his schoolboy days he practised—apparently with complete success—this compensatory telling of stories about himself, always in his own favour, and always to a greater or less degree an improvement of the reality, if they were not wholly invented. Lawrence was not singular in this, except that he did it so persistently, so cunningly and so successfully. . . .

It has been said that Lawrence had "no real self," that he was merely an actor who played many parts. But there was "a real self," which is fairly plainly shown both in *Seven Pillars* and in the letters to Lionel Curtis and Charlotte Shaw—an unhappy, wistful, tortured, hag-ridden self, floundering between heights and depths, aspiring to the rôle of a knight of the Round Table and tumbling with Hibernian awkwardness into grotesque and even terrible accidents and misfortunes—who can think of that flogging at Deraa without a shudder of pity for the victim? Yet he had the courage, the skill—the cunning, if you like—and the force of will and character to impose on the world his over-valued persona as reality, and to receive worldwide acclaim—for what? for the clever patter and pictures of a glib showman untroubled by the majesty of truth. And having triumph in his grasp he throws it all away, to escape the mother who now turned instinctively to the brilliant son for comfort. Let him be, as he dreamed, exalted like another Joseph to be ruler of Egypt, she could still follow and madden him with female efficiency and prayer. There was one place where neither she nor any woman could follow him—a barrack-room. And what a supreme punishment for the abhorred but inexorably shared Guilt—the baronet's son "gone for a soldier," the "Prince of Mecca" in the ranks! No wonder that, lacking the clue, the world was puzzled, and that the inventive powers of journalists flowered into ever more fatuous absurdities. —RICHARD ALDINGTON, *Lawrence of Arabia: A Biographical Inquiry*, 1955, pp. 34–35, 313–14, 345–50

I have endeavoured to make a fair assessment of the Arab military effort. Not wishing to exaggerate its value and its effect on the final outcome of the war, I would only say that it should receive the appreciation it deserves, particularly when we include the political side, acknowledged by the Allies to be more important than the military aspect, and view the whole Revolt as part of the campaigns in the East. . . .

It is important that we take into consideration the divergence between the Arab and British viewpoints. The Arabs considered the Revolt a basic and vital factor, regarding the British in Egypt and Palestine and the British fleet as a catalyst which would help them win their war and earn their freedom. The British, on the other hand, regarded the Arabs as a contributory element in bringing about the defeat of Germany's junior ally, Turkey. Allenby, therefore, thought of Feisal's army as his own right flank, while Feisal looked at the British Army as the left flank of the Arab liberation movement.

Anybody attempting to assess with fairness Lawrence's role on the battle-fields of the Revolt ranging from Mecca in the south to Aleppo in the north, cannot escape the conclusion that it was a modest one. What raids could Lawrence or anybody else have carried out without the permanent base at Aqaba, Gueira and Wadi Musa, which was the centre of gravity, and maintained by the Arabs? Putting aside Lawrence's eloquence and descriptive powers, and comparing the operations in which he took part with those led by Maulud Mukhlis at Wadi Musa, Gueira, and Shobek, we are immediately struck by the absurdity of the claim that Lawrence was the hero of the Revolt. But Lawrence had the advantage of his pen, while the bedouin and Arab regulars enjoyed no such gift. And here lies the secret of his magnified stature, which he earned at the expense of others.—SULEIMAN MOUSA, *T. E. Lawrence: An Arab View*, tr. Albert Butros, 1966, pp. 263–65

In any consideration of Lawrence the most striking characteristic to emerge is the complexity of the man, not only as an individual but in the effect he had on others. Was he the charlatan as perceived by Richard Aldington, or the prophet described by Eric Kennington as one who 'has lived with us in the flesh, as one of us, and, dying, has left us quickened by his spiritual message'? The truth probably lies somewhere in between, but the difficulty of ascertaining it is in part due to Lawrence, who in the words of Robert Graves, 'fought coherence. I could not, and cannot, do for him what he had set his face against doing for himself.''

This lack of coherence is the fascination that is Lawrence; his complexities provide the material for the interest he arouses. The further one delves into the legend the more there seems to be to discover about the man, with each writer exploring a different facet. It is because of this that interest in Lawrence has persisted. . . .

Any study of Lawrence involves one in a series of complex situations coloured by personal feelings, nationalistic fervour, politics and psychological questions. The majority of these questions have more than one answer or interpretation, and as yet the real Lawrence has escaped scrutiny—or, it would be truer to say, each writer has revealed something of the Lawrence that he personally has discovered. The position is perhaps best summed up by Margot Hill:

He was faceted to a thousand different angles, and the particular facet one caught and called Lawrence depended on the angle at which one caught it. That, I think, is why no satisfactorily homogeneous individual emerges, as sculptors say, 'in the round', either from his own writings or the many concerning him. One can only try to describe the Lawrence one knew, without pretension that it was any more real a Lawrence than the next man's.

—FRANK CLEMENTS, "Introduction" to *T. E. Lawrence: A Reader's Guide*, 1973, pp. 13–22

E. M. FORSTER
From "T.E."
Listener, 31 July 1935, pp. 211–12

The little fellow who is labelled for posterity as Lawrence of Arabia detested the title. He often asked people to call him T.E., and perhaps it is fitting to respect that wish when writing about him now. T.E. did not think very well of these *Seven Pillars*. 'Not good enough, but as good, apparently, as I can do' was inscribed in my own copy of it. He compared the thing to a builder's yard, he called the style gummy, and he advised beer to be spilt freely upon the binding. A public edition of the sacred volume now appears. It is a noble and a scrupulous reprint, and the multitudes who are expecting it will not go empty away. . . .

What is this long book about?

It describes the revolt in Arabia against the Turks, as it appeared to an Englishman who took part in it; he would not allow us to write 'the leading part'. It opens with his preliminary visit to Rabegh and understanding with Feisul; then comes the new idea: shifting north to Wejh and harrying thence the Medina railway. The idea works, and he leaves Feisul for a time and moves against Akaba with Auda, another great figure of the revolt. A second success: Akaba falls. The war then ceases to be in the Hejaz and becomes Syrian. Henceforward he co-operates with the British Army under his hero Allenby, and his main work is in Trans-Jordania; it leads up to the cutting of the three railways round Deraa. Deraa isolated, the way lies clear to the third success, the capture of Damascus; the united armies enter Damascus, the revolt has triumphed.

That is what the book is about, and it could only be reviewed authoritatively by a staff officer who knows the East.

That is what the book is about, and *Moby-Dick* was about catching a whale.

For round this tent-pole of a military chronicle T.E. has hung an unexampled fabric of portraits, descriptions, philosophies, emotions, adventures, dreams. He has brought to his task a fastidious scholarship, an impeccable memory, a style nicely woven out of Oxfordisms and Doughty, an eye unparalleled, a sexual frankness which would cause most authors to be run in by the police, a profound distrust of himself, a still profounder faith. The 'seven pillared worthy house' was in his judgment never finished; the peace settlement of Versailles and some personal loss combined to shatter it and 'the little things crept out to patch themselves hovels in its shadow'. But the fabric propped by the tent-pole of the military chronicle survives, stretched taut against the sun. As we penetrate its vast interior and are bewildered by contrary effects; it is natural that we should ask for a guide, and I would suggest for that purpose not the explosions of gun cotton and cries of dying Turks, not the cracklings of councils, not even the self-communings, but some such passage as this:

From this rock a silver runlet issued into the sunlight. I looked in to see the spout, a little thinner than my wrist, jetting out firmly from a fissure in the roof, and falling with that clean sound into a shallow, frothing pool, behind the step which served as entrance. The walls and roof of the crevice dripped with moisture. Thick ferns and grasses of the finest green made it a paradise just five feet square.

Upon the water-cleansed and fragrant ledge I undressed my soiled body, and stepped into the little basin, to taste at last a freshness of moving air and water against my tired skin. It was deliciously cool. I lay there quietly, letting the clear, dark red water run over me in a ribbly stream, and rub the travel-dirt away. While I was so happy, a grey-bearded, ragged man, with a hewn face of great power and weariness, came slowly along the path till opposite the spring; and there he let himself down with a sigh upon my clothes spread out over a rock beside the path, for the sun-heat to chase out their thronging vermin.

He heard me and leaned forward, peering with rheumy eyes at this white thing splashing in the hollow beyond the veil of sun-mist. After a long stare he seemed content, and closed his eyes, groaning, "The love is from God; and of God; and towards God'.

T.E. was a very difficult person, and no one who knew him at all well would venture to sum him up. But he certainly possessed the three heroic virtues: courage, generosity, and compassion. His courage and generosity he could not conceal, though he perversely tried to do so. Compassion is more easily hidden, and this passage is valuable because it reveals it. The little unhusked body, so happy in its baptism, the half-witted prophet contemplating it, lift us up into a region of tenderness and unselfish love which was probably his real world. A world unknown to the Arabs, he thought, and the mumblings of the old man quite upset his theories about them.

If we take compassion as a lodestar, it may lead us through the psychology of the *Seven Pillars* as surely as Damascus led us northward through the geography. Here is a young man, describing himself as he was when still younger. He has discovered that he can lead an Arab army, fight, bluff, and spy, be hard and disciplinary, and this is exhilarating; but the course of his inner life runs contrary. That course is turbid, slow, weighted by remorse for victory, and by disgust against the body. Personal ill-luck and ill-health, particularly a horrible masochistic experience, emphasise this, so that when he analyses himself it is as a spiritual outcaste, on the lines of Hermann Melville's Ishmael. To the attentive reader, something has gone wrong here, the analysis has reached one conclusion, the text keeps implying another. Does it imply that 'the love is from God and of God and towards God'? Nothing as theological as that, but there is a latent unselfishness, a constant good will which are fundamental, and which the fires of his own suffering fuse into compassion.

Whatever his inner life, he yearned to create a single work of art out of that life and out of his military experiences. He was rather superstitious about works of art, and spoke of them as if they belonged to a special category. The *Seven Pillars* to him was a failure, a 'builder's yard', where wealth of material did not compensate for absence of form. The romantic evocations of Rumm and Azrak, the masterly character-sketches of Auda and other chiefs, the episode of Farraj and Daud, the gargantuan mutton-feast—he regarded them as bricks for a future and better architect. Perhaps when the subscribers' edition came out and all sorts of people thought it good, he worried less as to whether it was a work of art, but he was so modest that he never grasped its greatness, or admitted that he had given something unique to our literature.

He has also contributed to sociology, in recording what is probably the last of the picturesque wars. Camels, pennants, the blowing up of little railway trains by little charges of dynamite in the desert—it is unlikely to recur. Next time the aeroplane will blot out everything in an indifferent death, but the aeroplane in this yarn is only a visitor, which arrives in the last chapters to give special thrills. A personal note can still be struck. It is possible to pot at the fat station master as he sits drinking coffee with his friends . . . good . . . got him . . . he rolls off his deck chair! Steal up behind the shepherds and score their feet, so that they do not carry the news! Hide under the bridge in the rain all night! This is not only agreeable to the reader, it is important to the historian. Because it was waged under archaistic conditions, the Arab revolt is likely to be remembered. It is the last effort of the war-god before he laid down his godhead, and turned chemist.

What T. E. himself thought of war it is impossible to say. He spent most of his life waging it or helping to prepare for it, but the military meditation which occupies Chapter 33 shows that he did not believe in killing people. Probably he was muddled and rattled like the rest of us, and cherished the theory that war is inevitable in order to steady himself. He was, of course, devoted to the Arab cause. Yet when it triumphed he felt that he had let down both his own countrymen and the foreigner by aping foreign ways, and became more English than ever. To regard him as 'gone native' is wrong. He belonged body and soul to our islands. And he should have been happier in olden days, when a man could feel surer that he was fighting for his own hearth, and this terrible modern mix-up had not begun.

ANDRÉ MALRAUX
From "Lawrence and the Demon of
the Absolute"
Hudson Review, Winter 1956, pp. 519–32

Nineteen-twenty-two. Colonel Lawrence—thirty-three years old—having become one of Winston Churchill's advisors for Arab affairs after the Arabian campaign, the Peace Conference and a temporary retirement, had just returned from the Hejaz, where he had been sent as minister plenipotentiary to the king who owed him his crown. For the first time, he felt himself "on the other side of the barrier". He had just read proofs of The Seven Pillars of Wisdom, *which he had hoped might become one of the "Titantic" books, on a par with* Moby-Dick, The Brothers Karamazov *and* Thus Spake Zarathustra.

What follows is not a critique of The Seven Pillars, *but an analysis of the feelings of the author in the presence of his book—feelings which are later to be modified.*

Lawrence had just submitted his resignation, writing to Churchill: "There are many other things I want to do". He had already decided to enlist as a private in the air force under an assumed name.

"There are many other things I want to do." There was only one, and he knew it perfectly well.

To give meaning to his life would involve subjecting it to some unequivocal value; values which carry in themselves this saving power (liberty, charity of heart, God) imply a sacrifice, or the appearance of a sacrifice, on behalf of mankind— whether the man who has chosen them believes in them or not. Whether or not they advertise it openly, they mean to change the order of the world, and on that account, values, like art, are the great allies of man against his fate.

If Lawrence had harshly protected the power which he had won and at first almost usurped, it was because a great action cannot be otherwise carried through. Without doubt, he had been profoundly concerned at times that this power takes its proper form. But a power whose form would be himself could not similarly attract him. Action for action's sake, power for power's sake were foreign to him. The instinct which pushes a politician towards a ministry, with politics playing the chief role, never made him want to direct the colonial politics of England: what he really wanted was to make sense, once again, of the confusion of what had so far been his fate.

Since the end of 1920, he had been finishing up his prodigious narrative. With half of it done, he reread it straight through, for the first time, between Jidda and Transjordania, with an anxiety which increased as he read. But was he able to judge this text which he knew by heart, where his memory always ran ahead of his writing? Did he read, or did he resume a restless dialogue with all that had passed since he had left the covetous and intractable king? One after the other the boat skirted Rabig, Yenbo, El Ouedj, Akaba. . . .

He had taken his manuscript, corrections made, to the press of the *Oxford Times*: to print up several copies would cost less than to have it typewritten. He had received the proofs in July, his decision to quit the ministry already taken. Now that all action was closed to him, he felt himself even more committed to this intellectual adventure than he had been to the Arabian adventure: imprisoned with the book for his decisive struggle with the angel, left more to himself by the decomposition of everything to which he had so far attached himself; more committed even than he had been by fear of defeat at the time of the Peace Conference and the flight of Feisal. He hoped to recover from these proofs the freshness of sight and judgment which his manuscript no longer could give him. He found them, in effect: a book a little better than those written by "the majority of retired army officers", with some hysterical passages.

The excitement of the Revolt had been as obvious to him as the comedy of the Peace Conference against which he had attempted rebellion: but the cupidity of the Arabs had never seemed any the less to him because, to Arab eyes, English wealth appeared inexhaustible and not to profit from it stupid, since all money won in combat was nobly won. Lawrence knew that his reader, whoever he might be, would expect purity from a national movement. An ordinary soldier might be alternately a hero and a plunderer; but from the leader, even from a mere participator in a revolt, national or social, the fraternal sentiments of the reader would accept nothing but exemplary actions. What runs counter to the revolutionary convention is, in revolutionary histories, suppressed more imperiously than embarrassing episodes in private memoirs, and by the same obscure forces.

Lawrence had written: *I saw an epic born before my eyes,*—and revealed an endless series of shady dealings. Of the leader of the Juheinas who had murmured while watching Feisal's army: *Now we are a people*. . . , Lawrence knew that several months later he had abandoned the Arab cause. The oath imposed by Feisal had been no more than a truce, even in the minds of those who prepared it. At every victory, at Akaba, at Deraa, the vendetta started up again; at Damascus this had not been merely the folly of Abd-el-Kader who had immediately forced the victorious army to fight with its allies. The Arabs had wanted less to create Arabia than to harass the Turks. The Syrians did not want to create Syria: the word Syria does not exist in Arabic. Nothing, apart from hatred of the Turks, had united the intellectuals of Beirut and the Druses. But to the eyes of a European, every national movement is first of all brotherhood. . . .

What was admirable in the Revolt was not that visionary campaign by which the Arabs were going to renew the birth of the Islamic epic; rather was it that men, by turn courageous and weak, greedy and generous, heroic and impure like all men (and more than most), should reconquer their historic capital in spite of all their weaknesses. Lawrence had expected to rediscover the enthusiasm which the Revolt had inspired among the crowds in the Albert Hall, but by grounding it in the truth: the same emulation which opposed him to "Lawrence of Arabia" opposed his narrative to the legend. In that respect he needed most of all lyricism, the great medium for the expression of enthusiasm. It was necessary, in spite of the dickerings, the defections, the treasons, that the reader be carried away by one of those exalting epics of generosity which make one believe that a few inspired days can hold all the beauty of the world. Lyricism alone could do it; not the descriptive lyricism which lives from what it carries away, but the transfiguring lyricism which lives from what it contributes. An artist's gifts, alas, are not always those he needs the most: and Lawrence behaved like a writer who wanted to write the kind of epic that Victor Hugo made of Waterloo, but who in fact possessed only the gifts which permitted Stendhal to make it into a comedy.

That the Revolt inspired in him feelings whose contradictions he had not overcome until he had first of all written a brief for the defense, he realized as soon as he began to write. The only way of not being paralyzed by them was not to impose on his book any premeditated structure. He had put his memory to work on the thread of his war diary or notes left on the margin of agendas: the very wording had been haphazard. The dynamiting of a bridge, an attack on a train—things which involved some preparation; his comrades in arms, his reversals of fortune—all this permitted lengthy exposition, for as far as his memory could carry him. But what of the organization of an intelligence service, made up of conversations all alike and which, carried on in another language, could not be used to describe the characters of those who held them? For everything involved in the secret service, for the execution of his major project—to make the Arabs arrive first at Damascus—Lawrence had chosen to be, if not secretive, at least swift. Hence a singular perspective in which all the aid brought to Allen by the breakthrough which had forced the Turks to sue for an armistice seemed less important than an attack on two trains, the discovery of Feisal's negotiations with the Turks less important than the treason of Abd-el-Kader. Lawrence now discovered that a detailed account of his acts was far from being the best means of expressing his action. He had wanted to bear witness to the revival of a people, and it sometimes seemed to him that he was rereading the memoirs of a dynamiter. . . .

So much so that having written to add grandeur to a vaguely legendary insurrection, he asked himself if the first question of his reader about the Revolt itself would not be: *Was that all it amounted to?*

At any rate, he would have written the only history of the Revolt. But he did not believe in history. He believed in art. And the implacable evidence that these agonized days forced on him, when he read the printed book as if it were the work of someone else, was that the book was not a work of art. . . . *The fact that it wasn't a work of art rose up and hit me in the face, and I hated it, because artist is the proudest profession.*

The writing of a journalist; *refuge in second hand words.* . . . If, by dint of work, he succeeded in giving this kind of writing the proper tone, he ceased to expect of it that regal gift which reconciles contradictions, which mixes strength and weakness in a transfigured whole.

His book was not a great narrative. The history of narrative technique for the last three centuries, like that of painting, has been essentially a search for a third dimension; for that which, in the novel, eludes narration; for what makes it possible not to narrate but to represent, to make present. Narration expresses a past whose total effect—scene by scene—is that of a present. Just as the painters developed perspective, the novelists found in dialogue and atmosphere a means of effecting this transformation. Even modern narrative art can boast of a just proportion between what is represented and what is related. What a vivid succession of scenes Dostoievski would have made of such memories! Lawrence's narrative predominated to such a degree in his episodes that he recovered nothing, in this stiff and linear book, of the passion that had made him write up to twenty hours a day. Was it enough that he had avoided banalities, coynesses, concessions? That he was confident of having escaped vulgarity? The absence of premeditated perspective, his submission to the diary, had handicapped him with an absence of artistic perspective, had restricted him to an action on a single plane. That whole background of evil in its obsessive opposition to every ideal, that absurdity which Lawrence so poignantly felt and which might have been so well expressed—the savagery of discipline amongst his bodyguard, those whipped men with never-healing scars, wandering about him while he read *Le Morte d'Arthur*, who never ceased wildly contradicting what was most pure in his will to victory and his determination not to let a single man be needlessly killed: all this he could only make into a bitingly picturesque vignette.

This book, considering it only as a book of memoirs, should at least have been able to recapture, in dealing with individuals, the mystery that possessed its author. What sort of existence did these people lead? That of the Arabs scarcely went beyond the picturesque, that of the English beyond a crude sketch. What reader, the book closed, "knows" Joyce, Young, Clayton? The most characterized person, Feisal, is he not a sort of official portrait?

One cannot reveal the mystery of human beings in the form of a plea for the defense. . . .

He questioned whether the knowledge of a man was a knowledge of his secrets, being eager to the point of mania not to be confounded with his own. But had he reached by other ways that pulse of irrationality by which a character comes alive, which fascinates the great memorialist as much as the great novelist, Saint-Simon as much as Tolstoi? These beings glimpsed during the action he instinctively brought into focus, caught in the meaning which the action so often imposed upon them. None of them carried the germs of his future destiny; the events seemed, not to bring out a part of these people so far merely touched on, but to transform them entirely. To what part of the knight Aouda belonged his negotiations with the Turks; to what part of Feisal, Saracen prince and judge of Israel, his negotiations for a separate peace?

Lawrence would have wanted in his book, as in those of his masters, unexpected actions what would illuminate the secret nature of the man from whom they sprung. But he, whose companions had almost never caught him off guard (once: when Zeid had squandered the money entrusted to him), leaned towards the conventional in the *portrayal* of individuals. The greed of Aouda surprised him less than it surprises the reader. Throughout this book in which complexity plays so large a role, has he really portrayed strongly any but simple, secondary beings? The soul of Abd-el-Kader was without doubt unintelligible, nor would the reader accept it unless he knew that Lawrence was reporting the facts. In a fiction the Algerian would have been unacceptable: but the characters of the great memorialists are people in whom the reader would believe even if he knew that the author had created them out of whole cloth. . . .

The whole ending is an anti-climax. Perhaps this was first of all because he was no longer unaware, at the time of writing, of where this epic would end. But a Melville, even a Conrad, would have found, beyond the atmosphere which Lawrence had perhaps achieved, the supreme source of poetry which makes of deception, of despair, not a paralysis but a tragedy. Solitude and inner defeat, the futility of epics, are also powerful means of art. What he failed to achieve was the transfiguration which should have been extended even to his memories in order to establish their meaning, to bring them on a level with the eternal.

And the Revolt was only a frame for an *Ecce Homo*, scourged like the other, lacerated like the other. Lawrence had begun to write after the speech of Feisal to the Conference, apparently in an appeal to history against injustice, actually in an appeal to art against the absurd. It was not only the Revolt he expected to save from absurdity, but his own action, his own destiny. The only means the spirit has for escaping the absurd is to involve the rest of the world in it, to imagine it, to express it. Little by little, without any change of frame, the Revolt began to take second place while the main interest passed to the absurdity of life for a man reduced to solitude by an irreducible inner conflict and the meditation it imposed. The subject of the book he believed he was writing had become the struggle of a being lashed without mercy by the scorn which he felt for certain appeals of his own nature, by a fatality acknowledged, with terrible humiliation, as a permanent failure of his will,— against the passionate resolution of this same being to kill his demon with great conquering strokes of lucidity. *I wrote my will across the sky in stars.* . . .

The Turks in retreat, Feisal at Damascus, he himself legendary with a legend both exalting and mocking—and weary of everything, weary to death, except for those pages which crumbled between his hands—was he wrong to believe such a struggle worthy of *The Brothers Karamazov?* That he had paid the heaviest price for his revelation, that this inner conflict may or may not have been due to some unsoundness in his character, reflects on neither its value nor its meaning; even the sanest man who tries to conduct his life intelligently loses control of himself once in a while. Man is absurd because he is master neither of time, nor of anxiety, nor of Evil; the world is absurd because it involves Evil, and because Evil is the sin of the world.

This drama might have been expressed by everything that separated Lawrence from the Arab movement; his narrative actually concerned itself with everything that should have bound him to it. What actually separated him from the Revolt, what he wanted to express in order to make his book great, is that every human action is defiled by its very nature. The portrait he wanted to paint was the anatomical sketch of a man who examines everything his own, or that might be his own, with the poisoned lucidity of the atheist of life.

He seemed as concerned to conceal this man as he had been to conceal the secret animator of the Revolt. To follow, as he had resolved, the order of his war diary, he had begun his narrative with his debarkation at Jidda: and, rereading it after having written the first six books, he felt so far removed from it that he added an introduction during his flight to Cairo. There, he said in clear but abstract language what he wanted to say: he was carried away at first by the appeal of liberty and was so completely committed to its service that he ceased to exist; he lived under the constant threat of torture; his life was ceaselessly crossed by *strange longings fanned by privations and dangers;* he was incapable of subscribing to the doctrines he preached for the good of his country at war; they knew the need for degradation; he ceased to believe in his civilization or in any other, until he was aware of nothing but an intense solitude on the borderline of madness; and what he chiefly recalled were *the agony, the terrors and the mistakes.*

What were the degradation, the terrors and the mistakes? Every priest knows that confession in the abstract costs little. The concrete admission, here, would have consisted in picturing himself *during* the mistake, in embodying himself in the phantom who said: *I*. His first narrative finished, he realized anew how much the matter discussed in this introduction was absent from the book. Throughout his text, it seemed to him that he was running after himself. *Then* he had described the introspective crisis of his thirtieth birthday, his portrait. A representation clear and cruel, but still abstract: the modesty born of his physique and of his dissimilarity; the constant split which made his inner life *a standing court martial*; his pride; his appetite for glory and deceit, his scorn of this desire; his implacable will; his distrust of ideas; his need for relief from his intelligence; his anguished self-consciousness which led him to try to see himself through the eyes of others; his lack of all faith and his search for the limits of his strength; his need for degradation (in the first person, this time); his disgust, so great that *only weakness delayed me from mind-suicide;* finally, and above all: *I did not like the 'myself' I could see and hear.* . . .

This was the man who said: *Feisal was a brave, weak, ignorant spirit trying to do work for which only a genius, a prophet or a great criminal, was fitted. I served him out of pity, a motive which degraded us both. The Seven Pillars* never ceased to demonstrate the opposite. . . . The introduction was an introduction to his secret memories much more than to his book; his drama, his portrait, were written in the margin; and only the incarnation of this portrait would have made *The Seven Pillars* not an historical fresco but a book of the order (if not of the genius) of *The Brothers Karamazov* and *Zarathustra*, the great accusatory work of which he had dreamed.

Little by little, because all the battles resolved themselves finally into a tardy and melancholy victory, and above all because, for him, art insensibly supplanted action, the Arab epic became in his mind the medium for a grandiose expression of human emptiness. Also, for *I wrote this to show what a man can do*, secret echo of his angers in Paris, was substituted, with the bitter sound of the two words A *Triumph* which he had added to the subtitle: *I wrote this to show what the gods are able to make of us.* . .

In the absolute, the triumph is a mockery—but so is the triumpher. Lawrence knew it quite well, and this was the secret meaning of such episodes as those in the hospital or at Deraa, accurate or not. A man's own lucid self-portrait—if there were in the world a single man lucid enough to recount his life— would be the most virulent indictment of the gods which could be imagined: as great as the man himself was great. The lucid hero, if he penetrates ever so little into this forbidden domain, can but choose between the absurd and original sin. But if one wants to express the human mystery by saying "Behold the man", one must offer something more than a close-mouthed confession. . . .

Lawrence's nature was opposed to confession both by the violence of his pride and by that of his modesty. At least, of that modesty born of the fear of giving a handle to the reader, that of characters in Russian novels whom the familiarity with public confession cannot free from an obsessive dread of ridicule; and also, of the fact that Lawrence considered almost everything he had achieved to be negligible—or certainly less important than what he had dreamed of achieving. His correspondence reveals, in general, strikingly more noblesse than he had admitted to in *The Seven Pillars* (with the exception of his will to save the lives of his fellow-fighters). He said that he remembered first of all his mistakes, and scarcely revealed any of them (defeats, yes: not without greatness); he said that he had undertaken his campaign for the love of one of his companions: this companion he suppressed.

For a moment he considered doing the whole book over again. But how could he have done it? These pages had been first written as he lashed his memory during bouts of insomnia, six months after the capture of Damascus. When they were lost, he recomposed them with exhausting effort. Corrections would not have changed the perspective: he would have been unable to rewrite it all, and would thus have lost the fine temper which, at least, was the reward of the historical witness that now seemed to him so vain. Why would the demon that had already twice paralyzed him have been defeated the third time? It was himself.

And a more subtle poison emanated still from those pages which crumbled between his fingers. Profoundly though he may have been involved in the artistic success of his book, he was not solely involved in that. Whoever writes his memoirs (except to deceive) judges himself. There were in this book, as in all memoirs, two *personae*: the one who said *I*, and the author. What Lawrence had done, was embodied in the person who acted: what he was, in the rectifier and judge of this other—in the writer. It was the writer (not as artist but as judge) who was to enable Lawrence to subordinate his legend to himself instead of remaining subordinated to it: who in the spiritual order was to serve the exemplary Lawrence as the rejection of all reward had served him in the moral order.

Literary talent was no longer in question; but being, human density. Lawrence knew that the greatness of a writer lies less in what he promulgates than in the place from which he speaks; that Tolstoi portraying a wounded person watching the night-time clouds at Austerlitz, or the banal functionary Ivan Ilych confronted by death, is no less great than Dostoievski making the Grand Inquisitor speak. A Tolstoi would have been able to draw from the death of the humblest Arab soldier the splendid and bitter meaning of the Revolt; because he had Tolstoi's talent, but first of all because he was Lev Nikolaevich. The power of Christ's reply in the presence of the adulterous woman is not a matter of the talent of the evangelists. And the demon of the absurd appeared in the cruelest guise: if Lawrence had not expressed the man he believed he was, was it not simply because he was not that man?

And if he was not that man, he was nothing.

IRVING HOWE

From "T. E. Lawrence:
The Problem of Heroism"

Hudson Review, Autumn 1962, pp. 333–64

Time has mercifully dulled the image he despised yet courted: T. E. Lawrence is no longer the idol of the twenties, no longer "Lawrence of Arabia." But for the minority of men to whom reflection upon human existence is both a need and a pleasure, Lawrence seems still to matter. He is not yet a name to be put away in history, a footnote in dust. He continues to arouse sympathy, outrage, excitement. If we come to him admiring whatever in his life was extraordinary, we

remain with him out of a sense that precisely the special, even the exotic in Lawrence may illumine whatever in our life is ordinary.

During the early twenties, after his return from Arabia, Lawrence became a national hero, the adventurer through whom Englishmen could once more savor the sensations of war and rescue from its filth emotions of sentimental grandeur. What he had done in Arabia—more important, what he had experienced—was epic in its proportions and even a glance at his life prompts one to speculate about the equivocal nature of heroism in our century. But transplanted from the desert to the lantern-slides of the Albert Hall, where Lowell Thomas was conjuring for the English their stainless version of "Lawrence of Arabia," the whole war-time experience shrank to farce. Partly to salvage it from vulgarities whch he himself had condoned, Lawrence wrote *The Seven Pillars of Wisdom*, a bravura narrative packed with accounts of battle yet finally the record of his search for personal equilibrium and value. By then, however, his public image had acquired a being and momentum of its own. So the book too, though in some ways esoteric, became popular—and helped sustain the image it was meant to subvert.

This sad comedy was to continue to the end. In *The Seven Pillars of Wisdom* the ideal of a forthright manly heroism, which Lawrence had supposedly rescued for an unheroic age, was soon transformed into the burden of self-consciousness, a burden he was never to escape. The dynamiter of railroads turned out to be an intellectual harassed by ambition and guilt. The literary man who had read Malory between desert raids and later worried over the shape and rhythm of the sentences in his book, made himself into a pseudonymous recruit tending the "shit-cart" of his camp. And these were but a few of his transfigurations. . . .

II

In the spring of 1916 Sherif Hussein of the Hejaz, descendent of the Prophet and protector of the faith, launched a revolt against the Turks. For some time the British had been tempting him with promises of post-war independence; but this shrewd fanatic had played a cautious game, rightly enough from his point of view, since he neither trusted the infidel British nor cared to risk the vengeance of the Turks.

At first the Arabs gained a few local victories, hardly decisive and, in their very success, exposing a poverty of purpose and leadership. But having lost the advantage of surprise and unable, with their irregular bands, to do more than harass entrenched Turkish posts, they now faced the danger of being wiped out by counterattack. The Arabs were ignorant of modern warfare; they had no master plan and barely an idea of why one might be needed; their main advantage lay not in any capacities of their own but in the sluggishness of the Turks. To provide help and soothe Hussein, British headquarters in Cairo sent an experienced official, Ronald Storrs, as envoy to the Hejaz. With him went T. E. Lawrence, who until then had spent the war months as an impudent and quite undistinguished staff captain in Military Intelligence.

In *The Seven Pillars of Wisdom* Lawrence has left a brilliant description of his first exploratory visit from one Arab camp to another, studying Hussein's three elder sons, each of whom led a body of troops. Ali, Abdullah, Feisal: which of these princes could become the focal point of rebellion, the embodiment of Arab desire? The picture of Lawrence plunging into the chaos of the Arab world, measuring the worth of its leaders and quickly bringing order to its ranks—this picture is surely overdrawn if one judges by the limited powers Lawrence actually enjoyed at the moment. Not until after his return to Cairo and his assignment as British Liaison officer to the Arab troops in the winter of 1917 did he even begin to command such authority. Yet the picture is essentially faithful if one grants Lawrence the right—he won it in the desert and then through his book—to treat his own experience as fable of heroism: the right, that is, to assign a scheme or purpose to hesitant improvisations which in the end did come to bear such a purpose. . . .

In regard to so complex and elusive a mind as Lawrence's, no simple distinction can be enforced between action and response, what "really" happened and what he made of it in memory. Lawrence neither was nor could be a detached observer; he was leader, follower, victim all in one. He tells us that his first commanding view of the revolt came to him in March 1917 when for ten days he lay sick in the camp of Abdulla. Perhaps, in writing *The Seven Pillars of Wisdom*, Lawrence gave dramatic form to his memories by condensing a long experience of discovery into a moment of sudden realization. But this possibility should not be allowed to blur the fact that there was discovery. Even in Arabia history is not all muddle or chance; there *is* intelligence, plan, purpose. And to the extent that these were present in the revolt, they were significantly Lawrence's: not his alone, but his most forcefully.

It is possible that the innovations in military tactics claimed for Lawrence were neither so revolutionary nor calculated as has been supposed—though by now only specialists and old friends will have strong opinions about Lawrence as commander. It is possible that a good many of his glamorous desert raids were of uncertain value—though in guerilla warfare bold acts can have consequences beyond their immediate military effects. It is possible that without British gold Lawrence could not have held together the Arab chieftains—though the crucial question is whether anyone else could have done it with twice as much gold. But one thing seems certain: it was Lawrence who grasped the inner logic of the revolt as a moral-political act and it was Lawrence who breathed into it a vibrancy of intention it had not previously known.

What his plunge into the desert meant to Lawrence he never fully said, perhaps because the main concern in his writings was to present his relations to the Arabs as a problem—a problem that could not be reduced to his private needs or desires.[1] From fragments of evidence left by Lawrence and those who were close to him, one may cautiously reconstruct some of his responses.

Lawrence, the cocky young officer who had been disliked so fiercely by the military regulars in Cairo, saw the Arabian campaign as an adventure in the simplest, most *English* sense of the word. This Lawrence took eagerly to the whole ritual-pageant of the Arab camps and Arab ceremonies and Arab pow-wows, though he knew that half the time they were mere displays veiling weakness. This Lawrence suddenly found himself cast in a role such as might satisfy the wildest fantasies of a middle class English youth raised on romantic literature. With a sharp eye for stylized effects, he continued in his own way the tradition of those English visitors to the mid-East who have managed to penetrate native life without ceasing to be immaculately English. . . .

Lawrence never wished to persuade the Arabs that he had become one of them. That would not only have been ludicrous, it would have threatened his mode of leadership. He did something more subtle and, in their eyes, impressive: he convinced the Arabs that in basic stoicism, outer bearing and daily practise he could become remarkably like them. The dream of "going back," of stripping to a more primitive self, which has so often fascinated Western man, was an authentic motive in his Arabian experience; but it was also consciously used by Lawrence to further his public role.

For a man who was so deeply drawn to the experience of *overcoming*—particularly a self-overcoming in the sense foreshadowed by Nietzsche—the war in Arabia came to be a test through radical humiliation and pain.

As he immersed himself in the life of the desert, repeating again and again the cycle of exertion—a moment of high excitement, a plunge into activity, then sickness, self-scrutiny, the wild desire to escape and finally a clenched return—Lawrence saw his experience as far more than a romantic escapade or fearful discipline. Since, in the bareness of the desert he had to remold his existence in order to meet an historical demand, he also found there the possibility of an action through which to carve out a chosen meaning for his life. From the trivia, the ugliness, the absurdity, the assured betrayal of events, he would snatch the trophy of freedom.

. . . Lawrence undertook the Arabian campaign as an adventure: the sense, in Simmel's words, that an adventure is like a work of art, "for the essence of the work of art is . . . that it cuts out a piece of endlessly continuous sequence of perceived experience, giving it a self-sufficient form as though defined and held together by an inner core. . . . Indeed, it is an attribute of this form to make us feel that in both the work of art and the adventure the whole of life is somehow comprehended and consummated." Exactly what Lawrence came to hope for in the desert: that somehow, through an unimaginable exertion, the whole of his life would be comprehended and consummated.

. . . By the summer of 1917 he knew about the Sykes-Picot treaty, a secret arrangement among Britain, France and Russia for perpetuating imperialism in the mid-East. This agreement made a farce of the promises of independence that had been given by Lawrence—though not by him alone—to the Arabs. Lawrence smarted under the knowledge that no matter what he would now say or do, he had no choice but to further this deceit. . . .

Had Lawrence been a principled anti-imperialist for whom sentiments of national pride were irrelevant, his problem might have been easier to bear. But he was not a principled anti-imperialist and he did retain sentiments of national pride. In fact, his shame and guilt derived precisely from a lingering belief in the British claim to fairness. Despite superb intuitions, he never reached a coherent view of the world political struggle in which, finally, he too was but another pawn. There were moments when he saw, but he could not long bear the vision, that his whole adventure had been absorbed by a cynical struggle for power. Lawrence was a man—hopeless, old-fashioned romantic!—who believed in excellence and honor; he came at the wrong time, in the wrong place.

On his thirtieth birthday, during a peaceful day shortly before the entry into Damascus, Lawrence tried to examine himself honestly, without delusion:

> Four years ago I had meant to be a general and knighted when thirty. Such temporal dignities (if I survived the next four weeks) were now in my grasp. . . . There was a craving to be famous; and a horror of being known to like being known. . . . The hearing other people praised made me despair jealously of myself. . . . I began to wonder if all established reputations were founded, like mine, on fraud. . . . I must have had some tendency, some aptitude, for deceit. Without that I should not have deceived men so well, and persisted two years in bringing to success a deceit which others had framed and set afoot.

As it now seemed to him, almost everything he had done was negligible in scale and value, a triviality of success. This judgment he would later express most forcibly in the preface he wrote for *The Seven Pillars of Wisdom*, and the summary of this preface that André Malraux has provided might almost have been written by Lawrence himself:

> . . . he was carried away at first by the appeal of liberty and was so completely committed to its service that he ceased to exist; he lived under the constant threat of torture; his life was ceaselessly crossed by *strange longings fanned by privations and dangers*; he was incapable of subscribing to the doctrines he preached for the good of his country at war . . . he ceased to believe in his civilization or in any other, until he was aware of nothing but an intense solitude on the borderline of madness; and what he chiefly recalled were *the agony, the terrors and the mistakes.*

When the British and Arabs marched into Damascus, the war came to an end for Lawrence. "In the black light of victory, we could scarcely identify ourselves."

III

. . . What Lawrence now felt came to far more than personal disappointment; it was a rupture of those bonds of faith that had made him a good and, in some respects, characteristic Englishman of his day. Now he "looked at the West and its conventions with new eyes: they destroyed it all for me." In the suppressed introduction to *The Seven Pillars of Wisdom* Lawrence poured out his heart with a bitterness that spoke for a generation:

> We were wrought up with ideas inexpressible and vaporous, but to be fought for. We lived many lives in those whirling campaigns, never sparing ourselves any good or evil: yet when we achieved and the new world dawned, the old men came out again and took from us our victory and remade it in the likeness of the former world they knew. Youth could win, but had not learned to keep, and was pitiably weak against age. We stammered that we had worked for a new heaven and a new earth, and they thanked us kindly and made their peace. . . .

Yet . . . Lawrence continued to behave like a tough and bouncy Irishman. Precisely during this period of failure, heartsickness and notoriety Lawrence kept working away with an insatiable ambition, often for whole days and nights, at *The Seven Pillars of Wisdom*. Largely written in 1919, the manuscript was lost, completely and painfully redone, and in 1922 set up in proof at the Oxford *Times*. How ambitious he was Lawrence revealed in a letter to Edward Garnett:

> Do you remember my telling you once that I collected a shelf of 'Titantic' books (those distinguished by greatness of spirit, 'sublimity,' as Longinus would call it): and that they were *The Karamazovs, Zarathustra* and *Moby-Dick*. Well, my ambition was to make an English fourth. You will observe that modesty comes out more in the performance than the aim.

"An English fourth" Lawrence did not quite make. Still, the book is one of the few original works of English prose in our century, and if Lawrence's name lives past the next half century it may well be for the book rather than the experience behind it. The book is subtitled "a triumph," and in regard to the Arabian campaign, formally its central action, this must surely be read as an irony. In another sense, however, it *is* a triumph: a vindication of consciousness through form.

As autobiography *The Seven Pillars of Wisdom* is veiled, ambiguous, misleading: less a direct revelation than a performance from which the truth can be wrenched. Nor can it be taken as formal history, since it focusses too subjectively, too obsessively, perhaps too passionately on its theme: which is the felt burden of history rather than history itself. Yet the book *as an act* has become part of the history of our politics, and is as necessary for comprehending the twentieth century as Brecht's poems or Kafka's novels or Pirandello's plays.

Primarily the book is a work of art, the model for a genre that would become all too characteristic of the age: a personal narrative through which a terrible experience is relived, burned out, perhaps transcended. This genre, to be perfected by the victims of totalitarianism, is a perilous one, succumbing too easily to verbal mannerism and tending to wash away the distinction between history and fable.

The Seven Pillars of Wisdom is a work of purgation and disgorgement. It is also, in order to resist the pressures of memory, a work of the most artful self-consciousness in which Lawrence is constantly "arranging words, so that the one I care for most is either repeated, or syllable-echoed, or put in a startling position." Robert Graves has said that "the nervous strain of its ideal of faultlessness is oppressive," and Lawrence himself found that the book is "written too hard. There are no flat places where a man can stand still for a moment. All ups and downs, engine full on or brakes hard on." The feverish state in which Lawrence composed the book, especially the early drafts—

> I tie myself into knots trying to reenact everything, as I write it out. It's like writing in front of a lookingglass, and never looking at the paper, but always at the imaginary scene.

—may help to explain why the book is "written too hard." . . .

To an age that usually takes its prose plain, Lawrence's style is likely to seem mannered. Unquestionably there are passages that fail through a surplus of effort; passages that betray the hot breath of hysteria; passages that contain more sensibility than Lawrence could handle or justify. But it is dangerous to dismiss such writing simply because we have been trained to suspect the grand. Lawrence was deliberately trying to achieve large-scale effects, a rhetoric of action and passion that may almost be called baroque; the style pursuing the thought. And while the reader has every reason to discriminate among these effects, it would be dull to condemn Lawrence merely for their presence.

Lawrence strives for a style of thrust and shock, and then, by way of balance, for passages of refined sensibility. He often uses words with a deliberate obliqueness or off-meaning, so as to charge them with strangeness and potential life. The common meaning of these key words is neither fully respected nor wholly violated; but twisted, sometimes into freshness and sometimes into mere oddity. All of this followed from conscious planning: "I find that my fifth writing . . . of a sentence makes it more shapely, pithier, stranger than it was. Without that twist of strangeness no one would feel an individuality, a differentness, behind the phrase."

It is a coercive prose, as it is a coercive book, meant to shake the reader into a recognition of what is possible on this earth. No one can end this book with emotions of repose; there is no pretense at conciliatory sublimation. The result, throughout, is a tensing of nerves and sensibility, a series of broken reflections upon human incompleteness. It is a modern book.

Notes

1. Some private desires there surely were. *The Seven Pillars of Wisdom* bears a fervid dedication in verse to "S.A.," who has generally been

taken to be an Arabian person Lawrence knew before the war. It has also been surmised, on the basis of teasing hints dropped by Lawrence to his biographers, that one motive for wishing to undertake the campaign in the desert was to reach "S.A." But whether this person was, as Robert Graves insists, a woman Lawrence had met in Syria or whether it was the Arab boy Sheik Ahmoud whom he had befriended at Carchemish, we do not know. There are other possibilities, but they are little more than guesses.

JOHN LE CARRÉ
David Cornwell

1931–

John le Carré was born David John Moore Cornwell in Poole, Dorset, on October 19, 1931. Though he began his education in England, he persuaded his father to let him go to school in Switzerland, where he learned German, French, and how to ski. After military service with the Army Intelligence Corps in Austria, he studied modern languages at Lincoln College, Oxford, graduating with first class honors in 1956. He taught at Eton College for two years, then in 1960 joined Her Majesty's Foreign Service and was posted to Bonn and Hamburg.

Since Foreign Service officials were discouraged from publishing under their own names, le Carré adopted the pseudonym by which he is known when he published his first novel, *Call for the Dead*, in 1961. The success two years later of *The Spy Who Came In from the Cold*, which won him the Somerset Maugham Award and the Crime Writers' Association Gold Dagger, enabled him to resign from the Foreign Service in 1964. After a few months on Crete and in Vienna he settled in England, where he has lived since.

Le Carré's series of highly successful novels includes *The Looking-Glass War* (1965), *Tinker, Tailor, Soldier, Spy* (1974), *The Honourable Schoolboy* (1977), which won the James Tait Black Prize, *Smiley's People* (1980), and *The Little Drummer Girl* (1983).

Le Carré's first marriage ended in 1971; he subsequently remarried. He was made an honorary fellow of Lincoln College in 1984.

Personal

Barber: Mr. le Carré, you once pointed out that spies spent a lot of their time pretending to be characters "outside of themselves." Isn't there an obvious analogy here with writers?

le Carré: Yes. I've certainly drawn that parallel in my own mind. It's part of a writer's profession, as it's part of a spy's profession, to prey on the community to which he's attached, to take away information—often in secret—and to translate that into intelligence for his masters, whether it's his readership or his spy masters. And I think that both professions are perhaps rather lonely.

Barber: Would you also agree that both thrive on tension?

le Carré: Well, certainly I don't think that there are very many good writers who don't live without a sense of tension. If they haven't got one immediately available to them, then they usually manage to manufacture it in their private lives. But I think the real tension lies in the relationship between what you might call the pursuer and his quarry, whether it's the writer or the spy. Graham Greene once referred to a chip of ice that has to be in the writer's heart. And that is the strain: that you must abstain from them. There you have, I think, the real metaphysical relationship between the writer and the spy.

Barber: I think Eric Ambler once said that there is a criminal and a policeman in all of us, and that this could account for the popularity of spy fiction and allied genres. Would you agree?

le Carré: I think there's something much more fundamental at work at the moment. We have learned in recent years to translate almost all of political life in terms of conspiracy. And the spy novel, as never before, really, has come into its own. There is so much cynicism about the orthodox forms of government as they are offered to the public that we believe almost nothing at its face value. Now, somehow or other the politicians try to convey to us that this suspicion is misplaced. But we know better than that. And until we have a better relationship between private performance and the public truth, as was demonstrated with Watergate, we as the public are absolutely right to remain suspicious, contemptuous even, of the secrecy and the misinformation which is the digest of our news. So I think that the spy novel encapsulates this public wariness. And I think also, in entertainment terms, it makes a kind of fable about forces that we do believe in the West are stacked against us.—JOHN LE CARRÉ, Interview by Michael Barber, *NYTBR*, Sept. 25, 1977, pp. 9, 44

General

Carré's talents are admirably fitted to his subject and its themes. He has learned from Greene how to take shabby, incompetent, squalid persons and make them interesting by virtue of the pathos of their unattractiveness.

He had that kind of crumpled, worried face which is only a hairs-breadth from the music halls and yet is infinitely sad; a face in which the eyes are paler than their environment, and the contours converge upon the nostrils. Aware of this, perhaps, Taylor had grown a trivial moustache, like a scrawl on a photograph, which made a muddle of his face without concealing its shortcoming. The effect was to inspire disbelief, not because he was a rogue but because he had no talent for deception. Similarly he had tricks of movement crudely copied from some lost original. . . . Yet the whole was dignified by pain, as if he were holding his little body stiff against a cruel wind. ⟨*The Looking-Glass War*⟩

His characters commit themselves to one another by creating "that strong love which only exists between the weak; each became the stage to which the other related his actions."

Moreover Carré's England is the outward counterpart of the souls of these characters.

They passed down Lambeth Road where the God of Battles presides; the Imperial War Museum at one end, schools the other, hospitals in-between; a cemetery wired off like a tennis court. You cannot tell who lives there. The houses are too many for the people, the schools too large for the children. The hospitals may be full, but the blinds are drawn. Dust hangs everywhere, like the dust of war. It hangs over the hollow façades, chokes the grass in the grave-yards; it has driven away the people. . . . ⟨*The Looking-Glass War*⟩

Such passages lead one to suggest that Carré's novels—all differences in talent and seriousness being allowed for—are in their way the opposite of Ian Fleming's, and his agents the opposite of James Bond. Bond emerges omnipotent; they are hopeless incompetents; he luxuriates in affluence, they grub along in minginess; he is in touch with all the powers of the world; they are sunk in bureaucratic miasma. Ian Fleming was a fantasist of England in the post-war period; Carré is a novelist. He is a novelist of small defeats and large disillusions, a novelist, in other words, of the periods we are living in. One is almost tempted to say that he is the first novelist of the Cold War, and in this novel he has read the Cold War in the light of World War II—which is, incidentally, a more sensible under-taking than Joseph Heller's *Catch-22*, which represented World War II as if it were already the Cold War.—STEVEN MARCUS, "Grand Illusions," *NYRB*, Aug. 5, 1965, p. 20

. . . ⟨O⟩nly John le Carré allows his spies to despair and only then for the failure of love, not the mission. For le Carré the failure of love is the spy's paradoxical triumph. It may be that the best lovers are not the most loving, or that the greatest need for love is felt by men disoriented and distorted by failure, men cut off from their community. Perhaps those who grasp feel the lack or loss of contact the most. Take it as axiomatic and it is not very flattering to the community. We have no love for traitors but traitors are the only ones who can love. They are dropouts whose love becomes only another perversion to be traded on and, by a kind of blackmail usually reserved for the homosexual, one more of war's cold faces.

For le Carré, who sees nothing glamorous in espionage, the spy is not autonomous. The spy is a thing, created in dull security meetings and controlled by a board of drab directors. Controlled (and therefore mechanical) he is as predictable to the opposition as to his own supervisors. Espionage establish-ments, knowing one another intimately (at a distance but their work throws them together), can force double and triple crosses by blackmail, blacklisting, or discovery: to turn traitor is not a free personal choice so often as it is determined for the spy by bureaus protecting a mission. The double and triple agent becomes the truly absurd hero because, as a puppet, his only choice is to be a comedian, to act out his empty loyalties in order to show contempt for each of them. Le Carré is the best of the espionage lot, probably the best writer in the form after Graham Greene. His conclusions are close to what other serious fiction has been telling us about the world we have made to live in, that it is physically shabby and seedy and

spiritually sterile, without love, faith, or hope.—ROBERT GILLESPIE, "The Recent Future," *Salm*, Summer 1970, pp. 57–58

It is right, I think, to see two traditions in the spy story as in the crime novel. The first is conservative, supporting authority making the assertion that agents are fighting to protect something valuable. The second is radical, critical of authority, claiming that agents perpetuate, and even create, false barriers between "us" and "them." Fleming belongs to the first tradition, le Carré to the second. The actual texture of le Carré's writing owes something to Maugham and Greene, but his material is most firmly rooted in the revelations about Soviet agents that shook Britain in the fifties. The messages of the unjustly neglected *Call for the Dead* ⟨1961⟩, of *The Spy Who Came In from the Cold* ⟨1963⟩, and of le Carré's later books are that authority is not benevolent but often destroys those who serve it, that espionage and counterespionage work is often fumblingly uncertain in its aims and effects, that "our" men may be personally vicious and "their" men decent human beings—and, most of all, that an agent is generally a weak and not a strong character, powerless once he has been caught in the spy net.

The special qualities of le Carré's books are their sense of place, their sense of doom, their irony. The irony is most powerful in the *Spy*, because there it is most closely associated with the fates of individuals. As layer after layer of deceit is lifted in the story, and the way in which "London" has cynically used its own agent is revealed, the effect is to show the two apparently opposed organizations on one side and helpless human beings like Leamas and Elizabeth on the other. Le Carré shows a strong sense, both here and in *The Looking-Glass War* (1965), that spying is a sort of game in which, without wearing comic noses or any kind of disguise, people pretend to be what they are not. The whole apparatus of the trial in the *Spy* is a game, and so of course are the ridiculous, out-of-date operations in the later novel. And the purpose of such party games is betrayal; this is what is required of human beings by the players "sitting round a fire in one of their smart bloody clubs." If none of le Carré's other admirably written novels comes up to the *Spy*, it is because here the story is most bitterly and clearly told, the lesson of human degradation involved in spying most faithfully read.—JULIAN SYMONS, "A Short History of the Spy Story," *Mortal Consequences*, 1972, pp. 243–44

Works

Mr. le Carré's first two tales of espionage were extremely well received; and now he has attempted a much more ambitious novel ⟨*The Spy Who Came In from the Cold*⟩ on a similar theme, which has already earned pre-publication tributes from J. B. Priestley and Graham Greene ("The best spy story I've ever read": high praise indeed from the author of *The Confidential Agent* and editor of *The Spy's Bedside Book*). The protagonist is a "vintage professional secret agent" of the type whose extinction was recently forecast by Mr. Eric Ambler, and the technicalities of network organization carry a stamp of authenticity seldom found in stories of this nature; but the subject-matter is basically sensational, and the dangers attached to the assignment itself are of a sort which we have encountered, vicariously, only too often. . . .

The author overstresses . . . the thriller element in his story: such compromises with the accepted canon as the double-bluff penultimate surprise and the spectacular cinemat-ic escape over the Western Wall which brings the operation to a predictably tragic close, nullify the careful build-up of back-ground detail and the publishers' belief, expressed in this autumn's *Bookseller*, that Mr. le Carré's latest provides an answer to the lack of "really realistic spy novels" complained of in these columns last February. The formidable Mundt, when finally encountered, bears a strong family resemblance to those cold Jew-baiting Nazis portrayed on the screen by Conrad Veidt; while, needless to say, Control himself—although presented initially as an almost contemptible figure—proves to be wily and ruthless to an extent exceeding even his "R"-type predecessors in fiction. It is to be feared that we still have to wait for the genuine unromanticized article foreshadowed by Mr. Somerset Maugham's *Ashenden* stories or the late Montagu Slater's little-known and much underrated novel, *Who Rules a Tiger*, published nearly two decades ago but unsurpassed since as an example of the realistic genre.—UNSIGNED, "Limits of Control," *TLS*, Sept. 13, 1963, p. 693

Le Carré is really dull and really pretentious in *Tinker, Tailor, Soldier, Spy*, plodding and gloomy. Eric Ambler gave the spy story good plots and well-observed exotic atmospheres; le Carré offers only boring shoptalk, in the name of telling it like it is, presumably, the spy business is just a business, see, so who is to complain if he sounds like Sloan Wilson in *The Man in the Gray Flannel Suit*. Where Joseph Heller tries, and tries and tries, to find edges and sadnesses to the clichés about big company bureaucracies, le Carré accepts them, literally, gloomily. I kept wondering if he were trying to find some way to fool all the people all the time.—ROGER SALE, "Fooling Around, and Serious Business," *HdR*, Winter 1974–75, p. 626

. . . ⟨P⟩art of the novelty of John le Carré's return to spy fiction in 1974, *Tinker, Tailor, Soldier, Spy*, lies in the complete refocusing of the reader's attention on the internal English situation. The Russian Secret Service, directed from Moscow Centre, has succeeded in planting a 'mole', a deep penetration agent, into the top echelons of the British Secret Service, called by le Carré's familiar nickname, the 'Circus'. But the Soviet assault on British espionage in *Tinker, Tailor, Soldier, Spy* is essentially long-distance string-pulling. A bogus cultural attaché called Polyakov is planted in London to 'service' the mole, and at the same time provide him with apparently vital Soviet bloc secrets. A special safe-house in London is financed by the Treasury, allegedly so that Polyakov can be debriefed by the mole. In fact it is the mole who is consistently milked for the entire picture of English Intelligence by Polyakov. The novel comes very close to the category of the 'democratic thriller' since it exploits on home soil the nightmare of any Intelligence organisation—the fear of being totally infiltrated at the top.

Le Carré turns his London 'inside out', just as Karla, the head of Moscow Centre, ties a knot to turn the Circus 'inside out'. Tailing and surveillance move to new jargons of institutionalised nomenclature: the novel repeatedly refers to espionage procedure as 'tradecraft', and to an individual agent's practice of it as his 'handwriting'. The surveillance units round a sensitive embassy or trade mission are 'lamplighters', and a single tail on the street is a 'pavement artist'. 'Scalphunters' go out looking for likely foreign agents to 'turn' or 'buy for stock', while 'talent spotters' buy up 'college boys' for the English game. A Soviet attaché who is watched for several months is finally graded 'Persil', clean as can be. This slang conceals the author's vision of his subject as totally serious, full of danger and tragedy, beyond the reach of irony. A little boy in a Cornwall prep school is permanently on the verge of breakdown because his favourite teacher has an incomprehensible secret: he is an ex-agent 'put out to grass', a cripple with two Czech bullets in his back as evidence of an abortive operation staged by Centre to protect the mole. This teacher, Jim Prideaux, had walked into a 'honey trap'. Now he talks to his

schoolboys with phrases like 'ju-ju man', which is Old Circus slang for ritualistic leadership.

Once again le Carré is dressing up the external motifs of a popular genre in order to create a peculiarly English tragedy. The trips to foreign countries made by his various and fully differentiated agents do not alter le Carré's basic situation: we are dealing in the currency of middle and upper class Englishmen striving to impress their colleagues and rivals in a London-based profession. This profession happens to be spying, and the target of the swelling disaster in British espionage is British security itself. The complexity of the mole's treachery is compounded by the ambition, greed, sexual infidelity, shiftiness, status anxiety, nostalgia for the way things were or plain deviousness of every other ranking Circus administrator. What is simple and clear-cut in the 'democratic thriller', or the run of cloak-and-dagger intrigue, becomes unfathomably deep in *Tinker, Tailor, Soldier, Spy*.

As in Conrad's more ambitious 'literary' presentation of espionage, le Carré seeks to broaden the human catchment area of the counter-Intelligence operation. Several times the phrase 'warts and all' happens to occur in the conversation of Circus figures, underlining at a minute meta-textual level that the writing itself is concerned to expose the most trivial negligence of the human soul. The protagonist shoulders most responsibility in the story because he is empowered to investigate an enemy penetration into the Secret Service. But dramatically he is on a par with the other main figures. He is the lonely, alienated, anti-hero George Smiley, familiar from le Carré's *A Murder of Quality*. He talks busily and fussily; in this respect his technique of interrogation is curiously similar to that of Kinderman, the detective in William Blatty's *The Exorcist*. Smiley is short, podgy, easily depressed by the rain or failure to find a taxi, betrayed by his wife, anguished by memories and uneasy in retirement. We know that he will eventually succeed in unmasking the double agent. The reader even senses that Smiley will succeed because of his manner and appearance rather than in spite of it. The inevitable unmasking takes place, and the mole turns out to be Bill Haydon, the brilliant Oxford product who had fascinated men and women alike (and arranged a camouflaging affair with Smiley's own wife). But the significant point is that Smiley admits to himself that they had known all along. Deep down he has 'unmasked' nothing: '. . . all of them had tacitly shared that unexpressed half-knowledge which like an illness they hoped would go away if it was never owned to, never diagnosed. This is the old English malaise, bred by years of confusion between amateurs and professionals, snobs and experts, queers and heteros, doubles and straights, the refusal to bring scandal and corruption out under a harsh light, the insistence on settling things behind doors, pulling strings for guilty friends, overlooking an admired colleague's fist in the petty cash.

This is the world and the ethos which le Carré investigates with ostentatious romanticism in *Tinker, Tailor, Soldier, Spy*, and the professionals agents who move in and out of the taint of treachery do so as fully rounded, nervous and fallible human beings. Like the common man, they coin their own proverbs to defuse the tension of living: 'Survival . . . is an infinite capacity for suspicion', 'A committee is an animal with four back legs' etc. Prideaux, the prep school master, takes time off to pursue the pursuers of the mole, and when they find Haydon with his neck broken outside a poorly-guarded Service Centre in the country, the reader senses, rather than knowing for certain, that the victim of the Czech operation has operated rough justice on his old friend and betrayer.

There is one small, internal key which associates this prep school microcosm with the outside macrocosm of espionage and international vengeance:

> he humped his way to Grenville dormitory where he was *pledged to finish a story by John Buchan.* (author's italics)

Otherwise the description is ample and colourful, unhurried by functional considerations of suspense or calculations of climax. The prep school is peopled by characters who owe more to the world of Evelyn Waugh than to thriller writing, characters like the '. . . late Mrs Loveday who had a Persian lamb coat and stood in for junior divinity until her cheques bounced' or the dreary picture of the former 'queen of research at the Circus', Connie Sachs, who lives out her retirement in a sprawling house full of undergraduate lodgers at Oxford: '. . . a wonderful mind which had never grown up. Her formless white face took on the grandmother's glow of enchanted reminiscence. Her memory was as compendious as her body and surely she loved it more, for she had put everything aside to listen to it: her drink, her cigarette, even for a while Smiley's passive hand.'

Le Carré leaves his novel with a moral, as well as a narrative, solution: spying destroys a man's capacity for self-appraisal. It nearly destroys his capacity for loving.—BRUCE MERRY, *Anatomy of the Spy Thriller*, 1977, pp. 210–13

Since le Carré wants to present espionage as actuality, he is not at liberty to invent fantastic schemes of global takeover, villains like Milton's Satan, mad ingenuities of torture or girls of lubricious voluptuousness. Admittedly, he has a very lovely girl ⟨in *The Honourable Schoolboy*⟩, Lizzie Worthington, but she sticks out like a sore thumb among the real-life ordinary and ugly; she ought to be qualified with a wart (now I come to think of it, the hero reflects that he is willing to take her "warts and all") or with (now I come to think of it) the broken noses and uneven leg-lengths that the Bond of the books (though not the films) finds not at all off-putting. Le Carré must also cling to real places, where real espionage situations are available. The world available to the British spy who (unlikely story) is not called in to assist the C.I.A. is shrinking very fast. Only Hong Kong seems to be left, and that is where the greater part of the action of this novel takes place. . . .

Le Carré is so concerned with planting his story in a wide field of credibility that he spends far more time in mowing the field than in spudding in his shoots. This is a very long book for its subject, and there is scene after scene—usually back in London where the Circus operates—in which the old fictional principle of Ockham's Razor (less is more) is relentlessly eschewed. On the other hand, le Carré has learned something about dialogue that is not apparent in the earlier books. His Hong Kong Chinese sound like the real thing, as do his Americans—the Cousins, as the Brits call them—and the horrible Bolshies and Yellow Perils of the Circus (so the specialists are facetiously called) speak like many varieties of Brit. But the dialogues go on forever, as if boredom were an essential adjunct of learning the real truth of how intelligence operations are set up. Le Carré is like the film director Stanley Kubrick of *2001: A Space Odyssey*: if you're bored in this fictional situation, therefore this fictional situation is real life. Sometimes, bizarrely, I seemed to be reading a novel, like those of Wyndham Lewis, in which every character is solid but not one of them moves.

From the very start, le Carré seems determined to put you off these characters: they're unattractive, therefore they must be real. The facetiousness—cliché-laden and often brutal—of much of their speech, and of the recit surrounding it, sets one's teeth aching. As we move with steamroller slowness to the dénouement, we move also toward the region of a conventional and satisfying spy story—with Jerry escaping death twice, Jerry hopelessly in love, guns and broken arms and fists on the windpipe, a Hong Kong beautifully if conventionally rendered all around. And before that, we've had some efficient evocations of Laos, Northeast Thailand and Phnom Penh. And, always, the marine, cartographical, ballistic and procedural technicalities are faultless.

This book is probably already a best seller. Does it have anything to do with literature? In the sense that literature is recognizable through its capacity to evoke more than it says, is based on artful selection, throws up symbols, suggests a theology or metaphysic of which the story itself is a kind of allegory, the answer has to be no. It has nothing to do with Conrad's *Under Western Eyes* or even Greene's *The Quiet American*. Even Ian Fleming has proved susceptible to esthetic analysis, but le Carré and Len Deighton remain ingenious, veridical, documentary rather than imaginative. There is nothing wrong with that, but it is probably better for a novelist's Soul. *Soul?* Souls are for the running dogs' Baptist missions.—ANTHONY BURGESS, "Peking Drugs, Moscow Gold," *NYTBR*, Sept. 25, 1977, pp. 9, 45

It has been said that whereas the traditional spy story is conservative, supports authority and accepts established values unquestioningly, le Carré's thrillers are radical, subversive of authority, question assumptions. In fact, the ideas they embody seem more complex and subtle than this opposition suggests. In the final pages of *The Spy Who Came In from the Cold* Leamas realizes that he and Liz have been sacrificed in order to bring down Fiedler, the honest and idealistic East German intelligence officer, and thus ensure the safety of his superior, Mundt, a murderer and antisemite (the contrast is a bit too neatly ironic), who is the Circus's agent. Leamas himself accepts that this is necessary; and though the author allows the reader to form his own judgment, he never allows him to forget that on the other side of the Wall the existence of the problem would be incomprehensible.

At a time when, in the West, simple loyalties are no longer possible (Haydon, in *Tinker, Tailor, Soldier, Spy*, it is hinted, becomes a traitor because he cannot be an Empire builder), le Carré seems to suggest that the only alternative to the amorality, the refusal to adopt a moral stance of the Deighton hero (indicated by his namelessness), is both to question and to accept; to see the dilemma but not to resolve it. His characters—Smiley above all—are torn between their inclinations and their duty; though they might wish to stand by Forster's dictum, in the last resort they will betray their friends rather than their country. In *Call for the Dead* Smiley kills Dieter Frey, a former pupil and close friend; in *Tinker, Tailor, Soldier, Spy* Haydon sets up his best friend (and possibly former lover), Jim Prideaux, to be captured by the Russians so that he himself may remain undetected. Only in *The Honourable Schoolboy* is there a break in the pattern: Jerry disobeys orders and returns to Hongkong to try to save Lizzie, wishing he could have a word with Smiley "about the selfless and devoted way in which we sacrifice other people". But his intervention achieves nothing; he can save neither Lizzie nor himself. In any case, he is only an Occasional; Smiley, the professional, the last of the Empire-builders, remains true to his code, even though he knows he will be stabbed in the back.—T. J. BINYON, "A Gentleman among Players," *TLS*, Sept. 9, 1977, p. 1069

Spy stories have a good deal of the farrago in them even when they are as accomplished as le Carré's and it would be impossible and unfair to give away his elaborate plot ⟨in *Smiley's People*⟩. Le Carré creates a manner which moves by suggestion, leaking a little at a time and gradually gathering all in, without reducing it all to a flat intelligence test or conundrum. He has got to make his implausible people plausible in their dirty and shabby game. In part, he belongs to the romantic school of spy literature, and has a blokey, speculative, disabused yet fateful manner which recalls Conrad's use of Marlow; he is good at loud talk, with an occasional apologetic leaning to the metaphysical. Le Carré is a romantic, for example, in joining the General and Smiley as the chivalrous and the good men, faced with the archfiend—discreetly referred to eventually as the Sandman—the legendary Baltic figure who puts even the strongest to sleep. He must convey that Smiley is sad, lonely, and haunted by a gnawing sense of failure, whereas the enemy has never failed and has indeed once gypped him, has once even inserted a defector in the British Service and into Smiley's private life.

There is a tendency in the literature of espionage to create the battered Saint. One sees the metaphysical view coming in when Smiley is moving away from the horrifying corpse on Hampstead Heath; a simple police superintendent flashes his torch on Smiley's face. Unlike your face or mine (the superintendent says to himself) it was not one face. More like a history of the human face.

> More your whole range of faces. More your patchwork of different ages, people, and endeavours. Even—thought the Superintendent—of different faiths.

The superintendent becomes eloquent, but his thought becomes Marlow-ish in the last sentence:

> An abbey, made up of all sorts of conflicting ages and styles and convictions. The Superintendent liked that metaphor the more he dwelt on it. He would try it out on his wife when he got home: man as God's architecture, my dear, moulded by the hand of ages, infinite in his striving and diversity. . . . But at this point the Superintendent laid a restraining hand upon his own rhetorical imagination. . . . Maybe we're flying a mite too high for the course, my friend.

A nice touch of British modesty and caution there, but we can guess that the superintendent's pause is an actor's: there is something even stranger to say about that face. As it looked down at the head of the dead émigré leader, himself a legend, the superintendent notices Smiley's face was oddly moist. This sometimes happened to the superintendent himself and the lads when they had to deal with the horrors of criminal assault or the rape of infants. You don't get a fit of histrionics, you don't throw up, as young policemen do: you put your hand to your face and find it is moist.

> You wondered what the hell Christ bothered to die for, if He ever died at all.

Marlow again: better take the day off if you start feeling like that or you'll start roughing up people. Fortunately fat little Smiley (who so often wipes his glasses and is red-eyed because he sits up half the night) is alive at the end of the book. If he died we might get a whiff of something like the odor of sanctity. It is knowing of le Carré to palm off the mystical suggestion on a cop. For Smiley's melancholy detachment is not godlike. He is a "case man" if there ever was one. Looking back in his lonely evenings on his private misery—his wife has "teams" of lovers and has injured his heart and career by going to bed with his closest colleague, who became a double agent and defector—he reflects that he has "sacrificed his life to institutions." If he is humane in a nasty trade and has seen a lot of dead men, he does not mourn for the dead. He mourns for the living. He is

patient and cunning in the minute detail; he looks into the human being first. He is a pluralist.

What a man like Smiley needs is an enemy, a fanatical monist who stops at nothing: there may be a moment when rigid fanaticism breaks down, overstrained by its inhuman excess. And there is one murderous absolutist whom he failed to trap in Delhi years ago, high up in the Moscow services. The professional Smiley burns to reverse that failure and, indeed, for revenge, but not murder. Slowly we scent this villain in the seemingly extraneous case of poor Ostrakova and the General.—V. S. PRITCHETT, "A Spy Romance," *NYRB*, Feb. 7, 1980, p. 22

Every age has its operative analogy, a mass interpretation of life. The Italians had the commedia dell'arte's succession of masks; the English during the Restoration saw life as a drama of manners. We seem to have adopted espionage as our analogy, as if, instead of masks, we all now have a second, narrower pair of eyes with which to view ourselves and others.

Espionage affects our politics not only in the billions of dollars spent by the CIA, the FBI, and the innumerable other intelligence divisions but in its spirit. Richard Nixon imagined a rabble out to get him; we imagine a government out to get us, not to mention credit agencies and the Warsaw Pact. The central concept of the Protestant Reformation was that each individual could commune directly, without intermediaries, with the Lord Almighty. The closest we come to direct access is the Freedom of Information Act, which we invoke to check on the size of our government dossiers. In the Age of Enlightenment, scientists studied orreries, wheelwork models of the solar system, to understand celestial mechanics. We study John le Carré for much the same reason: to better understand the murk we live in.

Writing about le Carré is chancy. Ever since 1962, when *The Spy Who Came In from the Cold* was published, he has been the standard by which other writers of the so-called international thriller are measured. A couple of years ago I got the garland "Le Carré of the Year." The next season it was passed to the succeeding pretender. Le Carré stayed the constant. With his new novel, *The Little Drummer Girl*, he remains ahead of us, dwelling at, exploring, the very end of espionage as the analogy he helped create.

Espionage is endless detail and paper-work, it is boredom and huge ignorances suddenly punctuated by violence that invariably goes out of control. It is a mosaic spotted with blood. There are no heroes, because heroes are the creation of crusades, not deceptions. In each new book, le Carré becomes more involved and entangled in espionage as the professional technique it really is. This is the context and lesson of his work as it has developed: ever more detailed means, ever more obscure ends.

The Little Drummer Girl is Charlie, a young English actress enlisted by Israeli intelligence to play the mistress of a Palestinian terrorist. The story, le Carré's orrery, is deliberately, ponderously complicated, full of gears and wheels turning at different paces, and populated by fifty or more characters, each with his own mass and orbit moving with strict consistency to the same gravity le Carré has traced in the real world.

This may be the best and most complete novel about espionage technique, about its psychoanalytical application, ever written. It's also the most balanced novel about Jews and Arabs, outrage for outrage and tear for tear, I've read. Still, for all that, there is no touch of le Carré's great characters—no Leamas, no Smiley—in *The Little Drummer Girl*. While there is much to be learned about how to tear apart the psyche of a second-rate actress and remake her into a spy, there remains a vacuum for a central human. Charlie is essentially an innocent bystander, a fellow traveler, and the willing slave of love; she is shrewdly observed but so suggestible as to give us no constant person we can live in. Leamas, *Spy's* centerpiece, has here developed into Gadi Becker, an Israeli intelligence officer, still middle-aged and scarred but smoother, handsomer, a deliberate seducer. He acts the part of a young Arab with painstaking exactness and utter denial of his own character and emotions, and he becomes more a blur the further we go into this long book. There are interesting secondary characters, but in the center no one alive. Espionage itself, with its self-deluding detail and obsession with manipulation, is the main character of *The Little Drummer Girl.*

It may be said that, when espionage no longer delivers new characters, only finer gears, it has ceased to be a creative metaphor. Yet this is a bleak and daring novel for all its hollowness, because of its hollowness, and because it delivers a message with no comfort. *The Little Drummer Girl* is in part a primer on what it means to be a spy. Klaus Fuchs, the "Atomic Spy," once said he could work with, admire, and be a close friend to the people he was betraying because he operated with a "controlled schizophrenia." That schizophrenia is what le Carré and Gadi teach; it is what all spies eventually must learn.—MARTIN CRUZ SMITH, "Season of Spies," *Esquire,* April 1983, p. 106

With *The Little Drummer Girl,* John le Carré has thrown off his winter cloak and let his limbs flex. Unlike the Smiley novels, which have a burrowing, circumspect determination, *The Little Drummer Girl* doesn't read as if it were written with mittens. The books feels as if it were dashed off with the zealous haste of a reporter filing for a deadline. Once the dread Karla had been flushed from his lair like a sick, shivering animal at the close of *Smiley's People* (". . . in the halo Smiley saw his face, aged and weary and travelled, the short hair turned to white by a sprinkling of snow"), le Carré must have sensed it was time to strike down the tents of the Circus and push on to a larger, more turbulent arena—the Middle East.

Yet this novel is far from a severe break from le Carré's previous preoccupations. Waiting on the bridge for Karla to show, Smiley "hung back, like a man refusing to go on stage," and once Karla moused into view, victor and victim had a brief moment in which to measure each other's depths—"They exchanged one more glance and perhaps each for that second did see in the other something of himself." With its secret sharers and frequent stresses on terrorism as the theater of the real, *The Little Drummer Girl* is a rugged elaboration on that moment when Smiley and Karla met as mirrors. Newsy as the novel is, it's also le Carré's go at writing a meditative adventure saga in the tradition of Joseph Conrad, and it's hardly a fluke that one of the characters here is named Joseph; another, Kurtz. A concealed bomb is this book's heart of darkness.

Not that le Carré succumbs to Conradian mystification. *The Little Drummer Girl* is very bold colored, very pop; it pares away the brooding ruminations of a Conrad adventure to reach instead the sinew of heroic romance. Reviewing *The Honourable Schoolboy* in these pages, Clive James lamented "the tone of myth-making portent" in le Carré's later fiction—the increasingly heavy tread of Smiley's legend. "'For nobody . . . quite dared to challenge Smiley's authority': In just such a way T. E. Lawrence used to write about himself. As he entered the tent, sheiks fell silent, stunned by his charisma." *The Little Drummer Girl,* too, rolls out legends capable of awing the sheiks.

. . . Where *The Little Drummer Girl* will prove controversial is in its rough thumping of Israeli policies. The Israeli agents in the book are depicted as seasoned, savvy pros with leather-hide skins and a fondness for homey proverbs: "Kurtz

said it too. Often. Grinning his pirate's grin, he said it now. 'You want to catch the lion, first you tether the goat.'" The success of Charlie's mission triggers a blood-scourge, and these amiably tough Israelis come to seem savagely efficient, almost kill-happy, as the bodies of Khalil's confederates are knifed, blown up, shot. And le Carré then brings in an event of far wider scope:

> . . . the long-awaited Israeli push into Lebanon occurred, ending that present phase of hostilities or, according to where you stood, heralding the next one. The refugee camps that had played host to Charlie were sanitised, which meant roughly that bulldozers were brought in to bury the bodies and complete what the tanks and artillery bombing raids had started. . . . Special groups eradicated the secret places in Beirut where Charlie had stayed; of the house in Sidon only the chickens and the tangerine orchard remained.

Le Carré has gone on record in the English press against the Israeli invasion of Lebanon, and in the novel he grafts onto Gadi Becker's conscience his own indignant qualms. "And [Becker] ended with a most offensive question, something he claimed to have culled from the writings of Arthur Koestler, and evidently adapted to his own preoccupation: 'What are we to become, I wonder,' he said. 'A Jewish homeland or an ugly little Spartan state?'" Well, at least le Carré had the presence of mind to label the question "offensive," but it does seem worth pointing out that if Israel resembles a garrison state it's hardly because it's thronged on three sides by imaginary foes.

Of course, the conflict between means and ends has always been the pricking tangle in le Carré's work. George Smiley couldn't savor his victory over Karla because the techniques he used brought him down to Karla's own level of ruthless cunning. And Becker can't really savor the snuffing out of these anti-Israel terrorists not only because of the Lebanon aftermath but because this triumph was brought about by the scooping out of Charlie's sensibilities, the husking of her heart. "I'm dead, she kept saying. I'm dead, I'm dead."

For all its waywardness, *The Little Drummer Girl* carries an exhilaration because it's le Carré's finest and most searching exploration of the dynamics of need, and how neediness is used, perverted. Love of his daughter toppled Karla, and love here is betrayal and submission, crippler and crutch. And the absence of love, le Carré seems to be saying in the novel's fade, is not hate but exhaustion. *I'm dead, I'm dead.* As in the best Smiley novels, le Carré poeticizes exhaustion in *The Little Drummer Girl,* and leaves you feeling that there are embers in the ashes of fatigue which will spark new obsessions, new betrayals. Hungry for reckoning, his burnt-out cases never find true rest.—JAMES WOLCOTT, "The Secret Sharers," *NYRB,* April 14, 1983, pp. 19–21

CLIVE JAMES
"Go Back to the Cold!"

New York Review of Books, October 27, 1977, pp. 29–30

L e Carré's new novel 〈*The Honourable Schoolboy*〉 is about twice as long as it should be. It falls with a dull thud into the second category of le Carré's books—those which are greeted as being something more than merely entertaining. Their increasingly obvious lack of mere entertainment is certainly strong evidence that le Carré is out to produce a more respectable breed of novel than those which fell into the first category, the ones which were merely entertaining. But in fact it was the merely entertaining books that had the more intense life.

The books in the first category—and le Carré might still produce more of them, if he can only bring himself to distrust the kind of praise he has grown used to receiving—were written in the early and middle Sixties. They came out at the disreputably brisk rate of one a year. *Call for the Dead* (1961), *A Murder of Quality* (1962), *The Spy Who Came In from the Cold* (1963), and *The Looking-Glass War* (1965) were all tightly controlled efforts whose style, characterization, and atmospherics were subordinate to the plot, which was the true hero. Above all, they were brief: *The Spy Who Came In from the Cold* is not even half the length of the ponderous whopper currently under review.

Elephantiasis, of ambition as well as reputation, set in during the late Sixties, when *A Small Town in Germany* (1968) inaugurated the second category. Not only was it more than merely entertaining, but it was, according to the *New Statesman's* reviewer, "at least a masterpiece." After an unpopular but instantly forgiven attempt at a straight novel (*The Naive and Sentimental Lover*), the all-conquering onward march of the more than merely entertaining spy story was resumed with *Tinker, Tailor, Soldier, Spy* (1974), which was routinely hailed as the best thriller le Carré had written up to that time.

The Honourable Schoolboy brings the second sequence to a heavy apotheosis. A few brave reviewers have expressed doubts about whether some of the elements which supposedly enrich le Carré's later manner might not really be a kind of impoverishment, but generally the book has been covered with praise—a response not entirely to be despised, since *The Honourable Schoolboy* is so big that it takes real effort to cover it with anything. At one stage I tried to cover it with a pillow, but there it was, still half visible, insisting, against all the odds posed by its coagulated style, on being read to the last sentence.

The last sentence comes 530 pages after the first, whose tone of myth-making portent is remorselessly adhered to throughout. "Afterwards, in the dusty little corners where London's secret servants drink together, there was argument about where the Dolphin case history should really begin." The Dolphin case history, it emerges with stupefying gradualness, is concerned with the Circus (i.e., the British Secret Service) getting back on its feet after the catastrophic effect of its betrayal by Bill Haydon, the Kim Philby figure whose depredations were the subject of *Tinker, Tailor, Soldier, Spy*. The recovery is masterminded by George Smiley, nondescript hero and cuckold genius. From his desk in London, Smiley sets in motion a tirelessly labyrinthine scheme which results in the capture of the Soviet Union's top agent in China. Hong Kong is merely the scene of the action. The repercussions are world-wide. Smiley's success restores the Circus's fortunes and discomfits the KGB. But could it be that the Cousins (i.e., the CIA) are the real winners after all? It is hard to tell. What is easy to tell is that at the end of the story a man lies dead. Jerry Westerby, the Honourable Schoolboy of the title, has let his passions rule his sense of duty, and has paid the price. He lies face down and lifeless, like someone who has been reading a very tedious novel.

This novel didn't *have* to be tedious. The wily schemes of the Circus have been just as intricate before today. In fact the machinations outlined in *The Spy Who Came in from the Cold* and *The Looking-Glass War* far outstrip in subtlety anything Smiley gets up to here. Which is part of the trouble. In those books character and incident attended upon narrative, and were all the more vivid for their subservience. In this book, when you strip away the grandiloquence, the plot is shown to

be perfunctory. There is not much of a *story*. Such a lack is one of the defining characteristics of le Carré's more recent work. It comes all the more unpalatably from a writer who gave us, in *The Spy Who Came In from the Cold*, a narrative so remarkable for symmetrical economy that it could be turned into an opera.

Like the Oscar Wilde character who doesn't need the necessary because he has the superfluous, le Carré's later manner is beyond dealing in essentials. The general effect is of inflation. To start with, the prose style is overblown. Incompatible metaphors fight for living space in the same sentence. "Now at first Smiley tested the water with Sam—and Sam, who liked a poker hand himself, tested the water with Smiley." Are they playing cards in the bath? Such would-be taciturnity is just garrulousness run short of breath. On the other hand, the would-be eloquence is verbosity run riot. Whole pages are devoted to inventories of what can be found by way of flora and fauna in Hong Kong, Cambodia, Vietnam, and other sectors of the mysterious East. There is no possible question that le Carré has been out there and done his fieldwork. Unfortunately he has brought it all home.

But the really strength-sapping feature of the prose style is its legend-building tone. Half the time le Carré sounds like Tolkien. You get visions of Hobbits sitting around the fire telling tales of Middle Earth.

> Need Jerry have ever gone to Ricardo in the first place? Would the outcome, for himself, have been different if he had not? Or did Jerry, as Smiley's defenders to this day insist, by his pass at Ricardo, supply the last crucial heave which shook the tree and caused the coveted fruit to fall?

Forever asking questions where he ought to be answering them, the narrator is presumably bent on seasoning mythomania with Jamesian ambiguity: *The Lord of the Rings* meets *The Golden Bowl*. Working on principle that there can be no legends without lacunae, the otherwise omniscient author, threatened by encroaching comprehensibility, takes refuge in a black cloud of question marks. The ultimate secrets are lost in the mists of time and/or the dusty filing cabinets of the Circus.

> Was there really a conspiracy against Smiley, of the scale that Guillam supposed? If so, how was it affected by Westerby's own maverick intervention? No information is available and even those who trust each other well are not disposed to discuss the question. Certainly there was a secret understanding between Enderby and Martello. . . .

And after a paragraph like that, you get another paragraph like that.

> And did Smiley *know* of the conspiracy, deep down? Was he aware of it, and did he secretly even welcome the solution? Peter Guillam, who has since had two good years in exile in Brixton to consider his opinion, insists that the answer to both questions is a firm *yes*. . . .

Fatally, the myth-mongering extends to the characterization. The book opens with an interminable scene starring the legendary journalists of Hong Kong. Most legendary of them all is an Australian called Craw. In a foreword le Carré makes it clear that Craw is based on Dick Hughes, legendary Australian journalist. As it happens, Australian journalists of Hughes's stature often *are* the stuff of legend. In the dusty little corners where London's journalists do their drinking, there is often talk of what some Australian journalist has been up to. They cultivate their reputations. After the Six Day War one of them brought a jeep back to London on expenses. But the fact that many Australian journalists are determined to attain the status of legend does not necessarily stop them being the stuff of it. Indeed Hughes has been used as a model before, most notably by Ian Fleming in *You Only Live Twice*. What is notable about le Carré's version, however, is its singular failure to come alive. Craw is meant to be a fountain of humorous invective, but the cumulative effect is tiresome in the extreme.

> "Your Graces," said old Craw, with a sigh. "Pray silence for my son. I fear he would have parley with us. Brother Luke, you have committed several acts of war today and one more will meet with our severe disfavour. Speak clearly and concisely omitting no detail, however slight, and thereafter hold your water, sir."

Known to be an expert mimic in real life, le Carré for some reason has an anti-talent for comic dialogue. Craw's putatively mirth-provoking high-falutin' is as funny as a copy of *The Honourable Schoolboy* falling on your foot. Nor does Craw do much to justify the build-up le Carré gives him as a master spy. The best you can say for him is that he is more believable than one of his drinking companions, Superintendent "Rocker" Rockhurst, the legendary Hong Kong Policeman. "Rocker" Rockhurst? There used to be a British comic-strip character called Rockfist Rogan. Perhaps that was the derivation. Anyway, it is "Rocker" Rockhurst's main task to preserve order among the legendary Hong Kong journalists, who are given to drinking legendary amounts, preparatory to engaging in legendary fist-fights. Everything that is most wearisome about journalism is solemnly presented as the occupation of heroes. No wonder, then, that espionage is presented as the occupation of gods.

Le Carré used to be famous for showing us the bleak, tawdry reality of the spy's career. He still provides plenty of bleak tawdriness, but romanticism comes shining through. Jerry Westerby, it emerges, has that "watchfulness" which "the instinct" of "the very discerning" describes as "professional." You would think that if Westerby really gave off these vibrations it would make him useless as a spy. But le Carré does not seem to notice that he is indulging himself in the same kind of transparently silly detail which Mark Twain found so abundant in Fenimore Cooper.

It would not matter so much if the myth-mongering were confined to the minor characters. But in this novel George Smiley completes his rise to legendary status. Smiley has been present, on the sidelines or at the center, but more often at the center, in most of le Carré's novels since the very beginning. In Britain he has been called the most representative character in modern fiction. In the sense that he has been inflating almost as fast as the currency, perhaps he is. His latest appearance should make it clear to all but the most dewy-eyed that Smiley is essentially a dream.

It could be, of course, that he is a useful dream. Awkward, scruffy, and impotent on the outside, he is graceful, elegant, and powerful within. An impoverished country could be forgiven for thinking that such a man embodies its true condition. But to be a useful dream Smiley needs to be credible. In previous novels le Carré has kept his hero's legendary omniscience within bounds, but here it springs loose. "Then Smiley disappeared for three days." Sherlock Holmes, it will be recalled, was always making similarly unexplained disappearances, to the awed consternation of Watson. Smiley's interest in the minor German poets recalls some of Holmes's enthusiasms. But at least the interest in the minor German poets was there from the start (*Vide* "A Brief History of George Smiley" in *Call for the Dead*) and was

not tacked on later á la Conan Doyle, who constantly supplied Holmes with hitherto unhinted at areas of erudition. Conan Doyle wasn't bothered that the net effect of such lily-gilding was to make his hero more vaporous instead of less. Le Carré, though, ought to be bothered. When Smiley, in his latest incarnation, suddenly turns out, at the opportune moment, to be an expert on Chinese naval engineering, his subordinates might be wide-eyed in worship, but the reader is unable to resist blowing a discreet raspberry.

It was Smiley, we now learn, who buried Control, his spiritual father. (And Control, we now learn, had two marriages going at once. It is a moot point whether or not learning more about the master plotter of *The Spy Who Came In from the Cold* leaves us caring less.) We get the sense, and I fear are meant to get the sense, of Camelot, with the king dead but the quest continuing. Unfortunately, the pace is more like Bresson than like Malory.

Smiley's fitting opponent is Karla, the KGB's chief of operations. Smiley has Karla's photograph hanging in his office, just as Montgomery had Rommel's photograph hanging in his caravan. Karla, who made a fleeting physical appearance in the previous novel, is kept offstage in this one—a sound move, since like Moriarty he is too abstract a figure to survive examination. But the tone of voice in which le Carré talks about the epic mental battle between Smiley and Karla is too sublime to be anything but ridiculous. "For nobody, not even Martello, quite dared to challenge Smiley's authority." In just such a way T. E. Lawrence used to write about himself. As he entered the tent, sheiks fell silent, stunned by his charisma.

There was a day when Smiley generated less of a nimbus. But that was a day when le Carré was more concerned with stripping down the mystique of his subject than with building it up. In his early novels le Carré told the truth about Britain's declining influence. In the later novels, the influence having declined even further, his impulse has altered. The slide into destitution has become a planned retreat, with Smiley masterfully in charge. On le Carré's own admission, Smiley has always been the author's fantasy about himself—a Billy Batson who never has to say "Shazam!" because inside he never stops being Captain Marvel. But lately Smiley has also become the author's fantasy about his beleaguered homeland.

The Honourable Schoolboy makes a great show of being realistic about Britain's plight and the consequently restricted scope of Circus activities. Hong Kong, the one remaining colony, is the only forward base of operations left. There is no money to spend. Nevertheless the Circus can hope to make up in cunning—Smiley's cunning—for what it lacks in physical resources. A comforting thought, but probably deceptive.

In the previous novel the Philby affair was portrayed as a battle of wits between the KGB and the Circus. It was the Great Game: Mrs. Philby's little boy Kim had obvious affinities with Kipling's child prodigy. But the facts of the matter, as far as we know them, suggest that whatever the degree of Philby's wit, it was the Secret Service's witlessness which allowed him to last so long. Similarly, in the latest book, the reader is bound to be wryly amused by the marathon scenes in which the legendary codebreaker Connie (back to bore us again) works wonders of deduction among her dusty filing cabinets. It has only been a few months since it was revealed that the real-life Secret Service, faced with the problem of sorting out two different political figures who happened to share the same name, busily compiled an enormous dossier on the wrong one.

There is always the possibility that in those of its activities which do not come to light the Secret Service functions with devilish efficiency. But those activities which do come to light seem usually on a par with the CIA's schemes to assassinate Castro by poisoning his cap or setting fire to his beard. *Our Man in Havana* was probably the book which came closest to the truth.

This novel still displays enough of le Carré's earlier virtues to remind us that he is not summarily to be written off. There is an absorbing meeting in a soundproof room, with Smiley plausibly outwitting the civil servants and politicians. Such internecine warfare, to which most of the energy of any secret organization must necessarily be devoted, is le Carré's best subject: he is as good at it as Nigel Balchin, whose own early books—especially *The Small Back Room* and *Darkness Falls from the Air*—so precisely adumbrated the disillusioned analytical skill of le Carré's best efforts.

But lately disillusion has given way to illusion. Outwardly aspiring to the status of literature, le Carré's novels have inwardly declined to the level of pulp romance. He is praised for sacrificing action to character, but ought to be dispraised, since by concentrating on personalities he succeeds only in overdrawing them, while eroding the context which used to give them their desperate authenticity. Raising le Carré to the plane of literature has helped rob him of his more enviable role as a popular writer who could take you unawares. Already working under an assumed name, le Carré ought to assume another one, sink out of sight, and run for the border of his reputation. There might still be time to get away.

DAVID MONAGHAN
"John le Carré and England: A Spy's Eye View"

Modern Fiction Studies, Autumn 1983, pp. 569–82

T he fact that John le Carré has worked almost exclusively within the popular genre of the spy thriller has not deterred reviewers and critics from according him a considerable literary reputation.[1] And in many cases these commentators have been most perceptive as to the source of his literariness. Free from any Leavisite prejudices about the inherent limitations of popular culture, they have located le Carré's achievement in his ability to manipulate the conventions of the spy novel toward artistic ends.[2] Thus, it becomes evident that a full appreciation of le Carré's novels will be based on an understanding of his simultaneous involvement in a tradition of patriotic British fantasy that includes Erskine Childers, John Buchan, "Sapper," and E. Phillips Oppenheim, and ironic distance from this tradition. Because of its national and international emphases, the spy novel always reveals something about a writer's vision of his own country, but because it is a popular form, the wish-fulfillment rather than the analytical aspects of the vision tend to come into sharpest focus. Hence, the world presented by the British spy novel, at least before Graham Greene, is composed of upright chaps defending the decencies of the British way of life from the threats posed by various unsavory foreigners. Le Carré is, in a quite fundamental sense, a romantic, almost a sentimentalist, possessed of a deep love for his country, and his novels belong, in some important ways, to this patriotic tradition. At the same time, though, le Carré is quite aware that English society is no longer, if it ever was, what John Buchan and Sapper claimed it to be, and the world of espionage he creates offers not only the satisfactions of escapism but also a very useful vantage point from which the reader can view the realities of contemporary English society. It is this latter aspect of le Carré's art that I intend to investigate in my paper.

John le Carré has made it quite clear that for him the world of spying functions as a metaphor: "The British secret services . . . are . . . microcosms of the British condition, of our social attitudes and vanities."[3] However, in suggesting that his secret world is a microcosm of the overt world, le Carré does not do full justice to the complex ways in which it interacts with the larger society, for the world of espionage not only mirrors contemporary England, it also offers an attractive alternative to a society that has become corrupt and loveless. Ultimately, though, le Carré shows this alternative to be a chimera and turns it on its head in such a way as to explain the necessity of and to provide some guidelines for continuing to engage the self in the world outside. The illusory nature of the appeal of espionage is bound up in its failure to cope with the full complexity of experience. Life, for le Carré, is made up of conflicting claims that are immensely difficult, if not impossible, to reconcile. The solution offered by the subculture of spying is to dismiss all those aspects of experience that le Carré, in imitation of Schiller, defines as naive or natural in favor of those he calls sentimental or learned.[4] The spy thus grants no value to feeling, spontaneity, or individuality and instead commits himself entirely to technique or tradecraft, as it is called in the jargon of le Carré's intelligence service. What le Carré's novels reveal, however, is that, as a price for refusing to behave complexly, the spy at best sacrifices any claims to maturity and at worst becomes totally dehumanized. The espionage world is, then, not just a mirror of contemporary society but is also, as le Carré comments in an interview with Teresa McGonigall, "a superb world with which to illustrate the various paradoxes in which we live."[5]

Le Carré's novels offer such detailed analyses of life beyond the confines of the Circus, the headquarters of British Intelligence, that the reader has little difficulty grasping the microcosmic implications of his depiction of the secret world. Traditional values such as love, trust, and close personal and family relationships receive no more respect in contemporary England than they do in the mocking jargon of the Circus, according to which "to make a pass" is to make contact with the target of an operation, "the Cousins" are the rival American Intelligence Service, and "to baby-sit" is to act as a guard. Consequently, betrayal, deceit, concealment, and isolation, those qualities we associate with espionage, prove to be equally applicable to the society at large.

The source of this rottenness lies, for le Carré, in the decadence of its ruling class. The great houses that were erected as visible symbols of the importance and dignity of an aristocracy that based its authority on a strict code of duty and a sense of obligation to others have either, like Millponds, been destroyed to make way for motorways[6] or turned into gambling clubs (*TTSS*, p. 196). Those that still stand, such as the Sercomb family home, aptly nicknamed "Harry's Cornish heap," are almost visibly disintegrating: "It was granite and very big, and crumbling, with a crowd of gables that clustered like torn black tents above the tree-tops. Acres of smashed greenhouses led to it; collapsed stables and an untended kitchen garden lay below it in the valley."[7] The ruling class itself, trained to administer an Empire that no longer exists, is at best directionless and at worst deceitful and self-seeking. Whitehall lies in the hands of people like Oliver Lacon, whose sole concern is personal power: "All power corrupts but some must govern and in that case Brother Lacon will reluctantly scramble to the top of the heap" (*TTSS*, p. 199). And the diplomatic service, le Carré shows in *A Small Town in Germany*, has been reduced to a time-serving aimlessness. In this "dream box,"[8] as Turner describes the Bonn Embassy, affairs are conducted according to a protocol that no one cares about (*STG*, pp. 24, 37) in pursuit of a "destination [that is] irrelevant" (*STG*, p. 28). Bradfield, the ambassador, whose career has run parallel to the final stages of the decline of the Empire, belongs, as his wife puts it, to "the humiliated generation" (*STG*, p. 237) and seeks nothing more than to keep up appearances: "I'm a great believer in hypocrisy. It's the nearest we ever get to virtue. It's a statement of what we ought to be. Like religion, like art, like the law, like marriage. I serve the appearance of things (*STG*, p. 299). His assistant, de Lisle, has the air of one who "had much rather not have been called at all (*STG*, p. 21) and operates according to an ethic of "Apathy is our daily bread" (*STG* 129).

This moral decay is nowhere more evident than in George Smiley's wife, the former Lady Ann Sercomb, who is bracketed with Lacon in being dominated by "the ego, demanding its feed" (*SP*, p. 45). Values such as loyalty, duty, and concern for others are anathema to Lady Ann, and she dedicates her life to the pursuit of sybaritic pleasure. The inevitable and repeated betrayals of her husband that this involves she justifies by glib and self-seeking epigrams such as "there is no loyalty without betrayal" (*SP*, p. 66).

Given that the ruling class has replaced the notion of the personal relationship founded on trust and mutual concern with one based on deceit, it is not surprising that the entire society is shot through with a sense of secrecy, betrayal, mistrust, and alienation. People characteristically spy on and gossip about rather than relate to each other. In *The Looking-Glass War* Mrs. Yates watches everyone "night and day" from behind her curtains;[9] Miss Crail, Leamas' superior in the Bayswater Library for Psychic Research, refuses to communicate with him and instead "conspired" into the telephone;[10] and the newspaper editor Stubbs, "listened to incoming calls from correspondents without telling them he was on the line."[11] Gossip and rumors are rife in a Whitehall populated by people like Roddy Martindale, and a sense of secrecy, which is epitomized by Maltby's trunk lurking ominously in the cellar at Thursgood's school, permeates even the most mundane corners of society:

> Maltby's trunk still lay in the cellar awaiting instructions. Several of the staff, but chiefly Marjoribanks, were in favour of opening the trunk. . . . But Thursgood set his creaseless face resolutely against their entreaties. Only five years had passed since he had inherited the school from his father, but they had taught him already that some things are best locked away. (*TTSS*, p. 9)

When people try to draw closer, they tend to repeat the pattern of betrayal that characterizes Ann's relationship with George Smiley. Lizzy Worthington nominates her husband as her "longstop" (*HS*, p. 214) and then simply walks out on him. Oliver Lacon's wife prefers men who beat her, presumably because they reflect more accurately the reality of the modern alienated relationship than does Lacon with his empty gestures at romantic love: " 'We were always taught that women had to be cherished,' Lacon declared resentfully. 'If one didn't make 'em feel loved every minute of the day, they'd go off the rails' " (*SP*, p. 288). And Alan Turner is first cuckolded and then deserted by his wife in favor of a man with a superior sexual technique. Even in relationships lacking an obvious exploiter, closeness seems almost impossible. Jerry Westerby is well-intentioned and longs for warmth and affection yet has left behind him a trail of broken marriages, and Aldo Cassidy, the hero of *The Naive and Sentimental Lover*, is unable to form a single fruitful relationship even though he devotes himself entirely to the pursuit of love.

Alienation is equally evident in areas of human interaction other than romantic love. Bill Roach has been betrayed and abandoned by his parents; Smiley is plagued by companions like Roddy Martindale and Oliver Lacon, men who demand his attention to satisfy their personal needs—Roddy's for gossip and Oliver's for emotional self-indulgence—rather than to establish any personal bond; and Westerby's editor greets him with a "hangman's smile" and questions about his expense account (*HS*, p. 98). As a result le Carré's novels are full of isolated and lonely men and women—Avery, Leclerc, and Haldane in *The Looking-Glass War*, Myra Meadowes and Jenny Pargiter in *A Small Town in Germany*, the Pellings in *The Honourable Schoolboy*, Mikhel in *Smiley's People*, and so on.

Although the world of spying serves throughout le Carré's work as a general metaphor for the quality of contemporary English life, it becomes most explicitly a microcosm in *Tinker, Tailor, Soldier, Spy*. The betrayal by its traditional ruling class—which, as in the case of Ann Smiley, usually manifests itself in moral terms—becomes more sinister and immediate in le Carré's account of Bill Haydon's work as a double agent. Haydon, who is indeed Ann's cousin, is firmly located in the upper reaches of English society: "His father was a high court judge, two of his several beautiful sisters had married into the aristocracy" (*TTSS*, p. 138). But even more than this, he once represented the best hopes of his class. At Oxford, Haydon was the golden boy, often compared with T. E. Lawrence and Rupert Brooke, symbols of the post-Victorian ideal of Englishness. To Peter Guillam, Haydon was "the torch-bearer of a certain kind of antiquated romanticism, a notion of English calling" (*TTSS*, p. 299). Yet it is he who betrays his country, not any of the other suspects, all of whom are in traditional class and racial terms more likely traitors—Esterhase is a polyglot European, Bland is working class, and Alleline is provincial middle class. Haydon himself underlines the extent to which old "truths" are being subverted here when, adopting with supreme irony the tone of a character out of Sapper or Oppenheim, he suggests that it is Percy Alleline who has been "turned" by the Russians: "Lower-class bloke with upper-class sources, must be a bounder. Percy's sold out to Karla, it's the only explanation" (*TTSS*, p. 140). Le Carré is unwilling to reduce Haydon entirely to a class metaphor, and he does suggest that the need to betray is an integral part of his personality: "Bill the born deceiver, whose quest for the ultimate betrayal led him into the Russians' bed, and Ann's" (*SP*, p. 142). At the same time, though, he makes it clear that Haydon is motivated by a need to revenge himself on his country for depriving him of the Empire he was trained to rule:

> Haydon had betrayed. As a lover, a colleague, a friend; as a patriot, as a member of that inestimable body which Ann loosely called the Set: in every capacity, Haydon had overtly pursued one aim and secretly achieved its opposite. Smiley knew very well that even now he did not grasp the scope of that appalling duplicity: yet there was a part of him that rose already in Haydon's defence. Was not Bill also betrayed? Connie's lament rang in his ears: "Poor loves. Trained to Empire, trained to rule the waves. . . . You're the last, George, you and Bill." He saw with painful clarity an ambitious man born to the big canvas, brought up to rule, divide and conquer, whose visions and vanities all were fixed, like Percy's, upon the world's game; for whom the reality was a poor island with scarcely a voice that would carry across the water. (*TTSS*, p. 297)

Thus, it would seem legitimate to take Bill Haydon's treachery

—which, as the above quotation underlines, is total because it involves Ann, Smiley, and Prideaux (lover, colleague, and friend) in addition to his nation and class—as emblematic of the betrayal of England by its upper classes.

For John le Carré, however, the world of espionage functions as more than a microcosm of English society; it also represents an alternative to it. The ways in which this is so are made evident by le Carré's exploration of his characters' motives for becoming spies. In the traditional spy thriller, the heroes find in espionage an excitement lacking in ordinary life, but they are also always acutely aware of serving the national interest and so in no sense feel they are turning away from English society. Thus, although Bulldog Drummond first becomes involved in espionage in an attempt to alleviate boredom and thinks of his adventures as going "on the warpath," he never forgets that he is working "for the good of the state."[12] The same combination of factors is at work in Oppenheim's *The Secret*. The hero, Courage, finds in espionage a much better outlet for his energies than anything possible in his life as a cricket-playing country gentlemen, but he becomes a spy in response to the appeal made to him by an ailing secret agent "as an Englishman—and a man of honour—to take my burden from my back, and carry it on—to the end,"[13] Patriotism and a desire to be of use to their country certainly motivate a number of le Carré's spies, most notably Smiley, Peter Guillam, Jim Prideaux, and Jerry Westerby. When called out of retirement to undertake Operation Dolphin, Westerby responds with the spirit of the British cavalry at Balaklava: "Ours not to reason why" (*HS*, p. 39).

But this is far from being all that attracts Smiley and Westerby does not seem to be a factor at all for most of the other members of the Circus. Spies, according to Alec Leamas, are "a squalid procession of vain fools" (*SCC*, p. 231), and Grigoriev calls them "criminals, charlatans and fools, a masonry of monsters" (*SP*, p. 329). These descriptions may be a little exaggerated, but they underline the central fact that for John le Carré spies are almost always social misfits who have been disappointed in their attempts at love and so have felt the alienation and betrayal of modern life particularly intensely. Smiley, Westerby, Leamas, Turner, and Esterhase have, for example, all failed in marriage. For men such as these the world of espionage offers an attractive alternative, because here love is not an ideal to be pursued but a weakness to be avoided in oneself and exploited in others. Furthermore, it is a world in which one is directed to betray rather than to be betrayed. As a private citizen, George Smiley suffers intensely as a result of Ann's repeated betrayals. However, when Ricki Tarr brings up Ann's infidelity in an attempt to distract him from his interrogation efforts, Smiley remains unmoved and continues to exploit the vulnerable spot created in Tarr by his emotional attachment to his daughter, Danny, and his Russian target, Irina (*TTSS*, pp. 171-173). Bill Haydon's much more calculating attempt to unbalance Smiley's professional equilibrium by involving himself in an affair with Ann is no more successful. The incident causes Smiley his greatest personal humiliation, but he retains sufficient detachment to extract from it the clue needed to expose Haydon as the mole Gerald. In the overt world Smiley feels and suffers; in the covert world he thinks dispassionately and triumphs. Oliver Lacon sums up the essential distinction between Smiley's personal and professional selves: "If Ann had been your agent instead of your wife, you'd probably have run her pretty well" (*SP*, p. 289).

The opportunity to escape from the demand to love and hence to suffer is clearly what also attracts Alan Turner to espionage. Haunted by his wife's unfaithfulness, Turner seeks as a spy to eliminate all considerations of feeling; his creed is "unreason will be your downfall. Make order out of chaos" (*STG*, p. 162). Thus, during interrogation he questions "emotive terms" because "they put me off" (*STG*, p. 65) and furiously attacks those who have allowed personal feelings to interfere with security.

"Sign the night book, did he?"

Gaunt faltered, waking at long last to the full menace in that quiet, destructive monotone. Turner slammed together the wooden doors of the cupboard. "Or didn't you bloody well bother? Well, not right really, is it? You can't come over all official, not to a guest. A dip too, at that, a dip who graced your parlour." (*STG*, p. 92)

Like Smiley also, Turner finds that as a spy he is able to switch from the role of the deceived to that of the deceiver. His method, as in the interview with Gaunt quoted in part above, is to lull his antagonist into a false sense of security out of which usually emerges the careless remark on which he can pounce. The relish with which Turner takes on the role of exploiter is particularly evident in his refusal to spare his victim any of the implications of his foolish or dishonest behavior. He taunts Gaunt with his vanity—"Look how grand having the dips in"—and his professional incompetence—"A guard they called you; he'd have charmed you into bed for half-a-crown" (*STG*, p. 93). Similarly, even after Jenny Pargiter admits she lent her keys to Leo Harting, Turner persists in reminding her of her sexual exploitation: "And after you'd given . . . he didn't want you any more, did he?" (*STG*, p. 150).

Escape into a world that denies value to feeling (as Control puts it, "in our world we pass so quickly out of the register of hate or love" [*SCC*, p. 22]) not only allows the individual to reverse his role completely but also introduces him to a code of conduct much simpler and hence more easily satisfying than that which operates in the larger society. In the course of his training at Sarratt, the spy acquires a set of techniques sufficient to guide him through all situations in a sphere of operation where "morality" has been reduced to "method" (*TTSS*, p. 65) or, to put it another way, where all value is placed on the sentimental and none on the naive. Instead of being called on to behave as a complex human being, the spy is encouraged to shrink comfortably into the guise of "Sarratt man and nothing else" (*HS*, p. 117). At dangerous moments "his twenty years of tradecraft rose in him and shouted 'caution,'" and any other considerations are "blanked out" (*HS*, pp. 117, 133).

Within this diminished framework, the individual can achieve something close to perfection. George Smiley, for instance, is so brilliant in two aspects of tradecraft, handling files (which at times he thinks of "as the only truth" [*SP*, p. 281]) and conducting interrogations, that he is transformed from a confused and pathetic little man into a figure of almost legendary proportions:

Whereupon the conversation returned once more to the topic of dear old George Smiley, surely the last of the *true* greats, and what was he doing with himself these days, back in retirement? So many lives he had led; so much to recollect in tranquility, they agreed.

"George went five times round the moon to our one," someone declared loyally, a woman.

Ten times, they agreed. Twenty! *Fifty!* (*HS*, p. 5)

The espionage world offers further satisfaction in that it substitutes close professional relationships for the unsatisfactory emotional bonds of the world outside. Whereas Smiley is betrayed by Ann and harassed by Martindale and Lacon, he is admired and trusted by Peter Guillam (his "cupbearer" [*HS*, p. 41]). Toby Esterhase, a sexual philanderer and crooked art dealer in the outside world, responds to the task of regathering his team of "pavement artists" in *Smiley's People* in the spirit in which a father might organize a family reunion. Craw's agents are also "his family, and he lavished on them all the fondness for which the overt world had somehow never given him an outlet" (*HS*, p. 195). Avery, in *The Looking-Glass War*, finds much more satisfaction in his relationship with the agent, Leiser, than with his unhappy and complaining wife: "Avery pressed his arm to his side, holding Leiser's hand captive, and they continued their walk in shared contentment" (*LGW*, p. 142). The character, however, for whom spying offers the most complete substitute for personal relationships is Connie Sachs. Connie, physically ugly and deeply eccentric, is rejected by an outside world she hates in return. For her, "all of human life" is to be found in "the double-double games" (*SP*, p. 194) played by the Circus, and she loves equally the "gorgeous boys" (*TTSS*, p. 101) who are her colleagues and Russian agents like "her lover" Aleks Polyakov (*TTSS*, p. 96) on whom she spies. Late in life Connie appears to have found real love with Hilary, but is quite willing to abandon her if Smiley will call her back to help in the final pursuit of Karla: "Take me with you, George, for God's sake! I'll leave Hils, I'll leave anything" (*SP*, p. 205).

To move from the overt to the covert world is so attractive that for many spies it has the force of religious conversion. In Grigoriev's words, "Conspiracy has replaced religion! . . . It is our mystical substitute!" (*SP*, p. 329). Smiley also sees espionage as an alternative faith: "Why are Scots so attracted to the secret world? Smiley wondered, not for the first time in his career. Ships' engineers, Colonial administrators, spies. . . . Their heretical Scottish history drew them to distant churches, he decided," (*SP*, p. 45). It is in the imagery of *The Looking-Glass War*, however, that le Carré most firmly establishes spying as a religion: "For its servants, the Department had a religious quality. Like monks, they endowed it with a mystical identity" (*LGW*, p. 66); "their strained faces fixed upon Leclerc as in the stillness of a church he read the liturgy of their devotion, moving his little hand across the map like a priest with the taper" (*LGW*, p. 183); "[Leiser] put the keys back in his pocket, and as he drew his hand away he felt the links slip between his thumb and finger like the beads of a rosary" (*LGW*, p. 192).

Attractive as spying may be, however, le Carré makes it clear that it is a false faith and not a genuine alternative to life in contemporary England. Rather than solving the problems posed by this loveless and decadent society, the world of espionage simply "provide[s] shelter from the complexities of modern life" (*LGW*, p. 66). The demands of the naive and sentimental aspects of experience are difficult, perhaps impossible, to reconcile, but to refuse to undertake the struggle, as the spy does when he strives to eliminate all feeling and spontaneity, is to opt out of the search for truth. Total dedication to tradecraft may be a way of creating "frontiers" (*LGW*, p. 66) in a world where they no longer seem to exist, but these boundaries are based on an arbitrary limitation of experience rather than on any genuine understanding of the nature of things. Because it is based on a false simplification of experience, life at the Circus is, as its name suggests, a performance, a construct of artifice and illusion, attended by men fated to remain always immature and thus children.

This sense of spying as an illusionary world inhabited by perpetual children is particularly strong in *The Looking-Glass War*. The novel's title and epigraph ("wouldn't mind being a Pawn, if only I might join") are taken from the Alice books, and it deals with a branch of the Secret Service that has been for all practical purposes redundant since the end of the Second World War. The operations of "The Department" are thus even further removed from reality than those of the Circus, and le Carré aptly titles it "the dream factory" (*LGW*, p. 101), a "sweet anachronism" that "gave them [its members] an illusion of nourishment" (*LGW*, p. 26). The realization that Operation Mayfly has ended is, for the members of the department, like "waking from a single dream" (*LGW*, p. 227).

Taylor and Avery both believe that their involvement in Operation Mayfly will help them each "become a man" (*LGW*, p. 66), but as the novel's imagery repeatedly asserts, anyone who fails to step back through the looking glass is fated to remain always a child. Leclerc's handwriting is "boyish and rounded." The staff gathered around a table are like "children at a meal." Leiser's training involves trying to turn "the skills of boyhood" into "weapons of war." And the conclusion of the training program is like "the end of term; the boys were going home" (*LGW*, pp. 30, 44, 138, 163).

The spy must, then, pay a big price for belonging to the world of espionage. Unfortunately it does not always even give him in return the control or freedom from loneliness he is seeking. Dedication to tradecraft, it turns out, is not always a guarantee of control. Ironically, it is George Smiley, the master of tradecraft, who reveals its limitations. The problem for the man who operates entirely in terms of learned techniques is, as Smiley realizes, that he becomes predictable and, hence, vulnerable. In *Call for the Dead*, for example, Smiley is first able to identify and then to manipulate the future behavior of his East German opponent, Dieter Frey, because he is still using the operational techniques with which Smiley became familiar when they worked together during the Second World War. As a result he is able to trap and then to kill him.

Smiley's own performance as a spy reveals that, although dependence on tradecraft may give a considerable degree of power, especially when dealing with civilians, it can never entirely replace instinct and spontaneity. At crucial points in all his cases Smiley looks for guidance not from Sarratt but from within himself: "He saw his last question, he recognised its logic, he sensed the wealth it promised. Yet the same life-time's instinct that had brought him this far held him back" (*SP*, p. 223). Thus, not even in the monistic world of espionage can the demands of dualism be entirely ignored.

The professional companionship the spy seeks as an alternative to difficult personal relationships is genuine enough. However, an essential part of the agent's role is to leave his secure home base and, assuming a false identity, penetrate the enemy's territory. Crossing the border is like cutting an umbilical cord, and once he finds himself "out in the cold" (*SCC*, p. 19) without a companion or secure identity, the spy experiences a loneliness so intense that nothing can alleviate it but the kind of complex emotional involvement to be found only in the overt world. Avery, for example, is so unnerved by his attempt to act out the role of "Malherbe's brother" against the backdrop of a cold and alien Finnish landscape that he looks forward eagerly to a reunion with the wife and child whose company he usually flees: "He was desperately tired. He wanted Sarah. He wanted to say sorry, make it up with her, get a new job, try again; play with Anthony more" (*LGW*, p. 93). Fred Leiser's experience is similar. A desire to belong motivates him to rejoin the Department he left after the War, and he continues to feel a strong sense of companionship with Avery, Leclerc, and Haldane right up to the moment the mission begins:

"It was us three. The Captain, you and me. It was all right, then. Don't worry about the others, John. They don't matter."

"That's right, Fred."

Leiser smiled. "It was the best ever, that week, John. It's funny, isn't it: we spend all our time chasing girls, and it's the men that matter; just the men."

"You're one of us. Fred. You always were." (*LGW*, p. 190).

However, once he enters enemy territory, dressed in the "unfamiliar thing[s]" (*LGW*, p. 187) of an East German workman, Leiser finds himself more alone than ever: "He caught himself thinking, it's all right for them, and he remembered that nothing ever bridged the gulf between the man who went and the man who stayed behind, between the living and the dying" (*LGW*, p. 199). His response is more or less to abandon attempts at security and to seek comfort in the very kind of heterosexual union from which he had fled by joining the masculine world of espionage: "they were weeping, laughing together, falling, clumsy lovers clumsily triumphant, recognizing nothing but each himself, each for that moment completing lives half-lived, and for that moment the whole damned dark forgotten" (*LGW*, p. 224)

By entering the secret world, then, the spy yields up the possibility of personal growth in exchange for a freedom from the demands of dualism and from difficult personal relationships that proves to be at least in part illusory. However, there is another and even more significant way in which the satisfaction offered by espionage turns out to be false. Espionage "is rooted in the theory that the whole is more important than the individual" (*SCC*, p. 124), which in practice means that "people don't matter" (*LGW*, p. 165) at all. As a consequence, a large part of the spy's tradecraft is based on the exploitation of the humanity of others. For a man like Alan Turner, who has been betrayed in his personal life, this obligation to betray is appealing. However, as Turner discovers when he begins to crack up "under the strain of being a pig" (*STG*, p. 229), it can also be damaging to the self. To seek escape from feelings guarantees that the spy will remain a perpetual child, but once he begins to exploit the feelings of others he is likely to end up completely dehumanized.

This tendency of spying to dehumanize is epitomized by Control, the head of the Circus. Just as he has replaced his real name with one describing his function, so Control appears to have yielded up all human considerations to the pursuit of successful technique, and for him ends have come totally to justify means. In both the novels in which he directs operations, *The Spy Who Came In from the Cold* and *The Looking-Glass War*, Control shows such a complete disregard for any kind of ethical laws that he betrays his own side even more than he does the enemy. In his final briefing of Leamas, Control tells two flat lies by assuring him that Liz Gold will not be brought into the operation and that Smiley has refused to be involved. Similarly, he repeatedly deceives Smiley about his real interest in the operation Leclerc is mounting. Even worse, in both operations Control strands the English agent in enemy territory, in the one instance to prevent the exposure of his double agent in the East German Intelligence Service, in the other merely to reinforce the Circus's ascendancy over Leclerc's department.

A number of other characters in le Carré's novels demonstrate a similar degree of dehumanization. Toby Esterhase has become so totally imbued with the Circus philosophy that he "would put the dogs on his own mother" (*TTSS*, p. 77); Leclerc regards the fact that to abandon Operation Mayfly means almost certain death for Leiser as "only a small point" (*LGW*, p. 229); Haldane has an equally inhuman attitude to

Leiser: "We sent him because we needed to; we abandon him because we must" (*LGW*, p. 229); and Martello considers Jerry Westerby as nothing more than "a rogue elephant" (*HS*, p. 498) who should be shot.

It is impossible to say with any certainty whether this kind of dehumanization is inevitable because few agents with any ethical sense remain in the Circus once they come to see it for what it is. Jerry Westerby's response is fairly typical. Westerby is one of le Carré's misfits, a man unable to communicate even with his beloved daughter, Cat. Consequently, he is deeply attracted by the role of "Sarratt man," which provides him with a sense of control lacking elsewhere in his life. However, even though he is not an introspective man, Westerby becomes increasingly conscious of the implications of following the dictates of his tradecraft. Operation Dolphin requires him to exploit a number of innocent people—Frost, Luke, Drake Ko, and Lizzie Worthington—and after two of them have been killed, he realizes that, saying, "others do the paying" (*HS*, p. 489). According to Circus morality, Frost's death by hideous torture is insignificant because "operationally nothing is amiss" (*HS*, p. 321). But so far as Westerby is concerned it does count, and he thus experiences the "temptation to gentleness" that is "the kiss of death to a fieldman" (*HS*, p. 165). As a consequence of his alienation from Circus morality, Westerby finally puts his "unscheduled affection" (*HS*, p. 481) for Lizzie Worthington ahead of the operation and allows Sarratt man to die in him.

John le Carré presents only one character who seeks to remain loyal to himself and to the Circus. However, because George Smiley is a man who engages in continual self-examination and is fully aware of the implications of belonging to a profession that demands that he "*be inhuman in defence of our humanity*" (*HS*, p. 461), his fate can be taken as particularly instructive. Because of his firm grasp on the paradoxical situation in which he has placed himself, Smiley is usually able to keep a delicate balance between his duty to the Circus and his obligation to be human. In *Call for the Dead*, for instance, a sense of duty directs him to hunt down and to kill Dieter Frey. Yet Smiley can also mourn him as a man who was once his friend and can acknowledge that in holding back at a crucial moment in their death struggle, Dieter, the Communist absolutist, had in fact "remembered their friendship when [he] had not," thereby proving himself the greater "gentleman."[14] Similarly, in *The Honourable Schoolboy*, Smiley is capable of cynically misrepresenting the realities of espionage to ensure that he retain Westerby's loyalty by claiming, "we're not necessarily in competition with affection" (*HS*, p. 105). And yet he feels genuine grief for his dead agents: "Guillam . . . found his master, to his embarrassment, sitting rigidly before an old volume of German poetry, fists clenched either side of it, while he silently wept" (*HS*, p. 51).

In *Smiley's People*, however, George Smiley experiences such a complete sense of self-betrayal in his betrayal of others that the delicate balance seems to have been finally lost. His lifelong pursuit of Karla, the head of Russian Intelligence, has been based on the conviction that he is a complete absolutist who poses an enormous threat to the freedom offered by the English way of life. However, the mistakes that bring about Karla's downfall derive from his love for his daughter, Tatiana, and in his willingness to exploit Karla's human weakness. Smiley changes roles with him. A significant indication of Smiley's descent into inhuman "fanaticism" (*SC*, p. 371) is that he rejects Ann, the lifelong focus of his willingness to feel, lest she distract him from his quest: "If that was so [that he was being given the chance to defeat Karla,] then no Ann, no false peace, no tainted witness to his actions should disturb his lonely quest" (*SP*, p. 143). Ultimately, as Smiley himself concludes, by "going off to blackmail a lover" (*SP*, p. 285) he becomes possessed by "the very evil he had fought against" (*SP*, p. 370). The fact that Smiley can still think in such moral terms implies that his corruption is not absolute. Nevertheless, it is real, and we are left with the conclusion that if Smiley can be dehumanized, it is unlikely that anyone can escape the corrupting effects of involvement in espionage. Thus, the individual who finally falls victim to the Circus philosophy that "the whole is more important than the individual" is, ironically, the spy himself.

The spy's journey of escape is then circular because, in experiencing dehumanization, he is ultimately sacrificed in defense of the very society he sought to escape. The obvious conclusion is that, difficult and painful as the overt world may be, it is there that the individual must seek salvation. Reality is by its nature dualistic, and to attempt a retreat into a monistic world is futile. Tradecraft or technique provides only the illusion of control and is vulnerable in the face of the person willing to combine training and instinct. Professional friendships present a tempting alternative to emotional entanglements, but when plunged into the total isolation encountered during his mission into enemy territory, the spy instinctively recognizes that real consolation can be found only in the love relationship. Because most of le Carré's attention is given to demonstrating the futility of trying to escape the complex demands of life in the real world, he does not offer any definitive portrait of how the individual can find fulfillment and happiness in what he has shown to be a society so corrupt that it mirrors many of the qualities of the secret world. However, through his analysis of the limitations of espionage as a way of life, he has at least pointed out a direction. Full humanity, le Carré argues, can be achieved only by accepting the dualistic nature of reality and by seeking a balance of the naive and the sentimental, the spontaneous and the disciplined, the emotional and the rational, the individual and the collective.

Notes

1 .In his review of *The Honourable Schoolboy*, "A Gentleman among Players," *TLS*, 9 September 1977, p. 1069, T.J. Binyon argues that le Carré has written a thriller that is at the same time "a substantial novel in its own right." Steven Marcus makes similar claims in his review of *The Looking-Glass War*, "Grand Illusions," *New York*

Review of Books, 5 August 1965, pp. 20-21, where he states that "Carré has written another spy story and thriller, but he has written something more as well." One notable dissenter from this view of le Carré is Clive James. In his review of *The Honourable Schoolboy*, "Go Back to the Cold," *New York Review of Books*, 27 October 1977, pp. 29-30, he claims that "Outwardly aspiring to the status of literature, le Carré's novels have inwardly declined to the level of pulp romance."

2. In the reviews cited above, T. J. Binyon suggests that le Carré "assimilates—if ironically—rather than rejects the former tradition of the spy novel," and Steven Marcus argues that "Carré has inverted the tradition; he shows how it has gone sour." For a more extended study of this aspect of le Carré's art, see Andrew Rutherford, "The Spy as Hero: Le Carré and the Cold War," in *The Literature of War: Five Studies in Heroic Virtue* (London: Macmillan, 1978), pp. 135-156.

3. "Introduction" to Bruce Page, David Leitch, and Philip Knightley, *Philby: The Spy Who Betrayed a Generation* (London: Sphere Books, 1969), p. 33.

4. Although this distinction underlies all of le Carré's novels, it is made explicit only in *The Naive and Sentimental Lover* (London: Pan Books, 1972). See particularly p. 64.

5. "Talk of Books and Writers," *Woman's Hour*, BBC Home Service, 13 August 1965.

6. *Tinker, Tailor, Soldier, Spy* (London: Pan Books, 1975), p. 102. Further references to this novel will be cited in the text, where the title will be abbreviated *TTSS*.

7. *Smiley's People* (New York: Alfred A. Knopf, 1980), p. 283. Further references to this novel, abbreviated *SP*, will be included parenthetically within the text.

8. *A Small Town in Germany* (London: Pan Books, 1969), p. 221. Further references in this novel, abbreviated *STG*, will be included parenthetically within the text.

9. *The Looking-Glass War* (London: Pan Books, 1966), p. 25. Further references to this novel, abbreviated *LGW*, will be included parenthetically within the text.

10. *The Spy Who Came in from the Cold* (London: Pan Books, 1964), p. 35. Further references to this novel, abbreviated *SCC*, will be included parenthetically within the text.

11. *The Honourable Schoolboy* (New York: Bantam, 1978), p. 98. Further references to this novel, abbreviated *HS*, will be included parenthetically within the text.

12. Sapper, *The Final Count* (London: Hodder and Stoughton, n.d.), pp. 803, 806.

13. E. Phillips Oppenheim, *The Secret* (London: Ward, Lock, 1935), p. 73.

14. *Call for the Dead* (Harmondsworth: Penguin, 1964), p. 145.

LAURIE LEE

1914–

Laurie Lee was born in Stroud, Gloucestershire, on June 26, 1914. Soon after his birth his father abandoned his wife, who moved with her large family to a nearby village. Lee was educated at Slad Village School and Stroud Central School, then from the age of fifteen worked as an errand boy and violin teacher. At twenty he journeyed on foot to London, where he worked for a year as a builder's laborer before setting off for Spain. There he lived as an itinerant fiddler, traveling after the outbreak of the Civil War around the Eastern Mediterranean. Returning to England, he became a scriptwriter, first with the G.P.O. Film Unit, and then with the Crown Film Unit, and from 1944 to 1946 was Publications Editor for the Ministry of Information. After the war he traveled as a scriptwriter to Cyprus and India, and in 1950 was Caption Writer-in-Chief for the Festival of Britain.

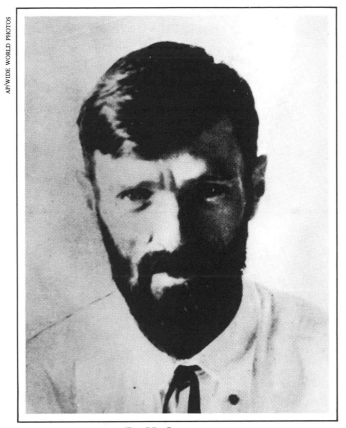

D. H. LAWRENCE

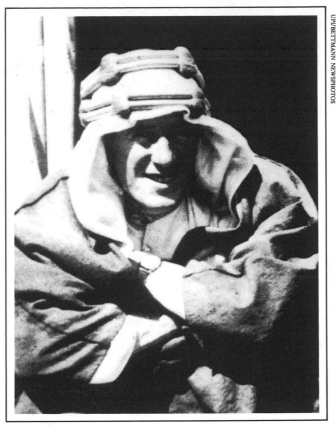

T. E. LAWRENCE

JOHN LE CARRÉ

LAURIE LEE

Wyndham Lewis

Malcolm Lowry

Rosamond Lehmann

C. S. Lewis

Lee's first poems were published in *The Sun My Monument* in 1944, followed in 1947 by *The Bloom of Candles*, which won him the Atlantic Award, and in 1955 by *My Many Coated Man*, which received the Foyle Award. However, Lee's reputation rests mainly on his memoirs, particularly *Cider with Rosie* (in America, *The Edge of Day*), 1959, which recalls his childhood in the disappearing world of an ancient rural community. *As I Walked Out One Midsummer Morning*, about his time in Spain, appeared in 1969, and *I Can't Stay Long* in 1975. His other publications include the play *Peasant's Priest*, produced in Canterbury in 1947, and *Two Women*, 1983, a book of prose and photographs about his wife, whom he married in 1950, and his daughter. *Selected Poems* was published in 1983.

Works

PROSE

The vogue for the highbrow travel-book shows no immediate signs of abating. At any rate, here are two more endeavours in that field ⟨Lee's *A Rose for Winter* and Peter Mayne's *The Narrow Smile*⟩. The usual characteristics of such books are, first, a leaning towards the more elaborate and unfashionable graces of prose—rightly unfashionable they seem to me, if I may show my hand thus early—and, secondly, a desire to get away from the exhausted sterilities of Western civilisation so feelingly alluded to from time to time by Mr. Priestley. In themselves, these two things may be all very well, though I judge it unlikely; in practice, however, the stylistic graces degenerate briskly into an empty and indecent poeticism, apparently based on a desire to get into the next edition of *The Oxford Book of English Prose*, while the escape-motive is only with difficulty to be distinguished from the feeling that the other fellow's grass is greener, that the really good time, or good life, is going on somewhere else. The two tendencies, in these degraded forms, find remarkably unalloyed expression in Mr. Laurie Lee's volume.

The experienced reader will know what to do with a book whose blurb announces, as if in recommendation, its author's claim to 'the enchanted eye . . . of a true poet,' but the reviewer must act differently. His part is to soldier grimly on, trying not to mind too much the absence of a verb in the opening sentence, the incessant din of adjective and poeticality ('the scarred and crumpled valleys,' 'the oil-blue waters'), the full close of the first paragraph, mannered as any Ciceronian *esse videatur*:

> And from a steep hillside rose a column of smoke, cool as marble, pungent as pine, which hung like a signal over the landscape, obscure, imperative and motionless.

(The effect is a little marred through having been anticipated, three sentences earlier, by a cadential 'raw, sleeping and savage.') Another item on the list of things to try not to mind too much is the prevalence of lists—cf. Mr. Auden's *Spain*, which Mr. Lee has perhaps been cf.-ing too—like 'the bright façades . . . the beggars . . . the vivid shapely girls . . . the tiny, delicate-stepping donkeys,' and so on; and yet another one is the 'striking' image—'fragrant as water'—which at first sight seems to mean almost nothing, and upon reflection and reconsideration is seen to mean almost nothing. One way of summing up this book would be to call it a string of failed poems—failed not-very-good poems too, for whoever said that bad poetry is much more like poetry than good poetry is, was in the right of it there.

This kind of objection, however, though compulsory for the reader of almost any highbrow travel-book, is here purely trifling. The really telling strictures emerge from a mulling-over of what Mr. Lee actually reveals to us about Andalusia. The figure of the narrator himself, having terrific fun with a drum in a wedding procession, carrying *two* guitars 'every-where,' carefully recording every pass made at his wife, drinking like mad at a party in a telephone exchange while the switchboard lights 'twinkled unheeded' (not too good for people who wanted to ring the doctor)—can safely be left on one side. One might even haul to the other side the bullfighting question, although the author's taste for 'the sharp mystery of blood' will remain unshared in some quarters, where, in addition, the use of the phrase 'the moment of truth' will appear a little worse than *naif*, and to upbraid a bull for having no grace or honour or 'vocation for martyrdom' will appear a lot worse; if we enjoined these duties upon a bull, he would not understand us. But the least attractive part of Mr. Lee's portrayal of Spain is his portrayal of Spaniards, so far as this can be debarnacled from rhetoric, generalisation and rhapsody. The effect is not what he evidently intends; where he seeks to show us gaiety, mere instability or hooliganism emerges, unselfconsciousness is detectable as coxcombry or self-pity, while the gift attributed to Andalusians of greeting others' misfortune with a shrug or a grin is neither mature nor admirable. I am sure these people are not as bad as all that, just as I am sure that they are not in touch with the 'pure sources of feeling' and the 'real flavours' of life, whatever these entities may be; Coleridge put Wordsworth right on peasants a long time ago. Perhaps too many people in England do watch television, or do they watch it too much of the time? Anyway, *nostalgie de la boue* is not the answer; it is silly to sleep on straw in the inn yard if you can get hold of a bed; and while it is no doubt better to be gay and have sores than to be un-gay and not have sores, it is better still to be fairly gay and not have sores.— KINGSLEY AMIS, "Is the Travel-Book Dead?," *Spec*, June 17, 1955, p. 774

Cider with Rosie is Mr Lee's celebration of his childhood in this Cotswold village. The book is written in prose—a luscious, evocative, poetic prose, with overtones from Wales. There is comedy as well as pathos. Some quiet drawings by John Ward illustrate the story.

In the Twenties an ancient rural culture was disintegrating: cars, buses, and charabancs were beginning to join the villages to the towns. But Mr Lee was born just early enough to have known the arduous, unsophisticated, self-sufficient, and sometimes dotty life of a community still dominated by the squire, the parson, and the horse. He conjures up this past, his own and the village's, in a number of beautifully composed pieces, some of which have already appeared in magazines. 'Grannies in the Wainscot,' for instance, a chapter about two witchlike nonagenarian neighbours, is a perfect short story. —MICHAEL RAMSBOTHAM, "A Gloucestershire Lady," *NS*, Nov. 7, 1959, pp. 634–35

Mr. Lee grew up in a small Cotswold village which remained remarkably self-sufficient, morally and socially, until late in the Twenties; and though the village was soon to 'break, dissolve, and scatter,' nevertheless when Mr. Lee looks back on his childhood ⟨ in *Cider with Rosie*⟩ he is able to feel that he witnessed 'the end of a thousand years' life.' The world which

Mr. Lee remembers was one of 'hard work and necessary patience, of backs bent to the ground, hands massaging the crops, of waiting on weather and growth; of villages like ships in the empty distance and the long walking distances between them, of white narrow roads, rutted by hooves and cartwheels, innocent of oil and petrol.' Thus, though Mr. Lee writes of nothing which he did not himself know or experience as a child, *Cider with Rosie* is a memoir which is more than personal in intention: it is, too, a memorial to a vanished way of life.

Much of the book is given to a description of the author's immediate family: kindly brothers and sisters; huge uncles and aunts; above all, the author's mother, to whom the best chapter in the book is devoted. There are neighbours, too, and glimpses of the local squire; there are local ghosts, school-teachers, madwomen; there are village outings and celebrations—all of them described in a style that would, one must say, be far more successful if it were less anxious to make its effects. So many of Mr. Lee's reminiscences are of charm and interest that one feels he should have had more trust in their power to speak for themselves; instead, again and again, they are over-decorated and over-elaborated. One cannot help feeling, indeed, that Mr. Lee's book is a memorial of a kind different from the one he intended it to be: the fact that Mr. Lee, who grew up in a village as remote and isolated as the one he describes, and was educated in the village school, should yet write a prose so mannered, willed, and metropolitan—this fact is in itself a sign of how dead is the old order he has tried to evoke.—Dan Jacobson, "To a Former Life," *Spec*, Nov. 13, 1959, p. 678

Suicide, said Camus, is the one really serious philosophical problem. The only simple answer to the questionable human condition is the act that ends all problems. Any other answer ignores the question or shelves the problem. And yet there is another sort of response, oblique as morning sunlight, irrational as joy, absurd as a human being—an acceptance of life that is also a welcoming and an embrace. Perhaps this response is less rare than we suppose, but only a poet can put it into words.

Laurie Lee has done it. Blessed be his name. These recollections of his country boyhood in the West of England ⟨in *The Edge of Day*⟩ are a testament to the wonder, joy and painful absurdity of being alive, a letter of thanks whose address is plain to be seen: to life, with love. *The Edge of Day* is funny, unsentimental and beautiful. Huck Finn would have given it his complete approval. . . .

Good books don't always sell; the best-seller lists are usually swamped by the second- and third-rate. But now and then, once in a blue moon, a book appears that deserves its success. This time the moon is blue, and *The Edge of Day* is the book.—T. S. Matthews, "An Acceptance of Life That Is Also an Embrace," *NYTBR*, March 1927, 1960, p. 4

One evening at his house in the high sierras of Kensington, Roy Campbell told me of an encounter he and his wife once had with a street-musician in Toledo. The fiddler turned out to be not a German, as they'd supposed, but a young man from Gloucestershire walking across Spain with a knapsack and a violin wrapped in a blanket. The Campbells asked him how he was getting on. Fine, he replied with surprising alacrity. Except for the wild dogs that occasionally woke him, sniffing and howling round at night. 'He thought they were dogs!' roared Campbell, delightedly. Then, *pianissimo*: 'They were wolves, man.'

Whether they were or not is irrelevant. In any case, Laurie Lee in his *As I Walked Out One Midsummer Morning* doesn't mention the wolves in connection with Campbell, but merely says 'they may have been'. To Campbell, always extravagantly and imaginatively generous, they had to be: for the same reason that he proudly introduced young Lee to his Toledan friends as: 'A champion, this boy. Walked all the way from Vigo. He walks a thousand miles a week. It's true, by God . . . The funny thing is—he's English.'

Laurie Lee's portrait of the good, gentle, fundamentally shy and uncertain Campbell—a poet shamefully neglected at the moment—is one of the best things in this new volume of autobiography. The encounter between the two poets—one established, the other to be—was unplanned, casual: like Lee's journey from Slad to London and the Mediterranean.

As I Walked Out One Midsummer Morning is a re-creation, after a gap of 30 years, of the sensations of late adolescence and early manhood. It's admittedly romantic, and the style is as juicily ripe as an autumn pear. There's a formidable, instant charm in the writing that genuinely makes it difficult to put the book down. (Conversely, some might find it difficult to pick up for a second reading in case the magic had flown.) Now and then one's conscious of a slightly overblown, Renoir-ish bloom on the text, an air of the extended set-piece, that comes dangerously close to choking the senses. But if there is a lot of sweetness, it's pure cane; not a trace of saccharin.

The book has the intensity, as well as the title, of a ballad. There's an undertone of menace as the story moves to the bloody climax of a community and a country exploding into Civil War. Mr Lee begins his journey as a political innocent; he ends it involved inextricably with a beautiful and sinister land, 'so backward and so long ignored . . . [where] . . . the nations of Europe were quietly gathering'.

As a self-portrait, it's a little muzzy: though perhaps this was the intention. Like many a clever peasant before him, Mr Lee doesn't give much of himself away; he remains peering from behind screens of glittering prose. Was he really the innocent he appears? One feels cheated, certainly, when our hero—crossing mountain and plain, hammered by hangovers and sunstroke, but never (apparently) diarrhoea or constipation—suddenly disappears into a post-office to see if there's any mail. Or, just as one gets used to him in an hotel attic, working as fiddler and odd-job man, he appears in the next chapter living in a room in the house of an unnamed expatriate English novelist. Sometimes, too, the observation seems slightly off-target. The characteristic smell of Gibraltar isn't, I'd say, that of provincial groceries. Cigar smoke, surely. And as an ex-Naafi busker myself, I've never heard of a song called 'Wales! Wales!' The title is 'The Land of My Fathers': a tune that Mr Lee rightly remarks will always call up its supporters from a crowd. So, I hope, will this lollipop of an autobiography.—Charles Causley, "On the Fiddle," *NS*, Sept. 26, 1969, pp. 428–29

Autobiography can be the laying to rest of ghosts as well as an ordering of the mind. But for me it is also a celebration of living and an attempt to hoard its sensations.

In common with other writers I have written little that was not for the most part autobiographical. The spur for me is the fear of evaporation—erosion, amnesia, if you like—the fear that a whole decade may drift gently away and leave nothing but a salt-caked mud-flat.

A wasting memory is not only a destroyer; it can deny one's very existence. A day unremembered is like a soul unborn, worse than if it had never been. What indeed was that summer if it is not recalled? That journey? That act of love? To whom did it happen if it has left you with nothing? Certainly not to you. So any bits of warm life preserved by the pen are trophies snatched from the dark, are branches of leaves fished out of the flood, are tiny arrests of mortality.

The urge to write may also be the fear of death—particularly with autobiography—the need to leave messages for those who come after, saying, 'I was here; I saw it too'. Then there are the other uses of autobiography; some less poignant than these assurances—exposure, confession, apologia, revenge, or even staking one's claim to a godhead. In writing my first volume of autobiography, *Cider with Rosie* (1959), I was moved by several of these needs, but the chief one was celebration: to praise the life I'd had and so preserve it, and to live again both the good and the bad.

My book was a recollection of early years set against the village background of my Cotswold upbringing. The end of my childhood also coincided by chance with the end of a rural tradition—a semi-feudal way of life which had endured for nine centuries, until war and the motor-car put an end to it. Technically the book was not so simple. It took two years, and was written three times. In remembering my life, even those first few years of it, I found the territory a maze of paths.

I was less interested, anyway, in giving a portrait of myself, than in recording the details of that small local world—a world whose last days I had seen fresh as a child and which no child may ever see again. It seemed to me that my own story would keep, whereas the story of the village would not, for its words, even as I listened, were being sung for the last time and were passing into perpetual silence.

The village was small, set in a half mile of valley, but the details of its life seemed enormous. The problem of compression was like dressing one tree with leaves chosen from all over the forest. As I sat down to write, in a small room in London, opening my mind to that time-distant place, I saw at first a great landscape darkly fogged by the years and thickly matted by rumour and legend. It was only gradually that memory began to stir, setting off flash-points like summer lightning, which illuminated for a moment some field or landmark, some ancient totem or neighbour's face.

Seizing these flares and flashes became a way of writing, episodic and momentarily revealing, to be used as small beacons to mark the peaks of the story and to accentuate the darkness of what was left out. So I began my tale where this light sparked brightest, close-up, at the age of three, when I was no taller than grass, and was an intimate of insects and knew the details of stones and chair-legs.

This part of the book was of course easiest. I had lived so near to it, with the world no larger than my legs could carry me and no more complex than my understanding. I ruled as king these early chapters. Then the book moved away from me—taking in first my family, then our house and the village, and finally the whole of the valley. I became at this stage less a character than a presence, a listening shadow, a moving finger, recording the flavours of the days, the ghosts of neighbours, the bits of winter, gossip, death.

If a book is to stand, one must first choose its shape—the house that the tale will inhabit. One lays out the rooms for the necessary chapters, then starts wondering about the furniture. The moment before writing is perhaps the most harrowing of all, pacing the empty rooms, knowing that what goes in there can belong nowhere else, yet not at all sure where to find it. There are roofless books in all of us, books without walls and books full of lumber. I realized quite soon, when writing my own, that I had enough furniture to fill a town.

The pains of selection became a daily concern, and progress was marked by what was left out. The flowing chatter of my sisters, for twelve years unstaunched, had to be distilled to a few dozen phrases—phrases, perhaps, which they had

never quite uttered, but bearing the accents of all that they had. A chapter about life in my village school also required this type of compression. Here five thousand hours had to be reduced to fifteen minutes—in terms of reading time—and those fifteen minutes, without wearying the reader, must seem like five thousand hours. In another chapter, about our life at home, I describe a day that never happened. Perhaps a thousand days of that life each yielded a moment for the book—a posture, a movement, a tone—all singly true and belonging to each other, though never having been joined before.—LAURIE LEE, "Writing Autobiography," *I Can't Stay Long*, 1975, pp. 49–51

Laurie Lee describes *I Can't Stay Long* as "on the whole a scrapbook of first loves and obsessions". He also records that some of the essays were written as long ago as twenty or thirty years. This no doubt accounts for the unevenness of the whole. In the chapter called "Love", for instance one has a curious sense of *déjà vu*. This is written in what seems in places a modernized version of the style of Rom Landau, who used the same high-flown language, and who was much admired in the 1930s by one's maiden aunts. Here is Mr Lee: "Love approves, allows and liberates, and is not a course of moral correction, nor a penitential brainwash or a psychiatrist's couch, but a warm-blooded acceptance of what one is." There is, too, a slickness which sets the teeth on edge. In the same essay he writes of the "drugfix of pop music (with its electronically erected virility)". Turning to the publisher's note at this point I read that some of these pieces have not appeared before except in the United States, which goes a long way to explaining the above but does not excuse it.

Yet when Lee drops his purple mantle he can write with a vivid, spare imagery that makes one realize how closely allied are the eyes of the poet and the painter: "the bright-backed cows standing along the dykes like old china arranged on shelves", "motionless canals, full of silver light, lap the houses like baths of mercury". One is no longer reading but looking at the work of an old Dutch master, for it is of Holland that Mr Lee is writing. "The Village That Lost Its Children", an account of the Aberfan disaster, is journalism at its best, factual and again vivid, the emotion directly conveyed through the words of the people of Aberfan. "Hills of Tuscany" is permeated with the heat and scents of the Italian countryside, and the evocation is such that the reader feels himself to be walking those fifty miles from Florence to Siena, drinking the black wine of Strada-in-Chianti, eating bread and fruit beside a valley stream and gratefully feeling its chill waters on his aching feet.

The genesis of *Cider with Rosie* is to be found in "Writing Autobiography", beside Mr Lee's thoughts in general on this hazardous occupation. While allowing that there are many reasons for embarking on such a project, and were in his own case, he sees it mainly as an act of celebration and preservation. As to what is truth where autobiography is concerned, it is—for him—what you remember, with the rider that there is no pure truth, "only the moody account of witnesses". Which serves as a very precise description of *I Can't Stay Long*, which has however the added interest of showing the progress of the writer as writer over a span of some thirty years.—SYLVIA SEEKER, "Writer on the Move," *TLS*, Jan. 30, 1976, p. 102

POETRY

Laurie Lee ⟨in *The Sun My Monument*⟩ is an impressionist poet. His poems have no structure, no technique beyond the immediate requirements of producing a brilliant impression. He evidently concentrates his mind on some vivid sensation and then produces words with the aim of fixing this sensation.

A too-marked metre, the necessity of searching for a rhyme, careful punctuation, would distract him from his aim, which is to create the sensation of an object by means of words, not to charm us with the delights of form and a sense of words. His poetry is also almost untouched by thought.

This is very hit-or-miss writing, and Mr. Lee is the poet whose future seems the most uncertain of the writers reviewed here (Edith Sitwell, Roy Fuller, Frederic Prokosch, Laurence Binyon, E. J. Scovell). For his stimulus is entirely in his sensations and not in language or in ideas: notoriously, our sensations grow weaker as we grow older. The great advantage of poets who care for poetry as such is that language itself gradually becomes for them an experience: words and metres and melodies are constantly passing through their minds, and what is called inspiration is only the impulse which precipitates the crystallization of a form which is already potentially there. Thus the growing sense of language in a poet's mind fully compensates for the weakening of sensation. Indeed, quite apart from this, I doubt whether sensations such as Mr. Lee describes are our most significant experiences.

The only powerful influence on Mr. Lee seems to be Lorca: a very bad influence on English poets, as Senor Barea has pointed out at considerable length: for English poets are attracted by what seems bizarre and unconnected in Lorca's dazzling imagery, and often they fail to see the hidden links of the Spanish tradition in his poetry.

Here is an example of the Lorca influence at its worst:

> I hear the girl beside me rock
> the hammock of her blood
> and breathe upon the bedroom walls
> white dust of Christmas roses.

Nevertheless, in many of these poems, Laurie Lee succeeds in doing what he sets out to do; producing, that is to say, a sharp sunlit impression:

> I watch a starling cut the sky
> a dagger through the blood of cold,

Unfortunately the next two lines are:

> and grasses bound by strings of wind
> stockade the sobbing fruit among the bees.

Stockade, which is commonly used as a noun, surely suits awkwardly with 'cut' in the first line? "The starling cuts, and the grasses stockade" is the use of two verbs in the same sentence, both of them objects of "I watch". This is the sort of objection a critic is bound to raise because poems are made out of words not out of clear eyes and intense passions. I am so conscious, though, of the eyes and the passions of Mr. Lee that it is an ungrateful task to have to criticize him. There are pure and lovely lines in his poems, such as the following:

> The hard blue winds of March
> shake the young sheep
> and flake the long stone walls;
> now from the gusty grass,
> comes the horned music of rams,
> and plovers fall out of the sky
> filling their wings with snow.

If he took more interest in words and in the formal qualities of poetry, his effects would be less precarious. As it is, their very uncertainty has a charm of its own.—STEPHEN SPENDER, *Horizon*, Oct. 1944, pp. 285–87

The war years saw in Britain (as they did in some of the Dominions, notably Australia) the rise of a number of "little magazines," among which Cyril Connolly's *Horizon* and John Lehmann's *Penguin New Writing* are best known on this side of the Atlantic. Laurie Lee has published poems in both these periodicals, as well as in the BBC magazine, *The Listener*, and in at least two anthologies of the newer verse; but *The Sun My Monument* is his first book publication. Mr. Lee is to be congratulated on the ready acceptance of his first book on these shores; and the American public for poetry now has another measure by which to appraise the new post-Auden generation of English poets.

Is there a greater freshness in the English air than here? At least, Mr. Lee dares to produce poetry that, by one of the standards now revered in local poetic circles, should be clearly "old hat." For example, he boldly backs his work with country, rather than urban, images. Is it that "England's green and pleasant land" provides greater justification for pastoral poetry than the less embraceable American countryside? Though, indeed, he has left his native Cotswolds:

> O the wild trees of my home,
> forests of blue dividing the pink moon,
> the iron blue of those ancient branches
> with their berries of vermilion stars,

with their fields ("that place of steep meadows"), he never really leaves them:

> But here I have lost
> the dialect of your hills,
> my tongue has gone blind
> far from their limestone roots.

When he writes of war, too, does he write more easily because his British audience, knowing the impact of war first hand, does not require the conscious strain of the poet's imagination to make the described experience its own?

> Fruit is falling in the city
> blowing a woman's eyes and fingers
> across the street among the bones
> of boys who could not speak their love.

Both the pastoral note and the ruined city assume an immediacy in the poems of this British writer that they can hardly possess for the self-conscious American poet.

He is an unashamed romantic, too. What poet of genuine talent in this country today would dare to write a line like "A boy is shot with England in his brain"? The sentiment of this is dangerously close to sentimentality. But, again, sentiment no less than romanticism is an old and honored part of the English literary scene. So we may accept this as a true report of an English war mood, even though we remember that between Rupert Brooke and Laurie Lee there was a Wilfred Owen.

In England, too—and this is a more universal note—death and war are still challenged by their eternal unconquerable enemy, love: love not only for the Wolds, not only for England, but love for a woman:

> Let me with vaporizing breath
> speak to my woman, while the frost
> makes up a grim metallic bed
> for me, and summer's broken head

There is hardly a poem in *The Sun My Monument* from which love is wholly absent.

Withal, the style is of our time—for Laurie Lee has not "snorted in the seven sleepers den" while modern poetry has been aborning. His association with advance-guard publications is one warrant of that. Another is his constant use of the metaphysical image. Now the metaphysical image, so popular today, is not simply a fashionable trick—though it can be, and has been, employed as such. The metaphysical image, which by violent shocking linking together of disparate objects makes us see resemblances and harmonies "that never were on sea or land," is *direct statement by metaphor*: that is, the metaphor is organic, structural—it more than advances the thought, it *embodies* the thought. By metaphor things are said which could not be said otherwise; and the emotion supplies the fusing force that brings far-fetched things together to make the new harmony.

The fact that Laurie Lee, who in another age might have been simply a pleasant pastoral poet, is writing metaphysical poetry, need not be charged to fashion. The background for metaphysical poetry is conflict, and we are certainly living in an age of many conflicts. The supreme metaphysical poet is supremely aware of the world about him—and within. Let it be said that Mr. Lee seems to be fully conscious of the world's disharmony, and the necessity to resolve the disorder. His weakness, *as a poet*, crops up in the impulse to find a resolution for these conflicts outside of poetry; a laudable impulse, but alien to the muse. Human love, and even love of humanity (as in "The Long War," where he writes:

> But as our twisted arms embrace
> the desert where our cities stood,
> death's family likeness in each face
> must show, at last, our brotherhood)

may stimulate, animate poetry; but provide no resolution within the poem. Paradoxically—and this is a conclusion which the poet may protest—there is greater promise of poetic health in the unpleasant but metaphorically more intense and satisfying "see how the sun rubs ulcers in the sky" in the Baudelairean second stanza of "Black Edge," his gloomiest poem, than in the more affirmative and lyrical, but weaker conclusion to the same poem:

> Wash me in happy air,
> restore me with the odor of rivers;
> then feed o feed my sight
> with your normal love.

—GERARD PREVIN MEYER, "Washed in Happy Air," SR, Sept. 6, 1947, pp. 23, 30

WILLIAM MAXWELL
"Bright as a Windblown Lark"

New Yorker, April 16, 1960, pp. 172–78

The common reader will put up with absolutely anything, but how like getting a stock split or finding a four-leaf clover it is to read a book by a writer who has managed to separate the material that is his from everybody else's, whose style is an approximation of his own manner of speaking, and who with some courage lays his cards on the table. *The Edge of Day*, by Laurie Lee, meets all three of these requirements, and is beautiful besides, as one would expect the autobiography of a poet to be—beautiful, rich, full of stories, full of the humor that fountains from unsuppressed human beings, full of intelligence and point, full of damn near everything.

I have a fondness for first sentences, and the first sentences of this book are "I was set down from the carrier's cart at the age of three; and there with a sense of bewilderment and terror my life in the village began. The June grass, amongst which I stood, was taller than I was, and I wept. I had never been so close to grass before."

He was rescued by his three big sisters, who came scrambling and calling up the steep, rough bank and, parting the long grass, found him. "There, there, it's all right, don't you wail anymore," they said. "Come down 'ome and we'll stuff you with currants." It was the summer of the last year of the First World War, and 'ome turned out to be "a cottage that stood in a half-acre of garden on a steep bank above a lake; a cottage with three floors and a cellar and a treasure in the walls, with a pump and apple trees, syringa and strawberries, rooks in the chimneys, frogs in the cellar, mushrooms on the ceiling, and all for three and sixpence a week."

Shortly before this, his father, "a knowing, brisk, evasive man, the son and the grandson of sailors," had decamped, leaving his mother to bring up their four young children and four more by his first marriage—on what it would be an exaggeration to call a shoestring. But at least he didn't abandon them entirely; he sent them a few pounds a year, and though they were always hungry, they never quite starved, for the simple reason that they had neighbors. "See if Granny Trill's got a screw of tea—only ask her nicely, mind," his mother would say. Or "Run up to Miss Turk and try and borrow half-crown; I didn't know I'd got so low." And the child spoken to would say, "Ask our Jack, our Mother! I borrowed the bacon. It's blummin'-well his turn now."

"Our Mother" is larger than life-size. She was descended from a long line of Cotswald farmers, and the village schoolmaster, finding that she had a good mind, lent her books and took considerable pains with her, until her mother fell sick and she was needed at home and her father put a stop to her education. At seventeen, wearing her best straw hat and carrying a rope-tied box, she went into domestic service and worked as a scullery maid, household maid, nursemaid, and parlormaid in the houses of the gentry—an experience that haunted her, because she saw luxuries and refinements she could never forget and to which, her son says, she in some ways naturally belonged. "Real gentry wouldn't hear of it," she would tell the children. "The gentry always do it like this"— with the result that they, too, were haunted by what she passed down to them. She had been more than pretty, and she was still a strong, healthy, vivid, impulsive woman. She was also extravagant and a dreadful manager.

> The rent . . . was only three shillings sixpence a week but we were often six months behind. There would be no meat at all from Monday to Saturday, then on Sunday a fabulous goose; no coal or new clothes for the whole of the winter, then she'd take us all to the theatre; Jack, with no boots, would be expensively photographed; a new bedroom suite would arrive; then we'd all be insured for thousands of pounds and the policies would lapse in a month. Suddenly the iron-frost of destitution would clamp down on the house, to be thawed only by another orgy of borrowing, while harsh things were said by our more sensible neighbours and people ran when they saw us coming.

Add to a love of finery unmade beds; add to her anger, which did not last, her gaiety, which was indestructible. To the old newspapers that were knee-deep all over the house add—in bottles, teapots, dishes, and jugs—all manner of leaves and flowers: roses, beech boughs, parsley, garlic, cornstalks. Add to her detailed knowledge of the family trees of all the Royal Houses of Europe her genuinely kind, genuinely compassionate heart. The bus driver is honking his horn and all the passengers are leaning out of the windows and shaking their umbrellas crossly, and a voice, sweet and gay, calls from down the bank, "I'm coming—yo-hoo! Just mislaid my gloves. Wait a second! I'm coming, my dears." She drove her children half crazy; she infected them with the wonder of life.

Here she is getting supper:

> Indoors, our Mother was cooking pancakes, her face aglow from the fire. There was a smell of sharp lemon and salty batter, and a burning hiss of oil. The kitchen was dark and convulsive with shadows, no lights had yet been lit. Flames leapt, subsided,

corners woke and died, fires burned in a thousand brasses. "Poke round for the matches, dear boy," said Mother. "Damn me if I know where they got to."

Here she is with a sick child:

Then Mother would come carolling upstairs with my breakfast, bright as a wind-blown lark. "I've boiled you an egg, and made you a nice cup of cocoa. And cut you some lovely thin bread and butter."

And here she is in bed:

My Mother, freed from her noisy day, would sleep like a happy child, humped in her nightdress, breathing innocently, and making soft drinking sounds in the pillow. In her flights of dream she held me close, like a parachute, to her back; or rolled and enclosed me with her great tired body so that I was snug as a mouse in a hayrick.

Though she bestrides the book, her largeness is not of the kind that results in somebody else's having to be small. The author says that there was no male authority in the house and that he and his brothers were dominated entirely by their mother and sisters, and yet he and the three other boys and every other man he writes about are thoroughly masculine. Somewhere, somehow, it all came out right.

They were not isolated. The stone house they lived in had once been a small manor house and was now divided into three cottages, in two of which lived two immensely old women who referred to each other spitefully as "Er-Down-Under" and "Er-Up-Atop" and lived only to outlive each other. One spent all her time making wine out of almost everything you can name, including parsnips. The other sat taking snuff and "biding still," and, if pressed, would take down the almanac and read about disasters to come, or tell the children about her father, who was a woodcutter and so strong he could lift a horse and wagon.

Gradually, little by little, the reader gets to know the people in other houses round about. The beautiful English landscape had a sufficient number of figures in it, and under the author's hand, one after another, they come to life. But not statically, not as set pieces or portraits, but as people who are being swept along in the current that flows only one way. Old people give up and die, children are picked up bodily, kicking and bawling, and carried off to school. The boys that were roaming the fields are lured under the hayrick and marry, all in good time, as trees come into leaf or shed their foliage, as plants come into flower. But not all of them, of course. For example, in the author's family there was another sister, who slipped away without warning when she was four years old, and every day of his mother's life she continued to grieve for and talk about that dead daughter, whose name is included, most touchingly, in the dedication of the book, among the living sisters and brothers.

The word I have been avoiding using all this time is "love." It is conveyed on virtually every page of this book. All kinds of love. And also, as might be expected of any place where love is amply present, murder and mayhem, fornication, incest, perversion, rape, suicide, grief, and madness. All of which the village managed in its own private way. Outsiders were not called in to punish or adjudicate, and when they came of their own accord, their questions were met by stares,

and the information they sought after was given to every man, woman, and child of the village, in detail, so that they would know what it was they were to hide.

On the brighter side, here is the Parochial Church Tea and Annual Entertainment:

The stage curtains parted to reveal the Squire, wearing a cloak and a deer-stalking hat. He cast his dim, wet eyes round the crowded room, then sighed and turned to go. Somebody whispered from behind the curtain. "Bless me!" said the Squire and came back.

"The Parochial Church Tea!" he began, then paused. "Is with us again . . . I suggest. And Entertainment. Another year! Another year comes round! . . . When I see you all gathered together here—once more—when I see—when I think . . . And here you all are! When I see you here—as I'm sure you all are—once again . . . It comes to me, friends!—how time—how you—how all of us here—as it were . . ." His mustache was quivering, tears ran down his face, he groped for the curtains and left.

His place was taken by the snow-haired vicar, who beamed weakly upon us all.

"What is the smallest room in the world?" he asked.

"A mushroom!" we bawled, without hesitation.

"And the largest, may I ask?"

"ROOM FOR IMPROVEMENT!"

"You know it," he muttered crossly. Recovering himself, he folded his hands: "And now O bountiful Father . . ."

The motorcar brought all this to an end. The last days of the author's childhood were also the last days of the village, the end of a thousand years' life, in that remote valley:

Myself, my family, my generation [Mr. Lee says] were born in a world of silence; a world of hard work and necessary patience, of backs bent to the ground, hands massaging crops, of waiting on weather and growth; of villages like ships in the empty landscapes and the long walking distances between them; of white narrow roads, rutted by hooves and cart wheels, innocent of oil or petrol, down which people passed rarely, and almost never for pleasure, and the horse was the fastest thing moving. Man and the horse were all the power we had—abetted by levers and pulleys. But the horse was king, and almost everything grew round him: fodder, smithies, stables, paddocks, distances and the rhythm of our days.

Granted that one has to live in one's own Age or give up all contact with life; nevertheless, one puts this book aside not with nostalgia but with a kind of horror at what has happened. There was perhaps no stopping it, one thinks, and at the same time as one thinks that, one thinks that it should never have been allowed to happen, that our grandparents would not have put up with it—with the terrible, heartbreaking impoverishment that is not confined to a single village in a remote valley of the Cotswalds, or to any one country. It is all but general, and very few of us know, at first hand, anything else. Like a fatal disease, it has now got into the blood stream.

ROSAMOND LEHMANN

1903–

Rosamond Nina Lehmann was born in London on February 3, 1903. After being privately educated at home, she attended Girton College, Cambridge, which provided the background for her highly successful first novel *Dusty Answer* (1927). Her career continued with A *Note in Music* (1930), *Invitation to the Waltz* (1932), *The Weather in the Streets* (1936), *The Ballad and the Source* (1944), *The Echoing Grove* (1953), and A *Sea-Grape Tree* (1976). She has also written a play, *No More Music* (1939), and short stories, collected in *The Gypsy's Baby* (1946). A volume of autobiography, *The Swan in the Evening*, appeared in 1967, and deals in large part with the life of her only daughter, after whose death at the age of twenty-four in 1958 she developed a serious interest in psychic and mystical experiences. She is vice-president of the College of Psychic Studies.

Like her brother John Lehmann, Rosamond Lehmann has shown a commitment to international literature, translating Jean Cocteau's *Children of the Game* (in America, *The Holy Terrors*), in 1955, and serving as international vice-president of P.E.N. She was made a CBE in 1982.

General

All Miss Lehmann's heroines have a sense of history that is both personal and general and are part of a past they are struggling to repudiate or recapture, sometimes both simultaneously as in *The Weather in the Streets*. A *Note in Music* takes its title from a quotation by Walter Savage Landor: "But the present, like a note in music, is nothing but as it appertains to what is past and what is to come." Throughout that novel, the characters try to seize the "moment," to crystallize an identity out of the flux of experience, a process like that sometimes achieved by characters in Virginia Woolf's novels, but, in Miss Lehmann's fiction, the "moment," the unique present, never appears or is illusory to immediately dissolves. Historical flux dominates. In *The Ballad and the Source* (1944), she uses the adolescent second sister to piece together the tales she hears from an old servant and members of a neighboring family to trace the "ballad," the story of corruption and resentment in the neighboring family that goes from elegance through madness to severe and tenacious competence in three generations, to its complicated "source," the combination of fascination, indifference, vitality, and narcissism in the character of Mrs. Jardine, the progenitor. Far from the "Edwardian Tremolo" or the "invitation to nostalgia" that one unperceptive reviewer called the novel when it was published, *The Ballad and the Source* links the personal history of one family to the more general decline of the English upper classes in the first twenty years of this century, providing the adolescents of 1920 with "reminiscent conversations" so that "their identity, to themselves so dubious, so cloudy, becomes clarified."

The extensions of the sensitive self into society and history give density and meaning to the fiction, but they give no permanence or consolation to the characters. A hard sense of the inconsolability of human experience dominates the fiction: all emotions change, no love is fully matched or requited, all human beings die. The version of the dying father in *The Weather in the Streets* is withdrawing into "the lifelong private integrity of his disillusionment." All the novels bring the characters to the recognition that death is the "dusty answer"—an answer that is both unsatisfactory and inescapable—to the human search that is "hot for certainties," to refer to the quotation from Meredith that reverberates throughout Miss Lehmann's work. Invariably, human sexuality is the principal means for an attempt to impose the self upon experience, to create an intense connection that can assuage the inevitable forces of time, history, death. And the sexual impulses described are sometimes, in a muted and secondary way, homosexual, particularly in *Dusty Answer*, *The Weather in the Streets*, and *The Echoing Grove*, for the sense of sexual connection, of expressing the self in close relationship, is more important than the nature of the relationship's object. Sex is primarily a release of self, not a search for an appropriate or particular kind of other. In all the novels, the sexual connections are transitory, defeated, the heroines left alone at the end with the recognition that they have nothing beyond themselves. In *The Echoing Grove*, in which two sisters have loved the same man, now dead, and in which the ending suggests that, for the mistress, her sister has always been more central, more loved, and more the adversary than has the man, the collapse of the affair is summarized with a line from Blake: "Go love without the help of anything on earth." Reviewers and critics have sometimes mentioned the disillusionment as a principal limitation of Miss Lehmann's fiction. Yet it is only a limitation from a perspective that asserts a human capacity to triumph over or in spite of time and death. And the simultaneously sharp and sympathetic refusal to console is also the "limitation" implicit in Housman's poems, in Chekhov's plays and stories, and in Arnold Bennett's serious fiction. . . .

Critics have always praised Miss Lehmann's prose, its clarity, its finish, its sensitivity, its "beauty," sometimes as a kind of minor compensation for the major limitations of her femininity and her disillusionment. . . . But there is also sometimes another note in the prose that I find less easy to accommodate as the instrument of a sensitive, lucid, and unconsoling human formulation. This is a kind of rhapsodic prose, an occasional flight into the mysteries of organic nature, connected with the moon, the trees, and water at night in *Dusty Answer*, with birds, gardens, and farms in a pastoral interlude for one of the women in A *Note in Music*. These interludes seem almost animistic, sensitive to spirits permeating the natural world, closer in ways to the prose of John Cowper Powys than to that of Katherine Mansfield. This rhapsodic prose is most apparent and given most room in *The Ballad and the Source*, the novel in which the attempt to discover the "source," the beginning of the mysteries that influence three generations, "the fount of life," is most conscious and articulate. The central figure of the novel, Mrs. Jardine, is seen as "savage," "unearthly," an "enchantress" of considerable charm or an "Enchantress Queen in an antique ballad of revenge." Although the novel—at times, as critics have noted, an almost Jamesian revelation of mystery to a perceptive adolescent—allows most scope for this kind of prose, it lacks, for me, the immediacy of the other novels, dissipates its force in long confessionals and melodramatic revelations. Animistic prose has its drawbacks and it does not, at least for Miss Lehmann, seem integrated well into the form of the novel. In fact, as apparent in *The Swan in the Evening* (1967), more recent experience has caused Miss Lehmann to focus more and more on the animistic and the mystical, and she has not written fiction at all. One kind of personal experience, most often that which refuses consolation, is transmuted into fiction; another kind of personal experience, less publicly communicable, more mysterious and more recondite, is transmuted into "fragments of an inner life." Yet hints of the mystical, bits of the animistic, are occasionally visible in all her prose.

The fact that implications that can be derived from her different kinds of prose are not fully integrated into a single kind of fiction might be one reason that Miss Lehmann's work has been so unjustly neglected. More probably, however, the reasons are less valid critically. Rosamond Lehmann is neither strident nor teachable; her work cannot easily be either extrapolated into a simplified and positive perspective, a message, or analyzed meaningfully in terms of an imagistic pattern or structure that yields what was not visible before. Unlike the novelists with whom she was most frequently compared, Virginia Woolf and Elizabeth Bowen, Rosamond Lehmann does not expand or reveal under the stress of rigorous analysis. Virginia Woolf, in her fiction, attempted to define identity, to say "there she was," in terms that dealt simultaneously with both individuals and a generalized essence of humanity. Although Miss Lehmann enthusiastically admired Woolf's fiction (an admiration expressed several times in critical prose and in a published letter to a sister, also a possible influence most visible in some of the technical devices in *Invitation to the Waltz*), she never strives for that kind of metaphysical coherence, never organizes a novel around reaching a lighthouse. Elizabeth Bowen's fiction, particularly her best-known work of the thirties and forties, carefully shapes and structures the moral dimensions of the characters she creates, has heroines, monsters, and various stages in between. Miss Lehmann's fiction relentlessly refuses to judge. Metaphysically and morally, although not stylistically, her novels are closer to those of Arnold Bennett than to those of either Virginia Woolf or Elizabeth Bowen.—JAMES GINDIN, "Rosamond Lehmann: A Revaluation," *CoL*, Spring 1974, pp. 205–10

Works

Miss Lehmann ⟨in *Dusty Answer*⟩ shows the clumsiness and lack of economy which so often accompanies freshness and exuberance in the work of inexperienced novelists. But both she and Miss ⟨Dorothy⟩ Edwards are born writers, natural creators of the curious world of fiction. You feel that a live hand has held the pen that wrote the words that have built up the book, and has quickened, with that subtle suppleness of what lives, the sentences, the conversations, the characters. . . . There is a quickness and subtlety of characterization, a spontaneous creativeness, which can be found in the work of so many of the best women writers of short stories or novels. But more important is the element of poetry. Neither Miss Lehmann nor Miss Edwards is a poet in the old sense, nor perhaps would they agree that they try to write poetry. Nevertheless both of them attempt to do in prose and as an accompaniment to the telling of a story or the development of character or what we now call "psychology," what the nineteenth century and all the centuries behind it left to the poet. . . .

It is a curious fact, which is worth a passing mention, that the philosophy of life in ⟨*Dusty Answer* and Edward's *Rhapsody*⟩ is that of the dusty answer. There is more rhapsody in Miss Lehmann's novel than in any of Miss Edward's stories, and the rhapsodical element is the cause of a good deal of its merits and of its ultimate failure. For nothing is so difficult to control by the artist as rhapsody and passion. *Dusty Answer* is a chaotic book; its author has tried to do too many things at the same time. There is a good story in it; there is, I am told, a very realistic picture of the life of the younger generation at Cambridge; there are detailed psychological studies of an interesting young woman and an extremely interesting family of cousins; there are vast conversations; there is a philosophy of life; there is the element of poetry. But Miss Lehmann never suceeds in getting all these elements to fuse; she has failed to find that invisible cement which alone can hold together the heterogeneous parts of a mere book and transform it into a work of art. Her poetry is often good poetry, but it seems to be superimposed upon her plot; her philosophy of life is often an interesting philosophy, but it does not, as with Miss Edwards, grow out of her story. There are terrible lapses. Some of the conversations in the modern novelist's style at Girton are distressing, and the scene when Martin shoots a rabbit is the kind of psychological melodrama which one expects only in a third-rate novel. But, despite its faults, the book has great promise. Miss Lehmann has the instincts of a writer and a story-teller; there is real beauty in some of the poetical passages. And, above all, both she and her book seem to be alive. —LEONARD WOOLF, "Rhapsody or Dusty Answer?," NA, Sept. 10, 1927, p. 749

. . . A *Note in Music* ⟨is⟩ a faintly snobbish book whose only attraction is its soothing, marbled prose. The present, like a note in music, may be (as Landor appropriately suggested on Miss Lehmann's title page) nothing, but as it appertains to what is past and what is to come; but there is no permission for the novelist, in this phrase, to write about nothing. That is virtually what Miss Lehmann has attempted. She takes two perfectly dressed, god-like creatures, utterly colourless in their London and Oxford sophistication, and watches their effect on the lives of two drearily married couples in a northern provincial town. Nothing happens. Everyone has been taken at the lowest ebb of his vitality. A banal, *blasé* and pretentious book about nothing.—V. S. PRITCHETT, "The Age of Speed?," *Spec*, Sept. 27, 1930, pp. 421–22

Miss Lehmann belongs to a generation that, for the most part, finds maturity difficult. Its emotion—congested, one cannot know how synthetic—is, though not pleasant to suffer, easier to suffer than to express: there has come to be perfected, for dealing with emotion, a frigid kind of bravado, irony with a current of mawkishness, in which the public school spirit has an unhappy counterpart. Many good novels show a muffled dismay. *One* sort of emotional novel is not, unhappily, rare: it is, as a rule, so shocking as to leave one with the impression that only second-rate people are uninhibited now. There is masochistic frankness, but almost no spontaneity.

Miss Lehmann is an exception to all this. The most remarkable, the most natural of her qualities is the power to give emotion its full value and play, to transcribe into prose emotion that is grown up and spontaneous, fatalistic but not abject, sublime without being high-pitched, infusing life but knowing its own isolation. She attempts to make no relation—

necessarily a false relation—between emotion, with its colossal, unmoving subjective landscape, and outside life with its flickering continuity of action and fact. She writes, in fact, to underline the disparity, which is the subject of *The Weather in the Streets*—its plot being the story of a love affair.

> Beyond the glass casing I was in the weather, were the winter streets in rain, wind, fog, in the fine frosty days and nights, the mild damp grey ones. Pictures of London weather the other side of the glass—not reaching the body. . . . In this time there was no sequence, no development. Each time was new, was different, existing without relation to before and after; all the times were one and the same. [And later.] Now I see what an odd duality it gave to life; being in love with Rollo was all-important, the times with him were the only reality; yet in another way they had no existence in reality. It must have been the same with him.

Circumstances increase this natural isolation of love. Olivia, sensitive, wary, tentative and a touch defiant, discouraged and in her own view declassed by a futile marriage, now over, becomes the mistress of Rollo Spencer—assured, charming, easy and essentially fortunate. The defensive husk she has acquired irks her a little and does not quite fit. Like most solitary people playing their own hand, she is absorbed, if not always fortified, by an intensive inner life. In any world— with her family, on the night she dines with the Spencers, with her London friends, so gentle, bleak, asexual, intimate— Olivia is alien, uncertain, nostalgic. She is like someone sitting a long way from the fire, but near a mirror reflecting the firelight. Whereas Rollo is more than an inmate of *his* world; his world is part of his nature; she sees in him the strong and happy flowering of it. From this world, now their love affair has begun, she is bound to know him apart; she is conscious that, in being with her, he is dissociated, however happily, from the major part of himself. Their love has for him the exhilaration of island life, whereas for her it is a continent.

The figure of Rollo Spencer, sometimes no more than a big, fatal silhouette, sometimes seen in strong light—with his "upper class charm," his intensities of purpose, his confusion of motive—is magnificently put in. Olivia's awareness of her lover never exceeds the bounds of love or art; she apprehends him rather than observes him; in thought, in the narrative of her consciousness, the idiom of love is never departed from— which, pitching the book so perfectly that there is never a drop in it, is in itself very fine art. The changes of person—from the third to the first in Part Two (giving the effect of blurred, too close-up, climactic, subjective vision), then back to the third again in Part Three, for sadder detachment, a sense of brutal collision with the outside world—are very telling. Apart from this, there is not a single intrusion of "technique"; though technically there are few flaws in the book. As a writer, Miss Lehmann's competence is so great that she has been able to sink her competence in her subject. There is no showing off— which is too rare. Her style has a sensuous, vital simplicity, to which her brain gives edge.

No one can write better than Miss Lehmann about the aesthetics, the intimate charm—much more than charm—of luxury, the unwary civility of the old world, privilege, ease, grace. She has always been able to place, and to evaluate, glamour. She has also a great command of contrast—between groups of people, settings, seasons of the year, moods, different idioms in talk. Olivia's solitary though gregarious life in London, her visits home, her times with Rollo Spencer make a strong triangle in the structure of the book. The Curtis family life, with its dialogue, is delicious. There are few "minor"

characters in *The Weather in the Streets*: Kate, now a cool young matron, Kate's children, Mrs. Curtis, Lady Spencer, Marigold, Etty and Anna are more than a mere supporting cast; they have an opposing reality of their own, and play a positive part in the plot. Miss Lehmann has accomplished a remarkably difficult thing; she has added, palpably, ten years of age to her characters since their first appearance in *Invitation to the Waltz*. Some features have hardened and others blurred; that first lyrical freshness has left Olivia and Kate.

Everything that went to make Miss Lehmann's three other novels is present in *The Weather in the Streets*, and still more has been added, which is as it should be. This book, which has lovely qualities that are inimitably its writer's, is outstanding as a sheer piece of good work.—ELIZABETH BOWEN, NSN, July 11, 1936, p. 54

One need not be a particularly accomplished Jamesian to recognize the dominant influence in Rosamond Lehmann's *The Ballad and the Source*. Miss Lehmann's new novel is a psychological mystery of the type that Henry James delighted in and from the precocious children who see and hear such a large part of the story, through the careful architecture of the narrative and its emphasis on psychological motive to its atmosphere of well-bred horror *The Ballad and the Source* reveals its distinguished ancestry. Even the names of the characters suggest the connection: there is not only the girl Maisie, as an obvious instance, but also such names as Mrs. Jardine and Mr. Charles Herbert, which ring an unmistakable note of familiarity. On the other hand, there is a factitious quality of Miss Lehmann's mystery, a growing sense of mystification for its own sake or the sake only of making a good dramatic yarn, which unfortunately reminds us less of Henry James than of a superior *Rebecca*.

But it is as much a part of the subtlety and delicate complication of *The Ballad and the Source* as of its mystification that it is very difficult to summarize. To say that Miss Lehmann is telling the story of a beautiful Edwardian lady the affirmation of whose will against the conventions of her society destroys her daughter's life and works its disastrous effects into the generation of her grandchildren is to make but a crude approximation of even the outline of the book; for the circles of circumstance generated by Mrs. Jardine's conduct in a very young-womanhood suggest an endless widening, like the circles started by a pebble on the smooth surface of a lake. In addition, any synopsis of *The Ballad and the Source* must be inadequate to the richly modulated character of Mrs. Jardine; and it is this character—its moral color and substance—with which Miss Lehmann is chiefly and best concerned. Even at the end of the novel, when all the clues to Mrs. Jardine are in and the consequences of her behavior have been shown in their full melodrama, we are warned against a simple judgment on so much complexity. Like the child Rebecca Landon, Rosamond Lehmann's author-person, the reader is left with the heavy burden of Mrs. Jardine's ambivalent morality; even in Mrs. Jardine's lies we have been taught to see a certain truth.

Among present-day novels, that is, *The Ballad and the Source* is unusually ambitious on the moral-psychological level. Miss Lehmann, running against the current of our time, refuses to be satisfied with absolute notions of right and wrong. She also avoids the great cliché of recent fiction, the substitution of psychopathology for moral and psychological understanding—and this quite despite the psychopathological nature of the novel's climax.

In method, too *The Ballad and the Source* is ambitious in a way that is uncommon in contemporary fiction. Miss Lehmann divides her novel into several parts, in each of which the character and history of Mrs. Jardine are presented in a fresh light; and the development of the story is handled in long narrative dialogues between Rebecca and some other person in a position to know what happened, often Mrs. Jardine herself. By the use of such devices she rejects both the internality which is so popular with present-day novelists and the straightway factuality of traditional fiction, in favor of the artificiality, if you will, of the "constructed" tale.

And yet when one has taken into account the moral and technical imagination of Miss Lehmann's novel, and also its high literacy, one wonders why the book as a whole swings so much less than its intended weight—and I suppose it is because moral imagination is not enough; it must always be supported with moral passion. I think that what finally exposes *The Ballad and the Source* to the accusation of factitiousness is the impression Miss Lehmann conveys of caring more about the outcome of a story than about the outcome of life itself. Whatever the high degree of consciousness with which Henry James went about the business of constructing his tales, this was an error of which he was of course incapable. The obsessive identification he made between art and life—his conviction, indeed, that art *was* life—saved James from such an act of inverse condescension. It also made him inimitable even by a writer who, like Miss Lehmann, brings to her study of him such considerable gifts of insight and taste.—DIANA TRILLING, *Nation*, April 14, 1945, pp. 422–23

Coincidence has produced, in this last week, two plays which, while they have no underlying resemblance, are alike in one thing: they both deal with emotion intensified by geographic conditions. In *Land's End* at the Westminster and *No More Music*, the London International Theatre Club production at the Duke of York's, the characters are, by isolation in the exact sense, driven in on each other and on themselves—Mr. F. L. Lucas's in a Cornish cliff-top house rocked by equinoctial gales, Miss Lehmann's in a West Indian island hotel. . . .

No More Music . . . falsifies nothing. The characters have all left what passes for life with them at the other side of the world. They have already detached themselves from their settings by the deliberate act of taking ship, in January, for the West Indies. . . . Jan and Miriam are both static characters: they drill down into themselves but do not proceed. The last morning, after a night electric with storm and tragedy, leaves them much as they were. Hilda, washed out to sea, has been too dynamic for them. Dramatically, all this is excellent.

Miss Lehmann has kept, throughout the play, a balance between the banal and the heroic. The mood is, with a few breaks, astringent; the dialogue is pointed, vivid, light. Some monologues could be shortened; more could be left implicit— for the characters make their momentum and their direction felt from the first.—ELIZABETH BOWEN, "Island Life" (1938), *Collected Impressions*, 1950, pp. 206–8

The problem of novel-writing is, how to convey.

. . . Rosamond Lehmann's handling of the problem is not the least of the triumphs of her novel *The Echoing Grove*. She has been so bold, in our time, as to picture the absoluteness, the entirety of love—its power to consume persons, and to consume itself. Her subject dominates, as the subject should—characters are taxed to the last inch, the time-continuity of the story is disrupted. Only consummate, considered, matured art on the part of a novelist could have achieved this—technical intricacy, sunk in the emotional power of the whole.

Scenes, incidents, radiate outward from the central factor—a man, Rickie, loved by his wife, Madeleine, has a love affair with Madeleine's sister, Dinah. The beginning of the story—in terms, that is, of Miss Lehmann's order of its narration—is in fact its end: the sisters, after fifteen years of estrangement, meet. Rickie is dead; years before his death there had been a break between him and Dinah, who has since then married, whose husband has been since then killed in the Spanish War. Madeleine is (on this late-autumn country afternoon when the widowed sisters go for a walk together) on the eve of a break with a lover, Jocelyn, the beginning of her relationship with whom had preceded Rickie's death. Rickie— though this is known to neither sister—had, within the last week of his life, become the lover of his friend's wife, Georgie. Madeleine once, by an ill-timed, well-meant call at her sister's flat, had inadvertently driven away the young man, Rob, with whom Dinah was making a desperate experiment in happiness. In the background had stood a refugee doctor, Selby, with whom Dinah's relationship is uncertain.

By being gradually given to know the whole, we are caused cumulatively to feel it. When, with the last pages of *The Echoing Grove*, we returned to the sisters alone together in the house by the river, in the autumn night, we feel the ring-after-ring of significance round each word which passes between them; we share (with two dead men) knowledge of the origin of the cigarette burn on the bedside table; we react to the irony of the extreme lightness of a pair of cuff-links, weighed on the palm of a woman's hand. What seems the more remarkable is that at the outset—when first we met these two women, as they meet on the porch—we should have been caused by Miss Lehmann to apprehend much that she had not even begun to tell us. She charges herself with the relation of incidents whose background cannot be estimated till we have gathered (through travelling back in time) what, and in what manner, had come before them. It is extraordinary that we should be, from the first, so deeply implicated in what we do not yet even know that there is to know.

Much of the strength is due to the placing—that is, to the order of the scenes and their illuminating relation to one another. Each scene is, in effect, a dialogue—A with B, A with C, B with C, C with D, and so on. Seldom are more than two of the protagonists on the stage, or page, together. Unspoken soliloquies link, or frame, the dialogues. What might most nearly be confusing is the movement to and fro in time; the actual action, or, one might more fittingly say, activity, extends over more than ten years. There is not, however, confusion; thanks, in a great part, to Miss Lehmann's unfailing grip on her own time-scheme, and her carefulness in making it clear to us. By a series of light, sure touches—hints, reminders, clues—she instigates or refreshes the reader's memory. She justifies her reliance on concrete detail—the jade links, the Berlin wool-work armchair, glazed flower-pots, a pound note, a blue cotton frock, a pink evening gown.

The novel is well named. More than one of the characters is aware of love's claustrophobia; and indeed we stand with them in a shaded place in which voices are multiplied, sometimes mocked, by their own echoes, or by echoes of others. The book, in spite of its length and fullness, is constructed with a most masterful economy, in itself tense. Rickie, Dinah, Madeleine, unfold, deepen, gain in living complexity with the addition of each revealing scene. They fail one another; they diminish before each other's eyes. What is wrong—or is something in Nature changing? Change in women as women, in men as men, in their needs, in their efficacy for one another, is the suggested answer—even, the submerged theme. We are brought face to face with the tragic contemporary predicament: Modern Love.—ELIZABETH BOWEN, Review of *The Echoing Grove* (1953), *Seven Winters and Afterthoughts*, 1962, pp. 218–23

The theme of victorious love is connected with that of life ⟨in A *Sea-Grape Tree*⟩, triumphing over the tenacity of the dead Mrs. Jardine as well as over the physical and spiritual paralysis from which Johnny suffers. He is continually associated with that primeval symbol of life, the tree. This image is central to the novel, just as in *The Ballad and the Source* there was the image "of a woman's figure in a blue cloak", an image which originated from the novelist's childhood memories and is still seminal in her latest novel.

Anonyma first takes a closer look at the tree through the Captain's binoculars:

> Stereoscopically vivid in the powerful lens, the sea-grape tree reared up its pale trunk twisting smooth and serpentine, its branches carrying a canopy of glaucous blue-fleshed leaves and pendent clusters of green berries, sterile and hard as stone. Beneath the tree the hut . . .

In the twilight every detail is sharply defined and the old tree looks petrified. Listening to the Cunninghams' conversation, Anonyma learns that the inhabitant of the hut is an invalid. A few moments later she has a vision of the tree suddenly changing:

> And that old stranded reptilian-vegetable growth had lost its petrification, had come alive, was coiling down violently into an explosion of undulating tentacles upon which floated a cargo of shimmering fruit and foliage. One great multi-fingered arm stretched across the hut, enfolding it in what seemed a tender gesture of protection.

Within the tent made by the tree's foliage the figure of a man appears. The dry tree, suggestive of death, comes to life, and the man entangled in its branches seems to smile at her. Anonyma is shaken by the vision; she withdraws from the conversation and lapses into a reverie. She remembers her last night's dream of another tree:

> in blossom, snowy, rose-flushed. It shoots a branch out, and on this branch a bird; a bird with a jewelled crest and irridescent feathers. A Bird of Paradise. A voice says: 'Love Bird!' She stretches out a hand. It bends its head and pecks with a cruel beak; vanishes. A voice says: 'This tree must be cut down. It's dead.' She cries out: 'No! No'!—starts up awake, in terror.

The tree in bloom, usually standing for the Tree of Life, was her false tree of love, the tree from which disappointment came. Because her lover was false and their love sterile, the tree, as in St. Matthew (3:10), must be hewn down. Anonyma realizes with terror that she has trusted in the bird of a false paradise. Later, on this paradisal island, true love and life come to her from a different tree, with which Johnny is identified.

On the same night Anonyma, going with Ellie to pay Johnny a visit, becomes aware of the sea-grape tree and the hut as objects with a mysterious significance for her. And later still, on the day they first kiss, Anonyma and Johnny meet in the evening under the sea-grape tree. It is the first time she has seen him walk a little, and, as he is standing afterwards propped against the tree, he seems to gain strength from its trunk. A great tree, the old symbol of human growth and development, implies the development of Anonyma's and Johnny's love. A unifying symbolism of the archetypal tree may be seen in the repeated image of the two lovers clasped in each other's arms under the sea-grape tree.

The meaning of the sea-grape tree, however, changes with Anonyma's shifting moods. On the day after their first night together, when Johnny went away in the fishing boat and she was watching the empty beach, she thought that the tree "had a menacing appearance, as if stonily encroaching upon a deserted human dwelling place." The lovers' last meeting before Anonyma's departure for England takes place under the tree. She runs to join Johnny who

> is standing underneath the tree, leaning against its trunk, dappled from head to foot with disks of leaf reflection, so that he looks half dematerialized in light and shadow. He has a cape slung over his shoulders: the blue cloak of Mrs. Jardine. When . . . she reaches him, he wraps it round them both.

They make plans for their future together in England and finally part. Anonyma cannot help looking back, and her last view of Johnny, suddenly seen as if from far away, is of "an archetypal Renaissance figure: Portrait of an Unknown Youth in a bower of leaves." But when a few hours later, in the morning sun, she looks down towards the beach for the very last time, "dissolved in light, the hut, the sea-grape tree have disappeared." What is now invisible is all the same real. It is yet another instance of the confusing nature of the reality-illusion relationship, Rosamond Lehmann's favourite theme. . . .

The problem of the clash of moral codes has been treated before by Rosamond Lehmann and is one of the chief concerns of *The Echoing Grove*. Another familiar theme in ⟨*The Sea-Grape Tree*⟩ is the emancipation of women, treated at some length in *The Ballad and the Source* and *The Echoing Grove*; here it is mentioned in passing and in a rather humorous way: Rebecca shocks the ghost of Mrs. Jardine—militant as always—by saying that on that subject she always considered her a bore! Rebecca seems to recognize the traps of the cause to which Mrs. Jardine had devoted herself so wholeheartedly. A minor theme, that of family likeness, with all its multi-layered implications in the *Ballad*, reappears in *A Sea-Grape Tree*. There are also echoes of another recurrent theme, that of personal isolation. In the latest novel, however, this human solitude is transcended by love. Anonyma cannot live without "being in a state of love. A loved and loving state"—and in the end she triumphs. Love appears in different guises but whatever form it adopts, it is a redeeming factor. On the paradisal though partly corrupted island, Johnny and Anonyma are like Adam and Eve after the fall (Johnny has literally fallen down from the sky!) and love is their way of coping with the world. The regenerative power of love gives them strength and hope. "The law of love" seems to operate on all levels of existence, even after death, as Mrs. Jardine explains to Rebecca. This is corroborated by both the pronouncements and the life of Miss Stay, the true psychic—in terms of the novel—who is a spiritual authority. Thus love, the main subject of *A Sea-Grape Tree*, is established as the governing principle of the universe: a message if not original yet certainly never out of date.—Wiktoria Dorosz, "Rosamond Lehmann's Novel *A Sea-Grape Tree*," MS, 1979, pp. 25–28

SIMON RAVEN
"The Game That Nobody Wins:
The Novels of Rosamond Lehmann"
London Magazine, April 1963, pp. 59–64

A young girl, beautiful, sensitive, intelligent *and* well educated, falls in love with a mature man of the world, who is either married already or otherwise heavily encumbered. Although he is incapable of feelings one tenth as intense or delicate as hers, he returns her love; he is an accomplished and assiduous performer in bed; and for the time being, despite the anxiety, the anonymous hotel bedrooms, the clock-watching, they are happy. But the god of love is a strict accountant; he may or may not defer the date of his bill, but sooner or later he renders it in full. There is not one tiny sigh of pleasure but what will have to be paid for in tears or even blood. Just as our heroine is supremely happy, just as her lover is talking of leaving his wife so that they can go away . . . tomorrow . . . anywhere. . . , the blow falls. Business or ill health intervenes; or perhaps somebody's old mother drops dead; or his wife, with whom he is supposed not to be sleeping, turns out to be pregnant. In any case, there it is: sorry, darling, but what can I do? He wipes the tears off her cheeks with the silk handkerchief she gave him for his birthday (I'll think of you, darling, every time I blow my nose), steps into his Bentley, and brmmm, leaving her faint, trembling, numb (etc.); probably penniless (she is too proud to ask); in the soup and, in one case at least, up the spout.

And so of course the stock thing to say about Rosamond Lehmann is that she writes, albeit with exceptional brilliance and penetration, the kind of story which is yearned after by the editors of women's magazines: guilty love, rapture, female steadfast, male fickle, retribution; the only difference being, you will be told, that in Miss Lehmann's case *nobody* ever lives happily ever after, for the good reason that in next to no time they'll all be at it again ('Nothink's ever over when it comes to this sort of a circus,' remarks Tilly in *The Ballad and the Source*). Nor can one altogether refute the charge. The resemblances between Miss Lehmann's work and the weekly woman's serial are obvious and numerous. It will be my business and pleasure, however, to insist on something much more important . . . on the qualities, technical, moral, poetic, even spiritual, which raise her work to a level, not indeed of classical permanence, but at least of intense and persisting interest. Miss Lehmann has taken the kitchen maid's basic fantasy and derived from it a theme pungent, elegiac and adult. How has she done it?

I have before me six novels and one book of short stories, which, apart from a play and some translations, constitute Miss Lehmann's *oeuvre*. I had read all of them, at intervals, any time between five and fifteen years ago; I have now read them all again, this time straight off one after the other. I remembered enjoying them in the past; but I did not expect to enjoy them in bulk, since to read seven books in a row by the same author, though necessary for practical reasons, would be to put her to a ridiculously unfair test. I can only say, however, that I have been consistently entertained, often exhilarated, occasionally very much moved; that while I have been irritated I have not for one moment been bored; and that I picked up the last book with an appetite as keen as that with which, two weeks before, I had picked up the first. Miss Lehmann, then, engages one's interest, one's intelligence and one's emotions: she is also a stayer. So much for the general; now to particular books and the more particular points of Miss Lehmann's morality and art.

Miss Lehmann's first book, published in 1927, was the famous best seller, *Dusty Answer*. It begins:

When Judith was eighteen, she saw that the house
next door, empty for years, was getting ready again.

To me this is a lyrical sentence; heralding a spring, a rebirth, stirring anticipation of the future yet at the same time hinting gently at the past, it is as good an example as I know of Miss Lehmann's gift for conjuring an atmosphere. Nor does she let her initial advantage go. After a few pages one has surrendered completely . . . to the children and their grandmother in the house next door, to the childhood they shared with Judith by the river, to the games and the laughter . . . and one has also

been made aware, not with insistence but by the occasional whisper, of . . . it is difficult to say quite what. . . . of the approaching winter, certainly, but also, let us say, of the snake in the grass which makes even the summer a time of peril. Here, then, as in the celebrated chapters about Cambridge which follow, we have an abiding element in Miss Lehmann's work: poetic evocation at once of the beauty and of the *threat*.

Dusty Answer also offers the first example of what is to be a recurring pattern: love offered, used, and then rejected. Judith loves Roddy, who is gifted, romantic, mercurial and possibly homosexual. Unlike Miss Lehmann's later heroine, she does not have to fight a wife, but the odds are slanted quite badly enough; and after brief, very brief, happiness comes the prototype betrayal. Judith wants to give too much; Roddy, embarrassed, glides smoothly and swiftly away. So far, if one were to ignore the bitterly sprung comment and the ingrowing despair, one might indeed be in the world of the woman's weekly. But in *Dusty Answer*, as in her later novels, it is *after* the disaster that Miss Lehmann is at her most powerful. For there are to be no facile consolations; there is not even anyone (least of all Miss Lehmann herself) to soften the heroine's grief by praising her magnanimity or congratulating her on her performance: there is simply a number of practical problems to be faced, about which Miss Lehmann writes with competence and unexpected precision, and, most important of all for our purpose, a statement of values to be made . . . or rather, to be inferred.

For consider the two following remarks, both of which are part of Judith's train of thought:

Then death, lovely death, lay at the heart of the enchantment.

She was rid at last of the weakness, the futile obsession of dependence on other people.

They add up to a philosophy but they also pose a question. 'This love,' they tell us, 'was an illusion which derived its power from our own frailty and mortality; the power could hurt as well as charm; best keep clear for the future.' Certainly. But the implied question remains. *Was it worth it?* You didn't . . . couldn't . . . win, but you did have the ecstacy of the game: does this compensate you for the pain and humiliation of the ultimate defeat?

At first sight *A Note in Music* (published in 1930) seems to give a tentative answer 'yes'. In this book two middle-aged and married women fall half unconsciously in love with a joyous, blond young man who spends a few months in their dreary provincial town and then leaves them, sorrowful indeed but with a vision to cling to and a better understanding of themselves and their husbands. But the trouble is that *A Note in Music*, beguiling tale though it is, does not really attempt to answer the question we are asking (the question, I suspect, which has always obsessed Miss Lehmann), for the good reason that neither of the women get to grips with the young blond; they merely weave a few dreams round him and keep their distance with care. All of which is well enough, but it is 'spectator' behaviour, like having one's emotions titillated by a drama of passion which, as one very well knows, can never come down off the cinema screen and really get at one. We, to say nothing of Miss Lehmann, are interested in people who palpably and purposefully take part in face to face engagements. We know what is going to happen in the end: they will all, even the least sensitive, be misled and cheated, and some will be viciously hurt. But, once again, will it have been worth it? For the sake of the good times, the high moments, when heart really did speak to heart?

In order to come closer to this question I must, with regret, pass by *Invitation to the Waltz* (1932 . . . a delicious study in innocence which, for our present purpose, remains insufficiently injured), and come straight on to *The Weather in the Streets* (1936), which, incidentally, presents the same characters as the previous book but presents them some years later . . . in their full maturity and with their talents for giving and receiving pain now tuned to the highest pitch. Olivia, poor, intellectual, professional middle class, separated from her poet husband, meets and falls in love with Rollo, who is rich, proper gentry, philistine but no fool, and has a beautiful, pampered and undersexed wife. The affair prospers in three star hotels in cathedral towns and reaches its height during a summer fortnight in Austria; but the violins have a warning note beneath their gaiety, and, sure enough, Rollo returns from Austria to find his wife pregnant. Half by chance and half on purpose he now eludes Olivia, who, though he does not know it, is pregnant too; and to make matters worse his mother, whose well trained upper class nose has scented trouble, appears on Olivia's doorstep to warn her off. Sold again; it was, of course, only a question of time. Nowhere has Miss Lehmann dealt with practical horrors (the lack of money, the muffed abortion) more skilfully and savagely than she does in the ensuing chapters; but what, one must ask, is her value statement to be this time? Will she, or will she not, answer the question, 'Was it worth it?'

She does answer; or rather, she demonstrates that the question has been put in the wrong terms and must be answered in different ones. Only slick and superficial Rollo, it seems, would ask it as coarsely as I have been doing, and his answer is typical: 'It *was* fun, wasn't it, darling?' For Olivia, for Miss Lehmann, there must be a deeper, a subtler, a much more terrible formulation: it is not, for them, a question of fun, of good value for money and effort, *because what has happened was in any case inevitable*. It was a solemn duty to obey the heart, which may not be denied. Love, indeed any personal relationship, is a matter of dedication. Given Olivia's love for Rollo, she must follow it up, live it out, take what comes for better or worse and never commit the blasphemy of counting the cost. She can do no other; and when it is all over, her only resource must be a Stoic withdrawal and the knowledge that she has submitted, with dignity and self-abnegation, to her allotted fate. These things are so. . . .

I would hazard, then, that what began as a decorative pagan philosophy had turned, by the time Miss Lehmann wrote *The Weather in the Streets*, to something nearer a religion. *Dusty Answer* is elegiac: love there is a fragile and beautiful thing, threatened, as the rose is threatened, by the hidden worm, and oh what a pity. *The Weather in the Streets*, on the other hand, is a declaration of faith: love between human beings is now the *only* thing, it must be followed wherever it calls, it will lead to hideous disaster, and this serves us right because we are unworthy. Devouring love . . . which has become, if anything, even more greedy in *The Ballad and the Source* (1944). This novel, apart from anything else, is a remarkable technical achievement, played out in conversations of dazzling versatility in which the past is rehearsed at the same time as the resulting present is enacted. As for its lesson, this is depressing and is rammed home without mercy: love, wherever it leads, is always right; and since it leads people of any sensibility to madness and death, there is your true end. The only people who can be happy are the callous and the frivolous, who sit on the sideline giggling cynically . . . and are therefore damned too. Which of the two alternative modes of damnation is to be preferred is a question which might perhaps give pause to anyone less dedicated than Miss Lehmann: for her there can only be the hissing snakepit hell of love, and it is therefore a relief to turn to the pleasant little tales of childhood and wartime in the country which make up *The Gipsy's Baby* (1946).

A relief, yes, but, one feels, rather an irrelevance. What one wants to know is what more Miss Lehmann has to say about her terrible vampire-god, and there is now only one more novel left in which to look . . . *The Echoing Grove* (1953). And here I must confess to being beaten. As a technical achievement, it is superior even to *The Ballad and the Source*: the switching of viewpoint, the shifts in time and sequence, are accomplished with a dexterity which leaves one gasping: piece by piece, layer by layer, the story is fitted together, a block from this angle, a small brick from that, until at last the whole complex structure is apparent. Yet what, apart from a subtly constructed but not very exciting story, is Miss Lehmann trying to tell us? A husband deceives his wife with the wife's sister; he goes back to his wife, who later starts deceiving him with a young schoolmaster; but not before the sister has taken on and been deserted by a boy from the gutter. The husband dies; the sisters are reconciled by their mother's death. Everyone, it seems, has both betrayed and been betrayed, the honours are just about even. And so what? There is nothing here of the elegiac melancholy of *Dusty Answer*, nor is there the fanatical sense of vocation which makes love such an awesome thing in *The Weather in the Streets* or *The Ballad and the Source*. There is just deceit after grubby deceit, excuses, rationalizations, reforms, broken promises . . . an endless process of hunt-the-bed, each bed turning out to have a dead toad at the bottom of it. No more sad farewells fading along the evening river; no more fierce damnations in the name of love; just a treacherous lump of decaying reptile at the bottom of the bed. What conclusion is invited? What now of love? Can it be that the game which nobody wins has become too formless and too foul even for the most obsessed of players?

A word more. It is now nearly ten years since Miss Lehmann published *The Echoing Grove*, which, though I stand by what I have said above, is by any measure a distinguished novel. I should like, if I may do so without impertinence, to say how grateful I for one shall be when she sees fit to break so long and so sad a silence.

LAWRENCE THORNTON
From "Rosamond Lehmann, Henry James and the Temporal Matrix of Fiction"

Virginia Woolf Quarterly, Spring 1973, pp. 68–75

II

*T*he Ballad and the Source consists of inter-related stories about Mrs. Jardine told from five points of view. They are sometimes violent and bizarre stories, related against the background of Rebecca Landon's adolescence which she recalls for us as an adult. The only technical flaw in the novel is that Rebecca is too often a spectator rather than a participant, a Jamesian *ficelle*, "the reader's friend." Although we are frequently aware of Rebecca as our "friend," we accept this limitation in order to learn about Mrs. Jardine and to follow her tragic fate.

Rebecca's lyrical description of adolescence also describes the form of the novel. "Looking back into childhood," she tells us,

> is like looking into a semi-transparent globe within which people and places lie embedded. A shake— and they stir, rise up, circle in inter-weaving groups. . . . Time is not movement forward or backward through them but simply that colourless globe in which they are all contained (p. 23).[1]

The action of the novel consists in a continuous shaking of this globe in the center of which, immovable and majestic, stands the figure of Mrs. Jardine. Everything in this microcosm coalesces in what Rebecca describes as "a shape too huge, too complex ever to see in outline . . . the monster: human experience (p. 43)." Isolated in this myriad of experience are the double strands of the novel's theme: freedom and sexuality.

The plot grows out of Mrs. Jardine's violation of the conventions of Edwardian society. The strength of her convictions about the rightness of this violation are clearly stated in an early interview with Rebecca which establishes the context in which we see her throughout the novel:

> Mrs. Jardine turned to the window, so that only her bleached stone profile was visible to us, and as if declaring herself, alone, before the judgment of the world, said:
>
> "I have never been a person to be frightened. Physically, I am exceptionally brave. I may say that I have never known physical fear. I have known great pain in my life, and great danger. Each time I have thought: 'How interesting! A first class experience. Not to be missed on any account.' As for those ignoble anxieties which rule the lives of most human beings—they have never touched me. The world is full of unhappy men and women who have feared the opinion of others too much to do what they wanted to do. Consequently they have remained sterile, unfulfilled. Now myself—once I was convinced of what was right for *me*, that was enough! I might suffer, but *nobody* could damage or destroy me (pp. 19–20)."

Ironically, the conviction expressed in this statement which leads to her attempt at personal freedom cripples her own life, destroys the sanity of her daughter, Ianthe, and has devastating and tragic consequences into the generation of her grandchildren who escape only partially what is very much like a curse on the house of Sibyl Anstey Herbert Jardine.

The principles which guide Mrs. Jardine are neither abstract nor bizarre, and they are deeply felt. In fact, they embody all that Lambert Strether knows he missed by the end of *The Ambassadors*. When Mrs. Jardine explains the essence of her views to Rebecca in a passage that explains the title of the novel, we are reminded of the interview between Strether and little Bilham when the older man urges his young companion to "live all you can." Similarly, Mrs. Jardine evokes the

> source . . . the fount of life . . . the quick spring that rises in illimitable depths of darkness and flows through ever living thing from generation to generation. It is what we feel mounting in us when we say: "I know! I love! I *am*! (p. 97)."

But this source is tapped only in Mrs. Jardine's young womanhood, for by following her principles based on a conception of individual freedom, the source becomes "vitiated" and "choked" (p. 97); and as it later flowed into the maturing life of her daughter, perverted and destroyed. This withering of potentialities is caused by the irresistible backlash of a society governed by rigid Edwardian moral conventions.

Mrs. Jardine's attempt at freedom came when she abandoned a hopeless marriage for a relationship with a painter she loved. "A bad marriage," she tells Rebecca, "is the most detrimental, most vicious of habits (p. 105)," and we approach the center of the globe, the theme of the novel, when she explains the consequences of having left her husband:

> I took a step which destroyed his prestige as a man of property. I was his property: he had lost it. Therefore he would destroy me (p. 106).

While the essence of the tragedy is contained in the implications of this chilling syllogism, it also illuminates her philosophical stature. Her abandonment of this man of property symbolizes the affirmation of the fully realized life in the emphatic "I *am*" of her speech to Rebecca as well as the act that "vitiated" and "choked" it. Never unaware of the consequences of her actions, she understands and accepts as inevitable what hapens to her:

> Do you know what goes to make a tragedy? The pitting of one individual of stature against the forces of society. Society is cruel and powerful. The *one* stands no chance against its combined hostilities. But sometimes a kind of spiritual victory is snatched from that defeat. Then the tragedy is completed (p. 103).

Her defeat is somewhat more complex and moving than Diana LeStourgeon's assertion that it "has come in the loss of Ianthe, her victory in the apparent recovery of her grandchildren,"[2] for of equal importance is the denial of her freedom by this society, of the chance to follow Strether's advice to "live all you can."

The consequences of this initial act move quickly and devastatingly into the lives of her husband, her daughter and her grandchildren. For almost immediately after she leaves him, Mrs. Jardine tells Rebecca that Ianthe's father became a singularly abnormal man:

> "Normal people send their energies and emotions out through a number of channels. He ceased to do this. He turned from life which had so disappointed him, and concentrated his whole being upon two objects: his daughter and his God. Naturally . . . the two got somewhat mixed up. The world was not to breathe upon her. It was to be a kind of spotless union—a Trinity. She was not to know any other fulfillment. He taught her that the natural love between a man and a woman, the love that makes them wish to live together and have children, was loathsome and degrading. Yes, he taught her that wickedness! He and she for God only and each for God in one another: that was how it was to be . . . every variation upon that theme. It involved—" She paused. "It seems that it involved watching over her day and night: a total absorption. Not one word or thought, not one instinct was to escape his possession. Waking or sleeping, she must be his—guarded—his miser's treasure."
>
> "Did he have her to sleep with him, then?" [Rebecca] asked, astonished at such intensity of fatherly concern.
>
> "Yes. That is what he did."
>
> ". . . . As she grew older, nearer to the time when a child normally begins to leave its parents' care and influence, his crazed love grew. At all cost he must isolate her from any future she might reach towards for herself—or that might open out for her through me. . . ."
>
> "She was rather old, wasn't she," [Rebecca] observed, "to sleep with somebody else?"
>
> "But in the ferment of adolescence!" she exclaimed, still thinking aloud, and disregarding [Rebecca's] suggestion. "The awakening instincts of sex all crushed, distorted—(pp. 121–122)."

The perversion and eventual insanity of Ianthe is absolutely convincing given this context of her adolescence which was the direct result of Mrs. Jardine's affirmation of freedom and love. This irony is an integral part of Miss Lehmann's thesis.

The decision by Mrs. Jardine to break away from the restrictive conventions of her time along with the perversion and destruction of her daughter's life which resulted from this attempt fuse the subjects of freedom and sexuality in the theme of the novel. It is stated in several places, but nowhere more succinctly than when Mrs. Jardine tells Rebecca:

> Englishmen dislike women: that is the blunt truth of it. I have no son. If I had, I should have seen to *him* all right. But why should a girl not receive a similar education? Oh, what an outrageous, what an indecent proposition! Do not you know that in England it is considered immoral to teach a girl the needs of her heart and body? . . . Dear me, dear me! Sometimes one is really led to conclude that material vindictiveness is at the bottom of it—imposed inferiority has bred it—as it will. "Let her go through what I did. Let her be unhappy, disappointed, shocked. She will get used to it. I had to: why should *she* not?" That seems to be the sort of idea. What a pass to be brought to! How long, I wonder, will ignorance spell purity and knowledge shame (pp. 136–37)?

Yet, while Mrs. Jardine suffers grievously, there is no intention on the part of Miss Lehmann to suggest only bitterness, only injustice, and it is here that the novel begins to diverge radically from the critical opinions of those writers I cited earlier. For Mrs. Jardine understands that she is part of an historical process. At times, she speaks prophetically of this role she has accepted. The following passage occurs shortly after her evocation of the life-force, and it is linked to the central image of the novel, the free-flowing source, which is the potentiality of Mrs. Jardine, as well as to the story of her life, which is the ballad:

> "Sometimes," she said, "the source is vitiated, choked. Then people live frail, wavering lives, their roots cut off from what should nourish them. That is what happens to people when love is betrayed—murdered." Her eyes flicked. Then looking at me sternly, she said: "One day, Rebecca, women will be able to speak to men—speak out the truth, as equals, not as antagonists, or as creatures without independent moral rights-pieces of men's property, owned, used and despised. It may begin to be so in your lifetime. What am I saying!—it has begun. When you are a woman"—her smile broke over me, full and tender, "living, as I hope and believe you will live, a life in which all your functions and capacities are used and *none* frustrated, spare a thought for Sibyl Anstey. Say: 'She helped win this for me (p. 97).'"

Surely Mrs. Jardine's use of her maiden name is no accident. She has a life of her own, as a woman, apart from her emotionless first husband or her kindly but alcoholic second one. And that is what the novel is all about.

III

Jamesian echoes in *The Ballad and the Source* are easily indentifiable. Intrigue, complex psychological motives, a strong character attempting to work her will, a prize to be won, the suggestion of the inexhaustibility of the concentric rings formed by human relationships—mention any of these elements and one thinks automatically of Henry James. And this is precisely the response of the critics I have cited. Mrs. Jardine calls up in their minds a panoply of James's women of a particular type perhaps best exemplified by Mrs. Gereth, whose aggression, anger and vindictiveness are symbolized in the pall of smoke rising over the spoils of Poynton, or Maud Lowder, or Madame de Vionnet. Portraits of these last two mature women

will clarify the kind of response I allude to. First, Maud Lowder, with her wonderfully onomatopoetic name:

> She would have meanwhile a wonderful lioness for a show, an extraordinary figure in a cage or anywhere; majestic, magnificent, high-coloured, all brilliant gloss, perpetual satin, twinkling bugles and flashing gems, with a lustre of agate eyes, a sheen of raven hair, a polish of complexion that was like that of well-kept china and that—as if the skin were too tight—told especially at the curves and corners.[3]

And we learn more about this "lioness" who, at the inevitable dinner table conversation, steers "a course in which she called at subjects as if they were islands in an archipelago," is satified, and begins again, "with a splash of the screw, her cruise among the islands." And here is Madame de Vionnet as the archetypal European woman:

> She had struck our friend, from the first of her appearing, as dressed for a great occasion, and she met still more than on either of the others the conception reawakened in him at their garden-party, the idea of the *femme du monde* in her habit as she lived. Her bare shoulders and arms were white and beautiful; the materials of her dress, a mixture, as he supposed, of silk and crape, were of a silvery grey so artfully composed as to give an impression of warm splendour; and round her neck she wore a collar of large old emeralds, the green note of which was more dimly repeated, at other points of her apparel, in embroidery, in enamel, in satin, in substances and textures vaguely rich. Her head, extremely fair and exquisitely festal, was like a happy fancy, a notion of the antique, of an old precious medal, some silver coin of the Renaissance; while her slim lightness and brightness, her gaiety, her expression, her decision, contributed to an effect that might have been felt by a poet as half mythological and half conventional. He could have compared her to a goddess still partly engaged in a morning cloud, or to a sea-nymph waist-high in the summer surge. Above all she suggested to him the reflexion that the *femme du monde*—in these finest developments of the type—was, like Cleopatra in the play, indeed various and multifold.[4]

Madame Merle, Mrs. Touchett, the invisible but felt presence of Mrs. Newsome could also sit for these portraits so clearly before the eyes of Miss Lehmann's critics. The point of this gallery tour is to suggest that Mrs. Jardine is distorted beyond recognition when she is implicitly compared to James's women. Granted that on first glance she may look like them, but the method of presentation is radically different, as different as the artists' intentions. While Mrs. Jardine is aggressive and could be called a *femme du monde* she is not presented as James's women are; i.e. our judgment of her is meant to be favorable, not unfavorable. And this sympathetic rendering violates the received ideas of her critics. Since she is aggressive, the argument subconsciously runs, she must be disagreeable, vicious, morally lax, for agressiveness in James is the objective correlative of these traits. The problem is that Miss Lehmann's critics have not been able to respond to a view of an aggressive woman that does not correspond with James's view. Male chauvinism informs their critical judgments as surely as staunch New England morality informs James's fiction. Ironically, these modes of limitation are at the center of Miss Lehmann's novel.

The implied competition for Mrs. Jardine is James's most perfect female character who demands our sympathy because of her delicacy and ill-health: Milly Theale, the dying fictional avatar of James's dead cousin, Minny Temple. And she is the most perfect because she is the least hardy, the least capable of that aggressive behavior that condemns any of his women who have an ounce of it in their souls. Innocence versus experience, James's favorite theme, was part of Mrs. Jardine's burden: "How long," we remember her saying, "will ignorance spell purity and knowledge shame?"

The resemblances between *The Ballad and the Source* and the fiction of Henry James can be discussed in terms of form, but not content as Mr. Basso, the *Newsweek* critic and, to a lesser degree, Mrs. Trilling argue both explicitly and implicitly. The aggressiveness of James's women is not that of Mrs. Jardine. With her it is only the force of a complete, complex, vigorous personality engaged in confronting her world, and her fate in that world is a reproach to a whole culture. "One day, Rebecca, women will be able to speak to men. . . ." Multiple ironies mount from this phrase whose speaker has been confounded with the black widows of Henry James—it says, among other things, that she is not, nor does she want to be, one of them. And her protest against not being heard has special meaning for us today. Rebecca has grown up.

Notes

Page numbers of *The Ballad and the Source* refer to the 1945 edition, published in New York by Reynal and Hitchcock.

1. This passage has striking parallels to Virginia Woolf's well-known statement that "life is not a series of giglamps symmetrically arranged: life is a luminous halo, a semi-transparent envelope surrounding us from the beginning of consciousness to the end."
2. Diana LeStourgeon, *Rosamond Lehmann* (New York, 1965), Twayne, p. 99.
3. Henry James, *The Wings of the Dove* (New York, 1958), Dell, p. 39.
4. ———, *The Ambassadors* (New York, 1964), Dell, pp. 201–02.

SYDNEY JANET KAPLAN
From "Rosamond Lehmann's
The Ballad and the Source:
A Confrontation with 'The Great Mother'"

Twentieth Century Literature, Summer 1981, pp. 127–32

A Book-of-the-Month-Club selection in 1945, Rosamond Lehmann's *The Ballad and the Source* received only a brief moment of critical acclaim before its reputation dwindled to the size of a footnote in studies of the modern novel.[1] Making its appearance toward the end of the Second World War, the novel must have seemed a curious relic, a charming throwback to the "innocent" sophistication of the Edwardians. Nearly every critic either delighted in or despaired over its "Jamesian" parallels.[2] The novel was known for its technique, its complexities in point of view. But Lehmann's elaborate narrative structure might have been the reason why so many of those pale-green copies languished in used-book bins over the years, their war-economy pages yellow and crumbling. It appears that Lehmann's readers were not sustained by Jamesian complexity nor by the novel's concern with feminist issues; after all, feminism was considered "old-fashioned" in the late forties. And since that also was a time when strong women were called "castrators," the novel's central figure, Sibyl Jardine, could only be treated with disdain. (One of the novel's first critics called it "The Turn of the Shrew.")[3]

As a consequence of such misplaced emphasis, the critics could not discover the meaning behind the extraordinary intricacies of female relationships in this novel. Lehmann's complex structure of narrative voices is not merely a "Jamesian" device, but a method for establishing the centrality of the novel's underlying myth: its access to the emerging consciousness of women. That myth of Lehmann is Demeter's long search for her daughter Persephone, so brutally abducted, now imprisoned in the underworld. Lehmann interweaves the myth into a subtle pattern in which archetypal images related to the basic core of that myth—the presence of "The Great Mother"—enhance and effect the story's emotional resonance.

The Demeter myth has always been seductive and is becoming even more so at the present time.[4] It offers us a certain sense of security in its inevitable movement from barrenness to fertility. Demeter suffers. She mourns. But sorrow is not her only response, and here lies part of the myth's present feminist appeal: Demeter is *enraged*. To use the words of Erich Neumann: "when she is angry, the Goddess . . . can close the wombs of living creatures and all life stands still."[5]

Beyond sorrow and rage is an even greater attraction. What finally captures us in the myth is the *power* of the ultimate rejoining of mother and daughter. In his well-known discussion of the Eleusinian mysteries (in which the myth was ritualized), Neumann emphasizes the centrality of this *heuresis*—the "finding again":

> Psychologically this "finding again" signifies the annulment of the male rape and incursion, the restoration after marriage of the matriarchal unity of mother and daughter. In other words, the nuclear situation of the matriarchal group, the primordial relation of daughter to mother, which has been endangered by the incursion of the male into the female world, is renewed and secured in the mystery.[6]

While timeless cycles of rebirth and decay were enacted repeatedly through participation in the Eleusinian mysteries,[7] Neumann suggests that there was another impulse, more hidden, which was to express the persistence of some level of femal power in a society where that power was already being undermined by the increasing domination of the patriarchy. For all their solemn beauty, the mysteries actually grew forth out of oppression and female misery. Neumann remarks that "abduction, rape, marriage with death, and separation are the great motifs underlying the Eleusinian mysteries."[8]

Obviously, the retelling of any myth in a modern novel gives voice to contemporary social and cultural pressures, values, and attitudes, as does Rosamond Lehmann's choice of the Demeter myth during the human catastrophe of the Second World War. This choice is also related to Lehmann's hope that a new kind of fiction might be created in the world emerging from war. She expresses that hope in an essay written shortly after the publication of *The Ballad and the Source*:

> Perhaps this great novel is still to be written. If it is to be born, I think it will not be in England but in some country whose inhabitants have undergone a great communal death and rebirth—that archetypal myth so fruitful for the writer throughout the ages.[9]

Yet it is startling to realize that the archetypal myths underlying so many "major" works of poetry and fiction of the twentieth century are predominantly masculine: myths of heroic encounters, father-son rivalry, the search for the father, and, most significantly, the myth of the fisher-king whose sterility needs to be reversed in order to restore fertility to a collapsing civilization. The figure of the fisher-king in Eliot's *The Waste Land* supplants the older power of the great mother as source of regeneration. Lehmann's return to the Demeter myth becomes even more suggestive in this context since mother-daughter relationships—let alone mythic versions of them—are so rarely a *central* theme in modern literature. (Of course Virginia Woolf's *To the Lighthouse* is an important exception.) Adrienne Rich has recently commented on this notable absence of the "mother-daughter passion and rapture" that provided the emotional force behind the rites of Eleusis.[10]

Such "passion," however, becomes increasingly evident in Rosamond Lehmann's writing, and is in keeping with the fact that the world of her fiction has always contained a decidedly matriarchal element. Mothers and children, sisters, even female communities such as the women's college in her first novel (*Dusty Answer*, 1927) provide the nourishment her female characters need in order to mature on their own terms even if the larger society surrounding them is assuredly patriarchal. Rosamond Lehmann's awareness of the subtleties of personal relationships has always been as astute as that of any novelist of our time, and this awareness is clearly most remarkable in her treatment of relationships among women—whether the passionate turbulence of the college friendship of Judith and Jennifer in *Dusty Answer*, or the contrasting mid-life blooming and fading of Grace and Nora in A *Note in Music* (1930), or the loving, disarming adolescent sisterhood of Olivia and Kate in *Invitation to the Waltz* (1932), or the troubled and competitive interaction of another two sisters, Dinah and Madeleine, in *The Echoing Grove* (1953), whose conservative mother "would surprise them all" by asserting "more than once in the bosom of the family that every woman had the right to have a child,"[11] married or not.

Yet it is painful to realize that the most intense portrayal of "mother-daughter passion and rapture" in Rosamond Lehmann's work appears in her autobiographical exploration of expanded consciousness, *The Swan in the Evening* (1967), where it reflects a great personal tragedy: the death of her own daughter in 1958. Years after her first fictional use of the myth of Demeter and Persephone to represent the essential nature of the mother-daughter bond, Lehmann is forced to turn to it once again and apply it to her own unbearable loss: "I was truly left behind to crawl on as best I could, eternal exile, through the stone streets full of other people's daughters."[12] She compares her daughter to "a young corn goddess," "particularly after her marriage": "Sometimes, though, her nimbus faded; sometimes she looked pale, with darkened eyes and bluish shadows in her skin, like an emerging, not yet sun-lit Persephone" (*The Swan in the Evening*, p. 101).

In this same book Lehmann refers to Jung's *Memories, Dreams, Reflections,* as one of her "bibles" (p. 121), and it should be apparent by now that her return to the "archetypal myth"[13] is in keeping with her underlying sympathy for Jungian concepts in general. Much earlier Lehmann had compared the source of images in the human mind to "an underground vat or generator with which we are all equipped—before our birth perhaps,"[14] a description that certainly echoes Jung's "collective unconscious." Moreover, Jung's explanation of "the creative process" as that which "consists in the unconscious activation of an archetypal image, and in . . . shaping this image into the finished work,"[15] is similar to Lehmann's belief that a novel originates from images "generated" by the unconscious:

> . . . [the novel's] genesis is the image, or isolated images which have become embedded in the mass of accumulated material in the author's "centre." When the moment comes (it cannot be predicted, but can be helped on by the right kind of passivity) these images will start to become pregnant, to illuminate one another, to condense and form hitherto unsuspected relationships. The characters will begin to emerge, to announce their names and

reveal their voices, purposes and destinies. The author does not "invent" his characters or know about them from the outset.[16]

In the same essay quoted above, Lehmann relates this generative process to the evolution of her own novel and reveals its central archetypal image:

> . . . my last novel *The Ballad and the Source,* sprang, in so far as I can analyze its long inception, from childhood memories of a round green hill with a church at the top and a garden wall with a small door in it; of a portion of a little French river choked with water-lilies, with a weir in it and an inn on its banks, which for some inexplicable reason impressed itself upon my imagination years ago as the place where something that I would one day cause to happen, would happen; and from the image (whose origins are lost to me) of a woman's figure in a blue cloak.[17]

. . . An awareness of this "Jungian" material also allows for a better explanation of Lehmann's peculiar narrative method than the critics' standard reliance on Jamesian influence alone. Lehmann's novel is presented to us through the reminiscences of its narrator, Rebecca Landon, who looks back from the vantage point of the 1940s at her girlhood in the years before the First World War, and her encounter with Sibyl Jardine, the enigmatic, older woman who had troubled her youth. Lehmann illuminates Rebecca's growth of awareness between the ages of ten and fourteen, and reveals her emerging adolescent sensitivity through the changes in her perceptions of Sibyl Jardine. The entire process allows for a series of juxtaposed contrasts between Rebecca's naïve responses to Sibyl's confidences and our own "sophisticated" awareness of what Rebecca is too young to understand. It gradually becomes apparent that Lehmann achieves those considerable effects of suspense, terror, and wonder (remarked upon by many critics) through an elaboration of the confrontation between Rebecca and the *archetypal* elements embodied in the figure of Sibyl Jardine.

Rosamond Lehmann does not merely impose mythic parallels, however. She uses them to comment upon a genuine conflict between social role and archetype, societal expectation and inner compulsion. Sibyl Jardine is a woman *consciously* attempting to live out the "great mother" role: Demeter in search of her lost daughter. But Sibyl never really submits to the mother role; she merely expresses it. Her efforts to play the role are self-defeating because her real drive is toward individuality, which is always in conflict with the archetypal. Sibyl's pursuit of personal freedom conflicts with the sublimation demanded by patriarchal society's definition of the mother role, which is, in essence, *total* acceptance of female process and submission to duty, tradition, and self-abnegation. Furthermore, Lehmann demonstrates that the character of Sibyl Jardine is torn apart by contradictions inherent in the nature of the archetype itself. She would live her life—if she could—as good mother, nurturer, and muse. But these are only the *positive* aspects of the archetype. Sibyl is blind to her own deficiencies; it is to the other characters, Rebecca in particular, that the *negative* aspects of the mother archetype are to be revealed: the "Terrible Mother," the witch, the devourer.

Notes

1. Rosamond Lehmann, *The Ballad and the Source* (New York: Reynal & Hitchcock, 1945). All subsequent references are to this edition. The novel first appeared in England in 1944. The most recent paperback edition. (New York: Harcourt Brace Jovanovich, 1975) duplicates the pagination of the 1945 edition.

2. Diana Trilling, "Fiction in Review," *The Nation*, 160 (Apr. 14, 1945), 422–23; "One of the James Girls," *Newsweek*, 25 (Apr. 9, 1945), 93–94; R. A. Scott-James, *Fifty Years of English Literature: 1900-1950* (London: Longmans, Green, 1956), p. 181; Diana LeStourgeon, *Rosamond Lehmann* (New York: Twayne, 1965). For an extended discussion of similarities to *What Maisie Knew*, see Wiktoria Dorosz, *Subjective Vision and Human Relationships in the Novels of Rosamond Lehmann*, Studia Anglistica Upsaliensia, no. 23 (Uppsala: ACTA Universitatis Upsaliensis, 1975), pp. 20–23. The widespread appeal of Henry James and the Edwardian period to British readers during the Second World War are noted by Robert Hewison, *Under Siege: Literary Life in London 1939–1945* (London: Weidenfeld and Nicolson, 1977), p. 91.

3. Christopher Morley's review for the *Book-of-the-Month-Club News*, Mar. 1945. For a more serious and reflective, yet finally equally negative, portrait of Sibyl, see Vida E. Marković, *The Changing Face: Disintegration of Personality in the Twentieth-Century British Novel, 1900–1950* (Carbondale: Southern Illinois Univ. Press, 1970), pp. 97–111.

4. Feminist reinterpretations of mythology have come a long way since Lehmann's use of the Demeter myth. One of the most extensive explorations is in Mary Daly, *Gyn/Ecology: The Metaethics of Radical Feminism* (Boston: Beacon Press, 1978).

5. Erich Neumann, *The Great Mother: An Analysis of the Archetype* (Princeton, N.J.: Princeton Univ. Press, 1963), p. 170.

6. Ibid., p. 308.

7. For descriptions of the mysteries see C. Kerényi, *Eleusis: Archetypal Image of Mother and Daughter* (New York: Bollingen Foundation, 1967); C. G. Jung and C. Kerényi, *Essays on a Science of Mythology: The Myth of the Divine Child and The Mysteries of Eleusis* (New York: Bollingen Foundation, 1949); Jane Harrison, *Mythology* (London: Harrap, 1924), pp. 63–64.

8. Neumann, *The Great Mother*, p. 306.

9. Rosamond Lehmann, "The Future of the Novel?," *Britain Today*, 122 (June 1946), 7.

10. Adrienne Rich, *Of Woman Born: Motherhood as Experience and Institution* (New York: Norton, 1976), p. 237. Of course there have been exceptions to this neglect; Rich mentions a highly unusual treatment of the myth in Margaret Atwood's *Surfacing*, and more than twenty years ago Joseph Blotner discerned Virginia Woolf's structural use of the Demeter myth in "Mythic Patterns in *To the Lighthouse*," *PMLA*, 7 (Sept. 1956), 547–62. The entire subject of mothers and daughters has recently provoked a great deal of interest. See also *Feminist Studies*, 4 (June 1978); the whole issue is devoted to this topic.

11. Rosamond Lehmann, *The Echoing Grove* (London: Collins, 1953), p. 94.

12. Rosamond Lehmann, *The Swan in the Evening: Fragments of an Inner Life* (New York: Harcourt, Brace & World, 1967), p. 118.

13. Allusions to Greek mythology surface frequently in Lehmann's later work. In "When the Waters Came," a short story in the collection of *The Gipsy's Baby and Other Stories* (New York: Reynal & Hitchcock, 1946), she mentions *The Golden Bough* and "the legend of Adonis, from whose blood the spring should blossom" (p. 96).

14. Rosamond Lehmann, "Rosamond Lehmann Reading," in John Lehmann, "New Soundings," *New World Writing*, 2 (1952), 47. I discuss Rosamond Lehmann's aesthetic theories more fully in *Feminine Consciousness in the Modern British Novel* (Urbana: Univ. of Illinois Press, 1975), pp. 110–35.

15. C. G. Jung, *The Spirit in Man, Art, and Literature* (New York: Pantheon Books, 1966), p. 82.

16. Lehmann, "The Future of the Novel?," pp. 9–10.

17. Ibid., p. 10.

ALUN LEWIS

1915–1944

Alun Lewis was born on July 1, 1915, in the mining village of Cwmaman, near Aberdare, South Wales. After attending Cowbridge Grammar School he studied at the University College of Wales in Aberystwyth, graduating with first class honors in history in 1935. A research fellowship at Manchester University enabled him to take an M.A. in 1937, after which he trained as a teacher in Aberystwyth, finding a position at a school in Pengam, Glamorgan, in 1938.

Despite pacifist scruples Lewis felt compelled by a sense of duty to join the army in 1940. He had already published work in national newspapers and magazines, including the *Welsh Review*, the *Manchester Guardian*, and *The Listener*, but became a more mature and productive writer as a soldier. His first book of poems, *Raider's Dawn*, appeared in 1942, and a collection of short stories, *The Last Inspection*, in 1943.

Lewis left England with the South Wales Borderers in October 1942 to sail to India, and died on active service on March 5, 1944. He had married in 1941, but had been able to spend little time with his wife. His posthumous works include the poems *Ha! Ha! Among the Trumpets* (1945) and *In the Green Tree* (1948), a collection of letters and stories.

RALPH HOUSTON

From "The Broken Arch:

A Study of the Poetry of Alun Lewis"

Adelphi, 1951, pp. 403–13

From the first few poems of *Raider's Dawn* it is clear that Lewis, possibly because of his life in the Army, was often unable to recognise the poetry and reject its by-products. Often the reader is almost overwhelmed by a smoky afflatus:—

The sunlight breaks its flashing wings
Imprisoned in the Hall of Mirrors;
Nightmare rides upon the headlines:
And summer leaves her green reflective woods
To glitter momently on peaks of madness.

This is not all bad; the first line is good, so are lines three and four. But the vagueness of lines two and five, and the lack of organisation of the whole, reminds one of Shelley at his worst; and the Shelleyan echoes are there, the "Hall of Mirrors" clearly being a subconscious echo of "Life like a dome of many-coloured glass." This passage comes from a poet who has temporarily lost control, and, although he recovers his sense of direction in the middle of this poem, Lewis finally collapses into self-pity:—

> Yet still
> I who am agonised by thought
> And war and love
> Grow calm again
> With watching
> The flash and play of finches
> Who are as beautiful
> And as indifferent to me
> As England is, this spring morning.
>
> (The Soldier)

This is slovenly and unconvincing; the word "indifferent" marks the invitation to pity him and indicates his self-pity, giving the lie to his calmness. The words do not convey "agony," primarily because the poet has blurted his feelings *at* us and does not allow us to *feel* them for ourselves. This, then, is the wrong kind of poetry of statement. That Lewis could write genuine poetry of statement is seen in the following:—

> I sat and watched the dusky berried ridge
> Of yew-trees, deepened by oblique dark shafts,
> Throw back the flame of red and gold and russet
> That leapt from beech and ash to birch and chest-nut
> Along the downward arc of the hill's shoulder,
> And sunlight with discerning fingers
> Softly explore the distant wooded acres,
> Touching the farmsteads one by one with lightness
> Until it reached the Downs, whose soft green
>   pastures
> Went slanting sea- and skywards to the limits
> Where sight surrenders and the mind alone
> Can find the sheeps' tracks and the grazing.
> And for that moment Life appeared
> As gentle as the view I gazed upon.
>
> (To Edward Thomas)

Here we are convinced of the poet's calm by the preparation that has soaked into us before the statement is made. This preparation makes *us* calm and thus the statement that follows is the only possible statement. One should, moreover, note the way the word "lightness"—the word that perhaps does most to bring calmness to us—is made to work, bringing into play the reader's sense of touch as well as that of sight. Though flawed in places, the assured movement of most of this poem testifies to Lewis's gathering strength, which, indeed, he gathers rapidly. From the unrealized "agony" of "The Soldier" we soon come to the realization of it:—

> Yet in this blood-soaked forest of disease
>   Where wolfish men lie scorched and black
> And corpses sag against the trees
>   And love's dark roots writhe back
> Like snakes into the scorching earth;
>   In this corrupted wood where none can hear
> The love songs of Ophelia
>   And the laughter of Lear,
> My soul cries out with love
> Of all that walk and swim and fly
> From the mountains, from the sky,
> Out of the depths of the sea
> Love cries and cries in me.
> And summer blossoms break above my head
> With all the unbearable beauty of the dead.
>
> (Odi et Amo)

Admittedly the rhythm stumbles at line eight, but here we do *feel* the agony, though it is nowhere stated, especially when it is reinforced by the bawdy songs of the pure Ophelia juxtaposed to the ambivalent ravings of Lear, and when one is forced, by the forest context, to recall the peaceful forests of Shakespeare's earlier plays. Moreover, the simple statement of love for all creatures is made to tell by contrast with the writhing roots of love in the convulsed world just described. And the whole passage is summarised by the final image, the phrase "unbearable beauty of the dead" turning the summer blossoms into a symbol. . . .

After these demonstrations of increasing skill, used to give direction to the conscious purpose expressed in "Prologue: The Grinder," it is not surprising that Lewis proceeds to "Threnody on a Starry Night," his first long flight. In this poem he uses to good purpose his skill at bringing together the distant past, the near past, and the present, thereby implying his sense of continual regeneration:—

> And on the broken arch of night
> The Babylonian planets tell
> The unromantic death of Keats.

This phrase, clipped and well modulated, might be used of his own death, for the deflation of emotion that deflects banal sentimentality implies his own determination not to turn aside from life; and this he carried into effect by refusing a staff post and returning to his unit. There follows:—

> Socrates on the frozen lake
> Sat awhile and heard, disconsolate,
> The blind unnerving harmonies of fate.
> And always in Shakespearian tragedy
> The foils are poisoned that the good may die.

Here the violence of the Elizabethan stage contrasts with the quiet, dignified death of Socrates; but "the foils are poisoned that the good may die" reminds us that the subtlety of killing, and the chances against the good surviving, remain the same today. . . .

In turning to *Ha! Ha! Among the Trumpets* the reader may feel some disappointment towards the end; this, I think, is due to the weight of reportage in the poems from India, pleasant reading though much of it makes. As a consequence, these poems suffer by contrast with the earlier work up to and including "On Embarkation" in the second volume, for they seldom demand so complex a response. Lewis was aware of the difficulties inherent in his situation, for he sub-heads the volume "Poems in Transit," and his publishers rightly comment: "The poems are a record of experience in England, at sea, and in India, and an attempt to control and clarify the swift succession of events that so often overwhelm the individual soldier." Let it be said at once that it was a gallant and far from unsuccessful attempt. But in England Lewis's mythopoetic imagination, his ability to move easily from experience to myth, recreating myth and thereby elevating and recreating experience, seems to have had freer play. It appeared in "Jason and Medea" once more before he sailed:—

> The night appeared to authorise it.
>   The snakes were curling in her tallow hair,
> And he stood in the weak and fascinating
>   Parlour of singing sexes, debonair,
> Knowing her hungry glance, her cool attraction,
> The cheap and placid aroma of her smile.
> Tomorrow was a carton of abstraction,
> A little debt he always could defer.
> And in a nest of snakes he courted her.

Clearly Jason is Jason and every man, especially modern man as lines 5, 6 and 7 indicate, who has "courted her" in a nest of snakes without a thought for the little debt he could defer. Yet if Lewis's mind was more restricted in this respect, it was also presented with greater opportunities to exercise its considerable power of pictorial description:—

(a)

The sun has sucked an beat the encircling hills
Into gaunt skeletons; the sick men watch
Soft shadows warm those bones of rock,
And the barefooted peasants winding back,
Sad withered loins in hanging dirty folds,
Mute sweepings from the disappointed streets,
Old shrunken tribes the starving dusk enfolds.
(In Hospital: Poona ii)

(b)

The valleys crack and burn, the exhausted plains
Sink their black teeth into the horny veins
Straggling the hills' red thighs, the bleating goats
—Dry bents and bitter thistles in their throats—
Thread loose rocks by immemorial tracks.
Dark peasants drag the sun upon their backs.
(The Mahratta Ghats)

(c)

Consider this silent disciplined assembly
Close squadded in the dockyard's hooded lamps,
Each blur a man with some obscure trouble
Or hard regret as bulky as the cargo
The cranking derricks drop into the hold.
(On Embarkation)

These passages exemplify the main difficulty with the second volume—that of distinguishing between vivid, stimulating reportage and that which is something more. Passage (a), I think, is good, especially the link between "Sad loins" and "disappointed streets;" but the last line of passage (b) seems to me to make the passage something more than pure description; and passage (c) is transformed into excellent poetry by the bodying forth of "hard regret" as bulky cargo dropped with sickening irrevocability into the ship's hold. . . .

Lewis had many obvious faults and his work could be pruned with advantage. Often he did not know when to stop and he marred many poems by tackling on trite endings; his rhythm sometimes stumbles or collapses into prose; sometimes he appeals to cheap sentiment. But he had had little time to polish his work and I think I have given sufficient reasons for believing that he had produced, in a short and harassed poetic life, a not inconsiderable body of good poetry. My title, moreover, implies that I feel he had more to give. Admittedly the muse deserted Wordsworth, for example, long before his death and reduced him to writing banal sonnets on the activities of free-enterprise railways in the Lake District; and she reduced Burns to writing in English. But there were sources of Lewis's power which, I think, would not have failed him.

First, there was his ability to evoke the rural scene, as in "To Edward Thomas," "On Embarkation," "The Mahratta Ghats" and others. In this he provides continuity in our pastoral tradition by taking from Thomas who, in turn bore a close affinity to much of Wordsworth's earlier poetry. Secondly, he had a power to contact, appreciate, absorb and profit by the past in both a historical and poetic sense, as can be seen in "The Captivity," "The Odyssey" and "Threnody on a Starry Night." Thirdly, his mythopoetic imagination, revealed, for example, in "To a Comrade in Arms," "Jason and Medea" and "From a Play" was strong, and, given the chance to exploit it, he might have helped us to penetrate that poetic continent where Blake and Yeats maintain their lonely outposts. On one level Lewis spoke for them, on another for his comrades, and thirdly for himself when he wrote these lines:—

We saw, moving along the line of hills,
The blond great-breasted goddess of pre-history
An in the stony glitter of her eyes
Divined our lonely destiny.

(From a Play)

IAN HAMILTON
From "The Forties"

London Magazine, April 1964, pp. 83–88

Alun Lewis . . . seems to me the most cruelly under-valued poet of the forties and it is interesting to see how a cliché estimate of him has descended from guide to guide so that is is now, apparently, established as solid ground for ignoring him. This estimate says that Lewis was not really a poet, but a prose writer. It seems to have been originally based upon an isolated remark of Lewis's and it first appears in the Penguin *New Writing* obituary notice by Jack Marlowe, where it receives minimal critical support. Since then it has gone into general currency and no longer needs support; one finds it repeated by Stephen Spender, in *Since 1939*, Kenneth Allott in his Penguin *Contemporary Verse*, and Anthony Thwaite in *Contemporary English Poetry*, in almost identical language and with an absolute identity of bald conviction. It might be argued that since Lewis is ignored completely in such general surveys as G. S. Fraser's *Vision and Rhetoric*, and Charles Tomlinson's contribution to the Penguin *Modern Age*, even these inac-curacies are something to be grateful for. But this indolent parroting is typical of a total attitude to the period that needs to be called in question.

One wonders, for instance, if the celebrated tact, restraint and commonsense of the fifties Movement would have seemed so revolutionary had a more balanced view of their forerunners been current at the time. It is certainly not difficult to trace such qualities in the best war poetry and to find them there upheld in situations where they seem not bleak and faintly preening but heroic and necessary.

'Acceptance seems so spiritless, protest so vain. In be-tween the two I live' wrote Alun Lewis, and this is a characteristic stance. One finds it echoed in another letter, by Keith Douglas: 'To be sentimental or emotional now is dangerous to oneself and to others. To trust anyone or to admit any hope of a better world is criminally foolish, as foolish as it is to stop working for it. It sounds silly to say work without hope, but it can be done; it's only a form of insurance; it doesn't mean work hopelessly.' To these poets the problem was to give practical meaning to Fraser's parenthesis 'not in ourselves' (quoted above and unsupported both by Fraser and by the Apocalyptics he was introducing; the point about them is precisely that they were seduced by chaos, they became a tiresome aspect of it); in Douglas, Fuller and Lewis there is certainly despair at the 'brittle systems', the empires breaking like biscuits and so on, but what one admires as much as anything else in their work is their determination to be sane in spite of all this; that is to say, to be articulate and intelligible, a sensitive participant. . . .

Lewis's stand against the futility of war can often be hysterical and trite; the resonant emblem usually eludes him: 'Nightmare rides upon the headlines', 'blood-soaked forest of disease', 'mass-rearming for mass-martyrdom', 'mutilated smile', 'wolfish men', and so on, are typical. He is, as he recognized, flabby and invalid when he gets 'too far away from the thing'. But working through particulars of barrack life, leave-taking, life in India, he is most impressive; subtle, exact, rhythmically various, he can allow his general indictment to emerge, climactic and proven, from the actual life it represents. He, too, is self-consciously the artist-soldier, 'sensitive and somehow apart', resentful of his 'crude trade', 'the rough immediate life of camp',

> the stench
> Of breath in crowded tents, the grousing queues,
> And bawdy songs incessantly resung
> And dull relaxing in the dirty bar;
> The difficult tolerance of all that is
> Mere rigid brute routine; the odd
> Sardonic scorn of desolate self-pity,
> The pathetic contempt of the lonely for the crowd.

But what he most passionately resists are the massively dehumanizing temptations of war; and even as he protests he is finely aware that the process has begun, is inexorable, and that he is included. The 'growing self-detachment' is necessary if one is to keep sane (as Lewis develops one senses how his irony becomes a kind of protective skin; his second book is a lot more measured and oblique than his first, and clings more desperately to local detail and sharp parenthesis). For some, this self-detachment engenders self-contempt, a kind of giggling heroism that is essentially a neurotic trivializing of the issues; it 'makes men toss their careless lives away' for the 'honour of the regiment', 'the flashy epaulettes of tradition'; for others, it can be a means of blurring the responsibility; 'we are the little men grown huge with death', 'stiff-backed and parrotwise with pamphlet learning':

> We had certain authority for this
> Not ours, but Anothers:
> Our innocence remained with us.

But whatever the motives, in poems like 'The Sentry' and 'Odi et Amo', Lewis brilliantly enacts the sensation of depersonalized, almost posthumous calm that both protects and reduces the humanity of the soldier:

> My body does not seem my own
> Now. These hands are not my own
> That touch the hair-spring trigger, nor my eyes
> Fixed on a human target, nor my cheek
> Stroking the rifle butt; my loins
> Are flat and closed like a child's.

It is perhaps from such impoverishment that he seeks asylum and renewal in nature, in its neutrality, and in the images it offers of unimpeded instinct. The war years produced a great deal of excellent loco-descriptive verse and one feels that this was not only because poets were being drafted abroad and confronted with new and exciting places, or because of the general historical and cultural self-consciousness, though these are clearly factors of importance. Another impulse—which one finds throughout Lewis—is of retreat into the permanent, the substantial, the disengaged:

> I sat and watched the dusky berried ridge
> Of yew-trees, deepened by oblique dark shafts,
> Throw back the flame of red and gold and russet
> That leapt from beech and ash to birch and chestnut
> Along the downward arc of the hill's shoulder,
> And sunlight with discerning fingers
> Softly explore the distant wooded acres,
> Touching the farmsteads one by one with lightness
> Until it reached the Downs, whose soft green
>   pastures
> Went slanting sea and skywards to the limits
> Where sight surrenders and the mind alone
> Can find the sheeps' tracks and the grazing.
> And for that moment Life appeared
> As gentle as the view I gazed upon.

In 'Lines on a Tudor Mansion' though and the excellent 'All Day It Has Rained'; it is the immediacy, the transience, of natural phenomena that soothes him; the unhistoric instant contrasted approvingly with the 'monumental homes', the 'marble cenotaphs'—this runs throughout also. Finches 'flicker and blossom', 'flash and play'; similarly, the 'dragonflies blue flicker', 'the soft silk flash of the swifts' are seen as images of the instinctual life that is no longer possible to the poet victimized by 'the horror of his century'.

Lewis's poems of separation are among his most memorable, ranging from the lyric intensity of 'Post-Script: For Gweno' to the terse despair of 'Goodbye,' in which—significantly—much of the exalted vigour of the love-poems in *Raider's Dawn* is deliberately frozen into a rhetorical posture and discarded. The final stanza represents the outcome of Lewis's struggle against impersonality:

> Yet when all's done you'll keep the emerald
> I placed upon your finger in the street;
> And I will keep the patches that you sewed
> On my old battledress tonight, my sweet.

Just as *Raider's Dawn* is often overheated into florid exaggeration, so *Ha! Ha! Among the Trumpets* can seem devitalized and prosy; in a sense it is an image of Lewis's personal predicament that this should be so. But totally he knew what was being done to him and what he was losing; between the two stylistic extremes there is a body of richly balanced verse whose effort is precisely that which finally distinguishes the significant poetry of the time—the complex but intelligibly managed effort to reconcile the dreamer and the soldier, and be sane.

JOHN PIKOULIS
From "Alun Lewis: The Way Back"

Critical Quarterly, Summer 1972, pp. 145–54

Alun Lewis was a poet in his twenties caught up in war. The war profoundly affected not only his attitudes to what in peacetime might equally have compelled his imaginative attention—love, community, the insights and relationships of the experiencing self—but also the very nature of his poetic talent. For such a young man to be excluded from the settled routines of daily life and to be pitched into an artificial arena of soldiery dominated by the very real presence of suffering and death involved a distortion both of his creative procedures and of their nourishing agents. Life importuned his art. The necessary development of his technique, the discoveries of his point of view and of his voice, the subtle inner processes of recording: all were foreshortened. This unnatural acceleration, this unwonted energy of the meeting between private and public worlds was as true of the man as of the writer, and the result was a poetry in which a real gift struggled to avoid being overwhelmed.

It was not as dramatic a situation as these remarks might imply. On the contrary, it may not have been dramatic enough. Lewis's war was no different from that of many others and his reactions to it (to the composition, behaviour and assumptions of the army, say) were unexceptional. He expressed a humane concern for his fellow-soldiers, a dislike of bureaucracy, the petty irritations (and worse) of army life and loving memories of home. The poems record these reactions and are affected by a persistent and pervasive sentimentality, a weakening indulgence in emotion. Deeply-felt, sincere and moving as a poem like 'All Day It Has Rained' is; the final result is gesture, a poem divided between a painful, honest and rhythmically exact impression of desultoriness and sadness and, in the last verse, an effective but flawed flourish of the imagination—flawed, that is, by an element of fantasy which strains after profundities it cannot sustain. The status of Edward Thomas and his relationship to the first section is nowhere deeply considered, despite the superficially striking effect and serious potential of the analogue. The subtle appeals of self-regard have not been mastered and, as in all poetic gesture, there is a gap between objective and subjective realities or between intention and achieved expression, on several occasions indicated by an uneasy air of circumlocution. The ghost of prose statement haunts the poetic line. If one points to the relative failure of diction to achieve a freshening rightness or if one complains of nerveless or insufficiently responsive rhythms, one indicates a general failure to transmute the discursive into the imaginative. But one still remains aware of a sensibility which is unmistakeably committed and fertile of possibility. Alun Lewis struggled in his too-alterable times to become coherent and then because his environment was double-edged, both that which fed, sustained, inspired, and that which weakened, irritated and divided.

Moreover, as he himself noted (in 'To Rilke'), he was not a 'natural' poet, one of 'Humanity's darlings' who 'never lack an occasion'. (Compare him randomly with Sidney Keyes and the point is quickly established.)

> But I have to seek the occasion.
> Labour, fatigue supervene.

There is indeed an attractive earnestness in the poetry, full of concentration and effort. No doubt Lewis's temperament inclined him that way, but his soldier's life emphasised the inclination excessively. The young poet needs his daring raids, the irresponsible magic of words, as part of his developing senses; for Lewis, wartime commanded ceaseless attention and imposed a preternatural sense of responsibility. Death and life were not for him letters on a page or counters of the imagination—they stalked him; rather their shadows stalked him, for it is a fact that he spent all his time on the periphery of combat: cleaning and maintaining railway engines, temporarily part of the Education Corps, and, once commissioned, Squadron Messing Officer, Advance Baggage Officer, Entertainments Officer, Intelligence Officer. (In 1943, he refused a Staff Officer's post.) It was a world of trenches, barbed-wire fences, boots, bread, driving tanks, buying pith helmets and drill shorts. This kind of army life is truly betwixt-and-between and is almost certainly more responsive to either the documentary or the comic. It is not readily amenable to poetic creation. At least it wasn't in Lewis's case, especially since his own short stories portrayed this sort of life, thus pre-empting some of the poet's options. The man who suffered the army and the mind which created grew disparate, as he well understood.

> It is easy to write prose in India, there is so much to satirise or hate or shrug one's shoulders at. But poetry is harder to command, mainly I think because everything is somehow remorseless here, arid, pellucid and incurable.[1]

II

These issues found their oblique expression in the one poem which marks Alun Lewis's final maturing into his poetic self and thus defines the nature of his achievement. 'The Way Back' is not only an extraordinarily packed, expressive and rewarding poem but also (because Lewis's dilemma touches the essential matter of a poet's being at several points) a classical paradigm of how the imagination works, an exciting and wholly neglected insight into the nature of literary creation, of the fertilizing tensions which sustain it and which it, in turn, dissolves and reforms.

> Six days and two thousand miles
> I have watched the shafted rain
> Feminise the burning land,
> Cloaking with a green distress
> The cerulean and the ochre
> Of the season's ruthlessness.
> Six days and two thousand miles
> I have gone alone
> With a green mind and you
> Burning in the stubborn bone.
>
> Soldiers quickened by your breath
> Feel the sudden spur and rush
> Of the life they put away
> Lest the war should break and crush
> Beauties more profound than death.
>
> I swam within your naked lake
> And breasted with exquisite ease
> The foaming arabesques of joy
> And in the sarabande of trees
> Of guava and papaya
> And crimson blown poinsettia,
> The millrace of my blood
> Beat against my smile,
> And were you answering my smile
> Or the millrace of my blood?
>
> But now the iron beasts deploy
> And all my effort is my fate
> With gladiators and levies
> All laconic disciplined men
> I pass beyond your golden gate.
>
> And in the hardness of this world
> And in the brilliance of this pain
> I exult with such a passion
> To be squandered, to be hurled,
> To be joined to you again.

. . . ⟨T⟩he 'I' of the poem is at once both autobiographical and a creative other self. Moreover, the human being who is a soldier and the human being who is a poet are set off against each other. One man's several selves respond to the equally disparate sources located in the 'you' addressed to the poem: the Indian land, the feminine watery world and the beloved. The poem's fictive task is to bind them all into a compelling unity.

Mrs. Lewis observes:

> It's a love poem—in a letter of August 26th he writes—'Wherever I am Love relates itself softly to the physical influences of the land and when the mood and the place are fully integrated I write . . .'

The dancing rhythms and exotic diction ('cerulean', 'arabesques', 'sarabande') especially of the critical fourth verse point to one thing above all others: the aroused imagination. It is the point of harmony, of nourished fulfilment, in the man. But it co-exists uncomfortably with a soldier's apprehension of death and destruction and may even, in the context of war, be defined by it. The whole poem rests on this confusion or ambiguity and tries to break free from it. The complex relates to the fact that Lewis's is a war poetry; even when it is most private, or relaxed, indirect pressures relate it to the larger effort. The poetry is thus dominated by (to borrow his terms) Beauty and the Beast, the affective man's devotions and the active man's responsibilities. 'The Way Back' is, then, in this particular sense the type of Alun Lewis's poetry, an attempt to explore and resolve an unholy interdependence of contrary realities, any one of which is expressed through or by sanction of or in despite of another. It ends with a vision of some tremendous disturbance whereby the essential self, caught up in a physical cataclysm, at last achieves the object of its desires.

The cataclysm is half-real, half-imagined, half-loved, half-loathed: the end cannot free itself from the means so that death-wish and life-wish are inextricably wedded. He longs to join the beloved but also the earth. The heavy successive stresses, the accumulating declamations and heightened feeling now seen triumphant cries from the heart, exhilarating and passionately yearning, liberatory, now oppressively emphatic, mechanically inhuman, menacing cries of despair. Just so, the joy of the fourth verse is ambiguous, both a true release and an escape, a sapping of human energies. There is both a 'smile' and 'the millrace of my blood', an ambiguity carried over to the last verse where it is resoundingly amplified. But there is something magnificent about those last lines (and about much of the poem) which is uncomplicated. It is the magnificence of achieved poetic utterance. Wilfulness and fantasy there may be but the expression is yet authentic. The poetic voice momentarily speaks.

> When I think of it, I think the poems are an act of daring, always daring, to plunge and tear and enter.[2]

The sexual desires of the man complement the creative drive of the poet. But as the man is separated from the object of his desires, so the poet's creativity is thwarted—and both by the agency of war.

> I want to write, though. It would be such a relief to write. I wait and hunger for the relief and the poetry.[3]

III

India is the scene both of revelling and of war, of joy and death, the extension of possibility and its conclusion.

> It's nice in this part of India just now. The rains have turned the burning cruel hills into green glades and the scorched wilted(?) *(sic)* valleys and plains into lush green pastures. The peasants are happier, their eyes are brighter, the rain gets into their vitals. I dread the next six months of sterility and heat.[4]

He writes of the peasants as of himself and thereby expresses an interdependence both factual and imaginative, as if the joy he feels, a strangely impersonal emotion, is an initiation into the death he half-fears, half-solicits.

> I pass beyond your golden state.

foreshadows

> the darkness that he knew would come.
> And bids him enter its deep gates alone.
>   ('Burma Casualty')

The 'you' of the poem is a reverberating and generalising vessel for his energies: the memory of his loved one 'burning' within and the memory of watching six days of rain on the 'burning' land typify the complex. His 'green mind', like the land's 'green distress' after the 'shafted rain', is thrown into turmoil by a process both cruel and productive. The 'green' of the mind is fertile and receptive; it is a temperament innocent and unprotected, unlike the age-old suffering of the burned land; it is also a vacancy, a suspension of ordinary faculties and the supervention of another, more powerful one. In what he sees of India he sees something of himself, particularly as what he sees stirs within him the promptings of a poem.

The conclusion is as double-edged. When he cries

> To be joined to you again.

he thinks of the woman who is impossibly distant; he also thinks of the 'naked lake' as his source of human delight and poetic power, now as distant from him as the woman. The exultant, emphatic rhythm of the last verse, no less than the language, provokes both ringing delight and something darkly

admonitory, in which love and death are combined in the pressure of release from constraint and suffering into a consummating joy which is not easy to distinguish from a final despair. The result is not confusion, for the competing emotions have been taken up and impersonalised in a poem, and the delight of achieved poetic expression transforms and supersedes them. The soldiers he mentions in the third verse share his delight and he speaks for the subdued poet in them when he talks (too loosely) of

> Beauties more profound than death.

That line reminds us that 'The Way Back' still show signs of its author's incomplete mastery, as in the accumulation of l's in lines 28–9, the circumlocution of 'iron beasts', the cliche of 'golden gate' and in the hesitant patterning of the lines. Yet the poem is clearly in the grip of genuine feeling as it emerges in the fourth stanza's wayward luxury, the sudden bloom of his genius, only to be succeeded by the feelings of the practical officer who must return to war. But he has been initiated, has passed into the golden realm and can see the war only through the self-conscious, sportingly archaic language of a faded tradition: 'iron beasts', 'gladiators and levies' (who in the third verse had been merely 'soldiers'). The poet in the lake must become again the soldier who is also a poet, and the gorgeous revelry and abundance of lacustrine man spills over uncomfortably into the world of 'laconic disciplined men' who can once more subdue, as he cannot, 'the life they put away' after its momentary revival. The quiet, controlled movement of the lines in this fifth verse suggests deliberate, even sacrificial, progression, but this residual tenacity of the soldier gives way to the positively buoyant conclusion with its resounding stresses. It is the poet's last cry before his fate claims him, and we hear it in the stresses (I read two to each line save for the last which admits of another on 'you' as prepared for by the brilliant caesura and end-stop of the penultimate line), in the modulated running metre, in the rhetorical syntax and its powerful movement towards climax.

What happens here is related to the experience of the 'little Vishnu of stone' in 'Karanje Village',

> Silently and eternally simply Being
> Bidding me come alone,
> And never entirely turning me away,
> But warning me still of the flesh
> That catches and limes the singing birds of the soul
> And holds their wings in mesh.

It is part of the Romantic theme in 'The Way Back'. The poetic self is that which alone can desire and achieve 'Being'—and that through the poetic imagination. The 'flesh' may meet the fate of levies and die but the 'singing birds of the soul' can live and die, thus achieving the immortality which is elsewhere seen in the land or the peasants. The experience also recalls one from Lewis's unpublished journal in which he confronts Buddha.

> *I felt the refusal.* A wall of darkness, hard, resistant, smooth-surfaced.

This refusal is followed by gross reminders of corporeality—picking a nostril, stomach rumbles, farting, stirring of the penis—and then

> *I forgot all those intimations of being a human being* once they had stated themselves.

Soldiering is temporarily forgotten and supplanted by a mystical mood of

> Love and poetry and a sense of rightness and of beauty

in which mood he enters into a unity with the Buddha. In a trance, he experiences 'service of perfect freedom' in space.

Also a sense of a journey I have long wished to
make . . . A journey through lands whose existence I did not know but whose location I had been
ignorant of till then. The map of the spirits geography (*sic*) . . .[5]

following which he senses great happiness and a desire to share
his feelings with his companions. This extraordinary episode
speaks again of poetry and the paths of the imagination. In the
poem, too, we have the rapt responses, the profound illumination, comradely emotions and a final exhilaration; even if it is
one which promises destruction ('squandered', 'hurled'), its
end is unity (as the land is 'feminised' by the 'shafted' rain in
some universal congress analogous to human sexuality). The
vicissitudes of time and flesh are left behind.

> To be squandered, to be hurled

bears comparison with his 'foaming arabesques of joy' in the
lake; in both, the self is defeated, taken up into a supra-personal
reality. When he writes—

> The millrace of my blood
> Beat against my smile,
> And were you answering my smile
> Or the millrace of my blood?

the lines have a gnomic suggestiveness, querying the nature of
the appeal made to him by the lake: is the vision a reward for
happiness of being or the cause of it? Once more, the man and
the poet are set in opposition. Is the experience of elevated ease
merely the lassitude which follows vigorous exercise, a delusion in which effort and responsibility are shed for childish
warmth and relaxation or does it represent an accession to a
different realm where creative pleasure holds sway? (The
'smile' is indicative of imaginative achievement made possible
by the lake which, like the jungle later, is 'A trackless
wilderness [dividing]/Joy from its cause . . .'). The question
corresponds to the moment before the Buddha in which bodily
presence gave way to a sublime euphoria. That moment had
been prepared for by his revival of spirits, 'the sudden spur and
rush/Of the life they put away', but he realises (as 'spur' and
'rush' indicate) the relationship between this recapture and the
'iron beats' which threaten (a relationship further extended by
the 'ruthlessness' which distresses the land). April is indeed the
cruellest month. Thus, in this rich complex, he finally comes
to exult in the imagined heightening of 'spur and rush' whereby
he will be destroyed in a moment of supreme imaginative
intensity that will permanently reclaim him for the world of
rain and land, of which the lake is the expression. The poet is
dedicated to the 'you' of the poem, which we may finally define
as his art, and, beyond that, to all he loves; and is created or
expressed by it. It is a fertile destruction.

    I see in the rampant last verse a discernible if not fully
realised instance of the dying god, especially as he has been
described by Anton Ehrenzweig in *The Hidden Order of Art*[6],
where he becomes the symbol of the poetic process, the
disintegration of the inner self, its fragmentation and ultimate
re-shaping in the work of art, which thus becomes an image of
the reconstituted, liberated self. He who describes and that
which is described unite in one compelling fiction. In the
interaction of nature and army life, Alun Lewis sought for his
creative self.

Notes

1. "Alun Lewis to Robert Graves: Three Letters," *Anglo-Welsh
Review*, Vol. 16, No. 37, Spring 1967, pp. 12–13.
2. Freda Aykroyd, "Some Letters of Alun Lewis," *Modern Reading*,
Summer 1952, p. 24.
3. Ibid., p. 19.

4. Brenda Chamberlain, *Alun Lewis and the Making of the Caseg
Broadsheets*, London, 1970, pp. 5–6.
5. Ian Hamilton, ed., *Alun Lewis: Selected Poetry and Prose*, London,
1966.
6. London, 1967.

VERNON SCANNELL
From "Alun Lewis"
Not without Glory: Poets of the Second World War
1976, pp. 56–69

Perhaps the view of Alun Lewis as a natural prose writer
rather than a poet is less of a 'cliché-estimate' than Ian
Hamilton supposes for it seems to me obvious that Lewis would
not allow the same kind of reach-me-down phrasing that
disfigures much of his poetry to appear in his prose which is
written with more care than a great deal of his verse. The
carelessness to be found in much of his poetry might be almost
deliberate, a consequence of a romantic attitude to the nature
and function of the poet, a blurred notion that authentic poetry
is 'inspired' and that it should come 'as naturally as leaves to a
tree'. His poems were written very quickly. In a letter to his
parents he writes:[1]

> Altogether they make 52 poems—17 written in
> England, 6 at sea and the remaining 30 out here. I
> suppose that's pretty good for twelve months.

In another letter, also to his mother and father, he speaks of the
writing of his short stories with a self-critical note that is not to
be found in any of his references to his own poetry:

> I've been working hard at the short stories: mainly
> some new ones I'm trying to write. My touch isn't at
> all sure: my thoughts wander instead of crystallizing
> and I can't imagine the people objectively enough.
> So I've had to scrap several versions. I've written one
> three times, another twice, and I'm still dissatisfied.
> It's good practice, even though it's rather dishearten-
> ing when I've got so little time for writing at all.

In fact I would suggest that Lewis's poetry is often at its best
when it is displaying virtues usually associated with good prose:
I would go farther and say that his approach to the raw material
of experience was often the way of the prose writer, and many
of his formal lyrics with their conventional ecstatics and
invocations of 'barefoot lovers', 'golden hair', 'roses', 'the
smiling moon', and suchlike properties are little more than
thin exercises whose poeticisms hope to disguise the essentially
prosaic cast of the mind which has produced them. . . .

    I cannot agree with Ian Hamilton[2] who finds Lewis's
second and last collection of poems, *Ha! Ha! Among the
Trumpets*, 'devitalized and prosy' compared with *Raiders'
Dawn*, and once Lewis gets away from the flatulent and
sentimental stuff in *Part One: England* and comes to grips with
the fresh experiences of leaving England and soldiering
overseas in *Part Two: The Voyage* and *Part Three: India* he
produces some of his finest work, poems which are less well
known than the widely anthologised pieces from *Raider's
Dawn* but are individual and memorable and long overdue the
recognition they deserve. . . .

    Far from finding the poems in *Ha! Ha! Among the
Trumpets* 'devitalized' I see them as developing a strength and
sinew of which there is not much sign in *Raiders' Dawn* and
poems like 'A Troopship in the Tropics' and 'Port of Call:
Brazil' maintain a steady contact with the situations they deal
with and show a steadfast rejection of the temptation to over-
exploit dramatic possibilities at the expense of total veracity, a

gritty honesty which reminds me of the best of W. E. Henley's sequence of hospital poems. The lyrical pieces, too, are far more skilfully managed, poems like 'Water Music' and 'Shadows', and in 'Song (On seeing dead bodies floating off the Cape)' Lewis achieves the fine synthesis of thought and feeling that he was groping for but infrequently finding in his first book:

> But oh! the drag and dullness of my Self;
> The turning seasons wither in my head;
> All this slowness, all this hardness,
> The nearness that is waiting in my bed,
> The gradual self-effacement of the dead.

The love poem, 'Ways', is also very effective, owing perhaps something to Edward Thomas in its ambivalence and imagery, but still an original and sensitive exploration of the way that love, to the exile, can be a burden as well as a precious gift:

> Love being gravel in the wound
> When the silent lovers know
> Swaying in the misty rain
> The old oppression of the burden
> Growing in them as they go,
> Though trees are felled and grow again,
> Far and farther each from each.
> Longing hardens like a stone.
> Lovers go but hardly, all alone.

Alun Lewis's most durable and original poems are, to my mind, the ones in which he treats the Indian landscape, especially its wilder reaches, as an external correspondence or emblem of certain attitudes and states of consciousness that he,

the Western invader, discovers in himself. In the best of these the physical details are sharply seen and the sense of place is strongly communicated but the poems are more than realistic pictures of an exotic country. He is able without strain or sleight of hand to universalise his personal dilemmas, the problems of coming to terms with the lover and the soldier, of preserving the creative virtues of imaginative sympathy, pity and love of justice while preparing to kill men, problems which he shared with every man in uniform and which he, as a poet, felt he had to articulate and explore. . . .

When he says in ⟨a⟩ letter to Graves '. . . I will have to abandon the vast for the particular, the infinite for the finite, the heart for the eye', he obviously speaks with regret as if, as a poet, he is accepting a necessary limitation but what has really happened is that he has arrived without knowing it at the salutary conclusion that the poet's job is to concentrate on the particular, something fully understood by men like Pound who said, 'Go in fear of abstraction' and Yeats who knew that 'Man can embody truth but cannot know it'. What Lewis did not seem to understand, at least in the letter quoted, is that concentration on the particular does not entail an abandonment of the vast but is a way of bringing it into focus and fixing it through correspondences, whereas an attempt to deal directly with the huge and abstract must end in myopia and impotence.

Notes

1. *In the Green Tree, Letters and Short Stories* by Alun Lewis. Preface by A. L. Rowse. London, 1948.
2. 'The Forties' by Ian Hamilton. *The London Magazine*, April 1964.

C. S. LEWIS

1898–1963

Clive Staples Lewis was born in Belfast on November 29, 1898. After the death of his mother in 1908, he saw little of his father, and spent several miserable years at private schools in England. A private tutor prepared him for Oxford, but he served in the army on the Western Front before taking up a scholarship at University College in 1919. After a successful undergraduate career he became a Fellow of Magdalen College, Oxford.

Lewis's literary debut was as a poet with his volume *Spirits in Bondage* (1919). At this time he was an atheist, but he became a reluctant convert to Christianity in 1929 and later exerted considerable influence as a Christian apologist in writings such as *The Screwtape Letters* (1942) and in radio broadcasts, collected in *Mere Christianity* (1952). His theological writings brought him stern disapproval and virtual social ostracism at Oxford, even though Lewis distinguished himself as a lecturer and a scholar, notably with *The Allegory of Love* (1936) and *A Preface to Paradise Lost* (1942). An outspoken and effective champion of older and neglected literature, he was appointed Professor of Medieval and Renaissance Literature at Magdalene College, Cambridge, in 1954.

At Oxford, Lewis played a leading part, with J. R. R. Tolkien, in the literary circle, the Inklings. Among his own works of fiction are the "Ransom" trilogy (*Out of the Silent Planet*, 1938; *Perelandra*, 1943; and *That Hideous Strength*, 1945), and the six books of the *Chronicles of Narnia*, for children, beginning with *The Lion, the Witch, and the Wardrobe* (1950) and ending with *The Last Battle* (1956), which won him the Carnegie Medal.

A thoroughly bookish man, Lewis appeared a confirmed bachelor until his marriage in 1956. After the death of his wife in 1960 he suffered considerable grief and illness, and died on November 22, 1963.

Like other thoughtful Christians, Lewis believed that a study of the Garden of Eden and the Fall of Man can yield valuable hints to the Christian, and this subject is recurrent in his works.

I have indicated that most of *Perelandra* is given to this topic, and that Mother Kirk repeats it briefly to John in *The Pilgrim's Regress*. A full chapter in *The Problem of Pain* is given to the practical implications of the Fall. Screwtape explains that Satan's ejection from heaven was a falsehood and insists that Satan removed himself because of what he considered God's cock-and-bull story about His disinterested love of man. . . . Lewis also has a fine poem called "Adam at Night," in which he tells of the joys of Adam and Eve before the Fall. Lewis sees man not only as fallen from his Edenic glory and happiness but also penetrated by a deep longing to return.

This longing or *Sehnsucht* permeates all of Lewis's writing. Perhaps the best single account of it is in "The Weight of Glory," the first essay in the book by that title. He calls it the inconsolable secret which inhabits the soul of every man, a desire which no natural happiness can ever satisfy, the lifelong pointer toward heaven, a nostalgia to cross empty spaces and be joined to the true reality from which we now feel cut off, the "faint, far-off results of those energies which God's creative rapture implanted in matter" and which give us such delight and yet are the meagre signs of the true rapture He has in heaven for redeemed souls. As the whole vegetable system of the country described in *The Pilgrim's Regress* was infected with the taste of wild apples, so longing is the God-like infection implanted in earthly joys like a drop of nectar in a glass of water which is sufficient to give it a new taste. The culmination of *Sehnsucht* in the rhapsodic joy of heaven is, for me at least, the strongest single element in Lewis. In one way or another it hovers over nearly every one of his books and suggests to me that Lewis's apocalyptic vision is perhaps more real than that of anyone since St. John on Patmos. I suspect that for most Christians the idea of attaining heaven means little more than coming within the golden gates, but for Lewis that stage is merely the start of a journey.—CLYDE S. KILBY, "Themes in Lewis," *The Christian World of C. S. Lewis*, 1964, pp. 186–87

Underneath all, I sense in his style an indefeasible core of Protestant certainties, the certainties of a simple, unchanging, entrenched ethic that knows how to distinguish, unarguably, between Right and Wrong, Natural and Unnatural, High and Low, Black and White, with a committed force, an ethic on which his ramified and seemingly conciliatory structures of argument are invisibly based; but the strength that they derive from this hard core deprived him of certain kinds of sympathy and perception. He had little sympathy, as I have said, for Mirabel, and little for what I have called the New Sensibility of the early 'twenties, for its flat bleakness, its lawless versification, its unheroic tone, its unintelligible images, its 'modernity' in short. It delighted him that he could find no use of the word *modern* in Shakespeare that did not carry its load of contempt. The new psychology was another of the advances of 'modernity' that he regarded with suspicion. None of these things were a part of the everlasting gospel; they were the quirks of fretful foreigners to good sense, sound poetry, and the known stuff of the soul. He did not feel at home in the poetry of Mr Eliot or in that of the Sitwells; I do not remember ever to have heard him speak of the poetry of D. H. Lawrence or Ezra Pound. But of all older poets he spoke gladly, learnedly, and often paradoxically, throwing out powerful assertions that challenged discussion. I remember, on one occasion, as I went round Addison's Walk, I saw him coming slowly towards me, his round, rubicund face beaming with pleasure to itself. When we came within speaking distance, I said 'Hullo, Jack! You look very pleased with yourself; what is it?'

'I believe,' he answered, with a modest smile of triumph, 'I *believe* I have proved that the Renaissance never happened in England. *Alternatively*'—he held up his hand to prevent my astonished exclamation—'that if it did, *it had no impor-*

tance!'—NEVILLE COGHILL, "The Approach to English," *Light on C. S. Lewis*, ed. Jocelyn Gibb, 1965, pp. 60–61

C. S. Lewis, in his 'Narnia' series which began with *The Lion, the Witch and the Wardrobe* in 1950 and ended with *The Last Battle* in 1956, was writing seriously for children, and his seriousness has not prevented his books from being greatly enjoyed. Peter, Susan, Edmund and Lucy enter the land of Narnia through the back of a wardrobe in the house of the old professor with whom they are staying, and are caught up in events of profound allegorical importance. The sources of the 'Narnia' books are literary. Lewis was learned in medieval allegory, in Norse myth and classical legend; besides these he was strongly influenced by George Macdonald and not a little by E. Nesbit. It is fair to say, without any adverse implication, that the 'Narnia' books are extremely derivative. The allegory is the most important element, and it is Christian allegory. Narnia has its special lord, Aslan the lion; and in a passage in *The Lion, the Witch and the Wardrobe* Aslan gives himself up to save the life of the child who has betrayed him. He is 'neither angry nor afraid, but a little sad'; he dies and afterwards he rises from the dead. Here of course the Lion represents Christ, and very effectively; for whereas the story of Jesus's death is so well known to us that even at Easter we find it hard to enter into it imaginatively, there is in C. S. Lewis's book a fresh and powerful rendering of the sacrifice. It is most moving.

At the end of the last book, Aslan tells the children that so far as the ordinary world is concerned they are dead; they have been killed in a railway accident.

> And as He spoke He no longer looked to them like a lion; but the things that began to happen after that were so great and beautiful that I cannot write them. And for us this is the end of all the stories, and we can most truly say that they all lived happily ever after. But for them it was only the beginning of the real story. All their life in this world and all their adventures in Narnia had only been the cover and the title page: now at last they were beginning Chapter One of the Great Story which no one on earth has read: which goes on for ever: in which every chapter is better than the one before.

The quality of the 'Narnia' books is not consistent. They are at their best when the author is at full stretch; I suspect that their most satisfactory strand comes from the fierce wild fantasy of George Macdonald, and the least satisfactory from the more homely and (for this purpose) less appropriate magic of E. Nesbit. The 'machinery', such as the magic wardrobe in the first book and the green and yellow rings in *The Magician's Nephew*, is unequal to the size and scope of Lewis's theme. Similarly, the Nesbit-like family of four children are too ordinary to sustain their important rôles as rulers of Narnia, and Edmund is more convincing as an unpleasantly greedy little boy than as the betrayer of Christ. I do not feel that the 'Narnia' books are quite as good as the author could have made them. But they are greatly liked, even by quite young children; they deal seriously with high and stirring themes, and they have faith, which is no common quality in our time.—JOHN ROWE TOWNSEND, "The New Fantasy," *Written for Children: An Outline of English Children's Literature*, 1965, pp. 122–23

. . . ⟨Lewis's⟩ first enthusiastic reading of medieval literature—and few men ever read so widely for a first book as he did for *The Allegory of Love*—led him to ascribe to Gower (in the *Confessio Amantis*) the qualities he most admired in human nature: 'The heart is insular and romantic, the head cool and continental: it is a good combination'. Lewis later found a scope for his own narrative writing in the space-fiction ('scientifiction', as he liked to call it) which, in the 'thirties and 'forties, was dealing still with possibilities so remote from actuality that there was an ample field for sustained imagination. In this, Spenser's confidence seemed to be vindicated:

> What if within the Moones faire shining spheare
> What if in euery other starre vnseene
> Of other worldes he happily should heare?
> He wonder would much more.

The last of the 'space' trilogy, *That Hideous Strength*, pits medieval wizardry against modern technological barbarism. Ransom, returned to Earth, is joined by Merlin, raised from his age-long sleep, and the planet Venus herself descends to take part in the final conflict. Is it fanciful to suppose that Lewis was prescient of the changes to come in the possibilities for science-fiction, once space flight became not only a serious possibility but an established fact? At all events, he turned from space-romance to children's stories, in which 'giants and magicians', if not 'genii', play their exhilarating parts and the whole sequence moves towards a profound climax. Perhaps it is more significant that his highest achievement in narrative is neither science-fiction nor fairy-tale, but the myth of *Till We Have Faces*. There, for once, we have an instance of the quality of 'myth' which Lewis himself defined better than anyone. Myth offers a pleasure which 'depends hardly at all on such usual narrative attractions as suspense or surprise. Even at a first hearing it is felt to be inevitable.' Lewis goes on to link anthropological investigation into myth with the 'impulse which makes men allegorise the myths. It is one more effort to seize, to conceptualise, the important something which the myth seems to suggest'.

Perhaps we have in this the explanation of his own misreading of Gower as a romantic. What the voyagings, the sorceries and the dreams suggested to Lewis's exalted imagination bore good fruit in his own narrative writing—not so much in particular felicities of science-fiction or fairy-story as in his constant awareness of that myth which he understood as prompting all curiosity and desire. It is the myth which he in part retells in *Perelandra*, when a new Fall of the divine creation appears imminent; and which achieves near-perfect expression in *Till We Have Faces*, where unassuming mortality puts on immortality. It is not strange that Lewis should have developed in this way. The myth he reverenced was to him expressive of ultimate truth, underlying, and constituting the only final justification for, the romantic impulse itself.—JOHN LAWLOR, "On Romanticism in the *Confessio Amantis*," *Patterns of Love and Courtesy: Essays in Memory of C. S. Lewis*, ed. John Lawlor, 1966, pp. 138–140

A labor of love, alas. Full of good things, but of a sort we already knew from his other books—Lewis the apologist, the critic, the spiritual adviser, the wit, the master of no-nonsense prose. We get ⟨in *Letters of C. S. Lewis*⟩ what the editor considers the highlights of his letters—"set-piece" paragraphs trimmed at either end; numbered, neatly argued answers to inquiring strangers; detachable portions that manifest the virtues of Lewis without giving away too much of his personal life. . . .

The book's title is misleading. We are not given many complete letters here—unless, that is, the letter happens to be an "instant essay" sent in answer to some question posed him (usually by a silly woman, her pen striking from afar like dreary lightning). Perhaps Lewis was not a good letter writer; there is, to date, no public evidence upon which to decide the matter.

For that one would have to read his *letters*, not a florilegium culled from them. . . .

Reviewers have, so far, been satisfied with the homiletic Lewis who blesses us in these bits and scraps of letters—because, I fear, they do not suspect the existence of any other. But it is the hidden Lewis we need. That man did have a gift for self-revelation; it came out in the pseudonymous diary published after his wife's death, *A Grief Observed*. There are hints in the present volume that uncut letters would show us more of this strange Lewis—the one who could not abide his father's company, yet adopted a surrogate mother twice as obnoxious and demanding, and twice as stupid, and lived with her, obeying her whims, till she died late in Lewis's life; the man who conceived what seems a quite genuine sexual passion for a victim of cancer soon to die and, for most of her time, unable to move except with severe pain; the man whose tastes were Victorian, whose life was uneventful even for a don, who wrote wild romances but seems to have perfected the most prosaic kind of life-style for himself. How did such a cramped parochial life open out on such sane, balanced, civilized work?

The answer lies, I think, in an objection I just heard from a very intelligent professor of philosophy. He said *The Screwtape Letters* are too pat; they have a shrewdness that calls men back from depths, a kind of creeping and formulaic spirituality. This or that temptation is to receive this or that "cure." I think there are two answers to be made to this acute criticism. One is that Lewis was writing his diabolic letters during the war in England, where the problem was not—as in the dreary rounds of teaching philosophy—to stay alive to the grandeur and menace of life, but to make the evil raining down everywhere seem minimally controllable. The devil is not a visible foe, but he is at least a foe—worthier of one's mettle than Hitler; one who must be fought even as one fights Germans if we are not ourselves to become Hitlers in the process.

So much for the external circumstances of the book. The real answer, though, lies in the fact that *Screwtape* joins the two thrusts in Lewis's work—toward argument, toward fantasy. All the professor could see in *Screwtape* is the rather conventional spiritual comfort; but what appealed to Lewis was the imagining of another world that inverts our own. The two aims conflict here, since the book is meant as an exorcism, and cannot make the devil too vivid. But there is no such inhibition in Lewis's masterpiece, the space trilogy.

The models for his romantic tales have been exhaustively studied—the obvious ones, classical and Arthurian myth, Wellsian science fiction. But the vital impulse behind them was closer to Poe than Wells. They are ghost stories—"tales of the supernatural." It is an oddity of the modern world that "supernatural" in that last phrase is normally *opposed* to religion; the supernatural of Poe and Baudelaire. Lewis was temperamentally on their side. But he kept up permanent war with his temperament. His "rationalism" was like that of Samuel Johnson or Gilbert Chesterton (two connoisseurs of the ghost tale)—the labors of a man whose head is hard at work keeping up the heart's defenses.

Lewis argued so meticulously to conclusions because he had, literally, to *reach* them; they did not come unsummoned, as ghosts do. He kept his life rigorously prosaic because his head tended to drift off into fairyland with the slightest encouragement. The best conservatives (think of Johnson) insist on order in life because they know chasms open around us; the best rationalists use their brain energetically because they know how little it can do, how urgent is the need that this little, at least, get done. Lewis says, in this volume, that he never felt less satisfied with a Christian doctrine than when he had just defended it with all the arguments he could think of. Reason, at full stretch, touches all its boundaries and rebuffs us:

> Might it be as if one were living in an infinite earth? Further knowledge would leave our map of the Atlantic, say, quite *correct*, but if it turned out to be the estuary of a great river—and the continent through which that river flowed turned out to be itself an island—off the shores of a still greater continent—and so on. You see what I mean. Not one jot of Revelation will be proved false; but so many new truths might be added.

Lewis kept, by duty, to our small plot of land; but his mind slipped off, when it could, across that infinite map. He was a ghostly man in every sense, a holy one.—GARRY WILLS, "Ghostly Wisdom," *NaR*, April 4, 1967, pp. 369–71

R. C. CHURCHILL
From "Mr. C. S. Lewis as an Evangelist"

Modern Churchman, January–March 1946, pp. 334–37

The writings of Mr. C. S. Lewis have been received with a degree of acclamation almost unique in our time, distinguished literary periodicals vieing with religious papers as diverse as the *Tablet* and the *Congregational Quarterly* in praising his wit, profundity, force, originality and brilliance. In expressing a dissenting opinion, I should like first of all to quote a remark made by Mr. S. L. Bethell in *Shakespeare and the Popular Dramatic Tradition*; although I quarrel with this interesting piece of criticism on several major points, I wholeheartedly concur with the sentiment of the author in his preface:

> Criticism is a co-operative function which thrives on controversy. The sharpest disagreement may be in the nature of a compliment: only a bland ignoring of the other person's point of view should bear the stigma of critical bad manners.

Throughout his religious writing, Mr. C. S. Lewis has announced, in the phrase of Leslie Stephen, that

> the old world is once more going to the devil, and that the evil principle, disguised as an angel of intellectual light, is seducing us to close our eyes to all that is elevating and purifying.

The ingenious method of *The Screwtape Letters*, for example, consists of a series of epistles written from hell by a senior official among the diabolical hierarchy, one Screwtape, to a very junior tempter, Wormwood, who has a certain human 'patient' in his charge. Wormwood is trying, with the aid of the advice of his 'affectionate uncle,' to bring the human being allotted him to moral catastrophe and eventually to the Throne of Our Father Down Below. It is an ingenious method, no more to be slated in itself than Butler's in *Erewhon* or Swift's in *Gulliver*; but it stands or falls, of course, by the use made of it.

What is initially puzzling is the extent to which these devils are intended literally and how far they are mere symbols of the Evil Principle. For we lack the clue given us in *The Problem of Pain*, where Mr. Lewis puts Satan into the Index like any other famous person and ranks him, indeed, between the distinguished Egyptian astronomer, Ptolemy, and the well-known Elizabethan dramatist, William Shakespeare. But two epigraphs and a preface introduce these Letters, and the place for a clue is evidently among them. The first epigraph is from

Luther: 'The best way to drive out the devil, if he will not yield to texts of scripture, is to jeer and flout him, for he cannot bear scorn.' The second is similar, but is from a Catholic writer, the noble martyr Thomas More: 'The devil . . . the prowde spirit . . . cannot endure to be mocked.' In his Preface, Mr. Lewis tells us that

> there are two equal and opposite errors into which our race can fall about the devils. One is to disbelieve in their existence. The other is to believe, and to feel an unhealthy and excessive interest in them.

But the Father of Protestantism, whose historical greatness is not in question, was grossly superstitious, and he believed in the devil and his angels in the most literal manner. Of a high wind, he said: ' 'Tis the devil who does this; the winds are nothing else but good or bad spirits'—a remark which might have been made by any Hottentot in Stanley's Darkest Africa. But this is merely fanciful, even charming. Where Luther did damage to a more civilized society is seen in his conception of bodily illness:

> Idiots, the lame, the blind, the dumb, are men in whom devils have established themselves, and all the physicians who heal those infirmities as though they proceeded from natural causes are ignorant blockheads who know nothing about the power of the demons.

I don't suppose for a moment that Mr. Lewis believes this nonsense himself, but it is clear from the foregoing that one of the two writers he has relied upon to introduce his book has fallen into the second error he denounces in his Preface.

Such muddles are, I suppose, inevitable in a work of this character, and my main criticism does not rest upon them; nor am I disputing the limited value of the book as entertaining paradox, in the G.K.C. tradition. But those reviewers, the majority, who saw in *Screwtape* 'a great religious classic' weren't thinking of the entertainment value, except as an added grace; they were thinking of the 'masterly denunciation' of the 'evil principle, disguised as an angel of intellectual light'—and this, too, is the use made of Judas in Miss Dorothy Sayers's radio plays about Christ. There Judas is supposed to be representative of the man who errs from intellectual pride. The jubilation of the more orthodox religious papers over both these curious productions is sufficiently explained.

Mr. Lewis covers his tracks, of course, as he has a perfect right to do. (We cannot accept this covering in *Gulliver* or *Erewhon* and boggle at it in *The Screwtape Letters*.) He warns us in the Preface that 'the devil is a liar' and that 'not everything that Screwtape says should be assumed to be true even from his own angle.' This is fair enough, for the reason stated; but where Mr. Lewis puts into the mouth of his devil some observations he makes elsewhere, we can be tolerably certain that the views expressed are his own and not the mendacious inventions of the Father of Lies. Sometimes, inevitably, it works the other way round, the implied Truth that contradicts Screwtape's catty observations being similar to Mr. Lewis's postulations in other books. I take but a slight delight in the fact that the malice of Screwtape is couched in exactly the same language (even to 'specially' throughout for 'especially' and the frequent feminine use of the italic phrase) as the radio talks given by Mr. Lewis *in propria persona*. This is not so important as the unconscious dishonesty of the orthodox propaganda which is also common to both.

To take a typical instance from the *Letters*: at one point Screwtape is taking an honest pride in the diabolical achievements of the past eighty years. 'In the last generation,' he says, 'we promoted the construction of a "historical Jesus" on liberal and humanitarian lines. . . . We first make Him solely a teacher, and then *conceal* [my italics] the very substantial agreement between His teachings and those of all other great moral teachers.' I read this latter sentence twice, to see if I had been mistaken at first over the word 'conceal'; but no, 'conceal' is the word used.

We are faced, then, with this alternative: either Mr. Lewis is atrociously ignorant or he is relying on his readers being uninformed. (Unless he has simply been led astray by the sheer delight of controversy.) For he could hardly have opened any book dealing with the unorthodox or historical treatment of Jesus without coming across a passage honestly setting out to prove, by parallel quotations, that not only were the noble teachings of Jesus 'in very substantial agreement' with those of Socrates, Mencius, etc., but that they were, in many cases, almost word for word the same. Mr. Lewis may, of course, as honestly believe that the world, save for the orthodox mind, is rapidly descending to the Throne of Our Father Down Below; but he goes almost out of his way to convince the sceptical reader that he is simply using the Church as an excuse for his dreary attacks on everything he hasn't bothered to understand. The *Letters* are full of vague references to Liberalism, Humanitarianism, the Life-Force, Modern Art, the Historical Point of View, Psycho-analysis, Progress, etc., all asserted to have their origin in the Evil Principle and to be winning over humanity to the devil in the guise of angels of intellectual light. This is what the reviewers are referring to when they say of Mr. Lewis's work in general (or of Miss Sayers's) that it 'traverses so many glibly repeated modern opinions' or 'clears away a mass of shoddy assumption.' They haven't stopped to think, these reviewers, whether to make a sneer do the work of a demonstration is not pretty 'glib' in itself, or whether it is not a 'shoddy assumption' to present the case against orthodoxy in a conveniently vague manner which leads to misrepresentation or as a mere reversal of the truth. What those ecclesiastics, who recommended *Screwtape* as eminently suited for the unorthodox mind, were thinking of, I don't quite know; for it should be clear enough that no conversion is likely to arise in the mind of one who is told that the whole of the unorthodox case springs from the Devil or that Evil Principle in which (by definition) he doesn't believe.

W. W ROBSON
From "C. S. Lewis"

Cambridge Quarterly, Summer 1966, pp. 252–71

An ambiguity overhangs the achievement of C. S. Lewis which the recent memorial volume, doubtless inevitably, does not clear up. Is he to be judged by high standards, or regarded as merely a parochial reputation which is already beginning to fade? More authoritative voices will have to pronounce on those regions of Lewis's work on which his scholarly fame depends, and where there is not even the ghost of a common reader. But much of his work, even when 'scholarly', is clearly addressed to a common reader; and this must be my excuse for writing. My motive is this: I am afraid that many of Lewis's books are going to suffer the fate which has already overtaken G. K. Chesterton's: and for much the same reasons. Before they suffer that fate, it seems desirable to try to disentangle what is of permanent value in them from what is ephemeral; not only in justice to the man himself, with his amiable personal qualities, but to his standing as a representative in recent English civilization of the Academy at its most brilliant. . . .

Lewis admired Chesterton, and they have obvious resemblances. They were both Christian apologists who reached large audiences, and they shared a point of view, at the same time hierarchical and democratic, which has now become rare, but which they expounded with gusto and conviction. As a critic, Chesterton was more original than Lewis, but Lewis with his greater knowledge and scholarship was much more responsible; Chesterton was a journalist, not a scholar. Their faults of style are not unlike: Chesterton is too highly coloured, Lewis too richly flavoured (he used too much quotation). Lewis was totally free from what is bad in Chesterton, that odious streak of old-fashioned anti-Semitism, and the fostering of sterile national hatreds. (Lewis might have said that Chesterton picked these up from Belloc, whom Lewis disliked.) On the other hand, Lewis did not have Chesterton's artistic gift; he never wrote a poem as good as 'The Secret People', and some of Chesterton's witty light verse has a way of running through one's head as Lewis's has not. But the main point of bringing Chesterton in is that he has 'dated'—whether this will prove a permanent characteristic need not now be discussed. We read him with the feeling that, for him, nothing has happened in literature since 1914—at any rate, nothing good, nothing that has modified the critic's sensibility. We get this feeling too when reading Lewis's criticism. But it is more understandable in a man of Chesterton's generation, born in 1874. Lewis was born in 1898; his *floruit* (to use a word he liked) was not the Edwardian age. What need not have been a conscious rejection on Chesterton's part must, then, have been so in a man of Lewis's age and Lewis's intelligence.

The short way of dealing with this Edwardianism of Lewis is to say that it was just a pose, put on to annoy contemporaries and juniors whom he thought *should* be annoyed. Besides being dull, this account is unlikely to be true. Even in men whom it is natural to call *poseurs* (and Lewis was not one of these) the pose has its basis in something real. What is difficult to decide is why he chose in particular to be Chestertonian, and so to involve himself in the contradiction one detects in so many of Chesterton's writings. For in Chesterton we have a writer who flamboyantly proclaims himself to be a traditionalist, who is breezily and belligerently opposed to most of the characteristic trends of modern secular society, and who yet seems to *belong* to it in one of its least attractive aspects: he himself is part of the age of advertisement and propaganda which he attacks. How did it come about that Lewis was attracted by this confusion? Like Chesterton, and like Ronald Knox, he is tempted to the clever-silly; readers of his literary criticism are often exasperated by his habit of spoiling his best insights by some puerile deviation; two examples out of many might be his suggestion, in the essay on Donne in the Grierson *Festschrift*, that a criterion of love-poetry is whether you could read it to Britomart; or his demand in the essay 'High and Low Brows' that a literary theory of general application must cover *The Tale of Peter Rabbit*. Neither of these essays as a whole is foolish; they both raise serious critical points. But they are stultified by this Chestertonianism. What is the explanation?

The same problem arises when we consider the readability on which Lewis rightly prided himself. We must do justice to a point Lewis was fond of making, that a tortuous jejune style is no more a guarantee of profundity than a lively, flowing, figurative style is necessarily a mark of superficiality. But readability can be bought at too high a price: the leaving out of the qualifications and the modifications which a scrupulous writer leaves in, if he is more concerned with expressing the exact truth than with removing grittiness from his prose style.

When Lewis is writing badly, his thought, if it enters the mind without resistance, does so because it is shallow, and ministers to complacency. But when he is writing well, as in the introductory chapter of his volume in The Oxford History of English Literature, *English Literature in the Sixteenth Century, Excluding Drama*, his readability is identical with his mastery of exposition. No one can impart information so painlessly as Lewis, and here of course he is far superior to Chesterton, since he had so much more; he almost ranks with Macaulay. Yet like Macaulay, and like Shaw and Lytton Strachey and Aldous Huxley, he is likely to be an author to whom the young are ungrateful; having instructed and entertained them, he will be left behind, they will feel that they have outgrown him, that somehow he is empty.

Again it is that lack of inwardness that seems to offer the hint of an explanation of why Lewis, with all his gifts, is so disappointing. It comes out very clearly in his autobiography, *Surprised by Joy*, and this is all the more painful because Lewis commits himself there to achieving it as he does not in most of his other writings. This book resembles Chesterton's autobiography in leaving us in doubt whether the author simply has not had the experiences that he claims to have been of transcendent significance in his life, or whether he has been unable to communicate them. Reticence, of course, is an old-fashioned quality which deserves respect. But if you want to be reticent, why write an autobiography? And, above all, why write it around what you claim to be the most important thing in your life—the discovery that Christianity is what gives it unity and meaning—and yet say so little about it? So little from the 'outside' even, let alone the 'inside'? Thus the book has a curiously self-conscious and patchy quality which resembles Knox's *Spiritual Aeneid* and distinguishes both these 'histories of religious opinions' from the great classic of the *genre*, Newman's *Apologia*. Not that Newman set out in the *Apologia* to *mettre son coeur à nu*; the *Apologia* originated in controversy, and is precisely what it sets out to be, a defence of Newman's consistency and intellectual honesty. But although Newman is not concerned with self-revelation, but with matters which to us are dry and churchy, he makes us interested in them because he convinces us that *he* was interested in them; and so we get a more vivid sense of his mind and character than Lewis or Knox give us of theirs, with their obvious concern about the picture, the impression, the emotional effect, they are conveying.

Was Lewis's Edwardianism a means of *guarding*, of *covering up* something? The contributors to this memorial volume sound oddly guarded themselves; Mr. Barfield hints at 'something *voulu*' about Lewis's literary personality, but he does not develop this theme. At any rate, Lewis had a formidable weapon for self-protection in his celebrated dialectic. He regarded this dialectic as a valuable educational discipline, and in his autobiography has given an amusing and vivid account of the man who taught it to him. Not that Lewis, of course, describes the dialectic as essentially self-protective. He saw it as intellectual armament in battles for impersonal causes. It is perhaps significant that it plays little part in Lewis's religious writings, contrary to what might be expected; perhaps Lewis did not feel the impulse to use it when he wanted to be serious down to the quick of life and death. But in literary matters the temptation to use it was strong, and Lewis often yielded to it. As a result, he won forensic victories which convinced nobody (did they even convince him?). I have some sympathy with his concern for the plain man who feels that modern literature and criticism are going wrong somewhere, but is too inarticulate to state his position cogently. But

sometimes, it must be confessed, the plain man for whom Lewis is acting as advocate seems to be a very plain man indeed, and in the controversy with Tillyard published as *The Personal Heresy* he allows himself to voice a hearty derision of the idea that a great writer's work *costs* him anything: 'what meditation on human fate could require more courage than the simple act of stepping into a cold bath?' Philistinism does not nullify a critic; we have a use for Walter Bagehot; and we can even find value in Macaulay's essay on Bacon as giving classic and amusing expression to the plain man's contempt for philosophy. But Lewis had an intellectual agility superior to that of Macaulay or Bagehot, and the element of philistinism in his critical writings is therefore all the more regrettable.

It might be said, however, that what I have discerned as a note of philistinism may have been no more than an unfortunate manner of expression, into which Lewis was sometimes betrayed by his promptness to defend the common man and common things against the facile contempt of literary intellectuals. Certainly it would be paradoxical to describe as a philistine a man so steeped in poetry as Lewis, so much a philologist in the older and richer sense of the word. He was not in the least like the kind of professor he mentions in *An Experiment in Criticism*, whose subject has become a mere routine which one doesn't discuss 'after hours'. Small talk, politics, and gossip had no attraction for him; he was always eager to proffer and to hear about literary experiences, to engage in controversial debate, and, if this was desired, to speak of 'serious matters' (in Jane Austen's sense). And his Chestertonian paradoxicality, tiresome as it could be, was often a way of stirring up stodgy minds; he liked a breeze to be blowing—and not usually a cold breeze, for the west wind nearly always prevailed over the east in Lewis's discussions. But his dialectic did not usually advance the cause of literary criticism—which I take to be the discovery of the truth about books. The most important questions could not be debated in Lewis's way; and indeed I suspect that one purpose of his mode of argumentation was precisely the exclusion of general issues. What is insidious is the suggestion conveyed in some of his writings that *his* way is the *only* way in which literature can be rationally discussed. This comes out in that disappointing book *An Experiment in Criticism*. I say 'disappointing' because this was a book (written late in his life) which Lewis wanted to be taken seriously, and which he regarded as a sort of critical testament. But the opponents he evokes in it are men of straw; the impression that Lewis is scoring bull after bull is not sustainable after inspection of his arguments, for everything has been so oversimplified that rational discussion—that is to say, discussion adequate to the complexity of the problems raised—has been ruled out. In this respect Lewis, like Chesterton, seems in tune with an age of political propaganda. The reader after a while sees the unfairness, and resents it. Would Lewis have been so unfair when 'serious matters' were in question? Would he have assumed, for instance, that Roman Catholicism is disposed of by rebutting the (reported) assertions of a half-witted seminarist from Connemara? Yet this is the sort of 'evidence'—of the opinions of critics influenced by literature written since 1920— which Lewis accepts in *An Experiment in Criticism* for his imaginary opponents' position; he takes on no foe more formidable than the Cambridge undergraduate who, he alleges, was deeply wounded because Lewis said that *The Miller's Tale* was written to make people laugh. How can literary questions be profitably or interestingly discussed at that level?

But here we have reached an area of Lewis's writings in which, except for his superior liveliness and energetic prose rhythm, he is indistinguishable from the voice of conventional academicism—though an academicism of an earlier vintage than that of to-day. In his attitude to the most influential critic of his time, T. S. Eliot, there is something sadly reminiscent of that academic campaign against original genius, which continued well into the nineteen-forties. An offence for which Eliot was long unforgiven was his essay on Gilbert Murray as a translator of Euripides. The reverberations of the official annoyance which this caused can be heard in Lewis's writings, and Eliot appears anonymously—and inaccurately, at that date—as 'a modern American critic' in *The Allegory of Love*, and is presumably glanced at as an importer of 'Franco-American' dandyism in the essay on Donne. What is depressing about all this is its conventionality, which appears even when Eliot was finally admitted into the fold of the respectable; Lewis, in making such *amende* as he ever did to Eliot, is quite frank about the part played by Eliot's religious orthodoxy is his own decision to accept him. But as a critic of modern literature, in so far as he was one, Lewis is not always so depressingly typical as this. For example, he had a respect for I. A. Richards as having set out the 'modern' theory of literature clearly, and frequently uses him as a starting-point for discussion. I think Richards' strong points and weaknesses were both of a kind which Lewis appreciated very well, and he was better in dealing with Richards, as a representative of the distrusted 'moderns', than when, later on, he attempted (in a regrettably oblique manner) to counter the influence of Leavis.

Once again, however, it is external, abstractable, theoretical issues that engage Lewis's mind; in the actual practice of criticism he is too often conventional. In urging, as he did, that matters of literary opinion should be forthrightly debated, and not confined to 'little senates', he laid too much stress (when he defined the requirements of a critic) on having the courage to say what one thinks, and not enough on having the intelligence to know what one feels. The first is vitiated without the second. Hence in his attacks on modern literature he is sometimes indistinguishable from a type Virginia Woolf was good at diagnosing, the clever detracting don who hates the creative literature of his time but has no secure basis of his own from which to judge it. Out of charity I abstain from examples, preferring to mention specimens of Lewis's criticism which seem to me good. His essay on Addison, in the Nichol Smith *Festschrift*, with its emphasis on Addison's 'good sense' and freedom from jargon, conveys at the same time that these were Lewis's own virtues as a critic. His remarks on Virgil in *Preface to Paradise Lost* make us feel that we ought to read Virgil, more than any of Eliot's pronouncements on that poet. And for all his twitting of Cambridge priggishness about Jane Austen (she writes *comedy!* he protests) his own essay on Jane Austen gives a more convincing, if not exceptionally penetrating, account of *Mansfield Park* than anything written by exponents of the cosy view. A certain community of outlook with the parson's daughter who wrote that novel steadies him and makes him serious in the right way.

For to Lewis 'seriousness' had to do with religion, the 'serious matters' of Jane Austen, the *Serious Call* of William Law. Literature belonged to rhetoric, to the realm of means; and so he often, though unwittingly, conveys the suggestion that it does not really matter. In his essay 'Christianity and Literature' he explicitly states that literature which claims to be important as literature is merely solemn triviality, and in writing of Scott he asserts, with apparent approval, that Scott would have acknowledged only the existence of 'conscience', not of 'artistic conscience' (for polemical purposes Lewis plays down the shame which Scott is constantly expressing in the *Journal* at having written so badly.) His stress on literature as merely a *means* results in the loss of a vital note in his criticism, the note that is heard in the impressive simplicity of Tolstoy's judgment that 'he alone can write a drama who has something to say to men—something highly important for them—about man's relation to God, to the universe, to all that is infinite and unending.'

On a less exalted plane of discourse, we may say that Lewis's literary criticism suffers from his having no secure base either in the modern world or out of it. His Edwardianism, as a country of the mind, was not adequate, because Lewis, at his deepest level of sincerity, could not identify himself wholeheartedly with it. And his fairy-tale country, which *did* embody things that Lewis was profoundly sincere about, was not adequate because so much in literature is not amenable to translation into its language—though we often feel that Lewis is doing his best, and with incongruous results, to make it so.

But I have begged a question in talking of Lewis's 'literary criticism'. We learn from this memorial volume that he associated 'literary criticism' with Cambridge, and insisted that what he himself was doing, in this region of his work, was literary history. It has been a much discussed question whether good literary history can be written without a critical purpose—that is, without a lively interest in, and engagement with, the problems of writing *now*. When speaking polemically on this subject Lewis was apt to give the impression that he accepted the 'academic' view of literary history, namely that it *can* be written without a critical purpose. But in practice, I think, he had not quite made up his mind what literary history was. In the book on the sixteenth century he argues that the literary historian should give more space to 'difficult' authors—that is, to authors who for one reason or another are uncongenial or inaccessible to modern taste—than he does to the 'important' ones, that is, to the authors who manifestly retain some kind of life in the present. This represents the antithesis of the position of the literary critic, and had Lewis carried out his programme consistently his Oxford History volume would have been somewhat curious. As it is, however, his common sense saved him from the grosser kinds of absurdity, and he does indeed set forth in his volume a critical view of the sixteenth century—as, in his less confused moments, he himself recognized that he was committed to doing. (How acceptable his critical view of that century may be found is another question altogether.) I venture to suggest an analogy which Lewis himself does not use, to bring out what I think he was doing as a literary historian, in so far as what he was doing is consistent. (I believe the analogy is used by Lytton Strachey.) Some books of the past seem to be *dead*; no doubt in their day they served their turn, but they now belong only to the history of taste of fashion; Lyly's *Euphues* is a standard example. The literary historian's duty is not to administer the kiss of life to such works, and to pretend that he has revived them; but rather to make us understand (perhaps by citing modern equivalents) how they ever came to be thought genuine works of art, why they were widely read and influential. But other books can be said to be *sleeping*; Sidney's *Arcadia* would for Lewis have been an acceptable example. The historian's object here, as he cuts through the thorn-hedges of the past, is to awaken beauty. The trouble is that Lewis's practice not only does not convince us that he has actually found which works are 'dead' and which are 'sleeping', but even makes us doubt sometimes whether he knows the difference. As a result, much in his Oxford History is more satisfactory if we interpret it as recording the history of taste and fashion. Of course *some* critical powers are required to write even that kind of history; but I take it that not even Lewis's harshest detractor will deny that he had some critical powers. What is disappointing about his Oxford History volume is that its best parts are clearly much more than history of taste and fashion; but the necessity of conscientiously covering so much ground has frequently reduced Lewis to a literary connoisseuring like Saintsbury's, and it is improbable that after drudging through vast masses of forgotten literature (say, after reading hundreds of Elizabethan sonnets) a historian is going to be in the mood in which critical discoveries are made. Neglected masterpieces have not usually been discovered in this way; they have been found when a reader was looking for something else, or was seeking to fulfil some other purpose (a creative one, perhaps) rather than making a chronicle.

The endeavour Lewis undertook for the Oxford History—and one cannot withhold respect from a man who took on and completed so vast and unrewarding a task, while maintaining his determination to read all the primary sources—this endeavour was bound to conflict, in practice, with the doctrine of historical imagination he preached with such eloquence. It is put simply, even baldly, in his *Preface to Paradise Lost*:

> To enjoy our full humanity we ought, so far as possible, to contain within us potentially at all times, and on occasion to actualize, all the modes of feeling and thinking through which man has passed. You must, so far as in you lies, become an Achaean chief while reading Homer, a medieval knight while reading Malory, and an Eighteenth-Century Londoner while reading Johnson. Only thus will you be able to judge the work 'in the same spirit that its author writ' and to avoid chimerical criticism.

Lewis here states with his usual clarity an assumption which lurks at the back of much academic work on creative literature. As always with Lewis, there is *some* element of good sense in what he says. Even to achieve a quite ordinary level of moral decency we have to have some capacity to 'see another person's point of view', 'put oneself in his place'; and something analogous must hold for the intelligent reading of literature. But the idea of *becoming* another person, entering the mind of someone in a remote age—does Lewis really recognize, even if we give full weight to his qualification 'so far as in you lies', the kind of task to which he is committing himself and his readers? Surely it is difficult enough, without any feats of impersonation, to find out and to articulate what *we ourselves* have felt; it may be nothing. I do not speak of the misleading suggestion that the audience of a writer was homogeneous at any time—though we are tempted to ask '*which* eighteenth-century Londoner should we become?' But the most suitable rebuttal is *ad hominem*: is there any reason to think that Lewis really entered into the point of view of a large number of his own contemporaries—let alone people in remote periods, of which we know so little, Achaean chiefs and so on? For example: did he really enter into the point of view of someone convinced, as he was not, that Pound and Joyce were not charlatans?

What is immediately relevant is that Lewis lends his prestige here to the notion that the 'mind' of another age—or even the mind of one individual in another age—is something we can go in and out of at will. This suggestion, so far from increasing the imaginative flexibility Lewis wishes to encourage, leads in practice to superficiality—at any rate in literary historians. Handling their huge mass of materials, they can only keep their sanity by putting most of their emphasis on what is picturesquely 'different' in the work of other men; to allow one's sense of a common human nature to be really involved in so miscellaneous and contradictory a *mêlée* of emotions as 'an age'—any age— is bound to be, imposes too

much strain: who has the right to demand it from a historian, or from anyone?

I feel that, with all their attractive qualities, books like the Oxford History volume and *The Allegory of Love* and *The Discarded Image* have more than a smack of antiquarianism about them. I do not think Lewis's doctrine of historical imagination really functions actively in his own practice; rather, that it is the transposition into general terms of some personal desire for self-transcendence which he was not able to express in any of the modes of his own writing. This is suggested by the tone of the eloquent conclusion to *An Experiment in Criticism*:

> Literary experience heals the wound, without undermining the privilege, of individuality. There are mass emotions which heal the wound; but they destroy the privilege. In them our separate selves are pooled and we sink back into sub-individuality. But in reading great literature I become a thousand men and yet remain myself. Like the night sky in the Greek poem, I see with a myriad eyes, but it is still I who see. Here, as in worship, in love, in moral action, and in knowing, I transcend myself; and am never more myself than when I do.

This gracious peroration was worthy of a better book. It certainly does not clinch the weak and superficial arguments of the *Experiment*. What it really does is to put us in touch with the frustrated minor poet in Lewis. I do not suggest that this was the 'real' C. S. Lewis; I doubt whether such a phrase has any meaning: a man is everything he is. But I do think this frustrated poetry is the key to both his strength and his weakness, as a man writing on behalf of creative work composed by other men.

The weakness can perhaps be localized by glancing at a writer of the past whom Lewis made four major attempts to 'put over' to a public he knew would not be initially sympathetic: I mean Edmund Spenser. Here, if anywhere, Lewis is fully involved in what he is doing; there is no mistaking the vibration of conviction in his writing. And yet I have never met anyone not professionally 'committed' to Spenser who could read Lewis's accounts of him, and his claims for the *Faerie Queene*, without astonishment. With Milton, or with Chaucer (to name two authors about whom Lewis still supplies critical currency) we feel that Lewis meets some resistance from the author he is 'rehabilitating'; with Spenser there seems to be none. Rather, there are many signs of self-identification; see for example, in the sixteenth century book, the account of the 'modern' Gabriel Harvey and Spenser's friendly ignoring of him. This consciously old-fashioned, serene, yet ambitious author Lewis presents may or may not be a true picture of Spenser. What Lewis does not make convincing is that 'his' Spenser is a great writer, one who deals centrally and vitally and effectively with things of deep and intimate concern to men and women. At times Lewis does not even seem to be trying to do this.

The point I am trying to make concerns Lewis, not Spenser. For all I know, the new 'arithmological' approach to writers of the Renaissance is going to supersede, in higher academic studies, the Lewises and the Hardin Craigs and the Theodore Spencers; their attempts to map the Renaissance mind for the twentieth century may already have become period pieces. I am not concerned with the question of just what was Lewis's contribution to cultural history. Though at this point I must remark that Professor Bennett, in what he says in this volume about Lewis the medieval scholar, has missed an opportunity; his *éloge* does not make it clear how Lewis compares in eminence with Huizinga or Burckhardt; or whether he really demolished 'the Renaissance' or discredited the 'humanists' as he supposed to have done; or whether in his most famous scholarly book, *The Allegory of Love*, while undoubtedly bringing out how much literature and literary convention influence 'real life', he was successful in establishing the decisive part played by poets in creating 'romantic' or 'courtly' love. These matters will have to await a fuller appraisal.

Lewis, so far as I know, has not convinced the common reader about Spenser; and this is not for technical reasons of Renaissance scholarship, but because for good or ill the common reader to-day rarely seems to share the boyish romanticism which I feel was Lewis's fundamental reason for liking Spenser—and many other authors. This boyish romanticism is responsible for some of Lewis's worst sillinesses; but it is also responsible for what was best and purest in his response to literature. Its perhaps least harmful feature was an insatiable appetite for juvenile balderdash. The survival of that appetite in the high culture of the English-speaking world is a phenomenon which deserves investigation[1]. Professor Coghill at the end of his tribute to Lewis suggests, though he does not press, a comparison between him and W. H. Auden; but it might well be pressed. There are a thousand differences between Lewis and Auden, but they both seem to share a wish to be reborn as Beatrix Potter in some other phase of the moon, and this hankering has a significant relationship with their work written for adults. Lewis, however, is a simpler writer than Auden, and there is no need to frown over his continued liking for the stories that charmed our childhood. It is where this natural nostalgia shades into something deeper—into Lewis's feeling for the 'joy' which he associated with his boyhood, and which he came to feel gave unity and significance to his life—that the critical problem becomes more problematic and more interesting.

I will put the problem in this way: what is *wrong* with having a boyish romantic taste? It would be a dull world if everyone had the same taste. Let a hundred flowers bloom! *That*, surely, is the position Lewis should have taken if he had been true to the principles of critical tolerance and eclecticism which he constantly preached. But why was he constantly impelled to *defend* a boyish romantic taste by so many ingenuities of sophistry? We sometimes feel that the whole dialectic Lewis was trained in, reinforced by an Oxford classical education, was elaborated just to do that. This might be said to be harmless enough. But there is always a danger that an academic figure so formidable and so justly respected may, with the best of motives, find himself institutionalizing his hobbies. We cannot help remembering the strong influence Lewis had on the English School at Oxford, which retains compulsory Anglo-Saxon and until recently ended the syllabus at 1830.

Lewis did not want to bully anyone, to force them to do what they did not want to do. His brief experience at a public school, which he describes in his autobiography, resembles that reported by Louis MacNeice in his posthumous book *The Strings Are Forced*, and (besides making us feel that those places should be instantly abolished) shows where Lewis acquired his lifelong hatred of bullying and forced conformity. Nor—though his controversial manner sometimes lends colour to this belief—was he a browbeater. His fault as an examiner was quite contrary to what undergraduates feared; he was too kind, being apt extravagantly to over-mark the papers of a candidate whose views he disliked. Why did a man with so great a love of literature, and such gifts of exposition, come to regard himself, as we are told in this book, as a failure? 'My medieval mission,' he remarked with typical candour, 'has

been a flop *d'estime.*' Why did he fail to reach so many people whom he would have liked to help?

The opponents of Lewis sometimes represent him as serving up academic clubmen's prejudices in various colourful disguises. But I do not think he was essentially a clubman of any kind. He was very much an individual, and a strange one. (That is well brought out in this volume.) In the academic world he was capable of an independence and courage which a conventional member of it would not have shown. I will merely mention his forthright objections to what passes for 'research' in the humanities; the attitude epitomized in his remark that there were three categories, the literate, the illiterate, and the B.Litt.-erate, and that he preferred the first two, may well have cost him a professorship at Oxford.

As a representative figure, Lewis may well have been right in his genial (or rueful) recognition that he was a back number. The Oxford classical education has lost the confidence it had in Lewis's younger days that it is *the* education for an intellectual *élite*. But was *his* classical education, acquired in the more confident days, the unqualified blessing he supposed it to be? How much of it was the 'trumpery' from which he prayed in a poem to be delivered before he died? Certainly it gave strength and solidity to his scholarship. But it also encouraged his propensity to dialectics; and in associating a taste for minor romantic poetry with a formidable ability to analyse and expound intellectual matters (this last being one of the strong points of the sixteenth century book) it provided another illustration of the curious alliance, in English academic life, between the 'dry' and the 'watery'; an alliance of which the symbolic representative is the scholar-poet A. E. Housman. The exact value of Lewis's education is, then, another of the ambiguities which it is hard to resolve, and which make it hard to see how he was representative. Perhaps he was significant for us because—in the closing words of *The Allegory of Love*, he was 'a highly specialised historical phenomenon—the peculiar flower of a peculiar civilization, important whether for good or ill and well worth our understanding'. But it is as a person that he may prove most memorable.

Notes

1. '. . . Certain people—especially, perhaps, in Britain—have a lifelong appetite for juvenile trash. They would not accept adult trash, but, confronted with the pre-teen-age article, they revert to the mental phase which delighted in *Elsie Dinsmore* and *Little Lord Fauntleroy* and which seem to have made Billy Bunter almost a national figure in England.' (Edmund Wilson: *The Bit between my Teeth*, pp. 331–2.)

CHAD WALSH

From "The Reeducation of the Fearful Pilgrim"
The Longing for a Form, ed. Peter J. Schakel

1977, pp. 65–72

When C. S. Lewis turned to science fiction in *Out of the Silent Planet*, he did not have to invent the genre or establish its traditions and conventions. A long line of worthy predecessors, some most frequently published in luridly illustrated magazines and others available in dignified hard covers, had done the pioneer work. Lewis could function in a world that had already been mapped out. I remember a former student of mine, Frank Robinson—who later helped create the scenario of *The Towering Inferno*—explaining these matters to me when he was at Beloit College. He pointed out that by long established tradition, Mars is an old planet, in process of desiccation, whereas Venus is usually warm and sensuous, with something of a Polynesian lifestyle. These comments were decades ago, before anyone knew how tropical Venus actually is.

C. S. Lewis, a traditionalist in so many things, was not a rebel against the great tradition of science fiction when he wrote the tale of Ransom's forced visit to Malacandra and his adventures and experiences there. As any science-fiction reader would expect, Ransom finds a network of artificial channels, and soon recognizes that the planet is slowly dying from lack of water, warmth, and air. The very colors that gently engage his eyes—lavender and pale green and pale rose—have a subdued quality, as though anything flamboyant would be out of place on a planet which has long since passed through the stages of its youth.

Lewis's faithfulness to the tradition of science fiction can lead at times to apparent symbolism which may be nothing more than obedience to a well-established literary convention. Take, for instance, the vertical quality of the Malacandran landscapes. Its inhabitants are elongated, the mountains rise at impossible angles, and slender vegetables soar higher than earthly trees. Some have seen in these details a symbology of spiritual aspiration and ascent, contrasting with the more earthbound landscape of Tellus. Possibly, but probably not. One of the canons of science fiction is to treat with respect whatever scientific knowledge is available at the moment, or at least the share that has somehow reached the writer at his desk. Lewis knew that Mars has low gravity. . . .

The trilogy is a three-act drama. In Act One, Malacandra is threatened by a greedy gold seeker and a half-demented scientist. Both are ready to subjugate or destroy the native inhabitants to win gold, or to conquer additional *Lebensraum* for the human race. Ransom, the Cambridge philologist with an evocative name, finds himself in a position where he can ally himself with the Martians and help them frustrate earth's imperialist designs. In *Perelandra* a fresh-made world, gleaming from the hands of God, is in danger of falling into disobedience and suffering the sad, alienated fate of the earth. Here again Ransom is a key figure in saving the beauty and innocence of the new creation. Finally, Ransom plays a central role in defeating the all-out assault of the powers of darkness against Tellus in the concluding volume, *That Hideous Strength.*

The cosmic drama runs through all three books, but it is possible to take *Out of the Silent Planet* by itself and to discern a subplot—the gradual reeducation of Ransom, as he is taught by his adventures and his contacts with various varieties of *hnau* whom he encounters on Malacandra.

When we first meet Ransom, he is a bachelor don, in early middle age, a philologist. He is pious in a quiet way; when expecting death on Malacandra he says his prayers, and at one point he worries about whether he should impart some elements of revealed religion to the Martians—who turn out to be worrying about the same question in reverse.

Ransom is one of the "new men" whom Lewis discusses in *Mere Christianity*. Basically, he is already on the side of God, but there is some further progress he needs to make. In particular, he is fearful. He doubts his own uncertain courage and his mind is filled with an appalling vision of space as void, dead, threatening. When he does think about the possibility of life on Mars, his science-fiction reading and fearful imagination conjure up "various incompatible monstrosities—bulbous eyes, grinning jaws, horns, stings, mandibles. Loathing of insects, loathing of snakes, loathing of things that squashed and squelched, all played their horrible symphonies over his nerves. But the reality would be worse: it would be an

extraterrestrial Otherness—something one had never thought of, never could have thought of."[1]

A fearful man (but one who turns out braver than he expects to be) and an academic slightly vain about his scholarship, Ransom is addicted at most to venial sins. He is about as "unbent" as a mortal can hope to be in this life. Fundamentally he is on the side of the divine forces of the universe; for his perfection he needs merely to lose his fears, which stem from an imperfectly vivid awareness that the cosmos belongs to God and is therefore not to be feared.

. . . On Malacandra all is clarity. Like a well-organized army, physical and spiritual beings exist in mutual love and harmony, all under the benign rule of Maleldil. There is nothing to fear. There is no need for inner agonizing. Obey and trust Maleldil, and all will be well. This is all mere common sense to the Martians, but they live on an unfallen planet. In their environment, an earthling like Ransom can achieve similar clarity of vision. But Ransom was basically on the side of truth and life before he came. The completely "broken" Devine and badly "bent" Weston undergo no spiritual awakening on Malacandra; their ignorance is invincible.

Ransom has favorable conditions for his reeducation. All around him are the three native species, illustrating by their daily lives what true life can be. He is also safer than he at first realizes. Oyarsa, the agent of Maleldil, is aware of his presence on the planet from the beginning, and mobilizes *eldila* to safeguard him. On such a planet, loss of fear and growth in grace come easy. There is, however, a price. Malacandra is a planned society, and the safeguards against the fallen powers of the universe are so systematically worked out that neither an individual nor society as a whole has much chance to launch a rebellion. Oyarsa's *eldila* could be regarded as a kind of benevolent C.I.A., on the lookout for subversive movements. And Oyarsa's unbodying rod is at the ready, in the event of a major emergency.

In any event, when Ransom returns to earth, walks into a pub, and orders a pint of bitter (the messianic banquet?), he is a far different man from the one who had been dragged into the spacecraft and sent on the terrifying voyage to Malacandra. He now *knows* the truths he once believed as an heroic act of faith. Never again will he listen to the Enemy's chatter about "cold, dead space," Never again will he blaspheme against the meaningfulness of God's universe.

The trilogy, however, is one vast myth, not three completely self-contained novels. Ransom is destined for further reeducation. The second stage is when he travels yet again through space, supernaturally transported by *eldila* to Perelandra. There he truly earns the name of Ransom, as he enacts the role of a kind of savior, a little Christ, in rescuing that virgin planet from the downfall that Tellus suffered. Everything has come to a sharper point in Perelandra. Malacandra had many safeguards built into its way of life; Perelandra is more like the earth before Adam and Eve listened to the bent Oyarsa of their planet. The new Adam and Eve are free to fall; there is no indication that heavenly hosts of *eldila* will attempt a last-minute blocking action. By comparison with Perelandra, Malacandra has something of the organization and discipline of a benign boarding school.

Good and evil confront Ransom more nakedly on Perelandra. Weston, who in the earlier book was badly bent but not completely broken (he still had some fellow feeling for his species, at least in the abstract), is now the Un-man, indwelt by the fallen Oyarsa. Obedient to his master, he is intent on tempting the new Eve into disobedience against God, with all the predictable consequences. A battle of words between the two men turns into a battle of bodies, and Ransom at last ransoms the new paradise by slaying the demonic Weston.

Eternally youthful from his stay on the blessed and unfallen planet, Ransom is summoned back to earth in *That Hideous Strength* to help lead the forces of good in their struggle against the diabolic powers striving for total and final victory on earth. The man who long ago, in the midst of his fumbling and fearful faith, was in principle already a "new man," now plays his full role as a "little Christ," for the salvation of his native planet.

The main structure of *Out of the Silent Planet* is now clear. By itself, it can be considered a tale of science-fiction adventures. But it is a tale in which religious and metaphysical realities are as important as marvels and strange adventures; indeed the two categories cannot really be separated. The central plot is the reeducation of the Ransom under the influence of an unfallen way of life. The book, however, does not stand by itself. It is one installment of a myth that demands three installments. And in each of these further volumes, the reeducation of Ransom continues, as he steadily becomes more attuned to the Maleldil who reigns over the solar system and indeed the entire cosmos.

As we have seen, *Out of the Silent Planet* is like a series of concentric circles, each with a greater diameter than the last. There is the science-fiction tale (the smallest circle). Then Ransom's reeducation, and new knowledge of the relation of God to *hnau*. Finally, the biggest circle, the cosmic drama that begins for us readers on Malacandra but does not end there. That smallest circle is crucial. By telling a superbly convincing science-fiction story, Lewis makes us willing to believe in, and explore, the ever-widening circles that issue from the narrative of Ransom's adventures.

Notes

1. From *Perelandra: A Novel* (1943; rpt. New York: The Macmillan Company, 1965), p. 35.

WYNDHAM LEWIS

1882–1957

Percy Wyndham Lewis was born on November 18, 1882, on his American father's yacht off Nova Scotia, Canada. After some years in Maine and Maryland his family moved to England, his mother's home. His parents separated in 1893, and Lewis stayed with his mother. Though an undistinguished schoolboy, he won a scholarship to study art at the Slade School in London, where he was considered a brilliant draughtsman. After leaving the school in 1901 he enjoyed a bohemian lifestyle in France, Holland, Germany, and Spain, and on his return to England rapidly established himself as a leader of the avant-garde in art and literature. With Ezra Pound he published the Vorticist organ *Blast* in 1914 and 1915, but his allegiances were always short-lived, and his taste for controversy and polemics drove him after World War I into self-imposed isolation.

Lewis' first novel, *Tarr*, published in 1918, was followed by several years of silence before a burst of creativity saw the appearance of *The Art of Being Ruled* (1926), *Time and Western Man* (1927), *The Childermass* (1928), and the immense satire *The Apes of God* (1930), in which he expressed furious opposition to almost all established positions. While most artists moved to the left in the 1930s, Lewis expressed a right-wing view in *Left Wings over Europe* (1936). In these years he painted portraits of many leading writers, and worked on the novel *The Revenge for Love* (1937).

Lewis spent World War II in Canada, but settled afterwards in London. From 1946 until his sight failed in 1951, he was art critic for *The Listener*. In his last years he was totally blind, but continued to write, completing the novels *Self Condemned* (1954) and *The Human Age* (1955). His art received a retrospective at the Tate Gallery in 1956. Lewis died on March 1, 1957.

Personal

Almost, by nature, I am the pure revolutionary: like Godwin, say. In me you see *a man of the tabula rasa*, if ever there was one (cf. *The Caliph's Design*). My mind is *ahistoric*, I would welcome the clean sweep. I could build something better, I am sure of that, than has been left us by our fathers that were before us. Only I know this is quite impossible.

This is the heart of what is, apparently, a political mystery—I have learnt my lesson, and, in spite of being the pure revolutionary, I am a bit of a realist too. Hence my extraordinary broadmindedness in politics, for instance. Otherwise I should be a man after Lenin's heart.—WYNDHAM LEWIS, "A Letter to the Editor," *TCV*, Nov.–Dec. 1937

And then one day Mr. Lewis who had penetrated into my drawing-room office with all the aspects of a Russian conspirator-spy . . . Mr. Wyndham Lewis (Percy) caught me mysteriously by the elbow, willed me out into Holland Street and, in his almost inaudible voice . . . said it. . . .

'You and Mr. Conrad and Mr. James and all those old fellows are done. . . . Exploded! . . . *Fichus!* . . . '*Vieux jeu!* . . . No good! . . . Finished! . . . Look here! . . . You old fellows are merely nonsensical. You go to infinite pains to get in your conventions. . . . *Progression d'effets.* . . . *Charpentes.* . . . Time-shift. . . . God knows what. . . . And what for? What in Heaven's name for? You want to kid people into believing that, when they read your ingenious projections they're actually going through the experiences of your characters. Verisimilitude—that's what you want to get with all your wheezy efforts. . . . But that isn't what people want. They don't want vicarious experience; they don't want to be educated. They want to be amused. . . . By brilliant fellows like me. Letting off brilliant fireworks. Performing like dogs on tight ropes. Something to give them the idea they're at a performance. You fellows try to efface yourselves; to make people think that there isn't any author and that they're living in the affairs you . . . adumbrate, isn't that your word? . . . What balls! What rot! . . . What's the good of being an author if you don't get any fun out of it? . . . Efface yourself! . . . Bilge!'

I often wonder what fun Mr. Lewis has got out of being an author since those old days.—FORD MADOX FORD, "There Were Strong Men," *Portraits from Life*, 1937, p. 219

My memory is a feeble one, whether for scenes or for conversations, and I envy Lewis's ability to conjure up pictures from the past. While we were on the Loire I provided myself with a sketch book; and under Lewis's critical eye, and guided by his tuition, made a number of sketches, which, feeble as they were, served to fix some of the landscape and domestic architecture in my mind. But one scene, which I had no opportunity of sketching, remains very clear in my mind. At Saumur Lewis and I hired bicycles for the day, with the intention of riding over to Chinon. It was Lewis's bicycle that caused all the trouble. We had hardly got out of the town when the chain came off; efforts to get it back in place proved fruitless, and I think we returned to the bicycle shop for repairs. On our second start we got further on the way, indeed, rather too far; for we were speeding along at a great pace, well beyond the town, when suddenly Lewis's handlebars snapped off, and he was precipitated violently on to the road. He was rather badly shaken, one trouser was torn and his knee badly bruised. There was an inn not far off; I managed to lead Lewis to a bench outside the door; and after some difficulty persuaded a rather unsympathetic hostess to provide brandy. Leaving Lewis on the bench, with his battered cycle beside him, I hastened back to Saumur and chartered an open barouche, which I led to the scene of the accident. The driver and I got Lewis into the barouche, hoisted his cycle behind, and returned to Saumur. As might be expected, a violent altercation with the bicycle-shop proprietor ensued: Lewis very angry at having been given so unreliable a machine, and the owner insistant that Lewis should pay for the damage to the bicycle. The dispute was terminated, in a hostile atmosphere, without any money changing hands.

The incident in itself is, up to this point, purely comic. But a good deal of dirt from the road had got into the wound on Lewis's knee, and he was firmly persuaded that there might have been some contamination which would lead to lockjaw. So much did this thought prey upon his mind, that he saw a doctor in Paris as well as a local practitioner in Saumur; and I do not think that his fears were appeased until the lapse of time, with no symptoms appearing, proved them to have been vain. This fear of tetanus, which surprised me, was, I came to think, indicative of Lewis's temperament. Many people may have thought of Lewis as "tough" and aggressive, with a tendency to persecution mania. He was rather, it now seems to me, a highly strung, nervous man, who was conscious of his own abilities, and sensitive to slight or neglect. To what extent, I still wonder, was the aggressiveness self-protective? His work was persistently ignored or depreciated, throughout his life, by persons of influence in the world of art and letters who did not find him congenial. Those who dislike such a man call him "neurotic"; but I do not think he was any more neurotic than other men of genius. He was independent, outspoken, and difficult. Temperament and circumstances combined to make him a great satirist: satire can be the defence of the sensitive.

I remember Lewis, at the time when I first knew him, and

for some years thereafter, as incomparably witty and amusing in company, with the same gift of phrase in conversation as is found in his writings. Later, I saw less of him; and on his return from Canada and America he was already a sick man, with the danger of blindness imminent. After the blindness had put an end to painting, and he was obliged to confine himself to writing, his conversation lost its brilliance, but his temper, I thought, was somewhat mellowed. (His essay describing the approach of blindness, printed in *The Listener* of May 10th, 1951, is a terrifying masterpiece of calm and detached self-observation.) Yet at no time do I remember his wit as having any savour of malice. His criticism was impartial. He had been a frank and merciless critic even of his friends, to whom indeed he devoted more attention than to his foes—witness his comments, in *Time and Western Man*, on Joyce and Pound, and elsewhere on myself.—T. S. ELIOT, "Wyndham Lewis," *HdR*, Summer 1957, pp. 168–69

. . . Visiting him one day I found him in his usual squalor, but I was surprised to note upon his desk a number of drawings of elephants. They were not ordinary elephants: *these elephants had beards!*

Expressing my astonishment, I taxed him with inconsistency: 'Elephants,' I said tentatively, 'do not, as far as I know, grow beards.' But Lewis, brushing me aside, answered rather sharply, 'You may be right, but I happen to *like* beards.' This was unanswerable, and I made no further cavil, zoological or otherwise, for I knew it was not a bit of good arguing with P.W.L. over questions of fact during one of his creative moods.

. . . Lewis was in favour of over-acting, for the truth is his view of life was based largely on the Commedia dell'Arte, a theatrical performance where everyone was allowed to invent his own gags or *lazzi*, and, provided he stuck to his role, could over-act as much as he liked, like clowns, who are, of course, in line with that incomparable tradition, the oldest in the world!

Unfortunately, he was a shy man and therefore could not himself take the lead in organizing a revival of this popular art; but how he revelled in any heaven-sent amateur of the tradition who might from time to time appear on the scene with his bag of tricks! Watching such performances attentively, he would applaud the miming, the postures and the bawdy witticisms, till, overcome with satisfaction, he would drop his mask and howl with laughter like a human being! . . .

After the calamity to his sight, living as I did in the country, I saw little of my old friend 'The Enemy', but would get him out to dinner on occasions when I was visiting London. I made a point of engaging some young female to join us, preferably a handsome Scandinavian or a nice middle-European girl I knew, as I had noticed my guest enjoyed the proximity of both and preferred to hear an honest foreign accent rather than the hideous vocables of the pseudo-genteel sub-dialect now cultivated in this country by all classes. Besides, the stricken man was grateful for a helping hand with his cutlery, etc. (His gastronomical tastes remained simple and conservative to the end: soup, a mutton chop or two followed by a trifle or an ice was all he asked for with his champagne.)

He still wrote, I knew; and when first I heard of his calamity I had wired him to bear up and above all stick to his art-criticism! This impertinence was received, as I had expected, with complete equanimity: he even seemed slightly amused. *Never once, during our subsequent meetings, did my afflicted friend allude to the disaster.* Instead of souring his spirit it seemed rather to have sweetened it.

The heart which he had so successfully disciplined was now allowed to make its appearance at moments, though never vocally. Lewis was incapable of pathos, and practised to the end the reserve of a philosopher.—AUGUSTUS JOHN, "Elephants with Beards" (1958), *Finishing Touches*, 1966, pp. 117–21

General

Space and Time, says Mr. Lewis, are now one, as the body is one with the soul; we worship the God of Time and all our present emotional life proves us Time-children. This reminder of mortality makes us live for sensations, hence the flabby, oversexed, undeveloped, pessimistic new democracy. The drab industrial mills grind our workers, the threadbare barbaric hedonism engulfs our millionaires. Our only defence against this is to deny Time—to return to a belief in the extra-temporal nature of the human mind, to a classical life and not a romantic, an optimistic rational virility and not a credulous and effeminate indulgence in every kind of superstitious awe. Admirable as this gospel sounds, it is yet open to a good deal of criticism. To begin with, it is a retrograde and rather Fascist enterprise based on the co-operation of that dreary creature the "I-am-afraid-I-am-a-very-conservative-young-man." So far Mr. Lewis has paraded one disciple—and what has become of Mr. Henry John, the baby Chang, whose gawky mysticism formed the only outside contribution to *The Enemy?* Secondly, the Greeks, whom Mr. Lewis wishes us to return to, were more abjectly under the domination of Time than any of us, and said so in passages of exceptional beauty. Then the half-baked lava flow of Jewish-American civilisation that is now engulfing us, despite its stupidity, cruelty, blankness and sentimentality, is far the most vital force there is, and can only be combated by a principle of equal activity: we can find sanctuary in some half-timbered Utopia, but we cannot expect our sanctuary to turn out an arsenal. Besides, this obsession with the passage of Time that Mr. Lewis would remove is really the nearest approach to a unity of conception that we have. A common philosophic outlook is the basis of every great age, and to this belief in Time we owe Proust, *Ulysses*, and the novels of Mrs. Woolf, to mention a few of the most typical productions of to-day. Compared with these, neo-classicism, however admirable in intention, must certainly appear a sterile force. Also passion, that bugbear of Mr. Lewis, is not necessarily a stunting food. He has taken the shabbiest collection of gutless half-wits, made them adore passion, and argued that passion has made them what they are. Leaving out all the philosophical aspects of Mr. Lewis's theories, which it requires a philosopher to judge, one can at least say that *Wuthering Heights* is likely to inspire more good literature in the future than, for instance, Jane Austen or *Candide*. The Romantic revival has given us birth, and in the machine age we have our being. We are free to rebel against either, but we are not free to remove them. The Age of Reason is past, and neither the balance of Greece, nor the detachment of China, the Action Française, the neo-Thomists, nor even Mr. Lewis and his virile desperadoes will ever put Humpty-Dumpty together again.

The great feature of Mr. Lewis's brave stand against modernity is that he fights the age with its own weapons. No living writer has the same aggressive intellectual vitality, or the capacity to express it in such leathery, whip-cracking prose. Behind this lies a mind and a sensibility which are among the most interesting of our time, and, one suspects, a colossal egotism to give them force. His peculiar merit, as a stylist, is his painter's vision of human beings, the vorticist eye which enables him to see them half as monsters, half as ridiculous automatons, before he proceeds to a diagnosis of their vanity and their faults. In spite of the die-hard background of his thought, his interests and his arguments are all magnificently *dans le vrai*. It is this modern quality in his sensibility and his

observation that makes one forget he is really a defender of the Faith. This book comes as a relief to those who pictured Mr. Lewis as a bullying pamphleteer, arriving late and heated at the queue of letter with no greater object than a desire ruthlessly to elbow his way to the top. All the same, one is tempted to suspect his passion for order. It is, after all, shared by Mussolini. The main point is that here is a superbly controversial section of a three-decker, ragged at first, but always alive, and deserving to be read by any intelligent follower of the social tendencies of to-day. The ring-craft, the "terrible punch" of Mr. Lewis have been already noted; add here his amazing chemical descriptions of scenery and human beings, his catchwords, his satire, and his superb vitality, and when irritated by his conceit or his dialectics, think of the majority of our living writers, whose only talent is the galvanic virtuosity by which they are enabled to walk and talk years after their heads have been cut off.—CYRIL CONNOLLY, "Chang!," NS, July 7, 1928, pp. 426–27

Mr. Lewis stands, in a paradoxically high-pitched and excited way, for common sense; he offers us, at the common sense level, perceptions of an uncommon intensity, and he is capable of making 'brilliant' connexions. But 'what we ordinarily call thinking' is just what he is incapable of—consider, for instance, the list of names brought together under 'Time-philosophy' in *Time and Western Man*. His pamphleteering volumes are not books; their air of sustained and ordered argument is a kind of bluff, as the reader who, having contrived to read one through, can bring himself to attempt a summary of it discovers.—F. R. LEAVIS, "Mr. Eliot, Mr. Wyndham Lewis and Lawrence," *Scy*, Sept. 1934, pp. 187–88

Ker-Orr the "narrator" of most of the stories in *The Wild Body* says in course of introducing himself: "Sex makes me yawn my head off; by my eye sparkles at once if I catch sight of some stylistic anomaly that will provide me with a pattern for my grotesque realism." This is a useful passage. It is a *stylistic* anomaly, one observes, that provides material for the author's "grotesque realism." Although Lewis's comedy, like Ben Jonson's, might be described as "intellectual," in that it is expressed in intellectual rather than emotional terms, it is not, like say Mr. Shaw's, a comedy of *ideas*. Its material is the *real*: its purpose is to entertain, and not to persuade or instruct. So far as ideas and morals come in at all, Lewis is not like Galsworthy painstakingly and painfully impartial: he doesn't care a hoot about being "fair to both sides"—he is just cheerfully *indifferent*, so long as his artistic purpose is served. This attitude is reflected in the relation between the author and his characters. Lewis never presents a character in such a way that the reader must look at the events through *his* eyes. Even when a story is told in the first person singular there is no identity between author and narrator—"I" always presents himself dramatically, and is seen just as much from the outside as the rest of his fellow actors.—GILBERT ARMITAGE, "A Note on *The Wild Body*," TCV, Nov.–Dec. 1937

. . . ⟨Lewis⟩ functions with equal brilliance in more than one medium and that is a dangerous thing to do in a country like ours. The English have a deep-rooted suspicion of professionalism and when they find a man is equally professional in two arts, then their suspicion is not only doubled but squared. If Lewis has been treated with increasing tolerance and respect during the last few years, it is partly because the English public have forgotten that he is not only a writer but a painter. Lewis himself is partly to blame for this and it is welcome news that we are to have a show of his recent paintings in December. In the meanwhile the illustrations to his autobiography *Blasting and Bombardiering* are a reminder that Lewis is not only one of our greatest prose-writers but one of our greatest draughtsmen. And it is important to remember this, for his prose is essentially that of a plastic artist (one deliberately avoids the phrase "a painter's prose," with its unfortunate evocation of the verbal equivalent of the juicy pigment of a Brangwyn.) It is that which primarily distinguishes it from the prose of Joyce and makes any attempt to derive one from the other so futile. For Joyce's prose is essentially musical in sentiment, rhythm and construction. Think of the negro spiritual rhythms at the end of *Anna Livia Plurabelle* or the curious construction of the second pub scene in *Ulysses*, so like the construction of Berlioz' *Romeo and Juliet*. Yet how difficult it is to form any visual image of the characters in Joyce. We know every detail of their stream of consciousness but it is impossible (except perhaps in the case of Bloom) to even speculate on the shape of their faces. Joyce creates everything and everyone from the inside. Lewis is the opposite. His approach is external (quite another thing from superficial) and his prose is definitely not musical. Much of it is like receiving a series of rather rude telegrams. But it has a most extraordinary visual impact, a physical "edge" which is without parallel in contemporary literature. The most painstaking description of a scene we already know could not have the nightmare realism of the landscape at the beginning of *The Childermass*. The opening pages of *The Apes of God* give us not only the externals of old age but its physical smell. We could tell exactly how a Lewis character would walk or order a drink from the other externals supplied. And the same applies to their moral and intellectual behaviour, though Lewis never expounds a character in the interior monologue fashion. He prefers the Ben Jonson manner and reveals the characters of these behaviourist tyros by setting them in action against each other.—CONSTANT LAMBERT, "An Objective Self Portrait," TCV, Nov.–Dec. 1937

. . . Lewis's painting usually makes sense; much of his writing does not, partly because writing with Lewis was a hobby, as painting was with D. H. Lawrence, though a hobby which he cultivated with such energy that it came to overshadow the main art. Many features of his writing are those of the amateur. He never mastered—never tried to master—the art of expository prose, and the insincerity in his journalism is mainly due to the fact that he does not have the technical equipment to be sincere. He cannot make words express a precise meaning: he showers his reader with a verbal offensive, with what the accurate schoolboy phrase calls shooting a line. A passage quoted by ⟨Geoffrey Wagner in *Wyndham Lewis: A Portrait of the Artist as the Enemy*⟩ reminds us how much of Lewis's prose is couched in the huff-snuff rhetoric which is a non-occult form of automatic writing:

> Ours has been in the West a generation of hypocrites . . . a generation that has shown less care for men in the mass than any for a great many centuries, combining this demonstrable indifference to the welfare of the generality with never-ceasing hosannas to the Common Man: a generation of power-addicts who put on a red tie with a smirk, climb upon the back of the Working Class and propose to ride it to a new type of double-faced dominion . . .

In reading even the best of expository works, one feels in contact with an acute, witty and erudite mind, yet these books are unusually difficult to finish. There are two reasons, I think, for this. One is their inconclusiveness: they never seem to make a memorable or rounded point except when they are attacking some other writer. The other is their lack of rhythm: one bores one's way along a deafening unaccented clatter of words until one can stand the noise no longer. . . .

In Lewis, as in others of the neo-Classical group, anti-Romanticism seems to be a late Romanticism fouling its own nest. The Romantic decadence glanced at in Lewis's *Diabolical Principle* seems merely to expand into a more political form of experimenting in sado-masochism. The genuine statements in neo-Classical theory are mainly of Romantic origin. Mr. Wagner shows that Lewis's theory of satire is lifted almost bodily from Bergson's *Le Rire*—an excellent place to go for a theory of satire, except that Bergson is one of the two philosophers most violently attacked in *Time and Western Man*. In any case the contrast between organism and mechanism is a Romantic commonplace, going back to Goethe and Coleridge. The other target of *Time and Western Man* is Spengler, and the framework of Lewis's pronouncements on contemporary culture comes straight out of Spengler. Lewis's polemical writings are in a relatively modern genre—Spengler calls it the diatribe—which was largely created by Victorian Romanticism, though Milton and Swift had practised the form earlier. It was Romanticism that brought in Lewis's notion of a special type of creative man, superior to others not simply in his particular expertise, but in general, in his whole attitude to life. This conception of the superior person is expounded particularly in Carlyle, whose Teufelsdröckh is a professor of things in general.

Our own age has inherited from this the conception of the "intellectual," who produces, in the line of duty, the "calling-for" book, the pseudo-political treatise that "calls for" various shifts of attitude in society, and is the modern form of Spengler's diatribe. It is based on the Romantic assumption that if one's expertise is in, say, poetry or fiction, one's reaction to the morning paper will show an infinitely more searching insight than the reaction of one whose expertise is in greasing cars or curling women's hair. I imagine that this assumption has still to be substantiated: in any case Lewis's political writings provide little evidence in its favor. Of the four men of 1914, Joyce, after his adolescence, remained almost entirely aloof from this kind of intellectualized journalism; Pound fell for it hard, which is one reason why he reads so like a late Victorian. Eliot has also yielded to the temptation to write the odd diatribe, but has had the literary tact to keep the musings of *After Strange Gods* and *Notes towards a Definition of Culture* at least overtly out of his poetry and drama. But even in this addled century there are few phenomena more strange than Lewis's fanatical addiction to the diatribe. . . .

What is one to make of a writer who hates everything, with the unvarying querulousness of a neurotic, that his own writing represents? The easy way out is to decide that Lewis must be some kind of phony. Even Mr. Wagner has twinges of wondering whether his subject has really been worth his pains, and speaks of Lewis's "constant, almost paranoid, lust for destruction". Certainly one cannot study Lewis in detail without exasperation, but that is true of many writers, and though he has uniformly substituted cleverness for wisdom, still no one can read *The Human Age* carefully and feel that its author has no real place in literature. The better solution is to take all Lewis's theories as projections, realizing that he is an almost solipsistic writer, whose hatreds are a part of him because he understands nothing of what goes on outside his own mind. As Stephen Spender pointed out in a hostile but shrewd critique of Lewis, that is what his external approach really amounts to. No one better manifests Yeats's dictum that we make rhetoric out of the quarrel with others, poetry (read satire) out of the quarrel with ourselves. Lewis's temporary admiration for Hitler thus becomes intelligible: here was someone else lost in a dream, yet with a medium's power of animating and imposing his dream. We come back to our figure of the Cartesian ghost caught in its own machine, which I have partly borrowed from Mr. Wagner. Lewis is the satirist of an age whose drama is a flickering optical illusion in a darkened room, whose politics is an attempt to make clichés into axioms of automatic conduct, whose spiritual discipline is a subjective exploring of the infantile and the perverted. Such books as *The Apes of God* or *The Human Age* can hardly be written without a personal descent into the hell they portray, and Lewis has made that descent, and taken the consequences of making it, with a perverse but unflinching courage. —NORTHROP FRYE, "Neo-Classical *Agony*," *HdR*, Winter 1957–58, pp. 592–98

Lewis's attempt to bridge the formalist and rebellious tendencies in modernism highlights an assumption that resonates through much of modern art: the idea that form can communicate directly, without reliance on interpretative convention. This faith in form's ability to communicate subliminally is a common assumption in Kandinsky's abstractions, in *Ulysses*, and Bauhaus architecture, as well as in the work of neoprimitives and the Fry circle. Their belief in universals—in a "psychology of style" as Worringer called it—led the most utopian-minded modern artists to believe that a unified style in all the arts could be created. But the variety of intentions, symbolisms, and attitudes toward the new age that artists brought to their work eluded the goal of expressing the new era with a coherent new style of art. And the proliferation of movements and experiments, the babel of verbal and painted languages, and the rebellious primitivism and love of technology that spring from the modernist impulse defy our attempts to find a stylistic key to the time.

Similarly, our view of Lewis supports Erwin Panofsky's contention that the arts follow their separate histories. Clearly there is no modern literary equivalent, for example, to abstract painting—a mode of art that banished the objective world itself along with traditional subjects and conventional associations. Moreover, the historical gaps and lags in change underline these differences. Lewis early complained that literature in London was not keeping pace with the revolution in visual art he had witnessed in Paris. Indeed, the most progressive writing in English in 1914 was as profoundly naturalistic as the painting was antinaturalistic. Joyce's *Dubliners*, Eliot's "Preludes" and the poems in *Des Imagistes* all stress disorderly realism, the depiction of everyday life, the voice of ordinary speech, and the sensation of how things look. The most advanced painting of the time, by contrast, was highly idealized, emphasizing the artificiality of art—its notational aspect dominating the sensational. If the literary efforts of the time have any plastic equivalent, it is in the Impressionist and realist painting of the previous century.

Lewis himself conceded that he could not manipulate language as he could blocks of color: "Writing [*Tarr*]—literature—dragged me out of the abstractist *cul-de-sac*," he claimed in his memoirs, noting that in literature he was forced to represent human beings engaged in human action. Yet, in *Tarr*'s stylizations of those humans, and in the stiltedness of their actions, Lewis may have succeeded better than any other English writer of the time in keeping pace with the radicalism of the painters. And though abstraction in particular failed him as a literary technique, Lewis nonetheless pursued the antinaturalistic course in his subsequent fictions, and borrowed images from the Expressionists and magic realists. He attempted to give his writings the apparitionlike, "perfectly inhuman" objectivity that he believed was the essence of painted representation. —THOMAS KUSH, "The Artist in the Modern Age," *Wyndham Lewis's Pictorial Integer*, 1981, pp. 119–20

Works

. . . ⟨*Tarr*⟩, for all its meticulous care in the matter of book-divisions, has some uncertainty of form and of goal. Its characterization is confident and pretentious, rather than sound. The physiognomy of the average page is annoying. Here and there one finds, necessarily, a lack of mere verbal decorum. The preface calls upon the artist's fellow citizens to allow him more freedom to develop his visions and ideas and to permit him to economize time by not having to circumvent the facts of existence. Mr. Lewis has written several pages with his eye doubtless on the English censor, but the deft training imparted by Paris has taught him how to "circumvent," even if not to use the facts as "simply and directly" as he would have wished.

In fine, *Tarr* is skittishly brilliant, indecorous, brash, bursting with vitality—a possible sign in the heavens for the younger generation, but somewhat unbridled and absurd to the older. Mr. Lewis appears to know his Paris—*his*, not mine, thank God. Nor yours, I hope. His presentation of it is full of swank and swagger—his own favorite words. Most of the time he seems as militant and arrogant as his own Prussian painter (or sculptor), a literary swashbuckler, a D'Artagnan of the pen. His book is a dashing and bizarre experiment, yet holding solid hopes for the future.—HENRY B. FULLER, "A Literary Swashbuckler," *Dial*, Oct. 5, 1918, pp. 261–62

The fact that Mr. Wyndham Lewis is known as a draughtsman and painter is not of the least consequence to his standing as a prose writer. To treat his writing as an outlet for his superabundant vitality, or a means on his part of satisfying intellectual passions and keeping his art healthy, cannot lead to accurate criticism. His prose must be judged quite independently of his painting, he must be allowed the hypothesis of a dual creative personality. It would be quite another thing, of course, to find in his writing the evidences of a draughtsman's training—the training to respond to an ocular impression with the motion of a line on paper; the special reaction to vision and especially the development of the tactile sense, recognition of emotion by the physical strains and movements which are its basis.

It is already a commonplace to compare Mr. Lewis to Dostoevsky, analogy fostered by Mr. Lewis's explicit admiration for Dostoevsky. The relationship is so apparent that we can all the more easily be mistaken in our analysis of it. To find the resemblance is nothing; several other contemporary novelists have obviously admired Dostoevsky, the result is of no importance. Mr. Lewis has made such good use of Dostoevsky—has commandeered him so efficiently for his purposes—that his differences from the Russian must be insisted upon. His mind is different, his method is different, his aims are different.

The method of Mr. Lewis is in fact no more like that of Dostoevsky, taking *Tarr* as a whole, than it is like that of Flaubert. The book does not comply with any of the accepted categories of fiction. It is not the extended conte ("Cantelman's Spring Mate" is not on the pattern of either Turgenev or Maupassant). It is not the elaboration of a datum, as *Madame Bovary*. From the standpoint of a Dostoevsky novel *Tarr* needs filling out: so much of Dostoevsky's effect is due to apparent pure receptivity, lack of conscious selection, to the irrelevances which merely happen and contribute imperceptibly to a total impression. In contrast to Dostoevsky, Mr. Lewis is impressively deliberate, frigid; his interest in his own personages is wholly intellectual. This is a peculiar intellectuality, not kin to Flaubert; and perhaps inhuman would be a better word than frigid. Intelligence, however, is only a part of Mr. Lewis's quality; it is united with a vigorous physical organism which interests itself directly in sensation for its own sake. The direct contact with the senses, perception of the world of immediate experience with its own scale of values, is like Dostoevsky, but there is always the suggestion of a purely intellectual curiosity in the senses which will disconcert many readers of the Russian novelist. And there is another important quality, neither French nor Russian, which may disconcert them still more. This is Humour.

Humour is distinctly English. No one can be so aware of the environment of Stupidity as the Englishman; no other nationality perhaps provides so dense an environment as the English. The intelligent Englishman is more aware of loneliness, has more reserves, than the man of intelligence of any other nation. Wit is public, it is in the object; humour (I am speaking only of real humour) is the instinctive attempt of a sensitive mind to protect beauty against ugliness; and to protect itself against stupidity. The older British humor is of this sort; in that great but decadent humorist, Dickens, and in some of his contemporaries it is on the way to the imbecilities of *Punch*. Mr. Lewis's humour is near to Dickens, but on the right side, for it is not too remote from Ben Jonson. In *Tarr* it is by no means omnipresent. It turns up when the movement is relaxed, it disappears when the action moves rapidly. The action is in places very rapid indeed: from the blow given by Kreisler in the cafe to the suicide is one uninterrupted movement. The awakening of Kreisler by the alarum-clock is as good as anything of the sort by Dostoevsky; the feverish haste of the suit-case episode proceeds without a smile. Bertha's impression of Kreisler is good in the same way:

> She saw side by side, and unconnected, the silent figure drawing her and the other one full of blindness and violence. Then there were two other figures, one getting up from the chair, yawning, and the present lazy one at the window—four in all, that she could not bring together somehow, each in a complete compartment of time of its own.

It is always with the appearance of Tarr, a very English figure, that Humour is apt to enter; whenever the situation is seen from Tarr's point of view. Humour invests him. He impressed you "as having inherited himself last week, and as under a great press of business to grasp the details and resources of the concern." Bertha's apartment, with the "repulsive shades of Islands of the Dead," is as it appeared to Tarr. Humour, indeed, protects Tarr from Bertha, from the less important Anastasya, from the Lipmann circle. As a figure in the book, indeed, he is protected too well: "Tarr exalts life into a Comedy," but it remains his (private) comedy. In one scene, and that in contact with Kreisler, Tarr is moved from his reserve into reality: the scene in which Tarr is forced out of Kreisler's bedroom. Here there is another point of contact with Dostoevsky, in a variation on one of Dostoevsky's best themes: Humiliation. This is one of the most important elements in human life, and one little exploited. Kreisler is a study in humiliation.

I do not understand the *Times* when it remarks that the book "is a very brilliant *reducto ad absurdum* not only of its own characters, but of its own method." I am not sure that there is one method at all; or that there is not a different method for Tarr, for Kreisler, and for Bertha. It is absurd to attack the method which produced Kreisler and Bertha; they are permanent for literature. But there is an invisible conflict in progress all the time, between Tarr and Kreisler, to impose two different methods upon the book. We cannot say, therefore, that the form is perfect. In form, and in the actual writing, it is surpassed by "Cantelman's Spring Mate." And "Inferior Reli-

gions" remains in my opinion the most indubitable evidence of genius, the most powerful piece of imaginative thought, of anything Mr. Lewis has written.

There can be no question of the importance of *Tarr*. But it is only in part a novel; for the rest, Mr. Lewis is a magician who compels our interest in himself; he is the most fascinating personality of our time rather than a novelist. The artist, I believe, is more *primitive*, as well as more civilized, than his contemporaries, his experience is deeper than civilization, and he only uses the phenomena of civilization in expressing it. Primitive instincts and the acquired habit of ages are confounded in the ordinary man. In the work of Mr. Lewis we recognize the thought of the modern and the energy of the cave-man. —T. S. ELIOT, "*Tarr*" (1918), *Shen*, Summer–Autumn 1953, pp. 65–68

⟨The Wyndham Lewis exhibition at the Redfern Gallery is⟩, in fact, a delightful proof that it doesn't matter what -ism a great artist subscribes to or invents. His work won't look 1913ish. It will just look satisfying, and the only relevant question is 'satisfying in what way?' If I were asked to define him I should call him *Gothic*, an adjective which doesn't belong to a period but to a temperament. He is hard, spiky, dynamic, full of thrusts and counter-thrusts, a bit tortured, very compact, and, above all, an inventor of shapes. Wherefore he is that very rare phenomenon in this century, a good (not a great) portrait painter whose portraits are also exciting pictures. His portraits are not only likenesses: they are shapes evolved from the sitter and his environment. This *is* the shape of Mr. X or Miss Y, not an inventory of their clothes and features. They bulge here and break out into little points there, they are vaulted and buttressed, fretted and smoothed till they achieve a queer, personal equilibrium so satisfying that it robs little words like 'Vorticism' of their meaning.

What applies to his portraits applies equally to his other pictures—'The Armada', 'The Mud Clinic', 'The Cubist Museum', etc. The shapes are smaller and more tightly packed, the pattern less closely bound to the bulk of a single human being, but the architecture is just as homogeneous. They vary in merit because the ideas behind them are not equally realisable in terms of architecture. The architect who is good at Town Halls might be bad at Railway Stations. But apart from their individual merits they serve a useful purpose by proving that the portraits are not different in kind from themselves. They are only different in function.

. . . Here is the man who occupies so much space in the last chapter of all our art histories—the precursor of Surrealism, one of the pillars of the edifice of 'Modernism'—suddenly presenting us with something that looks rather like Delacroix and rather like Rubens with strangely distorted echoes of Chirico, and proclaiming that 'Modernism' is bankrupt. The solemn moonlight on the deserted arcades, the football-headed figures, the pale ghosts of dream-horses have gone, and their place has been taken by an earthy, hearty world of Classical nudes, equestrian warriors in fancy dress, and rhetorical self-portraits: 'Surely a little vulgar: and surely more than a bit out of date' thinks the critic, not daring to say so in case he might be wrong and fearful lest this might be the dawn of another -ism.—ERIC NEWTON, "Emergence of Mr. Wyndham Lewis," *LT*, May 19, 1949, p. 852

⟨The⟩ parallel of his style with contemporary film technique reveals how vital Lewis's perceptions are today. But it also indicates a weakness in his style that we must consider before we can evaluate the achievement of *The Apes of God*. The problem is that Lewis approaches literature with the portrait painter's devotion to the details of appearance. "Dogmatically", he writes when explaining his satiric techniques, "I am for the Great Without, for the method of the *external* approach—for the wisdom of the eye . . ." He places his victims in what Ezra Pound called a "Kleig light of ridicule" to reveal their mindless, mechanized natures. Yet the very vividness of these descriptions makes the return to the conventional narrative pace needed to progress to the next description seem forced and awkward. A brief cut to inanimate objects in a film need not disturb the narrative flow. In a film, the object is immediately present; in prose, the object emerges only as the writer pauses to assemble its parts. In *The Apes*, the prose too often moves in a deadening slow motion.

Through the middle episodes of the satire, Lewis attempts to breathe some life into his narrative with a picaresque plot. The picaresque episodes begin as Horace Zagreus, another nephew of the Folletts, introduces his hulking young protégé Dan Boleyn (the picaro) to the world of artistic apes in order to alert him to the danger they pose for the true artist. Since Zagreus is a fool himself, he cannot recognize the pretensions of his brother apes—it's a case of the blind leading the blind. But Zagreus can make Dan follow the program his own master, Pierpoint, once set for him. The mysterious Pierpoint (whose private life and opinions correspond to Lewis's) never appears in the satire. He is the observer at the still centre of the Vortex—in it but not of it.—TIMOTHY MATERER, "The Great English Vortex," *Agenda*, Autumn–Winter 1969–70, pp. 58–59

At times he suggests, as in *The Art of Being Ruled*, that freedom is an illusion, a desire merely for the absence of responsibility which should really be equated with the wish for slavery, or at least the wish to be ruled. Since this is what most people want, and since we shall shortly have "a world-state and a recognized central world-control" (Lewis was writing in 1926), let us acknowledge this fact so that we may find "more profitable occupations for everybody" in which the "soft and peaceable" generality of human beings will "be left alone and allowed to lead a peaceful, industrious and pleasant life". The vision is similar to that in one of Auden's early poems:

> The few shall be taught who want to understand,
> Most of the rest shall love upon the land;
> Living in one place with a satisfied face
> All of the women and most of the men
> Shall work with their hands and not think again.

The view of man's desires and possibilities implied is not very high. "How Much Truth Does a Man Require?" Lewis asks, and his reply is that most people cannot endure very much. This note is struck often in the years before the War. It is contradicted, however, by the assertion made almost as frequently that "people should be compelled to be freer and more individualistic than they naturally desire to be." The whole question is important in the context of Lewis's social and philosophical ideas, and he never resolved it. Which freedoms are real and which shams like those "ancient liberties", who can endure genuine freedom, who would truly benefit by it, who deserves it? He is always discussing these questions, sometimes at one remove, and he gives different answers at different times. It has been suggested, to me dismayingly, that at the end of his life the answer would have been made in religious terms.

I am not making a case against Lewis, but pointing out that what he offers us as social critic is not a coherent system of ideas. *Time and Western Man* and *The Art of Being Ruled* are masterly books, the first full of insights into the current and still prevalent obsession with time, flux and movement, the second offering a blueprint for human behaviour in a possible future

society: but with all the original things that are in them, the things that nobody else was saying at the time about feminism and the child-cult, or the attack on Whitehead's thought, the battles fought in the books on behalf of Western man (that is, for a different kind of society and form of social thinking) have been lost. *Time and Western Man*, Lewis acknowledged in 1950, was a fortress now silent, "a place where bats hang upside down and jackals find a musty bedchamber". He was too deprecating. The *ideas* in both books are of permanent value, it is their practical application that now has no relevance. —JULIAN SYMONS, "Introduction" to *Wyndham Lewis in Canada*, ed. George Woodcock, 1971, pp. 3–4

He began his North American experience by finishing a novel—*The Vulgar Streak*—about a man who discards his identity and makes a new one, supported by a new trade, that of counterfeiter. He finished with that experience by recreating it from a decade's distance, back in London, in a novel—*Self Condemned*—about a man who discards his identity (that of British professor) and exists in Momaco, Canada, as an exacerbated nervous system merely, until after some years he claims a new identity (that of American professor) and is free to carry on "insect-like activity" in a "Cemetery of Shells." His Canadian years, his years as a nervous system, expose him to shock and psychic reduction and tragedy. Canada, projected from the author's experience there, is the book's synecdoche for limbo, a frigid province remote from a forgotten sun.

This novel about Canada—Canada as experienced by a stranded Martian—derives its insidious power from the recognition it elicits that we all to some extent share that condition. This recognition emanates from chilling crystals embedded in the intimate texture of the prose. When you are nobody, nowhere, arrived out of nowhere, unknown, then anything at all that touches your attention does so with uncanny aggressiveness. A squirrel for instance is neither an entrancing fellow-creature, as for a child, nor a frisking detail in the continuum of things, as for the urbanite, nor a reveller on the largest mown lawns he has ever seen, as for the Varsity freshman, nor even a professional problem, as for the rodent control operator. No, it is something suddenly perceived staring "with one large popeye through the window, his head, like a neolithic axe-head, pressed against the glass, standing on his hind legs": an alarming apparition that does not recur.

These moments of hallucinatory encounter we have all experienced when we are most wholly cut off from all we normally are: in our dreams. *Self Condemned* is like an immense bad dream—the psychedelic fan would say a bad trip—implacable, engulfing, unnervingly paced, voices and blurs and acts of madness and over and over those moments of eerily heightened awareness, so randomly related to what is there to be aware of: the vertigo of a man without an identity on which he can rely. A distinguished critic not long after its publication assured the readers of an American journal that Toronto was not in fact like that at all. He wryly suggested that they consider the testimony of one who merely lived there. Quite: no place is like that if you live there.

But who, Lewis would ask (had asked repeatedly since 1910)—who really lives anywhere? No one does who lives, as Lewis did, in his mind, accumulating sharp acts of elaborated perception. The mind can always demand an order of sense to which the real is unequal. Lewis exploited this situation, one might say, all his life: it gave him reasons to be active: "Most of my books," he wrote in 1940, "are merely a protest against Anglo-Saxon civilization, which puts so many obstacles in the way of the artist." He had been some time discovering these obstacles. "I started life as what is called a 'revolutionary'

. . . : a man of the *tabula rasa*. I thought everything could be wiped out in a day, and rebuilt nearer to the heart's desire. I designed an entirely new London for instance." You can make these rapid changes in your mind, as fast as you can whisk your thoughts about. Outside your mind you cannot. It was not merely Anglo-Saxon civilization that was recalcitrant, not merely the sluggish inhabitants of London, glancing comfortably at the Albert Memorial. It was reality, the created actual: that against which the hand bumps, or the head.

He thought not, however; he tended to suppose every named thing, every encountered distraction, as provisional as the painter's reputation. So his fictions specialize in dismissals of reality: in voids where people like the Communists of *The Revenge for Love* are designing wholly new Londons (a capitalist hung from each lamp-post) or painting wholly new Van Goghs (since his tricks, authenticated by bought experts, will sell); or where Vincent Penhale in *The Vulgar Streak* is making for himself a new self, supported by new money, which though skilfully made in the basement is every bit as "real" as the output of the Royal Mint. And the texture of his novels, right from *Tarr* onward, was made up of details like that hallucinatory squirrel, fixed on the page with arbitrary irrelevance.

This was a habit of mind appropriate to painting, where one may elaborate a passage which the eye may choose to pause on or not, or which may lie in wait to gratify the ripe seeker after local felicities. In prose, which exacts sequential attention, it frequently ministered to clutter, a vice of style. The painter of a squirrel, his mind stocked with shapes, may well elaborate its skull's resemblance to a neolithic axe-head. The describer of a squirrel impedes attention by such a remark; it takes us away from the squirrel. The describer of a squirrel presented by a state of semi-dream, a squirrel not part of nature's continuum but thrust against the consciousness of a man deprived of any scale of familiarity, can by invoking the axe-head and the pop-eye touch on the nearly primitive terrors of such an apparition.

And this was Lewis's feat in *Self Condemned*, to discover the use of his mannerisms: to manage with their aid that the provincial banal should menace like an apparition, and that a man should plausibly be driven mad by it. He had often patrolled the borders of madness before. His previous novels had repeatedly plunged into vertigo: the duel in *Tarr*, for instance, or the killing of the civil guard in *The Revenge for Love*. Their notation for vertigo is a sudden slowing-down of time, in which particulars follow one another at molasses speed and with stroboscopic vividness. People are tricked into such abysses by misfortune, or by a presumptuous disregard for the rules of a communal game. The books are controlled by a theory about the communal: that it is a game, beset with savage penalties, and a rather silly game because it is controlled by silly people. The losers, like Victor Stamp in *The Revenge for Love,* have not mastered the game, as Lewis never quite mastered the painting game (he could paint, but that was only part of the game, and not the most important part).

Self Condemned, however, is not about a game. It is about the meaning of identity, amid the great convulsions that render meaningless millions of lives. And it does not contain an episode of vertigo; it is from end to end a prolonged vertigo, a slow-motion picture of very little happening, appraising the power of that very little by its very slowness to destroy René Harding implacably. When near the end he is shown his wife on a morgue slab he sees her much as the squirrel was seen: "Top-most was the bloodstained head of Hester, lying on its side. The poor hair was full of mud, which flattened it upon

the skull. Her eye protruded: it was strange it should still have the strength to go on peering on in the darkness." This is a moment of appalling, disorienting shock; the nauseous intensity of its random detail (a corpse as still life) is evidently right. But in being continuous with the texture of so much else in the book it clarifies the nature of the book's less lurid passages: they document the continuous disorientation of the political prisoner, the man displaced, the survivor (there have been millions) of a community elsewhere in space or mislaid in time: a nightmare state of being no-one nowhere. Everyone alive today knows something about this. The break-up of Europe, the subsequent great privations and migrations, transposed whole peoples into a sort of life-long Momaco.

. . . The New World has tended to suppose that the order of nature does dominate its arrangements, that its opening arms of welcome symbolize (however scorched the earth elsewhere) access to all that man's heart can desire: mountains and fir-trees, water and wheat and sunlight. Do men need men? Do they need cities? The New World inclines to think not. Her sage is Thoreau. She feels that her cities are her problem areas; that some economic process, no doubt related to the concentrations of capital, makes them exist and metabolize thought and wealth; but that they turn cancerous.

But Europe is a place of cities, and the reliance of a Wyndham Lewis on his city is so complex that a city on a lower plane of organization than London's deprived him virtually of existence. He was not like the millions whose gratitude has confirmed the New World in its hypotheses, who deprived by war and famine of everything took life and hope from the gift of elements in an elemental continent. It was not for elements that he expressed so strident a hunger but for community: for all that can cross neither frontiers nor oceans: the established web of relationships, indescribably fragile, that made his life as painter and writer possible. Even his enmities were such relationships.

Despite many acts of particular kindness such a life was impossible to him in New York and equally impossible in Toronto, for he had left behind what it is to be a European, and so stepped out of himself. He stepped into the kind of nightmare for which he had been all his life perfecting the notation: phenomena become apparitions, charged with random detail. Back in England (and blind) he applied that notation to the Canadian experience: *Self Condemned.* Then he generalized the case and reapplied it; he repeated the fictive experiment of cutting a man loose from Europe, but this time set him, as René Harding had not been set, in alliance with the centres of power. The centres of power were successively the Bailiff and Sammael, and the book was *The Human Age.* It showed that power was not the nutriment René's soul perished for lack of it. It also opened up theological issues Lewis was still expecting to confront in 1956. In 1957 he died.—HUGH KENNER, "The Last European" (1968), *Wyndham Lewis in Canada,* ed. George Woodcock, 1971, pp. 14–20

<hr>

V. S. PRITCHETT
"The Eye-Man"
Books in General
1953, pp. 248–52

Art was the religion of the Twenties; originality was its attempt to invent rituals. It was a time of calculated disorientation, of the impertinent even perverse occupation of new sites, a time of disconnection and energy in the arts. What would a total reconsideration of everything, from the word upwards, reveal? The result—as we glance back over the works of the period—was a good deal of physical glitter and exhibition and some pomposity; but, now time has ebbed away, some of the carefully constructed ruins of the time remain impressive—in their strange way, like paralysed and abandoned machines, the works of Wyndham Lewis most curious of all. They do not rust or decay, no ivy grows about them, they cannot be used and have never been assimilated into the landscape; old block-busting guns and tanks skewed on the abandoned field, they stand still, fantastic without their thunder. Their interest lies in their massive detail, for their purpose has become academic; we wonder why such rage was worked up in *The Apes of God*, why such electric flashes were sent out by *The Childermass*; until it dawns on us that these peculiar objects were machines for destructive laughter, whose target was really less interesting or, at any rate, harder to pinpoint than the glorious noise they made.

I do not mean that Mr. Wyndham Lewis's thought-war was useless; apart from anything else it was provocative, and its attempt to recondition classicism was interesting, though it led to political folly. But every artist understands himself. Mr. Wyndham Lewis wrote of his character Tarr that the "curse of humour was on him, anchoring him at one end of the see-saw whose movement and contradiction was life", and that he was "a sort of quixotic dreamer of inverse illusions" who, unlike Quixote, "instead of having conceived the world as more chivalrous and marvellous than it was, had conceived it as emptied of all dignity, sense and generosity." It is the laughter that has remained and the curse has been removed from it. After twenty or thirty years *Tarr* is still an exposure of sentimental German romanticism—and ought to have warned Mr. Lewis and ourselves of the silly nastiness of Fascism—but it has become a considerable comic novel, a masterpiece of the period. It hangs round the company of Nashe, the Butler of *Hudibras*, the professional butchery of Smollett. Though it intellectualises in the cosmopolitan manner of the period, and does its best to look like a foreign book—and I suppose it might be called a piece of Welsh exhibitionism—it is restrained by the fundamental good sense, the lack of final intellectual cruelty, in our tradition.

The new note in *Tarr* was the notion of human relation-ships as mere fodder for a new master-race, the artists, those distorted Martians, all eye and brain and the will to power. This brought back the physical grotesque to our comic writing. *Tarr* is theatrical in the Celtic way; it is the savage comedy of small things made large—hence the proper comparison with Swift. But when one critic in the Twenties called the portrait of Otto Kreisler "almost Dostoevskian" there was an unconscious exactness about the description, for we are reminded of the comic Dostoevsky in his short, Westernised, civilised and expatriate phase, when he wrote *The Eternal Husband*. In a sense, Mr. Wyndham Lewis has always been an expatriate and that condition enormously stimulates the brain at the expense of feeling; yet perhaps the tendency to continual over-stimulus in his writing was only a new version of the Welsh obsession with fantastic verbal image and the behaviour of giants. We can even imagine a thesis on his debt to Meredith. The common dangerous Germanic ingredients are obvious.

The early success of *Tarr* was partly due to its shrewd penetration of the German character at the right moment, after the first world war. The raw, beastly, foolish, mad and simple cry-baby Otto Kreisler, the eternal hysterical student, is almost a tragic character. Lack of feeling on the author's part, Mr. Wyndham Lewis's high suggestibility, hold Kreisler back from the tragic apotheosis: he is ludicrous, detestable, pathetic. He

comes, interestingly enough, very close to the character of the husband in Dostoevsky's Western novel. The memory of the second world war revives the accidental interest of *Tarr*, but Otto Kreisler and Montparnasse are so far away by now, that they begin to have the picturesque, sentimental charm of an old-fashioned Bohemianism, rather than a disturbing psycho-logical point. I would not undervalue the nostalgic quality *Tarr* has acquired in the course of a generation; but what strikes one still is that its originality in description, episode and attitude to character, is more than innovation. It is an enlargement of the novelist's means; a new territory has been subdued: the *terrasse*.

Mr. Wyndham Lewis's originality lies in his use of a non-literary eye, the eye of the painter. He does not judge by experience, association, feeling or cogitation, before he has first considered all the physical implications of what he has physically seen. An eye, promoted in this way to an uncom-mon, even perverse position of power, becomes inevitably sardonic, expert in false, freakish, intuitive juxtapositions. It is almost certain to be brutally funny; it will sometimes hit upon important general truths. And so we get his gift for fresh generalisation:

> "Well then, well then, Alan Hobson—you scarecrow of an advanced fool farm——"
> "What is that?"
> "You voice-culture practitioner——"
> "I? My voice? But that's absurd! If my speech . . ."
> Hobson was up in arms about his voice al-though it was not his.
> Tar needed a grimacing, tumultuous mask for the face he had to cover. He had compared his clowning with Hobson's pierrotesque vanity; but Hobson, he considered, was a crowd. You could not say he was an individual, he was in fact a set. He sat there, a cultivated audience, with the aplomb and absence of self-consciousness of numbers. . . .
> A distinguished absence of personality was Hobson's most personal characteristic.

The descriptions can be more precise, the more they are picturesque. Kreisler is shaving:

> His face, wearing, it is true, like a uniform the frowning fixity of the Prussian warrior, had a ne-glected look. The true Bismarckian Prussian would seek every day, by little acts of boorishness to keep fresh this trenchant attitude; like the German student with his weekly routine of duels which regimen is to keep courage simmering in times of peace.

A dancer:

> A rather congested, flushed and bespectacled young woman, her features set in a spasm of duty. It was a hungry sex in charge of a flustered automaton.

And, in action, the figures become as grotesque as clowns in a circus, enlarged by the coarse fancy of a child's eye:

> She crossed her legs. The cold grape-bloom mauve silk stockings ended in a dark slash each against her two snowy stallion thighs which they bisected, visible, one above the other, in naked expanses of tempting undercut, issuing from a dead-white foam of central lace worthy of the Can-Can exhibitionists of the tourist resorts of Paris-by-night.
> Tarr grinned with brisk appreciation of the big full-fledged baby's coquetry pointing the swinish moral under the rose and mock-modesty below stairs, and he blinked and blinked as if partly dazzled, his mohammedan eye did not refuse the conventional bait.

The descriptions of people, of places and scenes are often surpassed for gritty vividness in *The Childermass* and *The Apes of God*; but in those books they are so piled on in the monotony of a morbid glitter that they eventually kill their effect. *The Apes of God* can be read for one or two fine broad scenes of libel—the dinner party with the Finnish poet bawling his French verse—and for its general blood bath in the literary society of the Twenties. Its fatal limitation is triviality of subject: it was topical to attack the cult of art, but there is a whiff of provinciality about the odd man out. Exciting sentence by sentence, image by image, it is all too much page by page. The note of sanity is excellent, but sanity that protests too much becomes itself a kind of madness. In *The Childermass*, a brilliant idea stands still and stuttering. The fact is that the influence of Joyce, the determination to be *avant garde*, was ruinous to Wyndham Lewis as he went on. To blow up Bloomsbury was an excellent idea: to sit out the long persecution mania of a cold war was too much.

But *Tarr* is a perfectly shaped and classical work. The characters are tried by the traditional and always rewarding test of their love affairs; and these are subjected to the scornful criticising of the brain. Like some repressed and arrogant savage, the brain is brought forward to make fun of the sogginess of human sentiment. Tarr does not apologise for being a two-girl man; he does not moralise, he does not torture himself, he is not even cynical. Human beings are enjoyed as the dangerous animals who are determined—whatever fairy tales they may tell themselves or others—to have their cake and eat it. They are dangerous because they dream, and dreams create an inflated physical world. Human nature is disgraceful; the only thing to be said for it is that it may produce a little, a very little, Art.

Mr. Wyndham Lewis's genius lies in his strange capacity for reducing mind to matter: "her lips were long hard bubbles . . . grown forward with ape-like intensity, they refused no emotion noisy egress if it got so far." Women for Kreisler are "vast dumping grounds for sorrow and affliction", huge pawnshops in which he deposits himself in exchange for "the gold of the human heart or any other gold that happened to be lying about." Anything in life which becomes unmanageable—*i.e.*, his failure as an artist—becomes converted into love. The pleasure of *Tarr* is that it wallows in the nature of the physical world: the butcher's shop provides many an analogy, not always coarse, indeed often comically delicate. The body is not respected; it is frequently insulted, especially if it is female, but the happiest love is where the laughter is loudest; on the other hand, it is recognised that we need a relief from the happiest love. We need—or at any rate Tarr in his sardonic way, and Kreisler in his suicidal way, need—something different from what we had before. The tail (when we become his character, the eye men) is invariably wagging the dog. There lies the virtue and the strain of his hard-hearted genius; he carries the burden of his laughter which has tipped the scale against life. But in Kreisler cadging, scrounging, loving, fighting, crawling back, breaking up parties and ending in murder and suicide, he has created a permanent character. (The fact is he created Hitler.) It is a strange experience to put down a masterpiece in which one has had the impression of not only knowing the characters but of giving them a pinch all over to see if they were ready for the comic pot of life on earth.

HUGH KENNER
From *Wyndham Lewis*
1954, pp. 14–17, 72–81

The War with Time
III. Vorticist Prose

In 1914 ⟨Lewis⟩ seems resolved never again to write a phrase that will betray a hint of literary antecedents; but that is only the most superficial of the ways in which his "Vorticist" prose abolished Time. It is in *Blast* that the Wyndham Lewis who appeared in silence on Ford's stairway finds an appropriate tongue. It is explosive in principle as well as in strategy; each sentence joins words by fiat, and the compound, though one cannot tell by what process it was arrived at, asserts as undeniably as a troop of Martians its right to corporate existence. It is, vastly elaborated, the style of its showpiece, the 1928 *Childermass*, and its mechanisms underlie the wonderfully expressive prose of Lewis's masterpiece, the 1937 *Revenge for Love*. We can observe it, not quite coming off, in the *Blast* account of a thunderclap:

> The great beer-coloured sky, at the fuss, leapt in a fête of green gaiety.
> Its immense lines bent like whalebones and sprang back with slight deaf thunder.
> The sky, two clouds, their furious shadows, fought.
> The bleak misty hospital of the horizon grew pale with fluid of anger.
> The trees were wiped out in a blow.

Thunderstorms happen in time and manifest duration; it is the necessity for placing things in succession, admitting sequence between paragraphs where the instinct at work within sentences is to abolish it, that makes this passage sound labored. Where nothing is happening, however, the effect is memorable. Here are the stars:

> The stars shone madly in the archaic blank wilderness of the universe, machines of prey.
> Mastodons, placid in electric atmosphere, white rivers of power. They stood in eternal black sunlight. . . .
> Throats iron eternities, drinking heavy radiance, limbs towers of blatant light, the stars poised, immensely distant, with their metal sides, pantheistic machines.

It is a style composed of phrases, not actions. The verb, inexorably the *time*-word, is where possible reduced to impotence ("shone" and "stood") or else simply omitted. Of course, there is no reason why there should not be more such phrases about the stars, or for that matter why a few of them should not be omitted, except that they seem, once achieved, too good to scrap. Sporadically conscious though he was of the necessity, Lewis didn't succeed in making his new prose *move* rather than accumulate, until, in the 1930's, he had struck his truce with Time.

He had only to abandon the posterish conventions of *Blast*, however, to possess a method for titling a book unforgettably or presenting any baroque stasis, whether of persons or places, with unflagging vigor. Its mechanisms can fix on paper with impartial efficiency New York sunbathers, "a collection of shabby baskers saluting the sun with many a caustic blink, the wreckage of Anglo-Saxon machine-mindedness"; the British grin, "conventionalizing like gun-shot, freezing supple Real in ferocious chemistry of Laughter"; or Gertrude Stein, "Teutonic music, *jazzed*—the German musical soul leering at itself in a mirror, and sticking out at itself a stuttering welt of swollen tongue." At greater length, here is the texture of a fake Van Gogh—

> Gnarled figures of peasants, with the striations of tree trunks, gathered in the foreground like hoboes in a hailstorm. But this hailstorm was the sunset. And the hailstones were the opaque particles showering down from the conflagration of the romantic solar disk, about to set, like a bloated firework.

And here is Ford himself—

> Hueffer was a flabby lemon and pink giant, who hung his mouth open as though he were an animal at the Zoo inviting buns——especially when ladies were present. Over the gaping mouth damply depended the ragged ends of a pale lemon moustache. This ex-collaborator with Joseph Conrad was himself, it always occurred to me, a typical figure out of a Conrad book—a caterer, or corn-factor, coming on board—blowing like a porpoise with the exertion—at some Eastern port.

This account of Ford was written in 1949. It is only a slightly more hurried application of the devices by which the stars and trees in *Blast*, or the characters of *Tarr*, were rendered thirty-five years earlier.

If anything extended could be done with it, this early style would be one of the most impressive inventions in the history of English literature. It remains one of the most fascinating. It may owe its origin in part to the impact on Lewis's sensibility of the compound nouns and participialized verbs peculiar to the German prose in which he has steeped himself: terms like *Blutsgefühl*, *Geldmensch*, *Judenfrage*, and *Leihkapital* merge with interesting casualness into the prose texture of his hastily written 1931 book on Hitler. The essential trick is worth isolating in a sentence of which the elements are conventional and only their mode of combination novel:

> Henry James: Ghost psychology of New England old maid: stately maze of imperturbable analogies.

Every word attaches itself to Henry James; but it was Lewis who attached them alchemically to one another. It isn't the maze that is stately, nor the analogies that are imperturbable; but by unhooking each of these words from its appointed object and joining them instead to each other, Lewis, in setting his signature on the combination, releases magnetisms that make its elements seem, once so joined, inseparable. The phrases thus arrived at are so condensed that their rightness grows wonderfully persuasive. Assonance and rhythm—not meaning—cause this particular ordering of the terms to snap together like a clock spring; any other arrangement, once we have seen this one, would hang open in flaccid incompetence. In this universe of words—precisely the "finely sculptured surface of sheer words" Lewis much later suggested discriminating readers should hunger for—we soon stop worrying about mere reality. It is a sort of dream-literature of unexampled energy. . . .

Polemics
III. The Gods of Time

In 1927 . . . Hitler was still in the future, and Lewis alone, with his image of Shakespeare to prop him, was busily opposing The Time. The liaison between The Time and "Time" is explained in the editorial to the second issue of *The Enemy* (1927):

> "History" is just what occurs, what gets into Time, as opposed to what does not, or what remains latent, unused or unexplored: that is the directest meaning of "history." And the "Destiny-idea," about which

Spengler makes so much fuss, is, again, just that: what is, is. . . . It is the religion of Fate, and it is called "History."

All rhetoric about "manifest destiny," about "modernity" or "the spirit of the age," comes down, for Lewis, to that: genuflection before the random visage discernible in what happens to have happened. He was exacerbated not so much by the events as by their succession being deified into a massive trend:

> All other times have bred criticism. . . . Only *this* time exacts an uncritical sleep of all within it. This, as elsewhere I am showing, is the sleep of the machine, or humanly, of the mass. . . . We have become so conscious of this obsessing "Time" that we tend to personalize it.

This was a discernment of great accuracy. Since Hanp by hypothesis seeks safety in numbers, Lewis in any age would have been in opposition. "Life" is what the herd is doing, and Art is the enemy of "Life," of what happens "naturally." Life passes through time and dies, whereas Art, as Tarr explained to Anastasya, "is ourselves disentangled from death and accident. . . . Anything living, quick and changing, is bad art, always." But with the momentum of his opposition, Lewis was enabled to discern as did no one else a special and unusual fact about the twentieth century: flux was not being taken for granted, it was being hypostatized. *La durée*, as Bergson had been explaining when the young Lewis visited his Paris lecture-room early in the century, was the only reality. The *Self* was being cut up into chronological compartments; Hanp was being told not only that he was a new man every morning, but that he was really not a man at all but a congeries of mental occurrences. "'It thinks here' is as good sense as 'it rains here,' the thought merely getting a certain colour from where it occurs. . . . We are the spot where a bundle of things is tied: we are the intersection of a multitude of paths." Simultaneously the pennies, chairs, and bricks of the *Not-Self* were being reduced to a series of "spatial apparitions made up of pure instantaneous sensations, enclosed in a temporal pen or corral." Everything, mental and physical, was being handed over to sensate "life," beyond the reach alike of the Intelligence and of Art. People didn't claim to be thinking, they claimed to be interpreting the sense of the age; nor did they claim that there was anything there to think about, only the sensations presented by one's "point of view."

This, reduced to essentials, is the argument of *Time and Western Man*, one of the dozen or so most important books of the twentieth century. The facts it surveys have become common knowledge; its value arises from its violently partisan tone. Disliking as he did the whole direction of contemporary philosophic thought, Lewis was able to expose its extraordinarily ramifying consequences in art, morals, and politics with a thoroughness and vividness denied to the submissive denizen of the time-stream. "Between Personality and Mankind it is always a question of dog and cat," said Arghol. So it didn't surprise Lewis at all that Science, with its cult of anonymity and impersonality, should be busily destroying, by means of behaviorist doctrines, the concept of the Person. A mass-mind, furthermore, offers advantanges to Machiavelli's devotee of Power:

> Politically, of course (and envisaging science as the supreme functioning of the consciousness of the crowd), 'consciousness' is equally objectionable. For so long as that, in any sense, and in whatever disguise, holds out, it is very difficult to get the *individual* firmly by the scruff of the neck, and seat of the trousers, and fling him into the 'Unconscious.'

How the 'Unconscious' comes to be the great democratic stronghold that it is, may require, in passing, a little further explanation.

The 'Unconscious' is really what Plato meant by the "mob of the senses," or rather it is where they are to be found, the mother region of "sensational" life. It is in "our Unconscious" that we live in a state of common humanity. There are no *individuals* in the Unconscious; because a man is only an individual when he is conscious.

It is because Lewis is so far from disinterested that *Time and Western Man* sparkles with epithetic vigor. The section on "Testers" is a minor comic classic.

Professor Watson is, however, the one who has most to say for himself—whose "testing" has a philosophy attached to it. It only consists of a few words repeated in various ways, like an opinionated but quite straightforward parrot: for if you deny the existence of everything except knee-jumps there is not much to say about life. It is a very austere position indeed, and you can become a man of few words.

Everything he touches in the book becomes animated in this way. The causation of Professor Alexander

. . . does not become its 'effect' with any *entrain*. It can be most accurately described as *falling into its effect*, or bursting into it gradually and blindly, with the weight of the oncoming change-stream behind it. It flops with a stagnant release, when sufficiently pushed into the neighbouring compartment, the next in temporal succession.

This is philosophic discussion conducted by an artist whose hyperconsciousness of the Self makes him unusually aware of the *will* (to call it that) behind the gray doctrines he has made it his business to anatomize. *Time and Western Man*, by connecting the most recondite thought with the most banal events, provides every necessary key to the controlling sensibility of our age. "Each man is *every man*, an abstraction, not a *concrete person*." In book, film, and daydream, this is the age of History; and "the historical writer, in every case, is distracting people from a living Present (which becomes dead as the mind withdraws) into a Past into which they have gone to live." Having conjured up a vision of Mr. and Mrs. Citizen of the Future switching on a sound-film and living again "the sandwiches, the tea in the thermos, the ginger beer and mosquitoes, of a dozen years ago," Lewis comments that "People have already somewhat that sense of things laid out side by side, of the unreality of time, and yet of its paramount importance, that the conditions indicated above would breed." This is "the sleep of the machine"; when Professor Norbert Wiener in 1948 announced with some unction that the supersession of Man by Cybernetics was underwritten by the philosophy of Bergson, he was supplying an unconsciously Swiftian footnote to a neglected book then over twenty years old.

The Art of Being Ruled, though genetically the parent book, is most accessible today as a discursive appendix to the book about Time. It concentrates on the political consequences of the modish exaltation of unconsciousness and discontinuity. In *The Diabolical Principle*, ostensibly an attack on the magazine *Transition*, Lewis goes further. The fate-ridden, destiny-worshipping, dogmatically romantic Kreislers of the literary avant-garde exploit a *communizing* frame of mind to which they are prostituting whatever original talents they have been able to corral. With Joyce as impeccable executant and Gertrude Stein ("a whale out of water") as ponderous comic relief, Messrs. Jolas and Paul were busy, he believed, promot-

ing the unconscious, the stream of consciousness, and the mongrelization of European languages, not, as they claimed, for highbrow amusement, but in the interest of an explicit political ideal. "Should *Transition* die tomorrow, there will in due course be another *Transition*, and another, until the Red sea is quite crossed."

Paleface links Sherwood Anderson's clumsy primitivism and D. H. Lawrence's visceral Dark Gods to the inferiority complex with which the conscious intelligence has been saddled. With Lawrence's account of Indians drumming—"There is no individual, isolated experience. . . . It is an experience of the blood-stream, not of the mind or spirit"—Lewis compares a paean to the beauties of Bolshevism. "The Unconscious: The Feminine: The Communist; those are the main principles of action in the mind of Mr. Lawrence, linked in a hot and piping trinity of rough-stuff primitivism, and freudian hot-sex-stuff." ("Communism" is Lewis's label for a state of mind which may or may not be articulated as a political philosophy.) With this welter he links the cult of jazz and the considerable literature of the late 1920's exalting the Negro for the spontaneous, rhythmic "Dark Laughter" it ascribed to him. The romanticization of the black man and the brown man he represents as part of the campaign to undermine the intelligence by making the white man ashamed of possessing so trashy an engine of apprehension. *Paleface* was Lewis's first serious tactical error. Having, as he has since put it, "crashed headlong into a political racket" which exploits for irrelevant purposes the American Negro's very real miseries, he was widely represented as a jack-booted racist. "It was my design to attack the Paleface sentimentalising about the dark skin, and the mysterious dark soul within it (as if all souls were not mysterious), and *not* the Asiatic or the African. . . . Send a peon to Yale or Oxford (as an experiment, not because this would be good for him) and you would find out his abdomen was the same as anybody else's. But he was dear to the avantgardist. I had sinned."

As for *The Doom of Youth* and its satellite *The Old Gang and the New Gang*, they document the familiar case in another area. Among the many groups into which Lewis saw individuals being herded in order to discourage their individuality, age-groups seemed to him the most factitious and the most explicitly political; was not the 1930's the decade of "youth-movements"? Like all Lewis's polemics, this anatomy of "government by inferiority complexes" is elaborately documented, this time, since the "age-war" was being staged for lower-middlebrows, chiefly with newspaper cuttings: *Open the Door to Youth*; *Is Forty Frightening?*; *Mocking the Moderns*; *Over-Eating, the Vice of Middle Age* (Lewis captions this one "Bath-chair article for the Roaring Forties").

The system behind the Enemy's campaigns is simple; assuming the existence of a vast conspiracy embracing everything that was happening in the modern world, he dealt seriatim with its manifestations in order of decreasing complexity. *The Art of Being Ruled* explains in all its details the master strategy by which, in Lewis's view, modern man is being governed: philosophy, literature, popular entertainment and all the engines of publicity are being used to reduce any recalcitrant lumps of individuality and render the world a gray mass to be shaped by power. "There have never been so many people entirely ignorant of everything that is happening to them." The succeeding books survey phases of this silent revolution; first time-philosophy, the most highbrow; then Stein, Joyce, and avant-garde letters; then the more popular modernism of Lawrence and Anderson; lastly, the amiable dramas staged by the press for the hypnotized delectation of

Mr. and Mrs. Everyman. The war was nearly lost by old generals, Everyman was being told; the peace was being gambled away by elderly politicians. (Mr. Eden's greatest political asset was his appearance of youth.) As for Everyman himself, he should be thankful, suffering as he does from prostate disorders, slowed reflexes, baldness, obesity, and obsolete patterns of thought, to draw his pension at forty and make way for a younger man. That eases the labor market too.

Now that we have achieved an alarmed consciousness of the adman, and can observe Mr. Gallup's reporters asking us how we choose to be exploited, it is difficult not to agree with nearly all of Lewis's particular diagnoses. It is more difficult to be satisfied about a conspiracy, since that involves knowing who the conspirators are. In *The Doom of Youth*, where he is dealing directly with the mechanisms governing the labor market, the standard of living, and the press, Lewis has little difficulty in establishing the Magnate as a personal devil. But though a Magnate might applaud an emotional equivalent of Bergson's philosophy if it were served up to him (of course, it is served up to him—for instance as Science Fiction), one has difficulty in imagining him presiding over the esoteric transformations described in *Time and Western Man*. In this difficulty Lewis has recourse to his old intuition that Hanp is a crowd.

> "Big Business" does not depend upon the *personal* initiative, energy, and resource of a *single person*: it is a group-system: and to that extent, certainly, it is more "impersonal" than the old individualist industry.

By analogy, it is a "group-system" that is breaking down the West; Bergson and behaviorism, Dale Carnegie and the Carnegie Libraries, *The Times* and *Transition*, all lean in the same direction though their intercommunication is virtually nil.

A group-system breaks down the personality because it is itself impersonal: the reigning Arghol makes Hanp in his own image. This fact didn't of itself attract Lewis to personal rule, even though the aim of the Vortex was "to create individuals, wherever found." He called Mussolini "a noisy ice-cream agitator," and has repeatedly made it plain that he regards the tyrants of history, enclosed in their monotonous ritual of power, as pretty depressing. Shakespeare, he points out, wasn't interested in them until they had lost the capacity for action and belatedly turned into persons. Regarding rule as inevitable, he didn't before the late 1930's much care what form it took, nor did he imagine that the sensual average man much cared either, so long as he was permitted his illusion of freedom. He attacked the *Zeitgeist*, he said, only because "from the standpoint of genius" he regarded the transformation of the outside world into a vast Nursery as undesirable; it would leave the artist no place to go on taking his leave of "the most oppressive and stuffy features of the traditional Family Circle."[1]

Notes

1. This is from *The Doom of Youth*, which is addressed to a large public by hypothesis uninterested in the arts. To the different public of *Time and Western Man* he didn't conceal his distaste for a set of critical values that conspired to exalt every sort of painting and writing but that of Wyndham Lewis. Lewis never conceals his personal interests, but he presents different ones to different publics. This must never be forgotten in any attempt to reconcile his various statements of principle. On the other hand it must not be forgotten that he has always tended to believe in the exhaustiveness of what he was writing at the moment.

THOMAS H. CARTER
"Rationalist in Hell"

Kenyon Review, Spring 1956, pp. 326–36

The opening volume of Lewis' singular fantasy, *The Childermass*, was issued early in 1928, and its publishers spoke hopefully of sections two and three being ready soon. Although its impact, then and later, was relatively negligible (unlike *The Apes of God*, it pilloried no recognizable victims), the book was not without readers. "I am delighted with the first 100 pages of *Childermass*," W. B. Yeats wrote Olivia Shakespeare, "interested and a little bored by the next. But these 100 pages are a masterpiece." Despite the publishers' optimism, however, the promised continuation failed to appear. Now, some twenty-seven years later, *The Childermass* is ostensibly being completed: *The Human Age* contains two more sections, and a concluding section is said to be in preparation. One says "ostensibly" for a reason: the two volumes are separated by a good deal more than time. *The Childermass*, seen from this distance, is a brilliant, exasperating curiosity; *The Human Age*—for which no American printing has been announced— is a serious, even profound work of art.

It would be as much a mistake, let me add, simply to dismiss *The Childermass* as it would be to accept it without reservation. Yeats was mostly right, though perhaps for irrelevant reasons (he liked the first hundred pages because they described "the first region of the dead as the ghosts everywhere describe it"). Wyndham Lewis has never, as far as I know, written anything that did not have, for varying reasons, some considerable interest; and *The Childermass* apotheosizes and exhibits permanently, as if under glass, what remains the best known, as it surely is the most dazzling phase in his development.

When *The Childermass* came out, Lewis was forty-four, a sometime associate of Pound, Joyce, and Eliot, and recognized as both painter and writer. He had published, rewritten, and published again his novel *Tarr*; his unusual short stories ("little monuments of logic," as he called them) had been collected in *The Wild Body*. The two great salutary polemics, *The Art of Being Ruled* and *Time and Western Man* (which one suspects of having had a greater influence than is nowadays acknowledged), were already in print; and the first half of *Paleface* had appeared in Lewis' own periodical, *The Enemy*. On Lewis' work of this period *The Childermass* depends heavily—so heavily, in fact, that I doubt its right to much independent existence at all.

The scene of *The Childermass*, we are told, is located "outside Heaven" on the "Plain of Death," which is "full of an empty whirling underneath—its movements signify nothing," where everything is undercut by a "fine angry senseless music . . . an unintelligible beating of the air. . . ." Gathered on this sorry plain, "living" in a sort of camp, are the disreputable dead, awaiting a possible admission into "Heaven"—into, that is, the Magnetic City separated from the plain by a river whose waters consist of "Time stuff." This way-station of the after-life is presided over by the Bailiff, an incredible grimacing, polemicizing, bloodthirsty little hunchback; a rude, sinister version of Mr. Punch who holds court once a day to determine the eventual fate of the dead men, who regard him as a great favorite.

As *The Childermass* opens, two old friends meet each other for the first time since death; it is implied that they have been out of touch even before that. (As Yeats complained, *The Childermass* is indeed obscure.) They are Pullman, a prim schoolmasterish figure, and Satterthwaite (commonly known as Satters), the former's ex-fag. Despite whatever may have happened to them since leaving school, they slip immediately into the old college relationship, in which Pullman is patently the master. (They have, in any case, practically no memory.) As they move about the indeterminate plain, they encounter the "peons"; these constitute a work force of pseudo-individuals who, although they were created by God and hence cannot be destroyed, possess such an indistinct reality that they can be said scarcely to exist at all. Pullman and Satters, of course, are not as far removed from the same state as they care to believe.

What we are getting, pretty clearly, is a poker-faced Lewisian parody of M. Bergson's notion of the human consciousness as a series of sense impressions linked merely by a temporal continuity, and persuaded by memory that they compose an intelligent being. Lewis' intention becomes evident as Pullman and Satters, their physical condition shuttling from youth to age and back (a shuttling, that is, in *time*), continue their exploration of the plain. The most vividly realized incident in *The Childermass* occurs when they wander into a "Time hallucination," which turns out to be a Hollywood-like re-creation of the England of some centuries ago, reduced to a diminished 3-D perspective. In it, exclaims Pullman, the perfect time-tourist, even the air is better to breathe!

The rationale of *The Childermass*, it is clear, must be sought in Lewis' polemical writing of the same period. In *Time and Western Man*, Lewis set himself, as we see today, squarely against the main drift of contemporary philosophic thought—specifically against the influence of Bergson, Whitehead, Alexander, James, Spengler, Russell, Croce, even Einstein, at the crucial point where their doctrines appeared to overlap, namely, their conception of Time. On the level of art, he attacked, as corollary manifestations of the same impulse, the work of Pound, Joyce, Robert McAlmon, Gertrude Stein (with whom he coupled, interestingly enough, Anita Loos), Bloomsbury, and the *Transition* coterie *en masse*. As alternative for what he considered the hypostatization of flux and change, Lewis held out for the classical, "spatializing" mind of antiquity, which offered, he contended, the only climate favorable to artistic creation—or, indeed, to thought in general.

The first hundred pages of *The Childermass*, then, are nothing more, as they are nothing less, than a sardonic dramatization of Bergson's *la durée*. It is as if Lewis had said: "You want a world without Space, a featureless world given over to Time? Very well; here is what it will be like!" This explains why, of course, the entire book is composed in the *present* tense.

Because of Lewis' purpose in *The Childermass*, it is useless to expect the book to conform to the structural demands of the conventional novel. Its over three hundred pages appear to encompass a period of not more than three hours in duration. Pullman's and Satters' excursion over the Plain of Death, beginning at what apparently passes for morning in a landscape composed of Time, lasts for but an hour (Satters thinks it longer, but Pullman is expert on such matters); it occupies a third of the book's space. Afterwards they return to camp to watch the Bailiff's court; the remainder of the space is devoted almost exclusively to the gyrations of this character.

The capering Bailiff seems quite without literary antecedents; and this is natural enough, since he is not, I think, strictly a *literary* creation: he is both more and less than a character in a book. With an exaggerated showman's delight, this sinister little figure cajoles and threatens his charges, expounding to them the Time-doctrines of their new existence,

and destroying them if they become rebellious. In rapid succession, he imitates the "stutter" of Gertrude Stein, parodies the "dark laughter" of Sherwood Anderson and D. H. Lawrence, and rehearses, in a take-off on *Work in Progress*, Lewis' own minor quarrel with Joyce. Like a sponge he absorbs all sides of a controversy, reducing distinctions to his own soggy substance. Then he spews them back perverted. His Marxism, for instance, is derived not from Marx but from the popular vulgarization of Marxist ideology. Likewise his Bergsonianism. *Eternity*, the Bailiff informs his admirers, *is in love with the productions of Time*:

> The Eternal loves Time if you do not! The only motive for His weakness for you is in your capacity as *factor of Time*, that is your principal not to say unique claim upon his interest. Some of you disregard your debt to Time in a really unaccountable way. Time is the mind of Space—Space is the mere body of Time. Time is Life, Time is Money, Time is all good things!—Time is God!

The Human Age (consisting of two regular-length novels, *Monstre Gai* and *Malign Fiesta*, bound together in a single handsome volume) differs radically in both intent and execution from its flashy, distant predecessor. (Its true affinities, though it continues in the broad outline of the earlier book, are with serious fictions like *The Vulgar Streak* and the recent fine *Self Condemned*.) What is most immediately apparent about this latest work is the remarkable austerity of Lewis' prose: his style here, finally purged of all that is merely showy, is an economical, transparent instrument devoted self-effacingly to rendering the somber action from which it takes its tone. One could not help feeling, in reading *The Childermass*, that its periodic verbal coruscations were studied to conceal a certain hesitation on the author's part—that somehow he didn't quite trust the capacity of his events and characters to stand by themselves, unsupported by a creator who didn't really believe in them himself. This is no longer true. Pullman and Satters, who have managed at last to sneak into the Magnetic City, are metamorphosed into people of indisputable reality. In fact Pullman, now restored to his earthly intellect, furnishes the central intelligence of the book; it is above all his story. The importance of Satters is correspondingly diminished, until he becomes finally little more than a token reminder of the inescapable ubiquity of mindless corporality, the eternal boy-man.

The Magnetic City itself, which they had trustfully believed was Heaven, turns out to be crushingly like the old earth, only (as we might say) more so. It is populated by a horde of vacuous idiots who, beneath the rims of identical *chapeaux melons*, spend all their time sunning themselves on innumerable cafe terraces, engaged in trivial conversation, or else grinning vacantly. No one works, or is even allowed to work: they are supported by the state, which furnishes them with money proportioned inversely according to their previous earthly condition. The street shops display garish, vulgar clothing suited precisely to their taste. The population, like that of the Bailiff's camp, is entirely male, and homosexuality is prevalent. (For Lewis, the matter of sexual perversion, which he defines primarily as a state of mind, is symbolic of a given society's internal decay: a particularly distasteful kind of dry rot.) Several characteristic Lewisian targets are potted in passing: the youth cult, the British clubman, the homegrown fascist.

We must not suppose, however, that the opening of *The Human Age* is merely another attack on the welfare state—although as an attack it is a considerable success; polemical tags, the bare bones of argument, are still visible, but they have been absorbed into the urgency of the narrative. When he composed *Rotting Hill* (1951), Lewis found himself, despite the characteristic *brio* he brought to his job, pretty well limited to what he observed around him; his imagination was not powerfully engaged, and the book, though full of good things, seemed at last to hang rather unsatisfactorily between fiction and fact. The scheme of *Monstre Gai*, on the other hand, imposes no such limitations: Lewis is free to seize on certain aspects of Clement Attlee's England and carry them to a logical extreme, thereby positing a peculiarly pointless society suspended over a void. The result is undeniably satirical, but only incidentally so; what emerges most solidly is a sense of nagging unreality, the familiar made strange. It should be remembered that Pullman and Satters are not Dantesque pilgrims who expect to return to a known world, but literally dead men; and it is their attempt to attach themselves to something concrete that brings out the underlying hollowness of the Magnetic City.

This element of strangeness, established early and firmly, helps make it possible, I think, for Lewis to reverse the trick and introduce its complement: to render the supernatural, that is, as immediate and natural, as available, to us as the air we breathe or the world we daily see. Power in the Magnetic City, as one would perhaps expect, is divided between two antagonistic factions, one headed by the subversive Bailiff, the other by an official governor known as the Padishah. Between these two and their supporters a deal of plotting and jockeying for position goes on, at times almost reminiscent of Conrad or the early Graham Greene. Lewis hasn't, as a matter of fact, so exploited his real knack as a reporter of action since *The Revenge for Love* (1937), which seems almost sprawling if we compare it to the stark compression of the present narrative. So in a way, *Monstre Gai* is a novel of political intrigue, but with this difference, the Bailiff is an emissary from Hell, the Padishah an angel dispatched by Heaven to rule over this "distant outpost." Their struggle—with Pullman caught unhappily in the middle, but drawn toward the Bailiff—is the ancient one between Evil and Good. Pullman's ethical position, as representative of intelligent mankind, may be ambiguous, but theirs is not.

Hell itself—that unfriendly foreign power—decides to "intervene," staggering the city first by a blight of insects, then an attack of huge dragons. Some of the harrowing *presence* of these scenes undoubtedly comes from Lewis' knowledge of London during the Blitz; but it is elevated by the clinical detachment of the prose to a point where it imposes its own vertiginous reality on the reader. It is not even necessary to insist that this is *not* London, but the Magnetic City: we accept it because it is set before us in all its shabby and painful detail, no more to be scoffed at than (say) a newspaper account of an air raid.

Monstre Gai, which closes as Pullman and Satters flee with the Bailiff from the Magnetic City, defines clearly the fundamental issues that are at stake. *Malign Fiesta* puts them into terms which we are not used to hearing in the 20th Century. It is set in Hell: not that little hell man carries around in him, but the genuine big Hell dedicated traditionally to deceased sinners. The subject itself is horrific, one which writers (nowadays unsustained by theology) tend to shy away from, or at best approach obliquely, like Sartre; and it is major. Wyndham Lewis no more than Dante shirks his vision of Hell.

Throughout *The Human Age* Lewis' steady invention of meaningful event seldom falters; he doesn't need to overwhelm us with a welter of indiscriminate horror: he can make his dramatic point with a single weighted incident though he knows very well that there is more than one kind of horror. There is, for instance, the lord Sammael, who is sometimes amused to call himself the Devil. The most civilized person in Hell, he supervises the punishment center with an awesome efficiency, as both a favor to his old friend God, and because he would like, if he could, to destroy the human race, sinners and saints impartially. He is very cordial to Pullman, however, who is after all something of a tourist in Hell, and conducts him into an inner office where there is a cradle containing the baby of two executed sinners; this manifestly innocent victim, Sammael has undertaken to raise. Pullman is puzzled but pleased.

> From the basket at the side of the fireplace came a scream so piercing that Pullman jumped: it was followed by the despairing cry of "Maman maman maman maman!" And there it stopped, for Sammael had sprung across the room like an enormous cat, and covered the child's mouth with his hand.
> "Alaine, tu fais de vilaines rêves, n'est-ce pas, ma petite?"
> Sammael, with wonderful alacrity, lifted a hypodermic syringe from a metal box, plunged it into the child's arm. "Te voila qui retrouve ta maman dans les songes, n'est-ce pas! Va, ma chatte, toujours de belles rêves et à tout l'heure, ma petite Alaine!"

There are scenes in *Malign Fiesta* more overtly awful; but here is the essence of the diabolic.

The punishment center itself, through which Pullman receives a courtesy tour, Lewis constructs with the grimmest possible logic. It is operated, as we by now expect, along the lines of an efficient welfare hospital, properly devoted to keeping its patients alive as long as possible, but inverted to inflict upon them the maximum amount of harm. Its showpiece is a crude parody—the quaking Pullman calls it a superior "critique"—of Dante's *Inferno*, based not on any principle of justice but merely that of "realism" (as witness the utterly debased version of Paola and Francesca). Lewis' distance from Dante, in fact, gives us something of a key towards understanding his Hell: in such a place, it is not merely the punishment that is meaningless, but the fact of human existence. When a sinner, for example, has been driven past the limits of his endurance, and even the marvels of medicine are insufficient to restore him to suffering, he is casually destroyed; the superintendent explains apologetically that, due to overcrowding, they can't manage anything so spectacular as a Judgment Day, but they do try to keep accurate records.

Our understanding of *The Human Age* depends to a great degree on our grasp of the character of James Pullman, who is a genuine if subdued Lewisian hero. When alive on earth, he was, as the flattery of the Bailiff early reminds him, the greatest writer of his day. In appearance and background, he is distinctly reminiscent of James Joyce, but the sharp analytic quality of his mind he shares with Lewis himself. Like the other Lewis heroes, he generates from within his own consciousness a set of brilliantly logical principles which he proceeds to apply to the external world; and like the other Lewis heroes, he miscalculates. *The Human Age* registers the stages of his enlightenment.

As a live man acting under the guise of disinterest, Pullman hastened to put his gift of intellect at the disposal of the wealthy and powerful. When we encounter him in the Magnetic City, gravitating almost inevitably into the Bailiff's orbit, he himself realizes that he is repeating the pattern of his previous existence, but with this terrible difference: that here "suddenly . . . you would find yourself involved with a powerful demon, whereas on Earth he would merely be dear old so-and-so, a rich patron of the arts, or a go-ahead publisher." Spurred by desperation, he brings into play his appalling powers of rationalization: as a man he is interested only in what is intelligent; and since all perfection, including God's, must by definition lack objective critical intelligence—must, in short, be stupid—he elects the Bailiff as being the supernatural element most favorable to man.

In Hell, he recognizes at once his error in coming, but still finds himself irresistibly attracted to Sammael, as Sammael apparently is to him; on the human and divine levels respectively, they represent intelligence. The Bailiff, the "monstre gai," stands somewhere in between: he is part human, part divine, and in him both orders are corrupted. In a very definite way, this figure indicates the thematic center of the book. (I hope it is clear that although these characters assume a schematic value in terms of structure, they are far, at any point in the narrative, from seeming abstractions.)

For what Sammael proposes to Pullman is nothing less than a liquidation of Hell; he is bored by the essential, tiresome stupidity of the average angel, and is prepared to mate those who followed him from Heaven with female sinners to overcome it; but he is not himself devious enough to put his grand design into effect. That is where Pullman fits in. Their Bailiff-like collaboration results in the "malign fiesta," intended to bring Sammael's charges and the available women together under propitious circumstances; it is a senseless mélange of pointless contests, incredible buffoonery and noise, jazz concerts, and insane displays of sex; an ironic apotheosis of the banal. As Sammael rises to open the festivities, Pullman is gifted with belated perception:

> How tremendously good looking he was, as he stood there dominating his fellow angels by his combination of legendary beauty and matchless intelligence—yet how false, thought Pullman. This was merely a defiance of God. In Sammael's heart there was no great purpose, but the old, cold pride. . . . Pullman . . . was smitten with a revelation. To save his skin, he had been actively assisting at the annihilation of the Divine.

As he concludes this disturbing meditation, Pullman meets the friendly glance of the Bailiff, and "As their eyes met the Gay Monster winked."

The success of the fiesta, and the attendant corruption of *both* human and divine, is apparently the one thing Heaven will not tolerate. While Pullman cowers in his room, a large body of militant white angels defeat with ridiculous ease the massed strength of Hell. In his pride and terror, Pullman has for the second time misjudged God. Before he has time even to think, he is seized gently but firmly by two of God's soldiers, told "No harm will come to you," and whisked off to—where?

We are told by the publishers that a final volume, called *The Trial of Man*, will take place in Heaven; its substance is to consist of a debate on the merits of the human as against the divine; and it is to be present at this debate that Pullman has been so unceremoniously spirited away. Whether Lewis can invest, or desires to invest, his Heaven with the indisputable actuality of his Hell, we must wait to see; in literature, one need hardly add, Heaven does not come easy. Wyndham Lewis has been, and I judge remains, one of the most determined rationalists of our age. Whatever its qualities, Heaven—if it is indeed Heaven—will be the home of God, therefore the intelligent center of the universe. And as Sammael readily admits, God—who conquered Hell to keep the divine order from being corrupted by and merged with the human—*values* man. His reason, at the end of *The Human Age*, has not been revealed to us.

Recent criticism has accustomed us to ask what transcendent *meaning* inheres in a literary work; in regard to a book like *A Fable*, it is the only question we can ask. *The Human Age* may be coerced into "meaning" many things. It can hardly avoid being read as a severe commentary on contemporary English life; it will adjust, surprisingly enough, into the scheme of a rigorously austere Calvinism; and certainly the characters become infected with the Demon of Progress. But none of these readings, nor any of the others readily available, begins to exhaust it. Speaking in 1922 of *Ulysses*, Lewis' friend Pound wrote:

> . . . for the first time since Dante the harpies, the furies are found living, symbols taken in the real, the contemporary; nothing depends on mythology or dogmatic faith. Proportions are reaffirmed.

In a sentence, Pound gives us perhaps the most impressive aspect of *The Human Age*: "Proportions are reaffirmed." It does what only the strongest books can do; even in its excesses, it helps put our lives into perspective.

VERNON YOUNG
"The Late Lamenting Wyndham Lewis"
Hudson Review, Autumn 1976, pp. 464–70

First Citizen: I say unto you, what he hath done famously, he did it to that end: though soft-conscienced men can be content to say it was for his country, he did it to please his mother, and to be partly proud; which he is, even to the altitude of his virtue.

(*Coriolanus*, I. 1)

Among these survivals of so-called criticism,[1] "André Malraux" (originally published in *The Writer and The Absolute*, 1952) is perhaps the exhibit *in extremis* of Wyndham Lewis' elliptical strategy—character assassination with sterilized instruments: the establishing of guilt by association (Malraux = revolution = life in action = T. E. Lawrence = execution of an Arab); the quoting (and distortion) of an isolated passage while disregarding the character of the whole work, the whole man; the imposition on one writer of the shortcomings of another with whom close affinities are alleged (Jean-Paul Sartre is the key scapegoat here) and, prominently in this instance, the employment of another critic (principally Claude Mauriac) to ratify one's own adverse judgement—and incidentally to rattle the reader by leaving him uncertain as to whether a given statement is a paraphrase of Malraux's thought or an obliquely edited version of it!

Briefly in another context Lewis had praised the concretely focused method of the novel, *Man's Fate*; in no single parenthesis of this essay is there such a concession, nor any other, for the man who by 1952 had published his major novels and his first masterpiece of another genre (to be reshaped as *The Voices of Silence*). Of the fewer than twenty paragraphs in this seven-page essay, not one independently encounters Malraux *on the page*; the accusations (analysis would be an impertinent synonym) are largely conveyed by others (even by anti-Malraux Communists!) engaged by Lewis to support his frivolous and defamatory charge that Malraux was merely a "political flirt," that he was violent to the extent of glorifying murder as a test of complete manhood and that although he never became a member of the Communist Party he was more reprehensible (to Lewis) than Sartre, who did so—and, at the moment of writing, the only identity Malraux visibly presented to Lewis was that of "publicity chief in the entourage of the French Franco, General Charles De Gaulle" (*sic*). I shall resist the temptation to cite the numerous expletives with which this incredible document is saturated. The destructive pivot is Lewis' philistine interpretation of a Malraux aphorism reworded by Mauriac: "In imposing his personality on the external world man finds the only outlet which remains open to him, his one and only chance of escaping—imperfectly—from Nothingness." Lewis, triumphant, proceeds to attribute Nothingness to the man, Malraux, when what Malraux (or Mauriac) had been contending was that Man, inhabitant of Nothingness, creates the destiny that rescues him from the anonymity of a mote in space. Lewis retorts:

> How this *action* theory [?] of "imposing your personality upon the world" may very easily develop into a quite substantial *power-complex* may be judged from pondering these further words of Malraux's (sic). "To lead, to be he who decides, to coerce. That is to live."

These "further words" I *have* pondered and find nothing in them with which to quarrel. "To lead" *is* a good thing, "to be he who decides, to coerce"; that *is* to live: it's one way, it's a way Lewis himself coveted; since, as a literary intellectual, he was seldom able to coerce anybody, could make nothing happen, he named the grapes as sour. Leadership *is* an admirable position; coercion is as much the prerogative of a teacher or critic as it is of a sergeant-major or a Minister of Propaganda. Lewis wanted it construed in one channel, negatively, as the symptom of brutality or autocracy. "How many people" he dared to ask, "were there in Western Europe between the wars nursing feverish power-complexes, beside the Duces and Führers?" We don't know how many there may have been but Wyndham Lewis was one—it's in his dossier forever.[2]

Lewis' animosity, ranging from medium rare to overdone, was not restricted to such as Malraux, Sartre, Orwell and Hemingway who sought political salvation or were cognizant at least that political action was a pregnant factor in the daily life of mankind. Sooner or later he vented his spite on anyone who wasn't going his way, even on D. H. Lawrence who, to a degree, was!—which Lewis failed to see, preoccupied as he was with the single aspect of Lawrence he loathed. As publisher and polemicist, Lewis was in the vanguard of those effecting a tidal movement in that oceanic inundation of literature and art which soon characterized the Modern Age, born in agony and earthquake with War I. That no one (in the literary world) except himself truly understood the nature of the Modernism Lewis shortly decided. What Erich Heller has aptly called the Discovery and Colonization of Inwardness—perhaps the best broad definition we have—would have been summarily rejected by Lewis (a Parnassian at heart), for he was speedily quarreling, at length or intermittently, and without shred of compromise, with all the writers of his day who shared many of his assumptions and whom he should have part-time admired, even if their aims were not in all particulars identical: Pound, Eliot, Joyce, D. H. Lawrence, Virginia Woolf, *ad infinitum. He would not share.* With no little sophistry in the argument, he proposed an "external approach to things"; for him this meant "relying upon the evidence of the *eye* rather than of the more emotional organs of sense . . . . And as for pure satire [his *sine qua non*] there the eye is supreme." Distinctions of aesthetic theory and practise were not seriously being defended here. He simply could not, or did not wish to, see people except through a distorting lens. Often, in his fiction, he wrote as if he had envisioned a scene with his *painter's* eye, then translated it into a verbal equivalent. Strictly read, his prose, excepting that of two or three novels and the short stories, more purely addresses the ear than the eye. His characters tend to

become magnetic fields, around which cluster *words*, barely contaminated by common associations of flesh or speech. The following passage, queerly splendid, is from *Childermass* (1928)—two men are traversing an unspecified landscape.

> The scene is steadily redistributed, vamped from position to position intermittently at its boundaries. It revolves upon itself in a slow material maelstrom. Satters sickly clings to his strapping little champion: sounds rise on all hands like the sharp screech of ripping calico, the piercing alto of the slate-pencil, or the bassooning of imposing masses, frictioning each other as they slowly turn in concerted circles.
>
> Never before have there been so many objects of uncertain credentials or origin: as it grows more intricate Pullman whisks them forwards, peering into the sky for lost stars twirling about as he has to face two ways at once on the *qui vive* for the new setting, fearing above all reflections, on the look-out for optical traps, lynx-eyed for threatening ambushes of anomalous times behind the orderly furniture of Space or hidden in objects to confute the solid at the last moment, every inch a pilot.[3]

For my part, I can no more read several pages of this with undivided attention than I can a comparable number from Lawrence Durrell or Vladimir Nabokov. The ostensible subjects of the narrative are blurred and discomposed by the opacity of the language; a day later I can't remember what [if] on earth I've been reading!

Since we learn much about a writing man if we find that he prefers Homer to Plato, Dante to Goethe, or Goethe to Rousseau, the backward reach of Lewis' admiration should be revelatory. His ancestral mentor, *he* fondly thought, was Montaigne, with whose temper he closely identified his own: pathetic identification, when you compare the Frenchman's moderate skepticism and his open-ended doubt of his own doubt—*Que sais-je?*—with the brook-no-argument salvos of Lewis. If not more comical, just as strange: Lewis' Shakespeare, a reluctant Elizabethan, compound of Montaigne and Machiavelli, who just *happened* to be born under the Tudors; suppressing a ferocious yawn, the man from Stratford tossed off thirty-odd plays, the best of which had as their subject Roman or British rulers whose problems and personalities actually bored him though he had a remote sympathy for his tiresome heroes when they were most nauseated by the weight of office, life and time. The greater number of his kings "had come to a violent and stupid end, clamoring about their divine right and their kingly ways, defiant or idiotically remorseful." He "probably" thought little more of these kings "than Gibbon did of his gallery of despots." While "tragically participating" in their experiences, he had no substantial confidence in their actuality in time and place, no more than he had for his commoners. "They were much more mirrors held up to his tired and baffled mind than they were the mirrors of any nature that he objectively could know." (We have Lewis' word for it!) Richard II's torrential grief and his image of the "little pin" penetrating so easily the life-wall and hence, "farewell King," was not conceivably an emotional concept to be entertained by the Plantagenet; it was merely "a reflection of the critical experiences of the poet." And so on until the end of Shakespeare's days (in the theatre) when, by Lewis' reasoning, he was equally uninvolved with the qualms of Macbeth, the deflation of Othello, the hyena scatology of Iago, the diatribes of Timon or the pride of Coriolanus; the despair, resentment and bleak disgust were Shakespeare's alone (for aught that Lewis says, he was born bleak!): they had no objective correlative in characters who might plausibly be expected to share such emotions! (Lewis is peculiarly diffident towards any conviction which *Coriolanus* should have conveyed to him and he was quite misguided, I'd say, in his refusal to find immense dramatic pathos in that great play.)

Naturally, it is Lewis, himself, who sees Shakespeare's kings as coming to a "stupid end . . . idiotically remorseful." As for the "little pin," *any* image might be described as "a reflection of the critical experience of the poet," without thereby being exempt as the probable experience of a Plantagenet—just as *Lewis'* images are reflections of *his* experience of Shakespeare! And that experience will permit no shade of political discernment in his subject. ". . . Nor was he [Shakespeare] innocent enough to suppose that he was living beneath a more oppressive system than the next, the next after that, or the one before it." I think we can safely conclude that Shakespeare was sufficiently "innocent" to be convinced that he was *not* living under as oppressive a system as Englishmen had been, let's say, between the mid-fourteenth century and the end of the fifteenth (*Richard III*, for example, displays a too ready acceptance of Richard's wholly malign character as reconstructed by Tudor historians). Shakespeare was in all breathing things a man of his time. Lewis' attempt to make him radically detached from his governing subject (the vicissitudes of the power-driven man) which, with passionate intensity, he pursued for forty years, is preposterous. Whatever else, Shakespeare was a Tudor propagandist—not a hired one, he didn't need to be: like most of his contemporaries he was fully aware that he was living at a crucial hour in the stabilization of the nation-state, prepared by Henry VII and maintained, despite reversals and calamity under Edward VI and Mary Tudor, by Henry VIII and Elizabeth. As much as, if not more than, his fellow Elizabethans, he must have had a wholesome dread of civil anarchy and a return to the lawless disunity of Richard II's reign and the decades of the York-Lancaster feuds. (One reason it took nearly a half-century to disseat the Stuarts was precisely because the English, until forced by royal obstinacy, were reluctant to plunge the country into another era of internecine warfare.)

Richard II is supposed by many to have been a warning to Essex and his party; whether or not this was so, the play was in any case an object lesson of the disaster which overtakes a monarch when recklessly indifferent to the obligations he has constitutionally inherited. That Shakespeare's Richard was driven by grief into reams of poetry does not alter Shakespeare's view of him as a fallible *man*, fallen from grace. That most of Shakespeare's later protagonists (and many of his earlier ones) discover at the ninth hour that they are, after all, mortal, that the glories of their blood and state are shadows, not substantial things, is scarcely an inference that *as* princes or tribunes they had negligible value for the playwright! Lewis drew nearly all his nutshell demonstrations of Shakespeare's "tired and baffled mind" from the late plays, relegating seven-eighths of the poet's production, belittling the diversity with which Shakespeare embodied throngs of common humanity, eluding the prevailing convention of "graves, worms and epitaphs" that permeated *all* Elizabethan and Jacobean literature and—most seriously, for Lewis' argument—suppressing the important circumstance that among these late plays (together with the world-weariness, the misanthropic outcries against human vanity and ingratitude and the suspicion that life is a sort of phantasmal dream—all these the natural heritage of any clear-sighted man approaching the end of his span—among these very plays which, for Lewis, illustrated nothing but anarchy and lordly indifference towards concepts of law and station) are two of the most eloquent expositions of a necessary order in the civil scheme, destroyed by political man at his peril, ever composed by Shakespeare: namely, his facetious adaptation of Plutarch on the primacy of the belly, argued by Menenius Agrippa (*Coriolanus*, I. 1.) and the magnificent discourse on "Degree" by Ulysses in *Troilus and Cressida* (I. 3.).

Why was it mandatory for Lewis to see Shakespeare as a man with no vital interest in the multitudes he animated, as a playwright of no visible development or trace of philosophy, as a poet of no viable connection with the peopled land which had fertilized him? We need not exert ourselves to find an answer, pardonably Freudian, to this riddle. The artist, especially in our time, frequently entertains a sense of himself as autonomous, unrelated, all but unconditioned: hence his normal fear of the *critic*, who minimizes his personal stature by *striving* to relate him—to his culture, his contemporaries or predecessors, his parental sources, whatever. Lewis suffered to an exaggerated degree, from the familar form of solipsism; he spent a lifetime, sweating to *dissociate* himself from anyone whom he might seem to resemble, anyone from whom he had learned anything, anyone who had committed the same errors as he or anyone who had contrived similar answers to the same vexed questions he asked: "as if a man were author of himself / And knew no other kin." Lewis' childhood situation was clearly the prime mover behind his unremitting effort to reject all upon whom he could be said to have leaned. Father, divorced from Mother, was virtually absent as the boy grew up, appearing once in a while, like an aloof God, to write a cheque, then disappearing into the blue. "Later," W. K. Rose has succinctly put it,[4] "as the boy became a young man, their contacts—and the cheques—dwindled." . . .

No father on the scene but happily a doting mother (to whom young Lewis, in letters from Paris, confided freely, if archly, his sexual conquests!). The sequel is classic. Lewis, growing to manhood fatherless, over-developed his superego and, further, expected the world to indulge him, as Mother had done, without reproof or limit. Whenever it did not oblige he expended a tireless amount of energy disputing and/or repudiating everyone who dared criticise a syllable of his work or take its character lightly. He seems never to have overlooked a slight, challenging all deprecations, however *en passant* (the letters make this abundantly clear.). At the same time, like so many male others deprived of fatherly authority, he not only lived his days searching for another father-figure and, of course, speedily impeaching all possibilities (especially among *living* candidates); he also craved to become a father-model himself (intellectually, at any rate); the evidence is plentiful in his correspondence with a young Finnish writer living in Canada, sustained over a surprising number of years because, it would appear, this chap listened to Lewis obediently, gave him no lip and, above all, was no professional threat to him whatever.

One of the few "modern" (but safely dead) writers Lewis positively admired was Flaubert. "To him almost everything and everybody are suspect, except the artist . . . . (At the mere sight of a politician he would turn aside and violently spit)." Here, then, was the Lewis ideal: a Shakespeare shaped in his own image with a tired, baffled and hating mind; a Flaubert who tolerated nobody and turned aside to spit. We can be sure that by "politician" Lewis meant the gamut, from statesman to local party hack. Never in his life had Lewis a glimpse of Disraeli's conception that "A nation was a work of art and of time." If he had such a glimpse, he found it expedient to bury it out of sight lest it impede his solitary, sacred progress across acres of nothingness. The nation did not exist; history had no mutations; the world at common large did not exist; nobody existed, if Lewis disallowed them. Inevitably he came to doubt his own existence. *Self Condemned*, his last novel, based patently on his miserable interlude in Canada (from which he personally escaped in relief to perfidious Albion), ends with its protagonist accepting That Teaching Job at an American university (the like of which Lewis had once begged for, though he despised academics as heartily as any other tribe) where, he closes his story, "the Faculty had no idea that it was a glacial shell of a man who had come to live among them, mainly because they were themselves unfilled with anything more than a little academic stuffing."

". . . and to be partly proud". A pity. Lewis could write with exalted acerbity when the bit was out of his mouth. We might have need of him now if we could more easily dismiss his foolishness and accept his sagacity. Not a critic to be durably relied upon, his occasional flash insights were memorable. In this volume, his tribute to the Russian novelists is the most sound. More pertinent than many of the more scandalous essays on his literary foes is a letter which might well have been included, in which, to the point and comprehensively, he exposed, in American circles, academic circles not least, "the ferocious and aggressive pride in the possession of money."[5] And after he had weathered his demented toleration of Hitler and Stalin he recognized, more explicitly than D. H. Lawrence, that Communism, "government by inferiority complex," was linked in our time with the cult of woman, the cult of youth, the cult of the colored skin, a quadrivium expressing a world-wide revulsion from maturity, from individual and ethnic self-confidence, from the sovereignty of hard-won intelligence—and from the alleviating grace of irony.

Notes

1. *Enemy Salvoes: Selected Writings on Literature*, by Wyndham Lewis. Edited by C. J. Fox. General Introduction by C. H. Sisson. Barnes & Noble.
2. January–April, 1931, Lewis wrote a defense of the Nazis in *Time and Tide*, later published in book form, wherein he announced, among other idiocies, that the Third Reich favored an "aristocracy of the intellect." From the subsequent damage his reputation suffered, Lewis learned slowly; thirteen years later he was defending Stalin, who had "a working state-system, with the air purged of humbug." (The air was purged, that's for sure!) See *The Letters of Wyndham Lewis* edited by W. K. Rose (Methuen, 1963). Letter to Gerty T. Cori, Aug. 20, 1944.
3. Quoted from the Methuen edition, *The Human Age*, Volume I, 1956, p. 48. Huge Kenner, in his *Wyndham Lewis* (New Directions, 1954)—a concise and commendably neutral study—traps the essence of this style when he writes that "Lewis' fiction as a whole concerns itself with gradations of unreality . . . with groups of people engaged in explicating by their actions some theorem in the Metaphysics of the Void." Of his own persona (unarguably) in a short story, Lewis opined, "He was very fond of reality; but he was like a man very fond of what did not at all agree with him." By a terrible stroke of irony, Lewis, before the end of his life, could no longer rely "upon the evidence of the *eye*." He became quite blind.
4. In his introduction to Part I. *The Letters*, op. cit.
5. *The Letters*, op. cit., pp. 497–8.

FREDRIC JAMESON

From *Fables of Aggression:*
Wyndham Lewis, the Modernist as Fascist

1979, pp. 1–4, 25–34, 179–85

Prologue

Wyndham Lewis is surely the least read and most unfamiliar of all the great modernists of his generation,

a generation that included the names of Pound and Eliot, Joyce, Lawrence and Yeats; nor can it be said that his painting has been assimilated any more successfully into the visual canon.[1] Lewis was a presence for his contemporaries, but we have forgotten their admiration for him. At best, in Britain today, he retains a kind of national celebrity and is read as a more scandalous and explosive Waugh; while internationally his name remains a dead letter, despite the diligent efforts of Hugh Kenner and others to make a place for him in some Pound-centered modern pantheon.[2]

Yet it has been my experience that new readers can be electrified by exposure to *Tarr*, a book in which, as in few others, the sentence is reinvented with all the force of origins, as sculptural gesture and fiat in the void. Such reinvention, however, demands new reading habits, for which we are less and less prepared. Anglo-American modernism has indeed traditionally been dominated by an impressionistic aesthetic, rather than that—externalizing and mechanical—of Lewis' expressionism. The most influential formal impulses of canonical modernism have been strategies of inwardness, which set out to reappropriate an alienated universe by transforming it into personal styles and private languages: such wills to style have seemed in retrospect to reconfirm the very privatization and fragmentation of social life against which they meant to protest. . . .

There were of course excellent and objective reasons for Lewis' neglect: reasonable motives, which it would be naive to ignore, for the resistance of sophisticated modern readers to that particular brand of modernism he had in store for them. A consistent perversity made of him at one and the same time the exemplary practitioner of one of the most powerful of all modernistic styles and an aggressive ideological critic and adversary of modernism itself in all its forms. Indeed, *Time and Western Man* (1927) diagnostically attributes the aberrant impulse of all the great contemporary artistic and philosophical modernisms to what he called the "Time Cult," to the fetishization of temporality and the celebration of Bergsonian flux. However illuminating this diagnosis may have been, it had the unfortunate effect of forcing his readership to choose between himself and virtually everything else (Joyce, Pound, Proust, Stein, Picasso, Stravinsky, Bergson, Whitehead, etc.) in the modern canon.

Meanwhile, at the very moment in which the modernisms of the mainstream discovered their anti-Victorian vocation and developed a battery of onslaughts on moral taboos and repressive hypocrisies, an analogous gesture finds Lewis affirming the oppressiveness of the sexual instinct and unseasonably expressing a kind of archaic horror at sexual dependency. The polemic hostility to feminism, the uglier misogynist fantasies embodied in his narratives, the obsessive phobia against homosexuals, the most extreme restatements of grotesque traditional sexist myths and attitudes—such features, released by Lewis' peculiar sexual politics and abundantly documented in the following pages, are not likely to endear him to the contemporary reader. . . .

"Hairy, Surgical, and Yet Invisible"

They were there in a confused mass before him. The thought of "settling everything before he went" now appeared fantastic. He had at all events started these local monsters and demons, fishing them out stark where they could be seen. Each had a different vocal explosiveness or murmur, inveighing unintelligibly against the other. The only thing to be done was to herd them all together, and march them away for inspection at leisure. Sudden herdsman, with the care of an antediluvian flock. (*Tarr*)

To face the sentences of Wyndham Lewis is to find oneself confronted with a principle of immense mechanical energy. Flaubert, *Ulysses*, are composed; the voices of a James or of a Faulkner develop their resources through some patient blind groping exploration of their personal idiosyncrasies from work to work. The style of Lewis, however, equally unmistakable, blasts through the tissues of his novels like a steam whistle, breaking them to its will.

For the mechanical, the machinelike, knows an exaltation peculiarly its own: "a motor-car roaring at full speed, as though bearing down upon the machine-gun itself, is more beautiful than the *Victory of Samothrace*," cried Marinetti, in words that echoed around the world like the pulsing telegraph waves upon the emblematic globe of the old newsreels, words that seem to furnish the program for the *scène-à-faire* of Lewis' finest single novel. But for Lewis, as for so many others, Marinetti's Futurism had the liberating effect of a mere slogan, a static and external caricature of what the new twentieth-century linguistic apparatus ought to register. For Lewis himself, indeed, there could be no question of opposing nature, or the organic, to the machine:

> Every living form is a miraculous mechanism . . . and every sanguinary, vicious and twisted need produces in Nature's workshops a series of mechanical arrangements extremely suggestive and interesting for the engineer, and almost invariably beautiful or interesting for the artist.

Nature itself as machine: such is the force of the preeminently typical opening page of one of Lewis' first great narratives, the (then) scandalous *Cantleman's Spring Mate* of 1917:

> Cantleman walked in the strenuous fields, steam rising from them as though from an exertion, dissecting the daisies specked in the small wood, the primroses on the banks, the marshy lakes, and all God's creatures. The heat of a heavy premature Summer was cooking the little narrow belt of earth-air, causing everything innocently to burst its skin, bask abjectly and profoundly. Everything was enchanted with itself and with everything else. The horses considered the mares immensely appetizing masses of quivering shiny flesh: was there not something of a 'je ne sais quoi' about a mare, that no other beast's better-half possessed?

So also for the sexual stimulation of birds, of sows and hogs, indeed of the very human animal itself, the primordial awakening of spring proving on closer inspection to be nothing but the effect of some terrific atmospheric pressure-cookery.

Yet this alarming demystification of the organic is conveyed in a paradoxical way: nothing is more characteristic of Lewis' style than the peculiar rotation of our inferential system around the adjective "strenuous"; than the peculiar slippage of the properties thus named from their official referent in the sentence. The fields, we tell ourselves, can in no case really be thought of as "strenuous": what is strenuous is at best the walk through them, or Cantleman's own exertions. Anthropomorphic projection seems an inadequate term for this shift, which classical rhetoric designated as *hypallage*, and in which "the adjective is grammatically referred to a different substantive in the context than that to which it ought semantically to be applied."[3] This minor figure of an essentially oratorical practice of language in the classical world most often stands as the sign of epic concision: we will see later that this distant affinity with Lewis' modernism is not fortuitous. Yet the classical figure is profoundly modified when, displaced, it comes to constitute the tropological infrastructure for a

properly modernist practice of *style*.[4] The alternate, purely negative, designation of a *mixtura verborum* testifies to the malaise of the rhetorical episteme as it registers such anomalous phenomena that threaten to explode its limits altogether. Lewis' hypallage, where the attributes of actor or act are transferred onto the dead scenery, generates a kind of contamination of the axis of contiguity, offering a glimpse of a world in which the old-fashioned substances, like marbles in a box, have been rattled so furiously together that their "properties" come loose and stick to the wrong places—a very delirium of metonymy of which, as we shall see, Lewis' subsequent writings provide some stunning examples.

Yet this transfer of adjectives is only the first moment of a far more complicated figural operation. No sooner do we register it, than it is itself withdrawn, undone, quite unexpectedly reversed, as though by the insertion of some new and unforeseeably more literal meaning beneath the first and figural one. It turns out, in this second moment or reversal, that Cantleman himself was nothing but a blind. Now the fields really are "strenuous" after all in their own right: overworked agents, they throw themselves enthusiastically into the business of giving off steam, perspiring from the effort of the summer's thermal preparations. Thus, what had on the story's literal level been a figure (the fields as the place of Cantleman's strenuous walk) has now, on the figural level of what the fields in spring are really like, been taken all too literally. Nor does the process stop there, for the metaphorical steam from Nature's kitchen then just as unexpectedly turns back into the steamy sweating surface of the flanks of "real" mares. Thus at length a veritable self-generating image- and sentence-producing machine comes into view behind the dextrous and imperceptible substitutions of literal and figural levels for one another.

From a somewhat different angle, we evidently have here to do with what in Roman Jakobson's influential distinction would be described as the substitution of a metaphor for a metonymy—with a metonymic figure subsequently transformed as though by sleight of hand into the complicated metaphor of nature as a single vast machine. Better still, since the spell of the initial metonymic gesture is finally never fully overcome, we have to do with a metaphoric process *concealed* behind the external trappings of a metonymic transfer; with a metaphor which can apparently emerge only disguised as metonymy; or, conversely, with an analytic, additive, mechanistic, essentially metonymic surface movement secretly powered by the natural energy of metaphoric creation. Meanwhile, if the figures themselves (metaphor/metonymy) are identified with the content of the passage (organism/machine), then it becomes clear that the passage is *autoreferential*, that is, that it laterally and unintentionally reflects back its own process of production and is in that sense "about" itself. Indeed, the entire text of this early story, which collapses sex and war or aggressivity—the organic and the machine—together into a single "ruse of Nature," can in this respect be read as a projection of the process of representation itself, or in other words, of the unnatural or artificial redoubling of "nature" by its expression, or by Language.

What is achieved by this peculiar linguistic substitution is thus essentially a demystification of the process of creation itself, from Aristotle to Proust, as the "hallmark of genius," a fundamental subversion of that still organic aesthetic ideology for which the very essence of the poetic process consists in the perception, or better still, the invention, of analogies. No doubt the primacy of metaphor is the projection of a literary hierarchy for which poetry and poetic inspiration are felt to be loftier and more noble than the humdrum referential activity of prose. As Jakobson has pointed out, in an influential passage, the fundamental mechanism of realistic prose is in fact not metaphor, but metonymy:

> Following the path of contiguous relationships, the realistic author metonymically digresses from the plot to the atmosphere and from the characters to the setting in space and time. He is fond of synecdochic details. In the scene of Anna Karenina's suicide Tolstoy's artistic attention is focussed on the heroine's handbag; and in *War and Peace* the synecdoches 'hair on the upper lip' or 'bare shoulders' are used by the same writer to stand for the female characters to whom these features belong.[5]

In Lewis, however, metonymy is read against metaphor, as its determinate negation: it thus becomes a sign of the devaluation of inspiration itself and of the art-sentence as a composed, subjectively ripe melodic unit in its own right. We have already suggested in our Prologue that in this respect the aggressive deconstruction of metaphor and the organic in Lewis can be seen as an anticipation of the poststructuralist assault on the Romantic valorization of organic form and the symbol. Indeed, three other features of Lewis' work about which we will have something to say shortly—his conception of the subject, his attack on the phenomenological view of time, and his practice of allegory—echo and reinforce this anti-Romantic stance on other levels than the purely stylistic one. Yet in his own social context, and in the codes of the period, this figural gesture would seem to have class, rather than theoretical, connotations. Lewis' futurism thus projects the symbolic value of an antitranscendental, essentially democratic option—the machine as against the luxury furnishings of the great estates, with their ideology of natural beauty, the sheer production of sentences as against the mysteries of poetic creation and the organic primacy of the beautiful or the masterpiece.

Politically, of course, Lewis was an elitist, committed to the great man theory of history and to the defense of "intelligence" in the face of the rising tide of mass mediocrity. What we have shown about the inner logic of his stylistic practice, however, allows us to detect, in some first anticipatory way, a fundamental contradiction in this work dramatized by a practice of "textual productivity" which stands in uneasy tension with Lewis' overt or official political positions. In protofascism this tension takes the form of a rivalry between "socialist" and 'nationalist" impulses, between the initial populist and anticapitalist thrust of the early fascisms, and their later vocation to secure the continuing privileges of the threatened middle-class and petty-bourgeois subject.

Yet this coexistence is itself dramatized by the dynamics of the production of Lewis' style, which is clearly a more complicated operation than the simple substitution of metonymy for metaphor, or indeed, the return to the "realistic" prose of Bennett or Wells and the outright repudiation of *fin de siècle* art language. The metaphoric content must itself be given in the text, in order to be cancelled: it is thus an initial figural richness which in some second "moment" is immediately restructured into metonymic forms and surfaces which anyone could make up for himself. Nowhere is this clearer than in those idling passages where the voice of metaphor remains silent, and metonymy functions on its own, motor wide open, in a kind of sheerly additive sentence production as accessible to the "common man" as carpentry or literacy itself.

In such purely metonymic passages, the machine in Lewis' style generates a whole painstaking and analytic dismemberment of the external world and of gesture, a kind of tireless visual inventory which reminds us of nothing so much

as the more famous bravura or antibravura descriptions of *Tristram Shandy*, and with which, given some initial object of representation, page upon page might effortlessly be filled:

> Don Alvaro could not have moved more slowly off the table had he been demonstrating the exercise to a slow-witted beginner in gymnastics: first he uncrossed his legs with a languourous slowness that suspended the leg he was thus translating for an appreciable accretion of seconds in mid-air; and he dropped it down beside the other with as much deliberation—as much inch by inch—as if the floor which was to receive it had been a hot brick, or an uncomfortable icicle. (*The Revenge for Love*)

This step-by-step dismantling of the body's gestural machine implies that reality is itself infinitely divisible, that its smallest atomic units can themselves be further and further subdivided by an infinitely expandable accretion of sentences, towards some unimaginable infinitesimality.

And like the body, the mind can be conceived as a mechanism also, which at its worst reproduces itself in the same additive fashion:

> Pulley has been most terribly helpful and kind there's no excusing himself Pulley has been most terribly helpful and kind—most terribly helpful and he's been kind. He's been most terribly kind and helpful, there are two things, he's been most kind he's been terribly helpful, he's kind he can't help being—he's terribly. (*The Childermass*)

This mindless babble is of course designed to represent what Lewis thought of as the gertrude "steining" of the modern child cult. Yet like the external anatomies, it projects a notion of the object as something decomposable ad infinitum, before which the writer places himself like a draughtsman, prepared to blacken "tireless" pages in frightening quantities. *The Apes of God* is indeed a kind of ambiguous monument to this illimitable sentence-producing capacity, which is itself a figure for human productive power in the industrial age.

It is therefore not surprising to find immense arid stretches in Lewis' often hastily composed works which are a deliberate provocation of the reader fully as much as they challenge a ritualistic cult of *belles lettres* or high style. Paradoxically, however, such "flaws," such sloppy writing, only confirm the immense and liberating energies of Lewis' style; for in such passages the principle of sheer sentence production is foregrounded and separates itself off as a now dominant force in its own right from all the individual sentences it leaves strewn behind it. The sentences of Joyce are composed according to a principle of immanence, God withdrawing from view behind his creation: in Lewis, however, sheer proliferation stands as the sign and ratification of his mechanistic enterprise.

In practice, of course, limits are placed on this infinite generation of empty sentences: from a contemporary standpoint, we would say that the textual impulse in Lewis is then strategically recontained by various devices, of which we will examine the narrative ones in our next chapter. But even the theoretical awareness of this production is carefully held in check: such is, for example, the function of a certain scientistic bias which presides over the systematic analysis and disjunction of the metonymic pole. "Burying Euclid deep in the living flesh,"[6] his characterization of the central impulse of his painting, was surely in his mind the motto for his linguistic practice as well.

Yet in the present day and age, in which scientific research has come to be understood as the construction of models, we are perhaps less intimidated by such invocations of the scientific absolute. From a stylistic point of view, even this scientific component of Lewis' language can be viewed as a single code or vocabulary field, a single terminological stock, among many other, equally distinctive, equally unprivileged sublanguages: the deliberately flourished anglicisms and British colloquialisms, for example ("fuss," "toddle," "beastly," "strapping"); or yet again the explicitly "painterly" and technical signals in certain descriptive passages, as though carefully blocked off by the expert's thumb extended to full distance.

The point to be made about these subcodes or idiolects is not their hierarchy but rather their sheer multiplicity, their jealously respected inconsistency with one another. No effort is made to fuse them into some more personal unity of tone. On the contrary, their very function is to interfere with each other, to clash visibly within the sentence itself in such a way that no surface homogeneity has time to reform: the words, unable to go together properly, end up projecting the warring planes and angles of a cubist painting. The sentence is thus an amalgam of heterogeneous forces which must not be allowed to congeal. Hence the ultimate and ineducable unruliness of the Lewis style, half-baked by design, and structurally too scandalous even for the most accommodating Pantheon, as, emblematically, in his well-known description of the Trolls ("hairy, surgical, and yet invisible"). That the composition of such sentences is a visual process, a juxtaposition and collage of word-objects felt to possess well-nigh tangible properties, may be judged from the effects of Lewis' blindness: unlike Joyce, the Lewis of the final years, able only to think or hear his language, reverts to an almost eighteenth-century sobriety, the fireworks of the earlier style now passing over into the content of the narratives themselves. . . .

Appendix: Hitler as Victim

The slapdash series of newspaper articles in which Lewis conveyed his impressions of Berlin immediately after the first great Nazi victories in the Reichstag in September 1930, and which were published as *Hitler* (London: Chatto & Windus, 1931), are as notorious as they are unread: the following brief account of this work, whatever its general usefulness, will indeed lead us to some unexpected conclusions.

With his satirist's feeling about cities, Lewis could hardly omit an initial tableau of Berlin ("Chicago, only more so if anything, but minus Bootleg, and with that great difference—that politics account for much of the street violence" [18]). The political point made here is that Nazi street violence is essentially a reaction to Communist violence and provocation; yet the inevitable narrative point is rather different: "But elegant and usually eyeglassed young women will receive [the tourist], with an expensive politeness, and he will buy one of these a drink, and thus become at home. . . . Then these bland Junos-gone-wrong, bare-shouldered and braceleted (as statuesque as feminine show-girl guardees) after a drink or two, will whisper to the outlandish sightseer that they are *men*. . . ." (24). With this characteristic and obsessive motif out of the way, we come to the political analysis proper, which I will resume as a series of theses:

1. "Adolf Hitler is just a very typical german 'man of the people'. . . . As even his very appearance suggests, there is nothing whatever eccentric about him. He is not only satisfied with, but enthusiastically embraces, his *typicalness*. So you get in him, cut out in the massive and simple lines of a peasant art, the core of the teutonic character. And his 'doctrine' is essentially just a set of rather primitive laws, promulgated in the interest of that particular stock or type, in order to satisfy its especial requirements and ambitions, and to ensure its vigorous survival, intact and true to its racial traditions" (31–32). This is

very different from the hero-worshipping tones with which Pound salutes Mussolini's "genius"; it also conveys the stance of Lewis' articles. He means to convey the spirit, to the British public, of a phenomenon culturally alien to it; he intends to translate and to explain the Nazi movement as a matter of some historical significance, but not necessarily to endorse it. "It is as an exponent—not as critic nor yet as advocate—of German National-socialism or Hitlerism, that I come forward" (4). It seems to me that this didactic stance is essential in grasping the symbolic value Hitler (and Germany) had for Lewis: not only are they doubly oppressed—by Marxist provocation and by the Versailles Treaty—but this oppression is formally inscribed within his text as the misunderstanding and miscomprehension of the British reader, against which Lewis must write.

2. The Nazi conception of race is a welcome antidote to the Marxian conception of class: "The Class-doctrine—as opposed to the Race-doctrine—demands a *clean slate*. Everything must be wiped off slick. A sort of colourless, featureless, automaton—*temporally* two-dimensional—is what is required by the really fanatical Marxist autocrat. Nothing but a mind *without backgrounds*, without any spiritual depth, a flat mirror for propaganda, a parrot-soul to give back the catchwords, an ego *without reflection*, in a word a sort of Peter Pan Machine—the adult Child—will be tolerated" (84).

3. Hitler's program is exemplary as a defense of Europe, at a time when Europe's intellectuals are at work undermining its legitimacy through their "exotic sense" (a "sentimentalizing with regard to the Non-White World" [121]). In effect, the Hitlerist has this message for the ruling classes of other European countries: "When, respected sir, and gracious lady, are you going—oh short-sighted, much indulging, sentimentally-renegade person that you are!—when may we hope that you will turn for a change to more practical interests? How about giving your White Consciousness a try for a little—it is really not so dull as you may suppose! A 'White Australia'—that may be impracticable. But at least there is nothing impracticable about a 'White Europe'. And today Europe is not so big as it was. It is 'a little peninsula at the Western extremity of Asia'. It is quite small. Why not all of us draw together, and put out White Civilization in a state of defense? And let us start by mutually cancelling all these monstrous debts that are crushing the life out of us economically" (121).

4. The Nazi program recapitulates many of Lewis' most deeply felt polemic themes: "A 'Sex-war', an 'Age-war', a 'Colour-line-war', are all equally promoted by Big Business to cheapen labour and to enslave men more and more. I do not like the present Capitalist system" (97). Hitlerism not only repudiates the call to hatred and division of Marxian class war, and the pernicious "trahison des clercs" of the "exotic sense," it also gives the welcome example of a transformation of Western "youth cults" into a genuine political movement (97).

5. "Race" essentially stands for the affirmation of the specificity of the national situation: this is the sense in which Lewis deals with Nazi antisemitism. The latter is, according to him, a German national characteristic, however unlovely, and must be understood as such. But here Lewis has a counter-sermon for the Germans themselves, as they try to explain themselves to other nations: "The Hitlerite must understand that, when he is talking to an Englishman or an American about the 'Jew' (as he is prone to do), he is apt to be talking about that gentleman's *wife*! Or anyhow *Chacun son Jew*! is a good old English saying. So if the Hitlerite desires to win the ear of England he must lower his voice and coo (rather than shout) *Juda verrecke*! if he *must* give expression to such a fiery

intolerant notion. Therefore—a pinch of malice certainly, but no 'antisemitism' for the love of Mike!" (42).

6. Hitlerian economics are those of the German peasant, essentially an anticapitalist attack on banks, loan-capital, and the War Debt. Hitler is a "Credit Crank." The Nazi opposition to Communism ("which has taken the mechanical ways of Megalopolis into the villages") "attacks the substitution, by the Communist, of the notion of quantity for that of *quality*. . . . Upon some points, of course, the Communist and the Nationalsocialist are in considerable agreement. Ultimately, the reason why their two doctrines could never fuse is this: the Marxist, or Communist, is a fanatically dehumanizing doctrine. Its injunctions are very rigidly erected against the continuance of 'the person'. In the place of 'the person' the Communist would put the thing—quantity in place of quality, as it is stated above. . . . So, even if Hitlerism, in its pure 'germanism', might retain *too much* personality, of a second-rate order, nevertheless Hitlerism seems preferable to Communism, which would have *none at all*, if it had its way. Personality is the only thing that matters in the world" (182–183). Thus, "the *Weltanschauung* of the Hitlerist or his near-relation (the egregious 'Credit-Crank') is laughing and gay compared to that of his opponent, the Communist. . . . On principle—for his is a deliberately 'catastrophic' philosophy (the word is Marx's)—the Communist views everything in the darkest colours. . . . The Hitlerist dream is full of an imminent classical serenity—leisure and abundance. It is, with them, *Misery-spot* against *Golden Age!*" (183–184).

Most discussions of this book (which is generally passed over in embarrassed silence) have centered on the false problem of whether, on the strength of this "misguided" assessment of Hitler before he came to power, Lewis is to be thought of as a fascist or fascist sympathizer. The reader is generally reminded that Lewis changed his mind, and on the eve of World War II wrote an anti-Nazi counter-blast, *The Hitler Cult and How It Will End* (1939). But Lewis' opinion of Hitler is by no means the most significant feature of the earlier work.

What is essential from our point of view is that *Hitler* is informed by *all* the ideological positions which will remain constant to the very end of Lewis' life: those fundamental themes do not change, even if his view of Hitler did. Among them, and far more central than his attitude towards Hitler as a historical figure, is his attitude towards *fascism* as a historical force. Here, but to the end of his career, fascism remains for Lewis the great political expression of *revolutionary* opposition to the status quo. This fundamentally historical vision of fascism—this structural place of "fascism" in Lewis' libidinal apparatus—is not altered by his later (and impeccable) anti-Nazi convictions, and is in fact recapitulated in *Monstre Gai*, published only two years before Lewis' death in 1957:

> Hyperides represented the most recent political phenomenon—hated or disliked by everybody. Here was the Fascist, the arch-critic of contemporary society. On earth this newcomer proposed to supplant the enfeebled Tradition, of whatever variety, no longer able to defend itself. So this enfeebled Power of Tradition, and its deadly enemy, the Marxist Power, joined forces to destroy this violent Middle-man (a borrower from both the new and the old).

Coming in the midst of the Cold War, and after the utter annihilation of Nazism as a presence on the world political scene, this retrospective evaluation of World War II may seem anachronistic, and the reader may be tempted to see it as a tired survival of thoughts that were alive for Lewis in the 20's and 30's. Yet the fact that fascism continued to stand as the political (and libidinal) embodiment of Lewis' chronic negativity, his oppositionalism, his stance as the Enemy, long after the defeat of institutional fascism itself, may, I think, be better grasped from a somewhat different perspective. The figural value of fascism as a reaction is determined by the more central position of Communism, against which the anticapitalist posture of protofascism (of which Lewis approved) must always be understood. We have touched on a number of reasons why Communism could not, for Lewis, be a satisfactory solution. The ultimate one now proves to be his feeling—paradoxical after all that has been said—that Communism was a historical inevitability, and thus, in a sense, the final and most irrevocable form of the *Zeitgeist*, that against which the oppositional mind must somehow always take a stand.

In this sense, and in the spirit of the present study, which has been an *immanent* analysis of Lewis' works, disengaging the self-critique always structurally implicit in them, we may allow his own truth-in-jest to have the final word:

> I know that at some future date I shall have my niche in the Bolshevist Pantheon, as a great enemy of the Middle-class Idea . . . I say: "I shall be among the bolshie prophets!" My "bourgeois-bohemians" in *Tarr*—and oh, my *Apes of God!*—will provide 'selected passages' for the schoolchildren of the future communist state,—of that I am convinced—to show how repulsive unbridled individualism can be.[7]

Notes

1. But the reader can now consult *Wyndham Lewis: Paintings and Drawings*, ed. Walter Michel (Berkeley and Los Angeles: University of California Press, 1971).

2. The first books on Lewis are still the best introductions: H. G. Porteus, *Wyndham Lewis: A Discursive Exposition* (London: Desmond Harmsworth, 1932); and Hugh Kenner, *Wyndham Lewis* (Norfolk, Ct.: New Directions, 1954), which should be supplemented by his more recent essays on *The Human Age* ("The Devil and Wyndham Lewis," in *Gnomon* [New York: McDowell, Obolensky, 1958]) and on Lewis' painting, his introduction ("The Visual World of Wyndham Lewis") in Michel, *Paintings and Drawings*. A brief listing of the meager critical literature is to be found in R. T. Chapman, *Wyndham Lewis: Fiction and Satires* (London: Vision Press, 1973). D. G. Bridson, *The Filibusterer* (London: Cassell, 1972), provides a useful review of Lewis' political positions in their historical contexts. My debt to Robert C. Elliott, *The Power of Satire* (Princeton: Princeton University Press, 1960), and in particular to the Lewis chapter, will become evident later on. The liveliest book on Lewis, however, remains his own autobiography, *Rude Assignment* (London: Hutchinson, 1950).

3. Heinrich Lausberg, *Elementi di retorica* (Bologna: Mulino, 1969), p. 169.

4. On the use of the distinction between rhetoric and style as a historical and periodizing concept, see Roland Barthes, *Writing Degree Zero*, translated by Annette Lavers and Colin Smith (London: Jonathan Cape, 1967), pp. 10–13, 41–52. The distinction is that evoked by Genette, following Lubbock's differentiation between *picture* (or "report") and *scene*, as "the opposition between classical *abstraction* . . . and 'modern' *expressivity*" (Gérard Genette, *Figures* III [Paris: Seuil, 1972], p. 131); and see Percy Lubbock, *The Craft of Fiction* (New York: Viking, 1957), especially pp. 251–254.

5. Roman Jakobson and Morris Halle, *Fundamentals of Language* (The Hague: Mouton, 1956), p. 78.

6. Quoted in Walter Michel, ed., *Wyndham Lewis: Paintings and Drawings* (Berkeley and Los Angeles: University of California Press, 1971), p. 40.

7. Wyndham Lewis, *Men without Art* (London: Cassell, 1934), pp. 267–268.

ERIC LINKLATER

1899–1974

Eric Robert Linklater was born on March 8, 1899, in Penarth, South Wales, and grew up in Cardiff, though for many years he fostered the impression he was, like his father, a native of Orkney. Childhood vacations there led to a lifelong fascination with the islands and their Viking and Scottish heritage. He was still at high school when his family moved to Aberdeen, Scotland, and it was at Aberdeen University that he chose to study on his return from military service at the end of World War I. After graduating in 1925 he took a position in Bombay on *The Times of India*, but left after eighteen months. In 1928 he won a two-year fellowship to study in America, where he worked on a scholarly study of Ben Jonson and traveled widely, gathering material for his very successful satirical novel, *Juan in America* (1931).

Settling in Scotland, Linklater was associated briefly with the Scottish National Party, though he later adopted a conservative and traditionalist position. He married in 1933, and from 1935 made his home in Orkney, where during World War II he served with the Royal Engineers for two years before being transferred to the Directorate of Public Relations. After the war he returned to the Scottish mainland, and was Rector of Aberdeen University from 1945 to 1948. In later years he made many lecture tours for the British Council, and received several honors, including a CBE in 1954.

Linklater's greatest successes as a writer included the novels *Magnus Merriman* (1934), *Juan in China* (1937), written after a trip to Shanghai, and *Private Angelo* (1946); the autobiography *The Man on My Back* (1941); and the children's book, *The Wind on the Moon* (1945), which won the Carnegie Medal. His reputation as a novelist later declined, and he enjoyed greater success with his non-fiction, including popular histories such as *The Conquest of England* (1966), but he remained a respected figure, especially in Scotland, until his death in Aberdeen on November 7, 1974.

General

And now for Mr. Linklater.

"What are the characteristics of middlebrow satire?"

"Sanity, sir."

"Not bad, MacDonnell."

"Being Scotch, sir."

"That's not funny, Collier."

"Topicality." "Ribaldry." "Tolerance."

"Don't speak at once, one at a time, you, Agate."

"Splendidly virile, robust, immensely readable, sir."

"Mackenzie!"

"Full-throated laughter, sir, a rousing bumper."

"And you, Priestley?"

"Zest and gusto, sir, the high spirits of a clever man."

"Very good, all of you, you avoided the trap. And you are quite right—for if you put irony, indignation, feeling—in short, wit—into this sort of thing you overdo it, like Swift, or merely irritate the public, like Joyce and Lawrence. You must be careful not to offend anybody. How are you going to manage? First: don't let your characters come to life—they must be types, you can abuse them freely. How do you create a type? You take a character and say he is a bridge bore or a golf bore or a poet or a colonel—and then whenever he appears he talks about bridge or golf or poetry or the army. Then you create a comic situation. You shut the poet and the colonel up in a stuck lift, you put the bridge bore on the golf links, or you let loose a pig at the vicarage garden party, like Linklater here. And then you put in the satire."

"How do you do that, sir?"

"The golden rule, I find, is to avoid the personal. Go in for something you really feel about and you endanger sanity. Endanger sanity and where is gusto? And, without gusto, what are royalties? No! Read the newspapers, and satirise what they satirise. Foreigners, Americans, D.O.R.A., fascists and spinsters. Never write a word you'd be ashamed to write for the *Daily Express*."

"And zest, virility, sir?"

"Get that eighteenth century feeling. Study sturdy common sense. Become a good trencherman. Make a few jokes about the way of a man with a maid, remember, the frankness of Fielding with the slyness of Sterne. And plenty of generalisation about humanity. Style? That will come with *Tom Jones* and practice. Show them, Linklater."

> Bugler Bliss's tongue was imperfectly taught, and that poignant call, that may summon the heart to a loneliness like the outer stars, brayed with his breath like a tinker's moke.
>
> Major Gander's life had not been happy, and the ceremonies attendant on his death were correspondingly mismanaged.

"Got the knack? If the major's life had been happier would the bugler have known the Last Post? No—but don't you smell the eighteenth century? Now once more, please, here's the chalk—and put some poetry into it."

But the Silver Trumpets sang:

> Blow, northern wind,
> Send thou me sweeting.

and a pizzicato, like the pin-prick pattern of April rain, softened all hearts and all desired that Daisy and Katherine and Bolivia should have twenty pink bottomed babies a-piece, a festoon of them, wreaths of them, troops of them, with no thought of prizes but simply to match May and fulfil the turning of the year. The triumph of all who'd begotten, and the travail of all who'd borne, were as warp and weft in their lot, and flute and fiddle, brass and drum, would join in a great cry, "Ripeness is All."

"Thank you very much. Time's up. Good night, boys. Happy Pens!"

"Yes, sir. Thank you, sir. Happy Pen, sir!"—CYRIL CONNOLLY, *NSN*, March 30, 1935, pp. 462–63

Works

Eric Linklater is a remarkably versatile Scotchman who has written with equal felicity novels and autobiographies that have conveyed his own zest for life, though he is capable of restraining his ebullient style to suit the mood of his story. In two of his earlier, and perhaps best-known, novels, *Juan in America* and *Juan in China*, he can be readily identified as the principal character traveling under a pseudonym across two continents. But no one could be more unlike Mr. Linklater than the reticent and introverted hero of his new novel, *The House of Gair*. Stephen Cougat is a mildly celebrated novelist who was living in solitary misanthropy in a tidy old cottage in the highlands, solitarily because his unfaithful wife had eloped with her latest lover. It is obvious that no intelligent young woman could have lived long with so arid a man as Steven without wanting to run away from him.

One fateful evening Steven's ancient car ran out of gas, and he had to spend the night in the home of Hazleton Crome, master of an ancient and remote mansion known as Gair House. Crome he was able to identify as the author of a late nineteenth-century satirical novel greatly admired by the devotees of the *Yellow Book* and the critics of the time. Old Mr. Crome had read Steven's work, and his effusive compliments won the younger man's affection. There were two servants in Gair House, the cook, a Spanish woman who had once been Crome's mistress, and a shy, red-headed maid who would have been strikingly beautiful if she had not had an atrociously ugly harelip. Crome proved to be a born midnight conversationalist whose anecdotes of the dead past were tinged with malice.

When Steven could escape, he took his host's only published book home with him to read. He asked himself why a man who in his youth had written so brilliantly had only one book to his credit and why he appeared to be so affluent. On his next visit he discovered the reason. Many of the wealthy and titled English men and women to whom he had access had scandals locked in their closets which they would pay any amount of money not to have revealed. Crome had written several malicious novels under various pen names, using the material he had at hand, and a confederate would then suggest to his victims that his next book would tell all. He had lived for years on blackmail; and when, after the World War, nobody was interested in scandals, he found another source of funds in the sale to wealthy Californians of spurious paintings, attributed to modern masters.

Crome's nephew was a charming and handsome young criminal who took large sums of money from rich old ladies, including, Steven discovered, his own aunt on whose bequest he was depending for his future security. When Steven returned to Gair House to confront the old man with his perfidy, he found him living in terror of his nephew, who was hiding there. The old house was charged with the threat of violence and death. When the explosion came, it swept everything away with it, the old man, his nephew, and his maid, and the house itself was burned to the ground.

Mr. Linklater's frightening termination of his story is a holocaust that would not be convincing if he had not led up to it so deftly in his previous chapters. In addition to its fascinating and odd characters and its tightly-knit plot, *The House of Gair* is one of the most convincing and well-written novels of suspense of the new year.—HARRISON SMITH, *SR*, March 20, 1954, p. 19

One of the great moments of my life was when I read Chapter One of Eric Linklater's *Juan in America*, which carries on from the point where Byron broke off in Don Juan. I felt, I remember, like some watcher of the skies when a new planet swims into his ken or like stout Cortez (or, as some say, Balboa) when with eagle eyes he stared at the Pacific. This, I said to myself, is the stuff to give 'em. And now Mr. Linklater has obliged with a long book in the same vein.

My Fathers and I starts in the world of today with Edward Vanbrugh (b. 1919), the unsuccessful proprietor of an antique shop, on the verge of bankruptcy, and ends with him taking the position of butler—major domo, he prefers to call it—in the home of a wealthy Texan. The rest of the book deals with Edward's forebears.

Mr. Linklater's method of introducing his explorations into the past is simple and ingenious. Edward Vanbrugh puts the blame for his failure in life on his father. We then get the story of his father also named Edward (b. 1891), who puts the blame for his failure in life on his father, Thomas (b. 1861), and so through Eustace (b. 1834), Jeremy (b. 1794), Francis (b. 1772), and Charles (b. 1750) right back to Moses, Baron Storleyford (b. 1705), the founder of the family. They all attribute their misfortunes to their fathers, except the last named, who never had one, being a foundling.

He was discovered one night in the carriage of the Earl of Lowestoft with nothing on but a theatre program advertising *The Confederacy*, by John Vanbrugh. So they called him Vanbrugh and a carriage being the next thing to bulrushes, added the name Moses. (Later he went to India and cleaned up there to the tune of £120,000, shaking the pagoda tree, it was called.)

Reading this book is like being escorted through the portrait gallery of some stately home in England by a kindly guide of immense charm and erudition. Mr. Linklater just goes on talking in a gentle voice, and it is impossible not to listen to his every word. He holds you, not with a glittering eye but by some subtle magic which it is difficult to analyze.

Highly recommended are the stories of Jeremy, the midshipman who became England's most expert coachman, and Eustace, who was a disciple of Thomas Huxley and had an unpleasant afternoon with the Gräfin von Huhnewasser und Münchengrätz, but they are eclipsed, in my opinion, by that of Francis (b. 1772).

It was of Francis (if, says Mr. Linklater, a local legend can be accepted) that Charles Lamb said, "The only measure he can tread is the faux pas, and his claim to nobility is descent from the old French family of De Trope." He was what a later generation was to call a buttinski or trailing arbutus, having much of the adhesive quality of Doctor Johnson's Boswell. He seeped into the homes of the eminent like oil. They would think they were alone and they would look around and there was Francis. He maddened Wordsworth to the point of homicide, and was actually, the "person from Porlock" who distracted Coleridge's mind from his "Kubla Khan."

We would have another one on these lines, Mr. Linklater.—P. G. WODEHOUSE, "The Descent of Unsuccessful Sons," *SR*, March 14, 1959, pp. 25, 60

FRANCIS RUSSELL HART
From "Novelists of Survival: Linklater and Jenkins"
The Scottish Novel from Smollett to Spark

1978, pp. 246–59

Shortly after the untimely death of Lewis Grassic Gibbon, Eric Linklater saluted him as "the only Scots writer of his generation to dare suppose that playing football with the cosmos was his chosen mission." It was a time when "social life in Scotland" had "no peculiar and individual significance" and was "derivative and provincial," and Scottish writers reacted in a way "likely to be evasive, or lacking in conviction, or minutely selective."[1] Yet the same year Linklater published in *The Lion and the Unicorn* a defense of the humane utility of small nations against modern bureaucratic imperialism. It is characteristic of him to have juxtaposed an adventurous manifesto and a hard-headed admonition of limitation.

Introducing his collected stories in 1968, Linklater wrote, "Critics, I am told, prefer an author who . . . will mark his territory and stay within it . . . I rarely write the same thing twice."[2] There may be a real clue here, for Linklater had extraordinary insight into literary decorum and his own relation to literary history. In his autobiography *Fanfare for a Tin Hat*, he identifies "the moment when I forfeited all claim to be recognized as a serious novelist" with the time (in 1931) when he declined the urgings of Jonathan Cape and Edward Garnett to follow up *Juan in America* with sequels, and sat down instead to write the ninth-century Orcadian saga of Thorlief Coalbiter and his sons, *The Men of Ness*.[3] In making such a switch—and he did it repeatedly—he gave up the way of the giants ("a true novelist is one who imposes his own character, his own way of thought and fashion of writing, on every page that leaves his table") for a "more humble and realistic way." In the belief that in literature, expression ultimately counts for more than content, he chose to vary his subjects widely as occasion and inspiration suggested and to allow "my subjects to determine the style and temper in which I have written of them." Linklater was a markedly occasional artist, trained in professional journalism. Yet among British novelists he was as well-read as Scott, whom he resembled in various ways: in his Scottish Toryism, his Episcopalianism, and the ease with which critics underrate his prodigious talent and confuse his creativity with potboiling or frivolity.

But while he may have denied it and critics may have missed it, the definitive quality is there in his twenty-three novels in thirty-eight years. The high points are the third (*Juan in America*, 1931) and the eleventh (*Private Angelo*, 1946), and these two ironic heroes—the Byronic-Aberdonian cosmopolitan aristocrat and the Italian peasant—have much in common, and are akin to the rest, not least in the romantic and ironic phenomenon of their will to survive.

White-Maa's Saga (1929), recalls Linklater, "had some of the virtues of green things," "most of the faults of inexperience," and "relied, like many first novels, on an autobiographical substratum which had to be raised, falsified, and decorated to make a good story."[4] It is a romance of *bildung* whose hero, Peter Flett, struggles in vain to pass his medical exams at "Inverdoon," spends his summers in Orkney, courts a crofter's daughter, engages in desperately witty and extended talks with his student friends, eats, drinks, fishes, and fights like the "etiolated Viking" he is, kills the despicable Orcadian villain, and finally agrees to sail to Vancouver with his Orcadian sweetheart.

For all the wit and exuberant evocation of local custom, it is a moody story of "the swift sadness of the beauty of youth" and "Greybeard Time wearing a cap and bells, and carrying a pig's bladder instead of a scythe." Peter and his friends are already old; they are filled with the war they have survived as "a lively memory" (it is 1921–22)—"most of the men who filled the Scots universities had seen death in stranger disguises than the frigid decency of the mortuary, and life painted more vividly than immaturity can paint it." One of Peter's girl friends says, "We're not really young, are we? We only have a kind of hard, make-believe youth that's lasting longer than the real thing would." But the make-believe youth is taken seriously for

the most part. The "raised, falsified" bouts of passion and wit and preening self-doubt mingle strangely with the vivid realism of Orkney's traditional life. The gypsy primitivism is falsified by idyllic sentimentality and complicated by Rabelaisian gusto. The germs and talents of later books are here but without the formal control, the fine decorum of mixed modes, or the characteristic episodes of fantastic farce.

Linklater spent the months following the completion of *White-Maa's Saga* partly in research for a thesis on Jacobean comedy and partly in writing a second novel which was "an exercise from which I hoped to learn something of the strategy and tactics necessary, as I believed, for the construction of a novel."[5] *Poet's Pub* (1929) is a comedy of southern English manners, a "fantastic idyl," located in a fashionable rural inn managed by a young Scottish poet whose zest for art in food, drink, and adventure is more robust than his talent for poetry. He has thought of writing "a Gargantuan epic of food, of inventing a young Gargantua who should eat his way through France and Eastern Europe to Russia . . . A gastronomic Tamburlaine." A mock spy-thriller plot intervenes: an American confidence man steals secret plans for converting coal to petrol; Nelly Bly, a gossip columnist, steals Keith's manuscript poem; the bartender believes his blue cocktail recipe has also been stolen; and the whole company drives wildly north to Scotland in a cavalcade of flight, chase, picaresque encounter, and coincidental victory. Much of the Linklater mixture is here: the Peacockian metier of elegance and wit; the Gargantuan mock-epic of gustatory orgy; the farcical, fantastic adventure; the artist-hero designing an art of life; the remotely-hinted-at real world of suffering and struggle. The tragic element has still to be assimilated. A suitable protagonist has not yet been conceived. A way of using the mixture to interpret the anxious contemporary world has still to be tried.

Linklater's genius for literary tradition and decorum led him to send an exiled descendant of Aberdonian Byron's Don Juan (Juan Motley) on a picaresque epic-farce foray across Prohibition America. Linklater claims that *Juan in America* (1931) is a historical novel, a vision of some "vestigial or stubborn remnant" of innocence beneath fabulous wealth, "remedial crime and sentimental well-being".[6] What suited him so perfectly was the discovery of a giant reality ripe for satire, yet patently fantastic and romantic. "Fantasy lived here. Satyrs walked in the woods and millionaires built with the large and unstudied imagination of Haroun-al-Raschid. America was the last home of romance and anything could happen there" (65). "America," Juan drunkenly tells a distinguished audience in Washington during Hoover (Bloomer)'s inaugural, "is really a quaint old-fashioned land. Personally I like it. But that does not blind me to the fact that it is the last abode of romance and other medieval phenomena" (285). The hero, generated out of an ironic saga of dynastic identity and suspect legitimacy (a Scottish mock-romance motif), in boyhood is a child satyr or gypsy Christ come to destroy respectability and humbug "with a keen perception of the grotesque and ridiculous." He falls temporarily into the seductions of romance—"I mean a certain kind of silliness on a large and pleasant scale; I mean a denial of tasteless common sense for the sake of pungent nonsense" (99)—and carries this propensity into a wild travelogue. He survives Manhattan's sudden violence, failure as a college football player, bootleg boating on the Canadian border, gang warfare in Red-eye Rod Gehenna's Chicago, the crushing passion of Olympia the amazonian operacrobat, the jealousy of a Negro rival in South Carolina swamps, the perilous idyll with his Haidee, Red-eye Rod's daughter, on an edenic Carolina island, parachute escape from his California-bound plane into the midst of an Oklahoma lynching party, and finally the complex unrealities of Hollywood, whence he escapes to join the beautiful Kuo Kuo in Dr. Salvator's mystical Arroyo Beach nudist colony. He sees himself sometimes boisterously, sometimes sadly, as a gypsy exile; he is moved by "something between fear and antic laughter." In his wildly drunken ecstasy, in the company of bootleggers, he has bawdy priapic visions of the many-wombed brotherhood of man, a "polychromatic but monogene world."

The cascading virtuosity of Linklater's grotesque is seen in the gangland murder Juan attends in a New York speakeasy:

> The first bullet, rising high, had missed Wenny altogether and smashed the aquarium tank above his head. It hit, indeed, the globular gaping fish that had so long and stupidly stared into the smoky room. Wenny disappeared under the deluge of water and broken glass and the unexpected draught of fishes, and the bullet-struck fish, its silver skin laced with its golden blood, lay on the floor unseen. It shining plump companions flopped and wriggled beside it, drowning in the hot air of the speakeasy, trampled on by the panic-feet of the men they had seen so often and so uncomprehendingly. Their fishy eyes stiffened into dead jelly, and their silver mail was broken on the floor where the customers had thrown the butts of their cigarettes. So, killed astonishingly by a gangster, one by one the silver fishes died, far from the cold native silence of their sea, and the jungle softness of waving weed, and the white labyrinthine shelter of coral reefs. And by-and-by a policeman spoke their epitaph in blasphemy as he trod on one, and slipped, and fell bluntly to the wet floor. [88–89]

George Blake writes that "this was not characteristically Scottish writing." Neither, to be sure, was Byron's *Don Juan*—and yet the peculiarly Scottish quality T. S. Eliot sensed at work in the first descends to its heir. "We may wonder," says Blake, "what such comic pieces as *Poet's Pub*, *Ripeness Is All*, and *Private Angelo* have to do with Scotland." Hugh MacDiarmid had found an answer when he placed the best of Eric Linklater in the company of Stevenson, Brown, Hay, Gibbon, and Sydney Goodsir Smith's *Carotid Cornucopius*; Smith, when he recalled goliardic Scots folktales, the satire of Dunbar, Byron's *Don Juan*, and MacDiarmid's *Drunk Man*.[7]

After *Juan*, Linklater went home literarily (and, not long after, domestically) to "pillage the Icelandic sagas" of *The Men of Ness* (1932)—his unique contribution to a brief flourish of archaic recreation in the novel (Gibbon, Gunn, Mitchison, and others)—and to chasten the stylistic exuberance of *Juan* into "a stark sismplicity that banished all Latinisms from its sentences and relied almost entirely on a vocabulary that could, with some latitude, be called Anglo-Saxon." He had read the Orkney Saga as a boy.

> Now Orkney was the southernmost home of that pagan heroism which had changed the shape and temper of all northern Europe, and in its heroism— destructive though it had been of much that was valuable—I was beginning to discern a principle that had little reference to the common motive of profit . . . a superior motive that showed itself in a code of behaviour dominated, not primarily by a prospect of material gain, but by wish or determination idealistically conceived . . . to complete an action in accordance with a pattern that was artistically satisfying.[8]

This historical thesis was to be worked out later in *The Ultimate Viking* (1955): the Vikings were unwitting "artists in conduct"; "they were unabashed by social obligation, undeterred by moral prohibition, and they could be quite contemptuous of economic advantage and the safety of their own skin. But they saw clearly a difference between right and wrong, and the difference was aesthetic"; "within the conventions of a brutal heroism would be disclosed the formative spirit of an artist."[9] It is akin to that quintessential Linklater manifesto, the 1945 Aberdonian rectorial address, "The Art of Adventure."

There is no critical language for the novel applicable to the terse matter-of-factness of *The Men of Ness*. One finds no thematic weight, no mythologizing, as in Gunn's *Sun Circle* or Mitchison's *The Corn King and the Spring Queen*: saga is the norm; unstudied brutality, proverbial admonition, and stark humor alternate. Ninth-century Viking history is broadly sketched without anachronistic interpretation; motives are limited to fame, property, security, and, most of all, atonement.

> Skallagrim said, "I will let you go free on this condition: when evening comes you will ride straightway to Ivar and tell him that Skallagrim Thorlief's son, Ragnar Hairybreeks' son, and Kol Cock-crow his brother, are come out of Orkney seeking him in the matter of that atonement which he did not pay for Bui of Ness, whom he killed, and also in consideration of certain wrongs he did to Signy my mother, Thorlief's wife and Bui's. Tell him that we shall wait here till he comes, for we have travelled far and do not mean to go bootless home.[10]

The saga comes of focus on the travels of Skallagrim and Kol, and the long chronicle of their stormy voyage in the North Sea is done with a magnificent simplicity equal to anything Linklater has written. Finally, both brothers must die, and only a lone survivor, their peasant neighbor Gauk of Calfskin, goes home to tell the tale. Gauk is not a hero but a little man content to hide in his little place. Gauk the little peasant, who survives at the end of the story, supplies something of a final comment on the heroic aesthetic of the men of Ness—a comment that will later be embodied in Linklater's most memorable hero, not a Viking bent on the art of adventure but an Italian peasant committed to the art of survival. For Linklater is no connoisseur of violence; while courage and beauty may be found in the horrors and absurdities of war, it is on the archaic will to survive that his notions of heroism ultimately focus.

This new focus produced in *Magnus Merriman* (1934) Linklater's first large-scale novel of modern Scotland. Magnus is White-Maa grown older, home from India and America, successful first-novelist, and Orcadian survivor of the Great War. He is a Juanesque victim of his own seductions, an epic drinker, and the first of Linklater's heroes to be conceived as a victim of a destiny that is both tragedy and farce: a fool, a brilliantly argumentative reactionary, an artist, and ultimately a peasant trapped into workaday Orkney domesticity by a beautiful, shrewd, and despotic farmer's daughter. His love for the very soil of Scotland is romantic enough, and the book characteristically and repeatedly deflates it. Yet it survives his ludicrous incursion into nationalist politics, and focuses at last on Linklater's view of the validity of small nations—that man at his most cosmopolitan remains a creature of local attachments, that "the human mind is essentially a village mind." "Life was the flowering of a single land, and love of country was no virtue but stark necessity. Patriotism and the waving of flags was an empty pride, but love of one's own country, of the little acres of one's birth, was the navel-string of life . . . life could not be whole save in its own place."[11] The long middle of the book carries Magnus through a thinly fictionalized satire of Edinburgh and the nationalist movement of the early thirties. The follies and crimes of his campaign and his manager are sketched in broad caricature. Some political and literary figures are caricatural portraits in a roman à clef, mingling with plausibly mimetic characters such as Magnus and his numerous paramours and with more typical manners figures. Satiric realism fuses with various kinds of fantasy—farcical, erotic, and even gothic—as when a mildly erotic episode in Edinburgh is bracketed by a reminiscence of frightening witchcraft, or when the manners comedy of Edinburgh respectability gives way to the mock-epic of international Rugby, or when Miss Beauly naively devastates the urbane Tarascon Restaurant by emptying Meiklejohn's snuffbox into the mouth of a nearby saxophone, producing a storm-ravaged orgy of sneezing. Such great setpieces of grotesque hilarity, erupting catastrophically in the midst of elegant manners milieux, will become one of Linklater's trademarks.

One of the most splendid examples occurs early in *Ripeness Is All* (1935). Lady Caroline Purefoy, wife of the Vicar of Lammiter, tireless patron of humane causes, gives a large garden party to benefit the Brackenshire Association for Improved Slaughterhouses and to demonstrate old and new ways of killing pigs. The demonstration pigs break loose in the lovely vicarage garden; the quality of the long, grotesque episode can only be suggested:

> The porker kicked its feet out of the rope and galloped headlong for the pergola. It was a fearsome sight. Its black body was convulsive with rage and speed, its huge ears flapped, and as it galloped it diabolically screamed . . . The scene of confusion in the garden was now almost indescribable. Most of the guests were women, and many of them were old . . . Brandishing their umbrellas like clubs, or stabbing with them as though they were assegais, they drove a resolute way to safety . . . The second pig had taken refuge among the rhododendrons, and though it could not be seen its progress might be marked by the shaking of the bushes and the occasional destruction of syringas and the remaining azaleas . . . In the meantime, the first pig, after a spirited pursuit round the garden by Miss Ramboise and several other athletic young women, was busily destroying the rose-garden. In such evident fury as to daunt even Miss Ramboise, it attacked a magnificent Golden Gleam, whose yellow petals fluttered in the air and fell like dapples of sunlight on its black satanic hide. Half a dozen ruined Duchesses of Athol lay behind it, their bloom an orange carpet for the soil, and the dark red blossom of l'Etoile de Holland lay like blood in the wasted snow of Madame Butterfly. The raging pig uprooted a fine Shot Silk; pink petals were mingled with the red, the creamy white, the yellow, and the gold, and the gross black brute, its swart ears flapping, trampled the lovely wreckage underfoot. Rain fell thick and steady now, and the least percipient was sensible of something awful in this sinister spectacle of wrath beneath a hostile sky.[12]

The pigs take refuge and are captured in the lily pond. Lady Caroline is soaked, takes cold, then pleurisy, then pneumonia, and in a few days is dead, leaving the poor vicar with six children. The hilarity of delicate patrician elegance devastated by gross beastliness leads to domestic tragedy. Yet this farcical novel celebrates life, fertility, ripeness. The episode is fitting: in an effete postwar pastorality, the gross will to survive tramples less fruitful orders into muddy chaos. A fantastic vitality crashes among the manners—it is a familiar motif of Scottish fable. And the ominous real world of 1935 is kept at an idyllic distance.

The book's occasion, Linklater remembers, was "exuberant delight" at the birth of his own first child. Shortly, the new father left his Orkney retreat, "returned to the clamorous world from which I pretended to have escaped," and sailed for China to develop a background for Juan Motley's only return appearance, in *Juan in China* (1937).[13] War is the main strand of Linklater's autobiography; he sees it as tragic folly emblematic of the absurd resilience of human destiny. His books so far had celebrated the delight of having survived a past war and the Primavera of renewed human vigor. The problem now was to adapt fantastic farce to the portents of renewed war. Sending Juan with his tireless wit and his amoral love of the adventurous, the free, the grotesque and heteroclite, to China's corrupt warlords and incipient Japanese invasion was a brave experiment.

The situation is appalling: internal corruption in the face of disaster, an early *Catch-22*. Juan's paramour Kuo Kuo seeks to recover a document of great price, which ultimately proves worthless, while Red-eye Rod Gehenna's former henchman Colonel Rocco and an obese Englishman arrange the sale of General Wu Tu Fu's Japanese-made tanks. The tanks in battle are discovered to have an armor plate of wood covered with tin. But they were paid for with bundles of phony money; and the battle that the tanks have lost Juan wins by throwing up the money to be blown over the Japanese lines, followed by hordes of avaricious Chinses.

The hilarious confusion on the battlefield is a variant on the devastated garden party or the murdered fish in the speakeasy, yet here humor wins an odd victory. "At first a very proper sympathy and decent feeling kept Juan from laughing. But laughter was like an acid that soon dissolved such soft metal, and presently his sobriety vanished, and from all over his body, as it seemed, there started small tides and currents of mirth that gathered and grew stronger" (356). The problem that pervades the book is the problem of laughter and of Juan's determined lack of seriousness. He is left overnight for safety in a Buddhist monastery and finds himself alone in a maze of idols. One is "a glaucous deity whose face was twisted in wild and diabolical laughter . . . Laughter that tore the very fabric of life. A god more evident than the others—despite his lineaments of the devil—for only a god could see such comedy in the world and have the courage to laugh at it . . . a god, but clothed in sackcloth and rags, heaven's outcast, perhaps, because he had mocked the foundations of heaven in the same breath . . . Or a god, it might be, who was God's jester" (138). From this "dreadful apotheosis of humour" Juan hastily retreats, coming next upon a "Chinese Gargantua" who amazes him with the realization that the Chinese have "no sense of sin" but instead a "gross and unpardonable innocence . . . capable of the most appalling misconduct." The stage is set for tragedy; the recurrent effect is of tragedy falling into farce.

When Juan is wounded, gives up the adventure, and goes home, the moments of triumphant laughter are underlain by a "stupid feeling of desolation," and it seems clear that the Juanism so marvelously suited to medieval Prohibition America has proved unfitted to a new tragic-farcical situation. The critics, Linklater recalls, found the book guilty of "heartless ill-taste." Juan was dead, and his true successor only emerged with Private Angelo nine years later. Meanwhile, the problem intensified and the experience multiplied with *The Impregnable Women* (1938) and *Judas* (1939).

But first came a brief picaresque tale, *The Sailor's Holiday* (1937).[14] The germ may be seen in *Juan in China*: "All men are sailors," says the narrator; "We men of action are incurably loquacious," says Juan. Henry Tippus, an impecunious English sailor home on holiday, is as loquacious and fertile a romantic liar as Arthur Gander of *Ripeness Is All*, and his adventures make a modern fabliau. Bawdy errors and providential accidents alternate with his fertile and nonsensical inventions, with gobs of speculative anecdote and dialogue. The effect is of Peacock shot with bawdy and farce: the blowing up of the demonstration model Little Beauty Washing Machine, overcharged with soap, in the market square of rural Whippleford; the lowering of the heroine, locked up with suspected appendicitis by her faith-healer father, out of her window in her bed. Indestructible, romantic Henry finds and loses again his own plain beloved and survives to complete his circle and to go back to sea, in his common blood the mingled blood of "princes and potentates" and in his name the echo of his mythic ancestor. The first of the sea-going Tippuses, his great-aunt Hannah had told him, sailed strange seas in the ship Argos; and "the story that Henry was telling, whether he knew it or not was a rude version of the voyage of Colchis and the Golden Fleece" (177). The survival of the archaic sailor, in his veins the illegitimate blood of kings, traveling in a world of bawdy adventure and poignant romance—here is the essential Linklater myth in an unpretentious gem of a book. It looks to *Private Angelo* and beyond to *Position at Noon*. Set entirely in England, it has the markings of Scottish folk fabliau.

The claims of serious comic art pulled Linklater back to more ambitious adaptations of legend. *The Impregnable Women* (1938), one of his least successful books, was "a novel inspired by angry revulsion against the prospect of war's renewal."[15] It supposes the renewal of European war sometime in the 1940s. The war begins with air raids, but an oil embargo sends the armies back into the grisly trench warfare of 1914–1918—and this, Linklater says accurately, he described "with sufficient realism . . . in a high, resounding style." . . .

After the long hiatus of World War II came *Private Angelo* (1946), out of Linklater's war experience in Italy. Following the fall of Rome he drove across Umbria to the Adriatic: "I had already given much of my heart to Italy, and now—though the local wine was bad—I renewed my dedication." The conception of his wry, wondering Candidean peasant hero—"no anti-hero, but a true one"—came a decade earlier, from observing and hearing about the peasants on the Villino Medici estate, particularly about one man who managed to survive and come home from war owing to his fortunate lack of the *dono di coraggio*.[16] Angelo has "the most useful of all accomplishments, which is to survive!" A deserter from the Italian army, he is dragooned into the German army, prevents his deportation by volunteering for the Italian front lines, deserts again and becomes attached to a commando group of the British Eighth Army, arrives in Rome for the liberation, is enlisted in one of the new Italian regiments, loses a hand and is discharged home to rule benignly over a menage of wife, mistress, sisters-in-law, and several polychromatic or international children, the waifs of foreign soldiers and increasing numbers of his own. Parallel to Angelo's fortunes run the fortunes of his patron, landlord, and evidently his natural father, the Count of Piccolograande, a refined, amoral patrician blackmailed into poverty by the despised Germans.

Angelo's happy penchant for flight keeps him out of major military events, and the book sedulously avoids narration of the Italian campaign—although Linklater was War Office historian of the campaign. It is a deliberate control, for Angelo is ideally suited to play naive ironic observer and might have been used primarily as a medium for ironic history. But Linklater has other designs:

> The subject of my novel was not only war and its capacity for destruction, but Italy and its genius for survival. War in Italy has a character all its own; it was tragical, as war inevitably is, but also ludicrous because its waste and folly were underlined, emphasized and thrown into toppling-high relief by the accumulated riches and beauty that Italy had created . . . War was hateful—anyone could see and say that—but war in Italy was also irrelevant because the forces of civilization, and the benignities of art, were clearly so much stronger, more informative and more permanent. War, in Italy, was a drunken, destructive and impertinent clown; to deal justly and truthfully with it one had to keep one's temper cool, one's judgment clear, and write a comedy."[17]

The effort is a triumph of tone. But the mode of drunken clownishness is absent, for the perspective of the book is either the count's poignant Panglossian urbanity, or Angelo's tongue-in-cheek Candidean irony. Amid the bloodshed and destruction their elegant dialogues go on, and the potentialities for grotesque farce are wisely muted. "Realism," Linklater recalls, he carefully avoided, but not in the interest of fantastic farce. The ironic lucidity of Angelo's sad bemusement is a little miracle of rational order:

> "Would you say that this village has been liberated?" asked Angelo.
> "Oh, properly liberated," said the soldier. "There isn't a roof left in it."
> "It makes me sad to look at such destruction," said Angelo. "I am Italian, you see." [82]

> "Do I, in any way, resemble Cassino?" he asked Simon, as soon as he was allowed to visit him.
> "There is no apparent similarity," Simon answered.
> "Then why was I bombed?"
> "We all make mistakes from time to time."
> "We do not all carry bombs. To make a private mistake in your own house is one thing, but to make a public mistake with a bomb of two hundred and fifty kilograms is different altogether."
> "Year by year," said Simon philosophically, "science puts more power into our hands."
> "So that we may throw bombs at the wrong people?"
> "Science, like love," said Simon, "is blind."
> "I prefer love," said Angelo. "It makes less noise." [90]

Angelo marvels at life, at survival, at the miracle of his own body; the count complements him with his own sad resignation to absurd misfortune:

> All the days of his life joined themselves together to make a Chinese scroll of the most rich and delectable entertainment . . . He saw himself swollen with the toothache and badgered by the ear-ache . . . Sleep-walking at seven, a clap at college, the piles at forty—he has fallen from his horse in the pincio, he had choked on a fishbone when dining with the Colonnas, he had gone to the races with his buttons undone. . . . And yet, though they were ten times as many, life would still be good. (100)

He is the indestructible patrician, the passionate individualist who speaks for Linklater's conservative antipathy to "Great Powers, great causes, great events—and how dull they are!" and sings Linklater's paean to the survival of man the phoenix in his smallness.

Notes

1. Eric Linklater, "The Novel in Scotland," *Fortnightly Review*, 144 (1935), 621–624; *The Lion and the Unicorn* is in the Voice of Scotland series (London: Routledge, 1935).
2. Eric Linklater, *The Stories of Eric Linklater* (London: Macmillan, 1968), p. 11.
3. Eric Linklater, *Fanfare for a Tin Hat* (London: Macmillan, 1970), p. 133.
4. Linklater, *Fanfare*, pp. 103–104; quotations from Eric Linklater, *White-Maa's Saga* (Harmondsworth, Middlesex: Penguin, 1963) are from pp. 57, 51, 10, 185.
5. Linklater, *Fanfare*, p. 104; quotations from Eric Linklater, *Poet's Pub* (London: Cape, 1933), are from pp. 22, 74, 77.
6. Linklater, *Fanfare*, pp. 121–122; references in the text are to Eric Linklater, *Juan in America* (London: Cape, 1931).
7. George Blake, *Annals of Scotland 1895–1955* (Edinburgh: Mac-Donald, 1964), p. 28; Sidney Goodsir Smith, *Carotid Cornucopius* (Edinburgh; MacDonald, 1964), p. 14; and see Kurt Wittig, *The Scottish Tradition in Literature* (Edinburgh: Oliver and Boyd, 1958), pp. 328–329.
8. Linklater, *Fanfare*, p. 132.
9. Eric Linklater, *The Ultimate Viking* (New York: Harcourt Brace, 1956), pp. 8–11.
10. Eric Linklater, *The Men of Ness* (London: Cape, 1932), p. 245.
11. Eric Linklater, *Magnus Merriman* (London: Cape, 1934), pp. 298, 352.
12. Eric Linklater, *Ripeness Is All* (New York: Farrar and Rinehart, 1935), pp. 41–44.
13. Linklater, *Fanfare*, pp. 149, 155; Eric Linklater, *Juan in China* (London: Cape, 1948).
14. Eric Linklater, *The Sailor's Holiday* (London: Cape, 1937).
15. Linklater, *Fanfare*, pp. 157–160; Eric Linklater, *The Impregnable Women* (London: Cape, 1938).
16. Linklater, *Fanfare*, pp. 300, 146; Eric Linklater, *Private Angelo* (New York: Macmillan, 1946).
18. Linklater, *Fanfare*, p. 316.

MALCOLM LOWRY

1909–1957

The son of a wealthy and respectable businessman, Clarence Malcolm Lowry was born near Liverpool on July 28, 1909. He attended the Leys School, Cambridge, but spent more time writing and perfecting his ukulele technique than studying. His early enthusiasm for the sea led to a spell as a sailor in the Pacific, after which he visited Germany and then traveled to America to visit Conrad Aiken, who became his literary mentor. He then entered St. Catherine's College, Cambridge, in 1929; graduating in 1932, he moved to London, where he became known in bohemian circles as a drunken young genius. His first novel, *Ultramarine*, was published in 1933.

In 1934 Lowry married an American, traveling to join her in New York later in the year. Alcoholism and periodic paranoia were already causing problems, and the marriage was a stormy affair. In 1936 the couple journeyed to Mexico, where Lowry's drinking problem worsened and his marriage failed. Leaving Mexico in 1938, he visited Los Angeles, where he met Margerie Bonner, who joined him the following year in Vancouver. They married in 1940 and settled in a shack in Dollarton, near Vancouver, where Lowry found peace for several years.

After many years of writing and revision, the novel *Under the Volcano* appeared in 1947. The success of the book proved almost overwhelming to Lowry, whose mental stability and productivity subsequently declined. In 1954 he left Canada for good, and after travels in Europe and treatment for alcoholism in London, he settled with his wife in the village of Ripe, in Sussex. On June 27, 1957, he died suddenly after heavy consumption of gin and barbituates; the coroner recorded a verdict of death by misadventure.

Lowry's various incomplete projects appeared posthumously as *Hear Us O Lord from Heaven Thy Dwelling Place* (1961), a collection of stories; *Selected Poems* (1962); *Lunar Caustic* (1963); *Dark as the Grave Wherein My Friend Is Laid* (1968); and *October Ferry to Gabriola* (1970).

Personal

It all began—of course—when Malcolm, as a result of reading my novel *Blue Voyage*, wrote to me at Rye in 1929, and proposed that we meet. In due course, his letter found me at Cambridge, Massachusetts, and, in turn, he crossed the Atlantic to spend three months with me, working together on *Ultramarine*. *Blue Voyage* he said he knew by heart. He did, too, and it became a great, and lasting, joke between us that he used so much of this—style, devices, &c.—in *Ultramarine* and in all the later work as well: the influence was permanent. Even the title *Ultramarine* was intended as a reference to *Blue Voyage*, and I suggested why not go a step further and call it *Purple Passage?* At one point he copied out a page of my novel, *Great Circle*, proposing to incorporate it, but I said No. (I have this in his handwriting—it is a description of the devouring of the father's skeleton by the son.) Just as the too loose Lowrytrek was *my* invention, not his. And I might add, for those who are interested, that the entire argument, between the Consul and the other, about Marxism in *Under the Volcano*, was a verbatim report of an argument between Malcolm and myself, with the positions reversed: what the Consul says, I said. Your writer observes that Malcolm could DO this. One might say that he was a *tope*-recorder. A great many of my remarks and turns of phrase are embedded in all his works, as also in letters.

And this brings us to another mystery. It has always been said that *Under the Volcano* was written *after* the Cuernavaca period. Not so. I read not only the "lost" novel, *In Ballast to the White Sea*, while we were there, but the whole of *Under the*

Volcano. The first draft, but complete, and with a different ending: the horse theme had not then been developed. In short, that book was going to be rewritten for the next nine years. No wonder, given his genius for language, that it is such a miracle of English prose, which, I think, is its chief virtue. He worked on it as one would on a patchwork quilt: every snippet of colour or serendipitous out-of-the-way knowledge that he found in his reading (he was always wanting me to send him old copies of *The Dial* or *Criterion*) was tucked in to enrich it, whether or not pertinent. But the novel was already substantially *there* in July, 1937.

Well, I can imagine him roaring with laughter about all this in his Ripe young grave in Sussex, and in this I join him. For to have manufactured such a myth, and turned himself into it, was perhaps a feat of literary *trompe-l'oeil* without parallel. He would have been particularly amused, I think, by your writer's quotation of the signature of his first—and so moving—letter to me:

te-thrum te-thrum
te-thrum te-thrum
Malcolm Lowry.

For the te-thrum te-thrum is not, as your writer says, characteristic of Lowry, but of me: it is in fact the running-theme of *Blue Voyage*, which he was quoting. And for Malcolm it was all just a great joke, even with the tragedy thrown in, which incredibly turned itself into a great book, or a great melodrama, as I said to him in a letter. And it *was* a great joke: his whole life was a joke: never was there a gayer Shaksperean jester. A fact that I think we must remember, when everyone is saying What Gloom, What Despair, What Riddles! Nonsense. He was the merriest of men. For some aspect of this, I recommend my novel, *A Heart for the Gods of Mexico*, where he appears as Hambo, and my autobiography, *Ushant: an Essay*, in which the relationship between us is gone into with considerable humour and precision. (Somehow the *TLS* never got around to reviewing this book.) When Malcolm read it, he said, simply, "A masterwork, but Ow how it hurts!"—CONRAD AIKEN, Letter to the Editor, *TLS*, Feb. 16, 1967, p. 127

The great problem of Lowry's life as a writer remains that of his loss of creativity. Why, after writing such a near perfect novel as *Under the Volcano*, did he leave no later novel that was complete or even comparable? ⟨Donald⟩ Day's explanation on this point ⟨in *Malcolm Lowry: A Biography*⟩ is, I feel, shrewd and worth quoting:

What destroyed Lowry's genius? If we refuse to agree with Freud that a writer's neuroses feed his art, then we may at least see that they can inhibit and disrupt it. Neurosis by definition is wasteful and destructive; it does not provide creative energy, it only expends it. I believe that Lowry's neuroses crippled him not only as a man, but also as an artist, in that they impeded him in his psychic journey between conscious discipline and unconscious experience. The root of neurosis is fear, and Lowry clearly feared his art; if its visionary aspect frightened him, so did its shaping aspect. He was, then, a man self-compelled to serve a vocation of which he was terrified; and this led him into the most elaborate and self-destructive ways of avoiding his art. Specifically, it led him ever deeper into introspection. Ultimately he was exhausted by this morbid self-absorption, and his art died.

This verdict certainly fits the pattern of Lowry's massive literary schemes that were never fulfilled. Most writers have experienced the occasions when they drive themselves to the desk, dreading the work ahead, or the more terrifying occasions when writing-blocks destroy or at least delay their productivity for months on end. In Lowry these common hazards of the writing life were gigantically exaggerated. And so *Under the Volcano* is a double miracle, both in itself as a novel, and as a work of self-liberation by a man who then returned to the prison of his tortured ego and never emerged alive.—GEORGE WOODCOCK, "The Myth of Malcolm Lowry," *Cmty*, March 1974, p. 73

Lowry is a one book author, everyone says, and the excellence of that book is accidental because he never learned how to write, he continually started and stopped, commenced and abandoned, caught in an endless proliferation of designs, so that the more evident it became that he would never complete his great work, the grander grew his schemes: everything he wrote would enter into them, one vast voyage, long as his life, just as confusing, just as deep, with ups and downs to rival Dante, yet he was wholly absorbed in himself and consequently could not create even an alter ego able to pull on socks ahead of shoes, at the uncork of a bottle he would fall into long dull disquisitions on the powers and bewilderments of alcohol, he hammered home themes like someone angry at the nail, yet buttered his bread on both sides and every edge; then, as if determined to destroy whatever mattered most, left manuscripts about like half-eaten sandwiches, and emptied Margerie of everything except the carton she came in.

However one thinks of the general sort of snacky under-earnest writers whose works like wind-chimes rattle in our heads now, it is easier to forgive Lowry his pretentious seriousness, his old-fashioned ambitions, his Proustian plans, his desire to pump into every sentence such significance as a Shelley or a Shakespeare had, to bring together on the page, like fingers in one fist, sense, sensation, impulse, need, and feeling, and finally to replace the reader's consciousness wholly with a lackaday magician's—drunk's, a fraud's—his own.

It was not glory or money, as a writer, Lowry wanted. He simply wanted masterpieces. He had no politics, particularly, no religion, no fastidious monkey-groomed morality, no metaphysics which would fancy up for him a world with more worth and order than a shelf of cheap sale books. It is hard to believe that he believed in much, though he read Goethe and Dante, dabbled in the occult, and used the Cabala as a symbolic scheme, though its choreography was an afterthought. Attitudes he had, but attitudes aren't philosophy. He was too eager to make use of what he read to be serious about it, and like Joyce he carried back to his books every tinshine thought he came across the way jackdaws break bright buttons off one's wash.—WILLIAM GASS, "Malcolm Lowry's Inferno: II," *NYRB*, Dec. 13, 1973, p. 28

Works

I do not think there is much doubt that Lowry has one foot well in the realm that is appropriate to *Canadian Literature*. It is not merely that on Canadian soil he produced the final, magnificent version of what many critics regard as the best novel written in our land; nor is it merely that much of his later work was set in Canada. We do not, after all, regard D. H. Lawrence as anything but an English writer, though he wrote many of his books abroad and set them in foreign countries. Try as he might to escape from his past, Lawrence remained the traveling Englishman, refracting all he saw through a personal and alien eye; his best writing on other lands was prompted by the lyrical observations of an outsider, and when he tried to enter into the heart of Mexico and portray it from within, he produced that literary monstrosity, *The Plumed Serpent*.

Lowry's relationship to his adopted home was quite

different. We read the poems he wrote on Burrard Inlet; we read the three Canadian stories in *Hear Us O Lord from Heaven Thy Dwelling Place*—"The Bravest Boat", "Gin and Golden Rod", and particularly "The Forest Path to the Spring". And we realise that he is not in fact writing about Canada as a transient outsider. He is writing about it as a man who over fifteen years lived himself into the environment that centred upon his fragile home where the Pacific tides lapped and sucked under the floorboards, and who identified himself with that environment—despite trials of flesh and spirit—as passionately as those other strangers who have rendered so well the essence of their particular corners of Canada, Grove and Haig-Brown. If Mexico stirred him through that combination of antagonism and attraction which so many Europeans feel there, Canada—or at least that fragment of it which stretches out from Burrard Inlet to embrace the Gulf of Georgia—stirred him through a sympathy that led towards total involvement.

It is for this reason, perhaps, that in his Canadian stories the Websterian hell of *Under the Volcano* never comes to view, though one gets a whiff of the sulphur in "Gin and Gold-enrod". No man goes down to destruction under Seymour Mountain, and along the beaches of Dollarton the phantoms with death's-head faces do not sing in the voices of demons as they did for Consul Firmin. On the contrary, here, in this closely and lovingly described land-and-inletscape, there is a sense of redemption; in "The Forest Path to the Spring" the mountain lion who sits in a tree over the path and embodies destruction runs away from the narrator's steady eye, and what the latter remembers about his trips to the spring—what he remembers most vividly—is the almost mystical experience of joy that at times seemed to carry him in a rhapsodic instant from the life-giving source back to the door of his cabin. Here, as in *Under the Volcano*, the self is immersed. But in the novel it drowns in the whirlpool of self-negation, whereas in "The Forest Path to the Spring" it bathes in a universal calm, the calm of a world of nature as sympathetic as ever Wordsworth wrote of, with which it identifies and from which it returns with joy enriched. It seems to me that it is in this almost rhapsodic identification with place that we find our best reason to claim much of what Lowry wrote for the literature of Canada. For it is not a sense of place that derives from mere observation, like that conveyed by a sensitive and competent travel writer; it is rather the sense of place that derives from a mental naturalisation which adds to a native's sense of identity the wonder of newness a native can never experience fully after childhood.

The stories in *Hear Us O Lord from Heaven Thy Dwelling Place* are all worth reading for themselves; some of the non-Canadian examples, while they do not attain the intensity of feeling of "The Forest Path to the Spring", are interesting for their experimental exploration of the problems of conveying multiple levels of meaning. "Through the Panama" is an example; the narrator, a transmuted Lowry figure, voyages to Europe by freighter, but his journey is also that of a modern Ancient Mariner, with the albatross of literary creation and its attendant curse hung around his neck as he considers his novels about novelists who are his own mirror images. For Lowry belonged in the early twentieth century cosmopolitan tradition that seemed to reach an end about the time of his death—the tradition of Proust and Gide, which came to the conclusion, inevitable after a century of introspection, that the proper study of the writer is the writer's mind.

But all these stories are also part of a great continuum, a vast Work in Progress that filled Lowry's life and was never completed—perhaps never could be completed. In this sense Lowry was of the Proustian rather than of the Gidian tradition.

The Gidians write many separate studies of experience, all related, but each self-contained; when one novel is finished a phase of investigation is ended, its record is terminated as quickly as possible, and then the writer is on to the next experience and the next novel. But the Proustians, and Lowry among them, conceive all their work as one great inter-related pattern on whose parts they work continuously and simultaneously. Proust could never leave the one great work of his life alone; he worked backwards and forwards over his manuscript, and only publication ever gave a final form to any of its parts; only death, one can be sure, put a period to the work itself, coming by coincidence at the point when Proust had reached the end of his original plan. So it was with Lowry. He worked on several novels, on stories and poems, all at the same time, and his revisions were multiple to the point of Flaubertian obsession. For this reason he spent many years over each novel, writing on others at the same time; his actually completed works are few out of all proportion to those he sketched out and started. Another decade of work might—and equally well might not—have presented us with a masterpiece in its own very different way rivalling *A la recherche du temps perdu*, perhaps even in one direction exceeding it, since Lowry possessed no cork-lined room and revised and added to his Work in Progress as the result, not of remembering a past now dead, but of experiencing and incorporating a lived present.

As it is, when *October Ferry to Gabriola* is published and the devoted labours of Lowry's editors have salvaged all that is publishable in fragmentary form from the other portions of the great cycle, we shall perhaps begin to see, at least in massive outlines, the modern Divine Comedy of which *Under the Volcano*, for all its portentous self-sufficiency, was intended only as a part.—GEORGE WOODCOCK, "Under Seymour Mountain," *CL*, Spring 1961, pp. 4–6

Perhaps all artists are born a little askant to life, but Lowry's angle of vision was no one else's. He knew it: it was one of the things that set him drinking and sent him looking for echoes of himself and his experience in Poe and Shelley and Keats and the early jazz artists he loved, Beiderbecke and Joe Venuti. A note that the Lowry-self, Wilderness, makes for a novel he is writing (or as he says "is enmeshed in") reads: "Martin had been on this planet for so long that he had almost tricked himself into believing he was a human being." Martin-Wilderness-Lowry, it will be seen, had strange visions which sometimes knit themselves into celestial puns.

These visions of Lowry's, where the world inside one's head and the world one kicks one's feet against penetrate each other, are not idle. They are visions of the reality behind the conventional habitual view we accept as life: they speak to us urgently of new meanings, like the trick bits of broken English overheard recurrently in Lowry's work which make odd, surrealist sense. Such bits of experience do not merely repeat each other; they reflect and heighten each other and connect the stories (in *Hear Us O Lord from Heaven Thy Dwelling Place*) making them a whole.

A whole, I almost wrote, which is more than the sum of its parts. And perhaps this is true. Lowry was not, in fact, an "easy" writer—as is evident not only from the two shorter stories here which are in part failures, but from the fact that his material needed to be worked, reworked, and worked again. His exact perception of nature and people and speech are not only profoundly individual, they must have come to him first as individual *events*, as small private explosions of meaning.

We can see him, in this book, working out their significance, mining them for what is public and communicable in them. Indeed he says himself, "Sometimes I had the feeling I was attacking the past rationally as with a clawbar and hammer, while trying to make it into something else for a supernatural end." (An excellent description, by the way, of exactly what it is that writers do when they write.)—ELIZABETH JANEWAY, "A Legacy, a Man and a Legend," *NYTBR*, May 21, 1961, pp. 1, 16

. . . Firmin ⟨in *Under the Volcano*⟩ is a compulsive drunkard (which is what Lowry himself became) and is clear-sightedly, almost Faustianly, bent on self-destruction. He has opted out of the world, rejecting both duty and love; when love and help are offered—by the wife who has returned to him and the half-brother who has come from the Spanish Civil War—he has to turn his face against them and elect for the hell of emptiness and the palliation of the mescal. It is a book about heaven and hell and the necessity of choice between them. On another level, it is a study of the choice that Europe, in the 'thirties, had already made. The most superficial level presents the self-enclosed world of the dipsomaniac, and this is the level that too many of the book's earliest readers saw to the exclusion of everything else. It was regarded as doing, rather more wordily and with far too many literary allusions, what had already been done in *The Lost Weekend*. . . .

Symbol-hunting could turn into a postgraduate sport if Lowry had not got in first. Laruelle goes to the local cinema during a thunderstorm and *Las manos de Orlac* (the film comes from Germany; the poster shows blood-stained hands) symbol-ises the guilt of mankind. In a similar storm Geoffrey Firmin releases a panic-stricken horse, which finally kills Yvonne, the wife who has come back to him. The careful planting of symbols and correspondences inevitably recalls *Ulysses*, but I think it would be wrong to call Lowry (as some critics have done) a disciple of Joyce. What it seems to me Lowry wrote is the kind of novel that Conrad Aiken wanted to write but lacked the architectonic skill to make structurally satisfying. Of course, *Blue Voyage*, *Great Circle* and *King Coffin* have such Joycean elements as interior monologue and recondite literary allusion, but they lack the Joycean lust for form. Lowry's first letter in this published selection is one he wrote at the age of nineteen to Aiken, and admiration for Aiken's work leads him not to the postures of the disciple but to the conversion of the master into a genuine father-figure. The father, as Stephen Spender indicates in his excellent introduction to the new edition of *Under the Volcano*, has to be destroyed by the son: this is one of the conditions of his own act of creation.

But the superiority of Lowry's book to any of Aiken's lies, among other things, in the fact that, where Aiken produced Prufrock figures, small Hamlets, Lowry created in Geoffrey Firmin a giant character whose sloth or accidie ironically suggests the Promethean rebel, whose total alienation from life etches the desired opposite, whose inability to love defines what love is. Firmin is perhaps the last exemplar of one of the forms of Liberal Man. He is civilised, sensitive, idealistic, and he cannot survive in the world of the ravine, dominated by the hands of Orlac. He stands in a phase of history which is also valid as myth, with the carious Mexico of Graham Greene mirroring the torn Spain of all the intellectuals of the 'thirties. Firmin is diseased, but the remedy sometimes seems to be in his own hands: he is an exact symbol of Europe.

At the same time, he is a human being who, though he contains within himself a picture gallery of all the tragic heroes, from Oedipus Tyrannus and Philoctetes (the names of two ships in the novel) to Faust and Hamlet, is a fresh tragic creation in his own right, since he is a product of our own period. His situation is hopeless, but he doesn't whine: he even maintains a courtesy proper to his rank. He doesn't lie in bed like Oblomov, waiting for the end of a régime; he drinks

steadily and, through the drink, achieves the poet's or saint's clairvoyance. He knows precisely what is going on. The attainment of self-knowledge, however cut off from the ability to act, is seen to be an aspect of the heroic. . . .

But the impression of Lowry we receive from ⟨*The Selected Letters of Malcolm Lowry*⟩ is of a restless, energetic man, incapable either of Firmin's accidie or his inability to love. He is garrulous, serious, yet given to self-mockery and a rather old-fashioned courtliness. He is one of those writers who, antithetical to Gilbert Pinfold, seem quite willing to write a student's thesis for him (American English departments were on to Lowry's importance pretty early). He knew the worth of *Under the Volcano*, was earnest about it but never pompous. The time is coming for a detailed appraisal of his later book, *Hear Us O Lord from Heaven Thy Dwelling Place*. It seems to me as remarkable, in its different way, as *Under the Volcano*, yet sensible reaction to it looks like being as long delayed. But that Lowry is one of the great dead major novelists there can no longer be any doubt.—ANTHONY BURGESS, "Europe's Day of the Dead," *Spec*, Jan. 20, 1967, p. 74

. . . ⟨T⟩here lies, behind the experimental and modernist spirit, a deep vein of romanticism. The signals of modernism are evident enough; the texture of deep literary allusiveness, the commitment to formal experiment, the quality of strain and anguish which itself, as Stephen Spender stresses in a useful introduction to the 1965 reprint of *Under the Volcano*, links Lowry with the other central modernists in his concern with the 'modern breakdown of values'. Yet, as Spender says, Lowry's view of life is individualistic in a way in which those of the leading moderns are not, since through them a con-sciousness that is ultimately historic and even collective speaks. (Spender quotes a revealing passage from Sigbjørn Wilderness's journal in 'Through the Panama' (in *Hear Us O Lord* . . .): 'I am capable of conceiving a writer today, even intrinsically a first-rate writer, who *simply cannot understand*, and never has been able to understand, what his fellow writers are driving at, and have been driving at, and who has always been too shy to ask.') But Lowry's work is primarily *self*-projection, and the surrounding world tends to be solipsistically merged into that of the hero. Lowry's essential assumptions about art thus tend to be purist romantic ones, art seen as imaginative voyage and representative suffering, all this in the cause of a final transcendence, the fulfilment of a paradisial opportunity. It is against this that he introduces, modernly, a sense of tragedy; his primary themes are then the despoliation of the world by man, and the tragic condition of the serious spirit in the modern world. His heroes move through landscapes of destruction and waste, landscapes of hell in which symbolic ruination abounds, seeking the restitution of the paradisial garden. To some extent, as in Fitzgerald's work, the tragic derives from a sense of necessary identification with that world, a need to know its nature; and in Fitzgerald this view is supported by a superb cultural and historical awareness. But in Lowry the tendency is rather towards an auto-destruction in excess of what conditions it; at the same time, the imagined world of his books approves the nobility of that destruction. He tended to associate this scaled-up romantic dream of the self with creativity, which he saw as the principle by which we compose our lives. In the later work, I think, he sees the difficulty, and the stories in *Hear Us O Lord* . . . are marked by situations in which fiction, or the created romantic view of the self, is violated by reality; or else romanticism is dissipated by a critique of it, as in 'Through the Panama', where the need for talent to be uncritical of itself is played off against the need for criticism, and a notion of equilibrium emerges: 'And yet there has never been a time in history when there was a greater necessity for the preservation of that seemingly most cold-blooded of all states, equilibrium, a greater necessity indeed for sobriety (how I hate it!).' The confession is surely crucial, and at the heart of Lowry's artistic difficulties throughout his whole *œuvre*. In consequence, Lowry's 'large' romantic heroes, both in battle with the universe and striving to attune themselves to what is transcendental in it, are at once somewhat overly regarded *personae* for Lowry himself, and the subjects of the author's own criticism and even his uncertainty. The result is an achievement that has a fascinating development, an achievement at once magnificent and incomplete.—MALCOLM BRADBURY, "Malcolm Lowry as Modernist," *Possibilities*, 1970, pp. 184–85

ROBERT B. HEILMAN
"The Possessed Artist and the Ailing Soul"
Canadian Literature, Spring 1961, pp. 7–16

To have been an original admirer of Malcolm Lowry's *Under the Volcano*, and to remain an admirer for almost a decade and a half, is very much like belonging to a semi-secret order with a somewhat odd, quite small, but widely dispersed membership. It is a very loose order, without adopted procedure and certainly without program. Membership is conferred by taste, not sought by will or exercised through evangelical rigor. Members become known to each other only when they discover each other by accident. The big point is that such discoveries do continue to be made, year after year, in more than one part of the English-reading world. Yet they are an insistent trickle rather than a growing stream that could be converted into a literary power system. Whoever has read Lowry has been unforgettably impressed, but readers have been, it appears, strangely few. The slender society of those who esteem him, whatever the strength of their convictions, have been given to contemplation rather than to promotion or even public debate: he remains a private possession rather than a public figure—far less established in a literary niche than, say, either Nathanael West or Djuna Barnes, whom in some way he brings to mind and who hardly have a greater claim upon our respect. Perhaps the disinclination of Lowry admirers to shout from the housetops is related to a certain meticulousness in their literary judgment: they customarily speak of *Under the Volcano* as a distinguished "minor" work or as a "minor classic". This reserve is understandable; despite the often kaleidoscopic movement of both outer and inner landscape, there is some limitedness of scope, some incompleteness of human range, some circumscribing of consciousness that is felt partly in the fewness of the dramatis personae and partly in the enclosing illness of the protagonist (though in saying this last, one must always be mindful that the ailing soul may have extraordinary visions). But the use of "minor" is not an inadvertent disparagement: it is an honorable by-product of that need to place which is felt only when the novel in question arouses the conviction that it is not an entertainment of the year but a work of art that will be valid for many other years.

If a historian leafed through the journals of 1947 and noted the new novels reviewed, he would not find another one written in English, I surmise, that has achieved a more durable quiet esteem than *Under the Volcano* (I exclude Mann's *Doctor Faustus*, to which I shall return later). It has survived in a "population" where the normal death rate is close to 100%. A minor irony: it has survived its own publishing house. It has survived, as we have noted, an apparent smallness of canvas, and it has also survived a quite opposite difficulty: a fecundity

of suggestive detail that tends to over-stimulate the imagination, that is, to set it off in more ways than can be decently encompassed within an overall design. Something survives beyond the sense of chaos that the fecundity is in danger of creating, beyond an impression of a tropical creative richness (this in itself, of course, is not to be disparaged, even when it is imperfectly controlled). What survives, again, is something beyond the quality usually called "intensity," though the stresses that Lowry images, luxuriantly and often fantastically, do induce the severe tautness that marks some kinds of aesthetic experience. Intensity is really a secondary virtue; it can be attached to superficial forms of action (of the order of fisticuffs, for instance), just as more profound experience can be transmitted in relatively un-taut moods such as the contemplative. The criterion is not the presence of intensity but the depth of the concern—the spiritual burden—that intensity accompanies. The less substantial the matter, the more the hard and gemlike flame will resemble ordinary flushed cheeks and fever that can be aspirined away. The fire in *Under the Volcano* is not easily put out.

The sense of a largeness that somehow bursts out of the evident constriction, the fertility that borders on the excessive and the frenzied, the intensity that is not a surrogate for magnanimity, and finally an apprehension of reality so vivid that it seems to slide over into madness—these are symptoms of the work of the "Possessed" artist. If he has not quite achieved majority, Lowry belongs to the possessed novelists, among whom the great figures are Dostoevsky and Melville and, some of the time, Dickens. They may be distinguished from the "self-possessed" artists: Thackeray and Trollope and, to snatch an example from current fashion, C. P. Snow. Or, since Lowry's theme is human disaster, a grievous, driving, frenetic disaster, let us take for contrast Hardy, who seems calmly to organize and impose disaster as if he were seated at some cosmic control panel. In an older writer like Hawthorne or a modern one like R. P. Warren, there is somewhat of a conflict, or even an alternation, of possession and self-possession, of an unbridled urgency and a controlling will. The possessed artist is in the tradition of Plato's Ion, and at the risk of too neat a polarity, it may be hazarded that the self-possessed artist has ties with Aristotle's Poetics: rational analysability of form appears to imply rational creatability of form. It is not altogether a parody to picture the self-possessed artist, deep browed at his drawing board, coolly planning plot and catharsis. In C. P. Snow the key line, a recurrent one, is surely, "May I have a word with you, Lewis?" "A word"—a council—a plan—logos and logistics: life is ordered, or, if it does not wholly accede to the order designed for it, what dissidence there is is reflected, not in unruly surges of action that in their way elude the author and his decorous creatures, but through the rational comment of observers. Things never get out of hand; no wild dogs tug at the trainer's leash. Perhaps the ultimate figure in the world of self-possession is Arnold Bennett: one of his major aims seems to have been to keep his characters down, to remain the unyielding bailiff on his huge Five Towns estate. Was not this—that he would never "let go"—a subtle ingredient in what Virginia Woolf had against him? That, really, he saw Mrs. Brown only in terms of attributes that were at his beck and call? Bennett illustrates the intimate relationship, the virtual identity, between self-possession and the rigorous domination of character and scene (or at least the air of this). In some way his sense of security seems to have been involved in his paternal tyranny: for his creatures, no out of bounds, no fractiousness, no unpredicted courses, no iddish cutting loose. And if V. S. Pritchett is right, Bennett sufferered accordingly: his self-possession was close to suicidal.

Such comparisons help us to place Lowry. In sum: the self-possessed artist—the one who uses his materials as an instrument. The possessed artist—the materials appear to use him as an instrument, finding in him, as it were, a channel to the objective existence of art, sacrificing a minimum of their autonomy to his hand, which partly directs and shapes rather than wholly controls. This is how it is with Lowry. If *Under the Volcano* is a more talented book than any one of the outstanding C. P. Snow novels and is still less well known, it is in part that the work of the self-possessed artist is more accessible, less threatening, farther away from anguish; even in Hardy the inimical and the destructive are in an odd way almost sterilized because for the most part they originate in an outer world that is unyielding or uncontrollable only by fits and starts, rather than in an inner realm of constants where catastrophe is always latent (Sue Bridehead is a rare exception). Snow works in a wider and more accommodating territory, Lowry in a very much more dangerous terrain. Possessed work may open up any depth before one, any abyss in other personalities or in one's own. It does not primarily contemplate, though it does not ignore, the ailing world, which is generally reparable in Snow, or traditionally irreparable in naturalist fiction. Rather its theme is the ailing soul. It is an ancient theme whose history concerns us here only in that in our day the theme is used with extraordinary frequency. Whether it is that illness is especially attractive to us because we find in it a novel window to reality, or an apparently better window to reality, than the less clinical ones that we have principally relied on; or that the culture is sick, as some critics aver with almost tedious constancy, and that as a consequence we must, to avoid self-deception and serve truth, contemplate only sickness—these differing conclusions are arguable.

In the contemporary use of illness, at any rate, we find quite different perspectives. In *Sound and Fury* there are various ailing souls: through them we have a complex view of decadence and of a contrasting vitality. In Robbe-Grillet's *Voyeur* clinical disorder of personality is itself the aesthetic object: despite all that has been said about Robbe-Grillet's innovations in the vision of reality, the final effect is one of a disturbingly ingenious tour de force. In *Magic Mountain* the ailment of the soul is intricately intertwined with that of the body; a host of theoretical salvations are examined, and the final note is one of hope through a surprisingly simple practical therapy. But in *Doctor Faustus* there is a more fundamental and violent illness of soul, a counterpart of a more fundamental and violent illness of body, one that is in effect chosen; we see a sick person and a sick era, sick thought that is a culmination of a tradition; yet a tradition in which the paradoxical affiliation of the destructive and the creative is terrifying.

Doctor Faustus offers some instructive parallels with *Under the Volcano*: both works belong to 1947; both recount the spiritual illness of a man that is in some way akin to the illness of an age; both glance at the politics of the troubled 1930's, but both are artistically mature enough to resist the temptations always offered by the political theme—the polemic tone, the shrill "J'accuse." Instead they contemplate the failures of spirit of which the political disorders are a symptom. They do this differently. Though both draw on the Faustian theme, Lowry introduces it less directly than suggestively, as one strand in a mythic fabric of considerable richness. Mann, by now an old hand at mythic reconstructions, revives Faustus in the grand manner. The mode of evil is affirmative: demonic possession, a rush into destruction in a wild flare of self-consuming, power-seizing creativity. In demonic possession there is a hypertrophy of ego; Lowry's hero, on the contrary,

suffers from a kind of undergrowth of soul. One leaps on life rapaciously; the other falls short of the quality that makes life possible. Both the rape and the agonizing insufficiency are done with hair-raising immediacy. But Mann's style is heroic, whereas Lowry's stage is domestic. Geoffrey Firmin (the infirm Geoffrey) is more of a private figure than Adrian Leverkühn; his life has less amplitude in itself; in the concrete elements of it there is not the constant pressure toward epical-allegorical aggrandizement. But this is a statement of a difference, not of a deficiency. Both novelists are possessed; both seem to be the instruments of a vision whose autarchy they do not impair as they assist its emergence into public form. This is true of Mann, despite his usual heavy component of expository pages; it is true of Lowry, despite some artifice and frigidity in the narrative arrangements.

If Lowry's work is, compared with Mann's, "domestic", nevertheless the implied analogy with domestic tragedy is slight at best. To make one important contrast: Lowry has a range of tone that household drama never had. In fact, even in the orbit of possessed artists, his range is unusual: in recording a disaster of personality that is on the very edge of the tragic, he has an extravagant comic sense that creates an almost unique tension among moods. Desperation, the ludicrous, nightmare, the vulgar, the appalling, the fantastic, the nonsensical, and the painfully pathetic coexist in an incongruous melange that is still a unity. The serious historian of the ailing soul may achieve the bizarre, but he rarely works through humor or finds the Lowry fusion of the ridiculous and the ghastly. With Lowry, the grotesque seems always about to trip up the catastrophic, the silly to spike the portentous, the idiotic to collapse the mad. When evil is present, it is more likely to be nasty than sinister. The assailing demons tend to be mean little gremlins; in a way, Geoffrey's disaster is the triumph of meanness, not as a case-history of an eccentric flop, but as a universal image of man in the smallness to which he is always liable. This can take on its own dreadfulness, partly because petty vice contains echoes of major failures, partly because nemesis is not trivial, and partly because there is always maintained a touching nostalgia for a large and noble selfhood. In *Lady Windermere's Fan* there is a very bad line about man's being in the gutter but looking at the stars; it is bad because the play contains no vestige of real gutters or real stars, so that words alone are being exploited. But these antithetical images could be used of *Under the Volcano* without bathos, for it contains some of the more plausible gutters in modern fiction while portraying the survival, even in them, of a dim and struggling consciousness of other worlds. Lowry is quite lucid about what is sickness and what is health, rather more so, indeed, than another possessed novelist usually credited with expertise in these polar states, D. H. Lawrence.

Lowry does not manage the cosmic texture of events that we find in *Doctor Faustus*, but there is an extraordinary texture of symbol and allusion. It is doubtless natural for the possessed novelist to call on many of the resources of poetry. The self-possessed novelist is not necessarily prosaic or shallow or one-dimensional, witness Henry James; but in the main we image him as forging steadily or deliberately ahead, on the direct prose route to his end. The possessed writer has an air of battling, not quite successfully, with a multitude of urgencies that come at him from all sides and fling off again on their own, not always forced into a common direction. If the overt action of *Under the Volcano* is slight, the metaphorical action is intense. Numerous objects, properties, occurrences, and even ideas, recollections, and observations not only exist in their own right but also work figuratively or symbolically. The nexuses are imaginative rather than casual, or logical, or chronological; hiatuses compel a high attention; dextrous leaps are called for. In such a sense the novel is "poetic," not in the sense that a mistily atavistic syntax and a solemn iambic hauteur, as often in the self-conscious experimental theatre, pass for poetic.

The "story," as I have said, is slight: Yvonne, the wife of alcoholic Geoffrey Firmin, returns, after a year's separation, to her husband in Mexico. The events all take place on the day of her return. Geoffrey's passing desires to pull out with Yvonne are overcome by a far more urgent passion for alcohol. A French movie-producer, former lover of Yvonne, is with them for a while and incredulously lectures Geoffrey. Geoffrey's brother Hugh, ex-reporter and sailor, now about to run arms to the Spanish loyalists, in love with Yvonne, spends the day with them. The chief event is an outing by bus—Lowry's own wayward bus ("making its erratic journey"), which stops for a while near a wounded Indian left by the roadside but leaves without anybody's having done anything. Late in the day Geoffrey, who has constantly been getting separated from Hugh and Yvonne, outrageously abuses Yvonne and runs into the woods near Popocatepetl. Yvonne and Hugh pursue. Yvonne and Geoffrey lose their lives by means symbolically associated with the episode of the unattended roadside Indian.

Hugh makes his boat for Spain: this we have learned from a retrospective prologue—the contents of which are certain words and thoughts of the French movie-man a year after the day of the main story. This prologue is supposed to introduce all the main themes; but there is too much there to assimilate, especially since most of the material is not dramatized. It is a cold beginning, and then one has to keep going back to it as a table of contents—which is not the kind of re-reading that a concentrated book may legitimately demand. Further, on technical matters: the retrospects on which a one-day story must rely tend to be flaccid in style (Hugh's) or foggy in detail (Yvonne's); and coincidence has a fairly large hand in things. But, once into the story, one is less aware of these things than of the imaginative richness. The minds of the characters are sensitive recording instruments, tenacious alike of facts and of their suggestive value. The book is a cornucopia of images; both the psychic and the outer world have a tangibility which a thoughtless slice of realism could never produce; humor and horror are never alleged but are moulded into a hard and yet resilient narrative substance. Always one is driven to follow through on the evocations that trail off behind the foreground facts.

So, besides reading the story as story, we are always aware of a multitude of implications which, in their continual impingement upon us, remind us of the recurrent images of Shakespeare. The action takes place in November, on the Day of the Dead; Geoffrey feels his "soul dying"; a funeral takes place; burial customs, the shipping of a corpse are discussed; an earlier child of Yvonne's is dead; Geoffrey thinks he is seeing a dead man; a cantina is called La Sepultura; Geoffrey recalls Dr. Faustus's death; a dead dog is seen in a ravine; a dying Indian is found by the roadside. Always there are vultures, pariah dogs, the noise of target practice. There are a decaying hotel, a reference to the House of Usher, the ruins of the palace of Maximilian and Carlotta. Geoffrey's soul appears to him "a town ravaged and stricken"; an imaginary "little town by the sea" burns up. Frustrations and failures are everywhere—engagements are missed, the light fails in a cinema. Always we are reminded of the barranca or ravine, near the town—a fearful abyss. Once it is called "Malebolge"; there are various allusions to Dante's *Inferno*; Geoffrey feels he is in hell, quotes Dante on sin, looks at Cocteau's *La Machine infernale*, takes a

ride in a Manquina Infernal, calls ironically-defiantly, "I love hell"; at the end he is in a bar "under the volcano". "It was not for nothing the ancients had placed Tartarus under Mt. Aetna. . . ." There are continual references to Marlowe's Faustus, who could not pray for grace, just as Geoffrey cannot feel a love that might break his love for alcohol, or rather, symbolize a saving attitude; as in the Faustus play, *soul* is a recurrent word. There is an Eden-Paradise theme: a public sign becomes a motif in itself, being repeated at the end of the story: "Do you enjoy this garden, which is yours? Keep your children from destroying it!" Geoffrey once mistranslates the second sentence: "We evict those who destroy." Geoffrey's own garden, once beautiful, has become a jungle; he hides bottles in the shrubbery; and once he sees a snake there.

The lavish use of such rich resources reveals the possessed artist. They might serve, perhaps, only to create a vivid sequence of impressions, feelings, and moods. But Lowry is possessed by more than sensations and multiple associations; there is a swirl of passionate thoughts and ideas as well as passions; thought and feelings are fused, and always impressions and moods seem the threshold to meanings that must be entered. It seems to me that he seizes instinctively upon materials that have both sensory and suprasensory values. How present the central conception—that of the ailing soul? There are endless symbols for ill-being, from having cancer to taking dope. But Geoffrey's tremendous drinking is exactly the right one, or by art is made to seem the right one. In greater or lesser extent it is widely shared, or at least is related to widely practiced habits; it is known to be a pathological state; it may be fatal, but also it can be cured. It lacks the ultimate sinisterness of dope, the irresistibility of cancer; hence it is more flexible, more translatable. And Lowry slowly makes us feel, behind the brilliantly presented facts of the alcoholic life, a set of meanings that make the events profoundly revelatory: drinking as an escape, an evasion of responsibility, a separation from life, a self-worship, a denial of love, a hatred of the living with a faith. There is an always pressing guilt theme: Geoffrey, who was a naval officer in World War I, is a kind of sinning Ancient Mariner, caught by Life-in-Death, loathing his slimy creatures, born of the d.t.'s, whom he cannot expiatorily bless but must keep trying to drink away). The horror of Geoffrey's existence is always in the forefront of our consciousness, as it should be; but in the horror is involved an awareness of the dissolution of the old order, of the "drunken madly revolving world," of which Hugh says, "Good god, if our civilization were to sober up for a couple of days, it'd die of remorse on the third." At the end Geoffrey, unable by act of will to seize upon the disinterested aid of two old Mexicans, is the victim of local fascists: fascism preys upon a world that has already tossed away its own soul.

The episode which most successfully unifies the different levels of meaning is that of the Indian left wounded by the roadside. He is robbed by a Spanish "pelado," a symbol of "the exploitation of everybody by everybody else." Here we have echoes of the Spanish Conquest and a symbol of aggression generally. Yvonne can't stand the sight of blood: it is her flaw, her way of acquiescing in the *de facto*. Geoffrey finds rules against doing anything; everyone feels that "it wasn't one's own business, but someone else's." It is modern irresponsibility and selfishness; the reader is prepared also to think of the "non-intervention" policy by the refrain which echoes throughout the book, "they are losing on the Ebro." But above all this is the story of the Good Samaritan—only there is no Samaritan. Devil take the least of these. (Geoffrey's ship, a gunboat disguised as a merchantman, has been named the "Samaritan"—a comment upon modern Samaritanism.)

Hugh, held back by Geoffrey, is almost the Good Samaritan—Hugh who is going to run arms to Spain. To Geoffrey and Yvonne, he is "romantic"; doubtless he is, and he has his own kind of guilt; but at least he insists on action, disinterested action. Here we come to what is apparently the basic theme of the book: man, in the words of a proverb repeated chorally, cannot live without love. Lowry flirts with the danger of the topical: the Spanish war might give the novel the air of a political tract. But ultimately, I think, the author does succeed in keeping the political phenomena on the periphery of the spiritual substance, using them for dramatic amplification of his metaphysic. It could be possible to read Geoffrey, always impersonally called the Consul, as dying capitalism, as laissez faire, or a sterile learning, like the speaker in Tennyson's *Palace of Art*. But such readings, though they are partly true, too narrowly circumscribe the total human situation with which Lowry is concerned.

The Consul's climactic acts of hate are a world's confession. Yvonne thinks of the need "of finding some faith," perhaps in "unselfish love." Whence love is to be derived, or how sanctioned and disciplined, is a question which the symbols do not fully answer. Yet it is the effect of Lowry's allusions—Dante, Faustus—to push the imagination toward a final reality that transcends all historical presents, however much each present may comment upon and even modify it. Most of all this effect is secured by his constant allusion to Christian myth and history—the crucifixion, Golgotha, the last supper, original sin. Lowry is hardly writing a Christian allegory; indeed, some of the Christian echoes are decidedly ironic. But his whole complex of image and symbol is such as to direct a dissolving order, in search of a creative affirmation, toward that union of the personal and the universal which is the religious.

The two extremes which are the technical dangers of this kind of work are the tightly bound allegory, in which a system of abstract equivalents for all the concrete materials of the story constricts the imaginative experience, and a loose impressionism, in which a mass of suggestive enterprises sets off so many associations, echoes, and conjectures that the imaginative experience becomes crowded and finally diffuse. It is the latter risk that Lowry runs. For the present account, to avoid excessive length, consistently oversimplifies the ingredients that it deals with, and it fails to deal with many other ingredients—for instance, the guitar motif, the cockfight motif, the theme of mystics and mysteries, the recurrent use of Indians, horses, the movie *The Hands of Orlac*, etc. Lowry has an immensely rich and vigorous imagination, and he never corks his cornucopia of evocative images and symbols. Some disciplinary rejections, some diffidence in setting afloat upon the imagination every boat that he finds upon a crowded shore, would have reduced the distractedness to which the reader is occasionally liable and would have concentrated and shaped the author's effect more clearly. This is to say, perhaps, that the possessed artist might at times borrow a little from the soul of the self-possessed artist. But if one might wish for a more ordered synthesis of parts, one would never want a diminution of the power in Lowry's possessed art. There is great life in what he has written—in his solid world of inner and outer objects in which the characters are dismayed and imprisoned as in Kafka's tales; and in the implicit coalescence of many levels of meaning that we find in Hermann Broch. Such a multivalued poetic fiction, with its picture of the ailing soul, its sense of horrifying dissolution, and its submerged, uncertain vision of a hard new birth off in clouded time, is apparently the especial labor of the artistic conscience at our turn of an epoch.

DOUGLAS DAY
"Of Tragic Joy"

Prairie Schooner, Winter 1963–64, pp. 354–62

There can be little doubt that Malcolm Lowry led as unfortunate and self-destructive a life as any writer one could name: for various psychoses, for drunkenness, for general inability to function as anything like a well-adjusted member of society, he was easily the equal of Poe, Rimbaud, or—to name a figure whose career more closely paralleled that of Lowry's—Dylan Thomas. There were the eye ailments, so foolishly ill-treated, that kept him nearly blind for four years of his childhood; the near-rejection by his parents, who never knew what to make of a son who refused to go into the family business; the disastrous first marriage with the flagrantly promiscuous Jan; the succession of lost manuscripts; the burning of his first shack in Dollarton, and the eviction from his second; the almost unrelieved poverty; the recurring fits of depression; the constant frustration of his attempts to write—and, above all, the really titanic struggle with alcoholism, which was (as Dr. Vigil of *Under the Volcano* diagnosed the illness of Geoffrey Firmin) "sickness not only in body, but in that part used to be called: soul." A perfect subject, one would say, for a biographer or critic with a fondness for depicting the pathology of genius.

Unless Lowry is luckier in his biographers than were Poe, Rimbaud, or Thomas (whose reputation is only now beginning to emerge from under the blight put on it by John Malcolm Brinnin's tasteless and irresponsible book), we are in danger of seeing him presented to posterity as morbid, wildly erratic, perhaps even suicidal. Such a picture would be cruelly unfair, and at least half-wrong; but we could scarcely blame the biographer who wished to dwell primarily on the sometimes pathetic and sometimes bizarre evidence supplied him by the many extant letters, diaries, and journals of Lowry's hallucinations, his conviction that he was the object of some monstrous and vaguely universal plot, his occasional fear that he was being spied upon by would-be assassins, and so on. This is, after all, the stuff that sells biographies. But there was another side to Lowry, however little it may interest sensationalists; and it is this side that I want to stress here: not only as a corrective to the biographies that are doubtless to come, but also as a way of suggesting that our blindness to this other side of Lowry's personality is liable to have as its corollary an inability to see a most important aspect of Lowry's work—its *humor*, its sense of being full of wry and self-mocking laughter.

When one reads the few brief essays that have been written by those who knew Lowry best—friends like Conrad Aiken, Earle Birney, Downie Kirk, William McConnell, Clarisse Francillon; his second wife, Margerie—one sees how these people could be perplexed and annoyed by the tendency of Lowry's critics to see him only as a tragic figure, self-absorbed and brooding. Aiken, for example, still stands by his characterization of Lowry as "Hambo" in his autobiographical *Ushant* (1952), when he called Hambo.

> that most engaging and volatile and unpredictable of geniuses: for surely of all the literary folk whom D. [Aiken] had ever encountered, there had been none among them who had been so visibly or happily alight with genius—not that Tsetse [T. S. Eliot] hadn't manifested something of the same thing, to be sure—controlling it, moreover, to better purpose; but in Hambo it had been the more moving, and convincing, and alive, for its very *un*controlledness, its spontaneity and gay recklessness, not to mention

its infectiously gleeful delight in itself. And why—he had always seemed to be in the act of asking—shouldn't genius damned well enjoy itself?—what was wrong with that—? Enjoy itself his genius did; here, there was never any secret hoarding, all was communicable and communicated, life itself was a picnic of genius in which everyone could share alike.

In his *A Heart for the Gods of Mexico* (1939), a *roman à clef* about a trip to visit Lowry in Cuernavaca, Aiken again used "Hambo" as a character, and described him as "good-natured," "shy," and "such a damned good fellow." Here, then, is a Malcolm Lowry very much different from the berserk who will surely fascinate the biographies: we see him, through Aiken, as an exuberant and cheery young man, rejoicing in his great physical strength, his obvious genius, his conviction that he was to become a great writer. We see him as an engaging *naïf*, arriving in Boston to study under Aiken, with a broken suitcase containing only his dirty socks, his ukelele, and the much-thumbed notebook in which were the first fragments of *Ultramarine*; we see him in England during his Cambridge years, whooping it up at Aiken's house over Christmas vacations. He is already an alcoholic past reclamation; he is shortly to endure the seedy humiliation of the years in Cuernavaca—but it never occurs to him that he has the slightest reason for self-pity or despair. He keeps on writing, and refuses to take himself seriously—except as writer.

Everyone else who knew Lowry well and who has written about him emphasizes this other side of the man. If Lowry (his friends wonder) had been as possessed, drunken, or demented as critics have said, how for one thing could he have produced so large a body of work in such a short time? (Granted that the *published* Lowry canon is small; yet observe what remains to be published; and observe the multiple drafts for every novel, every story.) How, for another, could his body have survived such mistreatment—not just the quantities of gin and scotch, but the countless illnesses and injuries that plagued him throughout his life? How, finally, could he have endured the poverty, the rejection, the humiliation by the Establishment of every country he lived in? Obviously, all these adversities, especially those that were self-imposed, would have been more than enough to silence and even to destroy any man who did not possess enormous reserves of spiritual and physical stamina. For Lowry to have survived even for as long as he did, and to have written as much as he did, was possible only because he was stronger than most men. To realize the truth of this, one needs only to read his letters, especially those written during any of his frequent dark nights of the soul; or better yet, one needs only to look at the photographs that were taken of him in England just before his death: his was the face of a man who had descended into the abyss, not once but many times—and who had emerged each time, his integrity, his fundamental innocence, and his humor intact. One realizes that his friends are right: Malcolm Lowry was not only a good man, but an essentially *happy* man. (Lest I seem to be going too far in the direction of making Lowry into a sort of beleaguered Pollyanna, let me hasten to add that Lowry's dark side *did* exist, and that at times his torments reached Promethean heights; but I still must maintain that there was another Lowry as well, just as sunny as the other self was dark.)

Once one is prepared to accept the complex nature of the man, he is ready to see what most critics have missed in the man's work: the saving grace of humor, the refusal to take too seriously the annihilation of the transparently autobiographical *personae* who serve as his heroes. This quality exists in all of Lowry's fiction, from the youthful *Ultramarine* to the un-

finished *October Ferry to Gabriola*. It must suffice here, however, to illustrate its presence in Lowry's masterwork, *Under the Volcano*, a novel of such symbolic complexity and such intricate design that its bedazzled critics have so far been unable to discern the very simple quality that makes it so profoundly moving: the quality that Yeats described as "tragic joy." What has hitherto been almost unobserved in that *Under the Volcano* is a novel about a brilliant and promising man who, because of some obscure but all-encompassing sense of guilt, is unable to love, unable to allow himself to be loved, and—finally—unable even to live; but who, throughout his headlong flight into hell, almost never gives in to maudlin self-pity—who seems, in fact, at times almost happily to embrace his destruction.

What is there in *Volcano* that obscures this basic theme? For one thing, there is the incantatory nature of Lowry's language (here, again, he is most like Dylan Thomas); for another, there is the whirling cerebral chaos that throws off images and symbols in almost insupportable profusion—the volcanoes, the dark forest, the demons that gnatter in Geoffrey Firmin's ears, the feculent barranca, the sinister Farolito, the ruined garden, the pariah dogs, the crumbling palace of Maximilian and Carlotta, the vultures, the branded horse, the snakes, the cleft rock, the chocolate skulls, and so on and on. There is, of course, the ingeniously developed cyclic structure of the book, which has seemed to some critics (those who have no conception of the part that occult correspondences play in the novel) too contrived, too repetitive, too coincidental. And there is also the wealth of literary allusion—so many references, occasionally obvious but mostly subtle, to so many authors and so many works, that at times one suspects that the less he knows about literature, philosophy, and pseudo-science, the better he can follow *Volcano*. How can we help but be distracted by so many tags, drifting in and out of every chapter, from the *Divine Comedy*; Marlowe's *Dr. Faustus* and Goethe's *Faust*; Pascal's *Pensées*; a Shakespeare sonnet; snatches of a song by Richard Strauss; poems by Marvell and Shelley; a German expressionist film; the *Mahabarata* and the *Rig Veda*; the Aztec legend of Quetzalcoatl and the Hellenic myths of Aphrodite, Hephaestus, and Prometheus; a play by Cocteau; and—especially—by constant references to several varieties of occultism: the Cabbala, Swedenborganianism, Rosicrucianism, astrology, and alchemy? If all these were not enough, there is, finally, Geoffrey Firmin's own library of arcana to ensnare the earnest student: from *Dogme et ritual de la haute magie*, *Serpent and Siva Worship in Central America*, *Goetia of the Lemegaton of Solomon the King*, down to *Peter Rabbit* ("Everything is to be found in Peter Rabbit," as Geoffrey Firmin was fond of proclaiming solemnly).

That all of these symbols, patterns, and allusions are joined organically to the whole Gestalt of the novel, and are not mere literary doodling, is one of the great strengths of Lowry's work; yet it is true that they cannot help but divert our attention from the real subject of *Under the Volcano*: the figure, dignified-ludicrous, of Geoffrey Firmin, drunk, failed consul, failed husband, failed poet—and happy man. We do not understand this novel until we realize that Geoffrey and his alter ego, his half-brother Hugh (who is Malcolm Lowry, no less than is Geoffrey) are presented to us not only as tragic victims, but also as the objects of our compassionate laughter.

In the formidable first chapter, we learn from Jacques Laruelle, the French film producer who had been Geoffrey's childhood friend, and who had acted more recently as the seducer of Geoffrey's lovely and slightly promiscuous wife, of two events that are, perhaps, at the bottom of the Consul's present overpowering guilt: that, during their adolescence in England, Jacques had come upon Geoffrey and a girl *in flagrante* at the bottom of the local golf course's "Hell Bunker" (a mild prefiguring of the cloacal barranca into which the lifeless body of the Consul is tossed at the novel's conclusion); and that, while in acting-command of a Q-Boat (named, with supreme irony, the *S. S. Samaritan*) during the First World War, Geoffrey might have had something to do with the burning alive in the ship's furnaces of some captured German officers. The earlier indiscretion had been, superficially at least, merely embarrassing; and we smile with Laruelle at "the expression on Geoffrey's face in the moonlight and the awkward grotesque way the girl had scrambled to her feet." But the second had been a more ominous hint of the destruction to come, and we are at first inclined to think of the Consul, years later in Mexico, as "a kind of more lachrymose pseudo 'Lord Jim' living in self-imposed exile, brooding . . . over his lost honour, his secret, and imagining that a stigma would cling to him because of it throughout his whole life." But Lowry will not let us off so easily, for he is quick to point out that

> No stigma clung to him evidently. And he had shown no reluctance in discussing the incident with M. Laruelle, who years before had read a guarded article concerning it in the *Paris-Soir*. He had even been enormously funny about it. "People simply did not go round," he said, "putting Germans in furnaces."

This qualification, this enforced drawing-back from conventional tragedy, is typical of Lowry's technique throughout the novel. When we first meet Geoffrey in the second chapter, after the long overture-cum-coda of the first, it is seven in the morning; and he is sitting at a bar, in evening dress (which he is not to discard for some hours) but sockless, trying to drink away a hangover from the preceding night's revelry. We have already learned, from a letter presented us in the first chapter, that Yvonne, his wife, had deserted him a year earlier, and that since her flight the Consul had plunged himself into a twelvemonth orgy of despair. But when Yvonne (who has returned to attempt a reconciliation) walks into the bar, Geoffrey can only make feeble jokes about his cuckoldry, his case of the shakes, the dismissal from his consular post. His attempt to achieve some sort of equilibrium is partially successful, and he and Yvonne return to the house they had once shared. But he needs alcohol to sustain this precarious balance, and runs from the house—only to fall flat in the street, where he lies in meditation until he is almost run over by a proper British type, who fortunately has a bottle of Irish whiskey in his car. Fortified by this encounter (partly because of the Irish, and partly because the Englishman's stiff-upper-lip stuffiness has reminded Geoffrey of his responsibility to the Empire), the Consul returns to his house with the intention of effecting a more physical reconciliation with Yvonne. In his weakened condition, however, he proves impotent; and, while Yvonne cries in the bedroom, he retires to the veranda, where he drinks himself into insensibility. The liquor exalts him, and he proclaims to himself pompously that "The will of man is unconquerable. Even God cannot conquer it"—then passes out, as the chair under him collapses. Here, once again, we have the pathetic and somehow ominous scene (the Consul's literal impotence here is only the outward and visible sign of his much larger spiritual impotence) cut off by the farcical conclusion.

When we meet Geoffrey next, he is awake again, and wandering about in the grossly deteriorated garden behind the house in search of a bottle of tequila he had slyly hidden there

days before. He stumbles about, fuzzily ponders a crude sign he notices on the edge of his property, drinks the tequila, and attempts to exchange pleasantries with his neighbor, a saturnine American named Quincey who mocks him for his drunkenness. The Consul has hiccups, and it is difficult for him to answer the neighbor's surly questions:

> "Hicket," answered the Consul simply. "Hicket," he snarled, laughing, and trying to take himself by surprise, he thwacked himself hard in the kidneys, a remedy which, strangely, seemed to work.

But Geoffrey's attempts to regain some semblance of sobriety and dignity do not work (because, for one thing, his fly is still unbuttoned from his earlier scene with Yvonne). When he whistles at his cat, and the creature's ears twirl in pleased response, he says that "She thinks I'm a tree with a bird in it." "I wouldn't wonder," retorts Quincey.

This garden scene is pure broad humor, and we must not fail to see it as such—even as we realize that, symbolically speaking, the garden is the ruined Paradise, and Geoffrey a forlorn and corrupted Adam, forced by a malevolent God to remain forever there, at the place of his sin.

When some time later we see the befuddled Geoffrey standing in the shower, still wearing his tuxedo trousers; or when he becomes trapped, inverted, at the top of a gigantic loop-the-loop machine, as all his possessions fall from his pockets into the hands of the children waiting below and laughing at him; or when he contrives to be enormously witty over the preposterous and unintentionally bawdy misspellings on a Mexican menu, for the benefit of Yvonne and his half-brother, the inevitable catastrophe is looming large, and our capacity to apprehend humor is correspondingly diminishing. For Geoffrey, the experience with the machine, say, is far from funny: he is horrified, and sees himself as Ixion, caught forever on a wheel turning in hell (the machine, not so strangely, is named *La Máquina infernal*—the infernal machine of Cocteau's play, that cruelly and inexorably unwinds, slowly destroying the human lives caught up in it); or as Prometheus, "that poor fool who was bringing light into the world." Yet even in the grips of this diabolical instrument, the Consul cannot help thinking, semi-facetiously, that this "was scarcely a dignified position for an ex-representative of His Majesty's government to find himself in"; and we realize that, however much Geoffrey is aware of the horror he has created for himself (and there is no novel in which horror is more palpable), he cannot help laughing at himself—at this stocky little man, his erect bearing, his dignified beard, and his occasional oh-so-Britishness not quite capable of offsetting the somewhat raffish effect of a slight but deplorable tendency to lurch and ramble, both physically and mentally. And because the Consul laughs, because he does not really *mean* to destroy himself, he is, in some unclear but nonetheless real way, indomitable. He is destroyed ultimately, in a nightmare scene that rivals Hieronymus Bosch for wild absurdity and ugliness; but his soul survives, ascending to the summit of the volcano that had always beckoned to him, even as his mutilated body is hurled into the barranca, to lie with offal and dead dogs.

To stop here is painful, for there is much more that ought to be said: about the Consul's wittiness, about his gentleness; about Lowry's fond mockery of himself as depicted in Hugh, the half-brother (an erstwhile soldier-of-fortune, who loves to wear cowboy outfits, imagines himself as taller than he really is, thinks of himself as protector of the martyred proletariat— all, we can reasonably suspect, poses that Lowry recognized, and laughed about, as parts of his own childlike ambitions). Lowry could not bring himself to finish a book, because there was always so much more to say; and the same difficulty obtains for his critics (myself included), who find that in Lowry they have someone rather much larger than life to deal with, someone who eludes definition and description. But, I must hope that I have succeeded if I have shown that a parable Geoffrey Firmin tells to himself in *Under the Volcano* is one which fits not only his own character, but Lowry's as well. According to this parable, man is a mountaineer whose way, either up or down, is fraught with danger, perhaps even impossible. "In life ascending or descending," the Consul thinks, "you were perpetually involved with the mists, the cold and the overhangs, the treacherous rope and the slippery belay; only, while the rope slipped there was sometimes time to laugh." The Consul had time to laugh, even while the rope slipped, and thereby becomes—in spite of his weakness, his irresolution, his failure to love—wholly admirable, in a way more so, even, than less-vulnerable tragic victims have been admirable. And Malcolm Lowry, for all his flaws, for all his sense of being slowly torn apart by the infernal machine that he took life to be, also had time to laugh.

E. V. LUCAS

1868–1938

Edward Verrall Lucas was born in Eltham, Kent, on June 11, 1868, and grew up in Brighton, Sussex. He attended eleven different private schools before being apprenticed at the age of sixteen to a Brighton bookseller, whose stocks allowed him to lay the foundations of his wide-ranging knowledge of literature. After two years he became a journalist, but the support of an uncle enabled him to go to London in 1892 to attend lectures at University College. The following year he joined the *Globe*, and he later became a regular contributor to *Punch*. He soon became known in literary circles, and was commissioned by Methuen to edit the *Works of Charles and Mary Lamb* (1903–05) and to write a new *Life of Lamb* (1905). He later worked as a reader for Methuen, and became chairman of the company in 1924.

Lucas' production was diverse and prolific, including the satire *Wisdom While You Wait* (1903) and a number of essayistic novels which he termed "entertainments," notably *Over Bremerton's* (1908), *Verena in the Midst* (1920), and *Rose and Rose* (1922). Travels in Europe led to the *Wanderer* series of travel books between 1905 and 1914. He also published books on art and tried his hand at drama, having a play, *The King's Visit*, produced in London in 1912. He was best known, however, as an essayist; his work in this capacity includes *Specially Selected* (1920) and *Lemon Verbena* (1932). A volume of reminiscences, *Reading, Writing, and Remembering*, appeared in 1932.

Lucas was a well-known figure in London society, a member of many clubs, and a noted bon vivant. He received honorary doctorates from Oxford and St. Andrews, and in 1932 was made a Companion of Honour. He died in London on June 26, 1938.

General

I called his output large. It is colossal. Nine times the space that measures industry in writing-men, namely, a page of the British Museum catalogue, he fills with his miscellanea. Nine pages!—with spaces (significant of popularity) for new editions and additions; and he is young enough, as literary years go, to fill another nine. The mere mass is remarkable; but what is really astonishing is its uniform excellence. Think, too, of its "infinite variety"—Verses, Essays, Novels (or "Entertainments," as he calls them), Topography, Biography, Editions of Lamb, Books for Children, Anthologies, Cricket, Satires, and Introductions innumerable! Nor does this take into account the contributions to *Punch* and other papers, not yet included in any volumes. Here, surely, is an illustration of Hazlitt's remark: "I do not wonder at any quantity that an author is said to have written; for the more a man writes, the more he can write." He might have added, "the better he can write." Lucas and Hazlitt can both be called as evidence.

He began with cricket—and verse; for the earliest surviving publication under his name is a little booklet called *Songs of the Bat*, a mere handful of verses, most of which were included in a later volume *Willow and Leather*. Not an inappropriate beginning. Cricket, the noble game, which appeals to purer passions than those inflaming the mobs who howl with glee or indignation (according to the side) over the fouls at football; cricket, which does not put its players up to auction and wax fat over transfer fees; cricket—for these desperate parentheses must come to an end—is one of the subjects that Mr. Lucas can never keep out of his pages. With cricket he began, and with cricket he will end. . . .

The public . . . have identified Lucas and Lamb in a way highly complimentary to Mr. Lucas the editor, but probably infuriating to Mr. Lucas the author. The worst of doing one thing very thoroughly is that you are not allowed to do anything else. True, the public like Mr. Lucas to write, as well as to edit; but its stupider members, who cannot get on without labels, insist on calling him a disciple of Lamb or even an imitator of Lamb, thereby proving that they can read neither Lucas nor Lamb, and probably cannot read anybody with intelligence. To find a likeness between the conversational simplicity of Lucas and the elaborated Gothic beauty of Lamb needs extraordinary obtuseness. The easy ripple of Lucas and the gyratory complexity of Lamb's digressions, progressions, retrogressions and circumgressions may be cited together for opposition, but for no other purpose. Moreover, there is such a thing as difference of scale, of plane, of intensity. Really, the comparison is too silly to discuss. The lunatics who call Lucas an imitator of Lamb are the kind of people who call Lamb "gentle."

Among Mr. Lucas's admirable achievements must be placed the invention of a humanised guide book. The usual book of this kind is either negatively dehumanised or positively priggish. One has the impression of earnest people painfully admiring what they are told to like and dutifully despising what they are told to dislike. Now the *Wanderer* volumes are remarkable for their absence of hortations and prohibitions, and their sense of wholesome personal enjoyment. They are utterly without pretence. They are not hectic even about the Primitives; they are rational even about the Renaissance. Mr. Lucas seems to be the only person who can write of Giotto without affectation and of Giorgione without preciosity. And the point is that these books are, in consequence, much more educative than all the ecstasies of the rapturous, who, in the end, do little more than transpose pictures into prose-poetry, a transmutation of which the bad pictures are often more capable than the good. In the best sense of the phrase, Mr. Lucas takes you with him; and, wandering in his friendly, healthy company, your range of enjoyment is so broadened that you will see beauty not only in the dome of Brunelleschi but in the steeples of Christopher Wren. The *Wanderers* are all excellent. They are good to travel with and good to sit at home with. Some day Mr. Lucas should travel in the realms of gold and gives us a "Wanderer in Shakespeare." But I hope he has not done with the merely bodily wanderings. . . .

There remain the essays and novels, increased just lately by *Cloud and Silver* and *The Vermilion Box*, that is, the pillar-box, an appropriate title for a story told in letters. Indeed, the names of Mr. Lucas's books are forty-and-four sweet symphonies; he has a positive genius for pleasant and intriguing titles. The novels, or entertainments, have the thinnest of plots and depend mainly upon quaint characters and current interests on which they serve as a humorous and really illuminating commentary. Future historians of social life in our generation will be able to learn much from Mr. Lucas. . . .

The character and comedy of life are Mr. Lucas's theme in nearly all the entertainments, whether stories or essays. Think of Mr. Ingleside's group of friends, of Miss Larpent and her epistolary injunctions, of Mrs. Washington Pink and her esoteric protégés, of Alf Pinto and his crucial name. The author's keen sense of idiosyncrasy in character is just his one point of affinity with Elia. Lucas, like Lamb, has an eye for the Sarah Battles and the George Dyers; I doubt, however, if Lamb would have been interested in Sister Lucie Vinken; but who can say; did he not love Quakers?

Very rarely does Mr. Lucas take us to the brink of tragedy; and he never plunges us into its depths. His pen is happier with life's little embarrassments than with life's greater ironies. In fact, his books have one essential quality of entertainments: they entertain. That is their *differentia*, and their value. It is good to be reminded in terrible times that life is not always terrible. The cloud upon the silver is sometimes all too visible; should we not rejoice, then, in a writer who shows us the silver of the cloud? In the Lucasian land it seems nearly always afternoon; but what a blessing to have this way of escape from the times when it seems nearly always ten o'clock on a foggy night and the way home lost.

To overpraise a writer so entirely unaffected, so pleasantly unmomentous, would be an insult which no one would resent more than he. The moving accident is not his trade. He does not vaticinate; he has never set up for a prophet; and he goes

upon his personal and literary way unparagraphed. Indeed, there are few writers of his enviable standing who have more sedulously shunned advertisement. His record is as clean as his art. The name of E. V. Lucas does not instantly occur to the mind when one counts up living writers of national importance. His work seems too slight to carry much weight. However, for my own part, I am inclined to think this slightness part of his real strength. His force lies in the fact that he is never forcible. The pleasant unruffled timber of his work is a national asset by being a national example.—GEORGE SAMPSON, "E. V. Lucas," *BkmL*, Feb. 1917, pp. 145–49

I cannot be certain whether *Listener's Lure* was the first of his stories, or novels, or "entertainments" as I seem to remember he once labelled them himself, but it was certainly one of the earliest. It arrived so long ago as 1906 and introduced a fresh and refreshing note into the fiction of its period. It adopted the old, well-worn method of telling a story in a collection of letters; but no method is too old in the hands of one who knows how to make it new again, and Lucas had the secret of doing that. Here, as in all his novels, the essayist and the novelist work in collaboration; the characters—Lynn Haberton, the literary man, his ward, Edith Graham, who is also his secretary, the delicate Albourne, the talkative, agnostic, Mrs. Pink, and the rest of the men and women, married and single, of their acquaintance—reveal themselves, or are revealed, and carry on the story in their correspondence; a story with no lack of love interests, abounding in humour, but with moods of deep seriousness, the letters digressing now and then into literary criticism, into gravely or whimsically shrewd comments on life and death and social and moral questions with which everybody is more or less concerned. These cunningly blended elements, and the skill and subtly humorous truthfulness with which the characters are drawn disguise the slightness of the story itself so that it keeps you as closely interested as if it were unravelling a powerful plot, and moves you to repeated chucklings of quiet enjoyment.

This same blend of delightful humour and occasional seriousness of thought, the same blend of essay and story, in varying proportions, the same deftness and lightness of touch and realistic art in characterisation are the irresistible lure of the witty and charming *Over Bembertons*, of *Advisory Ben*, *Genevra's Money*, *Verena in the Midst*, *The Vermilion Box* (another tale told in letters, the vermilion box being the familiar pillar-box), *Mr. Ingleside*, *Landmarks* (which has a good deal of autobiography in it), and of the Lucas novel in general. Some have more fantasy, or more sentiment, a more everyday homeliness or a more settled plot than others, but the same gracious Lucasian whimsicality and philosophy, acute and sympathetic understanding of men and women and charm of style link them each to each, and would seal them as distinctively his even if no name were printed on their title pages.

As for the essays, their very number and infinite variety reduces me to despair of saying anything of them in the space that remains to me that shall be sufficiently comprehensive. They have all the airy magic of the novels, sometimes are a compromise between tale and essay, and whether they take a theme that drifts into thought that is deep enough for tears, or is lively with burlesque laughter, or lighter in idea than thistledown or almost as intangible as the air, they are as delicately done as any filagree carving in ivory, but have a genial, friendly, companionable warmth of humanity in them that makes the comparison with ivory inadequate. His admirers used to be amazed that Swift could sit down and write an essay on a broomstick; but Lucas does not require a broomstick, he can write a delightfully quaint, witty or wise essay on nothing at all. He has not been contented to travel the great highways of literature, but has an extensive and peculiar acquaintance with its byways, and a special weakness for oddities of literary character, and can fascinate a reader with his cunning recreations of them. I remember his "Boswell of Baghdad", and, for example, his "Philosopher that Failed" (in "Character and Comedy")—which takes that old Barnard's Inn solicitor, Oliver Edwards, who had been at Pembroke College with Dr. Johnson and is a transitory figure in Boswell's *Life*, and reconstructs his character, his one meeting with Johnson when they were both old, and by sly little deductions and reasonable amplifications makes the man and the scene more vivid and intimately alive than Boswell himself has made it.

See how the manner and tone, the geniality, and variableness of the essays get into their very titles—*Urbanities, Fireside and Sunshine, One Day and Another, Loiterers' Harvest, Giving and Receiving, Luck of the Year, Encounters and Diversions, Events and Embroideries*—you know what to expect as soon as you read the names on the covers, and they do not disappoint you. Probably because of his association with Elia, Lucas is occasionally spoken of as if he had chosen Lamb for his model, but he is no more an imitator of Lamb than Lamb was of Addison and Steele; he is his own man, his humour, fantasy, pathos, and general outlook on men and things are his own, his subjects his own and his manner of treating them, and if he has affinities with Lamb, Leigh Hunt, Addison and Steele, it is simply because, as an essayist, he is in the legitimate line of descent from them. But to put this opinion on broader, more responsible shoulders than mine, I will leave the last word with the late Sir Edmund Gosse, who has said in one of his essays: "Unless my judgment is much at fault, there has written in English, since the death of R. L. Stevenson, no one so proficient in the pure art of the essayist as Mr. E. V. Lucas. . . . There have not been many true essayists, even in English, but Mr. Lucas is one of them."—ARTHUR ST. JOHN ADCOCK, "E. V. Lucas," *The Glory That Was Grub Street*, 1928, pp. 198–201

Works

Mr. Lucas . . . is a highly mysterious man. On the surface he might be mistaken for a mere cricket enthusiast. Dig down, and you will come, with not too much difficulty, to the simple man of letters. Dig further, and, with somewhat more difficulty, you will come to an agreeably ironic critic of human foibles. Try to dig still further, and you will probably encounter rock. Only here and there in his two novels does Mr. Lucas allow us to glimpse a certain powerful and sardonic harshness in him, indicative of a mind that has seen the world and irrevocably judged it in most of its manifestations. I could believe that Mr. Lucas is an ardent politician, who, however, would not deign to mention his passionately held views save with a pencil on a ballot-paper—if then! It could not have been without intention that he put first in ⟨*One Day and Another*⟩ an essay describing the manufacture of a professional criminal. Most of the other essays are exceedingly light in texture. They leave no loophole for criticism, for their accomplishment is always at least as high as their ambition. They are serenely well done. Immanent in the book is the calm assurance of a man perfectly aware that it will be a passing hard task to get change out of *him!* And even when some one does get change out of him, honour is always saved. In describing a certain over of his own bowling, Mr. Lucas says: "I was conscious of a twinge as I saw his swift glance round the field. He then hit my first ball clean out of it; from my second he made two; from my third

another two; the fourth and fifth wanted playing; and the sixth he hit over my head among some distant haymakers." You see, the fourth and fifth wanted playing.—ARNOLD BENNETT, "E. V. Lucas and G. K. Chesterton" (1909), *Books and Persons*, 1917, pp. 153–54

. . . ⟨I⟩t is the very essence of his work to display his own temperament in all its varied associations. The occasional essay, such as he affects, depends for its very life upon the revelation of temperament; it is a swift record of experiences imbued with the personal impression that holds the secret of its charm. And to touch high-water mark in the art, a writer must be happily free from self-consciousness, or must at least know how to convey the suggestion of absolute ingenuousness and private confidence. The art that secures this effect may be ever so deliberate, but it is the natural reflection of personality; "the adventures of a soul among" trivialities; meditation (so to speak) overheard; and directly the speaker grows conscious of his audience, the charm evaporates.

Few literary arts are more difficult. It is a fact, known to all whose business obliges them to dictate their correspondence, that a letter spoken aloud is seldom so sincere as a letter written by hand. The medium of the recording stenographer distorts the speaker's attitude. No man of honest feeling could possibly dictate a love-letter. And the same risk haunts the occasional, or personal essay. Most people, when they begin to write about themselves, assume involuntarily the airs of the peacock, and preen their plumage in the sunlight of observation. But Mr. Lucas never makes any such mistake. Almost alone among his contemporaries he can write about himself without the assumption of the egoist. He is self-revealing, but not self-exposing. He never steps over the broad white line which separates personality from conceit. And the reward of his instinctive discretion is that he neither shocks his reader, nor bores him. The charm and the interest of his soliloquies are impregnable.—ARTHUR WAUGH, "Mr. E. V. Lucas," *Tradition and Change: Studies in Contemporary Literature*, 1919, pp. 293–94

Mr. Lucas in *Rose and Rose* has written what may be called his first "straight" or, possibly, "legitimate," novel; and one may be permitted to doubt whether the effort which it must have cost him was worth the trouble. Mr. Lucas is nothing if he is not the prince of digressions; and for him deliberately to pass by opportunities for digressing, as he so obviously has done here, is merely to renounce the use of his chief gift. Rose is an orphan adopted by a bachelor country doctor. He brings her up and watches over her, and, with sorrow, sees her make an unfortunate marriage. She runs away from her stiff and priggish husband. The husband brings the younger Rose to the doctor to be brought up.

Mr. Lucas would not find it easy to write uninterestingly, and he does not achieve that feat here. His wisdom and knowledge of the world are immense: his judgments on humanity are as firm and precise and unalterable as they are tolerant. His characters are well drawn and alive. But some of them, in a book by Mr. Lucas, make one a little lift one's eyebrows. There is an elderly Irish lady, one of Dr. Greville's favourite patients, to whom he goes for advice on the affairs of the two Roses. She is sharp-tongued and warm-hearted: she abuses and loves both Dr. Greville and her companion. She is witty and playfully cantankerous: she delights in making herself seem worse-natured than she is. We have met her in innumerable novels before, and, even if we are fated to meet her in innumerable novels again, Mr. Lucas, who is capable of more originality, ought not to thrust her on us. But the greatest disappointment in the book is its inexorable "straightness." Dr. Greville must have had hobbies on which he would have liked to discourse: he must have met odd persons whom he would have liked to describe. Why should he not have done so? There is, indeed, no more story in this book than there was in *Mr. Ingleside*; but here the digressions, which never got in the way of the story there, have been severely trimmed away. One has the feeling that one is being hurried down a long corridor. The proportions and the panelling both please the eye, but the locked doors which one regretfully passes take away from their effect.—EDWARD SHANKS, *LM*, Nov. 1921, p. 97

EDMUND GOSSE
"The Essays of Mr. Lucas"
Books on the Table
1921, pp. 105–10

Unless my judgment is much at fault, there has written in English, since the death of R. L. Stevenson, no one so proficient in the pure art of the essayist as Mr. E. V. Lucas. In saying so, I do not forget how much excellent prose is constantly being produced among us, nor what a variety of stimulating merit labours for our entertainment. But the particular thing which Montaigne invented in the second story of the Tower of his Castle in the month of March 1571, is delicate and rare. It has not been cultivated with great success anywhere but in England—except, of course, by its immortal French inventor—nor in England save occasionally and by a few select pens. I confess to the heresy of not being able to consider Bacon's highly ornamented chains of didactic wisdom "essays" in the true sense, there being so little in them that is personal or even coherent. On the other hand, Cowley, who first understood what Montaigne was bent on introducing, is a pure essayist, and leads on directly to Steele and Addison, and to Charles Lamb. If we read Cowley's chapter "On Myself," we find contained in it, as in a nutshell, the complete model and type of what an essay should be—elegant, fresh, confidential, and constructed with as much care as a sonnet. There have not been many true essayists, even in English, but Mr. Lucas is one of them.

That Mr. Lucas has learned much from his long and intimate communion with the text of Charles Lamb is manifest, but he is a disciple, not an imitator, of that admirable man. He early felt that it was an error to copy the tricks and the archaisms of even so exquisite a master, and that there is a danger in producing a mere pastiche of the quaintnesses of Lamb, or of such an earlier model as Addison. How cleverly this can be achieved, when it is done of set purpose, may be seen in Sir James Frazer's marvellous *Sir Roger de Coverley* (Macmillan & Co.), but this has not been Mr. Lucas's aim. He has perceived that much of the "colour" of Steele and Addison was actual colloquialism in their own age, and that the charm of the Tatlers and Spectators lay, not in their oddity, but in the unaffected grace with which they said perfectly simple things in the straightforward language of well-bred people.

Lamb made a perilous experiment when he determined to secure a whimsical effect by imitating the speech of a century and a half before his time. His genius enabled him to carry the adventure off with complete success, but none the less it was dangerous. Less adroit writers simply fall into affectation in their effort to be fantastic, especially if they happen also to have adopted the fashionable contortions of George Meredith. The essay does not achieve genuine success unless it is written in the language spoken to-day by those who employ it with the maximum of purity and grace. It should be a model of current cultivated ease of expression and a mirror of the best conversation. The essays of Mr. Lucas fulfil this requirement.

Possibly the fecundity of Mr. Lucas, which is astonishing, has stood in the way of his reputation. Readers become restive, or tend to turn ungrateful, when a favourite writer makes his bow to them with a book too often. The abundance of Mr. Lucas is certainly surprising. His present publishers announce twenty-nine volumes issued by themselves alone, and I know not how many more are in other hands. The fluency is more apparent than real, for most of these are slender books, and some are scarcely more than brochures. A rigid calculation would probably show that, while Mr. Lucas's bindings are very numerous, the bulk of his printed matter does not exceed that of rarer visitants. His earliest "book of wayfarers," that delightful collection happily named *The Open Road*, is now more than twenty years old, and is still, no doubt, the volume of his which has penetrated the greatest number of households. But of works entirely his own, *Listener's Lure* is probably that which has been most universally appreciated. His essays, pure and simple, have, I conjecture, enjoyed a very uniform welcome, modified only by the more or less popular or amusing nature of the subjects he treats. Some day I hope he will find time to rearrange his writings in that "collected" form which is the Mecca to which every pilgrim-author looks pathetically forward.

The little volume (*The Phantom Journal, and Other Essays*) which gives me a thread on which to hang these wandering remarks, is wholly miscellaneous in character. It strings together specimens of Mr. Lucas in each of his moods, and offers therefore a good opportunity for the comparative study of his mind. We see that, with all his versatility, he avoids (as Lamb contrived to avoid) the purely didactic. This successful resistance to the instinct for teaching amounts to a positive, not a mere negative, quality. The desire to instruct, to occupy a pulpit, has been one of the greatest snares in the path of British essayists, and they have fallen the more inevitably into it because of the curious fact that, at the start, nothing is more eagerly—and even greedily—welcomed than the didactic. Moral reflections, especially if introduced with a certain polite air of solemnity, are to the British public what carrots are to a donkey; they cannot be resisted, the audience runs to read. But the appetite is satiated as quickly as it was aroused, and no form of literature fades out of sight more suddenly or more completely than do volumes inculcating Magnanimity in Humble Life or the Combating of Error by Argument.

A curious example is the fate of *Lacon*, a book first published over one hundred years ago—that is, early in 1820. It was a series of essays by a clergyman, the Rev. Caleb Colton, the success of which was sudden and overwhelming. The printing presses could not turn out copies of *Lacon* fast enough to satisfy the demand. Mr. Colton was so uplifted by his popularity that he took to gambling on a large scale and had to fly his incumbency and the country. He made a fortune by cards, and lost it, and blew out his brains in the Forest of Fontainebleau. Meanwhile, thousands of infatuated readers were drinking in moral truth from the pages of *Lacon*, which suddenly lost all its attraction for everybody, and is now deader than the deadest of the dead books that "Solomon Eagle" has been bewailing. Such is the fate of the didactic essay.

The two sections of the present volume which have entertained me most are those which deal, very irregularly, with the little town of Monmouth. Mr. Lucas visited that borough, as I gather, during the war, and made inquiries regarding two objects—the Man of Ross's armchair and a comely work entitled *The Elegant Girl*. Each of these is a subject which suits the genius of Mr. Lucas to perfection, and the consequence is that we have here two of the most typical essays which his entire writings are able to present to us. The first is informing—for Mr. Lucas, though never didactic, is willing, and even anxious, to share his information with the reader—the second is simply entertaining. Mr. Lucas went to Ross itself, which, indeed, rewards a visitor. Unhappily, he entered it at a moment when Ross could not have been looking its best, for "intensity and density of rain" are no embellishments to landscape.

I have a happier memory of my first sight of the little embattled town much more than fifty years ago, for we approached it, as I suppose visitors infrequently do, by boat, sailing and rowing up "pleased Vaga," as Pope called the Wye. I still recall the dark and velvet woods that ran down to the lustrous river, and then, at a turn, the sudden apparition of the sunlit spire of the famous church of Ross. How much depends on the hour of view, as well as on the point of view! Later, on a second visit, I felt as much as Mr. Lucas does the squalor and the commercialism of Ross, which, for all its teashops and its postcards, has no honest appreciation of John Kyrle. As an easy and yet careful and deliberate investigation of a point of literary and historical psychology nothing could be more adroit than this delightful study.

Our essayist is always happy when some by-way of literature invites him to saunter down it. He loves to dwell on the oddities of Borrow, as all good souls do, and will, until the old man of Qulton has been over-praised and over-analysed into a commonplace. In *An East Anglian Bookman* Mr. Lucas expatiates on Green's *Diary of a Lover of Literature*, which he introduces as a new discovery. Of this interesting diary (1796–1800) I was the first person to analyse the merit, in a causerie first published thirty years ago. I grieve that Mr. Lucas has forgotten that fact, and I administer to myself this little advertisement, as a lozenge, to take away the taste of my disappointment. An enchantingly whimsical essay "On Epitaphs" was manifestly started by a perusal of that very strange miscellany *Spoon River Anthology*. The inscription on the tomb of Mrs. Jones is singularly pleasing:—

> Here lies
> MARY JONES,
> the Wife of William Jones.
>
> Honour her memory, for she
> was lenient when her husband
> was in liquor.

The churchyards of our country villages would be far more inviting than they are now, and would even be more instructive, if they contained more sincere and more vivid epitaphs than local habit now thinks decorous. It is impossible to believe that the entire population of a village has lived and died resigned to unbroken tribulation and unsullied by a single fault. Our cemeteries are like the pastorals of M. de Florian, of which M. de Thiard said that they were charming, but that a wolf would improve them.

GRANT OVERTON
From "That Literary Wanderer, E. V. Lucas"
Cargoes for Crusoes
1924, pp. 214–19

II

In providing his "entertainments," as he terms his novels, Mr. Lucas has had in mind a structure always consistent, always graceful, generally amusing but of very real strength. His fictions may be compared to trellises set up with care to support as a rule no more serious burden than rambler roses or some other innocent vine. But it has occasionally happened that the trellis has been climbed upon by a plant of more rugged growth and heavier weight, and the trellis has never failed to sustain the spreading story. It might be apter to say that the plant has sometimes put forth an unexpected flower—instead of the unpretending rambler blossom a rose more disdainful—and still the frame has seemed eminently in keeping with the whole design. For there is this about such brightly elaborated, cheerfully artificial story structures: like the trellis they are never concealed, though completely hid, their outline or form remains exposed to every eye; yet both the eye and the mind receive them naturally. The truth is, of course, that their absence or apparent absence would throw us off. A climbing vine unsupported and unformed, its tendrils thrown about distractedly and frozen in mid-air, would freeze us with repulsion. And an ingenious, expanding, flowering tale without its evident slight pretexts, its amiable excuse of ingenuity, would be an equal monstrosity. Even artifice may be an art.

Characteristic is the device employed by Mr. Lucas in his most recent book of this sort, *Advisory Ben*. Benita Stavely is an attractive girl who struggles with cooks and other domestic matters until her father remarries, when she finds herself free to select an occupation. She starts an advisory bureau to assist harassed householders. The Beck and Call, as her office is styled, soon justifies Ben's venture by its popularity. It is approached through a bookshop below and to it come all manner of persons for counsel as to dogs, cooks, birthday presents and matrimony. The bookshop is kept by two young men. Ben's crowning performance before she says "Yes" to one of the young men in the bookshop is the finding and furnishing in three weeks of a large house for a rich American. Now there are present in this engaging novel the two requisites of Mr. Lucas's art as a fictioner: first, the amiable pretext or excuse for the tale, the slight but bright invention, which is of course the notion of The Beck and Call itself, and second, the strength, erectile, tensile and otherwise in the elaborated structure. For although the scheme of the story is slender and the design of a gay simplicity, the situations developed by Ben's venture sometimes enable the author to touch considerable depths of human feeling. But the airy scheme, the graceful trellis, does not break. I do not mean that no strength is due to the character portrayal; much is due to it. Obviously, if Ben were a flitter-brain, if Mr. Lucas could give her no depth of feeling or not enough personal sincerity, his story would crash. But Ben without The Beck and Call would be Ben without opportunities to enable us to realize her quality. An idea is at the bottom of all.

The same virtue of idea or scheme is the technical triumph of *The Vermilion Box*, in which Mr. Lucas uses the familiar red letter box of England as his device. He says, secretly, Open Sesame, and the mail box opens to give us a series of letters between friends, acquaintances, lovers, relatives who are all entangled in the web of the World War. . . . But this is much more than a love tale told in letters; behind that and behind the often occurring and charming humor of the book there is a seriously conceived and accurately painted picture of public opinion and feeling. A correspondent has been telling of a clergyman friend who has enlisted as a combatant, but who intends to resume his clerical duties after the war is over. The writer has composed some verses satirizing the view that Christianity is something thus to be put off or on, as circumstances dictate:

"'Three or four men to whom I have shown these verses have complimented me on the effort which they make to get at the truth. But none of these men would sign a document calling for a close time for the creeds until the war is over, or suggesting that our archbishops were not at the moment earning their not inconsiderable salaries. That is one of the odd things about England—that private conscience and the public conscience are so different. In France a typical private individual's view of things is, when multiplied indefinitely, also the view of the State. Not so here, where as individuals we practice or subscribe to many liberties which would not be good for the general public.'"[1]

III

Verena in the Midst also employed effectively the device of interchanged letters to develop the tale, and surely not even the expedient of The Beck and Call in *Advisory Ben* is more well-conceived than the tale of the adventures of Uncle Cavanagh in giving away his wife's property (*Genevra's Money*). There are bits about the Barbizon school of painting and there is a surprising deal about religious concepts in *Genevra's Money*, but I have yet to hear it said that this informative and speculative matter obtrudes itself or over-weights the book. It dwells comfortably alongside the high comedy of Uncle Giles (whose sole intellectual accomplishment is the verdict, general and specific, upon persons he doesn't understand: "He's a nasty feller") because Mr. Lucas had the courage, not of his convictions but of his ingenuity.

That he has convictions can scarcely be doubted by the careful reader; the nature of them can scarcely be missed by the thoughtful one. They may now and then be stated more plainly in his books of essays, for the nature of the essay exacts that, but they cannot be put with more poignancy. In the excellent Introduction to his *Essays of To-day: An Anthology* (itself a worthy essay), Mr. F. H. Pritchard reminds us of Montaigne's instruction that an essay must be "consubstantial" with its author, of Mr. Gosse's dictum that its style must be "confidential," and adds—what is true and striking—that the lyric and the essay are both "the most intimate revelations of personality that we have in literature." He adds: "The difference, indeed, is one of temperature."[2] But the material, or at least its base, is identical.

It would not be difficult—it would, in fact, be ignobly easy—to indicate this essay of Mr. Lucas's as typical of his power of pathos, that one as showing the exercise of comedy, another as the evidence of a controlled irony which is his. So one might make a swift and triumphant recapitulation of the

gifts and qualities of a literary personality among the most rounded of its time. But I had rather not be facile, for the sake, if possible, of going more surely. "Most of the other essays are exceedingly light in texture," observes Arnold Bennett, in a comment on *One Day and Another*. "They leave no loophole for criticism, for their accomplishment is always at least as high as their ambition. They are serenely well done." But—"it could not have been without intention that he put first in this book an essay describing the manufacture of a professional criminal."[3] Nor, I think, was it without intention that *Giving and Receiving* closes with that quietly-expressed but piercing account of a bullfight, "Whenever I see a Grey Horse . . ." The word "whimsical" has come to have a connotation exclusively buoyant or cheerful, although the habit of fancy— it is far more habit than gift—may be indulged in any direction congenial to one's nature. Mr. Lucas is whimsical enough in the series of tiny fables ("Once Upon a Time") composing the last section of *Cloud and Silver*. But one of his "whimsies" is savage in its scorn of the hunters of pheasants, another calmly reckons the totals of five years' expenditure on cloak-room fees for a hat and stick, and a third of the twenty, called "Progress," is so brief it is better quoted than characterized:

> Once upon a time there was a little boy who asked his father if Nero was a bad man.
>
> "Thoroughly bad," said his father.
>
> Once upon a time, many years later, there was another little boy who asked his father if Nero was a bad man.
>
> "I don't know that one should exactly say that," replied his father: "we ought not to be quite so sweeping. But he certainly had his less felicitous moments."

Notes

1. See pamphlet, *E. V. Lucas: Novelist, Essayist, Friendly Wanderer*, published in 1916, the excerpt being taken from Mr. Llewellyn Jones's article therein.
2. "The metal bar, cold or lukewarm, will do anywhere, but heat it to melting point and you must confine it within the rigid limits of the mold or see it but as an amorphous splash at your feet." This vivid metaphor of Mr. Pritchard's is surely one of the most inspired explanations and justifications of poetic form ever set down. It can hardly be cited except by the supporters of traditional verse forms, as in a preceding sentence of his eloquent passage Mr. Pritchard speaks of "rime" and "metre" as well as of rhythm.
3. *Books and Persons*, page 153. The notice first appeared in *The New Age*, London, 7 October 1909.

ROSE MACAULAY

1881–1958

Emilie Rose Macaulay was born on August 1, 1881, in Rugby, where her father was a teacher. In 1887 the close-knit family moved to Italy, where a relatively undisciplined childhood preceded a return to the conventions of England in 1894. Macaulay attended Oxford High School, then studied at Somerville College, Oxford. After graduating in 1903, she lived with her parents, first in Aberystwyth, and later in Cambridge, and, partly to entertain herself, wrote a novel, *Abbots Verney*, published in 1906.

After the success of *The Lee Shore* (1912), Macaulay lived mainly in London. During the First World War she worked in the Italian Section of the Ministry of Information, and began a life-long attachment to the section head, a married man.

Potterism (1920), was Macaulay's first best-seller, and was followed by *Dangerous Ages* (1921), *Told by an Idiot* (1923), *Crewe Train* (1926), and *Keeping Up Appearances* (1928). She also published many articles and reviews, and achieved considerable prominence in London literary circles. She travelled widely in Europe and in America, and was an enthusiastic, though reckless motorist.

The war, the destruction in a bombing raid of her London home, and the death of her lover in 1942, made the 1940s a difficult decade for Macaulay. Seeking distraction, she travelled in Portugal and Spain, producing the travel books *They Went to Portugal* (1946), and *Fabled Shore* (1949). After her pessimistic novel *The World My Wilderness* (1950), she regained much of her vitality and optimism, and became a practicing Anglican again, after a lapse of some thirty years. A trip to Turkey led to her twenty-third and final novel, *The Towers of Trebizond* (1956), which was awarded the James Tait Black Prize. In February 1958 she was created a D.B.E., and after a final journey to the Mediterranean, died at her London home of a heart attack on October 30, 1958.

Personal

She wrote from her earliest infancy, with the greatest zest, and began to publish the sprouts of her fancy at a young age. Descended on both sides from long lines of eloquent and well-informed clergymen, few of whom had denied themselves the indulgence of breaking into print, she busily wrote down from her earliest days those little thoughts that occurred to her childish fancy. Her novels and essays, if not widely read, appealed to certain thoughtful and well-regulated minds. They were written in pure and elegant English, almost devoid of that vulgarity which degraded so much of the literature of her period, and inculcated always the highest moral lessons. Those who called her a flippant writer failed to understand the deep earnestness which underlay her sometimes facetious style and the sober piety which she had inherited from her ecclesiastical forbears. She was much interested in religions; the voluminous calf-bound theological works of past centuries were among her reading, and no curious heresy, or antique doctrinal squabble, failed to intrigue her fancy. She was sometimes, and with too much truth, accused of having an old-fashioned mind, and indeed the nineteenth and twentieth centuries never seemed to her, in their literature or their history, so interesting as many others. No one could—anyhow no one ever did—call her a great writer, in any of the many literary spheres in which she experimented; she was called limited, finicking, lacking in vigour or robustness of imagination; she was accused of caring more for manner than matter, for words (in which she was somewhat morbidly interested) than for what they represented. The content of her writing (which may be unearthed, dusty relics of a lost age, from the unvisited shelves of libraries) and possibly also of her mind, even in its prime, was thin and somewhat negligible.

She never had any strong link with her age, or was much interested in social questions, such as the position of women, and so forth, though international affairs, disastrous as they have invariably been, never failed to entertain and shock her. She was seldom bored by the spectacle of life, though, as she complained, the older she got the more barbarous and shocking this spectacle became. Through one barbarous phase after another, through Capitalism, Toryism, World War, Fascism, Communism, and the present Anarchy, she picked her complaining way, making would-be facetious and quite ineffectual comments on the strange conditions in which all countries habitually found themselves. She was a strong pacifist and libertarian, with a passion for being let alone; like Lord Falkland and the Rajah of Bhong, she went about ingeminating 'Peace! Peace! Beautiful peace! I think all this bustle is wrong'. These sentiments endeared her to no recent régime.—ROSE MACAULAY, "Full Fathom Five" (Auto-obituary), *LT*, Sept. 2, 1936, p. 434

What fascinated me most about Rose Macaulay, apart from the shining arrows of her mind, was her passion for bathing. I remember that once when she was staying with us in the country during those ice-days that mark an English Easter, she manifested a desire to swim. We told her that, apart from the English Channel which was sixteen miles away and cold in April, all we could offer her was our pond. It was a muddy pond, not very deep, and thick with weeds and water-snakes. We told her of these disadvantages. "Oh, I never mind things like that," she answered, and within ten minutes there she was swimming happily in the viscous pool. She made us all feel middle-aged.—HAROLD NICHOLSON, "The Pleasures of Knowing Rose Macaulay," *Enc*, March 1959, p. 23

She was forever in transit, physically, intellectually, spiritually; energetically not eating, not drinking or sleeping, so it seemed; yet such was her transparency and charity of spirit that she seemed universally available to her friends. She has been called child-like; but to me she suggested youth, a girl, of that pure eccentric English breed which perhaps no longer exists, sexless yet not unfeminine, naïve yet shrewd; and although romantic, stripped of all veils of self-interest and self-involvement. I cannot write of her tenderness and understanding of the grief of others, fruit of deep personal suffering triumphantly surmounted. No one had better cause than I to know and value it. Her last letter arrived the morning before the morning of her death. One of the things it discussed was "our corrupting profession." I was meditating on her incorruptibility when the news reached me. With the first piercing pang came the thought: "But we have all just seen her, just been talking to her! How like her to slip off and run lightly, unhampered, without backward glance, straight into her death. Straight through it."—ROSAMOND LEHMANN, "The Pleasures of Knowing Rose Macaulay," *Enc*, March 1959, pp. 24–25

⟨*The Towers of Trebizond*⟩ is personal to Rose herself. She laughs her way through the absurdities of the journey as she might have done in gay letters home; for the style she adopted in this book allowed of all sorts of quipping and merry nonsense. She ridicules her own romantic adoration of old cities and ancient landmarks. She sports with variations of religious practice. And at the very kernal of the book is Rose's own heart, open to be understood by readers who say, with the dwarf in the fairy tale, "Something human is dearer to me than all the wealth of all the world," and to those other readers who appreciate candor in whatever form it is expressed.

I say "Rose's own heart" because at several points in *The Towers of Trebizond* she discusses her religious beliefs and disbeliefs, which she describes as anglo-agnosticism, saying "Once Anglicanism is in the system, I think one cannot get it out; it has been my family heritage for too many centuries, and nothing else, perhaps, is ultimately possible for us. I was a religious child, when I had time to give it thought; at fourteen or so I became an agnostic, and felt guilty about being confirmed, though I did not like to say so. I was an agnostic through school and university, then, at twenty-three, took up with the Church again; but the Church met its Waterloo a few years later when I took up with adultery; (curious how we always seem to see Waterloo from the French angle and count it a defeat) and this adultery lasted on and on, and I was still in it now, steaming down the Black Sea to Trebizond, and I saw no prospect in its ending except with death—the death of one of three people, and perhaps it would be my own. Unless, one day, the thing should relax its hold and peter out. So really agnosticism (anglo or other) seemed the only refuge, since taking the wings of the morning and fleeing to the uttermost parts of the sea is said to provide no hope, only another confrontation."

Death did in fact end an association lasting, if we may accept literally a passage in the last chapter, for ten years; and she looked back with casual regret upon the ruin of a wife's happiness, remembering only that "each year was better than the one before, love and joy gradually drowning remorse, till in the end it scarcely struggled for life." However, Rose was led to make a further attempt at this time to reach peace of soul; and the letters she wrote to a friend in America, Father Johnson, between 1950 and 1958 testify to the effort. She did not wholly clear her spirit; but she made a courageous assault upon faith, and was only defeated, I think, by what she described as the subjectivity of her mind or nature.

That nature had been strongly influenced by several things. First, her mother's urgent desire that she should be a boy; then the carefree life at Varazze, which made her half the dreamer who recited poetry to herself during solitary rambles and half the gauche, hockey-playing girl who could not adapt herself to conventional society; then the intellectual pride which caused her to be "rather riled" when she saw people "behaving in what strikes me as—well, as a foolish manner of behaving, you know"; and finally the restriction of her social contacts to a set or class which did not know, or wish to know, what went on in the minds of 99 per cent of the population of Britain.

She was thrown back upon herself, upon books, upon travel in which she indulged "my personal limitation of taste, which finds buildings and landscapes more aesthetically pleasing than the animal creation." She loved to go abroad; she loved anything in the shape of ruins; she drove like a demon in her little car (and one day, when Compton Mackenzie and J. B. Priestley were sitting rather apprehensively behind her, Mackenzie murmured to his companion, "At any rate, we shall make a good headline in tomorrow's papers"); and altogether was a brave, kind, honest woman who wrote much that was amusing, much that was beautiful, and one classic book, *The Towers of Trebizond*, in which all these influences, and all her virtues, were given a chance to demonstrate what they had done to form a character admirable in its simplicity. —FRANK SWINNERTON, "Rose Macaulay," *KR*, Nov. 1967, pp. 607–8

Works

PROSE

In this new novel by Miss Macaulay ⟨*Potterism*⟩ it is not only her cleverness and wit which are disarming. It is her coolness, her confidence, her determination to say just exactly what she intends to say whether the reader will or no. We are conscious, while the dreadful truth escapes us, of a slightly bewildered feeling, of, almost, a sense of pique. After all, what right has the author to adopt this indifferent tone towards us? What is the mystery of her offhand, lightly-smiling manner? But these little, quick, darting fishes of doubt remain far below our surface until we are well into the book; we are conscious of them, and that is all. The rest of us is taken up with the enjoyment of 'Potterism,' with the description of the Potter Press and what it stands for. It is extraordinarily pleasant to have all our frantic and gloomy protestations and furies against 'Potterism' gathered up and expressed by Miss Macaulay with such precision and glittering order—it is as though she has taken all those silly stones we have thrown and replaced them with swift little arrows. 'How good that is, how true!' we exclaim at every fresh evidence of Potterism and every fresh exposure of a Potterite. . . . But then there is her plot to be taken into account. It is very slight. She has simply traced a ring round the most important, the most defined anti-Potterites and Potterites. Potterism is the strongest power that rules England to-day; the anti-Potterites are that small handful of people, including ourselves, whose every breath defies it. And what happens to them? Here those small fishes begin to grow very active, to flirt their fins, flash to the surface, leap, make bubbles. This creates a strange confusion in our minds. For the life of us we can't for the moment see, when all is said and done, which are which. Is it possible that we ourselves are only another manifestation of the disease? Who has won, after all? Who shall say where Potterism ends? It is easy to cry: 'If we must be flung at anything, let us be flung at lions.' But the very ideas of ourselves as being flung at anything is an arch-Potterism into the bargain.—KATHERINE MANSFIELD, "A Springe to Catch Woodcocks" (1920), *Novels and Novelists*, ed. J. Middleton Murry, 1930, pp. 208–9

With Miss Macaulay at her best one is captured, irresistibly, by sheer delight in good workmanship: art, which does not, as it happens, at all depend on the special characteristics which we associate with quite modern fiction. The distinction, in fact, touches the heart of things: because, in her work, one is as much, if not more, interested in individual characters, as in thought or manner. Under the spell of her art we forget artifice.

It is true that Miss Macaulay has a marked style of her own: the antithesis of Miss Richardson's. Few writers, since Jane Austen, have achieved so compact a treatment of English: and the later novelist is the more abrupt. The peculiarity, at its best, is most noticeable in her introduction of a new character, whereby she conquers one of the chief difficulties in narrative. Some introduction is generally regarded as necessary; but a long preliminary analysis always defeats its own end. It bores the reader, and sacrifices the secret of good fiction: that character should reveal itself. All lengthy comment is a mistake. Miss Macaulay, however, has the gift of an ideal hostess who, in almost an epigram, says just what is needed to put two talkers at ease. She accomplishes it no less skilfully for a group of arrivals as with one visitor: "Professor Denison was a quiet person, who said little, but listened to his wife and children. He had much sense of humour, and some imagination. He was fifty-five. Mrs. Denison was a small and engaging lady, a tremendous worker in good causes: she had little sense of humour, and a vivid, if often misapplied imagination. She was forty-six. Her son Arnold was tall, lean, cynical, intelligent, edited an University magazine (the most interesting of them), was president of a conversation society, and was just going into his uncle's publishing house. He had plenty of sense of humour (if he had had less, he would have bored himself to death) and an imagination kept within due bounds. He was twenty-three. His sister Margery was also intelligent, but, notwithstanding this, had recently published a book of verse, some of it was not so bad as a great many people's verse. She also designed wallpapers, which on the whole she did better. She had an unequal sense of humour, keen in certain directions, blunt in others: . . . the same description applies to her imagination. She was twenty-two."

The assured decision of this paragraph is almost unique. It reveals personality.

Much the same may be said about her management of dialogue; which has distinguished courage.

Conducting a spirited discussion upon Women's Suffrage, for example, she introduces the disputants with stark, and surprising simplicity: "Mr. Robinson said. Benje said. Louie said. Jerry said. Cecil said. Mr. Robinson said. Louie said."

Here is a daring repudiation of the rules against repetition, of which the dramatic value is obvious. We feel at once how one after the other drops in his contribution to the controversy: the quick response, the ready tongue, the appreciation of each other's point of view. Talk reported in this manner becomes revelation of character.

Miss Macaulay, in fact, sees her people dramatically; she visualizes their personality: producing its full significance in a graphic word-picture. There is no blurring nor hesitation, no fumbling after the sub-conscious. It is not, of course, that she depends only on surface values, or paints from the outside. She has plenty of penetration and much subtlety; but her mind is made up: she writes as a spectator, not identifying herself with the creatures of her imagination, trusting rather to insight than instinct. Her understanding, indeed, is as truly a question of deliberate art as the crisp narrative interpretation.—R. Brimley Johnson, "Rose Macaulay," *Some Contemporary Novelists (Women)*, 1920, pp. 65–68

Miss Macaulay has a great talent for putting herself into her characters. So much so, that she may be accused of superficiality, when the correct accusation would be that she was "superficial" because she was writing about a superficial character. She is superficial in the cause of realism, inasmuch as other writers are tragic in the cause of tragedy. When critics write professionally and therefore quite often without caring *very much* what they say, demand that a novelist is superficial, they should realise that realism may quite easily put a novelist in a false position.

. . . Miss Macaulay writing about love . . . is sympathetic, reasonable, smart and quite nice. I have now to say something about her when she writes about religion, she is not nearly so sensible and is often not quite nice, but religion is the one great theme to bring out the worst in a woman writer. No woman is ever reasonable about religion, it is often for her a substitution for sexual starvation or so firm a belief that mere man has no chance of understanding the attraction it has for her.

In writing about religion Miss Macaulay succeeds in showing quite plainly her limitations. She tries to be clever and flippant and fails, now and again as though by accident she says a reasonable thing or two. But women are never theologians, the Almighty being far too sensible to trust their very doubtful powers of logic! . . .

I rather imagine that Miss Macaulay admires the licence that is allowed in novels in these days. I rather imagine that she thinks nothing need be hid in the very admirable cause of realism. And she is right, nothing should be hid, so long as it makes the artistic presentment of truth more true. Prudes will always object to realism because the real must in many cases be offensive to them. Yet the prude easily shocked and horrified at many of the obscenities of life cannot view life as a whole without at least realising that these obscenities are present.

But when realism is not materially helped, I see no particular merit in reference to matters which, if not coarse, are not at their best in the publicity of cold print.

I am referring to a passage when Miss Macaulay writes with an extreme frankness about poor Denham when she is undergoing the trying process of preparing to have a baby.

Denham felt, and often was, sick in the mornings.

Really how appallingly dull Miss Macaulay is sometimes, as if it is of any interest to know that Denham is very earnestly sick in the cause of having a baby. After all some thousands of women are daily sick in the good cause, but the matter is merely one of discomfort to the person concerned. . . .

Miss Macaulay is a very peculiar kind of novelist. She can and does at times write brilliantly, yet now and again she falls into the banal. Her greatest fault is a certain superficial flippancy, especially about the matters of religion, to which some reference has been made. She has great powers of "smart" writing and perhaps this is her most outstanding characteristic. Her characters, generally speaking, seem to be natural, though perhaps Miss Macaulay is a little liable to exaggeration in an attempt to make the characteristics of her characters outstanding. Her realism is tinged with an obvious pandering to the disgusting licence that certain women novelists take such a pernicious delight in exhibiting.

Miss Macaulay is more clever than charming or perhaps it is, that she is too clever or not clever enough to be charming. Using the word in the popular and therefore most easily understood application, Miss Macaulay is "interesting."

Perhaps Miss Macaulay is clever and therefore rather inclined to be superficial, perhaps she is flippant without realising that flippancy has no effect on serious matters, perhaps Miss Macaulay is a strange contradiction a smart novelist and at times a very shallow thinker.

But Miss Macaulay is a modern woman writer, she could not under the circumstances be expected to avoid a certain shallowness. She seems to be characteristic of her type, the woman novelist who must write modern books, mention that women are sick before they have babies. It is a type that will die out when modern woman, having travelled in a vicious circle, comes back to realise that modernism in literature and fiction is but a reaction from the standpoint of the last century. —Patrick Braybrooke "Miss Rose Macaulay," *Some Goddesses of the Pen*, 1928, pp. 33–47

In the case of *The Towers of Trebizond* the name of the narrator was the source of much argument. The whole point, ⟨Rose Macaulay⟩ argued, was that no one should know Vere's sex. The name was changed almost weekly from Vicky to Nicky to Evelyn to Vere, and at one time it seemed that in writing the book Rose's main purpose was to confuse the reader on this point. By the reader, she really meant the reviewer. The blurb had to be carefully drafted so that no clue should be given, and when the Book Society made it their monthly choice, I was told to persuade them to preserve a similar discretion in their appreciation. She was always much concerned with what appeared on the dust-jacket. She did not like picture covers though she sometimes produced one of her own rather small and very crowded drawings for this purpose. She detested being described as "witty" and quotations which employed this adjective were on her Index. With *Trebizond*, there was the problem of the Imprimatur. This read:

> *Nihil Obstat*
>
> ✠ Raymond Long Crichel
>
> *Imprimatur*
>
> Johannes Betjeman, *Decanus*

It was in her view a good joke, and none of her Roman Catholic friends thought it in bad taste. Would we include it?

Eventually it was printed in a limited number of copies for distribution to her friends.—MARK BONHAM CARTER, "The Pleasures of Knowing Rose Macaulay," *Enc*, March 1959, p. 28

Written, if not in the contemporary style which Rose Macaulay deprecates, at any rate in what we must now recognize as the contemporary method of Christian apologetic, the hero of *The Towers of Trebizond* is really the Church of England towards which all the characters are orientated in varying attitudes of loyalty, disloyalty, hostility or ignorant indifference, and that hero, Anglicanism, is seen, and this is the unique character of the book and of Rose Macaulay's mind, both from outside and from inside, both critically and compassionately. It is a powerful *apologia* for the Anglican position.

That may appear a strong statement to make about a book apparently so lightly written but we must not ignore Rose Macaulay's own plea about "the deep earnestness which underlay her facetious style", nor must we fall into the critical error of imagining that wit can only be a vehicle for triviality, and that humourless solemnity is an invariable sign of deep religious feeling, the *sine qua non* of serious purpose. The trouble lies perhaps in the kind of wit which Rose Macaulay possessed. It is both satirical and farcical and neither of these seems (except in her) to accord well with ecclesiastical devotion. One might dare to prophesy that Rose Macaulay will take her permanent place among the English satirists of the gentler sort and in *The Towers of Trebizond* she gives full rein to her gift. Billy Graham, preaching about Immorality, "He said it happened continually everywhere, in the streets and in the fields and on the beaches", the Seventh Day Adventists going to Mount Ararat to await the Second Coming and collecting pieces of Noah's Ark while waiting, the jealousies and dishonesties of writers, the idiosyncrasies of the Sunday newspapers, the strange things appearing in foreign language phrase-books, Americans abroad, the B.B.C. and especially its religious department, "it's a popish plot to reclaim England for Rome", are all reviewed with delightful irony without deflecting the author in the least from her main target which is the Anglo-Catholic branch of the Church of England. We are listening to an erudite and witty woman thinking aloud, meditating on the immense oddity of existence, human and animal, ancient and modern, secular and sacred. This satire is only possible to someone who has a visionary detachment from, as well as a charitable attachment to, this world. It is the counterpoise of that other striking element in the book, the element of vision.—DOUGLAS G. STEWART, "Rose Macaulay: Anglicanism," *The Ark of God*, 1961, pp. 100–101

Fiction gave her more scope for the play of her varied powers than did poetry or journalism. Early in her career she evolved a type of fiction that freely makes use of other resources than those of the "novel" in its narrowest definition. Her fiction deals primarily with ideas, preferences, and attitudes rather than with actions, decisions, and emotions; the characters are almost always of the social class traditionally most concerned with the play of ideas—her own. If Northrop Frye's terms are employed, she drew upon the Menippean satire or "anatomy" (*Anatomy of Criticism* ch. II, n. 9) for the device of a crew of characters who, although in the main realistic, could yet be seen to represent a selection of human follies and stupidities—or merely quirks. Her characters are a combination of authentic representation and the imaginative projection of some human potentiality. The situation at the opening of her books is often mildly fey—another aspect of the Menippean satire. She gathered her persons together for a confrontation of ideas—a "Menippean *cena*"—and through this device her

irony worked in what a recent critic called "her mocking, generous, exuberant approach" to human follies (Alan Pryce-Jones, Introduction to 1960 edition of *Orphan Island*).

Fascinated by language, Rose Macaulay used it with extraordinary versatility: she moved at ease from eighteenth-century elegance ("wit flatters the reader into borrowed discernment") to Edwardian, Georgian, and mid-century colloquialism ("What I mean is, he kind of likes me—"). Etymology was one of her favorite pursuits. For a time, in the 1930's, she overindulged her taste for donnish preciosity; but, as World War II approached, she abandoned this style. Her skill with rhythms, one of the chief elements of charm in her poems, is a constant delight in her prose, whether she is placing the key-words in an epigram, leading a sinuous discussion through surprising turns, or making a simple statement in monosyllables. Her effects are produced economically: "Few writers, since Jane Austen, have achieved so compact a treatment of English."

In all of Rose Macaulay's work the presence of the "implied author" is strongly felt. In fiction she follows Jane Austen and George Eliot in this respect. "The real pleasure of Rose Macaulay's novels," wrote one critic, "lies principally in the personality of their writer. . . . throughout her novels, we are conscious of a brisk and entertaining companion, who at intervals talks to us herself." . . .

Distinguished though Rose Macaulay's writing is, there is truth in the judgment of one of her life-long admirers: "Her very great natural gifts . . . would seem to have fitted her for greater deeds than any she has performed." Like most writers, she could have pruned to advantage. She sometimes diluted her work with irrelevancies and occasionally introduces bits of over-facile comedy. A tone of archness sometimes appears at what seems an ill-chosen moment. Probably, however, a basic difficulty was that she belonged to a class of gifted amateurs of living who expressed themselves in commentary. She enjoyed using language and found amusement in forming it into novels and essays, but she was more concerned with the presentation of thoughts and with the play of ideas than with creating formally constructed artifacts. Thus, Ellen Green, the mermaid—a triumphant invention—is given room in the novel in hand, *And No Man's Wit*; comments on various minor matters are permitted in *Keeping Up Appearances*; and the amusing ape is given long passages in *The Towers of Trebizond*.

It may be hazarded that her presentation of life, primarily at the level of thought (while not denying its sensuous delights); her complex of tragic awareness and ironic amusement; her constant recognition of the open-endedness of discussions of value; and her care to use language with regard to the authority of its tradition will give much of her work a long contemporaneity.—ALICE R. BENSEN, "An Assessment," *Rose Macaulay*, 1969, pp. 165–69

Surely nobody could ever talk about 'problem novels' and Rose Macaulay in the same breath, yet there were few problems she did not write about. She introduced her ideas with no prejudice and the minimum of discussion, just enough to whet the reader's appetite, and then stopped before she could be accused of causing boredom. The nature and status of women fascinated her, a preoccupation she showed in endless ways. For instance, like Iris Murdoch so much later, she enjoyed giving her heroines names which were either masculine (part-reflection of a Twenties fashion) or else sexually mysterious—like Derham in *Crewe Train* (1926), who could accept neither social convention nor basic femininity. Stanley in *Told by an Idiot* (1923) has been described by Ramond Mortimer as expressing a disbelief in any innate differences between the sexes. . . .

Those who are addicted to Rose Macaulay in general will obviously enjoy everything she wrote and if the atmosphere of her work changed after 1930 this is hardly surprising. She was too intelligently creative to spend the rest of her life producing what is regarded as light fiction, even if it was obviously not as light as all that. . . .

⟨*The World My Wilderness*⟩ was not a mere continuation of what she had written in the 1920s, but the themes which had always preoccupied her now came to the surface. The technique was highly professional and it was not intended to amuse. The author had lost her companion Gerald O'Donovan in 1942, she had lost her apartment and all her possessions in the London blitz, and this novel shows her concern at the collapse in moral standards which had begun in the 1930s. Family life had broken down, and the behaviour of the young people in the book, who become adept at stealing in the ruined city of London, reflects the mentality of the French collaborationists. The crazed priest who celebrates mass in the bombed church is too much of a 'symbol' but in 1950 there was every reason for using symbols, even obvious ones, for most serious writers felt that western civilization was in danger. . . .

Rose Macaulay saw the early struggles of women (individuals rather than the members of a movement) as preoccupied less with votes than with living, more with the possibility of love-making outside marriage than with the Married Women's Property Act. She spent middle and later life travelling, but the longest journey she undertook was from her early family life to those years of deeply spiritual existence, involving retreats and confession, that she crystallized in her last book. Only someone so immensely English could have entitled a volume of her articles 'A Casual Commentary'. Her novels also might seem casual on the surface, but they're still some of the most stimulating fiction written by anyone, and not only by women, this century.—MARGARET CROSLAND, "Laughing (1)," *Beyond the Lighthouse: English Women Novelists of the Twentieth Century*, 1981, pp. 49–52

POETRY

There is one small volume of poems by Miss Macaulay, called *The Two Blind Countries*. It is curiously interesting, since it may be regarded as the testament of mysticism for the year of its appearance, nineteen hundred and fourteen. That is, indeed, the most important fact about it; though no one need begin to fear that he is to be fobbed off with inferior poetry on that account. For the truth is that the artistic value of this work is almost, if not quite, equal to the exceptional power of abstraction that it evinces. Poetry has really been achieved here, extremely individual in manner and in matter, and of a high order of beauty.

One is compelled, however, though one may a little regret the compulsion, to start from the fact of the poet's mystical tendency. Not that she would mind, presumably; the title of her book is an avowal, clear enough at a second glance, of its point of view. But the reader has an instinct, in which the mere interpreter but follows him, to accept a poem first as art rather than thought; and if he examine it at all, to begin with what may be called its concrete beauty. I will not say that the order is reversed in the case of Miss Macaulay's poetry, since that would be to accuse her of an artistic crime of which she is emphatically not guilty. But it is significant that the greater number of pieces in this book impress the mind with the idea they convey, simultaneously with the sounds in which it is expressed. And as the idea is generally adventurous, and sometimes fantastic, it is that which arrests the reader and on

which he lingers, at any rate long enough to discover its originality.

But though the mystical element of the work is suggested in its very title, one discovers almost as early that it is mysticism of a new kind. It belongs inalienably to this poet and is unmistakably of this age. The world of matter, this jolly place of light and air and colour and human faces, is vividly apprehended; but it is seen by the poet to be ringed round by another realm which, though unsubstantial, is no less real. Indeed, so strong is her consciousness of that other realm, and its presence so insistently felt, that sometimes she is not sure to which of the two she really belongs. In the first poem of the book, using the fictive 'he' as its subject, she indicates her attitude to that region beyond sense. In the physical world, this 'blind land' of 'shadows and droll shapes,' the soul is an alien wanderer. Constantly it hears a 'clamorous whisper' from the other side of the door of sense, coming from the

> muffled speech
> Of a world of folk.

But no cry can reach those others: no clear sight can be had of them, and no intelligible word of theirs can come back.

> Only through a crack in the door's blind face
>   He would reach a thieving hand,
> To draw some clue to his own strange place
>   From the other land.
>
> But his closed hand came back emptily,
>   As a dream drops from him who wakes;
> And naught might he know but how a muffled sea
>   In whispers breaks.
>
> . . .
> On either side of a gray barrier
>   The two blind countries lie;
> But he knew not which held him prisoner,
>   Nor yet know I.

This poem may be said to state the theme of the whole book.—MARY C. STURGEON, "Rose Macaulay," *Studies of Contemporary Poets*, 1919, pp. 181–83

When *The Two Blind Countries* appeared in 1914 some thought it a most lovely and original book, but some were angry because it seemed to them like a pot-pourri of the styles of Walter de la Mare, Rupert Brooke, Frances Cornford, and certain others. Its author, Rose Macaulay, was already a writer of experience, having published six or more novels. Whatever influences may have affected her, her verse is sure enough of its own purpose, and delightful enough to please the sourest critic. This is what the title of the book means:—

> On either side of a grey barrier
>   The two blind countries lie;
> But he knew not which held him prisoner,
>   Nor yet know I.

She is certainly of the school of Walter de la Mare. For the rest, several of her poems have a strong flavour of Cambridge, and thus incidentally of Rupert Brooke and Frances Cornford. But Mrs. Cornford wrote in early youth and then appears to have stopped, while Rose Macaulay brought the skill and depth of maturity to the making of her verses. She is somewhat of the *clever* type, but has more intellect and modesty than others of that class. *The Two Blind Countries* contains at least a dozen things that most readers of modern poetry may enjoy, and, of these, particularly "The Alien," "Trinity Sunday" and "The Thief," should be mentioned.

Her second volume, *Three Days*, published in 1919, is more free from influence. It seems to represent a transition stage.—HAROLD MONRO, *Some Contemporary Poets*, 1920, pp. 179–80

STUART SHERMAN
From "Rose Macaulay and Women"
Critical Woodcuts
1926, pp. 84–93

Once started on logical courses, women, I surmise, run through them faster than men. Consider the mad speed with which Rose Macaulay has run through the bright hopes of the feminist program. Her course was slowly prepared and her lamp was trimmed by such poor, old, patient plodders as Samuel Butler, G. B. Shaw and H. G. Wells. Forty years it took these fumbling iconoclasts to get the Victorian candelabra thoroughly junked and the clean cinder path laid out for the Ann Veronicas of the present age. With *Potterism*, 1920, Rose Macaulay caught up what for brevity we may call the Wellsian torch, and in four short years she burned it out and tossed us the charred wick in *Told by an Idiot*. . . .

Just what was it in ⟨*Potterism*⟩ that cried "come hither" to so many readers? The gospel of Wells, the ideas of Wells, with the rose color rubbed off, the sentiment squeezed out. The Anti-Potterite League for the Investigation of Fact, for the destruction of cant, the slapdash, the second-rate, pomposity, mush, shellacked propriety and every hollow, plausible form of words employed to mask and blur the hard, sharp edges of actuality. Youth was there, shameless, fearless, uncompromising youth, truculently showing up the base compliances of parents. Above all, young women were there, with Cambridge honors, scientifically trained, tempered, edged, going into the world fully prepared to compete with their brothers, and bent on getting some of the important jobs, and demonstrating that "woman's work" is a disgusting Potterism.

Dangerous Ages, which followed hard upon *Potterism* in 1921, is the only book of Rose Macaulay's which wrings the heart, or, indeed, much recognizes the existence of that organ. It is my impression that no dozen novels of my time have given me so much authentic information about womankind as this one.

There are girls of twenty here, clean, fine and candid, who have read Freud and Ellis and don't wish to marry, but, open-eyed, to take the risks of a free companionship, in a "keen, jolly, adventuring business, an ardent thing, full of gallant dreams and endeavors." There are women of thirty who write—experienced, brilliant, gay, with a cynical twist, with no religious illusions, yet "with a queer desire, to put it simply, for goodness, for straight living and generous thinking, even, without reason, for usefulness." There are women of forty-three, with satisfactory husbands and promising young children—women turning, at forty-three, to the medical career interrupted twenty years before, turning back to the career, in horror of the threatening vacancy of the rest of life. There are grandmothers and great-grandmothers who have ceased to rebel at their wrinkles, and who stave off the ennui of age by reading Russian fiction and consulting the psychoanalyst.

Pathos broods over them all. For they are all hungry for some more adequate self-expression than they are ever likely to attain. They are bitten with a desire to leave behind in the world some more record more permanent, more personal, less undistinguished than—merely children! They are so sick of this self-sacrificial song! They want to live their own lives—for a little while, before they descend into the eternal nothingness. There is a hard core of egotism in them—just as there is in every *man* who sticks to his career. But one likes these girls and these women, so deliberately clean and fine and slim and taut; and one pities them, too. The intellectual life? Not many of them, one fears, want it, as men of their class want it—as the

first indispensable life choice. And a career chosen on any other basis is bitter with relinquishment.

In *Dangerous Ages* as it appears to me, Rose Macaulay let herself go as in none of her other books. She is more or less in love with all these women who are trying to make something satisfactory out of the little interval which is theirs before the swiftly shifting bright dance of the earth shall know them no more. Consequently she has here for once revealed her poignant emotional as well as her pungent intellectual qualities, and she has expressed intensely and adequately the consciousness of existence which her persons feel within themselves—the courage and verve with which they take up life's gauntlet.

If you scrutinize the story, however, you see that she has few illusions about the capacity of her sex to live the "life of reason." Her perception is lucid that the great majority of her sisters, struggling for "emancipation," are inextricably in the grip of the life-force, the passionate admiration of men remains still the secret ultimate object of their heart's desire and at a pinch they will fight for it with the crude ferocity of savages.

She has seen through them.

From the first, therefore, she has been anxious to make known that she is by no means committed to the positions in which her dramatis personæ are found. In *Potterism*, for example, she gave us a long epigraph from Evelyn Underhill on that "disinterestedness" of the artist which enables him to see things "for their own sakes." The point of view at which she philosophized upon the pangs of the feminine heart at the ages of twenty, thirty, forty, sixty and eighty is indicated by this epigraph in *Dangerous Ages*: "Reflecting how, at the best, human life on this minute and perishing planet is a mere episode and as brief as a dream."

She has, however, a personal register in one of the characters in *Dangerous Ages*. In the final chapter we are told that Pamela has the "key" to the door against which various of the other women bruise their eager hands. The key is not an important job, not a career, nor yet a man, but a philosophic attitude—an attitude of blithe philosophic despair. I will quote a passage which makes a close link between this book and *Told by an Idiot* and *Orphan Island*: "Pamela, going about her work, keen, debonair and detached, ironic, cool and quiet, responsive to life and yet a thought disdainful of it, lightly holding and easily renouncing, the world's lover, yet not its servant, her foot at times carelessly on its neck to prove her power over it—Pamela said blandly to grandmama, when the old lady commented one day on her admirable composure, 'Life is so short, you see. Can anything which lasts such a little while be worth making a fuss about?'"

One sees at a glance that Rose Macaulay has flung aside the torch with which Mr. Wells started the Ann Veronicas of 1909 marching toward the earthly kingdom of "God, the Invisible King." She has reverted to a mood nearer the "blithe paganism" of George Moore and Oscar Wilde and old Samuel Butler, with his seductive maxim: "We have all sinned and come short of the glory of making ourselves as comfortable as we easily might have done." . . .

Told by an Idiot is saturated with the pitiless, disintegrating, depressing irony of one who conceives that she has seen through "the illusion of progress." "Why so hot, little man, little woman?" she seems to inquire, with a frosty detachment which I find extraordinarily exasperating. "What we are doing and planning and hoping so hotly, with such an elate sense of its novelty, is very old stuff, my children. Come, peep in here at my little puppet show. Here you shall see the generations pass, one by one—Victorian, Fin-de-siècle, Edwardian and

Georgian. Mark them well and four times you shall see history mimic the vain spectacle of your anxious progress from the cradle to the grave, with all your empty mouthings and ineffectual gestures. Come, let us amuse ourselves. As the whirling of dead time spins past us I will mention for you all of the score or so of odd little 'interests' which constituted life and its zest for each of our little marionettes, as, for examples, the untimely death of the Duke of Clarence, the alarming increase of female bicyclists and the prevalent nuisance of that popular song, 'Ta-ra-ra-ra-boomdeay.'"

I should like to call *Told by an Idiot* a heart-breaking tale, but if I did that its author would turn her cool, frosty intelligence in my direction and inquire exactly what physiological change I conceived to take place when I spoke of the rupture of that organ. Let us say nothing of the heart. *Told by an Idiot* is a satire of great wit and even of erudition, but I find it horribly depressing, because it systematically belittles life and denies the possibility of progress.

Fancy becoming so superior to mundane events that in a chronicle of forty years you can tuck such an event as the World War into a couple of pages. On a scale of that sort the individual dwindles to a pin point, and births, marriages and deaths become of infinitesimal consequence. I ask, Whose is this sublime point of view? Where does the observer sit who whiffs all our human affairs into the air like a puff of cigarette smoke? No longer, certainly, at the point of view of the artist, according to Evelyn Underhill's definition, for she no longer is making any effort to see people "for their own sakes." She is no longer expressing the consciousness of existence which her persons feel within themselves.

I search again for Rose Macaulay's "register," and I find it in Miss Garden, a wholly disillusioned feminist—"a little cynical, a little blasé, very well dressed, intensely civilized, exquisitely poised, delicately, cleanly fair.

. . . *Orphan Island* is a picture of Victorian England, and how as intelligent a woman as Rose Macaulay can fail to regain her faith in progress after painting it is past my comprehension. As for myself, I find that my faith and hope and charity are all restored to me when I let my imagination dwell for an hour or so with that tippling, pedantic bigot, Charlotte Smith, and then turn swiftly to the description of Neville's forty-third birthday in *Dangerous Ages*.

I see that adorable woman, mother of two grown children, waked from her dream-broken sleep at sunrise of a summer dawn, "roused by the multitudinous silver calling of a world full of birds." She cups her tanned face in her sunburnt hands and, looking out of sleepy violet eyes, she shivers and says, "Another year gone and nothing done yet." She decides to change all that. She hops out of bed, spreads two chunks of bread with marmalade, trots across the lawn in her pajamas and down through the wood to the broad swirling pool in the stream. There she strips, has her swim, eats her bread, "resumes" her pajamas, swarms up the smooth trunk of a beech tree to a limb in the sun and sits there, whistling.

If that doesn't represent progress I give it up.

UNSIGNED
From "Miss Macaulay's Novels"

Times Literary Supplement, May 12, 1950, p. 292

A survey of Miss Rose Macaulay's past work shows that it has almost consistently ignored sensibility and concentrated instead on sense. In this it is rare, if not unique, among the works of contemporary women novelists; "sensitive" is an adjective worn thin and almost meaningless by the critics' pens, while "sensible" is one they seldom apply to modern fiction. Perhaps they hesitate to do so; it has about it an antiseptic flavour, a suggestion of the schoolmistress, and some authors might take it as a backhanded compliment. One can be sure that Miss Macaulay is not afraid of it; sane and stimulating, her novels and essays have a bracing effect on their readers, and appear to be dictated by liberal opinions and a rational view of life. Her humour is founded on a balanced mixture of tolerance and clear sight; too kind to be savage, she is yet too indignant to be urbane. Appealing to the intellect rather than to the emotions, she is distinguished as a witty and impartial recorder of changing fashions in thought and behaviour.

Miss Macaulay is the author of a penetrating analysis of *The Writings of E. M. Forster*, and Mr. Forster's influence is noticeable in some of her earlier novels. *Potterism* appeared in 1920; although it was not her first book, it is perhaps the first with a serious claim to survival. Describing itself as a "semi-farcical tract," and characteristically dedicated "to the unsentimental precisians in thought, who have, on this confused, inaccurate and emotional planet, no fit habitation," its general scheme bears a resemblance to that of *Howards End*. The style, like Mr. Forster's, is personal, informal, but never untidy; it is constructed with technical brilliance; and the central struggle between the Potters, who stand for sham and muddled thinking, and the anti-Potters, who are genuine and clear-sighted, recalls the clash in *Howards End* between the sensitive Schlegels and the unreflecting Wilcoxes. A fault in this book, however, is the inability of the author, in spite of the elasticity of her technique, to assimilate into her semi-farcical tract a plot with some of the unspontaneous atmosphere and reliance on coincidence of a machine-made detective story. When Miss Macaulay disappoints—as she occasionally does—it is with errors entirely contradictory to the nature of her best work. The merit of her books consists largely in the evidence of an unusually balanced mind responsible for them, in a delicate sense of proportion; but there are moments even in the most successful when Miss Macaulay seems to lose her balance, totter, and tumble into exaggerations and unreality. Her criticism, made in 1938, of the love affair between Helen Schlegel and Leonard Bast in *Howards End* applies to the murder story in *Potterism* and to some incidents in her other novels:

> The affair is possible; all the same, one does not quite believe in it. The episode has about it a flavour of device, of contrived drama; it is too sudden and too odd; we are not led skilfully towards it; we feel that these people, whom we thought we knew, have betrayed our confidence, have become two other people. . . . To forget themselves and what they are really like is one of the things that people in novels should try and remember not to do.

. . . In *Crewe Train* . . . it is the barbarian who unconsciously exposes the civilized and the cultured as ridiculous; Miss Macaulay's satire is at its most brilliant when it is directed at the chattering, bookish set into which she plunges the primitive Denham. *Crewe Train*, which was first published in 1926, is dedicated "to the Philistines, the Barbarians, the Unsociable, and those who do not care to take any trouble." This is a contrast to the earlier dedication, but it is only a variation of the same anti-social sentiment. Denham arrives by instinct at that point of truth at which Arthur Gideon, the "precision of thought" in *Potterism*, arrives intellectually; society interferes with them both, destroying one and sentencing the other to a pointless existence unnatural to her philistine simplicity. Miss Macaulay is impatient of society, but not intolerant of it, she laughs at it, but does not condemn it. The targets of her ridicule are muddled thinking, facile sentimentality and false values; she implies that there are two possible refuges from these: one, in the life of the mind, and the other in a happy ignorance such as Denham's.

Happy ignorance is a state which Miss Macaulay can imagine and can even, in the case of Denham, respect; but it is one that she would seldom recommend. The intellectual family who cannot understand Denham is presented as absurd, but it is not implied that its god of culture is a false one. Denham herself, whose untutored gaze lays bare the folly of an educated society, could only be the product of an intensely literary imagination. Miss Macaulay's talent has been nourished on learning and letters; she is indeed so well-read that there are times when she seems to be showing-off her erudition, including in her books references and information unnecessary to her point. Some of her novels are really animated essays; extracts from *A Casual Commentary* are to be found almost unaltered in *Told by an Idiot*, and they appear more at home in the volume of essays than in the novel. She uses comedy, not as an end in itself but as a medium for treatises on travel and religion, love and literature, politics and history; triumphantly achieving the light touch, she is careful never to sacrifice readability to her serious intention.

Running parallel with Miss Macaulay's keen objective curiosity about facts and theories, behaviour and ideas, there is a wide humanity, an interest in life of general rather than particular application, which eventually flattens and minimizes the differences between her characters, so that their pleasures and reverses seem almost unimportant. She invites her readers to share this bird's-eye view. Is life, after all, no more than "a rather absurd comic film"? That is Sir Arthur Denzil's tentative summing-up of the lively holiday in *Going Abroad*. But the bishop cannot agree:

A comic film . . . No; it would never do to let oneself think that life in this world was anything of that nature. No; dear me, that would never do at all.

The bishop, having thus definitely rejected his brother-in-law's phrase, felt happier and less perplexed.

Sir Arthur, no doubt, found freedom from perplexity in his own less serious view of life; Miss Macaulay's might be gauged as somewhere between the two. Never superficial, she acknowledges an inner dignity in human nature; and while her alert and inquiring mind links her with the follies of this world, her sense of humour leads her towards a serene and enviable detachment. . . .

In spite of her sad story ⟨in *The World My Wilderness*⟩ Miss Macaulay does not lapse from the high standard of entertainment that her former work has set, although some of her admirers may be disappointed to find *The World My Wilderness* less consistently funny than her lighter novels. The comedy is kept short of satire, and the drama is moderated, so that the two elements complement each other and do not clash. Her ambitious theme provides a solid pretext for the lively, well-informed discussions in which she loves to exercise her characters; these debates, which in her other books were often brilliant diversions, here illuminate the central point. Contemporary as always, she crystallizes an atmosphere of bewilderment prevalent to-day, stating the predicament of a generation that can only react to its unhappy time with stupefied passivity or defiant lawlessness. (A third reaction, that of the escapist, is represented by Richie, who is older than Barbary and Raoul and, with his rather pathetic conservatism, tries to keep past standards alive.) Miss Macaulay is too much an artist to suggest an easy solution beyond adding to our understanding of the problem with this stimulating and perceptive study.

HUGH MACDIARMID
Christopher Murray Grieve

1892–1978

Hugh MacDiarmid was born Christopher Murray Grieve on August 11, 1892, in Langholm, Dumfriesshire, near the Scottish-English border. He attended Langholm Academy, then went to Edinburgh to train as a teacher, but in 1911 turned to journalism. During World War I he served with the Royal Army Medical Corps, returning to Scotland wounded in 1918. That year he married and settled in Montrose, Angus, as a journalist.

MacDiarmid's first writings were in English, his first book, *Annals of the Five Senses*, appearing in 1923. However, believing in the need for a "Scottish Renaissance," he began in his periodical *The Scottish Chapbook*, founded in 1922, to experiment with Braid Scots, or Lallans, as a serious medium for poetry. Unlike the Celtic language Gaelic, spoken in the Highlands, Lallans draws on various regional dialects of spoken Scots, related closely to English, and was enriched by MacDiarmid with the language of older writers such as William Dunbar. His first collections of poems in Lallans, for which he adopted his pseudonym, were *Sangschaw* (1925) and *Penny Wheep* (1926), followed by the long poem sequences *A Drunk Man Looks at the Thistle* (1926) and *To Circumjack Cencrastus* (1930).

MacDiarmid was co-founder of the Scottish Centre of P.E.N. in 1927 and of the National Party of Scotland in 1928, but his relations with both were stormy, and he was expelled from the latter in 1933. He joined the Communist Party, but was expelled in 1938 for his Nationalist beliefs, rejoining in 1956. His first marriage foundered in 1931, but he remarried, and settled, almost destitute and in poor health, in Whalsay, Shetland, in 1933. *First Hymn to Lenin* (1931) was followed by *Stony Limits* (1934) and *Second Hymn to Lenin* (1935), but after this he produced no major work in Scots, reverting to English in *Lucky Poet* (1934), *In Memoriam James Joyce* (1955), and *The Kind of Poetry I Want* (1961).

After many years of extremism and isolation, MacDiarmid received a Civil List pension in 1950, enabling him to settle in Biggar, Lanarkshire, and began to be seen as a Scottish institution. The issue of his *Collected Poems* (1962) marked a breakthrough, and his later publications include *The Company I've Kept* (1966), *The Uncanny Scot* (1968), and *Dìreadh* (1974). His *Complete Poems* appeared posthumously, after his death on September 9, 1978.

The tide goes over.
Not on my knees
These poems lie,
But the floor of existence.

Whelk and razorshell,
Delicate weight-lifters,
Supporting and made by
The crush of fathoms.

—NORMAN MACCAIG, "MacDiarmid's Lyrics," *Hugh MacDiarmid: A Festschrift*, eds. K. D. Duval, Sydney Goodsir Smith, 1962, p. 9

How far have the newer men recreated Scots poetry? The nineteenth-century Scots bards would hardly recognise their progeny and would probably disclaim paternity. The newer poets certainly disclaim relationship. For in the past few years there has been a significant change in Scots poetry.

The first necessity had been cerebration—the introduction of an intellectual element—and the introducer was C. M. Grieve. With the publication, under the *nom-de-plume* of "Hugh MacDiarmid," of *Sangschaw* (1925) and of *Penny Wheep* (1926), Grieve established himself in the front rank of Scots lyric poets. Even in these volumes Grieve was a rebel, and he has rebelled ever since—against Kailyarders, Burns Clubs, and the music-hall edition of the Scotsman—and much of this rebellion found its way into *A Drunk Man Looks at the Thistle* (1926), where he dropped the self-contained lyric and adopted the discontinuous dramatic monologue form of Lawrence and Joyce and T. S. Eliot, though several inset lyrics are still retained in the body of the poem. Since then he has published another and more involved cerebral monologue: *To Circumjack Cencrastus*, and several volumes of lyrics (for example, *First Hymn to Lenin*). Unfortunately there has been a progressive decline in poetic power. Grieve is the finest lyric poet in Scotland, but his inability to separate art and life, his confusion of a thought or a movement with a totally different affair—a poem about these things—has led him from his early lyric style to a style that is inconsequent always, incoherent very often, and is all too seldom poetry. No matter how important one considers the message of one's verse, poetry requires more than simply statement of one's attitude. And if the message becomes of more importance than the poetry, why write in verse?

Even in the earlier poems there was the essential element of thought. But it was thought under control, allied to a new orientation of the Scots verse. Poems like "The Watergaw," "The Bonnie Broukit Bairn," and "Crowdieknowe" signalised a new age in Scots lyric poetry. But tracts of *Cencrastus* might well have been written in prose; and the thought-stream method is frankly a failure in a long satirical poem. Above all satire calls for clarity and a reasonable chance of knowing what the poet is attacking. The parts are better than the whole and it is only now and again that the old belligerent and concise Grieve appears. Grieve now sounds like a poet with a grouch.

Not that that might matter. A poet is sometimes all the better for something to grumble at. But when the grouch gets the better of the poetry, the loss is serious.

Yet Grieve's achievement is great. Whether or not he wins his way back to poetry, he has written lyrics that will last. He brought back thought to Scottish poetry. And though occasionally one wishes he would take it away again, its introduction was essential. The pendulum swung too far, and we must now look for balance.—IAN GORDON, "Modern Scots Poetry," *Edinburgh Essays on Scots Literature*, 1933, pp. 133–35

It is a great tribute to Hugh MacDiarmid to say that we find nothing either amusing or offensive in his characteristic attitude, which is that of the inspired Poet—the nobly indignant genius—of the Romantic tradition. But 'Romantic' is an unfortunate word if it suggests the usual self-dramatizing vanity, the petty egotism enjoying its *saeva indignatito*, the feminine gush of stoic pride and self-pity. ⟨In *Second Hymn to Lenin and Other Poems*⟩ MacDiarmid exhibits a truly fine disinterestedness and convinces us that we have here rare character if not rare genius. This disinterestedness, this character, this profound seriousness, distinguishes him again from the better-known of the young Left-wing poets. The title-poem, 'Second Hymn to Lenin,' is sufficiently a success to deserve inclusion in the ideal anthology (which would be a very small one) of contemporary poetry. It is an impressive product of the endeavour to recreate a tradition—to find some equivalent for the advantages that Burns enjoyed.

Had there been such a tradition actually alive MacDiarmid might have done a great deal more with his talent. As it is, the variety of manners he uses and of influences he reveals in this small collection shows what a difficult *ad hoc* achievement was the Scottish manner of the Hymn. The most important of the influences apparent are the later Yeats (see, e.g., 'With a Lifting of the Head,' 'At the Graveside') and D. H. Lawrence (see, e.g., 'One of the Principal Causes of War,' 'The Wild Duck'). Among his epigrammatic pieces 'Another Epitaph on an Army of Mercenaries' deserves noting: it ought, in fact, to be permanently coupled with Professor Housman's famous 'Epitaph.'—F. R. LEAVIS, *Scy*, Dec. 1935, p. 305

The baiting of Anglo-Scots and English apart, MacDiarmid's nationalism is not at all narrow but is rather conceived as the necessary condition of internationalism. For him, it is the veneered cosmopolite who lacks understanding of the differing points of view of different peoples, because he does not proceed from an adequate understanding of his own people. On the other hand, one of MacDiarmid's principal reasons for urging complete independence from England is that he believes the English to be inveterately insular while the Scots are (or were, and will be again) international-minded.

Even linguistically, MacDiarmid's greatest hope for Scotland lay, not in the vernacular Braid Scots—a northern development of what in the south has become "standard" English—but in Gaelic. In his pamphlet, *Scotland in 1980*, he envisaged the re-establishment of the ancient Gaelic Commonwealth in Scotland, with "80 per cent of all the creative literature of any value" being written in Gaelic.

His conception of the "Gaelic Idea" was, from the first, international—a sort of Pan-Celtism that would counterpoise an ancient culture, at once aristocratic and popular, against the dictatorship of the proletariat as that was manifesting itself in Russia. It might be as far-fetched as Dostoevsky's "Russian Idea," but he conceived it to be, like the latter, a "dynamic myth"—and at least it suggested a nobler prospect for Scotland's future than was offered by the Decline and Fall of the British Empire. In MacDiarmid's later conception, the need to "polarize Russia effectively" is replaced with the discovery of a common cause by the Slav and the Celt, in both of whom East and West are said to meet; and he sees it as his personal task to "work for the establishment of Workers' Republics in Scotland, Ireland, Wales and Cornwall, and, indeed, make a sort of Celtic Union of Socialist Soviet Republics in the British Isles."

In the words of Edwin Muir, MacDiarmid is "everything that is out and out." A life-long extremist on principle, he "despises scruples," as his most loyal friend has said, and yet he cannot resist any opportunity for self-justification. In the "Prelude" to *Scottish Scene* (1934), a book in which he collaborated with "Lewis Grassic Gibbon" (James Leslie Mitchell—another of the curious tribe of pseudonymous Scots), he wrote that

> He sees his land as a unity too,
> And creation in terms of it.
>
> The future concerns him even more
> Than the past or the present do;
> He boasts of his proleptic power
> —And is entitled to!

Typically, the truth that is here expressed is obscured by the truculent tone, which is an habitual part of his role as an intellectual tough. That truth is concerned, not as it might seem with simple futurity, but rather with *possibility*, which is of course referable to past, present, and future. And the unity he lays claim to is imaginative, not logical:

> I am a poet; our fools ask me for logic not life!

He has always been "immensely more interested in the vaguest adumbration of what we might have been than in any possible development of what we are." His premises are not amongst those to which we have become comfortably accustomed. The free play of conflicting and contradictory ideas is for him the most vital intellectual exercise whereby consciousness is extended; and his work from first to last may best be understood in the light of a statement he made in 1926: "The function of art is the extension of human consciousness."—KENNETH BUTHLAY, "Introductory," *Hugh MacDiarmid (C. M. Grieve)*, 1964, pp. 10–11

Much can be forgiven a man who is, at one and the same time, the Grand Old Man and *enfant terrible* of Scottish literature. And, for many admirers of his poetic achievement, there is quite a lot to be forgiven—an anglophobia that doesn't disdain a Civil List pension, a willingness to celebrate the Russian invasion of Hungary by getting back into the communist party, a smugness rather unseemly in a writer of seventy-four, an unashamed capacity for dealing out some of the worst prose of the decade. On the other hand, the one thing most Sassenachs will find hardest of all to forgive becomes, in Grievean logic, the most laudable aim of his whole career. Hugh MacDiarmid led Scotland into a literary renascence; he wants now to lead her into independence. He is right. The Union killed Scottish culture. MacDiarmid cherishes no Stuart dream. He wants a clean sweep, with a Scottish Communism that will breed epic poets, great painters, voluble talkers, robust comedians, composers like F. G. Scott.

There are no half-measures with Dr Grieve. When he hates, he hates. But his testimony here is mainly one of love, and the love, most readers will think, is well bestowed—on Ezra Pound, for instance, and Sean O'Casey, Willie Gallacher, John MacLean and Kaikhosru Shapurji Sorabji. I was both delighted and disturbed to meet Sorabji again after all these years. There are many who regard him as one of the greatest composers of the century, but few people have had a chance to hear his works. In the 'thirties, I read in the *Musical Times* a long account of his three-hour piano *Opus Clavicembalisticum*, and have been fired ever since with a desire to hear it. But his works are not to be played in public, the times being unpropitious.

MacDiarmid is bold enough to make statements that he must know won't hold water—such as, for instance, that religion never did any poet any good; that the English are terrible fish-like people with a poor literature, and that the Scots are a great race held down, presumably, by fins: that the Russians use the same word for 'beautiful' and 'red' (a nice political twisting of linguistic fact). His arrogance doesn't go well with a boyishness he should long have got over (but a poet must keep the clear eyes of a child, mustn't he?).

He is usually unassailable when he inveighs against philistinism, both in England and in Scotland, and one is willing to bow one's head under his sweeping dismissal of the contemporary English novel, sinde he lauds Scottish novels that one hasn't read but now wants to read—Sydney Goodsir Smith's *Carotid Cornucopius* and Fionn MacColla's *The Albannaich*. Still, the character that emerges is not all that endearing, and the prose style creaks like Tennyson's braces. The man who could, in his Scots poetry, evoke the uninhibited quasi-continental world of Burns's Caledonia, handles his secondary medium with very blunt tools. Where is the gaiety, invention, dionysiac verve we had a right to expect? Still, it's the friends that count, and he's had, and still has, many. He must be *simpático*. It would have been nice if he'd demonstrated that he is.—ANTHONY BURGESS, "His Ain Folk," *Spec*, Nov. 11, 1966, p. 621

If I were asked are there important issues about which I have changed my opinion since 1943, I would have to reply, I spoke then as I speak now, but I do not speak now as I spoke then. I am accustomed to being accused of all sorts of contradictions, to which I have often merely answered, like Walt Whitman, 'I contradict myself. Very well! I contradict myself.' But I am interested to note that many of those who have written about me and my work now tend to agree that under the apparent inconsistencies and contradictions there is a basic unity, and they refer their readers to my first book, *Annals of the Five Senses* (1930), in which I express the main ideas of all my subsequent work. I have demonstrably pursued these undeviatingly through my whole career—not only in my writings (including, in addition to my books, the enormous mass of my journalistic outpourings), but in my speeches and broadcasts in Great Britain and in a score of other countries. . . .

The principal theme of *Lucky Poet*, and of all my other books, has been my unqualified opposition to the English ethos. I do not claim to have originated the growing belief that English literature is petering out—but I certainly anticipated that it would. I agreed fully with my friend the French poet and philosopher, the late Professor Denis Saurat, when he wrote that unless the Second World War was to have been fought in vain there must be a profound change in English mentality (and he did not mean that availability of Yankee trash-culture which has since developed apace). Saurat used his terms with scrupulous care. (He also pointed out that he was not referring to Scottish mentality but strictly to English mentality.)

Everything that has happened since—and is happening now—has shown how right he was. He perfectly understood why I agreed with Henry Miller's statement in *The Cosmological Eye*, namely, 'as for English literature, it leaves me cold, as do the English themselves; it is a sort of fish-world which is completely alien to me. I am thankful to have made a humble acquaintance with French literature, which on the whole is feeble and limited, but which, in comparison with Anglo-Saxon literature today is an unlimited world of the imagination.' And he would have endorsed Cecil Gray's statement, which I have said should be hung up in large print in the vestibule of every library in Scotland, namely, 'Even today the whole hierarchy of the English novelists from Fielding and Smollett, through Dickens and Thackeray up to Hardy and Meredith means precisely nothing to me. I simply cannot read them. I have tried hard. I have tried several books of each. I have given them all a fair trial, but it is no use.'

. . . A great deal has happened since ⟨Lucky Poet⟩ first appeared. A dozen books about me and my work have been published, and scores of theses and doctoral dissertations accepted by many European, American, and Canadian Universities. There is a consensus of opinion that I have achieved a miracle—inventing a new language out of the dialects into which Scots has disintegrated; and, along with that, reviving large elements of vocabulary obsolete since the sixteenth century, and writing indisputably great poetry in this unlikely, if not impossible, medium. It is claimed that I have written the only high poetry attempted or achieved in Scots for over three hundred years, and won a place for myself as one of Scotland's three greatest poets along with Burns and Dunbar—and probably as the greatest of the three. It is claimed, too, that my work has had, and is increasingly having, political consequences—that I am largely responsible for the great escalation of the Scottish Nationalist movement of which I was one of the founders in 1928. Maybe! But I do not belong to the Scottish National Party. I am a Communist, a Scottish separatist, and republican—and I do not believe I have any idea in common with ninety-nine percent of these so-called Scottish Nationalists, who seem to me simply sitting on their butts and giving an imitation of a respectable democratic bowel movement.

Lucky Poet saw me embarked on a course which I have pursued assiduously ever since, in the teeth of all the opposition of those who hate versatility, since it takes most men all their time to master one line of work or thought, and who in particular hate omnivorous readers (and especially readers of foreign literature not available to Tom, Dick, and Harry), since their own reading, when they have any, is so severely restricted as to be virtually non-existent for purposes of literary discussion. Two phrases from my long poem *In Memoriam James Joyce* (1955) adequately described my practice in this matter. They are: 'Jujitsu for the Educated' and 'Jerqueing every idioticon'.—HUGH MACDIARMID, "Author's Note 1972," *Lucky Poet* (1943), 1972, pp. xi–xvi

Scotland's greatest living poet, and arguably the very greatest of all the makars who have written in the Scots tradition, Hugh MacDiarmid is also one of the great poets of the world, for he has succeeded in his early aim to 'aye be whaur/Extremes meet', and his work is both national and international, his aim to nourish 'the little white rose of Scotland' co-existing with his resolution 'to bring Scottish literature into closer touch with current European tendencies in technique and ideation'. . . .

MacDiarmid was the first modern Scots poet whose original verse expressed a post-romantic sensibility; and he was the first to be acutely aware of the contemporary world. The eight short lines of 'The Bonnie Broukit Bairn' contain immensity, for the poem's concern is not confined to a single local parish, as in the fashion of the followers of Burns, but extends to the whole of creation, as the individual stands alone in the darkness, confronting the world around him and the stars above. Again, in 'The Seamless Garment', where MacDiarmid seeks to express his conception of how society should be woven into an integrated and harmonious whole, he uses images derived from the weaving of cloth in a Border textile-mill, the images of a predominantly industrial world, not—as in nearly all earlier Scots verse—those of a community almost entirely rural.

In *Sangschaw* and *Penny Wheep*, the short lyrics possess intensity of passion, audacity of imagery, and original and often profoundly-haunting rhythmical patterns. MacDiarmid had the power to create in a few lines an emotional force of extraordinary strength, and to evoke scenes and situations which, while they are perfectly precise and definite in themselves, nevertheless suggest a whole world of experience behind and beyond them. Yet the latter volume also contains some longer poems on philosophical themes which anticipate much of MacDiarmid's later work, from *A Drunk Man* onwards. No Scottish poet has ever had a finer command of the lyric cry; and none has been less content with it. . . .

How novel and individual an achievement *A Drunk Man* was at the time of its original publication, almost half a century ago, may be in some danger of being overlooked now, when MacDiarmid's success has spurred three generations of younger poets to attempt verse in Scots which seeks to be universal rather than parochial in theme. The departure which MacDiarmid made from the Scots tradition as interpreted during the first two decades of the century was radical. That tradition, still content to follow the folk-song comedy and pathos of Burns and the glamourie of the ballads, still accepting a narrowness of intellectual scope and a limitation of theme to the local concerns of everyday, had been dominant but decadent in Scotland for at least a century. MacDiarmid broke with it; he made 'a new thing', a poem at once popular and profound, a work written mainly in Scots—which he had spoken as a boy in his native village—but which, far from limiting itself to village affairs, ranged over the whole world and all the heavens, tussling and teasing those mysteries which have tormented the minds of men in all ages and in every country, and plundering the literature of the present and the past, of other nations and of his own, to add the treasure of their words to the richness of his own vocabulary. He made Scots what it had not been since medieval times, a tongue capable of expressing the immensities. For behind MacDiarmid, as behind Gregory Smith, stands that other great poet, Coleridge, with his belief in the Imagination as 'the balance or reconciliation of opposite or discordant qualities'. This imaginative power makes *A Drunk Man* a work for the whole world. The drunk man is humanity, and its voice is MacDiarmid's.

The poem remains his supreme achievement in the synthesis of vernacular and literary elements which the French critic Denis Saurat called 'synthetic Scots'. Although MacDiarmid was to continue writing in Scots for most of another decade, and to extend his range of themes, he was never again to weave so many aspects of existence into a living unity. . . .

As a poet in English, MacDiarmid is in direct descent from his boyhood hero, the poet John Davidson—the subject of one of his most moving, and most concentrated, elegies. Davidson, in the work of his last decade, rejected the religious interpretation of life impressed upon him in childhood by his father, an evangelical minister, and expressed in his epics and tragic dramas a gospel proclaiming that the whole universe is explicable in terms of matter alone. Like his hero, MacDiarmid conceives much of his later work on an epic scale, banishes God from the universe, rejects most—if not all—mysticism, and bends his power towards the expression of what he calls 'a poetry of facts', the facts being of the kind that can be tested by the scientific intelligence. As he writes in his autobiography, *Lucky Poet* (1943): 'I am all for the driving, restless movement of the critical intellect. I want a poetry of fact and first-hand experience and scientific knowledge that is right about every technical detail. What my ideal amounts to is the poetical equivalent of one of nature's annual miracles—the flowering of Daphne Mezereum, the sudden burgeoning of beauty from the bare brown twigs.' The realization of MacDiarmid's ideal, the flowering of poetry from the bare facts, can be seen in such a poem as 'Crystals like Blood', which has the apparent artlessness that conceals the highest art.

Nevertheless, 'Crystals like Blood', in its brevity, expresses only one aspect of existence, and—generally speaking—MacDiarmid in his later work wishes to express the whole of it, to collect and arrange such a tremendous assembly of facts that 'their fineness and profundity of organization . . . is the condition of a variety great enough/To express all the world's.' Small wonder that, elsewhere, he describes the kind of poetry he seeks to create as 'such poems as might be written in eternal life'—for it would seem that only the God who has been expelled from MacDiarmid's universe could experience and express the simultaneous synthesis of all knowledge which is the poet's aim. The range of reference in the later poems is wider than that in any other modern poetry in English, but it is still scarcely wide enough for MacDiarmid to qualify as the exemplar of Rilke's dictum that 'the poet must know everything', and nothing less than such a totality of knowledge would appear to be able to achieve MacDiarmid's purpose.

Even as things are, however, the weight of his erudition—whether earned or borrowed—threatens not infrequently to crush the poetry and bury its emotional impetus under an accumulation of technical details. What MacDiarmid calls 'The terrific and sustained impact/Of intellect upon passion and passion upon intellect', which the later work seeks to express, is sometimes replaced by a kind of passionless recollection, or—even less satisfactorily—by a painstaking catalogue of scientific references which appear to have been culled from text-books. His manner of expression, too, often seems perfunctory, as if he were so intent on what he has to say as to have only a lesser interest in how it gets said. However, the above criticisms are only interim judgments, for all of MacDiarmid's late poems, even the bulky *In Memoriam James Joyce*, are eventually intended to be seen as parts of a mammoth 'work in progress', *Mature Art*, and it may be that in the perspective of the complete epic—should it ever take form as such—the more prosaic passages will find their own level and play their part in the total effect, whatever that may turn out to be. Certainly, on the occasions when MacDiarmid's own passions are directly involved, the rhythms of the verse quicken and cohere, and the recital of facts becomes charged with a potent energy whose effect is all the more powerful for the complete absence of any element which approaches conventional poeticizing.—ALEXANDER SCOTT, "MacDiarmid: The Poet," *The Hugh MacDiarmid Anthology*, eds. Nicholas Grieve, Alexander Scott, 1972, pp. xvii–xxiii

Walter Perrie: What role does contradiction play in your thought? It is often said that you present frequent contradictions.

Christopher Grieve: Like Whitman I would say "I contradict myself? Very well, I contradict myself". The variety and the enormity of the world and the infinite possibilities of the human mind are such that contradictions are inevitable for anyone who has a certain depth of intellectual perception. Only shallow minds fancy that they are being consistent. And they can only be consistent within a very narrow ambit. As soon as they endeavour to take in the whole, they are lost, completely lost, unless they have learned to juggle with contradictions.

WP: That, of course, is very much a neo-Hegelian view. Have you been influenced directly by the Neo-Hegelians? I am thinking of Bradley and Bosanquet.

CG: Oh, I read them long ago—before I became a convinced Marxist. They are a very fertile influence, a wonderful breeding ground for poets—unlike those who are opposed to them.

WP: Would you agree that there is a chasm today between sensibility and sensuality so that we no longer have any genuinely sensual poetry—such as the sonnets of Michelangelo, or Yeats' last poems? All that we have is a poetry of the senses.

CG: Inevitably, the kind of poetry I'm interested in has tended, in the last half-century, to become more and more highly intellectual—more mathematical. I find the same tendency in ultra-modern music and I think the two things are marching together. But it brings me back again to the rarity of poetry. The great majority of people who write verse haven't got to that stage at all. They are full of sensuality—which isn't a bad thing—but it cannot be associated with any sensibility they have without a loss. If they could conjoin the two, or penetrate the one with the other, without losing power, then it would be a very good thing. But they can't do that and there is that lack, as you say, of genuine sensuality in modern poetry. Even those poets to whom I attach most importance in the modern world show that. There's no English poetry of course, we're ruling that out completely—it doesn't exist.

WP: I take it that you regard communism as essentially a spiritual force rather than in materialist terms?

CG: Yes, I do.

WP: Given the nature and the trends which are evident in the contemporary world, do you see spiritual forces developing coherently in that world? When society is going through a period of great fragmentation, do you see communism as a spiritual force and the practice of poetry developing along fruitful lines?

CG: It may take time. We are living at a very critical period in world history. But it was, I think, an American who said that the main task confronting the poet today is a great task of assimilation. I agree with that. If poetry is to reassert itself as the Queen of the Arts then what Ezra Pound called 'poppy-cock', that's to say that store of outworn theories and superstitions, must be swept clean away. Very few poets are attempting to do that. They're still thirled to the 'poetic' which is the worst enemy of poetry. I'm brought back to that by thinking of perhaps the greatest technical change I've seen in poetry. Heine wrote a couple of volumes of song lyrics which were enormously popular—and still are. And then, at a given juncture, he said 'I'm not going to write any more of that kind of damned thing!' and he spent the remaining years of his life trying to break up the tonality of the lyric and introduce into his work elements up to then considered non-poetical. He succeeded, but his later poetry has, of course, never been popular—and never will be. Pasternak was in the same position. He said 'the lyric is hopeless in the modern world.' And I've done the same thing, followed the same example. I still adhere to that. One of the reasons is that the lyric, by its very nature, cannot reflect the complexities of modern life. But, apart from that, it necessarily ignores something even more important, and that is the enormous new perspective of the sciences. That can't be encapsulated in a short lyric. It's because of that enormous variety (which ought to be the pre-occupation of poetry and so seldom is) that most modern poetry is trivial and worthless.

WP: You would agree then that an important poem is necessarily a long poem?

CG: I think so. The epic is the only form which can discharge the duties of the poet in the modern world. . . .

WP: Which literary influences have you consciously rejected?

CG: I suppose it was inevitable that I should be influenced by most of the English lyric poets, because it was on English lyric poetry that we were fed at school. It wasn't until I turned to the great Scots poets of the fifteenth and sixteenth centuries that I began to see that I had no affiliations whatsoever with English poetry—and rejected it. In my early development I was influenced by the Arbeiter poets of Germany, Richard Dehmel and others, but I think that the greatest influence on my ideas about poetry, if not reflected in my actual poetry, was Paul Valéry and the Italians who followed in his wake: Montale and Ungaretti and Quasimodo. I knew both Montale and Quasimodo myself—I've been very lucky that way. It cuts both ways of course. I also knew Yeats and Eliot so there are flaws in my luck. Yeats was very nice to me but I soon got what I regarded as his measure. He wanted to know about Douglas' social credit. I hadn't said but a few things to him about it when I discovered that he knew nothing about how the present banking system worked and therefore couldn't possibly understand how the other would work. I told him so. We parted amicably.

WP: You have said that there is no English poetry. Why not?

CG: The whole framework of English society has been against it. Their schooling system kills the imagination—their whole system is opposed to the emergence of aesthetic values. They claim that there is a great tradition of English poetry. Where did it come from? Very little of it was English in an exact sense. In modern times you have two Americans, an Irishman and a Welshman. There are none at the moment. . . .

WP: In the thirties and later you exercised an obvious influence over a number of writers. Among younger writers that influence is now perhaps less obvious. What effects or influence do you think that you have exercised in this area?

CG: It's very difficult to tell. I've had this effect, that up until a few years ago there was no systematic teaching of Scottish literature in universities or in senior secondary schools and there's a good deal of it now in all these quarters. Now that's a big change, and it means that those who are students and pupils today will in ten or twenty years time show the benefit of that change. They will know the stuff. Now all these poets who followed my example, who looked up Scots words in dictionaries and so on, they've all faded out. They hadn't got it natively and that's where I had the advantage. I was born into a Scots-speaking community and my own parents and all those round about spoke Scots. But these poets hadn't that advantage and, of course, I have antagonised them—politically and

otherwise. I don't think that any of them has really followed my example—certainly not technically. Their poetry has no resemblance to mine excxept at the mere level of vocabulary and in some uses of the language. But they don't seem to me to be using the language creatively at all. So I don't think I've had a good influence on them. But then, one doesn't expect influences to be good. Basically, I don't think I've been influenced by anybody at all. I'm a great admirer of Valéry and others but I haven't been influenced by them. I'm not writing the kind of stuff they were writing at all. At least, I don't think I am. . . .

WP: The supernatural, the larger than life, do you agree that it's essential for poetry?

CG: I think it's essential for life. Human life itself implies a belief in, a desire to participate in, the transcendental. It's inherent in us without reference to any religious belief. That is the answer to your question.

WP: And how does that square with your materialism?

CG: The transcendental, if I am right, comes out of the seeds of things. It's inherent in the original substance—it's part of the materialism.—HUGH MACDIARMID, Interview by Walter Perrie, *Metaphysics and Poetry*, 1975

Grieve's mind . . . held two distinct possibilities: that the potential of Scotland could be expressed in poetry written in English with European terms of reference; or that Scotland could best parade her possibilities by exploring all the nuances of Scots, so that words floating around in the oral atmosphere could be allied to the literary vocabulary preserved in Jamieson's *Etymological Dictionary of the Scottish Language*. Never a man to limit himself to one *via media*, Grieve managed to get the best of both worlds by adopting Hugh MacDiarmid as his *alter ego*. Hence MacDiarmid was launched by Grieve in his new periodical *Scottish Chapbook* which bore the relevant motto "Not Traditions—Precedents". The first number appeared on 26 August 1922 and the third number (October 1922) included a poem by Hugh MacDiarmid. This was "The Watergaw", which has since become recognised as one of the greatest lyrics in Scots and the quintessence of MacDiarmid's early style.

It is as well, at the outset, to establish that MacDiarmid's Scots was not quite so dictionary-based as his propaganda suggested. He did, after all, grow up in the Borders where many of the great traditional ballads had been preserved in oral transmission thus ensuring that spoken Scots was still strong. MacDiarmid's educational platform—which insisted on the teaching of Scots, or at least Scots poetry, in schools—led him to condemn bitterly the reliance on English in schools (and before MacDiarmid's achievements made educationists rethink the matter, English *was* used rather exclusively in the classroom while Scots was tasted, with the flavour of forbidden fruit, outside school hours). MacDiarmid thought his native Langholm was "the bonniest place I know" and it was natural that his treatment of it should have been in Scots of a sort. Border Scots was unusually rich, perhaps because the Borderers like to underline their differences with their English neighbours. . . .

So MacDiarmid began with a reservoir of Scots words he had absorbed from his Border childhood; his development of this familiar speech into synthetic Scots was motivated by a desire to make Scottish culture into the mainstream of contemporary modernism. Helping him along the way was the precedent of Lewis Spence's poetic imitations for the Middle Scots style. Spence, however, did not go far enough for MacDiarmid's liking.

In the "Hitherto Uncollected" section of MacDiarmid's posthumously published *Complete Poems 1920–1976* (ed.

Michael Grieve and W. R. Aitken, London 1978) there is an early poem in conventional Scots, "The Blaward and the Skelly", which has some similarities with Burns's first poem "O, Once I Lov'd a Bonnie Lass". Both heroines are called Nelly (Burns's song was written for Nelly Kilpatrick) and both have their virtues recounted in lilting quatrains. Burns's Nelly is exceptionally delicate:

> As bonnie lasses I hae seen,
> And mony full as braw,
> But for a modest gracefu' mien
> The like I never saw.

Grieve's Nelly is more robust:

> The gowden hair that glamoured
> To wan weeds turned the skelly
> And bluer than the blaward
> Were your eyes, Nelly.

On internal evidence we could safely assume that the Grieve poem, though dated 1922, stylistically predates the first MacDiarmid poems. It is derivative and derives mainly from the Burns tradition and the oral Scots of Grieve's youth. If, as he claimed, his earliest poetry was in Scots then it was in a Scots similar to that employed in "The Blaward and the Skelly":

> the fact is that Scots was my native tongue.
> . . . And, above all, it should be understood that
> my earliest literary efforts were all in Scots, for in
> those days many Scottish papers ran a 'Doric' (i.e.
> Scots vernacular) column, and the influence of Sir J.
> M. Barrie . . . and the other writers of the Kailyard
> school was in the land, and more people spoke
> Scots—or spoke more (i.e. richer) Scots than do so
> today.

Grieve was not, then, converted to Scots; he had been converted to English because of a desire to dismiss Kailyardism and to avail himself of the international range of poetry in English (a theme he returned to in his "Mature Art" sequence comprising *In Memoriam James Joyce, The Kind of Poetry I Want* and the eventually abandoned *Impavidi Progrediamur*). What persuaded him to return to Scots was the realisation that the language could be shaken to its linguistic roots by an application of modernist theory. Taking as his poetic ingredients oral Scots, literary Scots and a shrewd contemporary mentality he self-consciously constructed an idiom that would be so alive with modern thought that it could not be construed as either reactionary or escapist. The distance between "The Blaward and the Skelly" to "The Watergaw" is an imaginative leap of unimaginable proportions. MacDiarmid was, at a bound, on a par with the pioneers of modernism. It should never be forgotten that "The Watergaw" first appeared in 1922, the *annus mirabilis* of modernism: the year of *Ulysses* and *The Waste Land*. MacDiarmid followed the careers of Joyce and Eliot closely. He emulated Joyce's liquid verbosity in "Water Music" and wrote *In Memoriam James Joyce* as a tribute to the Irish master. Eliot never fascinated him in quite the way Joyce did, but he respected him enough to refer to him with affectionate humour in *A Drunk Man Looks at the Thistle*:

> T.S. Eliot—it's a Scottish name—
> Afore he wrote 'The Waste Land' su'd ha'e come
> To Scotland here. he wad ha'e written
> A better poem syne—like this, by gum!

A scientific experiment is an exploration of a possible world; a literary experiment is a tentative research into life. MacDiarmid's "The Watergaw" was an experiment that succeeded triumphantly enough to look like the pinnacle of a long tradition rather than the renewal of a lost language. Themati-

cally the poem is a memory of the death of the poet's father, an instant that is also alluded to in the poem "Kinsfolk" (from *Work in Progress*):

> Afore he dee'd he turned and gied a lang
> Last look at pictures o' my brither and me
> Hung on the wa' aside the bed, I've heard
> My mither say. I wonder then what he
> Foresaw or hoped and hoo—or gin—it squares
> Wi' subsequent affairs.

However synthetic the language the experience was a basic one, and it is MacDiarmid's evocation of the mystery of reality that makes the poem so memorable. It uses imagery for philosophical purposes; it takes a symbol and invests it with an other-worldly significance. In the second stanza MacDiarmid refuses to spell out the vital light that is both watergaw and life itself. Instead he let the conclusion, like the symbol, hang in the air:

> There was nae reek i' the laverock's hoose
> That nicht—an' nane i' mine;
> But I hae thocht o' that foolish licht
> Ever sin' syne;
> An' I think that mebbe at last I ken
> What your look meant then.

That "mebbe" is not inserted in the interests of prosodic regularity; it is there to stress human fallibility and the possibility that there might be a perspective that transcends the three-dimensional human outlook. Stylistically, MacDiarmid had introduced a new note to Scots poetry. He had abandoned both the rigid quatrain and the Standard Habbie measure (which had been *de rigueur* in Scots poetry since Burns popularised it in the eighteenth century) in favour of a more fluid stanza which concluded with a clinching couplet. Finally, MacDiarmid had intellectualised Scots poetry by isolating a particular image and then seeking out its cosmic implications. . . .

Because MacDiarmid had always made himself *au fait* (to use one of his favourite expressions) with verbal advances in contemporary poetry, he was able to invest his early lyrics with the electrifying shock-effect of the new. His range of reference was remarkable and few poets have been able to command such a diversity of stylistic mannerisms. Moreover, no nationalist was ever more internationally minded, and MacDiarmid, though pugnaciously Scottish, usually confined his interest in Scottish poetry to the work of the great Makars, to a few poems by Burns (whom he regarded as a great songwriter rather than a great poet) and to the neglected genius of John Davidson. In the early 1920s he was more interested in the state of European poetry in general than in the facetious tone of contemporary Scottish poetry. MacDiarmid felt that his fellow Scottish poets merely wished to *conserve* the Scots language for antiquarian purposes and there was nothing conservative about his own thinking. He was, in 1922, working in isolation in Scotland but could not resist the temptation of thinking in the royal plural and hinting that there was a movement when there was really just one man making a new beginning. In 1923 he spoke of:

> the possibility of a great Scottish Literary Renais-
> sance, deriving its strength from the resources that lie
> latent and almost unsuspected in the Vernacular.

What MacDiarmid omitted to mention was that, in 1923, he *was* this "great Scottish Literary Renaissance". Later he attracted disciples who wrote outstanding poems in the Mac-Diarmid manner—I think of Soutar, Goodsir Smith, Garioch and others—but he remained unique because he could never be contained by a movement. He was too large for that.—ALAN BOLD, "Dr Grieve and Mr MacDiarmid," *The Age of Mac-Diarmid*, eds. P. H. Scott, A. C. Davis, 1980, pp. 42–48

DAVID DAICHES
"Introduction"
A Drunk Man Looks at the Thistle (1926)
1953, pp. xiii–xx

It is over a quarter of a century since this gallimaufry ⟨*A Drunk Man Looks at the Thistle*⟩ first appeared, breaking on a startled and incredulous Scotland with all the shock of a childbirth in church. Since then we have grown more used to "modern" poetry; when our author refers to Eliot's *Waste Land* we nod our appreciation, and the sudden transitions in mood and pace which confront us so often are accepted on the analogy of Pound's *Cantos* or Auden's discursive pieces. Most of us no longer regard MacDiarmid and his poetry as still dangerous. The state of culture has caught up with him, perhaps even overtaken him, we are inclined to think, and his methods are orthodox enough now.

But if we think this, we are dreadfully mistaken. In the first place, there is less in common between MacDiarmid and Eliot or Pound or Auden than there is between MacDiarmid and many an older classic. His technique is not "modern" in the sense in which expositors of modern poetry now use the term; his obscurity is quite unlike the obscurity of *The Waste Land* or the *Cantos* (if indeed obscurity is the proper word at all); he has not Eliot's interest in the poetic potentialities of religious faith or Yeats's concern about symbols or Auden's gift for metaphysical clowning or Dylan Thomas's cunning cultivation of the elemental. His ancestors are not Hopkins and Laforgue and the Jacobean dramatists or any of the other well known sources of modern poetic idiom; but Chaucer and Dunbar and Villon and Skelton, the Goliardic tradition of the Middle Ages, the flyting tradition of mediaeval Scotland, the humanist polemics of Renaissance Europe. Indeed, there is more of Milton's sonnets "I did but prompt the age to quit their clogs" and "On the New Forcers of conscience under the Long Parliament" in much of MacDiarmid than there is of the French symbolists or the seventeenth century metaphysical poets. MacDiarmid, in fact, remains wholly original in the sources of his poetic inspiration and the special qualities of his poetry. He is still original, and he is still dangerous.

I do not mean that MacDiarmid has consciously and deliberately gone to the poets I have mentioned for his inspiration; but I know that if you come to *A Drunk Man Looks at the Thistle* after reading some of Milton's Latin polemical pamphlets or Skelton's "Speak, Parrot" or some of the Goliardic songs of the Middle Ages you have the sense of being in the same world. Of course, MacDiarmid recognized a kinship with all contemporary poets who were endeavouring to extend the frontiers of their art, and he hailed Yeats and Eliot and Pasternak and others for that reason; but he cannot be ticketed as part of any generalized modern movement. His sensibility remains perversely different, and, for all the breadth of his interests, Scotland plays a curious and central part in it.

One might perhaps say that MacDiarmid's poetic objective is to extend the normal boundaries of relevance through powerfully suggestive incongruity. He juxtaposes the homely and the fantastic, the popular and the learned, the reverent and the blasphemous, the tender and the cruel, with deliberately explosive intention. Consider, for example, how in this volume he plays with the notions of divine birth, of Christ, of

maternity, of womanhood and childhood. The tone varies from the conversational, casual

> Wull ever a wumman be big again
> Wi's muckle's a Christ? Yech, there's nae sayin'.

—that last phrase is an extraordinary example of the verse shrug—through the more conventional

> Aye, this is Calvary—to bear
> Your Cross wi'in you frae the seed,

to the deliberately shocking

> I'm fu' o' a stickit God,
> *That's* what's the maitter wi' me,
> Jean has struck sic a fork in the wa'
> That I row in agonie.

MacDiarmid keeps shifting his contexts: a serious theological reference turns at last into a dig at the Presbyterian Church; a picture of the Holy Family becomes a discussion of sexual love. The poet himself turns into the divine infant or the dying God ("What tho'ts Montrose or Nazareth?"). This is an extension of the technique used traditionally in the Scottish pulpit ("We thank thee for the safe ingathering of the harvest, except for twa-three fields atween here an' Stonehaven") but it is employed here not so much to domicile religion among the daily affairs of men as to shock and arrest the reader into seeing new meanings in traditional symbols.

"The shock of recognition." Put a familiar abstraction into an all too familiar physical context, and you realize the implications of what you have been mechanically saying for years. God is indeed with us—but his tread is that of a policeman in a slum alley—

> And heard God passin' wi' a bobby's feet
> Ootby in the lang coffin o' the street.

This is a mild example of that clash of imagery in which MacDiarmid delights. The same clash is seen in the shift of imagery from the sublime to the ridiculous which goes on intermittently throughout the poem. The light by which the poem moves is moonlight, and moonlight is effectively linked not only with the slightly unfamiliar appearance of the natural world in the eyes of the drunken speaker but also with the meditative strain in the poem, the constant urge to work things out, the stumbling towards the inner meaning of things. But this meditative strain is constantly being broken by the intrusion of a comic reality:

> The munelicht ebbs and flows and wi't my thocht,
> Noo' movin' mellow and noo lourd and rough.
> I ken what I am like in Life and Daith,
> But Life and Daith for nae man are enough . . .
>
> And O! to think that there are members o'
> St. Andrew's Societies sleepin' soun',
> Wha to the papers wrote afore they bedded
> On regimental buttons or buckled shoon,
>
> Or use o' England whaur the U.K.'s meant,
> Or this or that anent the Blue Saltire,
> Recruitin', pedigrees, and Gude kens what,
> Filled wi' a proper patriotic fire!

This shift from meditation to cosmic satire, with its deliberate incongruities and the resulting shock of recognition, is made dramatically appropriate by the situation in which the speaker is presented. It is, after all, a drunk man speaking, and drunkenness serves for MacDiarmid the same purpose that the mediaeval poet found in the dream. The logic of dreams and the logic of drunkenness are similar; both give poetic probability to those violent transitions of mood and *tempo* which play such an important part in giving life to the poem as a whole. For it must not be forgotten that this is a dramatic poem, or poem-sequence, and the ebb and flow of drunken speculation, interspersed with physical observations as the drunken man's eye falls on some part of his environment and with concrete memories as they rise unbidden in the uninhibited mind, weave a dramatic whole as the poem moves forward to its superb lyrical conclusion punctuated with the final dry parenthesis.

The temptation is to pick out the incidental lyrics—many of which are, indeed, admirable poems in their own right— and regard the discursive portions as so much padding. But it is the discursive part of the poem which provides its logic and its dramatic unity. The opening has a fine, slow movement, distilling perfectly that sense of utter fatigue from which (as with Leopold Bloom in Joyce's *Ulysses*) the drunkenness really springs:

> I amna' fou' sae muckle as tired—deid dune.
> It's gey and hard wark' coupin' gless for gless
> Wi' Cruivie and Gilsanquhar and the like,
> And I'm no' juist as bauld as aince I wes.

That first line is absolutely right in its movement, ending as it does with those two heavy, weary monosyllabic words. The rhythm is deftly sustained, yet the accent of conversation is never lost. I remember Robert Frost once assuring me that all great poetry has the accent of conversation, and quoting—of all poets—Milton to prove it. MacDiarmid keeps this accent going, and when he deliberately inverts normal prose usage, as he often does, it is not through clumsiness or an effete traditionalism, but to make us look at the meaning of the words more closely through having them presented in an unexpected order. Similarly, all the "cultural" references, the dragging in of cumbersome foreign phrases and fancy scientific terms, springs not from exhibitionism but ironic violence.

And violence is the word; when MacDiarmid allows the poetic temperature to rise the tone is violent rather than mystical. His vocabulary, like Dunbar's, ransacks Middle Scots and other sources to get the arresting word:

> In wi' your gruntle then, puir wheengin's saul.
> Lap up the ugsome aidle wi' the lave,
> What gin it's your ain vomit that you swill
> And frae Life's gantin' and unfaddomed grave?

Or consider:

> What gin the gorded fullyery on hie
> And a' the fanerels o' the michty ship
> Gi'e back mair licht than fa's upon them ev'n
> Gin sic black ingangs haud us in their grip?

One does not need (I hope) at this time of day to defend MacDiarmid's "synthetic Scots." The power of his vocabulary speaks for itself: there is simply no other way of getting this kind of effect. True, a vocabulary of this sort if used merely to weave pallid ingenuities can sound monstrously artificial. A stream can rise no higher than its source, and a poet's vocabulary can do no more than the scope of his talent will allow. That is what makes nonsense of academic arguments about the proper language for a Scots poet. The proof of the pudding is in the eating, and the best language is that which *works*.

I have noted that the drunkenness of the hero is part of the dramatic scheme of the poem; I might add that it also provides a justification for that special kind of exuberance in which MacDiarmid delights. The concern with Scotland is passionate, but never jingoistic; the exaggerated terms in which it is expressed derive from the drunkard's expansiveness. There is no offence in his grotesque pictures of other nationalities; it is all part of the slight distortion of perspective which he employs in order to compel the reader's attention. It would be absurd to protest against such a description as "some wizened scrunt o' a

knock-knee Chinee" on the ground that it shows race prejudice or an anti-Chinese attitude. MacDiarmid is protesting against the monstrous absurdity of modern Burns suppers, and the distorted caricature of Chinese is part of his criticism not of China but of Scotland. Distortion and exaggeration constitute the norm of much of the idiom of the poem, just as they do in, say, Dante's *Inferno*. But MacDiarmid's is a profane and irreverent Inferno, deliberately profane and irreverent in order to test the staying power of the stereotypes of thought and diction which he is concerned to expose.

Scotland is, of course, the central theme of the poem; the title is, after all, *A Drunk Man Looks at the* Thistle. And Scotland is treated in two different ways. At some points it is the microcosm of the world, and problems of life and death, of the progress of civilisation, of fate and destiny, are illustrated with reference to Scotland:

> And as at sicna times am I,
> I wad ha'e Scotland to my eye
> Until I saw a timeless flame
> Tak' Auchtermuchty for a name,
> And kent that Ecclefechan stood
> As pairt o' an eternal mood.

At other points Scotland is not a microcosm of all history and geography, but a little country fixed in time and space, bound to a specific destiny, a country with its own special problems and its own special faults. The ambiguity in the treatment of Scotland is deliberate and characteristic. On the one hand MacDiarmid is concerned only with the regeneration of his own country; on the other, his wide ranging curiosity, his concern with what man has made of man on every part of this planet, leads him to search constantly for parallels and illustrations of the Scottish predicament. But this shifting of perspective is not arbitrary: it reflects the hero's changing moods as he moves between speculation, perception and memory.

1926 was a pretty shabby moment in Scotland's history, and it is astonishing to think that it was in that confused and apathetic year that this challenging poem-sequence on Scotland first appeared. It is a kind of dream allegory where the poet visits Hell and finds that every feature of its landscape reminds him of home. Grotesque, passionate, meditative, violent, plangent and reminiscent by turns, the poem moves with a fine assurance and a rich vitality. And, for all its severity about modern Scotland, this is not a hopeless poem; time and again the poet seeks refreshment in the recollection of physical sensation, and the challenging beauties of the physical world, the glories of sensation, remain. The silence invoked at the end is not the silence of the inanimate world or of death, but the silence of the man who has lost speech in experience. A nice piece of irony on which to end a dangerous poem.

ANN EDWARDS BOUTELLE
From "'Trembling Sunbeams':
The Vision and the Poetry"
Thistle and Rose:
A Study of Hugh MacDiarmid's Poetry
1980, pp. 23–30

The task that faces me—the delineation of the relationship between MacDiarmid's paradoxical vision of synthesis and his poetry—is anything but easy. As MacDiarmid wrote in 1926, "Comprehensibility is error: Art is beyond understanding," and "The ideal observer of art—as against art-at-work—is

God, conscious of all that has been and *will* be achieved."[1] While Duncan Glen has given a fine historical account of MacDiarmid's contributions to the Scottish Renaissance and Kenneth Buthlay has done pioneer work in his treatment of the entire opus,[2] no critic has yet produced a sufficiently detailed study of the poetry as a whole. The temptation has always been to concentrate on his Marxism, or his Scottish Nationalism, or his use of Lallans, or his "poetry of fact," or individual lyrics, to the exclusion of a consideration of his poetry as a whole. The Gargantuan size and the chameleon-like movements of the total work are sufficiently daunting. At the very moment when his poetry seems within human grasp, it wriggles away like the most slippery of fish, and the critic wishes more and more that he possessed the qualities of the "ideal observer of art." While I make no claims to be such a divinity, I bring to this study an awareness of my shortcomings, a conviction of the importance of MacDiarmid's poetry, and a gratitude to him for many hours of excited thought, joyful discovery, and the "extension of human consciousness."[3]

The recognition that MacDiarmid's vision is essentially paradoxical is the Ariadne's thread through the labyrinth of his poetry. To the service of this vision he subjects all the other elements in his poetry—language, politics, form, image, myth, theme, and moral standards. He is willing for the sake of this vision to risk boring, or confusing, or infuriating his readers. Everything he writes takes the paradoxical vision as a central point of reference.

Before I attempt to trace in detail the relationship between the vision and the poetry, it will be necessary to identify the major components of the vision, to suggest the basic connections between the vision and the poetry, and to establish some points of reference in the Scottish, Romantic, and modern traditions. This chapter, I hope, will provide the framework for the subsequent detailed study of the poetry.

The paradox that lies at the centre of his work manifests itself in many different ways and absorbs many varied ingredients. One of the most long-lasting influences upon this thought, as Duncan Glen has recently noted,[4] has been his early study of Solovyov, in particular his *La Russie et l'Eglise Universelle*. As early as 1923 he was noting a "Russo-Scottish parallelism" between J. Y. Simpson's *Man and the Attainment of Immortality* and Solovyov's work. Approvingly he draws attention to Simpson's suggestion that "with the origin of man there emerged the possibility of some new relationship, 'a moral linkage' with God; and only in so far as this possibility is realized does man attain the true 'individuality which is immortality'."[5] This "moral linkage" between man and God, a possibility that is inherent in man, provides MacDiarmid with a pattern of his vision of synthesis. Through the paradoxical vision of the poet, man and God meet. Like Solovyov's Sophia, the poet "plays before God, evoking before God images of possible extra-divine existence, shapes of chaotic multiplicity, and reabsorbing them again into herself."[6] Not only does this early and devoted acceptance of Solovyov's theory go a long way towards explaining MacDiarmid's rather idiosyncratic religious impulse, several steps removed from the orthodox Church of Scotland and the religion of his parents, but it also explains much of his fascination with all things Russian. Solovyov has given to the paradoxical vision a link between Scotland and Russia and between man and God.

MacDiarmid's unshakeable belief that poetry provides the "moral linkage" between the human and the divine emerges over and over again in his writing and indicates perhaps that in his own way he is as "devout" and as uncompromising as the "little mother" of his childhood: "As I have said, in one of my poems, I . . . would sacrifice a million people any day for

one immortal lyric,"[7] where the horrifying phrase is "any day." The romanticism of this view, coupled with the uncompromising and tough acceptance of the logical consequences and with an aristocratic disgust for what man at present is, gives to his poetry a strange and powerful tension as brute and angel are brought forcibly together under the aegis of paradox. His muse has both a divine halo and feet of clay.

Part of the responsibility for this paradoxical combination (the major source lying in Grieve's psyche and in his reaction to his childhood experiences) belongs to an as yet unrecognized source—namely Ouspensky's *Tertium Organum*. Its influence on MacDiarmid and on his poetry has been enormous. It began early: "A Moment in Eternity," written in 1921,[8] with its Ouspenskian concentration on unity and infinity, indicates that MacDiarmid had already read *Tertium Organum*: the 1926 essay "Art and the Unknown" presents Ouspensky's ideas with very little disguise and no acknowledgement. The essentially paradoxical nature of Ouspensky's theory of a "higher logic" must have fitted naturally and easily into the MacDiarmid paradox:

> *A is both A and Not-A*
>
> or
>
> *Everything is both A and Not-A.*
>
> or
>
> *Everything is All.*[9]

Ouspensky's "logic of the infinite" is the intellectual source of MacDiarmid's paradox.

Ouspensky, however, gives him more than the basic paradox. Solovyov's theory of Sophia gains definition from Ouspensky: man reaches God by the extension of consciousness. MacDiarmid's claim that the "function of art is the extension of human consciousness"[10] comes directly from *Tertium Organum*: "Poetry endeavors to express both music and thought together. The combination of feeling and thought . . . leads to a higher form of psychic life. . . . Art anticipates a psychic evolution and divines its future forms"; "the entire body of teachings of religio-philosophic movements have as their avowed or hidden purpose, *the expansion of consciousness*."[11]

Probably because of the attraction of his "logic of the infinite," Ouspensky bequeaths to MacDiarmid other related concepts. The importance of art ("the most important of human activities," according to MacDiarmid) had been stressed earlier by Ouspensky: "At the present stage of our development we possess nothing so powerful, as an instrument of knowledge of the world of causes, as art."[12] He is also responsible for MacDiarmid's belief, reinforced by his need to prove himself a hero, in the concept of an intellectual élite: an "infinitesimal minority of the people," those with higher consciousness who are on their way to a Nietzschean "linkage" with God, "the only real and important evolution for us—the evolution into superman."[13] Accompanying this idea is a vast scorn and distrust of what MacDiarmid calls "the vast majority o' men," and what Ouspensky had viewed as an active threat to evolution: "The enormous majority of the population of this globe is engaged . . . in destroying . . . and falsifying the ideas of the minority. The majority is without ideas."[14] The appeal of this theory to Grieve, an insecure minority faced with the combined forces of mother and brother, must have been irresistible.

Even the concept of the "ideal observer of art . . . conscious of all human experience up to the given moment" in the 1926 "Art and the Unknown" comes from *Tertium Organum*, although this time Ouspensky is quoting Bucke's *Cosmic Consciousness*: "The cosmic vision or the cosmic intuition, from which what may be called the new mind takes its name, in thus seen to be . . . complex and union of all prior thought and experience—just as self-consciousness is the complex and union of all thought and experience prior to it."[15] Here lies the intellectual origin of the basic thrust in MacDiarmid's paradoxical vision—the movement back into the past, the recapturing of the past, in order to reach the future and the "new mind."

His work has proved as faithful to Ouspensky's theories as to Solovyov's. Key concepts ("diversity in unity," "synthesis in differentiation," "unity of all opposites," "wonderment," "the voice of the silence," "the spur of love," "the marvellous and the mystic," and the belief that there can be "nothing dead or mechanical in nature") originate in *Tertium Organum* and remain throughout all his work as a solid core of ideas, major points of reference.[16] The ideas of Solovyov and Ouspensky have proved sufficiently suggestive, paradoxical, and all-embracing for MacDiarmid to build upon them many different kinds of poetry.

Ouspensky had also emphasized both the importance of language and its limitations. He saw language in relation to concepts as a limiting force and recognized the need for a new kind of language to transmit the new concepts.[17] At the same time he looked to the artist as a "clairvoyant . . . a magician [who would possess] the power to make others see that which they do not themselves see, but which he does see."[18] MacDiarmid, in his approach to language, seems to have amalgamated these two ideas with Solovyov. Words become magic, the incantation to summon up the God, the means of achieving the "moral linkage."

As early as 1923 he wrote, "We have been enormously struck by the resemblance—the moral resemblance—between Jamieson's Etymological Dictionary of the Scottish language and James Joyce's Ulysses,"[19] where the significant link between the two is a *moral* one. He continued: "A *vis comica* that has not yet been liberated lies bound by desuetude and misappreciation in the recesses of the Doric: and its potential uprising would be no less prodigious, uncontrollable, and utterly at variance with conventional morality than was Joyce's tremendous outpouring." This faith in words, this conviction that language holds within its recesses forces capable of unsettling the world, is close to Faustus's discovery in Marlowe's play. Significantly in 1952 MacDiarmid is quoting Blake's "All poets are of the devil's party."[20]

Paradoxically and appropriately, however, they are also members of the divine company: Lucifer before his fall, or Lucifer about to fall, as suggested by the name-changing from the devout "Christopher" to the proud "Hugh" of "divine wisdom." Language links the poet with God.

His delight in language goes far beyond seeing it as an intrinsically important component of the poem, or even recognizing, as Pound did, the relationship between language and society. In *Lucky Poet* MacDiarmid states explicitly the dependent relationship he sees:

> . . . the act of poetry being the reverse of what it is usually thought to be; not an idea gradually shaping itself in words, but deriving entirely from words— and it was in fact (as only my friend F. G. Scott divined) in this way that I wrote all the best of my Scots poems.[21]

Even the use of the word "divined" in this quotation is indicative of the magic relationship he sees between language and poetry. The core of his poetic theory (that man can be united with God, that poetry is the means by which this synthesis can happen, that language is the force that shapes poetry) explains the importance he attaches to the word. Like

St John he could cry, "In the beginning was the Word." And through the magic word the paradoxical synthesis is incarnate. All MacDiarmid's rummaging around in dictionaries, his delight in discovering a new or an arcane word, his incantatory catalogues of words, all spring from this belief in the magical, holy, shaping power of language. It has given us some of his best poetry and some of his worst. It has continually led him into both new and ancient areas of consciousness, and it has rarely been satisfied with standard English. Language, like Browning's "sunset touch," can disturb and extend human consciousness. It can force man to "look at things from an unaccustomed angle, see the unfamiliar and unsuspected aspects of all the everyday familiar things that in the sinful arrogance of his individuality he had taken as fixed and fundamental, given and unchanging."[22] Through language he reaches the paradoxical vision and forms the "moral linkage" with God.

Central to his concept of paradoxical synthesis is a belief in the extreme, the extreme without which the paradox could not take shape. Only the élite can reach it; the "vast majority o' men" retreat from extremes: "Heaven an' Hell's no' nice eneuch for some fowk. They want a' sorts o' half-wey hooses to suit their particular requirements."[23] To MacDiarmid any real progress is impossible if one is not willing to venture beyond the known into the unknown, to dare the extreme in order to make the paradox possible. His belief is essentially Blakean: "The road to excess leads to the palace of wisdom"; "If the fool would persist in his folly he would become wise"; "Without contraries is no progression."[24] And by becoming more human, by freeing himself from all that binds him, man becomes more like God. On this Blakean attempt to bring together opposites and to achieve a synthesis between man and God, heaven and hell, the past and the future, the particular and the universal, MacDiarmid's poetry rests.

The result of this belief in paradox and in the cultivation of the extreme to make possible a unity is often startling: a weird distortion of size and time (the world like an old white bone, the tears of a child appearing like a second flood, a glass of water containing the universe); or a shocking juxtaposition of tone (gross bawdiness shattering an ambience of wonder). The unexpected bursts into his poetry, reversing direction or changing focus without warning—a movement that forces the reader to take part in the central paradox and to move with it from one extreme to the other. The meeting place of his extremes is often painful, or shocking, or horrifying. In his poetry extremes never meet at the "still point of the turning world," but rather at a moment of tension and movement, whether violent, or trembling, or "twinklin' and fizzin' wi' fire," the human more human, and the inhuman or superhuman more true to its own nature. The satire that springs from his deep disgust with the Yahoos of the world, their physical grossness often as appalling to MacDiarmid as to Swift, counterbalances the Blakean innocence of his vision: "The new city must be a city of friends and lovers."[25] From the unexpected synthesis of disgust and wonder his most powerful poetry emerges: the early lyrics, *A Drunk Man Looks at the Thistle*, "Harry Semen," and later poems like "The Two Parents." I can think of no other poet who has so effectively made disgust and wonder touch each other. The combination of these two elements in precarious and dynamic balance is the most exciting and unique feature of his poetry, a manifestation of the central paradox in his vision of man.

Perhaps this paradoxical combination of elements is ultimately of a sexual origin. The combination of disgust and wonder is closer to the most intimate moments in Lawrence's novels or short stories than to anything else. Certainly in the early poems a sexual context is usually present either explicitly or implicitly, with the moment of pure vision emerging orgasmically from the disgust that precedes or surrounds it. For example, the brutal drunkenness of "The Looking Glass" suddenly soars into the pure ecstasy of "The Unknown Goddess":

> But what aboot it—hic—aboot it
> Mony a man's been that afore.
> It's no' a fact that in his lugs
> A wund like this need roar! . . .
> *I ha'e forekent ye! O I ha'e forekent.*
> *The years forecast your face afore they went.*

This in turn moves to the climactic

> *And generations that I thocht unborn*
> *Hail the strange Goddess frae my hert's-hert torn!*
> (p 71)

Immediately the sexual connotations of the vision ("generations that I thocht unborn," and the release of the Goddess "frae my hert's-hert") are converted into unredeemed physical terms as the speaker resumes the tone of disgust he had established in "The Looking Glass": "Or dost thou mak' a thistle o' me, wumman?" Disgust and wonder are continually touching each other, emerging from each other.

Characteristically the moment of vision is concentrated in a trembling or flickering movement: the "yow-trummle" (ewe-tremble) and "chitterin' licht" (shivering light) of "The Water-gaw"; the trembling of the moonlight in the thistle's branches in *A Drunk Man*; the "tiny hardly visible trembling of the water. / This is the nearest analogy to the essence of human life" of "The Glass of Pure Water." In this same poem MacDiarmid links this movement with Sacco and Vanzetti in the death cell, with "talking to God," and with the Recording Angel's report on human life: "the subtlest movement—just like that—and no more; / A hundred years of life on the Earth / Summed up, not a detail missed or wrongly assessed, / In that little inconceivably intricate movement" (p 470). This "little inconceivably intricate movement" is frequently the hallmark of his most suggestive poems—the trembling, miraculous movement of life, seen for an instant in its entirety, perfect in its paradoxical synthesis of all that is. It suggests, of course, the "queer swntherin' look" that links father and son together in "Andy." And it also suggests the trembling moment of sexual climax. While the sexual implications drop away in his poetry of the thirties, the quivering moments of paradoxical vision remain—as in the "Glass of Pure Water" section quoted above.

Notes

1. *Selected Essays of Hugh MacDiarmid,* ed. Duncan Glen (London: Jonathan Cape, 1969), p 44.
2. Duncan Glen, *Hugh MacDiarmid and the Scottish Renaissance* (Edinburgh and London: Chambers, 1964); Kenneth Buthlay, *Hugh MacDiarmid* (Edinburgh and London: Oliver and Boyd, 1964).
3. *Selected Essays,* p 44.
4. "The Word Which Silence Speaks," *Akros* 4 (Jan. 1970), p 58.
5. *Selected Essays,* p 39.
6. *Selected Essays,* p 40.
7. *The Uncanny Scot: A Selection of Prose by Hugh MacDiarmid,* ed. Kenneth Buthlay (London: MacGibbon and Kee, 1968), p 161.
8. See J. K. Annand's evidence for this date in *Early Lyrics of Hugh MacDiarmid* (Preston: Akros, 1968), p 10.
9. P. D. Ouspensky, *Tertium Organum: The Third Canon of Thought: A Key to the Enigmas of the World,* second American edition, authorized and revised (New York: Knopf, 1922), p 262.
10. *Selected Essays,* p 44.
11. *Tertium Organum,* p 83 and p 86.

12. *Tertium Organum,* p 161.
13. *Tertium Organum,* p 97.
14. *Tertium Organum,* p 228.
15. *Tertium Organum,* p 319.
16. *Tertium Organum,* p 134, p 265, p 158, p 161, p 171, p 199.
17. *Tertium Organum,* p 122.
18. *Tertium Organum,* p 162.
19. *The Scottish Chapbook,* 1 (Feb. 1923), p 183.
20. *Uncanny Scot,* p 97.
21. *Lucky Poet: A Self-Study in Literature and Political Ideas* (London: Methuen, 1943), p xiii.
22. *Uncanny Scot,* p 15.
23. *Uncanny Scot,* p 67.
24. See Blake's *The Marriage of Heaven and Hell.*
25. *Uncanny Scot,* p 23.

ALAN BOLD
From "To Prove My Saul Is Scots"
MacDiarmid: The Terrible Crystal
1983, pp. 85–101

A *Drunk Man Looks at the Thistle* is MacDiarmid's masterpiece; it is the poem he was apparently destined to write for all his interests and artistic talents merge in this poem. It is the poem in which the Synthetic Scots experiment proves amenable to an extended visionary treatment, the poem in which the subject is big enough to be the target for sustained assault by MacDiarmid, the poem in which he creates a persona idiosyncratic enough to suit himself, the poem in which MacDiarmid's staggering range of reference produces thematic variety rather than confusion. . . .

A Drunk Man Looks at the Thistle is a mould into which MacDiarmid pours all his cerebral conceptions, all his personal insights, all his philosophical conclusions, all his political passions. Little wonder, then, that the mould threatens to shatter under so much poetic pressure. As MacDiarmid is interested in visionary unity rather than psychological fragmentation this persistent attempt to find a form flexible enough to carry all MacDiarmid's ideas becomes a subject of comment throughout the poem:[1]

> I doot I'm geylies mixed, like Life itsel',
> But I was never ane that thocht to pit
> An ocean in a mutchkin. As the haill's
> Mair than the pairt sae I than reason yet.
> (87)

and

> O ilka man alive is like
> A quart that's squeezed into a pint
> (A maist unScottish-like affair!)
> (122)

and again

> And liquor packed impossibly
> Mak' pint-pot an eternal well
> (125)

So MacDiarmid is aware that the form has to emerge from the poetic experience and not vice versa; his reliance on couplets, quatrains and tercets in a modernist composition is his way of investing the familiar with the unexpected. The most familiar form that came to hand in Scotland was the ballad measure, especially appropriate in view of MacDiarmid's Border origins in Langholm. In one sense *A Drunk Man* is the biggest Border Ballad the world has ever seen. If we think of a ballad as a narrative poem intended for oral circulation then we must give MacDiarmid credit for taking this traditional technique and extending it into a speculative infinity. In the traditional ballad, story is raised to the musical level of song; in MacDiarmid's poem the narrative notion is enlarged into a rich compositional pattern capable of great variation. The poem presents a theme with its own variants and with metaphysical variations. Still, the essential rhythm is reassuring as MacDiarmid emphasised (in an 85th birthday broadcast on Radio Scotland on 11 August 1977):

> Largely, the engine that motivates the whole poem and keeps it going is the ballad measure, of course. It varies—there's a lot of variation of metre and so on in the *Drunk Man*—but underlying all the variations there's that continuing ballad metre. It comes back to the ballad all the time.

The poem unfolds on several levels of significance; it is a basic notion raised to a complex issue by the intensity of MacDiarmid's vision of a Scotocentric universe. On a purely narrative level the poem is the first-personal account of a Drunk Man's nocturnal adventures as he wakens from a hard-drinking session to find himself on a hillside confronted by the formidable flora of Scotland. The Drunk Man, as protagonist, is a representative Scot whose inviolable individuality gradually dawns on him. In this sense A *Drunk Man* is a demonstration of MacDiarmid's evolutionary idealism in action since the hero begins as a stereotypical Scottish drunk who, by a process of cerebration and emotional identification with the destiny of Scotland, moves away from the influence of alcoholic spirit into a unity with a universally creative spirit. In the beginning the Drunk Man looks at the thistle and he ends by tapping the wordless eloquence of the universe. MacDiarmid's great triumph is in allowing the spiritual aspects of the poem to develop, persuasively, from a convincing situation. As the poem opens the hero is exhausted, like Scotland. Punning on the associations of the word 'waun'ert' MacDiarmid then sets the Drunk Man on a hillside where he is ready to hold an argument with himself:

> But that's aside the point! I've got fair waun'ert.
> It's no' that I'm sae fou' as juist deid dune,
> And dinna ken as muckle's whaur I am
> Or hoo I've come to sprawl here 'neth the mune.
>
> That's it! It isna me that's fou' at a',
> But the fu' mune, the doited jade, that's led
> Me fer agley, or 'mogrified the warld.
> —For a' I ken I'm safe in my ain bed.
>
> *Jean! Jean! Gin she's* no' here it's no' *oor* bed,
> Or else I'm dreamin' deep and canna wauken,
> But it's a fell queer dream if this is no'
> A real hillside—and thae things thistles and bracken!
> (86)

It is, indeed, a strange dream that makes such spectacular advances on reality.

This Drunk Man is partially made in the image of his creator since he makes references to Montrose, (88) where the poem was executed; to the Muckle Toon of Langholm (97) where the poet was born; and to

> that upheaval in which I
> Sodgered 'neth the Grecian sky
> And in Italy and Marseilles
> (159)

Such autobiographical allusions are incidental since the main purpose of the poem is not self-portraiture but the creation of a new visionary unity that begins by being rooted in Scotland (like a thistle) and ends by reaching out into the stars. The process involves a startling metamorphosis for the Drunk Man is, ostensibly, a typically Scottish drunk—an argumentative creature who knows he must eventually creep home shame-

facedly to his nagging wife. Yet, in the course of the poem, he becomes something that is both unique and exemplary. When, having left his boozing cronies Cruivie and Gilsanquhar, the Drunk Man introduces himself his individuality is merely an assertive orthodoxy, a tiresome wha's-like-us affair:

> I'll bury nae heid like an ostrich's,
> Nor yet believe my een and naething else.
> My senses may advise me, but I'll be
> Mysel' nae maitter what they tell's
> (87)

With the slow dawning of sober spirituality the Drunk Man realises it is not enough to claim uniqueness since individuality is a quality that transcends a feeling of self-importance. It is a state of mind that enables the representative individual to project himself as an ideal embodiment of a national ideal:

> And let the lesson be—to be yersel's,
> Ye needna fash gin it's to be ocht else.
> To be yerself's—and to mak' that worth bein'.
> Nae harder job to mortals has been gi'en.
> (107)

As he acquires philosophical responsibility the Drunk Man understands that evolutionary idealism requires a creativity that transcends the domestic routine of reproduction:

> I dinna say that bairns alane
> Are true love's task—a sairer task
> Is aiblins to create oorsels
> As we can be—it's that I ask.
> (113)

So the Drunk Man wills himself upwards into a mystical union with the universe, this being the direction MacDiarmid himself wanted to take:

> The general (as beyond the particularly Scottish) theme of A *Drunk Man Looks at the Thistle* is to show 'a beautiful soul in the making'—to trace, that is to say, its rise through all struggle and contradiction till its stands out a self-conscious, self-directing personality—a purified person.[2]

MacDiarmid's own intellectualism is integrated into the cerebral texture of the poem which is ingeniously explained by a reference to the scholastic tradition of Scotland. The erudition of the Drunk Man is taken as a positive part of the Scottish educational heritage:

> Gin you're surprised a village drunk
> Foreign references s'ud fool in,
> You ha'ena the respect you s'ud
> For oor guid Scottish schoolin'.
> (97)

This village drunk translates from the Russian of Alexander Blok (88) and Zinaida Hippius (94), from the French of George Ramaekers (92) and Edmond Rocher (102) and from the German of Else Lasker-Schüler (95); or rather he adapts to his own ends extant English translations.[3] He also cites various intellectual and Scottish historical figures in the interests of contrast and counterpoint: Jascha Heifetz, Sir Harry Lauder, Mary Garden, Duncan Grant (84), G. K. Chesterton (85), Robert Burns (85), Sigmund Freud (93), T. S. Eliot (94), Arnold Schönberg (96), Leopold von Masoch, Marquis de Sade (99), William Dunbar, Oswald Spengler, Dostoevski, Nietzsche (106), Mallarmé (117), Herman Melville, Nathaniel Hawthorne (135), Tolstoi (153), Plato (157), Euclid, Einstein (159), Knox, Clavers, Mary Queen of Scots, Wallace, Carlyle (164). The display of booklore is part of the general assault on the reader's complacency for MacDiarmid makes it clear that he intends to lift up the reader's spirit and also brutally bring him down to the earth that sustains him. So he explains in a two-quatrain parenthesis:

(To prove my saul is Scots I maun begin
Wi' what's still deemed Scots and the folk expect,
And spire up syne by visible degrees
To heichts whereo' the fules ha'e never recked.

But aince I get them there I'll whummle them
And souse the craturs in the nether deeps,
—For it's nae choice, and ony man s'ud wish
To dree the goat's weird tae as weel's the sheep's!)
(83)

The Thistle *qua* thistle and Drunk Man *qua* drunk man are intellectually provocative items in their own right. To extend the Thistle and the Drunk Man from physical objects to metaphysical emblems MacDiarmid uses a multi-referential approach that leads to a Synthetic Symbolism (to match his Synthetic Scots). The eclecticism is energetic and the poetic synthesis of all the elements is MacDiarmid's triumph. From Socrates he takes the idea of a dynamically unfolding dialectic; from Plato the concept of earthly objects as imperfect copies of eternal Ideas; from biblical Christianity the figure of the saviour and the notions of crucifixion and resurrection; from neo-platonism the three hypostases of Soul, Mind and One; from Solovyov he borrows the figure of Sophia, the feminine personification of the wisdom of God; from Nietzsche the belief in an evolutionary idealism; from Freud the importance of phallic symbolism and lunar cycles. The Drunk Man tends ever upwards towards a union, through the mystical bride (or Sophia), with the universe which is the source of all creativity, the object of MacDiarmid's poetic search. This intellectual vision is a cerebral conception developed in an emotional matrix in aid of a metaphysical nativity. At the end of the poem the Drunk Man, who has already seen the eternal feminine principle assume the shape of both Sophia and the Virgin Mary, goes back to his earthly mate. At the beginning of the poem he is physically exhausted, at the end he has attained a Silence which is abruptly broken by Jean who closes the poem by speaking for the first time. The Drunk Man's odyssey is also an obsessive quest, as references to Moby-Dick (108) and The Flying Dutchman (111) confirm, and from all the internal evidence we are made to realise that the coming of 'A greater Christ, a greater Burns' (86) announced at the beginning of the poem has been accomplished by the end of it.

MacDiarmid concentrates a mass of conceptual, artistic and symbolic material into this poem of 2,685 lines and does so with reference to a small country whose visions are, proverbially, alcoholically induced nightmares. It is MacDiarmid's ability to make preconceptions rebound on the reader that provides the poem with its enduringly novel quality. At one point, aware of investing his native land with a universal importance, the Drunk Man asks a rhetorical question:

Is Scotland big enough to be
A symbol o' that force in me,
In wha's divine inebriety
A sicht abune contempt I'll see?
(145)

The answer is in the affirmative. Scotland, in this poem, is as big as the mind of the man who describes it. It is a world in itself but also a crucial part of the cosmos; in MacDiarmid's imaginative vision the universe is Scotocentric. Scotland's traditional symbol is the thistle and in looking at one the other is involved. At various points in the poem the thistle is described as something fundamentally alien and apart: it is 'Gurly' (90), 'Gothic' (93), 'Shudderin'' (105), 'nervous' (128), 'Infernal' (132), 'monstrous' (147), 'rootless' (147), 'epileptic'

(149), 'Presbyterian' (152), 'grisly' (153), 'Grugous' (156). These epithets conjure up a series of metamorphoses. MacDiarmid's thistle is clearly not the picture-postcard symbol of Lauderesque Scotland. At least, not by the time MacDiarmid has finished with it. It has a constantly changing quality as it seems to alter before the Drunk Man's eyes which are bleary before the vision comes. It carries the traditional connotations of defiance and austerity and its thorns relate it, figuratively, to the passion of Christ. MacDiarmid's Drunk Man is a saviour anxious to recreate Scotland in a spiritually appropriate image, aware that such an effort involves self-sacrifice on the altar of Scotland's defeatist history:

'A Scottish poem maun assume
The burden o' his people's doom,
And dee to brak' their livin' tomb.'
(165)

which is a tragic, though ultimately triumphant, consequence of the situation prefigured at the beginning of the poem:

A greater Christ, a greater Burns, may come.
The maist they'll dae is to gi'e bigger pegs
To folly and conceit to hank their rubbish on.
They'll cheenge folks' talk but no their natures, fegs!
(86)

The Christian symbolism does not, however, exhaust the poem which has layers and layers of meaning as it expands outwards from an explosive centre. For example the Christian concept of the saviour involved in spiritual struggle is complicated by being overlaid with the Nietzschean belief in the artist-as-redeemer. MacDiarmid isolates 'the Scots aboulia' (93) and proposes to deal with it by means of a Nietzschean will to (creative) power:

Or gin ye s'ud need mair than ane to teach ye,
Then learn frae Dostoevski and frae Nietzsche.
(106)

In the propagandist period leading up to the composition of A *Drunk Man*, MacDiarmid showed an enthusiastic interest in Freud who is undoubtedly an important figure in the structural and symbolic interpretation of the poem. From the Freudianism rampant in the art of the 1920s MacDiarmid derived two important ideas for application to A *Drunk Man*: the principle of free association *(freier Einfall)* developed by Freud in the 1890s to describe the preconscious shaping of human thought; and the psychological relevance of sexual symbolism. From the Freudian viewpoint, A *Drunk Man* can be seen as an enormous free association session as the fertile symbol of the thistle provokes multiple associations in the mind of the poet. MacDiarmid once referred to his own method of composition in these terms:

As keen students of the Vernacular will appreciate, he was making scores of little experiments in Doric composition and style even as he spoke—subtle adaptations of ancient figures of speech to modern requirements, finding vernacular equivalents for Freudian terminology—all infinitely difficult work but infinitely necessary if the Doric is again to become a living literary medium.[4]

In A *Drunk Man* he refers to how '*This* Freudian complex has somehoo slunken/Frae Scotland's soul'. (93) Throughout the poem the thistle, personifying Scotland as a thrusting aggressive force, becomes a phallic symbol of great power. Just as the full moon, the mystical bride (Sophia), and the conspicuously absent Jean represent the feminine principle of receptivity and creative congress, the thistle stands (phallically) for the masculine principle of thrust and procreation. This strong sexual image is sustained throughout the poem as the Drunk Man's spirit rises to the occasion, falls as the alcoholic spirit wears off, then rises again under the influence of a metaphysical spirit. Having found himself on the hillside under the full moon (and how MacDiarmid enjoys punning on the moon being 'fu'' in the Scottish colloquial sense of being full of drink), the Drunk Man is aware of stirrings that link him to Jean who is his own moon goddess and earthly representative of the eternal feminine ideal personified as Sophia, the mystical and universal bride:

> Or doest thou mak' a thistle o' me, wumman? But for
> thee
> I were as happy as the munelicht, withoot care,
> But thocht o' thee—o' thy contempt and ire—
> Turns hauf the warld into the youky thistle there.
> (91)

After brooding, in the 'fickle licht' (92), on the intimate appearance of the thistle the Drunk Man thinks back on his childhood days in Langholm, 'the Muckle Toon', (97) when the Common Riding celebrants carried an 'aucht-fit thistle' (97) through the Walligate. This memory of vitality provokes a memory of his wife Jean as she was on her wedding day and, at the erotic thought, the thistle seems to rise sexually before his eyes:

> Nerves in stounds o' delight,
> Muscles in pride o' power,
> Bluid as wi' roses dight
> Life's toppin' pinnacles owre,
> The thistle yet'll unite
> Man and the Infinite!
> (98)

It is the contention of the poem that the thistle can penetrate deep space, shoot out seeds like stars into the universe, and thus create a new metaphysical nativity, a Scottish spirit that comes back to the earth in a beautiful gesture of unity. So many images and allusions blend in MacDiarmid's poem that the symbols begin to acquire an autonomous power and at two sections—the climactic and miraculous nativity (101–6) and the closing triumph of Silence (166–7)—no amount of paraphrase or interpretation can detract from the element of mystery MacDiarmid creates.

Notes

1. The edition of *A Drunk Man Looks at the Thistle* is that of Castle Wynd, Edinburgh 1956.
2. Duncan Glen, *Hugh MacDiarmid and the Scottish Renaissance*, Edinburgh, Chambers, 1964, p. 91, quoting MacDiarmid's address to the Edinburgh University Nationalist Club, April 1958.
3. Kenneth Buthlay, in *Hugh MacDiarmid*, Edinburgh, Oliver & Boyd, 1964, discloses that the MacDiarmid translations in *Sangschaw*, *Penny Wheep* and *A Drunk Man* are in fact adaptations from books of translations by Babette Deutsch and Avrahm Yarmolinsky, and by Jethro Bithell: 'There can be no doubt that [MacDiarmid] has a remarkable facility in picking up a working knowledge of diverse languages, but there is no convincing evidence to show that he is in full command of any foreign tongue.' (p. 75)
4. *The Scottish Chapbook*, vol. 1, no. 3, October 1922, p. 70.

ALAN BOLD
From "Hugh MacDiarmid"
Modern Scottish Literature
1983, pp. 26–40

During his lifetime MacDiarmid was such a massive presence in Scottish literary affairs that his work had an unsettling influence: his followers lavished praise on his poetry without considering it in a global context, and his enemies dismissed him as a virulent polemicist who used poetry for political ends. It is now possible to see what MacDiarmid actually achieved. He began writing after the First World War and wanted to help Scotland take her place in a radically new world in which independence would be granted to both individuals and nations. Although he was a nationalist he detested chauvinism and cultivated international contacts. He was convinced that Scotland needed saving from her own worst excesses and had the justifiable immodesty to assume that he could be a cultural saviour. As his work shows, he believed that poetry was an immensely more important force than politics so he began to revitalise Scotland by giving it a new poetic voice. He came to the conclusion that 'most of the important words were killed in the First World War' ('Talking with Five Thousand People in Edinburgh'), so set about liberating language from convention and complacency. He regarded the use of dialect Scots by poets such as Charles Murray as a manifestation of mindlessness; therefore he put in the place of dialect Scots an *ad hoc* idiom called Synthetic Scots, as it used the resources of the etymological dictionary and the expressive sound of the spoken language. MacDiarmid wanted Synthetic Scots to be as modernistic as Eliot's allusive English or Joyce's textured prose. In fact MacDiarmid's Synthetic Scots was the Scottish contribution to the literary experimentalism of the twentieth century.

. . . MacDiarmid's lyrics constantly jumped from the particular to the general and then came back, lovingly, to earth. In the lyrics in *Sangschaw* and *Penny Wheep* MacDiarmid exhaustively pursued his method of opening up an image to cosmic consequences. He suggests a multi-dimensional view of reality by contrasting an earthly viewpoint with a God's-eye-view of the universe; this cosmic outlook simultaneously shrinks the world to socially manageable proportions and suggests the imaginative majesty of man who is capable of possessing the cosmos through creativity. MacDiarmid used God as an instantly accessible image of a meaningful universe and avoided the theological stereotype. In 'Crowdieknowe' God is not an omnipotent patriarch but an odious observer who has to contend with the truculent force of humanity in the shape of the unwillingly resurrected Langholm locals. MacDiarmid saw no point genuflecting before an abstract deity. In his poem 'Empty Vessel' he compared a girl crooning over a dead child to the intergalactic light that unfeelingly illuminates the universe:

> Wunds wi' warlds to swing
> Dinna sing sae sweet,
> The licht that bends owre a' thing
> Is less ta'en up wi't.

Paradoxically 'Empty Vessel' demonstrates how deeply MacDiarmid's modernity is rooted in tradition for the poem is a creative completion of a folk fragment. . . .

In the thistle (of *A Drunk Man Looks at the Thistle*) MacDiarmid has found an all-purpose symbol sufficiently familiar to provoke responses in all Scots and suggestive enough to sustain the poet's astonishingly inventive genius. For his next long poem *To Circumjack Cencrastus* (1930), he employed the Celtic symbol of eternity: the snake, or serpent, with its tail in its mouth. *Cencrastus* is inferior to *A Drunk Man*, but then so are most Scottish poems. It came as an anticlimax only because MacDiarmid had set himself such impossibly high standards in his masterpiece. It has generally been supposed that *Cencrastus* was weaker than its predecessor because the central symbol did not suit MacDiarmid's muse the way the thistle did. It is more basic than that. MacDiarmid never liked to repeat his successes. His whole career is a series of dramatic shifts in emphasis linked by the power of his personality; the dialectical motion of *A Drunk Man* corresponded to the contrary nature of MacDiarmid's own personality. In *A Drunk Man* MacDiarmid had sublimated his personality in the device of the dramatic monologue; in *Cencrastus* he decided to do without a poetic persona and, instead, expatiated on the state of the Scotocentric universe. *Cencrastus* is a series of autonomous poems and so regarded amounts to a splendid achievement. Poems like 'The Parrot Cry' and 'I'm the original/Plasm o' the ocean' search and satirise Scotland and the Scot. They are likely to be remembered without the benefit of the serpentine context. MacDiarmid's lyric gift was in evidence in the finest parts of the book although it had taken on a melancholy tone of uncharacteristic resignation:

> Nae wonder if I think I see
> A lichter shadow than the neist
> I'm fain to cry: 'The dawn, the dawn!
>   But ah
>   —It's juist mair snaw!¹

Equally impressive is MacDairmid's command of an elegiac English idiom in his translation of Rilke's 'Requiem für eine Freundin'. Yet the sequence is, overall, richer in opinion than in imagery and thereby demonstrates that MacDiarmid no longer took as his priority the revitalisation of Scots. He had personally fought that battle in his two collections of lyrics and *A Drunk Man*. During the next decade he was to be increasingly involved in personal survival and the embattled expression of his unpopular opinions.

The 1930s is remembered, in literary history, as a political decade; the era of the English pylon poets who took a fancy to Marxism and reinterpreted political comradeship in terms of public school chumminess. MacDiarmid bitterly dismissed them in a poem 'British Leftish Poetry, 1930–40':

> Auden, MacNeice, Day Lewis, I have read them all.
> Hoping against hope to hear the authentic call . . .
> And know the explanation I must pass is this
> —You cannot strike a match on a crumbling wall.

Yet Day Lewis acknowledged² that it was MacDiarmid who inspired the political poetry of the 1930s with his collection *First Hymn to Lenin* (1931). Although MacDiarmid did not join the Communist Party until 1934, the year after his expulsion from the Scottish National Party, this volume vividly revealed the colour of this politics. In the title poem the Synthetic Scots of the early 1920s is replaced by what is basically English with a Scottish accent. The poem, as the title makes abundantly clear, deifies Lenin (not individuality as in *A Drunk Man*) as the hope for the future of mankind. MacDiarmid, originally alive to the heroic individual, goes over to hero worship and the unMarxist assumption that Lenin personally orchestrated history by the force of his personality. In this poem MacDiarmid subscribes to the opportunist notion that the means justify the ends and that Lenin's policies, all of them, can be excused on pragmatic grounds:

> What maitters 't wha we kill
> To lessen that foulest murder that deprives
>   Maist men o' real lives?

MacDiarmid's rhetorical question was answered by bitter hostility on the part of the readership who had seen him as the great white hope of Scotland. Now he was cast as the red terror, a man publicly committed to the overthrow of bourgeois society. That society took a terrible revenge on him.

Nevertheless, delighted by the impact of his secular first hymn to Lenin, MacDiarmid published his *Second Hymn to Lenin* in 1932. In the short satirical poems printed alongside the 'First Hymn' MacDiarmid had shown himself a master of succinctly expressed malice. The 'Second Hymn', again written in a Scottish-accented English, reduced politics to the first step in a long road of human emancipation which would ultimately depend on poetry:

> Sae here, twixt poetry and politics,
> There's nae doot in the en'.
> Poetry includes that and s'ud be
> The greatest poo'er amang men.
>
> —It's the greatest, *in posse* at least,
> That men ha'e discovered yet
> Tho' nae doot they're unconscious still
> O' ithers faur greater then it . . .
>
> Unremittin', relentless,
> Organized to the last degree,
> Ah, Lenin, politics is bairns' play
> To what this maun be!

MacDiarmid believed in the practical role poetry would play in the classless society that is the aim of theoretical Marxism. He was also painfully aware that, in the real world he lived in, poetry was the concern of a tiny minority. While he was making ringing statements on the state of the world his personal life was breaking down into various crises.

In 1929 MacDiarmid had been invited, by Compton Mackenzie, to go to London to edit the periodical *Vox*. The magazine, devoted to radio, collapsed after three months and the poet almost went down with it. He left his wife, Margaret, in London while he found a job as a Publicity Officer in Liverpool. After a catastrophic year he returned to London to be divorced in 1932. From that period dates his intense hatred of England and he was 'desperately anxious not to leave Scotland again.'³ Ironically the collection MacDiarmid published in that miserable year of 1932, *Scots Unbound*, contains some of his most delicate poems. 'Milk-Wort and Bog-Cotton' is a lyrical triumph. Its beautifully hushed majesty nevertheless contains a confessional reference to the poet's 'darkness':

> Wad that nae leaf upon anither wheeled
> A shadow either and nae root need dern
> In sacrifice to let sic beauty be!
> But deep surroondin' darkness I descern
> Is aye the price o' licht. Wad licht revealed
> Naething but you, and nicht nocht else concealed.

In complete contrast there is the onomatopoetic extravaganza 'Water Music' which, as the introductory stanza affirms, was inspired by the Anna Livia Plurabelle section Joyce worked into *Finnegans Wake*. MacDiarmid's delight in the sensuous possibilities of Scots was never more joyously expressed than in this poem:

> Archin' here and arrachin there,
>   Allevolie or allemand,
> Whiles appliable, whiles areird,
>   The polysemous poem's planned.
>
> Lively, louch, atweesh, atween,
>   Auchimuty or aspate,
> Threidin' through the averins
>   Or bightsom in the aftergait.

Such ecstatic moments were isolated, though, for MacDiarmid was taking up the challenge of a more bookish poetry, a verse entirely devoted to linguistic exploration. The result was poetry in which verbal grandeur alternated with passages reflecting the poet's lexical obsessions. MacDiarmid had evolved in his art and his life. After his divorce he married a Cornish girl, Valda Trevlyn, and the couple moved, with their baby, Michael, to an abandoned cottage on the Shetland island of Whalsay. MacDiarmid has described his condition bitterly:

> I could not have lived anywhere else . . . without recourse to the poorhouse. We were not only penniless when we arrived in Whalsay—I was in exceedingly bad state, psychologically and physically . . . I had no books. Indeed, we had practically no furniture . . . I have forgotten what the first winter was like; no doubt my wife remembers all too well—it must have been one long nightmare of cold and damp and darkness and discomfort.[4]

With island exile imposed on him by economic and psychological circumstances he began to investigate his environment and the poetry he wrote then was neither Synthetic Scots nor everyday English. It was (as the opening of 'On a Raised Beach' shows) an erudite dictionary-based diction made poetic by the pressure of the poet's personality:

> All is lithogenesis—or lochia,
> Carpholite fruit of the forbidden tree,
> Stones blacker than any in the Caaba,
> Cream-coloured caen-stone, chatoyant pieces,
> Celadon and corbeau, bistre and beige,
> Glaucous, hoar, enfouldered, cyathiform,
> Making mere faculae of the sun and moon
> I study you glout and gloss, but have
> No cadrans to adjust you with, and turn again
> From optik to haptik and like a blind man run
> My fingers over you, arris by arris, burr by burr,
> Slickensides, truité, rugas, foveoles,
> Bringing my aesthesis in vain to bear,
> An angle-titch to all your corrugations and coigns,
> Hatched foraminous cavo-rilievo of the world,
> Deictic, fiducial stones.

MacDiarmid began to expand on even that idiom. He believed it was imperative that the poet should express the potentialities of the epic age he lived in and devoted his poetic efforts to the completion of a truly massive work that would include *In Memoriam James Joyce* (1955), *The Kind of Poetry I Want* (1961) and the projected *Impavidi Progrediamur*. Although he was Scotland's most distinguished living poet he refused to adopt any Grand Old Mannerisms but cherished his independence and idiosyncracy. He left Whalsay in 1942 and did warwork first as a fitter on Clydeside and then as a deckhand on a Norwegian ship. When the war ended he was technically unemployed. In 1951 he moved to a derelict, rent-free cottage in Biggar, Lanarkshire, and continued to plan the epic that was to be called *Mature Art*. Although critics despaired of the regurgitated bookish passages the poem is rich in personal moments perfectly expressed, as this extract from *In Memoriam James Joyce* shows:[5]

> In this realistic mood I recognise
> With a grim animal acceptance
> That it is indeed likely enough that the 'soul'
> Perishes everlastingly with the death of the body,
> But what this realistic mood, into which
> My mind falls like a plummet
> Through the neutral zone of its balanced doubt,
> Never for one single beat of time can shake or disturb
> Is my certain knowledge,
> Derived from the complex vision of everything in me,
> That the whole astronomical universe, however illimitable,
> Is only one part and parcel of the mystery of Life;
> Of this I am as certain as I am certain that I am I.
> The astronomical universe in *not* all there is.

> So this is what our lives have been given to find,
> A language that can serve our purposes,
> A marvellous lucidity, a quality of fiery aery light,
> Flowing like clear water, flying like a bird,
> Burning like a sunlit landscape.
> Conveying with a positively Godlike assurance,
> Swiftly, shiningly, exactly, what we want to convey.
> This use of words, this peculiar aptness and handiness,
> Adapts itself to our every mood, now pathetic, now ironic,
> Now full of love, of indignation, of sensuality, of glamour, of glory,
> With an inevitable richness of remembered detail
> And a richness of imagery that is never cloying,
> A curious and indescribable quality
> Of sensual sensitiveness,
> Of very light and very air itself,
> —Pliant as a young hazel wand,
> Certain as a gull's wings,
> Lucid as a mountain stream,
> Expressive as the eyes of a woman in the presence of love,—
> Expressing the complex vision of everything in one,
> suffering all impressions, all experience, all doctrines
> To pass through and taking what seems valuable from each.
> No matter in however many directions
> These essences seem to lead.

Although the idiom has altered the concerns are recognisably MacDiarmidian: language, individuality, unity-in-diversity. There is an artistic wholeness to his achievement in spite of, or because of since he was proud of his dialectical abilities, the contradictions. His poetry has the authority of a man who knows what it is to be possessed by imaginative powers, to be occasionally at the mercy of his material. Contrary to orthodox opinion, MacDiarmid did not take up Scots and then abandon it for English or vice versa. He used the two languages with a poet's indifference to dogmatic theory. He always hovered between Scots and English and in 1966, years after his supposed desertion of Lallans, could publish a poem like 'A Change of Weather' with its description of the sun 'strugglin' airgh and wan i' the lift'. The fact is that all MacDiarmid's work is cerebral: his Scots lyrics revealed an informed consciousness of the cosmos and his *Mature Art* project is a monumental exhibition of one man's erudition. Significantly enough, the first piece in Christopher Grieve's first book, *Annals of the Five Senses* (1923), is revealingly entitled 'Cerebral'. It is a prose composition delineating the thoughts that pass through the mind of a journalist as he writes a column on 'The Scottish Element in Ibsen'. It attempts to map the contours of a mind that free associates in a remarkably imaginative manner: 'His sense of actual cerebral disposition was acute and constantly employed.'[6] As MacDiarmid said in another context, 'That's me to a T.'[7] He was, after all, entitled to boast in 1972:

> I am accustomed to being accused of all sorts of contradictions, to which I have often merely answered, like Walt Whitman, 'I contradict myself. Very well! I contradict myself.' But . . . under the apparent inconsistencies and contradictions there is a basic unity . . . [In *Annals of the Five Senses*] I express the main ideas of all my subsequent work. I have demonstrably pursued these undeviatingly through my whole career.[8]

It was because of his determination to be utterly himself, albeit in a national context, that MacDiarmid spent so much time exposing as a cruel travesty the Lauderesque image of the

Scot as a sentimental and silly fool. MacDiarmid rained down polemical words as hard as hail on the heads of his fellow Scots because he wanted Scotland to recognise itself so other nations would follow suit and recognise it as something worthwhile. He continually urged Scottish writers to show more responsibility, to be an exceptional part of the national community, to eschew the derivative and embrace the essential. In *Lucky Poet* he criticised his contemporaries for being 'hopelessly muddle-headed, anti-intellectual'[9] and the charge was repeated some twenty years later in *The Company I've Kept*: 'Most of our writers are backward-looking, consumed by a repetition complex, afraid to face up to and grapple with contemporary realities.'[10] In making his own subject-matter the total substance of Scotland he answered with a defiant negative his own rhetorical question in 'Direadh I': 'Scotland small? Our multiform, our infinite Scotland *small?*' Scotland is, MacDiarmid maintained, as large as the imagination can make it. MacDiarmid never claimed his was the only way; what he did was open up a world of possibilities and restore a sense of purpose to the national community. When he was buried in his native Langholm on 13 September 1978 there was no way his work would rest in peace. All his life he had welcomed criticism and combined celebration with cerebration. His hope was for a nation of individuals capable of thinking for themselves. If MacDiarmid's work was to have an influence then the process would recall the motto of *The Scottish Chapbook*—'Not Traditions—Precedents'. If, for example, Synthetic Scots was to survive then it would support a Scottish national poetry. MacDiarmid, the self-styled saviour of *A Drunk Man Looks at the Thistle*, had little use for disciples, as his credo stressed individuality. To their credit the best of his followers attempted to adapt his idiom to their own needs.

Notes

1. Michael Grieve and W. R. Aitken (eds), *Hugh MacDiarmid: Complete Poems 1920–1976*, 2 vols., Martin Brian and O'Keeffe: London 1978, p. 205.
2. Hugh MacDiarmid, *Lucky Poet*, Methuen: London, 1943; Cape reprint (1972), p. 158.
3. Ibid. p. 41.
4. Ibid. p. 45.
5. Hugh MacDiarmid, *Complete Poems*, pp. 822–3.
6. C. M. Grieve, *Annals of the Five Senses*, Porpoise Press: Edinburgh 1930, p. 18.
7. Hugh MacDiarmid, *Lucky Poet*, p. 58,
8. Ibid. p. xi.
9. Ibid. p. 44.
10. Hugh MacDiarmid, *The Company I've Kept*, Hutchinson: London 1966, p. 20.

THOMAS MACDONAGH

1878–1916

Thomas MacDonagh was born on February 1, 1878, in Cloughjordan, a village in County Tipperary. He left home in 1892 to enter Rockwell College, where for a time he aspired to the priesthood. After completing his own studies he remained at the College as a teacher, but left in 1901 having decided he had no religious vocation. In 1902 he joined the Gaelic League, and became active in its campaigns for the revival of the Irish language, which he himself barely knew.

MacDonagh continued to work as a teacher, and began to publish poetry, in *Through the Ivory Gate*, *April and May* (both 1903), and *The Golden Joy* (1907). His play *When the Dawn Is Come* was performed at the Abbey Theatre in 1908, and that year he moved to Dublin. As a critic he contributed essays to the *Leader* and *T. P.'s Weekly*, while a fourth book of poems, *Songs of Myself*, appeared in 1910, and another play, *Metempsychosis*, in 1912. He played an important part in the founding of the *Irish Review* in 1911, and in 1914 was a co-founder of the Irish Theatre Company.

After joining the Irish Volunteers in December 1913, MacDonagh gravitated increasingly towards its militant revolutionary wing. Though apparently not involved in planning the Easter Rising of 1916, he commanded the Second Battalion of the Volunteers, and after the failure of the revolt was executed by the British with other Irish leaders on May 3, 1916. After his death his *Literature in Ireland* and *Poetical Works* were rushed into print, easing the circumstances of his widow and two children.

Personal

MacDonagh called to-day. Very sad about Ireland. Says that he finds a barrier between himself and the Irish-speaking peasantry, who are 'cold, dark and reticent' and 'too polite'. He watches the Irish-speaking boys at his school, and when nobody is looking, or when they are alone with the Irish-speaking gardener, they are merry, clever and talkative. When they meet an English speaker or one who has learned Gaelic, they are stupid. They are in a different world. Presently he spoke of his nine years in a monastery and I asked what it was like. 'O,' he said, 'everybody is very simple and happy enough.

There is a little jealousy sometimes. If one brother goes into a town with a Superior, another brother is jealous.' He then told me that the Bishop of Raphoe had forbidden anybody in his See to contribute to the Gaelic League because its Secretary 'has blasphemed against the holy Adamnan'. The Secretary had said, 'The Bishop is an enemy, like the founder of his See, Saint Adamnan, who tried to injure the Gaelic language by writing in Latin'. MacDonagh says, 'Two old countrymen fell out and one said, "I have a brother who will make you behave", meaning the Bishop of Raphoe, and the other said, "I have a son who will put sense into you", meaning Cardinal Logue.'—W. B. YEATS, "The Death of Synge" (1909), *Autobiographies*, 1955, pp. 505–6

E. V. Lucas

Rose Macaulay

Ian McEwan

Hugh MacDiarmid

ARTHUR MACHEN

JOHN MASEFIELD

COMPTON MACKENZIE

LOUIS MACNEICE

It is strange to look back to the time when I first knew Thomas MacDonagh. What with the present great war in Europe, and our own small war in Ireland, that time has so faded and retreated that one recalls it with difficulty and regards it with something of astonishment—yet it is only six years ago. Was there that peace, that gentleness, that good-humour? And was the MacDonagh of April, 1916, the same man with whom I walked and talked and quarrelled in 1910? One could quarrel with MacDonagh, but not for more than three minutes at a time, and if he were ruffled the mere touch of a hand or the wind of a pleasant word appeased him instantly. I have seldom known a man in whom the instinct for friendship was so true, nor one who was so prepared to use himself in the service of a friend. He was intensely egotistic in his speech; so, it seems to me, were all the young Irishmen of that date; but in his actions he was utterly unselfish.

At that time he lived a kind of semi-detached life at the gate-lodge of Mr. Houston's house in the Dublin hills. To this house all literary Dublin used to repair, and there MacDonagh was constantly to be seen. He was a quaint recluse who delighted in company, and he fled into and out of solitude with equal precipitancy. He had a longing for the hermit's existence and a gift for gregarious life. At Grange House both these aptitudes were met, and I think he was very content there. Out on the hills, walking across the fields, or along the narrow roads curving to this side and that, but always running upwards, he would repeat his verses to me, and accompany them and follow them with a commentary that seemed endless as the bushes that lined our road. Just then I was so interested in my own verse I could not afford to be interested in anyone else's, and I should say that my impression of his poems agreed absolutely with his impressions about mine.

In literary ways he was very learned, and would quote from English and French and Latin and Irish; but in worldly ways he was an infant, and he preserved that freshness of outlook and candour of bearing until the end—an end that in those days he did not dream of, or if he did, he who reported everything did not report this dream. I do not think he had any other ambition than to write good verse and to love his friends, and the pleasure he found in these two arts was the sole profit I ever knew him to seek or to get.

There was a certain reserve behind his talkativeness. Often, staring away at the hills or at the sky, he would say, "Ah me!"—an interjection that never expressed itself further in words. Yet that interjection, always half humorous, always half tragic, remains with me as more than a memory. I think that when he faced the guns which ended life and poetry and all else for him, he said in his half humorous, half tragic way, "Ah me!" and left the whole business at that.

Poor MacDonagh! There went a good man down when you went down.

About three weeks before the Insurrection I met him for the last time. We walked together for nearly an hour, and I remember he was saluted in Grafton Street by three young men—three of his Volunteers. At that time I am sure he did not intend any rebellion. I did not ask him much about the plans of the Volunteers, for when one is not in a movement one has no right to ask questions about it, and the only point we spoke of was the possibility of their arms being seized. His remark on that contingency was stern enough. But I can find nothing in his speech with the implication of rebellion. I think if he had meditated this he would have emphasised some phrase with his tongue or his eye, so that afterwards I could remember it. Indeed he was so free from all idea of immediate violence that he arranged to ask me later on to talk to some of

his boys about the poetry of William Blake. One thing that he said smilingly remains with me: "When are you lads going to stop writing stories and do something?" said he.

He had reserves to fall back on when the end came—reserves of pride and imagination and courage. An officer who witnessed the executions said, "They all died well, but MacDonagh died like a prince."—JAMES STEPHENS, "Introduction" to *The Poetical Works of Thomas MacDonagh*, 1916, pp. ix–xii

> He shall not hear the bittern cry
> In the wild sky, where he is lain,
> Nor voices of the sweeter birds
> Above the wailing of the rain.
>
> Nor shall he know when loud March blows
> Thro' slanting snows her fanfare shrill,
> Blowing to flame the golden cup
> Of many an upset daffodil.
>
> But when the Dark Cow leaves the moor,
> And pastures poor with greedy weeds,
> Perhaps he'll hear her low at morn
> Lifting her horn in pleasant meads.

> —FRANCIS LEDWIDGE, "Thomas MacDonagh" (1916), *The Complete Poems of Francis Ledwidge*, 1919, p. 210

General

Among the modern Irish poets MacDonagh strikes one, perhaps, as the most Irish in his character and the least so in his mentality. In the man, one finds the courage and warm-heartedness (the best of friends, as Stephens calls him), the fierce patriotism and gentle simplicity, which one has come to associate with the name of Irishman; in the poet, we find a tendency to pure speculation, to abstract philosophy, to mere intellectualism, which are qualities more common as a rule in Göttingen than in Dublin. We have to lift those wrappings from his work to find the warm fervour, the spiritual passion, the other world atmosphere, which are characteristic of Irish character and Irish thought.

There is altogether a strange dualism in Thomas MacDonagh. The professor who lectured daily on English literature as if he had no other thought in the world, and the patriot who was one of the most active organisers in the political movement—what had these two in common? The poet, rhetorical, learned, over-charged with ideas, and the poet who, occasionally lifting the veil from his inner soul, gives us a glimpse of intense feeling in words brief and simple—how are these two to be reconciled? Much of his poetry might be taken as subjective, the *Songs of Myself* might be taken as wholly so; yet they seldom reveal anything of this inner soul. With true artistic instinct he saved his poetry by this intended or unintended duplicity; his own nature was too passionate to attain to the aloofness necessary to poetic subjectivity. To live a poem, and to write one, are very different things, and art demands that the living be kept very much in subjection to the writing.

"Death in the Woods" is, perhaps, more expressive of the whole man, and also of the Celtic spirit, than any other of his poems. Here we find that fierce delight in the voice of the wind which is peculiar to the Irish. "For the baying of winds in the woods to me was music sweet." To the Irish poet, nature always means the voice of nature, nature speaking to the ear rather than to the eye. This is quite peculiar to the Irish. In no other poetry do we find the sounds of nature interpreted with such skill, and chief among these sounds is the sound of the wind. In an ocean-washed, wind-swept island, all the other voices of nature are often drowned by the voice of the storm, carrying its eternal messages of fear, of sorrow, of exultation. It is the note of exultation that appeals to MacDonagh's fiery, wind-swept heart.

> Oh, for the storms again, and youth in my heart
>   again,
> My spirit to glory strained, wild in this wild wood
>   then.

What an intolerance of life's calms, of nature in its placid moods in the lines, "But no wind stirs a leaf, and no cloud hurries the moon," etc.—"a night for a villager's death"—but not for the death of a patriot or poet! Then comes the inevitable speculation, the questioning as to the nature of death, lost for a moment in the heart's passionate cry:

> Gladly I'd leave them this corpse in their churchyard
>   to lay at rest,
> If my wind-swept spirit could fare on the hurricane's
>   kingly quest,

the finest lines in the poem, and perhaps in all his poems, one of the truest expressions of the poet's mind.

Poor Thomas MacDonagh, when you faced the bullets on Holy Cross day did your spirit then truly fare on the hurricane's kingly quest?

After this cry he again lapses into speculation, bringing our thoughts with him into the land of pure ideas, to emerge again towards the end of the poem into realms of simple faith, the faith of a soul that despises death, knowing that it will pass "to mingle with God's own breath."

In this poem we find the passionate nostalgia for some world other than this world of our sorrow, for some life other than that of earth's flats and calms, that nostalgia of the infinite and the perfect, which is peculiar to the Celtic mind.

In the *Songs of Joy* we have intellectual visions almost too obscure for the ordinary reader. The themes, though treated with strength and delicacy, leave us often unconvinced because of the subtlety of the thought. Take, for instance, "The Tree of Knowledge"; the ideas are so illusive, the symbols so remote, that the subject matter escapes each instant from our grasp. What is the subject matter? The vision of innocence, lost through sin? The Holy Grail seen by the pure of heart, lost through weakness of will; and recovered through painful purification? Or the Faust motif of the pursuit of knowledge, its impotence to satisfy the soul, the moral struggle, fall and repentance, and final redemption through toil, when through action the fruit of knowledge is made good to the soul?

The poem tantalises because of its obscurity. Were it less beautiful it might be passed over with a shrug, but the beauty of the thoughts and their poetic expression rivet the attention and force one to seek some solution.

It is possible that most of MacDonagh's poetry is influenced by his early religious life and by the acquired habit of religious meditation, and that, what makes it difficult to understand is that the unity of outlook, proper to the true mystic, is lacking. His visions are intellectual visions, not such as are awarded to simple faith, or are the result of a love that sees itself and all things mirrored in the love divine. To the vision of the saint faith can always give us a key, but to the vision of the intellectual poet there can be no key but that of a kindred intelligence. For this reason probably not many of Thomas MacDonagh's poems will appeal to a general public; but a few, such as the "Ballad of John John," "Of a Poet Patriot," and some others are bound to make a universal appeal.

In "John John," the simple human note, the unerring psychology—the typical woman who desires sympathy, even pity for herself but scorns such pity for the man she loves—strike a chord that must go straight to every heart. Add to this the swinging metre, the slight air of mystery, the quaint humour, and we have all the elements of not only a true, but a popular ballad.

In "Of a Poet Patriot," which in the light of after events reads like MacDonagh's own epitaph, we find the intenser vein of feeling, the white fire of subdued passion expressing itself in simplest words, which is the truer expression of the man, if not of the poet, the man, whose deed must echo down the ages, even if a time may come when his songs have lost their power to thrill.—A. RAYBOULD, "Thomas MacDonagh," *IM*, Sept. 1919, pp. 476–79

In 1917, with the posthumous publication of Thomas Mac-Donagh's *Literature in Ireland*, the convention of "peasant realism" was given the imprimatur of scholarly criticism. By then the dream of a Gaelic people with a literature of their own had faded. Hyde, Pearse, Sigerson, Joseph Campbell, and others had composed prose and poetry in Irish; and Hyde's play, *Casadh an tSúgáin (The Twisting of the Rope)*, performed by members of the Gaelic League, had led to the establishment of a Gaelic theater; but, clearly, the embryonic Gaelic literature could not be compared with the burgeoning Anglo-Irish literary movement. What MacDonagh proclaims in his study is not a revival of Gaelic letters but rather the emergence of a new national literature that "could come only when English had become the language of the Irish people, mainly of Gaelic stock," a literature written in English but devoted to the expression of Irish manners, customs, traditions, and outlook as they affect social manners, religion, and morality. Mac-Donagh also provides aesthetic justification for the new literature; he discusses at great length the ways in which the peculiarities of Irish speech and the transference of techniques of rhyme and meter from Gaelic prosody give to the new Anglo-Irish poetry distinctive cadences. Unique subject matter and unique sound combine into what he terms the "Irish Mode" of verse.

MacDonagh was not himself a narrow critic; for instance, he recognized Yeats' achievement as a poet and, in fact, cites certain of Yeats' poems—although, significantly, the earliest poems as a rule—to illustrate his own ideas concerning the new literature. Nevertheless, in his book MacDonagh affirms the popular, middle-class attitude toward art. In the context of his essay the assertion that the Irish poets should express various facets of the Irish heritage as "they *affect* social manners, religion and morality" [my italics] comes to mean that the poets should express their heritage as it is *determined* by social manners, religion, and morality. What is most noteworthy about MacDonagh's criticism is that he all but ignores the question of the poet's individual vision. He implies that for the Irish poet both the nature of his vision and the means for giving it expression are predetermined. The poet has only to give himself to the convention and the convention in turn will guarantee his art.—RICHARD J. LOFTUS, "For Houlihan's Daughter," *Nationalism in Modern Anglo-Irish Poetry*, 1964, pp. 15–17

Thomas MacDonagh's place in the literary revival will always be a minor one; as a poet he never developed beyond the point of showing promise, and only a few of his later poems are anthologized. Yeats's final assessment was accurate:

> This other his helper and friend
> Was coming into his force;
> He might have won fame in the end,
> So sensitive his nature seemed,
> So daring and sweet his thought.

MacDonagh's plays are ignored (and very likely will always be so) by the theater movement, and *Literature in Ireland* continues as a required or recommended text on academic syllabi, though not as a work that is much more important than for its statement of the "Irish Mode." There is some evidence of a general move toward reassessing MacDonagh's work, but this move has not gone much further than oblique statements in journals to the effect that such reassessment is needed. Donagh MacDonagh's view of his father—with Pearse and Plunkett—as one of the "young revolutionary writers of the time" will probably for long remain the standard view of Thomas MacDonagh's work.

MacDonagh's position as a minor figure casts a great deal of light on the nature of the literary revival, particularly with respect to Yeats and his influence on the literary scene. Yeats was, of course, the central figure of the revival, and for MacDonagh he was the epitome of the successful poet, a model for all younger poets to follow. MacDonagh dedicated his first book of poems to Yeats and sought the older man's advice on poetry generally; Yeats's influence is discernible in MacDonagh's earlier poetry. For most of his life MacDonagh strove to be as successful as Yeats by constantly rushing into print with whatever poems were available; though he believed in himself as a poet, it was important for him to be seen and respected as a poet.

It is as a dramatist, however, that MacDonagh's attempts to emulate Yeats's success become most apparent. As early as 1904 he tried to have a play produced by Yeats's theater, the Abbey. Unsuccessful at first, he pursued the matter until Yeats and Synge accepted, with reservations, *When the Dawn Is Come.* He emended that play at their suggestion until it no longer resembled his original intention. The whole experience of the play's final form and its production left him bitter and disillusioned, so much so that he determined to rewrite *When the Dawn Is Come* and vindicate its poor reception; but the rewritten version—if it was ever completed—was never given to the Abbey. *Metempsychosis*, a satire on the Abbey's managing director, was done by the Theatre of Ireland, a rival company established by Abbey dissidents. Again unsuccessful, Mac-Donagh took the only course left open to him: the establishment of his own theater. The new theater—the *Irish* Theatre—by its very name would become the expression not only of the nation's drama but of international drama as well; it would soon overshadow Yeats's theater and become, in effect, the centerpiece of the Irish dramatic movement. MacDonagh's experience with Yeats was exactly like that of Edward Martyn, with whom he joined in founding the Irish Theatre. In comparison with Yeats, both were men of slender talents; whether, finally, Yeats was scornful of these talents or of their personalities, their experience with him shows how pronounced the forces of personal rivalry and enmity were within the literary revival.

MacDonagh's rejection of Yeats, of the literary revival's model figure, was not in itself a bad thing; literature thrives on the rejection of established styles and ideas. But once he was committed to this rejection, MacDonagh had little else to fall back on. He was always a derivative thinker, one who relied on the more powerful forces and personalities around him. Both *Thomas Campion* and *Literature in Ireland* show how much he borrowed the ideas of his cultural milieu; it is only MacDonagh's synthesis of these ideas (and his impassioned argument for them) into unique and striking theses—song-verse, speech-verse, and chant, in *Thomas Campion*, the "Irish Mode" in *Literature in Ireland*—that gives his scholarly work a sound ring.

A man of too many parts, in a sense, MacDonagh could never give to any single aspect of his life the concentration it deserved. He turned to what was reliable, to what was easy. To the literary movement he made the only contribution a minor figure can; he was, in effect, one of its offshoots, and he reflected its ideas in a different form.—JOHANN A. NORSTEDT, "Epilogue," *Thomas MacDonagh: A Critical Biography,* 1980, pp. 142–44

PADRAIC COLUM
"Thomas MacDonagh and His Poetry"
Dublin Magazine, Spring 1966, pp. 39–45

> The songs that I sing
> Should have told you an Easter story
> Of a long sweet Spring
> With its gold and its feasts and its glory.
> Of the moons then that married
> Green May to the mellow September,
> Long moons that ne'er tarried
> Life's hail and farewell to remember—
> But the haste of the years
> Had rushed to the fall of our sorrow,
> To the waste of our tears,
> The hush and the pall of our morrow.

This is the poem of Thomas MacDonagh's that comes into my mind as I begin to write about the man and his poetry. It is not one of his memorable poems, but it has a sweetness that belonged to his nature; it has, too, a quality of reconciliation that is haunting in poetry.

To write about his poetry is for me to write a bit of his biography. We were a good deal together when he was working on the book published in 1910, *Songs of Myself,* and we discussed what one or the other of us was writing, now and again amending a word or changing a line. It was he who gave me the title for my first book of verse, *Wild Earth,* from a line of my own overlooked by me.

I met him at a time—it is more easy for me to define it by movement than by chronology—when the Gaelic movement was at its most hopeful and its most uplifting. The generous minded of the young men and women who were not of the West British persuasion, belonged to the Gaelic League, and were continually finding ways of expressing their ardour. Literary and musical festivals were igniting minds that were from all parts of the country and outside it. The young men and women who were to make a drastic change in Irish history were 'feeling the forces'. Yeats and A.E. were holding youthful poets to their vocation. Young men wearing kilts were to be met in the streets and in Dublin drawingrooms.

The occasion of my meeting Thomas MacDonagh was an excursion to some historic site—the Hill of Uisneach, I think. We did not spend all our time on the site; there was rain and we retreated to the railway platform. An efficient Gael gathered us into the platform shelter and called on anyone who could sing or recite or play a handy instrument to entertain the wayfarers. I recited a poem. Then a young man came to us, mentioned his name to myself and the young lady who was with me, and then, with an authority that was not always present in Gaelic League performers, recited a piece in Irish. He was Thomas MacDonagh.

In the interval of waiting for the train the three of us became happily disposed to each other. MacDonagh was a poet, and a freemasonry established itself; he was by profession a teacher in a well-known college and was one of the stirring figures in the Gaelic movement. With him was a young lady named Veronica who hardly entered the circle that was so promptly formed. My companion was Mary Catherine Maguire whom, because she afterwards took my name, I shall refer to as M.C.M.

MacDonagh's knowledge and fluency made an impression, and M.C.M. and myself kept making discoveries about him on the way back to town. Soon each of us received a copy of the book he had just published, *The Golden Joy*. As I now take it in my hand I am surprised how well the publisher and printer got it out—blue cover enclosed in gold lines: D. J. O'Donoghue, M. H. Gill 1906. And here is a fair specimen of its content:

> And now the poet heart is calling too,
> And called aloud by every voice divine
> Behind the wall and through the lattices—
> Now is the season of the Golden Joy,
> Now is the season of the birth of Love—
> The perfect passion of the Heart of God,
> The rapture of the Beauty of the World,
> The rapture of Eternity of bliss.

Too much of it was scholastic verse in which nothing of the exceptional personality we encountered on the railway platform appeared.

After the publication of *The Golden Joy*—he had published two booklets of verse before—he settled in Dublin. He was then, I should say, a man of thirty-six, low sized, with a wide mouth and a strong nose, hair crispy at the forehead, with an open and friendly approach. He had spent a good deal of his life in schools and was well read in Latin and French, as well as English, and knew what was to be known in Irish. Poetry he knew as people in those days knew it—by heart. He had, as James Stephens was to note, 'a longing for the hermit's existence and a gift for gregarious life.'

MacDonagh, M.C.M. and, to a small extent, myself, took positions under Padraic Pearse, educationalist. He had taken over a big house in Rathfarnham to which he had transferred, from his first foundation in Cullenswood Avenue, the name St. Enda's, making the first house into a girls' school under Miss Gavan Duffy, St. Ita's. MacDonagh became an assistant in St. Enda's while M.C.M. took a position with Miss Gavan Duffy. I occasionally gave a lecture in St. Enda's or St. Ita's.

The three of us spent a good deal of our leisure together. MacDonagh was not attracted to the gatherings at A.E.'s Sunday evenings nor to poets who had other haunts, such as Seumas O'Sullivan and Oliver Gogarty. But soon after he had started in St. Enda's, another house attracted him, Grange House, close to the school. The man of this house was David Houston, a North of Ireland man, taken over from a job in England by the College of Science to direct something in agriculture. As an enterprise of his own he brought out a monthly, *Irish Gardening*. David Houston was an outgoing, enthusiastic, hospitable man, with a tinge of Orangism that was provocative. Now his house open on Sunday afternoons was crammed with Irish Revivalists. Thomas MacDonagh from the school down the road appeared amongst them. So did James Stephens, who was now a cherished guest at every reception in Dublin. I would come with M.C.M., who was a favourite in the Houston household.

One evening the sanguine householder announced to the four of us that he had the establishment of an Irish monthly in mind. It is a measure of the faith that obtained in those days that this disclosure was discussed, not merely seriously, but eagerly. Houston, MacDonagh, Stephens and myself were to conduct it. We named the future publication—at my suggestion, I think—*The Irish Review*. M.C.M. was to have the office

of critic-in-chief. And the Review, mind you, was not to be quarterly, but monthly, with the same number of pages as a quarterly of today, and to be sold for sixpence.

In a couple of weeks we had assembled the first number of *The Irish Review*. James Stephens' contribution to its contents was outstanding: It was the story he had just finished, his first important one, 'The Charwoman's Daughter', which he bestowed on the publication as a serial. George Moore, A.E. and Padraic Pearse gave us material. As for Thomas MacDonagh, I am thinking now not of the literary contributions he made to it but of the effects its career had on him. It brought him out of a scholastic environment. A wider companionship grew for him as we considered, sought for, discussed contributions. James Stephens and he became close friends. He made the poems for the book that succeeded *The Golden Joy*, named, perhaps challengingly, *Songs of Myself*.

While there is still some of the scholastic verse of *The Golden Joy*, *Songs of Myself* are personal. They are poems of love and loss. Amongst these is that poem of reconcilement:

> The songs that I sing
> Should have told you an Easter story

And there is also 'John-John', 'The Night Hunt', 'The Yellow Bittern', 'The stars stand up in the air'. These are poems in which Thomas MacDonagh discovers himself.

The image that the man who had 'a longing for a hermit's existence and a gift for gregarious life' was wont to project of himself was that of one with a destiny. The destiny was of a poet of high vision:

> The prelude thus of all my after-play
> These variant notes, most wayward, hesitant—
> The groping of blind fingers that will stray
> Over the stiff strange keys ere the bold chant
> Breaks from the organ, sudden, resonant,
> And men that murmured waiting, silent stay.

About the hero of his play *When the Dawn Is Come* he was very serious—he has a poem whose title is in a very high style—'Of the Man of my First Play'. It ends:

> How may I show him? How his story plan
> Who was prefigured to the dreaming eye
> In term of other being?—May he fill
> The mask of life?—or will my creature cry
> Shame that I dwarf the sequel and the man
> To house him thus within a fragment still?

But if Thomas MacDonagh was always in this vein, always the visionary of this kind, he would not be the man his surviving friends keep in memory. A longing for the hermit's existence and a gift for the gregarious life! As a gregarious man he was discursive, a good storyteller, the one who circulated 'I thank you, ma'am, said Dan'.[1] As the man who, a hermit, came among the people to inspire them he wrote self-regarding poems. I will put it this way: he was a man of the little town and a man of the seminary. He knew the humours of the little town and its characters, but he had to be jogged by non-seminarians to write about them. He was so jogged when he wrote 'John-John', 'The Night Hunt', 'The Man Upright' (in this last people of Cloughjordan recognised themselves and were indignant about the portraiture):

> whether they straggle
> Up and down, or bend to haggle
> Over a counter, or bend at a plough,
> Or to dig with a spade, or to milk a cow,
> Or to shove the goose-iron stiffly along
> The stuff on the sleeve-board, or lace the fong
> In the boot on the last, or to draw the wax-end

Tight cross-ways—and so make or to mend
What will soon be worn out by the crooked people.
The only thing straight in the place was the steeple.

The three poems mentioned, with 'The stars stand up in the air' showed the humour and sweetness that were in Thomas MacDonagh.

I put my boots and bonnet on,
And took my Sunday shawl,
And went full sure to find you, John,
To Nenagh fair.

The boots and bonnet and Sunday shawl perfectly renders the lone house-dweller who turns her back for a while on her possessions. The life of the people of the roads, glorified in *The Shadow of the Glen* and *The Tinkers' Wedding*, is not for her. She sees them with the eyes of the people of the little town:

For there again were thimble-men
And shooting galleries,
And card-trick men and Maggie men
Of all sorts and degrees.

There is no romance. For those with memories of the end of *The Shadow of the Glen*, the parting between the householder and the tinkerman is an anti-climax:

But there now it is six o'clock
And time for you to step.
God bless and keep you far, John-John,
And that's my prayer.

'The stars stand up in the air' is a translation, but it is a translation that embodies a mood. The mood is a loneliness that is deeply felt. Ferguson translated this poem, but there is no personal mood in his translation. In MacDonagh's, the loved one who is never described might be only a dream as remote as the stars; though he declares that his love for her has put him under sorrow, sin and death, we take them as part of the alienation that includes the stars and the bare strand. The versification has a rare beauty:

The strand of its water is bare,
And her sway is swept from the swan.

or:

I wish that all music was mute,
And I to all beauty were blind.

Here MacDonagh has achieved that 'Irishness' in English verse which he advocated in *Literature in Ireland*. 'The Yellow Bittern' is also in the Irish mode and perhaps we could regard it as the poet's admonishment to himself as the hermit and seminarian:

The yellow bittern that never broke out
In a drinking bout, might as well have drunk.

As in 'John-John', we are transported from the hermitage to the village street. Beside these three I put 'The Night Hunt'. It is the hunt that watchers don't know of, the night hunt of the village dogs. It is a poem that is charming for its sense of the mystery of the night and of the fields that have lost their boundaries.

I have entitled this essay 'Thomas MacDonagh and His Poetry', and I find I have reduced the poems to five. Others may find I have unduly reduced them. But poetry has little to do with number. Blanco White's one sonnet uplifts us even though it does not come like its 'Hesperus and all the stars of Heaven'.

Notes

1. 'What brings you into my room, into my room, into my room
    'What brings you into my room?' said the mistress unto Dan.
    'I came to court your daughter, ma'am, sure I thought it no great harm, ma'am.'
    'Oh, Dan, my dear, you're welcome here.' 'I thank you ma'am,' said Dan.

    This is the first verse of a song of delightful fatuousness that he circulated in Dublin.

IAN MCEWAN

1948–

Ian Russel McEwan was born on June 21, 1948, in Aldershot, Hampshire. His father was a soldier, and McEwan's early years were spent in various British possessions, including Singapore, before he was sent to a state-run boarding school, Woolverstone Hall, in England. He studied at the University of Sussex, where he gained a B.A. in English in 1970, and at the University of East Anglia. He began writing seriously in 1970, and presented a collection of short stories as his master's thesis in 1971; when published as *First Love, Last Rites* in 1975, it won the Somerset Maugham Award.

McEwan's subsequent books, the stories *In Between the Sheets* (1978) and the novels *The Cement Garden* (1978) and *The Comfort of Strangers* (1981), have established him as one of the leading writers of his generation, and he has been elected a Fellow of the Royal Society of Literature. He has also worked extensively as a scriptwriter. Three of his television plays appeared in *The Imitation Game* (1981), and he wrote the screenplays for the films *The Ploughman's Lunch* (1982) and *Last Day of Summer* (1984). His oratorio *Or Shall We Die* was performed at the Royal Festival Hall, London, in 1983, and at Carnegie Hall in 1985.

Ian McEwan married in 1982 and has three children.

British writing is so habitually dependent on social poise and tone, on knowing, usually rather too precisely, what can be taken for granted, that we tend to be more astonished than perhaps we should be at the appearance of an English writer who takes nothing for granted. Every so often someone comes along whose prose style is so alert and fresh, so remote from the mainstream idiom of English social fiction, that it seems miraculous that they should be able to write like that and be British too. Jean Rhys is such a writer, though her West Indian background has helped to exile her from the fatal knowingness that goes with being English. Ian McEwan is another. His first collection of stories, *First Love, Last Rites*, oozes with talent as wayward, original and firm in vision as anything since Miss Rhys's early novels about being alone and young in Paris and London.

McEwan's characters are adolescents; they bristle with the sudden violent consciousness of selfhood like hatching pupae. Or they are children, prematurely burdened with egos that give them the wizened gravity of infants in Renaissance paintings. Or they are men whose bodies have grown but whose minds have never broken free of the appalling second womb of puberty. Cruelty comes easily to them: they can wound or kill with the offhand grace of animals for whom the self is the only reality. They are profoundly disturbed by their own capacity to love another, which creeps up on them from behind like a pad-footed intruder on their barred and bolted rooms. They are endlessly curious about the world, but their curiosity has the roving neutrality of creatures in a zoo, unsure of what to focus on. They belong to no society. They are alarmingly in touch with blood and slime.

In the title story of *First Love, Last Rites*, two teenagers copulate through a Norfolk summer while a rat steadily scratches its way towards them from behind the skirting-board of their room. The boy goes eel-fishing with the girl's father, while her younger brother, a playful rat himself, invades the room, furious at his sister's departure from childhood into an inaccessible sexuality. These separate elements—the lovemaking, the rat, the eels, the child—are woven by McEwan into a miniature symphony which mounts in pace and volume to a conclusion that is at once natural and tender, and appalling.

But the great strength of McEwan's writing is that it is constitutionally incapable of being appalled. Taking nothing for granted, it is surprised by nothing and observant of everything. His style is wonderfully supple, open to experience, and certain in its movements. At its frequent best, it has a musical purity matched to music's deep indifference to the merely moral. McEwan's narrators are—in the world's terms—an unsavoury crew . . . child-murderers, emotional cripples, brutally self-centred teenagers. Most of his characters are amply qualified for permanent residence in a prison or asylum. Yet they are all granted a Mozartian lucidity, a gift of clarity which turns them into angels despite the weight of the world's disapproval.

In "Solid Geometry" (its previous publication both in the pulp sci-fi mag, *Amazing Stories*, and in *The New Review* suggests something of McEwan's unplaceability as a writer) a man discovers how to make his wife disappear. Following a sequence of diagrams in his great-grandfather's diary, he persuades her that he has found a new love-making position, then folds up her naked body, turns the shape inside out, and she's gone. Just on the level of anecdote—the only level that most science fiction ever aspires to—the story is satisfyingly ingenious. What lifts it way above science fiction is the tone of the narration and its steady movement from inquisitive scientific cool to the wonder and joy of the experimenter at the moment of discovery. Yet Maisie, the wife, is such a thoroughly explored and observed character in her own right that the story has to win her disappearance by enlisting the reader as an accomplice to an outrageous act. It does so brilliantly, and in the process it teaches a dark truth about the abundant innocence of what is usually called evil.

McEwan does pay occasional penalties for being so confidently *sui generis*. Idiomatic writers are able to rely on the established standards of their idioms, but McEwan (and he shares this with Jean Rhys, too) sometimes lurches, apparently unconsciously, into stretches of bathos and carelessness. The first story in the book, "Homemade", is too close for its own comfort to "Whacking Off" in *Portnoy's Complaint*. And one story, "Cocker At The Theatre", is hardly more than an extended snigger. But these are niggles. *First Love, Last Rites* is one of those rare books which strike out on a new direction in current English fiction. The most important question is what will McEwan do next? His abilities as a stylist and a storyteller are profuse, and these stories are only the first harvest.
—JONATHAN RABAN, *Enc*, June 1975, pp. 81–82

It is customary to speak of Ian McEwan as a writer who is "out to shock". His two collections of short stories, *First Love, Last Rites* and *In between the Sheets*, have been widely acclaimed, but reservations have been expressed about their author's intentions. Some readers have wondered why so many of the tales should be, in Mr McEwan's own phrase, "histories of perversions", and why the typical McEwan narrator is in some way "abnormal"—a child-molester, a man who lives in a cupboard, an academic who keeps a "beautifully preserved" penis in a jar. Other readers have worried over the seeming implausibility of such stories as "Dead as They Come" in which a man buys a shop dummy, and takes it home to be his mistress. What has proved most troubling of all, though, is some of the casual detail in the stories—green snot hanging from the ends of noses, boiling fat poured over someone's lap, a teenage gang preparing to roast a cat.

Ian McEwan is certainly aware that his work sometimes produces feelings of dismay and revulsion. A section from "To and Fro", one of the stories from his last collection, looks as if it may have been intended as a sort of apologia: "I claim waking status in my dreams. Nothing exaggerated but fine points of physical disgust and those exaggerated only appropriately." A more substantial answer to his critics is to be found in *The Cement Garden*, Mr McEwan's first novel, and one which, though it may at times shock, could not be accused of doing so gratuitously. There are waking dreams here, and not a little physical disgust (a frog is accidentally trodden on, "a creamy green substance . . . spilling out of its stomach"), but the overall impression of the book is not one of a writer revelling in the fantastic or the grotesque; it is, rather, an impression of care and restraint. *The Cement Garden* should make clearer that the characteristic quality of McEwan's writing is a tension between precise narration and preposterous narrative.

The novel examines the individual developments of, and interaction between, four children left alone following the death first of their father, and then, not long afterwards, of their mother. Worried that, as orphans, they may be separated and taken into care, the children decide to conceal the fact of their mother's death from the outside world. Her corpse is carried down into the cellar, put in a trunk, and covered over with cement. The children struggle to fend for themselves, but it seems only a matter of time before they are found out. As it turns out, they are betrayed by the one intruder into the family, Derek, snooker-playing boyfriend of the elder girl, Julie.

It is a short and devastatingly simple story. Several familiar McEwan elements are present—a teenage male narrator, a strong evocation of adolescent sexuality, an interest in confinement and liberation—but this is a more austere work than his earlier stories. The austerity is discernible not only in the style of the novel (metaphors are so rare that the few allowed into the text—the dead mother "frail and sad in her nightdress lying at our feet like a bird with a broken wing"—come over with real force), but in its tone, McEwan allows himself few jokes; only when Jack is warned about the dangers of masturbation ("Every time . . . you do that, it takes two pints of blood to replace it"), or when the prissy Derek is observed holding the steering wheel of his car "at arm's length and between finger and thumb as if the touch of it disgusted him", is there any clear invitation to laughter.

There is austerity, too, in McEwan's refusal of the more sensational possibilities which the narrative initially seems to offer. Jack's reaction to his mother's death is to feel, as well as loss, "a sense of adventure and freedom", and it seems likely for a time that the novel will develop into a 1970s version of Golding's *Lord of the Flies*, the children running amok in the urban wilderness surrounding their house. But the author imagines quieter and more subtle changes taking place, and concentrates attention on Julie's assumption of authority, on Jack's resentment and lassitude, on Sue's private grief, on the deterioration of the younger boy, Tom. So cool and accurate is this attention that the more disquieting elements in the story—Jack's feeling that he has contributed to his father's death (the death occurs while Jack is masturbating), the girls' habit of dressing Tom up in clothes of the opposite sex, the smell of mother drifting up from the cellar—seem entirely plausible. This is McEwan's art: flat narration of the absurd or grotesque, the morally extraordinary made ordinary by the indifference or perfunctoriness of the telling.

It may be said that the virtues of *The Cement Garden* are those of a short story: there is a compelling central image (the cement cracking to reveal the mother's corpse), but little relish for plot. Whatever its status as a text, however, it should consolidate Ian McEwan's reputation as one of the best young writers in Britain today.—BLAKE MORRISON, "Paying Cellarage," *TLS*, Sept. 29, 1978, p. 177

There are novels so generally alert and involving that, if they reveal some dubious point of construction, this possible weakness itself becomes suspenseful. "What is the author doing?" "Why is the author doing it?" "Will the author pull it off?" Questions like these merge with the fundamental "What happens next?" (A reader is a person in a state of hope.)

The Comfort of Strangers, Ian McEwan's second novel, is such a book, well worth reading despite its sometimes arbitrary and implausible nature. It is the price one pays for the book's originality, vividness, wit and power to intrigue. Mr. McEwan's previous novel, *The Cement Garden* (he is also the author of two short-story collections), shows a more natural and a more complete dovetailing of subject and story than the new book does. But he is an alluringly gifted writer, whose future work it is a pleasure to anticipate.

The Comfort of Strangers is a nightmare about travel and evil, as it might have been conceived by a Harold Pinter, descended from a Henry James. Colin and Mary, presumably British, are on "holiday" in an Italian city, unnamed but presumably Venice. They are not married, these tourist lovers. Mary has children, whom she guiltily misses, from a marriage now ended. The couple do not relax on their vacation so much as they unravel, together and separately. They get lost all the time, saying, "We should have brought the maps." But the maps themselves are no help. Colin and Mary get lost merely studying the maps. Their personalities are somewhat melted.

So, lost late one night, famished and unable to find an open restaurant, they allow themselves to be taken over by a stranger on the street. Though the stranger's name is Robert, he is evidently Italian. (He says he has lived in England.) Robert "wore a tight-fitting black shirt, of an artificial, semitransparent material, unbuttoned in a neat V almost to his waist. On a chain around his neck hung a gold imitation razor blade. . . ." Myself, I would have insisted on staying lost, but Robert knows just the place, a very good place, and Colin and Mary, only a bit irritated and reluctant, go with him. The place is a bar Robert owns. He brings to the table a bottle of wine, three glasses, "and two well-fingered breadsticks, one of which was broken short." The cook is ill, Robert explains.

A wonderful thing now happens to the reader, if not to the helpless and hungry couple. Robert tells them a psychologically gruesome and somewhat comic story, more or less true, of his childhood as the son of a diplomat stationed in London, a story of the father playing off Robert, the only son, against two of Robert's sisters. The father is a sadist, a family fascist. Robert's intricate, dramatic tale stimulates one's curiosity and makes for unforgettable reading.

Colin and Mary eventually leave the bar, but they still cannot find their way back to their hotel. And they encounter Robert again. (He has, indeed, been following them—and worse.) This time, he brings them to his home and his wife, Caroline, allegedly the daughter of a former Canadian ambassador to England, where Robert had first met her. The remainder of the novel is an increasingly sinister, macabre, even "ghoulish" account of the reception that Robert gives the tourists. Robert has inherited, in a violent form, his father's cruelty, and Colin and Mary become ruined victims of his pathologically punitive personality (Caroline, already his victim, is a pathetic accomplice).

The Comfort of Strangers is Ian McEwan's nasty answer to our comfy adage "travel is broadening." The novel has an epigraph from Pavese: "Traveling is a brutality. It forces you to trust strangers and to lose sight of all that familiar comfort of home and friends. You are constantly off balance. Nothing is yours except the essential things—air, sleep, dreams, the sun, the sky—all things tending toward the eternal or what we imagine of it." I think it is impossible to resist the interest and challenge of the observation; and, even if the observation is untrue or incomplete, it is impossible to deny the interest and challenge of Mr. McEwan's novelistic elaboration.

The book, as it develops, requires the reader to accept a questionably large amount of innocence and acquiescence in Colin and Mary, and what almost seems like a careless overdose of perversity in Robert and Caroline. On the literal level, while not actually unbelievable, *The Comfort of Strangers* is hard to go along with at every moment. As a nightmare, however, it is convincing and clinging. Its details are so imaginative and precise as to be a source of delight.—RICHARD P. BRICKER, "Traveling in Peril," *NYTBR*, July 5, 1981, p. 7

Ian McEwan's new novel ⟨*The Comfort of Strangers*⟩ has only four characters: Colin and Mary, a young English couple holidaying in Venice, and Robert and Caroline, a slightly older couple who live there. It is not clear why the story is set in Venice, except that it is an easy place to get lost and Colin and Mary frequently do so. They smoke marihuana throughout the day, their lovemaking is friendly but perhaps bored, and they converse in commonplaces, he over-employing words like 'incredible' to describe things and she reiterating feminist platitudes. When they come across a poster put up by Italian feminists approving castration as a punishment for rapists Mary is excited but Colin is too distracted to argue with her and explain (if he could) the flaws and contradictions in her thinking. So they simply get lost again.

It is their lostness which in every sense delivers Colin and Mary into the hands of Robert, who rescues them as they stumble blindly from point to point and takes them to dine at his own bar and then later leads them to his house. The son of a diplomat, Robert is a powerful man who, when they first meet, is wearing an imitation razor blade round his neck. His view of life appears to be fairly simple: whereas his father and grandfather understood themselves perfectly, he explains to Colin, today men hate themselves for their weakness in the face of women; as for the women, they 'talk of freedom and dream of captivity'. But the fact of their talk, and the fact that men have listened to it, has confused everything. When they eventually meet Caroline, Robert's wife, they find that she is a semi-invalid, confined to the house with a bad back, although she shies from telling what is wrong with it. She apparently colludes with Robert's views on the status of women: if two women are sitting on a balcony talking, she explains to Mary when they are doing just that, nothing will 'happen' until a man arrives. Mary is lost for words.

Their embroilment with Robert and Caroline, if at first a little frightening, seems irresistible to Colin and Mary. They also find—although with characteristic lack of self-scrutiny they do not discuss these matters—that their contact with the strange, older, perhaps slightly sinister couple has regenerated their capacity for lovemaking, and they now stay in bed for most of the day. When the liaison is mentioned, it is only for Mary to remark that a framed, grainy photograph she had seen on Robert's bookcase was—inexplicably but definitely—of Colin. Shortly afterwards, the younger couple are mysteriously drawn back to Robert's house.

The final encounter with Robert and Caroline is a grisly one and it is treated masterfully by McEwan. A reviewer owes it to a novel as good as this one not to reveal exactly what happens, but the imitation razor blade hanging round Robert's neck has a very sharp counterpart in his sideboard and he uses it amid talk of his hate and scorn of women, and Caroline's talk of sex and pain and how she got her broken back. Meanwhile, Mary passes out and Colin realises, too late, that his limited means of argument and response will not get him out of this one. It is a fine novel, excellently told in slow, only occasionally mannered prose, with hardly a sentence too many. McEwan carries into the novel the short story teller's need for precision.

One thing worries me about *The Comfort of Strangers*, however. At the end, Mary, having discovered that her feminist simplicities will not enable her to unravel the real cords that bind people, is said to have a new theory,

> tentative at this stage, of course, which explained how the imagination, the sexual imagination, men's ancient dreams of hurting, and women's of being hurt, embodied and declared a powerful, single organizing principle, which distorted all relations, all truth.

The weight of the novel seems to me to depend heavily on this sentence; it may be true but it cannot be the whole truth and I dread to think that poor Mary, having undergone such a trauma as she has done, would come to believe it so and then proceed along yet another false trail guided by imaginary signs. I take it that it *is* only Mary's credo and not the author's (although that, I confess, is what worries me) for McEwan's ineffable but deeply understood morality has previously emerged not from what he revealed about his gruesome scenarios but from what they revealed about themselves. Men's ancient dreams of hurting and women's of being hurt may indeed

distort the truth, but even if men and women could awaken from these dreams the truth could not be conceived simply. What seals the fate of the wretched Colin and Mary is that they suppose it can be.—JAMES CAMPBELL, "Dreams of Pain," *NS*, Oct. 9, 1981, p. 22

LORNA SAGE
"Dreams of Being Hurt"

Times Literary Supplement, October 9, 1981, p. 1145

Ian McEwan is often talked about as if his was a precocious talent—as if he was, somehow, unnaturally old for his years. Actually, though, what's most distinctive about his acrobatically perverse fictions is his refusal to grow up or suppress the fantasies of childhood, and it's this, I think, that has produced the impression of mutant youth. He is thirty-three after all, and he can still get his big toe in his mouth: a most disconcerting variant on writing tongue-in-cheek, especially when it's done with a cool economy of style.

Ordinary, full-size people have usually come off rather badly in his books. They loomed Brobdingnagian in the first two collections of stories ("brown tissues", old dugs, red eyes) and even in more naturalistic settings they are strikingly awful. In his first novel, *The Cement Garden*, there was one called Derek who might have blossomed into quite a "character" in some more congenial context—he's a dandy and a professional snooker player—but who's merely a cardboard adult and moral policeman in the world McEwan contrives. Derek—all Dereks—are the reality principle in disguise, the ones who woo your big sister (for instance) and interrupt your incestuous idyll:

> As I closed my lips around Julie's nipple a soft shudder ran through her body, and a voice from across the room said mournfully,
>   'Now I've seen it all.'

It's also Derek, naturally, who finds what's in the cellar, and puts an end to the squalid rapture of childhood without parents.

However, his main role is to deflect the reader's "moral" responses. Who would be a Derek? Well, some would, like the BBC Television Drama Head who banned a McEwan play on the eve of production (*Solid Geometry*, 1979) because of its "grotesque and bizarre sexual elements". But most wouldn't.

In other words, Ian McEwan has exactly touched the obscure nerve that registers "newness" in English fiction, and it may be a measure of the oddness of the cultural climate—it ought to be a measure of something—that this is all about regression. One of the most memorable lines from his first book of stories, *First Love, Last Rites* (which won the Somerset Maugham Award in 1975) was "I want to climb in the pram". It helped that his I-figures were never messily confessional, but impersonally weird. The incestuous, onanistic, transvestite, infantile monsters he imagines belong, as Paul Bailey wrote, to "the recognizable world of private fantasy and nightmare—a world, despite our protestations to the contrary, we are all involved in". There haven't though, except at BBC Television (haunted, one imagines, by the thought of Mary Whitehouse) been many "protestations". This is, in part, a tribute to McEwan's persuasive strategies, for he has had from the beginning that instinct for protecting and presenting his own talent that does sometimes seem—as in the case of Philip Roth—to accompany obsessive nasty habits.

However, self-consciousness has threatened at times to narrow down the room for manoeuvre to the point where acrobatics—even getting your toe in your mouth—become unnecessarily abstruse. His second book of stories had a mirror-reversed piece ("Reflections of a Kept Ape") about a woman writer trying to start her second book:

> For two and a half years Sally Klee has grappled not with words and sentences, not with ideas, but with form, or rather, with tactics. Should she, for instance, break silence with a short story, work a single idea with brittle elegance and control?

What she produces, after long labour, is an exact reproduction of her first book, every word in its place. This kind of nightmare, fed doubtless by critical acclaim, must have made growth or development even more problematic than they would anyway be for a writer whose essential material was immaturity. It can't have helped, either, that his first venture, away from short stories, *The Cement Garden* (short, but a novel) irresistibly reminded Anthony Thwaite and some other reviewers of another novel years before, which had a similar plot about happy families. As indeed you might expect, given the amorphous, un-individual nature of fantasy life—private fantasies are common property.

Ironically enough, it seems to have been television that provided a clue to the path he's following now—not the trouble with *Solid Geometry* (based anyway on an early short story) but the experience of writing *The Imitation Game*, a play broadcast last year. McEwan's own account of the matter is uncharacteristically explicit:

> I felt I had written myself into too tight a corner; I had made deliberate use of material too restricted to allow me to write about the ideas that had interested me for some years. The Women's Movement had presented ways of looking at the world, both its present and its past, that were at once profoundly dislocating and infinite in possibility. I wanted to write a novel which would assume as its background a society not primarily as a set of economic classes but as a patriarchy. The English class system, its pervasiveness, its endless subtleties, had once been a rich source for the English novel . . . men and women have to do with each other in ways economic classes do not. Patriarchy corrupts our most intimate relationships with comic and tragic consequences. . . . But my narrators were frequently too idiosyncratic or solipsistic to allow me the freedom to explore.

What emerged from these ruminations was not, immediately, a novel, but *The Imitation Game* which, despite its title, got him out of his solipsistic and self-conscious corner into the (comparatively) breezy climate of sexual politics. Its setting, in 1940, provided—just—a link back to childhood ("the war . . . was a living presence throughout my childhood. Sometimes I found it hard to believe I had not been alive in the summer of 1940") but the central figure was an ATS girl, and the structure was not dictated by private fantasy, but by the organization of the "Ultra" project for breaking German codes at Bletchley Park. An army of women transcribed unintelligible signals, and fed them at Bletchley through proto-computers, while a central core of men jealously guarded their "official secrets" and actually broke the code. It was a splendid microcosm of the equivocal freedoms the war offered women, and by this accident of built-in symbolism, the play could be, on the surface, entirely naturalistic.

This might sound like another writer altogether, but it was the "old" one (acrobatics again) turned inside out: ATS Cathy as big sister; her useless lover, a member of the Ultra inner circle who finds her sexiness obscene and her curiosity treasonable, as an even wetter Derek. What's missing is "I", the brother/child/lover, who obviously has trouble in the land of Dereks (and in getting on television). There may be a connection between wanting to sleep with your sister and Women's Liberation, in short, but *The Imitation Game* doesn't make it. McEwan's new novel, *The Comfort of Strangers*, does, and if I seem to be approaching it via an inordinate preamble, that's because its interest and its problems are very much to do with Ian McEwan's search for ways of "placing" private fantasy in a context of public issues. That he should be engaged so deliberately in such a search is a symptom of a familiar contemporary dilemma—there being no *automatic* context, the tradition of social realism being ruinous and uninhabitable, and so on.

The Comfort of Strangers is set in Venice, a decaying labyrinth, and an appropriate place for the placeless. Mary and Colin get lost every time they leave their hotel, and their mutually apologetic wanderings isolate them neatly in their semi-detached relationship:

> Alone, perhaps, they could have explored the city with pleasure. . . . But they knew each other much as they knew themselves, and their intimacy, rather like too many suitcases, was a matter of perpetual concern; together they moved slowly, clumsily, effecting lugubrious compromises.

Mary has been married, has children she's left behind to go on holiday: her affair with Colin is a near-androgynous conspiracy; they don't live together, theirs is "no longer a great passion":

> When they looked at each other they looked into a misted mirror. When they talked of the politics of sex, which they did sometimes, they did not talk of themselves. It was precisely this collusion that made them vulnerable and sensitive to each other, easily hurt by the rediscovery that their needs and interests were distinct.

This composite "person" is a splendid comic characterization of the liberated couple: there's no "I"; Colin is described physically (his slightness, his baby-soft curls and so on); Mary is not, but does strenuous Yoga and can swim a lot further; "they" fit together perfectly.

Something has to go wrong, but before that happens it goes blissfully, suddenly right. They've been picked up in their wanderings by a dreadful couple. One half is garrulous, Italian Robert, who regales them with his macabre family history (how he came to hate his sisters), his views on men ("My father and his father . . . were proud of the sex. . . . Now men doubt themselves, they hate themselves") and on women ("They lie to themselves. They talk of freedom, and dream of captivity"). When Robert takes them home to meet his browbeaten Canadian wife Caroline, they're at first merely embarrassed and distressed to see sado-masochism flourishing so routinely, but when they get back to their hotel, they find their own relationship has taken on a new erotic urgency. Locked away together for days, they embark on a complex and incestuous (or nearly, they're so close) sexual odyssey—a tireless celebration of intertwined lives and fantasies, so different (they're rather complacent about this) from the prison of sex they've glimpsed in Robert and Caroline. They talk endlessly, too, even about themselves, and are full of passionate curiosity.

What they don't talk about is the matter of Robert and Caroline. But gradually things about that encounter surface to consciousness—suggestions hidden from themselves and each other: Robert punching Colin in a way that wasn't playful, Caroline's whispered entreaties, and most ominously and inexplicably, a grainy, much-enlarged photograph among Robert's trophies that, Mary's now convinced, was of Colin, though it can't be, they've never met before. . . . These buried memories take them back to the nightmare couple, and back into the perverse history of sexual cruelty they were so sure they'd transcended. Their rediscovery of each other has opened up an ancient chamber of horrors, and the novel's climactic scenes, in which Robert and Caroline take *their* kind of pleasure, have an appropriate sense of *déjà vu*—watching a foul old dream unfold itself—which I shan't enhance by telling the story any further.

The central tension (in part an equivocation, I think) is about how far Colin and Mary invite their fate: by being too close, too innocent of violence? by repressing their aggressions, and so secretly wanting horrors? Mary has all big sisters' erotic appeal, Colin is deliberately portrayed as sexily childlike (which is why they get along so well) but is an idyll what they want, or is it something nastier—which is certainly what they get? A rather overexactly planted clue during their paradisal spell—a set of uneasy "jokes" about mutilation and bondage—suggests that Ian McEwan wants us at least to toy with the idea that they're working out their own fantasies all along. Mary's final, numbed mental soliloquy tries for a "correct" point of view—

the sexual imagination, men's ancient dreams of hurting, and women's of being hurt, embodied and declared a powerful single organizing principle, which distorted all relations.

But Mary (mother/sister/lover) hasn't shown much sign of dreaming "of being hurt", though Colin has. What I'm saying, I suppose, is that the solipsistic logic of dreams, desires and fears, and the theories about patriarchy overlap uneasily. Loving one's sister may be a way of flirting with father, even; in

dreams begin responsibilities, and hideous Robert is a lot more powerful and interesting than the Dereks.

The Comfort of Strangers is not as claustrophobic as this would suggest—quite. I should before ending offer a longer quotation, a quiet "outside" scene that performs an elegant variation on the theme of spontaneity and role-playing:

Now and then a couple stopped to stare approvingly at the customers on the pontoon drinking against their gigantic backcloth of sunset and reddened water. One elderly gentleman positioned his wife in the foreground and half-knelt, with thin, trembling thighs, to take a picture. The drinkers at a table immediately behind the woman raised their glasses good-naturedly towards the camera. But the photographer, intent on spontaneity, straightened and with a sweeping gesture of his free hand, tried to usher them back on the path of their unselfconscious existence, . . . But now his wife . . . was turning her back to the camera in order to encourage the last rays of the sun into her handbag. Her husband called to her sharply and she moved smartly back into position. The closing snap of the handbag clasp brought the young men to life. They arranged themselves in their seats, lifted their glasses once more and made broad innocent smiles.

When he does a cool, comic vignette like this so well, it's hard to see why McEwan should have problems getting out of his corner, and tempting to think that he shouldn't bother his head with sexual politics. I don't think so, though his novel seems to me dislocated in ways he didn't intend. It will be interesting to see whether the readers who've enjoyed his polymorphous fantasies will now read him as he reads himself, as an explorer of patriarchy, or whether they'll want him to climb back in the pram.

ARTHUR MACHEN

1863–1947

Arthur Machen was born Arthur Llewelyn Jones at Caerleon-on-Usk, Wales, on March 3, 1863; he adopted his mother's maiden name Machen in grade school. Fascinated from youth by the Roman ruins of Isca Silurum near his birthplace, Machen would later give them an important place in his novels and tales. He attended Hereford Cathedral School, but failed the examination for the Royal College of Surgeons in 1880; he went to London as a tutor, cataloguer, and editor. Just before leaving Wales he privately printed the poem *Eleusinia* (1881) in an edition of 100 copies; he later claimed that his systematic destruction of this early work left only two copies of the pamphlet in existence. Aside from translating the *Heptameron* of Marguerite of Navarre (1886), Machen wrote the curious pseudo-philosophical treatise *The Anatomy of Tobacco* (1884) and the picaresque novel *The Chronicle of Clemendy* (1888).

The death of his father in 1887 ensured Machen economic independence for the next decade and a half, and it was at this time that he not only produced the standard translation of Casanova's *Memoirs* (1894) but wrote the supernatural tales that would bring him immediate notoriety and ultimate fame: *The Great God Pan* (1894), *The Three Impostors* (1895), *The House of Souls* (1906). These works—as well as the heavily autobiographical novels *The Hill of Dreams* (1907) and *The Secret Glory* (1922)—were condemned as the outpourings of a diseased imagination; Machen gathered the early reviews of these works in the volume *Precious Balms* (1924).

In 1901, his inheritance depleted, Machen was forced to seek employment. He worked as a bit player in Frank Benson's Repertory Company (1901–9) and wrote voluminously for newspapers and literary journals—*The Academy, London Evening News, T. P.'s Weekly, John O'London's Weekly, Independent, Daily Mail*, and many others. A small amount of his journalism was collected in *Dog* and *Duck* (1924), *Notes and Queries* (1926), and two volumes edited by Vincent Starrett, *The Shining Pyramid* (1923) and *The Glorious Mystery* (1924). Starrett played an influential role in introducing Machen to American readers, and Machen's work was very popular in the 1920s, thanks largely to the many reissues of his early volumes by Alfred A. Knopf.

By the late 1920s Machen had again fallen into poverty; but efforts by his friends secured a Civil List pension of £100 a year for him. In 1929 Machen finally left the London that had exercised his imagination for fifty years. He produced few notable works in his old age: the poorly received novel *The Green Round* (1933) and the two collections of tales *The Cosy Room* (1936) and *The Children of the Pool* (1936). Arthur Machen died on March 30, 1947.

Machen's most memorable works are *The Hill of Dreams* and his horror fiction, posthumously collected in *Tales of Horror and the Supernatural* (1948). *Hieroglyphics* (1902), a treatise on aesthetics, is a key to Machen's philosophy of literature, and his two autobiographies, *Far Off Things* (1922) and *Things Near and Far* (1923), speak poignantly of his career as fantaisiste and man of letters.

Personal

I was seventeen ⟨in⟩ the year 1880. I had left Hereford Cathedral School at the end of the Easter Term. I had spent most of the summer at Wandsworth and had seen London, then a rare and wonderful town. I had failed by reason of defective elementary arithmetic to pass the preliminary examination of the Royal College of Surgeons, and here I was at Llanddewi Rectory with nothing particular to do, and less to expect. I loafed about, wandering all over the country round Llanddewi, taking peculiar delight in turning into bridle-paths—narrow ways, with high hedges on each side—and following them till they brought me out into unknown country. I would go walking on and walking on, and the dusk fell and it grew dark, and I, with the vaguest notions of the lie of the land, would somehow find my way back to the Rectory and tell the story of my traffics and discoveries. And I wandered also in and out of the books in that unselected library which I have described elsewhere; and on the whole, I suppose, got the education, apart from the Humanities, which was most to my purpose.

I believe it was in November of that Autumn of 1880 that I set out one morning to walk to Newport; for no particular reason that I can remember. Probably, there had been a slight frost in the night; the day was shining and splendid, and there was a briskness in the air that made the walk—it would kill me now—go very well. I had climbed up the long hill from Llantarnam, and was on my way towards Malpas when I saw the mountain, from Twyn Barlwm to the heights above Pontypool, all a pure, radiant blue under a paler blue sky; and the sun shone on the farm houses and cottages of the mountain side, and made the whitewashed walls shine gloriously as if they were marble. I experienced an indescribable emotion; and I always attribute to that moment and to that emotion my impulse towards literature. For literature, as I see it, is the art of describing the indescribable; the art of exhibiting symbols which may hint at the ineffable mysteries behind them; the art of the veil, which reveals what it conceals.—ARTHUR MACHEN, *Beneath the Barley*, 1931

When we look at the difficult business of growing up, most of us, I imagine, can pick out one or two people whose influence on our young lives was far greater than we understood at the time. There was something about them, or some casual remark they made, that took root in our minds and grew. I remember with particular gratitude one very old gentleman, with a mane of white hair touching the collar of his ancient Inverness cape. He was half blind, half deaf—but wholly alive.

I was about fifteen then, and I was just beginning to make all sorts of exciting new discoveries in the world of books. I liked what the Americans call 'off-beat' stories—strange stories—and I had recently come across some very strange stories indeed. They were not ghost stories in any ordinary sense, but they were all the more frightening because they dealt with horrors that were never quite described. They hinted at dark things, at half-remembered rituals and evil powers which might still be lingering among the foxgloves and hawthorn around some mossy stone. They were finely and flawlessly written, and their author's name was Arthur Machen.

During the summer holidays, I happened to have lunch with John Betjeman, who was an old friend of my parents. I asked him if he had ever heard of this man Machen. Yes, he said, he knew him well. Machen was now almost eighty, and lived in complete retirement at Amersham. Why did I not go and see him? The old gentleman would be delighted.

A few weeks later I walked down from the railway station through the woods to the wide village street of Old Amersham. Machen lived in a small flat on the first floor of a rather ugly red-brick house. He answered the bell himself, looking dishevelled and surprised to see me. I am sure he had made little of Betjeman's letter and had no idea who I was. But he received me with great courtesy, gave me tea, and talked to me as one gentleman to another, both men of the world, equal in age and understanding.

After that I used to go and see him every two or three months. Usually we would lunch together at an old coaching inn; and, as a rule, my parents and Machen's wife came too. Machen used to sit by the fire, puffing away at an evil-smelling pipe and sipping gin and pale ale. It was always gin and pale ale in those days, though I have heard that long ago in his wild youth he preferred absinthe at the Café Royal. 'What's the time, Arthur?' my father asked him once. 'Time for a drink', he answered, in his beautiful deep voice.

Mrs. Machen was a small wrinkled woman, some years younger than her husband. Her name was Purefoy. Once upon a time she had been a chorus lady and she had a fund of anecdotes about eccentric theatrical landladies. Nowadays her whole life was devoted to looking after Arthur. One day, while Machen was holding forth in the grand manner, I remember hearing her whisper to my mother: 'Just think. I've had all these years of that splendid company'.

Arthur Machen *was* splendid company. He took conversation seriously as an art. When he raised his hand and announced, 'Literary anecdote', everyone within earshot stopped to listen. The local chatter about tractors and turnips died away and he held the whole room spellbound. He talked often about the giants of literature, particularly his favourites—Dickens, Rabelais, and Cervantes. 'When I was a young man', he said, 'I used to read *Pickwick Papers*, *Don Quixote*, and Rabelais once each year. Now I can read *Pickwick* once a year,

Don Quixote only once every two years, and Rabelais every three years—but I think that is the inverse order of their true importance'.

About his own work he had less to say. He was never really satisfied with it. Always, he felt, he had been on the verge of a masterpiece, but the vision half-perceived vanished when he stretched out his hand to take it. His quality had been recognised by the award of a small civil-list pension on which he lived; but by the standards of popular success he was a failure. His stories had—and, indeed, still have—a small and secret following. But his books of criticism and autobiography, into which he put his best work, were not the stuff to make either best-sellers or a highbrow fashion. They belonged to a time in the eighteen-nineties when Machen lived in seedy London lodgings, dining on crusty bread and green tea, earning a meagre living by making a catalogue of books on occultism, and trying to escape from his loneliness into dreams of the Welsh hills where he was born.

Some years later, he became a journalist on a national newspaper, and a most unusual journalist he must have been. He once overheard his news editor discussing which reporter should be sent out on an assignment. 'If we send Smith', said the harassed editor, 'we shall get a story. If we send Machen we *may* get a very good story'. No doubt it was Smith who went.

His one real commercial success came to him by accident and he was rather ashamed of it. In September 1914 he wrote a short story called 'The Bowmen'. It was about a section of British soldiers in France, hard-pressed by a German attack. One of them, a scholarly fellow, calls upon St. George for help, and they are saved by a ghostly company of English archers from Agincourt. It was not even a very good story, but its effect was remarkable. The story was talked about, quoted in sermons, and reprinted as a pamphlet. That was a time of rumours and credulity. No sooner had the story of Russians with snow on their boots been abandoned than the story of a supernatural army took its place. Soldiers wrote from France claiming to have taken part in the battle and to have seen it all themselves. The idea of archers gave way to the simpler one of angels. Machen's story was forgotten and the legend of the Angels of Mons passed into history. Machen himself was greatly surprised. He tried in vain to check the extraordinary rumour he had started, but only succeeded in acquiring some notoriety and even a little money. In the long run, it did him more harm than good. He was labelled and remembered as the man who invented the Angels of Mons, the author of a sharp journalistic trick, not to be trusted by respectable editors.

Soon after our first meeting, I had to write a prize essay on the subject of tradition. I asked his advice, and he wrote me a long letter in his firm, angular script. Tradition, he said, is a wonderful subject: and he went on to give examples from his own experience. One told of a mound in Scotland, which simple people said was the grave of a knight in shining armour. Nobody believed them, until one morning the mound was found to have been opened by thieves. All that was left was some bones and two or three of the silver *laminae* from the armour. Another told of a certain church with a blank wall before which the local peasants always bowed. The vicar was curious and scraped at the surface of the wall. He found a picture of the Virgin which had been covered over at the Reformation.

Machen's scholarship was wide rather than deep—except in a few curious places. He loved to roll church Latin round his tongue. 'I can't part with my beloved Latin tags', he said, 'as dark with antiquity and as well-worn as old farmhouse furniture'.

He hardly ever repeated a story, and he told a great many. He had never been able to accept wireless or cards as a substitute for talk. 'Cards,' he boomed, 'are a confession of inability to maintain conversation'. His own conversation would linger sometimes round Caerleon-on-Usk, and the countryside where he spent his childhood. He loved its deep lanes and dark woods and its memories running back to Roman times. He told me of one village where each cottage had a candle in its window at night. The candles were put there to keep the Little People away. Sometimes—less often—he talked about London, which he saw as a place full of mystery lurking beneath drab façades. He lived for most of his working life in Verulam Buildings, just off the Gray's Inn Road. Saturday night was always his 'at home' day, and scores of famous people had been his guests. The only one he seemed in the least proud of having known was Amundsen, the explorer. He liked to recall how Amundsen stood warming himself at the hearth one winter night and said: 'You know, Arthur, nobody who hasn't been up to his waist in the freezing slush of the Arctic can properly enjoy a fire like this'.—ANTHONY LEJEUNE, "An Old Man and a Boy," *LT*, March 29, 1956, pp. 315–18

General

There are those who will call him a novelist of Sin, quibbling about a definition. With these I have no quarrel; the characterizations are synonymous. His books exhale all evil and all corruption; yet they are as pure as the fabled waters of that crystal spring De Leon sought. They are pervaded by an ever-present, intoxicating sense of sin, ravishingly beautiful, furiously Pagan, frantically lovely; but Machen is a finer and truer mystic than the two-penny occultists who guide modern spiritualistic thought. If we are to subscribe to his curious philosophy, to be discussed later, we must believe that there is no paradox in this.

But something of what we are getting at is explained in his own pages, in this opening paragraph from his story, "The White People," in *The House of Souls*: " 'Sorcery and sanctity,' said Ambrose, 'these are the only realities. Each is an ecstasy, a withdrawal from the common life.' " And, a little later, in this: " 'There is something profoundly unnatural about sin . . . the essence of which really is in the taking of heaven by storm.' "

Nothing, it may be supposed, is more completely misunderstood than sin; but from the general vagueness on the subject one gathers that it is unpopular. To be sure, there are innumerable catalogued sins of varying degrees of wickedness, a chromatic scale, as it were, fixed by the state and by the church, and the sins of one are not always the sins of the other. There are new sins and advanced sins and higher sins, all intensely interesting and not a little puzzling to the lay mind, since they are neither new, advanced and high, nor particularly sinful. The sin with which Arthur Machen is concerned is an offense against the nature of things, it has to do with evil in the soul, and has little or nothing to do with the sins of the statute book. This Ambrose, whom I have quoted, would tell you that sin is conceivable in the talking of animals; if a tree were to wish you "Good morning," that would be sinful, or if a chimney-pot were to leap down and accompany you upon a walking-tour.

To quote: "What would your feelings be, seriously, if your cat or dog began to talk to you, and to dispute with you in human accents? You would be overwhelmed with horror. I am sure of it. And if the roses in your garden sang a weird song, you would go mad. And suppose the stones in the road began to swell and grow before your eyes, and if the pebble that you noticed at night had shot out stony blossoms in the morning?"

Our misconception of sin, thinks Ambrose, arises in large part from our looking at the matter through social spectacles. . . . The average murderer, *qua* murderer, is not a sinner in the true sense of the word; rather, he is a tiger. He murders not from positive qualities but from negative ones; he lacks something which non-murderers possess. "Evil, of course, is wholly positive—only it is on the wrong side. . . . Sin in its proper sense is very rare; it is probable that there have been far fewer sinners than saints. . . . It is harder to be a great sinner than a great saint. . . . We over-rate evil, and we under-rate it. We attach such an enormous importance to the 'sin' of meddling with our pockets (and our wives) that we have quite forgotten the awfulness of real sin." And so on.

Sin then is, simply, "an attempt to penetrate into another and higher sphere in a forbidden manner. . . . Holiness requires almost as great an effort; but holiness works on lines that *were* natural once; it is an effort to recover the ecstasy that was before the Fall. But sin is an effort to gain the ecstasy and the knowledge that pertain alone to angels, and in making this effort man becomes a demon." Obviously, this is not the sin of the legal code.

Ambrose I conceive to be Arthur Machen. There are only two realities; sorcery and sanctity—sin and sainthood—and each is an ecstasy. Arthur Machen's is a curious blend of both.—VINCENT STARRETT, "Arthur Machen: A Novelist of Ecstasy and Sin" (1917), *Buried Caesars*, 1923, pp. 4–7

In his earlier stories Mr. Machen revealed the mystery of horror. In a sense all horror appeals most strongly to youth. We get blunted as we get older, and even Poe does not thrill, except at his best, as he thrilled us in boyhood. Except Poe's stories, I know nothing so terrible as *The Three Impostors*. In that book Mr. Machen not only achieves some perfectly new thrills of his own; but he was and is reading among the odd books of the Middle Ages to give to his horror a secular air of ancient awe which indescribably heightens the effect. The effect is strengthened too by the commonplace circumstance of much of the book—the scene in Chandos Street when Headley is found in the mummy case; the terrible beginning when Rose Leicester laughs herself into the story. Rose Leicester is indeed one of the most cheerful "bad women" in fiction. Her brightness, her devilish humour, her recondite mirth make the adventures of Walters even more terrible than the horrors which Mr. Machen so ingeniously contrives.

The debt to Stevenson in form is obvious; but Mr. Machen's fancy is as fertile as Stevenson's, and his fancies have an imaginative background which is lacking from *The New Arabian Nights*.

There is at the moment a reaction against what its opponents call "fine writing." No one wishes to defend, except in purely artificial prose such as Beardsley's, the use of deliberately external ornament; but it is easy to say too much in denigration of an ornate style. An ornate style can be perfectly natural—Ruskin's style is as natural and normal as Swift's. Mr. Machen does not indulge in the purple episode. He can write a very muscular, sinewy narrative style when he pleases, as he shows both in *The Great God Pan* and in that excellent parable *The Terror*; but he can also enjoy writing a more elaborate descriptive prose. In his fascinating essay *Hieroglyphics* Mr. Machen claims that great literature, great art, is always distinguished by ecstasy; and he agrees with Mrs. Meynell in denying the title of great artist to Jane Austen, because of her deliberate acceptance of the commonplace, her zest to abide in the ordinary and the seen. Art is, in short, not a substitute for, but a form of, religion; and the artist who does not believe in some pattern in the heavens is no artist at all, but a very skilful

craftsman. Realism in the old-fashioned sense of the word is impossible; because nothing that is, is what it seems. The whole universe is a gateway to the unseen world, and every sunrise and sunset shows the pathway of imagination and desire. Mr. Machen's own work illustrates his creed. Even in his lightest things, in such an essay as "The Bowmen," he is true to his faith, and that unfortunate satire, *Dr. Stiggins*, can only be excused on the ground that Mr. Machen is in it defending, though mistakenly, what he values more than life.—R. ELLIS ROBERTS, "Arthur Machen," *BkmL*, Sept. 1922, p. 242

Arthur Machen has never been, and never will be, a popular god of literature. His name is carved in the inner, not the outer, courts of the temple; so if you want to burn incense before one who has never written a popular book, either in the best or the worst sense of the word, you must go beyond the obvious portals of the Temple. You must pass through the Meredithian maze, through the Jacobean labyrinth, through the gardens beyond Sunrise, and when you come to the pleasant courts where Rabelais and Boccaccio are enshrined, just beyond the dim Lake of Auber, you will find a statue of the great God Pan and you will know that you are where you would be. The worshippers will not be many, perhaps, but there will be that acute and honorable minority in which another author preferred to be remembered.

No, Machen will never live in the affections of the populace. His style, the cadence of his sentence, the studied art in his arrangement of words, these things are arcana and the man in the street cares not a fig for them. And if you do not care for such things, then you, like Smith, who wants a story with his reading, will not care for Machen. Then there's his subject matter!—Poe, Baudelaire, Stevenson, with a dash of Rabelais. What can 100 per cent Americanism, whether it flourish here or abroad, have to do with that? What, pray, has our great go-getting commonwealth in common with an Inmost Light and the Great God Pan? With such mooning calves as Ambrose Meyrick and Lucian Taylor? What concord has this healthy minded populace with those terrible White People and those infamous Three Impostors? And that volume of criticism! What can you make of a man who finds the secret of fine literature in the single word Ecstasy?

Well, for one I make a great deal of him. I find in his style a captivating beauty and I like the people that have their being in his books. I was going to write "live and move," but they hardly do that, since they are the creations of a mind that dwells upon the hills of dream, that knows the pathway to the terrible wood of unspeakable sins and unutterable sanctities. I find in such books as *The Hill of Dreams*, *The Secret Glory*, such stories as "The White People," "A Fragment of Life," the thing I always look for in books—beauty. Yes, and I find that "ecstasy" which Arthur Machen deems the true test of fine literature. His books *are* ecstatic! They have been written from an inner necessity. . . . From that itch that only genius knows to be at the work of putting words on paper in such a way that—to express it according to the Cabellian gospel—"one writes perfectly of beautiful happenings." Arthur Machen does that very often. He does it most perfectly in those two volumes of autobiography, *Far Off Things* and *Things Near and Far*. He does it again, a bit less perfectly, perhaps, in those two novels, *The Hill of Dreams* and *The Secret Glory*, wherein he portrays the torment of souls attuned to the mystical beauty of sin and sanctity moving amid souls that live on bread alone. He does it again in that strange book of criticism, *Hieroglyphics*, a record of thoughts upon the ecstatic beauty that dwells in fine literature. And since in all of his books there is always this element of ecstasy and the writing perfectly of beautiful happenings I find in Arthur Machen one of the great artists of all time.

Oh, yes! I know quite well that Arthur Machen has his faults as a writer. I am not unmindful of the fact that his *The Terror* is only a "shilling shocker," that his present vogue is due to a fate even more ironic than Mr. Cabell's, that *The Three Impostors* has been discovered by the critics (*post confessionem auctoris*, however) to be bad Stevenson, that the *Great God Pan* is an "incoherent nightmare of sex and the supposed mysteries behind it," that *The Hill of Dreams* portrays a namby-pamby weakling and that *The Secret Glory* is marred by the satiric goad with which the author prods the English public school system. Grant it all, since Mr. Machen himself does not deny it! What then? There still remains the thrill of horror which even bad Stevenson can give and the magic of a prose which even Stevenson might envy. What if there is a satiric goad in *The Secret Glory*? I like it none the less for that; rather more. And the beauty of his descriptions of the mystical Mass of the Grail, of the mountains, and of the tavern is surely not dimmed by that. And if Lucian Taylor *is* a namby-pamby—which I don't at all admit—does that mar the loveliness of the opening and closing sentences of that novel of the soul? Does that destroy those passages of passionate beauty in which the mystical glory of the country in summer and the desolate splendor of the city in winter are made manifest? And that "maddening volume," as Mr. Cabell calls it, *Hieroglyphics*, even if the solution of the enigma be not yours, does that hurt the wit and the subtlety with which it is presented? Then there are those two volumes of autobiography, *Far Off Things* and *Things Near and Far*. It seems to me, prejudiced Macheniac that I am, that in them Arthur Machen has reached the heights towards which he has all along been climbing. Wistful memories, evoked with a saddened smile; rambling reminiscences of days that are gone, when sometimes he sustained the life within literally upon the food of beauty; sly little digs at the comfortable stupidities that go to and fro among us, which we reverence as the gods of the Philistines—and all this in that prose of his which seems every moment about to change into poetry and yet which never quite does.—FREDERICK B. EDDY, "On the Heights," *LR*, July 21, 1923, p. 843

> There is a glory in the autumn wood,
> The ancient lanes of England wind and climb
> Past wizard oaks and gorse and taigled thyme
> To where a fort of mighty empire stood:
> There is a glamour in the autumn sky;
> The reddened clouds are writhing in the glow
> Of some great fire, and there are glints below
> Of tawny yellow where the embers die.
>
> I wait, for he will show me, clear and cold,
> High-rais'd in splendour, sharp against the North,
> The Roman eagles, and through mists of gold
> The marching legions as they issue forth:
> I wait, for I would share with him again
> The ancient wisdom, and the ancient pain.
>
> —FRANK BELKNAP LONG, "On Reading Arthur Machen," *A Man from Genoa and Other Poems*, 1926, p. 28

I'd a great deal rather have Machen as he is than not have him at all! What Machen probably likes about perverted and forbidden things is their departure from and hostility to the commonplace. To him—whose imagination is not cosmic—they represent what Pegana and the River Yann represent to Dunsany, whose imagination *is* cosmic. People whose minds are—like Machen's—steeped in the orthodox myths of religion, naturally find a poignant fascination in the conception of things which religion brands with outlawry and horror. Such people take the artificial and obsolete concept of "sin" seriously, and find it full of dark allurement. On the other hand, people like myself, with a realistic and scientific point of view, see no charm or mystery whatever in things banned by religious mythology. We recognise the primitiveness and meaninglessness of the religious attitude, and in consequence find no element of attractive defiance or significant escape in those things which happen to contravene it. The whole idea of "sin", with its overtones of unholy fascination, is in 1932 simply a curiosity of intellectual history. The filth and perversion which to Machen's obsoletely orthodox mind meant profound defiances of the universe's foundations, mean to us only a rather prosaic and unfortunate species of organic maladjustment—no more frightful, and no more interesting, than a headache, a fit of colic, or an ulcer on the big toe. Now that the veil of mystery and the hokum of spiritual significance have been stripped away from such things, they are no longer adequate motivations for phantasy or fear-literature.—H. P. LOVECRAFT, Letter to Bernard Austin Dwyer (1932), *Selected Letters: 1932–1934*, eds. August Derleth, James Turner, 1976, p. 4

Works

THE HILL OF DREAMS

I had just moved into chambers at 4 Verulam Buildings, Gray's Inn, and so, by way of Theobald's Road, I had easy access to the old, grave squares where life moved quietly and peaceably as if it were the life of a little country town. Grey square opened into grey square, silent street into silent street; all was decorous and remote from the roar of traffic and the rush of men. But few people ascended the steps of the dim old houses, but few descended them; the local tradesmen, all old established, old-fashioned, steady and good, called for orders and purveyed their wares in a sober way; Bloomsbury was silence and repose; and in its grey calm I pursued my anxious studies, and submitted my problems to myself.

The required notion came at last, not from within, nor even from Bloomsbury, but from without. I am not quite sure, but almost sure, that the needed hint was discovered in an introduction to *Tristram Shandy* written by that most accomplished man of letters, Mr. Charles Whibley. Mr. Whibley, in classifying Sterne's masterpiece, noted that it might be called a picaresque of the mind, contrasting it with *Gil Blas* which is a picaresque of the body. This distinction had struck me very much when I read it; and now as I was puzzling my head to find a spring for the book that was to be written, Mr. Whibley's dictum occurred to me, and applying it to another eighteenth century masterpiece, I asked myself why I should not write a *Robinson Crusoe* of the soul. I resolved forthwith that I would do so; I would take the theme of solitude, loneliness, separation from mankind, but, in place of a desert island and a bodily separation, my hero should be isolated in London and find his chief loneliness in the midst of myriads of men. His should be a solitude of the spirit, and the ocean surrounding him and disassociating him from his kind should be a spiritual deep. And here I found myself, as I thought, on sure ground; for I had had some experience of such things. For two years I had endured terrors of loneliness in my little room in Clarendon road, Notting Hill Gate, and so I was soundly instructed as to the matter of the work. I felt, in short, that I had my notion firmly by the tail; and so at once set to work.

. . . one happy night the whole matter of that famous

second chapter was manifested to me. As far as I remember, in the original design, Lucian was at this point to be packed off to London to the miseries of the inevitable garret; now it seemed that there were further adventures for him in his native country. I thought of these and wrote them and so got the opportunity of dwelling a little longer among the dear woods and the domed hills and the memorable vales of my native Gwent, of trying once more to set down some faint echoes of the inexpressive song that the beloved land always sang to me and still sings across all the waste of weary years. Then I found somewhere or other the recipe for the "Roman Chapter," an attempted recreation of the Roman British world of *Isca Silurum*, Caerleon-on-Usk, the town where I was born, and soaked myself so thoroughly in the vision of the old golden city—now a little desolate village—and listened so long in the deep green of Wentwood for the clangour of the marching Legion and for the noise of their trumpets that I grew quite "dithery" as they say in some part of England. I would go out on my dim Bloomsbury strolls, deep in my dream, and would "come to myself" with a sudden shock in Lamb's Conduit Street or Mecklenburgh Square or in the solitudes of Great Coram Street, realizing, certainly, that I was not, in actuality, in the Garden of Avallaunius or delaying in the Via Nympharum or on the Pons Saturni—it is called Pont Sadwrn to this day—but utterly at a loss to know exactly where I was or what I was doing, without the faintest notion of the various positions of north and south, east and west, and not at all clear as to how I was to get home to Gray's Inn and my lunch. And it was in this queer way that the fourth chapter was accomplished. I was somewhat proud of it, and went on gaily through Chapters Five, Six and Seven, and had a month's holiday in Provence, and came back to finish my book, feeling confident and in the best of spirits.

Alas! my pride had a deep fall indeed. I read over those last three chapters and saw suddenly that they were all hopelessly wrong, that they would not do at any price, that I had turned, unperceiving, from the straight path by ever so little, and had gone on, getting farther and farther away from the true direction till the way was hopelessly lost. I was in the middle of a black wood and I could not see any path out of it.

There was only one thing to be done. The three condemned chapters went into the drawer and I began over again from the end of Chapter Four. Five and Six were done, and then again I struggled desperately for many weeks, trying to find the last chapter. False tracks again, hopeless efforts, spoilt folios thick about me till by some chance or another, I know not how, the right notion was given me, and I wrote the seventh and last chapter in a couple of nights. Once more the thought of the old land had come to my help; the book was finished. It had occupied from first to last the labour of eighteen months.—ARTHUR MACHEN, "Introduction" to *The Hill of Dreams*, 1923, pp. vii–xiv

I never met Arthur Machen, and when I read this book over forty years ago, when I did not read very many books, I was deterred by some trifle from reading more of his. I think that what deterred me was a practice of the hero of this story of lacerating himself with thorns, a practice that seemed to me unwholesome. But, though I still do not like it, I look on it in my more tolerant years as merely one of those activities that I do not understand, like that of chopping tails off dogs. I see, now, that there was nothing unwholesome in Machen, and that this book records a fine struggle he made against poverty and materialism, both to hold his vision in his mind's eye, and get it down on paper so that others might see it. For perhaps all books ever written contain something of autobiography, and it

is an interesting sport to trace it, provided that one has not spoiled the sport by reading a crib, as I have done, for I have seen Machen's own later *Autobiography*. Is there anything more in literature than seeing one's vision and remaining true to it, and then putting it on to paper clearly and beautifully? Machen's vision was mainly that of a Roman encampment, where legend and old mounds still remember the Romans among the hills of Wales. And somehow fastening his vision to earth was a young man's love of a farmer's daughter; and, when she married someone else, his love somehow turns to dreams and is not lost, and the encampment of the Romans becomes more real to him than ever. And then comes the agony of the struggle to get his dream on to paper, without encouragement, without money for sufficient food, and even without the ability to write. And much of this book tells of the vision forcing its way past all these barriers, for there is a power in visions to overcome material things. How a vision comes cannot be told, for nobody knows; but surely it must bring comfort to many to know that when it does come it is more powerful than the obstacles that would stop it, and that it will even force its way past an inability to write and will clothe itself in appropriate words. That it is a hard struggle for a vision to be revealed this book shows, and many would have despaired where Machen kept on. But to those who do keep on it is possible. The obstacles that Machen's hero overcomes, and that he must have experienced himself, so vividly are they told, were poverty, lack of sympathy, some harsh criticism, and the surroundings of mean streets that were so unlike the Roman city which he dreamed, or the hills of his home whence that dream had arisen. Lack of sufficient food is an obstacle too huge and menacing for comment on it to be necessary, especially in this age whose stormy events must at one time or another have shown short rations to most of us. Lack of sympathy is the next great obstacle; but no writer will ever find another to see his vision with quite the glory in it that he sees, so that the writer must be prepared for a lonely task. As for harsh criticism, he must expect that if he writes badly; and if he writes well he must be prepared to face jealousy. . . .

Towards the end of the book the young man returns to his countryside and to his dream, which is not always clearly distinguishable from a nightmare, and ends in despair, dead over a manuscript that nobody can read. And yet the book is no product of despair, but rather a triumph over it. For, however much bitterness was engendered in Machen by the contrast between his imaginative self and his practical neighbours and relatives, and however hard such a spirit shaped by the country found the streets of the west of London, still he persevered to write this and his other books, with their delicate rhythms and a beauty drawn from the hills and the valleys he knew; and whether it be a dream or a nightmare that he pursued, he provides perhaps a lesson in hard work and resolute purpose to an age in which too many writers and painters are too ready to slap down any thought that strays into their heads without any of the hard work or resolution that went to writing *The Hill of Dreams*. For it is a triumph of the imagination over harsh reality, an imagination that built a city without marble and planted it with vineyards and ilexes, and brought back to Avallaunius an old Roman population, and girls who had danced with satyrs, from out of the dark of past ages. An architect has also such dreams, and when he can get marble his dream is soon accepted. For Machen it was a longer and harder struggle.—LORD DUNSANY, "Introduction" to *The Hill of Dreams*, 1954, pp. 5–10

ESSAYS AND CRITICISM

It is, perhaps, to be expected that Mr. Arthur Machen, having determined to arrive at some standard of judgment whereby literature, "fine literature," "literature with a capital L," might be distinguished from "mere literature," has succeeded in giving us nothing but an apology for his own books. Indeed, it would be strange if such were not the case considering Mr. Machen's emotional bias against any form of rationalism.

"I suppose there are only two parties in the world: the Rationalists and the Mystics, and one's vote goes with one's party," Mr. Machen tells us in the last chapter of ⟨*Hieroglyphics*⟩, having tried to convince us, in the previous five chapters, that he was arguing by a Coleridgean "cyclical mode of discoursing" in an attempt to arrive at deducible truths. He admits that he belongs with the mystics. Like most of the tribe he has a faculty for so mystifying the commonplace that it takes on the semblance of wisdom.

Like a good mystic Mr. Machen starts out with a premise which he defines in terms of itself and then proceeds to justify it on the basis of certain examples which he selects to prove it. The acid test of literature in the highest sense is "ecstasy." And ecstasy is "rapture, beauty, adoration, wonder, awe, mystery, sense of the unknown, desire for the unknown." Ecstasy is, in brief, that quality of literature which makes it "fine literature" you know not why. A rather shaky foundation on which to build a critique.

Nevertheless, it affords the critic a magic wand of dogmatism which he has merely to wave to separate the sheep from the goats at first reading. Take, for instance, *Pickwick Papers* and *Vanity Fair*. The first titillates Mr. Machen to a sense of ecstasy; the second does not. Ergo, to the junk heap with Thackeray along with "poor, draggle-tailed George Eliot" and unspeakable Gustave Flaubert, while Dickens is raised among the lower order of saints.

Moreover, there is no need to make such a fuss about the desire of the unknown in the *Odyssey*, which raises it, in the critic's estimation, to incredibly lofty heights. There is really nothing so mysterious about it. Given the early Greeks, a people dwelling by the vast and inexplicable sea, and given the ocean that reaches none knows where, teeming with all sorts of unknown possibilities, the adventures of Ulysses follow with all the logical certainty of Euclidean geometry.

To say, also, that writers like Rabelais wrote of giants to achieve the heroic and to avoid the commonplace stature of mankind and so differ noticeably from modern authors who take ordinary men and women and treat their symptoms realistically, is not sufficient. Rabelais exaggerated, probably, not because he wished for the unknown, the unheard-of, but because, by the simple process of applying a magnifying lens, a greater clarity could be achieved. In the same way contemporary authors writing of the diseased, the abnormal, are able to achieve a greater clarity of insight into human nature. Mr. Machen would have us believe that literature brings us closest to the heart of life when it removes us as far away from it as possible.

Artifice, he maintains, has nothing to do with art and the less we have of it the better. Now it is impossible to conceive of the spirit except in terms of the body. He is compelled, therefore, to concede begrudgingly that artifice is of some utility. Indeed, it is conceivable that artifice is the whole of art and that, as Miss Dorothy Richardson pointed out some time ago, genius is the usual thing, talent the rarity. For Mr. Machen to say that the lyric is the purest example of art hardly contaminated with artifice is to give himself away completely. For the lyric is the clearest example of the perfection of artifice to such a degree that the most intangible subtleties may be expressed thereby. If art approaches its maximum intensity

through a minimum of artifice, the finest book in the world would be a book with nothing in it.

But of course Mr. Machen doesn't mean that. After all, he is a mystic and we are criticizing him from the camp of the rationalists. "Art is by its very definition quite without the jurisdiction of the schools and the realm of the reasoning process, since art is a miracle, superior to the laws." When a critic believes that, criticism of him is futile.—EDWIN SEAVER, "Mystical Criticism," *Nation*, Sept. 26, 1923, pp. 329–30

In *The London Adventure*, as in the author's two former volumes of autobiography—*Far Off Things* and *Things Near and Far*—we are given to see the magnificent conquest of poverty and sordidness by one whose Act of Faith in the things of the spirit never wavered, nor sanctioned those paltry compromises wherein weaker men take timid refuge. With a quiet humor that all but conceals the underlying pathos, Mr. Machen relates the picaresque tales of his days as a Fleet Street reporter.

One is not surprised to learn that, to this alchemistical mystic, the most absurd errands and most foolish of reportorial assignments were but baser matters to be transmuted into the gold of high adventure. Thus was the everlasting search for "copy" turned into a quest for that strange beauty that the artist's eye is given the light to see even in the most squalid of London's slums. Just such an eye had Dickens, and the rare discoveries—æsthetic, dramatic, and historical—in *The London Adventure* are not unlike those odd flashes of vision of the author of *Pickwick Papers*.

The London of Arthur Machen is a far cry from the eternal museums and traditional relics beloved of Cook's tours. The reader will journey through Islington and Clapton, he will hear mention of Edmonton and Spa Fields, and, if he be a knowing and appreciative soul, he will sigh with relish at the good hearty ale in certain small taverns of Soho. Then there is the author's love of antiquity for its own sake—a characteristic affection omnipresent in his work:

> I can look with a kind of pleasure on a very doorstep, on a doorstep approaching a shabby grey house of 1810 or thereabouts—if the stone be worn into a deep hollow by the feet of even a hundred years and a little over. . . . The feet of the weary and hopeless, the glad and the exultant, the lustful and the pure have made that hollow; and most of those feet are now in the hollow of the grave; and that doorstep is to me sacramental, if not a sacrament, even though the neighborhood round about Mount Pleasant is a very poor one. For, it seems to me that here you have the magic touch which redeems and exalts the dull mass of things, by tingeing them with the soul of man.

> —MYLES TIERNEY, "The Highway to Avalon," *Bkm*, Oct. 1924, pp. 225–26

H. P. LOVECRAFT
From "The Modern Masters"
Supernatural Horror in Literature (1927)
1973, pp. 88–95

Of living creators of cosmic fear raised to its most artistic pitch, few if any can hope to equal the versatile Arthur Machen, author of some dozen tales long and short, in which the elements of hidden horror and brooding fright attain an almost incomparable substance and realistic acuteness. Mr. Machen, a general man of letters and master of an exquisitely lyrical and expressive prose style, has perhaps put more conscious effort into his picaresque *Chronicle of Clemendy,* his refreshing essays, his vivid autobiographical volumes, his fresh and spirited translations, and above all his memorable epic of the sensitive aesthetic mind, *The Hill of Dreams,* in which the youthful hero responds to the magic of that ancient Welsh environment which is the author's own, and lives a dream-life in the Roman city of Isca Silurum, now shrunk to the relic-strewn village of Caerleon-on-Usk. But the fact remains that his powerful horror-material of the nineties and earlier nineteen-hundreds stands alone in its class, and marks a distinct epoch in the history of this literary form.

Mr. Machen, with an impressionable Celtic heritage linked to keen youthful memories of the wild domed hills, archaic forests, and cryptical Roman ruins of the Gwent countryside, has developed an imaginative life of rare beauty, intensity, and historic background. He has absorbed the mediaeval mystery of dark woods and ancient customs, and is a champion of the Middle Ages in all things—including the Catholic faith. He has yielded, likewise, to the spell of the Britanno-Roman life which once surged over his native region; and finds strange magic in the fortified camps, tessellated pavements, fragments of statues, and kindred things which tell of the day when classicism reigned and Latin was the language of the country. . . .

Of Mr. Machen's horror-tales the most famous is perhaps *The Great God Pan* (1894) which tells of a singular and terrible experiment and its consequences. A young woman, through surgery of the brain-cells, is made to see the vast and monstrous deity of Nature, and becomes an idiot in consequence, dying less than a year later. Years afterward a strange, ominous, and foreign-looking child named Helen Vaughan is placed to board with a family in rural Wales, and haunts the woods in unaccountable fashion. A little boy is thrown out of his mind at sight of someone or something he spies with her, and a young girl comes to a terrible end in similar fashion. All this mystery is strangely interwoven with the Roman rural deities of the place, as sculptured in antique fragments. After another lapse of years, a woman of strangely exotic beauty appears in society, drives her husband to horror and death, causes an artist to paint unthinkable paintings of Witches' Sabbaths, creates an epidemic of suicide among the men of her acquaintance, and is finally discovered to be a frequenter of the lowest dens of vice in London, where even the most callous degenerates are shocked at her enormities. Through the clever comparing of notes on the part of those who have had word of her at various stages of her career, this woman is discovered to be the girl Helen Vaughan, who is the child—by no mortal father—of the young woman on whom the brain experiment was made. She is a daughter of hideous Pan himself, and at the last is put to death amidst horrible transmutations of form involving changes of sex and a descent to the most primal manifestations of the life-principle.

But the charm of the tale is in the telling. No one could begin to describe the cumulative suspense and ultimate horror with which every paragraph abounds without following fully the precise order in which Mr. Machen unfolds his gradual hints and revelations. Melodrama is undeniably present, and coincidence is stretched to a length which appears absurd upon analysis; but in the malign witchery of the tale as a whole these trifles are forgotten, and the sensitive reader reaches the end with only an appreciative shudder and a tendency to repeat the words of one of the characters: "It is too incredible, too monstrous; such things can never be in this quiet world.

. . . Why, man, if such a case were possible, our earth would be a nightmare."

Less famous and less complex in plot than *The Great God Pan,* but definitely finer in atmosphere and general artistic value, is the curious and dimly disquieting chronicle called "The White People," whose central portion purports to be the diary or notes of a little girl whose nurse has introduced her to some of the forbidden magic and soul-blasting traditions of the noxious witch-cult—the cult whose whispered lore was handed down long lines of peasantry throughout Western Europe, and whose members sometimes stole forth at night, one by one, to meet in black woods and lonely places for the revolting orgies of the Witches' Sabbath. Mr. Machen's narrative, a triumph of skilful selectiveness and restraint, accumulates enormous power as it flows on in a stream of innocent childish prattle, introducing allusions to strange "nymphs," "Dols," "voolas," "white, green, and scarlet ceremonies," "Aklo letters," "Chian language," "Mao games," and the like. The rites learned by the nurse from her witch grandmother are taught to the child by the time she is three years old, and her artless accounts of the dangerous secret revelations possess a lurking terror generously mixed with pathos. Evil charms well known to anthropologists are described with juvenile naïveté, and finally there comes a winter afternoon journey into the old Welsh hills, performed under an imaginative spell which lends to the wild scenery an added weirdness, strangeness, and suggestion of grotesque sentience. The details of this journey are given with marvellous vividness, and form to the keen critic a masterpiece of fantastic writing, with almost unlimited power in the intimation of potent hideousness and cosmic aberration. At length the child—whose age is then thirteen—comes upon a cryptic and banefully beautiful thing in the midst of a dark and inaccessible wood. In the end horror overtakes her in a manner deftly prefigured by an anecdote in the prologue, but she poisons herself in time. Like the mother of Helen Vaughan in *The Great God Pan,* she has seen that frightful deity. She is discovered dead in the dark wood beside the cryptic thing she found; and that thing—a whitely luminous statue of Roman workmanship about which dire mediaeval rumours had clustered—is affrightedly hammered into dust by the searchers.

In the episode novel of *The Three Impostors,* a work whose merit as a whole is somewhat marred by an imitation of the jaunty Stevenson manner, occur certain tales which perhaps represent the highwater mark of Machen's skill as a terror-weaver. Here we find in its most artistic form a favourite weird conception of the author's; the notion that beneath the mounds and rocks of the wild Welsh hills dwell subterraneously that squat primitive race whose vestiges gave rise to our common folk legends of fairies, elves, and the "little people," and whose acts are even now responsible for certain unexplained disappearances, and occasional substitutions of strange dark "changelings" for normal infants. This theme receives its finest treatment in the episode entitled "The Novel of the Black Seal," where a professor, having discovered a singular identity between certain characters scrawled on Welsh limestone rocks and those existing in a prehistoric black seal from Babylon, sets out on a course of discovery which leads him to unknown and terrible things. A queer passage in the ancient geographer Solinus, a series of mysterious disappearances in the lonely reaches of Wales, a strange idiot son born to a rural mother after a fright in which her inmost faculties were shaken; all these things suggest to the professor a hideous connection and a condition revolting to any friend and respecter of the human race. He hires the idiot boy, who jabbers strangely at times in a repulsive hissing voice, and is subject to odd epileptic seizures.

Once, after such a seizure in the professor's study by night, disquieting odours and evidences of unnatural presences are found; and soon after that the professor leaves a bulky document and goes into the weird hills with feverish expectancy and strange terror in his heart. He never returns, but beside a fantastic stone in the wild country are found his watch, money, and ring, done up with catgut in a parchment bearing the same terrible characters as those on the black Babylonish seal and the rock in the Welsh mountains. . . .

Mr. Machen returns to the daemoniac "little people" in "The Red Hand" and "The Shining Pyramid"; and in *The Terror*, a wartime story, he treats with very patent mystery the effect of man's modern repudiation of spirituality on the beasts of the world, which are thus led to question his supremacy and to unite for his extermination. Of utmost delicacy, and passing from mere horror into true mysticism, is "The Great Return," a story of the Graal, also a product of the war period. Too well known to need description here is the tale of "The Bowmen"; which, taken for authentic narration, gave rise to the widespread legend of the "Angels of Mons"—ghosts of the old English archers of Crécy and Agincourt who fought in 1914 beside the hard-pressed ranks of England's glorious "Old Contemptibles."

ROBERT S. MATTESON
From "Arthur Machen: A Vision of an Enchanted Land"

Personalist, Spring 1965, pp. 261–64

In . . . every story that he wrote, Machen pursues his one theme—the mystic vision—and employs his one plot—the rending of the veil to show his characters experiencing whatever lies beyond in the hidden world. The vision achieved by Lucian Taylor in *The Hill of Dreams* is one of unutterable horror. Certain of the meanness of society and this world, Lucian yearns "to win the secret of words," to capture the magic music of nature in a literary masterpiece. Moving on his quest from Wales to London, he turns his thought ever inward, retires from the paths of the Welch hills to a small room in a boarding house, loses the "art of humanity," reaches his spiritual climax in a vision of a decayed and rotting house north of London, and finally dies, leaving behind him a "terrible manuscript" which no one can read. The vision achieved in "The White People" is much the same, only it is more essential. Exploring the essence of evil, the text is an impressionistic painting in words, an account of a young girl who half remembers ghostly stories told to her by her nurse and who wanders through endless tunnels and hollows, along oozy paths, amidst gray rocks, thorny brakes and bushes in search of white people, beautifully evil people with whom she had seen her nurse dance. The account of her quest is prefaced by a dialogue concerning the essence of evil, which was for Machen "a passion of the solitary individual soul," "an infernal miracle," an attempt to penetrate into another and higher sphere in a forbidden manner. The unnamed girl in "The White People" attempted just this, and at the end of her journey she was found dead before a glowing white idol beneath a bush in an area where Adam and Eve might have roamed.

The malefic visions of *The Hill of Dreams* and "The White People" picture Machen at his evil best and form a rather useful contrast with *The Secret Glory* and "A Fragment of Life," both of which explore the other side of the coin by suggesting the essence of saintliness. Ambrose Meyrick in *The Secret Glory*, a book which combines a mystical quest with a satiric attack on the English public school system, attains red martyrdom in his attempts to restore the Holy Grail to its final resting place somewhere in the East. The book ends with a report of Meyrick's crucifixion by Turks, his face shining with rapture. Unlike Lucian in *The Hill of Dreams*, who conducted an inner search for beauty and truth, Ambrose Meyrick turns his thoughts away from himself. His quest takes him from the narrow confines of Lupton, a hideous public school, to the comparative freedom of London and a love affair with Nelly Foran, a maid in the house of the Lupton headmaster. Perhaps the most telling difference between Lucian and Ambrose can be seen in the manner of their searchings. Whereas both of them believed life to be a rite and a ceremony, the end of which was the attainment of mystic sanctity, they went about their rites and ceremonies in vastly different manners. Lucian fell in love with Annie Morgan, his distant neighbor in Wales. In his ecstasy he composed a poem, adorned the majuscules of the text with gold, and ornamented the margins with vermilion. His ultimate act of love was to lie upon a midnight bed of thorns and spines while he "tenderly repeated the praises of his dear, dear Annie." Later in life he again practiced this symbolic mortification and confinement as he worked on his "terrible manuscript" surrounded by the tattered walls of his London room. In contrast Ambrose Meyrick celebrated his love for Nelly Foran by drinking wine with her in London restaurants, by talking with her of their possible journey to France—by cultivating the art of humanity. Meyrick's ultimate success in cultivating this art is measurable in terms of his spiritualization of his love for Nelly. His reward is the San Graal, which he must carry to its final resting place, a reward which could come only to one approaching sainthood.

The last work, "A Fragment of Life," is concerned less with the achievement of the beatific vision than is *The Secret Glory*. Rather it seems to represent Machen's attempt to portray the process by which men begin to see the world as it really is. The hero of the story, Edward Darnell, and his wife Mary are depicted as living day after day in the "grey phantasmal world, akin to death, that has, somehow, with most of us, made good its claim to be called life."[1] They are enmeshed in problems of whether or not to furnish an extra room and thus attract overnight guests, in questions about the purchase of a new kitchen stove (should it be a Raven or a Glow?), and in innumerable petty concerns of household economy which force their marriage of one year into a rigid pattern of respectability and distant politeness. Both sense that there is more to life and begin consciously to realize that something more when Edward, in what must have been his first unveiling of himself, tells his wife of his earlier wanderings in London, of his first "voyage of discovery." Mary is moved by the account, but remains rather securely moored in her unwillingness to see life and living from any but a common sense point of view. Darnell's account of his wanderings fairly rings with overtones of a journey through an archetypal city, complete with greyred, silent, echoing courts, a moon that glows like a great rose, blue mists, and a celestial city on a distant hill. Listening to the account, Mary feels that she is seeing her husband for the first time; but she soon lapses back into twaddle about the cook, the stove, and the dreadful neighbors. The second half of the story pictures Edward turning more often to the past and to his own childhood in order to make his drab life bearable. As he does so, he begins to realize more acutely that "the whole world is but a great ceremony or sacrament, which teaches under visible forms a hidden and transcendent doctrine"; he senses that he must enact his part in the great mystery of life;

and he writes a book of autobiographical verse, which ends with the idea that he has begun to see for the first time the world as it really is. Mary is less active in pursuit of true vision and remains to the last concerned primarily about the morning bacon; however, she senses that she has embarked upon a great adventure in her marriage and when the story ends there is the suggestion that she too may rend the veil of useless little things and join her husband in his search for the essence of life. The meaning of the story may be seen in the movement from one awakening in the first paragraph to a second awakening at the end of the story. When the story opens, Edward Darnell awakes from "a dream of an ancient wood, and of a clear well rising into grey film and vapour beneath a misty, glimmering heat."[2] The dream fades and his first thought is that he will be late for the morning bus at 9:15. At the end of the story Edward describes himself as awaking from a dream of weary, useless,

little things. When fully awake, he finds himself in an ancient wood, where a clear well rises into grey film and where he and his love (Mary) are united. In "A Fragment of Life," as in the other works, the Machenian pattern is a familiar one: a sense of the mystery of life, a civilization that has suppressed and disguised but not obliterated the spiritual life, the basic motif of the quest or voyage of discovery, a searching of the past ending inevitably in visions of childhood, an awareness that mystic vision can easily be perverted if wrongly conducted, and, finally, either an infernal miracle or a sense of ineffable peace, both intended to convey ecstasy.

Notes

1. "A Fragment of Life," in *The House of Souls* (New York: Alfred A. Knopf, 1923), p. 37.
2. Ibid., p. 3.

COMPTON MACKENZIE

1883–1972

Edward Montague Compton Mackenzie was born on January 17, 1883, in West Hartlepool, County Durham. His parents were successful actors, and his background cultivated, and he read widely in childhood. After attending St. Paul's School, London, he studied history at Magdalen College, Oxford, where he was active in dramatic and debating societies, and founded a literary review.

After beginning as a poet and playwright, Mackenzie rose to prominence with the novels *The Passionate Elopement* (1911), *Carnival* (1912), and *Sinister Street* (1913–14). During World War I he served with the Royal Marines, and after being invalided worked with Intelligence in the Aegean. His experiences there were recorded in *Greek Memories* (1932), for which he was prosecuted under the Official Secrets Act. His conversion to Roman Catholicism in 1914 was reflected in several novels in the 1920s, though his most notable works in this period were the satires *Vestal Fire* (1927), and *Extraordinary Women* (1928). In 1923 he founded *Grammophone* magazine, remaining its editor until 1962. His continuing success as a novelist enabled him to buy several islands in the Outer Hebrides, and he settled on the island of Barra. He helped found the National Party of Scotland in 1928 and remained a keen nationalist the rest of his life. From 1931 to 1934 he served as Rector of Glasgow University.

Altogether Mackenzie wrote over one hundred novels, biographies, and plays. His later works include *The Four Winds of Love* (1937–45), *Whiskey Galore* (1947), and the autobiography *My Life and Times*, published in ten volumes between 1963 and 1971. He was president of the Croquet Association from 1954 until 1966, and his enthusiasm for cats is recorded in several books on the subject. Though his critical reputation varied, he remained a popular figure on a national scale into old age. He received an OBE in 1919 and was knighted in 1952. He outlived two wives and was survived by the third, dying on November 30, 1972.

Personal

I shall be bold enough to claim that as a precocious boy in ⟨the 1890's⟩ I was better able to apprehend the life-giving quality of the ambient intellectual air than those who were actually in their prime of productive energy, and certainly better able than those who looking back at its externals from the present can see in it nothing more than an interlude played in the not too dim past before life was as real as it became after the Great War. I hope there are some schoolboys of fourteen now who are experiencing the intellectual ecstasy which was to be experienced by the schoolboy of 1897 when beneath the huge pomp of the Diamond Jubilee he discerned the old world crumbling. I recall from the mid-'nineties one schoolfellow older than myself actually, but at fifteen or sixteen still in Etons

and displaying no hint externally of his real age, a small and handsome Jew, to whom as a kindred spirit I was presented by another brilliant youth two years younger than myself. Three boys of twelve, fourteen and sixteen are wandering across the great green expanse of the St. Paul's playing-fields, and I can recall how the eldest spoke with an enchanting gravity words of prophetic wisdom, in the course of which I was, as you might say, converted to divine the change that was coming. That boy was Leonard Woolf, and when I occasionally feel sceptical about progress, and when I feel inclined to let my reactionary prejudices harden into an immovable negative, I try to recapture that abundant sense of life which made nothing seem impossible upon that green playground not far from forty years ago, and in recapturing the memory of it I regain an assurance of life's purpose. It is hard without a suggestion of sentimentalization to re-conjure an episode like this which by its very nature possesses that dreamlike quality of importance to him who experienced it, but which is, like a dream, ultimately incommunicable. And the reader may well ask what bearing in any case such a reminiscence has upon the business in hand, since a similar experience must have happened to many schoolboys year after year back through time. My only reply can be that in the previous decade of the 'eighties I do not believe three schoolboys could have been filled with such a sense of a collapsing past, such an awareness of an incommensurable future.—COMPTON MACKENZIE, "The Last Decade of the Nineteenth Century," *Literature in My Time*, 1933, pp. 70–72

General

Mr. Compton Mackenzie, for the moment, has eschewed serious achievement. Nevertheless he has achieved the most genuine personal success, not only of the season, but of the year. *Poor Relations* has been everybody's diversion, and it has been everybody's diversion because it has been Mr. Mackenzie's. There is plenty of time to take Michael Fane and his Sylvia through the rest of the war; in the meantime Mr. Mackenzie is out for a holiday. This very sound instinct of Mr. Mackenzie's has been so heartily endorsed by his public that it becomes permissible to doubt whether Michael Fane and his Sylvia ever will be taken through the rest of the war. But sufficient for a season are the novels thereof; and Mr. Mackenzie has achieved a success which may incline his extremely individual gifts, we feel, into any direction, even into that of the theatre. *Poor Relations* already has all the air of running an uncountable number of nights—as long as anything, more soberly romantic, of John Touchwood's. Mr. Mackenzie's dramatist, who achieves affluence by the simple and unblamable power he has of writing "rosified" plays, and then finds his family on his back, is a figure of comedy quite ripe for the stage. But if John Touchwood's creator turns aside to shine in another *milieu*, who is there that will not deplore the characteristic effects we shall miss?—

> "Keep your eye on the ball," John gruffly advised him. "And don't shift your position."
>
> "One, two, three," murmured Laurence, raising the club above his shoulder.
>
> "Fore!" John shouted to a rash member of the household who was crossing the line of fire.
>
> A lump of turf was propelled a few feet in the direction of the admonished figure, and the ball was hammered down into the soft earth.
>
> "You distracted me by counting four," Laurence protested. "My intention was to strike at three. However, if at first you don't succeed . . ."

In Mr. Mackenzie's comic pages a kind of exemplified pun has come into its own, and it is an instrument very proper for the expression of exuberant vitality. It would be but a part of this book—but a part, for example, of the Rev. Laurence Armitage, cleric and stage neophyte—that would get into the theatre, however vigorously that part seems to clamour at times for entrance; and one is very glad to see the whole of it on the printed page, where for the most part it heartily justifies itself.—P. P. HOWE, "Fiction: Autumn, 1919," *FR*, Autumn 1919, pp. 66–67

Mr. Compton Mackenzie did not invent the English realistic-autobiographic novel. That goes back to Defoe; but Mr. Mackenzie has given it a local habitation and an Oxford accent. He did not invent the picaresque-picturesque, which was flourishing under Elizabeth. But he has adapted it to modern conditions—not very successfully. And he has wedded the two types by the rites of Bohemia.

The vogue of *Sinister Street* is certainly due in great degree to its literary merit. It is excellently written. But it also had luck. Rarely has a book fitted so precisely into the niche prepared for it by circumstance. The universities of Oxford and Cambridge came, in the years immediately preceding the war, into a double prominence of comfort and despair. On the one hand, Grub Street had flowed into Fleet Street, and scholarship had abandoned the garret for the club; literary journalism was in fine fettle; there were movements in it, as there were in poetry, in music, in all the fine arts; and a large number of the moving spirits appeared to come from the older universities. On the other hand, the dons were—it was implied by the haughty young—played out. The home of lost causes had become the antechamber to the cafés of Soho. And Mr. Compton Mackenzie was the Groom of the Antechamber. His scorn of a grand tradition was prodigious, symptomatic, and topical. So was his sympathy with undergraduates. Undergraduates at that time seemed to be more articulate and more influential than they are likely to seem again. They all read *Sinister Street*; and ever since they have all been writing it.

Most of them, unhappily, lack Mr. Mackenzie's chief weapon. He is master of a particularly fascinating style, at once smooth and various, which gives the quality of poetry to his explication of ordinary things. He has, moreover, some creative power. But there is no doubt that one part of *Sinister Street*, and the part that has been most assiduously imitated, is not creative at all. How much of the plot is taken from real life it would be impertinent to inquire; but the photographic reproduction of the setting is as easy to discern as it must have been to do. And it is this point of weakness that most of the imitators have fastened upon and exploited. There is a formula: public school, University, "night life." What is forgotten is that neither public school nor University nor night life has, for fiction, any significance in itself. The interesting thing is the individual. When Sir Philip Sidney's muse instructed him to look in his heart and write, the advice was excellent, because it was addressed to Sir Philip Sidney, and he had Stella in his heart. But the notion that everybody has at least one good book in him is misleading. To draw out from one's own interior the material for a book, and to objectify it *as* a book, requires more literary skill than is given to most of us, and more courage than is discoverable in the whole history of indiscretion. Even the most ruthless artists transmute and idealise; that is, indeed, the function of their art; if they were more ruthless they would the less be artists. But to transmute is not to ignore or to shirk; and it must be confessed that, since the publication of the second volume of *Sinister Street* in 1914, a great number of young men have repeated the formula while shirking or ignoring the spirit. They have imagined themselves to be giving us the secrets of their souls when they were really giving us, under thin disguises, the names of their schools and colleges. If any one of them had been brought up by a wolf, like Romulus or Mowgli, it would at least have made a change in the externals. But one school is desperately like another. I must not say that Oxford is like Cambridge: but books about the one resemble books about the other. And the delineation of living people becomes daily more daring and less tolerable.

Mr. Compton Mackenzie, having meanwhile dashed about the world in narratives like *Sylvia and Michael*, which do not call for detailed criticism, has reverted to the biographical form in *The Altar Steps*, *The Parson's Progress* and *The*

Heavenly Ladder—a trilogy of which the second volume is somewhat dull and the third, though exciting enough, somewhat incoherent. Indeed, Mr. Compton Mackenzie, in the last resort, must base his claim to fame upon *Guy and Pauline*, in which practically nothing happens but every least thing matters. That book is like a dream, a dream how melancholy but how exquisite! Pauline's shining and youthful simplicity, Guy's restless and ineffective egoism, alike degenerate into hysteria under the strain of their relationship. But their love, while it still has beauty, has so much, and is so deliciously accompanied by the music of woodland and water!—GERALD GOULD, "Compton Mackenzie," *The English Novel of To-day*, 1924, pp. 41–45

Of course you remember Michael Fane. He was a rather unusual boy, who went to St. Paul's for about three hundred pages. Michael's father was poor dear Saxby. But Michael's mother was not Lady Saxby. He was brought up by a governess, who was a Good Influence and got engaged to a simple soldier with one of those large, hair moustaches. Then (since Michael went to school in the Nineties) there were the bad influences as well. One remembers a wicked Anglo-Catholic and an extremely "period" gentleman who smoked puce cigarettes. Then our young friend went to Paddington and caught the second volume to Oxford; and the pleasing coincidence, which had led Mr. Mackenzie to select St. Paul's for his school, sent him to Magdalen for his college, masked under the simple-minded alias of "St. Mary's." This device is no protection for the purposes of a libel action, and can afford satisfaction to no one except Mr. Arnold Bennett, who is the leading exponent of the method: one is really profoundly grateful to Mr. G. R. Sims for not writing about *The Lights of Lonbridge*. The exquisite shadow of Oxford fell across the scene and inspired Mr. Mackenzie to the titular ejaculation, "Dreaming Spires": that, one feels, is the sort of thing that Cambridge men say about St. Pancras Station.

Yet Michael's journey from the cradle to the end of his second volume remains, for many of us, the most abiding relic of Mr. Mackenzie's industry. In his beginnings he walked delicately between a sense of form and a fastidious vocabulary. Undergraduates read his verses between paper covers, and exquisite young gentlemen caught in *The Passionate Elopement* a flattering echo of their own affectation. The bright beam of his observation shifted a century or so nearer to his own times; and *Carnival* seemed to promise a new school of the Picaresque, in which pretty girls in hansom-cabs trundled across a background of real beauty. But quite suddenly he surprised his contemporaries with the promise (or was it the threat?) of a new *Comédie humaine*. His imagination was engaged in a vast tangle of fictitious biographies in *Sinister Street* and its immediate neighbourhood. The little ladies of the new Picaresque were induced to enlist in a larger army; and he set out to draw the *état civil* of the West End of London, the older universities, a few streets in Chelsea, and a country parsonage or so. A wise old gentleman, who had once written for Edward Compton a supremely unsuccessful play called *The American*, was filled with wild alarms by his "waste and irresponsibility—*selection* isn't in him." But in the loose-limbed chronicle he had formed (or escaped from) his method; and he plies it to the general enjoyment on the various islands of his affection. For, like Sir James Barrie, he is an *amateur* of islands. But happily, in the case of Mr. Mackenzie, they are excluded from his work, which clings firmly to the mainland and almost to the metropolis, where there is traffic and the light of street lamps and altars and music-halls.—PHILIP GUEDALLA, "Compton Mackenzie," *A Gallery*, 1924, pp. 153–55

Compton Mackenzie, whose parents were well known and highly esteemed under their stage names of Edmund Compton and Virginia Bateman, showed early signs of literary versatility. He had become an editor (of the *Oxford Point of View*) before he left Magdalen College in 1904, and within a few years after had produced a comedy, published a volume of poems, and written an Alhambra revue. After his marriage he retired to Cornwall, and from this rustic seclusion sent his first novel, *The Passionate Elopement*, to one publisher after another until it was accepted in 1911 and scored an immediate success. It is "an eighteenth century exercise in concentration and flexibility," and gives little hint of the very different style and manner he adopted in *Carnival*. This is a realistic study of the life and character, especially in her childhood and youth, of a London ballet girl, conducted with admirable skill and verve until the author whisks her away from the glare of the footlights to meet an untimely death by the Cornish sea. There seems no call or excuse for this hurried ending, as the character might just as well have been taken over, as some of the others were, into the author's subsequent work. His plan of detailed realistic incident demands extensive space, and though it is difficult to bring a novel written on this scale to a satisfactory conclusion, sudden death is not a solution of the problem. The story really breaks into two parts, and the second part is out of proportion and out of tone with the first.

In *Sinister Street* the novelist took a much larger canvas and found himself more at ease. The two parts relate with abundant detail the childhood and youth, school days and love affairs of Michael and Stella Fane, the offspring of an irregular union in the English upper class. The development of the characters of the two children under their peculiar social conditions is wonderfully done, and the conflict in Michael's nature between the sensualist and the ascetic is movingly presented. *Guy and Pauline* is a detached idyll arising out of Michael's life at Oxford, but even at the end of this third novel the young people, after rich and varied experiences, are left still at the beginning of their careers. The author's task was twice interrupted, in 1913 by a physical breakdown, which drove him to Capri for a rest, and in 1915 by volunteering for the ill-fated expedition to the Dardanelles. In *Sylvia Scarlett* he made a fresh start, with an entirely new set of characters, but about halfway through the book the old ones begin to come back again, and by the end it is evident that the real crisis in the lives of Michael Fane and Sylvia Scarlett is still to come. It does come in *Sylvia and Michael*, which rounds out the series, with the help of a minor appendix in *The Vanity Girl*.

The detailed method adopted by Compton Mackenzie has obvious dangers, and he does not altogether escape them. He has inexhaustible inventiveness of incident, but his versatility betrays him at times into the irrelevant and the insignificant—not the loose, easy-going scheme of the Russians, which is not at all motiveless, but the merely episodical manner of Smollett, the multiplication of incident for its own sake. Take for instance the battle royal between two of Sylvia's early lovers, in the course of which Danny Lewis knocks Jay Cohen into a slop-pail: "Danny kicked off the slop-pail, and invited Cohen to stand up to him; but when he did get on his feet, he ran to the door and reached the stairs just as Mrs. Gonner was wearily ascending to find out what was happening. He tried to stop himself by clutching the knob of the baluster, which broke; the result was that he dragged Mrs. Gonner with him in a glissade which ended behind the counter. The confusion in the shop became general: Mr. Gonner cut his thumb, and the sight of the blood caused a woman who was eating a sausage to choke; another customer took advantage of the row to snatch a side of bacon and try to escape, but another customer with a finer moral sense prevented him; a dog, who was sniffing in the entrance, saw the bacon on the floor and tried to seize it, but getting his tail trodden upon by somebody, he took fright and bit a small boy, who was waiting to change a shilling into coppers." In the midst of the hubbub, Sylvia makes her escape, but one fails to see what all this has to do with the development of her character or what influence it has on her future career. It may excite the laughter of the groundlings, but it makes the judicious grieve, for the author had shown himself capable of better things. *Sinister Street* was a very solid and remarkable accomplishment for a novelist of Compton Mackenzie's years and experience, and it seemed a pity for so fine a talent to waste itself on such mere *tours de force* as *Poor Relations* and *Rich Relatives*.

The *Altar Steps* is a study of the Anglo-Catholic movement in the Church of England, centred in the life-history of a boy, who, at the age of fifteen, vows himself to the priesthood, and on his seventeenth birthday is vouch-safed what the author describes as "the miracle of St. Mary Magdalene's intervention" in the summary taking-off, by the fall of her image, of the blasphemous and too ardent lover of a girl the young hero admires. Up to the point of this crudely melodramatic episode, Mark Lidderdale's boyhood is charmingly recounted, with many delightful touches of humour, and the novelist holds the scales fairly even between the Anglo-Catholic party and its opponents, though his sympathies are obviously on the side of his hero's faith.

The character of Mark Lidderdale is carefully and sympathetically developed, not only in his youth, but in the further unfolding of the inner life and struggles with the world in *The Parson's Progress*.—J. W. CUNLIFFE, "Compton Mackenzie," *English Literature in the Twentieth Century*, 1938, pp. 236–39

JOHN FREEMAN
From "Compton Mackenzie"
English Portraits and Essays
1924, pp. 199–222

I

I make no attempt to disguise the fact that Mr. Mackenzie appears to be a writer who is not an imaginative artist, yet who might have been an imaginative artist; a novelist who has not concerned himself with life at all save in its external and mechanic motions. He has not confined himself to a single manner: his first book, *The Passionate Elopement*, was an eighteenth-century story in a style familiarised by less capable and less versatile practitioners. Little indeed was to be expected from an author whose first book contained such writing as:

> Presently he saw her join a blue mask and lose herself in the flickering throng. Last time he had remarked particularly that her *vis-à-vis* wore brown and gold, yet the two figures were alike in movement and gesture, and he could swear the hands were identical. It was the same without a doubt. Charles bit his nails with vexation, and fretted confoundedly.
>
> "My dear boy, my dear Charles, pray do not gnaw your fingers. Narcissus admired himself, 'tis true, but without carrying his devotion to cannibality."
>
> Charles turned to the well-known voice of Mr. Ripple.
>
> "A thousand pardons, dear Beau, I was vexed by a trifle. The masquerade comports itself with tolerable success."

—and the glitter and varnish of an upholstered narrative casually spangled with Meredithean brightness. But Mr. Mackenzie's second novel, *Carnival*, disappointed expectation by being readable. Like some of its successors, it might be mistaken for realistic, while another, *Guy and Pauline*, might be termed idyllic by those who love the phrase. He moves and changes, he is a part of all that he has met; and you wonder at length what *he* is. For myself, I am reminded frequently of an ingenious character seen in provincial music-halls, who to the eyes of a happy audience swiftly and imperceptibly invests and divests himself of many costumes of marvellous hue—one growing plain as another is impetuously flung off, blue gloves giving place to pink, a crimson shirt to an emerald, a shooting-jacket to a dinner-jacket—until I laugh unrestrainably.

II

Mr. Mackenzie has not sought a fugitive and cloistered virtue; his characters, as Johnson said of Gilbert Walmsley, mingle in the great world without exemption from its follies and its vices. He loves their activities; he sets them going and follows their whirring motion with the ruthless gaiety of a child playing with toys, who stops them, breaks them, and sometimes sets them going again. He understands mechanics and they must move, and when they are run down in one book he winds them up again for another; he hurries hither and thither, clutching at the skirts of perpetual motion like that other pageant master, Time. His scene is the capitals of Europe or a railway train between them, and he shares with his characters, of whatever age, their brilliant and childish youth. He invents untiringly, and seldom vexes himself or his readers with description; but if he pauses to paint he paints with unmistakable bright colours. He writes clearly: there is seldom a slovenly sentence, never a memorable one. He has a cruelly accurate ear for slang, and presents vulgarity with fond verisimilitude. Femininity haunts him, his flowers, even, remind him of frills; for something of extreme youth clings to his books—its zestfulness, curiosity, indiscriminateness, and its unregretful volatility. But when, you may ask, remembering at once his gifts and his opportunities, his gifts and the world amid which they are exercised, when will he grow up? When, rather, will he grow down and strike first roots into the dark earth of the mind? When, amid all his brisk preoccupations with men and women, will he touch life?

Leaving generalisation, it is interesting to look at one of the simplest of Mr. Mackenzie's novels, *Guy and Pauline*, published in 1915, and conspicuously dedicated to the Commander-in-Chief and the General Staff of the Mediterranean Expeditionary Force. It is the story of Guy Hazlewood (wound up again after *Sinister Street*) and a rector's daughter. Guy, returned from Macedonian Relief Fund work, is charmed by a watery Oxfordshire house called Plashers Mead, and settles there to write poetry. The rectory family are his neighbours, and with the rector's daughters, Margaret, Monica, and Pauline, he quickly obtains a brotherly footing, and then becomes engaged to the youngest. The rector is a shadowy gardener with a singular fondness for answering every question, upon whatever subject and of whatever importance, by a reference to a blossoming or decaying plant; an idiosyncrasy which is supposed to endear him to his family. And it is an "endearing" book, for everybody is unvaryingly sweet; the adjective is as common and as adhesive as mud. The three girls form a group of the kind for which the far more finely observant and delicate art of Miss Viola Meynell (among living novelists) has already obtained and exhausted our sympathy; and ungracious as the comparison must seem to both writers, it is irresistible and fatal. Linked sweetness too long drawn out becomes tiresome, and the indistinct softness of the style makes the book something more than tiresome.

> Pauline hurried through a shower to church on Easter morning, and shook mingled tears and raindrops from herself when she saw that Guy was come to Communion. So then that angel had travelled from her bedside last night to hover over Guy and bid him wake early next morning, because it was Easter Day. With never so holy a calm had she knelt in the jewelled shadows of that chancel or returned from the altar to find her pew imparadised. When the people came out of church the sun was shining, and on the trees and on the tombstones a multitude of birds were singing. Never had Pauline felt the spirit of Eastertide uplift her with such a joy, joy for her lover beside her, joy for summer close at hand, joy for all the joy that Easter could bring to the soul.

Elsewhere:

> The apple trees were already frilled with a foam of blossom; and on quivering boughs linnets with breasts rose-burnt by the winds of March throbbed out their carol. Chaffinches with flashing prelude of silver wings flourished a burst of song that broke as with too intolerable a triumph: then sought another tree and poured forth the triumphant song again. Thrushes, blackbirds, and warblers quired deep-throated melodies against the multitudinous trebles of those undistinguished myriads that with choric pæan saluted May; and on sudden diminuendoes could be heard the rustling canzonets of the gold-finches, rising and falling with reedy cadences.

The story is clogged by Guy's meditations upon "poetical ambition"—he is in the early 'twenties—and yet, with all these grievous handicaps, it survives with sufficient force to express the poignancy with which an incomplete passion may sink to oblivion. In Pauline, Mr. Mackenzie has succeeded in showing with simplicity and truth the quick development of a child to a passionate, then a despairing, and at last a forsaken woman; and in Guy the æsthetic frog swollen to a fraction larger than his nature and then relapsing into insignificance. I am not sure that the best of this novelist's achievement is not seen in the isolation of these characters, the sufficiency of quiet incident, and the sense—faintly yet perceptibly communicated—that the tragedy of separation is implicit in the persons of his story. The atmosphere may seem close, the setting fanciful, scenes, characters, and action diminished and slightly prettified; yet there is genuine movement, rise and decline. The occasion of Guy's last parting from Pauline is worth noting, if only because Guy happens to be but the present name of Mr. Mackenzie's invariable young man from Oxford; let it be remembered, however, that Guy reappears years after in *Sylvia and Michael* as a larger shadow and dies with the Serbians before Nish.

> "Even if temporarily I were interested in another girl, you may be quite sure that she would always be second to you."
>
> "But you might be interested?" Pauline asked breathlessly.
>
> "I must be free if I'm going to be an artist."
>
> "Free?" she echoed slowly.

There remains a negative merit. If the artist, as a hundred critics have asserted and a thousand authors forgotten, is proved by what he omits, it must be counted to Mr. Mackenzie for a virtue that this book of four hundred pages does not contain a single seduction, and that, despite the obvious piquancy of a contrast between Plashers Mead and a London night-club, he has so easily and so blessedly avoided it.

III

. . . *Sinister Street* is vast in size and meagre in content; it is packed with superfluities. Three-fourths of it is inessential to the author's declared intention; it is no more than a guide-book cleverly designed (*e.g.* the first week at Oxford) to evoke an illusion of Oxford in Pimlico and Shepherd's Bush; and concentrating upon the remaining fourth, you feel that your author has been aware of little more than the physiology of adolescence and the usual facile religious reactions. Boys from seventeen to twenty-three, girls from sixteen to any age, may find in Henry Meats *alias* Brother Aloysius, in Arthur Wilmot the last of the Decadents, in the Lilys and the Daisys of the streets, in the whole rank multitude of Mr. Mackenzie's "underworld," the irritation of sensation which adolescents naturally seek. Here may curiosity be half-satisfied, half-stimulated. A Guide to Prostitution could add little to the informations of *Sinister Street*: the dress, the habitation, even the finances of those who have "gone gay," are meticulously recorded. Passed, I am afraid, are the Orient promenade and the underground gilded sty, but their glory is not departed, it is merely transferred, and *Sinister Street* remains sufficiently lively and up to date to provoke the youngest and make the oldest feel young again. Do you ask why God gives brains for such a use? I cannot even guess. Mr. Mackenzie astonishingly blazons his book with Keats's famous analysis: "The imagination of a boy is healthy, and the mature imagination of a man is healthy; but there is a space of life between, in which the soul is in a ferment, etc."—an astonishing phrase for index to this book; whether used in simplicity or in subtle defiance, this also I cannot guess. Clear enough is it that what passes for imagination is no other than the froth of yeasty waves of youth. . . . It is a book written, if offence may be disavowed and avoided, by a boy for boys. Mr. Mackenzie himself, in his introductory letter, refers to his study of Russian writers (this in explanation of the length of his novels), and in his epilogical letter he apparently regards the book as a work of art. An author's opinion of his own intention is to be respected, for who shall challenge it? It does but afford an additional ground for judgment and surprise.

IV

To consider *Sinister Street* a mere aberration is an extravagant possibility, but possibility itself is left panting behind *Sylvia Scarlett*. Here, again, the author is generous of space, and here he has not been content to write a guide-book; he has chosen a woman for his central figure, and she, unlike the male protagonists of the other books, is no coloured cloudy reflection of a reflection. She is no minikin Michael or Guy or Maurice, but a semblable moving figure. Sinister Street is her place of origin, Vanity Fair her scene of action—a world of music-halls where farce passes for fantasy and women's dress for an exciting theme. Farce? Sylvia is not only farcical in herself, but is, like Falstaff, creative—the cause of farce in others; and though Book One opens so admirably with a paragraph showing how well the author can follow a good model, farce ensues and recurs and makes her chronicle an amusing thing.

But it is amusing only so long as coarseness is not strained through a child's mind, coarseness of phrase only or more significant coarseness of invention. I say more significant, for whether that worse coarseness is intended or involuntary must be immaterial, save as indicating the particular code against which the offence is primarily committed, the code of manners or the code of art. There is here no such gentleness in the treatment of childhood as distinguishes the earlier chapters of *Carnival.* . . . The point need not be stressed. I dislike the current practice of setting one's wits against the author whose work happens to be the subject of discussion; I do not want to produce an artificial dilemma and pretend that Mr. Mackenzie is inevitably trapped by it. Put it, then, that there are certain obligations of civilised life, and certain obligations of that flower of civilised life which we call art; put it that an irrelevant coarseness of phrase or incident outrages the former, and that an intention to commit such an outrage, or an insensibility of having committed it, is equally an offence against the less assertive but not less imperative obligations of art. In a word, the sin is vulgarity, two-edged vulgarity it may be, an offence against both canons or, if you will, both conventions; and the further weight hangs on the charge that it is here committed in the person of a child and is, therefore, wanton. Shall I add that the immanence of farce just spoken of does in a little degree mitigate the cruelty by generalising the vulgarity? Here is rude, healthy Smollett out-Smolletted, reduced to the uncostly and only half-odious horseplay of a music-hall:

> The encouragement put a fine spirit into Danny's blows; he hammered the unfortunate Cohen round and round the room, upsetting table and chairs and washstand until with a stinging blow he knocked him backwards into the slop-pail, in which he sat so heavily that when he tried to rise the slop-pail stuck and gave him the appearance of a large baboon crawling with elevated rump on all fours. Danny kicked off the slop-pail, and invited Cohen to stand up to him; but when he did get on his feet, he ran to the door and reached the stairs just as Mrs. Gonner was wearily ascending to find out what was happening. He tried to stop himself by clutching the knob of the baluster, which broke; the result was that he dragged Mrs. Gonner with him in a glissade which ended behind the counter. The confusion in the shop became general; Mr. Gonner cut his thumb, and the sight of the blood caused a woman who was eating a sausage to choke; another customer took advantage of the row to snatch a side of bacon and try to escape, but another customer with a finer moral sense prevented him; a dog who was sniffing in the entrance saw the bacon on the floor and tried to seize it, but getting his tail trodden upon by somebody, he took fright and bit a small boy, who was waiting to change a shilling into coppers. Meanwhile Sylvia, who expected every minute that Jubie and her pugilistic brother would come back and increase the confusion with possibly unpleasant consequences for herself, took advantage of Danny's being occupied in an argument with Cohen and the two Gonners to put on her hat and escape from the shop. She jumped on the first omnibus and congratulated herself when she looked round and saw a policeman entering the eating-house.

Sylvia herself is capable enough as well as universally attractive. The citation just made is from a passage following the second amorous attack upon her, when Danny Lewis threatens her with a knife, and she parries with the water in her bedroom. An earlier lover had retired from a similar contest with his underlip bitten through. When, some time after the knife-and-water episode, Sylvia meets the Oxford type in Philip Iredale, she is sent by him (being still but sixteen) for a year's schooling and then marries him. Coquetting with the Church is followed by flight—alone, it must be added; and indeed Sylvia's whole recorded life is fugitive, a pilgrimage between this world and some other. Three months later her husband's Oxford composure is shocked by:

> "You *must* divorce me now. I've not been able to earn enough to pay you back more than this [ten pounds] for your bad bargain. I don't think I've given any more pleasure to the men who have paid less for me than you did, if that's any consolation."

Adventures repeat themselves. A huge Russian officer bursts into Sylvia's room one night and is pitched out of the window by a couple of acrobats. The war begins and spreads itself over Europe as a background for her passages and parleyings; and maybe the Commander-in-Chief and the General Staff of the Mediterranean Expeditionary Force have beguiled many a tiresome after-war hour in pursuing Sylvia's wanderings between places familiarised by their own late anxieties. Sylvia is differentiated from the other women of these novels, not only by her superior capacity for experiences, but even more by her superior volubility. She is, consciously, mind as well as body, and as the narrative goes on and on she develops a passion for monologue—terrifying in any woman, and rare among women whose occupation Sylvia Scarlett's own name is perhaps meant assonantally to suggest. These monologues, recurrent as the farce and more deadly, might be called shortly the jargon. "I represent the original conception of the Hetæra," she asserts.

> "He'll think of me, if he ever thinks of me at all, as one of the great multitude of wronged women. I shall think of him, though as a matter of fact I shall avoid thinking of him, either as what might have been—a false concept, for, of course, what might have been is fundamentally inconceivable—or as what he was—a sentimental fool."

She meditates upon the art of Botticelli, whose appeal she seems to think is only childlike, upon the conflict of nationality with civilisation. She reads Tolstoi and Dostoieffsky, putting Apuleius by, goes to confession, analyses her sensations, details the errancy of her parentage, and seeks to shock the priest who, when Sylvia acutely suggests that God is "almost vulgarly anthropomorphic," can only murmur, "Are not five sparrows sold for two farthings, and not one of them is forgotten before God?" But here is a brief specimen of the almost unbroken monologue to which the priest of the wisest of the churches can make no answer but a profession of the power of the Church:

> "I suppose my running away was the direct result of my bringing up, because whenever I had been brought face to face with a difficult situation I ran away. However, this time I was determined from some perverted pride to make myself more utterly myself than I had ever done. It's hard to explain how my mind worked. You must remember I was only nineteen, and already at thirty-one I am as far from understanding all my motives then as if I were trying to understand somebody who was not myself at all. Anyhow, I simply went on the streets. For three months I mortified my flesh by being a harlot. Can you understand that? Can you possibly understand the deliberate infliction of such a discipline, not to humiliate one's pride but to exalt it? Can you understand that I emerged from that three months of incredible horror with a complete personality? . . ."
>
> Sylvia did not wait for the priest to answer this question, partly because she did not want to be disillusioned by finding so soon that he had not comprehended anything of her emotions or actions, partly because there seemed more important revelations of herself still to be made.

—Farce at least is unpretentious, but this crude jargon, this retroverted intellectualism, is offensive beyond farce, odious beyond "delicate indecency."

V

It may not be wholly due to perversity if the characteristics of these long biographical novels should overshadow the sharp merits of, say, *Carnival*. *Carnival*, even better than *Guy and Pauline*, may serve as a measure of Mr. Mackenzie's decline from his promise; since although its conclusion is a disharmony, its best chapters are good enough to cause a reader to sigh over the later novels. Was it, indeed, quite a worthless aim to follow in the footsteps of George Gissing? *Carnival* suggests that a new Gissing might have grown up before our eyes, with a touch of the same veracity, the same mordancy, and a little less than the same humourless and dishumoured regard for what is wry and hapless; but *Carnival* stands alone, and the exactions of that difficult sincerity have been put by. . . . Or take, again, *Poor Relations*, one of Mr. Mackenzie's later inventions. With its ease and brilliant vivacities, with the comedy of its conception, what a delightful play it would make! But might not the comedy have depended—as comedy must—more surely upon character and less upon incident? The author of *Sylvia Scarlett* has imposed a too-swift facility upon the author of *Poor Relations*. If practice makes perfect, then nothing was wanting to the completeness of *Poor Relations*—but how much is wanting! Admirable are the opening notes, but of the rest too much is a brisk falsetto. There is excess in the situations, excess in the characterisation, excess in the style:

> When he looked at the old lady he could not discover anything except a cold egotism in every fold of those flabby cheeks where the powder lay like drifted snow in the ruts of a sunless lane.

It is equally the virtue and the fault of Mr. Mackenzie that he provokes melancholy regrets, even in the middle of frequent chuckles; and when the chuckling has died away the shadow of *Sylvia Scarlett* falls upon the book, just as with the same unhappy denigration it is flung backwards over the better qualities of the earlier *Carnival*.

Yet *Poor Relations*, like *Guy and Pauline*, is free from what we have seen to be the worst flaw of the longer novels, the crude determination to shock, which breaks most starkly through the superficialities of *Sylvia Scarlett*. That, to revert to our broad and primitive distinction, is a breach of the code of art rather than the code of morals, an eruptive *épatisme* which would disfigure a better book, if it could be found there. Can you conceive a more attractive subject, if you are but three-and-twenty, than the philosophic harlot? Or an easier? I do not suppose that it is less interesting to be on the streets than to be in the Ministry of Labour; neither occupation can be objectionable as subject of a novel. It would be untrue to say that the subject of a novel is a thing of complete indifference, and that the treatment is everything; for a writer would not do wisely to forfeit the advantage which a subject might offer him. But neither would he do wisely in exploiting a subject only to excite the curiosity or astonish the simplicity of his reader. Merely adventitious at best is the gain. It is to reduce subject and treatment to their lowest terms, and reject the implicit conditions which confront every writer who would explore the imaginative world where there can be no laws save honour,

loyalty, and delicacy. The scientific writer is secured against deceiving himself or his readers for long; his assumptions can be verified, his deductions precisely analysed, his whole professions rationally weighed. The imaginative and the quasi-imaginative writer have no such security, nor their readers such protection. Traditional values may be inapplicable, and it is hard to discriminate novelty from originality; a book that shocks may be as profoundly conceived as *Jude the Obscure*, as cheaply fashioned as *Sylvia Scarlett*. Incident may be prodigal equally in Dostoieffsky and Mr. Compton Mackenzie, but significance of incident may vary infinitely. Mr. Mackenzie's incidents have no significance; they remain incidents. His thoughts are significant only in so far as they indicate a modern intellectual disvertebration; his view of character is significant only in so far as it betrays an adolescent apprehension. Who is Sylvia? you ask, and your author is silent. What is she? and the answer is dispersed among eight hundred garrulous pages.

VI

Yes, it must be repeated, Mr. Mackenzie has conspicuous gifts, and as the letters with which *Sinister Street* opens and closes indicate, he is aware of them, and has not undertaken these enormous fictions without a sense of his task. But he has too often accepted the easier way. He can invest his scene with an illusion of activity, if not of reality, but he is unable to picture reality, for he does not distinguish; neither does he create a reality, a world for himself, amenable to its own laws, establishing its own consistency. That would be a wonderful but a hard thing. Amid the booths of his Vanity Fair he moves, not soberly and critically as Christian and Faithful moved, but as one swiftly enchanted by externals. He approaches the field of imaginative art, and I cannot say that his powers and pretensions are such as must discourage entry; but for imagination he learns to substitute invention, chooses the superficial, and does not even trouble to secure the consistency of his characters. He might have chosen otherwise. His alertness, his preoccupation with externals, his fullness of incident, his soft fluency of style might have been flogged into subordination; he need not have been very serious to have taken his work seriously. But all that he promises now is, if the tempting derangement of a line by a modern poet be pardonable:

> A torment of intolerable tales.

Mr. Mackenzie has divagated. The task of presenting reality is left to the scientific mind, and the task of creating another reality is left to the poetic mind.

All this, I must frankly say, was written before *The Seven Ages of Woman* appeared, with its reminder that Mr. Mackenzie's instability makes expectation foolish. *The Seven Ages of Woman* shows a happy avoidance of the shocking, for he has compelled his hand to the simplest of chronicles, the chronicle of a life that opens in 1860 and has not closed with the story in 1920. The simple narrative is a pleasure to read, even when it is remembered that precisely the same chronological device was used by Miss May Sinclair (in *Harriet Frean*) a year or two ago, with a touch far firmer and an effect, it must be owned, much more gloomy. A falsetto note still pierces the dialogue, the development is still unsteady, but there are passages of truth and tenderness which one is surprised and thankful to discover.

Louis MacNeice

1907–1963

The son of an Anglican clergyman, Louis MacNeice was born in Belfast on September 12, 1907. His mother died when he was seven, and at ten he was sent to school in England. After attending Marlborough College he studied at Merton College, Oxford, from 1926 to 1930. In 1929 he edited *Oxford Poetry: 1929* with Stephen Spender, and had his first solo publication with the poems *Blind Fireworks*. In the 1930s he taught classics at Birmingham University and Bedford College, London, and was associated with Spender, C. Day Lewis, and W. H. Auden, with whom he visited Iceland in 1937 and published the travel book *Letters from Iceland*. His poetry in these years included the volumes *Poems* (1935), *The Earth Compels* (1938), and *Autumn Journal* (1939). His translation of the *Agamemnon* by Aeschylus was produced in London in 1936.

In 1941 MacNeice joined the BBC as a scriptwriter and producer, remaining in this capacity until 1954. His feature programs were at first aimed at clarifying the moral issues of World War II, and his application to radio as a medium led to such dramas as *The Dark Tower* (1947), with music by Benjamin Britten, and *Prisoner's Progress*, which won the Premio Italiano in 1954. His translation with Ernst Stahl of Goethe's *Faust* was broadcast in 1949, and published the following year. In 1950–51 he was director of the British Institute in Athens, Greece, and in 1954 he toured America with his second wife, a singer, giving poetry readings and song recitals. He was made a CBE in 1958, and died in London on September 3, 1963.

MacNeice's later poetry includes *Ten Burnt Offerings* (1952), *Autumn Sequel* (1954), *Visitations* (1957), *Solstices* (1959), and, posthumously, *The Burning Perch* (1963). *Collected Poems* appeared in 1966.

Personal

. . . ⟨I⟩n 1948, after seven years in the BBC, MacNeice was one of its most distinguished writer-producers. From the start, Archie Harding and Laurence Gilliam felt that they had a great 'catch', and by 1948 the official *Year Book* accorded him a 'Profile'. 'At the coming of peace he . . . continued to explore broadcasting as a medium of publication without ceasing to write and publish poetry and criticism. It was an important decision, and on its results depend to a large extent the direction and quality of original imaginative writing for radio in this country.' There are some personal touches too: 'one who walks by himself . . . his stillness, as he watches and listens at Lord's or Twickenham, in a Delhi bazaar or a Dublin pub . . . some are perturbed by his presence, call him aloof. Actors love the sinewy quality of his writing for speech, the sharp contemporary tang of his scholar-poet's idiom.' The picture is supplemented by other people's memories.

Auden made an acute comment, after MacNeice's death: 'On anybody who did not know him well and had never witnessed his powers of concentration and the rapidity of his mind, the first impression must have been of a lazy over-gregarious man who spent more time than he should pub-crawling.' He did enjoy the pubs, but he would peer carefully around the door of the Stag or the George before entering, so that he would not be saddled with the company of some bore. He might stay silent for hours, but his presence added something positive to the company. Another Features producer was Michael Barsley who wrote *Those Vintage Years of Radio*, in collaboration with John Snagge. 'Louis was one of the quietest and best-mannered of a rowdy bunch of writers and producers, and since he was Irish this seemed a remarkable thing. He would as soon have beer as wine or spirits, and was often to be found at lunch-time in "The George". . . . His voice was slow and rather nasal, and he had a way of curling his lip in argument as if slightly contemptuous, which was quite

unlike him, unless the contempt was deserved. His passionate hobby was, of all things, following and watching Rugby football.' MacNeice looked distinguished, usually elegant in tweeds; his sense of humour was real, though often slow to reveal itself, and it could be laconic and caustic. Some people thought him shy, some aloof; neither adjective is quite accurate.

Despite appearances, he was able to work hard and meticulously, and he could work anywhere, cutting himself off from surrounding noise and distraction. He enjoyed the company of all kinds of people, if they were not boring or pretentious. He kept his poetry private, but he was always observing. He could communicate a warmth, but he could take a long time to get to know someone. The writer Dan Davin first met MacNeice late in 1948, introduced to him by Jack Dillon; he recalls this in *Closing Times*. 'There was no instant exchange of liking, no immediate synapsis. He was wary of new men. . . . When he talked it was, as it were, through interpreters, distanced by formal courtesy and protocol.' Even after a night of drinking in company with Bertie Rodgers and Dylan Thomas, in Oxford in 1949, the distance persisted. 'They were all three very tight. . . . Dylan boisterous, Bertie portentously grave, and Louis' normal vigilant taciturnity betrayed by the fixture of his smile.' It was Louis who realised that Dan Davin was uneasy, probably because he was sober, and who tried to redress the imbalance by getting him a quick succession of drinks.

In September 1948 MacNeice went to Ireland for the reburial of Yeats in Sligo, in Drumcliffe churchyard. Maurice Collis's lively account of this tells how his brother gave MacNeice a lift in his car. 'MacNeice had many friends in Dublin and was lavishly entertained by them on the evening of the 16th.' So he turned up an hour late in FitzWilliam Square, his eyes not quite open. He sat in the back of the car with Maurice Craig: 'for all the poets of Ireland, great and small, were setting out for Yeats's funeral that day.' After lunch in

Sligo the cortège started for Drumcliffe, in pouring rain; a clouded Ben Bulben provided a backcloth for a desolate scene. The occasion was not as solemn, Collis says, as Yeats would have liked, what with the rain, and the umbrellas and a slight difficulty in lowering the coffin into the grave. MacNeice added a bizarre touch by insisting that it was the wrong body—a Frenchman with a club foot, he maintained, had been dug up by mistake. 'Can't do anything now, he said. Everyone then went back to the hotel for tea.'—BARBARA COULTON, "From India to 'Faust,'" *Louis MacNeice in the BBC*, 1980, pp. 105–7

General

If you read current literary journalism you will be able to rattle off a string of names—Day Lewis, Auden, Spender, Isherwood, Louis MacNeice and so on. They adhere much more closely than the names of their predecessors. But at first sight there seems little difference, in station, in education. Mr. Auden in a poem written to Mr. Isherwood says: Behind us we have stucco suburbs and expensive educations. They are tower dwellers like their predecessors, the sons of well-to-do parents, who could afford to send them to public schools and universities. But what a difference in the tower itself, in what they saw from the tower! When they looked at human life what did they see? Everywhere change; everywhere revolution. In Germany, in Russia, in Italy, in Spain, all the old hedges were being rooted up; all the old towers were being thrown to the ground. Other hedges were being planted; other towers were being raised. There was communism in one country; in another fascism. The whole of civilization, of society, was changing. There was, it is true, neither war nor revolution in England itself. All those writers had time to write many books before 1939. But even in England towers that were built of gold and stucco were no longer steady towers. They were leaning towers. The books were written under the influence of change, under the threat of war. That perhaps is why the names adhere so closely; there was one influence that affected them all and made them, more than their predecessors, into groups. And that influence, let us remember, may well have excluded from that string of names the poets whom posterity will value most highly, either because they could not fall into step, as leaders or as followers, or because the influence was adverse to poetry, and until that influence relaxed, they could not write. But the tendency that makes it possible for us to group the names of these writers together, and gives their work a common likeness, was the tendency of the tower they sat on—the tower of middle-class birth and expensive education—to lean.

Let us imagine, to bring this home to us, that we are actually upon a leaning tower and note our sensations. Let us see whether they correspond to the tendencies we observe in those poems, plays and novels. Directly we feel that a tower leans we become acutely conscious that we are upon a tower. All those writers too are acutely tower conscious; conscious of their middle-class birth; of their expensive educations. Then when we come to the top of the tower how strange the view looks—not altogether upside down, but slanting, sidelong. That too is characteristic of the leaning-tower writers; they do not look any class straight in the face; they look either up, or down, or sidelong. There is no class so settled that they can explore it unconsciously. That perhaps is why they create no characters. Then what do we feel next, raised in imagination on top of the tower? First discomfort; next self-pity for that discomfort; which pity soon turns to anger—to anger against the builder, against society, for making us uncomfortable. Those too seem to be tendencies of the leaning-tower writers.

Discomfort; pity for themselves; anger against society. And yet—here is another tendency—how can you altogether abuse a society that is giving you after all a very fine view and some sort of security? You cannot abuse that society wholeheartedly while you continue to profit by that society. And so very naturally you abuse society in the person of some retired admiral or spinster or armament manufacturer; and by abusing them hope to escape whipping yourself. The bleat of the scapegoat sounds loud in their work, and the whimper of the schoolboy crying 'Please Sir it was the other fellow, not me.' Anger; pity; scapegoat beating; excuse finding;—these are all very natural tendencies; if we were in their position we should tend to do the same. But we are not in their position; we have not had eleven years of expensive education. We have only been climbing an imaginary tower. We can cease to imagine. We can come down.

But they cannot. They cannot throw away their education; they cannot throw away their upbringing. Eleven years at school and college have been stamped upon them indelibly. And then, to their credit but to their confusion, the leaning tower not only leant in the thirties, but it leant more and more to the left. Do you remember what Mr. MacCarthy said about his own group at the university in 1914? 'We were not very much interested in politics . . . philosophy was more interesting to us than public causes'? That shows that his tower leant neither to the right nor to the left. But in 1930 it was impossible--if you were young, sensitive, imaginative—not to be interested in politics; not to find public causes of much more pressing interest than philosophy. In 1930 young men at college were forced to be aware of what was happening in Russia; in Germany; in Italy; in Spain. They could not go on discussing æsthetic emotions and personal relations. They could not confine their reading to the poets; they had to read the politicians. They read Marx. They became communists; they became anti-fascists. The tower they realized was founded upon injustice and tyranny; it was wrong for a small class to possess an education that other people paid for; wrong to stand upon the gold that a bourgeois father had made from his bourgeois profession. It was wrong; yet how could they make it right? Their education could not be thrown away; as for their capital—did Dickens, did Tolstoy ever throw away their capital? Did D. H. Lawrence, a miner's son, continue to live like a miner? No; for it is death for a writer to throw away his capital; to be forced to earn his living in a mine or a factory. And thus, trapped by their education, pinned down by their capital they remained on top of their leaning tower, and their state of mind as we see it reflected in their poems and plays and novels are full of discord and bitterness, full of confusion and of compromise.

These tendencies are better illustrated by quotation than by analysis. There is a poem, by one of those writers, Louis MacNeice, called *Autumn Journal*. It is dated March 1939. It is feeble as poetry, but interesting as autobiography. He begins of course with a snipe at the scapegoat—the bourgeois, middle-class family from which he sprang. The retired admirals, the retired generals and the spinster lady have breakfasted off bacon and eggs served on a silver dish, he tells us. He sketches that family as if it were already a little remote and more than a little ridiculous. But they could afford to send him to Marlborough and then to Merton, Oxford. This is what he learnt at Oxford:

> We learned that a gentleman never misplaces his
> accents,
> That nobody knows how to speak, much less how to
> write
> English who has not hob-nobbed with the great-
> grandparents of English.

Besides that he learnt at Oxford Latin and Greek; and philosophy, logic and metaphysics:

> Oxford he says crowded the mantelpiece with gods—
> Scaliger, Heinsius, Dindorf, Bentley, Wilamowitz.

It was at Oxford that the tower began to lean. He felt that he was living under a system—

> That gives the few at fancy prices their fancy lives
> While ninety-nine in the hundred who never attend
> the banquet
> Must wash the grease of ages off the knives.

But at the same time, an Oxford education had made him fastidious:

> It is so hard to imagine
> A world where the many would have their chance
> without
> A fall in the standard of intellectual living
> And nothing left that the highbrow cares about.

At Oxford he got his honours degree; and that degree—in humane letters—put him in the way of a 'cushy job'—seven hundred a year, to be precise, and several rooms of his own.

> If it were not for Lit. Hum. I might be climbing
> A ladder with a hod
> And seven hundred a year
> Will pay the rent and the gas and the phone and the
> grocer—

And yet, again, doubts break in; the 'cushy job' of teaching more Latin and Greek to more undergraduates does not satisfy him—

> the so-called humane studies
> May lead to cushy jobs
> But leave the men who land them spiritually
> bankrupt,
> Intellectual snobs.

And what is worse, that education and that cushy job cut one off, he complains, from the common life of one's kind.

> All that I would like to be is human, having a share
> In a civilized, articulate and well-adjusted
> Community where the mind is given its due
> But the body is not distrusted.

Therefore, in order to bring about that well-adjusted community he must turn from literature to politics, remembering, he says,

> Remembering that those who by their habit
> Hate politics, can no longer keep their private
> Values unless they open the public gate
> To a better political system.

So, in one way or another, he takes part in politics, and finally he ends:

> What is it we want really?
> For what end and how?
> If it is something feasible, obtainable,
> Let us dream it now,
> And pray for a possible land
> Not of sleep-walkers, not of angry puppets,
> But where both heart and brain can understand
> The movements of our fellows
> Where life is a choice of instruments and none
> Is debarred his natural music . . .
> Where the individual, no longer squandered
> In self-assertion, works with the rest

Those quotations give a fair description of the influences that have told upon the leaning-tower group. Others could easily be discovered. The influence of the films explains the lack of transitions in their work and the violently opposed contrasts. The influence of poets like Mr. Yeats and Mr. Eliot explains the obscurity. They took over from the elder poets a technique which, after many years of experiment, those poets used skilfully, and used it clumsily and often inappropriately. But we have time only to point to the most obvious influences; and these can be summed up as Leaning Tower Influences. If you think of them, that is, as people trapped on a leaning tower from which they cannot descend, much that is puzzling in their work is easier to understand. It explains the violence of their attack upon bourgeois society and also its half-heartedness. They are profiting by a society which they abuse. They are flogging a dead or dying horse because a living horse, if flogged, would kick them off its back. It explains the destructiveness of their work; and also its emptiness. They can destroy bourgeois society, in part at least; but what have they put in its place? How can a writer who has no first-hand experience of a towerless, of a classless society create that society? Yet as Mr. MacNeice bears witness, they feel compelled to preach, if not by their living, at least by their writing, the creation of a society in which every one is equal and every one is free. It explains the pedagogic, the didactic, the loud speaker strain that dominates their poetry. They must teach; they must preach. Everything is a duty—even love.—VIRGINIA WOOLF, "The Leaning Tower," *FNW*, Autumn 1940, pp. 20–26

Mrs. Woolf, in her article 'The Leaning Tower,' looks forward to a classless society which will give to writers 'a mind no longer crippled, evasive, divided. They may inherit that unconsciousness which . . . is necessary if writers are to get beneath the surface, and to write something that people remember when they are alone.' With this general aim or hope I sympathize. 'Literature,' I would agree with her, 'is no one's private ground.' I find it, therefore, both inconsistent and unjust that she should dismiss not only so lightly, but so acidly—as 'the embittered and futile tribe of scapegoat hunters'—that group of younger writers who during the Thirties made it their business to stigmatize those all too present evils which Mrs. Woolf herself considers evil and to open those doors which she herself wants opened. She seems to understand these junior colleagues of hers no better than Yeats understood Eliot. This mutual misunderstanding of the literary generations is one of the evils of our times; my own generation has too often been unjust to its immediate predecessors.

Mrs. Woolf's literary history is over-simplified. She writes of the social divisions of the nineteenth century: 'the nineteenth-century writer did not seek to change those divisions; he accepted them. He accepted them so completely that he became unconscious of them.' Confining ourselves to our own literature and leaving aside all foreigners—the Russians, for example, or Zola—we might ask her what about Shelley whom she herself has mentioned by name. Or what about Wordsworth whose early inspiration was 'Nature' admittedly but Nature harnessed to a revolutionary social doctrine? And even with the great Victorians 'All's well with the world' was not their most typical slogan; is *In Memoriam* a poem of placid or unconscious acceptance? 'Life was not going to change,' writes Mrs. Woolf; Tennyson said something different in 'Locksley Hall.' And what about William Morris? Or Henry James, for whom (according to Mrs. Woolf) as for (according to her too) his predecessors the social barometer was Set Fair for ever? Mr. Spender put forward a different, but at least as plausible a view of James in *The Destructive Element*.

Mrs. Woolf assumes that a period of great social and political unrest is adverse to literature. I do not think she produces adequate evidence for this; we could counter with the Peloponnesian War, the factions of Florence in the time of

Dante, the reign of Queen Elizabeth, the Franco-Prussian War; but, even if she is right, she should not attack my generation for being conditioned by its conditions. Do not let us be misled by her metaphor of the Tower. The point of this metaphor was that a certain group of young writers found themselves on a leaning tower; this presupposes that the rest of the world remained on the level. But it just didn't. The whole world in our time went more and more on the slant so that no mere abstract geometry or lyrical uplift could cure it. When Mrs. Woolf accuses the Thirties writers of 'flogging a dead or dying horse because a living horse, if flogged, would kick them off its back,' her point seems to me facile. No doubt we spent too much time in satirizing the Blimps, but some of those old dead horses—as this war shows every week—have a kick in them still. And the ruling class of the Thirties, the people above the Blimps, our especial *bête noir* or *cheval noir*, did manage to kick us into the jaws of destruction. But it remains to be seen who will be proved to have died; we'll hope it was the horse.

She proceeds to a surprising sentence: 'How can a writer who has no first-hand experience of a towerless, of a classless society create that society?' How can a larva with no first-hand experience of flight ever grow wings? On the premises implied in this sentence human society is incapable of willed or directed change. Because, quite apart from the intelligentsia and the privileged classes, there is nobody in the whole population of Great Britain who has had first-hand experience of that kind of society which nearly everybody needs. Mrs. Woolf is making the same mistake as some of the very writers she is attacking. For some of those writers were hamstrung by modesty. It all, they said to themselves, depends on the proletariat. And in a sense they were right. But they were wrong to assume that the proletariat itself knew where it was going or could get there by its own volition. These intellectuals tended to betray the proletariat by professing to take all their cues from it.

Mrs. Woolf deplores the 'didacticism' of the Thirties. But (1) if the world was such a mess as she admits, it was inevitable and right that writers should be didactic (compare the position of Euripides), (2) she assumes that this writing—especially the poetry—of the Thirties was solely and crudely didactic—which it was not. She makes an inept comparison between a morsel of Stephen Spender and a morsel of Wordsworth as exemplifying 'the difference between politician's poetry and poet's poetry': this ignores the fact that the great bulk of Wordsworth is pamphleteering and that Spender's poetry is pre-eminently the kind—to use her own words—'that people remember when they are alone.' Politician's poetry? Look at Spender's professedly political play, *Trial of a Judge*: it failed as a play just because it was not 'public' but rather a personal apologia; it displeased the Communists just because it sacrificed propaganda values to honesty.

It is often assumed by the undiscriminating—among whom for this occasion I must rank Mrs. Woolf—that all these writers of the Thirties were the slaves of Marx, or rather of Party Line Marxism. Marx was certainly a most powerful influence. But why? It was not because of his unworkable economics, it was not because of the pedantic jigsaw of his history, it was because he said: '*Our job is to change it.*' What called a poet like Spender to Marx was the same thing that called Shelley to Godwin and Rousseau. But some at least of these poets—in particular Auden and Spender—always recognized the truth of Thomas Mann's dictum: 'Karl Marx must read Friedrich Hölderlin.' Even an orthodox Communist Party critic, Christopher Caudwell, in his book *Illusion and Reality*, insisted (rightly) that poetry can never be reduced to political advertis-

ing, that its method is myth and that it must represent not any set of ideas which can be formulated by politicians or by scientists or by mere Reason and/or mere Will—it must represent something much deeper and wider which he calls the 'Communal Ego.' It is this Communal Ego with which Auden and Spender concerned themselves.

Politician's poetry? Yes, there was some of it; and some of it was bad. Rex Warner, for example, lost his touch when he turned from birds to polemics. Day Lewis's social satire cannot compare with his love lyrics. Auden and Isherwood's *On the Frontier* was worse than a flop. Mr. Edward Upward ruined his novel, *Journey to the Border*, with his use of the Deus ex Machina—i.e. 'the Workers'—at the end. But these mistakes are nothing to their achievements and it is grotesque to dismiss someone like Auden as a mere 'politician's poet' and an ineffectual one at that; was it not Auden who repudiated the Public Face in the Private Place? It is carrying the Nelson eye too far to pretend that Auden and Spender did not bring new life into English poetry and what was more—in spite of what Mrs. Woolf says about self-pity—a new spirit of hopefulness (see some of Spender's early lyrics). As for the novel, Mrs. Woolf suggests that, whereas her own generation could create objective character and colour, her successors can manage nothing but either autobiography or black and white cartoons. I would ask the reader—with no disrespect to *Mrs. Dalloway*, a book that I like very much—to compare Mrs. Woolf's 'Mrs. Dalloway' with Mr. Isherwood's 'Mr. Norris.'

Self-pity? Of course our work embodied some self-pity. But look at Mrs. Woolf's beloved nineteenth century. 'Anger, pity, scapegoat beating, excuse finding'—she intones against the poor lost Thirties; you find all those things—in full measure and running over—in the Romantic Revival and right down from *Manfred* or Keats' Odes through Tennyson and Swinburne and Rossetti to the death-wish of the Fin de Siècle and even to Mr. Prufrock. My generation at least put some salt in it. And we never, even at our most martyred, produced such a holocaust of self-pity as Shelley in *Adonais*.

Mrs. Woolf deplores our 'curious bastard language,' but I notice that in the next stage of society and poetry she looks forward to a 'pooling' of vocabularies and dialects. Just one more inconsistency. And Shakespeare wrote in a bastard language too.

This is no occasion to put forward a *Credo* of my own, but I would like to assure Mrs. Woolf (speaking for myself, but it is true of most of my colleagues) that I am not solely concerned with 'destruction.' Some destruction, yes; but not of all the people or all the values all the time. And I have no intention of recanting my past. Recantation is becoming too fashionable; I am sorry to see so much self-flagellation, so many *Peccavis*, going on on the literary Left. We may not have done all we could in the Thirties, but we did do something. We were right to throw mud at Mrs. Woolf's old horses and we were right to advocate social reconstruction and we were even right—in our more lyrical work—to give personal expression to our feelings of anxiety, horror and despair (for even despair can be fertile). As for the Leaning Tower, if Galileo had not had one at Pisa, he would not have discovered the truth about falling weights. We learned something of the sort from our tower too.—LOUIS MACNEICE, "The Tower That Once," *FNW*, Spring 1941, pp. 37–41

Works

The remarkable and important thing about MacNeice's poems is the style, not the substance. His style, his way of handling his subjects, at first seems a careful imitation of doggerel. One

notices the rocking-chair rhythm, the lines in which extra feet
are tucked in so that the rhyme can occur, and the almost naive
tone. Thus one poem begins:

> Down the road someone is practising scales,
> The notes like little fishes vanish with a wink of tails.

But it is soon clear that much is gained by this way of writing.
MacNeice is able to make his subject more and more explicit
and attain a full presentation, directness and clarity. The
contrary habit of most serious contemporary poetry, its obliqueness and allusiveness, and its effort to make everything
implicit, seems to have had its theoretical basis in the belief
that only through such means is the dramatic level attained.
This has led to a contempt for reflective experience, and
devotion to immediately felt experience, in contemporary
poetry. The lesson that MacNeice's poems make clear is worth
emphasizing. Style is crucial, particularly in its aspect of
rhythm. Much in the back of a poet's head is prevented from
coming to the page by certain styles, and much is released and
brought forth by other ways of writing. For example, Milton's
sonnets have little brilliance of metaphor, the ideas, though
respectable, are not discoveries, but through a mastery of
diction and metre, the sonnets are made to seem as if cut into
rock. Conversely, Hart Crane seems to have been muscle-
bound on the level of apostrophe because he wrote a "pre-
Websterian blank verse": he seems, that is, to be unable to
write about anything which he cannot become enormously
excited about. And MacNeice at times seems to be able to write
about everything. Such general statements as

> That people are lovable is a strange discovery

and

> The excess sugar of a diabetic culture
> Rotting the nerve of life and literature

fit in with

> I who was Harlequin in the childhood of the century,
> Posed by Picasso beside an endless opaque sea

and

> The lights irritating and gyrating and rotating in
>   gauze.

That is to say, MacNeice is able to step from judgment and
wide reference to the most concrete of impressions.

MacNeice is apparently a "student" of philosophy and of
modern painting. Several passages remind us that "Time is not
stone nor still his wings", and not to part asunder "The
marriage of Cause and Effect, Form and Content." And
repeatedly he uses painters: "I, like Poussin, make a stillbound
fête of us;" not only explicitly, but also in his mode of
description, which has thick bold strokes, as of Van Gogh or
Rouault, so that the traffic lights are *crème de menthe* or bull's
blood, the moon's glare is orange, the sheep are like grey stones
and clouds are like Zeppelins. MacNeice also tends to have his
own variety of despair, and the old sentimentality about how
life escapes the scholar but not the gardener, is present more
than once. In trying to maintain his tone, he falls to such
appalling usages as "consumptive Keatses," and in trying to use
brusque and broad metaphors, he even becomes silly:

> May his good deeds flung forth
> Like boomerangs return
> To wear around his neck
> As beads of definite worth.

MacNeice is perhaps too emphatically contemporary,
insisting again and again upon the wireless, the factory
chimneys, the policemen and the busses. Yet this is the main
interest of the substance of his poems, that the circumference is
always social and the center is always personal. And we find the
intrinsic half-known motive of all these poems to be the way in
which

> In your Chardin the appalling unrest of the soul
> Exudes from the dried fish and the brown jug and the
>   bowl.

—DELMORE SCHWARTZ, "Adroitly Naive,"
    Poetry, May 1936, pp. 115–17

Louis MacNeice is an exact contemporary of Auden's, but at
thirty has been far less prolific. He offers now a collection
which retains only four poems from his first volume, *Blind
Fireworks*, 1929, and adds to his volume of 1935 about fifteen
poems more. He showed his Irish sense of humor in choosing
the title for his early poems 'because they are artificial and yet
random; because they go quickly through their antics against
an important background, and fall and go out quickly.' The
short musical exercises that he has decided to keep from these
pieces possess what Eliot, in talking about Blake, recognized as
the more likely kind of promise; instead of crude efforts to
encompass something grandiose they are 'quite mature and
successful attempts to do something small.' The distance he
traveled between the less distinct remainder of that volume and
the *Poems* of 1935 is considerable. In the two years preceding
his second book he developed a distinguishing style, a rhythm
unmistakably his own. He seems to have profited most from
Hopkins in learning how to give to the conventional line a
more resilient conversational tone. But his feeling that Hopkins
was wrong to bind his sprung rhythm to the arbitrary frame of
an equal number of accented syllables for every line has
enabled MacNeice to gain a greater fluency, and a very deft
approximation to an actual speaking voice.

Although he was at Oxford at the same time as the group
of young English poets who have hitherto been more widely
discussed, MacNeice's course has been fairly independent of
theirs. His is not 'fighting' poetry. His impulse has not been
contentious and hortatory like Auden's; he has not joined
Spender in romantic proclamations of faith. He has recently
remarked: 'Poets are not legislators (what is an "unacknowledged legislator" anyway?), but they put facts and feelings in
italics, which make people think about them and such thinking
may in the end have an outcome in action.' Such an attitude
may seem too passive for much contemporary taste; and it has
not brought into poetry the wide subject matter of economics
and science which Auden's unflagging curiosity has explored,
nor the more mechanically manipulated culverts and pistons
and other modern properties of Day Lewis. In 'Turf-Stacks,'
written in 1932, MacNeice formulated his lack of political
position:

> For we are obsolete who like the lesser things
> Who play in corners with looking-glasses and beads;
> It is better we should go quickly, go into Asia
> Or any other tunnel where the world recedes,
> Or turn blind wantons like the gulls who scream
> And rip the edge off any ideal or dream.

But he has not embraced either of the alternatives offered in
that stanza, though ironically bitter contemplation of his own
country has brought him closer to the last one. He has never
made of poetry an easy vehicle for evasion, for although he has
a warm feeling for landscape, he knows that he always carries a
city-bred mind with him. He has, however, set himself fairly
deliberately to writing descriptive poetry, as when he states in
'Train to Dublin':

> I give you the incidental things which pass
> Outwards through space exactly as each was.

He knows that this demands an exacting discipline. Unlike
most other poets who have been influenced by Eliot he has

learned and declared that 'You must walk before you can dance; you can't be a master of suggestion unless you are a master of description.' He has consequently evolved the neat craft of making the inner coherence of a poem depend on the subtle and precise interrelationships of a series of things observed. But success in this kind requires tightrope technique, for if any image asserts itself too vividly, the balance is quickly upset, and the whole effect falls into obtrusive fragments.

Nor is it conceivable that a poet could describe anything exactly as it was without betraying some point of view towards his material. MacNeice's frequent fascination with catching the effects of sunlight and smoke suggests that he has the eyes of a painter, but his interest is never confined merely to recording surface textures. In some passages he may reveal that

there is beauty narcotic and deciduous

in the very midst of the sinister chaos of a modern city. But though his subject matter is seldom political, he is increasingly aware of the social implications of what he sees. He quoted last fall: '"Other philosophies have described the world; our business is to change it." Add that if we are not interested in changing it, there is really very little to describe.' And the close of 'Eclogue from Iceland,' 1936, to which he traveled with Auden, finds him in a much more positive mood than that of the young Irish intellectual who, in 'Valediction,' had two years previously turned away from his own country in the manner traditional to the *Portrait of the Artist as a Young Man*. For in the 'Eclogue' the ghost of Grettir tells the two summer visitors that they had better go back to where they had come from, and that in spite of the enormous odds against their being able to make anything prevail:

Minute your gesture but it must be made—
Your hazard, your act of defiance and hymn of hate,
Hatred of hatred, assertion of human values,
Which is now your only duty . . .
Yes, my friends, it is your only duty.
And, it may be added, it is your only chance.

Notwithstanding the dramatic tension here, MacNeice's talent so far seems fundamentally lyrical. In saying that I bear in mind that he has already published a translation of the *Agamemnon* and a two-act play of his own, *Out of the Picture*. But whereas the translation displays a firm controlled simplicity that recreates much of the original passion, his own play is the one occasion where MacNeice seems to have collapsed into being affected by the least valuable elements in Auden, and has produced a loosely blurred mixture where it is hard to say whether the intention is satire or farce, since nothing comes through clear. Moreover, in his poems, MacNeice's continual subject is Time, conceived wholly in the lyric mode of dwelling on the moment's evanescence, as when he advises a Communist that before he proclaims the millennium, he had better regard the barometer—

This poise is perfect but maintained
For one day only.

Both his mind and imagery are so possessed with this theme that he finally tries to shake off his preoccupation by affirming that he does not always to be stressing either flux or permanence, that he does not want to be either 'a tragic or a philosophic chorus,' but to keep his eye 'only on the nearer future.' From the stuff of that 'nearer future' he makes his most balanced and proportioned poems.

In an ode for his son, which owes something to Yeats' 'A Prayer for My Daughter,' he would ward off from him the desire for any absolute 'which is too greedy and too obvious.' MacNeice cannot accept the 'easy bravery' of being 'drugged with a slogan,' and can hand on to his son neither decalogue

nor formula but only symbols, and those only so far as he can feel them emerge from close and concrete samples of experience. Most of all he would pray:

let him not falsify the world
By taking it to pieces;
The marriage of Cause and Effect, Form and
Content,
Let him not part asunder.

The desire for such fusion has found fulfillment in the architectural structure of many of his longer poems, and it is the chief evidence for MacNeice's skill as an artist that his clearest successes are in their complex harmonies rather than in his simpler short pieces. In 'Homage to Clichés,' for instance, he has devised and developed a series of repeated images to celebrate his delight in the familiar: the expected response of his companion is elicited as though by stroking a cat, or is angled from the stream of their conversation as the fish swim into the net and the drinks swim over the bar. Here his observations intermesh so intricately that even though you can take surprised delight in a single example:

an old man momentously sharpens a pencil as
though
He were not merely licking his fur like a cat,

it becomes the best tribute to the unity which the poet has created that no adequate illustration is possible short of the entire poem. For here his attitude is less bald than in the somewhat stagy declaration in his 'Epilogue' that he drinks Auden's health before 'the gun-butt raps upon the door.' For, in 'Homage to Clichés,' the perishable stuff of the everyday life which he relishes is embodied with such warm resilience that the undertone of the menacing future which he expects reverberates far more movingly than it would by means of any bare direct statement.

Where his dependence on oblique and symbolic images can fail him is when they are not reinforced by sufficiently mature experience. This is the trouble with the pictures of contemporary man and woman near the end of the 'Eclogue from Iceland.' The details by which they are presented do not bite deeply enough into actuality, they are too private and trivial. The fact that this can be the case in one of MacNeice's latest poems will be disturbing to those readers who believe that the artist must progress and offer with each new year a better-appointed model. But, despite the clarification and firming of his social attitude, it cannot be said that MacNeice's graph has gone continually upward. He seems to have remained on about the same level from the time that he hit his individual stride five years ago, and he may not yet have written a solider poem than the sardonic conversation between a city-dweller and a country-dweller, 'An Eclogue for Christmas,' in 1933. It must also be added that in spite of his realization, on the Iceland trip, that further travel could be productive only of more souvenirs and 'copy,' 1937 found him, not following Grettir's advice, but in the Hebrides, evolving another detached and sensitive descriptive poem about those islands.

It is undoubtedly true that MacNeice's conversational style is less socially useful to the needs of our day than the public speech that may be developed from Auden's exciting rhetoric. Nor does MacNeice possess the exuberance and inventiveness which Herbert Read believes Auden to have brought back into English poetry for the first time since Browning's death. On the other hand, MacNeice's richest resource is suggested in a curious remark which he made about Day Lewis, that he is an inferior poet to Auden 'perhaps because his vision is purer and more consistent.' He recognizes that Lewis, though doctrinally correct, can fall into both priggishness and diffuseness by his humorless preaching for the cause. MacNeice's own awareness that life 'is incorrigibly plural,' his deeper immersion in its complexities, his more unchecked reliance on the evidence of his senses, at times result in a vague softness. He does not have anything like the extraordinary range of technical dexterity with which Auden seemingly can take up or burlesque almost any kind of tradition from Skelton to Tennyson and Kipling. But MacNeice's control is far more matured, he rarely indulges in thin tours de force or slipshod virtuosity. And if the measurement is not by 'promise,' by brilliant passages standing out from obscurity, but by whole poems, which can be tested line for line and reread with accruing satisfaction, MacNeice's performance so far is ahead of that of his contemporaries.—F. O. MATTHIESSEN, "Louis MacNeice," *PR*, Feb. 1938, pp. 56–60

Louis MacNeice is one of the best poets of the present century, and one of the most neglected. Reading his *Collected Poems 1925–1948*, one asks oneself why this is. One also wonders why the collection, which first appeared in England fifteen years ago, has not been brought up to date for its first U.S. publication.

The probable reasons for the neglect of MacNeice throw some light on the state of poetry and criticism today. Although his poems are learned and rich in references to Latin, Greek, and other literatures—as well as to other arts, particularly painting—they offer no difficulty that is special to their being poems about these subjects. MacNeice maintains a tone of eloquent, elegant, witty, and erudite discourse, and such difficulties as may occur are due simply to the ignorance of the reader or the superior knowledge of the poet, who is a fine classical scholar. There are metaphors in his poetry, but they do not crystallize into opaque symbolism. The general treatment of the material is that of a man living in this time but with intelligence and sympathies that reach beyond it, using all his wit and imagination to translate it intelligibly and even gaily into the terms of his own temperament and pose.

In short, MacNeice is an "honest" poet, in much the same way that Robert Graves sets out to be and usually is. MacNeice does not consider his poetry to be a system outside his own personality. Poetry remains personal, his way of understanding the world. What we find in it is an intelligent man living in this world, not a philosophy or theology transformed into a symbolic, objective-seeming poetry that demands to be criticized as symbolism and not as the philosophic or theologic system from which it derives.

One way of putting all this would be to say that MacNeice employs great poetic gifts, and projects a genuinely poetic personality, to surround ideas and situations that are essentially those of prose. Although in many of his qualities he is superior to the world, he never ceases to belong to it; he is a worldly poet. By this I don't mean that he is "materialistic," but that the idea of happiness imagined in his best poetry is of a society in which sensual, esthetic-minded, amusing, scholarly people are able to communciate with one another, without mystification and with perfect tolerance and understanding. One of his best poems, "The Kingdom," begins:

> Under the surface of flux and of fear there is an
>   underground movement,
> Under the crust of bureaucracy, quite behind the
>   posters,
> Unconscious but palpably there—the Kingdom of
>   individuals.

The members of this Kingdom are those who have eyes that can

>   see each other's goodness, do not need salvation
> By whip, brochure, sterilization or drugs,
> Being incurably human.

To come down to it, then, MacNeice is a classically trained, Renaissance-admiring, rationalist, individualistic humanist. Yet this is to leave out his very real vein of idiosyncratic fantasy, has individualism, which is not merely theoretical but shows in his rhythms, his imagery, his lightness of touch that reminds one at once of Latin poetry and of the painting of Matisse. This color and ability to think beyond images, composing pictures that one could take up a pencil and draw, show from the first:

> The dogs' tails tick like metronomes,
> Their barks encore the sticks you throw,
> The sallow clouds yawn overhead,
> The sagging deck-chairs yawn below.
> I wish I had my marble clock
> To race those minatory tails

MacNeice has responded intelligently to such movements as the politics of the Thirties and surrealism, without ever having become subject to them. His long poem *Autumn Journal* (included in this selection) is an interesting experiment in poetic diary-making which conveys the climate of the Thirties better than any other poem of that time.

First and last, MacNeice is an immensely skilled technician. His poems rank very high in the work of this century, and it is a pity that they are not more read; in addition to being very good, they give real pleasure.—STEPHEN SPENDER, "An Unsung Classicist," *SR*, Sept. 7, 1963, pp. 25, 33

JULIAN SYMONS
"Louis MacNeice: The Artist as Everyman"
Poetry, May 1940, pp. 86–94

What is immediately obvious about the poems of Louis MacNeice is their simplicity. Simplicity is a rare quality in poetry. There are as few simple poets as there are difficult poets. To write simply is to write directly, in words that in themselves and in their aggregate may be understood and appreciated by an unsophisticated reader, a reader unfamiliar with the verse mannerisms of the time. Campion is a simple poet, but not Shelley: Wordsworth's early poems were simple, but not Wordsworth's later poems. There is little that is *difficult* in Shelley or the later Wordsworth: but their poems are not simple, they do not describe an event or feeling directly, but interpret it in terms of the poet's moral or philosophical imagination. When I say that Mr. MacNeice does not do this, I mean that he is not a moralist, as was Wordsworth, or an amateur philosopher, as was Shelley: I mean that he writes as an Ordinary Man.

"I would have a poet able-bodied, fond of talking, a reader of the newspapers, capable of pity and laughter, informed in economics, appreciative of women, involved in personal relationships, actively interested in politics, susceptible to physical impressions." That is a summing-up in Mr. MacNeice's *Modern Poetry: A Personal Essay*. We may feel that this is going much too far: that a good poet may be as physically feeble as Leopardi, as ill-informed economically as Rimbaud, as little interested in politics as Keats; but there is no question that Mr. MacNeice's words describe perfectly the man who writes most of Mr. MacNeice's poems. His words also described very well the Ordinary Man; the degree to which the Ordinary Man is informed in economics (which seems an odd requirement) will depend on his education and intelligence: otherwise most men possess, in varying degrees, the interests and faculties required; and most men would be able to understand and appreciate Mr. MacNeice's poems. They would not appreciate the technical skill with which the poems are constructed; but that is a matter for the specialist, a matter of knowing how the machine works.

It is necessary to illustrate these statements. In Mr. MacNeice's collection of poems, *The Earth Compels*, I would say that more than two-thirds of the poems may rightly be called simple. Here are some quotations—from "Carrickfergus":

> I was born in Belfast between the mountain and the
>   gantries
> To the hooting of lost sirens and the clang of trams:
> Thence to Smoky Carrick in County Antrim
>   Where the bottle-neck harbor collects the mud
>   which jams
> The little boats beneath the Norman castle,
>   The pier shining with lumps of crystal salt;
> The Scotch Quarter was a line of residential houses
>   But the Irish Quarter was a slum for the blind and
>   halt.

From "The Sunlight on the Garden":

> The sunlight on the garden
> Hardens and grows cold,
> We cannot cage the minute
> Within its nets of gold,
> When all is told
> We cannot beg for pardon.

From "Hidden Ice":

> And I would praise our inconceivable stamina
> Who work to the clock and calendar and maintain
> The equilibrium of nerves and notions,
> Our mild bravado in the face of time.

These are fair samples: the thought they contain is simple, and the words in which the thought is expressed are appropriate. The first extract is a fragment of the Ordinary Man's autobiography; the second is an expression of his weakness in a harsh time; the last an indication of his courage in a harsh time. The other third of the poems in this book are another matter (notably "Chess," "Circus," "Homage to Clichés," "Eclogue between the Motherless"); the ordinary man would not like them: they are written in language which is not too difficult, but too strange for him. Mr. MacNeice differs from his ideal poet in being, first a scholar, and second a literary man who lives, as most scholars and literary men do, a little apart from the run of people. It is the scholar and the literary man who have written Mr. MacNeice's other poems, with their gleaming Bloomsbury wit and sophistication. It has taken some time for the Ordinary Man in Mr. MacNeice to gain the upper hand over the scholar. Here is the scholar writing in the foreword to Mr. MacNeice's first book of poems, *Blind Fireworks*:

> Several of these poems are founded on an esoteric mythology. For instance Pythagoras is, for me, not the historical Pythagoras, but a grotesque, automatic Man-of-Science, who both explains and supports the universe of counting, having thus an affinity to Thor and Time-God.

Poems, published six years after *Blind Fireworks*, shows the Ordinary Man struggling with the literary scholar: in *The Earth Compels*, as I have indicated, he has the upper hand, and he is not likely to lose it.

II

So far I have stated, and illustrated, a theory about Louis MacNeice's poems. The reader is assumed to have read the poems, or some of the poems, already, and to have made up his mind about them. In the rest of this essay I take the correctness of my theory for granted. I assume, that is to say, that the theory will make it possible to judge accurately the value of Mr. MacNeice's poetry; there are, naturally, other possible approaches to his poetry which might give the same result.

In estimating the worth of Mr. MacNeice's poetic work, then, we have to ask: what is an Ordinary Man, what is his attitude to current events, and how will that attitude affect his poetry? The Ordinary Man is not the violently class-conscious worker; the number of violently class-conscious workers in England just now is small. The Ordinary Man is the manual worker who is not violently class-conscious, who aspires to be a black-coated petty bourgeois, the black-coated petty bourgeois who aspires to be a bourgeois with a little property, the bourgeois with a little property who would like to be a big landlord. The Ordinary Man is everybody *except* the violently class-conscious working class and what we still call the "upper class." He is at least three-quarters of the people of England. It is this great "class"—this "class" which desires social change, but is terrified by the violent instruments of social change—of which Mr. MacNeice is involuntarily the perfect representative. MacNeice's poems are the expression of this attitude (the Liberal attitude) on a very high level of skill and feeling. The most honest and intelligent adherents to this attitude (like Mr. MacNeice) see themselves as the lost in a changing world. In *Poems* the long, magnificent lament of *An Eclogue for Christmas* is brought to a conclusion by the realization that there is nothing to be done; all the town-dweller and the country-dweller can do is to go on till Doomsday. They perfectly realize that "it is time for some new coinage," but they realize also that *they* are not the new coinage. They are the lost. All they can do is to pretend that the life they appreciate, the life of action and talking, of reading the newspapers, of eating and drinking and seeing friends, will go on for ever. The highest reach of Mr. MacNeice's poetry is to pretend that it will go on for ever. Near the end of *An Eclogue for Christmas* he says:

> A Let the saxophones and the xylophones
>   And the cult of every technical excellence, the
>   miles of canvas in the galleries
>   And the canvas of the rich man's yacht snapping
>   and tacking on the seas
>   And the perfection of a grilled steak—
>
> B   Let all these so ephemeral things
>   Be somehow permanent like the swallow's
>   tangent wings.

He knows that these things are not permanent: today especially they are not permanent. Yet only by pretending that they are permanent is he able to escape, in poetry, from the full realization of their impermanence.

The desperation and hopelessness which finds a compensation in praising what is here now—a grilled steak, a picture or a yacht, things one can see, touch, and even, in one case, eat—is repeated throughout the poems. Sometimes it takes the form of an affirmation of faith in the virtues of Mr. MacNeice as a representative of his class. Sometimes it takes the form of a question—if we can apprehend perfectly with the greatest tact and sensitiveness, things we see, touch and eat, if we are friendly and generous, if we experience deep physical love,—is not that enough? The affirmation of the importance of the petty bourgeois, or alternatively the dismay of the petty bourgeois, in a society which he dimly or acutely feels to be unfriendly to him and aimed at his destruction, is the open or disguised theme of (in *Poems* alone) *An Eclogue for Christmas*,

"Eclogue by a Five-Barred Gate," "Morning Sun" (in which everything in the streets is alive in the sun, but becomes colorless—dead—when the sun goes in), "Turf Stacks" ("For we are obsolete who like the lesser things/Who play in corners with looking-glasses and beads"), "The Individualist Speaks," "Train to Dublin" ("I will not give you any idol or idea, creed or king,/I give you the incidental things which pass/Outwards through space exactly as each was.") What is important occurs *now*, we do not want any nonsense about "tomorrow" or "ideas", "Sunday Morning," "Birmingham" (a purely descriptive poem, in which the importance of the people and things described is assumed), "Snow," "An April Manifesto" (the devil-may-care mood—"Before the leaves are heavy and the good days vanish/Hold out your glasses which our April must replenish"), "Insidiae," "Wolves," ("Join hands and make believe that joined/Hands will keep away the wolves of water/Who howl along our coast"), "August," "Aubade," "The Glacier," "Museums," "Mayfly" and the final "Ode." The poems I have named make up more than half the book; they are the best poems in the book; and I think they are unsatisfactory poems.

When I say these poems are unsatisfactory, I do not mean they are poorly written; I do not wish to discuss Mr. MacNeice's poems technically, but I think it is indisputable that he writes with care and skill: I mean that they have no moral basis. Mr. MacNeice, who is an intelligent man as well as a skillful poet, knows that the gentle hedonism, a relic of nineteenth-century Liberalism, which is his creed, is bound to disappear in the coming clash of classes. He cannot accept the tenets of Communism or Fascism, yet he is dissatisfied with his present position: and his indecision is reflected in his poems. In order to justify this indecision Mr. MacNeice would have to give it a moral basis: he is unable to do so because there is no moral basis for such an attitude. One must be careful nowadays about using the word "belief": but belief in some external driving force outside himself and his own feelings seems to be what is lacking to make Louis MacNeice a very fine poet. He is wholly self-centred, stuck in a world in which the virtues of the Ordinary Man are the cardinal virtues: generosity, friendliness, physical love.

III

The political events of the last two years have affected MacNeice keenly: the dilemma in which he is placed as a "man of good will" has become acute: and his long poem, *Autumn Journal*, might be called "The Bourgeois's Progress." It was written from August 1938 to the New Year, in the form of a journal—that is, roughly a verse diary, in which the poet put down some of his thoughts and feelings during those months. *Autumn Journal* covers public and private events, the September crisis and MacNeice's own affairs. The poem shows a shift of attitude, a concern with (but still, a detachment from) politics. Politics, indeed, are now everybody's concern; and Mr. MacNeice is concerned with them accordingly. He is amazed, and shocked, that an alien scale of values should threaten his existence:

But posters flapping on the railing tell the fluttered
World that Hitler speaks, that Hitler speaks
And we cannot take it in and we go to our daily
Jobs to the dull refrain of the caption 'War'
Buzzing around us as from hidden insects
And we think 'This must be wrong, it has happened
    before,
Just like this before, we must be dreaming.'

Still, we know we are not dreaming. We (the Ordinary Men the poet represents) feel hopeless, and feel guilty:

And the individual, powerless, has to exert the
    Powers of will and choice
And choose between enormous evils, either
    Of which depends on somebody else's voice.

What can we do? is the question Mr. MacNeice poses to himself indirectly through ninety-six pages. His conclusion (the conclusion of his class) is that we can do nothing: the poem ends with a valediction on the past year—a valediction which is a fine piece of verse, but a manifest evasion of the matter of the poem. Mr. MacNeice blesses everybody:

You, who work for Christ, and you, as eager
For a better life, humanist, atheist,
And you, devoted to a cause, and you, to a family,
Sleep and may your beliefs and zeal persist.

He dreams of "a possible land"

Where nobody sees the use
Of buying money and blood at the cost of blood and
    money . . .
Where the people are more than a crowd.

And he ends with a dramatic promise to cross the Rubicon—tomorrow.

Sleep to the noise of running water
    Tomorrow to be crossed, however deep;
This is no river of the dead or Lethe,
    Tonight we sleep
On the banks of Rubicon—the die is cast.

These are admirable sentiments: but they are meaningless, or at best contradictory. If you feel sympathy with both Christian *and* atheist, with the Communist who would destroy the family *and* the bourgeois who would preserve it, you cross no Rubicon at all: you wish to cross the Rubicon, but in fact you stay just where you are.

The reader may object that he is not concerned with Mr. MacNeice's words or actions, but with his poem. That is true: but on occasion we are bound to question a poet's belief in what he writes, his faith in the values he professes. There is a vagueness and slackness in *Autumn Journal*, which represents a slackness in its author's mind: and this slackness does not make for good writing. It was very well in 1934 to write of "the perfection of a grilled steak": Mr. MacNeice is too honest not to realise that today, for him at least, there can be no writing about grilled steaks when Hitler is on the menu. But his lack of a moral sanction makes it impossible for him to be anything but bewildered and shocked: like the Ordinary Man he is merely appalled by the threatened pestilence from the sky.

We cannot require (or it is useless to require) of a poet that he *should* do this or that: a critic can only point out the probable (poetic) consequences of a given attitude. From *Autumn Journal* we may extract the comfort that its author is fully aware of his own weaknesses and errors. It is impossible to make prophecies: one can only say that if MacNeice is able to cross the Rubicon, if he is able to take the step of adherence to some (not necessarily political) belief objective to himself, that will probably be a good thing for him as a poet; while he remains in his present position, hesitating unhappily on the edge of a half-a-dozen Rubicons, he is unlikely to write anything better in the future than he has done in the past.

G. S. FRASER
"Evasive Honesty: The Poetry of Louis MacNeice"
Vision and Rhetoric: Studies in Modern Poetry
1959, pp. 179–92

I t is probably an error, at least of tact, to bring into an appraisal of a living poet one's impression of his personality as a man. But there is a real sense, as Roy Campbell once remarked about Dylan Thomas and about William Empson, in which good poets are, when you meet them, like their works; they talk and behave in a way you expect them to. And it follows, conversely, that one's impression of the personality of a notable poet may throw some light on his work.

In any case, this personal impression will be a superficial one; I have talked or listened to Mr. MacNeice, at B.B.C. pubs, at his friend William Empson's, at the Institute of Contemporary Arts when I have taken the chair for him, I suppose half a dozen times in the last ten years; and I have seen him often in pubs or at parties without talking to him. He gives a paradoxical impression of at once extreme and genial sociability, and remoteness. His talk flows easily and wittily, and his remarks on people, on ideas, on works of literature come out with an unpremeditated spontaneity. At the same time, one has often the impression that he is thinking at the back of his mind about something else; that the alertness and the sparkle are very much on the surface of his mind, that his *ripostes*, however apt, are almost absent-minded, that a whole elaborate apparatus of thinking and feeling is behind a fire curtain.

Something like this I feel also about his poetry. Nothing could be more vivid, more frank, more candid, even in a sense more indiscreet than some of his best poetry. All the cards seem to be, even casually, on the table. At the same time, reading his poems one has the feeling sometimes that one has been subjected to an intelligence test; or that his hands, as he deals the cards on the table, move with disquieting speed. To use another metaphor, he is both in life and in poetry a man whose manner, at once sardonic and gay, suggests that he is going, perhaps, to let one in on a disquieting secret about something; one finds that he hasn't. The quality that one is left remembering, the poetic as well as the personal quality, is a kind of evasive honesty. Both the strength and the weakness of his best poems, like the strength and the weakness of the personal impression he makes, rest on the sense that a good deal is held in reserve. What it is, I have only a faint idea; but I have a feeling that he would be a more important poet, if it were less fully held in reserve, yet that the strength even of his slighter poems depends on one's intuition that there is so much of it.

He is a poet, I think, whom it is sensible to discuss in terms of his conscious attitude to life, his moral tastes and preferences, what he feels about the problematical world we are living in, since that mainly, and only occasionally deep personal feelings, seems to be what his poems are about. When his *Collected Poems* came out in 1948, he was the one poet of the 1930s in whose work the years of the Second World War did not seem to have brought about a sharp break. Mr. C. Day Lewis, for instance, in the 1930s was often writing, to my mind rather unsuccessfully, either in a manner diluted from Hopkins or in a manner taken over from Mr. Auden's coarser scoutmaster vein. He was writing about the 'state of the world', rebelling against it. At some period in the 1940s, one noticed that he was writing, much more successfully, in a manner that owed something to Hardy, something to Browning and Clough, and that he was writing about the personal life. As for Mr. Auden himself, he has run through styles almost as Picasso has, he has reminded one of Laura Riding, Byron, Rilke, Yeats, he has perversely forced interesting matter into what seems a strangely inappropriate mould, like the Anglo-Saxon alliterative metre of *The Age of Anxiety*; the very beautiful purely personal manner with its long lines and its florid vocabulary which he has forged for himself in recent poems like 'In Praise of Limestone' is composite, not simple; through the kaleidoscope of successive

styles, we now see that he has had a more consistent attitude all along than we thought. Mr. MacNeice's attitude has always been a firmly fixed one, and his style has changed only from a young man's concentration on images to an older man's care for structure. His short poems have been much more often successful than his poems of a certain length (the only two of his longer poems that I admire quite whole-heartedly are two from the middle of the 1930s, *Eclogue for Christmas* and *Death and Two Shepherds*.) In this again, he is not exceptional; the number of poems of more than three or four pages which are completely successful in their way is, I suppose, a very small fraction indeed of the number of poems of three or four stanzas which are completely successful in theirs. There is a case, in fact, for thinking of Mr. MacNeice as a poet who has sacrificed an unusual gift for concentration to a misguided ambition to deploy himself at length. But, failures or successes, Mr. MacNeice's poems express from his beginnings to now an attitude to life which is admirably coherent: that of the left-of-centre Liberal, and, morally, that of the man who is out at once to enjoy life and to shoulder his social responsibilities. The typical attitude is one of a sane and humorous, and sturdily self-confident, social concern.

What may put some readers off is that this is so much (polished, learned, alarmingly witty though Mr. MacNeice is) the decent plain man's attitude. Decency, measure, courage, a lack of pretence, a making of the best of good things while they last, and a facing up to bad things when they have to be faced, these are the good insider's virtues. Mr. MacNeice's standpoint is the standpoint of common sense. He is subtle enough, however, to realize that the standpoint of common sense can be defended only through dialectic and paradox; he does not try to fight the plain man's battles with the plain man's weapons. It is on an acceptance of paradox that his own consistency is based (he was very interested in his youth in the paradoxes of the modern Italian idealists, not only Croce, but Gentile):

> Let all these so ephemeral things
> Be somehow permanent like the swallow's tangent
>   wings.

Thus one of Mr. MacNeice's favourite figures (as he has noted in a lively and perceptive essay on his own work) is oxymoron: the noun and epithet that appear to contradict each other. He might himself be described in that figure as an intolerant liberal or a large-hearted nagger. He wants a world in which all sorts and conditions of men can have their say; but when their say, as so often, proves slack, or insincere, the say of

> The self-deceiving realist, the self-seeking
> Altruist, the self-indulgent penitent,

he loses his patience. It takes all sorts to make a world, certainly, but making is an activity, and the sorts he approves of must really put their shoulders to the wheel, must really creatively work to *make* it. More broadly, to underline yet again this paradoxical consistency, one might that it is Mr. MacNeice's taste for variety, contrast, obstinate individuality— combined with his feeling that all these things, all 'the drunkenness of things being various', must somehow join in the 'general dance'—that unifies his vision of the world. (The problem of the One and the Many, like the problem of Essence and Existence, crops up again and again in Mr. MacNeice's poetry. The swallows are ephemeral existents but the pattern their tangent wings make seems to claim to be an eternal essence. Perhaps the submerged nine-tenths, both of his poetry and his personality, is a speculative metaphysician, of an unfashionably ambitious sort).

The danger of Mr. MacNeice's liberal, humanistic attitude, so admirable in so many ways in itself, is that it is too often, especially in his longer poems, liable to slacken down into mere moralizing. Take such a passage as this:

> it is our privilege—
> Our paradox—to recognize the insoluble
> And going up with an outstretched hand salute it.

One agrees, of course, at some though not at all levels, with what is being said (one does not agree, but this is certainly not an application Mr. MacNeice will have had in mind, that one should greet the apparently insoluble political divisions of our time, as Browning greeted the Unseen, with a cheer). One is unhappy about the way of saying. Is not the tone of voice, too flat in one sense, and too stretched in another, the orator's tone rather than the poet's? When, in a long, ambitious poem, full of such moralistic passages, I come for instance on this,

> The paradox of the sentimentalist
> Insisting on clinging to what he insists is gone,

I do feel, I confess, a sense of relief. The tone is right, there, these two lines are tight, witty, hit straight home. The moral *fact* is presented, the moral judgment is left (as I think it should be) to the reader.

Readers of that collected volume of 1948 often found themselves, I imagine, like myself, lingering a little wistfully over the dash, vividness, and gaiety of the earlier poems. But the later poems also deserved careful reading. Mr. MacNeice was tired, as he explained in a prose piece written about that time, of 'journalism', and tired of 'tourism', tired of the poem as a mere footnote to experience; he aimed now at making all the parts of a poem fit coherently together, even if that involved the sacrifice of the brilliant inorganic image and the witty irrelevant sally. 'Thus the lines', he wrote, 'that I am especially proud of in my last book are such lines as these (of the aftermath of war in England):

> The joker that could have been at any moment
> death
> Has been withdrawn, the cards are what they say
> And none is wild

or (of a tart):

> Mascara scrawls a gloss on a torn leaf

(a line which it took me a long time to find).' Both passages are essentially exploitations of the poetic pun. A card in a gambling game that can become any other card is called 'wild'; the joker, which is not really a proper member of the pack, is often used in this way as a 'wild' card. But the wider connotations of death as a cruel practical joker, or as a wild beast in the jungle waiting to spring on one, emotionally reinforce what might have been a mere piece of knowingness. The second pun, I think, is even subtler. Mascara scrawls either a sheen on a torn piece of foliage (the tart's sad eyelid shaped like a leaf) or a commentary on a torn page (from a diary say, a record of illicit self-indulgence to be destroyed). And the tart herself is like a leaf torn from the living tree of life, and the false gloss of the mascara on her eyelid is a commentary on her fate. Such Empsonian economies certainly demanded harder work from Mr. MacNeice's readers than his old pieces of 'tourism',

> impending thunder
> With an indigo sky and the garden hushed except for
> The treetops moving,

or his old pieces of 'journalism', his shrewd remarks in passing,

> that a monologue
> Is the death of language and that a single lion
> Is less himself, or alive, than a dog and another dog.

The danger, however, that Mr. MacNeice at the end of the 1940s seemed to be facing was that of sometimes relapsing—as a relaxation from the strain of much close writing and as a sop

to his sense of moral urgency—into the very 'monologue' which in these lines he deplores. How far, in the last ten years, has he surmounted that danger?

Perhaps he did not wholly surmount it. In 1952, he brought out *Ten Burnt Offerings*, a set of fairly longish poems which had been originally conceived for radio (they took about fifteen minutes each to broadcast). In that book, one had a sense of an inner flagging battling with an obstinate ambition. The relevance of the themes of these ten poems, both to common problems of our day and to what one took to be Mr. MacNeice's personal predicaments, seemed real but oddly oblique. The themes of the poems were themes that might have suited a prose essay: the paradox of Elizabethan culture, the dung and the flower: the harsh roots of modern ethics in Greek and Hebrew guilt and sacrifice: Ulysses and Jacob as twin competing symbols of searching and driven man: Byron as the romantic for whom the conscious pursuit of liberty becomes the subconscious pursuit of death. Such a range of topics was impressive; but it had a touch about it, also, of the Third Programme Producer with his fatigued fertility in 'new approaches'. The language showed, sometimes, that fatigue. When Mr. MacNeice wrote about the Elizabethans,

> Courtier with the knife behind the smile, ecclesiastic
> With faggots in his eyes,

it was impossible to forget how much more freshly they said the same sort of thing about themselves:

> Say to the Court it glows
> And shines like rotten wood;
> Say to the Church it shows
> What's good and doth no good.

A wider reach can imply a shallower local penetration. As if aware of the dangers of a stretched thinness, Mr. MacNeice was fecund in metaphor:

> because your laugh
> Is Catherine wheels and dolphins, because Rejoice
> Is etched upon your eyes, because the chaff
> Of dead wit flies before you, and the froth
> Of false convention with it.

Nothing could be gayer than the 'Catherine wheels and dolphins'. But were the more painful connotations of 'etched' (a needle on the iris?) intended or relevant? Are 'chaff' and 'froth', themselves examples of conventional dead metaphor, appropriate because 'dead wit' and 'false convention' are what they refer to—but, even if so, is there not still an unpleasant though faint clash between the 'froth of false convention' and the real and beautiful sea-froth churned up, three lines back, by 'dolphins'? The ornamentation, in fact, in this book had often the air not of emerging spontaneously from the theme, but of being trailed over it, like roses over a trellis. A trellis, to be sure, would be nothing without roses, but the gaunter outlines of Mr. MacNeice's thought, often half-hidden here, were interesting in themselves. His language was best where it was barest: as in the section on Byron in Lowland Scots,

> I maun gang my lane to wed my hurt,
> I maun gang my lane to Hades,

or the aside about history,

> the port so loved
> By Themistocles, great patriot and statesman,
> Great traitor five years on,

or the statement of the poet's own predicament:

> This middle stretch
> Of life is bad for poets; a sombre view
> Where neither works nor days look innocent
> And both seem now too many, now too few.

Even in these fine lines, there was something to question about the texture. 'A sombre view of the situation' is a worn politician's phrase; was it being accepted with a sort of fatigue, or alluded to with a sort of irony? Bareness, at least, seemed in the early 1950s to be Mr. MacNeice's growing-point: his danger, that facility of the practised writer which is so very different from spontaneity—the temptation to write because one can, not because one must.

In *Autumn Sequel,* which came out in 1954, it seems to me that he yielded almost fully to that temptation. Certainly in calling these twenty-six Cantos of that very intractable metre in English, *terza rima,* 'a rhetorical poem', Mr. MacNeice rather cunningly anticipated one's own verdict, that the poem was a triumph not only of skill but of determination. Of course, for Mr. MacNeice 'rhetoric' is not, as for Sir Herbert Read, the natural enemy of poetry, but, in the traditional sense of the word, the art of eloquent and persuasive writing, or, as for Hopkins, 'the common teachable element in poetry'. *Autumn Sequel* was partly an exercise, a deliberate display of skill. And it was an exercise written with a particular medium in view (though it had not, in fact, been commissioned in advance by that medium). The bulk of the poem was, in fact, broadcast on the Third Programme before it was published, and a passage from the fourth Canto, about the dangers and rewards of radio for the creative writer, is both an example of the tone of the poem at its most effective and partly a definition of that tone:

> as Harrap said
> Suggesting I might make an air-borne bard
> (Who spoke in parentheses and now is dead),
> "On the one hand—as a matter of fact I should
> Say on the first hand—there is daily bread,
> At least I assume there is, to be made good
> If good is the right expression; on the other
> Or one of the other hands there is much dead wood
> On the air in a manner of speaking which tends to
>   smother
> What spark you start with; nevertheless, although
> Frustration is endemic (take my brother,
> He simply thinks me mad to bother so
> With people by the million) nevertheless
> Our work is aimed at one at a time, you know."

Throughout the poem Mr. MacNeice was at his best in the recording, as there, of conversation, Harrap's mannerisms of hesitation and deviousness, partly *mere* mannerisms, partly a technique for checking 'stock responses' in himself, are caught more fully than either a novelist or a realistic prose dramatist could afford to catch them. Mr. MacNeice makes us listen for the sake of listening, listen for the essential quality of something, instead of listening to see what comes next.

Harrap's remarks also suggest why *Autumn Sequel* makes a paradoxical, and in the end rather disturbing and unsatisfying, combined impression of impersonality and intimacy. A poem written for the ear—and though the poem was not commissioned in advance, it cannot have come as a very great surprise to Mr. MacNeice that the Third Programme should decide to broadcast it—must take every trick as it comes and some tricks, the less obvious ones, two or three times over. It must be painted in poster-colours. Its visual images should have the punch and the concentrated exaggeration of good descriptive journalism. Its shifts from one topic to another must be as smooth as a change of gears. Its moral reflections must be made explicit, must be hammered in, even at the cost of stridency. Its human characters must establish themselves at once in clear outline even at the cost of over-simplification and flattening out. All the goods must be in the shop-window; for the listener, with no text in front of him to go back over and puzzle about

has not, even ideally, access to the rest of the shop. Technically, *Autumn Sequel* is exactly what a long poem conceived primarily in terms of radio ought to be. Criticisms of it, therefore, must fundamentally be criticisms of the limitations of radio as a primary medium for poetry. The paradoxical 'limiting judgment' about *Autumn Sequel* is that the more Mr. MacNeice apparently succeeds in taking us into his confidence, the more we admire his public skill in 'putting himself over'. The poet throughout, even and perhaps especially at his moments of most extreme genial informality, has been on parade. *Autumn Sequel* was not only, as Mr. MacNeice himself rightly commented, less 'occasional' than its predecessor of the late 1930s, *Autumn Journal;* it was also much less the poetic equivalent of a journal, like Amiel's, written primarily for the writer's own eyes.

The poem's nearest traditional equivalents, perhaps, were those poems of the late eighteenth and early nineteenth centuries which mingled moral reflections, natural descriptions, and sketches of human character in a blank verse subdued to the tone of polite conversation, like *The Task* or *The Excursion. Autumn Sequel* is, in a slightly brittle way, much *brighter* reading than such poems. The easy amble of pedestrian blank verse does not keep many modern readers alert; and the very difficulty of *terza rima,* and its apparent unsuitability for a sustained conversational use enable Mr. MacNeice to keep us waiting restlessly for the next rhyme, the next glide at a tangent to a new topic. Yet perhaps readers will not return to *Autumn Sequel* as they find themselves returning even to the flatter patches of Cowper or Wordsworth. Everything, here, is on the surface. No nail is not hit on the head; and what we miss—in spite of what I have said earlier about my feeling that there is a great bulk of Mr. MacNeice that is permanently submerged, that never surfaces in poetry—is the sense of an area of unused resource outside the poem. (Of unused *conscious* resource: that may explain my apparent contradiction of myself, for it is the unconscious sources, probably, that Mr. MacNeice is always scary of tapping.) This, for all its abundant and sometimes too facile archetypal imagery, the sinister Parrot gabbling the cult of flux, the Garden, the Quest, the mountain which must be climbed 'because it is there', is above all a poetry of consciousness, as also of an admirable social conscientiousness. It lacks the beauty of necessity.

A few short quotations may illustrate, in a more particularized fashion, some of the poem's flaws and felicities. Mr. MacNeice is at his best a witty writer, but his wit can lapse into a pointless allusive facetiousness:

> Oxford in October
> Seems all dead stone (which here hath many a
>   Fellow.

'Stone dead hath no fellow': our memories are jogged flatteringly, but then we reflect that 'stone dead' does not mean 'dead stone' and that the impeachment of the Earl of Strafford has nothing really, at all, to do with what Mr. MacNeice is talking about. A similar fault is a recurrent facile smartness. Visiting Bath, Mr. MacNeice tells us at length that he does not like the eighteenth century:

> Accomplishments were in, enthusiasm out,
> Although to our mind perhaps it seems a pity,
> That prose and reason ran to fat and gout.

A deeper and today a more usual observation would be that in its greatest writers, in Swift, in Pope, in Gray, in Cowper, in Johnson, the prose and reason ran to spleen, melancholia, or actual madness; Mr. MacNeice is attacking an Austin Dobson view of the eighteenth century which nobody now holds.

Here and there also in the descriptive passages of *Autumn*

Sequel one feels that Mr. MacNeice is very much the Third Programme feature-writer, mugging up the background in advance, and determined to discover something quaint. But more usually Mr. MacNeice is at his best in the descriptive passages, as here, on Oxford stone:

> I roll on
> Past walls of broken biscuit, golden gloss,
> Porridge or crumbling shortbread or burnt scone,
> Puma, mouldy elephant, Persian lamb.

I have noted already his excellence in the recording of conversation. Some passages expressing personal feeling, notably those on the character, death and funeral of the poet Gwylim (an archetypal joyous maker, modelled, with the warts rather carefully left out, on Dylan Thomas) are genuinely moving, though, because Mr. MacNeice is shy about the direct expression of feeling, when he does express it directly he often seems just on the verge of becoming sentimental. One respects also the passages of moral exhortation, on the importance of being and making, of struggling and giving and loving, of not yielding to drift. The whole poem is extremely readable, but it is in these personal and moral passages that one gets farthest way from the sense of something extremely skilful, but also too consciously and too wilfully 'contrived'.

Both *Ten Burnt Offerings* and *Autumn Sequel* gave me, then, the sense that a fine talent was forcing itself. I read with far more genuine pleasure Mr. MacNeice's most recent volume, *Visitations*, in which he seemed to have got back for the first time in ten years or so the bite that he had in the 1930s; and in which he got away also from the snare of the blown-up, big poem, of a length suitable for broadcasting. In these new short poems or sequences of short poems he had freed himself from the twin temptations of moralizing at the drop of a hat, and of ad-libbing. His mood, from the beginning of the book, was agreeably cantankerous (it is very difficult to discuss him, except in oxymorons!):

> Why hold that poets are so sensitive?
> A thickskinned grasping lot who filch and eavesdrop.

He attacked snooty reviewers (or the snooty reviewer in himself):

> Yet the cold voice chops and sniggers,
> Prosing on, maintains the thread
> Is broken and the phoenix fled,
> Youth and poetry departed.
> Acid and ignorant voice, desist.
> Against your lies the skies bear witness.

It is time, perhaps, that I did stop prosing on about him, that my own acid and perhaps ignorant voice did desist. I have said already, I think, all the general things I want to say. I should say finally that one would not have registered so sharply the degree of one's dissatisfaction with some of Mr. MacNeice's recent poetry unless one had a very high respect for, and therefore made very exacting demands on, the range and flexibility of his art and the integrity and scope of his mind. He has tried, with a strain of conscious effort, to make himself into the wrong sort of major poet. I think that if he had only waited a little more patiently for the pressure to gather, for the poem to force itself upon him, he might have been a major poet of the right sort. He has brought intelligence and poetry together; but the intelligence has too often seemed something superadded to the poem, rather than something used up in its proper shaping.

D. B. MOORE
"Retrospect"
The Poetry of Louis MacNeice
1972, pp. 237–50

MacNeice defined a poet as "an ordinary man with specialised gifts". His own gifts were an acute sensory, and especially visual, perception; colour, shape, light and shade, sound, smell, touch and taste, lend to his verse an immediacy closely connected with time and place. For him emotional recollection was bound up with where and when, as in the whole of *Autumn Journal*, in 'Birmingham' and 'Belfast'. He exploited the pathetic fallacy for all it was worth, not as a mere device, but because his experiences were bound up with actual times and places, as we see clearly in 'Solitary Travel', in Canto III of *Autumn Journal* and, above all, in 'Snow'. This external sensory perception was an integral part of the deeper emotional or intellectual feeling he was trying to express. So when he had to try even harder to convey an emotion whose validity he doubted, as in 'Flowers in the Interval', he relied on the association with places both to recall and heighten it.

One criticism of MacNeice, related to his keen sense of place and time, and repeated from reviewer to reviewer, remains to be dealt with. It is a charge that he brought upon himself, that he was more journalist than poet. In *Modern Poetry* he had said:

> My own prejudice . . . is in favour of poets whose words are not too esoteric. I would have a poet able-bodied, fond of talking, a reader of the newspapers, capable of pity and laughter, informed in economics, appreciative of women, involved in personal relationships, actively interested in politics, susceptible to physical impressions.

Though this is a Romantic concept, it is likely to be an enervating one. He recognized the danger himself: "Those who take the whole modern world for canvas are liable to lapse into mere journalism." In spite of this awareness he still maintains: "It is my own opinion . . . that the normal poet includes the journalist." This offered too easy a handle to those critics who could not envisage the lesser contained in the greater, the newsman in the poet. His descriptions of the urban and suburban world, and the occasional passages, as in *Autumn Journal*, dealing with headline news, could be superficially written off as 'journalism'. The critics are rarely specific. In the descriptive pieces like 'Sunday Morning' or despatches from the front like Canto XXIII of *Autumn Journal* that can be compared to 'special articles', surely the poetic craftsmanship is sufficient to give the lie to the description of 'journalism' used in a perjorative sense. Although we can reject the jibe as not applying to most of his poetry, it remains true that because he clung to the idea that the poet contains the journalist, his subject was occasionally ephemeral and too smartly on target, as in Canto X of *Autumn Sequel*:

> Daily news. And today? There is not so much to
>   note.
> Much talk in Cairo of the Suez Canal,
> Much talk in Capetown of the Coloured Vote
> (And Kaffirs have rallied sharply—Fal-de-lal!),
> Much talk in Margate where the dextral faction
> Of Labour has outplayed its left cabal,
> Much talk throughout the world of action and
>   reaction
> And explanation centres and isotopes

And interzonal permits; for distraction
Much talk of football pools and Britain's hopes
On the greens of Virginia Water.

But if we criticize this we should perhaps pause for a moment and recall Wordsworth's lines: "I've measured it from side to side:/'Tis three feet long, and two feet wide" or "These hedge-rows, hardly hedge-rows, little lines/Of sportive wood run wild". In other words, it is not balanced criticism to dismiss the minutiae of daily life as being unsuitable stuff for poetry; though we must recognize the skill required not to fall into banality, for all inspiration weakens at times. On the other hand there is, as we have seen, reportage that is true poetry. It ranges from:

Man's heart expands to tinker with his car
For this is Sunday morning, Fate's great bazaar;
Regard these means as ends, concentrate on this Now,
And you may grow to music or drive beyond Hindhead anyhow,
Take corners on two wheels until you go so fast
That you can clutch a fringe or two of the windy past

to the clear-cut topical descriptions of 'Christmas Shopping':

Spending beyond their income on gifts for Christmas—
Swing doors and crowded lifts and draperied jungles—
What shall we buy for our husbands and sons Different from last year?

. . .

The great windows marshal their troops for assault on the purse
Something-and-eleven the yard, hoodwinking logic,
The eleventh hour draining the gurgling pennies Down the conduits

. . .

While over the street in the centrally heated public
Library dwindling figures with sloping shoulders
And hands in pockets, weighted in the boots like chessmen,
Stare at the printed
Columns of ads,

Perhaps one of the most evocative of all these descriptions taking his world for canvas, but not lapsing into journalism, is in *Autumn Journal* VII:

They are cutting down the trees on Primrose Hill.
The wood is white like the roast flesh of chicken,
Each tree falling like a closing fan;
No more looking at the view from seats beneath the branches,
Everything is going to plan;
They want the crest of this hill for anti-aircraft,
The guns will take the view
And searchlights probe the heavens for bacilli
With narrow wands of blue.
And the rain came on as I watched the territorials
Sawing and chopping and pulling on ropes like a team
In a village tug-of-war; and I found my dog had vanished
And thought 'This is the end of the old régime,'
But found the police had got her at St. John's Wood station
And fetched her in the rain and went for a cup
Of coffee to an all-night shelter and heard a taxi-driver
Say 'It turns me up
When I see these soldiers in lorries'—

This is a picture that combines the objective and subjective effect of momentous news and it is brilliantly continued in the next canto. In the last three books this element of reportage becomes absorbed into the more universal nature of his poetry. We can see this most clearly in the compassion and precision of 'The Suicide':

There are the bills
In the intray, the ash in the ashtray, the grey memoranda stacked
Against him, the serried ranks of the box-files, the packed
Jury of his unanswered correspondence
Nodding under the paperweight in the breeze
From the window by which he left; and here is the cracked
Receiver that never got mended and here is the jotter
With his last doodle which might be his own digestive tract
Ulcer and all

He had learnt from Eliot how to absorb into his poetry the impedimenta from the everyday life of our urban civilization. For MacNeice was an urban man. From 'Turf-Stacks' onwards, his rural landscapes were those of the visitor; his sympathetic, almost 'natural' response was to the town. Although Pound and Eliot, and to some extent Auden and Spender, preceded him in admitting urban and industrial images into poetry, it was MacNeice who had the true romantic relationship with the City. This kind of relationship is not entirely new in English poetry; Milton's "Tower'd cities please us then/And the busy hum of men", and Wordsworth's

This City now doth, like a garment, wear
The beauty of the morning; silent, bare,
Ships, towers, domes, theatres, and temples lie
Open unto the fields, and to the sky;

both express the same kind of elated reaction. MacNeice brought it up to date. The escalators of the Underground Railway, the vacuum cleaners in Lyons' Corner House, the moving advertisements of Piccadilly Circus, cars and their headlights and windscreen wipers, buses, traffic lights, telephones, all the paraphernalia of modern life were his landscape and provided his images. He belonged to the town as Wordsworth belonged to the landscape of the Lakes, and if the town failed to provide him with an equivalent to a pantheistic philosophy, it provided him with sparkling words and images fit to be used in his poetry. He loved the music of words. He had a sense of rhyme that made him free with all the variations that Hopkins and Owen and their predecessors had explored—half rhyme, bad rhyme, pararhyme, internal rhyme, assonance, alliteration, were his to command. He rarely departed from what he described in *Modern Poetry* as "the running trochees and dactyls of ordinary English speech". He had in fact what G. S. Fraser in *The Modern Writer and His World* calls "a way with words"; and Fraser points out that:

It was this disturbing, uncomfortable use of language, the supple closeness to the rhythms of intelligent speech, that poets of a later generation, like Auden and MacNeice, were to take over from Eliot and from the Pound of *Mauberley*;

but MacNeice had the defect of his virtues. He could be misled into inept punning, as in "Was he that once, the sole delight of my soul?" He could give the impression of building a whole poem to make appropriate a clever phrase of conclusion. One wonders, for example, whether 'Off the Peg' was written to accommodate the last line: "And off the peg means made to measure now"; or 'Déjà Vu' for "It does not come round in hundreds of thousands of years", or 'Birthright' for "My gift horse looked me in the mouth". There is occasionally a certain slickness in his work, but it is the obverse of his prosodic and verbal facility. He was early aware of the danger: "Any world" he says "is itself a trick to start with . . . We should not show the works, and our tricks should be suited to our subject matter." He could also be tedious; and the efficient versification of some of his agnostic sermonizing does not rescue it from banality; but he had a subtle command of rhythm from the heaviest of hymnal metric beats to the finest sense of stressed line. He had thought long about imagery and his metaphors and similes were apt, striking, illuminating, and drawn from scholarship and observation. He had resources of scholarship and deployed them with ease. With this equipment he passed rapidly through the early experimental stages in a poet's development. After 1929, except in the less successful parts of *Ten Burnt Offerings* and in *Autumn Sequel*, he progressed fairly steadily to the sparse, clear poetry of the last three books.

By 1932 he is writing 'Turf-Stacks', which we have already recognized as central to the nostalgic elements in his thought and which meets the need of the reader for reassurance that he is not alone. "For *we*" (note the plural) "For we are obsolete who like the lesser things". A year later he is describing these "lesser things" in 'Birmingham' in great swinging lines of four stresses rhymed, or half-rhymed couplets (and metrically, as we have seen, in all likelihood derived from Noyes) and the thought anticipates much of *Autumn Journal*. In the same collection, *Poems* (1935), he distils in the sonnet 'Sunday Morning', of contemporary construction (lines of irregular length syllabically, but with four stresses rhyming in couplets), something of the essence of the suburban life which he half criticized and half loved, in words sufficiently striking to be echoed by Eliot in 'The Rock'.

In 1935 he wrote 'Snow', a poem which attracted, as we saw in Chapter One, much misplaced critical attention, but which has a sharp appeal, both sensual and visual. So by way of 'The Jingles of the Morning' and the inexpressibly sad 'The Sunlight on the Garden', where the wrought craftsmanship of the poem matches perfectly the nostalgic despair, he reaches, as the threshold to *Autumn Journal*, the ironical 'Bagpipe Music' in which the music is such fun that the deep satirical undertone is in danger of being overlooked.

Here then is his poetry of the first decade. The threads that run through those of the poems that we have admired are the sharp impact of the world of the senses upon him, the inability to choose a political stance, the realization both as observer and participant of the limitations of urban life, the sadness of life passing, and the impossibility of catching the golden moment. Step by step his craftsmanship had kept pace with his subject matter and he was ready to begin the long poem which John Waterhouse told me he had suggested that MacNeice should attempt.

So we have *Autumn Journal*, Larkin's "brilliant quotidian reportage", and praised by other critics as among the best pictures of the Munich crisis, and of the immediate pre-war days. This surely is a poem which will live because we have one man, harassed by those who would wish him to accept a political view, but prevented from doing so by an intellectual honesty and natural scepticism, who sets out in diary-form the daily impact upon his senses of a civilization ill at ease and filled with foreboding. "The blue smoke rising, and the brown lace falling in the empty glass of stout" in *Autumn Journal* III is a picture that in two lines says as much as all the "false friend" sequence of *The Waste Land*. Of course there are inequalities

in *Autumn Journal*. Of course we must not demand that it is more than it sets out to be. Its very modesty ensures that it revives memories of those small and intimate moments when great disaster threatens the individual; the recognition that these moments, common to us all, have an element of universal truth, makes the poem live; and if, in this instance, this truth is based on uncertainty and insecurity, its appeal is no less; as in Clough's 'Amours de Voyage', human inability to decide, to achieve, to be complete in understanding, reaches in *Autumn Journal* the stage of being a truth in itself. The prosody matches the impotent casualness of the commentary; the discipline of the rhyme and the latitude of the rhythmic stress are in constant balance.

When we consider the poetry that followed *Autumn Journal* we would do well to recall Auden's lines:

> Intellectual disgrace
> Stares from every human face,
> And the seas of pity lie
> Locked and frozen in each eye.

We must realize that it is in the atmosphere of intellectual shame that the poetry of the war had, inevitably, to be written. MacNeice, writing at the time, first took refuge in personal poetry. 'Meeting Point', the converse of 'The Sunlight on the Garden' (since he now "cages the minute/Within its nets of gold") turns the intensely personal into a moment of truth by the simplicity of the language, the breadth of the imagery contained within a deliberately claustrophobic moment outlined by the cunning use of a one-line refrain in each stanza. Then, rather like a child hiding his head in his mother's bosom when danger threatens, he gives us two more poems dwelling on the psychological burdens of early experience, 'Christina' and 'Autobiography', again with skilful use of refrain. When he turns from this to a subject relevant to the times, we have 'Barroom Matins', neat, simple, ending with the apt line "Give us this day our daily news", from which it is impossible to divorce the too easy cynicism.

At this point he is in danger of dying poetically from a surfeit of craftsmanship over subject. This is not surprising, for he had 'sold himself' to the Establishment. Impressed into the service of the B.B.C. in war-time, all truth, all doubt, all feeling had to be employed in total war, and the end-product, if not confined to the personal, had to be propaganda, not art. The wonder is not that within the intellectual suffocation of these demands he could not do better, but that he could do at all well. Nor should it be surprising that from the midst of this inevitably schizophrenic situation should come such an intimately personal poem, so full of universal despair, as 'Prayer before Birth' on the one hand, or such shrewd extrovert observation as 'The Mixer' and 'The Libertine' on the other, and so little truly 'war' poetry. What is perhaps surprising and only to be understood in the context of general relief from conscripted conformism at the end of the war, is a poem such as 'Bluebells', with its deep psychological understanding of the problems of renewal of normal life. The third stanza of this poem has a noble simplicity of language wrought into a calm certainty of rhythm, assonance and rhyme; and the other poem of the same period that compares with it in prosody is 'The Drunkard', which also has the same relationship of universal to particular and the same simplicity of expression.

Then came the difficult years. Not too long, only 1950 to 1953, and not all of the last. They were at first cerebral years, as though in *Ten Burnt Offerings* he had set himself the task of writing only intellectual scholarly poetry related to the places in which he found himself. They have, as we have seen, their felicities; though *Autumn Sequel* is but passable. True poetry returns only with *Visitations*. From then until his death, we have poems which combine the early music, the craftsmanship of the middle years, and the compulsive themes, but shorn of self-pity and introspection. Here is a fiercer MacNeice. 'April Fool' is a better poem than 'Bagpipe Music', for the avenues of thought and dream imagery that are opened to us in it are at once more coherent and more controlled. "Sooner let night-mares whinny" is a stark opening to 'Dreams in Middle Age', a poem of psychological self-knowledge. *Solstices* has, as we have seen, much good poetry set around three memorable, possibly great, poems. 'Apple Blossom' has the strong effect that comes from embodying a simple but hitherto not clearly perceived statement in the simplest of verse forms, and the most natural language. 'Hold-up' in 15 lines of four-stress unrhymed verses, sets in amber a universal experience, and 'All Over Again' we have already praised as a great poem of middle-aged love. If we turn back from any of these poems to earlier ones such as 'Sunday Morning' or perhaps more appositely, 'Hidden Ice', we cannot but be struck by the economy and force of the later poetry compared with the looseness of expression and conse-quent dissipation of effect of the earlier. Even 'Meeting Point' has an almost artificial and repetitive effect if it is read side by side with the control, the internal rhyme, assonance and alliteration of 'All Over Again'. When we turn to the last volume, there are more memorable poems than in any single section of his work of equal size. If the thought is embedded in a kind of nostalgic inevitability, the craftsmanship has met the theme and is spare and direct, so that the overall effect is one of earnest and slightly deprecating fatalism. 'Soap Suds', 'Déjà Vu' and 'Off the Peg', granted an element of artificiality in their construction, escape sentimentality by a straightforward, al-most stark, mode of expression. 'Birthright' and 'The Habits' in stanzas of equal simplicity seem, at last, to perform the act of catharsis he had sought in his prose autobiography; while the lyric aspect comes to fruition in the determined surrender of 'Charon' and the hopeless hope of 'Thalassa'. In each of these poems the marriage of form and content, in the first group a little contrived, in the second as inevitable as in all good art, is its highest achievement.

In considering the progress of MacNeice's verse in all its aspects to its apogee in *The Burning Perch*, we have omitted that portion which explored the philosophical aspects of his thought. When we look back upon it this is not surprising. The longer works of vague philosophizing or agnostic sermonizing, such as 'Plurality' or 'The Stygian Banks', even when pleasing or interesting to read, make no deeper impact.

In *Modern Poetry* he had written: "I have already maintained that major poetry usually implies a belief", though he tries to qualify this by the view that by the poet "any belief . . . should be compromised with his own individual observation". Three years later in *The Poetry of W. B. Yeats* he came nearer to expressing in words the dichotomy which he never resolved in poetry: "The faith in the *value* of living is a mystical faith. The pleasure in bathing or dancing, in colour or shape is a mystical experience." By using the word "mystical" in both phrases, he was attempting to overcome the age-old dilemma of equating emotional apples with sensual pears. He knew, and expressed again and again in his poetry, the delights of the senses and he experienced them so fully that he could half deceive himself into believing that they were a "mystical experience" and half way to faith, or belief. A quarter of a century later, in *Varieties of Parable*, he could still say of belief: "This, as always, is a puzzler", but having recognized this, he avoids the issue which, for him, was unpalatable. He lacked, in the last analysis, the moral fibre, the capacity for intellectual achievement, or the single-mindedness, to attain belief, even

in disbelief. The question of belief and poetry is one of considerable difficulty. In general terms it is surely true to say that poetry must be based on conflict and passion, and whether it is employed to support or resist belief, the conflict and passion are all-important to the poetry. MacNeice came no nearer to a passionate resolution of philosophical or religious conflict than the expression of doubt in 'Didymus', the regression of 'Prayer before Birth', and the terrible fear that lies at the heart of 'Charon'.

We approached the poetry of MacNeice expecting to find, as he had himself indicated that we should, a poet in the Romantic tradition, and this indeed we have found. We may compare his achievements with Raymond's definition of the Romantic poet with which we began our study. His primary "form of knowledge" as displayed in his poetry, is self-centred. Every shift of ground, every alteration of emphasis is, in his verse, a contribution to the "metaphoric" or "symbolic" portrait of himself, pored over, again and again, with the nostalgic longing for the moment it embodies. His metamor-phoses range from the lonely child, cursed with a lifelong Oedipus complex, the schoolboy and student, then the townsman, the deserted lover, the husband, father, academic and author. The word "enjoyment" is echoed in the use of "mystical" to cover the experiences of the senses. Only when we come to the phrase "a feeling of the universe, experienced as a presence" are we forced to pause. A feeling of the minutiae of the universe, its colour, sounds, touch and smell, was indeed an integral part of his poetry and gives it an immediacy, a sense of heightened reality, that might at first sight satisfy the requirement of this definition, but the pleasure in colour or shape is not enough. It is not "a mystical experience". "A feeling of the universe, experienced as a presence" calls for a transcendental understanding of which he was only occasion-ally capable, as in the last few poems.

MacNeice remained the prisoner of his childhood. He could never escape the nostalgic chains this placed upon him either as lover or thinker. That his love for his mother rested, not unusually, on so profound a sexual base that her early death was permanently crippling emotionally, he half realized, as we see from the story of the twig that he tells in *The Strings Are False*. In prose that comes near to poetry, he describes the occasion:

> That had been a fresh spring morning and everyone well and gay and my father was perched on a ladder clipping the arbour which was made of little trees we called poplars. The long sprays fell on the ground with light green lively leaves and I gathered some of them up to arrange in a jam-jar. But one of my twigs was too long, whenever I put it in the jar the jar fell over. My mother came up smiling, folded the twig double, put it in the jar and the jar stayed upright. And I was outraged, went off in a sulk.

In *Experiences with Images* he comments in a note:

> Almost the most disastrous experience of my child-hood is for ever associated in my mind with a doubled-up poplar twig—but I have never yet used this image as a symbol of evil. Were I to do so, I should certainly elucidate the reference.

The importance of this lies in the last phrase. He never brought himself to "elucidate the reference". His ambivalent attitude to this story, so that he must tell it, shows that he realized that it contained a significance which it was difficult to face. His inability to use it in his poetry constituted in a major degree a moral failure in one for whom self was a major source of interest and inspiration. A parallel and not dissociated failure lay in his inability to make the intellectual effort either to achieve faith, to deny all belief, or to systematize his agnosticism. This ethical and intellectual weakness led to a certain sentimentality in his approach to social criticism and equally made any firm political attitude impossible. So MacNeice could find neither spiritual faith, political belief, or personal love and understanding to form the basis of his poetry, but relied instead on the conflicts of indecision. In so far as it lacks a passionate attempt to cope with the conflicts that arise from doubt and indecision, the poetry of MacNeice sometimes falls short of greatness. The tragedy is that he could not escape from within himself to wider exploration.

Perhaps the last words should be allowed to rest with two admired fellow-poets, both his friends. Auden has been included in the group of 'thirties poets in what he described as the "customary journalistic linkage". Eliot was at first Mac-Neice's inspiration, then his publisher, and finally his friend and admirer. In his memorial address Auden said:

> Louis MacNeice was clearly a poet who shared Cesare Pavese's belief that 'the only joy in life is to begin', that, from the poet's point of view, the excitement of tackling a problem, whether of technique or subject matter, which one has never attempted before, is even more important than the result. I am confident that posterity will sustain my conviction that his later poems show an advance upon his earlier, are more certain in their craftsmanship, brilliant though that always was, and more moving; but, even if I thought otherwise, I should still admire him for risking failure rather than being content to repeat himself unsuccessfully.

T. S. Eliot, speaking 'ex cathedra' (as we said at the very beginning of our study of MacNeice's poetry), had this to say in *The Times* of 5 September 1963:

> There is little that I can add to the encomiums of Louis MacNeice which have already appeared in the press, except the expression of my own grief and shock. The grief one must feel at the death of a poet of genius, younger than oneself . . .
>
> MacNeice was one of several brilliant poets who were up at Oxford at the same time, and whose names were at first always associated, but the difference between whose gifts shows more and more clearly with the lapse of time. MacNeice in particular stands apart. If the term 'poet's poet' means a poet whose virtuosity can be fully appreciated only by other poets, it may be applied to MacNeice. But if it were taken to imply that his work cannot be enjoyed by the large public of poetry readers, the term would be misleading. He had the Irishman's unfailing ear for the music of verse, and he never published a line that is not good reading.

There is, indeed, so much that is good and so much more that is satisfying. There is high craftsmanship and a developing capacity to achieve an almost classical clarity. His imagery gains its force from a precise expression of the impact of the world upon his senses. Just occasionally when this is married to deeper feelings, when for example he explores true doubt, true defiance of "God or whatever means the Good", when he faces true despair, and truly accepts the consequences of ultimate nothingness, of ultimate inability to contact other human beings, we salute the high genius of his poetry.

Derek Mahon

1941–

Derek Mahon was born on November 23, 1941, in Belfast, and was educated at the Belfast Institute and Trinity College, Dublin, where he received his B.A. in 1965. His *Twelve Poems* were published that year, winning him the Eric Gregory Award. He taught at high school for a year, and then became a lecturer at the Language Centre of Ireland in Dublin. From 1970 until 1974 he was co-editor of *Atlantis*, and in the later 1970s he held positions as writer-in-residence at colleges in America, Northern Ireland, and England. Since 1981 he has been poetry editor of the *New Statesman*.

Mahon's publications have all been verse, and include *Night-Crossing* (1968), *Ecclesiastes* (1970), *Lives* (1972), *The Snow Party* (1975), *Light Music* (1977), *Poems 1962–1978* (1979), and *The Hunt by Night* (1983). He edited *Modern Irish Poetry* in 1972.

Mahon is married, with two children, and lives in London.

If events in Ireland have been thought malefic in their relations to the art of poetry (as they are to almost everything else) then that may be the reason why Heaney and Derek Mahon have both maintained two distinct styles apiece. One can be used for the racial-*cum*-archaeological manoeuvres of their imaginations, or simply the lyricism towards which they are drawn by temperament, and another for more direct utterance, for the kind of poem which, in their Irish circumstances, is expected of them.

The formula is too simple, and suggests a similarity between Heaney and Mahon which doesn't exist. Mahon's art is one of elegance, in which the assurance of his skill aspires to

suavity, to an ease of writing in which the labour of making will be inconspicuous but impressive. Heaney's poems on the other hand are hewn, as if he wants to give the impression that, like Gaelic poets of old, he composes in the dark with a boulder on his chest. Mahon is also less immersed in the culture and history of Ireland. He appears to be re-enacting the Irish gesture of flight from possible parochialism towards a more sophisticated milieu of Europe complicated by home-looking, by the love-hate affections of the literary exile.

Yet it is these glances towards home, or, rather, intense stares productive of irascibility or melancholy, that, at present, predominate. This happens virtually on account of the over-literariness of many of his other poems. "Hommage to Malcolm Lowry", "After Nerval", or "Epitaph for Flann O'Brien" are examples. No matter the sincerity of these genuflections, Mahon's cleverness, wit, and grace are preferable when working against less literary subjects. "Cavafy", for instance, though literary enough in its origins, is an exhilarating series of poems.

Mahon's image of enchantment is summarised for him in the life of the gipsies. He has written about this in his earlier books. In the new collection he imitates a poem by Philippe Jaccottet, "Les Gitanes." A world of bandana and banjo, sing-songs under the stars at places with no disheartening historical associations—it looks like self-indulgence, though Mahon is too alert to allow his writing to create anything so inept.

Mahon's consciousness controls his imagination, as it must, to save the integrity of imagination and prevent it from being the repository of mere longings.

> I wake in a dark flat
> To the soft roar of the world.
> Pigeons neck on the white
> Roofs as I draw the curtains
> And look out over London
> Rain-fresh in the morning light.
> This is our element, the bright
> Reason on which we rely
> For the long-term solutions.

So begins "Afterlives." Like many of his poems it is addressed to a particular recipient. By 2050 the Californians will be writing *Irish Verse Letters: The 20th-century Moment.* Yet there is something humane and significant about the fact that Irish poets swap poems so frequently. For the opening of "Afterlives" soon warps to

> The orators yap, and guns
> Go off in a back street

while the poem goes on to be explicit in its reply to the Troubles, their intrusions on the creative psyche, and the unease, at once affectionate and accusatory, of not being there to live through it. That, too, is summed up in the title poem—

> Thousands have died since dawn
> In the service
> of barbarous kings—
> But there is silence
> In the houses of Nagoya
> And the hills of Ise.

Japanese mythology might here coincide with the Irish legend used in "The Last of the Fire Kings." Ise is the shrine to the Japanese Sun-Goddess, while the "Fire-King" poem presumably refers to the Irish feast of Beltane. This celebration of summer by fire—and the god of it, significantly, is as much associated with death as fertility—explains the "ancient curse" mentioned in the poem. Again, however, it's a poem of posited escapes reconsidered as unworthy or impossible. In this case personified Irish history cannot escape from what it has itself contrived.

> Last of the fire kings, I shall
> Break with tradition and
> Die by my own hand
> Rather than perpetuate
> The barbarous cycle.
> Five years I have reigned

The "cold dream" which the fire king perfects is "a place out of time, a palace of porcelain" populated by fruit eaters—that is, a characteristic dream of the South by those who live in the North. The fire-loving people won't allow it, "rightly perhaps"—

> Demanding that I inhabit,
> Like them a world of
> Sirens, bin-lids,
> And bricked-up windows

(an earlier version of the poem had "And consensus politics")

> Not to release them
> From the ancient curse
> But to die their creature and be thankful.

"Thammuz" is a revision of "What Will Remain" in *Lives.* The new title is a clue to a poem I had only half understood. Thammuz is a Babylonian god who dies at the end of summer and is born again in spring—you can read about him in *Paradise Lost*, Book 3. The chance of rebirth and its association with persistence are standard themes in Mahon's imagination.

The finest poem in *The Snowy Party* is "A Disused Shed in Co. Wexford." The poem starts with a literary occasion, but Mahon leaps over the possible limitations of that; the poem blazes off the page, and is the consummation of his writing so far, simply one of the finest poems of the decade. There is nothing wrong with it; and the same can be said for "The Banished Gods."

To say of a poem that there's "nothing wrong with it" might sound as grudging as the terms of praise said to be characteristic of the great jazz player, the late Pee Wee Russell—"it doesn't bother me." But I think it's true praise. Neither Mahon nor Hugo Williams, though, is a poet of negative virtues, writing tight little syntactical perfections which protect, lovingly, a single precious image. Mahon's "elegance" is more significant than that; he is not playing for safety but living up to a subjectively formed stylistic ideal within which he can be seen to *perform* in language without sacrificing what he feels for his concerns.—DOUGLAS DUNN, "Mañana Is Now: New Poetry," *Enc*, Nov. 1975, pp. 78–81

In a verse letter by Michael Longley, a fellow Ulsterman, Derek Mahon is addressed approvingly as one of the "poetic conservatives". He might well take umbrage; for the spirit that emerges from his poems is one which, while it hungers for ceremony and inherited order, has only the wannest faith that ceremony survives or that such order has relevance. Wistful, reticent, resigned, the poems in *The Snow Party* sound like the fastidious reflections of self-imposed exile. Like Seamus Heaney, he has "escaped from the massacre", but he is not "a wood-kerne . . . Taking protective coloring/From bole and bark"; Mr. Mahon's escape route has been even more tentative. In the first poem in the book, "going home by sea/For the first time in years", he comes to the conclusion:

> Perhaps if I'd stayed behind
> And lived it bomb by bomb
> I might have grown up at last
> And learnt what is meant by home.

The final stanza of the poem that follows this, "Leaves", pushes beyond that "perhaps":

> Somewhere in the heaven
> Of lost futures
> The lives we might have led
> Have found their own fulfilment.

Lost futures, rather than Mr. Heaney's lost pasts, are the substance of Mr. Mahon's poems. "The Last of the Fire Kings", "Thamuz", "The Banished Gods" and (a beautifully judged stroke of minimalism) "Flying" are all hesitant reachings forward to possibilities just beyond the range of understanding. In these, and in other poems such as "The Snow Party" and in parts of the *Cavafy* sequence, there is a sardonic aestheticism, a diffident acknowledgement that art can arrest and fix at least something in what would otherwise be mere noise and flux. Two prose-poems, "A Hermit" and "The Apotheosis of Tins," play humorous variations on the theme. "A Hermit" ends:

> I am an expert on frost crystals and the silence of crickets, a confidant of the stinking shore, the stars in the mud. There is an immanence in these things which drives me, despite my scepticism, almost to the point of speech. Like sunlight cleaving to the lake mist at morning, or when tepid water runs cold at last from the tap. I have been working for years on a four line poem about the life of a leaf. I think it may come out right this winter.

For all its circumstantial wryness, this is tenuous stuff, however, and it seems to me, reading *The Snow Party*, Mr. Mahon's third book, that there is some danger of his talent thinning itself away into arbitrariness and whimsy. As if to show that he can indeed manage something more solid, he ends the collection with its most impressive poem, a meditation with the bleak title, "A Disused Shed in Co. Wexford." Here "A thousand mushrooms crowd to a keyhole", and are celebrated as dumb survivors whose tenacity spells out a hard-won lesson.—ANTHONY THWAITE, "At the Point of Speech", *TLS*, Nov. 7, 1975, p. 1327

TERENCE BROWN
From "Four New Voices: Poets of the Present"
Northern Voices
1975, pp. 192–201

In Derek Mahon's poetry it is possible to see what can be made of the Irish urban and suburban experience which Simmons rarely transcends. Mahon, born in 1941 and educated in Belfast and at Trinity College, Dublin, has produced a small body of remarkable verse, developing out of a sense of the complex, aesthetically uninspiring tensions of Northern Protestant middle-class identity. Mahon has spoken of the difficulties of writing out of such a background, from a 'suburban situation which has no mythology or symbolism built into it':

> The suburbs of Belfast have a peculiar relationship to the Irish cultural situation inasmuch as they're the final anathema for the traditional Irish imagination. A lot of people who are regarded as important in Irish poetry cannot accept that the Protestant suburbs in Belfast are a part of Ireland, you know. At an aesthetic level they can't accept that.[1]

Those suburbs are, of course, the suburbs of a major British industrial city (in the sense that Belfast played a significant role in the industrial revolution in the British Isles), and the fabric of experience there must inevitably differ from that in what has, until very recently, been the less industrially developed part of the country. Mahon therefore suggests:

> To the extent that the Northern poet, surrounded as he is by the Greek gifts of modern industry and what Ferlinghetti called 'the hollering monsters of the imagination of disaster', shares an ecology with the technological societies his rulers are so anxious to imitate, he must, to be true to his imagination, insist upon a different court of appeal from that which sits in the South.[2]

This is, of course, a note we have heard before, implicitly in the work of Louis MacNeice, explicitly in the manifestos issued by McFadden and Greacen in the early 1940s. And indeed, Mahon is taking up problems which exercised those poets, coping with them, I would suggest, through writing poems so tensely controlled as to recall MacNeice's own work. Mahon's poetry is a force-field of unresolved tensions and ironies explored in a verse of elegant, exact eloquence.

In 'Glengormley' and 'As It Should Be' Mahon considers the implications of suburban existence in a country whose past has been heroic, dramatic, mythological. 'Glengormley' recognises the new heroism of suburban survival, contrasting it, a little too predictably, with Ulster's prehistoric titanism:

> Now we are safe from monsters, and the giants
> Who tore up sods twelve miles by six
> And hurled them out to sea to become islands
> Can worry us no more.
>
> . . .
>
> And much dies with them. I should rather praise
> A worldly time under this worldly sky.[3]

The tone throughout is ambivalent, suggesting only partial acquiescence in suburban order: 'By / Necessity, if not choice, I live here too.' 'As It Should Be' is more openly regretful of the mythological past. 'The mad bastard' has been hunted 'Through bog, moorland, rock, to the starlit west' and gunned down

> in a blind yard
> Between ten sleeping lorries
> And an electricity generator.

The quality of life has no doubt superficially improved:

> Since his tide-burial during school-hours
> Our kiddies have known no bad dreams.
> Their cries echo lightly along the coast

but the poem concludes with ironic deflation:

> They will thank us for it when they grow up
> To a world with method in it.[4]

For Mahon is no eulogist of suburban possibilities nor of industrial society's blessings. He cannot even rise to Mac-Neice's excited response to its bright surfaces, sensing rather a new barbarism beneath a façade of materialist disregard for ideology, social hierarchy and commitment:

> Now it is night
> And the barbarians have not come.
> Or if they have we only recognise,
> Harsh as a bombed bathroom,
> The frantic anthropologisms
> And lazarous ironies
> Behind their talk
> Of fitted carpets, central
> Heating and automatic gear-change.[5]
>
> ('After Cavafy')

So he has Raftery, blind poet-representative of an older order, playing for time on campus in the global village:

> I am Raftery, hesitant and confused among the
> cold-voiced graduate students and inter-
> changeable instructors. Were it not for the
> nice wives who do the talking I would have
> run out of hope some time ago, and of love.
>
> . . .   Is it
> empty pockets I play to? Not on your life,
> they ring with a bright inflationary music—
> two seminars a week and my own place reserved
> in the record library. Look at me now,
> my back to the wall, taking my cue from a
> grinning disc-jockey between commercials.[6]
>
> ('I am Raftery')

An antipathetic reaction to the conditions of advanced capitalism is, of course, a fairly commonplace response in modern poetry. Often the poet who responds in this fashion turns to a local tradition in quest of roots, identity, fragments that he may shore against what he feels is the contemporary ruin. Mahon rejects such a strategy, such imaginative Jacobinism, since the local tradition he knows in his bones is not one with which he feels much ready sympathy. Mahon's 'hidden Ulster' is no Gaelic pastoral-aristocratic idyll, but the Protestant planter's historical myth of conquest, and careful, puritan self-dependence frozen to a vicious, stupid bigotry which constricts personal identity, crippling the possibility of change, growth and excellence:

> We could *all* be saved by keeping an eye on the hill
> At the top of every street, for there it is—
> Eternally, if irrelevantly visible—
> But yield instead to the humorous formulae,
> The spurious mystery in the knowing nod.
> Or keep sullen silence in light and shade,
> Rehearsing our astute salvations under
> The cold gaze of a sanctimonious God.[7]
>
>   ('In Belfast')

So 'Ecclesiastes' is a powerful, impassioned rejection of the tradition that lies beneath the surface life of Belfast's superficially emancipated suburbia. It is a denunciation of the Northern Protestant's self-understanding and a call to him, to abandon a stance of intolerant rectitude and ridiculous isolationism which is the fruit of an assertive, black-minded self-dependence:

> God, you could grow to love it, God-fearing God-
>   chosen purist little puritan that,
> for all your wiles and smiles, you are (the
>   dank churches, the empty streets,
>   the shipyard silence, the tied-up swings)
> . . .
>   Yes you could
> wear black, drink water, nourish a fierce zeal
>   with locusts and wild honey, and not
> feel called to understand and forgive
>   but only to speak with a bleak
> afflatus, and love the January rains when they
>   darken the dark doors and sink hard
> into the Antrim hills, the bog meadows, the heaped
>   graves of your fathers.[8]

Recognising, as McFadden did before him, the impossibility of any simple regional loyalty Mahon, like McFadden, is drawn to romantic outsiders, individuals, who assert their individuality not in dour, provincial self-satisfaction but in bohemian excess, rhetorical panache, by style in the face of metaphysical bleakness. So he celebrates De Quincey, Van Gogh, Dowson and the tragic generation, a forger who works in agony and fanaticism 'beyond criticism / And better than the best'[9] ('The Forger'). He identifies with the poet Villon:

> In the year fourteen fifty-six
> Right at the very dead of winter,
> The wolves hungry and the nights dark[10]
>   ('Legacies')

often adopting the role of bohemian goliard:

> Curled up in armchairs
> Or flat out on the floors
> Of well-furnished apartments
> Belonging to friends of friends[11]
>   ('The Poets Lie Where They
>   Fell')

or with

> one crumpled Gauloise touting for a lift
> where Paris flamed on the defining dark.[12]
>   ('A Tolerable Wisdom')

There is something in these poems of that fabricated cosmopolitanism we have detected in earlier poets, suggesting Mahon's insecurity, caught between a narrow society he dislikes and the larger world outside his province, where he must make his life. What is not fabricated is the note of loneliness, bordering on terror, that informs his work. Some of his poems treat journeys by car, train and plane, as essentially solitary, if not quite so finally desperate, as those in MacNeice's late work:

> Now we are running out of light and love,
> Having left far behind
> By-pass and fly-over.
> The moon is no longer there
> And matches go out in the wind.
> Now all we have
> Is the flinty chink of Orion and the Plough
> And the incubators of a nearby farm
> To light us through to the land of never-never.
> Girls all, be with me now
> And keep me warm
> Before we go plunging into the dark for ever.[13]
>   ('Girls in Their Seasons')

Like MacNeice, as this extract reveals, Mahon not only experiences cultural dislocation, but moments of metaphysical *frisson*. He knows

> First there is darkness, then somehow light.
> We call this day and the other night[14]
>   ('Four Walks in the Country near Saint
>   Brieuc')

while his poetry is full of 'frosty starlight', empty, cold regions of the universe and of the imagination. Like MacNeice also, he senses an interdependence of dark and light knowing that life's moments of vision and ecstasy are set against the dark and cold:

> Where winter is so long
> Only a little light
> Gets through, and that perfect.[15]
>   ('Epitaph for Robert Flaherty')

For Mahon some of those moments of vision occur in the Irish landscape. In an interview with Serge Ferchercau, Mahon reported that as a child and youth in Belfast the countryside was a foreign land of which he knew almost nothing: 'Elle me semblait très mystérieuse, tout aussi mystérieuse que le quartier catholique de Falls Road que je traversais le matin à bicyclette pour aller à l'école. C'était quelque chose d'irréel que l'on traversait, et c'est tout.'[16] As an adult he discovered the West of Ireland, Donegal and Aran. Aran offered him

> A dream of limestone in sea-light
> Where gulls have placed their perfect prints.
> Reflection in that final sky
> Shames vision into simple sight—
> Into pure sense, experience.[17]
>   ('Recalling Aran')

While on a visit there he begins to comprehend an Ireland quite other to the one he has known:

> Scorched with a fearful admiration
> Walking over the nacreous sand,
> I dream myself to that tradition,
> Fifty winters off the land.[18]
>   ('In the Aran Islands')

The Irish landscape could provide Mahon, as it did Allingham and Hewitt, with the means whereby he might personally resolve his ethnic and cultural tensions, allowing him an uncomplicated, if limited, relationship with Ireland. But Mahon's political education has included essays such as Conor Cruise O'Brien's study of Albert Camus,[19] with its subtle delineation of the psychic effects of colonialism on the coloniser. He senses his own dissociated sensibility[20] too profoundly to find such an apolitical ahistorical resolution of tension wholly satisfying. For history in its political aspect is one of Mahon's central imaginative concerns, whereas with Allingham, Hewitt and Michael Longley one suspects that, in spite of the intrusion of history upon their work, they would primarily prefer to concern themselves with other matters.

History, it is important to make clear, does not mean for Derek Mahon that complex of Irish linguistic, ethnic, religious and geographic truths sensed as permanencies which it is in the poetry of John Montague or Seamus Heaney. History for Mahon is no saga of land and people but a process, 'the elemental flux'[21] ('Rocks') which casts one man as coloniser, another as colonised, and man in innumerable roles. So Mahon's second volume, *Lives* (1972), must be read as a series of experiments in perspective, in which modern Irish and European political and historical experience are viewed from different spatial and temporal angles.

'Edvard Munch', for example, contemplates one of the Norwegian artist's canvases, considering the mysterious relationship of material things to historical and political process— comparing the relationship implied in the painting to that in experience itself. 'The Archaeologist', 'What Will Remain' and 'Entropy' step into post-history and into gigantic landscapes to see man's life *sub specie aeternitatis*, the planet littered with capitalism's banal bric-à-brac. He takes us

> after
> The twilight of metals,
> The flowers of fire,
> when Nature 'without ideas' will move
>   in a slow dance
> Of the purist energy,
> Intent on a reiterative
> Exercise of known powers
> Under the mineral stars.[22]
>   ('What Will Remain')

'Consolations of Philosophy' and 'Gipsies Revisited' balefully regard the assumed security of modern bourgeois life from the grave and from the tinkers' roadside, while the bright searching images of 'An Image from Beckett' reveal a landscape and city of some unlikely human future hopefully immune to death, irony and absurdity:

> Still, I am haunted
> By that landscape,
> The soft rush of its winds,
>
> The uprightness of its
> Utilities and schoolchildren—
> To whom in my will,
>
> This, I have left my will.
> I hope they had time, and light
> Enough, to read it.[23]

'A Dark Country' tests the possibility, by contrast, of local, personal attachments in a lyric of moving, tentative affirmation

> Recognizing,
> As in a sunken city
> Sea-changed at last, the surfaces
> Of once familiar places.
> With practice you might decipher the whole thing
> Or enough to suffer the relief and the pity[24]

while 'Lives' is a witty series of perspectives on Being itself, in its unlikely manifestations.

Two things raise these perspectivist experiments above the level of clear mannerism: the poet's depth of humane feeling and his imaginative range. In these poems the poet has made a virtue of necessity. Accepting a dissociated sensibility as the inevitable possession of a Protestant Ulsterman, he has exploited his understanding of fragmentation and flux in a series of richly imaginative poems, in which confusion or triviality might so easily have resulted. Derek Mahon has expressed admiration for writers of the American South, who managed to write, as he sees it, good poems out of a 'morally ambiguous situation'.[25] In *Lives* and in his more recent poem 'A Disused Shed in County Wexford' Mahon has given good grounds for belief that he has the necessary imaginative and intellectual gifts to emulate them.

'A Disused Shed in County Wexford', employing a hauntingly poignant image, addresses itself to an act of rescue; its subject, the victims of history and nature. They wait like mushrooms in forgotten places for our necessary attention. Mahon opens a door on their fate, allows them their proper say in a poem of remarkable, tender power and authority that comprehends Ireland's civil wars, German concentration camps, the acts of God and the casual corruption of an advanced, morally neutral technology:

> A half-century, without visitors, in the dark—
> Poor preparation for the cracking lock
> And creak of hinges. Magi, moon-men,
> Powdery prisoners of the old regime,
> Web-throated, stalked like triffids, racked by drouth
> And insomnia, only the ghost of a scream
> At the flash-bulb firing-squad we wake them with
> Shows there is life yet in their feverish forms.
> Grown beyond nature now, soft food for worms,
> They lift frail heads in gravity and good faith.
>
> They are begging us, you see, in their wordless way,
> To do something, to speak on their behalf
> Or at least not to close the door again.
> Lost people of Treblinka and Pompeii!
> Save us, save us, they seem to say;
> Let the god not abandon us
> Who have come so far in darkness and in pain.
> We too had our lives to live.
> You with your light meter and relaxed itinerary,
> Let not our naive labours have been in vain.[26]

Notes

1. In an interview with Harriet Cooke, *Irish Times*, 17 Jan. 1973.
2. Mahon, "Poetry in Northern Ireland," *Twentieth-Century Studies*, No. 4 (Nov. 1970), 90.
3. Mahon, *Night Crossing*, London, Oxford University Press, 1968, 5. Henceforth NC. This poem thematically parallels MacNeice's "Hidden Ice" very closely. See MacNeice, *Collected Poems*, p. 76.
4. Mahon, *Lives*, London, Oxford University Press, 1972, p. 25.
5. Ibid., p. 24.
6. Ibid., p. 32.
7. NC, p. 6.
8. *Lives*, p. 3.
9. NC, p. 20.
10. Ibid., p. 35.
11. Ibid., p. 34.
12. *Lives*, p. 20.
13. NC, p. 2.
14. Ibid., p. 17.
15. Ibid., p. 29.
16. *Les Lettres Nouvelles* (Mars 1973), p. 195.
17. NC, p. 28.
18. *Lives*, p. 5.
19. Conor Cruise O'Brien, *Camus*, London, Fontana Collins, 1970.

20. In his essay "Poetry in Northern Ireland," Mahon applies the
    terms 'diffuseness' and 'dissociation' to his own first book and to
    those of Simmons and Michael Longley. See *Twentieth-Century
    Studies*, No. 4 (Nov. 1970), 92.
21. *Lives*, p. 6.
22. Ibid., pp. 26-7.
23. Ibid., pp. 9-10.
24. Ibid., p. 18.
25. Interview with Harriet Cooke.
26. *The Listener*, 27 Sept. 1973, p. 412.

BLAKE MORRISON
"An Expropriated Mycologist"

Times Literary Supplement, Feb. 15, 1980, p. 168

Ten years ago, when the strength of contemporary North-ern Irish poetry was beginning to become evident, but before it had become fashionable to talk of a "renaissance" Derek Mahon wrote a short essay called "Poetry in Northern Ireland" for the periodical *Twentieth-Century Studies*. Still the best introduction to the subject, Mahon's essay described the origins of the Belfast grouping in the 1960s, as well as providing a roll-call of the key figures—"John Montague (b. 1929), James Simmons (b. 1935), Seamus Heaney (b. 1939), Michael Longley (b. 1939), myself I suppose (b. 1941), and a number of younger fellows". That I "suppose" is no doubt chiefly a matter of tact, a necessary check against the charge of immodesty. But it would not be entirely fanciful to read into it Mahon's quite genuine uncertainty about whether to place himself in that company.

His verse-letters and his dedications to poets like Hewitt, Heaney and Longley put Mahon firmly within the community; and he uses the word "we" in his verse with a confidence that no English contemporary could command. But the more common guise in which he appears in his poems is as a rootless and restless outsider, lonely in flats or on beaches; and there is a poem called "Afterlives" in which he speaks of "going home by sea/For the first time in years" and of being unable to "recognize/The places I grew up in". Of all the poets to have emerged from the North, Mahon seems the least locally attached.

Whether this makes him a better or worse poet than his fellow-Northerners is not an easy question to answer, but it is one which the publication of *Poems 1962-1978* at least puts us in a better position to consider. The collection brings together most of the poems in Mahon's first three books, *Night-Crossing* (1968), *Lives* (1972) and *The Snow Party* (1975), as well as a certain amount of new work. Looking back over the contents of the first two books, one might wonder why they aroused so much interest at all, for though consistently decent and well made few suggest any very striking talent. "Glengormley", rightly brought forward to the front of the collection, has a brisk assurance brought about by its near bathetic opening rhymes— "Wonders are many and more wonderful than man'/Who has tamed the terrier, trimmed the hedge/And grasped the principle of the watering-can"—but strikes many poses, some of them Yeatsian ones, in what follows. "The Poets Lie Where They Fell" provides a witty account of the poet as scrouger and misfit, but is too cosy in its Bohemian ("We were born to this", "Forgive us, we mean well").

As the title of the second book implies, the overall impression of the early work is of a series of interesting "Lives", with Mahon imagining himself into the the place of relatives, artists, even a child in the womb, but coming up with very little in the way of profundity or insight. Mahon has considerable

sympathy with a post-Movement tradition of the poem as anecdote-and-moral, but in that kind of poem he is at his least interesting.

The turning-point in Mahon's career comes in the poem "Lives" itself, where he does not offer, as it sounds he might do, more in the line of human case-studies, but turns instead to the anonymous, inanimate and non-human. The "lives" in question are ones Mahon imagines himself having in a former, mineral existence—"First time out/I was a torc of gold", "Once I was an oar", "The time that I liked/best was when/I was a bump of clay":

> So many lives,
> So many things to remember!
> I was a stone in Tibet,
>
> A tongue of bark
> At the heart of Africa
> Growing darker and darker

The poem is one of a remarkable cluster in which Mahon appears a kind of anthropologist or archaeologist, rediscovering past cultures, recording the decline of present ones, or simply absenting himself from human populations altogether to picture a place where "seas sigh to themselves/Reliving the days before the days of sail."

Among these poems are "Entropy", "Going Home", "The Snow Party", "The Last of the Fire Kings", "The Golden Bough", "The Apotheosis of Tins", "The Banished Gods" and "Matthew V. 29–30", and behind several of them runs an apocalyptic impulse, a dream of "a twilight of cities" after which "there will be silence, then/A sigh of waking/As from a long dream". In the weaker of the poems, Mahon allows his fascination with the abandoned and out-of-the-way to be diverted to moralistic ends: there are smacks at modern technology and a far from convincing attempt to affirm the value of self-sufficiency and retreat. Even in the failures, however, one can see the imagery and the tone of voice to be found in Mahon's master-work, "A Disused Shed in Co. Wexford", a poem which has already a justifiable reputation as one of the finest British poems of the decade. Here, too, is a lost world happened on by the poet: the "mushrooms crowd[ing] to a keyhole" in a burnt-out hotel become a symbol of past human aspirations (not the least of those from "civil war days" in Ireland) striving to be remembered and redeemed:

> They are begging us, you see, in their wordless way,
> To do something, to speak on their behalf
> Or at least not to close the door again.
> Lost people of Treblinka and Pompeii!
> 'Let the gods not abandon us
> Who have come so far in darkness and in pain.
> We too had our lives to live,
> You with your light meter and relaxed itinerary,
> Let not our native labours have been in vain!'

It is understandable that having written "A Disused Shed . . ." Mahon should want to revise some of his earlier work in its light. *Poems 1962-1978* isn't just a collecting but a reworking, with many changes being made to titles and dedications, some of them apparently trivial: 'Dowson and Company' is retitled, less specifically, "Poets of the Nineties," whereas "Death of a Film Star" becomes, more specifically "The Death of Marilyn Monroe"; "In Belfast" is renamed "The Spring Dedication" and is now dedicated to Michael Longley, whereas Paul Smyth no longer has "Day Trip to Donegal" dedicated to him. Other changes are more important. "A Hermit" and "The Apotheosis of Tins", previously prose-poems, reappear in strange, indented stanza-forms; suggestions of terseness and telegraphese are smoothed over with prose connectives; risk-taking ugliness or slang is deleted, an at times too easy lyricism coming in instead; and there's a discernible shift to the six-line stanza—"What Will Remain", for example, already rewritten once to become "Thamuz", now has its three line stanzas doubled up and is retitled "The Golden Bough".

Whether these revisions are generally for the good is not at all clear. What is clear, and somewhat discouraging, is the pattern they follow: that of an older poet tidying up his younger self, sometimes with the result of greater technical competence, but sometimes, too, at the cost of vigor.

Tidiness is not exactly a vice, but its presence sometimes indicates that Mahon has not probed sufficiently far, that he has been too insistent on mastering language and has not allowed himself to be in some degree mastered by it. Certain poems from *The Snow Party* augered well in this respect, suggesting that Mahon was beginning to trust language to do his work for him—there was "Leaves" for example:

> Somewhere there is an afterlife
> Of dead leaves,
> A stadium filled with an infinite
> Rustling and sighing.
> Somewhere in the heaven

> Of lost futures
> The lives we might have led
> Have found their own fulfilment.

What new work we have here does not, unfortunately, bear out that promise. The "Autobiographies" have authentic period detail, but remain flat; the "Light Music" fragments do not achieve the resonance needed to make them more than fragments; and the long and ambitious "The Sea in Winter", though it has its (Audenesque) moments—"The good, the beautiful and the true/Have a tough time of it; and yet/There is that rather obvious sunset"—does not in the end hit the right note: the verse-letter has always seemed too cozy and companionable a form for an essentially solitary figure like Mahon.

It is in its gathering up of previous (and now out-of-print) books, then, rather than in its new work, that *Poems 1962-1978* is most useful. The collection shows the steady growth of a poet who, having a substantial body of work behind him, some of it a high quality, could now take several possible directions. It would be a pity if the remarkable finds he chanced on during his period as poet-archaeologist or "expropriated mycologist" should be forgotten, for it is there that his real imagination seems to lie.

OLIVIA MANNING

c. 1913–1980

Olivia Manning was born in Portsmouth, Hampshire, on March 2 of a year sometime between 1911 and 1915. Though she grew up in Portsmouth, her Anglo-Irish background was accentuated by childhood vacations in Ulster. She sold her first stories while still at school, and at eighteen moved to London to further her writing career. She supported herself by working at various menial jobs, while working on her first novel, *The Wind Changes* (1938).

In 1939 Manning married, and went to live with her husband, a British Council lecturer, in Bucharest. After a year they were forced by the war to evacuate via Greece to Egypt, and then spent three years in Jerusalem, returning to England in 1945. These experiences form the basis of her best-known work, the Balkan trilogy, made up of *The Great Fortune* (1960), *The Spoilt City* (1962), and *Friends and Heroes* (1965). The story is continued in *The Levant Trilogy*, comprising *The Danger Tree* (1977), *The Battle Lost and Won* (1978), and *The Sum of Things* (1980). Among her other novels are *School for Love* (1951) and *The Rain Forest* (1974). She also wrote two books of short stories, *Growing Up* (1948), and *A Romantic Hero* (1967). Her fascination with cats, especially Siamese, is expressed in *Extraordinary Cats* (1967).

Manning was made a CBE in 1976. She died on the Isle of Wight on July 23, 1980.

Whom is (Manning) like exactly? Well, she isn't quite like Elizabeth Bowen, although sharing some of that writer's sensibility, and not quite like Margaret Kennedy, though she writes with charm, and she isn't as caustic or satiric as a few other English lady writers who might be named. There is no pretension in her writing, and no bitterness—and yet her view of life is not in the least warped with sentimentality, although love is largely the subject of this book, as the title might indicate. I think what she is mainly is a solid professional, concerned with keeping her story interesting, her characters real, and her attitudes mature. She can evoke pity, describe the shame and the reality of poverty, and she can be delightfully entertaining. A light novelist? By no means. Let us say she is a modest novelist, in the sense that she keeps her aims fairly small and circumspect. Having circumscribed her subject she proceeds to reveal it with deftness and near-perfection.

—HOLLIS ALPERT, "London Bohemians," *SR*, Nov. 17, 1956, p. 18

(Manning's Balkan trilogy) seems to me perhaps the most important long work of fiction to have been written by an English woman novelist since the war; it seems also (in the wider sense that was not applicable to my chapter on the war-novels of servicemen) to be one of the finest records we have of the impact of that war on Europe. Miss Manning's two chief characters, Harriet and Guy Pringle, are living in Bucharest at the beginning of *The Great Fortune*: Guy is working for a British cultural mission in Rumania. In the first year of the war Harriet (who is the observer of the two; she observes her own husband as well as the big public events in which both are caught up) watches the slow corruption of a doomed civilization. The observation finds comic, as well as poetic, expression: the Rumanians are drawn with exasperated tenderness and are sometimes caricatured, but they remain real and rounded. In *The Spoilt City* we move towards the occupation of the city by the Germans after the fall of France; in the final novel Harriet and Guy are in Athens, in a fresh centre of disturbance, though accompanied there by a preposterous *émigré* aristocrat, their friend.

The minute and accurate record of the Balkans under the stress of war is only one aspect of the trilogy; the other aspect, perhaps more important, is Harriet Pringle's attempt to understand her husband—a process which is incomplete even at the end of *Friends and Heroes*. He is a complex character, big, cultured, quixotically helpful, vital, often foolish, demanding—indeed, one of the most fully created male leads of contemporary fiction. He needs three large volumes for his setting forth and, summing up the variable contradictoriness of man, he balances the Balkan civilizations which are breaking up, though only, as we know, to be remade. He is a kind of civilization in himself.

Miss Manning's talent is very considerable, and her Balkan trilogy is the important work towards which her earlier novels—*The Wind Changes, School for Love* and *A Different Face*—have been leading. It is rarely that one finds such a variety of gifts in one contemporary woman writer—humour, poetry, the power of the exact image, the ability to be both hard and compassionate, a sense of place, all the tricks of impersonation and, finally, a historical eye.—ANTHONY BURGESS, "Other Kinds of Massiveness," *The Novel Now,* 1967, pp. 94–95

Olivia Manning's *The Rain Forest* is one of those novels often described as 'old-fashioned': it gives all the satisfactions of a thoroughly planned and developing structure, a generally unobtrusive (but all too conscious) symbolism, an extensive roll of sharply outlined characters, subplots which refract and distortedly echo the principal story, and—most 'old-fashioned' of all, I suppose—a wholly professional and detached authorial voice, serenely encompassing the upsets and explosions it describes, arranging effects and set-pieces and settling accounts with impersonal calm. It's the novelist's grand, disposing narrative manner, and when it works as well as it does in *The Rain Forest*, it exists above fashion, old or new, as a particularly lucid way of getting a novel written and a story told.

In this case, the story concerns Hugh and Kristy Foster, who leave London when Hugh's script-writing career has slumped and take their wobbling marriage to Al-Bustan, an island in the Indian Ocean where the Empire is slowly and pompously winding down. Half of the island is the steamy mixture of British colonial snobbery and incompetence, rich Western decadence (at the exclusive Praslin hotel), Levantine plotting, seedy nightclubs and the Residency garden, which this sort of setting invariably suggests in fiction; the other half of Al-Bustan is the primeval rain forest of the title, territory forbidden to the island's inhabitants. This said, any longtime reader of novels will know that a revolution is in the offing, that the Fosters will suffer estrangement but rescue their marriage, and that some of the cast will penetrate the forest and—because it's primeval—in some way be renewed by it. Yet this summary, close enough to the events of the novel, does not suggest the delicacy of Olivia Manning's evocation of Al-Bustan, nor the effective eccentricity of her imagination: the world of plum-faced British residents, mummified by the conventions of a century before, takes on an oddly surreal and vivid awfulness, as in a film by Buñuel.—PETER STRAUB, "Detachment," *NS,* April 5, 1974, pp. 486–87

The Sum of Things might have looked like a different novel if Olivia Manning hadn't died this summer. With the prospect of more novels to come, this concluding volume of her Levant Trilogy might have seemed mainly about adjustment, compromise, experience. The trilogy ends, as it began, with Guy and Harriet Pringle (who were also the protagonists of Manning's Balkan Trilogy) continuing their contingent lives in Cairo during the second world war. Their lives must be contingent because, as Harriet realises, war is a special case of life: you have to do what you're told. The comings and goings of the North African campaign mimic and exaggerate Harriet's female powerlessness and ironically set off Guy's self-absorbed ebullience. Meanwhile other people are killed. *The Sum of Things* significantly ends in the midst of war with only local victories.

Now, since *The Sum of Things* must stand as the last novel in Olivia Manning's long and well-used career, it is still about contingent manouevres, but it is also, powerfully, about duration. In Manning's humane irony all events in life are radiantly fresh, but they are over quickly, their fulness is never quite used, and they never yield the knowledge which they tantalisingly might give if one knew where to look. So life continues until it is sliced off by death. Olivia Manning has managed to write that modern rarity, a philosophical novel formed entirely out of fragments of felt life. In *The Sum of Things* everything happens through people, even though the flares and barrages of history have put these people where they are. The rich filth of Cairo and the overpowering desert landscape are always seen by someone, often by Harriet, who comes closest to being Manning's mouthpiece, but also by others, including the youthful soldier Simon Boulderstone, whose recuperation into banal maturity forms one of the subplots.

The Sum of Things is a novel of incomplete recognitions. Vaguely trying, and equally vaguely failing, to understand, is the mark of a serious Manning character. The failure is almost always not recognized by the character and is usually not underlined by authorial comment; otherwise life couldn't go on. Beyond the more fully alive characters are the Egyptians, whose unstressed but repeatedly described object-status adds up to Manning's cold-eyed critique of the colonial world-view:

> As the heat slackened, a safragi came to pull back the jalouisies and they could watch for the pyramids on the western horizon. When it became dark, the safragi returned to open the windows and admit the evening air.
>
> It was a pleasant routine but on the night that Italy surrendered there was a disturbing break.

In the expatriate microcosm, the 'break' is the ill-health of the passive poet Castlebar. He has contracted typhoid, which his lover Angela, whose young son had died partly through her neglect, treats solicitously by offering him nice excursions, extra sex, ice-water and aspirin until he dies.

Whatever Harriet, Guy, Angela, and Castlebar can learn and whatever they can feel for each other doesn't begin to free them from what Manning, in an earlier volume, called 'the bewildering inexpedience of life'. Life, however, isn't experienced as a trap. The sheer sensation of being young and alive in wartime is so strong that *The Sum of Things* reads like a thriller, in spite of what is at times a fairly sluggish plot. You want to know what will happen to these people. For the new reader, *The Sum of Things* functions as an independent novel. For other readers, the curiosity built up through *The Danger Tree* and *The Battle Lost and Won* is pleasurably resolved.

All the major characters except Simon turn out to have extra resources, even if, as in life, explanations are few.

Manning makes characters drift in and out of focus without precisely clarifying their dramatic or thematic function for the whole trilogy because they have an experiential function here and now. After suddenly changing her mind about boarding an evacuation ship, Harriet heads for Damascus partly because she thinks handsome, troubled Aidan Pratt is stationed there but when she arrives, he's been sent to Cairo: there's no meeting, no affair. I resented this bad timing. But Harriet's deeper impulse has been to disobey Guy and live her own life for once. Later Aidan kills himself, partly because he thinks Harriet has died on the torpedoed evacuation ship, but mainly, impenetrably, because he would have done so anyway. Though Manning, with her usual tact, doesn't say so, the point is that through nobody's fault, even the most fascinating and promising friend may turn out to have a fate elsewhere.

Olivia Manning's best novels take place out of England. The Balkan Trilogy and the Levant Trilogy are set during the second world war in Bulgaria, Egypt, Greece, Syria and Palestine, all underused by novelists. Because she has resisted Durrellesque exoticism, these settings give Manning's realism its characteristic combination of distance and ordinariness. In the Levant Trilogy's brilliant battle scenes, life's natural incoherence accelerates into a terrifying but supernaturally purposive chaos. In Manning's foreign settings each detail is special, so it can be presented economically, then met with again. Conversely the predictability of friends and lovers takes on a supportive familiarity. Castlebar will always stand up his pack of cigarettes so that the next one is near at hand.

Being in wartime Cairo makes Guy and Harriet's young married life extraordinary, but what is being condensed and intensified is ordinary life. In the central irony of *The Sum of Things*, Guy thinks that Harriet is dead. Meanwhile she is having an existential vacation in Syria and Palestine. While Harriet is 'dead', Guy realises how unhappy he has made her. When by a Levantine miracle (precipitated by a travesty-miracle in the Holy Sepulchre), Harriet is restored to him, Guy's recognitions evaporate. 'Harriet was safely back and so there was no reason why life should not resume its everyday order.' Extrovert Guy bursts into tears but a few hours later he's too busy to take Harriet to dinner. 'Defeated by his belief in his own reasonableness', Harriet quietly goes to the Semiramis Suite with Angela and Castelbar. The story continues, as most lives do, quietly and unpeacefully, with the important things never getting enough stress. Olivia Manning picked a good note on which to end.—HELEN McNEIL, "Last Word," *NS*, Sept. 26, 1980, pp. 20–21

JAMES PARKHILL-RATHBONE
"Olivia Manning's Dilemmas"

Books and Bookmen, August 1971, pp. 22–23

There is a crag on the south coast covered with seabirds. This wedge of rock, pointing obliquely towards France, is divided both vertically and horizontally: the families nesting on the western precipice will have nothing to do with those on the eastern side; nor do they find it easy to move their lodging further up either cliff face without opposition: the upper regions, just below human reach at the cliff edge, are the top of this society. The sea that faces them both sustains and overwhelms them. One has the illusion, from a certain position at sea and observing the cliff closely, that it is perpetually covered with a coarse-textured, pulsating white cloud. Only when one is walking along the beach, turning over the wrack and rubbish cast up by the receding tide, does one occasionally come across the body of a dead bird, the feathers stroked in the direction of the sea. One lifts the head that contains the tiny brain and observes, in the outline of it, the evolutionary lines from predatory reptile to predatory bird. And 50 yards off, just beyond the water's edge, those that are still alive, for superiority and survival swoop and tear.

This place seems to resemble strongly the world of which Olivia Manning writes. Her acuteness of observation, with more than a hint of George Eliot in it, seems to arise from her being part of that community of which she writes, defending, as she may remind us, not that perch from which she came but the higher perch she has reached. She has an awareness of the oddity, tragedy and comedy—the fundamental strangeness—of a highly structured, fractured society, a personal consciousness of the precariousness of maintaining a position anywhere at all as an individual. It seems easier, in her world, to lose one's identity. The occasional crumbling of whole portions of the cliff into the sea is disturbing, but she returns to her place: this she knows—knows that it is not safe; nor are the positions of her companions, those she describes.

For many of us, whether we were born into her kind of world or reached it by one means or another, her novels have a documentary quality. If we do not recognise the warmth and sympathy at least we recognise the slashing beaks. And though the sharp cries of the birds have, in her world, analogues in the innuendoes of scandal and gossip and rumour in the quiet rooms of some of the main capital cities of Europe (even when there is a crowd rioting outside), they touch the nerve-endings of the mind . . . now, or at any time. Had not *Middlemarch* been a literary lode for academic mining some parallels might here be made. For Olivia Manning is here on the same ground describing in geological detail the strata of a society. She asks questions similar to those asked by George Eliot—her own questions echo back at her: there is no answer but disenchantment.

We recognise in what has been called Olivia Manning's Balkan Trilogy the men of the British Council of that time, clad in their hairy tweed jackets, seeking to subdue darkening Europe with productions of Shakespeare and *Maria Marten in the Red Barn*; in this pre-Second World War Europe we have heard the shyly apologetic women, their wives, steering the conversation from these subjects into the comfortable channels of strange food and the difficulties in getting suitable accommodation. If we are simple enough to ask why liberal men of culture are not liberalised in their lives, we have to remember a view expressed by William Shirer in particular and lately discussed in a radio broadcast that the civilising process called culture can be diverted into any channel: it is a tool and not, like a disease, infectious or contagious. While we are beating our wives the works of Shakespeare seem to have less relevance than usual. But this we have learned already.

There is a sense in which her characters are often 'typical', but in her clear characterisation Olivia Manning never 'types' anyone: it is possible to 'walk all round' nearly all her creations, from her first book *The Wind Changes* (1938) through *Artist among the Missing* (1949) and the trilogy *The Great Fortune* (1960); *The Spoilt City* (1962) and *Friends and Heroes* (1965) to some of her more recent works, such as *The Playroom* (1969) and others. *The Wind Changes*, written about the 'Irish troubles', has perhaps more background written into it; but her characters have a clarity, a separateness from the author, that distinguish Olivia Manning as a 'born' writer. The consistency of observation from the first book to the latest is possibly rare among authors, certainly among women authors.

With his elbows close to his side, his knees clenched, Lush sat as though compressed inside his baggy sports jacket and flannels. He sucked and gasped, gasped and spluttered, then said: 'When the Russkies took over Bessarabia, I told myself: "Toby, old soul, now's the time to shift your bones." There's always the danger of staying too long in a place.' *(The Spoilt City)*.

The Balkan trilogy takes place in Bucharest, in the first two books, and in Athens in the third. There is an economy in the painting in of the background, a skill and panache: 'The end of June brought a dry and dusty heat to Bucharest. The grass withered in the public parks. Up the Chassee, the lime and chestnut leaves, fanned by a breeze like a furnace breath, curled, brown and papery, and started falling as though Autumn had come. . . . People ate breakfast on the balconies. . . .' *(The Spoilt City)*.

Nothing could be more definite than that. And yet, if one looks more closely, as perhaps one is not supposed to do with Impressionism, one does not understand the detail. The 'people' eating on the balconies are those who can afford balconies, or are able to find enough to eat. The Roumanians, in the book in crowds, appear singly to provide foils for the main characters, who, with few exceptions, seem to have the English attitude towards 'foreigners'. If the reader wishes to understand the 'alarums and excursions' of the Roumanians of this time, he must go to a novel such as Petru Dumitriu's *The Prodigal* (1960), where they seem to be, if characteristically foreign, perfectly reasonable. The same may be said for many of the Middle Eastern characters who appear (and disappear) in *Artist among the Missing*, which is about the conflicts that arise between the callings of art and war, of creation and destruction. In the latter book Olivia Manning combines clarity with a compassion that, present in all her work, is particularly difficult to disguise here.

In *The Playroom* there is a particularly sensitive portrait of a young girl, Laura, who is so real that we almost feel we know her. Towards her and her friend, boasting, illusioned, both frightened and frightening, emerges a young man from the lower depths. Mud, rape and death are the endings in this novel . . . the dead bird on the sea-shore, victim of what used to be called the class struggle. For this author it is obvious that some gulfs cannot be bridged without fearful consequences, no 'moving up' without the shouldering of somebody off his perch—and the semi-psychopathological fascination of creatures from the lower abyss. . . .

Who, of course, don't exist—at least, not as monsters. These people are also persons. Driven to extremes, they also will kill, marry, make love; some shall die ignoble, some glorious deaths. The education and the new literacy of the workers may be seen as an opportunity or a challenge; it is a different thing from the education and literacy of the cultured middle classes in that, because it is concerned with technology, it has mostly to do with making things work. It seems significant that the main symbol threading this novel together is a motorcycle journey during which Laura's brother has been killed.

Olivia Manning offers no solutions, posing her dilemmas, asking her questions. She is worth reading, at the very least, because she writes of things that lie under the surface of all our lives, that other novelists gloss over with blood or sex or both. What is certain is that unless her questions are answered very soon, the cliff-face of which we have written will become uninhabited: it is either to be a solution of a community tolerably understanding, or a dark, lifeless, birdless sea, without end.

HARRY J. MOONEY, JR.
"Olivia Manning: Witness to History"
Twentieth-Century Women Novelists
ed. Thomas F. Staley
1982, pp. 40–58

Olivia Manning knows her history so well that she can recreate it with quiet control. Crucial to our reading of these novels is our developing sense that their atmosphere is something which we, like the characters themselves, are constantly experiencing—until we are in fact saturated in it. Secondly, the characters in ⟨Balkan⟩ trilogy witness as well as experience the history enclosing them. In the above passage, for example, it is characteristic that the weather, the 'frost-hard wind that blew from Siberia straight into the open mouth of the Moldavian plain', is for a group of English men and women and, surely, for their English author as well, unique. All kinds of sharply defining, particularising details are, in Olivia Manning's work, evocations of place, and therefore of a time in history. The reason why a taxi, *here*, is almost as cheap as a bus is a fine illustration of one part of her method.

But the November of 1939 is not merely November; it is, for many of the characters in *The Great Fortune*, the occasion of a new, historic fear; for some of them, because they are corrupt, it is the occasion of no fear, but rather of impending alliance. For the academic, buoyant, faithful Guy Pringle, it is the beginning of what might be a long challenge to his left-progressive political beliefs; for his wife Harriet it is her 'first real encounter with the enemy', suddenly, boldly present in the group of Germans, and especially so in the person of Gerda Hoffman, source of that terrible 'whispering campaign'. Places and events unfold simultaneously because the characters of course experience them simultaneously, scenes and occurrences dramatic with abnormality yet always threatening to become merely ordinary. Moreover, they retain hidden and ominous qualities with which the characters are forced to grapple. To make this last statement, however, is to recognise the extent to which Harriet Pringle is the novel's true and constant centre. Of Harriet's grapplings we are certain: we know their nature because we know her mind so well.

. . . ⟨T⟩wo other important qualities ⟨are⟩ fundamental to Olivia Manning's work. The first is a kind of understatement which, to an American at least, seems characteristically British. Historic occasions are deliberately rendered in terms personal, casual, very nearly unhistoric. (When, early in *The Great Fortune*, Harriet speaks to Clarence Lawson of Stendhal, she perhaps provides a clue to Olivia Manning's treatment of the historic; the author of the Balkan trilogy clearly understands the implications for the development of the novel of the opening sections of *The Charterhouse of Parma*.) And the second is the special quality of auctorial witness which Olivia Manning embodies in these novels. To the laminating, accreting experience of the characters is added a reinforcing sense of the writer's own mind and eye. Though the author never intrudes directly, and though her narrative presence seems deliberately restrained, I often experience in reading her work an odd, unsettling sense of George Orwell; she impresses me as a writer whose experience as historical witness compels her to creativity, though in a very different way from him. Her commitment is, after all, completely to the world of fiction, whereas such an observation concerning Orwell would not begin to suggest the nature of his achievement.

. . . Olivia Manning's characterisations . . . are the work of a novelist determined to tip no balance in order to achieve some point. The Balkan trilogy therefore succeeds brilliantly in doing what all fine fiction should do, in creating the impression of a writer who always allows her characters the freedom to speak for themselves. Consequently, her Jewish characters in part betray themselves, and Harriet, herself a distinctive combination of judgement and compassion, is simultaneously dismayed by and fearful for them. Drucker's subsequent arrest, the dispersal of his family, and Harriet's own affecting relationship with the boy Sasha, whom, in *The Spoilt City*, the second volume of the trilogy, she hides out both in her apartment and on its roof, embodies both the history of a family and the moral challenge Sasha brings to Harriet. For Harriet herself must respond as best she can to what is perhaps at first merely surprising and mysterious to an Englishwoman suddenly living in Rumania, and yet soon turns out to be a dreadful, self-confirming reality. This dire Rumanian political and social sickness takes many forms: an antisemiticism long latent but now free to emerge actively; the corruption of the dispossessed and effete Rumanian aristocracy, attenuated now to its principal role as collective customer in the bar of the Athenee Palace Hotel; a government equally corrupt and, like the aristocrats, distasteful and ineffectual; a vast peasantry steadily neglected, on the one hand, and cynically exploited, on the other; and, in Bucharest, people of all classes long devoid of faith in any political institution and now dangerously adrift. In fact, what the first two volumes of the trilogy largely analyse are the complex (yet in the end clear) reasons why Rumania should emerge as the Germans' natural prey; here, at least, Hitler does not simply embody some uniquely German pathology. And, politically at least, these two novels have a second significant concern. Among their characters, only one excuse is ever offered for the Rumanian government's behaviour: its sponsorship, so to speak, by the British themselves. Towards the end of *The Great Fortune*, David Boyd, of the legation, is asked by Clarence Lawson, of the Propaganda Bureau, whether any change of official British policy might still be effective. His response carries weight, here and elsewhere in these novels, simply because he is the clearest, least compromised or deluded, of their political thinkers and talkers:

> 'Now, very little. We've left it too late.' David's argument was heated. 'But we need not play Germany's game for her.' Taking possession of the talk, David spoke with force and feeling. 'We support a hated dictatorship. We snub the peasant leaders. We condone the suppression of the extreme left and the imprisonment of its leaders. We support some of the most ruthless exploitation of human beings to be found in Europe. We support the suppression of minorities—a suppression that must, inevitably, lead to a breakup of Greater Rumania as soon as opportunity arises.'

Unlike so many of the other voices in the trilogy, this one is authentic, compassionate, indignant in relation to larger causes. It is of course the voice of the traditional British left, and also, I feel fairly certain, that of the implied narrator of the novels. . . .

If I have suggested that it is Olivia Manning's method to write civilised comedy about the dismal end of a major period of our civilisation, two observations about the novelist's method are, I think, in order here. First, her comic sense in no ways prohibits her from arriving at a swift and devastating articulation of the awful. Here is Sasha Drucker, speaking to Harriet of the rapid triumph of antisemitism in the army from which he has just run away:

> We were on the train and he [Sasha's army friend, Marcovitch] went down the corridor and he didn't come back. I asked everyone, but they said they hadn't seen him. While we were waiting at Czernowitz—we stayed on the platform three days because there were no trains—they were saying a body had been found on the railway-line half-eaten by wolves. Then one of the men said to me: 'You heard what happened to your friend, Marcovitch? That was his body. You be careful, you're a Jew, too.' And I knew they'd thrown him out of the train. I was afraid. It could happen to me. So in the night, when they were all asleep, I ran down the line and hid in a goods train. It took me to Bucharest.

Here, as elsewhere in the Balkan trilogy, all experience is sharply particularised, individualised. General observations about antisemitism or about anything else occur rarely. Moreover, the narrator of the novels is master of a broad range of experience and is on unblinkingly knowledgeable terms with evil. In the middle of *The Spoilt City*, in what I find the most shocking passage in the three novels, Yakimov appears in Hungarian-occupied Cluj, where he has gone on assignment, loosely speaking, for the English newsman, Galpin, who knows all too clearly the danger of the territory. But Yakimov has another reason for going to Cluj: to recapture his friendship with a man 'in an important post', the Nazi Gauleiter, Count Freddy Von Flugel, and thus to secure his safety from the other side. He does not hesitate to report the Pringles, the suspicious-looking young man they are harbouring, and the plan to destroy an oil well (given to Guy by Sheppy) which he has purloined from the Pringles' desk. The encounter between Yakimov and Von Flugel is a metaphor for the final stage of the collapse of the terminally enfeebled European aristocracy. And yet, complex and ironic as these novels are, we will occasionally sympathise with 'poor old Yaki', as he calls himself, although our sympathy probably has an edge of desperation to it.

Concerning my second point, I have already said that I find it appropriate that Harriet Pringle should have spoken, early on, of Stendhal. 'Politics in the novel is like a pistol shot at a concert. . . .' But of course Stendhal's famous comment really means that no novel worth the name will steer clear of the topic. And, although she does not of course achieve the depth or intensity of the author of *Le Rouge et le noir* or *La Chartreuse de Parme*, a similar sense is at the heart of Olivia Manning's novels. Not only are they centrally about politics and its consequences, they also appear to explore the topic from as many angles as possible. Moreover, she shares the great Frenchman's conviction that large, public forces and even the events that embody them are best recorded through the chaos they impose on private life, a chaos too complex to be measured totally by either a comic or a tragic vision. When, in one of many intimidating gestures, the Germans summon the Rumanians to Salzburg, a large group of Rumanians meet in the salon of the Athenee Palace. The meeting is in fact an Iron Guard reception, attended by some of Rumania's wealthiest citizens, and it terminates in a demand for the abdication of the king. Harriet, her bleak education proceeding apace, perceives the reality clearly: 'Here was Bucharest's wealthiest and most frivolous society standing, grave-faced, almost at attention, singing the Nazi anthem'. But the context of the passage is dense and ambiguous, for it opens with Dudebat, 'taciturn when sober, garrulous when drunk', indicting for Toby Lush the poverty of his own early years and indeed of the life of half the world; conscience and social protest are reduced to a drunkard's diatribe. In the crush following the meeting, it is Harriet, not the men, who leads her party out of the lobby; she does so by thrusting the pin of her brooch into the principal backside in the crowd before her, simultaneously recognising that an important-looking woman in the group is the wife of the ex-Minister of Information, 'who had been pro-British no longer'. Finally, in the street before the hotel, she sees Dudebat and Toby Lush running off like desperate children, fleeing without shame. It is Harriet's intelligent mind, antic but dependable, which orders, often if only by perception, the diverse experience of the novels, and Harriet's mind is the mind of spirit. . . .

I have said that I should return to what is for me the one weakness of these splendid novels. It is simply this: at far-too-frequent moments Harriet ponders, rather formally, her evolving relationship to Guy and her own shifting response to it. Although these passages become more and more repetitive, they are clearly, by their rhythm, quite deliberately intended by the novelist. Since, however, Guy and Harriet's relationship is acutely analysed in the spontaneous development of the trilogy, these expositions are unnecessary. Moreover, they tend to suspend Harriet (and occasionally Guy) in an unnatural posture of pure thought.

And *Friends and Heroes* demonstrates once more how well that relationship is dramatised. Disappointed in the extent, the inclusivity and indeed the randomness of Guy's concerns, Harriet finds herself attracted to a young English soldier, Charles Warden, and tempted to yield to what she hopes might be a developing relationship with him—except that Charles has been assigned to join the fighting. Now competing for Guy's attention with an impeccably left-wing journalist, Ben Phipps, who seems to her to 'have taken over Guy', Harriet recognises that she has stepped beyond her husband and sees around him:

> She remembered when she had wanted him to take over her life. That phase did not last long. She had soon decided that Guy might be better read and better informed, but, so far as she was concerned, her own judgement served her better than his. Guy had a moral strength but it resembled one of those vast Victorian feats of engineering: impressive but out of place in the modern world. He had a will to believe in others but the will survived only because he evaded fact. Life as he saw it could not support itself; it had to be subsidised by fantasy. He was a materialist without being a realist; and that, she thought, gave him the worst of both worlds.

Appropriately, if at first surprisingly, it is Clarence Lawson, just returned from Turkey where Sophie has remained behind ('She really was a little trollop'), who indignantly questions Harriet about her walking out with that 'bloody little pongo', and who asserts, as he quickly tells Guy, who, within earshot at the same table, is curious about their conversation, that he considers her husband '. . . the finest man I've ever known, . . . a great man, . . . a saint. And she's not satisfied. . . .' But Harriet's feelings for Guy do not clarify themselves until, getting ready to leave Athens and unable to find her cat in the woods near the villa where they have been living, she startles her husband into a cry of distress by referring to the cat as 'all I have'. Now, for the first time, she is aware of Guy as a man who suffers. 'Reluctantly she moved over to him. During the last weeks she had almost forgotten his appearance: his image had been overlaid by another image. Now, seeing him afresh, she could see he was suffering as they all suffered.' Harriet, perhaps with less excuse since her concerns are *not* so random, has been nearly as guilty as Guy of overlooking the claims and needs of the other.

Near the close of *Friends and Lovers* (and that it is the close of the trilogy as well is indicated by the death of Yakimov, characteristically understated, as a careless victim of martial law), when Harriet briefly entertains the idea of flight from her husband, she feels 'the tug of emotions, loyalties and dependencies'. Finally, filled with dread and fear at having witnessed the return of wounded soldiers—'a smell of defeat came from them like a smell of gangrene'—Harriet finds Guy in Constitution Square:

> At first she could not speak, then she tried to describe what she had seen but, strangled by her own description, sobbed instead. He opened his arms and caught her into them. His physical warmth, the memory of his courage when the villa was shaken by gunfire, her own need and the knowledge he needed her: all those things overwhelmed her and held her to him, saying: 'I love you'.

At the end, amidst the moral squalor of self-concern which constitutes a large part of the desperate British departure from Athens, Harriet, aboard ship for Cairo, finds in Guy a tentative hope, a small sense of the future which, by its very limitation, seems appropriate to their circumstances and to themselves: 'If Guy had for her the virtue of permanence, she might have the same virtue for him. To have one thing permanent in life as they knew it was as much as they could expect.'

Such a passage, restrained, coolly and acutely realistic, properly contingent, marks a fitting conclusion to the world of the Balkan trilogy and to the marriage which stands at its centre. And that marriage, we now realise, has become more and more important to us in the moral decay, the timid compromises, the fearful threats and the small margins for hope that comprise the terrain of a certain corner of Europe between the fall of 1939 and the beginning of 1941.

JOHN MASEFIELD

1878–1967

John Masefield was born on June 1, 1878, in Ledbury, Herefordshire. A happy childhood was brought to an abrupt end by the death first of his mother and then of his father. In 1891 he was sent by his guardian, an uncle, to the school-ship H.M.S. *Conway*, moored near Liverpool, in preparation for a career in the Merchant Navy. However, in 1895 he abandoned ship in New York, and after a few months of vagrancy, farmwork, and bar-tending in Greenwich Village, found employment in a carpet mill in Yonkers, New York. In 1897 he worked his passage back to England and became a clerk in London. There he was able to make literary friendships, and was encouraged in his writing by W. B. Yeats. His first book of poems, *Salt-Water Ballads*, was published in 1902.

Masefield married in 1903 and settled to a life of journalism and professional writing. He enjoyed some success with plays, notably *The Tragedy of Nan*, staged in 1908, and the novels *Captain Margaret* (1908) and *Multitude and Solitude* (1909), but the real breakthrough came with his long narrative poems *The Everlasting Mercy* (1911), *The Widow in the Bye Street* (1912), and *Dauber* (1913). By this time he had become a public figure, and after serving with the Red Cross in France early in World War I he worked as a British propagandist, making lecture tours of America in 1916 and 1918.

After the war Masefield settled at Boars Hill, near Oxford, and began to live the life of a country gentleman. He produced more long poems, *Reynard the Fox* (1919), *Right Royal* (1920), and *King Cole* (1921), and a steady flow of novels, essays, and plays on biblical subjects. In 1930 he was appointed Poet Laureate, a role he filled with responsibility and sincerity. He received a number of honorary degrees, the O.M. in 1935, and a C.Lit. in 1961. He remained productive until the end of his life, though after the death of his wife in 1960 became something of a recluse. He died on May 12, 1967; his ashes are deposited in the Poets' Corner, Westminster Abbey.

Among Masefield's later works are the novels *The Square Peg* (1937) and *Badon Parchments* (1947); the autobiographical volumes *In the Mill* (1941) and *So Long to Learn* (1952); and the volumes of poetry *On the Hill* (1949), *The Bluebells* (1961), and *In Glad Thanksgiving* (1967).

Personal

What sort of a man was John Masefield? Gentle, generous, courageous, unassuming, over-sensitive. The last English edition of the *Encyclopaedia Britannica* gives his birthplace as Liverpool; whereas *The Times* Obituary column gives it as Ledbury, Hereford. Take your choice. Seven cities disputed Homer's birthplace; and if Masefield was not born in Liverpool, City of Surprises, he was at least reborn there while being trained for the sea in H.M.S. *Conway*, anchored in the Mersey.

When we first met, half a century ago, he had at last settled down, after years of knock-about adventure at sea and abroad, as a prosperous writer. His first book, *Salt-Water Ballads* (1902), owed much to Rudyard Kipling; but though Kipling as a master-journalist could dramatically impersonate tinkers, tailors, soldiers or sailors, he never quite got inside their skins. Masefield *was* a sailor, had served before the mast, and wrote from the heart. To his grief, however, he had been forced to abandon the seas as a profession—like Nelson, he was constantly prostrated by sea-sickness.

It was in 1911 that he set the Thames on fire with a long rhymed narrative poem *The Everlasting Mercy*. He told me later that while seated on a tree-stump in a wood—I think at Ledbury—he had been caught by a sudden trance-like compulsion to write, and it came out in a rush. *The Everlasting Mercy*, which concerns a ne'er-do-well country boy's conversion, carried us out of the poetic doldrums of the Edwardian age. Those pungent, urgent, violent lines, with their breaches of long-standing taboos, exhilarated us youngsters. Delightedly we quoted at one another his hero's:

> I'll bloody you a bloody fix,
> I'll bloody burn your bloody ricks

—an innovation, by the way, which drew from Max Beerbohm the gentle tribute:

> A swearword in a rustic slum
> A simple swearword is to some,
>   To Masefield something more,

and which, a year later, emboldened George Bernard Shaw to make this in fact innocent adjective the dramatic climax of *Pygmalion*.

War-time Oxford was where I first met Masefield. He had since written *The Widow in the Bye Street* and *Dauber*, in much the same personal style as *The Everlasting Mercy*, though with rather less abandon. I was then on sick leave from the Western Front, and training officer cadets at Wadham College. He had been introduced by Dr Robert Bridges, Masefield's predecessor as Poet Laureate, chosen in 1913— forgive the digression—by Asquith the Liberal Prime Minister, in replacement of Alfred Austin, whose appointment as Tennyson's successor had been generally regarded as a bad Tory joke. The truth was that a Poet Laureate needed to be presentable at Court, and in 1892 few of the better-known poets could have been, say, admitted to the Royal Enclosure at Ascot. Morris was a Socialist, Swinburne a drunkard, Hardy an atheist, Watson had once assaulted the Prince of Wales in a park, Kipling had earned Queen Victoria's anger by disrespectfully calling her 'the widow of Windsor'. So the Queen was asked to settle for Alfred Austin—a respectable Tory journalist, but very small beer as a poet. Bridges, by contrast, was an eminent physician, of unblemished personal life, a sound scholar, an expert of English prosody, and the author of fine rhetorical verse.

> Whither, O splendid ship, your white sails crowding,
> Leaning into the bosom of the urgent west,

survives in anthologies today. The self-educated Masefield—who, though a married man in his middle thirties and the father of two children, had recently served with the R.A.M.C. in a hospital ship at the Dardanelles—looked up to Bishops with a huge respect.

After one costly victory he published two more narrative poems: *Reynard the Fox*, about hunting, *Right Royal*, about horse-racing—to take people's minds off the war—and the peace. It is dangerous as a rule to attempt poems on set themes—who was it tried to interest Dr Johnson in a great poem in heroic stanzas on the Mediterranean Sea?—but Masefield was a born story-teller and these were rattling yarns and sold widely.

I returned to Oxford in 1920 as a married undergraduate, and Masefield, hearing that I could find no rooms for my family in the crowded City, nobly rented me a cottage at the bottom of his garden at Boars Hill. I grew greatly attached to my new landlord, as also did my neighbour, the poet Edmund Blunden, another young battle-shocked ex-officer. Though members of the rebellious new generation, we refused to ally ourselves with the modernistic Sitwells, Eliot, Pound, H. D., Flint, Read and the rest. Theirs was a Franco-American movement, and we remained as patriotically rooted in pre–eighteenth-century tradition as Masefield himself. He was Chaucer's man, and is being now laid near him in Poets' Corner.

On Bridges' death, Ramsay Macdonald, the first Labour Premier, proposed Masefield to King George as the new Laureate. King George, an old salt himself, approved. He also, it appears, had looked upon the rum when it was brown, and chuckled over Masefield's 'Old Bold Mate of Henry Morgan':

> Now some are fond of Spanish wine and some are
>   fond of French
> And some will swallow tea and stuff fit only for a
>   wench
> But I'm for right Jamaica till I roll beneath the
>   bench,
>   Said the old, bold mate of Henry Morgan.

These islands have fostered several different poetic traditions. First came the early Celtic master-poets, justly called Druids, ministers to the Kings, skilled in law, arts and magical sciences, ranking high above soldiers, stewards and others, avoiding feuds and politics. Their persons were sacrosanct, their satires destructive, and their sole appearance on the field of battle was to part combatants. Later came the *joculators* (*jongleurs* in French) who sang heroic lays and praises of their king mingled with jokes and acrobatic feats, and went singing into battle like William the Conqueror's Tallifer, or Thomas Moore's 'Minstrel Boy'. Then the anonymous Border Balladists; and also the University Scholars; for Poet Laureate originally meant someone on whom a University Senate had conferred a degree for proficiency in Latin and Greek verse-composition, his brow being thereafter ritually encircled with Apollo's laurel garland. And until Masefield's time, Laureates, so far as I can find out, had all been University graduates. The worst of their line had been the eighteenth-century court lacqueys, who composed sycophantic birthday odes and poems on Royal Occasions. Indeed, so much odium clung to the title even after Wordsworth's and Tennyson's tenures of office, that Bridges had refused to write any verses at all at the Royal request. I will remember the 1913 *New York Times* news heading: KING'S CANARY WON'T SING.

For Masefield, however, a job was a job. A jongleur, rather than a druid, he felt bound to celebrate Royal occasions with short, loyal, carefully rhymed verses for publication in the centre page of *The Times*, always sending a stamped return envelope in case of rejection. He was, I think, underscoring the continuity of the Royal tradition with which our poetic tradition has been bound for more than two thousand years. I respect him for that, even when his loyal addresses grew more and more laboured down the years, as I also respected Bridges' view that no true poem can be written at request, even at Royal request.

By the outbreak of the Second World War, when modernism had won, when verses were no longer expected to scan, rhyme, or even make grammatic sense, and when long narrative poems had long gone out of fashion, Masefield the poet became, for all but a few of his contemporaries, one of A. E. Housman's

> Runners whom their fame outran
> And the name died before the man.

But he concentrated on novels and poetic drama, and as President of the Authors' Society battled hard to keep his fellow-writers from exploitation by Mr Barabbas the publisher, or from oppression by Mr Bloodsucker of the Inland Revenue.

And yet once, at an earlier otherwise dark period, the fierce live flame of poetry had truly burned in him; and though it had seldom since reappeared, he had never lost the supreme poetic quality: of unselfish love for all and sundry . . . and I recall his shy smile of greeting in 1921 when, spade and refuse-bucket in hand, I used to come up from my cottage and pass his workshed half hidden among gorse trees in the garden. Though assumed by his energetic Ulster wife to be working hard on *Right Royal* for the family's support, he was, as often as not, idly engrossed in a favourite foc'stle occupation: carving and rigging model sailing-ships.

Nor can I ever forget the still earlier days when I was a sixteen-year-old rebel and he my hero.—ROBERT GRAVES, "Chaucer's Man," *PoR*, Autumn 1967, pp. 241–46

General

Time was when the present Laureate's passion for bringing into his verse a great many "common objects" and even unparliamentary expressions aroused considerable argument; brother ceased to clasp the hand of brother, literary societies broke up in sinister mood, under the shadow of the Masefield problem. It was usually in vain that the admirers appealed to the others for a large view, maintaining that all the realistic detail, the noises from the tap-room and the odours from the mud-flat, served a romantic purpose. The others merely cited parody or unfolded caricature; or, naming works in which beauty exists without any complication of man's cruder circumstance, they wished Mr. Masefield's works and their devotees elsewhere.

Those storms are past. Almost everyone now is willing that literature, poetry not excepted, should be invigorated with—how shall one define them?—"the facts." Many have almost persuaded themselves that even poetry should be factory-minded and stop-press-conscious, or else be dismissed as useless. Meanwhile Mr. Masefield has not altered remarkably. He still endeavours to outdo Crabbe himself in the accumulation of commonplace things and terms for poetical purposes; and he is seen through all he writes as the idolater of a high, supernal, essential Abstraction. Of course he observes less spiritedly, and meditates more willingly, than he did in his younger phase. But he remains wondering at the peculiarities, the intricacies and the energies of mankind and nature, and doggedly asserting the immortal arch-poet beyond these shows.

> You are still that, O Beauty, you are ours
> As Hope, as some wild knocker at the door,

Entering, dropping snow upon the floor,
With word of Kingdoms never known before:
And strong hearts kindle, and the watch-dog cowers.

Persistent in his main argument, the Laureate is also much the same as formerly in the characteristics of his style. He still attracts with his bright novelties, his little pictures, his promising directness of approach to themes which might have seemed remote. He still mars his handiwork with awkward slackenings, or sometimes plunges into bathos. In spite of his zeal for spoken verse, he seems inattentive to the sound of many passages, and even where the brevity of a poem demands that it should be uncommonly melodious (as well as lucid) he may produce a strange harshness. The first stanza of two which form "1176 Hours" is of this kind:

Oh, ticking Time, when wilt thou pass?
A thousand never-ending hours
Before the HAS TO BE is WAS
And all the desert IS is flowers.

In weird coinages of words, which the language neither needs nor can accept, Mr. Masefield continues to invest: with such results as

All winter through they ravenge
The salprey's glitter, for scavenge,
Any findings are havings.

With all this, his devotion to the round earth and her inhabitants, his pleasure in making heroic figures human and common humanity heroic, his ingenuity as a narrator, and his gift for communicating aspects of the earth and sky perceived in solitude, combine to lure his critical reader on through each new collection of his verses. His topics are agreeably various, even in the point of geography. ⟨A *Letter from Pontus and Other Verse*⟩ finds him depicting his memories of Australia, of the Spanish Main, and of England (he joins the list of poets who have versified a long journey in this country, like Braithwaite, Gay and Prior). Then, he adds several items to his already extensive list of stories in verse. His title-poem is a sort of memoir of Ovid, with details of the episode ending in Ovid's groans from the Danube. His humour has its scope in "Nets," a parallel to some of Mr. H. M. Bateman's pictures, purporting to satirize red tape. His patriotic, yet cheerful vein is shown in compositions on Drake and Whittington, and the anonymous captain S.S. *Mayblossom*. Among the shorter pieces there are such titles as "The Will," "Hope," "Beauty"; and country scenes and seasons, with more than one protest against blood-sports, have their turns. In "The Wild Geese," Mr. Masefield writes spasmodically and cryptically, aiming through his visions of the world of those birds, and the recollection of the Great War, at something like a parable of current nationalism.

Detach passages from the longer poems, and you will almost certainly find that they do not altogether bear the strain. Even the short poems must be taken without too much scrutiny. Here is one, which if I am right, achieves much of the intended effect, in spite of the poet's own attempt to shatter it with minor eccentricity. It is entitled "November the Sixth."

I face North-West upon a grassy hill,
Green ant-heaps under foot, behind me, briars,
With leaves like embers in decaying fires;
The sun is in blue sky, the clouds are still.

Over the valley facing me, a tump
Topped by a hawthorn bush, intensely shines;
A leafless wych-elm lifts her dainty lines,
A greenest ivy wreathes an oak-tree stump.

It is ten-forty, a November morning;
Two goldfinches upon the thistle kex
Cling to dig seed, a thrush is cracking snail,

Two pigeons pass, a rook caws between pecks;
The finches watch me as I watch the vale,
The owl within his yew-tree utters warning.

After many years as one of Mr. Masefield's army of readers, I can open his latest collection of poems with something of expectancy—but that expectancy is no longer dealing with permanent creations, except so far as the Laureate's work is embodiment of a distinct personal quality. The immediate scattered charm is not lost, but the uncertainties of substance and utterance which perplex it do not diminish. Their company is ominous; but one may at least be glad that the future fate of poems is not everything.—EDMUND BLUNDEN, "The Poet Laureate," *LM*, July 1936, pp. 257–59

John Masefield's early verses tell plain tales of the sea in the jargon of plain sailormen, after Kipling's fashion. Such pieces as "Fever Ship," "Hell's Pavement," the dialogue between a crimp and a drunken sailor on Liverpool Docks called "A Valediction," are salt-water parallels to the frankest and most tuneful of the *Barrack-Room Ballads*. At least one poem matches in harsh irony Hardy's lines about the dog scratching on its mistress' grave for the bone it had buried there; when the dead sailor has been wrapped up in rotten sailcloth weighted with holystone and dumped into the sea, "It's rough about Bill,' the fo'c'sle said, 'we'll have to stand his wheel.'" It was not for nothing that young Masefield had studied Chaucer and delighted in Kipling's verse, nor yet that he had a friend in John Synge. In the preface to his one thin book of lyrics, almost half of which is given over to racy translations, the Irish playwright showed what was wrong with most of the verse in the first decade of the century. He set the poetry of exaltation above any other, but he insisted that poetry needed the strong things of life, to prove that what is noble or tender is not the product of weakness, and he added that "before verse can be human again it must learn to be brutal." These words, written in December, 1908, were largely prophetic. Synge wrote with terrible simplicity of his own broken life. Padraic Colum was sensitively setting down the commonplaces of sufferings endured and small pleasures relished by the Irish peasantry in their smoky cabins and on their boggy roads. Yeats, though scarcely the poet of ordinary things, was soon to turn from the proud, high-flown style of his early lyrics to the proud, severe style of his middle period, and to recall in his own verse, as sharply as James Stephens in his translations from the Gaelic, the savagery of O'Bruadair and of Swift. These poets, among others, helped to set the tone. It remained for Masefield to produce a narrative poem abounding with brutality and yet emulous of tenderness and exaltation, *The Everlasting Mercy*, and its companion piece, *The Widow in the Bye Street*.

Both poems deal with the crasser aspects of life, both are realistic not only in their recital of unpleasant facts but in their freedom from any moral lesson. The everlasting mercy is extended to Saul Kane, drunkard, bruiser, fornicator, through no virtue of his. The widow lives to see her only son hanged for murder—"'*Crime passionel*' in Agriculture Districts" the lawyers list it—to have her heart broken, her life wasted, through no fault of hers. Although these poetic narratives are inept and sentimental in their lyrical passages, the dialogue has the vigor of the language of the prize ring and the public house. The drunken hired man's threat to the farmer in the famous couplet:

"I'll bloody him a bloody fix,
I'll bloody burn his bloody ricks"

is a use of common diction in a common situation that would have lifted the hair from Wordsworth's horrified head, but would also have assured him that poets had achieved the courage of his convictions.

A less ambitious but in some ways more satisfactory piece is *Reynard the Fox.* This Chaucerian verse narrative has much of the color and excitement of a fox hunt, and gives life to the fox himself. But like the bulk of Masefield's work, the poem suffers from his carelessness in matters of technique. He hoped that his verse would be spoken rather than read, that it would become part of the heritage of the simple folk about whom and for whom it was composed. In the prefatory remarks to the American edition of his *Collected Poems* he observes somewhat wistfully of himself and his fellows, that "Whatever their faults and shortcomings, these poets have been a school of life instead of a school of artifice. However harshly the next school may treat them, that school must be a little livelier for their efforts." The words "lively" and "harsh" recur in the two short pages of this introduction. To look at life closely, as he at first tried to do, was to see it as harsh—for the great majority of mankind squalid in its circumstances, cruel in its processes, meaningless in its conclusion. Within his limitations Masefield sought to make his readers enter more fully into the daily life of the sailor and the farm hand. It meant noting such details as "the stink of bad cigars and heavy drink" in the public house, "the fag-ends, spit and saw-dust" on the floor, the "filthy hut . . . without a drain" where mangy chickens with sore necks search the room for crumbs, the gale at sea in which the sails are "whirled like dirty birds." It meant dealing with raw lust, savage stupidity, brutish work, empty deaths.

There is some food for irony in the fact that the man who was to become Laureate of England should have opened his career with a poem consecrating his song not to the ruler, not to the bemedaled commander, but to "The men with the broken heads and the blood running into their eyes." If he has achieved a place not generally accorded those who choose such unsavory subjects, it may be because, for all his knowledge of and sympathy with the deprived, his attitude was not one of rebellion against their evil case, but one of simple tenderness and pity, and his usage was largely conventional. It is worth contrasting Masefield's narrative poems with the brief piece by Norman Nicholson on "Whitehaven." The young contemporary uses the same short couplets that Masefield did, and his theme is related to that of *The Everlasting Mercy.* Nicholson pictures the seaport mining town and its history in hard, muscular language, free of adjectival rot, and rendered livelier by the use of slant rhymes. His is the unorthodox Christianity of the revolutionary, and his clear-eyed, hot-hearted understanding, no less than his virile craftsmanship, is beyond that of Masefield, who has not to the same degree felt what the younger poet, in a lyric called "Waiting for Spring 1943," rightly calls "the anger of love."

Masefield has been uncritical alike of the established political and economic order and of the familiar forms in poetry. It remained for poets with keener eyes and ears, wilder blood, quicker minds, to write the short and ugly annals of the poor in a more compelling fashion. A strain of weakness runs through his performance. He lacks the skill exhibited by his masters. Here is neither Kipling's magnificent vocabulary nor his incantatory manipulation of the refrain. Instead, Masefield offers a dulling repetition of phrase. For all the rough speech in his early work, he does not have the ear for the vernacular of John Synge, who said he got more aid than any learning could have given him from a chink in the floor of an old Wicklow house that let him hear what the servant girls in the kitchen were saying. Yet if his verse wants the craftsmanship of his elder compatriot and the earthiness of the Irishman, Masefield's work shows that respect for the school of life with which he was

to inspire his own successors.—BABETTE DEUTSCH, "Farewell, Romance," *Poetry in Our Time,* 1952, pp. 38–41

BERTRAM HIGGINS
"John Masefield"
Scrutinies, ed. Edgell Rickword
1928, pp. 96–108

Mr Masefield stepped in with his *Salt-Water Ballads* at the moment when the nation's conscience, too roughly salved by Kipling for the humiliations of the Boer War, was in need of a little warm restorative. The *Ballads* sound a thin trumpet-note of romance, rather boyish-manly, like a Scout's, though the idealism of the sentiment is beaten down by the drum-taps of the borrowed idiom. Attitude and art are tentative in the next volume, with a falling inclination towards Celtic fatalism, gratified later in the prose rhythms of *A Mainsail Haul* and *A Tarpaulin Muster:* a poem like "Fragments" is an indication of something individual under this facility and swerve of style. And then something happens to Mr Masefield. So far, his work might have been called promising: the imitativeness of a young technique is no bar to future achievement unless the failures in the personal construction are on a lower level of vitality than the borrowed pattern. Perhaps Masefield does not quite come through this test, but there are signs of an uneasy sensibility and an emotional force which, if directed by the self-criticising faculty ("the artistic conscience"), may be fulfilled in art. Psychologists tell us that during adolescence incidents which at any other period would be minor in their effect on personality readily turn into primary ones. "Writer's adolescence" is a period of still more delicate adjustments, because it concerns developments which, being less amenable to the conventions governing conduct, are guided mainly by inner processes. Masefield's early indecision between two attitudes, as exemplified in his first two volumes of verse, should in the ordinary course have been settled by the emergence of a predominating creative desire, the imaginative equivalent of an effort of will. The drama of his adolescence was the clash between his "heroic" and "æsthetic" tendencies, represented by Kipling and Yeats respectively—a conflict which he could have solved by defining it. That problem was never solved; and for all his output Masefield to-day remains an adolescent writer.

Consider the general characteristics of his work. The Beauty-hunt to which he spurs himself is a purely reactive ritual, inspired by youth's desperate shame for the bodily initiations of puberty. The image he chases over Lollingdon Downs is a tribal fiction with a blurred face; he never gets near her, and, if he did, personal lineaments are the last thing he would look for in a goddess for whom his feelings are strictly generalised. "She was something too pure and gentle for a wild man like himself. His nature knelt to her." Thus Heseltine and Rhoda in *The Street of To-day.* Masefield's spirit of reverence has never outgrown its attachment to the crude hypotheses which are society's compromise with nature in the equivocal stages of the individual's development.

Woman, beauty, wonder, sacred woman.
Spirit moulding man from brute to human.

Even if it were not execrable technically, the invocation would be ineffectual because it is cast in the terms of an archaic need—and it comes from a poem called "Imagination." The world goes on unravelling its multiplicity to Roger Naldrett, in *Multitude and Solitude,* but "it was his duty to beat back the world before it fouled his inner vision. If he were not careful he would find that his next work would be tainted with some feverish animosity, some personal bitterness or weakness of contempt. It was his duty as a man and as an artist to prevent that, so that his mind might be as a hedged garden full of flowers, or as a clear, unflawed mirror, reflecting only perfect images." Masefield has perhaps by now discarded the letter of such an æstheticism, but its spirit persists as a determinant of the form in which his later work is conceived. Experience is piled up in successive books (the "heroic" inclination of the author satisfying itself by an eager-seeming cataloguing of external detail), but the heroes themselves are held back from any vital adjustment to their environment by the limitations of the interpretative ideas they bring to bear on it. Sard Harker is a pseudo-naïve, a parody of Conrad's dangerously simplified Lord Jim: his romantic sense of honour, interesting in itself, becomes pitiable when Masefield flourishes it in the face of the tropics as man's strongest weapon against natural evil. Father Garsinton, personifying intellectual evil, is the sullen creation of a mind which, morally uncertain itself, resents responsible action in others. The foil to this figure is the little Susan Jones of *Melloney Holtspur*. In this play Masefield leads the characters into situations which demand a fine sense of good and evil for their proper *dénouement*, but though the scene is filled with prompting spirits and the dialogue lets off a heavy incense of consecration, the shoddiness of the solutions shows how insincere was the asssumption of values on which the action depends. Lonny Copshrews, the "ill-living" genius who breaks Melloney's heart, is the prospective victim of the supernatural machinery, but the dramatist, finding himself unable to justify his anathema, contrives a *deus ex machina* in the person of Susan, who is a sort of "salvation-kid." In the same way that Conrad's Lord Jim does not at all points survive the test of his banal "afterthought," Sard Harker, so here the figure of little Susan makes Shakespeare's tightrope performance with little Arthur in *King John* seem more of a disaster than it really is. Susan is conveniently endowed with the gift of mystical clairvoyance so that she may clear up the intellectual muddle in which the ambitious theme has landed itself; and her omniscient innocence, backed by a vision of young love, charms away the malice of the ghostly revenge. The muddle of moral categories is complete when Lonny's Spirit, before Melloney's Spirit has been appeased, is allowed to turn his apology into self-justification. "For all my wickedness, I cared for truth and beauty and colour; three things which have never let man down. I was taunted and despised. I was ragged and starved. But I called those things noble with all my strength, all my life long." The Spirit of Myrtle West, who was seduced by Lonny's friend, does not even stay for an apology: dazzled by Mr Masefield's skill in "slipping" Gordian tangles as though they were sailors' knots, *"she goes out in ecstasy Front Left."*

> O joy of trying for beauty, ever the same,
> You never fail, your comforts never end;
> O balm of this world's way; O perfect friend!

This is Mr Masefield addressing us directly through the narrative of *Dauber*. Dauber has a similar ambition; he goes to sea in search of experience and "copy," but his paintings are destroyed by the sailors. Concealing his vexation, he gives up his unpopular habit of staring at the sea ("My Lord, my God, how beautiful it is!") and determines to prove himself a man at the masthead.

> It's not been done, the sea, not yet been done,
> From the inside by one who really knows;
> I'd give up all if I could be the one. . . .
> This is the art I've come for, and am learning,
> The sea and ships and men and travelling things.
> It is most proud, whatever pain it brings.

He encounters storm and distinguishes himself, but later falls while furling a sail. Before he dies he exclaims, " 'It will go on,' not knowing his meaning rightly"; and, his canvasses extinct, is buried at sea. Dauber's plight would win our sympathy if his creator, at least, knew his meaning rightly. Set down in the midst of a company whose rough natural ways Mr Masefield's spleen has perverted into brutalities of Philistinism, his appeal is falsened; we take sides against the unanalysed prepossession which exalts him and the hysteria with which the claim is enforced. *Dauber* has been called a great poem—"great," says one critic, "because of its pictures of the storm, the sea night, the ship entering the calm bay at day-dawn." Such judgments come from a complaisance with the emotional intention which, in all imperfect poetry, perceptibly accompanies the æsthetic achievement. The careless reader is only too likely to mistake the first for the second, and in Masefield this game of substitution assumes the proportions of downright bluff.

> Then from the hidden waters something surged—
> Mournful, despairing, great, greater than speech,
> A noise like one slow wave on a still beach.
>
> . . . .
>
> "Whales!" said the mate. They stayed there all night
>   long
> Answering the horn. Out of the night they spoke,
> Defeated creatures who had suffered wrong,
> But still were noble underneath the stroke.
> They filled the darkness when the Dauber woke;
> The men came peering to the rail to hear,
> And the sea sighed, and the fog rose up sheer.

These are more than average lines from the descriptive passages which have called forth so much enthusiasm. It does not need much alertness to find the cause of their failure: Masefield may have seen whales, but he has never imagined them. "Mournful, despairing, great, greater than speech." The tritely associative first pair of adjectives provide emotionalised comment where the narrative requires an image, and the comment is so deficient in vital force as to depress the curiosity stimulated by the "something" of the preceding line. The comparative construction which follows is a good example of the substitution-process mentioned above. The careless reader, seeing the germ of an idea in the phrase "greater than speech," feels that the idea is a poetic idea; in other words, that its relations have been explored and expressed. But the imageless "greater" aspires to a moral prestige which will be allowed only by facile victims of a poetic hypnosis. What actually happens here is that the reader, instantaneously creating for himself some of the more superficial relations between the two subjects, the appearance of the whales and the idea of speech, passes on under the impression that these relations have been established by the poet, and that, as the overt emotion in the versification is due to the poet's perception of them, his own responsive emotion is for the same reason proportionate and proper. This vicious circle which bad verse describes in the mind of its reader could be equally well illustrated, from the quotation given, by the sentence "Out of the night . . . underneath the stroke"—a sentence devoid of poetic significance and even obscure in meaning till we realise that, having nothing to say about the subject he has introduced, the poet is using words to evoke an abstract compassion which, with a little luck, may kindle the reader for reception of his next subject. What is the whole lumbering, half-minded passage worth, next to this little flash in Job?

> Leviathan maketh a path to shine after him;
> One would think the deep to be hoary.

Or Milton?

> There Leviathan
> Hugest of living creatures, in the deep

Stretched like a promontory sleeps or swims,
And seems a moving land; and at his gills
Draws in, and at his breast spouts out the sea.

Or Rimbaud?

J'ai vu fermenter les marais, énormes nasses
Où pourrit dans les joncs tout un Léviathan,
Des écroulements d'eaux au milieu des bonaces,
Et les lointains vers les gouffres cataractant!

Or the most casual description of *Moby Dick?*

From this height the whale was now seen some mile
or so ahead, at every roll of the sea revealing his high
sparkling hump, and regularly jetting his silent spout
into the air.

The poem of Masefield's in which perhaps he comes nearest to discarding these unsavoury devices is *The Everlasting Mercy*. It has been hailed by his biographer as "one more of the world's great sudden original poems and one of the greatest religious poems ever born"; but the effect of that eulogy is qualified by the critic's report of his reactions—"At first we gasped 'Oh!' What blasphemy! What indecency! Phew! Then, dazed and unbelieving, one read the long poem again—and again—and again. . . . A challenge to all that mistakes respectability for righteousness . . . a torrent of inspiration," etc. The "indecency," of no interest in itself, is noteworthy in as much as it produces many instances, rare in Masefield, of a feeling, immanent not aspirant, prolonged beyond a few lines. The social satire of which Saul Kane is made the mouthpiece, though it is weakened by an alliance with the poet's familiar self-pitying exasperations, is protected, to a degree, against the familiar preciosity by the short-winded metre. The question of greatness need not be raised. Taken as a whole, it is impossible to call *The Everlasting Mercy* even a *true* poem, for the reason, referable to the popular verse of the past hundred years, that it aims to have an emotional effect disproportionate to the poetic means that are employed.

In *Reynard the Fox*, published in 1919, we saw Mr Masefield reaching a point at which the preference for a completely objective theme might have been expected to assist in the liberation of his writings from those moral perplexities, about which it is not easy to decide whether he has remained more persistently aggressive in the presentation or pusillanimous in the treatment. It is certainly a far cry from the ethic of Saul Kane, social outcast, to that of Charles Copse, M.F.H.; and the poet is obliged to inject more frequent doses of his mild æsthetic serum to tone up the moribund social code with which his sympathies are identified in the later poem. There is a large public in England so enamoured of the theme of *Reynard the Fox* that its almost unprecedented sales are not to be wondered at. And though it might be thought that since Baudelaire moral clarity, if not a prerequisite, is at least a desirable quality in a poem about manners, it is perhaps not surprising that few critics could be persuaded to see anything hateful in the author's substitution of an anonymous fox at "the kill" for the endeared original one of the chase. Masefield's style has always been more suggestible than assimilative, and several of the critics have gone so far as to liken the first Part of this poem, which introduces the personages of the meet, to Chaucer's *Prologue*. Those who have read and taken in ten lines of Chaucer will be spared the pain of verifying this comparison, which partakes somewhat of the metaphysical horror of animism, of death parodying life. It would have been more to the point to remark that the second Part, the description of the actual hunt, compares not too favourably with Adam Lindsay Gordon and "Banjo" Patterson.

Instances have been given to show the faulty principle of

life from which the lyricism of the greater part of Masefield's work derives, and the insecure basis of its inspiration. The fundamental defect of *Dauber* we have already noticed, in the falsification of the issues between Dauber and the crew. This falsity is no less apparent in the recent *Melloney Holtspur* than in the early *Tragedy of Nan*, where Nan and Melloney, with an hysterical persistence which wins them a place among the most distasteful figures in contemporary literature, prolong out of all measure their spiteful persecution of Dick Pargetter and Lonny Copshrews. The expressed charge against both these characters is one of sexual brutality; but their real sin, it is only too apparent, is in lacking reverence for their creator's vague and self-conscious representations of the meaning of life. Lonny was more fortunate than Dick in having little Susan as an intermediary; but then, Dick is only a village lout and Lonny, as we have seen, is a devotee of Beauty: "For all my wickedness I cared for truth and beauty and colour . . . I called those things noble with all my strength, all my life long." The nervous substitution of *colour* in Lonny's case for the third of the Abstract Entities is a fair example of Masefield's unparalleled evasiveness when really confronted with one of the problems which, for a quarter of a century, he has never ceased to pose in his writings. It is not his failure to find solutions (which are not the essential business of a work of art), or even the insincerity which the continuous pretence of having done so implies, that invalidates all his more ambitious work, if we except a few of the shorter non-lyrical poems like "Biography." It is the artistic consequences of this attitude, from which only the small class of work just mentioned escapes, that monotonously continue to deface everything in his output that is either lyrical or long. If the subject of the present study were a writer of more genuine achievement it would have been necessary to devote more space to a consideration of the instrument of expression in his work, and less to its psychological conditions; that is, to have criticised him primarily as poet. As the case stands, this extreme test need hardly be applied. Henry James condemned Whitman's verse on the ground that "it pretends to persuade the soul while it slights the intellect; because it pretends to gratify the feelings while it outrages the taste." When this has been said of Whitman there is still a great deal left that, whether in point of achievement or simply of interest, cannot be dismissed. When it is said of Masefield, there is no such scope for qualification: once the first spontaneous act of criticism has been made, next to nothing of any value remains.

MURIEL SPARK
From "John Masefield's Achievement"
John Masefield
1953, pp. 11–23

The truest thing that has been said of Mr. Masefield, and the most frequent, is that he is a 'born story-teller'. In an address on Chaucer, he once said:

Let me speak to you of Chaucer to-day not as a learned man nor as one interested in the fourteenth century; but as one fond of stories and interested in all ways of telling them and in all systems of arranging them when told.

People tell stories because they have a genius for it. People listen to stories because life is so prone to action that the very shadow of action will sway the minds of men and women: any purpose will arrest no purpose.[1]

That he is a born story-teller is apparent, not only from the fact that he is at his best when telling a story, but from his confident way—whether in the form of verse, novel or historical record—of attacking a tale and spinning it out, his way of bringing a story immediately before his audience. He takes for granted a larger and more receptive audience than most men of letters have the courage or justification to do. He addresses, not only the inquiring, the bookish or the purposive minds, but those with no particular purpose, and does so with effect. This alone makes for uniqueness. As one who adapts a story-telling capacity to several art-forms, he is distinctive in our time, when the art of narrative is almost entirely confined to the novel, which at its best has become confined to the narrative of ideas. His own novels I look upon as aspects of a poet; and as a narrator in prose and verse he can best be compared with other narrative poets. In this sense, he is unique not only in our own time, but in the period extending back to Chaucer, for though during that time the novel form has evolved and developed, though poetic narrative is by no means scarce in our literature following Chaucer, there is nowhere—not in Spenser, in Crabbe, Burns, Byron, Browning or William Morris (to name but a few narrative poets)—such purity of motive and in such abundance, as in Chaucer and in John Masefield. There are likewise refinements in the narrative verse of the six centuries which lie between these poets, which both lack; and there are differences between Chaucer and John Masefield which demand examination; but I am concerned here with Mr. Masefield's historical importance, so far as he possesses this purity of motive combined with abundance which had disappeared from English poetry for so long a time. 'He brought us to reading Chaucer over again,' Mr. Middleton Murry admitted in the course of differentiating between Chaucer and John Masefield.[2]

The *motive* behind Mr. Masefield's narrative art is pure because it is apparently designed simply to convey a story in the most pleasurable and memorable form, without emphasis on moral, political or religious issues or issues personal to the poet. That is not to say that moral, political, religious or personal themes do not exist in his work; only that they are not emphasized by a didactic intention.

The *abundance* of Mr. Masefield's work is something that must be reckoned with, not in a spirit of quantitative judgment, but with the thought in mind that the abundance, in such variety as Mr. Masefield has given, is by itself a telling thing. In my own opinion he has produced a superfluity of writing; but there remains an abundance which is not superfluous and which betokens the uniqueness I speak of when allied to a sustained purity of narrative method. From well over a hundred publications which include poems, plays, historical episodes of the two world wars, verse and prose anthologies, essays, lectures; books on agriculture, on Shakespeare, on Rossetti, on ships and shipping, he emerges as a later type of epic writer; in which respect, of course, his resemblance to Chaucer ends.

In his documentary account of the evacuation of Dunkirk,[3] Mr. Masefield writes, 'The people of this island . . . have cared a good deal for what will look well in a ballad.' And that, too, is really the essence of John Masefield's writings; he cares a good deal for what will look well in a ballad, no matter what form of writing he uses for the purpose. (He seldom, in fact, uses the ballad form.) He is an objective, comprehensive and liberal observer of humanity and all the activities of man. He is not concerned with putting forward those individual impressions of society which have indeed enriched European literature; he is occupied with a vision of things—not a vision in the idealized sense, but a vision of things as they are as

distinct from things as they sound in factual reportage. He concentrates therefore on those aspects of man and nature which signify, which look well in a ballad. Not that his work is stamped with the heroic spirit, as we take the phrase from the vocabulary of the critics; but that the poet evokes an heroic spirit nearer the life-size than the heroic spirit proper; and he does this through his reverence for man's powers of endurance, imagination and skill.

Now this high sense of man's vocation is the sort of thing politicians and suchlike are always talking about and so we are not to be blamed if we regard with boredom, if not with suspicion, the talking about it by anyone else. There is also poetry in plenty to express these humanist sentiments, but it has been difficult for any poet since the eighteenth century to get away with it. Mr. Masefield does not always get away with it, but predominantly he does; and this is because he manages to steer between classical heroics and the spirit of the age as interpreted by, for example, Mr. J. B. Priestly.

Mr. Masefield re-introduced flesh-and-blood into poetry. It will be said, what of Kipling? Kipling, it is true, dealt in flesh-and-blood but, with all respect to the recent and timely tendency inaugurated by Mr. T. S. Eliot, to do Kipling's verse justice, I do not mean, with regard to Mr. Masefield, the kind of flesh-and-blood Kipling dealt in. For Kipling had little respect for flesh-and-blood, and you may argue in his favour that his respect was for God, not man. But if you say this, you must remember that it was reverence tainted with pride, tempered only intermittently by an humble and a contrite heart: the humility was expressed after the bombast had been elaborated upon with evident relish. Kipling's God, moreover, is not a God of immanence, but is remote and judicious, somewhat like Kipling. The flesh-and-blood remains, with Kipling, as carnal as those bare words sound and therefore up to no particular good, as he, uniquely in his own way, saw it. But 'flesh-and-blood' is not as carnal as it sounds. And so when I say it was John Masefield who brought flesh-and-blood back into poetry, I mean also that he has a sense of the will of man, directing the flesh-and-blood for good or evil. Kipling's verse demonstrates the activities of man as observed from a distant vantage-point; he saw man collectively, and his individuals are just one of the collection; he recognized Free-Will intellectually but he did not embrace it imaginatively. That is why an element of ridicule can be detected in Kipling's attitude to man's endeavours, and as such is undoubtedly edifying. But it is a one-sided view of flesh-and-blood. The purpose Kipling recognized was the purpose of the community, and it was not even a universal community: John Masefield is nothing like so abstract; he is aware of the will of man, and can be criticized so far as he does not sufficiently recognize the will of God. Still, it is the human species he is out to represent, and the human species is very seldom conscious of the will of God. It was an exclusive sense of the will of God operating outside of man, and almost no sense of man's freedom and purpose which makes Kipling's flesh-and-blood something of a caricature.

Some of Mr. Masefield's people can also be possessed of a will outside of them, good or evil. I am thinking not only of Saul Kane in *The Everlasting Mercy*, but of the Dauber, marked as an outsider by his obsession with his art, and of the fanatical Captain Duntisbourne in the novel *Bird of Dawning*. Such characters are there because it takes all kinds to make a world; because by their rareness, they illustrate how truly flesh-and-blood are their fellow-men. But, save in the poem *Dauber* to which I will return presently, it is not Mr. Masefield's 'extraordinary' people who make the story, they only vary it. But these 'ordinary' people are not too ordinary to be true; Mr.

Masefield has understood the tremendous diversity of ordinary people. No two of his characters are alike. They do extraordinary things and yet they are not extraordinary beings. Compare these fictitious people, however, with the real ones in documentary works like *Gallipoli* and *The Nine Days Wonder*, or in an autobiographical work like *In the Mill*, and it will be found that these are ordinary people too, doing extraordinary things. Mr. Masefield has been interested, all along, in the things of a certain magnitude done by ordinary people, and that is what he has selected from his real or imaginative experiences, to celebrate; it is just the sort of thing that will 'look well in a ballad'.

But because, in the last fifty years, ordinary people are doing less and less of the extraordinary, it is improbable that there will be another poet of Mr. Masefield's kind for a very long time indeed. For this reason alone, he is important in the history of our literature. For this reason, too, it is probable that for our own time the work of his which we shall feel most sympathetic towards, is *Dauber*, the poem in which the unique man is offset against the common run of men. For the Dauber's isolation is become a universal condition—it portrays not only the soul of the artist but the soul of the sensitive man existing in a state of transition between an individualist and a regimented society. In this sense, the poem is not the most typical of John Masefield's work; if we are looking for a typical poem, we must look to *Reynard the Fox*, where what I have called the poet's historical importance and where the uniqueness I have spoken of, are consummately shown.

The reasons for my own preference for *Reynard the Fox* are concerned more strictly with his literary, rather than historical importance. This poem, I believe, attains the point at which intensity of vision and artistic certainty are equally balanced, and it is a great poem. The intensity of John Masefield's vision is manifest throughout his work; artistic certainty is another thing. Where there is, as with Mr. Masefield, a plenitude, even an over-abundance of work, we are forced to judge material which a more cautious or self-critical author would have left unpublished. With seven volumes of Wordsworth before him, Matthew Arnold marvelled that 'pieces of high merit are mingled with a mass of pieces very inferior to them'. 'It seems wonderful,' said Arnold, 'how the same poet should have produced both.' Mr. Masefield's critic is in something of this position. Mr. Masefield has never been a cautious poet. Self-critical he must be to some degree, as his writings on the nature of poetry reveal. But he has never been self-critical enough. Therefore we find, as we do with all poets who give in plenty—with Browning, with Tennyson—we find, particularly among the poems, a great many that do not come off, along with the undoubted successes. But Mr. Masefield's lapses seem to differ in kind from those of Browning or Tennyson. If *dull* verse and plain *bad* verse can be distinct, then it is dull verse that bores us in Tennyson and Browning, and it is plain bad verse that shocks us in Mr. Masefield. For the great must always be dull at times—not only did Homer nod but St. Paul put a young man to sleep with one of his sermons. Dull work has its own sort of badness, but the quality of technical badness that comes sometimes from Mr. Masefield is truly incredible. . . .

This intermittent falling-off can for the most part be located in careless rhyming, that is, rhyming which is accurate so far as it is a rhyme, but imprecise or incongruous where meaning is concerned. But hear Mr. Palmer on this subject:

> Masefield has been attacked as a slipshod poet, for being careless and slapdash in his diction. But the Aunt Sally stone-flingers have rather overstated their

grievance. It is true that he is sometimes disconcertingly uneven, and sometimes inserts nonsensical or inept words for the mere sake of effecting a correct rhyme. But this does not occur on every page, and it is better to be like that than to be merely bloodlessly competent. [4]

'No,' Mr. Palmer says again, 'Masefield does not bother himself sufficiently, and gets on with the next job.' That is the truth of the matter. John Masefield is not a reflective craftsman. No doubt he has revised his work, but without a reflective attitude. He relies on instinct which frequently leads him to do things of great skill in the way of poetic technique; but his instinct sometimes fails him badly.

Having made these observations, I feel it necessary to say that, granted the unevenness, one of the great delights of Mr. Masefield's poetry comes from the way he uses language. The vigorous sweep and naturalness strike a direct contrast to the stylization of Robert Bridges and to the 'poetic' poetry of the nineties; and makes small matter indeed of the Georgians, stylized as they too were, in their quasi-natural, Housmanesque manner. Such conversational ease in poetry had not appeared before Mr. Masefield, since Arthur Hugh Clough—that most neglected and rare of nineteenth-century poets. Anyone who can enjoy as poetry the language of 'Amours de Voyage' and 'The Bothie' will find the same satisfying effortless style (though not the sophisticated tone) in John Masefield. I do not mean the rhetorical parts of Mr. Masefield's poetry (nor of Clough's)—they are here for another purpose. But in the substantial functionary parts of any of the narrative poems; and in the shorter pieces too, the idiom has the same relation to common speech in Mr. Masefield's time as Clough's idiom had to the common speech of his day.

This naturalness was not easily acquired by John Masefield. It grew from experiments in prose, much influenced by Yeats and Synge; from the experiments in verse—the closest Mr. Masefield has come to Kipling—in *Salt-Water Ballads*. It finds full expression in such narrative poems as *The Everlasting Mercy*, *Dauber*, and *Reynard the Fox*. His prose style has developed in quite a different way; not vigour, but patience, precision, grace inform the prose of his later novels and essays. The vigour of the poems and the 'sweetness and light' of the prose seem to me to meet in *Reynard the Fox*. *Dauber* is perhaps the most dramatically penetrating of the narrative poems; but *Reynard* is the most technically accomplished, the widest in range of characterization and action.

I have been speaking mainly of the narrative poems because I see him first as a narrative poet. But to speak of these is to represent only one of the numerous branches of Mr. Masefield's genius. There are to be considered his prolific writings about the sea, about seamen and practical seamanship, ships and voyages. In a later chapter I will devote some time to considering his vision of the sea, how vivid it is in every detail, how objective and yet how passionate. And we shall have to consider his pictorial sense and how skilfully he paints a landscape; also his historical sense and his talent for bringing the past to the present. Therefore, when we have said that John Masefield has advanced his art as a story-teller, as a portrayer of humankind, as one who has developed the language of poetry, there is a great deal left unsaid.

You cannot get an idea of his mind only from his poems, you must also know his novels; nor from his book on Shakespeare—you must know his essay 'On Rigging Model Ships' as well. His work on Rossetti reveals one aspect of him; his history of the training-ship *Conway*, another; his anthologies yet another. He has translated poems from the Spanish; he has translated Racine. He has described himself, as we have seen, 'not as a learned man', and yet his capacity for knowledge about life, in no way a superficial knowledge, is truly amazing, and is combined with a far-reaching experience of literature. I would not have it thought that, because I have narrowed the limits of this study to one aspect of John Masefield—the most important aspect—I do not value the others. Indeed, I believe that all these activities of his mind are, in a sense, part of John Masefield, the supreme story-teller.

I have suggested earlier that Mr. Masefield's work is not of the kind which should affect us as an interpretation of the author's life. Some types of writing, the more subjective types, call for a search for their original meaning in the personal aspects of the author's life. Mr. Masefield's work is not, in this sense, a projection of himself. It would not, for example, reward us to seek for the origins of the people who appear in *Reynard the Fox*; these people are self-explanatory. But we shall appreciate the poem better if we have read Mr. Masefield's essay on fox-hunting, and if we know that his imagination has been involved in that sport since childhood.

Where a knowledge of John Masefield's experience of life can enrich our experience of his work, is perfectly displayed in the poet's autobiographical writings. There he speaks of the friendships, the events, the places and books which matter to him imaginatively, and which formed his attitude to life. It is not a complex attitude but it is at once a broad and sensitive one.

Notes

1. From an essay on Chaucer published in *Recent Prose* by John Masefield (revised ed., 1932).
2. 'The Nostalgia of Mr. Masefield' in *Aspects of Literature*, J. Middleton Murry (1920).
3. *The Nine Days Wonder* (1941).
4. *Post-Victorian Poetry* (1938).

G. WILSON KNIGHT
From "Masefield and Spiritualism" (1967)
Neglected Powers
1971, pp. 265–72

T he artist-hero of *Dauber* (1931) qualifies painfully as a seaman, battling mast-high in a storm of 'devilish' malice (VI). Later he has a fatal accident and dies with the words: 'It will go on'. So it does, for the great ship comes safe to port: 'onwards she thundered, on', 'the new-come beauty stately from the sea', moving 'like a queen' (VII). The implications are pure Masefield. The word 'devilish' is important. Man's conflict with the elements on the material plane of skill and science is part of a wider elemental conflict of demonic and angelic powers. At moments of crisis those greater powers may be sensed.

Two of the best prose narratives, *The Bird of Dawning* (1933) and *Victorious Troy: or The Hurrying Angel* (1935), make contact with these powers. In the first a ship engaged in the homeward race of the China traders meets disaster and sinks; and we are sixteen men in a small boat commanded by the young second mate, Cyril Trewsbury. We follow their fears, angers, hunger, thirst, and thwarted hopes, all demanding of the hero every resource of leadership. The situation is new: 'In all his previous sea-service the wrestle had been with the wind, to use it and master it'; now it is only the 'appalling water so close at hand'. The ocean assumes an evil quality: its waters are 'devils', a great wave crests 'like the Judgement Day', sharks draw near, foreshadowing death. Against these antagonists stands man's will.

In half-sleep the men are 'haunted' by evil 'shapes'; but to Trewsbury on his waking the stars promise a greater power, and he has a conviction of 'someone much greater than a human being' who is 'trying to convince him that all would be well', a guardian 'spirit of blessing', maternal, saintly, and loving. Then they find the newly deserted *Bird of Dawning*, man her, and win the race home. The relation of the two parts is loose, but in Masefield's world meaningful: disaster, endurance in a small boat, spirit-help, and the winning through to victory. The elemental antagonist is regarded as evil.

Yet more powerful is *Victorian Troy*. The ship *Hurrying Angel* is commanded by an experienced but tyrannical captain given to drink who runs improper risks to make better time. A cyclone approaches. Through the mind of our eighteen-year-old apprentice hero, Dick Pomfret, we have a succession of sickly atmospheric experiences leading to associations of 'the Enemy', 'hell', and devils. The ship seems to be 'suffering' and 'crying' for help. Impressions of horror accumulate. The water is 'malevolent' and the air devilish. There is a fiendish quality about it all: 'like a revolution or a war, it had drawn into its madness all the sanity near it'. There is no sensation of 'majesty' or 'power', no 'big, determined evil, but limitless hordes of selfish evils . . . determined each to rend his neighbour, even if it rent himself'. We are told that men have been known to go mad 'from the sight of a cyclone sea'.

The descriptions attain amazing feats of startling, fantastic, lurid light and colour: 'a flash of bluish, searing fire' leaps down the mast into the sea, burning, as it seems, 'a hole' in it:

> Instead of collapsing, the mizen-mast shone out conspicuously with balls or fuzzes of luminousness, which crowned the snapped cap, went down the lifts to the yard-arms, and stuck like globes there. . . .
> One greenish globe flopped across the poop close to Dick: it was like a fish that he had caught in a night of phosphorescence.

Pressure and suspense are maintained by a descriptive colouring the more cogent for its entanglement with very relevant detail of ship and navigation and the psychology of men in peril. When a vast wave threatens destruction, one is not 'scared' but just 'interested'.

The cyclone is a living entity: 'it *is* dogs; nothing else could make that noise'; or 'guns'. Its appalling abnormality is driven home: 'This noise could not be wind. This was some new, untested, unknown force coming into the world for the first time'. It is alive and it is evil. Its intended victim, the ship, is also alive, 'like an animal cruelly hurt, kicking in death'.

As in *The Bird of Dawning*, there is help from beyond. The hero, Dick, late from college, has to assume control and, when exhausted, dreams that he is being questioned by an ironically contemptuous Examiner as to the correct procedures to be followed in such a crisis. Dick answers as best he may. During the interrogation the Examiner gives advice which is eventually followed. It is more than a dream: 'Dick was in a state between sleep and stupor. In that state the figure of the Examiner seemed present just in front of him'. The spirit-powers use Dick's college memories to get a message through.

The ship loses two of her three masts; she is a hopeless derelict, foundering. The officers are overboard or out of action. Dick finds the captain, grievously hurt. Hitherto he has been unreasonable and brutal, but he is a fine sailor and a man of authority. He at first curses Dick, but later softens and ratifies his position in command. The first sign of his softening comes at the moment when, the cyclone's centre being cleared, the danger is passing. The elemental drama is for an instant reflected into the human soul. The stars as 'Sons of God', now again clear, herald salvation. The *Hurrying Angel* is saved, the hero acclaimed, and his professional future assured. Never was a happy ending more convincingly won.

In these two narratives elemental evil is mastered by human will, courage and efficiency, with the aid of spirit-powers greater than the antagonist. Calamity is not always so averted: the title *Victorious Troy* refers to the book's sonnet epilogue on the contrasted sufferings of ancient Troy.

The elemental antagonist may be either sea or land. *Sard Harker* (1924) and *ODTAA* (1926) are adventure stories set in tropical America within a surrounding action of imaginary politics, but our main interest is again in man's contest with nature, with evil through nature, and in spirits of help.

The sailor Sard, guided by a recurring dream, gets into trouble on land preventing his return to his ship, the *Pathfinder*. Nature is horrible. Once he has to fight through vegetation 'sickly with the forms and the smell of death', 'evil' in its 'over-abundant life'; among poisonous plants and swarming insects; and through a sucking bog which 'chuckles' in triumph. Later, after escaping from a prison, Sark comes on a house among foothills which radiates goodness. Good people must once have lived there. He calls but gets no answer, and yet 'he felt quite certain that the thicket was full of people looking at him'. He finds a ruined chapel with faded painted heads in fresco. For Masefield childhood is a strong power; and in his sleep Sard hears and sees a boy friend, who had died eleven years before, calling as from a vast 'distance'. Above the altar stand blessed figures and a trumpeter, pointing and urging him to be gone:

> 'What is it, Peter? What is it, you great spirits?'
> But the woman faded from him, Peter faded from him into the wall, but he could still see the shining trumpet and notes like flakes of fire falling all around him. The trumpet dwindled slowly and resolved itself into the blossoming branch that had grown through a crack in the wall.

As he wakes, the figures are again the old frescoes. A smell of burning mingles with his memory of the command to be gone. Warned in time, he escapes a brush fire.

Later, lost among mountains, he sees in 'dream or fever' a female figure like the 'spirit' of his ship, the *Pathfinder*, 'fierce, hard and of great beauty'. It says: 'I am the *Pathfinder*. I can find a path for you'. He is directed to safety. Afterward 'it was in his mind all blurred, like the events of a fever, sometimes it seemed the only reality among things dreamed'. In such events Masefield works on the borderline of sleep and waking.

In *ODTAA* the eighteen-year-old hero, Highworth Ridden, is plunged into a succession of appalling jungle experiences, again in South America. Alone with his horse he comes up against a horrible bog and a pool of reddened water like 'stagnant blood', with hundreds of dead trees standing in it (XII). He is starving, blistered, nearly blind (XIV).

Once earlier he had awakened by night in mid-jungle: an impulse 'from the heart of things was calling him to rise'. His horse is staring at something he himself cannot see, and 'a wave of fear' passes from animal to man. Whether the enemy is beast or ghost he cannot tell. The tension lessens, and the horse's eyes follow the enemy as it moves slowly round. It again returns: 'When it deliberated, its will hardened against them, the horse knew it, and Hi knew it from the horse'(XII). There is in or behind nature a more than natural evil, compared with which nature's normal evils are a relief:

> Then the night, which for some minutes had seemed to hold her breath, began again to speak with her myriad voices out of the darkness of her cruelty. The

whisper and the droning of the forest sharpened into the rustlings of snakes, the wails of victims, the cry of the bats after the moths, and the moan of the million insects seeking blood (XII).

Dawn brings the brighter energies of daylight nature. Meanwhile, Hi 'had never understood what night was, now he knew' (XII; for another account of a ghostly night, see 'Ryemeadows' in *Old Raiger and Other Verse*, 1964).

There are good spirit-powers also. Hi hears voices advising him, as from a flock of invisible birds (XIV). He wins through to comparative safety. In a hut with a stranger, Anselmo, he senses the spirit of a former occupant, Dudley Wigmore (XV) and in the 'fiery mist' (XV) of sleep is aware of its distress. Later in a dream and also *after waking* Hi sees him 'distinctly', and, as he fades, see the wall too, through him (XVI). Wigmore, who had been murdered by Anselmo, urges Hi to escape. Words come unmediated without sound: 'a sentence floated into his mind as clearly as though a voice had spoken in his ear' (XVI). On the way to his escape, Hi sees Dudley Wigmore clearly, by day, and under his direction eludes Anselmo (XVI).

Afterward, again in dire straits, Hi is visited in sleep by a figure known in his *childhood* dreams: 'all peace, courage, goodness and happiness were in her 'face' and 'hope so bright' that danger pales. As on certain other occasions, but even more powerfully, the spirit-reality is not confined to sleep. She helps him to rise, leads and accompanies him, gives him medicaments, and empowers him with a song. 'What happened to him in these hours he never knew, save that he was miraculously helped'; 'they were among the intensest hours of his life' (XVII).

Other novels show similar tendencies. In *The Hawbucks*, the hero, battling by night against snow, senses, as in *ODTAA*, his horse's fear and then hears a cry which later turns out to have come *either* from a girl then dying at a distance *or* from an intuition of that death received by a woman within call; and in *Eggs and Baker* and *The Square Peg* tragedy is averted by conclusions of spiritualistic tone. In *Martin Hyde* the boy-hero is encouraged by a sense of the presence of his dead father, who had believed in the rightness of Monmouth's cause (XVIII, XXIV). In *Conquer* an inspiration from some 'spirit' enables Origen to save Byzantium.

In our four adventure narratives we have watched heroes faced by hostile nature, together with an evil coming from or from behind nature, and the advent of help from spirit-powers. The conditions of their breaking through are in Masefield's valuations the hero's will and hope; he does not use the word 'faith'. In the sonnet epilogue to *Victorious Troy* we read of 'Hope the living Key unlocking prison'; and 'Helper' are grouped with 'Hopes' in the Epilogue to *Grace before Ploughing* (1966).

That such powers attend human adventure is witnessed by Homer, Vergil, and the Old Testament. There are other and recent evidences. In *My Early Life* (1930 and reprints, XXI) Winston Churchill tells us how, when at a loss during his escape from a prison camp in South Africa, he was 'led' by an 'unconscious or sub-conscious' power, which recalled the power he had known when writing with a 'Planchette pencil', to an Englishman's house, and safety.[1] Another interesting experience is recorded in Charles Lindbergh's account of his Atlantic flight in *The Spirit of St. Louis* (1953; VI, Twenty-Second Hour). Troubled by drowsiness and uncertain of his navigation, he became aware of spirits around him—just like the spirits in *ODTAA*—speaking with human voices, 'conversing and advising on my flight, discussing problems of my navigation, reassuring me, giving me messages of importance unattainable in ordinary life'. He was 'on the border-line of life and a great realm beyond', and death was known as an entry to a greater freedom. In Harold Owen's *Journey from Obscurity* (1965) there is a comparable account of ancestral spirits functioning as saviours from an 'incalculable distance' (as in *Sard Harker*) during the author's nightmare experience when alone on an evil-impregnated hulk in the South Seas. Since then he has been convinced of a reality transcending 'all earthly happenings' (Vol. III). Even more impressive is his account of how, on entering his cabin in South Africa, he learned of Wilfred Owen's death, finding his poet brother seated there with soft eyes 'trying to make me understand': in *Good-bye to All That* (xiv) Robert Graves reports a similar experience. In a note to *The Waste Land* (V. 360) T. S. Eliot wrote: 'The following lines were stimulated by the account of one of the Antarctic expeditions (I forget which, but I think one of Shackleton's): it was related that the party of explorers, at the extremity of their strength, had the constant delusion that there was *one more member* than could actually be counted'.

Masefield had himself had a major experience of the paranormal. In *So Long to Learn* (1952) he describes how, years before, when his work was not progressing, he heard a male voice say, 'The spring is beginning'. Soon after, *while crossing a fence separating a wood from open ground*, the spirit-helpers apparently using that action for their purpose, he knew that he was to write 'a poem about a blackguard who becomes converted'; the poem appeared 'in its complete form, with every detail distinct', and he started writing it down *at once*. That night, alone in a country house, he continued hour after hour until the door of his room 'flung itself noisily wide open'.

He took the warning and went to bed. *The Everlasting Mercy* (1911) proved the turning point of his literary career.

Such help is perhaps most usually, and certainly most strikingly, experienced by men of action who risk death. Will, courage, hope, and perhaps loneliness and the dark, appear to be favourable conditions. It may happen to a whole community in war-time. When in *St. George and the Dragon* Masefield writes of 'the dead' creating a nation's 'great soul', able to guide it in 'trouble' and 'calamity', or calls the victory at the Marne a 'miracle', the phrases are more than decoration. In *The Nine Days Wonder*, on the sea rescue at Dunkerque, after observing the 'will to help from the whole marine population of these islands', he continues:

> It is hard to think of those dark formations on the sand, waiting in the rain of death, without the knowledge that Hope and Help are stronger things than death. Hope and Help came together in their power into the minds of thousands of simple men, who went out in the Operation Dynamo and plucked them from ruin.

On a national scale the event was of similar quality to those which we have been discussing. The belief in the Angels of Mons arose from a similar recognition.

Notes

1. Churchill appears to have received similar help twice during the Second World War; see Jack Fisherman's biography of Lady Churchill, *My Darling Clementine*, 1963; 132–3, 134–5. For a simultaneous recognition of spirit-helpers by two temporarily entombed miners, see *Psychic News*, 6 March 1965.

ADDITIONAL READING

GEOFFREY HILL

Bedient, Calvin. "Absentist Poetry: Kinsella, Hill, Graham and Hughes." *Poetry Nation* 4 (1976): 18–24.

Browne, Merle E. *Double Lyric: Divisiveness and Communal Creativity in Recent English Poetry.* New York: Columbia University Press, 1980.

Dodsworth, Martin. "Geoffrey Hill's New Poetry." *Stand* 13 (1971–72): 61–63.

Falck, Colin. "Borrowed Days." *Delta* 60 (1980): 1–5.

Fuller, Roy. Review of *For the Unfallen. London Magazine* 7 (January 1960): 73–76.

Hall, Donald. "Poet of Stones and Fields." *Nation,* 6 December 1975, pp. 600–602.

Hamilton, Ian. "Loosening the Screws." *Observer,* 25 August 1968, p. 22.

Hill, Geoffrey. "Letter from Oxford." *London Magazine* 1 (May 1954): 71–75.

———. "Geoffrey Hill Writes . . ." *Poetry Book Society Bulletin* 98 (Autumn 1978): 1.

Wainwright, Jeffrey. "'The Speechless Dead': Geoffrey Hill's *King Log.*" *Stand* 10 (1968): 44–49.

RALPH HODGSON

Aiken, Conrad. "Three English Poets." *Dial,* 30 August 1917, pp. 150–52.

Fraser, G. S. "I, My Ancestor." *New Statesman,* 18 August 1961, p. 218.

Lucas, E. V. *Nation,* 17 September 1914, pp. 341–43.

Neame, Alan. "London Chronicle I." *Poetry* 94 (1959): 124–27.

Spens, Maisie. "Ralph Hodgson." *Poetry Review* 20 (1929): 247–57.

Sturgeon, Mary C. "Ralph Hodgson." In *Studies of Contemporary Poets.* Rev. ed. New York: Dodd, Mead, 1919, pp. 108–21.

Sweetser, Wesley D. *Ralph Hodgson: A Bibliography.* Rev. ed. New York: Garland, 1980.

A. E. HOUSMAN

Carter, John A., and John Sparrow. *A. E. Housman: An Annotated Hand-List.* London: Hart-Davis, 1952.

Graves, Richard Perceval. *A. E. Housman: The Scholar-Poet.* London: Routledge & Kegan Paul, 1979.

Haber, Tom Burns. *A. E. Housman.* New York: Twayne, 1967.

Hawkins, Maude. *A. E. Housman: Man behind a Mask.* Chicago: Regnery, 1958.

Leggett, B. J. *Housman's Land of Lost Content.* Knoxville: University of Tennessee Press, 1970.

———. *The Poetic Art of A. E. Housman.* Lincoln: University of Nebraska Press, 1978.

Marlow, Norman. *A. E. Housman: Scholar and Poet.* Minneapolis: University of Minnesota Press, 1958.

Page, Norman. *A. E. Housman: A Critical Biography.* New York: Schocken Books, 1983.

Richards, Grant. *Housman: 1897–1936.* New York: Oxford University Press, 1942.

Ricks, Christopher, ed. *A. E. Housman: A Collection of Critical Essays.* Englewood Cliffs, NJ: Prentice-Hall, 1968.

Robinson, Oliver. *Angry Dust: The Poetry of A. E. Housman.* Boston: Bruce Humphries, 1950.

Scott-Kilvert, Ian. *A. E. Housman.* London: Longmans, 1955.

Watson, George L. *A. E. Housman: A Divided Life.* London: Hart-Davis, 1957.

LAURENCE HOUSMAN

Balmforth, Ramsden. *The Problem-Play and Its Influence on Modern Thought and Life.* New York: Henry Holt, 1928.

Nevinson, H. W. "War Tales and Truth." *New Statesman,* 30 August 1930, pp. 649–50.

Repplier, Agnes. "The Brothers Housman." *Atlantic* 165 (January 1940): 46–50.

Williams, Harold. *Modern English Writers.* London: Sidgwick & Jackson, 1918.

Unsigned. Review of *Trimblerigg. New York Times Book Review,* 8 February 1925, p. 6.

W. H. HUDSON

Charles, R. H. "The Writings of W. H. Hudson." *Essays and Studies* 20 (1934): 135–51.

Fletcher, James V. "The Creator of Rima." *Sewanee Review* 41 (1933): 24–40.

Frederick, John H. *William Henry Hudson.* New York: Twayne, 1972.

Hamilton, Robert. *W. H. Hudson: The Vision of Earth.* London: J. M. Dent, 1946.

Payne, John R. *W. H. Hudson: A Bibliography.* Folkestone, Eng.: Dawson, 1977.

Reid, Forrest. "W. H. Hudson." In *Retrospective Reviews.* London: Faber & Faber, 1941, pp. 110–23.

Roberts, Morley. *W. H. Hudson: A Portrait.* London: Eveleigh Nash & Grayson, 1924.

Ronner, Amy Debra. "W. H. Hudson: The Man, the Novelist, the Naturalist." Ph.D. diss.: University of Michigan, 1980.

Tomalin, Ruth. *W. H. Hudson: A Biography.* London: Faber & Faber, 1982.

RICHARD HUGHES

Bosano, J. "Richard Hughes." *Études Anglaises* 16 (1963): 262–69.

Brown, Daniel R. "*A High Wind in Jamaica:* Comedy of the Absurd." *Ball State University Forum* 9 (1968): 6–12.

Henighan, T. J. "Nature and Convention in A *High Wind in Jamaica.*" *Critique* 9, No. 1 (1967): 5–18.

Miller, Richard Hugh. "History and Children in Richard Hughes' *The Wooden Shepherdess.*" *Antigonish Review* 22 (1975): 31–35.

Poole, Richard. "Morality and Selfhood in the Novels of Richard Hughes." *Anglo-Welsh Review* 25 (1975): 31–35.

Sullivan, Walter. "Old Age, Death and Other Modern Landscapes: Good and Indifferent Fables for Our Time." *Sewanee Review* 82 (1974): 138–47.

Thomas, Peter. *Richard Hughes.* Cardiff: University of Wales, 1973.

TED HUGHES

Adams, John. "Dark Rainbow: Reflections on Ted Hughes." In *The Signal Approach to Children's Books,* ed. Nancy Chalmers. Harmondsworth: Penguin, 1980.

Faas, Ekbert. *Ted Hughes: The Unaccommodated Universe.* Santa Barbara, CA: Black Sparrow Press, 1980.

Gifford, Terry, and Neil Roberts. *Ted Hughes: A Critical Study.* London: Faber & Faber, 1980.

Hirschberg, Stuart. *Myth in the Poetry of Ted Hughes*. New York: Barnes & Noble, 1981.

Lodge, David. "Crow and the Cartoons." *Critical Quarterly* 13 (1971): 37–42.

Newton, J. M. "No Longer 'Through the Pipes of Greece'?" *Cambridge Quarterly* 7 (1977): 335–45.

Raban, Jonathan. *The Society of the Poem*. London: Harrap, 1971.

Sagar, Keith, and Stephen Tabor. *Ted Hughes: A Bibliography 1946–1980*. London: Mansell, 1983.

Weatherhead, A. K. *The British Dissonance*. Columbia: University of Missouri Press, 1983.

T. E. HULME

Bayley, John. *The Romantic Survival*. London: Constable, 1957.

Coffmann, Stanley. *Imagism: A Chapter for the History of Modern Poetry*. Norman: University of Oklahoma Press, 1951.

Davie, Donald. *Articulate Energy: An Enquiry into the Syntax of English Poetry*. New York: Harcourt, Brace, 1955.

Hynes, Sam. "Introduction" to *Further Speculations* by T. E. Hulme. Minneapolis: University of Minnesota Press, 1955.

Jones, A. R. *The Life and Opinions of T. E. Hulme*. Boston: Beacon Press, 1960.

Nelson, Francis. "Valet to the Absolute: A Study of the Philosophy of T. E. Hulme." *University of Wichita Studies* 22 (1950): 1–30.

Read, Herbert. *The True Voice of Feeling: Studies in English Romantic Poetry*. London: Faber & Faber, 1953.

ALDOUS HUXLEY

Atkins, John. *Aldous Huxley: A Literary Study*. London: John Calder, 1956.

Bass, Eben E. *Aldous Huxley: An Annotated Bibliography of Criticism*. New York: Garland, 1981.

Bedford, Sybille. *Aldous Huxley: A Biography*. London: Chatto & Windus, 1973.

Birnbaum, Milton. *Aldous Huxley's Quest for Values*. Knoxville: University of Tennessee Press, 1971.

Clark, Ronald W. *The Huxleys*. London: Heinemann, 1968.

Eschelbach, Claire John, and Joyce Lee Shober. *Aldous Huxley: A Bibliography 1916–1959*. Berkeley: University of California Press, 1961.

Ferns, C. S. *Aldous Huxley: Novelist*. London: Athlone Press, 1980.

Firchow, Peter. *Aldous Huxley: Satirist and Novelist*. Minneapolis: University of Minnesota Press, 1972.

Ghose, Sisirkumar. *Aldous Huxley: A Cynical Salvationist*. Bombay: Asia Publishing House, 1962.

Holmes, Charles M. *Aldous Huxley and the Way to Reality*. Bloomington: Indiana University Press, 1970.

Huxley, Julian, ed. *Aldous Huxley 1894–1963: A Memorial Volume*. New York: Harper & Row, 1965.

Huxley, Laura Archera. *This Timeless Moment: A Personal View of Aldous Huxley*. New York: Farrar, Straus & Giroux, 1968.

May, Keith M. *Aldous Huxley*. New York: Barnes & Noble, 1972.

Meckier, Jerome. *Aldous Huxley: Satire and Structure*. London: Chatto & Windus, 1969.

Watts, Harold H. *Aldous Huxley*. New York: Twayne, 1969.

Woodcock, George. *Dawn and the Darkest Hour: A Study of Aldous Huxley*. London: Faber & Faber, 1972.

DOUGLAS HYDE

Coffey, Diarmid. *Douglas Hyde: President of Ireland*. Dublin: Talbot Press, 1938.

Conner, Lester. "The Importance of Douglas Hyde to the Irish Literary Renaissance." In *Modern Irish Literature*, ed. R. J. Porter and J. D. Brophy. New York: Iona College Press/Twayne, 1972, pp. 95–113.

Daly, Dominic. *The Young Douglas Hyde*. Totowa, NJ: Rowman & Littlefield, 1974.

Gregory, Lady. *Poets and Dreamers*. Dublin: Hodges, Figgis, 1903.

Jeffares, A. Norman. *Anglo-Irish Literature*. New York: Schocken Books, 1982.

Murphy, Gerard. "Douglas Hyde: 1860–1949." *Studies* 38 (1949): 275–81.

O'Hegarty, P. S. A *Bibliography of Dr. Douglas Hyde*. Dublin: Thom, 1939.

CHRISTOPHER ISHERWOOD

Bliven, Naomi. *New Yorker*, 1 September 1962, pp. 77–80.

Forster, E. M. *Two Cheers for Democracy*. London: Arnold, 1951.

Fryer, Jonathan. *Isherwood: A Biography of Christopher Isherwood*. London: New English Library, 1977.

Gunn, Thom. *London Magazine* 1 (October 1954): 81–85.

Halpern, Daniel. "A Conversation." *Antaeus* Nos. 13–14 (Spring–Summer 1974): 366–88.

Kermode, Frank. *Puzzles and Epiphanies*. London: Routledge & Kegan Paul, 1962.

Mayne, Richard. "The Novel and Mr. Norris." *Cambridge Journal* 6 (1953): 561–70.

Spender, Stephen. *World within Word*. New York: Harcourt, Brace, 1951.

Wickes, George. "An Interview with Christopher Isherwood." *Shenandoah* 16 (1965): 23–52.

Wilde, Alan. *Christopher Isherwood*. New York: Twayne, 1971.

W. W. JACOBS

Hutchinson, Percy. "A Master Spinner of the Humorous Yarn." *New York Times Book Review*, 27 September 1931, p. 5.

Muir, Percy H. *Points: Second Series*. London: Constable; New York; R. R. Bowker, 1934.

Ward, Alfred C. "W. W. Jacobs: *Many Cargoes*." In *Aspects of the Modern Short Story*. London: University of London Press, 1924, pp. 227–39.

M. R. JAMES

Butts, Mary. "The Art of Montagu [sic] James." *London Mercury* 29 (1933–34): 306–17.

Cox, J. Randolph. "Montague Rhodes James: An Annotated Bibliography of Writings about Him." *English Literature in Transition* 12 (1969): 203–10.

Cox, Michael. *M. R. James: An Informal Portrait*. Oxford: Oxford University Press, 1983.

Lubbock, S. G. A *Memoir of Montague Rhodes James*. Cambridge: Cambridge University Press, 1939.

Penzoldt, Peter. *The Supernatural in Fiction*. London: Peter Nevill, 1952.

Pfaff, Richard William. *Montague Rhodes James*. London: Scolar Press, 1980.

Warren, Austin. "The Marvels of M. R. James, Antiquary." In *Connections*. Ann Arbor: University of Michigan Press, 1970, pp. 86–107.

STORM JAMESON

Adcock, Arthur St. John. "Storm Jameson." In *The Glory That Was Grub Street*. London: Sampson Low, Marston, 1928, pp. 169–79.

Behrend, Hanna. "Storm Jameson: Decline of a Fellow-Traveller." *Zeitschrift für Anglistik und Amerikanistik* 26 (1978): 232–40.

Butcher, Fanny. Review of *Three Kingdoms*. *Forum* 76 (1926): 157–58.

Gray, James. "Storm Jameson." In *On Second Thought*. Minneapolis: University of Minnesota Press, 1946, pp. 215–21.

Greene, Graham. Review of *Company Parade*. *Spectator*, 20 April 1934, p. 634.

Marble, Annie Russell. *A Study of the Modern Novel*. New York: D. Appleton, 1928.

Phelps, William Lyon. "Has the Drama Gone to Pieces?" *New York Times Book Review*, 24 April 1921, p. 5.

JEROME K. JEROME

Carter, John. "Jerome K. Jerome Tells What He Learned from Life." *New York Times Book Review*, 26 December 1926, p. 8.

Faurot, Ruth. *Jerome K. Jerome*. New York: Twayne, 1974.

Mansfield, Katherine. *Novels and Novelists*. Ed. J. Middleton Murry. New York: Knopf, 1930.

Markgraf, Carl. "Jerome K. Jerome: An Annotated Bibliography of Writings about Him." *English Literature in Transition* 26 (1932): 83–132.

Moss, A. *Jerome K. Jerome: His Life and Work*. London: Selwyn & Blount, 1928.

My First Book. London: Chatto & Windus, 1897. See Jerome K. Jerome, "On the Stage and Off."

PAMELA HANSFORD JOHNSON

Borowitz, A. *Innocence and Arsenic: Studies in Crime and Literature*. New York: Harper & Row, 1977.

Dick, Kay. "Pamela Hansford Johnson." In *Friends and Friendships: Conversations and Reflections*. London: Sidgwick & Johnson, 1974.

Miles, Rosalind. *The Fiction of Sex: Themes and Functions of Sex Difference in the Modern Novel*. New York: Barnes & Noble, 1974.

Newquist, Roy. *Counterpoint*. New York: Simon & Schuster, 1964.

Rabinovitz, Rubin. *The Reaction against Experiment in the English Novel, 1950–60*. New York: Columbia University Press, 1967.

Raymond, John. *The Doge of Dover*. London: MacGibbon & Kee, 1960.

Unsigned. "Interview with C. P. Snow and Pamela Hansford Johnson." *Publisher's Weekly*, 30 November 1959, pp. 28–29.

DAVID JONES

Agenda 5, Nos. 1–3 (1967). Special issue on David Jones.

——— 11, No. 4/12 No. 1 (1973–74). Special issue on David Jones.

Blamires, David. *David Jones: Artist and Writer*, Toronto: University of Toronto Press, 1972.

Hague, René. *David Jones*, Cardiff: University of Wales Press, 1975.

Hooker, Jeremy, *John Cowper Powys and David Jones: A Comparative Study*. London: Enitharmon Press, 1979.

Raine, Kathleen. *David Jones and the Actually Know and Loved*. Ipswich: Golgonooza Press, 1978.

———. *David Jones, Solitary Perfectionist*. Ipswich: Golgonooza Press, 1974.

Rees, Samuel. *David Jones*. Boston: Twayne, 1978.

Silkin, John. *Out of Battle: The Poetry of the Great War*. London: Oxford University Press, 1972.

HENRY ARTHUR JONES

Cordell, R. A. *Henry Arthur Jones and the Modern Drama*. New York: Ray Long & Richard Smith, 1932.

Moore, Charles Leonard. "A Deliverance on the Drama." *Dial*, 1 May 1913, pp. 374–76.

Unsigned. *Times Literary Supplement*, 10 September 1931, p. 679.

JAMES JOYCE

Beckett, Samuel. "Dante . . . Bruno. Vico . . Joyce." In *Our Exagimination round His Factification for Incamination of* Work in Progress. Paris: Shakespeare & Co., 1929.

Budgen, Frank. *James Joyce and the Making of* Ulysses. New York: Harrison Smith & Robert Haas, 1934.

Burke, Kenneth. *Joyce's Voices*. Berkeley: University of California Press, 1978.

Cross, Richard L. *Flaubert and Joyce: The Rite of Fiction*. Princeton: Princeton University Press, 1971.

Curtius, Ernst Robert. *Essays on European Literature*. Tr. Michael Kowal. Princeton: Princeton University Press, 1973.

Eliot, T. S. "*Ulysses*, Order and Myth." *Dial* 75 (1923): 480–83.

Givens, Seon, ed. *James Joyce: Two Decades of Criticism*. New York: Vanguard Press, 1948.

Hart, Clive. *Structure and Motif in* Finnegans Wake. Evanston, IL: Northwestern University Press, 1962.

Hawkins, Marguerite. *The Aesthetics of Dedalus and Bloom*. Lewisburg, PA: Bucknell University Press, 1984.

MacCabe, Colin. *James Joyce and the Revolution of the Word*. London: Macmillan, 1979.

Manganiello, Dominic. *Joyce's Politics*. London: Routledge & Kegan Paul, 1980.

Schutte, William M. *Joyce and Shakespeare: A Study in the Meaning of* Ulysses. New Haven: Yale University Press, 1957.

Staley, Thomas F., ed. *James Joyce Today: Essays on the Major Works*. Bloomington: Indiana University Press, 1966.

Tindall, W. Y. *A Reader's Guide to* Finnegans Wake. New York: Farrar, Straus, & Giroux, 1969.

PATRICK KAVANAGH

Boland, Eavan; Heaney, Seamus; Hartnett, Michael; and Miller, Liam. "The Future of Irish Poetry: A Discussion." *Irish Times*, 5 February 1970, p. 14.

Colum, Padraic. "A Note on P. K." *Kilkenny Magazine* 4 (1962): 33–36.

Donoghue, Denis. "Irish Writing." *Month* 17 (1957): 180–85.

Kennelly, Brendan. "Patrick Kavanagh." *Ariel* 1 (1970): 7–28.

O'Brien, Darcy. *Patrick Kavanagh*. Lewisburg, PA: Bucknell University Press, 1975.

Warner, Alan. *Clay Is the Word*. Dublin: Dolmen Press, 1973.

Weber, Richard. "The Poetry of Patrick Kavanagh." *Icarus* 6 (1956): 22–25.

SHEILA KAYE-SMITH

Cowley, Malcolm. "The Woman of Ihornden." *Dial* 68 (1920): 259–62.

Doyle, Paul A. "Sheila Kaye-Smith: An Annotated Bibliography of Writings about Her." *English Literature in Transition* 15 (1972): 189–98.

Ellis, S. M. "A Novelist of Sussex: Miss Sheila Kaye-Smith."

In *Mainly Victorian*. London: Hutchinson, 1925, pp. 170–73.

Hopkins, R. Thurston. *Sheila Kaye-Smith and the Weald Country*. London: Cecil Palmer, 1925.

Kernahan, Coulson. "Sheila Kaye-Smith as a Poet." *Nineteenth Century* (1920): 910–24.

Walker, Dorothea. *Sheila Kaye-Smith*. Boston: Twayne, 1980.

MARGARET KENNEDY

Birrell, Augustine. Reveiw of *The Constant Nymph*. *New Statesman*, 6 December 1924, pp. 269–70.

Field, Louise Maunsell. Review of *Together and Apart*. *New York Times Book Review*, 4 April 1937, p. 6.

Lawrence, Margaret. "Margaret Kennedy." In *The School of Femininity*. New York: Frederick A. Stokes, 1936, pp. 296–98.

Loveman, Amy. "Mischief before Dawn." *Saturday Review*, 5 November 1927, p. 278.

Powell, Violet. *The Constant Novelist: A Study of Margaret Kennedy*. London: Heinemann, 1983.

Stuart, Henry Logan. "Taut and Frugal Art of Margaret Kennedy." *New York Times Book Review*, 22 February 1925, p. 5.

THOMAS KINSELLA

Clark, David Ridgley. *Lyric Resonance*. Amherst: University of Massachusetts Press, 1972.

Harmon, Maurice. *The Poetry of Thomas Kinsella*. Dublin: Wolfhound Press, 1974.

Kellner, Bruce. "The Wormwood Poems of Thomas Kinsella." *Western Humanities Review* 26 (1972): 225–27.

Moore, John Rees. "Thomas Kinsella's *Nightwalker*: A Phoenix in the Dark." *Hollins Critic* 5 (1968): 12–13.

Rosenthal, M. L. *The New Poets: American and British Poetry since World War II*. London: Oxford University Press, 1967.

RUDYARD KIPLING

Beresford, G. C. *Schooldays with Kipling*. London: Gollancz, 1936.

Birkenhead, Lord. *Rudyard Kipling*. London: Weidenfeld & Nicolson, 1978.

Bodelsen, C. A. *Aspects of Kipling's Art*. New York: Barnes & Noble, 1964.

Brown, Hilton. *Rudyard Kipling*. New York: Harper & Brothers, 1945.

Dobrée, Bonamy. *Rudyard Kipling: Realist and Fabulist*. London: Oxford University Press, 1967.

Gerber, Helmut, and Edward Lauterbach. "Rudyard Kipling: An Annotated Bibliography of Writings about Him." *English Fiction in Transition* 3 (1960) 1–235.

Gilbert, Elliot L. *The Good Kipling*. Athens: Ohio University Press, 1970.

Gross, John, ed. *The Age of Kipling*. New York: Simon & Schuster, 1972.

Harrison, James. *Rudyard Kipling*. Boston: Twayne, 1982.

Hopkins, R. Thurston. *Rudyard Kipling's World*. London: Robert Holden, 1925.

Le Gallienne, Richard. *Rudyard Kipling: A Criticism*. London: John Lane/Bodley Head, 1900.

Mason, Philip. *Kipling: The Glass, the Shadow and the Fire*. New York: Harper & Row, 1975.

Moore, Katharine. *Kipling and the White Man's Burden*. London: Faber & Faber, 1968.

Moss, Robert F. *Rudyard Kipling and the Fiction of Adolescence*. New York: St. Martin's Press, 1982.

Rao, K. Bhaskara. *Rudyard Kipling's India*. Norman: University of Oklahoma Press, 1967.

Stewart, J. I. M. *Rudyard Kipling*. London: Gollancz, 1966.

Wilson, Angus. *The Strange Ride of Rudyard Kipling: His Life and Works*. New York: Viking Press, 1977.

ARTHUR KOESTLER

Davis, Robert Gorham. "The Sharp Horns of Koestler's Dilemmas." *Antioch Review* (1944–45): 503–17.

Hamilton, Iain. *Koestler: A Biography*. London: Secker & Warburg, 1982.

Harris, Harold, ed. *Astride the Two Cultures: Arthur Koestler at 70*. London: Hutchinson, 1975.

Hoffman, Frederick J. "*Darkness at Noon*: The Consequences of Secular Grace." *Georgia Review* (1959): 331–45.

Merleau-Ponty, Maurice. "Koestler's Dilemmas." In *Humanism and Terror*. Tr. John O'Neill. Boston: Beacon Press, 1969.

Pritchett, V. S. "Koestler: A Guilty Figure." *Harper's* 196 (January 1948): 84–92.

Sperber, Murray A., ed. *Arthur Koestler: A Collection of Critical Essays*. Englewood Cliffs, NJ: Prentice-Hall, 1977.

Toulmin, Stephen. "Koestler's Act of Creation." *Encounter* (July 1964): 58–71.

PHILIP LARKIN

Alvarez, Alfred. *Beyond All This Fiddle*. London: Allen Lane, 1968.

Bateson, F. W. "Auden's (and Empson's) Heirs." *Essays in Criticism* 7 (1957): 76–80.

Browne, Merle E. *Double Lyric: Divisiveness and Communal Creativity in Recent English Poetry*. New York: Columbia University Press, 1980.

Davie, Donald. "Landscapes of Larkin." In *Thomas Hardy and British Poetry*. New York: Oxford University Press, 1972.

King, P. R. *Nine Contemporary Poets: A Critical Introduction*. London: Methuen, 1979.

Motion, Andrew. *Philip Larkin*. London: Methuen, 1982.

Petch, Simon. *The Art of Philip Larkin*. Sydney: Sydney University Press, 1981.

Ricks, Christopher. "A True Poet." *New York Review of Books*, 28 January 1965, pp. 10–11.

———. "The Words and Music of Life." *Sunday Times*, 7 January 1968, p. 34.

Timms, David. *Philip Larkin*. Edinburgh: Oliver & Boyd, 1973.

MARY LAVIN

Bowen, Zack. *Mary Lavin*. Lewisburg, PA: Bucknell University Press, 1975.

Dunleavy, Janet Egleson. "The Making of Mary Lavin's 'A Memory.'" *Éire-Ireland* 12 (Autumn 1977): 90–99.

Murray, Thomas J. "Mary Lavin's World: Lovers and Strangers." *Éire-Ireland* 7 (Summer 1972): 122–31.

Peterson, Richard F. *Mary Lavin*. Boston: Twayne, 1978.

Scott, Bonnie Kime. "Mary Lavin and the Life of the Mind." *Irish University Review* 9 (1979): 262–79.

D. H. LAWRENCE

Bedient, Calvin. *Architects of the Self: George Eliot, D. H. Lawrence, and E. M. Forster*. Berkeley: University of California Press, 1972.

Cavitch, David. *D. H. Lawrence and the New World*. New York: Oxford University Press, 1969.

Coombes, H., ed. *D. H. Lawrence: a Critical Anthology.* Harmondsworth· Penguin, 1973.

Gilbert, Sandra M. *Acts of Attraction: The Poems of D. H. Lawrence.* Ithaca, NY: Cornell University Press, 1972.

Goodheart, Eugene. *The Utopian Vision of D. H. Lawrence.* Chicago: University of Chicago Press, 1963.

Hough, Graham Goulden. *Two Exiles: Lord Byron and D. H. Lawrence.* Nottingham: University of Nottingham Press, 1956.

Innis, Kenneth. *D. H. Lawrence's Bestiary.* The Hague: Mouton, 1971.

Joost, Nicholas, and Alvin Sullivan. *D. H. Lawrence and* The Dial. Carbondale: Southern Illinois University Press, 1970.

Lawrence, Frieda. *Frieda Lawrence: The Memoirs and Correspondence.* Edited by E. W. Tedlock, Jr. London: Heinemann, 1961.

Levy, Mervyn, ed. *Paintings of D. H. Lawrence.* New York: Viking Press, 1964.

Murry, John Middleton. *Love, Freedom and Society.* London: Jonathan Cape, 1957.

Oates, Joyce Carol. *The Hostile Sun: The Poetry of D. H. Lawrence.* Los Angeles: Black Sparrow Press, 1973.

Tindall, W. Y. *D. H. Lawrence and Susan His Cow.* New York: Columbia University Press, 1939.

T. E. LAWRENCE

Aldington, Richard. *Lawrence of Arabia: A Bibliographical Enquiry.* London: Collins, 1955.

Arendt, Hannah. "The Imperialistic Character." *Review of Politics* 12 (1950): 303–20.

Clements, Frank. *Lawrence of Arabia: A Reader's Guide.* Newton Abbot, Eng.: David & Charles, 1972; Hamden, CT: Archon Books, 1973.

Garnett, David, ed. *The Letters of T. E. Lawrence.* London: Jonathan Cape, 1938.

Graves, Robert. *Lawrence and the Arabs.* London: Jonathan Cape, 1927.

Hart, B. H. Liddell. *T. E. Lawrence in Arabia and After.* London: Jonathan Cape, 1965.

———. "T. E. Lawrence: Through His Own Eyes and Another's." *Southern Review* 2 (1936): 22–40.

Howe, Irving. "T. E. Lawrence: The Problem of Heroism." *Hudson Review* 15 (1962): 333–64.

Nonopoulos, James A. "The Tragic and the Epic in T. E. Lawrence." *Yale Review* 24 (1935): 331–45.

Rutherford, Andrew. *The Literature of War: Five Studies in Heroic Virtue.* London: Macmillan, 1978.

Toynbee, Arnold J. *Acquaintances.* London: Oxford University Press, 1967, pp. 178–97.

Weintraub, Stanley. *Private Shaw and Public Shaw.* London: Jonathan Cape, 1963.

JOHN LE CARRÉ

Bell, Pearl K. "Coming In from the Cold War." *The New Leader,* 24 June 1974, pp. 15–16.

Boucher, Anthony. "Temptations of a Man Isolated in Deceit." *New York Times Book Review,* 12 January 1964, p. 5.

Halperin, John. "Between Two Worlds: The Novels of John le Carré." *South Atlantic Quarterly* 79 (1980): 17–37.

Rothberg, Abraham. "The Decline and Fall of George Smiley." *Southwest Review* 66 (1981): 377–93.

Rutherford, Andrew. "The Spy as Hero: Le Carré and the Cold War." In *The Literature of War: Five Studies in Heroic Virtue.* London: Macmillan, 1978, pp. 135–56.

Wood, Michael. "Spy Fiction, Spy Fact." *New York Times Book Review,* 6 January 1980, pp. 1, 16.

LAURIE LEE

Cavalerie, Nicole, and Françoise Cavalerie. "Conversations with Laurie Lee." *Caliban* 13 (1976): 149–60.

Finn, Stephen. "Contrasts in Laurie Lee's *A Rose for Winter.*" *CRUX* 12 (1978): 33–36.

Pritchett, V. S. "In Spain It's Like That." *New York Times Book Review,* 8 April 1956, p. 6.

Weeks, Edward. "The Peripatetic Reviewer." *Atlantic* 224 (September 1969): 3.

Unsigned. "A Winter in Andalusia." *Times Literary Supplement,* 1 July 1955, p. 366.

ROSAMOND LEHMANN

Allen, Walter. *Tradition and Dream.* London: Phoenix, 1964.

Burgess, Anthony. *The Novel Now: A Student's Guide to Contemporary Fiction.* London: Faber & Faber, 1971.

Coopman, Tony. "Symbolism in Rosamond Lehmann's *The Echoing Grove.*" *Revue des Langues Vivantes* 40 (1974): 116–21.

Crosland, Margaret. *Beyond the Lighthouse: English Women Novelists in the Twentieth Century.* London: Constable, 1981.

Dorosz, Wiktoria. *Subjective Vision and Human Relationships in the Novels of Rosamond Lehmann. Studia Anglistica Upsaliensia* 23 (1975).

Gindin, James. "Three Recent British Novels and an American Reprise." *Michigan Quarterly Review* 17 (1978): 223–46.

Lerot, Jacques, and Rudolf Kern, eds. *Mélanges de linguistique et de littérature offerts au Professeur Henri Draye à l'occasion son éméritat.* Louvain: Bibliothèque de l'Université, 1978.

LeStourgeon, Diana E. *Rosamond Lehmann.* New York: Twayne, 1965.

Sackville-West, Victoria. "The Eternal Game." *Spectator,* 10 April 1953, p. 454.

ALUN LEWIS

Graves, Robert. "War Poetry in This War." *Listener,* 23 October 1941.

Jones, Gwyn. "Alun Lewis, 1915–1944." *Welsh Review* 3 (1944): 118–21.

Lehmann, John. "A Human Standpoint." In *The Open Night.* London: Longmans, 1952.

Rowse, A. L. "Poets of Today." *Listener,* 13 July 1944.

Symes, Gordon. "Muse in India: An Aspect of Alun Lewis." *English* 6 (1947): 191–95.

C. S. LEWIS

Christopher, Joe R., and Joan K. Ostling. *C. S. Lewis: An Annotated Checklist of Writings about Him and His Works.* Kent, OH: Kent State University Press, 1977.

Gibb, Jocelyn, ed. *Light on C. S. Lewis.* London: Geoffrey Bles, 1965; New York: Harcourt, Brace & World, 1966.

GoodKnight, Glen ed. *Mythcon I Proceedings.* Los Angeles: Mythopoeic Society, 1971.

———. *Mythcon II Proceedings.* Los Angeles: Mythopoeic Society, 1972.

Hillegas, Mark R. ed. *Shadows of Imagination: The Fantasies of C. S. Lewis, J. R. R. Tolkien, and Charles Williams.* Carbondale: Southern Illinois University Press, 1969.

Keefe, Carolyn. *C. S. Lewis: Speaker and Teacher.* Grand Rapids, MI: Zondervan, 1971.

Kilby, Clyde S. *The Christian World of C. S. Lewis*. Grand Rapids, MI: William B. Eerdmans, 1964.

Lawlor, John. *Patterns of Love and Courtesy: Essays in Memory of C. S. Lewis*. London: Edward Arnold, 1966; Evanston, IL: Northwestern University Press, 1967.

Murray, Patrick. *Milton: The Modern Phase: A Study of Twentieth-Century Criticism*. New York: Barnes & Noble, 1967.

Urang, Gunnar. *Shadows of Heaven: Religion and Fantasy in the Writings of C. S. Lewis, Charles Williams, and J. R. R. Tolkien*. Philadelphia: United Church Press, 1971.

Walsh, Chad. *C. S. Lewis: Apostle to the Skeptics*. New York: Macmillan, 1949.

WYNDHAM LEWIS

Allen, Walter. "Lonely Old Volcano." *Encounter* 21 (September 1963): 63–70.

Bridson, D. G. *The Filibuster: A Study of the Political Ideas of Wyndham Lewis*. London: Cassell, 1972.

Chapman, Robert T. *Wyndham Lewis: Fictions and Satires*. London: Vision Press, 1973.

Eliot, T. S. "The Lion and the Fox." *Twentieth Century Verse* Nos. 6/7 (November–December 1937): n.p.

Holloway, John. "Wyndham Lewis: The Massacre and the Innocents." *Hudson Review* 10 (1957): 171–88.

McLuhan, Herbert Marshall. "Wyndham Lewis: His Theory of Art and Communication." *Shenandoah* 4 (1953): 77–88.

Meyers, Jeffrey. *The Enemy: A Biography of Wyndham Lewis*. London: Routledge & Kegan Paul, 1980.

Michel, Walter, ed. *Wyndham Lewis: Paintings and Drawings*. Berkeley: University of California Press, 1971.

Morrow, Bradford and Bernard Lafourcade. *A Bibliography of the Writings of Wyndham Lewis*. Santa Barbara, CA: Black Sparrow Press, 1978.

Symons, Julian. "The Thirties Novels." *Agenda* 7 (Autumn–Winter 1969–70): 37–48.

Wagner, Geoffrey. *Wyndham Lewis: A Portrait of the Artist as the Enemy*. New Haven: Yale University Press, 1957.

ERIC LINKLATER

Linklater, Eric. *A Year of Space: A Chapter in Autobiography*. London: Macmillan, 1953.

McCarthy, Mary. *Nation*, 19 June 1935, p. 720.

Plomer, William. *Spectator*, 29 March 1935, p. 549.

Pritchett, V. S. "How Much Artist?" *Spectator*, 21 March 1931, p. 478.

MALCOLM LOWRY

Bradbrook, M. C. *Malcolm Lowry: His Art and Early Life*. Cambridge: Cambridge University Press, 1974.

Costa, Richard Hauer. *Malcolm Lowry*. New York: Twayne, 1972.

Cross, Richard K. *Malcolm Lowry: A Preface to His Fiction*. Chicago: University of Chicago Press, 1980.

Day, Douglas. *Malcolm Lowry: A Biography*. New York: Oxford University Press, 1973.

Edmonds, Dale. *"Under the Volcano: A Reading of the 'Immediate Level.'"* *Tulane Studies in English* 16 (1968): 63–105.

Gass, William H. "In Terms of the Toenail." *New American Review* 10 (1970): 51–68.

Grace, Sherrill E. *The Voyage That Never Ends: Malcolm Lowry's Fiction*. Vancouver: University of British Columbia Press, 1982.

Hirschman, Jack. "Kabbala/Lowry, etc." *Prairie Schooner* 37 (1963–64): 347–53.

Markson, David. *Malcolm Lowry's Volcano*. New York: Times Books, 1978.

New, William H. *Malcolm Lowry: A Reference Guide*. Boston: G. K. Hall, 1978.

Smith, Anne, ed. *The Art of Malcolm Lowry*. New York: Barnes & Noble, 1978.

E. V. LUCAS

Ellis, S. M. Review of *Edwin Abbey*. *Fortnightly Review* 117 (1922): 159–60.

Farrar, John. *E. V. Lucas: Appreciations*. New York: George H. Doran, 1925.

Lucas, Audrey. *E. V. Lucas*. London: Methuen, 1939.

ROSE MACAULAY

Inglisham, John. "Rose Macaulay." *Bookman* (London) 72 (1927): 107–10.

Nicolson, Harold. "Spanish Journey." *Observer*, 6 May 1949, p. 291.

Pryce-Jones, Alan. "Introduction" to *Orphan Island*. London: Collins, 1960.

Schelling, Felix E. *Appraisements and Asperities*. Philadelphia: Lippincott, 1922.

Swinnerton, Frank. New York: Farrar & Rinehart, 1934.

HUGH MACDIARMID

Ackerman, Diane. "Hugh MacDiarmid's Wide-Angle Poetry." *Parnassus* 9 (1981): 129–39.

Agenda 5/6 (Autumn–Winter 1967–68). Special double issue on Hugh MacDiarmid.

Akros 7 (August 1972). Special issue on Hugh MacDiarmid.

Duval, K. D., and Sydney Goodsir Smith, eds. *Hugh MacDiarmid: A Festschrift*. Edinburgh: K. D. Duval, 1962.

Glen, Duncan. *Hugh MacDiarmid and the Scottish Renaissance*. Edinburgh: W. R. Chambers, 1964.

Law, R. S., and Thurso Berwick, eds. *The Socialist Poems of Hugh MacDiarmid*. London: Routledge & Kegan Paul, 1978.

MacDiarmid, Hugh. *Selected Essays of Hugh MacDiarmid*. Ed. Duncan Glenn. London: Jonathan Cape, 1969.

Wand Zuoliang. "Reflection on Hugh MacDiarmid." *Studies in Scottish Literature* 19 (1984): 1–16.

Wittig, Kurt. *The Scottish Tradition in Literature*. Edinburgh: Oliver & Boyd, 1958.

THOMAS MACDONAGH

Bourke, Marcus. "Thomas MacDonagh's Role in the Plans for the 1916 Rising." *Irish Sword* 3 (1968): 178–85.

Colum, Padraic. "The Dead Irish Poets." *Poetry* 8 (1916): 268–73.

O'Hegarty, P. S. *A Bibliography of Books by Thomas MacDonagh and Joseph Mary Plunkett*. Dublin: Thom, 1931.

O'Neill, George. "Thomas MacDonagh." In *Poets of the Insurrection*. Dublin: Maunsel, 1916, pp. 14–22.

Parks, Edd Winfield, and Aileen Wells Parks. *Thomas MacDonagh: The Man, the Patriot, the Writer*. Athens: University of Georgia Press, 1967.

IAN MCEWAN

Lee, Hermione. "First Rites." *New Statesman*, 29 September 1978, p. 415.

Mewshaw, Michael. *New York Times Book Review*, 28 September 1975, p. 32.

Tyler, Anne. *New York Times Book Review*, 26 November 1978, p. 11.

ARTHUR MACHEN

Gekle, William Francis. *Arthur Machen: Weaver of Fantasy.* Millbrook, NY: Round Table Press, 1949.

Goldstone, Adrian, and Wesley Sweetser. *A Bibliography of Arthur Machen.* Austin: University of Texas Press, 1965.

Hillyer, Robert. "Arthur Machen." *Atlantic* 179 (May 1947): 138–40.

Jordan-Smith, Paul. "Black Magic: An Impression of Arthur Machen." In *On Strange Altars.* New York: Albert & Charles Boni, 1924, pp. 214–35.

Reynolds, Aidan, and William Charlton. *Arthur Machen.* London: Richards Press, 1963.

Scarborough, Dorothy. *The Supernatural in Modern English Fiction.* New York: G. P. Putnam's Sons, 1917.

Sewell, Brocard, ed. *Arthur Machen.* Llandeilo, Wales: St. Albert's Press, 1960.

Sweetser, Wesley D. *Arthur Machen.* New York: Twayne, 1964.

COMPTON MACKENZIE

Adcock, Arthur St. John. "Compton Mackenzie." In *The Glory That Was Grub Street.* London: Sampson Low, Marston, 1928.

Goldring, Douglas. *Reputations: Essays in Criticism.* London: Chapman & Hall, 1920.

James, Henry. *Notes on Novelists.* London: J. M. Dent, 1914.

Johnson, Reginald B. "Compton Mackenzie." In *Some Contemporary Novelists (Men).* London: Leonard Parsons, 1922.

Swinnerton, Frank. *The Georgian Scene.* New York: Farrar & Rinehart, 1934.

LOUIS MACNEICE

Furbank, P. N. "New Poetry." *Listener,* 19 September 1963, p. 439.

Gregory, Horace. "The New January." *Poetry* 75 (August 1949): 301–4.

Larkin, Philip. "Memoranda to Horace." *New Statesman,* 6 September 1963, p. 294.

McKinnon, William T. *Apollo's Blended Dream: A Study of the Poetry of Louis MacNeice.* London: Oxford University Press, 1971.

Rosenthal, M. L. "Everything Is Subject for Good Talk." *New York Times,* 12 November 1961, sec. 8, p. 4.

Southworth, James G. *Sowing the Spring: Studies in British Poets from Hopkins to MacNeice.* Oxford: Basil Blackwell, 1940.

Symons, Julian. "Louis MacNeice: The Artist as Everyman." *Poetry* 55 (1940): 86–94.

DEREK MAHON

Brownjohn, Alan. "A Cold Wind Blows: Recent Poetry." *Encounter* 55 (August–September 1980): 60–61.

Holland, Jack. "A Searing Objectivity." *Nation,* 20 September 1980, p. 260.

Motion, Andrew. Review of *Poems 1962–1978. New Statesman,* 14 December 1979, p. 948.

OLIVIA MANNING

Emerson, Sally. "Olivia Manning Interviewed." *Books and Bookmen* 17 (November 1971): 30–31.

Glendinning, Victoria. "Ordeals of Solitude." *Times Literary Supplement,* 19 September 1980, p. 1012.

Jamal, Zahir. "Rooting." *New Statesman,* 17 November 1978, p. 665.

Morris, R. K. "The Balkan Trilogy: The Quest for Permanence." In *Continuance and Change: The Contemporary British Novel Sequence.* Carbondale: Southern Illinois University Press, 1972, pp. 29–49.

JOHN MASEFIELD

Biggane, Cecil. *John Masefield: A Study.* Cambridge: Heffer, 1924.

Fisher, Margery. *John Masefield.* London: Bodley Head, 1963.

Hamilton, W. H. *John Masefield: A Popular Study.* London: George Allen & Unwin, 1922.

Lamont, Corliss. *Remembering John Masefield.* Rutherford, NJ: Fairleigh Dickinson University Press, 1971.

Simmons, Charles H. *A Bibliography of John Masefield.* New York: Columbia University Press, 1930.

Smith, Constance Babington. *John Masefield: A Life.* Oxford: Oxford University Press, 1978.

Sternlicht, Sanford. *John Masefield.* Boston: Twayne, 1977.

Strong, L. A. G. *John Masefield.* London: Longmans, 1952.

Thomas, Gilbert. *John Masefield.* New York: Macmillan, 1933.

ACKNOWLEDGMENTS

Accent. BREWSTER GHISELIN, "The Unity of Joyce's *Dubliners*," Vol. 16, No. 2 (Spring 1956), copyright © 1956 by *Accent*.

Adelphi. RALPH HOUSTON, "The Broken Arch: A Study of the Poetry of Alun Lewis," 1951, copyright © 1951.

Agenda. JOHN BAYLEY "A Retreat or Seclusion?," Spring 1979, copyright © 1979. TIMOTHY MATERER, "The Great English Vortex," Autumn–Winter 1969–70, copyright © 1969. C. H. SISSON, "Geoffrey Hill," Fall 1975, copyright © 1975.

D. Appleton & Co. GRANT OVERTON, "That Literary Wanderer, E. V. Lucas," *Cargoes for Crusoes*, copyright © 1924.

Archon Books. FRANK CLEMENTS, "Introduction" to *T. E. Lawrence: A Reader's Guide*, copyright © 1972 by Frank Clements. JOHN HOLLOWAY, "A Perpetual Showing: The Poetry of David Jones," *The Colors of Clarity*, copyright © 1964.

Fytton Armstrong. ARTHUR MACHEN, *Beneath the Barley*, copyright © 1931.

Arion. J. P. SULLIVAN, "'The Leading Classic of His Generation,'" Summer 1962, copyright © 1962.

Arkham House Publishers, Inc. H. P. LOVECRAFT, Letter to Bernard Austin Dwyer (1932), *Selected Letters: 1932–1934*, ed. August Derleth and Donald Wandrei, copyright © 1976 by Arkham House Publishers, Inc.

Edward Arnold. JOHN LAWLOR, "On Romanticism in the *Confessio Amantis*," *Patterns of Love and Courtesy: Essays in Memory of C. S. Lewis*, ed. John Lawlor, copyright © 1966 by Edward Arnold.

The Athenaeum. UNSIGNED, Feb. 1, 1913, copyright © 1913.

Atheneum. LAURIE LEE, "Writing Autobiography," *I Can't Stay Long*, copyright © 1975 by Laurie Lee.

The Atlantic. LORD DUNSANY, "Four Poets," Vol. 201, No. 4 (April 1958), copyright © 1958. CHRISTOPHER ISHERWOOD, "Aldous Huxley in California," Vol. 214, No. 3 (Sept. 1964), copyright © 1964.

Australasian Medical Publishing Co. IAN R. MAXWELL, "A. E. Housman," *Some Modern Writers*, copyright © 1940.

Barnes & Noble. G. WILSON KNIGHT, "Masefield and Spiritualism," *Neglected Powers*, copyright © 1971 by G. Wilson Knight. HARRY J. MOONEY, JR., "Olivia Manning: Witness to History," *Twentieth-Century Women Novelists*, ed. Thomas F. Staley, copyright © 1982 by Thomas F. Staley.

Bobbs-Merrill. LAURENCE HOUSMAN, "Bubble Reputation," *The Unexpected Years*, copyright © 1936 by Laurence Housman.

The Bodley Head. WILLIAM ARCHER, "Laurence Housman," *Poets of the Younger Generation*, copyright © 1902. J. B. PRIESTLEY, "Mr. W. W. Jacobs," *Figures in Modern Literature*, copyright © 1924.

Boni & Liveright. LEWIS MUMFORD, *The Story of Utopias*, copyright © 1922 by Boni & Liveright

The Bookman (London). R. ELLIS ROBERTS, "Arthur Machen," Sept. 1922, copyright © 1922. GEORGE SAMPSON, "E. V. Lucas," Feb. 1917, copyright © 1917.

The Bookman (New York). DOROTHEA BRANDE, "Five Novels," Jan. 1933, copyright © 1933. JAMES DOUGLAS, Nov. 1902, copyright © 1902. MYLES TIERNEY, "The Highway to Avalon," Oct. 1924, copyright © 1924. UNSIGNED, July 1900, copyright © 1900.

Bookman Associates. RICHARD E. HAYMAKER, "Novels and Tales," *From Pampas to Hedgerows and Downs: A Study of W. H. Hudson*, copyright © 1954 by Richard E. Haymaker.

Books and Bookmen. JAMES PARKHILL-RATHBONE, "Olivia Manning's Dilemmas," No. 191 (Aug. 1971), copyright © 1971 by Hansom Books Ltd.

Bromsgrove School. A. W. POLLARD, "Some Reminiscences," N. V. H. SYMONS, "Farewell to A. E. H.," *Alfred Edward Housman: Recollections*, copyright © 1936.

Bucknell University Press. GARETH W. DUNLEAVY, "The End of a Ship Is Wreckage," *Douglas Hyde*, copyright © 1974 by Associated University Presses, Inc.

Caledonian. DAVID DAICHES, "Introduction" to *A Drunk Man Looks at the Thistle* by Hugh MacDiarmid, copyright © 1953.

Cambridge Quarterly. J. M. NEWTON, "'. . . And a More Comprehensive Soul,'" Winter 1965–66, copyright © 1965. W. W. ROBSON, "C. S. Lewis," Summer 1966, copyright © 1966.

Cambridge University Press. STEPHEN HEATH, "Ambivalences: Notes for Reading Joyce," *Post-Structuralist Joyce*, ed. Derek Attridge and Daniel Ferrer, copyright © 1984 by Cambridge University Press. D. H. LAWRENCE, Letter to Edward Marsh (Oct. 28, 1913), *The Letters of D. H. Lawrence*, Vol. 2, ed. George J. Zytaruk and James T. Boulton, copyright © 1981 by the Estate of Frieda Lawrence Ravagli. ALLARDYCE NICOLL, *English Drama 1900–1930: The Beginnings of the Modern Period*, copyright © 1973 by Cambridge University Press.

Canadian Literature. ROBERT B. HEILMAN, "The Possessed Artist and the Ailing Soul," No. 8 (Spring 1961), copyright © 1961. GEORGE WOODCOCK, "Under Seymour Mountain," No. 8 (Spring 1961), copyright © 1961.

Jonathan Cape. W. H. DAVIES, "A Poet and His Dog," *Later Days*, copyright © 1925. AUGUSTUS JOHN, "Elephants with Beards," *Finishing Touches*, copyright © 1964 by the executors of the late Augustus John. PERCY WITHERS, A *Buried Life: Personal Recollections of A. E. Housman*, copyright © 1940.

Carcanet Press. JOHN SILKIN, "The Poetry of Geoffrey Hill," *British Poetry since 1960: A Critical Survey*, ed. Michael Schmidt and Grevel Lindup, copyright © 1972. ANDREW WATERMAN, "The Poetry of Geoffrey Hill," *British Poetry since 1970: A Critical Survey*, ed. Peter Jones and Michael Schmidt, copyright © 1980.

Cassell & Co. H. RIDER HAGGARD, *The Private Diaries of Sir H. Rider Haggard 1914–1925*, ed. D. S. Higgins, copyright © 1980 by The Trustees of the Estate of the late Sir Henry Rider Haggard.

John Castle. GERALD GOULD, "Compton Mackenzie," *The English Novel To-day*, copyright © 1924.

The Centennial Review. JAMES GINDIN, "Storm Jameson and the Chronicle," Vol. 32, No. 4 (Fall 1978), copyright © 1978.

Chatto & Windus. ARNOLD BENNETT, "E. V. Lucas and G. K. Chesterton," "W. W. Jacobs and Aristophanes," *Books and Persons*, copyright © 1917. HUGH KENNER, "The Portrait in Perspective," *Dublin's Joyce*, copyright © 1955. WYNDHAM LEWIS, "Love? What Ho! Smelling Strangeness," *Paleface*, copyright © 1929. V. S. PRITCHETT, "The Eye-Man," "W. W. Jacobs," *Books in General*, copyright © 1953 by Chatto & Windus.

Chicago Review. DONALD T. TORCHIANA, "Contemporary Irish Poetry," 1964, copyright © 1964.

Chilmark Press. FRANK KERMODE, "T. E. Hulme," *Romantic Image*, copyright © 1961.

Cobden-Sanderson. EDMUND BLUNDEN, "Fallen Englishmen," *Votive Tablets*, copyright © 1931.

Collins & Harvill Press. STORM JAMESON, *Journey from the North*, Vol. 2, copyright © 1970 by Storm Jameson.

Columbia University Press. CAROLYN HEILBRUN, *Christopher Isherwood*, copyright © 1970 by Columbia University Press. PAUL PIAZZA, "The Hero," *Christopher Isherwood: Myth and Anti-Myth*, copyright © 1978. W. B. YEATS, "Old Gaelic Love Songs," *Uncollected Prose*, Vol. 1, ed. John Frayne, copyright © 1970 by John P. Frayne and Michael Yeats.

Commentary. GEORGE WOODCOCK, "The Myth of Malcolm Lowry," Vol. 57, No. 3 (March 1974), copyright © 1974 by the American Jewish Committee.

Contemporary Literature. JAMES GINDIN, "Rosamond Lehmann: A Revaluation," Vol. 15, No. 2 (Spring 1974), copyright © 1974 by the University of Wisconsin Press.

Contemporary Review. ROBERT BUCHANON, "The Voice of 'The Hooligan,'" Vol. 76, No. 6 (Dec. 1899), copyright © 1899.

Constable. MARGARET CROSLAND, "Laughing (I)," *Beyond the Lighthouse: English Women Novelists of the Twentieth Century*, copyright © 1981 by Margaret Crosland.

W. Paul Cook. FRANK BELKNAP LONG, "On Reading Arthur Machen," *A Man from Genoa and Other Poems*, copyright © 1926 by W. Paul Cook.

Covici-McGee Co. VINCENT STARRETT, "Arthur Machen: A Novelist

Holt, Rinehart & Winston. BABETTE DEUTSCH, "Farewell, Romance," *Poetry in Our Time*, copyright © 1952 by Henry Holt & Co.

Horizon. STEPHEN SPENDER, Vol. 10, No. 4 (Oct. 1944), copyright © 1944.

Houghton Mifflin Co. FORD MADOX FORD, "These Were Strong Men," "W. H. Hudson," *Portraits from Life*, copyright © 1936, 1937 by Ford Madox Ford. EDMUND WILSON, "The Kipling That Nobody Read," *The Wound and the Bow*, copyright © 1941 by Edmund Wilson.

Hudson Review. HAYDEN CARRUTH, Summer 1971, copyright © 1971. T. S. ELIOT, "Wyndham Lewis," Summer 1957, copyright © 1957. MONROE ENGEL, "The Continuity of Lawrence's Short Novels," Summer 1958, copyright © 1958. NORTHROP FRYE, "Neo-Classical Agony," Winter 1957–58, copyright © 1957. DANA GIOIA, Winter 1980, copyright © 1980. ANTHONY HECHT, Spring 1968, copyright © 1968. IRVING HOWE, "T. E. Lawrence: The Problem of Heroism," Autumn 1962, copyright © 1962. ANDRÉ MALRAUX, "Lawrence and the Demon of the Absolute," Winter 1956, copyright © 1956. ROGER SALE, "Fooling Around, and Serious Business," Winter 1974–75, copyright © 1974. MARK SCHORER, "Technique as Discovery," Spring 1948, copyright © 1948. VERNON YOUNG, "The Late Lamenting Wyndham Lewis," Autumn 1976, copyright © 1976.

Hutchinson & Co. LOWELL THOMAS, "A Modern Arabian Knight," *With Lawrence in Arabia*, copyright © 1924 by The Century Co.

International Literary Annual. A. ALVAREZ, "Poetry of the Fifties: In England," 1959, copyright © 1959.

The Irish Monthly. A. RAYBOULD, "Thomas MacDonagh," Vol. 47 (Sept. 1919), copyright © 1919 by M. H. Gill & Son.

Irish University Review. JANET EGLESON DUNLEAVY, "The Fiction of Mary Lavin: Universal Sensibility in a Particular Milieu," Vol. 7, No. 2 (Autumn 1977), copyright © 1977 by *Irish University Review*. MARY LAVIN, Interview by Catherine Murphy, Vol. 9, No. 2 (Autumn 1979), copyright © 1979 by *Irish University Review*.

Herbert Jenkins. FRANCIS LEDWIDGE, "Thomas MacDonagh," *The Complete Poems of Francis Ledwidge*, copyright © 1919.

Johns Hopkins University Press. MARGOT NORRIS, "Technique," *The Decentered Universe of Finnegans Wake: A Structuralist Analysis*, copyright © 1974, 1976 by Johns Hopkins University Press. RICHARD WILBUR, "Round about a Poem of Housman's," *The Moment of Poetry*, ed. Don Cameron Allen, copyright © 1962 by Johns Hopkins University Press.

The Kent State University Press. CHAD WALSH, "The Reeducation of the Fearful Pilgrim," *The Longing for Form*, ed. Peter J. Schakel, copyright © 1977 by The Kent State University Press.

The Kenyon Review. THOMAS H. CARTER, "Rationalist in Hell," Spring 1956, copyright © 1956. WILLIAM EMPSON, "The Throne of Ulysses," Winter 1956, copyright © 1956. GERALD HEARD, "The Poignant Prophet," Winter 1965, copyright © 1965. RANDALL JARRELL, "Texts from Housman," Summer 1939, copyright © 1939. ARTHUR MIZENER, "Spring Fiction," Summer 1957, copyright © 1957. FRANK SWINNERTON, "Rose Macaulay," Nov. 1967, copyright © 1967.

Carey Kingsgate. DOUGLAS G. STEWART, "Rose Macaulay: Anglicanism," *The Ark of God: Studies in Five Modern Novelists*, copyright © 1961.

The Kipling Journal. C. S. LEWIS, "Kipling's World," Sept. 1958, copyright © 1958.

Alfred A. Knopf. SIMONE DE BEAUVOIR, "D. H. Lawrence or Phallic Pride," *The Second Sex*, tr. H. M. Parshley, copyright © 1953. MAX BEERBOHM, "A Deplorable Affair," *Around Theatres*, copyright © 1930 by Max Beerbohm. ELIZABETH BOWEN, "Island Life," *Collected Impressions*, copyright © 1950. ELIZABETH BOWEN, *Seven Winters and Afterthoughts*, copyright © 1953 by Elizabeth Bowen. ERNEST BOYD, "Douglas Hyde," *Ireland's Literary Renaissance*, copyright © 1916, 1922 by Alfred A. Knopf. F. R. LEAVIS, "Lawrence and Art," *D. H. Lawrence: Novelist*, copyright © 1956. ARTHUR MACHEN, "Introduction" to *The Hill of Dreams*, copyright © 1922 by Alfred A. Knopf. KATHERINE MANSFIELD, "A Landscape with Portraits," "A Springe to Catch Woodcocks," *Novels and Novelists*, ed. J. Middleton Murry, copyright © 1930 by Alfred A. Knopf.

John Lane. FRANCIS ADAMS, "Mr. Rudyard Kipling's Verse," *Essays in Modernity*, copyright © 1899. G. K. CHESTERTON, "On Mr.

Rudyard Kipling and Making the World Small," *Heretics*, copyright © 1905 by John Lane.

Leicester University Press. D. B. MOORE, "Autumn Journal," *The Poetry of Louis MacNeice*, copyright © 1972.

David Lewis. HELENE CIXONS, "The Language of Reality," *The Exile of James Joyce*, tr. Sally A. J. Purcell, copyright © 1972 by Helene Cixons, translation copyright © 1972 by David Lewis, Inc.

J. B. Lippincott Co. PATRICK BRAYBROOKE, "Miss Rose Macaulay," *Some Goddesses of the Pen*, copyright © 1928.

The Listener. JOHN BAYLEY, "Smash and Bash," June 2, 1977, copyright © 1977 by British Broadcasting Corporation. ANTHONY BURGESS, "Why, This Is Hell," Oct. 1, 1964, copyright © 1964 by British Broadcasting Corporation. E. M. FORSTER, "T.E.," July 31, 1935, copyright © 1935 by British Broadcasting Corporation. ROY FULLER, "Gilding by the Ruolz Process," March 18, 1971, copyright © 1971 by British Broadcasting Corporation. ANTHONY LEJEUNE, "An Old Man and a Boy," March 29, 1956, copyright © 1956 by British Broadcasting Corporation. ROSE MACAULAY, "Full Fathom Five," Sept. 2, 1936, copyright © 1936 by British Broadcasting Corporation. ERIC NEWTON, "Emergence of Mr. Wyndham Lewis," May 19, 1949, copyright © 1949 by British Broadcasting Corporation.

The Literary Review. FREDERICK B. EDDY, "On the Heights," July 21, 1923, copyright © 1923.

Little, Brown & Co. T. H. DICKINSON, "H. A. Jones," *The Contemporary Drama of England*, copyright © 1920. LORD DUNSANY, "A Preface" to *Tales from Bective Bridge* by Mary Lavin, copyright © 1940, 1941, 1942 by Mary Lavin.

London Magazine. JUDITH CHERNAIK, "Sacred Cows," Dec.-Jan. 1978–79, copyright © 1978. ROY FULLER, Jan. 1958, copyright © 1958. IAN HAMILTON, "The Forties," April 1964, copyright © 1964. PHILIP LARKIN, Interview by Ian Hamilton, Nov. 1964, copyright © 1964. SIMON RAVEN, "The Game That Nobody Wins: The Novels of Rosamond Lehmann," April 1963, copyright © 1963. CHRISTOPHER RICKS, "Cliche as 'Responsible Speech': Geoffrey Hill," Nov, 1964, copyright © 1964. EVELYN WAUGH, "Youth at the Helm and Pleasure at the Prow," July 1955, copyright © 1955. JOHN WHITEHEAD, "Christophananda: Isherwood at Sixty," July 1965, copyright © 1965. DAVID WRIGHT, "Patrick Kavanagh," April 1968, copyright © 1968.

London Mercury. EDMUND BLUNDEN, "The Poet Laureate," July 1936, copyright © 1936. EDWARD SHANKS, Nov. 1921, copyright © 1921. UNSIGNED, July 1927, copyright © 1927.

Longman Group Ltd. ALAN BOLD, "Hugh MacDiarmid," *Modern Scottish Literature*, copyright © 1983 by Alan Bold. ISABEL QUIGLEY, *Pamela Hansford Johnson*, copyright © 1968 by Isabel Quigley. GAMINI SALGADO, "Story and Fable: The Biblical Framework," *A Preface to Lawrence*, copyright © 1982.

Lothlorien. HUGH MACDIARMID, Interview by Walter Perrie, *Metaphysics and Poetry*, copyright © 1975 by Lothlorien.

Lovell, Coryell & Co. HENRY JAMES, "Introduction" to *Mine Own People* by Rudyard Kipling, copyright © 1891.

MIT Press. THEODOR W. ADORNO, "Aldous Huxley and Utopia," *Prisms*, tr. Samuel and Sherry Weber, copyright © 1967 by Theodor W. Adorno.

MacDonald. ANN EDWARDS BOUTELLE, "'Trembling Sunbeams': The Vision and the Poetry," *Thistle and Rose: A Study in Hugh MacDiarmid's Poetry*, copyright © 1980 by Ann Edwards Boutelle.

McGill-Queen's University Press. BRUCE MERRY, *Anatomy of the Spy Thriller*, copyright © 1977 by Bruce Merry.

Macmillan & Co. Ltd. (London). BERNARD BERGONZI, "Remythologizing: David Jones' In Parenthesis," *Heroes' Twilight: A Study of the Literature of the Great War*, copyright © 1980. LOUIS L. CORNELL, "A Vision of India," *Kipling in India*, copyright © 1966 by Louis L. Cornell. ALAN SANDISON, "Rudyard Kipling: The Imperial Simulacrum," *The Wheel of Empire*, copyright © 1967 by Alan Sandison. W. B. YEATS, "The Death of Synge," "Dramatis Personae," *Autobiographies*, copyright © 1955.

Macmillan Publishing Co. (New York). CYRIL CONNOLLY, "The New Mandarins," "Predicaments," *Enemies of Promise*, copyright © 1938, 1948 by Cyril Connolly. J. W. CUNLIFFE, "Compton Mackenzie," *English Literature in the Twentieth Century*, copyright © 1933. A. S. F. GOW, *A. E. Housman: A Sketch*, copyright

"Mescalin," "Mescalin Interpreted," *Mysticism, Sacred and Profane,* copyright © 1957 by Oxford University Press.

Leonard Parsons. R. BRIMLEY JOHNSON, "Rose Macaulay," *Some Contemporary Novelists (Women),* copyright © 1920. HAROLD MONRO, *Some Contemporary Poets,* copyright © 1920.

Partisan Review. BERNARD CRICK, "Koestler's Koestler," Vol. 44, No. 2 (1982), copyright © 1982 by Partisan Review, Inc. ALFRED KAZIN, "Sons, Lovers and Mothers," Vol. 29, No. 3 (Summer 1962), copyright © 1962 by Partisan Review, Inc. F. O. MATTHIESSEN, "Louis MacNiece," Vol. 4, No. 3 (Feb. 1938), copyright © 1938 by Partisan Review, Inc.

The Personalist. ROBERT S. MATTESON, "Arthur Machen: A Vision of an Enchanted Land," Spring 1965, copyright © 1965.

Philosophy. W. R. INGE, "Discussion: *The Perennial Philosophy,*" Vol. 22, No. 1 (April 1947), copyright © 1947 by Macmillan & Co. (London).

Poetry. HAYDEN CARRUTH, Sept. 1968, copyright © 1968. GALWAY KINNELL, June 1958, copyright © 1958. EZRA POUND, "Love Poems, and Others," July 1913, copyright © 1913. ADRIENNE RICH, "Reflections on Lawrence," June 1965, copyright © 1965. DELMORE SCHWARTZ, "Adroitly Naive," May 1936, copyright © 1936. JULIAN SYMONS, "Louis MacNeice: The Artist as Everyman," May 1940, copyright © 1940.

The Poetry Review. ROBERT GRAVES, "Chaucer's Man," Vol. 58, No. 3 (Autumn 1967), copyright © 1967.

Prairie Schooner. DOUGLAS DAY, "Of Tragic Joy," Vol. 37, No. 4 (Winter 1963–64), copyright © 1964 by the University of Nebraska Press.

Proceedings of the British Academy. STEPHEN GASELEE, "Montague Rhodes James," Vol. 22 (1936), copyright © 1936.

G. P. Putnam's Sons. PHILIP GUEDALLA, "Mr. Compton Mackenzie," *A Gallery,* copyright © 1924.

Quarterly Review. SHANE LESLIE, "Montague Rhodes James," Vol. 304 (Jan. 1966), copyright © 1966 by John Murray.

Random House, Inc. A. ALVAREZ, "Prologue: Sylvia Plath," *The Savage God,* copyright © 1972. W. H. AUDEN, "A. E. Housman," *Collected Shorter Poems 1927–1957,* copyright © 1966 by W. H. Auden. W. H. AUDEN, "D. H. Lawrence," *The Dyer's Hand,* copyright © 1962 by W. H. Auden. JOHN GALSWORTHY, "Foreword" to *Green Mansions* by W. H. Hudson, copyright © 1916. GORE VIDAL, "Christopher Isherwood's Kind," *The Second American Revolution,* copyright © 1982 by Gore Vidal.

The Review of English Literature. FRANK O'CONNOR, "The Girl at the Gaol Gate," Vol. 1, No. 2 (April 1960), copyright © 1960 by the Review of English Literature.

Reynal & Hitchcock. GEORGE ORWELL, "Arthur Koestler," "Rudyard Kipling," *Dickens, Dali and Others,* copyright © 1946 by George Orwell.

Richards Press. LORD DUNSANY, "Introduction" to *The Hill of Dreams* by Arthur Machen, copyright © 1954 by Richards Press.

Routledge & Kegan Paul. ALAN BOLD, "To Prove My Saul Is Scots," *MacDiarmid: The Terrible Crystal,* copyright © 1983 by Alan Bold. ALEXANDER SCOTT, "MacDiarmid: The Poet," *The Hugh MacDiarmid Anthology: Poems in Scots and English,* copyright © 1972 by C. M. Grieve.

Rowman & Littlefield. GLEN CAVALIERO, "Literary Regionalism: Hugh Walpole, Sheila Kaye-Smith," *The Rural Tradition in the English Novel 1900–1939,* copyright © 1977 by Glen Cavaliero.

St. Martin's Press. JOHN HALPERIN, "Appendix: A Conversation with Lady Snow," *C. P. Snow: An Oral Biography,* copyright © 1983 by John Halperin. GEOFFREY THURLEY, "The Legacy of Auden," *The Ironic Harvest,* copyright © 1974.

Salmagundi. ROBERT GILLESPIE, "The Recent Future," Summer 1970, copyright © 1970 by Skidmore College.

Sampson Low, Marston & Co. ARTHUR ST. JOHN ADCOCK, "E. V. Lucas," "Jerome K. Jerome," "William Wymark Jacobs," *The Glory That Was Grub Street,* copyright © 1928. ARTHUR WAUGH, "Mr. E. V. Lucas," *Tradition and Change: Studies in Contemporary Literature,* copyright © 1928.

Saturday Review (London). L. P. HARTLEY, "New Fiction," Nov. 5, 1927, copyright © 1927. UNSIGNED, Oct. 5, 1889, copyright © 1889.

The Saturday Review. HOLLIS ALPERT, "London Bohemians," Nov. 17, 1956, copyright © 1956. GERARD PREVIN MEYER, "Washed in

Happy Air," Sept. 6, 1947, copyright © 1947. HARRISON SMITH, March 29, 1954, copyright © 1954. STEPHEN SPENDER, "An Unsung Classicist," Sept. 7, 1963, copyright © 1963. P. G. WODEHOUSE, "The Descent of Unsuccessful Sons," March 14, 1959, copyright © 1959.

Science-Fiction Studies. WILLIAM W. MATTER, "The Utopian Tradition and Aldous Huxley," Vol. 2, No. 2 (July 1975), copyright © 1975.

Scientific American. MAX BLOCK," Aldous Huxley's View of the 'Two Cultures,'" Vol. 210, No. 3 (March 1964), copyright © 1964.

Charles Scribner's Sons. A. E. MORGAN, *Tendencies of English Drama,* copyright © 1924. STUART SHERMAN, "Rose Macaulay and Women," *Critical Woodcuts,* copyright © 1926 by Charles Scribner's Sons. WILLIAM YORK TINDALL, "Myth and Symbol," *James Joyce: His Way of Interpreting the Modern World,* copyright © 1950 by Charles Scribner's Sons. EDMUND WILSON, "James Joyce," *Axel's Castle,* copyright 1931 by Charles Scribner's Sons, copyright © 1959 by Edmund Wilson.

Scrutiny. F. R. LEAVIS, "Mr Eliot, Mr Wyndham Lewis and Lawrence," Vol. 3, No. 2 (Sept. 1934), copyright © 1934. F. R. LEAVIS, Vol. 4, No. 3 (Dec. 1935), copyright © 1935.

Seabury Press. HAROLD BLOOM, "Geoffrey Hill: The Survival of Strong Poetry," *Figures of Capable Imagination,* copyright © 1976.

Sewanee Review. HOWARD NEMEROV, "Seven Poets and the Language," 1954, copyright © 1954. WALKER PERCY, "Hughes' Solipsism Malgré Lui," July-Sept. 1964, copyright © 1964.

Shenandoah. T. S. ELIOT, "Tarr," Vol. 4, Nos. 2/3 (Summer–Autumn 1953), copyright © 1953 by *Shenandoah.*

Colin Smythe Ltd. LADY GREGORY, *Seventy Years: Being the Autobiography of Lady Gregory,* copyright © 1974 by the Lady Gregory Estate.

South Atlantic Quarterly. FRANK BALDANZA, "*Point Counter Point:* Aldous Huxley on 'The Human Fugue,'" Vol. 58, No. 2 (Spring 1959), copyright © 1959.

Southern Illinois University Press. MARK SCHORER, "Lawrence and the Spirit of Place," *A D. H. Lawrence Miscellany,* ed. Harry T. Moore, copyright © 1959.

Southern Review. JOHN HAZARD WILDMAN, "Beyond Classification: Some Notes on Distinction," Vol. 9, No. 1 (Jan. 1973), copyright © 1973 by *Southern Review.*

The Spectator. PETER ACKROYD, "Agonising," June 11, 1977, copyright © 1977. KINGSLEY AMIS, "Is the Travel-Book Dead?," June 17, 1955, copyright © 1955. C. M. BOWRA, "The Scholarship of A. E. Housman," June 19, 1936, copyright © 1936. ANTHONY BURGESS, "Europe's Day of the Dead," Jan. 20, 1967, copyright © 1967. ANTHONY BURGESS, "His Ain Folk," Nov. 11, 1966, copyright © 1966. PETER FLEMING, "The Stuff of Nightmares," April 18, 1933, copyright © 1933. BENNY GREEN, "Wapping Lies," July 19, 1975, copyright © 1975. GRAHAM GREENE, "High Wind in the Caribbean," July 8, 1938, copyright © 1938. DAN JACOBSON, "To a Former Life," Nov. 13, 1959, copyright © 1959. JULIAN MITCHELL, "Everyman's Island," Oct. 6, 1961, copyright © 1961. V. S. PRITCHETT, "The Age of Speed?," Sept. 27, 1930, copyright © 1930. V. S. PRITCHETT, "Three Exceptional Novels," Sept. 28, 1929, copyright © 1929. GEORGE BERNARD SHAW, "The Latest from Colonel Lawrence," March 12, 1927, copyright © 1927. EVELYN WAUGH, "Author in Search of a Formula," March 25, 1938, copyright © 1938. EVELYN WAUGH, "Mr. Isherwood and Friend," March 24, 1939, copyright © 1939.

Frederick A. Stokes Co. MARGARET LAWRENCE, "Matriarchs," *The School of Femininity,* copyright © 1936 by Frederick A. Stokes Co.

Studies. JOHN JORDAN, "Mr. Kavanagh's Progress," Fall 1960, copyright © 1960. AUGUSTE MARTIN, "A Skeleton Key to the Stories of Mary Lavin," Winter 1963, copyright © 1963.

Studies in Short Fiction. JOSEPH H. HARKEY, "Foreshadowing in 'The Monkey's Paw,'" Vol. 6, No. 5 (Fall 1969), copyright © 1969.

Studies in the Novel. WALTER ALLEN, "*Point Counter Point* Revisited," Vol. 9, No. 4 (Winter 1977), copyright © 1977.

Talbot Press. JAMES STEPHENS, "Introduction" to *The Poetical Works of Thomas MacDonagh,* copyright © 1916.

Thought. MARSHALL MCLUHAN, "James Joyce: Trivial and Quadrivial," No. 108 (Spring 1953), copyright © 1953.

Twentieth Century Literature. SYDNEY JANET KAPLAN, "Rosamond

Lehmann's *The Ballad and the Source*: A Confrontation with 'The Great Mother,'" Vol. 27, No. 2 (Summer 1981), copyright © 1981.

Twentieth Century Verse. GILBERT ARMITAGE, "A Note on *The Wild Body*," Nos. 6/7 (Nov.-Dec. 1937), copyright © 1937. CONSTANT LAMBERT, "An Objective Self Portrait," Nos 6/7 (Nov.-Dec. 1937), copyright © 1937. WYNDHAM LEWIS, "A Letter to the Editor," Nos. 6/7 (Nov.-Dec. 1937), copyright © 1937.

Times Literary Supplement. CONRAD AIKEN, Letter to the Editor, Feb. 16, 1967, copyright © 1967 by *Times Literary Supplement*. T. J. BINYON, "A Gentleman among Players," Sept. 9, 1977, copyright © 1977 by *Times Literary Supplement*. BLAKE MORRISON, "An Expropriated Mycologist," Feb. 15, 1980, copyright © 1980 by *Times Literary Supplement*. BLAKE MORRISON, "Paying Cellerage," Sept. 29, 1978, copyright © 1978 by *Times Literary Supplement*. LORNA SAGE, "Dreams of Being Hurt," Oct. 9, 1981, copyright © 1981 by *Times Literary Supplement*. SYLVIA SECKER, "Writer on the Move," Jan. 30, 1976, copyright © 1976 by *Times Literary Supplement*. ANTHONY THWAITE, "At the Point of Speech," Nov. 7, 1975, copyright © 1975 by *Times Literary Supplement*. UNSIGNED, "A Corvo of Our Day," Jan 9, 1959, copyright © 1959 by *Times Literary Supplement*. UNSIGNED, "Limits of Control," Sept. 13, 1963, copyright © 1963 by *Times Literary Supplement*. UNSIGNED, "Miss Macaulay's Novels," May 12, 1950, copyright © 1950 by *Times Literary Supplement*.

UMI Research Press. THOMAS KUSH, "The Artist in the Modern Age," *Wyndham Lewis's Pictorial Integer*, copyright © 1981 by Thomas Kush.

Frederick Ungar Publishing Co. CLAUDE J. SUMMERS, "Evil Mothers and Truly Weak Men," *Christopher Isherwood*, copyright © 1980.

University of British Columbia Publications Centre. HUGH KENNER, "The Last European," JULIAN SYMONS, "Introduction" to *Wyndham Lewis in Canada*, ed. George Woodcock, copyright © 1971 by the University of British Columbia.

University of California Press. FREDRIC JAMESON, *Fables of Aggression: Wyndham Lewis, the Modernist as Fascist*, copyright © 1979 by The Regents of the University of California. HUGH MACDIARMID, "Author's Note 1972," *Lucky Poet: A Self-Study in Literary and Political Ideas*, copyright © 1972 by Hugh MacDiarmid.

University of Minnesota Press. MURRAY KRIEGER, "T. E. Hulme: Classicism and the Imagination," *The New Apologists for Poetry*, copyright © 1956 by the University of Minnesota Press.

University of Oklahoma Press. WILLIAM C. FRIERSON, "Diffusion, 1929–1940," *The English Novel in Transition: 1885–1940*, copyright © 1942 by the University of Oklahoma Press; copyright reassigned 1965 to Mrs. William C. Frierson.

University of Pittsburgh Press. DAVID A. WHITE, "The Reality of Flux," *The Grand Continuum: Reflections on Joyce and Metaphysics*, copyright © 1983 by the University of Pittsburgh Press.

University of Toronto Quarterly. MERVIN NICHOLSON, "'What We See We Feel': The Imaginative World of W. H. Hudson," Vol. 47, No. 4 (Summer 1978), copyright © 1978. LIONEL STEVENSON, "The Ideas in Kipling's Poetry," *The University of Toronto Quarterly*, Vol. 1, No. 4 (July 1932), copyright © 1932.

University of Tulsa. UMBERTO ECO, "The Early Joyce," *The Aesthetics of Chaosmos: The Middle Ages of James Joyce*, tr. Ellen Esrock, copyright © 1982 by the University of Tulsa.

The University of Wisconsin Press. ROBERT S. BAKER, "The Descending Road of Modern History," *The Dark Historic Page*, copyright © 1982 by The Board of Regents of the University of Wisconsin System. RICHARD J. LOFTUS, "For Houlihan's Daughter," *Nationalism in Modern Anglo-Irish Poetry*, copyright © 1964 by the Regents of the University of Wisconsin.

University Press of Virginia. JOHANN A. NORSTEDT, "Epilogue" to *Thomas MacDonagh: A Critical Biography*, copyright © 1980 by the Rector and Visitors of the University of Virginia.

Victorian Poetry. B. J. LEGGETT, "The Poetry of Insight: Persona and Point of View in Housman," Winter 1976, copyright © 1976.

Victorian Studies. NOEL ANNAN, "Kipling's Place in the History of Ideas," Vol. 3, No. 4 (June 1960), copyright © 1960.

Viking Penguin, Inc. A. ALVAREZ, "Beyond the Gentility Principle," *The New Poetry*, copyright © 1962 by Penguin Books Ltd. JOHN BAYLEY, "The Puzzles of Kipling," *The Uses of Division*, copyright © 1976 by John Bayley. ISAIAH BERLIN, "Aldous Huxley," *Personal Impressions*, copyright © 1965, 1980 by Isaiah Berlin. ANTHONY BURGESS, "Introduction" to *D. H. Lawrence and Italy* by D. H. Lawrence, copyright © 1972. ALDOUS HUXLEY, "Introduction" to *The Letters of D. H. Lawrence*, ed. Aldous Huxley, copyright © 1932 by the Estate of D. H. Lawrence. FRANK KERMODE, *D. H. Lawrence*, copyright © 1973. JOHN LEHMANN, "Refitting the Novel," *New Writing in Europe*, copyright © 1940.

Virginia Woolf Quarterly. LAWRENCE THORNTON, "Rosamond Lehmann, Henry James and the Temporal Matrix of Fiction," Vol. 1, No. 3 (Spring 1973), copyright © 1973 by California State University.

Wishart & Co. BERTRAM HIGGINS, "John Masefield," *Scrutinies*, ed. Edgell Rickword, copyright © 1928 by Wishart & Co.

Woburn Press. VERNON SCANNELL, "Alun Lewis," *Not without Glory: Poets of the Second World War*, copyright © 1976 by Woburn Press.

The Yale Review. G. B. STERN, "The Heroines of Sheila Kaye-Smith," Vol. 15, No. 1 (Oct. 1925), copyright © 1925.